	WESTERN ASIA	SOUTH ASIA	EAST ASIA	EUROPE	AFRICA	AMERICA
A.D. 200–300			Fall of Han Dynasty	Military Anarchy in Rome		Rise of Mayan Culture
300–400		Rise of the Guptas		Age of Constantine	Ethiopia Adopts Christianity	
400–500				Western Roman Empire Collapses	Augustine	
500–600		Collapse of Gupta Rule	Buddhism in Japan	Age of Justinian		
600–700	Rise of Islam		Rise of T'ang Dynasty			Teotihuacán Destroyed
700–800	Abbasid Caliphate Founded		Nara Period	Rise of the Franks	Muslims Go to Ghana and Sudan	
800–900				Charlemagne's Empire		Decline of Mayans
900–1000			Rise of Sung Dynasty	Holy Roman Empire Begins	Fatimids Conquer Egypt	
1000–1100	Avicenna	Islamic Invasions	*Tale of Genji*	Norman Conquest	Almoravid Conquest of Morocco	
1100–1200	Crusades		Kamakura Shogunate Founded	Romanesque Age		
1200–1300	Latin Kingdom in Constantinople	Founding of Delhi Sultanate	Yuan Dynasty Founded	Gothic Age	Rise of Mali and Kilwa	
1300–1400	Rise of Ottoman Turks	Age of the Tughluqs	Ming Dynasty Founded	Black Death		Rise of Aztecs
1400–1500	Conquest of Constantinople by Turks		Expeditions of Cheng Ho	Renaissance	Decline of Mali	Rise of Incas; Columbus
1500–1600	Suleiman	Age of Akbar	Hideyoshi Unites Japan	Reformation		Conquest of Aztecs and Incas

CIVILIZATIONS OF THE WORLD

The Human Adventure

Richard L. Greaves
Florida State University

Robert Zaller
Drexel University

Philip V. Cannistraro
Drexel University

Rhoads Murphey
University of Michigan

1817

Harper & Row, Publishers, New York
Grand Rapids, Philadelphia, St. Louis, San Francisco,
London, Singapore, Sydney, Tokyo

Sponsoring Editor: Lauren Silverman
Development Editor: Mary Lou Mosher
Project Editor: Susan Goldfarb
Art Direction: Teresa J. Delgado
Text and Cover Design: Delgado Design Inc.
Cover Coordinator: Mary Archondes
Text Maps: Burmar Technical Corp.
Photo Research:. Elsa Peterson
Production: Willie Lane

Cover Illustration: The Granger Collection

Part-opening art: Part One: From Egyptian papyrus of mouth-opening ceremony, New Empire (Giraudon/Art Resource); Part Two: From Koran, Maghribi script, c. 1300 (Metropolitan Museum of Art, Rogers Fund); Part Three: From Gutenberg Bible (Innervisions/Rare Books and Manuscripts Collection, New York Public Library, Astor, Lenox, and Tilden Foundations); Part Four: From preface to *Alzire, ou les Américains,* by Voltaire, Amsterdam, 1736 (Innervisions/Rare Books and Manuscripts Collection, New York Public Library, Astor, Lenox, and Tilden Foundations); Part Five: From contemporary rendering of traditional Japanese Zen Buddhist daily chant (courtesy of Dai Bosatsu Zendo).

The authors are indebted to Princeton University Press for permission to reprint the poem "Ithaka" by C. P. Cavafy in the front matter for this book. The poem appears in *Selected Poems by C. P. Cavafy,* translated by Edmund Keeley and Philip Sherrard (Princeton, N.J.: Princeton University Press, 1972).

Title page photo: Alison Frantz

Civilizations of the World: The Human Adventure

Library of Congress Cataloging-in-Publication Data

Civilizations of the world : the human adventure / Richard L. Greaves
. . . [et al.].
p. cm.
ISBN 0-06-047359-2
1. Civilization—History. I. Greaves, Richard L.
CB69.C565 1990b 89-24559
909—dc20 CIP

90 91 92 93 9 8 7 6 5 4 3 2 1

Stockton and Darlington Railway (1825)
Lancaster
York
Hull
Liverpool and Manchester Railway (1830)
Holyhead
Crewe
Lincoln
Norwich
Ruabon
Birmingham
Rugby
Cambridge
Gloucester
Colchester
Merthyr
Oxford
Cardiff
Bristol
London
Dover
Salisbury
Brighton

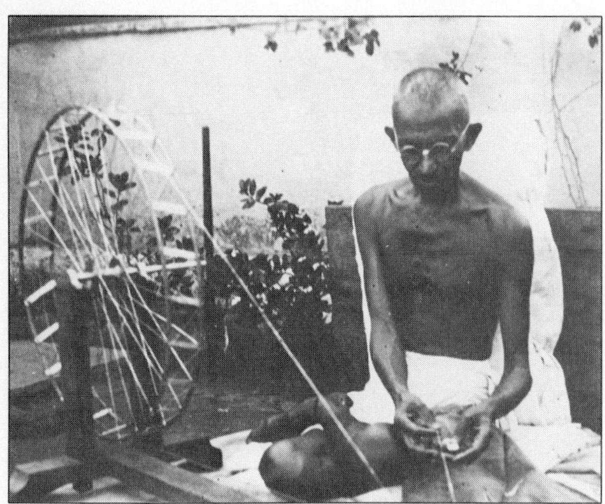

- Harper & Row Film Rentals. A wide selection of films is available on topics from Western Europe, Africa, and Asia.
- *World History Media Handbook.* Specially prepared for adopters of *Civilizations of the World,* this brief guide provides descriptions and ordering information for available media resources as well as numerous practical strategies for incorporating media in the classroom.

ACKNOWLEDGMENTS

The authors are grateful to Marianne Russell, Editorial Director at Harper & Row, who not only signed this book but enthusiastically supported it from its inception to its publication. The authors would also like to thank Lauren Silverman, history editor; Mary Lou Mosher, senior development editor; Susan Goldfarb, project editor; and Bruce Emmer, copy editor. This book could not have been completed without the invaluable assistance of Judith Dieker Greaves, editorial assistant to the authors. The authors wish additionally to thank the following persons for their assistance and support: Lili Bita Zaller, Philip Rethis, Kimon Rethis, Robert B. Radin, Julia Southard, Robert S. Browning, and Professors Eric D. Brose, Roger Hackett, Victor Lieberman, William W. Rogers, Donald F. Stevens, Ralph Turner, Thomas Trautmann, and Edward D. Wynot, Jr.

The following scholars read the manuscript in whole or in part and offered many helpful suggestions:

Dorothy Abrahamse
California State University, Long Beach

Winthrop Lindsay Adams
University of Utah

George M. Addy
Brigham Young University

Jay Pascal Anglin
University of Southern Mississippi

Charmarie J. Blaisdell
Northeastern University

William A. Bultmann
Western Washington University

Thomas Callahan, Jr.
Rider College

Miriam Usher Chrisman
University of Massachusetts, Amherst

Jill N. Claster
New York University

Cynthia Schwenk Clemons
Georgia State University

Allen T. Cronenberg
Auburn University

John Dahmus
Stephen F. Austin State University

Elton L. Daniel
University of Hawaii at Manoa

Leslie Derfler
Florida Atlantic University

Joseph M. Dixon
Weber State College

John Patrick Donnelly
Marquette University

Mark U. Edwards, Jr.
Harvard University

Charles A. Endress
Angelo State University

Stephen Englehart
California State Polytechnic University, Pomona

William Wayne Farvis
University of Tennessee

Jonathan Goldstein
West Georgia College

Edwin N. Gorsuch
Georgia State University

Joseph M. Gowaski
Rider College

Tony Grafton
Princeton University

Coburn V. Graves
Kent State University

Janelle Greenberg
University of Pittsburgh

Udo Heyn
California State University, Los Angeles

Clive Holmes
Cornell University

Leonard A. Humphreys
University of the Pacific

Donald G. Jones
University of Central Arkansas

William R. Jones
University of New Hampshire

Thomas Kaiser
University of Arkansas at Little Rock

Thomas L. Kennedy
Washington State University

Frank Kidner
San Francisco State University

Winston L. Kinsey
Appalachian State University

Thomas Kuehn
Clemson University

Richard D. Lewis
Saint Cloud State University

David C. Lukowitz
Hamline University

Thomas J. McPartland
Bellevue Community College

Elizabeth Malloy
Salem State College

John A. Mears
Southern Methodist University

V. Dixon Morris
University of Hawaii at Manoa

Marian Purrier Nelson
University of Nebraska at Omaha

William D. Newell
Laramie County Community College

James Odom
East Tennessee State University

William G. Palmer
Marshall University

William D. Phillips, Jr.
San Diego State University

Paul B. Pixton
Brigham Young University

Ronald R. Rader
University of Georgia

Leland Sather
Weber State College

Kerry E. Spiers
University of Louisville

Paul Stewart
Southern Connecticut State University

Richard G. Stone
Western Kentucky University

Alexander Sydorenko
Arkansas State University

Teddy Uldricks
University of North Carolina
at Asheville

Raymond Van Dam
University of Michigan, Ann Arbor

John Weakland
Ball State University

David L. White
Appalachian State University

Richard S. Williams
Washington State University

Glee E. Wilson
Kent State University

John E. Wood
James Madison University

Martin Yanuck
Spelman College

About the Authors

RICHARD L. GREAVES Born in Glendale, California, Richard L. Greaves—with Robert Zaller general editor of this text—is a specialist in Reformation and British social and religious history. Greaves earned his Ph.D. degree at the University of London in 1964. After teaching at Michigan State University, he moved in 1972 to Florida State University, where he is now Robert O. Lawton Distinguished Professor of History and Courtesy Professor of Religion. A Fellow of the Royal Historical Society, Greaves has received fellowships from the National Endowment for the Humanities, the American Council of Learned Societies, the Andrew Mellon Foundation, the Huntington Library, and the American Philosophical Society. The eighteen books he has written or edited include *John Bunyan* (1969), *Theology and Revolution in the Scottish Reformation: Studies in the Thought of John Knox* (1980), *Saints and Rebels: Seven Nonconformists in Stuart England* (1985), *Deliver Us from Evil: The Radical Underground in Britain, 1660–1663* (1986), and *Enemies Under His Feet: Radicals and Nonconformists in Britain, 1664–1677* (1990). The Conference on British Studies awarded Greaves the Walter D. Love Memorial Prize for *The Puritan Revolution and Educational Thought: Background for Reform* (1969), and his *Society and Religion in Elizabethan England* (1981) was a finalist for the Robert Livingston Schuyler Prize of the American Historical Association. He has been named president of the American Society of Church History for 1991.

ROBERT ZALLER Robert Zaller was born in New York City and received a Ph.D. degree from Washington University in 1968. An authority on British political history and constitutional thought, he has also written extensively on modern literature, film, and art. He has taught at Queens College, City University of New York; the University of California, Santa Barbara; and the University of Miami. He is Professor of History and former Head of the Department of History and Politics at Drexel University. He has been a Guggenheim fellow and is a member of the advisory board of the Yale Center for Parliamentary History. His book *The Parliament of 1621: A Study in Constitutional Conflict* (1971) received the Phi Alpha Theta prize for the best first book by a member of the society, and he was made a Fellow of Tor House in recognition of his study *The Cliffs of Solitude: A Reading of Robinson Jeffers* (1983). His other books include *Lives of the Poet* (1974) and *Europe in Transition, 1660–1815* (1984). He has edited *A Casebook on Anaïs Nin* (1974), and coedited, with Richard L. Greaves, a *Biographical Dictionary of British Radicals in the Seventeenth Century* (3 vols., 1982–1984). Zaller's most recent publications include studies of Samuel Beckett, Philip Guston, Bernardo Bertolucci, and the English civil war. With Richard L. Greaves he is general editor of this text.

PHILIP V. CANNISTRARO A native of New York City, Philip V. Cannistraro, an authority on modern Italian history and culture, received the Ph.D. degree from

New York University in 1971. Currently Professor of History and Head of the Department of History and Politics at Drexel University, Cannistraro taught at Florida State University and has been a visiting professor at New York University and St. Mary's College, Rome. He has lectured widely in Italy and in the United States and is American editor of the Italian historical quarterly *Storia Contemporanea*. The recipient of two Fulbright-Hays fellowships, Cannistraro is an active member of the Society for Italian Historical Studies and the American Italian Historical Association. His numerous publications include *La Fabbrica del Consenso: Fascismo e Mass Media* (1975), *Poland and the Coming of the Second World War* (with E. Wynot and T. Kovaleff, 1976), *Italian Fascist Activities in the United States* (1976), *Fascismo, Chiesa e Emigrazione* (with G. Rosoli, 1979), *Historical Dictionary of Fascist Italy* (1981), and *Italian Americans: The Search for a Usable Past* (with R. Juliani, 1989). Cannistraro is currently writing biographies of Generoso Pope and Margherita Sarfatti.

RHOADS MURPHEY Born in Philadelphia, Rhoads Murphey, a specialist in Chinese history and in geography, received the Ph.D. degree from Harvard University in 1950. Before joining the faculty of the University of Michigan in 1964, he taught at the University of Washington; he has also been a visiting professor at Taiwan University and Tokyo University. From 1954 to 1956 he was the director of the Conference of Diplomats in Asia. The University of Michigan granted him a Distinguished Service Award in 1974. Currently president of the Association for Asian Studies, Murphey has served as editor of the *Journal of Asian Studies* and *Michigan Papers in Chinese Studies*. The Social Science Research Council, the Ford Foundation, the Guggenheim Foundation, the National Endowment for the Humanities, and the American Council of Learned Societies have awarded him fellowships. A prolific author, Murphey's books include *Shanghai: Key to Modern China* (1953), *An Introduction to Geography* (4th ed., 1978), *A New China Policy* (with others, 1965), *Approaches to Modern Chinese History* (with others, 1967), *The Scope of Geography* (3rd ed., 1982), *The Treaty Ports and China's Modernization* (1970), *China Meets the West: The Treaty Ports* (1975), and *The Fading of the Maoist Vision* (1980). *The Outsiders: Westerners in India and China* (1977) won the Best-Book-of-the-Year award from the University of Michigan Press.

Ithaka

As you set out for Ithaka
hope your road is a long one,
full of adventure, full of discovery.
Laistrygonians, Cyclops,
angry Poseidon—don't be afraid of them:
you'll never find things like that on your way
as long as you keep your thoughts raised high,
as long as a rare excitement
stirs your spirit and your body.

Laistrygonians, Cyclops,
wild Poseidon—you won't encounter them
unless you bring them along inside your soul,
unless your soul sets them up in front of you.

Hope your road is a long one.
May there be many summer mornings when,
with what pleasure, what joy,
you enter harbors you're seeing for the first time;
may you stop at Phoenician trading stations
to buy fine things,
mother of pearl and coral, amber and ebony,
sensual perfume of every kind—
as many sensual perfumes as you can;
and may you visit many Egyptian cities
to learn and go on learning from their scholars.

Keep Ithaka always in your mind.
Arriving there is what you're destined for.
But don't hurry the journey at all.
Better if it lasts for years,
so you're old by the time you reach the island,
wealthy with all you've gained on the way,
not expecting Ithaka to make you rich.

Ithaka gave you the marvelous journey.
Without her you wouldn't have set out.
She has nothing left to give you now.

And if you find her poor, Ithaka won't have fooled you.
Wise as you will have become, so full of experience,
you'll have understood by then what these Ithakas mean.

C. P. Cavafy

A Note on the Spelling of Asian Names and Words

Nearly all Asian languages are written with symbols different from our Western alphabet. Chinese, Japanese, and Korean are written with ideographic characters, plus a phonetic syllabary for Japanese and Korean. Most other Asian languages have their own scripts, symbols, diacritical marks, and alphabets, which differ from ours. There can thus be no single "correct spelling" in Western symbols for Asian words or names, including personal names and place names—only established conventions. Unfortunately, conventions in this respect differ widely and in many cases reflect preferences or forms related to different Western languages. The Western spellings used in this book, including its maps, are to some extent a compromise, in an effort to follow the main English-language conventions but also to make pronunciation for English speakers as easy as possible.

Chinese presents the biggest problem, since there are a great many different conventions in use and since well-known place names, such as Peking or Canton, are commonly spelled as they are here in most Western writings, even though this spelling is inconsistent with all of the romanization systems in current use and does not accurately represent the Chinese sounds. Most American newspapers and some journals now use the romanization system called *pinyin,* approved by the Chinese government, which renders these two city names, with greater phonetic accuracy, as Beijing and Kwangzhou but which presents other problems for most Western readers and which they commonly mispronounce.

The usage in this book follows the most commonly used convention for scholarly publication when romanizing Chinese names, the Wade-Giles system, but gives the pinyin equivalents for modern names (if they differ) in parentheses after the first use of a name. Readers will encounter both spellings, plus others, in other books, papers, and journals, and some familiarity with both conventions is thus necessary.

In general, readers should realize and remember that English spellings of names from other languages (such as Munich for München, Vienna for Wien, and Rome for Roma), especially in Asia, can be only approximations and may differ confusingly from one Western source or map to another.

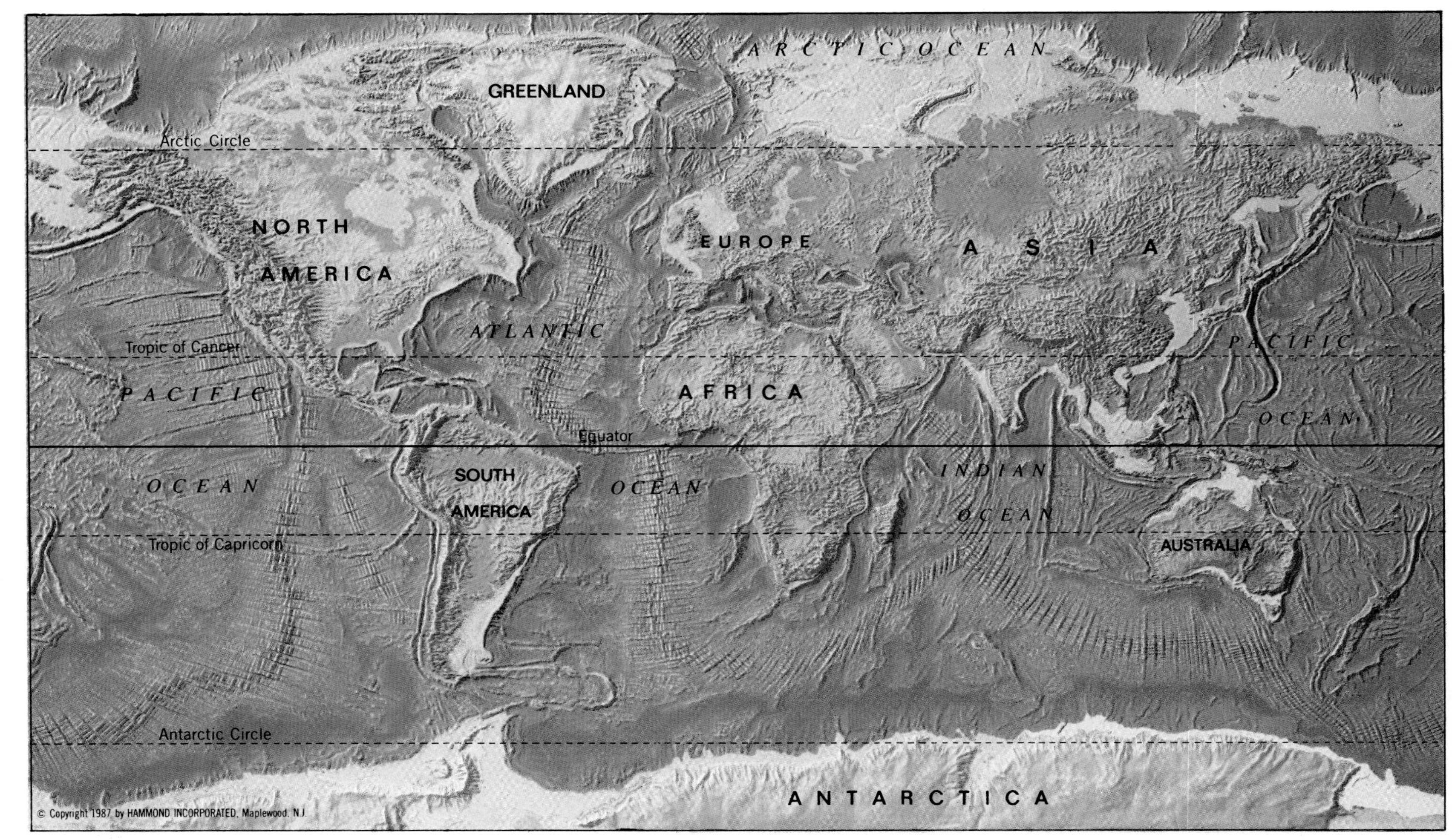
ARCTIC OCEAN
GREENLAND
Arctic Circle
NORTH AMERICA
EUROPE
ASIA
ATLANTIC
Tropic of Cancer
PACIFIC
PACIFIC
AFRICA
OCEAN
Equator
OCEAN
SOUTH AMERICA
OCEAN
INDIAN OCEAN
Tropic of Capricorn
AUSTRALIA
Antarctic Circle
ANTARCTICA
© Copyright 1987 by HAMMOND INCORPORATED, Maplewood, N.J.

EUROPE

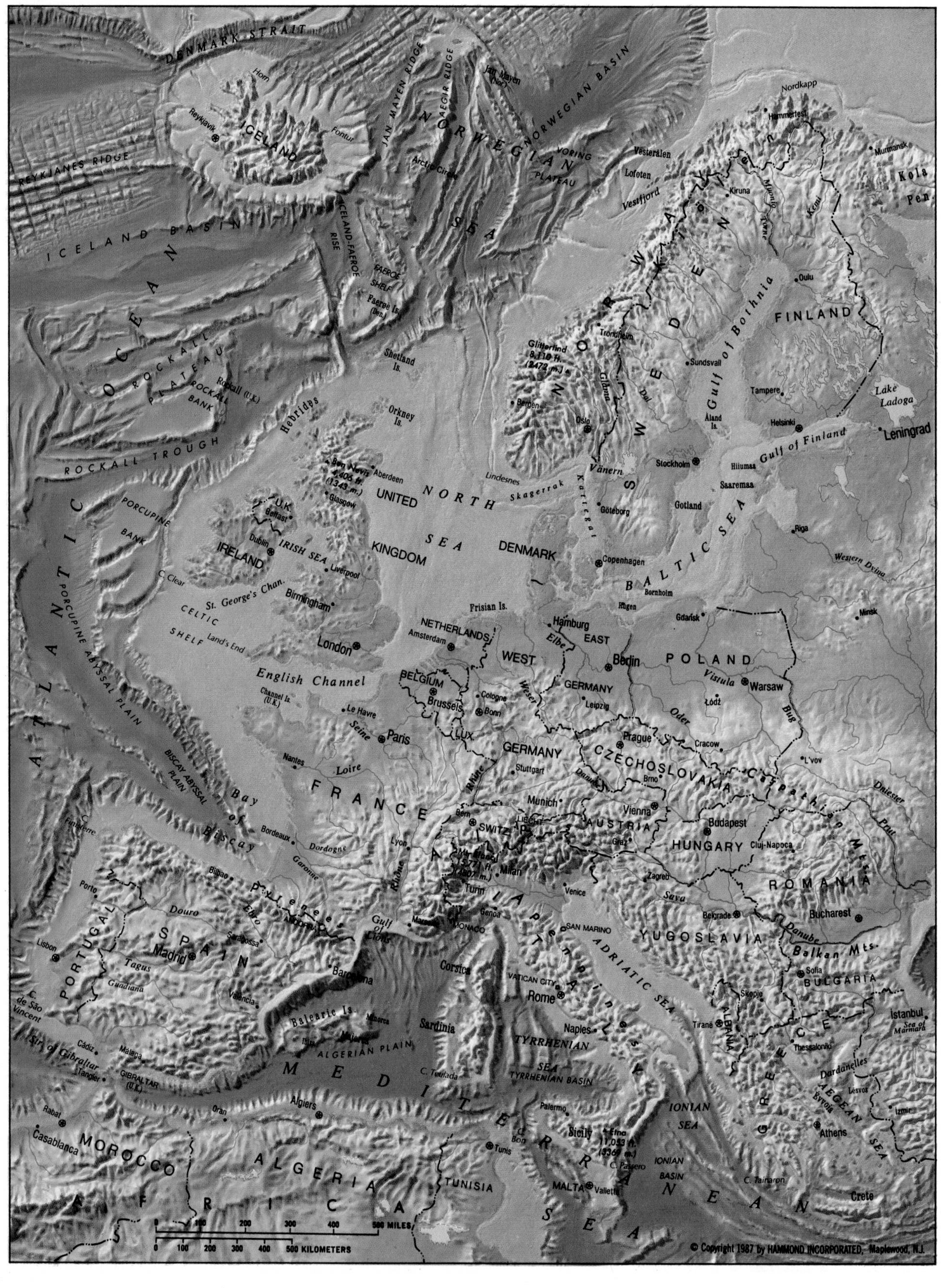
DENMARK STRAIT
ICELAND
Reykjavík
REYKJANES RIDGE
ICELAND BASIN
JAN MAYEN RIDGE
AEGIR RIDGE
NORWEGIAN BASIN
NORWEGIAN SEA
VORING PLATEAU
Arctic Circle
ICELAND-FAEROE RISE
FAEROE SHELF
Faeroe Is. (Den.)
ROCKALL PLATEAU
ROCKALL BANK
Rockall (U.K.)
ROCKALL TROUGH
ATLANTIC OCEAN
PORCUPINE BANK
PORCUPINE ABYSSAL PLAIN
BISCAY ABYSSAL PLAIN
Shetland Is.
Orkney Is.
Hebrides
Nordkapp
Hammerfest
Murmansk
Kola Pen.
Vesterålen
Lofoten
Vestfjord
Kiruna
NORWAY
SWEDEN
FINLAND
Oulu
Gulf of Bothnia
Trondheim
Glittertind 8,110 ft. (2472 m.)
Sundsvall
Tampere
Lake Ladoga
Bergen
Oslo
Åland Is.
Helsinki
Leningrad
Gulf of Finland
Stockholm
Hiiumaa
Saaremaa
Vänern
Lindesnes
Skagerrak
Kattegat
Göteborg
Gotland
Riga
Ben Nevis 4,406 ft. (1343 m.)
Aberdeen
Glasgow
UNITED KINGDOM
NORTH SEA
DENMARK
BALTIC SEA
Western Dvina
U.K.
Belfast
Dublin
IRELAND
IRISH SEA
Liverpool
Copenhagen
Bornholm
Rügen
C. Clear
St. George's Chan.
Birmingham
CELTIC SHELF
Land's End
London
Frisian Is.
NETHERLANDS
Amsterdam
Hamburg
Gdańsk
Minsk
EAST GERMANY
Berlin
POLAND
WEST GERMANY
Vistula
Warsaw
English Channel
BELGIUM
Brussels
Cologne
Bonn
Leipzig
Łódź
Channel Is. (U.K.)
Le Havre
Seine
Paris
LUX.
Oder
Bug
Prague
Cracow
GERMANY
CZECHOSLOVAKIA
L'vov
Nantes
Loire
Stuttgart
Brno
Carpathian Mts.
Dniester
Bay of Biscay
FRANCE
Munich
Vienna
AUSTRIA
Budapest
Prut
Bern
SWITZ.
HUNGARY
Cluj-Napoca
Bordeaux
Dordogne
Lyon
Graz
Garonne
Milan
ROMANIA
Bilbao
Zagreb
Porto
Turin
Venice
Sava
Douro
Pyrenees
Ebro
Genoa
Belgrade
Bucharest
PORTUGAL
SPAIN
Gulf of Lions
MONACO
SAN MARINO
YUGOSLAVIA
Danube
Lisbon
Madrid
Balkan Mts.
Tagus
Barcelona
Corsica
ADRIATIC SEA
Sofia
BULGARIA
Guadiana
VATICAN CITY
Rome
Skopje
Valencia
C. de São Vincent
Balearic Is.
Minorca
Sardinia
Naples
Tiranë
ALBANIA
Istanbul
Sea of Marmara
Cádiz
Málaga
Str. of Gibraltar
ALGERIAN PLAIN
TYRRHENIAN SEA
TYRRHENIAN BASIN
GREECE
Thessaloníki
Dardanelles
Tangier
GIBRALTAR (U.K.)
C. Teulada
MEDITERRANEAN SEA
Lesvos
Rabat
Oran
Algiers
Palermo
IONIAN SEA
Evvoia
AEGEAN SEA
Izmir
Casablanca
MOROCCO
Tunis
Sicily
Etna 11,053 ft. (3369 m.)
Athens
ALGERIA
TUNISIA
MALTA
Valletta
C. Passero
IONIAN BASIN
C. Tainaron
AFRICA
Crete
0 100 200 300 400 500 MILES
0 100 200 300 400 500 KILOMETERS
© Copyright 1987 by HAMMOND INCORPORATED, Maplewood, N.J.

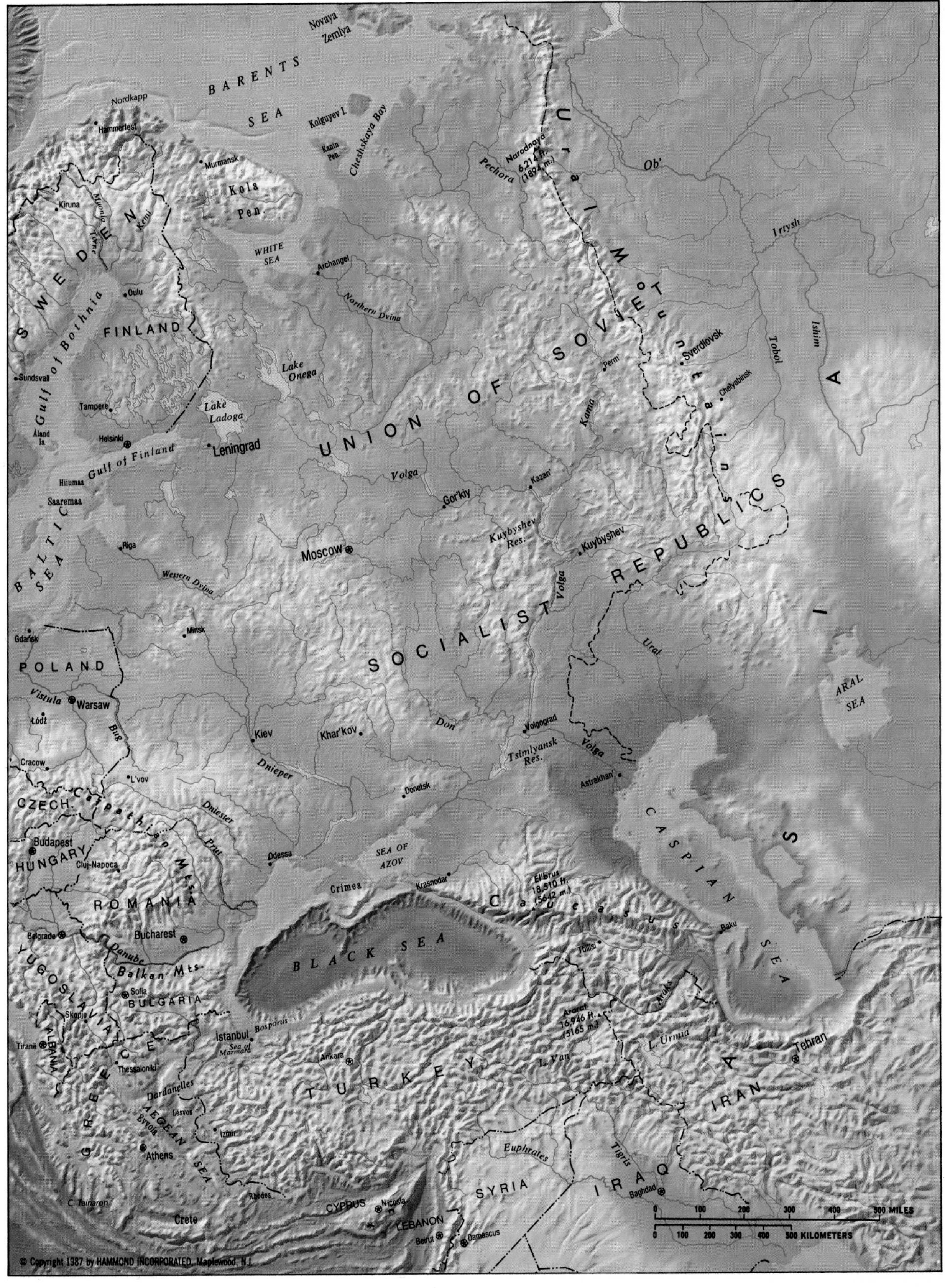
Novaya Zemlya
BARENTS SEA
Nordkapp
Hammerfest
Murmansk
Kola Pen.
Kolguyev I.
Cheshskaya Bay
Kanin Pen.
Narodnaya 6,214 ft. (1894 m.)
Pechora
Ob'
Ural Mts.
Kiruna
Muonio
Torne
Kemi
SWEDEN
WHITE SEA
Archangel
Oulu
Northern Dvina
FINLAND
Gulf of Bothnia
Sundsvall
Tampere
Lake Onega
Lake Ladoga
Helsinki
Åland Is.
Leningrad
Gulf of Finland
Hiiumaa
Saaremaa
BALTIC SEA
Riga
Western Dvina
UNION OF SOVIET SOCIALIST REPUBLICS
Volga
Gor'kiy
Kazan'
Kama
Perm'
Sverdlovsk
Chelyabinsk
Irtysh
Tobol
Ishim
Kuybyshev Res.
Kuybyshev
Moscow
ASIA
Gdańsk
Minsk
POLAND
Vistula
Warsaw
Łódź
Bug
Ural
ARAL SEA
Kiev
Khar'kov
Don
Volgograd
Tsimlyansk Res.
Astrakhan'
Dnieper
Cracow
L'vov
Donetsk
CZECH.
Carpathian Mts.
Dniester
Prut
Budapest
HUNGARY
Cluj-Napoca
Odessa
SEA OF AZOV
CASPIAN SEA
Crimea
Krasnodar
El'brus 18,510 ft. (5642 m.)
Caucasus
ROMANIA
Belgrade
Bucharest
Danube
Baku
BLACK SEA
Tbilisi
YUGOSLAVIA
Balkan Mts.
Sofia
BULGARIA
Skopje
Araks
Ararat 16,946 ft. (5165 m.)
Tiranë
ALBANIA
Istanbul
Bosporus
Sea of Marmara
L. Urmia
Tehran
GREECE
Thessaloniki
Ankara
TURKEY
L. Van
IRAN
Dardanelles
Lesvos
AEGEAN SEA
Evvoia
Izmir
Athens
Euphrates
Tigris
SYRIA
IRAQ
Baghdad
C. Tainaron
Rhodes
CYPRUS
Nicosia
LEBANON
Crete
Beirut
Damascus
0 100 200 300 400 500 MILES
0 100 200 300 400 500 KILOMETERS

AFRICA

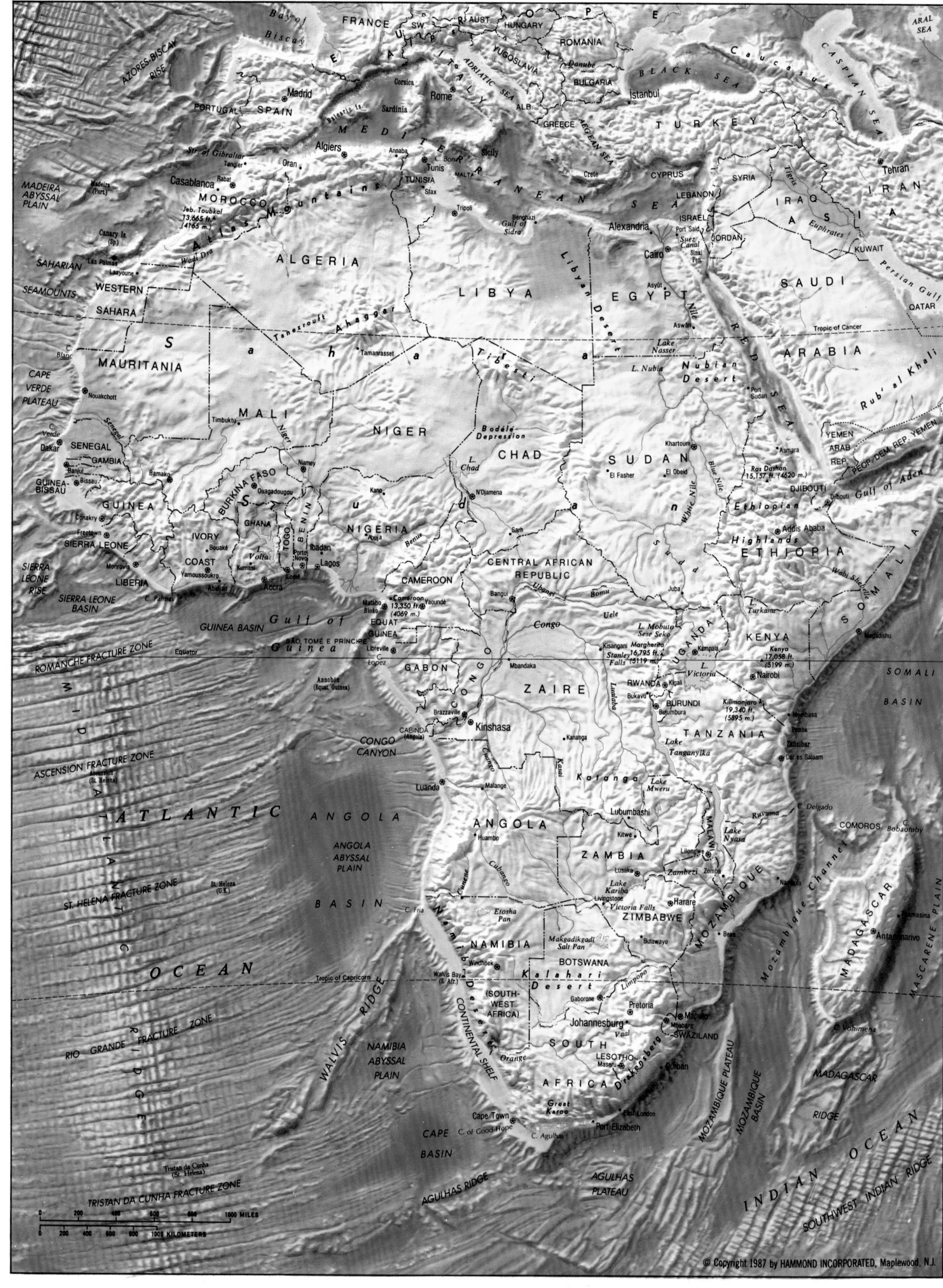

EUROPE
FRANCE
SW.
AUST.
HUNGARY
ROMANIA
YUGOSLAVIA
BULGARIA
ITALY
SPAIN
PORTUGAL
GREECE
TURKEY
Bay of Biscay
AZORES-BISCAY RISE
ARAL SEA
CASPIAN SEA
Caucasus
BLACK SEA
Danube
ADRIATIC SEA
AEGEAN SEA
Istanbul
Madrid
Rome
Corsica
Sardinia
Balearic Is.
Sicily
ALB.
Crete
CYPRUS
MEDITERRANEAN SEA
Str. of Gibraltar
Tangier
Oran
Algiers
Annaba
C. Bon
Tunis
TUNISIA
MALTA
Sfax
Tripoli
Benghazi
Gulf of Sidra
Rabat
Casablanca
MOROCCO
Atlas Mountains
Jeb. Toubkal 13,665 ft. (4165 m.)
Madeira (Port.)
MADEIRA ABYSSAL PLAIN
Canary Is. (Sp.)
Las Palmas
Laayoune
Wadi Dra
SAHARIAN SEAMOUNTS
WESTERN SAHARA
ALGERIA
LIBYA
EGYPT
Libyan Desert
Alexandria
Cairo
Port Said
Suez Canal
Sinai Pen.
Asyût
Aswân
Lake Nasser
L. Nubia
Nubian Desert
Nile
RED SEA
Port Sudan
SYRIA
LEBANON
ISRAEL
JORDAN
IRAQ
IRAN
Tehran
Tigris
Euphrates
KUWAIT
ASIA
Persian Gulf
QATAR
SAUDI ARABIA
Tropic of Cancer
Rub' al Khali
YEMEN ARAB REP.
PEOP. DEM. REP. YEMEN
Gulf of Aden
DJIBOUTI
Djibouti
Asmara
Ras Dashan 15,157 ft. (4620 m.)
Tanezrouft
Ahaggar
Tamanrasset
Tibesti
Sahara
C. Blanc
MAURITANIA
Nouakchott
CAPE VERDE PLATEAU
C. Verde
Dakar
Senegal
SENEGAL
GAMBIA
Banjul
Bissau
GUINEA-BISSAU
GUINEA
Conakry
Freetown
SIERRA LEONE
Monrovia
LIBERIA
C. Palmas
SIERRA LEONE RISE
SIERRA LEONE BASIN
MALI
Timbuktu
Niger
Bamako
BURKINA FASO
Ouagadougou
Niamey
NIGER
Bodélé Depression
L. Chad
CHAD
N'Djamena
Sudan
Kano
NIGERIA
Abuja
Benue
IVORY COAST
Bouaké
Yamoussoukro
Abidjan
GHANA
L. Volta
Kumasi
Accra
TOGO
Lomé
BENIN
Porto-Novo
Ibadan
Lagos
Gulf of Guinea
GUINEA BASIN
ROMANCHE FRACTURE ZONE
Equator
CAMEROON
Cameroon 13,350 ft. (4069 m.)
Yaoundé
Malabo
Bioko
EQUAT. GUINEA
SÃO TOMÉ E PRÍNCIPE
Libreville
C. Lopez
GABON
Annobón (Equat. Guinea)
Sarh
CENTRAL AFRICAN REPUBLIC
Bangui
Ubangi
Bomu
Uele
Congo
Mbandaka
ZAIRE
Lualaba
Kisangani
Stanley Falls
SUDAN
Khartoum
El Fasher
El Obeid
Blue Nile
White Nile
Sudd
Juba
Ethiopian Highlands
Addis Ababa
ETHIOPIA
L. Turkana
SOMALIA
Wabi Shebelle
Mogadishu
KENYA
Kenya 17,058 ft. (5199 m.)
Nairobi
L. Mobutu Sese Seko
Margherita 16,795 ft. (5119 m.)
UGANDA
Kampala
L. Victoria
RWANDA
Kigali
Bukavu
BURUNDI
Bujumbura
Kilimanjaro 19,340 ft. (5895 m.)
TANZANIA
Lake Tanganyika
Mombasa
Pemba
Zanzibar
Dar es Salaam
SOMALI BASIN
Brazzaville
Kinshasa
CABINDA (Angola)
CONGO CANYON
Kasai
Kananga
Katanga
Lake Mweru
Lubumbashi
Luanda
Malange
ANGOLA
Huambo
Cubango
Cunene
ASCENSION FRACTURE ZONE
Ascension (St. Helena)
ATLANTIC OCEAN
MID-ATLANTIC RIDGE
ANGOLA BASIN
ANGOLA ABYSSAL PLAIN
St. Helena (U.K.)
ST. HELENA FRACTURE ZONE
C. Frio
Etosha Pan
ZAMBIA
Lusaka
Zambezi
Lake Kariba
Livingstone
Victoria Falls
Harare
ZIMBABWE
Bulawayo
MALAWI
Lilongwe
Zomba
Lake Nyasa
Ruvuma
C. Delgado
COMOROS
C. Bobaomby
Nacala
MOZAMBIQUE
Beira
Mozambique Channel
MADAGASCAR
Antananarivo
Toamasina
MASCARENE PLAIN
NAMIBIA
Windhoek
Walvis Bay (S. Afr.)
Namib Desert
Makgadikgadi Salt Pan
BOTSWANA
Kalahari Desert
Tropic of Capricorn
Limpopo
Gaborone
Pretoria
Maputo
Mbabane
SWAZILAND
Johannesburg
Vaal
(SOUTH-WEST AFRICA)
SOUTH AFRICA
Orange
LESOTHO
Maseru
Drakensberg
Durban
Great Karoo
East London
Port Elizabeth
Cape Town
C. of Good Hope
C. Agulhas
C. Vohimena
WALVIS RIDGE
CONTINENTAL SHELF
NAMIBIA ABYSSAL PLAIN
RIO GRANDE FRACTURE ZONE
CAPE BASIN
AGULHAS RIDGE
AGULHAS PLATEAU
MOZAMBIQUE PLATEAU
MOZAMBIQUE BASIN
MADAGASCAR RIDGE
INDIAN OCEAN
SOUTHWEST INDIAN RIDGE
Tristan da Cunha (St. Helena)
TRISTAN DA CUNHA FRACTURE ZONE
0 200 400 600 800 1000 MILES
0 200 400 600 800 1000 KILOMETERS

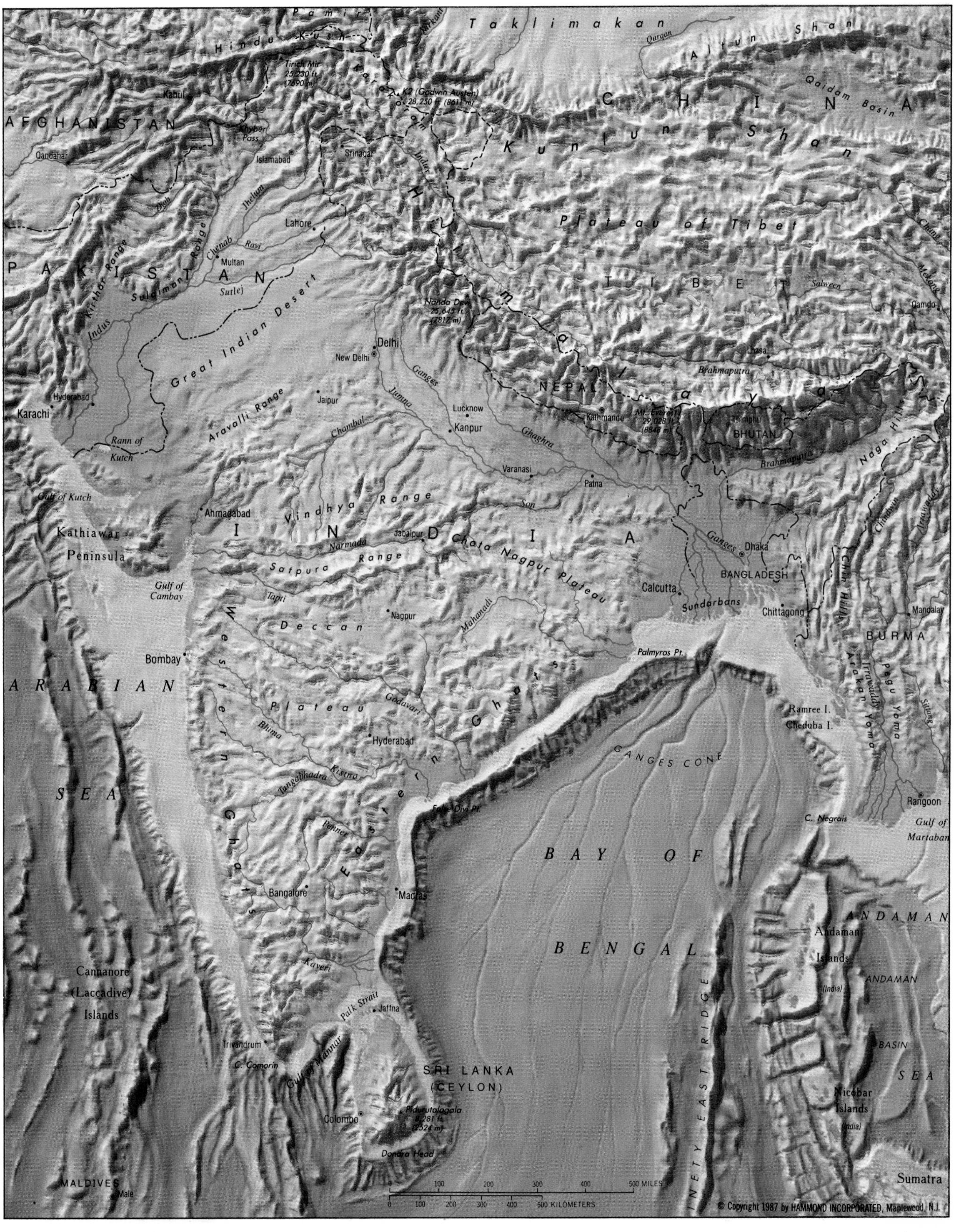
Pamir
Hindu Kush
Tirich Mir
25,230 ft.
(7690 m)
Karakoram
K2 (Godwin Austen)
28,250 ft. (8611 m)
Taklimakan
Qargan
Altun Shan
Qaidam Basin
CHINA
Kunlun Shan
Kabul
AFGHANISTAN
Khyber Pass
Qandahar
Islamabad
Srinagar
Indus
Jhelum
Lahore
Chenab
Ravi
Multan
Sutlej
PAKISTAN
Kirthar Range
Sulaiman Range
Plateau of Tibet
TIBET
Salween
Mekong
Qamdo
Himalaya
Nanda Devi
25,645 ft.
(7817 m)
Great Indian Desert
Delhi
New Delhi
Ganges
Lhasa
Brahmaputra
NEPAL
Kathmandu
Mt. Everest
29,028 ft.
(8848 m)
Thimphu
BHUTAN
Hyderabad
Karachi
Jaipur
Aravalli Range
Jumna
Lucknow
Kanpur
Chambal
Ghaghra
Rann of Kutch
Varanasi
Patna
Naga Hills
Gulf of Kutch
Ahmadabad
Vindhya Range
Son
Chindwin
Irrawaddy
Kathiawar Peninsula
INDIA
Jabalpur
Narmada
Chota Nagpur Plateau
Dhaka
Satpura Range
BANGLADESH
Gulf of Cambay
Tapti
Calcutta
Sundarbans
Chittagong
Chin Hills
Mandalay
Nagpur
Deccan
Mahanadi
BURMA
Bombay
Palmyras Pt.
Arakan Yoma
Pegu Yoma
Sittang
ARABIAN SEA
Western Ghats
Plateau
Godavari
Eastern Ghats
Ramree I.
Cheduba I.
Bhima
Hyderabad
Kistna
GANGES CONE
Tungabhadra
False Divi Pt.
Rangoon
C. Negrais
Gulf of Martaban
Penner
BAY OF BENGAL
Bangalore
Madras
ANDAMAN SEA
Andaman Islands
(India)
ANDAMAN BASIN
Kaveri
Cannanore
(Laccadive)
Islands
Palk Strait
Jaffna
Trivandrum
C. Comorin
Gulf of Mannar
SRI LANKA
(CEYLON)
NINETY EAST RIDGE
Nicobar Islands
(India)
Pidurutalagala
8,281 ft.
(2524 m)
Colombo
Dondra Head
MALDIVES
Male
Sumatra
0 100 200 300 400 500 MILES
0 100 200 300 400 500 KILOMETERS
© Copyright 1987 by HAMMOND INCORPORATED, Maplewood, N.J.

EAST AND SOUTHEAST ASIA

Bering Strait
St. Lawrence I.
BEAUFORT SEA
CANADA BASIN
Pt. Barrow
BEAUFORT SHELF
Brooks Range
Alaska Range
Queen Elizabeth Islands
Ellesmere I.
GREENLAND (Den.)
ICELAND
Reykjavík
Denmark Strait
ICELAND BASIN
IRMINGER BASIN
REYKJANES RIDGE
Melville I.
Banks I.
Parry Channel
Devon I.
Baffin Bay
Baffin I.
Davis Strait
Arctic Circle
Nuuk
C. Farewell
Victoria I.
Great Bear L.
Mackenzie
Gulf of Alaska
Yellowknife
Great Slave L.
Alexander Arch.
Prince Rupert
Queen Charlotte Is.
L. Athabasca
Athabasca
Peace
Churchill
Nelson
CANADA
Hudson Bay
Ungava Peninsula
LABRADOR BASIN
LABRADOR SEA
C. Chidley
Smallwood Res.
Churchill
Newfoundland
Gander
St. John's
C. Race
GRAND BANKS OF NEWFOUNDLAND
Gulf of St. Lawrence
Cape Breton I.
Laurentian Plateau
James Bay
Rupert
Albany
North Saskatchewan
Edmonton
Saskatchewan
South
Calgary
Saskatoon
Regina
L. Winnipeg
Winnipeg
Red
Vancouver I.
Victoria
Vancouver
Columbia
Seattle
Mt. Rainier
Portland
Missouri
Thunder Bay
L. Superior
Duluth
Sudbury
St. Lawrence
Québec
Montréal
Ottawa
St. John
Halifax
Minneapolis
Mississippi
L. Michigan
L. Huron
Toronto
L. Ontario
Buffalo
Boston
GEORGES BANK
C. Cod
Milwaukee
Detroit
L. Erie
Cleveland
New York
Chicago
Pittsburgh
Philadelphia
Columbus
Washington
Indianapolis
Cincinnati
Ohio
Norfolk
C. Hatteras
C. Mendocino
Great Basin
Great Salt Lake
Salt Lake City
San Francisco
Sierra Nevada
North Platte
South Platte
Omaha
Denver
Pikes Peak 14,110 ft. (4301 m.)
Kansas City
UNITED STATES
St. Louis
Mt. Whitney
Las Vegas
Colorado
Arkansas
Wichita
Ozark Plateau
Nashville
Mt. Mitchell 6,684 ft. (2037 m.)
Tennessee
Charlotte
Memphis
Tulsa
Los Angeles
San Diego
Phoenix
Albuquerque
Oklahoma City
Red
Birmingham
Atlanta
Appalachian Mts.
CONTINENTAL SHELF
HATTERAS ABYSSAL PLAIN
BERMUDA RISE
Bermuda (U.K.)
Tucson
Gulf of California
El Paso
Ciudad Juárez
Rio Grande
Fort Worth
Dallas
Jacksonville
Guadalupe (Mex.)
MOLOKAI FRACTURE ZONE
San Antonio
Houston
New Orleans
Florida
C. Canaveral
Tampa
Pen.
NARES ABYSSAL PLAIN
Tropic of Cancer
Chihuahua
Sierra Madre Occidental
Corpus Christi
Gulf of Mexico
Miami
Nassau
BAHAMAS
West Indies
PUERTO RICO TRENCH
Turks and Caicos Is. (U.K.)
Culiacán
Monterrey
C. San Lucas
SIGSBEE DEEP
Havana
CUBA
Sierra Madre Oriental
MEXICO
Tampico
CAMPECHE BANK
Bay of Campeche
Mérida
Yucatán Pen.
YUCATAN BASIN
CAYMAN TRENCH
Greater Antilles
HAITI
DOM. REP.
Santo Domingo
San Juan
PUERTO RICO
CLARION FRACTURE ZONE
Guadalajara
Mexico City
Veracruz
Revillagigedo Is. (Mex.)
JAMAICA
BELIZE
CARIBBEAN SEA
NICARAGUA RISE
Acapulco
MIDDLE AMERICA TRENCH
GUATEMALA
Guatemala
HONDURAS
Tegucigalpa
EL SALVADOR
San Salvador
NICARAGUA
Managua
COLOMBIA BASIN
NETH. ANT.
ARUBA (Neth.)
Curaçao
VENEZ. BASIN
Caracas
VENEZUELA
Orinoco
Barranquilla
Panama Canal
Panama
PANAMA
COSTA RICA
San José
SOUTH AMERICA
Magdalena
Bogotá
COLOMBIA
CLIPPERTON FRACTURE ZONE
Clipperton (Fr.)
MILES
KILOMETERS
GUATEMALA BASIN
Cocos I. (C.R.)
PACIFIC OCEAN
ATLANTIC OCEAN
© Copyright 1987 by HAMMOND INCORPORATED, Maplewood, N.J.

SOUTH AMERICA

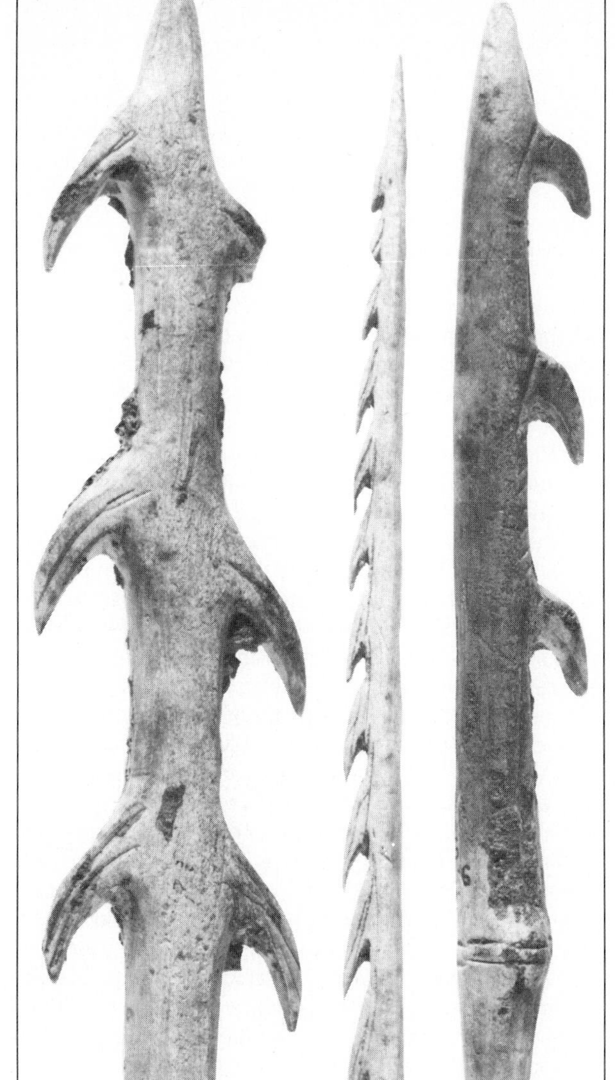

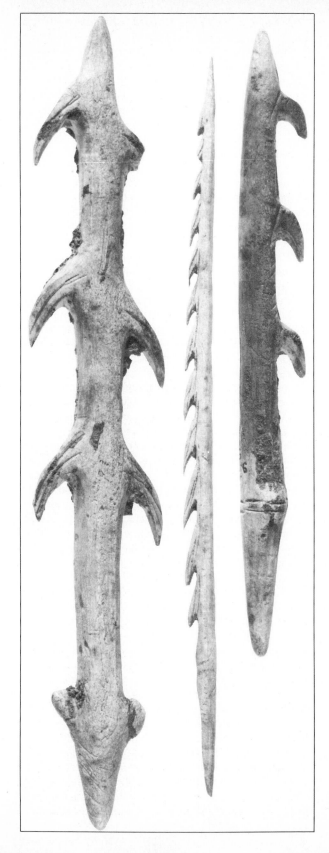

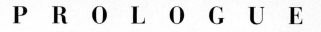

PROLOGUE

History and the Origins of Civilization

This book tells the story of humans through their experience in civilizations throughout the world. The human species has existed for some millions of years, and human cultures for tens and perhaps hundreds of thousands of years. Only within the past 6,000, however, have these cultures exhibited the form that we call civilization. A civilization is a culture characterized by the building of cities, the development of a social and political structure through class differentiation, and the evolution of an economic structure through a formalized division of labor. Civilization implies the growth of familial groups to embrace outsiders, although clan and kinship patterns may remain important even in the most highly developed civilizations.

Civilization also entails the keeping of records, and for this purpose the development of a system of writing. The first records were kept for the everyday purposes of levying taxes, compiling inventories, and setting down business transactions. But they were also kept for compiling royal genealogies, ordering sacred texts, and preserving the accounts of military expeditions. From these latter functions slowly evolved the idea of keeping chronologies of major events, particularly of religious or political significance, and, in time, the notion of binding these together

Bone harpoons from western France, about 14,000 years old. [British Museum]

in the form of a narrative. Such narratives of past events came to be called histories. History as a human activity thus grows out of the basic processes of civilization itself and, in its most developed form, is not just the record of civilization but of civilization's way of reflecting upon itself. In this sense, history and civilization are inseparable.

The Nature of History

The uses of history have been understood in many ways. Herodotus, the classical Greek historian, declared that his purpose in publishing a history of the Persian wars of the early fifth century B.C. was "to preserve from decay the remembrance of what men have done, and of preventing the great and wonderful actions of the Greeks and the barbarians [i.e., the Persians] from losing their due meed of glory."[1] For Herodotus, history was the record of deeds of valor, a view that necessarily excluded much of human experience, particularly that of women.

Although Herodotus emphasized the importance of remembering great heroes, his aim was not merely to encourage passive recollection but to inspire emulation in his readers. Later historians would argue that the study of the past was essential to understanding the present and predicting the future. In its most radical forms, history has been presented as envisioning the end of the world in a day of judgment or other apocalyptic event or as revealing inevitable progress toward a perfect society. Even for those whose claims are more modest, history has almost always been presented as an essential part of the knowledge of educated women and men.

History therefore consists of far more than the simple chronicle of past events. The historian is not the mere conservator of the past but in an important sense its active shaper. To study the past is to help mold the future by providing the basis for informed judgments. The cultural memory of societies that have not developed civilized forms, such as the aborigines of Australia or the Indians of Brazil, appears to be largely an effort to preserve traditional skills, stories, and folkways. The historical consciousness of modern civilized society, even when it results in an attempt to return to past values, is inseparable from the attempt to consider options and to make choices.

In this sense, history is a living process that involves the discussion and interpretation of issues that affect the lives of millions. Not surprisingly, therefore, historians often differ in the philosophical approach they bring to their material. Even with the best of intentions it is virtually impossible to remain neutral in discussing human affairs. Some historians reflect a predetermined ideological position. Others have written either in defense of or in opposition to a particular political regime or point of view. All historians necessarily reflect their time and culture and their own position in that culture.

A major factor in the response of historians to past events has been their religion. The Christian and Islamic historians of the Middle Ages, for example, viewed the past through the lens of their faiths, whereas the secular, rationalistic outlook of the eighteenth-century British author Edward Gibbon led him to discuss Christianity in largely negative terms. Others, such as Herodotus and the sixteenth-century Florentine Niccolò Machiavelli, seem to have been motivated by curiosity about the mainsprings of human behavior. Still others, from the Greco-Roman Polybius to the twentieth-century historian Arnold Toynbee, have sought to find patterns and cycles of repetition in past events. In contrast to this has been the conviction, especially strong since the early Christian period, that a study of history reveals a constant improvement in human life in accordance with a divine scheme.

The concept of human progress, so characteristic of the modern industrialized world, itself raises fundamental questions. The rapid technological developments of the twentieth century have encouraged the belief that people somehow live better than they used to, but this is by no means universally true. Nor is the idea of progress basic to all human cultures; most civilizations have looked back to a supposed golden age, of which they were the humble descendants, or have seen history as a series of ups and downs rather than a forward progression. This was the historical perspective of most of the great Asian civilizations, for example. Improvement, moreover, is often in the eye of the beholder. Few people would dispute that the abolition of slavery in most of the world is a great gain or that today's medical care is superior to that of the eighteenth century. These same advances, however, have also contributed to a world population explosion and the actual decline of basic living standards in the poorer regions of the globe. It would be hard to argue that contemporary Chinese art and architecture are better than those of 1,000 years ago, and many of the results of industrialization, including air and water pollution, have worsened rather than improved the quality of life.

We should expect history neither to determine our future nor to impose neat patterns on the past. The aim should rather be to establish as clear an understanding as possible of past events and cultures. This is, needless to say, no easy task. Political conquerors of all ages have manipulated the truth for their own ends, making it vitally necessary for the historian to weigh the surviving evidence with great care. Furthermore, vast numbers of people—the slaves of ancient Egypt or nineteenth-century America, women in the Muslim world, peasants everywhere—lived lives that are difficult to document individually. The result is a historical picture that depends on sources that are inevitably biased. In the case of more recent times there is some possibility of setting the record straight: the true nature of the forced labor camps of Stalinist Russia or the Nazi extermination camps has emerged despite attempts to conceal or destroy the record. In assessing the history of the distant past, historians can try to speculate, to read between the lines, to make use of new discoveries and advanced research techniques to refine the traditional picture. Nor is nearness or remoteness in time the sole criterion for historical accessibility. Much more is known about life in Athens or China of the fifth century B.C. than of Africa or North America in the fifteenth century A.D.

Sources

In seeking to understand the past, historians have a wide range of materials on which to draw. There are the accounts by their predecessors and the commentaries on them. Second, there are descriptions of events by those who took part in them; although these are hardly likely to be impartial, they provide valuable insights. Third, there is a wide spectrum of documentary records, ranging from the imperial bureaucratic records of the Han or T'ang dynasties in China to the archives of modern cities and the parish registers of churches. In many cases these documents are still lying unstudied in libraries or public offices, and many of the new historical discoveries being made today come from diligent research in the bureaucratic and archival records of the past. Buildings and monuments are records of the past as well. Clothing styles and common utensils tell us much about the tastes and even the social structure of bygone times. Even fecal remains have taught us much about ancient and prehistoric diets. Few surviving objects cannot tell us something of importance about the past, and although written records have always had a special importance for the historian, other evidence can, to the trained observer, often be as revealing.

In addition, there is the evidence produced by art. A tendency exists today to draw a distinction between the arts and other social, political, and economic pursuits. For most earlier ages such a separation would have been meaningless. The cathedrals of medieval Europe and the Buddhist sculptures of classical India, to cite but two examples, had a profound effect on all levels of the societies exposed to them and a cultural significance that penetrated every aspect of social activity. Through music we can come into contact directly with the emotional experience of bygone times. Every work of art has much to tell the historian about the age and the people who created it.

To the sources just described must be added those produced by the related disciplines of archaeology, anthropology, and psychology. The archaeologist seeks to study the past by retrieving and analyzing its material remains, whether they be ruins, inscriptions, pots, or graves. Anthropologists have used present models of social behavior in an attempt to reconstruct those of the past. Far more controversial is "psychohistory," the attempt to apply psychological theories and models to account for the behavior of historical personalities.

The historian of more recent times has a wide range of additional material in the form of films, recordings, and other products of the era of mass communication. Magazines, newspapers, film, photography, popular literature, and songs are valuable sources of historical evidence. In the case of recent events, oral accounts can provide significant information. If ancient historians must often literally dig in the dirt for their information, or struggle to infer the technology and commerce of an entire culture from a handful of coins, modern historians are frequently inundated with data, much of which they must learn to sift rapidly and discard. If the evidence available to ancient historians is almost always less than they would like, the material available to modern historians is often more than they can use.

Time

The ordering of time is basic to any study of the past. Events must be examined in relation to those that precede and follow them. Yet even the simplest chronology often poses a challenge. The dating of events in ancient cultures, for example, is dependent on our knowledge of their calendar systems, which are often extremely complex, both numerically and symbolically. Such calendars are not mere units of convenience, but semisacred codes that touch on the most basic questions of ordering human experience. Traces of this remain in our modern religious calendars and in such customs as observances of the equinox and Halloween.

At the same time, all notions of time are relative. Our most common experience is the alternation of light and dark that we call a day, yet the periods in this alternation vary from one latitude to another, and at the poles the sun at times never sets. We mark the seasons by periods of recurrent temperature, rainfall, vegetation, and the progression of the stars, yet these too vary with geography.

All of these experiences have a circular character, in which we periodically return to a point of observation from which we had moved away. At the same time, we are conscious of the linear aspect of time in the biological facts of birth, aging, and death. Our conception of time is thus a compound of circular and linear elements that combine into larger patterns of passage and recurrence. We must take account not only of things that appear to change little if at all, such as the regular phases of the moon or the annual positions of the stars, but also of those that change rapidly and unpredictably, such as the forms of life.

A calendar is a compromise that combines both circular and linear patterns of our experience into a single system. It is based on the most immediate patterns of recurrence (days, months, seasons, years), but it imposes a linear progression on them by the device of numbering and counting. Our most general ideas about history, too, tend to be either circular or linear, or an attempt to combine the two. Circular theories of history tend to emphasize the theme of recurrently rising and falling civilizations, while linear theories stress the idea of progress, whether along an indefinite path or toward a final destination.

The Western world has used the birth of Jesus and thus of Christianity as the principal dividing point in history; all historical dates are commonly expressed as B.C. (before Christ) or A.D. (Anno Domini, "Year of our Lord"). This system, so familiar to us (although its actual use dates only from the seventeenth century), has far less cultural significance for much of the non-Western world, yet it is now universally understood and widely accepted. Nonetheless, it is by no means the only historical reference point in use today. Jewish and Muslim history have their own dates of origin and continue to keep their own calendars. We have adopted the Western convention in this work.

Fields of History

Chronology is only one tool of history. It is especially important for the study of political or military history, where a grasp of the sequence of events is essential. Some historians prefer to deal with different areas of human experience. Social history is concerned with the general question of social organization and behavior in the past. Interaction between the sexes, attitudes toward death, the rearing of children, class and kinship structure, patterns of mobility, the rules of inheritance and property, and the formation of elites are all concerns of the social historian. A special aspect of social organization is the study of urban life, one of the key distinguishing marks of civilization. Here, too, the material evidence is generally more plentiful, and shifting social patterns are easier to discern than in the more slowly changing life of the countryside. Most of the following chapters include portraits of individual cities and their lifestyles. Cities have changed greatly in size and structure through the centuries, and yet they exhibit many common characteristics and functions over time. A modern walker in ancient Rome, with its crowded apartment buildings and narrow traffic-clogged streets, would find many parallels with the urban capitals of today.

Economic, demographic, and environmental history, too, is crucial to an understanding of the past. The movement of people, the flow of trade, the development of technology and its diffusion by contact and exchange, the fluctuations in population and in the rates of birth and death, and the changing patterns of climate all contribute to our perception of human dealings with the world, with each other, and with survival, creating and sustaining the uniquely human construct we call civilization.

The history of ideas also casts light on the general principles and assumptions of society, the transmission of elite norms, the interplay and conflict of cultural values, and the common threads that unite such diverse cultural products as religion, art, science, and law. Indeed, virtually no aspect of human behavior can fail to cast some light on the period from which it comes to the attentive observer, since few people have ever lived isolated or cut off from their times. A historian might well quote the words of the Roman dramatist Terence, writing in the second century B.C.: *Nihil humanum alienum a me puto*—"I regard nothing human as alien to me."

Human Origins

General scientific consensus places the age of the earth at 5 or 6 billion years. The appearance of human beings was comparatively recent, perhaps 2 to 4 million years ago, and the development of civilization occupies only the past 6,000 years or so.

The evolution of *Homo sapiens*, beings with the same physical characteristics that we possess, was a long and complex process that is still imperfectly understood. The earliest evidence for the existence of *Australopithecus*, or "southern ape," dates from approximately 2 million years ago and comes from the temperate regions of Africa and western Asia (now known as the Middle East). These remote ancestors of the human race stood and walked on their back feet and had a brain large and complex enough to make use of tools. Some anthropologists do not recognize *Australopithecus* as a hominid, or humanlike creature, but all scholars accept *Homo erectus* as one. *Homo erectus* probably originated in Africa and then migrated into western and southern Asia and Europe.

The principal material of the tools hominids used was stone, and the first (and by far the longest) period in human history is therefore known as the Stone Age. Human culture evolved slowly in this period: the Paleolithic, or

Skull of *Australopithecus boisei*, an early hominid, found in the Olduvai Gorge, Tanzania. [David Brill]

Old Stone Age, lasted from the earliest appearance of hominid forms to around 15,000 years ago. The slow development of tools from primitive chips of stone to sophisticated small tools known as microliths was accompanied by important global climatic and topographical changes caused by movements of the polar ice cap.

Toward the end of the Paleolithic Age, a new species of hominid appeared, *Homo neanderthalis*, so named because his remains were discovered in the Neander River valley in modern Germany. Like their ancestors, Neanderthal people probably lived on food they could gather or hunt—roots and berries, birds, fish, and the few larger mammals, such as goats and deer, that they could trap. Yet in the midst of this precarious existence a major development occurred in the patterns of human behavior, for the Neanderthal people were apparently the first to bury their dead in graves and cemeteries; it is conceivable that the objects they left with the bodies indicate belief in an afterlife. Furthermore, the caves in and around which much of Neanderthal life took place, with their huge stone fireplaces, suggest some kind of communal existence and organized group activity.

Our picture of Neanderthal people is based on the tools they made and the caves and holes in which they lived, in addition, of course, to the study of their skeletal remains. The end of the Paleolithic period is suddenly illuminated by the first works of art in human history. *Homo neanderthalis* became extinct about 30,000 to 35,000 years ago, and the human culture that replaced it is traditionally known as Cro-Magnon, from the name of the cave in southwestern France where important discoveries about these people were made. A number of the caves inhabited by the Cro-Magnon people were decorated with wall paintings, dating to around 16,000 years ago, that depict animals—some being chased in the hunt, others quietly grazing. The scenes were clearly not intended to give visual pleasure; indeed, their location in remote, dark caverns means that few except their makers would have seen them, and their purpose was probably related to some kind of magical ritual involving the hunt. Yet in its vivid expression of movement and elegance of line, the cave art of Lascaux and other sites shows a strong urge to artistic expression. For the first time humans left a record of the way they observed the world around them.

The earliest representations of the human figure date to the same period. Almost all of them are of women whose sexual characteristics are depicted in enlarged or exaggerated form. This suggests that women's role as the source of birth and life played as important a cultural role in the late Paleolithic world as the male-dominated hunt.

Cro-Magnon culture was marked by important technological advances. The use of materials other than stone, such as ivory and deer antlers, permitted the construction of tools such as darts, fishhooks, and the bow and arrow. The sewing together of animal skins provided Cro-Magnon people with clothing. Most significant, evidence from the cave sites where they lived suggests that they occupied them for periods of several years: earlier nomadic ways had begun to change into more settled patterns of domicile.

The Laussel Venus, a stone relief carving from Les Eyzies. [Musée d'Aquitaine, Bordeaux]

Recent archaeological research suggests that some of the people of this age, although hunter-gatherers, were the first to settle in permanent communities, with facilities for the storage of food, patterns of trade that extended over long distances, and social and political hierarchies. The existence of such hierarchies is suggested by standardized beads and pendants made by western European foragers as long as 32,000 years ago. These people also knew how to fire clay to make ceramics. In central Russia archaeologists have found the remains of elaborate settlements constructed of mammoth bones; the people who lived here some 20,000 years ago traded for materials from the Black Sea region, 500 miles away. Presumably they stored their food because their population was expanding, although this practice limited their mobility. As they settled into permanent communities, internal conflicts must have occurred, leading to the development of social and political organization to maintain order. Probably because of climatic changes, this society came to an end some 12,000 years ago, when the Europeans broke up into small bands and returned to a nomadic life.

The last period of the Stone Age, the Neolithic, or New Stone Age, saw the discovery of new techniques of production, including tools for grinding and polishing. Far more significant for the development of civilization, however, was the invention of new methods of agriculture and animal breeding that occurred in various parts of the world beginning some 10,000 years ago. The changes in lifestyle they made possible represent one of the most revolutionary developments in history.

The Agricultural Revolution

Agriculture was the principal technological advance that made civilization possible, but the process of its development was a long one. Neolithic culture eventually spread throughout the entire world, taking different forms in varying regions, but always with the same basic characteristics. For the first time humans began to manipulate the local environment and to create systems of selective food production. It is generally believed that farming techniques were first developed in Asia, where wheat and other cereal grains have been found growing in a wild form and where wild pigs, sheep, and goats were relatively common. None of these animals was native to Europe, and the same is true of wheat and barley. The only cereal native to the Americas is maize (corn).

The theory that farming techniques originated in Asia has received further support from excavations in Iraq and Palestine. Around 7000 B.C., sites such as Jericho and Jarmo supported populations of some 3,000 people who had already developed food production techniques to provide self-sufficiency. Jericho, with its round mud-brick houses and 20-foot-high defense wall, may have been the earliest city in history. From this area the revived concept of permanent settlements, together with the agricultural methods that made them possible, spread westward to Europe. The earliest buildings at Karanovo, in modern Bulgaria, date to the end of the sixth millennium B.C., around the time that settlers had arrived on what was to become the Greek mainland.

The spread eastward was somewhat slower. The earliest settlements in India were small farming villages in Baluchistan and lower Sind that date to the fourth millennium B.C., and it may have taken another millennium before crop growing became established in China. North Africa, by contrast, physically close to Europe and western Asia, soon acquired the new techniques. Fully developed Neolithic culture existed in Egypt by 5000 B.C., and from

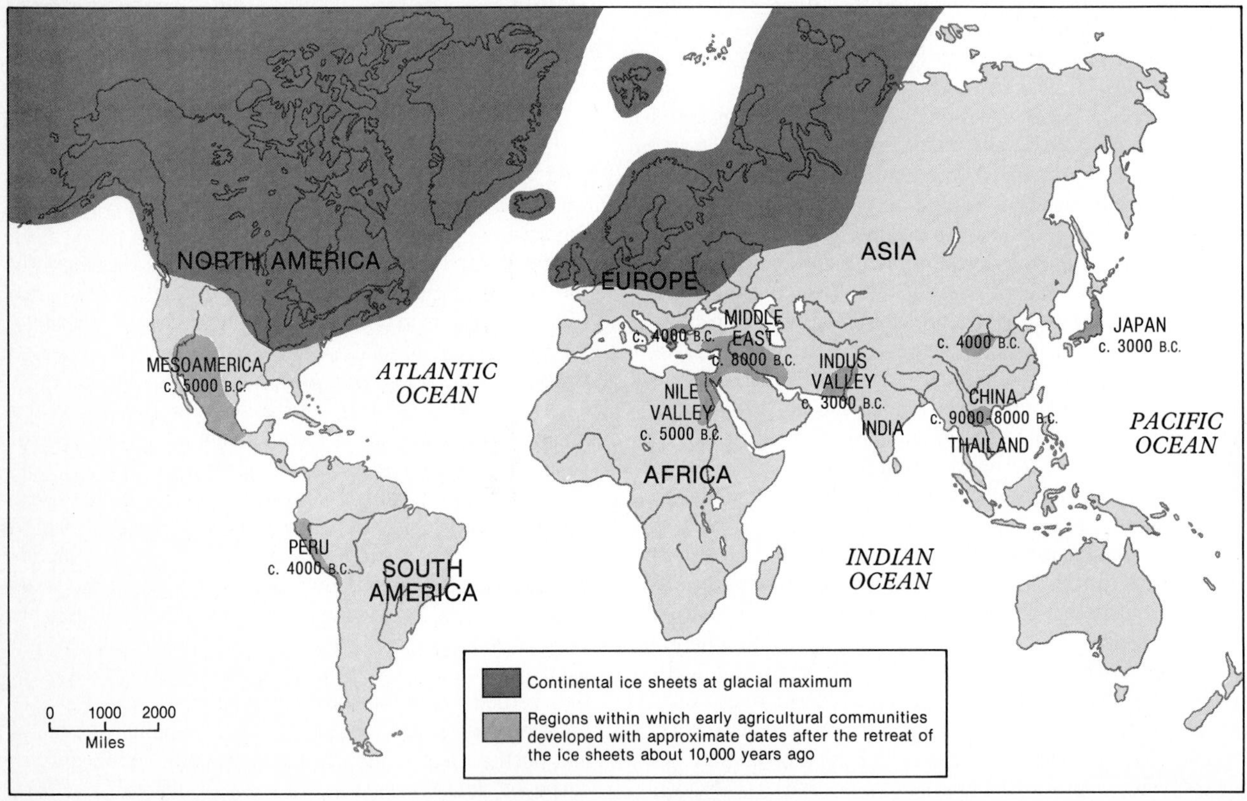

P.1 The Development of Agriculture

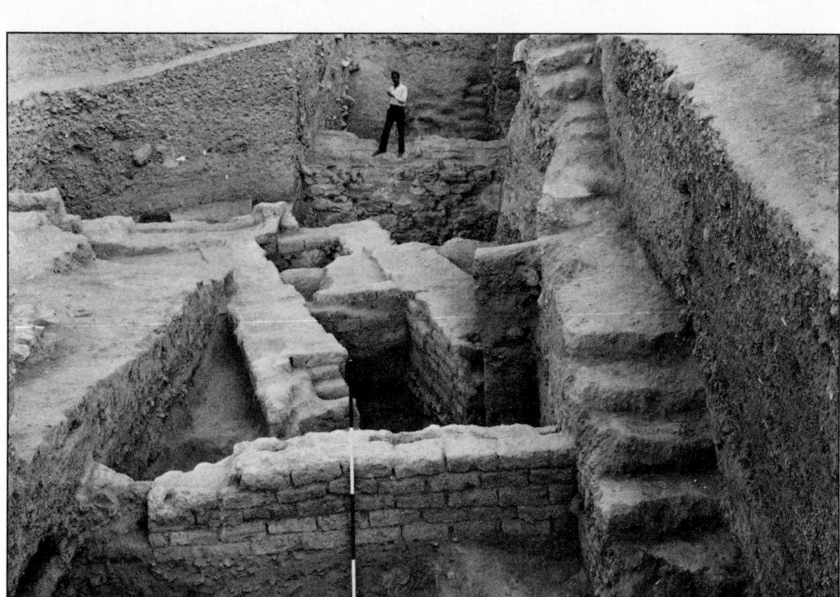

The ruins of Jericho, the oldest city to have been excavated. [British School of Archaeology at Jerusalem]

there farming spread gradually through the African continent. In the Americas agricultural communities developed more slowly than in Asia and Europe, but by about 2000 B.C. sufficient amounts of food were being grown to make permanent settlements possible.

Agriculture based on tropical crops, especially root crops, appeared in Southeast Asia by 5000 B.C., and was almost certainly independent of the beginnings of grain agriculture in western Asia, many thousands of miles away. The year-round warmth and moisture of most of Southeast Asia gave it strong advantages for sustained cultivation. Rice was native to this area also. Originally a swamp plant, it was adapted to upland fields or to irrigated paddies with relative ease. Pigs, chickens, and water buffalo were native to the region, and the former two soon spread among the late Neolithic cultures elsewhere in Eurasia.

Food supply could be supplemented by fish and shellfish at or near the many coastal sites. Gathering cultures began the transition to planted and tended fields and the return to permanent settlements by 8000 B.C. or so. By about 5000 B.C. these developments had spread into southern and central China, and northern China developed agriculture based on the indigenous crop plant of millet by around 4000 B.C.

Effects of the Agricultural Revolution

With a more settled existence came a host of developments. No longer entirely at the mercy of the weather or forced to seek shelter in caves, Neolithic people lived in houses constructed of mud-brick and wood that gradually formed villages. The domestication of sheep and goats provided milk, meat, and wool, the last of which led to the invention of weaving. The greater range of available food, including surplus grain, may have been the stimulus that led to the production of pottery, since food could be easily prepared, cooked, served, or preserved in pots.

Among other Neolithic innovations were the domestication of animals and the distillation of spirits. One of the first animals to be domesticated was the dog, not for food but as a hunting companion and guard. Another form of satisfaction was discovered around 8000 B.C., when Neolithic people realized that by allowing cereals to ferment they could begin the process of brewing beer. As Neolithic culture moved westward to the area around the Mediterranean, where vines were common, wine production was similarly begun.

These specific improvements in the quality of daily life were naturally accompanied by much broader changes in living patterns. The communities of the Neolithic period needed special forms of social organization to function. Given the scanty evidence, it is possible only to speculate about the nature of society in Neolithic times, based in part on probability and in part on the study of peoples whose culture is still Neolithic, as in the case of the jungle tribes of Brazil. The family unit may well have been important in the Paleolithic period; it almost certainly became the principal social institution for Neolithic culture. Yet the necessity to ensure the discipline of labor in the fields and the specialization introduced by such functions as herding, sowing, and weaving, not to mention defense, must have required broader forms of organization. Thus the need to protect the wealth of the community led to a more elaborate form of government than mere tribal leadership and the establishment of a communal authority.

Although Neanderthal people had probably begun to develop some elements of religion, the complex rituals of

Neolithic culture marked a significant change in its development. It is probable that Neolithic religion was principally concerned with nature and the cycle of the seasons and with the animal and plant world. There has been much speculation as to when it was first realized that human conception was the result of sexual intercourse; certainly the process of birth must have seemed miraculous to Neolithic peoples and their predecessors. From this may have developed the widespread worship of the Earth Mother, who symbolized both human and agricultural fertility and who figured prominently in religions that developed over the succeeding millennia.

The manufacture of decorated pottery and textiles—works of art as well as of utility—may well have been related to the growth of trade, since objects that were distinctive as well as practical would have had obvious attraction. The decoration on Neolithic pottery is sometimes painted or cut and sometimes added in the form of strips or bands of clay. It is always abstract in design, although artists were no doubt inspired by natural forms.

Raw materials as well as manufactured objects were exchanged during the Neolithic period. A study of obsidian (a natural volcanic glass used for flaking and grinding) found at Neolithic sites throughout western Asia has revealed a widespread trading network. Obsidian from central Turkey was discovered at villages within a radius of 200 miles and in smaller quantities farther afield in Syria and the Jordan valley. Presumably, the valuable raw material was exchanged for food or manufactured goods. No doubt there was a great deal of trade or exchange between neighboring communities. Thus the settled character of Neolithic life formed a basis for the development of patterns of economic growth and interdependence.

The Birth of Civilization

The giant strides taken in the Neolithic period dramatically changed the material character of human existence. After millennia of nomadic hunting and gathering, the basis was laid for the development of civilization and the organization of society. Around 4000 B.C. the Neolithic cultures of Mesopotamia and Egypt had reached a point at which they were transformed from agricultural communities into urban cultures that were focused economically and politically around cities. The development of cities was critical to this emergence. The story of Mesopotamian and Egyptian civilization is told in Chapter 1, but it is worth noting some of the reasons that caused civilization to develop first in these two regions.

Among many factors, geography and climate were crucial. Both controlled the nature of food production and determined the avenues for travel, migration, and the transportation of goods and ideas. The discovery of metal and the ability to work it into tools and weapons were also critical in the emergence of Egypt and Mesopotamia. By 4000 B.C. irrigated agriculture had been established in both areas, taking advantage of the rich alluvial (river valley) soils, warm climate, and annual floods of the river valleys and deltas. Production became great enough to support growing numbers of urban, nonfarm people, and the rivers provided an easy means to transport food and other goods to and from the cities.

Metalworking was only one of a number of technological developments that promoted the production and trade that supported urban culture. In both Egypt and Mesopotamia the wheel was introduced, together with the

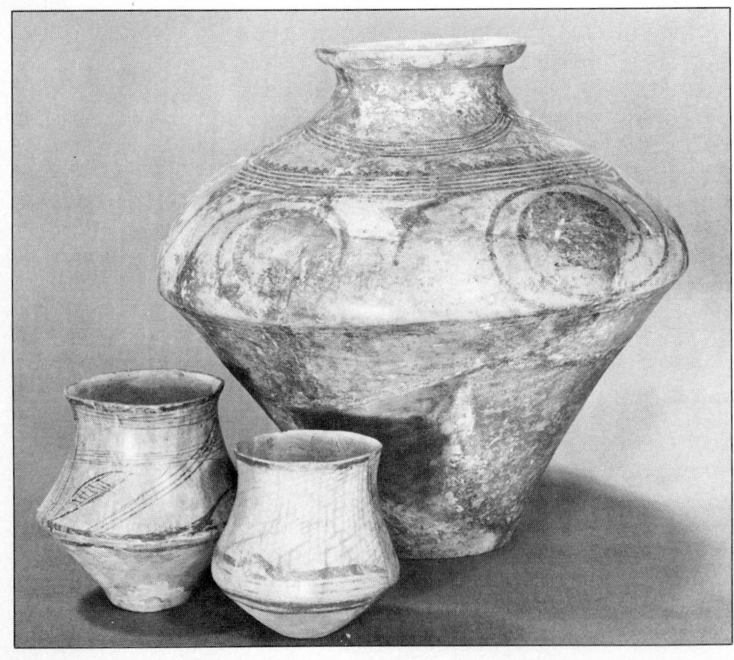

Neolithic pottery from Shipenitsi, USSR. Notice the curvilinear painted decoration. [Ashmolean Museum, Oxford, England]

plough, and oxen were used to till the fields and to transport goods and produce by cart. Both civilizations were dominated by rivers, Egypt by the Nile and Mesopotamia by the Tigris and the Euphrates. By devising methods of boatbuilding and sailing, their peoples learned to transport cargoes by water over large distances and thus began to develop complex trading systems.

The final breakthrough was the Mesopotamians' development of writing in the third millennium B.C. With the possibility of keeping records came all the other uses of a written language, from the inscribing of laws to the creation of literature and the writing of history.

The period of human history covered in these few pages is immeasurably longer than that of the whole of the rest of this book. The principal reason for the apparent lack of balance is, of course, the absence of information for most of the first 2 million years of human existence, although it is surely true that less "happened" for us to be informed about. Viewed from the standpoint of Mesopotamian, Egyptian, Indian, and Chinese history, and the subsequent development of civilizations elsewhere in the world, the Neolithic period and its consequences seem to have laid the course for our own lives today. Yet the 2 million years of human existence that preceded civilization serve as a reminder that modern culture did not simply grow by itself, as a phenomenon of nature, but was produced by the active engagement of humans in social, economic, artistic, and spiritual activities. In that respect, at least, we have much in common with our remote human ancestors.

Notes

1. M. I. Finley, ed., *The Portable Greek Historians* (New York: Penguin Books, 1977), p. 29. See Chapter 4.

PART · ONE

The Peoples and Cultures of Antiquity

By discovering techniques for the organized cultivation of food, the world's first farmers made possible the development of civilization. By producing enough to feed a settled community and leave a surplus, they provided a basis for trade and barter. Other people, freed from the necessity of feeding themselves, could engage in different activities—administration, the organization of religion, and warfare. With the development of specialized crafts, new agricultural methods made possible large urban communities and led to the formation of states. With the need to record transactions came the invention of writing. Stratified social structures appeared together with the division of populations into rulers and ruled. As commerce developed, individuals were better able to communicate wealth and use it as a means to acquire power and influence.

In widely separated parts of the world this process produced the earliest human civilizations—in the river basins of the Tigris and Euphrates in western Asia, the Nile in Egypt, the Indus in India, and the Yellow River in China. If the causes that produced civilization were similar in each case, the characteristics of individual cultures were very different. Conditioned by factors of geography and climate, accessibility to outside influences, and, in some cases, pure chance, the forms of language, art, religion, and almost all aspects of daily life varied widely from region to region.

The application of bronze-working techniques—first in western and southeastern Asia and then in India, China, and Europe—led to further technological progress. With the notable exception of the Chinese, few other Bronze Age cultures had sizable deposits of both copper and tin, the two alloys necessary to produce bronze. This stimulated foreign trade, which was made easier by improved means of transport. Greater wealth led to aggressive economic and territorial expansion.

With the invention of iron smelting, civilization took a new turn. Discovered by the Hittites in western Asia in the mid-second millennium B.C., the technique spread to Europe and to sub-Saharan Africa, where it was possibly diffused from contacts through the upper Nile. New geographic areas began to develop in importance. In western Asia the center of civilization moved from the river basins to what is now Iran, where the Persians flourished. In India culture spread south and east. In Europe civilization gradually expanded westward to Greece and then to Italy.

By the end of classical antiquity in Europe, the world had become sufficiently small for most of the leading civilizations to be in contact with one another. At the peak of their power, the Romans controlled large tracts of Europe and Asia and traded in India and Africa and through central Asian intermediaries with China. Only the Americas and Australasia remained isolated from contact with outside culture.

The first 4,500 years of civilization saw a great variety of artistic and literary creations, much of which not only illuminates remote periods but also retains its power to move and delight. The chief religions of the ancient world serve as a reminder of the common ground of human experience, addressing the eternal problems of existence. ■

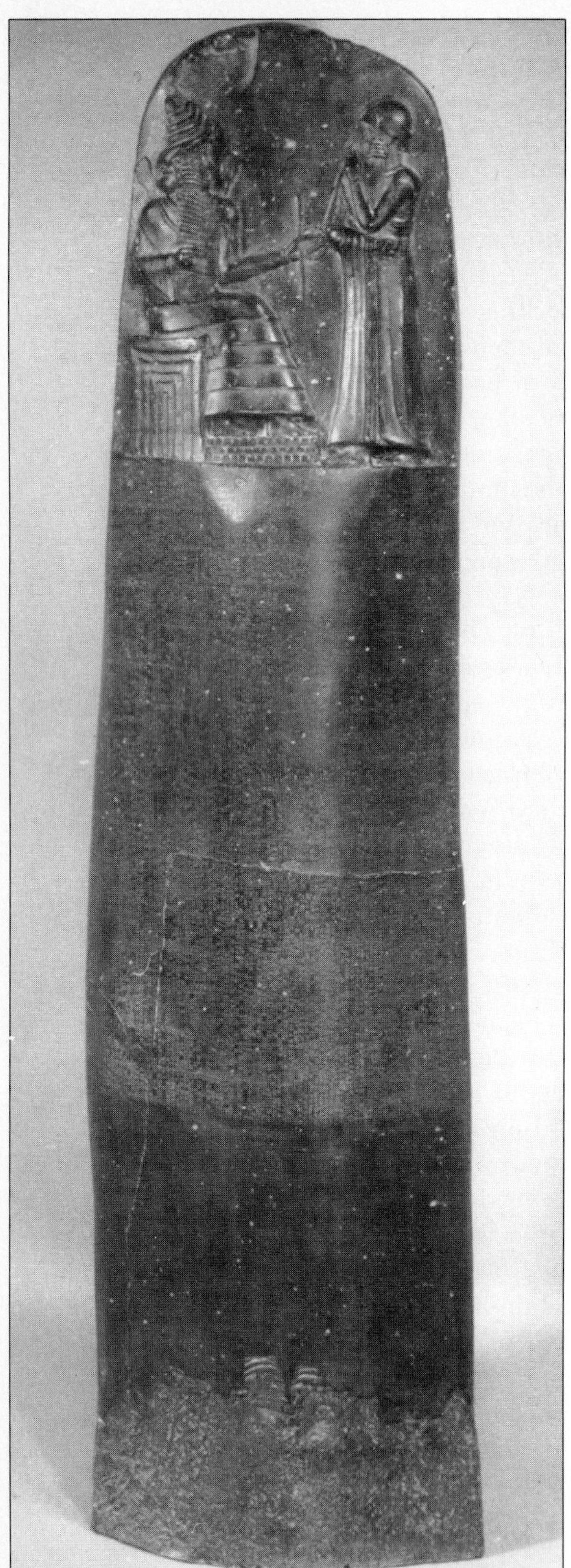

C H A P T E R · 1

The Societies of Western Asia and Egypt

The first civilizations developed in one of the birthplaces of the agricultural revolution, western Asia (now known as the Middle East), and ancient Egypt. Village-level agriculture had appeared earlier, in the uplands west of Mesopotamia and in mainland Southeast Asia. But the peoples of ancient Egypt and Mesopotamia were the first who systematically organized the growing of food in large permanent fields under irrigation, developed improved techniques of mining and metal processing, founded cities, and devised social, legal, and ethical systems as well as institutions of government and religion.

Such large-scale developments were greatly advanced by the discovery and use of new materials. Pottery was produced by at least 5000 B.C. in western and southeastern Asia, and soon afterward metal rather than stone began to be used in the manufacture of tools and weapons. Copper was the earliest material employed, but the technique of alloying copper with tin to produce bronze was soon discovered, probably around 3000 B.C. It was at the fortified settlements of this new Bronze Age in Egypt and Mesopotamia that civilization began. In the centuries that followed, other peoples began to form their own distinctive

Stele of Hammurabi, showing the king in front of the sun god Shamash. Hammurabi's code of law is carved below. [Art Resource, Louvre, Paris]

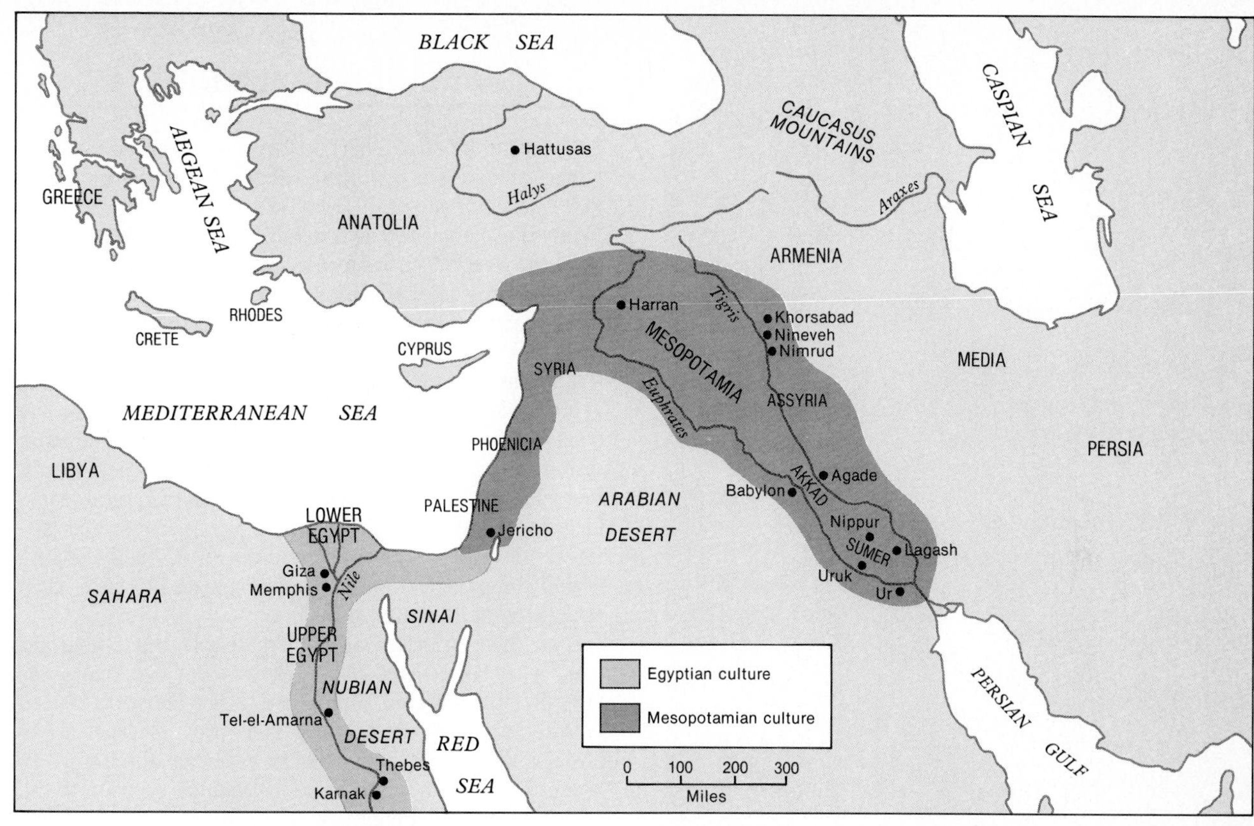

1.1 Western Asia and Egypt

cultures, the most important of which included the Jews, the Hittites, and the Persians.

Egypt and Mesopotamia are dominated by great rivers—Egypt by the Nile, which regularly floods each year, and Mesopotamia by the Tigris and the Euphrates. The annual flooding of the Nile was consistent and predictable, both in its timing and in the configuration of the land that was inundated. As the floodwater receded, seeds were planted in the wet soil; the new surface of fertile silt retained enough moisture to bring the crop to harvest. The Tigris and Euphrates rivers were far more irregular in their flooding, and often wreaked destruction. Protection for farmland was therefore essential, as were means to irrigate the fields. Owing in part to these differences, the cultures of Egypt and Mesopotamia developed in distinctive ways, making a special contribution to the development of civilization.

Life Between the Rivers: The City Dwellers of Mesopotamia

The history of ancient Mesopotamia consists of a series of independent peoples, each having its separate culture. This diversity makes generalization difficult. To complicate the picture, a number of other peoples played a part in Mesopotamian history, notably the Hittites to the northwest and the peoples of ancient Iran to the east, both of whom had periods of prosperity and cultural importance. For the most part, however, the neighboring peoples were overshadowed by the more powerful states of Mesopotamia. The lack of natural barriers opened Mesopotamia to invaders, who used the element of surprise, superior leadership, and technology to establish domination over the area. The political history of the region reflects this susceptibility to invasion both in the unpredictable rise and fall of local empires and in the development of an eclectic civilization. The foundations of this civilization, however, rested clearly on the advanced culture of Sumer.

Sumer

The first Sumerian settlements were farming communities that had developed around 4000 B.C. in the region between the Tigris and Euphrates rivers. The land in this region is flat, and dikes and canals had to be constructed to limit erosion during the rainy months and to collect water for the arid season. The only way for the early settlers to acquire the means for such large-scale building projects was to pool their resources and work together

Cuneiform tablet recording the foundation of the city of Aanepadda, c. 2600. [British Museum]

for their common benefit; thus villages began to merge and new towns were born.

The need to organize and administer complex projects of this kind led to centralized control. The same necessity led the Mesopotamians to develop a system of writing by using images of tokens that had hitherto been used for record keeping (see the essay "Writing and Communication (I)" on pp. 193–198). The images were marked on soft clay tablets with a split reed, and the tablets were then baked. The reeds made the distinctive wedge-shaped marks of the Mesopotamian system, known as cuneiform. With the ability to write came possibilities for trade and administration on a broader scale. The economic development this permitted led to the growth of powerful cities. The city where modern excavation has uncovered the most spectacular treasures was Ur.

URBAN LIFE IN SUMERIA: UR

Ur was the most southerly of the great Sumerian cities, lying just to the south of the Euphrates River and about 200 miles northwest of what we call the Persian Gulf. From the early third millennium B.C. its citizen-traders used the river as a means of navigating to the outer world, and the wider markets they could reach helped to account for the extraordinary wealth the city accumulated. In describing Ur as a city, however, it is important to remember that in the third millennium B.C. a Sumerian city was more like a regional complex than a densely inhabited core. Ur consisted of the city itself, suburbs, and smaller and more distant villages that depended on the central administration. The whole was surrounded with agricultural lands, including barley and wheat fields, palm groves, and gardens. The exact size of Ur is not known, but Lagash, a city of comparable importance, is estimated to have had a population of 30,000 to 35,000.

For their principal building materials the Sumerians used what lay at hand. The valley of the two rivers has virtually no supplies of stone, and the builders of Ur used unbaked bricks made from clay and straw. Because these are not durable, it is difficult to ascertain the nature of Sumerian urban architecture. Excavations reveal that the center of the community was the temple, the dwelling place of the god who protected the town. The temple was surrounded by flat-roofed houses, the largest of which contained shrines and family burial plots.

The greatest monument at Ur is the ziggurat, the present form of which dates to around 2100 B.C. The word *ziggurat* means "pinnacle" or "mountaintop," and these layered artificial mountains were built from early Sumerian times throughout the Tigris and Euphrates valleys. The ziggurat at Ur consisted of a huge platform, measuring 190 by 130 feet, surmounted with terraces. Its great central staircase led to the upper terrace, which housed a temple.

It was presumably on this pinnacle that Nanna, the moon-god and patron deity of Ur, appeared to the ruler, who acted as the interpreter and conveyor of divine wishes to the citizens and as the principal servant of the gods. One of his chief duties was the building and maintenance of the temples. Several monuments show Sumerian and later Mesopotamian rulers carrying baskets on their heads with bricks for the construction of a new sanctuary. Nonetheless, any impression that Sumerian rulers lived austere lives is quickly dispelled by treasures retrieved from the Royal Cemetery.

In early Sumer the ruler and the chief priests shared responsibility for governing the city. But a gradual separation of palace from temple took place, and at times conflicts developed between the two sides. Nevertheless, the temple owned about a third of the land around the city of

Ur, a part of which was cultivated to provide food for priests and temple employees. Some temple property was allotted to farmers, and some was leased to tenants who were required to hand back a proportion of their harvest as dues, or "tithes." The bulk of land under secular control was probably owned by the ruler, but individuals owned their own houses, fields, and gardens. The disparity of ownership reflected social status. A high government official might own estates of as much as 500 acres, while a simple builder owned perhaps 5 acres. Apart from slaves, Sumerians of all classes could buy, sell, exchange, or rent privately owned houses, property, and livestock.

Private citizens constructed and manufactured both for the state and for one another. From Ur's earliest days its citizens had exported their manufactured products both overland and by sea. Most foreign trade was organized by the state, but on occasion wealthy private contractors were licensed to export their goods.

The population of a city such as Ur was diverse, consisting of nobles, commoners, and slaves. Most slaves were prisoners of war or kidnapped foreigners, although some were children who had been sold into slavery by their parents. Owners could beat or brand their slaves, but if the slaves worked hard, they might earn profits and in some cases purchase their freedom. They were also permitted to marry free persons. A wide range of people worked for the temples, on farms, and in workshops, engaged in activities as diverse as spinning and weaving wool and brewing beer. Other inhabitants worked for the state, either in the standing army or in one of the state building projects, digging canals or constructing fortifications.

Much of this wide range of social and economic activity involved women as well as men. At the lower end of the scale, enslaved women served as domestic servants, cooks, concubines, and gardeners, while among the upper classes the ruler and his wife were surrounded by a retinue of elaborately attired court ladies. The remains of a number of these, together with their jewelry and costumes, were found in the Royal Cemetery at Ur. The ruler's wife played an important part in public life; in cities where the principal deity was a goddess, the queen often took charge of temple affairs.

Thus, in spite of obvious differences, life in a city such as Ur must have been closer to our own than might have been expected, not least in the all-pervading presence of professional administrators. Citizens today would recognize many of the attributes of a modern civil service in the bureaucrats of ancient Sumer. On the clay tablets, inscribed in cuneiform, they systematically recorded the lists of workers, payrolls, inventories, vouchers, revenues, taxes, and other details for a functioning city. Like their modern counterparts, they sought to impose their vision of order on the variety of life. They divided fishermen, for example, into three separate groups: those who fished in fresh water, those who fished in salt water, and those who fished in brackish water.

Mesopotamian Religion

Sumerian civic life was permeated by religion. Heaven and earth, the sun and the moon, and natural phenomena such as lightning and storms were all regarded as manifestations of deities. The principal holidays marked the change of the seasons. The chief annual event was the New Year, when the blistering heat of the previous summer and the winter's cold yielded to the fertile spring. The Great Mother symbolized the earth's abundance, and the sterility of the winter was attributed to the death of her partner, Dumuzi (Tammuz). His disappearance was mourned annually as the New Year festival began. At the festival's culmination, his resurrection was celebrated, together with the sacred marriage of god and goddess, renewed each spring as a symbol of hope for the coming year.

The Mesopotamians received little comfort from their religion. Life in the valley of the two rivers was harsh, and it posed a continuous struggle against the natural disasters of drought and flood. If nonetheless inhabitants preferred it to the afterlife, it was because their religion offered only darkness and dust after death, even for kings. Mesopo-

Ziggurat at Ur, c. 2100–2000. Note the huge staircases that led to a shrine at the top. [Hirmer]

tamian religion advanced the notion that the pantheon of gods was demanding and that humans were servants to the deities. As in many religions, failure to obey the wishes of the gods was thought to bring punishment.

The Mesopotamians' grim vision of life is reinforced by the great Sumerian poem *The Epic of Gilgamesh*. Gilgamesh himself was an actual historical figure who ruled the city of Uruk around 2700 B.C. A series of legends grew up around his name, and these oral traditions were eventually set down in writing to become the world's first epic poem. Written in Sumerian about 2000 B.C., the poem was inscribed afterward on clay tablets in their own languages by the Babylonians, the Hittites, and others in western Asia.

The general vision of *The Epic of Gilgamesh* is pessimistic, although the early scenes, which chronicle the exploits of Gilgamesh and his beloved friend Enkidu, are fresh and vivid. When Enkidu perishes, Gilgamesh sets out to find a way to avoid death. His quest fails. He returns home to record his adventure on a stone and by that means finds immortality. With Gilgamesh's assistance, Enkidu returns at the end of the poem with an account of the ways of the underworld, affirming the Mesopotamian belief in a shadowy but unappealing life after death. The existence of similar tales among other peoples, including the Hebrews and the inhabitants of Asia Minor and the Pacific islands, underscores the common human interest in questions of divine punishment, death, and immortality. The story of the flood recounted in the *Epic*, for instance, has numerous points in common with the later version in the biblical book of Genesis, although the tone of the scriptural account is very different. The God of the Hebrews is motivated by moral disapproval, whereas the Sumerian gods apparently send the flood to punish mortals for making too much noise and keeping the gods awake.

Akkadian and Babylonian Culture

Between approximately 2350 and 2130 B.C. the whole of Mesopotamia fell under the rule of King Sargon and his descendants; his capital city of Akkad gives the period its name. The Akkadians were Semitic peoples who had originally come from the fringes of the Arabian desert. Their new home base was to the north of the principal Sumerian cities, and their conquest and unification of Mesopotamia

A Mesopotamian Account of Creation

The Sumerian poem The Epic of Gilgamesh *circulated widely in Mesopotamia in a variety of versions and languages. This is how it begins.*

O Gilgamesh, lord of Kullab, great is thy praise. This was the man to whom all things were known; this was the king who knew the countries of the world. He was wise, he saw mysteries and knew secret things, he brought us a tale of the days before the flood. He went on a long journey, was weary, worn-out with labor, and returning engraved on a stone the whole story.

When the gods created Gilgamesh they gave him a perfect body. Shamash the glorious sun endowed him with beauty, Adad the god of the storm endowed him with courage, the great gods made his beauty perfect, surpassing all others. Two-thirds they made him god and one-third man.

In Uruk he built walls, a great rampart, and the temple of blessed Eanna for the god of the firmament Anu, and for Ishtar the goddess of love. Look at it still today: the outer wall where the cornice runs, it shines with the brilliance of copper; and the inner wall, it has no equal. Touch the threshold, it is ancient. Approach Eanna the dwelling of Ishtar, our lady of love and war, the like of which no latter-day king, no man alive can equal. Climb upon the wall of Uruk; walk along it, I say; regard the foundation terrace and examine the masonry: is it not burnt brick and good? The seven sages laid the foundations.

Source: The Epic of Gilgamesh, trans. N. K. Sandars (Harmondsworth, England: Penguin Books, 1960), p. 59.

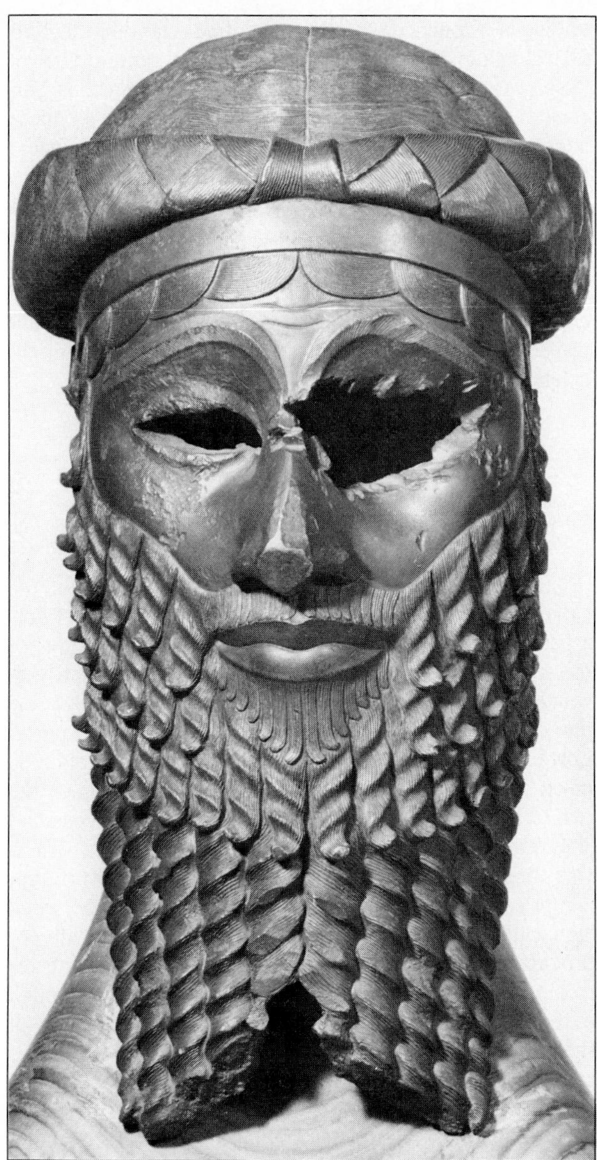

This portrait of a Akkadian king could well be of Sargon himself. [Hirmer]

had a lasting effect on its political and cultural life. They also introduced a new language, of the Semitic family, which includes Hebrew, Arabic, and Aramaic. At the same time, however, the Akkadians preserved some aspects of Sumerian culture, including their system of writing.

Whereas earlier Sumerian rulers had governed large parts of Mesopotamia, Sargon was the first to create a unified kingdom. In the reign of his grandson, Naramsin, rulers of individual cities were called "slaves of the king," who himself assumed the title of King of the Four Quarters of the Universe. This emphasis on human might rather than submission to the gods is clearly visible in a portrait of an Akkadian king, perhaps Sargon himself, that radiates pride and self-confidence.

With the sudden and violent end of Akkadian rule produced by the Guti, nomadic invaders from Iran, the cities of Mesopotamia revived earlier cultural practices. Renewed religious devotion can be seen in the many temples of this so-called Neo-Sumerian period (c. 2130–c. 2030 B.C.), especially in the statues of Gudea, the governor of the city of Lagash around 2100 B.C. Gudea is shown in an attitude of devotion, hands tightly clasped, as he stands respectfully before the gods. The humility of the figure contrasts strongly with the earlier Akkadian portrait.

By 1800 B.C. Mesopotamia had once again been unified, this time under another Semitic group, the Amorites. The reign of their most famous king, Hammurabi (c. 1792–1750 B.C.), was marked by the formulation of a law code that aimed to achieve social justice by royal pronouncement. Hammurabi's code is one of the earliest surviving law codes. It sought to regulate the rights and obligations of the three classes—free people, state dependents, and slaves—by establishing laws and providing specific punishments for their transgressions. The penalties, which differed according to social status, included not only fines but corporal punishment, mutilation, and execution.

As in most early legal systems, the provisions were harsh. A surgeon whose patient died in the course of a major operation was sentenced to have a hand cut off, and architects whose faulty work caused a building to collapse and kill a client were themselves put to death. On the whole, however, the code shows a concern for human relationships: the rights of husbands and wives, of parents and children, and of masters and workers. The laws pertaining to property and family were designed to protect the interests of women and children. Hammurabi, who formally pronounced the code, had copies of its provisions inscribed on stone slabs set up in temples to attest to the gods' approval.

The Assyrians

Yet another people was to dominate Mesopotamia for a brief period, the Kassites. Formerly nomadic, they occupied Babylon sometime after 1700 B.C., only to fall in turn under the rule of the militaristic Assyrians, who evolved the last great culture of Mesopotamia. The peak of Assyrian power was between 1000 and 612 B.C.

The four centuries of Assyrian domination were marked by powerful and aggressive rulers. The general impression of Assyrian history, in fact, is of periods of violent imperialistic warfare punctuated by the relatively calm reigns of less vigorous kings. Assyrian armies were frequently on the march throughout western Asia and even crossed the Sinai desert to invade Egypt in 671.

The central bases from which these military expeditions were dispatched were the cities designated as royal capitals. In the course of Assyrian history, different places served this purpose at different times. In the reign of Ashurnasirpal (884–859 B.C.), a huge palace was constructed at Nimrud and decorated with elaborately carved reliefs. Under Sargon II (722–705 B.C.) a new city was built at Khorsabad, where enough has been preserved and excavated to give a good idea of how Sargon's city would have looked. Although abandoned under his successor, the remains show evidence of careful planning. Khorsabad, which covers almost a square mile, is surrounded by defensive walls. The gates were placed to satisfy the two requirements of symmetry and convenience for traffic; they were provided with guard posts that could serve for defense in time of war and as customs and police posts in peacetime. Both the outer gates and the entrance doors into the palace were also protected by huge statues of the Assyrians' most powerful demons, the Lamassu, splendidly depicted as winged, human-headed bulls. These massive figures, assured and forbidding, are among the most imposing representations of political power in history.

The palace itself was built around a large open court, with separate quarters for officers and servants, a number of temples, and the king's residential apartments. Most impressive were the state rooms, where the king would receive foreign ambassadors. The throne room was approached through an open courtyard lined with greater than life-size statues of the king and his courtiers. Its entrance was provided with a collection of demonic figures, again of vast size. The Assyrian kings hoped by intimidation to deter their neighbors from attacking and their own subjects from rebelling. The ambassadors or petitioners who had made their way through the ceremonial halls into the throne room faced the carved base of the king's throne, which showed Sargon standing in his war chariot over heaps of dead bodies while his soldiers made piles of severed heads in front of him.

The emphasis on the violence of war, both at Sargon's palace and elsewhere, imparts a somewhat forboding air to our impression of the Assyrians and their culture. Nor do the Assyrians off duty, so to speak, seem any more relaxed. To judge from the relief carvings in the palace at Nineveh, built by Ashurbanipal (669—630 B.C.), the principal peacetime activity seems to have been hunting. Perhaps slaughter would more accurately describe the process, for the carvings show the king killing lions in a space closed off by a wall of soldiers carrying shields.

Nineveh fell in 612 B.C., and with it the Assyrian empire. Western Asia Minor came under the control of the Medes (from Media, the ancient name for northwestern Iran) and then the Persians (from Persis, in southern Iran), while the Chaldeans of southern Babylonia dominated Palestine, Syria, and the whole of Mesopotamia. Yet even at this point the cultural fertility of Mesopotamia was not exhausted. The ancient kingdom of Babylon came under the rule of a dynasty of monarchs of whom the best-known is Nebuchadnezzar, familiar from the Bible, and for 70 years or so underwent a remarkable cultural revival. This period, which lasted from 612 to 539 B.C., is generally called the Neo-Babylonian period, and its art harks back across the period of Assyrian domination to that of the Babylon of 1,000 years earlier.

The greatest building project of the age was Nebuchadnezzar's palace at Babylon. Although little of it has survived, its construction and decoration differ considerably from Sargon's palace at Khorsabad. The gates of the city around the palace were decorated with painted and glazed bricks, giving an impression of considerable splendor.

The Beginnings of Egyptian Civilization

Egypt is a desert country, most of which can support only a pastoral economy. That it served as a breadbasket for the ancient world is due to the 4,000-mile-long Nile River, which flows north from central Africa, and provides a fertile delta. Ancient Egypt was divided into two parts. Lower or northern Egypt occupied approximately 150 miles of broad, flat land in the Nile delta, from which the rest of the Mediterranean region was easily accessible. The region had twice as much land as Upper Egypt, which was more remote from the outside world. Upper Egypt comprised a narrow band of fertile soil that ran between high cliffs and desert on either side of the Nile for approximately 525 miles. The sparseness of rain in both regions meant that agriculture was possible only through extensive irrigation systems and by taking advantage of the annual flooding of the river. The Greek historian Herodotus called Egypt "the gift of the Nile," which remains an apt description. Here, as in Mesopotamia, it was possible to produce an agricultural surplus on river alluvium (silt), continually deposited by annual floods. Water from the Nile could also be manipulated to provide a controlled supply to arid areas throughout the year, and the Nile, like the Tigris and the Euphrates, also served as a vital avenue of transport to the cities, especially for the supply of food, fuel, and building materials. The Nile valley was separated from other civilizations by deserts, so Egypt was seldom menaced by outside aggressors. This allowed it to develop a homogenous civilization of its own. Thus political and economic life in Egypt, as in Mesopotamia, was profoundly affected by the character of its geographic position.

Some of the rock carvings on the cliffs of the Nile valley date back to around 6000 B.C. Their depictions of hunters and animals, weapons and traps, illustrate the conditions of life before the development of civilization. As Neolithic culture began, drawings of cattle and boats appeared, but at this early period the small village communities were subject to damage caused by the floodwaters of the Nile even as they bestowed fertility. Starting around 4000 B.C. larger villages were built on higher ground out of reach of the flooding Nile. The efforts of several neighboring communities to cooperate in constructing canals and dikes to channel the waters seem to have been the original stimulus for the growth of organized districts. As the villages joined together, the regions began to unite into two main kingdoms, Upper and Lower Egypt, and shortly before 3000 B.C. the two united under a single ruler. An Egyptian priest, Manetho, the author of a history of Egypt (c. 280 B.C.), divided the vast span of Egyptian history into 31 dynasties. Today scholars group that history into five periods, each of roughly 500 years' duration: the Archaic Period (c. 3100–c. 2686 B.C.); the Old Kingdom (c. 2686–c. 2181 B.C.); the Middle Kingdom (c. 2133–1603 B.C.); the New Kingdom (1567–c. 1085 B.C.); and the Late Period (c. 1085–c. 525 B.C.), after which Egypt was absorbed into the Persian Empire. These dynastic periods were separated by times of instability and disturbance.

Unification: The Age of the Pyramids

The Old Kingdom was an age of prosperity and innovation. New technical skills were used to construct the massive religious and funerary monuments for which ancient Egypt is renowned. The central authority of the divine ruler, or pharaoh, maintained the unity of the state while providing a focus for Egyptian religion and the development of a large bureaucracy of priests and officials. The Egyptians of the Old Kingdom undoubtedly had trading contacts with the Syrians and other peoples of western Asia, but these appear to have had little effect on their culture; there is scant evidence of contacts with Mesopotamia, except at the beginning, as suggested by similarities between the Mesopotamian ziggurat and the Egyptian pyramid. The prosperity of the early dynasties collapsed at the end of the Old Kingdom, primarily the result of rivalries among members of the provincial nobility that had developed under the earlier dynasties.

Throughout the Old Kingdom a strong pharaoh was both the symbol of and the principal reason for national unity; some of Egypt's earliest pharaohs had pyramids constructed to serve as their tombs and as sites of worship and devotion. The pharaoh Zoser commissioned the architect Imhotep to build the first pyramid during the Third Dynasty (c. 2686–c. 2613 B.C.) as Zoser's tomb and memorial. Imhotep himself is the first architect known to history and was in later ages regarded as a god. Zoser's successors continued the tradition of building pyramids for their tombs. The great pyramid of Khufu at Giza (c. 2600 B.C.), which rises to a height of nearly 500 feet, was constructed of more than 2 million limestone blocks weighing as much as 30,000 pounds apiece.

Egyptian Society and Religion

The monumental architecture that characterizes the Old Kingdom reveals much about Egyptian society. Such structures were made possible by the use of forced labor, which was also used for other large projects such as the

Great Pyramids at Giza. They were constructed between 2650 and 2550. [Holton/Photo Researchers]

construction of canals. The surviving images, inscriptions, and documents perpetuate the memory of the ruling classes, while the anonymous laborers go, for the most part, unrecorded except for their appearance in scenes painted in the tombs and on the coffins of the great. Although Egyptian society was stratified, some upward mobility was possible. The ruling family was drawn from the hereditary nobility, whose principal aim was to retain political power and pass it on to descendants. This required a firm grip over the two elite groups: the nobility and the priests, guardians of Egypt's religious traditions. The pharaoh's person was regarded as divine, his authority as equal to that of any other deity. His power was theoretically absolute; his commands were carried out by the advisers, scribes, and others who made up the ever growing bureaucracy of governing officials. At the head of the bureaucracy was the vizier, who served as the intermediary between the pharaoh and local officials, tried cases, appointed magistrates, entertained foreign envoys, and supervised agriculture, road and building maintenance, record keeping, the army and the police, and tax assessment and collection. The pharaoh's family formed the center of a royal court that the hereditary nobility attended. He could demand taxes ranging up to 20 percent of annual income, which were typically paid in kind, for example, in grain.

The priests who served the pharaoh regarded themselves as the preservers of traditional religious doctrines, the most fundamental of which was the concept of divine kingship. By the time of the New Kingdom, the priests, whose office was hereditary, had become a separate caste. Each temple had a priestly hierarchy responsible for undertaking a wide variety of tasks, ranging from menial duties to performing religious rites. Priestesses, however, were not professionals but wives of the nobility who assisted in some of the rituals. Some priests wore special clothing that reflected their status.

Religion was woven into the very fabric of Egyptian political and social life, and society reflected the Egyptian view of creation. Just as the sun god, Amon, had created the universe by bringing order to the primeval chaos, so the pharaoh ruled the physical world. The upper class, formed by the royal court, the priests, and other wealthy landowners, maintained strict control of financial resources and commerce.

The lowest level in the social order was occupied by the numberless court servants and workers and the agricultural laborers who farmed the Nile valley. A few laborers may have been independent and self-supporting, but the vast majority were serfs who were virtually bound to the land and were also forced to work on state building projects. The use of slaves was widespread in the New Kingdom. In the absence of a middle class of nonaristocratic merchants and traders, there was relatively little possibility for the humble to rise above their origins by acquiring financial independence, although some used their talent to improve their social rank. In general, the state controlled both the production and distribution of agricultural and manufactured products. The government had enormous granaries and warehouses and was normally able to provide for the people when harvests were bad.

The social status of the humble is aptly illustrated by the difference between their burial rites and those of the nobility. Even a minor royal official would spend much of

Hairdressing scene carved on the coffin of Kawit. [Egyptian Museum, Cairo]

The Technique of Mummification

Since Egyptian literature provides little information about the technique of mummification, we have to rely on ancient travelers' accounts. The following one is by the Greek historian Herodotus, who visited Egypt around 450 B.C. *Modern research has confirmed the accuracy of his information.*

There are a set of men in Egypt who practice the art of embalming, and make it their proper business. These persons, when a body is brought to them, show the bearers various models of corpses, made in wood, and painted so as to resemble nature. The most perfect is said to be after the manner of him whom I do not think it religious to name in connection with such a matter; the second sort is inferior to the first, and less costly; the third is the cheapest of all. All this the embalmers explain, and then ask in which way it is wished that the corpse should be prepared. The bearers tell them, and having concluded their bargain, take their departure, while the embalmers, left to themselves, proceed to their task. The mode of embalming, according to the most perfect process, is the following: they take first a crooked piece of iron, and with it draw out the brain through the nostrils, thus getting rid of a portion, while the skull is cleared of the rest by rinsing with drugs; next they make a cut along the flank with a sharp Ethiopian stone, and take out the whole contents of the abdomen, which they then cleanse, washing it thoroughly with palm wine, and again frequently with an infusion of pounded aromatics. After this they fill the cavity with the purest bruised myrrh, with cassia, and every other sort of spicery except frankincense, and sew up the opening. Then the body is placed in natron for seventy days, and covered entirely over. After the expiration of that space of time, which must not be exceeded, the body is washed, and wrapped round, from head to foot, with bandages of fine linen cloth, smeared over with gum, which is used generally by the Egyptians in the place of glue, and in this state it is given back to the relations, who enclose it in a wooden case which they have had made for the purpose, shaped into the figure of a man. Then fastening the case, they place it in a sepulchral chamber, upright against the wall. Such is the most costly way of embalming the dead.

Source: Herodotus, *The Histories*, vol. 2, trans. G. Rawlinson (New York: Library of Living Classics, 1928), pp. 85–86.

his life and income preparing an elaborate tomb for himself in which he would be buried with various treasures, and the burials of the ruling family were to become legendary for their sumptuousness. Corpses were mummified because Egyptians believed that the *ka*, the spirit of life in each person, would periodically return to the body. Yet the corpse of a poor Egyptian was typically wrapped in a piece of linen and left in a cave or a pit or even in the open sand of the desert, with only a staff and a pair of sandals for the journey to the next world. Beginning in the Middle Kingdom, however, some members of the lower classes had their corpses mummified. Relatively little documentary evidence has survived about living standards among the lower classes, and they are visible to us mostly in the painted and carved scenes of the tombs, going about their work as domestic servants or farm laborers. The concept of a future life was the only shared experience that united nobles, peasants, and slaves, since the Egyptian obsession with immortality offered the hope of a good life after death to all Egyptians, regardless of status.

However orderly Egyptian society may have been, traditional Egyptian religious beliefs involved a bewildering variety of deities, whose rights and privileges were jealously guarded by their priests. At the time of Egypt's unification, local guardian-deities were merged into Re (or Ra), the sun god, who sailed the skies in his boat by day and combated the forces of darkness in the underworld by night. Because of the political importance of Thebes, this god absorbed the identity of the Theban deity Amon, associated with the welfare of the state, and became known as Amon-Re.

The worship of Osiris, the god of the Nile, came to offer the hope of immortality to the masses. The cult of the afterlife involved elaborate funeral rituals at which the dead would be judged and move on to the next life. Each person, it was thought, would be judged by Osiris, who would assess the good and evil that had been done in life and then determine whether the person deserved punishment or admittance into the realm of bliss. Texts were written on papyrus and placed in the graves to assist the deceased in the examinations that marked their entrance into the afterlife; these texts are known as *The Book of the Dead*. The following excerpt suggests the standards of ethical and social behavior to which Egyptians were supposed to aspire:

> **I have not done evil to mankind. I have not oppressed the members of my family, I have not wrought evil in the place of right and truth. . . . I have not brought forward my name for exaltation to honors. I have not ill-treated servants. . . . I have not defrauded the oppressed one of his property. . . . I have made no man to suffer hunger. . . . I have done no murder. . . . I have not committed fornication. . . . I have not encroached upon the fields of others. . . . I have not caught fish [with bait made of] fish of their kind. . . . I am pure.[1]**

Osiris, the god who presided over funeral rituals, was the symbol of death and rebirth. The worship of Osiris, his wife Isis, goddess of the fertile earth, and their son Horus came in time to symbolize a sense of the afterlife beyond simple material survival; it represents the closest that Egyptian religion came to the notion of a true spiritual state. According to one common belief, Osiris was killed by his evil brother, Seth, who cut the corpse into pieces; Isis gathered them up, wrapped them in linen, and thereby brought Osiris back to life. A different Horus, the sky god, eventually defeated Seth. This Horus was typically depicted as a hawk, the form in which pharaohs were believed to ascend to heaven after they died. The Egyptians worshiped a great variety of other divinities and spirits of nature, who were responsible for all aspects of existence. The mythology and ritual they inspired affected the lives of all Egyptians on a daily basis. Several animals, such as the jackal and the cat, also had religious importance; their mummified remains have been found at a number of sanctuaries.

Egypt in the Middle Kingdom: Consolidation, Expansion, and Decline

The ordered world of the Old Kingdom was brought to an abrupt end around 2181 B.C. as a result of rivalries among the nobility, who now claimed offices by hereditary right. Members of the royal court began to claim religious and political privileges that had formerly belonged only to the pharaoh, whose position had been weakened by lavish building schemes and temple endowments. By challenging the unique status of the pharaohs, the courtiers provoked conflicts that led to the collapse of the monarchy. In the absence of a central authority, provincial governors attempted to seize power in their region and maintain their independence, and not until about 2040 B.C., when Mentuhotep conquered Lower Egypt and succeeded in reuniting the country, did peace return. The new royal capital was situated at Thebes, and the decorations of the tomb complex built there for the pharaoh and members of his entourage provide a vivid picture of private life at the court of a Middle Kingdom pharaoh.

The principal rulers of the Twelfth Dynasty maintained Theban domination of Egypt by a combination of determination and brute force. Their successes at home included a massive drainage project that reclaimed 27,000 acres of arable land south of Memphis. They also developed a vigorous, aggressive foreign policy. Part of Nubia, the land to the south of Egypt, was occupied, and the pharaoh Sesostris III himself led a military expedition into Palestine, opening up a fresh sphere of influence and new commercial frontiers. Trade links were probably established at this time with the Minoans of Crete, and evidence appears of renewed contact with Mesopotamia, perhaps through the mediation of the Syrians. Although Egyptian art and culture remained relatively untouched by foreign influence, the Egyptians were eager to appropriate the wealth of their neighbors, by trade or by conquest.

The successes of the Middle Kingdom pharaohs were followed by collapse and by the invasion around 1720 B.C. of the Hyksos, a nomadic or pastoral people from western Asia with horses and war chariots. Our knowledge of the period of the Hyksos' invasion and occupation is incomplete, partly because the invaders left little in the way of written evidence and partly because the Egyptians of the New Kingdom were understandably reluctant or perhaps unable to document life under occupation by foreigners.

For most of the seventeenth century B.C. the Hyksos apparently controlled Palestine and Syria as well as Egypt, where their power was strongest in the north. In contrast to the Egyptians, with their desire to maintain a closed society, the Hyksos seem to have encouraged the presence of foreign immigrants like themselves. It was possibly under Hyksos rule that Jewish immigrants, led by Joseph, arrived in Egypt and prospered there. Not until the sixteenth century B.C. were the Hyksos driven out of Egypt and back to Palestine.

The early pharaohs of the New Kingdom, which began with the Eighteenth Dynasty in 1567 B.C., involved Egypt internationally for the first time on a broad scale. Among the most remarkable of them was Queen Hatshepsut, who initially wielded power as regent to her stepson, the future Tuthmosis III, and then proclaimed herself pharaoh with the support of the priests of Amon. Although in general Egyptian society was male-oriented, it was by no means unusual for a pharaoh's mother to take charge of government during his younger years or absence at war. Indeed, the custom whereby the pharaoh generally married his sister or half-sister strengthened such family connections, and Egyptian religion, with its many gods and goddesses, meant that Egyptians were accustomed to respect female figures. Women were sometimes active in government at the local level too. Even so, Hatshepsut was an unusual case. Taking the title of king, she ruled for over 20 years and left as her principal legacy one of the most massive Egyptian temples. A funerary monument for herself and her father, Tuthmosis I, it was designed by one of the greatest figures in Egyptian art, the architect Senmut. The temple combined opulence of effect with extreme care for detail; its facade was decorated with colossal statues of Hatshepsut herself, which her stepson Tuthmosis III, who loathed her, destroyed when he became pharaoh.

Tuthmosis III proved to be an aggressive and forceful ruler, leading campaigns in western Asia and to the south in Nubia. By the end of his reign Palestine and Syria as far as the Euphrates were under Egyptian control, and a huge temple complex had been constructed in Nubia near Napata. The conquered territories were controlled by Egyptian garrisons, and inspectors were sent to supervise the shipping of raw materials and manufactured objects back to Egypt. Tuthmosis is said to have waged 17 successful campaigns; on the first one alone, 1,000 chariots and more than 400,000 bushels of wheat were captured.

The effects of the Egyptians' imperial expansion on their economy were considerable. During the Old and Middle Kingdoms, manufacturing and foreign trade had played a relatively small part in the development of Egyptian society. In part, as we have seen, this had resulted from the lack of a commercial class whose activity might have proved a threat to the hereditary nobility. The Egyptians' agricultural self-sufficiency, too, eliminated the need to look elsewhere for basic provisions. With their new possessions throughout western Asia, however, they operated on a wider economic scale. The New Kingdom's elite, with its opulent lifestyle, provided willing customers for the foreign luxury goods that were traded for Egyptian products, including stone vessels, pottery, colored glass, and fine linens. Egyptian artisans were especially noted for their production of luxury items, including jewelry, carved ivory, enamel work, pearl inlay, perfumed oils, ointments, and even cosmetics, such as hair dyes, rouge, and eye shadow.

Akhenaton and Religious Reform

The general pattern of consolidation and expansion was abruptly broken by the pharaoh Amenhotep IV (1379–c. 1362 B.C.), who tried to impose a complete reform of Egyptian political and religious institutions. In place of the innumerable deities of traditional religion, he encouraged the worship of a single one, the sun god Aton. In the words of the *Hymn to Aton*:

> ***O sole god, like whom there is no other!***
> ***Thou didst create the world according to thy desire,***
> ***Whilst thou wert alone.***

Amenhotep himself took the name of Akhenaton, "servant of Aton." To implement these revolutionary changes and to reduce the power of the priests at the royal court of Thebes, he transferred the capital to Tel-el-Amarna, which he called Akhetaton.

Akhenaton's attempt to impose monotheism is reflected in the culture of the Amarna period. The monumentality and idealized features of traditional art were replaced by a new lightness, in which for the first time detailed physical features were shown. A stone relief depicting Akhenaton, his wife Nefertiti, and three of their children reposing beneath the sun disk is remarkably different from the formalized style of previous eras.

Clearly, so revolutionary a change in culture and religion posed a serious threat to the priests, whose interests lay in the preservation of traditional ways. After Akhenaton's death, he was condemned as a heretic and his name was removed from the monuments of his era. His son-in-law and successor, Tutankhamen, is perhaps the most famous of all Egyptian rulers, although for reasons that have nothing to do with his religion or politics; his unopened tomb, excavated in 1922, contained the richest hoard of Egyptian artifacts ever recovered. Tutankhamen's sweeping restoration of the old religion was carefully recorded in the temple at Karnak:

> **Then his majesty made monuments for the gods, fashioning their cult-statues of genuine fine gold from the highlands, building their sanctuaries anew as monuments for the ages of eternity, established with possessions forever, setting for them divine offerings as a regular daily observance, and provisioning their food-offerings upon earth. He surpassed what had been previously. . . . He inducted priests and prophets from the children of the nobles.[2]**

Akhenaton's lack of interest in foreign policy had weakened Egypt's control of conquered territories. Revolts in Egyptian possessions in Syria and Palestine were fomented by the Hittites, another imperial power in western Asia. From the accession of Ramses I in 1320 B.C. to the end of the New Kingdom around 1085 B.C., pharaohs were involved in constant wars in which they tried, unsuccessfully, to maintain control of their overseas possessions. Shortly after 1200 B.C. Egypt itself was threatened by a new wave of migrants, known to us only as the Peoples of the Sea. Their invasions were repelled, but only at great cost, and Egyptian imperial power continued to decline.

Akhenaton, Nefertiti, and three of their children. The naturalism of this relief is characteristic of late Amarna art. [Egyptian Museum, State Museums, West Berlin]

The ever-larger building projects of the later New Kingdom seem as much attempts at restoring self-confidence as triumphal monuments.

In the last centuries of independent Egyptian history a succession of invaders attacked and occupied various parts of the country, from the Assyrians in the seventh century B.C. to Alexander the Great (331 B.C.). With its conquest by Alexander, Egypt at last became absorbed into the larger Mediterranean world.

The Legacy of Egyptian Culture

Ancient Egyptian religion and language were lost for centuries, only to be recovered by the archaeologist's spade. The earliest Egyptian writing was in the form of hieroglyphics, or pictorial symbols, which represented individual objects or actions. As early as the Old Kingdom, the Egyptians had a system of alphabetic characters for the 24 consonants, although they had no way to indicate vowels. The Frenchman Jean Champollion finally deciphered the Egyptian hieroglyphic script by means of a trilingual inscription, the Rosetta Stone, found in the Nile delta in the early nineteenth century. Champollion compared the three languages on the stone—hieroglyphic, the demotic script of the common Egyptian people, and ancient Greek. The Rosetta Stone is, among other things, a monument to the passing of ancient Egyptian culture. The Egyptians had ceased to use their script in the last stages of their history, whereas the Greek that was largely replacing it has never fallen out of use from ancient times to the present day. Similarly, the beliefs that sustained the ancient Egyptians for millennia had begun to disappear along with their language.

Yet the monuments remain, and ever since their rediscovery some two centuries ago, they have fascinated the modern world. Part of the continuing appeal of Egyptian art lies in the extraordinary technical skill it often displays. In seeking to record the world around them, Egyptian artists developed techniques in painting and sculpture that permitted them to achieve a perfection of finish and a beauty of surface that remain unsurpassed. Living in or with easy access to the rocky upper valley of the Nile, they learned to use stone to produce everything from vast temple complexes to tiny figurines. Their skill at rendering the human form was adopted by the Greeks when Greek colonizers moved to Egypt shortly after 700 B.C. Comparison proves instructive: when the Greeks went to Egypt, they found the Egyptians producing statues not very different from those of 2,000 years earlier. The Greeks borrowed their style and in just over 100 years developed it into the finest the world had known.

Aton, the One God

This extract from the Hymn to Aton *composed by Akhenaton illustrates the pharaoh's belief in a single divine force.*

Thou appearest beautifully on the horizon of heaven,
Thou living Aton, the beginning of life!
When thou art arisen on the eastern horizon,
Thou hast filled every land with thy beauty.
Thou art gracious, great, glistening, and high over every land;
Thy rays encompass the lands to the limit of all that thou hast made;
As thou art Re, thou reachest to the end of them;
Thou subduest them for thy beloved son.
Though thou art in their faces, no one knows thy going.

When thou settest in the western horizon,
The land is in darkness, in the manner of death.
They sleep in a room, with heads wrapped up,
Nor sees one eye the other.
All their goods which are under their heads might be stolen,
But they would not perceive it.
Every lion is come forth from his den;
All creeping things, they sting.
Darkness is a shroud, and the earth is in stillness,
For he who made them rests in his horizon.

At daybreak, when thou arisest on the horizon,
When thou shinest as the Aton by day,
Thou drivest away the darkness and givest thy rays.
The Two Lands are in festivity every day,
Awake and standing upon their feet,
For thou hast raised them up.
Washing their bodies, taking their clothing.
Their arms are raised in praise at thy appearance.
All the world, they do their work. . . .

Source: J. B. Pritchard, ed., *Ancient Near Eastern Texts Relating to the Old Testament,* trans. J. Wilson (Princeton, N.J.: Princeton University Press, 1969), p. 370.

The Egyptians' art as a whole was primarily conditioned by the character and requirements of their religion. In addition to the images of deities, artists were required to provide temples and shrines for religious ceremonies. Even the buildings or sculptures that commemorated the images, names, or deeds of real people generally served religious purposes. The largely undeviating style that resulted from the joint control of state and religion seems to have appealed to the Egyptians' cultural conservatism. In troubled times during the Middle Kingdom or the Late Period with its foreign invaders, artists tended to turn back to the certainty and security of Old Kingdom art. As late as the Roman period, architects at Meroë, an Egyptian city in Nubia, were still building pyramids as funerary monuments.

Although the Egyptians maintained their social and political structure substantially unchanged over thousands of years, they were not completely immune to outside influences. Among them was the idea of writing, probably borrowed from the Sumerians; the adoption of the chariot, the horse, and long-range bows from the Hyksos; and the use of luxury items imported from Asia and Europe. Nevertheless, apart from the widespread use of slaves, the economic expansion of the New Kingdom had little social effect on one of the most static and rigidly stratified societies that has ever existed.

Lord Carnarvon (left) and Howard Carter opening the door to Tutankhamen's burial chamber on February 17, 1923. [Ashmolean Museum, Oxford, England]

Our knowledge of Egyptian history and society was literally dictated by the ruling class in the form of the inscriptions that decorate their monuments. The awkward silence that hangs over the period of Hyksos rule serves as a reminder of how many other aspects of Egyptian life were never recorded. There is a certain irony in the fact that material objects have survived in remarkable numbers: furniture, clothes, utensils, and, of course, enough mummified ancient Egyptians to fascinate museumgoers throughout much of the world today. Yet the society that made use of the couches and footstools and makeup boxes remains a mystery to us in many respects.

The Hebrews

The history of the Hebrews is continuously intertwined with that of the other peoples of ancient Egypt and western Asia, including the Canaanites and the Phoenicians, both of whom had settled in Palestine from very early times. Much of Canaanite culture was influenced by Mesopotamia, while the trade-oriented Phoenicians developed an early version of an alphabet (though without vowel signs) and founded colonies as far away as North Africa and the Iberian peninsula.

The Hebrews too had early links with Mesopotamia. The family of Abraham, the traditional founder of the nation of Israel, came from Ur, and we have already met its descendants in Egypt at the time of the Hyksos. Yet the study of the early history of the Hebrews differs significantly from that of the other peoples of western Asia and Egypt. A particularly crucial difference is the role played by written as well as archaeological evidence. Our picture of ancient Egypt and Mesopotamia is reconstituted from material remains, supplemented and at times amplified by inscriptions and surviving documents. Our principal source for the early history of the Hebrews, by contrast, is the first five books of the Old Testament, known as the Pentateuch. According to tradition, the author of the Pentateuch was Moses, a participant in the later stages of the story it tells, though the consensus of scholars is that the text we have was completed in the fifth century B.C. from oral and written traditions and laws. In places, archaeological discoveries have confirmed or filled out the biblical account; elsewhere they provide information that is missing from the Bible.

From the time of the first patriarch, Abraham, the covenant between God and the Hebrews was the dominant theme of their history. Abraham believed he had made a covenant or agreement with God that placed the Jews in a special relationship with the Creator as a "chosen people." The biblical book of Exodus records that Moses reconfirmed this covenant and on Mount Sinai received the tablets of the law from God.*

Abraham's family settled for a while near the city of Harran in northern Mesopotamia; his descendants moved southward, living as pastoral nomads. Taking their flocks with them, they crossed the desert from one water source to the next, in general avoiding the major urban centers, always following what they perceived to be divine instructions.

At some point after 2000 B.C. these wandering nomads, driven perhaps by hunger, settled in the Nile delta. It is difficult to establish a precise date for the events that brought the Hebrews and the Egyptians into contact. Egyptian texts fail to record the presence of the Hebrews, and Old Testament accounts make no reference to a specific Egyptian ruler or time period. Egyptian tomb paintings of around 1900 B.C. show nomads, described in the accompanying inscription as "Asiatics," who may well be among the descendants of Abraham. It is generally agreed, however, that the period of Hebrew prosperity in Egypt described in the story of Joseph is related to the period of Hyksos rule in the century or so following 1700 B.C. The

*The following account focuses on Hebrew history; Judaism as a religion is discussed in Chapter 7.

Hyksos, themselves foreigners, were more likely to look with favor on an immigrant community. Furthermore, the Hebrews' connection with the Hyksos would help to explain the Egyptian silence, both on the period itself and on the events that led to the Hebrew exodus described in the Old Testament.

The exodus from Egypt, under the leadership of Moses, probably occurred during the reign of Ramses II (1304–1237 B.C.). Paintings of the period show "Asiatics" being used as slaves in brickmaking and other building labors, and there is archaeological evidence for a period of migration into Palestine around 1200 B.C. For the Hebrews, and for subsequent Jewish tradition, the exodus became the basis for the foundation of Israel. It demonstrated the intervention of their God, Yahweh, and was the occasion for the renewal of the covenant under the leadership of Moses.

Following Moses, the migrants traveled northeast toward their "promised land," although the final crossing of the Jordan and the conquest of Palestine were accomplished only after Moses' death under the leadership of Joshua. The details of the subsequent foundation and growth of the kingdom of Israel are far from clear. The biblical account is incomplete, and archaeological excavations have generally complicated rather than clarified matters. The picture is of almost two centuries of struggle between the Jews and other migrant peoples, particularly the Philistines, before the establishment of a Hebrew monarchy. Even then the new kingdom of Israel was far from secure. Saul, its first king, was killed in battle, and only with the accession of David, his successor (c. 1000–c. 970 B.C.), was stability established.

David was first proclaimed king by the Hebrews who lived in Judah, an arid frontier region in southern Palestine that Saul had never effectively governed; it took some seven years before David could take advantage of internal dissension in the north to unite all of Israel. Displaying considerable talent as a political and military leader, he conquered Jerusalem from a local tribe known as the Jebusites and defeated the Philistines. Jerusalem, in a nearly impregnable geographic position, became his new capital and eventually the historic center of the nation of Israel.

Unsatisfied with these achievements, David used his victorious troops to expand the frontiers of his state until it extended from the Euphrates to the Gulf of Aqaba at the head of the Red Sea; even Damascus was occupied by Hebrew troops. In a symbolic attempt to unify the disparate peoples of his empire, David married wives from the various groups; ultimately this contributed to substantial dissension within his own family and the rebellion and death of his son Absalom.

To solidify his authority, David interpreted kingship in distinctly religious terms. At his command, the ark, a fundamental symbol of the covenant between the Hebrews and their God, was enshrined in Jerusalem. There it signified the renewal of the covenant through David, "the anointed (messiah) of the Lord," and established Jerusalem as the religious as well as the political capital of Israel.

Under David's successor, his son Solomon, who reigned from around 970 to 930 B.C., Israel reached its greatest prosperity. This was in part the result of an absence of competing powers in western Asia at this time. The power of Egypt was on the wane, and the Assyrians had yet to embark on their foreign campaigns and con-

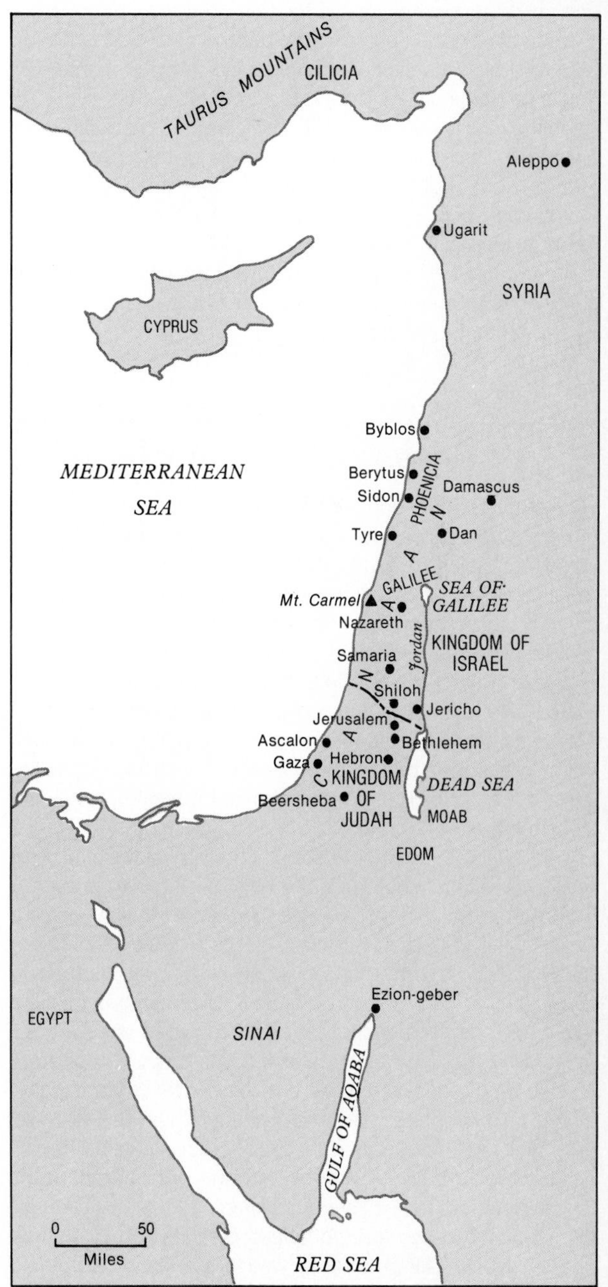

1.2 Ancient Palestine

quests. That Solomon was aware of the necessity of coming to terms with his neighbors is suggested by the fact that one of his wives was an Egyptian, daughter of the reigning pharaoh.

Solomon sought to consolidate and extend the power of his kingdom. He expanded foreign trade by building up a large merchant fleet, manned by Phoenician sailors, that imported gold from Arabia and Ethiopia. Excavations at the port of Ezion-geber on the Gulf of Aqaba suggest the existence of a large-scale metal industry. Objects manufactured there were traded for imported foreign products and raw materials, including the famous cedars of Lebanon used in the construction of Solomon's temple, a majestic building that housed the Great Sanhedrin (the supreme rabbinic court) and served as the center of national worship. He also strengthened the power of his army by the use of iron, which was introduced throughout the Mediterranean shortly after 1000 B.C. His building projects both in Jerusalem and elsewhere in the kingdom are evidence of his ambitious intentions; the fortified city of Megiddo, with its stables for almost 500 horses, is just one of the cities he rebuilt.

The Society of Ancient Israel

The wealthy and sophisticated city of Jerusalem provided a very different lifestyle from that experienced by the Hebrews in their long journeys and hard-won conquests. Jerusalem itself had been a small town of little importance. Now it became a major international capital, its population swollen by the crowds of workmen involved on Solomon's building projects; over 200,000 are said to have participated in the construction of the temple. Camels replaced asses as the principal means of transporting goods such as spices from Arabia, while Sardinia, with its copper refineries, and Spain, a source of mineral wealth, were accessible by sea.

Throughout their wanderings, the Hebrews had been under strict injunction from the Law of Moses to preserve rigorous standards of hygiene. In almost every private house built at Jerusalem in the years following Solomon, there was a cistern to collect rainwater in the winter and keep it cool and clean throughout the summer. Unlike many of their contemporaries, who collected water at the nearest spring and who were accustomed to pouring refuse into open street drains, Israelite women could count on a continued fresh water supply, and the city was provided with underground drains. The houses themselves were constructed of two stories, a ground floor for storage and an upper level for living.

The introduction of iron helped farmers and craftsmen in their work. The iron-tipped plough, probably introduced during the reign of Solomon, made possible increased food production, and iron sickles speeded harvesting. Carpenters were now able to replace their bronze saws and axes with sharp and efficient iron ones. The ensuing improvements in production served both the needs of Solomon's growing city and the increasing export trade.

In later ages Solomon was remembered not so much as an efficient administrator as a man of wisdom. As the biblical account notes, however, toward the end of his life he began to give way to foreign influences, and the extravagance of the greatest of his monuments, the temple in Jerusalem, proved fatal to the kingdom's survival. His death was followed by a period of bitter civil war, leading to the division of the kingdom into two parts, Israel to the north and Judah, with its capital at Jerusalem, to the south.

Solomon's reign was the high point in Israel's political history, but it also marked the beginning of the kingdom's collapse. Fatally divided, it was a tempting prize. The Assyrians invaded and by 721 B.C. destroyed the northern kingdom of Israel. The kingdom of Judah lasted until 587 B.C., when Jerusalem was destroyed by the Babylonians and the Hebrews were herded into captivity in Babylon. Some 40 years later they were permitted to return to Palestine by the intervention of the Persians, a new force on the international scene. It was during these trying centuries that the great Hebrew prophets, including Isaiah and Jeremiah, explored the religious implications of Israel's trials in terms of divine punishment and the promise that a remnant of the Hebrew nation would be preserved. Although the pharaoh Akhenaton had professed a belief in a single creator-god, it was the Hebrew prophets who first fully enunciated ethical monotheism.

The Hittites

Unlike the Hebrews and the other Semitic peoples of western Asia, the Hittites were Indo-Europeans, members of a large group of peoples who spoke a language related to Greek, Latin, and Persian. The Hittites first migrated into Anatolia, probably from central Europe, no later than 2700 B.C. By the middle of the second millennium B.C. the Hittite kings of Asia Minor were among the most powerful of all rulers in western Asia, equals of the monarchs of Babylon and Assyria or the Egyptian pharaohs. Yet with the fall of their empire around 1200 B.C., the Hittites virtually disappear from history. Apart from being mentioned in the Old Testament as one of the Palestinian tribes with whom the Hebrews came into contact, they remained unknown and undiscovered until the end of the nineteenth century. The exploration of their cities, with their palaces and royal archives, has revealed them as one of the most fascinating of ancient peoples.

The principal Hittite territory was located in what is now modern Turkey. Its capital was at Hattusas (sometimes called by the modern name of the site, Bogazkoy). From there, beginning around 1650 B.C., the Hittite kings embarked on aggressive military campaigns, pushing south across the formidable natural barrier presented by the Taurus Mountains into the more fertile territory of their southern and eastern neighbors. Sometime after 1600 B.C. they captured Babylon.

These initial successes were eroded by internal feuding, and the apparent obscurity of the following century may imply that the Hittites were more concerned with defending their territory against invaders than with empire building. The powerful military leader Suppiluliumas (c. 1375–c. 1335 B.C.) put Hittite armies once again on the attack. They conquered Syria, and even the Egyptians made peace overtures. The widow of the pharaoh (probably Tutankhamen, who had just died at the age of 18) sent a letter to Suppiluliumas begging him to send one of his sons to provide her with a new husband. Such an attractive alliance could hardly be turned down, and a Hittite prince was duly dispatched, only to be murdered en route to the Egyptian court. Suppiluliumas thus lost the opportunity to place his son on the Egyptian throne, an event that would have firmly linked the two empires.

HATTUSILIS III AND PUDUHEPA

The career of King Hattusilis III (1275–c. 1250 B.C.) and his queen, Puduhepa, provides an even more vivid picture of power and politics in the ancient world. This is in part due to the fact that Hattusilis wrote the earliest surviving political autobiography. Like many public figures after him, Hattusilis gave a biased picture, the principal purpose of which was to justify murky dealings on his part. He was an experienced military commander in his late forties when he deposed the reigning king, his nephew, in a coup. Hattusilis described his childhood as dogged by ill health and an early youth surrounded by jealous enemies. Yet the events of his reign show him to have been a powerful and ruthless leader, engaged in incessant fighting to protect his kingdom's northern frontiers and negotiating with Egypt to retain control of Syria. His principal strength, he claimed, lay in the support of the goddess Ishtar, who protected him from his enemies. In fact, Ishtar herself, he declared, had encouraged him to declare war on his nephew by appearing in a dream.

The goddess chose not to appear to Hattusilis himself, however, but to his wife. Puduhepa was by no means the first Hittite queen to emerge as a powerful personality in her own right; in the previous century, the widow of Suppiluliumas had caused so many problems for her son that he finally drove her out of the palace. Puduhepa clearly played an important part in her husband's career. Both their names regularly appear on state documents, and Puduhepa apparently carried on an independent correspondence with the queen of Egypt.

It is, in fact, from their letters that we best know the Hittite rulers, since the palace bureaucrats inscribed on clay tablets copies of outgoing correspondence as well as incoming documents. In many cases the language used was Akkadian or Babylonian, the international language of western Asian diplomacy at the time. One of the tablets found at Bogazkoy, in fact, was a letter from Ramses II to Hattusilis about conflict in Syria, written in Babylonian. The discovery of what has justly been called the Hittite equivalent of the State Department archives throws intriguing light on remote events and personalities.

Hattusilis' uncertain claim to the throne seems to have made him particularly sensitive to the way he was addressed by his fellow rulers. A letter to Ramses complains of being treated as an inferior and not as a fellow "Great King." Ramses' reply was intended to remedy any unintended insult, although it reproaches Hattusilis for his touchiness; addressing Hattusilis as his brother, Ramses reassures him of his great accomplishments but concludes by saying that Hattusilis, instead of good wishes, had written "incomprehensible words not worthy to be sent." Yet when an Assyrian king addressed him as brother in seeking an alliance, the Hittite ruler was quick to reply: "What is this you keep repeating about 'brotherhood'? Were we born of the same mother? Stop writing to me about brotherhood. I do not wish it." Presumably the professional diplomats who kept these documents on file were able to smooth over whatever ruffled feelings may have resulted.

Hittite Society and Religion

The Hittite kingdom over which Hattusilis and Puduhepa ruled was basically agricultural. Many of the documents from the royal archives consist of land deeds, together with laws governing farming mishaps—the escape of a pig or an accidental fire in an orchard, for example. Unlike the Mesopotamians, the Hittites could cultivate the vine, and wine, olive oil, and grain figure prominently in their records. The Hittites were also the first people to discover the technique of iron smelting, but, as we have seen, iron remained a precious metal, in short supply until about 1000 B.C. In a letter to a contemporary ruler, probably an Assyrian king, Hattusilis refused to provide supplies of iron, with the excuse that it was "a bad time for production," although he enclosed an iron dagger blade as a personal gift.

Hittite trading was widespread throughout western Asia, and much of the royal correspondence deals with trade concessions and the protection of merchants traveling abroad. Egypt and Syria provided the principal markets, although the Hittites also traded with the Babylonians and were probably in commercial contact with the Mycenaeans, the principal Bronze Age people of the Greek mainland. Hittite objects sold or traded included

Hittite Laws

Hittite laws were designed for reparation rather than retribution, as these examples demonstrate.

If anyone breaks a freeman's arm or leg, he pays him twenty shekels of silver and he [the plaintiff] lets him go home.

If anyone breaks the arm or leg of a male or female slave, he pays ten shekels of silver and he [the plaintiff] lets him go home.

If anyone steals a plough-ox, formerly they used to give fifteen oxen, but now he gives ten oxen; he gives three oxen two years old, three yearling oxen, and four sucklings(?) and he [the plaintiff] lets him go home.

If a freeman kills a serpent and speaks the name of another [a form of sorcery], he shall give one pound of silver; if a slave does it, he shall die.

If a man puts filth into a pot or a tank, formerly they paid six shekels of silver; he who put the filth in paid three shekels of silver [to the owner?], and into the palace they used to take three shekels of silver. But now the king has remitted the share of the palace; the one who put the filth in pays three shekels of silver only and he [the plaintiff] lets him go home.

If a freeman sets a house on fire, he shall rebuild the house; but whatever perishes inside the house, be it a man, an ox, or a sheep, for these he shall not compensate.

Source: O. R. Gurney, *The Hittites* (Harmondsworth, England: Penguin Books, 1954), p. 96.

bronze and iron vessels, and among the commodities Hittite merchants tried to buy was lapis lazuli, a precious blue stone mined in northeastern Afghanistan.

Like the Babylonians and other ancient peoples, the Hittites developed legal codes to organize their society. Detailed provisions were made for cases of homicide, theft, and arson as well as general conditions governing employment, property holding, and the treatment of slaves. Many of the provisions reflect the agricultural nature of Hittite society: rulings on crimes related to vineyards and orchards, offenses related to cattle, and accidents at river crossings.

In spite of exceptions such as Puduhepa, Hittite society was clearly patriarchal. Fathers "gave away" their daughters, and marriage was principally regarded as a financial contract. Nevertheless, young Hittite women seem to have been allowed a little more independence than their Babylonian counterparts. The initial betrothal was accompanied by a present from the future bridegroom, but if the young woman decided that she would prefer to marry someone else, she could do so, with or without her parents' consent, provided that she returned the engagement present. Various other regulations governed the treatment of widows and children; they included a provision that if a man died childless it was the responsibility of his brother, father, or other male relative to marry and take care of his widow. Any children born of such a marriage took the name of the dead man and thus perpetuated his line. Although Babylonian law did not make this provision, a similar law existed in the ancient Jewish tradition, so that the dead man's name would not be "blotted out of Israel."[3]

As might be expected among an agricultural people, the principal Hittite deity was a weather god. In contrast to the predictability of the Mesopotamian cycle of seasons, the weather in the Taurus Mountains in southern Asia Minor is stormy and uncertain. The son of the weather god, Telipinu, was one of the gods of agriculture, who may have become the center of a cult similar to that of Osiris in Egypt, symbolizing death and rebirth. As Hittite society developed, a complicated interweaving of various deities, local and statewide, came into being, but the weather god remained the dominant figure. The language of a treaty guaranteeing security throughout western Asia during the reign of Hattusas III describes the agreement as being between "the Sun God of Egypt and the Weather God of Hatti."

The End of the Hittite Empire

The treaty with Egypt may have secured the Hittites' eastern frontiers, but trouble soon developed in the west.

Local governors there had revolted, and when the mass migrations of the so-called Peoples of the Sea, who were repelled with such difficulty by Ramses III, swept across western Asia, the Hittites were unable to keep the invaders out. With the collapse of their capital at Hattusas around 1190 B.C., the population scattered. A version of Hittite culture continued in a few cities in the extreme south, in what is now Syria, but these were soon taken over by the Assyrians. The heirs of the Hittites in Asia Minor were the Phrygians, whose worship of Cybele, the Great Mother, became widespread in the Roman world, and the Lydians, who were probably the inventors of coinage.

The Rise of Persia

The land of the Persians had been inhabited for millennia, perhaps from as early as 15,000 B.C. Persia itself, or Iran as it is now called, lies at a crossroads between the rugged lands of western Asia, the plains of central Asia, the great steppes to the northeast, and Afghanistan and the Indus valley to the east. At the heart of Persia is a high central plateau surrounded by mountains, which separate the plains of the interior from the Caspian Sea to the north and the Persian Gulf to the south. Two extensive deserts, virtually impassable in the summer, lie in the center of the immense plateau; from time immemorial they have diverted nomads from central Asia into India to the east or the Tigris-Euphrates valley to the west. The lowlands beyond the mountains receive most of the region's precipitation and thus contrast sharply with the dry interior. The land is rich in minerals, particularly iron, copper, and brilliant blue lapis lazuli. Early in its history western Iran, known then as Elam, fell under Sumerian influence. Persia as a whole, however, was only sparsely settled by prehistoric peoples throughout the centuries of Sumerian and Babylonian rule.

Around 1000 B.C., as we have seen, conditions in western Asia were generally unstable. The Egyptians had begun their decline, the Assyrians had not yet established firm rule, and the mass movements of the Peoples of the Sea had created havoc, destroying the Hittites in the process. Nor was the situation simplified by the fact that at about the same time tribes of nomadic, horse-riding warriors migrated from central Asia into Iran, bringing their flocks and herds. Without horses, the prehistoric inhabitants were no match for them. Among the invading tribes were the Indo-European Medes and Persians, both of whom were related to the Aryans who settled India. The Medes and Persians were soon joined by the warlike Scythians, who had in turn been driven from the far eastern steppe, where the Huns, a people from central Asia, were at war with the Chinese.

This carved Hittite relief, which comes from Zinjirli, shows the weather god. [State Museum, East Berlin]

The Medes and the Persians established a number of small kingdoms, each of which was ruled by a king who was little more than a warlord supported by a band of warriors. Below this elite group, early Iranian society was comprised of free farmers, skilled craftsmen, peasants who owed labor to the king, and slaves. Trade was conducted with other peoples in the region, particularly the Assyrians to the west, who were attracted by Iranian horses and minerals. The Medes, who had settled in northern Iran, united in the late eighth century B.C., after which they imposed their rule on the Persians in the south.

An alliance of Medes and Scythians together with the help of other nomadic tribes sacked Nineveh in 612 B.C. and put an end to the Assyrian Empire. Throughout these tumultuous events the Persians retained their tribal identity and through a process of intermarriage and aggression established their rule over most of Iran. In 550 B.C. the Medes, weakened by their struggles to the west, were resoundingly defeated by Cyrus (559–530 B.C.), chief of the Persian tribes. The land of the Medes became Cyrus' first province, or satrapy.

About 546 B.C. Cyrus conquered prosperous Lydia and the Greek cities on the Anatolian coast, in what is now Turkey. This gave him possession of the ports that marked the western terminus of the trade routes extending from the Aegean Sea deep into Asia. After securing his eastern frontiers by fighting that extended as far as Afghanistan and western India, he turned to the southwest and in 539 B.C. captured the venerable city of Babylon. That city, which had recently witnessed the splendid reign of Nebuchadnezzar, became an important symbol of Persian success. Cyrus included the title "king of Babylon" in his inscriptions and spent considerable time in residence there. As a conqueror he distinguished himself by his appreciation of the cultures of his new subjects; local customs and religious beliefs were not suppressed.

Cyrus' son and successor, Cambyses (530–522 B.C.), conquered Egypt in 525 B.C., and even tried to reach Carthage (modern Tunis). He failed, however, to persuade his Phoenician allies to attack their Carthaginian kinsmen. His plan to conquer Ethiopia also remained largely unfulfilled because of inadequate supplies. Cambyses was said to have been mentally unbalanced, and he was cruel enough to kill his own brother.

The accession of Darius I (522–486 B.C.) returned stability to the Persian Empire, and his reign inaugurated nearly two centuries of peaceful Persian rule. Among his accomplishments were the introduction of a uniform system of gold and silver coinage, standard weights and measures, a postal service, an imperial law code based on Mesopotamian principles, and a common calendar derived from the Egyptians'.

Darius' reign saw further attempts to extend the empire. Around 513–512 B.C. he sent expeditions into southeastern Europe, reaching as far as the River Danube, and into India, the northwestern portion of which became the satrapy of Hindush. Darius wanted to improve communications and trade, and to that end supported an expedition, led by the Greek sailor Scylax, that sailed from the Indus River to the northern end of the Red Sea. Darius also became embroiled with the people to the far west, the Greeks, against whom he and his successor Xerxes launched three unsuccessful expeditions. Despite his failure to conquer the Greeks, Darius' empire enjoyed trade relations with people as far away as India to the east and Phoenicia on the Mediterranean. The Persians planned to construct a canal from the Nile to the Red Sea; had they succeeded, Alexander the Great might have conquered India, and fifteenth-century explorers might not have sought a passage across the Atlantic Ocean to East Asia.

Life and Government in the Empire

The Persian Empire at its height was both wealthy and cosmopolitan. Foreign artisans worked with materials that came from Greece, Lebanon, and India to decorate the royal palaces. The Persians traded widely, using their gold coin, the daric, and maintained contacts throughout western Asia. Many of the people under their control did not speak their language, and the monuments on the Royal Road, the principal highway to cross part of the empire, were accompanied by inscriptions in Babylonian and Elamite as well as Persian. Some 1,600 miles long (the distance from New York to Dallas), the Royal Road extended from Susa in western Persia to Sardis, near the port of Ephesus, a Greek city on the Aegean. It took caravans three months to travel this road, although royal couriers, using fresh horses provided at the 111 post stations along the route, could make the trip in a week.

For all the power of their ruler, the "King of Kings," the Persian view of their monarchy differed from that of the Assyrians. The king was not an instrument of fear but a righteous leader, elected by all the gods. The empire was in general ruled with efficiency, justice, and tolerance. It was so large that it had to be divided into some 20 satrapies, each of which was administered by a governor (or satrap), aided by a military force under a separate commander. The governors, who were Mede or Persian nobles, were prevented from exercising inordinate power by the presence of both military officials and royal agents and spies. From the satraps the king was primarily interested in receiving appropriate tribute and recruits for the military; if those demands were fulfilled, the governors enjoyed a good deal of autonomy.

Persian Capitals: Susa and Persepolis

The principal centers of the empire were at Susa, eastern terminus of the Royal Road; Ecbatana, the former Mede capital; and ancient Babylon. Susa, which had been inhabited since Neolithic times, was situated at the foot of the Zagros Mountains, near the bank of the River Karkheh. Beginning in 521 B.C., Darius made it his principal capital for most of the year, leaving only in the summer to escape the intense heat. He ordered the construction of a citadel and a sumptuous palace as well as walls and a moat for protection. His workers were imported from many lands: stonecutters from Greece and Asia Minor, goldsmiths from Egypt, brickmakers from Babylon. So were his materials, including cedar from Lebanon, gold from Bactria,

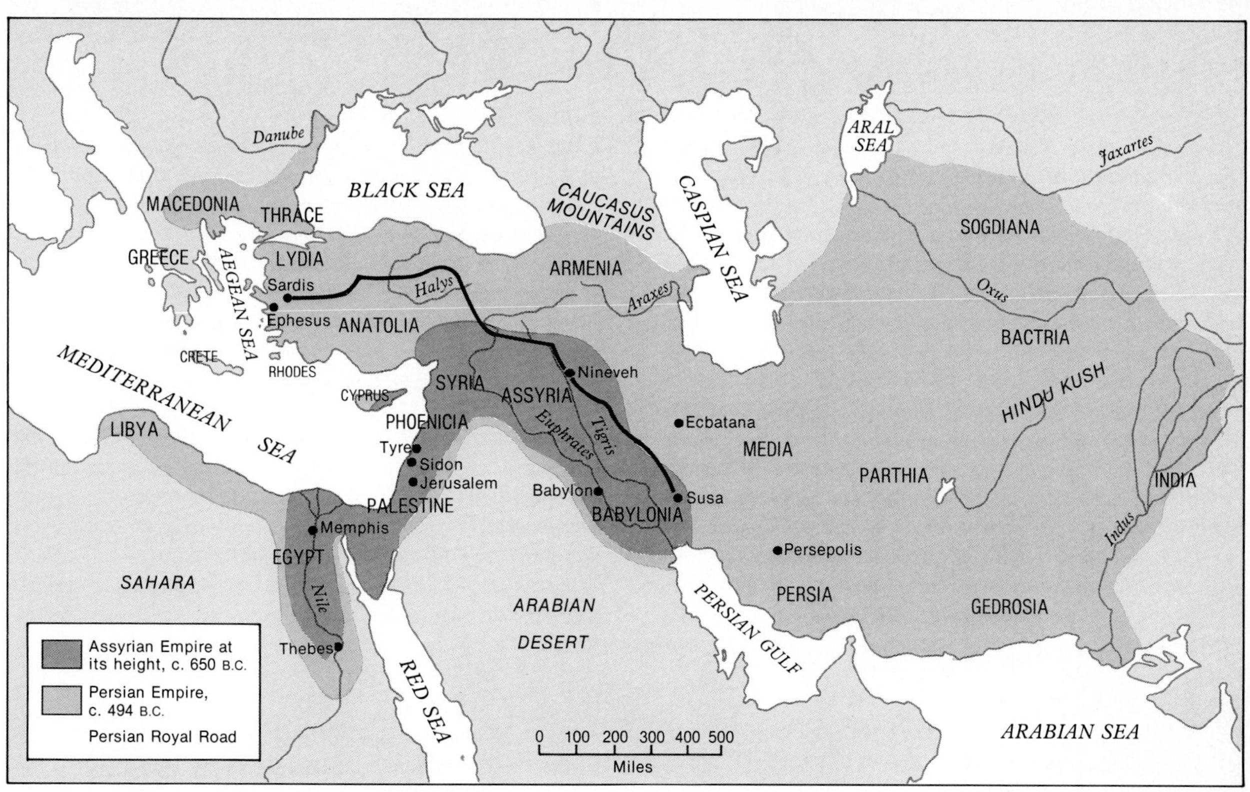

1.3 The Empires of Assyria and Persia

and ivory from Ethiopia. Susa became a cosmopolitan center; the Jewish book of Esther is set there.

In 518 B.C. Darius began the construction of a new capital at Persepolis, a remote site in an alpine region southeast of Susa. The style of architecture and sculpture that developed at Persepolis, like that at Susa, was highly eclectic. Lacking their own architectural traditions, the Persians drew on those of others. Like the Sumerians, they employed mud brick and constructed their palaces on terraces, although they used the kind of glazed decoration found on Nebuchadnezzar's palace at Babylon. Assyrian human-headed bulls, Egyptian doorways, and even Greek columns can be found at Persepolis; some of the decorative sculpture was almost certainly produced by visiting Greek and Egyptian artists. The total effect is striking in the extensive ruins that remain.

The site of Persepolis was topped by a citadel. The lower slopes of the mountain on which it stands were leveled to allow construction on a terrace 14 to 41 feet above the ground. The terrace was reached by a stairway broad enough to be used by groups of riders. Upon it were monumental public buildings, each intended to reinforce the general impression of splendor. The vast audience hall of the royal palace built by Darius and Xerxes between 520 and 460 B.C. was approached by an elaborate staircase lined with sculptural decoration. The reliefs showed a procession of officials, soldiers, and representatives of the assorted peoples of the empire bringing tribute to the king. The great hall was 60 feet high and contained three dozen 40-foot columns. On a retaining wall, Darius inscribed a prayer for his subjects: "God protect this country from foe, famine, and falsehood."

Darius' successors maintained the Persian Empire until it was conquered by Alexander the Great between 334 and 326 B.C. The arrival of Alexander and his troops thrust Europe and Asia into the long period of mutual influence that has lasted, despite interruptions, to our own time.

The peoples of western Asia achieved some of the greatest artistic and cultural innovations in history. The invention of metalworking and writing and the development of architectural techniques and draining and irrigation systems are only the most obvious of the many technological advances of the period. These made possible the development of cities, and with them came the growth of legal systems and complex urban relationships that remain, in one form or another, the basis of our daily lives.

Growing economic prosperity, coupled with technological developments such as wheeled vehicles and seagoing ships that simplified long-distance travel, encouraged the expansion of trade. This in turn led, on the one hand, to stimulating contact with foreign ideas as well as goods and, on the other hand, to conflict, since what could be bought peacefully could also be taken in war. It is no accident that much of the new technolgy was devoted to making better weapons and stronger fortifications. Internal and external expansion required professional planners and administrators, which produced the new profession of bureaucrat.

The same drive that laid the foundations of civilized life in western Asia was responsible for the art that helps us to interpret the varied character and world view of the peoples who produced them. Some monuments are more familiar than others. The pyramids of Egypt, for example, were known to Roman soldiers and to Napoleon, whereas the Hittites have been rediscovered only in our century. Time after time, works of art that were created in a world remote from our own succeed in communicating to us with vividness and power. The fascination they continue to exert confirms the underlying unity of human experience.

Notes

1. *The Book of the Dead According to the Theban Recension*, trans. E. A. Wallis Budge, in *Egyptian Literature*, ed. E. Wilson (London: Colonial Press, 1901).
2. J. B. Pritchard, ed., *Ancient Near Eastern Texts Relating to the Old Testament,* trans. J. Wilson (Princeton, N.J.: Princeton University Press, 1969), pp. 251–252.
3. Deut. 25:6.

Suggestions for Further Reading

Ackroyd, P. R. *Israel Under Babylon and Persia*. London: Oxford University Press, 1970.

Bengston, H. *Introduction to Ancient History*. Berkeley: University of California Press, 1976.

Bright, J. *A History of Israel*, 3d ed. Philadelphia: Westminster Press, 1981.

Burney, C. *The Ancient Near East*. Ithaca, N.Y.: Cornell University Press, 1977.

Davies, W. D., and Finkelstein, L., eds. *The Cambridge History of Judaism*. Vol. I: *The Persian Period*. Cambridge: Cambridge University Press, 1984. Vol. 2: *The Hellenistic Age*. Cambridge: Cambridge University Press, 1987.

De Boer, P. A. H. *Fatherhood and Motherhood in Israelite and Judean Piety*. Leiden, Netherlands: Brill, 1974.

De Gobineau, J. A. *The World of the Persians*. London: J. Gifford, 1971.

De Vaux, R. *The Early History of Israel*, trans. D. Smith. London: Darton, Longman & Todd, 1978.

Finley, M. I. *The Ancient Economy*. Berkeley: University of California Press, 1973.

Gurney, O. R. *The Hittites*, 2d ed. New York: Penguin, 1972.

Hallo, W. W., and Simpson, W. K. *The Ancient Near East: A History*. New York: Harcourt Brace Jovanovich, 1971.

Harden, D. *The Phoenicians*, 2d ed. New York: Praeger, 1971.

Hawkes, J. *The First Great Civilizations: Life in Mesopotamia, the Indus Valley, and Egypt*. New York: Knopf, 1973.

Jacobsen, T. *The Treasures of Darkness: A History of Mesopotamian Religion*. New Haven, Conn.: Yale University Press, 1976.

Kitchen, K. A. *The Third Intermediate Period in Egypt, 1100–650* B.C., 2d ed. Warminster, England: Aris & Phillips, 1986.

Kramer, S. N. *History Begins at Sumer*, 3d ed. Philadelphia: University of Pennsylvania Press, 1981.

———. *The Sumerians: Their History, Culture, and Character*. Chicago: University of Chicago Press, 1963.

Laessoe, J. *The People of Ancient Assyria*, trans. F. S. Leigh-Brown. London: Routledge & Kegan Paul, 1963.

Manniche, L. *City of the Dead: Thebes in Egypt*. Chicago: University of Chicago Press, 1987.

Nissen, H. J. *The Early History of the Ancient Near East, 9000–2000* B.C. Chicago: University of Chicago Press, 1988.

Oppenheim, A. L. *Ancient Mesopotamia*, rev. ed. Chicago: University of Chicago Press, 1977.

Redford, D. B. *Akhenaten: The Heretic King*. Princeton, N.J.: Princeton University Press, 1984.

Redman, C. L. *The Rise of Civilization: From Early Farmers to Urban Society in the Ancient Near East*. San Francisco: Freeman, 1978.

Sandars, N. K. *The Sea Peoples*, rev. ed. London: Thames & Hudson, 1985.

Silver, M. *Economic Structures of the Ancient Near East*. Totowa, N.J.: Barnes & Noble Books, 1987.

Smith, W. S. *The Art and Architecture of Ancient Egypt*. New York: Penguin, 1958.

Wells, E. *Hatshepsut*. Garden City, N.Y.: Doubleday, 1969.

CHAPTER · 2

Ancient India

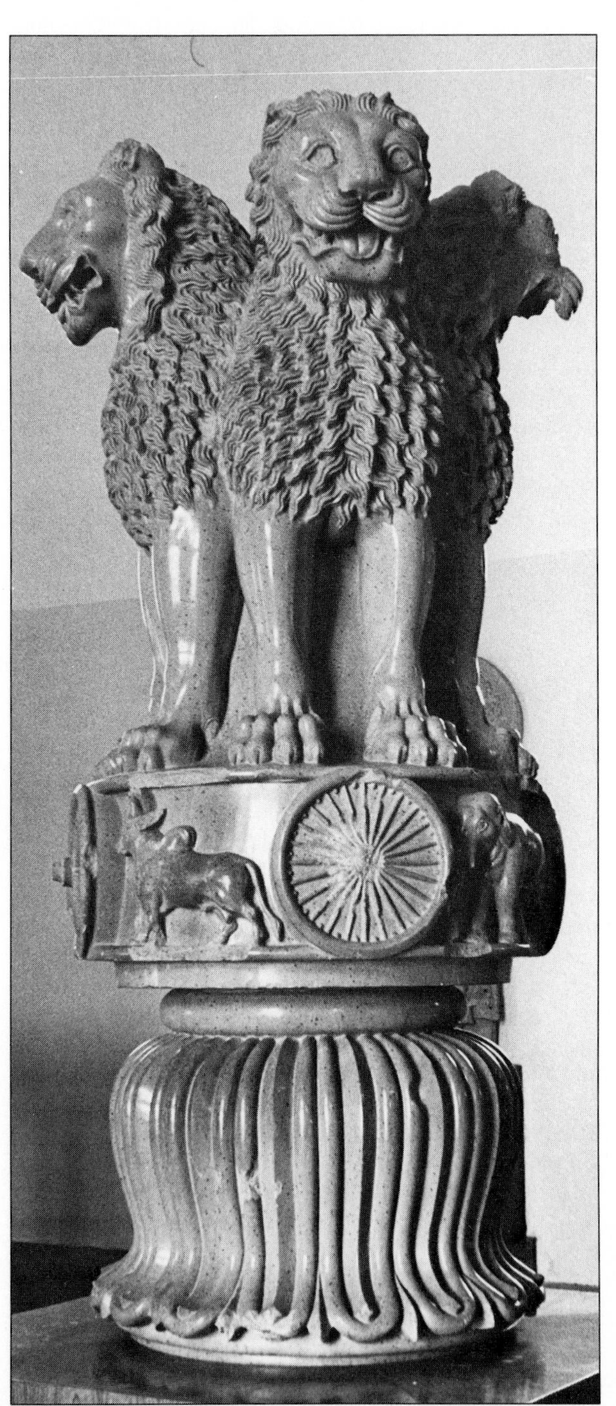

Perhaps the best-known samples of Mauryan art are the pillars erected by the emperor Ashoka, usually bearing Buddhist edicts and surmounted by sculptured figures. This triad of royal lions in stone, still used as an official symbol of India, formed the capital of one of Ashoka's columns and effectively captures the splendor of Mauryan India. [Stella Snead/ Archaeological Survey of India]

India's civilization is the oldest in continuous existence. If one defines civilization as involving a writing system, metal working, and some concentration of settlement in cities where most of the inhabitants are not farmers, the earliest such developments seem to have occurred in Mesopotamia by about 4000 B.C. and about the same time in Egypt. By about 3000 B.C. civilization in these terms had emerged in the Indus valley of India, and by about 2000 B.C. in China. Mesopotamian and Egyptian civilizations came to an end by Roman times and were later superseded by the Arab conquest. The present cultures of these areas have little or no connection with ancient Sumer or the time of the pharaohs, leaving India as the oldest survivor. The Indus civilization is the clearly traceable direct ancestor of subsequent Indian civilization, and the continuities are strong.

The Indian subcontinent, as it is called, from the mountain borders of Afghanistan to the Bay of Bengal on the east and from the towering Himalayas to the southern tip of the peninsula, is about the size of all of Europe (excluding Russia) and is even more varied physically, linguistically, and culturally. This huge and diverse area has only briefly during its long history been united under a single ruler, and then only partly so. It is now composed of the separate states of Pakistan, India, Nepal, Bangladesh, and Sri Lanka, but within each of these political divisions remain major regional differences. For every period of Indian history it is thus difficult to generalize about this vast and varied part of the world, containing about a fifth of the world's people. Nevertheless, an underlying culture shared by inhabitants of the subcontinent, periodically enriched by new infusions, gave and still gives Indian civilization its basic identity.

Although a literate urban culture was in existence in India by around 3000 B.C. and lasted about 1,000 years, we know relatively little about it. We cannot yet decipher the texts its people inscribed on clay tablets and seals, and the evidence we have is mainly the partly excavated ruins of the very large cities they built. After the collapse of the Indus civilization, northern India was invaded, over many centuries, by a central Asian people who called themselves Aryans. They gradually became the dominant group in the north, although they intermarried with the indigenous people. By the time Alexander the Great invaded India in 326 B.C. many regional kingdoms had arisen. These were welded together into an empire by the Maurya dynasty (c. 322–c. 180 B.C.) after Alexander withdrew, which unified most of the north. A new group of invaders reunified the north under the Kushan dynasty from 100 B.C. to about A.D. 200. In the following century the indigenous Gupta dynasty restored most of the Mauryan accomplishments in the north from A.D. 320 to 550, while the south remained divided among flourishing rival kingdoms. Gupta rule collapsed around 550, as did the short-lived northern empire of Harsha by 648. Once more, India became a complex pattern of separate states. But in most of its basic elements, Indian civilization has remained continuous from the third millennium B.C. to the present.

Origins of Civilization in India

Agriculture had evolved much earlier than civilization, probably independently in a number of places including tropical Southeast Asia, western Asia (what is now eastern Turkey, Syria, and northern Iraq), Africa, and, by about 2000 B.C., in Central and South America. Agriculture in permanent fields, as opposed to a food-gathering culture, requires permanent settlement. Villages or even small towns of this sort inhabited by farmers began to emerge soon after 10,000 B.C. in western Asia.

It was not far from Sumer to India, and the way was relatively easy: by ship along the sheltered coasts of the Persian Gulf and thence still following the coast to the mouth of the Indus River. The route by land across Iran and Baluchistan ran through desert with few oases, but it was used too. Neolithic developments in agriculture and the beginnings of large settled villages or towns were taking place at several locations along this land route and in the upland Baluchistan borderlands west of the Indus during the fifth millennium B.C. These developments were probably independent of Sumer but may have benefited indirectly from early Sumerian achievements. Agriculture had also appeared on the Indus floodplain by the fifth millennium and may thus have developed independently there. By 3000 B.C. or so true cities had arisen in the Indus plain and in tributary river valleys, much as early agriculture in the highlands around Mesopotamia later spread onto the riverine lowlands. As in Mesopotamia, the floodplain presented new challenges to early agriculturists: how to control river flooding, manipulate irrigation, and drain swampy land. The long experience with an evolving set of agricultural techniques ultimately made it possible to exploit the potentially rich agricultural resources of the lowlands. Consistent agricultural surpluses provided the basis for real cities, as opposed to towns; the cities were literate, metal-using, food surplus–storing centers with a division of labor and great sophistication in the arts, in building, and in planning.

The Indus Civilization

The chief urban centers so far discovered are Kalibangan in modern Rajasthan (probably the oldest city site yet found in India), Harappa in what is now the Pakistani part of Punjab, and Mohenjo Daro on the lower course of the Indus. All three, plus nearly 200 smaller town or village sites from the same period, scattered over an immense area from the Indus valley east to the upper Ganges and south to near modern Bombay, show similar forms of settlements, pottery, seals (for marking pieces of property), and artwork. This vast complex, extending over by far the largest area of any ancient culture, is called the Indus civilization. It clearly had a close relationship to the river and its tributaries, a situation very similar to that in Sumer and in Egypt. Like the Nile and the Tigris and Euphrates, the Indus is an "exotic" river, that is, one that originates in a well-watered area. Rising with its tributaries in the Himalayas, the source of snowmelt and heavy summer monsoonal rains, it flows across lowland Punjab and arid Rajasthan into the desert of Sind to reach the sea near modern Karachi. All of this lowland area is dry, and the lower half of the Indus valley is virtually desert, as in Sumer and Egypt, so that agriculture is dependent on irrigation. Annual river floods provided both water and highly fertile and easily worked alluvium, or silt. Combined with a long growing season of high temperatures and un-

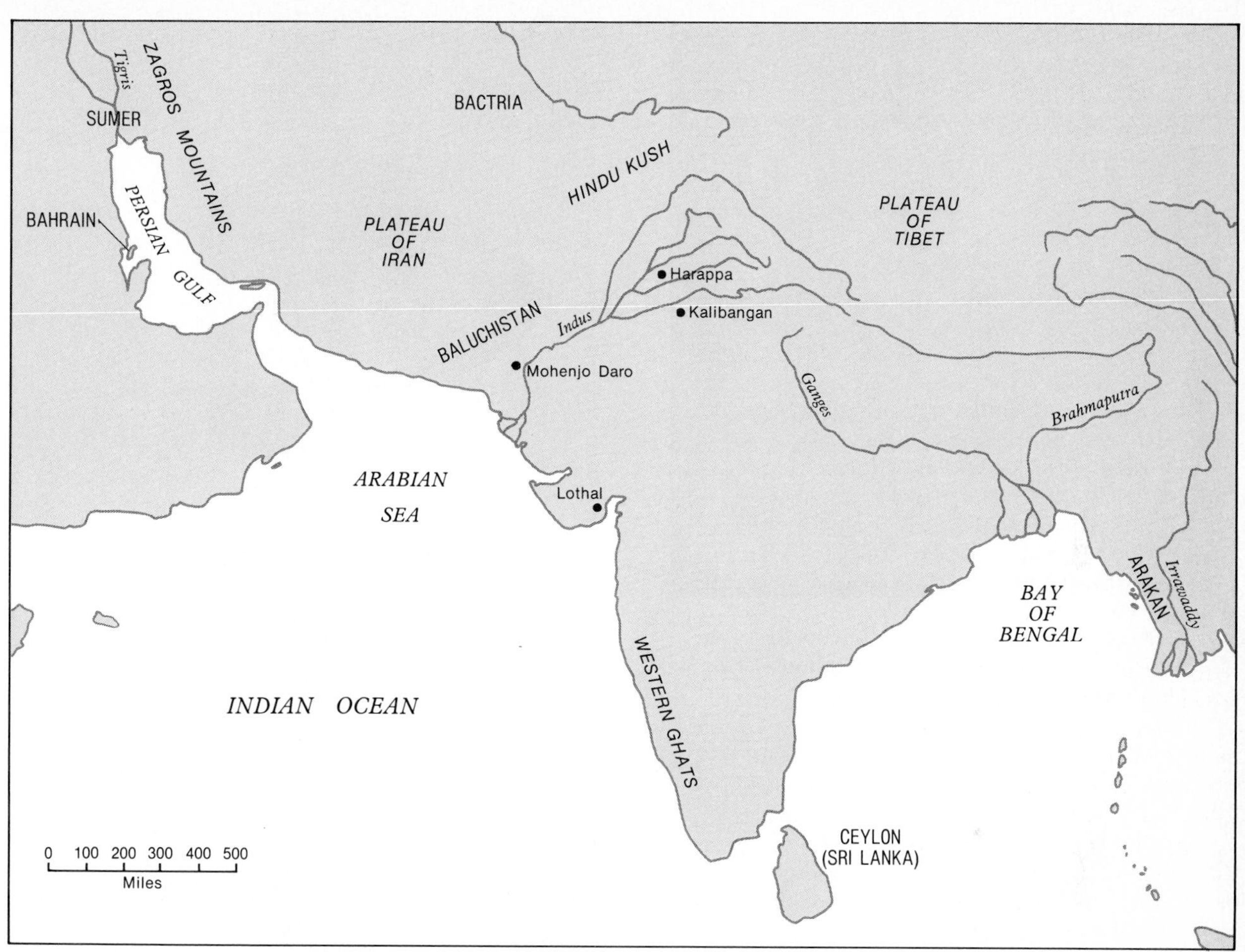

2.1 South Asia

broken sunshine, this was the same set of agricultural advantages that helped to explain the early prominence of Egypt and Sumer after the management and use of floodwater had been mastered. The river also offered cheap, easy transport for bulky goods such as grain or building materials and together with the treeless and level plain created the access for transport that is essential for exchange and hence for the division of labor.

Relations with Sumer

We know much less about the Indus civilization and its cities than about Sumer or ancient Egypt, in part because the Indus script has not yet been deciphered. The texts we have are incised on clay tablets and seals, as in Sumer, and contain over 300 different symbols. They may help provide some clue to who the writers were. It is plausible to assume that they were part ancestors of the present inhabitants of South India, for which there is some linguistic evidence. But the Indus script has no resemblance to cuneiform, which by at least 3200 B.C. had replaced pictographic writing in Sumer, almost certainly before the beginnings of city-based civilization in India. The clear superiority of cuneiform ensured its rapid spread. If the Indus civilization had been an outgrowth of Sumer, it would surely have used cuneiform or at least shown some connection with earlier Sumerian writing systems.

The art of the Indus people and their remarkable city planning are also completely distinctive and show no relation to Sumerian equivalents. The seals that they used are very similar to those of earlier and contemporary Mesopotamia, and we know that from at least 2500 B.C. there was trade between them. Objects from India at this period have been found in Sumer, and Sumerian objects in India. It seems likely that since seals were probably used primarily to mark property or goods, they were adopted by the Indus people in the course of their trade with Sumer. But in all other respects, their civilization was distinctively their own.

When the Indus civilization emerged is difficult to determine exactly, but it was probably around 3000 B.C. The

Seal from Mohenjo Daro. The bovine figure at top right suggests the early veneration of cattle. [Borromeo/EPA; Art Resource]

The famous bronze dancing girl from Mohenjo Daro. [Scala/Art Resource; Karachi Museum, Pakistan]

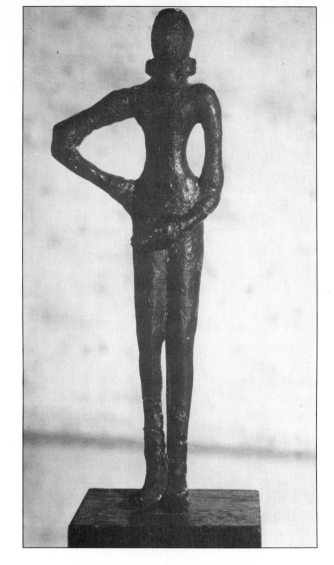

city sites, including the three major ones at Kalibangan, Harappa, and Mohenjo Daro, were necessarily close to the Indus or its tributaries. Water levels and stream courses have changed since these cities were built some 5,000 years ago. Flooding and silt deposition have carried away, buried, or drowned most of the earliest archaeological evidence. As in the case of the Nile delta and for similar reasons, we can no longer see beginnings that may be considerably earlier than we can now prove. The earliest objects dated so far cluster around 2500 B.C., but they come necessarily from upper site levels and from a period when the urban culture was already well advanced. Especially in the emerging phase of civilization, development is relatively slow. One must assume that it began many centuries before 2500, during which it evolved, built the first city levels, and acquired the form and quality evident by 2500.

We do not know what the builders of these cities called themselves or their settlements. The place names we use for them are modern—Mohenjo Daro means "place of the dead." The Greeks called the land they encountered in Alexander's time "India." This was derived from the Sanskrit *Sind,* the Aryan name for the river and by association the river's valley and the land beyond it. From *Sind* comes the Persian and modern Indian name for the country, *Hind,* and its derivatives, *Indus, Hindu,* and *Hindustan* (*stan* means "country").*

Trade with Sumer took place both overland and through the port of Lothal on the coast near the mouth of the

**India* is the label commonly used for the entire subcontinent, including the present states of Pakistan, India, and Nepal, which date in this form only from 1947, and Bangladesh, which was founded in 1971.

Indus, where the remains of large stone docks and warehouses have been found. These were associated with a city that was clearly part of Harappan culture (a convenient shorter label for the Indus civilization). Goods from Sumer have been found there and elsewhere in Harappan India, and Harappan goods in Sumer. A site along the route between them, on Bahrain, has yielded both sorts of objects and seems to have supported a major trade center where many routes to and from Sumer met. Sumerian texts speak of a place called Dilmun, which was probably Bahrain, a number of days' sail southward from the mouth of their river, where were found goods from a place they called Meluha, to the east: ivory, peacocks, monkeys, precious stones, incense, and spices, the "apes, ivory, and peacocks" of the Bible. Meluha must have been India, but it is not clear whether people from Sumer went there or whether the Indus people, or some intermediary, carried their cargoes to Dilmun.

The Cities of the Indus

Perhaps the most remarkable thing about this civilization was the planned layout of its cities, including wells, a piped water supply, bathrooms, and wastepipes or drains in nearly every house. There is no parallel for such planning anywhere in the ancient world, and indeed one must leap to the late nineteenth century in western Europe and North America to find such achievements on a similar scale. The rivers that nourished these cities were the source of their water supply, led by gravity from upstream, a technique later used by the Mughal emperors for their palaces in Delhi and Agra. The importance attached by the Indus people to personal use of water already suggests the distinctively Indian emphasis on both bathing or washing and on ritual purity. Religious remains are varied, but they include many figures that suggest an early representation of the Indian god Shiva, Creator and Destroyer, god of the harvest, of the cycle of birth, life, death, and rebirth, and also the primal yogi,* represented even then seated with arms folded and gaze fixed on eternity. Figures of a mother goddess, phallic images, and the worship of cattle are other elements that provide a link with classical and modern Indian civilization. Some scholars have suggested that the distinctively Indian ideas of reincarnation and the endless wheel of life were Harappan beliefs. Indeed, the roots of most of traditional and modern Indian culture can be found or guessed at in what we can piece together from the Indus culture.

The houses in these cities were remarkably uniform, suggesting an absence of great divisions in the society, arranged along regular streets in a semigrid pattern. There were a few larger buildings, including in most of the cities a large public bath, and others that were probably municipal granaries or storehouses. The art these still unknown people have left behind is strikingly varied and of high quality. Its variety may suggest that it was produced over a very long time, during which styles changed, as anywhere else in the world over 1,000 years: abstract, realistic, idealized, and so on. One of the most appealing forms is the enormous number of clay and wooden children's toys, including tiny carts pulled by tiny oxen or little monkeys that could be made to climb a string. This suggests a relatively prosperous society that could afford such nonessential production—a tribute to the productivity of its irrigated agriculture—and one whose values seem admirable. Complementing the picture, very few weapons or other indications of warfare have been found at these sites. The Indus civilization seems to have been notably peaceful and humane as well as organized and sophisticated. Cotton, indigenous to India, was woven into cloth earlier here than anywhere else. The animal sculpture and bas-relief, including the figures on many of the seals, were superbly done and include very large numbers of bovines, mainly the familiar humpbacked cattle, which suggests the importance attached to cattle and their veneration ever since in India. This and other evidence indicates that the reverence for life and the quest for nonviolent solutions that mark the consistent Indian stress on the great chain of being and the oneness of creation had emerged by Harappan times.

The chief Indus food crop was wheat, probably derived originally from areas to the west, augmented by barley, peas, beans, oil seeds, fruits, and vegetables, and by dairy products from domesticated cattle and sheep. Tools were made of bronze, stone, and wood, but in later centuries iron began to appear and was used, for example, in axle pins for wheeled carts. Rice appeared as a minor crop only toward the end of the Indus period, imported from its Southeast Asian origins as a crop plant via contact with the Ganges valley, to which it had spread earlier. Riverine location was essential for irrigation but also made for recurrent problems from irregular and occasionally disastrous flooding. The remains of successive dikes speak of efforts to protect even the cities themselves against floods and major course changes, not always successfully. There was no building stone in this flat and semiarid or desert region, and the cities were built of brick, as in Sumer, some of it sun-baked and some kiln-fired, using fuel from riverside stands of trees (which must soon have been exhausted), or brought down the rivers from forested hills and mountains upstream. The ruins of Harappa were first investigated in the 1850s by a British military engineer whose sharp eye noticed the strange dimensions of the bricks and other fragments brought to him by Indian contractors for railway ballast and the equally strange markings on some of them, samples of the Indus script, which

*One who practices yoga, the Hindu philosophy that entails a strict spiritual and physical discipline in order to attain unity with the Universal Spirit.

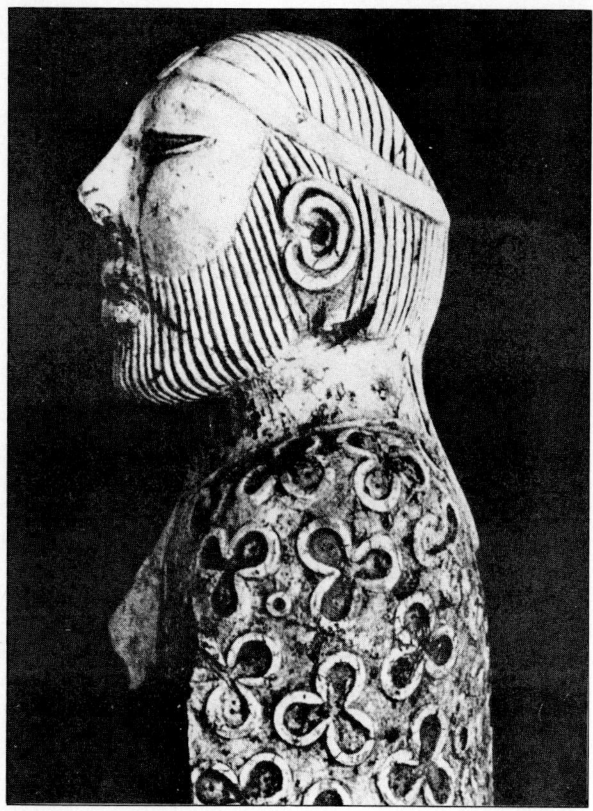

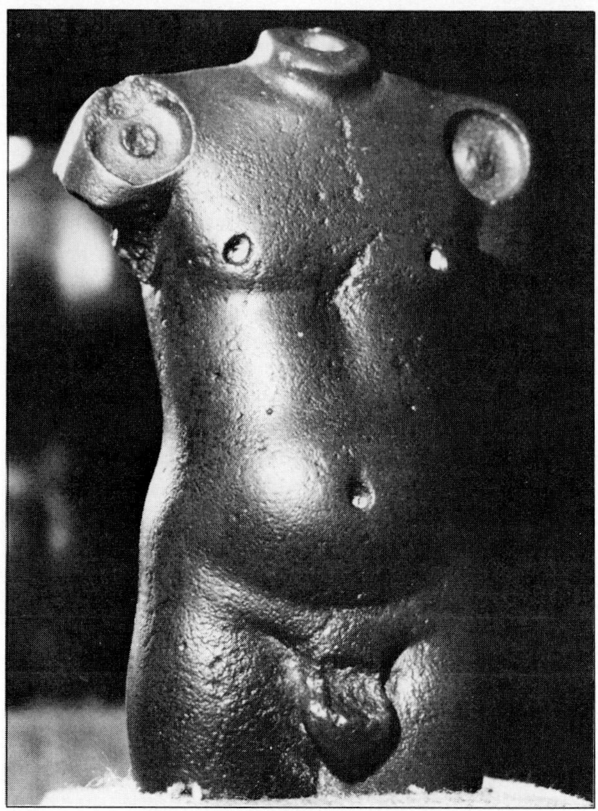

Two strikingly different objects from the Indus civilization, the priest-like figure from Mohenjo Daro and the torso from Harappa. The highly stylized "priest" suggests comparison to Minoan (Cretan) art, the torso to classical Greece. That both come from the Indus civilization may suggest that they were produced at different periods and reflect stylistic changes over time. [*Left:* Stella Snead/Archaeological Survey of India; *right:* Art Resource/National Museum of India, New Delhi]

he traced back to the site of Harappa and realized were the remains of a civilization earlier than any in India then known.

Decline and Fall

Toward the end of the third millennium B.C. the Indus civilization began to decay. We can only guess at the reasons, but there is clear evidence of progressive shrinking of the area under cultivation or irrigation and of the urban area occupied. The port of Lothal was abandoned by about 1900 B.C., and the other major centers probably supported only a fraction of their earlier populations, huddled in a small part of the decaying city. There is also evidence of violence at some of these sites: ashes and unburied or headless corpses, victims perhaps of bandit raids against nearly defenseless cities. But the Indus people encountered some specific problems resulting from their desert or semiarid environment, problems that may quickly have become overwhelming. Continued irrigation of any arid area leads to the progressive buildup of salts and alkalines left behind by the evaporating water and not washed away adequately by rainfall. Irrigation also raises the water table, which may drown crop roots. When accumulated salts and alkalines reach levels toxic to plants or when the root zone is flooded, agriculture may rather suddenly come to an end. We have modern experience with both problems in many arid irrigated areas, including the drier parts of the United States.

In the Indus valley large parts of the areas cultivated in ancient times appear to have been abandoned for these reasons, as the telltale white deposits on the ancient surface indicate. In addition, recurrent flooding and course changes not only menaced the cities directly but also indirectly undermined their agricultural base by destroying or choking with silt the irrigation channels that fed the fields. Course changes could also deprive a city or an irrigated area of its water. All of this is characteristic of the behavior of "exotic" rivers, rising in the mountains and then flowing across a treeless desert. There is no evidence that the climate changed, as has often been asserted despite clear evidence to the contrary, but plenty to suggest that the agricultural surpluses that had built the cities and nourished their culture shrank and then disappeared, leaving only a remnant population living on a relatively primitive level in the ruins of the once great cities on what they could still wring from the remaining but far less productive fields, plus hunting and gathering. In this reduced state, they were less and less able to defend themselves against raiders. The Aryan invaders, arriving later, could never have seen the Indus civilization in its prime and are thus unlikely causes for its decline. The people who built it, or their descendants, probably dispersed eastward into the Ganges valley and southward into peninsular India, taking their culture and technology with them.

The Aryans

Aryan is, strictly speaking, a linguistic term, but it has been used (and widely misused) to mean a people or, even more inappropriately, a race. In the centuries after about 2000 B.C. a series of migration waves moved out from south-central Asia, including what is now Iran, to richer areas both eastward and westward. One such group was probably the Mycenaean invaders of Greece, another the Kassites who invaded and conquered Sumer, and another the Hittites who occupied northern Anatolia, while still another group moved eastward through passes in the Hindu Kush range into India sometime after about 1800 B.C. and called themselves Aryans. They spoke an early form of Sanskrit but were still preliterate, preurban, seminomadic tenders of cattle, sheep, and goats who also lived in part from hunting, from plough agriculture of wheat and barley, and from raiding more highly developed agricultural settlements and trade centers or routes. What little we know about them comes from their ritual hymns, the Vedas, and from the later epic poems of heroic deeds and warfare, the *Mahabharata* and the *Ramayana*, which were written down many centuries later in Sanskrit, the classical language of India. By that time the Aryans had acquired literacy, plus the arts of agriculture, city building, and other aspects of civilization, presumably from contact and intermarriage with the more highly developed people already in India.

Vedic period culture (c. 1000–c. 500 B.C.) was, like its people, a combination of originally Aryan, Harappan, and other indigenous Indian strains. Sanskrit is the oldest written language among the ancestors of modern European languages, and it is also the direct ancestor of the languages of modern North India.* The connection was not realized until the pioneering research of a British judge in Bengal in the late eighteenth century, Sir William Jones, who established the clear link among the Indo-European tongues—Greek, Latin, Celtic, Persian, and Sanskrit, as well as their modern derivatives—all of which had originally stemmed from the great migration of linguistically related peoples both eastward and westward from south-central Asia beginning around 2000 B.C.

Aryan Domination

The Aryans had a telling advantage, despite their more primitive culture: by the time they reached India they had acquired not only metal-tipped weapons but a light, fast war chariot with spoked wheels drawn by two or more horses, equivalent to the Greek war chariots of Homer's time, with a driver and an archer or spear thrower. Their culture glorified war, and they made a disproportionate military impact on a more peaceful Indian population. The Kassites, Hittites, Hyksos invaders of Egypt, and Mycenaeans, all possibly coming originally out of central Asia, made a similar impact with the same tactics. The horse had been known to the Indus people but was not used in fighting. The Vedas and the epics tell the story of Aryan victories over "alien" peoples, whose cities they besieged and conquered, led often by their warrior God Indra riding in his chariot with his great war bow. Like most history written by the victors, the Vedas and the epics portray the Aryans as godlike heroes and the conquered as "irreligious," inferior people. The archaeological record of the Indus civilization abundantly disproves such propaganda, but the Aryan language triumphed, presumably because, though a minority numerically, the Aryans became the ruling class of ancient India. *Arya* means "noble" or "pure" in Sanskrit; the same root word appears in the Greek *arios* ("good quality"), and in the names of Iran and Eire (Ireland), illustrating the Indo-European connection.

We do not know exactly when the institution of caste first appeared, the division of Indian society into ranked status groups that could marry or eat only within the group. One possibility, however, is that it evolved later out of distinctions made in Vedic times between a conquering group of Aryans, insecure because of its numerical weakness, and a conquered people, although such distinctions must in time have been submerged by intermarriage and by cultural hybridization. In any case, caste distinctions and rules, including bans on intermarriage, seem not to have been widely observed until much later, perhaps

*Sanskrit *nava*, "ship"; *deva*, "god"; *dua*, "two"—these and many other Sanskrit words are easily recognizable as the roots of Latin and related English words (*naval, divine, dual*, for example).

as late as the fifth century A.D. The Aryan immigrants brought with them their male and warlike gods and their male-dominated culture, which slowly blended with the female goddesses and matriarchal culture of early India.

By around 1000 B.C. these Aryan-speaking groups had conquered or absorbed most of India north of the Vindhya range, which divides and protects the peninsular south and the Deccan plateau from the Ganges and Indus valleys of the north. Their language never prevailed in the south, which still speaks mainly four non-Indo-European languages collectively known as Dravidian, each with its own extensive and ancient literature. The south has also tended to resist what it still refers to as "Aryan" pressures or influences, but in fact interactions with the "Aryan" north have been a heavily traveled two-way street for thousands of years now, in religion, art, literature, philosophy, and many other aspects of culture. There is a clear north-south distinction in Indian culture, but Indian civilization is a generic whole. We can only guess at what the south was like in Vedic times. The great epics, the *Ramayana* and the *Mahabharata*, speak of the south and Ceylon (now Sri Lanka) as inhabited by savages and demons with whom the Vedic heroes were at war, in keeping with their pejorative descriptions of the people they conquered in the north. But although there were probably battles and raids, the south remained beyond Aryan control except where coastal plains at the western and eastern ends of the Vindhyas allowed easier access. Ceylon was, however, invaded by sea and settled by an Aryan-speaking group in the fifth century B.C. and about the same time by Dravidians from South India.

Vedic Culture

The basis of traditional Indian culture and most of its details evolved in the Vedic period. We know little of that process or of worldly events. The Vedas and the epics are concerned with romantic adventure involving gods and demons, or with philosophical and religious matters rather than with accounts of actual events or daily life. We know only that these centuries saw the maturation of a highly sophisticated culture, no longer simply Aryan or Aryan-dominated but Indian, which we can see in worldly terms for the first time in any detail through the eyes of Greek observers after 326 B.C., following Alexander's invasion of northwestern India. They show us a culture remarkable for its absorption in philosophy and metaphysics but also for its achievements in more mundane respects. The later classical West, like the Chinese, acknowledged India as the home of the most advanced knowledge and practice of medicine; of mathematics, including the numbering system we still use, miscalled "Arabic"—the Arabs got it from India—and of working iron and steel. Indian steel was later to be transmitted to the West, also through the Arabs, as "Damascus" or "Toledo," though the steel itself was Indian. The Indian practice of medicine, known as Ayurveda, enriched both Greek and Chinese knowledge and was widely disseminated, although it also benefited from Greek and Chinese medical practices.

These and other elements of Indian science had something to do with Vedic period assumptions about the universe and the physical world. Like some of the Greek philosophers, but even more consistently, Vedic India thought in terms of universal laws affecting all things—a supreme principle or indwelling essence, an order of nature that they called *Rta*. This order, unlike the Greek conception, was thought to exist above and before even the gods, and to determine all observable and nonobservable phenomena. Modern science and technology are not conceivable without such an assumption of universal physical laws. The Greeks were on the right track in those terms, but the Indians anticipated the Greeks and probably influenced them.

The Rise of Empire: Mauryan India

By about 500 B.C. kingdoms had emerged in the Ganges valley, already established as India's primary center of population, productivity, and commerce. This was the area traditionally known as Hindustan, which stretched from Delhi in the upper valley to Bengal near the river's mouth. Population had multiplied many times since the fall of the Indus civilization, and agriculture had spread from the Indus valley into the Ganges, a potentially more productive area watered far more plentifully by monsoonal rains and with the advantage of rich alluvial soils and a long growing season. In Harappan times the Ganges valley was still heavily forested and probably only thinly settled by hunter-gatherers. With the increasing use of iron tools after about 1000 B.C. and the rise in population, the forest was progressively cleared and most of Hindustan settled and cultivated. Growing numbers and surplus production provided the basis for the emergence of territorial states with revenue bases, officials, cities, roads, and armies.

Alexander the Great and the Greek Impact on India

When Alexander, fresh from his conquest of the Persian Empire and eager to add what the Persians had earlier controlled in northwestern India, burst through the northwestern passes in 326 B.C. (providing thereby the first certain date in Indian history), India was composed of many rival states covering both the north and the south. Alexander encountered and defeated some of them in the Indus valley and Punjab and heard accounts of others. His

Greece in India: standing Buddha from Gandhara, a Greek-ruled kingdom of the second and first centuries B.C. in the northwest. Notice the close similarity in style to Hellenic sculpture, including the conventional representation of the folds of the garment and the generally realistic portrayal. [Lahore Museum, Pakistan]

campaign against Porus, king of West Punjab, with his large army and his battalions of war elephants, was the most difficult of his career. When the proud but wounded and defeated Porus was brought before him, Alexander asked how he wished to be treated. Though barely able to stand, Porus boldly replied: "As befits me—like a king!" Alexander was so impressed that he gave him back his kingdom as an ally, a pact that Porus kept to his death. Alexander's invasion was undertaken with a strong sense of mission, to unite East and West and to create a cosmopolitan fusion of cultures, a plan he had already begun to carry out by merging Greek, Persian, and Medean elements and by taking a wife and a male companion from Persia. He encouraged his 10,000 Greek and Macedonian soldiers to take Persian and Indian wives, in keeping with his larger vision, although, like most soldiers far from home, his men probably needed little urging.

The Greek impact is symbolic of the continuous link between India and the West, not only in common linguistic roots but in physical and cultural terms too. Hellenic-style art continued to be produced by the post-Alexandrian Greek kingdoms in the northwest, such as Bactria, and influenced the evolution of Buddhist art in India. Indian philosophical ideas circulated more widely in the West as a result of the link that Alexander's invasion strengthened. He was himself a widely curious person. Realizing the Indian penchant for philosophy, he summoned Indian scholars to instruct and debate with him and recorded much of what he learned and observed for his own teacher, Aristotle. One Indian sage whom he summoned refused at first to come, saying that Alexander's evident preoccupation with conquest and empire could leave little place for philosophy. Alexander had him brought in, and the two men apparently impressed each other enough that they became friends and companions until Alexander's untimely death in 323 B.C. Before his homesick and rebellious troops obliged him to turn back, far short of his goal of descending the Ganges to the Bay of Bengal, he made several alliances (as with Porus), set up several Hellenic kingdoms in the northwest, and received a number of Indian princes, among them the young Chandragupta Maurya, who was to found the first Indian empire and the Maurya dynasty.

The Mauryan Conquest

By 322 B.C. Chandragupta had emerged as head of an empire that included the whole of Hindustan and most of the northwest, with its capital on the Ganges at Pataliputra, near modern Patna in what is now the state of Bihar. The age of heroic chivalry, as recorded in the Vedas and the epics, was long passed, and the time of ruthless power politics had arrived. We may also guess this from the book attributed to Chandragupta's prime minister, Kautilya, the *Arthashastra*. This is one of the earliest samples we have of what was to become a genre, a handbook for rulers with advice on how to seize, hold, and manipulate power, of which the most famous in the West is Machiavelli's *The Prince*. The *Arthashastra* also deals with the wise and humane administration of justice, but the text we have was composed by many hands over several centuries after Kautilya's time, although he may well have been the author of a now lost original. In any case, empire building is a rough game everywhere, and the writing of such a manual fits the circumstances of the time. It is paralleled very closely by a similar text, the Book of Lord Shang, and the doctrines of Li Ssu, prime minister to China's first imperial unifier, Ch'in Shih Huang Ti, about a century later as warring states were welded into an empire by conquest.

In both India and China in the sixth century B.C. warfare and political rivalries had begun to break up the institutions and values of an earlier age. This period saw the emergence of new philosophical and religious efforts to restore the social order (Confucianism in China) or to provide an escape from worldly strife through contemplation, mysticism, and other-worldly salvation (Taoism in China, Buddhism and the Hindu revival in India). These religious and philosophical developments are dealt with in Chapter 7. We know very little about actual political forms or events in India during these centuries before the rise of the Mauryan Empire. The documents we have are, as indicated earlier, concerned almost exclusively with heroic deeds or with metaphysical and religious matters. Politics and the rise and fall of kingdoms, by their nature transitory, were perhaps considered not important enough to record by comparison with the eternal quest for the mysteries of man and the universe, the consistent emphasis of Indian thinkers. We know the names of some of the states immediately preceding the Mauryan conquest, including the kingdom of Magadha in the central Ganges valley, which seems to have been Chandragupta's original base. But even for Mauryan India we are dependent for actual descriptions largely on Greek sources, including surviving fragments of the Book of Megasthenes, who was posted by Alexander's successor Seleucus Nicator to Chandragupta's court at Pataliputra. The book itself is lost, but later Greek and Latin writers drew on it extensively. It is the earliest description we have of India by an outsider.

PATALIPUTRA AND THE GLORY OF MAURYAN INDIA

In Megasthenes' time and for some two centuries or more after, Pataliputra was probably the largest and most sophisticated city and center of culture in the world, rivaled in its later days perhaps only by the Han dynasty capital at Ch'ang An and larger than anything in the West, as the Greek accounts state. It was the seat of a famous university and library, to which scholars came, reputedly, from all over the civilized world, a city of magnificent palaces, temples, gardens, and parks. Megasthenes describes a highly organized bureaucratic system that controlled the economic and social as well as political life of Mauryan India, complete with a secret service to spy on potential dissidents, suspected criminals, and corrupt or ineffective officials. But he clearly admired Chandragupta for his conscientious administration of justice and for his imperial style. The emperor presided personally over regular sessions at court, where cases were heard and petitions presented, and ruled on disputes in similar fashion on his travels around the empire. His enormous palace at Pataliputra was a splendid complex, and visitors were awed by its magnificence and by the throngs of courtiers, councillors, and guests at state receptions.

Advice to Indian Princes

The Arthashastra, *in addition to its advice to princes on how to seize and hold power and to outwit rivals by often unscrupulous means, also stressed the responsibility of the king to take care of his people.*

The king's pious vow is readiness in action,
his sacrifice the discharge of his duty. . . .
In the happiness of his subjects, his welfare.
The king's good is not that which pleases him,
but that which pleases his subjects.

Therefore the king should be ever active,
and should strive for prosperity,
for prosperity depends on effort,
and failure on the reverse. . . .

A single wheel cannot turn,
and so government is possible only with assistance.
Therefore a king should appoint councillors
and listen to their advice.

Source: A. L. Basham, *The Wonder That Was India,* 3d ed. (New York: Grove Press, 1959), pp. 89, 98.

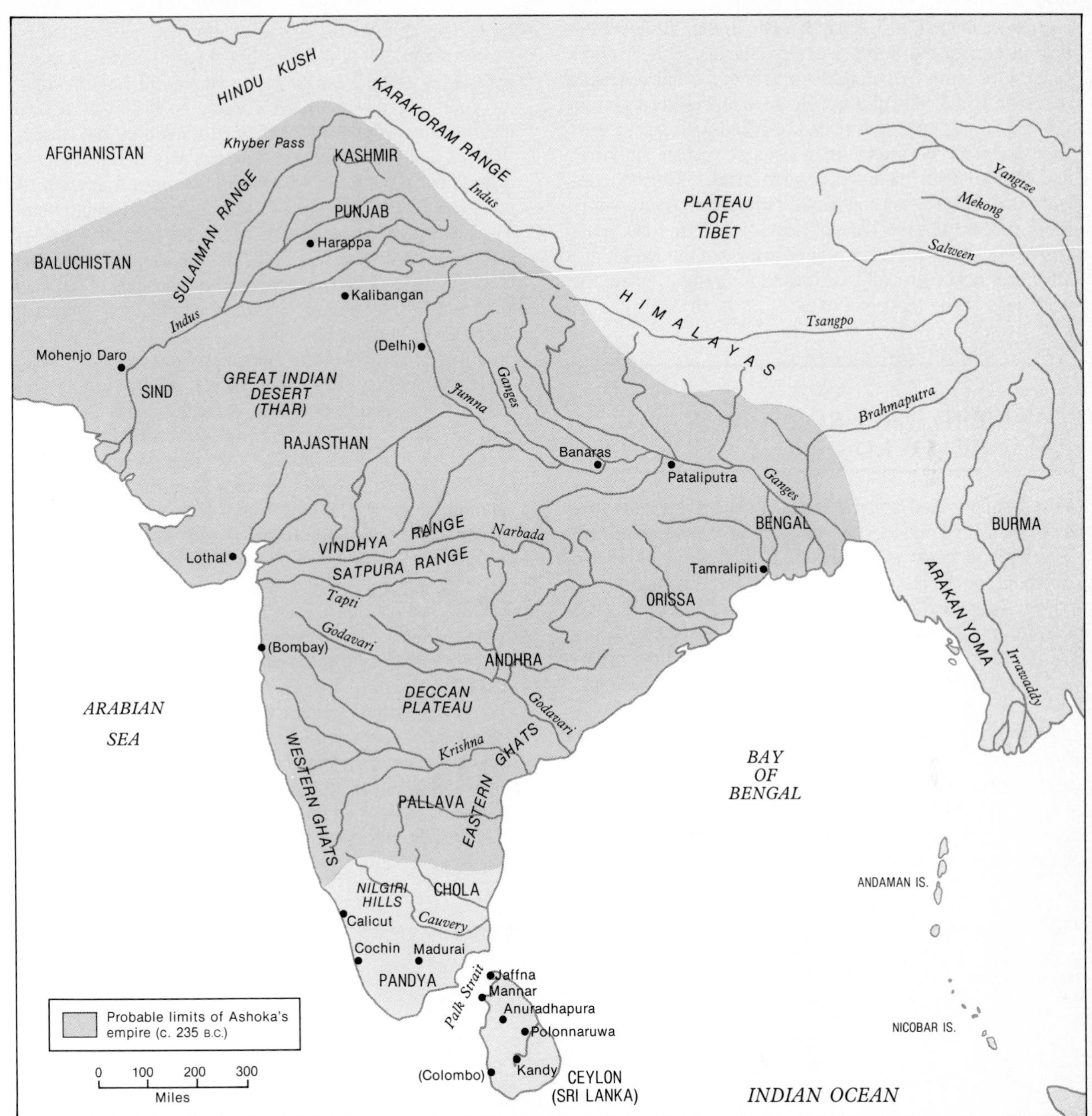

2.2 Ancient India

Pataliputra was surrounded by a huge wall with 570 towers and 64 gates. All mines and forests were owned and managed by the state, and there were large state farms and state granaries, shipyards, and factories for spinning and weaving cotton cloth, all supervised by appropriate government departments. To guard against corruption and favoritism, departments were supposed to be headed by more than one chief, and officials were to be transferred often. Even prostitution was controlled by the state. Megasthenes describes Mauryan India as a place of great wealth and prosperity and remarks on the bustling trade and rich merchants. By this time, if not before, there was already an extensive seaborne trade as well, perhaps extending to Southeast Asia, and a large seaport city in Bengal, Tamralipiti, close to the mouth of the Ganges not far from modern Calcutta. Roads were essential to hold the empire together, and by Mauryan times the main trunk road of India had been built from Tamralipiti along the

Ganges valley to Pataliputra, Banaras, Delhi, through Punjab, and on to the borders of Afghanistan. Other routes branched southward, on to the mouth of the Indus, linking together all the chief cities of Hindustan. The road system was apparently well maintained, marked with milestones, provided with wells and resthouses at regular intervals, and planted with trees to provide shade. Megasthenes says that famine was unknown, although it seems more likely merely that he did not hear of it during his years there. Famine was endemic everywhere in the world, and northern India especially was prone to drought, given the fickleness of the monsoon rains.

THE EMPEROR ASHOKA, "BELOVED OF THE GODS"

Chandragupta died about 297 B.C.; we do not know the exact year, and one legend has it that he wearied of affairs of state and became a wandering ascetic, in the Indian tradition, for the last few years of his life. The empire was further expanded and consolidated by his son Bindusara, who maintained the Greek connection and exchanged gifts with Antiochus I, the Seleucid king of Syria. But the greatest Mauryan ruler was Chandragupta's grandson Ashoka, one of the great kings of world history. Here, however, is another reminder of the traditional Indian lack of interest in political history. Ashoka was perhaps the greatest Indian ruler ever, yet he was all but forgotten until his rediscovery by British antiquarians and archaeologists in the late nineteenth century, thanks to Ashoka's habit of inscribing his name and imperial edicts on rocks and pillars, which he set up all over his immense empire. He came to the throne about 269 B.C. and spent the first several years of his rule in military campaigns to round out the empire by incorporating the south. According to his own rock-cut inscriptions, Ashoka saw and was grieved by the carnage that his lust for power had brought about. His campaign against the Kalingas of Orissa and northern Andhra in the northern Deccan plateau was apparently a turning point. The following year he foreswore further territorial aggression in favor of what he called "the conquest of righteousness." Ashoka was converted to the teachings of the Buddha, who had died four centuries earlier, and vowed to spend the rest of his life, and his great imperial power and prestige, in spreading the Buddhist message.

The beautifully carved stones and pillars that presumably marked Ashoka's empire extend far into the south, well beyond Andhra, and may suggest that he added to his military conquests those of the spirit. We do not know to what extent the south was ruled from Pataliputra during his time, although we know that a Mauryan governor was appointed for the southern provinces. Ashoka clearly felt a sense of mission, not only to spread Buddhism but also to set an example of righteousness in government that could persuade others elsewhere to follow it. He declared that all people everywhere were his children, and he softened the harsher aspects of Chandragupta's police state methods of control. He advocated the ancient Indian ideal of nonviolence (adopted also by the Buddha), urged pilgrimages as a substitute for hunting, and encouraged the spread of vegetarianism. But he kept his army, law courts, and systems of punishment, including execution for major crimes, and remained an emperor in every sense, with his feet firmly in the world of politics. Nevertheless, his reign was remarkable for its humanity and its vision. The mod-

Ashoka's Goals

Ashoka had edicts inscribed on rocks and pillars at widely scattered locations all over India, stating official policy and giving instructions and advice. In one he recounts his conversion and outlines his new goals.

When the king, of gracious mien and Beloved of the Gods, had been consecrated eight years, Kalinga was conquered. 150,000 people were taken captive, 100,000 were killed, and many more died. Just after the taking of Kalinga, the Beloved of the Gods began to follow righteousness, to love righteousness, to give instruction in righteousness. When an unconquered country is conquered, people are killed. . . . That the Beloved of the Gods finds very pitiful and grievous. . . . If anyone does him wrong it will be forgiven as far as it can be forgiven. The Beloved of the Gods even reasons with the forest tribes in his empire and seeks to reform them. . . . The Beloved of the Gods considers that the greatest of all victories is the victory of righteousness.

Source: A. L. Basham, *The Wonder That Was India,* 3d ed. (New York: Grove Press, 1959), pp. 53–54.

ern Republic of India appropriately adopted for its state seal the sculptured lions from the capital of one of Ashoka's pillars. Ashoka also sent explicitly Buddhist missions to Ceylon, and missionaries later went to Burma and Java. They converted the first two countries almost entirely to that faith, which they still hold, while establishing Buddhism as a new religion in much of the rest of Southeast Asia. Indian traders and adventurers, as well as priests and scholars, also carried Indian high culture in art, literature, written language, and statecraft to Southeast Asia. This cultural diffusion from India marked the beginning of literate civilization, in the Indian mode, in much of that extensive region, an origin still evident in many respects.

Kushans and Greeks

Soon after Ashoka's death around 232 B.C., the Mauryan Empire seems to have disintegrated into civil war among provincial governors, although the Mauryan name continued through several successive rulers at Pataliputra. By 180 B.C. or so India had returned to its more traditional pattern of separate regional kingdoms. The northwest was again invaded by Greeks, descendants of groups left behind by Alexander. Northern India was subsequently invaded by new groups of outsiders, the Sakas (Scythians) from west-central Asia, and other originally nomadic peoples from east-central Asia who were driven from their pasture lands by the ancestors of the Mongols and by the rise of the first Chinese empire, the Ch'in, in the late third century. One such group around 100 B.C. crossed the passes into Kashmir and down onto the Indian plain, where they defeated the Greek, Saka, and Indian kingdoms and welded most of the north into a new empire, the Kushan dynasty. The Kushans restored much of the former Mauryan grandeur, ruling also from Pataliputra, but they too declined after some three centuries, and by A.D. 200 the north was once again, like the south, a regional patchwork. The Kushans adopted and promoted Buddhism and disseminated it to their former homelands in central Asia, from which it later reached China. In other respects, like nearly all invaders or conquerors of India, they became thoroughly Indianized, including not only their adoption of the other aspects of Indian culture and language but also widespread intermarriage, adding still further to the hybrid character of the population. The most obvious and enduring legacy of the Kushans is probably the magnificent Buddhist sculpture produced under their rule and patronage. It is interesting also for the clear traces of Hellenistic artistic influence, still important in India in the time of the Kushans, deriving both from the remaining Greek-style kingdoms in the northwest and from direct contact with the Hellenic world by sea.

Throughout the centuries after Alexander, Greek traders and travelers visited India on a regular basis. Greek ships carried Indian goods to the Mediterranean: spices, precious stones, incense, brasswork, fine cotton textiles, ivory, peacocks, monkeys, and even larger wild animals. Indian philosophers visited Mediterranean and Levantine cities, perhaps making some contribution to the Western intellectual heritage. In return, there seems little reason to doubt the claim of Indian Christians that their early church was begun by Thomas the Apostle, who probably reached India and founded there what may well be the world's oldest Christian community. The trip from Suez—or from Alexandria, where we know the apostles preached—was routine in the first century A.D. India was connected to the Greco-Roman world, and one of the apostles probably preached there in carrying out the command recorded in Mark 16:15: "Go ye into all the world and preach the gospel to every creature." To this day, a large proportion of Indian Christians, clustered in the southwest near the ports the Greeks and Romans used, carry the surname Thomas.

Our most important source for this period of Indian history is a Greek handbook for traders and travelers to India called the *Periplus of the Erythrean Sea*, dated about A.D. 80, which gives sailing directions, information on prices and sources for Indian goods, and brief descriptions of Indian culture. Large hoards of Roman coins, to pay for India's exports, and Roman pottery have been found at many ports along the west coast, from Mannar in Ceylon through Cochin and Calicut to the Bombay area and now abandoned ports south of the Indus mouth.

Southern India

The south was protected against pressures from successive states or empires in the north by the uplifted plateau of the Deccan and its fringing mountains, the Vindhya and Satpura ranges, punctuated by the Narbada and Tapti rivers as further barriers. There was also fierce southern resistance to the repeated attempts at conquest from the north. We know very little about the lower half of India before about the time of Ashoka. By then it is clear that southern cultures and states, though divided into often rival groups, were fully as rich and sophisticated as those of the Aryan-influenced north. They shared what was by the third or second century B.C. a common Indian civilization, including Hinduism, philosophy, values, art forms, and material culture. The three largest political states of the south were Chola, Pandya, and Pallava, which vied with each other for regional dominance but were never able to unite the whole area under the control of any one of them. Each maintained extensive trade relations by sea, mainly with Southeast Asia, and the cultural, economic, religious, and political life of each centered in their respective capitals, which were dominated by temple complexes.

The City of Madurai

Probably the largest and best-preserved temple complex is the former Pandya capital of Madurai. The fullest and most detailed account of any ancient Indian city is included in an early Tamil poem of the third century A.D. called *The Garland of Madurai*, which may be summarized in part as follows:

> **The poet enters the city by its great gate, the posts of which are carved with the images of the goddess Lakshmi. It is a festival day, and the city is gay with flags; some, presented by the king to commemorate brave deeds, fly over the houses of captains; others wave over the shops which sell toddy [a fermented drink made from the blossom of the palm tree]. The streets are broad rivers of people of every race, buying and selling in the market place or singing to the music of wandering minstrels.**
>
> **The drum beats and a royal procession passes down the street, with elephants leading and the sound of conchs [shell trumpets]. An unruly elephant breaks his chain and tosses like a ship in an angry sea until he is brought under control. Chariots follow, with prancing horses and fierce footmen. Stall keepers ply their trade, selling sweet cakes, garlands of flowers, scented powder, and rolls of betel nut [to chew]. Old women go from house to house selling nosegays and trinkets. Noblemen drive through the streets in their chariots, their gold-sheathed swords flashing, wearing brightly dyed garments and wreaths of flowers. The jewels of the perfumed women watching from balconies and turrets flash in the sun.**
>
> **People flock to the temples to worship to the sound of music, laying flowers before the images. Craftsmen work in their shops, bangle-makers, goldsmiths, cloth weavers, coppersmiths, flower sellers, wood carvers, and painters. Foodshops are busily selling mangoes, sugar candy, cooked rice, and chunks of cooked meat. [At this period, only the more pious Hindus were strict vegetarians.] In the evening, the city's prostitutes entertain their patrons with dancing and singing to the accompaniment of the lute. The streets are filled with music. Drunken villagers, in town for the festival, reel about in the streets. Respectable women visit the temples in the evening with their children and friends, carrying lighted lamps as offerings. They dance in the temple courts, which resound with their singing and chatter.**
>
> **At last the city sleeps . . . all but the ghosts and goblins who haunt the dark and the housebreakers, armed with rope ladders, swords, and chisels. But the watchmen are also vigilant, and the city passes the night in peace. Morning comes with the sounds of brahmins intoning their sacred verses. The wandering bands renew their singing, and the shopkeepers open their booths. The toddy-sellers ply their trade for thirsty early morning travelers. The drunkards stagger to their feet. All over the city the sound is heard of doors opening. Women sweep the faded flowers of the festival from their courtyards. The busy everyday life of the city is resumed.[1]**

This gives a vivid picture of what urban life must really have been like; with few adjustments, it could serve as a description of a festival day in a small Indian city even today.

Ceylon

The island of Ceylon (called Sri Lanka since 1975, reviving an ancient name for the country) lies within view of the tip of South India, only some 20 miles across the shallow Palk Strait via a disconnected chain of islands. Nevertheless, the two countries have always been separate politically, and Ceylon developed a distinctive culture and sense of separate identity even though it remained, understandably, a part of greater Indian culture. Sometime in the fifth century B.C. a Sanskrit- or Aryan-speaking prince named Vijaya came to Ceylon by sea from northwestern India with a large band of followers and established a kingdom. It is likely that Indian merchants had visited Ceylon earlier and perhaps settled there, but we have no record of such earlier contact. The followers of Vijaya called themselves Sinhala ("lion people") and became the dominant inhabitants of Ceylon as the Sinhalese (Singhalese). This is also the name of their Indo-European language, which is related to those of North India. The Sinhalese brought with them not only the literacy, writing forms, and religion of late Vedic North India but much of the rest of its culture and technology, including the knowledge of irrigation and the cultivation of rice. They were probably joined shortly by a second wave of settlement from Bengal, which merged with them. The Sinhalese soon displaced the earlier and far less technically developed Neolithic inhabitants of the island, the Vaddas, a few survivors of whom still live in the remoter jungles, although in the earlier centuries there was considerable intermarriage.

Beginning no later than the first century B.C. the Singhalese constructed an extensive system of irrigated rice agriculture, centered in the northern half of the island with its capital at Anuradhapura and a secondary urban center at Polonnaruwa. This area was part of the so-called Dry Zone of Ceylon, where permanent field agriculture is impossible without irrigation but where fertile soils, level land, and an unbroken growing season of strong sun and high temperatures can produce high crop yields if water is available. Considerable rain falls there in a brief period of three months during the northeast monsoon of winter, leaving the rest of the year mainly dry. The Singhalese kingdom constructed large reservoirs to catch the winter rain and stream runoff and then to distribute it to rice fields through an intricate system of canals. Dams also diverted water from the few year-round streams that flowed through the area. The population of the Dry Zone grew substantially, and Anuradhapura at its height about the tenth century A.D. may have contained 100,000 people or

The art of ancient Ceylon: divine nymphs dropping flowers on the earth, from a mural painting of the fifth century A.D. on the rock face of the fortress of Sigiriya in the southern Dry Zone, and preserved there better than most Indian painting of this period, which it closely resembles. [Stella Snead/Archaeological Survey of Sri Lanka]

more, while Ceylon as a whole may have had as many as 3 or 4 million. Only with such a large population, controlled by the state through corvée (conscript labor), could the massive irrigation works be built and maintained and the many large palaces and temples at Anuradhapura constructed. Nowhere else in the premodern world was there such a dense concentration of irrigation facilities at such a high technical level, but it was dependent on maintaining state control over mass labor.

Ceylon was the first area beyond India to which Buddhism spread. The pious legend is that Ananda, a disciple of the Buddha, brought the message himself in the Buddha's own lifetime, but Buddhism probably did not extend beyond North India, and almost certainly not to Ceylon, until Ashoka's time in the third century B.C., when missionaries were specifically dispatched to Ceylon and Burma. The Sinhalese rapidly accepted and have retained Buddhism. They produced beautiful works of sculpture and architecture in the Buddhist-Indian tradition, including the world's largest mound temples or stupas and colossal statues of the Buddha and his disciples. The great stupa at Anuradhapura is bigger than all but one of the pyramids of ancient Egypt and is surrounded for miles by others nearly as big and by a host of beautiful and monumental stone buildings and large baths. All of this gorgeous display suggests large and consistent surpluses from the agricultural system to pay for the costs of construction and art and an economy that could spare labor for such purposes. The classical Sinhalese chronicles, compiled and preserved by Buddhist monks, deal mainly with the pious acts of successive kings, especially their building or endowing of temples, but indirectly they reflect a prosperous and generally controlled society.

Given the short and easy journey from southern India to Ceylon, continuous interaction probably began before the fifth century B.C. By or before the Christian era, the northern tip of Ceylon had been settled by people from the Dravidian Tamil-speaking area of South India, who practiced their own form of irrigated agriculture based mainly on wells. They became the dominant inhabitants of the Jaffna peninsula and the immediately adjacent parts of the north but retained their cultural ties with South India as well as their Hinduism. Immigration from South India continued for several centuries, and there was some intermarriage with the Sinhalese. These two groups of Indian immigrants, Sinhalese and Tamils, coexisted for most of Ceylon's history, until their differences exploded into a violent political issue in the 1950s (described in Chapter 39).

The Sinhala kingdom based on Anuradhapura periodically controlled the Tamil areas of the north but had to protect itself against intermittent raiding from the far larger Tamil kingdoms in South India. These raids often stimulated or increased internal dissension when rival Sinhalese claimants to the throne made common cause with the invaders, especially after about the sixth century A.D.

The Port of Puhar

A graphic passage in the Tamil epic the Silappatikaram, *of uncertain date but probably fourth or fifth century* A.D., *describes the port city of Puhar, not far from modern Madras, in this period a great center of foreign trade.*

The riches of Puhar shipowners made the kings of faraway lands envious. The most costly merchandise, the rarest foreign produce reached the city. . . . The sunshine lighted up the open terraces, the harbor docks, the towers with their loopholes like the eyes of deer. In various quarters of the city the homes of wealthy Greeks were seen. Near the harbor seamen from far-off lands appeared at home. In the streets hawkers were selling unguents, bath powders, cooling oils, flowers, perfume, and incense. . . . Each trade had its own street in the workers' quarter of the city. At the center of the city were the wide royal street, the street of temple cars, the bazaar, and the main street where rich merchants had their mansions . . . with warehouses of merchandise from overseas. . . . Near the sea, flags raised high toward the sky seemed to be saying: "On these stretches of white sand can be found the goods that foreign merchants, leaving their own countries to stay among us, have brought here in great ships." . . . All night lamps were burning, the lamps of foreigners who talk strange tongues, and of the guards who watch over precious cargoes near the docks.

Source: A. Danielou, trans., in M. Singer, "Beyond Tradition and Modernity in Madras," *Comparative Studies in Society and History* 13 (1971): 169–170.

The Chola empire, which arose in the early centuries of the Christian era in South India, launched a particularly destructive invasion of Ceylon in the eleventh century that sacked Anuradhapura in 1017. The Sinhalese capital was moved to Polonnaruwa, from which the local forces finally drove the Cholas out of the country by 1070. In the following century King Parakrama Bahu (1153–1186) unified the whole of Ceylon from his capital at Polonnaruwa, invaded South India and Burma, and constructed huge new irrigation works and public buildings that made his capital almost as impressive as Anuradhapura had been. But his death was followed by civil war and by new and especially destructive invasions from South India, which led by the thirteenth century to the virtual abandonment of the Dry Zone, whose vital irrigation works could no longer be maintained. The much reduced population clustered from then on in the protection of the hills and mountains of southeastern Ceylon, centered around the medieval capital of Kandy, and later in the lowlands around the port of Colombo.

The Guptas and the Empire of Harsha

An imperial revival of the Mauryan model in India, the Gupta dynasty, ruled the north from about A.D. 320 to about 550. Pataliputra was again the imperial capital and seems once more to have played the role of cultural center for surrounding areas. Contact with the West appears to have diminished or ceased by this time, as the eastern Roman Empire was largely cut off from India by the rise of the Sassanid dynasty in Persia. Trade and cultural exchange, however, was still extensive with Southeast Asia, although most of it probably took place from the South Indian kingdoms of Chola, Pandya, and Pallava and from ports on the southeast coast, beyond Guptan imperial control. For much of what we know about the Gupta period, as for earlier periods, we are dependent on foreign observers. The chief source is the diary of Fa Hsien, a Chinese Buddhist monk who made the long and arduous journey to India via central Asia and the Himalayas to seek true copies of the Buddhist sutras (scriptures) and who lived and traveled there for six years in the early 400s. A typical literate Chinese, he carefully recorded what he observed, at Pataliputra and elsewhere, and gives a picture of a rich and sophisticated society and of its culturally brilliant capital in the early fifth century, when it was probably at its height.

Life and Culture in the Guptan Period

Fa Hsien noted the peacefulness of Guptan India and the mildness of its government. His journal remarks that crime was rare and that one could travel from one end of the empire to another without harm and with no need for travel documents. He made special note of the free hospitals for treatment of the sick, supported by private donations. He also says that all "respectable" people (by which he probably means those of high caste) were vegetarians, a trend that seemed to have picked up momentum from the time of Ashoka, but that the lower orders ate meat and hence were regarded as sources of "pollution," an aspect of caste that he was the first outsider to describe. Buddhism he describes as still flourishing, but apparently in the process of being reabsorbed into the Hinduism from which it had originally sprung. In general, Fa Hsien's account shows us a prosperous, tranquil, and smoothly operating society, which probably contrasted with the turbulent China of his time.

The Gupta period was the golden age of Sanskrit literature and of classical Indian sculpture and monumental building, although unfortunately only fragments have survived. This cultural flowering was equally vigorous in the south, beyond Gupta control, and in both south and north seems to have taken the form of a renaissance of Mauryan grandeur. Kalidasa, widely acclaimed as India's greatest poet and playwright, lived and worked in the late fourth and early fifth centuries, near the peak of Gupta vigor. Many of his works have survived, as have fragments of some others. They still make fresh and enchanting reading, as well as moving commentaries on the foibles of human existence.

Seated Buddha from fifth-century Guptan India. Here one can see the complete Indianization of sculptural style. There is no garment or Hellenic-style folds, and the whole figure is turned inward in meditation, seated in a yogic posture. [Sarnath Museum of Archaeology/ Archaeological Survey of India]

The Collapse of Gupta Rule

By A.D. 550 or so the Gupta power was destroyed by new invaders, the so-called White Huns (probably Iranians or Turks from central Asia), one more group in the long succession of ethnically and culturally different outsiders drawn to India by its wealth and sophistication and then woven into the hybrid Indian fabric. Like earlier and later invaders, they came from the west, through the only easy entrance into the subcontinent, the passes that punctuate the northwest frontier. As the linguistic tie still reminds us, India's relations were and remained overwhelmingly with the West since at least Harappan times and, except for the sea connection with Southeast Asia, hardly at all with the East and with China, the other major cultural center of Asia. Buddhism did move from India, first into central Asia and then into China by Han times, but it seems to have carried very little of Indian culture with it except for some art forms, and almost nothing of Chinese culture seems to have penetrated into India. Cotton, native to India and first woven into cloth there, spread to China only some 3,000 years later. Trade between the two societies, the other common vehicle of cultural exchange, was minimal and indirect. The reason is clear from a glance at the map: the world's highest mountains lie between India and China, and behind them the desert or alpine wastelands of Sinkiang and Tibet. It is in fact a very long and exceptionally difficult way between the centers of Indian and Chinese civilizations, from the plains of Hindustan to the lower Yellow and Yangtze River valleys. The shorter route from eastern India through Burma and into mountainous southwest China (still a long way from the Chinese center) has proved even more difficult, with its combination of mountains, deep gorges, and rain forest, and has never carried more than a trickle of indirect trade.

With the collapse of the Gupta empire, India reverted once more to its regional structures. The new invaders from central Asia did not succeed in building their own empire, and for a time there was political chaos, but the first half of the seventh century saw a final indigenous effort at unification. This was the reign of Harsha (606–648), who in a series of campaigns joined the separate kingdoms of the north together and presided over a notable reflowering of Sanskrit literature and art. Harsha also encouraged Buddhism, and the Chinese Buddhist monk Hsuan Tsang visited his court, leaving a valuable account of it and of the contemporary India through which he traveled. His journal gives an admiring picture of Harsha as a charismatic, energetic, and able administrator and an impressive emperor of his domains, through which he made repeated tours to supervise its government. Like earlier and later Indian emperors, he held court wherever he went, to hear complaints and dispense justice. Like them, he lived in luxury and pomp but loved literature and philosophy and was a generous patron; he even found time to write plays himself. By this time Hsuan Tsang's account shows Buddhism declining and Hinduism again dominant, but, perhaps because of the brevity and idiosyncrasy of Harsha's rule, law and order were not as well kept as in Guptan times. Hsuan Tsang reports banditry and was himself robbed twice on his travels. Harsha's empire was so much his own creation that when he died in 648, leaving no heirs, it disintegrated into factional fighting.

Women in Ancient India

Medieval and early modern India tended to fit the popular stereotype applied to most traditional Asian societies: heavy male dominance and female subservience or even servitude. That has been changing fast in twentieth-century Asia and was, like most stereotypes, not totally accurate even for the past. In particular, it overlooks the major part nearly all women played in the basic Asian institution of the family, a private as opposed to public role but often critically important, and it also overlooks the many women writers and performers of other public roles, including political ones. However, ancient India was substantially different from the later period of Indian history in this respect. There is much evidence to show that pre-Mauryan Indian society, especially in the south, was matriarchal; women held important economic power, and property, status, and family names often descended through the female line. Survivals of this ancient pattern remain in parts of South India today. The Aryan north was from Vedic times more clearly patriarchal, and women were conventionally

Virtues of an Indian Wife

A passage in the Mahabharata *extolls the virtues of a wife.*

The wife is half the man, the best of friends,
the root of the three ends of life,
and of all that will help him in the other world.
With a wife a man does mighty deeds,
with a wife a man finds courage.
A wife is the safest refuge;
a man aflame with sorrow in his soul or sick with disease
finds comfort in his wife as a man parched with heat
finds relief in water.
Even a man in the grip of rage will not be harsh to a woman, remembering that on
her depend the joys of life, happiness, and virtue.
For a woman is the everlasting field
in which the self is born.

Some centuries later the Laws of Manu, written about the second century A.D., reflected the growing emphasis on the domesticity and dependency of women.

She should always be cheerful, and skillful in her domestic duties with her household vessels well cleaned and her hand tight on the purse-strings. In season and out of season her lord, who wed her with sacred rites, ever gives happiness to his wife, both here and in the other world. Though he be uncouth and prone to pleasure, though he have no good points at all, the virtuous wife should ever worship her lord as a god.

Source: A. L. Basham, *The Wonder That Was India*, 3d ed. (New York: Grove Press, 1959), pp. 180–182.

seen as subject to their parents, husbands, and male relatives. But they had some control over personal property, and a number of women even owned businesses. Women could not serve as priests but were free to become nuns, several of whom were notable poets and scholars. The *Upanishads*, treatises dating from about the seventh century B.C., tell the story of an exceptionally learned woman, Gargi Vacaknavi, who took an active part in discussions with the sage Yajnavalkya and outdistanced all her male counterparts. Other women attended lectures by sages and mastered the Vedas. Goddesses were as important as gods in Vedic religion, and a goddess's name was commonly recited before that of a god, a practice which still persists.

By the Mauryan era, however, the scope for women in religious and intellectual pursuits seems to have been reduced. Convention shifted to an emphasis on marriage and care of the family as the proper female role, although many upper-class women continued to be taught privately, or to educate themselves, and several wrote poetry and drama that was widely read. Others learned music—both performance and composition—dancing, and painting. In early Vedic times (we know too little about society in Harappan times to speculate about it), unmarried men and women seem to have mixed freely. By the time of the *Arthashastra* (third century B.C.), upper-class women were more circumscribed by convention, although widows were still free to marry. By late Gupta times (sixth century A.D.), restrictions on women had increased, and widows could no longer remarry. Women were to be cherished, but protected—and restricted— a trend which apparently had begun under Mauryan rule, at least in the north. In the south, women remained freer and less submissive.

The freest women in ancient India were probably the courtesans (high-class prostitutes). In many traditional societies, including India, they were usually well educated and well versed in the classics, the arts of music, dance, poetry and its composition, flower arranging, the composition of riddles and other mental puzzles, and even fencing. There were lower grades of prostitutes, but the standard was generally high. Such women were often praised for their learning and quick verbal wit, sometimes even more than for their beauty, as in China and Japan. Even the Buddha is said to have chosen to dine with a famous courtesan rather than with the city fathers, no doubt duller company. Many of the courtesans were celebrated poets, but most of them were considered especially sensitive and as having "great souls."

Another group of women were hereditary dancers in the service of temples; most of them also served as prostitutes, but in any case they never married, having dedicated themselves to the god, like the temple priestesses and Vestal Virgins of classical Greece and Rome. Dance was a particularly important religious ritual in India, as well as a beautiful art form. The god Shiva was thought to have created the world through his cosmic dance and to dance on the harvest floor as the spirit of life and of creation. From at least the Gupta period, classical Indian dance came to be associated with the temple dancers. They were honored and admired for their art but socially discriminated against. Other women were discouraged from dancing because of this association until recent years, when the classical dance forms have seen a national revival and have once again become respectable.

The custom of *sati* (suttee), wives burning themselves to death on their husbands' funeral pyres, does not seem to have extended to most widows at any period in Indian history. Although it was known in ancient India, Sumer, and China, it was uncommon. When it was practiced, it was mainly as part of the custom of burning or burying all the followers, retainers, horses, and prized possessions of a dead ruler or aristocrat with him. *Sati* was relatively rare until late Gupta times, when widow remarriage had begun to be strongly discouraged or prohibited, as it had not been before. It became more common thereafter, although it was supposed to be voluntary, as a mark of exceptional fidelity. Social and family pressure, plus the emptiness and often the material hardship of a young widow's life, doubtless added other incentives. *Sati* horrified early Western observers, and the British tried to suppress it in the nineteenth century. Many ancient and even medieval Indian writers and poets condemned it, and in the end the Hindu renaissance and reform movement of the later nineteenth century turned educated Indian opinion against it. There is some evidence that *sati* is occasionally practiced even now.

The Indian Heritage

The building and maintaining of empires exacts a heavy human cost everywhere. India's return to its more normal regionalism after the collapse of the Gupta empire and the death of Harsha was hardly a tragedy. But it leaves the historian, whose data are only fragmentary, to try to deal with a confused tapestry woven, like India's history and culture as a whole, of many threads. The revival of regional kingdoms did, however, encourage the continued development of the rich regional cultures that make up the Indian fabric.

Given India's size and diversity, it is not surprising that the subcontinent has only very briefly been united into a single empire, and even under Ashoka and the later rule of the British some areas remained outside imperial control. We are accustomed to thinking of Europe as properly composed of a large number of separate states and cultures, despite the heritage of common Roman rule over much of it for some four centuries and despite its common membership in the Greek, Roman, and Christian traditions. India too has long shared common traditions, including the universal spread of Hinduism, and like Europe has experienced successive efforts at unification by conquest. But the strength of separate regional cultures and states remained at least as great as in Europe, reinforced by different languages, literatures, and political rivalries. India's more recent success in building a modern state—or rather the three states of Pakistan, India, and Bangladesh—contrasts with the continued political division of Europe but still encompasses regional differences, each with its own proud tradition reaching back before Ashoka. In these terms, there is nothing improper or backward about regional separatism, for India, Europe, or any other area of the size and variety of the subcontinent. India, like Europe, would be the poorer without its array of different cultural and regional traditions. Their separate contributions in literature, philosophy, and the arts in the centuries of political disunity after the death of Harsha continued to enrich the varied tapestry of Indian civilization. But our political picture of those centuries is confusing, frequently changing, and plagued by a severe shortage of information.

Ancient and classical India as a whole had a deep respect for learning and for education, beginning with literacy and mathematics and continuing to philosophy and the study of the Vedas. But education was a privilege enjoyed only by the upper classes, and after the Vedic age for the most part only by males, as in nearly all premodern societies. As mentioned earlier, courtesans frequented by the elite classes were highly educated and widely read in addition to being accomplished dancers, singers, musicians, and poetesses; their role was to entertain their patrons in the fullest sense of the word. However, most people were peasant villagers, uninvolved with any of these upper-class matters and intent on their own active communal life. The several Greek and Chinese travelers to classical India who have left accounts describe the rural scene as productive and prosperous and compare it and the lot of villagers favorably with their own homelands. India during these centuries may have been less burdened by mass poverty or communal tensions than it is now, but we have no way to measure that. Contemporary accounts from that period can of course make judgments only in terms of what they knew of conditions elsewhere. Our modern perspectives are different. But the classical accounts we have nearly all stress the relatively high level of material well-being, the orderliness of the society, and its impressive achievements in science, technology, philosophy, and the arts. It is a tradition of which modern Indians are justly proud.

From the modern perspective, classical India seems especially noteworthy for its scientific accomplishments. Mathematics had by Gupta times been brought to a high level of sophistication, including a rudimentary algebra and a numeration system using nine digits and a zero, far more efficient than the cumbersome Roman numerals. The Arabs, who transmitted it to the West, called mathematics "the Indian art" (*Hindisat*). Later European science would have been impossible without it. Medieval Indian mathematicians after Harsha's time developed the concepts of negative and positive quantities, worked out square and cube roots, solved quadratic and other equations, understood the mathematical implications of zero and infinity, worked out the value of pi to nine decimal places, and made important steps in trigonometry, sine functions, spherical geometry, and calculus. Earlier Indian scientists anticipated the classical Greeks in developing an atomic theory of elements, basic to twentieth-century Western science, by the sixth century B.C. Traditional Indian medicine had a very extensive pharmacopoeia and used a variety of herbal remedies and drugs discovered and used only much later in the West. Physicians appear to have understood the function of the spinal cord and the nervous system, and successful surgery included cesarean section, complicated bone setting, plastic surgery, and the repair of damaged limbs. Doctors were highly respected, and the textbook of the famous physician Caraka in the late first century A.D. includes a passage reminiscent of Hippocrates, the classical Greek physician:

> **If you want success in your practice . . . you must pray every day on rising and going to bed for the welfare of all beings . . . and strive with all your soul for the health of the sick. You must not betray your patients, even at the cost of your own life. . . . You must be pleasant of speech . . . and thoughtful, always striving to improve your knowledge.**
>
> **When you go to the home of a patient you should direct your words, mind, intellect, and senses nowhere but to your patient and his treatment. . . . Nothing that happens in the house of the sick man must be told outside, nor must the patient's condition be told to anyone who might do harm by that knowledge.[2]**

It is more than possible that the political turmoil of invasions and internal struggles did not greatly affect the lives of most people of South Asia most of the time. For the Indians it was not particularly important to record the details of empires, kingdoms, rivalries, and political changes. We do have enough evidence to show us a sophisticated civilization, a remarkably humane set of values, and enough glimpses of the life of the common people to establish ancient and classical India as a great tradition, one of the major achievements of the human experience.

The Indus civilization, with major urban centers at Kalibangan, Harappa, and Mohenjo Daro, arose, flourished, and declined between 3000 B.C. *and 2000* B.C. *The migration of Aryan-speaking peoples from central Asia into North India after about 1800* B.C. *produced Vedic culture, which became dominant in most of the north. Regional kingdoms had emerged by 500* B.C., *some of which Alexander encountered when he invaded the northwest in 326* B.C. *By 322 the Mauryan empire had emerged under Chandragupta Maurya and unified most of the north from the imperial capital at Pataliputra in the central Ganges valley. Chandragupta's grandson Ashoka ruled as emperor from around 269 to 232* B.C., *and extended the empire southward. Troubled by the slaughter occasioned by his conquests, he converted to the nonviolent faith of Buddhism and devoted the rest of his reign to spreading its message. The Mauryan power faded after his death, and both North and South India reverted to regional rule. New Greek and Scythian invaders in the north yielded to another dynasty of conquest, the Kushans, from around 100* B.C. *to* A.D. *200, while the south and Ceylon supported separate flourishing kingdoms and built impressive architectural monuments. The Gupta dynasty restored much of the Mauryan grandeur in the north from about 320 to 550, based again at Pataliputra, and Harsha from 606 to 648 reunited the Guptan empire. After his death India resumed its more typical political pattern of separate regional kingdoms, where art, learning, philosophy, and commerce continued to thrive.*

Notes

1. A. L. Basham, *The Wonder That Was India,* 3d ed. (New York: Grove Press, 1959), pp. 203–204.
2. Ibid., p. 500.

Suggestions for Further Reading

Allchin, B., and Allchin, R. *The Rise of Civilization in India and Pakistan*. Cambridge: Cambridge University Press, 1982.

Auboyer, J. *Daily Life in Ancient India*. London: Weidenfeld & Nicolson, 1965.

Basham, A. L. *The Wonder That Was India*, 3d ed. New York: Grove Press, 1959.

De Silva, K. M. *A History of Sri Lanka*. Delhi: Oxford University Press, 1981.

Dutt, A. K., and Selb, M. *Atlas of South Asia*. Boulder, Colo.: Westview, 1987.

Fa Hsien. *Travels of Fa-hsien*, trans. H. A. Giles. London: Trubner, 1877.

Gokhale, B. G. *Asoka Maurya*. New York: Twayne, 1966.

Kalidasa. *The Cloud Messenger*, trans. F. Edgerton and E. Edgerton. Ann Arbor: University of Michigan Press, 1964.

Kautilya. *The Arthasastra*, trans. R. Shamasastry. Mysore, India: Raghuveer Printing Press, 1951.

Kosambi, D. D. *Ancient India: A History of Its Culture and Civilization*. New York: Pantheon, 1966.

Lingat, R. *The Classical Law of India*. Berkeley: University of California Press, 1973.

McCrindle, J. W., trans. *Ancient India as Described in Classical Literature*. New Delhi: Today and Tomorrow Press, 1972.

Murphey, R. "The Ruin of Ancient Ceylon," *Journal of Asian Studies* 16 (1957): 181-200.

Nilakanta, S. *The Cholas*, 2d ed. Madison: University of Wisconsin Press, 1955.

———. *A History of South India*, 4th ed. Madras: Oxford University Press, 1976.

Piggott, S. *Prehistoric India to 1000* B.C. London: Cassel, 1962.

Possehl, G. L., ed. *Ancient Cities of the Indus*. Durham, N.C.: Carolina Academic Press, 1979.

Rapson, E. J., ed. *The Cambridge History of India*, vol. 1. Cambridge: Cambridge University Press, 1922.

Singhal, D. P. *A History of the Indian People*. London: Methuen, 1983.

Tarn, W. W. *The Greeks in Bactria and India*. Cambridge: Cambridge University Press, 1951.

Thapar, R. *Asoka and the Decline of the Mauryas*. London: Oxford University Press, 1961.

———. *A History of India*, vol. 1. Baltimore: Penguin Books, 1966.

Van Buitenen, J. A. B., trans. *The Bhagavadgita and the Mahabharata*. Chicago: University of Chicago Press, 1981.

Warmington, E. H. *Commerce Between the Roman Empire and India*. Cambridge: Cambridge University Press, 1928.

Wolpert, S. *A New History of India*, 3d ed. New York: Oxford University Press, 1989.

Woodcock, G. *The Greeks in India*. London: Faber, 1966.

C H A P T E R · 3

The Formation of China

Chinese civilization arose largely independent of contact with or influence from other areas and early developed its own distinctive form and style. China was effectively isolated by high mountains and deserts along its northwestern, western, and southwestern borders and by the distance across the great breadth of arid central Asia. Northward lay the desert and steppe of Mongolia and the subarctic lands of Siberia and northern Manchuria. In part because of its isolation until recent centuries, the Chinese civilized tradition was more continuous, coherent, and slow to change over a longer period than any other in history.

Interaction was much easier with areas to the east, and the model of Chinese civilization later spread to Korea, Vietnam, and Japan, where it still forms a basic part of the literate cultures of those areas. East Asia as a whole is accordingly sometimes called the *Sinic* culture (from the Latin word for China).

An extraordinarily lifelike pottery figure from a Han dynasty tomb in Szechuan shows a groom whistling up his horse. [Innervision/Overseas Archaeological Corporation]

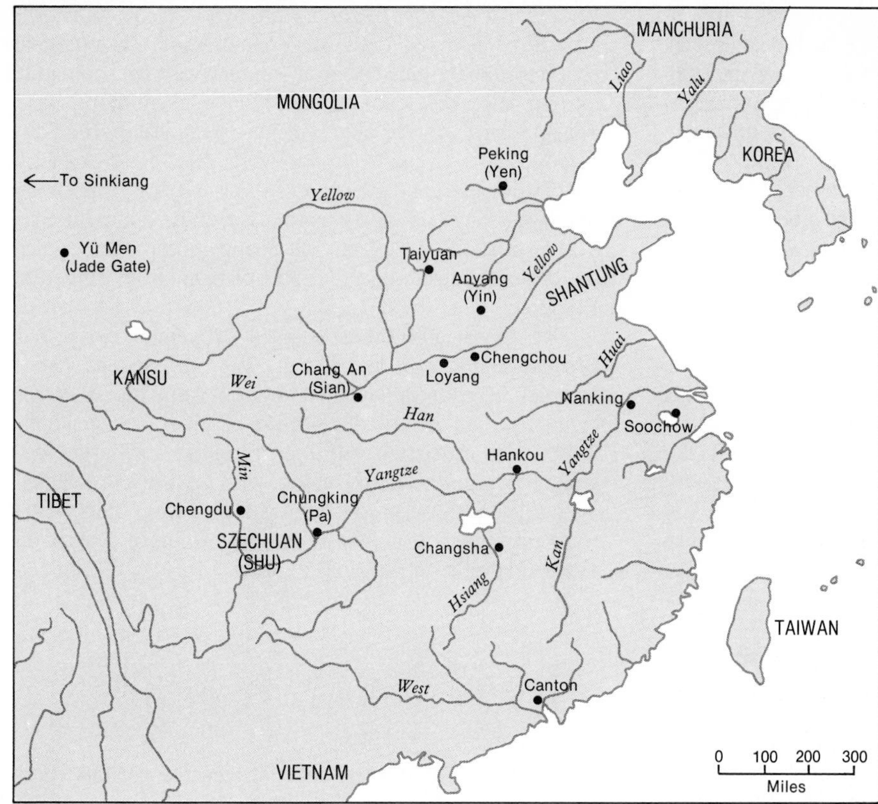

3.1 East Asia

The area also inherited much of the tradition of Chinese agriculture as well as systems of writing, philosophy, literature, political and social institutions, and art forms. This diffusion took place, however, 2,000 years or more after Chinese civilization first began, and after the establishment of the first empire in the third century B.C. This empire discarded some elements developed in earlier centuries and added others to create the model of imperial Chinese culture that subsequently spread to the rest of East Asia. But long before the beginning of the Christian era in the West, China had already produced one of the world's major civilized traditions, and the model of the Han dynasty (202 B.C.–A.D. 220) was to be reaffirmed by successive Chinese dynasties for the next 2,000 years.

The Origins of China

We cannot fix a precise date for the emergence of a city-based, literate, metal-using civilization in China. As everywhere else, it happened over a long period of transition out of Neolithic beginnings. By about 2000 B.C., however, the late Neolithic culture we call Lung Shan, or Black Pottery, had begun to build walled settlements larger than villages, to make bronze tools, weapons, and ornaments, and to use a pictographic and ideographic script clearly recognizable as the ancestor of written Chinese. The towns and cities included large groups of nonfarmers: scribes, metallurgists, artisans, and perhaps officials, and already the Lung Shan people had learned the art of silk-making, long an exclusive Chinese skill and trademark. Approximately four centuries later, around 1600 B.C., the first authenticated Chinese dynasty, the Shang, was established in the area at or near the great bend of the Yellow River where the major Lung Shan settlements had also clustered, on the North China plain. The Shang probably consolidated or arose from a combination of the previously distinct Lung Shan and Yang Shao (Painted Pottery) cultures, but they and other late Neolithic cultures may well have begun to merge considerably earlier, perhaps to form the dynasty of Hsia (Xia), which was recorded as such by traditional Chinese texts but has not yet been confirmed by archaeological finds.

Whether the Hsia was a real state and dynasty or not, the name was certainly used, and a culture of the Shang's complexity could not have appeared without a predecessor. The existence of the Shang was also discounted by modern historians despite its mention in the traditional texts giving the names of kings, until archaeological discoveries in the 1920s began to reveal its capitals and inscriptions that listed Shang kings exactly as the traditional texts had. Hsia may still be a convenient label for late Lung Shan–Yang Shao culture in the last stages of its evolution. By about 2000 B.C. Lung Shan towns were large and were surrounded by pounded-earth walls with heavy gates, clearly no longer farmers' villages and possibly organized into one or more kingdoms. What may have been a capital from this period near modern Chengchou (Zhengzhou), perhaps of the Hsia, had a wall 20 feet high and a mile square, with two bronze foundries outside the walls.

Lung Shan settlements with a similar material culture extended eastward to the sea and southward into the Yangtze valley and the south coast. The traditional Chinese texts give the names of five pre-Hsia "emperors" who are recognizable as mythological culture heroes, credited with the "invention" of fire, agriculture, animal domestication, calendrics, writing, and flood control. The last of these, the great Yü, is said to have founded the Hsia dynasty, which may tentatively be dated 2000–1600 B.C., but we know almost nothing more about it. The earliest texts we have were written many centuries later.

By Shang times in any case, many of the elements of a distinctively Chinese culture are present. How much Shang or its Chinese predecessors owed to earlier achievements farther west has long been debated. There seems no question that wheat and later donkeys, alfalfa, grapes, and some elements of mathematics were carried to China from western Asia, but well after 2000 B.C. (The chief crop of Shang China was millet, probably an indigenous grain.) Rice, water buffalo, chickens, and pigs, also not native to northern China, came considerably earlier, but from Southeast Asia via southern China. Indeed, China owed far more to diffusion from the south than from the west, especially if we consider the basic place in its economy later occupied by these originally southern imports.

In Neolithic times South China was culturally and linguistically closer to adjacent Southeast Asia than to dry, cold North China. Recent archaeological finds in the lower Yangtze valley and south of the great river suggest that the beginnings of civilization may have emerged there as early as or even earlier than in the better-surveyed and better-preserved north. The first East Asian bronzes and the first evidence of rice cultivation so far discovered come from what is now northern Thailand and Vietnam and presumably spread from there relatively easily into neighboring South China probably long before Shang times. By the early Shang period, there already seems to have been a good deal of cultural mixing between North and South China, although the people were ethnically and linguistically distinct.

No aspect of Shang culture suggests any connection with Mesopotamia or India, including Shang art and two further basic and conclusive elements, writing and bronze technology. Both were developed earlier in Sumer and then in India, but the earliest Chinese writing resembles neither. It is highly unlikely that the Chinese, like the Indians, would have failed to adopt or adapt cuneiform instead of developing far more cumbersome ideographic characters if they had been in contact with Mesopotamia or had imported ideas or techniques from there. And Shang China stands alone in the technical perfection, beauty, and style of its bronze work, the result of a long history of experimental progress using varying proportions of copper, tin, lead, and zinc to achieve the optimum mix. The farther one goes from the Shang centers, the cruder the bronze artifacts become; no trail leads from Sumer or Harappa.

For these and other reasons it seems clear that Chinese civilization, like Indian, was an independent innovation, already well formed before it came into effective contact with other or older centers of equal sophistication. This is also consistent with the Paleolithic and early Neolithic record, where the stone tools of China remained distinct from those produced in the area from India westward through central Asia to Europe. Chinese civilization evolved largely on its own.

The Shang Dynasty

The Shang ruled from several successive capitals, first near modern Loyang (Luoyang), then near modern Chengchou (both close to the Yellow River), and finally, for about the last two centuries, at Anyang, which they called Yin. We do not know the extent of the Shang political domains, but cultural remains suggest that they were limited to the central Yellow River floodplain, although the Shang had or claimed vassals to the west, east, northeast, and possibly the south, who shared much of Shang material culture. By this time wheat was beginning to share prominence with millet, and rice was also grown, though mainly in the Yangtze valley and the south. Hunting remained a subsidiary source of food in addition to domesticated cattle, pigs, and poultry. The Shang kept slaves, mainly war captives from less highly developed or subjugated groups on their borders. Slaves may have been an important part of the agricultural work force; they were also used extensively to build the cities and palaces, and perhaps as troops.

Especially at Anyang, monumental building was impressive, and the city at its peak may have covered as much as 10 square miles, with nearly a dozen elaborate royal tombs complete with a variety of grave furniture. The tombs provide evidence of surplus production that could support extravagant display, including richly decorated chariots with bronze fittings and caparisoned horses to draw them; the horses had been harnessed, backed down a ramp into the underground tombs, and killed. Royal or aristocratic dead were accompanied in their burials not only by objects of use and value but also by tens or even hundreds of followers, buried as human sacrifices

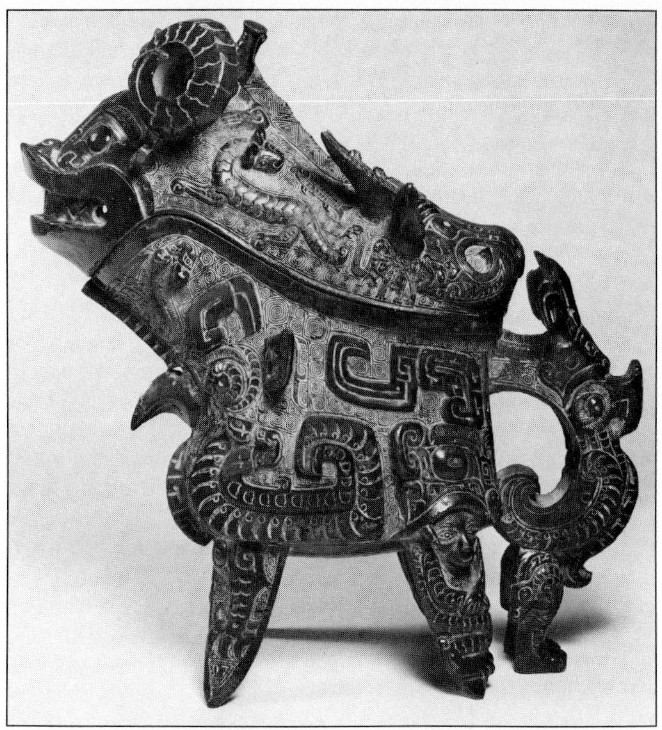

Shang bronzes were technically sophisticated and are dominated by ritual vessels in a variety of forms. This sample, with its removable lid, probably served as a pitcher for pouring ceremonial wine. Like other Shang objects, it shows a mythical beast in abstract form and is covered with abstract designs. [Freer Gallery, Washington]

to serve in the afterlife and probably also as a mark of the dead person's status.

The only Shang texts we have are inscriptions used for divination, most of them incised on the flat shoulder bones of cattle or on tortoise shells. These were heated until cracks appeared from which answers to questions were somehow formulated. Others of the so-called oracle bone inscriptions, like the divination texts using characters so close to classical Chinese that most can still be read, provide lists of the Shang kings and brief accounts of royal activities.

Altogether this inscriptional material gives a picture of a hereditary aristocratic society in which warfare against surrounding groups was chronic; archers used a powerful compound bow, there were ranks of spearmen, and nobles rode in light, fast war chariots similar to those of the Indo-Europeans. The royal hunt remained important and was usually a very large affair in which hundreds took part and thousands of animals perished. The inscriptions make it clear that the spirits of royal and perhaps all aristocratic ancestors demanded respectful service from the living and could intercede for them with a supreme deity—the roots of traditional Chinese "ancestor worship." Slaves were not thought to have souls or spirits and thus could safely be killed; the Shang aristocrats seem not to have thought about what might happen if they became war captives themselves. Although those at the top lived in great luxury, the houses of the common people seem to have been quite crude, often simple pit dwellings, certainly not in a class with those of the Indus civilization. Many of the divination questions ask about the weather and suggest that the North China climate then, as now, was semiarid and prone to both drought and river flooding, but there is little evidence of any large-scale irrigation, apart from what one may assume was the possible use of floodwater. North China was not as dry as the Indus valley, and the agriculture there seems to have been primarily rain-fed except perhaps in small areas adjacent to the river or on a small scale from local wells in long dry spells. The great agricultural advantage of North China was its *loess* (wind-laid alluvium), a highly fertile soil that is easily worked, and the level expanse of the largely treeless plain, which allows easy transport and exchange.

The Chou Dynasty

Relations between the Shang and their vassals were uneasy, and chronic warfare with other groups on the margins strained Shang resources. So too did the extravagant demands of royal building and display, much of it extorted from slave laborers. The last Shang king is said to have been a physical giant and a monster of depravity who, among other cruelties, made drinking cups of the skulls of his vanquished enemies. The dynasty ended in a great slave revolt, which was joined by one of the Shang vassals, the Chou (Zhou, pronounced like *Joe*), who guarded the western frontier in the Wei valley with their capital near modern Sian (Xian). The Chou were probably an original barbarian group taken over by the Shang, tough frontiersmen who seem to have been awaiting their chance to take over the whole kingdom. About 1050 B.C. they succeeded, together with the slave rebels, defeating the last Shang king and sacking Anyang (where the king died in the flames of his own palace). By that time the Chou had absorbed most of Shang culture and technology. The victorious Chou, now fully literate, gave their own account of the excesses and oppression of the Shang as justification for their conquest and first voiced what was to become a standard Chinese justification for change: "The iniquity of Shang is full; Heaven commands me to destroy it." The Shang had lost what they called the "mandate [approval] of Heaven" by their misgovernment, and it was the duty of responsible people to overthrow them.

The Chou set up their new capital in the Wei valley, their old base. They continued and extended the Shang system of dependent vassals whereby surrounding groups and areas, soon to begin emerging as states, were linked to the Chou king by oaths of fealty that acknowledged him as sovereign. The parallel with medieval European feudalism is not exact in details, but the basic system and the reasons for it were the same: a central kingdom with ambitions to control or administer a large area beyond its own immediate territory, which it thus arranged for by contracting with local chieftains. In addition, there were needs for joint defense against surrounding enemies or raiders. The Chou appear to have subdued by means of this system a much larger area than they inherited from the Shang, from the Wei valley to the sea, north into southern Manchuria, and south into the Yangtze valley. Mutual interest among evolving kingdoms, or dukedoms, as the Chou called them, may also have led them to join together in the defense of the "civilized" area against the outer barbarians and to keep order internally.

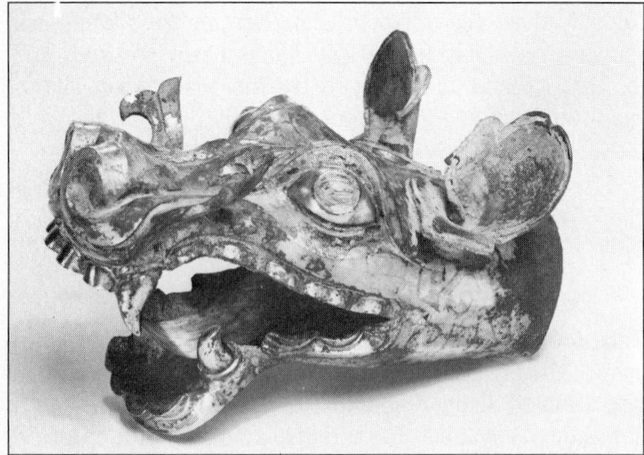

Early Chou bronzes show a trend away from abstraction and toward more lifelike representation, although the pieces are still highly ornamented. [Freer Gallery, Washington]

For a time this system seems to have worked reasonably well, based also on what appears to have been an institution like serfdom by which most land was cultivated under the ownership of hereditary lords, perhaps with some irrigation from shallow wells in a center plot. As in parts of medieval Europe, serfs were bound to the land and could not leave, becoming virtually the property of their lords. At both the royal Chou court and increasingly at the courts of other dependent states there was an unbroken evolution of technological and artistic development. Bronze remained the chief metal, and magnificent ritual vessels, often of great size, increasingly bore long texts recording events or decrees.

Although most writing was by now done with brush and ink on silk or on strips of bamboo, none of these perishable texts has survived, and we are dependent on much later and perhaps substantially altered copies. It is generally assumed that the central body of the Chinese classics originated in early Chou, including the Book of Changes (*I-ching*, a cryptic handbook for diviners), the Book of Songs, the Book of Rituals, and collections of historical documents. Among the collections were the texts that give the story of the five culture-hero emperors and the Hsia dynasty, as well as a now confirmed account of the Shang and of the Chou conquest. The Chinese were already writing history and attaching characteristic importance to the keeping of records.

But fundamental changes were at work that were gradually to disrupt and then destroy the Chou structure. Iron was becoming slowly cheaper and more plentiful as technology improved, and it began to be available for agricultural implements, including iron-tipped plows, which the Chinese developed more than 1,000 years before the West. Helped by better tools, irrigation was spreading, especially in the semiarid north of China, and more and more land was being brought under cultivation. Iron axes speeded the attack on the remaining forests in the hilly margins of the north and in the Yangtze valley. Spurred by rising agricultural output, the population began to grow much more rapidly, perhaps to 20 million by the mid-Chou period. Except for recurrent years of drought, the population did not apparently outrun food supply, and surpluses were common, providing the basis for increasing trade.

New agricultural productivity freed increasing numbers from farm labor to serve as artisans, transport workers, soldiers, officials, scholars, and merchants. More and more towns, now more important as centers of trade than of royal or feudal control and dominated by merchants, began to dot the plain and the richer lands to the south in the Yangtze valley, where easier transport by water further stimulated the growth of trade and of urban centers. Fixed and hereditary serfdom and the domination of a

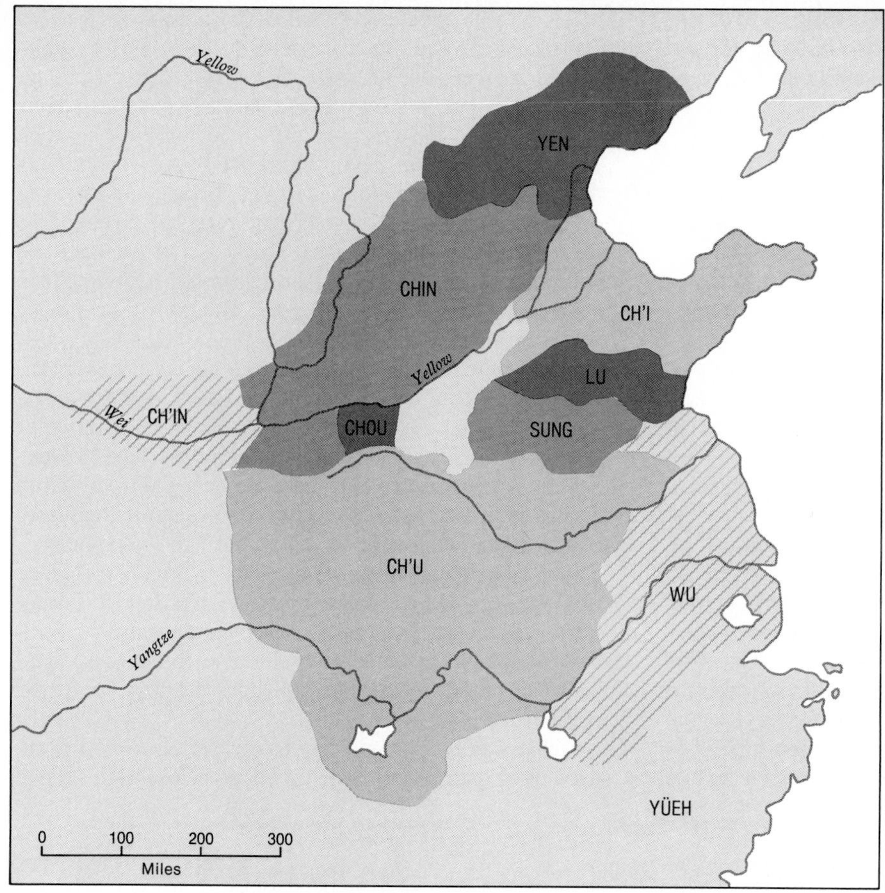

3.2 China in the Sixth Century B.C.

landed aristocracy came to seem less and less suited to the changing conditions, a situation that may have been in some ways similar to that in the later periods of the medieval European feudal order. At the same time many of the original Chou vassals were evolving into separate states, each with a distinctive culture. After some four centuries of Chou rule the political, social, and economic structure began to show strains, and eventually it disintegrated.

Warring States

In 771 B.C.* the royal capital in the Wei valley was sacked by a barbarian group from the north and the Chou king was killed. His son was installed as king the next year, but in a new and better-protected capital at Loyang, in the hope that a control point closer to the center of the royal domains would be more secure and more effective in holding the kingdom together. It was to be a vain hope. To guard the northwest borders, the old Chou base in the Wei valley was given as a fief to a loyal noble of the Ch'in (Qin) clan; five centuries later the Ch'in were to sweep away the crumbled remnants of Chou rule to found the first empire.

After 770 B.C. royal authority over the surrounding dependencies had dwindled and vassals became rival states: Ch'in to the west, Jin to the north, Yen to the northeast in the area around modern Peking (Beijing), Ch'i (Qi) to the east in Shantung (Shandong), Ch'u (Qu) to the south in the central Yangtze valley, and a number of smaller states including Shu in Szechuan (Sichuan) and Lu in Shantung, where Confucius was born and served for a time as an adviser. It is still too early to speak of any of them, even of the Chou, as "China"; each was culturally and linguistically as well as politically and perhaps even racially distinct. China as we know it emerged only under the empire of Ch'in (Qin) in the third century B.C. The

*From this time on, traditional Chinese dates, almost certainly inaccurate for earlier periods, are fully reliable. The earliest surviving books come from the ninth century B.C., and by the eighth century the Chou were recording eclipses of the sun, which we now know did in fact occur exactly when their records state.

Ch'in empire put its own overpowering stamp on what was to become the dominant Chinese style in statecraft and social organization for the ensuing two millennia. Our name *China* comes, appropriately enough, from the Ch'in, as the creator of the first imperial Chinese identity.

Until then no one strand dominated the assortment of people, cultures, and states that occupied what is now China. They warred repeatedly among themselves and against the various groups around their edges, still well within the borders of modern China. Technology probably passed relatively easily and quickly from group to group, and by mid-Chou most seem to have shared achievements in metallurgy, agriculture, and irrigation, as well as other arts. But in spoken and written language, in many aspects of culture, and in political identity they were as different as, say, the evolving states of late medieval Europe.

Ch'u was one of the largest such states. Its location astride the central Yangtze valley made it probably the most productive of the rival states, since its agriculture benefited from the more adequate and reliable rainfall and the longer growing season of central China as well as from the greater ease of irrigation. But it was different in character too, in particular in the size and importance of its merchant group and the role of waterborne trade and towns in its economy. Ch'u had evolved far beyond the earlier Shang pattern where power had been held by a hereditary landowning nobility and virtually the sole source of wealth was agriculture worked by slaves or serfs. Ch'u was also a naval power, with fleets on the Yangtze and its tributaries and adjacent lakes, in contrast to the land armies of the north, and even larger numbers of trading junks (riverboats). Ch'u was ultimately defeated by a coalition of northern states in a great battle in 632 B.C., and though it continued to exist, its power and further growth were greatly reduced while those of the other states rose. This may have been one of those battles that changed the course of history. A China that followed the Ch'u pattern would have been very different from what eventually emerged.

With increasing crop yields came changes in warfare. It was now possible to field large armies of men who could be spared from agriculture at least for parts of the year and could be fed on surpluses. Warfare became broader and more ruthless, and its character changed from that of earlier chivalric contests of honor between aristocrats to one of more wholesale conquest and fights for survival. The crossbow with a trigger mechanism greatly increased firepower, range, and accuracy, and by the fourth century B.C. foot soldiers were supported by armed cavalry. Such developments combined to undermine the earlier dominance of hereditary aristocrats, their chariots, and their personal retinues.

What was happening in China during this period paralleled the Indian pattern a century or so before as described

Reflections on Social Reform

The philosopher Mo-tzu (Mozi), who was born in the fifth century B.C., while Confucius was still alive, was more interested in reforming society.

It is the sage's business to regulate the world; he must thus know whence disorder comes in order to be capable of regulating it. . . . The origin is the lack of mutual love. . . . All the disorders of the world have this cause and this alone. . . . If mutual love prevailed universally throughout the world, no state would attack another state; no family would trouble another family; thieves and brigands would not exist; princes and subjects, fathers and sons, would all be filial and good. Thus the world would be well governed. . . . Where do ills come from? They come from hatred of others, from violence toward others. . . . The love which makes distinctions among persons causes all the ills of the world. . . . This universal love is very advantageous, and far more easy to practice than you imagine. If it is not put into practice, that is because the rulers take no pleasure in it. If the rulers took pleasure in it, I believe that men would throw themselves into it. . . . Nothing on earth could stop them. . . . To kill a man is called an unjust thing; it is a crime deserving death. To kill ten men is ten times more unjust, to kill a hundred men a hundred times more unjust. Today every prince in the world knows that this must be punished; they declare it unjust. Yet the greatest of injustices, the making of war, they do not punish. On the contrary, they glorify it and declare it just! Truly they do not know how unjust they are.

Source: After H. Maspero, *La Chine antique* (Paris: Presses Universitaires de France, 1927), pp. 253–254.

The Path of the Sage

One of the most influential followers of Confucius was the philosopher Hsun-tzu (Xunzi, c. 300–c. 235 B.C.), who assembled his own teachings in a book that faithfully pursues the path of the sage, as the following sample indicates.

When his horse is uneasy harnessed to a carriage, a gentleman is not comfortable in it. When the common people are uneasy under a government, a gentleman is not comfortable in his post. When a horse is uneasy, nothing is as good as calming it. When the common people are uneasy under a government, nothing is as good as being kind to them. Recruit the worthy and respectable and appoint the sincere and humble. Support filial piety and human heartedness. . . . It is traditionally said that the ruler is like a boat and the common people are the water. Water supports the boat but may also upset it.

Source: After C. O. Hucker, *China's Imperial Past* (Stanford, Calif.: Stanford University Press, 1975), p. 101.

in Chapter 2, where a chivalric age gave way to power struggles between states and the emergence of the Mauryan empire, based on the spread of iron, improvements in agriculture, and a population boom. As in India, bronze and copper coins minted by the state became common in this period in China, trade and cities grew rapidly, roads were built, standing armies proliferated, and the bureaucratic apparatus of the state began to appear. All of this offered a range of new opportunities for able commoners. For many it was a positive and welcome change, but for others the passing of the old order and the great disruptions and sufferings of warfare engendered only chaos and moral confusion. Confucius, who lived at the beginning of the period of warring states, offered his prescriptions as an effort to reestablish order and what he referred to as "harmony," in an attempt to restore the values of an earlier "golden age."

CONFUCIUS THE SAGE

Confucius was born about 551 B.C. in one of the smaller states which arose out of the Chou domains in Shantung province, and died about 479. He was a contemporary of the Buddha and died only a few years before the birth of Socrates. His family name was K'ung, and Chinese refer to him as K'ung Fu-tze (Kongfuzi, "Master K'ung"), which Europeans Latinized as Confucius. The K'ung family were low-ranking aristocrats in reduced circumstances, but they were able to arrange for their son's education. Confucius made a career out of teaching, periodically serving as consultant or counselor to various feudal lords. To his pupils he taught not only literacy and the classics but also his own philosophy of life and of government. Some of his pupils won high-level jobs in state administration, but Confucius himself was never very successful in such terms, and he apparently thought of himself as a failure. In reality, he was the founder of the most successful philosophical, moral, and ethical system in human history, measured by the number of people in China, Korea, Japan, and Vietnam who followed his precepts for more than 2,500 years and who are still profoundly influenced by them.

We have nothing that the sage himself wrote and not very much direct information about him or his teachings. All we know for certain comes from a collection of discourses, or sayings, known as the *Analects*, put together rather unsystematically after his death by his disciples and hence probably not wholly accurate. Later commentaries expanded on the meaning and application of his teachings.

The picture we derive from the *Analects*, though incomplete, is of a thoughtful but very human person. He complained that he could never seem to get the right kinds of students or the kinds of appointments he yearned for. In discussing his lack of success, he commented loftily: "I don't mind not being in office; I am more concerned about being qualified for it. I don't mind not having recognition; I strive to be worthy of recognition." Yet at the same time he complained about being treated "like a gourd fit only to be hung on the wall and never put to use." He seems to have been so eager for a post as adviser that he considered working even for rebel groups, believing that, given any kind of opportunity, he could remake men and states in line with his philosophy—an attitude that Plato was to share a century later. But he also had a keen sense of the ridiculous and could even enjoy jokes on himself.

The basic message of all Confucius' teachings is that people can be molded and elevated by education and by the virtuous example of superiors. "Civilized" people so formed will *want* to do what is morally right, rather than what is merely expedient; hence they will preserve the harmony of society, which is what distinguishes humans from animals. Force and threats are ineffective controls, he asserts; only internalized values can produce correct behavior. Behavior should be modeled on that of people of superior status, beginning with the family and extending to the ruler, who thus must match power with responsibility and uprightness. For all relationships, he counsels in a variant of the Golden Rule, "Do not do unto others what you yourself would not like."

Confucianism is a prescription for benevolence in human affairs and in government, with an essentially conservative stress on order. Nevertheless, the focus on benevolence meant that bad government should rightly be rejected, despite the threat to civil order, a point that the *Analects* repeats in several contexts. The Confucian model is the upright man who unswervingly pursues the right moral course whatever the consequences, even at the expense of his own self-interest. Master K'ung's life seems to have conformed to the model he preached. Perhaps he was, like Socrates, too outspoken to win the favor of the powerful men of his day. But his teachings and his example have far outlived the petty politics of the age in which he lived.

The Ch'in Conquest

Ch'in, originally one of the poorest, smallest, and most remote of the Chou dependencies, seemed easily outclassed by the other contending states. Its succession of able rulers made a virtue of its relative poverty, its peasant base, and its frontier location by stressing the importance of hard work, frugality, and discipline and emphasizing agriculture and peasant soldiery rather than trade or the development of an intellectual elite. The Ch'in rulers blended these elements to create a strong military power. Its tough armies defeated those of rival states in a long series of campaigns that were kept away from the mountain-ringed Ch'in home base in the Wei valley but often devastated the more fragile economies of its trade-dependent enemies. Opponents saw the menace of rising Ch'in power too late to unite against it and were picked off one by one. Ch'in generals and statesmen were masters of strategy and tactics who used diplomacy, propaganda, treachery, espionage, and various forms of psychological warfare adroitly.

A series of victorious campaigns during the 230s and 220s culminated in the final defeat of all the other states in 221 B.C. North China and the Yangtze valley were united politically for the first time, and the Ch'in ruler, who now took the title of emperor (Huang Ti) as Ch'in Shih Huang Ti (Di), applied to his entire empire the systems that had built Ch'in power. Further conquests after 221 began the long Chinese absorption of the south with the acquisition of the kingdom of Yüeh (Yue) centered in the Canton (Guangzhou) delta and the route to it southward from the Yangtze, together with Yüeh territory in what is now northern Vietnam. Throughout the new domains, as in the former state of Ch'in, primogeniture (the custom whereby the eldest son inherits all of the father's property and status) was abolished, as was slavery except for minor domestic servants. The former feudal and land tenure arrangements were dissolved. Land became privately owned and was freely bought and sold. The state levied a tax on all land in the form of a share of the crop. A new uniform law code was applied to all subjects without discrimination, ending many centuries of aristocratic privilege, a reform that clearly appealed to most people. Currency, weights, measures, and forms of writing, which had varied widely among what had been separate cultures as well as states, were also unified by imperial fiat to follow the Ch'in mode, a change essential for governing a large empire. An imperial system of roads and canals was begun, and a splendid new capital was built near modern Sian (Xian) in the Wei valley. Even axle lengths for carts were standardized, so that all carts would fit the same ruts.

Probably the most spectacular and best known of the new public works projects was the Great Wall, which Ch'in Shih Huang Ti ordered consolidated from a series of much earlier walls along the northern steppe border and reconstructed as a uniform barrier with regularly spaced watchtowers. It and subsequent reconstructions (the remains currently visible date from the Ming rebuilding in the fifteenth century A.D.) constitute probably the largest single works project in human history; the Great Wall is said to be the only human construction visible from the moon. A million men reportedly died in building the Ch'in Great Wall, working as conscript labor. Ironically, the wall was never very effective in its supposed purpose of preventing nomadic incursions; end runs around it and intrigues that opened the gates made it often quite permeable. But it did serve as a symbolic affirmation of empire and as a statement of territorial and sovereign limits. The new state control over mass labor tempted the emperor to plan more and more projects of monumental scope, including the road system, the new canals (useful for transporting troops and their supplies as well as for irrigation), and his own magnificent palace and tomb, in addition to fresh conquests.

Ch'in Authoritarianism

Agriculture was stressed as the basis of the economy and the state, with hardy peasants available in off seasons for conscript labor or for the army. Merchants were regarded as parasites and as potentially dangerous power rivals to the state. The removal of primogeniture also reduced the

The Great Wall was probably Ch'in Shih Huang Ti's most famous, or infamous, project. Here it is shown west of Peking snaking along the mountain ridges separating northeastern China from Mongolia. The wall was built wide enough to allow two war chariots to pass abreast. The sections of it that remain standing now date from its most recent wholesale reconstruction under the Ming dynasty in the fifteenth century. [Werner Forman Archive]

threat from hereditary landed power. But the chief target of the Ch'in system was the independence of intellectuals, people who ask questions, consider alternatives, or point out deficiencies. China already had a long tradition of scholars, philosophers, and moralists, of whom Confucius and his later disciple Mencius were honored examples. The Ch'in saw such people as potential troublemakers. It was an openly totalitarian state, and its sense of mission made it even more intolerant of any dissent.

Ch'in Shih Huang Ti persecuted intellectuals, buried several hundred scholars alive for questioning his policies, and ordered all books burned that could promote what he considered undesirable thoughts. In practice this meant most books other than trade manuals and the official Ch'in chronicles. The documents destroyed included valuable material accumulated from earlier periods. There was to be no admiration of the past, no criticism of the present, and no recommendations for the future, except the state's. These policies were profoundly contrary to the Chinese reverence for the written word and the preservation of records. They earned the emperor the condemnation of all subsequent Chinese scholars. Certainly he was a cruel tyrant, inhumane and perhaps even depraved in his lust for absolute power. But his methods, harsh though they were, built an empire out of disunity and established most of the bases of the Chinese state all the way to the present.

The emperor's policies were actually in large measure the work of his prime minister, Li Ssu, whose career closely paralleled that of Kautilya in Mauryan India and who is credited with founding a new school of philosophy called Legalism, which embodied the Ch'in policies of strict state control through the application of harsh laws. This control was augmented by a greatly expanded state bureaucracy and by rigid supervision of all education. Only values that supported the state design were taught, and practical skills were stressed over critical inquiry. As in Mauryan India, there were a highly developed police system and a secret service to ferret out and punish dissidents. Travel, within the realm or abroad, was forbidden except by special permit.

China, once unified by the Ch'in, even by such ruthless means, was to cling to the idea of imperial unity ever thereafter. Each subsequent period of disunity following the fall of a dynasty was regarded as a time of failure, and each ended in the rebuilding of the empire. But one must also acknowledge the appeal of the new order that even the totalitarian methods of the Ch'in represented. By its time most people were clearly ready to break with their feudal past and to move toward a system based on achievement rather than birth. The Ch'in believed firmly that their new order was progress; they had a visionary conviction that they were creating a better society. The parallels with Communist China are striking, and indeed Ch'in Shih Huang Ti was praised as a model during the Cultural Revolution in the late 1960s. Sacrifice for an inspiring national goal has its own appeal; the end is seen to justify the means, including treachery, cruelty, and inhumanity toward the people, who are nevertheless seen as the supposed beneficiaries of the new order.

Lord Shang, an earlier Ch'in official and the true progenitor of the Legalist school, summarized state policy in classic totalitarian terms:

Punish heavily the light offenses. . . . If light offenses do not occur, serious ones have no chance of coming. This is said to be "ruling the people in a state of law and order." . . .

A state where uniformity of purpose has been established for ten years will be strong for a hundred years; for a hundred years it will be strong for a thousand years . . . and will attain supremacy. . . .

The things which people desire are innumerable, but that from which they benefit is one and the same. Unless

> **the people are made one, there is no way to make them attain their desire. Therefore they are unified, and their strength is consolidated. . . .**
>
> **If you establish what people delight in, they will suffer from what they dislike, but if you establish what they dislike, they will be happy in what they enjoy.**[1]

Nevertheless, there was merit in the new equality under the law propounded by the Ch'in, new opportunities for advancement, and allure in its ambitious projects. The best illustration of the more constructive aspects of the Ch'in is the figure of Li Bing, provincial governor of the former state of Shu (Szechuan) and famed as a hydraulic engineer on many Ch'in projects, including the control works on the Yellow River. It was Li Bing who devised the best formula for minimizing the floods that had already made the Yellow River notorious: "Dig the bed deep, and keep the banks low." This helped to prevent the buildup of silt in the river's bed, which over time had raised it above the level of the surrounding country and greatly worsened the destructive consequences of floods. Li Bing's sound advice was finally acted on effectively only under the present Communist government after 1949.

Li Bing is credited with designing and constructing the famous irrigation works at Kuan Hsien (Guanxian) in western Szechuan (Sichuan), diverting the Min River where it emerges from the mountains and enters the wide plain around the capital city of Chengdu. These works, much visited by tourists, still stand, with Li Bing's statue overlooking them. They are reputed to have saved millions of people on the Chengdu plain from drought and famine ever since. Like all big projects, they took enormous labor and hardship, mainly from conscript workers under iron discipline. According to the great Han dynasty historian Ssu Ma Ch'ien (Simaqian), Li Bing said toward the end of his life:

> **People can be depended on to enjoy the results, but they must not be consulted about the beginnings. Now the elder ones and their descendants dislike people like me, but hundreds of years later let them think what I have said and done.**

Li Bing's memory is still honored, while that of his emperor is reviled.

The Han Dynasty

Ch'in Shih Huang Ti died in 210 B.C., leaving the throne to his eldest son, but Li Ssu and other counselors suppressed the news of his death for fear of uprisings and then installed the second son as their puppet. But the harshness of Ch'in rule had left the country in turmoil, exhausted the people, drained the treasury, and alienated the educated upper classes. Without their cooperation, the regime was in trouble. Rebellion had already begun in several provinces. This was soon joined by the desertion of several army commanders. In 206 B.C. rebel armies occupied the capital and burned the emperor's splendid new palace. Rival forces contended for power in the ensuing struggle, in which large groups of soldiers, workers, and former officials roamed the country. Out of this chaos there had emerged by 202 B.C. a new rebel leader, Liu Pang (Liu Bang), who founded a new dynasty, which he named the Han. Under Han rule China took the political, social, and territorial shape it was to retain until the present century. The Chinese still call themselves "People of Han," a label they carry with much pride as the heirs of a great tradition. Han imperial success, and that of later dynasties, depended, however, on retention of many of the techniques of control used by the Ch'in. The administration of an empire the size of Europe with a population of probably about 60 million could not have been managed otherwise.

Beginning with the Han, the harsher aspects of the Legalist approach of the Ch'in were softened by both common sense and the more humane morality of Confucianism. Liu Pang, who took the title Han Kao-tsu ("High Progenitor") as the first emperor, emphasized the Confucian precept that government exists to serve the people and that unjust rulers should forfeit both the mandate of Heaven and the support of the ruled. He abolished the hated controls on travel, education, and thought, lowered taxes, and encouraged learning so as to build a pool of educated men whose talents, in the Confucian mode, could be called on to serve the state. Conscription for the army and forced labor for public works such as road and canal building were, however, retained, as was the administrative division of the empire into hsien (xian, counties), each under the control of an imperial magistrate. The imperial state superimposed its model in all things, including currency, weights, measures, script, and orthodox thought, on a vast and diverse area that had long been politically and culturally varied. Under beneficent rule, this system could be made to work successfully and could command general support. Early Han was a time of great prosperity and of enthusiasm for the new order.

Expansion Under Wu Ti

The new power of the Han empire, on Ch'in foundations and with the boost of economic and population growth, tempted successive emperors to further conquests and imperial glory. Liu Pang's son and grandson continued his frugal and benevolent model as rulers, but the bitter memories of Ch'in had faded by the time of the emperor Wu Ti (141–87 B.C.). He first tightened imperial control, removed the remaining power of the lords created by Liu Pang for faithful service, and imposed regulations on trade and merchants, new taxes, and new controls over salt, iron, and the supply of grain. The last measure, which

The Perils of Mindless Traditionalism

Han Fei (died 233 B.C.), a Legalist philosopher, was a contemporary and sometime colleague of Li Ssu, who ultimately poisoned him as a rival. Han Fei's writings, however, survived, including the following story illustrating the folly of mindlessly following old ways instead of adapting policies to fit new circumstances.

In a plowman's field was a tree stump. When a rabbit ran into the stump and broke its neck, the plowman left his plow and watched over the stump, hoping to pick up more rabbits. But he got no more and became the laughingstock of the whole kingdom. Wanting to apply the policies of former kings to govern people in these times belongs in the same class as watching over that stump.

Source: After C. O. Hucker, *China's Imperial Past* (Stanford, Calif.: Stanford University Press, 1975), p. 94.

created what came to be known as the "ever-normal granary system," was intended to prevent famine by state collection of grain in good years or surplus areas, which could then be sold at low rather than inflated prices when lean years came. It was a good idea and was practiced with some success by subsequent dynasties, but, like Li Bing's projects, it was not always popular with the local producers or merchants.

Having put the imperial house in order and increased state revenues and power, Wu Ti began an ambitious program of new conquests in 111 B.C., beginning in the southeast against Yüeh in the Fukien and Canton areas, which had broken away after the fall of the Ch'in. The Yüeh kingdom had included the related people and culture of what is today northern Vietnam, and this too was now again added to the Chinese empire. Over the centuries the Vietnamese were to reassert their separate identity despite their adoption of much of Chinese culture. In Han times the people and culture of Yüeh were regarded as foreign and were very different from those of the north. More than traces of these differences remain even now, including the Cantonese language and cuisine, but the south has been an integral part of China for 2,000 years and has been largely remade in the greater Chinese image.

Turning northward after the successful southern campaign, in 109–108 B.C. Wu Ti's armies conquered Manchuria and northern Korea for the empire, while other campaigns established looser control over the still non-Chinese populations of Yunnan and Kweichou (Guizhou) in the southwest. Southern Manchuria was to remain solidly a part of the Chinese system, with large colonies, originally garrisons, planted there by Wu Ti. These became agricultural settlements in the fertile valley of the Liao River.

Similar garrisons were established in northern Korea, where there was heavy Chinese influence from Han times on. But Koreans, like the Vietnamese, remained eager to reclaim their cultural identity and independence. As in Vietnam, Korea had already developed its own civilization and was linguistically and ethnically distinct from China despite Chinese cultural influence. After the Han collapse in A.D. 220 both areas broke away from Chinese control, Korea as a nominally tributary state, Vietnam to endure later Chinese reconquest under the T'ang and then successive wars of independence until modern times, which created a heavy legacy of mutual mistrust.

China's northern and northwestern frontiers had been and were to remain troublesome for other reasons. The Great Wall had been built as a barrier, but it could not prevent infiltrations by the horse-riding nomads who occupied the steppe border zone and who periodically harried Chinese agricultural areas and trade routes. The major route for international trade was the famous Silk Road through the Kansu (Gansu) Corridor and along the northern and southern edges of the Tarim Desert in Sinkiang (Xinjiang, Chinese Turkestan), where there are widely separated oases fed by streams from the surrounding mountains. The two routes met at Kashgar at the western end of the Tarim Desert and then crossed the Pamirs into central Asia, where the trade passed into other hands on its long way to the Levant and eventually on to Rome. Silk was the main export, a Chinese monopoly since Lung Shan times and in great demand westward, especially in luxury-loving imperial Rome. The Romans were obliged to pay for it largely in gold, a drain that Pliny and other Roman historians felt weakened the economy and contributed to Rome's ultimate collapse in the West. It was profitable to China, and Wu Ti's pride in his new imperial power made him less willing to accept nomad interruptions of the trade and raids on Chinese territory.

The chief nomad group at this period was the Hsiung-nu (Xiung-nu), a Turkish people whose mounted mobility

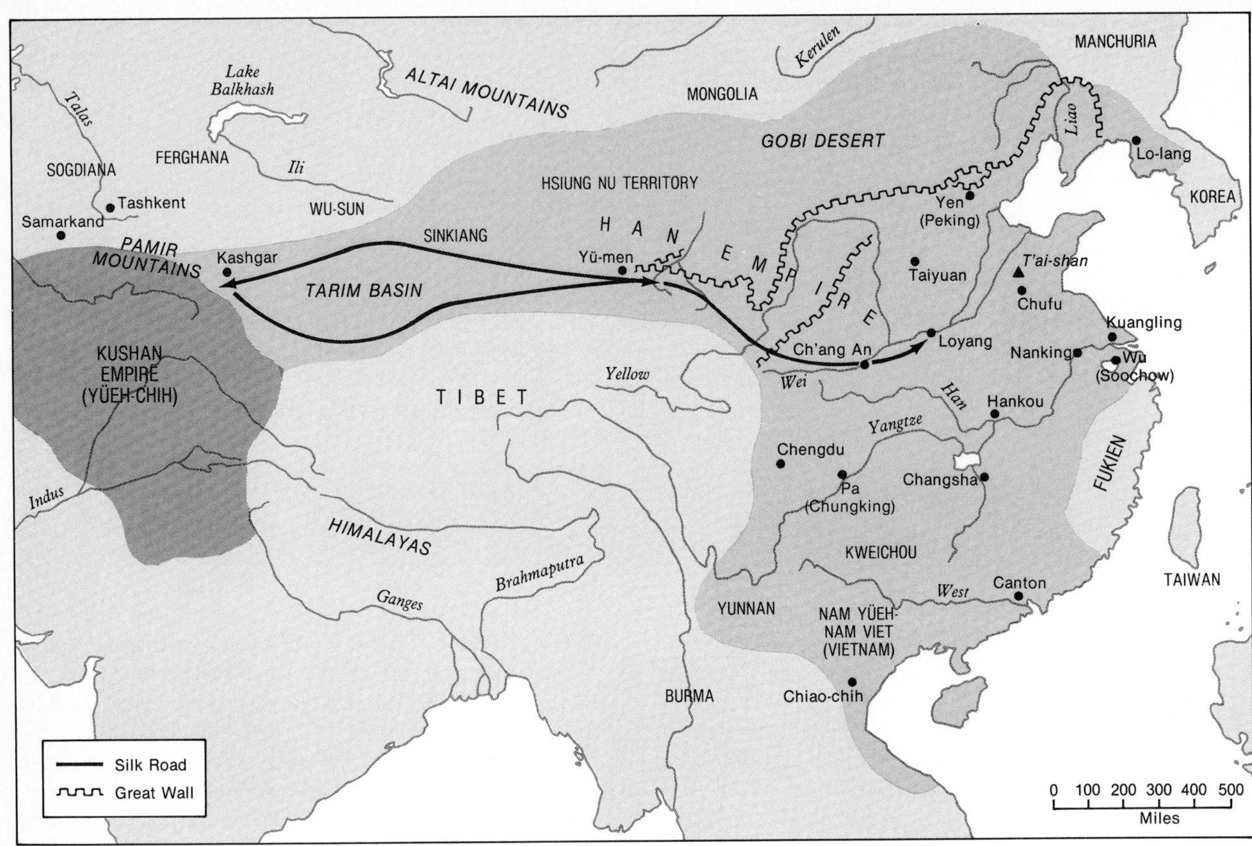

3.3 The Han Empire

and cavalry tactics gave them the kind of military effectiveness later used by the Mongol leader Chinghis Khan. The Han generals complained that the Hsiung-nu "move on swift horses, and in their breasts beat the hearts of beasts. They shift from place to place like a flock of birds. Thus it is difficult to corner them and bring them under control." One can understand the frustration of the Han, but in a series of major campaigns Wu Ti defeated the Hsiung-nu, drove them for a time out of most of Inner Mongolia, Kansu, and Sinkiang, and planted colonies and garrisons in those areas and along the Silk Road, which is still marked by ruined Han watchtowers. Sinkiang and Inner Mongolia were to fall away from Chinese control in later periods whenever the central state was weak but were reclaimed by most subsequent strong dynasties as part of the empire. Non-Han groups like the Hsiung-nu and the Mongols remained the major steppe inhabitants until the present century, and another Turkish people, the Uighurs, remained the dominant oasis farmers in the desert region of Sinkiang. The Uighurs later embraced Islam and helped to transmit it to China proper, where there are still a number of Chinese Muslims, concentrated in the northwest.

China and Rome

Wu Ti sent an ambassador westward in 139 B.C., a courtier named Chang Ch'ien (Zhangqian), to try to make an alliance with other nomads against the Hsiung-nu and to scout out the country more generally. He was captured instead by the Hsiung-nu but escaped after ten years. He returned to the Han capital at Ch'ang An (Qangan) in the Wei valley, where the Ch'in had ruled, in 126 B.C. with an account of central Asia that included bits of information about India and a great empire far to the west, where the silk went. This was China's first news of Rome, but they were never to learn much more. Travelers who said they had been to Rome turned up much later at the Han court with their own tales in the second century A.D., as recorded in the Han annals. The Romans knew China only as the source of silk and called it, accordingly, Seres, the Latin word for silk.

Wu Ti was tempted by Chang Ch'ien's report to add central Asia to his conquests, partly out of vainglory and partly to secure supplies of the excellent horses to be found there, which he wanted for the imperial stables and his cavalry. If he or his successors had done so, the

Chinese and Roman empires or their forward troops might have met and perhaps learned from each other. In the first century A.D., with the Han still in power and still occasionally probing westward, Rome was campaigning against the Parthian kingdom in Persia. If the Romans had conquered Parthia, they might have encountered at least Han patrols or might have followed the Silk Road, which they knew about, from central Asia to the borders of China. But both armies were very far from home. Moreover, the Parthians and other central Asian groups were formidable opponents and were eager to retain their profitable role as intermediary in the silk trade rather than allow the two empires to meet. Han envoys reached the Parthians but were advised to return home, which they did.

Wu Ti's endless campaigns and his impositions on the people exhausted the country's patience and resources. One of his earlier reforms had been the establishment of imperial censors whose job it was to keep officials, even the emperor, faithful to their duty to serve the people. The censors finally convinced Wu Ti that he had neglected this basic precept and persuaded him to issue a famous penitential edict apologizing for his excesses and promising to be a better ruler, more deserving of the mandate of Heaven—and less likely to be overthrown by rebellion, which was already brewing. The institution of the censorate remained a regulatory feature of all subsequent dynasties.

Wu Ti's immediate successors, while largely abandoning further conquests, continued to press the Hsiung-nu as a defensive strategy and even sent an expeditionary force across the Pamirs into the Samarkand region in pursuit. There, in 42 B.C., on the banks of the Talas River near Tashkent in central Asia, they defeated a Hsiung-nu coalition that included mercenary troops who from the Chinese description may have been Roman auxiliaries; they had learned the Roman *testudo* formation with shields overlapping above their heads to ward off arrows and spears. The Han armies in central Asia, having marched across deserts and high mountains, were farther from their capital than regular Roman troops ever were from Rome. But this was the high point of Han power, and the empire that Wu Ti welded together was not to be significantly enlarged or altered in subsequent centuries.

Wider Trade Patterns

Contacts across Eurasia had probably been important since the prehistoric period: Sumeria may have contributed to Indian civilization (and vice versa) and to the emergence of Chinese civilization. We have no adequate archaeological data to permit more than speculation about such interchanges. Given the multiplicity and often the mutual hostility of the various cultural groups and political alliances in central Asia during the ancient and medieval periods, the passage of goods and ideas through this area, in either direction, was necessarily slow and difficult. There was certainly trade linking China and India to western Asia, Greece, and Rome. From at least 600 B.C. there was also sea trade bringing Indian and Southeast Asian spices to the Mediterranean and Europe. But except for the visits of Greek and Roman traders to the Indian west coast, the travels of a few Indian philosophers to Greece and Rome, and Alexander's invasion of India, there was no direct contact between Eastern and Western civilizations from then until the time of Marco Polo in the thirteenth century. Arab ships traded by sea, and a chain of various central Asian peoples transmitted ideas as well as goods across Eurasia, but the transmission was incomplete, and understandably some of the ideas were garbled in the process.

The Chinese and Roman empires thus remained largely in ignorance of each other except for travelers' tales, although both were of comparable size, sophistication, power, and achievements. China might have developed a different and more open attitude to the rest of the world if it had had some experience with another culture, Roman or Indian, at its own level of sophistication. Like the Chinese, the Romans were builders of roads, walls, and planned cities, synthesizers of varied cultures under an expansionist and cosmopolitan system, and contenders with "barbarians" along the fringes of their empire. The Han empire was larger, and probably richer and more populous, than either the Roman or the Indian empires, but its level of cultural and technical sophistication was probably matched by the others.

Roman traders, and before them Greeks, regularly reached the west coast of India, as mentioned in Chapter 2. Roman goods, including pottery and coins, have been found as far east as Malaya but were probably carried there by Indian or Arab merchants. Before the time of the Greeks, there was trade by both sea and land between India and Mesopotamia, but we know little or nothing about the goods shipped from west to east in that exchange; Indian exports may have been paid for largely in gold, as the Romans paid for Chinese silk. Commerce between China and the rest of Eurasia almost certainly developed later than India's trade with Mesopotamia, and there is no evidence of Chinese exports westward until the beginning of the silk route, probably during the Chou dynasty.

Chinese merchants took the silk only as far as Sinkiang, handing it over there to a long series of central Asian traders who passed it along through the thousands of miles of central and western Asia to the shores of the Mediterranean, where Syrian, Greek, and Roman merchants picked it up for transport farther west. This trade continued after the fall of the Han dynasty and was later augmented by the export of porcelain and lacquer goods, all high-value commodities that could bear the very heavy costs of such long-distance transport. The camel caravans carrying them were also exposed to frequent raids from other central Asian groups along the route, risks that further increased the prices charged for Chinese exports when they finally reached their destinations. By the eleventh century much of the Chinese export trade was also being carried by ships westward to India (and later to Africa), while Indian exports westward—fine cotton textiles, spices, gems, and other goods—continued from the earliest period through the Middle Ages to move mainly by sea, from ports on the west coast.

Han Culture

The first two centuries of Han rule were a time of great cultural flowering, in poetry, painting, music, philosophy, literature, and the writing of history. Confucianism was more firmly established as the official orthodoxy and state ideology, and the famous Chinese imperial civil service system recruited men of talent, schooled in classical Confucian learning, to hold office through competitive examination regardless of their birth. Liu Pang, the founder of the Han, had been born a peasant, and thus ability and education were stressed rather than inherited status. This approach was to remain a source of strength and effectiveness for the state for the next 2,000 years. Office-holding by the scholar-gentry, who were enriched each generation by new blood rising from peasant or commoner ranks and entering the elite through the imperial examinations, became the most prestigious of all occupations. That in turn generally helped to ensure that able people went into the administration and often preserved the political arena and government service from corruption, mediocrity, and ineffectiveness.

Bronze casting continued its development under the Han. This magnificent bronze horse from the second century A.D. shows the sophistication of Han technology and art. [Granger Collection]

China was not free from the common problems of bureaucracy, but each new dynasty reestablished the system begun under the Han and on the whole probably managed the task of government better than many other states. Confucius, with his emphasis on duty, learning, "human-heartedness," and virtue, is to thank for this. Chinese society continued to choose that way and periodically reaffirmed the teachings of an obscure consultant to a small feudal lord in the sixth century B.C. who lived long before there was any thought of empire. Great landed-gentry families remained and periodically formed power cliques, together with court aristocrats, eunuchs, and ambitious generals—a pattern familiar from imperial Rome, Persia, and elsewhere. But the original Han ideal endured, through the rise and fall of successive dynasties, and with all its imperfections built a long and proud tradition of power combined with service that is still very much alive in China. The People's Republic is the conscious heir of an imperial past.

Han rule was briefly broken by the rebellion of Wang Mang (A.D. 9–23), who tried, as a model Confucian emperor, to curb the resurgent power of merchants and landowning gentry. He also extended new state controls over the economy, in an effort to reestablish the egalitarianism he claimed to derive from the sage's teaching. His reforms included the abolition of private estates, which had increasingly avoided paying taxes, and the nationalization of land. Such policies bitterly alienated the rich and powerful, and Wang Mang was murdered by a rebel group called the Red Eyebrows, with support from both distressed peasants suffering from a drought-induced famine and from merchant and gentry groups.

Landowning and its abuses were, of course, problems for all ancient and medieval empires. Ownership of land usually meant power and was usually (except in post-Ch'in China) passed on within the family by inheritance. Even in China the abolition of primogeniture (inheritance by the eldest son) did not always prevent powerful families from accumulating large blocks of land. Large landowners built up wealth but also threatened the supremacy of the state by their growing political power. By manipulating their influence, they often managed to reduce or avoid paying state taxes on their lands and would often also support or even constitute in themselves powerful political factions. Their tenants, the peasants who farmed the land, were often cruelly exploited, paying far more in rent and services to the landowner than the latter paid to the state. As these practices were carried to extremes, rebellion brewed, and reformers in government periodically tried to check the abuses of the large landowners, as in Wang Mang's abortive reforms. Throughout the empires of the ancient and medieval world, similar problems and similar efforts at solution can be observed, as in the case of the revolt of the Gracchi in Rome (see Chapter 6) or the reforms of Wang An-Shih in Sung China.

In A.D. 25 the Han dynasty was reestablished, under

Han dynasty scientists in the second century A.D. calculated the value of *pi* as 3.1622 and developed a highly accurate calendar, the wheelbarrow, and a bronze seismograph for recording earthquakes. The model shown here is based on detailed description of the original. Eight dragons at major compass points along the outer edge of the vessel responded to tremors from the appropriate direction by spitting a pearl into the mouth of the frog below. [Sheridan/Ancient Art and Architecture Collection]

new rulers and with a new capital at Loyang, following the earlier model of the Chou and for the same reasons. It is thus known as the Eastern or Later Han, while the Ch'ang An period from 202 B.C. to A.D. 9 is called Western or Former Han. A succession of strong and conscientious emperors restored the power, prosperity, and cultural vigor of Wu Ti's time. Learning, philosophy, and the arts flourished once more, and elite society reached new levels of affluence, elegance, and sophistication. Peace was reestablished along all the imperial frontiers by reconquest. In A.D. 97 a Han army marched all the way to the Caspian Sea, and its advance scouts reached either the Persian Gulf or the Black Sea. In A.D. 89 a Han army invaded Mongolia and again defeated the Hsiung-nu, probably contributing to the start of the latter's subsequent migration westward and their ultimate role as invaders of Europe as the Huns. Sinkiang, northern Vietnam, northern Korea, southern Manchuria, and Inner Mongolia were all reincorporated into the empire, trade flourished, and China gloried in its confidently reasserted power and cultural leadership.

The Latter Han produced some of the most famous generals in Chinese history; those generals had repeated successes against rebellious groups on the northwest frontier. One of the best known of these is Pan Ch'ao (Ban Qao), whose brother and sister were joint authors of a famous history of the Han dynasty. In the words of the French historian René Grousset, Pan Ch'ao is said to have asserted that "only he who penetrates into the tiger's lair can carry off the cubs." In A.D. 73 he was sent with a detachment of troops to pacify the area south of Sinkiang. Surrounded by enemy tribal forces with whom he was attempting to negotiate, he said, "Let us profit from the

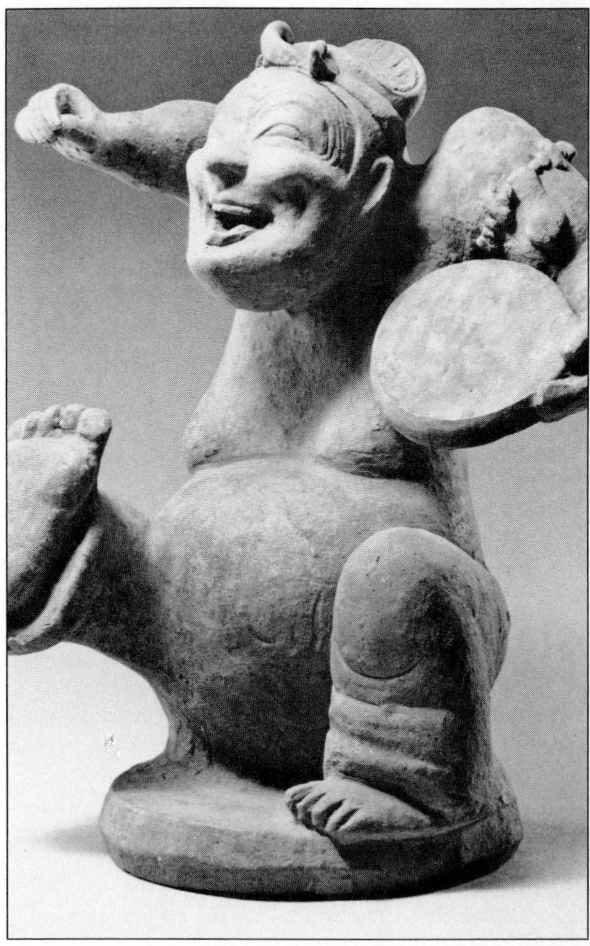

Pottery figure titled "Balladeer," part of the grave furniture from a Han dynasty tomb in Szechuan Province. The afterlife was clearly supposed to be a happy time, replete with worldly pleasures. This figure beautifully captures the human quality of Han folk culture. [Innervisions/Sichuan Provincial Museum, China]

Raised ceramic tile from a Han dynasty tomb showing a festive scene with jugglers, dancers, and musicians. [Asian Art Archives, University of Michigan; Private Collection, Chengtu, China]

darkness and take the barbarians by surprise." When his men asked how he was to take this initiative without getting permission from the civil authorities, he said, "Our life or death is to be decided; what do we care for the opinions of a civil servant? If we inform him of our plans, he will certainly take fright." Night had fallen and the wind blew up a gale. Pan Ch'ao ordered some of his men to take up drums and hide behind the barbarian camp. It was agreed that as soon as they saw flames rising, they would start beating their drums and shouting. The remainder of his men were concealed before the gates of the barbarian fortress.

> **Then Pan Ch'ao started a great fire, leaving the wind to carry it, while a clamor of drums and war cries broke out behind the fortress. The barbarians were taken by surprise. Pan Ch'ao killed three of them with his own hands, his soldiers beheaded thirty others, including the barbarian envoy, and another hundred died in the flames. This done, Pan Ch'ao summoned the one who called himself "king," and without a word showed him the head of his emissary. The king, who had been on the point of betraying them, now in abject fear renewed his vassalage to China.[2]**

After the first century, landlord power and oppression grew again; Wang Mang had been right to try to curb them. Imperial relatives and powerful families jockeyed for position or influence, peasant revolts were growing, and the elite, especially those at court surrounding weak emperors, indulged themselves in luxurious living heedless of the problems around them—all echoes of the problems Rome was facing at the same time. Palace intrigues grew out of control, and eunuch groups acquired more and more power. Generals in the provinces became rival warlords after suppressing peasant uprisings. The entire imperial structure was crumbling, and in A.D. 220 the last Han emperor abdicated.

The French historian Jacques Gernet has suggested as well that, as the expansion of Han China was based on economic growth and trade with Mongolia, Korea, central Asia, South China, and northern India, so its gradual incorporation of these areas within its empire gave it secure frontiers beyond which there was little incentive to expand.[3]

Chinese control over Sinkiang was lost with the fall of the Han, by which time nearly all Chinese originally settled there as garrison troops had withdrawn, although their watchtowers and fortified bases remained, to crumble away in succeeding centuries. With the reassertion of empire under the T'ang, Sinkiang was reclaimed as imperial territory, only to fall away again with the collapse of the T'ang order, a pattern repeated under the Ch'ing (Manchu) dynasty (1644–1911). Only with the advent of modern means of communication have large numbers of Chinese again settled in Sinkiang, but the dominant inhabitants remain, as they were well before Han times, Turkish and other central Asian peoples.

The Collapse of the Han Order

A new dynasty called Wei was proclaimed in 220, but it failed to hold the empire together, and rival dynasties soon emerged. In ensuing years the north was progressively overrun by barbarians, Hsiung-nu and other steppe nomadic groups, who sacked both Ch'ang An and Loyang by the early fourth century. The north disintegrated into a bewildering series of minor rival kingdoms under barbarian control, while the south was similarly divided into rival Chinese states.

The period from the fall of the Han in 220 to the ultimate reunification in 589 is sometimes rather misleadingly called the Six Dynasties (there were many more than six) but is better described as a long interval of disunity, invasion, disruption, intrigue, and warfare that shattered the imperial image and left most Chinese disheartened. Much of the former high culture survived, especially in the arts, and little of it was forgotten by educated Chinese, but the period was a time of troubles. Except among the elite, many of whom fled south, most people suffered. These centuries suggest comparison with what began only a little later in the breakup of the Roman Empire and the Germanic and Hun invasions of southern Europe. In China too the period was thought of as a Dark Age, and as in Europe confidence was lost. As Europe saw the spread of a new mass religion of otherworldly salvation, Christianity, so Buddhism took root in China. But the imperial idea continued to appeal to Chinese pride, and in time it was to be

The Fall of the Han

The popular Chinese novel Romance of the Three Kingdoms, *first written down in the fourteenth century A.D., tells of the fall of the Han and the civil war that ensued. The account begins as follows:*

Empires wax and wane; states cleave asunder and coalesce. When the rule of Chou weakened, seven contending principalities sprang up, warring one with another until they settled down as Ch'in, and when its destiny had been fulfilled there arose Ch'u and Han to contend for the mastery. And Han was the victor. . . . In a short time the whole empire was theirs, and their magnificent heritage was handed down in successive generations till the days of Kuang-wu, whose name stands in the middle of the long line of Han. . . . The dynasty had already passed its zenith. . . . The descent into misrule hastened in the reigns of the two emperors who sat on the dragon throne about the middle of the second century. They paid no heed to the good men of the court but gave their confidence to the palace eunuchs. . . . The two trusted advisers, disgusted with the abuses resulting from the meddling of the eunuchs in affairs of state, plotted their destruction. But the chief eunuch was not to be disposed of so easily. The plot leaked out and the two honest men fell, leaving the eunuchs stronger than before. . . . [Some years later] the earth quaked in Loyang, while along the coast a huge tidal wave rushed in, which, in its recoil, swept away all the dwellers by the sea. . . . Certain hens developed male characteristics, a miracle that could only refer to the effeminate eunuchs meddling in affairs of state. Away from the capital, a mountain fell in, leaving a great rift in its flank. . . . But the eunuchs grew bolder. Ten of them, rivals in wickedness, formed a powerful party. One of them became the emperor's most trusted adviser. The emperor even called him Daddy. So the government went from bad to worse, till the country was ripe for rebellion and buzzed with brigandage.

Source: After C. H. Brewitt-Taylor, trans., *Romance of the Three Kingdoms* (Tokyo: Charles Tuttle, 1959), vol. 1, pp. 1–2.

reestablished in a new birth of unification, power, and glory, the T'ang.

CITIES IN ANCIENT CHINA

The Shang capitals, and their immediate Lung Shan predecessors, were primarily ceremonial centers, symbols of royal authority. The late Lung Shan city on the site of modern Chengchou and the Shang capitals there, at Loyang, and at Anyang were massively walled and gated. The walls enclosed royal palaces and tombs, royal residences, quarters for priests, slaves, or kept artisans, and military guards, but much of the enclosed area was not built on. Most nonroyal inhabitants and most of the workers lived in unplanned villagelike settlements outside the walls. By at least the late Shang period, the Chinese character and the spoken word for "city" were the same as those for "wall," and this has remained so to the present. Cities, in other words, were designed as statements of authority; the wall was a symbol of state or, later, imperial power and thus distinguished cities from villages or market towns. Apart from the capitals, imperial and provincial, most cities first arose as county seats, the lowest rung of national administration and, from Han times, the base of an imperial magistrate.

Chinese cities were built predominantly of wood, which is why little evidence remains from this early period to show what they looked like. Some written documents surviving from Chou times describe the precise planning of all walled cities and their ritual or symbolic importance, including their exact north-south orientation, and the arrangement and dimensions of the royal or imperial buildings within the walls. Religious cults such as ancestor worship and the worship of what the Chinese called Heaven, or the Supreme Deity, were represented in every walled city by carefully placed temples.

By the time of the Han dynasty, China had nearly 2,000 years of urban experience; much of it was reflected in the Han capital at Ch'ang An. The site was carefully chosen by Liu Pang, the first Han emperor, but it was not until the reign of his successor, in 192 B.C., that the city walls were begun, of pounded earth 52 feet thick at the base, 27 feet high, and over 3 miles long on each of the four sides. The walls enclosed imperial palaces, tombs, and temples to the ancestors among other temples. The government regulated and supervised market areas inside as well as outside the walls, and the city was divided into 160 wards. Straight broad avenues led from each of the major gates at the main compass points, with an apparently less planned growth of lanes and alleys in the wards. The ideal city form was a square, which Ch'ang An approximated, with one major central gate and two lesser ones on each of the four sides.

The Han now ruled an immense territory, much of it newly conquered, especially in the south. The imperial stamp on these new lands was achieved primarily through the building of walled cities, county seats on the imperial model but on a far smaller scale. Once the original inhabitants had been subdued and the land cleared, settled, and farmed, garrison towns or fortresses gave way to such walled county seats from which the imperial magistrate could keep order, dispense justice, and supervise the collection of taxes and the exactions of forced labor and military conscription.

In the hilly south such cities often had to accommodate to the terrain and sometimes altered the square shape somewhat. But the imperial model was apparent in all of them, including their official buildings, temples, military barracks, and regulated market areas inside and outside the walls. One can in fact chart the southward spread of Han occupation and the growth of Chinese-style agricultural settlement by noting the successive establishment of new walled county seats. They appeared first along the rivers leading south from the Yangtze and then progressively inland from the rivers. They were linked with each other and with the imperial and provincial capitals by the imperial road system begun under the Ch'in and greatly extended under the Han.

The Han Legacy

China by Han times was highly developed technologically as well as culturally. Ch'ang An and Loyang were built of wood, and little has survived to tell us much about them, but what accounts we have suggest that they rivaled imperial Rome in size and splendor. It is symptomatic of this vast bureaucratic empire, whose culture also put a high value on education and learning, that paper was first made there, before A.D. 100 (more than 1,000 years passed before the knowledge of papermaking spread to Europe). Another Han innovation was an early form of porcelain, one more Chinese gift to the world known everywhere simply as "china." Water-powered mills were invented in Han China, as was the basis of the modern horse collar, which made it possible for draft animals to pull much heavier loads more efficiently and without being choked. Lacquer had made its appearance by Wu Ti's time, and samples of fine lacquer ware have been found in Han tombs.

Probably the greatest literary achievement of the Han was in the writing of history. Many Chou records destroyed by Ch'in Shih Huang Ti were reconstructed by Han scholars from memory, and the texts we have date largely from this period. New pride in empire and tradition produced the man called China's Grand Historian, Ssu-ma Ch'ien (Simaqian, died c. 85 B.C.). His massive *Historical Records* put together materials from earlier texts in an effort to provide an accurate record of events dating back before the Shang. He added summary essays on geography, culture, the economy, and biographies of important people. A century later Pan Ku (Bangu, died A.D. 92) compiled a similarly comprehensive *History of the Han Dynasty*, which became the model for the standard histories commissioned by each subsequent dynasty, another respect in which the Han set the pattern for later centuries.

Han writers set a high standard for historical scholarship that many scholars feel was not equaled until the eighteenth century in the West. Here is another point of comparison between Han China and imperial Rome, where the writing of history also reached a high degree of cultivation and reflected a similar pride in accomplishment and the tradition that had led to it. The Roman ideal remained appealing to the European mind, and still underlies much of the modern West, while in China the state system, the imperial model, and most of the other institutions and forms first established under the Han endured to shape the course of the next 2,000 years.

Modern civilization in China can be traced through the rise of the Shang, the first authenticated dynasty, about 1600 B.C., *its conquest by the Chou about 1050* B.C., *the warring-states period in the last centuries of nominal Chou rule, the Ch'in empire from 221 to 206* B.C., *and the rise, flourishing, and decline of the Han from 202* B.C. *to* A.D. *220. The pattern of subsequent Chinese history was largely set by the achievement of the Han empire, much of it based in turn on the teachings of Confucius, who lived in the sixth century* B.C. *From local beginnings on the northern China plain under the Shang, the Chinese state and empire had grown by the end of the Han to incorporate most of the area within the borders of modern China. During the same centuries the traditional model of Chinese civilization was established, a model that was largely adhered to for the next 20 centuries.*

Notes

1. J. J. L. Duyvendak, trans., *The Book of Lord Shang* (London: Arthur Probsthain, 1928), pp. 193–194, 203, 209, 211, 229.
2. R. Grousset, *The Rise and Splendor of the Chinese Empire* (Berkeley: University of California Press, 1953), pp. 71–72.
3. J. Gernet, *A History of Chinese Civilization*, trans. J. R. Foster (Cambridge: Cambridge University Press, 1985), p. 129.

Suggestions for Further Reading

Bodde, D. *China's First Unifier.* Hong Kong: Hong Kong University Press, 1967.

Chang, K. C. *The Archeology of Ancient China.* 4th ed. New Haven, Conn.: Yale University Press, 1987.

Creel, H. G. *The Origins of Statecraft in China.* Chicago: University of Chicago Press, 1970.

Dawson, R., ed. *The Legacy of China.* Oxford: Clarendon Press, 1964.

De Barry, W. T., ed. *Sources of Chinese Tradition.* New York: Columbia University Press, 1960.

De Crespigny, R. *Northern Frontier Policies and Strategies of the Later Han Empire.* Canberra: Australian National University Press, 1985.

Elvin, M. *The Pattern of the Chinese Past.* Stanford, Calif.: Stanford University Press, 1973.

Fairbank, J. K. *China: Tradition and Transformation.* Boston: Houghton Mifflin, 1978.

Gernet, J. *A History of Chinese Civilization,* trans. J. R. Foster. Cambridge: Cambridge University Press, 1985.

Hsu, C. Y. *Ancient China in Transition: An Analysis of Social Mobility.* Stanford, Calif.: Stanford University Press, 1965.

Hucker, C. O. *China's Imperial Past.* Stanford, Calif.: Stanford University Press, 1975.

Li Chi. *Anyang.* Seattle: University of Washington Press, 1976.

Liu Xinru. *Ancient China and Ancient India: Trade and Religious Exchange,* A.D. *1–600.* New York: Oxford University Press, 1988.

Loewe, M. *Everyday Life in Early Imperial China.* New York: Putnam, 1968.

Meskill, J., ed. *An Introduction to Chinese Civilization.* Boston: Heath, 1973.

Needham, J. *Science in Traditional China.* Cambridge, Mass.: Harvard University Press, 1981.

Owen, S. *Remembrances: The Experience of the Past in Classical Chinese Literature.* Cambridge, Mass.: Harvard University Press, 1986.

Rubin, V. A. *Individual and State in Ancient China.* New York: Columbia University Press, 1976.

Sullivan, M. *The Arts of China.* Berkeley: University of California Press, 1977.

Watson, B. *Courtier and Commoner in Ancient China.* New York: Columbia University Press, 1977.

Watson, W. *Ancient China: Discoveries of Post-Liberation Archeology.* London: British Broadcasting Corporation, 1974.

Yu, Y. S. *Trade and Expansion in Han China.* Berkeley: University of California Press, 1967.

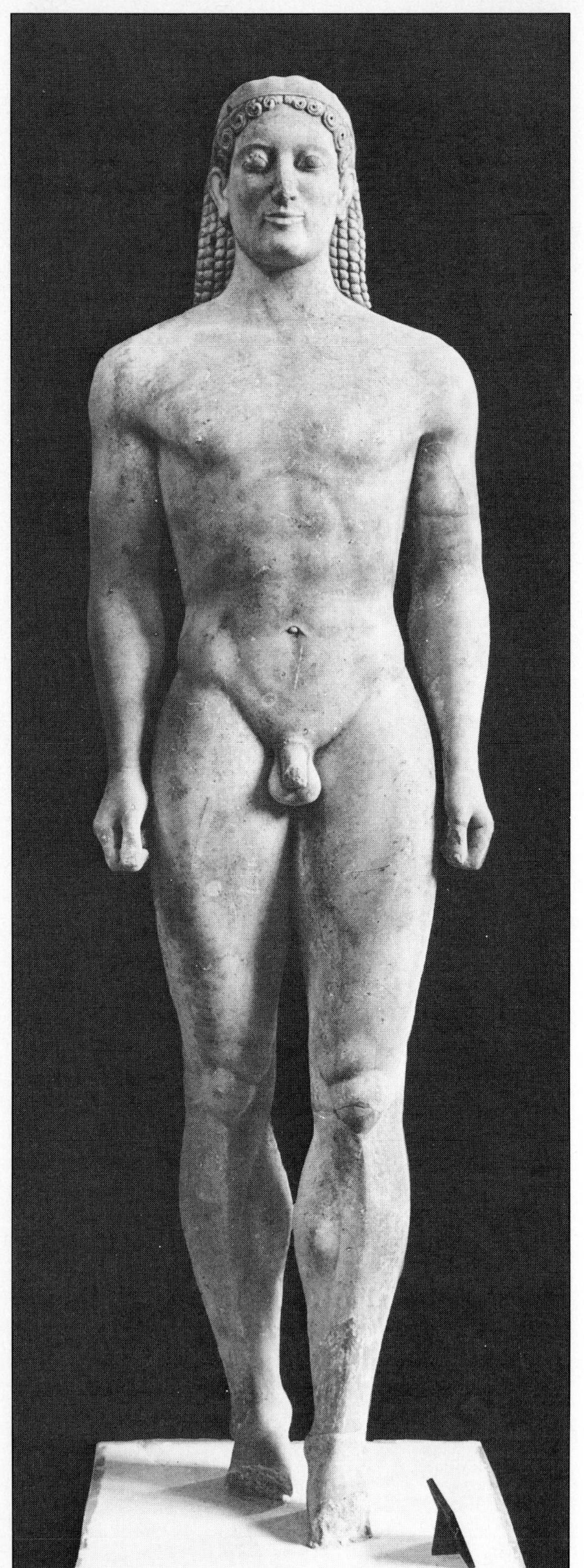

CHAPTER · 4

Early and Classical Greece

Immigrants from the East arrived in the area around the Aegean Sea approximately 6000 B.C., bringing with them the newly developed agricultural techniques of the Neolithic period. Unlike the Egyptians of the Old Kingdom or the Sumerians, these small Neolithic communities developed neither an elaborate culture nor complex life patterns, and for some 3,000 years life continued on a simple pastoral basis.

Around 3000 B.C., however, a brilliant and sophisticated Bronze Age culture began to develop first among the Minoans of Crete and then, about 1650 B.C., among the Mycenaeans who inhabited the Greek peninsula. The Greeks of later ages knew little of these peoples because of the centuries of confusion and disorder that preceded the dawning of the Iron Age around 1000 B.C.; they were the stuff of myths and legends, rather than historical predecessors. Many Greek tales of later times are set in Bronze Age surroundings such as Thebes and Mycenae.

Kouros from Anavuysos, c. 530 B.C. Marble, height 1.93 m. The base bears an inscription saying that the statue represents a young man, Kroisos, who died heroically in battle. The figure's pose is rigid, but note the realism with which the muscles are carved. [Marburg/Art Resource; National Archaeological Museum, Athens]

Furthermore, the earliest Greek literary masterpieces, the works of Homer, reflect a legendary interpretation of the Mycenaean past.

One of the major turning points of history in the Mediterranean region is the period around 1100 B.C., which marked the change from the Bronze Age to the Iron Age. Over the centuries that followed, a new culture began to develop in Greece that was to form the foundation of Western civilization. By the fifth century B.C. Greek culture reached its zenith in the Classical Age.

Neolithic Greece

Western civilization begins with the arrival on the Greek peninsula of people from Asia who were looking for new farming land and were experienced enough to develop the farms they founded. Crossing to Europe by means of the Bosphorus, these earliest of Western pioneers settled in northern Greece. From here some spread northwest into central Europe, while others moved south to central Greece and the rich plains of Thessaly.

In Thessaly, where the land is well watered and fertile, they built villages that in some cases grew into small towns. At the largest, Sesklo, the houses were built of mud bricks on stone foundations with rectangular rooms and were arranged close together in straight rows. The dead were buried outside the settled area. In their earliest stages these communities had no defensive fortification walls, since, for a while at least, there was enough good land for all. Pottery of fine quality was made throughout the Neolithic period, often with painted decorations. These early settlers may have already related the fertility of the earth to human fertility, for a number of little statues have been found, almost always of female nudes. As we shall see, the figure of a divine female, the Mother Goddess, is one of the most striking aspects of Bronze Age religion and was probably introduced from the East by Neolithic farmers.

On the Greek mainland, settlements such as Sesklo and its neighbor, Dimini, continued to thrive in relative isolation. Meanwhile, on the island of Crete other settlers from the East had founded their own communities. In many cases they chose to live in caves rather than construct drafty huts. Their pottery was elaborate and stylistically different from that of the mainland. The animals they reared included pigs, cattle, and sheep. None of these previously existed on Crete, and the transport of the original herds by sea from Asia must have presented a considerable challenge for their owners. The largest Neolithic settlement on Crete was at Knossos, the future site of the grandest of Bronze Age palaces.

The continuity of civilization at Knossos underlines the fact that the transition from stone to metal tools was gradual, producing no immediate revolution in ways of life. The Bronze Age on Crete began shortly after 2900 B.C., and different regions developed at various speeds. On the islands of the Cyclades in the eastern Aegean, bronze tools were certainly in use by that date, and with them came other changes. The inhabitants of the Cycladic communities cut tombs in the rock or built them of stone, and with the dead they often buried weapons, a sign that the peace of the Neolithic farms was beginning to erode.

Figurine, c. 3000 B.C. This female figure may symbolize fertility. [Leonard von Matt/Photo Researchers]

The people of the Cyclades also produced elegant sculpture, including marble statues that in many cases were buried with the dead together with weapons. These figurines, most of which represent women, vary in height from a few inches to 5 feet. The function of the statues is not clear. They may have been used as part of the funeral ceremony, and the fact that the overwhelming majority are female suggests that they too, like the earlier Neolithic figures, were forerunners of the cult of the Earth Mother.

Shortly after 2000 B.C. a new wave of invaders from the east moved into the Cyclades and eventually the Greek peninsula, to be followed by immigrants from the Balkans. The newcomers caused considerable disruption to the earlier settlers, and many of the mainland communities of this period constructed massive walls and towers to defend themselves. It appears, from the numerous warriors' graves, that life on the mainland consisted of perpetual warfare waged between rival settlements. On Crete, however, the picture is different. Far from retreating behind walled settlements, the population of the island, isolated from the troubles farther north, began to gather in large urban centers. Here developed the richest and most durable Bronze Age culture, that of the Minoans.

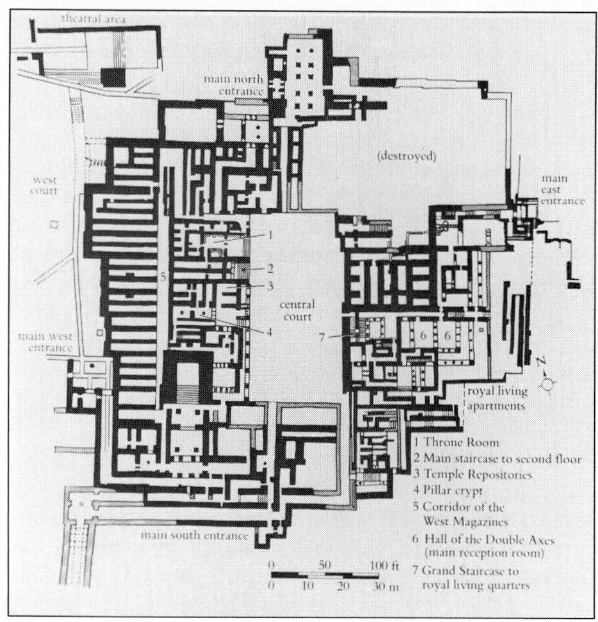

Plan of the Palace of Minos at Knossos, c. 1600–1400 B.C. The building is ranged around a central courtyard, with the public and religious rooms to the west and royal living quarters to the east. [After S. Marinatos, *Kreta und das Mykenische Hellas,* Hirmer Verlag, Munich, 1959, fig. 4]

The Minoans

In the Classical Age of the fifth and fourth centuries B.C., Crete's fame was due to its mythic past. The legendary King Minos had ruled there, from his great palace at Knossos. The myths said that within the palace, at the center of a labyrinth, dwelt the Minotaur, a monster part man and part bull. To keep the monster alive Minos exacted an annual tribute from the mainlanders of seven youths and seven maidens, who were dispatched to Crete to feed the Minotaur. Other places in Crete appeared in Greek legends. Homer's *Odyssey* mentions "Crete of a hundred cities." By the fifth century no visible evidence remained of Minos or his palace, yet subsequent generations continued to believe that Minos had indeed existed.

In 1906, while excavating Knossos, the British archaeologist Arthur Evans discovered ancient remains. Five years later, after further excavations, he determined that the discoveries were those of a hitherto unknown Bronze Age civilization of extraordinary richness. The quantity and quality of the finds was overwhelming: ceramics, frescoes, inscriptions, and jewels. In one room Evans found a raised seat with high back set against elaborate paintings, which he identified as the throne room of King Minos. These and later finds on Crete documented the ancient tales of its prosperity and power. The civilization that Evans had discovered was named Minoan, after the legendary king.

The Early Minoan period (2900–2100 B.C.), which corresponded with the early Bronze Age elsewhere in Greece, was a time of slow expansion. In southern and eastern Crete small towns appeared, and contacts were made with Egypt and Mesopotamia. The first major development in Minoan civilization occurred at the beginning of the Middle Minoan period (2100–1575 B.C.). Inhabitants of earlier communities abandoned them and gathered together in large urban centers. Following Evans, scholars have called these centers "palaces," although they provided more than a royal residence and included storerooms, workshops, and chapels.

In the years following the discovery of Knossos, royal centers were found at other Cretan towns. The typical main structure, built around an open rectangular courtyard, contained religious shrines, public halls for banquets, and quarters for administrators. Other parts of the structure held royal living quarters and working areas for slaves and artisans. Surrounding the palace were the private houses of the aristocrats and the chief religious leaders. The construction of these palaces was remarkably sophisticated. They contained drainage systems and were designed to provide shade in the hot summer months and insulation against the winter cold.

Around 1700 B.C. the palaces suffered severe damage, probably due to an earthquake, only to be reconstructed in an even more grandiose manner. About a century later they were rebuilt again, probably for the same reason. These later palaces represent Minoan culture's highest achievement, and their wall paintings illustrate the richness and elaboration of court ceremonial. The Minoans left only a small amount of written material, some of which is in hieroglyphics and the remainder in a script called Linear A. Although scholars cannot yet decipher more than a few words of Linear A, they believe it was derived from either a Semitic or an Anatolian script.

The rulers of these communities were apparently male, but some scholars have suggested that the principal Minoan deity may have been a mother-goddess. Like the Great Mother of the Mesopotamians, she may have been a fertility figure, taking on a variety of forms, associated at times with animals, at times with vegetation. The most famous religious image in Minoan art is the figure known as the Snake Goddess.

At the beginning of the Late Minoan period (1575–1150 B.C.), Minoan artistic styles began to make an impact on the Greek mainland. The political and military power of the Minoans, however, was beginning to decline, and mainlanders seem to have occupied Knossos around 1460. Archaeologists have discovered signs of destruction at Knossos and the other palaces that occurred around 1590, 1500, and 1400, after which only small impoverished mountain settlements survived the remaining centuries of the Bronze Age. The reasons for these calamities are hotly debated; natural disasters (a volcanic explosion on the nearby island of Thera, tidal waves, earthquakes, and fire), a Hyksos invasion around 1590, or the incursion of Mycenaeans may have played a part.

"Mask of Agamemnon," from Shaft Grave V, Mycenae, c. 1550 B.C. The death mask of one of the earliest Mycenaean rulers, this was one of five such masks found in the Royal Grave Circle. [Hirmer]

The Mycenaeans

The Mycenaeans, dominant in mainland Greece during the Bronze Age, are so called because the greatest and richest of their settlements was named Mycenae. Other Mycenaean communities in central Greece included Athens and Thebes, but most of their settlements were in southern Greece, an area known as the Peloponnesus. The Mycenaeans, like the Minoans, owed their fame to Greek legends long before the discovery of their cities. Their principal claim to fame was the war they launched against Troy, on the eastern shore of the Aegean Sea. The Trojan War and its consequences were the subject of subsequent Greek literary works attributed to Homer. For centuries, however, it seemed that the Trojan War, and even Troy, were mythical.

The German Heinrich Schliemann (A.D. 1822–1890) devoted much of his life to demonstrating that the myths were based on real events. In 1870 he began work at the site of what he believed to be Troy, in modern Turkey. During the next three years he uncovered the city's walls and gate as well as gold, silver, and bronze jewelry and weapons. On the basis of his finds at Troy, Schliemann then set out to discover the Mycenaeans who had been responsible for the Trojan War. In 1876 he excavated inside the walls of Mycenae, where he discovered the cemetery known as the Royal Grave Circle, consisting of impressive pits cut into the rock. The gold treasures in the shafts date to 1550–1500 B.C., a time when Mycenaean power had begun to expand.

Mycenaean culture was influenced by the Minoans, particularly in its artistic style and possibly with respect to writing as well. The Minoans' Linear A script may have helped to inspire the development of a Mycenaean script, Linear B, an early form of Greek. But unlike the Minoans, the Mycenaeans built their principal cities, including Mycenae, Tiryns, and Pylos, on hills for defensive purposes. Their palaces were surrounded by walls, and even Mycenaean art emphasizes military motifs as well as hunting. Mycenaean kings amassed considerable wealth and governed with the aid of bureaucrats who kept records of taxes, the property and livestock of their subjects, and the stocks of assorted commodities. As the principal power in the western Mediterranean world after the decline of the Minoans, the Mycenaeans traded not only with the peoples of the Italian peninsula and Sicily but also with those of Egypt and western Asia. They even established trading colonies in the eastern Mediterranean. It may have been as a result of commercial rivalry that the Mycenaeans attacked Troy, probably around 1200 B.C.

Shortly after the assault on Troy, some Mycenaean cities, including Pylos and Mycenae, were destroyed, possibly by sea raiders. In the century that followed, the remaining Mycenaean cities met with a similar fate, partly at the hands of outside invaders but possibly also because of fighting among themselves.

Homer and the Dark Age

In most important areas the Greeks of the ensuing Dark Age (c. 1100–c. 800 B.C.) had to develop afresh almost all the techniques of the visual arts, architecture, literature, and the ability to write. All but the simplest manufacturing disappeared, numerous villages were abandoned, and many people presumably adopted a nomadic life. Much of this decline has been blamed on the movement of Dorian-speaking Greeks into the southern part of the peninsula, an event better understood as a migration than as an invasion. There was also a migration of Greeks of all dialects—Aeolian, Ionian, and Dorian—to the islands of the Aegean and the coast of Asia Minor. Despite these movements, however, there was at first little trade with western Asia or even between Greek settlements themselves.

Although there are no written or artistic sources from the Dark Age, we can reconstruct something about life in this period from two great epic poems. The *Iliad* and the *Odyssey* are generally thought to have been written by Homer, a ninth-century poet. The Greeks were not certain when he had composed the works, where he had lived, or if the same person had written both epics. The first version of these poems was probably produced about 800 B.C.; the earliest known written version dates probably to the late 500s. Although many people may have contributed to its final shape, at an early stage in this process the poems must have passed through the imagination of the genius whom we, like the Greeks, call Homer.

Both works have the Trojan War as their background. Throughout them are fitful glimpses of the world of the

Homer's World

In describing the scenes decorating the shield Hephaistos made for Achilles, Homer paints a picture of his own early Iron Age world.

On it he wrought in all their beauty two cities of mortal
men. And there were marriages in one, and festivals.
They were leading the brides along the city from their maiden chambers
under the flaring of torches, and the loud bride song was arising.
The young men followed the circles of the dance, and among them
the flutes and lyres kept up their clamor as in the meantime
the women standing each at the door of her court admired them.
The people were assembled in the market place, where a quarrel
had arisen, and two men were disputing over the blood price
for a man who had been killed. One man promised full restitution
in a public statement, but the other refused and would accept nothing.
Both then made for an arbitrator, to have a decision;
and people were speaking up on either side, to help both men.
But the heralds kept the people in hand, as meanwhile the elders
were in session on benches of polished stone in the sacred circle
and held in their hands the staves of the heralds who lift their voices.
The two men rushed before these, and took turns speaking their cases,
and between them lay on the ground two talents of gold, to be given
to that judge who in this case spoke the straightest opinion.

Source: Homer, *The Iliad*, trans. R. Lattimore (Chicago: University of Chicago Press, 1961), b. 18, ll. 490–508, p. 388.

Dipylon Amphora, c. 750 B.C. Originally a grave marker, the vase shows on its main band a funeral scene; the mourners, painted in silhouette, are tearing their hair. [Hirmer]

Bronze Age, and some of the tales may well have been passed down from that earlier period. For the most part, though, Homer's world reflects life in Greece during the Dark Age, combined with fantasy. Toward the end of the *Iliad*, at the funeral games in honor of Patroclus, the friend of the poem's hero, Achilles, two of the principal prizes are lumps of iron. Achilles himself points out their usefulness for a farmer in need of a new plow. The voice is that of a Mycenaean prince, but the words and the audience to whom they are implicitly addressed are both clearly of an agricultural community of the early Iron Age, which began in the eleventh century B.C.

Like *The Epic of Gilgamesh* and the Vedas, these two poems were at first transmitted orally. In their early stages the poems were recited by itinerant professional bards who traveled throughout the Greek world. Their audiences consisted of the small groups of aristocrats who ruled each community in the Dark Age. Our impression of the lives of these communities is limited, for the most part, to the objects buried with the dead. Certainly some of the graves of the ninth and eighth centuries in the Dipylon Cemetery at Athens suggest a considerable concentration of wealth and power in the hands of a few. The pottery of the period is of a style called geometric. Much of the decoration consists of severe, abstract patterns of often striking power, but from around 800 B.C. onward human figures appear.

Greece and the Mediterranean

By 800 B.C. Greek civilization had entered a new phase. Literacy had been recovered, with an alphabet borrowed from the Phoenicians and adapted to the Greek tongue. Extensive trade resumed, and the pressures of a growing population led to both social conflict and colonization. Ambitious Greeks traveled overseas in search of wealth. A number of the cities they founded, such as Syracuse in Sicily and Croton in southern Italy, grew richer and more powerful than their mother cities. Cities were also founded in Egypt and around the Black Sea. It was perhaps inevitable that intercity rivalries accompanied the settlers, often creating tension in their relations with each other and with the communities of the Greek homeland.

Simultaneously, along the coast of Asia Minor the Greek settlements founded in the Dark Age established trade links with much of western Asia; these were to have important consequences for Greek culture. After several centuries of isolation, the Greeks came into contact with the developed cultures of western Asia and Egypt, which they rapidly assimilated. So profound was the effect of western Asian art on the Greeks from the late eighth century to around 600 B.C. that the artistic style of this period is called "orientalizing."

As the Greeks continued to expand, they gradually shaped the characteristic sociopolitical institution that they called the *polis*. Each of the *poleis* was an independent political unit consisting of a town or village and the surrounding territory, the inhabitants of which were bound together in a community of "relatives." Geographic conditions in Greece played a crucial role in shaping these small political units, for the mountainous terrain encouraged communities to develop in relative isolation. Communication was difficult; unlike Mesopotamia and Egypt, the Greek peninsula has no major rivers, although many communities had ready access to the sea and to the myriad islands that dot the Aegean.

The polis provided the basis for social, political, religious, and cultural life. The loyalty of its citizens toward

4.1 Classical Greece

their city was far more powerful than any sense of fellowship with other Greeks. The resulting competitive spirit eventually produced fierce rivalries. The polis was thus both the highest achievement of Greek civilization and its most destructive element, responsible for nurturing both unrivaled intellectual and cultural achievement and a tendency to intercommunal rivalry.

Many poleis sent out colonizers as a way to release tensions and population pressures at home. The wealth made possible by colonial trade, however, created unsettled conditions both abroad and in the mother cities in Greece. The more prosperous the polis, the more likely a political upheaval created by the newly powerful traders, manufacturers, and farmers, who challenged the traditional elites. In these unstable conditions, power in many of the poleis was seized by local leaders with popular support. The Greeks called these revolutionary leaders "tyrants." The term was not derogatory; it meant simply those who attained office through insurrection or, sometimes, consensus. Indeed, many tyrants became famous for their public works and enlightened rule, although there was no shortage of those whose behavior explains the modern use of the word.

The experience of Corinth was typical of many poleis that submitted, not unwillingly, to tyrants. Corinth was among the richest Greek cities in this period. Corinthian colonies were established in the west, and Corinthian vases, oil, and perfume were exported throughout the Mediterranean. This growth of the trading class undermined the old aristocracy, and around 655 B.C. Cypselus overthrew them and became tyrant of Corinth. Supposedly related to the ruling family he had overturned, he governed for 30 years. It was a mark of his popularity that he never had a bodyguard.

The success of Cypselus illustrates the basic conditions that made possible the phenomenon of the tyrants. On the one hand, tyranny was a form of monarchy. Not only did the tyrants wield power, but they passed it on to their descendants; Cypselus was succeeded by his son, Periander. On the other hand, the tyrants could continue to rule only if they maintained popular support. The citizen-militia that often gave them power in the first place could, and did, dislodge them if that proved necessary.

These citizen-armies were made possible by a new form of warfare that had developed in the late eighth century. Previously, fighting had been undertaken by small troops of mounted horsemen and Homeric-style champions, who dueled with spears and swords. The new military style involved large numbers of armed infantrymen, called *hoplites,* who fought in a tightly organized block, or *phalanx*. As long as the phalanx remained intact, it was virtually indestructible. Because the hoplite needed only a shield, a sword, and a pike, it was economically feasible to organize citizen-armies. The absence of a standing professional army that could be used by an oppressive ruler against his people was the ultimate guarantee of popular control. Paradoxically, therefore, the concentration of power in the hands of one person, checked by the citizen-militia, made possible a general move toward wider community participation in the affairs of government.

The social and economic discontents that gave rise to the tyrants were not always resolved as in the case of Cypselus. At Miletus in Asia Minor, the center of the earliest school of Greek philosophy, the common people rose up against the aristocrats who ruled them and slaughtered their wives and children; when the aristocrats regained power, they roasted their opponents alive.

A number of the tyrants were famous for their public works. Polycrates, tyrant of Samos, commissioned a long protective harbor mole and a new water system cut through the rock, as well as an enormous temple to Hera. The aqueduct ran over 3,000 feet and carried a waterpipe in a channel 3½ feet high. At many cities, as on the island of Samos, outer defensive walls were constructed for the first time since the Mycenaean era, thereby defining the urban core, as well as reflecting the increased rivalry of the poleis.

The new merchant traders and the tyrants who ruled them were often patrons of artistic projects intended to perpetuate their memory and fame. The sculptures they commissioned were the first life-size stone figures in Western art. The earliest surviving figures, dating to the mid- and late seventh century B.C., are stiff and formalized, with flat planes and rigid stances. By the middle of the next century, however, sculptors had learned to produce works with individual character and in doing so developed a new style in art that reached its fulfillment in the Classical Age. The intermediate period beginning around 600 B.C., during which the Greeks gradually eliminated orientalizing elements from their art and developed their own style, is known as the Archaic period. It was during this period as well that pottery and vase-painting reached their highest development. Most subjects represented were mythological scenes, but many showed everyday activities and events, including games and revels, and some depicted erotic acts with considerable frankness.

In literature too new forms emerged. The heroic verse of Homer had served the ruling class of an aristocratic society, with the leisure to hear about the deeds of mighty leaders such as Achilles. The poets of the age of the tyrants were more interested in individual feelings and emotions, and the medium invented to express their feelings about life, death, and love was lyric poetry. One of the earliest lyric poets was Archilochus (c. 708 B.C.), whose work exhibited antiheroic elements, as in these lines:

> ***Some Thracian is proudly wearing the shield I left behind;***
> ***It was a fine one, but I had to throw it into a bush.***
> ***Anyway I saved my life, so why worry about the shield?***
> ***I can always get another one just as good.***[1]

Dionysus in a boat, c. 525 B.C. The god is shown in the center of the cup, surrounded by grapes and dolphins. [Antikensammelungen, Munich]

Sappho's Poetry

This poem by Sappho gives a fair example of her work.

Seizure

To me that man equals a god
as he sits before you and listens
closely to your sweet voice

and lovely laughter—which troubles
the heart in my ribs. For now
as I look at you my voice fails

my tongue is broken and thin fire
runs like a thief through my body.
My eyes are dead to light, my ears

pound, and sweat pours down over me.
I shudder, I am paler than grass,
and am intimate with dying—but

I must suffer everything, being poor.

Source: Sappho, trans. W. Barnstone (New York: Doubleday [Anchor Books], 1965), p. 11.

SAPPHO AND THE POETRY OF LOVE

Although women played an important part in Greek mythology and religion, we have almost no account of their experiences from their own hands. Virtually all of our knowledge is derived from sources written by men, and Sappho, the first Greek woman to enshrine her personal experiences in literary form, is therefore an important exception.

Sappho was born around 612 B.C. on the island of Lesbos, where she lived most of her life. She apparently combined the domestic functions of wife and mother with her writing and teaching. She earned considerable admiration as a poet during her own lifetime and taught younger women on Lesbos. The warm bond between Sappho and her students was deep, for it recurs as a constant theme in her poetry. Her appearance itself is uncertain: one ancient authority described her as a "beautiful day," while a less complimentary commentator said that "physically she was very ugly, being small and dark, like a nightingale with misshapen wings enfolding a tiny body." A contemporary poet described her as "violet-haired, pure and honey-smiling." In the ancient world the women of Lesbos were notorious in the popular imagination for shameless, uninhibited sexual behavior. Sappho's poetry makes clear her sexual feelings for other women, but we have no evidence that her contemporaries thought this unseemly. Erotic friendship played an important role in Greek society, both between women and between men.

The principal topic of Sappho's poetry is love; the only one of her poems to survive intact is a prayer to Aphrodite, the goddess of sexual love, expressing Sappho's fondness for an unnamed young woman about to be married. In other works Sappho expresses the conflicting but equally painful distress of isolation and of intense erotic involvement. Her tone is distinctive, but her theme, the celebration of sexual love, is quite common in Greek culture.

Sappho's writing shows a remarkably objective self-awareness, and she makes it clear that the agony her love often causes her is worth the price. Her most outstanding gift is her skill in understanding the complexity of her own responses and achieving that understanding at least in part by describing it. In the same way as sixth-century sculptors and painters understood the workings of the human body by portraying it, Sappho revealed the process of her emotional development. In so doing, she learned to temper her feelings, and much of her work expresses the kind of resignation that is the fruit of deep self-understanding. Throughout antiquity Sappho's work evoked the highest praise. Plato described her as "the tenth muse," and the Hellenistic poet Meleager said of her poems that they were "few but roses." In Roman times poets such as Catullus and Horace imitated her forms, and from there they were passed down into the long history of European lyric poetry.

The Growth of the City-State

The political ideals inherent in the concept of the polis involved the devotion of the citizens to their city-state at the expense of any broader perspective and had practical consequences wherever the Greeks settled. A city that represented the collective image of its citizens needed to have impressive public buildings and, if possible, an organized town plan. In the case of the older cities of the Greek mainland, cluttered by the buildings of several centuries, planners and architects were constrained by the work of their predecessors. Where new sites were settled, however, as at Poseidonia in southern Italy (better known by its Roman name, Paestum), streets were laid in straight lines to form city blocks, intersected by other streets running at right angles. At a convenient flat space within the city was the main square, or *agora*, surrounded by the principal public buildings, where the citizens could meet both formally and informally. The inhabitants of Paestum embellished their city with impressive temples, constructed between 550 and 450 B.C.

If great buildings could give visible character to a city, so could coinage. The coins each city minted bore a figure or design that identified its origins. Corinthian coins, for example, showed Pegasus, the legendary winged horse, which, according to the myth, was born at the fountain in Corinth's main square. The citizens of Metapartum, the fertile plain of southeast Italy, chose an ear of grain as their symbol.

Coins and manufactured objects such as pottery and terra-cotta statues were used to pay for raw materials the Greeks lacked. One basic commodity, iron, was close at hand in central and northern Italy, and a thriving trade developed between the western Greek colonies and the Etruscans. The individual cities often established their own trade patterns. The citizens of Aegina in central Greece transported grain from their colonies on the Black Sea back to the mother city. In some cases cities were founded precisely to serve as trading exchange ports, as in the case of Naucratis in Egypt.

The most complete demonstration of the sense of the Greeks' pride in their own cities was provided by the athletic festivals at which they came together to compete against one another. Olympia, Delphi, and Nemea were

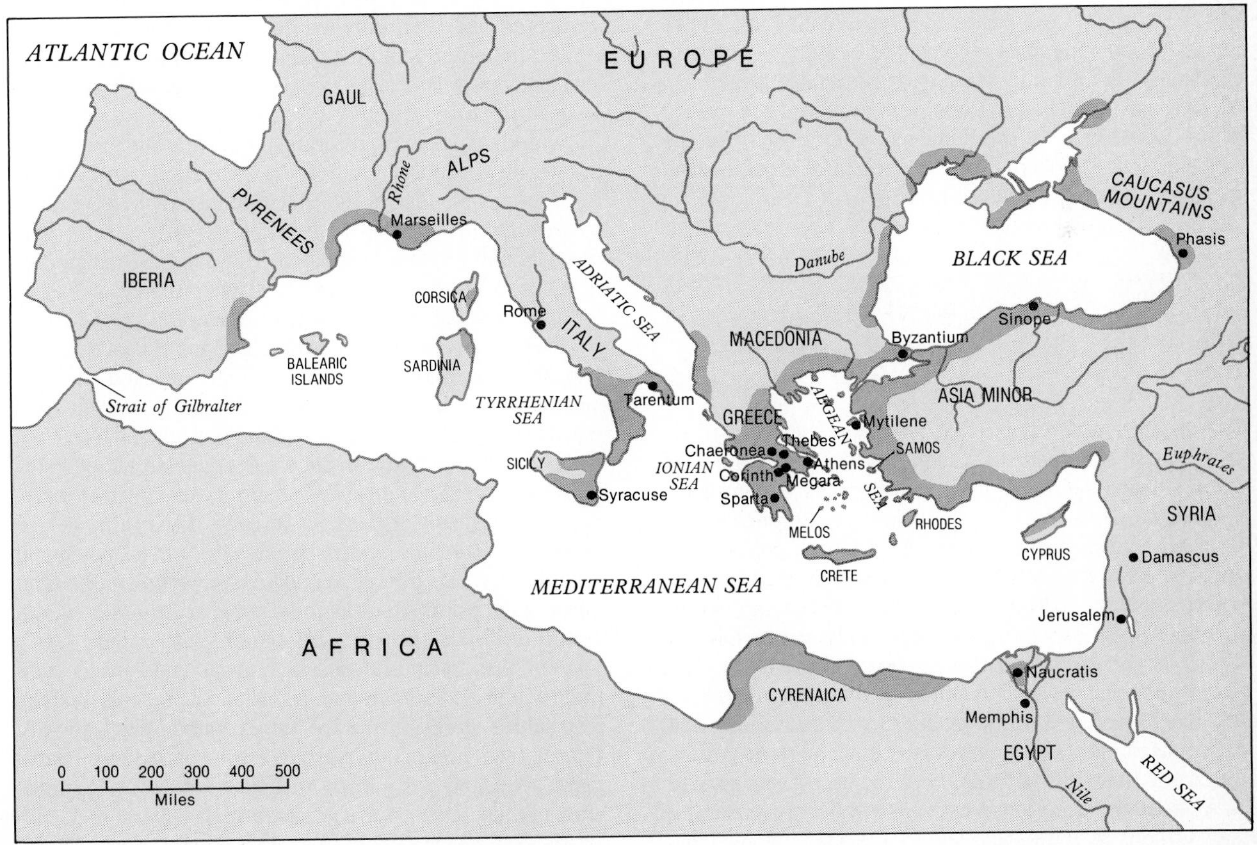

4.2 The Classical Greek World (c. 550 B.C.)

known as Panhellenic (all-Greek) shrines, and games were held at each of them. Victors, upon their return home, were given a civic welcome at public expense.

In all these ways individual citizens were constantly reminded of the differences between themselves and their fellow Greeks. Certain shared characteristics were never lost. The Greek language and alphabet varied slightly from one part of the Greek world to another, but not enough to prevent communication. Indeed, one of the few "national" attitudes of the Greeks was their contempt for foreigners—"barbarians"—whose language sounded to the Greek ear like "ba-ba," the bleating of goats. Furthermore, although there were certainly regional variations in Greek religious practices and beliefs, there was enough common ground to sustain the great Panhellenic sanctuaries such as Delphi. Yet apart from these common events and observances, and a shared artistic taste, even neighboring poleis failed to develop a sense of community until after the Macedonian conquest of the fourth century B.C. That conquest was a direct result of divisive civic pride and of the great fifth-century civil war that had fatally weakened them.

Yet however flawed in practice, the Greek civic ideal was a distinctive concept in the development of civilization. From the earliest history of Egypt and Mesopotamia, the city had represented the focus of political, economic, and technological development. For the Greeks, their poleis took on a moral significance that transcended any sense of nationhood. The polis represented a complete and self-contained way of life in which each adult male citizen had his civic and moral being. During the relatively brief period of its ascendancy as the dominant political body of the eastern Mediterranean, it nurtured a culture of astonishing fecundity, diversity, and brilliance.

Athens and the Birth of Democracy

The greatest of the poleis was Athens, situated strategically on the Attic peninsula at the confluence of the Gulf of Corinth and the Aegean Sea. To later ages Athens symbolized the pinnacle of Greek civilization. Its beginnings, however, were modest. While other Greek poleis were founding colonies abroad and developing politically at home, Athenian society in the eighth and seventh centuries underwent no dramatic changes. There was little or no rise in population and virtually no overseas trade. The would-be tyrant Cylon attempted to overthrow the aristocratic government in 632 or 628 B.C. but failed for lack of popular support. However, the continuing power of the wealthy aristocracy combined with the increasing poverty of the peasant farmers was ominous. Growing numbers of poor Athenians were reduced to the state of pledging themselves and their families as security against their debts. When they were unable to pay, they were sold into slavery, often abroad, a fate that many avoided by fleeing into exile.

The Athenian solution to this social and economic problem was characteristically daring and farseeing. Solon was appointed sole archon (magistrate) around 594 B.C., with the power to introduce sweeping reforms. A poet and a man of wide cultural interests, but also a trader with extensive experience abroad, he gave shape to the development of an Athenian constitution that was to last 200 years. Solon abolished all debts and restored freedom to all Athenians who had been sold into slavery. In addition, he devised a more broadly based system of government. Athens had traditionally had a popular assembly as well as an upper council of wealthy citizens (the Areopagus) and an executive of nine archons, but the assembly had had little effective power. Decision making had rested in the hands of the aristocratic magistrates and the Areopagus. Under Solon's reforms, all citizens received the right to vote in the assembly, although only landowners could qualify as citizens. At the other end of the scale, high offices were no longer limited to males born within the old aristocracy but opened to all wealthy men.

Although hindsight suggests that these reforms were essential to the stability of Athens, Solon was by no means uniformly popular. The aristocrats feared for the erosion of their power, and the poorer citizens were at first disappointed and then enraged at the absence of any real redistribution of wealth. Like many a later moderate reformer, Solon had failed to please the groups at either extreme.

Moreover, Solon's reforms, in solving old problems, created new political rivalries. As competing factions jockeyed for power, Pisistratus, an aristocrat, twice attempted to seize control, failing both times. Returning with new financial resources accumulated from his gold-mining operations in northern Greece, he finally attained power in 546 B.C. and ruled as tyrant until 527.

The tyranny of Pisistratus and his sons Hipparchus and Hippias, who ruled after him until 510, marked the first sustained period of peace and economic growth in Athenian history. Pisistratus maintained and administered Solon's constitution and introduced an equitable tax system. Increasing wealth at all levels of society did much to eliminate the problem of debt. Externally, Pisistratus established ties elsewhere in the Greek world, most notably in Asia Minor. The peaceful conditions enjoyed at this time encouraged cultural developments, and at Athens itself the period of Pisistratus' rule was one of great artistic development. Vase painters such as Exekias and Amasis used their fine skills as draftsmen and their expressive abilities to produce works that were increasingly sought abroad. In sculpture, artists continued to move toward more naturalist styles, applying their techniques not only to free-standing figures but to relief carving.

Pisistratus' sons failed to maintain their father's legacy of civil peace. After Hipparchus was assassinated in 514,

Solon on Injustice

In this fragment of verse, Solon, the reformer of Athenian political life, expresses his own perplexity at the injustices of the world.

In every activity there is danger, nor does anyone know,
at an enterprise's start, where he will end up.
One man, striving to do what is right, but lacking foresight,
falls headlong into great folly and great hardship,
while to another who acts wrongly, God in all things gives
pure good luck, redemption from his own thoughtlessness.

• • •

The immortals bestow rich profits upon men,
but folly often appears as the result, which when Zeus
sends it to punish, strikes now this man, now that one.

Source: J. J. Pollitt, *Art and Experience in Classical Greece* (Cambridge: Cambridge University Press, 1972), p. 4.

Hippias introduced a policy of repression to protect himself. In 510, however, he was driven into exile by a group of Athenian nobles led by Cleisthenes, a reformer who looked to the people for his political support. His return was made with the assistance of Athens' archrival, Sparta, whose army, led by King Cleomenes, helped to expel Hippias. Presumably Cleomenes hoped that Hippias would be replaced by a friendly government that would be more to the Spartans' aristocratic taste. Cleisthenes, however, proved to be democratic. The Spartans, together with the more conservative Athenian aristocrats, drove him out of Athens for a brief period. In the end, however, popular will triumphed. Cleomenes and his allies reluctantly withdrew, and in 508 Cleisthenes returned to Athens.

Like Solon, Cleisthenes set out to produce a more broadly based government. The citizens were given membership in *demes*, or local districts, that were then combined in such a way as to cut across the old tribes and factions. Under Cleisthenes' new constitution all adult male citizens continued to serve as members of the Popular Assembly. The day-to-day business of running the state was entrusted to the *Boule*, or People's Council, consisting of 500 members. Fifty were chosen by lot from each of the city's ten new tribes and served a term of one year. The origins of this body may have gone back to Solon, but it now became effective for the first time. By rotating membership and offices, Cleisthenes ensured that a large number of Athenian citizens would have practical experience in civic administration. In addition, all laws were debated and ratified in the Popular Assembly, thus providing for a direct exercise of sovereignty by all citizens. The Areopagus and the magistrates retained their aristocratic character, but with decreased authority.

When Solon had been called to power around 594 B.C., Athens was a polis of relatively minor significance. By the end of the century the Athenians had become a major political force. With the prosperity acquired during the years of Pisistratus and their newly won political freedom, they were soon to become the most energetic and influential power in the Greek world. First, however, both they and their fellow Greeks had to face a threat from a source well beyond their borders: Persia.

The Persian Wars

The Greeks had been aware of the Persian Empire ever since their early days of colonization and trade. In the seventh century B.C. the two principal powers to their east were Lydia and Persia. The Lydian kings were generally well disposed toward the Greeks, some of whom settled in colonies on the coast of Asia Minor, an area known as Ionia. The Greeks learned much from contacts with their eastern neighbor; coinage, probably invented in Lydia, had first been introduced into Europe around 625. Greek relations with the Persians were less friendly, although trade contacts apparently existed.

In 546 the kingdom of Lydia fell to Cyrus the Great of Persia, who added to his conquests the Greek colonies in Ionia and installed Persian governors. The situation was volatile. In 513 and 512 the Persian king, Darius (522–486 B.C.), led a great campaign to subdue southeastern Europe. The expedition was unsuccessful, however, and for the moment the Persians withdrew, preoccupied with problems in central Asia.

Discontented with their Persian governors and the taxes levied to support Persian interests, the Ionians took advantage of the temporary relaxation of imperial control. In 499 they launched a rebellion and called on their fellow Greeks to the west for help. Only the Athenians and their allies the Eretrians, a minor polis on the island of Euboea in the western Aegean, sent ships and men. Their support could not save the Ionians from defeat. By 494 the last city to hold out, Miletus, was sacked after a decisive naval battle off its shore.

Darius, displeased by the interference of Athens and Eretria, reportedly ordered a servant to say to him three times every day before dinner: "Sire, remember the Athenians." Revenge was not long in coming. In 490 the king's troops sailed across the Aegean and sacked Eretria. Proceeding south toward Athens, they landed at Marathon Bay north of the city to face an outnumbered Athenian army. The Athenians had desperately sought support from other Greeks in their struggle against mighty Persia, particularly from Sparta. When the Athenians appealed to the Spartans for help, however, they offered the convenient excuse that the celebration of a religious festival prevented them from leaving their borders.

The Persians, despite their greater number, were less flexible in their tactics than the Athenians. Under the brilliant generalship of Miltiades, the Athenian soldiers outflanked the Persians and drove them back to their ships or into the marshy shore, where thousands were trampled to death.

The Persians had been stopped only temporarily. Before they could return, the Athenians, under the leadership of the archon Themistocles (527–460 B.C.), built new warships. By the time the Persians, now led by Darius' son Xerxes, returned in force to Greece in the fall of 480, they found a combined Greek army with some semblance of unity. The subsequent battles and the final Greek triumph represent one of the high points of Greek history. Having marched virtually unopposed through northern Greece, the Persians were blocked at the pass of Thermopylae by 300 Spartans, together with several thousand other Greek soldiers. Only treachery on the part of local Greeks enabled the Persians to circle from the rear and wipe out the defenders. The fifth-century Greek historian Herodotus describes the last stage of the battle:

> **The Greeks under Leonidas [the Spartan general], as they now went forth determined to die, advanced. . . . [They] carried slaughter among the barbarians, who fell in heaps. Behind them the captains of the squadrons, armed with whips, urged their men forward with continual blows. Many were thrust into the sea, and there perished; a still greater number were trampled to death by their own soldiers; no one heeded the dying. . . . They defended themselves to the last, such as still had swords using them, and the others resisting with their hands and teeth; till the barbarians . . . overwhelmed and buried the remnant left beneath showers of missile weapons.[2]**

According to legend, the Spartan defenders were massacred to a man. Victorious, the Persians proceeded toward Athens, still the object of their vengeance. They found the city abandoned, occupied it, and destroyed many of its buildings. The final confrontation was on the sea. The two fleets fought in the narrow straits between the Attic mainland and the island of Salamis, where Athenian experience proved decisive. A few months later, in 479 B.C., the remaining Persian land forces were defeated at Plataea.

The details of the Greeks' success were chronicled by Herodotus, whose account is the earliest surviving prose record in the West of historical events. Herodotus is often called the "father of history." His explanation of the Greek victory in his *History of the Persian Wars* shows how the Greeks explained their success: the Persian defeat was the result not only of Greek arms but also of the Persians' moral flaw—*hubris,* or excessive ambition. The Greek victory thus demonstrated the triumph of justice over brute force and proof that the gods, who had helped determine the war's outcome, were on the side of right. In Herodotus' mind, the war had been fought to preserve not only the independence of the Greek poleis but the rule of law, which had been directly threatened by the invaders from the east. Thus the conflict was important not only for its immediate outcome but also as a source of future Greek perceptions about Asiatics. The war sharpened the Greeks' sense of their separate identity, and that notion of Western distinctiveness was subsequently inherited by the Romans.

Herodotus also saw the war as the beginning of three generations of trouble for the Greeks, caused at least in part by disputes among themselves. Nevertheless, the Greeks' victory had been made possible by the fact that they had managed to unite in the face of a common enemy. Their success marked the high point of Greek political unity, but unity proved only temporary. The events of the following years were to show the Greeks becoming prey to *hubris* as well.

Athens in the Age of Pericles: Democracy and Imperialism

The Athenian leader during much of the late fifth century was Pericles, whose name now symbolizes the glories of

Athens' Golden Age. Born to an aristocratic family around 495 B.C., Pericles entered politics and by 457 had become the unofficial leader of Athens, although he ran for public office every year like other magistrates. He devoted his efforts to glorifying Athens by constructing the majestic buildings on the Acropolis that still testify to the grandeur of his age.

Pericles did not "lead" Athens in the sense that a modern head of state does. The Athenians governed themselves by the participation of every adult male citizen in the Popular Assembly. Any member of this body could address it and try to convince it of his point of view. Frequently the Assembly would follow Pericles' advice, but his authority was personal, not constitutional.

Few Athenians, presumably, would have disagreed with Pericles' conviction of the superiority of their city. He claimed, according to the historian Thucydides, that Athens was "the school of Greece," its natural political and cultural leader, and his plans were devoted to maintaining and increasing its greatness. His patriotism inspired him and his fellow citizens to combine political liberty at home for all but the slaves with control of an empire abroad.

LIFE IN PERICLEAN ATHENS

Not only could every citizen play a part in determining the Assembly's decisions, but each could also be called on to participate in the daily running of Athens. By the mid-fifth century the male citizen population of Athens was about 40,000 to 45,000. With women and children the total population was probably around 170,000, with perhaps the same number of slaves. In 451, however, a law was passed limiting citizenship to those whose parents were both Athenian. The new decree may have prevented a flood of immigration from Athens' allies. It did not, however, help to soothe the allies' resentment of Athens' military and political domination.

The Assembly met three or four times a month, and major business could not be transacted unless at least 6,000 members were present. Proposals were submitted to it by the Boule, or Council of 500. The Council, broken down into smaller units, also supervised the routine work of running the state: control of expenditures, organization of religious festivals, supervision of magistrates, and superintendence of buildings and other public works. Citizens also had the duty to serve as magistrates. The nine archons, who in Solon's time had been drawn from the aristocracy, were now chosen by lot. They had been supplemented as chief magistrates by ten generals, who were elected by the ten tribes. The post of general was the office Pericles held for many years, and during his tenure the generals played as large a part in domestic affairs as in military operations. With the exception of the generals and those in charge of the treasury, virtually every magistrate was chosen by lot. As a consequence, even the obscurest citizen could find himself in a top administrative position.

Trials were held in popular courts, or *dikasteria,* before juries whose members were also selected by lot. Treason was prosecuted before the Assembly, and homicide was tried by one of the few survivals from predemocratic days, the Court of the Areopagus. All other cases were conducted before large juries in the popular courts. Even in criminal cases the prosecutors and defenders had to speak for themselves; there were neither judges nor professional lawyers.

Clearly, a government in which so many of its citizens could participate required very special conditions. The average Athenian was expected to maintain a detailed

Cresilas, "Pericles." Roman copy after original of c. 440 B.C. Marble. An idealized image rather than a realistic portrait, the sculpture shows Pericles wearing a helmet, symbolic of his office as general. [Alinari/Art Resource]

Pericles on the Government of Athens

In a speech on the occasion of the public funeral of the Athenian war dead, delivered in the fall of 430 B.C., Pericles describes his view of the Athenian system of government.

Let me say that our system of government does not copy the institutions of our neighbors. It is more the case of our being a model to others, than of our imitating anyone else. Our constitution is called a democracy because power is in the hands not of a minority but of the whole people. When it is a question of settling private disputes, everyone is equal before the law; when it is a question of putting one person before another in positions of public responsibility, what counts is not membership of a particular class, but the actual ability which the man possesses. No one so long as he has it in him to be of service to the state, is kept in political obscurity because of poverty. And, just as our political life is free and open, so is our day-to-day life in our relations with each other. We do not get into a state with our next-door neighbor if he enjoys himself in his own way, nor do we give him the kind of black looks which, though they do no real harm, still do hurt people's feelings. We are free and tolerant in our private lives; but in public affairs we keep to the law. This is because it commands our deep respect.

Source: Thucydides, *History of the Peloponnesian War*, trans. R. Warner (Harmondsworth, England: Penguin Books, 1954), p. 117.

knowledge of current affairs and of the workings of the law. Financial hardship was no obstacle to holding public office, for the state paid almost all public servants an allowance to compensate for their loss of regular earnings. Thus even the poorest citizen was expected to serve as juror, member of the Council, or magistrate; only the elected officials, the generals and the treasurers, were not paid. Furthermore, all magistrates, even the generals,

Ostraka **from the Athenian Agora, fifth century B.C. *Ostraka* are votes for the banishment of the individuals whose names are scratched on the potsherds; the names include Themistocles and his principal opponent, Aristides. [American School of Classical Studies at Athens: Agora Excavations]**

were fully accountable to the Assembly for their conduct in office. A crude system known as *ostracism* prevented the ambitious from acquiring too much power and reviving tyranny. Any political figure could be forced to undergo ten years of exile by means of this institution. The names of potential tyrants were inscribed on fragments of pottery known as *ostraka,* and if one name appeared often enough, that person was forced to leave. Themistocles, the hero of the resistance to Persia, was one of those proscribed; he ended his days in the Persian camp.

Athenian democracy—the word literally means "rule by the people"—was a remarkable and unprecedented experiment. It coincided with Athens' political and economic hegemony in Greece, and its great cultural flowering as well. It remains the wellspring of the Western democratic tradition, and although it had severe critics even in its own day, it has remained the ideal of a political community of free, equal, and self-governing persons. It did not embrace the entire community, however, for it excluded two large groups that together made up the majority of the adult population: women and slaves.

Women in Classical Athens

The first literary and dramatic representations of women we have from the ancient Western world, apart from the Hebrew Bible, are those of classical Greece. The Greeks added what the Hebrews lacked, the visual representation of women in paint and stone. The great tragic figures of the Greek stage—the avenging queen, Clytemnestra; the betrayed wife, Medea; the martyred princess, Antigone; and many others—are still the prototypes of Western drama. The magnificent representations of the female figure, including the first life-size nudes in Western art (beginning with those of Praxiteles in the fourth century B.C.), are still the acknowledged ideal of feminine beauty in Western culture. In mythology, too, women played a crucial and often commanding role, and the very name of Athens was derived from its patron goddess, Athena, whose 40-foot-high statue sat enthroned within the Parthenon.

The actual position of women in classical Greek society fell far short of these idealized images. Aristotle reflected the prevailing view when he described women as the natural inferiors of men, born to serve and obey; he even denied them a full share in the procreation of children, which was seen as women's chief function, arguing that the male seed alone contained the full germ of the child, with the womb serving only as its receptacle. The role and status of women were far closer to those of slaves than those of citizens. Women had no independent legal standing and could have legal rights exercised for them only through male guardians. Marriages were generally arranged by the bride's father, who was also responsible for the wedding celebration and, of course, the dowry. Husbands could divorce their wives at will, whereas women had to find magistrates to represent them. Husbands could even dispose of their wives in their wills, and the orator Demosthenes describes the case of a widow ordered to marry her husband's former slave in his will. The double standard was also applied to adultery; tolerated for men, it was regarded as automatic grounds for divorce in the case of women.

Only inside the home did women exert any authority. Within her house a woman was responsible for domestic finances, duties such as spinning and weaving, and the supervision of slaves. Even here, however, the sexes were socially segregated, with women consigned to their own part of the house while men entertained their visitors (including prostitutes and concubines) elsewhere. The women's part of the house, the *gynaeconitis*, varied in size and complexity with the scale of the home. In small residences it consisted of one or two rooms, divided from the main section by a door that could be locked, apparently to keep the male and female slaves apart. In larger houses the woman's quarters had a separate dining room, an open courtyard, and occasionally additional suites of rooms.

The sexual life of most women was as restricted as their social lives. The open eroticism of Greek vase paintings is very misleading. Procreation rather than pleasure was the aim of marital sexuality. The Greco-Roman historian Plutarch cited a law of Solon's that required married couples to have intercourse at least three times a month, "for the same reason that cities renew their treaties from time to time." Athens and most other Greek cities supported a large population of male and female prostitutes; Corinth is said to have had 1,000 of the latter. These included the famous *heterae,* or courtesans, who in Hellenistic times had the reputation of being cultivated companions as well as women skilled in the art of pleasure. Their position in Periclean times was less prestigious. It is they who are largely represented in the vase paintings, often performing acts that were frowned upon in the marriage bed. They were also occasionally represented as being beaten, raped, or otherwise abused.

Domestic occupation was viewed as good for women, but any kind of work for pay was considered socially demeaning. Women of the lower classes hired out as weavers, spinners, and wet nurses; many worked as vendors in the public market. Athenian women seldom worked at agriculture, but in times of duress they sometimes went into the field or picked grapes in the harvest. A very few served in temples. Most respectable women simply stayed home, and only those of prominent families could venture forth socially. It is unclear whether they were even able to attend the theaters where the tragic heroines were portrayed, but we do know that they were prohibited from acting the parts, which were played by men and boys.

Lacking rights, women were of course excluded from political life. As in many folk cultures, however, they were permitted to turn the tables on men once a year in the festival known as the Thesmorphoria, satirized in Aristophanes' play *The Parliament of Women*. In Aristophanes' portrayal—most probably taken from life—women dressed up as men, even pasting on false beards, and convened for a day in their own assembly to pass "laws." The more serious satire of the same playwright's *Lysistrata*, which depicts a sex strike aimed at bringing the Peloponnesian War to an end, as well as the sensitive and thoughtful examinations of women's role in society in the works of Euripides, betokened the coming of a new attitude. But in classical Athens women were still second-class persons.

Slaves and Metics

Slaves were a necessary part of the Athenian way of life, since by doing much of the work, they left the citizens free to devote themselves to politics and law. At Athens alone the number of slaves in the late fifth century B.C. amounted to between 100,000 and 200,000 people, or roughly half the population. Almost none of these were of Greek origin; many, either captured in war or bought at slave markets in Greece and western Asia, came from Asia Minor or southern Russia. They were owned by individual citizens or by the state. Those who were skilled in a craft were allowed to produce work for sale, on condition that their masters received a share of the profit. Many worked in industries such as mining and quarrying, or in farming. About half worked as domestic servants. Since the wealthier households had several slaves—a fa-

A Critical View of the Athenians

An extremely unsympathetic view of Athenian life is expressed by an anonymous writer of the late fifth century B.C. known simply as the "Old Oligarch."

Another point is the extraordinary amount of license granted to slaves and resident aliens at Athens, where a blow is illegal, and a slave will not step aside to let you pass him in the street. I will explain the reason of this peculiar custom. Supposing it were legal for a slave to be beaten by a free citizen, or for a resident alien or freedman to be beaten by a citizen, it would frequently happen that an Athenian might be mistaken for a slave or an alien and receive a beating; since the Athenian people is not better clothed than the slave or alien, nor in personal appearance is there any superiority.

Or if the fact itself that slaves in Athens are allowed to indulge in luxury, and indeed in some cases to live magnificently, be found astonishing, this too, it can be shown, is done of set purpose. Where you have a naval power dependent upon wealth we must perforce be slaves to our slaves, in order that we may get in our slave-rents, and let the real slave go free.

For my part I pardon the people its own democracy, as, indeed, it is pardonable in any one to do good to himself. But the man who, not being himself one of the people, prefers to live in a state democratically governed rather than in an oligarchical state may be said to smooth his own path towards iniquity. He knows that a bad man has a better chance of slipping through the fingers of justice in a democratic than in an oligarchical state.

Source: C. Starr, *The Ancient Greeks* (London: Oxford University Press, 1971), pp. 199–201.

mous shield manufacturer, Cephalus, owned 120—many Athenian households of the poorer classes must have functioned without slave labor.

The daily life of a domestic slave differed little from that of the average Athenian housewife. It was not possible for an outsider to distinguish between slaves and free workers by their dress or their treatment. Slaves were generally considered members of the family. They were allowed to marry and produce children, who then became the property of their owners; they were allowed to save money for their old age; and when they died they were buried in the family tomb. Although no laws existed to protect them from abuse, they could seek refuge from cruel masters in various legal sanctuaries. There were even cases where slaves were given their freedom, went into business, and became Athenian citizens. The lot of agricultural or mine workers was far grimmer. The quarriers and miners were often worked to death, and farm laborers shared the generally uncertain and penurious conditions of their farmer-masters.

In addition to citizens and slaves there was another class in Athens, the resident aliens, or *metics*. These were immigrants from other parts of the Greek world and their descendants, freed slaves and their descendants, and, after 451 B.C., the children of marriages between citizens and noncitizens. Like the slaves and female relatives of citizens, they could not vote, nor could they own houses or land. Nonetheless, they were in general socially accepted, had freedom of religious beliefs, and were able to follow their chosen trade or profession. Many of them, in fact, played an important part in Athenian business and industry.

The Spartan Ideal

Sparta, Athens' principal rival in the Greek world, was based on very different premises. The champion of conservative forces in Greece, the Spartans had been warlike from the beginning of their history. Gradually they evolved a way of life based on the military ideal, to which they subordinated all other aspects of social, economic, and cultural life.

The Spartans dominated the region around them, known as Laconia. Because all adult Spartan males were soldiers, the work of cultivation was done by the neighboring population, the *perioikoi,* and the large class of serfs, or "helots," who were owned by the Spartans, bound to the soil, and kept under strict control. Together these groups gave the Spartans an abundant supply of forced or semifree labor. This system also surrounded them with a permanently hostile population. The perioikoi enjoyed personal freedom and a measure of local self-government, but they were subject to Spartan governors and to conscription in the Spartan army. They were probably the descendants of former allies who had been reduced to subservience. The helots, descended from conquered peoples, were restive and frequently rebellious. Unlike the Athenian slaves, who were in large part integrated into the families of citizens or at work beside them in the fields, they had little incentive to identify themselves with the harsh and exclusive rule of their masters.

Sparta's military ideal was thus both a cause and an effect of its pattern of conquest, which left the Spartans an elite minority among a disaffected mass of serfs and subjects. But if the Spartans were hard on those they ruled, they were hard on themselves as well. Spartan babies were inspected at birth, and those deemed unfit were exposed to die. Children were taken from their mothers at the age of 7 to be trained in martial arts and athletics. Their clothes were scanty, their beds were hard, and their food was monotonous and strictly rationed. The training they received was calculated to increase their powers of endurance and inspire them with patriotic fervor. Students were encouraged to steal, because foraging was a military virtue, and were punished only if caught, not for the act itself but for failing at it. At the age of 20 each male enlisted in the army and spent the next ten years living in barracks. For the rest of his life he remained a member of a small peer group, with whom he took his meals, even though he was expected to marry by the age of 30. Girls were given a similar, though less rigorous, military education. In contrast to Athenian women, those in Sparta had legal standing, could inherit property and represent themselves in court, and played a major role in managing the large estates of the Spartan aristocracy.

At the age of 30 Spartan males were divided into two classes, "equals" and "inferiors." The equals made up the Assembly, whose principal function was to elect the 30 members of the Council. These comprised two kings, who shared power and ruled jointly, and 28 elders. The chief magistrates were the five ephors (overseers), who had almost unlimited powers; they could arrest and prosecute any citizen, including the kings.

In embracing this social and political system, the Spartans of classical times believed they were following a code of laws introduced by Lycurgus, a shadowy and perhaps mythical figure in early Spartan history. Even the Oracle at Delphi was uncertain whether Lycurgus was a man or a god, and it is probably safer to assume that the Spartan system of government developed over a period of time.

The Spartans' concern with military affairs tended to limit their contacts with the rest of Greece and left them in relative economic and cultural isolation. Their self-sufficiency was, of course, voluntary. Indeed, the profound differences between the Athenian and Spartan interpretation of civic ideals underscore the diversity of the polis. The Athenian version of democracy produced a spirit of commercial and imperial aggressiveness and stimulated a rich culture. The Spartans left behind no art or architecture of consequence, nor did they develop a literary or dramatic tradition. Yet many Greek cities feared and mistrusted Athens' expansionism and looked to Sparta for leadership as Athenian power grew.

The Spartans' attachment to tradition, the austerity of their lives, and their rigorous adherence to the military ideal were widely admired. Many of the poleis were far more attracted to Spartan stability than to the democratic experiments of Athens. Powerful but staunchly conservative, the Spartans rarely undertook any kind of political initiative and therefore seemed less threatening to their neighbors. If they lived on the labor of serfs, they often lived less well, materially, than those who served them. Their standards of courage, loyalty, endurance, and honor were high, and the penalty for failing them was severe: disgrace and loss of citizenship. The Spartans deliberately contrasted their ascetic way of life with what they considered the self-indulgence and reckless individualism of the Athenians; one of their kings, Agesilaus, asked what the greatest Spartan virtue was, is said to have replied, "Contempt of pleasure."

The imperial aggressiveness of Periclean Athens finally roused the Spartans to concerted action. In 431 B.C., at Corinth's urging, they declared war on Athens, leading to a civil war of 27 years' duration and the eventual defeat of the Athenian empire.

The Peloponnesian War

By the end of the Persian Wars, Athens was the most powerful polis in the Greek world, not least because it had played a decisive part in defeating the Persians. Moreover, its essentially democratic government had proved stable and effective. Athens organized a defensive alliance of Greek city-states to repulse any future Persian attack. This was the Delian League, so named because the money contributed by the member states was stored in a treasury on the island of Delos, sacred to Apollo and politically neutral.

Other city-states, including Sparta, Thebes, and Corinth, soon became suspicious that the league was intended primarily to enhance Athenian power. The Athenians, they believed, were transforming an association of free states

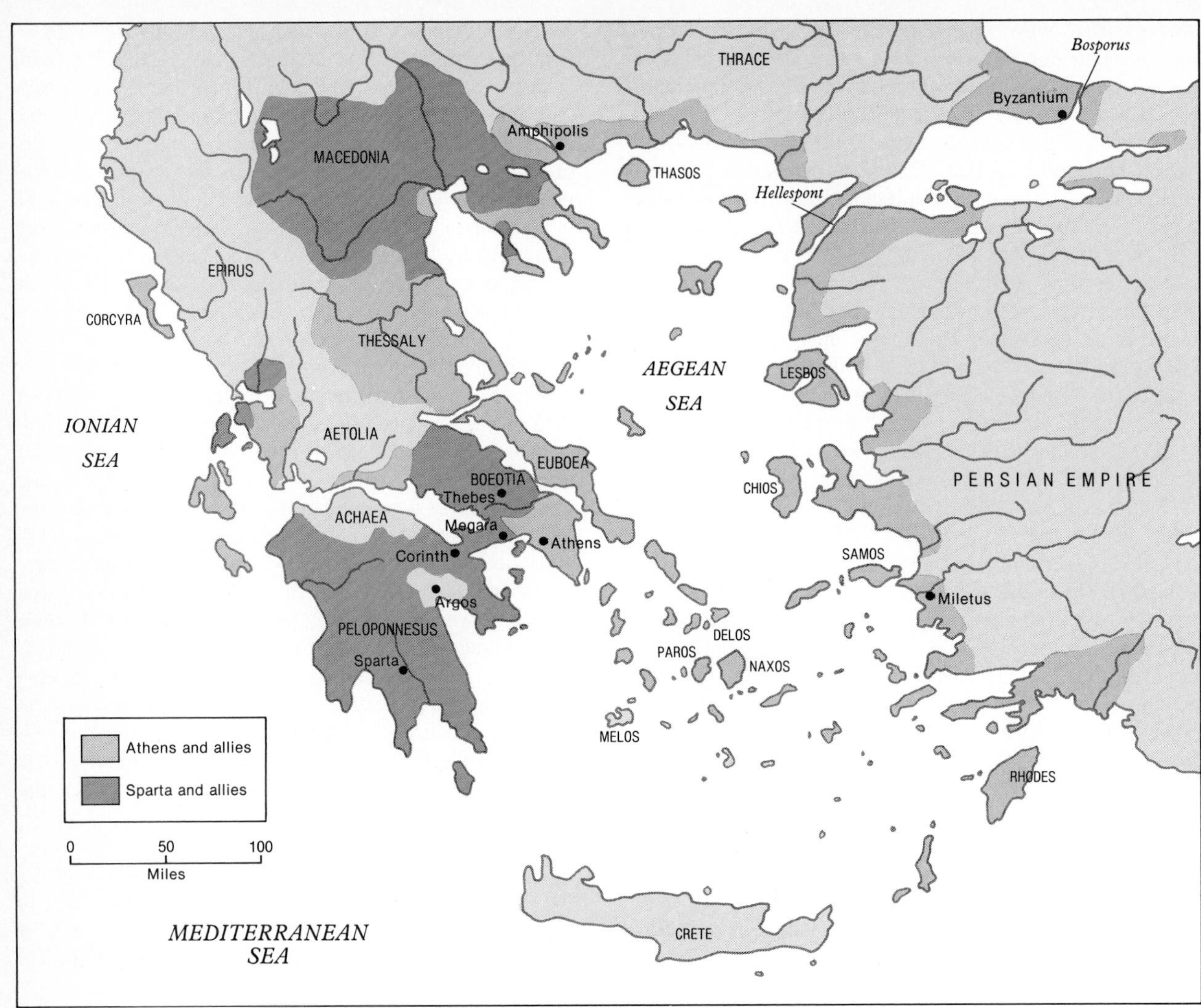

4.3 Allies in the Peloponnesian War

into an empire. Their concerns were intensified in 454 B.C. when the league's funds were moved to Athens and some of the money was diverted to pay for new buildings. The Greek world largely divided into competing camps, with Athens and the city-states that remained in the league arrayed against Sparta and its supporters. Conflict was inevitable. The Peloponnesian War, so called after the homeland of the Spartans and their principal supporters, broke out in 431 and lasted until 404 B.C., when it ended in the defeat and occupation of Athens.

The Peloponnesian War, although it involved virtually the whole of Greece in a generation of bitter conflict, did not result in more satisfactory and stable conditions. It served principally to hasten the decline of the independent city-states, which had proved themselves incapable of co-existence. If the significance of the war seems somehow greater than mere events suggest, that is probably because our understanding of its course owes much to the account by the great historian Thucydides, who lived through its calamitous events.

Thucydides, born about 460–455 B.C., had been active in Athenian politics before the war. Elected general in 424, he was responsible for the defense of Amphipolis in northern Greece. When Sparta seized Amphipolis, Thucydides was tried in absentia and exiled. Not until 404 did he return to Athens. The purpose of his *History of the Peloponnesian War* was to narrate the events of the war to 404, but he was able to finish it only down to 411 before his death. Thucydides was not content with a mere narrative of events. Through the use of set speeches, he analyzed the motives and reactions of the principal personalities of the struggle to give future generations an understanding of its causes. At the heart of his examination was the contrast between the restless, revolutionary Athenians and the confident, conservative Peloponnesians. Thucydides was also intrigued by the contest between Athens, a naval power, and Sparta, whose strength was on land; and by the technical problems of siege warfare, troop landings, and nighttime battles. Unlike Herodotus, he deliberately avoided digressions, and like modern historians he made a scrupulous effort to verify his facts, fully aware of the presence of bias in his sources. With Herodotus, he ranks as one of the fathers of historical study.

Strife and Stalemate

The Athenian war effort went badly at first. The Persian Wars had demonstrated the power and efficiency of the Athenian navy, but no land army in Greece was a match for the Spartans. Trusting to the strength of Athens' fortifications and the richness of its treasury, Pericles allowed the Spartans to ravage the countryside outside Athens and wear themselves out. Thucydides vividly depicted the strain on the Athenians:

> **When they saw the army . . . barely seven miles from the city, they felt the presence of the invader to be intolerable. The devastation of their country before their eyes, which the younger men had never seen at all, nor the elder except in the Persian invasion, naturally appeared to them a horrible thing, and the whole people, the young men especially, were anxious to go forth and put a stop to it. Knots were formed in the streets, and there were loud disputes, some eager to go out, a minority resisting. . . . The people were furious with Pericles, and, forgetting all his previous warnings, they abused him for not leading them to battle, as their general should, and laid all their miseries to his charge.[3]**

Meanwhile, Pericles sent the Athenian navy to do what damage it could to the Peloponnesus. For two years the Athenians withstood a Spartan siege, guaranteed food supplies by their access to the sea. The devastation of the farmlands around the city, however, drove thousands of people inside the walls. In 430 a terrible disease, still unidentifiable, ravaged the city. Perhaps as much as a quarter of the population, including Pericles himself, had perished by the time the contagion finally abated in 427.

The Athenians found themselves with no able leader to take his place. The city split into two main factions, a war party and a peace party. The latter were led by Nicias, a wealthy Athenian who used his money to provide public entertainments. His opponent was the fiery Cleon, a self-styled "watchdog of the people" and the son of a tanner. After ten years of reverses for both the Athenians and the Peloponnesians, the peace faction at Athens gained the ascendancy. In 422 Cleon was killed in action, and in 421 the so-called Peace of Nicias was signed. It was supposed to last for 50 years, but few had much confidence in its durability.

By now a new generation had come to power in Athens. Chief among its leaders was the brilliant but erratic Alcibiades (c. 450–404 B.C.); handsome, wealthy, intelligent, he was called ambitious and extravagant by his enemies. An aristocrat by birth, he seems to have despised the lower classes, although he was mistrusted by his fellow conservatives. As long as his aims seemed in the city's interest, his charm won him popular support. Even his admirers, however, learned to fear him.

The Sicilian Expedition and the Collapse of Athens

When war resumed in 415, Alcibiades was one of the principal promoters of a daring scheme to invade Sicily. The Athenians' intention was twofold: by conquering the Sicilian Greek cities they could enrich themselves with treasures and crops; at the same time, they could disrupt Sicilian trade with the Peloponnesus, especially Corinth, thereby weakening its alliance with Sparta.

A string of disasters dogged the Sicilian expedition. When Alcibiades was recalled to Athens to answer trumped-up charges by his political enemies, he defected to Sparta and helped the Spartans against his own polis. By painting a menacing picture of a growing Athenian empire in the west, he induced the Spartans to send the Sicilians a volunteer force. In the spring of 414 the Athenians found themselves trapped between the Syracusans and the Spartans. The Athenians dispatched more troops, but when they arrived late in the spring of 413, it was too late. A rout occurred, and the expedition surrendered.

The Athenians were so disheartened by this reversal that they temporarily abandoned their greatest achievement, the democracy they had created. In 411 a revolution brought a Council of 400 to power, although after a few months it too split into various factions, and by 409 democracy was restored. Alcibiades returned briefly to Athens, where, despite his earlier defection, he was welcomed as a savior. When his enemies revived the old suspicions, he again retired into exile, this time for good.

The war's end came in the late summer of 405, when the Spartan navy ambushed the Athenians in the Hellespont. Of 179 Athenian ships only 9 escaped, and 4,000 Athenian prisoners were executed. Even then the city resisted a siege. By the spring of 404 the situation was hopeless, and Athens surrendered unconditionally.

The long-term causes of the Peloponnesian War are to be found in the nature of Greek political life, which encouraged confrontation rather than unity. The temporary alliance against the Persians had proved only an exception to the tradition of intercommunal rivalry. The defeat of Athens was hailed as a victory for Greek independence, but it did nothing to foster unity among its divided states.

By the end of the Peloponnesian War the concept of the polis as the dominant force in the lives of its citizens, inspiring and fulfilling them, had been damaged beyond repair. The internal divisions within the Greek world ultimately produced wounds far more serious than those inflicted by the Persian invasions. In the years that followed, the Greeks moved in new political and cultural directions but failed to solve the fundamental dilemma of their disunity. That dilemma remained part of its legacy, along with the magnificent achievement of its classical age.

Notes

1. Archilochus, "My Goodly Shield," trans. W. R. Castle, in *Classics in Translation*, ed. P. MacKendrick and H. M. Howe (Madison: University of Wisconsin Press, 1966), vol. 1, p. 94.
2. Herodotus, *The Persian Wars*, trans. G. Rawlinson (New York: Modern Library, 1942), pp. 587–588.
3. Thucydides, *The Peloponnesian War*, trans. B. Jowett (New York: Bantam, 1960), p. 109.

Suggestions for Further Reading

Austin, M. M., and Vidal-Naquet, P. *Economic and Social History of Ancient Greece*. Berkeley: University of California Press, 1978.

Boardman, J. *The Greeks Overseas*. Baltimore: Penguin, 1973.

Bury, J. B., and Meiggs, R. *A History of Greece to the Death of Alexander the Great*, 4th ed. New York: St. Martin's Press, 1975.

Cargill, J. *The Second Athenian League: Empire or Free Alliance?* Berkeley: University of California Press, 1981.

Charbonneaux, J., Martin, R., and Villard, F. *Archaic Greek Art, 620–480 B.C.* London: Thames & Hudson, 1971.

Cook, R. M. *Greek Art*. Baltimore: Penguin, 1976.

Dover, K. J. *Greek Homosexuality*. New York: Random House, 1980.

Finley, M. I. *Early Greece: The Bronze and Archaic Ages*, 2d ed. New York: Norton, 1982.

———. *Economy and Society in Ancient Greece*, ed. B. D. Shaw and R. P. Saller. London: Chatto & Windus, 1981.

Flaceliere, R. *Daily Life in Greece at the Time of Pericles*. New York: Macmillan, 1965.

Hood, S. *The Arts in Prehistoric Greece*. Baltimore: Penguin, 1978.

Hooker, J. T. *The Ancient Spartans*. London: Dent, 1980.

Kagan, D. *The Fall of the Athenian Empire*. Ithaca, N.Y.: Cornell University Press, 1987.

———. *The Peace of Nicias and the Sicilian Expedition*. Ithaca, N.Y.: Cornell University Press, 1981.

Kitto, H. D. F. *The Greeks*. Baltimore: Penguin, 1957.

Lacey, W. K. *The Family in Classical Greece*. Ithaca, N.Y.: Cornell University Press, 1968.

Luce, J. V. *Homer and the Heroic Age*. New York: Harper & Row, 1975.

Marinatos, S., and Hirmer, M. *Crete and Mycenae*. New York: Abrams, 1960.

Page, D. L. *Sappho and Alcaeus*. Oxford: Clarendon Press, 1955.

Pomeroy, S. B. *Goddesses, Whores, Wives, and Slaves*. New York: Schocken Books, 1975.

Schaps, D. M. *Economic Rights of Women in Ancient Greece*. Edinburgh: Edinburgh University Press, 1979.

Snodgrass, A. M. *An Archaeology of Greece*. Berkeley: University of California Press, 1987.

———. *Archaic Greece*. Berkeley: University of California Press, 1980.

Strauss, B. *Athens After the Peloponnesian War*. Ithaca, N.Y.: Cornell University Press, 1986.

Vermeule, E. *Aspects of Death in Early Greek Art and Poetry*. Berkeley: University of California Press, 1981.

Willetts, R. F. *The Civilization of Ancient Crete*. Berkeley: University of California Press, 1977.

Zinserling, V. *Women in Greece and Rome*. New York: Schram, 1972.

CHAPTER · 5

The Greek Achievement and the Hellenistic World

The Peloponnesian War and the fall of Athens devastated Athenian dreams of political and cultural supremacy. No other Greek polis filled the vacuum left by the Athenians' defeat. The ensuing period of confusion was brought to an end only by the appearance of a new power, the northern kingdom of Macedon. Yet the ultimate failure of the Greek political system could not wipe out the cultural achievements of Greek civilization. The Greeks were pioneers in many aspects of Western culture and provided the basis for subsequent accomplishments in fields as varied as history and sculpture, urban planning and medicine, drama and mathematics.

The world in which Greek ideas were developed was a period of war and disturbance, and the Greek concern for order in all things must be seen against that background. The Greek conviction that the pursuit of reason could provide a basis for order in human affairs governed

Alexander the Great. Note the strained position of the head and the emotion expressed by the eyes and the mouth. [Alinari/Art Resource; Musée du Louvre]

the artistic achievements of the classical period. The essence of this classical belief was the quest for an ideal balance between mind and body and for harmony between the individual and society. The Greeks summed this up in the adage "Nothing in excess."

This classical concern for balance and proportion was reflected in everything from religious belief to architectural and artistic forms. The Greeks believed that humans could achieve order in their lives by comprehending the causes not only of other people's actions but also of their own. This faith in reason and self-understanding was as central to Greek spiritual life as belief in divine forces. The Parthenon, the principal temple on the Athenian Acropolis, was intended to celebrate Athens as much as to honor the goddess Athena. Even in the worst of times, this belief in human potential remained central to the Greeks' vision of life. At the same time they understood the powerful forces of the irrational that were part of human nature and had to be acknowledged and pacified. If Apollo, god of the sun, represented clarity and order, he was balanced by the figure of Dionysus, god of wine, sexuality, and abandonment.

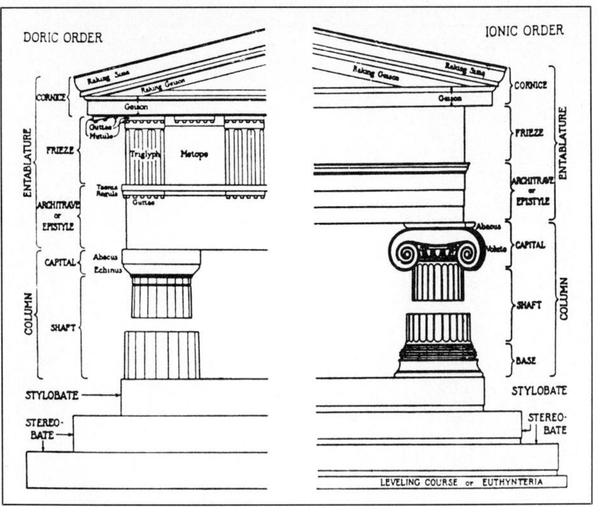

The Doric and Ionic orders (after Grinnell). [H. W. Janson, *History of Art*, Prentice-Hall, 1970]

The Visual Arts: In Search of the Human Ideal

The buildings on the Acropolis were the culmination of artistic developments at Athens and elsewhere in Greece. The two principal styles of Greek architecture, Doric and Ionic, which were both represented on the Acropolis, had begun to develop centuries earlier. The Doric style was widespread by 600 B.C.; the Ionic, though used in the Archaic period, was not common until the fifth century B.C.

The Doric order is more austere and majestic than the Ionic. A number of its features may be based on building techniques employed in the wooden structures of an earlier period. The Ionic order, by contrast, is more delicate and makes use of complex architectural details; its surface decoration is as important as its structural design. When, after the Persian Wars, the Greeks collaborated to construct the Temple of Zeus at the Panhellenic shrine of Olympia, they chose the Doric order. Built between 470 and 456 B.C., it was the largest Doric temple in Greece. Libon of Elis, its designer, was concerned to render the classical sense of order in architectural form. The positioning of the columns and other architectural elements follow precise mathematical formulas. A similar concern for proportion can be seen in the temple of Apollo designed by Ictinos and built at Bassae in the western Peloponnesus around 450–425 B.C.

Sculptors of the classical age were also concerned with harmony. They sought to produce a fresh notion of human beauty by presenting the human form through the application of principles of symmetry and proportion. Polyclitus of Argos, one of the most important classical sculptors, invented a mathematical system of proportion in order to depict the ideal male form. His book, *The Canon* (c. 440 B.C.), argued that ideal beauty is achieved by an exact correspondence of proportion between all parts of the human anatomy. His bronze statue of a youth holding a spear, the *Doryphoros*, was intended to demonstrate this principle. Neither the book nor the original statue has survived, although later copies of the *Doryphoros* exist.

One of the great achievements of fifth-century Greek sculptors was the depiction of movement in conjunction with proportion and gracefulness. Figures such as a woman fastening her sandal or a charioteer gripping his reins convey motion in a satisfyingly natural fashion. Such figures contrast sharply with the formal, rigid statuary of the archaic period. The classical sculptors were largely successful in this endeavor because of their careful observation of human anatomy, particularly musculature. Subjects such as Zeus hurling a thunderbolt or an athlete poised to throw a discus were obviously chosen at least in part to explore the artists' anatomical interests. Naturalism was heightened by the skillful depiction of bones and muscle as though under living skin. Artists had manifestly become more sensitive to and appreciative of the natural world.

Toward the end of the fifth century B.C. both sculpture and vase painting began for the first time to exhibit an interest in portraying individuals rather than idealized beauty. Conditions of war were starting to take their toll, and artists began to depict the reactions of individual people to mortality. Thus the subject of death and the human response to it came to be treated frequently in works of art.

Detail of Apollo from the center of the west pediment of the Temple of Zeus at Olympia. [Alinari/Art Resource; Olympia Museum, Greece]

The *lekythoi,* or oil flasks, used for funeral ceremonies are decorated with scenes that are among the most moving in classical art. Many show grieving figures or funerals; the background is generally white instead of the black or red favored in other painted pottery. Although the figures retain the composure of the classical style, they frequently display deep emotions. A similar individual reaction to death also characterizes the *stelai,* or grave markers, of the late fifth century, which reveal a sense of loss and resignation as well as depth of feeling.

The Athenian Acropolis

The most famous buildings of the classical period are the structures on the Athenian Acropolis. The magnificence of their design and execution is still visible. The Parthenon, the great temple to Athena, remains an unsurpassed symbol of classical achievement. Nevertheless, it was constructed in a period of conflict and division among the Greeks, its sculptures completed only months before the outbreak of the Peloponnesian War. The Erechtheum, the last temple on the Acropolis to be finished, was completed in 406 B.C., scarcely a year before Athens' disastrous defeat in the Hellespont. Despite the political tensions of the classical period, the temples serve as a memorial to its highest ideals.

The natural stone outcrop known as the Acropolis made an ideal location for the temples. The site, which rises more than 400 feet above Athens, had dominated the city's life from the Bronze Age, when it was occupied by a fortress. During the Archaic period a number of temples were built there, but the Persians destroyed them in 480 B.C. The new building program was begun in 449 under the general supervision of Phidias, the leading sculptor of the day. The most important building, the Parthenon, was begun in 447 and completed in 438. Its designers were Ictinos and Callicrates, and its name is derived from the Greek word *parthenos,* or virgin. This honored the city's patron goddess Athena, one of whose imputed qualities was virginity. Built on an even grander scale than the early fifth-century temple of Zeus at Olympia, it displays both Doric columns (17 on the sides and 8 on the ends) and Ionic characteristics, including a band of sculptural decoration within the outer colonnade.

Grave stele of Heges. [Hirmer; National Archaeological Museum, Athens]

Equestrian group, detail of Parthenon frieze (west face), c. 442–432. The speed and vigor of the horses' movement is in strong contrast to the calm, typically classical expressions of their riders. [Sheridan; The Ancient Art and Architecture Collection, British Museum, London]

Sculpture was used in three sections of the building. The Ionic running band, or frieze, shows a ceremony that was held every four years at the time of the Great Panathenaic festival. It depicts some Athenians walking and riding in procession and others at the climax of the religious ceremonies. The contrast, motion, and rhythm in this sculpture make it one of the most impressive masterpieces of classical art. The extant freestanding figures originally on the east and west pediments are no less striking despite their damaged condition. The group of three goddesses from the east pediment blends ideal form and natural observation, particularly in the harmony of limbs and flowing drapery. The rectangular slabs decorating the outside of the building, which are called *metopes,* show various legendary battles, including the conflict between the Lapiths, a tribe of northern Greece, and the half-human, half-animal Centaurs, which for the Greeks represented the clash of civilization and barbarism.

Work on the entrance to the Acropolis, the Propylaea, began in 437 B.C. and lasted six years, although the war probably forced its architect, Mnesicles, to modify his original design. He used both Doric and Ionic columns, an uncommon practice for a classical building. The little Ionic temple of Athena Nike (goddess of victory), built between 427 and 424, is decorated with carvings that depict the earlier Athenian triumph over the Persians. The purpose of showing historical figures instead of legendary ones was no doubt intended to recall Athenian successes at a time when the city was faced with renewed crisis.

The Erechtheum, an Ionic temple of unusual and striking design, was built between 421 and 406 B.C. It was the site of a variety of religious ceremonies and commemorated several gods. The Erechtheum's most famous element is the south porch, whose roof is supported by the Caryatids, statues of young women, rather than traditional columns.

Late Classical Art

Nothing comparable to the scope and ambition of the Acropolis was attempted in Greece during the century that followed Athens' defeat. The shrines at Olympia and Delphi were expanded, and new forms were devised, such as the *tholos,* or circular building. The grandest project of the age was perhaps the reconstructed Temple of Artemis at Ephesus. Many of the principal fourth-century sculptures are lost, although surviving Roman copies enable us to trace the principal stages of development in this field. The heroic, idealized facial expressions of fifth-century works gave way to a new and often inward sense of individualism. The sculptor Praxiteles, for example, was famous for the gentle melancholy of his figures, a mood aptly characterized by the *Hermes* at Olympia often attributed to him. Lysippus, his younger contemporary, who developed a more elongated approach to proportion and a greater naturalism, had a significant influence on later Hellenistic art.

Tragic Drama and the Meaning of Existence

The fifth century B.C. also gave rise to the tragic drama, a form invented by the Greeks. The plays written for performance in the sanctuary of Dionysus at Athens rep-

Erechtheum, Athens. As a result of pollution and the deterioration of the stone, the statues have now been moved to the Acropolis Museum. [Wim Swann]

resent classical literature at its height and the birth of theater as we know it. The three great playwrights of the era, Aeschylus, Sophocles, and Euripides, not only created a new form of human expression but also set a standard in their works that has never been surpassed.

The extant works are religious, in two senses. In the first place, the theater for which they were written was regarded as sacred to the god Dionysus, who was honored at the festival at which they were performed. In the second place, their plots, usually derived from legend, frequently deal with the interaction between mortals and gods in search of the meaning of existence. To achieve an appropriate seriousness, the style of performance was lofty and dignified. The actors, all of whom were male, thought of themselves as priests of Dionysus and wore masks, intricate costumes, and high shoes.

Greek tragedy had its origins in choral hymns honoring Dionysus, and the chorus, a group of supplemental actors who commented on the actions of the main actors, remained an important element in classical plays. In earlier works, such as Aeschylus' *Suppliants,* the choral group is at the center of the action. Generally, the chorus reflects on the action and its implications for the moral law, whose affirmation is the function of tragedy.

The three principal dramatists illustrate the evolution of fifth-century Athenian cultural history. Aeschylus (525–456 B.C.) lived at a time when the ideals of the early classical period were still unshaken by disaster. His plays reveal an intense sensitivity to human frailty and the corrupting influence of power; he had been a soldier at Marathon in 490 B.C. Aeschylus did not abandon his belief that justice would always prevail; he recognizes, however, the difficulties of gaining knowledge, for only suffering can teach the errors of human ways. Moreover, even after the lessons have been learned, they do not alter the conclusion—only a divinely inspired justice, represented by Zeus, chief of the Olympian gods, can determine the outcome.

Aeschylus' optimism persists even when he depicts scenes of violence and blood. His greatest achievement is the group of three plays, or trilogy, known as the *Oresteia,* first performed at Athens in 458 B.C. Its theme is sweeping: the evolution of civilization from a primitive state ruled by blood vengeance to a society governed by reason.

Sophocles (c. 496–406 B.C.), a personal friend of Pericles, enjoyed great acclaim. His plays reveal a more somber view of life than those of Aeschylus, although it is more difficult to extract a consistent philosophy from his work. He is interested chiefly in showing how each of his characters changes rather than in presenting a general theme, but he tempers the tragic results of human error with a belief in the dignity and capacity of people.

However splendid human achievement may be, Sophocles asserts, each individual is responsible for deciding between good and evil. Yet in his plays the choice is often obscured or difficult and at times impossible to make. Sophocles was more insistent than his fellow dramatists on human helplessness in the face of divine will or destiny. Moreover, he demanded such respect and reverence for forces beyond human understanding that he is generally considered the most religious of the Greek tragedians. The play for which he is most widely known, *Oedipus the King,* has remained the most enduring symbol of classical tragic drama. First performed in 429 B.C., it combines a unity of time, place, and action with a story that inevitably moves toward a tragic conclusion. Its poetic language is beautiful and controlled. The play is universally regarded as a work of genius, yet its meaning remains ambiguous.

The play tells the story of Oedipus, who is doomed before birth by divine decree to murder his father and marry his mother and who finally discovers that he cannot avoid his fate. The simplest conclusion to be drawn from Oedipus' story is that humans must meet their destinies, but it is unclear as to whether such fates are deserved. Oedipus did not consciously decide to kill his father or marry his mother, although unknowingly he did both. Why

Human Destiny: A Greek View

This chorus from Sophocles' Antigone *expresses his complex view of human destiny.*

Chorus. Happy the life that tastes not lamentation!
But when with the curse of God a lineage shakes,
From generation down to generation
Comes no surcease of sorrow; so, when breaks
The Thracian tempest and the dark surge wakes,
Up from the deeps it whirls the sable sand,
While groan, in answer to the waves, the capes of the wind-vexed land.

Lo, from of old the Labdacids are stricken—
On the sorrows of their dead new sorrows fall.
Each generation sees the same curse quicken,
Some God still ruins them, helpless. In the hall
Of Oedipus one hope lit, last of all,
One root yet living. Now, this too lies slain
By Hell's red dust, by a reckless tongue, by a Fury in the brain.

Thy power, O Zeus, who can master? What pride of man's endeavor?
Sleep binds Thee not (that snares all else to rest),
Nor the tireless months of Heaven—Time leaves Thee ageless ever,
Throned in the dazzling glory of high Olympus' crest.
But for Man, from long ago
Abides through the years to be
This law, immutably—
All over-greatness brings its overthrow.

For Hope, that wanders ever, comes oft to Man as blessing;
For oft she cheats, till his giddy lusts are stirred.
Nearer she creeps, the deceiver, till he stumbles, all unguessing,
In the hot fires hid beneath him. Wise is the ancient word—
That he whom God hath planned
To ruin, in his blinded mood
Sees evil things as good—
And then the coming doom is hard at hand.

Source: F. L. Lucas, *Greek Tragedy and Comedy* (New York: Viking, 1968), p. 144.

then should he bear the consequences of his actions? Perhaps the meaning of the play is that much of human life is inexplicable and lies beyond ordinary experience. In this sense, Sophocles chronicled the impotence of human will in the context of destiny and warned that humans should not expect self-reliance to provide an escape from fate.

The plays of Euripides (c. 485–406 B.C.), Sophocles' contemporary, reflect the profound impact of fifth-century Greek political conflict and its social repercussions. Perhaps as a consequence, his work has the most direct meaning for us. Euripides was bent on exposing the social and political injustice of his time. He acknowledges that irrational forces, symbolized by the gods, affect human life, but he refuses to respect and worship them. Indeed, his open skepticism made people suspect him of impiety. The characters in his plays often reach the limits of their endurance, and his depiction of their response reveals a keen sense of psychological portraiture. More than any of his predecessors Euripides displays a deep sympathy for the problems of women in a male-dominated society. Characters such as Medea and Phaedra, who seek vengeance and passion outside the norms of social life, challenge many of the fundamental assumptions of Athenian society.

In a world that admired Spartan militarism, Euripides hated war and its attendant misery. His play *The Suppliant Women* was apparently written in 421 B.C., when a decade of inconclusive struggle in the Peloponnesian War was temporarily halted by the Peace of Nicias. The play deals with the return of the bodies of dead warriors to their families, in particular to their wives and mothers. The scenes of mourning that he depicted were undoubtedly grimly familiar to his audience. Furthermore, the grief does not terminate the violence. In the last scene, Athena announces that the heirs of the dead soldiers will launch a war of vengeance. Euripides has rejected the optimism of Aeschylus; the cycle of violence cannot be broken.

Euripides lived long enough to see his fears fully realized. Driven from Athens by a public that had little taste for reminders of their folly, he ended his days at the court of the king of Macedon. There he wrote *The Bacchae,* a work that shows the limits of the rational mind in confronting the darkness of experience. This profoundly disturbing work, which describes the killing of Pentheus, the young king of Thebes, at the hands of his mother, acknowledges that emotion can overturn the sense of balance and proportion and that religious intoxication can release powers of destruction.

Pre-Socratic Science and the Physical World

The curiosity that characterized the Greeks' exploration of the physical, mental, and emotional character of human beings in their art and literature drove them to try to understand the world around them. Early Greek thinkers did not distinguish between philosophy and science. Their quest was for an understanding of how the universe operated, and they tried to explain nature by looking for broad fundamental principles.

By the sixth century B.C. the traditional religious ideas of Homer, with his depiction of gods and goddesses in human form, were being called into question. In the mid-sixth century, Xenophanes of Colophon wrote that if cows and horses had the ability to draw, they would depict gods in the shape of cows and horses. The various schools of thought that developed between the early sixth and the end of the fifth century B.C. are generally described as pre-Socratic, that is, prior to the time of the philosopher and teacher Socrates (469–399 B.C.).

Perhaps the most remarkable aspect of the pre-Socratics' work was the sheer breadth of the questions they sought to answer: What is the nature of matter? How did the world begin? What is our place in it? Lacking all the resources of modern scientists, often unconstrained by a lack of methodical observation and a willingness to test their theories by practical experimentation, they passionately debated the nature of the physical world.

The first scientific school was represented by the *Materialists*, who described physical reality in terms of elements. Thus Thales of Miletus (c. 585 B.C.), commonly called the "father of philosophy," believed that nature was composed of or convertible into water. He was thus the first to posit that all matter was reducible to a single substance, thereby challenging the evidence of the senses. Known for his practical ingenuity, Thales invented a system for measuring the distance of ships at sea. Empedocles (c. 493–c. 433 B.C.) taught that nature is composed of four elements, fire, air, earth, and water, which continuously combine and separate under the influence of the basic forces governing all matter, attraction and repulsion, which he called love and strife. By all accounts a colorful character, he claimed miraculous powers, and is said to have leaped to his death into the crater of Mount Etna in Sicily. Anaxagoras of Clazomenae (c. 500–c. 428 B.C.) argued that matter was composed of countless tiny particles, each consisting of dominant substances such as water along with other random ingredients. His claim that the sun was not an emanation of divinity but merely a large white-hot stone led to his condemnation for sacrilege.

The most famous of the pre-Socratics was Pythagoras of Samos, who lived in the late sixth century B.C. *Pythagoreanism* was to flourish throughout the fifth century, and many of its doctrines may have been developed by later followers. As a religious cult, Pythagoreanism taught the transmigration of souls, according to which souls passed into new bodies at the time of physical death, and the essential unity of all living things; the latter belief led to the practice of vegetarianism. Pythagoras himself was a mathematician, whose fame now rests on the geometric theorem named for him but previously known to the Babylonians. His interest in numeric relationships led him to discover their significance for musical harmonies, and our modern musical scale derives ultimately from his research. Inspired by his discoveries, he further asserted that mathematical relationships formed the basic principle of the universe, the reputed "harmony of the spheres."

Whereas Pythagoras believed in universal harmony, the *Dualists* posited the existence of two disparate universes, a constantly changing physical world and an ideal realm that is perfect and immutable and can be understood solely through the mind. Heraclitus of Ephesus (flourished c. 500 B.C.), the major advocate of the Dualist view, expressed the ever-changing flux of material nature in the axiom "One cannot step twice into the same river." Parmenides of Elea (flourished c. 460 B.C.), a later Dualist, distinguished between two ways of comprehending experience, those of opinion and truth. The way of opinion is that of our senses, which mislead us into believing in the reality of change, motion, and what we call nature, while the way of truth, based on contemplation, reveals a reality that is motionless, indivisible, and finite.

The *Atomists* were the most famous school of pre-Socratic thought. Democritus (c. 460–c. 370 B.C.), its leader, claimed that invisible atoms separated by empty space were at the core of all unchangeable things. Atoms, Democritus hypothesized, are indivisible, infinite in number, indestructible, and solid; in different combinations, they make up all the phenomena our senses perceive. The Atomists believed that all the processes of nature were mechanical and unchangeable; as we shall see, their work provided the scientific basis for the system of philosophy developed a century later by Epicurus (341–270 B.C.).

The pre-Socratics were distinguished by the boldness of their speculation about the nature of the physical world, which they neither accepted at face value nor repudiated as mere illusion, as Buddhist thought was to do. The categories they introduced—space and matter, stability and flux, monism and dualism—remained fundamental in Western thought. Their sense of the world as a product of harmony, proportion, and even strict mathematical ratio contributed to the classical culture that finds its expression in the ordered columns of the Parthenon and the balanced cadences of the tragic playwrights. Above all, they are striking in their rejection of any mythological explanation of the world or of divine caprice in its governance. In this they sharply challenged received tradition and religious orthodoxy and set up a new standard of truth based on rational examination.

Philosophy and the Quest for the Good

Just as Greek achievements in literature and the visual arts have influenced the development of later Western art, so Greek philosophy forms the basis for much of the Western intellectual tradition. Whatever their interests, few philosophers in the West have been able to ignore the ideas of the two most important figures of fourth-century Greece, Plato and Aristotle, both of whom were indebted to Socrates.

Socrates

Socrates was born in 469 B.C. His father was a sculptor and his mother a midwife, and later in his life he liked to say that he himself was a "midwife to ideas." After studying natural science, he became interested in human behavior and ethics. Unlike the sophists, who were professional teachers of discussion and debating skills, Socrates did not charge his pupils, nor did he found a school. Rather, his fame rested on his consistent discussion and argument and his challenging of ideas through logically constructed questions. His method consisted of extended oral discussions in which apparently simple questions allowed him to reveal logical inconsistencies in his pupils' responses, leading to a debate that clarified his own beliefs and exposed errors. This Socratic method, which involved no written argument, proved influential for later thinkers and became a standard teaching device. Socrates attracted a band of loyal admirers as well as numerous enemies among people whose ignorance he exposed.

His supporters included members of an unpopular political group who had seized power in Athens after the city's defeat in 404 B.C. Known as the Thirty Tyrants, a brutal group of oligarchs set up by the Spartans, they ruled for only a few months. Many of these leaders were subsequently executed or exiled. Socrates' enemies seized the opportunity to turn popular feeling against him. Tried in 399, he was charged with impiety and corruption of the young. The purpose of the trial seems to have been principally to use Socrates as a scapegoat, and few expected that he would actually be executed. Socrates' friends urged him to escape, and the prison officials actually gave him an opportunity to flee. But he refused, arguing that his flight would be an admission of guilt and a defiance of the law, and he was executed by a lethal dose of hemlock.

Because Socrates never wrote anything, our knowledge of him is derived from the surviving accounts of two disciples, Xenophon and Plato. Xenophon (c. 430–354 B.C.) was a historian best known for his account of a Greek expedition in Asia Minor, the *Anabasis.* Plato (428–347 B.C.), along with his pupil Aristotle, remains one of the major figures of the Western intellectual tradition. Plato asserts that his dialogues reflect the thought of Socrates, who appears as a character in most of them, arguing his controversial ideas. We cannot know how much of the content of these discussions is genuinely Socratic. In the early dialogues Plato probably presented his teacher's ideas and methods with more fidelity, whereas the later dialogues mirror primarily his own views.

Plato

Socrates' life and death powerfuly influenced Plato. Born of an aristocratic family, Plato soon gravitated to the Socratic group. He attended Socrates' trial and reported the speech Socrates gave in his own defense in the *Apology,* though how accurately it is impossible to know. Although not present at the execution, Plato records Socrates' final hours in the *Phaedo,* which also expounds ideas Plato later expanded. His conviction of the soul's immortality is derived in part from his belief that the soul is imprisoned in a living body and thus cannot achieve its potential: "The body is the tomb of the soul." Plato's idealism, that is, his belief in the primacy of a world of immaterial forms beyond the reach of the senses, also derived from Parmenides. It had a major effect on the development of Western philosophy and later helped to provide an intellectual framework for Christian theology.

In 387 B.C. Plato, who had left Athens after Socrates' death, returned home to found the Academy, the earliest educational institution in the West. Focusing on law, mathematics, and political theory, it aimed at training government officials. Plato had the chance to try out his political theories in 368, when he was asked to apply them to Syracuse, a Sicilian polis, and to train Dionysius II, its youthful sovereign, as a philosopher-king. The effort failed, and he was back in Athens by 366.

Plato's works touch on a wide variety of topics, from metaphysics to love. Among the recurring themes is his theory of forms. Briefly put, this claims that the phenomena we see in the material world are only distorted reflections of perfect forms beyond space and time, to which the soul instinctively aspires. *The Republic,* one of his most famous dialogues, is largely concerned with politics and the creation of a perfect society. After an examination of the concept of justice and how it operates, Plato defined an ideal state as one ruled by philosopher-kings who would be both experts in his theory of forms and persons seasoned by practical experience. Without doubt his vision of an ideal society is far too extreme for most tastes, involving among other restrictions the state-sponsored breeding of children, the censorship of music and poetry, and the abolition of private property. In fairness to Plato, however, it must be remembered that *The Republic* was not intended as a set of instructions to be followed literally but as a challenge to his readers to think seriously about how their lives should be organized. In any case, the last years of the fifth century B.C. in Athens presented an unhappy picture of democracy at work, and fourth-century Greek politics were to remain largely chaotic. Thus what may seem drastic in Plato's proposed solutions was in part a reflection of the intractability of the problems he saw.

Aristotle

Aristotle (384–322 B.C.), Plato's most distinguished pupil, initially built on his master's teachings but then repudiated Plato's radical separation of form and matter. In 335 Aristotle established the Lyceum, a school that competed with Plato's Academy, thereby openly breaking with his mentor. Aristotle was a systematizer of immense range

Platonic Love

In this extract from The Symposium *Plato describes what has often been called platonic love.*

It is necessary for the one proceeding in the right way toward his goal to begin, when he is young, with physical beauty, and first of all, if his guide directs him properly, to love one person and in his company to beget beautiful ideas and then to observe that the beauty in one person is related to the beauty in another. If he must pursue physical beauty, he would be very foolish not to realize that the beauty in all persons is one and the same. When he has come to this conclusion, he will become the lover of all beautiful bodies and will relax the intensity of his love for one and think the less of it as something of little account. Next he will realize that beauty in the soul is more precious than that in the body, so that if he meets with a person who is beautiful in his soul, even if he has little of the physical bloom of beauty, this will be enough and he will love and cherish him and beget beautiful ideas that make young men better, so that he will in turn be forced to see the beauty in morals and laws and that the beauty in them all is related.

Source: M. P. O. Morford and R. J. Lenarden, *Classical Mythology* (New York: Longman, 1977), p. 126.

who delved into virtually every topic. In the *Metaphysics* he argued, contrary to Plato, that all matter was an inseparable unity of form and substance, and he sought to explain the concept of a single God, whom he characterized as "thought thinking of itself" and "the Unmoved Mover." The elements that make up the universe, together with the laws by which they operate, he described in the *Physics,* while in *Poetics* Aristotle delineated the nature of poetry. In the *Organon* he explored two means to acquire knowledge: the deductive method, which derives specific facts from general truths, and the inductive method, which formulates general truths from particular facts. Aristotle also developed the first theory of logic, including the syllogism, a form of argument in which a conclusion is deduced from two propositions. The range of his interests was encyclopedic; he investigated everything from the motions of the stars to the gait of animals, from meteorology to ethics.

Although he shared Plato's interest in politics, Aristotle avoided the temptation to construct an ideal state; instead he analyzed existing forms of government. The state, he argued, ought to serve the good of all citizens; when it is subjected to special interests, it becomes perverted. Thus an aristocracy may degenerate into an oligarchy governed by a wealthy elite, monarchy into tyranny under the rule of men of low character, and democracy into mob rule. He believed that the best rule was one that combined the best of each form of government and preserved itself by balancing them. Similarly, his system of ethics sought not a dogmatic solution to moral dilemmas but a mean between two extremes.

Aristotle had a profound impact on later ages. During the medieval period his writings were translated into Latin and Arabic and provided a philosophical foundation for systematic Christian theology in the West. His world view was considered authoritative, as were his scientific treatises. Through the Renaissance, some of Aristotle's views on philosophy and science were widely accepted, as many still are. The Middle Ages called him simply "the Philosopher," and he was justly described by the poet Dante as "the master of those who know."

Power Passes North: The Rise of Macedon

Despite the intellectual brilliance of the fourth century B.C., the Greeks failed to sustain the political coalition that had defeated Athens in the Peloponnesian War. No single state could fill the vacuum left by the collapse of Athenian power, and peaceful cohabitation proved as elusive as before. The early years of the fourth century saw divisive skirmishes among Sparta, Thebes, Corinth, and Argos that were interrupted only by the intervention of the Great King of Persia. By the so-called King's Peace of 387 B.C. the Greeks bought a brief respite, but the price was high; many of the Greek cities of Asia Minor, whose freedom had supposedly been achieved by the victories in the Persian War of 100 years earlier, were handed back to the Persians. It was not long before Thebans and Spartans were once again fighting. In 371 B.C. the Thebans defeated the Spartans at Leuctra and became for a few years the dominating force in Greek politics.

Such instability was bound to attract outside intervention. The Persians were too far away and had problems in their own empire. Just to the north of the Greeks, however, lay the kingdom of Macedon, hitherto a backward land of farmers and agricultural laborers. Although the Greeks considered them barbarians, the Macedonians in fact spoke a rough Greek dialect; and if they managed to avoid becoming entangled in Greek political feuding, it was principally because they were kept occupied defending themselves from raiders from the north.

In 359 B.C., with southern Greece still divided, Philip became king of Macedon. Over the following 20 years he gave ample evidence of his powers as an orator, general, and statesman, but perhaps his greatest asset was his ability to manipulate and outmaneuver even the most cunning Greek politicians. By negotiating with his enemies secretly and singly, Philip soon unified virtually the whole of Greece under his rule.

Before he could challenge the Greeks, however, Philip needed to secure Macedonia's northern borders and restore the morale of his troops. By 356 he had already begun to look south to Athens and Thebes. After a trial expedition into Greece met with defeat, Philip retreated to Macedon to recoup. Like a battering ram, as Philip himself said, he drew back to hit harder the next time. By 349 he was ready to return to the offensive. Two half-brothers of his, possible contenders for his throne, were living in the northern Greek town of Olynthus. As a pretext for action he demanded their surrender, and when they refused, he attacked and razed Olynthus in 348. In 346 Philip turned to Delphi, one of the most venerated sanctuaries in the Greek world, and seized control of the governing council. The message to the rest of Greece was clear.

Yet Philip himself always denied that he had plans to conquer Greece. There was even talk of an Athenian-Macedonian alliance that could unite the Greeks and lead them against Persia. The Athenian orator and politician Isocrates (436–338 B.C.) publicized the project in a pamphlet called *Philip*. Disunity in Athens, however, undermined the scheme. The pro-Macedonian faction at Athens found itself increasingly under pressure from a conservative majority that could not conceive of Athenian power subordinated to a barbarian king. The success of Philip's opponents at Athens unquestionably owed much to the fact that their principal spokesman was also the greatest Greek orator of the day, Demosthenes (384–322 B.C.).

A Call to Arms

Demosthenes tries to shame his Athenian audience into taking action against Philip of Macedon.

What is the cause of these events? Not without reason and just cause were the Greeks of old so ready to defend their freedom but now so resolved on servitude. Men of Athens, there was then something in the spirit of the people which is not there now, something which overcame even Persian gold and kept Hellas free, something which admitted defeat on neither land nor sea. Now the loss of that has ruined everything and made chaos of our affairs. What was that thing? Nothing involved or tricky. It was just that one and all hated those who accepted bribes from men who aimed to rule or ruin Hellas. To be convicted of taking bribes was a most grievous crime; yes, they punished the guilty one with the utmost severity, and there was no room for intercession or pardon. Therefore the right moment for achieving each enterprise, the opportunity Fortune often extends even to the indifferent at the expense of the vigilant, could not be bought from statesman or from generals, any more than could our mutual good will, our distrust of tyrants and foreigners, or any such thing at all. But now these possessions have been sold off like market wares, and in exchange there have been imported things which have brought ruin and disease to Hellas.

And what are these things? Envy, if a man has received a bribe; laughter, if he admits it; indulgence for a man proved guilty; hatred for his critic; and all the other things that come from bribery. As for warships, troops, abundance of funds and equipment, and all else that may be held to form the strength of our cities, in every instance they are present in greater abundance and extent than in days gone by. But all this is being made useless, unavailing, unprofitable because of those who traffic in them.

Source: P. MacKendrick and H. M. Howe, eds., *Classics in Translation* (Madison: University of Wisconsin Press, 1966), vol. 1, p. 288.

Demosthenes proved a formidable opponent to Philip. A stern politician, he urged the Athenians to resist the Macedonian monarch in order to maintain their freedom. The power of his orations persuaded the Athenians to levy taxes and pour money into military preparations. In 341 the Athenians sent troops to northern Greece to attack territory held by the Macedonians, and over the following two years they continued to clash with Macedonian troops and allies; Philip could no longer delay. When the Athenians learned of the Macedonians' advance south, the city was mobilized, and Demosthenes himself went to Thebes to seek an alliance with his former enemy. At Chaeronea in 338 Philip defeated a combined Greek army, although the Spartans, no longer the force they once had been, were not present. In a congress at Corinth the same year a league of all Greek cities except Sparta proclaimed Philip its captain-general.

A year later Philip began plans to enlarge his empire even further by attacking Persia, but he was never to carry them out. In 336 he was assassinated under mysterious circumstances, perhaps through the jealousy of Olympias, Alexander's mother, for Philip's new wife. Alexander, tutored by Aristotle himself, succeeded him. His career was to prove even more spectacular, but the loss of Philip at so delicate a stage in the reestablishment of peace was fateful for the Greeks. The new king had little interest in establishing good terms with his Greek neighbors; he was eager to invade Asia and pursue his dreams of world conquest.

The Conquests of Alexander the Great

With the accession of Alexander in 336 B.C. the history of the Greeks was transferred to a wider stage. The spread of Greek culture throughout much of Asia was, in fact, one of Alexander's principal achievements and, unlike the empire he sought to build, one of long duration. Yet Alexander himself, however well disposed to Hellenic ideas, was not reluctant to use force to dominate the Greeks. When in 335 the Thebans took advantage of trouble in the north to stage a revolt, Alexander and his troops stormed the city, razed it, and sold the population into slavery. Thereafter the horrified Greeks provided no more opposition to him, and he was free to turn his attention to the campaign against Persia. By the time of his death in 323 B.C. at the age of only 33, he had extended Macedonian rule from the Adriatic to the river Indus.

The great expedition left for Asia Minor in 334 B.C. Success came quickly with a lightning victory over the forces of the Persian governors at the river Granicus, although Alexander himself was almost killed in the confusion. Pausing only to liberate the Greek cities of Asia Minor, in 333 he pushed south into Syria, where he defeated the Persians at Issus. Most of the next year was spent in a siege of Tyre. Alexander's troops finally destroyed it in time to reach Egypt by the winter. Not only did the Egyptians give way without fighting, but the oracle of Zeus Ammon greeted him as son of God and rightful pharaoh of Egypt. While in that country Alexander founded Alexandria, later to be one of the greatest cities of the ancient world. In 331 he moved east of the river Tigris, where he scored one of his greatest victories at Gaugamela; although vastly outnumbered, his forces penetrated the enemy lines and drove the Persian king Darius into flight. At Persepolis, the old Persian capital, Alexander burned the royal palace, seized the treasury, and began to enlist the young men of Persia in his army.

Over the next three years Alexander battered the rugged northern and eastern sections of the Persian Empire into submission. In 326 he reached northwestern India, but after a desperate battle against the warrior king Poros and his forces (which included 200 elephants), his men would go no further. Even Alexander's drive would not persuade them to take on the kingdoms of the Ganges, and he was compelled to turn back to Persia. The main part of the expedition took the route they had followed on the outward journey, but Alexander, with a small contingent, set out to explore the desert wastes of the coast while another group went by ship. They made it back to Persia, but only with heavy losses and terrible suffering, first from thirst and then from flood. Even Alexander's iron constitution was not proof against such continued ordeals. While preparing yet another campaign, against southern Arabia, he became sick and died within ten days.

Such a life was made possible in part by the remarkable personality and restless energy that characterize his portraits and that certainly marked his career. At the same time, Alexander had other virtues. Often against the wishes of his followers, he rejected the traditional Greek contempt for foreigners. From the beginning he meant his empire to be governed by principles of tolerance. The peoples whom he conquered were encouraged to retain their native laws, religions, and customs, and he himself set an example of "the marriage of east and west" by

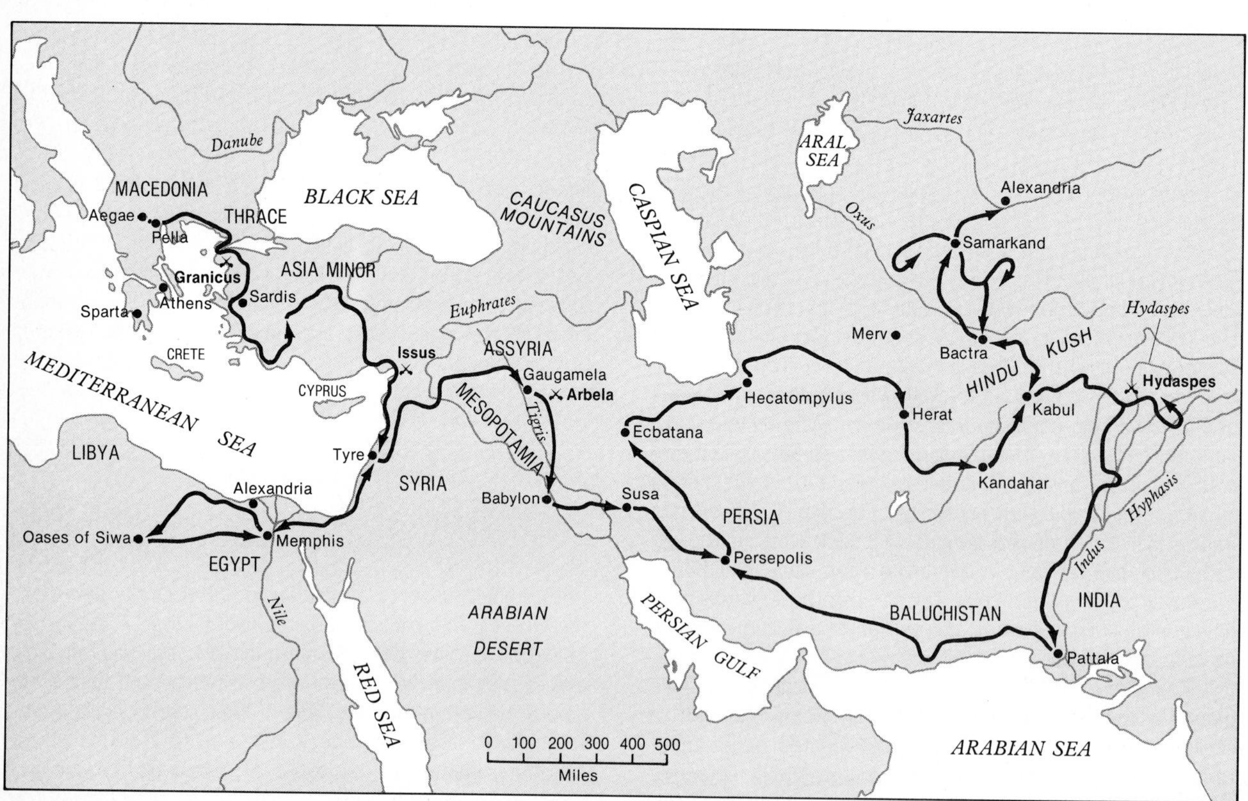

5.1 Alexander's Conquest of the Persian Empire, 334–323 B.C.

taking a Persian bride. At the same time, to unite the enormous variety of peoples involved in his conquest, he founded more than 70 cities, all of them called Alexandria or Alexandropolis (one in Egypt and another in northern Greece still survive) and all embodying the principles of Greek urban planning, architecture, and institutions. Through these strongholds many of his conquests survived the confusion that followed his death.

Alexander's critics have often observed that he never seems to have paid any regard to who would succeed him or how his empire would have been ruled on a permanent and stable basis. Apart from the cities he founded, he retained, for the most part, the administrative structure of the Persian Empire. He often employed former Persian governors, several of whom betrayed him, although in the army most of the principal officers remained Macedonian. In the detailed planning and execution of a campaign, however, he functioned efficiently. Lines of communication were kept open over very long distances with the arrival of reinforcements and medical supplies from Macedon. Such careful organization, coupled with his personal charisma, held his troops together under the most arduous conditions. Yet toward the end of his life he began to play the part of the great king with too much enthusiasm. To the discomfort of his Macedonian old guard, he wore Persian dress, required them to make obeisance before him, and even assigned Persian brides to them. It is by no means certain that, had he survived his illness, his empire would have been more permanent. His achievements still stand: the spread of Greek culture from a small corner of southeastern Europe to most of the Mediterranean and central Asian world and the memory of his life—the scope and daring of his conquests, his heroic personality, and the new world that he sought to create.

The Hellenistic Kingdoms and the Cosmopolitan World

In the absence of a successor nominated by Alexander, disagreements among his generals after his death resulted in the breakup of the Macedonian empire. The most important of the new states were Egypt, Pergamum, Macedon, and the kingdom of the Seleucids, each of which fought the others until the Romans conquered them all. They continued to "Hellenize", or spread Greek civilization (*Hellas* is the Greek name for Greece).

The Ptolemies and the Seleucids

The Egyptian city of Alexandria remained the most significant center of Greek learning. There Ptolemy, a former officer of Alexander's, proposed the creation of an institute for study and research called the Temple of the Muses—the "Museum." Ptolemy himself had bolstered his claim for power by snatching Alexander's body and burying it at Alexandria, although the tomb has never been discovered. In 305 B.C. he took the title of king and, on his death in 283, was succeeded by his son. The dynasty of the Ptolemies continued to rule Egypt until Rome's absorption of it after the reign of Cleopatra (died 31 B.C.).

Ptolemaic rule had little of the multiracial character of Alexander's original design. Egypt was primarily run by a Greco-Macedonian elite, and Greek remained the official business language. Cleopatra was the only Ptolemaic ruler who learned Egyptian.

The wealth accumulated by the Ptolemies became legendary—not surprisingly, given the elaborate taxing and licensing system of the state. Even beekeepers had to have a license from the king, and fishermen were required to pay a part of their catch to a representative of the royal treasury. Little or nothing of the money raised from the peasants in the form of such levies as taxes, death duties, sales taxes, and transit dues was used to improve their lot. Some was spent on maintaining the strongest navy in the Mediterranean, and the rest ended up in the royal coffers.

The former Persian territories in Asia were seized by the commander of Alexander's footguard, Seleucus, who by the time of his murder in 280 had sufficiently consolidated his power to be succeeded by his son, Antiochus. The Seleucids ruled until 83 B.C., when they were briefly replaced by Armenian kings and then annexed by Rome. Even Seleucus himself, however, had to give up Alexander's Indian conquests, and the Seleucid portion of the empire shrank rapidly. As early as 275 Antiochus held off with great difficulty an invasion of the Gauls, a tribe that had migrated from western Europe, only to become involved in futile wars with Egypt. The sheer size of the Seleucids' territory precluded the establishment of a Ptolemaic-style bureaucracy, and much of it was ruled by local governors. Antioch, the royal capital, was designed on Greek lines, and Greek continued to be spoken in Seleucid cities as far east as the river Tigris for centuries following the fall of the kingdom.

Macedonia and the Hellenistic Greeks

Macedon acquired a permanent dynasty only in 275 B.C., after several generals had fought for its possession. The eventual victor was Antigonus, a grandson of one of Alexander's commanders. His successors spent most of their time fighting with neighboring kingdoms for influence in central and southern Greece, where two competing leagues of poleis, the Aetolian and Achaean, battled each other as well as external enemies.

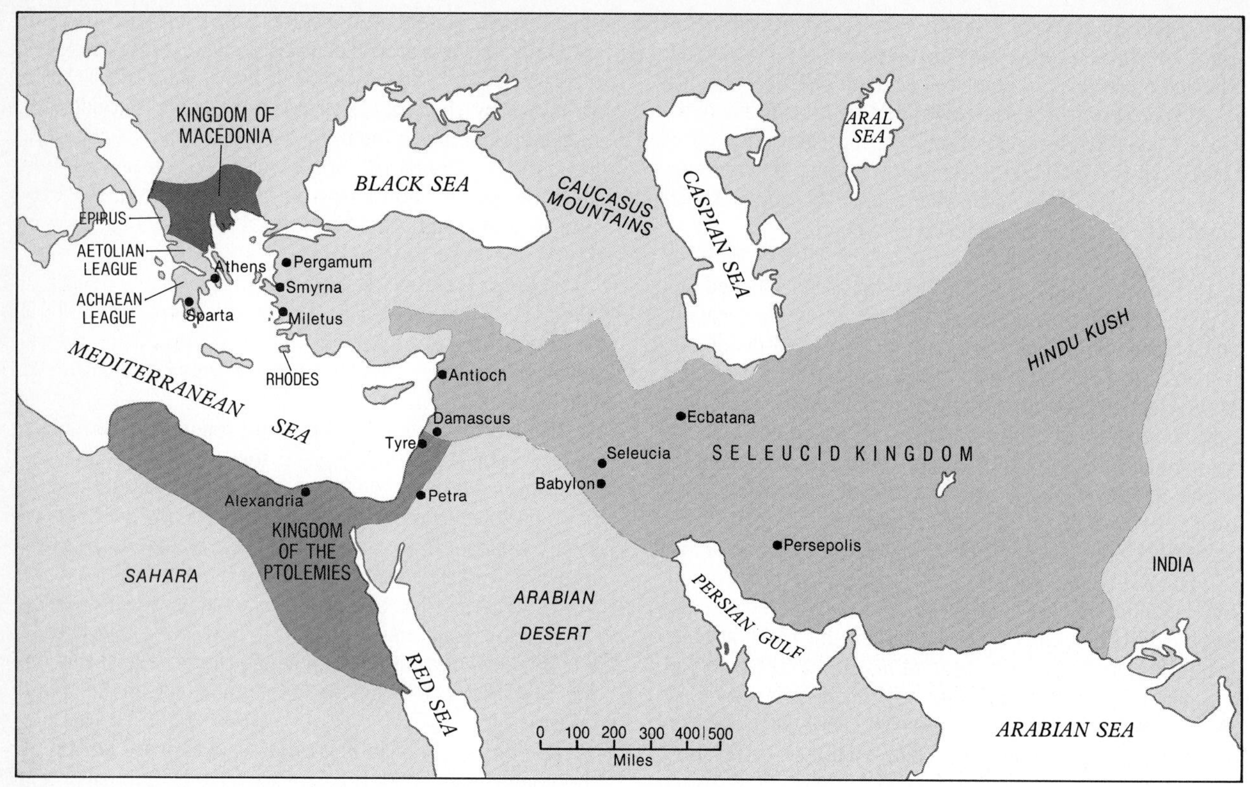

5.2 Hellenistic Kingdoms, c. 275 B.C.

The vision of a single great state, Hellenic in culture but multiethnic in character, did not die with Alexander but remained alive as an ideal until the Romans unified the eastern Mediterranean and western Asia two centuries later. Alexander had prayed at a celebrated banquet for a union of all hearts and a commonwealth of Macedonians and Persians; the philosopher Zeno envisioned a universal city under one divine law; and the word derived from this, *cosmopolitanism,* originally taken up by the Cynics to indicate their attachment to no state, was finally adopted in the Hellenized world to signify world citizenship. This remained (as it does today) an ideal rather than a reality, but it had some practical consequences for the old Greek poleis themselves, now under Macedonian domination but enjoying a certain degree of autonomy.

Honorary citizenship was increasingly conferred on foreigners, and whole cities exchanged citizenship as a mark of friendship and alliance, as in the case of Athens and Rhodes. Arbitration was extensively adopted in the third century B.C. as a means of settling boundary claims, and foreign commissioners were frequently invited to adjudicate intracity disputes, a practice that would have been almost unthinkable among the jealously divided and fiercely independent poleis of the fifth century. Leagues grew up among cities, which shared a joint army, pursued a common foreign policy, and introduced a common system of taxes, tariffs, weights, and measures.

The best known of these leagues, the Aetolian and Achaean, developed innovative federal structures that were models of cooperation. The Aetolian League, centered in the region north of the Gulf of Corinth, had organized as a federation of states by 367 B.C. Beginning in the 270s it incorporated additional states, the peoples of which retained their own citizenship even while receiving full Aetolian citizenship, a system known as *sympolity.* More distant states were linked to the league by *isopolity,* according to which their citizens enjoyed Aetolian civil but not political rights. The latter could be acquired, however, simply by relocating in a community that possessed full Aetolian citizenship. In the Achaean League, based in the northern Peloponnesus, the mutual exchange of citizenship was rare. Members of the federation shared a common coinage and uniform standards of measurement and used a system of federal courts. Both leagues had relatively democratic constitutions, with power vested in each case in an assembly, a representative council, and an elected general. The federal governments could levy taxes, raise armies, and conduct foreign policy. These and other Greek leagues of this period illustrate a trend away from the distinctive autonomy of the polis in favor of a significant degree of cooperation and unity.

Temples and sanctuaries, such as Delphi, had long been considered neutral ground, but after 270 B.C. whole cities, including Smyrna and Miletus, proclaimed their permanent neutrality, and more and more places sought the status of *asyla* (asylums), which were immune from reprisal. Obviously, these claims were not always respected, but they had a certain deterrent force. War itself became milder, at least temporarily; the old practice of slaughtering the males in a conquered city and selling the women and children into slavery was first modified into a general sale of both sexes and finally abolished altogether; when it was revived, as against Mantinea in 223 B.C., it roused a storm of protest. In short, international public opinion had begun to develop, at least among the older Greek cities, and the idea of a world without borders, of a universal city of the spirit, persisted through Roman times until it was given its final expression in antiquity by the fifth-century A.D. Christian philosopher Augustine in his book *The City of God.*

Pergamum and Bactria

Pergamum, an ancient Greek polis in Asia Minor, was the most influential Hellenistic kingdom in Greek affairs. For a time it had been a Seleucid possession. Its local governor, a eunuch called Philetaerus, had used the money in the treasury to hire his own army; he was succeeded by a nephew, Eumenes I (263–241 B.C.), who governed Pergamum with the support of the Seleucids' great rivals, the Ptolemies. Under later rulers Pergamum won a reputation as a great cultural and artistic center, reaching a high point in the reign of Eumenes II (197–159 B.C.). Its chief religious shrine was the immense altar to Zeus erected by Eumenes II around 180 to commemorate the victories of his father Attalus I over the Gauls during the preceding century. The tangled, writhing bodies of the figures on the frieze, with their intensity of gesture and facial expression, represent one of the high points of Hellenistic art. Other Pergamene rulers reinforced their reputation as champions of Hellenism by contributing money and building projects to Athens and other Greek cities.

Head of Buddha from Gandhara. Note the classical expression. [SCALA/Art Resource; Victoria and Albert Museum, London]

***Athena Slaying Giant,* detail of frieze in altar to Zeus, showing the head of the giant Alcyoneus, whose hair is grasped by Athena. [Staatliche Museen, East Berlin]**

At the opposite end of Alexander's conquests, on the northeastern frontier of India, a new kingdom, Bactria, broke off from Seleucid rule around 250 B.C. Its control of trade routes throughout central Asia lasted until the middle of the following century and brought the descendants of Alexander's Greek mercenaries into contact with the peoples of India. Even after Bactria had been overrun by central Asian nomads, Greek-style cities such as Begram and Taxila continued to exert a cultural influence: Gandharan Buddhist sculpture, the earliest monumental Buddhist art, made use of Greek styles and techniques. Thus in the two centuries following Alexander's death the various Hellenistic kingdoms each contributed to the Hellenization of vast tracts of Asia.

In the meantime, a new political force had begun to make its presence felt in the western Mediterranean: Rome. In 133 the last king of Pergamum died childless and willed his kingdom to Rome; by 31 B.C. the defeat and death of Cleopatra left almost the whole of Alexander's empire in Roman hands. Thus the history of the Hellenistic world became fused with that of Rome.

Changing Economic Patterns

Although in some ways the Hellenization of western Asia produced significant social and economic changes for both natives and new arrivals, it did not cause a total revolution. The Greek poleis were, after all, famous for being able to maintain their independent character under the most trying circumstances. The citizens of the newly founded cities of the Hellenistic period continued to own the land in and immediately around the city and used slaves or resident aliens to work for them. The rest of the land belonged to the king and was worked by peasants as it had been for centuries. The basic level of agricultural production thus remained fairly constant.

Some rulers did try to make improvements. Both the Ptolemies and the Seleucids encouraged the introduction of more sophisticated agricultural equipment, such as iron plows and more efficient oil and wine presses, and introduced new fruit and crops. One of the Ptolemies' successes was a new quick-growing wheat that gave a double harvest and a higher yield. On occasion, the extra supplies were sent to feed the urban poor, although in general the kings, or their local representatives, were unwilling to subsidize the urban population at their own expense. In some cases the cities tried to solve the problem of subsistence on their own. Samos, for example, set up a fund for making loans; the interest on the loans was used to purchase grain, which was then distributed free to the citizens.

Within each independent city-state, industry and manufacturing developed according to the needs and abilities of the resident artisans. Sidon was famous for its glassware, Tarsus for its linen, and Antioch for its gold and silver, as might be expected for a royal capital. The volume remained small, and there is no evidence of mass production. Most businesses were family run, with perhaps two or three slaves. Economic power was concentrated in the hands of the royal family and a small minority of wealthy landowners who, rather than providing food to the urban centers, preferred to ornament them with new temples, porticoes, and theaters that would perpetuate the memory of their donors.

In one significant respect, however, Alexander's conquests did change economic patterns. Trade, both in manufactured goods and in raw materials, became increasingly international, and the descendants of Alexander's Greeks found themselves in commercial contact with the people of the East. The kingdom of Bactria continued to serve as a center for Greek interests in central Asia, but other trade routes were also developed.

The principal route, which ran through Seleucid territory, followed the river Tigris to the Persian Gulf and then the coast of Baluchistan to the mouth of the river Indus. Although under Seleucid control, the route was used for a while by the Ptolemies, but in time they developed their own trade route. This involved sailing around the south coast of Arabia to the Gulf of Aden. Although the route was longer, it opened up the Arabian spice market as well as that of India. The Sabaeans, the ancient inhabitants of modern Yemen, produced myrrh and cinnamon that was highly regarded and expensive in the west.

More complicated was the importation of elephants. After Alexander's Indian campaign, the strategic value and prestige of having elephants in a royal army appealed to his successors. The Ptolemies had a source fairly close to home, for they captured their elephants in what is now Somalia; the Seleucids, on the other hand, had to import theirs from India. Nor was this ancient form of military extravagance without its problems. On a famous occasion in 217 B.C., at a battle fought between Ptolemy IV and Antiochus III, Ptolemy's forest elephants were no match for the larger Indian elephants of the Seleucid army. Terrified by their smell and trumpeting, according to the Greek historian Polybius, the African elephants fled. (Today's larger African elephants are of a different variety.)

Trade contacts such as these were sufficiently important to the Seleucids for them to station a permanent ambassador at the court of one of the Indian kingdoms, the Mauryan empire. One of the ambassadors, Megasthenes, wrote a detailed account of India, now lost, that circulated widely in the Greco-Roman world (see Chapter 2).

Although the cultural exchange resulting from these commercial links was limited, some mutual influence undoubtedly occurred. Many of the Greek coins minted in India have an inscription in Greek on one side and in a local script on the other. Western theories of medicine and astrology were imported into India, and some Greek settlers became assimilated into the native populations. Some were said to have become Buddhists, while others were described by a later writer as the equivalent of the warrior class in Hindu society.

All such contacts throughout Asia in the Hellenistic period were originally motivated by the desire to establish trading relations, but they also awakened curiosity in some Greek minds as to the nature of the wider world. Polybius,

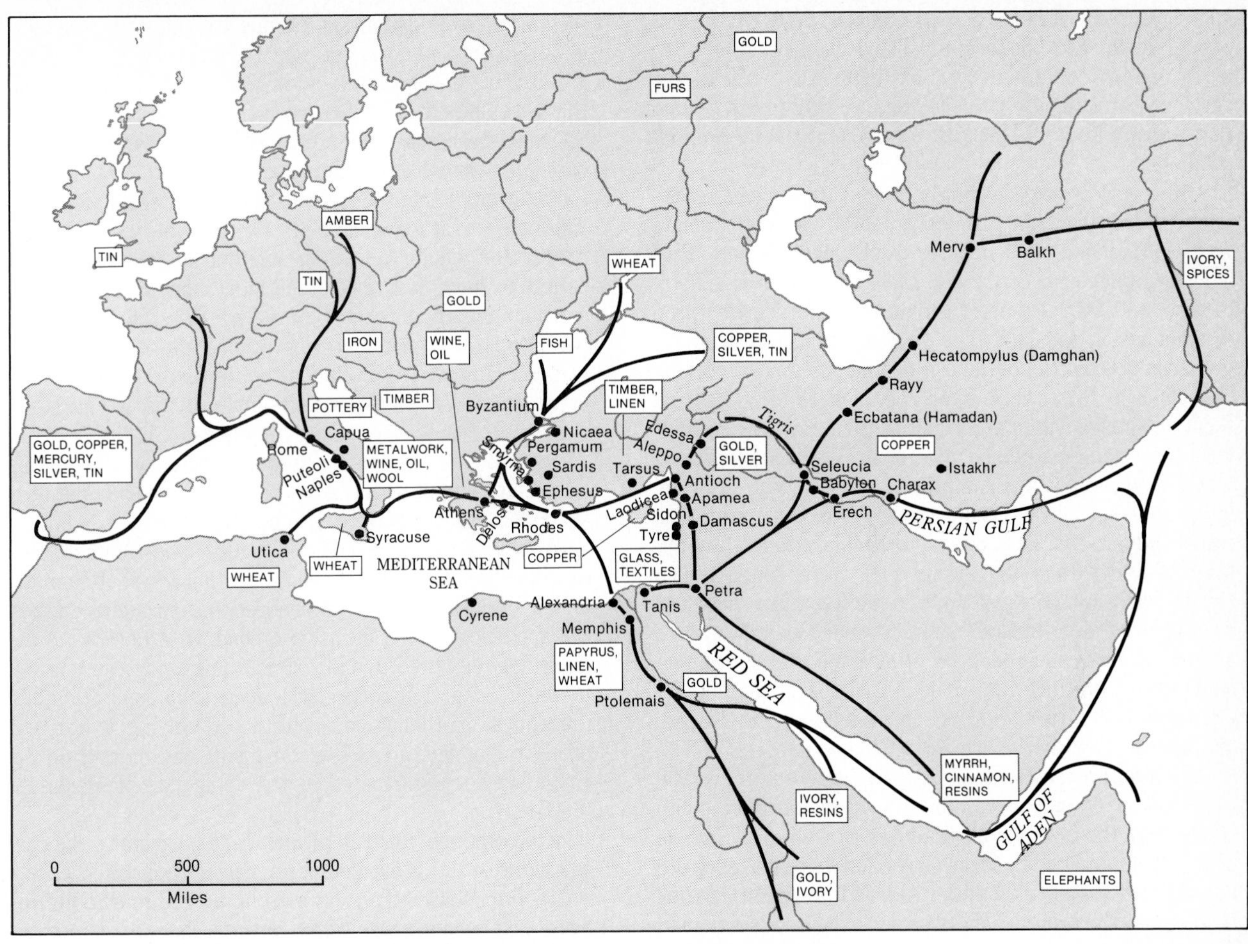

5.3 Trade in the Hellenistic World, c. 145 B.C.

the Greek historian, joined a military expedition that seems to have sailed down the western coast of Africa as far as southern Morocco. Another traveler, Pytheas, set off on a journey from the Greek city of Massilia (modern Marseilles) in 320 B.C. that took him as far north as the Arctic. From his description he seems to have reached either Iceland or the northern coast of Norway.

ALEXANDRIA: CAPITAL OF THE PTOLEMIES

From the time of its foundation by the great conqueror in 332 B.C., Alexandria became a natural meeting place for the cultures of Europe and Asia. Its planner was Deinocrates, like Alexander a Macedonian. Laid out on a grand scale, its main street was said to be 100 feet wide and lined with shops and bazaars. The principal building complex was the royal palace, which served both as residence of the Ptolemies and seat of government. Surrounded by gardens and fountains, it was principally occupied by the Greek-speaking bureaucrats who administered Ptolemaic Egypt.

The center of Greek culture at Alexandria was the Museum, one of the major intellectual institutions of the ancient world. Within its walls were lecture halls, laboratories, observatories, a dining hall, a park, and a zoo. Its library was said to have contained over half a million scrolls, and its principal librarian was also the head of the whole organization and thus one of the most powerful figures in Alexandria. In some ways the Museum resembled a modern university, except that the scholars and scientists who worked there had no obligation to teach. They were supported by the Ptolemies to pursue their own research and to glorify the royal family.

At first the Greek community tried to keep out the native Egyptians, but as intermarriage became more common, Alexander's dream of fusing cultures became at least in part fulfilled. The Alexandrians came to think of themselves, and be thought of by others, as cosmopolitans, citizens of the world that revolved around their city. They were notorious for their rowdiness, always ready for a spectacle, fond of noisy demonstrations, rude to foreigners, arrogant and opinionated. The Ptolemies kept them more or less contented by constructing race tracks and parks and staging lavish public festivals and sports events that were often the pretext for violent street demonstrations.

Only the Jews of Alexandria, one of the largest settlements of the Diaspora (the settlement of the Jews outside Palestine), maintained their cultural independence. Ptolemy I had encouraged the establishment of a Jewish community, and by the time of Ptolemy III there were three synagogues in the city. The Jewish population lived together in one district of the city and had its own governing council. The Jews were given the right to be judged by their own magistrates according to their own law, a privilege that brought some hostility from Greek Alexandrians who felt that religion was a private matter. With time the Jews came to speak Greek, and the Old Testament was translated into that language, a version known as the Septuagint. Services at the synagogues were conducted in Greek, and many Jews took Greek names, such as Theophilus ("lover of God"). The Jews of Alexandria were allowed to own land and were often employed as tax collecters but were rarely involved in trade or moneylending. On several occasions Jewish generals led Egyptian forces, and Jewish mercenaries were not unknown.

Much of the activity at Alexandria centered around the harbor, one of the most international of its times, with traffic from the Nile and the Red Sea as well as the whole of the Mediterranean. Great quays and warehouses were constructed there, as well as Alexandria's most famous monument, the Pharos. This was a vast lighthouse, named after the small island on which it stood at the mouth of the harbor. The Pharos was 440 feet tall, and the beam of light from its lantern was intensified by a series of reflectors. A marvel of the latest technology, it became an apt symbol of the city whose port it illuminated.

There are few traces of Ptolemaic Alexandria today; owing to a change in sea level, most of the ancient city is underwater. The tomb of Alexander, a pilgrimage center for centuries, has never been found, and the Pharos was destroyed by an earthquake in the fourteenth century A.D. Yet the memory of the city's glamor and cultural activity has not altogether faded, nor has its power to fuse different cultures. One of the greatest modern Greek poets, Constantine Cavafy (A.D. 1863–1933), lived there, and much of his work evokes the cosmopolitan world of Hellenistic Alexandria.

Hellenistic Science and Religion

By the time of Alexander, the Greeks had discovered two basic principles of science: the use of mathematics as a means of investigating natural phenomena and the idea of establishing general truths by practical research. Both of these were applied, if at times somewhat haphazardly, in the development of Hellenistic science.

The astronomer Aristarchus of Samos (early third century B.C.) wrote a treatise on the size of the sun and the moon, arguing that the sun was the center of the universe. This was regarded as impiety by most of his contemporaries, for whom the earth and human existence were central to their view of life. The most influential Hellenistic astronomer, Hipparchus (flourished 161–126 B.C.), proposed a rival theory involving cyclical movements of the planets. Hipparchus produced the first work on trigonometry, *The Table of Chords;* discovered the irregular occurrence of equinoxes; and compiled a catalog of some 850 stars. The geocentric theory eventually received its classic statement in the *Almagest* of Claudius Ptolemy, a second-century A.D. Greek scholar.

An even more remarkable figure was Eratosthenes (c. 275–194 B.C.), the head of the library at Alexandria under Ptolemy III, who measured the circumference of the earth, calculated by using a shadow to determine the angle between the Egyptian cities of Alexandria and Aswan to within 1 percent accuracy, a successful application of a theoretical mathematical system for solving a practical problem. Interest in accurate mapping and measuring the earth had been stimulated by the conquests of Alexander the Great.

Eratosthenes' calculation was made possible by the earlier work of the great geometer Euclid (flourished c. 300 B.C.). Euclid also wrote on astronomy and music, but his major achievement was *The Elements,* the most important work on geometry in antiquity. One of the most popular textbooks of all time, it was translated into Hebrew, Latin, Arabic, and western languages and has remained useful up to our time. A little later Archimedes of Syracuse worked on the geometry of cylinders and spheres and in the process established the mathematical value of pi (3.14), as had been done in India.

ARCHIMEDES OF SYRACUSE: PRACTICAL SCIENCE IN THE ANCIENT WORLD

Perhaps the greatest figure in Hellenistic science, Archimedes (c. 287–212 B.C.) was born at Syracuse in Sicily. After spending a period of research at Alexandria, he returned to Syracuse to become chief scientific adviser to King Hieron II (265–215 B.C.). He wrote on geometry and calculus and considered that his greatest work was in theoretical mathematics. On his tomb was engraved the figure of a sphere within a cylinder, a symbol of his concern for pure, abstract form.

Yet Archimedes' chief claims to fame—he is surely the only mathematician in history to have acquired a legendary reputation—are based on the practical use to which he put his knowledge. The inventor of the science of hydrostatics, the measurement and use of waterpower, he made a planetarium, worked by water, to represent the movements of the sun and planets around the stationary earth. He developed pulleys and a drilling system to pump out ships and to drain the fields of the Nile delta after flooding. The archetypal absentminded scientist, he was, it was said, too forgetful to eat; and when he allegedly discovered the concept of gravity by noticing the water he displaced in his bathtub, it is said that he leaped out and ran naked through the streets, crying "Eureka," Greek for "I have found it." When Hieron had constructed a huge ship, the *Syracusia,* Archimedes found a way of launching it and then said to the king: "Find me a place to stand and I shall move the world."

In mathematics his achievements include the invention of a system for expressing extremely large numbers and the solution of various problems relating to the cube. Although most of his work was done at Syracuse, he corresponded with the mathematicians working at Alexandria. A letter to Eratosthenes there included a complex mathematical analysis described in the form of an elegaic poem. Like many of his contemporaries, he applied his theories to the study of astronomy, and his planetarium still survived in the time of Cicero, 200 years later.

All Archimedes' skill was needed in 215 B.C., when Syracuse was besieged by the Romans. He spent his time inventing ways to defend the city, including iron gates that caught up the Roman soldiers as they advanced toward the walls and lifted them into the air and pulleys for raising huge stones or lumps of lead to be dropped on enemy ships. Finally, in 212 an outbreak of malaria undermined the morale of both Romans and Syracusans, and the city, which the Athenians had failed to take 200 years earlier, was forced to surrender. It is said that when Archimedes realized that his beloved Syracuse was about to fall, "he wept much." The Roman soldiers, storming the city, killed him by accident. Archimedes' career became symbolic of the achievements of the Hellenistic scientists; a profoundly original thinker, he was also famous for his patriotism.

Health and Medicine

The father of Greek medicine, Hippocrates, was born on the island of Cos in the mid-fifth century B.C. and traveled widely in the Greek world. His writings include case studies of various illnesses that show his concern with the practical details of curing invalids. Doctors still subscribe to the Hippocratic Oath, which prescribes a physician's ethical responsibility. Hippocrates' successors were more interested in research, which often involved dissection. According to the Roman scholar Celsus (early first century

Greek Medicine

In the following extract, taken from his work on epidemics, Hippocrates describes his approach to the treatment of illness.

These are the things observed in disease from which we have learned to judge them, studying the general nature of mankind as well as the peculiarities of the individual, the disease as well as the patients, the measures taken and the physician who prescribed them. Our judgment is easier or harder in proportion to our knowledge of these matters. First of all, there is the general climate and any local peculiarities of geography and weather. Then there is the particular patient—his habits and way of life, his occupation, his age; his words, manner of speaking, talkativeness, silence; his disposition; his sleep or lack of it, the time and nature of his dreams, his gestures, his tears. Thirdly, from the onset of the disease we must consider the movements of the bowels and the urine, the spitting and vomiting; we must observe the causes of each stage in the progress of the disease, and likewise their effects, and how it finally reaches a favorable end or death. During its course we must study the patient's sweats and chills, coughs and sneezes, hiccoughs and breathing, belching and gas, and bleeding and piles. From our observation of these we must then decide what course the disease will take next.

Source: P. MacKendrick and H. M. Howe, eds., *Classics in Translation* (Madison: University of Wisconsin Press, 1966), vol. 1, p. 311.

A.D.), who wrote a book about Hellenistic medicine, doctors not only dissected corpses to study their entrails but also practiced human vivisection on criminals. Whether this is true or not, Hellenistic doctors made important discoveries concerning digestion and the vascular system.

Ruler Cults and Mystery Religions

Interest in the workings of the body did not preclude a concern for more spiritual matters, and the Hellenistic age saw a number of fundamental changes in the nature of Greek religion. From the time of Homer, traditional beliefs had centered around the 12 Olympian gods, deities such as Zeus and Athena, who were thought to live on Mount Olympus in northern Greece. The Greeks thought of their gods as like themselves, distinguished only by their powers and their immortality, and they came to symbolize various human attributes: Ares, the war god, personified aggression; Aphrodite, sexual love; and so on. Over time a wide variety of local cults sprang up, and the concept of the original deities became blurred by the variations of regional practices. By the fifth century B.C. educated Greeks had begun to doubt the existence of the traditional gods. Temples were still built and rituals celebrated, but the old beliefs began to lose their power. When the Greeks came into contact with the enormous variety of Asian religions, fundamental changes occurred.

The first major development was initiated by Alexander, who claimed to be descended from Hercules and Achilles and in 324 B.C. ordered the Greek states to pay him "godlike honors." The subsequent practice of ruler worship became a feature of many Hellenistic kingdoms. In Egypt, where from time immemorial the people had been accustomed to think of their pharaoh as the incarnation of the sun god, Ptolemy I began by deifying Alexander, and his son deified both his father and himself. From then on the reigning monarch automatically became a god, and the Seleucids soon followed the example of their Egyptian rivals.

Clearly, these ruler cults served political purposes, reinforcing the power and prestige not only of the kings but of their dynasties as well. It is doubtful that they satisfied religious needs on any broad scale, and the conquering Macedonians and Greeks, far from exporting Greek religion to Asia, found themselves subscribing to Asian and Egyptian religions, which in many cases they carried back to Greece. The most popular cult was that of the Egyptian deities Sarapis and Isis. Sarapis was invented by Ptolemy I, who adapted the cult of Osiris, the Egyptian god of the underworld, to Greek tastes. Sarapis was a god of healing and a protector of travelers, and by the second century he was worshiped as far west as Sicily. Isis, his wife, was even more important, offering the promise of life after death to all of her initiates who had undergone certain mysterious rituals.

Other "mystery cults" also flourished, as did the practice of magic and astrology. The Greeks, with their tendency to religious eclecticism, were naturally attracted by the emotional emphasis in much of what they found. Others were drawn to the mystery cults, with their focus on the afterlife, because they offered hope in a period when the economic condition of many people had deteriorated. At the same time one of the few Greek cults that developed and spread throughout the Hellenistic period was that of Tyche, or chance, a force beyond control or understanding that dictated the fate of human existence. Yet paradoxically, the sheer variety of cults and religions, from the Syrian Hadad to the Phrygian Sabazios to the Anatolian Great Mother Cybele, made the ground fertile for the development of monotheism. Hadad, after all, represented Zeus in another context, and the sun god Apollo and the Egyptian sun god Helios were clearly two versions of the same idea. Thus all gods, Greek and non-Greek, might be regarded as aspects of a single universal deity.

These various strands of belief encountered the monistic world view of Aristotle and his successors, particularly Zeno of Elea, to produce the philosophical conception of a single god. This god, as developed by the school of philosophy known as Stoicism, was an object of contemplation rather than worship. Nonetheless, Stoic divinity was a significant element in the idea of universal salvation.

The one people in the Hellenistic world who already practiced a monotheistic religion were the Hebrews. Following the period of Babylonian captivity described in Chapter 1, the Hebrews had scattered throughout Asia, a process of dispersal known as the Diaspora, and had established settlements alongside those of other religions. Orthodox Jewish belief was essentially exclusive, however, and Hebrew communities were appalled at the concept of ruler worship, which inevitably brought them into conflict with the authorities. One of the consequences was the uprising of Judas Maccabaeus and his followers from 173 to 164 B.C. against their Seleucid rulers, a rebellion still commemorated in the annual Jewish festival of Hanukkah. Elsewhere in Asia, Jewish settlements were more peaceful. We have already met the Jews of Alexandria, and earlier Seleucid rulers had encouraged Jewish immigration into the western part of their kingdom, Lydia and Phrygia. The Jewish community of the Greek island of Delos was able to build its own synagogue on land that had once been dedicated to Apollo. In general the Jews of the Diaspora continued to look to Jerusalem as their holy city and to pay an annual tax for the upkeep of the temple there. Nevertheless, contacts between the wide range of Hellenistic religious thought and Orthodox Judaism inevitably affected both sides; in turn, each was to play a part in the formation of Christianity.

The Changing Status of Women

As we have seen, the social life of women in classical Greek society was essentially restricted to the household. Even in fifth-century art, there seems to have been little interest in women or their lives. The ideal form of beauty was largely represented by the male nude, and women were rarely depicted nude before the fourth century. It is true that at the performances of Greek tragedies the audience, which may have included women, would see powerful female characters such as Clytemnestra and Electra who often behaved more forcefully than the men whom they dominated. Yet their roles were played by males.

By the end of the fifth century the general upheaval at all levels of society brought forward new artistic and intellectual concerns. Yet it cannot be said that women's role changed to any significant degree; indeed, the turmoil of the age, together with the population movements of Alexander's time and the subsequent Hellenistic period, probably strengthened the traditional patriarchal family unit. However, late classical art and literature began to show interest in women as women.

One of the earliest examples of this can be found in Euripides' play *Medea,* probably first performed in 431 B.C. The play describes how Medea, abandoned by her husband Jason for a new bride, avenges herself by killing first the prospective wife and then her own two children. In the eyes of an Athenian audience, Medea labors under two crushing disadvantages: she is both a woman and a foreigner. As such she is denied her basic rights; she is married to a Greek, Jason, and has two children by him, but Athenian law did not recognize children by foreign wives as citizens. Thus Jason has no responsibility when he abandons her for a Greek wife and thereby legitimizes his children. The deserted Medea expresses all the rage, frustration, hopelessness, and loneliness that she feels as a woman. Ironically, Euripides' contemporaries, anxious to preserve the status quo, branded him as a mysogynist, or hater of women.

By the fourth century B.C. sculptors had begun to turn to the naked female form to express concepts of ideal beauty. The most famous example was Praxiteles' much imitated Aphrodite of Cnidus. The statue combines a goddess's dignity with a clearly erotic message. We see her while she is bathing; recognizing the intrusion, she covers herself modestly with one hand—thereby drawing the viewer's attention precisely to what she seeks to conceal.

Throughout the Hellenistic period the female nude remained one of the most popular artistic subjects. In smaller statuettes, Hellenistic artists seem to have enjoyed showing various aspects of the private lives of women, from the two girls intent on their game of knuckleball to the elegant lady from Tanagra, out for a stroll. Women in public are described as well by Theocritus (c. 310–250 B.C.) in a poem set in Alexandria. Two women from Syr-

Women with a fan. The figurine comes from Tanagra in Boeotia, where examples of these clay statuettes were first found. [Staatliche Museen, East Berlin]

acuse have moved to the big city and become suburban housewives; Theocritus describes their walk around town on a festival day and records their gossip and their comments on the various sights. It is inconceivable that so witty, realistic, and familiar a note could have been sounded in the fifth century, whose writers show little or no interest in women's daily life.

Change in the status of women was thus slow but perceptible. In terms of their legal and economic rights, the old barriers remained, but the Hellenistic kingdoms, with their constant evolution, made it possible for women of extraordinary character to achieve power. Arsinoe II, the wife of Ptolemy II (283–244 B.C.), instituted the custom of having the queen's portrait appear on the coinage as well as her husband's, and both she and her mother wore crowns. In the wars between Egypt and the Seleucids (276–272 B.C.) her generalship apparently succeeded in leading the Egyptian forces to victory. Not only was Arsinoe deified, but she also had a separate priestess for her own worship. Arsinoe and other Hellenistic queens and princesses began to play an increasing cultural role as well. Berenice, wife of Ptolemy III (246–221 B.C.), corresponded with the leading poet of the day, Callimachus (c. 305–c. 240 B.C.), and Stratonice, the wife of Antiochus I (280–261 B.C.), helped to build the art collection at Delos.

Following such aristocratic examples, other women began to write and publish and even to appear in public. The poetess Aristodama of Smyrna traveled throughout Greece in the mid-third century, giving recitals and receiving honors; her brother went along as business manager. By the end of the Hellenistic period there were even clubs for women, on the lines of similar organizations for men, at Alexandria and Athens. Perhaps most important was the development of two new schools of philosophy that actively encouraged the participation of women at their meetings and made no distinction between the sexes: Stoicism and Epicureanism.

Hellenistic Women

These Hellenistic inscriptions throw light on the improving status of women in that period. The first records the gratitude of the city of Lamia to the poetess Aristodama for her public readings; in the second, King Antiochus III establishes a state cult in the name of his wife.

Good fortune. The people of Lamia decreed: Whereas Aristodama, daughter of Amyntas of Smyrna in Ionia, an epic poetess, came to the city and gave several readings of her own poems in which she made appropriate mention of the Aetolian nation and the ancestors of the people . . . , showing zeal in her declamation, that she be a *proxenos* [protector and informal diplomatic representative] of the city and a benefactor, and that citizenship, the right to acquire land and property, grazing rights, exemption from reprisals, and safety by land and sea in peace or in war be granted to her and her children and her property for all time together with all the grants made to other *proxenoi* and benefactors. To . . . her brother and his children there shall be rights of *proxenia,* citizenship and freedom from reprisals.

King Antiochus to Anaximbrotus, greeting. As we desired to increase still further the honor of our sister-queen Laodice . . . we have now decided that, just as there are appointed throughout the kingdom high-priests of our cult, so there shall be established in the same districts high-priestesses of her also, who shall wear golden crowns bearing her image and whose names shall be mentioned in contracts after those of the high-priests of our ancestors and of us.

Source: F. W. Walbank, *The Hellenistic World* (Cambridge, Mass.: Harvard University Press, 1982), pp. 73, 216.

Later Greek Philosophy: Stoicism, Epicureanism, and Cynicism

The three major schools of philosophy to emerge from the Hellenistic age are important not only for their own period but also for their subsequent effect on the development of Roman intellectual life. All represent attempts to see human existence in terms that avoid the anthropomorphic deities (gods portrayed in human form) of traditional religions and seek to appeal to the intellect rather than the emotions. Furthermore, they all address the same problem: how to relate to the universe when the traditional values symbolized by the polis have disintegrated. The end they seek is the same, oneness with the universe, but their means are different. Stoicism aimed at achieving balance and self-control, Epicureanism favored the contemplative life, and Cynicism rejected the world and worldliness completely.

The most influential of the three was Stoicism. Its founder, Zeno (335–263 B.C.), came to Athens in 313 and set up a school in a lecture hall of the Painted Stoa, or portico, of the Athenian marketplace, from which the word *Stoic* derives. The Stoics believed that reason ruled the universe and that divine providence protected the good from suffering evil. The path to virtue lay in wanting only things that a human was capable of controlling. As a result, wealth, power, or good health—all of which are affected by the accidents of fate—had to be shunned. To the Stoics all individuals were to be regarded as equal, and equally dependent on divine providence.

One of the most important later Stoic writers is Epictetus (A.D. c. 55–c. 135), a former slave who established a school of philosophy first in Rome and then in Greece. In his *Handbook* Epictetus advocates total trust in providence, even in the face of misfortune. He saw the philosopher as speaking for providence, "taking the human race for his children." One of his followers, the Roman emperor Marcus Aurelius (A.D. 121–180), shows us how difficult it was to live up to such high expectations. An active military campaigner and effective imperial administrator, Marcus Aurelius tried to combine the practical nature of his work with his Stoic theories. In his *Meditations,* written when he was on military service, he wrote: "Tell yourself every morning, 'Today I shall meet the officious, the ungrateful, the bullying, the treacherous, the envious, the selfish. All of them behave like this because they do not know the difference between good and bad.' "

The system of philosophy expounded by Epicurus (341–270 B.C.) was very different. In 306 he settled in Athens and founded his school. Its pupils included women and slaves, and all students shared a common life including regular discussions and a monthly banquet. The school was designed not only to teach an integrated curriculum but to function as a publishing house, distributing textbooks as a means to spread Epicurean views.

For Epicurus, the guiding principle and aim of human actions is to maximize pleasure and avoid pain. Deities, should they exist, have no role in human affairs or in nature. Consequently, our lives unfold without fear of such unknown forces as divine retribution. His view of matter, which followed that of the Atomists of the fifth century, offers an exclusively physical explanation of the universe as composed of atoms and space. Atoms, which are solid, have size, shape, and mass but cannot be divided or destroyed. (The Greek work *atomos* means "unsplittable.") Atoms join together by random movements in space to form complex structures free from divine interference. Our power to affect or change our lives is therefore extremely limited; hence we should serenely accept what life brings—including disasters such as earthquakes and disease, for they are beyond human control. Epicurus believed that when we die, the atoms of which our bodies are composed separate, leaving intact neither body nor mind. Because no aspect of humanity is immortal, we should not fear death. Unlike Stoics such as Marcus Aurelius, who was actively engaged in the world, the Epicureans believed in acquiring happiness by leading lives of worldly renunciation and tranquillity. Epicurean "pleasure" consisted of freedom from pain and anxiety through the loss of attachment to success or ambition. Epicurus taught that the highest aim in life is *ataraxia,* or freedom from disturbance.

The founder of the Cynic movement, which was never strictly a school of philosophy, was Diogenes of Sinope (c. 400–c. 325 B.C.). He taught by his own example the virtues of an ascetic life, complete freedom of speech, and shamelessness of action; this last won him his nickname of the Cynic ("the dog"). Diogenes had a number of followers in the early Hellenistic period, but interest in Cynicism declined in the second and first centuries. It revived during the Roman Empire, when it was cultivated as an alternative to Stoicism.

Unlike the other two philosophies, Cynicism has little intellectual content, for its very point was to demonstrate that life can be lived at a minimum level of material, emotional, and spiritual needs. Diogenes' disciple Crates of Thebes expressed it thusly:

> ***There is a city Pera [a beggar's bag] in the***
> ***midst of wine-dark vapor,***
> ***Fair, fruitful, passing squalid, owning nought,***
> ***Into which sails no fool or parasite***
> ***Or glutton, slave of sensual appetite,***
> ***But thyme it bears, garlic, and figs and***
> ***loaves,***
> ***For which things' sake men do not fight with***
> ***each other***
> ***Or stand to arms for money or for fame*** [1]

The social effect of Cynicism was considerable in the increasingly unstable world of the later Roman Empire, and it may have served as the forerunner of the ascetic, monastic life of the early Christian church.

The cultural and artistic developments described in the first part of this chapter had mostly occurred in fifth- and fourth-century Athens, a polis with a citizen body of no more than 50,000. Greek culture was fundamentally urban, and thus it spread rapidly throughout Egypt, western Asia, and even into India during the cosmopolitan Hellenistic Age. The conquerors, rulers, traders, and colonizers who flocked to the east were themselves transformed by the rich cultural traditions of their subject peoples and allies, and the result was cultural blending on a scale hitherto unknown in history. By the time the main center of power moved to the western Mediterranean and, more specifically, to Rome, Hellenic culture had become familiar to millions of people throughout southern Europe, Asia, and North Africa. Indeed, the Roman Empire, in enlarging and uniting the diverse kingdoms and peoples of the Hellenistic world, continued the spread of a cultural tradition formed in classical Greece and established it firmly as the foundation of Western civilization.

Notes

1. Diogenes, *Laertius,* 6:85, trans. R. D. Hicks (Cambridge, Mass.: Harvard University Press, 1931), vol. 2, p. 89.

Suggestions for Further Reading

Barnes, J. *Aristotle.* Oxford: Oxford University Press, 1982.

Burkert, W. *Greek Religion.* Cambridge, Mass.: Harvard University Press, 1985.

Casson, L. *Travel in the Ancient World.* London: Allen & Unwin, 1974.

Cawkwell, G. *Philip of Macedon.* Boston: Faber & Faber, 1978.

Finley, M. I., ed. *The Legacy of Greece: A New Appraisal.* Oxford: Clarendon Press, 1981.

Hammond, N. G. L. *Alexander the Great: King, Commander and Statesman.* London: Chatto & Windus, 1981.

Haynes, D. *Greek Art and the Idea of Freedom.* London: Thames & Hudson, 1981.

Kirk, G. S., and Raven, J. E. *The Pre-Socratic Philosophers: A Critical History with a Selection of Texts,* 2d ed. Cambridge: Cambridge University Press, 1983.

Lefkowitz, M. R., and Fant, M. B. *Women in Greece and Rome.* Toronto: University of Toronto Press, 1978.

Lesky, A. *Greek Tragic Poetry,* 3d ed., trans. M. Dillon. New Haven, Conn.: Yale University Press, 1983.

Lloyd, G. E. R. *The Revolutions of Wisdom: Studies in the Claims and Practice of Ancient Greek Science.* Berkeley: University of California Press, 1987.

MacDowell, D. M. *The Law in Classical Athens.* London: Thames & Hudson, 1978.

Marrou, H. I. *A History of Education in Antiquity.* Madison: University of Wisconsin Press, 1982.

Morford, M. P. O., and Lenardon, P. J. *Classical Mythology,* 2d ed. New York: Longman, 1977.

Onians, J. *Art and Thought in the Hellenistic Age: The Greek World View, 350–50 B.C.* London: Thames & Hudson, 1979.

Pollitt, J. J. *Art and Experience in Classical Greece.* Cambridge: Cambridge University Press, 1972.

Rist, J. M., ed. *The Stoics.* Berkeley: University of California Press, 1978.

Staveley, E. S. *Greek and Roman Voting and Elections.* Ithaca, N.Y.: Cornell University Press, 1972.

Walbank, F. W. *The Hellenistic World.* Cambridge, Mass.: Harvard University Press, 1982.

Wycherley, R. E. *The Stones of Athens.* Princeton, N.J.: Princeton University Press, 1978.

CHAPTER · 6

The Romans

Throughout much of Asia and North Africa as well as the West, the Romans have left an indelible mark. In law, politics, religion, language, and the arts, Roman culture spread throughout an empire that stretched from the Atlantic to western Asia and from North Africa to England. The alphabet in use throughout much of our world was derived from the Roman alphabet, and the various Romance languages, such as Italian and French, are derived from Latin. The Western calendar is a modified form of one adapted from an Egyptian calendar by Julius Caesar in 46 B.C. Rome advanced fundamental political concepts, especially the republican form of government, that have influenced numerous modern states. The Romans developed sophisticated law and jurisprudence that served as the foundation of modern continental European legal systems as well as those of the areas Europeans colonized, especially in Africa and Asia. Roman law had an impact on the English common law; much of it was employed in formulating the canon law of the Roman Catholic church; and all international and maritime law is based on it. Even the road network of modern Europe and the Middle East is based on one planned and built 2,000 years ago by the Romans.

Detail of lower bands of Trajan's Column, Rome, showing the bearded river god of the Danube and the Romans' pontoon bridge. [Leonard von Matt/Rapho Guillumette/Photo Researchers]

Rome's tremendous influence on world culture was in part due to the hardworking and dedicated temperament of the Romans, who from the beginning of their rise to power envisioned their task as one of divinely inspired world domination. In fulfilling this vision, they carried their culture throughout much of the ancient world. Through the Romanization of diverse peoples and cultures, the Romans were able to transmit ideas they had acquired from others as well as those that they developed themselves. In particular, the two great streams of Western culture, the classical and the Judeo-Christian, spread throughout the empire. In assessing their own cultural achievements, the Romans were uncharacteristically modest. They seem to have believed that their virtues lay in efficient rule and success on the battlefield rather than aesthetic and intellectual achievements. Rome's self-appointed task was to rule the known world.

The history of Rome began with the traditional foundation of the city in the mid-eighth century B.C., but almost at once it fell under the domination of another people of ancient Italy, the Etruscans. Rome's subsequent rise to power was made possible by the impact of Etruscan rule.

Italy Before Rome

Although it was a rich period culturally in the eastern Mediterranean world, in the Bronze Age Italian settlements remained small agricultural communities untouched by outside contacts save for an occasional Mycenaean expedition in search of minerals. With the dawning of the Iron Age around 1000 B.C., however, manufacturing communities began to develop that generally shared a common culture. This culture is called Villanovan, after the village of Villanova outside Bologna in central Italy, where the first discovery of an early Iron Age settlement in Italy was made in the nineteenth century A.D. Among the characteristics of Villanovan culture was cremation of the dead; ashes were placed in urns, which were then buried in pits dug in the ground, together with funerary objects such as bronze and iron jewelry, harness parts, tools, and utensils.

The gradual emergence of civilization in Italy was given new impetus around the late eighth century B.C., when Greek colonizers arrived in the south and on Sicily. In the valley of the river Tiber, in central Italy, farmers and shepherds belonging to a group of tribes known as the Latins founded small villages. One of them was Rome. Meanwhile, to the north of this area a new culture, the Etruscan, emerged.

6.1 Etruria

The Etruscans

As early as Roman times scholars began to question the identity, origins, and language of the Etruscans. By 700 B.C. these people had settled in central Italy, in what was later called Tuscany. There is considerable doubt, however, as to whether they were of foreign origin or a native Italian people with a more highly developed culture. In most cases the principal Etruscan cities developed where Villanovan communities had previously existed, which would seem to support the latter opinion. Yet the ancient Greeks and Romans, with few exceptions, were convinced that the Etruscans had migrated to Italy from western Asia, perhaps from Lydia, an ancient kingdom in what is now Turkey. Much of their social life and art was strikingly Eastern in character.

As is clear from the ornate funerary objects found in mid-seventh-century tombs, the Etruscans were a rich and technologically sophisticated people from the beginning of their history. Their commercial connections included the Greek cities of southern Italy and the Phoenician colony of Carthage in North Africa. Indeed, throughout the seventh and sixth centuries in the western Mediterranean, the three principal trade rivals, the Etruscans, the Greeks, and the Carthaginians, formed a constantly changing series of alliances. The high point of Etruscan success came in 540 B.C. when, with Carthaginian help, they defeated the Greeks at Alalia and drove them out of the island of Corsica, off the coast of Tuscany. The price of their victory, however, was that their erstwhile collaborators, the Carthaginians, obtained control of the nearby island of Sardinia, a rich source of iron and other minerals that had formerly been in Etruscan hands.

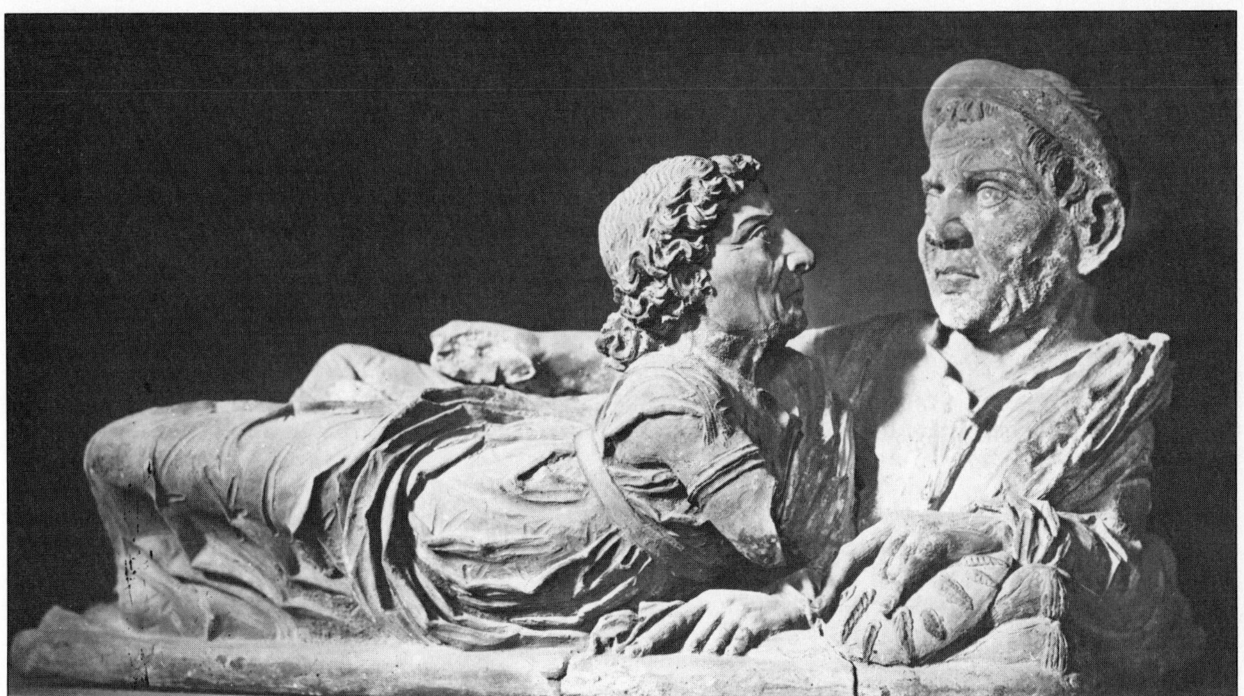

Lid of an Etruscan funerary urn depicting the couple whose ashes it contains. Note the characteristic Etruscan concern for vividness of facial expression and lack of interest in proportions. [Allinari/Art Resource]

The Greeks had their revenge when, in 474 B.C., a Syracusan fleet destroyed Etruscan forces off the coast at Cumae and effectively put an end to any Etruscan influence in southern Italy.

By then the Etruscans had already lost one of their strongholds in central Italy, Rome itself, which they had occupied from around 616 B.C. In 510 the Etruscan rulers of Rome were driven out by the Romans, and centuries of Etruscan decline began. The principal Etruscan cities nearest to Rome were conquered one by one: Veii in 396, Cerveteri in 353, and Tarquinia, the richest Etruscan center, in 351. The northern Etruscans submitted to the Romans without resistance, and in the wars of the third century in which the Romans fought and finally destroyed Carthage, the Etruscans provided support.

By the first century B.C. the Etruscans had been awarded the right of Roman citizenship and became absorbed into the Roman state. It is perhaps surprising that a people who had once been one of the richest and most active in the Mediterranean should have declined so rapidly. A partial explanation may be found in the nature of Etruscan society, which was divided into a small hereditary aristocracy in control of the wealth and a large body of slaves and peasant farmers. Such a social structure, lacking flexibility, functioned successfully in the relatively stable conditions of the seventh and sixth centuries. With the changing economic conditions produced by Roman expansion, however, the small number of rich Etruscan families were unable to hold their own, let alone compete against the increasingly prosperous Romans. The pronounced gloominess of late Etruscan art suggests that the people feared their own demise.

Early Rome

The early history of Rome is shrouded in legend and tradition. The Romans themselves celebrated the foundation of their city on April 21, although there were different and irreconcilable accounts of who the actual founders had been. Modern archaeological research has done much to clarify the early stages of Roman history, but uncertainties remain, and it may never be possible to establish the precise chronology.

From Monarchy to Republic

Recent archaeological finds of Bronze Age pottery have shown that a small community probably existed on or near Rome's Capitoline hill in the second millennium B.C., but there is no real evidence of continuity of occupation, and the Iron Age settlements of the eighth century probably represent a new beginning. The Romans of later times, with characteristic attention to detail, dated the foundation of their city to 753, and the tradition coincides closely with the archaeological evidence. Like other Latins, the first Romans were probably farmers and shepherds, and the simple huts discovered on the seven hills that surround Rome are similar to those of other Latin tribes to the south and east. The fertile land below was left for grazing.

As the community grew, the slopes of the hills, which were formerly used only as burial sites, became inhabited, and by the end of the seventh century the grazing land had been partially drained and settled. There are also signs of contact with the outside world, notably the importation of pottery and metalwork from neighboring Etruscan cities. Roman historians later endowed their city with a legendary founder, Romulus, who, together with his twin brother Remus, was said to have been born to Rhea Silvia, the daughter of a local king, and the war god Mars. For more than two centuries, according to tradition, the city was ruled by seven kings, first Latin and then Etruscan.

Rome as the Etruscans found it was a small country town. The new rulers built it up considerably. Etruscan engineers drained the marshy central valley and built temples, shrines, and roads. Etruscan craftsmen introduced and developed new skills and established guilds, including those of the bronze workers, goldsmiths, and carpenters. Most important of all, under Etruscan rule the Romans came into contact for the first time with the outside world. From the simple village life of a small community under the leadership of tribal chiefs they took their place in a larger cultural and political context that extended beyond Italy. It took only a century for the Romans to learn the principles of Etruscan technology, expel their former rulers, and begin their climb to power.

The Republic: Conflict and Accommodation

With the expulsion of the Etruscans, the Romans devised a new form of government, abolishing the monarchy and founding a republic. The two principal magistrates, or consuls, were elected by all the male citizens to serve one-year terms. Throughout the first century and a half of the republic they had to be members of the Roman aristocracy. This tradition of rule by the nobility seems to have developed during the period of the monarchy, although its basis is not clear. When Rome's last king was overthrown, the closed groups of families, known as *patricians,* assumed control of the primary political and religious offices and comprised the Senate, the principal advisory body.

The remaining citizens, regardless of their wealth or education, were known as the *plebeians,* or common people. Prosperous and ambitious plebeians, who resented the patricians' political domination, joined with poorer exploited plebeians to force change on the ruling order, although the struggle proved bitter and protracted. By the end of the fifth century a plebeian assembly had evolved that met alongside the Senate in the Forum. The leaders elected by this body, the tribunes, represented plebeian interests and protected them from unjust treatment by state officials.

It was not until 367 B.C., with the passage of the Sexto-Licinian Laws, that plebeians could stand for the consulship. Any man elected to the office automatically ennobled his family, and a mixed patrician-plebeian aristocracy began to develop that encouraged the support of the poorer plebeians by distributing some of the land won in Rome's conquest of Italy. The final recognition of the plebeians' formal political equality came in 287 B.C., when the Hortensian Law made decisions of the plebeian assembly binding on the Senate and the Roman people. The patricians' slow and reluctant acceptance of the need for compromise had significant consequences for the growth of Roman power; without adjustment Roman expansion abroad would have been impossible.

The Unification of Italy and the Conquest of the Mediterranean

Between 509 and 266 B.C. the Romans extended their control over the Italian peninsula, aided by a number of factors. The Etruscans failed to mount any serious or organized opposition and, as we have seen, were defeated city by city. The Greeks in southern Italy, like their fellow Greeks in the homeland, were so rent by intercity feuding that they offered little unified resistance. Finally, the Romans turned an event that could have proved catastrophic to their own advantage. In 390 B.C. the Gauls, a northern Celtic people, crossed the Alps and moved into Italy. In the course of their rampaging they laid waste much of central Italy and sacked Rome. By the speed of their recovery, particularly in comparison with their Etruscan and other neighbors, the Romans proved to themselves and their fellow Latins that only they could mount a real defense of the peninsula in the face of foreign invasion.

The Latins had signed a treaty with Rome as early as 493 B.C. The formation of the Latin League in that year guaranteed the Romans some security on their immediate borders and allowed them to deal with the Etruscans and the other peoples of central Italy. The Aequi and the Volsci were defeated in 431, and with the fall of the city of Veii in 396 the collapse of the Etruscans seemed assured.

There remained, however, one of the fiercest of Italian peoples, the Samnites. This warlike tribe came originally from the rugged mountainous country to the east of Rome, but during the fifth century B.C. they had moved south into the rich land in the region below Naples abandoned

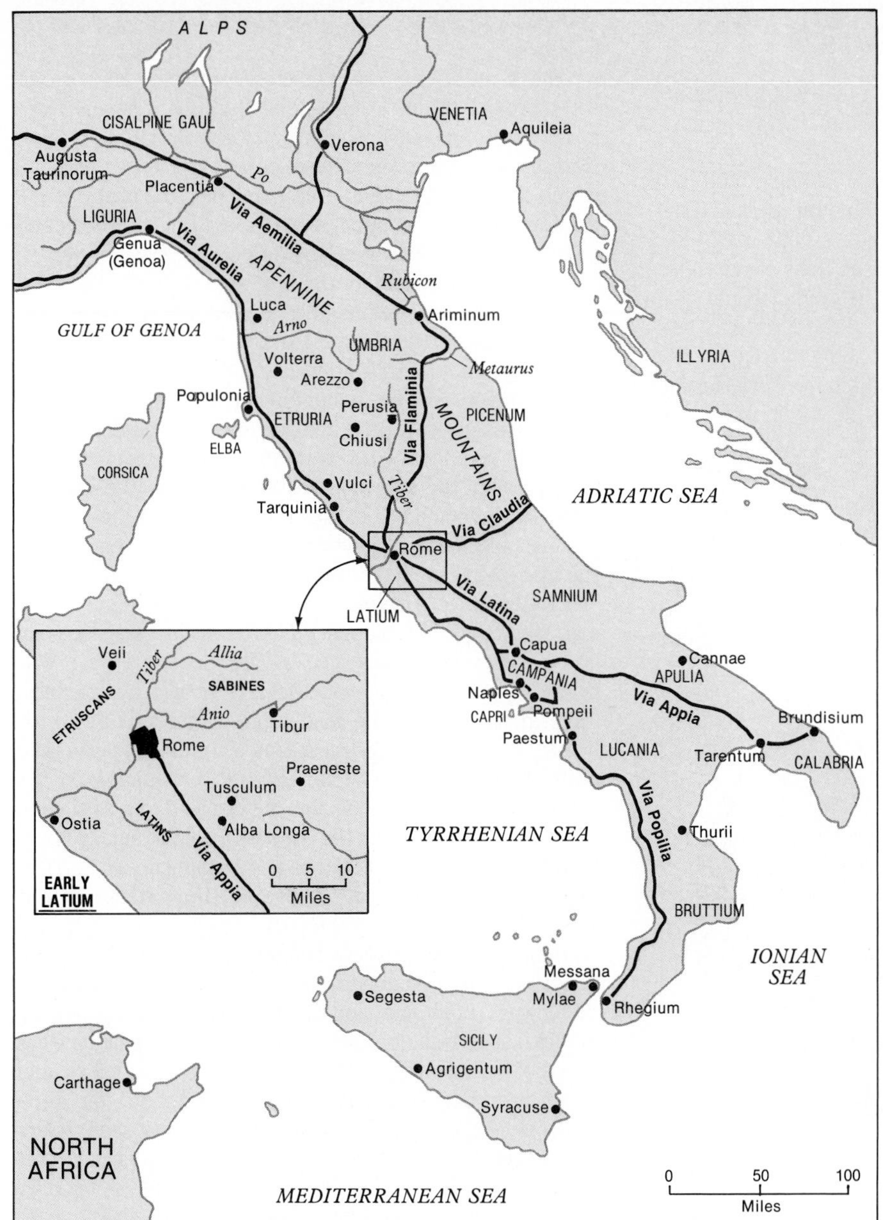

6.2 Roman Italy

by the Etruscans after the battle of Cumae in 474. For a while both Romans and Samnites were sufficiently distracted by problems elsewhere to leave each other in peace, but conflict was inevitable. The Samnite Wars, which lasted intermittently from 325 to 290, constituted the most serious challenge Rome had yet faced to its growing power. By 290, however, the Samnites had been crushed and their principal cities turned into Roman colonies.

That left the Greeks of the south the only independents on the peninsula. Unable to agree on a plan of common defense, they turned to outside help. The city of Tarentum (modern Taranto) invited Pyrrhus, the Greek ruler of the Adriatic Confederation of Epirus, to aid them. One of the other Greek cities in southern Italy, Thurii, appealed for Roman aid against this outside intervention, thereby giving the Romans an excuse to attack. The wars with Pyrrhus lasted from 281 to 272, and by 267 the whole of southern Italy, Greeks and native tribes alike, had submitted to Roman domination.

The Punic Wars

Even the most dedicated Roman soldiers might have been forgiven for seeking a breathing space after so continuous and so complete a conquest. Yet almost immediately the Romans found themselves in a decisive struggle with the most powerful state in the western Mediterranean, Carthage. The Carthaginians, active traders who were dependent on conditions of peace to pursue their commercial enterprises, had made a treaty with the young republic as early as 509 B.C. During the course of the Pyrrhic Wars the Carthaginians in 279 B.C. made another treaty with the Romans in the hope of deterring them from interfering with Carthaginian settlements in Sicily. It was in vain. The inhabitants of the Sicilian Greek city of Messana (modern Messina), a group of Campanian mercenaries formerly in the pay of Syracuse who had deserted some 20 years earlier, invited the Romans to intervene; they accepted. The first of three wars with Carthage began when in 264 the Romans sent a force to Messana. They are called the Punic Wars because Carthage had been founded as a Phoenician colony, and the Latin for Phoenician is *Punicus*.

Gold coins minted at Carthage. [Sheridan/Ancient Art & Architecture Collection, London]

The First Punic War, which lasted from 264 to 241 B.C., proved to the Romans that the Carthaginians were formidable opponents. Fighting for the first time at sea, Roman forces suffered severe losses, and it was only the development of an effective Roman fleet that finally drove the Carthaginians to seek peace. The Romans were in no mood to negotiate a face-saving compromise. A war in which the Romans had for the first time to face the serious possibility of defeat seems to have reinforced both the best and worst aspects of their character. Brave, efficient, self-sacrificing, they won by virtue of their persistence and determination. Having won, though, they arrogantly dictated terms of peace that humiliated Carthage, demanding both the surrender of territory and the payment of a large indemnity. In the following years, moreover, the Romans did what they could to cause trouble between the Carthaginians and their allies, while expanding along the eastern Adriatic shore of Illyria (modern Yugoslavia).

In 218 B.C., hearing that a Roman expedition was marching to Spain to support a revolt against Carthaginian allies, Carthage struck back. The Second Punic War (218–201 B.C.) began with the arrival of a Carthaginian force in Italy under the leadership of perhaps the most brilliant and certainly the most famous of Carthaginian generals, Hannibal (247–183 or 182 B.C.). Counting on the support of the local population, he crossed into Spain and descended on Italy over the Alps with a huge supply train, including elephants, inflicting several painful defeats on Roman forces. The last, at Cannae in 216, virtually annihilated a Roman army.

Hannibal, victory within his grasp, besieged Rome, but he was unable to sustain his momentum. His forces were a long way from home, and the Romans effectively blocked the arrival of reinforcements. The Italian population was still too fearful of Roman reprisals to aid Hannibal, and Rome remained a formidable opponent fighting on home territory. As a result, Hannibal and his troops spent years waiting for the formation of an anti-Roman alliance that never materialized. The Romans seized the opportunity to rebuild their forces and sent a counterexpedition to North Africa to invade Carthaginian territory under the young and ambitious general Scipio.

When the victorious Romans demanded uncompromising peace terms, Hannibal returned with his troops to reinforce the Carthaginians. In 202 the entire Carthaginian army was defeated at Zama in North Africa and forced to surrender, and peace was concluded the following year. Carthage was divested of its entire empire, including Spain, and was left with only a small strip of territory around the city itself, in modern Tunisia. It was forced to pay a crippling indemnity and permanently to disband its armed forces. The once proud Carthaginians were reduced to impotence, and the expression "Carthaginian peace" entered the language, denoting a dictated settlement designed to crush an opponent permanently.

Hannibal: A Roman View

Livy's description of Hannibal was written some 200 years after the Second Punic War, yet it vividly conveys the Romans' wary respect for the Carthaginian general.

Hannibal was dispatched to Spain and on his first appearance attracted the interest of the army. The old soldiers thought that a younger Hamilcar had come back to them. They saw in him the same features, the same liveliness of expression, the same fire in the eyes. But shortly his resemblance to his father was only the least among their reasons for devotion to him. Never was an individual more perfectly suited both to obedience and to command. It would be hard to say whether the commander or the army loved him more. There was no one whom Hasdrubal preferred to put in charge of any assignment which demanded bravery and vigor; nor was there any leader under whom the army fought with greater confidence and daring. When danger was to be faced it was Hannibal whose spirit was the boldest, and in a crisis his strategy was the shrewdest. Under no hardship did his energy wane or his spirits flag. He could face heat or cold with equal endurance. His appetite for food and drink were controlled by hunger and not by pleasure. His waking and sleeping were not fixed by day and night. What time remained after the task in hand was done he gave to sleep, and this without any need of soft bed or quiet. Many a time he could be seen lying on the ground among the sentries and pickets off duty, covered only with a soldier's cloak. His dress was no different from that of his fellow-soldiers, but his weapons and his horses were of the finest. He was the best among cavalry and infantry alike, always the first to go into battle and the last to leave any clash of arms.

These qualities were matched by equally great flaws of character: inhuman cruelty and a worse than Punic treachery which had no regard for the truth, held nothing sacred, was stopped by no fear of the gods or scruple at breach of faith. With such an endowment of faults and virtues he served for three years in Spain under the command of Hasdrubal, omitting no experience or training suitable for a man destined to become a great military leader.

Source: P. MacKendrick and H. M. Howe, eds., *Classics in Translation* (Madison: University of Wisconsin Press, 1966), vol. 2, p. 296.

Conquests in the East

Throughout the following century the Romans continued to fight sporadically in Spain, where a series of brutal campaigns established Roman control. The helpless Carthaginians, who had attracted Roman enmity by regaining some of their former prosperity, were completely destroyed in the Third Punic War of 149–146 B.C. Their city was leveled, and its inhabitants were sold into slavery.

In theory, Roman involvement in the affairs of Greece and the Asian kingdoms was for the purpose of defending and even "liberating" the Greeks from their Hellenistic rulers. Already by the end of the third century B.C. Greek art and literature had become fashionable at Rome. Victory over the Carthaginians had fed the Romans' pride and arrogance. Triumphant in the western Mediterranean, they looked to the rich kingdoms of Asia as both potential enemies and attractive conquests. Allegedly advocating the cause of Greek freedom, first in Macedon and then in Asia, Roman forces fought a series of wars to gain control there.

The first step was to secure the Adriatic Sea, which was begun in the First Illyrian War of 229–228 B.C. In the following years the Romans became involved in a series of wars with Philip V of Macedon and Antiochus III of the Seleucid empire, and by 200 B.C. they were committed in the Hellenistic east on a massive scale. The next half century saw complex battles and negotiations in western Asia, in which territories of the Hellenistic kingdoms either gained their independence or were merged with other states. The Greek poleis threw off Macedonian domination in 197 B.C., thanks to Roman assistance.

In the case of Pergamum, King Eumenes decided that

collaboration offered better prospects than opposition. Pergamum continued to serve Roman interests in Asia as a client state until 133 B.C., when Attalus III willed it to Rome in a last attempt to win favorable treatment for his people. Any belief the Greeks may have had that Roman campaigns against Macedon or the Seleucid empire of Syria were for their benefit was shattered when a defensive league of Greek poleis was crushed at Pydna in 168 B.C. In 146 B.C. another Greek army that refused to accept Roman "liberation" was defeated at Corinth. The Romans razed the city and shipped its artworks to Rome. Other temporary beneficiaries of Roman aid also paid with their freedom. The Romans supported the Jewish revolt of the Maccabees in 167 B.C.; two centuries later, a Roman army would destroy the last vestiges of Jewish independence and burn the temple in Jerusalem.

The Crisis of the Republic

By the end of the second century B.C. the Romans had constructed a huge empire of subject regions, client states, and nominally free kingdoms that stretched from Spain to western Asia. They had been so busy acquiring their empire, however, that they had failed to develop effective systems of administration, and the consequences were often chaotic. Provincial governors were frequently inefficient and corrupt. To complicate matters, political instability was mounting at Rome. The patricians and wealthy plebeians, enriched by their conquests, began to compete in piling up fortunes derived either from property in Italy or from the provinces.

The victories in the Punic Wars had enhanced the Senate's prestige. During the many years of fighting it had been necessary for some authority to make decisions quickly and efficiently, and that task had fallen to the Senate. Among the powers it assumed was the right to prolong magistrates' terms of office when conditions of war made it necessary. Furthermore, by the end of the wars the Senate had taken control of foreign policy, and the provincial governors it appointed thus had unofficial license to extort what they could from their subjects. Laws against bribery were passed in 181 and 159, but to little effect; Rome's opponent in North Africa, King Jugurtha, was advised that "at Rome everything is for sale."

The poorer plebeians had lost rather than gained from the continued warfare. Rome's new territories had been won by part-time soldiers, eager to return to their farms or businesses. In order to hold on to their conquests, the Romans now needed to maintain conscript troops outside Italy, but in many cases plebeians were unwilling to serve. On some occasions the tribune, as defender of plebeian rights, stepped in to arrest the consul conducting the conscription. In other cases the conscript had little choice. Many small plebeian farms had been swallowed up by the growth of large estates or *latifundia,* whose wealthy owners bought public land and worked it by means of slaves made available by the wars. Thus the poorer plebeians who had survived economically by cultivating their plots had little choice other than to serve abroad or to join the growing number of unemployed in Rome. The urban mob that these social conditions produced was to prove a new and powerful force in Roman political life.

As the government of the empire grew ever more complex, divisions began to appear among the wealthy as well, both patrician and plebeian. Public contracts for tax collecting, construction work, or other projects were issued by the Senate. Because they were supposed to oversee the contracted work, senators were debarred from appointing themselves and undertaking these contracts in their own name. The rich landowners who were not members of the Senate thus became the principal group to benefit from the large sums of money spent in and received from the provinces. This new social and economic class was known as the *equestrians,* or cavalry. The provision of a horse at public expense had been a mark of honor from earlier times; now it became a property qualification to distinguish between senators, with their inherited wealth, and the new class of equestrians. Of course, the formal exclusion of senators from lucrative work in the provinces, especially tax collecting, scarcely impeded their own accumulation of wealth through bribery, payoffs, and the like. With the spoils of three continents at their disposal, the patrician and equestrian classes reaped immense fortunes. Meanwhile, the gap between the propertied elite and the plebeians continued to widen.

The Gracchi and the Rebellion of Spartacus

By the last third of the second century B.C. Rome faced a number of serious and interrelated problems. The great estates required increasing numbers of slave workers, while free agricultural laborers were all but disappearing as a class. There was little chance of agrarian reform as long as the members of the Senate saw it as contrary to their own interests. In 133 B.C., faced with apparent deadlock, the tribune Tiberius Gracchus attempted to introduce major changes. He recommended that the government reclaim state land that had been illegally occupied, mostly by owners of large estates. A proposed commission would distribute the repossessed farmholdings to the landless. Tiberius' plan was approved by a plebeian assembly made unusually large by the crowds of poor ex-farmers who had poured into Rome to vote for the measure. To achieve this, however, Tiberius had bypassed the Senate and illegally blocked the veto of a fellow tribune. Wealthy landowners claimed that he had acted unconstitutionally. He ran for a second term to implement the new law but was clubbed to death in street fighting on election day.

At the Niaux cave in what is now southwestern France, prehistoric hunters apparently threw spears at this painting of a bison, probably in the expectation of ensuring a successful hunt. [c. 15,000–13,000 B.C., 50″ (127 cm.) long; Sheridan/Ancient Art and Architecture Collection]

THE VISUAL EXPERIENCE

From Antiquity to the Early Middle Ages

The peoples of the world's earliest civilizations shared many common experiences, including a search for the meaning of life and the hidden workings of nature. Their religious beliefs, literature, and social customs bear witness to this quest, but nowhere is it more penetratingly revealed than in their art. From the cave paintings of prehistory to the statuary of classical China and Greece, the peoples of antiquity expressed their varied beliefs in such transcendental forces as gods and evil spirits. At the same time, however, they exhibited a marked interest in things natural and human, as reflected in their fascination with animals and the heavens, fate and responsibility, music and death. The determination to tame nature and understand human existence, so vividly depicted in their art, is not only a priceless heritage but also the driving force of our own civilization.

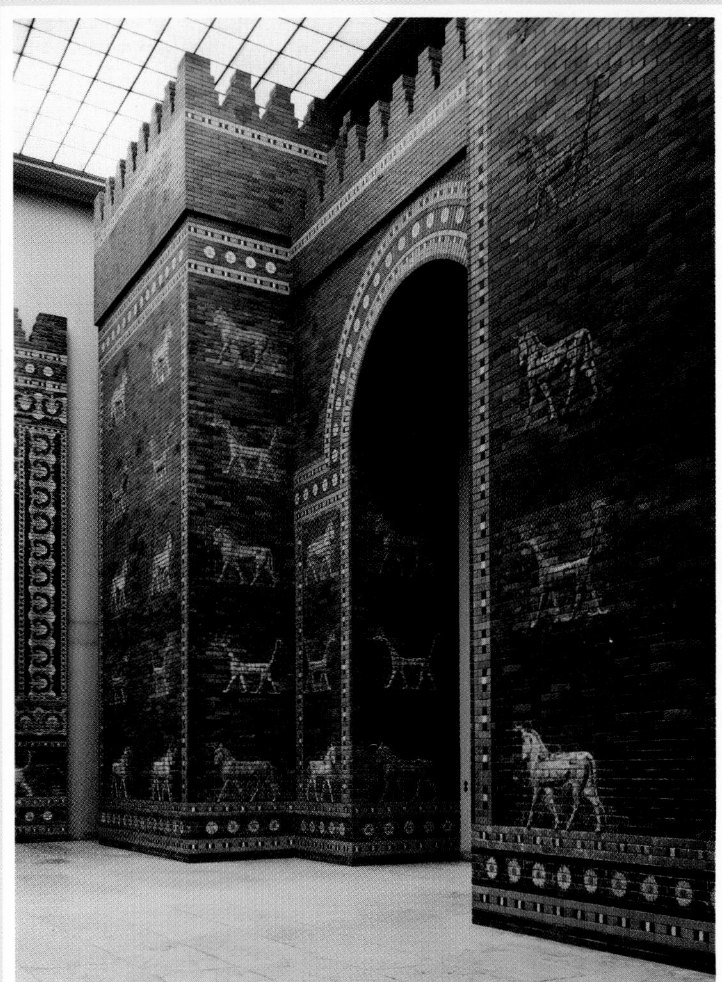

Worshippers in ancient Babylon passed through the Ishtar Gate (now restored) en route to the temple complex. The glazed figures of the bull and the dragon depict the gods who were the objects of worship. [c. 575 B.C.; Staatliche Museen zu Berlin, D.D.R.]

The pharaoh Chefren commissioned the Great Sphinx at Giza to guard his tomb. A millennium later, Egyptians revered the 65-foot-tall sculpture as an image of the sun god. [c. 2350 B.C.; Werner Forman Archive, London]

In contrast to some of the rigid and grandiose Mesopotamian and Egyptian statues, those of the Minoans were small and animated. This priestess holds snakes, possibly reflecting Minoan religious rituals. [c. 1600 B.C., $13\frac{1}{2}''$ high; Hirmer Fotoarchiv, Munich]

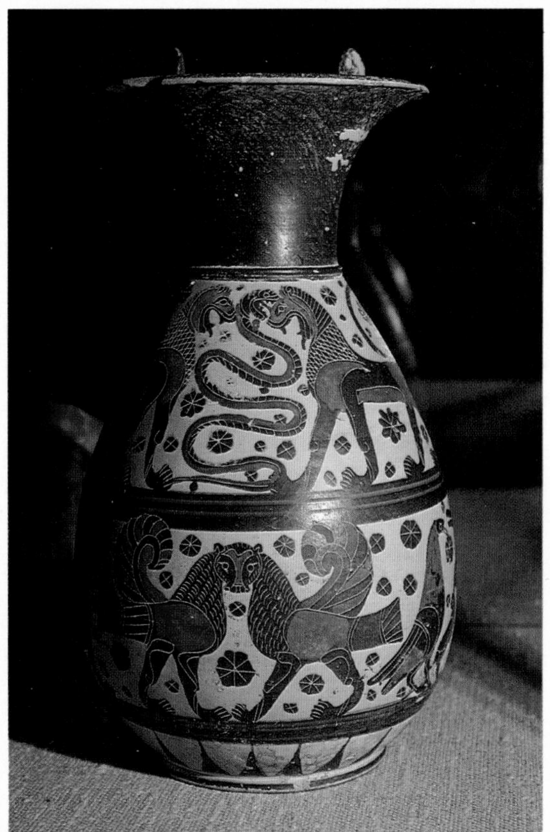

Greek artists shared the interest in animals common among other ancient peoples, and their earliest art forms show the influence of western Asia and Egypt. [7th century B.C.; Sheridan/Ancient Art and Architecture Collection]

This figure of a tree goddess is a fine example of the grace and voluptuousness that Indian sculptors were able to create in stone, even under alien Kushan rule in the second century A.D. [C. M. Dixon, Canterbury, England]

Ch'in Shih Huang Ti was buried in a huge underground tomb near modern Sian with an army of life-size clay figures to guard the approaches. Excavations in the 1970s brought them to light again after more than 2,000 years; each figure is a faithful representation of a real individual. [Chinese Overseas Archaeological Exhibition Corp.]

This painting of a Chinese scholar viewing the moon from his pavilion reflects the Chinese interest in the beauty and wonder of the natural world. [In the tradition of Ma Yuan, Ming dynasty, 15th century; Susan Dirk/Seattle Art Museum]

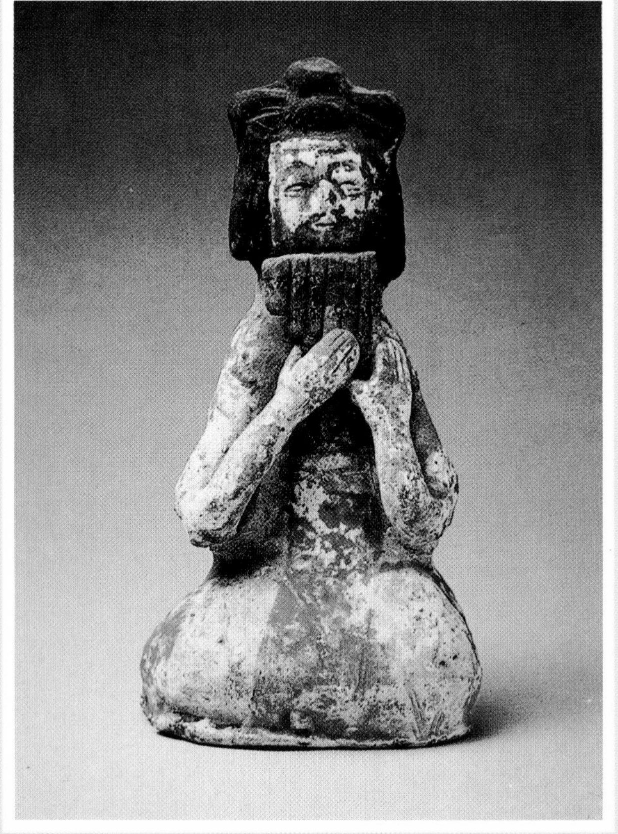

The artistic creativity of ancient cultures was manifest in their music. From paintings and sculpture, such as this pottery figure of a woman playing bamboo pipes, musicologists can learn much about ancient music. [Northern Wei period; Chinese Overseas Archaeological Exhibition Corp.]

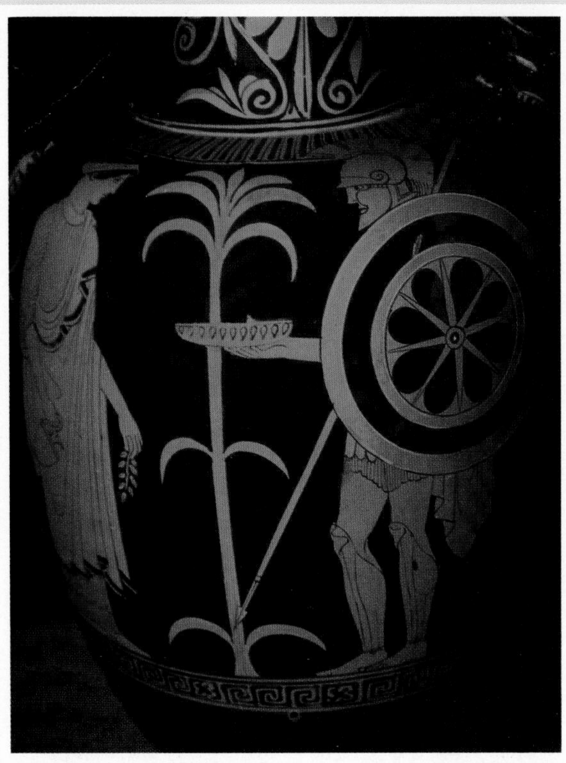

Paintings on classical Greek vases commonly treated religious, military, and social themes, as in this depiction of a warrior about to depart for battle facing a girl with a wine jug and olive branch, the symbol of peace. [5th century B.C.; Sheridan/Ancient Art and Architecture Collection]

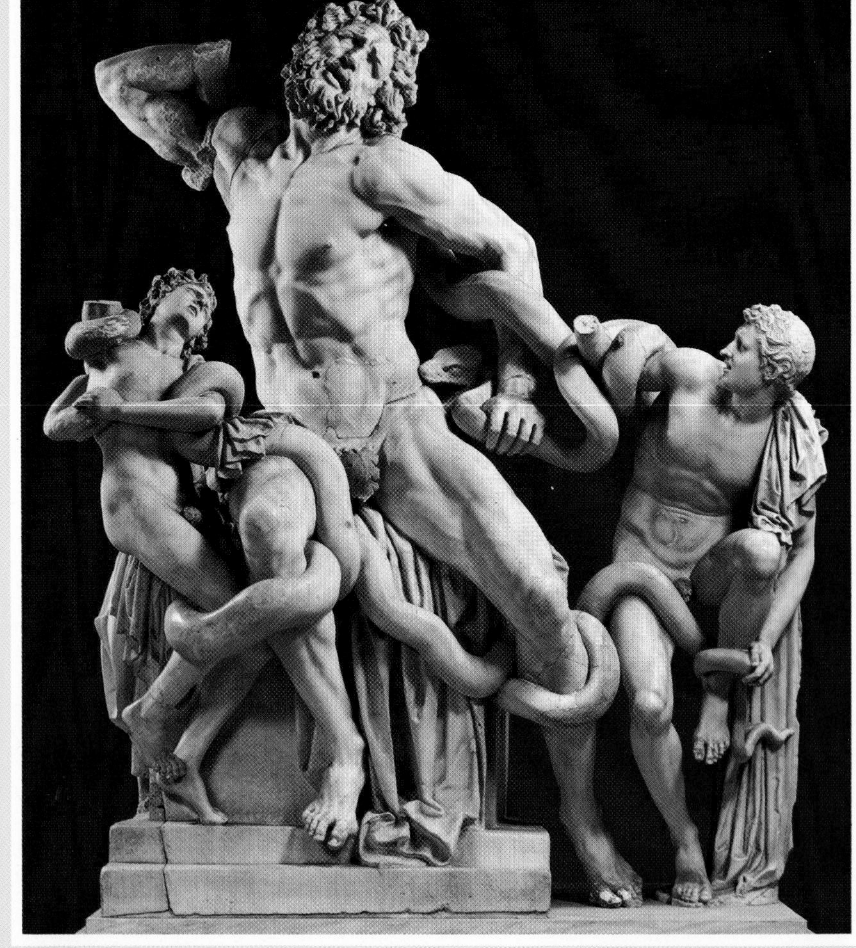

The Greeks were keenly interested in questions of responsibility, fate, and the role of the gods in human affairs. In this sculpture Laocoön, a priest of Troy, and his sons are strangled by serpents, presumably because he angered the god Poseidon by warning the Trojans that the Greeks intended to smuggle themselves into the city in a hollow horse. [c. 100 B.C., marble, 8′ (244 cm.); Scala/Art Resource]

The ancient world regularly blurred the distinction between the human and the divine, usually by describing the gods in human terms. The Byzantines tended to reverse that process by according their rulers an almost divine aura in their art. This mosaic in the church of San Vitale in Ravenna, Italy, depicts the empress Theodora with her attendants. [6th century A.D.; Sheridan/Ancient Art and Architecture Collection]

The blurring of the human and the divine is also apparent in this horseman from Mali in Africa; the statue probably represents a minor deity. [Minneapolis Institute of Arts, gift of Aimee Mott Butler Charitable Trust et al.]

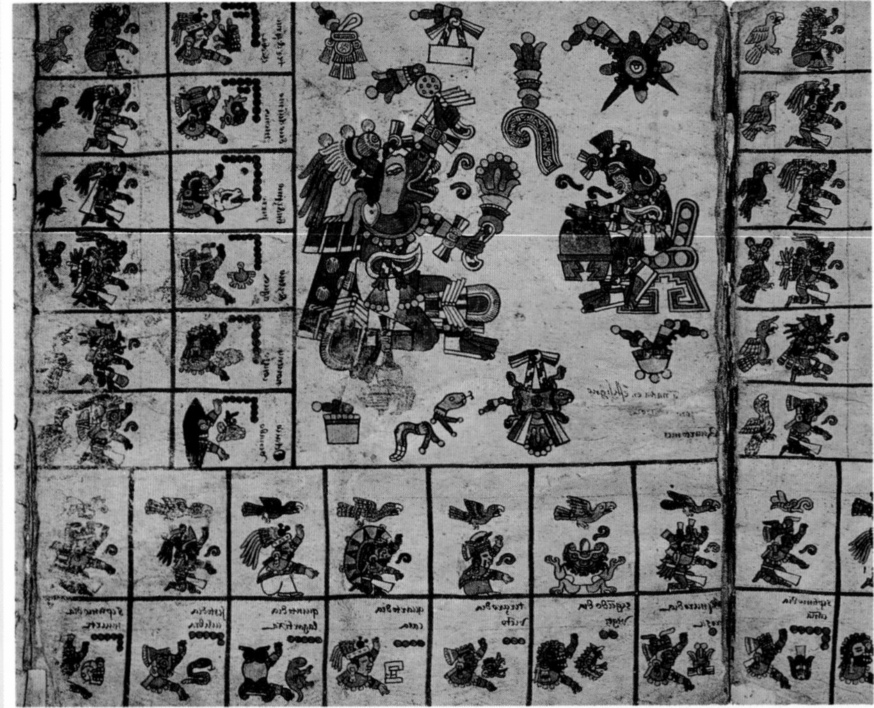

The human quest to understand the natural world soon led to attempts to mark the passage of time, and thus eventually to calendars. Shown here is a detail from an Aztec calendar. [Assemblée Nationale/Bibliothèque de la Chambre des Deputés]

Tiberius' younger brother, Gaius, was elected tribune for 123 B.C., and again for the following year. More cautious than Tiberius, he buttressed his appeal to the plebeians by seeking the support of the equestrians. The right to collect taxes in Roman territory in Asia was for the first time put up for auction at Rome rather than meted out by the Senate, providing equestrians with the opportunity to compete for highly profitable monopolies. At the same time the membership of juries that tried provincial governors for corruption was, at Gaius' suggestion, limited exclusively to equestrians. Governors had always been drawn from the Roman Senate, and this gave the equestrians the chance to play watchdog over provincial administration and protect their own interests. Gaius was threatening the wealthy senatorial landowners, as his brother had done, and despite his attempt to broaden his political base, he met with the same fate: early in 121 he and perhaps as many as 3,000 of his supporters were killed by mobs openly encouraged by the Senate.

The Gracchi demonstrated only too well that a political system that had been devised for a small city 400 years earlier was inadequate for the governance of a vast empire. Furthermore, no ambitious politician could leave out of account two new forces on the political scene: the urban mob and the standing army. The first had been used against the Gracchi. The second, a professional fighting force whose primary loyalty was not to Rome but to whichever general led and paid it, was to play a crucial role in the careers of the next generation of politicians. Indeed, the men who struggled for power right up to the end of the republic—Marius, Sulla, Pompey, and Caesar—were all highly successful field commanders in their own right and could count on the loyalty of their troops.

Two figures, Marius the populist and Sulla the aristocrat, dominated Roman political life from Marius' first consulship in 107 to Sulla's retirement in 79. Fierce opponents, each could claim military successes, Marius in Africa and Sulla in Italy, where the latter played a large part in crushing a revolt by Rome's Italian allies in the so-called Social War of 90–88. Marius' principal contribution to Rome was his reform of recruitment procedures. During his first consulship he abolished the need for members of the army to own property; the poverty-stricken could enlist and be armed at public expense. Those who joined did so not only for the pay but also in the hope that they would receive a grant of land at the end of their service.

Both Sulla and Marius, together with their followers, were responsible for bloody purges among their opponents, which plunged Rome repeatedly into civil war; neither provided even a temporary solution to Rome's real problems. Sulla ruled as dictator until he retired in 79 B.C. This was, in fact, a constitutional position, first created after Hannibal's victory at Cannae; the holder was appointed for six months by the two consuls, with the Senate's advice, to rule the state during an emergency. Sulla imposed a new constitution that attempted a return to the conservative and elitist concepts of the early republic. He doubled the size of the Senate and strengthened its powers, limited the tribunes' right of veto, and abolished their ability to legislate and take legal action. After Sulla stepped down, chaos resumed.

In 73 B.C. a major slave revolt erupted, led by the Thracian gladiator Spartacus. An initial band of 74 men quickly swelled to an army of 70,000, and only massive intervention by the Roman army crushed the rebels. Some 6,000 of them were crucified as a warning to others.

Enslaving prisoners had been a Roman practice since 396, when the citizens of the captured city of Veii were taken to Rome. Throughout the second century B.C. thousands of prisoners were shipped to Italy and put to work on the great estates. Plantation workers generally toiled in chain gangs and were locked up in underground barracks at night, but it was harder to control herdsmen, who had to be left free to tend their flocks. Slave uprisings such as the one led by Spartacus were therefore a continuous threat and made travel through remote agricultural areas unsafe.

In general, the Romans were liberal in granting freedom to domestic slaves, if not in their treatment of them during the years of servitude. Throughout the first century B.C. thousands of slaves were freed by their owners through a process called manumission, which required them to purchase their freedom. Many of them became shopkeepers, artisans, or clerks, although some practiced their skills as teachers or doctors. The freed slaves, or *liberti,* were subject to certain legal restrictions, but their children became full citizens.

Julius Caesar

The principal political contest of the generation following Sulla was between Pompey (106–48 B.C.), who called himself Pompey the Great and appointed himself defender of the Senate, and Julius Caesar (c. 102–44 B.C.). Both men were military commanders as well as politicians. Pompey combined the virtues of his military calling—efficiency and good planning—with lack of principle, deviousness, and personal vanity. Caesar's talents were much more complex and versatile; some have called him Rome's greatest mind. A successful politician and orator and a lucid, elegant prose writer, he was also, as Pompey was not, a genuine political thinker. He was ruthless enough to realize that the only sure way to achieve power was through military force. After making his mark in the politics of the capital between 65 and 62, he left Rome, first to serve as governor in Spain and then, in 58, in Gaul. He remained there for almost ten years and completed the conquest of the region, thereby bringing much of continental Europe north of the Alps into the orbit of Roman civilization.

Before leaving Rome, Caesar ensured his continuing influence by concluding a secret agreement in 59 B.C. to divide the power and patronage of the capital with Pompey and the wealthy businessman Crassus; this pact is known

as the First Triumvirate. Pompey and Caesar cemented their alliance by the marriage of Caesar's daughter, Julia, to Pompey—a match that proved unexpectedly happy, although Julia was considerably younger than her husband. During his period in Gaul, however, Crassus and Julia died, and Pompey, distrustful of the increasingly popular Caesar, forged close ties with the aristocrats in the Senate. When in January 49 B.C. the Senate commanded Caesar to relinquish his command, he illegally ordered his army to cross the Rubicon River, the boundary between Gaul and Italy.

Caesar's march to Rome with his victorious army made civil war inevitable. After a brief period of indecision, Pompey and his followers fled to Greece. Caesar followed him and defeated his forces at Pharsalus (48 B.C.). Pompey himself escaped to Egypt, whose ruler decapitated him and sent the embalmed head to Caesar as a means of currying favor. Caesar turned this to patriotic advantage by executing Pompey's murderers and erecting a statue to him in the Senate. Caesar spent the winter in Alexandria, where he entered into a liaison with the young queen of Egypt, Cleopatra. By the time he left, Cleopatra was pregnant. She named her son Caesarion and sent him to Rome. Although Caesar showered Cleopatra with presents and honors, he never returned.

By 46 Caesar had been appointed dictator, which gave him emergency powers to govern for up to six months. As dictator, he set about reorganizing the government both at home and in the provinces. Among his most lasting achievements was the creation of a unified code of civil law. Produced with the help of eminent legal experts, it served as a model for later times. His reformed calendar, based on the research of astronomers at Alexandria, was used in the West until the eighteenth century, and our present one is a modified form of it.

Caesar also launched an ambitious and wide-ranging program of reform. He began an extensive public works program designed in part to take citizens off the welfare rolls and make them less susceptible to the violence that had become commonplace in Rome. To that end also he instituted a police force and relieved the overpopulation of the capital by sending 100,000 citizens into the provinces. He subsidized Italian farmers to restore the agricultural self-sufficiency of the peninsula and undertook the reform of provincial administration. To reduce political opposition, he packed the Senate with his own followers. But his plans had little time to take effect. On March 15, 44 B.C., he was assassinated by a band of senatorial conspirators, and the agony of the republic was prolonged for another 13 years.

A portrait bust of Julius Caesar (late first century B.C.) made in Egypt, perhaps during Caesar's stay with Cleopatra. [Staatliche Museen zu Berlin, German Democratic Republic]

The End of the Republic

In the turmoil that followed Caesar's assassination, Mark Antony (83–30 B.C.), his former lieutenant, organized the attempt to avenge his death. He was joined by Caesar's young great-nephew, Octavius (63 B.C.–A.D. 14), whom Caesar had named in his will as his heir. On Caesar's death Octavius had arrived in Rome from the provinces to assume power. It was soon clear that Antony and Octavian (the name he now took) were bound to clash. After the defeat of Caesar's assassins in 42 B.C. at Philippi in western Greece, an uneasy settlement placed Octavian in charge of the western provinces while Antony was dispatched to the east. To strengthen their ties and to protect Antony from the enticement of Cleopatra, whom he had met on an earlier tour of duty, he was persuaded to marry Octavia, Octavian's sister. A woman of firmness and tact, she seems to have curbed Antony's tendencies to sen-

View of the Roman Forum, with the Arch of Titus in the distance. [Graziano Paiella, Rome]

suality and self-indulgence and maintained peaceful relations between her new husband and Octavian. From 39 to 37 Octavia and Anthony administered the eastern provinces from their base in Athens.

Three years of domestic tranquillity were enough for Antony. After a disastrous military operation in Syria, he escaped to Alexandria, where in 34 B.C. he made his union with Cleopatra official by the so-called Donations of Alexandria. This news was predictably exploited at Rome by Octavian, who depicted his rival as degenerate and corrupt. With Antony out of Rome, Octavian declared war on Egypt.

Cleopatra had become a symbol of Eastern beauty, seductive and therefore dangerous, yet she was concerned more with power than with love. She was a Macedonian by birth and thus the successor of Alexander the Great, and her native language was Greek. Yet she also considered herself to be the successor of the pharaohs and a descendant of the sun god Re. Like Alexander, she dreamed of uniting East and West in one great empire. Her plan was to conquer Rome and with its aid create a global kingdom. But Egypt, though wealthy, had virtually no military strength. It was her hope to overthrow the Roman Empire by provoking civil war among the Romans, but to achieve this goal she needed a Roman ally. Her liaison with Mark Antony was a gamble that, without the equally strong resistance of Octavian, might well have produced military success.

The end for Cleopatra and Mark Antony came in 31 B.C. at the naval battle of Actium in western Greece. When Antony's forces deserted, he and Cleopatra escaped to Egypt, where Antony saw no honorable alternative to suicide. Cleopatra hesitated. A meeting was arranged between her and Octavian, perhaps so that she could make a final desperate attempt to win him over, but she failed. Knowing that Octavian wanted only to display and humiliate her at Rome, she killed herself with a deadly serpent smuggled to her in a basket of figs. Octavian was left as sole leader of the Roman world, and his victory marked the end of the republic.

The Accession of Augustus and the Pax Romana

By the time of the battle of Actium, Rome had suffered more than a century of civil and external war. Political institutions had in large part ceased to function effectively, and much of Italy was in chaos. By the time of Octavian's death in A.D. 14, Rome had acquired a political stability and a commercial success unsurpassed in its history. Augustus—to use the title he assumed in 27 B.C.—formally inaugurated the empire, a period that lasted some 500 years in the West and nearly 1,500 in the East.

Augustus' political achievement was to transform the nature of Roman government while retaining the formal offices and institutions of the republic, including the Senate. He ran for the consulship every year until 23 B.C. and thereafter retained the power of a tribune. Augustus wanted to avoid the impression of authoritarian rule and thus never took the title of king or dictator. Had he retained his title of general, or *imperator,* he would have seemed to rule through military power. He was therefore known simply as *princeps,* or first citizen of the state. His acts were legitimated by the appropriate assembly or magistrates—although Augustus himself controlled the nomination of those whose approval he sought. In his autobiography he claimed that he "transferred the state back into the hands of the Senate and the Roman people." He clearly did nothing of the kind, but his care for preserving the institutions of Roman political life while in fact taking personal command did much to smooth the transition. Moreover, his tactful diplomacy was supported by the moral authority he wielded because of his restoration of stability in the empire.

The economy clearly needed attention. One of the chief problems was the system of taxation that had developed during the last two centuries of the republic. The principal sources of revenue were the provinces, and Augustus authorized new censuses to assess population, assets, and resources. By this means population shifts, agricultural conditions, and commercial enterprises could be regularly evaluated and the tax burden shifted accordingly.

In Italy the principal occupation remained farming. Owners of latifundia were encouraged to diversify their crops to guard against poor years or changes in the market. Many medium-size farms specialized in the production of wine or olive oil, both of which were popular abroad and easy to export. The general rise in living standards produced by the Augustan peace led to a demand for luxury products such as peacocks or pheasants, so even a modest poultry ranch could be profitable. Augustus encouraged agriculture not only for its practical benefits but also as a symbol of the bounty guaranteed by political stability.

Italian industry flourished under Augustus, partly for obvious economic reasons and partly because the emperor seems to have favored businessmen and manufacturers rather than the ingrown, snobbish aristocracy. A style of pottery called Arretine was developed in the ceramics factories of Arezzo and other centers in central Italy; Arre-

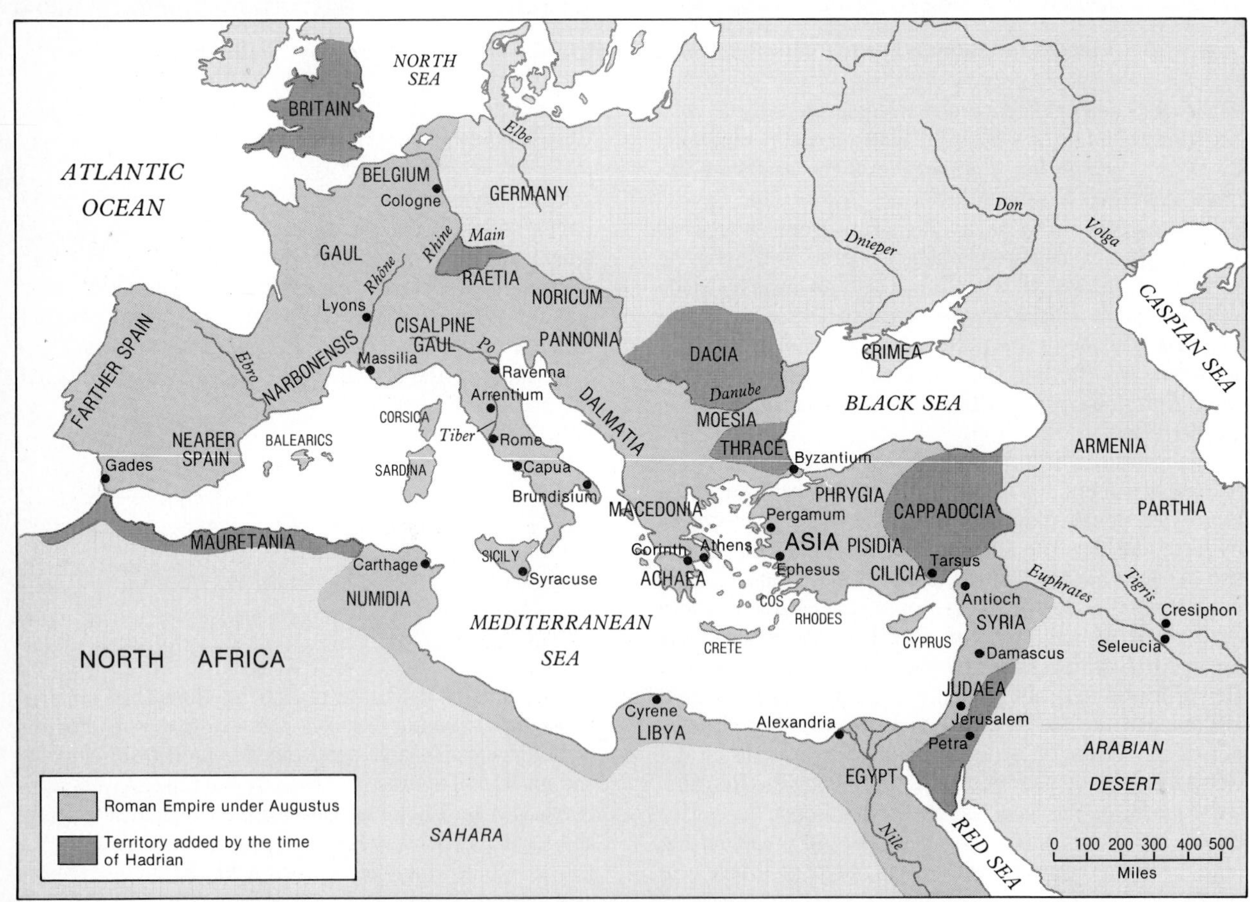

6.3 The Roman Empire

tine vessels were exported throughout the empire. Such demand required new, more efficient methods of production. One of the factories at Arezzo could mix 10,000 gallons of clay at a time, and similar mass production techniques were used for the extraction and working of metals. Furthermore, Augustus' building program throughout Italy stimulated demand for bricks, tiles, and other construction materials.

Augustan legislation stimulated industry and commerce throughout the provinces. Egypt, with its fine sand, became a center for glass manufacture, while Alexandria retained its importance as an international port for the buying and selling of raw materials. With a return to prosperity, the demand for luxury goods such as silk, rare fruits, and fine wines rose sharply. To some extent this could be satisfied by products from the provinces; the Greek island of Cos was famous for its silks, and dates, figs, and plums were imported from Spain. Supply stimulated yet more demand, and Roman traders found themselves exploring ever more distant markets.

In the late first century B.C. Roman sailors discovered that monsoon winds greatly aided the sea journey from Egypt to India. The trip there took some 40 days, and the speed with which commercial links grew is demonstrated by the large quantities of Arretine pottery discovered at ports on India's east coast. The Indian connection was valuable in itself, providing spices, jewels, ivory, and other exotic commodities. More important, it gave the Roman world better access to China, with its production of high-quality silk, than the dangerous overland route that passed through the territory of the warlike Parthians, the inhabitants of northeastern Persia. From the time of Augustus it was possible to transport Chinese products through Afghanistan, down the river Indus, and across the Indian Ocean to Syria and then Rome. Fashionable Romans were thus assured of luxury products, although some political leaders were concerned that the trade in luxury items seriously depleted stocks of gold and silver.

One of Augustus' chief priorities was to stabilize the empire's military and administrative structures. He fixed the permanent size of the army at 25 legions (300,000 men), all directly responsible to himself, and regularized pay, pensions, and length of service to make the military an attractive career. He divided the empire into an inner ring of provinces administered by civil magistrates and officials and frontier provinces under direct military control. Augustus retained Egypt, Rome's vital granary, as a direct imperial estate; he assumed the title of pharaoh and prohibited any senator to set foot on its soil without his consent. But he also restored the Senate to its former standards of birth, wealth, and conduct and gave it a genuine share in the administration of the empire.

Augustus drew a clear distinction between political and administrative control. The former he kept in his own hands; the latter he dispersed as widely as the security of the empire permitted. Thus provincial autonomy and local self-government were stressed, as was respect for ethnic customs and cultures. This enabled Rome to control a very large empire with a minimum of centralized bureaucracy, and that in turn kept taxation at tolerable levels. Local self-government proved Augustus' happiest and most enduring innovation. It enabled the provinces to withstand the effects of erratic or tyrannical rulers and to prosper until the empire weakened in the third century A.D., and the Augustan system began to break down.

Social Legislation

Much of Augustus' social reform was intended to correct the general societal laxity that had developed during the last century of the republic. Comprehensive laws on marriage were introduced that rewarded large families and penalized the single, the childless, and those whose marriages took place after childbearing age. In part the legislation reflected Augustus' attempt to promote the family as a social unit and his concern with the falling population of native Roman citizens. The slaves who had been freed during the previous century represented a foreign element in Italy that the emperor saw as a potential threat. Thus in addition to his encouragement of large families, he had laws passed that specifically limited the number of slaves who could be freed by their masters.

Augustus himself lived simply and unostentatiously, at least in public, and laid great emphasis on duty to the state as well as traditional values and morality. He even exiled his daughter Julia for wanton conduct. High society must have found the new austerity difficult to adapt to, and Augustus' successors had little success in maintaining his high moral tone—nor, in most cases, much inclination to do so.

Augustan Literature and Art

A masterful propagandist, Augustus made full use of the arts to reinforce the impression of peace and prosperity. Much of the art produced at Rome during his reign was official, commissioned by the state to serve government purposes. Yet if he can justly be accused of cultural manipulation, it must be admitted that the art and literature of his age are of the highest quality.

The literary period of Augustan Rome is known as the Golden Age. Perhaps the greatest poet of the age, and one of the most influential figures of the Western literary tradition, was Publius Vergilius Maro, called Vergil (70–19 B.C.). His principal work, the *Aeneid,* an epic poem in 12 books, was commissioned to give the Romans their own national epic, worthy to stand alongside the *Iliad* and the *Odyssey.* It contains passages of patriotic fervor, recounting the mythical founding of Rome by Aeneas, son of Venus, after he fled from the ruins of Troy. Inspired by Homer, Vergil consciously made his epic a Roman counterpart of Homer's works, thus firmly linking the glories of Rome to the Hellenic cultural legacy. An earlier work of Vergil's, the *Georgics,* deals with one of the emperor's favorite themes by praising agriculture and the virtues of family life on the farm, as well as including practical advice on farming, forestry, and raising cattle and horses.

Among the other Roman poets of the period to praise country life was Horace (65–8 B.C.), a personal friend of both Vergil and Augustus, whose private secretary Horace became. A more worldly man than Vergil, Horace combined passion with irony to create a series of short odes that illuminated both Roman politics and his own refined sensibility. The leading prose writer of the time was Livy (59 B.C.–A.D. 17), whose *History of Rome,* also sponsored by Augustus, told the story of Rome's growth from its earliest days.

Just as Vergil consciously evokes memories of the Greek Homer, so Augustan sculptors sought inspiration by transforming Greek themes. The *Augustus of Prima Porta* recalls Polyclitus' *Spearbearer* of almost five centuries earlier, made more active and dominating and clothed, literally and figuratively, in imperial authority. It also tells us how Augustus wanted us to remember him. Carved in the year of his death, when he was 76, it shows him with an almost ageless poise, calm yet alert.

If one word could sum up the many complex aspects of Augustus' legacy to the Roman Empire, it would be peace. Peace is, in fact, the subject of one of the most complex works of art produced during his reign, the *Ara Pacis,* or Altar of Peace. The scenes carved on it combine episodes from Rome's mythic past with depictions of the emperor and his family making their way to the dedication ceremony, at which the altar will be consecrated—not to Jupiter or Mars nor to Augustus himself but to the goddess Peace. It was a fitting monument to his reign, which inaugurated two centuries of relative civil security—the Pax Romana, or Roman Peace.

Augustus' Successors: The Julio-Claudians

The one problem for which Augustus was unable to find a satisfactory solution was the choice of his successor. In the end he was forced to nominate his able but unpopular stepson, Tiberius (A.D. 14–37). The first five emperors, including Augustus himself, were related to one another as members of the Julian and Claudian clans. Thus the principle of hereditary succession was implicitly established, although as early as the reign of Claudius (A.D. 41–54) the right to select the family member was temporarily seized by the army, a precedent that was to prove dangerous.

The Julio-Claudian emperors do not make a particularly good case for the hereditary system of government. Claudius himself was effective enough. A dedicated administrator, he also achieved what even Julius Caesar had failed to do by adding Britain to the empire. Nor did Tiberius altogether deserve the hatred with which his contemporaries regarded him. Whatever his personal idiosyncrasies, which are spelled out in lurid detail by the historians Tacitus (c. 55–117) and Suetonius (c. 69–c. 160), the Augustan peace was maintained throughout his reign.

The other two Julio-Claudians, however, were a very different matter. Gaius, better known as Caligula, or "Little Boots" (a nickname he acquired as a child), came to the throne in A.D. 37 amid general relief at the passing of Tiberius. By the time of his assassination in 41, he had a reputation for criminal insanity that has endured; among his more whimsical acts was declaring a horse his prime minister. If Nero (54–68) surpassed the excesses of Caligula, as in certain respects he did, the greater length of his reign is at least in part responsible. Protected from his worst instincts for the first five years by his mother, Agrippina (whose killing he ordered in 59), he organized a reign of terror that has become legendary. He may not have deliberately started the great fire that destroyed Rome in 64 as legend states, but he certainly took advantage of it to build an immense palace, the so-called Golden House of Nero, and to persecute the Christians, whom he accused of starting the conflagration.

The Flavians and the "Good" Emperors

Nero's assassination was followed in 69 by a year of confusion in which no fewer than four generals made themselves emperor. The final victor, Vespasian (69–79), was the first emperor to die peacefully since Tiberius. A professional soldier, hardworking and conscientious, he did much to repair the economic confusion wrought by Nero and reasserted the Augustan emphasis on peace in the provinces. He also gave Rome one of its most famous monuments by turning an artificial lake that had been made for Nero within the walls of his Golden House into the Colosseum.

Vespasian had little better luck than Augustus in finding a successor. His two sons, Titus and Domitian, were groomed to succeed him. Titus, the elder son, served his father as general in the Roman province of Judea, where disturbances had broken out in the last years of Nero's reign. Vespasian himself had commanded Roman forces in 66, when the Jews of Caesarea and Jerusalem protested their lack of civil equality. The revolt at Caesarea was suppressed, but at Jerusalem the protestors remained active. In 70 Roman forces under Titus finally crushed the revolt, destroyed the temple of the Jews, and abolished the Jewish national council, the Sanhedrin.

By the time of his accession, Titus was known for his cruelty, and his well-publicized love affair with Berenice, sister of the Jewish king Julius Agrippa II, had given Rome a subject for gossip. When he came to power, he proved a modest and popular ruler, but a fever cut short his reign barely two years later. Domitian (81–96) continued his father's policies of maintaining efficient government and improving provincial defenses and administration, but, victim of his own paranoia, he constructed the apparatus of a police state, instituting a complex system of state spies and informers.

Prominent Roman political leaders could take no more. With the approval of the Senate, a group of conspirators determined that an elderly senator of unimpeachable character would be chosen to serve as immediate successor to Domitian. Aided by the Senate, he would select as his successor someone who seemed qualified for the position and adopt him as his son. The scheme worked well. Domitian was assassinated in 96 and replaced by Nerva (96–98), who was doubly qualified by his age (66) and by the fact that he was childless. Nerva in turn adopted one of the most distinguished generals and provincial administrators of his day, Trajan (98–117).

Thus merit rather than birth or brute force was responsible for two outstanding Roman emperors, for Trajan in his turn was to adopt as his successor the able and cultivated Hadrian (117–138). The system of adoption continued in the selection of the next two emperors, Antoninus and Marcus Aurelius. With Trajan and Hadrian, they provided an extended and much needed period of stability. Under Trajan the borders of the empire expanded to their fullest extent, and Hadrian successfully consolidated them. He traveled tirelessly throughout the provinces to see that imperial defenses and administration were strengthened. The reign of Hadrian, perhaps the most gifted and complex of all the emperors, marks a high point of Roman civilization.

LIFE IN THE ROMAN CAPITAL: IMPERIAL POMP AND URBAN SQUALOR

By Hadrian's reign Rome's center had become filled with temples, monuments, and public buildings, many of which have partially withstood the ravages of time, of fifth- and sixth-century invaders, and of Renaissance builders looking for bricks or marble for their own palaces and churches. Roman architecture and engineering have had a lasting effect on later styles. In particular, the Roman use

Life in Imperial Rome

An embittered description of life in imperial Rome was penned by the Roman satirist Juvenal.

So the day goes by with a lovely order of business:
First, this handout; then the forum, the courts of Apollo,
And the triumphal statues, including some lousy Egyptian's,
At the base of which only pissing's permitted.
There they go, the poor souls, old clients, weary and hopeless,
Though the last hope to leave is always that of a dinner,
They must buy cabbage now, and a little kindling to cook it.
Meanwhile, all by himself, on a couch unshared, their good king will
Gobble and guzzle the choicest products of land and ocean.
Down goes a whole estate; from such luxurious tables,
Broad and antique, down goes a whole estate at one sitting.
This will kill parasites off, at least; but who can endure this
Luxury, grudging and cheap? A whole roast boar for one gullet
When good custom decrees this is the fare for a party?
You will get yours pretty soon, when you go and undress in your bathroom,
Trying to ease your gut's distending burden of peacock.
Hence come sudden deaths, too sudden for old men to make wills.
What a good laugh for the town at all of the dinner tables!
Hear the disgruntled friends cheer at the funeral service!

Source: Juvenal, *The Satires*, trans. R. Humphries (Bloomington: Indiana University Press, 1958), p. 22.

of columns, arches, and domes has been widely imitated since the eighteenth century in public building in Europe and the Americas.

One of the greatest domed buildings, the Pantheon, designed by Hadrian himself, was constructed around 126. Its imposing portico (or porch), containing 16 monolithic granite columns, leads into the central rotunda, the roof of which consists of a huge concrete dome. The building is lit only by a central *oculus,* or eye, in the top of the dome. As the sun moves across the sky, its rays travel around the inside of the Pantheon, whose form thus became symbolic of the world itself.

The Forum, where the early political life of the young republic had been concentrated, remained at the heart of the city's activities. During the empire, however, effective political control passed to the emperor and his staff, who lived on the Palatine (from which our word *palace* is derived), the hill overlooking the ancient assembly place of the people. Augustus' house there (which can still be visited) is a surprisingly, if characteristically, modest structure. Domitian, with his obsessive need for protection, began the construction of a huge imperial palace, the Domus Augustana. This palace, extended by his successors, contained its own race track and incorporated a private viewing stand from which the emperor could watch the races in Rome's principal public stadium, the Circus Maximus.

According to tradition, racing and blood sports had been introduced into Rome by the Etruscans. By the time of the empire chariot races and gladiatorial combats were held on a massive scale before a vast public; in its heyday the Circus Maximus had places for more than 300,000 people. Public performers such as charioteers, musicians, and fighters were generally slaves or criminals, since no respectable citizen would perform or compete in public. Of the scandals that helped to turn popular opinion against Nero, the most serious was not his murder of his mother or his wife but his appearance in public as a musician. Prizes were very large; a successful charioteer could easily amass a fortune and become the idol of a rabid fan club. There were four teams, the Reds, Whites, Blues, and Greens, each with its fan club, and rivalry was intense.

The principal stage at Rome for individual gladiatorial contests was the Colosseum, which held 50,000 spectators. Of the three types of gladiators, the Samnite was heavily armed with a long oblong shield, the Thracian re-

The Pantheon, Rome. The inscription, which dates the building from the third consulship of Agrippa (27 B.C.), must have been intended by Hadrian as a tribute to Agrippa's master and friend, Augustus. [Marburg/Art Resource]

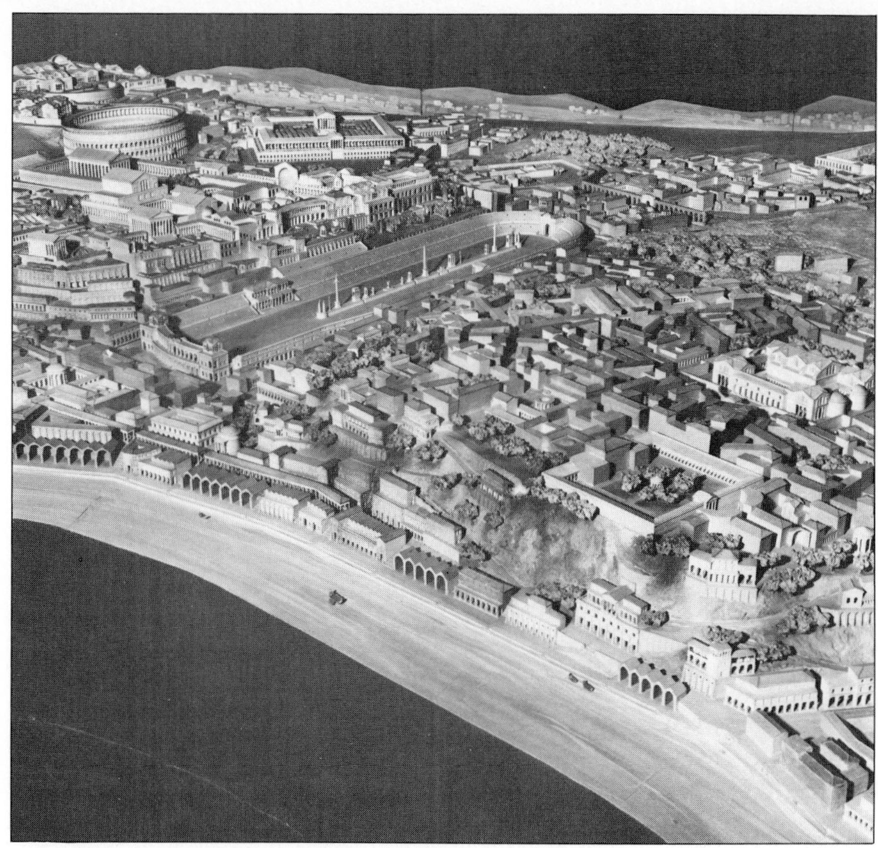

Part of a large plastic scale model of Rome in A.D. 350 showing the Circus Maximus in the center and the Domus Augustana behind. Note the arches of the aqueduct. [Alinari/Art Resource]

lied on a small round shield, and the Retiarius carried only a net and dagger in one hand and a short pronged spear in the other. In general, combats ended with the death or surrender of one of the participants. In the case of surrender it was up to the crowd (or the emperor, if he was present) to decide the loser's fate. As the empire grew and the Romans had access to more exotic creatures, animal contests (either against gladiators or between animals) became increasingly popular. In the "games" of 249 a thousand pairs of gladiators fought, and among the animals killed were 32 elephants, 10 elks, 10 tigers, and 60 lions. Such entertainment reveals a darker side of Roman culture.

Emperors exploited popular tastes by organizing special games, such as the one just described, to keep the urban masses content. This policy of "bread and circuses," by which rulers attempted to control their often unruly subjects, also entailed the construction of centers for the distribution of grain and the sale of basic commodities such as wine and oil at subsidized prices. The provision of cheap grain for the Roman masses had begun as early as the tribunate of Gaius Gracchus (123–122 B.C.). By 58 B.C. free grain was being provided for any citizen who needed it, and this remained the case throughout the history of the empire. The magistracy in charge of the distribution of the grain dole, the Annona, was one of the most important public offices.

Rome also was provided with a plentiful supply of fresh water. A huge system of aqueducts carried pipes through which millions of gallons of water flowed each day; the water provided public fountains and baths as well as the private homes of the well-to-do. The street drains were covered, thereby avoiding the open sewers of earlier times (which, after the fall of Rome, were to become the norm again until the nineteenth century).

For all the ingenuity of its public works, however, imperial Rome was overcrowded, and life must often have been uncomfortable. Most Romans lived in apartment blocks, of which there were some 45,000. Laws regulated the height of these buildings to discourage the construction of unsound structures, but buildings sometimes collapsed, and fire was a continual hazard. The streets were crowded and noisy, and traffic jams were a constant problem: descriptions of the squabbling and brawling between carriage drivers sound all too familiar to the modern big-city dweller. It is little wonder that at weekends and in summer, affluent Romans escaped to their rural villas. Hadrian imported all the convenience of the city to his immense villa at Tivoli, which contained libraries, theaters, baths, and quarters for hundreds of servants.

Life in the Provinces and on the Frontier

The same dependable engineering that provided the capital with water linked it, by means of a vast road network, to the farthest corners of the provinces. Good communications were essential for maintaining efficient government, and Roman roads are the most visible remains of the Roman achievement. The principal roads connecting Rome to other parts of Italy were begun in the fourth century B.C. Rome's armies included builders who surveyed and laid roads for supplies and reinforcements in conquered territories and provinces. By the time their conquest was complete, each province was thus provided with an effective network of communications. The thousands of miles of roads were well maintained and provided with milestones, and in the time of Augustus a column was erected in the Roman Forum that recorded the distances between Rome and the principal cities of the empire.

Provincial Life in Southern Europe, North Africa, and Asia

An empire as vast as that ruled by Trajan and Hadrian encompassed enormous diversities of people, culture, language, and religion. The average Roman soldier or administrator probably felt most at home in Greece or the Greek cities of Asia Minor, where he was surrounded by art and architecture of the kind that had conditioned Roman taste. Athens, although no longer of political significance (its former rival, Corinth, was the capital of the Roman province of Achaea), was always a cultural and intellectual center. Augustus provided it with a fine new marketplace, and Hadrian had a public library built there. Even in the Greek world, however, there were cultural differences. The Greeks, for example, were fond of serious music, which held little interest for the Romans, and they exhibited no enthusiasm for gladiatorial contests. Even Greek theaters had to be adapted for the performance of Roman plays by the construction of a permanent stage set.

Elsewhere in the provinces, where local culture was less developed and new cities were built, the Romans created an environment more to their taste. Many cities in southern France and Spain still have their Roman amphitheaters, and Roman public baths were built throughout the empire. One of the most elaborate sets of baths were those at Lepcis Magna in North Africa that rival even those of the capital for size. Like many other public works, they were paid for by a wealthy private citizen rather than by the state.

The generally mild climate of the Mediterranean region meant that life in the Roman provinces of North Africa, Spain, or western Asia was in many respects similar to that in Italy. Large public squares were adorned with temples and public buildings such as baths and theaters, and private houses often included gardens. The best preserved of these houses can be seen at Pompeii.

POMPEII: LIFE IN A PROVINCIAL TOWN

On August 24, A.D. 79, the volcano Vesuvius that stands above the Bay of Naples erupted. The lava that flowed from it and the pumice and ash that were spewed out buried a number of small towns. The most famous of these is Pompeii, located 10 miles southeast of the volcano. The finds excavated there in the past 250 years provide detailed evidence about life in a provincial town of the period—from the shrines of the religious cults and the houses and gardens to the meals Pompeiians had prepared at the time of the eruption.

Lying some 150 miles south of Rome, Pompeii was a prosperous town of 20,000 people that served both as a commercial center for its region and as a holiday resort for Romans of modest means who sought to escape the heat of summer. It provides an impressive picture of the pleasant but modest lifestyle of the provinces. Houses were spacious and comfortable, and the frescoes that decorated them were often of high quality. Many houses had private gardens, sheltered from the noise of the streets. The furniture, tableware, and other household goods were often elaborately designed.

Pompeii's layout followed the Greek system of town planning, adapted to the irregularities of its hillside. Long, narrow residential blocks were separated by narrow access roads running at right angles to the main avenues. As in all town plans of this kind, there are two principal arteries, the *cardo,* running north-south, and the *decumanus,* running east-west.

The town contained three public baths, a concert hall, a theater, and an amphitheater capable of accommodating all the citizens, as well as houses of prostitution; a famous sign in the form of an erect phallus pointed to the red-light district. The main square or forum was closed to vehicular traffic; about it were grouped public buildings, including a *basilica,* or large hall, that was the setting for Pompeii's legal and financial activities. At the opposite end of the forum was the principal temple, dedicated to Jupiter. Just beyond it was another temple, consecrated to the emperor Augustus, whose memory by the first century A.D. was revered throughout the empire.

Excavation at other towns buried by Vesuvius suggests that Pompeii was far from the most prosperous site in the region. Some of the villas at nearby Herculaneum are grander than anything at Pompeii, particularly the lavish waterfront homes with large windows that opened on the view. Recent excavation at Oplontis has revealed a magnificent villa.

In addition to serving the needs of tourists, Pompeii and the neighboring towns had their own commercial life. The largest building in Pompeii's forum, for example, was neither religious nor political; it was a large hall for the clothmakers and dyers that combined storage and sales facilities with a meeting place for fabric manufacturers. Nearby was a large open market, the Marcellum, at which farmers sold their produce. At its center, where fishmongers had their stands, was a pool connected to underground sewers, in which the sellers cleaned their fish; it was found filled with scales. Other shops in the city sold utensils, wine and olive oil, and bread, including flat loaves that look like modern pizza bases. In addition to the usual artisans, Herculaneum boasted a colony of artists.

A number of toilet facilities, including a communal one across from the Marcellum, were found in Pompeii. The provision of such facilities throughout the empire was one of Vespasian's contributions to Western culture. To this day in Italy a public urinal is known as a *vespasiano.*

Provincial Life in the North

The northern provinces present a different picture. In the rich farmland of northern France, life was concentrated not in cities but around country villas. The largest of these contained not only farming establishments but small factories, producing pottery, bricks, ironwork, and other materials useful for the armies guarding the northeastern frontier against hostile Germanic tribes. The grain and wool produced by the smaller establishments served the farms themselves, which seem to have been run by slaves, and the neighboring troops.

Britain, one of the remotest provinces, was the northern frontier, for the Romans never gained control over what is now modern Scotland. Agricola, who governed Britain from A.D. 78 to 84, did what he could to Romanize the local population, and in the south Roman ideas and customs took root fairly quickly. The capital, Londinium (most of which lies beneath modern London), developed into a city of some size, and Roman villas and baths have been uncovered throughout southern England. The north, however, presented a more formidable challenge. One of the military encampments Agricola built was in modern Perthshire. Shortly after being occupied, it was abandoned and destroyed lest it fall into enemy hands. The buildings, principally made of wood, included a headquarters, barracks, granaries, a drill hall, and a hospital.

The Romans' last major extension of their frontiers is recorded in detail on the monument known as Trajan's Column. In 101 and again in 104 Trajan led expeditions to subdue the Dacians, whose territory in modern Rumania lay to the east of the river Danube, previously a frontier. To celebrate Trajan's victory and the submission of the Dacians to Rome, a 125-foot column was erected in Trajan's Forum in Rome that shows the campaigns in vivid detail: the crossing of the Danube, the Roman army building camps and bridges, the harangues of Trajan, and scenes of battle and torture. Here is carved no mere celebration of Roman triumph but an almost photographic record of the endurance needed by emperor and foot soldier alike to create and maintain the empire.

Women in Roman Society

With the growth of empire and of contact with the Hellenized East, the position of upper-class women became freer. Wealthy and aristocratic women were able to preside over literary salons and to dabble in high politics. The salons appear to have been of some cultural importance from the days of the Flavian dynasty to the empress Julia Domna (died A.D. 217). Some women won fame as orators, and political demonstrations by women were not unknown. In 195 B.C. the women of Rome gathered to demand repeal of the Oppian Law, which, having confiscated most of their gold for the war effort against Hannibal, had been prolonged into peacetime. On a similar occasion in 42 B.C., when women were taxed to pay the expenses of the civil war, a group of them burst into the Forum, and their spokeswoman, Hortensia, made an impassioned speech:

> **Why should we pay taxes when we do not share in the offices, honors, military commands, nor in short, the government, for which you fight between your selves with such harmful results? . . . Let war with the Celts or Parthians come, we will not be inferior to our mothers when it is a question of common safety. But for civil wars, may we never contribute nor aid you against each other.**[1]

Hortensia's speech made her famous, and it was quoted with approval by later male commentators. But the official ideal of matronly virtue was Cornelia, the daughter of the hero of the Second Punic War, Scipio Africanus, and the mother of the famous reformers Tiberius and Gaius Gracchus. Cornelia, who endured a long widowhood as well as the assassination of her sons, was praised for her fidelity, her fortitude, and (in a period of declining aristocratic birthrates), her fertility as well; her letters were published after her death, and a statue was erected in her honor. Not all women of the noble classes lived up to this standard; Caesar divorced his wife for adultery.

The legal position of Roman women was, as in Greece, strictly subordinate. In the intensely patriarchal culture of early Rome, the male head of the family literally had life and death powers over the members of his household. Adult males were emancipated at their father's death, but women were subject, at least in theory, to the guardianship of a male relative until marriage. Roman law assumed the incapacity of women to deal with matters of contract, property, and inheritance.

There were two kinds of marriage, with or without *manus,* the equivalent of a transfer of paternal authority to the husband. Marriages without *manus* left the bride freer but also with fewer rights. The consent of both partners was required for betrothal, but a woman could refuse a prospective husband only if she could show that he was morally unfit. With or without *manus,* the bride's father continued to exercise considerable supervision over his daughter and could, as in Greece, initiate divorce.

Divorce among the upper classes in the late republican and imperial periods was surprisingly casual. No reason was legally required for it, and no particular stigma attached to it unless scandal was involved. Despite the official exhortations to increase childbearing, infanticide and abortion were commonly practiced; in fact, infanticide, did not become a moral offense until the third century A.D. Among the many advertised techniques for contraception was the suggestion that a woman hold her breath at the moment of male ejaculation.

Roman matrons were expected to master such traditional domestic skills as spinning and weaving. In practice, they left these tasks to their slaves, exercising only a general supervision of the household. With little restriction on their movements, they were able to visit, shop, and attend public functions. In this and other respects they enjoyed far greater freedom than their Greek counterparts.

At the apex of the social scale, some women enjoyed extraordinary honors. The erection of statues to the women of prominent Roman families was imitated by provincial governors, who put up likenesses of their wives. Some women were granted citizenship and even held public office in late Hellenistic Greece, a practice that continued into Roman times. A number of empresses were deified after their deaths, becoming part of the official state religion.

For the great majority of Roman women, life was quite different. The majority fell into three broad categories: slaves, freedwomen, and the freeborn poor. The slaves of well-to-do families were perhaps the best off economically; they were permitted to accumulate property and even to buy other slaves. Their duties were varied, including cooking, cleaning, clothesmaking, and the care and nursing of children. More specialized slaves might serve as secretaries, ladies' maids, masseuses, entertainers, and midwives. Some acquired considerable education. Because there was always more demand for male slaves, however, slave daughters were often left to die of exposure or sold. All female slaves, whatever their function, were used sexually by their masters; Cato the censor, in addition to exercising his own prerogatives, gave his male slaves access to the women of the household in return for a fee.

Slaves might buy their freedom or be manumitted through marriage. Freedwomen comprised a large part of the Roman working class, serving as laundresses, shopkeepers, waitresses, and prostitutes, or working at artisanal trades or as domestics. Some attained prosperity, but many continued to work for their former masters. Freeborn women enjoyed a higher status than any slave, even slaves who worked in the imperial household and often wielded considerable influence. They were discouraged from marrying slaves, and in A.D. 52 a senatorial decree reduced those who did to the status of slaves of their husbands' masters. Some freeborn women purchased the freedom of male slaves in order to marry them, but this practice too was subsequently outlawed. Under Constantine, finally, it was made a capital offense for a woman to cohabit with a slave, and the slave himself was to be burned to death.

Unlike notable women of the upper classes, whose lives were often commemorated, we have little biographical information about the great mass of Roman women. Their position, restricted as it was, did offer some opportunity for mobility and self-expression and in these terms compared favorably with that of the women of Han China. The epitaph of one woman, Claudia, must serve for the anonymous history of many:

> **Stranger, what I have to say is short. Stop and read it through. This is the unlovely tomb of a lovely woman. Her parents named her Claudia. She loved her husband with her whole heart. She bore two sons, one of whom she leaves on earth; the other she has placed beneath the ground. She was charming in conversation, yet her conduct was appropriate. She kept house; she made wool.[2]**

The Roman Achievement

The Romans' mission, as defined by Vergil, was to "rule the world, show mercy to the defeated, and strike down the proud." Their intellectual contribution to the human heritage is significant. From the beginning, Roman culture was imitative rather than original. The first Roman poet of whom anything is known is Ennius (239–169 B.C.), a writer the Romans themselves called the father of Roman poetry. Ennius adapted tragedies from Greek and used Greek metrical schemes to write his *Annals,* an epic chronicle of Rome; almost all his work is lost. The first writers whose work has survived in any quantity, the comic playwrights Plautus (c. 251–184 B.C.) and Terence

(c. 195–159 B.C.), turned Greek comedies into Latin and generally adapted them to Roman tastes, with results that were lively and often earthy.

The last years of the republic produced a rich body of literature. The poetry of Catullus (c. 84–c. 54 B.C.) is renowned for its uninhibited satire and eroticism, and his account of an unhappy affair with the girl he calls Lesbia is painful and candid. *On the Nature of Things,* by Lucretius (c. 94–55 B.C.), expounds the materialist teachings of Epicurus in one of the world's greatest philosophical poems. Caesar himself left us the history of his military campaigns in Gaul, written in a simple but gripping style.

Perhaps the most representative literary and political figure of the late republic was Marcus Tullius Cicero (106–43 B.C.). A successful lawyer, Cicero published many of his speeches, the rhetorical power of which serves as a reminder of the Romans' cultivation of oratory. Cicero also wrote philosophical works and took an active part in politics, but he is best remembered for the personal correspondence that he kept to be published after his death. His nearly 900 letters provide an incomparable picture of the man and his world, his political judgments, his literary tastes, and his personal relations. If they often reveal Cicero's weaknesses—his vanity, his reluctance to make decisions, and his stubborness—they confirm his humanity and sensitivity.

The Romans also paid a good deal of attention to practical matters. Cato (234–149 B.C.) published a guide to farming, as did Varro (116–27 B.C.), Rome's first public librarian, who also wrote on language and grammar. A work from the late first-century B.C., Vitruvius' *On Architecture,* influenced Renaissance architects such as Bramante and Michelangelo. Sextus Frontinus (c. A.D. 30–104), who directed Rome's water system, wrote a fascinating treatise on aqueducts.

If the Augustan Age saw in Vergil the high point of Roman poetry, the so-called Silver Age that followed found its historian in Cornelius Tacitus. Many of the historical characters of the period spring to life in his works. Tiberius, Nero, and Domitian are unforgettably portrayed by one who observed at first hand the consequences of their deeds. Tacitus' world is one of continuous action, moving from the imperial court to the battles on the frontiers. He was married to Agricola's daughter, and his biography of his father-in-law (one of the few people for whom he had anything good to say) includes an account of Roman Britain. He also provides us with the best contemporary account of the Germans in his *Germania,* based on reports related to him by travelers.

Among the greatest Roman contributions to literature was the Latin language itself. Latin was the language of the early writers of the Christian church and remained the common link between people of culture in the West virtually until our own time. It is still used for scientific nomenclature and remains the official language of the Roman Catholic church. It evolved into all the Romance languages, including French, Italian, Spanish, Portuguese, and Rumanian, and was a root of English and German as well.

The Romans were awed by the brilliance of Greek visual art, and many of their own chief monuments are marked by a dependence on classical models. Yet in at least two major fields the Romans broke new ground. Roman portraiture broke with the idealizing classical style.

Cicero on His Daughter's Death

Cicero's letter to his friend Atticus conveys the effect on him of his daughter's death.

To Atticus — Astura, 15 May 45 B.C.

I think I shall conquer my feelings and go from Lanuvium to my house at Tusculum. For either I must give up my property there for ever—since my grief will remain the same, though I shall become able to conceal it better—or if not it does not matter in the least whether I go there now or in ten years' time. The place will not remind me of her any more than the thoughts which consume me all the time, day and night. You will be asking me if there is no comfort to be derived from books. I am afraid that in this situation they have the contrary effect. Without them I might have been tougher; an educated man is not insensitive or impervious enough.

So do come as you wrote you would, but not if it is inconvenient. A couple of letters will be enough. I will come and meet you, if necessary. Whatever you can manage, so be it.

Source: Cicero, *Selected Works,* trans. M. Grant (Harmondsworth, England: Penguin Books, 1960), p. 87.

Taking their cue from Hellenistic examples, Roman artists learned to use physical appearance to convey character. Many of the best Roman portraits are revealing psychological documents; that of Cicero, for example, reveals his self-satisfaction as well as his humanity.

In architecture most of all, the Romans could express their need to construct and to dominate. Whereas Greek buildings were generally meant to be seen from the outside, Roman buildings consciously enclose their occupants. The Pantheon is a striking example of this, as are the imperial baths or, on an even grander scale, monumental complexes such as Trajan's Forum, which could accommodate thousands of people. The invention of concrete in the first century B.C., and the growing mastery of the principles of stress and counterstress enabled architects to experiment with forms—arches and vaults—that passed into the Western architectural tradition. The theaters, stadiums, libraries, markets, temples, and other public buildings constructed on three continents are proof of the high quality of Roman engineering.

The Empire in Crisis

The changing character of the army, whose principal task was to guard the frontiers of the empire against attack, altered the nature of imperial rule. The larger the army became, the more necessary it was to recruit troops from the more distant provinces, whose cultural ties and loyalty to Rome proved tenuous in times of stress. Military anarchy had left its mark as early as A.D. 69, when only the decisive action of Vespasian put an end to the depredations of rival armies fighting for the throne of Nero. A similar period of chaos followed the assassination of the deranged emperor Commodus (180–192), when the members of the imperial bodyguard auctioned the empire to the highest bidder. It was only a matter of months before Roman legions from various parts of the empire had marched on Rome and proceeded to fight for the right to impose their own candidate.

Only in 197 did Septimius Severus (193–211) defeat his last rival and end the civil war. Septimius was born in North Africa at Lepcis Magna and spoke Latin with a strong Punic accent; his wife, Julia Domna, was from Syria. The authority of his reign produced a brief economic revival and restored stability in the provinces, where he spent much of his time campaigning.

JULIA DOMNA, MOTHER OF EMPERORS

The life of Julia Domna (c. 169–217) was exceptional. The younger daughter of a wealthy Syrian high priest from Emesa, she was married at the age of 16 to Septimius Severus, then a magistrate in Gaul and 26 years her senior. His nickname, "the Severe," coupled with accounts of his pompous dignity, suggests that he made a difficult companion for a young woman who was both beautiful and high-spirited, but the marriage must have seemed sensible in practical terms. Septimius was an officer serving the empire, and one whose career seemed on the rise.

Their life at Lugdunum (modern Lyons) in provincial Gaul was very different from the relative freedom of Syria, where Julia was used to the discussions of religion, literature, and science between her father and his many visitors. Her first task was to produce a family; in 188 her son Antoninus was born. When Septimius' appointment in Gaul expired in 189, he was sent as governor to Sicily, where she gave birth to their second son, Geta. Julia seems to have been even more ambitious than her husband, but even she could hardly have predicted the speed with which he was to become emperor in the disorders following Commodus' death in 192.

Julia accompanied Septimius on his imperial missions, traveling in a litter that was carried on the shoulders of six bearers. Undeterred by the rigors of military life, she was once acclaimed by the soldiers as *Mater Castrorum*—camp mother. The imperial travels often included sightseeing; on one trip to Egypt she visited Alexander's tomb at Alexandria and journeyed to Upper Egypt, where Septimius performed the annual sacrifice to the Nile, encouraged, no doubt, by his wife's interest in eastern religion.

Under Julia's influence, the imperial court became a center for scholars of religion and philosophy. Her close friend Philostratus composed a biography, the *Life of Apollonius,* that borrowed from the Christian Gospels to describe a saintly figure of the first century A.D. Although not herself a Christian, Julia was generally sympathetic to Christians and employed them in her household. Her curiosity about the world can be seen in the work of writers she encouraged. Foremost among them was Galen (c. 129–c. 199), whose work on human anatomy remained the basic text on the subject in the West until the sixteenth century.

On his deathbed in 211 Septimius left the empire to his two sons. It was proposed to split the empire in two, leaving Antoninus in Europe and sending Geta to Asia. Julia, who favored Geta, opposed this plan: "You might as well try to divide my living body between you." Soldiers, however, killed Geta, wounding Julia in the process.

Antoninus (better known Caracalla, as from the Gallic word *caracal,* for the short cloak that he habitually wore), purged everyone suspected of having supported his late brother. Julia, however, remained untouched, and Caracalla became increasingly dependent on her for advice. She took a major part in policymaking and the day-to-day conduct of affairs. Among the most important aspects of Caracalla's reign was the passage in 212 of a decree granting Roman citizenship and equal rights to all communities throughout the empire. When Caracalla was assassinated in 217, Julia moved to Antioch and then to Emesa, her birthplace. Because Caracalla's successor, Macrinus, was far from popular, an attempt was made at Rome to place Julia on the throne. The plot was unsuccessful, and Julia spent the remaining months of her life under virtual house arrest. She had helped provide the empire with the respite of her husband's reign and protected it from the worst excesses of her son. In the circumstances, her achievement was considerable.

The Germanic Invasions

In the 50 years from 235 to 285, more than 25 emperors were officially recognized by the Senate. Almost all were raised to power through, and sooner or later killed by, the army. These rulers had little reason to feel loyalty to Rome. They were themselves generally not of Roman origin; selected by an army that was itself increasingly non-Roman, they were unlikely to see beyond their own interests and those of their men to the state as a whole.

The empire was now under serious threat from outside. Germanic, partly Romanized tribes such as the Goths and the Alemanni penetrated its defenses. As early as 231 marauding Franks crossed the river Rhine. In 259 the city of Rome itself was almost invaded by the Alemanni. In many parts of the empire it became clear that Rome could provide no help against invaders, and some of the provinces tried to establish themselves as independent states with their own armies. Although the attempts of Gaul in 260 and Palmyra in 267 to win their freedom were crushed, they presaged the fragmentation of the empire. By 271 the reigning emperor, Aurelian (270–275), began the construction of a defensive wall around the city of Rome, the first since the time of Hannibal. Meanwhile, in the east, Roman armies were continually involved in repelling the Persians. In 274 Aurelian regained Roman territory in Asia, but he was assassinated before he could deal effectively with the Persian threat.

These problems had a devastating effect on the economy. Taxes increased as the value of money plunged. The constant threat of invasion or civil war made trade difficult. What funds there were went for the support of the army, and the general standard of living steadily declined. The former Hellenistic kingdoms in the east suffered less than the western provinces, since they were protected in part by their prosperity. Much of Italy's farmland ceased to be cultivated, the loss of export markets played havoc with industry, and the population of Rome diminished.

The heroic efforts of the emperor Diocletian (284–305) brought a real, if temporary, recovery. The length of his reign enabled him to address the disorganization that had become endemic throughout the empire. A masterful if rigid administrator, he believed that the only way to save the empire was to impose stringent controls on every aspect of life—social, administrative, and economic. In 301 he issued an edict establishing wage and price controls. A vast bureaucracy was set up to collect taxes and administer the provinces. To deal with the mass of administrative problems, Diocletian appointed an old army colleague, Maximian, first as his deputy, or Caesar, and then as his coemperor. He subsequently divided the empire into east and west, took charge of the east himself, and appointed two more Caesars, one for each half of the empire. Thus Rome was governed by the Tetrarchy, or rule of four men.

Diocletian also succeeded in reestablishing the authority of the emperor by claiming a semidivine status. He never appeared in public but developed an elaborate court with complex rituals. He also tried to provide for a peaceful succession when he retired in 305, but his attempt failed. His designated successors battled for power until 312, when Constantine emerged as the principal victor. In the meantime Diocletian himself had retired to a rustic life at Split in Dalmatia, where he died in 313.

Constantine and His Successors

Constantine (died 337) changed the course of Roman history in two decisive ways: he transferred the imperial capital to the great new city he consecrated on the Bosporus, Constantinople, and he adopted Christianity as his personal religion. (The growth and early development of Christianity are discussed in Chapter 7.) The Christians had been mostly ignored by the Romans for the first two centuries after Christ, except where breaches of the peace brought them to the attention of magistrates. By the third century the number of Christians and the influence they exerted had grown sufficiently to bring them increasingly to the notice of the authorities. Sporadic persecutions resulted, not in the name of religion but in what was perceived as the interest of imperial unity. The most forceful attempt to purge Christian influence was made by Diocletian, whose persecutions began in 303.

Constantine, an adherent of the popular solar cult, was converted to Christianity in 312 just before he won the battle of the Milvian Bridge and, with it, control of Italy. He claimed to have seen a cross against the disk of the sun in a vision, accompanied by the words, "In this sign you will conquer." This he interpreted as a command to worship the Christian God together with the sun deity. In 313, by the Edict of Milan, he proclaimed toleration for all religions. Under Constantine churches were constructed, and a move was planned from pagan Rome to a new Christian capital at Byzantium, a location purportedly revealed to the emperor in another vision. He renamed the new capital after himself.

By the end of his reign Constantine had succeeded in establishing an imperial Christian city in the east, which was to last until 1453 and which maintained Greek, the language of the east, as its official tongue. The west, which

The Christian Empire

In this speech, delivered in 336 to celebrate the thirtieth year of Constantine's reign, the church historian Eusebius works out a theological justification for the existence of a Christian emperor and empire.

The divine Logos [Word], which is above, throughout and within everything, visible and invisible at once, is the lord of the universe. It is from and through the Logos that the emperor, the beloved of God, receives and wears the image of supreme kingship, and so guides and steers, in imitation of his Lord, all the affairs of this world. . . . Constantine, like the light of the sun . . . illuminates those farthest from him with his rays . . . and harnessing the four Caesars like spirited coursers beneath the single yoke of his royal quadriga, he molds them to harmony with the reins of reason and unity, guiding his team like a charioteer, controlling it from above and ranging over the whole surface of the earth illuminated by the sun, and at the same time present in the midst of all men and watching over their affairs. . . . God is the model of royal power and it is he who has determined a single authority for all mankind. . . . Just as there is only one God, and not two or three or more, since polytheism is really atheism, so there is only one emperor. . . . He has received the image of the heavenly monarchy, and his eyes lifted on high he governs the affairs of this world in accordance with the ideas of his archetype, fortified by the imitation of the sovereignty of the heavenly king.

Source: R. Browning, *The Emperor Julian* (Berkeley: University of California Press, 1976), p. 22.

Head of the colossal statue of Constantine from the Basilica of Constantine in Rome. [Werner Forman Archive, London]

remained Latin in language and culture, was plagued by the problems of the previous centuries: attack from without and corruption within. Both Persians and Germans continued to press their attacks on opposite ends of the empire, while Constantine's sons fought a fratricidal civil war for control. In 378 the empire suffered a major defeat when an army of Visigoths, Ostrogoths, and escaped slaves annihilated a Roman army at Adrianople. The Germans from the north who defeated the Romans were fleeing from yet another, more ferocious people who had moved into their territory, the Asiatic Huns.

Apart from Julian (361–363), known as "the Apostate" because he tried to strengthen paganism and check the spread of Christianity, the remaining emperors of the fourth century actively supported the church while fighting an increasingly rearguard action to retain the western provinces. In 394, meanwhile, the final enshrinement of Christianity as the official state religion came when Emperor Theodosius (379–395) prohibited all other worship and closed all pagan temples.

By the reign of Theodosius the empire had been divided in two, and the fate of the west was sealed. In 410, for the first time since the Gallic invasions of 800 years earlier, Rome was sacked by an enemy army, the Germanic Visigoths under the leadership of Alaric. The Asiatic Huns, under Attila, and the Germanic Vandals completed the task. By the time the last Roman emperor in the west, Romulus Augustulus, was deposed in 476, the western empire had already been shattered by barbarian migrations.

The eastern half of the empire, subsequently known as Byzantium, was sufficiently far from the invaders' concentration on the Rhine and Danube frontiers to remain relatively intact. In the west, where the principal cities had never really recovered from the strain of the previous two centuries, there were no resources of money or manpower to withstand the invasions.

The reasons for the so-called decline and fall of the Roman Empire (a phrase coined by the eighteenth-century British historian Edward Gibbon) have long been debated. But the question has perhaps been wrongly posed. What is remarkable is not that Rome at last succumbed but that it survived so long, encompassing the cultures of three continents within a single system of law and government.

The dissolution of Rome was in reality a process rather than an event. If the empire's political center of gravity was the city of Rome, its economic and cultural base had always been in the eastern Mediterranean, a fact that Constantine recognized when he built his new capital on the shore of Asia. In a sense, then, the stronger, more viable half of the empire survived there, its history and culture continuous down to the Turkish conquest of 1453.

If the Byzantine Empire was, historically, a half sister of Rome, its traditions evolved in an independent direction after the collapse of the western empire in the fifth century. Indeed, from the point of view of the Hellenized east, the long centuries of Roman rule were an episode of foreign dominion in a region whose civilizations stretched back thousands of years. To be sure, the passing of Rome was painfully felt, but the traditions and cultures that Rome had so freely borrowed for its own only reverted to their native soil, and everyday life went on much as before. The major difference between the pre- and post-Roman periods was the advent of Christianity, itself a product of the east; and the major change to come was the rise of the latest of the great world religions, Islam, and the rival civilization it was to build in the ancient lands of western Asia and North Africa.

Notes

1. Appian, *Civil Wars,* 4.33.
2. S. B. Pomeroy, *Goddesses, Whores, Wives, and Slaves: Women in Classical Antiquity* (New York: Schocken Books, 1975), p. 199.

Suggestions for Further Reading

Balsdon, J. P. V. D. *Roman Women*. Westport, Conn.: Greenwood Press, 1975.

Birley, A. *Marcus Aurelius: A Biography*, rev. ed. New Haven, Conn.: Yale University Press, 1987.

Bradford, E. *Cleopatra*. New York: Harcourt Brace Jovanovich, 1972.

Bradley, K. R. *Slaves and Masters in the Roman Empire*. Berkeley: University of California Press, 1987.

Brendel, O. *Prolegomena to the Study of Roman Art*. New Haven, Conn.: Yale University Press, 1979.

Christ, K. *The Romans: An Introduction to Their History and Civilization*. Berkeley: University of California Press, 1984.

Cornell, T., and Matthews, J. *Atlas of the Roman World*. New York: Facts on File, 1982.

Crawford, M. *The Roman Republic*. Cambridge, Mass.: Harvard University Press, 1982.

Cunliffe, B. W. *Rome and Her Empire*. London: Bodley Head, 1978.

D'Arms, J. H. *Commerce and Social Standing in Ancient Rome*. Cambridge, Mass.: Harvard University Press, 1981.

Deiss, J. J. *Herculaneum: Italy's Buried Treasure*, rev. ed. New York: Harper & Row, 1985.

Duncan-Jones, R. *The Economy of the Roman Empire: Quantitative Studies*. Cambridge: Cambridge University Press, 1982.

Finley, M. I. *The Ancient Economy*. Berkeley: University of California Press, 1973.

Gardner, J. F. *Women in Roman Law and Society*. Bloomington: Indiana University Press, 1986.

Garnsey, P., and Saller, R. *The Roman Empire: Economy, Society and Culture*. Berkeley: University of California Press, 1987.

Goodenough, S. *Citizens of Rome*. New York: Crown, 1979.

Grant, M. *Cities of Vesuvius: Pompeii and Herculaneum*. New York: Penguin Books, 1971.

———. *The Etruscans*. New York: Scribner, 1981.

Hanfmann, G. *Roman Art*. New York: Norton, 1976.

Heurgon, J. *The Rise of Rome to 264 B.C.*. Berkeley: University of California Press, 1973.

Hooper, F. A. *Roman Realities*. Detroit: Wayne State University Press, 1979.

Hopkins, K. *Conquerors and Slaves*. Cambridge: Cambridge University Press, 1981.

Kampen, N. *Image and Status: Roman Working Women in Ostia*. Berlin: Mann, 1981.

Lefkowitz, M., and Fant, M. B., eds. *Women's Life in Greece and Rome*, rev. ed. Baltimore: Johns Hopkins University Press, 1982.

Luttwak, E. N. *The Grand Strategy of the Roman Empire*. Baltimore: Johns Hopkins University Press, 1976.

Macmullen, R. *Roman Social Relations 50 B.C. to A.D. 284*. New Haven, Conn.: Yale University Press, 1981.

Millar, F. *The Emperor in the Roman World, 31 B.C.– A.D. 337*. Ithaca, N.Y.: Cornell University Press, 1977.

Pallottino, M. *The Etruscans*. Baltimore: Penguin Books, 1976.

Potter, T. *The Changing Landscape of South Etruria*. New York: St. Martin's Press, 1979.

Scullard, H. H. *Roman Politics, 220–150 B.C.* Westport, Conn.: Greenwood Press, 1982.

CHAPTER · 7

The Ancient World Religions

The earliest evidence for religious beliefs dates back to the Neanderthal people of the late Paleolithic period. Even in its most primitive forms, religion helped humans to explain their natural environment, to the point of providing means, such as prayer, sacrifices, or offerings, intended to control the world around them. Appeasing the gods, for instance, was seen as a way to ward off illness or famine or perhaps to enjoy the blessings of children and fertile fields. Religion also provided a way for people to relate to each other, often hierarchically within their own society, especially since priests usually enjoyed substantial social and political status. Religious beliefs could be used as well to persuade people to obey their secular rulers and perform their vocational responsibilities. Eventually, many religions developed codes of ethical conduct to guide adherents in their dealings with each other. Thus religion was often the bond that bound a society together.

All of the religions discussed in this chapter took their particular character from the environment in which they evolved. The Hindu concept of *dharma* and the Christian

A classic representation of the Buddha from Japan made of bronze and dating from the Nara period in the eighth century A.D. [Mega Press, Tokyo]

practice of monasticism paralleled the social and political realities of their respective societies. Most religions try to influence the nature of society, with varying success, and it is important to remember that none of them exists in a vacuum as pure theology. Yet by considering the principal world religions as entities and by comparing their aims and characteristics, it is possible to cast fresh light on some of the oldest human needs, hopes, and fears.

All of the world's major religions, including Judaism and Christianity, had their origins in Asia. All of them go back roughly 1,500 to 2,500 years, yet they still affect the lives of most people today. Most Communist states have substituted a secular belief system, but in China, the biggest of them, much of both Confucianism—like Taoism, more of a moral philosophy rather than a religion—and traditional folk religion survive, while even in the Soviet Union and eastern Europe, traditional religion remains popular.

Hinduism

Hinduism is the oldest world religion, and India has remained the most religiously oriented of all major cultures. Hinduism is often called a way of life, which is true but not very helpful. It is hard to define; its name means simply "Indianism," and the religious element is hard to sort out from more general cultural practice. The caste system is a good illustration. It is a Hindu practice, but it is also observed by South Asian Muslims and Buddhists. Caste has some minor religious connection but is primarily a system of social organization and is discussed as such in Chapter 21. There is no single body of writings for Hinduism like the Koran, the New Testament, or Buddha's sayings, and Hinduism had no single founder.

Hindu Beliefs and Writings

In the broadest sense, we can define Hinduism as developing out of the complex of religious beliefs held by the people of the Indus civilization, which included the cult of Shiva, still the dominant god of Hinduism. The Aryans brought their own tribal gods, including the war god Indra and the fire god Agni,* but by the time the Vedas were first written down, many centuries later, Vedic religion was becoming a mixture of Harappan, Aryan, and Dravidian (southern Indian) elements. Composed cumulatively between about 1500 and 600 B.C., first orally and later written down, as a set of hymns, spells, and mystic poems used at sacrifices, the Vedas are the world's oldest religious texts still used in worship. The last of the Vedas, the Upanishads (seventh century B.C.), deal mainly with the nature of the universe and the place of humans in it. The Upanishads involve a sophisticated metaphysics that is characteristically Indian, a far cry from the earlier anthropomorphic (humanlike) gods of the Aryans. Asceticism and mysticism are seen in the Upanishads as paths to wisdom and truth.

The Upanishads deal also with good and evil, law, morality, and human duty and are often seen as the core of classical Hinduism. But Hinduism's main ethical text is the much later Bhagavad Gita (second century A.D.), which tells the story of Prince Arjuna. Arjuna is faced with a rebellion led by disloyal friends, relatives, and teachers, people he has loved and respected. He knows his cause is just but cannot bring himself to fight and kill those so close to him. He stands in his chariot awaiting battle and talks to his charioteer, who turns out to be Krishna, an incarnation of the Vedic god of creation, Vishnu. Krishna tells him that bodily death does not mean the death of the soul and is thus unimportant. For any individual's life, what is important is duty, and action in accordance with duty, without attachment, personal desires, or ambition. Each person has a special role in society, and morality lies in faithfulness to that prescribed role.

This concept of *dharma,* or the selfless execution of one's prescribed duty on earth, applied also to the faithful following of caste rules. Arjuna was a ruler and had to follow the ruler's dharma, which included the duty to fight to uphold his rightful power. Other roles in society entail their own, different dharmas, including that of lower castes to serve and defer to those above them and the rules associated with wives, students, parents, and others. *Karma* is the result or consequence of one's actions; faithfulness to one's dharma produces good karma or reward, while behavior contrary to dharma yields bad karma and punishment. There is much universal human wisdom in this, but it also clearly supported the social status quo of India and its maintenance by force if necessary. It has accordingly been much criticized, even by leading Hindus. In many ways it is inconsistent with other parts of Hinduism, especially the doctrine of *ahimsa,* or nonviolence and reverence for all life. Mahatma Gandhi, the leading religious figure of modern India, saw no conflict between the Gita and ahimsa and took the former simply as emphasizing duty.

A broad variety of doctrine, however, is characteristic of Hinduism. Hinduism has cumulatively incorporated various ideas, texts, and practices and combines what may seem excessive emphasis on ritual with much genuine spirituality. But the concepts of dharma and karma have remained basic to Hinduism, as has the tradition of meditation and asceticism. Moral uprightness lies in faithfulness to dharma, and dharma is rightly different for everyone. This has helped to create the tolerance for which

*Compare the Latin *ignis,* "fire," and the English *ignite.*

Creation: Hindu Views

These selections from the Rig Veda illustrate early Hindu concepts of creation. Compare them with the biblical accounts in Genesis and John.

Let me proclaim the valiant deeds of Indra,
The first he did, the wielder of the thunder,
When he slew the dragon and let loose the waters,
And pierced the bellies of the mountains. . . .

When Indra, you slew the firstborn of dragons,
And frustrated the arts of the sorcerers,
Creating sun and heaven and dawn,
You found no enemy to withstand you. . . .

At first there was only darkness wrapped in darkness.
All this was only unillumined water.
That One which came to be, enclosed in nothing,
Arose at last, born of the power of heat. . . .

But who knows, and who can say
Whence it all came, and how creation happened?
The gods themselves are later than creation,
So who knows truly whence it has arisen?

Source: A. L. Basham, *The Wonder That Was India* (New York: Grove Press, 1983), pp. 248, 400.

Hinduism is noted. All faiths and all ascetic or mystic disciplines are seen as paths to truth, which is held to be universal. Gandhi said he did not object to the message of Christian missionaries but wished they could be more faithful to their dharma—that is, true Christians.

Reincarnation

The belief in reincarnation and the immortality of the soul, probably first held by the Harappans, had reappeared by late Vedic times and became a further basic part of Hinduism. The karma produced by one's mortal life determined the next rebirth of the soul, which might be in a person of higher or lower status or even in an animal or insect. Special piety, meditation, asceticism, and understanding of eternal truth could bring escape from the endless cycle of birth and rebirth. The soul was then liberated from the cycle and achieved *moksha,* not a bodily heaven but a blissful spiritual rejoining with the godhead, whose essence was love.

Belief in reincarnation heightened reverence for all life. One's relative might have been reborn as a horse or a spider. Bovine animals were especially revered from Harappan times onward, both for their basic usefulness to people and for the obvious relation of the cow's milk with creation and motherhood. Bulls and oxen, too, were valued natural symbols of patient strength and virility, as also in Mediterranean cultures. But to Hinduism all life is sacred, and all creatures are part of the great chain of being that manifests the divine. Accordingly, pious Hindus are vegetarians, and all but the lowest castes particularly avoid eating beef. Milk, curds, clarified butter, and yogurt are also used ritually in religious ceremonies.

By late Vedic times (c. 600 B.C.) the Hindu pantheon was dominated by the trinity of Vishnu, Shiva, and Brahma, all supreme deities. There developed as well, however, a bewildering variety of consorts, divine incarnations, and lesser gods, each with his or her own cult, as Hinduism continued to incorporate regional and folk religious figures and traditions. These included, among the more prominent, Ganesh, the benevolent elephant-headed son of Shiva and of his consort Parvati; Hanuman the monkey god; Lakshmi, wife of Vishnu and goddess of good fortune; and Kali or Durga, another consort or female equivalent to the grimmer aspect of Shiva, sometimes called the goddess of death.

Hinduism accepted the presence of evil and suffering in the world to a greater extent than other religions and recognized that people, themselves a mixture of good and evil, love and hate, petty and noble, selfish and altruistic, must come to terms with their own nature and with the nature of the cosmos. The major Hindu gods and goddesses thus represent both aspects, destroyers as well as creators, makers of suffering as well as bliss, true representations of the world as it is. Nevertheless, most devout Hindus, especially literate ones, have always been basically monotheistic, stressing the oneness of creation and the majesty of a single creative principle above the level of a humanlike god figure, to which access was possible without cults or intermediaries but through devotion, meditation, and mystical understanding of eternal truth. As a Hindu proverb put it, "God is one, but wise people know it by many names."

Jainism and Sikhism, reformist offshoots of Hinduism that arose respectively in the sixth century B.C. and the late fifteenth century A.D., centered on monotheism. So too did the teachings of the Buddha, in which universal truth was given no material identity, as is it not in pure Hinduism. A similar tension has existed in Christianity between concepts of the Christ as a godhood and the worship of saints and other cults.

Hinduism never developed a fixed or uniform ritual comparable with those of Christianity or Judaism. Pious Hindus recite specified prayers daily before the simple altar found in nearly all Hindu homes and may make frequent offerings of prayer, food, and flowers at one of the many temples throughout India, which are tended by people called priests. But there is no formal "service," no established ordination or clergy comparable with Christianity, and no special day for worship like the Sabbath. Brahmins—the highest and supposedly priestly caste and the exclusive keepers and reciters of the sacred rituals, mainly texts from Sanskrit Vedas and epics—are the only people who perform the rituals for death, marriage, coming of age, and intercession with the divine. These are certainly priestly functions, but such people are not seen as necessary intermediaries for lay persons. Not all Hindu Brahmins are priests, and although Hindu priests may tend temples and receive offerings, they are a far more informally constituted group than in Christianity or Judaism. There are a number of Hindu festivals, most of which are as much cultural as religious, such as the autumn Diwali, or festival of lights, and the spring festival of Holi, and there is an ancient tradition of religious pilgrimage to famous temples and sacred sites.

Hinduism is deeply rooted in the Indian tradition and in the modern sense of Indian identity, and it remains the basic guide for over 600 million people. But despite its strong elements of spirituality, Hinduism has also long recognized the importance to human life of achieving material well-being (*artha*), the responsibility of individuals to provide for their families, and the importance of interpersonal love and of sex (*kama*). Such matters are basic parts of human nature and hence accepted as good. Hinduism in effect rejects nothing that God has made but celebrates and enshrines all of life, including its creation through sex, while making much less distinction than in the West between the sacred and the profane; all are part of creation, which is divine. Hinduism's acknowledgment of the bad as well as the good things of life may perhaps have made things easier or psychologically healthier for its followers, who accept the tragedies and sufferings of life without feeling that they are somehow being "punished."

Buddhism

The preoccupation of the Upanishads with eternal truth reflected a troubled world. A new hybrid India was emerging, and the rise of larger states brought an increase in the scale of warfare. Many people sought solace or escape from a harsh reality through otherworldly quests. The founders of Buddhism and Jainism, roughly contemporary figures in the sixth century B.C., pursued such a path, as they also reacted against the growing ritualization of Hinduism and its dominance by the priestly caste of Brahmins. Both urged independent access to truth through meditation and self-denial without the aid of priests or ritual, and both taught the equality of all in these terms, rejecting caste distinctions. But Buddhism and Jainism were developments within the tradition of Hinduism, and they also share the Hindu beliefs in dharma, karma, *samsara* (reincarnation), moksha (union with the godhead), devotion, and nonviolence or reverence for life. Both rejected the folk panoply of Hindu gods but reaffirmed Hinduism's basic monotheism, its nonpersonalized worship of the infinite and of the "great chain of being."

GAUTAMA BUDDHA, THE ENLIGHTENED ONE

The founder of Buddhism was born around 563 B.C. in the Himalayan foothills region of Nepal, the son of a minor raja ("king"; compare the English word *royal*) of the Sakya clan. His family name was Gautama and his given name Siddartha, but he was also later called by some Sakyamuni ("Sage of the Sakyas"), as well as Gautama or Prince Siddartha. Until he was 29 years old, he led the conventional life of a prince, filled with earthly pleasures. At 19 he married a beautiful princess, and in due time they had a son, or so say the pious legends elaborated in great detail long after his death, as with so many religious figures. We know that he subsequently became an ascetic, wandered and taught for many years, acquired a number of disciples, founded a religious order, and died at the age of about 80 somewhere between 485 and 480 B.C. This is all we know of his life for certain. The later embroidered story of his life, replete with miraculous tales, is important as it has influenced the lives of many millions among successive generations of Asians, from India eastward.

According to this story (in its briefest form), Prince Siddartha, filled with nameless discontent, wandered one day away from his walled palace and met in quick succession an old man broken by age, a sick man covered with boils and shivering with fever, a corpse being carried to the cremation ground (Hindus have always burned their dead), and a wandering saddhu (holy man) with his begging bowl and simple yellow robe, but with peacefulness and inner joy in his face. Overwhelmed by this vision of the sufferings of mortal life, the emptiness of worldly pleasure, and the promise of ascetic devotion, Siddartha shortly thereafter left his palace, abandoning his wife and son. He became a wandering beggar, seeking after the truth and owning nothing but a rag of clothing and a crude wooden bowl to beg the bare essentials of food. For several years he wandered, wasted from fasting, until he determined to solve the riddle of suffering through intense meditation under a great tree. After 49 days, during which he was tempted by Mara, the prince of demons, with promises of riches, power, and sensual pleasures, he perceived the truth and attained enlightenment. From this moment, he was known as the Buddha, or the Enlightened One. Soon after, he preached his first sermon, near Banaras (Varanasi) in the central Ganges valley, and spent the rest of his life as an itinerant preacher with a band of disciples.

A modern *saddhu,* or holy man, who has renounced the world and lives by begging for food. He stands in front of a temple frieze in South India. [Stella Snead, New York]

The Four Noble Truths, announced in that first sermon, formed the basis for the new faith: (1) Life is filled with pain, sorrow, frustration, impermanence, and dissatisfaction. (2) All this is caused by desire, by wanting, and by the urge for existence. (3) To end suffering and sorrow, one must be released from desire. (4) Release from desire can be gained by the eightfold path of "right conduct." The "right conduct" of the eightfold path was later defined as kindness to all living things, purity of heart, truthfulness, charity, and avoidance of faultfinding, envy, hatred, and violence. To these were added specific commandments not to kill, steal, commit adultery, lie, speak evil, gossip, flatter, or otherwise wander from the path.

Followers of the path may attain *nirvana,* or release from the sufferings of worldly existence through the endless cycle of rebirth, and achieve blissful reabsorption into the spiritual infinite, as the Buddha did on his death. Such perfection was, however, rare, and although the Buddha did not say so, Buddhism incorporated the Hindu concept of karma. In accordance with this, less dutiful individuals were reborn in successive existences in forms appropriate to their behavior in their most recent incarnations. Accounts of the Buddha's own teachings were recorded in a collection of texts called the Tripitaka ("three baskets"). In addition, a literature of moral tales about the life of Buddha grew up, together with commentaries on the teachings, which are comparable in many ways to the stories of the Christian New Testament.

As with Christianity too, Buddhism remained for its first several centuries a minority religion, although the difficult discipline of the original teachings was softened somewhat so as to accommodate more followers. The conversion of Emperor Ashoka (c. 269–c. 232 B.C.) helped to transform it into a mass religion, and it began to spread from India, first to Ceylon and Southeast Asia and later to China, Korea, and Japan. Within India, Buddhism survived for many centuries, although its following slowly declined from a peak reached around A.D. 100. For many, its distinction from Hinduism was gradually blurred, and except for its several monastic orders and some lay devotees, Buddhism was slowly reabsorbed into Hinduism. The remaining Buddhist centers and monasteries in the central Ganges heartland were destroyed, most of the monks slaughtered, and the few survivors driven into exile by the Muslim invaders of the twelfth century. That holocaust largely extinguished Buddhism in the land of its birth.

Hinayana and Mahayana Buddhism

Soon after Ashoka's time, Buddhism divided into two major schools known as Hinayana ("the lesser vehicle") or Theravada and Mahayana ("the greater vehicle"). Theravada Buddhism remained closer to the original faith, although it too was necessarily popularized to some extent as it spread and included more scope for the doctrine of good works. By performing good works, one could acquire

Buddhist Teachings

Many of the teachings attributed to the Buddha are almost certainly later additions or commentaries. Here are two rather striking passages from such Buddhist scriptures, whose closeness to the Christian Gospels is remarkable.

A man buries a treasure in a deep pit, thinking: It will be useful in time of need, or if the king is displeased with me, or if I am robbed, or fall into debt, or if food is scarce, or bad luck befalls me. But all this treasure may not profit the owner at all, for he may forget where he hid it, or goblins may steal it, or his enemies or even his kinsmen may take it when he is not on his guard. But by charity, goodness, restraint, and self-control man and woman alike can store up a well-hidden treasure—a treasure which cannot be given to others and which robbers cannot steal. A wise man should do good; that is the treasure which will not leave him.

Brethren, you have no mother or father to care for you. If you do not care for one another, who else will do so? Brethren, he who would care for me should care for the sick.

Source: A. L. Basham, *The Wonder That Was India* (New York: Grove Press, 1983), p. 284.

"merit," which could even offset bad conduct in the building of karma; thus, for example, pious donations could make up for the bad karma of unethically acquired money. Theravada was the form of Buddhism transmitted to Southeast Asia, where especially in Burma, Thailand, Cambodia, Laos, and much of Vietnam as well as Ceylon it has remained the dominant religion and is paid far more than lip service even today. Nearly all young men in these countries traditionally spent two years in a Buddhist monastery, as many still do, with shaven heads, a yellow robe, and a begging bowl.

Mahayana Buddhism developed a little later, during the Kushan period in India in the second century A.D. What had begun as a spiritual discipline for a few became a mass

The great stupa (temple) at Sanchi in Central India. Begun by Ashoka in the third century B.C., it was enlarged during the century after his death, when the outer ring and gateways were added. The stupa represents the universe as the great bowl of the sky. The small three-tiered structure on top became the basis for the pagoda form as Mahayana Buddhism spread from India to China, Korea, and Japan. [Giraudon/Art Resource]

religion for all, popularized, humanized, and provided with a variety of supports. The Buddha himself was made into a supernatural god, and there were also innumerable other Buddhas called *bodhisattvas,* saints who out of compassion delayed their entrance into nirvana in order to help those still on earth to attain deliverance. Faith in and worship of a bodhisattva also offered comfort to those who felt they needed divine help for any purpose. This in turn promoted the worship of images, including those of the original Buddha, and the development of elaborate rituals and cults. Such worship by itself, it was held, could produce salvation, as well as help in solving worldly problems.

Some forms of Mahayana Buddhism acquired a magic overlay. Bodhisattvas and their attendants were believed capable of flying through the air. Sanctity could be obtained, some held, merely by repeating ritual phrases or worshiping supposed relics of the Buddha. The Mahayana school also developed details of a bodily heaven to which the faithful would go, filled with recognizable human pleasures, while to match it, there was a gruesome hell, presided over by a host of demons, where the wicked or unworthy suffered an imaginative variety of hideous tortures. One may again compare this with analogous changes in Christianity. As with Christianity too, the popularization of Buddhism led to extensive artistic representation in painting, sculpture, and architecture, including a number of often profoundly beautiful paintings and statues of the Buddha and his attendants and a great variety of temples. The latter included the pagoda form in the Mahayana countries and the dagoba in Theravada lands.

Mahayana Buddhism was transmitted to China, Tibet, Korea, and Japan, because by that time it had become the dominant form in India. From China it spread to Tibet and Korea and from there to Japan by A.D. 500. A number of new Mahayana monastic orders and sects that developed originally in China, including the contemplative and mystical school of Ch'an Buddhism, were diffused to both countries; in Japan, the term *Ch'an* was corrupted into *Zen,* and other schools and monastic orders of Buddhism also flourished. The growth of Japanese Buddhism accelerated greatly during the period of direct Japanese contact with T'ang dynasty China (eighth century A.D.), when many Japanese Buddhist monks visited the country. In Japan and Korea too, Buddhist art flourished in a variety of forms. In the 840s the Chinese state, concerned about and covetous of the growing wealth and power of Buddhist temples and monasteries, confiscated much of it and suppressed Buddhism except as a small minority religion within a dominantly Confucian context. That was to be its fate until modern times, but in Japan Buddhism remained proportionately far more important. Buddhism is today, at least nominally, the major religion of Japan, although most Japanese are either wholly secular or very casual followers in their adherence to any religious faith. In Korea Buddhism survived the T'ang persecution and remained vigorous, though losing ground in the modern period to secularism, as in Japan.

Confucianism

Many people argue that Confucianism is not a religion but merely a set of ethical rules, a moral philosophy. It is true that it specifically avoids any concern with theology, the afterlife, or otherworldly matters and true as well that most Chinese, Korean, Vietnamese, and Japanese Confucianists supplemented it with Buddhism, Taoism, or Shinto (traditional Japanese animism or nature worship), which provide a greater otherworldly structure. In the end it does not perhaps matter whether one calls Confucianism religion or philosophy; it is the creed by which millions of East Asians, close to a third of the world, have lived for over 2,000 years. Confucianism has probably made more impact on belief and behavior than any of the great religions, in the sense that most East Asians accept and follow the teachings of Confucius more thoroughly than the ethical teachings of any other system of belief. Those teachings contain much common sense about human relations, but they are a good deal more than that, reflecting and shaping a highly distinctive set of values, norms, and sociopolitical patterns. Confucianism has its temples too, which serve as monuments to the doctrine even though it lacks a prescribed ritual or organized priesthood.

Confucius and Mencius

Confucius (551–c. 479 B.C.), the son of a minor official in one of the smaller states of eastern China long before the first imperial unification, became a teacher and later an adviser to various local rulers. He never had a definite official post, and he had no discernible political influence. Like Plato, he looked for rulers who might be shaped by his advice, and like Plato, he never really found one. Several of his students became his disciples, though never as organized as in Plato's Academy; after his death, they and their students began to write down his teachings and to expand on them.

The most famous of his later followers and commentators was Meng-tzu (Mengzi), or Mencius (c. 372–c. 289 B.C.). Confucius and Mencius lived in the chaotic period of warring Chinese states and sought means for restoring order and social harmony through individual morality. Society in East Asia has always been profoundly hierarchical. The social order was seen in terms of a series of status groups and graded roles, from the ruler at the top through officials, scholars, and gentlemen to the father of the family, all of whom possessed authority over those below them but also had the responsibility to set a good example. The key element was "right relationships," carefully defined for each association: father-son, subject-ruler, husband-wife, elder brother–younger brother, and so on. Confucius and Mencius provided what became doctrinal support for such a system. It left small place for the individual but at the same time stressed the vital importance

Confucius: A Ch'ing dynasty ink rubbing, made over two thousand years after the death of the sage, of whom there are no contemporary portraits. [**Granger Collection**]

of self-cultivation and education as the only true guarantee of morality, or "virtuous behavior."

The Confucian View

According to Confucianism, people are born naturally good and inclined to virtue but need education and the virtuous example of superiors to stay that way. Confucius emphasized "human-heartedness," benevolence, respect for superiors, filial loyalty, and learning to prevent anarchy and to achieve the "great harmony" between self and society that was his chief objective. Force and law were no guarantee of individual virtue or of social harmony, and indeed they were seen as ineffective as well as unnecessary in a properly run society. People must *want* to do right, and that can be achieved only by internalizing morality. When force or punishment have to be used, the social system has broken down.

Confucianism offered a highly pragmatic, this-worldly, and positive view of people and of society; it provided little scope for metaphysical speculation, for the supernatural, or for concepts like sin or salvation. Although Confucius and Mencius were certainly conservatives and supporters of a hierarchical social order, their doctrine also allowed for individual ability and dedication. They taught that everyone is born with the seeds of virtue and that by self-cultivation and by following virtuous examples, anyone can become a sage. This concept was incorporated later in the imperial examination system and the selection of officials from the ranks of the educated, regardless of their social origins. Confucianism also reaffirmed the right of the people to rebel against immoral or unjust rulers who had forfeited the "mandate of Heaven" by their lapse from virtue. Thus loyalty to superiors was ultimately subordinate to moral principle. This often presented individuals with a severe dilemma, especially in family situations; fathers, for example, however unjust, were rarely defied.

Natural calamities like floods, droughts, or earthquakes were commonly taken as portents of Heaven's displeasure at the unvirtuous behavior of rulers and as pretexts for rebellion, especially since they disturbed the Confucian sense of order and harmony. The natural world was seen as the model for the human world. Both ran by regular rules. Nature was a nurturing power, not a hostile one, grander and more to be admired than human works, something to which people should harmoniously adjust rather than attempt to conquer. But it was not to be looked to except as a pattern. As Confucius said, "Heaven does not speak"; it merely shows us a model of order and harmony to emulate.

Such occasional references to Heaven as an impersonal force superior to humanity are about as far as Confucius went beyond the human world. When disciples asked about the suprahuman world or life after death, he merely said that we had enough to do in understanding and managing human affairs without troubling about other matters. Although he did not explicitly say so, he did approve, however, of what is rather misleadingly called "ancestor worship." In folk religion, ancestors were prayed to as if they could intervene as helpers. Confucian practice merely extended respect for one's elders to those who had gone before, valuing them as models and performing regular rituals in small household shrines to keep their memory alive. It was the duty of the eldest son to perform rituals on the death of his father, keeping the ancestral chain intact through succesive generations and thus ensuring family continuity. Mencius underlined this by saying that of all sins against filiality (respect for one's parents), the greatest was to have no descendants, by which he meant male descendants, since women left their parental family at marriage and became members of their husband's family. This attitude still militates against current Chinese efforts to reduce the birthrate.

In the twelfth century A.D. the Confucian philosopher Chu Hsi (Zhuxi, 1130–1200) went somewhat further in speculating about the nature of the universe, in whose operation he saw the working of abstract principles, rather

Sayings of Confucius

Sayings attributed to Confucius and printed in the Analects *are usually brief and pithy. Here are some examples.*

- Learning without thought is useless. Thought without learning is dangerous.
- Shall I teach you the meaning of knowledge? When you know a thing to recognize that you know it, and when you do not know to recognize that you do not know, that is knowledge.
- Not yet understanding life, how can one understand death?
- The gentleman is concerned about what is right, the petty man about what is profitable.
- The gentleman's quality is like wind, the common people's like grass; when the wind blows, the grass bends.
- If one leads them with administrative measures and uses punishments to make them conform, the people will be evasive; but if one leads them with virtue, they will come up to expectations.

The following are from the Book of Mencius.

- Between father and son there should be affection; between sovereign and minister, righteousness; between husband and wife, attention to their separate functions; between young and old, a proper order; and between friends, fidelity.
- Nature speaks not, but the ongoing of the seasons achieves the nurturing of the ten thousand things of creation. . . . [The moral laws of society] form the same system with the laws by which the seasons succeed each other. . . . It is this same system of laws by which all created things are produced and develop themselves, each in its order and system, without injuring one another, that makes the universe so grand and impressive.

Source: Translated by R. Murphey.

like those of Plato, and a Supreme Ultimate, or impersonal cosmic force. From his time on it is appropriate to speak of Neo-Confucianism, which also sets before every person the goal of becoming a sage through self-cultivation. Like classic Confucianism before it, Neo-Confucianism spread to Korea, Vietnam, and Japan, where it became the dominant philosophy, especially among the educated.

Confucianism in general strikes a balance between individual self-development and achievement on the one hand and the subjection of the individual to the greater good of the family and society on the other. Unfettered individualism and freedom, basic values to Americans, connote in East Asia selfishness and the absence of rules or essential constraints, the result of which is social chaos, from which everyone suffers. For Confucianism, chaos is the greatest of all evils. Though officially rejected, Confucianism remains in many ways the basis of Chinese society today. It has persisted because it works, as the ethical code of probably the world's most successful society over so long a time. It is said to be a basic factor also in the phenomenal success of modern Japan and Korea.

Taoism

The second important moral or religious philosophy of traditional China was Taoism (or Daoism), from the Tao (Dao), or Way. Taoism is hard to define since one of its basic axioms is silence, even inaction. It holds that the observable, rational, human world does not matter; the far greater cosmic world of nature does. Accordingly, one must seek guidance from the cosmos, which is beyond the realm of words. The chief text of Taoism, the *Tao te Ching* ("Classic of the Way"), is a cryptic collection of mystical remarks whose meaning even in Chinese is far from clear. The famous opening line is typical and may be translated as "The name that can be named is not the eternal name" or "The Way that can be spoken of is not the true Way, which is inconstant," implying, one supposes, that truth can only be expressed in language, if at all, through riddle and paradox. Much of the content is attributed to a contemporary of Confucius' known simply as Lao-tze (Laozi, "The Old One"), although the present text is not older than the third century B.C. and was probably compiled by several hands. Lao-tze is said to have debated with Confucius and to have disappeared in old age, traveling westward, where he somehow became immortal.

On one point the *Tao te Ching* is clear: "Those who understand don't talk; those who talk don't understand." This comment may well have been aimed at the Confucians, but although Taoist figures did occasionally speak or write, it was usually in riddles or in metaphors drawn from nature. All make the point that worldly strivings, especially attempts at political control, are futile and wrong. Their message is to relax, "go with the flow," stop trying to improve things, as the Confucians were always doing. The Taoists' favorite model was water, which flows around obstructions, adapts itself to what is, and seeks the lowest places. Whatever is, they said, is natural and hence good.

The other major figure of Taoism was the philosopher Chuang-tze (Zhuangzi; died c. 329 B.C.), whose still intriguing essays and parables further expound the ideas already associated with the school. One of his most delightful stories tells that he dreamed he was a butterfly and when he awoke could not be sure whether he was himself or was the butterfly now dreaming that it was Chuang-tze.

Taoism grew into a religion as it merged with folk beliefs, earlier animistic and nature worship, belief in the supernatural, and a variety of mystical practices. Taoist priests, temples, and monastic orders developed (however inconsistent with the earlier message), and the originally rather esoteric philosophy became a mass religion. Later Taoists, especially after the Han dynasty, practiced magic and alchemy and pursued the search for elixirs of immortality. Such activities put them in bad repute with proper Confucians, as did their habit of irresponsible hedonism or pleasure seeking. However, the Taoists' search for medicinal herbs and their experimentation contributed importantly to the growth of Chinese medicine and other technology. They deviated from their supposed founder's injunctions to accept nature without questioning and began instead to probe for its secrets.

As it acquired a mass following, Taoism also developed a pantheon of gods and "immortals" who offered help to people in trouble and eased the way to a Taoist version of the Buddhist heaven. Taoism became in many ways an important supplement to Confucianism, and Confucians often found parts of it attractive. It was aptly said that most Chinese were Confucian when things went well and Taoist when things went badly and in retirement or old age. Confucianism's activist and social reformist postures were well complemented by Taoism's passivity and inwardness. This dualism appealed to the old Chinese distinction between yin and yang, where yang is the strong, assertive, masculine principle of existence and yin is the passive, intuitive, feminine one. Taoists and Confucianists alike agreed that both nature and humans must approximate a balance of yin and yang elements and that nature should serve as a model for humanity. But where Confucians sought to shape the world through education, Taoists urged acceptance of things as they are, confident that human meddling could not improve on cosmic truth. For them, the human world was terribly petty.

Asian Religions: Some Reflections

Most East Asians have always been eclectic in religion, weaving into their beliefs and practices elements from different religious traditions. Confucianism and Taoism are dominant except in Japan, where Confucianism, Buddhism, and Shinto predominate. Shinto is similar to Taoism but remained closer to animism and nature worship. These complementary parts form a whole, representing the religion or philosophical outlook of nearly a third of the world. Each part of the combination has its undeniable appeal, and it is easy to understand why most people selected from all of them in their beliefs and practices. When Christian missionaries arrived in the sixteenth century, they found the religious ground already thoroughly occupied in Asia not only by Confucianism, Taoism, and Shinto but by Hinduism, Buddhism, and Islam as well. All were old and sophisticated religions or philosophies with long literate traditions.

All of these Asian religions recognized that there is evil in the world, and even evil people, but none of them ever developed the sharp dichotomy (or dualism) between good and evil that is characteristic of Zoroastrianism, Judaism, Christianity, and Islam. In the Indian and Chinese view, all of creation is the work of God ("Heaven," the creative principle), which thus necessarily includes what is perceived by humans as both good and bad. Consequently, there was no conception of "original sin" inherent in individuals, no Garden of Eden or early innocence from which people then fell into error and suffered punishment because they had broken God's rules. Evil was understood as part of God's created world, not as some human aberration. The Christian idea of sin thus had little meaning in Asia; as has often been said, "Eden was preserved in the East." Bad behavior was acknowledged and might be punished in this world and the next, but the basic presumption was that people were born and remained intrinsically good, not with built-in inclinations to "sin."

Misbehavior was seen as a failure of society, which God created imperfect, and the result of an individual's straying from the teaching and model of her or his elders or superiors, as in Confucianism, or from the established rules of her or his dharma in Hinduism and Buddhism, as made clear by priests and sages. People were seen not as morally lost when they strayed from the path but as always redeemable, through education or renewed efforts at right behavior, aided by piety, meditation, and so on. Return to virtue, or "merit," might also be won by good deeds, including charity, or simply by leading (in Christian words) "a godly, righteous, and sober life," but never by having one's "sins" magically forgiven by priestly or other ritual, since no concept of sin existed. Nor was faith or the acceptance of any creed ever seen as paramount, if important at all; people were judged by their actions.

One further distinction between all of these eastern Asian religions on the one hand and Christianity, Judaism, and Islam on the other is their acceptance of the natural world as good, as part of divine creation that is greater and more powerful than humankind but like them a part of the cosmos. People occupy a humbler place in God's creation, and it behooves them therefore to adjust, while seeking in nature the image of God, rather than in themselves. The sages and holy men who sought wisdom and the understanding of God or of the cosmos looked for it in nature, in the mountains, far from human distractions. There was no conception of the natural world as an enemy, to be fought against or overcome, as in later Christianity. Nature was instead seen as a nurturing mother or as an inspiring model. Adapting to it and understanding it were the keys both to earthly success and to spiritual and moral truth.

Such a thread runs deeply through Hinduism, Buddhism, Confucianism, Taoism, and Shinto and is far weaker, absent, or explicitly opposite in Judaism, Christianity, and Islam, as in the Book of Genesis call to the human world to "have dominion" over all the world of nature or in the nineteenth- and twentieth-century Western drive for the "conquest of nature." One might perhaps argue that Judaism, out of which Christianity and later Islam grew, were conceived in a harsher environment than the great religions of Asia, where it may be easier to see nature as beneficent and nurturing and people as prospering by adjusting to, accepting, and admiring it. Whatever the reasons, Asia west of India followed a different religious path.

Zoroastrianism and Mithraism

We know less about Zoroastrianism, the dominant religion of ancient and classical Persia (Iran), than about any of the others described in this chapter. Zoroaster, its founder, lived and preached long before the advent of preserved written records in Persia, probably between 800 and 600 B.C., and the incomplete texts we have on the belief and practice of the religion he founded come mainly from the thirteenth century A.D., although earlier texts were probably written down by the sixth century B.C. The founder's name in Persian was Zarathustra (Zoroaster was the Greek version), and his teachings are recorded and embroidered in the Avesta, but the form of the Avesta we have is only a fragmentary remnant of earlier texts and includes much later material and doctrine. To the Greeks and Romans, Zoroaster was famous as the founder of the wisdom of the Magi, mythical Iranian priest-kings. In his youth he is said to have had celestial visions and conversations with divine beings, after which he became a wandering preacher. Later he interested an eastern Iranian prince in his teachings; the prince became his protector and advocate, and the new religion became a state church.

Zoroastrian Beliefs

Zoroastrianism was rooted in the old Iranian or Aryan folk religion, and there are some striking similarities between it and the religion of Vedic India. Both are polytheistic (professing many gods), and both worshiped Indra as well as natural forces, especially fire. Both believed in the supremacy of moral powers and of an eternal natural law and creative principle. The major difference lay in the pronounced dualism of Zoroastrianism, which divided creation into the powers of good and evil, light and darkness. Vedic India called all their gods and goddesses *deva,* and although many of them had destructive aspects, in general they were seen as good. Zoroastrianism used the closely related term *daeva* in Persian to refer to evil spirits only, which are opposed and kept in check by the forces of good and light, incorporated in the supreme deity, the sexless Ahura-Mazda. In one of several striking parallels with Judeo-Christian theology, Ahura-Mazda's original twin Ahriman was, like Lucifer, banished from heaven to hell, where he or she reigns as the principle of evil. Earlier cults, such as the cult of Mithras, the god of day, survived within Zoroastrianism and later spread to the Mediterranean.

Zoroaster is reported to have said that he received a commission from God to purify religion, in effect by transcending the earlier cults, introducing moral laws, and constructing a theory of the universe embodying the dualist principle. By his time Iranian society was based mainly on agriculture rather than hunting, gathering, or nomadism; had developed cities and towns; and was ready for a more sophisticated theology than nature worship alone or ritual cults. Ahura-Mazda is the personification not only of power and majesty but of ethical principles for the guidance of human behavior. She or he is described in the Avesta as assisted by her or his creatures, "immortal holy ones," the forces of good sense or good principle, truth, law, order, reverence, immortality, and obedience. The history of the conflict between these good forces and the forces of evil is the history of the world. All creation is divided between these two forces, whose endless conflict has as its object the human soul. People are creations of Ahura-Mazda, but they are created free to decide and to act and can be influenced by the forces of evil. All human life and activity are part of this conflict. By a true confession of faith, by good deeds, and by keeping body and soul pure, any individual can limit the power of the evil forces and strengthen the power of goodness. Evil deeds, words, and thoughts strengthen the power of evil.

After death, each person is judged in heaven, according to the Book of Life in which all deeds, thoughts, and words are recorded. Wicked actions cannot be undone but can be balanced by good works. If the balance is favorable, the person enters paradise; if unfavorable, the eternal pains of hell. If the account is equally balanced, a kind of limbo or intermediate stage is provided, with the final lot to be decided at the last judgment. The Avesta tells us almost nothing about ceremonial worship, but it appears from early times to have centered on a sacred fire. Later development of the religion added the doctrine of repentance, atonement, and the remission of sins, administered by priests.

Zoroaster saw himself as a prophet and believed that the end of the present world and the coming of the Kingdom of Heaven were near. But for most people his doctrines were too abstract; both old and new popular deities became part of Zoroastrianism in later periods, and a priesthood developed that organized and conducted worship and laid down detailed laws for the purification of the body and soul, the conduct of good works, the giving of alms, the pursuit of agriculture, and the prohibition against either burning or burying the dead. Both soil and fire, as well as water, were considered sacred and not to be defiled by death. Bodies were to be exposed in appointed places, sometimes an elevated platform, for consumption by vultures and wild dogs. Originally there seem to have been no temples, but in later periods fire altars came into use, and these slowly evolved into more elaborate temples where sacrifices and other rituals were performed by priests. Priests were the teachers and keepers of the religion; every young believer, after being received into the religion, was supposed to choose a spiritual guide, usually a priest. Most of the changes mentioned here seem to have come about by approximately the sixth century B.C. and to have begun considerably earlier.

With the rise of the Persian Empire in the sixth century, Zoroastrianism was further confirmed as the national and state religion of Iran. Under the Achemenid dynasty and its conquests, the religion spread over most of western Asia and what is now the southern USSR. After the collapse of this first empire, Zoroastrianism languished and then was restored to new vigor under the Sassanids from the third to the seventh centuries A.D., when it was again the state church; compliance with its religious laws was even enforced by the state. The Arab conquest of Iran, complete by 637, and the persecutions that followed largely extinguished Zoroastrianism in the land of its birth. In modern Iran there remain only a very few followers, now under new pressure from the rigid fundamentalism of its Muslim rulers. The chief survivors are the Parsees of the Bombay area (the name is a corruption of *Persian*), who came originally from Persia to India about the eighth century A.D., primarily to escape Muslim persecution; they still maintain most of the doctrine and practices of classical Zoroastrianism.

Zoroastrianism, as well as the cult of Mithras, which it incorporated, had a profound influence on both Eastern and Western thinking during the time of its flourishing. It has obvious similarities both with Hinduism and with Judaism and Christianity and in part even with Islam, especially its doctrines on life after death. Its basic dualistic emphasis helped to shape early Christian theology, and more than traces of what was eventually labeled the "dualistic heresy" remain even in modern Christian thought, like its pre-Christian ideas about the judgment of the dead, the relationship between faith and good works, and the role of the priesthood. Arising out of more primitive cults, especially the worship of fire and of the sun, it nevertheless became through the teachings of Zoroaster and his successors a sophisticated theological, cosmological, and ethical system that was known to and admired by both Eastern and Western civilizations before or during the period when they were working out their own transition from tribal cults to mature religious thought. Although Zoroastrianism largely ceased to exist nearly 14 centuries ago, many of its ideas live on in the other great religions, a further reminder of the central role that Persian civilization played in the evolution of Eurasian culture.

Mithraism

The worship of Mithras began as far back as the fourth century B.C. Originally Ahura-Mazda's chief aide in the battle against the powers of darkness, Mithras became the central figure in a cult that spread rapidly throughout western Asia and into Europe, arriving in Rome in the first century B.C. In the years following A.D. 100 it acquired many new adherents in Italy and other parts of the Roman Empire, attracting the lower classes, slaves, and soldiers, who took their religious customs with them when they served abroad—a temple to Mithras has been discovered in the Roman remains of London. By the late third century A.D. Mithraism was vying with Christianity to replace the old paganism, although Constantine's support of the Christians caused Mithraism's rapid decline.

Mithraism's broad appeal was probably due to the fact that it combined the spirituality of its origins with humanizing detail. Unlike Ahura-Mazda, the remote god of light, Mithras, god of day, was born in human form on December 25 in a cave. When he grew up, he slaughtered a mythical sacred bull, whose blood fertilized the earth. After a time the god returned to heaven, where he constantly interceded with Ahura-Mazda on behalf of his followers.

Ceremonies in honor of Mithras were held in special temples known as Mithraea, which often took the form of underground caves in memory of his birth. Among the rites of initiation was baptism in the blood of a bull, which formed one of the seven stages of induction; others included the recitation of various miracles that Mithras had performed, such as ending a drought and averting a flood.

It is a measure of Mithraism's appeal that Christianity adopted a number of its external characteristics, including the symbolic date of December 25 as the birthday of Jesus—the day marks the approximate period of the winter solstice, when the sun, returning from south of the equator, is "reborn." Yet in the end Mithraism was to gain no lasting hold. One reason for this may well be that women were not accepted as initiates and played no part in the rituals or the myths. By contrast, many of the early converts to Christianity were women, and tradition has it that Constantine himself was much influenced by his mother Helena, herself a Christian.

Judaism

Unlike Buddhists or Christians, the Jews have maintained a strong sense of ethnic as well as spiritual identity. That this identity has survived so lengthy and so tragic a history is an indication of the strength of Jewish convictions.

From the very beginning of their history the Jews saw themselves as special instruments of a unique providence. The vision of Abraham, whose family fled from Ur around 2000 B.C., was twofold. Abraham, the traditional founder of the Jewish people, put his faith in a God who operated in the world on principles of righteousness. At the same time he saw the Jews as appointed by his God to communicate this vision to the world. To transmit their message, the Jews found it essential to maintain their separateness from the peoples with whom they came in contact. This did not preclude the possibility of others joining the Jewish nation, but those who did so had to give tangible proof of their conversion. The symbolic representation of this was the rite of circumcision, a tradition that probably goes back to the time of Abraham. In addition, as Judaism developed, customs evolved that were intended to strengthen the sense of ethnic distinctness.

The Covenant at Sinai

Abraham's message had stressed a universal obligation for the Hebrews to serve humanity as a "kingdom of priests." The more precise terms and conditions of this service were spelled out by Moses in the Sinai desert after the exodus from Egypt, particularly in the Ten Commandments, which laid out the basic tenets of the Jewish ethical system. The first four dealt with human obligations to God and described how Yahweh was to be worshiped. The remaining six were concerned with relationships between peoples, parents and children, husbands and wives; they also prohibited certain crimes, such as perjury, theft, and murder, which might involve strangers. Other ancient religions produced codes governing conduct, but the Ten Commandments were unique in that they were directed not only at the Jews but all peoples. They underlined the special character of the Jewish message, moreover, by forbidding the worship of nature or of images and by emphasizing that the piety and morality they outlined constituted a duty. All who abided by them would be rewarded; the disobedient would be punished.

By subscribing to the Covenant, the Jews acquired a special historical consciousness. The Ten Commandments were universal in their application, yet the Jews alone bore the responsibility of communicating the message to the rest of the world. This sense of special identity proved crucial to the survival of Judaism, and the Jews, throughout centuries of persecution.

The Torah

The teachings that evolved from the Covenant at Sinai are known as the *Torah,* or Law. The Torah laid out the religious and moral requirements of Judaism in prescriptions and prohibitions; one of its special characteristics was the importance laid on negative commands: "thou shalt not." Jewish law aimed to cultivate a holiness that would influence not only the spiritual life of individuals but also their relationship to society. Just as the pious Buddhist was enjoined not to wander from the path by injunctions that were intended to regulate human relationships, so Jews were taught by the Torah not only about their religious duties but also about their earthly responsibilities, including an injunction to "love thy neighbor as thyself" that could apply to Jews and non-Jews alike.

As in Hinduism and Buddhism, Jewish law paid special attention to the poor and the weak. Employers were forbidden to exploit their workers. There were complex regulations about the making and repaying of loans that were designed to protect the borrower. Unlike the Law

A section from the scrolls found near the Dead Sea in 1947, probably dating from the first century B.C. [Zev Radovan, Jerusalem]

Code of Hammurabi and the laws of the Hittites, which were intended to safeguard property, the Torah sought to protect the individual. This concern extended also to animals. Although Jews were not required to be vegetarians, as pious Hindus were, they were instructed to treat oxen and other work animals with kindness and to allow them the same rights as humans to rest on the Sabbath, the weekly day of repose. Detailed instructions concerned the preparation and consumption of food and drink and other aspects of daily life. The dietary regulations covered both foods that could and could not be eaten and the dishes and utensils with which they were prepared and consumed. This tradition, often loosely referred to as "keeping kosher," is still observed by many Jews today. In general, the aim of the Torah's social legislation was to eliminate distinctions based on rank, wealth, or birth; in the eyes of the law, all people were equal and enjoyed the same rights. This was in strong contrast to the hierarchic caste system of Hinduism or the graded society of Confucius.

In later centuries Judaic traditions often had the effect of alienating the Jews from other people among whom they lived. Even in cosmopolitan Alexandria, as we have seen, the Jewish community lived apart from the rest of the population, a tradition that, by unhappy irony, became a requirement in the ghettos of the Middle Ages in Europe. It is therefore important to remember that the Torah exhorts Jews to follow the example of their God and love all persons equally. Only by doing so, while maintaining their own Jewish character, could they truly love God. Tradition, together with the experience of prolonged exile following a brief period of nationhood, may have accentuated the Jews' sense of distinctiveness. Furthermore, their belief that they were the people divinely chosen to reveal God's love for all was often interpreted by non-Jews as a conviction of moral superiority. Yet from its beginning the message of Judaism was intended to be applicable not to the Jews alone but to all societies.

The Prophets

The injunctions of the Torah left no doubt that people who violated the Law would be punished. Formal warning, however, was in itself insufficient to instill righteousness, and throughout the history of the foundation and subsequent collapse of the kingdom of Israel there appeared religious figures known as prophets. The word is derived from the Greek word *profetes,* meaning "one who speaks for another"; the prophets of the Old Testament thought of themselves as spokesmen for God. Inspired by their visions of God's will, they counseled and rebuked their contemporaries on every aspect of religious, moral, and political conduct.

The earliest prophets were probably unofficially attached to shrines or, during the kingdom, to the royal household. From the eighth century B.C., however, figures such as Jeremiah vigorously expressed their opposition to corruption in official religion. Calling his people to a rigid observance of ethical monotheism, Jeremiah railed against the emptiness and hypocrisy of formal religious observance. Speaking on behalf of his God, he thundered: "Why have they provoked me to anger with their graven images and with their foreign idols?"[1] Other prophets, such as Isaiah, reminded the Jews of their unique historical mission: "Give thanks to the Lord, call upon his name; make known his deeds among the nations, proclaim that his name is exalted."[2]

Although the prophets affirmed their belief in the special destiny of the Jews, they underlined the universal nature of their message and insisted on the necessity of rigorous monotheism. The God of Israel was the only God, destined to be the God of all people. Furthermore, their messages were directed against not only religious error but also social injustice. In language that was frequently sharp, they reproved an errant people for breaking their covenant with God. In the words of Amos: "Seek the Lord and live, lest he break out like fire in the house of Joseph, and it devour, with none to quench it for Bethel [the northern kingdom's chief sanctuary], O you who turn justice to wormwood, and cast down righteousness to the earth!"[3]

The role of the prophet as unofficial mediator between God and humanity is a special characteristic of the Jewish religion and was partly embraced by Christianity and Islam. It profoundly influenced the life and teachings of Jesus, whose fierce denunciations of the Jewish religious leaders of his day were in the tradition of Jeremiah and other prophets.

With the destruction of Solomon's temple at Jerusalem in A.D. 70 by Roman forces, the Jews lost the focal point of their worship. The temple was never forgotten; indeed, to this day pious Jews pray at the western wall of the building, known as the Wailing Wall, the only part still standing. Jewish tradition advises observant Jews to leave a tiny part of their house unfinished, perhaps a small piece of wall unplastered, in memory of Jerusalem and its temple. The very need to remember Jerusalem underlines the sense of dispersal that has permeated the past two millennia of the Jewish Diaspora ("scattering").

JERUSALEM: THE HOLY CITY

The historic center of Judaism, Jerusalem, is today the crossroads of three great world religions, Judaism, Christianity, and Islam, and remains sacred to each. The historic city of Jerusalem is situated dramatically on a series of hills north of the Negev desert. From its very beginnings it appears to have been a sacred city; its name derives from Shalem, a western Semitic deity of the second millennium B.C. King David captured it from a local tribe, the Jebusites, about the year 1000 B.C., and made it the capital of ancient Israel. David's successor, Solomon,

A Prophet Calls for Social Reform

Typical of the prophetic message is the following passage from Amos, written in the eighth century B.C. The prophet is incensed by the social injustice he sees among the Hebrews.

Listen to this, you that trample on the needy and try to destroy the poor of the country. You say to yourselves, "We can hardly wait for the holy days to be over so that we can sell our grain. When will the sabbath end, so that we can start selling again? Then we can overcharge, use false measures, and fix the scales to cheat our customers. We can sell worthless wheat at a high price. We'll find a poor man who can't pay his debts, not even the price of a pair of sandals, and we'll buy him as a slave."

The Lord, the God of Israel, has sworn, "I will never forget their evil deeds. And so the earth will quake, and everyone in the land will be in distress. The whole country will be shaken; it will rise and fall like the Nile River. The time is coming when I will make the sun go down at noon and the earth grow dark in daytime. I, the Sovereign Lord, have spoken. I will turn your festivals into funerals and change your glad songs into cries of grief. I will make you shave your heads and wear sackcloth, and you will be like parents mourning for their only son. That day will be bitter to the end.

"The time is coming when I will send famine on the land.

People will be hungry, but not for bread; they will be thirsty, but not for water. They will hunger and thirst for a message from the Lord. I, the Sovereign Lord, have spoken."

Source: Amos 8:4–11a, *Good News Bible* (New York: American Bible Society, 1976).

greatly enlarged it and built a massive temple for the Ark of the Covenant, which David had brought with him.

The temple was a thick-walled rectangular building of squared stones and cedar beams laid out east to west, 110 feet long, 48 feet wide, and more than 50 feet high. A huge porch extended on its eastern side, and side chambers were built against the other three sides. An interior wall marked off the main hall from the sanctuary of the ark, a 30-foot cube paneled with richly carved cedar that admitted light through high lattice windows and contained a single lamp. The ark itself was surmounted by two cherubim carved from olive wood, each standing 15 feet high.

Over the centuries the city and especially the temple became the primary focus of the Jewish faith. Psalm 137 still rings with the passionate sense of loss felt by the Jewish people during their first exile from the city during the Babylonian captivity of the sixth century B.C.:

> ***If I forget thee, O Jerusalem, let my right***
> ***hand lose its cunning.***
> ***If I forget thee, O Jerusalem, let my tongue***
> ***cleave to the roof of my mouth.***

After the return to Zion, a second temple, completed around 515 B.C., was built on the ruins of the first. The city too was rebuilt and flourished under successive domination by the Persians, the Ptolemaic dynasty of Egypt, and the Romans. During the Hellenistic period the Jews became widely dispersed throughout the eastern Mediterranean world, but Jerusalem remained their spiritual capital, the site of their pilgrimages, and the direction they turned to in prayer. All pious Jews, wherever they were, sent a half shekel of tribute each year for the upkeep of the temple.

Ancient Jerusalem reached the height of its splendor under the otherwise repressive rule of the Roman client-king Herod (37–4 B.C.), who undertook a restoration and expansion of the temple that was completed only shortly before both the city and the temple were razed in the wake of the Jewish rebellion of A.D. 70. Despite Herod's unpopularity, even his Jewish subjects marveled at the reconstruction of their temple; one rabbi commented, "He who has not set eyes upon the structure of Herod has not seen a structure of beauty in his life." But few guessed that the fame of Herod would rest not on his public works but on the birth, late in his reign, of Jesus of Nazareth. Jerusalem was where Jesus came to preach his gospel and where on the small hillock of Golgotha outside the city walls he was crucified in A.D. 29.

Christianity made little headway in Jerusalem in the decades after Jesus' death and slow progress even after the city was once again rebuilt. It was not until its adoption by the Roman emperor Constantine that the sites associated with his life were identified. The magnificent Church

Following the Jewish revolt against Roman rule in A.D. 66, Roman troops looted Jerusalem, taking such religious objects from the temple as the *menorah,* or seven-branched candlestick, and the sacred trumpets. The scene is depicted here on the Arch of Titus in Rome. [Alinari/Art Resource]

of the Resurrection, completed in A.D. 335, marked the beginning of Jerusalem as a Christian capital, and by the end of the fourth century it was crowded with churches, shrines, and monasteries, as well as hospices for the many thousands of pilgrims who now thronged to it. Within the church Jerusalem was elevated to the status of a patriarchate, equal in rank to the far larger cities of Alexandria, Antioch, and the new imperial capital of Constantinople. Under the Byzantine emperors, its position was unrivaled. But after a brief Persian occupation (A.D. 614–629), it surrendered to Muslim forces, ushering in the city's third phase as a religious center.

The Talmud

With the temple gone and its priests scattered, Jewish worship centered on local synagogues and their teachers, or rabbis. The term *rabbi* is often applied to individuals who have undergone special study and training in religious matters. In more recent times rabbis have come to serve as the equivalent of priests or ministers of congregations, with a wide range of social and counseling responsibilities. In its original sense, however, the term was applied to anyone who impressed fellow Jews by the wisdom and insight with which he expounded Jewish Law.

The principal source of the Law was to be found in the biblical texts. The transformation of the written and oral accounts into a fixed canon was long and complex; the work that came to be known among Christians as the Old Testament had probably received its final form by A.D. 100. Rabbinical teachings on these biblical texts, together with legal judgments, religious duties, and other aspects of Jewish life, began to be collected and written down by the scattered Jewish communities of the Diaspora. By the middle of the fourth century B.C. the Jews of Palestine had put together a compilation of religious and ethical teachings known as the *Talmud,* which, together with another version of the Talmud produced slightly later in Babylon, has served ever since as the single most cohesive force in Judaism. The aim of the Talmud's creators was to use biblical interpretation and discussion as the basis for religious, moral, and legal practice that could serve all Jewish communities.

The rituals of modern Judaism still derive from the Talmud, as do marriage laws and other social customs. Until the nineteenth century religious services made use of the Hebrew liturgy, which included psalms and other readings from the Bible, established by Talmudic scholars; Orthodox Jewish worshipers continue this practice today. The custom of the "bar mitzvah" (the confirmation of boys at the age of 13) and the principal holy days of the year, together with the manner in which they should be kept, all derive from the Talmud. Yom Kippur, the day of atonement for sins, the most solemn day of the year, is marked by fasting.

Firmly anchored in a tradition that goes back to the Torah and Moses' exposition of the Covenant, the Talmud is a practical guide to conduct rather than a theological treatise. Unlike the early Christian writers, who sought to provide a sound theological basis for the principles of their religion, the Talmudic rabbis concentrated almost exclusively on religious practice and questions of morality in human relationships. The Talmud teaches that faith is valuable only if it leads to ethical action. In this way Judaism has avoided many of the theological controversies that characterize the history of Christianity. In its insistence on God as pure spirit, Talmudic doctrine reaffirms a belief as old as Abraham. The Hebrew Scriptures, it is true, refer to God as one who addresses Moses and the prophets, but this manner of speaking is used only to make communication possible between God and humans: "We describe God by terms borrowed from the divine creation in order to make [God] intelligible to humans." Judaism is thus the only ancient religion that avoids the use of the visual arts and condemns the worship of "graven images." Centuries later Islam adopted similar strictures.

The goal to which obedience to God will lead is an age of righteousness on earth. Judaism believes that this period of universal peace will be ushered in by the Messiah, who will preside over the spiritual regeneration of humanity. In the words of Isaiah, "Of the increase of his government and of peace there will be no end, upon the throne of David, and over his kingdom, to establish it, and to uphold it with justice and with righteousness from this time forth and for evermore."[4]

Judaism remains a minority religion outside of Israel. If its ethical influence remains strong, that is in part because such principles have proved relevant to people in a wide variety of circumstances, often adverse, from the Babylon of Nebuchadnezzar to the concentration camps of Nazi Germany. At the same time Judaism's principal religious texts, the Hebrew Scriptures, have had a profound influence on every aspect of Western culture. Many of its principles have entered the mainstream of Western culture through the religion that sprang from it, Christianity.

Christianity

From the time of its adoption by Constantine, the history of Christianity has been inextricably linked with that of Western culture. During the centuries of its diffusion and transmission by missionaries throughout virtually the entire world, it has taken on a variety of forms. If the range of Christian belief is less varied than that of Hinduism, it is more eclectic than Judaism or, probably, Buddhism. Yet its founder, Jesus of Nazareth, was a Jew who regularly attended the synagogue on the Sabbath and on the principal Jewish religious festivals and who declared that his purpose was not to destroy but to fulfill the Jewish Law.

Virtually all that is known about the life of Jesus is contained in the Gospels of Matthew, Mark, Luke, and John. Even the date of his birth is uncertain; most modern authorities place it between 4 and 2 B.C. The Gospel writers give little information about his early life; only Matthew and Luke describe the nativity (the birth of Jesus) and his childhood.

Near the age of 30 Jesus was baptized by John "the Baptist," a religious ascetic in the style of the earlier prophets. Fervent in denouncing the ways of his contemporaries, John predicted that one greater than he would come after him as an agent of divine judgment and identified that figure as Jesus. In taking up the life of an itinerant rabbi, Jesus continued to preach John's message that the Jews should mend their ways and return to a strict observance of the Law. He was assisted in his mission by a band of 12 male followers, who were called the apostles.

By the time of Jesus' baptism Jerusalem had become the capital of the Roman province of Judea and the center for a wide variety of Jewish religious movements. The teachings of the Pharisees, who advocated strict observance of the Law, were at one extreme. The Sadducees combined Jewish traditions with those of the Greco-Roman world in a blend typical of the Hellenistic period, while the Zealots advocated violent revolution against the Romans. These groups were united in one respect: opposition to the teachings of Jesus.

The ideals that emerge in the Gospel accounts stress the importance of love and the avoidance of anger or violence. In the Sermon on the Mount, Jesus extends the traditional Jewish sympathy for the poor and the helpless: "Blessed are the meek, for they shall inherit the earth." His teaching was explicitly based on the Law; his insistence on the importance of following its ethical content rather than merely observing its outward forms drew the anger of the Pharisees. Their attempts to trap him in a simple solution to moral dilemmas are described by the Gospel writers. When Jesus was reproached for preaching against divorce, which was permitted by Mosaic Law, he replied: "For your hardness of heart Moses allowed you to divorce your wives, but from the beginning it was not so."

Jesus' declaration that the Kingdom of God was at hand was interpreted by some of his followers as referring to contemporary political events; they believed him to be predicting the expulsion of the Romans and the refounding of David's old kingdom of Israel. The use of David's title of Messiah (*Christos,* in Greek) by Jesus' followers thus implied that he was the successor of the great Jewish king;

The Sermon on the Mount

The essence of Jesus' teaching is found in the Sermon on the Mount.

Now when he saw the crowds, he went up on a mountainside and sat down. His disciples came to him, and he began to teach them, saying:

"Blessed are the poor in spirit,
for theirs is the kingdom of heaven.
"Blessed are those who mourn,
for they will be comforted.
"Blessed are the meek,
for they will inherit the earth.
"Blessed are those who hunger and thirst for righteousness,
for they will be filled.
"Blessed are the merciful,
for they will be shown mercy.
"Blessed are the pure in heart,
for they will see God.
"Blessed are the peacemakers,
for they will be called sons of God.
"Blessed are those who are persecuted because of righteousness,
for theirs is the kingdom of heaven.

"Blessed are you when people insult you, persecute you and falsely say all kinds of evil against you because of me. Rejoice and be glad, because great is your reward in heaven, for in the same way they persecuted the prophets who were before you. . . . Do not think that I have come to abolish the Law or the Prophets; I have not come to abolish them but to fulfill them. . . .

"You have heard that it was said, 'Love your neighbor and hate your enemy.' But I tell you: Love your enemies and pray for those who persecute you, that you may be sons of your Father in heaven."

Source: Matt. 5:1–12, 17, 43–45a. Taken from the *Holy Bible: New International Version* © 1978 by the New York International Bible Society. Used by permission.

it was for this reason that he was condemned for blasphemy by the high priest and crucified by the Romans.

The apostles' belief in Jesus' physical resurrection was the prime factor in the foundation of a church to promote his teachings. The message of the apostle Peter's first sermon was that Jesus had died and risen to be with God and that the adherence of those who accepted his resurrection was marked by the rite of baptism. These first Christians were Jewish by birth and continued to follow the basic Jewish Law, but their belief in the divine as well as the human nature of Jesus inevitably aroused hostility and suspicion among their contemporaries. When one early convert, Stephen, was stoned to death, many of the others left Jerusalem and traveled throughout Asia, preaching and seeking converts. One of them, Thomas, is even credited by tradition with having carried Christianity to India.

Paul and the Expansion of Christianity

The most important figure in the development and spread of Christianity was Paul (died A.D. 67), a Pharisee who had been present at the stoning of Stephen. Converted to Christianity by a vision, Paul was the first and greatest theologian of the early church. As a Jew he spoke Aramaic, the language of Jesus and his followers, but he had been brought up in the Greek city of Tarsus and was at home in the world of Greco-Roman culture. His exposition of

One of the earliest (c. 460) surviving depictions of Jesus' crucifixion and resurrection. At the foot of the cross Roman soldiers gamble for Jesus' robe. From the "Rabula Gospels." [Alinari/Art Resource]

the principal beliefs of Christianity, together with his subsequent preaching in Greece and Italy, played a major part in Christianity's rapid spread. The cohesion of the early church and its teachings, for which Paul is largely responsible, is in strong contrast to the variety of traditions that accumulated about the Buddha after his death.

According to Pauline doctrine, human failure to follow God's law was the consequence of Adam and Eve's disobedience, which corrupted all their descendants. Thus humans could achieve salvation not by living in accordance with any set of laws, Jewish or other, but only by the grace of God. The life and death of Jesus were intended, Paul taught, as a manifestation of this grace; as God's son, he suffered in order to show God's love for humanity. All who accepted Jesus' sacrifice through faith, said Paul, could thus achieve reconciliation with God.

Paul was the virtual creator of Christian theology, and his views were debated and generally accepted throughout the early church. Yet the austerity of his view of proper relations between men and women caused problems for future theologians. Women played an important part in the life of Jesus and were among his most loyal and devoted supporters; a majority of those who followed him to his crucifixion were women. Nonetheless, for Paul they were required to play a subordinate social role. The devout man, he taught, should avoid them as much as possible: "It is well for a man not to touch a woman." Those who were single should remain so, Paul urged, as he himself did. Marriage was counseled in cases where sexual abstinence was impossible, but Paul warned that it tended to distract from spiritual duties by tempting the couple to think in worldly terms. Elsewhere in his writings, however, Paul compares marriage to Christ's relationship with the church. Paul's teachings have profoundly influenced social relations and sexual ethics in the West up to our time.

Paul saw Christianity as a universal religion. Unlike Judaism, it involved no traditional or ethnic barriers, and unlike Hinduism or Buddhism, its followers could become Christians only by rejecting their earlier religious beliefs. In expressing these ideas Paul used what was the universal language of his day, Greek, which had been spoken since the Hellenistic period from Italy to India. The use of Greek helped transform Christianity from an offshoot of Judaism to a universal religion by placing it on the vast stage of the Roman Empire. The other crucial factor in the transformation was Paul's insistence that converts to Christianity were not bound to follow the customs prescribed in the Jewish Law or to undergo the rite of circumcision. Paul's opinion was much debated in the first century of Christianity, but its general acceptance facilitated the conversion of Gentiles to the early church. (*Gentile* is derived from a Latin word meaning "non-Roman," thus "foreign," "pagan.")

The rich and complex character of many Hellenistic cults, with their blend of ancient Greek and Asian features, had in many ways prepared the West to accept a new religion from Asia. Throughout the Roman world, as we have seen, philosophical systems of belief such as Stoicism and Epicureanism provided satisfaction only to an elite few, while traditional Roman religion was largely an instrument of the state. Provided that they said or did nothing to question the state's authority, Paul and other Christian missionaries were free to preach their doctrines in public. Nor was there any serious chance of Jewish opposition, since the Roman forces that destroyed the temple in Jerusalem in 70 effectively ended the city's role as a religious center. Indeed, some Hellenized Jews throughout the Roman world became enthusiastic converts, and the network of synagogues throughout the Mediterranean area and western Asia often provided a valuable platform for Paul and the other missionaries.

For its first decades the new movement functioned on a relatively informal basis, with preachers, teachers, and evangelists either self-appointed or selected by individual congregations. The community at Jerusalem remained "first among equals," while Paul continued to exercise supervision over the churches he founded. Conflict with the Roman authorities was usually avoided; Paul himself instructed Christians to obey the laws and pay taxes.

As Christian communities grew and became more active, the need for greater organization arose. Around the end of the first century the principal seat of religious authority was transferred from Jerusalem to Rome, where according to tradition Peter and Paul had founded a church. Each community had a leader, or bishop, but beginning in the fourth and fifth centuries the bishops of Rome claimed supreme authority by virtue of their reputed succession from Peter.

In addition there remained a constant need to define and explain Christian doctrine as it came into contact with adherents of other beliefs. The Gnostics, who followed a Hellenistic blend of Greek and Roman religious beliefs, posed a particular challenge. They despised the world of matter and sought salvation by escape from the flesh, like Hindu and Buddhist ascetics. Many of them eagerly adopted the belief in a divine Christ but could not accept that the divinity had become flesh in the person of Jesus. To avoid the confusion of dogma presented by Gnostic Christians and others like them, the leaders of the early church formalized their teachings.

It was in response to a Gnostic opponent of the church, Marcion (died c. 160), who refused to acknowledge the Old Testament as a source of revelation, that the Christian canon evolved. From the time that the content of the New Testament was established, this canon served as a binding force for Christians throughout the Roman Empire and has remained central to Christianity ever since. Judaism and Christianity are therefore "religions of the book" in a way that Hinduism and Buddhism are not.

The earliest Christian preachers were the apostles themselves, who chose and ordained their successors. Throughout the history of the church, its leaders have traced their mission back to the earliest Christians, and the concept of apostolic succession represents a major difference between Christianity and Judaism. The religious ceremonies conducted by the early ministers of the church were in the vernacular, and the rites included the celebration of the sacraments, visible ceremonies intended to bestow divine grace on worthy recipients. Two sacraments are retained by nearly all Christians today in one form or another: the rite of baptism and the commemoration of the Last Supper. The precise nature and number of these sacraments, however, was the subject of long debate. The Catholic church finally established the definitive number at seven, but this was repudiated by Protestant reformers in the sixteenth century.

The Church and the Roman Empire

During the reign of Septimius Severus (193–211) figures such as Julia Domna began to take an interest in the theoretical bases of Christianity. One of the principal Christian writers of the age was Tertullian (c. 160–c. 225), who was the first to formulate the doctrine of the Trinity, whereby one God is simultaneously conceived of as Father, Son, and Holy Spirit. The detailed philosophical implications of this doctrine provided thorny problems for the church for centuries.

Two other major figures of the third century, Clement (c. 150–c. 214) and Origen (c. 185–c. 254), both of Alexandria, continued the process of synthesizing the original Jewish content of Christianity with Greek ideas and culture and making the result available to their Roman readers. Origen, however, fell victim to the first major systematic persecution of Christians, initiated by Emperor Decius (249–251). After Decius' death, Christians were able to resume their worship, but the persecution had created a new theological issue: should those Christians who had saved themselves by making public sacrifices to local gods be forgiven and admitted back into their congregations? To deal with such cases, a system of penance evolved that was to prove one of the most striking characteristics of medieval Christianity.

Christianity's impact on the Roman Empire during its first three centuries was through the effects of personal example and moral witness rather than systematic organization and conversion. The high moral standard maintained by most Christian leaders, coupled with the willingness of many to die as martyrs, elicited reluctant admiration. The subtleties of Christian theology attracted the interest of many prominent intellectuals. Furthermore, both church and empire depended for their success on careful organization and concern for administrative detail; some church leaders, in fact, saw the empire as a force for order, making possible the performance of their own work.

By the beginning of the fourth century one out of every ten Roman citizens was at least nominally a Christian. The emperor Diocletian (284–305) attempted to control the growing faith by a series of persecutions that lasted from 303 to 311. Although the policy produced thousands of martyrs, it failed in its aim, and in 313 Diocletian's successors, Constantine and Licinius, signed the Edict of Milan, granting all citizens of the empire freedom of religious worship. Constantine subsequently introduced legislation that protected the church. Writing in the aftermath of this new partnership between church and state, the Christian writer Eusebius (c. 260–c. 339) claimed that the empire and the church were both the work of God.

Constantine's toleration for Christianity doubtless owed much to the fact that his mother, Helena, was a Christian who devoted her influence to its promotion. As an elderly woman she visited the Holy Land and helped to found numerous churches there. By the late fourth century writers began to credit her with the discovery of the "true cross" on which Jesus had been crucified.

The Early Church and Heresy

Unlike Hinduism or Buddhism, Christianity presented a single body of doctrine, together with the requirement that adherents accept the faith in the form in which it was handed down and interpreted to them by their religious superiors. Indeed, from the time of Paul the growth of Christian influence had been aided by careful, consistent leadership. With Constantine, victory had been won, but the church paid a price for its success. Its new power and security encouraged the development of alternative views about basic Christian teachings, which had to be discussed and in most cases were prohibited in church councils. Throughout the fourth and fifth centuries various theological interpretations were proposed, only to be declared heresies. The words *heresy* and *heretic* are now often used to describe an unconventional opinion and its holder; they were originally coined to describe someone whose beliefs were contrary to the teaching of the church and whose immortal soul was thus in danger. In this way Christian theological orthodoxy was defined in relationship to views that were deemed unacceptable. In contrast, Judaism never attempted to define heresy; Hinduism has always embraced seemingly inconsistent ideas; and Buddhism, Confucianism, and Taoism, in their different ways, were intended to be adapted to the individual's moral and spiritual needs.

The first dispute was caused by the problem that had occurred after the persecutions of Decius: namely, how people who had betrayed their faith at the time of Diocletian should be treated. The most delicate cases were those of priests who had, at the imperial command, handed over the Scriptures to be burned. A group of rigid opponents to reinstatement developed at Carthage, in North Africa; they were known as the Donatists from their leader, Donatus. In an effort to solve the controversy, Constantine summoned a council of bishops in 314 at Arles in Gaul. Although the council decided against the Donatists, it was unable to enforce its opinion. The principle of using church councils to debate and rule on theological issues, however, had been established.

Among the earliest heresies to be denounced was Arianism, first propounded by a priest from Alexandria named Arius, whose teaching concerned the divinity of Christ and the relation between God the Father and God the Son. Arius claimed that Christ was divine but did not have the same nature as the Father, who had created him. In 325, at the Council of Nicaea (an ecumenical rather than a regional gathering, as Arles had been), the Arian view was rejected; the Nicene Creed asserted that the Father and Son were fully equal, sharing one being and, together with the Holy Spirit, constituting the Trinity. This formulation met with opposition, and the debate about the Trinity and the nature of Christ still continues.

Monasticism

Even before the establishment of Christianity as the state religion, individual Christians had turned to asceticism and solitude as a source of spiritual discipline. The tradition of withdrawal from the world to an austere life of religious devotion is also a characteristic found in Hinduism, Buddhism, and Taoism. In all three religions, monks have tended to live in communities, although solitary mystics or hermits inaugurated the Christian tradition. (*Monk* is derived from the Greek word *monos,* meaning "alone.") Anthony (c. 251–356), generally acknowledged as the father of Christian monasticism, spent some 20 years after 285 alone in the desert of Egypt. As the practice spread and communities began to develop, monastic life was organized according to a set pattern or rule. Such rules were established in Asia as early as 358 by Basil (330–379) and later in Italy by Benedict (480–547). Throughout the subsequent history of Christianity the religious orders of men and women who retired to monasteries and convents exerted a considerable influence in secular as well as sacred matters. It was through monks in the West that the Latin language and classical Latin texts were preserved, carefully copied for monastery libraries.

Augustine

If Paul was the first great leader in the history of the early church, Augustine (354–430) was its culminating figure and one who influenced Christian thought for centuries after his death. His writings, which draw on both Christian theology and Greco-Roman thought, deal with the most complex questions: human nature and destiny, the work of Christ as savior, and the relationship of the church to the world. His *Confessions,* an autobiographical account of his spiritual life, reasserted the teachings of Paul, in particular the unique importance ascribed to God's mercy as a means of forgiveness. In *The City of God,* written between 413 and 426 when Roman power was rapidly crumbling, Augustine claimed that God was punishing the Romans for the violence and corruption of their empire. The new order to emerge from this chaos should, he argued, be a Christian society, governed by principles of love and justice.

A portion of Augustine's theological writing was inspired by his opposition to Pelagius, whose writings had brought him a number of enthusiastic followers. The Pelagians believed that humans did not inherit original sin and that free will was sufficient to attain salvation. Divine grace was not limited to the preordained elect but was given to all persons; hence Pelagius' view of human nature was not pessimistic like that of Augustine. In works such as *On Original Sin* and *On Grace and Free Will* Augustine attacked the Pelagian view. To some of Augustine's contemporaries and successors, however, his refutation presented an equally extreme picture: a world ruled by a God so omnipotent that lives were predestined, where individual acts of goodness were insignificant in the face of dependence on divine grace. Medieval theologians generally tried to steer a middle course between the two extremes, but the debate was to be renewed in the sixteenth-century

Augustine, Bishop of Hippo, author of *The City of God;* a detail from a painting by Simone Martini. [Fitzwilliam Museum, Cambridge, England]

Protestant Reformation, which saw the revival first of Augustinian and then of Pelagian views.

Augustine's views on sex and marriage have remained central to Catholic thought ever since his time. The only justifiable purpose of sexual relations, he believed, was the creation of children, and only within the institution of marriage. Marriage thus serves the divine will, even though people who abstain from sexual relations are of a spiritually higher order. This concept of the flawed state of the human condition is a fresh assertion of the Pauline belief in human sinfulness. Augustine remained unrivaled as an expositor of Christian theology until Thomas Aquinas in the thirteenth century. The theologians of the Protestant Reformation were inspired by the influence of Augustinian principles to seek fundamental changes in Christian practice. Martin Luther and John Calvin were both dedicated readers of Augustine.

Women in the Ancient World Religions

The role of women in ancient and classical religious practice was roughly consistent throughout Eurasia. Most priestly functions were reserved for men, and women were often excluded from the inner sanctum of the temple, especially in Judaism. Judaism and to a degree the teachings of Paul contain an underlying bias against women, seeing them as "unclean" and hence as profaning religious ritual. In many orthodox Jewish congregations, women were obliged to sit apart from men, concealed behind a screen. In India by classical times, priests were exclusively male, and this was also true of Buddhism and most of Taoism. Confucianism, which largely lacked a priestly order, was explicitly male-dominated and preached the subjection of women to their husbands. Shinto, the Japanese partial equivalent of Taoism, similarly reflected the heavy male dominance of Japanese society. Nevertheless, some women played major religious roles, separate from the male priestly order, as soothsayers and priestesses in ancient and classical Greece and Rome and similarly in ancient and classical India. The Tantric version of Hinduism, in its celebration of sex as the embodiment of the life force and hence a celebration of the divine mystery, made a central role for women as the chief focus of its rituals and doctrine. In this, Tantrism may be seen as echoing very early religious veneration of women as symbols of fertility and life. Perhaps it was also, like the acceptance of temple priestesses and soothsayers in both East and West, an acknowledgment of the spiritual and intuitive qualities of women. Especially in the earlier periods, most religions (except Judaism and Islam) have imputed to women special access to the mysteries and special spiritual powers.

As Buddhism and Christianity developed, so did female devotion, and various orders of nuns were organized, counterparts to the monks of both religions and with a similar discipline. Women had in fact played a far more prominent part in the early growth of both religions than the established order recognized. The Buddha and Jesus seem to have paid as much attention to women as to men and apparently made little status distinction between them; both may indeed have been said to favor them or to regard them as more open to the message. For whatever reason, both religions quickly produced female saints in great numbers, of which the best known are the Virgin Mary and the Buddhist goddess of mercy, Kuan Yin (Kannon in Japanese), among a host of others to whom people prayed for help probably more often than to male saints. In our own time women generally (except in Judaism and Islam) play a more active role than men in religious faith and practice everywhere, as perhaps they have always done, and the Christian priesthood is in the early stages, at least within Protestant Christianity, of admitting them on equal terms.

Hinduism has always had more or less equal numbers of female and male deities, and even Shiva was provided with a female consort of equal powers, although by classical times the priesthood was closed to women and currently shows few signs of removing that bar. But Hindus still give at least equal attention to female deities and hence continue to acknowledge the special powers and insights of women. Confucianism has no deities, no saints, and no organized priesthood, although since Han times a small number of people calling themselves Confucian priests have tended the temples and conducted services centered on the veneration of Confucius the sage. These have always been men, and Confucianism barely acknowledges the existence of women. Women in Confucian countries seek religious involvement in Taoism or Buddhism, where their role is more accepted—another aspect of East Asian eclecticism in religion.

From very early times in China there was an explicit assertion of the need for balance in all things between yin (female) and yang (male); this was incorporated into Taoism and accepted by nearly all Chinese, including Confucians, although most Chinese followed both religious traditions. The persistence of this idea even in modern China indicates an acceptance of the equal importance of male and female characteristics and the essential role of both.

Religion seems to have evolved away from its earliest emphasis on women. With the rise of the first states and empires, the coming of bureaucracy, the increase in large-scale warfare, and the consequently greater importance of the warrior, males and male roles may have become more dominant, and religion may have changed accordingly. Most of the great religions subordinate or even exclude women, and most tended to justify male domination. Judaism, Confucianism, and Islam are probably the clearest examples, but only Judaism and Islam speak explicitly, and pejoratively, about women. Christianity, to some degree a blend of Judaism with other Eastern religious traditions, was clearly male-dominant. Only Buddhism and to some extent Taoism approach the ideal of gender equality.

In spite of the obvious differences between the various religions and moral philosophies discussed in this chapter, they share some important characteristics. Each continues to influence the lives of millions of people. Whereas the worship of the gods of ancient Egypt, Assyria, or Greece has largely vanished without trace, all the major religions and philosophies described here provide at least partial solutions to the problems of life for their followers, even though they originated in times and cultures remote from our own. The major world religions share a number of attitudes. Nonviolence and reverence for life are urged by Hindu and Christian doctrine alike. The important role played by the religious mystic and teacher is typical of virtually all present world religions. Moreover, each attempts to order human relationships in society as well as individually. In this, however, they share another common characteristic, the fact that the ideal visions they propose remain, for the most part, unfulfilled.

In an age of rapid communications, the ancient world religions have inevitably, and often profitably, been brought into direct contact with one another. Christian priests and teachers continue to work in Asia, and in India Mother Teresa of Calcutta, herself an Albanian, has become a symbol of practical Christian charity. At the same time Western culture has become increasingly open to the religions of the East, with their emphasis on spiritual rather than material values. In the 2,000 years since the foundation of Christianity, only one other religion has established itself on the same global scale: Islam, whose formation and growth is discussed in the next chapter.

Notes

1. Jer. 8:19.
2. Isa. 12:4.
3. Amos 5:6–7.
4. Isa. 9:7.

Suggestions for Further Reading

Religions of South and East Asia

Basham, A. L. *The Wonder That Was India,* rev. ed. New York: Grove Press, 1983.

Bowker, J. *Problems of Suffering in Religions of the World.* Cambridge: Cambridge University Press, 1975.

Brown, W. N. *Man in the Universe: Some Continuities in Indian Thought.* Berkeley: University of California Press, 1970.

Campbell, J. *The Masks of God: Oriental Mythology.* New York: Viking, 1962.

Chandhuri, N. C. *Hinduism: A Religion to Live By.* New York: Oxford University Press, 1979.

Creel, H. G. *What Is Taoism? and Other Studies in Chinese Cultural History.* Chicago: University of Chicago Press, 1970.

De Bary, W. T., ed. *Sources of Chinese Tradition.* 2 vols. New York: Columbia University Press, 1964.

———. *Sources of Indian Tradition.* New York: Columbia University Press, 1958.

Eliot, C. *Hinduism and Buddhism.* London: Routledge & Kegan Paul, 1954.

Embree, A. T., ed. *The Hindu Tradition.* New York: Modern Library, 1966.

Hopkins, T. *Hindu Religious Tradition.* Encino, Calif.: Dickenson, 1971.

Humphreys, C. *Buddhism.* London: Cassell, 1962.

Munro, D. J. *The Concept of Man in Early China.* Stanford, Calif.: Stanford University Press, 1969.

Schwartz, B. I. *The World of Thought in Ancient China.* Cambridge, Mass.: Harvard University Press, 1985.

Sharma, A., ed. *Women in World Religions.* Albany: State University of New York Press, 1987.

Thompson, L. G. *Chinese Religion.* Encino, Calif.: Dickenson, 1969.

Waley, A. *Three Ways of Thought in Ancient China.* Garden City, N.Y.: Doubleday, 1956.

Welch, H. *The Parting of the Way.* Boston: Beacon Press, 1957.

Wright, A. F. *Buddhism in Chinese History.* Stanford, Calif.: Stanford University Press, 1959.

The Judeo-Christian Tradition

Bright, J. *A History of Israel,* 2d ed. Philadelphia: Westminster Press, 1972.

Coggins, R., Phillips, A., and Knibb, M., eds. *Israel's Prophetic Tradition.* Cambridge: Cambridge University Press, 1984.

Frend, W. H. *Martyrdom and Persecution in the Early Church.* New York: New York University Press, 1967.

Grant, M. *The Jews in the Roman World.* New York: Scribner, 1973.

Halpern, B. *The Constitution of the Monarchy in Israel.* Chico, Calif.: Scholars Press, 1981.

Hengel, M. *Acts and the History of Earliest Christianity.* London: SCM Press, 1986.

Jacobs, L. *The Talmudic Argument.* Cambridge: Cambridge University Press, 1984.

Knowles, D. *Christian Monasticism.* New York: McGraw-Hill, 1969.

Negev, A. *Archaeological Encyclopedia of the Holy Land.* New York: Putnam, 1972.

Renko, S. *Pagan Rome and the Early Christians.* Bloomington: Indiana University Press, 1986.

Sanders, E. P. *Jesus and Judaism.* Philadelphia: Fortress Press, 1985.

Segal, A. *Rebecca's Children.* Cambridge, Mass.: Harvard University Press, 1986.

Smallwood, E. M. *The Jews Under Roman Rule,* rev. ed. Leiden, Netherlands: E. J. Brill, 1981.

Watson, F. *Paul, Judaism, and the Gentiles.* Cambridge: Cambridge University Press, 1987.

Witherington, B., III. *Women in the Earliest Churches.* Cambridge: Cambridge University Press, 1988.

PART · TWO

The Middle Ages

The millennium that stretched from 500 to 1500 witnessed the golden age of the civilizations of China and Byzantium and the continuation of classical civilization in South India. Particularly in China and the Byzantine Empire, the great advances of the classical era flowered and spread to other societies. In Arabia, however, a new civilization, rooted in the Muslim religion, emerged in the seventh century and rapidly expanded from its Middle Eastern base into North Africa, Iberia, Iran, North India, and parts of Southeast Asia. During the mid-fifteenth century the Turks, themselves Muslims, overwhelmed the remnants of the Byzantine Empire, widening their wedge between Hindu and Buddhist Asia and Christian Europe. Thus much of the vast area from the Atlantic Ocean to Southeast Asia acquired a degree of social and cultural unity, though throughout most of India and Southeast Asia Islam failed to supplant Hindu and Buddhist traditions.

In East Asia China was dominant throughout this era, particularly after the T'ang dynasty began to restore Chinese unity and imperial power in the seventh century. China, however, fell under the rule of the Mongols in 1279. This Asiatic people established an enormous empire that stretched from the Pacific Ocean to the Baltic Sea, opening up vast new opportunities for trade and cultural exchange. Less than a century later, in 1368, the Chinese regained control of their land through a new dynasty, the Ming. Chinese influence extended to Korea and Japan, whose civilizations were modeled after China's. Southeast Asia, because of its uniquely important position on the trading routes, served as the principal meeting place for Buddhist and Islamic culture.

The collapse of the Roman Empire in the West left North Africa and Europe vulnerable to the Muslim invaders. Although North Africa and Iberia were lost, the reorganization of Europe, first along feudal lines and later through more centralized states, contributed to its ability to repel the Muslims despite repeated attacks that occurred as late as the seventeenth century. The politically fragmented European societies slowly recovered from the effects of Muslim and Viking invasions, while relearning much of their classical heritage from their Islamic neighbors and from Jewish scholars. Such unity as there was in Europe was provided largely by the Catholic church, which played a major creative role in areas as diverse as education, agriculture, governmental organization, and the arts. Despite the stunning crises of the fourteenth century—famine, the arrival of the Black Death from Asia, and war—western Europe was sufficiently strong by the fifteenth century to launch voyages of discovery that took the European adventurers to South and East Asia, Africa, and the Americas. They came into contact with the ancient civilizations of the Sudanese and Swahili kingdoms in Africa as well as the Incas and Aztecs in America. Without realizing it, these explorers had taken the first steps that would eventually lead to the integration of the peoples of the world. ■

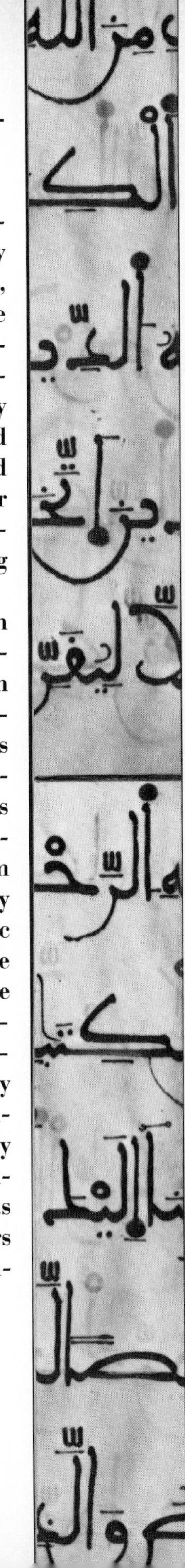

C H A P T E R · 8

Byzantium and Islam

In almost every corner of the world, with the major exception of western Europe and India, the period from the seventh to the tenth centuries saw the rise and development of powerful cultures and empires—the T'ang dynasty in China and the related Nara culture of Japan; Arab civilization in the Middle East, North Africa, and Spain; the Christian empire of Byzantium in the eastern Mediterranean; and the Mayan civilization of the Americas. This same period also saw the emergence and spread of the last of the great world religions, Islam. Perhaps at no other moment of history had so many independent civilizations experienced so remarkable a flowering at once. Some of these cultures flourished in virtual ignorance of one another, while others, thrown together by geography, lived in troubled proximity, sometimes engaging fruitfully in a commerce of goods, ideas, and values but periodically erupting into conflict and attempted conquest. This latter pattern is best exemplified by the uneasy coexistence of Byzantium and Islam.

A detail from one of the eighth-century mosaics that line the walls of the Great Mosque at Damascus. [Sheridan/Ancient Art & Architecture Collection, London]

Byzantium

Founded in A.D. 330, Constantinople was one of the wealthiest cities in the world for nearly a millennium. Its harbor was filled with merchant ships from East and West, and its buildings were magnificent and grandiose. After imperial power was transferred to Constantinople from Rome, a new blend of Greco-Roman culture, infused with Christianity, developed in western Asia. That culture is known as Byzantine, from the city that had formerly occupied the site of Constantinople, Byzantium. At the beginning of its independent existence in the late fifth century A.D., this "new Rome in the East" controlled virtually the entire eastern Mediterranean world and large areas of western Europe.

Yet by the time the Byzantine Empire fell, with the capture of Constantinople by the Ottoman Turks in 1453, its power was virtually limited to the space within the city walls. For all the splendor of their achievements, Byzantine rulers found themselves involved in an almost constant struggle to hold on to their possessions throughout their thousand-year reign. Asiatic tribes such as the Huns, which had operated so successfully in the west, were among the first to turn their attention to the potential new prize at the entrance to the Black Sea. Throughout the fifth century the Balkans were ravaged by Alaric and the Goths and by Attila and the Huns. Constantinople itself was protected by its fortifications and managed to survive the indolent rule of the emperor Arcadius (395–408). After a period of civil war, peace was restored in the reign of Anastasius (491–518), who also did much to revive the Byzantine economy.

Byzantine power was reasserted in Asia Minor in the sixth century during the reign of Justinian (527–565), but his successors found themselves facing challenges from the Persians, the Slavic peoples, and the Arabs. Beginning in the early seventh century the Arabs rapidly advanced from their original homeland to become one of the principal powers throughout the Mediterranean region and much of Asia. They carried with them a new religion, Islam, and spread it as they extended their conquests. When the Turks, originally a central Asian people, finally took Constantinople, they brought Islam with them. The day after the city fell, its principal church, Hagia Sophia, was converted into a mosque, a house of Muslim worship.

Byzantine Society

In the 200 years between the foundation of Constantinople and the reign of Justinian, successive emperors warded off invasions from east and west while continuing to enrich the imperial coffers. The incursions of the Huns, sporadic wars with the Persians, and even a brief period of rule by the Isaurians (474–491), an Asiatic tribe that had moved west, only temporarily halted the growth of Constantinople and the spread of the Byzantine bureaucracy.

The strength of Byzantine government lay in its sound economic base, since the parts of the empire that contributed most in taxes, notably Syria and Egypt, were relatively unaffected by the wars of the fifth and sixth centuries. The burden of taxation fell principally on peasants and farmers as international trade declined owing to difficulties in transport and commerce among the various parts of the empire. Constantinople itself continued to thrive economically. Apart from Constantinople itself and Thessalonica in northern Greece, the second city of the empire, there were few other Byzantine towns of note; even Athens shrank to a virtual hamlet. With the notable exception of a few provincial regions, most of the western territories reverted to the agricultural economic level of the period before their conquest by the Romans. In the east as well, land in northern Syria was turned into farms to supply food for the inhabitants of Constantinople. A decline in population in the west further reduced the potential market for goods manufactured elsewhere in the empire.

Even in the eastern provinces financial control remained in the hands of the emperor and his court; although individual cities such as Antioch maintained their commercial importance, they never acquired independence as trading centers. The imperial army drained surplus manpower, thus limiting the potential for agricultural exploitation. Nor did the emperors encourage wealthy individuals to increase their income (and potential power), since most surplus revenues were siphoned off into taxes. It was clearly in the interests of the commercial monopoly of Constantinople to maintain most of the working population as farmers and peasants living in village communities and dutifully paying taxes, while always ready to serve in the imperial army when needed.

Thus completing a process first set in motion by Diocletian and Constantine, landowners and farm laborers replaced the industrial and business classes of the Roman Empire as the principal sources of state income. For the most part, products such as bricks, pottery, and clothing were made and sold locally by small businesses operating in the remaining towns or on the great farming estates. The tax system was, moreover, extremely complicated, involving three separate treasuries, and the system of collection encouraged fraud and embezzlement at all levels, from the provincial governors who supervised collection to the official state auditors.

The same combination of elaborate complexity and rampant corruption characterized much of Byzantine public life. The nominal head of state was the emperor, who increasingly became the focal point of court ceremonials designed to make him appear lofty and remote. His power was exercised principally through the appointment and supervision of the empire's chief administrators, who in turn controlled a vast bureaucracy notorious for its graft. Access to the emperor or his chief ministers could be obtained only by means of a direct bribe, a gift, or a return favor. The various officials in public works, finance, and provincial adminstration were not highly paid, even though they had often been required to buy their appointments. It was thus a matter of personal interest to make as much money as possible by embezzlement and accepting bribes so as to acquire the funds to buy yet higher offices. A system that often proved oppressive for its clients nevertheless perpetuated itself through the crises of the empire. Corruption functioned as an indirect form of taxation by means of user fees, and to that extent it contributed to the functioning of government.

Justinian and Theodora

The emperor Justinian (527–565) was the nephew of a Macedonian peasant, Justin, who had achieved imperial power (518–527) by a successful military career. Justinian was born in Illyria (modern Yugoslavia) and spoke Latin. His Western origins seem to have been an important factor in his drive to reconquer former Roman territory and restore the empire. Tireless in his care for detail and devotion to duty, he had a formidable helpmate in his wife, Theodora, who was humbly born. Between them they sought to correct much of the inefficiency and corruption of Byzantine public life.

Under the direction of Tribonian, Justinian's judicial minister, a commission was appointed to organize the mass of Roman imperial edicts that had been issued since the time of the emperor Hadrian into a code. Their work eliminated outdated and conflicting legal provisions. In 529 a collection of laws was published that became known as the Code of Justinian. This was followed in 533 by the Digest, which summarized and reconciled the canon of often contradictory Roman judicial opinion, together with the Institutes, a handbook for law students. Although these documents were written in Latin, still the official language of the empire, new laws, the Novels, were composed in Greek, the language of most citizens in the east. A compilation of these was issued later in the reign. Collectively, these four compilations were known as the *Corpus Juris Civilis,* or "body of civil law"; more familiarly, they are referred to as the Code.

The organization and circulation of the Code of Justinian did not, of course, resolve the issues it addressed on a lasting basis. Throughout Byzantine history successive emperors put out amended editions, reflecting new constitutional developments. Its influence, which was profound, spread to the West, where the principle of mutual interest—enshrined in the phrase "That which touches all concerns all"—provided much of the basis for Western

Theodora: A Critical View

In his Secret History, *Procopius paints this extremely unflattering portrait of the empress Theodora.*

Theodora had a lovely face and was generally beautiful, but she was short and pale—not completely, but enough to seem pallid—and her expression was always serious and frowning. All time would not be enough for anyone who tried to record most of her past life on the stage. . . . Now I must speak briefly of what she and her husband did, for they never acted separately in their life together. For a long time they gave everyone the impression that they were constantly at odds in opinions and mode of life. But later it was realized that this was deliberately cultivated by them so that their subjects, far from joining together and rebelling against them, would all have different views about them. . . .

Of her body she took more care than was necessary, though less than she herself desired. She went very early to her bath and left it very late, and after her bath she went to breakfast. After breakfast she rested. At lunch and dinner she took all kinds of foods and drinks and would sleep for long periods from morning until night, and at night until sunrise. And after this self-indulgence for such long stretches of the day, she saw fit to rule the Roman Empire. If the emperor gave orders to someone for an action against her wishes, the man's affairs stood at such a state of fortune that soon afterwards he would be dismissed from his office in ignominy and destroyed in a most shameful manner.

Source: Procopius, *History of the Wars,* trans. A. Cameron (Boston: Twayne, 1967), pp. 311, 323.

medieval law, both religious and secular. This led ultimately to the development of representative institutions in the fourteenth century and eventually to modern parliamentary government. Justinian advanced other reforms to eliminate the sale of offices and reform provincial government, but his lasting monument was the Code, the most significant single body of legal documents in Western history and the chief means by which the great Roman legal heritage was preserved and transmitted.

Justinian was less successful in fulfilling another of his ambitions, that of permanently reconquering all the former territories of the Roman Empire. Aided by the skill of his principal general, Belisarius, his armies secured control of much of Italy from the Ostrogoths, Roman North Africa from the Vandals, and southern Spain from the Visigoths. Once again, his achievements barely survived his death, and the revolts and wars that wracked the regained western provinces proved financially ruinous. Justinian could not prevent East European tribes, the Avars and Slavs, from moving into the Balkans, and he could only temporarily check Persian aggression on his eastern frontier.

Nevertheless, Justinian's conquests left a legacy in the monuments erected in his honor. The most famous of these are the churches built at Ravenna, which had become the capital of Roman Italy during the fifth century. The glittering mosaic decorations, which form one of the high points of Byzantine art, include resplendent portraits of the royal couple, each of them surrounded by courtiers and priests of their entourage. Other major churches were erected at Ephesus in Anatolia and at Jerusalem. The greatest of Justinian's artistic achievements, however, was his building program in Constantinople.

CONSTANTINOPLE IN THE AGE OF JUSTINIAN

Justinian's capital boasted a population of perhaps a million people, excluding the suburbs, a combination of commercial centers, residential villages, and, along the shores of the Bosporus, resorts for the wealthy. Constantinople enjoyed a strategic location at the point where the waters of the Black Sea, after passing through the Bosporus straits, emptied into the Sea of Marmora en route to the Aegean

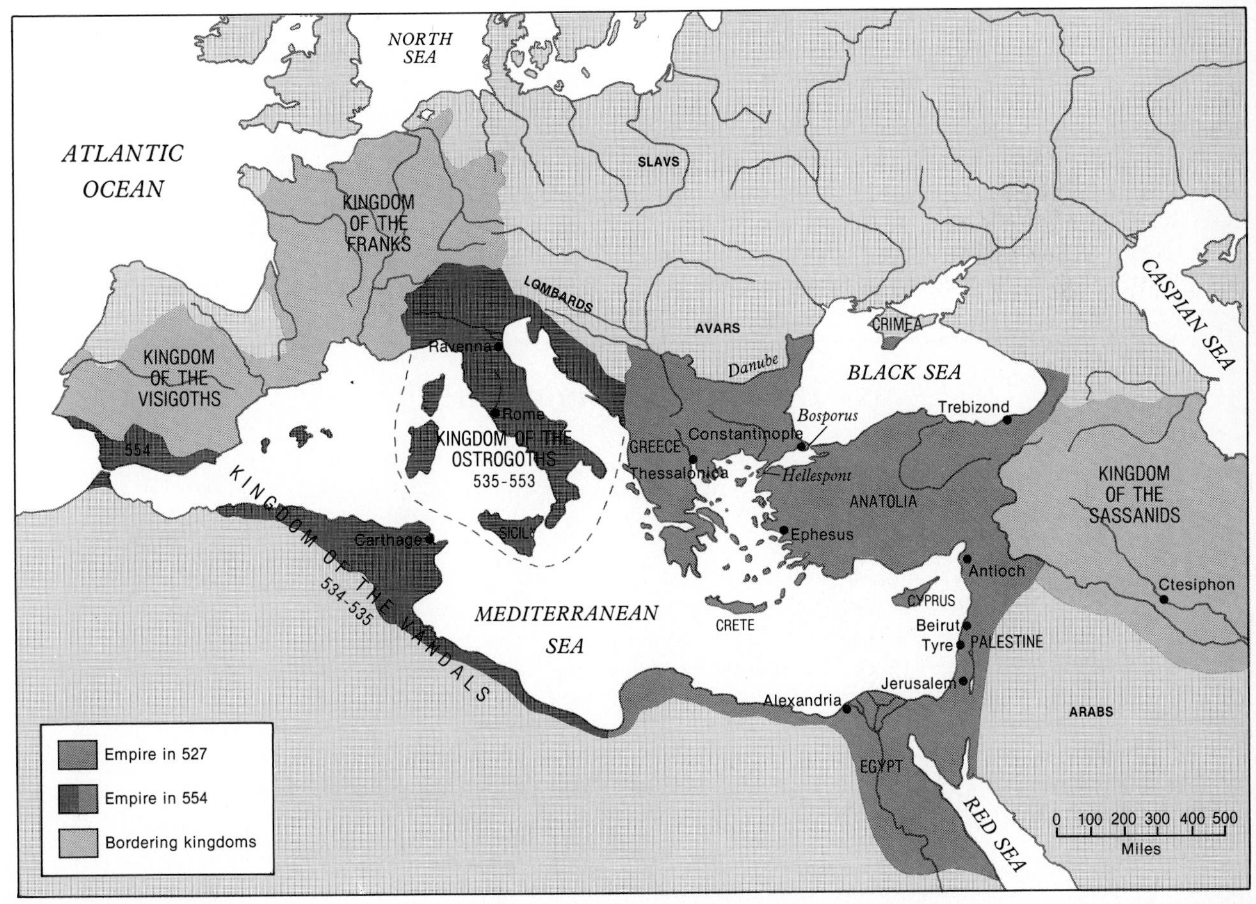

8.1 The Byzantine Empire Under Justinian

by way of the narrow Hellespont. Protected on three sides by water, the Byzantines built two mammoth walls on their northwestern flank to defend themselves from a land attack. "The sea," enthused the Byzantine historian Procopius, "encircles the city like a crown, the interval consisting of the land lying between it in sufficient quantity to form a clasp for the crown of waters."[1] So secure was this location that for centuries the Byzantines referred to Constantinople as "the city protected by God."

At the heart of Constantinople was a great public square, the Augusteion, surrounded by the principal public buildings: the royal palace, the Senate house, and a huge race track, the 40,000-seat Hippodrome, to which the poor were admitted without charge. The citizens were devotees of chariot racing, although their frequent riots in the Hippodrome were often inspired by political as much as sporting considerations. A particularly violent demonstration in 532 was quelled only by the personal intervention of Theodora. When Justinian was cowed by the ferocity of the mob, the empress took charge and sent Belisarius and his troops into action; according to contemporaries, 30,000 rioters were killed.

The main avenue of Constantinople, Central Street, led westward from the Augusteion through a series of districts, each with its own public square and market. The line of bazaars and shops stretched 5 miles and ended at one of the city's 11 gateways, the Golden Gate. The city walls, built during the early fifth century, were 15 feet thick and 40 feet high; they remained intact until 1453, when they were breached by Turkish cannon fire.

Constantinople had no fashionable residential districts; as in Renaissance Florence, its grand homes were scattered among modest dwellings and hovels. Like the Romans, affluent Byzantines constructed their homes around inner courtyards, many of which had fountains. More modest houses typically had balconies overhanging the street. As early as the fifth century, efforts were made at town planning, with the imposition of regulations for drainage, street width (12 feet), and balcony height (15 feet minimum), and the prohibition of outside staircases. Churches were numerous. Most were small, but some had monasteries attached. The church provided hostels, hospitals, and orphanages, while the city itself maintained sizable public gardens. The southeastern section of Constantinople was dominated by the sumptuous imperial palace, adjacent to which was the palace of the patriarch of Constantinople, the most important religious leader among eastern Christians. In the city too were the urban residences of the nobility, each of which sought to reflect something of the splendor of the imperial court.

The royal palace was not only the repository of the empire's treasures but also the storehouse of the finest collection of relics in Christendom. In addition to regulating the economic life of the empire, the palace became the heart of a vast silk trade for which the crown maintained a monopoly. Indeed, the looms on which the silk was woven were located in the women's quarters of the palace. Silk manufacture was a secret the Byzantines had acquired from the Persians. The imperial monopoly extended as well to gold embroidery and purple dye. It contributed to the prosperity of both the imperial family and the merchants and artisans involved in the trade and indirectly to the people of the empire as a whole, since income from the monopolies presumably reduced the tax burden.

Among the buildings in Constantinople destroyed by the rioters of 532 had been the church of Hagia Sophia (Holy Wisdom), originally constructed in the fourth century. Its replacement, intended by Justinian to serve as the enduring monument of his reign, remains one of the greatest of all architectural achievements. One hundred

Rich Man, Poor Man

This extract from the Life of St. John the Almsgiver, *quoting the saint's own words, conveys something of the gap between rich and poor at Byzantium.*

Who shall say that humble John was lying under a coverlet costing 36 nomismata whilst Christ's brethren are pinched with cold? How many are there at this minute grinding their teeth because of the cold? and how many have only a rough blanket half below and half above them so that they cannot stretch out their legs but lie shivering, rolled up like a ball of thread? How many would like to dip their bit of bread into the soupwater which my cooks throw away? How many would like even to have a sniff at the wine which is poured out in my wine-cellar? How many strangers are there at this hour in the city who have no lodging-place but lie about in the market-place, perhaps with the rain falling on them?

Source: J. M. Hussey, *The Byzantine World* (London: Hutchinson, 1967), pp. 128–129.

The church of Hagia Sophia, completed in 535; the minarets were added a thousand years later by the Turks. [Wim Swaan, New York]

thousand men are said to have worked for five years under the supervision of the emperor himself, who visited the building site almost daily. Justinian evidently wanted the church to represent the richest and most elaborate building ever constructed. At its dedication on December 27, 537, he is said to have exclaimed: "Solomon, I have surpassed you." Unlike Greco-Roman buildings, Hagia Sophia's exterior is generally plain. By contrast, the interior, a rectangular space surmounted by a dome, is decorated with mosaics, gold, silver, and multicolored marble. The effect of this, illuminated both by natural light and by gold and silver lamps, must have been stunning. The solemn religious ceremonies at which the participants were dressed in rich embroidered robes and the church filled with clouds of incense do much to explain the enduring mystique of Byzantine power.

Although Hagia Sophia still stands as a monument to the glory of early Byzantium, its extravagance severely depleted the imperial treasury. Later emperors succeeded in restoring the city's splendor and, at least partly, the empire's prestige, but the immediate consequence of Justinian's acquisition of the western provinces and his ambitious building plans was a period of enforced retrenchment. In part this was due to Justinian's spendthrift ways, but the years following his death were also marked by the start of a long and exhausting war against the Persians, an old enemy. The emperor Heraclius (610–641) finally defeated the Persians in 627, retaking Syria, Palestine, and Alexandria after years of foreign occupation. His achievement was all the more impressive because the Avars and Slavs were simultaneously assaulting Byzantine territory in Europe. An even greater challenge to Byzantine power, however, was a new force in the Mediterranean, the Arabs. Their zeal to conquer produced a series of radical changes in Europe, Asia, and Africa that were to have wide-ranging and long-lasting consequences.

The Arabs

Arabia, the "Island of the Arabs," lies in southwestern Asia, a rocky peninsula cut off from Persia and India by the Persian Gulf to the east and from Egypt by the Red Sea to the west. With the exception of the mountain slopes of southern Arabia, the land is unfertile and rainfall sparse. Such unpromising conditions were no doubt responsible for a series of Arab emigrations to the north from as early as the third millennium B.C. Peoples such as the Babylonians and the Assyrians were descended from Arab immigrants and spoke languages related to Arabic. The general linguistic group, called Semitic, includes Hebrew, and the Jews themselves were probably descendants of early immigrants from Arabia to Mesopotamia.

The passing of former empires had left Arabia divided into separate states and kingdoms, relatively untouched by the outside world. The Assyrians established a kingdom there in the eighth century B.C., which lasted only 50 years. Alexander the Great died before he could carry out his project of invading Arabia, uniting it, and including it in his empire. With the development of trade routes during the Hellenistic period, a small state, Nabatea, sprang up at the head of the Red Sea. Controlling the caravan road from the south, its capital was at Petra, in what is now Jordan. As the Romans expanded into Asia they initially formed an alliance with the Nabateans, but in A.D. 106 Roman forces conquered the kingdom and turned it into the Roman province of Arabia.

The small neighboring kingdom of Palmyra, which lay on the trade route between Syria and Babylon, was more fortunate. Its Arab rulers preserved strict neutrality in the wars between the Romans and the Parthians (the inhabitants of present-day Afghanistan) and enjoyed special Roman favor during the reign of the Severi. For a brief period, from 262 to 267, the Palmyran king Odaenathus was even acknowledged as ruler of Rome's eastern provinces. His wife, Zenobia, succeeded him after his murder, for which she may have been responsible. A woman of intense ambition and restless energy, she led her army throughout Egypt and Asia Minor until the Roman emperor Aurelian finally drove her back to Palmyra, where in 272 he besieged her capital and captured her. The Arabian queen was taken back to Rome, where she was exhibited in Aurelian's triumphal procession and then pensioned off to live in a country villa. Memory of her abrupt change of fortune endured in the Arab world, in the saga of Queen Zaynab, and in the West, where the fourteenth-century authors Boccaccio and Chaucer refer to her melancholy fate.

Mecca

With the gradual erosion of Roman power in Asia, the Sassanid rulers of Persia made sporadic attempts to fill the vacuum, but the Arabs succeeded in maintaining their independence. As the West fell into economic decline and Byzantine power provided a new focus for financial prosperity in Asia, Arabian cities prospered by exploiting their geographic position. One such commercial center in western Arabia was Mecca, through which passed much of the trade between the Mediterranean and the Indian Ocean. Ancient Mecca had been an oasis on the old caravan route linking southern Asia, eastern Africa, and the southern kingdom of Arabia with the principal markets of the Hellenistic world. During the Roman Empire's commercial expansion, the city grew into an important center in its own right, developing business ties with its Arabian neighbors as well as with commercial centers throughout the Mediterranean.

Prosperous and bustling, Mecca was also famous in the ancient world for its religious shrines, at which various nature deities were worshiped. Among the holy places was a rectangular stone structure known as the Kaaba, with a black stone built into its eastern corner. Mecca remains to this day one of the world's principal religious centers, and the black stone in the Kaaba is still visited by millions of pilgrims, but for reasons very different from those of its pagan worshipers. Mecca was the birthplace of Muhammad, founder of Islam, who incorporated the ancient symbol into his new religion. The development and spread of Islam, which literally means "acceptance" or "submission," explains the Arabs' emergence as a world power.

Muhammad and the Rise of Islam

As in the case of Buddha and Jesus, little is known about the early life of Muhammad, and it is often difficult to separate historical fact from the mass of tradition that inevitably accumulates around the life of any great spiritual leader. Muhammad was born about 570 into a branch of one of Mecca's leading families, although it was declining economically. His father had died before Muhammad's birth, and he was orphaned at the age of 6. He was then raised by an uncle, who allowed him to travel with some of the caravans that journeyed to Syria and Yemen. This experience served him in good stead when a wealthy widow, Khadija, employed him to manage her business affairs. At the age of 25 he married her and devoted the ensuing 15 years or so to commercial activities.

A devout man, Muhammad went regularly into the hills near Mecca to pray, and there, on Mount Hira in 610, he had a vision in which the archangel Gabriel revealed the word of God to him. Nearly three years passed, however, before Muhammad felt fully assured that his vision was real and that he indeed had received a divine command to preach. He was inspired as well by a sense of the social injustice and corruption that had developed in Mecca.

The fundamental principle of Muhammad's religious ideas was firmly monotheistic: he affirmed one supreme deity, known as Allah, the Arabic word for God. There is debate as to how much Muhammad directly drew on Jewish and Christian beliefs in formulating this concept. Organized Jewish and Christian communities certainly existed in Arabia, but there appears to have been a strain of monotheism in Arabian religion even before Muhammad's time.

A more direct link to Christianity can be found in Muhammad's belief in the resurrection of the physical body in the afterlife and an eventual Last Judgment. Unlike Christianity, however, which emphasized God's love, Islam stresses the "wrath of God to come," fear of which should compel good behavior. A Muslim is thus one who submits to the will of God. Allah (God) is omnipotent, Muhammad asserted, and humans can only win forgiveness by his grace, but to be worthy they must dedicate their lives to prayer, good works, and the giving of alms.

Having failed to find many supporters at Mecca, Muhammad moved 200 miles north in July 622 to the town of Yathrib, later called Medina. This journey is known as the Hejira ("emigration"), and 622 was soon recognized as the first year of the new Muslim era. At Medina Muhammad established a distinctive Islamic community (*Umma*) and refined and developed his teachings, which eventually took written form.

The Koran

The principal sacred text of Islam, the Koran, consists of statements and discourses that Muhammad and his followers believed were of divine origin. To devout Muslims, therefore, the Koran represents the words of Allah, which were directly communicated to Muhammad as parts of a "heavenly book." The final form of the text of the Koran was established around 650. The text was accompanied by commentaries that explained and interpreted its contents. Over the centuries theologians continued to compile their explanations and elucidations; the one produced in the thirteenth century by al-Baidawi (died 1286) remains the standard commentary for most modern Muslims.

The Koran, like the Hebrew Scriptures and the Christian Bible, does not consist of a logically ordered exposition of beliefs, though certain general doctrines and injunctions run through it. These have remained as the central teachings of Islam. First, and most important, Allah is worshiped as the only deity, existing eternally, infallibly foreknowing all things, the giver of life and death. Muhammad specifically rejected the Christian doctrine of the Trinity, even while according respect to Jesus:

> **The Messiah, Jesus son of Mary, was only the Messenger of God, and His Word that He committed to Mary, and a Spirit from Him. So believe in God and His Messengers, and say not, "Three." . . . God is only One God.[2]**

Thus humans, while adoring and worshiping Allah, must also fear him and live in awe of him. He communicates with mortals by means of angels and archangels; the main one is Gabriel, who is said to have brought the Koran to Muhammad.

The second fundamental doctrine of Islam is that throughout history Allah has sent prophets to preach his unity and to warn of the Last Judgment. Such figures included Abraham—father of Ishmael, the reputed founder of the Arab race—Moses, Alexander the Great, and Jesus. All prophets before Muhammad had been in possession of only part of God's message, and it was to the last, Muhammad, that the full and perfect religion was revealed. In short, Islam, it is claimed, is a perfection of all existing religions, including Judaism and Christianity. Muhammad was thus the "Seal of the Prophets." His life provided an example that was to be followed by the faithful.

The Last Judgment, preceded by the physical resurrection of the dead, is a key concept in Islam. As in much of the Christian tradition, the good will enter paradise and the bad will be cast into everlasting fire. The Koran explicitly describes both the silken couches and dark-eyed beauties of the first and the boiling water and bronze cauldrons of the second. Of hell (Gehenna) Muhammad wrote:

> ***Behold, Gehenna has become an ambush,***
> ***for the insolent a resort,***
> ***therein to tarry for ages,***
> ***tasting therein neither coolness nor any drink***
> ***save boiling water and pus***
> ***for a suitable recompense.[3]***

All Muslims perform mandatory observances and are required to live in accordance with the teachings of the Koran. The observances, or "pillars of faith," are fivefold: profession of the creed, prayer, almsgiving, fasting, and a pilgrimage to Mecca. In contrast to typical Christian creeds, that of the Muslims is strikingly simple: "There is no God but Allah, and Muhammad is the prophet of Allah." The importance of a daily prayer ritual for all believers is greater in Islam than in most of the other principal world religions, where the practice of offering worship several times a day is generally limited to religious communities or solitary contemplatives. Faithful Muslims are called to prayer five times daily by a *muezzin,* or reciter, a ritual observed throughout the Islamic world. Other duties include fasting during daylight hours in the lunar month of

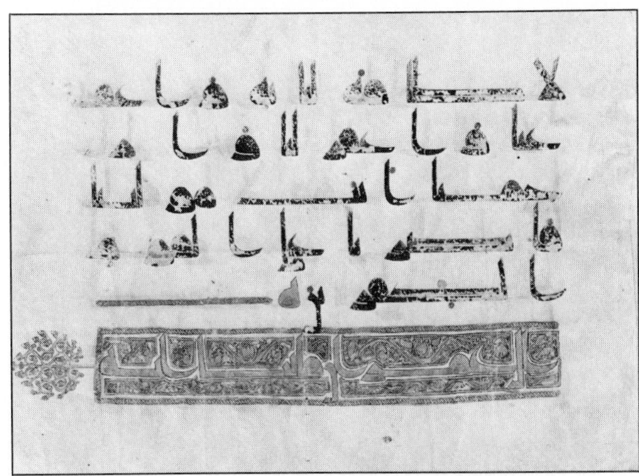

A page from the Koran, written in Kufic script. The text reads: "And pardon us and grant us protection and have mercy on us, thou art our patron, so help us against the unbelieving people." [Metropolitan Museum, New York]

Ramadan and giving alms to the needy. When paid, the alms, in the form of a mandatory tax called the *zakat* ("purification"), render the rest of the believer's property religiously acceptable. Perhaps the most striking prescription in the Koran is the obligation of every able-bodied Muslim to make a pilgrimage, or *hajj,* to Mecca to visit the Kaaba with its Black Rock once in one's lifetime. All these responsibilities are viewed by most Muslims as essential if one is to be saved. It is also necessary that one adhere to high moral precepts in all personal dealings and relations.

The Koran also provides instruction and guidance in social affairs. Laws for dowries, divorce, and inheritance are given in detail. Women are thereby assured of some guarantee of their status, but the Koran openly claims that men, as both fathers and husbands, have superior rights, and it permits polygamy up to a maximum of four wives. Slavery is allowed, although specific regulations control the owners' treatment of their slaves.

> **Those your right hands own who seek emancipation, contract with them accordingly, if you know some good in them; and give them of the wealth of God that He has given you. And constrain not your slavegirls to prostitution, if they desire to live in chastity.[4]**

Fraud, slander, and perjury are severely condemned. Gambling and moneylending are forbidden, as is the consumption of alcohol or pig's flesh. Some Islamic social teaching is found in the Hadith, a collection of traditional sayings and acts of Muhammad.

Muslim relations with those who do not accept Islam can be affected by the concept of the *jihad,* or holy war. This can be waged by four means: the heart, the tongue, the hand, and the sword. The first involves self-purification by the cleansing of the heart, or conscience. The second and third involve supporting what is right and correcting what is wrong. The last sanctions physical war against unbelievers and enemies of Islam. Martyrs in defense of the faith are assured of paradise.

Because a Muslim was required to read the Koran in Arabic, in the beginning it could not be translated. The spread of Islam, together with the teachings of its sacred text, therefore provided a unifying cultural element in the countries in which it became established. Throughout the Muslim world its teachings, along with those of the Hadith, were codified into the *Shari'a,* or Islamic Law, which still governs the lives of hundreds of millions of people.

In the eighth and ninth centuries a mystic movement within Islam known as Sufism developed at Baghdad. Sufism taught that individuals could find salvation only by living a contemplative life outside society, by studying the Koran, and by constant practice of spiritual exercises. Following this method the mystic hoped to proceed by way of remorse and patience to intimacy with God and a vision of the pure truth. Sufism was an important Islamic movement, playing a considerable role in the spread of the faith in Africa, India, and Southeast Asia, where the practice of meditation was already part of religious custom. Its devotees were distinguished by a white woolen garment called a *sufi,* similar to that worn by some Christian monks.

The Umayyads at Damascus

Even within the lifetime of Muhammad, warfare was the means by which the faith was spread. Caravans to Mecca, the scene of the prophet's first rejection, were repeatedly

Holy War

These extracts are from the Koran on the subject of the jihad, *or holy war.*

Fight in the Way of God against those who fight against you, but do not commit aggression. . . . Slay them wheresoever ye find them, and expel them from whence they have expelled you, for sedition is more grievous than slaying. . . . Fight against them until sedition is no more and allegiance is rendered to God alone; but if they make an end, then no aggression save against the evildoers.

When the Sacred Months are over, kill those who ascribe partners to God wheresoever ye find them; seize them, encompass them, and ambush them; then if they repent and observe prayer and pay the alms, let them go their way.

Fight against those who believe not in God nor in the Last Day, who prohibit not what God and His Apostle have prohibited, and who refuse allegiance to the True Faith from among those who have received the Book, until they humbly pay tribute out of hand.

Source: H. A. R. Gibb, *Mohammedanism* (New York: Oxford University Press, 1962), p. 67.

attacked, and the city itself was taken in 630. Islam increasingly began to provide the focus for Arab unity, and in 632, the year of his death, Muhammad seems to have been planning a military attack on the Byzantine province of Syria to the north.

In the following decade Arab forces launched a series of brilliant campaigns that resulted in the conquest of Syria, much of Persia, and Egypt. In 642 Alexandria was abandoned by a weakened Byzantine state to Arab forces. A Byzantine naval contingent reoccupied the city briefly in 645, only to be driven out again the following year. Nor were these victories disorderly routs, motivated only by plunder. Wherever the Islamic forces established themselves, they sought to combine the laws of their faith with orderly government in a way that would permit a peaceful existence. Thus the peoples of western Asia, who from the Hellenistic period had become accustomed to absorbing and being absorbed by new cultures, now began to integrate with their Arab rulers and to adopt their religion.

The Islamic leaders after Muhammad were known as the caliphs, or "successors." As the Arabs' territory grew, local governors were appointed to oversee the collection of taxes. Other administrative duties were carried out by the army, which acted simultaneously as garrison and government, while also representing Islam. From the beginning there was no attempt at enforced conversion of the local populations. In many places, in fact, native magistrates continued to operate, subject to the supervision of their Muslim overlords.

Between 661 and 750 the principal caliphs were drawn from the influential Umayyad family, whose prosperous ancestors had been related to Muhammad. The seat of the caliphate was moved to Damascus in Syria, where much of the local population was Christian. The first Umayyad caliph, Muawiya (661–680), did much to establish good relations between the Christians and their Arab rulers; one of the principal financial advisers at his court was a Christian. Muawiya's reign was stable and prosperous, successfully balancing the rivalries that had begun to develop among the leading families of the Arab ruling class and maintaining equitable government throughout the provinces. In organizing the tax system he returned to the methods used by the Romans in their provincial government and set up a series of regional collection agencies. Each region was encouraged to develop agricultural or industrial projects that provided a solid base for local prosperity. These schemes were carefully controlled by local administrators, working under the supervision of central offices in Damascus. The result was a broadly based economic growth that, unlike Byzantium, was not limited to the capital. In consequence, the Muslim empire soon developed one of its greatest strengths, a thriving commercial life that could draw on widespread prosperity.

Muawiya was the first Arab ruler to attempt not only the annexation of Byzantine territories but also the conquest of Constantinople itself. From 674 to 678 his troops besieged the city, which was saved by its massive fortifications. The Arabs were compelled to withdraw, but the strength of their attack was a warning of the formidable threat they presented to Byzantine power. It marked as well the first serious appearance of Arab naval power in the Mediterranean.

Later Umayyad caliphs continued to harry Constantinople, attacking the city again in 716–717, while in the west the spread of Arab power throughout North Africa provided access to Spain. In 711 an Arab expedition crossed to Europe and assembled on Gibraltar, a mountain later named for their leader, Tariq (Gibraltar is the corruption of Jabal Tariq, "Mount of Tariq"). Spain, which had been one of the Roman provinces conquered by the Goths and Visigoths, came wholly under Arab control within seven years. With Spain secured, the Arabs attacked the former Roman province of Gaul, now the kingdom of the Franks, or France, but they were temporarily brought to a halt in 732, when an army led by Charles Martel (see Chapter 12) repulsed them between Tours and Poitiers.

The Umayyad caliphate was also marked by important cultural developments. In the early years of Islam the faithful had gathered for prayer in mosques, or Muslim places of worship, that were simple courtyards with roofed porticoes. In 691 the Muslims built the towering Dome of the Rock in Jerusalem as a shrine for pilgrims to the Holy City; from this rock Muhammad had reportedly ascended into heaven. Work was begun in 705 on converting the main church of Damascus into an elaborate temple generally known as the Mosque of the Umayyads. In the absence of any tradition of Islamic religious architecture, its builders borrowed from Byzantine design. The mosaic decoration was actually made by workers from Constantinople, some 1,200 of whom were reportedly engaged on the building project.

The austerity Muhammad imposed had originally discouraged the development of secular literature, but the elaborate court life of later Umayyad rulers proved fertile ground for the growth of love poetry and even drinking songs. Muhammad had prohibited the consumption of wine, but he could not abolish it, and court poets vied with each other to produce songs that celebrated the pleasures of companionship and the good life. The love poems reflect the elegant life of aristocratic Damascus, with their tales of flirtation and intrigue.

At court, complex tribal and family rivalries, combined with religious dissent, undermined the Umayyads' power. Their opponents turned to another venerable family, the Abbasids, one of whose ancestors had been a cousin of Muhammad. After bitter conflict (the caliph who conquered the Umayyads and ruled from 750 to 754 was given the nickname al-Saffah, or Blood Pourer), the rule of the Abbasid caliphs was firmly established in the reign of Abdullah al-Mansur (754–775).

One of al-Mansur's first decisions was to construct a new imperial capital. Moving eastward, he settled on the site of a small Christian village, Baghdad, located on the

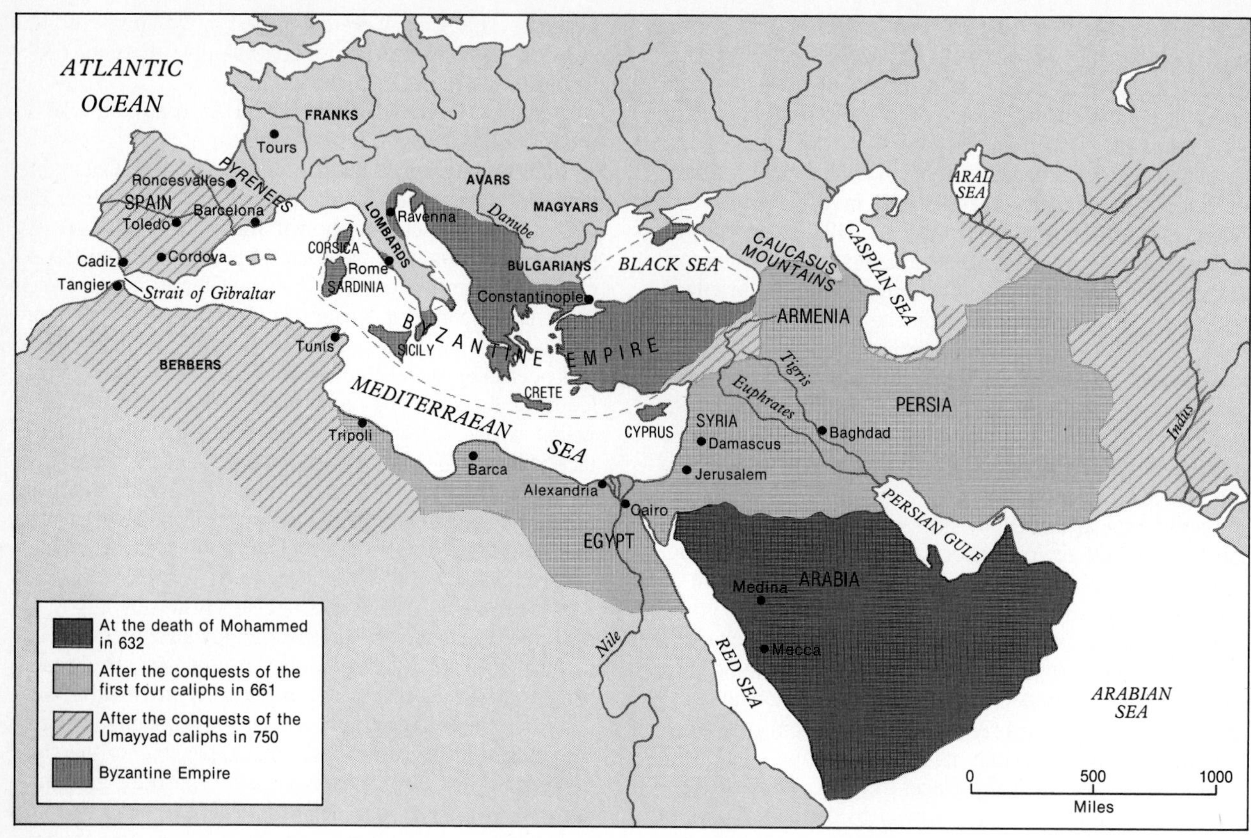

8.2 The Expansion of Islam

west bank of the Tigris River in what is now Iraq. The city was renamed Dar as-Salam, or House of Peace, but its old name remained in use then, as now.

BAGHDAD: LIFE IN THE ABBASID CALIPHATE

Al-Mansur intended the move to Baghdad to inaugurate a fresh era in Islamic history; the new city was planned as the setting for an opulently ceremonial court. The ground plan of the city was unusual in being circular. No trace of its walls still stands, although they probably resembled that of the city of Raqqah, which was constructed at about the same time. On the west bank of the Tigris, within the walls, were the palace buildings for the caliph and his court, government offices, and mosques. Across the river al-Mansur's son, al-Mahdi, had a camp, while the various other family members, followers, and officers were assigned locations around the city, outside the walls.

Thus the plan of Baghdad intentionally isolated the caliph from the outside world. Court officials and dignitaries, who had hitherto come from the most important families, were now appointed by the caliph himself. One of their major functions was to keep strict control of who was admitted to an audience with him.

From this central location al-Mansur could rule both the life of the capital and the affairs of the provinces through his officials. A network of postal directors throughout the main centers had already been established under the Umayyads. From the time of al-Mansur these inspectors were required to report to the caliph on the success or failure of provincial governors, as well as to provide general information about local affairs. Al-Mansur's son helped to streamline this communication system by commissioning the construction of a road network from Baghdad to the provincial centers. The city's location made it an ideal way station for trade between western Asia and India, and the improved highways thus also served a sound economic purpose.

As the empire expanded under Abbasid conquest, trade played an increasing role in Baghdad's importance. Bazaars were not permitted within the city walls, and consequently an entire merchants' district developed just outside one of the main gates. The traders of Baghdad imported goods from regions as far apart as North Africa and central Asia to satisfy the court's demand for luxury goods. Intense agricultural development of the area immediately outside Baghdad provided the means of feeding the lower classes.

The central dome of the mosque at Cordova, Spain; the dome is supported by a series of intercrossing arches. [MAS, Barcelona]

During the reign of the most famous Abbasid caliph, Harun al-Rashid (786–809), Baghdad was famous for its poetry and music. The world reflected by the art of this period is primarily that of Baghdad high society. The court of Harun became notorious as a center for intrigues and adventures, many of them involving courtships and seductions. Some of the tales of Abbasid Baghdad turn up in the famous collection of stories known as the *Thousand and One Nights,* into which earlier traditions were absorbed. They include accounts of escapades involving Harun himself, together with his favorite poet, the Persian Abu Nuwas (c. 756–c. 813), one of the greatest figures in Arabic literature. His elegant drinking songs reflect the gaiety of Baghdad society.

Spreading the Word: The Expansion of Islam

During the Abbasid caliphate Islamic culture was transformed from its austere desert origins into a rich, cosmopolitan civilization. This change was effected primarily by Persian converts to Islam, and Baghdad itself was situated in the heart of the ancient Persian Empire. Yet although the Abbasids and their successors spread the faith both east and west, they failed to establish a united Islamic empire. Spain, for example, which had been conquered in 711, never accepted rule by Baghdad and returned to Umayyad rule in 756. Persia itself split into several kingdoms ruled by local dynasties.

Yet if Islamic political unity proved elusive, the period from the mid-eighth to the mid-eleventh centuries was marked by a profound cultural and economic expansion. In general, local rulers encouraged trade and industry rather than indulging in profitless military struggle. The result of this was an international market that provided an economic base for the spread of Islam.

The increasing territory accessible to Islamic traders produced an expansion of trade in both raw materials and manufactured goods, in turn promoting the development of one of the main resources of the Islamic economy, a banking system. The empire's financial operations had been complicated by the fact that two currencies were in general circulation: the Persian silver dirham of the east and the Byzantine gold denarius of the west. Because the value of gold and silver was in constant flux, the coins fluctuated in value. As a result, moneychangers were required to participate in all financial transactions in order to establish the exchange rate and facilitate payments.

These bankers became integral to the smooth operation of the Muslim economy. They developed many of the concepts that three centuries later were applied to financial management in the West. Operating out of central banks with branch offices, they issued letters of credit and checks that could be honored from one country to another.

The merchants who took advantage of the services of these new professional financiers were thus able to travel to remote regions and purchase goods without having to carry cash and then easily negotiate sales on their return. The trade often involved long journeys; the great marine and overland caravans connected western outposts such as Spain and North Africa with India, China, and the East Indies. The risk and expense of such journeys were high, but profits were considerable: never less than 50 percent for a successful trip, according to one account.

Thus supported by thriving economic conditions and based on the twin strengths of a single religion and a common language, a series of Muslim kingdoms ruled from Spain in the west across North Africa to Persia and Syria in the east. An important base in western Europe was secured in the years from 830 to 875, when Sicily was conquered. Arab influence in Sicily was to have a profound effect on the island's later Norman conquerors.

Egypt proved a tempting prize to military leaders. It was taken in 969 by the Fatimid family, who ruled it for the next two centuries. Parts of Persia, together with the territories to the east of the river Oxus, in central Asia, fell with relative ease under the control of the Samanid dynasty. The court of the Samanids, the first great native dynasty in Persia after the Arab conquest, became famous for its patronage of writers and scientists. Paradoxically, the least stable of all Muslim kingdoms was Arabia itself.

Much unrest was caused by the growth of a split between Sunni (or orthodox) Muslims and a breakaway group known as Shi'ites. The dispute began as a political quarrel among Muhammad's successors, but it was to have lasting consequences for the development of Islam. Even today most Muslims are either Sunni (about 90 percent) or Shi'ite.

The dispute revolved around the figure of Ali, Muhammad's son-in-law, who was recognized as caliph in 656 by rebellious Muslims in Egypt. The rebels had assassinated the previous caliph, Uthman (644–656), largely in retaliation for his authoritarianism and his attempt to establish an official version of the Koran to the exclusion of others. Ali himself was soon opposed by some of his former followers, the Kharijites, a group of radical idealists who condemned Ali for submitting his claim to be caliph to arbitration. Ali's principal rival was Muawiya, the governor of Syria, who succeeded in deposing him and taking over as caliph. Ali's followers, however, challenged Muawiya's claims.

The murder of Ali in 661 by a Kharijite and the defeat of a band of his supporters led by his son Husein led to open division between the Sunni, or the "followers of custom," and the Shi'ites (*shi'a* means "party," in this case Ali's party). The death of Husein, the grandson of the Prophet, which is still commemorated in an annual passion play, became the rallying point for the Shi'ite cause, and the two sides remain to this day bitterly opposed. Whereas the Shi'ites regard Ali as the first of Muhammad's successors, the Sunnis accept the three men who preceded Ali. Modest differences in belief and practice also divide the Shi'ites and the Sunnis. The former, for instance, believe that the text of the Koran is incomplete and that a Muslim can perform the pilgrimage to Mecca by proxy or can substitute a visit to the tomb of a Shi'ite saint, such as Ali.

By the eleventh century the Islamic states were so decentralized and divided that they were vulnerable to attack by a unified outside force. The Seljuk Turks were a nomad people, originally from Samarkand in central Asia. Moving westward and adopting the Islamic faith in the process, they swept through Persia, Syria, Iraq, and most of western Asia. By 1055 they had conquered Baghdad, and in 1071 they won a commanding victory against Byzantine forces at Manzikert. Their control over the Islamic kingdoms was subsequently weakened by dynastic rivalries and family disagreements. Nonetheless, a system of political administration that left supreme power in the hands of one ruler—the sultan—and his court gave the Seljuk empire a brief period of stability before it too fell to invaders from the east, the most powerful of whom were the Mongols.

Islamic Society and Economy

The principal force that shaped the character of Islamic society was, of course, the religion itself. Yet as we have seen, as early as the period of the caliphates the original austerity and simplicity of the Arab way of life was changed and enriched by contact with the peoples the Muslims conquered and those with whom they traded.

Many of Muhammad's teachings remained fundamental to Islamic society. The family maintained its role as the central social unit. It was ruled by its patriarch, the oldest male, who controlled the family's collective property and whose approval was necessary for marriage. Although the development and spread of sophisticated court society gave a few women scope for a life beyond family duties, in general Muslim wives and daughters had to be subordinate and obedient to their male relatives. We have no evidence of women playing a significant role in public life, even as writers.

Muhammad had found the practice of slavery well established in the Arabia of his time, and though he taught that slaves should be treated humanely, he did not condemn slavery itself. As the Muslim conquests of the succeeding centuries produced vast numbers of foreign slaves, many of them originally prisoners of war, the slave trade became an important and lucrative industry. Slavery was permitted by Islamic law until as recently as the mid-nineteenth century, when it was abolished except in Arabia. The acquisition of substantial numbers of slaves facilitated large-scale agricultural, manufacturing, and construction projects, thereby strengthening the economy. But the possibility of slave uprisings always presented a political and social threat.

For the most part the Muslims avoided the worst excesses of gang work in the fields, industry, or mines, which had been common in Roman times, and employed their slaves as domestic servants, treating them in accordance with the provisions of the Koran. Nor did Muslim society discriminate on grounds of color or race. If liberated, slaves of any origin could take their places as equal members of the community and could rise to high positions. The most famous case was that of the Mameluke dynasty, descended from slaves, that ruled Egypt from 1250 to 1517. Male domestic slaves were sometimes emasculated, however, and females could be required to act as their owners' sexual partners. In some cases such concubines were eventually granted the status of legitimate wives.

The geographic spread of Islam produced, over time, considerable social mobility. The conquerors were obliged to accept as administrators and bureaucrats men of a wide variety of backgrounds, only some of whom converted to Islam. The period was marked by the growth of cities, first Damascus and Baghdad, then Palermo (conquered 831), Cairo (founded 969), and others throughout the Mediterranean region and western Asia.

In contrast to the Byzantine Empire, which never encouraged the growth of urban life, the Muslim caliphates actively promoted the foundation of new cities as a stimulus to trade and industry. Cairo, which began as a new section for the city of al-Fustat, soon developed its manufacturing and plantations to become a formidable rival to Damascus and Baghdad. The conquest of Palermo strengthened Arab contacts with Mediterranean culture and left an artistic legacy that is still visible.

Such widespread urbanization created new possibilities for economic and social mobility by trade, land speculation, and professions such as teaching. Whereas the early Islamic leaders had been drawn from the aristocratic class, the principal figures in the urban centers of the ninth and tenth centuries were businessmen, bankers, and manufacturers.

Thus a civilization with no centralized rule, with the Byzantine Empire as its constant rival to the west and with the periodic threat of nomad invasion from the east, forged for itself a period of almost unprecedented economic prosperity. The merchants of Baghdad and the other major cities bought and sold commodities from India and Ceylon, Russia, Sweden, and Spain. Carpets and textiles were exchanged for gold from central Africa or furs and amber from the Baltic.

As in Roman times, China supplied many of the luxury goods, including silk, peacock feathers, porcelain, and spices. Trade caravans to the east generally made use of maritime routes. Elsewhere Arab merchants continued to use Roman and Persian overland roads, which local rulers generally kept in good condition. Muslim governors maintained an efficient road network to promote trade, and the stopping places along the routes, where the caravans and their owners could find overnight rest in a *caravanserai*—a kind of camel motel—became prosperous centers in their own right.

In addition to trade and manufacturing, the Muslim economy depended on successful agricultural production. The original Arab conquerors had come from a land where water was scarce and precious. Irrigation and water conservation techniques were widely and skillfully used, not only for farming but also for the construction of ornamental gardens, an important feature of Muslim urban life. Fruit trees and fountains appear frequently in Persian and other Muslim art of the period. To this day in Spain, Muslim agricultural and ornamental irrigation systems are in use.

The economy of Islam prospered despite political corruption and inefficiency. As the provincial centers began to prosper, they found it increasingly unnecessary to look to a central administration. At Baghdad factions soon developed, and the seizure of property, the taking of bribes, and the buying and selling of official positions became commonplace. Provincial governors became increasingly lax in sending taxes to Baghdad. Local administrations were often as corrupt as that of Baghdad, but in time they came to be controlled by the business class rather than the landed aristocracies. It was in the interests of the merchants that the roads were kept usable, that the financial markets worked efficiently, and that international trade remained possible. In this way the financial prosperity of the Islamic world militated against political unity. Nor was it difficult to justify the exalted position of commerce in Islamic life: Muhammad, a merchant himself, had urged pious Muslims to trade during their pilgrimage to Mecca.

Islamic Civilization

The cohesion of Islamic culture lay in a shared language, religion, and economic strength. It was also characterized by important intellectual and scientific developments. Quite apart from the growth of specialized theological studies, based initially on the Koran, Arab scholars explored a wide variety of secular fields. Arab geographers, for example, accumulated vast amounts of data about both Islamic and non-Islamic countries, from travelers, traders, and explorers. Perhaps the most influential Muslim intellectual contribution to the modern world, however, was in science and medicine.

Scientists and Doctors: The Muslim Synthesis

The starting point for many Arab scientists was the works of ancient Greek scientific writers such as Galen and Ptolemy. As early as the seventh century many of these works were translated, first into Syriac, the dialect of the Umayyad court at Damascus, and later into Arabic.

With the move to Baghdad and the increasing importance of Persian scholars, both Persian and Indian scientific writings began to circulate. The development of the Islamic tradition was highly eclectic. The Islamic world's first acquaintance with astronomical theory was derived from Sanskrit texts. The system of mathematics that made astronomical calculations possible was based on a synthesis of Greek mathematics and Indian notation. Around 830 Muhammad ibn-Musa al-Khwarazmi, who had translated a number of mathematical and astronomical works from the Sanskrit, published two collections, *Arithmetic* and *Algebra,* which were translated into Latin in the twelfth century. The first introduced Western scholars to what is generally called the Arabic system of numbers, although it was in fact Hindu in origin; the second was a popular textbook in western Europe until the sixteenth century.

In addition to astronomy, geography, and zoology, Arab scholars were interested, like their counterparts in the West, in the pseudosciences of astrology (the interpretation of the effects of the movement of the stars and planets on human affairs) and alchemy. By manipulation of chemical elements, alchemists sought to transform base metals into gold and alter other substances. Many of their experiments had little practical value, but by isolating and distinguishing between various metals and solid chemicals they developed valuable knowledge and procedures.

In the field of practical technology Muslim scientists absorbed and ultimately passed on many of the innovations of the cultures to their east, notably India and China. Among these were the magnetic compass, gunpowder, and paper, which were Chinese inventions. The use of a glass lens for magnification was an Arabic discovery, from which the science of optics developed.

Arabic medicine combined the theory of Greek medical texts with the practical study of patients and their ailments; such study was facilitated by the relatively high quality of Muslim hospitals. Islam forbade the dissection of corpses, so advances in surgery were limited. Considerable progress was made, however, in the classification of diseases and in understanding their interrelationships.

The Persian physician and philosopher Ibn Sina (Avicenna; 980–1037) published the *Canon of Medicine,* in which he identified the contagious nature of tuberculosis and described certain skin diseases and psychological disorders. He also pointed out that water and soil could act as spreading agents for disease. Probably no other work of its period was more widely studied; the basis for Arab medical research, it was also used in European universities as the chief guide to medical science from the twelfth to the seventeenth centuries. Like many other Arabic texts, it was first introduced into Europe through the universities of Cordoba, Granada, and other cities in southern Spain. By this means, much Arabic scholarship was diffused throughout the Christian West. Ibn Sina's knowledge and use of the philosophical methods of the classical Greek Aristotle also played a major part in the development of another branch of Muslim intellectual inquiry, philosophy.

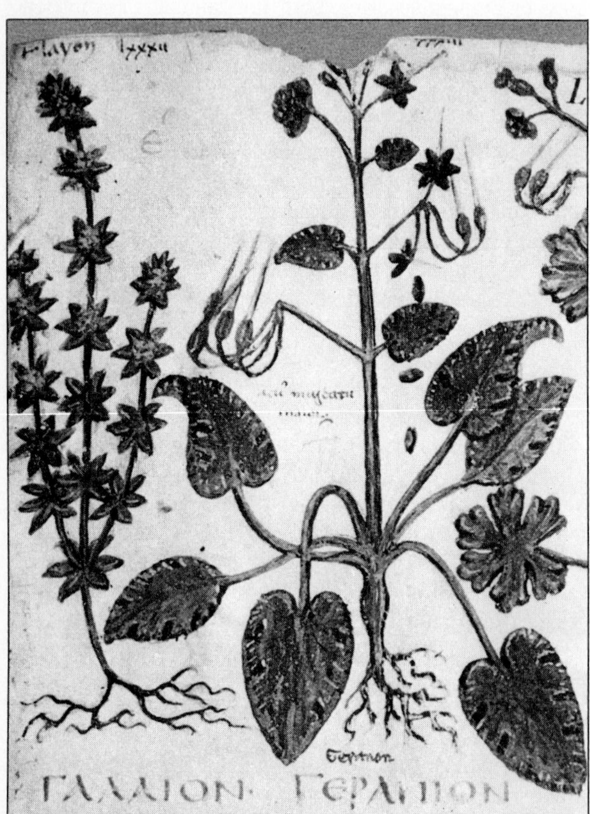

A page from an Arabic medical manuscript depicting the cultivation of medicinal herbs. [Granger Collection]

Philosophy: The Search for Order

As in the case of science, the initial inspiration for much Islamic philosophy was found in translations of Aristotle and other Greek philosophical writers. Unlike science, however, philosophy often came into direct conflict with the religious teachings of the Koran and its intepreters. In general, Islamic theologians were opposed to philosophical inquiry. Al-Ashani, (873–935), for example, warned that Allah's will was entirely free and impossible to know, rendering completely useless any philosophical speculation. Most Muslim philosophers, consequently, were not professional theologians, as in the medieval West, even though they were in many cases devout believers.

The center of scholarly inquiry was the library at Baghdad known as the House of Wisdom, constructed in the early ninth century. It contained the major works of Aristotle and Plato and other Greek philosophical and scientific texts, all translated into Arabic. Some original manuscripts were Byzantine that had been seized by Muslim forces in attacks on Byzantine strongholds. Others were acquired by more peaceful means: emissaries were sent to Byzantium to purchase copies.

No Greek thinker aroused more passion and controversy than Aristotle, whose teachings seemed to many Muslims to be in conflict with their own tradition. Muslim theologians conceived of a personal, unpredictable Allah who could be perceived only by spiritual revelation. By contrast, Muslim students of Greek philosophy claimed that the force governing the universe was both rational and fully comprehensible. Its power was entirely impersonal and could be understood by contemplation and reason. These teachings were to prove as problematic to later Christian theologians as they did to strict Muslims.

The most appealing of Aristotle's doctrines to Muslim thinkers was his insistence that by cataloging information it was possible to impose order on apparent chaos. In this way people could come to grips with the nature of knowledge in a concrete way. The Islamic writer Alkindi (died 872) discussed the distinction between our way of knowing and what we know. Ibn Sina examined the relationship of knowledge to existence. Though he was an orthodox Muslim, his concept of Allah nonetheless owed much to Aristotle's idea of God as the "Unmoved Mover" and as "thought thinking of itself." Because God was already perfect, Ibn Sina argued, existence followed unyielding laws, rendering human intercession with God pointless.

The greatest Muslim philosopher was the Spanish-born Averroës (Ibn-Rushd; 1126–1198), whose versatile career combined the pursuits of the law, astronomy, and medicine. Averroës is often accused of having taught "the double truth," namely that while the faithful may hold one unchanging set of beliefs, philosophers are entitled to speculate for themselves. His writings are aimed at a sophisticated audience rather than at pious but literal students of the Koran, principally because he denied that faith and reason could be reconciled. However secure Averroës' own religious convictions, certainly no other Muslim thinker had a higher regard for Aristotle, whom he believed to have been "a rule in nature and an example which nature has devised to demonstrate supreme human perfection."

Islamic Literature: Love and Morality

In addition to the large body of theological literature devoted to expounding the Koran, a number of authors were inspired by Sufism. The principal Sufi writer was Muhammad ibn-Muhammad al-Ghazzali (1058–1111), who rejected attempts to reconcile Islam and Greek philosophy in *The Incoherence of the Philosophers,* which called forth a rebuttal from Averroës, *The Incoherence of the Incoherence.*

We have already seen something of the development of secular Arabic literature at the courts of the caliphates. Like Abu Nuwas, the favorite of Harun al-Rashid, many of the most famous and most popular poets of the Islamic world were Persian. The greatest Islamic epic poet was perhaps Firdawsi (c. 935–c. 1020). His tomb at Tus, in modern Iran, is venerated as a national shrine, but almost every event in his career is hotly debated. The work on which his fame rests is the *Shah-Nama* (Book of the Kings), which tells the history of Persia's rulers from legendary times to the fall of the Sassanians, the last dynasty of native Persian rulers, in 651; its stories provided a favorite source of inspiration for Persian miniature and manuscript illustrations.

The most beloved of lyric poets, Shams ud-din Hafiz (c. 1325–1389 or –1390), lived most of his life in poverty at Shiraz, where he composed some 500 *ghazals,* short lyric poems on the subject of love. Although they deal with conventional erotic themes and include frequent references to drinking and drunkenness, the poems were often interpreted as mystical allegories, in which references to the "Beloved" were assumed to refer to God, as in the Hebrews' Song of Songs. Modern scholarship is more inclined to take them literally. In the seventeenth century Hafiz was "discovered" by European poets, and he had a great impact on the German Romantic poet Goethe.

Hafiz' audience was accustomed to the easy lifestyle and luxury of the royal courts. Sa'adi (c. 1215–1292) addressed a broader public; his homely and practical wisdom

Love and Being in Islamic Poetry

These are Sufi poems, the first by the woman saint Rabia al-Adawiya and the second by the great Persian poet Jami.

I love Thee with two loves, love of my happiness,
And perfect love, to love Thee as is Thy due.
My selfish love is that I do naught
But think on Thee, excluding all beside;
But that purest love, which is Thy due,
Is that the veils which hide Thee fall, and I gaze on Thee,
No praise to me in either this or that,
Nay, Thine the praise for both that love and this.

The Eye of the Beloved, seeing what was not, regarded nonentity as existent.
Although he beheld His attributes and qualities as a perfect whole in His own
 Essence,
Yet He desired that they should be displayed to Him in another mirror
And that each one of His eternal attributes should become manifest accordingly in
 a diverse form.
Therefore He created the verdant fields of Time and Space and the life-giving
 garden of the World,
That every branch and leaf and fruit might show forth His various perfections.

Source: H. A. R. Gibb, *Mohammedanism* (New York: Oxford University Press, 1962), pp. 133, 151–152.

remains much esteemed in the Muslim world. Although he wrote ghazals, his reputation is based on two longer works, *The Orchard* and *The Rose-Garden,* collections of anecdotes and advice on such subjects as "submissiveness, contentment, and other excellences." One of the greatest Islamic poets, the Sufi Jami (1414–1492), was influenced by Hafiz. Jami's lyrics explore the world of Islamic mysticism and deal with such fundamental themes as ethics and existence. His contemporary, the Indian poet Kabir (died 1518), was also a mystic. Raised as a Muslim and influenced by Hindu teachings, Kabir taught the equality of all persons and their ability to achieve unity with God through personal devotion.

By far the most famous literary work from the Muslim world is *The Thousand and One Nights.* It is a collection of stories assembled over a period of several centuries, and no standard text was produced until the fifteenth century. The tales themselves provide a wide-ranging view of Muslim society, including as they do Persian and Indian fairy stories, Egyptian romances, and Arab anecdotes. Many of the earlier ones provide a vivid picture of urban life at Baghdad or Cairo, blending luxury and courtly intrigue. Some of the later ones deal with the lower strata of society and describe the antics of rogues, vagabonds, and tricksters.

The simple Arabic of the tales, unlike the sophisticated language of Hafiz and Firdawsi, has wide appeal. Many Muslim scholars did not regard them as serious literature, relegating them to the level of popular storytelling. They found, however, a warm reception in western Europe when they were translated into French and English in the eighteenth and nineteenth centuries.

Byzantium and the Islamic Challenge

The Islamic cultural and economic achievements were won during a period in which the Arabs' principal rival in the eastern Mediterranean and western Asia, the Byzantine Empire, lurched through a series of increasingly serious crises. To some extent these were the result of Arab pressures. Constantinople itself was attacked by Muslim forces as early as 717, but Emperor Leo III (717–741), a native of Syria, successfully defended the capital and repulsed the Arabs from Asia Minor. The assault on Constantinople was nevertheless a traumatic experience, as reflected in the reaction of its patriarch:

> **Such dangers our city had never before experienced, and not our city only, but the whole world that is inhabited by Christians. For it may be acknowledged without any doubt that Christ's entire flock would have been in the same peril as ourselves had the godless Saracens attained the goal of their expedition against us [the capture of Constantinople].[5]**

The Arabs did, however, retain their conquests in Syria, Palestine, Egypt, and North Africa, and in the ninth century they captured Crete and Sicily, from which they periodically raided Byzantine territory in Greece and southern Italy. In the meantime the Lombards had overrun Ravenna (751), and the Bulgars and other Slavs advanced in the Balkans.

Defensive needs prompted Byzantine rulers to organize their territories into military districts, called *themes,* each of which was headed by a general in charge of civil and military affairs. Troops were recruited locally and rewarded with grants of land in return for their military service. The land could not be sold but in turn passed to their sons, who assumed responsibility for military duty. Many of those who served in the Byzantine army under this system were migrants, particularly Armenians and Slavs. This pattern of recruitment was similar to that in the late Roman Empire.

The development of the theme system, coupled with the impact of enemy invasions, destroyed much of the traditional aristocracy, which had been based on service rather than hereditary titles. Large landowners suffered extensively, especially beginning in the seventh century when the emperor Phocas I (602–610) and several of his successors executed nobles and confiscated their lands. Yet some aristocrats, who were needed in the civil administration and the church, survived. The theme system gave rise to the development of a new military aristocracy, which was generally less educated and less culturally refined than the old nobility. The emperor Michael II (820–829), a product of the theme system, was, for instance, infamous for his dislike of Greek education as well as for his personal ignorance. Many of the succeeding crises that the empire experienced were the result of such internal problems as the inadequacy of its economic base and the poor training of its elite.

Byzantium and Christianity

Like Muslim culture, Byzantine civilization was rooted in religion. Yet the Christianity that it promoted resulted in dissension and periodic outbreaks of violence. From the time of Justinian, debate on religious matters had played a major part in political affairs. In theory, the moral and ethical code of Islam was at least as strict as that of Christianity, but the wide cultural diversity of successive waves of Muslim converts led to considerable flexibility in its practice. By contrast, each Byzantine emperor sought to impose his own views on orthodox Christianity, which frequently differed from those of his predecessor.

Imperial legislation on matters of religious doctrine had a profound effect on a society permeated by religion at all levels, from the official life of the court to the peasants' world of popular Christianity. The emperor himself was alleged to be the representative of God on earth. His authority was absolute, and the oaths of loyalty sworn to him were sacred. The people he ruled were required to sub-

Ivory panel showing the Byzantine emperor Constantine VII being crowned by Christ. [Giraudon/Art Resource]

scribe to the orthodox faith. Pagans were ordered to attend church services and accept baptism; from the time of Justinian the number of non-Christians in Constantinople was carefully limited, and missionaries were sent to convert those of western Asia. Among the penalties for failure to adopt Christianity was prohibition of inheritance. Thus a pagan father could not pass his property on to his sons unless they became Christians.

Successive emperors attempted to control the official representatives of Christianity, the priests and monks, by regulating the size of churches and limiting their financial income. The monasteries formed an enduring center for Byzantine religious culture. The primary means of spreading Christianity was by missionaries and traveling holy men, whose lives became the subjects of popular biographies. Healing the sick, feeding the hungry, and purportedly driving out demons, these itinerant proselytizers represented Christianity on a far more popular level than the official religious culture of the court.

The function of the emperor as supreme interpreter and guardian of the faith meant that Byzantine rulers could not accept decentralization of their empire, as the Abbasid caliphs had. Their concept of Constantinople as the new, Christian capital of the ancient Roman Empire remained fixed, even as the empire dwindled in size.

This attitude came under increasing challenge as Christianity spread throughout western Europe. As early as 800, with the coronation of Charlemagne in Rome, the Byzantine claim to universal Christian sovereignty was undermined. The growing power of western, or Latin, Christianity led in 1054 to a dispute that finally divided the "Orthodox" Christians of the east from the "Roman Catholics" in the west. At its basis was the struggle between secular and ecclesiastical authority. The Latin church, with its concept of the universal role of the papacy, was in fundamental conflict with the Byzantine belief in the authority of the emperor. Disputes over theology and ritual that had been brewing for more than a century thus came to a head in the mid-eleventh-century schism, or split in the church, that produced a turning point in east-west Christian relations. One of the consequences was that the Byzantines reserved for Latin Christians a hatred even more implacable than that with which they viewed the Muslims. A late twelfth-century patriarch of Constantinople expressed this feeling clearly:

> **Let the Muslim be my master in outward things rather than the Latin dominate me in matters of the spirit. For if I am subject to the Muslim, at least he will not force me to share his faith. But if I have to be under the Frankish rule and united with the Roman Church, I may have to separate myself from my God.[6]**

It was an eloquent comment on the intolerance of Christianity and the greater freedom of Islam in this period.

Even in the final struggles to maintain the independence of Constantinople against the invading Turks, when only massive intervention on the part of western European Christian forces could have helped, Byzantine rulers were reluctant to ask for help from those whom they perceived as enemies. The Latins were equally disinclined to offer assistance, and their temporary conquest of the empire between 1204 and 1261 gave point to the Byzantines' suspicions.

Early symptoms of the Byzantine obsession with religious dogmatism can be found in the icon controversy of the eighth and ninth centuries. The emperors Leo III and Constantine V (741–775), among the ablest of Byzantine rulers, banned the use of icons—painted or carved representations of Christ and the saints—because abuses relating to them were deemed idolatrous. Leo took down the icon of Christ that had hung over the imperial palace and in 730 ordered all icons destroyed. The violence that followed lasted for over a century, as iconoclast (anti-icon) and iconodule (pro-icon) factions vied for power, and emperors were judged less for their ability to defend the empire from Bulgarian and Slavic invaders than for their position on icon worship. Only in 843 was iconoclasm finally proscribed with regulations for the proper use of images, after which icons were again freely produced.

An icon from the seventh century showing Jesus as Pantocrator, or ruler of all. [©Sheridan/Ancient Art & Architecture Collection, London]

If the Christians of western Europe seemed increasingly alien—they were, in fact, strongly opposed to the iconoclastic policy—the Byzantines could at least spread their religion farther east. The first important contact between the Byzantine Empire and Russia occurred in 860, when the Rus, the Viking rulers of the Slavs of Russia, sailed to Constantinople. One of the consequences was a missionary campaign, led by two brothers, Cyril and Methodius, that succeeded in converting the Russians to Christianity. The brothers devised a special religious literature for the Russians, using a version of the Greek alphabet; the Cyrillic script, named after one of them, is still in use today in Russia and other Slavic countries, all of which were heavily influenced by Byzantine civilization.

Yet once again Byzantine religious policy failed to accomplish more practical goals: the Bulgarians, who posed a much more serious threat to Byzantine security than the more distant Russians, decided that the Latin church could offer them Christianity on more favorable terms. Bulgarian troops continued to harass the empire, even after they were reclaimed by the Byzantine church. Only in 1018 did the emperor Basil II (976–1025), known as Basil the Bulgar Slayer, finally succeed in annihilating the Bulgarian army; in a ferocious act of revenge, he had some 15,000 captured troops blinded.

The Comnenian Revival

Although the Bulgarian threat had been eliminated, by Basil's death the empire had lost most of its former glory. Much of the empire's foreign trade was by now conducted by Muslims, Jews, and Italians. Moreover, the Muslims controlled the Mediterranean and made periodic raids on the Greek mainland and islands. Although the Arabs had conquered Sicily in the ninth century, they were displaced two centuries later by the Normans from northern France, who also attacked the few remaining Byzantine settlements of southern Italy. The victory of the Seljuk Turks at Manzikert in 1071 left the whole of western Asia vulnerable to Turkish attacks. Fortunately for the Byzantines, the able Alexius Comnenus (1081–1118) and his successors recovered some of Byzantium's territory and prestige. On coming to power, he remarked, "I found the empire surrounded on all sides by barbarians and absolutely deficient in resources." By the time he was succeeded by his son John (1118–1143), he had defeated Turkish forces and withstood western Europe's First Crusade.

ANNA COMNENA: CONSPIRATOR AND HISTORIAN

Much of our knowledge of Alexius' reign and of Byzantine court life of the period comes from the writings of Anna Comnena (1083–c. 1153), his eldest child. From her youth this remarkable woman came into contact with the leaders of the empire and acquired an education in literature and philosophy that was unheard of for girls at that time. Married to the son of Alexius' rival for the throne, Anna assumed that her new husband would succeed her father; when in fact her brother John did so, she was involved in a plot to assassinate him. As a consequence, she was forced to retire to a convent for the rest of her life. Having failed to gain political power, she turned to scholarship and organized a group of philosophers who revived the study of Aristotle, as their near contemporary Averroës was doing in the Muslim world.

Anna herself wrote a history of her father's reign, *The Alexiad.* She had lived through many of the events she chronicled and was a woman of strong feelings, fully capable of nursing a grudge for 30 years. Her father, whom she idealized, is the hero of her story, and the principal villains are not so much his Turkish opponents as the Latin Christian leaders of the First Crusade. Her brother is barely mentioned, and only in the coldest of tones.

Anna's precocious youth and elite education made her something of a snob. She wrote in an elaborately stylized form of Greek that aimed to recapture the classical language of 1,500 years earlier. Her work is filled with literary references and archaic words, and she apologized for even mentioning the names of the western European characters who appeared in her story. Yet her passionate, committed account, filled with details from her own observation, provides a remarkable picture of her father's times, most vividly in her reconstruction of her own youth.

Unlike many of her contemporaries, Anna avoided

theological dispute. Her contempt for the Crusaders was political rather than religious, and her interest in Aristotle came two centuries before a similar rediscovery in western Europe. Indeed, her passionate defense of reason places her intellectually with the great classical historians whom she revered. Of a bishop who had committed a theological blunder, she remarked with characteristic haughtiness that it was only to be expected, "for he was incapable of making a precise statement with conviction, as he was absolutely untrained in the science of reasoning."

Anna thought of her work as a great responsibility. In preparing it she consulted documents from the state archives and diplomatic correspondence, and in its prologue she explained that "history alone can save the memory of events from oblivion." Her devotion to truth, tempered only by her passionate family pride, marks her as one of the greatest Byzantine historians.

The Byzantine Achievement

The Byzantines maintained the symbolic value of their city and empire for over 1,000 years. In practice, however, Constantinople could never, like Rome, govern a unified, broadly based territory. This was due in part to the fact that despite the fame of its capital, Byzantine culture was basically nonurban. Apart from Constantinople and Thessalonica, as we have observed, there were few other Byzantine towns of note. Thus there was no centralized infrastructure that would strengthen the defense of territories under attack.

Nevertheless, the Byzantine record of defending the empire is impressive. For much of their history, the Byzantines were a beleaguered people who spent much of their wealth on defensive wars. Indeed, the Byzantine Empire served as a bulwark, protecting the West against waves of nomadic Asian attackers, beginning with the Huns in the fifth century and followed by Avars, Bulgars, and Magyars, and finally Pechenegs and Cumans. There were also assaults from the Persians and the Arabs beginning in the seventh century, and ultimately from the Turks. Pressure came as well from the Russians and the western Europeans. The Byzantines' survival depended on their economic strength, their military organization and adaptability, and their navy, which employed a chemical weapon known as "Greek fire" that set enemy vessels aflame.

The theme system, which for a time had been very successful, became a destructive force in the mid-eleventh century. Ambitious, self-centered generals increasingly turned insubordinate, ignoring commands from Constantinople and allying themselves with large landowners for personal gain. The emperors unwittingly furthered this trend by rewarding state servants with large grants of land, technically in return for military service. With the breakdown of the theme system the emperors found themselves facing not loyal armies but increasingly rebellious and powerful subjects. Attempts to counter this trend by hiring mercenary troops were unsuccessful, and mercenary forces were expensive, causing additional financial pressure on the government, which was ultimately forced to begin devaluing its gold coinage in the eleventh century.

The empire was, of course, not without resources. The two major cities had great ports, and the empire itself straddled some of the world's great trade routes. Byzantium exported a variety of products, notably jewelry, glassware, and fine cloth. The wine of southern Greece was much in demand, and carpets were exported from the Peloponnesus. Only the Chinese produced luxury items that could equal those of the Byzantines. There was a brisk trade in spices and luxury goods from Syria, Arabia, India, Ceylon, and East Asia, including porcelain and silk from China. Ivory and slaves were imported from Africa, mulberry leaves to feed the silkworms came from plantations in Syria, and papyrus came from Egypt. Wine and furs as well as grain, hides, slaves, timber, and salt arrived from the Black Sea region and Russia. Imports from western Europe included wool, linen, and wrought iron. Until the Arab conquest, Africa provided the Byzantines with wheat, but Asia Minor and Thrace, within the empire, took over in the tenth century as the chief suppliers of that commodity as well as meat. The decreased supply of food was probably a factor in Constantinople's declining population. Exports and imports alike were subject to a tax of 10 percent that eventually hurt Byzantine commerce. Moreover, commencing in the eleventh century, upheavals in the lands bordering the empire and beyond also curtailed trade.

Almost all surviving Byzantine art is religious, underscoring the fundamental role Christianity played in Byzan-

Main apse of the cathedral in Cefalu, Sicily, dominated by the figure of Christ the Pantocrator. [SEF/Art Resource]

tine life. The art underwent remarkably little stylistic development over the centuries but rather concentrated on perfection of technique. Unlike Western art, where paintings illustrated religious themes or inspired spiritual meditation, Byzantine icons were worshiped. As a result, Byzantine art was extremely conservative, concerned with the preservation and repetition of familiar images. After the defeat of the iconoclasts, the decoration of churches became similarly repetitive, with particular scenes assigned to specific parts of the building: the figure of Christ as Lord of the Universe, for example, generally occupied the crown of the dome. But if Byzantine art lacked the inventiveness of classical Greece, the absence of experimentation was intentional. The blue and gold backgrounds set with richly dressed figures were meant to evoke on earth the unchanging brilliance of heaven.

In many ways the culture of the Byzantines was very different from that of their Muslim contemporaries. Islamic poetry and art celebrate the delights of love and wine, subjects unthinkable in a Byzantine context, and Islamic scholarship and science far surpass Byzantine achievements in such fields. Yet in other respects both cultures made a lasting impact on the world. Byzantine law, as codified by Justinian, remained one of the bases for the political and legal systems in force throughout much of the West, while the law of Islam is one of the principal influences in the life of the Middle East and North Africa. Byzantine religion, in the form of Orthodox Christianity, and the Islamic faith continue to affect the lives of hundreds of millions of people. Both civilizations preserved and passed on the achievements of classical Greece, the Muslims in science and scholarship, the Byzantines in literature and the arts. Islam, more broadly based as a culture and more dynamic as a religion, subsequently exerted enormous influence in the Indian subcontinent and remains to this day the dominant culture in Pakistan, the Middle East, Southeast Asia, and North Africa.

Notes

1. Procopius, *The Buildings of Justinian* (London: Palestine Pilgrims' Text Society, 1896), p. 24.
2. *The Koran Interpreted,* trans. A. J. Arberry (New York: Macmillan, 1955), 1:125.
3. Ibid., 2:320.
4. Ibid., 2:50.
5. P. Whitting, ed., *Byzantium: An Introduction,* 2d ed. (Oxford: Basil Blackwell, 1981), p. 57.
6. Ibid., p. 103.

Suggestions for Further Reading

Andrae, T. *Mohammed: The Man and His Faith.* London: George Allen & Unwin, 1956.

Bishai, W. B. *Humanities in the Arabic-Islamic World.* Dubuque, Iowa: Brown, 1973.

Cameron, A. *Circus Factions: Blues and Greens in Rome and Byzantium.* Oxford: Clarendon Press, 1976.

Daniel, N. *The Arabs and Medieval Europe,* 2d ed. London: Longman, 1978.

Donner, F. M. *The Early Islamic Conquests.* Princeton, N.J.: Princeton University Press, 1981.

Downey, G. *Constantinople in the Age of Justinian.* Norman: University of Oklahoma Press, 1960.

Endress, G. *Islam: A Historical Introduction,* trans. C. Hillenbrand. New York: Columbia University Press, 1987.

Every, G. *The Byzantine Patriarchate, 451–1204,* 2d ed. New York: AMS Press, 1978.

Grabar, A. *Byzantine Painting,* trans. S. Gilbert. Geneva: Skira, 1953.

Hussey, J. M. *The Byzantine World.* Westport, Conn.: Greenwood Press, 1982.

Kitzinger, E. *Byzantine Art in the Making.* Cambridge, Mass.: Harvard University Press, 1977.

Le Strange, G. *Baghdad During the Abbasid Caliphate.* New York: Barnes & Noble Books, 1972.

Lewis, B. *Islam: From the Prophet Muhammad to the Capture of Constantinople.* 2 vols. New York: Oxford University Press, 1987.

Maclagan, M. *The City of Constantinople.* New York: Praeger, 1968.

Magoulias, H. J. *Byzantine Christianity: Emperor, Church, and the West.* Detroit: Wayne State University Press, 1982.

Mottahedeh, R. P. *Loyalty and Leadership in Early Islamic Society.* Princeton, N.J.: Princeton University Press, 1980.

——. *The Mantle of the Prophet.* New York: Simon & Schuster, 1985.

Nicol, D. M. *Church and Society in the Last Centuries of Byzantium.* Cambridge: Cambridge University Press, 1979.

Obolensky, D. *The Byzantine Commonwealth: Eastern Europe, 500–1453.* New York: Praeger, 1971.

Rahman, F. *Islam,* 2d ed. Chicago: University of Chicago Press, 1979.

Robinson, M. *Mohammed,* trans. A. Carter. New York: Pantheon, 1971.

Runciman, S. *The Byzantine Theocracy.* Cambridge: Cambridge University Press, 1977.

Sherrard, P. *Constantinople: Iconography of a Sacred City.* New York: Oxford University Press, 1965.

Watt, W. M. *Muhammad: Prophet and Statesman.* New York: Oxford University Press, 1974.

Wiet, G. *Baghdad: Metropolis of the Abbasid Caliphate,* trans. S. Feiler. Norman: University of Oklahoma Press, 1971.

Ziadeh, N. A. *Damascus Under the Mamluks.* Norman: University of Oklahoma Press, 1964.

Writing and Communication (I)

One of the major elements in the development of civilization was the invention of writing. Its original purpose was probably to leave messages and to keep track of financial and other transactions, but with the ability to accumulate and preserve knowledge almost every aspect of human life was transformed. The power of the written word became vastly extended with the invention of printing, and the twentieth century has seen the discoveries of new technologies and an almost unimaginable proliferation of means of communication. These three stages—writing, printing, and mass communications—have affected the history of virtually every human civilization.

The earliest known writing system was devised by the people of Uruk (now Warka), one of the principal Sumerian city-states. In the late Neolithic period, records had been kept using small tokens in the shape of disks, spheres, half spheres, cones, and other figures, some of which were marked with incisions. Usually kept in clay containers, such tokens might be used, for instance, to represent animals in a palace herd. Late in the fourth millennium B.C., as cities and large-scale trade developed, the use of tokens to maintain records became too cumbersome. The Mesopotamians substituted written images known as ideographs for the tokens. During the third millennium B.C. these ideographs evolved into a series of wedge-shaped marks that could be impressed on a clay tablet quickly and easily with a split reed. The Sumerians also wrote on stone and metal, but clay, which was plentiful in their country and was already used for building and pottery, was much easier to make marks on. Mistakes could easily be smoothed out, and the record could be made permanent by leaving the clay to dry in the sun or baking it slowly in an oven. In this form it was light and easy to carry as well. The system of wedge-shaped marks on clay is known as *cuneiform,* after the Latin word *cuneus,* which means "wedge."

Statuette of the goddess Ningal from Ur (2080 B.C.). The figure can be identified by the cuneiform inscription on the side of the throne. [University Museum, University of Pennsylvania]

Cuneiform combined the use of pictographic signs (representing objects) and phonetic signs (representing sounds) with a total of some 350 characters. It was adopted by the Sumerians' Akkadian successors and was in general use in western Asia and Persia until around the middle of the first millennium B.C. Cuneiform signs formed the basis of the earliest known alphabet, which was devised around 1400 B.C. at the Canaanite city of Ugarit. An *alphabet* is a system using only phonetic symbols. The Canaanite writing system, known as North Semitic, gave rise to a large number of later alphabets, including the Arabic, Hebrew, Greek, and Latin.

Around 3000 B.C., shortly after the Sumerian invention of cuneiform, the Egyptians introduced a system of writing that is somewhat misleadingly known as *hieroglyphics.* The word means "sacred carved text," but Egyptian hieroglyphs were used for funerary and commemorative inscriptions as well as religious ones and were often painted or written on papyrus, a material woven from the reeds that grew along the Nile River. Whether the Egyptians were directly influenced by the Sumerians is uncertain. The sudden appearance and rapid development of hieroglyphic writing cer-

Relief from the Old Kingdom tomb of Ptahhotep at Saqqara, showing agricultural scenes with hieroglyphic inscriptions above. [George Holton/Photo Researchers]

tainly suggests contact, but the Egyptians never developed a simplified sign system like cuneiform; throughout their long history no attempt was made to change the basic hieroglyphic signs, although the cursive forms of hieratic and, later, demotic (a script devised for secular use) were introduced for speedier writing with brush-pen on papyrus for business, tax, and other nonmonumental purposes.

The earliest writing in India dates back to the Indus valley civilization, which flourished between 3000 and 2000 B.C. in what is now Pakistan. Small, square seal-stones were carved with picture signs, often accompanied by animals. The script has never been deciphered, however. With the disappearance of the Indus valley culture, knowledge of writing seems to have been lost for a few centuries. By 600 B.C. the Aryan invaders of India had developed an alphabetic script. Under the Maurya dynasty (third century B.C.) the *Brahmi,* ancestor of all modern Indian scripts and of many others elsewhere, was firmly established and was used for numerous rock-carved edicts of the emperor Ashoka (269–232 B.C.).

Attempts have been made to link the Brahmi script with the Indus valley pictograms and thus provide it with a native origin. Most experts, however, believe that a Semitic alphabet was imported into India. Given the remarkable way the alphabet was adapted to Indian needs, this must have occurred sometime before the third century B.C., although no traces of earlier inscriptions have survived. We shall look at the early history of Brahmi when we consider the other descendants of the Semitic alphabets.

The beginning of writing in China is difficult to trace. Its first surviving appearance is in the form of divination inscriptions on shells and bones worked by the Lung Shan people around 2000 B.C. and found in far greater numbers at Anyang and other Shang sites of the late second millennium B.C. The bones were carved with divinations relating to the public and private life of the ruler: building projects, military campaigns, tribute payments, sickness, royal excursions, the weather. These oracle bones were then burned, and the position of any cracks that occurred was carefully studied, since the patterns they formed and their position in relation to the inscriptions were supposed to reveal the wishes of the sacred spirits and to predict the future. The system is known as *scapulimancy.* It was used in a simpler form as early as the fourth millennium B.C. both in China and elsewhere in the eastern Neolithic world. The Anyang rulers were the only people in Chinese history to add inscriptions, however; all other instances of scapulimancy were produced by drilling holes around which the cracks could form.

The writing was a highly developed series of characters that are clearly related to those still in use today. It appears already well developed on the Anyang bones, and its origins are thus obscure. The objects of everyday life were represented by simple pictures. The abstract ideas of "above" and "below" were conveyed by a short line above or below a longer line. Each character was given a phonetic sound, consisting of one syllable. In time the signs came to be used phonetically, although to avoid ambiguity picture signs remained in use. Thus a sign group conveying an action will include a hand, one conveying an emotion includes a heart, and one naming a tree includes a tree.

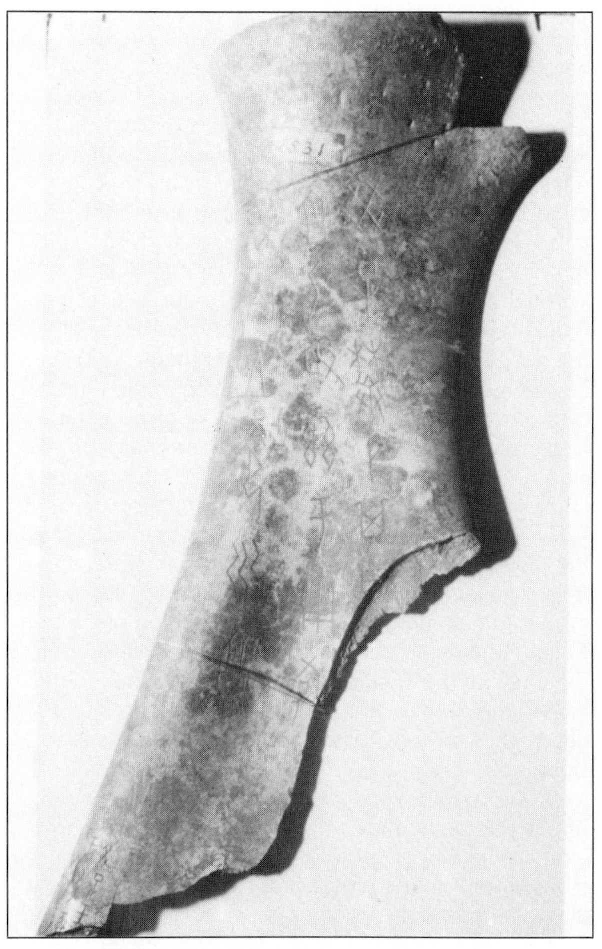

A Chinese oracle bone with writing, from the Shang period. [©Sheridan/Ancient Art and Architecture Collection, London]

These composite characters, combining pictographic and phonetic signs, soon became the most common type. Most of the pictographic elements were recognizable, but many of the old phonetic signs were only approximate, and the spoken language has changed completely over such a long period, as it has everywhere. Speakers of different languages or dialects sound the characters quite differently, but the meaning is the same. By the eighth century B.C. characters had evolved beyond simple pictographic and phonetic elements and included abstract ideas in an often multiple mix of signs or in two-character combinations. The Chinese script is accordingly best labeled *ideographic.* The educated Chinese reader or writer, even of a newspaper, has to master several thousand characters to be literate. Furthermore, since each character represents a concept rather than a sound, there is a dissociation between the written and spoken language. But this feature had an important benefit: the fact that the standardized written language did not vary with regional dialects proved of immense value in unifying a country of such pronounced diversity. Only in the twentieth century, with the diffusion throughout China of the standard written and spoken language of Peking (Beijing) made possible by methods of mass communication, has speech become more uniform.

The Chinese system of writing remains virtually unique in retaining its nonalphabetic form. Even cultures that borrowed Chinese characters to write their own languages, such as Korean, Vietnamese, and Japanese, added a separate phonetic system for many purposes. But the Chinese characters are still used, their meaning unaffected by differences in spoken language. Most other written languages in the world developed an alphabetic system, many of them directly or indirectly based on the earliest alphabet of all, the North Semitic.

One of the earliest decipherable inscriptions in alphabetic writing is the calendar found at the Canaanite site of Gezer, dating to the eleventh century B.C.—approximately the biblical period of Saul and David. The words, roughly scratched on a schoolchild's tablet of soft limestone, consist of a poem describing the principal agricultural occupations of the seasons.

Other Semitic languages used versions of the origi-

The Gezer calendar. [Palestine Exploration Fund]

nal North Semitic alphabet, with the exception of Akkadian, which continued to employ cuneiform. Aramaic writing goes back to the beginning of the first millennium B.C. and by 500 B.C. had become the most important and widespread script of western Asia. It served as the diplomatic writing system for the western provinces of the Persian Empire and continued to be used until around the second century A.D. The square Hebrew script that is still in use today was derived from Aramaic. The Jews adopted the Aramaic language, the common tongue of the region, during the period of the Babylonian captivity. With their return, Aramaic became the vernacular of the Jews in Palestine.

After the conquest of Persia and the introduction of Greek as the official business language there, Aramaic scripts began to develop local variations; one of them, Nabatean, was to give birth to Arabic. The Hebrew version seems to have split off around 200 B.C. and began to attain uniformity in the years between 30 B.C. and A.D. 70. In the subsequent period the script was widely used in the production of biblical manuscripts and occasionally for nonliterary documents such as letters and accounts. Detailed rules developed regulating the copying of synagogue scrolls and the manner in which they should be set out. As a result, Hebrew writing has changed little since the first century A.D.

The primary diffusers of the Semitic alphabet in the Mediterranean region were the descendants of the Canaanites, the Phoenicians, who occupied the narrow coastal plain of what is now Lebanon and Syria during the first half of the first millennium B.C. The greatest traders and seafarers of their time, the Phoenicians set up commercial posts from the Atlantic to the Tigris; they are even reputed to have circumnavigated Africa. To assist their financial and trading activities they developed a form of Aramaic script for the Phoenician language that they then spread in the course of their commercial activities.

Among the peoples who came into contact with the Phoenicians were the Greeks. A form of writing had existed in the Bronze Age world of the Minoans and Mycenaeans (second millennium B.C.), but with the collapse of Mycenaen culture, knowledge of it died out. The earliest works of Greek literature, the epic poems attributed to Homer, had begun their history as oral compositions, passed from speaker to speaker without being written down, but as Greek culture developed in the eighth century B.C., an efficient writing system became necessary. The Greeks may have learned the Phoenician alphabet from contacts in the eastern Mediterranean, but it is just as likely that the transmission occurred in the west, in Italy. Both Greeks and Phoenicians had set up trading posts there, partly to sell to Italian customers and partly to exploit the rich mineral wealth of the Italian peninsula. Throughout the seventh and sixth centuries Greek colonies were founded in southern Italy and Sicily, and the new writing system was diffused there.

Italy was to prove an important site in the transmission of the original alphabet. Italic peoples such as the Oscans and the Umbrians began to use their own versions of the Greek alphabet, as did the Etruscans of central Italy. During the Etruscan occupation of Rome (616–510 B.C.) the Greek alphabet was picked up by the Romans, who spread it throughout their empire as it grew. Every modern European language uses a form of the Roman alphabet, with the exception of Russian, Bulgarian, and Macedonian, which use a version of the Greek. Thus by the fall of the Roman Empire the Greek and Roman alphabets had become standard for all Western cultures. They have remained so ever since.

In the Arabic world there is little evidence of writing before the coming of Islam. The Nabateans, who lived in the Sinai region, used a version of the Aramaic script, but the oldest Arabic inscription in Nabatean characters dates only to A.D. 267. In the early period of their culture the Arabs had little need for writing, even though they were highly language-conscious and poetically gifted. Arab poets preferred to hand down their compositions orally, and each bard had at least two young companions whose task it was to memorize their master's works and continue the tradition.

With the appearance of Islam in the seventh century A.D., however, a writing system was urgently needed. Muslims felt it essential to record every syllable of the Koran with the utmost precision, and the ability to write became a skill of the highest importance. Furthermore, since strict Muslim law discouraged the painting of pictures, the Arabs began to develop the art of calligraphy (fine, ornamental writing). Within less than two centuries after the time of Muhammad, Arabic calligraphy had reached a sophistication that has been surpassed only in China, where it was highly valued as early as the Han period and was in fact considered a basic art form. Like Chinese calligraphy, several kinds of Arabic script were developed, ranging from monumental angular lettering, preferred for copying the Koran and other important works, to more cursive letters used for decorative displays. Today both types are in use, and in China calligraphic ability remains the mark of an educated person.

As Islam spread it carried the new writing with it. The enormous diversity of peoples and territories that fell under Arab rule, from North Africa and parts of Spain in the west to India and the border of China in the east, encouraged the development of local forms of Arabic script. The western style is known as Maghribi ("Western"), and a version of it was introduced into central and western Africa by Muslim traders. Other forms were adopted in Iran and Turkey.

When the Arabs carried their culture with its writing system to India, they found there, as we have seen, yet another alphabet descended from the Semitic, the Brahmi. In the strictest sense, Brahmi is not a true alphabet, since each basic consonant is accompanied by the vowel *a*. This syllabic device is due to the fact that in the early northern Indian languages, the best known of which is Sanskrit, *a* was the most common vowel sound. Other vowels were represented either by their own signs when they began a word or by signs that modified the consonants. Modern Indian scripts for the most part still use this system, although the languages of South India belong to a completely different family.

For the first centuries of its use the form of Brahmi seems to have been fairly consistent throughout India, although no manuscripts survive and the only extant examples of writing are on coins, seals, and inscriptions. Under the Gupta dynasty of the fourth century A.D., northern India developed its own version, which in due course was exported to the Buddhist centers of Chinese Turkestan. Beginning under the emperor Ashoka in the third century B.C. and in subsequent centuries, versions of the Brahmi script were also diffused, via Buddhist texts, to Ceylon (Sri Lanka), Burma, Thailand, Cambodia, and Vietnam. Each of these countries in time developed its own form of Brahmi, alphabetical systems written with added flourishes and curves that remain in use there today, although Chinese characters later displaced the Brahmi-based script in Vietnam. Thus while Muslim culture introduced one version of the Semitic alphabet into India, Buddhism was the vehicle whereby another form was transmitted even farther east.

In the New World the Mayans had formed a complex system of hieroglyphic writing as early as the fourth century A.D. The signs were based on pictures, and most of the surviving examples take the form of monumental inscriptions carved in stone. Not all of

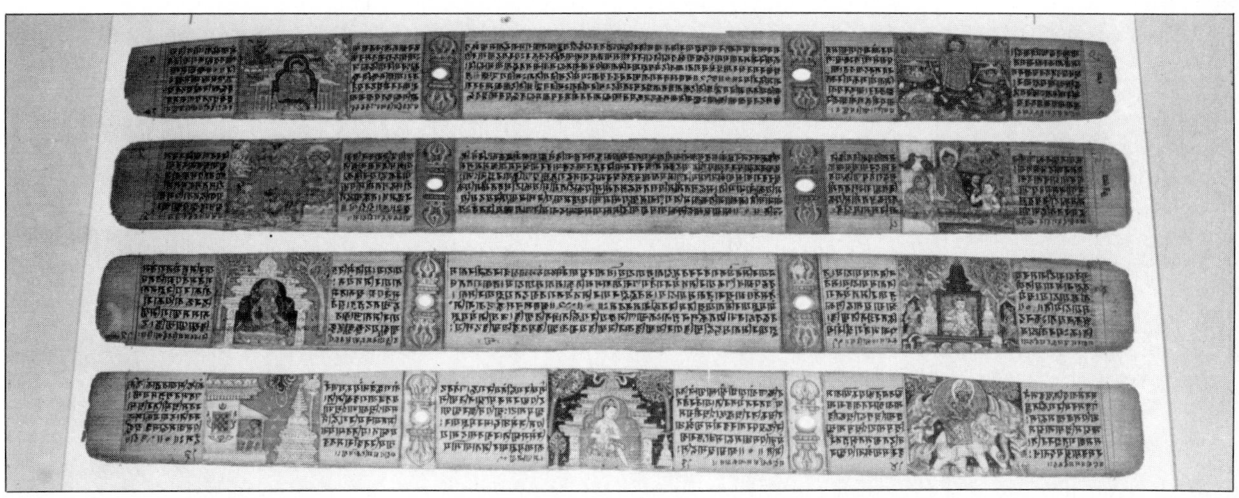

An eleventh-century Sanskrit northern Buddhist work written in the Nepalese version of Brahmi. [©Sheridan/Ancient Art & Architecture Collection, London]

them have been deciphered, but for the most part they consist of archival records or religious texts, and a number attest to the Mayan interest in astronomy and the calendar. Other Mesoamerican peoples developed their own scripts, notably the Aztecs and the Mixtecs, and used them in extended manuscripts known as *codices.* These consist of long strips of animal hide or tree bark, which were folded concertina fashion, like a modern map. Most of them record mythological events, and some were preserved by the conquering Spanish of the sixteenth century. With the arrival of Europeans the Roman alphabet replaced hieroglyphic systems.

Before the invention of printing, the many systems of writing so far described provided only a limited kind of literacy. Inscriptions erected in public places were, of course, available for all to read. The Roman Emperor Augustus wrote an autobiography, *Res Gestae* ("Things I Have Done"), shortly before his death in A.D. 14, and had copies distributed throughout the empire; it was also inscribed on the bronze doors of his tomb. Muslim rulers often used the public display of passages from the Koran as a means of spreading and reinforcing the faith.

Yet such examples confirm the general limitations of literacy. Administrators, priests, and sometimes merchants—the elite in the various cultures described—required the ability to read and used it both for business and governmental purposes and for preserving sacred texts such as the Bible, the sayings of the Buddha, and the Koran. Plays and poems were popular in the Greek and Roman world, and a few romantic stories were written in Greek in the second and third centuries A.D., but there is little evidence of the circulation of written literature beyond the elite in the ancient world.

Suggestions for Further Reading

Craig, J. *Thirty Centuries of Graphic Design: An Illustrated History.* New York: Watson-Guptill, 1987.

Diringer, D. *The Alphabet.* 2 vols. London: Hutchinson, 1973.

Goody, J. *The Logic of Writing and the Organization of Society.* Cambridge: Cambridge University Press, 1986.

Gordon, C. H. *Forgotten Scripts: Their Ongoing Discovery and Decipherment,* rev. ed. New York: Basic Books, 1982.

Hosking, R. F., and Meredith-Owens, G. M. *A Handbook of Asian Scripts.* London: British Museum, 1966.

Hutchinson, J. *Letters.* New York: Van Nostrand Reinhold, 1983.

Lasswell, H. D., Lerner, D., and Speier, H., eds. *Propaganda and Communication in World History,* vol. 1. Honolulu: University Press of Hawaii, 1980.

Lockwood, W. B. *A Panorama of Indo-European Languages.* London: Hutchinson, 1972.

Logan, R. K. *The Alphabet Effect: The Impact of the Phonetic Alphabet on the Development of Western Civilization.* New York: Morrow, 1986.

Pope, M. *The Story of Archaeological Decipherment.* New York: Scribner, 1975.

Roberts, C. H. *The Birth of the Codex.* London: Oxford University Press, 1983.

Sampson, G. *Writing Systems.* London: Hutchinson, 1985.

Schmandt-Besserat, D. "The Earliest Precursor of Writing," *Scientific American,* June 1978, pp. 50–59.

Whalley, J. I. *Writing Implements and Accessories: From the Roman Stylus to the Typewriter.* Detroit: Gale Research, 1975.

CHAPTER · 9

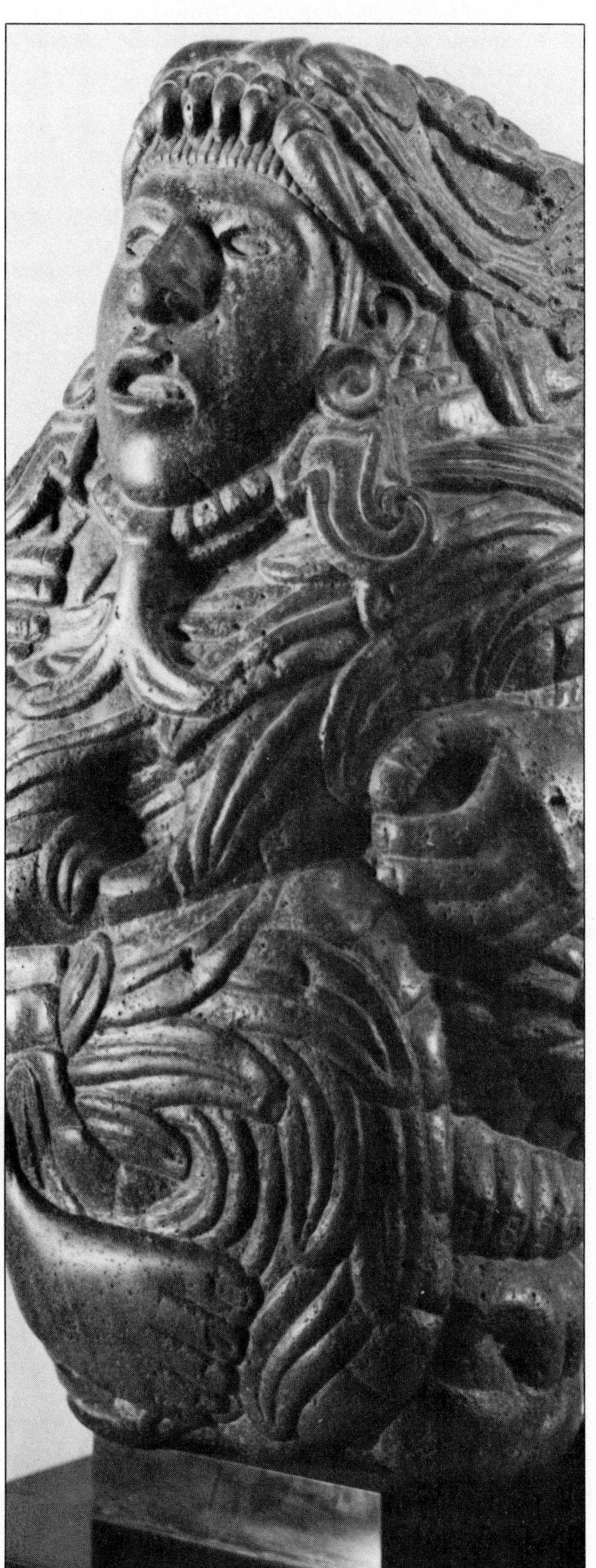

Africa and the Americas Before 1500

The relatively large amount of information that has survived from the early stages of the major European and Asian cultures in the form of written accounts or objects recovered by excavation enables us to form a fairly coherent picture of their growth and development. The same cannot be said for Africa and the Americas, although the scarcity of written or archaeological evidence is misleading. In the case of Africa, in particular, the false impression of a continent that has only recently enjoyed the benefits of civilization has been disproved. Whereas, for example, the indigenous peoples of Australia, the Aborigines, were still using stone tools when they were first discovered by European explorers in the seventeenth century, African farmers began to use iron implements around 500 B.C. In the succeeding centuries the peoples of the northern third of Africa were brought into contact first with the Romans and later with Islamic culture, while in central and southeastern Africa states and kingdoms of considerable size developed. Indeed, it was through the strength of these

Aztec statue of the god Quetzalcoatl in the form of a feathered serpent with a human head. [Musée de l'Homme, Paris]

communities that the indigenous populations of West Africa, among others, were able to resist European attacks on their gold mines until the eighteenth century.

Yet it is still true that a relative lack of historical evidence, coupled with the fact that archaeological exploration of Africa and the Americas on a wide scale is comparatively recent, means that early developments there often remain obscure. In the case of Central and South America the surviving evidence is almost exclusively archaeological and anthropological, most written documents having been destroyed by European conquerors in the sixteenth century. For the kingdoms of Iron Age Africa, the written accounts of European and Muslim travelers and traders help to supplement the picture.

Africa: From Stone to Iron

It was probably in Africa that the ancestors of the human species first became differentiated from the other primates. Throughout the Old Stone Age, Africa was the center for the development of stone tools known as hand axes, which may have served for skinning and chopping. Rich deposits of these tools have been found in eastern Africa, and their use spread from Africa to western Europe and as far east as India.

The African Land

Despite this early evidence of cultural diffusion, however, life in Africa has always been affected by its relative geographic isolation. It is true that the Sahara was not always the formidable barrier it is today. Indeed, between 5500 and 2500 B.C. open grassland areas now covered with sand were used not only by hunters but also by animal breeders and farmers. Even when changes of climate returned these grasslands to their desert state, devoid of fish and game, caravans of traders used routes that crossed the central Sahara or made their way through Nubia and Egypt to and from the Mediterranean. Nonetheless, for most of recorded history the Sahara has prevented the movement of quantities of people or goods and kept contacts to a minimum.

This rock shelter painting in Tanzania, Africa, probably dates from the late Stone Age. [John Reader, Richmond, England]

Similarly, much of central and southern Africa is inaccessible by sea because there are few good natural harbors. Even within the continent, transport from one region to another is difficult. Few rivers are navigable, and deserts and rain forests form further barriers to travel. As a result, many African communities tended to stay in one region, developing their own language and culture and making little contact with other indigenous peoples. One of the consequences of this is that a great number of independent languages developed throughout the continent, as in Mesoamerica.

To the difficulties presented by geography must be added other natural problems. Unlike Mesopotamia or India, which experienced a predictable alternation of dry and wet spells each year, the African climate is extremely irregular. Two or three years of drought may be followed by prolonged rainfall that erodes the soil and washes away important nutrients. Furthermore, the regions that are hot and humid provide breeding grounds for insects such as mosquitoes, tsetse flies, and other parasites. Regular food production under such conditions poses formidable problems. Without it the inhabitants of Africa were unable to establish on a widespread basis the kind of urbanization that, as we have seen in Asia and Europe, is normally the precondition for social and economic development and technological innovation. The only place on the African continent where the introduction of farming techniques led to an early appearance of urban civilization was Egypt, where the fertility of the Nile valley made comparatively large population concentrations possible.

Africa's First Farmers

The earliest peoples of Africa supported themselves by hunting and gathering. Agriculture arrived on the continent around 5000 B.C. in Egypt, when crop farming and animal breeding were introduced to the northern African coastal regions, probably from western Asia. The relative fertility of the sub-Saharan region permitted the slow spread southward of agricultural techniques. In eastern Africa, particularly in Ethiopia and along the Nile, local cereals such as millet and sorghum were laboriously developed from native wild grasses, while in the west the Bantu began to occupy the coastal rain forests, attracted there by the abundance of yams and oil palms. Farther south, in Kenya, animal breeding was introduced by the people of the so-called Stone Bowl culture before 1000 B.C.

Throughout the whole of Africa, however, with the notable exception of Egypt, the transition from hunting to farming was very gradual, and in many regions both food systems probably coexisted for centuries. Two factors in addition to climate account for the slow growth of agriculture. First, the native forest food plants were limited in range; only after the importation of crops from abroad such as the banana and the yam, both native to Southeast Asia, were dependable staple crops developed, around the beginning of the first century A.D. Second, unlike the Chinese or the peoples of the Mediterranean and western Asia, the inhabitants of Africa never worked in bronze. Until the introduction of iron around 500 B.C., farmers were limited to stone and wood tools.

Like agricultural skills, ironworking techniques developed first in Egypt and subsequently spread to other regions. By the middle of the first millennium B.C. the great days of Egyptian civilization were over, but a powerful kingdom had emerged at Meroë. The population was predominantly Negro, a term used to describe the people indigenous to the woodlands in the Sudan, south of the Sahara. Tall, slender, and dark-skinned, most Negro groups spoke languages that belong to the general linguistic family known as Bantu. Iron was plentiful in the Sudan, and smiths were quick to develop techniques for the manufacture of tools and weapons.

Throughout the following centuries, as ironworking spread throughout Africa, Bantu Negroes expanded over much of the farmable territory, either absorbing other indigenous groups such as the Bush people and the Khoikhoi, both of whom were native to eastern and southern Africa, or driving them into the forests of the Congo. Whether the Bantu were able to spread south in the period after 500 B.C. because of their technological superiority or whether Bantu migrations had occurred at an earlier date and the Bantu's new techniques had been used to consolidate and extend their territory is not known. In either case, by the third century B.C., perhaps even earlier, iron was in regular use in northern Nigeria. The people who mined during this period in the Nok hills also produced baked clay figurines that are among the earliest surviving works of art from sub-Saharan Africa.

The lively character of the Nok figurines serves as a reminder of how sparsely documented is this first period of settled population and development. Anthropologists have tried to reconstruct early African rural life from later urban forms of society. People probably lived in family compounds, three or four generations together, forming a compact village community. Settlements like these were established in clusters, forming larger communities in which everyone was involved in farming, while within each community different families specialized in various arts and crafts—some in pottery, others in woodwork or medicine. Neighboring villages spoke the same language and followed the same social and religious patterns. A much later document that describes the foundation of the West African city of Kano, the Kano Chronicle, talks of 11 chiefs, each the head of a large clan; their professions included blacksmith, brewer, doctor, hunter, miner, and chief of the dancers.

Africa in the Iron Age: Mediterranean Contacts

Perhaps the most important conduits of new ideas into Africa were the Phoenicians, whose North African colonies, founded in the eighth century B.C., introduced Syrian culture to the continent. Carthage, the most significant Phoenician colony, was destroyed by the Romans in 146 B.C., but the people of the region, the Berbers, continued to pose a threat to the Romans' southern frontier. To control them, the Romans colonized the coastal plain of North Africa, establishing farms, cities, and military outposts. This colonial population consisted mainly of soldiers, bureaucrats, and businessmen from all over the empire, who in many cases intermarried with Berber women. The children of these unions spoke Latin but adopted many Berber customs.

Christianity came early to North Africa, and Carthage and Alexandria became two of its leading centers; the latter was the home of the Arian heresy described in Chapter 7. The most influential of all early church fathers, Augustine, was a Berber from Libya who was brought up and educated at Carthage. With the erosion of Roman control, North Africa was conquered in 429 by the Vandals, a Germanic tribe that had embraced Christianity, and then, in the sixth century, by the Byzantines. Had it not been for the arrival of Islam with the Arab conquests of the seventh century, much of Africa might well have been Christianized. In 639 the first Muslims entered Egypt, and by the beginning of the following century they were in control of virtually all Africa north of the Sahara. The sole exception to the Islamic tide in this region was Ethiopia, which remained Christian after the conversion of its rulers in 333. The desert remained a formidable barrier to the diffusion of Islam, but over the following centuries the Sudan and the trading cities of the East African coast were absorbed into the Islamic world.

The Sudan Kingdoms

When the Muslims first crossed the Sahara into the Sudan in 753, they found a number of kingdoms already established, particularly the Berbers'. The origins of these states lay in the farming communities of the early Iron Age, but other forces had in the meantime also appeared in central Africa. Bands of migrants, perhaps from Meroë or East Africa, had taken control of much of the Sudan from the Red Sea to the mouth of the river Senegal on the west African coast. These mounted warriors, armed with iron-tipped spears, won control of the open country south of the Sahara, keeping the local populations under subjugation while raiding for slaves. Thus the arrival of the horse in central Africa, coupled with the stability made possible by the settled agricultural communities, provided the basis of the first urban communities in sub-Saharan Africa. Their growth, however, was limited to the Sudan, since horses could not survive the effects of the tsetse flies that were endemic to southern Africa.

The Kingdom of Ghana

One of the earliest documented African kingdoms is Ghana, in the western Sudan. According to later traditions, there had been 22 kings of Ghana before the arrival of the Muslims in the mid-eighth century A.D. By the time the Arabs appeared, Ghana was already prosperous; as early as the eighth century it was known as "the land of gold." Other exports included salt, copper, and horses. Gold was sold north of the Sahara in exchange for salt, and the other commodities to other peoples of the Sudan. Imports included glass, ceramic oil lamps, and fine tableware. Trade thus played a major role in the state's growth. Although there are conflicting later traditions, most of the population was almost certainly Negro, of the group known as Soninke, who spoke a language belonging to the family known as Mande. Both economically and culturally their kingdom made a profound impression on Muslim visitors. An Arab writer of the tenth century refers to a trade contract for 20,000 gold coins, and a century later the Muslim geographer al-Bakri, who lived at Córdoba in Spain, noted the customs duty levied by the king of Ghana on copper, salt, and other goods exported from or imported into the country. The Arabs, themselves expert and enthusiastic traders, were clearly impressed by the commercial sophistication of Ghana.

Little is known about the cities from which the kingdom was ruled. Among the areas to which access was controlled was that of Bambuk, between the upper Senegal and Faleme rivers, where much of the gold was mined. The capital of ancient Ghana has been tentatively identified as the modern Kumbi Saleh; excavations have been carried out both there and at Tegdaoust. These and other major sites controlled either natural resources, as in the case of Bambuk, or highways. Some were resting places for the desert caravans, or intersections of overland and river transport, providing sites for customs posts. The cities were probably constructed of mud brick and surrounded with a defensive wall within which rulers, artisans, and servants were housed. Each was supported by nearby farming villages.

In spite of contact with the world of Islam, Ghana maintained its cultural and religious independence until the eleventh century. Al-Bakri described a foreign enclave 6 miles from the capital where most Muslims lived; its mosques were built in stone, in contrast to the mud-built structures of the native population. Although he underlined the fact that many of the king's advisers were Muslims, he described the religion of Ghana as "paganism and the worship of idols." The picture al-Bakri provides is of an aristocratic society, dominated by the king and his court, that was the focus of elaborate rituals. The royal dwelling was surrounded by horses whose bridles were decorated with gold, and when the king's subjects were summoned to an audience, they approached him on their knees and with dust on their heads, to express their respect.

The fundamental importance of the king is reminiscent of similar cultural patterns in ancient Egypt. According to al-Bakri, when a king died, a huge dome of wood was constructed over the site of his tomb. The body was placed within this, together with the dead man's weapons and ornaments and the plates and cups he had used, which were filled with foods and beverages.

The period described by al-Bakri marked the end of Ghana's independence. By the eleventh century the tribesmen of the Sahara had been converted to Islam. Known as the Almoravids, or "those who fight to establish true Islam," they swept out of the desert in two great waves. One went north, conquering Morocco and southern Spain. The other wave moved south against Ghana, where in 1076–77 the Almoravids imposed their rule, perhaps by conquest, perhaps by the imposition of a Muslim king. Subsequent Almoravid squabbles enabled Ghana to reestablish its independence for a while, but the invasion had disrupted trans-Saharan trade and damaged local agriculture. With its economic strengths blighted, the kingdom of Ghana broke up into tribal units, and power passed to the upper Niger valley, where the kingdom of Mali began to flourish.

The Empires of Mali and Songhay

The collapse of ancient Ghana led many of its inhabitants to flee to the south, where they were safer from Saharan marauders and where the land was more productive. There they found other Mande-speaking clans, who, originally subject to Ghana, had established an independent kingdom in the twelfth century. This was to become the empire of Mali, which remained the most powerful force in West Africa for 200 years (c. 1250–c. 1460).

SUNDIATA: FIRST MONARCH

The founder of the empire of Mali was Sundiata (c. 1230–c. 1255), one of 12 brothers who claimed the throne of the small kingdom of Kangaba. A neighboring ruler who aspired to take control of Kangaba murdered 11 of the royal brothers but spared Sundiata because he had been born a cripple and seemed unlikely to survive. On being cured, he became a hunter and a wandering soldier. Accompanied by a small group of followers, he traveled

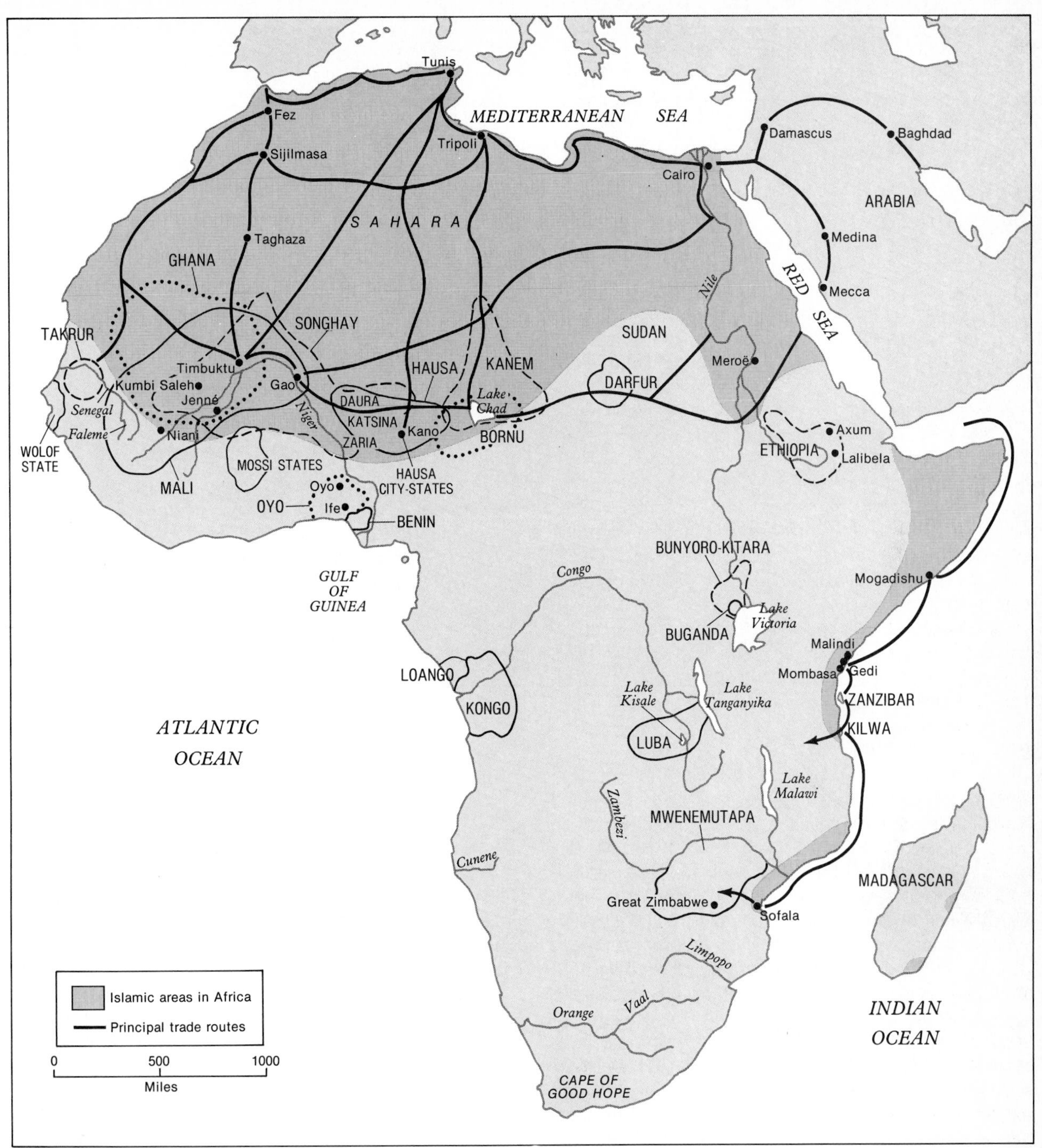

9.1 Africa, 1000–1500

from country to country and thus escaped the massacre of his fellow citizens that followed the invasion of Mali by a rival clan, the Susu, that had gained power in southern Ghana.

Sundiata returned home to lead the resistance. After winning a decisive victory in 1235, he put together a federal state in which local governors maintained their positions while acknowledging Sundiata as their monarch. With the conquest of the Susu and adjacent territory, the new kingdom combined the southern half of Ghana with Mali and parts of what is now Guinea. Sundiata thus controlled not only major gold-producing areas but also the commu-

West African Fetishes

This description of fetishism in Dahomey, West Africa, was written by Geoffrey Gorer in 1936, but it reflects centuries-old religious practices.

A man called Epiphane had had a silver bracelet stolen. Instead of going to the police about his loss he called in a fetisher. The fetisher took up a position just off the main road a little way out of Abomey [where the bracelet had been stolen] and had a chicken brought to him. He held the chicken by the claws in his left hand above his head, so that the bird's beak was level with his mouth, and started talking to it quietly. He was telling it about the theft, repeating the same words over and over again. After some little time the chicken began to bleed from the mouth, a drop every few minutes. The fetisher went on talking quietly. This had been going on for more than half an hour when a man suddenly arrived desperately out of breath and with his pagne [loincloth] torn; he fell panting on the ground by the fetisher. The fetisher went on talking to the bird, which suddenly gave a sort of strangled squawk, at which the exhausted man confessed that he had stolen the bracelet and explained how he had taken it and where it was. The fetisher put the chicken on the ground; it started pecking rather uncertainly.

Prince Aho explained that this was the usual method of dealing with stolen property. When the chicken started to bleed the thief was forced to come to where the fetisher was, wherever he might be and whatever he was doing. Only certain fetishers knew how to do this. I wanted to see it repeated, but never had another opportunity.

Source: J. J. Norwich, ed., *A Taste for Travel* (London: Macmillan, 1986), p. 382.

nications network provided by the upper Niger River and its tributaries. From Timbuktu, the great trading city on the southern fringes of the Sahara, to the Atlantic coast, a secure base for economic prosperity was established.

The importance of the rivers in uniting the Mali empire is underlined by the fact that toward the end of his life, Sundiata inaugurated the construction of a new capital at Niani, on one of the Niger's tributaries, where it was out of range of Almoravid intrusions. Although Niani has not been systematically excavated, it seems to have been an urban center surrounded by a sizable agricultural population, resembling the earlier cities of Ghana but on a larger scale. Potential profits from the gold trade, together with the peaceful conditions Sundiata imposed on Mali, attracted traders and merchants. Consequently, Niani soon became one of West Africa's most important commercial centers.

Although tradition claims that Sundiata came to power as a pagan with magical powers, he was nominally a Muslim. Sundiata kept the support of both the predominantly Muslim merchants and the non-Muslim rural population. In this way he fulfilled the traditional religious function of West African kings, who simultaneously served as religious and political leaders.

The Adoption of Islam

Sundiata's son and successor, Uli, was a pious Muslim. Even before his time Islam had begun to make converts throughout western Africa, and most subsequent rulers of kingdoms there professed at least allegiance to the Muslim faith. Among the practical benefits was the establishment of goodwill with the Arab states of North Africa, and hence good trading relations.

In addition to these economic gains, the adoption of Muslim culture brought political rewards. The kingdom of Ghana had maintained control over its territories by vigorous military supervision of local governors, many of whom saw no reason to remain loyal to the king. The survival of an empire as large as that of Mali required a stable central administration and an effective communication system. With the spread of Muslim education and Arab texts, a class of scholars who could also serve as administrators began to develop. Putting aside their tribal loyalties, these public servants were concerned primarily with maintaining efficient government and trade and with preserving the empire.

To organize an economy of increasing complexity, the governing classes devised a currency system that made use of standarized weights of gold dust for large amounts and cowrie shells for everyday transactions. Expenses were defrayed by taxes, collected by local treasuries and then paid to the central administration. Some of the money was used to purchase arms abroad; the Malian army was by far the best equipped in sub-Saharan Africa. Other expenses included the feeding and maintenance of sizable urban populations. Like their neighbors, the Malians used slave labor to increase food production. Prisoners taken in war, neighboring peoples kidnapped on raids, and the offspring of current slaves provided sources of labor. They were assigned to villages in key positions along the rivers and sent to work in the fields.

The key to Mali's prosperity was the success of its merchant traders. Taking their cue from Muhammad, himself a merchant, they used their pilgrimages to Mecca and other holy cities of the Muslim world as a means of building trade connections. Furthermore, Mali's products were sold through North African outlets in European markets around the Mediterranean. Ivory, animal skins, and slaves were exchanged for European textiles, glass, and timber. Above all, the economy of Mali benefited from the fact that since the twelfth century most European communities had begun to replace copper and silver with gold as the principal unit of currency. The Christian kings of northern Spain began to use gold in imitation of the Almoravids of the south, and during the thirteenth century most of the banking centers of western Europe adopted gold coinage. It has been calculated that at least two-thirds of the gold that made this possible was mined in territory controlled by Mali. A map produced in Spain in 1375 depicts the king of Mali holding a gold nugget; the caption describes him as "the richest and most noble king in all the land."

This immense wealth was concentrated in the hands of the ruling class, which lived in cities such as Timbuktu and Jenné. These urban centers distributed salt and other imported goods throughout the empire and engaged in the manufacture of textiles. The majority of the population worked in the mines or on the land. In the drier north they bred cattle and goats, while in central Mali, with its more abundant rainfall, they grew millet and sorghum. As might be expected in a country geographically united by its river system, fishing was also an important industry.

Our picture of Mali at the height of its prosperity is enlivened by the account by Ibn Battuta, the Arab traveler and observer, of a journey he made there in 1352–1353. Sophisticated and tireless, Ibn Battuta was no casual sightseer; by the time he made his tour of Mali he had already visited China. Among other things, he was struck by the general safety of traveling conditions among the Mali people, asserting that there was "complete security in their country." The Mali, he said, had a greater horror of injustice than any other people and showed no mercy to those guilty of it. Part of this could presumably be ascribed to the influence of Islamic law, and Ibn Battuta comments on the zeal with which law and theology were studied. On visiting the chief judge of Niani at his home, he saw the judge's children in chains, from which they would be able to win release only by reciting the Koran from memory.

Bearded male figure from Djenne/Mopti, dating from the fourteenth century. [Founders Society, Detroit Institute of Arts, African, Oceanic and New World Cultures]

Journey to Mali

The following passage comes from Ibn Battuta's account of his travels in West Africa to visit the Muslim rulers there.

I was at Malli during the two festivals of the sacrifice and the fast-breaking. On these days the sultan takes his seat on the *pempi* [ceremonial chair] after the midafternoon prayer. The armor-bearers bring in magnificent arms—quivers of gold and silver, swords ornamented with gold and with golden scabbards, gold and silver lances, and crystal maces. At his head stand four amirs [attendants] driving off the flies, having in their hands silver ornaments resembling saddle-stirrups. The commanders . . . and preacher sit in their usual places. The interpreter Dugha comes with his four wives and his slave-girls, who are about a hundred in number. They are wearing beautiful robes, and on their heads they have gold and silver fillets, with gold and silver balls attached. A chair is placed for Dugha to sit on. He plays on an instrument made of reeds, with some small calabashes [gourds] at its lower end, and chants a poem in praise of the sultan, recalling his battles and deeds of valor. The women and girls sing along with him and play with bows. Accompanying them are about thirty youths, wearing red woollen tunics and white skull-caps; each of them has his drum slung from his shoulder and beats it. Afterwards come his boy pupils who play and turn wheels in the air, like the natives of Sind. They show a marvellous nimbleness and agility in these exercises and play most cleverly with swords. Dugha also makes a fine play with the sword. Thereupon the sultan orders a gift to be presented to Dugha and he is given a purse containing . . . gold dust, and is informed of the contents of the purse before all the people. The commanders rise and twang their bows in thanks to the sultan. The next day each one of them gives Dugha a gift, every man according to his rank. Every Friday after . . . prayer, Dugha carries out a similar ceremony to this that we have described.

Source: Ibn Battuta, *Travels in Asia and Africa, 1325–1354,* trans. H. A. R. Gibb (London: George Routledge & Sons, 1929), p. 328.

Ibn Battuta did not approve of all aspects of life in Mali. The elaborate court ceremonials, with their hymns in praise of the king and the ritual groveling of the courtiers, met with his contempt. In general he was treated courteously, but on at least one occasion a provincial governor kept him and his merchant companions standing and refused to speak to them except through an interpreter.

Ibn Battuta sheds light on the role of women in Mali society. Much to his horror, women were free to circulate as they chose, without wearing a veil. They selected their own companions and could go about their business outside the home. Even worse, the female slaves of the king and the provincial governors were naked. Ibn Battuta's extreme reaction, and perhaps even a touch of exaggeration in his description, may have been the result of his own Muslim upbringing. Nor, it must be added, is there any concrete historical evidence that women played any important role in Mali's political and economic life. Nonetheless, Ibn Battuta's observations suggest a radical difference between traditional Islamic society and that of sub-Saharan Africa.

Mali was at the zenith of its powers when Ibn Battuta saw it. Under Mansa Musa (1312–1337) it extended from Lake Chad to the Atlantic Ocean and from Morocco to what is now southern Nigeria. Both north and south, local kingdoms paid regular tribute and in some cases accepted Malian governors. Shortly after Ibn Battuta's visit the empire began to crumble. Around 1375 the Songhay fishermen, who had resented Mali domination, ceased to pay tribute to the central government. Soon thereafter they began to raid Mali-controlled territory, and the first great Songhay leader, Sonni Ali (ruled c. 1464–c. 1492) mobilized his armies to conquer Mali itself. The empire that his successors assembled had its capital at Gao, 700 miles east of Niani. Larger even than the empire of Mali, the Songhay territories extended from the upper Niger almost to Morocco and included the salt mines of the Sahara.

Events elsewhere in Europe and Asia were to prevent the Songhay empire from repeating the successes of Mali. The Arab rulers of Morocco, fresh from victories over the Portuguese and the Turks, were eager to gain control over West Africa's gold supplies. During the period from

Bakota figure—a reliquary head—from Gabon, West Africa. Statues like this were originally set over urns containing the skulls and bones of ancestors in order to keep evil spirits away. [Werner Forman Archive, London]

1590 to 1618 small bands of Arab mercenaries, armed with gunpowder and firearms, made their way across the Sahara and defeated the Songhay forces. The collapse of central government that ensued destroyed Songhay unity. The entire gold-producing area of West Africa fragmented once more into tribal kingdoms, as the Europeans found on their arrival at the end of the eighteenth century.

Southeast Africa: The Swahili City-States

Unlike remoter regions to the west, the coast and offshore islands of eastern Africa were visited and settled by foreigners from the earliest recorded times. The indigenous population, like that of West Africa, was black, but early settlers included Arabs, traders from western India, and Indonesians; around the seventh century the Indonesians introduced bananas, rice, and coconuts to Africa. Thus the natives were in continuous contact through trade with the outside world. Their language was Swahili, a Bantu tongue heavily influenced by Arabic and Persian. In many other respects too Swahili culture was strongly influenced by Islam from the time of the earliest Muslim expansion.

Little concrete evidence has survived for the period before the ninth century. Prehistoric peoples who were probably Bantu speakers spread throughout eastern Africa. Blacks from the southeastern coastal regions, who were known as Zenj, were sold into slavery and recruited as soldiers by the Umayyad and Abbasid caliphs, and as early as 696 there are references to revolts by Zenj slave-soldiers. The main commodity that traders sought was ivory, which was hunted south of what is now Mozambique, a region that early travelers tell us was ruled by the "great king of the Zenj."

One of the earliest town sites to have been identified in the southeast is that of Manda, one of the islands of the Lamu archipelago, off the coast of modern Kenya. Its prosperity began in the ninth century and continued for over 200 years. The town covered about 45 acres; its population of some 5,000 citizens lived in sturdy houses made of blocks of coral. The settlement was protected from the sea by defensive walls made of huge coral slabs weighing approximately a ton each. Almost a third of the pottery excavated there was imported, much of it of high quality. Most of it came from Iran, but a few examples from China have been found. No mosque has yet been discovered at Manda, but most of the population was probably Muslim, trading in ivory and slaves and perhaps selling wood to the builders of western Asia.

The greatest settlement in East Africa at this period was at Kilwa, which consisted of two offshore islands to the south of Zanzibar. Around 1200 they were united under the rule of Abi bin Hasan, whose name appears on the copper coinage minted by the new state, the first of its kind in East Africa. The principal town, Kilwa Kisiwani, was constructed during his reign; its buildings, many of them of stone, include the Great Mosque.

Kilwa continued to prosper, deriving much of its wealth from its position on the main trade route to the southeast coastal regions of what is now Zimbabwe, with their supplies of gold and ivory. In return, its citizens probably imported luxury goods from China, the Persian Gulf area, and India. A new dynasty, the Mahdali, remained in power from the end of the thirteenth century until the arrival of Portuguese colonizers two centuries later. Under Mahdali rule, elaborate building programs were initiated. The Great Mosque was enlarged and an immense palace was constructed, its vast courtyard illuminated by hundreds of oil lamps. Large warehouses were built to store the cargoes shipped through Kilwa. In 1331 Ibn Battuta visited the ruler of Kilwa, who impressed him as a modest man and a pious Muslim who distributed alms to beggars. The city itself, he wrote, was "one of the most beautiful and well-constructed towns in the world." Its inhabitants were mostly Zenj; one of them, a merchant, told Ibn Battuta that the journey to the gold mines in the south, presumably in what is now Zimbabwe, took about a month.

Thus for much of the period before the arrival of the Europeans, the main centers of East Africa formed part of a Muslim commercial network that stretched to India and China. By the mid-thirteenth century the Muslims had consolidated their commercial monopoly in the Indian Ocean. Kilwa and other centers maintained Muslim influence in the western zone of this trading empire, while also acting as a link between Islam and the indigenous peoples of Africa. The citizens of city-states such as Kilwa, although Muslim, continued to speak Swahili.

The conical tower and part of the ruins of the city of Zimbabwe, inhabited from the sixth to the twelfth centuries. [Robert Aberman/Barbara Heller Collection, London]

Early Southern Africa

Our knowledge of the history of southern Africa is limited by physical conditions that make exploration difficult. Heavy forestation impedes both traditional excavation and aerial photography. Moreover, the destructive acids in forest soils have caused metals to corrode and bone to dissolve. Nonetheless, a sketchy picture of developments is emerging.

The earliest inhabitants of southern Africa were the Bush people, who spoke a language unrelated to Bantu called Khoikhoi; some tribes still speak it in southern Angola and parts of South Africa today. Hunter-gatherers, they depicted both themselves and their prey in rock paintings that are among the finest achievements of prehistoric African art.

Historians are unable to date the establishment of ironworking techniques and food production in the area. They are fairly certain that these innovations were brought by the Bantu, as they had been elsewhere in Africa, but the chronological evidence is scanty. White colonists of South Africa at the end of the eighteenth century preferred to believe that the Bantu migrations southward occurred more or less simultaneously with the establishment of white settlements. That historical picture might be seen to justify European claims to the land or at least to deny the Bantu, whom the Europeans had conquered and subjugated, any historical rights of their own. The evidence, however, indicates that groups of Bantu had introduced ironworking into the south long before modern times. At the cave of Castle Cavern, in Swaziland, pottery, smelted iron, and iron-mining tools have been found, dating to approximately A.D. 400. This and other proof of metalworking south of the Limpopo River suggests that Bantu farmers and smiths had begun to work their way down the continent relatively early, coexisting with rather than conquering the hunting peoples whom they found there.

By the eleventh century hundreds of villages had been built on the high plateau of the Transvaal. Some were still inhabited in the nineteenth century and were seen by early missionaries to southern Africa. Their buildings, made of stone, were circular, as were the fences that surrounded each house and the outer wall of the village itself. The clay floors were so polished that they appeared to be varnished. The doorways were framed, and the roofs were supported by pillars. At Melville Koppies, the site of a village that now lies in the center of Johannesburg, iron-smelting furnaces have been discovered.

tinctive customs and art. By 200 B.C. two peoples had begun to emerge as the dominant powers. The first were the Mayans, the heart of whose territory was the Yucatán Peninsula and Guatemala. The second are named after their capital city of Teotihuacán, which lies on the high plateau of central Mexico, 20 miles from modern Mexico City. The people of Teotihuacán traded widely with the Mayans and other peoples, developing the first great urban civilization in the New World. Indeed, it may well have been as a result of an attempted Teotihuacán conquest of the Mayans that the city of Teotihuacán was destroyed around 650 B.C., and with it the influence of its inhabitants.

Archaeologists have divided the early period of Mesoamerican history into two main time spans: the Early Classic (A.D. 100–600) and the Late Classic (600–900). Throughout much of the Early Classic period, the Teotihuacán people were the dominating force in much of Mesoamerica, and the products of their artisans have been found by the thousands over a wide area. Among the finest of their manufactured goods are cylindrical pots, often covered with plaster and painted. Small figurines were mass-produced by means of clay models. Examples of both have been found throughout Mesoamerica.

Much of Teotihuacán's commercial preeminence came from its control of obsidian mines near the modern city of Pachuca, which supplemented the stone mined near Teotihuacán itself. In addition to production for home use, knives, blades, scrapers, and dart points were manufactured for export.

Because no written inscription has been discovered at their city, it is not known whether the Teotihuacán people were literate. By the fourteenth century the name Teotihuacán meant "place of the Gods" in the Aztec language, and some scholars believe that the people of Teotihuacán were the precursors of the Aztecs. Both groups cremated their dead and worshiped some of the same deities, including Tlaloc, the rain spirit, and Quetzalcoatl, the Feathered Serpent, god of the wind.

TEOTIHUACÁN: THE FIRST GREAT CITY IN THE AMERICAS

The most remarkable achievement of this active urban people was the construction of their city. In the absence of other documentation, its ruins provide some indication of the lifestyle of its inhabitants. Shortly before 600, when it was at its height, it covered 8 square miles and housed a population of about 150,000.

Construction was begun in the first century A.D., when two great avenues were laid out at right angles to each other, dividing the area into quarters. The Aztecs later called the north-south road the Avenue of the Dead. As the city grew, it was laid out on a grid plan based on the two principal arteries, with the chief ceremonial structures on the Avenue of the Dead. At the southern end stood the Pyramid of the Sun, one of the largest constructions of the ancient world, almost four times the size of the Great Pyramid of Cheops in Egypt. Its name derives from the Aztecs, who believed it to be the sun's birthplace, although it may have had an entirely different significance for the people of Teotihuacán. Recent exploration indicates that there may be a huge tomb at its base, although this has never been excavated. At the opposite end stands a similar construction, the Pyramid of the Moon.

Almost at the center of the city is a sunken courtyard known as the Citadel. It is surrounded by temples; in the middle of the square is another temple, dedicated to Quetzalcoatl, the sides of which are decorated with representations of the Feathered Serpent, together with the Fire Serpent, bearer of the sun across the sky.

Square residential compounds lined much of the Avenue of the Dead. Within the simple walls were luxurious dwellings, probably the homes of the ruling class; in them, rooms decorated with paintings of ritual processions were arranged around a central courtyard. Workers and artisans lived on the outskirts of the city in more crowded conditions; some of the outlying districts were reserved for foreigners.

The vast scale of the city, coupled with the presence of Teotihuacán culture over a geographic area that includes most of Mexico, indicates a people with expansionist aims. At some point they apparently became embroiled with the Mayans. Even the Aztecs never tried to gain control of Mayan territory, and the destruction of Teotihuacán may have been a reprisal by the Mayans for an invasion of their territory. Yet the city was still inhabited for centuries, even though the temples had been abandoned and the great houses burned to the ground. Throughout the Classic period people lived in hovels constructed in corners of the former palaces, and the pyramids became places of pilgrimage for the Aztecs.

The Mayans

Around the time of the early building at Teotihuacán, the greatest prehistoric New World civilization began to develop in southern Mexico and Central America. Throughout the Early Classic period, the Mayans constructed enormous ceremonial sanctuaries, involving novel architectural features such as the vault. Their painting, unlike that at Teotihuacán, is naturalistic, concerned with depicting the real world and taking a special interest in portraiture. By the time of the decline of Teotihuacán, Mayan culture and civilization had reached a height that was to last until its mysterious collapse around the year 900.

Although it is possible to deduce much about various aspects of Mayan life, many of the most basic features of their culture remain imperfectly understood. Only a hand-

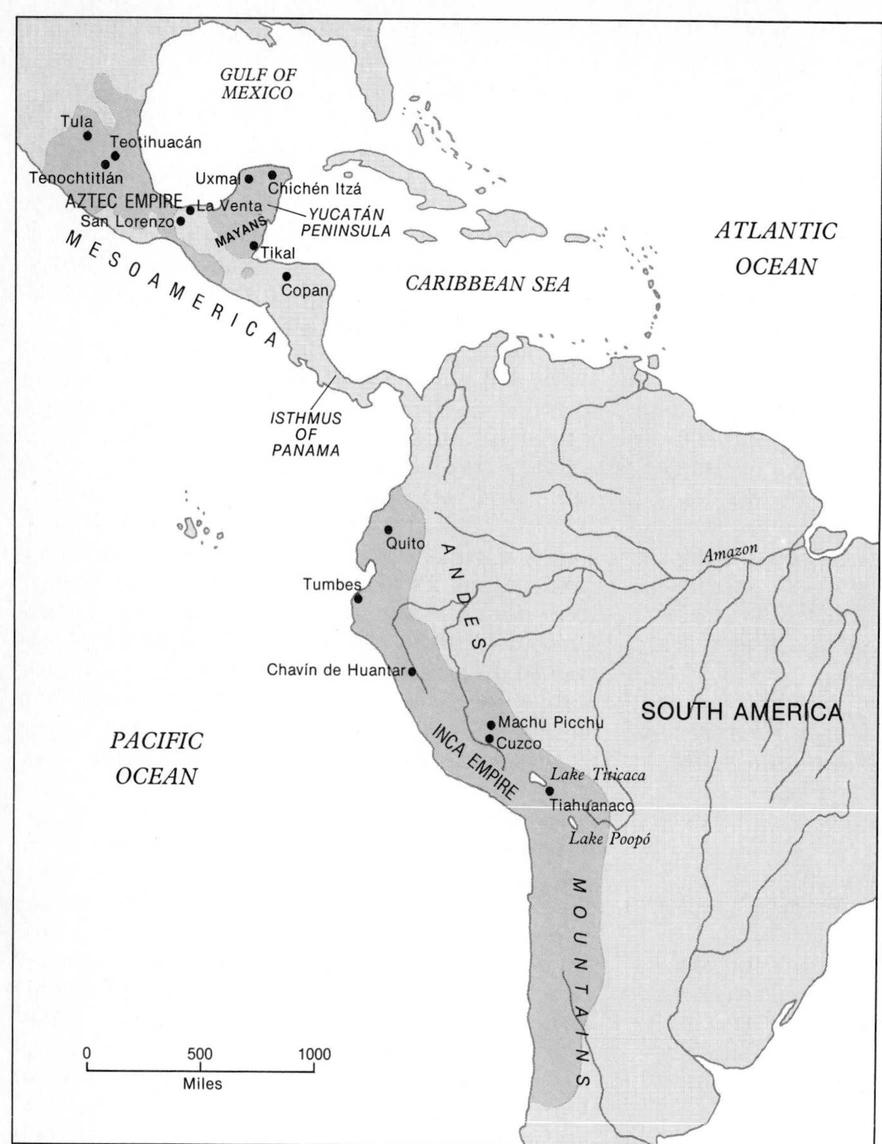

9.3 The Mayans, the Aztecs, and the Incas

ful of Mayan sites have been fully excavated or even mapped, and the results present an incomplete picture of Mayan life. The largest Mayan center to have been uncovered so far, Tikal, contains some 3,000 buildings within an area of 6 square miles. Unlike Teotihuacán, Tikal shows no evidence of town planning, and many scholars believe that it was a ceremonial center rather than a city, serving the needs of the Mayan villages in the region. Its inhabitants would have been the ruling classes and their servants rather than a cross section of the Mayan population.

If this is true, Mayan civilization, like that of the Olmecs, represents the exception to the general rule that cultural developments are the result of urbanization. Even at the 50 or so principal Mayan sites, it seems unlikely that the Mayan aristocracy put in long periods of residence. The so-called palaces, large structures divided into many small, cramped rooms, are uncomfortable and damp, and there are few traces of permanent occupation. The other structures are almost exclusively religious: great stone processional ways, temples, and the pyramids that are the most famous characteristic of Mayan architecture. At Tikal the highest pyramid is 229 feet tall and decorated with sculptures of Mayan warlords. The only constructions of importance at Tikal besides the temples, pyramids, and palaces are tombs dating to the Late Classic period, yet on occasion the center supported a regular population: ten large reservoirs were constructed to supply drinking water.

In Search of the Mayans

John Lloyd Stevens (1805–1852) describes early excavations at the Mayan city of Copan.

Monument "T", a buried image. It was one of the most beautiful in Copan and in workmanship is equal to the finest Egyptian sculpture. . . . It stands at the foot of a wall of steps, with only the head and part of the breast rising above the earth. . . . When we first discovered it, it was up to the eyes. Arrested by the beauty of the sculpture and by its solemn and mournful position, we commenced excavating. As the ground was level up to that mark, the excavation was made by loosening the earth with the machete, and scooping it out with the hands. As we proceeded, the earth formed a wall around and increased the labor. The Indians struck so carelessly with their machetes, that, afraid to let them work near the stone, we cleared it with our own hands. It was impossible, however, to continue; the earth was matted together by roots which entwined and bound the monument. It required a complete throwing out of the earth for 10 or 12 feet around; and without any proper instrument and afraid of injuring the sculpture, we preferred to let it remain, to be excavated by ourselves at some future time, or by some future traveller. Whoever he may be, I almost envy him the satisfaction of doing it.

Source: C. W. Ceram, *A Picture History of Archaeology* (London: Thames & Hudson, 1963), pp. 308–309.

Society and Religion

The archaeological evidence for Mayan life is enriched by the survival of written or carved texts. The Mayans devised a complex system of hieroglyphic writing, as yet not completely deciphered, which they used to record historical and astronomical information organized by means of an elaborate calendar. The urge to record the passing of the seasons seems to have been common to many Mesoamerican peoples, but the Mayan calendrical system outstrips all others in its intellectual complexity. The events recorded include the births, marriages, and military triumphs of Mayan rulers and their ancestors, as well as accounts of the lives of the most important gods.

The importance ascribed to the Mayan ruling classes continued after their deaths. Virtually every pyramid contains a tomb in its base, presumably of a member of the aristocracy. Ancestor worship seems to have played a major role in Mayan court religion, each ruler being associated with the god from whom he claimed descent. Mayan warlords launched military campaigns with the help of these divine patrons, not so much to take control of enemy territory as to capture prisoners for slavery and sacrifice.

The lives of the Mayan peasants who lived in the villages were very different from those of the ruling class. Indeed, measurement of the skeletons found in royal tombs and in village graves shows that the nobility were much taller than their farm laborers. This may reflect a difference in ethnic origin or may simply be the result of superior nutrition; for the Mayans it was proof that rulers and ruled were created separately by the gods. The villages that have been studied had no elaborate ceremonial sanctuaries, although they did have shrines. A survey of the countryside around Tikal has revealed that for every 50 to 100 dwellings there was a small religious center, dividing the residential areas into zones.

These residential areas must have constantly shifted, since the Mayan lowlands were not suitable for intensive cultivation and the farming communities were probably in constant search of new land—a factor that may explain the lack of developed urban life. Nor is there any evidence of large-scale manufacture or trade with the other peoples of Mesoamerica. Unlike the people of Teotihuacán, the Mayans do not seem to have been interested in commercial expansion. One of the results is that their painting, pottery, and sculpture are totally different from that of their neighbors. The Mayan style is elaborate and complex, and the stone and wooden carvings that have survived often feature scenes of rulers accompanied by their divine protectors, together with lengthy hieroglyphic inscriptions.

It has sometimes been said that Mayan society was dominated by its priests, but there is no evidence to prove the existence of a priestly class distinct from the nobility. It seems more likely that some of the aristocracy performed religious functions. Much of the evidence for Mayan religion is derived from later sources, but given

Creation: A Mayan View

The Popol Vuh, *the Mayan creation epic, opens with these lines.*

This is the account, here it is:

Now it still ripples, now it still murmurs, ripples, it still sighs, still hums, and it is empty under the sky.

Here follow the first words, the first eloquence:

There is not yet one person, one animal, bird, fish, crab, tree, rock, hollow, canyon, meadow, forest. Only the sky alone is there; the face of the earth is not clear. Only the sea alone is pooled under all the sky; there is nothing whatever gathered together. It is at rest; not a single thing stirs. It is held back, kept at rest under the sky.

Whatever there is that might be is simply not there: only the pooled water, only the calm sea, only it alone is pooled.

Whatever might be is simply not there: only murmurs, ripples, in the dark, in the night. Only the Maker, Modeler alone, Sovereign Plumed Serpent, the Bearers, Begetters are in the water, a glittering light. They are there, they are enclosed in quetzal feathers, in blue-green.

Thus the name, "Plumed Serpent." They are great knowers, great thinkers in their very being.

And of course there is the sky, and there is also the Heart of Sky. This is the name of the god, as it is spoken.

And then came his word, he came here to the Sovereign Plumed Serpent, here in the blackness, in the early dawn. He spoke with the Sovereign Plumed Serpent, and they talked, then they thought, then they worried. They agreed with each other, they joined their words, their thoughts. Then it was clear, then they reached accord in the light, and then humanity was clear, when they conceived the growth, the generation of trees, of bushes, and the growth of life, of humankind, in the blackness, in the early dawn, all because of the Heart of Sky, named Hurricane. Thunderbolt Hurricane comes first, the second is Newborn Thunderbolt, and the third is Raw Thunderbolt.

Source: Popol Vuh, trans. D. Tadlock (New York: Simon & Schuster, 1985), pp. 72–73.

the conservatism of Mayan culture, there is good reason to think that it reflected traditional beliefs. Numeric subdivisions played an important role: there were four world directions, each with its own color and with a tree on which sat a particular bird; the heavens were divided into 13 levels and the underworld into 9.

The stone processional ways at Tikal and elsewhere were symbolic of the divine roads that led from the "green tree of abundance," which stood at the center of the earth; they formed a setting for ceremonies in praise of the gods. The supreme deity was Itzamna, creator of the world and lord of fire, who is frequently depicted as a snake. The Feathered Serpent of the Teotihuacán people and the Aztecs was worshiped by the Mayans under the name of Kukulcan; the most commonly portrayed of all Mayan deities, recognizable by his large nose, is known only as God K.

The Mayan underworld, a sinister and frightening place, was ruled by gods associated with the jaguar, itself a symbol of night. To provide companions and attendants in the next world for their rulers, the Mayans performed human sacrifices, using prisoners as their victims. The most common method was decapitation following torture. The Mayans also practiced self-mutilation, drawing blood from wounds in ear, penis, or tongue and splashing it on pieces of bark as offerings to the gods.

The Collapse of Mayan Civilization

Around the year 800 this conservative, elitist culture went into a decline. The causes are unknown. No evidence has been found for foreign invasion or internal revolts; overpopulation and misuse of agricultural land may have been contributing factors, yet they seem insufficient to account for so precipitous a collapse. The last Mayan calendar date to be inscribed was in 889, and by 900 most sites were abandoned and their populations scattered. When the Spanish arrived in the early sixteenth century they found people who identified themselves as Mayans and who traced their origins back to the Classic Mayan period; even today people speaking a language related to Classic Mayan live in the Mexican highlands. Yet the complex hierarchical culture of that period has disappeared, and until the last hieroglyphic inscriptions are more fully understood, there seems little chance of identifying the causes of the Mayan collapse.

The Aztecs

The final period of independent Mesoamerican history, the Post-Classic, is dated from 900 to 1519, the year of the arrival of the Spanish general Hernando Cortés and his troops. By 1521 the Aztecs, the last great people of Central America, had been conquered by the Europeans.

At the time of its fall the Aztec empire covered some 80,000 square miles and united about 6 million people. The original Aztecs were probably a nomadic tribe from northern Mexico, hunters and gatherers who migrated southward. The surviving Aztec histories describe their ancestors as the chosen people of the sun god, destined to conquer and rule in his name, but their origins were probably relatively humble. The first major recorded act of their culture was the foundation of the city of Tenochtitlán (the present Mexico City) in 1325, and by 1428 they had begun their conquest of most of Mexico.

The Aztec ascendancy was preceded by the rule of the Toltecs, whose own defeat and dispersal was followed by a period of general anarchy. The exact dates of Toltec power and the details of their history have been disputed, and some scholars have even doubted their existence as a people. The site of their capital, referred to by the Aztecs as Tollan, has been located at modern Tula, although the small scale of the buildings has led some to question its identification as an imperial capital. The city of Chichén Itzá in the Mayan territory of the Yucatán has similar architecture but on a more monumental scale, suggesting that the Yucatán may have been an independent Toltec kingdom.

Whatever the extent of the Toltecs' rule, their power had long disappeared by the time of the Aztecs' ascendancy. The century or so of the Aztec empire is well documented, both by Spanish visitors and missionaries and by the Aztecs' own books, or codices, some of which escaped destruction. The latter include calendars, historical texts, and a magnificent botanical work with drawings of medicinal plants. Further information is provided by Spanish administrative records.

The high density of population in the capital and in other cities was supported by the most intensive of all Mesoamerican farming systems. Plant and animal fertilizers were employed to enrich the soil, and complex irrigation systems were developed, using terraces and canals. The Aztecs even managed to reclaim swamplands and drain lakes in order to create productive agricultural terrain. Their homeland was not rich in natural resources, and one of the principal motives for conquest seems to have been to gain possession of commodities such as cotton, incense, metal, and—most prized of all—jade. Thus military aggression as much as trade was the principal means of economic development. The only large-scale industry that manufactured objects for export was the production of tools made of obsidian, a kind of natural glass that was one of the few materials abundant in the region.

Society and Urban Life

Like the Mayan, Aztec society was strictly divided into upper and lower classes. The distinction was underlined in a number of ways. The elite lived in large stone palaces, wore cotton clothes, and ate a wide range of imported foods. Commoners' houses were small huts built of mud or stone and mud, their clothing was made of fiber, and their diet was limited to food produced locally.

Each household contained a number of related families living in a small multiroom home. The buildings were divided into separate apartments and surrounded by compound walls. Peasant households were small, generally consisting of up to three families, but the homes in the towns were considerably larger, and the royal residence contained several thousand people.

Groups of these households, sometimes several hundred, were organized into units of political administration known as *calpulli.* Serving as the basis of land division as well as social organization, the calpulli paid tax to the central government and provided labor and military service. They also possessed a school where military and moral instruction was provided.

Above the calpulli were the states. The Aztec empire comprised 50 or 60 of these. Most consisted of a central town, with a population of several thousand, and a rural district. The state's governor lived in splendor, wore golden sandals, and traveled in a sedan chair. Many of his duties were discharged by professional administrators who worked under him, including accountants, tax collectors, and judges. The governor retained final power, organized military campaigns, levied taxes, headed the state religious cult, and controlled Aztec markets. Merchants transported goods such as tobacco, honey, and hides from one part of the empire to another. The markets were held daily in the cities and every fifth day in the smaller towns. According to Spanish observers, just one of the several market squares in the capital had some 60,000 buyers and sellers on a busy day.

Tenochtitlán was the largest city in Mesoamerican history, surpassing even Teotihuacán; the population in 1519 was estimated at about 400,000. When the Spanish arrived, the king, Montezuma II (1502–1520), lived in a palace of 300 rooms, the grounds of which occupied 10 acres and included not only the royal living quarters but workshops, libraries, and a zoo. The city contained hundreds of temples, including the central complex made up of three large pyramids. The dedication of this shrine was marked by the sacrifice of 20,000 prisoners, three entire tribes captured for the purpose in the mountains of central Mexico.

Aztec Women

The Aztecs' preoccupation with war was coupled with a strict morality. Girls were brought up at home to assist in domestic duties. Marriages were arranged by the families, each of which paid a dowry. If the girl's family expected compensation for the loss of a cook and cleaner and a potential potter or weaver, the boy's parents had to do without their son's services as a worker or a warrior who would bring home plunder. The marriage ceremony lasted about half a day; the service was followed by a banquet and lengthy speeches.

After marriage the couple were helped by their kin to build and furnish their house. Husbands and wives were expected to be faithful: women who were accused of immorality were physically punished by their husbands, and prostitution was permitted only in the military camps. The women who worked there, however, were taken away and strangled as soon as they showed signs of illness or weakness, and their bodies were thrown into the swamps.

Women were not permitted to hold public office and played no formal part in running the calpulli. They helped plant the fields. Because large numbers of men were involved in almost endless military campaigns, the women also took care of the land during the growing period, camping by the fields in brushwood huts, clearing the weeds, and driving off animal predators.

The Gods of Human Sacrifice

Female participation in agricultural labor was undoubtedly related to the worship of the great earth goddess, Coatlicue, and the goddess of maize, Xilonen, who also protected the home. Much of Aztec religion, including the worship of Quetzalcoatl, was derived from earlier Mesoamerican cultures, and its breadth of range reveals its varied origins. The year was filled with ceremonies held at the temples and performed by priests.

Human Sacrifices

This description of Aztec sacrifices was written by Bernard Díaz del Castillo, who accompanied Cortés to Tenochtitlán in 1519. The victims are captured members of Cortés' expedition.

When we had retired almost to our quarters, across a great opening full of water, their arrows, darts, and stones could no longer reach us. . . . The dismal drum . . . sounded again, accompanied by conches, horns, and trumpet-like instruments. It was a terrifying sound, and . . . we saw our comrades who had been captured in Cortés' defeat being dragged up the steps to be sacrificed. When they had hauled them up to a small platform in front of the shrine where they kept their accursed idols we saw them put plumes on the heads of many of them; and then they made them dance with a sort of fan. . . . Then after they had danced [the Aztecs] laid them down on their backs on some narrow stones of sacrifice and, cutting open their chests, drew out their palpitating hearts which they offered to the idols before them. Then they kicked the bodies down the steps, and the Indian butchers who were waiting below cut off their arms and legs and flayed their faces, which they afterwards prepared like glove leather, with their beards on, and kept for their drunken festivals. Then they ate their flesh with a sauce of peppers and tomatoes. They sacrificed all our men in this way, eating their legs and arms, offering their hearts and blood to their idols as I have said, and throwing their trunks and entrails to the lions and tigers and serpents and snakes that they kept in the wild-beast houses.

Source: J. J. Norwich, ed., *A Taste for Travel* (London: Macmillan, 1986), p. 305.

The lives of these priests conformed to the harsh character of Aztec culture. Required to be celibate, they performed daily self-punishment by passing barbed cords through their tongues and ears to draw blood. They sacrificed humans by extracting the hearts of their victims. These latter were almost always prisoners who, after their capture, were placed in wooden cages and fattened for the ceremony. The cult of war and capture appears at its most bizarre in the custom of staging a "war of flowers," in which warriors of neighboring cities tried to take their opponents captive. Those imprisoned on both sides could then be sacrificed with a clear conscience.

Great events rarely occur at a single stroke, but, as in the case of Byzantium, the fall of the Aztec empire can be dated precisely. The Spanish entered Tenochtitlán on November 8, 1519. Within a year Montezuma died under mysterious circumstances, and the whole of Mexico was ravaged by smallpox brought from Europe by Cortés' soldiers. In August 1521 Tenochtitlán was razed, and Aztec rule was over.

This view from a cliff overlooks the Inca city of Machu Picchu, built around the time of the arrival of the Spanish. [Elsa Peterson, New York]

The Incas

The development and collapse of Aztec civilization in Mexico was paralleled by the history of the Incas in South America. Like their contemporaries to the north, the Incas dominated their neighbors to form a sizable empire under authoritarian rule, but it too fell quickly to European conquerors.

Incan Civilization and the Spanish Conquest

Shortly after Cortés' conquest of Mexico, another Spanish soldier of fortune, Francisco Pizarro, arrived in Peru. The Inca empire he found there in 1527 stretched along the Pacific coast and through the Andes Mountains to central Chile, covering an area of more than a million square miles and embracing a population of over 12 million. The most powerful of all South American peoples, the Incas passed on their history verbally from generation to generation by means of professional memorizers. The Spanish versions of these traditional accounts form the basis for a study of Inca history, but they need to be treated with care, since Inca historians produced a selective version of the facts in order to buttress the power of the ruling classes, and the Spanish may have introduced distortions themselves.

The Andes region, where the Incas originated, is an area of varied resources. Fertile river valleys supported the cultivation of corn, potatoes were grown on the slopes, and the high mountain plateaus provided grazing land. The early Incas were nomads who settled throughout the Cuzco valley, moving from village to village in search of fertile land. By 1100 they had established their hegemony over the region. The history of the early emperors is probably legendary, but archaeological evidence confirms that the mid-fourteenth century was marked by an Inca expansion beyond the Cuzco valley. The cause may have been related to a global weather change that occurred in the mid-fourteenth century, a period known as the Little Ice Age. A diminution of rainfall in the Andes area drew the Incas to seek land elsewhere. At the same time they began to raid more distant peoples in search of plunder. By the early fifteenth century such casual raids had been converted into an aggressive policy of conquest. Territories, once subdued, were left under the control of Incan officials and garrisons. Family rivalries within the ruling class led to further conquest, and Emperor Topa Inca Yupanqui (c. 1471–c. 1493), one of the most powerful Incan rulers, led his armies into what is now highland Bolivia, northern Chile, and most of northwestern Argentina. The last years of his reign were spent traveling throughout the territory he had conquered, establishing local administrations, and organizing systems of tribute. One of these systems was a scheme whereby each district provided women to serve as temple attendants in state shrines or to become the brides of soldiers who had distinguished themselves by their courage.

On the eve of the Spaniards' arrival, the Incan royal family was once again racked by feuds. Huáscar (1525–1532), the reigning emperor, was challenged by his brother, Atahualpa (1532–1533). In the civil war that followed, Huáscar maintained control of the southern part of the empire, while his brother conquered Ecuador and parts of northern Peru. Atahualpa's army defeated the imperial army outside Cuzco in April 1532, capturing Huáscar and executing his entire family; the latter were fastened to poles along the road, while Huáscar himself was imprisoned. Within months Atahualpa ordered his brother killed, only to fall victim himself to the Spaniards, who had by now arrived. After a brief interval, Pizarro and his men embarked on an undisguised conquest of their empire. By 1535 the last rulers of the Incas were driven into the remote mountains of the interior, where their independent state lasted until 1572.

State and Society Under the Incas

Inca society was highly stratified. The noblest aristocrats were those who could claim descent from an emperor and were called "Incas by blood." The emperor, who ruled by divine right, was allegedly descended from the sun and was worshiped during his lifetime. Because there was no clear-cut system of imperial succession, however, squabbling among descendants was not uncommon.

Incan government was organized in a clear chain of command. Immediately beneath the emperor, from whom all authority derived, were the four prefects of the principal territories of the empire. Often members of the imperial family, they lived in Cuzco, from where they supervised the work of the provincial governors; all had to be Incan by birth. The bureaucrats beneath them were generally the leaders of the states that the Incas had conquered. Their sons were often taken to Cuzco to be trained in administration, thereby providing a constant supply of personnel while guaranteeing their fathers' loyalty.

The central government imposed two forms of taxation. The first consisted of service in the army or labor on public works projects; the second involved agricultural work, either in the fields or tending flocks of llamas and alpaca. The products of this farming were sold, and the money was used to run the government. In general, Inca rule was relatively beneficent. As in China, state warehouses throughout the empire were used to store food, which was distributed to the needy in time of famine. Religious differences were tolerated, although local cults were also used as a means of political control: when new peoples were conquered, their most sacred statue or religious object was taken to Cuzco and placed in an Incan temple as a hostage.

Public order was enforced by the army. Numbering 200,000, with auxiliary labor and supply units, it was efficient and disciplined and could rely on supplies from the state warehouses. Permanent garrisons maintained order, and revolts were met by fierce reprisals. The skulls of rebels were fashioned into drinking cups, and drums were made from their skins. As the empire expanded, however, rebellions became more common, and many of the peoples whom the Incas conquered later supported the Spanish.

Among the achievements of the Incan empire was the diffusion of metal tools and the creation of an effective road network. Two main roads ran through Inca-controlled territory, one along the coast and the other in the mountains. The importance of apportioning land and taxes required complex devices that calculated distance and area, while time was measured by a calendar that divided the year into 12 months of 30 days divided into 10-day weeks. The remaining five days of the year were devoted to religious ceremonies in December and June.

The Incas maintained their tightly organized empire without a written alphabet, just as their splendid stone temples and fortresses were joined without mortar; records were kept by a system of knotted cords. Much of their culture centered on religious ritual, which involved an elaborate priesthood that numbered in the hundreds of thousands. These functions, which culminated in the display of mummified emperors on state occasions, also enhanced the power of the ruling dynasty.

Like the Aztecs, the Incas proved easy victims for the better-armed Spanish, and their conquest marked the beginning of the subjugation of South America and its indigenous peoples. Nonetheless, vestiges of earlier times survive in the forms that European culture and Western religion have taken there. In particular, South American popular Christianity has preserved something of the color and fervor of pre-Hispanic times, and in the remoter regions tribes continue to speak a language descended from Incan.

The societies described in this chapter were untouched by contact with Asian and European culture until late in their development. In the case of Africa, Islam provided a bridge, while the Americas were isolated by their geographic position. Both in Africa and in the Americas, prosperous and sophisticated civilizations developed, although the relative absence of written records make them more difficult to document. Over the past 500 years the effect of foreign ideas on Africa has been slow, some parts of the continent remaining virtually untouched before the nineteenth century. In the Americas the arrival of the Europeans produced massive changes that in a matter of decades radically affected both conquered and conquerors.

Suggestions for Further Reading

Bernal, I. *The Olmec World,* trans. D. Heyden and F. Horcasitas. Berkeley: University of California Press, 1975.

Clark, J. D. *The Cambridge History of Africa,* Vol. 1: *From Earliest Times to 500 B.C.* Cambridge: Cambridge University Press, 1982.

Cobo, B. *A History of the Inca Empire.* Austin: University of Texas Press, 1979.

Coe, M. D. *The Maya,* 2d ed. London: Thames & Hudson, 1980.

———. *Mexico.* London: Thames & Hudson, 1984.

Conrad, G. *Religion and Empire: The Dynamics of Aztec and Inca Expansionism.* Cambridge: Cambridge University Press, 1984.

Crowder, M., and Ade Ajayi, J. F., eds. *A History of West Africa.* New York: Columbia University Press, 1972.

Curtin, P., Feierman, S., Thompson, L., and Vansina, J. *African History.* Boston: Little, Brown, 1978.

Davidson, B. *Africa: History of a Continent.* New York: Macmillan, 1972.

———. *The African Genius.* Boston: Little, Brown, 1970.

———. *A History of West Africa, 1000–1800.* New York: Doubleday, 1966.

———. *The Lost Cities of Africa,* 2d ed. Boston: Little, Brown, 1970.

Davies, N. *The Toltecs: Until the Fall of Tula.* Norman: University of Oklahoma Press, 1977.

Fage, J. D. *A History of Africa.* New York: Knopf, 1978.

Hammond, N. *Ancient Maya Civilization.* New Brunswick, N.J.: Rutgers University Press, 1982.

Hull, R. *Southern Africa: Civilization in Turmoil.* New York: New York University Press, 1981.

July, R. W. *A History of the African People,* 3d ed. New York: Scribner, 1980.

———. *Precolonial Africa: An Economic and Social History.* New York: Scribner, 1975.

Labouret, H. *Africa Before the White Man.* New York: Walker, 1963.

Levitzion, N. *Ancient Ghana and Mali.* London: Methuen, 1973.

Mason, J. A. *The Ancient Civilizations of Peru.* New York: Penguin Books, 1957.

Mokhtar, G., ed. *Ancient Africa.* Berkeley: University of California Press, 1980.

Niane, D. T., ed. *Africa from the XIIth to the XVIth Century.* Berkeley: University of California Press, 1984.

Olaniyan, R., ed. *African History and Culture.* Ikeja: Longman Nigeria, 1982.

Oliver, R. *The African Middle Ages, 1400–1800.* Cambridge: Cambridge University Press, 1981.

Oliver, R., and Mathew, G., eds. *History of East Africa.* Oxford: Clarendon Press, 1963.

Shaw, T. *Nigeria: Its Archaeology and Early History.* London: Thames & Hudson, 1978.

Soustelle, J. *Daily Life of the Aztecs on the Eve of the Spanish Conquest,* trans. P. O'Brian. Stanford, Calif.: Stanford University Press, 1970.

———. *The Olmecs.* Garden City, N.Y.: Doubleday, 1984.

Trimingham, J. S. *A History of Islam in West Africa.* New York: Oxford University Press, 1962.

———. *Islam in East Africa.* Oxford: Clarendon Press, 1964.

Turnbull, C. M. *Man in Africa.* Garden City, N.Y.: Anchor/Doubleday, 1976.

Weaver, M. P. *The Aztecs, Maya and Their Predecessors.* New York: Academic Press, 1981.

Zantwijk, R. A. M. van. *The Aztec Arrangement: The Social History of Pre-Spanish Mexico.* Norman: University of Oklahoma Press, 1985.

CHAPTER · 10

Medieval India and Southeast Asia

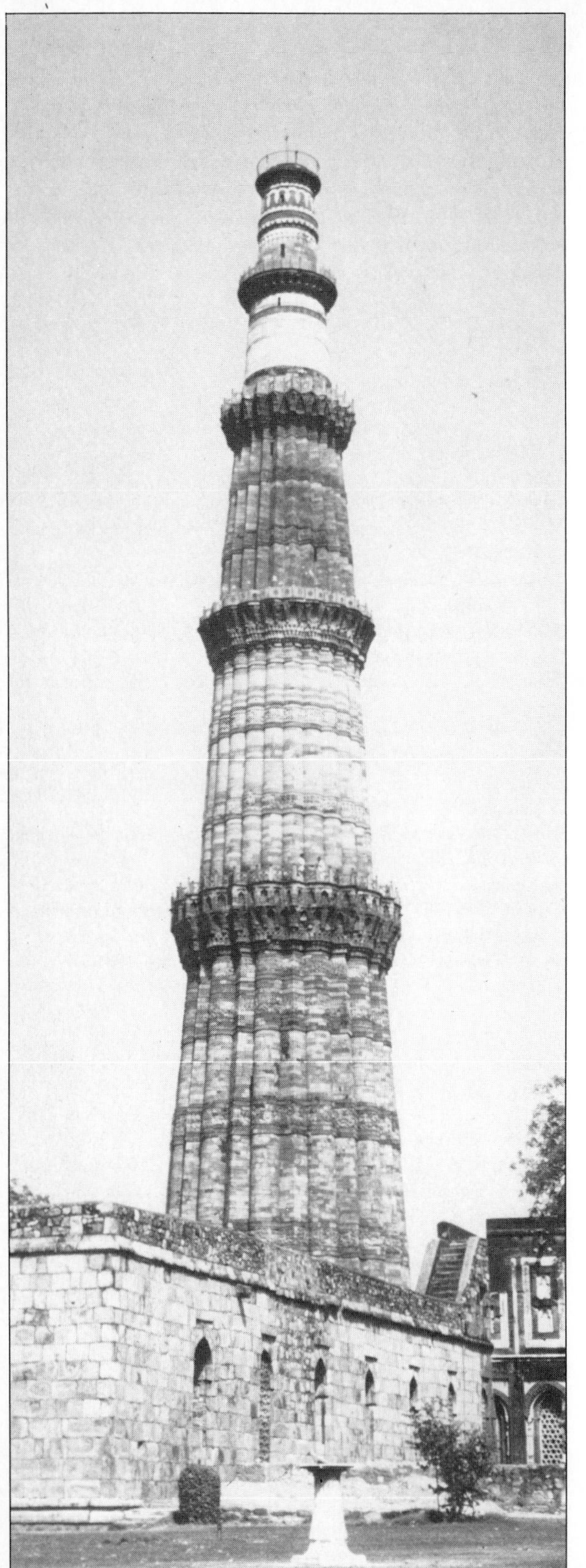

From the mid-tenth century, about three centuries after the collapse of the Gupta dynasty and the death of Harsha, North India endured a long period of disunion, conflict, and renewed invasions from central Asia. This era culminated in 1526 with the establishment of the Mughal Empire and a new flowering of unity and cultural brilliance. The medieval centuries of disorder and conquest, comparable in some ways to the situation in Europe after the decline of the western Roman Empire, were, however, in no way a period of universal disaster. Invasion and conquest were limited to relatively short periods of disturbance in the northern half of the subcontinent. Most people in most parts of India went on with their lives in the usual way

The Qutb Minar—begun in 1199 by Sultan Qutb-ud-din Aibak, completed by Sultan Iltumish (1211–1236), and repaired by Firuz Tughluq—was built to celebrate the victory of the new rulers of Delhi and also as a minaret to the adjacent mosque, since largely destroyed. The tower, 73 meters high and beautifully decorated in each segment, is one of the few monuments preserved in reasonable condition from the centuries of the Delhi Sultanate. [Giraudon/Art Resource]

most of the time. These centuries also saw the vigorous continuation of the Indian artistic tradition patronized by the Guptas and by Harsha, including the construction of a great many magnificent temples and their sculpture, especially in the south. Trade flourished, particularly with Southeast Asia; wealthy merchants subsidized temple complexes and the arts in the rich urban culture of medieval India, and great literature continued to be produced. The south remained largely peaceful, but in much of the north, invasion, conquest, and warfare brought periodic misery.

Early Islamic Influence

The new invaders from the north were part of the general expansion of Islam, and they brought with them an often harsh and intolerant version of the new religion. But they also brought Islamic and, in particular, Persian culture, including many educated Iranians, who served as scribes for the largely illiterate conquerors as well as administrators, artists, writers, and other elites. India, with its wealth, numbers, and sophistication, was an irresistible target, and both Hinduism and Buddhism were seen as pagan creeds, to be conquered by the faith of the Prophet. The invaders' early motives and ruthless behavior were similar to those of the sixteenth-century Portuguese and Spanish invaders of Asia and Latin America in their search for riches, such as gold and spices, and for converts to Catholic Christianity. For the Muslim invaders of India, Hinduism, with its "idolatrous" worship of many gods, its tolerance, and its lack of precise scriptural doctrine, was seen as an evil to be eliminated. Their attitude to the closely related faith and practice of Buddhism was much the same. Probably the chief original motive for their invasion of India was, however, simple plunder. Many of these central Asian groups contented themselves at first with pillaging India's wealth and slaughtering "infidel" victims before withdrawing across the passes with their loot.

In time, however, Muslim kingdoms with a largely Persian courtly culture were established in much of northern India, which had far more to attract and support them than their dry, barren, and mountainous homelands. In time this new infusion of alien vigor blended with older strands of the Indian fabric.

Since the time of Ashoka and the first Buddhist missions (see Chapter 2), there has been a close connection between India and Southeast Asia. We know very little about Southeast Asian systems before this time. It is possible that Indian influence there began before Ashoka, but our earliest data for Southeast Asian kingdoms come from the centuries after his reign and show a political, literate, and religious or philosophical culture already Indianized. Following the Muslim conquest of northern India, Islam was also carried to insular Southeast Asia by converts among Indian traders. These and other aspects of Indian civilization were, however, overlaid onto a well-developed preexisting base whose character was distinctly different.

Indian and Chinese influences have continued to operate on Southeast Asia up to the present. But this immense area, which embraces the present-day nations of Burma, Thailand, Laos, Cambodia, Vietnam, Malaysia, Indonesia, and the Philippines, has retained, despite regional differences, its own indigenous social and cultural forms. These evolved separately before the coming of Indian and Chinese elements. Only writing and various literary, artistic, political, and religious forms came in from India, Vietnam, and China. The social base and most other aspects of culture were less affected and indeed helped to shape many aspects of the new culture. The latter part of this chapter deals with the civilization of Southeast Asia during the medieval period, after the fall of the Gupta Empire in India, when we can see for the first time in any detail the evolution of separate kingdoms and cultures in that region.

The Muslim Advance

India at first lay beyond the wave of Islamic conquests of the seventh century, which engulfed most of the Middle East and North Africa, but Arab traders continued to bring back samples of Indian wealth. Sind, the lower half of the Indus valley, was conquered by Arab forces in the eighth century, primarily as a rival trade base. But the major advance came nearly three centuries later, from the newly converted Turks of central Asia, who had been driven westward and into Afghanistan by earlier Chinese expansion under the Han and the T'ang dynasties.

Approaches to the Khyber Pass near the eastern border of Afghanistan. The Hindu Kush mountain range is a formidable barrier, but it is penetrable through several passes. Through them have come a long succession of invaders of India, including the Turkish-Afghan carriers of Islam and Persian cultures. [Rhoads Murphey]

The Turkish leader Mahmud of Ghazni (971–1030), known as the "Sword of Islam," mounted 17 plundering expeditions between 1001 and 1027 from his eastern Afghan base at Ghazni into the adjacent upper Indus and western Punjab, destroying Hindu temples, sacking rich cities, killing or forcibly converting the inhabitants, and then returning to Ghazni with jewels, gold, silver, women, elephants, and slaves. His remote mountain-ringed capital became by the eleventh century a great center of Islamic culture, thanks in part to stolen Indian riches. Pillage and slaughter in the name of God did not make a good impression for Islam among most Indians, but the austere new religion, with its promise of certainty and of equality, did appeal to some. And India attracted Mahmud's successors, as well as rival central Asian Turkish groups.

The military effectiveness of these invaders depended importantly on their mastery of cavalry tactics, true to their nomadic heritage, and their use of short, powerful

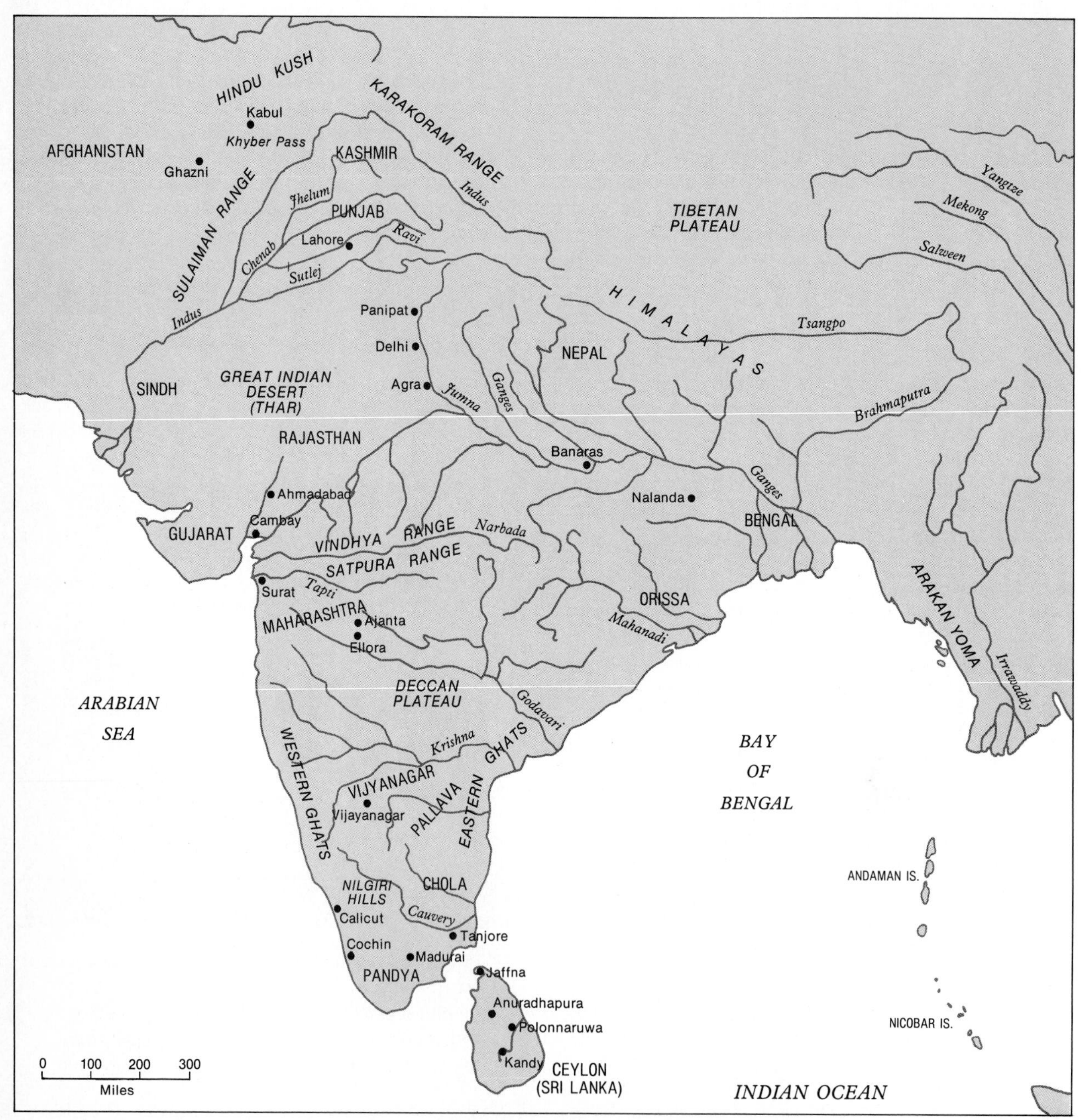

10.1 Medieval India

compound bows of laminated wood, horn, and sinew that they could fire at a gallop on horseback. The Rajputs of Rajasthan, on the flank of the Islamic invasion route, fought relentlessly from their desert strongholds and fortified cities against these Turco-Afghan armies, which the more peaceful inhabitants of Hindustan were less able to resist. Some of the Rajputs had central Asian origins too, some centuries earlier, and hence shared an originally nomadic tradition of mounted, mobile warfare, but all Rajputs were part of a military culture of great tenacity, nurtured in the desert of Rajasthan. They were never completely overcome, but most of the rest of the north, seriously weakened by continual political division and internal conflict, was progressively conquered.

By the end of the twelfth century, Punjab and most of Hindustan (the valley of the Ganges) had been incorporated into a Turco-Afghan empire with its capital at Delhi. Delhi controlled an easy crossing place on the Jumna River where a range of hills stretched southwest and provided protection. Northward lay the barrier of the Himalayas; westward, the Thar desert of Rajasthan. Eastward the broad Ganges valley led into the heart of Hindustan, but for access to it and for routes southward, Delhi had first to be secured; all invaders from the northwest, the repeated route of entry via the Punjab, were obliged to maintain control of Delhi. Bengal was overrun in 1202, and in 1206 the Delhi sultanate was formally inaugurated. As a series of successive Islamic dynasties, it was to dominate most of North India for the next 320 years, until the rise of the Mughal Empire in 1526.

Bengal had prospered as a separate kingdom after the fall of the Gupta order. It remained the chief Indian center of Buddhism, including a great university and monastery at Nalanda, where some 10,000 monks lived and studied,

Marco Polo on India

Marco Polo visited South India on his way back from China by sea in 1293. Given his fulsome descriptions of the wealth and splendor of China, it is notable that he nevertheless called India "the noblest and richest country in the world." His account of what he saw and heard otherwise has the ring of truth and is easily recognizable as an accurate picture of many aspects of Indian society and culture.

The people go naked all the year round, for the weather here is always temperate. That is why they go naked, except that they cover their private parts with a scrap of cloth. The king wears no more than the others, apart from certain ornaments: a handsome loin cloth with a fringe set with precious stones, so that this scrap of cloth is worth a fortune. . . . It is his task every day, morning and evening, to say 104 prayers in honor of his idols. Such is the bidding of their faith and their religion. . . . He also wears bracelets of gold studded with precious stones, and three anklets adorned with costly pearls and gems.

The people of this kingdom worship idols. Most of them worship the ox. . . . No one would eat beef for anything in the world, and no one would kill an ox. . . . They daub all their houses with cow dung. . . . Another of their customs is that they wash their whole body in cold water twice a day, morning and evening. . . . In this kingdom justice is very strictly administered to those who commit homicide or theft or any other crime. . . . It is a proof of the excellent justice kept by the king that when a nocturnal traveller wishes to sleep and has with him a sack of pearls or other valuables—for men travel by night rather than by day because it is cooler—he will put the sack under his head and sleep where he is; and no one ever loses anything by theft.

The Brahmans live longer than anyone else in the world, due to their light feeding and great abstinence. . . . Among them are certain men living under a rule who are called *yogis*. They live even longer than the others . . . and their bodies remain so active that they can still come and go as they will and perform all the services required by their monastery and their idols and serve them just as well as if they were younger. This comes of their great abstinence and of eating very little food and only what is wholesome.

Source: R. Latham, trans., *The Travels of Marco Polo* (Baltimore: Penguin Books, 1959), pp. 233–252.

and similar Hindu centers of learning and piety. Both religions and their followers were targets for the Muslim invaders. Tens of thousands of monks and other Hindus and Buddhists were slaughtered and the universities and monasteries destroyed. This catastrophe marked the effective end of Buddhism in the land of its birth. The few surviving Buddhists fled from the slaughter to Nepal and Tibet. Hindu monuments also suffered, for they violated Islamic principles forbidding the artistic representation of divine creation, including the human form.

Unfortunately for its people, northern India remained hopelessly divided among rival kingdoms, most of them small and nearly all of them in chronic conflict. In total, their armies were huge, but they seem never to have considered a united or even partially united stand against the invaders who, like Alexander before them, defeated the few forces sent against them one by one. Even after Mahmud and his successors had established their rule over most of the north, little opposition was organized against them or against their repeated efforts to spread their conquests southward into central India and the Deccan.

The Delhi Sultans

Successive Turco-Afghan rulers were more accepting, if not of Hinduism, then of Hindus, who remained the vast majority of the Indian population. But Hindus were treated as decidedly second-class citizens and forced to pay a special tax as "infidels" if they refused, as most did, to convert. This was an improvement on the atrocities of the earlier raiders and followed the original Islamic practice of recognizing in other established religions a justified but inferior status.

There was no shortage of Hindu religious texts, and it was not hard in time to accept Hinduism as a sophisticated religion, not simply as "paganism." With more knowledge it was also recognized that Hinduism was basically monotheistic, like Islam, and could not be judged only on the basis of the many gods of Indian folk religion. This distinction was comparable to that between unadorned Christianity and folk practice involving many saints and local cults, as, for example, in Latin America. The head tax (*jizya*) paid by protected non-Muslims (*dhimmis*) was heavy—about 6 percent of an individual's total net worth annually—but it bought a degree of freedom to practice one's own religion. Moreover, the later Delhi sultans agreed to leave many of the original Hindu Indian local rulers and petty rajas in control of their domains. The sultanate thus slowly became more an Indian order and less an alien occupation. It came in time to depend increasingly on the support of India's indigenous people and, under the best of its rulers, to try to govern rather than merely to exploit.

Raids and plundering expeditions went on under the stronger rulers of the Delhi sultanate into the Deccan, south of the Ganges plain of Hindustan, but no permanent position was ever won there or elsewhere in the south. The landscape favored the Hindu defenders, beginning with the double range of mountains that mark the northern edge of the Deccan—the Vindhyas and the Satpura—and including the Narbada and Tapti rivers, which run between the two ranges.

The Deccan itself is deeply eroded and in many areas cut up into steep ravines and river valleys, with easily defended hills or smaller mountains in almost every part. It has seen many bloody campaigns but never a complete or permanent victory for any of the successive invaders from the north, including both the Delhi sultanate and the Mughal dynasty as well as the Guptas and Mauryas long before. The chief and most consistent Hindu defenders against the Muslim attackers were the warlike Mahrathas of Maharashtra, the arid northwestern quarter of the Deccan. They were protected by their strategically located plateau base and its mountain fringes and, like the Rajputs, had a proud martial tradition of resisting northern invasions.

The Delhi sultanate was also weakened by the internal power struggles and political intrigues, which similarly plagued their Ottoman Turkish cousins later in their far larger empire. Most of the Delhi sultans were absolute rulers who tolerated no dissent and demanded total submission; most of them consequently provoked chronic revolts and plots against them, and many died by assassination, by poisoning, or in the dust of a coup or a civil war. There was no agreed method of succession, and the death of each sultan was the occasion for fighting among rivals for power.

The armies of the sultans, like those of the Ottomans and other Turkish states, owed their strength in large part to *mamelukes*, usually Turks bought in their youth as slaves and then trained as full-time professional fighters. They were an outstandingly disciplined force, but like many lifetime mercenaries, they were not above an interest in power and its rewards. Their commanders were often formidable contenders for political power. The ruthlessness and frequent cruelty of many of the sultans provided additional motives for revolt.

In general, the sultanate succeeded only fitfully in becoming an effective administration for the areas it controlled in the north. The records we have tell of power rivalries, intrigues at court, tax policies, coups, civil wars, and the abortive efforts to invade the south, but we have little evidence of the effect of these affairs on the lives of ordinary people. Political power was highly concentrated in Delhi, leaving much of the sultanate's domains under local rulers who had a good deal of autonomy. It seems likely that after the first half century or so of ruthless plunder, conquest, slaughter, and intolerance, most people in North India were left largely to themselves as long as they paid both land taxes and the *jizya*.

The main impact of the sultanate on India was probably to implant a deep mistrust of politics, government in general, and Islam in particular, where it was used as the basis of state policy. Few monuments remain from this period of northern Indian history. In broader cultural terms, however, these centuries did witness a fusion of originally Hindu elements with the Iranian influences brought in by the Turkish conquerors. Like the Mughals who followed them, they were the agents of a largely Persian culture, whose richness and variety found acceptance among many Indians. What we now think of as "traditional" Indian language, poetry, music, architecture, and painting in fact took their present forms from this fusion. Islam, and Hindu-Muslim differences, proved not to be either a bar to such cultural hybridization or a source of conflict, except where it was made an issue in political and military matters. Religious differences were ultimately far less important than other aspects of culture and proved no barrier to cultural mixing.

Islam was progressively Indianized, and over the centuries it won some converts on its own merits and through the agency of a long line of Sufi mystics (see Chapter 8) whose vision was broad enough to appeal to the Indian mystical tradition.

ALA-UD-DIN KHALJI, OPPRESSIVE SULTAN

The power of the Delhi sultans was severely tested by the Mongol invasion of the early fourteenth century. By this time the Turco-Afghan invaders had been partly Indianized, like so many conquerors before them, and depended more on the support of the indigenous people. It was fortunate that on the throne of Delhi was a capable ruler , Ala-ud-din Khalji (1296–1316), who, augmenting his forces with mameluke troops, drove the Mongol horsemen back into Afghanistan in a rare Mongol defeat. Ala-ud-din had usurped the throne by having his uncle murdered, after raiding the Deccan and bringing back loot, which he used to buy the loyalty of those around his uncle, Sultan Jalal-ud-din.

Ala-ud-din paid his army officers in cash and kept tight personal control over his forces. He could neither read nor write and had no tolerance for intellectuals, sophisticated courtiers, or other elites. He abolished all regular stipends and grants to the Muslim nobles, eliminating their political influence and leaving them wholly dependent on him. He outlawed wine-drinking parties, which were in any case against Muslim doctrine, fearing that revelers might plot against him. Ala-ud-din's power base was fueled by a land tax, which he raised to 50 percent of the value of each crop, and by new taxes on milk cows and houses. The crop tax tended to impoverish especially Hindus, most of whom were engaged in agriculture. Barani, the fourteenth-century Arab historian of India, quoted Ala-ud-din as saying:

> **I am an unlettered man, but I have seen a great deal. Be assured that Hindus will never become submissive and obedient until they have been reduced to poverty. I have therefore given orders that just enough shall be left them of grain, milk, and curds from year to year, but that they must not accumulate hoards or property.**

Hindus were also forbidden to possess any weapons or to ride horses. Loyalty and conformity with the sultan's decrees were further ensured by a network of spies, harsh penalties, and intricate court duplicities. He also imposed wage and price controls in Delhi and prohibited the private hoarding of gold and silver, while at the same time requiring all merchants to be licensed and their profits restricted. Peasants could sell their crops only to licensed

The Mongols: An Eyewitness Account

Even the Turco-Afghan rulers of the Delhi sultanate were appalled by the Mongols, whose invasion of India they managed to repel. Here is a description of them by a Turkish eyewitness.

Their eyes were so narrow and piercing that they might have bored a hole in a brazen vessel. Their stink was more horrible than their color. Their faces were set on their bodies as if they had no neck. Their cheeks resembled soft leather bottles, full of wrinkles and knots. Their noses extended from cheek to cheek and their mouths from cheek bone to cheek bone. Their nostrils resembled rotten graves, and from them the hair descended as far as the lips.

Source: H. G. Rawlinson, *India: A Short Cultural History* (New York: Praeger, 1965), p. 224.

merchants and at set prices and could retain only fixed amounts for their own use. These measures kept most prices low enough to permit soldiers and workers to live adequately on their pay, at least in the Delhi area, though merchants and peasants everywhere resented them bitterly. But the controls and taxes made it possible for Ala-ud-din to field an army that could meet and repulse the Mongol invasion.

With the Mongols defeated, Ala-ud-din resumed his looting raids in the Deccan, overcoming even some of the Rajputs and penetrating briefly as far as Pandyan territory farther south. But at his death in 1316 not only these efforts but his own family line as well came to an end; his first son was murdered by his own soldiers, and a second son abandoned all efforts at maintaining the controls established by his father and gave himself up to pleasures at court. Ala-ud-din, ruthlessly cruel and oppressive, was understandably hated and feared. His system died with him, but during his lifetime it permitted Hindustan to avoid the fate of subjugation by the Mongols. His economic controls were remarkable for their thoroughness and extensiveness, but they rested on absolute power and severe taxation, both bound to provoke resistance and ultimately to destroy them. He had bought and murdered his way to the throne with the help of the plunder brought back from his Deccan raids, but he and his successors failed to hold any part of the south or its wealth. They could maintain their authoritarian rule in the north only by bleeding the agricultural base of the economy—a prescription for ultimate disaster.

The Tughluqs

With the collapse of Ala-ud-din's order, a new Muslim dynasty succeeded to power in the Dehli sultanate, the Tughluqs, whose founder was the son of a Turkish court slave and a Hindu woman. His son and successor, Muhammad Tughluq (1325–1351), came to the throne when a pavilion he had erected for his father collapsed and killed him. Muhammad's regime of strict piety and his renewed efforts at carrying Islam southward may perhaps be interpreted as an attempt to expiate his sense of guilt. He ordered everyone to observe the Koranic ordinances for ritual, prayers, and Islamic doctrine and forced large numbers of troops and officials to man his drive into the Deccan, where he briefly established a secondary capital.

The endless campaigns, and taxes to support them, provoked growing rebellion as well as southern resistance. From 1335 to 1342 North India endured a seven-year drought and famine, one of the worst such periods in its history, but Muhammad was too busy with fighting, tax collecting, and the promotion of strict Islam to respond, and there was no organized effort by the state to provide tax relief or food distribution. Well over a million people died, and revolts became even more widespread, in the north as well as in the south, and even in Delhi itself. Bengal broke away and declared its independence in 1338, retaining it for the next three centuries.

Muhammad was killed fighting a rebellion in Sind in 1351, and his cousin Firuz Tughluq claimed the throne, which he held until his death in 1388. Firuz proved a more constructive ruler, who largely abandoned the earlier efforts at conquest and warfare and concentrated instead on the rebuilding of Delhi, with splendid new gardens, mosques, hospitals, and colleges for the study of Islam. He also supported the construction of new irrigation schemes, including dams and reservoirs, that brought new land into production. Although a Muslim zealot like Muhammad, he cut back the sultanate's system of spies and informers, abolished torture, and tried to improve the material welfare of his subjects. But his Islamic orthodoxy and intolerance, his insistence on payment of the *jizya* tax by all "infidels," and his clear message that Hindus were second-class citizens alienated the majority. Soon after his death, the sultanate's domains broke up into warring factions.

This chaos in North India invited, as so often before, a catastrophic invasion by central Asian armies, this time led by the brutal Tamerlane (1336–1405), a Turkish leader who had already ravaged much of Central Asia and the Middle East. After looting the Punjab, he entered Delhi in 1398 and systematically slaughtered those inhabitants he did not take away as slaves or force to carry his booty. Famine and pestilence followed in his wake. The Delhi sultanate never fully recovered from this devastating blow, and its political fragmentation accelerated. Gujarat declared its independence in 1401 and flourished under its own rulers, especially in the Gujarati capital of Ahmedabad. Gujarat had always depended on its maritime trade, westward across the Arabian Sea and the Indian Ocean, eastward to Southeast Asia, and this trade now increased still more. Many Gujaratis, including their rulers, had converted to Islam, which proved useful in trade connections both westward and eastward and made Gujarat prosperous. With their commercial profits the Gujaratis built luxurious new palaces and mosques in Ahmedabad.

Sikandar Lodi and Ibrahim

In what remained of the Delhi sultanate, an Afghan clan, the Lodis, took the throne in 1450 and produced an effective ruler, Sikandar (1489–1517). A patron of culture and a poet, Sikandar encouraged scholarship and the compilation of books on medicine and music. Though a highly orthodox Muslim, he fell in love with a Hindu princess, and his reign saw the continued blending of the Islamic and Hindu mystical traditions. Sikandar himself was not, however, an adherent of Sufism, and perhaps to prove himself orthodox despite having a Hindu mother, he continued the Muslim policy of destroying temples and other Hindu religious art.

In North India, Sikandar's successor, Ibrahim (1517–1526), was a far less compelling figure than his father had been and was confronted by revolts in many parts of the remaining sultanate territories. The rival Rajput Confederacy grew and threatened to extinguish the sultanate altogether. Lahore, chief city of Punjab, was in rebellion, and its governor unwisely invited a new group of central Asian Turks to strengthen his hand against Sultan Ibrahim. This was the army of Babur (1483–1530), known as "the Tiger," who claimed descent from Tamerlane through his father and from Chinghis Khan through his mother. For 20 years, as his own account of his life tells us, he had "never ceased to think of the conquest of Hindustan." India's wealth and its political divisions chronically tempted Afghans, Turks, and others. Babur's outnumbered but brilliantly led forces defeated those of Ibrahim at Panipat, northwest of Delhi, in 1526, and in the next year similarly vanquished the Rajput Confederacy, now plagued by internal divisions. North India was again under alien domination, but the Mughal dynasty that Babur founded was to reach new levels of splendor and imperial achievement.

In the troubled centuries after A.D. 1000, with their shifting and periodically disastrous political changes, punctuated by invasion and bloody warfare, it is understandable that people turned even more fervently to religion. A new Hindu movement known as *bhakti* ("devotion") developed in the south in the tenth century, spread gradually north, and by the fourteenth century reached Bengal, where at the ancient sacred city of Banaras on the Ganges a latter-day disciple, Ramananda, preached the bhakti message of divine love. Its universal appeal as well as its solace attracted a mass following in all parts of India, including many Muslims, with its emphasis on the simple love of God and the abandonment of sectarian or rival causes. This was the Sufi message also, and Muslim Sufis helped to spread the bhakti movement while they also increased the appeal of a more humane yet more mystical Islam. It was celebrated by a long series of poet-saints, probably the most beloved of whom was the blind and illiterate Muslim weaver-poet Kabir of Banaras (died 1518), a disciple of Ramananda whose moving verses on the bhakti theme have inspired many millions since his time.

Hindu Devotion

Here are some samples of the Hindu bhakti devotional literature of medieval South India.

I am false, my heart is false, my love is false, but I, this sinner, can win Thee if I weep before Thee, O Lord, Thou who art sweet like honey, nectar, and the juice of sugar cane. Please bless me so that I might reach Thee. . . . Melting in the mind, now standing, now sitting, now lying, and now getting up, dancing in all sorts of ways, gaining the vision of the Form of the Lord shining like the rosy sky, when will I stand united with and entered into that exquisite Gem? . . . Without any other attachment, I cherished with my mind only Thine holy feet; I have been born with Thy grace and I have attained the state whereby I will have no rebirth. O benevolent Lord, worshipped and praised by the learned! Even if I forget you, let my tongue go on muttering your praise. . . . Lighting in my heart the bright lamp of knowledge, I sought and captured Him. Softly the Lord of Miracles too entered my heart and stayed there without leaving it. . . . He is not male, He is not female, He is not neuter, He is not to be seen. He neither is nor is not. When He is sought He will take the form in which He is sought, and again He will not come in such a form. How can one describe the nature of the Lord? . . . The name of the Lord will bless one with high birth and affluence; it will obliterate all the sufferings of the devotees; it will endow one with the heavenly state; it will bring success and all good things; it will perform for one more beautiful acts than one's own mother. . . . The lamb brought to the slaughterhouse eats the leaf garland with which it is decorated. The frog caught in the mouth of the snake desires to swallow the fly flying near its mouth. So is our life. . . . He who knows only the sacred books is not wise. He only is wise who trusts in God.

Source: W. T. de Bary, ed., *Sources of Indian Tradition*, vol. 1 (New York: Columbia University Press, 1964), pp. 349–352.

The Bhakti Synthesis

Kabir, the blind Muslim weaver-poet of the fifteenth century, is the best-known representative of the Hindu-Muslim fusion in the bhakti movement.

O servant, where dost thou seek me? Lo, I am beside thee.
I am neither in the temple nor in the mosque,
Not in rites and ceremonies nor in yoga and renunciation.
If thou art a true seeker thou shalt at once see Me;
Thou shalt meet Me in a moment of time.
It is needless to ask of a saint the caste to which he belongs,
For the priest, the warrior, the tradesman and all the other castes
Are all alike seeking God. The barber has sought God,
The washerwoman, and the carpenter.
Hindus and Muslims alike have achieved that end,
Where there remains no mark of distinction.
O Lord, who will serve Thee?
Every supplicant offers his worship to the God of his own creation;
None seek Him, the perfect, the Indivisible Lord.
Kabir says, "O brother, he who has seen the radiance of love, he is saved."
When I was forgetful, my true guru showed me the way.
Then I left off all rites and ceremonies, I bathed no more in the holy water.
I do not ring the temple bell, I do not set the idol on its throne
Or worship the image with flowers.
The man who is kind and who practises righteousness, who remains passive
Amidst the affairs of the world, who considers all creatures on earth
As his own self, he attains the Immortal Being;
The true God is ever with him; he attains the true Name whose words are pure,
And who is free from pride and conceit.
Look within your heart, for there you will find the true God of all.

Source: W. T. de Bary, ed., *Sources of Indian Tradition*, vol. 1 (New York: Columbia University Press, 1964), pp. 355–357.

The modern historian D. P. Singhal sums up the history of the Delhi Sultanate as follows:

> **The history of the sultanate of Delhi is full of dynasties which were short-lived and weak. Of the thirty-five sultans belonging to the five dynasties who sat on the throne of Delhi during a period of 300 years, nineteen were assassinated by Muslim rebels. It is almost a catalogue of kings, courts, and conquests, but it was the richest of all the Islamic states during the period. An important feature of the period was the Hindu-Muslim cultural fusion. It was not an Islamic state; it charged more than the one-fifth land tax prescribed by Muslim law, and also interest. Kingship was hereditary and not elected. The sultans were unlimited despots. Even agriculture did not flourish; no attempt was made to better the lot of the cultivators. . . . Rebellions and military expeditions were common and their political fortunes varied. The Turko-Afghan rulers lacked national support and a sound administration based on tradition, so essential for any government to survive and flourish. There was no well defined, well regulated administrative machinery under their rule. The authority of the central government, which was dominated by the ruler and military aristocracy, hardly extended beyond the capital, court, and fort. The rest of the country was in the hands of ambitious provincial governors who, having sent tribute or presents to Delhi, felt free to continue their autocratic rule. Their rule in turn rarely extended beyond their own courts. . . . The disintegration which began toward the close of the reign of Muhammad Tughluq was completed by [Tamerlane's] invasion and the following anarchy. The recovery of northern India under the Lodi kings was too brief to alter the picture materially.[1]**

South India

Most of India remained in fact under native control during the Delhi sultanate, including the ancient kingdoms of Pallava, Pandya, and Chola, whose rule, cultures, and literary and artistic traditions continued largely unbroken. In much of the Deccan and the south, however, with the exception of the Chola kingdom, central state control was relatively loose, and the Hindu monarchies were organized on a semifeudal basis. Lands were held by lords as fiefs, in return for military assistance, payments in kind, and periodic attendance at court, a system similar to that in Chou dynasty China and medieval Europe. Rulers also granted tax-free estates as rewards for service. In India, as in medieval Europe, the tax burden was made heavier by grants of tax-free domains to religious orders, monasteries, and temples. These were often in fact the richest groups in the country and also received large voluntary donations, especially from merchants eager to demonstrate their piety.

The chief cities of medieval India, as of Europe, served as religious centers, grouped around a complex of temples, although supported by profits from trade, farming, and the production of artisans. The great Indian tradition of monumental architecture and sculpture flourished, during these centuries, especially in the south. The major southern kingdoms alternated in their efforts to dominate all of the south, but trade continued between South India and Southeast Asia. Commercial ties served, as they had since Mauryan times, as a channel for Indian influence in the parts of Southeast Asia close to the sea. There was also some settlement by Indian colonists, who brought both Hinduism and Buddhism together with other aspects of Indian culture.

Preoccupation with the violent political scene in the medieval north, for which we have more detailed records, should not obscure the unbroken continuance and evolution of indigenous Indian civilization in the south. The south remained politically divided and periodically involved in warfare among contending states, but such problems were chronic in most societies of the time elsewhere, as in Europe. The medieval South Indian record of temple building alone, including many immense and beautiful complexes, tells a more positive tale of agricultural and commercial prosperity, a relatively orderly society and government, and a continuing emphasis on religion. Much of the urban culture was supported by merchants, and this too provides some evidence of the scope and wealth of commerce, including the maritime trade with Southeast Asia from a series of ports on the southeast coast.

The Temple Builders

The history of South India during these centuries is in fact recorded largely in the building of temples and their records and inscriptions. Through them we know the outlines of rival and successive kingdoms; their conquests, rise, and decline; and the names of rulers and rich donors. Perhaps the greatest temple builders were the Pallavas of the western and central Deccan, who reigned from the fourth to the tenth centuries, but all of the South Indian kingdoms built temples. It was an age of faith, like the European Middle Ages, and as in Europe, Indian builders worked in stone, although many of the temples were hewn out of solid rock and consist of a series of adjoining caves, ornately decorated and with ceilings supported by carved stone pillars.

The best known and most extensive of these rock-cut temples is the complex of 27 caves at Ajanta in the central Deccan, which stretch in a crescent across an entire mountainside, and the nearby 34 cave temples at Ellora, both constructed between the fifth and the eighth centuries. The Ajanta caves were partly buried by a landslide and were rediscovered in the early nineteenth century in excellent condition by British amateur archaeologists, who marveled at the beautifully ornate friezes, sculptures, bas-reliefs, monumental figures of elephants and deities, and wall paintings.

The Pallavas and other southern dynasties who also patronized the arts built a great number of other temples. Many of them were freestanding, including the enormous complex at Madurai built by the Pandyan kingdom, the temples at Tanjore built by the Cholas, and similar clusters in other South Indian cities in a variety of styles.

Revenues from trade and productive agriculture, plus donations from the pious, helped to make this extensive building possible. They also supported political power and imperial ambition. The Cholas were the most successful conquerors, fanning out from their base in southeastern peninsular India. Their economic strength depended in part on their organized success in constructing a system of excavated tanks or reservoirs to hold the monsoon rains and then distributing water to fields via canals during the long dry periods. Originally a feudatory dependency of the Pallavas, the Cholas emerged as the dominant power in South India by the tenth century and even absorbed much of the earlier Pandyan kingdom, including its capital at Madurai. They further developed the Pallavan style of temple building. The revived Pandyan kingdom continued the tradition when it supplanted Chola domination after the thirteenth century, and in the seventeenth century it completed the Madurai temple complex in the form we see today.

Throughout the classical and medieval periods, temples were the scenes of frequent festivals that included music, drama, elaborate processions, and dance. These forms of religious worship were also often combined with markets, as in the fairs of medieval Europe, and offered attractions for secular as well as religious interests. Pilgrimages to temple centers were popular, with the same mixture of devotion or piety and social entertainment, complete with storytellers and itinerant actors and jugglers as well as vendors of food, trinkets, and religious objects. Chaucer's *Canterbury Tales* could have been set in medieval South India, and pilgrimages and religious festivals of much the same sort remain an important feature of modern Indian culture.

The Cholas

What gave the Cholas additional power for expansion during their centuries of dominance was their profitable involvement in maritime trade and their navy. Chola armies conquered most of South India, from the central Deccan to the tip of the peninsula. The Chola navy was the greatest maritime force of the surrounding oceans. It even defeated the fleet of the Southeast Asian empire of Sri Vijaya in 1025, intervening again in 1068 to defend the Malayan dependencies it had acquired.

With the help of their navy, the Cholas also invaded the northern half of Ceylon (now Sri Lanka) and occupied it for more than 50 years in the eleventh century. The Cholas were finally driven out of Ceylon by a great revival of Sinhalese power, which lasted until the thirteenth century. The Sinhalese capital was moved from its classical

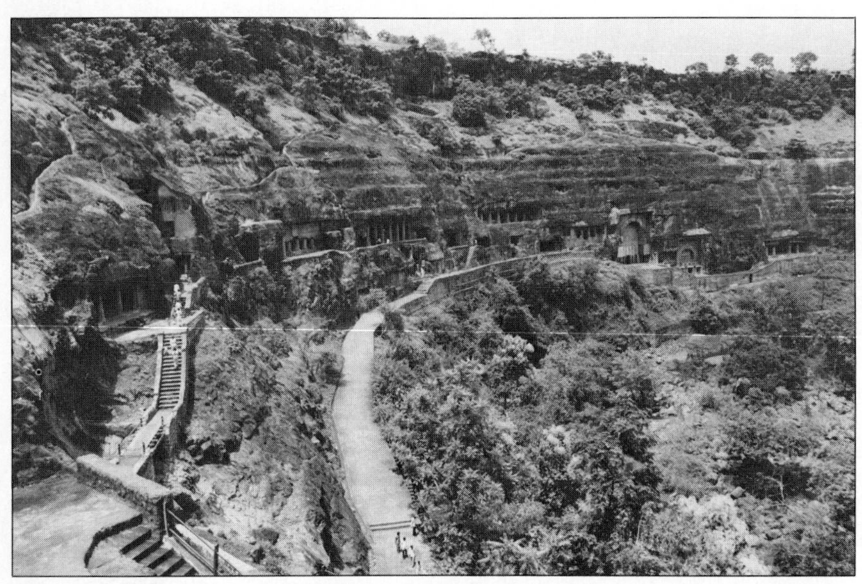

General view of the entrances to the Ajanta caves. [Gregory Griffin, New York]

Classical Indian sculpture; a wall of figures from the temple complex at Kajuraho in Central India, c. 1000. [Lucas/Art Resource]

site at Anuradhapura to a new monumental capital at Polonnaruwa, and its armies in turn briefly invaded the Tamil country of the Cholas and temporarily occupied Madurai in the late twelfth century. The Sinhalese took advantage of a Pandyan revolt against the Cholas, which in itself symptomized the overall decline of Chola power and of the resurgence of rival South Indian kingdoms. By the thirteenth century Chola power had faded and the south resumed its more typical pattern of political fragmentation, although a reduced Chola kingdom remained and continued to patronize Tamil culture and to prosper economically. The kingdom's administration was remarkable for the role played by village and district councils, which were under central supervision but retained a large measure of local autonomy.

The development of bronze casting and sculpture reached new levels of perfection in medieval South India, especially in Chola domains. The famous and exquisite figure of the dancing, many-armed Shiva was cast in eleventh-century Chola, and the form was widely copied by other Indian artists. Other pieces from this period have the same grace and beauty. These artistic accomplishments bespeak the wealth and confidence of the period.

Shiva as Lord of the Dance. With one foot crushing the demon dwarf, he is poised in the cosmic dance of life, holding in one hand the drum of awakening and in another the fire of creation as well as destruction. With still another hand he gives the gesture whose meaning is "fear not." Cast in the eleventh century in the Chola Kingdom of South India. [Cleveland Museum of Art]

But until modern times Indians have never deemed most events of the everyday world important enough to record. Consequently, we have few accounts of day-to-day life beyond inscriptions and temple records. Indian writers concentrated on religion, philosophy, and literature. In comparison with the eternal questions, politics and material details seemed of little consequence.

Vijayanagar, Empire of Victory

Recurrent raids into the Deccan by the Delhi sultanate, which began in the thirteenth century, helped to stimulate the rise of a new Hindu kingdom in 1336, the empire of Vijayanagar ("city of victory"). Having organized to resist the sultanate's incursions southward and the pressures of their Muslim associates in the northern Deccan, the founders of Vijayanagar went on to unify most of the peninsular south under their rule. Their capital, which bore the same name as their empire, impressed European travelers in the fifteenth and early sixteenth centuries as the most splendid in India, both larger and more populous than contemporary Rome. The capital depended on a huge excavated reservoir and was adorned with numerous magnificent temples. A textbook on government written by the last great Vijayanagar king, Krishna Deva Raya (1509–1529), suggests part of the reason for the empire's success in its advice on how to deal with minority subjects: "If the king grows angry with them, he cannot wholly destroy them, but if he wins their affection by kindness and charity they serve him by invading the enemies' territory and plundering his forts."[2] The Portuguese traveler Domingos Paes visited Vijayanagar in Khrishna Deva Raya's time and described him as follows:

> **He is the most feared and perfect king that could possibly be, cheerful of disposition and very merry. . . . He is a great ruler and a man of much justice. . . . He is by rank a greater lord than any, by reason of what he possesses in armies and territories, but he has nothing compared to what a man like him ought to have, so gallant and perfect is he in all things.[3]**

Thirty-six years after the king's death, in a great battle in 1565, a coalition of the Islamic sultanates of the northern Deccan defeated Vijayanagar with the help of the new Mughal conquerors of North India, sacked and destroyed its capital city, and ended its period of greatness.

The Eastward Spread of Islam

Buddhism and trade provided the links between India and Southeast Asia in the classical and early medieval periods, and both served as vehicles for the spread of Hinduism and other aspects of Indian civilization. But Arab traders had been active in inter-Asian trade well before the time of Muhammad and had extended their commercial networks throughout most of maritime Southeast Asia and as far east as the China coast. However, Indian converts to Islam after the founding of the Delhi sultanate were primarily responsible for carrying the new religion to insular Southeast Asia, following the long-established trade routes by sea. This included Indian merchants from Gujarat on the northwest coast and its major ports of Surat and Cambay, which had probably been India's principal base for overseas trade since at least Mauryan times, including the trade with the Hellenic and Roman world.

These enterprises continued under the Delhi sultanate, which for some two centuries ruled Gujarat and converted some of its inhabitants to Islam. Many merchants, eager for official favor, probably chose conversion for their own financial benefit. In Southeast Asia, while there was resistance to conversion by Arabs, the long tradition of learning from Indian civilization meant that Islam was more readily accepted from Indian hands. In any case, both Indian and Arab traders spread Islam eastward along the sea routes, as earlier Indian merchants had spread Hinduism and Buddhism. Burma, Siam (Thailand), Cambodia, and Laos on the mainland remained dedicated to Buddhism, but the coastal areas of peninsular Malaya as well as insular Indonesia and the southernmost Philippines, where trading fleets had easier access, were gradually converted to Islam.

Local merchants in many of these Southeast Asian kingdoms also adopted Islam as an advantage in dealing with Muslim traders from India. In several cases local rulers were converted or chose Islam, perhaps for similar reasons, and their subjects were obliged to do likewise. Insular Southeast Asia became a patchwork of Islamic sultanates. By the late fourteenth century Indian and Arab Muslims largely controlled the trade of this enormous area and made converts first in Sumatra and Malaya, closest by sea to India, and in coastal ports through the far-flung archipelago. Malacca, on the west coast of Malaya, where it dominated the routes through the Malacca Strait, became a great center of commerce and a spearhead for the advance of Islam eastward. Nearly all trade eastward from India has always passed through the strait as the shortest and safest route, avoiding the treacherous southwest coast of Sumatra and the difficult Sunda Strait between Sumatra and Java.

In the course of the fifteenth century the new religion incorporated most of Malaya, north coastal Java, and coastal parts of the rest of the archipelago, including Mindanao, the southernmost large island of the Philippines,

Islamic Ideals

The Key to Paradise, *a guide to the good Muslim life, was compiled in the fourteenth century as an aid to newly converted Indians:*

The Prophet said that whoever says every day at daybreak in the name of God the Merciful and the Compassionate, "There is no god but Allah and Muhammad is his Prophet," him God most high will honor with seven favors. First, He will open his spirit to Islam; second, He will soften the bitterness of death; third, He will illuminate his grave; fourth, He will show the recording angels his best aspects; fifth, He will give the list of his deeds with His right hand; sixth, He will tilt the balance of his account in his favor; and seventh, He will pass him over the eternal bridge which spans the fire of hell into Paradise like a flash of lightning. . . . Keep your lips moist by repeating God's name. . . . The servant of God should make the Qur'an [Koran] his guide and his protection. On the day of judgment, the Qur'an will precede him and lead him toward Paradise. Whoever does not stay diligently close to the Qur'an but lags behind, the angel will come forth and striking him on his side will carry him off to hell. One's rank in Paradise depends upon the extent of one's recitation of the Qur'an. Everyone who knows how to read a small amount of the Qur'an will enjoy a high position in Paradise, and the more one knows how to read it, the higher one's status in Paradise. . . . The Prophet said that on the night of his ascent to heaven he was shown the sins of his people. He did not see any greater sin than that of him who did not know and did not read the Qur'an.

Source: W. T. de Bary, ed., *Sources of Indian Tradition*, vol. 1 (New York: Columbia University Press, 1964), pp. 386–387.

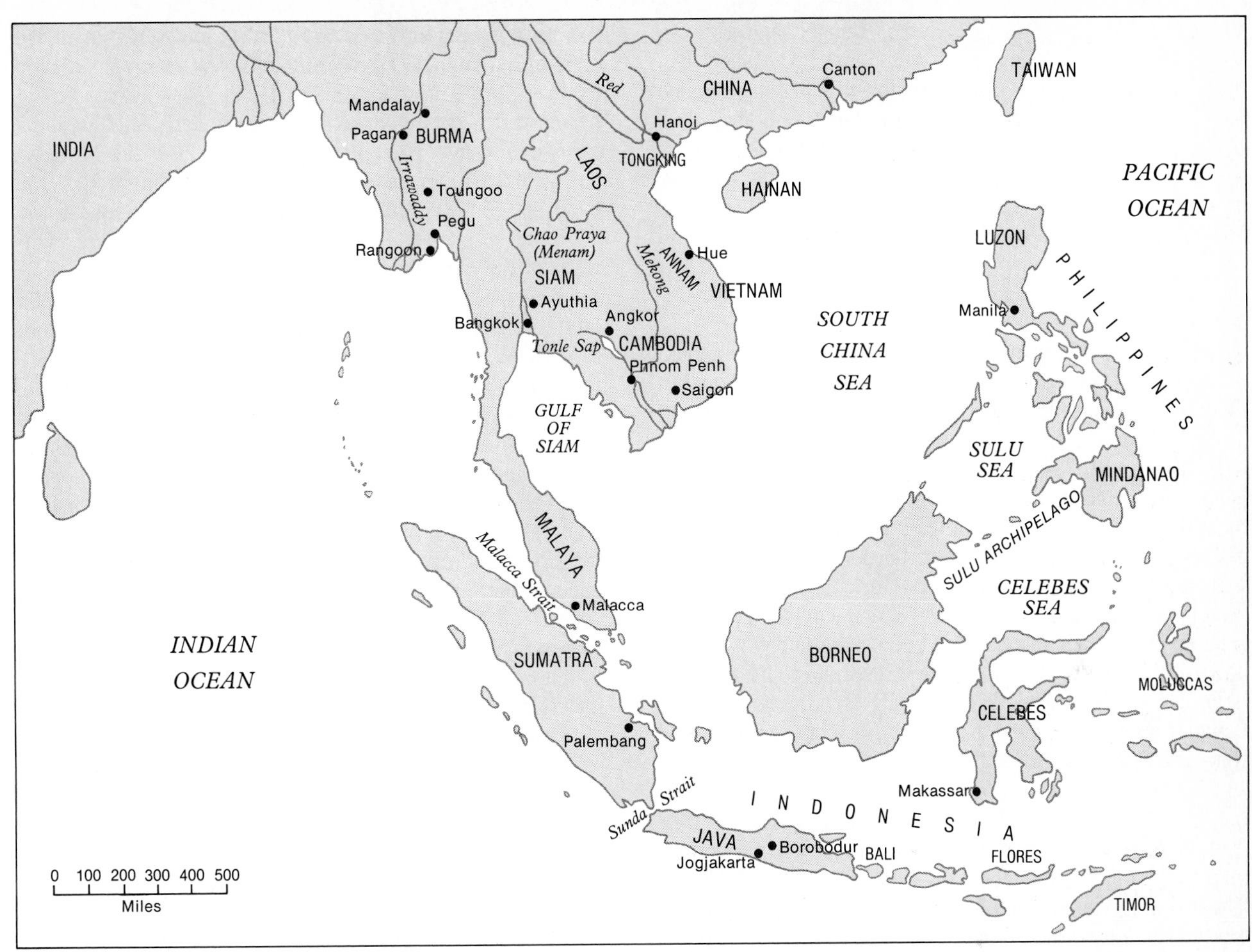

10.2 Southeast Asia

where it seems to have arrived early. Islam's further spread was checked in part by the almost simultaneous arrival of the Spanish in the Philippines and of the Portuguese and the Dutch in Indonesia, although away from the coast, inland Java remained Hindu-Buddhist for another century or so, even under some nominally Muslim rulers.

By the sixteenth century only a few small and isolated areas of Indonesia outside Java retained their original animism or tribal religion, while the island of Bali, east of Java, remained Hindu, as it still is. The very different context of Southeast Asian culture, however, softened some of the more rigid aspects of Islam. This was particularly the case with regard to the treatment of women, for Southeast Asia has always been closer to gender equality than any other major culture. At the same time Islam brought, as in India, a new emphasis on the equality of all before God. In India, the Islamic practice of purdah (literally, "curtain"), whereby women must not be seen by men outside the family and must cover themselves completely when outside the house, spread also to Hindus in many parts of the north ruled by Muslim conquerors. In Southeast Asia, with its far more open society and its tradition of female equality, this custom was rejected. Many other Koranic injunctions were modified in practice, including dietary prohibitions, strict fasting during Ramadan, and rigid observance of the rule to pray five times a day facing Mecca. Indonesia has for some time been the world's largest Muslim country, but the Indonesian (and much of the Malaysian) practice of Islam is recognizably different from that in Saudi Arabia, Iraq, or Iran.

Medieval Southeast Asia

Indian forms of dance, music, literature, art, and dramatic versions of the great Hindu epics, the Mahabharata and the Ramayana, dominated the culture of insular Southeast Asia during the medieval period, as they still do. Meanwhile, Chinese traders became more active and more numerous from the tenth century, especially in the eastern half of the area, and founded permanent settlements of merchants in the major port cities of the Philippines and Java. Peninsular Malaya at this period was very thinly settled, and although Malay-related languages and culture were widespread throughout the archipelago, Malays remained a small group on the mainland. The traditional Buddhist monarchies of Burma, Siam, and Cambodia, centered in the productive cores of their economies in the mainland deltas and lower valleys of the great rivers, were more self-contained. They too built magnificent temple complexes in the Indian-Buddhist style, such as those in the later abandoned Cambodian capital of Angkor built by the Khmer Empire, which flourished from the ninth to twelfth centuries.

The people of Burma and Siam include large infusions of stock originally from southwestern China, where many of their close ethnic relatives still live. The spoken languages of both countries are distantly related to Chinese but written with an Indian-derived script. The majority inhabitants of Siam, the Thais, probably moved down over many centuries into the delta from a homeland that originally straddled the mountainous border zones of China. The origins of the people of northern Burma and to a lesser extent the lowland Burmans are similar. The civilization of both countries has been profoundly shaped, however, by the Indian models which spread to them from Ashoka's time on, including not only Buddhism but also Indian systems of writing, art, literature, philosophy, kingship, and government.

Burmans became the dominant inhabitants of Burma only after A.D. 800 and the Thais of Siam after about 1100, each displacing earlier groups who had followed the same migratory route southward from western China and Tibet. These earlier inhabitants were either assimilated or remained as minorities, a problem particularly severe in Burma and still a source of chronic tension. The Burmans and Thais occupied the productive lowlands and floodplains of the Irrawaddy in Burma and the Chao Praya (Menam) in Siam, where they founded successive capitals. Indian cultural influences were welcomed, especially since they came without political conditions or ambitions. Local rulers invited Indian advisers, priests, and administrative councillors as well as philosophers, artists, and musicians. Trade was an important source of revenue along the sea routes, but in the great river valleys of the mainland, agriculture and its revenues were the heart of the economy and the chief support of the state. The early medieval capital of Burma was at Pagan, founded about 850 in the central Irrawaddy valley, which by 1057 had incorporated the Irrawaddy basin and an upland perimeter within its boundaries.

Included in the new empire were several minority groups. Some of these were in fact culturally more advanced, especially those in the south, which had been influenced by Indian culture. The most important among them were the Mons, who gained dominion over the court and culture at Pagan until the late twelfth century and played a prominent role in Burma's overseas trade. It was via the Mons that Theravada Buddhism spread to the Burmans, together with the rest of the Mon legacy of Indian civilization. But the Pagan kingdom was utterly destroyed by the Mongol invasion of the 1280s. New waves of migrants and raiders poured into Burma, and rival kingdoms struggled against each other for control after the Mongols had withdrawn. A new Burmese dynasty emerged in the early sixteenth century at Toungoo in the southwest. By 1555, after prolonged civil wars, Toungoo had brought most of the country again under one rule.

Successive kingdoms in Burma were strongly Buddhist after the region's initial conversion, and kings competed, as in Siam, in building temples and endowing religious enterprises. Their piety did not prevent them from engaging in internal military struggles, efforts at territorial expansion, and brutal campaigns against alleged heretics, followers of Buddhist sects that were considered unorthodox. From the sixteenth century there was chronic warfare as well between Burma and Siam. But despite the denial by monarchs and armies of the Buddha's teaching of reverence for life, most people in both countries were genuinely committed to Buddhism as a culture as well as the path to personal salvation.

The Toungoo dynasty was vigorously expansionist, mainly at the expense of the Thais. The rising importance of maritime trade, in which lower Burma played a growing role, provided increased revenues to fuel conquests, and the locus of political authority shifted toward the coast. Improved guns brought in by the Portuguese gave new and often devastating firepower to Burmese expansionism. But the Toungoo order proved fragile and overextended. Its capital, now at Pegu in lower Burma, fell to rebellion and invasion in 1599, and later Toungoo rulers abandoned their claims to Thai territory, although Thai-Burmese warfare continued intermittently.

Meanwhile, the Thais had formed a state that grew in power, began eventually taking over much of the decaying Khmer Empire, and in 1431 captured the Khmer capital at Angkor. Thais had probably spilled southward across the present border of southwestern China before 1200, but the trickle became a flood after the Mongol conquest of their homeland in the late thirteenth century. By the fourteenth century they were the dominant inhabitants of the Chao Praya basin. They pushed southward and eastward against the Khmers, from whom they adopted Indian art forms, writing, and political systems while accepting Buddhism from Burma and from the earlier Mon inhabitants of the Chao Praya basin. The Thai capital was established in the mid-fourteenth century at Ayuthia on the edge of the delta, then close to the Khmer frontier and with easy access both to the Gulf of Siam and to the Mon area of lower Burma.

Ayuthia consolidated its hold on the delta and continued the Thai push southward into the thinly settled Malay peninsula and eastward into Khmer Cambodia. Thais were also a major part of the invasion that sacked the Toungoo capital at Pegu in lower Burma in 1599, but for the next two or three centuries Burmese armies generally had the upper hand in their wars with the Thais and finally sacked and destroyed Ayuthia in 1767. After a period of disorder and confusion, a new Thai dynasty, the Chakri, emerged in 1782 with a new capital at Bangkok, the same dynasty that still rules present-day Thailand. Bangkok, near the seaward edge of the delta, was originally a place of marshes and tidal creeks on the Chao Praya, and the site was chosen in part because of the protection it offered against Burmese raids. With the rapid growth of maritime trade in the nineteenth century, it became a major economic center as well as the chief Thai city.

Cambodia, Laos and Vietnam

The Khmer people had also probably come originally from southwestern China (or northeastern Himalayan India) and were ethnically related to the Mons. They followed the Mekong River into what is now Cambodia, probably by 100 B.C., but before they had had any lasting contact with Chinese or Indian civilizations. In Cambodia they may have founded Funan, which is described as a kingdom in Han Chinese records but was partly Indianized as well. By the third century A.D. Funan seems to have covered what is now southern Vietnam, eastern and central Thailand, northern Malaya, and southernmost Burma. Its large fleets dominated the sea lanes and carried much of the trade moving eastward from India to China, of which it became a tributary state. Funan was probably several small loosely organized states that were overthrown by a later group of Khmers in the seventh century. They inherited its domains, and in the ninth century began to build a magnificent capital and temple complex at Angkor Thom, which for several centuries was thereafter the most important city in Southeast Asia.

ANGKOR: CITY OF MONUMENTAL SPLENDOR

The Khmer king Yasovarman I (889–900), who began building the new capital, designed it with the help of Brahmans invited from India to legitimate his claim to divine kingship. The plan of the city reflected the structure of the world according to Hindu cosmology. It was surrounded by a wall and a moat, as the universe was thought to be encircled by rock and ocean. In the exact middle of the city, on an artificial mound, a pyramidal temple represented the sacred Mount Meru in the high Himalayas, where Shiva was said to be perpetually meditating for the eternal maintenance of the cosmic order. Numerous other temples were grouped on and around the mound, which was regarded as the center of the universe. The king declared himself Ruler of the Universe, a title, together with attendant symbols and rituals, passed on to his successors. Angkor Thom reached its final and completed form at the beginning of the thirteenth century, after the Khmers and their rulers had adopted Mahayana Buddhism. New Buddhist temples and sculptures were added, but the earlier Hindu elements remained, and the Khmers seem to have accepted both religious traditions and symbols. The financial drain of such large scale building probably contributed to the decline and conquest of the empire only a few decades later.

The whole urban complex was a symbol of the union between king and god and of harmony between the human

The temple complex at Angkor in Cambodia, dating from the twelfth century. [Wim Swaan, New York]

and divine worlds, and it was intended to ensure prosperity for the kingdom and its people as well as the authority of the ruler. Water, a further symbol of life-giving nurture, was led from the Mekong to keep the moat full and was in turn part of a much larger system of irrigation. The city formed a square about 2 miles on each side, enclosed by its walls and moat, and was entered by five huge monumental gates. Inside was the large royal palace as well as the temple complex, but little evidence remains of the other buildings, which housed the court, its officials, clerks, engineers, workers, artisans, and other inhabitants of the city. We know from surviving inscriptions that there was a large and highly organized bureaucracy.

Less than a mile to the south Suryavarman II (1113–1150) built another major temple complex a century later known as Angkor Wat (*wat* means "temple"), which replicated the arrangement and style of the temples at Angkor Thom and like them was surrounded by a moat, although Angkor Wat was smaller than the capital. Both sites were largely abandoned after the Thai invasion of 1431, and Angkor Thom itself was left in ruins. Angkor Wat was better preserved, since it was not so central a target, and remains one of the chief monuments of Southeast Asian art and architecture, reflecting the glory of the Khmer Empire at its height.

The city, and Cambodia as a whole, may have had a larger population in the thirteenth century than in the twentieth. The Mekong floodplain's fertile alluvial soil was made still more productive by an intricate hydraulic network of canals, dams, and dikes for both irrigation and flood control. Fish from the nearby Tonle Sap lake in the middle Mekong valley added to the food supply. The monsoon rains were heavily concentrated in a short summer season, when the Tonle Sap tended to overflow, leaving much of the rest of the year too dry. Flood prevention works, storage tanks, and reservoirs were carefully engineered, and canals were constructed to direct water to rice fields while protecting them from too much water. Canals were also used to transport the stone used to build Angkor Thom and Angkor Wat. The construction and maintenance of these extensive works required enormous amounts of planning and controlled labor. As the authority of the Khmer kings began to weaken and the country was invaded, dams, tanks, and canals could not be maintained. Without the productive agriculture they made possible, the kingdom's economic base was severely reduced. In 1434, after the capture of Angkor three years earlier, the capital was moved to Phnom Penh on the lower Mekong. The Khmer Empire never recovered its former power and glory, however, and jungle invaded the ruins of Angkor Thom and Angkor Wat. They were revealed again when French explorers stumbled on them in the late nineteenth century. The French colonial government later cleared the sites, although the turmoil in Cambodia again isolated them after 1975.

The southern part of the landlocked and mountainous state of Laos had been included in the Khmer Empire during its centuries of power. It then came under Thai domination until the whole of Laos was absorbed by the French colonial empire at the end of the nineteenth century. The dominant population groups of Laos are related to the Thais and Burmans. Like these, the Laotians originally migrated from southwestern China and adopted Buddhism, but their language and culture are distinctive. The three small Lao states had to contend with Thai, Burmese, and Vietnamese incursions. Buddhism spread to Laos from Mon and Khmer sources, but Laos was chronically squeezed between expansionist states on all sides.

Vietnam: Expansion to the South

The northern part of Vietnam, known as Tongking, in the productive basin of the Red River with its capital at Hanoi, had been part of the pre-Han South China kingdom of Nan Yueh, or Nam Viet, which included the Canton area and was then incorporated in the Han and T'ang empires. It thus acquired a heavy overlay of Chinese civilization, becoming the only Southeast Asian state to be Sinified rather than Indianized. Below the elite level, however, Vietnamese culture remained distinctively Southeast Asian and maintained its identity.

Vietnam regained its independence after the fall of the T'ang dynasty, although it had to repel efforts at reconquest by the Mongols, the Ming, and the Manchus. During these centuries the Vietnamese were engaged in their own expansion southward, down the narrow coastal plain of Annam and eventually into the agriculturally rich delta of the Mekong in what is now southern Vietnam, a process that took nearly 1,000 years. Southward movement took place at the expense of the Indianized Champa kingdom in Annam with its capital at Hue, and then of the Khmers, who originally controlled the Mekong delta and the surrounding plain.

In this long struggle, the Vietnamese drew strength from a fervent nationalism originally engendered by their efforts to resist and finally to throw off Chinese control, a 2,000-year ordeal of chronic war. But their growing empire was managed on Chinese bureaucratic lines, and their later rulers even adopted the title of emperor, although they prudently accepted the status of tributary to China. Like the Koreans and the Japanese, the Vietnamese accepted aspects of Chinese culture while resisting Chinese political control. By the early nineteenth century their empire included essentially all of the modern state, including territories conquered or detached from Cambodia and Laos, with the central and southern areas ruled from subsidiary capitals at Hue and Saigon. The delta of Tongking in the north around Hanoi and of the Mekong around Saigon, as well as the coastal plain of Annam joining them, were fertile and became highly productive under a Chinese-style system of intensive irrigated agriculture. This lent further strength to the state, helping it to maintain control over a mountainous western borderland inhabited by a variety of non-Vietnamese tribal minorities in addition to Laotians and Khmers.

Malaya, Indonesia, and the Philippines

Malay-style culture and the Malay language family are dominant not only in the Malay peninsula but also in most of insular Southeast Asia, especially the coastal areas easily accessible by sea. The peninsula itself, however, has never supported a very large population, especially compared to the larger and more productive areas of Indonesia and the Philippines, and probably did not reach half a million until the late nineteenth century. Its mountainous and rain-forested landscape contained no extensive river valleys or productive agricultural plains, and settlement was most concentrated on the coast, where small ports were engaged in regional trade. There is no evidence of a highly developed indigenous civilization until the rise of Malacca in the fifteenth century, and Malacca itself was part of a larger system in greater Malay Southeast Asia. During the medieval period most of Malaya was first controlled by the Indonesian trading empire of Sri Vijaya, with its capital on nearby Sumatra, and later by the Thai state. Malaya was politically unified only under twentieth-century British colonial control, and most of its growth dates only from the tin and rubber booms of the same period.

In Indonesia the central island of Java, with its richly productive volcanic soils, has remained the heart of the sprawling island country. Rival kingdoms arose in Java, while larger empires based on maritime trade grew to control and profit from the sea lanes. The first and most enduring of these was the empire of Sri Vijaya, with its capital at Palembang on Sumatra, from which it could dominate the Malacca Strait, the crucial passage between east and west. It was the chief power of the archipelago from the seventh to the thirteenth centuries, despite a brief conquest by the Chola navy from southern India in the eleventh century. Mahayana Buddhism spread early to Sri Vijaya, and Palembang became a major center of Buddhist learning. Meanwhile, in central Java the Sailendra dynasty in the eighth century built a land-based state on prosperous agricultural revenues, which were also used to construct one of the world's great architectural monuments, the immense Buddhist temple at Borobodur, completed by around 825.

Borobodur, like Angkor, was a symbolic representation of the sacred Mount Meru, built up in a series of nine terraces some 3 miles in circumference and including about 400 statues of the Buddha. Indian artists and sculptors were probably involved, along with Javanese craftsmen. Other Javanese states built many similar temples, which combined Buddhist and Hindu iconography and symbols, as at Angkor. Interstate rivalry and the final blow of the Mongol invasion broke the empire of Sri Vijaya in the 1290s, though it survived in Sumatra. But a resurgent new Javanese state expelled the Mongols and founded the empire of Majapahit in the early fourteenth century, which succeeded to the far-flung commercial interests of Sri Vijaya and at the same time unified much of eastern and central Java.

Majapahit was the last of the great Hindu-Buddhist states of Southeast Asia. Within a century it faced aggressive competition from the new trading state of Ma-

The eighth-century Buddhist stupa at Borobodur in Central Java, chief remaining monument to the Indianization of Southeast Asia before the arrival of Islam. [Brian Brake/ Photo Researchers]

lacca and newly Islamicized ports on the north coast of Java, which soon wrested from it control of the strait and nibbled away at its domination of the maritime trade eastward and of Majapahit client states in the archipelago. Islam had earlier spread to Sumatra along the trade routes from India, and the rulers of Malacca and north coastal Java adopted the new religion as a means of enhancing their commercial connections, through which they made further converts. Majapahit became merely one of many small Javanese states.

The recorded history of the Philippines begins only with Magellan's voyage in 1521, in which he claimed the islands for Spain, although a settlement was not made on Luzon, the main island, until 1565. The Philippines consist of 7,000 islands, many more than Indonesia's 3,000. Although speakers of Malay-related languages have long been dominant in the Philippines, other and probably earlier cultural groups remained in relative isolation, especially in the mountainous and heavily forested parts of the larger islands. Differences of dialect, language, and culture divided the inhabitants of most of the islands, and until recent times they lived in largely separate worlds despite a degree of trading. No recognizable state emerged in any area before Spanish times, and there was no well-established or widely used form of writing, although Indian writing systems and some aspects of the Hindu tradition did have a minor effect over many centuries.

There was also trade contact with China, probably from Han times, but little cultural evidence remains from that early period, apart from Chinese coins and pottery shards. Islam penetrated most of Mindanao in the south, but until the Spanish occupation the religious pattern of the rest of the Philippines was dominated by a great variety of local animistic cults in the absence of any text-based religious tradition. This and the lack of anything approaching Filipino national coherence or identity made for ready conversion to Islam and to Christianity and contributed to the relative ease of the Spanish conquest. Four and a half centuries of Spanish control left the Philippines in many ways culturally, socially, and politically closer to Latin America than to Asia.

From the late tenth century to the foundation of the Mughal dynasty in 1526 India was divided as waves of invaders from the north brought in both a new religion, Islam, and a new cultural infusion. It was nevertheless a period of great artistic creativity, especially in the south, and though the records we have tell mainly of battles, kings, and conquests, they tell also of monumental building, a flourishing of the arts, and growing and profitable trade. Surpluses from this trade helped to support these creations as well as the political structures and armies of numerous states. Southeast Asia was similarly divided and engaged in chronic warfare, but there too these centuries saw the building of majestic temples and the flowering of the arts, supported as in India by extensive maritime commerce and the taxes on yields from the fertile river valleys and deltas of the mainland and the rich volcanic soils of Java. Religion too was periodically a source of conflict, as Buddhism developed new sects and Islam spread eastward over India and most of Southeast Asia, profoundly changing its social and cultural character.

Notes

1. D. P. Singhal, *A History of the Indian People* (London: Methuen, 1983), pp. 173–174.
2. A. L. Basham, *The Wonder That Was India* (New York: Grove Press, 1959), p. 198.
3. Ibid., p. 76.

Suggestions for Further Reading

Andaya, B., and Andaya, L. *A History of Malaysia*. New York: St. Martin's Press, 1982.

Auboyer, J. *Daily Life in Ancient India*. New York: Macmillan, 1965.

Aung-Thwin, M. *Pagan: The Origins of Modern Burma*. Honolulu: University Press of Hawaii, 1985.

Basham, A. L. *The Wonder That Was India*. New York: Grove Press, 1959.

Briggs, L. *The Ancient Khmer Empire*. Philadelphia: American Philosophical Society, 1951.

Chand, T. *The Influence of Islam on Indian Culture*. Allahabad: Indian Press, 1954.

Chandler, D. P. *A History of Cambodia*. Boulder, Colo.: Westview, 1983.

Coedes, G. *The Indianized States of Southeast Asia*, ed. W. F. Vella. Honolulu: East-West Center Press, 1968.

Gesick, L., ed. *Centers, Symbols, and Hierarchies: Essays on the Classical States of Southeast Asia*. New Haven, Conn.: Yale University Press, 1983.

Groslier, B. P., and Arthaud, J. *Angkor: Art and Civilization*. New York: Praeger, 1966.

Hall, D. G. R. *A History of Southeast Asia*, 4th ed. London: Macmillan, 1981.

Hall, K. R. *Maritime Trade and State Development in Early Southeast Asia*. Honolulu: University Press of Hawaii, 1985.

Ikram, S. M. *Muslim Civilization in India*. New York: Columbia University Press, 1964.

Lieberman, V. *Burmese Administrative Cycles: Anarchy and Conquest, 1580-1760*. Princeton, N.J.: Princeton University Press, 1984.

Miller, H. *A Short History of Malaya*. New York: Praeger, 1965.

Osborne, M. *Southeast Asia: An Illustrated Introductory History*, 3d ed. London: George Allen & Unwin, 1985.

Qureshi, I. H. *The Administration of the Sultanate of Delhi*. Lahore: Mohammad Ashraf, 1942.

Rawlinson, H. G. *India: A Short Cultural History*. New York: Praeger, 1965.

Ricklefs, M. C. *A History of Modern Indonesia*. Bloomington: Indiana University Press, 1981.

Sastri, A. N. *The Cholas*. Madison: University of Wisconsin Press, 1955.

Singhal, D. P. *A History of the Indian People*. London: Methuen, 1983.

Stein, B. *Peasant, State, and Society in Medieval South India*. Berkeley: University of California Press, 1980.

Taylor, K. W. *The Birth of Vietnam*. Berkeley: University of California Press, 1983.

Thapar, R. *A History of India*, vol. 1. Baltimore: Penguin, 1969.

Van Leur, J. C. *Indonesian Trade and Society*. The Hague: W. van Hoeve, 1955.

Vlekke, B. *Nusantara: A History of Indonesia*. The Hague: W. van Hoeve, 1960.

Wolters, O. L. *Early Indonesian Commerce: The Origins of Srivijaya*. Ithaca, N.Y.: Cornell University Press, 1967.

Woodside, A. *Vietnam and the Chinese Model*. Cambridge, Mass.: Harvard University Press, 1971.

Wyatt, D. *Thailand: A Short History*. New Haven, Conn.: Yale University Press, 1984.

Yazdani, G., ed. *The Early History of the Deccan*. London: Oxford University Press, 1960.

CHAPTER · 11

A Golden Age In East Asia

The period from the sixth to the fourteenth centuries saw the reunification of China following a long period of division. After 600 years of renewed imperial splendor under the T'ang dynasty and its successor, the Sung (Song), China was overrun by the Mongols and ruled as part of their short-lived empire from 1279 to 1368, when a new Chinese dynasty, the Ming, restored Chinese power. During the same period, Korean civilization matured, produced a series of effective dynasties, and added innovations to the Chinese culture it had adopted from the earlier Han dynasty in China. In the eighth century Japan evolved a literate civilization on the model of T'ang China and in subsequent centuries produced a highly sophisticated court culture. Japan slowly dissolved into chronic fighting between rival clans until unity was reimposed by the founders of the Tokugawa shogunate by 1600.

Samurai armor from the Muromachi period (c. 1550) made of steel, silk, and bronze, with a hard lacquer mask and gauntlets. [Granger Collection]

Reunification in China

For nearly four centuries after the fall of the Han dynasty in A.D. 220 China was divided into many separate kingdoms, with much of the north under barbarian control. Buddhism flourished, perhaps as a response to the troubled times, and was promoted also by the Sinicized rulers of the north. The chief such kingdom, known as the Northern Wei, controlled most of North China from 386 to 534. It built a number of splendid Buddhist cave temples with statues of the Buddha and his devotees whose style, though Chinese, reveals Indian influence, as do the many pagodas, a temple form adapted from the Indian stupa.

The Chinese cultural and political tradition proper was carried on by a succession of rival dynasties vying for supremacy in the south, which was enriched by a flood of wealthy and educated refugees from the north. Nanking (Nanjing) was the chief southern capital and major urban center, but none of the southern dynasties or kingdoms was able either to unify the region or to provide strong government. Literature, philosophy, and the arts continued vigorously despite the absence of political unity, and Buddhism also became popular in the south. This was the period of both Indian Buddhist missions to China and Chinese pilgrim visits to India; it was also a time of new technological achievements, including gunpowder, advances in medicine, refinements in the use of a magnetized needle for indicating direction (the forerunner of the compass), and the use of coal as a fuel.

Most politically conscious Chinese wanted to see the Han model of greatness restored, but first the country had to be reunified and the imperial machine rebuilt. This was primarily the work of the short-lived Sui dynasty, which in 589 welded contending Chinese states together by conquest. Interestingly, the Sui base was the same Wei valley from which the Ch'in had erupted, and like the Ch'in, the Sui built roads and canals to connect their empire, radiating out from their capital at Ch'ang An.

The second Sui emperor, Yang Ti (604–618), heady with new power, is often compared to Ch'in Shih Huang Ti. He too rebuilt the Great Wall, at a cost of a further million lives, and reconquered northern Vietnam as well as much of Sinkiang and Mongolia, although his campaign in Korea was defeated by fierce resistance. Yang Ti built a magnificent new capital at Loyang, following the model of the Chou and the Han, but at heavy expense. Perhaps his most notable project was the building of the Grand Canal, from Hangchow (Hangzhou) in the south to Peking (Beijing) in the north, to bring rice from the productive Yangtze delta for troops and officials in semiarid northern China. But his megalomaniacal behavior caused great suffering to his exhausted troops, forced laborers, taxpayers, and tyrannized officials. Rebellion spread, as in the last years of the Ch'in, and Yang Ti was assassinated by a courtier in 618 after only 14 years on the throne. A frontier general swept away the pretensions of the Sui heir and proclaimed a new dynasty, the T'ang. Although the new dynasty was to last nearly 300 years, it owed its success in large part to the foundations laid by the Sui, as the Han had rested on those of the Ch'in.

The T'ang Dynasty

Under T'ang rule China achieved a new high point in prosperity, cultural sophistication and greatness, and imperial power. The cosmopolitan T'ang capital at Ch'ang An (Qangan), where the Han had ruled, was the world's largest city with about 2 million inhabitants. The imperial civil service and the examination system were reestablished, and learning and the arts flourished. The T'ang is still seen as the greatest period of Chinese poetry, especially in the work of Li Po (Li Bo, 701–762) and Tu Fu (Du Fu, 712–770).

Some 1,800 samples of Li Po's 20,000 poems survive, including these lines:

Beside my bed the bright moonbeams glimmer
Almost like frost on the floor.
Rising up, I gaze at the mountains bathed in moonlight:
Lying back, I think of my old home.

A girl picking lotuses beside the stream—
At the sound of my oars she turns;
She vanishes giggling among the flowers,
And, all pretense, declines to come out.

Amid the flowers with a jug of wine
The world is like a great empty dream.
Why should one toil away one's life?
That is why I spend my days drinking. . . .
Lustily singing, I wait for the bright moon.

I drink alone with no one to share
Raising up my cup, I welcome the moon. . . .
We frolic in revels suited to the spring.

The legend, almost certainly untrue but appealing, is that Li Po drunkenly leaned out of a boat to embrace the reflection of the moon and drowned, happy in his illusion.

Tu Fu (712–770) was a more sober poet than Li Po, but equally admired. Here are some samples of his lines:

Frontier war drums disrupt everyone's travels.
At the border in autumn a solitary goose honks.
Tonight the hoar frost will be white. . . .
I am lucky to have brothers, but all are scattered. . . .

The letters I write never reach them.
How terrible that the fighting cannot stop.

Distant Annam sends the court a red parrot,*
Gaudy as a peach blossom and as talkative as we are.
But learning and eloquence are given the same treatment:
The cage of imprisonment. Is one ever free?
The capital is captured, but hills and streams remain.
With spring in the city the grass and trees grow fast.
Bewailing the times, the flowers droop as if in tears.
Saddened as I am with parting, the birds make my heart flutter.
Army beacons have flamed for three months.
A letter from home now would be worth a king's ransom.
In my anxiety I have scratched my white hairs even shorter.
What a jumble! Even hairpins cannot help me.

Tu Fu's poetry, concerned as it is with human troubles, reminds us that the rebuilding of the empire exacted a price, for all its glory. Most of the Han-ruled territories were reclaimed by conquest after they had fallen away at the end of the Sui, including northern Vietnam, but Tibet, Sinkiang, Mongolia, and southern Manchuria were wisely left as tributary regions, after their inhabitants had been defeated in a brilliant series of campaigns by the emperor T'ang T'ai-tsung (Tang Taizong, 626–649). Korea again fought the Chinese armies to a standstill but accepted tributary status, and much of the mountainous southwest, home of the Thai and other groups, remained outside imperial rule. T'ai-tsung is remembered as a model ruler who fostered education and encouraged conscientious officials. In his cosmopolitan time, Buddhism was still tolerated and widely popular.

The gradual Sinification of the originally non-Han south below the Yangtze valley continued apace under the new imperial momentum. By the late T'ang most of the empire's revenue came from the more productive south, including the Yangtze valley, and most Chinese lived in that area. The north, where the empire had been born, suffered as always from recurrent drought, erosion, and the silting of its vital irrigation works. But now the south, progressively cleared of its earlier forests, more than made up the difference. Agricultural techniques were slowly adapted to the wetter and hillier conditions and the far longer growing season of the south. The growing use of human manure ("night soil") improved the less fertile soils outside the alluvial river valleys, supporting a continued increase of population, which thus provided still more night soil. Many northerners had fled south after the fall of the Han dynasty; now they and their descendants were joined by new streams seeking greater economic opportunity than in the overcrowded and often marginal north. Imperial tradition and the defense of the troublesome northwest frontiers kept the capital in the north, but the south was the empire's principal economic base.

*Annam is central Vietnam, beyond the empire's direct rule, but, as implied here, tributary.

The poet Li Po (701–762), perhaps the most appealing T'ang figure. His poetry is still learned and quoted by successive generations of Chinese. [Tokyo National Museum, through courtesy of the International Society for Education Information, Inc., Tokyo]

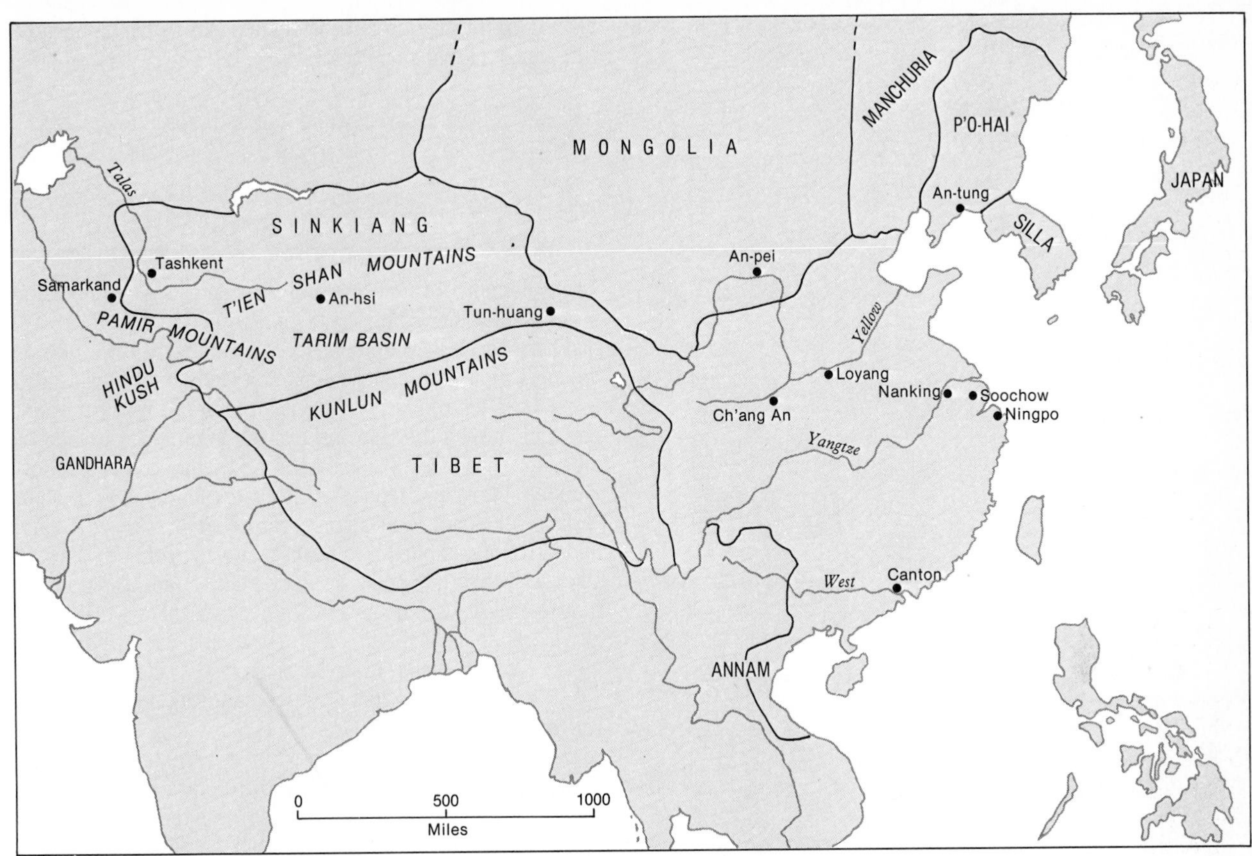

11.1 China Under the T'ang

Renewing their contacts with more distant lands westward, the Chinese found no other civilization that could rival the Celestial Empire. The Son of Heaven, as the emperor was called, was seen as the lord of "all under heaven," meaning the four corners of the known world, within which China was clearly the zenith of power and sophistication. Did not all other people the Chinese encountered acknowledge this, by tribute, praise, and imitation of Chinese culture, the sincerest form of flattery?

In fact, even beyond the world the Chinese knew, they had no equal. Rome was long gone, and the Abbasid Caliphate was no match for the T'ang or its great successor, the Sung. A coalition of Arabs and western Turks did repulse a T'ang expeditionary force at the battle of the Talas River near Samarkand in 751, but the battle is perhaps more significant in that some captured Chinese transmitted the recently developed T'ang arts of printing and papermaking to the West. The mass production of paper dated from the late first century A.D., although it had been invented a century earlier. Printing, which began about A.D. 700, was first done from carved wooden blocks a page at a time, but by 1030 the Chinese, and only slightly later the Koreans, had developed movable-type printing, with individual characters made of wood, ceramics, or metal. Only in the fifteenth century would this technique reach Europe.

Paper and printing were typical creations of the Chinese, with their love of written records and of learning, literature, and painting. They were only two of China's basic gifts to the West, along with cast iron, the crossbow, gunpowder, the compass, the use of coal as fuel, the water wheel, paper currency, the wheelbarrow, wallpaper, and porcelain, to mention only a few. Porcelain had appeared by T'ang times, and from it were made objects of exquisite beauty whose refinement was never matched elsewhere. Porcelain, silk, and later tea became China's chief exports to the cruder world abroad.

The secret of making silk had been supposedly smuggled out of China by two monks at the time of the eastern Roman emperor Justinian (527–565) in the form of cocoons concealed in hollow walking sticks. But later Western silk production in Italy and France never equaled the Chinese quality, just as European porcelain, developed in the eighteenth century, never reproduced the perfection of form and finish of the Chinese models. Silk remains a staple export to this day, although the Chinese lost ground to more uniform Japanese and later Korean silk in the nineteenth century.

The T'ang Emperor T'ai-tsung (626–649), an able man and brilliant field commander but also an astute administrator. His campaigns reestablished Chinese control over Sinkiang and northern Vietnam, conquered Tibet, and even extended imperial rule into Central Asia. T'ai-tsung also restored and extended the imperial bureaucratic system of the Han. [Granger Collection]

Tea, largely unknown in Han times, was introduced from Southeast Asia as a medicine and an aid to meditation and began to be drunk widely in fifth-century China. It became the basic Chinese drink during the T'ang, grown in quantities in the misty hills of the south. By the eighteenth century it was a major item of export to the West. Seeds and cuttings of the tea plant were smuggled out of China by the English East India Company in 1843 to start plantation production in India and Ceylon, and tea became the world's most popular drink.

CH'ANG AN IN AN AGE OF IMPERIAL SPLENDOR

The splendor of the T'ang and its empire was symbolized in its capital at Ch'ang An, where the Han and the Ch'in had also ruled. It was the eastern terminus of trade routes linking China with central Asia and lands beyond and also presided over the largest empire the world had yet seen, exceeding even the Han and Roman empires. People from all over Asia—Turks, Indians, Persians, Syrians, Vietnamese, Koreans, Japanese, Jews, Arabs, and even Nestorian (eastern) Christians—thronged its streets and added to its cosmopolitan quality. It was probably also the largest wholly planned city ever built, covering some 30 square miles and including within its massive walls about a million people. The imperial census also recorded nearly another million living in the urban area outside the walls.

Like all Chinese administrative centers, Ch'ang An was laid out on a checkerboard pattern, with broad avenues running east-west and north-south to great gates at the cardinal compass points. These were closed at night, and the main avenues leading to them divided the city into major quarters. These were further subdivided by other principal streets into groups of 110 blocks, each constituting an administrative unit, with its own internal pattern of alleyways. The emperor's palace faced south down a 500-foot-wide central thoroughfare to the south gate, the one used by most visitors and all official envoys and messengers. This arrangement was designed to awe and impress all who came to Ch'ang An with the power and greatness of the empire. Kaifeng and Peking were later designed similarly, and for the same purpose.

Within the city, people lived in rectangular wards, each surrounded by walls with gates closed at night. The West Market and the East Market, supervised by the government, occupied larger blocks to serve their respective halves of the city. There and elsewhere in the city, in open spaces and appointed theaters, foreign and Chinese players, acrobats, and magicians performed dramas, operas, skits, and other amusements. Women of fashion paraded their fancy clothing and coiffures. For men and women alike, one of the most popular pastimes was polo, which had been adopted from Persia; T'ang paintings showing polo matches make it clear that women played too. As later in India, the wealthy prided themselves on their stable of good polo ponies and their elegant turnout for matches.

Artists and sculptors also found horses popular subjects; despite their apparent mass production, T'ang paintings and clay figurines of horses are still full of life and movement. Another favorite subject for art was the endless variety of foreigners in this cosmopolitan center, depicted faithfully in both painting and figurines so that one can easily recognize, by dress and physical features, which people are being represented.

T'ang culture was worldly, elegant, and urbane, but Buddhism was still in vogue and in official favor. Buddhist temples and pagodas also gave Chinese architects an outlet for their talents, and the first half of the T'ang was a golden age of temple architecture and sculpture, the latter showing clear artistic as well as religious influences from the Indian home of Buddhism. A cosmopolitan center for all of Asia, Ch'ang An was also, like China, the cultural model for the rest of East Asia. Official emissaries and less formal visitors and merchants or adventurers came repeatedly from Korea, Japan, and lesser states to the south and west to bask in the glories of Ch'ang An and to take back with them as much as they could for building their own versions of T'ang civilization.

Persian Zoroastrians, Muslims, Jews, Indian Buddhists and Hindus, and Nestorian Christians from the eastern Mediterranean, representing nearly all of the great world religions, were among the city's permanent residents, all welcomed in this center of world culture and all leaving some evidence of their presence. Ch'ang An flourished for two and a half centuries, from the early seventh to the mid-ninth, when the capital, like the empire, fell into chaos. But from 618 to around 860 it shone with a cosmopolitan brilliance perhaps never equaled until modern times.

Cultural Achievement and Political Decay

Relatively little T'ang painting and literature has survived, apart from a few tomb walls and a few texts, but we have many accounts of the great painters of the time and of writers of whose work we have only a few samples. What has survived in great abundance is the magnificent glazed pottery figures used to furnish tombs and adorn houses and palaces, probably the best known aspect of T'ang art.

Tax Reform: A Chinese View

Yang Yen (727–781), a high official of the T'ang dynasty, wrote a memorial to the throne proposing tax reforms, which were carried out and lasted several centuries.

When the dynastic laws were first formulated there was the land tax, the labor tax on able-bodied men, and the cloth tax on households. But enforcement of the law was lax; people migrated or died, and landed property changed hands. The poor rose and the rich fell. The Board of Revenue year after year presented out-of-date figures to the court. Those who were sent to guard the frontiers were exempted from land tax and labor tax for six years, after which they returned from service. Yet as Emperor Hsuang-tsung was engaged in many campaigns against the barbarians, most of those sent to the frontier died. The frontier generals, however, concealed the facts and did not report their deaths. Thus their names were never removed from the tax registers. When Wang Kung held the post of Commissioner of Fiscal Census during the T'ien Pao period [742–755] he strove to increase revenue. Since these names appeared on the registers and yet the adults were missing, he concluded that they had concealed themselves to avoid paying taxes. . . . The way to handle all government expenses and tax collections is first to calculate the amount needed and then to allocate the tax among the people. The income of the state would be governed according to its expenses. All households would be registered in the places of their actual residence, without regard to whether they are native households or not. All persons should be graded according to their wealth. . . . Those who have no permanent residence and do business as travelling merchants should be taxed in whatever prefecture they are located at the rate of one-thirtieth of their wealth. All practices which cause annoyance to the people should be corrected. . . . Everything should be under the control of the President of the Board of Revenue and the Commissioner of Funds.

Source: W. T. de Bary, ed., *Sources of Chinese Tradition* (New York: Columbia University Press, 1960), pp. 414–416.

Learning and the arts enjoyed a further blooming under the emperor Hsuan-tsung (Xuan Zong, 712–756) and at his elegant court. But in his old age Hsuan-tsung became infatuated with a son's concubine, the beautiful Yang Kuei-fei, who with her relatives and protégés gained control of the empire but ran it badly. Rebellion resulted, and the capital was sacked in 755. Hsuan-tsung fled south with Lady Yang, but his resentful guards strangled her as the cause of all the empire's troubles, and Hsuan-tsung abdicated in sorrow. The rebellion was finally put down, and order was restored.

Although there were to be no more outstanding T'ang emperors and the power of court factions and great families grew, the economy thrived, and culture flourished. A Confucian revival occurred in the ninth century, and partly as a result, the state moved to confiscate the wealth and destroy the political power of Buddhist temples, monasteries, and monks in the 840s. Most temple and monastic properties and tax-free estates, which had grown to immense size, were taken over by the state, and most monasteries were destroyed. The move was similar to that undertaken by King Henry VIII of England seven centuries later, and with similar motives—the need to regain undivided power and control over lost revenues (see Chapter 16). Chinese Buddhism never recovered from this blow and remained thereafter a small minority religion in a Confucian and Taoist society (see Chapter 7). Buddhism was also resented by many Chinese because of its foreign origins, especially orthodox Confucianists and dedicated Taoists, as Christianity was to be later.

Like its Han predecessor, the T'ang lost effectiveness over time and was weakened by corruption. A series of rebellions broke out after 875, prompted first by a great drought in the north but spreading quickly among disaffected subjects all over the country. Rival generals or their puppets succeeded one another on the throne after 884,

The "Ever-Normal Granary" System

Po Chu-i (772–846), one of China's greatest poets, was also a T'ang official. While serving as an imperial censor in 808 he wrote a memorial criticizing the "ever-normal granary" system.

I have heard that because of the good harvest this year the authorities have asked for an imperial order to carry out Grain Harmonization so that cheap grain may be bought and the farmers benefitted. As far as I can see, such purchases mean only loss to the farmers. . . . In recent years prefectures and districts were allowed to assess each household for a certain amount of grain, and to fix the terms and the date of delivery. If there was any delay, the punitive measures of imprisonment and flogging were even worse than those usually involved in the collection of taxes. Though this was called Grain Harmonization, in reality it hurt the farmers. . . . If your majesty would consider converting the taxes payable in cash into taxes payable in kind, the farmers would neither suffer loss by selling their grain at a cheap price, nor would they have the problem of re-selling bales of cloth and silk. The profit would go to the farmers, the credit to the emperor. Are the advantages of that commutation in kind not evident? . . . I lived for some time in a small hamlet where I belonged to a household which had to contribute its share to Grain Harmonization. I myself was treated with great harshness; it was truly unbearable. Not long ago, as an official in the metropolitan district, I had responsibility for the administration of Grain Harmonization. I saw with my own eyes how delinquent people were flogged, and I could not stand the sight of it. In the past I have always wanted to write about how people suffered from this plague [but] since I was a petty and unimportant official in the countryside, I had no opportunity to approach your majesty. Now I have the honor of being promoted to serve your majesty and of being listed among the officials who offer criticism and advice. [If] my arguments are not strong enough to convince . . . order one of your trustworthy attendants to inquire incognito among the farmers. . . . Then your majesty will see that my words are anything but rash and superficial statements.

Source: W. T. de Bary, ed., *Sources of Chinese Tradition* (New York: Columbia University Press, 1960), pp. 423–425.

and in 907 the dynasty dissolved. After a period of confusion, a young general proclaimed a new dynasty in 960, the Sung, which was to last more than three centuries.

The Sung Dynasty

In many ways, the Sung is the most exciting period in Chinese history. Later Chinese historians have criticized it because it failed to stem the tide of barbarian invasion and was ultimately overwhelmed by the hated Mongols. But it lasted from 960 to 1279, roughly the 300-year average for most dynasties, and presided over a period of unprecedented growth, innovation, and cultural flowering. For a long time the Sung policy of defending the empire's essential territories and appeasing neighboring barbarian groups with money and Chinese brides worked well. It made sense to give up the exhausting Han and T'ang effort to hold Sinkiang, Tibet, Mongolia, Manchuria, Vietnam, and even the more marginal arid fringes of northern China. These areas were all unprofitable from the Chinese point of view; they never repaid, in any form but pride, the immense costs of controlling them. Most of them were arid or mountainous wastelands thinly settled by restless nomads who took every chance to rebel and who were very effective militarily.

Vietnam and Korea had been chronic drains on China's wealth and military strength; both were determined to fight relentlessly against Chinese control but willing to accept a more or less nominal tributary status, which satisfied Chinese pride and avoided bloody struggles. The Sung wisely concentrated on the productive center of Han Chinese settlements south of the Great Wall and even accepted barbarian control of what is now the Peking area and a similar arrangement with another barbarian group in the arid northwestern province of Kansu (Gansu). Little of value was lost by these agreements, and the remarkable flowering of Sung China had much to do with its abandonment of greater imperial ambitions. What remained under Chinese control was still roughly the size of non-Russian

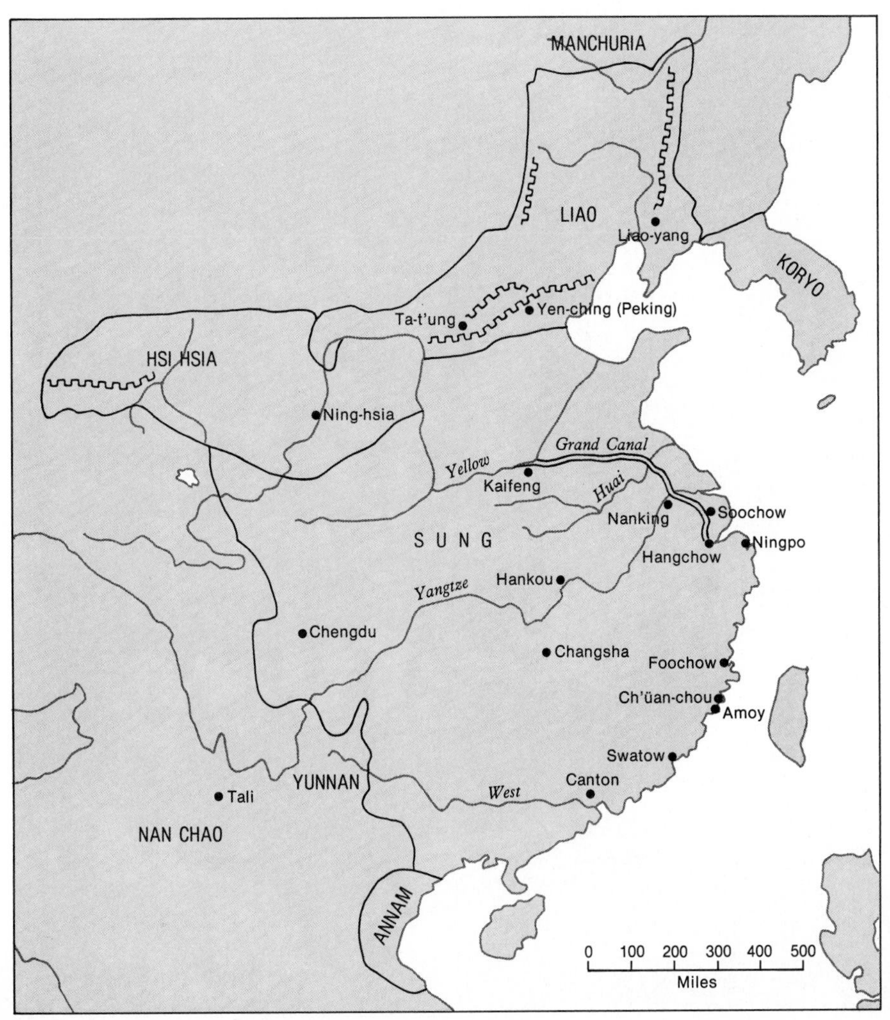

11.2 China and Korea in 1050

Europe and, with a population of some 100 million, was by far the largest, most productive, and most highly developed state in the world.

The Sung capital was built at Kaifeng, near the great bend of the Yellow River. In addition to its administrative functions, it became a huge commercial entrepôt and also a center of manufacturing, served in all respects by the Grand Canal, which continued to bring rice and other goods from the prosperous south. There was a particular boom in iron and steel production and metal industries, using coal as fuel. China in the eleventh century probably

Life along the river near Kaifeng at spring festival time. These are two scenes from a long scroll that begins with the rural areas and moves through suburbs into the capital itself, giving a vivid picture of the bustling life of Kaifeng, then the largest city in the world. The painting, by Chang Tse-tuan, was done in the early twelfth century. [Werner Forman Archive, London]

produced more iron, steel, and metal goods than the whole of Europe until the mid-eighteenth century and similarly preceded Europe by seven centuries in smelting and heating with coal. Kaifeng was better located to administer and to draw supplies from the Yangtze valley and the south than Ch'ang An, whose role in frontier pacification was in any case no longer so necessary. The Sung army was large, mobile, equipped with iron and steel weapons, and well able for some time to defend the state's new borders. Kaifeng probably exceeded a million inhabitants, with merchants and artisans proportionately more important than in the past, although there were also swarms of officials, soldiers, providers, servants, and hangers-on of various sorts.

The early Sung emperors prudently eliminated the power of the court eunuchs and the great landed families and reestablished the scholar-officialdom as the core of administration. Civil servants recruited through examination had no power base of their own but did have a long tradition of public service and could even check the abuses of the powerful. To ensure their loyalty to the empire, their local postings were changed every three years, and they never served in their native places, lest they become too identified with the interests of any one area. In each county and at each higher level the emperor appointed both a civil administrator—a magistrate or governor—and a military official, each with his own staff, who with other officials such as tax collectors and the imperial censors or inspectors had overlapping jurisdictions and could check on each other. It was an efficient system that ensured good administration most of the time. The spread of mass printing promoted literacy and education and opened wider opportunities for commoners to enter the elite group of the scholar-gentry from whom officials were recruited or to prosper in trade.

The eleventh century was in many ways a golden age of good government, prosperity, and creativity. Paper promissory notes and letters of credit, followed by mass

The Confucian Revival

The Sung poet, official, and historian Ou-yang Hsiu (1007–1070) was one of several leading figures who promoted the revival of Confucianism and criticized Buddhism as alien.

Buddha was a barbarian who was far removed from China and lived long ago. In the age of Yao, Shun, and the Three Dynasties [the golden age of China's remote past], kingly rule was practiced, [and] government and the teachings of rites and righteousness flourished. . . . But after the Three Dynasties had fallen into decay, when kingly rule ceased and rites and righteousness were neglected, Buddhism came to China, [taking] advantage of this time of decay and neglect to come and plague us. . . . If we will but remedy this decay, revive what has fallen into disuse, and restore kingly rule in its brilliance and rites and righteousness in their fullness, then although Buddhism continues to exist, it will have no hold upon our people. . . . Buddhism has plagued the world for a thousand years. . . . The people are drunk with it, and it has seeped into their bones and marrow so that it cannot be vanquished by mouth and tongue. . . . There is nothing so effective in overcoming it as practicing what is fundamental. . . . When the way of Confucius [is] made clear, the other schools [will] cease. This is the effect of practicing what is fundamental in order to overcome Buddhism. . . . These days a tall warrior clad in armor and bearing a spear may surpass in bravery a great army, yet when he sees the Buddha he bows low and when he hears the doctrines of the Buddha he is sincerely awed and persuaded. Why? Because though he is indeed strong and full of vigor, in his heart he is confused and has nothing to cling to. . . . If a single scholar who understands rites and righteousness can keep from submitting to these doctrines, then we have but to make the whole world understand rites and righteousness and these doctrines will, as a natural consequence, be wiped out.

Source: W. T. de Bary, ed., *Sources of Chinese Tradition* (New York: Columbia University Press, 1960), pp. 442–445.

government issue of paper currency, served the growth of commerce. Government officials distributed printed pamphlets and promoted improved techniques in agriculture: irrigation, fertilization, ingenious new metal tools and mechanical equipment, and improved crop strains. Population grew even beyond the T'ang levels. Painting had a glorious development, often supported by rich urban merchants as well as by the Sung court. Literature also flourished, aided by the spread of cheap printing. Fiction proliferated, some now in the vernacular. The most famous Sung literary figure is the poet-painter-official Su Shih (Su Tung-p'o—Su Dongpo, 1037–1101), perhaps the best known of China's long tradition of poetic nature lovers. It was a confident, creative time.

Su Shih was, like so many of the scholar-gentry, a painter as well as a poet. In several of his poems he tries to merge the two media, inviting the reader to step into the scene and be immersed in a mind-emptying union with the great world of nature. He also used dust as a symbol for both official life (dead files and lifelessness, as in our own culture) and for the capital on the dusty plains of the north, where he served for many years as an official.

> ***Foggy water curls and winds around the brook road;***
> ***Layered blue hills make a ring where the brook runs east.***
> ***On a white moonlit shore a long-legged heron roosts.***
> ***And this is a place where no dust comes.***
> ***An old man of the stream looks, says to himself:***
> ***"What is your little reason for wanting so much to be a bureaucrat?***
> ***You have plenty of wine and land;***
> ***Go on home, enjoy your share of leisure!"***

Advice to a Chinese Emperor

The Sung official Ssu-ma Kuang (1019–1086) was also part of the Confucian revival and wrote a monumental general history of China. Here is part of one of his memorials to the emperor, urging the abolition of Wang An-shih's reforms.

Human inclinations being what they are, who does not love wealth and high rank, and who does not fear punishment and misfortune? Seeing how the wind blew and following with the current, the officials and gentry vied in proposing schemes, striving to be clever and unusual. They supported what was harmful and rejected what was beneficial. In name they loved the people; in fact they injured the people. The crop loans, local service exemptions, marketing controls, [the] credit and loan system, and other measures were introduced. They aimed at the accumulation of wealth and pressed the people mercilessly. The distress they caused still makes for difficulties today. Besides, there were frontier officials who played fast and loose, hoping to exploit their luck. They spoke big and uttered barefaced lies, waged war unjustifiably, and needlessly disturbed the barbarians on our borders. . . . Officials who liked to create new schemes which they might take advantage of to advance themselves . . . changed the regulations governing the tea, salt, iron, and other monopolies and increased the taxes on families, on business, and so forth, in order to meet military expenses. . . . They misled the late emperor, and saw to it that they themselves derived all the profit from these schemes. . . .

Now the evils of the new laws are known to everyone in the empire, high or low, wise or ignorant. Yet there are still some measures which are harmful to the people and hurtful to the state. These matters are of immediate and urgent importance, and should be abolished. Your servant will report on them in separate memorials, hoping that it may please your sage will to grant us an early decision and act upon them. . . . The best plan is to select and keep those new laws which are of advantage to the people, while abolishing all those which are harmful. This will let the people of the land know unmistakably that the court loves them with a paternal affection.

Source: W. T. de Bary, ed., *Sources of Chinese Tradition* (New York: Columbia University Press, 1960), pp. 487–489.

A boat, light as a leaf, two oars squeaking
frighten wild geese.
Water reflects the clear sky, the limpid waves
are calm.
Fish wriggle in the weedy mirror, herons dot
misty foreshores.
Across the sandy brook swift, the frost brook
cold, the moon brook bright.
Layer upon layer like a painting, bend after
bend like a screen.
Remember old Yen Ling long ago—"Lord,"
"Minister"—a dream,
Now gone, vain fames.
Only the far hills are long, the cloudy hills
tumbled, the dawn hills green.

Drunk, abob in a light boat, wafted into the
thick of flowers,
Fooled by the sensory world, I hadn't meant
to stop here.
Far misty water, thousand miles' slanted
evening sunlight,
Numberless hills, riot of green like rain—
I don't remember how I came.

Defeat in the North

But trouble was brewing on the northern frontiers. A barbarian group, the Jurchen, spilled over from their homeland in southern Manchuria in the early twelfth century. In alliance with the Sung, in 1122 they defeated another barbarian group that had ruled the northeastern border area, returning it to Chinese control. The warlike Jurchen were not overly impressed by the army of their Sung allies, and the Sung foolishly treated them as inferiors. The Jurchen advanced southward, besieged Kaifeng, starved it into surrender, and sacked the city in 1127 after the Chinese failed to pay them an extravagant indemnity. The war continued for a decade, with Jurchen armies briefly penetrating south of the Yangtze. But the Sung armies regrouped and drove them back into northern China, finally concluding a treaty that left the Jurchen in control of the area north of the Yangtze valley as a tribute-paying vassal of the Sung. Now called Southern Sung, the dynasty built a new capital at Hangchow at the southern edge of the Yangtze delta. The Sung had lost the north, but now they could concentrate on China's heartland, the Yangtze valley and the south. Another century of brilliance and innovation ensued, with no loss of momentum.

The Southern Sung Period

Cut off from normal overland trade routes through the northwest, the Sung turned in earnest to developing sea passages to Southeast Asia and India. Permanent colonies of Chinese merchants grew in many Southeast Asian trade centers, and ports on China's southeast coast, from Hangchow south, flourished. These included large numbers of resident foreigners, mostly Arabs, who lived in special quarters under their own headmen. Foreign accounts agree that these were the world's largest port cities at the time. Taxes on maritime trade provided a fifth of the imperial revenue, an unheard-of proportion that betokened new commercial prosperity. There was a striking advance in the size and design of oceangoing ships, some of which could carry over 600 people plus cargo, far larger than any elsewhere until modern times. The earlier Chinese invention of the compass was a vital navigational aid, and these ships also pioneered in the use of multiple masts (important for manageability as well as speed), separate watertight compartments (not known elsewhere until much later), and the stern-post rudder, which replaced the awkward and unseaworthy steering oar. In all these respects, Sung ships predated modern ships by many centuries. Ironically, they helped make it possible much later for Europeans to undertake the sea voyage to Asia using the compass, rudder, and masts—plus gunpowder—originally developed by China and to record their conquests and profits on Chinese-invented paper.

Domestically, too, commerce and urbanization flourished. The Yangtze delta and the southeast coast had long been China's commercial centers, thanks to their high productivity and the easy movement of goods by river, sea, and canal. An immense network of canals and navigable creeks covered the Yangtze and Canton deltas, serving a system of large and small cities inhabited increasingly by merchants managing a huge and highly varied trade. The capital at Hangchow, with its additional administrative role, grew to giant size and may have reached a million and a half in population, making it one of the world's largest cities before the age of railways. Water transport made this possible for Hangchow and other big cities, including Pataliputra, Rome, Ch'ang An, Istanbul, Edo (Tokyo), and eighteenth-century London.

We know a good deal about Hangchow, both from voluminous Chinese sources and from the accounts of several foreigners who visited it, including Marco Polo, who saw it only under Mongol rule after its great period had long passed. Nevertheless, he marveled at its size and wealth and called it the greatest city in the world, by comparison with which even Venice, his hometown and probably then the pinnacle of European urbanism, was, he says, a poor village. The great Arab traveler Ibn Battuta, 50 years later in the fourteenth century, says that even then Hangchow was three days' journey in length and subdivided into six towns, each larger than anything in the West. His approximate contemporary, the traveling Italian friar John of Marignolli, called Hangchow "the first, the biggest, the richest, the most populous, and altogether the most marvelous city that exists on the face of the earth."

These were all men who knew the world; even allowing for the usual hyperbole of travelers' tales, they were right about Hangchow. Its rich merchant and scholar-official community and its increasingly literate population of shopkeepers, artisans, and the upwardly mobile supported an exuberance of painting, literature, drama, music, and opera, while for the unlettered there were public storytellers in the ancient Chinese oral tradition. Southern Sung (and the Yuan or Mongol dynasty that followed it) is the great period of Chinese landscape painting, with its celebration of the beauties of the misty mountains, streams and lakes, bamboo thickets, and green hills of the south.

Innovation and Technological Development

The Southern Sung period was also a time of technological innovation. The philosopher Chu Hsi (Zhuxi, 1130–1200), the founder of what is called Neo-Confucianism, was in many ways a Leonardo-like figure, interested in and competent at a wide range of practical subjects as well as philosophy. This was in the tradition of the Confucian scholar-gentleman, but Chu Hsi and some of his contemporaries carried what Confucius called "the investigation of things" still further into scientific inquiry. Chu Hsi's journals record, for example, his observation that uplifted rock strata far above current sea level contained marine fossils. Like Leonardo, but three centuries earlier, he made the correct deduction and wrote the first statement of the geomorphological theory of uplift. But Chu Hsi was primarily concerned with personal development. He argued that through the Confucian discipline of self-cultivation, every man could be his own philosopher and sage, a doctrine similar to Plato's.

Rapid developments in agriculture, manufacturing, and transport led to a great variety of new tools and machines for cultivation and threshing, for water lifting (pumps), for carding, spinning, and weaving textile fibers, and for windlasses, inclined planes, canal locks, and refinements in traction for water and land carriers. Water clocks were widespread, as were water-powered mills, to grind grain and to perform some manufacturing functions. Superficially at least, thirteenth-century China resembled eighteenth-century Europe: commercialization, urbanization, a widening market (including overseas trade), rising demand, and hence both the incentive and the capital to pursue mechanical invention and other measures to increase production.

Would these developments have led to a true industrial revolution, with all its profound consequences? We will never know, because the Mongol onslaught cut them off, and later dynasties failed to replicate the conditions of late Sung society. The great English historian of early modern Europe, R. H. Tawney, warns us against "giving the appearance of inevitableness by dragging into prominence the forces which have triumphed and thrusting into the background those which they have swallowed up."[1] It is tempting to think that if the Sung had had just a little longer—or if Chinghis Khan had died young (as he nearly did many times)—China might have continued to lead the world and modern Europe might never have risen as it did.

The Mongol Conquest and the Yuan Dynasty

The Mongols overran Southern Sung because they were formidable fighters, but they were aided by some serious Sung errors. The Mongol leader, Chinghis Khan (1155–1227), first attacked the Jurchen territories in the north and then the other non-Chinese groups in the northwest. In 1232 the Sung made an alliance with the Mongols to crush the remnants of the Jurchen and within two years reoccupied Kaifeng and Loyang. A year later they were desperately defending northern China against an insatiable Mongol army, other wings of which had already conquered Korea, central Asia, the Near East, and eastern Europe.

For 40 years the fighting raged in the north, where the heavily fortified Chinese cities were both defended and attacked with the help of explosive weapons. Gunpowder had been used much earlier in China for fireworks and for warfare too as an explosive and a "fire powder." Fire arrows using naphtha as fuel and part propellant had been known in early Han times, and by the tenth century fire lances, spear-tipped bamboo tubes filled with a gunpowder propellant, were in use. In the struggle between the Chinese and the Mongols, cast-metal barrels using gunpowder to propel a tight-fitting projectile appeared, marking the first certain occurrence of cannon in warfare. This devastating new technology, especially helpful in sieges, quickly spread to Europe and was in use there by the early fourteenth century.

By 1273 the Mongols had triumphed. They soon poured into the south, where Hangchow surrendered in 1276. Resistance continued in the Canton area until 1279, when the Sung fleet was defeated in a great sea battle. During much of the long struggle it was touch and go, but the Mongols made few mistakes and the Sung many, although they put up a far longer and more effective resistance to the Mongols than any of their many other continental opponents except the Delhi sultanate of Ala-ud-din Khalji and his mameluke troops. (The Mongol seaborne expeditions to Japan left them at a serious disadvantage; their fleet was twice scattered by major storms at critical points, and their invasion attempts were abandoned.)

The Mongols could indeed never have conquered China without the help of Chinese technicians, including siege engineers, gun founders, artillery experts, and naval specialists. Chinghis died in 1227, but he had already planned the conquest of Sung China, which was completed by his grandson Kubilai (1260–1294), who fixed his capital at Peking as early as 1264 and adopted the dynastic title of Yuan. Korea, northern Vietnam, and the previously non-Chinese southwest were also conquered; southern Vietnam, Siam, Burma, and Tibet were forced to accept tributary status as vassals. The Mongol conquest of China's southwest included the defeat of the Thai kingdom of Nan Chao based at Tali (Dali) and forced a major wave of Thais out of their homeland southward into Siam, where they joined earlier migrants (see Chapter 10).

China, for all its size, constituted only a small part of the vast empire built by the Mongols (see Chapter 12). It is astounding that an area of such extent was conquered by a people who probably numbered only about a million, supplemented by a few other steppe nomads. The simple reason is that they were uniquely tough warriors, almost literally born in the saddle, used to extreme privation and exposure, and welded into an unbeatable fighting force by the magnetic leadership of Chinghis Khan, who consolidated the many warring Mongol and related tribes into a single weapon. Chinghis was born clutching a clot of blood in his tiny fist. The Mongols in his time were Shamanists (animists and believers in magic), and his mother hurriedly called a soothsayer, who declared, "This child will rule the world."

The Mongols' great military advantage was mobility. Their brilliant use of cavalry tactics, controlled by the ingenious use of signal flags, plus the short but powerful compound reflex bow, which they could load and fire from a gallop, maximized their striking force. They could cover 100 miles a day in forced marches, unencumbered by a baggage train since they carried their spartan rations of parched grain and mares' milk in their saddlebags. They always traveled with spare horses, and they knew how to open a vein in the necks of the wiry steppe ponies and drink some blood, closing it again so that horse and rider could continue. Through Kubilai's time, the Mongols rarely lost an engagement, and even more rarely a campaign. Those who resisted were commonly butchered, and their women and children raped, slaughtered, or enslaved.

The terror of the Mongols' record demoralized their opponents, who described them as inhuman monsters. They were expert practitioners of psychological warfare and even employed spies or agents to spread horrifying stories of their irresistible force and their ruthlessness toward any resisters. Chinghis, as a true steppe nomad, especially hated cities and city dwellers and made a series of horrible examples of them, often leaving no one alive. The Mongols loved the violence and pride of conquest but had little understanding of or interest in administration, and their empire began to fall apart within a few years of its acquisition.

The Mongols' rule in China, the so-called Yuan dynasty (1279–1368), lasted a little longer only because by that time they had become considerably Sinified and had realized as well that they could not manage China without employing many thousands of Chinese. They also used many foreigners whom they felt they could trust, including the Venetian Marco Polo, who served as a minor Mongol official in China from 1275 to 1292. He and others of his contemporaries were able to reach China in this period because for the brief years of the Mongol Empire, unified control was imposed on most of Eurasia and people could travel more or less safely across it.

Marco's famous journal, like all medieval tales, includes some supernatural stories, and it was dismissed by many because it speaks in such extravagant terms about the size and splendor of Yuan China. Indeed he soon became known as "Il milione," someone who told tall tales of millions of this and that. But when his confessor came to him on his deathbed and urged him to take back all his lies, Marco is said to have replied, "I have not told the half of what I saw."

Yuan China

The Mongols ran China largely through Chinese officials, aided by a few Sinified Mongols and foreigners. The Chinese bureaucratic system was retained, leaving only the military entirely in Mongol hands. For the years of Mongol rule, Chinese culture continued its development on Sung foundations, once the country had recovered from the profound devastation of the Mongol conquest. A number of new Chinese artists restored and extended the glories of Sung landscape painting, and drama and vernacular literature flourished anew. People, especially of the scholar-gentry-official group, were understandably disheartened by the political scene and turned for solace to art and literature. Mongol rule from the new capital at Peking was exploitive and often harsh. The Mongols rebuilt the Grand Canal, neglected since the fall of the Northern Sung, and extended it to feed and supply Peking, but at a heavy cost in lives and revenue.

Kubilai proved an able ruler of his new empire but concentrated on China and became almost entirely Chinese culturally. Marco Polo gives a flattering account of his sagacity, majesty, and benevolence, a portrait that was probably no more or less accurate than his more general accounts of Yuan China. But Kubilai was followed on his death in 1294 by increasingly inept figures. Smoldering Chinese hatred of their conquerors had flared into widespread revolts by the 1330s, and by 1350 Mongol control of the Yangtze valley was lost, while factions of their once united front fought one another in the north. A peasant rebel leader welded together Chinese forces, chased the remaining Mongols back into the steppes north of the Great Wall, and in 1368 announced the foundation of a new dynasty, the Ming, which was to restore Chinese pride and grandeur.

Chinese Culture and the Mongol Empire

By the late T'ang period, Chinese culture had largely acquired its present form. With the occupation and Sinification of most of the south, begun under the Han dynasty and completed under the aegis of the Mongols in the southwest, the state also assumed essentially its modern form. Tibet was more permanently incorporated by the Ch'ing (Qing or Manchu dynasty) in the eighteenth century, which also added Manchuria to the empire. By Sung times, the institutions of government and society had taken on outlines that persisted until the twentieth century. Civil administration was divided among six ministries, plus the censorate, and a military administration under ultimate civil control. At the top of the pyramid was the emperor, assisted by high officials. The empire was divided into provinces within the Great Wall, 18 of them by the seventeenth century, each under a governor and subdivided into prefectures and counties.

Paper flowed to and from the capital, transmitted along a network of paved roads and canals. Most decisions ultimately had to be made or approved by the emperor, which often created a bottleneck at the top. An equally important limitation was the small number of officials of all ranks. Probably no more than 30,000 governed an area the size of Europe and a population that had reached 100 million by Sung times. These administrators were indirectly augmented by unofficial but effective gentry leadership and management, even in the vast rural areas, which were beyond the power of the county magistrate to govern alone.

Still more important in the ordering of society was the family, which not only controlled people's lives but settled most disputes and ensured harmony by virtuous example. Government controls were thus less essential. A peasant proverb summed up the self-imposed discipline of Chinese society: "Work when the sun rises, rest when the sun sets. The emperor is far away." Dynasties rose and fell, but the fundamental order of Chinese civilization persisted.

Chinese history can be readily divided into dynastic periods and into what is called the dynastic cycle. The typical dynasty lasted about three centuries, sometimes preceded by a brief whirlwind period of empire building such as the Ch'in or the Sui. The first century of a new dynasty would be marked by political, economic, and cultural vigor, expansion, efficiency, and confidence; the second would build on or consolidate the achievements of the first; and in the third vigor and efficiency wound wane, corruption would mount, banditry and rebellion would multiply, and the dynasty would ultimately fall. A new group would come to power from among the rebels but would rarely attempt to change the system, only its management and supervision.

Chinese culture was continuous, even during the political chaos that followed the fall of the Han. By T'ang times most of the elements of contemporary Chinese society were present. Rice was the dominant food in the diet, supplemented or replaced in the more arid parts of the north by wheat noodles, which Marco Polo is said to have brought back to Italy in the thirteenth century in a form later to become spaghetti, and steamed bread or, among poorer people, millet. Food was eaten with chopsticks, a technique adopted early by Korea and Japan, while the rest of the world ate with its fingers.

Given the size and density of population and the consequent pressure on land, poultry, eggs, meat, and fish were relatively scarce. The diet consisted largely of rice or wheat with a variety of vegetables, including beans and bean products such as curd (tofu) as a source of protein. Oxen or water buffalos were needed for ploughing and were usually eaten only when they died naturally. Pigs, chickens, ducks, and fish, however, could scavenge for their own food and thus could be more easily raised.

The Chinese cuisine is justly famous, including as it does such a wide variety of foods (the Chinese have few dietary inhibitions), flavors, and sauces. Ingredients were sliced small so as to maximize and distribute their flavor and also so that they would cook very quickly over a hot fire. As the burgeoning population cut down the forests, fuel became scarce, and people were reduced to using twigs, branches, and dried grass for cooking. The universal utensil was the thin cast-iron saucer-shaped pot (*wok* in Cantonese), which heated quickly but held the heat and distributed it evenly in a technique we now call "stir frying."

The Chinese landscape was more and more converted into an artificial one of irrigated and terraced rice paddies, fish and duck ponds, and market towns where peasants sold their surplus produce or exchanged it for salt, cloth, tools, or other necessities not produced in all villages. From T'ang times, teahouses became the common centers for socializing, relaxation, gossip, and the negotiation of business or marriage contracts. Fortune tellers, scribes, booksellers, itinerant peddlers, actors, and storytellers enlivened the market towns and cities, and periodic markets with similar accompaniments were held on a smaller scale in most villages. All this made it less necessary for people to travel far from their native places, and most never went beyond the nearest market town. Beyond it they would have found for the most part only more villages and towns like those they knew, except perhaps for the provincial capital and of course the imperial capital.

In the south most goods and people in the lowlands moved by waterways, in the dry north by pack animals, carts, and human porters, which also operated in the mountainous parts of the south. The wheelbarrow and the flexible bamboo carrying pole were Chinese inventions that greatly enhanced the ability to transport heavy weights, carefully balanced as they were to enable porters to wheel or trot all day with loads far exceeding their unaided capacity. All these and many other aspects of Chinese culture remain essentially unchanged today.

Korea

Korean culture, though adopting much from China, added its own innovations and retained a strong sense of separate identity, together with a fierce determination to preserve its political independence. The Korean peninsula, set off from the mainland of Asia, is separated by mountains along its northwestern frontier adjacent to Manchuria and by the gorge of the Yalu River, which marks the boundary. The Korean people probably came originally from eastern Siberia and northern Manchuria, as their spoken language, which is unrelated to Chinese, suggests. They brought with them or evolved their own culture, which was already well formed before they were exposed to heavy Chinese influence at the time of the Han occupation in the late second century B.C.

Rice, wheat, metals, written characters, paper, printing, lacquer, porcelain, and other innovations spread to Korea after they appeared in China. As in Vietnam, literate Chinese-style culture in Korea was an elite phenomenon that rested on an already developed indigenous cultural base that remained distinctive. A Chinese-style state arose in the north around Pyongyang in the century before Han Wu-ti's conquest. On the withdrawal of the Chinese military colonies after the fall of the Han in A.D. 220 Korea regained its freedom and was thenceforward self-governing (except for the brief Mongol interlude) until the Japanese takeover in 1910, although Chinese cultural influence continued and was openly welcomed.

Three Kingdoms: Paekche, Silla, and Koguryo

Three Korean kingdoms arose after 220: Paekche in the southwest, Silla in the southeast, and Koguryo in the north, the largest and closest to China. Confucianism and Chinese forms of government, law, literature, and art spread widely throughout the peninsula, followed by Buddhism as it grew in China. But Korea's long tradition of a hereditary aristocracy in a hierarchically ordered society of privilege prevented the adoption of China's more open official system of meritocracy based on examinations. Like the Japanese, the Koreans also departed from the Chinese pattern in providing an important place for a military aristocracy.

In 669, with help from the T'ang, Silla succeeded in conquering Koguryo, after having earlier demolished Paekche. With its now united strength, Silla repelled T'ang efforts at reconquest, a remarkable feat given the power and proximity of T'ang China. As a formal Chinese vassal, Silla presided over a golden age of creativity. T'ang culture was a natural model, but in many respects Korean adaptations were at least the equal of their Chinese models. Korean ceramics, fully as accomplished as anything pro-

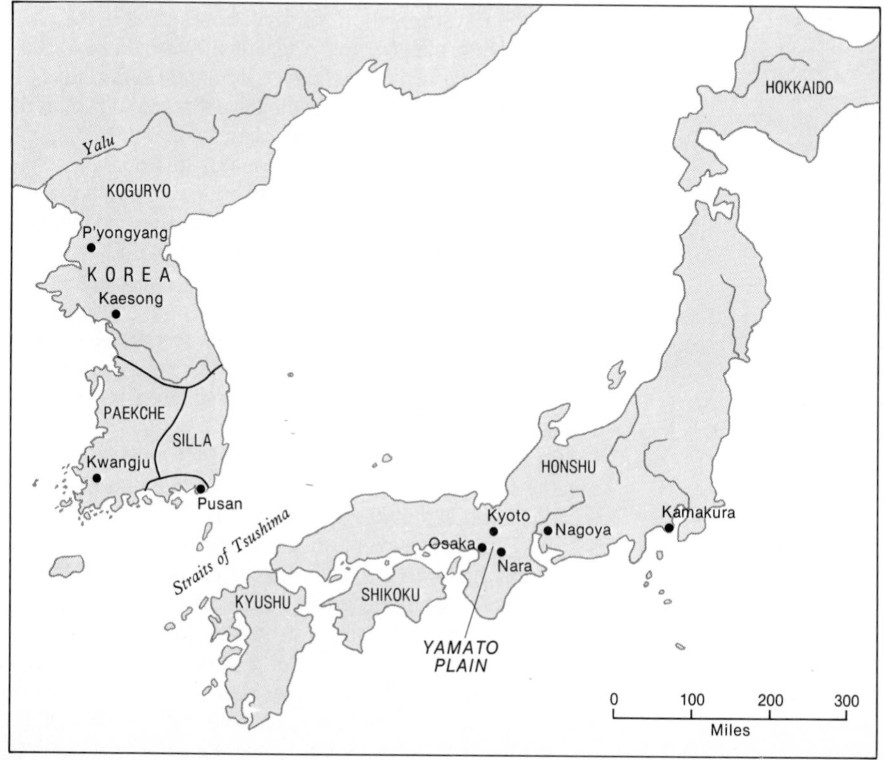

11.3 Korea and Japan, c. 500–1000

A masterpiece of Korean art in bronze, Silla period, sixth or seventh century A.D. This seated figure is Maitreya, "Buddha of the future." [National Museum of Korea, Seoul]

duced in China, had a magnificent development, particularly in pottery and fine porcelain. This included the beautiful celadon ware with its subtle milky green jade-colored glaze, whose secret formula was admired and envied by the Chinese, though it was extinguished by the Mongol conquest of the thirteenth century. Silla Korea also went beyond Chinese written characters and began a system of phonetic transcription, derived from the sound of characters but designed to reproduce spoken Korean. By the fifteenth century this had been further refined into the *han'gul* syllabary.

Silla control weakened by the tenth century. The kingdom was taken over by a usurper in 935, who named his new united state Koryo, an abbreviation of Koguryo and the origin of the name Korea. The Koryo capital at Kaesong, just north of Seoul, was built on the planned imperial model of the T'ang city of Ch'ang An and incorporated most of the Chinese system of government. Interest in Buddhism and its texts, as well as a refinement of Sung techniques, stimulated a virtual explosion of woodblock printing in the eleventh century, and magnificent celadon pieces were again produced. Koryo rule dissolved into civil war on the eve of the Mongol invasion, and Chinghis Khan easily overran the peninsula in 1218. The Mongols exacted heavy tribute and imposed an iron rule, including forcing Koreans to aid them in their later expeditions against Japan. But in the 1350s the Mongol empire collapsed, and in 1392 a new dynasty arose, the Yi, which was to preside over a united Korea until 1910.

The Yi Dynasty

Under the Yi dynasty Korea continued the adaptation of Chinese civilization to a greater extent than any of its predecessors, including the incorporation of the imperial examination system, the Confucian bureaucracy, and the division of the country into eight centrally administered provinces on the Chinese model. Although Confucian ideology spread, in practice officeholding was still dominated by hereditary aristocrats. From their capital at Seoul, Yi rulers continued to accept the formal status of a Chinese tributary state, a relationship that both parties spoke of amicably as that between "younger brother and elder brother." Buddhism declined almost completely, while Confucianism and Chinese-style painting and calligraphy flourished. A group called the *yangban*, originally landowners, acquired most of the functions and status of the Chinese gentry as an educated elite but remained a hereditary class, providing both civil and military officials, unlike the Chinese model.

Korean economic development was retarded by the country's mountainous landscape, which like that of Japan is divided into separate small basins, and by its long harsh winter, especially severe in the north. Only about one-seventh of the total land area could be cultivated, and trade and concentrated urban growth were also disadvantaged. But although most Koreans remained materially poorer than most Chinese, elite culture, technology, and the arts prospered in distinctively Korean styles, including the still superb ceramics. Korean dress, house types, diet, life-styles, marriage and inheritance customs, and the volatile,

11.4 Yi Dynasty, Korea

earthy, robust, spontaneous Korean temperament remained their own as well. Food was flavored by the peppery pickled cabbage called *kimch'i*, as it still is. Korea's indigenous cultural fabric was basic and showed through the Chinese overlay. There was thus no risk that Korea would be absorbed into Chinese culture, and Koreans remained proud of their independence and of their own sophisticated cultural tradition.

The first century or so of Yi rule was a brilliant period in Korean and East Asian history. The fifteenth century saw a new explosion of printing, now vigorously supported by a Confucian state that put a high value on texts and learning. The Koreans further perfected the art of movable metal type, which was used among other things to reproduce the libraries burned by the Mongols and the wooden plates from which those books had been made. Eight other ambitious printing projects were carried out between 1403 and 1484. This was the first extensive use of movable type anywhere in the world. The technique originated in eleventh-century Sung China and was further developed in Korea a century or so later. In contrast, movable type printing began in Europe only in the mid-fifteenth century.

The same century in Korea also saw important new developments in mathematics and in the manufacture of astronomical instruments. More closely related to printing was the perfection of the *han'gul* alphabet and syllabary, not only to write Korean but to give the Korean pronunciation of Chinese characters as well. Traditional characters continued to be used for official documents and elite literature, but the development and popularity of *han'gul* was an affirmation of Korea's proud and confident distinctiveness.

The vigor of the Yi order was slowly weakened by bureaucratic factionalism, which the throne never really overcame. No strong rulers emerged after the early sixteenth century, and toward its end a divided and enfeebled Korea had to face the invasion of the Japanese warlord Hideyoshi between 1592 and 1598. His army overran and ravaged the country, until with aid from China the invaders were driven back almost to the coast and there stalemated. The gifted Korean admiral Yi Sun-sin then repeatedly defeated Japanese naval detachments and disrupted their supply lines with his ingenious "turtle ships." These vessels, covered with overlapping plates of iron and copper and armed fore and aft with beak-shaped metal prows that could ram and sink any ship, were the first armored warships. They were powered by rowers protected by the outer "turtle shell." The invasion was abandoned when Hideyoshi died in 1598, but Korea never fully recovered from its devastation.

The Yi dynasty continued, plagued by perennial factional fighting, although it still supported learning, the arts, and major new printing projects. Considerable economic growth resulted from improved agriculture and a rising commercial sector, and population probably doubled between 1600 and 1800. Merchants began to buy their way to *yangban* (gentry) status, as did prosperous farmers. Korea thus followed the path of Sung, Ming, and Manchu China and of Tokugawa Japan. But its political and administrative health was poor, ultimately inviting Japanese intervention after 1894.

Japan

Composed of four main islands off the southern tip of Korea (see Map 11.3), Japan had been protected by its insularity from turmoil on the Asian mainland and to a degree also isolated from its development. The Straits of Tsushima between Korea and Japan are approximately 120 miles wide, and although Japan has been periodically involved with the mainland, the connection has never been as close as between China and other areas of East Asia or between Britain and Europe. Japan has had the advantage of a clearly separate identity and as a result of its insularity has been able to make its own choices at most periods about what it wanted to adopt from abroad. Japan too is mainly mountainous, and settlement has remained heavily concentrated on the narrow coastal plain between Tokyo and Osaka, an area roughly equivalent to the coastal corridor between Boston and Washington, D.C. Overall, Japan is about the size of California. Mountains also retarded Japanese economic development and political unification. As in Korea, only a little over a seventh of the country is cultivated even now, although the climate, conditioned by the surrounding sea, is far milder and better watered. Coastal sea routes have also helped to link settled areas and to carry trade.

Early Culture and Development

The Japanese spoken language, unrelated to Chinese but in the same linguistic group as Korean, suggests that they too came originally from the Asian mainland north of China via the sea passage from Korea, although other migrants and cultural influences may have come into Japan from the tropical Pacific. The migrants slowly defeated, displaced, or absorbed the islands' original inhabitants, including a physically very different group called the Ainu, who now live as a tiny and dwindling minority on reservations on the northernmost island of Hokkaido. Early Japanese history is cloudy, in part because written records do not begin until the eighth century A.D., after Japan had adopted the Chinese art of writing from Korea. We have no firm dates before that time and can only guess when the people we now call Japanese arrived or when they emerged as a separate culture, but it was probably sometime between the second century B.C. and the second century A.D. Earlier preliterate and premetallic cultures had developed in Japan, producing pottery perhaps as early as in any part of Asia. Bronze tools and weapons from China entered via Korea about the first century B.C., and implements made of iron, a technology also imported from Korea, were being produced by around A.D. 200.

It seems clear that Korea played an important role in Japan until the fifth century A.D. By the time of the first Japanese records in the eighth century, a third of the nobility claimed Korean or Chinese descent, and clearly such lineage was perceived as a mark of superiority. Close interaction with Korea continued, with large numbers of Korean artisans, metallurgists, and technologists living in Japan as well as Korean nobles and perhaps even rulers. There were also invasions and raids in both directions, until by about 400 such violent interactions faded and the Japanese continued to move northward from the southernmost island of Kyushu, closest to Korea, onto the main island of Honshu. There they established a central core on the Yamato plain in the Nara-Kyoto-Osaka area, where it was to remain for approximately the next 1,000 years. The imperial capital, however, was not moved northeast to Tokyo until 1868, and the frontier with the Ainu lay just north of Kyoto for some centuries.

The Nara Period

Chinese cultural infusions continued from Korea, including, sometime before 500, Chinese written characters and an increasing knowledge of Chinese culture and of Buddhism. By the end of the sixth century and increasingly in

Traditional Japanese stone garden, Ryoanji Temple, Kyoto. Also originally from T'ang China, this orderly and peaceful form of landscaping became characteristically Japanese and is still widely practiced. [Jack Deutsch, New York]

the seventh, missions were dispatched to China to observe and to bring back to Japan as much of Chinese civilization as possible. In the mid-seventh century a sweeping series of reform measures called the *Taika* ("Great Reform") began the process of transforming Japan and the Japanese imperial administration into a facsimile of China's. By 710 the first permanent capital was inaugurated at Nara, a smaller-scaled copy of Ch'ang An, which presided over a modified Chinese-style government.

The ensuing century (until 794) is known as the Nara period, during which the transplantation of Chinese civilization continued, helped by successive Japanese missions to China. Currency and coins on the Chinese model were introduced. The Chinese habit of recording everything they observed was transmitted too, and important accounts of T'ang China come from Japanese sources of this period, as well as the first official histories of Japan. Buddhism spread, but Confucianism also entered from China and became important for the upper classes. As Taoism was retained in China, the original animistic and naturalistic Japanese religion of Shinto remained, in part no doubt as an assertion of Japanese distinctiveness but also because of its close connection with the imperial family. Beautiful wood-crafted Shinto shrines remain in "natural" areas even in contemporary Japan.

Artistic styles, gardens, court and official clothing, and sophisticated tastes all strove to replicate the Chinese model, and although they slowly diverged from that standard, Japanese high culture still retains the unmistakable marks of its seventh- and eighth-century Chinese origins. Korean and Chinese artists, artisans, and technicians remained important in the Nara period as teachers and implementers of cultural reform. But Japan was a very different place, and the cultural transplant was never complete, nor did it ever penetrate very deeply into the mass of the people, most of whom remained peasants until the late nineteenth century. Unlike Chinese society, but as in Korea, descent and inherited status continued to be important, and society as a whole remained more tightly organized and more hierarchically controlled. Feudal-style lords and hereditary nobles remained the chief wielders of power. Japan tried the Chinese examination system, but, as in Korea, hereditary aristocrats undercut it by reserving most official positions for themselves. The Japanese emperor, considered divine and hence the bearer of a sacred mandate, was above politics or even administration.

The Heian Era

In 794 a vigorous young emperor, Kammu, moved the capital to Kyoto (then called Heian), in part to break away from the growing influence of Buddhist institutions in Nara. With the support of the powerful Fujiwara family, he and his successors began to modify or discard some aspects of the Chinese model so enthusiastically adopted earlier. Art and architecture increased their characteristically Japanese concern for textures and the use of natural materials. T'ang China was in turmoil, and Japanese missions stopped going there, while new interest arose in indigenous cultural patterns. Chinese written characters were increasingly supplemented and later somewhat displaced by a phonetic system known as *kana*. Most of its symbols combined a consonant and a vowel and made it possible to transcribe spoken Japanese accurately, as Chinese characters could not do. Chinese characters remained important among the educated elite and for official use, but the *kana* system was understandably preferred for most purposes, including popular literature.

The effort to follow Chinese patterns of government was largely given up, and power came increasingly into the hands of the Fujiwara clan and its appointees or hereditary officeholders. Because the new capital was called Heian, the centuries from 794 to 1185 are called the Heian era. The period is famous for its aristocratic and court culture, where noble gentlemen and ladies devoted their lives to aesthetic refinement. The best-known Heian work is Lady Murasaki's *Tale of Genji*, considered the world's first psychological novel.

LADY MURASAKI AND HEIAN COURT LITERATURE

Lady Murasaki's birth date is not known precisely, though it was probably around A.D. 978, and we are also not sure of the date of her death, probably around 1015. We do not even know her real name, since in Heian Japan it was considered improper to record the personal names of aristocratic women outside of the imperial family. It is known that she came from a junior branch of the great Fujiwara clan and that her father was a provincial governor. The name Murasaki may derive from that of a major figure in her novel, *The Tale of Genji*, or from its meaning of "purple," a pun on the *Fuji* of Fujiwara, which means "wisteria." She was far from being alone as a woman author; mid–Heian period literature is dominated by women, who, particularly at court, were apparently less conventional than men. The absence of harems and extensive concubinage in Japan left women freer to express their talents in other ways.

Lady Murasaki's journal is our only source of information about her life. It records that she was a precocious child and became literate early:

> **My father was anxious to make a good Chinese scholar of [my brother], and often came to hear him read his lessons. . . . So quick was I at picking up the language that I was soon able to prompt my brother. . . . After this I was careful to conceal the fact that I could write a single Chinese character.[2]**

But she acquired a wide knowledge of both Chinese and Japanese works and also became a talented calligrapher, painter, and musician, attainments considered suitable for an aristocratic girl. At about age 21 she was married to a much older man, a distant Fujiwara cousin, and bore a daughter. The next year her husband died, and in her grief she considered becoming a Buddhist nun but turned instead to reflection on the problem of human happiness, especially for women. Around that time, approximately the year 1001, she began work on her masterpiece, *The Tale of Genji*, which was probably nearly finished when, some six years later, she became a lady-in-waiting at the imperial court.

Her journal describes the refined and colorful life at court, as well as its less glamorous rivalries and intrigues. Both are the subject of her great novel, which combines a romantic as well as psychological approach with realistic detail and subtle insight into human behavior. *Genji* is still praised as the masterpiece of Japanese literature. Her people are real, despite the highly mannered world in which they lived, and through her journal we also have a picture of her as an extraordinarily alive, imaginative, and compelling person. A collection of her poems has also survived, which further mark her as an accomplished stylist.

The Tale of Genji deals with the life of a prince and his seemingly endless affairs with various court ladies. It includes careful attention to manners, dress, and court politics—perhaps not the most rewarding of subjects, but in the hands of Lady Murasaki they become not mere details but a means of revealing character. Although the hero is idealized, this is far more than a conventional romantic tale, and the portrayal of Genji as he grows older is a subtle one. Toward the end of her journal, Lady Murasaki gives us a candid glimpse of herself: People think, she wrote, that "I am very vain, reserved, unsociable . . . wrapped up in the study of ancient stories, living in a poetical world all my own. . . . But when they get to know me, they find that I am kind and gentle."[3] Perhaps she was all these things. Bold as she was in her writings, when describing herself Lady Murasaki still felt compelled to present her character in terms of the traditional "feminine" virtues.

Political Disorder and the Rise of Feudalism

Heian court culture was delightful no doubt, but may suggest a lack of adequate Fujiwara concern with the real world of politics. Elite life at the capital was deeply involved with elegance, refinement, and aesthetic sensitivity but gave little thought to increasingly pressing economic problems, the poverty of most Japanese, or a growing political disorder. In the end Fujiwara power was undermined and finally destroyed by new families who used their private armies to become de facto rulers over lands they had originally guarded for noble families. Some of these armies, and the new group of warriors (*samurai*) with their pronounced military ethic, had developed out of frontier wars as Japanese settlement spread slowly northeastward beyond the Yamato area after the ninth century. Armed followers of Buddhist temples increasingly took part in political struggles. Armies began to interfere in factional conflicts at court or were called in by different factions, including clans within the Fujiwara family. By the twelfth century, armies had become the real powers.

The Kamakura Period

In 1185 one of the warrior lineages, the Minamoto clan, set up a rival capital in its then frontier base at Kamakura (now a southern suburb of Tokyo). The refined culture and court-based politics of Heian was now supplemented by a less cultivated but far more politically effective system based on a combination of new bureaucratic methods, military power, and the security offered by the samurai. The samurai leaders were hereditary aristocrats who became both literate and educated and were more administrators than fighting men. Through them and other educated aristocrats Heian culture spread and in time influenced even the warrior clans. However, the rise of noble families and the samurai armies under their control led to the emergence of Japanese feudalism, a phenomenon parallel to that of medieval Europe but different from the imperial civil bureaucracy and meritocracy of China.

The emperor became increasingly a figurehead during this period, and real power rested with whoever could grasp and hold it—first the Fujiwara and then the Minamoto and other military clans. The Kamakura-based administration presided over a feudal hierarchy of warriors and nobles who were bound in fealty assured by oaths, financial and service obligations, and promises of military support. In return, the Kamakura ruler granted his vassal-lords hereditary rights to their lands. As in medieval Europe, this was a symptom of limited central state power, an arrangement of mutual convenience; but it was also inherently unstable, as ambitious or upstart vassals sought to improve their positions or rebel against the central authority. Political power was seldom unified under any single control for long. Each vassal maintained both his own group of samurai and his army, but the loyalty of these forces could not always be ensured, whether to local lords or to the center. The patterns that emerged in the Kamakura shogunate (1185–1333) were to dominate Japan until the nineteenth century.

In 1268 the Mongol emperor Kubilai Khan demanded the submission of the Japanese, and when they refused, the Mongols forced the recently conquered Koreans to build and man a fleet for the invasion of Japan, which arrived in 1274. Soon after the first landings a great storm wrecked many of their ships and forced their withdrawal. The Japanese executed subsequent Mongol envoys, and in 1281 a far larger expedition manned by both subject Koreans and Chinese arrived, only to be swept away by an even greater storm. This storm was typical of the late summer typhoons along the coasts of East Asia, though the Japanese can perhaps be forgiven for attributing their double deliverance to a "divine wind," or *kamikaze*. However, the costs of meeting the terrible Mongol threat and of the preparation that went on against an expected third expedition drained Kamakura resources and diverted large numbers of people from productive occupations. With the weakening of Kamakura power, political divisions and open revolts multiplied. In 1333 an unusually active emperor, Go-Daigo, whom the dominant faction at Kamakura had tried to depose, gathered support and attracted dissidents from the crumbling Kamakura structure. One of his commanders overran Kamakura and ended its power. But another of his supporters turned against him, put a different member of the imperial line on the throne, and had himself declared shogun, the real power holder, although officially he remained the emperor's chief military commander.

The Ashikaga Shogunate

The Ashikaga shoguns, who established themselves in Kyoto from 1339, were never able to build effective central control. A rival faction supporting another member of the imperial family remained in power in southwestern Honshu and could not be dislodged, while Kyushu continued under the control of one or more other groups. Civil war became endemic, and as one consequence feudal lords beyond the reach of central control supported highly profitable piracy along the coasts of China. This caused chronic trouble between the Ashikaga and the Ming dynasty. The government tried to suppress piracy, but its power to do so was inadequate. For a time the Ming felt obliged to abandon large stretches of their own coast and pull settlements back to more easily protected sites up rivers and estuaries. From the mid-fifteenth century, political chaos in Japan was endemic, despite the country's small size and the even smaller dimensions of its settled areas. By 1467 effective Ashikaga rule was ended and much of Kyoto had been destroyed, although the emasculated shogunate continued in name. Rival Buddhist sects and their monasteries also fought bloody wars against each other with armed monks as troops. Peasant revolts and bitter conflicts among petty feudal lords continued to ravage the countryside.

Yet despite the growing political disorder, especially after 1450, the last century of the Ashikaga shogunate saw a remarkable flowering of culture. In part this was the result of a conscious fusion of aristocratic Heian traditions with those of the newer samurai culture. Millions also found solace in Buddhist sects, including Shin, Nichiren, and Zen, originally Chinese but adapted to Japanese tastes and styles. These popular and egalitarian or, in the case of Zen, contemplative and mystical approaches concentrated on salvation, self-cultivation, and the apprehension of eternal truths rather than on the turmoil of political life. The discipline of Zen appealed to the warrior class but also stressed unity with nature, a traditional Japanese interest. Less detached but clearly related to a turning away from worldly strife were the further blossoming of temple and palace architecture, consciously and ingeniously integrated with their peaceful natural settings, of landscape gardening, and of nature painting, much of it in the Southern Sung mode. The literature of the period meanwhile commented on the shifting fortunes of politics and the foibles of those grasping for power or gloried in the simple beauty of nature and the joys of untroubled rural life. The shogunate patronized Zen as it supported art and literature, continuing the Heian tradition.

Even more specifically Japanese was the Ashikaga evolution of the tea ceremony as a graceful, soothing, contemplative, and aesthetic ritual. Although its origins too were in T'ang China, it became and remains a distinctively Japanese assertion of cultural identity and personal serenity. Delicate teahouses set in a naturally landscaped garden in unobtrusive elegance provided havens of tranquillity and aesthetic enjoyment for samurai and other members of the elite, who took additional pleasure from the exquisite beauty of the teacups. It was a striking and thoroughly Japanese counterpart to the bloody and often ruthless life of the times.

Finally, the Ashikaga era saw the evolution of traditional dances into a stylized and distinctively Japanese form, the *Noh* drama. This subtle, Zen-inspired blending of dance, gesture, speech, and costume evolved into a unique theatrical style capable of communicating rich meaning and emotion. Every step and every movement are precisely measured to achieve a state of controlled tension, a slow-moving, concentrated experience of understatement and disciplined expression.

The production of artisans, too—including, appropriately, the making of fine swords—developed still further. The arrival of the Portuguese early in the sixteenth century stimulated trade, already growing for some time, as the Europeans' more powerful vessels supplanted those of local pirates.

The Ashikaga shogunate dissolved completely into still more chaotic civil war in the 1570s, and Japan was torn by rival clans and their armies until the end of the century. In 1568 a minor but able and determined feudal lord, Oda Nobunaga (1534–1582), won control of Kyoto. He broke the military power of the major Buddhist monasteries and their fortified strongholds in the capital region, including the great fortress of the Shin sect at Osaka. As a counterweight against Buddhism, Nobunaga encouraged Portuguese and other Jesuit missionaries, but his tactics against opponents were ruthless, including the burning alive of captives and the slaughter of noncombatants.

Troubled Times in Japan

Political conflicts in Ashikaga Japan were echoed in literature but did not prevent continued cultural growth. This period saw the development of the haiku poetic form, evolved from an originally Chinese model but becoming in time a distinctively Japanese mode, still much used. Here are some samples, spanning roughly a century but all reflecting troubled times.

In the hills the cries of deer,
In the fields the chirping insects.
In everything
What sadness is apparent
This autumn evening.

Nijo Toshimoto (1320–1398)

The clouds still possess
Some semblance of order:
They bring the world rain.

Shinkei (1407–1475)

To live in the world
Is sad enough without this rain
Pounding on my shelter.

Sogi, a pupil of Shinkei (1421–1502)

Source: J. W. Hall, ed., *Japan in the Muromachi* (Berkeley: University of California Press, 1977), pp. 254, 257.

When Nobunaga was murdered by one of his own commanders in 1582, his chief general, Toyotomi Hideyoshi (1536–1598), seized power and by the early 1590s controlled most of Honshu, Kyushu, and Shikoku, thus unifying most of Japan for the first time. A peasant by birth, Hideyoshi tried to disarm all nonsamurai to ensure that commoners were kept down and unable to challenge his authority. He nationalized and centralized the taxation system and further separated warriors from cultivators. Hideyoshi seems to have succumbed to megalomania, as evidenced by his grandiose plan for the conquest of China, for which he carried out an invasion of Korea as a first step in 1592. The story of that misadventure has already been told. In the chaos following Hideyoshi's death in 1598, Tokugawa Ieyasu (1542–1616), originally a vassal of Nobunaga, emerged victorious in 1600 to found the far more effective and lasting order of the Tokugawa shogunate, which was to rule Japan under a centralized feudal administration until 1868.

This chapter has summarized the renaissance of Chinese civilization after the time of troubles following the fall of the Han dynasty in A.D. *220 and the golden ages of the T'ang and the Sung until those impressive developments were cut off by the Mongol conquest late in the thirteenth century. Despite Mongol brutality, Chinese civilization continued under alien domination, and the hated invaders were eventually thrown off. Korean culture had arisen before the Han conquest and retained its distinctiveness. It borrowed heavily from Chinese civilization at the elite level while creating innovations in ceramics and printing by movable type, and shaping to the Korean tradition institutions adopted from*

China. Korea was first unified by the Silla dynasty from 669 to 995 and continued under the Koryo dynasty until it was destroyed by the Mongol invasion in 1218. Yi dynasty Korea from 1392 to 1910 saw a new burst of cultural and technological growth, although its political vigor was slowly eroded by factionalism.

Japanese civilization, having been largely created on the Chinese model and with Korean help, in time asserted its own separate cultural identity and produced a graceful elite culture that coexisted with rural poverty and chronic political division and conflict. Japanese feudalism and the role of the samurai evolved after the Heian period (794–1185) under the Kamakura and Ashikaga shogunates (1185–1568), but such methods were unable to unify the country or to end endemic civil war until the emergence of the Tokugawa clan in 1600. Despite political turmoil, Japan also produced great art, literature, and architecture and a refined culture for the upper classes. Chinese influence on the major East Asian societies was thus limited. Koreans and Japanese made what they took from China their own and went on to modify or develop it further in distinctive ways while retaining and building on their own indigenous culture.

Notes

1. R. H. Tawney, *The Agrarian Problem in the Sixteenth Century* (London: Longman, Green, 1912), p. 177.
2. All quotations from Lady Murasaki's journal are taken from Arthur Waley's Introduction to his translation of *The Tale of Genji* (New York: Doubleday, 1955), pp. ix, xxi.
3. Ibid., p. xxi.

Suggestions for Further Reading

China

Carter, T. F., and Goodrich, L. C. *The Invention of Printing in China and Its Spread Westward*. New York: Ronald Press, 1955.

Chaffee, J. W. *The Thorny Gates of Learning: A Social History of Examinations in Sung China*. Cambridge: Cambridge University Press, 1987.

Dawson, R. S. *Imperial China*. London: Oxford University Press, 1972.

De Crespigny, R. *Under the Brilliant Emperor: Imperial Authority in T'ang China*. Canberra: Australian National University Press, 1985.

Fitzgerald, C. P. *China: A Short Cultural History*. New York: Praeger, 1961.

Gernet, J. *Daily Life in China on the Eve of the Mongol Invasion*, trans. H. M. Wright. London: Macmillan, 1962.

Hymes, R. *Statesmen and Gentlemen: Elites of the Southern Sung*. New York: Cambridge University Press, 1986.

Lo, W. W. *An Introduction to the Civil Service of Sung China*. Honolulu: University Press of Hawaii, 1987.

Meskill, J. *An Introduction to Chinese Civilization*. Boston: Heath, 1973.

Olschki, L. *Marco Polo's Asia*. Berkeley: University of California Press, 1960.

Philip, E. D. *The Mongols*. New York: Scribner, 1969.

Schafer, E. *The Golden Peaches of Samarkand: A Study of T'ang Exotics*. Berkeley: University of California Press, 1963.

Spuler, B. *History of the Mongols*. Berkeley: University of California Press, 1972.

Waley, A. *The Poetry and Career of Li Po*. London: Allen & Unwin, 1960.

Korea

Henthorn, G. *History of Korea*. Glencoe, Ill.: Free Press, 1971.

Lee, K.-B. *A New History of Korea*, trans. E. Wagner. Cambridge: Harvard University Press, 1985.

Japan

Dunn, C. J. *Everyday Life in Traditional Japan*. London: Batsford, 1969.

Duus, P. *Feudalism in Japan*. New York: Knopf, 1969.

Hall, J. W., ed. *Japan Before Tokugawa*. Princeton, N.J.: Princeton University Press, 1986.

Hane, M. *Japan*. New York: Scribner, 1972.

Keene, D. *No: The Classical Theatre of Japan*. Stanford, Calif.: Stanford University Press, 1966.

Mass, J. P. *Warrior Government in Early Medieval Japan*. New Haven, Conn.: Yale University Press, 1974.

Morris, I. *The World of the Shining Prince*. Oxford: Oxford University Press, 1964.

Reischauer, E. O. *Japan: The Story of a Nation*. London: Duckworth, 1970.

Rossabi, M. *Kubilai Khan: His Life and Times*. Berkeley: University of California Press, 1987.

Sansom, G. B. *A History of Japan*. Stanford, Calif.: Stanford University Press, 1963.

———. *Japan: A Short Cultural History*. New York: Appleton-Century-Crofts, 1962.

Tiedemann, A. E., ed. *An Introduction to Japanese Civilization*. New York: Columbia University Press, 1974.

Totman, C. *Japan Before Perry: A Short History*. Berkeley: University of California Press, 1981.

Weinstein, S. *Buddhism Under the T'ang*. New York: Cambridge University Press, 1988.

CHAPTER · 12

The Rise of Europe

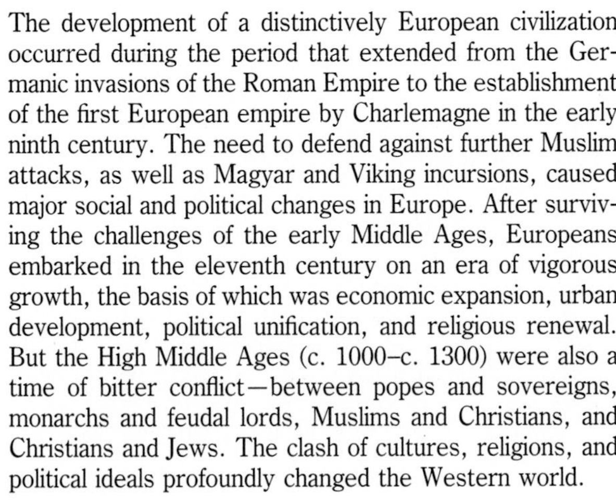

The development of a distinctively European civilization occurred during the period that extended from the Germanic invasions of the Roman Empire to the establishment of the first European empire by Charlemagne in the early ninth century. The need to defend against further Muslim attacks, as well as Magyar and Viking incursions, caused major social and political changes in Europe. After surviving the challenges of the early Middle Ages, Europeans embarked in the eleventh century on an era of vigorous growth, the basis of which was economic expansion, urban development, political unification, and religious renewal. But the High Middle Ages (c. 1000–c. 1300) were also a time of bitter conflict—between popes and sovereigns, monarchs and feudal lords, Muslims and Christians, and Christians and Jews. The clash of cultures, religions, and political ideals profoundly changed the Western world.

The Byzantine emperor Alexius Comnenus is best known for his appeal to the West for help in fighting the Turks, thus inaugurating the crusades. [Vatican Library, Rome]

Migration and Transformation

Generally the invasions that transformed Europe between the fifth and ninth centuries pitted nomads against the inhabitants of settled communities and were thus a clash of distinctive lifestyles and cultures. Much of Europe and Asia was threatened by the nomads; only remote southern China and southern India eluded their grasp. The impact of the incursions was greatest in the West, partly because the nomads tended to migrate westward, where the land was more fertile and water was more plentiful, and partly because the more advanced cultures of China and India resisted transformation.

The eastern Roman Empire, with its well-defended capital at Constantinople, its thriving economy, and its strong navy, survived the invasions, but by the end of the fifth century its western counterpart was gone, its lands fallen into the hands of Germanic rulers: the Visigoths in southern Gaul and Spain; the Ostrogoths in Italy; the Franks in northern Gaul; the Angles, Saxons, and Jutes in England; the Burgundians in the Rhône Valley; and the Vandals in North Africa and the western Mediterranean.

Unlike the Romans whom they conquered, the Germans were at first organized in social units, as tribes based on kinship rather than a state founded on political rights and obligations. Whereas Roman laws were written, those of the Germans were unwritten and grounded in custom. German families were responsible for the conduct of the members of their household and thus played a crucial role in upholding the laws. The Germans elected their kings or tribal leaders as well as the chiefs who led the warriors into battle. In return for serving those chiefs, the warriors received weapons, subsistence, and a share of any spoils.

The Germans were superstitious people who feared chopping down trees because they were sacred or building bridges lest they anger river spirits. As nomads, their livelihood revolved around cattle raising, but as they settled on their new lands, they turned to farming, raising grain, beans, peas, and other vegetables. Over time the Germans assimilated some aspects of classical culture, including Roman language, law, and principles of government, thus creating a distinctively European society. The fusion of Germanic and classical elements was eased by the fact that the Visigoths, Ostrogoths, and Vandals had been introduced to Christianity before they migrated into Europe. They were, however, disciples of Arian Christianity, and it was not until about 500 that the Nicene Christianity of the Latin church began to make headway among the Germans following the conversion of Clovis, king of the Franks (481–511). With the support of the Gallo-Roman population, which was loyal to Nicene Christianity, Clovis expanded the Frankish kingdom until it extended from the Pyrenees to the Rhine and beyond.

The Franks

The dynasty Clovis founded, called the Merovingian in honor of a legendary ancestor, was undermined by the physical weakness of his successors. With kings too young to rule, authority was exercised by aristocratic mayors of the palace. For much of the sixth and seventh centuries the kingdom was plagued by civil war and conflicting loyalties. Fortunately for the Franks, unity had been restored by the early eighth century, when western Europe was threatened by new invaders, the Islamic Moors from North Africa. By 711 the Iberian peninsula was theirs. Turning next to Gaul, the Moors were finally rebuffed by the Frankish mayor of the palace, Charles Martel ("the Hammer"), near Tours in 732. The battle was less significant for the Muslims, who in crossing the Pyrenees had overextended themselves, than for the Franks, whose military prowess attracted papal attention.

In 741 Charles' son and successor, Pepin the Short (741–768), deposed the Merovingian monarch and claimed the Frankish throne as his own. After the fact, he obtained papal approval for his action to make his usurpation seem legitimate. He repaid the debt in 752 by defending Rome from Lombard aggression and in addition granted certain Italian lands to the papacy. By this "donation" Pepin laid the foundation for a papal state in central Italy.

Charlemagne

The dynasty founded by Pepin became known as the Carolingian (from *Carolus*, Latin for Charles). Its greatest ruler was Pepin's son Charlemagne ("Charles the Great," 768–814). An extraordinary ruler, this warrior-king established an empire larger than any in Europe between that of Rome in the third century and that of Napoleon in the nineteenth. He crushed the Lombards and claimed their crown for himself when they tried to regain the land Pepin had given to the papacy. Against the Moors his gains were modest but strategic, consisting of a *march*, or frontier district, on the southern slopes of the Pyrenees. Repeated campaigns against the Saxons gave him control of much of what is now northern Germany, and in the southeast he overran Bavaria and then pushed back the nomadic Avars, from whom he seized the tribute they had exacted from the Byzantines. The Abbasid caliph in Baghdad sent him gifts that included spices, monkeys, and an elephant.

Despite his expanding empire, Charlemagne had no capital to rival Baghdad or Constantinople, so he determined to create a "second Rome" at Aachen (Aix-la-Chapelle) in the heart of his kingdom. Its layout and principal buildings were inspired by Rome, its royal chapel by the Byzantine church of San Vitale in Ravenna. The new capital became the center of a cultural renaissance Charlemagne sponsored not only to enhance the reputation of

12.1 The Empire of Charlemagne

his realm but also to improve the quality of the clergy. To direct his palace school, Charlemagne recruited one of the foremost scholars of the age, Alcuin (c. 735–804), from Anglo-Saxon England. Charlemagne chose well, for Alcuin employed a curriculum inspired by Classical Rome and refined by European writers that became the model for education throughout medieval Europe. The seven liberal arts were divided into the *trivium*, comprising grammar, rhetoric, and logic, and the *quadrivium*, consisting of arithmetic, geometry, music, and astronomy. Other scholars were lured to Aachen, and Charlemagne acquired manuscripts of legal and religious works for his scribes to copy and distribute to the monasteries of the realm. His scholars issued new editions of learned works and even developed a new, more readable script, called the Carolingian minuscule, from which modern scripts are derived. The manuscripts produced by these writers were discovered by fifteenth-century scholars and thus influenced that later, more famous renaissance.

Charlemagne's apparent interest in being the equal of the Byzantine emperor culminated on Christmas Day in 800, against a background of political intrigue. Three years earlier the emperor's mother, Irene, had blinded her son in order to rule herself. Charlemagne and Pope Leo III (795–816) seem to have regarded the Byzantine throne as vacant on the basis of Irene's sex. Some thought was apparently given to a marriage between Irene and Charlemagne, though nothing came of it. Then, in 799, the pope was kidnapped by political enemies; after he escaped, he sought Charlemagne's help to restore his control in Rome. Thus it was that the Frankish sovereign was in Rome on December 25, 800, when, following mass, Leo crowned him emperor of the Romans. The coronation strained relations with Constantinople, which claimed the imperial title solely for its own ruler. Not until 813 did both parties agree that Charles would be recognized as emperor of the Franks and the Byzantine sovereign as emperor of the Romans. For the West, the semantics were of little import, for the real significance of the Christmas coronation was the revival of the imperial tradition in the West and the question of ultimate authority raised by the way in which the crown was bestowed—from the pope to the emperor.

Disintegration and Invasion

Had Charlemagne adhered to the Byzantine tradition, he would have bequeathed his empire to his eldest son. Instead, following the Frankish custom, he intended to divide his realm among his sons. Only one, however, survived him. Hoping to preserve most of the empire intact, Louis (814–840), Charlemagne's successor, designated his eldest son heir to the imperial title and promised his other two sons royal titles and the territories of Aquitaine and Bavaria. Unsatisfied with this and egged on by their stepmother, the younger sons revolted against their father. By the time peace was agreed on in the Treaty of Verdun (843), Louis was dead and the empire was irrevocably fragmented. Between the western and eastern kingdoms, out of which eventually emerged France and Germany, was a middle kingdom that retained the imperial title and extended from the modern Netherlands into Italy. The middle kingdom was divided into three realms in 855.

As the Frankish states struggled to survive, new waves of invaders struck Europe. From North Africa, Arab raiders, emboldened by improved naval power, began attacking the islands of the Mediterranean and even southern France, Italy, and the great Alpine passes in what is now Switzerland. The revived militance stemmed from newly independent Muslim states in Egypt, Tunisia, and Spain following the decline of the Baghdad caliphate. Before the ninth century was over, the Mediterranean was virtually a Muslim lake.

Byzantine miscalculation was responsible for the invasion of eastern Europe by the Magyars, a nomadic people from central Asia. In 896 the Byzantines encouraged the Magyars to attack the troublesome Bulgars, but the latter outwitted the Byzantines by persuading the Pechenegs, Turkic nomads from the area around the Volga River, to attack the Magyars. Instead of fighting the Bulgars, the Magyars moved west, invading Germany, France, and Italy and plundering virtually at will. Not until 955 were they defeated by the German army of Otto I, but they retained control of the great Hungarian plain. There they gradually settled down, established their own kingdom, and converted to Christianity.

A third group of invaders, the Norsemen or Vikings, came from Scandinavia, not on horseback like the Asian nomads but in swift, mobile ships. As early as 793, Viking raiders had destroyed the monastery at Lindisfarne, which had been instrumental in converting northern England to Christianity. In the century that followed, the Vikings struck freely, sacking the coastal regions of Europe and sailing up rivers to reach such cities as Paris and Hamburg. They even plundered the Muslim city of Seville in Spain and Italian towns reached by ships that sailed into the Mediterranean. Vikings struck out across the Atlantic to Iceland and Greenland, both of which they settled, and North America. The reasons for this activity varied: some Vikings were clearly in search of land for new settlements, but others apparently regarded the raids as an appropriate prelude to a settled life or as a means to establish new trade routes. Norsemen from Sweden, in fact, used the rivers of Russia to make contact with the Byzantines and the Persians.

The Vikings established settlements at Kiev in Russia, on the coast of Ireland, in northeastern England, and along the lower Seine River in northwestern France, a region later called Normandy. In the eleventh century descendants from that area seized control of southern Italy and Sicily, and in 1066 William, duke of Normandy, conquered England. As the Normans settled, they embraced Christianity and European culture.

Feudal Society

The breakup of the Carolingian empire and the impact of the various invasions caused changes in European lifestyles and governments. As royal authority ebbed, landowners were forced to turn elsewhere for protection, thereby providing the nobility with the opportunity to increase its power. The nobles ruled their districts with miniature governments of their own, dispensing justice, collecting fees, raising troops, and sometimes minting money. The heart of this way of governing was the personal bond: whereas in modern society we owe allegiance to a state, in the early medieval world allegiance was rendered to a person, and that person was in turn bound to fulfill his or her part of the contractual arrangement.

Lords and Vassals: The Feudal Aristocracy

In the Merovingian age free landowners seeking protection offered their lands to more powerful men and agreed to serve them. The former were known as vassals. In return for their service, they were allowed to live in the lord's household or were given money or the use of land, called fiefs. Normally the most important service was mil-

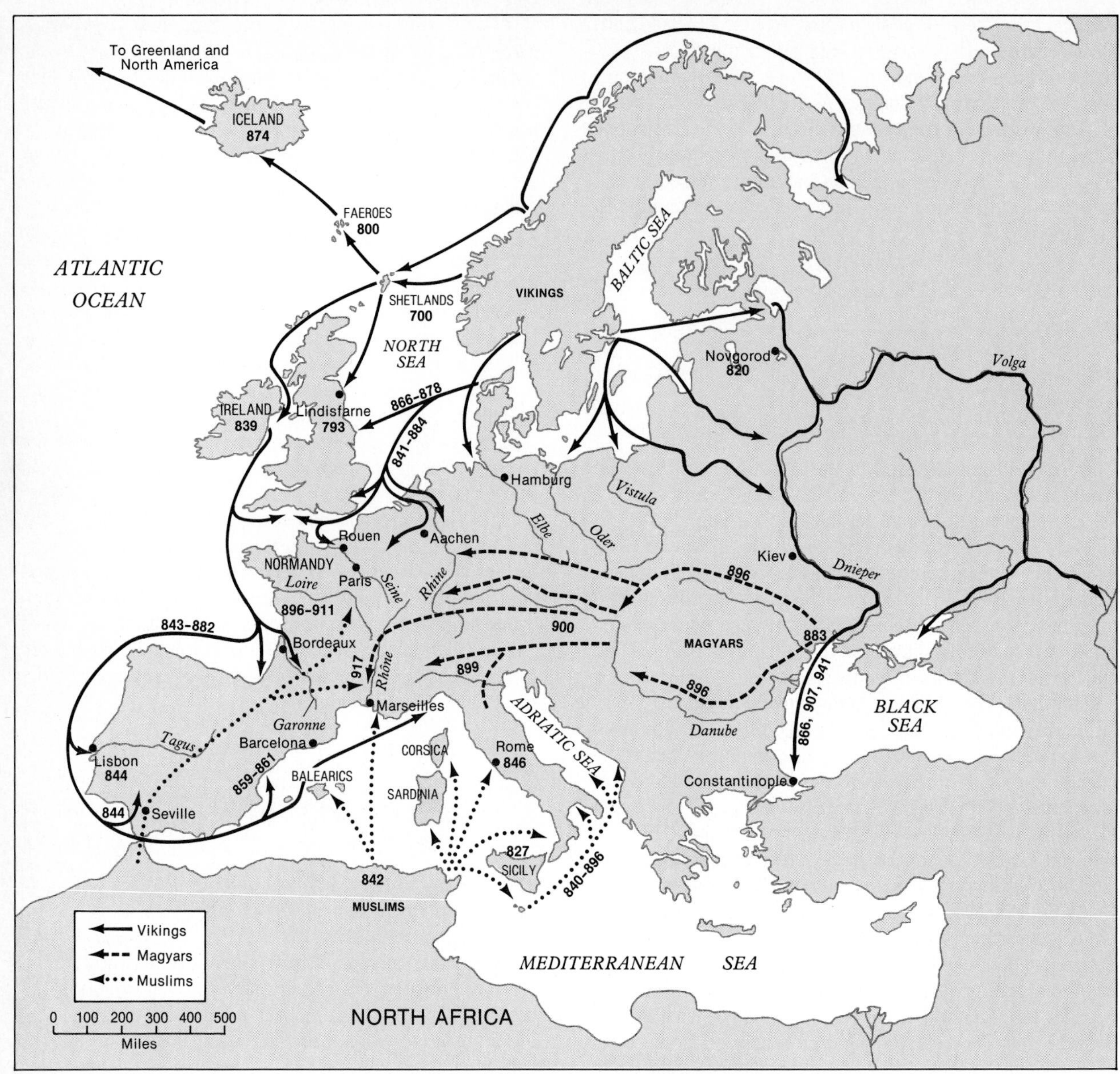

12.2 Viking, Magyar, and Muslim Invasions

itary, for together the vassals comprised the lord's private army, which offered protection to its collective members. Vassals were also expected to perform other duties, such as serve on the lord's court or provide him with hospitality. As these feudal arrangements developed, various safeguards were added. In eleventh-century France, for example, the normal amount of military service required of a vassal each year was 40 days. A vassal could receive fiefs from a variety of lords, thereby raising the question of which lord had first claim on his obedience. This was resolved by designating a liege lord as the one to whom primary obedience was due. Vassals with substantial landholdings could create vassals of their own. Thus the feudal order was not a neat hierarchical arrangement but a complex web of loyalties and obligations, the total effect of which was to decentralize power.

Because fiefs were normally inherited, they could be acquired by women. Yet a woman could not perform the required military service, so she had to have a husband. Younger sons, who normally had no fief to inherit, often married such an heiress as a means of acquiring a place in the feudal order. Women exercised an important role in feudal society, managing the family estates while their husbands were away and sometimes even defending their castles or fortified manor houses if they were attacked. Legally, however, a woman could not buy or sell property or even appear in court in her own right. Yet as the wife of a noble or a knight, she enjoyed considerable status in the community and could normally expect the deference of her social inferiors, male or female.

The impact of the feudal order on monarchs was considerable. Although kings were normally the most substantial landowners, with vassals who owed them military and other forms of service, in some states the nobles were more powerful than their monarchical lords. In such places a king was only as dominant as his great vassals allowed him to be, for as long as they collectively refused his bidding, he had no other army to enforce his will. In Germany the substantial size of the Magyar armies meant that the nobles could not marshal adequate defenses; hence the kings actually increased their influence, as exemplified by Otto I's revival of the imperial tradition. In western Europe, by contrast, the smallness and swiftness of the Viking raiding parties enhanced the power of local lords, who could respond more quickly to the threat than the kings could. Japan experienced a similar development beginning in the twelfth century, as the emperors increasingly lost power to hereditary warrior-aristocrats; the latter's power was based, as in Europe, on the vassals who comprised their armies. In both systems, the personal bond of loyalty was crucial, and the power of the central government was clearly limited.

The Early Medieval Economy

Beyond their impact on government, the invasions altered the economy of Europe. Muslim domination of the Mediterranean did not eliminate Europe's trade with the East, but it did substantially reduce shipping and profits. This in turn adversely affected European towns, particularly in coastal areas. The population of early medieval Europe became overwhelmingly rural, with peasants comprising up to 90 percent of the population.

Seeking protection and a livelihood from the large landowners, the free peasants gradually lost their lands and became dependent. Most peasants worked on large estates or manors, which became the basic social and economic unit at the local level. These manors were essentially descended from the Roman *latifundia* (see Chapter 6). In return for labor services for the owner, peasant families received the right to till tracts on the manor for their own sustenance and profit. Such arrangements allowed them considerable security—housing, land, and food—but bound them to the land; serfs (villeins) could not leave the manor without prior permission from their lord. In addition to the agricultural labor and other services that peasants owed, they were obliged to pay fines (often in produce or livestock) to the lord of the manor for the opportunity to marry someone from another manor, for a son to inherit the right to his father's lands on the manor, or for the use of the lord's mill to grind grain.

The conditions of peasant life varied greatly. Many peasants retained their freehold farms and their freedom and were quite prosperous, while others possessed few rights and were forced to endure abject poverty. The peasant diet was invariably simple, with black bread the primary staple. There was normally little meat, though poaching wild game was fairly common, and the more fortunate peasants occasionally ate pork. Fish was available fresh to those who lived near water or otherwise in salted form. The basic vegetables were beans, cabbage, peas, and onions; fruit, apart from wild berries and nuts, was rarely available. Peasants lucky enough to have sheep, goats, or cows could make cheese, and those with chickens could eat eggs.

Peasant women not only had to perform the typical childrearing and household duties but also worked in the fields with the men and cared for the animals. They endured a life of hard toil with little amusement other than drinking, perhaps watching cockfights, and amusing themselves on the numerous holy days that dotted the church calendar. Their lives, like those of their families, must in some cases have begun to improve, however marginally, as the result of better economic conditions in the High Middle Ages.

New Foundations: Economic Expansion

The dramatic achievements of the High Middle Ages—urban growth, the organization of guilds and universities, the construction of majestic cathedrals and guildhalls, and the revival of monarchical authority—were possible only because of the large-scale economic expansion that grew out of an agricultural revival that began in the tenth century. The development of the three-field system and crop rotation; the use of horses, properly harnessed and shoe-clad, and fertilizer; the recovery of new land by deforestation and drainage; and the increased use of heavy wheeled plows, metal tools, and windmills permitted Europeans to produce more food with less human labor. This in turn opened up possibilities for some people to specialize in manufacturing or commerce and for some landowners to plant crops, such as flax and hemp, that were not needed for basic sustenance. Others converted their land from tillage to pasturage, specializing in sheep, cattle, or horses, sometimes even cross-breeding to improve their stock.

Agricultural and pastoral developments spurred both a rise in population and the growth of manufacturing and commerce. In the year 1000 the population of Europe, including Russia, was approximately 38 million—small in comparison to Sung China's 100 million. By the early fourteenth century, however, Europe's population had doubled. No town in western or central Europe, with the exception of several in Muslim Spain, had as many as 50,000 people in the year 1000, though in the East, Constantinople had a population of some 300,000. In the ensuing three centuries, however, agricultural and commercial advances and the economic boom fostered by the crusades made it possible for towns to develop rapidly throughout Europe. Europeans again began to participate extensively in the major trade routes that extended from England and Scandinavia to India and China, especially the commerce that had developed in the Mediterranean in the tenth and eleventh centuries. Byzantine, Muslim, and Jewish merchants remained active throughout much of Europe, but they were soon surpassed by western Europeans, especially the Italians.

Much of the commerce of the High Middle Ages was conducted at annual fairs that lasted up to six weeks. Local markets handled weekly retail sales; the international fairs involved primarily wholesale transactions and were carefully regulated. The most influential of these were held under the aegis of the counts of Champagne six times a year. Merchants from as far away as Italy and the Balkan region were attracted to these fairs because of their strategic location at the crossroads of the European trade routes and the protection they were offered by the counts. Transactions at the fairs required the development of more sophisticated business practices, including the use of standard weights and measures, and the evolution of an international mercantile law.

Because the fairs were international in scope, moneychangers were also needed. Customarily seated on benches (*bancs*), these exchange specialists became known as bankers. They accepted deposits and were instrumental in instigating the use of paper credit, which was especially helpful in facilitating the distribution of goods over long distances and in encouraging commercial transactions when bullion and coins were in short supply. Eventually governments found it advantageous to finance some of their activities by credit. These developments collectively led to the emergence of capitalism.

Commercial expansion stimulated the development of new organizations to meet the demand for products of all types and to facilitate international trade. Partnerships became commonplace, despite one serious limitation: the responsibility of each partner for the total indebtedness of the firm in the event of default. Because of this drawback, partnerships such as the Bardi and Peruzzi of Florence were usually formed only by family members, perhaps with a few close associates. An alternative was the *commenda*, a business association in which an investor provided capital to a merchant in return for a share of the profits but which limited the investors' potential loss to the funds he had invested. Merchants and artisans also organized in guilds. On a much larger scale, beginning in the twelfth century various cities joined forces in commercial leagues designed to promote their interests. On occasion such a league, or *hansa,* became embroiled in political and military affairs. Among the most important of these confederacies were the Hanseatic League of North German cities and the Rhenish League, the leader of which was Cologne.

The increase in trade stimulated industrial production, particularly cloth manufacturing. English and Frisian cloth was sold throughout Europe by the ninth century, in Russia by the eleventh. The major textile centers of the High Middle Ages were in Flanders and eventually northern Italy. By 1300 Florence had some 200 workshops devoted to the manufacture of woolens. Less advanced than the sophisticated metal industries in China, those in Europe, which produced weapons, armor, tools, and cutlery, nevertheless expanded in this period, thanks especially to renewed interest in mining. The old Roman mines had had shafts as deep as 500 feet, but work in them had ceased in the sixth century. Until the tenth and eleventh centuries most of the digging was in shallow pits, but during the High Middle Ages mining was again pursued seriously, especially along the eastern Alps and in Bohemia, England, and northern Spain. In addition to gold and silver—crucial for the expansion of coinage—European mines produced tin, copper, mercury, iron, and coal. Productivity was gradually improved by the adoption of such technological devices as pulleys, cranks, and pumps and the harnessing of waterpower to crush the ore. Larger supplies of bullion made it possible to mint coins in higher values; pennies were increasingly coined out of copper instead of silver. Gold coins were issued by the emperor Frederick II in Sicily in 1231, followed shortly thereafter by Florence (1252), Genoa (1254), and other Italian cities.

In addition to textiles and metals, European craftsmen manufactured such items as leather goods, paper (primarily in Italy and Spain, although it was a Chinese invention), plate and blown glass (especially in Venice), and stained glass (France). Maritime states had shipbuilding industries, and some coastal cities, such as Venice and Marseilles, produced salt by evaporating seawater. Throughout Europe the food industry developed as people specialized in salting fish, curing meat, brewing, making wine, and milling grain. The building industry flourished, particularly beginning in the eleventh century, when it became fashionable north of the Alps to use stone instead of wood and plaster for major construction, such as cathedrals, castles, and town halls.

The manufacture of textiles and metals as well as the construction of large buildings required capital, reliable transportation, adequate supplies of raw materials, and a skilled labor force. All of this was possible only in a climate that could offer reasonable security and legal protection; hence industrial expansion and the reappearance of reasonably stable governments went hand in hand. Trade and industry provided the revenues without which effective governments could not exist, and the authorities, in turn, had to maintain conditions conducive to the further development of commerce and manufacturing. The High Middle

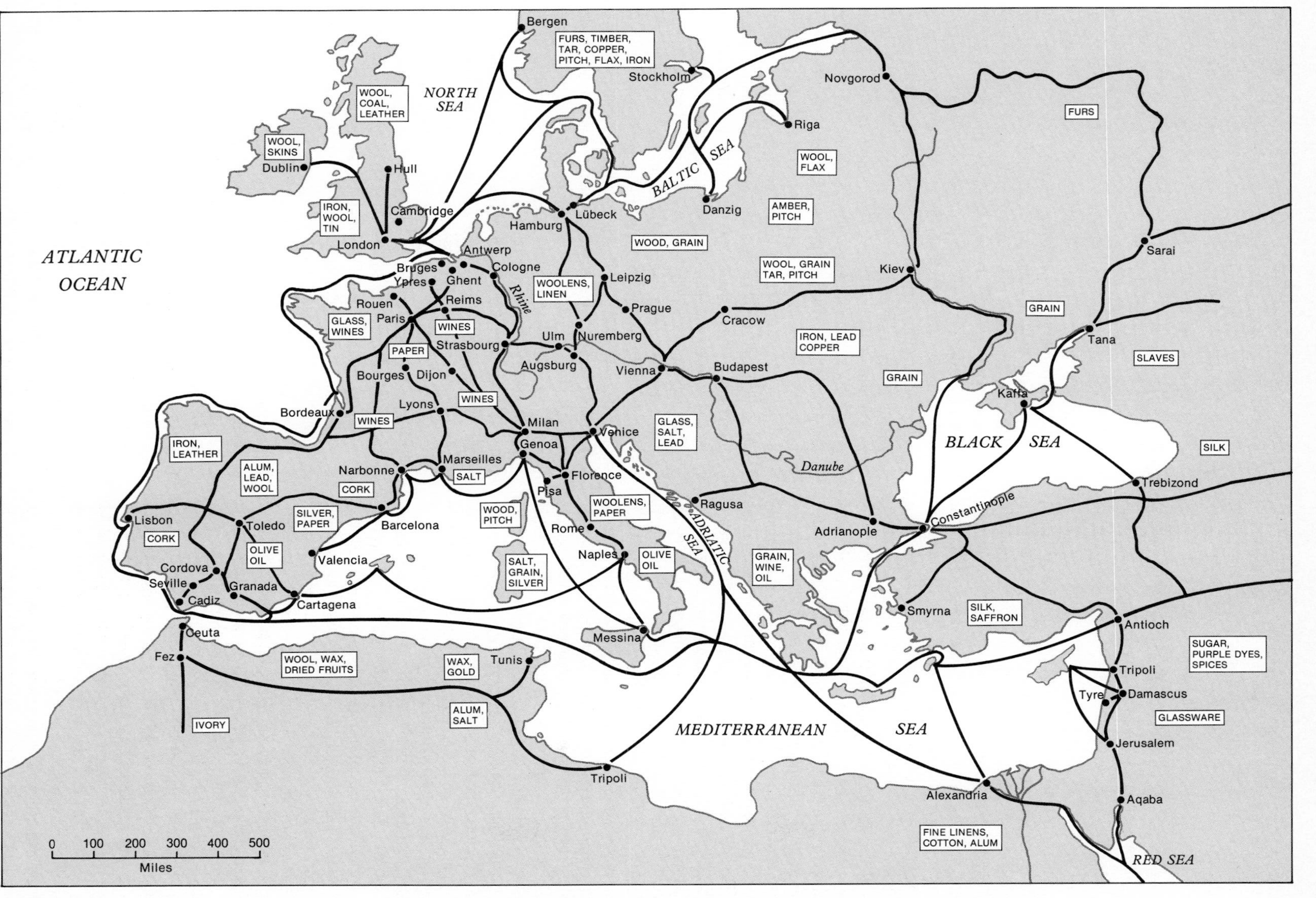

12.3 Primary Trade Routes of Europe, c. 1300

Ages achieved dramatic progress because of the fortunate combination of agricultural expansion, technological and commercial development, and increasing political stability.

Urban Development and Town Life

The eleventh through the thirteenth centuries witnessed extraordinary urban growth in western and central Europe that provided many people with an alternative to rural living. This growth was prompted by the expansion of trade and manufacturing to meet the needs of a rising population, which was fostered in turn by the agricultural revolution and the revival of extensive commerce throughout the Mediterranean.

No single factor accounts for the development of medieval cities. Some, such as Rome, Marseilles, and Bordeaux, were rebuilt on the decayed foundations of old Roman cities and administrative centers. Ports such as Pisa and Genoa recovered in the aftermath of Lombard and Arab domination, particularly once their fleets had increased. Because the growth of cities reflected the expansion of trade, many were located at the sites of natural harbors, such as Barcelona or Naples, on major rivers, such as London (on the Thames) and Cologne (on the Rhine), or at strategic locations astride major trade routes, such as Milan, Prague, and Vienna. Some cities, such as Bruges and Cambridge, emerged where key bridges crossed rivers. Many towns developed where people congregated for protection in fortified settlements, a trend commemorated in names ending in *fort* or *furt, burg,* or *borough:* Frankfurt, Hamburg, Augsburg, and Edinburgh are examples. An ecclesiastical center could serve as the nucleus of an emerging town; Paris and Rouen were not only seats of bishops but also sites of important monasteries.

The largest medieval cities—Paris, Venice, Florence, Naples, Milan, and Genoa—probably never exceeded 100,000 inhabitants in the High Middle Ages, and the Flemish cities of Bruges, Ghent, and Ypres, as well as London and Cologne, were roughly half their size. Apart from Cologne, the largest German towns, such as Hamburg and Augsburg, had fewer than 30,000 people. Asian cities were much larger: in the twelfth century, China had 52 cities with more than 100,000 *households*! Ch'ang An, the imperial capital of T'ang China, the world's largest city, had some 2 million residents. In the Middle East, Cairo's population reached 500,000 by 1300, and the largest Muslim cities of late medieval Spain were nearly as big.

The traditional description of medieval European cities as overcrowded is often an exaggeration, though space within the city walls soon came to be at a premium. Beyond the walls there was open space adjacent to the city where residents could farm or build homes. Some cities erected new walls as necessary, but wall construction and maintenance consumed a considerable portion of the urban budget. It was also possible to expand vertically, and medieval builders typically made each successive story wider than the one below, with the result that many streets received little sunlight. Pollution was common, as refuse of all types, including human excrement, was routinely dumped in the streets. Horses, dogs, and oxen added their own dung. The popularity of ale was no doubt partly due to the prevalence of contaminated water (a phenomenon sometimes blamed on Jews because of the myth that their shadows polluted wells). Fires were a severe hazard wherever buildings were made of wood. In the absence of urban planning, medieval cities were like mazes, their winding streets and narrow alleys a bizarre mixture of fortified houses, shops, and the ramshackle shanties of the poor.

Whatever their drawbacks, the towns were the achievement of a new social order, the burghers or bourgeoisie—the urban merchants who took their place beside the aristocracy, the clergy, and the peasants. In some circles the newcomers were by no means welcome: a fourteenth-century English preacher thundered that "God made the clergy, knights, and laborers, but the devil made townsmen and usurers." The point, of course, was that the traditional social orders had little understanding of the merchants' role in the economy, for they neither tilled the land, provided military protection, nor ministered to spiritual needs. Although merchants and artisans originally came from humble backgrounds, in time some of them acquired substantial wealth and eventually rivaled the aristocracy. Wedded to the land and steeped in tradition, however, most nobles treated the merchants with disdain, though in Italy the lesser aristocracy moved to the towns and allied with their inhabitants against the greater nobility and the bishops.

The lure of the towns was due in no small measure to the privileges set forth in their charters. These were usually granted by lords, nobles as well as monarchs, who were interested in potential tax revenues or income from the sale of charters. In cities such as Cologne, Mainz, and Liège, however, the townspeople had to rebel to secure their charters. The heart of the typical charter was the assurance of personal freedom for anyone who lived in the town for a year and a day. Charters typically guaranteed the people the right to hold markets and often to govern themselves, even to the point of making and enforcing their own laws to regulate commerce. Towns normally had to pay a stipulated sum to their overlords each year, but usually the citizens determined the taxes they would levy on themselves.

Although townspeople were personally free, urban governments were not democratic. Power customarily rested with the prosperous merchants and master artisans. Control was exercised not only through town councils but also through the guilds, groups of persons pursuing the same economic activity that were organized first by merchants in the eleventh century and then by craftsmen in the 1100s. As the craft guilds developed, they insisted on at least sharing city government with the merchant guilds. Because the guilds were so well organized, they virtually dominated government affairs, particularly since they could vote as a bloc and thereby elect their own leaders to city offices. Town government thus perpetuated the power of the guilds.

The guilds were designed to protect the interests of their members by restricting membership, limiting competition, and setting prices. In effect, a guild enjoyed a monopoly over a particular craft or trade and controlled prices; yet consumers benefited too in that the guild regulated quality. Guilds performed important social functions, such as training apprentices to become journeymen and possibly master craftsmen and guild members. Some guilds also provided basic education for members' children. The guilds aided needy members or their families, providing health care and financial assistance, particularly for victims of fire and flood as well as for widows and orphans. Some guilds, especially those involved with textiles or brewing, included women. Religion often played an important part in guild life, whether in activities honoring their favorite saints, in charitable donations to local churches, or in the construction and maintenance of their own churches and chapels. Guilds rivaled the church in their pageantry, particularly by their great feasts and public processions. Modern-day visitors to Venice can still see some of these pageants reenacted, complete with medieval costumes.

The guilds could not absorb all those who wished to enter; hence, as peasants kept flocking to the towns, many could find employment only as unskilled laborers. Poorly paid, devoid of political rights, and often barely able to survive, they constituted the proletariat. Although they were nominally free, few had any chance of improving their social status.

The Growth of Monarchy: England and France

No sovereigns made more effective use of the improved economic conditions to enhance their power than the rulers of England and France, particularly through their efforts to establish internal security and their interest in legal reform. In both countries the dominant political

The Rights of a French Town

The attractiveness of medieval towns was based in large part on the charters that set forth their privileges. A representative sample is found in the charter granted to the French town of Lorris, near Orléans, by Louis VII in 1155.

1. Every one who has a house in the parish of Lorris shall pay . . . sixpence only for his house, and for each acre of land that he possesses in the parish.
2. No inhabitant of the parish of Lorris shall be required to pay a toll or any other tax on his provisions; and let him not be made to pay any measurage fee on the grain which he has raised by his own labor.
3. No burgher shall go on an expedition, on foot or on horseback, from which he cannot return the same day to his home if he desires. . . .

6. No person while on his way to the fairs and markets of Lorris, or returning, shall be arrested or disturbed, unless he shall have committed an offense on the same day. . . .

9. No one . . . shall exact from the burghers of Lorris any tallage, tax, or subsidy. . . .

16. No one shall be detained in prison if he can furnish surety that he will present himself for judgment. . . .

18. Any person who shall dwell a year and a day in the parish of Lorris, without any claim having pursued him there, and without having refused to lay his case before us or our provost, shall abide there freely and without molestation.

Source: F. A. Ogg, *A Source Book of Mediaeval History* (New York: Cooper Square, 1907), pp. 328–330.

theme of the High Middle Ages was the struggle of the crown to establish a position of authority reasonably secure from the claims of the church on the one hand and the powerful feudal aristocracy on the other. Simultaneously, the seeds were also sown for the bitter conflict between the two countries that lasted for centuries.

The Norman Conquest

One of the most significant dates in English history is 1066, the year William, duke of Normandy, defeated the last Anglo-Saxon monarch, Harold, at the battle of Hastings to seize the English crown. The Norman Conquest brought some fundamental changes to England, principally the imposition of a Norman-French feudal aristocracy that owed military allegiance directly to the new king and was thus more centralized than its French counterpart. The Anglo-Saxon nobility disappeared, and England was henceforth governed by Normans. Nevertheless, William shrewdly opted to retain most Anglo-Saxon laws and institutions, including some of the traditional courts and the sheriffs. The royal council, the Witan, however, was replaced by the Great Council, an advisory body and court of feudal law, and its nucleus, the Small Council, composed of the king's principal advisers and officials. One of William's most remarkable accomplishments was a detailed survey of landed property in England—the Domesday Book—probably undertaken with a view to assuring a complete collection of taxes. William also extended royal control over the church, gradually replacing Anglo-Saxon bishops and abbots with Normans.

During the reign of William's great-grandson, Henry II (1154–1189), the territory in France under English control increased dramatically. In addition to Normandy, Henry inherited Maine, Touraine, and Anjou from his father, the count of Anjou, and added Aquitaine and Poitou by virtue of his marriage to Eleanor, duchess of Aquitaine. The Angevin empire, as all this was called, stretched from the Scottish border to the Pyrenees and included more than half of France. In feudal terms, however, Henry held his French lands as a vassal of the French king.

ELEANOR OF AQUITAINE: COURT POLITICS AND COURTLY LOVE

In her life Eleanor linked several of the major themes of the High Middle Ages—the political struggles of France and England, the crusades, and the courtly love tradition.*

Born in 1122, Eleanor, the daughter and heiress of William X, duke of Aquitaine, inherited the ducal title at the age of 15. Her guardian, King Louis VI, arranged her marriage to his son, who succeeded to the French throne as Louis VII in August 1137. When Louis, a deeply pious man, set out on the Second Crusade in the summer of 1147, Eleanor too "took the cross" as her grandfather, William IX, had done in the First Crusade. At Antioch, after long conversations with her uncle Raymond, Eleanor shocked Louis by announcing that their relationship was illegitimate because of their blood ties. Whether Eleanor was now sexually unfaithful, as the king's friends charged, is impossible to prove, but Louis forced her to remain with him, and she undoubtedly was with the crusaders when they reached Jerusalem.

Papal intervention kept the royal couple together until March 1152, when their marriage was finally annulled. Happy to be rid of Louis, who was "more monk than king," Eleanor married Henry Plantagenet two months later. When Henry succeeded to the English throne in 1154, she was crowned queen of England. Having already had two daughters by Louis, she gave Henry eight more children, among them two future kings of England, Richard I and John. As a political force to be reckoned with during her first decade in England, Eleanor served as regent when Henry was out of the country. Beginning in 1163, however, she was largely reduced to ceremonial functions, and in 1168 Henry dispatched her to Aquitaine to govern her duchy. Eleven years her junior, Henry was left free to pursue an affair with his mistress. Eleanor schemed to use her children to get revenge on Henry. Unwittingly, he played into her hands in 1169 by dividing his continental lands among his sons, giving them a base from which to oppose him. An exasperated Henry finally placed Eleanor in captivity in 1174, thus keeping her from actively supporting her sons when they rebelled against him in 1183. Henry even seems to have toyed with the notion of forcing her into a convent. She appeared in court on rare occasions in the mid-1180s, but her official release came only when Henry died in July 1189.

At Poitiers in the 1160s Eleanor presided over the beginnings of the courtly love tradition, with its exaltation of women. Although experts debate the extent of her role as a patron of literature and art, the roots of courtly love were undoubtedly in her court; the tradition really flourished for the first time at the court of her eldest daughter, Marie of Champagne, patroness of Chrétien de Troyes, author of the Arthurian romances. This emphasis on love, music, and poetry was something of a family tradition that dated back to Eleanor's grandfather, William IX, reputedly the first troubadour. The troubadours who gathered at her court to sing her praises eventually spread their passionate lyrics throughout much of France, England, Spain, and Sicily.

Eleanor virtually governed England until Richard I (1189–1199), who had been estranged from his father, arrived in the country. Close to Richard, she exercised considerable power throughout his reign, especially after

*The crusades are discussed later in this chapter, and the courtly love tradition in Chapter 13.

Effigy of Eleanor of Aquitaine at Fontevrault Abbey, Normandy. [Giraudon/Art Resource]

he was captured while returning from the Third Crusade. In addition to raising funds for his ransom, she called on the pope to help free Richard, whom she depicted as "the soldier of Christ." Four months after Richard's return, she retired to Fontevrault Abbey in western France in June 1194. She was buried there ten years later in a nun's habit.

Law and Monarchy in Norman England

Significant reforms in law and administration were undertaken during the reigns of Henry I and Henry II. The former shifted administrative authority from feudal barons to persons of lesser rank who operated under the direction of a new official called the justiciar. The justiciar's court, known as the Exchequer, performed judicial and administrative tasks but became noted for its role as the royal treasury and the accounting arm of the government. The two kings were instrumental in the emergence of common law, a body of legal principles based on custom and judicial precedents, uniformly applicable throughout England and administered by royal judges. In contrast, the civil law that increasingly prevailed throughout much of the European continent was derived from Roman law, especially as set forth in Justinian's *Corpus Juris Civilis*. English royal justice was not only legally superior to that dispensed in the local courts but more popular as well, and people were willing to purchase writs (legal orders) to have their cases decided by panels of jurors over which the crown's judges presided. In addition to operating a court at Westminster, the kings dispatched justices on regular circuits throughout the country. Because of the crown's role as the source of justice, the itinerant judges claimed the right to intervene in both feudal and local courts, thus furthering the notion of a common law. Henry II required residents to appear before these justices to report alleged criminals, a practice that later evolved into the modern grand jury. Henry also instituted the grand assize, which gave persons whose land titles were challenged the opportunity to have their cases judged by a jury in a royal court rather than by compurgation (the oaths of neighbors) or ordeal (trial by combat) in a feudal court.

Henry II's efforts to impose legal reforms on the church provoked a major confrontation. He was troubled in particular that the clergy had the right to be tried and sentenced in church courts, where the penalties were considerably less severe than those imposed in secular courts; a bishop's court, for instance, did not impose the death penalty. The Constitutions of Clarendon, which he issued in 1164, prohibited legal appeals to Rome without the king's permission, required that clergy convicted of a secular crime be sentenced in a royal court, and provided basic rights to laity tried in ecclesiastical courts. Thomas à Becket (1118–1170), whom Henry had appointed archbishop of Canterbury, rejected any notion of clerics being subject to a secular court. After spending six years in exile because of his opposition, Becket was allowed to return to England, only to incur more of Henry's wrath when he excommunicated bishops loyal to the king. When Henry, in a fit of anger, asked if no one would rid him of "this troublesome priest," four knights murdered Becket in Canterbury Cathedral. In the storm of outrage that ensued, Henry was forced to yield on two crucial points: clergy would be tried and sentenced in church courts, and appeals could still be made to the papal court.

The church and the barons each won a major victory during the reign of King John (1199–1216), who quarreled with Pope Innocent III (1198–1216) over a disputed election to the archbishopric of Canterbury. The pope, rejecting the candidates of both the king and the cathedral chapter at Canterbury, insisted on the appointment of a third candidate, Stephen Langton. When John balked, In-

Knights of King Henry II murdered Archbishop Thomas à Becket in the cathedral at Canterbury in 1170. This illustration is from a fourteenth-century manuscript. [British Tourist Authority]

nocent excommunicated him and placed England under an interdict, severely restricting religious services to the people. Faced with widespread unrest and the threat of a French invasion, John capitulated, even agreeing to the pope's demand that he hold England as a papal fief.

With the church controversy settled, John determined to invade France to regain the territory north of the Loire River that Philip II had taken. Although John had the support of the Holy Roman Empire and Flanders, his French vassals refused to fight against Philip, their supreme lord, and Philip crushed the imperial and Flemish forces at Bouvines (1214). The financial demands of the war had forced John to use extreme measures to raise money, thereby violating the feudal rights of his barons. In June 1215 at Runnymede, on the banks of the Thames River, the barons resorted to their feudal right of armed force to compel him to accept a charter—the Magna Carta—affirming their rights. Far from being a charter of rights in the modern sense, the Magna Carta served as an affirmation of feudal principles, though some of its provisions touched the clergy, the peasants, and the townsfolk. Among other things, the charter limited feudal payments, promised the church freedom from royal interference, restricted fines on peasants, and confirmed the special privileges of London and other boroughs. The real significance of the Magna Carta was its embodiment of the principle that monarchs are subject to the law and can be constrained if they violate it. Beginning in the seventeenth century creative interpreters argued that it contained such principles as due process of law and the right of representation for those being taxed. Although John himself subsequently ignored the charter—with Innocent III's blessing—his medieval successors were repeatedly obliged to confirm revised versions of it.

Another important legal precedent was established in 1295 when Edward I (1272–1307) broadened the Great Council of nobles and prelates by summoning knights and representatives from the towns. The purpose of this Parliament, as it came to be called, was to secure support for taxes to fund a war against France. Edward justified his decision to consult this wider group on the basis of a principle used by the church in convening a general council: "What touches all should be approved by all." This principle also influenced the development of representative bodies in France and elsewhere.

Capetian France

When Hugh Capet was elected king of France in 987, France was a patchwork of fiefs largely independent of royal authority. Hugh's own territory, the Île de France around Paris, was considerably smaller than that of the two vassals who flanked him, the duke of Normandy and the count of Champagne. Hugh, however, had two advantages over his vassals: his lordship over them in feudal theory and his consecration by the church in the coronation ceremony. The Île de France, moreover, was centrally located and the site of Paris, which in time became the greatest medieval city north of the Alps. The early Capetian monarchs improved their political fortunes by cultivating support from the church and by having their heirs crowned and given some governmental responsibility before they assumed the throne. The Capetians were fortunate in that they produced male heirs, most of whom reigned for relatively long periods. Although early Capetian authority in France was hardly extensive, it was stable. Beginning in the twelfth century the kings also wisely began to rely less on the greater nobles in the Île de France for their officials, preferring lesser nobles, clerics, and burghers whose loyalty to the throne was stronger.

By the time Philip II (1180–1223)—Philip Augustus, as he was called—became king, the gravest threat to the monarchy was posed by the English because of their extensive holdings in western France. Philip therefore devoted much of his attention to reducing English influence, an endeavor made easier by King John's domestic problems. French troops forced John to surrender everything but Aquitaine and Gascony, more than trebling the territory under Philip's control. John's hope of winning his lands back with the help of imperial and Flemish allies was crushed on the battlefield at Bouvines in 1214.

The Magna Carta

The Magna Carta, to which King John of England affixed his seal, guaranteed the rights of nobles and others in a largely feudal society, but subsequent centuries interpreted the passages quoted here as guarantees of fundamental legal rights for all.

1. In the first place, we have granted to God, and by this our present charter confirmed for us and our heirs forever, that the English church shall be free, and shall hold its rights entire and its liberties uninjured. . . .

12. No scutage [tax] or aid shall be imposed in our kingdom save by the common council of our kingdom, except for the ransoming of our body, for the making of our oldest son a knight, and for once marrying our oldest daughter; and for these purposes it shall be only a reasonable aid. . . .

13. And the city of London shall have all its ancient liberties and free customs. . . . Moreover we will and grant that all other cities and boroughs and villages and ports shall have all their liberties and free customs. . . .

20. A free man shall not be fined for a small offense, except in proportion to the gravity of the offense; and for a great offense he shall be fined in proportion to the magnitude of the offense, saving his freehold [i.e., except for the land he held without servile obligations]; and a merchant in the same way, saving [except for] his merchandise; and the villein shall be fined in the same way, saving his wainage [harvested crops set aside for seed], if he shall be at our mercy; and none of the above fines shall be imposed except by the oaths of honest men of the neighborhood. . . .

39. No free man shall be taken, or imprisoned, or dispossessed, or outlawed, or banished, or in any way injured . . . except by the legal judgment of his peers, or by the law of the land.

40. To no one will we sell, to no one will we deny or delay, right or justice.

Source: J. H. Robinson, ed., *Readings in European History*, vol. 1 (Boston: Ginn, 1904), pp. 234–237.

Philip's domestic policies contributed significantly to the growth of monarchical power. Earlier kings had conferred land on local officials in return for their service, thus making many of their offices hereditary; many subsequently became venal and self-seeking. Philip restored greater royal control over local affairs by appointing new officers—known as bailiffs in the north and seneschals in the south—who worked for a salary and thus could be replaced as necessary. Moreover, they reported directly to Philip. He was careful, however, to insist that local customs be respected, a characteristic of French law until the nineteenth century. To fund his enlarged government, the king insisted on the full payment of feudal dues by his vassals, including special fees from those who did not render military service. By the end of his reign, his increase of royal revenues was no less impressive than his enlargement of the royal domain. He further enhanced his authority by issuing 78 town charters, thereby forging strong links between the townsfolk and the crown.

Philip's grandson, the saintly Louis IX (1226–1270), was distinguished by his devotion to Christian principles, symbolically represented by his washing of lepers' feet during Holy Week and his bestowal of alms to the poor. Few rulers have been as dedicated to justice, both in the workings of the royal courts and in his personal capacity as the source of French justice. One of the endearing images of medieval Europe is that of Louis sitting under an oak tree dispensing justice to all comers. More formally, Louis encouraged appeals from lower courts to the Parlement of Paris, which the king recognized as the highest tribunal in France. A concern for justice and good government also prompted Louis to appoint special commissioners to monitor the work of the bailiffs and seneschals. When conflict between wealthy merchants and artisans erupted in the towns, the king intervened to preserve order, an action that resulted in a decrease in the number of privileges the towns enjoyed. Louis made effective use of *ordonnances*, or royal decrees, to prohibit private warfare and dueling and to require the acceptance of royal money throughout France. But for all his accomplishments, Louis failed to continue Philip II's policy of reducing English influence in France.

Louis' grandson, Philip IV (1285–1314), "the Fair," was a cunning sovereign who sought to expand royal authority, in part by the vigorous use of itinerant members of Parlement to extend royal justice throughout the realm at the expense of feudal courts. He also resumed hostilities against England, prohibiting Flemish towns from importing English wool. This endeavor failed, however, when Philip's army proved unable to defeat the rebellious Flemish cities. As military expenses mounted, Philip sought more revenue, imposing forced loans, debasing the coinage, and taxing the clergy.

This last policy sparked an explosive controversy with Pope Boniface VIII, which pitted French national interests against traditional claims of papal supremacy. In his quest for funds, Philip not only expelled Jews and Italian moneylenders as a pretext to confiscate their property but also launched a vicious assault on the Knights Templars, a crusading order that had prospered from the donations of the pious and involvement in banking activities. Accusing the Templars of assorted crimes ranging from heresy to black magic and homosexuality, he extracted confessions by torture and had the leading Templars burned at the stake. Although the papacy refused to allow Philip to take the Templars' lands, he avoided having to repay the substantial debts he owed them.

The need for funds was also behind his decision to summon urban representatives to meet with his council of nobles and clergymen in 1302, thus marking the beginnings of a more representative assembly that later became known as the Estates General. In contrast to the English Parliament, the Estates General never became powerful enough to establish permanent control over the levying of taxes and thus to serve as an effective check on monarchical power. By the early fourteenth century, then, the French monarchy had substantially centralized authority at the expense of the feudal nobility, and in England, despite the success of the nobles in checking the growth of royal power in the 1200s, legal reform had done much to lay the foundation of a unified state.

The Holy Roman Empire and the Church

Unlike their French and English counterparts, the German emperors of the High Middle Ages failed to lay the foundations of a unified German state. In part this was due to the strength of the feudal nobility and the emperors' quest to dominate Italy, but perhaps the most crucial factor was a furious struggle with the papacy that culminated in the disintegration of the Holy Roman Empire. The church's victory was made possible by reforms in the tenth and eleventh centuries that gave it new vigor and a stronger claim to moral leadership (see Chapter 13).

Germany and the Imperial Revival

When the Carolingian empire declined in the ninth century, essentially independent duchies were established in the eastern Frankish lands. Out of this territory the Saxon duke Henry the Fowler founded the medieval German monarchy, which he governed as Henry I (919–936). His success in controlling the dukes was due partly to the freedom he allowed them in their duchies and partly to his ambitious foreign policy. He annexed Lorraine, strengthened Saxon defenses against the Magyars and Norsemen by encouraging the building of fortified towns, and urged Saxon expansion in the Slavic lands beyond the Elbe River.

The policies of Henry's son, Otto I (936–973), were basically an extension of his father's, but on a grander scale. His efforts to centralize royal power incited no less than four rebellions, all of which he repressed. When the Magyars took advantage of the civil strife to invade Germany, Otto crushed them at Lechfeld, near Augsburg, in 955. Like his father, he appointed churchmen to offices of state, knowing they could not undermine royal authority by passing their positions to their sons. The clergy, moreover, were better educated. For its part, the church welcomed the alliance with the state, which brought not only greater influence but grants of land as well. The ecclesiastics who held those estates were responsible for providing Otto with many of his soldiers and much of his revenue.

When political turmoil in Italy offered Otto the excuse to intervene in 951, he claimed the Lombard throne as his own. Renewed conflict brought a call for his assistance from Pope John XII (955–964), who rewarded him with the imperial crown in February 962. That crown had several advantages, including the legal title to the Carolingian middle kingdom and reinforcement of Otto's supremacy over the German dukes, but it also thrust his successors into an untenable relationship with the head of a church that they had to dominate to maintain their power. The imperial policy of relying on ecclesiastical officials as the primary servants of the crown was effective so long as the papacy did not insist on appointing only those who had its approval.

Beginning in the late eleventh century the papacy attempted to assert the church's independence from secular control. The first of these popes, Leo IX (1049–1054), deposed corrupt bishops and reasserted papal supremacy over all the clergy. In 1059 a church council took a major step in freeing the papacy itself from imperial control by establishing the right of the College of Cardinals to elect future popes, a practice still in effect. In 1075 Gregory VII (1073–1085) attempted to restore the election of bishops and abbots to the church by terminating the practice of lay investiture—the bestowal of the insignia of an ecclesiastical office by a layperson. Practically speaking, lay investiture entailed the right of the laity, such as emperors or kings, to select bishops and abbots, though this was in violation of church law and tradition. A vigorous, reformed church could hardly be established if its key officials were selected with a view to political, monetary, and family considerations rather than spiritual qualifications and if the loyalty of such persons was ultimately to the sovereign who appointed them rather than to the pope.

The immediate target of Gregory's decree was the emperor Henry IV (1056–1106), who enjoyed the support of his bishops but not the German territorial princes. The latter stood to gain by any reduction of imperial power. Recognizing the implications of the decree, Henry had his prelates declare Gregory deposed, to which the pope responded by excommunicating Henry, absolving his subjects from their duty to obey him, and depriving the imperial bishops of their offices. Delighted with this turn of events, the renegade princes in Germany called for a council, over which Gregory would preside, at Augsburg in February 1077; its task would be to ascertain the validity of Henry's claim to the imperial crown. Unprepared to cope with a rebellion, the emperor intercepted Gregory at Canossa in Italy to seek absolution. As a priest, Gregory had to forgive the penitent Henry, thereby giving the emperor the upper hand in the civil war that ensued in Germany. Henry was in a much stronger position when Gregory again excommunicated him in 1080. Four years later Henry's troops occupied Rome, driving Gregory into exile and installing an "antipope," Clement VII, on the papal throne.

The investiture struggle dragged on until 1122, when Henry V (1106–1125) and Pope Calixtus II (1119–1124) agreed in the Concordat of Worms that the church would henceforth give prelates their offices and spiritual authority but that the emperor could be present when German bishops were elected and invest them with fiefs. In theory, at least, the clergy were now more independent of secular control, though in practice their selection and work were still very political. The real winners in the investiture struggle were the powerful territorial princes, who consolidated their hold over their own lands while imperial attention focused on Rome, and the emerging urban communes of northern Italy, which seized this opportunity to

Gregory VII on Papal Authority

The principles on which Pope Gregory VII and his supporters acted to reform the church and assert the supreme authority of the papacy are set forth in the Dictatus papae *("Sayings of the Pope"), which was probably composed about 1075.*

The Roman church was founded by God alone.
The Roman bishop alone is properly called universal.
He alone may depose bishops and reinstate them.
His legate [direct ambassador], though of inferior grade, takes precedence, in a council, of all bishops and may render a decision of deposition against them. . . .
The pope is the only person whose feet are kissed by all princes.
His title is unique in the world.
He may depose emperors.
No council may be regarded as a general one without his consent.
No book or chapter may be regarded as canonical without his authority.
A decree of his may be annulled by no one; he alone may annul the decrees of all.
He may be judged by no one.
No one shall dare to condemn one who appeals to the papal see.
The Roman church has never erred, nor ever, by the witness of Scripture, shall err to all eternity.
He may not be considered Catholic who does not agree with the Roman church.
The pope may absolve the subjects of the unjust from their allegiance.

Source: J. H. Robinson, ed., *Readings in European History*, vol. 1 (Boston: Ginn, 1904), pp. 274–275.

achieve a semi-independent status. In the end the biggest losers were not only the emperors but the German people, who were increasingly subjected to feudal conflict at a time when the French and English were laying the foundations of unified states.

Papal Triumph and the Imperial Challenge

The papacy reached the zenith of its political power in the thirteenth century, but only after a renewal of its struggle with the empire. The emperor Frederick I (1152–1190), called "Barbarossa" because of his red beard, made domination of northern Italy (Lombardy) a cornerstone of his policy. Together with Burgundy, which he acquired by marriage, and his native Swabia, Lombardy would give him a solid territorial base from which to dominate Germany and Italy. Recognizing this, the pope joined with the cities of the Lombard League and the Normans in Sicily to thwart Frederick's ambitions, an end they achieved in the Peace of Constance (1183), which forced Frederick to relinquish virtually all meaningful power in the Lombard cities. The imperial cause in Italy received new life when Barbarossa's son, Henry VI (1190–1197), married Constance, heiress of Sicily and southern Italy. The papacy was now caught in the imperial vise, but rather than so-

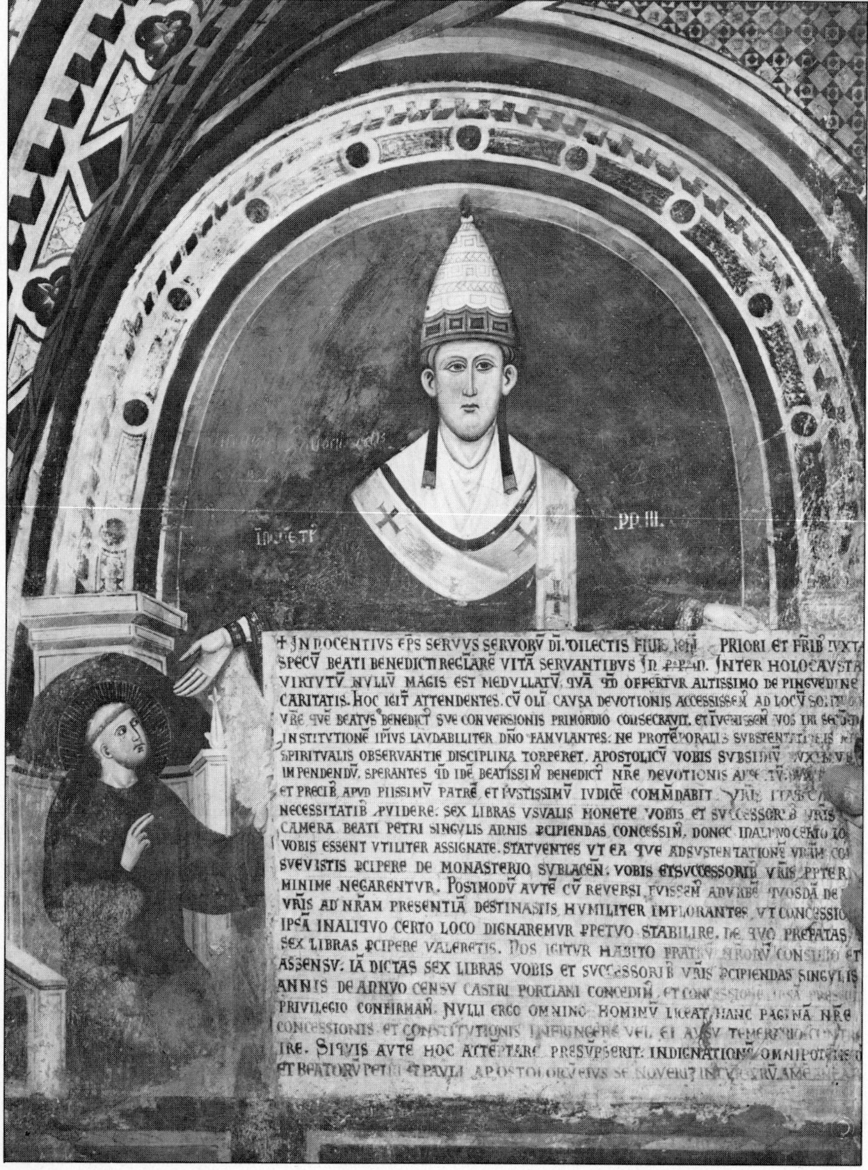

Innocent III, perhaps the most powerful of the medieval popes, made King John of England his vassal and helped establish Frederick II as Holy Roman Emperor. This portrait is a thirteenth-century fresco in Sacro Speco Church, Subiaco. [Alinari/Art Resource]

lidify his Italian holdings, Henry prepared to attack the Byzantine Empire. Simultaneously, he gave many of the German princes hereditary rights to their fiefs in return for their recognition that the imperial crown would likewise be hereditary rather than elective, a scheme bitterly opposed by the papacy.

Innocent III (1198–1216), arguably the most powerful of the medieval popes, took advantage of the chaos that followed Henry's untimely death to undermine the link between Germany and Sicily. Germany was thrust into civil war when the leading Hohenstaufen candidate for the imperial throne, Philip of Swabia, Henry VI's brother, was challenged by Otto of Brunswick. Although Innocent crowned Otto in 1198, the latter's attempt to control Sicily prompted the pope to excommunicate him. At the urging of the French king, Philip Augustus, Innocent recognized the hereditary claim of Henry's son, Frederick II, as king of the Romans in 1212. Philip's victory over Otto at Bouvines (1214) decided the struggle in Frederick's favor, though Frederick continued to fight with the popes over Sicily for the rest of his reign.

After Frederick's death in 1250, the papacy encouraged civil strife in Germany so successfully that between 1254 and 1273 there was no generally recognized emperor. Moreover, the Hohenstaufen line itself died out in 1268. The Great Interregnum, as the period without a recognized emperor was called, marked the triumph of the papacy over the empire—a victory achieved with French support. Yet half a century after the interregnum began, the French monarchy delivered a crippling blow to papal power and prestige.

Boniface VIII and the End of Papal Hegemony

The century between the pontificates of Innocent III and Boniface VIII (1294–1303) witnessed a dramatic change in the political fortunes of the major European states, with France and England now the dominant powers. Boniface, a short-tempered, elderly man of aristocratic background, seriously blundered when, in 1296, he issued the bull (or edict) *Clericis laicos*, rejecting the right of monarchs to tax the clergy without papal authorization. Neither Philip IV nor Edward I, who were on the verge of war with each other, would tolerate such a challenge. While Edward denied legal protection to clerics who refused to pay, Philip prohibited the export of funds from France to Rome, crippling papal finances. Boniface retreated, allowing Philip the right to tax the clergy in an emergency and canonizing Louis IX for good measure.

Emboldened by the jubilee in 1300, when tens of thousands of pilgrims flocked to Rome, Boniface was ready when a new crisis erupted in 1301. When Philip had a

The Church's Claim to Supremacy

The bull Unam sanctam, *issued by Pope Boniface VIII in 1302 during the course of his struggle with King Philip Augustus, is the classic statement of the medieval church's claim to spiritual and temporal supremacy.*

The true faith compels us to believe that there is one holy Catholic Apostolic Church, and this we firmly believe and plainly confess. And outside of her there is no salvation or remission of sins. . . .

By the words of the gospel we are taught that the two swords, namely, the spiritual authority and the temporal, are in the power of the Church. . . . The former is to be used by the Church, the latter for the Church; the one by the hand of the priest, the other by the hand of kings and knights, but at the command and permission of the priest. Moreover, it is necessary for one sword to be under the other, and the temporal authority to be subjected to the spiritual; for the apostle says, "For there is no power but of God: and the powers that be are ordained of God" [Rom. 13:1]; but they would not be ordained unless one were subjected to the other, and, as it were, the lower made the higher by the other. . . .

Submission on the part of every man to the bishop of Rome is altogether necessary for his salvation.

Source: F. A. Ogg, *A Source Book of Mediaeval History* (New York: Cooper Square, 1907), pp. 385–388.

French bishop tried in a royal court on charges of heresy and treason, the pope protested that this violated the clergy's privilege to be judged in a church court and warned Philip to submit to his authority as the vicar of Christ. Philip countered by summoning the first Estates General (1302), which protested to Rome. Boniface responded with a new papal bull, *Unam sanctam* (1302), in which he argued that God had given the church two swords: the spiritual sword, which was superior, was retained by the church, but the temporal was bestowed by the church on secular authorities to be wielded on behalf of the church and at its direction. The bull also flatly asserted that "submission on the part of every man to the bishop of Rome is altogether necessary for his salvation."

Whether *Unam sanctam* was a desperate ploy or the logical culmination of medieval papal claims is debatable, but Philip was undaunted. He dispatched his chief minister to Italy to arrest the pope, whom Philip hoped to try on fabricated charges ranging from heresy to sodomy and sorcery. Boniface was rescued by Italian loyalists, but not before he had been physically abused and the prestige of the papacy badly tarnished. In a matter of weeks Boniface was dead, and with him perished the heady days of papal supremacy. A French pope, Clement V (1305–1314), formally praised Philip's devotion, heralding the beginning of a long period in which the papacy found itself in the shadow of the French monarchy.

The Waning of the Byzantine Empire

While western Europe was achieving remarkable political progress in the High Middle Ages, the Byzantine Empire was plagued by internal decay and external assault. In many respects the eleventh century was pivotal in its decline. The emperor Basil II (976–1025) had secured the frontiers and brought the Balkans under Byzantine domination by defeating the Bulgars. From 1028 to 1056, however, the empire was ineffectually governed by Basil's nieces, Zoe and Theodora, who unwisely allowed imperial military strength to be sapped by supporting large landowners in their acquisition of smaller holdings. The result was the growth of a body of powerful magnates capable of fielding their own armies and posing a threat to imperial control. In effect, the empire was being feudalized.

In 1056, when the Macedonian dynasty died out, civil strife erupted until the military aristocrat Alexius I Comnenus (1081–1118) finally imposed control. In addition to weak emperors, much of the internal instability of the eleventh century was attributable to a fierce power struggle between the cultured bureaucratic elite and a wealthy aristocracy, the effects of which not only weakened the army but also undermined the government's financial stability. The lavish expenses of the imperial court and the increasing exemption of the aristocracy from taxation forced the government to devalue its coins in the mid-eleventh century.

The internal crises made it difficult for the Byzantines to cope with the pressure on their frontiers. The peoples of west-central Asia, particularly the Pechenegs who lived along the northern coasts of the Black Sea, regularly raided Byzantine territory. An even graver danger was posed by the Seljuk Turks, whose destruction of a Byzantine army at Manzikert in 1071 meant the loss of eastern Anatolia and Armenia. In the same year the Normans of Sicily drove the Byzantines out of southern Italy and attacked western Greece. Alexius Comnenus regained some of the lost territory by allying with the Venetians against the Normans and by successful military campaigns against the Pechenegs and the Turks. His military needs were so great, however, that he had to appeal to the papacy for western volunteers to fight the Turks, thus setting the stage for the crusades.

The Clash of Faiths: Muslims Against Crusaders

The Turks had moved from the Asian steppes into the Islamic empire to serve in its armies. By 1055 one group of Turks, the Seljuks, had established themselves as the real rulers of the Abbasid caliphate. In the two centuries that followed their victory at Manzikert, they extended their control over most of Asia Minor, permanently changing it from a Christian to an Islamic civilization. Turkish domination extended into Armenia and Palestine as well, making it difficult for Christian pilgrims to visit the Holy Land. The Byzantine emperor, Michael VII, appealed to Pope Gregory VII for western assistance in 1073, and though the pontiff was willing to proclaim a holy war, not least because it might reunite Christendom under his authority, the outbreak of the investiture controversy delayed the plan.

Twenty-two years later, against a background of alleged hostilities against Christian pilgrims, Byzantine envoys from Alexius Comnenus urged Pope Urban II (1088–1099) to dispatch military aid. At the Council of Clermont (1095) in southern France, the pope proclaimed a crusade to liberate the holy places, free the persecuted Christians of the East, and acquire wealth and power in a land of "milk and honey." It was better to slaughter the infidel than fellow Christians, Urban argued, and if a Christian died in the process, he would receive a plenary indulgence exempting him from the necessity of rendering satisfaction for his sins—in other words, immediate entry into heaven. To the pope's message, directed against a "pagan race," his audience responded with gusto: "God wills it! God wills it!"

The motives of the church and the crusaders varied. For the papacy the crusades offered the possibility of lead-

A Call to Crusaders

The crusades to bring the Holy Land under Christian control were launched by Pope Urban II's speech to the Council of Clermont in November 1095. Note the appeal to spiritual, material, and racial motives as well as the emotional tone.

From the confines of Jerusalem and from the city of Constantinople a grievous report has gone forth and has been brought repeatedly to our ears; namely, that a race from the kingdom of the Persians, an accursed race, a race wholly alienated from God, . . . has violently invaded the lands of those Christians and has depopulated them by pillage and fire. They have led away a part of the captives into their own country, and a part they have killed by cruel tortures. They have either destroyed the churches of God or appropriated them for the rites of their own religion. They destroy the altars, after having defiled them with their uncleanness. . . .

On whom, therefore, rests the labor of avenging these wrongs and of recovering this territory, if not upon you—you, upon whom, above all other nations, God has conferred remarkable glory in arms, great courage, bodily activity, and strength to humble the heads of those who resist you? Let the deeds of your ancestors encourage you and incite your minds to manly achievements. . . .

Let none of your possessions restrain you, nor anxiety for your family affairs. For this land which you inhabit, shut in on all sides by the seas and surrounded by the mountain peaks, is too narrow for your large population; nor does it abound in wealth; and it furnishes scarcely food enough for its cultivators. Hence it is that you murder and devour one another, that you wage war, and that very many among you perish in civil strife. . . .

Enter upon the road of the Holy Sepulcher; wrest that land from the wicked race, and subject it to yourselves. . . . Undertake this journey eagerly for the remission of your sins, with the assurance of the reward of imperishable glory in the kingdom of heaven.

Source: F. A. Ogg, *A Source Book of Mediaeval History* (New York: Cooper Square, 1907), pp. 284–287.

ership in Europe and the opportunity to heal the breach between the eastern and western churches that had been formalized in 1054. While some crusaders were moved by spiritual considerations, including the promise of a plenary indulgence (a complete discharge of punishment for sin), others were motivated by stories of atrocities purportedly inflicted on pilgrims by the Muslims, the hope of material gain, the lure of adventure, the chance to escape from daily cares, or the desire to participate in an activity that quickly became fashionable. Most of the crusaders came from France, Italy, and Germany.

When the emperor Alexius appealed for assistance, he wanted western knights trained and equipped to fight, but instead the first group of crusaders, some 15,000 to 20,000 strong, were largely commoners, including women and children, devoid of military experience or suitable weapons. Inspired by faith and led by Peter the Hermit, the unruly force was hurriedly shipped from Constantinople to Asia Minor by alarmed Byzantine officials. The sultan of Nicaea's army annihilated or enslaved most of the crusaders, leaving the bones of some as a grisly warning to others who might follow. Fired by hopes of founding the New Jerusalem, the Peasants' Crusade ended in disaster, not only for the crusaders but also for the thousands of Hungarians and Jews they killed en route and the Byzantines they robbed or whose homes they burned.

Later in the same year, 1096, a much more impressive effort was made in the Crusade of the Princes, traditionally called the First Crusade. Although no monarchs participated, some of Europe's most illustrious princes were involved, including Godfrey of Bouillon, duke of Lower Lorraine; Raymond II, count of Toulouse; Robert, duke of Normandy, brother of the English king, William II; Hugh, count of Vermandois, brother of King Philip I of France; and Stephen, count of Blois, son-in-law of William the Conqueror. In all there were 5,000 to 10,000 knights, more than 25,000 soldiers, and at least that many noncombatants, both male and female, including servants, pilgrims, and prostitutes. In the hope of gaining control over whatever lands the crusaders conquered, Alexius bribed and

Crusaders besieging Nicaea in 1097 catapult human heads at their enemies. [Bibliothèque Nationale, Paris]

cajoled the princes to take oaths of fealty to him, making them his vassals.

Although the Turks used scorched-earth tactics, the crusaders pushed relentlessly eastward. One branch of their army, under the command of Godfrey's brother Baldwin, captured the ancient Syrian city of Edessa, which had been ruled by Armenians, making it the first crusader state (1098). The heavily fortified city of Antioch, surrounded by 7 miles of walls, was besieged for seven months before it was finally betrayed from within and became the second crusader state. In July 1099 Jerusalem itself was conquered with the aid of equipment and supplies provided by an English-Genoese fleet. Once inside the city the crusaders massacred the inhabitants, whether Muslims or Jews, sparing neither women nor children. It was, the victors thought, a "splendid judgment" of God.

The crusaders offered the crown of Jerusalem to Godfrey of Bouillon, who agreed only to serve as protector in deference to the kingship of Christ. Following Godfrey's death in 1100, however, his brother Baldwin became king of Jerusalem and nominal overlord of the three other crusader states, Edessa, Antioch, and Tripoli, which together formed a 500-mile strip along the coast of the eastern Mediterranean. Defending this outpost of European civilization from the hostile powers on its frontiers was therefore a matter of overriding concern, particularly since the subjects of the crusader states viewed their new rulers with hostility. Feudal knights had to be used to defend the states, but at the cost of developing a strong central government. Imposing castles were built, and the crusaders founded military orders in which the knights took the monastic vows of poverty, chastity, and obedience while dedicating their lives to the defense of the Holy Land. The Knights Hospitalers and the Knights Templars wore distinctive dress, defended castles, and generally distinguished themselves as warriors. A third order, the Teutonic Knights, was established by German crusaders in 1198, though most of its efforts were devoted to campaigns in Hungary and the Baltic region.

The conquests of the first crusaders were possible largely because the Muslims had been disunified. In the early twelfth century, however, they began to regroup, initially under the leadership of Zenghi, governor of Mosul on the Tigris River. His capture of Edessa in 1144 sparked the call for the Second Crusade (1147–1149), which was led by King Louis VII of France and the German emperor Conrad III. Most of the crusaders were annihilated as they moved through Asia Minor, and the remnant, without the effective support of the suspicious defenders already in the Holy Land, failed to capture Damascus. Instead the city, which had been an ally of the crusader states, was conquered by Zenghi's successor, Nurredin, in 1154, placing Syria firmly in Muslim hands. Nurredin's forces imposed their control over Egypt in the late 1160s, setting the stage for the triumphal exploits of Saladin (1138–1193), who established himself as the master of much of the Muslim Middle East, particularly Egypt and Syria, after Nurredin's death in 1174. Thirteen years later he launched a holy war of his own to recover Palestine, taking Jerusalem in October 1187. By 1189 the Christians held only Antioch, Tripoli, and Tyre.

The loss of Jerusalem roused Europe to launch yet another crusade, a formidable expedition led by the emperor Frederick Barbarossa, King Philip II of France, and King Richard I of England. But the emperor drowned in Asia Minor and Philip returned home after the crusaders captured the port of Acre, leaving Richard "the Lion-Hearted" to negotiate an agreement with Saladin permitting Christian pilgrims the right to visit Jerusalem. This was not enough for Pope Innocent III, who called for a fresh crusade, the Fourth (1202–1204). In return for food and transport, the crusaders acquiesced to a Venetian demand to help them reconquer the Dalmatian port of Zara, an act that resulted in the crusaders' excommunication because Zara was a Catholic city. The crusaders subsequently embroiled themselves in a disputed succession to the Byzantine throne that ended with their sack of Constantinople and the establishment of a Latin kingdom there that lasted until 1261.

As disreputable as the Fourth Crusade was, it did not quench the crusading fever. Among the later crusades, only the Sixth (1228–1229), led by Frederick II, was successful, thanks to the emperor's diplomatic skills and rapport with the Muslims. A treaty with the Egyptian sultan left Jerusalem in Christian hands, but Frederick's running feud with the papacy forced him to return to Italy. Turkish forces in the employ of Egypt recaptured Jerusalem in 1244. Later crusades failed to regain the Holy Land, and in 1291 the last of the crusader possessions, Acre, was lost.

In terms of their stated objective—the conquest of the Holy Land—the crusades were a failure. The heavy expenditure in lives and resources as well as the undercutting of spiritual motives by worldly considerations cast a pall over the crusading movement. One of the most significant long-term legacies was the incitement of deep-seated religious hostility between Christians and Muslims and of Christians toward Jews. Nor did the crusades heal the breach between eastern and western Christendom, which, if anything, hardened as a result of them. In the short term the papacy probably enhanced its prestige as the spiritual leader of the West, but in the end its use of crusades to eradicate heresy in France and its deepening involvement in secular affairs began to erode its influence. The monarchs of Europe improved their position by gaining the right to levy direct taxes in order to obtain cru-

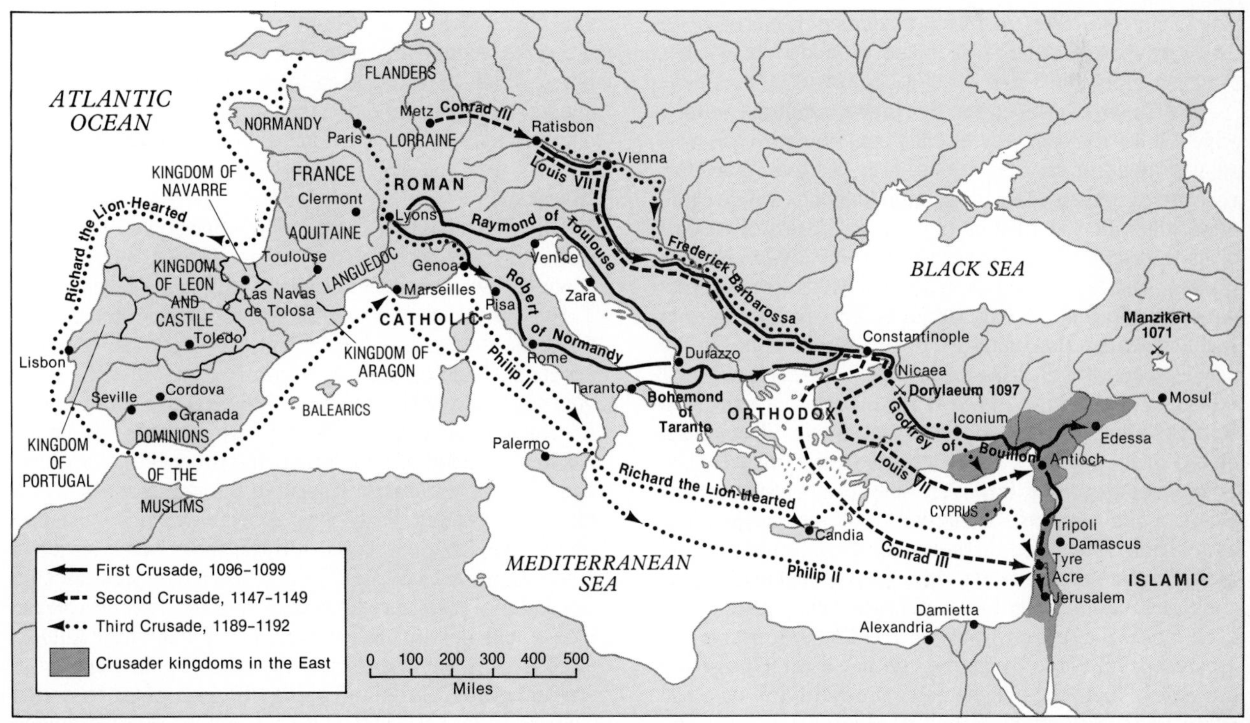

12.4 The Crusades

sading funds, and perhaps Europe was subjected to a little less fighting because so many lords and knights directed their militancy against the Muslims.

There were a number of benefits from the crusades, particularly of an economic and cultural nature. The heightened contact between Europe and the Middle East stimulated commerce, especially in such commodities as fine textiles, spices, and perfumes. Expanded commerce in turn encouraged improvements in shipbuilding and banking, including greater use of letters of credit and bills of exchange. Although Islamic culture was already spreading to the West through the Iberian peninsula and Sicily, the crusades facilitated the exchange of ideas and the increase of geographic knowledge. The notion of "crusading" for a worthy cause lived on well past the last crusade and is still a frequently encountered concept, usually in secular guise, as well as in the Islamic notion of the *jihad.* The crusades were also significant as a chapter in the history of Western expansion and the backdrop for the great voyages of exploration that began in the fifteenth century, in part as a means of renewing the crusading movement.

Byzantium After the Crusades

While the Europeans ruled Constantinople as a Latin kingdom, Greek refugees established a rival government at Nicaea in Asia Minor. In 1261 the Nicaean regime, aided by the Genoese, who were jealous of the privileges accorded to the Venetians by the Latin kingdom, regained Constantinople. The restored Byzantine Empire, however, was territorially smaller and economically weaker than it had been in 1200.

The empire survived for two more centuries, during which time its economy eroded and its strength was sapped by bitter social divisions. External threats were a recurring problem. A revived Latin kingdom was averted only by accident in 1282 on the eve of Charles of Anjou's planned assault. The younger brother of King Louis IX of France, Charles wanted to establish a Mediterranean empire by combining the kingdom of Sicily, which he already ruled, with the Byzantine Empire. Charles' hopes were dashed when the Sicilians massacred his French supporters during an uprising known as the Sicilian Vespers. With Byzantine financial support, an Aragonese fleet from Spain seized Sicily, ending Charles' threat to the empire. The Byzantines were not, however, able to repel the periodic incursions of the Serbs in the west and the Turks in the east. Their diminished territories in the aftermath of the Latin kingdom meant decreased resources and manpower, and the government at Constantinople was further weakened by debilitating civil wars in the 1300s. Perhaps the greatest cause of the Byzantines' decline was their inability to recover their once phenomenal prosperity, in no small measure because much of their commerce had fallen into the hands of northern Italian merchants.

The Iberian Peninsula and the Reconquista

Although the crusaders failed to achieve a permanent hold in the Holy Land, in Europe a much longer campaign against the Muslims for the control of the Iberian peninsula was slowly being won. The *reconquista* ("reconquest") had begun in the ninth century, but by the dawn of the High Middle Ages only a thin band across the north of the peninsula was in Christian hands. Three centuries later the Muslims held only Granada at the peninsula's southern tip. Christian progress was due largely to the collapse of the caliphate of Córdoba in 1031, which had been torn by bitter internal dissension among Arabs, Jews, Berbers, and native Spaniards. As the caliphate, once the most prosperous state in Europe, disintegrated into petty principalities, the task of the knights of the cross was greatly simplified.

During the course of the High Middle Ages, three major Christian kingdoms developed in the peninsula: Castile, the largest; Aragon, in the northeast; and Portugal in the west. In addition there was a tiny Basque kingdom of Navarre in the north. During the reign of Sancho the Great of Navarre (1005–1035), Christian Spain was largely united, but Sancho viewed his state in personal terms and divided it among his four sons. Out of their inheritances eventually emerged the kingdoms of Navarre, Castile, and Aragon. The kingdom of Portugal was the result of a decision by Alfonso VI of Castile (1065–1109) to reward a Burgundian count in 1095 for his services against the Muslims. In 1143 Alfonso VII and the papacy officially recognized the count's son as a king, and Portugal henceforth pursued its own historical path. The reconquista proceeded more rapidly there than in the other Iberian kingdoms, the most crucial event being the capture of Lisbon in 1147 with the aid of an English fleet en route to the Holy Land.

The reconquista became a holy crusade in 1063, more than 30 years before Urban II proclaimed a crusade to conquer the Holy Land. In 1085 Alfonso VI conquered Toledo, the ancient Visigothic capital. Large numbers of Muslims, Jews, and Mozarabs, or Christians who had adopted Arabic culture, were incorporated into the kingdom of Castile, which promised Muslims the right to practice their religion and preserve their customs. Although Alfonso intended to be tolerant, the prospects of a Christian-Moorish civilization similar to the one that existed in thirteenth-century Sicily was doomed when the militant Almoravids invaded southern Spain from North Africa in 1096. Relations between Christians and Moors became increasingly embittered, in part because French Cluniac monks inflamed Spanish emotions and pressured Alfonso to adopt a harder line toward the Muslims. The spread of crusading zeal contributed to the Christian victories, which culminated in 1212 with the rout of the Muslims at Las Navas de Tolosa by the forces of Castile, Aragon, Navarre, and Portugal. As in the battle for the Holy Land, the crusades led to the creation of military orders in Spain. The knights of the Calatrava, Santiago, and Alcantara orders took the vows of poverty, chastity, and obedience but interpreted them in the loosest possible manner; chastity, for example, did not mean abstinence from sexual relations but marital fidelity. The orders acquired considerable power during the High Middle Ages.

The reconquista not only provided the context in which the Iberian kingdoms emerged but also helped to shape their ideals and institutions. Iberian culture, especially in the Spanish states, combined Arabic influence with a fanatical religious zeal born in northern Spain of the crusading spirit. The need for fighting forces and the funds to support them during the long campaign against the Muslims resulted in the appearance of representative institutions, or Cortes, in the states of Leon (1188), Castile (1250), and Portugal (1254) well before the development of similar institutions in France and England, although they never acquired the power of the English Parliament. In Castile, which supplied the bulk of the men for the reconquista, the need for urban support also brought charters for the towns. Above all, the reconquista paved the way for the establishment in the fifteenth century of a unified Spain, which concluded the reconquest with the acquisition of Granada in 1492.

GRANADA, THE "GARDENS OF PARADISE"

Situated on the slopes of the Sierra Nevada and the banks of the Genil River, the Islamic city of Granada developed rapidly following the disintegration of the caliphate of Córdoba in 1031. As late as the ninth century Granada had been little more than a fortified village distinguished by its large Jewish population, which was so numerous that contemporaries called it "Granada of the Jews." Blessed with fertile soil and a Mediterranean climate, the population of the city grew rapidly in the High Middle Ages, rising from 20,000 in the tenth century to 26,000 in the eleventh century, about one-third the size of neighboring Seville. As the reconquista picked up speed, growing numbers of Muslim refugees fled south to Granada, enriching the city with an influx of artisans and merchants. When the monarchs of Castile and Aragon expelled thousands of Muslim agricultural workers in the 1260s, many moved to the kingdom of Granada. By the fifteenth century the population of the state had probably reached 350,000, of whom at least 50,000 resided in the capital, by then the wealthiest city in Spain.

The development of Granada began in earnest after the fall of the strife-ridden Zirids, a dynasty of North African Berbers from Tunis who had governed Granada for most of the eleventh century. They were followed by two dynasties of Berbers, the Almoravids (1090–1154) and the Almohades (1154–1228), the latter of which began the construction of major new fortifications. The city reached the peak of its glory during the rule of the Nasrid dynasty (1231–1492), which conquered Granada in 1238 and made it the capital of a new kingdom. For two and a half centuries Granada remained the only Islamic state in Iberia, but only by becoming a vassal of Castile, which exacted a tribute of 20 to 50 percent of the royal revenues and also required the Nasrid sovereigns to provide military assistance to Castile, even in the work of the reconquista. Thus the Granadans were forced to help the Castilians end Muslim rule in Seville in 1248.

As the city expanded, the role of the Jews declined. Their influence had peaked in the early eleventh century, when many Jews held fiscal and administrative offices and were prominent in the merchant community. Two Jewish financiers—Samuel ibn-Naghrilah and his son Yusuf—even served as viziers, or key administrators, for Zirid kings in the 1000s. In 1066, however, there was a violent reaction to Yusuf and other Jews in government office, which resulted in the massacre of as many as 4,000 Jews. Unlike Mozarabs, Jews were still to be tolerated in Granada, though their numbers were small by the fifteenth century.

Throughout the medieval period, Granada retained the appearance of a Middle Eastern city; one contemporary likened it to Damascus. Because of the influx of immigrants in the Nasrid period, it was extremely crowded; devoid of systematically planned open spaces, most of its maze of streets were no more than 3 to 4 feet wide. The narrow, crooked streets at least offered some protection from the intense sunlight, as did an abundance of shady gardens and courts. Aqueducts brought water to the city, including its numerous Roman-style baths. Artisans, who were grouped according to their craft in distinct quarters or streets, produced linen and silk, much of it for export. Fruits, sugarcane, and almonds were also exported to pay for the grain that had to be imported to supplement inadequate domestic crops.

The Nasrids were noted patrons of education and the arts, and their court attracted numerous learned Muslims. Mathematics, science, medicine, and literature flourished. A university was founded in the mid-1300s, and the city had no less than three important libraries. A hospital for the sick and insane was founded in 1365–1366. But perhaps the greatest monuments of Granada's golden age are the Alhambra and the Generalife. The former, constructed mostly between 1238 and 1358, was a palatial fortress replete with barracks, stables, mosques, and gardens. Built on a hilly terrace overlooking the city, the palace is richly decorated in an ornate Arabesque style with colored tiles and marble, geometric figures, and floral motifs. Its horseshoe arches, delicate columns, and graceful arcades are the culmination of Islamic architecture in Iberia. The nearby Generalife beautifully illustrates the description of paradise in the Koran as "a garden flowing with streams." Intended for summer use, the Generalife, with its pools, fountains, and rows of trees, perfectly blends building and

The Court of the Lions in the Alhambra is not only an exceptionally exquisite walled garden but also a symbol of paradise. The four waterways that converge at the fountain represent the four rivers of paradise, while the twelve lions on the fountain symbolize the signs of the zodiac. [MAS, Barcelona]

landscape architecture. Justifiably, a fourteenth-century observer described Granada in glowing terms: "No city can be compared to it as to its exterior or interior, and no country is like it with respect to the extent of its buildings, and the excellence of its position."[1]

Russia and the Mongol Conquest

While Christians were launching their crusades against the Muslims in the Iberian peninsula and Palestine, the Mongols invaded Russia, which they ruled for two centuries. Just as the initial success of the crusaders in Palestine and the advances of the Christians in Iberia were facilitated by the internal weaknesses of their Muslim enemies, so the Mongol advance was made easier by Russian disunity.

The last of the great Kievan princes, Yaroslav the Wise (1019–1054), had been a very effective ruler, extending the territory of his state, issuing the first written codification of East Slavic law, building numerous churches including the Kiev Cathedral, and supporting the translation of religious literature from Greek into Slavic. He had also strengthened ties between Russia and western Europe, in part by marrying his daughter Anna to the French King Henry I. But Yaroslav made a fatal mistake by implementing the rota system to determine succession to the throne. According to this system, the crown passed to the senior member of the ruling family rather than to the eldest son of a deceased ruler; brothers, in other words, normally had preference over sons. The situation was complicated by the stipulation that each prince in the royal family would be assigned to a town suitable to his place in the line of succession. When the grand prince died, each prince moved up one step to the next highest town. Instead of providing for the peaceful succession of experienced rulers, the rota system fostered dissension and occasionally violent feuding. Rather than evolving into a centralized state, Russia disintegrated into a loose confederation of essentially independent principalities.

Long before the Mongols struck, Kiev was crippled by the assaults of the militant Cumans, a nomadic people who lived in the steppes. Their attacks, which began in the 1060s, eventually severed Kiev's access by the Dnieper River to the Black Sea and trade with Byzantium. In 1203 the Cumans even sacked Kiev, already weakened by the ravages of a rival Russian prince in 1169. The attacks of the Cumans and the Pechenegs had the effect of directing Russian expansion to the forests of the north and west, away from the steppes and from contact with the Byzantine Empire. Thus already by 1200 the Russians were experiencing less and less contact with the rest of Christian Europe.

The Mongols who invaded Russia in the early thirteenth century were militant nomadic tribesmen from Mongolia who had been united into a powerful confederation by Chinghis Khan (1155–1227). They had already launched assaults on China and Korea, while other military units pushed westward until they attacked the Cumans in southern Russia. In 1223 the Mongols defeated a joint Cuman-Russian army, after which they held a victory banquet on a platform beneath which they crushed the captured Russian princes. At the death of Chinghis Khan in 1227 these Mongol units withdrew to their homeland to participate in the selection of his successor, but in 1237 they returned under Chinghis' grandson, Batu, who had a huge army of 50,000 Mongols and 50,000 auxiliaries, mostly Turks. By 1240 they had overrun Russia, slaughtering all who resisted. From there they invaded Poland, Silesia, Bohemia, Moravia, and Hungary, only to pull back to Russia when another khan died in 1241. In the late thirteenth century, under the leadership of Kubilai Khan, Chinghis' grandson, the Mongol Empire included not only Russia but also Iran, China, and part of Southeast Asia—the largest empire known to this time. Within its borders new possibilities existed for peoples of different cultures to communicate with and learn from each other.

The Mongols, commonly called Tartars, Tatars, or the Golden Horde, established their western capital at Sarai on the Lower Volga River, north of the Caspian Sea. The princes of southern and eastern Russia had to pay tribute to the khans, but in turn they received charters, or *yarliks*, authorizing them to act as deputies of the khans. In general, the princes were allowed considerable freedom to rule as they wished. One of them, Alexander Nevsky (died

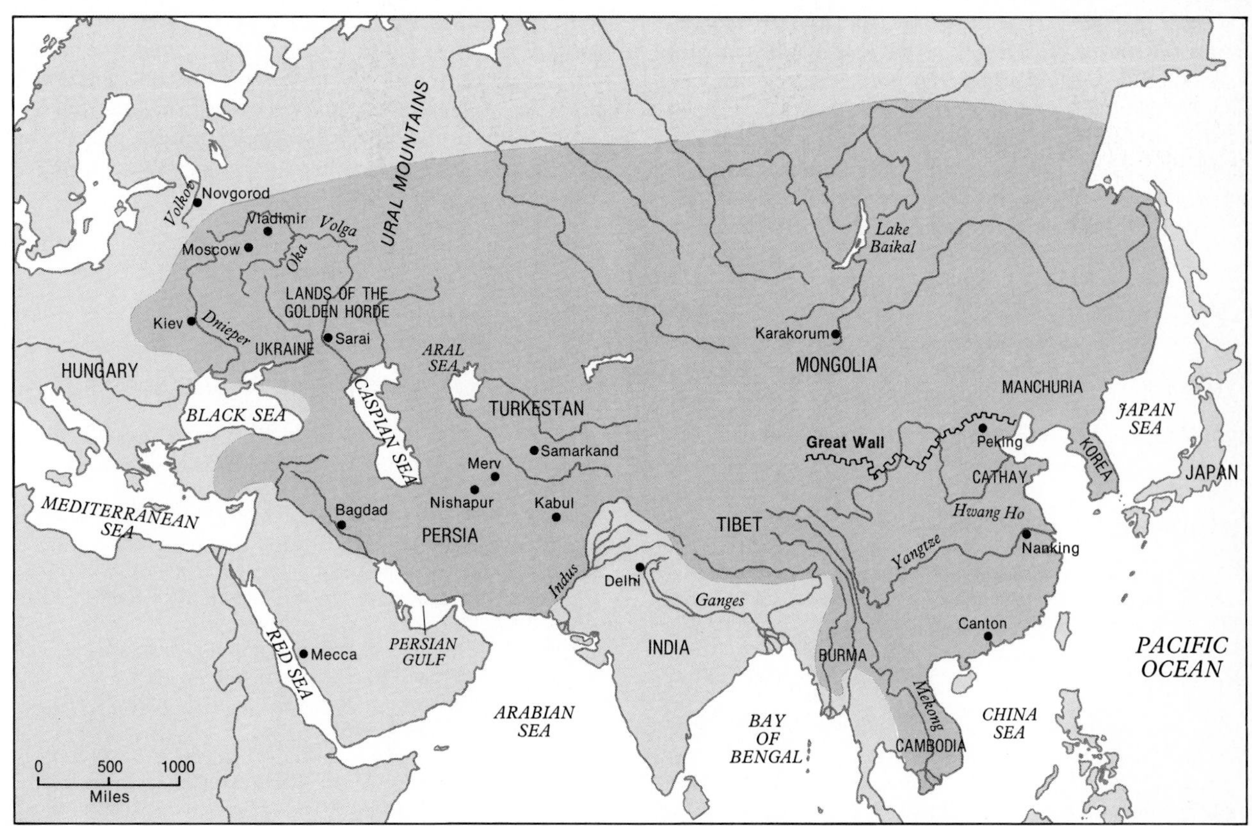

12.5 Mongol Empire, c. 1300

1263), prince of Vladimir, acquired heroic status as the result of major victories over the Swedes, the Teutonic Knights, and the Lithuanians.

The Mongol incursions destroyed the last remnants of Kievan power, and henceforth medieval Russia was essentially divided into four regions. The Mongols dominated the southern steppes, but exercised only moderate control over Great Russia, the region between the Volga and Oka rivers, which included the principalities of Vladimir and Moscow. Western Russia, including the Ukraine, freed itself of Mongol control in the late medieval period, only to fall under the sway of Lithuania. The Tartars had the least influence in northern Russia, where the vast principality of Novgorod extended from the Baltic Sea to beyond the Ural Mountains. Novgorod enjoyed the advantage of a strategic commercial site on the Volkov River, but most of its territory was thinly populated because of its poor soil. Immigrants who left southern Russia to escape the Mongols gravitated mostly to the northeast, where the soil was better and the rivers were more conducive to commercial development. It was this region that provided the nucleus of the modern Russian state in the late medieval period. By that time the Mongols had left their impact on the Russians in such areas as military dress and tactics, manpower levies, and the development of new trade routes. Eastern influence remained strong well into the eighteenth century, when Russian rulers made a conscious effort to westernize their country.

In political terms, the Middle Ages witnessed the transition of England and France from decentralized feudal states to emerging national monarchies, but the course of German and Italian history was strikingly different because of the imperial ambitions of the German rulers and the determination of the papacy to rejuvenate the church by controlling episcopal appointments. Although the popes won the struggle, destroying the Hohenstaufens in the process, they in turn succumbed to growing secular concerns and the forceful resistance of the French and English monarchs.

The century between the pontificates of Innocent III and Boniface VIII, though one of brilliant cultural achievement, nevertheless saw the beginnings of a process that eroded papal prestige and power over secular rulers. The change in papal fortunes was mirrored in the history of the crusading movement over which they tried in vain to preside. The early successes were more than offset by subsequent failures as well as the increasingly materialistic motives of the participants. In the end, only the Iberian crusades achieved their objectives. The accomplishments of the High Middle Ages were nevertheless significant, not only with respect to the political achievements in France and England and the reforms in the church but also in terms of commerce and urban development, the founding of universities, scholastic and scientific thought, and the construction of majestic cathedrals. It is to these religious, intellectual, and cultural achievements that we turn in Chapter 13.

Notes

1. A. G. Chejne, *Muslim Spain: Its History and Culture* (Minneapolis: University of Minnesota Press, 1974), p. 156.

Suggestions for Further Reading

Baldwin, J. W. *The Government of Philip Augustus: Foundations of French Royal Power in the Middle Ages*. Berkeley: University of California Press, 1986.

Barlow, F. *Thomas Becket*. London: Weidenfeld & Nicolson, 1986.

Barraclough, G. *The Origins of Modern Germany*. New York: Norton, 1984.

Brand, C. M. *Byzantium Confronts the West, 1180–1204*. Cambridge, Mass.: Harvard University Press, 1968.

Chapelot, J., and Fossier, R. *The Village and House in the Middle Ages*, trans. H. Cleere. London: Batsford, 1985.

Chazan, R. *European Jewry and the First Crusade*. Berkeley: University of California Press, 1987.

Chibnall, M. *Anglo-Norman England, 1066–1166*. New York: Blackwell, 1986.

Dillard, H. *Daughters of the Reconquest: Women in Castilian Town Society, 1100–1300*. Cambridge: Cambridge University Press, 1984.

Ennen, E. *The Medieval Town*, trans. N. Fryde. New York: Elsevier North-Holland, 1979.

Fawtier, R. *The Capetian Kings of France: Monarchy and Nation, 987–1328*, trans. L. Butler and R. J. Adam. New York: St. Martin's, 1960.

Hanawalt, B. A. *The Ties That Bound: Peasant Families in Medieval England*. New York: Oxford University Press, 1986.

Hillgarth, J. N. *The Spanish Kingdoms, 1250–1516*, 2 vols. Oxford: Clarendon Press, 1976–1978.

Hohenberg, P. M., and Lees, L. H. *The Making of Urban Europe, 1000–1950*. Cambridge, Mass.: Harvard University Press, 1985.

Holt, J. C. *Magna Carta and Medieval Government*. London: Hambledon, 1985.

Imamuddin, S. M. *Muslim Spain, 711–1492 A.D.* Leiden: Brill, 1981.

Kelly, A. *Eleanor of Aquitaine and the Four Kings*. Cambridge, Mass.: Harvard University Press, 1950.

Leyser, K. J. *Medieval Germany and Its Neighbours, 900–1250*. London: Hambledon, 1982.

Little, L. *Religious Poverty and the Profit Economy in Medieval Europe*. Ithaca, N.Y.: Cornell University Press, 1978.

Lopez, R. S. *The Commercial Revolution of the Middle Ages, 950–1350*. Cambridge: Cambridge University Press, 1976.

Mayer, H. E. *The Crusades*, trans. J. Gillingham. London: Oxford University Press, 1972.

Morgan, D. *The Mongols*. New York: Blackwell, 1986.

Nicholas, D. *The Domestic Life of a Medieval City: Women, Children, and the Family in Fourteenth-Century Ghent*. Lincoln: University of Nebraska Press, 1985.

Obolensky, D. *The Byzantine Commonwealth: Eastern Europe, 500–1453*. New York: Praeger, 1971.

Petit-Dutaillis, C. *The Feudal Monarchy in France and England, from the Tenth to the Thirteenth Century*, trans. E. D. Hunt. New York: Barnes & Noble Books, 1964, 1980.

Postan, M. M., and Miller, E. *The Cambridge Economic History of Europe*, vol. 2: *Trade and Industry in the Middle Ages*, 2d ed. Cambridge: Cambridge University Press, 1987.

Reynolds, S. *An Introduction to the History of English Medieval Towns*. Oxford: Clarendon Press, 1977.

Rossabi, M. *Khubilai Khan: His Life and Times*. Berkeley: University of California Press, 1988.

Strayer, J. R. *The Reign of Philip the Fair*. Princeton, N.J.: Princeton University Press, 1980.

Vernadsky, G. *The Mongols and Russia*. New Haven, Conn.: Yale University Press, 1953.

Warren, W. L. *King John*, 2d ed. Berkeley: University of California Press, 1978.

CHAPTER · 13

Life and Culture in Medieval Europe

The culture of Europe was forged primarily from a combination of Judeo-Christian values, classical ideals and concepts, and Germanic traditions. Yet as it developed, European culture also owed much to the Islamic world. By the High Middle Ages, European culture was vigorously creative. Commercial developments were instrumental in shaping the new outlook, as the burgeoning cities became the setting for the cathedral schools and the first universities as well as for the great symbols of the High Middle Ages, the Romanesque and Gothic cathedrals. Troubadours, university professors and students, affluent merchants, and crusaders took their place in a Europe hitherto largely confined to feudal aristocrats, peasants, and parish clergy. This was an age of spiritual renewal, as reflected in the growth of papal power, the founding of new religious orders, and the intellectual brilliance of scholastic thought. Theologians such as Thomas Aquinas attempted nothing less than a synthesis of all knowledge, both earthly and spiritual, for the greater glory of God. But although the age was one of brilliant artistic and intellectual achievement, it was no less an age whose darker side boded ill for Jews. If love, service, and civic pride inspired the build-

St. Clare of Assisi, disciple of St. Francis and founder of the Poor Clares, as painted by the fourteenth-century Italian artist Simone Martini. [Bildarchiv Foto Marburg; Chapel of St. Martin, Church of St. Francis, Assisi]

ing of the great cathedrals, bigotry and hate found their outlet in ruthless anti-Semitism. Nor did the status of women appreciably improve despite the overall achievements of the age and their contribution to them.

The Medieval Church

Although Christianity was the dominant religion and played a pivotal role in the development of Europe throughout the Middle Ages and beyond, its adherents struggled to overcome a widespread belief in primitive natural forces and magic. Early medieval priests were in effect missionaries in their own parishes, though in the course of time they were successful in winning at least nominal adherence to Christianity. With its warnings of eternal damnation and its message of salvation through the sacraments, the church gradually shaped a code of conduct and a basic system of belief that was common to much of Europe. The church was, then, a key unifying force.

In their efforts to win the adherence of the people, church leaders periodically clashed with their secular counterparts when their policies conflicted. The tendency of secular authorities to rely on educated churchmen to help administer their governments raised the question of authority: To whom did such officials owe their ultimate obedience? It is, however, erroneous to think of secular and ecclesiastical rulers as being in perpetual conflict, for they were commonly allies in maintaining control over their subjects. Most rulers governed with the church's blessing, while secular authorities in turn used the machinery of government and the military force at their disposal to protect the church and assist it in carrying out its policies. When conflicts did erupt, church leaders could seek support from their secular allies or have recourse to two spiritual weapons, excommunication and the interdict. Excommunication technically prohibited an offender from participating in church rites or maintaining contact with other Christians, and if the sentence was not lifted prior to one's death, the offender was eternally damned. An interdict, which could be imposed on a particular area, barred all church services with the exception of baptism and extreme unction (last rites). To be effective, these penalties had to have popular support and could not be overused.

Monastic Communities

One of the characteristic features of medieval Christianity was the founding of religious communities in which men and women lived in relative isolation from the rest of society. Such communities were initially established in Egypt and then spread throughout the Roman Empire, including such places as Constantinople and Jerusalem. The first monastic communities in the West appeared in the late fourth and fifth centuries, the most famous of them being the two founded by John Cassian (385–440) near Marseilles in Gaul. Other monastic experiments were tried as far afield as Spain, England, and Ireland, but it was a monastery founded in Italy in 529 by Benedict of Nursia (480–547) that eventually had the greatest impact on European monasticism.

As a guide for the monks who joined him at Monte Cassino, south of Rome, Benedict wrote a rule, the intent of which was to provide for an orderly existence conducive to the complete dedication of one's life to God. Unlike some of the other early monastic leaders, Benedict did not call for extreme forms of self-denial but insisted on moderation in a life of prayer, contemplation, study, communal worship, and labor. Monks vowed to follow a life of poverty, to be chaste, to obey their superiors, and to be stable, that is, not to leave the monastery without permission. Responsibility for the direction of the monastery was placed in the hands of an abbot, elected for life by the monks and consecrated by a bishop but accountable only to the Rule and to God. The monastery was intended to be self-sufficient; hence its members had to perform a variety of tasks that ranged from farming to cooking and making clothes. Benedict's Rule did not direct monks to teach or copy manuscripts, but such tasks became necessary as novices had to be educated and as the monks required service books, Bibles, and other religious literature. By the seventh century there were communities for Benedictine nuns, who regarded Benedict's sister Scholastica as their patroness. Like the monasteries of the men, their convents spread throughout Europe in the ensuing centuries.

The Papacy

No less important than monasticism for the history of Latin Christendom was the growth in the early Middle Ages of the power and prestige of the bishop of Rome, more familiarly known as the pope (the Latin *papa* is derived from *pappas*, the Greek word for "father"). The claim to papal primacy, though based on Jesus' allusion to the apostle Peter as the rock on which the church would be built, was in fact asserted much later and only in response to the growing authority and claims of the patriarch of Constantinople. Pope Leo I (440–461), the beneficiary of an imperial Roman decree recognizing his sole jurisdiction over the Latin church, claimed to have fullness of power, presumably over the church as a whole. If, however, Justinian's successors had been able to continue the expansion of Byzantine rule, such claims might have proved worthless. But the internal problems of the Byzantine Empire and the external challenge of the Muslims destroyed whatever chance the patriarch of Constantinople had to establish himself as universal head of the Christian church and contributed to its growing split into eastern and Latin communions. The ability of the popes to maintain their independence was momentous, for they claimed to have authority superior to that of monarchs. In Eastern Orthodoxy, however, the prevailing theory of caesaropapism placed ultimate authority in the hands of the emperor. In practice, of course, in both east and west, challenges to the authority of emperors and popes were successful from time to time.

The greatest of the early medieval popes, Gregory I (590–604), enhanced papal power by sponsoring a mission to convert the pagans of Anglo-Saxon England. The success of the mission was partly due to his instructions that pagan festival days and shrines be adapted to Christian use rather than repudiated outright. He was concerned as well with the conversion of the Lombards and with the expansion of Christianity in Spain. Contemporaries called him "God's consul" because of his administrative reforms, particularly the reorganization of papal revenues. A monk himself, Gregory wrote a biography of Benedict of Nursia, thereby helping to provide the impetus that made the Benedictine Rule the dominant form of monastic life by the ninth century.

Apostolic Renewal: The New Religious Orders

Although the imperial revival under Otto I in the mid-tenth century threatened the independence of the papal office, a contemporary reform movement helped restore its vigor and spiritual leadership in the High Middle Ages. In 910 Duke William "the Good" of Aquitaine founded a monastery at Cluny in Burgundy, with a charter guaranteeing independence from secular control. By this time control over other monasteries had fallen into the hands of feudal lords, who stripped their revenues and sold their offices. To prevent this from happening at Cluny, William placed the monastery under papal protection before he died; henceforth its abbots owed their allegiance only to Rome. They insisted on major reforms in the church, including renewed emphasis on the Rule of Benedict and the monastic liturgy, an end to the sale of church offices, and the enforcement of clerical celibacy, which, though widely disregarded, had been church policy since the sixth century. The call to reform received a stunning response: new foundations and converted Benedictine houses swelled the total of institutions based on the Cluniac model to more than 300, all of which were administered by priors subordinate to the abbot of Cluny. The renewed sense of spiritual devotion radiated well beyond the cloister as lay believers were inspired by the Cluniac monks. The heightened devotional interest was appropriately manifested in the appearance of the first prayer books for the laity. Inspired by the prayers of Cluniac monks, the prayer books began a tradition that culminated in the production of the beautifully illustrated books of hours in the late medieval period.

The Cluniacs were the first wave of a series of reform-oriented monastic movements that swept the Latin church in the High Middle Ages. The Cistercians, founded in the twelfth century, were a Benedictine reform movement that emphasized individual devotion rather than public worship and agricultural labor rather than other forms of work. The Cistercians tended to settle in remote areas to avoid corruption by secular influences. With austerity as their ideal, the Cistercians followed a rigorous vegetarian diet that even excluded dairy products. They seldom spoke, and they worshiped in churches devoid of ornamentation. The Cistercians achieved a well-deserved reputation for their skills in making marginal lands productive. The movement reached its peak under the leadership of Bernard of Clairvaux and his successors. There were nearly 350 Cistercian abbeys by the time Bernard died in 1153, and more than 700 by 1300. Like other monastic orders, the Cistercians were less than enthusiastic about the thousands of women who wanted to become Cistercian nuns, though in the end the church resolved the issue by placing the convents under monastic supervision as a subordinate branch of the male order.

The richness of medieval Christian religious life is illustrated in the variety of orders that were founded. The Carthusians were far more rigorous than the Benedictines, insisting, for example, that each monk live in a separate cell, fast every Friday, and eat with his fellow monks only

St. Francis of Assisi, founder of the Franciscan order of mendicants, as depicted by the thirteenth-century Italian painter Cimabue. [Alinari/Art Resource]

Holy Poverty: The Ideal of Francis

The ideals of Francis of Assisi are clearly reflected in his will, prepared shortly before his death in 1226. His emphasis on holy poverty contrasts with the growing wealth of the church.

When the Lord gave me the care of some brothers, no one showed me what I ought to do, but the Most High himself revealed to me that I ought to live according to the model of the holy gospel. I caused a short and simple formula to be written, and the lord pope confirmed it for me.

Those who presented themselves to follow this kind of life distributed all they might have to the poor. They contented themselves with one tunic, patched within and without, with the cord and breeches, and we desired to have nothing more. . . .

We loved to live in poor and abandoned churches, and we were ignorant, and were submissive to all. I worked with my hands and would still do so, and I firmly desire also that all the other brothers work, for this makes for goodness. Let those who know no trade learn one, but not for the purpose of receiving the price of their toil, but for their good example and to flee idleness. And when we are not given the price of our work, let us resort to the table of the Lord, begging our bread from door to door. The Lord revealed to me the salutation which we ought to give: "God give you peace!"

Let the brothers take great care not to accept churches, habitations, or any other buildings erected for them, except as all is in accordance with the holy poverty which we have vowed in the Rule; and let them not live in them except as strangers and pilgrims.

Source: J. H. Robinson, ed., *Readings in European History*, vol. 1 (Boston: Ginn, 1904), pp. 393–394.

on Sundays and the major holy days. In sharp contrast to this solitary life, "canons regular" combined the monastic concept of living according to a rule with the duties of a secular priest. Thus the Augustinians ministered to the needs of the laity, both spiritually and materially. Unlike the Benedictines and Cluniacs, they refused to amass large endowments and impressive buildings, preferring instead to follow a humble lifestyle and aid the needy.

A third form of religious vocation originated in the thirteenth century with the founding of mendicant or begging orders, so called because their friars depended on alms for their living. Like the monks and canons regular, they took vows of poverty, chastity, and obedience, and they lived in communities; but unlike the monks, they devoted their lives to ministering to the laity. One of the principal mendicant orders was founded by the Spanish Augustinian Dominic (1170–1221) to fight the spread of heresy in southern France. The Dominicans, formally constituted in 1216, intended to combat heresy by preaching, education, and holy living. Their enormous contribution to Western education stems from their rule: "Day and night, whether at home or traveling, let the brethren ever be occupied with reading or meditation."

The other major mendicant order, the Franciscans, was established by Francis of Assisi (1182–1226), the son of a well-to-do Italian cloth merchant. Motivated by a religious vision, Francis sold much of his father's possessions, gave the proceeds to the church, and renounced material goods. Francis and his followers, whose ideal was absolute poverty and humility, obtained papal approval for their order in 1209. The friars devoted themselves to the spiritual and material needs of the lowly, particularly in the towns. At first the Franciscans shunned learning in preference to apostolic simplicity, but their growing competition with the Dominicans gradually persuaded them to engage in scholarly endeavors. Before the century was over, both mendicant orders became prominent in the universities. Similarly, both became actively involved in missionary work among the Muslims and the Mongols.

ST. CLARE AND THE POOR SISTERS

The life of Clare of Assisi illustrates the problems experienced by women attracted to the new religious movements. For most, including Clare, the lure was undoubtedly spiritual, though some may have been drawn to the religious life because they had little prospect of marriage, shunned the dangers of childbirth, or sought spiritual status to compensate for their declining role in medieval society. But churchmen were generally troubled by the prospect of separate female orders. How could they support themselves? Because women were excluded from the priesthood, who would provide cloistered convents with pastoral care? Women, moreover, were thought to be unusually susceptible to heresy. The problem became acute by the early thirteenth century as female groups began to organize, particularly in Italy and Flanders.

Born into a pious aristocratic family at Assisi in 1194, Clare was influenced by a mother known for her charitable deeds and pilgrimages. While her parents were arranging her marriage, Francis of Assisi secretly met with Clare to persuade her to pursue a more rigorous spiritual life. One night in March 1212, at the age of 18, she fled to a nearby chapel, where Francis received her vows to lead a life of poverty and to imitate Christ and Mary. The "Poor Clares" or "Poor Sisters" date their origins from that event. The sisters were housed in the church and convent of San Damiano, near Assisi, where Clare formally acquired the title of abbess in 1216, a position she retained until her death in August 1253. She attracted many followers, including two of her sisters and, after her father's death, her mother.

The problem of procuring a rule for her order, already difficult because of antifemale sentiment, was compounded by the decision of the Fourth Lateran Council in 1215 not to allow any new orders. Francis had given Clare only verbal advice and a brief "way of life," but this had not been officially recognized. In 1219, therefore, Cardinal Ugolino, the future Pope Gregory IX, provided a rule based on Benedictine and Cistercian principles: an austere life, strict seclusion from the world, and the right of the community as a whole to own property. Having already taken a vow of absolute poverty, Clare was adamantly opposed to the property provision, an issue that remained a sore point until the last days of her life. Ugolino's intent was to place all the female groups under papal protection, with a single uniform rule and with pastoral care provided by the Franciscans. Francis, however, refused to be associated with any female community apart from that of Clare at San Damiano: "God has taken away our wives, and now the devil gives us sisters," he fumed, afraid that Ugolino's scheme would ruin his order.

Despite Francis' reluctance to accept pastoral responsibility for convents, he maintained close relations with Clare, who seems to have been his confidant. On one occasion she nursed him back to health at San Damiano, during which period he wrote his famous *Canticle of the Sun*, reflecting his remarkable sense of oneness with and love of nature. Her own writings, particularly her *Testament*, reveal her strong commitment to poverty: "I was ever anxious with my sisters to preserve the holy poverty which we promised to God and the blessed Francis."[1] This commitment was especially striking since Clare and most of her followers came from aristocratic backgrounds. As she lay dying in 1253, she was visited by Pope Innocent IV, who at last approved the rule she had sought for more than three decades, which embraced a concept of poverty that allowed neither personal nor communal possessions apart from enough land on which to grow food. The continuation of the Poor Clares to the present day is largely due to the persistence and devotion of Clare, who was canonized in 1255.

Dissidents and Heretics

The spirit of reform that swept the church substantially increased lay interest in religion, but one unintended result of this was the rapid growth of beliefs the church considered heretical (unorthodox). In the 1170s the French merchant Peter Waldo of Lyons attracted disciples by his emphasis on poverty and simplicity as well as his attack on the moral corruption of the clergy. The Waldensians, or "Poor Men of Lyons," insisted on the right of laymen to preach, rejected some of the sacraments, and accepted the Scripture alone as authoritative in religion. Moreover, they wanted translations of the Bible in the language of the people. Although they were excommunicated by the pope in 1184, the Waldensians remained popular in southern France and northern Italy.

A more serious threat to the church was posed by the Albigensians, so called because their center was the town of Albi in southern France. Their teaching viewed the universe in terms of a struggle between the forces of good and evil.* The Cathari, or "pure ones," were therefore supposed to abstain from most material things, including marriage, worldly possessions, and meat, in their quest to attain a state of perfection. Some rejected the mass, infant baptism, and even the church itself; voluntarily starving oneself to death was highly praised. Not only were the Albigensians condemned by the church, but Pope Innocent III called for a crusade to exterminate them. Knights from northern France rallied to the call, more interested in the possibility of seizing land than uprooting heresy. The harshest fighting lasted 20 years (1209–1229) and ultimately eradicated many of the heretics.

Another weapon to combat heresy was the Inquisition, instituted by Pope Gregory IX in 1231. The inquisitors' task was to convert the heretics if possible, but in any case to prevent the deadly "disease" of heresy from spreading. The Inquisition embraced the principles of Roman law, including the use of torture, such as the rack or holding the feet of the accused to hot coals. Suspects had no right to counsel, no opportunity to question witnesses, nor even the right to know the charges against them.

*Such views were called Manichaean, after the third-century Mesopotamian prophet who advocated such a dualistic view of the universe.

Those who refused to relinquish their heretical beliefs or were convicted a second time were subject to severe penalties, including imprisonment, loss of property, or burning at the stake. Although some inquisitors were notoriously severe, such as a Dominican who had 180 people burned on a single day in 1239, most of the accused escaped execution. Because the inquisitors were not allowed to shed blood themselves, the executions were carried out by the state, but the church nevertheless left itself open to condemnation by relying on force rather than moral suasion to maintain its spiritual supremacy.

The World of Learning

The need to staff expanding governments with educated officials and the growth of towns, with their increasingly sophisticated businesses, their law courts, and their collection of taxes and fees, led to a greater demand for literate persons. This was a major cause of the educational revolution of the late eleventh century and the twelfth century, as was the Gregorian stress on the importance of a better-educated clergy. From the sixth century to the tenth, most schooling in Europe had been provided by the monasteries, though there were also a few cathedral and secular schools, the latter mostly in northern Italy and southern France. These early schools were insufficient, both in number and in curriculum, to meet the needs of the towns, the expanding royal courts, and the growing ecclesiastical bureaucracy. The monastic schools, with a curriculum oriented toward biblical interpretation and commentary, were never intended to serve society as a whole.

Urban developments not only increased the demand for educated persons but also made cathedral schools accessible to more people, particularly sons of the laity. The better cathedral schools, such as those at Chartres, Rheims, and Paris, included a music school, a school for the seven liberal arts, and a more advanced school for theological studies. The seven liberal arts—grammar, rhetoric, logic, arithmetic, geometry, astronomy, and music—were regarded as the fundamental branches of knowledge. Some ecclesiastical schools even provided education in law, medicine, philosophy, and the natural sciences. At a humbler level, parish priests sometimes taught reading, writing, mathematics, and the other liberal arts. The church's growing interest in education was especially evident in the late twelfth century, when it became mandatory for every cathedral to have a school and for each to be provided with funds sufficient to educate the children of the poor without charge. In Italy, Germany, and the Netherlands merchants took the lead in establishing municipal schools; Hamburg, Munich, and Lübeck had them by 1300. In the towns young people could also be trained as apprentices by surgeons, barbers, dentists, lawyers, notaries, architects, and artists.

In addition to the establishment of new schools, the educational revolution of the High Middle Ages also involved curricular changes. Before the eleventh century the curriculum was heavily oriented toward biblical studies, but in the 1000s the emphasis shifted to logic. As more Latin translations of Arabic and Greek works on philosophy and natural science became available, these subjects too were the object of greater attention. Writers such as the Augustinian friar Egidio Colonna, author of *On the Governance of Rulers*, called for a comprehensive curriculum that included the seven liberal arts, classical and Christian literature, philosophy, politics, economics, natural science, and etiquette. Colonna also advocated the education of women. At one level the educational revolution increased lay literacy, though only a small minority could read and even fewer could write, while at another level the revolution culminated in the founding of the first universities.

Scholarly Guilds: The Medieval University

As growing numbers of students traveled to cities such as Paris, Bologna, and Salerno in search of the best teachers in the arts, theology, law, and medicine, formal organization became necessary to secure the rights and privileges of students and teachers. There was also a need for some form of academic recognition—a "degree"—that would enable qualified persons to teach in other cities. In a society accustomed to craft and merchant guilds, the natural solution was an academic guild, a *universitas* or corporation, that could protect the interests of faculty and students as well as issue licenses to teach. Organization was essential to assure academic standards, provide protection from townspeople inclined to overcharge students for board and room, and obtain the right of faculty and students to be tried in church rather than local courts. In southern Europe universities were initially guilds of students; in northern Europe, guilds of teachers.

The earliest universities evolved at Bologna and Paris in the mid-twelfth century, and Salerno had a medical school. In the early 1100s Bologna's reputation as the leading center of legal studies was firmly established through the work of Irnerius, who wrote commentaries on contemporary legal codes based on his familiarity with the Byzantine *Corpus juris civilis*, and of Gratian, whose *Decretum* became the standard text for the study of canon (church) law. At Bologna students first organized into regional groups called "nations," and these in turn eventually united to form the University of Bologna, chartered by the emperor Frederick Barbarossa in 1158. Students established regulations to govern the number, length, and content of lectures and fined or boycotted teachers who failed to cover the specified material or missed classes. The faculty, however, controlled the granting of degrees and, because of their permanence, gradually increased their authority in the university.

At Paris teachers formed a guild to control the granting of licenses to teach, at least in part because the chancellor of the archdiocese of Paris had been selling them to unqualified persons. Following a "town-gown" conflict in which several students were killed, King Philip II gave the university its charter in 1200, and the papal bull *Parens scientiarum* (1231) subsequently established institutional independence by exempting the university from the jurisdiction of the local church.

Paris was famous for its teachers of logic, philosophy, and theology. English students were among those attracted to Paris, but in 1167 worsening relations between England and France forced King Henry II to order them home. They settled at Oxford, which had its own chancellor by 1214. The growing demand for educated people in church and state, national and urban rivalries, and the search for more hospitable environments led to the founding of more universities—over 20 by 1300, more than 75 by 1500. A number of these were royal or papal foundations: that of Naples, which absorbed the medical school at Salerno, was established by the emperor Frederick II; those of Rome, by Pope Innocent IV; of Toulouse, by Pope Gregory IX; and of Seville, by King Alfonso X of Castile. Others were the result of migrating students, as in the case of Cambridge (from Oxford) and Padua (from Bologna).

Most universities were organized into four faculties: the arts, which comprised the *trivium* (grammar, rhetoric, and logic) and the *quadrivium* (arithmetic, geometry, astronomy, and music), theology, medicine, and civil and canon law. The standard form of instruction was the lecture, which consisted of reading and expounding on a Latin text. A typical student listened to lectures for about seven hours a day, beginning at 6 A.M. Formal debates were also a standard pedagogical tool, but because of the expense there were few books and no libraries. Students were not examined at the conclusion of a series of lectures but at the end of a program of study, when examinations were oral and usually public. A bachelor of arts degree typically took three to six years of study and qualified one to instruct others under a master's supervision. A license to teach required several more years of study. In order to lecture as part of the arts faculty one had to become a master of arts, which required the preparation and defense of a thesis. Substantial additional study was required for a doctorate in law (up to seven years) or theology (up to 15 years).

At first universities had no permanent campuses or buildings but made do with rented rooms. To assist needy students, residence halls or "colleges" were endowed, and these eventually acquired their own instructional staff. Among the best known are the Sorbonne, founded at Paris in 1257 or 1258 by Robert de Sorbon, a royal chaplain, and Merton College, established at Oxford around 1263 by Robert Merton, who acquired the buildings from the local Jewish community. Such colleges provided the nucleus of a permanent campus. By the end of the thirteenth century the number of students—all male—at Paris exceeded 4,000, while Oxford had more than 2,000. As centers of learning, the universities attracted some of the greatest minds of the High Middle Ages.

PARIS: MONKS, MERCHANTS, AND STUDENTS IN THE ROYAL CITY

By the time the University of Paris received its charter from Philip II in 1200, the city was in the midst of a period of dramatic growth. At the beginning of the eleventh century its outskirts had still been in ruins as the result of ninth-century Viking raids, but by 1300 the city's population had reached 100,000 and gloried in a majestic new cathedral, imposing new walls, and a flourishing commerce in addition to its university. In part the growth reflected the increasing power of the French monarchy, in part the city's strategic location at the crossroads of the trade routes between southern Europe and Flanders, or, by way of the River Seine, between eastern France and the English Channel. Because the Capetian monarchs made Paris their capital, the city attracted both the nobility and ecclesiastical and educational institutions, thereby increasing the demand for luxury items and other goods. Parisian artisans produced a wide range of jewelry, swords, saddles, linens, and wine barrels. Merchants in turn traded these goods at the great Champagne fairs in northeastern France for Flemish and Italian woolens, Asian spices and sugar, Byzantine silks, Spanish leathers, and English tin.

The heart of Paris was the Île de la Cité, an island in the Seine whose western half was dominated by the royal palace and the exquisite Gothic chapel of Sainte-Chapelle, built by Louis IX to house a collection of relics that allegedly included the crown of thorns, a piece of the cross, and a sample of Christ's blood. The eastern portion of the Île de la Cité became the site of the magnificent Gothic cathedral of Notre Dame ("Our Lady"), first begun in 1163. The city's commercial center, site of its guilds and principal markets, was on the right bank of the Seine, extending in a rough semicircle from the Grand Pont, the great bridge, to the Île de la Cité, on which the Jewish and Lombard moneychangers had their shops. To the south, the Left Bank, or Latin Quarter, was the home of the university and of several religious orders, including the Dominicans, the Augustinians, and the Carmelites. The ancient Roman walls, which were still standing in the twelfth century, enclosed only some 25 acres and were thus totally inadequate for the burgeoning city. Philip II ordered the construction of new ramparts on both banks. The resulting walls, which enclosed approximately 625 acres, were up to 20 feet high and 10 feet thick and featured 33 towers on the north bank and 34 on the south.

Just beyond the wall, where the rampart met the river, stood the Louvre, a fortified palace that also functioned as a treasury, an armory, and a prison. Philip's ambitious building program also included three new hospitals to care for the needy and three aqueducts to supply the city with fresh water. He even launched a project to pave the city's main streets with 3-foot-square blocks of sandstone.

The Paris of Philip II and Louis IX was a colorful amalgam of the secular and the sacred, the royal and the common. The enforcement of the law was the responsibility of the provost of Paris, who was appointed by the crown, but in general city affairs were handled by a municipal council presided over by the master of the corporation of river merchants, the *marchands de l'eau*. Despite the presence of the crown and major religious orders, Paris was far from a puritanical city. Prostitutes were so abundant that two streets were named after them, the Rue Val-d'Amour and the Rue Pute-y-muce ("whore-in-hiding"). The churchmen of Paris themselves sometimes behaved bawdily, and in 1212 a council convened in the city tried to curtail their more outlandish behavior, including the keeping of mistresses, the Feast of the Drunken Deacons on December 26, and the Feast of Fools on January 1, when they parodied the liturgy, burned old shoes instead of incense, and marched through the streets wearing grotesque costumes.

In the thirteenth century university students added to the local color, particularly when they demonstrated on behalf of a favorite cause, battled with the civic guards, or fought with the townsfolk or among themselves. Although lectures began at 5 A.M. and continued, with appropriate breaks, well into the afternoon, there was time in the evening for conversation and a few drinks in a tavern before retiring to modest rooms, typically in the attics of Left Bank houses. Classes met in rooms rented by the faculty, and only gradually did the university begin to acquire buildings, notably the privately endowed colleges, such as the Sorbonne, established to house, teach, and control the students. Although these were arduous years, the students lived in one of the most exciting European cities and studied under the foremost faculty of their day.

The Scholastics

Well before the evolution of the first universities, the schoolmen, or scholastics, of western Europe were engaged in a heated debate over a number of philosophical and theological issues. The scholastics, who used Aristotelian methodology and adopted the Aristotelian world view, were especially concerned with three fundamental and intimately related problems: the proper study of theological knowledge, the nature of ultimate reality, and the relationship of faith and reason.

Although the roots of Christian theology go back to the first century, only in the 1100s did the discipline of systematic theology emerge through the application of logic to the most fundamental religious questions. The leaders in this endeavor were Peter Abelard (1079–1142) of Brittany, a master in the cathedral school at Paris, and his disciple Peter Lombard (c. 1095–1160), who eventually became bishop of Paris. Their technique, known as the dialectical method, consisted of juxtaposing seemingly contradictory statements in order to encourage students to seek a logical resolution. Abelard applied this technique to theology in his book *Sic et Non* ("Yes and No"), a compilation of contradictory statements by early church fathers on a variety of religious issues. Students were encouraged to resolve the conflicts by taking into account the way words change meaning over time, the possibility of inaccurate texts, historical context, and the need to weigh the credibility of different authorities. Peter Lombard followed the same pedagogical method in his *Four Books of Sentences*, which analyzed such fundamental Christian doctrines as the Trinity, creation, the Incarnation, and the sacraments. From the thirteenth century to the sixteenth Peter Lombard's book served as the standard theological text in the universities. Traditionalists, however, condemned the logical approach to theology on the grounds that divine mysteries could not be probed by human reason, and that such a method could easily lead to unorthodox thought.

The famous debate over the nature of reality reflected the indebtedness of the scholastics to classical Greek philosophy. In the eleventh century the French scholar Roscellin rejected the Platonic notion that universal concepts are real and instead insisted that reality consists only of individual things. Individual men and women are real; humanity is simply the name (*nomen*) for a mental category or concept. Roscellin and his followers thus came to be called nominalists. Because they attached primary significance to the experience of individual things through the senses, the nominalists radically altered traditional theology, which had relied heavily on philosophical concepts. Accordingly, nominalists had to assert most religious beliefs solely on the basis of faith and biblical teaching, not rational demonstration.

In contrast to the nominalists, Realists such as the Italian monk Anselm (1033–1109) asserted that individual things are knowable only because they reflect universal ideas, which are accessible by reason. Realists agreed that initially an act of faith is required for things beyond the reach of the senses. "I believe," said Anselm, "so that I may know." Once beyond this, however, reason could demonstrate the existence of universal ideas and even of God. It is impossible, Anselm argued, to conceive of a being greater than God; a being who exists is greater than a being who does not exist; therefore, the idea of God must include the existence of God. The importance Anselm attached to reason did not negate Scripture but helped to make logic and philosophy a fundamental part of the new systematic theology.

A middle ground in the debate over universals was advocated by a group of Moderate Realists that included

The scholastic theologian Thomas Aquinas was influenced by Aristotle (lower left) and Plato (lower right) as well as the earlier Christian thinkers shown above him. The Islamic philosopher Averroës lies vanquished at his feet. [Alinari/Art Resource]

Abelard and his student, John of Salisbury. Influenced by Aristotle, they accepted the reality of both individual things and the general ideas after which they were patterned. The idea of humanity was thus as real as the experience of individuals. The greatest of the Moderate Realists, Thomas Aquinas (c. 1225–1274), taught that each particular thing has the universal within it, as that which gives it its essence; by studying individual things, one can rationally discover the essence and thus formulate valid general concepts.

At the heart of the debate over universals and the dialectical method was the fundamental question of the relationship between faith (or revelation) and reason. The scholastics generally agreed that theology and philosophy are intimately related, but Franciscan and Dominican thinkers disagreed over the nature of that relationship. The great Franciscan theologians Alexander of Hales (died 1245) and his pupil Bonaventure (1221–1274), both of whom taught at the University of Paris, respected reason but put their real emphasis on revelation. To them faith was an act of the will by which one accepts revealed truth; reason is useful only to explain the truth gleaned from revelation. The leading Dominican theologians, Aquinas and his teacher Albertus Magnus (died 1280), who also taught at Paris, accorded reason a greater role than the Franciscans in the discovery of knowledge but stopped short of making revelation subordinate to reason. Because faith and reason are complementary paths, Aquinas believed that by rational processes an unbeliever can be led to the point of making a commitment of faith.

Both Alexander of Hales and Aquinas wrote lengthy *summae* (summations) in which major theological issues were rationally analyzed through a process that included the meticulous refutation of opposing viewpoints. The blending of theology and philosophy is nowhere more evident than in Aquinas' *Summa Theologica*, particularly in the sections devoted to rational proofs for the existence of God, such as the argument from an orderly universe to the existence of a Great Designer or the argument from motion to the existence of a Prime Mover, derived from Aristotle. For Aquinas, faith and reason are fully harmonious, for both are avenues to seek the one truth. The work of Aquinas thus represents the culmination of the attempt to synthesize the revealed tenets of Christianity with the rational principles of classical philosophy. Christian scholastics such as Aquinas, Jewish theologians such as Maimonides, Muslim philosophers such as Averroës, and contemporary Neo-Confucian scholars in China all stressed the importance of logical analysis to bolster traditional values. Apart from the Neo-Confucianists, they shared a heavy indebtedness to the thought of Aristotle, but in a more general sense all of them reflect the basic human quest to order existence and reaffirm basic ideals through the use of reason.

Law and Political Thought

While the scholastics established the discipline of systematic theology, other scholars were responsible for reviving the study of Roman law in the late eleventh and early twelfth centuries. The revival began in southern France and northern Italy as teachers and attorneys turned increasingly to the sixth-century *Corpus juris civilis* of Justinian for guidance. At Bologna, Irnerius and his successors lectured on the *Corpus* using the same dialectical method popularized in theology by Abelard. Their work was largely confined to glosses or comments on the *Corpus*, but commencing in the mid-twelfth century legal scholars became more creative by exploring the general principles on which the laws were based and adapting the laws to the specific conditions of their own time and locale. There was thus a gradual blending of ideas in Roman and customary law, even in Germany and England, where customary and Roman law continued as separate entities. Ro-

Proving That God Exists

The compatibility of faith and reason in scholastic thought is reflected in Thomas Aquinas' arguments to prove the existence of God.

God's existence can be proved in five ways. The first and clearest proof is the argument from motion. It is certain, and in accordance with sense experience, that some things in this world are moved. Now everything that is moved is moved by something else. . . . We are therefore bound to arrive at a first mover which is not moved by anything, and all men understand that this is God.

The second way is from the nature of an efficient cause. We find that there is a sequence of efficient causes in sensible things. . . . We are therefore bound to suppose that there is a first efficient cause. And all men call this God.

The third way is from the nature of possibility and necessity. There are some things which may either exist or not exist, since some things come to be and pass away, and may therefore be or not be. . . . We are therefore bound to suppose something necessary in itself, which does not owe its necessity to anything else, but which is the cause of the necessity of other things. And all men call this God.

The fourth way is from the degrees that occur in things, which are found to be more and less good, true, noble, and so on. . . . There is therefore something which is the cause of the being of all things that are, as well as of their goodness and their every perfection. This we call God.

The fifth way is from the governance of things. We see how some things, like natural bodies, work for an end even though they have no knowledge. . . . There is therefore an intelligent being by whom all natural things are directed to their end. This we call God.

Source: Thomas Aquinas, *Nature and Grace*, trans. and ed. A. M. Fairweather. *Library of Christian Classics*, vol. 11 (Philadelphia: Westminster Press, 1954), pp. 54–56.

man influence was especially evident in the work of codifying and systematizing the law, such as was carried out in Saxony and southern Germany in the 1200s. The Roman influence was not entirely positive, for it also resulted in the reintroduction of judicial torture. The impact of Roman law was greatest in the Italian states and the Iberian peninsula.

Roman principles and procedures also heavily influenced the development of the church's own law, called canon law, which was codified in the twelfth century by Gratian, an Italian monk who taught at Bologna. His influential text, the *Decretum* (c. 1140), used the dialectical method to organize and reconcile approximately 3,900 laws. Canon law in this period involved not only such religious matters as sacraments and church property but also slander, libel, morals, tithes, wills, and oaths. Gratian's codification was the prelude to a whole series of commentaries on canon law and an increasingly judicial relationship between the church and its members. In the thirteenth century legal studies became as complex and sophisticated as scholastic theology.

The discussion of legal questions was relevant to a growing interest in political theory sparked in large measure by issues raised in the investiture controversy. As the debate over investiture intensified, theorists sympathetic to the papacy claimed ever broader papal powers until at last they asserted the pope's right to intervene in secular matters as part of his responsibility to supervise temporal sovereigns. This, of course, was unacceptable to secular rulers, whose own theorists obligingly extended the claim of royal authority until it included the duty to intervene in ecclesiastical affairs should the papacy prove incapable of reforming the church. Whereas papal writers contended that temporal sovereigns received their right to govern through the church as a divine agency, monarchical theorists insisted that such power was bestowed on the rulers directly by God. Manegold of Lautenbach (died 1085) even went so far as to argue that God's agency was not the church but the people, who were therefore entitled to withdraw their support from a tyrannical ruler. Although Manegold's theory had democratic implications, no medieval thinker espoused a philosophy of popular government. Most, in fact, would have accepted Aquinas' assertion that monarchy is preferable to other forms of government because it is the most stable.

Monarchical government was made to seem natural by the depiction of society in organic terms. The English scholar John of Salisbury (c. 1115–1180) developed the notion of the body politic, in which the sovereign is the head; the judges and governors are the ears, eyes, and tongue; the magistrates and soldiers are the hands; and the peasants are the feet. As an apologist for papal supremacy, John was then able to argue that the church is the soul of the body. Although the organic theory was often used to underscore the naturalness and stability of hierarchical society, John accepted the right of people to overthrow a tyrannical ruler on the grounds that tyranny was an abuse of the power bestowed on a ruler by God. Despite the democratic implications of this theory, however, John refused to consider rulers responsible to their subjects; if tyrants were overthrown, people acted only as divine agents and not in their own right. In general, medieval thinkers preferred monarchical government but expected sovereigns to rule justly in accord with divine law. The tendency was to see society and government in positive, natural terms: the state, said Aquinas, was a natural institution, not a necessary evil as Augustine had taught in the fifth century.

Science and Medicine

Although medieval thinkers failed to free science from its subservient position as a handmaiden to theology, they succeeded in pointing the way to a more accurate understanding of the physical universe. Scientific knowledge came to be seen not only as a reflection of divine handiwork but also as a means to improve living conditions. The expanding availability of Greek and Arabic treatises on science in Latin translation gave strong impetus to scientific study in Europe. One of the earliest interpreters of Arabic science was the twelfth-century English scholar Adelard of Bath, whose translation of Euclid's *Elements* from Arabic became the principal textbook for the study of geometry in the West. His own *Natural Questions* gave European students an insight into Arabic knowledge in such fields as astronomy, botany, zoology, and meteorology.

One of the most important contributions of medieval science was the gradual awareness of the significance of observation and experiment as the best means to acquire knowledge of the physical world. Among the early advocates of this methodology were Albertus Magnus of Paris and Robert Grosseteste (c. 1175–1253) of Oxford, both influenced by Aristotle. Grosseteste was convinced that optics, or the study of vision, was the foundation of all other scientific knowledge because light was the most basic physical substance. Accordingly, he employed an early form of the experimental method to study the rainbow. His famous pupil, the English Franciscan Roger Bacon (c. 1220–1292), proposed the dissection of pig and cow eyes in order to understand optical principles. Bacon learned that light travels faster than sound, and he was interested in the use of magnifying glasses and eyeglasses. However, he is more noted for his advocacy of experimental study than for specific contributions to scientific knowledge, and like his contemporaries he continued to attach credibility to the pseudosciences of alchemy and astrology. Bacon's oft-quoted anticipation of airplanes, submarines, and machine-powered ships were flights of fantasy, not concepts based on scientific principles like those of Leonardo da Vinci two centuries later. However, medieval scientists such as Grosseteste and Bacon did make a significant contribution by advocating the importance not only of the experimental method but also of mathematics as a key toward understanding the natural world.

Medical knowledge, too, was highly dependent on translations of Greek and Arabic works, among them the Arabic treatises of the Jewish physician Maimonides (1135–1204), much of whose career was spent in Cairo, and Avicenna, whose *Canon of Medicine* went through numerous editions. Arabic doctors had made major advances in the use of drugs, and this knowledge passed to Europeans, especially through the famous medical school at Salerno. Until it was surpassed by Montpellier in France about 1200, Salerno was the leading center of medical education in Europe, thanks largely to the presence of Greek and Arabic physicians. Among those who taught at Salerno were a number of women, including Trotula, author of the treatise *On Feminine Disorders*. Students at Salerno learned surgical techniques, though medieval operations were generally crude affairs in which modified butchers' instruments were used and amputation was common. Although anesthetics were coming into use, many patients suffered through operations deadened only by alcohol or opium. Death from shock or infection was common. The first illustrated guide to surgery was written by the Muslim Abul Kasim of Córdoba, Spain (c. 936–c. 1013), but there was no handbook of anatomy until 1316, when one was prepared by Mondino de' Luzzi, who taught at Bologna. The advance of medicine was reflected in the growth of hospitals; England had 18 in 1123 but 428 by 1300. Quarantine, however, was introduced only in 1346. Because of the interest in optics, eyeglasses became fairly common in Italy in the thirteenth century, and there were even operations for cataracts. A good deal of medieval practice, of course, was still grounded in superstition, such as the belief that sexual intercourse with a virgin would cure a man of various illnesses. Medicine remained primitive, not least because of its reliance on the Hippocratic theory of disease. The best treatment was often that administered by folk doctors who used herbal remedies and commonsense practices.

The Medieval Vision

Between the eleventh and the fifteenth centuries European artists developed new styles that reflected not only their Christian faith but also the outlook first of the monastic and feudal orders and then of the expanding cities. The rampaging Vikings, Normans, and Magyars in the preceding period had destroyed many wooden churches, hence the eleventh and twelfth centuries had ample incentive to rebuild—in stone wherever possible. Perhaps even greater motivation to build stemmed from the expanding economy, the need to provide churches for pilgrims on their way to holy places, and the pious spirit engendered by the religious reforms. The cathedrals and abbey churches erected in the High Middle Ages stand as a silent but pictorially eloquent monument to the faith, resolve, and urban pride of medieval Christians.

The Age of the Romanesque

The artistic style of the eleventh and twelfth centuries was largely shaped by the monastic revival and the militant ideals of the feudal order. The monastic reforms that commenced in the tenth century revitalized the church, giving it a new resolve to glorify God. The great abbey churches that epitomize the Romanesque style reflect the monastic values of order, simplicity, and otherworldliness. But the religious revival also led to a substantial increase in the number of people who undertook pilgrimages to the shrines of the saints, such as that of St. James at Compostela in northwestern Spain. The churches along the pilgrimage routes had to be larger than the traditional basilicas in order to accommodate the throngs of pilgrims. In the aftermath of the Viking and Magyar invasions, there was also a desire to make the churches stronger, with stone instead of wooden ceilings and with facades in certain cases that were reminiscent of feudal castles. Some Romanesque churches, such as that of Notre-Dame-la-Grande in Poitiers, look almost like fortresses because of their towers and thick walls.

Romanesque churches were constructed throughout Europe, although the greatest number were in France. There were regional differences as the form developed, but the Romanesque—or Roman-style—buildings shared fundamental characteristics, including a floor plan in the shape of a cross, the use of round arches and barrel (tunnel) vaults, and heavy buttresses to support the legs of the arches. The weight of the stone ceiling made it virtually impossible to cut windows into the sides of the barrel vault; hence the interior of early Romanesque churches was dark. Later Romanesque architects revived the Roman principle of the groined vault, by which intersecting arches distribute the weight of the ceiling to specific points along the wall. These points must be heavily buttressed, but windows can then be cut in the intervening spaces to illumine the interior of the church. One of the earliest Romanesque churches to use this principle was the cathedral at Durham in northern England.

To adorn the new churches, Romanesque artists revived the technique of stone sculpture, which had largely been forgotten during the eighth and ninth centuries. The figures they sculpted were intended to teach as well as to adorn, a function especially significant in an age when the overwhelming majority of the population was illiterate. Rich in symbols easily remembered by the faithful, Romanesque sculpture was a constant visual reminder of the fundamental teachings of the church. One of the most common locations for Romanesque sculpture was the semicircular space, called a tympanum, above the door of a church, which was often used to show Christ at the Last Judgment. Moreover, the columns of churches and cloisters alike were regularly topped by carved capitals depicting everything from vegetation to monsters. To some of the godly, the artists had gone too far: "I say naught of the vast height of your churches," thundered the Cistercian monk Bernard of Clairvaux, "their immoderate length, their superfluous breadth, the costly polishings, the curious carvings and paintings which attract the worshipper's gaze and hinder his attention."[2]

The monastic spirit of the Romanesque was also reflected in the paintings of the period, the most important of which were either murals in abbey churches rendered in a Byzantine style or miniatures that "illuminated" (illustrated) manuscripts. The latter were often painted by monks and nuns already devoted to copying manuscripts. Some miniaturists depicted religious scenes, while others created elaborate, intricate capital letters. Some of their work reveals a sense of humor, as in the case of the nun who depicted herself swinging on the tail of an elaborate

The nave and choir of the pilgrimage church of St. Sernin in Toulouse, France (c. 1080–1120) were built using a barrel, or tunnel, vault. The interior lighting is dim and indirect. [Marburg/Art Resource]

The Romanesque sculpture in the tympanum of St. Trophime in Arles, France, is symbolic rather than naturalistic. The winged figures around Christ represent the four evangelists. [Marburg/Art Resource]

Q. The miniatures in turn served as models for murals and later for the stained glass windows that decorated Gothic churches.

The Gothic Achievement

The world of the Gothic artist was no longer primarily that of the monastic and the pilgrim but of the city and the scholastic theologian. Gothic cathedrals were triumphs of the urban spirit, a testimony to the civic pride that manifested itself in rivalries between the cities. But the Gothic achievement was equally a testimony in stone to the synthesis of theology and philosophy that the scholastics were forging. Just as reason became the handmaiden of faith to bridge the gap between heaven and earth, so the soaring spires and lofty vaults of the Gothic cathedral carried the vision of the worshiper logically and compellingly heavenward. The principles of scholastic theology and Gothic architecture share the conviction that reason and nature are not stumbling blocks but pathways to spiritual truth. In the Romanesque the material and the spiritual exist in an uneasy tension; in the Gothic they unite in praising God.

The principles of the Gothic style were initially worked out in the abbey church at St. Denis, near Paris, in the 1130s and 1140s. Under the direction of Abbot Suger, the goal of the architects was to construct a church that "would shine with the wonderful and uninterrupted light of most luminous windows."[3] The key was to construct a skeletal framework strong enough to support the stone roof and yet airy enough to permit the extensive use of stained glass. By using pointed instead of round arches, the architects could achieve greater height and enclose rectangular as well as square spaces. At Beauvais the groined vaulting with its supporting ribs soared to the incredible height of 157 feet, only to collapse and have to be rebuilt. The Gothic architect also introduced the flying buttress, a support that carried the horizontal thrust of the arch to heavy piers outside the church. The purpose was twofold: placing the massive piers outside the church created a more spacious interior, while the flying buttress, like the pointed arch, guided the eye of the beholder heavenward.

The abundant stained glass windows, some of which may have been done by women, give the interior of a Gothic cathedral an ethereal quality. One writer of the period likened the windows to the Bible: "Since their brilliance lets the splendor of the True Light pass into the church, they enlighten those inside."[4] Like sculpture, the windows had a pedagogical as well as an aesthetic function, and to the degree that they encouraged worship, they had a liturgical role as well. To create a window, the artist first sketched a design in chalk and then fit together cut pieces of glass. Details, such as facial features, were created by using metal oxides on the glass and firing them in a kiln. The pieces of glass were joined with lead strips, and the window was strengthened by the addition of black iron bands, which also served to separate the colors to keep them from blurring in the viewer's eye. The finished window took the place of the mosaics and murals that had decorated earlier churches. The windows were costly, but royalty, nobility, prelates, and guilds donated them as marks of their piety.

As in the Romanesque period, sculpture adorned the cathedrals, only more lavishly. The cathedral at Chartres, for instance, has more than 2,000 carved figures. In keeping with the attempt to unite the physical and the spiritual, Gothic statuary became increasingly more naturalistic both in its representation of people and in its rendering of plants and animals. Unlike their Romanesque predecessors, Gothic artists, some of whom were women, began to use human models for their statues so that their work captured elements of individual personality. Simultaneously, convention required the continued use of traditional iconographic symbols, which restricted artistic freedom but assured the ability of viewers to interpret the art's religious meaning. The range of subject matter was even more extensive than that of the Romanesque era, so much so that Gothic cathedrals, with their myriad statues and surrounding stained glass, have been likened to visual encyclopedias. In its comprehensive treatment of the natural and spiritual worlds, the Gothic cathedral was akin to the ambitious *summae* of Thomas Aquinas.

The Gothic statuary on the exterior of Rheims Cathedral is more naturalistic than that of the Romanesque period (compare St. Trophime). On the left, the Archangel Gabriel informs Mary that she will give birth to the Messiah; on the right, Mary visits Elizabeth, mother of John the Baptist. [Marburg/Art Resource]

Vernacular Culture and the Age of Chivalry

Apart from the Anglo-Saxon tradition, the literature of the early medieval period was nearly all in Latin, though a rich oral tradition created and preserved stories and poems in the vernacular, the language of the people. Easily the most important vernacular work from the early medieval period is *Beowulf*, a lengthy poem about a Swedish hero who saved the Danes from a monster and his mother. Written in England by a monk around the eighth century, *Beowulf*

A view of the apse of Amiens Cathedral. A series of tiny chapels radiate around the exterior. [Marburg/Art Resource]

The story of Roland's heroism in battling the Muslims as recounted in the *Song of Roland* was a favorite theme in medieval art. Roland is shown here about to be ambushed by the Muslims at the lower right. [(West) Berlin, Staatsbibliothek Preussischer Kulturbesitz, Handschriftenabteilung]

reflects the values of the period: loyalty, valor, and a strong sense of aristocratic worth. Surviving poems written by other authors about the same time in northern England cover both sacred and secular themes. The greatest of these writers, who were influenced by monks from Ireland, was Bede (c. 673–735), a Benedictine monk commonly called "the Venerable" because of his piety and learning. Most of what he wrote was in Latin, including his masterpiece, the *Ecclesiastical History of the English Nation*, the primary source of our knowledge about English history from the time Christianity was introduced in 597 until 731. His classic was translated into Anglo-Saxon by King Alfred the Great (871–899) and the scholars at his palace school. During Alfred's reign another major historical source was begun, a vernacular compilation of documents known as the *Anglo-Saxon Chronicle*. Thus the early medieval writers resorted to the vernacular to explain their past as well as to entertain.

During the High Middle Ages much of the material that had only been transmitted orally was written down, still in the vernacular, and to this body of material were added new works, both secular and religious. The richness of this body of vernacular literature is reflected in the fact that it appeared in no fewer than eight major literary forms: heroic epics, minstrel songs, courtly romances, allegorical romances, mystery and miracle plays, pious writings, historical works, and popular stories. Although the French took the lead in developing vernacular literature, important contributions were made as far afield as Russia, Scandinavia, and Spain. Latin was the language of the learned—of lawyers, ecclesiastics, and scholastics—but beginning in the eleventh century the vernacular tongues increasingly became the language of literary entertainment. Although literacy rates remained low, these works undoubtedly reached wide audiences as the literate read them aloud to others.

The earliest heroic epics were the *chansons de geste*—"songs of heroic deeds"—composed in the northern French vernacular. In oral form they go back to the ninth and tenth centuries, when they were used to entertain French pilgrims traveling to the religious shrines of southern France and northern Spain. Of the more than 80 *chansons de geste* that survive, the most popular is the *Song of Roland*, the legendary account of a Muslim attack on Charlemagne's rear guard as it retreated across the Pyrenees in 778. The forceful lines of the poem exalt the simple virtues of the feudal order: personal loyalty, militant Christian faith, and individual honor. Because Roland failed to summon help in time to save his men, he is praised for his valor and loyalty but not his wisdom. The conflict with Islam is also the setting for the famous Spanish *chanson* of the twelfth century, the *Poem of My Cid*, the fictionalized account of a chivalric lord noted for his defeat of the Moorish rulers of Andalusia and the heroic exploits that led to his conquest of Valencia. The great German epic, the *Nibelungenlied* (c. 1200), has a strikingly different flavor as it recounts the mythical quest for a hoard of Rhine gold in an atmosphere of love, treachery, and violence. Although the written version was given a Christian veneer, at root it reflects pagan Germanic mythology. In spirit it is akin to the twelfth- and thirteenth-century Scandinavian *Eddas*, which recount the stories of pagan gods and heroes, such as Thor, the god of thunder, and Frigga, the goddess of marriage, after whom Thursday and Friday are named. The counterpart of these works in Kievan Russia was the twelfth-century *Song of Igor's Campaign*, another account of heroic exploit. Together such works represent a simple historic interest in a largely mythical past dominated by valiant heroes and heroines, a sharp contrast to the theological and metaphysical concerns of the scholastics.

French poets also took the lead in composing minstrel songs, particularly in the south, where troubadours sang their lyrical lines in the Provençal dialect. These *chansons d'amour*, or "songs of love," were immensely popular in the twelfth and thirteenth centuries throughout western Europe. Nearly 2,500 Provençal lyrics survive. Whereas the *chansons de geste* helped establish the code of knightly conduct called chivalry, the *chansons d'amour* were instrumental in popularizing the concept of courtly love. The key to this concept is the exaltation of women and love, sometimes in a platonic rather than a physical sense. The minstrels encouraged the virtual worship of the wife of someone of a higher social degree, expecting in return at least simple kindness and inner joy if not physical pleasure. A cult of courtly love was presided over at Poitiers by Eleanor of Aquitaine, wife of the English King Henry II, and in Champagne by her daughter, the Countess Marie. The Germans had their counterpart to the troubadours in the *Minnesingers* ("love singers"), whose lyrics were more spiritual than those of the French *chansons*. The best known of these minstrels was Walther von der Vogelweide (Walter of the Birdmeadows, c. 1170–c. 1230), so named because birds are prominently featured in his love lyrics. A number of women similarly wrote romantic lyrics, though they did not exalt men as the male poets did women in the literature of courtly love.

The courtly love of the minstrels was united with the *chansons de geste* to create the courtly romance, the most famous of which are the late-twelfth-century works of Chrétien de Troyes about King Arthur. In these stories the adventurous knight sought his identity in the dangerous world beyond the royal court, but if successful he could receive his just acceptance by recounting his deeds before that court. Cistercian influence in the thirteenth century led to the addition of the theme of the Holy Grail, purportedly the chalice used by Christ in the Last Supper and later taken to Britain. Thus, as the Arthurian legends spread throughout Europe, knights such as Sir Galahad and Perceval were recognizably Christian heroes. In the 1200s two French authors, William de Lorris and Jean de Meun, combined allegory and satire with the romance to create the popular *Romance of the Rose*. William's portion treats traditional troubadour themes of love in an allegorical mode—the "Rose in the Garden of Delight" is the poet's sweetheart—but Jean uses his pen to satirize everything from women to clerical celibacy.

Although most religious literature continued to be written in Latin, vernacular works began to win a wider audience. Mystery plays—religious dramas about biblical subjects, especially Christ's life—were often in Latin and in fact originated as part of the Latin liturgy. As fictitious matter was added, the plays acquired a separate identity, opening the way for vernacular versions, such as the twelfth-century French play, *The Mystery of Adam*. Beginning in the fourteenth century these plays were no longer the province of the clergy but community productions typ-

Courtly Love

One of the more intriguing documents in the courtly love tradition is the treatise on love, De amore, *by Andreas Capellanus, who was associated with the court of Eleanor of Aquitaine's daughter, Marie de Champagne. There is considerable debate as to whether this twelfth-century work was intended to be taken seriously or humorously.*

1. Marriage cannot be pleaded as an excuse for refusing to love.
2. A person who cannot keep a secret can never be a lover. . . .
7. If one of two lovers dies, love must be foresworn for two years by the survivor. . . .
11. It is not becoming to love those ladies who only love with a view to marriage. . . .
14. Too easy possession renders love contemptible. But possession which is attended with difficulties makes love valuable and of great price. . . .
17. A new love affair banishes the old one completely. . . .
22. When one of the lovers begins to entertain suspicion of the other, the jealousy and the love increase at once. . . .
29. Too great prodigality of favors is not advisable, for a lover who is wearied with a superabundance of pleasure is generally as a rule disinclined to love.

Source: J. F. Rowbotham, *The Troubadours and Courts of Love* (New York: Macmillan, 1895), pp. 245–247.

ically performed, by women as well as men, during such church festivals as Whitsun or Corpus Christi. A variation of the mystery play, the miracle play, took as its theme the life of a saint; one such was the twelfth-century English drama about St. Catherine, which must have been particularly interesting to women. The miracle and mystery plays in turn gave rise to morality plays, such as *Everyman*, which personified vices and virtues in the context of a struggle for the soul. A variety of pious literature was also composed in the vernacular during the High Middle Ages, including Francis of Assisi's *Canticle of the Sun*, a lyrical praise of God for creation, and a thirteenth-century collection of stories about Francis titled *The Little Flowers of St. Francis*.

In a more secular vein, the vernacular literature of this period included several historical works of note. Geoffrey of Monmouth's *British History* is largely given over to retelling the legendary stories of King Arthur and other fictitious tales and thus hardly qualifies as history. In contrast, Geoffrey de Villehardouin provided a historical account of the capture of Constantinople by the crusaders in 1204, which he titled *The Conquest of Constantinople*, and Jean de Joinville wrote the *History of St. Louis*, the story of the French King Louis IX. Various German chroniclers also wrote in the vernacular. French writers in particular were interested in recording popular tales—*fabliaux*—that had long been current in oral form. Alternately satirical, coarse, and amusing, the intent was usually to entertain, though some stories had a didactic purpose as well. Some were animal fables, such as the *Romance of Reynard the Fox*.

The variety of vernacular literature provides a healthy corrective to the common notion that medieval people were inordinately concerned with religious issues. Instead they demonstrated a pronounced interest in such themes as chivalry, courtly love, the mythical and mysterious past, bawdy stories, and tales of violence and romance.

Medieval Jewry

No discussion of medieval life and culture can fail to acknowledge the significant contribution of the Jews. During the period of the Roman Empire they had migrated throughout Europe as far afield as Spain, France, Dalmatia, and the Crimea. Small Jewish communities also established themselves to the east, from Arabia and Persia to India and China. Many of the earliest Jewish settlers in the West were farmers, an occupation in which they continued for centuries in southern Europe, but most of the Jews who settled farther north engaged in commerce as town life developed. Charlemagne's government welcomed Jewish immigrants by granting them charters that guaranteed protection and privileges. The Capetian kings of France continued this policy, making France a center of medieval Jewry. The German Jewish communities were founded by immigrants from France and southern Europe beginning in the ninth century; by 1100 there were numerous Jews in the Rhineland. Few Jews emigrated to Scandinavia, and England was the last major European country where they settled, mostly after the Norman Conquest in 1066. The extensive Jewish settlements in Europe and their contributions to Jewish culture ensured that in the future the Jews would be fundamentally European in outlook.

As Europeans turned increasingly to commercial activities in the High Middle Ages, Jewish merchants found themselves slowly squeezed out of commerce and into moneylending. Because the Christian church prohibited usury—lending money at unjust rates of interest—many people had to obtain their loans from Jewish businessmen. When the Lombards introduced systematic banking, many Jewish moneylenders were forced to become pawnbrokers.

The crusades had a devastating impact on European Jews, thanks to the religious hatred fostered by some church leaders against non-Christian groups generally and by the anti-Semitic sermons of the friars in particular. In Europe the Jews were a tempting target, particularly to Christians inflamed by recurrent charges that Jews had murdered Christ and were sacrificing Christian children at the Passover feast. The first persecution occurred at Metz in Lorraine and then spread from the Rhineland into France and England. Christian bigotry reached as far as Palestine, where the crusaders burned an entire synagogue full of Jews in 1097. Some Jews preferred to die

Interior of the synagogue at Worms in Germany, built in 1034. [Bildarchiv Foto Marburg]

with swords in their hands, but many chose to commit suicide rather than be killed by Christians. In the English city of York in 1189, Jewish men killed their wives and children before turning their swords on themselves. The pattern of persecution was reinforced in the 1300s when Jews became scapegoats for the Black Death, for which they continued to be blamed well into the sixteenth century.

The climate of hostility against the Jews was furthered by the Third and Fourth Lateran Councils. Despite the fact that the Councils' decrees were not thoroughly implemented, henceforth Gentiles were not supposed to be servants of Jews, nor were they allowed to live in the same districts, a regulation that encouraged the development of separate Jewish quarters. Jews were required to wear identifying badges and attend Christian sermons designed to convert them. Christian officials censored or confiscated Jewish books and forced Jews to be present at public disputations intended to demonstrate the errors of their ways. English authorities seized synagogues on trumped-up charges that Jewish chanting disrupted Christian church services. The Holy Roman Empire asserted proprietary rights over its Jews, making them virtually the property of the crown, and other states followed suit. Many Jews fled to Poland and Lithuania, only to become the legal property of the nobility. In practice, proprietary rights had little effect on Jewish life or freedom of movement, but they provided the justification for special taxes, and finally for the expulsion of the Jews from several countries. When Edward I banned the Jews from England in 1290, as many as 16,000 emigrated. Louis IX had decreed their exile from France in 1249, but the order was not implemented then. In 1306, however, Philip IV ordered their arrest, the confiscation of their property, and their ouster from France. Twice they were allowed back, only to be banned again in 1394. Because of political disunity in Germany, there was no general expulsion, but many local governments forced the Jews to flee. Spain and Sicily followed suit in 1492, Portugal in 1497, Naples in 1510 and again in 1541, and Milan in 1591. The expulsions forced the Jews eastward, particularly to Poland—where King Boleslav the Pious granted them a charter in 1264 to guarantee their liberties—and to the Ottoman Empire.

Between Two Cultures: The Jews in Spain

One of the principal centers of Jewish culture in the medieval era was Spain, where the pre-Islamic community was strengthened by Jewish colonists and traders who followed

The Expulsion of the Jews from France

The animosity of medieval Christians toward Jews is apparent in this account of Philip II's expulsion of the Jews from France in 1182.

When the faithless Jews heard this edict some of them were born again of water and the Holy Spirit and converted to the Lord, remaining steadfast in the faith of our Lord Jesus Christ. To them the king, out of regard for the Christian religion, restored all their possessions in their entirety, and gave them perpetual liberty.

Others were blinded by their ancient error and persisted in their perfidy; and they sought to win with gifts and golden promises the great of the land . . . that through their influence and advice, and through the promise of infinite wealth, they might turn the king's mind from his firm intention. But the merciful and compassionate God . . . so fortified the illustrious king that he could not be moved by prayers nor promises of temporal things. . . .

The infidel Jews, perceiving that the great of the land, through whom they had been accustomed easily to bend the king's predecessors to their will, had suffered repulse, and astonished and stupefied by the strength of mind of Philip the king and his constancy in the Lord, . . . prepared to sell all their household goods. The time was now at hand when the king had ordered them to leave France altogether, and it could not be in any way prolonged. Then did the Jews sell all their movable possessions in great haste, while their landed property reverted to the crown. Thus the Jews, having sold their goods and taken the price for the expenses of their journey, departed.

Source: J. H. Robinson, ed., *Readings in European History*, vol. 1 (Boston: Ginn, 1904), p. 428.

in the wake of the Arab conquests. Jews enjoyed considerable freedom in Islamic Spain, in part because of their key role in commerce, including the slave trade, but also because of their intellectual attainments. One of the key patrons of Jewish learning was Hasdai ibn-Shaprut (c. 915–970), himself a Jew and the confidant of two caliphs. Trained in medicine and skilled in Latin as well as Arabic, Hasdai supported Jewish poets and Hebrew scholars, initiating a brilliant era of Jewish culture. The poetic revival culminated in the hymns to Zion by the physician Judah ha-Levi (1086–1141). Jewish scholars played an important part in translating Greek classics into Arabic and, beginning in the twelfth century, from Arabic into Latin. Their linguistic skills paved the way for advancements in such fields as mathematics, medicine, astronomy, and cartography. Some of the more enlightened Christian rulers, such as the Emperor Frederick II and Alfonso the Wise, king of Castile, recognized the significance of these contributions and extended their patronage to Jewish scholars. Thus one of the principal avenues for the revival of classical learning in Europe came by way of the Arabs and the Jews.

The greatest of the medieval Jewish scholars was Moses ben Maimon (1135–1204), popularly known as Maimonides. Although a native of Córdoba, Spain, he spent most of his life in Cairo, where he served as court physician. As a philosopher his contributions to Judaism are comparable to those of Thomas Aquinas in Catholic theology. His major work, the *Mishneh Torah* ("Repetition of the Law"), was intended to be a *summa* of Judaism—a systematic presentation of rabbinic teachings that earned him the reputation of being a second Moses. Maimonides' approach to religion was highly rational, reflecting the influence of Aristotle and Avicenna. His *Guide to the Perplexed* includes rational arguments for the existence of God, among them the thesis that there must be an Unmoved Mover. Although his views influenced Christian scholastics, the Dominicans were finally persuaded by conservative rabbis that Maimonides' works endangered the Christian faith, and they were banned in 1234.

In Judaism, as in Christianity, there was a mystical reaction to the rationality of Maimonides and his disciples. The mystical tradition in Judaism, of course, was much older than this, dating back to the first century A.D. In the twelfth and thirteenth centuries Jewish mystics known as *Hasidim* ("Pietists") were active in the Rhineland. Probably influenced by Christian monks, they combined a penitent's life with the conviction that God can be found through humility rather than ecstatic visions. Much of the opposition to Maimonides came from mystics in Provence and Spain known as Cabalists ("Traditionalists"), who believed that every letter of the Law has some mystical meaning that can be revealed only to the initiated. Jewish and Christian mystics were one in their conviction that the deepest meaning of religion is profoundly spiritual and cannot be attained by rational processes. Thus, despite the intense animosity of many Christians toward the Jews, Christianity and Judaism were strikingly similar in the search for a rational synthesis and the subsequent reaction of those who favored a mystical approach to God. But their common quest was not strong enough to prevent the onset of bitter persecution—the dark side of the age of faith.

Women and Medieval Society

Although medieval women were rarely subjected to the kind of persecution experienced by the Jews,* their social position began to decline around the late eleventh century, a pointed reminder that the history of civilization is not one of unbroken progress. In the early medieval period, wives of clergymen and warriors often enjoyed substantial social prominence and economic responsibility because they managed their households or estates while their husbands were away. Women were not only managers but often also owners of land, particularly in southern France and Spain, where there were no legal restrictions on a woman's right to administer family property. Within the feudal order, the development of the chivalric ideal reinforced the role of women as managers of domestic and estate affairs by stressing the male's role as a warrior and a vassal. This was truer in France and Germany, where chivalry had the greatest impact, than in Italy, where chivalric ideas were slow to win acceptance.

Throughout the medieval era women tended to enjoy greater power and prominence in periods of heavy military activity or vigorous expansion into new regions. The military campaigns of Charlemagne, the crusades to the Holy Land, and the lengthy efforts to drive the Moors out of the Iberian peninsula took men from their homes for lengthy periods and exposed them to the hazards of war and disease. Medieval records indicate that during such periods substantial amounts of property were left in the care of wives and sisters as well as the church. It was against the background of the crusades that western Europeans developed the cult of courtly love and troubadours devoted their songs to the exaltation of aristocratic ladies.

Simultaneously, however, developments in the religious and political sphere began to undermine the position of clerical wives and women of the feudal order. In religion the decline was sparked by the Gregorian reforms of the late eleventh century, which had an adverse effect on women by insisting on clerical celibacy, thereby weakening the role of women in parish activities, and by seeking to curtail the ability of laymen and women to nominate candidates for church offices. These reforms were not fully

* The main exception was the persecution of women in southern France during the Albigensian Crusade.

Women: A Western Medieval View

The tendency of Christian thinkers to regard women as inferior is reflected in the influential Decretum *of the jurist Gratian, written about 1140.*

Women should be subject to their men. The natural order for mankind is that women should serve men and children their parents, for it is just that the lesser serve the greater.

The image of God is in man and it is one. Women were drawn from man, who has God's jurisdiction as if he were God's vicar, because he has the image of the one God. Therefore woman is not made in God's image.

Woman's authority is nil; let her in all things be subject to the rule of man. . . . And neither can she teach, nor be a witness, nor give a guarantee, nor sit in judgment.

Adam was beguiled by Eve, not she by him. It is right that he whom woman led into wrongdoing should have her under his direction, so that he may not fail a second time through female levity.

Source: Gratian, *Corpus Iuris Canonici*, in *Not in God's Image*, ed. J. O'Faolain and L. Martines (New York: Harper Torchbooks, 1973), p. 130.

effective until well beyond the medieval period, but the attempts to enforce them boded ill for women. So too did the growing importance of the bishops in the High Middle Ages, a development intimately related to the revival of urban life. Bishops had no female counterparts, whereas during the period when the church had been dominated by monasteries women had achieved positions of leadership as prioresses and abbesses. Monastic life continued, of course, but power gradually shifted into the hands of the bishops. The trend toward more exclusively male leadership was encouraged by the growth of cathedral schools and universities, neither of which were open to females. Unless they had private tutors, girls could hope for education only in the convents, but from the twelfth century on these establishments were primarily interested in religious rather than academic pursuits.

The church's repressive attitude toward women became especially apparent in the thirteenth century. The religious zeal of the preceding century, which had led to the appearance of such new orders as the Cistercians, also affected women, and thousands of them organized themselves into religious communities. The male orders reluctantly agreed to provide some form of discipline, but instead of being allowed to become independent, female orders were forced to remain subservient branches of their male counterparts. In general this was because women were thought to be undisciplined, prone to heretical ideas, and less than serious in their commitment to the religious life. The Franciscans, Dominicans, and Cistercians bitterly resisted the attachment of subordinate convents, though they were overruled by the papacy. Faced with a church hierarchy determined to relegate them to subordination in all things spiritual, some women joined heretical groups such as the Waldensians, where they were permitted to preach and administer the sacraments.

Yet the influence of Christianity on medieval women was in other respects highly positive, as in the case of the attention given to the Virgin Mary, whose influence extended throughout the High and late Middle Ages. The devout exalted Mary as the Universal Mother whose love for her son was a manifestation of her love for humanity and on whose behalf she acted as an intermediary with God. The faithful credited her with performing miracles and commemorated her life with special festivals. Revered as the queen of heaven and one who was "exalted above the choirs of angels," Mary symbolized the dignity to which women could aspire. Pilgrims flocked to her shrines at such places as Chartres and Mont-Saint-Michel in France and Ipswich in England, and many churches, most notably the cathedral of Notre Dame ("Our Lady") in Paris, were dedicated to her. Numerous other churches had lady chapels in her honor. Expressions of love to the Virgin increasingly paralleled those to aristocratic women in the literature of courtly love, so that the practical effect of both movements was a tendency to idealize women.

In the secular realm, the development of stronger governments did not necessarily diminish the status of women, but it effectively blocked them from many areas of political involvement. As long as state governments were ineffectual and real power resided in the great aristocratic families, women had an opportunity to assert themselves in political affairs. But as the state governments revived, particularly in the 1100s, they required the services of lawyers and clerks to staff their treasuries and courts, and women had no access to the training that prepared people for such positions.

Changing inheritance laws also adversely affected women. A woman in the feudal order was generally allowed to inherit a fief, subject to her ability to meet the feudal obligations. In practice this meant the lord's right to arrange her marriage to a suitable vassal. Because a fief typically involved military responsibilities, her husband usually assumed control of the estate. But aristocratic families were increasingly determined to preserve their power by excluding females and younger sons from any substantive inheritance in order to keep their estates intact. This was accomplished by the principles of primogeniture and the indivisibility of patrimony, by which an estate had to pass to the eldest son. Daughters received dowries and dowers, the latter being the assurance of an income during widowhood, but in turn they were excluded from inheriting a portion of the family estate. If she had no brothers, the eldest daughter could usually inherit the estate. In the thirteenth century the French awarded two-thirds of an estate to the eldest son and allowed the other children to divide the remaining third. In varying degrees, most women of the propertied order were victims of legal discrimination.

For women of humbler status, fundamental economic needs often mandated a relative equality between men and women, particularly those in rural areas who worked beside their husbands in the fields or who devoted some of their time in the home to brewing ale or making cloth to sell. In the countryside women regularly hired themselves out to bailiffs on the greater estates, where they performed virtually every form of labor except heavy plowing. Much of the sheep shearing was done by women, as were the dairy and poultry chores. Even in the towns medieval women were found in virtually all crafts—as butchers and bakers, haberdashers and shoemakers, goldsmiths and embroiderers. Masters' wives were active in many guilds, often training female apprentices. Widows regularly carried on their husbands' crafts, and those who had been married to merchants sometimes took over their business dealings. English records mention "widows of London who make great trade in wool and other things."[5]

In medieval society the range of occupations in which women were engaged was very extensive. Some women even worked in the coal and iron mines, although their pay was less than that of the men. Many women were employed in domestic service, while others managed their own shops. Urban life clearly expanded career opportunities for women, whether married or single. Whereas a landed aristocrat might leave directions in his will to place his daughter in a convent or find her a suitable spouse, an artisan was more likely to leave funds to train his daughter in a trade, usually because he could afford neither a dowry nor the funds required to place her in a monastic house. Many women continued to pursue their crafts after marriage, even when their husbands pursued a different occupation. Without doubt, the female labor force was crucial to the medieval economy. The scholastic Peter Lombard may have reflected the sentiments of the commoners when he observed that God created Eve from Adam's rib rather than his head or foot because they were intended to be companions.

On balance, the High Middle Ages was a period of notable intellectual and cultural achievement. The growth of cathedral schools and the rise of universities brought new intellectual vigor to European life and made possible the training of a better-educated clergy and officials more adept at meeting the needs of government. Scholastics made a daring attempt to synthesize all knowledge, a development that focused attention on natural science. The growth of medical schools set the stage for improved health care. Virtually all of these developments occurred in the context of an urban revival made possible by an expanding economy. The cities provided the setting for brilliant artistic achievements, particularly the age of the Gothic, which owed so much to the Romanesque era. The Gothic cathedrals, resplendent with their towering spires, soaring vaults, flying buttresses, and stained glass, were the perfect visual symbol of the age of faith.

But for two groups—women and Jews—the High Middle Ages brought a relative deterioration in their position. Excluded from the cathedral schools and the universities, women increasingly found themselves shunted aside in politics as well. Law, medicine, and theology were forbidden areas, and women were banned from the parsonages they had once served as priests' wives. The exalted status they received in the courtly love tradition was scant compensation. The Jews, whose intellectual accomplishments influenced and were the equal of scholastic thought, were thrust into a nightmarish world of expulsion, exile, and massacre.

Notes

1. R. B. Brooke and C. N. L. Brooke, "St Clare," in *Medieval Women*, ed. D. Baker (Oxford: Blackwell, 1978), p. 287.
2. E. G. Holt, ed., *Literary Sources of Art History* (Princeton, N.J.: Princeton University Press, 1947), p. 17.
3. E. Panofsky, *Abbot Suger on the Abbey Church of St. Denis and Its Art Treasures* (Princeton, N.J.: Princeton University Press, 1951), p. 101.
4. H. Gardner, *Art Through the Ages*, 7th ed., ed. H. de la Croix and R. G. Tansey (New York: Harcourt Brace Jovanovich, 1980), p. 337.
5. E. Power, *Medieval Women*, ed. M. M. Postan (Cambridge: Cambridge University Press, 1975), p. 57.

Suggestions for Further Reading

Andreas Capellanus [André le Chapelain], *Andreas Capellanus on Love*, ed. and trans. P. G. Walsh. London: Duckworth, 1982.

Artz, F. B. *The Mind of the Middle Ages, A.D. 200–1500*, 3d ed. Chicago: University of Chicago Press, 1980.

Baker, D., ed. *Medieval Women*. Oxford: Blackwell, 1978.

Baldwin, J. W. *The Scholastic Culture of the Middle Ages, 1000–1300*. Lexington, Mass.: Heath, 1971.

Ben-Sasson, H. H., ed. *A History of the Jewish People*. Cambridge, Mass.: Harvard University Press, 1976.

Berman, H. *Law and Revolution: The Formation of the Western Legal Tradition*. Cambridge, Mass.: Harvard University Press, 1983.

Bogin, M. *The Women Troubadours*. New York: Paddington, 1976.

Bony, J. *French Gothic Architecture of the Twelfth and Thirteenth Centuries*. Berkeley: University of California Press, 1983.

Brooke, C. N. L. *The Monastic World 1000–1300*. New York: Random House, 1974.

——. *The Twelfth Century Renaissance*. New York: Harcourt Brace & World, 1969.

Bynum, C. W. *Holy Feast and Holy Fast: The Religious Significance of Food to Medieval Women*. Berkeley: University of California Press, 1987.

Cobban, A. B. *The Medieval Universities: Their Development and Organization*. London: Methuen, 1975.

Copleston, F. Charles. *Aquinas*. Harmondsworth, England: Penguin Books, 1959, 1965.

Erickson, C. *The Medieval Vision*. New York: Oxford University Press, 1976.

Fell, C. *Women in Anglo-Saxon England*. Oxford: Blackwell, 1987.

Ferruolo, S. C. *The Origins of the University: The Schools of Paris and Their Critics 1100–1215*. Stanford, Calif.: Stanford University Press, 1985.

Fitchen, J. *The Construction of Gothic Cathedrals*. Oxford: Clarendon Press, 1961.

Frankl, P. *Gothic Architecture*, trans. D. Pevsner. Baltimore: Penguin Books, 1963.

Gies, F., and Gies, J. *Women in the Middle Ages*. New York: Crowell, 1978.

Grodecki, L., and Brisac, C. *Gothic Stained Glass, 1200–1300*. Ithaca, N.Y.: Cornell University Press, 1985.

Haskins, C. H. *The Renaissance of the Twelfth Century*. Cambridge, Mass.: Harvard University Press, 1971.

Herlihy, D. *Medieval Households*. Cambridge, Mass.: Harvard University Press, 1985.

Jackson, W. T. H. *Medieval Literature: A History and a Guide*. New York: Collier, 1966.

Keen, M. *Chivalry*. New Haven, Conn.: Yale University Press, 1984.

Kirshner, J., and Wemple, S. F., eds. *Women of the Medieval World*. Oxford: Blackwell, 1985.

Lawrence, C. H. *Medieval Monasticism: Forms of Religious Life in Western Europe in the Middle Ages*. White Plains, N.Y.: Longman, 1984.

Leff, G. *Paris and Oxford Universities in the Thirteenth and Fourteenth Centuries: An Institutional and Intellectual History*. New York: Wiley, 1968.

McInerny, R. *Romanesque*. New York: Harper & Row, 1978.

Moore, R. I. *The Formation of a Persecuting Society: Power and Deviance in Western Europe 950–1250*. New York: Blackwell, 1987.

Moorman, J. R. H. *A History of the Franciscan Order*. Oxford: Clarendon Press, 1968.

Nicholas, D. *The Domestic Life of a Medieval City: Women, Children, and the Family in Fourteenth-Century Ghent*. Lincoln: University of Nebraska Press, 1985.

Panofsky, E. *Gothic Architecture and Scholasticism*. New York: Meridian, 1957.

Power, E. *Medieval Women*, ed. M. M. Postan. Cambridge: Cambridge University Press, 1975.

Ross, J. B., and McLaughlin, M. M., eds. *The Portable Medieval Reader*. New York: Viking, 1949.

Russell, J. B. *A History of Medieval Christianity: Prophesy and Order*. New York: Crowell, 1968.

Shahar, S. *The Fourth Estate: A History of Women in the Middle Ages*, trans. C. Galai. New York: Methuen, 1983.

Talbot, C. H. *Medicine in Medieval England*. London: Oldbourne, 1967.

Death and the Human Experience (I)

To every thing there is a season . . . :
A time to be born, and a time to die. (Eccles. 3:2)

Throughout history death has been defied or embraced, an object sometimes of fear, sometimes of hope. The earliest human ritual of which we have a record, developed by Peking man some 500,000 years ago, was associated with death, perhaps in the hope of preserving the memory of the deceased and soliciting their assistance for the living. More than 50,000 years ago Neanderthal people prepared elaborate funeral rites to deal with the needs of those who had died and presumably lived in some afterlife. Bodies were interred in graves filled with shells and ornaments made of ivory and bone, while the skin or bones of the deceased were colored with red ocher, apparently to commemorate life. The corpses themselves were buried in a fetal position, possibly to facilitate rebirth or to restrict the movements of the dead and thereby prevent them from returning to haunt the living. Thus the first human societies sought to explain death and in the process developed primitive conceptions of an afterlife.

A Neanderthal skeleton discovered in France in 1909 reveals that corpses were interred in the fetal position. [Collection Musée de l'Homme, Paris]

The earliest civilizations coped with death in strikingly different ways. The Mesopotamian *Epic of Gilgamesh* (c. 2000 B.C.) suggests that the people of that region conceived of a hinterworld that existed just below the surface of the earth, a House of Darkness in which the dead were made of clay, ate dust, and endured a wretched existence. This world was neither heaven nor hell but a place bereft of light where ghostly beings, dressed like birds, fluttered their wings. To prevent the spirit of the dead from haunting the living, the Sumerians took pains to bury the corpse and provide food and drink in the grave. Offerings and prayers were made to the Mesopotamian deities, but these were intended to benefit the living rather than to obtain access to a decent afterlife. To escape his destiny in the shadowy underworld, Gilgamesh resolutely searched for immortal life but failed to find it. The sense of resignation before death was reflected in the Mesopotamians' willingness to embrace a life of physical pleasure; as Gilgamesh is advised in the poem, it is best to live the merry life, dancing and playing night and day, for old age and death are inevitable.

The Egyptians too believed in life after death, as reflected in the Pyramid Texts of the third millennium B.C., the Coffin Texts of around 2000 B.C., and later papyrus inscriptions, documents collectively known as the *Book of the Dead*. Here we find the earliest expression of belief in the idea of a divine judgment after death. The Pyramid Texts relate the story of Osiris and his resurrection, but by the time of the Coffin Texts belief in the notion of a general judgment after death was widespread. Convinced that specific fates awaited different people, the Egyptians came to fear death because of the uncertainty of their position in the afterlife. The specter of divine judgment not only spurred some to moral living but also encouraged the development of elaborate funeral rituals designed to influence the final verdict. These included lengthy prayers repudiating sin as well as artwork designed to stress the goodness of the deceased's life. One of the most common symbols of Egyptian funerary art was the scale of judgment, depicting the soul as pure enough to balance the feather of truth. A similar symbol was later used in Christian art.

The earliest Greeks viewed death as the separation of the soul (or "shade") and the *thymos*—the seat of emotions—from the body. At death the *thymos* simply disappeared, leaving the soul to enter Hades, the Land of the Dead, once the corpse had been buried or had decomposed. Existence in Hades was thought to entail anything from a senseless state to associations akin to those in life. The earliest Greeks accepted death as an inescapable evil. One could hate but not fear death, which was part of the life cycle of the community. There was no reason to dread either contact with the deceased or one's own death.

The Greek attitude began to shift in the seventh and sixth centuries B.C. in the face of changing circumstances. The tightly knit communities broke up, a sense of individuality developed, philosophers speculated about salvation and a last judgment based on morality, and economic expansion and political upheaval increased feelings of insecurity and disorder. Consequently the specter of death caused anxiety and stimulated a concern to perpetuate one's memory, often by inscriptions or by gravestones or other monuments. At first the depictions of the deceased on statues and gravestones followed conventional types, but gradually these evolved into actual portraits of the dead, reflecting the heightened sense of interest in the individual that was characteristic of later Greek art.

This depiction on a fifth-century B.C. tombstone of a woman holding her grandchild underscores the extent to which the Greeks, unlike the Egyptians, concentrated primarily on the beauty of life. [Deutsches Archäologisches Institut/Kerameikos Museum, Athens]

The Greeks initially believed that only a few aristocratic heroes escaped Hades, but over time the idea was broadened to include others, until finally a happy afterlife was possible for all who lived morally or were initiated into the mystery cults associated with such gods as Dionysus. Increasingly death was perceived as less a part of the community's cycle of existence than a threat to an individual.

Grappling with the meaning of death produced equally varied responses among Asian peoples. In ancient India the Vedas and the epics offered two conflicting views of death. On the one hand, death was seen as inescapable, its rule over everyone invincible. On the other, death's hold was only conditional, for each person could in theory choose from among a variety of means to attain *moksha*—release from the cycle of rebirth. Yet all but a few sages were thought to be bound to the endless wheel of such rebirth. The nature of each reincarnation was determined by the individual's behavior in the present life, and could be favorably influenced by such things as an ascetic life, the acquisition of wisdom, the performance of sacrifices, and the pursuit of morality. At the very least adherence to such means enabled the Hindu to avoid "death in life"—living in perpetual fear of death. The Hindu sages occasionally linked death with evil—a theme common in later Christianity—but in general death was accorded a natural and indispensable role in the cosmic order, for without it there would be no room for new life. Death should therefore be celebrated, the Hindus felt, not mourned; "for death is a certainty for him who has been born, and birth is a certainty for him who has died. Therefore, for what is unavoidable thou shouldst not grieve."[1]

The ability to embrace death, or at least quietly to resign oneself to it, was complicated by the Hindu belief in *samsara*, the transmigration of souls through reincarnation, which is first explicitly stated in the *Upanishads* (c. 800–c. 500 B.C.). According to this concept, death is followed by rebirth in another worldly existence, although whether this is to be viewed in positive or negative terms was largely a personal matter. Certainly for many Hindus, *samsara* was tantamount to endless "redeath." Most Hindus sought to improve their status in the next round of existence by embracing morality and social responsibility, whereas some sought escape from physical existence through asceticism. For them, death could be the culmination of the journey along the Way of the Gods to the world of Brahma, the absolute. This quest for release and the joyful union with the infinite in Nirvana subsequently became a dominant theme in Buddhism.

Perhaps none have been more willing to embrace death than the Taoists in China, for whom the death of

The Hindu god Shiva and his wife, Parvati, aided by their sons, string together the skulls of the dead. One of Shiva's responsibilities was to preside over cremation grounds. [C.M. Dixon/Photoresources]

an individual was insignificant in the face of the workings of the universal cosmos. Seeing themselves as a mere part of the unity of all things, they could accept death tranquilly as a manifestation of the ongoing operation of nature. "If one once recognizes his identity with this unity, then the parts of his body mean no more to him than so much dirt, and death and life, end and beginning, disturb his tranquility no more than the succession of day and night."[2]

For most Chinese, however, death was explained in the context of an extended family group that embraced the deceased, the living, and the generations yet unborn. Because the dead were seen by some to have the same needs as the living, they must be provided for, and their activities in the afterlife could in turn aid the living. Funeral ceremonies were intended to ease the passage of the spirits into the next world, yet they would symbolically dwell in graveyards, in ancestral shrines in the homes, and in temples dedicated to specific clans. It was the task of the living to make offerings to the memory of the dead, to undertake pilgrimages to their places of burial, and to worship or commemorate them as a family. Ancestor worship, as it is somewhat misleadingly called, was by no means unique to China but was practiced by peoples as diverse as Persians, Indians, Russians, Scandinavians, and the Bantu of southern Africa. Through ancestor worship, death was prevented from cutting the ties between the deceased and their families; hence the dead could be dealt with in traditional human ways, such as paying respect or making offerings. Unless the dead were thought to be angry or vindictive, the continuation of the familial relationship eased both the physical separation imposed by death and apprehensions about what lay beyond the grave.

The ideas discussed to this point treat death in one of three ways: as an inevitable part of the natural process, following which souls exist in a shadowy and normally unpleasant underworld; as part of an endless cycle of rebirth; or as part of an ongoing familial relationship between past, present, and future generations. A fourth way of viewing death, which originated in Judaism and was subsequently adopted by Christianity and Islam, associated it with resurrection and the notion of salvation. Like the Sumerians, the early Hebrews thought of the dead as existing in a shadowy underworld, called *sheol*, commonly linked with the tomb. Originally this was the common fate of all, good or bad, Jew or Gentile, apart from the patriarch Enoch, who "walked with God," and the prophet Elijah, who was said to have been carried to heaven in a chariot of fire. But in the late eighth century B.C., the prophet Isaiah proclaimed the resurrection of all the righteous, and nearly six centuries later the Book of Daniel asserted that even the wicked would be resurrected in order to face judgment. For the Jews, then, death became a temporary state, less important than the judgment that followed the resurrection. Thus the Hebrews, like the ancient Egyptians but unlike the Mesopotamians, stressed the importance of moral living as the necessary preparation for death and the afterlife.

Early Christianity built upon this Judaic foundation, making death and resurrection only the prelude to an eternal heaven of blissful existence for the saved and endless torture in hell for the damned. Death was a foe to be conquered, but the victory came with the physical resurrection of Christ, belief in which became a cardinal tenet of the Christian faith. Because of that triumph, wrote the apostle Paul, "the dead shall be raised incorruptible. . . . O death, where is thy sting? O grave, where is thy victory?"[3] But for those who died alienated from God, death and judgment were but the fearful prelude to eternity in a lake burning with fire and brimstone.

This fourteenth-century A.D. Japanese Buddhist scroll shows the Buddha, lying on a bier, ready to enter Nirvana as he is mourned by gods, humans, and animals. [Museum für Ostasiatische Kunst]

Apart from the idea of Christ's resurrection, Islam adopted the essential features of the Christian belief in death, judgment, and reward or punishment. Death was viewed as a divinely determined act, executed by an Angel of Death or other messengers of Allah. Death itself was akin to sleep, though for unbelievers this involved agony. At the appointed time the dead would be awakened, the godly to receive the pleasures of paradise and the unbelievers to face a torment so unbearable that they would plead to be destroyed. Thus Islam, like Judaism and Christianity, regarded death as a transitory state, for which the proper preparation was righteous living.

Attitudes toward death affected decisions regarding the disposal of corpses. Cremation was common in India, Burma, and Japan, though not in China, where the people preferred to be buried in their native soil. The Etruscans, Greeks, and Romans practiced cremation (though not exclusively), but in the West it died out as the Christian belief in the physical resurrection of the body took hold. Not until the late nineteenth century did the practice again revive in Europe and America.

Christianity also introduced changes with respect to burial. The Romans, like the other peoples of antiquity, kept the dead separate from the living. In Rome and Pompeii, for example, the deceased were buried outside the gates or beside the roads leading into the cities, but close enough to maintain the tombs and make the requisite offerings. Burial within the towns was prohibited by Roman law and the early Germanic Theodosian Code and in the teachings of the early Christian theologian St. John Chrysostom.

The prohibition of entombment within the towns began to change as Christians were martyred in North Africa. Buried in the traditional necropolises outside town walls, their tombs soon became the sites of basilicas where devout pilgrims worshiped. Other Christians wanted to be buried nearby, thus leading to the association of churches and burial plots. By the mid-sixth century it was possible to inter a corpse within a church, thus reversing the ancient attempt to separate the living from the dead. In fact, in medieval Europe cemeteries were not only places of burial but also sites for dancing, gambling, concerts, and business transactions. Sometimes homes were even built in cemeteries. The proximity of the living and the dead in medieval Europe was also manifest in charnel houses, normally galleries that bordered churchyards and housed skulls and bones stacked neatly or arranged artistically for the living to contemplate.

Such customs point to a society in which life and death were viewed harmoniously—a society willing to accept the inevitability of death rather than depict it as a frightening event. The calmness of the deathbed ritual reflected a fundamental faith in the church's ability to care for the souls of the deceased and in the ultimate triumph of resurrection over death. A leading historian has called this view "tamed death," an attitude prevalent among the common people of the West into the nineteenth century.

Beginning in the eleventh and twelfth centuries a new attitude began to take hold among the intellectual and social elite. In part this stemmed from a desire to have funerals reflect material wealth and status. More important, the new outlook in Europe manifested a growing attention toward individuals, as reflected in the revival of funeral inscriptions, which had fallen into disuse around the fifth century; the popularity of requiem masses for individuals; and the reappearance of effigies and death masks. Individual responsibility was also emphasized, as special stress was placed on the Last Judgment, with the deeds of each person weighed on the great scales. This outlook was also accompanied by a change in funerary art, as decomposing cadavers—worm-ridden corpses—began to appear, mostly in the fifteenth century. Against the background of the Black Death, there was thus a new horror of dying and a longing for earthly life that had previously been manifest only rarely in the medieval West. This preoccupation with the fate of the individual has been called the "death of the self," an attitude that persisted in elite circles until the eighteenth century.

Notes

1. Bhagavad Gita, 2.27, in *Religious Encounters with Death: Insights from the History and Anthropology of Religions*, ed. F. E. Reynolds and E. H. Waugh (University Park: Pennsylvania State University Press, 1977), p. 92.
2. *Chuang Tzu*, 2.48, in H. G. Creel, *What Is Taoism? and Other Studies in Chinese Cultural History* (Chicago: University of Chicago Press, 1970), p. 42.
3. 1 Cor. 15:52, 55.

Suggestions for Further Reading

Ariès, P. *The Hour of Our Death*, trans. H. Weaver. New York: Knopf, 1981.

——. *Images of Man and Death*, trans. J. Lloyd. Cambridge, Mass.: Harvard University Press, 1985.

——. *Western Attitudes Toward Death: From the Middle Ages to the Present*, trans. P. M. Ranum. Baltimore: Johns Hopkins University Press, 1974.

Boase, T. S. R. *Death in the Middle Ages*. New York: McGraw-Hill, 1972.

Bowra, C. M. *The Greek Experience*. New York: World, 1957.

Brandon, S. G. F. *The Judgement of the Dead: An Historical and Comparative Study of the Idea of a Post-Mortem Judgement in the Major Religions*. New York: Scribner, 1967.

Creel, H. G. *What Is Taoism? and Other Studies in Chinese Cultural History*. Chicago: University of Chicago Press, 1970.

Harrah, B. K., and Harrah, D. F. *Funeral Service: A Bibliography of Literature on Its Past, Present and Future, the Various Means of Disposition and Memorialization*. Metuchen, N.J.: Scarecrow Press, 1976.

Miller, A. J., and Aeri, M. J. *Death: A Bibliographical Guide*. Metuchen, N.J.: Scarecrow Press, 1977.

O'Shaughnessy, T. *Muhammad's Thoughts on Death*. Leiden: Brill, 1969.

Reynolds, F. E., and Waugh, E. H. *Religious Encounters with Death: Insights from the History and Anthropology of Religions*. University Park: Pennsylvania State University Press, 1977.

Vermeule, E. *Aspects of Death in Early Greek Art and Poetry*. Berkeley: University of California Press, 1979.

Whaley, J., ed. *Mirrors of Mortality: Studies in the Social History of Death*. London: Europa, 1981.

CHAPTER · 14

Crisis and Recovery in Europe

Famine, pestilence, war, and death—the four horsemen of the Apocalypse—ravaged Europe with unprecedented fury in the fourteenth century. The devastation inflicted by the bubonic and pneumonic plague, recurring famine, and the Hundred Years' War contributed to serious economic decline and a change in people's outlook. The prestige of the papacy suffered too when its headquarters shifted to Avignon, which proved to be the prelude to the most scandalous schism in the history of the western church. Nevertheless, about 1450 Europe began to experience a dramatic revival as population growth resumed, commerce and manufacturing expanded, and the states of western Europe and Russia attained greater unity and built strong central governments. In Italy, Germany, Hungary, and Poland, however, territorial princes and cities prevented the growth of centralized states. Europe in the fourteenth and fifteenth centuries moved from an age of adversity to one of recovery and in doing so laid the foundations for the early modern era.

The fourth horseman of the Apocalypse: "And I saw, and behold, a pale horse, and its rider's name was Death, and Hades followed him; and they were given power over a fourth of the earth, to kill with sword and with famine and with pestilence and by wild beasts of the earth" (Rev. 6:8). To the people of the fourteenth and fifteenth centuries, this prophecy seemed to be coming true in their own age. [Giraudon/Art Resource]

Famine and the Black Death

From the late tenth through the thirteenth centuries the population of Europe grew as farmers expanded the amount of land under cultivation and increased the supply of food. But neither the population growth nor the food supply increased uniformly, and marginal settlements, where the possibility of extreme hunger was always high, arose throughout Europe. Even in the more prosperous agricultural regions, poor distribution facilities often resulted in pockets of famine. By 1300 the population had expanded so rapidly that most Europeans faced grave peril should the fragile agricultural economy be disrupted by unfavorable changes in the weather patterns. The warming trend that characterized the period from the mid-eighth to the mid-twelfth centuries was reversed as Europe entered what climatologists call the Little Ice Age, which lasted approximately two centuries. In the late thirteenth century heavy rains and unexpected freezes began to wreak havoc with the food supply. The threat of famine, which became more pronounced in the 1290s, culminated between 1315 and 1317 in the greatest crop failures of the Middle Ages. Soaring grain prices placed food beyond the reach of many, especially in urban areas, where sometimes as many as one in ten died from starvation or mal-

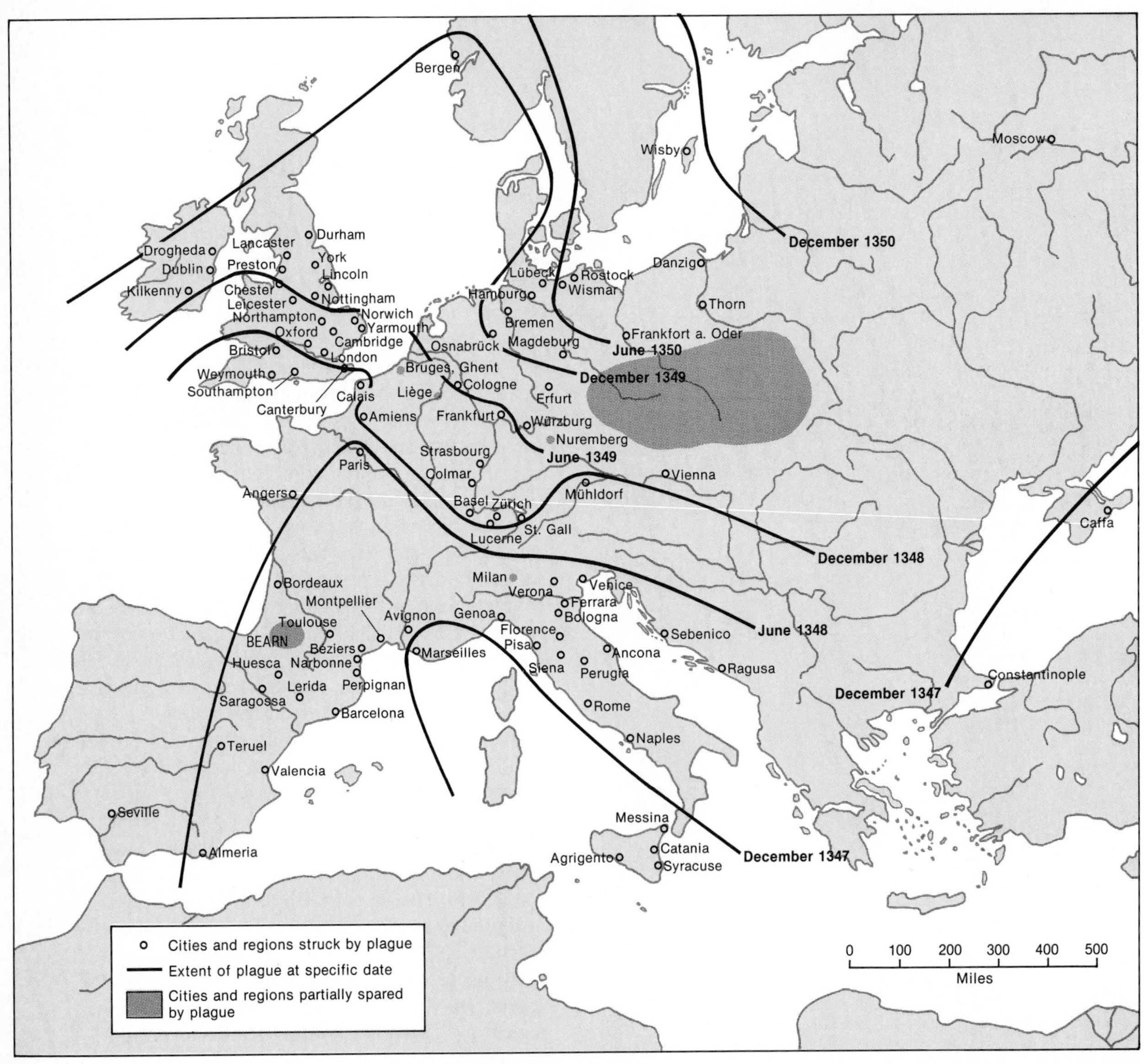

14.1 Spread of the Plague in Europe

nutrition. Marginal lands had to be abandoned as the poor sought relief in towns or in more productive regions, thereby increasing the strain on the food supply. As famines continued to recur throughout the fourteenth century, the most serious consequence was the debilitating effect of chronic and severe malnutrition on much of the population. Physically weakened, most Europeans were highly vulnerable to disease, especially tuberculosis.

The bubonic plague is caused by bacteria that live in an animal's blood or a flea's stomach and is thus easily transmitted, particularly by fleas on rats. The first symptom in a human is a small, blackish pustule at the point of the flea bite, followed by the swelling of the lymph nodes in the neck, armpit, or groin. Then come dark spots (buboes, for which the plague is named) on the skin caused by internal bleeding. In the final stage the victim, convulsed by severe coughing spells, spits blood, exudes a foul body odor, and experiences severe neurological and psychological disorders. Bubonic plague, however, was not always fatal, especially if the pus was thoroughly drained from the boil; up to half its victims survived. A more virulent form of the plague—the pneumonic variety—was transmitted by coughing and was nearly always fatal. Both forms devastated Europe.

Plague had ravaged the Byzantine Empire in the 540s and eventually extended from central and southern Asia to Arabia, North Africa, and the Iberian peninsula and north as far as Denmark and Ireland. Some 200,000 people may have died in Constantinople alone between the fall of 541 and the spring of 542. When this outbreak finally ended in 544, more than 20 percent of the people of southern Europe had died. Further outbreaks followed for another 200 years, after which Europe was free of most epidemic diseases until the mid-fourteenth century. But the bacterial strains responsible for the plague continued to survive in the Gobi Desert of Mongolia. From there the plague was transmitted both east and west by nomadic tribesmen, perhaps forced to move their flocks to new regions when hot winds began drying up the pastures of central Asia.

The plague reached epidemic proportions in the Gobi Desert in the late 1320s and from there may have spread first to China. The Chinese had already been weakened by famine brought on by drought, earthquakes, and then flooding in the early 1330s. The Black Death followed, reducing the population nearly 30 percent (from 125 million to 90 million) before the end of the century. By 1339 the plague had begun its westward march, carried slowly but widely by migrating central Asian rodents and more rapidly by traders along the caravan routes and shipping lanes.

The impact on Asia and the Middle East was devastating. According to one chronicler, "India was depopulated; Tartary, Mesopotamia, Syria, [and] Armenia were covered with dead bodies; the Kurds fled in vain to the mountains."[1] Constantinople and Alexandria were struck in 1347; both cities suffered heavy losses, with the latter witnessing perhaps 1,000 deaths a day in early 1348. It was worse in Cairo, one of the largest cities in the world with its population of 500,000; there some 7,000 probably died each day at the peak of the plague. By 1349 it had spread throughout the Muslim world, killing a third of the people and possibly as many as half of those who lived in towns.

A procession of flagellants during the Black Death. Note the bare backs and the whips. [Lauros-Giraudon/Art Resource]

The Black Death was brought to western Europe when a Genoese ship carrying infected rats from the Crimea docked at Messina, Sicily, in October 1347. Within months the plague struck the great ports of Venice and Genoa, then spread throughout the rest of Italy, devastating Florence especially. By the end of 1348 most of France and the southern tip of England had been hit, and a year later the infected areas stretched from Ireland and Norway to Würzburg and Vienna. The plague moved relentlessly through northern Germany and Scandinavia, finally reaching western Russia in 1351 and 1352. Severe outbreaks again struck Europe in 1362 and 1375. Until the end of the fifteenth century no decade passed without at least one outbreak, and the plague continued to pose a serious threat to Europeans for two centuries after that. Surviving records are inadequate to determine accurate mortality figures, but the Black Death of the late 1340s probably claimed 25 million lives, perhaps a third of Europe's population. No war in history has destroyed so large a percentage of the people.

Europeans had no knowledge of the cause of the plague, though many attributed it to something mysterious in the atmosphere; many Christians were convinced it was divine punishment for their sins. Some fled from the towns to the countryside, where the pestilence was less frequent. Officials of port cities tried in vain to turn away ships carrying signs of the infection. Reaction among the people varied considerably. Convinced of imminent death, some opted for the unbridled pursuit of sensual pleasures, while others turned to ascetic extremes, such as the itinerant flagellants, who ritualistically whipped themselves, wore penitential dress, and bore crucifixes. Others turned to black magic and witchcraft, while some shunned anything Asian or blamed the Jews, many of whom were massacred. At Basel the bodies of slain Jews were floated down the Rhine in wine casks; 2,000 were slaughtered in Strasbourg, 600 in Brussels. Many physicians fled, whereas the clergy often ministered to the sick and thus suffered extensively themselves. Entire Dominican friaries in Tuscany and Languedoc were decimated, and perhaps a third of the German clergy perished.

The social and economic effects of the plague were profound. In several respects the Muslim response to the Black Death differed from that of Christians. Whereas the latter were preoccupied with guilt and fear, Muslims tended to regard the plague, like the *jihad,* or holy war, as an opportunity to achieve martyrdom and thus as a vehicle of divine mercy. "Their wounds had been similar" to those of holy warriors, said one Islamic tradition, "so they joined the martyrs."[2] Unlike the Christians, the Muslims therefore thought it was wrong to flee from a plague-stricken area, though in part this may also have involved some realization that flight could spread the disease. Theologically, however, Muslims denied that the plague was contagious, inasmuch as it was supposed to be divinely bestowed on a community deserving of special favor. Europeans, in contrast, were firmly convinced that the plague was infectious. The practical result was that Christians feared the Black Death, whereas the Muslims tended to accept it as they accepted such disasters as droughts and floods.

In the Middle East the immediate effect of the plague was a sharp rise in wages for laborers and a decrease in rents and income for the propertied classes. Yet there was no long-term improvement in the living standards of rural workers, particularly in Egypt and Syria, because a large increase in military needs to defend the region meant heavier taxes. Only in the case of urban workers did income rise sufficiently to bring an increase in real wages. In Europe hundreds of villages were severely depopulated or disappeared altogether, reducing the value of land and driving up wages as the labor supply plummeted. As in the Middle East initially, peasants who survived found their services in greater demand and could obtain better terms from their landlords or find more accommodating ones elsewhere, while others moved into the towns as artisans. Falling rents and rising wages prompted landowners to seek legislation fixing wages at low levels and restricting access to urban occupations. A French ordinance of 1351 limited wage increases to no more than a third of the preplague level, while the more ambitious English Statute of Laborers of the same year fixed wages at the pre-1349 rates and prohibited the employment of cheap female workers in place of men. Spanish, Portuguese, and German governments made similar attempts to control wages, but none was very effective. The French and English also enacted measures to curtail the rising cost of food.

Catastrophe and Rebellion

In Europe the dislocation caused by the plague coupled with the restrictive measures against the peasants and the artisans contributed to explosive unrest in the late fourteenth century. In 1358 many peasants in northern France joined in uprisings known as the Jacquerie (*jacques* was a name nobles used to address a peasant). Already embittered by efforts to limit their wages, the peasants were angered by heavy financial exactions to support French forces in the Hundred Years' War and by marauding bands of mercenaries from whom the nobles offered them no protection. The peasants began their rampage in May, killing, raping, burning, and destroying a number of castles. They had, however, neither strong leaders nor a program of reform. Priests, craftsmen, and lesser merchants joined them before the nobles ruthlessly suppressed the rebellion throughout the summer by means of widespread massacres. In the end, some 20,000 died.

Social revolt erupted in England in 1381, fueled by the peasants' resentment at efforts to restrict their economic advances, long-standing bitterness over aristocratic cruelty toward them, and governmental efforts to impose a poll or head tax to pay for the war against France. Peasants in the south, where the rebellion broke out, were also upset by French raids on their lands. Led by the priest John Ball and the journeyman Wat Tyler, the revolt soon spread throughout much of the country as urban workers joined the peasants. The killing and destruction was stemmed only when the young king, Richard II (1377–1399), met with the rebels and promised reform. Instead the nobles regrouped and carried out a campaign of retribution. Radical rebel demands—the equality of all men before the law, the granting of most church property to the people, and the end of mandatory peasant labor on

Peasant Rebellion: A Call for Communalism

The English peasants who rebelled in 1381 were motivated in part by resentment against the landed aristocracy. One of those who encouraged such hostility was the priest John Ball, whose views reflect a basic communalism.

Ah, ye good people, the matters goeth not well to pass in England, nor shall not do till everything be common, and that there be no villains [serfs] nor gentlemen, but that we may be all [made one] together, and that the lords be no greater masters than we be. . . . We be all come from one father and one mother, Adam and Eve: whereby can they say or show that they be greater lords than we be, saying by that they cause us to win and labor for that they dispend? . . . They dwell in fair houses, and we have the pain and travail, rain and wind in the fields; and by that that cometh of our labors they keep and maintain their estates: we be called their bondmen, and . . . [unless] we do readily them service, we be beaten; and we have no sovereign to whom we may complain, nor that will hear us nor do us right. Let us go to the king.

Source: G. C. Macaulay, ed., *The Chronicles of Froissart*, trans. J. Bourchier, Lord Berners (London: Macmillan, 1924), p. 251.

the lords' demesnes (personal lands)—were not met, though the government ceased collecting the head tax.

The Jacquerie and the Wat Tyler rebellion are but the most famous examples of the revolts that swept parts of Europe in the century after the Black Death first appeared. The peasants of Languedoc rose up in 1382 and 1383, Catalonian peasants were frequently in arms, and peasants and miners rebelled in Sweden in 1434. Much of the unrest erupted in the cities, where artisans demanded more political power and where the working poor were chained in poverty by repressive guilds. The greatest urban revolt was that of the *ciompi* (cloth workers) in Flor-

On the left the English rebel Wat Tyler is slain as Richard II watches, while on the right the king calms a mob of angry peasants. [The British Library]

ence in 1378, but there were uprisings as well in Paris and Rouen in France, at Ghent in Flanders, at Brunswick and Lübeck in the Holy Roman Empire, and at Barcelona and Seville in Spain. No other period in the Middle Ages experienced as much social unrest as the century 1350–1450.

The Hundred Years' War

Between 1337 and 1453 the English and French engaged in a series of armed conflicts collectively known as the Hundred Years' War, though in fact the two countries spent less than half this period in actual fighting. Each side went to war because it felt the other threatened its security and blocked its rightful ambitions. The war began when King Edward III of England (1327–1377) claimed the French throne as his own. The last three Capetian monarchs, the sons and heirs of Philip IV, had died without leaving a male heir. Although Edward III, Philip's maternal grandson, was the closest male heir, the French nobles supported the claim of Philip of Valois, a nephew of Philip IV's sons. At first Edward accepted the decision and even swore the vassal's oath of fealty to Philip at Amiens for his holdings in Aquitaine. English involvement in France, however, stood squarely in the way of the ambition of the French sovereigns to extend their authority throughout the country. No less important as a cause of the war was Anglo-French rivalry over Flanders. Its count was Philip's vassal, but Flemish towns depended on English wool for their textile industry. English support for the Flemings when they rebelled against their count threatened French domination in the region, whereas French control jeopardized English trade. Another grievance was France's support for the Scots, which prevented the English from exercising lordship over their northern neighbors.

As the two sides embarked on war, France was seemingly the stronger, with greater wealth and a population three times the size of England's. The French had the advantage of fighting on terrain they knew, but this in turn subjected their peasants to the ravages of war. The French kings, moreover, had to cope with the fact that some of their own subjects—the Burgundians, the Flemish, and the Gascons of Aquitaine—allied with the English at various times during the war. For most of its duration the French monarchs were unable to provide either strong military leadership or sound fiscal policies to finance the fighting. The English, despite the popular support marshaled by Edward III and a string of impressive military victories, were unable to inflict a total defeat on France because they had neither the manpower nor the funds to dominate such a vast land. In the end the English were largely reduced to a policy of intimidation, which failed in the face of renewed French resolve.

England's early victories were the result of the military superiority of its longbowmen, who could lay down a barrage of arrows powerful enough to pierce French armor at a distance of up to 200 yards. The effectiveness of the English archers was demonstrated at Crécy in 1346, at Poitiers a decade later, and at Agincourt in 1415. Although the French also had longbows, they failed to use them effectively. The turning point of the war came in 1429 as the English besieged Orléans. Charles, the sickly dauphin (crown prince), his plight desperate, gambled on an illiterate peasant girl from the village of Domrémy who claimed to have been sent by heavenly messengers. Accompanied by fresh troops dispatched by the dauphin, Joan of Arc, though only 17, inspired the French with a vision of victory. The English in any event were on the verge of withdrawing from Orléans, but Joan's sense of divine mission and the dauphin's decision to accept the royal crown as Charles VII in May 1429 gave the French new life. When the Burgundians captured Joan a year later, the English hoped to discredit her by having her tried and executed as a heretic, but instead they created a martyr. A posthumous trial found her innocent in 1456, and in 1920 she was canonized as a saint. In the years that followed her death in 1431, the French, with the Burgundians at their side after 1435, relentlessly drove the English out of France, leaving them in 1453 with only Calais.

The French victory was facilitated by the growth of national feeling and the effective use of gunpowder and heavy artillery. Not only were the new cannons useful in besieging fortifications, but they also demoralized enemy forces and frightened their horses. In the end the war was beneficial to the French monarchy, for during its course the kings acquired both a monopoly on the sale of salt, the *gabelle* or tax on which became a major source of royal income, and the right to impose other taxes, including a direct tax called the *taille*, without the approval of the Estates General. These funds were necessary to support the standing army introduced in the war. In contrast, the English monarchs were able to maintain the war only by repeatedly seeking parliamentary approval for taxation, thereby making Parliament an indispensable part of the government. By the war's end the principle was established that neither taxes nor other forms of legislation could be implemented without parliamentary approval, and Parliament had taken the first steps to hold royal officials accountable to them or risk impeachment. England and France thus began to follow strikingly different paths of monarchical government, the former eventually culminating in constitutional monarchy, the latter in absolute rule.

The social consequences of the war were profound. In both countries the rural economy was hit hard by the loss of men to the recurring campaigns, especially as the population fell sharply because of the Black Death. In addition to the soldiers killed in battle, the English callously murdered thousands of French civilians. The war brought higher taxes, disrupted trade, and contributed to the shortage of manpower on the farms of both countries. The change in the manner of fighting had significant long-term effects. Both the longbow and the use of guns enhanced

Joan of Arc as she may have looked, shown here holding a banner with the fleur-de-lis, the royal emblem of France. [Giraudon/Art Resource]

the value of commoners on the battlefield and thus encouraged the development of larger armies. Those armies in turn required greater and greater financial support from the state in contrast to the smaller feudal forces. The cannons meant major changes in the construction of city walls, which had to be much thicker. At the same time, however, siege trains capable of attacking towns were generally beyond the reach of all but sovereigns and the greater princes; the military changes thus contributed to the evolution of more unified states. Economically, the demand for cannons, guns, and ammunition sparked the growth of the armaments industry and the mining companies that provided it with the necessary raw materials. Thus in the long run the socioeconomic effects of the war were more important that its territorial consequences.

The Spiritual Crisis of the Late Medieval Church

Against a backdrop of widespread misery caused by famine, pestilence, and war, the medieval church was rocked by scandal and division in the late fourteenth and early fifteenth centuries, precisely at a time when strong spiritual leadership was desperately needed. The French king, Philip IV, emboldened by his earlier victory over Pope Boniface VIII, successfully pressured Pope Clement V (1305–1314), himself French, to move the seat of the papacy from Rome to Avignon in 1309. Although an imperial city under papal control, Avignon was not only on the French border but was French in language and culture. The papacy remained at Avignon until 1377, a period usually referred to as the Babylonian Captivity, an allusion to the period in which the ancient Hebrews were held captive in Babylon. Avignon had the advantage of freeing the popes from the turmoil then disrupting Rome and the Papal States, but it also placed the papacy under a greater degree of French influence. Of the 134 cardinals appointed during the Avignon period, 111 were French. The English, the Germans, and many Italians were displeased at the specter of a papacy in the shadow of French power, and Rome was particularly hard hit because its economy had rested so heavily on papal revenues. But perhaps most of the resentment against the Avignon popes stemmed from their efforts to create new sources of income to offset decreased revenue from the Papal States. The collection of annates, usually the first year's income from an ecclesiastical position, or expectatives, a fee for the right to be appointed to a particular ecclesiastical position when it became vacant, created the impression that the popes were more concerned with material than spiritual matters.

Disillusion with the papacy became even more pronounced as a result of the great schism that scandalized the church from 1378 to 1417. In 1377 Pope Gregory XI (1370–1378), persuaded by Catherine of Siena and Bridget of Sweden, moved the papal court back to Rome. When he died a year later, Roman mobs intimidated the cardinals to elect an Italian pope who would keep the papacy in Rome. The cardinals obliged with the reform-minded Urban VI (1378–1389), but five months later a group of mostly French cardinals declared Urban's election void and elected a rival pope, Clement VII, a cousin of the French king, Charles V. Europeans had witnessed schisms before, but nothing like the spectacle that now divided Christendom, largely along political lines. Clement, ruling from Avignon, had the support of France and its allies, Castile, Aragon, Naples, and Scotland, whereas Urban was backed by England, Portugal, Flanders, and the Holy Roman Empire. The Bohemians, Hungarians, Poles, and Scandinavians also supported the Roman pope. As each pope claimed to be the true vicar of Christ and condemned the other, the schism raised serious questions about the validity of priests' authority and the sacraments they administered. In addition to casting disrepute on the leaders of the church, the schism encouraged the spread of heresy and mysticism, with its stress on the inner life of the spirit rather than church matters and liturgy.

When it became apparent that neither the Roman nor the Avignonese pope would yield to his rivals in the interest of unity, reformers called for a church council to end the scandal. Advocates of reform contended that a council

Marsiglio on the Power of the People

In his Defender of the Peace, *Marsiglio of Padua makes a strong case for the people as the fundamental source of authority and the maintenance of peace as the primary task of a government.*

The authority to make laws belongs only to the whole body of the citizens . . . or else it belongs to one or a few men. But it cannot belong to one man alone . . . for through ignorance or malice or both, this one man could make a bad law, looking more to his own private benefit than to that of the community, so that the law would be tyrannical. For the same reason, the authority to make laws cannot belong to a few; for they too could sin . . . in making the law for the benefit of a certain few and not for the common benefit, as can be seen in oligarchies. . . . Since all the citizens must be measured by the law according to due proportion, and no one knowingly harms or wishes injustice to himself, it follows that all or most wish a law conducing to the common benefit of the citizens. . . .

It is hence appropriate . . . that the whole body of citizens entrust to those who are prudent and experienced the investigation, discovery, and examination of the standards, the future laws or statutes. . . . After such standards, the future laws, have been discovered and diligently examined, they must be laid before the assembled whole body of citizens for their approval or disapproval. . . . The laws thus made by the hearing and consent of the entire multitude will be better observed, nor will anyone have any protest to make against them.

Source: Marsilius of Padua, *Defensor Pacis,* trans. A. Gewirth (Toronto: University of Toronto Press, 1980), pp. 48, 54–55.

of the church exercised authority superior to that of a pope and was ultimately responsible for faith and unity. In its attempt to limit papal power, this Conciliar theory drew on a medieval intellectual tradition that in the past had been very controversial. In 1324, for instance, Marsiglio of Padua, the rector of the University of Paris, had argued in his *Defender of the Peace* that because the people are the ultimate source of authority in church and state, a church council is superior to the pope. Marsiglio went even further, insisting that the church's power was entirely restricted to spiritual matters; hence the pope had no claim to temporal authority. By reducing the church to a community within the state, he challenged its traditional claim to superiority. Although the church condemned Marsiglio's theories in 1327, his ideas provided a useful arsenal for those intent on disputing papal primacy. Among the most important of these were theologians at the University of Paris, especially Jean Gerson and Pierre d'Ailly, who espoused Conciliar arguments as the means to end the papal schism.

With the support of most monarchs, a group of cardinals representing Rome and Avignon summoned a council to meet at Pisa in 1409. There both popes were deposed and a new one chosen, but because neither pope accepted the council's action, there were now three claimants to Peter's chair. The embarrassing schism was resolved only when a new council met in the Swiss city of Constance beginning in 1414. It took three years and the energetic support of the Holy Roman Emperor Sigismund to restore unity through the election of an Italian cardinal as Martin V 1417–1431). One of the three feuding popes resigned, but the others had to be deposed. The church subsequently regarded the Roman popes as the legitimate line. In addition to ending the schism, the Council of Constance issued two decrees supporting Conciliar views, the first of which asserted that a general council of the church derived its authority directly from Christ and thus could compel the obedience of popes "in matters pertaining to the faith, the extinction of the schism, and the form of the church." The second decree called for the next two councils to meet after intervals of five and seven years and subsequent ones every decade. The council also addressed the question of heresy, particularly the problem of John Hus.

The Challenge of Heresy: Wyclif and Hus

Symptomatic of the church's problems in the fourteenth and early fifteenth centuries was the enthusiastic reception in England and Bohemia of ideas that challenged the very core of orthodox teaching. The Oxford professor John Wyclif (c. 1330–1384) not only denied papal claims to temporal power, as Marsiglio of Padua had done, but also demanded that prelates (cardinals, archbishops, and bishops) relinquish their political offices and that the church divest itself of its property. In the tradition of Francis of Assisi, he insisted that the clergy should devote themselves to poverty and piety. On the crucial question of authority, Wyclif insisted that it rested in the Bible alone, which, he argued, should be in the language of the people. In this spirit he began preparing an English version of the Bible. Wyclif also called for the abolition of many traditions, including pilgrimages, the sale of indulgences, the veneration of saints, and the doctrine of transubstantiation. Convinced that the true church was composed only of people divinely predestined to believe in God, Wyclif daringly argued that salvation was independent of the institutional sacraments, and he denied both papal and clerical power to excommunicate the righteous from the true church. Wyclif's clear distinction between the spiritual church of true believers and the corrupt temporal institution presided over by the popes appealed to Christians disgusted by the events of the 1300s. Wyclif enjoyed powerful support among aristocrats in England, who saw in his teachings the possibility of acquiring the church's wealth. Although many of his ideas were condemned and he was expelled from Oxford, Wyclif had enough influential friends to escape death as a heretic. His followers, known as Lollards, kept his ideas alive in England well into the sixteenth century despite heavy persecution. Ultimately they helped prepare the ground for the Protestant Reformation.

Wyclif's ideas were carried to Bohemia by Czech students studying at Oxford and by members of the household of Anne of Bohemia, who married King Richard II of England in 1381. The leader of the Bohemian reformers, John Hus (1369–1415), rector of the University of Prague, embraced some of Wyclif's teachings, especially his concept of the true church as a body of saints and the need for sweeping reforms. Hus, whose views struck a responsive chord among Czech nationalists resentful of the domination of foreign ecclesiastics, enjoyed the backing of King Wenceslas, brother of the Emperor Sigismund. When Sigismund offered Hus a guarantee of safe conduct in order to discuss his views at the Council of Constance, Hus accepted, though he had already been excommunicated. The Council, which had previously condemned Wyclif's tenets, accused Hus of heresy. He was tried and convicted, turned over to Sigismund's officials, and burned at the stake in 1415; promises made to heretics, Sigismund was assured, were not binding. A year later Hus' disciple, Jerome of Prague, met the same fate. Their militant followers, fired in part by Czech patriotism, mounted a fierce rebellion that lasted from 1421 to 1436. In the end the Bohemians were left with considerable authority over their own church, an example that was not lost on Martin Luther a century later as he pondered the need for reform in the German church.

The Late Medieval Outlook

The crises of the fourteenth and early fifteenth centuries had a striking effect on people's outlook: famine, plague,

A Corrupt Clergy: Wyclif's Indictment

John Wyclif's attack on the moral evils of the clergy struck a responsive chord among many Englishmen.

We should put on the armor of Christ, for Antichrist has turned his clerks to covetous and worldly love, and so blinded the people and darkened the law of Christ, that his servants be thick, and few be on Christ's side. And always they despise that men should know Christ's life, . . . and priests should be ashamed of their lives, and especially these high priests, for they reverse Christ both in word and deed. . . .

O men that be on Christ's half, help ye now against Antichrist! for the perilous time is come that Christ and Paul told [of] before. . . . For three sects fight here, against Christian[s]. . . . The first is the pope and cardinals, by false law that they have made; the second is emperors [and] bishops, who despise Christ's law; the third is these Pharisees [i.e., friars]. . . . All these three, God's enemies, travel in hypocrisy, and in worldly covetousness, and idleness in God's law. Christ help his church from these fiends, for they fight perilously.

Source: J. H. Robinson, ed., *Readings in European History*, vol. 1 (Boston: Ginn, 1904), pp. 497–498.

and war on the cult of death and decay; the Hundred Years' War on the cult of chivalry and the growth of national literature; and the Babylonian Captivity and the papal schism on social criticism and the views of nominalists and mystics.

The Cult of Death

The preoccupation with death induced by the massive fatalities resulting from famine and plague manifested itself in various ways. In the minds of the pious, greater attention was given to the Last Judgment, a popular motif in both art and literature. A few church walls still feature murals of the Last Judgment dating from this period. Others found solace in the Pietà, a depiction of Mary holding the dead Christ in her arms—a poignant symbol for grieving parents who shared her sense of personal loss and the hope of resurrection. Painters commonly depicted figures of death, and sculptors placed skeletal figures instead of traditional effigies on tombs. Nothing, however, more graphically reveals the fascination with death than the *danse macabre*, the dance of death that was not only portrayed in art but acted out as an eerie drama and celebrated in poetry. The *danse macabre* may, in fact, be related to the psychological and neurological disorders that accompanied the plague. A recurring theme in these representations is the equality of all persons in death, a sharp counterpoint to a society preoccupied with social hierarchy. There was no more vivid reminder of this than the Churchyard of the Innocents in Paris, where skulls and bones were heaped by the thousands along the cloister walls.

The Chivalric Ideal

Juxtaposed with this cult of death and decay, with its democratic implications, was another cult, more positive in outlook and restricted in its social appeal—the cult of chivalry. Here was a code for knights and nobles, the last gasp of a way of life and warfare gradually being pushed into the shadows by new methods of fighting, the rising mercantile order, and a gradual shift in importance from ancestry to talent as the key to a successful political career. The late medieval cult of chivalry, with its idealized knights and exalted ladies, was the swan song of the old order. The chivalric code exalted war, but there was nothing particularly glorious when England's peasant archers cut down the cream of the French knighthood at Crécy, Poitiers, and Agincourt. Efficiency, technology, and discipline replaced bravado, loyalty, and dignity on the battlefield, a change that ultimately revolutionized and depersonalized warfare by shifting the burden from the landed elite to the masses. As if to protest the passing of the old order, the aristocracy put greater emphasis on the trappings of chivalry: pageants, tournaments, and glitter. When Francis I of France and Henry VIII of England met

This sixteenth-century Flemish illustration depicts the churchyard of the Church of the Innocents in Paris. On its walls was a painting of the Dance of Death, below which skulls and bones were neatly stacked for public viewing. [Giraudon/Art Resource, Musée Carnavalet, Paris]

in 1520, chivalric trappings were so extravagant that contemporaries described the scene as a "field of cloth of gold." Extravagance and overstatement were indicative of the fact that chivalry, once primarily a military code of conduct, had been transformed into an elegant charade, a form of escapism.

National Literatures

The Hundred Years' War encouraged the further development of national vernacular literature. There are, of course, earlier examples of medieval literature in native tongues, such as the *Song of Roland*, the *Nibelungenlied*, and the poetry of the troubadours, but the contributions of Dante, Chaucer, and Villon were critical in shaping national languages out of regional dialects. All three writers sharply criticized late medieval society and the church.

Dante Alighieri (1265–1321), who held various civic offices in his native Florence before being forced into exile in 1301 by a rival political faction, spent the last two decades of his life traveling throughout Italy in search of patrons. Embittered by the divisiveness of the Italian states, Dante used these years to write in defense of the vernacular and to compose his epic poem, *The Divine Comedy* (1310–1321), so named because it progresses from a fearsome vision of hell in the first part, the Inferno, to a happy ending as the reader is guided through Purgatory to Paradise. The scenes from hell, peopled with everyone from actual popes and priests to politicians and queens, are used by Dante to condemn such evils as ecclesiastical corruption, political treachery, and immorality. On other levels the journey is an allegory of the Christian life and a pictorial *summa* of medieval ethical and religious teachings akin in spirit to the scholastic *summae* of Thomas Aquinas.

Disenchantment with the defects in contemporary society, especially the church, is also reflected in Geoffrey Chaucer's *Canterbury Tales* (1387–1400). The son of a wine merchant, Chaucer (c. 1340–1400) fought in the Hundred Years' War before serving in various capacities as a royal official. It was probably on a mission to Florence that he learned of Dante's work, which influenced his own writings. Many of his poems, such as *The Legend of Good Women*, deal with the theme of love, while others, such as *The Parliament of Fowls*, may reflect contemporary political events. In the characters, anecdotes, and moral fables of *The Canterbury Tales* he probed English society, making particularly incisive and satirical comments about the foibles and hypocrisy of ecclesiastics. The thrust is similar in a nearly contemporary work entitled *The Vision of Piers Plowman*, usually attributed to William Langland (c. 1330–c. 1400). The work's 11 poetic visions reflect the crises of the 1300s, especially as they affected the peasants, and are highly critical of the failings of the church even while reaffirming faith in Christian principles.

The poetry of the Frenchman François Villon (1431–c. 1463) is the voice of the downtrodden and criminal element in a society thrown into turmoil by the Hundred Years' War. A convicted murderer, thief, and brawler as well as a graduate of the University of Paris, Villon was in and out of jail and was for a time under sentence of death. The themes of his ballads range from the ways of the Parisian underworld and his drinking companions to meditations on the beauty of life as he contemplated the skeletons in the Churchyard of the Innocents. The specter of death stalks much of his work, reflecting the popularity of this theme in the fifteenth century.

Nominalists and Mystics

While the great vernacular writers criticized their social and religious world, William of Ockham (c. 1290–1349), an English Franciscan theologian, mounted a sweeping challenge to the scholastic teaching that prevailed in the universities. Ockham asserted that only individual things, not essences or universals, were real and knowable, a philosophical theory known as nominalism. Knowledge could therefore be attained by direct experience rather than by philosophical speculation. Contrary to the scholastics, he argued that the principal doctrines of Christianity, such as the existence of God and the immortality of the soul, were incapable of rational proof and had to be affirmed on the basis of faith alone. By removing the rational basis for Christian belief, Ockham opened the way to scepticism, a path followed by some of his disciples. Ockham's principles convinced him that the popes could not possess absolute authority, even in matters of faith; hence he contributed to Conciliar theory by insisting on the supremacy of general councils.

The rational and institutional approach to Christianity was also challenged by mystics, who urged the importance of seeking God within oneself. One of the most influential mystics was the Dominican friar Meister Eckhart (c. 1260–1328), a German, who taught that the mystical union of the human and the divine could be achieved in the soul through the purifying work of divine grace. Because the views of both Eckhart and Ockham were sufficiently different from traditional teaching, they had to defend themselves against charges of heresy before the papal court at Avignon, and Eckhart had to recant.

The real strength of late medieval mysticism was among the laity, particularly in Germany and the Netherlands. There the Dutchman Gerhard Groote (1340–1384) founded a movement known as the *devotio moderna* ("modern devotion,"), which combined a strong sense of morality with an emphasis on the inner life of the soul rather than liturgy and penitent acts such as fasting and pilgrimages. After his death his followers established the Brethren and the Sisters of the Common Life—lay believers who lived in strictly regulated religious houses and devoted themselves primarily to the education of young

Death and Decay

François Villon's poetry reflects not only his own experiences among the lowly and the criminal in France but also the fifteenth century's fascination with death and decay.

Death makes one shudder and turn pale,
Pinches the nose, distends the veins,
Swells out the throat, the members fail,
Tendons and nerves grow hard with strains.
O female flesh, like silken skeins,
Smooth, tender, precious, in such wise
Must you endure so awful pains?
Aye, or go living to the skies.

The following lines were written while Villon was under sentence of death; he describes the fate that awaits his body.

The rain has washed us through as through a sieve,
And the sun dried us black to caricature;
Magpies and crows have had our eyes to rive
And made of brows and beards their nouriture.
Never we pause, no moment's rest secure,
Now here, now there, as the winds fail or swell,
Always we swing like clapper of a bell.
Pitted as thimble is our bird-pecked skin.
Be not of our ill brotherhood and fell,
But pray to God we be absolved of sin!

Source: The Complete Works of François Villon, trans. J. U. Nicolson (New York: Covici Friede, 1931), pp. 32, 108.

boys. Some of the most influential religious leaders of the late fifteenth and sixteenth centuries, including Erasmus of Rotterdam, studied in these schools. The literary classic of this movement, Thomas à Kempis' *Imitation of Christ*, was a devotional handbook that emphasized personal piety and ethical conduct. Its message that "a humble husbandman who serves God is better than a proud philosopher" reflected a widespread desire among the laity to find relief from the material problems of their age through simple piety.

Economic Recovery

Europe recovered from the calamities of the fourteenth and early fifteenth centuries in large measure because of renewed population growth, economic diversification, and technological inventions spurred by the labor shortages resulting from the Black Death. As the population began to return to its former levels in the late fifteenth and sixteenth centuries, there was once again an abundant labor supply as well as improved productivity and greater economic diversification. Merchants increasingly branched out into fields as varied as banking, textile and weapons manufacturing, and the mining of iron ore and silver. The Germans modernized the mines by harnessing horsepower and waterpower to crush ore, operate their rolling mills, pump water from mine shafts, and run the lifts. Blast furnaces were constructed to make cast iron. Dutch fishermen learned to salt, dry, and store their fish while at sea, thus enabling them to stay out longer and increase their catch. The Hundred Years' War, as we have seen, stimulated the armaments industry, and the invention of movable metal type not only led to a new industry in printing but also greatly encouraged the manufacture of paper.

The textile industry experienced some growth in this period. The production of woolens in Flanders and the cities of northern Italy, however, declined in the fifteenth century, primarily because the English monarchs made a concerted effort to build up their native woolen industry by imposing low export duties on cloth and high ones on raw wool. Woolen manufacturing also expanded in France, Germany, and Holland, and new textile industries such as silk and cotton began to develop. In Venice some 3,000 persons were involved in the production of silk, 16,000 in the manufacture of cotton. Several thousand were employed in the Venetian arsenal, the greatest shipyard and probably the largest industrial establishment in Europe.

The growth in manufacturing went hand in hand with a dramatic increase in commerce and the rise of great merchants and their organizations. The latter included the seven major guilds in Florence, the six merchant corporations known as the *Corps de Marchands* in Paris, and the 12 Livery Companies in London. Firms in Europe's leading commercial centers established branch offices in other cities, and exchanges or bourses were opened to facilitate financial transactions. Banking houses developed rapidly; Florence had 33 in 1472. There were state banks in such places as Genoa, Venice, Augsburg, Hamburg, and Barcelona. As rulers as well as merchants found themselves in need of loans, the demand for credit grew, thus undermining the hostility of the medieval church to most interest charges. The Genoese pioneered the development of insurance, especially for merchants engaged in seaborne trade. The dominant role of northern Italians in banking was aided by the fact that the most stable coins of this period were Florentine florins and Venetian ducats.

Ships in the Mediterranean trade called at the Italian ports of Pisa and Genoa as well as at Marseilles and Narbonne in France and Barcelona in Aragon, but the heart of this commerce was really Venice. Its 3,300 ships, some of them capable of carrying as much as 250 tons of cargo, plied the waters from the North Sea and Spain to North Africa, Syria, and the Black Sea. In contrast, Genoa, itself a major maritime power, had 2,000 ships. Cloth from Europe was traded in the East for spices, dyes, sugar, silks, and cotton. Shipping in northern Europe was mostly the province of the Hanseatic League, whose members included Lübeck, Danzig, and Hamburg. Their ships ranged from Scandinavia and Russia to England, Flanders, and northern Italy. From the states of the Baltic and the North Sea they obtained fish, timber, naval stores, grain, and furs in exchange for wine, spices, and cloth. Much of the commerce moved through the ports of the Low Countries; in 1435 an average of 100 ships a day docked at Bruges. In the late fifteenth and sixteenth centuries the power of the Hanseatic League began to wane, partly owing to internal problems but mostly because of the growing power of states such as England and Denmark, whose merchants demanded an end to Hansa privileges and a greater role in the carrying trade.

Political Renewal: The Quest for Unity and Authority

Economic revival was accompanied in western Europe and Russia by the development of relatively strong centralized states. The political crises of the era of adversity had increased the need for state governments to raise substantial tax revenue. Such revenue made it feasible to think in terms of a professional army rather than a feudal levy, but this in turn increased the costs of government. So too did the growth of royal bureaucracies, which were essential not only to raise the revenue but also to administer the more unified realms. Greater unity was in general beneficial to the business community; hence the monarchs typically found important allies in the towns. Urban support was translated into tax revenues (though many French towns enjoyed exemptions), an enlarged pool from which government officials could be selected, and political backing in the drive for sovereignty.

The decline of particularism—the dominance of local and regional authorities rather than a central government—was in most respects a blow to the landed aristocracy, but they were appeased by exemptions from most taxes and frequent appointments to political office. The landed elite were also prominently represented in the national assemblies, where they enjoyed power and prestige greater than that bestowed on urban delegates. The achievement of national sovereignty was possible in large measure because the power of the landed aristocracy was not so much crushed as altered: in the new system, many of them became staunch supporters of the crown, not its traditional enemy. In the case of Russia and Spain, the development of a centralized state was carried out as part of a drive to expel hitherto dominant invaders—the Mongols in Russia and the Muslims in Spain.

The Rise of Muscovy

During the period of Mongol domination, Russia was a conglomeration of feudal principalities, but in the fourteenth century the princes of Moscow began to "gather the Russian land" by expanding their borders through marital alliances, inheritance, purchases, and conquests. In this process they were aided by three factors: the strategic location of Moscow near tributaries of the Volga and Oka rivers; Mongol reliance on the Muscovites to collect tribute from other Russians; and the support of the Russian Orthodox church, whose metropolitan archbishop made Moscow the religious capital of the Russians in the fourteenth century. As Mongol power declined late in that century, the Muscovite princes ceased to be agents for the Mongols and took up the mantle of patriotic resistance. Their new role was made abundantly clear when Grand Prince Dimitri defeated the Tatars, as the Russians called the Mongols, in 1380 at Kolikovo, southeast of Moscow. The war of liberation continued well into the fifteenth century, during which time Moscow was besieged numerous times.

The foundation of a strong Russian state was laid by Ivan III, known as Ivan the Great (1462–1505), who was determined to prevent the recurrence of the factional struggles that had plagued his father's reign. To counterbalance the power of the hereditary boyars, or nobles, Ivan created a class of serving gentry by offering them lifetime grants of land in return for their service, a practice somewhat akin to that used earlier in the feudal states of western and central Europe. Ivan also enhanced his status as the result of his marriage to the Italian-educated Zoë, niece of the last Byzantine emperor, Constantine XI (died 1453). Henceforth Ivan began to refer to himself as the successor of the Byzantine emperors, adopting the Byzantine double eagle as the symbol of Russia, introducing Byzantine ceremonies at court, and calling himself Autocrat and Tsar ("Caesar"). At Zoë's urging, Italian architects were commissioned to design the Kremlin, a fortresslike palace befitting the tsar's pretensions to grandeur. Russian scholars contributed to the new image by asserting that Moscow was the third Rome (after Rome and Byzantium, each of which had fallen) and thus the center of Christianity.

Ivan expanded the boundaries of his state, first by conquering the republic of Novgorod (1477–1478). In 1500 he invaded Lithuania, hoping to conquer Smolensk; although he failed in this objective, by 1503 he had successfully expanded his borders to the west. Above all, Ivan consciously advanced his claim to be ruler "of all the Russias," a title that even the prince of Lithuania had recognized in 1492. It was in this context that Ivan issued a new code of laws—the Sudebnik—for the Russian people in 1497. Ivan can justly be regarded as the founder of the modern Russian state.

The Spain of Isabella and Ferdinand

The unification of Spain was made possible by the marriage in 1469 of Isabella, the future queen of Castile (1474–1504), and Ferdinand, the future king of Aragon

The marriage of Ferdinand of Aragon and Isabella of Castile made the unification of Spain possible. [MAS, Barcelona]

(1479–1516). Of the two kingdoms, Castile was by far the more populous and wealthy. It was, moreover, an expanding state as it continued the campaign to reconquer Granada from the Muslims, a goal finally achieved in 1492. The marriage of Isabella and Ferdinand did not effectively unite the two countries, each of which spoke a different language and retained its own laws, taxes, monetary system, military, and customs. The two sovereigns left Aragon largely alone, free to keep its provincial assemblies, the Cortes, although royal supervision was exercised through viceroys appointed by the crown. Understandably, the monarchs concentrated on Castile, whose Cortes supported their quest for order and whose new council was the principal agency for the implementation of royal policy. In the work of centralization the sovereigns had the support of the towns, which were liberally represented in the Cortes, and of the hidalgos—knights who did not enjoy the tax-exempt status of the nobles and therefore sought employment from the crown. A number of the hidalgos served as *corregidors*, administering local districts, performing judicial functions, and supervising urban affairs. Although the role of the nobles in the government was somewhat reduced, they still exercised considerable influence through the powerful military brotherhoods established in the twelfth century, the Santiago, Calatrava, and Alcántara. To bring them under greater royal authority, Ferdinand became the head of each of the three great brotherhoods. The Mesta, the organization of large sheep farmers, also had to be controlled, for its payments were a primary source of royal revenue in the period before Spain began importing large quantities of American bullion.

The deeply devout Isabella and the pragmatic Ferdinand made the Catholic church a key instrument in their centralizing work. Isabella's most important minister, Cardinal Francisco Ximenes (c. 1436–1517), carried out a program of reform centering around the restoration of ecclesiastical discipline, thus reinforcing central authority. In 1482 Pope Sixtus IV granted the sovereigns the *Real Patronato* ("Royal Patronage"), giving them the right to make the major ecclesiastical appointments in Granada; this was later extended to Spanish America and then to Spain as a whole, a development akin to the assertion of the "Gallican liberties" in France (discussed below). Even more striking as a demonstration of royal authority in religion was the campaign of Isabella and Ferdinand to enforce religious orthodoxy. Although the Inquisition had been introduced into Spain by a papal bull in 1478, it soon became an instrument controlled by the crown and run by the queen's confessor, Tomás de Torquemada (died 1498). In 1492, the year Isabella and Ferdinand entered Granada in triumph, the Jews were given the option of being baptized as Christians or losing their property and going into exile; approximately 150,000 left. Ten years later Ximenes persuaded Isabella to expel professing Muslims. Jews and Muslims who converted—*conversos* and *Moriscos* respectively—were subject to the terrors of the Inquisition if their sincerity was doubted. Spain achieved religious unity, but at the cost of expelling or alienating productive minorities, curtailing intellectual freedom, and destroying toleration.

England: The Struggle for the Throne

By the time England concluded the Hundred Years' War in 1453, royal authority, already checked by the growth of parliamentary power in the areas of legislation and taxation, had been undermined by bastard feudalism. By this practice a small group of powerful nobles who controlled much of the country's landed property used their wealth to employ private armies through a practice known as livery and maintenance. The retainers in their hire wore distinctive clothing (or livery), served primarily for pay rather than for the use of land as in the traditional feudal arrangement, and could expect legal assistance—often involving intimidation or bribery—if they got in trouble while serving their lord. Many of these retainers were recruited from the ranks of soldiers who had fought in the Hundred Years' War. The powerful magnates who hired these private armies exerted enormous influence on the monarchs through the royal Council and commanded strong support from their followers in Parliament. These circumstances made it possible for Henry of Bolingbroke, a nephew of Edward III, to force the abdication of Edward's grandson, Richard II, in 1399. Parliament dutifully confirmed Bolingbroke's assumption of the crown as Henry IV (1399–1413), the first ruler of the house of Lancaster.

The reign of Henry IV's grandson, Henry VI (1422–1461), who became king at the age of 9 months, was conducive to the further growth of the magnates' power during his regency and then during the bouts of insanity that afflicted him as an adult. The result was the outbreak of civil war between the feuding factions, the houses of Lancaster and York. In the sixteenth century this came to be known as the Wars of the Roses when William Shakespeare, in *Henry VI*, assigned the symbol of the Tudor dynasty, a red rose, to the Lancastrians; the Yorkist symbol was a white rose. Henry's queen, Margaret of Anjou, was unwilling to see power pass to Richard, duke of York, great-grandson of Edward III and heir apparent before the birth of Henry's son. Richard's son, Edward IV (1461–1483), finally succeeded in capturing the throne in 1461 and forcing Henry VI to abdicate. The house of Lancaster staged a brief comeback in 1470–1471, though Edward soon regained control, after which Henry VI mysteriously died in the Tower of London.

The Wars of the Roses were over, giving Edward the opportunity to improve his position by carefully shepherding his finances, establishing firm control over the Council, and expanding royal authority in Wales and northern England. At his death in 1483 his brother Richard, regent for the young Edward V, had the new king and his brother imprisoned. They too died mysteriously, possibly at the instigation of their uncle, who assumed the throne as Richard III (1483–1485). Although Richard suppressed one rebellion provoked by the renewal of factional strife, in 1485 Henry Tudor, who was remotely related to the house of Lancaster, invaded England with French backing and defeated Richard in the battle of Bosworth Field. Once again Parliament willingly recognized the victor's claim to the throne, and Henry's marriage to Edward IV's daughter, Elizabeth of York, helped heal the reopened wounds dividing the English ruling order.

Henry VII (1485–1509) resumed the task of strengthening royal authority that Edward IV had begun, notably by making the crown financially secure and building up a modest surplus in the treasury. Instead of increasing taxes, he made effective use of income from crown lands, judicial fees and fines, and feudal dues such as wardship rights. He also avoided costly foreign adventures, with the exception of a brief and futile invasion of France in 1492 in an attempt to keep Brittany independent. Apart from token forces, Henry had no standing army, but he made good use of unpaid justices of the peace drawn from the ranks of the gentry to maintain order in the counties, thereby reducing the crown's dependence on the nobility. Henry also used his Council, which could sit as a court (called the Star Chamber), to maintain order and impose swift justice; people cited before it had no right to legal counsel and could be compelled to testify against themselves. Like Edward IV, he selected men for the Council because of their loyalty to him rather than their status as magnates. He negotiated two strategic alliances, one of which involved the marriage of his daughter Margaret to James IV of Scotland. From that line came the Stuart dynasty, which governed both countries in the seventeenth century and unified them in the kingdom of Great Britain in 1707. The second alliance involved the marriage of Henry's elder son, Arthur, to Catherine of Aragon, daughter of Ferdinand and Isabella. After Arthur died of tuberculosis, Henry arranged for Catherine's marriage to his younger son, Prince Henry. When in the late 1520s the latter tired of Catherine, who had failed to provide him with a male heir, he set in motion the events that led to England's break with the Catholic church. By the time of his death in 1509, Henry VII had imposed substantial order and unity on England and, in the Statutes of Drogheda (1495), had made the Parliament and laws of Ireland subject to English control as well.

Valois France

Charles VII (1422–1461) laid the foundation for the recovery of the French monarchy in the late fifteenth century, not least by his victory over the English in the Hundred Years' War. Despite the large size of the kingdom, the continued presence of feudal traditions and local privileges, and the existence of a representative assembly, the Estates General, the French kings were at last in a position to unify the country, aided by a new spirit of national feeling. Because of the war Charles had been able to form the first French standing army, supported by the *taille*, a direct tax for which he did not have to seek the approval of the Estates General after 1439. In fact, meetings of the Estates were very rare between 1441 and 1614, after which there were no sessions until 1789. In 1438 Charles had also brought the French church firmly under royal control in a pronouncement called the Pragmatic Sanction of Bourges. It set forth such "Gallican liberties" as the right of the French church to choose its own prelates and an end to the payment of annates to Rome.

Once England was defeated, the greatest threat to the French monarchy was the duchy of Burgundy, whose dukes, Philip the Good (1419–1467) and Charles the Bold (1467–1477), entertained thoughts of making their state a powerful middle kingdom between France and the Holy Roman Empire. Their lands included not only the duchy of Burgundy in eastern France but also the Franche-Comté, Flanders, and other areas of the Netherlands. To establish a viable middle kingdom, Charles the Bold attempted to conquer Alsace and Lorraine, thereby linking Burgundy with the Low Countries, the major source of his extensive wealth. The French king, Louis XI (1461–1483), responded to this threat by subsidizing the armies of the Swiss Confederation, who defeated and killed Charles in 1477. In the absence of a male heir, his Burgundian lands were seized by France, though Charles' daughter Mary and her new husband, Maximilian of Habsburg, retained possession of the Low Countries. The royal domains were increased again in 1480 and 1481 when Louis inherited the Angevin lands of Anjou, Maine, and Provence. Only Brittany remained beyond the pale of his authority, but that was remedied in 1491 when his son and heir, Charles VIII (1483–1498), employed military force to compel Anne, duchess of Brittany, to marry him.

Although the crafty Louis XI had shunned war wherever possible in favor of diplomacy and intrigue, Charles VIII recklessly involved France in a disastrous attempt to dominate Italy. The stage had been set when Louis succeeded not only to the Angevin lands in France but also to the Angevin claim to the throne of Naples, now occupied by the Aragonese. Louis had wisely done nothing about the claim, though he had involved himself in the political affairs of northern Italy. Charles, however, was determined to assert his Neopolitan claim, and in 1494 he invaded Italy, thus precipitating a great power struggle for control of the Italian peninsula that lasted 65 years. By February 1495 he had reached Naples, where he was crowned in May. Although the duke of Milan, Ludovico il Moro (1451–1508), had encouraged the French invasion as a means of weakening his own enemies—Naples, Florence, and the papacy—he soon recognized that a French presence in Italy threatened everyone. He threw his support to the newly formed League of Venice, consisting of the empire, the papacy, and the Venetians, which forced Charles out of Italy.

The French king Louis XI was a homely man who enjoyed a game of chess. He significantly expanded the royal domain by acquiring the duchy of Burgundy. [Sheridan/Ancient Art and Architecture Collection]

Charles' successor, Louis XII (1498–1515), was likewise determined to pursue his Italian ambitions. This time the French had papal support, for Pope Alexander VI (1492–1503) was primarily interested in weakening the Venetians, who were competing with him for domination of central Italy. Louis obtained the support of Ferdinand of Aragon by offering to partition Naples with him. Louis' primary goal was the conquest of Milan, which he claimed as his own because his mother had been a member of the Visconti family, which ruled the duchy until 1447. Ludovico was accordingly accused of usurping the ducal title and imprisoned for the rest of his life by the French—perhaps a fitting end for the man who had first encouraged French intervention in Italy.

Once Pope Julius II (1503–1513) had secured the Papal States, he enlisted Spain, Venice, the Swiss Confederation, and the Holy Roman Empire in a Holy League to drive France out of Italy, an end they accomplished in 1513. Under Francis I (1515–1547) the French returned again in 1515, this time sparking a series of wars with the Habsburgs that financially drained France and damaged the prestige of the monarchy. Nevertheless, as in the case of the Hundred Years' War, military needs and financial demands led to the continued expansion and centralization of the royal administration, thus strengthening the king's hold on the realm.

Italy: Papal States and City-States

While Russia and the western European states were developing stronger, more centralized governments in the fifteenth century, in Italy, Germany, Hungary, and Poland regional states and princes consolidated their power, effectively blocking the emergence of national states. The struggle in the High Middle Ages between the papacy and the Hohenstaufen emperors left the Italians without a strong government capable of extending its sway throughout the peninsula. Nor did any state possess a theoretical claim to serve as the nucleus for a unified nation. From Rome the popes governed the Papal States, a band extending across central Italy, but their claims to authority were international in scope. The popes themselves did not acquire their position by hereditary succession but by an elective process that was not limited to Italians. The papacy's temporal authority in Italy was severely reduced during the Avignon period and further damaged during the great schism. Beginning with Martin V, the fifteenth- and early sixteenth-century popes were therefore preoccupied with reestablishing their temporal power. Popes such as Alexander VI of the Spanish Borgia family and Julius II were less spiritual leaders than temporal princes willing to use any means to extend their power. Alexander relied heavily on his son Cesare, who had few moral principles, while Julius personally led his forces into battle.

In the fourteenth and fifteenth centuries the communal governments of northern Italy experienced substantial internal tensions resulting from economic and social changes. Rapid urban growth, the development of textile industries, and the rise of a sizable proletariat excluded from the hope of prosperity by privilege-conscious guilds created such strife that Milan and Florence turned to men who were virtually despots to preserve order. So too did some of the smaller cities, such as Mantua. Often these despots were *condottieri*, mercenary generals whose hired armies provided them with the force necessary to keep order. In the south the kingdom of Naples and Sicily had problems of a different nature because of foreign domination. In 1282 the Sicilians revolted against their French Angevin rulers and turned for assistance to Aragon. Throughout the fourteenth century the Angevins and Aragonese contested southern Italy until, in 1435, Alfonso the Magnanimous of Aragon drove the Angevins out of

Naples. As we have seen, it was the decision of Charles VIII of France to reassert the Angevin claim that led to the French invasion of Italy in 1494.

The Duchy of Milan

From its strategic position in the heart of the Po valley and at the base of the trade routes leading across the Alps into northern Europe, Milan developed rapidly as an industrial center specializing in textiles and arms. The medieval commune suffered, however, not only from social tensions but also from a struggle for power between Guelph (propapal) and Ghibelline (proimperial) factions. Under the leadership of the Visconti family the Ghibellines triumphed in 1277, effectively ending communal government and establishing despotic rule. The Visconti—dukes of Milan beginning in 1395—employed *condottieri* to extend their control in the Po valley. The last of the Visconti dukes, Filippo Maria, introduced the mulberry plant, laying the foundation for Milan's silk industry.

When Filippo died without a male heir in 1447, the Milanese revived communal government, but their so-called Ambrosian Republic proved unable to govern effectively. Thus in 1450 the *condottiere* Francesco Sforza, Filippo Maria's son-in-law, reestablished ducal rule. Apart from extending Milan's control over Genoa, Francesco attempted to maintain a balance of power in Italy among the five principal states: Milan, Venice, Florence, Naples, and

***14.2** Italy, c. 1494*

the Papal States. To this end he was an architect of the Italian League (1455), which also included some of the lesser states and was in part designed to prevent French aggression. Thus when his son Ludovico connived with Charles VIII of France to intervene in Italian affairs, he foolishly undermined his father's policy, thereby contributing not only to the devastating wars that ensued but to the demise of the Sforza dynasty as well. After the French were ousted, the family's rule was briefly restored between 1512 and 1535, at which time the Holy Roman Emperor Charles V acquired Milan.

CATERINA SFORZA, THE DESPOT OF FORLÌ

The duplicitous world of fifteenth-century Italian politics is reflected in the career of the sensuous and beautiful Caterina Sforza (c. 1463–1509), daughter of Francesco Sforza's son, the second duke of Milan. Although she received a humanist education (see Chapter 15), she displayed no interest in classical authors or philosophical issues, but she was intrigued by history as well as riding and dancing. For political reasons Caterina's father arranged her marriage to Pope Sixtus IV's nephew, Girolamo Riario. The pope subsequently gave them control of the towns of Forlì and Imola, northeast of Florence, but Caterina's husband was assassinated by political rivals in 1488. She retained power by ruling in her son's name, thanks to assistance from the armies of Milan and Bologna, and avenged her husband's murder by staging a spectacle of brutality in which the bodies of some of the conspirators were dismembered and scattered in the piazza of Forlì. That done, she sought to restore unity to her possessions by launching an extensive program of public building in Forlì, including a lavish park.

Although a campaign to extend her territory to the northeast failed because of opposition from Venice, her importance was such that she was courted by all the major Italian states. When the French invaded Italy in 1494, Caterina, fearful of Venice, refused to join the Holy League against France, opting instead for a neutrality that favored the French and their Florentine allies. The brutal assassination of her lover in 1495 prompted her to instigate another bloody vendetta, but it also opened the way for her secret marriage a year or two later to Lorenzo the Magnificent's second cousin, Giovanni de' Medici. About this time she underwent a period of spiritual searching in which she wrote to the reformer Girolamo Savonarola, who urged her to seek redemption through pious works and just rule.

Caterina's final period of political crisis began in 1498 when the Venetians raided her lands, but she was saved by military aid from Milan and the outbreak of fighting between the Venetians and the Florentines. While Caterina was occupied with Venice, Pope Alexander VI and his son, Cesare Borgia, plotted to increase their control over the Papal States, particularly the region that included Caterina's lands. Her main ally, Milan, was preoccupied in 1499 with the threat of a new French invasion, thanks to a pact between France and Venice signed in February. A month later the pope, calling Caterina a "daughter of iniquity," claimed her lands. Negotiations with Niccolò Machiavelli, the Florentine envoy, failed to achieve an effective alliance, nor were the assassins she dispatched to kill Alexander VI successful. Cesare Borgia's army struck in the autumn, forcing Caterina to send her children and treasures to Florence for safety. She retreated to a fortress with her troops, destroying all buildings in the area that might shelter the enemy, cutting down the trees, and flooding the marshes. Italy watched as the papal army relentlessly attacked until she was finally captured—and raped by Cesare—in January 1500. For a year she was imprisoned in a Roman dungeon. Without support from any major Italian state, her efforts to regain her territories failed, forcing her to seek refuge in Florence. Her last years were spent attending to her household, her garden, her horses, and her soul. Contemporaries called her the

Caterina Sforza, countess of Forlì. [Bildarchiv Foto Marburg]

"Amazon of Forlì," a tribute to her ability to hold her own in a political world governed by deceit and the ethics of power.

Florence and the Medici

Bitter social conflict disrupted Florence throughout the fourteenth and early fifteenth centuries. Thanks to its banking houses and textile industry the city was typically prosperous in this period, though it suffered severely when England's Edward III repudiated his debts and caused major banking houses to fail and again when 50,000 of its 80,000 inhabitants died in the plague. The periodic crises intensified social tensions that were already present. In part the turmoil was caused by an unusual degree of social mobility in Florentine society. The older nobles, the *grandi,* had been effectively excluded from power in 1293 through a constitution called the Ordinances of Justice, the work of the newly rich capitalists who dominated the seven greater guilds. In 1343 they in turn were successfully challenged by the craftsmen of the lesser guilds and their allies, the shopkeepers and small businessmen. The *ciompi* had their turn in 1378, when they revolted and won the right to organize their own guilds and have a say in political affairs. Feuding between the lesser guilds and the *ciompi* enabled the wealthy merchants to regain control in the early 1380s under the leadership of the Albizzi family. When the Albizzi blocked the rise of new capitalists to power but could not win a war against neighboring Lucca, they were exiled in 1434 by partisans of the Medici family.

Cosimo de' Medici (1389–1464) and his successors, who dominated Florentine politics except for brief intervals until 1737, governed as despots by manipulating republican institutions, often from behind the scenes. In addition to working with Francesco Sforza to create a balance of power in Italy and prevent French aggression, Cosimo introduced a graduated income tax and curried favor among the lesser guilds and workers. His grandson, Lorenzo the Magnificent (1449–1492), was the object of an assassination plot by the Pazzi family that killed his brother Giuliano while the two were worshiping in the cathedral at Florence in 1478. The plot had the support of Girolamo Riario, Caterina Sforza's husband, as well as Pope Sixtus IV. The pope resented the Medici's alliance with Venice and Milan, which was intended to block the extension of his authority in the northern Papal States. Although the assassination attempt failed, Lorenzo had to defend Florence against an attack by papal and Neapolitan forces. His son Piero was less able, and as a result of territorial concessions made to the French in 1494, he was ousted by the Florentines. Republican government was restored and for four years a spirit of religious frenzy prevailed under the sway of the fiery Dominican Girolamo Savonarola (see Chapter 15). The republic's alliance with France isolated Florence from other Italian states, but in 1512 Pope Julius II persuaded the Florentines to join the Holy League against Louis XII and allow the Medici to return.

VENICE: THE REPUBLIC OF ST. MARK

In sharp contrast to the Florentines and Milanese, the Venetians enjoyed a remarkable degree of social and political stability, in large measure because the merchant oligarchy that governed the republic was a closed group limited to families listed in the Golden Book. This register of more than 200 names included only families represented in the Great Council prior to 1297. Venice had neither a landed nobility nor a large industrial proletariat to challenge the dominance of its wealthy merchants, and the republic, because of its relative isolation, had not become embroiled in the Guelph-Ghibelline feud that left cities such as Florence with a tradition of bitter factionalism. There was never a successful revolution in Venice.

The Venetian government was a tightly knit affair. The approximately 240 merchant oligarchs who sat in the Great Council elected the Senate, the principal legislative body, as well as the ceremonial head of state, called a *doge*, and other government officials. The most powerful body in the state was the annually elected Council of Ten, which met in secret, focused on security, and in an emergency could assume the powers of all other government officials. To the Venetians' credit, the merchant oligarchy disdained despotic rule, thereby maintaining the support of those excluded from the political process.

In the fourteenth and fifteenth centuries the Venetians engaged in a program of expansion that made them a commercial empire. This involved a bitter contest with Genoa for control of trade in the eastern Mediterranean, a struggle that ended with Genoa's defeat in 1380. In the meantime, the Venetians embarked in 1329 on a campaign to acquire territory in northern Italy in order to assure an adequate food supply and access to the Alpine trade routes. Conquering such neighboring states as Padua and Verona brought the Venetians face to face with Milan and the Papal States, both of which were also expanding, as well as with the Habsburgs and the Hungarians, who were unsettled by Venetian expansion around the head of the Adriatic. The struggle on the mainland diverted crucial resources from the eastern Mediterranean, where Turkish expansion in the late fifteenth century gravely threatened Venetian interests. More dangerous than the lengthy war with the Turks (1463–1479) was the threat posed to Venice by the League of Cambrai, formed in 1508 and 1509 by Pope Julius II to strip Venice of its territorial acquisitions. Members of the league included the emperor Maximilian, Louis XII, and Ferdinand of Aragon. Although the league seized some of Venice's Italian lands, a reprieve came when the pope, increasingly fearful of French ambitions, negotiated peace preparatory to forming a Holy League against France. Venice was still an important state, but Turkish expansion coupled with the discovery of new trade routes to Asia eroded its role as a Mediterranean power.

At the peak of its influence in the fifteenth and early sixteenth centuries, Venice was a city of striking contrasts. The fabulous wealth of the merchant oligarchy was reflected in the palatial houses that lined the Grand Canal, none more glittering than the Ca' d'Oro (1421–1440), with its polychrome marble and gilded paint. Living space in the city was at a premium, hence not even the wealthiest patricians could acquire spacious lots. Away from the Grand Canal there was no special residential district for the merchant oligarchy, whose homes were scattered throughout the city. Venice had its poor, but generally there was employment for them, particularly in the shipbuilding, textile, and fishing industries. Food prices were regulated, and grain was periodically distributed without charge to the needy, but there was considerable reluctance to provide regular relief until 1528, when the city was inundated with refugees because of famine and war. The Venetians traded in slaves, and some blacks were kept in Venice as household servants, though the slave trade declined as the Turks pushed the Venetians out of the Mediterranean. The Venetians were mostly tolerant of the foreign minorities who settled in the city, but that attitude did not fully extend to the Jews. In the late fourteenth century the Jews of Venice were required to wear yellow badges, and beginning in 1423 they could not own real estate. Finally, in 1516 the Jews were forced to live in a special district known as the ghetto. It was, however, unthinkable to exclude them from the republic, as they had been from Spain, for the community required their medical expertise and their ability to provide monies, particularly in time of war. Venice was more tolerant of the Jews than were other Italian states.

The Holy Roman Empire

The destruction of imperial power in the thirteenth century during the struggle between the Holy Roman Empire and the papacy left Germany badly divided. When the princes ended the Great Interregnum (1254–1273) by placing Rudolf of Habsburg (1273–1291) on the imperial throne, they were not interested in creating a strong centralized government that would diminish their own influence. Although the Habsburgs dreamed of creating a strong dynastic state, their own dominions were limited to Austria, thus giving them little control over the princes

The Glories of Venice

The civic pride of the Venetians is manifest in the 1423 deathbed oration of the Doge Tommaso Mocenigo, which was delivered to a group of senators.

This our city now sends out in the way of business to different parts of the world ten millions of ducats' worth yearly by ships and galleys, and the profit is not less than two million ducats a year. . . . Every year there go to sea forty-five galleys with eleven thousand sailors, and there are three thousand ship's carpenters and three thousand caulkers. . . . There are one thousand noblemen whose income is from seven hundred to four thousand ducats. If you go on in this manner you will increase from good to better, and you will be the masters of wealth and Christendom; everyone will fear you. But beware . . . of waging unjust war. . . . Everyone knows that the war with the Turks has made you brave and experienced of the sea; you have six generals to fight any great army, and for each of these you have . . . enough [men] to man one hundred galleys; and in these years you have shown distinctly that the world considers you the leaders of Christianity. You have many men experienced in embassies and in the government of cities, who are accomplished orators. You have many doctors of divers sciences, and especially many lawyers, wherefore numerous foreigners come here for judgment of their differences, and abide by your verdicts. You mint coins, every year a million ducats of gold and two hundred thousand of silver. . . . Therefore, be wise in governing such a State.

Source: P. Lauritzen, *Venice: A Thousand Years of Culture and Civilization* (London: Weidenfeld & Nicolson, 1978), p. 87.

and towns in other regions. The virtual independence of the more powerful princes was confirmed in 1356 when the emperor Charles IV issued the Golden Bull, affirming that the empire was an elective monarchy. Henceforth new emperors were chosen by four hereditary princes, each of whom was virtually sovereign—the count palatine of the Rhine, the duke of Saxony, the margrave of Brandenburg, and the king of Bohemia—and three ecclesiastical princes—the archbishops of Cologne, Mainz, and Trier. In the century and a half that followed, lesser princes emulated the seven electors by establishing a strong degree of authority within their own states, a process that involved them in a struggle with the knights and administrative officials who wanted virtual independence for their fiefs. In Germany the territorial princes triumphed over both the emperor and the knights. Their power was reflected in the Imperial Diet, a representative assembly whose three estates comprised the electoral princes, the lesser princes, and the imperial free cities. Similar assemblies existed in the principalities. The Swiss took advantage of weak imperial authority to organize a confederation of cantons or districts—13 by the early 1500s—that were essentially independent.

Although Habsburg power within the empire was weak, Maximilian negotiated a series of strategic marriage alliances that vastly increased the family's power. His own marriage to Charles the Bold's daughter, Mary of Burgundy, led to the acquisition of the Low Countries, and the marriage of his son Philip to Ferdinand and Isabella's daughter Joanna made it possible for Maximilian's grandson Charles to inherit Spain and its possessions. The emperor Charles V (1519–1556) thus ruled the Habsburg lands in Germany, the Low Countries, Spain, Spanish territories in the New World, and the Aragonese kingdom of Naples and Sicily. No larger dominion had existed in Europe since the time of Charlemagne.

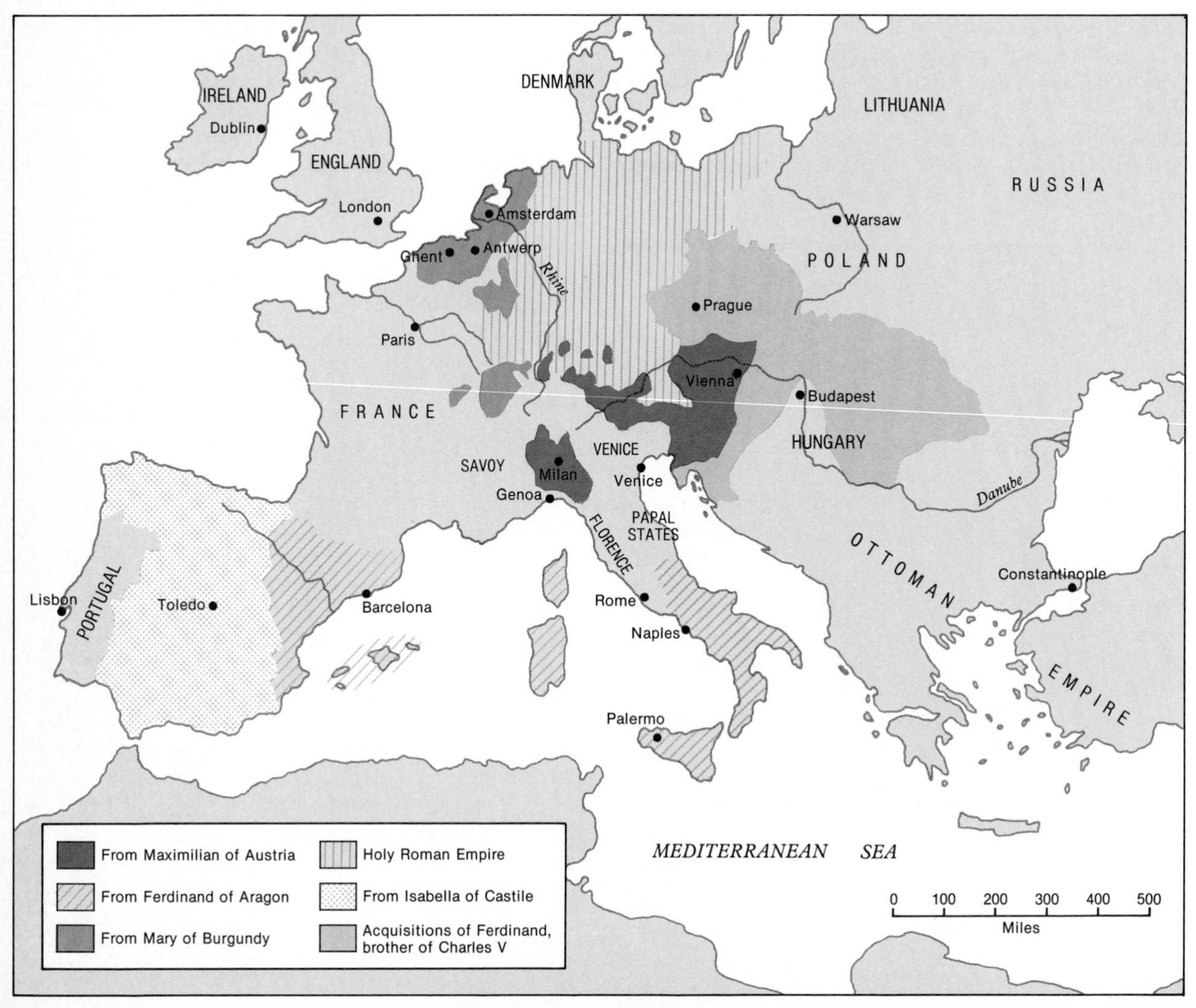

14.3 The Empire of Charles V

Spanish possessions in Italy brought Charles V into a bitter confrontation with the French king, Francis I, who was no less determined to press his own Italian claims. Although Charles was also concerned with the threat of advancing Turkish armies on the Danube, in 1525 he crushed the French at Pavia, near Milan, capturing Francis and forcing him to relinquish both his Italian claims and the duchy of Burgundy. Francis quickly reneged and allied with the Turks, who defeated the Hungarian army at Mohács in 1526. When the major Italian states (except Naples) allied with France in the League of Cognac, the imperial armies again invaded, this time sacking Rome in 1527 when their pay was late, an event that was widely regarded as the major atrocity of the sixteenth century. Louise of Savoy and Margaret of Austria negotiated a peace, the terms of which restored Burgundy to France. A year later, however, Pope Clement VII recognized Habsburg domination in Italy by crowning Charles both emperor and king of Italy, the last time the two crowns were bestowed on the same person. Although Francis renewed the war against Charles twice more (1536–1538, 1542–1544), not even an alliance with the Turks and German Protestant princes was sufficient to achieve a decisive military victory. When the Habsburg-Valois wars finally ended in 1559, Milan and Naples remained under Habsburg control. The Habsburgs, however, had failed to establish a unified state in Germany.

Eastern Europe

Although the Hungarians had developed a reasonably strong state in the 1200s, during the following century they were weakened by a dynastic struggle involving Bavarian, Bohemian, and Angevin claimants; the Angevins triumphed with the support of the papacy. There were further problems due to the frequent absences of King Sigismund (1387–1437) from the country, partly because of his campaigns against the Turks and partly because of his responsibilities as Holy Roman Emperor (1433–1437). In 1458 the nobles gave the crown to Matthias Corvinus (1458–1490), son of the great military leader János Hunyadi, who had successfully repulsed the Turks. Matthias increased royal authority through administrative and judicial reforms, higher taxes, and the creation of a standing army. Abroad he used Hungary's new power to conquer Bohemia, Moravia, and Austria. Following his death, however, a disputed succession enabled Maximilian to regain Austria and to bring Hungary into the imperial orbit by two dynastic marriages involving his grandchildren, Anne and Ferdinand. The nobles subsequently took advantage of weak rulers to disband the standing army. As in Germany, the real struggle in Hungary then took place between the magnates and the lesser nobility. Although the latter won their claim to equality in the eyes of the law, in practice the magnates were dominant.

Poland was an immense state—the largest in Europe after its union with Lithuania in the late 1300s—but it too failed to establish a strong central government. The position of the nobles was enhanced when King John Albert (1492–1501), in need of funds, allowed a national diet composed only of nobles to impose taxes on the towns and peasants. His successor accepted a statute requiring the diet's approval of all new legislation, further eroding royal authority. Although Sigismund II (1548–1572) allied with the lesser nobles in order to curtail the power of the magnates, his death without an heir enabled the nobles to assert their right to elect a successor. Henceforth Poland was in fact as well as in theory an elective monarchy in which real power rested in the hands of the nobility.

Politically, the fifteenth and early sixteenth centuries were a major watershed in European history. The failure of the Italians, Germans, Hungarians, and Poles to establish strong centralized states left them vulnerable to their neighbors and a perpetual source of temptation to expansionist-minded states. In contrast, the newly unified states of western Europe found themselves in an excellent position to take advantage of the economic possibilities opened up by the great voyages of discovery. It took the combined economic and military resources of these states to prosper in the expanding global trade. Nevertheless, although the Italian states failed to unify, their impressive economic growth, historical tradition, and sense of civic independence enabled them to provide intellectual and cultural leadership for Europe in the Renaissance.

Notes

1. R. S. Gottfried, *The Black Death: Natural and Human Disaster in Medieval Europe* (New York: Free Press, 1983), p. 36.
2. M. W. Dols, *The Black Death in the Middle East* (Princeton, N. J.: Princeton University Press, 1977), p. 113.

Suggestions for Further Reading

Aston, M. *The Fifteenth Century: The Prospect of Europe*. New York: Harcourt, Brace & World, 1968.

Barraclough, G. *The Origins of Modern Germany*. New York: Norton, 1984.

Becker, M. B. *Florence in Transition*, 2 vols. Baltimore: Johns Hopkins University Press, 1967–1968.

Contamine, P. *War in the Middle Ages*, trans. M. Jones. New York: Blackwell, 1984.

Dollinger, P. *The German Hansa*, trans. D. S. Ault and S. H. Steinberg. Stanford, Calif.: Stanford University Press, 1970.

Dols, M. W. *The Black Death in the Middle East*. Princeton, N.J.: Princeton University Press, 1977.

Gillingham, J. *The Wars of the Roses: Peace and Conflict in Fifteenth-Century England*. London: Weidenfeld & Nicolson, 1981.

Goodman, A. *A History of England from Edward II to James I*. New York: Longman, 1977.

Gottfried, R. S. *The Black Death: Natural and Human Disaster in Medieval Europe*. New York: Free Press, 1983.

Guenee, B. *States and Rulers in Later Medieval Europe*, trans. J. Vale. Oxford and New York: Blackwell, 1985.

Hale, J. R. *Florence and the Medici: The Pattern of Control*. London: Thames & Hudson, 1977.

Hall, L. B. *The Perilous Vision of John Wyclif*. Chicago: Nelson-Hall, 1983.

Holmes, G. *Europe: Hierarchy and Revolt, 1320–1450*. New York: Harper & Row, 1975.

Hook, J. *Lorenzo de' Medici*. London: Hamilton, 1984.

Huizinga, J. *The Waning of the Middle Ages*. New York: Doubleday, 1954.

Kenny, A. J. P. *Wyclif*. New York: Oxford University Press, 1985.

Lane, F. C. *Venice: A Maritime Republic*. Baltimore: Johns Hopkins University Press, 1973.

Larner, J. *Italy in the Age of Dante and Petrarch, 1216–1380*. London and New York: Longman, 1980.

Leff, G. *The Dissolution of the Medieval Outlook: An Essay on Intellectual and Spiritual Change in the Fifteenth Century*. New York: New York University Press, 1976.

McNeill, W. H. *Plagues and Peoples*. Garden City, N.Y.: Anchor/Doubleday, 1976.

Mollat, M., and Wolff, P. *The Popular Revolutions of the Late Middle Ages*, trans. A. L. Lytton-Sells. London: Allen & Unwin, 1973.

Perroy, E. *The Hundred Years' War*, ed. W. B. Wells. London: Eyre & Spottiswoode, 1962.

Post, R. R. *The Modern Devotion*. Leiden: Brill, 1968.

Renouard, Y. *The Avignon Papacy, 1305–1403*, trans. D. Bethell. London: Faber & Faber, 1970.

Seward, D. *The Hundred Years' War: The English in France, 1337–1453*. London: Constable, 1978.

Tierney, B. *Foundations of the Conciliar Theory*. Cambridge: Cambridge University Press, 1955.

Tuchman, B. *A Distant Mirror: The Calamitous 14th Century*. New York: Ballantine, 1979.

Warner, M. *Joan of Arc: The Image of Female Heroism*. New York: Knopf, 1981.

CHAPTER · 15

New Horizons: The European Renaissance

Petrarch is usually recognized as the first of the Renaissance humanists. [Bildarchiv Foto Marburg]

The social, political, and economic developments of the Renaissance era described in Chapter 14 were most apparent in the changes they wrought on the culture of the Middle Ages: a fresh approach to the heritage of "pagan" antiquity and an attempt to blend its values with those of Christianity; the rise of court- and city-sponsored scholars known as humanists, whose espousal of ancient values was linked to the secularization of political power; and a new style in the arts that reflected these changes. At the heart of the cultural renaissance was a shift in the way people viewed themselves, based on a fresh evaluation of the legacy of classical antiquity. Yet the new intellectual and artistic expression of the Renaissance was not only deeply rooted in the past but coexisted with a centuries-old medieval vision. Construction of the largest Gothic cathedral in Italy was still under way in Milan in the mid-1490s when

Leonardo da Vinci, working nearby, painted the Last Supper. By then the new developments in thought, education, and the arts we call the Renaissance had been developing for a century and a half. Interpreting the Renaissance has always posed a special but intriguing challenge to students of history, particularly in light of the fact that no comparable phenomenon occurred in the advanced Asian societies, which enjoyed cultural continuity.

The Urban Setting of the Renaissance

The Renaissance originated in fourteenth- and fifteenth-century Italy, which, unlike the rest of Europe, had an essentially urban culture. In Italian towns, where wealth was crucial in establishing one's social status, the emergent capitalists increasingly sought to patronize persons of intellectual and aesthetic talent, partly as a demonstration of piety, partly as an indication of cultural refinement, and partly as a manifestation of civic pride. When these conditions combined in Florence with a special sense of civic and historical awareness, particularly of the value of humanistic ideals as a unifying element in the face of external dangers from rival city-states, the stage was set for the Renaissance.

It is easy to understand why the Renaissance, inspired by the classical world, should have begun in Italy, with its abundance of classical monuments; but at first glance it is somewhat more difficult to explain why it first developed in Florence. Unlike Rome, Florence had few classical remains, nor did it possess the advantages of a port and a maritime economy like Genoa and Venice, which might bring it into contact with new currents of thought. The Venetians enjoyed not only a lucrative trade with the eastern Mediterranean but also close cultural ties with the Greeks. Even Milan was better situated because of its strategic position for transalpine trade.

Florence's principal advantage was its location astride the trade route between Rome and the north, a route familiar to the many pilgrims who flocked to the Holy City. Because of its location, Florence was coveted by the expansionist Visconti rulers in Milan, and Florentine efforts to preserve the independence of their city fostered civic pride and a stronger awareness of their historical heritage. In turn, their interest in Greek and Roman politics reinforced their fascination with classical ethics, literature, and education. Writers and artists tested themselves against Roman models, hoping to find in a glorious past the inspiration to meet the challenges of the present. The humanists, moreover, saw themselves as living in a postmedieval world, reuniting themselves with the ancient world. In so doing, they created the notion of the thousand-year Middle Ages.

FLORENCE: A PANORAMA

The thirteenth century had been one of economic growth for Florence, especially in the fields of finance and textiles. Florentines established themselves as the preeminent bankers of Europe as well as tax collectors for the papacy. Using wool imported from England and Spain, they manufactured high-quality cloth for the markets of western Europe and the eastern Mediterranean. Two major catastrophes in the fourteenth century—the bankruptcies caused when King Edward III of England repudiated his debts and the devastation of the plague—failed to destroy the city's determination to prosper. Its economy was organized around 21 guilds, of which the most important were the wool manufacturers, the wool finishers, the silk manufacturers, and the bankers.

The political, social, and economic life of the city was dominated by the patricians, whose wealth enabled them to purchase land and contract marriages with the landed aristocracy, thus expanding the city's sway over the countryside. As we saw in Chapter 14, the traditional aristocracy had been ousted from its domination of the city by the great guilds in 1293, but in the late fourteenth century the guilds were in turn challenged by an alliance of artisans, shopkeepers, and owners of small businesses. Throughout this period of turmoil the patricians and guilds patronized humanists and artists, in part to encourage civic unity. When the conservative patricians feuded among themselves in the 1430s, a faction led by Cosimo de' Medici triumphed, leaving the Medici family in control of Florence for the rest of the Renaissance era, except for the brief republican periods of the 1490s and 1512–1527. Even during these periods the Medici continued to support scholars and artists.

Florence underwent striking changes during the Renaissance period. Located on the banks of the Arno River—torrential in the winter, a trickle in the summer—the city was surrounded by fertile fields and picturesque hills. Beyond them to the north lay the Apennines, while Pisa and the sea lay down the Arno to the west. The city had the appearance of a walled forest, particularly after the last of its three walls was erected between 1284 and 1328. Nearly 40 feet high and 6 feet thick, the outer wall had 73 towers and was surrounded by a moat. By the mid-1200s there were over 275 other towers and tall buildings within the city, partly because of the need for space but mostly because towers were symbols of aristocratic power as well as refuges during the vendettas that plagued Italian society. Some towers were as high as 230 feet, roughly the equivalent of a modern 20-story building. On the eve of the Renaissance the towers were reduced in size when the patricians, who dominated the urban economy, triumphed over their landed aristocratic rivals. From the late thirteenth century the more substantial homes were built for merchants with different needs and tastes. The great fire of 1304, the result of feuding between rival Guelph factions, destroyed some 1,700 houses and resulted in a major rebuilding effort. After the bubonic plague killed perhaps 55,000 of the city's 95,000 inhabitants in the mid-1300s, recovery was slow, and by 1500 Florence had only grown to between 50,000 and 70,000 inhabitants, or roughly half the size of Venice and Milan.[1]

Well into the Renaissance period Florence's main buildings made it visually a Gothic city. The great cathedral, begun in 1296, was Tuscan Gothic, apart from the innovative dome added in the fifteenth century, which heralded the beginning of Renaissance architecture. The cathedral manifested civic pride and reflected Florence's rivalry with Pisa and Siena, each of which was also building a cathedral. The Florentines were determined to exceed the greatest classical monuments:

The Florentine Republic, soaring ever above the conception of the most competent judges, desires that an edifice should be constructed so magnificent in its height and in its beauty that it shall surpass anything of the kind produced in the time of their greatest power by the Greeks and Romans.[2]

Two of Florence's most beautiful churches, Santa Croce and Santa Maria Novella, were rebuilt in the Gothic style by the Franciscans and Dominicans, respectively, in the 1200s. The two major palaces, the Palazzo del Popolo and the Palazzo della Signoria, are also Gothic and fortresslike in appearance. Erected in 1255, the former (now called the Bargello) was the residence of the captain of the people, who commanded armed societies representing the people's interests during periods when they exercised political dominance over the nobility. The Palazzo del Popolo

The Cathedral of Santa Maria del Fiore dominates the skyline of Florence. Begun in the Tuscan Gothic style, the church, with its gleaming marble exterior, is crowned by Brunelleschi's dome, a triumph of Renaissance architecture. The campanile (bell tower) was designed by Giotto. [Wim Swann]

was also a meeting place for the city's councils. The Palazzo della Signoria (commonly known as the Palazzo Vecchio or "old palace") was begun in 1299 to house the guild representatives who governed the city. The palaces and chapels constructed during the Renaissance contrast sharply with the Gothic structures, symbolizing a new outlook and a changing set of values.

The Patronage of Arts and Letters

Support for humanists and artists in the Renaissance came principally from guilds and religious confraternities, the state, and wealthy families and oligarchs. Clergymen and merchants of more modest means also provided some backing, but their support appears to have had no significant impact on the development of the new scholarship and artistic styles. Persons with newly acquired wealth patronized artists and scholars as a means of demonstrating their status and enhancing their reputation. This meant commissions for painters to depict religious themes that incorporated portraits of the donors, for architects to design funeral chapels, and for sculptors to create impressive tombs.

As guild and civic patronage declined in the early fifteenth century due to an economic recession, families and individuals increasingly supported artists, writers, and scholars, thus increasing the scope for innovative themes and styles, particularly ones that reflected the values and interests of the patrons. All of this helped to improve the artists' own social and economic status. In the medieval period they were commonly regarded as mere artisans, but by the early sixteenth century some artists had become well-to-do. The best known were much in demand, and a highly sophisticated appreciation had developed of their individual styles and talents. Some became famous and acquired a wide following, thus inaugurating the modern Western cult of the artist. Giorgio Vasari recorded anecdotes about them and facts about their careers in his book of biographical sketches, *The Lives of the Painters*. Florence, with its status-conscious patricians, its deep-rooted civic pride, its historical interest in classical Rome, and its willingness to embrace new concepts and styles, became the first setting for the Renaissance.

Before long, Rome and Milan also became important centers of patronage. Because the economy of Rome relied for the most part on the papacy, it had suffered a period of decline when the popes and their vast bureaucracy resided at Avignon. Without major manufacturing and removed from the principal trade routes, Rome stagnated economically, its population declined, and its government proved unable to control the lawless. The early fifteenth-century popes thus had their hands full trying to restore order, though prosperity returned with the papal administration. Pope Nicholas V (1447–1455), himself a humanist, used church funds to beautify the city. Papal patronage brought Renaissance painters such as Fra Angelico (1387–1455) to Rome from Tuscany, sponsored the philologist Lorenzo Valla (1405–1457), and established a major library of classical authors. With Pope Sixtus IV (1471–1484) and his nephew, Pope Julius II (1503–1513), providing patronage to the greatest artists of their age, Rome supplanted Florence as the heart of the Renaissance during Julius' pontificate.

The Renaissance spread to Venice under strikingly different circumstances. The Venetian merchant oligarchy, primarily concerned with affairs of the republic and lucrative foreign trade, was still heavily influenced by Byzantine taste in the fourteenth and early fifteenth centuries. Because merchants returning from the Middle East brought art objects for St. Mark's Cathedral, the styles of the eastern Mediterranean were familiar. Byzantine mosaics adorned the interior of St. Mark's as well as the churches of neighboring Ravenna. Nevertheless, Renaissance ideals began to make headway as Florentine artists worked in nearby Padua, which the Venetians dominated politically, and as humanists won the support of the Venetian Senate for their printing press. Two technical developments—the introduction of oil-based paints from the Flemings about 1475 and the use of canvas—were important to the development of Renaissance painting. The new canvases were far more adaptable to the humid Venetian climate than the traditional wood or plaster and thus could readily be used to decorate religious and civic buildings. The Senate, churches, and charitable societies patronized painters such as Giovanni Bellini (c. 1430–1516) and his family. In Venice the Renaissance adapted to the merchant oligarchy's luxurious tastes and fondness for pageantry, thereby setting a rather different course from the Renaissance in Florence and Rome.

The Humanists

The bond that knit humanists together was a commitment to study classical literary texts for their own sake rather than as handmaidens to Christian theology. The goal of such study, basic to the Renaissance, was nothing less than the revitalization of political, social, and religious institutions through the infusion of classical values. Humanists were engaged less in sponsoring a rebirth of the classics than in a reorientation of their approach toward them. An awareness of the thought and art of classical antiquity had never been completely lost in the medieval period and in fact had grown substantially since the late eleventh century. The reorientation that began in the 1300s entailed a shift in emphasis from the study of theology and metaphysics to the study of grammar, rhetoric, poetry, ethics, and history.

The humanists generally espoused two basic ideals: reverence for the full scope of "pagan" as well as Christian antiquity and belief in the distinctiveness of the individual, though the civic humanists of the early fifteenth century tended to subordinate the individual to the city-state. In contrast to the medieval tendency to seek virtue through solitude, the humanists sought virtue in the public sphere. Although Italian humanists focused almost exclusively on secular things, and some even assumed a personal attitude of religious skepticism, most remained traditional Catholics. Their interest in pagan literature gave way to a concern for early biblical and patristic literature, especially north of the Alps, where they were determined to blend humanistic and Christian concerns. Many Italian humanists deemphasized ritual and sacrament. Instead they stressed such temporal concerns as the performance of civic duties, the fulfillment of which brought a civic renown that pushed the medieval quest for spiritual immortality into the shadows.

The Age of Petrarch

The earliest humanists addressed the needs of the social groups that emerged triumphant in the political struggles within the Italian city-states in the fourteenth century. As these groups consolidated their hold on power, they were ready to embrace a new psychological consciousness oriented toward worldly ends rather than the otherworldly ideals that had dominated the medieval outlook. The humanists provided the flattering self-image the patricians sought by praising the worth of the individual, the dignity of political affairs, secular accomplishments, and even the pursuit of personal glory. The success of the humanists was directly related to the existence of a responsive audience of the social and political elite, an audience warmly receptive to the humanist use of eloquence to validate the lifestyle and public role of the patriciate.

The most prominent of the early Renaissance humanists, Petrarch (Francesco Petrarca, 1304–1374), son of a political exile from Florence, gave up the study of law to devote himself to a public literary career, a vocation that he virtually invented. Fascinated by classical antiquity, he wrote biographies of famous Romans and composed *Africa*, a Latin epic in the style of the *Aeneid* to honor the Roman general Scipio Africanus. He even penned letters to his classical heroes—Horace, Livy, Vergil, and especially Cicero—and published them as *Letters to the Ancient Dead*. His best-known work is a charming collection of love sonnets to Laura, a married woman in Avignon. For more than 20 years he idealized her beauty, always from a distance, until she died in the plague in 1348. Although much

Petrarch on Petrarch

As an elderly man, Petrarch pondered his life and the values of a humanist. Like many humanists, he developed a strong interest in religion in his later years.

I have always possessed an extreme contempt for wealth; not that riches are not desirable in themselves, but because I hate the anxiety and care which are invariably associated with them. . . . Nothing displeases me more than display, for not only is it bad in itself and opposed to humility, but it is troublesome and distracting. . . .

The greatest kings of this age have loved and courted me. They may know why; I certainly do not. With some of them I was on such terms that they seemed in a certain sense my guests rather than I theirs. . . . I fled, however, from many of those to whom I was greatly attached; and such was my innate longing for liberty that I studiously avoided those whose very name seemed incompatible with the freedom that I loved.

I possessed a well-balanced rather than a keen intellect—one prone to all kinds of good and wholesome study, but especially inclined to moral philosophy and the art of poetry. The latter, indeed, I neglected as time went on, and took delight in sacred literature. Finding in that a hidden sweetness which I had once esteemed but lightly, I came to regard the works of the poets as only amenities.

Among the many subjects that interested me, I dwelt especially upon antiquity, for our own age has always repelled me, so that, had it not been for the love of those dear to me, I should have preferred to have been born in any other period than our own.

Source: F. A. Ogg, ed., *A Source Book of Mediaeval History* (New York: American Book Company, 1907), pp. 471–472.

of Petrarch's work was secular, he made some efforts to harmonize classical and Christian teachings. Cicero's Stoic concepts, he thought, were compatible with the Gospel, and he used a series of dialogues with St. Augustine to explore his own feelings of sin and guilt. Contemptuous of both scholastics and the uneducated, committed to the critical study of manuscripts, and concerned about his reputation with posterity, Petrarch was an exemplar for later humanists.

Petrarch's divergence from an essentially medieval outlook is evident when he is compared with the greatest figure of the previous generation, Dante Alighieri (1265–1321). Exiled from Florence with Petrarch's father, Dante foreshadowed one aspect of the Renaissance by using vernacular Italian for his masterpiece, *The Divine Comedy*. Petrarch subsequently expressed the ideal of a unified Italian motherland in the poem *Italia Mia* ("My Italy"). But Dante's *Divine Comedy* more closely reflects the spirit of Thomas Aquinas' *Summa Theologica* than the ideals of the humanists. Its three-line stanzas symbolizing the Trinity, its treatment of the present life as a preparation for eternity, and its traditional interpretation of sins and virtues are evocations of the medieval world. The subordinate role of classical knowledge in Dante's scheme is apparent when Vergil, after guiding Dante through hell and purgatory, is replaced for the journey through paradise by Beatrice, a symbol of revelation. Beatrice also figures prominently in Dante's *Vita nuova* ("New Life"), his spiritual autobiography. Unlike Petrarch's love for Laura, which is intensely personal and secular, Dante's lifelong passion for Beatrice is symbolic of Christ's love for his church. The two types of love reflect the difference between the medieval and Renaissance outlooks.

Petrarch's friend and student, Giovanni Boccaccio (1313–1375), is remembered for his *Decameron*, a collection of 100 short stories related by ten young people who fled the plague that ravaged Florence in 1348. The racy tales were mostly borrowed from classical, medieval, and Eastern sources. Unlike Geoffrey Chaucer, who used some of the same material in *The Canterbury Tales*, Boccaccio gave his work a more secular flavor by omitting the usual moral commentary. Boccaccio's most substantive work, an encyclopedia of classical mythology titled *Genealogy of the Gods*, maintains the medieval fascination with allegory but is humanistic in its praise of poetry and its assertion that learning remakes the natural person into the civil person. Like other humanists, Boccaccio was convinced that he was part of a new age, for Petrarch, he said, had "cleansed the fount of Helicon," the abode of the mythical classical muses, "swampy with mud and rushes, restoring its waters to their former purity."[3]

Civic Humanists

The second stage of humanism, which lasted from approximately 1375 to 1460, was staunchly committed to the proposition that humanistic scholarship must be brought to bear on public affairs. Cicero, one of the humanists' heroes, had after all been an active statesman in the Roman republic. Civic humanists held community service in high regard as a justification for the positions and privileges of the patriciate. Learning thus became a tool to benefit society as well as a means to assert political influence. Taking note of their predecessors' interest in rhetoric, the civic humanists extolled it as the basis for a new standard of nobility to which patricians were urged to aspire. Rhetoric, which entailed not only eloquence but also the application of knowledge to specific problems, could reputedly preserve society and mold good citizens by making law and morality effective. Eloquence became a way of life, as relevant to princes and ruling elites as to poets and teachers, not least because it made possible a strong degree of self-confidence.

The civic humanists espoused a belief in political liberty for a broadly defined elite and in civic patriotism, which in Florence involved a concerted attempt to preserve the city's freedom from Milanese aggression. In the late fourteenth and early fifteenth centuries Florence had three chancellors who were civic humanists: Coluccio Salutati, Leonardo Bruni, and Poggio Bracciolini. During his 31-year chancellorship, Salutati, a disciple of Petrarch, boasted that Florence was the "mother of freedom," a theme echoed by Bruni and Poggio. Bruni's *History of Florence* was written in the conviction that history involves the use of examples to teach philosophy and that "the careful study of the past enlarges our foresight in contemporary affairs." The political liberty extolled by the civic humanists was never fully realized in Renaissance Florence, however, and such liberty as did exist was sharply reduced after Cosimo de' Medici began to dominate city politics in 1434. Faced with the realities of the Medici oligarchy, which effectively undermined constitutional government, the humanists accepted Medici patronage and generally retreated from the political arena to their scholarship and contemplation.

The Florentine Academy and the Neoplatonists

The decline of the civic humanists and the flowering of Neoplatonism in late fifteenth-century Florence marked the beginning of humanism's third stage. Instead of a primary concern with the problems and duties of civil life and a preoccupation with such works as Aristotle's *Ethics* and Plutarch's *Lives*, interest shifted to Plato and the ideal of the contemplative life. The seeds of this transformation had been planted in the 1390s when the Greek scholar Manuel Chrysoloras taught Greek in the city; among his pupils was the civic humanist Bruni. Bruni subsequently translated Plato and other classical and Christian authors. Greek studies received a further impetus in 1439 when hundreds of Greeks came to Ferrara and Florence to attend an ecumenical council. At the urging of one of them, Cosimo de' Medici eventually endowed an academy near Florence in 1462. The academy provided the setting for philosophical discussions presided over by Marsilio Ficino (1433–1499). The atmosphere was semireligious: the disciples sang hymns praising Plato, burned a lamp before his bust, and adopted as their motto "Salvation in Plato." Ficino himself prepared editions of the works of Plato and Plotinus.

Renaissance Neoplatonism was a fascinating, eclectic mixture of ideas from classical thought, Christian dogma, and astrology. Ficino and his followers stressed the uniqueness of humankind, including personal worth and dignity as well as the power to transform oneself spiritually by choosing the good. Above all, each person was free, though one's sphere of action was circumscribed by the stars. Those who chose to pursue the higher things of life aspired to the release of their souls from the perishable world of matter. The Neoplatonic ideal was otherworldly, and the Neoplatonic experience emotional. Its moving force was love, and its direction was the rational life. To know God was the ultimate goal, attainable only by separating from the material world. The Neoplatonists were deeply sensitive to beauty, which they intimately associated with truth and goodness, all of which were earthly manifestations of Platonic Forms. The Neoplatonic love of symbolic allegory, Christian mysticism, and beauty made the philosophy attractive to such Renaissance artists as Botticelli, Raphael, and Michelangelo.

Through their eclectic, mystical philosophy, the Florentine Neoplatonists effectively moved beyond the range of traditional humanists. The latter's shift of emphasis from metaphysics to ethics was reversed by the Neoplatonists, but without returning to the traditional and orthodox philosophical views of the medieval scholastics. The Neoplatonists also broke with the civic humanists by turning their backs on public affairs and the campaign for political freedom—perhaps a prudent choice in the treacherous political atmosphere of Medici Florence. Nevertheless, something of the original humanist ideal remained in their respect for human dignity and the freedom to choose one's destiny. This ideal was expressed most eloquently in the *Oration on the Dignity of Man* by Ficino's disciple, Pico della Mirandola (1463–1494). Drawing on his vast reading in Jewish, Christian, and Arabic works, the erudite Pico accorded humans a special rank in the universal chain of being where they could ponder the plan of the universe and marvel at its beauty. Although Renaissance Neoplatonism was quietist in its avoidance of political activism, it was nevertheless radical in its rejection of church hierarchy in favor of an emphasis on individual enlightenment.

Education and Scholarship

The central goal of a humanist education was to develop the virtuous individual, one who would live a moral, disciplined life not only for personal enrichment but also for the benefit of society. This education, however, was intended for the socially elite, not commoners. A number of humanists urged major changes in the educational curriculum, particularly at the secondary level, in order to accomplish this end. An education focusing on the humanities was deemed to have the greatest practical relevance for daily living because it addressed the whole person. The humanist ideal in education was neatly summarized by Pietro Paolo Vergerio (1370–1444), a student of Chrysoloras and a friend of Bruni:

> **We call those studies *liberal* which are worthy of a free man; those studies by which we attain and practice virtue and wisdom; that education which calls forth, trains, and develops those highest gifts of body and of mind which ennoble men, and which are rightly judged to rank next in dignity to virtue only. . . . Amongst these [studies] I accord the first place to history, on grounds both of its attractiveness and of its utility.[4]**

For the humanists virtue entailed not only the fundamental principles of morality but also an ethical ideal that encompassed both self-determination and an awareness of personal worth. Vergerio and his colleagues drew extensively on classical authors such as Quintilian in developing this concept of a humanist education.

One of the leading Renaissance educators, Vergerio's friend Vittorino da Feltre (died 1446), established a model secondary school at Mantua called the Happy House. Scholarships enabled the children of the poor to attend, and unlike many other schools girls too were welcome. The curriculum included the humanities, religion, mathematics, drawing, and physical education—riding, fencing, swimming, and martial skills. Appropriate attention was given to proper diet and dress, so that education was concerned with the whole of life.

The ideas of the humanist educators are reflected in the Renaissance's most influential handbook of manners, *The Book of the Courtier* (1527) by Baldassare Castiglione (1478–1529). Deliberately limited in scope as a guide for aristocrats in the service of their prince, the book depicts the ideal courtier as someone knowledgeable in Greek, Latin, and the vernacular. His accomplishments would also range from music and poetry to dancing and sports. In sharp contrast to the image of a courtier as a hard-drinking, arrogant swordsman, Castiglione's courtier is a well-mannered, cultivated, and versatile gentleman, as much at home in the salon and the concert chamber as in the halls of power. The courtier, moreover, must be an educator—not of young people but of the prince, who must be taught the ways of virtue, especially temperance. Many of the same qualities are to be found in the aristocratic lady who, said Castiglione, should be adorned with "admirable accomplishments." Nevertheless she was to shun "manly" sports such as riding and tennis as well as musical instruments that required ungainly physical effort, such as

Aristocratic Women

Baldassare Castiglione's Book of the Courtier *reflects the humanist interest in shaping the aristocratic woman to please the men. Note here how the courtier is expected to teach her as well as to revel in her beauty.*

Many faculties of the mind are as necessary to woman as to man; likewise gentle birth, to avoid affectation, to be naturally graceful in all her doings, to be mannerly, clever, prudent, not arrogant, not envious, not slanderous, not vain, not quarrelsome, not silly, to know how to win and keep the favor of her mistress and of all others, to practice well and gracefully the exercises that befit women. . . . Beauty is more necessary to her than to the courtier, for in truth that woman lacks much who lacks beauty. Then, too, she ought to be more circumspect and take greater care not to give occasion for evil being said of her. . . .

Let him obey, please and honor his lady with all reverence, and hold her dearer than himself, and prefer her convenience and pleasures to his own, and love in her not less the beauty of mind than of body. Therefore let him take care not to leave her to fall into any kind of error, but by admonition and good advice let him always seek to lead her on to modesty, to temperance, to true chastity. . . .

In such fashion will our courtier be most acceptable to his lady, and she will always show herself obedient, sweet and affable to him, and as desirous of pleasing him as of being loved by him.

Source: B. Castiglione, *The Book of the Courtier,* trans. L. E. Opdycke (New York: Scribner, 1901), passim.

trumpets, fifes, and drums. While Castiglione idealized women as objects of courtly love, in practice he expected them to maintain an appropriate degree of subservience to men. *The Book of the Courtier* was immensely influential throughout Europe and was still widely consulted as a guide to aristocratic bearing in the eighteenth century. It marked a turning point in the refinement of manners that left a permanent mark on the European upper classes.

Another fundamental concern of the humanists was the search for accurate texts from classical Greece and Rome. This quest encouraged the humanists to ransack archives to find as many early manuscripts as possible. To produce good texts they had to develop critical tools, especially philology (the study of the origins of language), paleography (the study of ancient manuscripts), and textual criticism. Lorenzo Valla used the principles of textual criticism to demonstrate that the eighth-century Donation of Constantine was a forgery. Some experts already suspected that this document, by which Emperor Constantine (died 337) allegedly endowed the papacy with vast lands, was fraudulent, but Valla laid any doubt to rest by demonstrating that it contained language and references unknown in Constantine's day. His exposure of the Donation was a triumphant exhibition of the powers of humanist scholarship in challenging tradition and the political authority that rested on it.

Valla also used his command of classical languages to prove that there were errors in the official version of the Bible, the Latin Vulgate. Because of his belief in the supremacy of faith over reason, however, his loyalty to the church was not shaken. Thanks to the patronage of Pope Nicholas V (1447–1455), himself a humanist, he was even appointed apostolic secretary. Valla's application of philological and historical techniques to the Donation and the Vulgate provided the foundation for major advances in textual criticism in the sixteenth century, particularly in the field of biblical scholarship, as reflected in the work of Desiderius Erasmus.

Humanists Outside Italy

The ideals of the Italian humanists were carried beyond the Alps in the late fifteenth century by students, scholars, and merchants. The rapid development of the printing industry, particularly in the Rhineland cities, also facilitated the spread of humanist scholarship. The great pioneers were the German Peter Luder (c. 1415–1474), a hard-drinking poet whose insistence on the importance of classics in the curriculum helped make the University of Heidelberg a leading center of humanist thought, and the Dutchman Rudolf Agricola (c. 1443–1485). After spending ten years in Italy, where he was deeply influenced by Petrarch's writings, Agricola gathered a group of humanist disciples at Heidelberg. His goal was to surpass the Italians in classical learning, wresting from "haughty Italy the reputation for classical expression which it has nearly monopolized . . . and aim to it ourselves." His wide-ranging interests extended from philosophy and Greek to mining, a subject on which he wrote a treatise.

In England, too, the humanists carried their message to the universities. Both William Grocyn (c. 1466–1519), who lectured at Oxford, and Thomas Linacre (c. 1460–1524), who taught at Cambridge and was interested in classical medicine, had studied in Florence. Among Grocyn's friends were three of the greatest humanists of the sixteenth century, his pupil Thomas More, John Colet, and Erasmus (all discussed in Chapter 16). The English were also acquainted with humanist ideals through the presence of Italian scholars at the royal court. Other Italian humanists took their views to the courts of Spain, Hungary, and Poland, where the University of Cracow achieved eminence as a center of humanist studies.

Humanist ideas had already begun to penetrate France before its armies invaded Italy in 1494, but the military adventure heightened interest in Italian scholarship and the arts. Early French humanists such as Guillaume Budé (1468–1540) and Lefèvre d'Étaples (1455–1536) knew Greek and had varied interests. In addition to writing about Byzantine law and ancient coinage, Budé persuaded King Francis I to found a library at Fontainebleau, the origin of the famous Bibliothèque Nationale in Paris. Lefèvre, who had studied at Florence and Padua, was noted for philological and biblical studies, particularly his *Commentary on the Epistles of St. Paul*. His emphasis on grace, faith, and predestination may have influenced the Protestant reformer John Calvin, though Lefèvre never left the Catholic church.

The literary accomplishments of the French humanists are exemplified by Marguerite d'Angoulême (1492–1549), sister of Francis I, and François Rabelais (c. 1495–1553), successively a Franciscan friar, a Benedictine monk, and a secular priest and medical doctor. Marguerite's prolific writing ranged from poetry to religious treatises, but her most famous work was the *Heptaméron*, a collection of 70 short, racy stories akin to Boccaccio's *Decameron*. Rabelais' *Gargantua* and *Pantagruel*, tales about giants enamored of life and drinking, offer a satirical portrait of sixteenth-century society peppered with humanist insights about the human condition. Gargantua's advice to his son Pantagruel is a fitting summary of the humanists' exhortation to their disciples: "I urge you to spend your youth making the most of your studies and developing your moral sense."

Women and Renaissance Culture

Although most Renaissance humanists were men, more than 30 women humanists have been identified, though few wrote major works. This may be more indicative of social barriers than creative talent. Women almost never attended a university. They thus had no opportunity to enter the learned professions, although there was a female doctor of medicine at Salerno, Italy, in 1422. Women humanists typically acquired their education from their fathers or private tutors, which effectively eliminated all but those of princely, aristocratic, or patrician status. During the early Renaissance their intellectual careers were confined to their late teens and early twenties if they opted to marry, for marital obligations and spousal pressure made intellectual commitments extremely difficult. The advent of printing, however, provided literate women with the opportunity to pursue a variety of studies, including medicine, religion, and the classics—a development often reflected in paintings of the Annunciation showing Mary reading a book. The usual alternative to marriage—entry into the religious life—was tantamount to rejecting the world in favor of a book-lined cell. For intellectually gifted young women the choice was difficult, more so because men typically regarded learned women as intellectual oddities, male minds in female bodies. An educated woman was often thought to have exchanged female symbols, such as needles and wool, for male symbols, such as pens and books.

Although male humanists praised women in general, they usually preferred that learned women remain safely unwed and likened them to Amazon queens and armed warriors or viragos. In the courtly love tradition of the Middle Ages men were supposed to please the ladies, whereas in the Renaissance women were molded to satisfy the gentlemen. As the Renaissance ideal of learning spread, girls and young women of the upper estates received better educations than their medieval counterparts, but the classical material they studied reinforced notions of male superiority. Their education was not to enable them to enter the learned professions but to act as ladies of the court, patronesses of the arts, and decorative presences who added gracefulness to their households.

The contributions of learned Renaissance women were varied. Many wrote Latin letters, orations, treatises, and poems. Alessandra Scala of Florence had a command of Greek equaled by few Western scholars. The ranks of humanist poets embraced such women as Christine de Pisan (c. 1364-c. 1431), a French writer of Italian descent whose works included a biography of the French King Charles V, and Lucrezia Tornabuoni, mother of Lorenzo the Magnificent and author of religious hymns. As the Renaissance extended north of the Alps, more young women received a humanist education and took up their pens to write literary, religious, and historical works. The range

After Christine de Pisan's husband died, when she was only 25, she successfully supported herself and her three children as a writer. Among her patrons were Philip the Bold, duke of Burgundy, and Queen Isabella of Bavaria. [Bayerische Staatsbibliothek, Munich]

of topics available to women was, however, restricted by social custom since most secular subjects were thought to be the province of men. Even in the religious realm women were expected to confine themselves to hymns and poems, devotional works, and translations. "Great things by reason of my sex," admitted the English translator Anne Locke, "I may not do." Thus humanist education tantalized bright young women even as society thwarted their ambitions by tightly hedging in their possibilities for intellectual expression. No wonder Christine de Pisan lamented that she had not been "born into this world as a member of the masculine sex." She found consolation in her prolific writings, for these enabled her to reflect that "now I am truly a man."

VITTORIA COLONNA, POET AND PHILOSOPHER

One of the most gifted Renaissance women, Vittoria Colonna belonged to a powerful Roman family with vast holdings in the Papal States and southern Italy. Among her relatives were a pope and 30 cardinals. Born in 1492 at Marino, near Rome, she was the daughter of Fabrizio Colonna, grand constable of the kingdom of Naples. Although her marriage at the age of 19 to the marchese of Pescara, a Spaniard, had been arranged for political reasons 15 years earlier, she nevertheless fell in love with him. Often absent on military service, the marchese died in 1525, leaving her childless. In his memory Vittoria wrote sonnets idealizing him as a saint despite the fact that he had been faithless to her, contemptuous of Italians, and treasonous in his political dealings. Imbued with Neoplatonic concepts, Vittoria envisioned a reunion with him in a better, spiritual life. Her love sonnets, written in the tradition of Petrarch, won her acclaim in humanist circles, particularly from the great literary stylist Pietro Bembo and from Castiglione, who gave her a manuscript of his *Courtier* to critique.

Vittoria's religious sonnets reflect both her ascetic piety and her Neoplatonism, which together sought to liberate the spirit by subduing the flesh. In Neoplatonic imagery she expressed her hope to "mount with wings" in order to reach true light and love. Hers was an intensely personal experience: "I write," she said, "only to free myself from my inner pain." Her sonnets manifest a keen interest in church reform, a concern she shared with a number of her friends, including Cardinal Contarini, a chief architect of the Catholic Reformation. Although one of her closest friends, Bernardino Ochino, ultimately defected to the Protestants, she remained loyal to the Catholic church.

Vittoria found a kindred spirit in Michelangelo, whom she met shortly after he had begun painting the Sistine Chapel ceiling in 1508. He was Vittoria's "most singular friend" and she his "love," capable of causing "a withered tree to burgeon and to bloom." Their intimacy, in which Michelangelo found spiritual solace and artistic inspiration, was not sexual. They corresponded extensively and exchanged sonnets, the tone of which is reminiscent of Petrarch's sonnets to Laura, but in an unmistakably Christian context. Michelangelo wrote madrigals and painted at least three works for her and probably a portrait as well. He must have been sympathetic to her ascetic convictions, which were so pronounced after her husband's death. She fasted and wore hair shirts until Cardinal Reginald Pole, a key figure in the Catholic Reformation, persuaded her to adopt a more moderate course. She spent much of the period between 1541 and her death in 1547 in monasteries, a reminder that many Renaissance humanists saw their religious and humanist principles as fully compatible.

Machiavelli and the Culture of Power

The evolution of the humanist movement is nowhere more apparent than in its attitude toward history. Initially the humanists were preoccupied with the recovery of classical

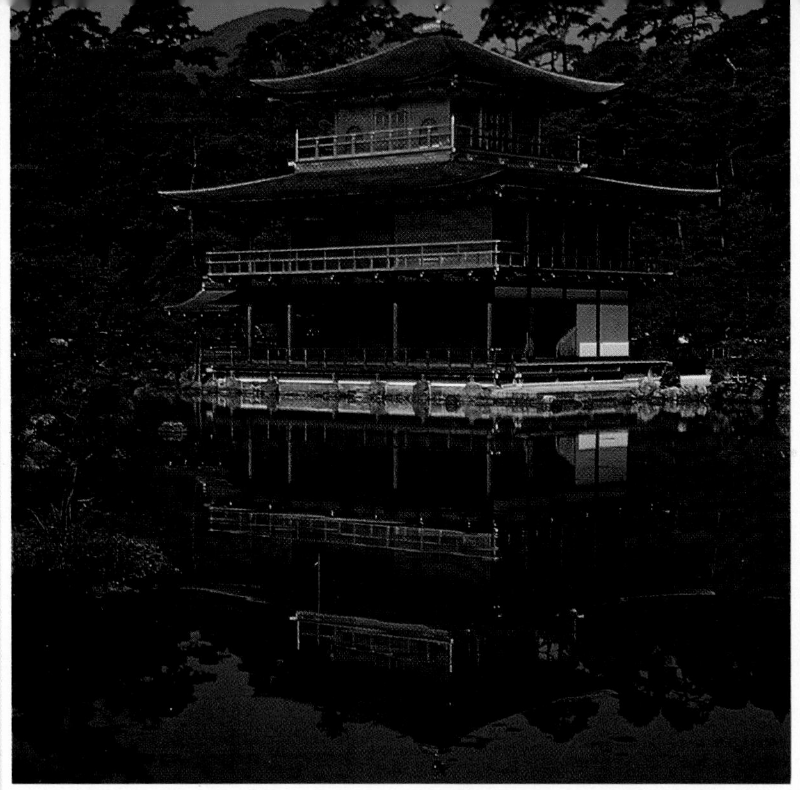

The Golden Pavilion in Kyoto is a Japanese adaptation of a Chinese original; note the careful blending of architecture with landscaping. The Pavilion dates from 1397 but has been restored several times after fires. [Wim Swaan, New York]

THE VISUAL EXPERIENCE

From the Late Middle Ages to the Early Modern World

As the art critic John Ruskin observed, "Great nations write their autobiographies in three manuscripts, the book of their deeds, the book of their words and the book of their art. Not one of these books can be understood unless we read the two others, but of the three the only trustworthy one is the last." Art is a mirror of humanity—a record sometimes poignant, sometimes humorous, but always instructive. This is especially true of those centuries which in Europe and India we call medieval—a time of urban growth, majestic building, and growing political unification. The continuing fascination with humanity and the natural world was reflected in countless ways, including the great Chinese and European voyages of exploration and the cultural exuberance of the Renaissance in the West.

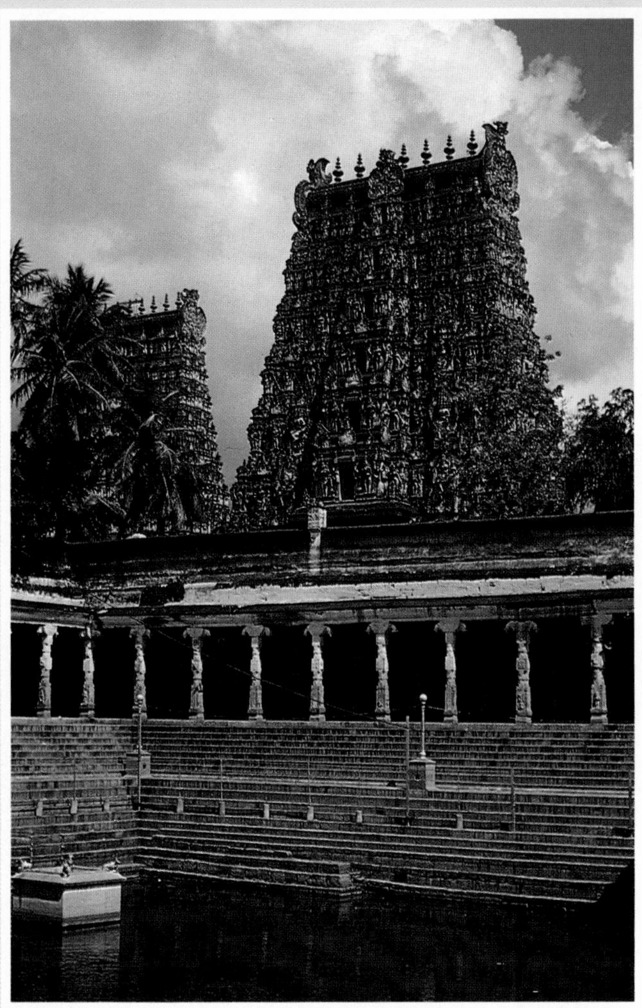

The temple complex at Madurai in southern India was one of the classic buildings preserved from the Muslim onslaught that swept northern India. This example dates from the seventeenth century. [Wim Swaan, New York]

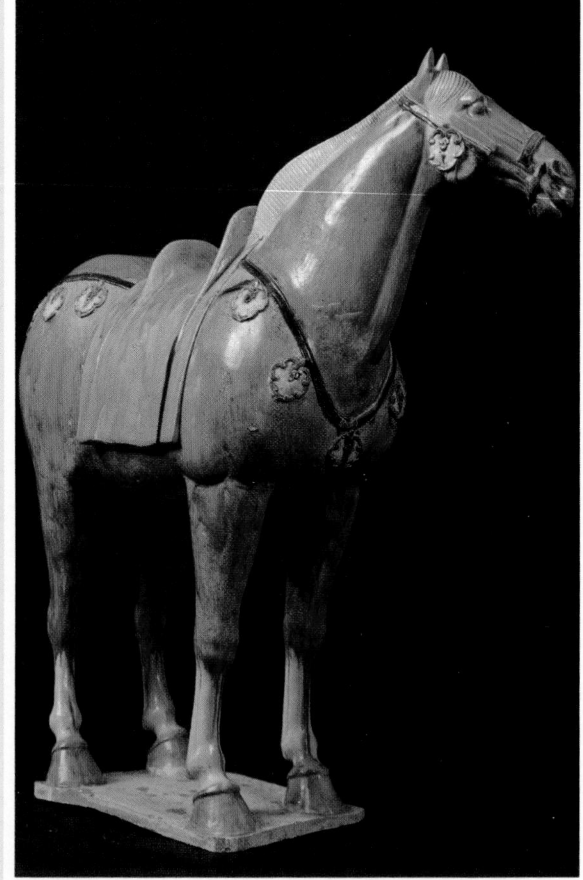

This glazed pottery horse, a manifestation of the ongoing interest in the natural world, is typical of the figures produced in huge quantities during the T'ang dynasty. [c. 30″ high; Cleveland Museum of Art, anonymous gift]

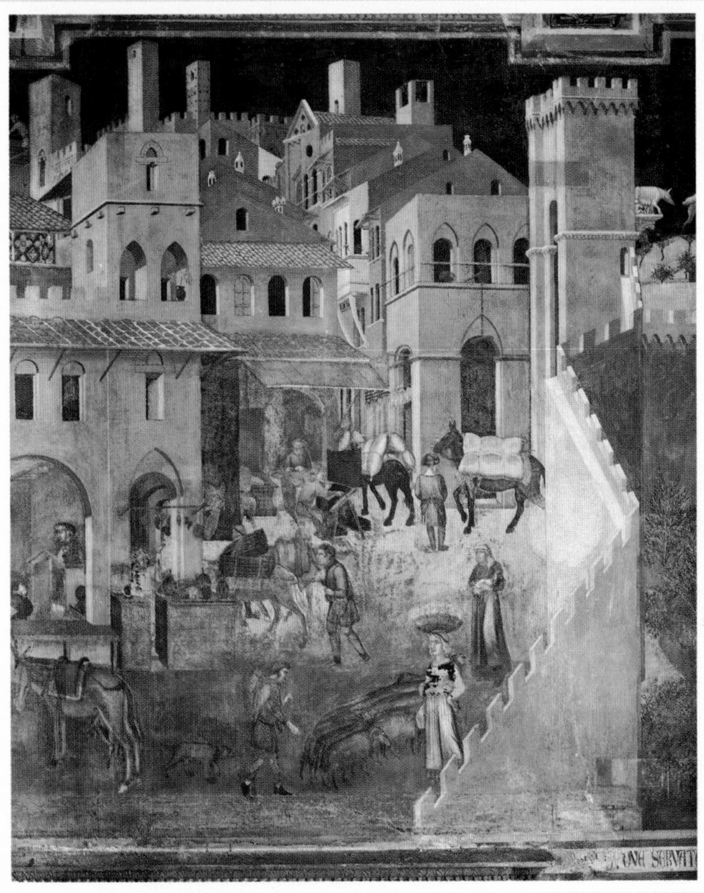

The crowded towns of the late medieval period were bustling centers of commerce, as illustrated in this fresco of the Italian city of Siena by Ambrogio Lorenzetti. Shops were usually on the ground floor, living quarters above. Note the classroom in the building on the lower left. [*The Effects of Good Government,* 1339; Colorphoto Hinz, Allschwill, Switzerland]

The Louvre dominates this scene of sowing and preparation for planting in the fields outside the walls of medieval Paris. The painting, by the Limbourg brothers, is from the *Très Riches Heures du Duc de Berry.* [Manuscript illumination, 1413–1416; Giraudon/Art Resource]

Giotto's *Lamentation*, painted for the Scrovegni Chapel in Padua, is one of the most eloquent depictions of grief in early Renaissance art. [Fresco, c. 1305, 7′7″ × 7′9″ (231 × 236 cm.); Scala/Art Resource]

Venetians were fond of pageantry. Members of the devotional confraternity of St. John the Evangelist carry a relic of the cross in the Piazza San Marco during the *Corpus Domini* procession in 1496. In the background is St. Mark's Cathedral; to the right, the Palace of the Doges. The painting is by Gentile Bellini. [Scala/Art Resource]

The Neoplatonic concern with beauty is apparent in this celebration of spring, *Primavera* by Sandro Botticelli. The Venus figure in the center represents spring; Mercury and the three Graces are to the left; at the right a nymph being chased by the wind god Zephyr is transposed into the goddess Flora (in the flowered dress), while Cupid hovers above. [c. 1478, tempera on canvas, 6′8″ × 10′4″ (203 × 314 cm.); Scala/Art Resource]

Leonardo da Vinci's *Virgin of the Rocks* masterfully combines the artist's intense interest in natural phenomena and human anatomy with traditional religious devotion. [c. 1485, oil on wood panel, 75 × $43\frac{1}{2}$″ (190.5 × 110.5 cm.); Giraudon/Art Resource]

Like all Mughal emperors, Akbar personally administered justice. Here he is shown by a contemporary court artist hearing a petition, surrounded by courtiers and nobles. The painting is in the style made famous at the Mughal court and shows characteristic Mughal architecture, including the pillared cupola in the background. [Freer Gallery of Art, Smithsonian Institution]

Carpets are Iran's best-known art form. This magnificent example in one of the many traditional Persian styles emphasizes floral motifs and was made under the Safavids at Tabriz, near the Turkish border. [Victoria and Albert Museum, London]

The Case for Educating Young Ladies

One of the most gifted women writers of the Renaissance, Christine de Pisan argued on behalf of offering girls the same educational opportunities as boys.

If it were customary to send little girls to school and to teach them the same subjects as are taught to boys, they would learn just as fully and would understand the subtleties of all arts and sciences. Indeed it may be they would understand them better . . . for just as women's bodies are more soft than men's, so too their understanding is more sharp. . . . If they understand less it is because they do not go out and see so many different places and things but stay home and mind their own work. For there is nothing which teaches a reasonable creature so much as the experience of many different things.

[Rectitude personified next speaks to Christine.] Your father, who was a natural philosopher, was not of the opinion that women grow worse by becoming educated. On the contrary, as you know he took great pleasure from seeing your interest in learning. Your mother, however, who held the usual feminine ideas on the matter, wanted you to spend your time spinning, like other women, and prevented you from making more progress and going deeper into science and learning in your childhood. But as the proverb says, what nature gives may not be taken away. So you gathered what little drops of learning you could and consider them a great treasure and are right to do so.

Source: J. O'Faolain and L. Martines, eds., *Not in God's Image* (New York: Harper Torchbooks, 1973), pp. 181–182.

Roman texts that they could use as a standard against which to measure their own society. They then broadened their horizon to the study of classical history with a view to using its lessons as a guide to human affairs and the improvement of political and social institutions. Lorenzo Valla's use of textual criticism exemplifies the humanists' refinement of scholarly techniques. Finally, in the sixteenth century, disillusioned by their inability to reshape the present by the application of historical ideals, humanist historians relinquished their belief in the ability of simple virtue to triumph over external forces. Those who thought in theological terms explained such forces as the will of God directing human history. Instead of examining the past with a view to improving the present, most historians and their readers increasingly used the historical record to justify their religious beliefs or the political ambitions of their respective states.

The disillusionment characteristic of the sixteenth-century humanist historians was a product of earlier conditions, particularly in northern and central Italy. The failure of republican government in Florence and the French invasion of 1494 virtually demolished the hopes of the earlier humanists. Power replaced virtue as the cardinal principle in the conduct of human affairs, particularly in the thought of Niccolò Machiavelli (1469–1527). He was in his twenties when the French invaded Italy, prompting the ruler of Florence, Piero de' Medici, to try to save the city by territorial concessions. For this the Florentines overthrew Piero, revived their republican government, and rallied to the reforming message of the impassioned Dominican friar Girolamo Savonarola (1452–1498). For four years the Florentines were caught up in a frenzy of revivalism directed against materialism, immorality, corruption, and godlessness. Bonfires claimed everything from sumptuous clothing and stylish wigs to books and works of art. By 1498 the zeal had ebbed and Savonarola, having infuriated the immoral Alexander VI by his candid criticism, was burned as a heretic on trumped-up charges. The Council of Ten, which assumed the direction of Florentine affairs, made Machiavelli its secretary and one of its diplomats. Fascinated by the practice of statecraft, the young official traversed Italy conducting the business of his republic. His career was abruptly terminated in 1512 when the Medici returned to Florence and ousted the republican government. Machiavelli himself was tortured and sent into exile.

In his enforced idleness he reflected on the political problems of Italy and its history in his principal works, *The Prince* and the *Discourses on Livy*. Machiavelli brought to his writing not only a knowledge of Roman history and the works of such humanist historians as Bruni and Poggio but also considerable firsthand experience of the realities of contemporary politics and diplomacy. *The Prince* (1513), dedicated to Lorenzo de' Medici, grandson of Lorenzo the Magnificent, has sometimes been interpreted as if it were

Machiavelli's Advice to a Renaissance Prince

The advice Machiavelli tendered in The Prince *reveals a degree of cynicism based on his experience in Renaissance politics.*

How praiseworthy a prince is who keeps his promises and lives with sincerity and not with trickery, everybody realizes. Nevertheless, experience in our time shows that those princes have done great things who have valued their promises little, and who have understood how to addle the brains of men with trickery; and in the end they have vanquished those who have stood upon their honesty. . . .

For a prince, then, it is necessary . . . to appear merciful, trustworthy, humane, blameless, religious—and to be so—yet to be in such measure prepared in mind that if you need to be not so, you can and do change to the contrary. . . . A prince, and above all a prince who is new, cannot practice all those things for which men are considered good, being often forced, in order to keep his position, to act contrary to truth, contrary to charity, contrary to humanity, contrary to religion. Therefore he must have a mind ready to turn in any direction as Fortune's winds and the variability of affairs require. . . .

Hate is incurred as much by means of good deeds as of bad. Therefore . . . if a prince wishes to keep his position, he is often forced to be not good, because when that group—whether the masses, the soldiers, or the rich—which you decide you need to sustain yourself, is corrupt, you have to adapt yourself to its nature in order to please it. Then good works are your enemies.

Source: N. Machiavelli, *The Chief Works and Others,* trans. A. Gilbert, vol. 1 (Durham, N.C.: Duke University Press, 1965), pp. 64, 66, 72.

a satire on the politics of despotism. On the contrary, it reflects the sober realism of a middle-aged diplomat and a theoretical brilliance that has earned Machiavelli a reputation as the founder of modern political science. *The Prince* has rightly been called "the greatest of all theoretical explorations of the politics of innovation";[5] its primary theme deals with the "new prince"—the political innovator who has just seized power—and his dealings with his subjects, some of whom have been ousted from power, while others expect rewards he cannot bestow.

The Medici now dominated not only Machiavelli's beloved Florence but even Rome, where Leo X (1513–1521), Lorenzo the Magnificent's son, had just become pope. Machiavelli intended to prod the Medici into embracing an ethic of power shorn of religious or ethical limitations as the only effective means to achieve a stable, secure Italy free of "barbarian" intervention. His was a creed of action, not reflection, of pragmatism rather than idealism. He praised Roman republicanism because it had been a successful tool of power and praised republican government in general if it embodied *virtù*, or inner strength. As he pondered the meaning of history, he concluded that it was shaped by a recurring cycle of events; instead of evolution and progress, there was mere repetition.

Although Machiavelli did not regard historical study as a quest for virtue, he reflected humanist influence in a variety of other ways; for him, as for Bruni, history is a storehouse of examples and should be studied to ascertain both the causes and the cures of current problems. Because history repeated itself, present ills could be treated by imitating solutions that were successful in the past. Everything in the present and the future had a counterpart in antiquity, the happiest time in history. Machiavelli's concept of the imitation of antiquity is an extreme application of the humanist tendency to venerate the classical world. One can find similar parallels in Confucian thought. In formulating his principles of statecraft, Machiavelli ransacked classical history to find material for his argument and also drew on his own practical experience in politics. Between them he found justification for the political principles that make *The Prince* famous: Be deceitful and cunning in dealing with rivals; do as people actually do rather than as they ought to do; regard the state—the prince—as supreme, recognizing that the end justifies the means; always place military security first; avoid neutrality, especially in dealing with other states; instill fear in one's subjects as the best means to compel obedience; undertake great enterprises to divert attention from internal problems. Such was the culture of power, and in espousing it Machiavelli broke with the traditional model of the good ruler, whether Confucian, Aristotelian, or Judeo-Christian.

Machiavelli's Florentine contemporary, Francesco Guicciardini (1483–1540), surpassed him as a historian, particularly in his determination to discover the reasons for human behavior and explore the way institutions work. His first *History of Florence*, written during the republican era, characterized Lorenzo the Magnificent as a tyrant, but two decades later he found Lorenzo's Florence preferable to the now discredited republic. His attitude changed even more in his last work, a *History of Italy*, in which Lorenzo was glorified, reflecting Guicciardini's disillusionment with the inability of the Italian states to unify in the face of foreign aggression. The optimism of the early humanists—their faith in the ability to shape states and their leaders—was abandoned in the face of hostile external forces and the assumption of power by men with the trappings of Renaissance culture but without the ideals of humanistic virtue. Although Guicciardini was the better historian, Machiavelli had a much greater historical impact because of the popularity—and notoriety—of *The Prince*, with its calculated disregard of traditional morality and its pithy, provocative appeal to political "realism."

The Printing Revolution

Machiavelli's *Prince* was too scandalous to be published during his lifetime, but other works of Renaissance scholarship were printed despite some humanist opposition to putting learned works in the hands of commoners. Movable metal type, developed in Germany in the fifteenth century, was vastly superior to the technique of block printing. The Chinese and Koreans, of course, had already invented movable type, but it had little appeal to them because their scripts consisted of thousands of different characters. Metal type was more durable as well as more flexible than wooden blocks because individual letters could be reused in new combinations. By 1300 linen paper, which had been introduced from East Asia through the Islamic world, was in common use, thus setting the stage for the new presses. Johann Gutenberg of Mainz, one of the pioneers of the new technology, published his first known work, an indulgence proclamation by Pope Nicholas V, in 1454. The first of his magnificent Bibles appeared two years later. The new press spread rapidly throughout western and central Europe; by 1500 there were 73 in Italy, 50 in Germany, 39 in France, 24 in Spain, and smaller numbers in other countries.

The fact that Italy had more presses than any other country was largely due to the impact of the Renaissance, despite humanist misgivings about putting learned works in the hands of the masses. The finest press was that of the humanist Aldus Manutius in Venice. His Aldine Press published at least 30 first editions of Greek classics, a tremendous benefit to Renaissance scholarship. Aldus also founded his own academy in Venice which was especially devoted to encouraging humanist authors and editors. Its nucleus was composed of Greek exiles whose knowledge of classical Greek civilization thus found its way into print and henceforth became available to scholars throughout the West. The influential northern humanist Erasmus of Rotterdam (c. 1466–1536) perfected his Greek during a stay with Aldus.

The changes brought about by the printing press reached virtually every aspect of life. As the price of books

In this sixteenth-century print shop the men to the left are setting type, their colleague at the center rear is inking a plate of type, the man at the right is printing a sheet on the press, and the youth in the foreground is setting the wet sheets out to dry. [Bettmann Archive]

fell and their number increased, there was a greater incentive to acquire and improve reading skills. The expansion of the literate population in turn offered new opportunities to writers and eventually freed some from the need to find and please wealthy patrons. Religious topics, works on astrology, and popular tales were prominent on the early book lists, as were editions of the Bible, especially once vernacular versions became common in the sixteenth century. The press proved a boon to scholarship by making more accurate editions possible, by standardizing maps and images as well as texts, and by encouraging cross-cultural interchange. Ideas spread with greater rapidity, and there was more inducement to develop new theories. Codifying and cataloging became commonplace, and the use of running titles at the top of each page, regular page numbering, and indexing helped order the thoughts of readers. Printing also increased the likelihood of a document's preservation. Through printing, collections of laws and ordinances became available to a wider public, with beneficial effects for the practice of law as well as for public discourse about political affairs. By the sixteenth century, however, both church and state found it necessary to step up their censorship. The advent of printing made propaganda possible, and in the seventeenth century newspapers began replacing the pulpit as the primary source of news in urban areas. Printing also increased the reputation—or infamy—of authors and eventually made it possible for some writers, such as the English dramatist Aphra Behn (c. 1640–1689), to earn a living by their pens alone. Gutenberg and his colleagues thus set in motion one of the most sweeping revolutions in history.

The Fine Arts

The Renaissance ushered in significant changes in artistic style and taste, reflecting the absorption of humanist ideals. The most prominent hallmarks of Renaissance painting and sculpture—fascination with classical themes, expressions of individualism, a more self-confident embracing of secular themes—reflected humanist concerns. Technical advances in painting were also possible after oil-based paints were brought to Italy from Flanders in the late fifteenth century. Painters had previously worked in fresco, which involved the application of pigment to wet plaster, and tempera, which entailed mixing pigments with a sizing, such as eggs. Oils enabled the painter to achieve a detail, clarity, and permanence of color not possible with fresco or tempera. Renaissance artists also achieved the ability to give the illusion of dimensionality by using gradations between light and dark to model their figures and by applying mathematical principles to create the visual illusion of objects receding into space.

The Renaissance in the fine arts was greatly facilitated by an expansion of patronage, especially by lay people. Not only did this lead to an increased demand for paintings and statues, but the expanded circle of patrons—towns, guilds, religious brotherhoods, patricians, aristocrats, and church leaders—broadened traditional tastes and themes, thus leading to a new richness and diversity in art. The dictates of patrons also popularized the intermingling of sacred and secular, instances of which are apparent earlier in the stained glass and statuary of the Gothic cathedrals. Some patrons wanted their portraits included alongside those of the Virgin and saints, as testimony to their piety as well as their wealth, though again there are instances of this in the Middle Ages. The blending of secular and sacred is also seen in the rather free interchanging of style and organization between classical and religious themes: Venus is represented as a secularized Mary, Mary as a spiritualized Venus. The inquiring spirit of the humanists combined with the sundry tastes of patrons encouraged greater artistic expression.

Early Renaissance Painting

In the Middle Ages, painting was the least developed of the principal fine arts. Giotto (c. 1266–1337), a Florentine, revitalized it and provided the bridge between the medieval era and the early Renaissance. Boccaccio overstated the case when he praised Giotto for reviving painting after it had "been in the grave" for centuries, but Giotto's contributions were rightly recognized when he was made head of the cathedral workshop in Florence, an honor previously accorded only to architects and sculptors. In a series of frescoes on the walls of a chapel in Padua depicting the life of Christ, Giotto's narrative power, evocation of human emotion, and use of spatial depth turned the chapel walls into a stage on which the central events of the Christian faith were acted out. His work was seen as the harbinger of a new era; in the words of Giorgio Vasari, he ushered in the "good modern manner." Although none of Giotto's immediate disciples equaled their master, his frescoes on the walls of Florentine chapels became textbooks for later generations of Renaissance painters, including Masaccio and Michelangelo.

The frescoes of the Florentine artist Masaccio (1401–1428) revolutionized painting. His treatment of the nude figures of Adam and Eve being expelled from the Garden of Eden displays a naturalism and psychological penetration very different in spirit from Giotto's paintings. Both here and in a masterly fresco of the Trinity, the Virgin, and St. John, Masaccio links the Christian and the classical by setting his scenes against a Roman arch. These two paintings demonstrate a dramatic advance in the ability to render a sense of depth, and the expulsion scene in particular is notable for its use of shading, a technique known as *chiaroscuro*, which enhanced the pictorial effect by conveying the reflection of light from three-dimensional surfaces. Masaccio's discoveries encouraged his contemporaries and successors to continue experimenting, and Michelangelo himself was among those who sketched Masaccio's work in order to learn his techniques.

The impact of Neoplatonism on Renaissance painting is manifest in the works of the Florentine Sandro Botticelli (1444–1510), a tanner's son. Through his Medici patrons he came into contact with Marsilio Ficino and the Florentine Academy. His famous paintings of Venus—emerging from the sea on a giant shell, celebrating the arrival of spring in the company of Mercury and Cupid, or reclining with Mars as mythological lovers—reflect the Neoplatonic notion of Venus as the source of divine love. But Botticelli, the poet of lyrical beauty, sometimes had to paint more mundane subjects at the behest of his Medici patrons. After they crushed the revolt of the Pazzi in 1478 they commissioned him to depict the execution of the rebels as a warning to others; the painting was destroyed after the Medici were forced into exile.

Masaccio, *The Holy Trinity*, 1428. God the Father holds the cross while the Holy Spirit descends in the form of a dove. Mary is to the left of the cross, St. John to the right, and below them are the kneeling donors. Masaccio's use of linear perspective gives the fresco a striking sense of depth. [Alinari/Art Resource; Santa Maria Novella, Florence]

Later Renaissance Painting: A New Phase

The early Renaissance achievements in rendering the human figure, three-dimensionality, chiaroscuro, and individualized portraiture became the foundation of the mature period of Renaissance painting that began in the late 1400s and lasted approximately a century. The late Renaissance is distinguished as an era in which the great artists combined creative talents with intense individuality, thereby producing a highly personal style. At the end of the fifteenth century there was a noticeable rise in the status of leading artists, the result of which was greater freedom from the dictates of patrons. Information about the artists was disseminated more widely, and the great ones were increasingly thought of in terms of genius and referred to as "divine." Leonardo da Vinci, said Vasari, manifested *grazia divina*—divine grace. Interest in and respect for the artist's personality grew, and two artists—the sculptor Benvenuto Cellini and the painter Albrecht Dürer—even wrote autobiographies, expressing the Renaissance fascination with the individual. It became increasingly common too for artists to paint their own portraits, and Dürer even depicted himself nude. The elite who could afford art valued the artist's development of a distinctively personal style, especially in the case of artists who acquired international reputations. When Titian left Venice in 1547 to paint the Holy Roman Emperor Charles V at Augsburg, he was besieged with requests from people who wanted to own one of his works. In the late Renaissance more people collected art, thus encouraging the notion that a cultured person should own a few paintings or bronze statues.

Leonardo da Vinci

Although no single painting or date marked a sharp cleavage between the early and late Renaissance, Leonardo da Vinci's depiction of the *Virgin of the Rocks*, done in the early 1480s, has a claim to be considered the first late Renaissance painting. By this point in his career Leonardo (1452–1519) had already developed a keen interest in nature. In the *Virgin of the Rocks*, for instance, he chose a semidark grotto with an abundance of plant life and a pool for his setting. Although the natural details are faithfully rendered, the total effect is one of mystery and poetic vision—of a psychological world. Coming as it did against a tradition of artistic development dedicated to rendering nature faithfully, the *Virgin of the Rocks* is an intensely personal statement by the artist, as is his famous portrait of the Mona Lisa (*La Gioconda*) with its dreamlike background expressive of the personality of the subject.

About the time he was working on the *Virgin of the Rocks*, Leonardo left Florence and his native Tuscany for Milan, where he acquired the duke's patronage. There he painted his masterpiece, *The Last Supper*, on the wall of a church refectory, unfortunately using an experimental paint that has decayed over the years. The key to this masterful study in human psychology lies in Leonardo's philosophy of art: "A good painter has two chief objects to paint—man and the intention of his soul. The former is easy, the latter hard, for it must be expressed by gestures and the movement of the limbs."[6] For Leonardo, gestures reveal the inner drama as the disciples react to Christ's stunning statement that one of them will betray him. Space is mathematically ordered through the use of recurring rectangles, especially on the walls and ceiling, and the placement of the disciples in groups of three, united by their gestures. The serene Christ, his arms outstretched and his head framed against a window of symbolic light, is in the shape of a pyramid, Leonardo's favorite organizing device, while Judas, his profile rendered in symbolic darkness, has not been separated from the rest of the disciples as had been usual in earlier paintings of the same theme, such as Giotto's famous fresco. The innovation is deliberate, the psychological insight unsurpassed.

Leonardo's genius as a painter was only one of his many interests. He is the supreme example of the Renaissance ideal—a virtuoso whose intellectual curiosity led him into a host of fields. His notebooks contain ideas and sketches for military inventions, many of which were not realized for centuries, including submarines, turbines, and prototypes of a tank and a helicopter. His studies of human anatomy were based on the dissection of more than 30 corpses. After examining fossils discovered in the mountains, he concluded that the biblical account of creation was inaccurate. An accomplished rider and a lover of horses, he sketched dozens of them preparatory to designing a gargantuan (but unfinished) equestrian statue for the Sforza family. Town planning, architecture, botany, music, and optics were among his wide-ranging interests. Above all he was supremely self-confident; after he listed his talents in military engineering for the duke of Milan, he added: "I can do in painting whatever may be done, as well as any other, be he who he may."[7]

Leonardo on Art and Nature

The Renaissance determination to return to the sources, whether in nature or in classical antiquity, is evident in Leonardo da Vinci's insistence that a painter must study the natural world rather than merely imitate the works of his predecessors.

The painter will produce pictures of small merit if he takes for his standard the pictures of others, but if he will study from natural objects he will bear good fruit. As was seen in the painters after the Romans who always imitated each other and so their art constantly declined from age to age. After these came Giotto, the Florentine, who—not content with imitating the works of Cimabue, his master—being born in the mountains and in a solitude inhabited only by goats and such beasts, and being guided by nature to his art, began by drawing on the rocks the movements of the goats of which he was keeper. And thus he began to draw all the animals which were to be found in the country, and in such wise that after much study he excelled not only all the masters of his time but all those of many bygone ages. Afterwards this art declined again, because every one imitated the pictures that were already done; thus it went on . . . [until] Masaccio showed by his perfect works how those who take for their standard any one but nature—the mistress of all masters—weary themselves in vain.

Source: E. G. Holt, ed., *Literary Sources of Art History* (Princeton, N.J.: Princeton University Press, 1947), pp. 178–179.

Raphael, Michelangelo, and the Roman Renaissance

After Julius II became pope in 1503, the center of the Renaissance shifted from Florence to Rome. Julius used his patronage to make the city the artistic and intellectual capital of the West. Raphael Sanzio (1483–1520), a native of Umbria in central Italy, studied various works of Leonardo and Michelangelo in Florence before going to Rome. Commissioned by Julius to paint frescoes in several rooms of the Vatican Palace, Raphael reflected the synthesis of the classical and the Christian in the Renaissance by juxtaposing two magnificent scenes, one linking the earthly and heavenly churches by the sacrifice of the mass, the other an assembly of classical philosophers and scientists grouped around Plato and Aristotle. The faces in the latter work include those of Leonardo and Michelangelo as well as his own, a characteristic late Renaissance touch. Raphael is also renowned for a series of gentle Madonnas that carefully blend naturalism with idealized beauty.

Michelangelo Buonarroti (1475–1564), another native son of Tuscany, was already in Rome to paint the ceiling of the Sistine Chapel when Raphael arrived in 1508. Deeply influenced by Neoplatonism, the temperamental Michelangelo created a massive work (128 by 44 feet) fusing Hebrew and classical themes. Christianity is only implicitly present in the sense that the pagan sibyls and the Hebrew prophets were thought to point to the advent of the Messiah. The work abounds in symbolism: the Neoplatonic contrast between light and darkness, spirit and matter; the recurring triads, basic to the numerical symbolism of Neoplatonism; the relationship of earthly knowledge (pagan sibyls) and divine revelation (Hebrew prophets); and the tree imagery in the central panels, which is both biblical, as in the tree of good and evil, and an allusion to Julius II's family name, Della Rovere ("of the oak tree"). Michelangelo's painting *The Last Judgment* on the east wall

Michelangelo, a portion of the Sistine Chapel ceiling, 1508–1512. In the central panel God gives the spark of life (a Neoplatonic concept) to Adam. [Marburg/Art Resource; Vatican Palace, Rome]

of the chapel was added much later, between 1532 and 1541, and reveals both the somber, deeply religious mood that characterized the final period of the artist's life and his fascination with Dante.

Titian and the Venetian Renaissance

In their basic conviction that art must transcend nature, Michelangelo and Titian (c. 1487–1576) were in full accord, yet their paintings are strikingly different. In contrast to Michelangelo's preoccupation with statuesque figures and Neoplatonic symbolism, Titian epitomizes Venice's fascination with light and color, reflecting the play of light on its waterways and palatial buildings. An immensely prolific and successful artist, Titian was appointed painter to the republic of Venice, and he enjoyed the patronage of numerous sovereigns and aristocrats, among them the Emperor Charles V. Titian's themes range from devout Christian subjects to sensuous reclining nudes, from classical mythology to contemporary portraits. His is an elegant art, befitting the clients for whom he painted. Only in his late paintings, such as his depiction of Christ being crowned with thorns, does he forsake vibrant colors and rich textures in favor of subdued tones and gloomy light. Like Michelangelo, Titian spent his last years engaged in deep religious introspection. At the personal level, both men manifest the Renaissance origins of the religious reform movements that swept Europe in the sixteenth century.

Sculpture: From Virtuosity to Introspection

In sculpture as in painting, Renaissance artists strove to achieve greater naturalism, individualization, and, in sculptural reliefs, a keen sense of depth. Sculptors such as Lorenzo Ghiberti (1378–1455) and Donatello (1386–1466) influenced contemporary painters as they pioneered these developments. Ghiberti's crowning achievement, the bronze doors of the baptistery in Florence, were intended to imitate nature in the classical Greek style. As Michelangelo later did on the Sistine Chapel ceiling, Ghiberti used only scenes from the Old Testament in his ten panels, flanked with portrait busts of pagan sibyls and Hebrew prophets as the heralds of Christ's coming. He succeeded brilliantly in fulfilling his commission from city officials and the guild of merchants to produce a work with "the greatest perfection, the most ornamentation, and the greatest richness."[8]

Ghiberti's pupil, the Florentine Donatello, exhibited a bold, revolutionary style that is evident in his bronze statue of David, the first freestanding nude sculpture since antiquity. Wearing only a shepherd's hat and military leggings, David, with his idealized face and physique, is the antithesis of Donatello's melancholy, emaciated figure of Mary Magdalene. In his portrayal of her as a time-ravaged penitent, there is no hint of the usual Renaissance preoccupation with beauty, for Donatello's outlook has become more introspective, his concern with matters of the spirit more predominant. In the works of Donatello, Leonardo,

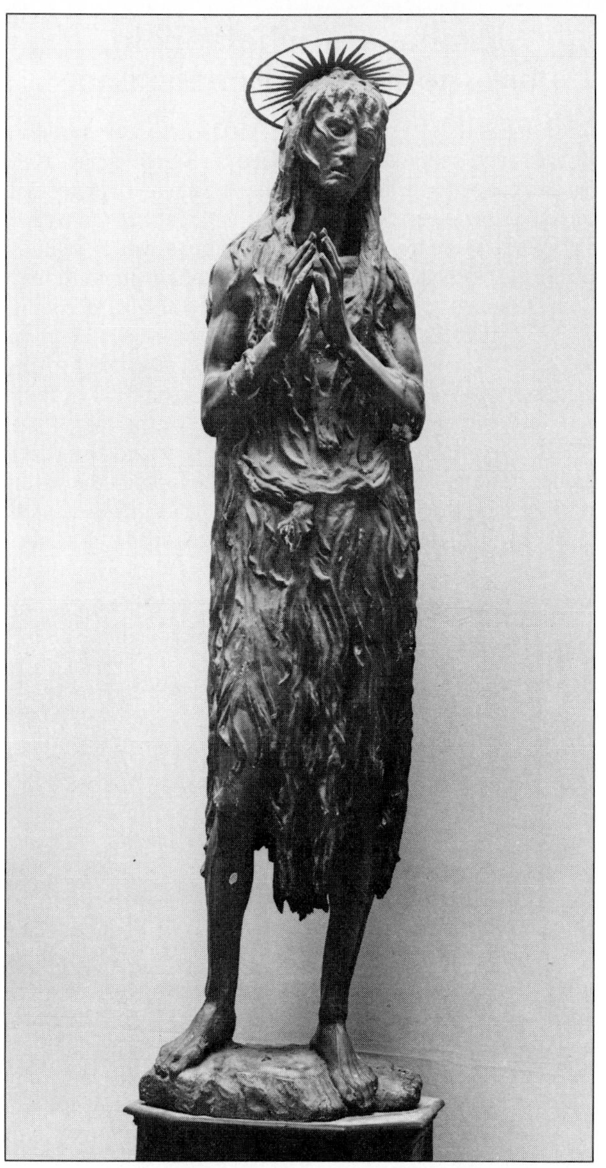

The vivid realism of Donatello's wood statue of the aged penitent Mary Magdalene (1454–1455) is roughly comparable to the realism of Japanese sculptors in the Kamakura period (thirteenth and fourteenth centuries). [Alinari/Art Resource; Cathedral Museum, Florence]

and Michelangelo a steady progression can be seen from an early concern with innovation and virtuosity to a later preoccupation with inward states and spiritual experience.

Michelangelo's first love was sculpting, an art he approached through his Neoplatonic convictions in the belief that his task was to liberate the living figure encased in a block of marble. Like Donatello, Michelangelo in his early years produced statues of sublime beauty, as if he were perfecting rather than duplicating nature. Instead of pursuing mathematically ordered perfection in the manner of Leonardo, he relied on inspiration to determine ideal proportions. His success is apparent in two majestic works completed in his twenties: the Pietà in which Mary's youthful face is as supremely beautiful as Raphael's Madonnas, and a towering statue of David, resolutely awaiting Goliath, the heroic physique in every sense an idealized rendition of male anatomy. To Vasari—as to the Florentine government which commissioned the work—Michelangelo's David was a political symbol indicating that Florence "should be boldly defended and righteously governed, following David's example." Michelangelo's last works stand in vivid contrast to these idealized, confident statues. The Pietàs of his final years are unfinished, two of them partially smashed by his own hand. One Pietà includes the figure of Nicodemus, the Pharisee who had asked Jesus how a person could "be born when he is old"; Nicodemus was in fact a self-portrait of Michelangelo, whose own searching in these years was for the assurance of spiritual rebirth. The late Pietàs were a plea for his own redemption, the culmination of the Renaissance quest for individual fulfillment at the deepest, most personal level.

Women Artists

Although relatively little is known about women artists in this period, some achieved both acceptance and a degree of fame. Michelangelo, for instance, took a special interest in the painter Sofonisba Anguissola (c. 1535–1625) of Cremona, whose five sisters also painted. Vasari visited their household and described the works of each woman. For nearly two decades Anguissola, who specialized in individual and group portraits, painted at the court of King Philip II of Spain. The English monarch Henry VIII patronized a number of women painters, paying one of them—Levina Teerling (c. 1515–1576), a manuscript illuminator—even more than the famous portraitist Hans Holbein for her work. Royal patronage was also bestowed on Catharina van Hemessen (1528–c. 1587) of the Netherlands, who enjoyed the support of Queen Mary of Hungary and painted some intriguingly introspective portraits. In the area of sculpture the leading woman artist was probably Properzia Rossi (c. 1490–1530) of Bologna, whose work is reminiscent of the sculptural reliefs of Ghiberti. That women artists were active and relatively prosperous during the Renaissance is unmistakable, although it is difficult to reconstruct their contributions because so many of their works were subsequently lost or destroyed.

Architecture and Classical Inspiration

Inspired by the architectural principles and motifs of classical antiquity, Renaissance architects rejected the Gothic style in favor of one that recalled the arches, columns, capitals, and ordered simplicity of Greco-Roman buildings. The artist who pioneered Renaissance architecture, the Florentine Filippo Brunelleschi (1377–1446), solved the greatest architectural puzzle of the fifteenth century—the design and construction of a suitable dome for the cathedral in Florence—by meticulously studying ancient Roman buildings, particularly the Pantheon. His solution was to build an inner dome to support the massive outer dome, thus avoiding the supports that had become unsightly to the tastes of his time, to use a drum below the dome to contain its outward thrust, and to place a lantern atop the dome to stabilize the entire structure. The result was not only technologically innovative but also aesthetically pleasing, as anyone who views Florence from the surrounding hills can attest. Brunelleschi's other designs, including a chapel for the Pazzi family and the Foundling Hospital in Florence, are even more distinctly Renaissance in spirit with their graceful arches and concern with classical order.

When Michelangelo set about to design the dome for St. Peter's Basilica in Rome, he studied Brunelleschi's dome. Other architects had already worked on St. Peter's, including Donato Bramante and Raphael, and Michelangelo's main contribution was the soaring dome. It was intended to crown a church in the shape of a Greek cross, with four equal arms, but in the early seventeenth century the western arm was extended into a long, traditional nave, upsetting the careful balance that Bramante and Michelangelo had envisioned. Michelangelo regarded his work on St. Peter's as both divinely commissioned and an offering of his talents to God: "It was God who laid this charge upon me. . . . I undertook it for the love of God, in whom is all my hope."[9]

Like Brunelleschi, Andrea Palladio (c. 1518–1580), the leading architect of the Venetian Renaissance, made a special trip to Rome to study classical buildings. Convinced that the numerical ratios basic to musical harmony were found throughout the universe and were thus derived from God, Palladio designed his buildings to embody mathematical symmetry. His specialty was the rural villa, of which his best known example is the Villa Rotunda near his native Vicenza, not far from Venice. The building, mathematically perfect, is cubical, with an interior cylinder, a saucer-shaped dome, and four matching Ionic porches reminiscent of Greek temple facades. Numerous eighteenth-century architects were influenced by Palladio, particularly in Italy, England, and North America. Renaissance architecture provided the inspiration for some of the most famous buildings in the new American republic, including the Capitol, which reflects the influence of Michelangelo's dome, and Thomas Jefferson's house at Monticello in Virginia, which is indebted to Palladio.

Northern Art

North of the Alps the transition from Gothic to Renaissance came in the fifteenth century. Pioneering Flemish artists took advantage of the discovery of oil paints to develop an artistic style that was primarily concerned with capturing realism by depicting intricate details; surface appearances mattered more than form, anatomy, and motion. The fascination with detail is evident in the work of Jan van Eyck (c. 1390–1441). In his portrait of the Medici banker Giovanni Arnolfini and his bride, his ties to the medieval world are still apparent in the painting's traditional symbolism: the dog represents fidelity, the single burning candle the all-seeing Christ; the statue on the bedpost is St. Margaret, patron saint of childbirth, and the shoes have been removed to symbolize the holy ground of the sacrament of matrimony. Although the work is suffused with religious meaning, in the last resort the painting is about the union of two individuals and the status they enjoy—concerns common to Italian Renaissance painters of this period.

Jan van Eyck, *The Arnolfini Wedding,* 1434. [National Gallery, London]

While these artists concentrated on external appearances, the Dutch painter Hieronymus Bosch (c. 1450–1516) created symbolic scenes so imaginative that specialists are still attempting to decipher his meaning. The world of his *Garden of Earthly Delights* is peopled with emaciated nudes, unnatural beasts, flying creatures, biting toads, burning ruins, couples making love, and exotic instruments of torture. At first sight the work appears medieval in its inspiration, but in fact Bosch was daringly individualistic in allowing his imagination to engage in flights of fantasy with unmistakable sensual and sexual overtones. The intent, however, was clearly to warn viewers of the consequences of erotic pleasure as their eyes moved from the Garden of Eden on the left, through the depiction of sensual joys in the center panel, to the fires of hell on the right. Artistic creativity triumphed over the bonds of tradition, but without sacrificing the customary moral message.

Renaissance art culminated in the Netherlands in the work of Pieter Brueghel the elder (c. 1525–1569), whose circle of friends apparently included some humanists. Although he visited Italy, he was never very impressed by classical art but instead was influenced by Bosch and other painters of the Netherlands. He was intrigued by peasant life and by landscapes, particularly the Alpine scenery he saw on his Italian trip. His delightful peasant scenes celebrate folk customs such as dances and wedding feasts, often with a touch of humor. There was a serious side to Brueghel, who used his works to condemn religious bigotry and Spanish barbarity in the Netherlands. The inscriptions on his copper engravings were so outspoken, in fact, that he had his wife destroy them as he neared death. Brueghel's almost total lack of interest in classical models and his continued use of traditional symbolism and moralizing underscore the fact that northern Renaissance artists retained far more of the medieval heritage than their counterparts in Italy.

Perspectives on the Renaissance

"Out of the thick Gothic night our eyes are opened to the glorious torch of the sun," wrote the French writer François Rabelais, reflecting the Renaissance belief in the birth of a new age of cultural brilliance following a millennium of darkness and ignorance. Petrarch contrasted the "ancient" world, the period before the Roman emperors adopted Christianity, with the "modern" era, which he described as a time of barbarism and darkness. Thus was born the

Pieter Brueghel, *The Wedding Dance.* Compare Brueghel's depiction of this rustic scene full of robust peasants with the bourgeois couple painted by van Eyck. Brueghel's paintings do not exhibit the usual Flemish concern with sharp detail. [Detroit Institute of Arts, City of Detroit Purchase]

unfortunate notion of the Dark Ages. To one fifteenth-century Florentine businessman the compendious writings of the medieval scholastics darkened learning by their "subtleties and confusion." It was thus a natural step to describe the new epoch as a *rinascita*—a rebirth or renaissance, a term adopted by Vasari to describe the renaissance of the arts. Vasari was on solid ground when he cited the dramatic changes that occurred in the fourteenth and fifteenth centuries in painting, sculpture, and architecture. The notion of the Renaissance was expanded by later historians to include not only developments in philosophy and literature but virtually every aspect of civilization from statecraft to the economy.

A tendency to exalt the Renaissance developed in the eighteenth century, as reflected in the French philosopher Voltaire's willingness to depict Italy as the successor to the glories of classical Greece. The corollary of this was the denigration of the Middle Ages, which appeared to Voltaire as a dark age of irrationality and superstition. The romantics who followed, however, evaluated the Middle Ages more positively, taking their inspiration from its religious culture and finding their historical roots in medieval states rather than the classical heritage. But the Renaissance was once again thrust to the fore in a remarkably influential book by the Swiss historian Jacob Burckhardt (1818–1897), *The Civilization of the Renaissance in Italy*. First published in 1860, Burckhardt's book develops the Renaissance as an age dominated by the revival of classical antiquity, the development of a pronounced individualism (the awareness and expression of personality), and a fresh discovery of the world of nature and man. This was possible, he argued, only because of the genius of the Italians, "the first modern people of Europe who gave themselves boldly to speculations on freedom and necessity." Thus, according to Burckhardt, the Renaissance as a distinctive epoch in the history of civilization was born in the political turbulence that engulfed Italy in the fourteenth and fifteenth centuries. By the time that Burckhardt had finished his wide-ranging exploration of this age, he had provided a synthesis in which the Renaissance amounted to nothing less than a major turning point in European history.

Burckhardt's emphasis on the glories of the Renaissance was taken a step further by the English literary critic John Addington Symonds, whose seven-volume study, *The Renaissance in Italy* (1875–1886), sharply distinguished between the Middle Ages, which he likened to the shores of the Dead Sea, and the Renaissance. The history of the latter he exalted as "the history of the attainment of self-conscious freedom." The Renaissance, he contended, was the seedbed of the essential qualities that distinguish the modern from the ancient and medieval worlds, especially the emancipation of reason from its medieval bondage.

The sharp break drawn by Burckhardt and Symonds between the Middle Ages and the Renaissance was challenged by medieval specialists, whose research demolished the stereotype of the Middle Ages as a time of ignorance and "semibarbarism." Claiming to find the roots of the Renaissance in the twelfth century, some medievalists asserted that it should be considered the last phase of the Middle Ages, not the beginning of the modern world. In 1927 the American historian Charles Homer Haskins published *The Renaissance of the Twelfth Century*. Pointing to such phenomena as the revival of the Latin classics and Roman law, the recovery of Greek science and philosophy, and the beginnings of the European universities—a revival of learning in the fullest sense—Haskins argued that the more famous Italian Renaissance was in reality the culmination of a movement that began in the late eleventh century and continued without a major break into the early modern period. We err, he argued, if we attempt to draw too sharp a distinction between successive periods of history. Haskins' attack on the Burckhardt-Symonds school did not deprecate the achievements of the Renaissance. Some medievalists did, however, pointing out that in many respects, such as its emphasis on magic and the occult, the Renaissance was actually less "rational" than the Middle Ages, and its science less advanced than in the thirteenth and fourteenth centuries. Even the term *Renaissance*, one medievalist contended, is detrimental to historical understanding because it has discouraged the study of the Middle Ages and obscured the truth that modern life owes far more to the medieval era than to classical Greece and Rome.

After World War II, Wallace Ferguson asserted a compromise interpretation according to which the Renaissance was an age of transition between the medieval and modern eras. Basic to this argument is the conviction that the changes that occurred in the Renaissance were profound, encompassing a transformation of institutions, outlook, culture, and economies. Although some critics objected that all periods involve transition, advocates of this view insisted that, taken together, the changes produced a distinctive cultural period that is neither medieval nor modern, though elements of both can be found in it.

The debate continues today. Much of the discussion has concentrated on the nature of Renaissance humanism, which has been variously defined as an educational system focusing on Greek and Roman classics, a cult of rhetoric and oratory, a philosophical method of rational inquiry, a philosophy of human dignity and individualism, or scholarly endeavor devoted to establishing new criteria of political liberty and civic responsibility.

In the face of so many interpretations, historians have come to realize that humanists were in reality a diverse group of individuals whose concerns were far from identical. The simplest definition of humanism, as suggested by Paul Kristeller, treats it as the *studia humanitatis*, the study of grammar, rhetoric, poetry, history, and ethics in classical texts as distinct from the scholastic emphasis on logic and metaphysics. By this interpretation, humanism is an academic movement rather than a philosophy or, as Federico Chabod has argued, a pattern of life based on the quest to imitate classical antiquity. Chabod recognizes the medieval interest in the classics but distinguishes the scholastics' selective approach—picking and choosing things that supported the Christian world view—from the humanist attempt to use all of antiquity as a means of challenging medieval assumptions and reconciling the full legacy of Western culture with its religion.

Another group of historians traces the origins of humanism to the political conditions in Italy and the need to develop a predominantly secular interpretation of government in order to throw off the bondage of the church. One exponent of this view, Walter Ullmann, contends that the evolutionary process of Renaissance humanism "began with the secularization of government itself and inevitably went on to engulf society at large."[10] Political conditions, particularly in Florence, provide the basis for a different interpretation advanced by Lauro Martines, who argues that the leaders of the city-states encouraged the emphasis on the glories of classical antiquity to assert their own political identity and to unite the people behind their rule. Humanistic ideals in this view were welcomed because they healed rifts between competing social groups and unified the community in the face of threats from other city-states. Whereas Burckhardt and Symonds highlighted the individual, Martines and David Herlihy stress the civic nature of humanism and the importance of social groups such as the patriciate.

Although initially the intellectual and artistic developments in the Renaissance were the province of the socially elite, in the long run many commoners enjoyed them as well. Statues and paintings were displayed in churches, civic buildings, and town squares, and such architectural gems as the Florence Cathedral and St. Peter's Basilica were of course open to the public. Michelangelo's statue of David was placed in front of the Palazzo della Signoria, while statues of Donatello were publicly displayed in Florence and Padua. As printing spread, books became less expensive, making it possible for the literary achievements of the Renaissance to reach a wider audience than anyone could have anticipated in 1400. Because husbands or wives could read to families, and masters to apprentices, the high levels of illiteracy were less a barrier to the dissemination of literature than might be imagined. As humanist ideas were accepted into the curriculum and new schools were founded, Renaissance teachings reached a wider and wider audience. Despite the un-

willingness of many humanists to support a liberal education for the masses, the Renaissance was the first step in an educational revolution that swept Europe beginning in the sixteenth century. The Renaissance concern with accurate texts, the keen interest in the classical world (the birthplace of Christianity), and the spread of the printed word also contributed to the Protestant Reformation in the same century. So did the humanist interest in reviving Christianity and integrating it with the culture of antiquity.

Notes

1. L. Martines, *Power and Imagination: City-States in Renaissance Italy* (New York: Knopf, 1979), p. 168.
2. P. G. Ruggiers, *Florence in the Age of Dante* (Norman: University of Oklahoma Press, 1964), p. 43.
3. J. B. Ross and M. M. McLaughlin, eds., *The Portable Renaissance Reader* (New York: Viking, 1968), pp. 124–125.
4. W. H. Woodward, *Vittorino da Feltre and Other Humanist Educators: Essays and Versions* (Cambridge: Cambridge University Press, 1912), pp. 102, 106.
5. J. G. A. Pocock, *The Machiavellian Moment* (Princeton, N.J.: Princeton University Press, 1975), p. 154.
6. A. Blunt, *Artistic Theory in Italy, 1450–1600* (London: Oxford University Press, 1964), p. 34.
7. E. G. Holt, ed., *Literary Sources of Art History* (Princeton, N.J.: Princeton University Press, 1947), p. 170.
8. Ibid., p. 90.
9. Ibid., p. 197.
10. W. Ullmann, *Medieval Foundations of Renaissance Humanism* (London: Elek, 1977), p. 9.

Suggestions for Further Reading

Antal, F. *Florentine Painting and Its Social Background*. New York: Harper & Row, 1975.

Baron, H. *The Crisis of the Early Italian Renaissance: Civic Humanism and Republican Liberty in the Age of Classicism and Tyranny*, rev. ed. Princeton, N.J.: Princeton University Press, 1966.

Brucker, G. A. *Renaissance Florence*, rev. ed. Berkeley: University of California Press, 1983.

Chabod, F. *Machiavelli & the Renaissance*, trans. D. Moore. London: Bowes & Bowes, 1958.

Clark, K. *Leonardo da Vinci: An Account of His Development as an Artist*. Baltimore: Penguin Books, 1967.

Eisenstein, E. L. *The Printing Press as an Agent of Change: Communications and Cultural Transformations in Early Modern Europe*, 2 vols. Cambridge: Cambridge University Press, 1979.

Ferguson, W. K. *The Renaissance in Historical Thought: Five Centuries of Interpretation*. Boston: Houghton Mifflin, 1948.

Gilbert, F. *Machiavelli and Guicciardini: Politics and History in Sixteenth-Century Florence*. Princeton, N.J.: Princeton University Press, 1965.

Goldthwaite, R. A. *The Building of Renaissance Florence*. Baltimore: Johns Hopkins University Press, 1980.

Hale, J. R. *Machiavelli and Renaissance Italy*. London: English Universities Press, 1961.

——. *Renaissance Europe: Individual and Society, 1480–1520*. Berkeley: University of California Press, 1978.

Herlihy, D. *Medieval and Renaissance Pistoia*. New Haven, Conn.: Yale University Press, 1967.

Holmes, G. *The Florentine Enlightenment, 1400–1450*. New York: Pegasus, 1969.

Hook, J. *Lorenzo de' Medici: A Historical Biography*. London: Hamilton, 1984.

King, M. L. *Venetian Humanism in an Age of Patrician Dominance*. Princeton, N.J.: Princeton University Press, 1986.

Klapisch-Zuber, C. *Women, Family, and Ritual in Renaissance Italy*. Chicago: University of Chicago Press, 1985.

Kristeller, P. O. *Renaissance Thought: The Classic, Scholastic, and Humanistic Strains*. New York: Harper & Row, 1961.

——. *Renaissance Thought and Its Sources*. New York: Columbia University Press, 1979.

Labalme, P. H., ed. *Beyond Their Sex: Learned Women of the European Past*. New York: New York University Press, 1980.

Levey, M. *Early Renaissance*. Baltimore: Penguin Books, 1967.

——. *High Renaissance*. Baltimore: Penguin Books, 1975.

Maclean, I. *The Renaissance Notion of Woman*. Cambridge: Cambridge University Press, 1980.

Martines, L. *Power and Imagination: City-States in Renaissance Italy*. New York: Knopf, 1979.

——. *The Social World of the Florentine Humanists, 1390–1460*. Princeton, N.J.: Princeton University Press, 1963.

Muir, E. *Civic Ritual in Renaissance Venice*. Princeton, N.J.: Princeton University Press, 1980.

Murray, P., and Murray, L. *The Art of the Renaissance*. London: Thames & Hudson, 1978.

Partner, P. *Renaissance Rome, 1500–1559: A Portrait of a Society*. Berkeley: University of California Press, 1977.

Ralph, P. L. *The Renaissance in Perspective*. New York: St. Martin's Press, 1973.

Ross, J. B., and McLaughlin, M. M., eds. *The Portable Renaissance Reader*. New York: Viking, 1953.

Ruggiers, P. G. *Florence in the Age of Dante*. Norman: University of Oklahoma Press, 1964.

Stinger, C. S. *The Renaissance in Rome*. Bloomington: Indiana University Press, 1985.

Ullmann, W. *Medieval Foundations of Renaissance Humanism*. London: Elek, 1977.

Weinstein, D. *Savonarola and Florence: Prophecy and Patriotism in the Renaissance*. Princeton, N.J.: Princeton University Press, 1970.

The Human Image (I)

Across the ages and around the globe, from the prehistoric cave dwellers of Europe and the rock painters of Africa to our own century of abstract painting and sculpture, every culture has represented the human figure in its art. Successive generations of artists in each civilization have used a rich variety of styles and techniques, but their efforts reveal the common concerns that underlie the human experience.

The meaning of a statue or a painting can be understood fully only in its historical context, for works of art have different functions, depending on the religions, the philosophies, and the values of the culture that produces them. Yet the focus of most artistic traditions has been on the human figure. How one culture has portrayed human beings in its art tells much about the society in which the artist worked. Thus while experts often debate the exact meaning or purpose of a particular work of art, broad cultural patterns can easily be discerned by comparing the artistic treatment accorded the human figure. In a very real sense, art serves as a language by which civilizations communicate their concerns and aspirations as they explore the meaning of existence.

The earliest known representations of the human figure were carved perhaps 30,000 years ago in central Europe. The exaggerated breasts and roundness of the body in these female figures suggest that they served as fertility images; they typically have no facial features. The remains of an ivory statue of the so-called Man from Brno in present-day Czechoslovakia dates from approximately the same period but reveals much more attention to the head, which has deep-set eyes and short hair. The Brno Man seems to have been part of a burial ritual.

The unknown sculptors who executed these early Paleolithic (Old Stone Age) works rendered the human figure with a naturalism that was not true of the cave art painted 15,000 years later. The powerful realism that makes the cave paintings of France and Spain famous was devoted almost exclusively to the depiction of animals, and human figures were rarely painted or carved on the walls. When humans were represented, they often appear as abstract forms such as boxes with sticks for arms and legs.

The Addaura finds of Sicily are a rare exception. These caves contain human figures dating from 10,000 to 8000 B.C. incised in outline into the rock face. The nature of the scene is unknown, but the images are exceptionally supple and expressive. Indeed, no earlier wall art renders the human figure with such grace, and, judging from surviving evidence, several thousand years passed before such skill in representing humans occurred again.

Man from Brno, Czechoslovakia. [Moravian Museum, Brno]

The shift from hunting and gathering to a farming culture that ushered in the Neolithic (New Stone) Age around 8000 B.C. saw the first permanent village communities created in western Asia. Humans began to view themselves and their world differently, and a much more sophisticated skill in depicting the human figure emerged. At Jericho, in Jordan, archaeologists have uncovered sculptured heads dated to 7000 B.C., made by refashioning human skulls with colored plaster and seashell eyes. These heads, which appear to have been placed above graves, were modeled with great skill, and some had painted features. They may represent the first attempts at individual portraiture.

When compared across many cultures and long stretches of time, all these representations of the human figure suggest the varieties of ritual and belief common to early civilizations. Indeed, clay statues of fertility goddesses made in Anatolia around 6000 B.C. bear a remarkable resemblance to figures from Romania produced 1,000 years later, and both appear quite similar to the Venus of Willendorf, carved 20,000 years earlier.

One of the most extraordinary representations of the human form in Neolithic art is a male figure, also from Cernavoda (c. 4000 B.C.). Modeled from dark clay, the features and limbs of the small statue are reduced to a stark, bold design that conveys a forceful sense of monumentality in miniature form. The man is seated on a stool and holds his head between his hands, a Neolithic "thinker" captured by the artist in the universal pose of contemplation 6,000 years before the French sculptor Auguste Rodin created his famous version of the same subject.

Ancient Egypt, which enjoyed political unity for more than 2,000 years, produced a remarkably consistent artistic culture obsessed with continuity and permanence. Statues of the pharaohs show the basic Egyptian approach to rendering the human figure: the anatomy and drapery are realistic, but the features are highly idealized, conveying not an individual portrait but the notion of divine power. Less formal portraits of ordinary people, however, are exceptionally lifelike, showing the facial features of a real person.

Egyptian artists adhered to strict rules for representing the human body. They generally rendered the body according to exact proportional ratios between its parts. The poses of the figures are often almost anatomically impossible, with shoulders facing the front while heads and legs face to the right. Despite this stylization, Egyptian artists were capable of achieving great naturalism, as in the relief of Akhenaton, Nefertiti, and three of their children.

The civilization of the Indus valley in the same period (c. 3000–1500 B.C.) stands in sharp contrast to Egyptian culture. Its cities developed no large-scale public art such as the pyramids or the monumental statues of the pharaohs, and the works that survive are small and delicate. A male torso found at Harappa, carved in limestone sometime between 3000 and 2000 B.C., suggests a civilization with markedly different values. The highly skilled sculptor has captured the texture of youthful flesh, softly and sensuously depicted in the swelling body. Contrasted to the rigidity of Egyptian statues, this torso appears to be a living, moving body. Nowhere else was the human figure represented at such an early date with such sensitivity.

In the ancient Aegean the human figure ultimately achieved what is probably its most famous representation. The painting and sculpture of Crete from around 1500 B.C. show influence from Egypt, yet very few human figures were depicted in explicitly religious or political postures in Minoan art. The major exceptions are the strange snake-goddess statues, which must have been worshiped by an unknown cult.

In depicting the human figure, Greeks soon became engrossed in the search for order and ideal beauty, which they saw as complementary aspects of life. Nowhere is this better illustrated than in the freestanding statues of nude young men known as *kouroi* ("youths") produced in Archaic Greece (see p. 76). The pose is stiff, with head held high, eyes focused straight ahead, broad shoulders, narrow waists, arms held down at the side with clenched fists, and one leg striding. The purity, simplicity, and balance of the anatomical form, almost abstract in its conception, must

Man from Cernavoda, Romania. [EastFoto/Sovphoto]

surely have been a deliberate effort to equate natural beauty with divine order through the representation of the human form—for the Greeks made no distinction between the physical features of humans and gods.

The principal subject and the greatest achievement of classical Greek art was its treatment of the nude body, which it presented with increasingly greater freedom and suppleness. Indeed, Greek artistic triumphs, such as Praxiteles' *Hermes with Dionysus* or the later *Venus de Milo* and the winged *Victory of Samothrace*, have so conditioned us to equate beauty with the human form that Western art has been concerned with the depiction of human beings ever since.

Because their art sought to achieve a sense of the ideal, the early Greeks left little in the way of actual portraiture, which was introduced into Western art during the later Hellenistic period. The Romans excelled at portraying not only the physical likenesses of real people but their character and psychology as well. Roman art generally lacked the universal sensuousness and idealized beauty of the Greeks and was more concerned with a straightforward rendering of civic and political values. Much Roman sculpture and statuary in the imperial period was devoted to representing the emperor, a practice begun by Augustus, who was keenly aware of its propaganda value. Roman imperial art was never as monumental as Egyptian art had been, but it contrasted strongly with that of the Greeks, who regarded statues of their rulers as vulgar and stamped their likenesses only on coins. But not all Roman art was official, and there was a particularly keen interest in portraiture. In relief sculpture and in portrait busts, Roman depictions of the human form are marked by a direct rendering of individual features and characteristics.

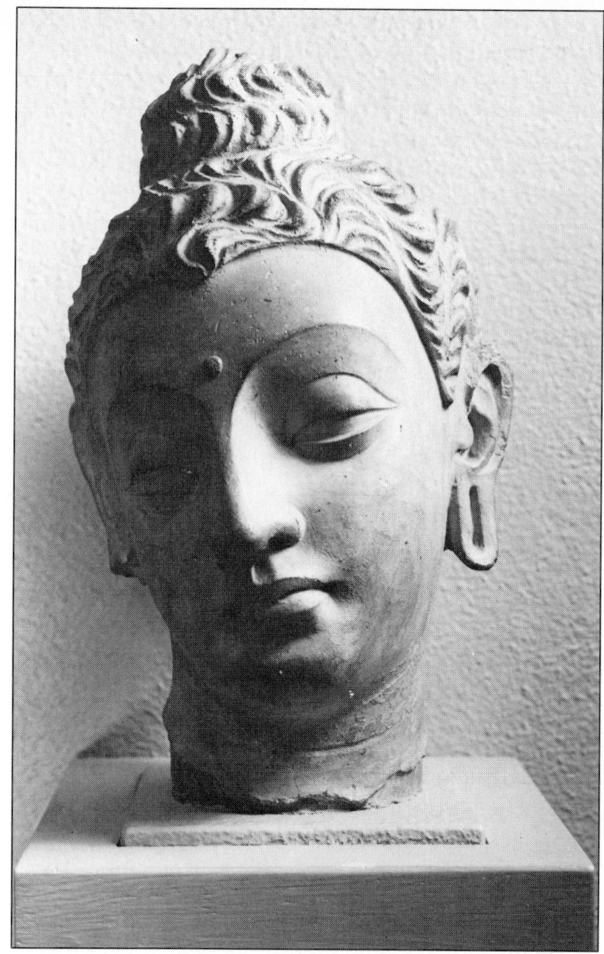

Head of Buddha, from Gandhara, third century A.D. [Victoria and Albert Museum, London]

The image of the Buddha, which was to dominate much of Asian art, was first depicted in human form at the time when the Romans were producing portraits of their civic leaders. Because doctrine held that the Buddha—the "enlightened one"—eventually achieved transcendence of the senses and of self, he had been depicted for centuries only by means of abstract symbols. But a new school of Buddhist thought that emerged in the first century A.D. conceived of the Buddha as an eternal god and provided him with a host of divinities, known as bodhisattvas, to assist him. The need for icons as visual aids to this new creed became apparent. Moreover, competition with Hinduism, which practiced the worship of personalized deities, also led to the adoption of a human image for the Buddha.

Among the earliest images of the Buddha were third-century statues produced in the border region comprising much of modern day Afghanistan and Pakistan, where Greek and Roman cultural influences were strong. The features of these Buddhas suggest a sensual spirituality that would be a trademark of Indian art. A more purely Indian classical style emerged in the fifth century under the Guptas, where statues that have no equivalent in the West portray the Buddha as more a divine essence than a real person. As Buddhist influences spread eastward into China, Southeast Asia, and Japan, images of the Buddha were fashioned according to local artistic conventions and styles.

Aside from Buddhist influences, early Chinese art generally avoided depictions of the human figure. Taoist philosophy stressed that humans were not dominant in nature but merely a part of it, so secular Chinese art preferred landscapes and animals to portraits. The excavation of imperial tombs from the Chin dynasty (221–207 B.C.) unearthed a stunning collection of more than 500 life-size clay warriors. From the Han dynasty on, emperors were painted in lifelike portraits, as were famous sages, such as Confucius and

Lao-tze. Portraits of courtiers and court ladies were also important, although often as part of large scenes of court life and the palace world.

In the millennium from the fifth to the fifteenth centuries, the human figure predominated almost everywhere in art, largely to serve religious or political purposes. The major exception was Islamic art, where Arab tradition and Muslim doctrine generally proscribed the representation of living things. The Koran, however, specifically prohibited only statuary, and some Islamic painting did portray human figures. After about 800, Muslim theologians launched a campaign against representation, arguing that an artist who made images of living things usurped the divine creative act. The human figure disappeared thereafter in large-scale art for public display, although it survived in miniatures, manuscript illuminations, and private art in large part as a result of the influence of non-Muslim artists.

In the medieval West and in Byzantium two religious images—Christ and the Virgin Mary—dominated painting and sculpture. Although these images varied greatly in artistic style and emphasis from century to century and from one region to another, they served to convey basic precepts of Christian belief. In the early sixth century mosaics of the Byzantine city of Ravenna, Christ still appears as the beardless and youthful miracle worker of early Christian art, but he was later transformed into the bearded, lean-faced image that became familiar throughout the Christian world.

A similar transformation occurred in representations of the Virgin Mary as the Madonna, the mother of Christ. Byzantine icons conformed to strict formal rules of design that were repeated over and over. They reveal a stiffness of treatment and an almost abstract quality that is related to mosaic art. The northern Gothic imagination transformed the serenity of the icon into a highly expressionistic *Pietà* whose agonized faces and grotesque wounds evoke the horror of Christ's grief-stricken mother. During the Renaissance, Italian painters produced serene and often sensual Madonnas that depict a mother and child with only muted reference to Christian symbolism.

Indian artists of the same period, intent on rendering an inner spirituality, ignored the Western obsession with the lifelike, giving their work instead a peculiar tension between spirituality and sensual beauty. A seventh century wall painting of a bodhisattva presents an exquisite vision of harmony, the personification of compassion and tenderness, that is in marked contrast to Western paintings of the Virgin Mary or of Christ from the same period. Similarly, Chinese statues of bodhisattvas from the T'ang dynasty reveal the beauty of the figure in the traditional Indian pose. Even in Hindu religious sculpture, so filled with symbolic images, Indian artists remained faithful to the sensuous quality of their artistic traditions. A bronze statue from c. 1000 A.D. shows the graceful four-armed figure of Siva Nataraja dancing within a flaming halo, creating a magnificent three-dimensional effect.

In Sung China, the major representation of a human figure, after the Buddha, was Kuan-yin, the bodhisattva of mercy, who is generally shown as a sexless deity in

Miracle of the Loaves and Fishes, **mosaic, c. 504 A.D. [Alinari/Art Resource]**

***Pietà*, German, early fourteenth century. [Rheinisches Landesmuseum, Bonn; Marburg/Art Resource]**

either male or female form. But a glazed pottery statue from the same period demonstrates that the Chinese were equally capable of the most straightforward representation.

No native deities were depicted in Japanese art before the Buddha, and the only earlier human likenesses were terra-cotta figures from the fourth to the sixth centuries consisting of human heads atop tube-like limbs and torsos. Large-scale figure sculpture came to Japan with the introduction of Buddhism, as can be seen in the enormous Buddha and bodhisattva statues from the eighth century.

Unique artistic cultures also developed in Africa and Central America. Near the village of Nok, in northern Nigeria, the discovery of terra-cotta sculpture testifies to a thriving civilization as early as 400 B.C. Besides representations of animals, startling human figures and large heads were produced. The heads are highly stylized, generally cylindrical or conical, but each one has expressive features that clearly suggest individual personalities. These clay works were no doubt modeled after wood carvings, for many suggest the carved masks so familiar in African art.

Although Nok culture disappeared after the third century A.D., it seems to have exercised an important and lasting influence on the later cultures of West Africa. Terra-cotta and brass heads were found at Ife, in southwestern Nigeria, dating probably from the twelfth century. Human features are brilliantly rendered in these masterpieces. These and similar heads are no doubt idealized forms rather than portraits. Such sculptural traditions apparently evolved in West Africa without outside influences; indeed, European artists produced no works of equal subtlety during this period.

In marked contrast to the refinement of African sculpture stand the early carvings of Central America. Although the Olmecs of Mexico were capable of sophisticated works, such as a stone wrestler that dates from around 400 B.C., or small jade figures of infants, nonetheless their culture seems to be more aptly characterized by the colossal monolithic heads made during the same period.

***Bodhisattva of Mercy*, Chinese, eleventh or twelfth century. [Nelson-Atkins Museum of Art, Kansas City, Missouri (Nelson Fund)]**

The Late Medieval Church

The medieval church derived considerable strength from its ability to renew itself from within. The Gregorian reform of the eleventh century, subsequent monastic reforms, and the founding of the mendicant orders in the thirteenth century all gave vitality to the church. In the early fifteenth century, reformers successfully ended the Papal Schism at the Council of Constance, but further reform attempts generally failed. The major reason was lack of effective papal leadership. Fifteenth-century popes were occupied not only with their roles as Italian princes and as patrons of the arts but also with the challenge to their power posed by the reformers. Renaissance popes proved unwilling to address the deep-rooted problems that reform movements, particularly that of John Hus in Bohemia, sought to redress. Although the better popes were capable administrators and notable patrons of the arts, none instituted major ecclesiastical reforms, and Pius II (1458–1464) even prohibited appeals to church councils.

Lay Piety

Demands for reform were made by persons intent on preserving the unity or spiritual supremacy of the church, not on destroying it; theology was not an issue for them, save in the cases of heretical groups such as the Hussites in Bohemia or the Lollards in England. Particularly in German-speaking lands, popular piety remained strong and was probably increasing. Visitors from Italy were impressed by the people's devotion, much of which was rooted in traditional family piety. The development of the printing press dramatically increased the circulation of religious material, though Bibles were still fairly expensive on the eve of the Reformation. Some 10,000 different sermons, mostly in Latin, were in print by 1500, and popular manuals for religious devotion encouraged spiritual training in the home.

The growth of piety was also reflected by the fact that more churches were constructed in German lands in the fifteenth century than in any preceding period. Religious clubs or organizations for laypersons were founded at a striking pace in the fourteenth and fifteenth centuries. Typical of these were the Brethren of the Common Life, established in the Netherlands in the fourteenth century, and the Brotherhood of the Eleven Thousand Virgins, founded at Cracow and Cologne a century later. While some brotherhoods, such as the Common Life, were involved in education, most were associations to foster piety through common praying and singing. In large measure, then, the Reformation was possible because the heightened sense of religious awareness among the people, often expressed outside the institutional church, was not matched by reform of the chronic problems.

Hans Holbein the Younger's rendering of the "Dance of Death" reflects the fifteenth- and early-sixteenth-century preoccupation with dying, which was in part responsible for the piety and religious concern of this period. In this panel a child is snatched by death. [Giraudon/Art Resource]

Institutional Decay

Two of the most critical problems of the church involved the quality and training of the clergy and ecclesiastical finances. Although the moral standards and educational preparation of the ministry did not substantially decline in the fifteenth century, many people, particularly north of the Alps, were growing impatient with priests who were sometimes flagrantly immoral or semiliterate, particularly as the educational level of many laypersons began to rise. The problem was compounded by the moral laxity of many of the church's leaders, including Pope Alexander VI (1492–1503) and numerous cardinals and prelates. In an age acutely conscious of mortality, there was a demand for spiritual shepherds capable of relieving fears and providing religious guidance. Sensitivity to such needs was often lacking among the higher clergy—notably the archbishops and bishops—who were normally younger sons from aristocratic families pursuing ecclesiastical careers for wealth and political power and had little contact with commoners.

At the level of the parish priesthood, minimal incomes made it difficult to recruit educated men, although some able individuals fostered the growth of popular piety. As a result, most parish priests were drawn from the lowest ranks of society. In the absence of seminaries, the parish priests received on-the-job training from neighboring colleagues and were ill-prepared to instruct parishioners in the complex teaching of the church. The church's future welfare required the recruitment of dedicated priests, an educational program to train them, their effective supervision by bishops, adequate salaries, and the expulsion of unfit men from the priesthood.

The problem of attracting able men at the parish level was directly related to defects in the church's economic structure and officialdom. Although the church was an immensely wealthy institution with vast landholdings, its riches were unequally distributed. In contrast to the opulent lifestyles enjoyed by the archbishops and bishops, most parish priests barely eked out a living; some administrators in the church improved their positions by holding multiple benefices (church livings), a practice that normally detracted from religious duties. Others never visited their parishes but hired poorly paid vicars to perform their duties. Beneficed priests were also in the awkward position of obtaining income from their parishioners by collecting tithes (usually paid in goods, such as wheat) and fees (for baptisms, marriages, and burials). Because tithes were mandatory, they often caused disputes and resentment, particularly among the poor or those dissatisfied with the absenteeism and the low moral and educational levels of the priests. In Germany and Switzerland, peasants and artisans in the fifteenth and sixteenth centuries often condemned these abuses. In addition to the abolition of serfdom and a decrease in rents, they demanded religious reforms, including a reduction of church lands and clerical wealth. In the resulting uprisings, flags depicting a peasant's shoe beside Christ on a white cross symbolically united religious and social protest.

Christian Humanists and the Quest for Reform

The need for institutional reform in the church was a dominant theme of the Christian humanists of northern Europe. To the principles of the Italian humanists they fused the teachings of primitive Christianity in the hope that they might achieve a return to the purity of the early church and its simple but deep-rooted faith. Many northern humanists placed special emphasis on the study of biblical languages and the publication of accurate scriptural texts. Likewise, the humanist attack on corruption and meaningless ceremony in the church prepared the way for Protestant demands for reform and a justification for the break with Rome. Yet the older generations of northern humanists generally remained loyal to Catholicism. In England, Sir Thomas More chose death over renunciation of the church when the latter was demanded of him by King Henry VIII. However, many in the younger generation, such as John Calvin and William Tyndale, found their humanist principles compatible with Protestantism. Indeed, humanists and Protestants each looked to the past as the basis for their proposed reforms—humanists to the classical world, Protestants to the early church—and both shared a deep interest in history.

The Challenge of Hebrew Scholarship: Reuchlin and Hutten

One of the leading biblical scholars among the Christian humanists was Johann Reuchlin (1455–1522), a German authority on Hebrew language and thought. He ran afoul of a converted Jew named Johann Pfefferkorn, who had the emperor Maximilian's authorization to examine Jewish materials in order to identify ones that attacked Christianity. With the support of Dominican scholastics in Cologne, Pfefferkorn attempted to suppress all Jewish literature on the basis of its hostility to Christianity, but Reuchlin objected because Jewish texts had religious and cultural value. When Maximilian condemned his attacks on Pfefferkorn in 1512, Reuchlin retaliated by branding his enemies "pigs" and "children of the devil." Pfefferkorn had the backing of several leading theological faculties, but Reuchlin was defended by a number of German humanists, particularly Ulrich von Hutten and Crotus Rubeanus. These two men wrote the satirical *Letters of Obscure Men* (1515), which purportedly came from the pens of Pfefferkorn's friends and made them appear ridiculous. Hutten, who had once condemned Pope Julius II as the "pest of the world," regarded the papacy as the source of Christendom's troubles. A German patriot, he applauded when Martin Luther attacked the pope's authority to issue indulgences in 1517.

Erasmus, Prince of the Humanists

The greatest Greek scholar among the northern humanists was Desiderius Erasmus of Rotterdam (c. 1466–1536), a pupil of the Brethren of the Common Life and later a student at the University of Paris. Much of his scholarly career was spent in Basel, though he was widely traveled and visited England several times. One of the great triumphs of Renaissance scholarship was his edition of the New Testament in Greek, first published in 1516. In its preface, he made an eloquent plea for Bibles in the ver-

A Bible for the People

In The Paraclesis, *Erasmus argued for the importance of having the Bible translated into the language of the people. This was directly related to his belief in the essential simplicity of the Christian message.*

I greatly dissent from those men who would not have the Scripture of Christ translated into all tongues that it might be read diligently by private and secular men and women, as though Christ had taught such dark and insensible things that they could only be understood by a few divines, or else as though the pith and substance of the Christian religion consisted chiefly in this, that it be not known. Peradventure it is most expedient that the counsels of kings should be kept secret, but Christ would have his counsels and mysteries spread abroad as much as possible. I desire that all women should read the Gospel and Paul's epistles, and I would to God they were translated into the tongues of all men, so that they might not only be read and known by the Scots and Irishmen, but also by the Turks and Saracens. Truly it is one degree to good living, yea the first . . . to have a little sight into the Scripture, though it be but a gross knowledge . . . and that some should err and be deceived. I would to God the plowman would sing a text of the Scripture at his plow, and the weaver at his loom. . . . I would that all the communication of the Christian should be of the Scripture, for in a manner we ourselves are such as our daily speech is.

Source: Erasmus, *An Exhortation to the Diligent Study of Scripture* (London, 1529), pp. 8–9 (edited to conform with modern usage).

nacular: "I would that even the lowliest women read the Gospels and the Pauline Epistles. . . . Would that . . . the farmer sing some portion of them at the plough."[1] Erasmus thus anticipated one of the major accomplishments of the Protestant Reformation, the bringing of the Bible to the common people.

Erasmus' religious beliefs are summarized in his idea of a "philosophy of Christ," by which he meant a disciplined life of love and service for God and other people. In contrast to the complexities of the scholastics, Erasmus stressed the simple teachings of Jesus; the heart of religion was faith and love in action, not ritualistic observance. In his great classic, the *Praise of Folly,* he mercilessly satirized such Catholic practices as pilgrimages, the veneration of relics, the sale of indulgences, and the mechanical use of the rosary. Erasmus condemned war as a denial of Christian love and insisted that peace was essential for the spread of education and scholarship. He even condemned war against the Turks on the ground that any

Hans Holbein's portrait of Erasmus of Rotterdam, the influential Christian humanist whose stinging criticism of abuses in the Catholic church helped set the stage for the Protestant Reformation. Erasmus himself, however, remained a Catholic. [Metropolitan Museum of Art, Robert Lehman Collection]

victories they might win against Europeans were divinely ordained as a means to chastise Christians. Nowhere is his repudiation of the philosophy of might more evident than in his *Education of a Christian Prince* (1516), written for Charles of Habsburg, the future emperor Charles V. Erasmus' ideal ruler—devoted to peace, guided by honesty and right religion, concerned for the welfare of his people—was diametrically opposed to Machiavelli's prince. Erasmus was the epitome of a Christian idealist: "We may shortly behold," he wrote in 1517, "the rise of a new kind of golden age. So great is the heaven-sent change we see in the minds of princes, who bend all their powers to the pursuit of peace."[2]

The Humanists in England

John Colet and Sir Thomas More, both friends of Erasmus, were the leading Christian humanists in England. Colet (c. 1466-1519) founded St. Paul's School for boys in London, with a curriculum devoted to the critical study of Latin and Greek as well as religion. Colet's scriptural expositions were noted for their attention to historical context and literal meaning, and some of his sermons fearlessly denounced corruption in the church.

More (1478–1535), an able diplomat and later Lord Chancellor for Henry VIII, depicted the model society of a Renaissance humanist in *Utopia* (1516), a shrewd work of social criticism coupled with autobiographical reflections. His book envisioned a communal society in which "life and work [are] common to all," education is universal and compulsory, and crime is largely nonexistent because there would be no extremes of wealth and poverty. Utopia ("nowhere" in Greek) was a tolerant society in which one enjoyed the freedom to believe as one wished, so long as one did not coerce others or use religion to promote sedition. There is tragic irony in the fact that More, who was beheaded for refusing to accept Henry VIII's headship over the English church, dreamed of a day when a ruler would recognize that it was "arrogant folly for anyone to enforce conformity with his own beliefs by means of threats or violence."[3] Yet More himself had supported the persecution of heretics in his capacity as Henry's chancellor. In the end, More, like Erasmus, found Protestant theology unacceptable, but his call for reform helped pave the way for the Reformation.

Luther and the German Reformation

The event which triggered the Protestant Reformation—or Revolt, as Roman Catholics often call it—was associated with the church's financial policy as well as popular piety. Late in 1514, Pope Leo X revived a campaign originally launched by Julius II to rebuild St. Peter's Basilica in Rome, the money for which was to be raised partly through the sale of indulgences. An indulgence cancelled or reduced the temporal punishment for sin. Retribution and forgiveness for one's sins were the central focus of the sacrament of penance, which included confession and the performance of prescribed penalties. Catholic theology advanced the belief that few people lived such exemplary lives that the remission was complete. Most Christians therefore had to be purified in purgatory after they died before they could enter heaven. Beginning in 1476, the papacy claimed the power to reduce the time that souls spent in purgatory by transferring to them the surplus good deeds of Christ and his saints (stored in the "treasury of merit"). This it would do for anyone who purchased indulgences, usually in return for monetary gifts to the church. As early as the thirteenth century, the papacy had sold indulgences as a source of income, though reformers at the Council of Constance in 1415 protested this practice. It continued, partly because so many shared in the profits and partly because many common folk sincerely believed that their money could speed their loved ones or themselves through purgatory.

In the spring of 1517, the papacy completed preparations for the sale of indulgences in northern Germany. However, a university professor in the Saxon town of Wittenberg, Martin Luther (1483–1546), raised serious questions about indulgences and soon challenged the authority of the papacy itself. No issue was more central to the Reformation than this question of authority.

Luther: The Early Years and the Attack on Indulgences

Luther's domineering father, an ambitious peasant who became part owner of a mine, provided a good education for his son, including a year's study with the Brethren of the Common Life. As Luther prepared to study law after graduating from the University of Erfurt, he was deeply troubled by religious doubts. Terrified by a lightning storm, he promised St. Anne, the patron of miners, that he would become a monk in return for his safety, and shortly thereafter he became an Augustinian friar. Although the rigors of the monastic routine brought no relief from his deep-seated fears of divine wrath, he remained in the order.

A trip to Rome on Augustinian business in 1510 confirmed Luther's feeling that the church was too worldly and needed reform. As he prepared lectures on the Bible at the University of Wittenberg, to whose faculty he had been assigned, he became convinced that no amount of human effort could save a person from the awesome judgment of God; salvation (or justification) could come only through the divine gifts of grace and faith. Luther vividly likened the human condition to that of a worm trapped in the ordure of the bowels, unable to escape unless God plucked the soul from the filth. From this conviction of salvation by faith alone, Luther gained the spiritual strength to become a religious leader, although personal fears continued to plague him. More than 15 years later he confessed that he was still terrified when he heard God called "just." It was this unusual sensitivity to human unworthiness and the need for divinely bestowed faith that made him rebel at the commercialism of the indulgence hawkers, particularly Johann Tetzel, who dramatically evoked the appeal of relatives suffering in purgatory: "Pity us, pity us. We are in dire torment from which you can redeem us for a pittance."[4]

Although Luther had criticized indulgences in 1516, it was not until the people of Wittenberg purchased them from Tetzel the following autumn that his views attracted serious attention. Intended at first only for academic debate, the 95 theses that Luther issued on October 31, 1517, challenged belief in papal authority to release souls from purgatory. Finding no scriptural authority for indulgences, Luther insisted that believers received full forgiveness for their sins through faith and repentance, not letters of indulgence. Within weeks, the theses were translated from Latin into German, printed, and distributed throughout Germany, creating a sensation. Summoned to Rome for examination on charges of heresy, Luther instead received a hearing in Augsburg, thanks to the intervention of his prince, Frederick of Saxony. As one of the seven electors of the Holy Roman Empire empowered to select a successor when the aged Maximilian died, Frederick was a man Pope Leo X dared not alienate. For political reasons, then, no effective action was taken to suppress Luther, who gained vital time to work out the implications of his views on authority and salvation by faith.

Toward a New Theology

In a debate at Leipzig with the papal spokesman Johann Eck in 1519, Luther moved closer to an open break with the church by rejecting the authority of the pope and the infallibility of church councils and by referring with approval to John Hus, the Bohemian heretic. Further reflection led Luther to write three reform manifestos in 1520. Their publication broadcast his views widely and was enormously effective in winning support for them. The first of the treatises was the *Address to the Christian Nobility of the German Nation*, an appeal to the emperor, the German princes and knights, and the imperial cities to cast off papal bondage. In a work with pronounced nationalistic overtones, Luther repudiated three fundamental papal claims: superior jurisdiction over temporal powers, the sole authority to interpret Scripture, and the exclusive right to summon a general council of the church.

In his second treatise, *On the Babylonian Captivity of the Church*, Luther rejected four of the sacraments for which he found no biblical basis, retaining only baptism, the Lord's supper, and penance (which he later dropped). Here too he set forth his concept of the priesthood of all believers, repudiating the traditional Catholic distinction between the clergy and the laity: "We are all equally priests . . . we have the same power in respect to the Word and the sacraments."[5] He conceded that to preach required the church's approval, thereby preserving a sense of order. Finally, in *The Liberty of the Christian Man,* Luther explained his doctrine of salvation by faith alone, insisting that good deeds were necessary fruits of this faith. On these principles Protestantism was founded.

Before the last two of these treatises appeared, Pope Leo issued a bull, *Exsurge domine*, commanding Luther to retract his assertions or be excommunicated. Luther and his supporters responded to this challenge by publicly burning copies of the bull and the canon law. Luther finally received a formal hearing in April 1521, three months after his excommunication, when he appeared before the imperial Diet at Worms. The decision to leave the safety of Saxony was an act of courage, despite a guarantee of safe conduct from the new emperor, Charles V. As Luther knew, a similar promise had not saved Hus from the flames a century earlier. Expecting to debate his views before the Diet, Luther was stunned when ordered to retract his statements without an opportunity to defend himself. To the emperor and the nobles Luther responded the following day: "I am neither able nor willing to revoke anything, since to act against one's conscience is neither safe nor honest."[6] The break with Rome was now complete, for Luther had rejected the fundamental Catholic doctrine of the combined authority of Scripture and tradition. Neither pope nor church councils could be the final court of appeal, as authority resided in the Bible and the conscience of the believer, duly enlightened by the Holy Spirit through Scripture. The emphasis on individual conscience became one of the most important elements in the Protestant tradition.

Although the emperor was unmoved by Luther's stand, he honored the safe conduct. Taking no chances, Frederick hid Luther in his castle at Wartburg, where Luther, disguised as "Sir George," translated Erasmus' Greek New Testament into German. Excommunicated by the church and outlawed by the empire, he could not return to Wittenberg for nearly a year. He remained there until his death in 1546, secure only because of political and religious rivalries within the empire and Charles' preoccupation with military campaigns against the French and the Turks.

Religion and Social Reform

Luther's program of reform had major religious and social consequences. Refusing to recognize the Roman church as the true church of Christ, he set out to establish an institution that conformed to his view of the New Testament. He and his supporters rejected prayers to the saints, the veneration of relics, indulgences, and pilgrim-

Luther on Justification by Faith

One of Luther's strongest statements of the doctrine of justification by faith alone appears in his commentary on Paul's epistle to the Galatians. First published in 1535, the commentary was based on lectures delivered at the University of Wittenberg four years earlier.

We imagine as it were two worlds, the one heavenly and the other earthly. In these we place these two kinds of righteousness, being separate the one far from the other. The righteousness of the law is earthly and hath to do with earthly things, and by it we do good works. But as the earth bringeth not forth fruit except first it be watered and made fruitful from above . . . even so by the righteousness of the law, in doing many things we do nothing, and in fulfilling of the law we fulfil it not, except first, without any merit or work of ours, we be made righteous by the Christian righteousness, which nothing appertaineth to the righteousness of the law, or to the earthly and active righteousness. But this righteousness is heavenly and passive: which we have not of ourselves, but receive it from heaven: which we work not, but apprehend it by faith; whereby we mount up above all laws and works. Wherefore like as we have borne (as St. Paul saith) the image of the earthly Adam, so let us bear the image of the heavenly (1 Cor. 15:49), which is the new man in a new world, where is no law, no sin, no sting of conscience, no death, but perfect joy, righteousness, grace, peace, life, salvation, and glory.

Why, do we then nothing? Do we work nothing for the obtaining of this righteousness? I answer: Nothing at all.

Source: Martin Luther, *A Commentary on St. Paul's Epistle to the Galatians*, ed. P. S. Watson (Westwood, N.J.: Revell, 1953), p. 25.

ages because they regarded them as superstitious and unscriptural. The monasteries in Lutheran territories were dissolved, resulting in a major redistribution of wealth that ultimately improved the social position of the wealthier urban citizens as well as the princes and the aristocracy. Mandatory celibacy for the clergy was also ended. Regarded by Catholics as a superior state, celibacy now was given no more importance than marriage, which gained a new dignity. Luther himself married a former nun, Katherine von Bora, who bore him six children. The effects of these changes on women were mixed, for although wives were no longer regarded as inferior to celibate women, the closing of nunneries deprived women of a vocational option. Fathers, however, could no longer place their daughters in convents to avoid providing dowries for them.

In most respects Luther's view of women was traditional, predicated on their subordination to men and a belief in the inferiority of their abilities. They should, he said, "remain at home, sit still, keep house, and bear and bring up children." But even though he regarded wives as subject to their husbands, he viewed them as partners in marriage. Because Luther made the family the focal point of society and church, wives had a new dignity. Thus Luther accepted women's spiritual equality with men, but he refused to allow them a formal role in the preaching or teaching ministry of the church or in politics. Nevertheless, some women became active in the spread of Lutheranism. Argula von Grumbach, who came from an aristocratic Bavarian family and had a humanist education, distributed Lutheran books, conducted religious services in her home, and corresponded with Luther. Elizabeth of Braunschweig converted people in Hanover and Göttingen to Lutheranism and furthered the Protestant cause in letters to political leaders. Argula's and Elizabeth's roles in the Lutheran movement, however, owed more to their aristocratic status than to Luther's encouragement of female activity.

In Lutheran churches the sermon was accorded a prominent place, services were conducted in the vernacular, and congregational participation was increased, especially through the singing of hymns. The more active role of the laity and the significance attached to the sermon led to greater attention to education. Luther wanted a primary school in every parish and a secondary school in every sizable town, with provision for the education of girls as well as boys. With his colleague Philip Melanchthon, he urged civil authorities to establish and support schools,

A Lutheran Woman Speaks Out

Argula von Grumbach, one of Luther's most prominent female disciples, was undaunted by the traditional domination of males in theological matters. In 1523 she wrote a stinging letter rebuking the faculty of the University of Ingolstadt for condemning a young Lutheran teacher.

Where do you read in the Bible that Christ, the apostles, and the prophets imprisoned, banished, burned, or murdered anyone? You tell us that we must obey the magistrates. Correct. But neither the pope, nor the Kaiser, nor the princes have any authority over the Word of God. You need not think you can pull God, the prophets and the apostles out of heaven with papal decretals drawn from Aristotle, who was not a Christian at all. I am not unacquainted with the word of Paul that women should be silent in church (1 Tim. 1:2) but, when no man will or can speak, I am driven by the word of the Lord when he said, "He who confesses me on earth, him will I confess and he who denies me, him will I deny" (Matt. 10, Luke 9). . . . I would be willing to come and dispute with you in German and you won't need to use Luther's translation of the Bible. . . . I send you not a woman's ranting, but the Word of God.

Source: R. H. Bainton, *Women of the Reformation in Germany and Italy* (Minneapolis: Augsburg, 1971), pp. 97–98, 100.

drawing especially on the wealth obtained by the closing of monasteries and other Catholic institutions. Because of the importance of the Bible, which Luther insisted must be in the vernacular, Protestantism became a major incentive to the growth of literacy.

Medallion depicting Argula von Grumbach, one of Luther's leading female supporters. [Staatliche Münzsammlung, Munich]

At first, the religious confusion of the opening years of the Reformation brought a reduction in the number of students, especially at the universities; enrollment at the University of Vienna fell from 661 students in 1519 to 12 in 1532. An alarmed Erasmus complained that "wherever Lutheranism prevails, there learning disappears." But Luther and his colleagues successfully pressed civic officials and territorial princes to establish new schools. The Lutherans had several outstanding educational reformers, including Johannes Bugenhagen, who organized school systems in Germany and Denmark that included separate institutions for girls. The most influential Lutheran educator was Johannes Sturm, whose secondary school (called a "gymnasium") at Strasbourg became the pattern for similar schools throughout Europe. Divided into ten grades, the curriculum included Latin, Greek, religion, and logic. Lutherans also founded new universities in Germany, including those at Marburg and Jena. Luther's own university at Wittenberg attracted 16,000 students between 1520 and 1560, of whom a third were foreigners.

The Growth of the Lutheran Movement

Luther's views spread rapidly, aided by the printing press, the reformer's own eloquence, the zeal of numerous German merchants, especially in the Hanseatic towns, and the prospects for material gain by people who coveted Catholic lands and wealth. Various German princes as well as cities such as Hamburg and Magdeburg requested that Luther's friends and pupils fill their pulpits and lecterns. The work of reform went forward by winning the support of established leaders, not by revolution. For this reason, Luther himself strenuously opposed any attempt to alter the political order.

In the German cities the reform typically followed a threefold course, beginning with the preaching of Protestant tenets, followed by the growth of popular support and finally by the backing of the magistrates. While the reformers recognized that the last step was critical, the magistrates were cautious, not wanting to introduce religious change until they were assured that it would not destroy traditional social ties. The magistrates were also pressured by Charles V to remain Catholic. When some finally decided to support Protestantism, they did so with deliberation, stretching out the work of reform over a period of years: 11 in Constance, 13 in Nuremberg, 21 in Osnabrück. Wary of creating new popes, the magistrates were frequently unwilling to grant the preachers all the changes they sought. In Strasbourg, for instance, Martin Bucer's attempt to transfer control of the city's religious and moral life to the church was rejected. Some magistrates inaugurated the religious change with debates rigged so that the Protestants prevailed, as happened at Nuremberg and Constance. Because of their concentration, urban populations were especially open to the influence of popular preaching and the Protestant works that flowed from the press, the results of which were evident in the demonstrations of voting support often accorded the Protestants in the early 1530s.

Luther himself corresponded with Hussite leaders in Bohemia, and his doctrines were preached as far afield as Hungary, Prussia, and the Netherlands. Beyond the German states, however, only the Scandinavian lands adopted Lutheranism, which suited the political needs of the kings of Denmark and Sweden as they worked to unify their countries. Adopting Lutheranism made it possible for them to confiscate ecclesiastical lands and assert greater authority over the clergy. As a province of Denmark, Norway too became Lutheran, and Protestant teachings spread as well into Finland. Within Germany, Luther's views provoked bitter divisions that ultimately led to social upheaval and civil war.

Initially the German peasants regarded Luther as a leader who would help them attain not only their religious goals but social reform as well. The success of Luther's movement was tied, however, to the support of princes, nobles, and wealthy burghers, without whose backing he would have been subjected to the power of the empire and the church. Thus despite his sympathy for many peasant demands—which included reduced rents, the abolition of serfdom, and an end to unlawful punishment—he preached patience when peasants rebelled in southern and central Germany in the summer of 1524. He refused to support their call for the termination of serfdom on the grounds that such action not only violated biblical respect for property but "would make all men equal, and turn the spiritual kingdom of Christ into a worldly external kingdom." As the Peasants' Revolt became increasingly violent the following year, Luther reacted against the killing, arson, desecration of churches, and destruction of property. In May 1525 he published his pamphlet *Against the Rapacious and Murdering Peasants*, urging the nobility in God's name to "cut, stab, and strangle" the rebels. The peasants were crushed with dreadful severity: some 300 were beheaded in front of the town hall at Frankenhausen, and altogether the Peasants' Revolt claimed between 70,000 and 100,000 lives.

Although Luther's support for the nobles tied his movement to the conservative social order, Catholics seized on the revolt to accuse Lutheranism of fomenting social rebellion. In 1525 and 1526 both sides organized defensive leagues, but Charles V, who remained steadfastly Catholic, was prevented from crushing the Protestants by hostilities with the French, with whom he fought four major wars over northern Italy and Naples between 1521 and 1559. He was preoccupied too by the advancing Turkish forces of Suleiman the Magnificent (1520–1566), which soundly defeated the Hungarians at Mohács in 1526 and advanced to the very gates of Vienna before retreating.

Political and military pressures forced Charles to allow the German princes a degree of religious toleration at the Diet of Speyer the same year. When he revoked this freedom in 1529, the Lutheran princes and urban delegates protested, giving birth to the term *Protestant*. In response to Charles' demand at the 1530 Diet of Augsburg that Lutherans return to the Catholic fold, the Protestant princes organized the Schmalkaldic League to defend themselves. Although the emperor defeated the league in 1547, his armies were in turn vanquished five years later, forcing him to return to a policy of religious toleration. Finally, in 1555 both sides agreed in the Peace of Augsburg that each prince had the right to determine whether the people of his territory would be Catholic or Lutheran. Only in some of the German cities where toleration was already practiced did the people themselves retain the right to choose their own faith. Northern Germany became mostly Lutheran, as did Württemberg and most of the cities of the south, though much of southern Germany remained loyal to Catholicism.

The Reformed Tradition

While Lutheranism developed in the German states, a different variety of Protestantism emerged in Switzerland. There, under the leadership of Ulrich Zwingli in Zurich and later John Calvin in Geneva, the Reformed tradition distinguished itself from Lutheranism by simpler forms of worship, emphasis on the weekly sermon rather than the celebration of the Lord's supper (undertaken only four times a year rather than weekly), greater stress on moral discipline, and a denial of Christ's physical presence in the Lord's supper. In Switzerland, a loose confederation of 13 independent states (cantons) and allied areas, there was widespread disenchantment with conditions in the church, stemming mostly from the impact of the Christian humanists and the reforming spirit kindled by the Councils of Constance (1414–1418) and Basel (1431–1449). Although the cantons were overwhelmingly Catholic, feelings against abuses in the church ran so strongly that in 1520 the Swiss diet ordered the execution of anyone selling church offices. Along with the desire for reform, there were mounting protests in the cantons against the recruitment of Swiss men for foreign military service.

Ulrich Zwingli and the Swiss Reformation

The son of a peasant and village magistrate, Ulrich Zwingli (1484–1531), the founder of the Reformed tradition, was educated by humanists at Bern, Vienna, and Basel. Intellectually he was a disciple of Erasmus. After serving as a chaplain to Swiss mercenaries, he was moved by their heavy losses to condemn such military service except on behalf of the church. As a priest in the Great Minster at Zurich, Zwingli became an outspoken critic of indulgences. While comforting the sick during an outbreak of the plague in 1519–1520, his own illness deepened his religious convictions and ultimately spurred his interest in reform. In 1522 he condemned fasting during Lent as unscriptural and reformed the liturgy. Finding no biblical evidence for clerical celibacy, he denounced it and married a poor widow. "I know of no greater scandal," he wrote caustically, "than that priests are not allowed to take lawful wives but may keep mistresses if they pay a fine."[7] In a series of public debates, he called for a return of the church to its original simplicity and for the removal of all images, relics, and altars. Because he allowed only psalm singing in church, the minster organ was chopped into pieces. For Zwingli, nothing was acceptable in religion unless it was revealed in Scripture.

From Zurich the reform movement spread by 1529 to Bern and Basel, as well as beyond the confederation to the German cities of Strasbourg and Constance. Civil war between Catholics and Protestants briefly erupted in 1529, after which Zwingli met with Luther to forge a Protestant union. At Marburg, however, the two leaders strongly disagreed on the nature of the Lord's supper. Zwingli, believing that Christ was present only spiritually in the sacrament, rejected Luther's insistence on a "real" (physical and spiritual) presence. The failure at Marburg was followed by renewed civil war in Switzerland when, despite Zwingli's protests, the Protestant cantons blockaded the Catholic districts in 1531, forcing them to fight or starve. Captured during the battle of Kappel that year, Zwingli was quartered and burned as a heretic. Leadership of the reform movement in Zurich was taken up by his son-in-law, Heinrich Bullinger. Following the war, the right of each canton to decide its own religion was recognized.

John Calvin

The Reformed tradition founded by Zwingli became a major international force under the guidance of John Calvin (1509–1564), the son of a French attorney and secretary to the bishop of Noyon. After a broad education in theology, law, classical languages, and humanistic studies at the Universities of Paris, Orléans, and Bourges, Calvin joined Catholic humanists in Orléans and Paris interested in religious reform in the late 1520s. Shortly after his conversion to Protestantism, he was briefly imprisoned in 1534 and then forced into hiding.

When the French government stepped up the persecution of Protestants that autumn, Calvin fled to Basel, where he met Bullinger and other reformers. There he wrote the classic of Reformation Protestantism, the *Institutes of the Christian Religion* (1536). In it he provided a thorough introduction to a Protestant view of the Christian faith, concentrating on the nature and work of God, the redemption of sinners, and the role of the church and sacraments in the Christian life. On a trip to Strasbourg later that year, he stopped in Geneva, which had just ended Catholic worship under the leadership of Guillaume Farel. Needing assistance, Farel pressured Calvin to stay, threatening him with God's wrath until he became "terrified and shook." Together they imposed a public confession of faith on citizens to distinguish the devout from the unfaithful, called for educational reform, and punished immorality. These measures, coupled with changes in worship and the abolition of holy days, provoked such strong resentment that the two men were exiled in 1538.

Settling in Strasbourg, Calvin became the pastor of a congregation of French exiles, lectured at Johannes Sturm's gymnasium, and revised his *Institutes*. Influenced by the teachings of Paul and Augustine, Calvin proclaimed that because human nature was totally corrupt, belief in God was impossible without the irresistible gift of faith. Only those chosen by God before creation—the elect—received this gift; all others—the reprobate—were left to their sins and condemned to eternal damnation. In his mind, the doctrine of predestination revealed not only God's justice and majesty but also his mercy in providing salvation for the elect despite their unworthiness. Too much inquiry into this doctrine was discouraged:

> **Let them remember that when they inquire into predestination they are penetrating the sacred precinct of divine wisdom. If anyone with carefree assurance breaks**

Eternally Chosen, Eternally Damned

Calvin's Institutes of the Christian Religion, *perhaps the finest theological work of the Protestant Reformation, put great emphasis on the sovereignty of God. The most famous manifestation of this was Calvin's insistence that God determined the eternal destiny of each person before the creation of the world.*

We shall never be clearly convinced as we ought to be, that our salvation flows from the fountain of God's free mercy, till we are acquainted with his eternal election, which illustrates the grace of God by this comparison, that he adopts not all promiscuously to the hope of salvation, but gives to some what he refuses to others. Ignorance of this principle evidently detracts from the Divine glory, and diminishes real humility. . . .

Predestination we call the eternal decree of God, by which he has determined in himself, what he would have to become of every individual of mankind. For they are not all created with a similar destiny; but eternal life is foreordained for some, and eternal damnation for others. . . .

We affirm that this counsel, as far as concerns the elect, is founded on his gratuitous mercy, totally irrespective of human merit; but that to those whom he devotes to condemnation, the gate of life is closed by a just and irreprehensible, but incomprehensible, judgment. . . .

The will of God is the highest rule of justice; so that what he wills must be considered just, for this very reason, because he wills it. When it is inquired, therefore, why the Lord did so, the answer must be, Because he would. But if you go further, and ask why he so determined, you are in search of something greater and higher than the will of God, which can never be found.

Source: John Calvin, *Institutes of the Christian Religion*, trans. J. Allen (Philadelphia: Presbyterian Board of Christian Education, 1928), vol. 2, pp. 140–165 passim.

into this place, he will not succeed in satisfying his curiosity and he will enter a labyrinth from which he can find no exit.[8]

Like Luther and Zwingli, Calvin accepted the authority of Scripture alone, which he regarded as "a declaration of the word of God," and refused to consider the teachings of the early church fathers and church councils as equally binding. He insisted, however, that only those enlightened by the Holy Spirit could properly understand the Bible. With other Protestants, Calvin recognized only two sacraments, baptism and the Lord's supper; his concept of the latter was closer to Zwingli's idea of a spiritual presence than to Luther's view. Influenced by the Strasbourg reformer Martin Bucer, Calvin developed a "democratic" plan for church government that called for the election of ministers by the congregation and the joint participation of ministers and popularly elected lay elders in running the church. Calvin's stress on the disciplined moral life and a godly society made his movement a potent force.

One of the most important themes in Calvin's thought was his treatment of vocation as a Christian duty, a concept he shared with other Protestants. He gave all legitimate professions a sense of Christian purpose, so that one's job became a principal means of serving God. To work was to worship. This outlook brought new dignity to occupations as diverse as business, the crafts, and agriculture. The artisan no less than the minister, Calvin insisted, was divinely called to his vocation.

Calvin's view of wealth was equally significant for economic development. In his judgment, God intended that money be used to better the human condition, and thus, within limits, usury (or interest) had a positive function. Like Luther, Calvin was conscious of the plight of debtors, but if charging interest was consistent with the good of the community, usury was acceptable. Interest rates, however, could never be excessive. Luther, by contrast, prohibited all usury as unscriptural with the exception of loans by which the borrower prospered. For Calvin the governing economic principle was always the mutual responsibility of citizens for the common welfare. Although he never sanctioned the unlimited acquisition of wealth or equated riches with godliness, his emphasis on work and discipline in the context of Christian vocation as well as his limited acceptance of usury were compatible with the growth of a capitalistic economy.

GENEVA IN THE AGE OF CALVIN

After the election of men favorable to his cause, Calvin returned to Geneva in 1541. The city was the largest in its region, with a population of approximately 10,000. Under Calvin, Geneva became the international center of Reformed Protestantism and attracted more than 5,000 religious refugees from France, Italy, England, and Scotland, many of whom were artisans and merchants who contributed to the city's prosperity. Among the newcomers were many booksellers and printers, who helped make Geneva one of Europe's foremost publication centers. Throughout most of the 1500s, books were the city's primary export and were only supplanted late in the century by the export of silk, an industry introduced by Italians. Because Geneva had little industry of its own apart from printing, the economy was based on commerce. Its artisans produced mostly for the local market rather than the export trade.

Genevans prized their independence, which they achieved on the eve of Calvin's arrival by rebelling from Savoy. The heart of Genevan government was its three councils: a 25-member Little Council served as an executive body, a Council of 200 determined municipal policy, and a Council of 60 conducted foreign relations. Under Calvin's leadership, these institutions protected the Protestant church, safeguarded property, and imposed moral standards on private behavior. Although Calvin himself never held political office, his advice was sought on such matters as foreign policy, taxes, and military defense.

The councils approved his ecclesiastical ordinances, establishing four offices in the church: pastors, teachers, elders, and deacons (who were responsible for poor relief and assisting the sick). Each of the 12 elders was assigned a district in Geneva and required to oversee its families. Through the Consistory, composed of the ministers and elders, Calvin imposed strict discipline on the people for such offenses as absence from church, sexual immorality, swearing, drunkenness, bawdy songs, card playing, and even criticizing Calvin himself. More serious offenses were turned over to the city government. Between 1542 and 1546, 76 persons were banished and 58 executed for heresy, adultery, blasphemy, and witchcraft. In the quest to make Geneva an example of godliness, the Consistory even questioned children about the conduct of their parents. Discipline and obedience were crucial.

As the years passed, Calvin, like Luther, grew even more intolerant of opposition and demanded that his critics be punished. The intolerance of the two leaders, like that of most of their fellow reformers, grew out of their belief in the need for a unified Christendom and was the practical result of the need to define the churches they had created. In 1552 Calvin persuaded the city councils to declare that his *Institutes* contained the "pure doctrine" and should not be questioned. The extent to which Calvin's supporters would go in defending his theology became apparent the next year when the Spanish physician and lay theologian Michael Servetus (1511–1553) visited Geneva, thoroughly scandalizing the citizens by his views. The author of works attacking the doctrine of the Trinity, the baptism of infants, and original sin, he was already a man whom the Catholics regarded as a heretic. After a trial in which he clashed with Calvin personally, Servetus was burned at the stake. Calvin's treatment of him was praised by Catholic and Protestant leaders alike. From 1555 until his death in 1564, Calvin ruled Geneva with little opposition.

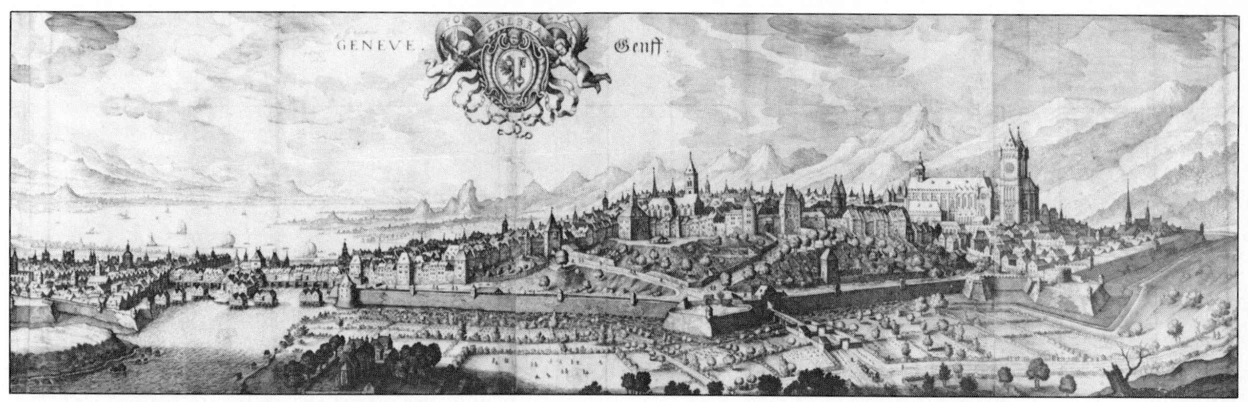

Geneva in the late sixteenth century, its skyline dominated by St. Peter's cathedral. [The British Library]

Geneva made a determined effort in this period to deal with the needy. Before Calvin's arrival, the small medieval hospitals were reorganized into the Hospital of the Holy Spirit, which cared for the elderly, the sick, the indigent, and widows and orphans. Outside the city walls was a smaller hospital for victims of the plague. Responsibility for the main hospital was vested in the deacons, who obtained funding from the city government as well as from private charity. Support for the hospital was sometimes the largest item in the city budget. In addition to providing free care for the needy in the hospital, every medical doctor was required, beginning in 1569, to treat the poor without charge.

Calvin supervised a sweeping reform of the school system that replaced the old secondary schools with a gymnasium patterned after Johannes Sturm's in Strasbourg. A new academy, established to train superior students for leadership in church and state, developed into the modern University of Geneva. Beginning in 1536, all children had to attend primary school, but girls were barred from the secondary level. No reformer was more aware than Calvin of the value of education to instruct young people in religious beliefs.

Like Luther, Calvin accepted the traditional notion of female inferiority and the subject position of women in marriage. He too recognized their spiritual equality but refused to allow women a ministerial role in the church. In the secular sphere, when a woman inherited a crown, Calvin interpreted the event as a divine reproach to men. Apart from their responsibilities in the home, women were assigned the task of educating the young. In practice, however, Calvinist women of aristocratic background were prominent in the movement. Jeanne d'Albret, mother of King Henry IV of France, was a leader of the Huguenots (as the French Calvinists were called), while Madeleine Mailly, Comtesse de Roye, worked on behalf of the Huguenot cause with both the French government and German Protestant princes. Yet in Geneva, Calvin neither allowed women to serve as deaconesses nor favored their participation in city government, although his own wife was virtually his partner in the work of religious reform.

Under Calvin, Geneva was the focal point of an expanding network of reformers who carried his message as far afield as France, the Netherlands, England, Scotland, and even Hungary. With its strict morality and religious fervor, Geneva was the nerve center of a militant, determined Protestantism.

The Radical Reformation

Although both the Lutheran and Reformed traditions appealed to Scripture as their authority and worked to restore the church to its original simplicity, as early as the mid-1520s radical critics expressed dissatisfaction with the extent and pace of reform. In their judgment, Luther and Zwingli had compromised their principles in order to win the support of the powerful. Most of the radical critics became known as Anabaptists ("Rebaptizers"), a group that quickly became an abomination to the propertied classes and the major religious groups.

The Anabaptists

In 1523 Conrad Grebel (1498–1526), a follower of Zwingli and a member of a prominent patrician family in Zurich, became impatient with the slowness of reform. The following year he attacked Zwingli's view of baptism, insisting that the rite must be confined to believing adults as a mark of their spiritual rebirth. After a public debate in January 1525, the Zurich town council ruled in favor of Zwingli, but Grebel and his followers—the Swiss Brethren—refused to conform. For their defiance, they faced banishment or execution by drowning, a cruel parody of their baptismal practices and a poignant reminder of how intolerant some Protestants could be toward others. The Brethren rejected the traditional concept of a state church in favor of congregations composed of believers alone. Accepting the Lord's supper as a simple meal to commemorate Christ's death, they celebrated it in private homes. Of more concern to the landed classes, the Brethren insisted that pastors must be chosen by individual congregations and supported by voluntary gifts, not tithes. Because so many tithes were now paid directly to laymen rather than to the clergy, the Anabaptist call for voluntary tithing was viewed by both clergy and laity as an attack on property rights. Equally radical was the Brethren's insistence on separating from the evil world, which entailed a refusal to participate in civil government or military service, both of which involved the taking of life. They also declined to pay taxes for military purposes and rejected oaths, which traditionalists regarded as basic to the maintenance of law and order. In the eyes of the authorities, the Anabaptists were dangerous social revolutionaries, while religious leaders not only detested their theological views but feared that the separation of church and state that the Anabaptists advocated would lead to the secularization of society.

The Kingdom of Münster and Its Consequences

Initially the Anabaptists were not identified with any social group, but in the aftermath of the Peasants' Revolt in Germany they attracted large numbers of peasants and artisans. In 1534 the Anabaptists seized control of the

German city of Münster, where they expelled or persecuted all who disagreed with them. Under the leadership of a charismatic Dutch tailor, John of Leiden, they founded a theocratic kingdom, based on the laws of the Old Testament. Polygamy was practiced, and John himself took 16 wives. Initially, an unmarried woman had to accept any marriage proposal, though female opposition finally became so intense that women were given the right to decline offers. A woman, however, could have only one husband and faced capital punishment for adultery. In Münster all property was held in common. Within the city walls there was wild anticipation that King John would soon rule the world in preparation for the second coming of Christ, but the rest of Europe was appalled. The armies of the Catholic bishop of Münster and the Protestant Philip of Hesse, acting together, recaptured the city in 1535, executed the Anabaptist leaders, and publicly displayed their bodies as a warning to others. The Münster fiasco intensified the persecution of Anabaptists throughout the Holy Roman Empire, which in 1529 had revived an old Byzantine law making rebaptism a capital offense. By the early 1600s, several thousand Anabaptists had been executed.

Persecution encouraged the migration of Anabaptists to other areas, particularly the Netherlands, Poland, Bohemia, and Moravia. Shunning the excesses of Münster, these groups distinguished themselves by their quiet piety and strict morality. The most prominent of these sects was that of the Mennonites, founded by Menno Simons (1496–1561), whose followers eventually spread as far as Russia and North America.

Spiritualists and Rationalists

During the heady days of the early Reformation, a handful of radicals claimed to be prophets bearing special revelations from God. One of the most prominent was the revolutionary Thomas Müntzer (died 1525), who accepted only the authority of the Holy Spirit and endorsed the use of violence to advance the Gospel. Offering to raise 30 squads to slaughter the ungodly, Müntzer urged the elector Frederick to establish a new kingdom for the faithful. Exiled from Saxony, he preached social revolution in southern Germany and helped incite the Peasants' Revolt, during which he was executed. Spiritualists from Zwickau near the Bohemian border favored the slaughter of all the ungodly in Europe, whether at their own hands or by the Turks. In contrast to such men, Sebastian Franck (c. 1499–c. 1542) was an intellectual who rejected Lutherans and Anabaptists alike for their dogmatism. Repudiating the authority of the Bible, he argued for a religion based entirely on the inner life of the Spirit and free from all dogma and sacraments.

Whereas the Spiritualists were essentially mystics, another group of Protestant radicals advocated a religion that was predominantly rational and ethical. Distinguishing themselves by their rejection of the Trinity, they criticized predestination and original sin and favored religious toleration. In addition to Servetus, the leading rationalists included Lelio Sozzini (1525–1562) and his nephew Faustus (1539–1604), whose followers, the Socinians, were found primarily in Poland and England. There they helped prepare the foundation for seventeenth-century Deism, the ancestor of modern Unitarianism. One of the greatest literary works of the radical Reformation was Sebastian Castellio's *Concerning Heretics and Whether They Should Be Punished by the Sword of the Magistrate.* Castellio (1515–1563) condemned Calvin for supporting Servetus' execution and offered a ringing defense of religious toleration. To burn a heretic, he asserted, "is not to defend a doctrine, but to kill a man."[9] The legacy of the religious radicals was the concept of religious freedom, an idea slow to win acceptance because of the conviction that religious diversity led to the breakdown of the social and political order.

The English Reformation

In contrast to the reform movements instigated by Luther, Zwingli, and Calvin, the Reformation in England was fundamentally an act of state rather than the work of a religious leader. The relative ease with which the break with Rome was accomplished owed much to widespread dissatisfaction with the Catholic church and to the work of early reform movements. Popular hostility toward the clergy had grown because of their tithes and fees, and many people were disillusioned by priestly ignorance and immorality. Animosity was particularly strong among the Lollards, an underground group whose radical views, inherited from John Wyclif in the fourteenth century, were spread by itinerant cloth workers. Many Lollards embraced Lutheran ideas in the 1520s, and their literature was published by Protestants to demonstrate that their own pleas for reform were firmly rooted in the English past. Lutheran cells were formed at Oxford and Cambridge, and from them Protestant theology began to infiltrate the clergy. In London a covert group of merchants known as the Christian Brethren spread the Protestant message, which they had learned as traders on the Continent. With their support, William Tyndale (c. 1492–1536) translated the New Testament and the Pentateuch into English, with marginal notes that stridently attacked the papacy and the Catholic priesthood. Many early Protestant leaders in England had been educated as humanists and were deeply influenced by Erasmus. Well before the Reformation, English humanists such as John Colet had made strong pleas for reform, helping—unwittingly—to prepare the way for the break with Rome.

The King's "Great Matter"

The state's decision to reject papal authority was not made primarily for religious reasons. The strong-willed King Henry VIII (1509–1547), the second of the Tudor rulers, had been married since 1509 to Catherine of Aragon, by whom he had one surviving child, Princess Mary. The prospect of leaving the new dynasty in a woman's hands raised fears of another dynastic struggle like the fifteenth-century Wars of the Roses. The fact that Henry had become infatuated with Anne Boleyn, a lady of the court, contributed to his decision to seek a new wife and produce a male heir. But to marry Anne required a church-approved annulment of his marriage to Catherine. The latter's position was strengthened by the fact that the army of her nephew, the emperor Charles V, controlled Rome in 1527 and temporarily held the pope prisoner. Unable to act freely, Clement VII delayed the annulment hearings. Exasperated, Henry summoned Parliament in 1529 to bring pressure on the pope, correctly anticipating

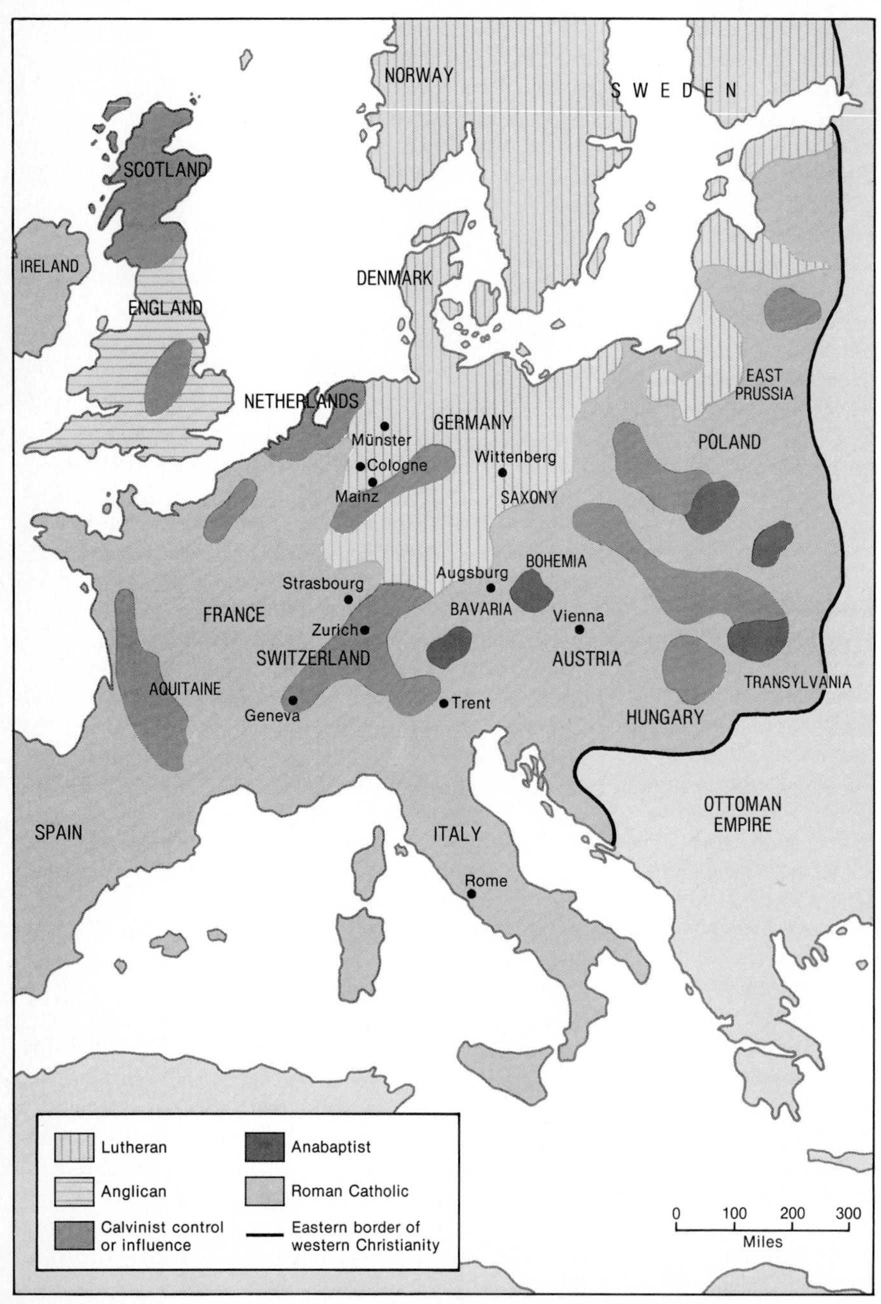

16.1 The Division of Christendom, c. 1550

Henry VIII of England. [National Portrait Gallery, London]

that it would demand reforms. But the pope remained unresponsive.

Henry cowed the English clergy by threatening to punish them for enforcing papal authority in the church courts. Giving in, they recognized the king as head of the English church "as far as the law of Christ allowed." Under the leadership of Henry's new adviser, Thomas Cromwell (1485–1540), a friend of the English Lutherans, Parliament renewed its complaints against religious abuses. When Henry learned in January 1533 that Anne was pregnant, he secretly married her without waiting to resolve the status of his marriage to Catherine. In March, Parliament passed the Act in Restraint of Appeals, drafted largely by Cromwell, which prohibited legal appeals to Rome without royal permission. Asserting that "this realm of England is an empire," the act affirmed the country's legal independence of all foreign authority. Two months later the new archbishop of Canterbury, the Protestant Thomas Cranmer (1489–1556), moved the Convocation of the Clergy to declare Henry's marriage to Catherine null and void, and on June 1 Anne Boleyn was crowned queen of England. Three months later she gave birth to Princess Elizabeth.

Royal Supremacy

Most of the changes during Henry's reign involved the seizure of papal authority by the crown rather than theological issues as on the Continent. Church funds previously paid to Rome now went to the English government. The king received the right to make appointments to all major church offices, as well as the final authority for all ecclesiastical legislation. In the 1534 Act of Supremacy, Parliament recognized the king as "the only supreme head in earth of the Church of England." To deny him this title was treason. An act of succession recognized the children of Henry and Anne as heirs to the throne. For refusing to accept the succession and the royal supremacy in the church, Sir Thomas More and Bishop John Fisher, Catherine's outspoken supporter, were executed in 1535. Catherine remained loyal to the Catholic faith until her death in 1536—an event celebrated by Henry and Anne, both brightly clad in yellow, with a banquet and a joust. Four months later Anne was executed on trumped-up charges of adultery and incest. In reality, Henry could forgive neither her arrogance nor her failure to bear him a son.

Although Henry generally remained loyal to Catholic dogma, Protestants welcomed certain changes in the Church of England. An officially approved translation of the Bible in English by Miles Coverdale was published in 1535, and the following year Cromwell ordered that every church have a copy of the Bible in English and Latin. Between 1536 and 1540 the monasteries were dissolved and their properties confiscated by the crown. Some of the land was sold, enabling the lesser aristocracy (or gentry) in particular to expand their holdings. Because the monasteries had been centers of education and hospitality, the social effects of their dissolution were profound. Although some theological concessions were temporarily made to Protestants for political reasons, the king's conservative religious ideals were reflected in the Six Articles of 1539. Except for papal supremacy, they supported Catholic teachings on the sacraments, the celibacy of priests, and vows of chastity. The religious position of the Church of England in this period is best described as Henrician Catholicism, or Catholicism without monastic institutions or obedience to Rome.

The Edwardian Reformation

After Henry's death in 1547, the Church of England became increasingly Protestant. Henry was succeeded by his 9-year-old son, Edward VI (1547–1553), whose mother, Jane Seymour, Henry's third queen, had died after childbirth. Real power rested at first in the hands of the king's uncle, Edward Seymour, duke of Somerset. Under his direction Parliament repealed the Six Articles and dissolved the chantries, which were endowments to support priests who said masses for the dead. In 1549 Parliament passed an act of uniformity requiring all ministers to use the *Book of Common Prayer*, an English liturgy prepared by Archbishop Cranmer. When Somerset failed to suppress rioting peasants in 1549, he was overthrown by John Dudley, soon to be duke of Northumberland. Under his leadership the English church became even more firmly Protestant. A second act of uniformity required clergy and laity alike to use the revised *Book of Common Prayer*, which simplified the worship service and required ministers to wear only a plain black robe and a white vestment. Communion tables replaced stone altars, and confession was made by the congregation as a whole rather than individually to priests. Royal approval was also given to the Forty-two Articles, a Protestant confession of faith.

The Edwardian Reformation, however, was secure only as long as the king lived, for the heir apparent, Princess Mary, was a determined Catholic. As Edward lay dying of tuberculosis in 1553, Northumberland tried desperately to save himself by preventing Mary from becoming queen. He persuaded Edward to name as his heir Lady Jane Grey, Northumberland's daughter-in-law and a great-granddaughter of Henry VII. But when Edward died in July, the English people overwhelmingly supported Mary as the rightful ruler. As Northumberland was brought into London following his capture, "all the streets [were] full of people, which cursed him, and called him traitor without measure."[10] A month later he died on the scaffold as the new queen prepared to introduce the Counter-Reformation, already under way on the Continent.

The Catholic Revival: A Church Militant

The spirit of reform prevailed within the Catholic church as well as outside it, partly stimulated by the shock of the Protestant secession. The demands for change were matched by a determination to maintain the ideals of the medieval church. Conciliarism, the major source for reform in the late medieval period, had lost much of its force by the early 1500s. The Fifth Lateran Council (1512–1517), meeting in Rome, adopted no significant reforms. Efforts to improve the church, however, were under way in various states, including France, where Cardinal Georges d'Amboise (died 1510) imposed more effective discipline on the monasteries. In Spain, Queen Isabella's confessor, Cardinal Francisco Ximenes (c. 1436–1517), the archbishop of Toledo, improved education for the clergy, placed tighter controls on errant priests and monks, and encouraged humanist learning at the new University of Alcala.

A characteristic feature of Catholic revival was the founding of new organizations, beginning with the Oratory of Divine Love, established in Italy in 1494. Composed of clergy and laity, its members emphasized piety and charitable work for the poor and the sick. The Capuchins (1528), inspired by Francis of Assisi's ideal of poverty, devoted themselves to helping the common people. Other new orders, such as the Barnabites (1530) and the Somaschi (1532), focused on the problems of poverty and disease. The Somaschi, who founded hospitals and orphanages, also took an interest in the plight of prostitutes. The role of women in the Catholic revival is reflected in the Congregation of the Holy Angels (an auxiliary of the Barnabites), the Capucines (the female counterpart of the Capuchins), and the Ursulines, who specialized in educating young women.

ANGELA MERICI AND THE URSULINES

The new sense of spiritual dedication that was reviving the Catholic church is exemplified in the life of Angela Merici, the daughter of a minor country gentleman. Born in 1474 in the republic of Venice, she was orphaned at age 10. As a young woman she was deeply influenced by the piety of local nuns and recluses as well as by the devotional activities of the Oratory of Divine Love. She took part as a layperson in the work of the Franciscans but did not take formal vows. Merici devoted herself to charitable work, helping the sick and the poor as well as teaching girls. While praying in the fields in 1506, she had a vision in which she was promised that "before your death, you will found a society of virgins." Ten years later she established a school for girls, primarily to teach the catechism.

At Brescia in 1531, Merici, now partially blind, recruited a dozen young women as teachers, and in 1535, when the group had grown to 28, she founded the Company of St. Ursula (Ursulines). Like the Franciscans, she rejected the concept of a cloistered order in favor of social activism, insisting that her religious sisters live and work among the people. Because of the novelty of this idea, the pope did not approve her order until 1565, after her death. Although no formal vows were required, Merici's rule demanded poverty, chastity, and obedience. Each sister was allowed to live in her own home and work with her family and neighbors. Until her death in 1540, she served as superior general of the Ursulines. Her *Testament and Souvenirs* expresses her ideals, especially gentleness and concern for others. Her movement had more than doubled in size by 1536 and became the greatest teaching order for women.

Ignatius of Loyola and the Jesuit Order

The most influential of the new orders, the Society of Jesus, was founded by Ignatius of Loyola (1491–1556), the son of a Basque nobleman. A French cannonball shattered his right leg as he fought in Charles V's army at Pamplona in 1521. Profoundly influenced during his recovery by biographies of Francis and Dominic, he dedicated his life to serving the Virgin Mary. After a period of meditation in monasteries and study at the Universities of Alcala and Paris, Ignatius and a small band of disciples vowed to go to the Holy Land to convert Muslims. Finding the way to Palestine blocked by fighting between the Venetians and the Turks, they preached instead to the Italians. Ignatius' constitution for a new order, which reflected the trend toward centralized government in this period, was approved by Pope Paul III in 1540. Governed by a general directly responsible to the pope, the order was highly structured in order to supervise its active, mobile apostles. Although the traditional monastic vows were required, Jesuits were exempt from the typical duties of monks, such as reciting the church offices. The society's purpose was to advance and defend the Catholic faith.

The Jesuits concentrated on four activities. To persuade secular rulers to suppress Protestantism, they served as confessors and propagandists in Catholic courts. To keep the masses loyal to the Catholic faith, the Jesuits stressed confession, achieving some popularity because of their principle that there is "no sin without specific intent" to commit it. The society was particularly successful in its efforts to improve education, especially at the secondary level, where strict discipline and obedience to the church were emphasized. After surveying the educational facilities of the church and finding the secondary schools wanting, the Jesuits launched a program to build new schools (or "colleges"). By 1640 there were approximately 520 of these secondary schools in Europe, teaching some 150,000 boys. Up to half of the students were the children of peasants and artisans, who paid no tuition. The curriculum was based on the *Ratio studiorum* ("plan of studies"), which sought to combine the best of humanist teaching with traditional Catholic beliefs, and to instill in students a strong sense of obedience to the church. Instruction was in Latin and occasionally Greek but not the vernacular. Classical texts were edited to remove "pagan" elements, and explanatory notes interpreted everything from the Catholic perspective. To motivate learning, competition was encouraged: student against student, class against class, school against school. Jesuit schools were highly successful in providing church and state with educated officials and in helping to check the expansion of Protestantism.

Ignatius of Loyola, founder of the Society of Jesus. This is an engraved copy of a portrait originally painted in 1584 by Alonzo Sanchez Coello under the direction of a former associate of Ignatius. [SEF/Art Resource]

Finally, the Jesuits, determined to carry their message throughout the world, dispatched missions to Asia, Africa, and North and South America as well as to such European states as England and Poland. Their leading missionary, Francis Xavier (1506–1552), who preached in India, Ceylon, the Moluccas, and Japan, died half frozen and starved as he prepared to enter China. By 1557 the Jesuits had missions in the Congo, Morocco, and Ethiopia, and they also worked in Florida (1566) and Virginia (1570) as well as Brazil, Peru, and Mexico. Late in the century the Jesuit Matteo Ricci established the nucleus of a Christian church in China at Peking (see Chapter 17), and another Jesuit, Benedict de Goes, disguised as an Armenian merchant, crossed the Khyber Pass and traveled through Afghanistan and Turkistan to China. Between 1581 and 1712 no fewer than 376 Jesuits sailed for China, although a third of them died en route. The most influential Jesuit missionary to India, Roberto de Nobili (1577–1656), who was knowledgeable in Sanskrit and the Vedas, permitted his converts to retain some of their cultural traditions, such as the celebration of Hindu feasts, as long as they embraced the fundamental principles of Christianity. At times he even wore the clothing of a Brahman ascetic. This willingness to tolerate non-Western cultures coupled with their knowledge of Western science and technology helped make the Jesuits very effective missionaries.

The religious experience of Ignatius provided the basis for his *Spiritual Exercises*, a handbook to develop self-mastery and spiritual discipline. The *Exercises* call for a period of intense self-examination and meditation, at the culmination of which the disciple experiences a sense of unity with God through the surrender of the mind and will. In contrast to Protestantism, which stressed the importance of the individual conscience, Ignatius emphasized the church's authority: "To be right in everything, we ought always to hold that the white which I see, is black, if the Hierarchical Church so decides it."[11] This unqualified devotion and obedience to the church was at the heart of the Catholic revival.

The Council of Trent and the Inquisition

Catholic reformers were anxious for the papacy to convene a general council to deal with the Protestant challenge and make needed changes, but the popes, fearing a loss of their power and preoccupied with political concerns, were slow to act. Pope Paul III, a humanist who appointed a number of reformers to the College of Cardinals and even offered a cardinal's hat to Erasmus, finally yielded to pressure from Charles V and summoned a council. Convened in 1545 at Trent in northern Italy, it met intermittently until 1563 and was dominated by conservative Italians loyal to the papacy, although in the early stages there was also some sympathy for the Protestants. Neither the laity nor the lower clergy were allowed to vote at its sessions.

In matters of theology, the council firmly reasserted all the doctrines challenged by the Protestants. On the crucial issue of authority, it reaffirmed the importance of both Scripture and tradition, "with an equal pious devotion and reverence" to each. It recognized the Latin Vulgate as the official version of the Bible, with the church having the sole right to determine its "true sense and interpretation." The doctrine of salvation by faith and good works was asserted. All seven sacraments were acknowledged, and the wine in the Eucharist was reserved for the clergy alone. The council reaffirmed the central Catholic doctrine of transubstantiation—the belief that the substance of the bread and wine miraculously become the body and blood of Christ in the Eucharist—thereby rejecting the Lutheran doctrine that the bread and wine coexist with Christ's body and blood and the Reformed emphasis on the spiritual presence alone of Christ in the Lord's supper. It insisted on celibacy for the clergy, reaffirmed the invocation of saints and the veneration of relics, and refused to abolish indulgences and the doctrine of purgatory, despite their role in igniting the Protestant revolt. The theological interpretation of the Thomists, the disciples of Thomas Aquinas, prevailed, and the council therefore marked the triumph of the tradition-minded scholastics over the reforming Catholic humanists in the church.

In addition to settling the church's theology, the council reformed church discipline. Henceforth, every bishop, unless he had a papal dispensation, was required to live in

Obedience: The View of Ignatius

One of the dominant features of Ignatius of Loyola's thought was his emphasis on discipline and order. In this 1553 letter to Jesuits in Portugal, he returns to the theme of obedience that was fundamental to his Spiritual Exercises.

We may the more readily allow other religious orders to surpass us in the matter of fasting, watching, and other austerities in their manner of living, which all of them devoutly practice. . . . But in the purity and perfection of obedience and the surrender of our will and judgment, it is my warmest wish, beloved brethren, to see those who serve God in this Society signalize themselves. . . .

Make it a practice to recognize Christ our Lord in any superior you may have, and with all devotion, reverence and obey the Divine Majesty in him. This will seem the less surprising if you take note that St. Paul bids us obey our civil and pagan superiors as we would Christ, from whom flows all legitimate authority. . . .

He who wishes to make an absolutely complete offering of himself must in addition to his will include his understanding, which is the . . . highest degree of obedience. The result will be that he not only identifies his will with that of the superior, but even his thought, and submits his own judgment to the superior's judgment, to the extent that a devout will can bend the understanding.

Source: Ignatius of Loyola, *St. Ignatius' Own Story: As Told to Luis González de Cámara, with a Sampling of His Letters*, trans. W. J. Young (Chicago: Regnery, 1956), pp. 111–115 passim.

The Council of Trent in session, 1562–1563. The cardinals and papal legates sit prominently on the left, flanked by archbishops on their right. [British Museum]

his diocese and supervise his clergy. To improve the education of priests, a seminary was to be established in every diocese. Selling ecclesiastical offices and appointing relatives to church positions were condemned. Such reforms brought a new spirit of determination to the church in its struggle with Protestantism.

As Catholicism regained the offensive, the church launched the Roman Inquisition in 1542 at the urging of Loyola and Giampietro Cardinal Caraffa (1476–1559). As head of the Inquisition, Caraffa directed a commission of six cardinals empowered under Roman law to use torture, accept hearsay evidence, and keep the accused ignorant of the charges against them. The Inquisition was especially effective in stamping out Protestantism in Italy, but it also stifled intellectual life and even closed down the University of Modena in 1546. One of the Inquisition's most notable victims was the Dominican monk Giordano Bruno, who was burned at the stake in Rome in 1600 for unorthodox views about God and for teaching that the universe is infinite and contains innumerable suns and planets like our own (see Chapter 23). The Sacred Congregation of the Holy Office, which oversaw the Inquisition, also imposed its *Index of Prohibited Books*. Among the works it banned were Erasmus' writings, vernacular translations of the Bible, Boccaccio's *Decameron*, and Machiavelli's *The Prince*. To Protestants, the *Index* and the Inquisition were further proof that Catholicism was the church of the Antichrist, as Luther had argued.

The Counter-Reformation in England

Mary Tudor's accession to the English throne in 1553 provided the Catholics with a golden opportunity to recover an entire state that had been lost to Protestantism. Following the advice of her cousin Charles V to proceed slowly, she began by having Parliament repeal the religious legislation of Edward VI's reign. This action, coupled with the announcement of her impending marriage to Charles V's son, Philip of Spain, provoked a Protestant rebellion led by Sir Thomas Wyatt. After the revolt was crushed, Parliament repealed the antipapal legislation of Henry VIII, and in November 1554 England was officially reconciled to the Catholic church. Most of the lands previously confiscated from the church were not, however, returned. Prodded by the zealous queen, Parliament also revived a fifteenth-century law allowing the church to condemn and the state to burn heretics. Nearly 300 Protestants died in the flames, most of them laborers and more than 50 of them women. The most famous victim, former Archbishop Cranmer, had been coerced into retracting his Protestant beliefs, but as the fire was lit his courage returned: holding the hand that had signed the retraction in the flames, he reaffirmed his Protestantism. Accounts of the martyrs hardened Protestant commitments. The words of the martyred Hugh Latimer were prophetic: "We shall this day light such a candle, by God's grace, in England, as I trust shall never be put out."[12]

Faced with persecution, some 800 Protestants fled to the Continent, where most settled in such Reformed cities as Geneva, Zurich, Strasbourg, and Frankfurt. In exile, John Foxe collected material for his *Acts and Monuments*, an immensely popular history of Christian martyrs from the early church to his own day. Other exiles prepared a new edition of the Bible in English—the Geneva version (1560)—complete with marginal notes attacking Catholicism and advocating Calvinism. Until it was finally supplanted by the Authorized (King James) version in the next century, the Geneva Bible was probably the most influential book in England. Three other exiles—John Ponet, John Knox, and Christopher Goodman—made lasting contributions to political theory by advocating the revolutionary idea that common people have the right to overthrow tyrannical and idolatrous rulers, a theory also espoused by the Jesuits against Protestant sovereigns. Knox, however, reflected traditional thinking in *The First Blast of the Trumpet Against the Monstrous Regiment of Women*, which argued that women normally have no right to govern.

The Counter-Reformation failed in England largely because of the intense revulsion the burnings caused and also because Mary had no Catholic heir. The unpopularity of Mary's marriage to Philip, symbol of Catholic orthodoxy and Spanish imperialism, also contributed to the failure. If Mary had been able to give birth to the heir she desperately wanted, Catholicism might have regained its dominance in England, but the accession in 1558 of Elizabeth I, Mary's half sister and the daughter of Anne Boleyn, destroyed the English Counter-Reformation. The foundation of the Elizabethan religious settlement was an act of supremacy that made Elizabeth supreme governor of the church and an act of uniformity that required the use of the *Book of Common Prayer*. In 1563 the queen issued the Thirty-nine Articles, a revised version of Edward VI's doctrinal statement. England thus moved firmly into the Protestant orbit, followed by Scotland under the leadership of John Knox in 1560. Throughout Catholic Europe, however, Catholicism was successfully reinvigorated by its new orders—especially the Society of Jesus—and by the reforms of the Council of Trent.

The Reformation and the Jews

The repressive side of the Catholic Reformation had an immediate and negative impact on European Jews. They were less affected by the Protestant Reformation, in part because they had been evicted from Geneva in 1490, well before Calvin's era, as many had been from German cities. In the earliest stages of the Reformation, Luther expected the Jews to convert to his movement, but when they failed to do so, he became increasingly hostile toward them. Finally he insisted that the German princes deport them to Palestine or at least force them to return to agricultural occupations and prohibit them from practicing usury. Luther even demanded that Jewish books be confiscated and synagogues burned. In the course of the Catholic Refor-

An attack on the Jews of Frankfurt in 1614 illustrates recurring anti-Semitism in Europe. [Bildarchiv Foto Marburg]

mation the plight of the Jews similarly worsened as the hitherto tolerant papal position was reversed. Beginning in 1553, the Talmud was publicly burned in Italy, and two years later Caraffa, now Pope Paul IV, issued a bull ordering that the Jews be segregated in their own quarter (the "ghetto"), which was to be enclosed with high walls and, at night, locked gates. Jews were banned from the professions, prohibited from employing Christian servants, refused the right to own real estate, and forced to wear yellow hats as a badge. Although the Jews were not expelled from the Papal States, they could live only in cities such as Rome and Avignon under close supervision. The ghetto concept gradually spread until it became a hallmark of European Jewish life.

As the persecution of the Jews intensified in Reformation Europe, substantial numbers migrated to Poland, where rulers such as Sigismund I (1506–1548) tolerated minorities. The number of Jews in Poland rose from 50,000 in 1500 to 500,000 in 1650. In some of the bigger towns, such as Cracow and Lublin, large ghettos developed. Polish Jews generally enjoyed far greater choice of occupation than Jews in western Europe, and they were permitted substantial self-government in matters involving Jewish law.

The Witchcraft Craze

In striking contrast to the idealism that characterized much of the Protestant movement and the Catholic revival, the Reformation also unleashed a terrifying new wave of cruelty and popular hysteria. The age of spiritual renewal paradoxically gave birth to the most extensive period of witchcraft persecutions in Western history, sparked in large measure by the breakdown of religious unity. Belief in witches originated in ancient times, and the medieval church had organized those ideas into a systematic demonology. Witchcraft persecutions began in the context of the thirteenth-century crusades against the Albigensians and were revived by the papacy in 1484. Within two years a handbook, the *Malleus Maleficarum* ("The Hammer of the Wicked"), appeared with instructions for the discovery and interrogation of witches. Twenty-nine editions were published by 1669, testifying to the continuing interest in witchcraft.

Reformers and Witches

At the heart of the witchcraft craze was an unquestioned acceptance of the reality of the Devil and the pervasive effects of his influence in the world. Luther, for instance, claimed to have had repeated confrontations with Satan, many of which he described in anal terms. On one occasion he threatened to defecate in his pants and hang them around the Devil's neck to drive him away. In Protestant propaganda the pope became the personification of the Devil. Determined to win and hold the people's allegiance, the reformers intensified the belief in the widespread presence of satanic influence by repeatedly linking Catholicism with Satan. To Luther, monasticism was the Devil's "sweet latrine," and monks were attacked on the grounds that they had made a pact with Satan to obtain supernatural powers. For this reason, Luther believed that witches must be burned. In Geneva, Calvin appealed to the Bible (Exod. 22:18) as a divine sanction for the execution of witches. As Protestant preachers took their gospel of justification by faith into new areas of Europe, they carried with them demands for the persecution of witches. Lutherans introduced the witchcraft craze to Denmark, northern Germany, and Bavaria, and Calvinists carried it to Scotland and Transylvania.

Catholic persecution of witches had begun, as we have seen, even before the Reformation. Protestant attempts to associate the papacy with Satan were countered by Catholic charges that Luther and his colleagues were tools of the Devil. Catholics also drew on late medieval demonology to justify their accusations of witchcraft. The persecution of witches increased as the intensity of religious hostility provoked by Catholics and Protestants grew. Persecution was especially vicious in areas, such as the Rhineland and Bavaria, that were reconquered from the Protestants. Chief among the Jesuits in this work was Peter Canisius (1521–1597), whose activities ranged from popular evangelism and the founding of Jesuit colleges to demands for the trial of witches. Witch burnings also followed in the wake of the Catholic recapture of Poland and Flanders, but in areas where Catholic uniformity was not effectively challenged, such as Italy and Spain, reported incidents of witchcraft were apparently fewer. Burning witches—like burning heretics—became a means of purging society of evil, of purifying the community while the reformers cleansed the church.

Choosing the Victims

Although men as well as women could be accused as witches, most victims were female, probably because of the medieval notion that as the "weaker sex" they were more susceptible to the Devil's enticements. In England women were apparently accused more often than men because they were more likely to resist economic and social change. Of the 291 persons accused of witchcraft in the English county of Essex in the period 1560 to 1680, fully 268 were women. Although many of the victims were stereotypical older widows or spinsters, younger women were often persecuted on the Continent, and there are cases of men and children suffering as well. To extract confessions, torture was often used (except in England), which led to more accusations and executions. Convicted witches were normally burned on the Continent and

Women and Witchcraft

The popular handbook on witchcraft, Malleus Maleficarum, *attempted to explain why so many women were accused of being witches. These deprecatory views of female inferiority and frailty were widespread in this period.*

As for the first question, why a greater number of witches is found in the fragile feminine sex than among men; it is indeed a fact that it were idle to contradict, since it is accredited by actual experience. . . .

For some learned men propound this reason; that there are three things in nature, the Tongue, an Ecclesiastic, and a Woman, which know no moderation in goodness or vice; and when they exceed the bounds of their condition they reach the greatest heights and the lowest depths of goodness and vice. . . .

Others again have propounded other reasons why there are more superstitious women found than men. And the first is, that they are more credulous; and since the chief aim of the devil is to corrupt faith, therefore he rather attacks them. . . .

The second reason is, that women are naturally more impressionable, and more ready to receive the influence of a disembodied spirit; and that when they use this quality well they are very good, but when they use it ill they are very evil.

The third reason is that they have slippery tongues, and are unable to conceal from their fellow-women those things which by evil arts they know; and, since they are weak, they find an easy and secret manner of vindicating themselves by witchcraft. . . .

To conclude. All witchcraft comes from carnal lust, which is in women insatiable.

Source: M. Summers, trans., *Malleus Maleficarum* (London: Rodker, 1928), pp. 41–44, 47.

hanged in England. During the course of the witchcraft hysteria, from the mid-sixteenth to the mid-seventeenth century, the number of victims probably reached 30,000. Only as religious passions waned, social upheaval receded, and a new spirit of rationalism took hold in the mid-1600s did the craze die down.

Although the witchcraft trials were in large measure due to the breakdown of religious unity, religion alone cannot account for the full force of the persecutions. The social and economic changes that occurred in the West beginning in the fifteenth century created enormous tension, adding to the uncertainties and hostility resulting from the religious upheavals. A growing population, increasing poverty, devastating crop failures, and a rising crime rate made many people fearful and insecure. They continued to find scapegoats for their problems in social nonconformists—witches, Jews, and homosexuals, all of whom were persecuted. The link between them was sometimes explicit: Jews, for instance, were often accused of witchcraft. The witchcraft craze was a result of credulity and uncertainty produced by widespread socioeconomic changes and group jealousies as well as passionate religious rivalries.

The Cultural Impact of the Reformation

Protestantism had a significant impact on the arts in the areas it dominated, whereas the effects of the Catholic revival on culture were not generally visible until the late sixteenth century. Because Protestantism, especially the Reformed tradition, adopted a negative attitude toward the use of images and the veneration of saints, artists in Protestant regions found virtually no demand for religious statues and little interest in paintings for churches. They adapted by catering to the growing secular market for paintings and providing artwork for the burgeoning publishing industry. Similarly, although architects initially were not needed by Protestant leaders, who took over their churches from the Catholics, they found an outlet for their talents by designing palatial residences for princes and nobles. Henry VIII's palace at Hampton Court and Francis I's château at Chambord, both of which reflected the growth of the centralized state, provided further impetus for such building. The Protestant rejection of the mass and the general simplification of the church service created a demand for suitable music, particularly hymns and psalm settings. The artistic impact of the Reformation on the Catholic church was more delayed, but its influence was strongly felt in the revival of the church after the Council of Trent and in the seventeenth-century movement known as the Baroque (see Chapter 23).

Grünewald, Dürer, and Holbein

The dilemma that the Reformation posed for the artist is illustrated by the career of Matthias Grünewald (c. 1460–1528), a German who became court painter for the archbishop of Mainz. A man of many talents in the Renaissance tradition, he supervised the rebuilding of the archbishop's castle. His major work, an altarpiece for the monastic church at Isenheim in Alsace, was finished on the eve of the Reformation. The massive altarpiece, with its flanking panels closed, depicts the anguish of Christ on the cross, his body discolored, his feet blackened, and his flesh lacerated. With the panels opened, however, the inner pane reveals the triumphant resurrected Christ bathed in the glow of an eerie red light. Other altar paintings followed for Catholic patrons. Yet Grünewald himself became a Lutheran, and in 1525 he participated in the Peasants' Revolt. The archbishop of Mainz dismissed him for his beliefs in 1526, and he spent his last years in Protestant Saxony. Only his skills as an artist and his willingness to paint traditional altarpieces had enabled him to obtain Catholic patronage despite his Lutheran sympathies.

Born in the German city of Nuremberg, Albrecht Dürer (1471–1528) became the greatest artist of the German Renaissance. Twice he went to Italy, bringing back to Germany an understanding of Renaissance ideals and techniques. He was one of the first non-Italian artists to acquire an international reputation and the first northern artist to provide a rich account of his life through self-portraits, personal correspondence, and a diary. In addition to his paintings, he produced superb woodcuts and engravings; his illustrations for books and his sale of prints to ordinary folk helped make him a wealthy man. His woodcut *The Four Horsemen of the Apocalypse,* done near the turn of the century, reflects the popular apocalyptic spirit of northern Europe.

A Christian humanist in the early 1500s, Dürer captured the spirit of his friend Erasmus' *Handbook of a Christian Knight* in his engraving of a *Knight, Death, and the Devil.* His own spiritual doubts were resolved when he embraced Lutheranism: "If God helps me to meet Martin Luther," he wrote in 1520, "I shall carefully draw his portrait and engrave it on copper as a lasting remembrance of this Christian who helped me out of great distress."[13] After his conversion, his style became more austere. His engraving of the Last Supper and his painting of four apostles (John, Peter, Paul, and Mark) reveal the simple style of his Protestant years. Quotations from Luther's German New Testament appear on the twin frames of *The Four Apostles.* Like Grünewald, Dürer continued to accept commissions from Catholic patrons after his conversion, although he hoped to establish a distinctively Protestant tradition of monumental art.

Albrecht Durer's engraving *Knight, Death, and the Devil* (1513) reflects the confidence of humanists in the ability of the Christian faith to triumph over the enemies of mankind. [Museum of Fine Arts, Boston, Harvey D. Parker Fund]

The son of an Augsburg painter, Hans Holbein the Younger (1497–1543) achieved prominence as the greatest portrait painter of the sixteenth century. Like Dürer, he was a friend of Erasmus (whose portrait is one of Holbein's masterpieces) as well as a book illustrator. Holbein settled in Basel, but when the Protestant reform created a hostile atmosphere for artists there, Erasmus recommended him to Sir Thomas More in England. Henry VIII commissioned some of his most famous portraits, including those of the king himself and of three of his six wives, Anne Boleyn, Jane Seymour, and Anne of Cleves. Among Holbein's most fascinating works are 41 woodcuts depicting the late medieval "dance of death" and a series of drawings satirizing abuses in the Catholic church. Holbein died of the plague in 1543, but his influence on English portraiture continued for decades.

Music and the Reformation

Although Protestant reformers repudiated the ornate polyphonic masses of the late medieval period, they retained music in the worship service. To Luther, music was "an endowment and a gift of God" that made people cheerful and chased away the Devil. Luther himself composed at least eight hymns, including the still popular "A Mighty Fortress Is Our God," and wrote sacred texts for German folk tunes. A Lutheran hymnal appeared in 1524. Although Zwingli's radical liturgical reform led to the destruction of church organs in Zurich, the year after his death a new organ was built in the cathedral, and congregational singing was introduced. In Geneva, Calvin approved of psalm singing, and the practice quickly spread throughout the Reformed churches. One of the main objections to traditional religious music was the difficulty of understanding the words, which prompted English reformers in the 1560s to condemn most choral music. To most people, however, the simplification of religious music was a matter of regret:

What shall we now do at church, since all the saints are taken away, since all the goodly sights we were wont to have, are gone, since we cannot hear the . . . chanting, and playing upon the organs, that we could before?[14]

The Catholics too were concerned that elaborate musical compositions were obscuring the sacred texts. The Council of Trent enacted regulations designed to encourage simplicity as well as to ban the use of secular themes in religious works. Polyphony, however, was not prohibited, so long as the words of the mass could be clearly understood. After the council, the Roman Curia urged an end to the use of lay singers as well as all instruments except the organ in religious services, but compliance was never complete. The challenge to blend simplicity with musical beauty was brilliantly met in the masses and motets, or sacred compositions, of the Italian composer Giovanni Palestrina (c. 1525–1594), whose works, often sung by unaccompanied choirs, manifest a sense of monumental grandeur. His work reflected the achievements of the Renaissance composers and remained the model for Catholic devotional writers down to the nineteenth century.

The changes in art and music that occurred in the first half of the sixteenth century reflect the effects of the religious convulsions that shook Europe. Henceforth the West was permanently divided in its religious beliefs and institutions. Yet out of that diversity eventually came the demands for freedom of religion and thought that are now fundamental to the concept of liberty. In other ways, too, the Reformation made significant contributions to the quality of Western life. Better education and improved care for the needy and the helpless were direct fruits of Protestant and Catholic idealism. But there was a dark side to the Reformation era, manifested in the religious wars to which the bellicose attitudes of Protestant and Catholic alike led. For more than a century the hostilities rooted in rival religious convictions parodied the love that was at the core of Christian teaching. This aspect of the Reformation was also reflected in brutal religious persecutions and in witchcraft trials and burnings. The Reformation era dramatically pitted the authority of religious institutions against the claims of individual conscience. Unresolved in the sixteenth century, this clash remained a source of tension well into modern times. The fervency of the religious debate had global implications as well, particularly as Catholic missionaries carried their message to Asia, Africa, and the Americas.

Notes

1. Desiderius Erasmus, "The Paraclesis," in *Christian Humanism and the Reformation: Selected Writings*, ed. J. C. Olin (New York: Harper & Row, 1965), p. 97.
2. *The Correspondence of Erasmus*, trans. R. A. B. Mynors and D. F. S. Thompson, vol. 4 (Toronto: University of Toronto Press, 1977), p. 261.
3. Sir Thomas More, *Utopia*, trans. and ed. R. M. Adams (New York: Norton, 1975), p. 80.
4. R. H. Bainton, *Here I Stand: A Life of Martin Luther* (New York: Abingdon-Cokesbury, 1950), p. 78.
5. Martin Luther, "The Babylonian Captivity of the Church," in *Three Treatises* (Philadelphia: Muhlenberg Press, 1960), p. 248.
6. V. H. H. Green, *Luther and the Reformation* (New York: Capricorn Books, 1964), p. 98.
7. G. R. Potter, *Huldrych Zwingli* (London: Arnold, 1978), p. 24.
8. John Calvin, *Institutes of the Christian Religion*, ed. J. T. McNeill, trans. F. L. Battles, vol. 2. (Philadelphia: Westminster Press, 1960), pp. 922–923.
9. Sebastian Castellio, "Contra libellum Calvini," in *Concerning Heretics*, ed. R. H. Bainton (New York: Columbia University Press, 1935), p. 271.
10. C. Wriothesley, *A Chronicle of England During the Reigns of*

the Tudors, from A.D. *1485 to 1559*, vol. 2, ed. W. D. Hamilton (London: Camden Society, 1877), p. 91.

11. *The Spiritual Exercises of St. Ignatius*, trans. E. Mullan, ed. D. L. Fleming (St. Louis: Institute of Jesuit Sources, 1978), p. 234.
12. D. M. Loades, *The Oxford Martyrs* (London: Batsford, 1970), p. 220.
13. W. Strauss, ed., *The Complete Drawings of Albrecht Dürer*, vol. 4 (New York: Abaris Books, 1974), p. 1905.
14. R. L. Greaves, *Society and Religion in Elizabethan England* (Minneapolis: University of Minnesota Press, 1981), p. 458.

Suggestions for Further Reading

Bainton, R. H. *Erasmus of Christendom*. New York: Scribner, 1969.

——. *Here I Stand: A Life of Martin Luther*. New York: Abingdon-Cokesbury, 1950.

——. *Women of the Reformation in Germany and Italy*. Minneapolis: Augsburg, 1971.

Benesch, O. *The Art of the Renaissance in Northern Europe: Its Relation to the Contemporary Spiritual and Intellectual Movements*, rev. ed. London: Phaidon, 1965.

Blaisdell, C. J. "The Matrix of Reform: Women in the Lutheran and Calvinist Movements," in *Triumph over Silence: Women in Protestant History*, ed. R. L. Greaves. Westport, Conn.: Greenwood Press, 1985.

Bossy, J. *Christianity in the West, 1400–1700*. New York: Oxford University Press, 1985.

Cohn, N. *The Pursuit of the Millennium*, rev. ed. New York: Oxford University Press, 1970.

Dickens, A. G. *The English Reformation*. London: Batsford, 1964.

Edwards, M. *Luther's Last Battles*. Ithaca, N.Y.: Cornell University Press, 1983.

Elton, G. R. *Reformation Europe, 1517–1559*. New York: Harper & Row, 1963.

Erikson, E. H. *Young Man Luther: A Study in Psychoanalysis and History*. New York: Norton, 1962.

Evennett, H. O. *The Spirit of the Counter-Reformation*. Notre Dame, Ind.: Notre Dame University Press, 1970.

Gäbler, U. *Huldrych Zwingli: His Life and Work*, trans. R. Gritsch. Philadelphia: Fortress Press, 1986.

Ginzburg, C. *The Night Battles: Witchcraft and Agrarian Cults in the Sixteenth and Seventeenth Centuries*, trans. J. Tedeschi and A. Tedeschi. London: Routledge & Kegan Paul, 1983.

Grimm, H. *The Reformation Era, 1500–1650*, 2d ed. New York: Macmillan, 1965.

Ives, E. W. *Anne Boleyn*. Oxford: Blackwell, 1986.

Jensen, D. *Reformation Europe: Age of Reform and Revolution*. Lexington, Mass.: D.C. Heath, 1981.

Kingdon, R. M., ed. *Transition and Revolution: Problems and Issues of European Renaissance and Reformation History*. Minneapolis: Burgess, 1974.

MacFarlane, A. *Witchcraft in Tudor and Stuart England: A Regional and Comparative Study*. London: Routledge & Kegan Paul, 1970.

McGrath, A. E. *The Intellectual Origins of the European Reformation*. Oxford: Basil Blackwell, 1987.

Midelfort, H. C. E. *Witch Hunting in Southwestern Germany, 1562–1684: The Social and Intellectual Foundation*. Stanford, Calif.: Stanford University Press, 1972.

Monter, E. W. *Calvin's Geneva*. New York: Wiley, 1967.

——. "Women in the Age of Reformation, " in *Becoming Visible: Women in European History*, ed. R. Bridenthal and C. Koonz. Boston: Houghton Mifflin, 1987.

Oberman, H. *The Roots of Anti-Semitism in the Age of Renaissance and Reformation*, trans. J. I. Porter. Philadelphia: Fortress Press, 1984.

O'Connell, M. R. *The Counter-Reformation, 1559–1610*. New York: Harper & Row, 1974.

Ozment, S. E. *The Age of Reform (1250–1550): An Intellectual and Religious History of Late Medieval and Reformation Europe*. New Haven, Conn.: Yale University Press, 1980.

——. *The Reformation in the Cities: The Appeal of Protestantism to Sixteenth-Century Germany and Switzerland*. New Haven, Conn.: Yale University Press, 1975.

Potter, G. R. *Zwingli*. Cambridge: Cambridge University Press, 1976.

Russell, P. A. *Lay Theology in the Reformation: Popular Pamphleteers in Southwest Germany, 1521–1525*. Cambridge: Cambridge University Press, 1986.

Scarisbrick, J. J. *The Reformation and the English People*. Oxford: Basil Blackwell, 1984.

Skinner, Q. *The Foundations of Modern Political Thought*, Vol. 2: *The Age of Reformation*. Cambridge: Cambridge University Press, 1978.

Spitz, L. *The Religious Renaissance of the German Humanists*. Cambridge, Mass.: Harvard University Press, 1963.

Sprunger, K. "God's Powerful Army of the Weak: Anabaptist Women of the Radical Reformation," in *Triumph over Silence: Women in Protestant History*, ed. R. L. Greaves. Westport, Conn.: Greenwood Press, 1985.

Strauss, G. *Luther's House of Learning: The Indoctrination of the Young in the German Reformation*. Baltimore: Johns Hopkins University Press, 1978.

Wendel, F. *Calvin: The Origins and Development of His Religious Thought*, trans. P. Mairet. London: Collins, 1963.

Williams, G. H. *The Radical Reformation*. Philadelphia: Westminster Press, 1962.

CHAPTER · 17

The Age of European Discovery

The century and a half from 1450 to 1600 was one of the most extraordinary periods in Western history. The religious convulsions that shattered Christian unity and helped spur a global missionary effort occurred in the context of daring voyages of exploration and the beginnings of extensive trade that laid the foundation for a world economy. By 1450 the West, which had long lagged behind the more culturally and technologically sophisticated Indians and East Asians, developed the technological innovations, forms of commercial organization, and spiritual and materialistic ideals that enabled it to dominate much of the world by the nineteenth century. Mastery of the high seas was the key to global expansion, and the financial support and incentives for this endeavor were made possible by the development of merchant capitalism and the increasing centralization of European states.

The greatest of the merchant-capitalists was Jakob Fugger of Augsburg, shown here with his chief accountant in 1519. The signs on the wall indicate Fugger branches in such cities as Lisbon, Cracow, Rome, and Innsbruck. [Herzog Anton Ulrich-Museum, Brunswick, Federal Republic of Germany]

Europe on the Eve of Exploration

By the mid-fifteenth century Europe was on the road to recovery after the demographic catastrophe caused by the Black Death. One of the most crucial elements in the revival was a new and rapid growth in population. Demographers are still analyzing evidence, but the broad outlines of this growth are now well established. Between 1460 and 1620 the population of Europe nearly doubled, to approximately 100 million people. In some places, particularly the cities of western Europe, the rise was even sharper. Antwerp grew from 20,000 in 1440 to 100,000 in 1560, and Rome doubled its population, also to 100,000, between 1526 and 1600. This demographic growth increased the pressure on land and food as demand outstripped supply, thus spurring inflation while preventing many Europeans from rising above the subsistence level. Demographic recovery also meant the end of the period of improved conditions for the peasantry brought on by the Black Death in the mid-1300s. Simultaneously, however, the rising population provided not only an abundant labor supply but also economic incentives for agricultural improvements, commercial expansion, and overseas exploration and settlement. Population growth thus provided much of the impetus for economic expansion.

Land Tenures and Agricultural Development

The decimation of the population by the Black Death and, in France, the Hundred Years' War (1337–1453) resulted in a shortage of peasant labor and a decrease in the amount of land under cultivation. For many peasants in western Europe the resulting demand for their services made it possible to escape the bonds of serfdom, trading the security of the old system for freedom and its attendant risks. Those who rented lands might profit by their industry, but they were also subject to potentially ruinous increases in rent. Whether the landlord or the tenant prospered was normally determined by the terms on which the land was held, as well as by tax obligations. Long-term leases, which some English peasants enjoyed, were usually beneficial to the holders. Tenants in parts of France and western Germany whose tenure could be inherited might likewise prosper, for they were free to farm the land and sell the produce as they saw fit in return for a fixed payment to their landlords. In parts of Italy and France, short-term leases, which required the peasants to pay a fixed share of their crops to landlords, were common and helped the latter keep pace with rising food costs. Peasants without secure tenure, however, faced a troubled future in which the value of their services was as uncertain as their ability to continue working the land. Such tenants were at the mercy of landlords, who had to choose between opportunities for economic advancement and traditional obligations for their tenants' welfare.

Landed aristocrats whose tenants could inherit tenure or had long-term leases suffered a loss in real income as prices rose faster than rents. The lesser aristocracy often reacted by supporting wars and overseas conquest because of the prospect of new lands and financial gain. When the reconquest of the Iberian peninsula from the Moors was completed in 1492, the interest of the Spanish hidalgos, or lesser nobles, shifted to the New World. Other aristocrats, especially in France and England, shored up their finances by forming strategic alliances—typically by marriage—with rising merchant families, who shared their wealth in return for social prestige. Although some of the old nobility bitterly resented this infusion of new blood into their ranks, those who formed such alliances brought the landed elite into a closer relationship with the emerging world of overseas exploration and capitalistic investment.

Landlords whose tenants did not enjoy secure tenure had a wider range of options. This was especially the case in Spain, Portugal, southern Italy, parts of England, eastern Germany, and Poland. Some lords were content simply to raise rents at will—"rack-renters," they were called by bitter peasants and social critics. The more enterprising, however, took advantage of their power to embark on new economic ventures. In some instances this meant enclosing their lands, evicting their tenants, and converting from tillage to the pasturing of sheep. More often it meant an end to the old open-field system of farming, in which land was divided into strips and production was largely for the local market, in favor of larger, more productive farms that produced commercially for the wider marketplace. These new farms required the employment of agricultural hands, usually for subsistence wages, in place of peasants with a degree of personal attachment in the land. In many places agriculture thus became a commercial endeavor. This pattern was not equally distributed. It occurred often in England but rarely in Spain, where most hidalgos thought anything pertaining to business was beneath their dignity as warriors. In eastern Germany, Poland, and Russia landlords took advantage of western Europe's inability to feed itself by enclosing their lands in order to produce large quantities of grain for export. Unlike the English, they did not evict their peasants but forced them into gradual serfdom. The extent of western Europe's inability to feed itself in the face of rising population is amply demonstrated by the fact that approximately 6 million tons of grain had to be imported from the Baltic region between the mid-1500s and the mid-1600s.

The changes in the period from 1450 to 1600 caused substantial agrarian unrest both in the English Midlands and eastern Europe, where large-scale commercial agriculture became commonplace, and throughout western Europe, where most peasants worked small plots and often worried about the security of their holdings. The Peasants' Revolt in 1524–1525, which Martin Luther denounced, was but one manifestation of this discontent. Commercial farming, however, was essential if the expanding population, particularly in the towns, was to be fed from the mid-sixteenth century on.

Commercial Innovation and Expansion

The economic depression that gripped Europe in the fourteenth and early fifteenth centuries had been beneficial to the towns in certain respects. Despite urban riots, declining production caused by the drop in population, and war, the price of manufactured goods and wages for skilled workers generally rose while the cost of grain declined, thus increasing overall urban prosperity.

Merchants adapted to the new conditions by developing stronger organizations, diversifying their activities, and improving business procedures. Temporary partnerships, neither efficient nor conducive to expansion, were replaced by permanent companies, often formed around prominent families such as the Medici in Florence or the Fuggers in Augsburg. These firms were vulnerable during recessions when borrowers defaulted on their loans. Businessmen who survived learned to break up their firms into several independent partnerships. The importance of diversification was also recognized, as merchants engaged in a combination of commerce, banking, manufacturing, and sometimes overseas trade. Diversification encouraged the development of new industries: linens in Cambrai, iron in Liège, and weapons in Milan, among others. Economic growth was enhanced by more widespread use of double-entry bookkeeping, which uses parallel columns to balance credits and debits, and bills of exchange, which facilitate the transfer of large sums of money without risking the shipment of currency or bullion. These developments helped provide the capital accumulation that made exploration and the growth of overseas trade possible.

No family better illustrates the success of the new merchants than the Fuggers of Augsburg. By the time Jakob Fugger became a merchant in 1478, the family had been conducting business in the city for a century, mostly trading in the spices and silks that came through Venice. Jakob Fugger branched out into banking and mining, acquiring virtual control of the silver mines in the Tirol through his loans to the Habsburg emperors Maximilian I and Charles V. His company also dominated the copper supply in Europe by its acquisition of Hungarian mines and the con-

Fugger Money: The Price of Power

Merchants who loaned money to princes often ran a considerable risk, but in addition to interest on loans they might acquire valuable favors or monopolies. When, in April 1523, Jakob Fugger had to press the emperor Charles V to repay his debts, the Habsburg ruler was reminded that he owed his crown at least in part to Fugger money.

Your Imperial Majesty doubtless knows how I and my kinsmen have ever hitherto been disposed to serve the House of Austria in all loyalty to the furtherance of its well-being and prosperity; wherefore, in order to be pleasing to your Majesty's grandsire, the late Emperor Maximilian, and to gain for your Majesty the Roman crown, we have held ourselves bounden to engage ourselves towards divers princes who placed their trust and reliance upon myself and perchance on no man besides. We have, moreover, advanced to your Majesty's agents for the same end a great sum of money, of which we ourselves have had to raise a large part from our friends. It is well known that your Imperial Majesty could not have gained the Roman crown save with mine aid, and I can prove the same by the writings of your Majesty's agents given by their own hands. In this matter I have not studied mine own profit. For had I left the House of Austria and had been minded to further France, I had obtained much money and property, such as was then offered to me. How grave a disadvantage had in this case accrued to your Majesty and the House of Austria, your Majesty's royal mind well knoweth.

Source: R. Ehrenberg, *Capital and Finance in the Age of the Renaissance: A Study of the Fuggers and Their Connections,* trans. H. M. Lucas (New York: Harcourt, Brace, n.d.), p. 80.

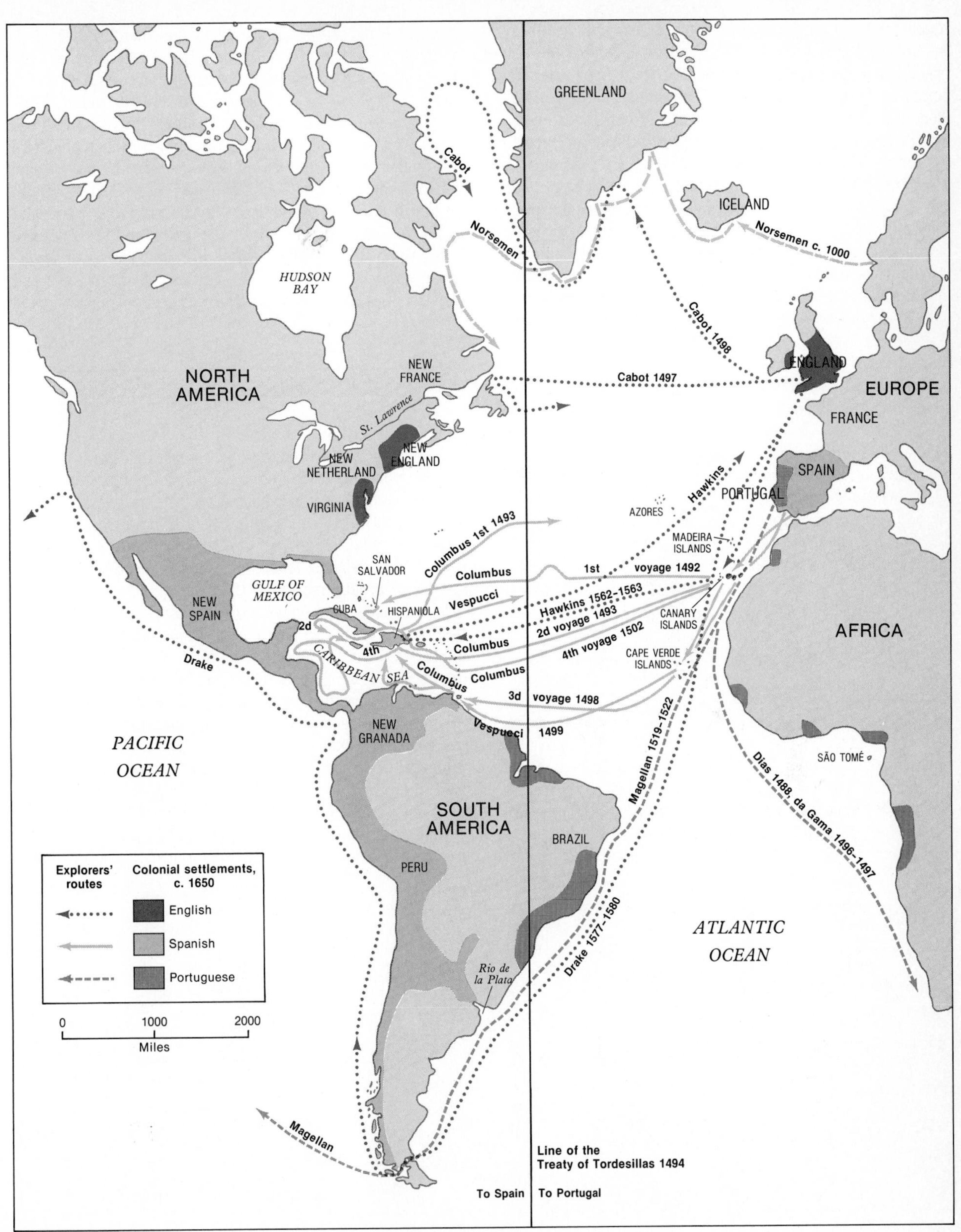
GREENLAND
ICELAND
Cabot
Norsemen
Norsemen c. 1000
HUDSON BAY
Cabot 1498
ENGLAND
Cabot 1497
EUROPE
FRANCE
NORTH AMERICA
NEW FRANCE
St. Lawrence
NEW ENGLAND
NEW NETHERLAND
VIRGINIA
SPAIN
PORTUGAL
Hawkins
AZORES
MADEIRA ISLANDS
Columbus 1st 1493
SAN SALVADOR
GULF OF MEXICO
NEW SPAIN
CUBA
HISPANIOLA
Columbus
1st voyage 1492
Vespucci
Hawkins 1562–1563
2d voyage 1493
4th voyage 1502
CANARY ISLANDS
CAPE VERDE ISLANDS
AFRICA
2d
4th
CARIBBEAN SEA
Columbus
Columbus
Columbus
3d voyage 1498
Vespucci 1499
Drake
NEW GRANADA
PACIFIC OCEAN
SÃO TOMÉ
Magellan 1519–1522
Dias 1488, da Gama 1496–1497
SOUTH AMERICA
BRAZIL
PERU
Explorers' routes
Colonial settlements, c. 1650
English
Spanish
Portuguese
0
1000
2000
Miles
Drake 1577–1580
Rio de la Plata
ATLANTIC OCEAN
Magellan
Line of the Treaty of Tordesillas 1494
To Spain
To Portugal

17.1 Voyages of Exploration to the Americas

tuguese as it attempted to sail back across the Pacific to Mexico. In this fashion Magellan's crew accomplished the first circumnavigation of the globe. It took three years to complete and imposed terrible hardships on the crews, who suffered from scurvy and were forced to eat rats, sawdust, and hides on the long passage across the Pacific.

For a time Spanish hopes to dominate the Moluccas quickened, but it soon became apparent that the Spaniards were no match for the Portuguese in the East. In 1529 the emperor Charles V, preoccupied by his wars with the French, sold Spain's rights in the Moluccas to Portugal. By that time Spain already had more than it could manage in America, although it retained the Philippines and began a 300-year link between Manila and its New World empire centered in Mexico. The Manila galleon, as it was called, carried yearly shipments of Mexican and Peruvian silver from Acapulco to Manila and Chinese silk, lacquer, and porcelain back to both New and Old Spain. Manila grew as an entrepôt, or intermediary center, for trade with China, and New World silver flowed into the Chinese market with major consequences for the Ming and Ch'ing dynasty economy and its growing commercialization. New World crops, especially potatoes and maize, also entered China via Manila and helped make possible subsequent major increases in population.

Westerners in Asia and Africa

Portuguese and later Dutch settlements in Africa were incidental to the drive into Asia but served as way stations and provisioning bases along the sea route. Although the Portuguese extended the slave trade from West Africa to Brazil and sought a few other African goods, including gold, they did not penetrate inland and their coastal bases were few and scattered. Access to the interior was made more difficult by mangrove swamps, rain forests, or steep cliffs as well as by hostile African states, and the few Portuguese settlements were confined to tiny footholds on the coast or offshore islands. Their primary objective was indicated by the names they gave to their two main African bases, Algoa Bay ("to Goa," now Port Elizabeth in South Africa) and Delagoa Bay ("from Goa," now Maputo in Mozambique). Both names were derived from Goa, the administrative center of Portugal's Asian enterprise established in 1510 on the west coast of India and for which the African bases were to serve as provisioning stops.

The Portuguese and Africa

The gold, and later the slaves, that the Portuguese obtained from scattered parts of the coasts of West and East Africa were important sources of profit, but the Portuguese established permanent African bases only in Angola on the southwest coast and at Algoa and Delagoa. In addition, they seized and occupied Madeira, the Azores, the Cape Verde Islands, and a few other offshore bases. Their presence greatly increased the slave trade, already thriving in Africa, by opening additional markets, especially in the New World. The Portuguese impact on several African societies went far beyond their relatively small power and numbers. They tried repeatedly to extend their power inland and on some occasions sacked and burned African towns or cities and pillaged overland trade routes. Although they could occasionally raid the interior, the Portuguese lacked the means for establishing control there, and their chief objective remained the Indies.

Cape Verde, where the city of Dakar now stands, was reached only after traversing the long, waterless desert coast of the northwest. Farther south, the kingdoms of

Situated on the Tagus River, Lisbon became one of Europe's busiest ports in the sixteenth century because of Portugal's trade with Africa and Asia. During the course of the century, however, much of this trade shifted to Antwerp. [Granger Collection]

Ghana and Benin offered trade at coastal ports, although the main commodities, gold and slaves, came from farther inland. Much of the interior of West Africa was controlled by the empire of Mali, centered at Timbuktu on the upper Niger River. Gold and slaves moved from Timbuktu north across the great desert by camel caravans to the Mediterranean. The arrival of the Portuguese at the coast marked a shift of trade routes toward West African ports, from which European and New World markets could be reached more easily and cheaply. Timbuktu and the Mali empire slowly declined as the coastal centers of trade grew more rapidly in the centuries following the start of European expansion.

Persisting southward in their long search for a sea route to the Indies, the Portuguese found the dense rain forests of the Congo region impossible to penetrate. Inland navigation on the great river was blocked by falls and rapids where the Congo tumbles off the steep escarpment that rises only a few miles from the coast around nearly the whole of Africa. The same problem hampered access from the east coast. Along the Congo coast, ivory and slaves were available to traders, but the coastal cultures were less highly developed than many of those inland, of which the Portuguese learned little except that they were the source of most of the trade goods. The coasts of Angola and Southwest Africa were part of the great southern desert and thus somewhat easier to penetrate, but also less rewarding. Having come this far south along the coast, however, the Portuguese badly needed a base for supply and refitting; they finally established one at Luanda in Angola by 1530. Once Bartholomeu Dias had made it around the Cape of Good Hope in 1488 and was followed a decade later by Vasco da Gama, the road to the Indies lay open and the bases in Mozambique on the east coast were more useful. The Portuguese traded and raided northward along the East African coast and for a time even tried to control Mombasa in what is now Kenya. Somali resistance, as well as competition and opposition from the long-established Arab traders in coastal East Africa, soon ejected the Portuguese except as traders. The Europeans were resented for their arrogance and aggressiveness. Their efforts to move inland from Mozambique and to open the area to Jesuit missionaries were ultimately repelled by the African kingdom of Vakaranga, although the Europeans continued to buy slaves and other goods on the coast.

Traders in Asia

For over two centuries after Europeans made contact with Asia by sea they remained insignificant on the Asian scene, a handful of people the natives dismissed as barbarians. At sea and along the Asian coasts they had the upper hand, but their power on land extended little beyond the range of their naval guns. The Portuguese and later the Dutch built a strong position in the spice trade, but in Asian commerce as a whole, even its seaborne component, their role was minor. They bought spices and a few other goods in preexisting markets at established ports, such as Calicut, where they had already been collected by Asian traders, and then hauled them to Europe. The Portuguese never and the Dutch only much later had any involvement in production, and both continued to compete as traders with numerous Chinese, Indian, Southeast Asian, and Arab entrepreneurs, who did the bulk of the assembly. Only in the transporting of Asian goods to Europe did they have a monopoly, and there the Portuguese in time faced intense competition from the Dutch and the English (see Chapter 18). As if to emphasize their role as ocean carriers with their improved ships for long voyages, the Portuguese developed a highly profitable trade between China and Japan, carrying Chinese silks and porcelains (and some Southeast Asian spices) from the Canton area to Nagasaki in southwestern Japan and bringing back Japanese silver and copper for China. They, and later the English, also found profit in hauling Southeast Asian and Chinese goods to India and exchanging them for Indian cottons, which had an even larger and more eager market in Europe.

Recognizing their weakness on land or in trade competition with Asian and Arab merchants, Europeans built on their strength at sea by occupying and fortifying coastal footholds at key points along the sea routes. Ideally these were in areas on the fringes of the great Asian empires or where the local power was weak or could be persuaded to grant privileges in return for favors. The latter often included Western naval help against pirates, rebels, or small rival states. The Portuguese seized Goa on the Indian west coast in 1510 and soon made it into their major Asian base. The small area around the city was not then part of any powerful Indian state. The Portuguese saw they had little hope of controlling the larger ports farther south, such as Calicut, although they did establish some smaller bases elsewhere on the Malabar coast in the west. From Goa, however, their ships could patrol the entire coast and essentially control Indian Ocean trade. Goa was a logical choice as the administrative center of the extensive Portuguese trade network farther east, and it prospered so much on the profits of that trade that it became known as "Golden Goa."

A commercial empire stretching another 6,000 miles east by sea, through all of Southeast Asia (except the Philippines) and on to China and Japan, required other bases too. The most obvious control points over the sea lanes eastward from India were Colombo in Ceylon (now Sri Lanka) and Malacca in Malaya. The Palk Strait between India and Ceylon was too shallow for shipping, and the route around Sumatra and through the Sunda Strait between Sumatra and Java was longer and plagued by reefs and currents, with no safe harbors along the Sumatran west coast. Traffic to and from East Asia was therefore funneled through the Straits of Malacca. The Portuguese seized the town of Malacca, commanding the straits, in 1511, but Malaya at that period was thinly settled and relatively unproductive. Malacca's role was primarily stra-

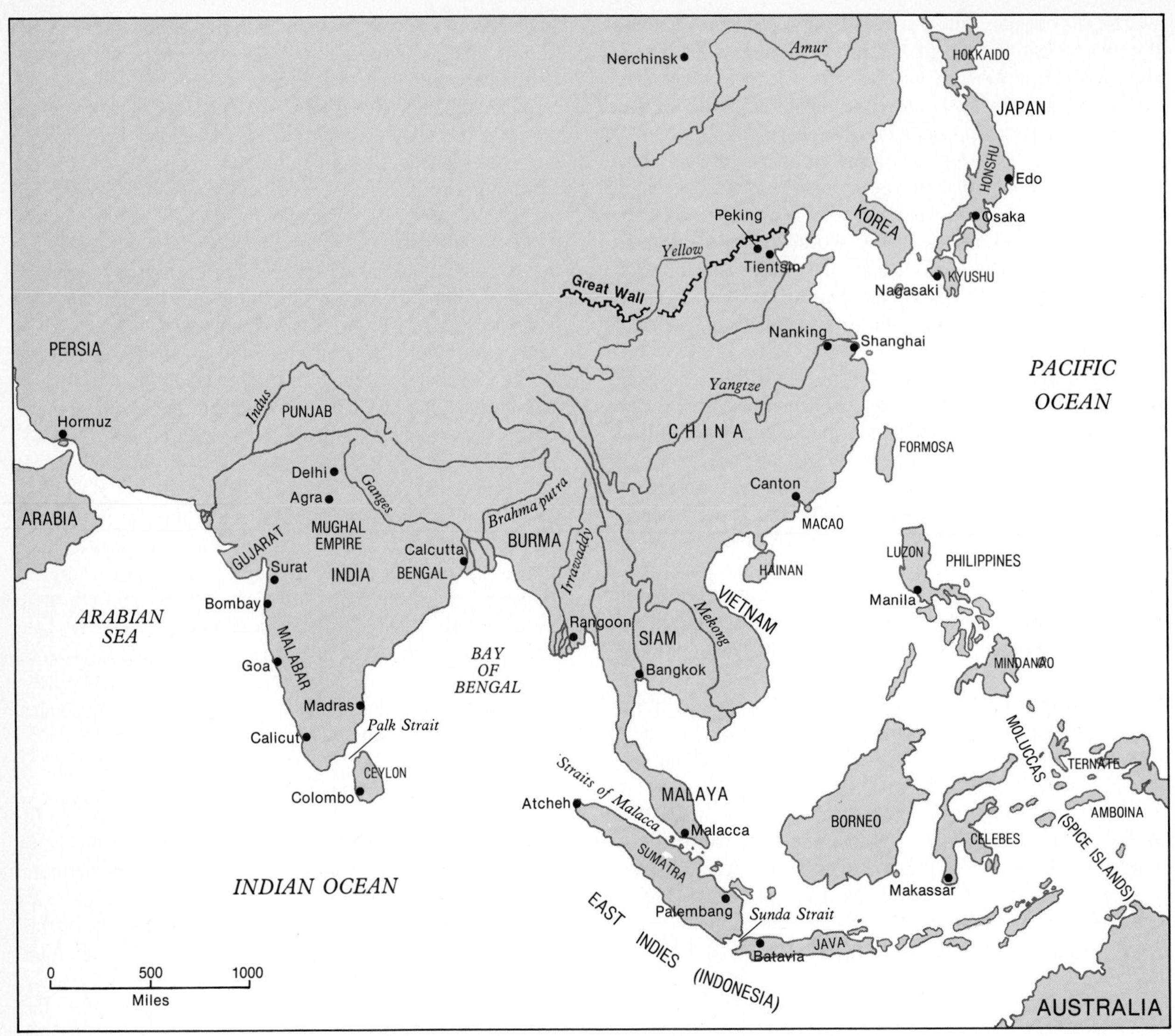

17.2 Asia in the Age of Early European Expansion

tegic, although it did some entrepôt business to and from Southeast Asia. Colombo, which the Portuguese also fortified after establishing themselves there about 1515, was able to draw on the nearby production of cinnamon, which the Ceylonese made from the bark of a rain forest tree, and thus played a commercial role as well.

For trade with China and Japan, the Portuguese somewhat later established their chief base at Macao, at the seaward edge of the Canton delta. There they could be a little freer of the restrictions imposed on foreign merchants at Canton by the Ming government and be tolerated by the Chinese authorities, enough to permit modest fortifications and a small permanent settlement. From the Chinese point of view, these unruly and barbaric foreigners were in any case better shunted off to such a remote neck of land and closed off by a wall (which still stands) where they could not make trouble and where they could govern themselves according to their own customs. In the sixteenth century the Ming were still close to the height of their power and effectively excluded all foreigners except for tribute missions and a handful of traders at the fringes. There was no comparable territorial base in Indonesia, where in any case no large state existed at this time. The Portuguese dominated the spice trade and excluded rival Europeans by intimidation of local sultans, alliances or treaties with others, and a scattered string of forts as far east as Ternate and Amboina in the Moluccas.

The shape and nature of the Portuguese commercial empire is clearly defined by its emphasis on strategically located ports, most of them already long in existence, and on domination of the sea lanes. The Portuguese controlled no territory beyond the immediate area of the few ports named, and traded in the hundreds of other ports in competition with Asian and Arab traders. Even so, their effort was overextended, and by the latter part of the sixteenth century they could no longer maintain what control they had earlier established. Their home base was tiny as well as poor; it could not provide either manpower or funds to sustain the effort required to maintain their overseas stations against competition. As the century ended, they were rapidly being ousted by the Dutch in Southeast Asia and were soon to be eliminated as serious competitors in the rest of the Asian trade by the other rising European power, the English. Many Portuguese stayed on, picking up crumbs of trade and also operating as pirates. As in Africa, they had from early days married local women, and from the seventeenth century virtually all of them in Asia were Eurasians, though commonly carrying Portuguese names and retaining the Catholic faith to which they had been converted. To this day names such as Fernando or de Souza are common in coastal South India, Sri Lanka, Malacca, and Macao. As the power of the Portuguese faded, their bases were no longer a threat, which is why Portugal retained formal sovereignty over Goa until it was forcibly reclaimed by India in 1961. The fiction of Portuguese control is maintained even today for Macao, an arrangement that suits the Chinese government for the present.

Religious Concerns

From the beginning, the crusade against Islam and the winning of souls for the Catholic church had been Portuguese goals equal to trade in importance. When Vasco da Gama arrived in Calicut in 1498 and was asked what he sought, he is said to have replied, "Christians and spices." His ships carried missionary priests, and their effort played a major role in the 1500s. After Affonso de Albuquerque (1453–1515), chief architect of the Portuguese commercial empire in Asia, was named viceroy of the Indies in 1508, he wrote of his plan to capture Malacca in 1511:

> **The first aim is the great service which we shall perform to our Lord in casting the Moors out of this country and quenching the fire of the sect of Mohammed. . . . And the other is the service we shall render to the king . . . in taking this city, because it is the source of all the spiceries and drugs which the Moors carry every year. . . . For I hold it certain that if we take this trade of Malacca away from them, Cairo and Mecca will be entirely ruined, and Venice will receive no spiceries unless her merchants go and buy them in Portugal.[4]**

When Albuquerque took Malacca, he massacred all the Muslims but tried to make allies or friends of the few other inhabitants. In insular Southeast Asia, by now predominantly Muslim, these were not attitudes or policies calculated to ingratiate the Portuguese. Their cruel practice of conversion by torture, their pitiless extortion, and their slaughter of "heathen" Hindus and Buddhists as well as their ancient Muslim foes earned them hatred. The Portuguese record during their century of power in Asia is at least as horrendous as that of the Spanish in the New World, and their decline was regretted by no one.

The Chinese remained aloof from these Western maritime and commercial rivalries and kept their distance at Canton, where European traders were not even permitted to enter the city but did their business outside the walls during the six-month trading season and then were obliged to depart until the next year. Successive Portuguese, Dutch, and English efforts to break these restrictions by trading elsewhere on the China coast were repelled, as Europeans did not have the means to challenge the Dragon Throne. (Dutch and English involvement in Asia are discussed in Chapter 18.) The sixteenth-century missionary effort to penetrate China was more successful, at least for a time. For the Jesuits, as for all later missionary groups, China was the chief goal, if only because of its immense population, its sophisticated culture, and the knowledge that it lacked an indigenous religion of salvation. Successive Jesuit efforts to enter the country failed after Francis Xavier died off the south China coast in 1552, still cherishing the dream of converting China's millions.

MATTEO RICCI: MISSIONARY TO THE MING COURT

The pioneer of the Jesuit effort in China was Matteo Ricci. He was born at Ancona in 1552, where he soon demonstrated his scholastic ability and magnetic personality. At the age of sixteen he went to Rome to study law and at 19 entered the Society of Jesus, where he distinguished himself in mathematics and geography. In 1577 he determined to pursue his career in the East and arrived in Goa the following year. After finishing his religious training, he taught in the college there until 1582, when he was called to Macao to prepare himself for the challenge of China. There he began diligent study of written and spoken Chinese and in 1583 became the first Jesuit to enter China, although at first only as a "guest" in Kwangtung province near Canton. There he continued his study of the Confucian classics and in 1589 built a church in the Chinese architectural style. By this time he had discovered that priests of any kind were associated with the now despised Buddhists, and he therefore adopted the dress as well as the manner and education of a Confucian scholar.

Ricci was a compelling person, tall and vigorous with flashing blue eyes, a curly beard (which assured the Chinese of his sagacity), and a resonant voice. What impressed them most, however, was his remarkable learning, combining as it did most of contemporary Western achievements, including cartography, and a thorough mastery of the classical Chinese corpus. He also had a phenomenal memory and made use of a variety of mnemonic devices to assist it. This was a tremendous help to a

Matteo Ricci with a Chinese convert to Christianity, Li Paulus, who translated European works on astronomy from Latin into Chinese. [New York Public Library]

scholar, especially for learning Chinese characters. Ricci was accordingly much sought after by Chinese who wanted to succeed in the imperial examinations or wanted their sons to do so. This enhanced his acceptability, as did his success in dissociating himself from the Portuguese traders at Macao. In 1595 he and his missionary colleagues were permitted to move north to the Yangtze valley and in 1601 to establish their permanent base at Peking.

The reigning emperor, Ming Wan-li, had become incompetent and concerned only with pleasures; the court was corrupt and full of scheming factions. Ricci finally caught the emperor's fancy by presenting him with two clocks and a clavichord, a precursor of the piano. When asked to demonstrate it, Ricci composed some "edifying" madrigals for his majesty to sing. Later he was given a special imperial stipend and was accepted at court as an outstanding and useful scholar. As the first missionary to China and one who fully understood how Chinese society worked, Ricci concentrated on the well-placed. To avoid alienating them and to make Christianity more understandable and appealing, he represented it as a system of ethics similar to and compatible with Confucianism, leaving out such potentially upsetting parts as the crucifixion, the virgin birth, and the equality of all persons. He also avoided discussion of Christian theology. This abbreviated version of the faith got the Jesuits in trouble with Rome later on, but it made excellent sense if the aim was to interest the Chinese. Ricci avoided preaching or overt efforts at conversion, and when he died in 1610, he was buried at Peking in a special plot granted by the emperor. He and his colleagues won few converts, but they saw their role as preparing the ground for a later assault by easing the Chinese into accepting the less controversial parts of Christianity and by masquerading as Confucian scholars. With his sharp mind, vast erudition, and winning personality, Ricci was an ideal person for such a role, but interest in him as a scholar never led to an equivalent interest in the religion he came to China to plant.

Such success as Ricci and his successors achieved was largely the result of their use of some of the new fruits of the European Renaissance as a lure, especially early clocks, improvements in the calendar, maps of the world, astronomy, and glass prisms. Such things intrigued the Chinese and ingratiated the Jesuits at court as learned men. By now they had necessarily learned not only the Chinese language but also the full deportment of the Confucian scholar as the vital credential for acceptance. They also understood that in this hierarchical society, the key to missionary success was to convert the people at the top, especially the emperor, and that preaching to the masses would only earn them a reputation as troublemakers. Aided by their Confucian guise as men of learning, they made some converts among gentry and court officials, but though they interested successive emperors, they never converted many Chinese. Western technology was more appealing than Western religion; this has remained true into our own times. In the end, the Jesuit effort was undermined by the pope, who refused to permit their softening of Catholic doctrine or the acceptance of some Confucian rites in order to avoid offending potential converts. The controversy simmered for years, but the ground had been cut out from under the Jesuits, and they were ultimately expelled in the early eighteenth century. Meanwhile, their accounts of China became an important source of Western knowledge.

The Russian Advance in Asia

Russian expansion across Siberia was slow but involved permanent Russian occupation and domination of this vast territory and its technologically less developed peoples, whose numbers were also small. By 1637 the Russians had reached the Pacific coast north of what is now Vladivostok, but they were behind the western Europeans in making direct contact with China. Early Russian explorers followed the major Siberian rivers, but these flow north-

A Jesuit View of India

Asians did not think much of Europeans, especially in this period, when they could easily be seen as a bunch of crude ruffians. An Italian traveler to early seventeenth-century India, Niccolò Manucci, recorded Indian views that agreed closely with those of the Chinese, Japanese, and other Asians. They believed that Europeans "have no polite manners, that they are ignorant, wanting in ordered life, and very dirty." The Europeans, however, were far more positive about Asia, which they had come so far to seek, in terms of both its wealth and its civilization. Here is a sampling of a Jesuit account of China in 1590.

There are such a number of artificers ingeniously framing sundry devices out of gold, silver, and other metals . . . and other matters convenient for man's use, that the streets of cities being replenished with their shops and fine workmanship are very wonderful to behold. . . . Their industry does no less appear in founding of guns. . . . To these may be added the art of printing . . . and with marvelous facility they daily publish huge multitudes of books. . . . You may add two more, that is to say navigation and discipline of war, both of which have been in ancient times most diligently practiced. . . . The people of China do above all things profess the art of literature, and learning it most diligently, they employ themselves a long time and the better part of their age therein. . . . Graduates of the second degree are elected in each province, and a certain number . . . ascend to the highest pitch of dignity. . . . Out of this order the chief magistrates are chosen. . . . Magistrates bear office for the space of three years, yet for the governing of each province men of another province are selected . . . [so that] judges may give sentence with a far more entire and incorrupt mind than if they were among their own kinsfolk and allies. . . . Over and besides all these there is an annual magistrate [the imperial censor] . . . whose duty it is to make inquisition of all crimes, and especially the crimes of magistrates. . . . Hence it is that all magistrates . . . are kept within the limits of their callings.

Source: N. Manucci, "An Excellent Treatise of the Kingdome of China," in *The Principal Navigations*, vol. 2, ed. R. Hakluyt (London, 1600), pp. 88–97 passim. The manuscript was written in Macao and captured by the English on its way to Lisbon.

ward into the Arctic. Gradually a network of fortified garrisons and trading posts spread eastward. When the Amur River was reached, it was eagerly used as an easier route leading to more productive areas and to the sea. Russian presence in the Amur valley came to Chinese attention when northern Manchurian tribes, tributary vassals of the Ch'ing dynasty, appealed for help. Mongol groups were also trading with the Russians, which further alarmed the Chinese. Two successive Russian embassies to Peking, in 1654 and 1676, requesting trade privileges, refused to perform the required prostrations before the emperor and were sent away. By the 1680s the Ch'ing, now having consolidated their power within China, began to establish new routes and military colonies in the Amur region and put naval ships on the river itself. The Russians were quickly chased out, and a large Ch'ing army besieged the one remaining Russian fortress. The Russians now agreed to negotiate and sent an ambassador to their major post at Nerchinsk, on an upper Amur tributary but still within Siberia.

The treaty concluded there in 1689 confirmed the Amur region as Chinese and obliged the Russians to destroy their remaining fortress but accepted limited Russian trade rights by camel caravan to Peking, in part because the Chinese court wanted to maintain the supply of fine Russian furs from Siberia. A later treaty in 1727 excluded Russia from Mongolia and further delimited the boundary between Russia and China, leaving the Russians only Siberia. The Ch'ing emperor K'ang Hsi would not deal directly with "barbarians," still less go to them, so he sent as his representatives two Jesuits from the court, whom he deemed appropriate agents for the management of such affairs. Nevertheless, the Treaty of Nerchinsk treated both sides as essentially equal sovereign states. It was the only such treaty China agreed to with a Western state until the nineteenth century, when China was forced to abandon the pretense of political superiority and accept inferior status. Until 1842 the various "sea barbarians" could be treated as savages, though Russia as a rival and adjacent land power had to be dealt with differently. Fear of Russia and its ambitions remained a fixture in the Chinese mind and was later intensified by Russian expansion into Manchuria.

The Catholic missionary drive in Asia met with the greatest success under the Spanish in the Philippines, where there was no sophisticated indigenous religious tradition to oppose it. The Japanese too, as a small, remote, and, in their own view, less developed people, were far more open than the Chinese or the Indians to new ideas, even of foreign origin. Where Chinese, and often Indians, with their cultural pride and self-confidence, tended to dismiss anything foreign as undesirable, the Japanese remained curious and sought opportunities to learn, as they had done from T'ang China. The sixteenth century, sometimes called "Japan's Christian century," saw significant numbers of Christian converts as well as a flourishing trade with Europeans, centered in Nagasaki but also at Osaka, Edo (Tokyo), and other ports. After missionary work in Goa and the East Indies, Francis Xavier spent two years (1549–1551) in Japan preaching, teaching, and disputing with Buddhist monks. But Christians were soon branded troublemakers. Rival Catholic religious orders contended with one another, often violently, as did the Portuguese, Spanish, Dutch, and English. Their ships and arms were often used in domestic Japanese factional fighting and intrigue, and Christianity was also seen as corrupting the Confucian loyalty of the Japanese and making converts potential subversives. Christianity was suppressed by 1640, thousands of converts crucified, and all foreigners expelled. The Japanese were forbidden to go abroad, and contact with the world beyond China was limited to one Dutch ship a year, allowed to trade only on an island in Nagasaki harbor.

The first burst of Western activity in Asia thus ended with only minor success. It was the Europeans who sought out the East, because Europe, poor and backward by comparison with the riches of Asia, was eager for contact. Columbus carried with him on his first voyage a copy of Marco Polo's journal, with its account of the immense wealth of Cathay; the riches of India and Southeast Asia were even better known via Arab traders. The discovery of the New World was thus an accidental incident on the road to Asia. In terms of power, the Europeans were no match for the great Asian empires or even for lesser states, and they had nothing desirable to offer in trade with the more sophisticated economies of the East. This was to inhibit European contacts for several more centuries. The Europeans had to be content with a few tiny and insecure footholds on the coast, where they competed with Asian and Arab merchants. Sometimes, at the whim of the Asian states, they were thrown out and had their goods confiscated.

Only at sea were the Europeans powerful—hence in part the Dutch success in controlling most of the trade of insular Southeast Asia—and there they tended to cancel one another out as rivals. Their chief commercial advantage was in the carrying trade, where their ships made them competitive but where they served mainly Asian markets. Soon after the Portuguese arrival, Asian shipbuilders on the Indian west coast began to adopt a Western-looking rig in the hope of scaring off pirates, sometimes adding dummy gun ports for the same purpose. Although Portuguese power subsequently faded in the face of Dutch and English competition, often forcing the Portuguese into piracy, the Asians continued to acknowledge Western superiority at sea. As the first British consul at Shanghai was to remark over three centuries later in 1843: "By our ships our power can be seen, and if necessary, felt."[5] This was to remain the principal basis of Western success in Asia throughout the centuries from 1498 to the end of colonialism in the ashes of the Second World War. In the early period, however, Asians saw Westerners as clever with ships but ignorant, dirty, contentious, drunken, uncivilized, and treacherous. To Asia's later cost, they were largely ignored. That seemed reasonable enough in the splendid and confident context of Mughal India, Ming and Ch'ing China, and Tokugawa Japan, and it remained so for another two or three centuries, until these Asian orders declined while Europe began to ride the wave of new industrial and technological power.

The European Conquest of the Americas

While the Portuguese fashioned a commercial empire in the East, the Spanish imposed a colonial empire on much of Mexico and South and Central America. Faced with uncertain economic prospects at home, the hidalgos who led the assault on the Aztecs and the Incas came in search of gold, but they were also deeply influenced by the crusading ideal and saw this adventure as a means of serving God. The combination of materialistic and spiritual motives was potent enough to provide them with the confidence to take on civilized peoples who vastly outnumbered them. In the end, however, the keys to their success were their technological superiority and the fact that both the Aztecs and the Incas were the overlords of a vast Indian population, some of whom actually fought on the side of the Spaniards. The Aztecs and Incas were also at a disadvantage because their empires, unlike those in Africa, were highly centralized and thus ill-suited to keep up resistance once their rulers had fallen.

Conquistadors, Aztecs, and Incas

The first of the great triumphs of the Spanish conquistadors began in 1519, the same year that Magellan set out on his historic voyage. Under the command of Hernando Cortés (1485–1547), a former law student who had participated in the conquest of Cuba, a force of some 600 men, 16 horses, and a few cannon landed in Mexico near Veracruz (which Cortés founded). Although the Indians resisted him at first, Cortés gradually won them over, aided by his Indian mistress and translator, Doña Marina. With the aid of 1,000 Tlaxcala Indians, the long-standing enemies of the Aztecs, he advanced on the capital at Tenochtitlán, an impressive city whose population of approximately 90,000 was nearly the equal of Europe's largest cities. Dominated by an enormous temple, pyramids, and the royal palace, the city was built on mud dredged from Lake Texcoco. Impressive for its orderly streets and canals, its open squares bustling with commerce, and its whitewashed public buildings, Tenochtitlán was ruled by the war-chief Montezuma from 1502 to 1520. In a society dominated by war, all able-bodied Aztec men received military training. So many warriors died in battle that the Aztecs had to practice polygamy. Bearing children was therefore highly regarded, and a woman who died in childbirth received the same ceremonial rites as a warrior who perished on the battlefield. The main motive for the warfare was the need to acquire victims with which to appease the sun god, who fed on blood obtained by ripping out the hearts of living people. Women were rarely among the sacrificial victims. In practical terms, human sacrifice functioned as a means to terrorize subject Indians, which helps to explain their unwillingness to defend the Aztecs against Cortés.

Despite initial threats from the Aztecs, Cortés was allowed to enter the capital peacefully, but in a matter of days he used the pretext of an attack on his garrison at Veracruz to imprison Montezuma. An Indian uprising in which Montezuma was killed forced Cortés to flee in July 1520, but thirteen months later he regained Tenochtitlán with the help of the Tlaxcalas. The fighting destroyed most of the city, but amid its ruins the Spaniards built Mexico City, complete with a Catholic cathedral and, in 1551, the University of Mexico.

The Splendors of Tenochtitlán

When Cortés' party entered the Aztec capital of Tenochtitlán, it was cordially received and given a tour of the city. An eyewitness account by a member of the party records the city's splendor and teeming life.

When we arrived at the great market place . . . we were astounded at the number of people and the quantity of merchandise that it contained, and at the good order and control that was maintained, for we had never seen such a thing before. Each kind of merchandise was kept by itself and had its fixed place marked out. Let us begin with the dealers in gold, silver, and precious stones, feathers, mantles, and embroidered goods. Then there were other wares consisting of Indian slaves both men and women; and I say that they bring as many of them to that great market for sale as the Portuguese bring negroes from Guinea. . . .

So we stood looking about us, for that huge and cursed temple stood so high that from it one could see over everything very well, and we saw the three causeways which led into Mexico. . . . We saw the bridges on the three causeways which were built at certain distances apart through which the water of the lake flowed in and out from one side to the other, and we beheld on that great lake a great multitude of canoes, some coming with supplies of food and others returning loaded with cargoes of merchandise; and we saw that from every house of that great city and of all the other cities that were built in the water it was impossible to pass from house to house, except by drawbridges which were made of wood or in canoes; and we saw in those cities Cues [temples] and oratories like towers and fortresses and all gleaming white, and it was a wonderful thing to behold.

Source: B. Díaz del Castillo, *The True History of the Conquest of New Spain*, ed. G. Garcia, trans. A. P. Maudslay, 5 vols. (London: Hakluyt Society, 1908–1933), 2: 70–71, 74–75.

The attack on the Incas was commanded by Francisco Pizarro (c. 1474–1541), a former associate of Balboa. With a force of only 180 men and 27 horses he set out in 1531 to conquer an empire ruled by Atahualpa with his army of 30,000. The overconfident Atahualpa agreed to meet with Pizarro, whom he seriously underestimated. Pizarro took him prisoner, extracted an enormous ransom, and then executed him for allegedly murdering his half brother. In 1533 Pizarro captured the Inca capital at Cuzco in the Peruvian Andes, after which the remaining Incas maintained a tiny but independent state high in the mountains at Machu Picchu. To maintain better communications with other Spanish authorities, Pizarro founded Lima on the coast of Peru in 1535. The University of San Marcos was established there 16 years later under a grant from the emperor Charles V. Conquest of the Incas was facilitated by the dissatisfaction of subordinate Indians with Inca domination, as well as by internal dissension among the Incas themselves.

Spanish Rule in the Americas

Virtually from the beginning, the Spanish confronted difficult legal questions concerning the status of the Indians. The problem was compounded by religious considerations, for the papal decision in 1493 that recognized Spain's claim to most of the Western Hemisphere also made the Spaniards responsible for the conversion of its inhabitants. As Spanish subjects and, in time, Christians, what legal rights did they possess? The conquerors, vastly outnumbered by their subject population, sought an essentially feudal form of government, with considerable local autonomy for their own colonists, and the right to treat the Indians as forced laborers. In sharp contrast, the influential Dominican friar Bartolomé de las Casas contended that as fellow Christians and subjects of the Spanish crown, the Indians were entitled to full legal rights and protection. Although the Spanish government was unwilling to provide the colonists much autonomy, it gave selected conquistadors and other Spaniards the right to collect tribute from specified villages and to impose forced labor. Those who exercised this power—the *encomenderos,* or protectors—were required to render military service and pay the salaries of the clergy. Because of abuses, this system was modified in the mid-sixteenth century. The authority to compel labor was transferred to colonial officials, and forced workers were paid according to a fixed rate. Legally, the Indians could not be enslaved, but in practice their situation was little different from slavery.

Administration of the Spanish empire in America was directed by two viceroys who received their instructions from the Council of the Indies in Spain. The viceroyalty of New Spain, with headquarters in Mexico City, embraced Spanish territories in North America, the West Indies, Venezuela, and the Philippines, whereas the viceroyalty of Peru, governed from Lima, included the rest of Spanish South America. Under the viceroys were lesser provincial governors. Both the viceroys and the lesser governors shared authority with conciliar courts known as *audiencias*, which gave them advice and had the power to overturn their decisions. This system of checks and balances safeguarded royal prerogatives, but it also deprived colonial government of administrative efficiency.

The Economy of Spanish America

Nothing was more important in determining the pattern of Spanish settlement than the sites of gold and silver deposits and the availability of native labor to mine them. On his first voyage, Columbus had found gold in Hispaniola, and more was soon discovered in Cuba and Puerto Rico. At first the gold was obtained from shallow diggings or extracted from stream beds. Such mining, however, was labor-intensive, and as the Indian population declined, it became more profitable to graze cattle or raise sugarcane. Many Indians soon died because of forced labor or diseases introduced by the Spanish. The conquest of the Aztecs and Incas, whose gold artifacts were seized and melted down, was of enormous economic importance because it led to the discovery of rich silver deposits in the 1540s. The greatest of these was an extraordinary mountain of silver at Potosí, in the Andes, discovered in 1545. By 1570 Potosí had a population of 120,000, nearly the same as Paris. The introduction of the latest technology by German miners—a water-powered stamp mill and a mercury amalgamation process that purified the silver—made the mines so productive that silver became the most important export to the mother country. By 1570 no less than 97 percent of the bullion shipped to Spain was silver. As the output of European mines declined in the late sixteenth century, the flow of silver from the New World continued to increase, rising in the 1590s to more than 10 million ounces a year. Altogether, according to official accounts, the Spanish treasure fleets transported 180 tons of gold and 16,000 tons of silver to Seville between 1500 and 1650. Much of the wealth, 20 percent of which went to the crown as the "royal fifth," was used to pay for imports, service the royal debt, and finance war.

No less significant, particularly for the future history of the Americas, was the introduction of large estates. Some, the *haciendas*, were used to rear animals or raise cereal crops, but in tropical regions sugar and tobacco plantations were established, patterned after the sugar plantations of Atlantic islands such as the Azores and Canaries, which in turn had been influenced by Genoese plantations in Cyprus and Crete. Unlike the haciendas, which used Indian workers, the primary laborers on the plantations were African slaves. Although both the plantation system and the trade in African slaves predated the Spanish conquests in the

The Cerro Rico, the fabulous mountain of silver at Potosí in Bolivia. Potosí itself, at an altitude of 13,700 feet, is one of the world's highest cities. Its population reached 160,000 in 1650 and then sharply declined. [Harvard College Library]

Americas, the success of the conquistadors opened up vast new markets for the sale of blacks. Africans were accustomed to working in tropical climates, possessed some immunity from the diseases that decimated the American Indians, and had lower mortality rates in the New World than even the Europeans. By the eighteenth century the British were the main suppliers for this slave market, followed by the French, but the Portuguese, Spanish, Dutch, Danes, and Americans also participated.

In Spain, the economic effects of its new colonial empire were a mixed blessing. Seville, which enjoyed a monopoly of trade with the colonies, prospered for several centuries. Ultimately, however, its prosperity and economic potential were undermined by the heavy hand of the Spanish government, which overregulated everything, and by the reluctance of the Spaniards to seize the commercial opportunities their empire made possible. The French historian Fernand Braudel has observed:

> **The latent defect in the Spanish imperial economy was that it was based on Seville—a controlled town rotten with dishonest officials and long dominated by foreign capitalists—and not on a powerful free town capable of producing and carrying through a really individual economic policy.[6]**

There was some new manufacturing in Spain, but in general Spaniards continued to rely on France and the Netherlands for their goods. Nor did large numbers of Spaniards emigrate to America, the total number amounting to some 100,000 in the entire sixteenth century. The influx of bullion into Spain, while seemingly a great economic advantage, was so badly mismanaged that for many Spaniards the most direct result was a spiraling cost of living. The quadrupling of prices in the 1500s, in part because of the increase in bullion, adversely affected the living conditions of many Spaniards.

The Impact of Spanish Imperialism

In retrospect, the most dramatic effect of Spanish domination in the New World was the catastrophic decline in the Indian population, one of the greatest demographic disasters in history. By 1510 nearly 90 percent of the Indians of Hispaniola were dead, while in Mexico the Indian population, which had numbered 11 million, fell by more than 75 percent. Famine and ruthless exploitation accounted for some of the deaths, but the biggest killer was disease, especially smallpox. The fact that Europeans introduced universities and printing to the New World and that Spanish law and Christianity ended the Aztec practices of human sacrifice and polygamy was small comfort in the face of such suffering. Although Aztecs and Incas suppressed other Indians, the Spanish exploitation of the native inhabitants and the introduction of slave plantations were hardly an improvement, though the Indians were treated better than the blacks. Because of the shortage of Spanish women, intermarriage with Indians was so frequent that the descendants of mixed marriages—the *mes-*

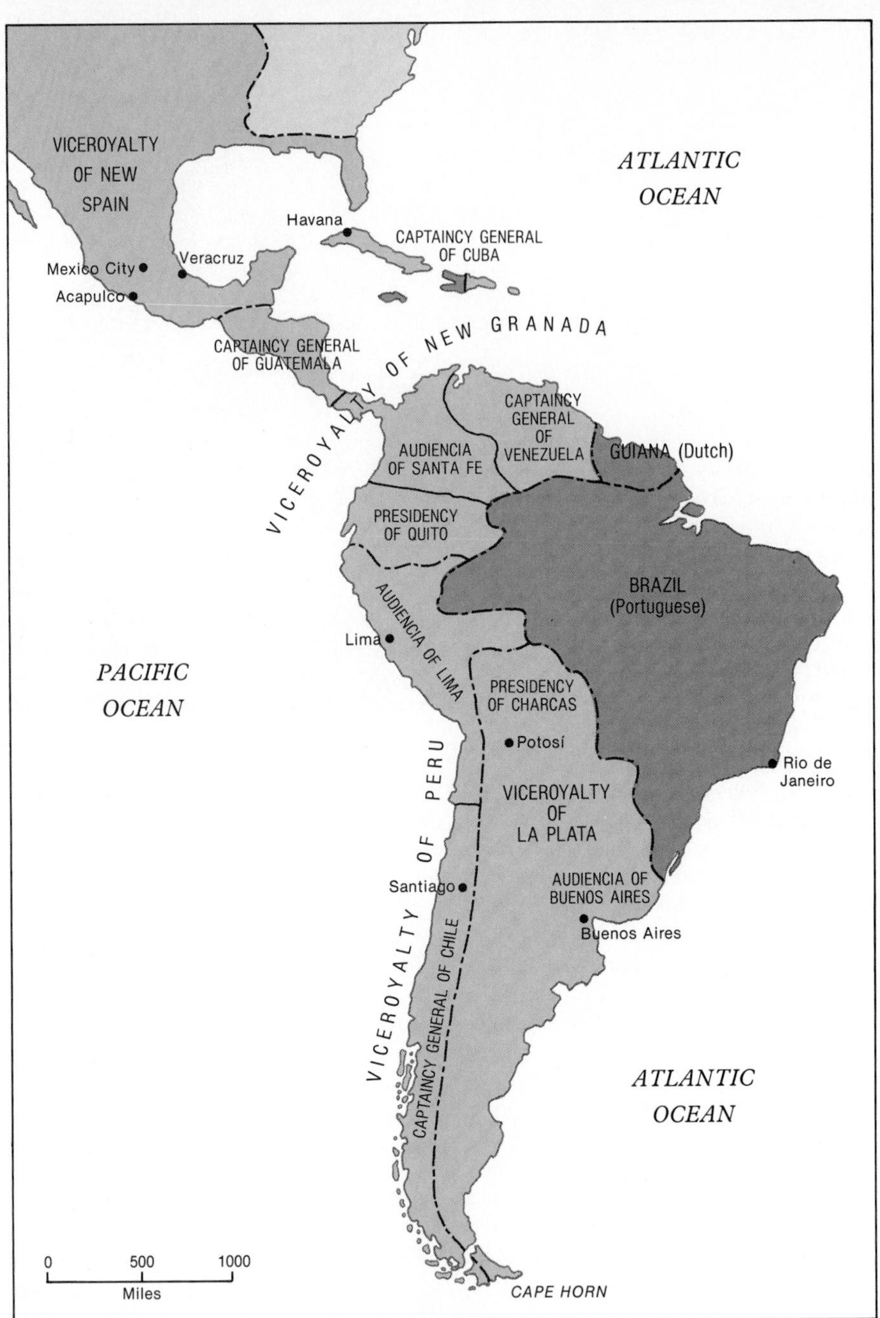

17.3 Colonial Empires in America, c. 1600

tizos—eventually outnumbered both the Spaniards and the Indians.

The Portuguese in Brazil

Portugal concentrated on its commercial empire in Asia and paid relatively little attention to Brazil in the early 1500s, particularly since no gold or silver was found there. The region, however, did produce brazilwood, used in making red dye. The threat of Spanish incursion and the intrusion of the French into the brazilwood trade forced the government in Lisbon to act in 1533. It organized Brazil into 15 hereditary fiefs, the holders of which—the *donatários*—enjoyed sweeping powers, including the right to levy internal taxes and bestow grants of land. When most of the *donatários* proved ineffectual, the Portuguese king imposed a centralized administration under the direction of a governor general, who took up duties in 1549. After Spain's conquest of Portugal in 1580, Spanish-style colonial administration, headed by a viceroy, was introduced in Brazil.

As in the Spanish colonies, there was controversy over the treatment of the Indians. Jesuit missionaries worked tirelessly to convert and settle them in Christian villages. Their efforts ran counter to the needs of settlers who established sugar plantations in northern Brazil in the late 1500s. Brazil, in fact, became the world's leading producer of sugar in the early seventeenth century. In 1574 the Portuguese government resolved the dispute between the Jesuits and the plantation owners by allowing the former to protect residents of their Christian villages, while giving settlers the right to enslave Indians captured in war. Unable to procure sufficient labor in this manner, the colonists increasingly relied on African slaves.

The French, too, were interested in Brazil, and in 1555 they occupied the harbor of Rio de Janeiro. When the colony refused to honor its initial promise of religious toleration, potential Protestant settlers in France and Switzerland lost interest. After the Portuguese captured the French garrison, they founded the town of Rio de Janeiro in 1567. Large numbers of Portuguese Jewish immigrants subsequently settled in Brazil, where they found some freedom for the exercise of their religion.

The North Atlantic States and the Americas

The Portuguese were the first to profit from John Cabot's discovery of the cod fisheries off Newfoundland. For the masses, salted fish was a vital item in the diet, particularly during the winter and on the frequent fast days throughout the year. Because the herring fisheries in the Baltic, monopolized by the Hanseatic League of North German merchants, were declining as the fish shifted their spawning grounds to the North Sea, there was a ready market for cod to feed the growing population. Although Portugal claimed Newfoundland, French and English fishermen were soon hauling in catches from its waters. In addition to providing needed food, the development of new fisheries led to the beginning of the fur trade with the Indians and to an increase in the number of ships and mariners capable of sailing the Atlantic.

As their naval expertise improved, the English were determined to participate in the spice trade, the immense profits of which were enjoyed by the Portuguese and the merchants of Antwerp. Unwilling to challenge Portugal's control of the route around the Cape of Good Hope, the English opted to search for a northeast or northwest passage to Asia, encouraged by Magellan's discovery of a southwest route. Accordingly, Sir Hugh Willoughby and Richard Chancellor set out in 1553 to find a northeast passage. Two of the ships became icebound and their crews froze to death, but Chancellor took the third ship through the White Sea to Archangel. From there he traveled overland to the court of Tsar Ivan the Terrible in Moscow. His trip resulted in the establishment of the Muscovy Company (1555), which pursued a small direct trade between England and Russia. Subsequent attempts by the English and the Dutch to find a northeastern passage were unsuccessful, as were English efforts beginning in 1576 to find a northwestern route. The latter, however, led to the discovery of Hudson Strait and Hudson Bay and to additional sources of fur in the adjacent territory.

As the search for a northern passage progressed, the English turned their attention to the possibility of trade with Spain's American colonies, notwithstanding the fact that the Spaniards considered unauthorized trade illegal. In 1562 John Hawkins, son of a Plymouth merchant, launched the English slave trade with the backing of a private syndicate. In Hispaniola he traded the 300 or 400 slaves he had acquired in Sierra Leone for hides and sugar. Impressed by the potential of this trade, Queen Elizabeth I and several of her privy councillors quietly helped finance his successful second voyage in 1564–1565. In the face of mounting Spanish hostility, Elizabeth permitted Hawkins to sail again in 1567, but this time the Spanish fleet captured or destroyed three of his five ships in the Mexican harbor of San Juan de Uluá. As relations with Spain worsened, the English restricted their activity in the New World primarily to privateering—government-approved piracy—for the rest of the century. During his circumnavigation of the globe in 1577–1580, Francis Drake challenged the Spanish sphere of dominion by claiming California, which he called New Albion, for England. In the 1580s Sir Walter Raleigh's pioneering attempt to found an English colony near Roanoke Island (now part of North Carolina) resulted in dismal failure, but the experience proved valuable for later colonial endeavors. The French, whose activities in the New World in the sixteenth century consisted largely of plundering Spanish shipping, were equally unsuccessful in attempting to establish a colony in Florida in the early 1560s.

The ability of the English, French, and Dutch to make inroads into Spanish America was largely determined by the economic and political events of the late sixteenth century. England's successful war with Spain (1585–1604) severely crippled the latter and provided substantial freedom of action to the Dutch. France, disrupted by a long and bitter civil war, began to build the strong monarchy and economy necessary for colonial expansion only in the 1590s. In all three states, a key to future success in colonial expansion and the emerging global economy was the development of aggressive capitalism.

The Economy in the Age of Exploration

In the fifteenth and sixteenth centuries the European economy underwent dramatic changes that helped to chart the course of modern economic development. The most important characteristics of this change involved not only the founding of commercial and colonial empires but also the rapid growth of capitalism and a price revolution triggered by an expanding population.

Merchant Capitalism

Capitalism involves three elements: (1) the acquisition and investment of capital to obtain profit, (2) private ownership of the principal means of production and distribution, and (3) a division in the productive and distributive process between the owners of the capital (the employers) and the laborers. Capitalism cannot exist without the capacity and the willingness to invest and to take risks, which in turn presupposes the possibility of significant profits. The medieval concepts of the just price and the wrongfulness of usury (interest on loans purely for profit) were thus impediments to capitalistic development. Medieval theologians had generally recognized the right of a lender to additional compensation beyond the principal if he incurred a loss by forgoing the use of his money. The acceptability of reasonable interest was gradually extended until, in the sixteenth century, bankers regularly paid interest of 5 to 12 percent on deposits and merchants routinely operated on credit. The expansion of capitalistic activities was also furthered by the increased use of bills of exchange, improved facilities for interregional trade, stable coinage, and an adequate and affordable labor supply. Finally, the rise in prices was a stimulus to capitalistic investment as merchants and others with surplus wealth opted to seek profits through investment rather than to spend their money on consumables.

As the European states centralized in this period, they exercised a threefold influence on capitalism. First of all, their own demands—for weapons, supplies, and luxury items—created an expanding market for merchant capitalists, who were quick to realize the potential for profits. Second, the encouragement of overseas commercial and colonial activity by the governments of the maritime states was a major incentive to invest in such ventures. Finally, these governments introduced economic policies intended to strengthen their respective states. Collectively, these policies constitute what is sometimes referred to as "mercantilism," or the "mercantile system," as Adam Smith called it in 1776.

At the heart of mercantile policy was the principle of state regulation, which was designed primarily for the benefit of the state itself. Free enterprise—the right of merchants and manufacturers to respond to market conditions as they deem best—was not part of mercantile capitalism. Both rulers and merchants who profited from business dealings with the state accepted economic controls as necessary. However, some of these controls, particularly those creating monopolies, became increasingly unpopular in the late sixteenth and seventeenth centuries among the people, who blamed them for high prices. Governments used controls to assure the availability of strategic items, to provide order in the economy, and to regulate commerce with other states. Economic regulation was thus an important facet of the campaign to impose greater order on the early modern state. The most common controls were tariffs on imported goods, subsidies (grants) to strategic industries, and monopolies, which conveyed the exclusive right to manufacture, sell, or trade in a specific commodity. Some also attempted to regulate the export of raw materials, such as wool and leather. In 1572 French royal edicts banned the export of various raw materials, and England tried a variety of expedients in the sixteenth and early seventeenth centuries to reduce the export of raw wool in order to encourage domestic manufacturing.

Some proponents of mercantile capitalism were convinced that the strength of the state depended on the acquisition of considerable supplies of bullion. To accomplish this, they favored strict controls on foreign commerce in order to produce a favorable balance of trade, whereby the value of exports exceeded the value of imports. The Dutch, who dominated the carrying trade, recognized the sterility of this concept and instead pursued a policy geared to maximize the volume and value of trade. Profit, they recognized, was obtained by increasing trade, not hoarding bullion. The English converted to this view for a time in the 1600s but then reverted to a protectionist policy. The Spanish, who wanted to amass bullion, had to use it instead to finance their wars and the conspicuous consumption of their elite and to import goods that they were unwilling to manufacture. Supporters of the bullionist theory tried to reduce the export of bullion by encouraging the immigration of skilled artisans, thereby reducing the need of the host country for imports and perhaps even creating new export commodities from the goods the immigrants manufactured.

Government intervention in the economy was not always beneficial, as in the case of most monopolies. An English scheme designed by the merchant Sir William Cokayne to dye and finish cloth before exporting it to the Continent, though supported by the crown, was so disastrous that it helped provoke a depression. Nevertheless, mercantile policies helped France build a stronger economy in the 1600s by expanding trade and assisting farmers, and both the English and the Dutch benefited by allowing religious refugees, especially Huguenots, to immigrate in the sixteenth and seventeenth centuries. Government intervention also had positive results as companies received charters to trade with Asia, Africa, and America; as internal barriers to trade gradually ended (though France was a major exception); and as new industries were subsidized. The implementation of policies was complicated not only by the lack of experience in dealing with a capitalistic economy but also by spiraling prices and corruption.

The Price Revolution

Inflation is a fact of modern life; Europeans in the sixteenth century were unprepared for the rises in prices that occurred, at varying rates, throughout Europe. By today's standards the inflation rate was low, often hovering around 2 percent per year, though in some years the rate was much higher. Moreover, prices varied greatly from region to region, especially over the short run. In Spain prices quadrupled in the sixteenth century, and the figure was nearly as great in England. Inflation began later in Italy, where prices doubled by 1600. The greatest increases came between the 1540s and 1570s when bad weather and crop failures added additional pressures to the inflationary spiral and when the impact of American bullion began to be felt. For a long time many historians attributed the rise in prices to the influx of bullion from the New World, but recent research has confirmed the fact that the main cause was a rise in population and thus in demand without a corresponding increase in output, thereby creating shortages of goods and services. The shortages in turn put pressure on prices, as did the expansion of the money supply because of the large quantities of imported bullion. War destruction, crop failures, and the requirements of expanding governments also contributed to a demand that outstripped production.

Food prices rose approximately twice as much as those of other goods, with wheat costing roughly five times more in the early 1600s than it had in the late 1400s. Rising food prices caused severe hardship for the poor and acted as a brake on population growth by the mid-seventeenth century, but they also spurred the development of the Atlantic fisheries and commercial agriculture. Prices, however, rose faster than agricultural yield. In England in the late 1500s rising grain prices curtailed the earlier trend of converting arable land to pasture. Economic conditions encouraged the Dutch not only to continue reclaiming land from the sea but also to develop the techniques of crop rotation. Traditionally, a third of the land had been left fallow each year on a rotating basis in order to restore fertility, but the Dutch discovered that the same end could be achieved by periodically planting beans or peas (to return nitrogen to the soil) and grazing animals, whose manure acted as fertilizer. The adoption of crop rotation by the English and the French in the late seventeenth and eighteenth centuries was crucial to the growth in agricultural productivity that made the Industrial Revolution possible.

Industrial and Commercial Development

The growth of merchant capitalism led to a major reorganization of the means of producing textiles, the demand for which increased as the population grew. In the cities of the Netherlands and northern and central Italy, merchant capitalists distributed raw wool from England or raw silk from Asia and western Europe to master artisans. These craftsmen, who still belonged to their own guilds, typically owned their shops, though not the materials on which they worked. Then, beginning in the late sixteenth century, English capitalists altered the system by distributing raw wool directly to village workers for spinning, dyeing, and weaving. From the merchants' standpoint, this system of "putting out" the work to villagers had the advantage of bypassing the traditional guilds with their controls over working conditions, wages, and prices. Because the labor was undertaken in the workers' cottages rather than in shops, the merchants' overhead was lower. In contrast to the guild system, however, the workers had no hope of improving their condition by completing an apprenticeship, and the division between employer and worker gradually became permanent. The price revolution provided additional incentive for the expansion of this system as the cost of goods outpaced the rise in wages. Thus the introduction of the domestic system of textile production could bring substantial profits to the merchant capitalists but increasingly sharpened the division between the haves and have-nots as workers were exploited. The domestic system, which regularly involved entire families working together in the home, gradually spread throughout western Europe until it was phased out by the introduction of factories in the Industrial Revolution. By that time rural workers were manufacturing not only textiles but cutlery, buttons, gloves, and household goods as well.

Merchant capitalists were also responsible for innovative new forms of business organization intended primarily to take advantage of the trade opportunities with Asia, Africa, and America. The partnerships and family firms of the medieval period were simply not in a position to raise sufficient capital to fund these voyages. With government approval, merchants began banding together as "regulated" companies with a monopoly on a particular item or trade with a given area. Even so, the amount of capital was limited to what the merchants themselves could raise. The solution was the formation of the joint-stock company, an organization of investors rather than an association of traders. Funds came not only from the business community but also from the aristocracy and government officials, and management was in the hands of directors experienced in commercial affairs. The firms were normally awarded monopolies and tended to concern themselves at first with overseas trade and colonization. The English (1600), Dutch (1602), French (1664), and others had East

India companies organized on a joint-stock basis by private businessmen with government encouragement. Other companies were formed for such endeavors as colonizing Virginia and Massachusetts and trading furs in North America.

ANTWERP'S GOLDEN AGE

No city more clearly reflected the opportunities and the glory of the age of exploration than Antwerp. In the late fifteenth and sixteenth centuries it stood at the crossroads of Europe, the hub of trade between England and the Continent, the Baltic and the Mediterranean. In terms of international commerce, Antwerp enjoyed the position formerly held by Venice. An awed Venetian envoy observed: "I was astounded and wondered much when I beheld Antwerp, for I saw Venice outdone."[7] Antwerp's dominant position among a host of secondary towns moved the Belgian historian Henri Pirenne to refer to the Netherlands —which in the sixteenth century included what is now Belgium as well as Holland—as its "suburb." Antwerp was a major cultural center as well. The German artist Albrecht Dürer was impressed by the city as well as by the "wonderful works of art" from Mexico that he viewed there on his last visit in 1521. The great Flemish painters Pieter Brueghel the Elder (c. 1525–1569) and Peter Paul Rubens (1577–1640) lived in Antwerp. Rubens, famed for his historical scenes, classical allegories, and sensuous nude figures, was the most eagerly sought-after painter of his time and the first to accumulate a substantial fortune through his art. He served as well as an ambassador from the archducal court of the Spanish Netherlands (later called Belgium), particularly to England.

Antwerp's rise to commercial greatness was facilitated by its geographic advantages. In the late 1400s the preeminence of Bruges as a trading center was undercut when the Zwyn River silted up. Antwerp, situated on the Scheldt River, thereupon became the leading port and commercial center in the Netherlands. Antwerp's rise was also aided by Bruges' insistence on maintaining outmoded commercial regulations; by its hostility to the Burgundian dukes, who turned their attention to Antwerp; and by Habsburg favoritism toward Antwerp in the collection of customs duties. Many of the city's major buildings were constructed in the period of prosperity that ensued, including the great Gothic cathedral of the Holy Virgin (begun in the 1300s), the castle, the Renaissance town hall, and the Bourse, the center of foreign exchange. So great was the expansion that in 1542 a third set of costly city walls had to be constructed. With a population of 100,000 in the mid-sixteenth century, Antwerp was one of the largest cities in Europe.

Commencing in the late 1400s, the shift in the center of European commerce from Venice and the cities of the Hanseatic League brought more than 1,000 foreign businesses to Antwerp. It became the hub of the Portuguese spice trade, the northern headquarters of the Fugger family, and the center for the import of English cloth. Its bustling harbor handled as many as 500 ships a day, and more than 1,000 freight wagons arrived in the city each week carrying the overland trade. Recognizing the amount of capital necessary to participate in the spice trade, as early as 1505 the king of Portugal allowed the merchants

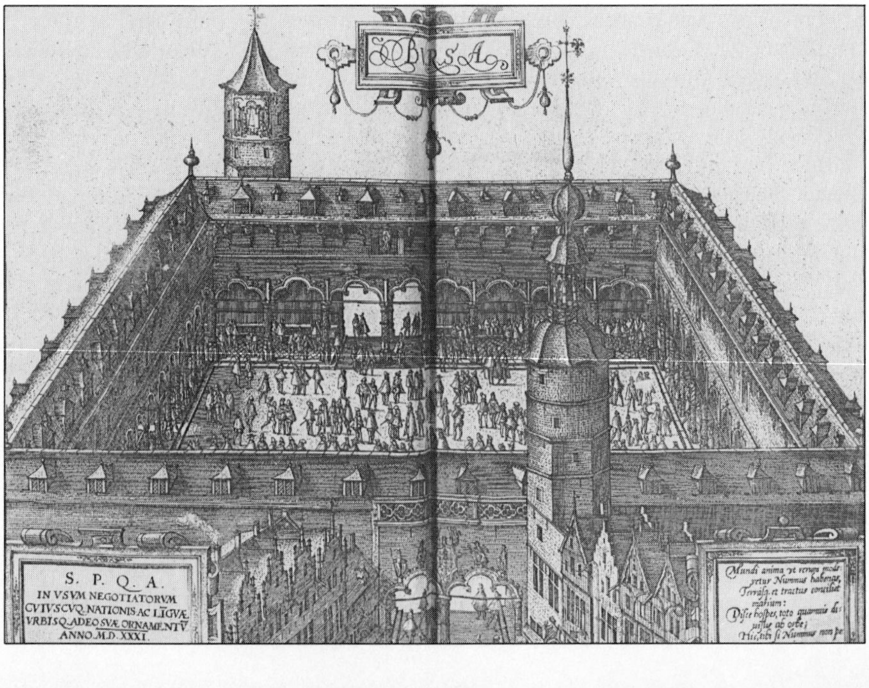

Merchants gathered at the Antwerp Bourse, built in 1531, to transact their business. The portico surrounding the courtyard rested on 38 sculptured columns, each of which was unique, and the upper level contained shops. The building was destroyed by fire in 1581. [New York Public Library]

Antwerp's Prosperity

When the Florentine traveler Ludovico Guicciardini visited Antwerp in the mid-1500s, he was thoroughly impressed by its commercial activity. Here he tries to explain why the city was so prosperous.

The causes of the great wealth that Antwerp is grown to, are three. The first [is] the two markets that are in Antwerp, the one whereof begins fifteen days before Whitsuntide. . . . The other . . . begins the second Sunday after Our Lady Day in August. . . . Each of these markets endures six weeks, all the which time no man is subject to any arrest for debt. . . . There are also at Antwerp besides these markets two great horse fairs . . . and likewise two of leather and skins of all sorts, which follow immediately after the horse fairs.

The second cause of the wealth of Antwerp is this . . . : The king of Portugal, having partly by love, partly by force, drawn all the traffic of spices in Calicut and the isles adjacent thereunto into his own hands, and having brought them to Lisbon, sent his factor [agent] with spices to Antwerp, by which means it drew all nations thither to buy spices. . . . Afterwards in the year 1516 divers [foreign] merchants . . . departed from Bruges to go and dwell at Antwerp, and after them others. . . .

The third cause of the wealth of Antwerp . . . [is that the citizens have] marvelously fortified their town, for the safety both of it and of all merchants trafficking to it, so that it is now free from all danger and thought impregnable, by means whereof, a great multitude of noblemen and gentlemen come to dwell in the town.

Source: L. Guicciardini, *The Description of the Low Countreys* (London: Peter Short for Thomas Chard, 1593), pp. 26–27 (edited to conform to modern usage).

of Antwerp to purchase a sizable cargo in the Indies and transport it directly to Antwerp in Portuguese ships. The Fuggers were among those who participated in this venture and the ensuing expansion of the spice trade. Antwerp also imported large quantities of raw materials for use in its own industries, especially cloth manufacturing and finishing. Antwerp craftsmen pioneered in the production of "new draperies," a lighter and less expensive material than traditional woolen broadcloth, and they also manufactured silk, velvet, and similar luxury goods. Antwerp designers determined European fashions. Like Geneva, Antwerp was a center of the printing industry, boasting approximately 50 print shops in the mid-1500s. The English Bible translators William Tyndale and Miles Coverdale worked for a time in Antwerp, and by the late sixteenth century its printers were among the leading publishers of Counter-Reformation literature.

Antwerp, facing growing commercial competition from the English, became a casualty of the religious wars that plagued much of Europe in the late sixteenth century (see Chapter 18). In 1576, as the Netherlands struggled against Spanish domination, Antwerp was plundered by Spanish troops and 6,000 of its citizens were slaughtered. The people rallied, expelled the Spaniards, and were governed by Calvinists until 1585, when the Spanish regained control and exiled the Protestants. Antwerp's troubles enabled Amsterdam to replace it as the leading commercial center of Europe in the seventeenth century.

By the time that Antwerp began to decline, the beginnings of a global economy had been established. Antwerp was the first city in the world to serve as the hub of such a commercial network. Compared to the tempo of economic change in preceding centuries, the speed with which a global economy developed in this period was striking. Europeans experienced a social and economic revolution in the late fifteenth and sixteenth centuries. The emergence of merchant capitalism provided striking opportunities for the acquisition of wealth and power. In England progressive aristocrats recognized this and profited by their association with the business community, whereas in Spain the hidalgos' resistance to com-

mercial activity contributed to that nation's declining economy. As European rulers centralized their states, they adapted to the economic changes by formulating policies designed to control or expand trade. The governments of France, England, and the Netherlands were especially successful, and the resulting wealth was the basis of their growing power in the late 1500s and 1600s. Indeed, one of the effects of the commercial revolution was the increased ability of states to field large, better-equipped armies.

The lives of countless ordinary people changed, slowly but dramatically. The domestic system of manufacturing eventually created significant numbers of workers who had no reasonable prospect of improving their position. Many continued to live at the subsistence level despite shifting from agriculture to manufacturing. To feed the expanding population, commercial agriculture blossomed, aided by the introduction of crop rotation and the further enclosing of land. For many, however, the general living standard declined in the face of bad harvests, higher taxes, the adverse effects of war on the economy, and capitalistic developments, especially on the farms. Colonial expansion, however, brought Europeans new foods—tomatoes (called "love-apples" and initially thought to be poisonous), lima beans, maize, squash, potatoes, and chocolate—and in turn the people of the New World were introduced to horses, cattle, and the Eurasian diseases that largely decimated them. The development of global trade patterns also gave Europeans readier access to such items as tea, coffee, chocolate, and sugar. As sugarcane cultivation spread from the eastern Mediterranean to the eastern Atlantic and then to the New World, so did the slave trade through the agency of the Portuguese and the Spanish. The slave trade was not a European invention, for it was already thriving among the Africans. Nevertheless, for the enslaved Africans and the decimated natives of America, European expansion often had cruel results. In Europe the discovery of new continents and the increased contact with Africa and Asia forced a rethinking of traditional views. As travelers and explorers documented their observations, a more accurate understanding of the physical world began to replace myth and superstition. The developments of this period also marked the first steps toward a Western hegemony in the world that has lasted into the twentieth century.

Notes

1. C. D. Ley, ed., *Portuguese Voyages 1498–1663* (New York: Dutton, 1947), p. 28.
2. P. M. Watts, "Prophecy and Discovery: On the Spiritual Origins of Christopher Columbus's 'Enterprise of the Indies,'" *American Historical Review* 90 (February 1985): 102.
3. D. B. Quinn, ed., *New American World: A Documentary History of North America to 1612*, Vol. 1: *America from Concept to Discovery: Early Exploration of North America* (New York: Arno Press and Hector Bye, 1979), p. 97.
4. G. F. Hudson, *Europe and China* (London: Arnold, 1931), p. 201.
5. R. Murphey, *The Outsiders: The Western Experience in India and China* (Ann Arbor: University of Michigan Press, 1977), p. 21.
6. F. Braudel, *Civilization and Capitalism, 15th–18th Century*, Vol. 1: *The Structures of Everyday Life: The Limits of the Possible*, trans. S. Reynolds (New York: Harper & Row, 1979), p. 514.
7. C. Wilson, *The Transformation of Europe, 1558–1648* (Berkeley: University of California Press, 1976), p. 62.

Suggestions for Further Reading

Andrews, K. R. *Trade, Plunder and Settlement: Maritime Enterprise and the Genesis of the British Empire, 1480–1630*. Cambridge: Cambridge University Press, 1984.

Ball, J. N. *Merchants and Merchandise: The Expansion of Trade in Europe, 1500–1630*. London: Croom Helm, 1977.

Boxer, C. R. *The Dutch Seaborne Empire, 1600–1800*. London: Knopf, 1965.

——. *The Portuguese Seaborne Empire, 1415–1825*. New York: Knopf, 1969.

Braudel, F. *Civilization and Capitalism*, trans. S. Reynolds. 3 vols. New York: Harper & Row, 1981–1984.

Cipolla, C. M. *Before the Industrial Revolution: European Society and Economy, 1000–1700*, 2d ed. New York: Norton, 1980.

——. *Guns and Sails in the Early Phase of European Expansion, 1400–1700*. London: Collins, 1965.

Cole, J. A. *The Potosí Mita, 1573–1700: Compulsory Indian Labor in the Andes*. Stanford, Calif.: Stanford University Press, 1985.

Curtin, P. D. *Cross-cultural Trade in World History*. Cambridge: Cambridge University Press, 1984.

Davis, R. *The Rise of the Atlantic Economies*. London: Weidenfeld & Nicolson, 1973.

Diffie, B. W., and Winius, G. D. *Foundations of the Portuguese Empire, 1415–1580*. Minneapolis: University of Minnesota Press, 1977.

Elliott, J. H. *The Old World and the New, 1492–1650*. Cambridge: Cambridge University Press, 1970.

Gibson, C. *The Aztecs under Spanish Rule: A History of the Indians of the Valley of Mexico, 1519–1810*. Stanford, Calif.: Stanford University Press, 1964.

Hemming, J. *The Conquest of the Incas*. New York: Harcourt Brace Jovanovich, 1970.

Kling, B. B., and Pearson, M. N., eds. *Europeans in Asia Before Dominion*. Honolulu: University Press of Hawaii, 1979.

Kriedte, P. *Peasants, Landlords and Merchant Capitalists: Europe and the World Economy, 1500–1800*. Leamington, England: Berg Press, 1983.

Lockhart, J. M. *The Men of Cajamarca: A Social and Biographical Study of the First Conquerors of Peru*. Austin: University of Texas Press, 1972.

MacLeod, M. J. *Spanish Central America: A Socioeconomic History, 1520–1720*. Berkeley: University of California Press, 1973.

Mannix, D. P., and Cowley, M. *Black Cargoes: A History of the Atlantic Slave Trade, 1518–1865*. New York: Viking, 1962.

Masselman, G. *The Cradle of Colonialism*. New Haven, Conn.: Yale University Press, 1963.

McAlister, L. N. *Spain and Portugal in the New World, 1492–1700*. Minneapolis: University of Minnesota Press, 1984.

Meilink-Roelofsz, M. A. P. *Asian Trade and European Influence in the Indonesian Archipelago, Between 1500 and About 1630*. The Hague: Nijhoff, 1962.

Mintz, S. W. *Sweetness and Power: The Place of Sugar in Modern History*. New York: Viking, 1985.

Morison, S. E. *The European Discovery of America: The Northern Voyages,* A.D. *500–1600*. New York: Oxford University Press, 1971.

——. *The European Discovery of America: The Southern Voyages,* A.D. *1492–1616*. New York: Oxford University Press, 1974.

Murray, J. J. *Antwerp in the Age of Plantin and Brueghel*. Norman: University of Oklahoma Press, 1970.

Nef, J. *The Conquest of the Material World*. Chicago: University of Chicago Press, 1964.

Nowell, C. E. *The Great Discoveries and the First Colonial Empires*. Ithaca, N.Y.: Cornell University Press, 1954.

Parry, J. H. *The Age of Reconnaissance*, 2d ed. New York: New American Library, 1966.

——. *The Discovery of the Sea*, 2d ed. Berkeley: University of California Press, 1981.

——. *The Establishment of European Hegemony, 1415–1715*. New York: Harper & Row, 1961.

——, ed. *The European Reconnaissance: Selected Documents*. New York: Walker, 1968.

Pearson, M. N. *Merchants and Rulers in Gujarat: The Response to the Portuguese in the Sixteenth Century*. Berkeley: University of California Press, 1976.

Ricci, M. *China in the Sixteenth Century: The Journals of Matthew Ricci, 1583–1610*, trans. L. J. Gallagher. New York: Random House, 1953.

Rice, E. F., Jr. *The Foundations of Early Modern Europe, 1460–1559*. New York: Norton, 1970.

Schurz, W. L. *The Manila Galleon*. New York: Dutton, 1939.

Souza, G. B. *The Survival of Empire: Portuguese Trade and Society in China and the South China Sea, 1630–1754*. Cambridge: Cambridge University Press, 1986.

Spence, J. D. *The Memory Palace of Matteo Ricci*. New York: Viking, 1984.

Wallerstein, I. M. *The Modern World System: Capitalist Agriculture and the Origins of the European World Economy in the Sixteenth Century*. New York: Academic Press, 1974.

Maps and Their Makers (I)

One of the most basic tasks of all human communities, from nomad bands to settled civilizations, is to orient the group to the locations of things. To situate resources, to mark off shelter and defense, to establish territorial limits—all are essential to group survival. The idea of accomplishing these tasks by drawing a map evolved long ago among many different peoples. Human beings were making maps long before they developed the ability to symbolize their speech in writing.

From early times, too, maps appear to have been used not only to mark off known places but to theorize, and sometimes fantasize, about unknown ones. Modern armchair travelers who open maps to stimulate their imaginations about faraway places are exercising the same faculty as ancient mapmakers who populated the scrolls and edges of their charts with dragons and monsters. Maps thus invite us not only to define but also to extend the world. They are the instruments of our curiosity as well as our knowledge, our dreams as well as our science.

The growth of our knowledge has made mapmaking—cartography—an ever more important part of modern civilization. Somewhere in the world at this moment, a topographical or geodesic survey is making our understanding of the earth more precise; somewhere, a telescope is scanning the heavens, and a satellite or a space vehicle is beaming back information about interstellar space that will go into a map. Scientists and physicians speak of mapping the brain and the living cell, and psychologists, the human mind. As a tool as well as a metaphor, mapping is one of the principal functions of our culture, in some ways as basic as speech.

The universality of mapmaking is one of its most striking characteristics. The Eskimos of North America carved coastal maps of extraordinary accuracy on animal skins and wood. The Marshall Islanders of the South Pacific lashed sticks and cane fibers together to indicate wind and wave patterns at sea, inserting stones or pieces of coral to designate islands. The Spanish conqueror Cortés made his advance through Central America only with the aid of native maps, and the British explorer James Cook navigated the South Seas with a chart made for him by a Tahitian that covered nearly 3,000 miles. Australian aborigines made rudimentary maps, and European cave dwellers incised maps on cave walls.

Perhaps the oldest surviving map is a clay tablet found at Nuzi in northern Iraq, dating from c. 2300 B.C. It is a cadastral survey, a map of property lots made for purposes of taxation. Many of the surviving maps from the second millennium B.C. are city plans, such as the highly detailed one for the city of Nippur on the Euphrates, which shows the major temples, the river itself, the central park and canal, moats, walls, and the city gates. There is no reference to a Chinese map before the seventh century B.C. and none extant before the second century, but the splendid examples excavated in Hunan province in 1974 suggest that Chinese cartography may be as ancient as any, and as sophisticated. Drawn on silk for the king of Changsha, they depict much of modern Hunan and regions as far south as the South China Sea. The first map gives the names of all cities and provinces and indicates major topographical features including more than 30 rivers. The second map, a military one, shows walled fortresses, military encampments, supply depots, and observation towers. Both the detail of the maps and the

The oldest surviving world map. Earth, ocean, and heaven are linked in this Babylonian vision of the cosmos, dating from the sixth century B.C. [British Museum]

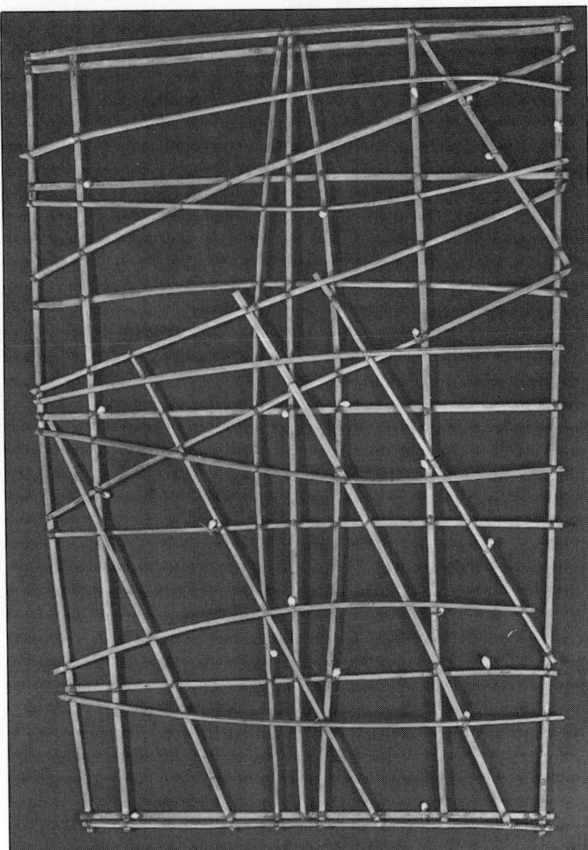

A chart of the South Seas. This ingenious map of the Marshall Islands in the South Pacific depicts wind and tidal patterns. The islands themselves are marked by inserts of coral stone. [British Museum]

intricate use of symbols and legends suggest a highly developed tradition of cartography.

The earliest maps, then, were local and functional. The first people to attempt to map the world as a whole appear to have been the Babylonians. Their interest in the earth may have derived from their fascination with the heavens, which had for them, as for most peoples, a deep religious significance. The Babylonians depicted the sky as a vast circle, charting some 5,000 stars. In doing so, they introduced the first systematic measurement into mapping. The Babylonians had long before devised a calendar of 360 days, which they had divided into 60-minute hours and 60-second minutes. They hit on the idea of applying the same number system for measuring the circle, dividing it into 360 degrees, the degrees into minutes, and the minutes into seconds. Applying this to the heavens, they were able to plot the locations of the stars.

The Babylonians likewise conceived of the earth as round. In what appears to be the earliest surviving world map, it is depicted as a flat circular disk with Babylonia in the center and its neighbors, the Assyrians and the Chaldeans, to the east and the southwest, respectively. Beyond that single landmass lay a great, globe-encircling ocean, from which rose seven islands. These in turn formed a bridge to an outer circle or Heavenly Ocean, the abode of the ancient gods. Fanciful and symbolic, this first world map was as much an exercise in cosmography as cartography.

Not long after, the Ionian philosopher Anaximander produced the first world map in the Greek-speaking world. The slightly later map of Hecataeus (c. 501 B.C.), who is credited with having compiled the first manual of geography, was used by Aristagoras of Miletus in soliciting the help of Sparta against the Persian Empire at the time of the Ionian revolt. The Spartan king, Cleomenes, was attracted by the prospect of spoil from Persia's neighbors, but when he learned that they lay three months' journey away, he ordered Aristogoras out of Sparta by nightfall.

Herodotus, the source of this story, himself proposed locating geographic sites by means of parallels and meridians. By the end of the fifth century B.C., the idea of maps had become familiar enough so that a character in Aristophanes' comedy *The Clouds* (produced in 423 B.C.), carried one on stage and pointed out Athens on it. In the next two centuries the geographic horizons of the Greeks expanded considerably, notably through the conquests of Alexander and the travels of Pytheas to Britain and the Low Countries. The actual size of the world remained a matter of conjecture, however, until Eratosthenes (276–196 B.C.), the librarian of Alexandria, conceived the brilliant scheme of measuring the angle of shadow cast by the sun at noon in Alexandria and computing it against the known distance to another site on the same meridian in Egypt, where the sun's rays were reportedly vertical at noon on the day of the summer solstice. Assuming (as the ancient mathematician Pythagoras had) that the world was a perfect sphere, Eratosthenes was able to calculate its circumference as 250,000 stadia, or about 28,000 miles. None of Eratosthenes' factual assumptions was quite right—the two sites were not precisely on the same meridian, the distance between them was not measured exactly, and the earth is not a perfect sphere—but his method was basically sound, and his result was only about 3,000 miles off. For the first time, human beings had a tolerably accurate notion of the size of their planet, based not on fancy or guesswork but on scientific measurement. The news was not especially pleasing to Hellenistic geographers, however. It meant that three-quarters of the globe was unknown to them.

This vast expanse, *terra incognita* ("unknown earth"), as the Romans called it, did not remain unpopulated for long. Solinus, a grammarian of the third century A.D., imagined a race of horse-footed men to the east in Asia with ears so long that the flaps covered their entire bodies, making clothes unnecessary. Other men were said to have only one leg with a giant foot. In Germany, Solinus asserted, there were birds whose feathers glowed in the dark, while Libya was the home of the cockatrice, which crept along the ground like a crocodile on its forequarters but was hoisted in the rear by lateral fins. Mythical kingdoms abounded as well, such as that of Prester (Elder) John, a Christian monarch reputedly descended from the Magi who ruled a land in which one of the rivers flowed directly from Paradise. When several expeditions failed to discover this kingdom in the east (Marco Polo reported it conquered by Chinghis Khan), cartographers obligingly shifted it to Africa, where it figured on maps for several centuries. A less benign vision was that of the land of Gog and Magog, whose terrifying hordes, first prophesied by Ezekiel, were feared by Christian and Muslim alike. Some mapmakers placed the savage tribes in southern Russia, while a Syrian tale held that Alexander the Great had sealed them off, presumably in India, behind a wall of iron and brass. Ibn-Khaldun, a fourteenth-century Arab geographer and historian, apparently confused the wall of Gog and Magog with the Great Wall of China.

As the Babylonians had placed themselves at the center of the earth and as medieval Christians placed Jerusalem there, so too did the Chinese regard their "Middle Kingdom" as the center of things. Legend had it that two men had walked from the court of the fabled Emperor Yu, first from north to south and then from east to west, and found the earth equidistant at all points from the imperial palace. We do not know how the Chinese may have embellished their own *terra incognita*, but their high standard of mapmaking was maintained and advanced. P'ei Hsiu (Bei Xiu, A.D. 224–271), author of the *Six Principles of Cartography*, constructed a map of China for the emperor Wu Ti on a scale of about a third of a mile to an inch; it covered 18 sheets. An even more finely detailed map was produced in the eighth century: measuring 33 by 30 feet, it took 16 years to complete. In the eleventh century, Shen Kuo (Shen Guo) produced the first relief map, modeled in wax.

The most important ancient cartographer in the West was Claudius Ptolemy (c. 90–c. 168), who, like Eratosthenes, was the librarian of Alexandria. In his two principal works—the *Almagest*, a compendium of astronomy and mathematics, and the *Geographia*, which, with its large world map and 26 regional ones showing some 8,000 places, was the world's first atlas—he attempted to survey the whole of the cosmos. Like Eratosthenes, Ptolemy had better ideas than information. He devised the notion of dividing maps into areas of latitude and longitude, and he was the first to orient maps to the north. But he lacked precise instruments for celestial angle measurement and timekeeping that were essential to accurate siting, and he was dependent for much of his information on travelers' reports that, as he well knew, were often both boastful and sketchy. The Ptolemaic world consisted of three continents—Europe, Asia, and Africa. Of these, only Europe was shown in full outline, and even here, guesswork or inaccurate reportage was evident; the shape of Britain (Albion), for example, was grossly distorted, and Scandinavia (Scandia) was shown as an island. Nonetheless, Ptolemy's map was by far the best representation of the known world available to Western or Islamic cartographers for more than 1,300 years, and it became the standard reference, particularly in Arab lands.

This huge, spendidly carved Aztec stone calendar, which stood atop the Aztec temple at Tenochtitlán, was used to make complex astronomical measurements, including the calculation of eclipses. [Paolo Koch/Photo Researchers]

Two of Ptolemy's errors were to have fateful consequences. Like most educated people of his time, he rejected the hypothesis of the third-century B.C. astronomer Aristarchus that the sun was the center of the universe and placed the earth there instead. He also underestimated the circumference of the globe, accepting Poseidonius' calculation of 18,000 miles instead of Eratosthenes' older but more accurate one. The result of this, amplified by the expanded idea of Asia brought home by Marco Polo, was to persuade Christopher Columbus that the Indies were relatively close to western Europe. That mistake uncovered the New World.

The first large map depicting the New World in its relation to Europe was made in 1500 by Juan de la Cosa, who accompanied Columbus on his second voyage. De la Cosa, like Columbus, was still unsure that the New World was not connected to Asia. But in 1507 a German cartographer, Martin Waldseemuller, produced the first map suggesting that "America," as he baptized the southern half of the New World in honor of the explorer Amerigo Vespucci, was actually a continent, separated by an unknown and unnamed ocean. Waldseemuller's truncated depiction of the Western Hemisphere was hopelessly inadequate, and his "Ocean Orientalis" was only a fraction of the actual Pacific Ocean. But his daring guess was right. For the first time, even if only in the roughest configuration, the true shape of the world was known. Six years later, Vasco Núñez de Balboa made the first sighting of the western Pacific, and six years after that Ferdinand Magellan undertook the first circumnavigation of the globe. Magellan's heroic voyage cost him his life (he was killed in a skirmish with natives in the Philippines); only one of his five ships survived, and 35 of his 280 sailors. With what they brought back, however, the Portuguese cartographer Diego Ribero was able to produce a map that conveyed not only the true shape but also an approximation of the true proportions of the world.

From this point on, discovery proceeded apace, as explorers and cartographers worked together. The dimensions of Africa had finally been realized in the fifteenth century, when Prince Henry of Portugal—the famous Henry the Navigator—had explored the west coast of Africa, partly in hopes of finding a sea route around it to India, partly in quest of the kingdom of Prester John. The daunting length of Africa had led Columbus to try a crossing of the Atlantic instead, but in 1498 Vasco da Gama sailed around the Cape of Good Hope and reached India. By the mid-sixteenth century the real dimensions of North and South America had begun to appear on maps, and the influence of Ptolemy at last faded. It was no longer permissible, as it had still been only a generation or two earlier, to mix fact and fancy, discovery and tradition. Rulers in quest of gold and merchants of silk and spices demanded accuracy and completeness of their maps. What the historian J. H. Parry has called the age of reconnaissance had begun.

The dependence of mariners on the accuracy of their maps for voyages of increasing distance and duration highlighted a problem that Ptolemy had grappled with: how to represent the reality of a three-dimensional globe on a flat, two-dimensional surface. Ptolemy had divided his world into lines of longitude and latitude, thus forming a grid whose intersections would enable one to plot any point on the globe; but on that globe itself, of course, the lines were curved, not straight, converging in the case of longitude at the two poles and varying widely in length in the case of latitude. Ptolemaic maps had attempted to compensate for this by drawing curvilinear lines, but while this was of some help with lines of latitude, it still left parallel rather than converging lines of longitude. Model globes themselves were helpful, but any large enough to show sufficient detail for navigational purposes were far too large to carry.

A practical solution was devised by a Flemish cartographer, Gerhard Kremer (1512–1594), better known as Gerardus Mercator. Mercator abandoned the Ptole-

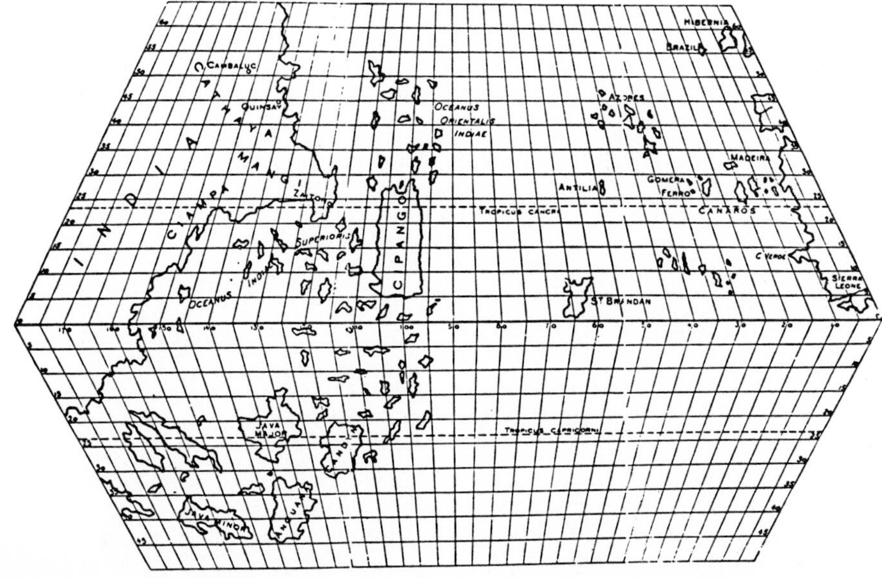

A sketch of the map used by Columbus on his first voyage to the New World in 1492. The cartographer estimated the distance to the "Indies" as being little more than that from Portugal to the Azores Islands. "India" and "Cathay" (China) were represented as part of a single undifferentiated land mass. The large island of "Cipango" represents Japan [Library of Congress]

maic compromise of curving lines to draw a grid of perfectly straight ones. At the same time, he extended the distance between the lines of latitude at an increasing rate from the equator to the poles. This widened the distortion both of distance and of representation, particularly in the polar regions: thus, on a Mercator map, the island of Greenland appears considerably larger than the continent of South America, although in reality it is only one-eighth as big. But the map was of vital advantage to mariners in one respect. It enabled them to plot direction and to chart their voyages from home port to final destination on a straight line. Mercator's new map was first published in 1569, and his system is still in use.

By the late sixteenth century, the shape, dimension, and much of the outline of the world had been revealed. Shortly thereafter, the shape of the heavens would begin to disclose itself as well.

Suggestions for Further Reading

Bagrow, L. *A History of Cartography*. London: Watts, 1964.

Bricker, C., and Tooley, R. V. *A History of Cartography: 2500 Years of Maps and Mapmakers*. London: Thames & Hudson, 1969.

Brown, L. A. *The Story of Maps*. Boston: Little, Brown, 1980.

Harley, J. B., and Woodward, D., eds. *The History of Cartography*. Chicago: University of Chicago Press, 1987.

Kopal, Z. *Widening Horizons: Man's Quest to Understand the Structure of the Universe*. New York: Taplinger, 1970.

Parry, J. H. *The Age of Reconnaissance*, 2d ed. New York: New American Library, 1966.

Schlee, S. *The Edge of an Unfamiliar World: A History of Oceanography*. New York: Dutton, 1973.

Thrower, N. J. W. *Maps and Man*. Englewood Cliffs, N.J.: Prentice-Hall, 1972.

Wilford, J. N. *The Mapmakers*. New York: Knopf, 1981.

CHAPTER · 18

State-Building and Revolution

Emboldened by the wealth of its new empire, Spain made a major bid in the late sixteenth century to establish domination in Western Europe. This was largely the outgrowth of the determination of both Charles V and Philip II to rule their inherited territories, and of the equally strong resolve of the English and French to prevent the expansion of Habsburg power. The Netherlands, Portugal, England, Italy, and France were all threatened by a militant Spanish imperialism imbued with the spirit of the Counter-Reformation. By the end of the century Philip II had largely failed in his quest, although fighting continued in the Netherlands, and Portugal remained firmly under Spanish rule. Two decades after Philip's death in 1598, the Thirty Years' War erupted. Most of Europe was involved in what proved to be one of the bloodiest wars in the continent's history. The wars, internal tensions and rebellions stemming from the increasing burdens of government centralization and taxation, and competing religious ideologies both within and across borders contributed to a series of crises in the mid-1600s that threw almost every major European state into turmoil.

A pious, brooding, bookish man, Philip II was described by an English admirer as "the most potent monarch of Christendom." [National Portrait Gallery, London]

Philip II and the Quest for Spanish Hegemony

Spain's bid for supremacy in the late 1500s was a natural outgrowth of earlier Habsburg policy, the development of political absolutism, the religious zeal of the Counter-Reformation, and the wealth and power created by its new colonial empire. It was also made possible by the division of the vast and unwieldly Habsburg domain between two crowns. When the emperor Charles V abdicated and retired to a monastery in 1556, the imperial crown was bestowed on his brother, Ferdinand I (1556–1564), along with the Austrian Habsburg territories. The Spanish throne went to Philip II (1556–1598), together with the territories of the Netherlands, Milan, Naples, Spanish America, and lesser places. His wife ruled England in her own right as Mary I (1553–1558). Vast though they remained, Spain's dominions still had a clear center of authority in the court of Madrid.

Spanish power in the reign of Philip II was made possible in part at the expense of France. Charles V's troubles with the Lutherans and the Turks had prevented him from attaining a permanent victory over his archenemy, King Francis I of France (1515–1547). For most of their reigns the two monarchs quarreled, particularly over northern Italy. After the Habsburg forces captured Francis at the battle of Pavia in 1525, Charles held him prisoner in Spain until he signed a treaty surrendering both the duchy of Burgundy and his Italian claims. When Francis repudiated the treaty, the struggle was renewed. Both rulers had died by the time this phase of the Habsburg quest for dominance ended in 1559 with the Treaty of Cateau-Cambrésis. The treaty, which confirmed Spanish possession of Milan and Naples, ended 65 years of fighting in northern Italy.

In 1559 Philip II's prospects for the extension of Spanish Habsburg hegemony were good. The Treaty of Cateau-Cambrésis, which recognized Spanish mastery in Italy, required Spain to yield nothing of consequence in return. Although Philip's attempt to win the hand of the English queen, Elizabeth I, had been politely rebuffed after Mary's death, the new treaty included a proviso for his marriage to Elizabeth of Valois, the 13-year-old daughter of the French king, Henry II (1547–1559). Henry's accidental death in a tilting match during the treaty ceremonies

18.1 Europe About 1560

brought his feeble son, Francis II (1559–1560), briefly to the French throne. Two of his equally weak brothers followed. Not until the late 1590s would a strong monarch again govern France. Spain was without peer in Europe.

Although the work of centralizing had been under way in the major western European states since the late 1400s, the Spain that Philip inherited was still far from unified. Unlike England, where a single Parliament served as a unifying bond, Spain had a separate assembly called a Cortes for Castile, each of the three regions of Aragon, and Navarre. France and the Netherlands similarly had regional states, but in both cases there was an Estates General, albeit weak, to represent the country as a whole. Philip made no attempt to create such a body in Spain but instead governed each of the three states—Aragon, Castile, and Navarre—independently. In Castile, the largest state with 7 million inhabitants, the aristocracy was tax-exempt and thus had little reason to strengthen the Cortes. Because the nobility of Aragon had a tradition of greater independence and political power, Philip seldom summoned its Cortes. The states of Aragon and Navarre, with a population exceeding a million, were in any event less important than populous Castile, whose townspeople and peasants bore the brunt of Philip's taxation. In the end, these taxes virtually destroyed Spanish manufacturing.

Although Philip had no Cortes for Spain as a whole, central authority was administered by local agents appointed by the crown. The English monarchs accomplished this function in the early Tudor period by expanding the authority of the justices of the peace. Similarly, in Castile, Isabella increased the responsibilities of the *corregidors*, who supervised the town councils.

The distinctive feature of Spanish government was the system of higher councils Philip used to supervise the affairs of his far-flung empire. Although the English sovereigns also used councils, the English conciliar structure was less elaborate and powerful than the Spanish. In England the Privy Council advised the monarch, helped administer the realm, and performed certain judicial functions, and there were councils for the north and for Wales. Philip, whose domain was much more extensive and scattered, had a major council for each region of his empire: Castile, Aragon, the Netherlands, Italy (Milan and Naples), and Spanish America. Viceroys carried out the instructions of these councils. There were also specialized councils to handle such matters as state affairs, finance, war, and the Inquisition. Although the councils convened in Madrid, there were so many of them that Philip rarely attended. Nevertheless, his bookish, bureaucratic temperament moved him to spend long hours poring over the mountain of paperwork his officials produced. Philip became heavily embroiled in the details of government, devoting enormous time to writing marginal comments on the papers he studied. Distrustful of his officials and jealous of his power, he played his officers against each other and set up a system of checks and balances that made Spanish administration ponderous and inefficient.

Although Philip apparently hoped to wield absolute power based on the idea that his subjects owed him unquestioning obedience as a right and a Christian duty, in practice both the top-heavy administrative system and limited revenues circumscribed his authority. The nobles paid only sales taxes, and though Philip taxed merchants and professionals, there were fewer of them proportionately in Spain than in other western European countries. The bulk of the taxes therefore fell on those least able to pay, the peasants. The result was insufficient revenue, forcing Philip to declare bankruptcy three times during his reign. Because the government protected the ships that transported New World bullion to Spain, it was entitled to a royalty of 20 percent, but smuggling decreased the potential value of this revenue, and the king mortgaged much of what he did receive to finance military campaigns. Like the English monarchs in the early 1600s, he raised some money by selling offices and titles, and he also received income from crown lands and the sale of papal dispensations. None of this, however, compensated for the loss of funds that would have been obtained by properly taxing the nobility. In Castile alone, 300 tax-exempt nobles owned more than half the land. The king's habitual indebtedness was thus a passive restraint on his power exercised by the nobility.

THE SPANISH CITADEL: MADRID AND THE ESCORIAL

The development of absolute government and the bureaucracy to administer it made a permanent capital necessary. "It was right," said one observer, "that so great a monarchy should have a city which could function as its heart—a vital center in the midst of the body, which ministered equally to every state in time of peace and war."[1] Unlike Charles V, who frequently moved around his empire, Philip favored a sedentary life, though when he settled the capital at Madrid in 1561, he had no apparent intention of making it permanent. Located on a plateau at an altitude of more than 2,000 feet, its major advantages were its healthy climate and its centrality. The city had a population of only 25,000 in 1561, but by the early 1600s it had quadrupled in size. Madrid's rise adversely affected Valladolid and Toledo, the latter a beautiful medieval city whose population of more than 50,000 decreased by two-thirds during Philip's reign. By the mid-seventeenth century Madrid was the only Spanish city whose population was substantially larger than it had been in the 1500s.

Madrid's growth was not the result of new industry but of bureaucratic expansion and the capital's attraction to younger sons of the nobility, declining hidalgos, and impoverished workers in search of a living. In a futile attempt to curb the growth of the city, the crown ordered the nobles to return to their estates in 1611, hoping the hangers-on would follow. Gypsies were also attracted to the city despite repeated attempts to expel them. Urban growth in Madrid was relatively easy because of ample space. The city was enclosed only with a mud wall to denote its boundaries, and as late as the nineteenth century there was still open space inside the walls. The city's importance as a financial center grew in the 1600s, particularly after the collapse of the large fairs at Medina del Campo. Although Madrid had neither a university nor a bishop, it became a leading cultural center in the early seventeenth century.

The site selected for Philip's massive new palace, the Escorial, was in the rocky hills some 30 miles northwest of Madrid. The building had been planned because of a provision in Charles V's will that his son construct a "dynastic pantheon" to house the bodies of Spanish sovereigns. In the octagonal Pantheon of the Kings, the gray marble coffins now rest four high along the walls. Philip, a deeply religious man, took a direct interest in the design, at one point admonishing one of the architects, Juan de Herrera, to remember the basic ideals of "simplicity of form, severity in the whole, nobility without arrogance, majesty without ostentation." The Escorial took two decades to build (1563–1584). Laid out in the shape of a gridiron, which probably reflected the influence of Italian Renaissance palace architecture, the gray stone building housed a Hieronymite monastery, a royal mausoleum where Charles V was interred, a large domed church inspired by Michelangelo's plan for St. Peter's in Rome, a library, and the royal palace and apartments. From a window in the apartments Philip could look out on the high altar in the chapel.

The Culture of the Spanish Counter-Reformation

The spirit of religious austerity revealed in the Escorial reflected the severer side of the Catholic Reformation. The Spanish Inquisition, founded in 1478, rigorously persecuted Protestants and other suspected heretics, even twice imprisoning Ignatius of Loyola, the Jesuit founder. The extent of its power was demonstrated when it jailed Bartolomé de Carranza, the archbishop of Toledo and primate of Spain, for 17 years on falsified charges of heresy. Obsessed with the need to keep the Spanish church pure, Philip supported the Inquisition and on five occasions even attended *autos-de-fé*, religious rites, or "pageants of faith," at which sinners and heretics performed acts of penance or were executed. The Spanish Inquisition averaged 1,000 cases a year during his reign. The Inquisition also supervised the converted Jews known as *Conversos* who remained in Spain. The king himself was anti-Semitic, as reflected in his belief that "all the heresies which have existed in Germany and France . . . have been sown by the descendants of Jews."[2]

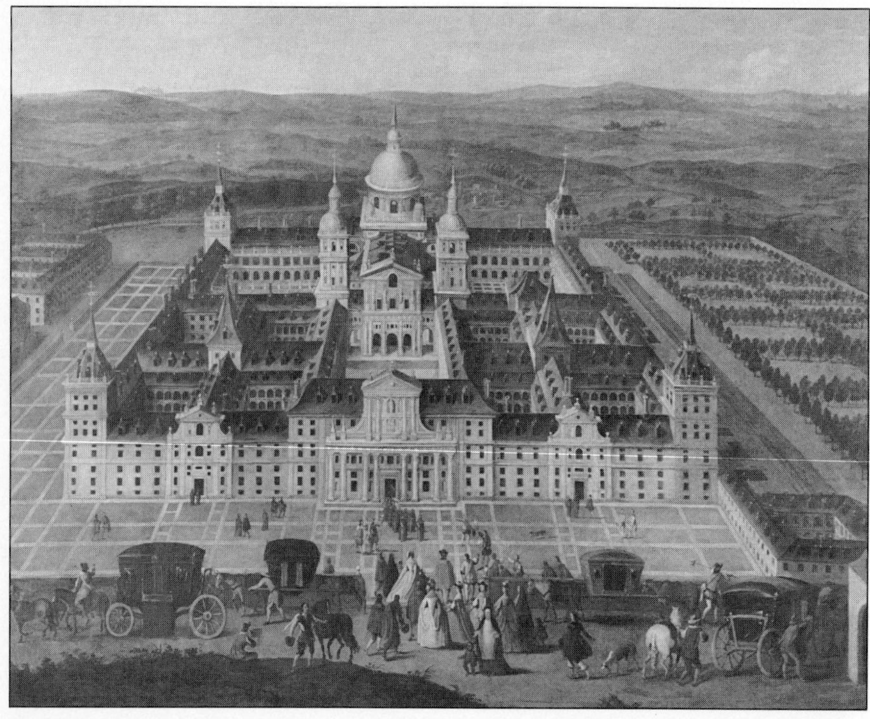

Philip II's palace, the Escorial, as it appeared in the seventeenth century. According to a popular legend, the ground plan symbolized the gridiron on which St. Lawrence, whom Philip admired, was martyred. Philip tried to find the martyr's head to keep as a relic at the palace. [Photo RMN; Musée du Louvre]

When Philip struck at the *Moriscos*—the christianized Moors of Granada—by banning their language, customs, and distinctive dress, he incited a rebellion in 1568 that lasted until 1570. Subsequent efforts to assimilate the Moriscos were largely unsuccessful, and in the early 1600s they were deported by the tens of thousands. Altogether the number of Jews and Moors expelled from Spain between 1492, when they were given the option of becoming Christians or going into exile, and 1609 probably exceeded half a million. Philip also exiled the Jews from northern Italy much as his father had expelled them from Naples in 1544. Some 300,000 Conversos survived the threat of the Spanish Inquisition and remained active in professional and commercial activities, though most lived in their own districts.

Despite the brutal repression that characterized Spanish religious policy and comprised an important facet of absolutism, there was a positive side to Spanish piety in this period. This is beautifully manifested in the work of the mystics Teresa of Avila (1515–1582) and John of the Cross (1542–1591), both of whom were of Converso ancestry. Teresa, whose father was a hidalgo and whose seven brothers were colonial officials in America, was a Carmelite nun. Much of her work was devoted to the Carmelite Reform, an order dedicated to recapturing the original spirit of Carmelite austerity. She shared her religious experience in an autobiography, and in writings such as *The Way of Perfection* and *Exclamations of the Soul to God* she described the progress of the Christian soul toward its goal of unity with the divine. John of the Cross, a Carmelite who assisted Teresa in her reforming work, expressed his mystical experiences in poetry and in a meticulous analysis of mysticism. Together they inspired humble Spaniards to maintain their devotion to the Catholic church; their emphasis on the spiritual life probably helped the masses to cope with their poverty.

Philip's favorite painter was Titian, the late Renaissance Venetian master famous for his sumptuous colors. For more than a quarter of a century Titian supplied Charles V and Philip with paintings. A number of these depicted mythological themes, often including sensuous female nudes. Like most of his contemporaries, Titian and presumably the pious Philip as well saw no contradiction between their veneration of the Virgin Mary and their appreciation of physical beauty in the Venus figures.

Directly as well as through his brilliant successor at Venice, Tintoretto (1518–1594), Titian influenced the painter whose work best captures the spirit of the Spanish Counter-Reformation, Domenico Theotokopoulos (1541–1614), known as El Greco ("the Greek"). Born in Crete, El Greco studied in Venice before moving to Spain in the 1570s. His first work for Philip allegorized the Holy League against the Turks by depicting Philip, the pope, and the doge of Venice kneeling before the "Holy Name" of Jesus. The king commissioned him to paint an altarpiece, the subject of which was the decision of St. Maurice, a commander in the imperial Roman army, to die rather than worship the traditional Roman deities. Displeased with the extent to which El Greco departed from the more straightforward Venetian style, Philip rejected the work. Most of El Greco's paintings convey the tension between the spiritual and material realms through spiral composition—swirling motion that drives the eye upward—and elongated figures. By accentuating color rather than form, he heightened the spiritual sense and created an art more emotional than intellectual or naturalistic. Thus the canvases of El Greco reflect the spiritual ecstasy expressed in the writings of Teresa and John of the Cross.

Although religion dominated much of the culture of Counter-Reformation Spain, other themes were popular as well, especially in literature and drama. The great masterpiece of Spanish literature, *Don Quixote*, was the work of Miguel de Cervantes (1547–1616), a surgeon's son who spent most of his creative life in Madrid. Captured while fighting against the Turks, he was enslaved in Algiers. Following his ransom, he finally turned to writing plays for the Madrid theater, but success eluded him until he published *Don Quixote* in 1605. A satire of the popular chivalric romances, the book entertained readers by humorously juxtaposing the idealist Don Quixote with the realist Sancho Panza. Despite Sancho's warnings, Don Quixote pursued his "righteous warfare" to rid the world of "accursed" giants, which in fact were windmills and sheep—the visions, said Sancho, of one who had "mills of the same sort in his head."

The success that eluded Cervantes on the stage was achieved by the prolific Lope de Vega (1562–1635), author of 1,500 plays by his own count. His works fall into two categories: heroic plays dealing with Spanish history and legend and comedies of manners and intrigue. Several of his plays break down the stereotyped image of the secluded Spanish lady. Some of Lope's women reject love and marriage, pursue careers, and even become outlaws. One of his most important themes deals with the king as the fount of justice and protector of the poor. Reflecting the spirit of his age, his plays demonstrate respect for the crown and the church.

Spain and the Mediterranean

The wars in which Cervantes and Lope de Vega fought—the former against the Turks, the latter against the English—represent the two spheres of military activity that occupied Philip. Attention was focused on the Muslims in the Mediterranean during the first part of his reign and later on the Protestants in the North Atlantic. With the Ottoman Turks already in control of three-quarters of the Mediterranean coastline, their seizure of Cyprus from Venice in 1571 alarmed Europe. Spain, Venice, and the papacy responded by forming the Holy League to attack the Turks. The league's fleet of 300 ships and 80,000 men,

The battle of Lepanto was the first major European naval victory over the Turks. Some 600 ships were involved. [National Maritime Museum, London]

most of them Spanish, engaged the Turks near Lepanto in Greece. The league won a decisive victory—the first major one in centuries over a Muslim fleet—in this last great battle between oar-propelled ships. The significance of Lepanto lay primarily in its impact on European morale and its check on Islamic expansion. The Turks, however, quickly rebuilt their fleet and refused to be driven from the western Mediterranean, though henceforth they concentrated on North Africa and never regained the superiority they had once enjoyed.

Philip's second major foreign policy triumph came in 1580 when he annexed Portugal and its empire. The death of the Portuguese king without a direct heir gave Philip, whose mother had been a Portuguese princess, his opportunity. After bribes and promises had won the support of the nobility and higher clergy for his own succession, the Spanish army completed the conquest. Philip ensured peace by leaving Portuguese officials to administer the realm and by generally leaving the people alone. The Spanish, however, failed to exploit their victory by coordinating the economic policy of the two countries and their empires. Spain's failure to unify the Iberian peninsula by anything more than a common crown made it possible for Portugal to recover its independence in the next century. During the period that the two crowns were united, large numbers of Portuguese Jews emigrated to Spain, where persecution had become less intense. The annexation also gave Philip additional ships and Atlantic ports, which were sorely needed for his campaigns in the Netherlands and France and for his armadas against the English.

Rebellion in the Netherlands

The revolt of the Netherlands was the first significant setback to Philip II's dream of Habsburg hegemony in western Europe and the New World. The Low Countries were the wealthiest region in Europe and the center of the developing global economy, and its people were accustomed to considerable local autonomy and religious diversity. Unlike Charles V, who had been raised in the Netherlands, Philip spoke no Dutch, disliked the Netherlands, and did not set foot there after 1559. The roots of the rebellion against Spanish authority were bound up in his attempt to impose a more centralized and absolute government. The first crucial step occurred when the Catholic church in the Netherlands was reorganized. By expanding the number of bishops from 4 to 18 and nominating them himself, Philip strengthened his hold over the church. Determined to impose religious uniformity in the Netherlands, Philip ordered that the decrees of the Council of Trent be enforced. The Protestants responded with the "Compromise," a covenant pledging to resist the decrees of Trent and the Inquisition. Leading members of the council of state, which helped Philip's regent, Margaret of Parma, govern the Netherlands, protested in vain. When several hundred nobles presented their grievances to Margaret in 1566, one of her courtiers derided them as beggars. Making the epithet a badge of honor, the rebel battle cry became "Long live the beggars!"

Although the nobles had set the stage for rebellion by their protests, initially they failed to lead it. Instead the first outbreak of violence came in the summer of 1566 when Calvinists attacked the symbols of Catholicism. In a frenzy of iconoclasm—the "Calvinist Fury"—they ransacked Catholic churches, shocking almost everyone by their destructiveness. Unable to keep order, Margaret was replaced by the ruthless duke of Alva, who professed a willingness to destroy the country rather than see it fall into the hands of heretics. Backed by an army of 10,000, he attempted to enforce absolute rule through a special tribunal called the Council of Troubles. Because it executed thousands of heretics, confiscated their property, and imposed heavy new taxes, Netherlanders called it the Council of Blood. Thousands fled.

The heavy-handed Spanish tactics were enormously expensive. With Alva and his successors finally mobilizing 65,000 men and more for their campaigns, the tax revenue from the Netherlands was diverted to the war. Even this was insufficient, but Philip could not provide additional funds from Spain. The result was chronically unpaid troops prone to rebel against their own officers; more than 45 mutinies occurred between 1572 and 1607.

Instead of cowing the Netherlanders, Alva's cruelty prompted them to rally around William the Silent, prince of Orange (1533–1584). William was a *politique*, someone who allowed political circumstances rather than religion to dictate his allegiance. Originally a Lutheran, he had converted to Catholicism as a child in order to receive his inheritance, but he returned to the Lutheran fold in 1567 and became a Calvinist in 1572. As *stadholder* or governor of the northern provinces of Holland, Utrecht, and Zeeland, where Calvinism was strong, he had a natural base of support. He also had the allegiance of a group of pirates and patriots who called themselves "sea beggars" and preyed on Spanish shipping. In the spring of 1572 they captured Brill and other ports in Holland and Zeeland, providing a haven to which Calvinists in other provinces fled. When the Spaniards besieged Leiden the following year, the rebels opened the dikes, forcing the Spanish army to flee before the advancing floodwaters.

The high point of rebel fortunes came in 1576 after unpaid Spanish troops sacked Antwerp. The "Spanish Fury" left more than 7,000 dead and persuaded the largely

The "Calvinist Fury"

The revolt in the Netherlands commenced with an outburst of violent iconoclasm in 1566. An English observer describes the "Calvinist Fury."

When . . . [the priests] should have begun their service, there was a company [that] began to sing psalms, at the beginning being but a company of boys, whereupon the margrave and other . . . lords came to the church and rebuked them. But all in vain, for . . . as soon as they turned their backs, they [went] to it again, and the company increased. . . . They broke up the choir. . . .

After that, they began with the image of Our Lady . . . and utterly defaced her and her chapel, and after [that], the whole church, which was the costliest church in Europe, and [they] have so spoiled it that they have not left a place to sit. . . . And from thence, part went to the parish churches and part to the houses of religion, and made such dispatch as I think the like was never done in one night. . . .

Coming into Our Lady church, it looked like a hell, where were above 1,000 torches burning, and such a noise, as if heaven and earth had gone together, with falling . . . images and beating down of costly works. . . . From thence I went . . . to all the houses of religion, where was the like stir, breaking and spoiling all that there was. Yet, they that did this never looked towards any spoil, but broke all in pieces and let it lay underfoot. So that, to be short, they have spoiled and destroyed all the churches, as well nunneries as others, but as I do understand they neither said nor did anything to the nuns. . . . In divers places in Flanders they have [done] and do the like.

Source: J. W. Burgon, *The Life and Times of Sir Thomas Gresham, Knt.*, vol. 2 (London: Jennings, 1839), pp. 138–140 (edited to conform to modern usage).

Catholic provinces in the south to ally with the primarily Protestant areas of the north. All but 4 of the 17 provinces united in the Pacification of Ghent (November 1576), and the others joined in the Union of Brussels (January 1577). The religious question was settled by leaving each region free to make its own policy. The Spanish, however, refused to quit, and by 1579 Philip's new commander, the duke of Parma (Margaret's son), had regained a large degree of control by combining military victories in the south with an appeal to Catholic Netherlanders to stand firm with Spain. The ten southern provinces, organized as the Union of Arras, made their peace with Philip, but under William's leadership the seven northern and largely Protestant provinces, the Union of Utrecht, declared their independence in 1581.

Even as Parma's forces advanced northward, the Dutch cause was jeopardized when a Catholic partisan assassinated William in 1584 with the pope's blessing. Unwilling to see the Protestant cause in the Netherlands crushed, the English stepped into the breach, sending a small army in 1585. The French too provided assistance. Whatever chance Philip had to destroy the Dutch rebels was lost when he became directly embroiled in war against England. By 1593 the Spaniards had been driven out of the northern provinces, though fighting continued until 1609. War resumed in 1621, and not until 1648 did the Spanish formally recognize the independence of the Dutch Republic.

The Armada portrait of Elizabeth I, painted by George Gower c. 1588. The upper left shows the English fleet, while the view in the upper right depicts the Spanish armada being destroyed by gales. Elizabeth often wore a stylish wig and covered her face with a white cosmetic that blanched the skin. [Marquess of Tavistock, Trustee of the Bedford Estate]

The English Challenge

Well before Elizabeth I's decision to send an army to the Netherlands, relations with Spain had been deteriorating. On the queen's part the reasons for the hostility were less religious than political and economic. The English wanted to trade with Spain's American colonies, and the attack on John Hawkins' third expedition had set off a series of hostile economic moves on the part of both states between 1568 and 1573. The Netherlands were also a source of friction. Although Elizabeth was reluctant to support rebels and was not committed to Dutch independence, she was unwilling to accept either a massive Spanish military presence in the Netherlands or Dutch reliance on the French, which could result in French domination of the entire Channel coast.

Relations between Elizabeth and Philip were further complicated by the problem of Mary Stuart, queen of Scotland (1542–1567), widow of the French king Francis II, and a member of the powerful French Catholic family of Guise. As the great-granddaughter of the first Tudor king, Henry VII, Mary claimed the English throne, insisting that Elizabeth, as Anne Boleyn's daughter, was illegitimate. Mary, however, had fallen on hard times in Scotland because of a scandalous marriage to the earl of Bothwell, the probable murderer of her husband, Henry Lord Darnley. Irate Scottish Protestants, including the reformer John Knox, forced Mary to abdicate in 1567. After her escape to England a year later, she remained under arrest for 19 years in remote castles. Although Elizabeth tried to negotiate her return to the Scottish throne, Mary supported plots for her overthrow. In 1584 a conspiracy involving the Spanish ambassador helped set the stage for English intervention against Spain in the Netherlands. When royal officials intercepted a letter from Mary in 1586 encouraging yet another assassination attempt, Elizabeth agreed to have Mary stand trial. She was unanimously found guilty, and Elizabeth reluctantly authorized her execution in February 1587. Philip had determined to invade England well before Mary's death, but her execution and the Protestantism of her son, King James VI of Scotland, gave him an excuse to claim the English throne as his own. He based that claim on his descent from a granddaughter of the fourteenth-century English King Edward III.

Because Philip had insufficient funds to mount a direct seaborne assault, his plan called for a fleet to control the English Channel while Parma's veterans invaded England from the Netherlands. Preparation of the armada was delayed when Sir Francis Drake's daring attack on Cadiz in April 1587 destroyed some 20 ships and crucial supplies. During the interval, Spain's experienced admiral, the marquess of Santa Cruz, died. His successor, the duke of Medina Sidonia, had neither confidence in himself nor adequate experience. "I am always seasick," he protested, "[and have] no experience of seafaring or war."[3] When the two fleets met in July 1588, they were roughly equal in size, though the English vessels had greater maneuverability and superior long-range guns. Because the Spaniards used a crescent-shaped formation, the English were unable to get into position to use their guns effectively until they finally broke up the enemy formation by launching six burning ships against it. The Spaniards fled north through the Channel, suffering major losses when they rounded northern Scotland and were struck by Atlantic gales. Philip lost nearly half his ships, but an English force sent by Elizabeth to destroy the rest disobeyed her orders, giving Philip a reprieve. In the ensuing years two more armadas were readied to attack England, but storms prevented either from reaching its target. Until peace was officially concluded in 1604, both sides concentrated on helping their allies in the French civil war.

The French Civil War

The struggle in France had begun in 1562 when soldiers of the duke of Guise slaughtered a congregation of Huguenots, or Reformed Protestants, at Vassy in Champagne. The Guise family—patrons of a militant, zealous Catholicism—were political rivals of the Bourbon and Montmorency-Chatillon families, both of whom supported the Huguenots. Because the crown of France was in the hands of a minor, Charles IX (1560–1574), his mother, Catherine de Medici, exercised authority. To preserve her power, she played a shrewd game of shifting alliances, working first with one and then the other of the factions. Although this helped to prevent either side from dominating the other, it also kept France in a state of political and religious instability.

The "wars of religion" in France were at root a struggle for political dominance in which religion, itself a potent and divisive factor, was used to justify the fighting and to attract adherents. The struggle was marked by intermittent periods of peace, assassinations, and the involvement of foreign troops, including English and German forces who aided the Huguenots in the early years.

The worst atrocity of the war—the St. Bartholomew's Day massacre in August 1572—grew out of Catherine's fear that the Huguenots were becoming too powerful. One of their leaders, Admiral Gaspard de Coligny, had persuaded Charles IX, who had come of age, to intervene in the Netherlands on behalf of the Protestants. Fearful of a Franco-Spanish war, Catherine was determined to reverse this decision. Huguenot power was also on the increase because of the marriage in August of the king's sister, Marguerite of Valois, to a prominent Huguenot, Henry of Navarre. Four days later an assassination plot that had Catherine's blessing wounded Coligny. Fearful of Huguenot reprisals, Catherine persuaded the king to sanction the execution of Protestant leaders on trumped-up charges that they were plotting his overthrow. Shortly before dawn on August 24, Coligny and other leading Huguenots were assassinated, and by daybreak militant Catholics were slaughtering Protestants. At least 3,000 were butchered in Paris, where bloody corpses bobbed in the Seine, and perhaps 20,000 in all of France. News of the massacre pleased Pope Gregory XIII and King Philip II, who celebrated with special religious services.

The massacre temporarily ended French intervention in the Netherlands but failed to destroy the Huguenot cause. As the Huguenots plotted revenge, Henry of Guise in 1576 organized the Catholic League, which soon received financial support from Philip II. By the mid-1580s the league controlled Paris, forcing King Henry III (1574–1589) to adopt desperate means to save his crumbling authority: the assassination of Henry of Guise and

The massacre of a congregation of Huguenots at Vassy by followers of the duke of Guise in March 1562 ignited a civil war in France that lasted until 1596. [Bibliothèque Nationale, Paris]

The St. Bartholomew's Day Massacre: Papal Reaction

News of the St. Bartholomew's Day massacre in August 1572 prompted rejoicing in Catholic circles, including the papacy itself. An observer describes Pope Gregory XIII's reaction.

Although it was still night, I immediately sent to his Holiness to free him from the tension, and so that he might rise to the wonderful grace, which God had granted to Christendom under his pontificate. On that morning there was a consistory court . . . and as his Holiness had such a good piece of news to announce to the Holy College, he had the dispatches publicly read out to them. His Holiness then spoke about their contents and concluded that in these times, so troubled by revolutions, nothing better or more magnificent could have been wished for; and that, as it appeared, God was beginning to turn the eye of his mercy on us. His Holiness and the college were extremely contented and joyful at the reading of this news. . . .

On the same morning . . . his Holiness with the whole College of Cardinals went to the church of Saint Mark, to have the *Te Deum* sung and to thank God for granting so great a favor to the Christian people. His Holiness does not cease to pray God, and make others pray, to inspire the Most Christian King [Charles IX] to follow further the path which he has opened and to cleanse and purge completely the Kingdom of France from the plague of the Huguenots.

Source: W. F. Reddaway, ed., *Select Documents of European History, Vol. 2: 1492–1715* (New York: Holt, n.d.), pp. 94–95.

his brother, a cardinal in the Catholic church. Although the king allied with Henry of Navarre in an effort to crush the Catholic League, he was assassinated in July 1589.

With Henry of Navarre now claiming the throne as Henry IV (1589–1610), the civil war entered its final stage. Unprepared to see France governed by Protestants, Philip II not only continued to back the Catholic League but also ordered his army to invade France. Elizabeth I, determined to prevent France from falling under Spanish hegemony, sent her troops to Henry's aid. A *politique* rather than a convinced Huguenot, Henry finally decided in 1593 that peace was possible only if he converted to Catholicism. The pope absolved him of his heresy, and Paris finally opened its gates to him, though Philip continued the struggle until 1598. In the latter year Henry provided some solace to his Huguenot allies by issuing the Edict of Nantes, giving Protestants liberty of conscience, full civil and political rights, and control of 100 fortified towns. Catholicism, however, was recognized as the official religion of France, and Protestant worship was prohibited in the Paris area.

Although France was saved for Catholicism, from Philip's standpoint the 1590s was a decade of military disaster. Spain had no power in France, the Dutch Netherlands were virtually irretrievable, and the English, exultant in their victory over the armada in 1588, had checked Spain on the seas. By the time of Philip's death in 1598, the Spanish quest for hegemony had been blunted, though the Spaniards retained the southern Netherlands and continued to battle the Dutch until 1609.

The Age of the Queens

The second half of the sixteenth century is notable as an age of unusual political prominence for women in western Europe. Mary I (1553–1558) and Elizabeth I (1558–1603) in England and Mary Stuart in Scotland (whose effective rule was from 1561 to 1567) governed as queens, while other women exercised power as regents: Mary of Guise in Scotland (1554–1560), Margaret of Parma in the Netherlands (1559–1567), and Catherine de' Medici in France beginning in 1560. Women, of course, had governed before, sometimes very successfully, as in the case of Queen Isabella of Castile (1474–1504), cofounder of a unified Spain. Although some Renaissance writers had recognized women's ability to govern, men were still quite reluctant to accept their authority. The classic statement of this view was a treatise by John Knox, architect of the Protestant Reformation in Scotland, titled *The First Blast of the Trumpet Against the Monstrous Regiment of Women* (1558), which argued that female rule was contrary to divine and natural law, though God occasionally made an exception. The queens had their defenders, but even supporters of women's right to rule were unwilling to admit women to governing bodies or deliberative assemblies. No woman sat in the English or Scottish royal councils or Parliaments during the reign of these queens; government remained an essentially male preserve throughout Europe.

Elizabeth I in particular exerted an enormous impact on England, not only by thwarting Spanish ambitions and supporting Protestantism but also by creating an atmosphere conducive to brilliant cultural achievements. The glorious image of her rule, which she assiduously cultivated, is reflected in the literary masterpieces of Edmund Spenser (c. 1552–1599), whose allegorical poem *The Faerie Queene* exalted "the most excellent and glorious person of our sovereign the queen, and her kingdom in Fairy Land," and William Shakespeare (1564–1616). The self-confidence and exuberance that radiated from England after the Spanish were repelled is eloquently expressed in Shakespeare's *Richard II*:

> ***This royal throne of kings, this scepter'd isle,***
> ***This earth of majesty, this seat of Mars,***
> ***This other Eden, demi-paradise,***
> ***This fortress built by Nature for herself . . .***
> ***This blessed plot, this earth, this realm, this England.***

In no small measure England's achievements were attributable to its queen. During the early 1600s the image of Elizabeth—more exalted in death than in life—proved to be more than her successors, James I and Charles I, could emulate.

Europe in Crisis

As Spanish ascendancy waned, Europe became preoccupied with the Thirty Years' War and the general crisis of authority that followed it in the mid-1600s. The two problems were directly related, for the unparalleled destruction inflicted in the Thirty Years' War, much of it by undisciplined troops, underscored the need to bring armies and warfare under strict control. Ultimately, monarchs and nobles found it to their advantage to work together to determine policy and implement discipline. By 1660 there was also a consensus that even religious convictions had to be subordinated to the maintenance of order. The period 1600–1660 was thus a major watershed in European history.

The Thirty Years' War

Germany, a patchwork land of some 360 independent political entities, became the killing field of Europe in a great war triggered by a dispute involving the role of the Austrian Habsburgs as Holy Roman emperors. The compromise Peace of Augsburg (1555) that had ended the first round of religious warfare in Germany had given no rights to Calvinists, whose growing strength, particularly in the Palatinate (see Map 18.1), alarmed the Lutherans. There was considerable tension too between Protestants and Catholics because of changes in religious allegiance. When the Catholic rulers of ecclesiastical principalities became Protestant, Catholics demanded that they surrender both their religious office and their lands, but Lutherans refused. After the Protestants organized the Evangelical Union in 1609 and their opponents responded with a Catholic League, Germany was divided into two armed camps.

The event that sparked the fighting occurred when the Habsburg Ferdinand of Styria, king of Bohemia, curtailed religious toleration for Protestants and Hussites. In May 1618 Bohemian nobles registered their protest by throwing two of Ferdinand's advisers out of a castle window in Prague; their lives were saved when they landed in a pile of manure. A year later the rebels deposed Ferdinand as their king and gave the crown to a Calvinist prince, Frederick V of the Palatinate, son-in-law of King James I of England. Had the rebels succeeded in establishing a Protestant on the Bohemian throne, Protestants would have had a majority of the seven votes needed to elect future emperors. Ferdinand, who had become emperor in August 1619, had little choice but to reassert his control over Bohemia.

At first the war went well for Ferdinand. In addition to receiving the help of Catholic armies from Spain and Bavaria, he got the assistance of Lutheran Saxony, whose elector was more interested in acquiring land in the Palatinate than in religious solidarity with his fellow Protestants. After Frederick was defeated at the Battle of White Mountain in 1620, he fled Bohemia, leaving his Protestant supporters to face Ferdinand's wrath. The Dutch, who were alarmed by Spain's presence in the area, provided Frederick with funds to keep fighting, but his small principality was overwhelmed. After the Danes entered the war in 1625, Ferdinand's new general, Albrecht von Wallenstein, invaded Denmark, leaving starvation and destruction in his wake. Danish lands were returned on the condition that Denmark refrain from intervening in Germany.

With Ferdinand on the verge of establishing total control over his empire, the Swedish king, Gustavus Adolphus, invaded Germany. He was supported militarily by Brandenburg and Saxony and financially by the Dutch and the French, both of whom were threatened by Habsburg

The French artist Jacques Callot (1592–1635) created a series of 24 etchings titled *The Miseries of War*, one of the most moving statements of the horror that gripped Germany in the Thirty Years' War. The etchings reflect a dramatic change of mind on Callot's part, for his earlier works glorify warfare. This etching depicts the hanging of thieves, a vivid reminder of the fate that awaited German peasants unlucky enough to get caught as they stole to stay alive. [New York Public Library]

expansion. Using innovative tactics that increased the mobility of his army, Gustavus Adolphus crushed the imperial forces in 1631. The fighting was carried into Catholic regions, especially Bavaria, whose residents were subjected to calculated brutality—rape, pillage, torture, and murder. In November 1632 the armies of Gustavus Adolphus and Wallenstein confronted each other at Lützen in Saxony in one of the bloodiest battles of the war. The Swedish king was killed, but neither side was strong enough to defeat its enemies in the ensuing months. Wallenstein was assassinated in 1634.

The final and most destructive period of the war (1635–1648) reverted to a dynastic struggle that pitted the Habsburg powers, Austria and Spain, against the French and the Swedes. The real victims were the German people. "Every soldier had his favorite method of making life miserable for peasants," noted one observer, "and every peasant had his own misery."[4] The city of Marburg was occupied no less than 11 times. As peasants fled before the marauding armies, the destruction of crops triggered famine. The loss of population was catastrophic: 40 percent in rural areas, 33 percent in the cities. The overall population of the empire decreased by as much as 8 million during the war.

An end to the fighting was finally achieved by the Peace of Westphalia in 1648. The sovereignty of each German state was recognized; altogether there were now some 300 entities with sovereign rights and nearly 1,500 minor lordships. Each prince, whether Catholic, Lutheran, or Calvinist, could determine the religious beliefs of his subjects, who had no choice but to accept or emigrate. The treaty also recognized the independence of the Swiss Confederacy and the Dutch Republic, but it did not end hostilities between France and Spain, which lasted until the Treaty of the Pyrenees in 1659. Just as Spain's quest for hegemony was doomed by Philip II's defeats in the 1590s and confirmed by the Treaty of the Pyrenees, so the bid of the Austrian Habsburgs to dominate central Europe was wrecked in the Thirty Years' War. Not until 1871 would the Germans achieve political unity. The war also had disruptive effects on the domestic politics of the major European states, thereby contributing to the midcentury crises.

Rebuilding France: Foundations of Bourbon Rule

France's ability to act decisively in the Thirty Years' War and ultimately to impose peace terms on Spain in 1659 was made possible by the rebuilding of its institutions in the aftermath of the Huguenot wars. Beginning with Henry IV, the first Bourbon monarchs pursued a course of absolutism in politics and mercantilism in economics. In the Bourbon view, stability mandated a thoroughly centralized state capable of maintaining order at home and fielding large armies. Centralization could be accomplished, however, only at the expense of local and special interests, which were sometimes strained severely by the burden of financing a war. The attempt to impose royal absolutism coincided with the costly struggle to prevent the establishment of Spanish or Austrian hegemony. By the 1640s grinding taxation, aristocratic discontent, and resistance to centralized control had built to the crisis point and erupted in a new civil war, the Fronde.

Although no monarch came close to achieving totalitarian power in this period, there was growing interest in the concept of absolute rule, particularly in its national, monarchical form. The French political theorist Jean Bodin had stressed the importance of a sovereign power whose authority was beyond challenge, though he also insisted that monarchs were responsible to God for their actions. Building on this traditional notion, various seventeenth-century thinkers asserted that kings and queens derived their right to govern directly from God and were therefore above human law. Seemingly, the apostle Paul had provided the foundation for this theory when he taught that earthly powers were ordained by God. The concept that sovereignty was divinely bestowed suited the needs of rulers intent on centralizing their control, for they were in a position to claim the unquestioning obedience of their subjects as both a right and a Christian duty. Political theorists such as Bodin and the Englishman Robert Filmer drove home the argument for divine right absolutism by likening the monarch to a father. While divine right theories were widely embraced, they were applied with more success in France than anywhere else in the 1600s, though even there not without a struggle.

When Henry IV temporarily ended the Huguenot wars in 1598, he revived the goals of the Renaissance sovereigns Francis I and Henry II, who had aimed at centralizing royal authority and expanding French territory. Although he opted not to summon the Estates General after 1593, he took care to secure the support of the more powerful aristocrats—the nobility of the sword—especially by strategic bribes. Offices were traditionally sold in France, but Henry took the practice one step further by allowing his principal bureaucrats, the nobility of the robe, to pay a voluntary annual fee called the *paulette* that made the offices hereditary. These men, most of them members of the bourgeoisie, were thus closely linked to the expansion of the government.

Henry faced daunting economic problems. He was nearly 300 million livres in debt, with annual revenues amounting to only half that amount. His finance minister, the clever duke of Sully, repudiated part of the debt, renegotiated a lower rate of interest on the balance, and rigorously sought new sources of revenue, such as the *paulette*. As a proponent of mercantile policies, Sully established monopolies on salt, gunpowder, and mining. France was already a food-exporting nation, and Sully strengthened agriculture by building more bridges, roads, and canals. To reduce the export of bullion for luxury items, new laws restricted the use of gold and silver, and royal factories were constructed to produce such luxury goods as silk, satin, tapestries, and crystal. By 1601 the budget was balanced.

When Henry was assassinated by a Catholic ideologue in 1610, the throne passed to his 9-year-old son, Louis XIII (1610–1643). The regency was in the hands of Louis' mother, Marie de' Medici. Because she relied on her Italian favorites for advice, disgruntled nobles and troubled Huguenots threatened a resumption of civil strife. Marie tried to defuse the crisis by summoning the Estates General in 1614, but internal feuding rendered it impotent, and it was not called again until 1789. For ten years France lacked an energetic government, but Marie maintained a semblance of peace by lavishing pensions and bribes on the nobles and allowing them a greater role in provincial affairs.

The appointment of Cardinal Richelieu (1585–1642) as the king's chief adviser in 1624 once more meant a strong hand at the controls of government. Nobles who defied royal edicts were imprisoned and some even executed, and their castles were destroyed. Responsibility for local administration was transferred from the nobles to *intendants*, commissioners appointed by the crown who held their posts at the king's pleasure. Their responsibilities included tax collection, the administration of justice, military recruitment, and local defense. To deal with the rebellious Huguenots, Richelieu besieged one of their key strongholds, La Rochelle, for 14 months until it surrendered. Other Huguenot towns were overrun by royal forces. In 1629 Richelieu ended the political and military rights given to the Huguenots in the Edict of Nantes, although they retained religious freedom. Richelieu also enhanced French power by building effective Atlantic and Mediterranean fleets. His policies, however, were expensive and required deficit financing. Occupied with his centralizing schemes and the Thirty Years' War, Richelieu failed to undertake desperately needed tax reform. As the cost of French military involvement in Germany increased, rising taxes underscored the unfairness of the burden on the peasants. Richelieu faced tax riots throughout France, to which he reacted with increased repression.

The death of Richelieu in 1642 and Louis XIII a year later left the 5-year-old Louis XIV on the throne and real power in the hands of Richelieu's protégé, Giulio Mazarin (1602–1661), a Sicilian cardinal and the illicit lover—or secret husband—of the regent, Anne of Austria. A foreigner and a powerful churchman, he was thoroughly disliked. Discontent was especially pronounced because of the effects of centralization on local authority and Mazarin's inability to pay interest on the loans that financed French participation in the Thirty Years' War. So depleted were royal finances that some officials had not been paid for four years. The situation was made worse by famine, especially in the late 1640s, when many peasants lost their holdings to bourgeois creditors.

Against this backdrop of economic dislocation and political unrest, the Parlement of Paris, France's main law court and a stronghold of the nobility of the robe, called for reform, including the abolition of the office of *intendant*,

A meeting of the Estates General at The Hague in the Netherlands in 1651, painted by Dirck van Delen. [Rijksmuseum, Amsterdam]

in the late 1570s, Amsterdam moved quickly to establish itself as the center of European commerce. By the mid-seventeenth century the Dutch operated more than half of the world's commercial vessels. Using raw materials from Scandinavia, the shipyards of Amsterdam built Europe's most efficient ships, including large vessels for the transoceanic trade and inexpensive flat-bottomed freighters known as *fluiten* ("flyboats"). In addition to trading and shipbuilding, the economy of Amsterdam was based on banking, insurance (including the first life insurance policies), printing, and manufacturing. Artisans finished cloth, made jewelry, brewed beer, dressed leather, processed tobacco, and cut diamonds. Other towns became famous for particular products, such as Delft for ceramics, Haarlem for linens, and Schiedam for gin. The Haarlem area also achieved fame by cultivating tulips, which were first imported from the Ottoman Empire. Jews, who benefited greatly by the normally tolerant religious atmosphere in the Netherlands, played a prominent role in the Dutch business community, especially banking. The Dutch, in short, were economically the most progressive Europeans in the seventeenth century, and the people of Amsterdam enjoyed the highest per capita income in Europe. Although there were a substantial number of poor, whose ranks were swollen by immigrants and refugees, the Dutch provided enough relief to stave off the misery that attended political crises in other European states in the mid-1600s.

Early Stuart England: From Consensus to Conflict

Alone among the European states, England experienced not only a severe crisis but a revolution in the 1640s and 1650s as well. Under Elizabeth I (1558–1603) and James I (1603–1625), who also governed Scotland as James VI (1567–1625), England attained religious stability and a reasonably effective working relationship between crown and Parliament. Elizabeth's Protestant settlement withstood the challenge of Catholics, nearly 200 of whom she executed for treason, and of a handful of radical Protestants who repudiated the state church. James, raised as a Calvinist, disappointed English Puritans who wanted further reforms in the established church, including a better-educated clergy, stricter sabbath observance, and an end to such "unscriptural" customs as the sign of the cross in baptism and the wedding ring. He did, however, agree to a Puritan request for a new translation of the Bible into English, the so-called King James version of 1611.

The work of centralization was carried forward, particularly through the appointment of lords lieutenant and their deputies in the counties. Because England had no standing army, local defense was in the hands of these men, but as long as the crown appointed local magnates, the system worked well. Central authority was also enhanced by the use of conciliar courts, especially the Star Chamber, which evolved out of the judicial activities of the king's Council, and the Court of High Commission, which originated in Elizabeth's reign and enforced the laws and doctrine of the Church of England.

Although the war against Spain (1585–1604) was popular, its cost forced Elizabeth to adopt measures that reduced future income, such as the sale of various crown lands. In most respects she handled her Parliaments superbly, though at the end of her reign a controversy over royal grants of monopolies embittered relations as anger over their abuse mounted. Finances were increasingly a problem for James, especially with respect to foreign policy. Dreaming of the glory of the 1580s, his Parliaments were willing to support a naval war against Spain but had little desire to become embroiled directly on the Continent in the Thirty Years' War on behalf of James' son-in-law, Frederick V. Nor did they understand the king's desire to establish an alliance with their traditional enemy, Spain, by means of a marriage involving Prince Charles and a Spanish princess. The proposed match was crucial to James' dream of a partnership between Catholic Spain and Protestant England that could serve as the vehicle to maintain peace in Europe.

James, who thought that kings were "God's lieutenants upon earth" and sat on "God's throne," heightened concern by actions that seemed to challenge traditional constitutional procedures. Chronically short of funds, he sought additional revenue by levying a special import duty, an "imposition," without parliamentary approval. Although the courts decided in his favor on the grounds that import duties were part of his prerogative to determine foreign policy, some members of Parliament were irate. James also provoked controversy by dismissing one of his chief justices, Sir Edward Coke, for attempting to assert judicial independence. The king subsequently imprisoned Coke and a fellow member of the House of Commons for drafting a "protestation" asserting Parliament's right to speak freely on such subjects as "the arduous and urgent affairs concerning the king, state, and defense of the realm, and of the Church of England," including areas that had traditionally been reserved to the crown.[6] Yet when James died in 1625, he left a country whose tensions were still largely contained beneath the surface.

The consensus that Elizabeth had achieved was rapidly undermined by the policies of James' son, Charles I (1625–1649). Unable to conclude an agreement to marry a Spanish princess, he was determined to go to war against Spain, though a distrustful Parliament refused to give him sufficient funds. An expedition that tried to repeat Sir Francis Drake's brilliant 1587 raid on Cadiz not only failed but provoked outrage when the unpaid, sick, and wounded troops returned to the streets of Plymouth. Charles blundered further by going to war against France while still fighting Spain. With his finances depleted, he tried to raise money by forced "loans," billeting his troops in private homes to compel payment. Led by Coke, critics in the House of Commons responded in 1628 with the Petition of Right, which demanded that no taxes be levied without parliamentary consent, no person be imprisoned without knowing the charge, no troops be billeted in private homes without the owners' consent, and martial law not be imposed in peacetime. The king accepted the document in principle in return for further taxes. In 1629, however, a bitter attack on newly appointed Arminian bishops who supported Charles led to Parliament's dismissal, although only after critics held the speaker of the House of Commons in his chair while they passed resolutions condemning Catholicism, Arminianism, and taxes that lacked parliamentary approval. The Arminian position that Puritans and others found so offensive rejected the Calvinist doctrine of predestination, insisted that Christ died for all persons rather than the elect alone, and affirmed the freedom of each person to accept or reject divine grace.

For 11 years Charles ruled without a Parliament, raising revenue by a variety of unpopular expedients that stretched his legal powers. One of these was "ship money," a tax traditionally levied on coastal areas for naval expenses but now extended to the entire kingdom. Charles also sold monopolies, titles, offices, and crown lands. During this period religious grievances continued to mount, with much of the hostility directed at Charles' French Catholic queen, Henrietta Maria, and his Arminian archbishop of Canterbury, William Laud. Committed to the principle that a unified state required unity in religion, Laud vigorously persecuted his Puritan critics. They in turn attacked his Arminian theology and his emphasis on liturgy

Charles I, by his ineptitude, and Henrietta Maria, by her Catholicism, contributed to the outbreak of civil war in England. In the cultural atmosphere of the royal court the leading painter was Rubens' disciple Anthony Van Dyck (1599–1641), whose twin portrait of the king and queen this is. [Bridgman/AA Resource]

rather than preaching. When Charles and Laud attempted to force the English liturgy on the Presbyterian Scots, the latter rebelled. The militia units Charles dispatched to restore order were woefully inadequate, and the king was forced to summon Parliament.

The English Revolution

Historians hotly debate the nature and causes of the English revolution. Some contend that it was only a civil war, while others perceive a full-scale revolution that altered the structure of government, religion, the economy, educational thought, and the fabric of society. Lawrence Stone has gone back to the early sixteenth century to find such preconditions of revolution as the crown's failure to establish a standing army and a paid local bureaucracy; Puritan criticism in the state church; the growing wealth and power of the gentry and the decline of many of the greater nobility; and a crisis of confidence in high government officials. Against this background, he argues, the crown precipitated a revolution by encouraging Laud's campaign against the Puritans, curtailing the political role of the gentry, restricting upward social mobility, and enforcing tighter economic controls. The outbreak of civil war was then triggered by military defeat at the hands of the Scots and financial bankruptcy.

Analysts who hold to the more limited notion of a civil war place the origins much later, either in 1637 and 1638, when the Scots rebelled against the English liturgy, or even in early 1642, when the king and Parliament failed to agree on control of the militia. According to this interpretation, the civil war was largely an accident that neither side intended. Marxist historians concentrate on economic factors as the primary cause of the revolution, observing that Parliament drew most of its support from the economically advanced south and east of England, while the king's strength was greatest in the more backward regions of the west and north. Marxists have also tried to demonstrate that most of the aristocracy supported the king, whereas the "middling sort" of tradesmen, merchants, and yeoman farmers allied with Parliament. On any interpretation, however, it is clear that the revolutionary period was the gravest and most sustained political and military crisis in English history.

The "Short Parliament" that met briefly in the spring of 1640 was dismissed when it refused the king's demands for money. After the Scots invaded England, Charles had to call another Parliament in the autumn, the so-called Long Parliament. In a series of striking constitutional measures, Parliament abolished courts such as the Star Chamber and the High Commission, whose authority derived directly from the king; outlawed ship money and other questionable forms of revenue that lacked parliamentary sanction; and provided that no more than three years could elapse between Parliaments. By circumscribing royal authority, this legislation prevented the establishment of absolute government. Parliament also imprisoned and tried the king's principal advisers, the earl of Strafford and Archbishop Laud; both were eventually executed for high treason. Although Charles had little choice than to agree to the constitutional reforms and even to the death of his friend Strafford, he refused to surrender control of the militia, his only real military force. Troops had to be raised to suppress a Catholic rebellion that had erupted in Ireland in 1641, but neither side trusted the other with command. This distrust finally persuaded both sides to take up arms, and the civil war began in August 1642.

The Cavaliers supported Charles, while the Roundheads (so called for their short hairstyles) fought for Parliament. They were roughly equal in strength, but the latter established military supremacy through an alliance with the Scots, more effective military organization, and greater wealth, owing to the support of London and the commercial southeast. Most members of Parliament were required to resign their commissions, promotion was based on merit rather than birth, and strict discipline was imposed. The Cavaliers were badly defeated at the battle of Naseby in 1645, and a year later Charles surrendered. The price of the Scottish alliance was a promise to make the Church of England Presbyterian, but this was unacceptable to the army, which favored religious toleration for Protestants. The army was also impatient over negotiations with the king. In 1648 civil war broke out again, this time with the Scots on Charles' side. Under the leadership of Oliver Cromwell (1599–1658), the parliamentarian army crushed its enemies. After the victorious army purged Parliament of moderates, the remnant—derisively called the Rump Parliament by its critics—appointed a special tribunal to try the king on charges of treason. Found guilty, he was beheaded in London on January 30, 1649. This act, which shocked all Europe, was, said Cromwell, a "cruel necessity."

The Rump proceeded to make England a republic—the Commonwealth—but refused to provide for new elections. In practice it allowed a good deal of religious toleration, particularly for radical Protestants such as the Congregationalists, Baptists, and Quakers. The Quakers were particularly controversial because they not only rejected the traditional ministry and sacraments but also allowed women to preach. The Rump used the army to crush the rebellion in Ireland and then to suppress the Scots when they rallied on behalf of Charles I's son, hoping to impose a Presbyterian state church on England. The Rump also dispatched the navy to fight an inconclusive trade war against Europe's other major republic, the Dutch Netherlands, in 1652. When Cromwell's patience with the Rump finally ran out in 1653, he forcibly dismissed it.

Although handpicked by army officers with the advice of Congregational churches, a new Parliament—nicknamed Barebones after a quaintly named member, Praise-

Who Should Vote? The Putney Debates

During the English revolution the radicals differed sharply among themselves on numerous political and religious issues, one of the most crucial being the extent of the parliamentary franchise. During a debate in the army council at Putney in the autumn of 1648, the crucial issue was whether the right to vote should be limited to male property owners.

Henry Ireton: It is not fit that . . . the persons who shall make the law in the kingdom . . . have not a permanent fixed interest in the kingdom. . . .

John Wildman: Our case is to be considered thus, that we have been under slavery. . . . Our very laws were made by our conquerors. . . . We are now engaged for our freedom; that's the end of Parliaments. . . . Every person in England has as clear a right to elect his representative as the greatest person in England. I conceive that's the undeniable maxim of government: that all government is in the free consent of the people. . . .

Ireton: If a foreigner comes within this kingdom . . . that man may very well be content to submit himself to the law of the land: that is, the law that is made by those people that have a property, a fixed property, in the land. . . . A man ought to be subject to a law [to which he] did not give his consent, but with this reservation, that if this man do think himself dissatisfied to be subject to this law he may go into another kingdom. And so the same reason does extend . . . to that man that has no permanent interest in the kingdom. . . .

Edward Sexby: We have engaged in this kingdom and ventured our lives, and it was all for this: to recover our birthrights and privileges. . . . We have had little propriety in the kingdom as to our estates, yet we have had a birthright. But it seems now [that] except a man have a fixed estate in this kingdom, he has no right in this kingdom.

Source: After C. H. Firth, ed., *The Clarke Papers*, vol. 1 (London: Camden Society, 1891), pp. 317–323.

god Barebone—proved ineffective. In 1654 army officers drew up a constitution called the Instrument of Government that made Cromwell Lord Protector. Cromwell, however, fared no better with his Parliaments than had the early Stuart kings. Dissension raged over the structure of the government, the question of religious toleration, the enormous cost of maintaining a standing army, and the appointment of major generals to maintain order throughout the country. A war with Spain brought England both Dunkirk and Jamaica but simultaneously made Cromwell's financial position desperate despite increased taxation. With the political and economic crisis unresolved at his death in 1658, his son Richard, the new Lord Protector, proved unable to govern. By 1660 the propertied classes, fed up with military rule, were prepared to accept the return of monarchy in order to achieve stability and security. Although a good deal of antimonarchical sentiment and popular support for the republic continued, most of the country was relieved when Charles II returned from exile in May 1660.

Although the monarchy was restored, its position was seriously altered. Absolutism such as existed in France had been rendered impossible. The despotic royal courts of the Star Chamber and the High Commission did not return, and the principle of parliamentary approval for taxes was firmly established. Religious toleration ended in the early 1660s, but the dissenters were now strong enough to survive the sporadic persecution that ensued. The Jews, who had been welcomed to England in the 1650s in the expectation that their return signaled the coming of a millennial age, were not expelled. Moreover, the shakeup in the universities left proponents of the new science firmly established and set the stage for the foundation of the Royal Society in 1660. New directions in political thought had also been initiated by the work of the Levellers, who advocated a moderate form of democracy;

by Thomas Hobbes, who developed a theory of secular absolutism; and by Gerrard Winstanley (1609–c. 1676), who advocated a commonwealth based on the abolition of property. Most important, the revolution established the principle in England that there must be a government of laws, not of men.

A WOMAN IN THE ENGLISH REVOLUTION: MARGARET FELL

The collapse of censorship, of the authority of bishops, and ultimately of the monarchy in revolutionary England enabled women who belonged to such Protestant sects as the Congregationalists, Baptists, and Quakers to preach and publish their views in a manner hitherto impossible. Of these groups, however, only the Quakers, with their rejection of a professional ministry and the sacraments, were relatively comfortable with active female participation in ministerial activities. Quaker women crisscrossed England carrying their message of the Inner Light, and the more daring extended their work as far afield as Ireland, Portugal, Malta, the West Indies, and the American colonies, including Massachusetts, which expelled or hanged them. Two Quaker women even went to Adrianople in a futile attempt to convert the Turkish sultan.

The most influential Quaker woman, as well as one of the key figures in the Society of Friends, as the Quakers called themselves, was Margaret Fell (1614–1702), daughter of a Lancashire gentleman. Although she and her first husband, the attorney Thomas Fell, were Congregationalists, the Quaker founder George Fox (1624–1691) persuaded her to adopt his views in 1652, after which she held Quaker meetings in her home. The mother of eight children, she was at first unable to become a traveling minister, but she provided the Friends with an even more important contribution by her extensive correspondence with Quakers of both sexes who sought her advice on religious questions. Enormously influential in shaping the Quaker movement and its ideals, she frequently argued the Friends' case in assertive letters to non-Quaker clergymen and judges.

Margaret Fell's wide-ranging activities included the authorship of numerous pamphlets, several of which were translated into Dutch, Hebrew, and Latin. She pleaded with Oliver Cromwell and King Charles II for religious toleration, petitioned the Rump Parliament with 7,000 other women for an end to mandatory tithing, and tirelessly worked for the release of imprisoned Quakers. She was jailed several times, once for four years, because of her religious beliefs. Among her special concerns was the conversion of the Jews to Christianity, a cause for which she wrote five pamphlets, including *A Call unto the Seed of Israel*. Her best-known work, *Women's Speaking Justified*, which argued for the right of women to preach and prophesy, helped lay the foundation for the establishment of Quaker women's meetings.

Soon after her husband died in 1658, Fell began traveling throughout England on behalf of the Society. In 1669 she married George Fox, partly to end unfounded rumors of an illicit relationship between them but also to symbolize the union of male and female Quakers. Until her death in 1702 she remained active in the Society's work, particularly its women's meetings. The example that she and other sectarian women set made it difficult to force them back into their traditional places in the home, the shop, and the field. Nevertheless, after 1660, with the revolutionary crisis in England essentially concluded, only the Quakers allowed women to preach. In the 1680s and 1690s a flurry of protofeminist works appeared in England by writers such as Mary Astell, but so successful was the restoration of traditional male authority in the 1660s that the new writers were content to plead only for their spiritual equality with men. Viewed in this context, the work and careers of Margaret Fell and her colleagues were an extraordinary product of the midcentury crisis.

Central and Eastern Europe

Although the institutions of the Holy Roman Empire survived the Thirty Years' War and the Peace of Westphalia, the more powerful German princes subsequently went their own way, leaving the emperors to govern the small German states and their own patrimony in Austria, Bohemia, and Hungary. Increasingly, they concentrated on ruling through ancestral institutions, especially the Austrian Chancellery—where Habsburg policy was formulated—rather than imperial institutions. The result was the gradual establishment of a Danubian state governed from Vienna and mostly Catholic in religion. Because the emperors shared power with the landed aristocracy, the peasant rebellions of the 1640s and 1650s were doomed, and the empire avoided a serious crisis.

Much of the unrest in central and eastern Europe was sparked by the gradual enserfment of the peasants in the sixteenth and seventeenth centuries. The process of enserfing, carried out by the landed aristocracy with the acquiescence of the monarchs, was intended both to increase agricultural production, particularly for the market in western Europe resulting from the increase in population, and to end the mobility of peasants by binding them to the land. Whereas peasants in western Europe might suffer from heavy debts and eviction from their lands, their counterparts in eastern Europe not only lost their freedom of movement but were saddled also with increasingly heavy burdens, including personal labor on landlords' estates and financial exactions that covered virtually every aspect of their lives. Widespread misery engendered social upheaval.

Social Unrest in Poland

In common with most of the major states in western Europe, Poland and Russia experienced crises in the mid-1600s. In the case of Poland, the centralization of royal authority was not a factor, for the country was thoroughly fragmented. Real power lay in the hands of the nobles, who secured the principle of elective monarchy in 1572. Their assembly, the Sejm, met at least every two years to determine policy. Poland was also religiously split between Catholics, Greek Orthodox, Jews, and adherents of the Uniate church, who recognized the pope but worshiped according to Greek rites. Under Sigismund III (1587–1632), known as the King of the Jesuits, Catholics tried to destroy Polish Protestantism, causing a civil war in which the Orthodox Cossacks allied with the Protestants. The Jews were cruelly victimized by the wave of religious persecution, with as many as 100,000 murdered in the pogroms, or organized massacres, of the decade 1648–1658.

The Cossacks, free herdsmen and peasants, were the major cause of unrest in both Poland and Russia. In 1648 one of the great Cossack leaders, Bogdan Khmelnitsky, ignited a major revolt against the Polish government, partly in defense of the Orthodox faith and partly because of economic grievances. In 1654 Khmelnitsky and his supporters in the Ukraine offered their allegiance to the Russian tsar and were incorporated into the Russian state. Refusing to accept the loss of the Ukraine, Poland went to war twice until peace was finally achieved in 1667 by partitioning the Ukraine between Russia and Poland.

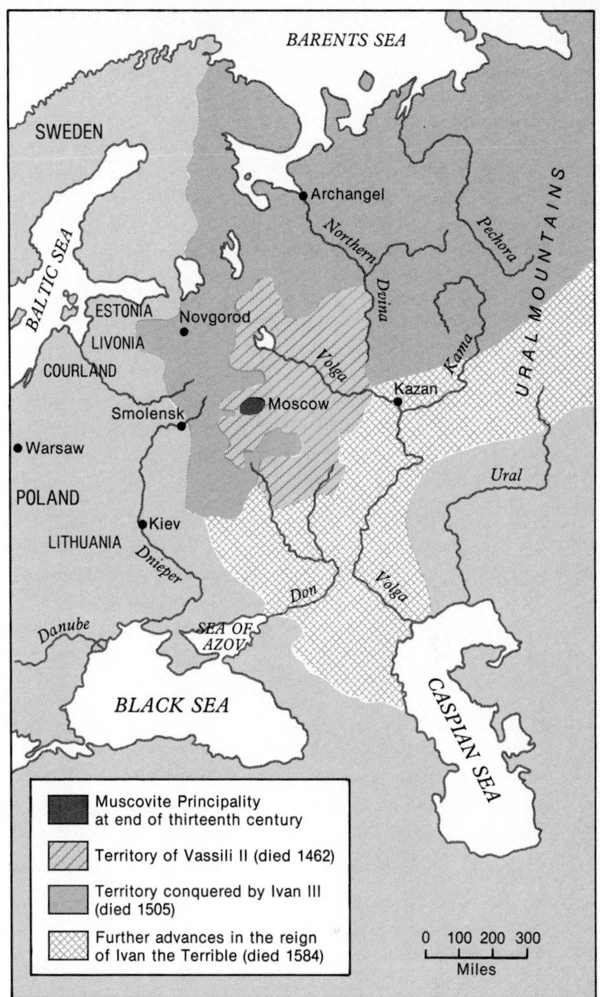

18.2 Russia: The Growth of Muscovy, 1300–1584

Russia: Centralization and Turmoil

The roots of Russia's troubles in the seventeenth century stemmed primarily from the imposition of serfdom and the centralizing work of Ivan IV, "the Terrible" (1533–1584). When Ivan assumed control of Russia in 1547 at the age of 16, he was crowned tsar ("Caesar") "of all the Russias." He ruled by divine right in a land dominated by an Orthodox faith that stressed the subservience of the church to the state. At first he governed well, consulting with the great nobles, or *boyars*, formulating a new law code, instituting direct trade with western Europe, and convening Russia's first consultative assembly, the *zemski sobor*. In the late 1550s, however, he became increasingly paranoid and vindictive. Setting aside a portion of Russia exclusively for himself—the *oprichnina*, or "separate realm"—he used the oprichnina's black-garbed military force of 6,000 to brutalize his opponents. Boyars who resisted him were summarily imprisoned and executed, and their estates were confiscated. Ivan tortured priests, slaughtered his enemies while they worshiped, and in a rage killed one of his own sons. Towns were burned, and large numbers of people were forcibly resettled on the frontiers. Following his death in 1584, he was succeeded by his weak son, Fedor I, who died in 1598 without an heir. Russia was plunged into a period of turmoil known as the "Time of Troubles." While the boyars struggled to regain their power, peasants rioted, and both the Poles and the Swedes intervened militarily.

Dismayed at the civil war and foreign intervention, the *zemski sobor* resolved the feuding over the crown by awarding it in 1613 to Ivan's grandnephew, 17-year-old

Ivan the Terrible

One of the earliest descriptions of the court of Tsar Ivan IV, "the Terrible," underscores the extent to which he ruled by inculcating respect and fear in his subjects.

This emperor uses great familiarity, as well unto all his nobles and subjects, as also unto strangers who serve him either in his wars or in occupations: for his pleasure is that they shall dine oftentimes in the year in his presence, and besides that he is oftentimes abroad, either at one church or another, and walking with his noble men abroad. And by this means he is not only beloved of his nobles and commons, but also had in great dread and fear through all his dominions, so that I think no prince in Christendom is more feared by his own [people] than he is, nor yet better beloved. For if he bids any of his dukes go, they will run; if he gives any evil or angry word to any of them, the party will not come into his majesty's presence again for a long time if he be not sent for, but will fain . . . to be very sick, and will let the hair of his head grow very long, without either cutting or shaving, which is an evident token that he is in the emperor's displeasure: for when they be in their prosperity, they account it a shame to wear long hair, in consideration whereof they used to have their heads shaven. . . .

He delights not greatly in hawking, hunting, or any other pastime, nor in hearing instruments or music, but sets . . . his whole delight upon two things: first, to serve God, as undoubtedly he is very devout in his religion, and the second, how to subdue and conquer his enemies.

Source: R. Hakluyt, ed., *The Principal Navigations, Voyages, Traffiques and Discoveries of the English Nation*, vol. 2 (Glasgow: James MacLehose & Sons, 1903), pp. 438–439.

Mikhail Romanov. The new dynasty would rule Russia until its overthrow in the 1917 revolution. Rather than risk their estates in more civil war, the boyars cooperated with the first Romanovs, enabling them to finish the work of bureaucratic centralization. In return the tsars allowed the boyars to complete the process of enserfing the peasants. Together they placed the overwhelming burden of taxation on the peasants, whose rate was 100 times greater in 1640 than it had been a century earlier.

In a period when peasant disorders were endemic, the greatest peasant uprising in seventeenth-century Europe erupted in 1667. Incited by the Cossack Stenka Razin, runaway serfs and Cossacks proclaimed a message of freedom, equality, and land for all. Stenka led his undisciplined followers up the Volga River, inciting peasant uprisings and replacing local governments with Cossack rule. His ships attacked Muslim villages on the Caspian Sea and even defeated a Persian fleet. The tsar's army finally

The Russian tsar Ivan the Terrible, as depicted in a contemporary portrait. The period between his reign and that of Mikhail I, the "Time of Troubles," was an age of turmoil. [Nationalmuseet, Copenhagen]

crushed his forces in 1670, a year before Stenka was captured and beheaded. The resulting repression that ended the last of the midcentury crises was the death of as many as 100,000 peasants.

Old World Rivalries in a Global Setting

The political struggles that enveloped Europe in the century from 1560 to 1660 had profound consequences for the entire world. By 1660 the two countries that had dominated European expansion in the preceding two centuries—Portugal and Spain—had largely been supplanted by the Dutch, the English, and the French. Spain retained control of most of South and Central America, and Brazil remained in Portuguese hands. North America, however, increasingly became the province of the northwestern European powers who would eventually extend their sway over much of the globe.

The Dutch and English in Asia

The union of Portugal and Spain in 1580 did not materially strengthen what was now their joint effort in the East, but it did highlight the enmity and rivalry between them as Catholic powers and the rising Protestant states of the Netherlands and England. All of the Iberian positions overseas became attractive targets, and Portuguese profits were newly tempting. The Dutch were the first to pick up this challenge effectively in Asia. At this period the Netherlands was a more important center of trade and shipping than England, and Dutch ships had the upper hand in the English Channel. There were more of them, backed by merchant capital earned in trade, and in the course of the sixteenth century they became larger and more powerful, as well as more maneuverable than the Portuguese caravels. Dutch seamen had traveled east on Portuguese ships and learned what they needed to know about sailing to Asia. By the late 1500s their ships began to outnumber those of the Portuguese in Asia, defeating them repeatedly and surpassing them as carriers. Unlike the Portuguese, they concerned themselves only with trade, avoiding any missionary effort or religious conflict, and were generally welcomed as efficient agents to replace the hated Portuguese.

Rival Dutch companies were amalgamated into the Dutch East India Company in 1602, which in the following decades built a highly profitable commercial empire centered on Java, controlling the trade of Southeast Asia far more effectively than the Portuguese had done. Much of this was the work of their able governor-general, Jan Pieterzoon Coen, appointed in 1618, who fixed the naval and administrative capital of the Dutch East Indies at Batavia (now Djakarta), with other bases at strategic points throughout Indonesia and Ceylon, which expelled the Portuguese in 1658. English competitors, excluded from this new empire, increasingly centered their attention on India, while the Dutch successfully competed with them for a share in the trade of mainland Southeast Asia and, more important, at Canton, Formosa, and Nagasaki. Coen and his successors recognized that the long-established trade of Asia would remain in able Asian and Arab hands. They also saw that greater profits could be won by taking whatever part in it they could win, especially in the carrying trade, than by hauling Asian goods to the far smaller European market. The Dutch spice monopoly, however, remained important. Meanwhile, the English East India Company had also been founded, its charter signed by Queen Elizabeth I in December 1600. England was still primarily a country of farmers, unlike the commercially advanced Low Countries, and the scale of its overseas effort was for some time small. The Dutch had little trouble repelling English efforts to break the monopoly of the Asian trade, but the English hung on as minor players at Canton, in some of the mainland Southeast Asian ports, and in India after Dutch attention had shifted to the more profitable East Indies.

The English first concentrated on Surat, where they were obliged to compete with a host of local, Arab, and rival European traders but where much of Indian trade westward was based (see Map 17.1). The Dutch were not prominent there, and the Mughal governor permitted the English to rent a warehouse. Their ships, though few, were now far more able and maneuverable than those of the Portuguese, and in successive naval battles off Surat in 1612 and 1615 they defeated Portuguese fleets decisively. In 1616 King James I sent Sir Thomas Roe as an ambassador to the Mughal court. Influenced in large part by recent English naval success against both Portuguese and pirates, the emperor Jahangir granted the English rights of residence at Surat and limited trade privileges. Roe, however, recognized that the trade goods at Surat were assembled there from all over India, mainly by local merchant networks, and that the most desirable of all, fine cotton cloth of the highest quality and much in demand in Europe, came from Bengal, where the Portuguese and some Dutch traders still had a strong position.

> **The number of Portuguese residing there is a good argument for us to seek it; it is a sign that there is good doing. An abbey was ever a token of a rich soil, and stores of crows of plenty of carrion. . . . We must fire them out and maintain our trade at the pike's end.[7]**

Thus was foreshadowed the English drive to establish a position in eastern India, the founding of Madras in 1639, and the subsequent rise of English power in Bengal.

Colonial Conflict in the Americas

The Spanish annexation of Portugal in 1580, which was so important for Asia, had less impact on the Americas, where the Portuguese held only Brazil. Because Portuguese settlers, mostly from the islands of the eastern Atlantic, went to Brazil in growing numbers in the seventeenth century, the colonists were strong enough to repulse Dutch and French attempts to establish permanent footholds. Although the Dutch renounced their Brazilian claims in 1661, the French continued their efforts into the eighteenth century, without success. In the meantime, the Dutch began colonizing Guiana, to the north of Brazil, in the 1610s. The Dutch West Indies Company, founded in 1621, subsequently supplied the settlers with slaves for their sugar plantations. The demand for sugar was also a major factor in the colonial efforts of the English and the French in Guiana, the only area in South America where these countries established settlements.

A much stronger challenge to Spanish domination was mounted in the West Indies, strategically important as bases for fleets sailing to and from Mexico and Central America and valuable as well for the raising of tobacco and sugar. The islands attracted so many privateers and smugglers in the late sixteenth century that the Spaniards were forced to build heavy fortifications and organize their shipping in convoys. Beginning with the voyages of John Hawkins in the 1560s, the English intruded themselves into the West Indies trade, though non-Hispanic colonies were not established there until the 1620s. By midcentury the English, Dutch, and French all had colonies in the West Indies, and England added to its holdings when a fleet dispatched by Oliver Cromwell seized Jamaica in 1655. The development of sugar plantations in the mid-1600s meant a growing demand for African slaves, who soon outnumbered Europeans in these "sugar islands."

Apart from Mexico and Florida, where St. Augustine was founded in 1565 to check French incursion, the Spaniards were unable to settle North America. Against a background of deteriorating relations with Spain in the early 1580s, Elizabeth I issued a charter to Sir Walter Raleigh authorizing him to found a North American colony, but his settlement at Roanoke Island lasted only a year. War with Spain prevented further attempts, and not until 1607 did the English establish a permanent colony at Jamestown in Virginia, soon to become famous for its tobacco. Puritan dissatisfaction with the Church of England provided crucial motivation for the founding of colonies at Plymouth (1620) and Massachusetts Bay (1629) in New England, whereas the settlement of Maryland in 1634 was largely made by Catholics. By 1670 English colonies stretched from Maine to South Carolina, the development of which angered Spaniards in Florida.

England's main competitors in North America—the Dutch and the French—could not keep pace. Rebuffed by the Spanish in Florida, the French concentrated their efforts in the north, establishing settlements at Port Royal, Acadia, in 1605, and at Quebec three years later. When France and England went to war in 1627, reverberations were felt in the colonies as Scots from Nova Scotia captured Port Royal and English ships forced Quebec to surrender. Once peace was restored at home, however, both settlements were returned to France in 1632. The decisive struggle for the domination of North America, still more than a century in the future, would not be resolved until 1763.

In the short term the English faced a graver threat from the Dutch, who established New Amsterdam at the mouth of the Hudson River in 1624 and subsequently ended Sweden's bid for a colonial stake on the Delaware River in 1655. Fortunately for the English, however, the Dutch were preoccupied with their Asian trade as well as their African colony on the Cape of Good Hope. The growing commercial and colonial rivalry between the Dutch and the English, which now extended from Asia to the Americas, culminated in a series of three wars, the first of which was instigated by the Rump Parliament in 1652. The Second Dutch War (1665–1667) brought New Jersey and New Amsterdam—henceforth known as New York—to the English and permanently removed the Dutch from North America as a colonial power, though Dutch settlers remained in New York and thousands more made homes in Pennsylvania later in the century. Thereafter, the contest for North America was among the English, the French, and the Spanish, who were exploring northward from Mexico into California. The next three centuries were to demonstrate repeatedly that the struggles for power in Europe could no longer be fought without major ramifications for the rest of the world.

The century that began in 1560 witnessed the failure of Spanish and Austrian attempts to impose hegemony, the former on western and the latter on central Europe. The frequent wars of the period, normally funded by deficit financing and the imposition of onerous taxes on the peasantry, were a major cause of domestic instability. By the mid-1600s every major state in Europe except the Dutch Netherlands underwent a severe crisis: the vicious destruc-

tion of the Thirty Years' War in Germany, the Catalan and Portuguese revolts against the government in Madrid, the Fronde in France, the English revolution, and the Cossack uprisings in Poland and Russia. Although the specific conditions differed in each country, certain common themes stand out: reaction against centralized government, the financial burden of war, and, in most areas, religious conflict. Order was restored when monarchs and nobles discovered a common self-interest, though this realization did not lead to political uniformity. Poland retained its feudal monarchy, England brought its sovereign under the rule of law, and France and Russia, their nobles pacified, were governed by absolute monarchs. Of the major European states, only the Dutch Netherlands was a republic, though even there the House of Orange remained very influential. In the end, except for Poland, the costly quest for centralization was successful. With order restored, Europe in the late seventeenth century was threatened by new visions of hegemony, this time in France, but at the same time European expansion around the world offered dramatic new opportunities for commercial and industrial development.

Notes

1. J. H. Elliott, *Imperial Spain 1469–1716* (New York: New American Library, 1966), p. 250.
2. G. Parker, *Philip II* (London: Hutchinson, 1979), p. 193.
3. D. Howarth, *The Voyage of the Armada: The Spanish Story* (New York: Penguin Books, 1982), p. 23.
4. T. K. Rabb, *The Struggle for Stability in Early Modern Europe* (New York: Oxford University Press, 1975), p. 120.
5. Elliott, *Imperial Spain*, pp. 322–323.
6. R. Zaller, *The Parliament of 1621: A Study in Constitutional Conflict* (Berkeley: University of California Press, 1971), p. 178.
7. J. N. Das Gupta, *India in the Seventeenth Century* (Calcutta: University of Calcutta Press, 1916), p. 212.

Suggestions for Further Reading

Ashton, R. *The English Civil War: Conservatism and Revolution, 1603–1649*. London: Weidenfeld & Nicolson, 1978.

Aylmer, G. E. *Rebellion or Revolution? England, 1640–1660*. New York: Oxford University Press, 1986.

Bergin, J. *Cardinal Richelieu: Power and the Pursuit of Wealth*. New Haven, Conn.: Yale University Press, 1985.

Braudel, F. *The Mediterranean and the Mediterranean World in the Age of Philip II*, trans. S. Reynolds. 2 vols. New York: Harper & Row, 1972–1973.

Buisseret, D. *Henry IV*. London: Allen & Unwin, 1984.

De Vries, J. *European Urbanization, 1500–1800*. Cambridge, Mass.: Harvard University Press, 1984.

Dominguez Ortiz, A. *The Golden Age of Spain, 1516–1659*, trans. J. Casey. New York: Basic Books, 1971.

Dunn, R. S. *The Age of Religious Wars, 1559–1715*, 2d ed. New York: Norton, 1979.

Elliott, J. H. *Europe Divided, 1559–1598*. New York: Harper & Row, 1969.

——. *The Revolt of the Catalans: A Study in the Decline of Spain, 1598–1640*. Cambridge: Cambridge University Press, 1963.

——. *Richelieu and Olivares*. Cambridge: Cambridge University Press, 1984.

Elton, G. R. *The Parliament of England, 1559–1581*. Cambridge: Cambridge University Press, 1986.

Fennell, J. L. I. *Ivan the Great of Moscow*. New York: St. Martin's Press, 1961.

Geyl, P. *The Revolt of the Netherlands, 1555–1609*, 2d ed. London: Benn, 1966.

Haley, K. H. D. *The Dutch in the Seventeenth Century*. New York: Harcourt Brace Jovanovich, 1972.

Hill, C. *The World Turned Upside Down: Radical Ideas During the English Revolution*. New York: Viking, 1972.

Hirst, D. *Authority and Conflict: England, 1603–1658*. Cambridge, Mass.: Harvard University Press, 1986.

MacCaffrey, W. T. *Queen Elizabeth and the Making of Policy, 1572–1588*. Princeton, N.J.: Princeton University Press, 1981.

——. *The Shaping of the Elizabethan Regime*. Princeton, N.J.: Princeton University Press, 1968.

Maltby, W. S. *Alba*. Berkeley: University of California Press, 1983.

Mattingly, G. *The Armada*. Boston: Houghton Mifflin, 1959.

Parker, G. *Europe in Crisis, 1598–1648*. Brighton: Harvester Press, 1980.

——. *Philip II*. London: Hutchinson, 1978.

——. *The Thirty Years' War*. London: Methuen, 1985.

Pennington, D. H. *Seventeenth-Century Europe*. London: Longman, 1970.

Rabb, T. K. *The Struggle for Stability in Early Modern Europe*. New York: Oxford University Press, 1975.

Rowen, H. H. *John de Witt: Statesman of the "True Freedom."* Cambridge: Cambridge University Press, 1986.

Russell, C. *Parliaments and English Politics, 1621–1629*. Oxford: Clarendon Press, 1979.

Smith, H. L. *Reason's Disciples: Seventeenth-Century English Feminists*. Champaign: University of Illinois Press, 1982.

Stone, L. *The Causes of the English Revolution, 1529–1642*. London: Routledge & Kegan Paul, 1972.

Stradling, R. A. *Europe and the Decline of Spain: A Study of the Spanish System, 1580–1720*. London: Allen & Unwin, 1981.

Tapié, V. L. *France in the Age of Louis XIII and Richelieu*, trans. D. M. Lockie. New York: Praeger, 1975.

Wedgwood, C. V. *The Thirty Years' War*. Gloucester, Mass.: Peter Smith, 1969.

Wilson, C. *The Transformation of Europe, 1558–1648*. Berkeley: University of California Press, 1976.

Zagorin, P. *The Court and the Country: The Beginning of the English Revolution*. New York: Atheneum, 1970.

——. *Rebels and Rulers, 1500–1660*. 2 vols. Cambridge: Cambridge University Press, 1982.

Zaller, R. *The Parliament of 1621*. Berkeley: University of California Press, 1971.

CHAPTER · 19

Islamic Empires in the Early Modern World

The sixteenth century witnessed extraordinary events in the Middle East and Asia. Under Suleiman the Magnificent (1520–1566), the Ottoman armies made dramatic advances in Syria and North Africa despite their failure to capture Vienna and strike into the heartland of Europe. Under Suleiman, Ottoman imperial power was rivaled only by the Chinese, and despite the Ottomans' later decline, especially in the eighteenth and nineteenth centuries, they remained a force to be reckoned with into the early twentieth century.

Meanwhile, in India the oppressive rule of the Delhi sultanate gave way early in the sixteenth century to a new Islamic dynasty of conquest, the Mughals, who ruled northern India as well as Afghanistan and parts of southern India from 1526 to 1707. At the height of their power, the Mughals restored and added to India's imperial tradition,

The coronation of the sultan Selim I, "the Grim". This is a detail from a sixteenth-century manuscript illustration. [Giraudon/Art Resource]

patronized a notable flowering of culture, and reestablished a large measure of political unity. The sixteenth century also saw the restoration of imperial grandeur in Iran under the Safavids, particularly Shah Abbas the Great (1587–1629), who freed western and northern Iran from Ottoman control. As in western Europe, the late sixteenth and early seventeenth centuries were a time of cultural brilliance in the Middle East, India, and Iran.

The Ottoman Empire

While the Delhi sultans were at the peak of their power in India, a new dynasty of sultans, the Ottomans, was established among another group of Turks who had moved westward into Asia Minor. For nearly three centuries the Ottomans expanded their conquests, until in 1683 they ranged from Hungary to the Persian Gulf and from the Crimea to North Africa and the coasts of Arabia. The followers of the Ottoman founder, Osman (1299–1326), were mostly *ghazis*, Islamic warriors who saw their sacred duty in extending the faith by attacking unbelievers. Motivated by religion and a thirst for booty, disciplined by a ghazi code of honor, and aided by the weakness of their enemies, the Ottomans were successful out of all proportion to their relatively small numbers. Their success was also aided by their tolerance of other faiths after their first conquests and by the disgust of many Byzantine subjects with the corrupt and oppressive imperial government (see Chapter 8).

From their newly conquered base in western Asia Minor, the Ottomans began in the 1300s by extending their sway over other Turkish states and Byzantine territories in the rest of Asia Minor and adjoining areas. A request for their help by one of the feuding political factions in Constantinople gave them an opportunity to establish a bridgehead on the European side of the Dardanelles, from which they later refused to retreat. Taking advantage of political chaos in the Balkans as well as their own military superiority, the Ottomans defeated the Serbs, Bulgars, and Macedonians in the late 1300s, opening up the Balkans to Turkish immigrants. Europeans were now sufficiently alarmed to send a crusading army. The Ottoman leader Bayezid I, "the Thunderbolt," who had allegedly threatened to feed his horse at the altar of St. Peter's Basilica in Rome, took only three hours to defeat the Europeans at Nicopolis in 1396. As Bayezid prepared to attack the Byzantine capital at Constantinople, the Ottomans themselves became the victims of a new Turco-Mongol invasion led by Tamerlane, who defeated them near Ankara in 1402.

After Tamerlane withdrew and order was restored, the Ottomans renewed their conquests, defeating the Greeks and finally taking Constantinople in 1453. Under Mehmet II, "the Conqueror" (1451–1481), the city, renamed Istanbul, was rebuilt and repopulated with new immigrants, including Jews and Christians as well as Muslims.

MEHMET THE CONQUEROR

Mehmet hoped to make his new capital the center of a world empire far greater than that to which Alexander the Great and Julius Caesar had aspired. In this imperial state Mehmet ruled supreme. He made war—the vehicle to expand his empire—the dominant preoccupation of Ottoman society.

Because of his imperialistic ambitions and his despotic rule, Mehmet's life was increasingly endangered by foreign agents as well as domestic zealots. The Venetian republic organized at least a dozen attempts to assassinate him, but Mehmet's espionage network successfully protected him. Despite the threats to his life, he frequently

Mehmet II, conqueror of Constantinople, as painted by a contemporary artist. [Topkapi Palace Museum, Istanbul]

rode through Istanbul accompanied by only two guards or walked the streets in the company of his slaves. But the strain eventually took its toll, turning the once affable sultan into a suspicious, reclusive despot, afraid even to eat with his viziers for fear of being poisoned. Stories of his cruelty abound. When the Italian Renaissance painter Gentile Bellini showed Mehmet his painting of the beheading of John the Baptist, Mehmet criticized Bellini for making John's neck extend too far and proved his point by having a slave beheaded in Bellini's presence. A serious offender against Mehmet's laws might have a long, sharp pole driven up his rectum with a mallet; if that failed to kill him, the pole, with the victim on it, was erected. Between his military campaigns and his domestic persecution, Mehmet may have been responsible for nearly 30,000 deaths a year during his reign.

Despite his undeniable vicious streak, Mehmet was tolerant when it came to matters of religion. Perhaps this was due in part to the fact that his mother, who was of Greek, Slavic, or Italian ancestry, had been raised a Christian. Mehmet himself made some effort to comprehend Christian teachings, at least as a means of understanding the faith of a substantial number of his subjects. His own preference was the Shi'ite version of Islam, but as the ruler of a largely Sunni state, he publicly embraced Sunni tenets. Mehmet treated the Jews well; his Jewish physician, Maestro Jacopo, was also a trusted financial adviser.

The Sufis' religious fraternities, or dervishes, did not fare as well. As mystical religious ascetics roughly akin to Christian monks or friars, they were popular with the masses because of their pastoral concerns, their poverty and charitable work, their mystical rites, and in some cases their cult of saints. Because their popularity made Mehmet suspicious, however, he curtailed their activity and occasionally even exiled their leaders, whom he denounced as insane, and confiscated their property.

Mehmet's personality combined intellectual curiosity with superstition and cold calculation. Given his vast imperial ambition—the state he ruled was roughly equivalent to the Byzantine Empire at its height—it was only natural that he should be interested in the study of geography, history, and military strategy. As he grew older, he increasingly enjoyed the company of poets and scholars. Yet he was also keenly superstitious and hired Persian astrologers to prepare horoscopes for him, sometimes even using their predictions as the basis for military decisions. To an artist such as Bellini, who painted his portrait (which the sultan commissioned in defiance of Islamic law), Mehmet attributed virtually supernatural power. Reinforcing the coldness of Mehmet's personality was the constant threat of assassination as well as his refusal to become involved in long-term relationships with women. Sexually, he enjoyed the company of women and boys, but domestic intimacy he deliberately shunned. Although his modern biographer calls Mehmet's personality "demonic," today many Turks regard him as the greatest of the sultans and a holy man who can still intercede with Allah on their behalf.

Selim the Grim, Suleiman the Magnificent, and Ottoman Expansion

In the decades after the fall of Constantinople the Ottoman armies completed the conquest of Greece and the Balkans. They also established a foothold in the Crimea by supplanting colonies founded by the Genoese so that by the late 1400s the Black Sea was virtually a Turkish lake. In the following century two of the greatest sultans, Selim I, "the Grim" (1512–1520), and Suleiman I, "the Magnificent" (1520–1566), made major new advances. Selim first had to turn his attention eastward, where the expansionist Shi'ite regime in Safavid Iran threatened the Ottomans and offended their Sunni orthodoxy. After pushing back the Safavids, Selim overran Syria, Palestine, and Egypt. These conquests forced the sultan to assume responsibility for protecting the Islamic holy places in Mecca and Medina, now threatened by the advance of the Portuguese into the Red Sea and the Indian Ocean in their quest for bases along the route to India.

Suleiman continued his predecessor's expansionistic program. In a series of brilliant campaigns he captured the island citadel of Rhodes; Belgrade on the Danube, gateway to central Europe; and much of Hungary. He besieged Vienna, but his forces lacked both the supplies and the resolve to take the city, and he was forced to retreat in 1526. Elsewhere his armies were victorious in North Africa as far west as Algeria, and in the Middle East, where they captured Baghdad. In the course of these campaigns Suleiman became an ally of France against the Habsburgs. As a consequence France gained special trade privileges in the Ottoman Empire, and later it acted as protector of Catholic subjects in the empire and of the Christian holy places in Palestine.

Ottoman expansion continued for another century, though at a much slower pace because of domestic conflict, a stronger European maritime presence in the Mediterranean, bitter rivalry with Iran, and a succession of ineffectual sultans. After the Ottomans conquered Cyprus in 1570, the Holy League, comprised of Spain, Venice, and the papacy, successfully challenged and defeated the Ottoman fleet in 1571 at Lepanto, off western Greece. The last major Ottoman conquest in the west was the island of Crete in 1664. A second assault on Vienna failed in 1683 (see Chapter 22), effectively marking the end of Ottoman expansion. From this point on, the Ottomans, now on the defensive and surpassed by European scientific and technological advances, repeatedly lost territory. The remains of their empire finally crumbled more than two centuries later after their defeat in World War I.

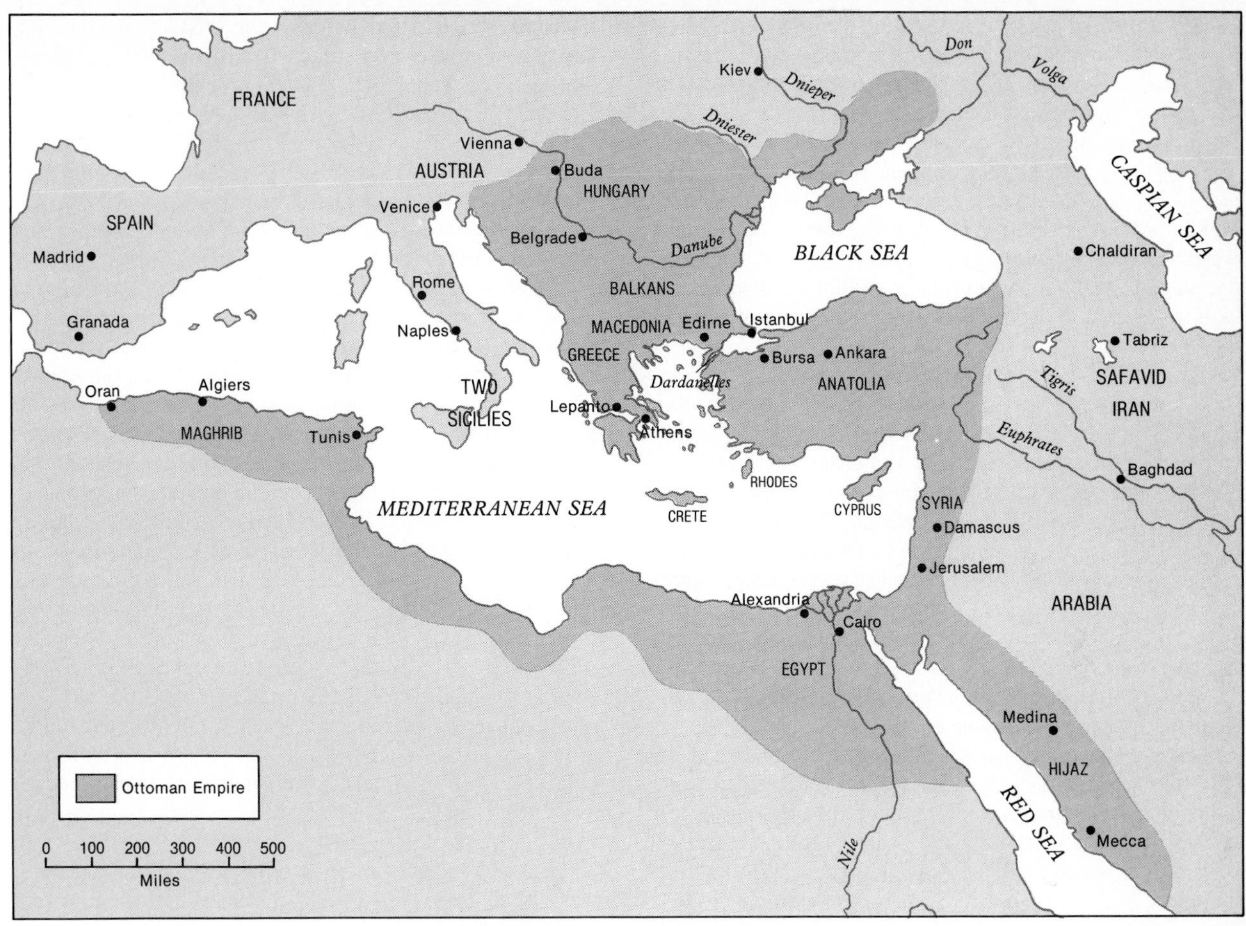

19.1 The Empire of Suleiman I

Ottoman Society

The sultans who presided over the empire had supreme authority in matters civil, military, and religious, subject only to divine law. Interpretation of that law was therefore critical, and for this the sultans turned to the grand mufti of Constantinople, a legal expert who interpreted sacred law and issued legal opinions on the secular decrees of the sultans, with the consensus of other religious leaders. Like their counterparts in Europe and Asia, the sultans ruled with the aid of an advisory council called the *divan*, which met regularly to handle petitions and to supervise the affairs of state. Beginning in the late 1400s, the sultans rarely met with the divan, though they sometimes listened to its proceedings behind a grille in the wall of the council chamber. Presiding over the sessions was the grand vizier, the highest-ranking official in the government after the sultan.

Below the divan a highly centralized and immense bureaucracy administered the affairs of state. Because the sultans had huge harems, the problem of succession was potentially explosive, as in Mughal India and Iran. Mehmet II solved the problem by creating the "law of fratricide," which necessitated that each new sultan execute all but one of his brothers and half brothers; one was usually left alive in case a sultan died without a surviving heir. Perhaps no sultan was more thorough in his adherence to this practice than Selim the Grim, who killed his brothers, nephews, and sons, with the exception of his designated heir, Suleiman. Beginning in the mid-1600s, the Ottomans ended the practice of fratricide in preference for selecting the sultan's eldest son as heir. Other sons were made prisoners in palace chambers called the "cage" and kept politically powerless.

A major responsibility of the sultan was to dispense justice, symbolized by a high "tower of justice" in the imperial palace from which the sultan could theoretically see officials acting unjustly and punish them accordingly. In the divan the grand vizier dispensed justice in the sultan's name. Because the empire was ruled chiefly according to Islamic sacred law, even the sultan's decrees had to be rendered in its spirit, and the judicial system in practice involved a close intermingling of legal and religious principles. The two chief justices, second in legal significance only to the grand mufti of Constantinople, were the leaders of the *ulema*, a body of learned men that included judges, teachers, prayer leaders known as imams, and muftis, who specialized in interpreting the law for judges and public officials. Although the grand mufti was originally not part of the judiciary in order to ensure his objectivity, in time he came to dominate it, even to the point of naming the chief justice.

These officials were drawn from the sultan's ruling class, and most belonged to an elite group known as the "true Ottomans." This group consisted solely of Muslims who served the state and "knew the Ottoman way"; that is, they were Turkish and conformed to Ottoman customs. Membership in the ruling class was not denied by reason of birth; regardless of origin, one could become an Ottoman by acquiring the stipulated qualifications. In an empire that included a wide variety of races and cultures, this was important in attracting support and conveying a sense of shared power.

Beneath the ruling class were the *reaya*, or "subjects"—peasants, townspeople, and nomads, both Muslim and non-Muslim. They were legally distinct from the ruling class. Because sons of that class generally inherited their father's social status, they perpetuated the oligarchy, provided that they acquired the necessary education to serve the state, although recruits from below could be promoted on merit.

The vast numbers of subject communities enveloped by Ottoman expansion were essentially allowed to govern themselves and to retain their institutions as long as they paid their taxes and provided the sultan with military and administrative personnel. The Ottomans even permitted their subjects to retain their traditional religious loyalties. Non-Muslims, including Jews and Greek Orthodox Christians, were organized into communities known as *millets*, which served as the main agencies for tax collection, education, and civil matters such as marriage and inheritance. To encourage the conversion of non-Muslims to Islam, the Ottomans imposed a special tax on all "infidels." Muslim men were permitted to marry non-Muslim women, who did not have to convert, but the children of such unions had to be raised as Muslims. In general the Ottomans proved more tolerant than Christian monarchs in Europe, who subjected heretics and Jews to forcible conversion and sometimes expelled and even executed them.

A characteristic feature of Ottoman society was the institution of slavery. Slavery, as the Ottomans practiced it, was substantially different from the brutal servitude Europeans imposed on blacks in the New World. It was less menial and offered greater opportunities. As elsewhere in the Middle East and parts of Asia, slaves were employed primarily as personal and household attendants or were given assignments in the military and bureaucracy. Some eventually established themselves as judges, philosophers, and poets. A sixteenth-century sultan typically had between 20,000 and 25,000 civil servants and troops in his household, all nominally slaves; the grand vizier had 1,700 in 1561. Slavery was not necessarily considered demeaning in all its circumstances, for some sultans were sons of slaves in their fathers' harems, and sometimes even the grand vizier was a slave.

Because Islamic law did not permit the enslavement of Muslims, slaves necessarily consisted of prisoners of war, people the Ottomans purchased in North Africa and Spain, and young males from Christian families within the empire who were recruited in a periodic levy. This levy, known as the *devshirme*, was imposed by the sultan's personal authority as a special tax, usually on one household in 40 in order to distribute the burden as equitably as possible. The youths selected had to be unmarried and typically between the ages of 8 and 18; orphans and only sons were exempt. Some parents offered bribes to keep their sons out of the levy; some young men resorted to similar means to get in. Once in Istanbul, the youths were forcibly converted to Islam and circumcised; the most promising were then designated to receive special education so that they might assume appointment to a high government office. Many acquired membership in the janissaries, the most elite unit of the Ottoman army; members became especially proficient in the use of firearms, and originally they were not permitted to marry.

Ottoman society, like nearly all societies of the time, was largely geared to benefit the males. Muslim custom permitted polygamy, and women usually wore veils. In sharp contrast with the Byzantine Empire and the western European states, women were excluded as rulers. Wives of the sultans were instead confined to harems, which were organized hierarchically like the rest of society. Presided over by the sultan's mother, who was assisted by mothers of the sultan's children and royal favorites, harems were guarded by eunuchs, men castrated as boys so as to assure no risk of their plotting to put their sons in power and to prevent them from engaging in sexual misconduct with harem members. From the 1500s onward, virtually all eunuchs in the empire were African blacks.

From their position in the harem, powerful women were sometimes able to dominate the government, particularly in the "sultanate of the women" in the mid-1600s. One of the most influential of these women was Turhan, mother of Mehmet IV (1648–1687), who seized power by having the boy's grandmother murdered. Beyond the upper reaches of the imperial harem, however, women were excluded from places of power and even from many of the Islamic religious ceremonies.

Despite their general exclusion from political power, Muslim women in the Ottoman world enjoyed a variety of rights, including the ability to hold and control property without interference from fathers, husbands, or male rela-

Devshirme: The Turks Draft Christians

Europeans were intrigued and horrified by the Turkish practice known as the devshirme, *by which Christian boys were drafted into slavery by the state. In 1585 a Venetian ambassador described it in these words:*

There are two types of Turks. One is composed of people native-born of Turkish parents, while the other is made up of renegades who are sons of Christians. The latter group were taken by force in the raids . . . on Christian lands, or else harshly levied in their villages from the sultan's non-Muslim subjects and taxpayers. They are taken while still boys, and either persuaded or forced to be circumcised and made Muslims. It is the custom . . . to send men throughout the country every fourth or fifth year to levy one-tenth of the boys, just as if they were so many sheep, and after they have made Turks of these boys they train each one according to his abilities. . . .

Not only is the Turkish army made up of these renegades, but at one time they used to win all the chief positions in the government . . . and the highest commands in the armed forces, because ancient custom forbids that the sons of Turks should hold these jobs. But the present Grand Signor ignores this custom and chooses whatever men he wants. . . .

After they have been taken away as young boys the renegades are sent to different places to be trained according to the jobs they will be given. The handsomest, most wide-awake ones are placed in the seraglio [palace] of the Grand Signor, or in one of two others . . . and there they are all prepared . . . to rise to the highest government offices. . . .

The other boys . . . [are] in a kind of seminary for the janissary corps. . . . They make them drudge day and night, and they give them no beds to sleep on and very little food. When these boys begin to shave they make them janissaries.

Source: J. C. Davis, ed. and trans., *Pursuit of Power: Venetian Ambassadors' Reports on Spain, Turkey, and France in the Age of Philip II, 1560–1600* (New York: Harper Torchbooks, 1970), pp. 135–136.

tives. This right extended even to property that was part of their dowry, a right not accorded to French women as late as the nineteenth century. Legally Ottoman women could be executors of wills, defend their rights in court, and testify, though technically a man's testimony was considered twice as valid. No Muslim woman could be forced to marry, although various pressures could be applied to attain the family's end. Although divorce was rare among Muslims, a woman who received one was entitled to retain her property. Thus, although Ottoman women shared the generally low status of women elsewhere, they did possess some basic economic rights and at least a degree of social choice.

ISTANBUL: "THIS PLACE THAT IS LIKE PARADISE"

Before the Muslim conquest in 1453, the population of Constantinople had declined to some 40,000 inhabitants, and it fell to 10,000 immediately after the conquests, but within 25 years it had rebounded to nearly 100,000, including its suburbs. By 1600 Istanbul, as the Turks called it, was larger than any city in Europe, with a population of at least 700,000. The initial impetus for the city's growth came from its conqueror, Mehmet II, who was determined to make his new capital the greatest in the world. To increase the population, he offered to return the property of refugees and to give them freedom to work and worship if they came back, which a great many did.

Mehmet also ordered nearby provincial governors to send 4,000 families to Istanbul (although this goal was never fully achieved), and he attracted merchants and artisans from such conquered cities as Corinth and Argos in Greece and towns in the Crimea. Because of their wealth and trading skills, Jews were also encouraged to emigrate to Istanbul. By 1478 they were the third largest group in the capital, comprising some 10 percent of the population behind Muslims (58 percent) and Greek Christians (23 percent). To help feed the burgeoning population, Mehmet settled 30,000 captive Balkan peasants, whom he virtually enslaved, in villages near the capital.

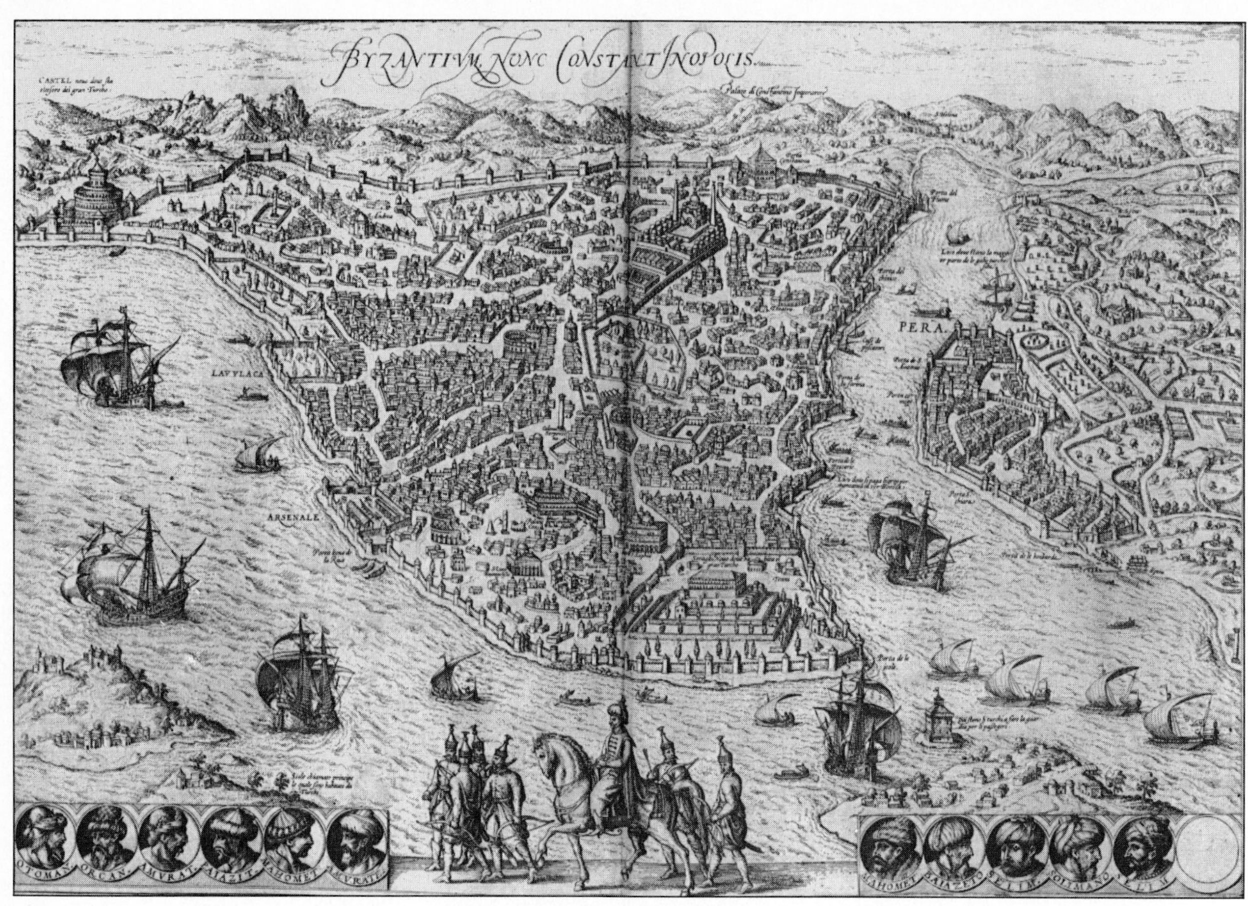

A view of Istanbul in the sixteenth century. Note the natural defenses of the city as well as the wall at the top of the painting. [British Library]

Because much of the city had been ruined during the siege, the Ottomans initiated a massive building program that included two palaces and a grand mosque. Around the latter there developed a hospital, an almshouse, and a major center of higher education that provided instruction in theology, law, medicine, and the sciences. The famous Christian church, Hagia Sophia, was transformed into a mosque, minarets were gradually added, the Byzantine mosaics were plastered with a gray limewash, and verses from the Koran were substituted as decorations. The grandest of the new mosques was constructed in the early 1550s at the behest of Suleiman, who employed the leading Ottoman architect, Sinan, designer of more than 300 buildings. When his masterpiece was finished, Sinan reportedly told Suleiman: "I have built for thee, O emperor, a mosque which will remain on the face of the earth till the day of judgment."[1] In addition to such grandiose structures, the Ottomans commissioned many public works, including new roads, bridges, and aqueducts.

The commercial heart of Istanbul was the grand bazaar or *bedestan*, built at Mehmet's command. Consisting of a monumental building with stone domes and iron doors—a secure depository for valuable goods, jewelry, and money—the bazaar was surrounded by groups of shops lining the roads that branched out into the city. Each group of shops housed merchants or artisans who specialized in a particular kind of goods. Mehmet's complex, including the 118 shops in the bedestan and the 984 surrounding it, is today known as Istanbul's covered market.

Crucial to the reconstruction of the capital were the *imarets*, each of which was typically an endowed complex consisting of a mosque, an institution of higher learning or *medrese*, a hospital, travelers' lodgings, and appropriate roads and bridges. In 1459 Mehmet required the most prominent citizens to establish imarets in Istanbul, and in time these complexes became the centers of new quarters or suburbs. Istanbul, in fact, grew so rapidly that in the seventeenth century the sultans tried to restrict its expansion and generally succeeded in slowing down the rate of growth. By comparison, the English monarchs Elizabeth I and James I were less successful in their efforts to halt the growth of London. A truly cosmopolitan city unlike anything in Europe, some 40 percent of Istanbul's population in the seventeenth century was non-Muslim.

Urban Life

While Istanbul was unmistakably the preeminent jewel in the Ottoman crown, a host of other cities contributed to the richness, productivity, and cultural heritage of the empire. Among them by the late 1600s were some of the great cities of antiquity: Alexandria and Baghdad, Athens and Jerusalem. Others, such as Sarajevo and Tatar-Pazarjik in the Balkans, developed from imarets founded in the fourteenth and fifteenth centuries by frontier lords. The largest Ottoman city and commercial center in the Balkans was Edirne (now in Bulgaria), which was strategically located on the major overland trade routes between Istanbul and Hungary, Bosnia, and Greece. Its counterpart in Anatolia—Bursa, center of a thriving silk industry—sat astride the overland routes from Europe and western Asia Minor to the Middle East, Iran, and India.

The heart of every major Ottoman city was a great mosque and a bedestan, around which trade centers developed. The endowment of imarets played a key role in the growth of such cities as Edirne and Bursa, underscoring the importance of substantive charitable giving in the expansion of Ottoman urban life and commerce.

Although the people were officially divided into two groups, Muslim and non-Muslim, in practice socioeconomic divisions had little to do with religion. Merchants and artisans in the towns had the same rights, though in theory non-Muslims were required to dress distinctively and were not allowed to ride horses or own slaves. In fact, however, such restrictions were ineffective. Each religious group—Muslim, Jewish, and Christian—was housed in its own quarter, as were the gypsies. Each quarter was typically organized around a religious center or a bedestan and was a community in its own right, its members linked most often by distinctive religious or economic ties. Normally the religious leader of each quarter—imam, rabbi, or priest—was responsible for contacts with the imperial government and would, for example, make the sultan's decrees known to the people. Each quarter had to provide for its own night watchmen, lamplighters, street cleaners, and volunteer fire fighters.

Although the Ottoman city was at root a collection of distinctive communities, there were municipal officials who coordinated common services, such as street paving and repair, water supply, building regulations, and refuse disposal. These officials were not, however, representatives of a formal municipal organization, as in modern America, but agents of the imperial government.

Economy and Culture

Economic life in Ottoman cities was organized around the guilds, whose members comprised a substantial part of the population. Like their medieval European counterparts, the Ottoman guilds regulated their activities, including standards, prices, and competition, and cared for the welfare of their members. They also engaged in a wide variety of social activities ranging from processions and festivals to the provision of relief to the needy. Some guilds were restricted to adherents of a particular religious group, while others embraced Muslims, Jews, and Christians. As in Europe, masters trained apprentices, who in time became journeymen and ultimately masters, so long as their number did not become excessive. Some guilds hired women, principally to wind silk and spin cotton. Other guilds, such as that of the weavers in Bursa, relied heavily on slave labor, promising freedom to slaves who wove a stipulated quantity of cloth. As in Renaissance Florence, these guilds also hired free labor.

The range of guilds was extensive, embracing the usual skilled craftsmen as well as fishermen, minters, scribes, and religious men. There were even guilds in Istanbul that provided snow, ice, and water from the mountains or made sherbet in such exotic flavors as rhubarb, rose, and lotus. All guilds were subject to strict regulations and substantial taxes.

Merchants in the Ottoman cities generally fell into two groups: those who dealt with local products and belonged to guilds akin to those of the artisans, and those engaged in caravan and overseas trade, who were essentially free to pursue their businesses as they wished. Some merchants organized partnerships or corporations, sometimes cornering the market in various commodities and driving up the prices to make substantial profits. Guild members were understandably hostile to such merchants, particularly since profit margins in the guilds normally did not exceed 15 percent. Moreover, the great merchants paid relatively little in taxes, though they used their wealth to benefit their communities in other ways. Some procured raw material for workers and exported their finished products, while others endowed charitable institutions.

Although charging interest under Islamic law was illegal, merchants of all religious persuasions found ways to provide loans. Among the borrowers were government officials who used the loans to procure higher offices and then rewarded the lenders with such benefits as monopolies or tax farms (the right of private parties to collect taxes for the government). Certain merchants received contracts to establish factories for the production of large amounts of armaments or woolens for the military, thereby depriving the smaller guild shops of business and increasing the friction between merchants and artisans.

The wealthier Ottoman merchants engaged in extensive international trade, particularly from the key centers

Jewish Life in the Ottoman Empire

On his tour of the Ottoman Empire in the sixteenth century, Nicolas De Nicolay, chamberlain and geographer to the king of France, described the Jews in this manner:

The number of Jews dwelling throughout all the cities of Turkey and Greece, and principally at Constantinople, is so great, that it is a thing marvelous and incredible. For the number of those who trade and traffic in merchandise, likewise who loan money at usury, doth there multiply so from day to day, that the great haunt and bringing of merchandise which arrives there from all parts as well by sea as by land, is such, that . . . they have in their hands the most and greatest traffic of merchandise and ready money that is in all [the] Levant. And likewise their shops and warehouses, the best furnished of all rich sorts of merchandise which are in Constantinople are those of the Jews. Likewise they have among them workmen of all arts and handicrafts most excellent, and especially of the Maranes [Moriscos] of late banished and driven out of Spain and Portugal, who to the great detriment and damage of Christianity, have taught the Turks divers inventions, crafts, and engines of war, as to make artillery, harquebusses [handguns], gunpowder, shot, and other munitions. They have also there set up printing, not before seen in those countries, by the which in fair characters they put in light divers books in divers languages, as Greek, Latin, Italian, Spanish, and the Hebrew tongue, being to them natural, but are not permitted to print the Turkish or Arabic tongue. They . . . speak and understand all other sorts of languages used in [the] Levant, which serves them greatly for the communication and traffic which they have with other strange nations, to whom oftentimes they serve for Dragomans, or interpreters. . . . They are abhorred by God and men, and more persecuted by the Turks . . . than by any other nation. [The Turks hold] them in such disdain and hatred, that by no means will they eat in their company, much less marry any of their wives or daughters, notwithstanding that oftentimes [Turks] marry Christians, whom they permit to live according to their law, and have a pleasure to eat and be conversant with Christians. . . . If a Jew would become a Muslim, he should not be received, except first leaving his Judaical sect he became a Christian. The Jews which dwell in Constantinople, Adrianople, . . . and other places of the dominion of the great Turk, are all apparelled with long garments, like unto the Greeks and other nations of [the] Levant, but for their mark and token to be known from others, they wear a yellow Tulbant [a turban].

Source: N. De Nicolay, *The Navigations into Turkie*, trans. T. Washington (London, 1585), fols. 130v–131v (edited to conform to modern usage).

of Istanbul, Bursa, Edirne, Cairo, and Salonika. Muslim merchants even had their own trading companies in the important cities of northern Italy. The textile merchants of Edirne exported their products as far afield as Florence, Paris, and London and in turn imported European cloth. Cotton from Anatolia, Egypt, Yemen, and India was sold throughout Europe, while the merchants of Bursa exported silk, timber, hides, and ironware to the East. Spices, jewelry, perfume, costly textiles, and dyes were the major commodities in overseas trade. Through the key North African cities of Cairo and Alexandria came ivory, gold, and slaves; Istanbul alone had some 2,000 slave merchants. One of the oddities of the empire was that foreign traders paid fewer taxes than their Ottoman counterparts and thus after the eighteenth century came to dominate international commerce.

Feeding the imperial population, especially the residents of the capital, was a major task. By the mid-seventeenth century Istanbul alone required 250 tons of wheat each day and 2,000 shiploads of food each year. Much of the food, of course, was produced within the empire: wheat from Egypt, Thrace, and especially the

Dobrudja region west of the Black Sea; livestock, fish, cereals, and honey from the area north of that sea; wine from the Aegean region; rice, spices, and sugar from Egypt; and cereals from Macedonia and Thessaly. So crucial was the need to find adequate food for the population and sufficient raw materials for the artisans that the imperial government imposed numerous controls. It fixed the price of the food at the point of production, licensed the middlemen who bought it, and supervised its distribution. Smuggling and profiteering were strictly prohibited, and violaters faced the loss of their ships and goods.

Until the end of the sixteenth century the food problem was aggravated by labor shortages in rural areas. The government responded to this by curtailing the mobility of peasants and by offering tax incentives and the right to sell surplus crops on the open market to farmers who brought unused lands under cultivation. Substantial population growth in the sixteenth century finally resolved the labor shortage.

During the golden age of Ottoman culture, which followed the conquest of Constantinople, most leading writers and thinkers belonged to the ulema. Their contributions were rich and varied, reaching a peak of excellence in the poetry composed for wealthy, powerful patrons. The leading Ottoman poets no longer imitated Persian writers but achieved a creativity of their own, even while extensively borrowing Persian and Arabic words.

The "sultan of the poets," as his contemporaries called him, was Muhammad Abd ul-Baki (1526–1600), a former appprentice to a saddlemaker and hawker of poems in the courtyard of a mosque. His major work was a moving elegy on Suleiman's death:

> ***Will not the King awake from sleep? The***
> ***dawn of day has broken.***
> ***Will not he come forth from his tent bright as***
> ***heaven's display?***
> ***Long have our eyes looked down the road,***
> ***and yet no news is come***
> ***From yonder land, the threshold of his***
> ***majesty's array.***[2]

Most of Baki's poems urged readers to enjoy the transitory pleasures of life. Almost as revered as Baki, Mehmet ibn Suleiman Fuzuli (1480–1556) explored the unity of creation and mystic love.

> ***Let your grace, my only Lord, forever be my***
> ***only guide;***
> ***Lead me not by any path that leads not to***
> ***where You abide.***[3]

There was also poetry for the masses, sung, as in medieval France and Germany, by itinerant troubadours; their themes, however, were mystical rather than secular, as in the West. The greatest of the folk poets was the seventeenth-century minstrel Karacaoglan, whose vigorous verse recounted the lives of the ordinary people of Anatolia.

> ***The cranes they circle in the air***
> ***The dreams I fear I see anew***
> ***Brave comrades, this I have to say***
> ***She does not love who is not true.***[4]

Novels, plays, and short stories became important literary forms in the Ottoman world only in the nineteenth century as the result of Western influence, but earlier prose authors made worthy contributions in essays, biographies, and learned treatises on history, geography, and religion. Recognizing the value of history to buttress their claims to expand the empire, Mehmet II and his predecessor, Murat II (1421–1451), sponsored the earliest Ottoman historians, including Ahmedi, whose *Epic of the Histories of the House of Osman* is the earliest source for the rise of the Ottomans. While the major historical writers of Suleiman's era were chroniclers, the distinguished court historian Mustafa Naima Efendi (1665–1716) not only recorded facts but analyzed them as well. "Historians," he insisted, "should speak frankly and fairly . . . , they should not exaggerate . . . , and if, to attain their end, they must criticize and censure great men of praiseworthy works, they should never be unjust."[5]

Two generations earlier, Mustafa ibn Abdullah, known as Katip-elebi (1609–1657), demonstrated equal respect for sources in compiling his *View of the World*, a compendium of geography that drew not only on Muslim works but also on such European authors as the Flemish geographer Gerardus Mercator. Western scholarship, which owed so much to the Muslim world, was now beginning to repay the debt.

In the area of religion, Muslim authors continued to debate the relationship between philosophy (reason) and religion (faith), in particular whether the two fields could be reconciled. During the late fifteenth century the ulema officially decided that reason could be used in the study of medicine and mathematics but not religion. Religious writers concentrated on the mystical notion of the unity of existence, a theme popular with many poets as well.

The medrese associated with the mosque founded by Suleiman was a boon to science because of its emphasis on mathematics and medicine rather than religion. Its influence is apparent in the large number of hospitals subsequently established in the empire. One of the most influential Ottoman physicians, Ahi Ahmet-elebi (1436–1523), founded hospitals in 40 villages, encouraged these institutions to train doctors, and established the first Ottoman medical school. Religious leaders, however, continued to threaten scientific inquiry, as in 1580, when their pressure prompted the sultan to destroy the astronomical observatory in Istanbul. Tensions between religious values and secular movements in education and society have continued in Islamic areas to the present day.

The Decay of the Empire

Beginning in the mid-seventeenth century, the rule of the sultans began to weaken. At the same time the janissaries, who could now marry at will, became more devoted to their families and personal fortunes than to the sultan's welfare. Discipline in the janissary corps eroded, demands for higher pay escalated, and there was a growing reluctance to fight extended campaigns in remote lands. Fortunately for the Ottomans, effective government was restored when Turhan appointed the Albanian Muhammad Kuprili as grand vizier in 1656. Determined to end graft and corruption in the empire, he and his successors dominated Ottoman politics until 1710.

After 1716 Ottoman officials, stung by the loss of Transylvania and most of Hungary to Habsburg armies (which had been confirmed in the 1699 Treaty of Karlowitz), began trying to reorganize their decaying army along European lines, but the forces of conservatism, led by the janissaries and the ulema, resisted change. The sultans and some factions at court regularly pressed for reform but were resisted by vested interests and conservative groups. The Ottomans were ultimately unable to stave off the European challenge to their empire. The Treaty of Passarowitz (1718), by which the Ottomans ceded much of Serbia to Austria and Dalmatia to Venice, was a foretaste of things to come.

The Mughals in India

After Tamerlane's bloody invasion of 1398 (see Chapter 10), the Delhi sultanate never regained its earlier control, and the north of India remained fragmented. An Afghan clan, the Lodis, seized power in Delhi in 1451 but could not extend their rule beyond neighboring Punjab. Their continued oppression of the Hindu population, including temple razing, sparked rebellions that could not be put down. These erupted eastward in the central Ganges valley, westward among the Rajputs of Rajasthan (who still defended Hindu India), and finally in Punjab itself.

Babur and the New Dynasty

A rebel governor in Punjab asked for help from the central Asian leader Babur (1483–1530), known already as "the Tiger" and by this time established also as ruler of most of Afghanistan. Babur claimed descent on his father's side from Tamerlane and on his mother's from Chinghis Khan. Like many other central Asian Turks, he had acquired a great deal of Persian culture and was a gifted poet in Persian. Babur's tough, mounted Turco-Afghan troops defeated the numerically superior Lodi forces and their war elephants at the battle of Panipat in Punjab, some 70 miles northwest of Delhi, in 1526. The next year Babur routed the Rajput army, which tried to eject him, and in 1529 crushed the Delhi sultanate's last effort to regain power. Babur was master of the north and proclaimed the Mughal dynasty (the name is derived, via Persian, from *Mongol*), which was to restore imperial grandeur in northern India for nearly two centuries.

The greatness of the Mughal period rested on a fortunate combination of able, imaginative rulers, especially the emperor Akbar (1542–1605), and the new infusion of Persian culture into North India. Under Akbar and his immediate successors, Persian, the official language of court, government, and law, merged with the earlier language of the Delhi-Agra area to form modern Hindi, now the largest single language of India, and Urdu, its close equivalent, now the official language of Pakistan. Persian artistic and literary forms blended with earlier traditions in the north and enriched all of Indian culture. The Mughals reestablished firm central control in the north. Within their empire, agriculture and commerce flourished again. Steady revenues and an efficient imperial administration enabled the Mughals to build a network of roads that linked the empire. This was no small task, given India's previous disunity and regional separatism, as well as its size.

The total population in the empire was probably over 100 million, on a par with China's and Europe's. To symbolize their power and wealth, the Mughal emperors built magnificent new capitals at both Delhi and Agra. Only 100 miles apart, the cities served alternatively as the seat of government. This area, between the Jumna and Ganges rivers, had long been the key to Hindustan, the Ganges valley, and routes southward (see Chapter 10). Successive Delhis had risen and fallen on the same strategic site, controlling, with Agra as its satellite, the heart of repeated imperial efforts. Both cities were built, like sentinels, on the west bank of the Jumna, which flows into the Ganges below Agra after running parallel to it, like a defensive moat, from well north of Delhi.

Each city was dominated by a great walled fort containing the palace and audience halls. Inside and outside the walls the Mughals also constructed great mosques, gardens, tombs (such as the Taj Mahal at Agra), and other monumental buildings in the Persian style, which they developed further and made distinctively Indian. Literature, music, and the graphic arts flourished under imperial patronage at both capitals. Strong imperial rule was often oppressive, but it helped to ensure an unprecedented period of unity and prosperity that most Indians shared. Hindus too could feel pride in the new imperial grandeur, for they were given an important role in it.

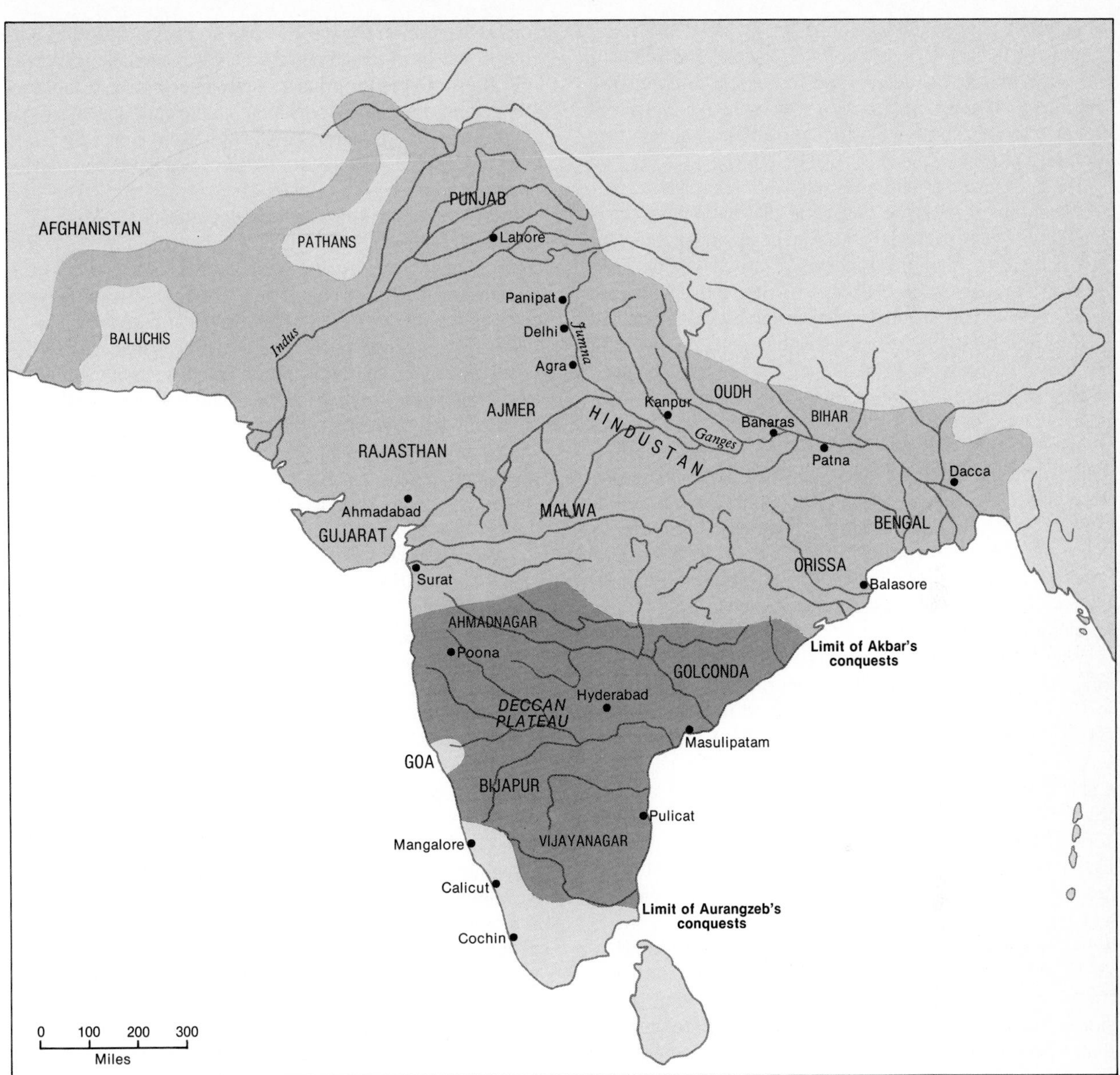

19.2 India at the Height of Mughal Power

Akbar and His Achievement

Akbar's success in building a truly Indian empire rather than just another alien conquest was the chief foundation of Mughal greatness, but he had first to establish his rule. Babur died prematurely in 1530, after offering his life to God in exchange for that of his son Humayun, who was deathly ill. But Humayun (1508–1556) was a weakling who was finally driven out of India in 1540 by one of Babur's Afghan generals and forced to take refuge in Iran. A year after he returned in 1555 at the head of a Persian army to reclaim his father's conquests, he fell on the stone steps of his private astronomical observatory and library, lightheaded from opium, and died, leaving the throne to his 13-year-old son Akbar, who had been born in exile in 1542.

Immediately challenged upon his accession in 1556, Akbar's army defeated yet another Hindu effort to drive out the invaders at Panipat. In 1562, at the age of 20, Akbar assumed full charge of the empire from his advisers. In the same year he married a Rajput princess, beginning what was to be a lifelong campaign to blend the many strands of India's ancient cultural, regional, and religious heritage. Akbar was determined to build both an empire and a new culture that was as nearly as he could make it truly Indian, uniting its various elements under firm Mughal control.

He saw himself as an Indian ruler, not a foreign despot, and understood from the beginning that his own success and that of the dynasty depended on commanding the support and participation of all Indians. But he could be ruthless too if his power was challenged. When the chief Rajput faction resisted his diplomacy, he sacked the Rajput capital in 1568 and massacred the surviving defenders. By 1570 all but a small remnant of the Rajputs had sworn allegiance to him; in return, he made a Rajput, whose military skills he knew well, one of his chief generals, and other Rajputs thereafter also played a strong role in the imperial army. This political wisdom solved what would have otherwise been his major military problem. Rajputs became his comrades rather than his implacable enemies. To mark his policy of religious toleration further, he chose for his four wives two Hindus (including his Rajput bride), one Christian, and one Muslim, thus symbolically embracing India's religious variety.

With his new Rajput allies, Akbar invaded wealthy Gujarat, capturing Surat, the chief seaport of the west coast, in 1573. Three years later he completed the conquest of Bengal in the east and by 1581 had added most of Afghanistan to his empire. For many years his armies raided south into the northern Deccan but were never able to win permanent control, a goal that also eluded his successors. But northern India and Afghanistan under Akbar and his successors remained until the end of the seventeenth century one of history's greatest empires in size, wealth, and splendor. It was divided into 15 provinces, each under a governor but with a separate set of officials responsible for revenue collection. Provinces were subdivided into districts, where representatives of the governor kept order and dispensed justice. Revenue demands were smaller than under the Delhi sultans, and the large number of Hindus employed in the revenue service, as well as at its head, helped to keep taxes from becoming exploitive or unfair. Hindu law was applied in disputes between Hindus. Revenue collectors were ordered to remit taxes in districts that had had a poor harvest.

One reform that endeared Akbar to his subjects was his abolition of two hated taxes: on Hindu pilgrims traveling to sacred sites and on all Hindus as infidels (the *jizya*, or poll tax), both of which had been collected by Muslim rulers for centuries. He abolished the practice of enslaving war prisoners and their families and forbade forcible conversion to Islam, long a bitter issue. Hindus were welcomed at court, and their advice was regularly sought. Akbar patronized Persian and Urdu art and literature, but he also appointed a court poet for Hindi and encouraged Hindu literature and art more generally. Most of the greatest court painters were Hindus, producing beautiful portraits, miniatures, and naturalistic bird, animal, and flower paintings. Orthodox Muslims challenged this defiance of the Islamic ban on the depiction of human or animal forms, but Akbar replied that he could not believe God, "the giver of life," would disapprove of the beauty he had made, which was portrayed in true art.

Like the other Mughal emperors after him, Akbar loved gardens, with which nearly all Mughal buildings, including palaces, forts, and tombs, were surrounded in magnificent blendings of green lawns, gaily colored beds of flowers with flowering trees for shade, and an ingenious use of water in fountains, pools, and fluted channels. These devices enhanced the atmosphere of coolness, restfulness, and greenness, creating an effect that was especially striking in the hot dry surroundings of the plains of North India. Akbar took a personal interest in the planning and care of the imperial gardens. He is often shown by court painters supervising the planting of flower beds and tending his roses.

Akbar was widely curious and loved to discuss philosophy and religion with all comers, including Portuguese Jesuits as well as Hindu Brahmins. He had the Christian Gospels translated into Persian and attended mass. But as he came to reject the dogma of Islam as the only true religion, he could not accept the exclusive truth of any one faith, except a universal faith in an all-powerful creator. In later life he increasingly became a Sufi, or Islamic mystic. He was a deeply religious person, but his departures from orthodox Islam shocked many Muslim leaders and provoked a revolt against him in 1581. He suppressed it by force and then in deference to Hindu values forbade the slaughter of cattle and became a vegetarian, even giving up hunting, of which he had been very fond. Akbar founded a new faith that he hoped could unite his varied subjects in the common love of God, without need for a sectarian priesthood, but it did not survive him. If he had been followed by rulers like him, his dream of a united India free of strife might have moved closer to realization.

Much has been written about the fascinating Akbar. He was a contemporary of Elizabeth I of England, Henry IV of France, Shah Abbas of Iran, and the Ming Emperor Wan-li. Europeans who had met them all agreed that as both a human being and a ruler, he towered over his contemporaries. He had great strength of intelligence, character, and will, but he also had the good sense to realize that compromise and cooperation work better than force. He was full of energy and imagination but highly sensitive and often prey to melancholy and fits of depression. He seems to have suffered from epilepsy as well, like Julius Caesar and Napoleon. Astonishingly, he also appears to have been illiterate. As a child he preferred hunting and other sports to lessons, but he had a phenomenal memory, like many unlettered people, and was a great listener. From adolescence he appointed courtiers to read to him several hours a day; he had over 24,000 manuscripts in

The Court of Akbar

One of the many accounts of Akbar and the India of his time is that of the Jesuit Antonio Monserrate, who visited the court from 1580 to 1583. Here are some excerpts from the Commentary on His Journey to the Court of Akbar.

This prince is of a stature and type of countenance well fitted to his royal dignity, so that one could easily recognize even at first glance that he is the king. . . . His forehead is broad and open, his eyes so bright and flashing that they seem like a sea shimmering in the sunlight. . . . He creates an opportunity almost every day for any of the common people or of the nobles to see him and converse with him. It is remarkable how great an effect this courtesy and affability has in attaching to him the minds of his subjects. . . . He has an accute insight, and shows much wise foresight both in avoiding dangers and in seizing favorable opportunities for carrying out his designs. . . . Unlike the palaces built by other Indian kings, his are lofty [and] their total circuit is so large that it easily embraces four great royal dwellings. . . . Not a little is added to the beauty of the palaces by charming pigeon cotes. . . . The pigeons are cared for by eunuchs and servant maids. Their evolutions are controlled at will, when they are flying, by means of certain signals, just as those of a well trained soldiery. . . . It will seem little short of miraculous when I affirm that when sent out they dance, turn somersaults all together in the air, fly in orderly rhythm, and return to their starting point, all at the sound of a whistle. [Akbar's] empire is wonderfully rich and fertile both for cultivation and pasture, and has a great trade both in exports and imports. . . . Indian towns appear very pleasant from afar; they are adorned with many towers and high buildings in a very beautiful manner. But when one enters them, one finds that the narrowness, aimless crookedness, and ill planning of the streets deprive these cities of all beauty. . . . The common people live in lowly huts and tiny cottages, and hence if a traveller has seen one of these cities, he has seen them all.

Source: D. Lach, *Asia on the Eve of Europe's Expansion* (Englewood Cliffs, N.J.: Prentice-Hall, 1965), pp. 63–69 passim.

his library, and the learned men who debated with him often found him better "read" than themselves. He had a broadly inquiring mind, but a complicated one; the Jesuits at his court, who came to know him well, could never fully understand it or predict what he might say or do. He kept his dignity with all but had the knack of making the humblest petitioner feel at ease, and he charmed everyone who met him, high and low.

He was remarkably versatile, not only in his interests but in his skills as well. He was an accomplished polo player, metal worker, draftsman (many of his beautiful drawings have survived), and musician. He even invented a lighted polo ball so that the game could be played at night and a gun with a new mechanism that could fire multiple rounds. But his main preoccupation shifted to religion, especially after he had completed his major conquests, and he spent many nights alone in prayer and meditation. In 1575 he built a Hall of Worship, to which he invited the widest range of philosophers and theologians for periodic discussions, first from Islamic schools of thought and then from all the religions he could gather, including individual holy men, ascetics and mystics, Hindu saddhus and Muslim Sufis, Jesuit priests and Iranian fire worshipers. In time, these "seminars on religion" were held regularly every Thursday evening, while Akbar continued his own private devotions at sunrise, noon, sunset, and midnight. It was typical of him that although he hoped earnestly that the new mystic religion he founded in 1581 to unite all people would attract a mass following, he never tried to force it on anyone.

Akbar was too intellectually alive and too religiously devout to lapse into the life of extravagant luxury that surrounded him at court, but he was no purist or prude. He enjoyed food and wine, the sherbet brought to him daily by runners from the snowy Himalayas, the dancing girls, the music and plays, and the flourishing literature

Akbar's planned capital at Fatehpur Sikri, near Agra. Shown here is part of the women's quarters, open to the view and the breezes, from which the women could overlook the courtyard in the left foreground, marked off as a giant pachisi (Parcheesi) board. The game was played with live pieces—court ladies and members of the harem—whose moves were directed by court or royal players throwing dice. [Stella Snead]

and art that he so generously patronized. He was, in other words, a truly regal monarch, but a most unusual one in the range of his vision and understanding. It was too much to ask for a succession of others like him, but India was not again to be served by a ruler of his quality until the first prime minister of its modern independence, Jawaharlal Nehru (prime minister, 1947–1964.)

Akbar was still without an heir after six years of marriage. He sought help from a Sufi saint who lived at a place called Sikri, 20 miles west of Agra. A year later his first son was born, and in gratitude Akbar built of red sandstone a magnificent new capital, which he called Fatehpur Sikri, next to the saint's humble cottage. Here he had fresh scope to blend Indian, Persian, Islamic, and Mughal themes in architecture, drawing also on traditional Hindu architecture in the south. But the water supply in this arid region proved inadequate, and Fatehpur Sikri had to be abandoned after only 15 years. The deserted stone city still stands much as Akbar left it, a monument to his vision that still can move visitors.

The last four years of Akbar's life were clouded by the rebellion of his eldest son, whose birth had been such a joyous occasion. The Mughals were never able to work out the problem of succession. From this time on, each emperor was plotted against in his old age by his many sons, who also tore the empire apart by their fighting until the most ruthless had disposed of his rivals. It was a pattern inherited from the Mughals' central Asian origins, and it blighted their otherwise great achievements while also draining the country's resources. In 1605 Akbar reasserted his authority, only to die of poison administered by his rebellious son, who took the throne that year under the name Jahangir ("world-seizer").

Jahangir and Shah Jahan

Jahangir's Persian wife, Nur Jahan, a power in her own right, further entrenched Persian culture at the court and throughout North India. The administrative system inherited from Akbar continued to run smoothly, and revenues flowed in to pay for the brilliance of the court. Jahangir and Nur Jahan preferred Agra to Delhi and adorned it further with new palaces, gardens, and tombs. Court life took on a more luxurious splendor; Jahangir was no mystic like his father. He and his courtiers delighted in silks and perfumes, jewel-decked costumes, wine, song, and the pleasures of the harem. State processions featured troupes of dancing girls and elephants covered with silk and jewels, and monthlong festivities were held to celebrate the marriages of Jahangir's many sons.

The painting of this era became more naturalistic, and the orthodox Islamic prohibition against representing human or animal forms gave way to older Indian traditions, even including nearly nude figures and embracing couples in classic Rajput and earlier Hindu styles, as well as portraits of the emperor, often in his beloved gardens. For all their use of Persian language, culture, and art forms, the Mughals had become Indian rulers and were increasingly seen as such by most Indians. They were following a traditional maharaja lifestyle, and their pretensions to

Festivals in Mughal India

Jahangir's Memoirs *include these descriptions of New Year and birthday festivals.*

The feast of the New Year was held near Agra, and at the time of transit of the sun I seated myself on the throne with glory and gladness. The nobles and courtiers all came forward with their congratulations. . . . I determined that this time I would enter Agra [to visit his father Akbar's tomb] and after that would go on foot on this pilgrimage to the shrine, in the same way that my father, on account of my birth, had gone from Agra to Ajmir [Fatehpur]. . . . At an auspicious hour, I returned to Agra, and scattering with two hands 5,000 rupees in small coins along the way, I entered the august place which was inside the fort. . . . On the ninth of the month the feast for my solar weighing, which is the commencement of the 38th year of my age, took place. According to custom, they got ready the weighing apparatus and the scales. At the moment appointed blessings were invoked and I sat in the scales. Each suspending rope was held by an elderly person who offered up prayers. The first time I was weighed against gold, and then against several metals, perfumes, and essences, up to twelve weighings. Twice a year I weigh myself against gold and silver and other metals, and against all sorts of silks and cloths and various grains, etc., once at the beginning of the solar year and once at that of the lunar. The weight of the money of the two weighings I hand over to the different treasuries for faqirs [holy men] and those in want.

Source: J. N. Das Gupta, *India in the Seventeenth Century* (Calcutta: University of Calcutta Press, 1916), pp. 104–105.

divine authority were familiar to their subjects; like luxurious living, these were expected of royalty.

A resurgent Iran under Shah Abbas began to challenge the Mughal Empire in the west and conquered most of Afghanistan, but Jahangir was too busy with his gardens, wine, and harems to lead his army over the mountains. He had given his son Shah Jahan command of the army, but Shah Jahan refused to leave the capital because he was plotting to seize the throne, having previously poisoned his elder brother. He knew that his real enemy was Nur Jahan, who had manipulated Jahangir, appointed her own father and brother to the highest offices, and even hoped to occupy the throne herself. Jahangir, entranced by her beauty and wit, had named her Nur Jahan, meaning "light of the world," but she became empress in all but name soon after he married her. She arranged the marriage of her brother's daughter, Mumtaz Mahal, to Shah Jahan as an extension of the power of her clan.

But Shah Jahan openly rebelled in 1623, and when Jahangir died late in 1627, he put to death all of his closest relatives and pensioned off Nur Jahan. He declared himself "emperor of the world," which is the meaning of his regnal name, with three weeks of extravagant coronation ceremonies. He ruled for three decades. His was the most lavish of all the Mughal reigns, especially visible in the royal passion for monumental architecture inlaid with precious stones. Court life under Shah Jahan was sumptuous, in the pattern set by his father, but he was even more attached to his harem, where 5,000 concubines awaited his pleasure. Nevertheless, he was genuinely devoted to his wife, Mumtaz Mahal, who bore him 14 children. When she died in childbirth in 1631 at the age of 39, he was desolated. "Empire has no sweetness, life has no relish for me now," he said when told of her death.

To honor her memory, he built what is probably the most famous structure in the world, the Taj Mahal at Agra, which took 20,000 workmen more than 20 years to complete. Designed by two Persian architects, it beautifully blends Iranian and Indian styles and Indian craftsmanship. The emphasis on water and gardens was characteristically Mughal, while the use of Rajput canopies around the base of the dome was traditionally Indian. Before it was finished, Shah Jahan had begun a new capital city at Delhi, site of so many capitals before, modeled on Akbar's Red Fort at Agra and built of the same red sandstone, with similarly massive walls and battlements but on an even larger scale. Inside were beautiful gardens, palaces, audience halls, harems, barracks, stables, and storehouses, and outside he built India's largest mosque, the Jama Masjid. Both still stand, little altered, and still dominate Delhi, the Mughal name of which was Shah Jahanabad ("Shah Jahan's city").

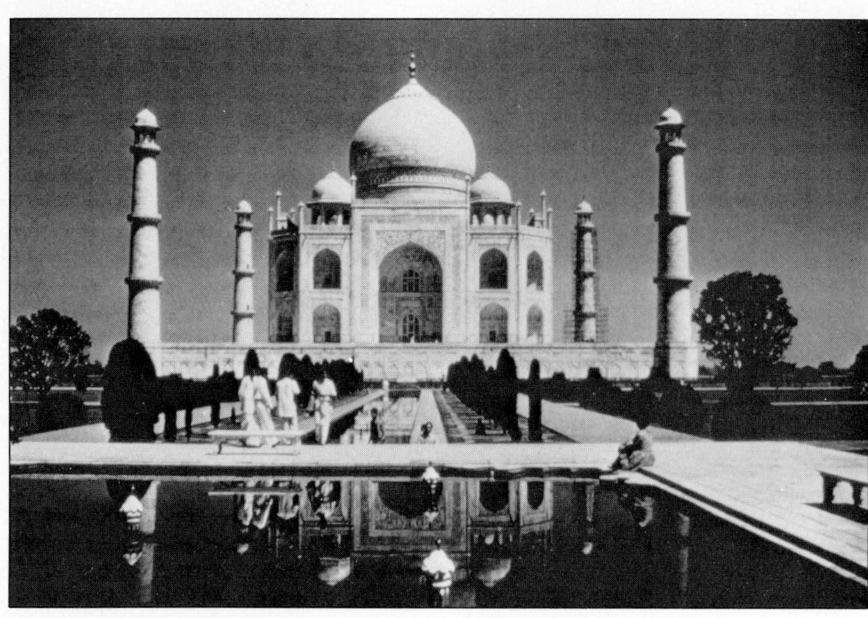

No photograph can do full justice to the Taj Mahal, whose great bulk seems to float weightlessly above the pool that holds its reflection. Mughal cupolas and domes are matched by minarets (the four slender towers on each side) in the Islamic tradition, while the central archway beneath the dome is reminiscent of the Persian (Iranian) models on which it was based. Inscriptions from the Koran and beautiful inlaid floral patterns cover much of the outer and inner walls. The entire structure is of glistening white marble. [Rhoads Murphey]

Monumental building and the opulent court were not Shah Jahan's only extravagances. He ordered campaigns to reclaim Afghanistan and to restore Mughal rule in central Asia. Both failed but exhausted the treasury. From his Red Fort palace, on his Peacock Throne, encrusted with the largest jewels ever found, the emperor doubled Akbar's revenue demands, and the empire groaned. Meanwhile, his many sons were already conspiring against one another, impatient to succeed the ailing ruler. His favorite son, Dara, a philosopher and mystic like his great-grandfather Akbar, might have made a fine ruler, but a younger son, Aurangzeb, was insatiably ambitious.

From 1657 open warfare prevailed among rival brothers. Aurangzeb imprisoned his father, Shah Jahan, in the dungeon of Agra's Red Fort while he completed his gruesome work and then sent the old emperor the head of his favorite son, Dara. The aged Shah Jahan could just see through the barred window of his cell a glimpse of his beloved Taj Mahal. Hearing that this gave the old man a little comfort, Aurangzeb is said to have had his father's eyes put out.

The Reign of Aurangzeb: Repression and Revolt

The cold-blooded Aurangzeb ascended the throne in 1658. By poison, intrigue, or assassination he had eliminated a dozen of his own brothers and half brothers, plus uncounted others. He gave as the reason for this slaughter his own devotion to orthodox Islam against the laxer or more tolerant views of his many rivals. But Aurangzeb was also a brilliant and single-minded ruler and administrator and a cunning statesman. Sunni Muslims revered him as much as Hindus hated him. He is said to have had no friends, only servile admirers and bitter enemies.

Civil war on top of Shah Jahan's extravagances had emptied the treasury, but Aurangzeb increased his revenue demands and at the same time extended his own puritanical tastes to the running of court and empire. He stopped all court luxuries, especially the wine, song, and dance forbidden by the Koran, and ended all monumental construction. He also appointed censors of public morals to enforce rigid Islamic law, ordered everyone to pray at the orthodox Islamic intervals every day, tried to abolish gambling and drinking, and began a lifelong campaign to demolish all surviving Hindu monuments and temples. Unfortunately, he largely succeeded in the north, and the only surviving samples of pre-Mughal architecture are in the south, where Aurangzeb never prevailed. Hindus were forbidden to carry arms, forced conversion was resumed for many, and Hindu festivals and public expression were outlawed. Aurangzeb knew the Koran by heart and copied it out twice in his own hand. But his piety and his zealous praying, which mark him as an Islamic zealot, sparked a keen sense of religious intolerance. To increase the revenue needed to maintain his army and to pay for new conquests in the name of Allah, he reimposed the hated *jizya* on Hindus, laid a new tax on Hindu pilgrims, and doubled the taxes on Hindu merchants. When crowds gathered outside the Red Fort in Delhi to protest, he ordered the imperial elephants to crush them to death.

The widespread revolts that arose within a few years merely increased Aurangzeb's pressure for more revenue to put them down. For many years he did so successfully, thanks to his superior generalship and to the fear-induced loyalty of most of his court and army. When revolt failed or the risks of defying Aurangzeb or his tax collectors seemed too great, growing numbers of peasants abandoned their homes and fields and became bandits or joined dissident groups or armies elsewhere, including explicitly Hindu forces such as the Sikhs of Punjab (particularly brutalized by Aurangzeb), the formerly loyal Rajputs, and the Marathas.

Relentless in suppressing rebellion, Aurangzeb was also determined to extend his empire into the south. The last half of his wearily long reign was consumed in bloody but ultimately unsuccessful campaigns into the Deccan, while at the same time his forces tried to stem the rising tide of Sikh, Rajput, Afghan, Bengali, and Maratha revolt. His brief conquests in the south, won at terrible cost in treasure and lives, quickly evaporated. From their mountain fortresses in the northwestern Deccan, the Hindu Marathas became increasingly powerful and took the field to harry Mughal forces retreating from the south near the end of Aurangzeb's reign. His campaigns exhausted the country and left it split among contending powers, who shared an implacable hatred of Mughal rule but were divided by their own differences and rivalries.

Sects and Rebels: Rajputs, Sikhs, and Marathas

Three groups stood out against Aurangzeb's intolerance and military conquests and as his most effective opponents: the Rajputs, the Sikhs, and the Marathas. Unfortunately for them, they never made a common cause, as they also failed to do later against the British.

Aurangzeb broke the alliance that Akbar had prudently made with the Rajputs and eliminated their role in the Mughal army. Throughout most of his reign they were in revolt, maintaining their reputation as courageous fighters, and were never effectively suppressed. The proximity of their base and its fortresses in Rajasthan to the center of Mughal power in the Delhi-Agra region made them highly vulnerable, and they suffered repeated "annihilation" campaigns, but Rajput resistance survived in the margins of Rajasthan. Each campaign against them bred new bitterness and new determination to fight. Aurangzeb's religious zeal and conquering ambition called forth resistance in the name of India and of Hinduism against a Mughal order now seen afresh as alien and hateful. It was a sad sequel to Akbar's vision of a multiracial, multicultural, and multireligious India. The Rajputs throughout their history had been quick to spring proudly to the defense of Hindu India, and now they took the field again, convinced of the rightness of their cause.

The Sikhs of Punjab emerged as a religious group with its own separate identity as an outgrowth of the bhakti movement late in the fifteenth century (see Chapter 10). As elsewhere in India where bhakti ideals spread, a series of nonsectarian saint-reformers preached a puritanical form of life and freedom from priestly domination, discarding the more dogmatic and hierarchical aspects of Hinduism, such as caste, but retaining its devotion to nonviolence. The founder of Sikhism, Guru Nanak (1469–1538), tried at first to work out a compromise between Hinduism and Islam and then to purify Hinduism. He preached the bhakti message of a universal God and his love, to whom everyone has access without the need for priests or rituals. Perhaps his best-known saying is "Man will be saved by his works alone; God will not ask a man his tribe or sect, but what he has done. There is no Hindu and no Muslim. All are children of God."[6] Nanak's rejection of priests as essential intermediaries was akin to the view of his European contemporary, Martin Luther, although Nanak was not a formal theologian and, unlike Luther, stressed good works rather than faith.

His disciple and successor Guru Angad (active 1530–1552) began the compilation of the Sikh holy book, the Granth Sahib, recording all he had learned from Guru Nanak and adding devotional reflections. Successive Sikh gurus continued their opposition to caste and to all forms of discrimination and met with Akbar, who listened to them with interest and granted them a site for their chief temple in Amritsar, near Lahore. The origins of Sikhism were thus wholly peaceful, but in the sixteenth century some Sikhs were drawn into support for one of Jahangir's rebellious sons, hoping that he would be more tolerant of non-Muslims. When the rebellion failed and Jahangir had the Sikh leader executed in 1606, the Sikhs began to develop a defensive military mentality, to maintain their own identity and their territorial base in Punjab.

By 1650 the Sikhs' numbers had greatly increased, and they began to see themselves as a separate state. Sikh gurus urged their followers to eat meat, in distinction from high-caste Hindus but also to give them strength. Martial skills, bravery, and physical strength began to be cultivated as Sikh hallmarks. Shah Jahan left them largely alone, preoccupied as he was with his ambitious building projects and with the luxurious pleasures of his harem and court. But when the Sikhs supported his favored son Dara's bid for the throne, they became Aurangzeb's enemies. His persecutions of them and his efforts to eliminate them as both a power and a community predictably strengthened their commitment and led to their further militarization. Aurangzeb cruelly tortured to death the ninth Sikh guru, Teg Bahadur, in 1675 when he refused to embrace Islam and ignored the guru's warning against the still tiny but foreboding European threat to India. Teg Bahadur's son and successor, Guru Govind Singh (1675–1708), first organized the Sikhs into a real political power and a great military fraternity. He urged them all to adopt the surname Singh ("lion") as he had done, to swear never to cut their hair (which came to be worn knotted up in a turban) or their beards, and to avoid tobacco and alcohol. The practices of *purdah* (the veiling and seclusion of women) and *sati* (the burning of widows) were rejected. Sikh women were freer and were seen more nearly as coequals than in most other Indian societies. Govind Singh's four sons were captured by Aurangzeb and tortured to death or executed, steadfastly refusing to convert to Islam.

When Govind Singh himself died in 1708, the line of ten guru leaders ended, and the Sikhs were thereafter ruled by political rather than religious leaders. Many Punjabis and others from neighboring areas had adopted Sikhism, and many more now joined its numbers. A former Rajput, Banda Bairagi, ravaged the Mughal forces as leader of the Sikhs until he was betrayed, captured, and executed in 1716. Nadir Shah's invasion from Iran in 1739 finally eliminated the remnants of Mughal power and gave the Sikhs new opportunity to extend their domination of Punjab. During the remainder of the eighteenth century the Sikh kingdom became still stronger and stood finally as the last major obstacle to British rule, overcome only in 1849 after two campaigns against it.

The Marathas were probably the most formidable and effective enemies of the Mughals, and for some two centuries they played a major role in India. For a time it seemed as if they would become the dominant power in the subcontinent and would found a new Indian empire. Their home base was well protected by a mountain range behind Bombay, the Western Ghats; by the hilly Deccan Plateau east of the Ghats; and by the central Indian mountain ranges of the Vindhyas and their spurs to the north and east, which were ideally suited to guerrilla warfare. The Marathas gloried in their hardiness, which they attributed to the relative barrenness of their mountain-girt homeland, rather like the Scots or the Gurkhas of Nepal, and like them had a proud military tradition.

The greatest Maratha leader was Shivaji (1627–1680), who rose to prominence as Hindus were beginning to take up arms against Aurangzeb. Shivaji was brought up as a zealous Hindu but combined Hinduism with his martial background and his determination to free India from the Mughals. From the beginning of Aurangzeb's reign, Shivaji and his commando cavalry raided Mughal territory. The Mughal general sent against him captured Poona, the Maratha capital, in 1663, but was surprised there by Shivaji in a daring night attack and routed. A few months later in 1664 Shivaji attacked and looted Surat, then the richest port in India, and carried off immense booty. A second major Mughal campaign against him ended in negotiations after some of Shivaji's feuding adversaries deserted to the Mughal cause. Shivaji visited Agra, expecting to be offered a high post, but when he complained that Aurangzeb's offer was not good enough, he was imprisoned. He smuggled himself out, concealed in a basket, and rebuilt his forces and resources for what he now saw as an inevitable conflict.

When Aurangzeb ordered all Hindu temples and schools demolished and all Hindu public teaching and practice suppressed, Shivaji renewed his raids in 1670 and over the next ten years more than doubled the territory under his control, rivaling the Mughal territory itself as a state to be reckoned with. This achievement inspired the Marathas with renewed pride, and Shivaji remains their greatest hero. Unlike his successors, he was not only a brilliant military strategist and tactician but also an effective organizer and political administrator. He ruled with a council of ministers, made Marathi and Sanskrit the court languages, and banned the use of Urdu and Persian. For nearly 20 years he defied a series of Mughal armies, a considerable accomplishment in itself. Aurangzeb called him "the mountain rat." "My armies have been employed against him for nineteen years," he said, "and nevertheless his state has always been increasing."

But Shivaji did not live to see the death of Aurangzeb and the collapse of Mughal power, and the son who succeeded him neglected the army and the state and spent his time enjoying the luxuries of court life. He was defeated and captured by the Mughals, who executed him and many other Maratha chiefs in 1689. Shivaji's grandson, the next Maratha ruler, defected to the Mughals and was made one of their high officials, but other Marathas renewed the struggle. A younger descendant of Shivaji reorganized the army and resumed his grandfather's devastating raids. In 1699, after his own generals had failed to put them down, Aurangzeb himself marched against the Marathas, but without success. By 1702 the Mughals were on the defensive, and the Marathas were now led by Tara Bai, the remarkable wife of the ruler, who had died in 1700, although she ruled in name through her son, Shivaji III. She rode a horse with fearless skill and led Maratha cavalry charges in battle.

After Aurangzeb's death, however, and the collapse of his crusade, the Marathas were torn by internal civil war, a continuation of the feuding that was also part of their tradition. Successive leaders after 1712 resumed campaigns to the north, south, and east, extending their territory close to Delhi, conquering most of the peninsular south, and raiding even into Bengal.

The Maratha Confederacy, as it was called, had become by far the greatest power in India, but it lacked the firm hand and the administrative skills of Shivaji. The Maratha army was used as much to raid and plunder as to fight major engagements, and raids or conquests were seldom followed up by responsible government of the areas acquired. In 1761 the army marched north to meet an Afghan invasion on the historic field of Panipat, northwest of Delhi, and was totally defeated. The short-lived Maratha "empire" was dissolved, and its power was never recovered. The real beneficiaries were the English, since the Marathas had been the only major defenders of India against foreign invaders and the only group with the potential to reunite the country. Internal feuding among themselves, lack of commitment to responsible administration, and the exhausting strain of chronic fighting against the Mughals left them unequal to that enormous task. India itself was exhausted by unending warfare, and the Mughals, Marathas, Sikhs, and Rajputs merely bloodied and drained each other and the country as a whole rather than taking any united stand.

The Mughals and India

By the beginning of the eighteenth century the order and prosperity that had flourished under Akbar and his immediate successors had been fatally weakened. Akbar's carefully designed revenue system, managed by Hindus, had been eroded by the excessive granting of tax-collecting rights for large areas, known as jagirs, to people whom the throne wanted or needed to pay off. Especially under Aurangzeb, Mughal attention was concentrated on military conquest, which meant mounting demands for revenue but also decreasing attention to normal administration or its supervision. Hindu revenue officials were eliminated; holders of jagirs (jagirdars) became more and more independent and more and more rapacious in extracting everything they could from an oppressed peasantry and merchant class, retaining for themselves any balance beyond the official government tax rates. The same was true for the group known as the *zamindars*, who were also granted tax-collection rights for smaller local areas and used them to enrich themselves, often acquiring the ownership of land from peasants who were unable to pay the tax. This was a disastrous formula for the well-being of most of the agricultural sector, the predominant basis of the economy and the major tax base. The Mughals had built an imperial road system, but it was used mainly for the movement of troops and supplies. Even so, it was not well maintained and became impassable in many sections, especially during the torrential rains of the annual monsoon.

In general, Mughal economic policy concentrated heavily on obtaining revenue and far too little on maintaining or enhancing the system's ability to generate production. In contrast to China, the state did almost nothing to increase irrigation, so badly needed in most of India, or to promote other agricultural improvements. Neglect of agriculture meant neglect of most of the country and its people.

Even before Aurangzeb, what was left over after paying the staggering costs of military campaigns was used primarily for gorgeous display at the capital and the court and for monumental building. The Mughals were at war on a major scale for much more than half of the years from Babur's victory at Panipat in 1526 to Aurangzeb's death in 1707, and fighting continued into the 1750s. Even a prosperous and well-run system would have been fatally weakened by such an outpouring of treasure to no constructive result and by devastation of the countryside on such a scale over two centuries.

Administration as well was increasingly neglected. Court life at Delhi and Agra was sumptuous and brilliant. Officials knew that their money and property would revert to the emperor when they died, and consequently they spent it freely in lavish consumption, with stables full of Arabian horses and harems filled with dancing girls. Massive entertainments and banquets occupied much of their time, complete with music, dance, and poetry readings. Courtiers and the upper classes dressed in magnificent silk outfits, or fine Kashmir wool in the brief northern winter, while the peasants wore coarse sackcloth woven from jute or locally made cottons, if they could afford them. Indian cotton cloth won extensive markets in the rest of Asia and much of Africa as well as in Europe; weavers benefited, but the state's tax collectors benefited still more.

For all the brilliant splendor of court life, however, science and technology were largely neglected after Akbar. What learning there was centered on the Koran and on the cultivation of the arts. There were no changes or improvements in the arts of production, and by the seventeenth century India had fallen behind Europe in science and technology and probably in the productivity of both its agriculture and manufacturing, while at the same time bleeding the economy by virtually continuous warfare. While Shah Jahan was building the Taj Mahal, at staggering expense, India suffered probably the worst famine in its history, from 1630 to 1632, and another nearly as bad took place in 1702 and 1703 in which over 2 million people died while Aurangzeb was campaigning in the Deccan with a huge army and supply corps.

Aurangzeb had personally moved south in 1683, and for the rest of his life he was primarily concerned with conducting military campaigns from a new capital he established in the Deccan. Annual losses were estimated at 100,000 men and over 300,000 transport animals, mainly requisitioned from the peasantry. Continued Maratha raids and fierce southern resistance sapped his forces. After 1705 he seems to have spent most of his time reading and copying the Koran, preparing himself for death. Until then, he had refused to recognize the destructiveness of his policies. At least one anonymous letter reached him after he had restored the poll tax on Hindus, which read in part:

> **Your subjects are trampled underfoot; every province of your empire is impoverished; depopulation spreads and problems accumulate. . . . If your majesty places any faith in those books called divine, you will be instructed there that God is the God of all mankind, not the God of Muslims alone.**[7]

In 1705 he confessed to his son: "I came alone and I go as a stranger. I do not know who I am, or what I have been doing. I have sinned terribly and I do not know what punishment awaits me."[8] The Mughals had come full circle from the inspiring vision of Akbar to the nightmare of Aurangzeb.

A Westerner Visits Delhi

François Bernier, a French traveler in India from 1656 to 1668, included the following description of Delhi in his Travels in the Mogul Empire.

It is about forty years ago that Shah Jahan, father of the present Great Mogul Aurangzeb, conceived the design of immortalizing his name by the erection of a city near the site of the ancient Delhi. . . . Owing to their being so near at hand, the ruins of old Delhi served to build the new city. Delhi is situated on the Jumna and built on one bank only in such a manner that it terminates in this place very much in the form of a crescent, having but one bridge of boats to cross to the country. Excepting the side where it is defended by the river, the city is encompassed by walls of brick. . . . The suburbs are interspersed with extensive gardens and open spaces. . . . The citadel [Shah Jahan's Red Fort] is defended by a deep ditch faced with hewn stone, filled with water and stocked with fish. . . . Adjoining the ditch is a large garden, filled at all times with flowers and green shrubs, which contrasted with the stupendous red walls produce a beautiful effect. Next to the garden is the great royal square, faced on one side by the gates of the fortress, and on the opposite side of which terminate the two most considerable streets of the city. The tents of such Rajahs as are in the king's pay, and whose weekly turn it is to mount guard, are pitched in this square. . . . In this place also, at break of day, they exercise the royal horses, which are kept in a spacious stable not far distant. . . . Here too is held a bazaar or market for an endless variety of things, which, like the Pont-neuf at Paris, is the rendezvous for all sorts of mountebanks [swindlers] and jugglers. Hither likewise the astrologers resort. These wise doctors remain seated in the sun, on a dusty piece of carpet, handling some old mathematical instruments and having open before them a large book. In this way they attract the attention of the passers-by and impose upon the people, by whom they are considered as so many infallible oracles. . . . Silly women, wrapping themselves in a white cloth from head to foot, flock to the astrologers, whisper to them all the transactions of their lives, and disclose every secret. . . . The rich merchants have their dwellings elsewhere, to which they retire after the hours of business.

Source: F. Bernier, *Travels in the Mogul Empire*, trans. A. Constable (London: Constable & Co., 1891), pp. 241–245 passim.

The effective power of the Mughals ended with Aurangzeb's death in 1707. India slowly dissolved into civil war, banditry, intergroup rivalry, and mounting chaos, a context in which the English traders, present on the fringes for well over a century, began their own path to ultimate power.

Aurangzeb, whose reign had spanned nearly 50 years, was a contemporary of the Manchu Emperor K'ang Hsi in China (Chapter 28) and of Louis XIV of France, the Glorious Revolution in England, Frederick I of Prussia, and Peter the Great of Russia. During these years Europe began its modern development of strong centralized states, continued its commercial and colonial expansion overseas, and rode a wave of unprecedented economic growth, which was reflected in the beginnings of major population increases. Manchu China in Aurangzeb's time also experienced a period of prosperity and vigorous economic growth, with major increases in trade and at least a doubling of agricultural output and population. The modern agricultural revolution was beginning at the same time in Europe, and the foundations were being laid for the later Industrial Revolution. European science and technology leaped ahead of the rest of the world with pioneering discoveries of scientists such as Isaac Newton and Robert Boyle. In these years Europe developed a lead that was to widen greatly in subsequent centuries.

If Akbar's open-minded curiosity and zeal for learning and experimentation had prevailed into Aurangzeb's time, India might have taken part in or at least benefited from these important advances. The early European visitors to India had, like Marco Polo, been drawn to and impressed by its wealth and sophistication. In Akbar's time there seems little question that India was not only richer than Europe but at least on a par with it and with China technologically, economically, and politically. Jahangir and Shah Jahan, however, were preoccupied with the pleasures of the court, monumental building, and intrigue. Aurangzeb was a single-minded zealot who cared nothing for the material welfare of his people and bled the empire to finance his wars. Instead of scholars, as at Akbar's court, Aurangzeb surrounded himself with sycophants, servile yes-men who dared not disagree or suggest alternatives and who flattered the emperor into thinking that he and his empire led the world. He did not deign to correspond with other monarchs, as Akbar had done, or to take an interest in anything but his endless military campaigns, undertaken in the name of Islam, to impose his tyrannical rule over all of India, a goal he never achieved. By the time of his death, India was economically and politically a shambles, and technological development was non-existent. This was to prove a fatal combination of weaknesses, resulting in a situation of virtual anarchy. The now far more effective and technologically advanced Europeans were able to establish footholds from which their power in India could grow.

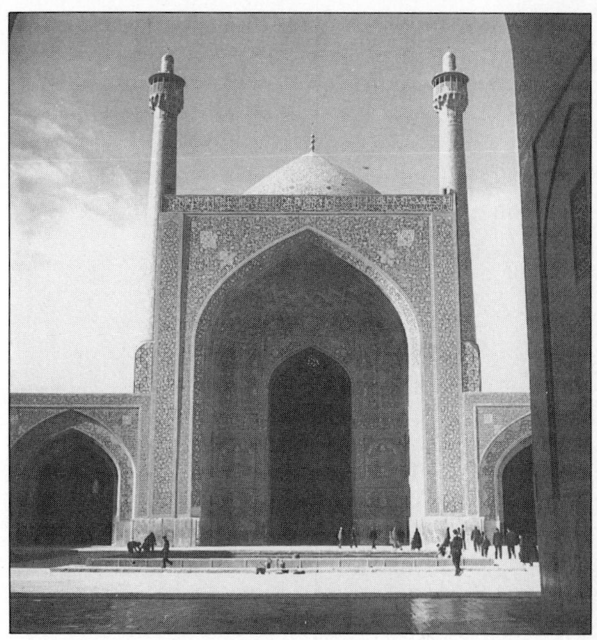

Part of the royal mosque at Isfahan, the capital of Safavid Iran. The influence of Mughal style is evident, but in Iran a great archway tended to dominate most monumental buildings, as here. [Bildarchiv Foto Marburg]

The Safavids in Iran

By about the year A.D. 1000 the Abbasid Caliphate began to break up into separate and rival states. At the eastern end of their former domains, a group of central Asian Turks, the Seljuks, took over Iran, accepted Islam, and even captured Baghdad in 1065. The Seljuk rulers of Iran embraced and furthered Persian culture, as did their separate Turkish successors, but all this was swept away by the Mongol onslaught, which also destroyed virtually every city in central Asia in the mid-thirteenth century. A hundred years later, Tamerlane laid waste most of the same area. Through all these catastrophes, Persia's culture and sense of identity survived, much as in China under Mongol rule. Finally, out of the chaos left in the wake of Tamerlane, a new group rose to control Iran and to preside over a new and vigorous period of growth and cultural revival—the Safavids (1501–1736), who claimed descent from a Sufi saint but were in fact founded by yet another central Asian Turkish tribe.

The first Safavid ruler, Ismail, assumed the ancient title of Shah of Iran and briefly incorporated parts of what is now Iraq and southern Russia into his empire. The Safavids were Shi'ite (Shia) Muslims; they forcibly converted the previously Sunni Iranians and came into chronic conflict with the orthodox Sunni Ottomans and with the Mughals in India and Afghanistan.

Shah Ismail's son, Tahmasp I, reigned for 52 years (1524–1576); defended the plateau of Iran, protected by its mountain borders, against continued Ottoman attacks; and presided over a great flowering of Iranian art, especially in miniature painting. In the familiar central Asian pattern, he was poisoned by his overeager son, who also killed off all his other relatives and rivals, only to die himself a year later, in 1577. After a period of civil war, there emerged the most outstanding of the Safavids, Shah Abbas the Great (1587–1629), who was to restore much of Iran's ancient glory. Its art, literature, and philosophy had long played the leading role in the Middle East, as China's had done in East Asia. Shah Abbas had the strength and vision needed to reunite the country and then to ensure economic prosperity and cultural vigor. He was an efficient administrator and a patron of the arts who made Persian culture once more a model for surrounding peoples. The beautiful capital he built at Isfahan in southwestern Iran remains perhaps the finest example of the medieval Persian style. In a series of campaigns between 1595 and 1612 he drove the Ottomans and their allies out of the parts of western and northern Iran they had occupied during earlier periods of disorder and kept them out for the rest of his reign.

Shah Abbas rebuilt much of the imperial structure originally laid down by Cyrus and Darius in the sixth century B.C., including the famous network of roads and bridges that crisscrossed the plateau, penetrated its mountain borders, and connected its cities with ports on the Persian Gulf and the Caspian Sea. Agriculture, trade, and cities grew rapidly under the new conditions. In 1617 Shah Abbas began commercial relations with the newly formed English East India Company, and with its help in 1622

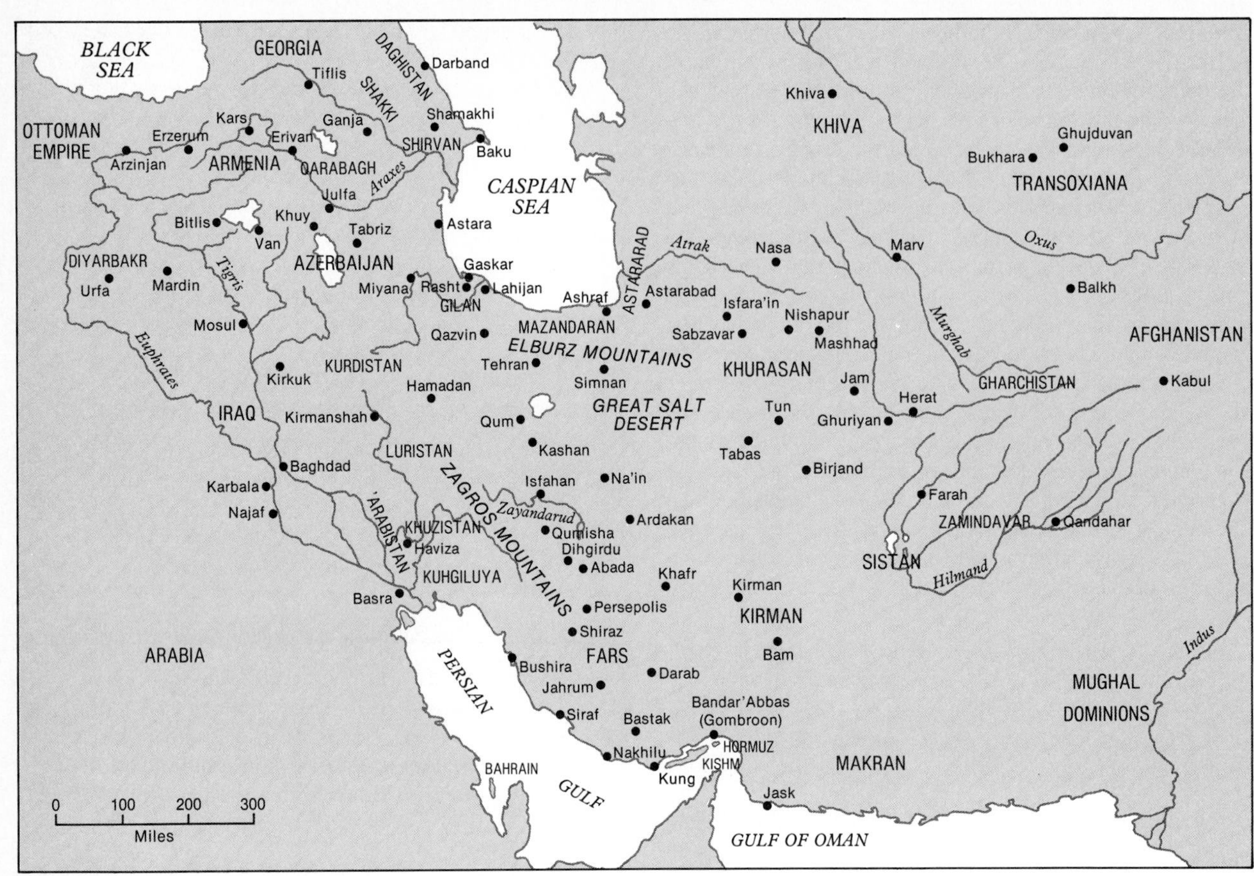

***19.3** Iran Under the Safavids*

drove the Portuguese from the port of Hormuz on the gulf. Silks, ceramics, tapestries, carpets, and other exports from Iran could now be sent directly to England and Europe by sea, avoiding the overland route through hostile Ottoman territory and the tolls exacted along it.

Iran under Abbas became the cultural center of the Islamic world. Persian architecture, painting, literature, and the minor arts flourished and exercised a strong influence on Mughal India and on the Ottoman Empire. Rulers in both countries wrote poetry in the Persian style, had their portraits and court scenes painted in the Persian mode, and built palaces, domes, fountains, pools, gardens, and mosques on Persian models. Much of the credit for Iran's revival must go to Shah Abbas. Persian culture was renowned long before his time, but he inherited a weak, poor, war-torn country and gave it new strength, prosperity, and pride.

By the late seventeenth century the Safavids, Mughals, and Ottomans were experiencing serious problems. The Safavid dynasty would collapse in 1736, yet despite Iran's weakened condition, the Ottomans were unable to subjugate their neighbor. In India the last Mughal emperor was not removed by the British until 1858, but for its final 150 years the dynasty increasingly ruled in name only over a progressively shrinking part of northern India. After the death of the emperor Akbar in 1605, successive rulers were more self-indulgent and more concerned with luxury and power than with responsible administration. With the reign of Aurangzeb, Islamic orthodoxy was reasserted, and the empire's wealth was squandered in bloody but fruitless campaigns to control the south and to subdue the rebellious Rajputs, Sikhs, and Marathas. At Aurangzeb's death India was exhausted, impoverished, and torn by civil war. So weak did India become that in 1739 an Iranian army not only defeated the Mughal emperor but stole the Peacock Throne (later captured by the Ottomans and taken to Istanbul). Thus the simultaneous flowering of western and south-

central Asia in the sixteenth century had turned to decline, and in India's case genuine disaster, by the eighteenth.

The French traveler François Bernier, who visited India in Aurangzeb's time, reported in his Travels *that the emperor, after belatedly realizing the potential strength of the Europeans, complained to him that his tutor had told him, "The whole of Feringustan [Europe] was no more than some inconsiderable island, that its kings resembled petty rajahs, and that the potentates of Hindustan eclipsed the glory of all other kings."*[9] *Bernier's contemporary, the Italian traveler in India, Niccolò Manucci, recorded his impression that Indians believed Europeans "have no polite manners, that they are ignorant, wanting in ordered life, and very dirty."*[10] *Crude and dirty or not, the Europeans were fast becoming the most effective groups in India, given the ruin of the Mughals and the disorganization of the Marathas and other possible Indian orders. The way was open for the rise of a British-dominated India.*

Notes

1. B. Lewis, *Istanbul and the Civilization of the Ottoman Empire* (Norman: University of Oklahoma Press, 1963), p. 110.
2. N. Itzkowitz, *Ottoman Empire and Islamic Tradition* (New York: Knopf, 1972), p. 36.
3. N. Menemencioglu, ed., *The Penguin Book of Turkish Verse* (New York: Penguin Books, 1978), p. 80.
4. Ibid., p. 150.
5. S. Shaw, *History of the Ottoman Empire and Modern Turkey*, Vol. 1: *Empire of the Gazis: The Rise and Decline of the Ottoman Empire, 1280–1808* (Cambridge: Cambridge University Press, 1976), p. 289.
6. D. P. Singhal, *A History of the Indian People* (London: Methuen, 1983), p. 206.
7. J. Sarkar, *History of Aurangzeb*, vol. 3 (Bombay: Orient Longman, 1972), p. 34.
8. W. Hansen, *The Peacock Throne* (New York: Holt, Rinehart and Winston, 1972), p. 485.
9. R. Murphey, *The Outsiders: The Western Experience in India and China* (Ann Arbor: University of Michigan Press, 1977), p. 54.
10. Ibid.

Suggestions for Further Reading

The Ottomans

Babinger, F. *Mehmed the Conqueror and His Time*, trans. R. Manheim. Princeton, N.J.: Princeton University Press, 1978.

Cook, M. A., ed. *A History of the Ottoman Empire to 1730*. Cambridge: Cambridge University Press, 1976.

Frazee, C. A. *Catholics and Sultans: The Church and the Ottoman Empire, 1453–1923*. London: Oxford University Press, 1983.

Inalcik, H. *The Ottoman Empire: The Classical Age, 1300–1600*. London: Weidenfeld & Nicolson, 1973.

Islamoglu-Inan, H., ed. *The Ottoman Empire and the World Economy*. Cambridge: Cambridge University Press, 1987.

Itzkowitz, N. *Ottoman Empire and Islamic Tradition*. New York: Knopf, 1972.

Lewis, B. *Istanbul and the Civilization of the Ottoman Empire*. Norman: University of Oklahoma Press, 1963.

——. *The Muslim Discovery of Europe*. New York: Norton, 1982.

Lewis, R. *Everyday Life in Ottoman Turkey*. London: Batsford, 1971.

Shaw, S. *History of the Ottoman Empire and Modern Turkey*, Vol. 1: *Empire of the Gazis: The Rise and Decline of the Ottoman Empire, 1280–1808*. Cambridge: Cambridge University Press, 1976.

Vyronis, S., Jr. *The Decline of Medieval Hellenism in Asia Minor and the Process of Islamization from the Eleventh Through the Fifteenth Century*. Berkeley: University of California Press, 1986.

Waddy, C. *Women in Muslim History*. London: Longman, 1980.

Mughal India

Bernier, F. *Travels in the Mughal Empire*, trans. A. Constable. London: Pickering, 1934.

Edwards, S., and Garrett, H. L. *Mughal Rule in India*. Delhi: Chand, 1962.

Gascoigne, B. *The Great Moghuls*. New York: Harper & Row, 1971.

Habib, I. *The Agrarian System of Mughal India, 1556–1707*. New York: Asia Publishing House, 1963.

——, et al. *The Cambridge Economic History of India*, Vol. 1: *1200–1750*. Cambridge: Cambridge University Press, 1982.

Majumdar, R. C., ed. *An Advanced History of India*. Delhi: Macmillan, 1973.

Prawdin, M. *Builders of the Mughal Empire*. New York: Allen & Unwin, 1963.

Sarkar, J. *Shivaji*. Calcutta: M. C. Sarkar & Sons, 1952.

——. *A Short History of Aurangzeb*. Calcutta: M. C. Sarkar & Sons, 1962.

Shelat, J. M. *Akbar*. Bombay: Bharatiya Bidya Bhavan, 1964.

Singhal, D. P. *A History of the Indian People*. London: Methuen, 1983.

Srivasta, A. L. *The Mughal Empire*. Agra: Agarwala, 1966.

Wolpert, S. *A New History of India*. New York: Oxford University Press, 1989.

Safavid Iran

Cambridge History of Iran. Cambridge: Cambridge University Press, 1983.

Savory, R. M. *Iran Under the Safavids*. Cambridge: Cambridge University Press, 1980.

Sykes, P. *A History of Persia*. London: Macmillan, 1930.

CHAPTER · 20

Imperial Revival in China

With the expulsion of the Mongols in the mid-fourteenth century, the Chinese imperial tradition was reasserted by the founding of the Ming dynasty in 1368. Pride in regained power and wealth led to the building of magnificent new capitals, first at Nanking (Nanjing) and then at Peking (Beijing), as well as to the resumption of the tributary system whereby lesser Asian states sent regular missions to China, acknowledging its superiority and prostrating themselves before the Son of Heaven. Ming armies reconquered the empire of the T'ang and the Sung, and early in the dynasty a series of seven naval expeditions toured Southeast Asia, India, the Persian Gulf, and as far as the east coast of Africa, acquiring new tributaries, trading in Chinese products, and bringing back curiosities from afar.

The growing commercialization of the economy, aided from the sixteenth century by imports of silver from the

Magnificent paintings of nature continued under the Ming dynasty in the now long established Chinese tradition. This lovely spray of white magnolia is part of a larger painting by the master Wen Cheng-ming (1470–1559). [The Metropolitan Museum of Art, bequest of John M. Crawford, Jr.]

Spanish New World, stimulated urban growth and a rich merchant culture. Literature, philosophy, and the arts flourished, and popular culture also expanded into vernacular writing, opera, plays, and woodblock printing. For at least its first two centuries Ming administration was effective and the country was prosperous. But the dynasty became increasingly conservative and traditional. It was plagued by court intrigues, and a series of weak emperors sapped its vigor. Popular unrest mounted as government became less and less able to provide an equitable order or to move with the times. Rebels took Peking and then were replaced by a new set of alien conquerors, the Manchus from Manchuria, who inaugurated the Ch'ing dynasty in 1644. Manchu rule nevertheless rested consciously and purposefully on the Ming heritage, and most of the trends that began under the Ming continued with little break once order was restored.

The Ming Dynasty

By the early 1300s Mongol control of China was weakening under the ineffective successors of Kubilai Khan. Chronic feuding within the imperial clan and pressures from rival clans enfeebled Mongol power, and by 1330 civil war had erupted. Beginning in 1333 successive drought-induced famines racked northern China, worsened by unchecked flooding in the Yellow River where the dikes had been neglected. Most Chinese interpreted these natural disasters as portents of divine displeasure and the loss of the Mandate of Heaven by the Yuan dynasty, a response typical of the declining years of all previous dynasties but further fed in this case by bitter Chinese hatred of the alien Mongols and their oppressive rule.

Banditry and rebellion spread rapidly in nearly every province, and rebel leaders vied for Heaven's mandate in efforts to eliminate their rivals. Many rebel groups were aided by or belonged to secret societies. The most important of these was the White Lotus, a Buddhist sect originating in the Southern Sung period that consistently opposed the ruling dynasty and hence had to remain secret, with its own private rituals. The White Lotus persisted underground or in association with banditry and rebellion until the twentieth century.

One of the rebel leaders, Chu Yüan-chang (Dzu Yuanzhang, 1328–1398), rose to a commanding position in the 1350s and went on to found a new dynasty. His forces swept the Yangtze valley by the end of the decade, set up a government at Nanking in 1356, and in 1368 captured Peking, proclaiming the Ming ("brilliant") dynasty, which was to last until 1644. The Ming achievement in rebuilding the empire and restoring Chinese pride ushered in a period of unprecedented economic and cultural growth that went far beyond where the Sung had left off. The population probably rose by at least 50 percent by the end of the Ming dynasty, stimulated by major improvements in agricultural technology promoted by the state. The entire economy commercialized rapidly, accompanied by a rise in the number and size of cities and perhaps a doubling of total trade.

HUNG-WU: THE REBEL EMPEROR

Chu Yüan-chang, the victorious rebel leader who became the first Ming emperor, took the name Hung-wu ("great military power"), by which he is mainly known. Life had been hard for him up to that point. Like Liu Pang, the founder of the Han dynasty, he had been born a peasant. Orphaned early, he entered a Buddhist monastery, where he became literate, and at age 25 joined a rebel band, where his native ability soon brought him to the top. As emperor his strong personality and high intelligence made a deep and lasting impression on the first two centuries of the Ming, whose foundations he largely built. He was an indefatigable worker, concerned with all the details of administering his new empire, but he had few close associates or friends and pursued an austere lifestyle that reflected his difficult and impoverished youth. Having risen to power over rebel rivals, he became paranoid about supposed plots against him and was given to violent rages of temper during which he often ordered harsh punishments for suspected disloyalty or trivial offenses. Irritated by continued Japanese piracy along the China coast, he also wrote to the Ashikaga shogun (see Chapter 11): "You stupid eastern barbarians! Living so far across the sea . . . you are haughty and disloyal; you permit your subjects to do evil." The Japanese replied simply: "Heaven and earth are vast. They are not monopolized by one ruler."[1] Hung-wu's reaction, perhaps fortunately, is not recorded. In his last will, he wrote of himself: "For 31 years I have labored to discharge Heaven's will, tormented by worries and fears, without relaxing for a day."[2] One wonders if he felt that the winning of the Dragon Throne had really been worth it!

Hung-wu increasingly concentrated power in his own hands and in 1380 abolished the Imperial Secretariat, which had been the main central administrative body under past dynasties, after suppressing a plot for which he blamed his chief minister. The emperor's role thus became even more autocratic, although Hung-wu necessarily continued to use what were called the Grand Secretaries to assist with the immense paperwork of the bureaucracy, which included memorials (petitions and recommendations to the throne), imperial edicts in reply, reports of various kinds, and tax records.

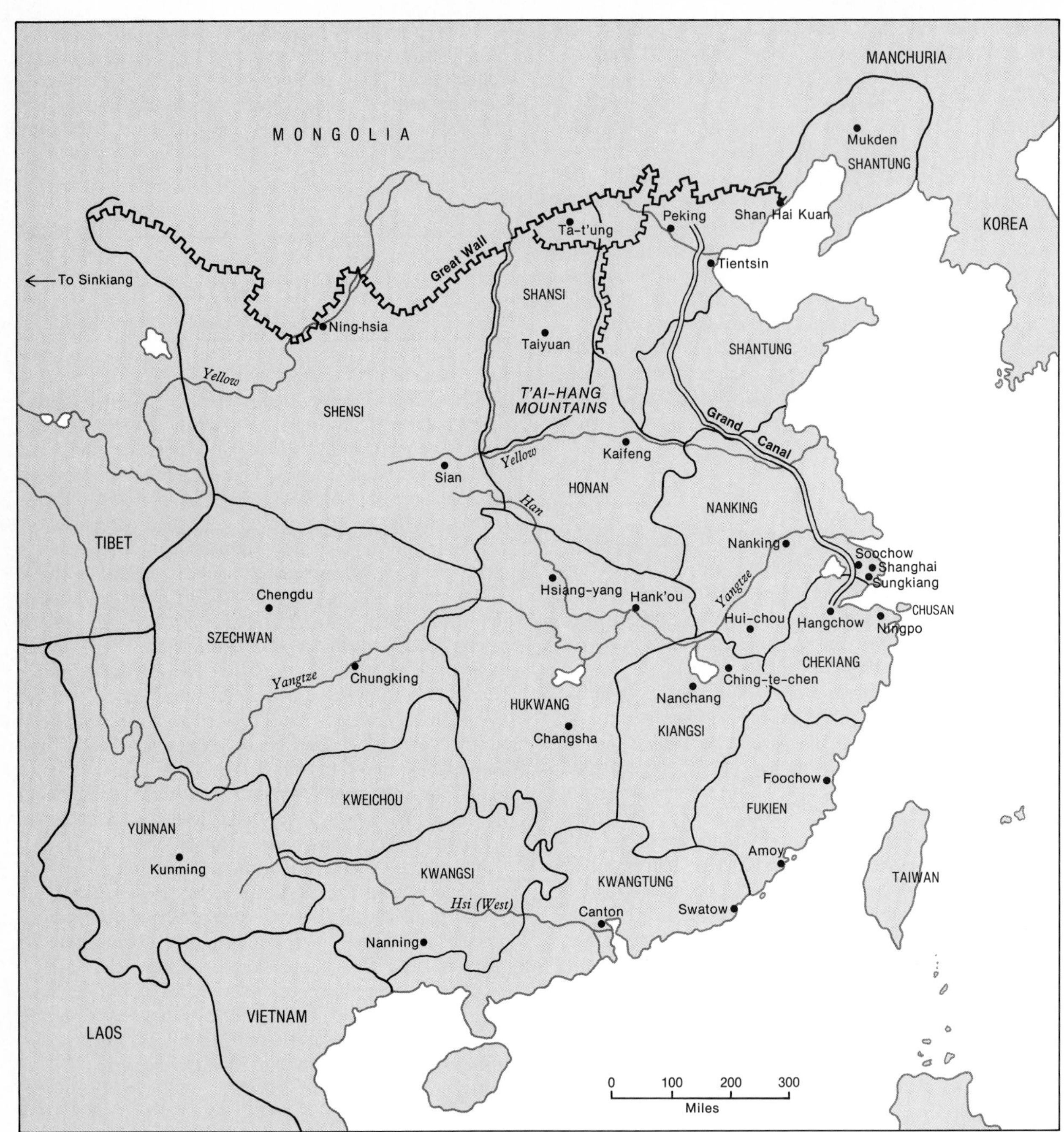

20.1 Ming China

This group was later more regularly established as the Grand Secretariat, a kind of cabinet, but in Hung-wu's time he supervised everything and made or approved all decisions. He was concerned about the power of eunuchs, remembering the trouble they had often caused in earlier dynasties, and erected a tablet in the palace that read, "Eunuchs must have nothing to do with administration."[3] He greatly reduced their numbers, forbade them to handle documents, insisted that they remain illiterate, and got rid of those who so forgot their place as to offer comments on government matters. Some eunuchs were considered necessary as guards and attendants for the imperial harem, which the emperor was thought to need so as to ensure male heirs. In time eunuch power was to grow

The emperor Hung-wu (1328–1398), also known more formally as T'ai-tsu ("Great Progenitor"), in a caricature by an unknown fifteenth-century artist, one of a series of caricatures of notable emperors. Hung-wu's rather piglike face, commented on by many of his contemporaries, was pockmarked from smallpox, which had nearly killed him as a younger man. The caricature conveys Hung-wu's forceful personality. [Collection of the National Palace Museum, Taiwan, Republic of China]

again, until in the later Ming period they became once more a scourge of good government.

One policy of Hung-wu's that shocked the Confucians was his resumption of the Mongol practice of having officials publicly beaten when they had displeased him. Confucian doctrine held that corporal punishment was only for the ignorant masses; the "superior man" was to be exempt, because with him one could reason and could expect him to mend his ways if necessary by following the virtuous example of those above him. Hung-wu was a tough ruler and demanded complete submission despite his praise for the Confucian classics. He also reorganized the army around a new system of elite guard units stationed at strategic points throughout the empire and along the frontiers. While some of his policies seemed extreme to many and his personality forbidding or fearsome, Hung-wu was a strong emperor whose work provided the Ming with a momentum of imperial power and effectiveness that lasted far beyond his time. His concentration of power in the emperor's hands worked well when the emperor was as able and dedicated as he was. When weaker and less conscientious men occupied the throne, the empire was in trouble, as was to happen disastrously in the last decades of Ming rule.

When Hung-wu died in 1398, the provinces within the Great Wall were secure and Chinese power was again dominant in eastern Sinkiang, Inner Mongolia, and southern Manchuria. Vietnam, Tibet, Korea, and Japan accepted tributary status. Hung-wu built a splendid new capital at Nanking with a city wall 60 feet high and 20 miles around. It was the longest city wall in the world, although like most Chinese city walls, it was intended more for symbolic affirmation of imperial power than for defense. Indeed, the Chinese word for "city" also means "wall," to distinguish it from a mere town. Peking was passed over as a capital because of its association with the Mongols and its location on the northern fringe of the country, far from major trade routes and agricultural centers. The Yangtze valley had long been the economic heart of the empire, and it made sense to put the capital there.

The second Ming emperor, Yung-lo (Yongluo, 1403–1424), was also an able and conscientious administrator. Continued prosperity, plus the new southern orientation of the Ming, stimulated the further expansion of trade. Commerce and city life grew rapidly. Ports on the southeast coast acquired new importance as links with the colonies of overseas Chinese in Java, the Philippines, Vietnam, and elsewhere in Southeast Asia.

Tributaries and Expeditions

To mark the resurgence of empire after the brief Mongol eclipse, the traditional tributary system was enlarged and made more formal. This helped to keep peace along the extensive borders as well as to assert Chinese overlordship. In theory, Chinese political and cultural superiority was a magnet for all lesser peoples or states. They would willingly acknowledge its greatness and, "yearning for civilization," as the official Chinese phrase went, would model themselves on it. In practice, there was just enough truth in this to warrant saying it. Although, of course, the tributary states had their own pride and culture, they freely recognized that Chinese civilization had a great deal to offer them. Near neighbors such as Korea or Vietnam, and later Burma, Laos, Tibet, and Mongolia, had reason, moreover, to fear Ming military power and hence to accept tributary status. Recognizing China's supremacy cost them little; as long as they did not try to challenge it, they were left to manage their own affairs.

The ritual obeisance to the Chinese emperor required of ambassadors was probably not seen as humiliating, as it might be by a modern diplomat, but in keeping with the way in which they had to deal with their own monarchs at home. Tributary states sent regular missions every few years to the imperial capital, where their representatives kneeled before the Son of Heaven in a series of prescribed prostrations known as the *k'e t'ou* (later Westernized as *kowtow*, literally "bang head," or placing the head to the floor, as a token of respect). They presented a long list of "gifts" and in return were given "presents," often greater in value and number. The missions were in part a polite cloak for trade, combining mutual benefit with diplomacy and the prestige of association with the Celestial Empire. It also fed the Chinese opinion of themselves as the only imperium, the only true civilization, the center of the world, compared with which all other people were barbarians.

At its height, first under the Ming and later in the early Ch'ing period, the tributary system involved over 40 states, including Korea, Vietnam, Tibet, Japan, Java, the Philippines, Burma, Siam, Ceylon, Malacca, and many central Asian kingdoms. The renewed Chinese interest in the wider world was a feature of the first few decades of the Ming, although the tributary system continued into the nineteenth century. The last half or more of Ming rule was, in contrast, a period of retrenchment, preoccupation with the defense of the land frontiers, and cultural conservatism. Such a shift fits the pattern of the dynastic cycle discussed in Chapter 11. All dynasties tended to be open-minded, cosmopolitan, and expansionist in their first century, complacent in their second, and overwhelmed by problems in their third and last, when the effectiveness and vigor of the imperial government deteriorated, corruption mounted, and rebellion spread. The Ming were no exception to this pattern, and the memory of the Mongol conquest tended in any case to make them antiforeign, conservative in their determination to reaffirm the great tradition of the Chinese past, and inward-centered. All this was understandable and probably benefited the country, at least in the short run, as much or more than foreign adventuring. China was a huge and productive world in itself. Until late in the 1500s things continued to go well, and general prosperity kept most people content.

Japanese and Korean pirate raids at places all along the coast did worry the Ming, and not only because of what the pirates stole or destroyed. The raids demonstrated that the Chinese government could not keep order locally or defend its people. The raids were regarded as equivalent to rebellion, and the government also knew that a good many renegade Chinese were involved, masquerading as Koreans or Japanese. After much pressure from Peking, the Ashikaga shogunate in Japan, now formally a Ming tributary, suppressed some of the Japanese pirate activity and sent some captured pirates to Peking for execution. A Ming document addressed to the Ashikaga in 1436 acknowledged this and went on to say, in the customary language of the tributary system:

> **Since our empire owns the world, there is no country on this or other sides of the seas which does not submit to us. The sage emperors who followed one another had the same regard and uniform benevolence for all countries far and near. You, Japan, are our eastern frontier, and for generations you have performed tributary duties. The longer the time, the more respectful you have become.[4]**

From Southeast Asia to Africa

What distinguished the early Ming period was the outreach of imperial pride, manifested especially in remarkable maritime expeditions. The eunuch admiral Cheng Ho (Zhenghe) mounted seven naval expeditions of Chinese fleets between 1405 and 1433, with up to 60 vessels. They toured much of Southeast Asia, the east and west coasts of India (including Calicut, where 90 years later Vasco da Gama was to make his Asian landfall), Ceylon, the Persian Gulf and the Straits of Hormuz, Aden, Jidda (from where seven Chinese went to Mecca), and East Africa. They may have gone as far as the Cape of Good Hope or even around it. They brought back giraffes, zebras, and ostriches to amaze the court and tributary agreements with gifts from a host of new states. When the king of Ceylon was considered not deferential enough, he was arrested and taken back to Nanking, while Yung-lo appointed a new king in his place.

Cheng Ho's many-decked ships carried up to 500 troops but also cargoes of export goods, mainly silks and porcelains, and brought back foreign luxuries such as spices and tropical woods. The economic motive for these huge ventures may have been important, and many of the ships had large private cabins for merchants. But the chief aim was probably political, to show the flag and command

A Ming Naval Expedition

Here is part of a text engraved on a stone tablet in 1432, commemorating the expeditions of Cheng Ho.

The Imperial Ming dynasty in unifying seas and continents . . . even goes beyond the Han and the T'ang. The countries beyond the horizon and from the ends of the earth have all become subjects. . . . Thus the barbarians from beyond the seas . . . have come to audience bearing precious objects. . . . The emperor has ordered us, Cheng Ho . . . to make manifest the transforming power of the Imperial virtue and to treat distant people with kindness. . . . We have seven times received the commission of ambassadors [and have visited] altogether more than thirty countries large and small. We have traversed immense water spaces and have beheld huge waves like mountains rising sky-high, and we have set eyes on barbarian regions far away hidden in a blue transparency of light vapors, while our sails loftily unfurled like clouds day and night continued their course, traversing those savage waves as if we were treading a public thoroughfare. . . . We have received the high favor of a gracious commission of our Sacred Lord, to carry to the distant barbarians the benefits of his auspicious example. . . . Therefore we have recorded the years and months of the voyages. [Here follows a detailed record of places visited and things done on each of the seven voyages.] We have anchored in this port awaiting a north wind to take the sea . . . and have thus recorded an inscription in stone . . . erected by the principal envoys, the Grand Eunuchs Cheng Ho and Wang Ching-hung, and the assistant envoys.

Source: J. J. L. Duyvendak, "The True Dates of the Chinese Maritime Expeditions in the Early Fifteenth Century," *T'oung Pao* 24 (1938): 349–355.

respect for the empire, as well as to enroll still more states as tributaries.

Some of the ships were larger than anything previously built in the world, 400 feet long and of 500 tons burden, with four decks. Despite their size, they were reported to be faster sailers than the Portuguese caravels or Spanish galleons of two centuries later, especially with a favorable wind, and they were designed in accordance with the monsoonal wind patterns of Asia and the Indian Ocean. Properly timed voyages could count on going with the wind for about half the year almost anywhere in that vast region and then returning with the opposite monsoon in the other half of the year.

The Expeditions in Retrospect

Cheng Ho's ships, like those of the Sung, were built with double hulls and up to a dozen separate watertight compartments. Despite their far-flung voyages and their many encounters with storms and unknown coasts, few were lost. They were provided with detailed sailing directions, at least for the waters near home, and compasses. Such exploits of seamanship and exploration were unprecedented in the world. Their grand scale and imperial pretension, as well, perhaps, as their commercial ambition, expressed imperial pride and vigor. However, they contributed little to the economy except temporary employment for shipbuilders and crew and luxuries for consumption, and they made no lasting impression on the Chinese except to confirm their sense of superiority as the only civilized empire in the world.

The expeditions were also very expensive. They were stopped after 1433, perhaps mainly for that reason, although abuses and corruption in procuring shipbuilding materials and in contracts with shipyards also attracted official criticism. The emperor may have felt that he had made his imperial point, and it is unlikely that trade profits covered the costs. Another factor was the decision to move the capital to Peking in 1421, better to command the chronically troubled northern frontier against the attempted revival of Mongol power and to assert the tradition of a northern capital. The monumental building of Peking also competed for shrinking sources of timber and labor, as well as for treasury allocations.

But the abandonment of the maritime expeditions, like the move to Peking, was a symptom of the Ming's growing interest in consolidation. There were understandable fears of a Mongol resurgence and deep concern as well about the central Asian conquests of the Turkish leader Tamerlane, who was apparently planning to invade China. Tamerlane's death had ended that threat, but the Mongols were still active. Yung-lo personally led five expeditions into the steppe to combat the Mongol revival and remained preoccupied with the northern defenses for the remainder of his reign. In fact, Mongol tribes were to harass the border areas and raid across the frontier until the mid-seventeenth century. The Ming also promoted the spread of Lamaistic Buddhism to the Mongols in an effort to pacify them, a strategy that seems in the end to have been more effective than military confrontation.

The cost of the anti-Mongol campaigns on top of the building of Peking was a strain, and the extravagant oceanic adventures were a logical item for retrenchment. These excursions had also become politically controversial. Cheng Ho's voyages had been supported by his fellow eunuchs at court and strongly opposed by the Confucian scholar-officials; their antagonism was in fact so great that they tried to suppress any mention of the naval expeditions in the official imperial record.

China's relations by sea had always been given a far lower priority than the empire's land frontiers, and this ancient pattern was now reasserted. The Ming expeditions did not, to the Chinese mind, discover anything worth making greater efforts to exploit, and conquest was never part of the plan. Nonetheless, the scale of Cheng Ho's voyages remains impressive. While the Portuguese were just beginning to feel their way cautiously along the West African coast in sight of land, Chinese fleets of far larger ships dominated the Indian Ocean and the western Pacific and traded in most of their ports. They did not try to cross the Pacific or continue westward to Europe, which they were clearly capable of doing, only because to their knowledge there was nothing in either direction to make such a voyage worthwhile.

If they had reached Europe, they probably would have been no more impressed by it than by what they saw in Southeast Asia, India, the Persian Gulf, or Africa, nor any more than they were to be a century later by the early European arrivals in China. Fifteenth-century North America would have seemed to them too primitive even to mention. Like earlier Chinese innovations in science and technology, these maritime achievements were not followed up. The conquest of the seas, global expansion, and a sea-based commercial revolution were left to the poorer and less complacent Europeans, who from both their own and the Chinese point of view had more to gain thereby. The chief early goal of the European expansion overseas was in fact China, whose riches and sophistication had attracted Europe's mind and ambitions since Marco Polo—indeed, perhaps since the first Roman imports of Chinese silk, that symbol of luxury and wealth.

Prosperity and Conservatism

Meanwhile, the Ming turned inward from their new capital at Peking, rebuilding the Great Wall and its watchtowers in the form it still has today and promoting the development of their own home base. Such domestic concerns had always been the center of Chinese attention. Since Shang times they had called their country the Middle Kingdom, meaning not only that it was the center of the world but also that it combined the advantages of a golden mean, avoiding the extremes of desert, jungle, mountains, or cold around its borders.

In whatever direction one went from China, the physical and cultural environment deteriorated. The Chinese attributed the lack of civilization they noted in all "barbarians" to their far less favorable geographic environment as well as to their distance from the only center of enlightenment. China was indeed the most productive area of comparable size anywhere in the world, especially its great river valleys and floodplains. The empire was bigger than all of Europe in size, held more people, and supported a far greater volume of trade. The Chinese saw their interests best served by embellishing their home base rather than pursuing less rewarding foreign contacts. Domestic and interprovincial trade, between provinces the size of many European states, was far greater than foreign trade and served the world's largest market. Revenues now went increasingly to support domestic projects and to glorify the empire's rulers.

Thus conservatism was growing even before the end of the Ming's first century. Partly this reflected a determination to reestablish the traditional Chinese way in all things after the Mongol humiliation, but it also stemmed from enhanced prosperity. With everything going so well, there was less incentive to seek change or to be innovative, at least in terms of official policy.

The emperors who followed Yung-lo were less able or imaginative and tended to leave policy and administration to the intrinsically conservative Confucian bureaucracy, once again entrenched in power. The imperial censors were revived to keep officials honest and responsible and to keep the capital informed of actual or potential problems. On the whole, this tried and true system worked well for another century. In time it became increasingly rigid and less able to respond to change or the need for change, but until the last decades of the Ming, as with other dynasties, it was an impressive form of government that kept order and ensured justice to an admirable degree.

Nor did official conservatism and Confucian-based anti-commercialism impede the basic changes at work in the economy. As in every Chinese dynasty, agriculture was regarded as the main source of wealth and worthy of official promotion. The government undertook many new projects to extend irrigation, build canals, pave roads, stock public granaries, and construct flood prevention works. Rice yields rose with the use of more productive and earlier-ripening varieties introduced from Southeast Asia and actively promoted by the state. New irrigation and better manuring, plus new land brought under cultivation to feed the growing population, produced a major rise in total output and a marked improvement in average material well-being.

In the sixteenth century new crops, especially maize and potatoes, reached China from Spanish America via the Philippines. This increased output still further since they did not replace rice or wheat but grew in hilly or sandy areas little cultivated before.

The Ming government and most of its Confucian magistrates executed duties conscientiously during this period. The tax system was reformed to make it less burdensome for peasants, although the bulk of imperial revenue came from taxes on land and grain in addition to customs duties and the official monopoly taxes on salt and tea. Regular labor service was also required of all districts and households for public works, including the building and maintaining of irrigation and flood prevention systems and the imperial road network.

A new, comprehensive code of administrative and criminal law was published in 1397. Food crops were still considered of prime importance, but the state encouraged a boom in commercial crops, such as mulberry (for silkworms) and cotton. Silk was produced in the densely populated Yangtze delta area, where its dependence on intensive hand labor could rest on the family, especially women and older children. The populous Canton (Kwangzhou) area and that of the Red Basin of Szechuan (Sichuan) were other important silk-making regions. All three were close to major urban markets and to navigable waterways to distribute their output throughout the empire at low cost.

Under the Ming, however, for the first time, cotton became the predominant fabric of daily clothing for most people. Cheaper and more durable than silk, it displaced coarser and more laboriously made hemp and linen. Silk remained a luxury item for the wealthy, but cotton became a far larger crop. It was grown and woven in the lower Yangtze, northeastern China, and central China, significantly adding to the income of farmers and providing new employment for weavers and merchants.

Commerce and Culture

For all the ambitious revival of the imperial bureaucracy, it remained a thin and superficial layer at the top. There were only about 2,000 officials outside the capital, far too few to touch most aspects of daily life in a vast country with a population now well over 100 million. Commerce was officially disparaged, but the most significant changes taking place in Ming China were in the expanding commercialization of the economy. Cheng Ho's expeditions were past, but trade with most of the places he had visited continued to increase, especially with eastern Southeast Asia. Although the largest trade was domestic, new supplies of silver and silver coins came into China to pay for the exports of silk, tea, porcelain, lacquer ware, and other goods, and heightened the pace of commercialization and monetarization. More and more production was undertaken for sale, in agriculture and in manufacturing. Most of it was consumed in the rapidly growing cities, but some found its way to Korea, Japan, Java, the Philippines, and farther abroad.

Some of the silver flowing back came from Japan, but more and more of it came from the Spanish base founded at Manila by the end of the sixteenth century, where it was brought from the mines of Peru and Mexico. Spanish-minted silver dollars began to circulate widely in the China market. Taxes too were commuted from a share of the grain harvest and periods of labor on public works projects to silver. A sweeping reform in the sixteenth and early seventeenth centuries attempted, with considerable success, to simplify the tax system. The reform lumped what had previously been a great variety of exactions into a few categories and collected them at fixed dates in silver, a major step toward a modern revenue system. At least for a time, this greatly reduced the confusion, corruption, and evasion that had bedevilled the former system, and it also increased the government's net income.

Merchant guilds acquired new though unofficial power in many Chinese cities, especially along the lower Yangtze and the southeast coast, the country's most urbanized and commercialized areas. Guilds controlled much nonagricultural production, marketing, and long distance trade, informally and often through family or native-place networks, but very effectively. Merchants were still considered parasitic rather than productive. They were formally subject to officials and periodically to special government exactions. However, they were able to secure protection, access to favors, and other informal means of assistance, usually through a member of an extended family who had acquired gentry or official status. Indeed, such contacts were the only secure basis for commercial success in this bureaucratic society. Despite the Confucian disdain for their activity, at least on the surface, many merchants grew rich in this expanding economy. Some were able to buy gentry rank, although they were almost never permitted to hold office. Their money enabled them to live in the style if not with the prestige of the scholar-gentry, as literate connoisseurs of sophisticated art and literature in their great townhouses.

After 1520 or so, capital investment increasingly moved away from the ownership and rental of land into commercial enterprises: trade and artisan production. Prices for land continued to fall, and coastal piracy did not apparently discourage the increase of maritime trade as charges rose to cover those risks, although the biggest growth was in domestic commerce. In agriculture too, commercial or industrial crops such as cotton, indigo (for dyeing fabrics), and vegetable oil for illumination became more important. Handicraft production of tools, furniture, paper, porcelain, and art objects for wider sale became common, distributing finished products to a regional or even national market. Some shops employed several hundred workers—another step toward industrialization. Large cotton mills producing cloth in major urban centers in the lower Yangtze valley and the highly commercialized delta area sold their output nationwide. Skilled workers were in great demand and were recruited over a very wide area. Silk, porcelain, and tea especially, among other products, were exported in growing volume and with great profit. Chinese silk sold in Japan, for example, at five or six times its price in the domestic market, and it continued to be sold in the West at even higher prices.

As would happen two centuries later in Europe, growing commercialization, a widening market, and rising demand for goods provided incentives for improving and speeding up production and the development of new technology to turn out more goods. In the last century of the Ming dynasty a number of technical handbooks were published that show impressive progress in production technology. Some of the new techniques are reminiscent of ones that appeared in eighteenth-century Europe, where the increase in trade and demand helped lead to technological innovation, rising output, and the beginnings of the Industrial Revolution. In Ming China, such innovations included mechanical looms with three or four shuttle winders for producing larger amounts of silk or cotton cloth in less time and without increasing labor requirements. New techniques emerged for the printing of woodblocks in three, four, and five colors to feed the booming market for books and prints. Movable type improved. An alloy of copper and lead made the type sharper and more durable so that it could be used for larger print runs and could be reused many more times. New procedures were worked out even for the manufacture of specially refined grades of sugar, to suit the tastes and the pocketbooks of the greatly increased numbers of the wealthy.

Suspension bridges, to carry the booming trade over rivers, made use of iron chains, had originally been developed by T'ang times. Such bridges were widespread under the Ming dynasty and greatly impressed the early European observers, although they were not successfully copied in Europe until the eighteenth century. The use of a mast and sail on wheelbarrows, important carriers of trade and raw materials on a local scale, especially on the North China plain with its wide expanses of level and treeless areas and its strong winds, also attracted European attention and was soon copied by the Dutch, although the wheelbarrow itself had been invented in Han China, and sails added soon thereafter. In agriculture, new machines were developed under the Ming for cultivating the soil, for irrigation, and even for mechanical sowing, planting, and harvesting. Crops imported from the New World continued to add to total agricultural output. After Hung-wu and Yung-lo, Ming population figures are increasingly unreliable—another symptom of the decline in governmental efficiency—but total population probably increased to something like 130 million by the end of the dynasty.

To serve the needs of an increasingly commercialized economy, guilds of moneychangers and bankers became more important, and some of them developed a national network, with representatives in most major cities and at the capital. Techniques for transferring money through the equivalent of letters of credit, referred to as "flying money," had been used in the Sung dynasty but were refined and greatly expanded in the second half of the Ming period, as were other aspects of banking and the financing of trade. These developments too suggest comparison with what was happening in Europe along similar lines. The Marxist historians of China in the 1970s identified these trends in the Ming era as "early sprouts of capitalism," a description that seems quite reasonable despite the official downgrading of trade and merchants and the state regulation of commerce. Many of the richest merchants in fact grew wealthy through managing what were officially state enterprises or monopolies: supplies for the army, the shipment of rice to feed the capital, and the trade in salt.

Patronage and Literature

Wealthy merchants patronized literature and the arts, decorated their houses lavishly with art objects, and supported an elegant urban culture. Vernacular literature, too, which had had its major beginnings under the Sung, took on new dimensions and variety, appealing now to a growing mass of urban readers. Ming painting was in general less imaginative or innovative than that of the Sung and tended to rework older themes and styles, but the later Ming produced its own great painters, especially gifted in their exquisite representations of birds and flowers. Ceramics reached a new level of perfection, and beautiful pieces were part of every rich merchant household. This was the period of the famous Ming blue-and-white porcelain, samples and copies of which were prominent among Chinese exports to the West.

Later Ming painters turned to a decorative portrayal of natural details, as in this silk scroll of peacocks by Lin Liang (1488–1555). [Cleveland Museum of Art, Mr. & Mrs. Severance A. Millikin Collection]

An example of the famous Ming blue-and-white porcelain. Pieces such as this are universally admired for their contours as well as their decoration. [Collection of the National Palace Museum, Taiwan, Republic of China]

Yung-lo commissioned an immense encyclopedia of all knowledge, on which 3,000 scholars worked for five years. It was followed later in the fifteenth century by a great medical encyclopedia and others devoted to geography, botany, ethics, and art. The medical volumes, completed in 1578, listed over 10,000 drugs and prescriptions, most of them unknown in the West, and recorded the use of inoculation to prevent smallpox, far in advance of this discovery in eighteenth-century Europe. A handbook of industrial technology printed in 1637, just before the dynasty collapsed, described methods and tools or machines in the production of rice, salt, porcelain, metals, coal, paper, weapons, and many other fruits of Chinese industry and ingenuity.

In the more popular realm, the theater flourished, but the major advance of Ming literature was in long popular novels and other stories of adventure and romance. They still make excellent reading and give a vivid picture of the

Part of the carved lacquer surface of a cabinet, with the figure of a dragon—an example of the elegant refinement of court life in the last century of Ming rule. [Granger Collection]

life of the times. Perhaps the best known now is titled *Water Margins* (translated by Pearl Buck as *All Men Are Brothers*), which tells the story of an outlaw band and its efforts to correct wrongs done by unjust officials. Bandits of the Robin Hood variety had the same romantic appeal in China as in the West, and their life as "men of the greenwood" (a phrase identical to that used in medieval England), meaning, of course, the forest, where they had their protected bases, was idealized. Several centuries later, Mao Tse-tung (Mao Zedong), the revolutionary Communist leader, said that *Water Margins* (the title came from the marshes that surrounded the outlaws' base) was his favorite book, probably because it glorified men attempting to defy and replace the existing government. Another still widely read Ming novel, *The Golden Lotus*, is an often pornographic satire about the amorous adventures of a druggist with servants, neighbors, and other people's wives that seems as fresh as today's best-sellers.

Most of the characters in *The Golden Lotus* are members of the leisure class, servants, or concubines in a wealthy household. The novel is generally interpreted as a critical portrayal of decadence, but since the characters are mainly well educated, including the concubines, it includes scenes in which they recite or improvise classical-style poems or songs. Here is one of them:

> ***It is evening.***
> ***The storm has passed over the southern hall,***
> ***Red petals are floating on the surface of the pool.***
> ***Slowly the gentle thunder rolls away.***
> ***The rain is over and the clouds disperse;***
> ***The fragrance of waterlilies comes to us over the distance.***
> ***The new moon is a crescent***
> ***Fresh from the perfumed bath, decked for the evening;***
> ***Over the darkening courtyard it wanes***
> ***Yet will not go to rest.***
> ***In the shade of the willow the young cicada bursts into song,***
> ***Fireflies hover over the ancestral halls.***
> ***Listen. Whence comes this song of Ling?***
> ***The painted boat is late returning,***
> ***The jade chords sink lower and lower;***
> ***The gentlefolk are silent:***
> ***A vision of delight!***
> ***Let us rise and take each other by the hand***
> ***And dress our hair.***
> ***The moon lights up the silken curtains,***
> ***But there are no sleepers there.***
> ***The mandarin duck tumbles the lotus leaves***
> ***On the gently rippling water***
> ***Sprinkling them with drops like pearls.***
> ***They give out fragrance,***
> ***And a perfumed breeze moves softly over the flower beds***
> ***Beside the summer-house.***
> ***How can our spirits fail to be refreshed?***
> ***Why crave for the islands of the blest, the home of fairies?***
> ***Yet when the west wind blows again, Autumn will come with it.***[5]

The bandit tales collected in *Water Margins* include a well-known story called "The Birthday Gift Convoy," part of which reads as follows:

> **The road had narrowed to mountain paths, but Yang Chih kept the carriers with their pole loads moving. It was almost noon and the sun [was] directly overhead. The men broke out with "Such hot weather! That deadly sun really kills!" but Yang Chih bore down on them shouting, "Hurry along! We have to cross that ridge. Time to worry about the weather later!"**
>
> **On attaining the top of the ridge, the men flung down their poles, loads and all, and stretched themselves at full length under the pine trees. Yang Chih tried to beat them into resuming the march, saying, "This very spot is the haunt of bandits, where even in the best of times robberies are committed in full daylight." Suddenly he dropped his cane, grasped his sword, and dashed into the woods, where he saw seven men with seven wheelbarrows. They said they were date sellers on their way to the capital, resting in the woods in the heat of the day. Soon another man appeared, with two buckets of wine hanging from his shoulder pole, who also sat down to rest in the shade. The carriers of the birthday gift convoy begged to be allowed to buy some wine, but Yang Chih adamantly refused, saying the wine might be drugged. Hearing the commotion, the date sellers came out of the woods, and, after some dickering, persuaded the wine seller to let them have one of his buckets, which they drank from with coconut shell ladles they had in their packs. Yang Chih watched all this and observed that even after some time the date sellers did not seem to be much affected by the wine. Realizing that he still had to get his convoy a long way that day and calculating that a little wine might help get his men back on their feet, he grudgingly permitted them to buy some, and even took a little himself. Within minutes, the date merchants, who had been watching these proceedings, pointed their fingers at the entire party and chanted in chorus, "Sink, sink, sink into heavy slumber!" Instantly the carriers and their guards wobbled at the knees and sank to the ground. The seven strange travelers now brought their wheelbarrows out of the woods, emptied out all the dates, transferred the eleven precious loads of gold, silver, and jewels to the seven wheelbarrows, and were soon out of sight.**
>
> **Yang Chih groaned with rage and bitterness, but his body seemed paralyzed and he could not struggle to his feet. Who were the seven men? Why, they were all famous bandits. How was the wine drugged? Why, by one of the date merchants when he playfully tried to steal another ladleful from the second bucket and in the process added the drug. It was all a carefully worked-out plan to convince Yang Chih and his men, by the date sellers' drinking the first bucket, that the wine was pure. Yang Chih's downfall was like the proverb: Though you**

Folk Wisdom: Maxims from the Chinese

- A wise man adapts himself to circumstances, as water shapes itself to the vessel that contains it.
- Misfortunes issue out where diseases enter in—at the mouth.
- The error of one moment becomes the sorrow of a whole life.
- The gem cannot be polished without friction, nor man perfected without trials.
- A wise man forgets old grudges.
- A mouse can drink no more than its fill from a river. [Enough is as good as a feast.]
- Who swallows quick can chew little. [Applied to learning.]
- What cannot be told had better not be done.
- The torment of envy is like a grain of sand in the eye.
- Dig a well before you are thirsty.
- Better be a dog in peace than a man in anarchy.
- To win a cat and lose a cow—the consequences of litigation.
- Forbearance is a domestic jewel.
- Kindness is more binding than a loan.
- Those who cannot sometimes be unheeding or deaf are not fit to rule.
- Parents' affection is best shown by teaching their children industry and self-denial.
- A truly great man never puts away the simplicity of a child.
- To obtain one leads to wishing for two—enough is always something more than a man possesses.
- If the upper beam be crooked, the lower will be awry. [The example of superiors.]
- One lash to a good horse, one word to a wise man.
- The man who combats himself will be happier than he who contends with others.
- Let every man sweep the snow from before his own door, and not busy himself about the frost on his neighbor's tiles.
- A man need only correct himself with the same rigor that he reprehends in others; and excuse others with the same indulgence he shows to himself.

Source: J. R. Davis, ed., *The Chinese,* vol. 2 (London: Charles Knight, 1845), pp. 235–240.

be as circumspect as the devil himself, you may unwittingly swallow your own bathwater. Yang Chih tore up his orders. "How can I go back to face my patron? I have no home to return to, no state to serve. Where can I go?" What eventually happened to Yang Chih you will find out in our next chapter.[6]

The West as a whole has still not acknowledged that the novel, in much the same form as we know it today, originated in Asia, as did detective stories. But a few Westerners were less parochial in their awareness and their tastes. Here is a conversation between the famous German writer Johann Wolfgang von Goethe (1749–1832) and a friend in 1827:

"During the days when I did not see you," he said, "I have read a great deal, in particular a Chinese novel with which I am still occupied."

"A Chinese novel," I said, "that must be rather curious."

"Not as curious as one might be tempted to think," replied Goethe. "These people think and feel much as we do, and one soon realizes that one is like them."

"But," said I, "perhaps this Chinese novel is a rather exceptional one?"

"Not at all," said Goethe, "the Chinese have thousands of the kind, and they even had a certain number of them already when our forebears were still living in the woods."[7]

Popular Culture

By the sixteenth century there was a large and growing number of people who were literate or semiliterate but were not members of any elite or of the official Confucian-style gentry. The latter probably never exceeded 2 percent of the population. These nonelite literates and semiliterates lived in the vast Chinese world that was little touched by the imperial system and its canons, most of them outside the big cities and the circles of the rich merchant elites. Popular literature, stories, novels, and plays produced by and for them probably exceeded in volume and circulation the output in the orthodox classical mode, extensive and varied as that was. Much of it was also read, in private, by the elite, who would hide any "undignified" book under the pillow if someone entered the room. For us today, too, most of it is more fun than the restrained, polished, or formal material that the scholarly gentry were supposed to read and write.

In addition were the number of puppet shows, shadow plays, mystery and detective stories (four or five centuries before they appeared in the West), operas, ballads, the oral tradition of itinerant storytellers, and a wealth of inexpensive woodblock prints, many of them dealing with aspects of daily life, others with mythology or folk religion. Opera, which combined drama, music, dance forms, singing, and gorgeous costumes, could appeal also to illiterates, still the large majority, as could storytellers, balladeers, and plays. Itinerant groups performed in all these media everywhere, even in small towns. Storytellers would be accompanied by musicians or provide their own music and would end each recital at a moment of suspense: "Come back next time if you want to hear the next episode" or "Pay now if you want to know how it all came out!"

Over 300 different local or regional genres of opera have been identified, intended mainly for nonelite audiences. Many operas, plays, and stories centered on the adventures of heroes and villains of the rich Chinese past, not always historically accurate but always entertaining, and appealing to the deep interest of the Chinese in their own history. Most of the common people learned their history from opera, theater, and storytellers, and they learned a great deal of it. The connection with folk religion was close, including folk versions of Buddhism and Taoism as well as local animist cults and deities, and many of the operas, plays, and stories focused on it.

Operas were commonly performed at festivals celebrating a local god or as part of temple rituals, and many of them, as well as shadow plays, had an explicitly religious or ritual content, like the medieval miracle plays of Europe. Still others satirized daily life: henpecked husbands, jilted or faithless lovers, grasping merchants, corrupt officials, overprotective or authoritarian parents, tyrannical landlords, and so on, set in villages or towns rather than in the more sophisticated and urbane world of the cities.

These operas and plays formed in effect a countertradition to the elite culture. They expressed strong sympathy for the powerless, the oppressed, and the underdogs, especially women, who were often major figures. The works express contempt for wealth without compassion, for power without responsibility, and for all forms of hypocrisy, opportunism, and moral compromise. In this extensive genre, individuals are valued and respected for their achievements and their moral virtue regardless of their social position, in contrast to the hierarchical ordering of individuals that Confucian doctrine supported. This rich and varied literature has a universal flavor and many parallels in the popular culture of most other societies around the world, past and present. But it also reveals the basic good sense, humor, and appealing human qualities of the common people of Ming China.

Elite Culture and Traditionalism

In monumental architecture the Ming created new glories in their capitals at Nanking and Peking and in temples in every city and many towns, a further indication of prosperity. But in general, particularly after their first century, the Ming looked to the past for guidance. This accounted for their interest in encyclopedias, which collected the wisdom and experience of previous generations as guardians of tradition.

Most Ming scholars and philosophers were traditionalists, mistrusting speculation or innovation. There were exceptions, of course, but orthodoxy tended to dominate thought, reinforced by the system of imperial examinations. As one Ming writer put it: "Since the time of Chu Hsi [the Sung Confucianist] the truth has been made clear. No more writing is needed. We have only to practice."[8] There were nevertheless some important developments in philosophy, especially in the thought of Wang Yang-ming (1472–1529), a scholar-official who went beyond the Neo-Confucianism of Chu Hsi in urging both a meditative and intuitive self-cultivation, much influenced by Buddhism, and an activist moral role in society. Wang's most famous aphorism stresses the organic connection between knowledge and behavior: "Knowledge is the beginning of conduct; conduct is the completion of knowledge"—a maxim still admired by Confucianists in China, Korea, and Japan.

Before Wang's time, Hung-wu had issued six brief imperial edicts that were posted in all villages and towns in 1397, a year before his death. They ordered people to be filial, to respect their elders and ancestors, to teach their children to do the same, and peacefully to pursue their livelihoods. Local gentry, not in office but functioning as local elites and keepers of order and morality, helped to see that these prescriptions were carried out. The orthodox Confucian denigration of trade and merchants and their subordination to officialdom helped to strengthen official disinterest in commerce. Foreign trade was left largely in private hands or was managed by powerful eunuchs at court, which further devalued it in Confucian eyes.

Grain had to be hauled north from the Yangtze valley to feed the swarm of officials, garrison troops, and commoners as well as the elite of Peking. Japanese piracy prompted Yung-lo to restore the Grand Canal and to abandon the coastal sea route after 1415. The cost was high, but the canal helped to stimulate further increases in interregional trade and in artisan and other consumer goods production to supply an enlarged market. Soochow (Suzhou), in the Yangtze delta just west of Shanghai and until the nineteenth century the major city and port of that area after Nanking, became a national financial and commercial center; it was noted for its fine silk goods, which were distributed to the wealthy all over China, especially in fashionable Peking. Cotton cloth, lacquer, magnificent porcelain pieces, iron cooking pots from Canton, and numerous other goods were carried, mainly by water routes, to an increasingly national market. Hankou (now part of the city of Wuhan) on the central Yangtze grew as a major junction of rivers and a national distribution center as well as a major market in itself. Private Chinese merchants went to Southeast Asia in great numbers and managed an increasing overseas trade from bases on the southeast China coast such as Canton, Amoy, Swatow, and Foochow (Fuzhou) despite official discouragement. Tientsin (Tianjin), the port of Peking, grew also as the chief port for trade with Korea. Other booming cities included Chengdu, the capital of the agriculturally rich province of Szechuan with its many rivers, and Changsha, the capital of Hunan on the Hsiang (Xiang) River, a tributary of the Yangtze, which flowed through the productive lowlands of central China known as "China's rice bowl."

Increasingly conservative official attitudes were reflected in the Ming reform of the imperial examination system. In 1487 a set form was established for the writing of examination papers in eight categories using no more than 700 characters altogether, following a prescribed style of polished commentary on the Confucian and Neo-Confucian classics. This was the notorious "eight-legged essay," which in all likelihood intentionally inhibited individual thought or innovation and encouraged a traditionalist orthodoxy.

Government schools at the county and prefectural levels and private academies and tutors for the sons of the wealthy (daughters were given no formal education) passed on the distilled wisdom of the ages to youngsters fortunate enough to attend and shaped their instruction to prepare them to conform to what the examinations now required. Nevertheless, the basic Confucian message of responsibility and human-heartedness continued to be stressed, with its conviction that human nature is fundamentally good and can be molded by education and by the virtuous example of superiors. The ultimate deterioration and collapse of the Ming, and in 1911 of the entire imperial system, should not obscure its positive aspects, especially during its many centuries of relative vigor. Even up to the last years of the Ming, the growing corruption and ineffectiveness of the court were not much reflected in the continued operation of the system elsewhere in the country, which rested far more on the basic Chinese social fabric of family, gentry, and Confucian principles than on the management or intervention of the few imperial officials. The lives and values of most people had their own momentum. Local freedom and good order had relatively little to do with imperial politics at most times and much to do with the traditional Chinese system of a self-regulating society based on respect for tradition and hierarchy.

IMPERIAL PEKING: AXIS OF THE MING WORLD

When Yung-lo decided to move the capital back to the north, Peking was the obvious choice, primarily for its nearness to the most threatened frontiers. It is only about

The Imperial Palace inside its own wall, looking south across the courtyards of the Forbidden City. The planned rectangular layout of imperial Peking is evident. [Paolo Koch/Photo Researchers]

Throne room in the Imperial Palace, Peking. Each building in the Forbidden City is fronted by sweeping marble stairs, and courtyards are linked by ornate marble bridges. The buildings are elaborately decorated inside but elegantly simple in their external lines. [Marc F. Bernheim/Woodfin Camp]

40 miles from the mountains that surround and protect the city on the west, north, and northeast. The Great Wall runs through them, crossing a narrow lowland strip of coastal plain east of the city that leads to Manchuria and is called Shan Hai Kuan ("mountain sea gate"). Passes to the northwest lead directly into Mongolia. Both areas had been identified by now as the chief trouble spots along the frontier, and it was mainly to guard against them that the Great Wall was rebuilt.

The Hsiung-nu menace that had plagued the Han had been replaced by that of the Mongols farther east and by early signs of what was to become the next alien conquering group, the Manchus of Manchuria. The gradual eastward progression of China's capital from Chou, Ch'in, Han and T'ang Ch'ang An (Sian) to Loyang, the Sung move to Kaifeng and Hangchow, and now the Ming choice of Peking reflected these military challenges. The growth of the south, the drought and agricultural deterioration of the northwest, and the provision of canals to bring food from the surplus areas of the Yangtze valley to feed successive northern capitals were also factors in determining where the imperial capital would be located.

The new Peking was designed to make a statement of imperial power and majesty. The older center of the city today is largely a Ming creation, replacing what had been left of the Mongol capital but on a much larger scale. The main outer city walls were 40 feet high and nearly 15 miles around, forming a rectangle pierced by nine gates with watchtowers and outer gates to deter attackers, check permit papers, and awe all who entered.

Inside was the Imperial City, within its own walls, 5 miles in circumference. These enclosed in turn the red inner walls of the Forbidden City, which contained the palace and was surrounded by a moat 2 miles around. Successive courtyards inside the Forbidden City, dominated by throne halls for different purposes, were set on terraces of white marble with gleaming gold-tiled roofs. These led along a north-south axis to the palace. Outside the Forbidden City (so called because it was closed to all except people with official business), a similar succession of elegant stone-paved courtyards, terraces, and audience halls led to the main gates. The outermost walls enclosed gardens, artificial lakes, and even an artificial hill.

The orientation of the city as a whole, based on astronomical principles, followed a north-south axis, thus aligning the court with the order of the universe. The plan and all its details were designed to awe and impress all who approached or entered its series of walls and courtyards. It still has that effect, and partly for that reason, it has been restored by the People's Republic as the centerpiece of the modern capital. The Ming design was accepted and embellished by their successors, the Ch'ing (Qing). That part of Peking remains one of the best-preserved and most impressive planned capitals anywhere. Its splendid courtyards, the gracefulness and yet strength of architectural and roof lines in all of its buildings, and the lavish use of colored porcelain tiles make it aesthetically as well as symbolically overwhelming.

A less planned city grew up outside the walls, where most of the common people lived, and it soon housed most of Peking's residents. The total population, inside and outside the walls, was probably a little over a million under both the Ming and the Ch'ing, fed in part with rice brought from the Yangtze valley by the Grand Canal. Some space was left clear immediately around the outer walls for better defense, and there were large military barracks. A maze of streets, alleys, and small courtyards covered most of the area outside the walls, including the small walled compounds with their tiny gardens and living space for extended families. Some of these too can still be seen.

The majestic Imperial City and Forbidden City were formally ordered on a grand scale, in sharp contrast to the unplanned alleys and irregular streets of the city around them. But above all Peking was—and remains—an imperial statement in wood, stone, brick, and tile that dominated the entire urban area physically as well as symbolically.

Complacency and Decline

Peking was built in the days of Ming power and pride, but as the decades went by, complacency set in, and a number

A Western View of China

Here is an excerpt from the journal of Matteo Ricci, who observed Ming China from 1583 until his death in 1610.

The Chinese are a most industrious people, and most of the mechanical arts flourish among them. They have all sorts of raw material and they are endowed by nature with a talent for trading, both of which are potent factors in bringing about a high development of the mechanical arts. . . . Their skill in the manufacture of fireworks is really extraordinary, and there is scarcely anything which they cannot cleverly imitate with them. They are especially adept in reproducing battles and in making rotary spheres of fire, fiery trees, fruit, and the like, and they seem to have no regard for expense where fireworks are concerned. When I was in Nanking I witnessed a display for the celebration of the first month of the year, which is their great festival, and on this occasion I calculated that they consumed enough powder to carry on a sizeable war for a number of years. . . . Their method of making printed books is quite ingenious. The text is written in ink, with a brush made of very fine hair, on a sheet of paper which is inverted and pasted on a wooden tablet. When the paper is thoroughly dry, its surface is scraped off until nothing but a fine tissue bearing the characters remains on the wooden tablet. Then with a steel graver the workman cuts away the surface following the outlines of the characters until these alone stand out in low relief. From such a block a skilled printer can make copies with incredible speed, turning out as many as fifteen hundred copies in a single day. . . . The simplicity of Chinese printing is what accounts for the exceedingly large number of books in circulation here and the ridiculously low prices at which they are sold. Such facts as these would scarcely be believed by anyone who has not witnessed them.

Source: M. Ricci, *China in the Sixteenth Century: The Journals of Matthew Ricci, 1583–1610,* trans. L. J. Gallagher (New York: Random House, 1953), pp. 18–21.

of growing problems were dealt with inadequately or left unattended. Japanese and Korean pirate attacks on the coast proved impossible to control, and the government's feeble response was to order the removal of all settlement 30 miles inland and officially to forbid maritime trade, although the ban was widely ignored. Guns had been in use for centuries, but China had begun to fall behind advances in Western gunnery. Late in the fifteenth century, when a touring censor asked for a demonstration of a garrison's long-neglected cannons, the commander said, "What, fire those things? Why, they might kill somebody!"[9] This may be an exaggerated example, and during most of the dynasty the Ming armies were reasonably effective in keeping the long peace at home and on the frontiers. Yet the failure to control raids by tributary states clearly presaged the decline of the dynasty.

China had now to deal with Western visitors as well. The Portuguese reached the South China coast by 1514, but their aggressive behavior led to their expulsion from Canton in 1522, where their envoy died in prison. To the Chinese, they were just another lot of unruly pirates, like the Dutch who followed them later, and their numbers and ships were small enough to be brushed off. The Chinese also found the Westerners offensively hairy, misshapen, and very smelly, and although a few military commanders noted that their guns were superior to China's, no one in the government took them very seriously.

The Westerners had different ideas. The Jesuits had their eye on China as an immense potential harvest of souls, and sent a series of missions there beginning with Matteo Ricci in 1582 (see Chapter 17). He and his successors, notably Adam Schall von Bell and Ferdinand Verbiest, were learned men with a good working knowledge of the rapidly developing science and technology of post-Renaissance Europe. Complacency and pride kept the Chinese from learning what would have been most useful from the Jesuits: new European advances in mathematics, geography (despite the great voyages of the fifteenth century, the Chinese picture of the world was still woefully inaccurate and incomplete), mechanics, metallurgy, anatomy, surveying, techniques and instruments for precise measuring and weighing, and gunnery.

The court was instead fascinated by the clocks and clockwork gadgets or toys that the Jesuits brought and

Social Customs in Ming China

Ricci also described a variety of social customs, as in these excerpts.

When relatives or friends pay a visit, the host is expected to return the visit, and a definite and detailed ceremony accompanies their visiting. The one who is calling presents a little folder in which his name is written and which may contain a few words of address, depending on the rank of the visitor or the host. These folders or booklets consist of about a dozen pages of white paper, with a two inch strip of red paper down the middle of the cover. . . . One must have at least twenty different kinds on hand for different functions, marked with appropriate titles. . . . Men of high station in life are never seen walking in the streets. They are carried about enclosed in sedan chairs and cannot be seen by passers-by, unless they leave the front curtain open. . . . Carriages and wagons are prohibited by law. . . . The whole country is divided up by rivers and canals. People here travel more by boat than we in the West, and their boats are more ornate and more commodious than ours. . . . Sometimes they give sumptuous dinners aboard their yachts and make a pleasure cruise of it on the lake or along the river. . . . Because of their ignorance of the size of the earth and the exaggerated opinion they have of themselves, the Chinese are of the opinion that only China among the nations is deserving of admiration. They look on all other people not only as barbarous but as unreasoning animals.

Source: M. Ricci, *China in the Sixteenth Century: The Journals of Matthew Ricci, 1583–1610,* trans. L. J. Gallagher (New York: Random House, 1953), pp. 61, 81, 167.

used to ingratiate themselves, while their most useful knowledge was passed over. Von Bell, a trained astronomer and mathematician, was able to decipher and explain the use of some remarkable astronomical instruments built under the Yuan dynasty in Peking; by the late Ming period, the Chinese had lost the secret. Their own astronomers had noticed that their calculations no longer accurately predicted the movements of the heavenly bodies, but instead of questioning their assumptions and methods, they concluded that "the heavens were out of order." All these were symptoms of an increasing tendency to ignore new ideas or troublesome problems or to gloss them over with confident-sounding pronouncements.

At the capital, decline in administrative effectiveness was clear by the end of the sixteenth century. The court was filled with intriguing factions, including the eunuchs. This was to become a curse of the imperial system. Because they had no heirs, eunuchs were often trusted, given the care of imperial sons, and granted ready access to the emperor and to powerful wives and concubines. Strong rulers, like Hung-wu, could control them, but under weaker ones the eunuchs often became the real powers, and they usually did not use their power responsibly. After Yung-lo came a succession of undistinguished emperors, most of whom kept to the pleasures of their palaces and left the running of the empire to the eunuchs and the bureaucrats, a disastrous pattern in a system where authority and responsibility had been so heavily centralized in the person of the emperor.

A briefly successful effort at reform was led by Chang Chü-cheng (Zhang Juzheng), who became Grand Secretary from 1573 to 1582. The emperor Wan-li had ascended the throne as a boy in 1572 and was guided for some time by Chang Chü-cheng, who as a distinguished Confucian scholar stressed the need for economy, justice, and responsibility. Chang tried to increase the now shrinking imperial revenue by once more reforming the tax system to restore exempted lands and families, which had slipped off the rolls after the earlier tax reform. He also tried to limit the special privileges and extravagant expenses of the court and the imperial family and to rebuild the authority of the censors to check abuses. But after Chang's death in 1582, Wan-li abandoned all pretense at responsibility and indulged in more extravagance and pleasures while leaving the court eunuchs to run the empire. He avoided even seeing his own ministers for many years and refused to make appointments, conduct any business, or respond to abuses.

Unfortunately, he lived and reigned until 1620, and the 15-year-old who succeeded him on the throne was mentally deficient and spent most of his time tinkering with carpentry in the palace. He gave control of the government to an old friend of his childhood nurse, a eunuch named Wei who had been a butler to his mother. Wei put together a small eunuch army to control the palace and set up a spy network all over the empire. By unscrupulous plotting and force he eliminated all his official enemies—most of the Confucianists at court—filled their places with his opportunist supporters, and extorted new taxes to pay for his luxurious lifestyle. Half the government offices were left vacant, and petitions went unanswered. A group of Confucian scholars calling themselves the Tung Lin (Donglin, from the name of a famous academy) attempted a moral crusade against these evils. Wei responded with terror tactics after the Tung Lin leader accused him of murders, of having forced abortion on the empress, and 24 other "high crimes." In the end Wei won out, and most of the Tung Lin scholars were disgraced, jailed, or beaten to death before he himself died in 1627.

It was late for reform, and the eunuch stranglehold on the palace was now too strong to break. Eunuch power at court undercut and then virtually eliminated the power and even the role of the imperial censors. Many censors were killed when they dared to speak up. Palace eunuchs went on making most policy, or not making it, after Wei's death. By the 1630s most of the country had lost confidence in the imperial order. The state treasury had been drained by the heavy expense of assisting the Koreans to repel an invasion by the Japanese warlord Hideyoshi in the 1590s (see Chapter 11), and even more by extravagances at court. The treasury never fully recovered. The results for the efficient operation of all state systems were disastrous.

Inflation aggravated the problem. Officials and local magistrates had to cope with a much larger population, increasingly troubled by discontent, banditry, and even rebellion. Their salaries were increased and special allowances given to discourage them from diverting official funds or taking bribes, but none of this made up for the far heavier work demands, which necessitated their hiring larger and larger staffs to assist them. These aides, though essential, were not official employees, and their wages were not provided by the state, leaving magistrates and other officials to meet the costs out of their own inadequate salaries and allowances. The inevitable result was increased corruption and bribery, since the greatest of all traditional Confucian virtues was responsibility for one's own family. More and more, the rest of the Confucian morality disappeared as individuals and families strove simply to survive.

The Ming army did not distinguish itself in Korea. It drove the Japanese back but then was ambushed near Seoul, the Korean capital, and the rest of the campaign was largely a stalemate until Hideyoshi providentially died and his army promptly returned to Japan. A few years later, Matteo Ricci found the Ming army unimpressive: "All those under arms lead a despicable life, for they have not embraced this profession out of love of their country or love of honor but as men in the service of a provider of employment."[10] Many Chinese were now saying, "Good iron is not used for nails or good men for soldiers."

Much of the Ming army by this time was composed of ex-prisoners, drifters, former bandits, and idlers. Its size had doubled since the beginning of the dynasty, but its effectiveness had diminished sharply. Military contracts had become an open and expanding field for graft and corruption, and the quality of equipment and other supplies had deteriorated, as had military morale and leadership. One of the reasons for the failure to drive the Japanese out of Korea was what had become the inferiority of most Chinese weapons, including swords, spears, and guns. The Japanese had quickly noted and copied the Portuguese improvements in cannons, and the development of an early version of the rifle, the harquebus, a cumbersome muzzle-loading weapon that was, however, devastating in close combat.

At the capital under the dissolute Emperor Wan-li, and progressively elsewhere in the empire, effectiveness and morale likewise declined. Despite Chang Chü-cheng's reforms, corruption had again removed much land and other wealth from the tax rolls, and the new taxes imposed by the eunuch Wei and his successors, together with a grow-

Street people of the Ming: beggars and hawkers, painted by Chou Ch'en (active c. 1500–1535). [Cleveland Museum of Art, John L. Severance Fund]

ing population, created widespread economic hardship and a rapid growth of tenancy, lawlessness, and regional famine. Banditry, local revolts, and secret societies, always a barometer of impending collapse, multiplied. There was open talk that the Ming had forfeited the Mandate of Heaven.

The incompetent government now faced two major revolts. A famine in Shensi (Shaanxi) in the northwest in 1628 led to arbitrary government economies instead of the needed relief. A postal clerk named Li Tzu-ch'eng (Li Zicheng) was laid off and joined his uncle, a bandit in the nearby mountains. Li and his forces raided widely among three or four adjoining provinces, attracted more followers, set up a government, distributed food to famine victims, appointed officials, and proclaimed a new dynasty. Early in 1644 he advanced on Peking, meeting only weak resistance. Hearing the news that the city had fallen, the last Ming emperor hanged himself in the palace garden, after failing to kill his oldest daughter with a sword.

A rival rebel leader named Chang (Zhang) had meanwhile been raiding and plundering much of northern China. In 1644 he invaded Szechuan, set up a government, and moved to claim the throne. His power plays and his terror tactics, however, lost him the support of the gentry, and without them his cause was lost. Neither Li nor Chang was fated to create a new dynasty; it came instead, as in Mongol times, from the steppe beyond the Great Wall.

The Manchu Conquest

A non-Chinese steppe people, the Manchus, had risen to power in Manchuria despite Ming efforts to keep them divided. A strong leader, Nurhachi (1559–1626), united several previously separate tribes and founded a Chinese-style state, taking the title of emperor and promoting the adoption of the Confucian system and its philosophy. His capital was established at Mukden (now called Shenyang) in southern Manchuria, where his two sons, also capable leaders, succeeded him and continued the Sinification of the Manchu state and culture.

An Earthquake at Peking, 1626

The Chinese interpreted earthquakes and other natural disasters as symbols of Heaven's displeasure. When they coincided with popular discontent and dynastic decline, they were seen as warnings. Here is a description of an earthquake in 1626 at Peking, in the last corrupt years of the Ming. The partisans referred to were palace eunuchs.

Just when the . . . partisans were secretly plotting in the palace, there was a sudden earthquake. A roof ornament over the place where they were sitting fell without any apparent reason and two eunuchs were crushed to death. In a moment there was a sound like thunder rising from the northwest. It shook heaven and earth, and black clouds flowed over confusedly. People's dwellings were destroyed to such an extent that for several miles nothing remained. Great stones hurtled down from the sky like rain. Men and women died by the tens of thousands [a phrase that in Chinese means "a great many"]. Donkeys, horses, chickens, and dogs all had broken or cracked limbs. People with smashed skulls or broken noses were strewn about—the streets were full of them. Gunpowder that had been stored in the Imperial Arsenal exploded. This alarmed elephants, and the elephants ran about wildly, trampling to death an incalculable number of people. The court astrologer reported his interpretation of these events as follows: 'In the earth there is tumultuous noise. This is an evil omen of calamity in the world. When noise gushes forth from within the earth, the city must be destroyed. . . . The reason why the earth growls is that throughout the empire troops arise to attack one another, and that palace women and eunuchs have brought about great disorder.'

Source: C. O. Hucker in D. Lach, *Asia on the Eve of Europe's Expansion* (Englewood Cliffs, N.J.: Prentice-Hall, 1965), p. 133.

By 1644 the Manchus were for all practical purposes politically and culturally indistinguishable from the Chinese, except for their spoken language. Their administration and army included large numbers of Chinese, who saw them as a coming power. The Manchus made vassals of the Mongols of Inner Mongolia and the Koreans after expeditions had conquered both. They were consciously building their power to take over China, and in 1644 they had their opportunity.

A Ming general invited the Manchu armies waiting on the border at Shan Hai Kuan to help him defeat Li Tzu-ch'eng, who with his army now occupied Peking. The Manchus did so and remained to found a new dynasty, rewarding a number of Chinese collaborators with grants of land. Some of these collaborators later rebelled but were suppressed in heavy fighting. Finally, in 1683 the new dynasty conquered the offshore island of Taiwan, which had clung to the defeated Ming cause, a situation with parallels in the twentieth century. It thus took nearly 40 years before the Manchu conquest was complete. Unlike the Mongols, however, the Manchus ushered in a long period of domestic peace and unprecedented prosperity.

The Manchus called their new dynasty Ch'ing (Qing), a title adopted by Nurhachi's son and continued by his grandsons. *Ch'ing* means "pure," and the name was intended to add legitimacy to an alien rule. But the Manchus had learned their Chinese lessons well. They honored and continued the best of the imperial tradition and could plausibly represent themselves as liberators restoring China's glorious past. While this made them, like the Ming, conservative stewards rather than innovators and in time helped to harden them against change, they too presided over a brilliant period in Chinese history for their first two centuries. Ch'ing was the China most Westerners first knew well. Although already in its declining years in the nineteenth century, Westerners still found it impressive, built as it was on the long foundation of imperial greatness that had preceded it.

The Ming dynasty ended in ineptness and disgrace, but the more positive aspects of its achievements were valued and preserved by its successors. Having begun with great vigor and success, the Ming went on to administer effectively for two centuries or more a new wave of prosperity, cultural growth, commercial and urban development, and the further refinement of taste. Popular culture, aided by cheap printing, enjoyed a notable boom, and in the larger cities rich merchants patronized and participated in elite culture. Although the dramatic maritime expeditions of Cheng Ho were abandoned, private Chinese trade multiplied with Southeast Asia, and domestic commerce thrived. Agriculture was made more productive, in part under state direction, and the population increased substantially. Ming Peking still stands as a monument to the dynasty's wealth and power. But the highly centralized system of government begun under Hung-wu helped to sap administrative effectiveness under later and weaker emperors, while power came increasingly into the hands of court eunuchs, with disastrous results. In the end the Ming dynasty was easy prey for the far better organized Manchus, who had learned the Confucian lessons that the Ming had forgotten.

Notes

1. J. K. Fairbank, E. O. Reischauer, and A. Craig, *East Asia: Tradition and Transformation* (Boston: Houghton Mifflin, 1978), p. 197.
2. Ibid., p. 182.
3. Ibid.
4. W. Bingham, H. Conroy, and F. Ikle, *A History of Asia*, vol. 1 (Boston: Allyn & Bacon, 1964), p. 459.
5. After W. McNaughton, *Chinese Literature: An Anthology* (Tokyo: Charles Tuttle, 1959), pp. 697–698.
6. After H. C. Chang, *Chinese Literature* (Edinburgh: Edinburgh University Press, 1973), pp. 166–177.
7. J. W. von Goethe, *Conversations with Eckermann*, in J. Gernet, *A History of Chinese Civilization*, trans. J. R. Foster (Cambridge: Cambridge University Press, 1985), p. xxvii.
8. C. O. Hucker, *China's Imperial Past* (Stanford, Calif.: Stanford University Press, 1975), p. 373.
9. C. O. Hucker, *China to 1850* (Stanford, Calif.: Stanford University Press, 1980), p. 139.
10. J. Gernet, *History of Chinese Civilization*, p. 431.

Suggestions for Further Reading

Berliner, N. *Chinese Folk Art*. Boston: Little, Brown, 1986.

Birch, C. *Stories from a Ming Collection*. New York: Grove Press, 1958.

Boxer, C. R., ed. *South China in the Sixteenth Century*. London: Hakluyt Society, 1953.

De Bary, W. T., et al. *Self and Society in Ming Thought*. New York: Columbia University Press, 1970.

Duyvendak, J. J. L. *China's Discovery of Africa*. London: Probsthain, 1949.

Eberhard, W. *Moral and Social Values of the Chinese*. Taipei: Chengwen Publishing Co., 1971.

Fairbank, J. K. *The Chinese World Order: Traditional China's Foreign Relations*. Cambridge: Harvard University Press, 1968.

Farmer, E. L. *Early Ming Government: The Evolution of Dual Capitals*. Cambridge, Mass.: Harvard University Press, 1976.

Gernet, J. *A History of Chinese Civilization*, trans. J. R. Foster. Cambridge: Cambridge University Press, 1985.

Hayden, G. *Crime and Punishment in Medieval Chinese Drama*. Cambridge, Mass.: Harvard University Press, 1978.

Hsia, C. T. *The Classic Chinese Novel*. New York: Columbia University Press, 1968.

Huang, R. *Taxation and Government Finance in Sixteenth Century Ming China*. Cambridge, Mass.: Harvard University Press, 1974.

Hucker, C. O., ed. *Chinese Government in Ming Times*. New York: Columbia University Press, 1969.

Idema, W. L. *Chinese Vernacular Fiction*. Leiden: Brill, 1974.

Johnson, A., Nathan, A., and Rawski, E., eds. *Popular Culture in Late Imperial China*. Berkeley: University of California Press, 1985.

Lach, D. F. *China in the Eyes of Europe: The Sixteenth Century*. Chicago: University of Chicago Press, 1968.

Levenson, J. R. *European Expansion and the Counter-example of Asia, 1300–1600*. Englewood Cliffs, N.J.: Prentice-Hall, 1967.

Parsons, J. B. *The Peasant Rebellions of the Late Ming Dynasty*. Tucson: University of Arizona Press, 1970.

Rawski, E. S. *Agricultural Change and the Peasant Economy of South China*. Cambridge, Mass.: Harvard University Press, 1974.

Ricci, M. *China in the Sixteenth Century: The Journals of Matthew Ricci, 1583–1610*, trans. L. J. Gallagher. New York: Random House, 1953.

So, K. W. *Japanese Piracy in Ming China During the Sixteenth Century*. East Lansing: Michigan State University Press, 1975.

Van Gulik, R. *The Chinese Bell Murders*. Chicago: University of Chicago Press, 1984.

CHAPTER · 21

The Societies of the Early Modern World

The richness and variety of the world's societies is abundantly revealed in the period of transition between the medieval and modern worlds that extends from approximately 1400 to 1800. Throughout the Western world in particular, social structures, behavioral patterns, and value systems underwent important changes that helped determine the character of today's societies. The institution of the family also altered, again mostly in the West, whereas in Asia the traditional family remained the bulwark of social hierarchy and stability. The age of women's rights lay in the future, but throughout the world women made significant contributions to their societies, sometimes in terms of political power at the highest levels of government. Women ruled, or were powers behind the throne, in societies as different as western Europe, Africa, and the Ottoman Empire.

The dress and many of the pursuits of the aristocracy—such as hunting, lawn bowling, and formal afternoon promenades—set them apart from the other social classes. This is a detail from *Le Rendez-vous pour Marly* by Moreau le Jeune. [The Metropolitan Museum of Art, Harris Bisbane Dick Fund, 1933]

The early modern period saw dramatic educational expansion in the West and a printing revolution in both the West and Asia. For the most part, neither Africa nor the Ottoman Empire effectively shared in these developments. Although patterns of trade became worldwide in the early modern period, most people lived at or near the subsistence level. To alleviate misery, Asians looked primarily to the family, Europeans to religious, civic, and charitable institutions. In many respects, however, people responded to their social needs in similar ways, as reflected, for example, in the resort of the desperate in virtually all societies to banditry. This was particularly so in areas where governmental power was weak and resentment of urban wealth was strong. Beyond the threads of common human experience, however, differing value systems, rooted in religion and tradition, shaped early modern societies into distinct entities.

Social Hierarchies

Traditional Asian civilizations were hierarchically based, marked not only by the uniquely Indian institution of caste but also by the status groupings associated with kingship, feudal-style relations, occupation, age, gender, and levels of literacy and learning. In general, apart from caste, the importance of the social hierarchy and the emphasis on achieving status through learning remains a distinctive aspect of Indian, Chinese, Korean, and Japanese civilizations to the present day. Perhaps more than any other characteristic, this emphasis on seeking status and advancement through education distinguishes them from most societies elsewhere. For many Asians, an individual's place in the hierarchy is still the most important single determinant of how to behave, and the proper observance of hierarchical rules remains the most basic means of preserving social and political harmony.

Southeast Asia has always been fundamentally different from China, Korea, India, and Japan, partly because of the influences of Buddhism and Islam, both of which stress equality, and partly because of the indigenous nature of Southeast Asian culture. Kingship and the hierarchies related to it, however, were common in Southeast Asia too.

Caste and the Social Order in India

In contrast to the merit system of China and its variants in Vietnam, Korea, and Japan, caste was decreed by birth

Aristocratic Behavior in Japan

The importance of hierarchical order in Japan is revealed in this 1615 decree of a shogun regulating the behavior of the feudal lords, or daimyo, *and their retainers, the* samurai. *Note the obligation to be aristocrats rather than mere soldiers.*

Literature, arms, archery, and horsemanship are to be the favorite pursuits. Literature first, and arms next to it, was the rule of the ancients. They must both be cultivated concurrently. . . . Drinking parties and gambling amusements must be kept within due bounds. . . . Offenders against the law are not to be harbored in the feudal domains. Law is the very foundation of ceremonial decorum and of social order. To infringe the law in the name of reason is as bad as to outrage reason in the name of the law. . . .

The distinction between lord and vassal, between superior and inferior, must be clearly marked by apparel. Vassals may not . . . wear silk stuffs. . . . Miscellaneous persons are not at their own pleasure to ride in palanquins. . . . Lately even sub-vassals and henchmen of no rank have taken to so riding. This is a flagrant impertinence. . . . The *samurai* throughout the provinces are to practice frugality. Those who are rich like to make a display, while those who are poor are ashamed of not being on a par with others. There is no influence so pernicious as this, and it must be kept strictly in check. . . .

Source: D. Lach, *Asia on the Eve of Europe's Expansion* (Englewood Cliffs, N.J.: Prentice-Hall, 1965), pp. 157–160 passim.

in India. Caste is a sociocultural practice with some religious concepts woven into it. Since it is also practiced by South Asian Muslims, Christians, and Buddhists (in Sri Lanka), it is clearly separable from Hinduism as a nonreligious system evolved later as a means of ordering an otherwise disordered society. The lack of a strong central state was accompanied by chronic disruption. Caste provided a system of social organization, a mutual-benefit society, a trade guild, and a sense of group identity. Ritual pollution and purity became the essence of caste, but its operative units were and are "subcastes," or *jatis*, commonly linked to occupation: potters, weavers, farmers, and so on. Each *jati* was and is endogamous (that is, it restricts marriage to fellow *jati* members), and members are forbidden to eat with or accept food or water from members of other *jatis*. One cannot change one's caste any more than one can change the place where one was born, although caste distinctions seem not to have been observed rigidly until relatively late in Indian history, well after the time of Harsha (seventh century A.D.). However, it has always been possible to escape from caste through religious devotion, again underlining the nonreligious nature of the caste system. The ascetic saddhu, or holy man, was beyond caste and honored by all, regardless of his earthly origins. Such mystics were, and like priests remain, far more numerous in India than elsewhere. South Asians have known for many centuries which *jatis* they were born into, but this is not really part of their religion, any more than genealogy, social class, or occupation are for Christians in the West.

Caste has remained a highly flexible system. Although individuals are born into a given *jati*, by sustained group effort the members of a *jati* can raise its status, often by adopting religious, dietary, and other practices of higher-status groups. This process is called "Sanskritization," from the use of Sanskrit rituals associated with the Brahmins. In addition, the power of group action can be a potent weapon, especially in politics. This is particularly characteristic of Asian societies, where the individual is important primarily as a member of a group, whether family, clan, caste, guild, or regional or linguistic division.

Caste also served the need for some form of hierarchical order in a region of complex divisions. As new religions, cultures, and languages came into India, no single one emerged as permanently dominant. In this bewildering context caste provided a sense of group identity, a means of support and defense, and a cultural vehicle as well, since each caste was necessarily local and shared a common language. Occupational associations for most subcastes meant that they also functioned as the equivalent of guilds and mutual-help societies, serving to arbitrate disputes. Caste was less a matter of religious than of social ordering, and the hierarchy it entailed was perhaps less important than the day-to-day support it gave and the social mobility it made possible for group members.

Social Hierarchy in East Asia

Despite the uniqueness of caste, Indian society conformed in other respects to the dominant Asian social model, of which China is the principal example. Under the empire in China, which lasted from the third century B.C. to 1911, power, responsibility, and status formed a pyramidal structure, with the emperor at the top as a truly absolute monarch. Below him were appointed officials in a series of grades: councillors, provincial governors, and generals, down to the district magistrates in some 2,000 counties, all of whom were selected from the ranks of the scholar-gentry who had passed the third level of the imperial examinations.

But this was not merely a political pyramid, and it did not act alone. The emperor and his officials had as their highest duty the setting of a good example, of "virtuous conduct." They were seen, and saw themselves, as fathers to the people, since the family was the basis of social order in all of Asia to an even greater extent than in most other societies. In theory, if the emperor and his officials behaved properly and responsibly, others in the social hierarchy would do so as well. In practice, social order—in Chinese parlance, the "Great Harmony"—was preserved primarily by the family system; this operated in much the same way in the rest of Asia. Younger people deferred to their elders, wives to husbands, and social "inferiors" to "superiors." This was the Confucian formula for human happiness and social harmony, but it was accepted in India, too, as well as in Korea and Japan as Confucianism spread.

Social Hierarchy in Europe

Europeans likewise attached a great deal of significance to a hierarchical society, which they believed was ordained by both divine and natural law. Civic and religious leaders alike insisted that the duty of each person was to accept his or her place in the social order, an ideal intended to promote social stability and domestic tranquillity. The hierarchical societies of early modern Europe were not, however, structured according to a class system in which groups were defined by similar levels of income and lifestyles, as in the modern West. In the early modern period the common basis of aristocratic power—landed wealth and the control of labor—was modified by the source of one's wealth, the antiquity of one's title, and the number of armed and paid retainers at one's disposal. A noble, though possibly not as rich as an urban businessman, outranked the latter in prestige—so much so that business families often tried to marry their daughters to landed aristocrats as a means of enhancing their social status.

The European system was divided, though less formally than in Asia, into *estates,* or social groups defined by degrees of fixed status. The aristocratic estate was generally expected to possess significant wealth in order to fulfill its social function as leader, exemplar, local ruler, maintainer of order, and reliever of the poor. Whereas in Asia many of these functions resided primarily with the family, in Europe—and among the Aztecs in Mexico—they were largely the province of the aristocracy. It was the duty of the lower orders, both religious and political, to accept the rule of the upper, though in reality there was often resentment and occasionally rebellion. Good behavior demanded deference to superiors, courtesy to equals, and kindness to inferiors. More was expected of, but also tolerated from, the higher orders, where gentility was supposed to entail a combination of birth and virtue.

There are some parallels between social hierarchy in the East and the West, including the importance attached to the idea that status entailed responsibility. Europeans too used the analogy of paternal authority to justify monarchical power, especially in the 1600s, but never to the same degree as in Asia, where the family exercised a greater role in the maintenance of social order. In the West the function of the extended family in this regard declined in the early modern period as the emphasis gradually shifted to the nuclear family on the one hand and the state on the other. Both Europeans and Asians tried to reinforce the social hierarchy by reserving distinctive styles of dress for the upper orders.

In Europe social distinctions were also reflected in numerous other ways, such as the number of a noble's retainers or clients or the number of coaches in his procession. Even funerals were distinctive pageants designed to reflect the social status of the deceased and their families.

The European Aristocracy

Prior to the mid-sixteenth century, the aristocracy generally improved its social position and became more involved in public affairs at the local or state level. Most nobility strove to acquire more land, usually by strategic marriages, or greater status, normally by obtaining more elevated titles of nobility. To meet the demand for status, titles such as duke, marquess, and viscount were created, and new chivalric orders, including the Knights of the Garter in England and the Order of the Golden Fleece in Burgundy, were founded. New nobles were usually recruited from the landed gentry rather than the bourgeoisie, especially in France and England. On the Continent an administrative aristocracy developed in the early modern period. In France and Milan, for example, officials acquired aristocratic privileges and became known as the nobility of the robe, after their gown of office.

Conditions among the gentry varied widely. Whereas the more successful among them could be as wealthy and powerful as some nobles, others, especially on the Continent, sometimes turned to banditry to improve their sagging fortunes. A notorious gang of English robbers followed the lead of two lesser aristocrats, Sir William Bussy and Sir John de Colseby, while in France similar groups tried unsuccessfully in 1560 to end the political dominance of the Guise family, the head of which, the duke of Guise, was the king's chief adviser. Disaffected knights often supported reform movements, including Lutheranism in Germany and Calvinism in France, hoping to better their position.

Beginning in the mid-sixteenth century, the aristocracy entered a period of difficulty. Incomes from landed estates did not keep pace with excessive expenditures on elaborate dress, rich food, fine jewelry, lavish hospitality, and luxurious buildings. Raising funds through the sale of lands only reduced the income from rents. Nor did rents keep pace with the rising cost of living due to inflation, especially since many rents were fixed by custom, and in some areas tenants held long-term leases. The political position of the aristocracy was further undermined by the growing reliance of governments on talent rather than rank, though no Western country came close to establishing a meritocracy such as existed in China.

The prestige of the older aristocracy was harmed when sovereigns in France, Spain, and England sold titles to raise funds and accommodate the demand for status among newly wealthy elites. The upper aristocracy normally suffered more from these problems than the lower; in England much of the lower aristocracy, or gentry, improved its position in this period through careful land management, advantageous marriages, and the purchase of lands from the monasteries dissolved during the Reformation.

Urban Society

The social eminence of urban merchants, or patricians, stemmed from their involvement with long-distance trade, their ownership of city property, and their control of town government. Patricians intermarried to preserve the exclusiveness of their privileges, though some married off their daughters to aristocrats merely to acquire the unique prestige that went with ownership of the land. Townsfolk treated the patricians as a noble class, particularly in republican Venice, where the absence of a monarch or a landed aristocracy elevated their status. In the Netherlands and the German states too the wealthy patricians were virtually a noble class, though their supremacy was disputed by the landed nobility.

In contrast to the patricians, the guildsmen continued, as in the medieval era, to concern themselves primarily with local production and services. In most towns they had considerably less influence than the patricians but were better off than the artisans and unskilled workers, who were poorly organized and had little voice in town government. Only by joining with the guildsmen could the artisans and laborers bring about change. Another urban

An arranged marriage, in this instance between the son of a financially strapped nobleman and the daughter of a wealthy merchant hungry for social prestige, is the subject of one of the scenes from William Hogarth's series of six paintings titled *Marriage à la Mode* (1744–1745). [National Gallery, London]

group, the lawyers, found their services in increased demand as commerce expanded, land transactions became more complex, and landowners sought ways to evade the fiscal payments that were still part of feudal land tenure. Together these middling and upper urban groups began insisting upon a greater share of political power in early modern Europe, particularly in France and England, where their demands contributed to the outbreak of civil war in both countries in the 1640s.

Marriage and the Family

The Family in Asia

The Asian family was a hierarchical structure in which group welfare took precedence over individual preferences. The father was like a little emperor, with absolute power but also with absolute responsibility. Filial obedience was the cardinal Asian virtue; loyalty and obligation to parents and elders was rigid and inflexible, but it produced a tight-knit unit. In family relations age was the major determinant. Three generations commonly lived under one roof, and the grandfather was thus the dominant figure, although his place might be taken after his death by his widow. Younger sons were subject to their older brothers, wives and sisters to their husbands and brothers, and all to the eldest male. Individual initiative other than by the patriarch was not tolerated; the welfare of the family as he interpreted it came first, and all decisions were accordingly made by the elder members.

A new Asian bride was the servant of the husband's family and was often victimized by a tyrannical mother-in-law. More so than in the West, Asian girls could be married against their wishes and had little or no right of refusal—except suicide. An entire genre of Asian stories was devoted to this theme. In a typical story, an unwilling bride is carried in an enclosed cart or sedan chair to her new husband's family; when the curtains are opened, she is found to have killed herself. Marriage was seen as a business arrangement between families, not as an individual choice or a love match. In later centuries the custom of foot-binding spread through the Chinese population, inflicting dreadful pain on growing girls and emphasizing their role as erotic playthings while reducing them to a hobble that effectively kept them at home. About the same period, the practice of purdah, the veiling and sequestering of women, spread with the Muslim conquerors even through Hindu northern India.

Few Asians questioned the family hierarchy. The family operated as a collective entity; each member was both socially and legally responsible for the behavior of all other members. Collective responsibility, family pride, and the shame of family disgrace are still credited for the relatively low rate of crime in much of Asia. Government from higher levels was far less necessary. Asian societies have been called self-regulating, and to a very large extent that is true. The price of this has been the sacrifice of individual initiative, independence, and self-fulfillment so prized by the modern West and now increasingly attractive in many parts of modern Asia.

Individuals moved through life only as members of families, as did members of larger groups such as castes, clans, or guilds. Yet there was a surprising amount of vertical mobility in Chinese society. Judging from the numerous biographies of successful examination candidates, as many as a third of the gentry group in each generation represented new blood. In Asian countries families and sometimes villages, clans, or guilds squeezed their resources to support promising boys through the lengthy education needed for entry to the scholarly ranks, in effect as their representative and as one who could bring prestige and profit.

The larger society offered few support mechanisms. Without a family or descendants to care for them, the sick, the poor, and the elderly could not survive. In the Hindu and Buddhist countries minimal shelter and food were available to all at temples, as they still are, but in all of Asia the production of offspring, especially sons, was the overriding goal for simple self-preservation. People who did well in life were bound to help not only siblings but also uncles, aunts, cousins, and their families.

The bonds of obligation and collective responsibility reached throughout the extended family, which in Asia included all parental and maternal relatives, or at least those with whom a given nuclear family was in touch. Each Asian society had a complex variety of name designations for each of these graded kin relationships; one did not refer merely to "brother," "sister," "uncle," "aunt," or "grandmother" but to elder or younger brother, first, second, or third paternal aunt, maternal grandfather, and so on. This extended network of relationships put a heavy burden on individuals, but also provided mutual support.

The Family in Europe

Extended family linkages were important in Europe as well at the level of the aristocracy, where patterns of ownership, inheritance, and status were complex. Below this level the conjugal or nuclear family was a more or less self-contained unit. Apart from eastern Europe, most couples married late, in their mid-twenties, by which time they were usually in a position to find living quarters and establish their own households. A widowed parent might subsequently take up residence with a married child, in contrast with the Asian practice of newlyweds moving in with the bridegroom's parents. The prevalence of the nuclear family pattern at the lower social levels was disadvantageous in the sense that mistreated spouses received less kin support, and smaller family units were more vulnerable to economic hardship if a spouse became unemployed.

The large family network common in Asia provided an important support system that commoners in the West often lacked. Conversely, however, the smaller family units in the West presumably made it easier for many couples to make the personal adjustments necessary for a successful marriage without the intervention of relatives and in-laws.

The nature of the Western family underwent a significant change in the sixteenth and seventeenth centuries, particularly among the aristocracy. The late medieval aristocratic family, in return for loyalty and personal attendance by its retainers and servants, provided patronage and hospitality. The aristocratic household was large because it included not only family members and relatives but also a collection of servants and retainers that might number in the hundreds. The importance of preserving the family's status and property led to the practice of the arranged marriage. Often a young person had no choice in the determination of a partner, for matrimony was a collective decision of the family and kin in which the key issues were property and power. Some parents allowed their children a veto over the proposed spouse, and occasionally headstrong young people defied the system by eloping, but only at the risk of losing their inheritance. Young men's acceptance of the arranged marriage was aided by the knowledge that once an heir was born, mistresses could be enjoyed. There was a double standard, however, for wives were denied such freedom and were expected to remain sexually loyal to their husbands.

Daughters were often an economic liability among the propertied classes since a dowry had to be provided for marriage; in return, the groom's father guaranteed the bride an annuity if her husband died before she did. As heirs and potential fathers of future heirs, firstborn sons usually married earlier than other young men. In sixteenth-century England men normally wed at about age 28, but aristocratic heirs typically married at 22 in order to facilitate property settlements and enhance the prospects of providing a male heir in the next generation. Because a younger son had considerably less property and wealth than his elder brother, who benefited from the practice of primogeniture, he faced a decline in social position unless he could find a wealthy bride.

About the middle of the sixteenth century the nature of the family began to change among the upper social orders. On the one hand, more significance was attached to the nuclear core (parents and children), and on the other, affection between spouses apparently became more important as a determinant of family relationships. The decline of kinship dominance is manifested in both decreasing hospitality and the diminishing sense of kin responsibility for individual acts. As states such as France, Spain, and England expanded their control of justice, protection, and the preservation of property, the responsibility for social control shifted from kin to state. Simultaneously, Protestantism increased the significance of the nuclear family by stressing marital affection and by treating the family as a miniature parish, with distinct religious responsibilities in

"Surplus" Daughters

In the eyes of both Asians and Europeans, daughters were much less desirable than sons. To avoid the expense of providing dowries, Catholic parents sometimes sought to dispose of "surplus" daughters by coercing them into becoming nuns. Some clergymen strongly protested this practice.

You have no right to dispose of your children by forcing a vocation on them. . . . It would cost money to establish this daughter: reason enough to consecrate her as a nun. . . . But she has no trace of religious calling: the present state of your finances is calling enough for her. . . . And so the victim is led to the temple, hands and feet tied: by which I mean against her will, dumb with fear and awe of a father whom she has always honored. Such murderous fathers are far from imitating Abraham . . . who was ready to sacrifice his son to God: instead they sacrifice their children to their own estate and to their own cupidity.

Source: L. Bourdaloue, *Œuvres complètes*, in *Collection intégrale et universelle des orateurs sacres*, vol. 15 (Paris, 1845), cols. 374 ff.; English translation in *Not in God's Image*, ed. J. O'Faolain and L. Martines (New York: Harper Torchbooks, 1973), p. 270.

instruction and worship. These changes brought about a greater and greater divergence from the Asian model and its associated lack of state control.

In contrast to the modern nuclear family, patriarchal authority was reinforced. The Renaissance state supported the domination of the husband-father on the grounds that his authority was analogous to that of a sovereign over his subjects. The decline of kinship could increase the wife's subordination to her husband by leaving her more exposed to exploitation in the nuclear family. Capitalizing on this, the state relied on husbands to keep their wives law-abiding. Yet the development of the nuclear family could also facilitate better relations between spouses by providing them with more time to be alone, away from the prying eyes of relatives, retainers, and servants.

Marriage in Asia

In the societies of early modern Asia marital patterns were similar in many ways to those in Europe, particularly with respect to the arranged marriage, the premium placed on sons, and the use of dowries, although considerably less so in areas such as divorce and remarriage. In Asia, however, the average age at marriage was lower than in the West—approximately 21 for males and 17 for females in China; 16 and 14, respectively, in India; and 20 and 16 in Japan and Southeast Asia.

Except for parts of Southeast Asia and a small region of South India, marriage was and remains patrilocal; that is, the bride, who was almost invariably recruited from another village to avoid inbreeding, left her family and became a member of her husband's family, where she was the lowest-status member until she had borne a son. She might visit her parents occasionally, but she was lost to them as a family member and cost them heavily in dowry. Girls were often loved as much as boys, but on practical grounds they were of far less value, although they were desirable domestic helpers to their mothers. Sons were essential for family continuity and security. Since life was an uncertain business and death rates were high, especially in the early years of life, most families tried to produce more than one son. Girls might be sold in hard times as servants or concubines in rich households.

The childless family was truly bankrupt and might even pay relatively large sums to acquire a son by adoption. A wife who failed to produce a son after a reasonable amount of time was commonly returned to her parents as useless, for the primary purpose of marriage was perpetuation of the male line. It was not understood until quite recently that the sex of a child is determined by the father or that childlessness may result as often from male as from female sterility. In time, however, most women became willing and even enthusiastic members of their husbands' families, passing on these attitudes to their children. Eventually they might become household heads and oldest survivors, thereby sometimes achieving considerable power.

All members of the society regarded marriage as a contract between families for the furthering of their interests. Virtually all marriages were arranged by the families, usually through a go-between. Bride and groom had usually not met before their wedding. Sometimes they might be allowed to express preferences, although these might be overruled in the family interest. Compatibility was rarely considered, and love marriages were extremely rare, although affection might grow in time.

There was a similar willingness to suppress individual wishes among the Incas of South America, where state officials chose mates for young people slow to act on their own. At times the Incas arranged mass marriages. The rulers themselves could marry only their sisters, making the royal family a product of considerable inbreeding.

Divorce in Asia and Europe

Divorce was rare in Asia, difficult but not impossible. Unlike the West, remarriage was even more difficult, and that knowledge probably helped people try harder to make their marriages work. It doubtless helped too that romantic expectations were not as high as in the modern West. People were trained to put individual wants second to family interest. Biographies, memoirs, popular literature, and legal records bear out that most marriages were successful on these terms and that husbands and wives valued and even loved each other and worked together in the family unit to reproduce the dominant social pattern. Divorce was relatively rare in the Islamic world as well.

There was no divorce in the modern sense in the medieval West since the canon law of the Catholic church deemed marriage an unbreakable sacrament. If the existence of an impediment or bar to a marriage could be demonstrated, the marriage could be annulled, but any children resulting from the union were thereby made illegitimate. Annulments were granted in such cases as marriage to relatives or in-laws, impotence, or forced marriage. The only other alternative, separation, did not bastardize the children, but neither did it leave the spouses free to remarry.

The Reformation reduced the grounds for annulment but established divorce in the modern sense only in certain geographic areas, including Geneva. Catholic states retained the medieval canon law, with its absolute prohibition of divorce until modern times, apart from a brief period during the age of the French Revolution and Napoleon. Among Europe's poor, some unhappy spouses ran away; others committed bigamy. From the medieval period into the nineteenth century a dissatisfied husband in England occasionally put a halter around his wife's neck, took her to the local cattle market, and sold her. The practice underscored the notion that a wife was the property of her husband, although common law never recognized this. In rural Greece well into the twentieth century, a bride might simply be returned to her family if she was discovered or believed to have lost her virginity before marriage.

Marriage and the Family in Africa

Like the Muslims, Aztecs, and Incas, many African tribes practiced polygamy. A man demonstrated his wealth by having several wives, although in reality women, who typically worked beside men, produced so much by their labor that they virtually supported themselves. The perception of wealth was derived from the fact that a man had to pay "bridewealth"—usually livestock—to a woman's father in order to marry her. As in western Europe, men married relatively late, usually about the age of 30, though brides were typically in their late teens. A new wife would be added at fairly regular intervals of a year or two, and because of the importance attached to fertility, the result was normally a large family.

The high birthrate helped to offset the large number of deaths of infants and children and also ensured support for parents in their old age, an ideal no less valued in Asia. Like the early Hebrews, many Africans accepted the practice of leviratic marriage, by which the brother of a deceased man married the widow. In the African family no function was more important for the wife than bearing children, but beyond that she exercised a critical role in providing the food supply and in some instances even conducting local and regional trade.

Throughout the early modern world, the family was the basic unit of social organization. The Western European aristocracy began to distinguish itself in this period by moving away from the extended family, which remained common in Asia and Africa, toward the conjugal or nuclear family, which was probably already the norm among the lower social orders in Europe. Although family structures varied substantially between Muslims and some Africans and Amerindians, with their polygamous marriages, and Asia and Europe, where monogamy prevailed, all societies valued children for a variety of reasons, including, among the lower orders especially, their function as laborers and eventually as providers for elderly parents. Protestant Europe, by establishing the principle of divorce as we now understand it, planted the seeds for the eventual weakening of the family as the fundamental social unit.

The Status of Women

Although many women might have been powers within their families, their role in general was highly subordinate. There is no question that theirs was a male-dominated world and that their chief claim to status was as producers of sons. They were less valued from birth virtually everywhere. Females were subject first to their fathers and brothers, then to their husbands and their husbands' male relatives.

Women in Asia

Unlike their counterparts in the West, Asian widows were not supposed to remarry or even to have male friends. Given the high death rate and the unpredictable fortunes of life, many women—often no more than girls—were thus condemned to celibacy, loneliness, and poverty for most of their lives. "Chaste widows" were praised, and though some managed a little life of their own, most conformed to the expected model and suffered. Some widows committed suicide in China and in the Islamic world; this was carried to its extreme in India, where it often came to be expected among the higher castes. Hindu funeral practice includes the burning of the corpse; a surviving widow was supposed to throw herself on her husband's funeral pyre, a ritual known as *sati* (suttee). Perhaps as many as one-fifth of all childless Indian upper-caste widows actually sacrificed themselves in this way.

As in the West, in hard times female infants might be killed soon after birth so that the rest of the family might survive; Asian female babies could also be sold as servants or potential concubines. The selling of children seems especially heartless, but such a girl might have a better life as a slave-servant or concubine in a wealthy household than starving to death with her own family. Women were rarely given any formal education, and although some acquired it, they were primarily instructed by their mothers and mothers-in-law in how to be good, subservient wives, mothers, and daughters-in-law.

Power within the family brought women rewards that were especially important in this family-centered society. Their key role in ensuring family continuity brought much satisfaction. In most families women, as the chief raisers of children, shaped the future. More directly, they managed most families' finances, as they still do in Asia. Some women achieved public prominence as writers, reigning empresses, and powers behind the throne as imperial consorts or concubines. In India, China, and Southeast Asia, as in England and Scotland, a few women became rulers in their own right, but only in India could one find women who were brilliant generals and cavalry fighters, such as the Rani of Jhansi. Admittedly, these were a tiny handful within Asia and Europe as a whole. In East and West alike, the crucial role of women in what mattered most—the family, its well-being, and its perpetuation—was, within clear status limits, recognized. Among the peasantry, the overwhelming mass of the population, women played a crucial role in helping with the agricultural labor and were usually the major workers in cottage industries, producing handicraft goods for sale or barter. Upper-class women lived a generally idle life and commonly turned their children over to nurses or tutors.

It remained for the twentieth century, spurred by Western influence, to discourage the traditional subjugation of women in Asia and begin the movement toward equality, or at least more equitable treatment. Southeast Asia has traditionally been freer of sex discrimination than India, China, Korea, or Japan, and most of its regional cultures included some matrilocal marriage, female control and inheritance of property, and female dominance within the family. In the rest of Asia the traditional patterns were formed 4,000 years ago and persisted largely unchanged until this century. (See Chapters 38 and 39.)

In this court scene, attributed to Ku Kai-chih (A.D. 344–406), an instructress is writing down directions for her pupils, ladies of the court. In China, as elsewhere, court ladies were expected to be literate and accomplished in several arts. [Trustees of the British Museum]

Women in the Middle East and Africa

In the Islamic societies of the Middle East and North Africa, women were discouraged from participating in activities outside the home by the conviction that females should be secluded as well as veiled. The latter practice was obviously a practical way of enforcing anonymity on them when they did appear in public. Women who engaged in trade or educational pursuits were rare exceptions. As in Asian cultures, the woman's primary task was to marry and raise children, especially boys.

Religion was used, as in the West, to legitimate the subordination of women. This point was succinctly stated by a seventeenth-century Iranian theologian, who asserted that a wife's principal spiritual duty was subservience to her husband: "A wife must obey her husband, never disobey his commands, never leave the house without his permission." As early as the 1200s Islamic society was characterized by a separate social life for men and women, though a small number of women were sometimes able to exert political power in both Ottoman Turkey and Safavid Iran.

In sub-Saharan Africa some tribal societies accorded prominent roles to women. In contrast to the Western world, West African tribes such as the Igbo and Yoruba in Nigeria were organized on a "dual sex" system, in which each sex governed its own affairs at all levels of society. One group of Igbo was ruled by dual monarchs, one female and the other male, each with its own advisory group. The female monarch, or *omu* (literally "mother"), was different from a queen in the Western sense, for she was neither the king's wife nor the reigning daughter of a deceased king who had no male heir. The *omu* represented all women and had special responsibility for the marketplace. Igbo women also had their own organizations at the village level, which functioned as political pressure groups.

Although most African societies were dominated by men, there were important exceptions. Women, for instance, could be chiefs among some of the tribes of West Africa. A number of other West African tribes followed the custom of female descent, by which the throne descended not to the king's son but to the son of his sister. In precolonial African societies, which had no permanent political structure, important matters were routinely decided by a meeting of the heads of households, but because women rarely exercised this responsibility, they were not prominent in making community decisions.

The subordinate role of most African women was underscored by the predominance of patrilineal and patrilocal customs, which traced lineage through the male line and required brides to live in the villages of their husbands. There were exceptions, such as the Senufo of West Africa, whose wives could remain in their native villages and whose divorced women retained custody of the children because the latter belonged to the maternal kin. Generally, however, the traditional African societies treated women as the economic and social dependents of males, as elsewhere.

Women in Europe

In late medieval Europe aristocratic women were regarded largely as bearers of children, sexual companions, and comrades in social functions. Few administered family estates or raised their own children, a task left to nurses and tutors. Nurturing an infant was turned over to a wet nurse, typically a peasant woman hired for the occasion and often blamed for subsequent medical or psychological problems. Wet nursing freed the mother from the inconvenience of nighttime feeding and did not interrupt her social engagements, but the practice largely died out in the 1700s.

Aristocratic women had relatively little to occupy their time apart from such leisurely pursuits as reading, social visits, card playing, and theatergoing, especially since many had stewards to run their households as well as nurses and tutors to care for their children. However, women of the landed gentry often played a major role in the household economy and managed the family estates when their husbands were away. Because of her social status, a gentlewoman or a merchant's wife had little choice of occupation, for manual labor was incompatible with her position, and the professions were closed to women. Some became ladies-in-waiting to aristocratic women, some governesses of children, and a few, such as the English dramatist Aphra Behn (c.1640–1689), authors. Two aristocratic English women—Margaret Cavendish, duchess of Newcastle, and Anne, Viscountess Conway—wrote about the new science, and Katherine Boyle, the sister of the chemist Robert Boyle, took an active part in it. Catholics, of course, had the option of joining a convent or a teaching order.

Near the lower levels of society, the wives of artisans and peasants had to join in their husbands' labor in order to survive, since most Europeans lived at or near subsistence. As in Asia, Africa, and the Americas, peasant women engaged in virtually every aspect of farming from plowing and spreading manure to reaping and threshing, and also handled the household chores and cared for any poultry or dairy animals. In both urban and rural areas many wives supplemented the family income by weaving or other side employments, occasionally even prostitution.

Late medieval craft guilds allowed masters' wives to share in their work, and they often carried on the business when the men died. Although women had been admitted to the guilds, the new forms of business organization were almost exclusively male, and there was mounting hostility to women in the trades because they worked for lower pay. Apart from the cloth industry, women were being pushed out of many trades, such as brewing, at one time largely a female preserve. In England men were even moving into the occupation of midwife. Women could practice folk medicine and compete with barber-surgeons, but they were generally excluded from the profession of physician as well as attorney and minister. Although women found it increasingly difficult to compete for jobs in most trades, they found employment in the cottage industry concerned with cloth manufacturing, but the pay was poor and the hours long. Life was also difficult for single women. Some worked in the coal and iron mines, where they typically received lower wages than their male peers. Most single women earned their living by spinning cloth, a practice that gave rise to the term *spinster* for an unmarried woman.

In certain respects the legal position of European women declined in the late medieval period. Frenchwomen could no longer participate in public affairs, testify before various courts, or even act in place of an absentee or insane husband. Women in Saxony and wives in England were prohibited from undertaking legal actions; an English wife had to be represented by her husband, while a Hamburg statute of 1603 stipulated that "women can neither bring a matter up before the court nor transfer or hand over property without a guardian." Bavarian law prohibited a woman from selling anything without her husband's consent, though beginning in 1616 an exception was made for goods specified for her personal use. In England a husband enjoyed absolute control over his wife's personal property and could profit by leasing her real estate to others. In the seventeenth century, however, marriage contracts guaranteed the wife "pin money" for her personal expenses, and the courts increasingly recognized the existence of her "separate estate," a handy device if her husband was sued for bankruptcy. French courts similarly began to demonstrate greater concern for a wife's rights, including control over her dowry. A French wife whose husband mismanaged her property could win a legal separation, the most she could expect in a society without divorce. By the eighteenth century Russian noblewomen and the wives of artisans and merchants became the heads of their households when their husbands died, although only in urban areas. Legally, then, the decline in women's rights bottomed out in Europe in the 1500s and improved slowly in the seventeenth and eighteenth centuries.

Sexual Customs

Asian women were expected to be modest and chaste. They seldom appeared in public, and any open display of affection with their spouses was taboo. At the same time, the elite Asian cultures, unlike those in the West, are famous for their erotic literature and art and for the development of a courtesan (prostitute) tradition older than any other living civilization. The geisha tradition of Japan and its original, the "singsong" or "flower boat" women of China, are well known, as is the cult of ritual sex among Indian temple priestesses and the orgies of Tantric Buddhism. Explicit portrayals of sex appear in Indian art, and the classic Indian sex manual, the *Kamasutra*, is world famous. But this behavior was reserved for the privileged few.

In contrast to the Judeo-Christian West, India, Tibet, and parts of Southeast Asia had a religious tradition in which sex was used as ritual, in some ways rather like the ancient cult of Dionysus in classical Greece. Representations of sex in Indian sculpture and painting use gods and goddesses as subjects, not ordinary mortals, and celebrate the divine life force, creation. Tantric Buddhist and some Hindu temple sex rites had the same purpose. Western art, beginning in the Renaissance, was less explicit than Indian art but depicted sensuous nudes in the guise of classical deities. All of this—the pleasures of the elite dallying with their concubines, singsong girls, erotic pictures, and the joys of Islamic rulers in their harems—was beyond the experience of the lower social orders, although at least in the West they might find an outlet for their sexual desires in traditional festivals, such as the May Day celebrations, when promiscuous behavior was reportedly common.

A relationship between sex and religious ritual existed in some African societies, especially in connection with puberty rites. The Kikuyu, who lived in the region of Mount Kenya, not only circumcised boys as part of such rites but also removed the clitoris from girls. This practice is still widespread in eastern Africa today. In both cases the act of cutting symbolized the rite of passage into adulthood. In the case of the Masai, however, puberty initiation for girls involved elongating the labia by massage and teaching the girls movements to enhance their sexual performance.

European attitudes toward sex were generally determined by the teachings of the church, although these were often merely a veneer imposed on centuries of folk custom. For the masses of East and West, sex appears to have been largely oriented toward procreation and usually confined officially to marriage or engagement, although Japanese, Southeast Asian, and Polynesian young people of both sexes were encouraged to experiment with sex before marriage. In the eyes of the medieval Christian church, sexual relations were acceptable only within marriage and were intended primarily for procreation. Little attention was attached to love in a sexual context, and lust was condemned.

During the Reformation, Protestants began to treat love and procreation as related and to regard sexual pleasure in marriage as a legitimate expression of the conjugal relationship. Among the propertied orders, sexual relations before marriage were regarded with disapproval, largely because of the importance of bearing a legitimate heir. Because a woman was regarded as the sexual property of a man, her value diminished if she had been "used" by another man. Despite the church's official disapproval, males of the propertied elite frequently engaged in premarital sex, normally with women from professional or merchant backgrounds whose families had fallen on hard times. The same freedom did not extend to women of their rank. A woman's honor was based on her reputation for chastity, a man's on his word. A wife who committed adultery insulted not only her husband's virility but also his ability to govern her, which resulted in dishonor. In this respect the elites of East and West shared the acceptance of a double standard that enhanced male dominance.

Among the lower orders in Europe, pressure for premarital sex was created by the late ages at which people wed—typically in their upper twenties. Late marriage helped hold down population growth, but figures for illegitimacy indicate relatively little sexual activity apart from engaged and married couples, probably due to religious and socioeconomic pressure. Infanticide may also have contributed to low bastardy levels. The bastardy rate was 3 percent in rural England in the 1590s and 2 percent at Frankfurt in the early 1700s. In contrast, there was considerable sexual activity by engaged couples. Approximately 21 percent of English brides were pregnant at their weddings in the late sixteenth century.

Because the Catholic church considered the sexual act primarily procreative, it regarded most attempts at contraception as mortal sin. By the sixteenth century, however, many Catholics accepted *coitus reservatus*—withdrawal before ejaculation—as a permissible technique for the economically destitute, and people did use a variety of physical contraceptives. The church condemned *coitus interruptus*—ejaculation outside the vagina—as unnatural on biblical grounds.

In Protestant lands religious leaders discouraged birth control methods, believing they were contrary to the biblical command to be fruitful and multiply. Instead, they argued, children should be accepted as blessings from God, a means to maintain the commonwealth and church, and the means for women to recover the honor lost when Eve disobeyed God.

For women with unwanted pregnancies, medical manuals provided information on how to induce an abortion. Interest in the use of birth control methods was undoubtedly strong among women who wanted relief from the repeated cycle of pregnancies that often brought death. In the sixteenth and seventeenth centuries, perhaps one out of every ten pregnancies ended in the mother's death, and 30 to 50 percent of all children died before the age of 5. In France as many as 30 percent were dead before their first birthday.

Because abortion could be so dangerous to the mother, infanticide was a popular alternative, particularly since it could be disguised as accidental "overlaying" or suffocation. The problem was so prevalent that in 1784 Austria made it illegal for parents to take children under 5 into bed with them. The punishment for infanticide was often harsh; in the German town of Bamberg a convicted person was drowned or buried alive and speared. Infanticide figures for Renaissance Florence indicate that more girls than boys died, presumably reflecting the greater value placed on males, though in eighteenth-century Paris there was no significant discrepancy among victims.

Many parents, already victims of poverty, simply opted to abandon their children in the streets. More foundling hospitals were built to deal with the problem. Milan and Venice had established theirs in the medieval period, and new ones were built in Florence (1445), Paris (1670), London (1739), and St. Petersburg, where two former palaces of the nobility were used to house the children. The availability of the houses seems to have encouraged more parents to abandon their infants. In the 1770s and 1780s the number of children abandoned in Paris reached 4,500 per year, more than double the number at the beginning of the century. By the 1770s more than one out of every five children baptized in Paris had been abandoned. Conditions were so bad in these homes that at times no more than 5 percent of the infants admitted in Paris survived to adulthood.

Catholic and Protestant leaders alike denounced homosexuality. In England the Tudor Parliaments of the sixteenth century made it a capital offense, though the statutes seem not to have been enforced. Magistrates there were more concerned with heterosexual intercourse outside marriage because it could lead to illegitimate children and thus pose a financial burden on the community. Homosexuals were found in the court of Elizabeth I, and especially in that of her successor, James I, himself a homosexual. Homosexuality was common in secondary schools, where boys often shared beds, and in universities. It was probably also common among servants and in tiny rural communities where access to persons of the opposite sex was severely restricted. In London there were homosexual prostitutes as well as "molly houses" where homosexuals gathered for entertainment. Although Islamic religious writings typically disapproved of homosexuality, the practice itself was generally treated with indifference.

By the 1600s organized prostitution was common in European cities such as Paris, Berlin, and Toledo, often with the tacit acceptance of authorities. In Seville brothel keepers and prostitutes were licensed by the city, which even leased houses for this purpose. Church officials tried to close down the brothels, but the city fathers would do no more than require the prostitutes to attend church on Sundays and holy days. In 1676 Cambridge had 13 brothels catering largely to the university community. Many women drawn into a life of prostitution were economically destitute, including unwed mothers and cast-off mistresses, while others opted for it in preference to a 14- to 16-hour day as a seamstress. Some domestics as well were forced out of service and into prostitution when their employers got them pregnant. Other prostitutes were

Brothels such as this one, which catered to the aristocracy, became commonplace in early modern Europe. Note that the nobleman is casually giving alms to a syphilitic beggar. This drawing by Thomas Rowlandson is titled *Charity Covereth a Multitude of Sins*. [Trustees of the British Museum]

wives from poor families. Prostitution was often a criminal offense, for which women were typically pilloried, flogged, imprisoned, and sometimes expelled from a city, though usually to little effect. Nor were punitive measures effective against operators of houses of prostitution.

The late ages at marriage as well as the proximity of family members in small houses tempted some Europeans to commit incest. Apprenticing male children and placing girls in other homes as servants were safety valves, but incest was still sufficiently common to trouble church authorities. Perpetrators caught in the act were usually punished by shaming (public penance), as in the case of other sexual offenses. Usually confined to the lower orders, shaming typically required the offender to appear before the local congregation clad only in a white sheet and to stand in a public place or ride through town in a cart with a sign proclaiming the offense.

Parents of bastards were treated more harshly because their misdeed was a potential burden on the community's funds; such persons were regularly stripped to the waist, whipped, and placed in the stocks. In keeping with the double standard of the age, mothers of bastards were often subjected to punishment while the fathers sometimes escaped, although efforts were made to hold fathers fiscally responsible for their illegitimate children. Whether suffering from the double standard or undergoing frequent pregnancies, sexual experience for the early modern woman was fraught with hazard and anxiety and was potentially life-threatening as well.

The dangers sexual intercourse posed to a woman were real whether she lived in Europe, Asia, Africa, or the Americas. Nevertheless, sex was widely valued as the means for procreation. The way in which sex was viewed varied considerably, depending especially on religious traditions. Whereas Roman Catholicism, for instance, exalted the celibate life, sexual elements were incorporated into religious ritual in parts of Africa, India, Tibet, and Southeast Asia, while Hindu elites embraced concubines and their Muslim counterparts had harems. Although all societies embraced sex as a life force, for procreative purposes, there was considerable disagreement as to whether it should properly serve as a vehicle for pleasure or religious expression.

Education, Literacy, and the Printed Word

Learning in Asia

Respect for learning was universal in Asia. Written texts in particular or even scraps of paper with writing on them were to be treated reverently and preserved. This was partly due to the importance of the philosophical, moral, and religious texts that played so great a part in each Asian cultural tradition but partly also because literacy and learning were the surest and most prestigious paths to worldly success. In the cultures where religion was more centrally important than in China, especially in India and Buddhist Southeast Asia, literacy and learning also led to an honored status as priest or monk; such persons were second only to the ruler in the status hierarchy. The Indian Brahmin combined the role of scholar and priest, while in Buddhist countries the monkhood has remained the most honorable calling of all. Scholars, priests, and monks were exempt from manual labor, whereas in Europe many clergymen farmed to make ends meet, and monastic labor was often a deliberate part of the ascetic regime. In East and West alike, lip service was paid to the worth and importance of peasant labor and agriculture, but the rewards and status went to people who had risen above the necessity of physical work. In Asia even kings and emperors deferred to the learned holy man or the upright scholar.

Freedom from manual labor for the educated was marked by dress, lifestyle, and the deference of others. In Europe and Asia alike, it was the duty of the rest of society to support monks and priests by regular donations and alms and to finance their temples and rituals. Their activities were connected with ordinary life, including weddings, namings of children, funerals, and religious festivals. Officials, drawn from the ranks of the learned, also wore distinctive clothing and enjoyed special privileges, including exemption from corporal punishment. Especially in China, the masses treated them with respect in deference to their awesome authority as the direct representatives of the emperor. The Chinese gentry, from among whom officials were selected, wore the long blue scholar's gown, hem touching the ground and loose floppy sleeves hanging from the arms. Since no physical exertion could be performed in such a garment, it was in effect a badge of their freedom from manual labor. The scholar-gentry also frequently let their fingernails grow to extreme length, sometimes protecting them with special covers, to make the same point.

There were three grades of gentry, reflecting the three levels of the examination system. Only members who had passed the third level could be selected as officials, but those in the two lower grades were also recognized as educated men and followed gentry lifestyles and dress. Many of them served as teachers of the next generation of candidates, running both private and government-financed schools where Chinese boys learned their characters and worked their way through the Confucian classics under stern discipline. Most gentry did not become officials but formed an unofficial local elite, serving as teachers, arbiters of disputes, and managers of local enterprises, deferred to by all below them.

Merchants too needed at least some literacy in all Asian cultures, especially since in most of them merchants also had to deal with the state and the official bureaucracy. In any case, they had to keep records and accounts and communicate over long distances. Some of them also acquired a good deal of classical education, and certainly they read poetry and fiction, both classical and popular, as did the scholars. We have no accurate means of measuring literacy in traditional Asian societies. It may have been as high as a quarter of the population, at least in terms of the most basic ability to read and write. Literacy was much higher in Japan after about 1600, and by 1800 it probably reached 50 percent for males. But even a literacy rate of 25 percent would be remarkable, considering the difficulty of learning Chinese characters, which were also the basis of the Japanese, Korean, and Vietnamese written languages.

The gentry group in China, and comparable elites in other Asian societies, probably never constituted more than about 2 percent of the population. To these must be added merchants and petty traders (who often had at least some degree of literacy), clerks and scribes, and some village elders. Despite the fact that they did not attend the regular schools, women sometimes acquired literacy from their brothers or fathers or occasionally on their own. The best evidence is probably the respectable number of female Asian authors, including the famous Lady Murasaki, Japanese author of the world's earliest psychological novel, *The Tale of Genji.* Court ladies such as Lady Murasaki had the leisure to learn to read and write. Literacy was expected of them, as were accomplishments in music, painting, and dance. In the Buddhist countries of Southeast Asia the monkhood claimed virtually all young men for at least two years and at any one time may have included, with older monks, 10 or 15 percent of the population, all of whom were literate. In India the Brahmins, as the sole performers of ritual and the keepers of the Great Tradition, had to be literate.

Paper and printing were both invented in China, the former by the first century A.D. under the Han, the latter by T'ang times. Movable type appeared in the Sung dynasty by about A.D. 1100, and shortly thereafter in Korea. These inventions spread rapidly to Japan, more slowly to India, Southeast Asia, the Islamic areas, and the West. The importance of sacred texts and commentaries for Hinduism, Buddhism, and Islam meant that even before printing, large numbers of copies were made by scribes. As in the West, the spread of printing greatly increased the reading public. The most important result was the increased circulation of literature, first in China, then progressively in other parts of Asia. This included copies of the classics; philosophical and religious texts; epic tales, such as the Indian *Mahabharata* and the *Ramayana;* and similar epics and accounts of heroic deeds from the classical traditions of China, Japan, and Korea.

Literature for a mass audience was being printed by T'ang times in China (A.D. 600–900) and soon thereafter in the rest of Asia, including plays, short stories, poetry, and the first novels. Well before the T'ang period in China, in the splendor of Guptan India (A.D. 300–500), the court poet and playwright Kalidasa had created a brilliant series of dramas. With the spread of printing, his plays and poems were made available to a mass audience. Throughout Asia printing also meant that what had long been present as an oral tradition of storytelling and drama took on new life. Much of it has been lost or is available only in much later printed versions, but from T'ang times on there was a vigorous popular literature in the vernacular, less lofty and more down-to-earth than the classics. Stories and plays about universal human foibles—akin to Chaucer's *Canterbury Tales* in the West—were read avidly by a growing number of people, including scholars to whom such works were supposedly prohibited and who hid them under their pillows. In China there were even detective stories. India produced similar tales, and some of the works of Kalidasa are in this genre. Accounts of adventure and intrigue flourished throughout Asia.

Learning in the West

Respect for learning in the West was not as pronounced as in the East, though in the early modern period there was a notable increase in literacy, in the number of schools, and in the continued development of the universities. In keeping with their broad range of intellectual and cultural interests, Renaissance humanists not only founded new schools but also reformed the traditional curriculum by challenging its heavy reliance on Aristotle. The success of Protestant reformers ultimately rested on the ability to educate younger generations in their religious principles, and in turn the Catholics relied heavily on education to thwart Protestant expansion and to provide the foundation for their missionary work.

Both religious groups looked to the universities to provide intellectual leadership. The Protestant stress on Bible reading, especially with the availability of new vernacular translations in the sixteenth century, was a powerful incentive to become literate. The scientific revolution, with its rapid communication of ideas, was also highly dependent on literacy, and the rapid growth of state bureaucracies increased the demand for skilled officials, particularly those with some legal training. In England the early modern period was the golden age of the Inns of Court, where aspiring young men studied the common law.

As in the East, many Western educational developments were closely linked to religion. Catholic orders such as the Jesuits and the Ursulines are famous for their educational work, but other groups were active too. The Oratory of Jesus, a society of secular priests, established colleges and seminaries throughout France, mostly for children of the French nobility, which rejected physical punishment as an educational tool. So did reforming Catholic Jansenists, whose "little schools" normally had no more than 25 boys in classes of six or less. Several Catholic organizations were established in France in the late 1600s to teach the children of the poor. Although Protestants had no teaching orders, they too actively founded schools, including "charity schools" for children of the poor; their curricula concentrated on reading, writing, and religion. One of the greatest Protestant successes was the founding of the University of Halle in eastern Germany in 1694 by Pietists, whose evangelical, devotional faith troubled orthodox Lutherans. By its emphasis on independent thinking, the faculty at Halle helped pioneer the development of modern academic freedom.

The Jewish communities of eastern Europe and Spain were keenly interested in education. At the elementary level, education was mandatory for all boys, and some girls were taught to read, especially after the appearance of printed vernacular literature. Gifted male students were directed into the fields of medicine and religion, the latter being a specialty of rabbinical academies. Because of the importance of rabbinical law in the ghettos, legal studies as well as religion were an important part of the curriculum.

Note the use of corporal punishment as a learning device in this 1592 woodcut of a German classroom. [Bettman Archive]

Progress in the founding of schools and the increase of literacy was pronounced in early modern Europe. Between 1580 and 1650 more than 800 schools were endowed in England and Wales. By the late seventeenth century the number of parishes with schools was near 90 percent in the diocese of Paris and the lowland counties of Scotland, though the figure was only 42 percent in the diocese of Verdun and even less in some areas. French literacy rates were perhaps 20 percent overall in the seventeenth century, but a third of the population was literate by 1789. The reformer John Knox proposed a program of universal education in the 1560s, but the Scottish Parliament refused to fund it. Nevertheless, a century later Scotland had an impressive system of parish schools where even the poor were welcome.

Universal education effectively began when Prussia made attendance at elementary school mandatory in 1717. The founding of new schools was accompanied by substantial increases in literacy. By 1800 the literacy rate for males approached 90 percent in Scotland and 67 percent in France, whereas in 1600 only one in six Frenchmen had been able to read. Among women, whose educational opportunities were more restricted, literacy rates generally rose more slowly. Only 5 percent of the women in the English counties of East Anglia were literate, compared to 35 percent of the men in the period from 1580 to 1640. In Amsterdam, where literacy greatly enhanced employment opportunities, the rates were 57 percent for men and 32 percent for women in 1630. Because the Swedes required literacy for confirmation and marriage, by the 1690s at least one Swedish diocese had achieved a rate approaching 100 percent, though for many this may have represented little more than the ability to sign one's name. As in the East, the growth of literacy helped spur the printing industry, which published inexpensive books, ballads, and newspapers, the latter appearing for the first time in the seventeenth century. The dramatic increase in Western literacy was not matched in Asia; in Japan, which had the best record, 45 percent of the men and only 15 percent of the women were literate as late as the mid-nineteenth century.

Education in the Ottoman Empire

Unlike eastern Asia or the West, the Turks, who opposed the publication of Islamic religious literature, did not allow printed books until 1728, with the exception of a small number of presses in the non-Muslim communities. The first Turkish newspaper did not appear until 1861. Religious influence dominated the Turkish educational system; most schools were attached to mosques, and the ulema typically supplied the teachers. The Jewish and Christian communities had some schools, but generally the Ottomans discouraged education for their subject peoples. Even among the Muslims, education was essentially the preserve of the well-to-do or the politically important, since the Turks were convinced that too much learning threatened Islam.

Beyond the elementary schools, the more capable Muslim students could pursue the study of Islamic theology, law, and some humanities and science in theological schools known as *medreses*. Here the curriculum lasted as long as 12 years. The sultan also maintained five preparatory and four vocational schools where a full course of study could be as long as 15 years. These palace schools had some Christian teachers, though most of the faculty belonged to the ulema. The curriculum included the study of Turkish, Persian, and Arabic as well as the liberal arts, physical education, calligraphy, and vocational training in such areas as architecture, shipbuilding, and military affairs. There was instruction too in Islam and Turkish etiquette. But the *medreses* and the palace schools were only for the few. The expansion of Islam into North Africa and the Sudan meant that there too education was not encouraged for the masses.

Thus attitudes toward education and learning varied sharply among early modern societies. Until the arrival of Europeans, schools were nonexistent in the Americas and sub-Saharan Africa, while in the Islamic world education was narrowly confined and provided to the few by schools linked to the royal palace or the mosques. The advent of the printing press and the Protestant and Catholic Reformations in Europe spurred the founding of schools, the growth of literacy, and a growing appreciation of learning that has generally continued in the West to the present. Yet nowhere in the early modern world was respect for learning greater than in Asia, both as a means to preserve its philosophical and religious traditions and as a path to achieve worldly success.

Poverty, Crime, and Social Control

It is impossible to measure levels of well-being for most periods in the past. We can calculate living standards only roughly, using such evidence as travelers' accounts, estimates of population and production, trade figures, stories reflecting lifestyles, famine records, and remedial measures. Before the modern period these records are fullest for China, where we have a wealth of official and local documents and an extensive literature. Generally, most Chinese seem to have been materially better off in diet, housing, and clothing than most people elsewhere in the world until perhaps as late as the mid-nineteenth century. But the only real defense against absolute poverty was the family system in Asia, which provided its own mutual-assistance network.

Authorities in France and England in the late 1600s probably exaggerated in estimating that over half of their people lived at or below the subsistence level, but the number was high. In the late 1400s more than two-thirds of the taxpayers in Basel and Augsburg were too poor to survive serious economic adversity. The large number of poor seriously strained the ability of religious and civic authorities to provide assistance. In the plague year of 1580, more than half the population of Genoa was on poor relief. In the last decades of the sixteenth century some 20 percent of the inhabitants of Lyons, France's second largest city, needed assistance.

For the poor the greatest problem was often the uncertainty of the food supply, which was frequently threatened by inflationary pressures as well as natural disasters. Malnutrition and disease were the principal reasons for a life expectancy of only 25 years as late as 1700. The bulk of the world's population still lived in rural areas in the early modern period, often in mud huts with thatched roofs. Living quarters were severely cramped; an entire family often lived in a single room. In towns the poor were victims of polluted water and filthy living conditions.

The diet of the poor was simple and, even in Europe, usually devoid of meat. The more fortunate peasants might occasionally have a little mutton or pork, but the poor usually had to survive on a diet of dark bread, peas, beans, and soup. Many European peasants kept stock simmering in a pot, adding to it whatever foods were available each day. Sometimes cheese, butter, or curds were consumed, but milk was shunned because it was thought to be unhealthy. In general, the lot of the rural poor was marginally better than that of their urban counterparts, since many of the former were able to raise some of their own food. This was not usually true of landless day laborers, who amounted to as much as half the population of some districts in Spain and Switzerland. As the general population increased, it was imperative to find means to relieve the destitute.

Causes of European Poverty

Various factors contributed to the severity of poverty in the early modern period. As the population grew, landlords improved the efficiency of their farms to provide additional food, but industry did not expand rapidly enough to absorb the surplus labor displaced as landowners switched from raising crops to grazing sheep. Inflation itself took a heavy toll as rents and prices rose faster than wages, leaving urban workers particularly vulnerable.

Peasant Poverty: France, 1696

The famous French military engineer, Sébastien Le Prestre, marquis de Vauban, wrote a moving description of the poor peasants in France in 1696.

All the so-called *bas peuple* [mean people] live on nothing but bread of mixed barley and oats, from which they do not even remove the bran, which means that bread can sometimes be lifted by the straw sticking out of it. They also eat poor fruits, mainly wild, and a few vegetables from their gardens. . . .

The general run of people seldom drink [wine], eat meat not three times a year, and use little salt. . . . So it is no cause for surprise if people who are so ill-nourished have so little energy. Add to this what they suffer from exposure: winter and summer, three fourths of them are dressed in nothing but half-rotting tattered linen, and are shod throughout the year with *sabots* [wooden shoes], and no other covering for the foot. . . .

The poor people are ground down in another manner by the loans of grain and money they take from the wealthy in emergencies, by means of which a high rate of usury is enforced, under the guise of presents which must be made after the debts fall due, so as to avoid imprisonment. After the term has been extended by only three or four months, either another present must be produced when the time is up, or they face the *sergent* [debtors' bailiff] who is sure to strip the house bare.

Source: Vauban, "Description géographique de l'élection de Vezelay," in P. Goubert, *The Ancien Régime: French Society, 1600–1750,* trans. S. Cox (London: Weidenfeld & Nicolson, 1973), pp. 118–119.

Short-term increases in poverty were caused by extreme fluctuations in the cloth industry, which was adversely affected by such things as plague, war, and bad harvests. Whereas rural textile workers might weather a slump by finding temporary farm work, urban laborers were typically reduced to poor relief or begging. When harvests failed, the plight of the poor often became desperate. In England from the late fifteenth to the early seventeenth century, harvests failed on an average of every four years. When the harvests were bad several years in a row, the problem was acute, and food riots were common. Finally, as the size of European armies expanded in the early modern period, the number of demobilized and often unemployable soldiers increased, adding burdens to relief rolls.

Poor Relief in Europe

Various attempts were made to deal with the poor in this period. In the late 1400s local authorities ordered beggars to leave their districts, although exceptions were sometimes made for local beggars who were handicapped, ill, or elderly. In Brabant, France, and Venice, vagabonds provided oarpower for the galleys, while in England a 1495 law ordered that the idle be whipped, placed in the stocks for three days, and then returned to their parishes of origin. Intended to keep the destitute from flooding into the towns, virtually all early measures to deal with the poor relied on some form of coercion but failed to provide organized means to relieve the needy.

The widespread social unrest sparked throughout Europe by the harvest failures of the 1520s brought major changes in social policy. Between 1531 and 1541 some 60 cities reformed their welfare policies, and there were state-imposed reforms in the Netherlands, England, France, Scotland, and Spain. The governments of the first three states prohibited begging and insisted that the able-bodied poor work. Funds for those unable to work were raised through taxes or donations, but there was a clear shift in emphasis from private charity to public welfare. The English Poor Law of 1601, for example, prohibited begging, required the able-bodied poor to work on local projects, centralized poor relief, and provided for the education of paupers' children. Where there was industry to employ the able-bodied at low wages, as in Flanders, France, and England, the new system achieved some success. In Scotland and Spain, however, there was little need for the labor of unskilled paupers, and licensed begging was used in an attempt to keep them under control.

Because employment could not always be found for the able-bodied poor, many European cities established workhouses to discipline the poor as well as to provide job training and moral instruction. Although these institutions could not accommodate all the able-bodied poor, officials hoped to coerce the remainder into finding employment. Some workhouses, such as Bridewell in London and those founded by the papacy in Rome, became little more than places of punishment, while others, such as those in the Netherlands, Scandinavia, and Germany, were sources of cheap labor for private employers. French workhouses at first were used to benefit private business, but after 1640 they were employed primarily to control rebellious peasants and workers. The inmates of these institutions rarely benefited from their enforced stays.

In early modern Europe many indigent persons took to the highways in search of employment, but in so doing they risked severe punishment as vagabonds. This 1520 engraving is by Lucas van Leyden. [Staatliche Museen Preussischer Kulturbesitz, Kupferstichkabinett, West Berlin/Jörg P. Anders]

Poor Relief Outside Europe

The towns of coastal West Africa similarly developed a system of poor relief in the late sixteenth and seventeenth centuries. As the rural poor fled to the towns in search of better opportunities, the number of the indigent was often as high as 40 percent, and in the port of Shama on the Gold Coast it reached 70 or 80 percent.

There were, however, no professional beggars because of a rather extensive system of poor relief. The wealthy took some of the poor into their personal service, while others received assistance from special funds raised by taxes or court fines. Some of the offerings given to priests made their way to the poor as well. Local authorities were required to provide gainful employment for young men, the physically handicapped, and the elderly, usually in the crafts, food processing, and market vending. Because the rural poor who faced severe economic hardship sometimes opted for banditry rather than migration to the towns, in the early 1600s brigandage reached near-epidemic levels in parts of West Africa. By striking at the trading caravans transporting rural produce to the towns, the brigands effectively symbolized the resentment of peasants at their growing subservience to urban merchants, a development that was also common in much of Europe.

In South America the Incas addressed the problem by systematic regimentation and care of the needy. The state itself owned the land and apportioned it to families based on their size, with a substantial portion of the crops going to storehouses to supply the nobility, the military, state workers, and priests. The government also took much of what the artisans produced. Although the masses were thus deprived of both freedom and initiative, in times of famine or natural disaster the state provided them with food from the public warehouses.

The larger Asian society had pitifully inadequate means beyond the family level to intervene on behalf of the poor. In China the imperial bureaucracy did what its limited local powers allowed, including the remission of taxes, the control of floods, the keeping of order, and the storing of grain for distribution in lean years at uninflated prices, a policy called the "ever-normal granary system." Such efforts flagged or failed when the dynasty was weak or collapsed—perhaps a third of the time—and even in strong periods the state could not cope with a major catastrophe. In India and Southeast Asia, and to a lesser degree in the Buddhist areas of Korea and Japan, temples provided some refuge for the destitute, but this too was inadequate. In general, the family system of mutual support could keep most people from total destitution most of the time, but no means were adequate to deal with the recurrent large-scale disasters to which all premodern societies were subject, such as drought-induced famine, major flooding, or long periods of civil disorder. In the Islamic world, the poor could look to social-service institutions funded primarily by charitable legacies and the obligatory tax, or *zakat,* which was one of the principal duties of a Muslim.

Crime and Poverty

One of the most striking differences between East and West was in the treatment of crime. In general terms, Asian thought made no place for the Judeo-Christian concept of sin. Correction and, if possible, reform through reeducation or renewed piety were stressed more than repayment or punishment, although these were certainly used and frequently harsh. The incidence of crime or social deviance was almost certainly less in Asia than in other areas, thanks to the self-regulating mechanism of the family and the deterrent power of the shame that individual misbehavior might bring on the group. It is sometimes said that whereas Western societies emphasized individual sin and guilt, the East stressed the unacceptability of antisocial behavior and used shame to enforce moral codes. In addition to the social stigma of misbehavior, public shaming was commonly used as an official punishment both in Asia and in Europe. Both Asian and European criminals were publicly exhibited, often paraded through the streets carrying placards indicating their offenses, and sometimes executed.

As the living standards of European workers and peasants deteriorated, criminal activity increased, especially after the mid-1500s. In rural areas there was a clear connection between crime and destitution. Records for the Spanish province of Toledo show that nearly all defendants in larceny cases came from the lower ranks of society. Theft was often the most common crime; in the English county of Sussex in the early 1600s stealing accounted for nearly two-thirds of all indictments. Theft was a capital offense, though the death penalty was rarely applied. Most rural felons were common laborers who did not repeat their criminal activity after once being caught.

Larceny changed somewhat in the early modern period. In medieval times thieves stole mostly subsistence items—food, clothing, and tools—but later they began to prefer luxury goods, increasingly available in the expanding towns. Whereas the poor had hitherto stolen mostly from other poor, they began more and more to rob the rich. A major exception to this pattern of crime occurred during the unsettled times of fourteenth- and fifteenth-century Europe when bands of lawless nobles and gentry engaged in robbery and extortion. Victims who refused to pay often had their crops destroyed and their homes burned. Not even the wealthy were immune, for they provided tempting targets for kidnapping and extortion. Known as "fur-collar criminals" because of their noble garb, the culprits thrived until governments were strong enough to stamp most of them out in the 1500s.

Banditry did not cease with the decline of fur-collar crime, but henceforth nearly all bandits were from the lower ranks and included many men unable to find employment. As major roads were more effectively patrolled by the seventeenth century, most of these bandits were forced into remote areas. Russia, however, experienced considerable turmoil throughout the 1600s because of large roving bands.

In Asia, too, banditry was a common response by people reduced to absolute poverty. It was especially frequent in periods of political disorder and hence virtually endemic in parts of India, while its incidence rose and fell in China with the changing effectiveness of the imperial government and the levels of peasant distress. Bandits operated most successfully on the fringes of state-controlled areas or in frontier zones between provincial jurisdictions, areas that were often mountainous or forested. Bandits exacerbated the poverty of their prey. Although their prime targets were the rich and the trade routes, these were often better protected than the common people and their villages. Some bandit groups turned into rebels, who built on the support of the disaffected majority to overthrow the government and found a new order that could better serve mass welfare. Much popular fiction dealt with the adventures of bandit groups, often depicted as Robin Hood–type figures but in any case regarded as heroes rather than criminals.

In the West a new literary form, the picaresque novel—celebrating the adventures of an urban rogue, or *picaro*—developed in connection with a trend toward more sophisticated urban crimes. In addition to the usual larceny, physical assault, homicide, and arson, early modern towns were increasingly troubled by business fraud and swindlers. By the mid-1600s novels about these rogues were popular in Spain, from whence they spread to Germany and England.

Another facet of urban crime was the growth in the larger European cities of neighborhoods where a genuine underworld existed. In Paris the criminal sector near the Porte St.-Denis was so extensive that officials dared not enter it until it was subdued by an army detachment in 1667. Curtailing crime in the cities was nearly impossible because the poor were packed into grossly overcrowded slums where shanties filled even the narrow alleys.

Controlling Crime

European states responded to the rise in crime by reorganizing the personnel and procedure necessary to control it. In the medieval period criminal control was based on the existence of small populations in compact, mostly isolated areas. As the population expanded and interregional contacts increased, it became imperative to develop more effective government controls beyond the local level. In France this need was met by expanding the powers of the royal *procureur*, who handled the prosecution in criminal proceedings. In England the Tudors, who had no police force, enlarged the role of the justices of the peace, who, as unpaid agents of the crown, had the authority to arrest, indict, and grant bail. They also enforced labor codes and social laws, which governed such things as alehouses and unlawful games. By the late sixteenth century justices of the peace were responsible for enforcement of the poor law.

Capital Punishment and Cruelty

European justice entailed not only the use of torture to extract confessions but also the application of capital punishment for various crimes against property as well as human life. Here is the account of a French observer sensitive to the cruel suffering inflicted on criminals in eighteenth-century Paris; note his opposition to capital punishment as contrary to natural law.

I went home by way of rue Saint-Antoine and the Place de Grève. Three murderers had been broken on the wheel there, the day before. . . . As I crossed the square I caught sight of a poor wretch, pale, half dead, wracked by the pains of the interrogation inflicted on him twenty hours earlier; he was stumbling down from the Hôtel de Ville supported by the executioner and the confessor. These two men, so completely different, inspired an inexpressible emotion in me! I watched the latter embrace a miserable man consumed by fever, filthy as the dungeons he came from, swarming with vermin! And I said to myself, "O Religion, here is your greatest glory! . . ." I saw the other as the wrathful arm of the law. . . . But I wondered: "Have men the right to impose death . . . even on the murderer who has himself treacherously taken life?" I seemed to hear Nature reply with a woeful no! . . . "But robbery?" "No, no!" cried Nature. "The savage rich have never felt they devised enough harsh safeguards; instead of being friends and brothers, as their religion commands, they prefer the gallows. . . ." This was what Nature said to me. . . .

Source: Nicolas-Edmé, Restif de la Bretonne, *Les Nuits de Paris, or The Nocturnal Spectator*, trans. L. Asher and E. Fertig (New York: Random House, 1964), pp. 7–8.

Throughout Europe revised criminal procedures had the effect of depersonalizing the judicial process and treating criminal activity as an offense against society rather than the individual. Punishment became more severe. In contrast to the relatively mild medieval system, where justice was intended to settle disputes between persons, the new criminal proceedings punished the guilty but ignored compensation for the victim. Unlike medieval justice, corporal punishment became more common, though a status distinction was generally made in meting out justice; the rich were often fined, the poor imprisoned or mutilated. The increased severity of punishments was intended to discipline the lower orders and curb the increase in crimes by the poor against the rich. Public punishment thus had a twofold purpose: to deter crime and to demonstrate the authority of the state to regulate the behavior and command the obedience of its citizens.

Chinese punishment for minor offenses. The heavy wooden collar, the *cangue*, was a burden to support and also prevented the criminal from reaching his mouth with his hands, which meant that he would starve if not fed by others. This man's crime is recorded on the inscription, but all that shows here is the official title and seal of the imperial magistrate at Shanghai in 1872. [Photo by John Thomson; Harvard-Yenching Library, Harvard University]

In both Asia and Europe criminals were tried and laws and punishments enforced by civil courts run by the state and presided over by magistrates, rulers or their representatives, community elders, or learned men. In both Asia and sometimes in Europe there was no prior assumption of guilt or innocence; judgment was made and sentences arrived at on the basis of evidence, including the testimony of witnesses. Asians had no lawyers standing between people and the law; plaintiffs and defendants spoke for themselves. In China and most of the rest of Asia, people charged with criminal behavior could be found guilty and punished only if they confessed their guilt. If they refused to do so despite the weight of evidence against them, they were often tortured to extract a confession. Torture was also used in early modern Europe, though confession was not essential for a conviction. Asian law and the system of official justice, like its European counterpart, was designed to awe all who appeared before its majesty. Plaintiffs, defendants, and witnesses knelt before the magistrate or judge and could be whipped if they were not suitably reverential—another expression of a strongly hierarchical, authoritarian society.

In both Asia and Europe punishment for major crimes of violence was almost invariably death, commonly by beheading or strangulation. Death could also be imposed for many minor crimes. For especially dreadful crimes, such as parricide, treason, rebellion, or, in Asia, other forms of filial and political disloyalty, more gruesome punishments were used: dismemberment, the pulling apart of limbs by horses, the Chinese "death of a thousand cuts," or in India impalement or trampling by elephants. In Europe dismemberment by "drawing and quartering" (sundering limbs from the body) was imposed for treason.

Punishments were seen as deterrents to would-be criminals; the heads of the executed were exhibited on poles until they rotted. For lesser offenses Asian criminals were displayed in painfully small cages or mutilated, practices also used in Europe, or forced to wear a heavy wooden collar that prevented them from feeding themselves. In East and West alike prisons were often dreadful places where inmates might starve if they were not fed by relatives. For what we might call misdemeanors, Asian sentences tended to stress reeducation and reform. Criminality, or at least misbehavior, was seen as potentially correctible, especially with family help.

People naturally worried about falling into the machinery of the law and courts, especially in criminal cases. Two important points need to be made. In Asia probably considerably fewer than 10 percent of disputes and minor crimes—perhaps most crimes of all sorts—ever reached the courts since they were settled through family, village, gentry, or other local networks. Second, modern Western scholars conclude that justice was done by that system, perhaps more consistently than in the West. Most magistrates were judicious, diligent with evidence, and concerned to see justice done, not only to avoid the censure that could ruin their careers but also because of the sense of responsibility they bore. But there was, particularly in the West, a double standard of justice, which was much harder on the poor, whose crimes generally stemmed from poverty, than on their social betters. Laws were made and administered by elite groups, whose interests in the preservation of their privileged status and property were at least as great as their devotion to justice.

Surveying the societies of the early modern world, perhaps most striking is the contrast between the relative stability of Asian society and the volatility of Europe. As Europeans made crucial economic, political, and educational advances in the early modern period, Western society altered substantially, beginning in western Europe and spreading to the Americas through colonization. Nevertheless, the strikingly numerous social parallels between the different parts of the world in this period underscore the commonality of much historical development and human experience. Societies were structured hierarchically and embraced the principle that social status entailed special responsibility. In Asia and Europe alike, arranged marriages were common, and precedence was accorded to sons. Capital punishment was commonly imposed for major crimes, and some of the poor in all societies periodically resorted to banditry. Moreover, in their treatment of women, most Asian and Western societies were alike in not granting even a modicum of social equality to women until the twentieth century.

Conflicting religious tenets were responsible for some of the most basic social differences in the early modern world. Religious considerations explain at least in part why Aztecs, Incas, Muslims, and some Africans practiced polygamy, whereas non-Muslim Asians and Europeans were primarily monogamous. Religion was also a key factor in views on sex. Many East Asians and Africans, unlike Christians, for instance, linked sex and religious ritual. Religious changes were responsible for altering the way some Westerners viewed marriage: divorce (other than through annulment) was not possible in Europe until the Protestant Reformation in the sixteenth century; in Asia, divorce did occur, though rarely. The relative importance attached to education, particularly in Asia, stemmed partly from the desire to preserve its religious and philosophical traditions. The same can be said of Judaism and later of Christianity.

Suggestions for Further Reading

Buxbaum, D., ed. *Chinese Family Law and Social Change*. Seattle: University of Washington Press, 1978.

Ch'u, T. *Law and Society in Traditional China*. Paris: Mouton, 1961.

Cohn, B. S. *India: The Social Anthropology of a Civilization*. Englewood Cliffs, N.J.: Prentice-Hall, 1971.

Davidson, B. *The African Genius: An Introduction to Social and Cultural History*. Boston: Little, Brown, 1969.

Dumont, L. *Homo Hierarchicus: An Essay on the Caste System*, trans. M. Sainsbury. Chicago: University of Chicago Press, 1970.

Forster, R., and Forster, E., eds. *European Society in the Eighteenth Century*. New York: Walker, 1969.

Foucault, M. *The History of Sexuality*, trans. R. Hurley. New York: Pantheon, 1977.

Fraser, A. *The Weaker Vessel: Woman's Lot in Seventeenth-Century England*. London: Weidenfeld & Nicolson, 1984.

Freedman, M., ed. *Family and Kinship in Chinese Society*. Stanford, Calif.: Stanford University Press, 1970.

Goubert, P. *The French Peasantry in the Seventeenth Century*, trans. I. Patterson. Cambridge: Cambridge University Press, 1986.

Greaves, R. L. *Society and Religion in Elizabethan England*. Minneapolis: University of Minnesota Press, 1981.

Hanawalt, B. A., ed. *Women and Work in Preindustrial Europe*. Bloomington: Indiana University Press, 1986.

Ho, P. *The Ladder of Success in Imperial China*. New York: Columbia University Press, 1964.

Hunt, D. *Parents and Children in History: The Psychology of Family Life in Early Modern France*. New York: Basic Books, 1970.

Kea, R. A. *Settlements, Trade, and Politics in the Seventeenth-Century Gold Coast*. Baltimore: Johns Hopkins University Press, 1982.

Ladurie, E. L. *The French Peasantry, 1450–1660*. Berkeley: University of California Press, 1986.

Lannoy, R. *The Speaking Tree: Indian Culture and Society*. New York: Oxford University Press, 1971.

Laslett, P. *The World We Have Lost Further Explored*, 3d ed. London: Methuen, 1983.

Le May, R. S. *The Culture of Southeast Asia*. London: Allen & Unwin, 1954.

Lerner, G. *The Creation of Patriarchy*. New York: Oxford University Press, 1986.

Lewis, R. *Everyday Life in Ottoman Turkey*. New York: Putnam, 1971.

Macfarlane, A. *Marriage and Love in England: Modes of Reproduction, 1300–1840*. New York: Basil Blackwell, 1986.

McKnight, B. *The Quality of Mercy: Amnesties and Traditional Chinese Justice*. Honolulu: University Press of Hawaii, 1981.

Mandelbaum, D. G. *Society in India: Continuity and Change*. 2 vols. Berkeley: University of California Press, 1970.

Maynes, M. J. *Schooling in Western Europe: A Social History*. New York: State University of New York Press, 1985.

Norberg, K. *Rich and Poor in Grenoble, 1600–1814*. Berkeley: University of California Press, 1985.

Ozment, S. *When Fathers Ruled: Family Life in Reformation Europe*. Cambridge, Mass.: Harvard University Press, 1983.

Pike, R. *Aristocrats and Traders: Sevillian Society in the Sixteenth Century*. Ithaca, N.Y.: Cornell University Press, 1972.

Pollock, L. A. *Forgotten Children: Parent-Child Relations from 1500 to 1900*. Cambridge: Cambridge University Press, 1984.

Prior, M., ed. *Women in English Society, 1500–1800*. London: Methuen, 1985.

Rawksi, E. S. *Education and Popular Literacy in Ch'ing China*. Ann Arbor: University of Michigan Press, 1979.

Rose, M. B., ed. *Women in the Middle Ages and the Renaissance: Literary and Historical Perspectives*. Syracuse, N.Y.: Syracuse University Press, 1986.

Schalk, E. *From Valor to Pedigree: Ideas of Nobility in France in the Sixteenth and Seventeenth Centuries*. Princeton, N.J.: Princeton University Press, 1986.

Shorter, E. *The Making of the Modern Family*. New York: Basic Books, 1977.

Stone, L. *The Family, Sex and Marriage in England, 1500–1800*. New York: Harper & Row, 1977.

——, and Stone, J. C. F. *An Open Elite? England, 1540–1880*. New York: Oxford University Press, 1984.

Traer, J. F. *Marriage and the Family in Eighteenth-Century France*. Ithaca, N.Y.: Cornell University Press, 1980.

Wakeman, F., ed. *Conflict and Control in Late Imperial China*. Berkeley: University of California Press, 1975.

Wiesner, M. E. *Working Women in Renaissance Germany*. New Brunswick, N.J.: Rutgers University Press, 1986.

Woodbridge, L. *Women and the English Renaissance and the Nature of Womankind, 1540–1620*. Champaign: University of Illinois Press, 1984.

CHAPTER · 22

The Age of Absolutism

The sixteenth century had witnessed the emergence of the nation-state in western Europe. The seventeenth and eighteenth centuries saw its consolidation. By the end of the Thirty Years' War, it was clear that the future lay with the powers capable of mobilizing their resources most effectively for both war and peace. From the middle of the seventeenth century to the end of the eighteenth, the major states of Europe embarked on a variety of programs designed to increase centralized political and economic control. On the political level, this process generally took the form of absolutism; on the economic level, that of mercantilism. Each of the major states took a somewhat different path to these ends. What proved workable in the France of Louis XIV required a different approach in England or in the Russia of Peter the Great. But by the mid-eighteenth century, every major power had succeeded in its program of centralization, or had paid the price of failure.

The professionalization of the military coincided with the growth of standing state-supported armies. The elaborate costume of the Prussian grenadiers, the most elite corps of the eighteenth century, set them distinctively apart from the civilian population, impressing the authority of the state on them in peace as well as in war. [Granger Collection]

This process was not accomplished without difficulty. Merchants generally welcomed the economic initiatives of the state, and in some cases actively sought them. The landed aristocracy, fearful of losing its privileges and jealous of its traditional authority, often opposed centralization. Workers demanded wage and price controls, a dependable supply of bread, and restrictions on cheap imported labor. Peasants sought relief from the onerous burdens of taxes and traditional obligations. Thus the state's quest for political unity and economic control raised a host of demands from competing constituencies. It sharpened the differences between the estates and led eventually to the demand for political representation. By the eighteenth century some European rulers frankly regarded themselves as arbiters between the competing interest groups in their countries. But the centralizing states were not always able to control the forces they had unleashed. By the late eighteenth century, absolutism had created the conditions that would lead to its demise and its replacement by the modern state.

France Under Louis XIV

Of all the absolute monarchs, none stamped his age as decisively as Louis XIV of France. No other Western European ruler exerted greater or more uncontested control of his country during the 1000-year period between the reign of Charlemagne and the French Revolution of 1789. Yet even Louis faced daunting obstacles and resistance in his efforts to bend the people and institutions of France to his will, and even he was forced to acknowledge the limitations of his power.

Provincial Autonomy and Central Control

The France of Louis XIV was not a unitary state but a patchwork of widely varying provincial customs and pow-

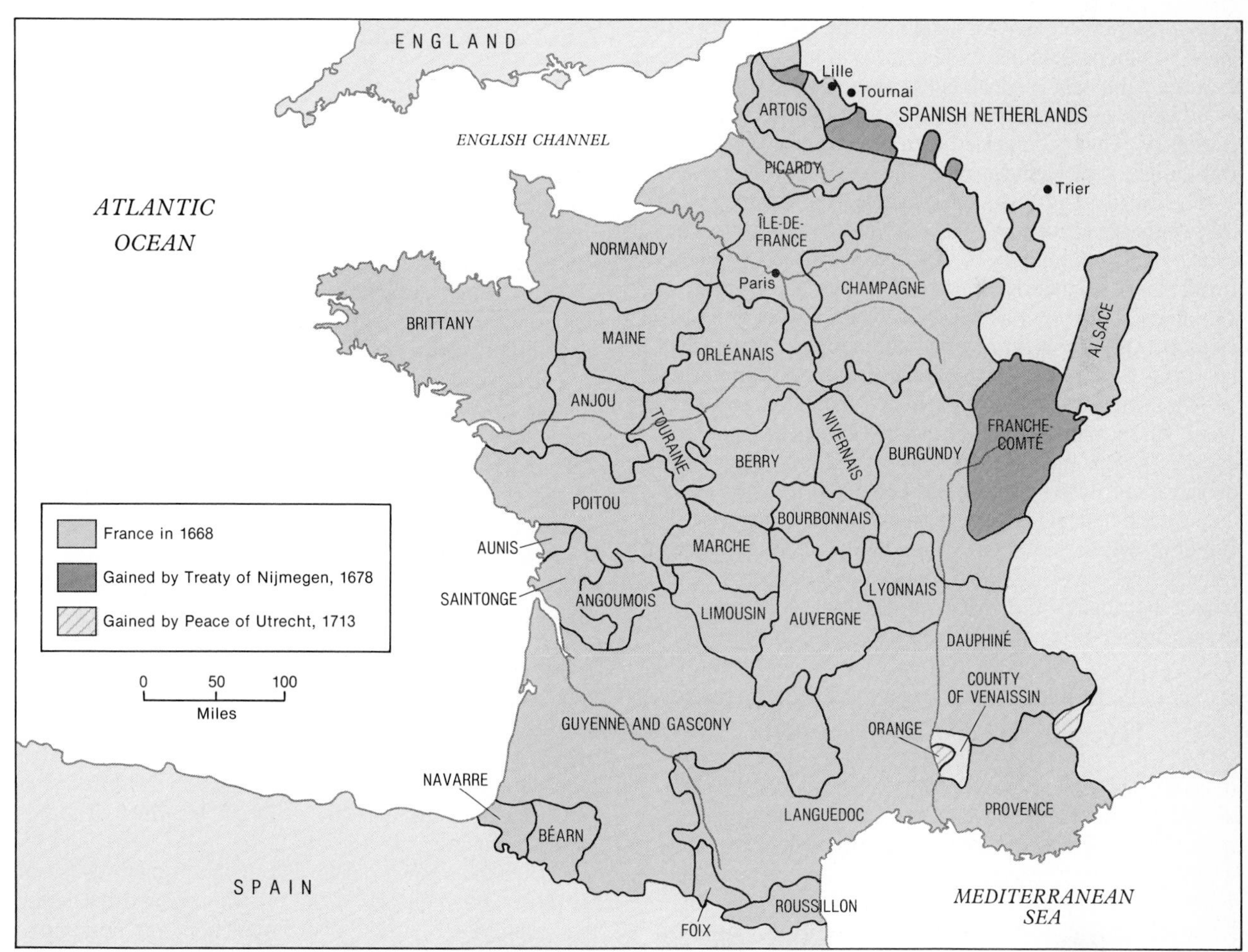

***22.1** France Under Louis XIV*

ers. In many respects, the crown's relations with the larger and older provinces, called *pays d'état* because they had their own representative assemblies or estates, resembled treaties with quasi-sovereign powers. These provinces set their own tax rates and passed laws independent of and often at odds with those of the central government. As late as 1661 Louis was acknowledged as no more than count of Provence and duke of Brittany in those two provinces. Many of the towns as well enjoyed not only their own councils and magistrates but also levied their own customs duties and raised their own militias. A good number of them were wholly exempt from the basic property tax of the realm, the *taille.* So were whole classes of the population, notably the clergy and, in at least some of the forms in which it was levied, the nobility. On the other hand, the taille was imposed directly and unilaterally on the newer provinces. The hated excise tax on salt, the *gabelle,* was applied so unequally that the price of this vital commodity was as much as 25 times higher in one province than in another.

Armed rebellions often broke out when the central government attempted to impose a new tax. Some of these rebellions went on for years and cost the government far more to suppress than it could ever have hoped to gain in revenue. The only constant in the system was that it bore most heavily everywhere on the poor, particularly the peasantry. Thus it combined both the greatest unfairness and the greatest inefficiency.

The basis for a policy of effective centralization was clear: standardization of laws and taxes, reduction of internal tariffs, promotion of key industries, and the neutralization of seigneurial courts and provincial legislatures. The foundations for this policy had been laid in the previous two reigns. Henry IV had curbed the power of the provincial estates and established government monopolies over mining and the production of gunpowder and salt. Louis XIII's minister, Cardinal Richelieu, had dispatched special agents, the *intendants,* to oversee provincial administration. Both Henry IV and Louis XIII had studiously ignored the national representative assembly, the Estates General, which met only twice during their combined reigns. The revolt of the Fronde (see Chapter 18), in which the nobility had made its last serious attempt to assert power on a national level, had ended in failure.

Divine Right Monarchy

It was Louis XIV, however, who most successfully exploited the powers of personal monarchy to create a centralized state. For Louis, increasing the power of the state was not merely a matter of policy. It was a natural consequence of his authority as a divine right king. Whether Louis actually made the famous statement attributed to him, "I am the state," he clearly lived by the thought. Louis identified himself wholly with the French state. Even his private life was lived in public, among a throng of courtiers; for him, there was no distinction between the man and the monarch. Fortunately, Louis had the ideal temperament for a king. He was highly conscious of his dignity; it was said that even as a child he seldom laughed. But Louis did not experience the cares of state as a burden. "The calling of a king is great, noble, and delightful," he said. Louis took his pleasures and his responsibilities with the same equanimity. In 54 years of active rule, he never lost his zest for governing.

For Louis, the aim of the state was *gloire*—glory. *Gloire* was both an attribute of persons—the dignity of a nobleman, the majesty of a king—and the collective aspiration of a nation. The glory of France was in its wealth and productivity, its technology and engineering, the splendor of its arts. Even more, in an age that valued military prowess above all else, its glory was measured by its power. France was already the richest and most powerful state in Europe at the accession of Louis XIV. For Louis that was only the measure of its potential for further achievement and greater *gloire.*

JEAN-BAPTISTE COLBERT, MINISTER OF FINANCE

The king assembled around him a small group of ministers recruited not from the nobility but the bourgeoisie. Chief among these was Jean-Baptiste Colbert. The son of a draper, Colbert shared his master's vision of glory. From 1661 until his death in 1683, he was the most important man in the kingdom after Louis himself.

Colbert had entered government service when not yet 20, and his talents and capacity for hard work soon commended him to the secretary of state for war, Michel Le Tellier, who made him his private secretary. By 1649, at the age of only 30, Colbert had become himself a councillor of state, and two years later he entered the service of Cardinal Mazarin, who had succeeded Richelieu as the dominant figure in French politics. Mazarin at first treated the upstart young bourgeois with reserve, if not disdain, but he soon found Colbert's services indispensable, as Le Tellier had. As the cardinal's health began to fail, Colbert took on more and more responsibility. By the late 1650s he was charged with suppressing a major revolt of the nobility in Normandy, Anjou, and Poitou, while at the same time he drafted an ambitious new plan for reform of the king's finances that directly undercut his chief rival, Nicholas Fouquet.

Fouquet learned of Colbert's scheme through his friend the postmaster general of Paris, who opened the letter that contained it. But Colbert's position was now unassailable, and at Mazarin's death in 1661 he had the professional and no doubt personal pleasure of arresting Fou-

Jean-Baptiste Colbert, the consummate bureaucrat, in a portrait by Lefebvre. Colbert's financial and organizational genius made the splendor of Louis' reign possible. [Giraudon/Art Resource)

quet. The fallen minister, who had grossly enriched himself, narrowly escaped execution. Colbert also used his position to enrich himself and his numerous family, but with a difference: he enriched the king as well.

Colbert's title was controller-general of finances, but his mandate embraced the economy as a whole, including trade and commerce, the merchant marine and the navy, the colonies, and internal security. Colbert found that the crown's deficit was nearly a third of its income and that its revenues were pledged as much as three years in advance. Worse still, barely a third of the taxes levied by the crown found their way into the treasury due to fraud and evasion.

While actually decreasing the taille, Colbert was able to double the overall tax yield within six years by curbing the abuses of tax collectors, tightening exemptions, exploiting the royal demesne more efficiently, and compelling the *pays d'état* to increase their share of taxes. He presided over a council of commerce consisting of prominent merchants, which charted a course for France's commercial and industrial supremacy. Disdainful of agriculture, he pointed to the example of the Dutch, who had gained wealth and world power by commerce despite a land area and population barely a tenth the size of France. He established and subsidized hundreds of new workshops and factories, either under direct royal control or licensed as monopolies. His agents scoured Europe to recruit the most skilled technicians—dyers, glassblowers, gun founders. At home, meanwhile, he tried to organize all French craftsmen into guilds, subject to minute regulations and supervised by an army of state inspectors.

The purpose of new industry was to provide material for commerce; the purpose of commerce was to amass wealth; and the purpose of wealth was power. Economic activity was thus for Colbert, as for Louis, both a preparation for war and a kind of warfare in itself. By fostering new trades and erecting tariff barriers, France would reduce its dependence on imports and prevent the drain of its bullion. By increasing production, expanding the navy, and creating large overseas trading companies, it would penetrate markets, drive off rivals, and extend French power on a global scale. To all of this, centralized organization and control was the key. "If your Majesty could constrain all your subjects into these four kinds of profession," Colbert wrote the king, "agriculture, trade, war by land or by sea, it would be possible for you to become the master of the world."[1]

Colbert was particularly active on behalf of maritime trade and warfare. Within France, he built canals and modernized ports. He created a flotilla of trading companies for both the West Indies and the East Indies that were designed to extend French power and wealth no less than its fleet. He was the real founder of the French navy, and he searched the prisons and poorhouses of France to man his new ships. In some cases he commuted death sentences to procure sailors, but in many others he arbitrarily lengthened prison terms, compelled judges to sentence convicts to the galleys, and forcibly impressed beggars and vagrants. Such actions showed the darker side of a man obsessed with the goals of power. Assiduous in cultivating his superiors, he seemed a tyrant to many when at last he had no superior but the king. When he died in 1683, his body was buried secretly lest his tomb be desecrated by his enemies. Yet he was France's greatest economic statesman, and perhaps its greatest cultural patron as well.

Louis XIV and the Bureaucracy

Ironically, the chief obstacle to the king's dreams appeared to be his own bureaucracy. According to one contemporary estimate, the number of government offices in France had increased by 50,000 during the first half of the seventeenth century. There were nearly 2,000 officers in the Court of Chancery, and almost 1,000 tax collectors for the taille (at least on paper) in the province of Normandy alone.

The reason for this explosion of bureaucrats lay in the nature of officeholding itself. Each occupant of a venal office bought and owned it. In return for his investment, he acquired a blue-chip property that yielded a handsome income in fees and whose resale value was very likely to appreciate. There was status value too, since even minor offices often entitled the holder or his heir to ennoblement.

The entire system constituted a form of indirect taxation. Purchasers advanced a lump sum to the crown, and recouped their outlay by charging the public for their "services." For the financially pressed monarchy, the lure of ready cash was irresistible. Administratively, however, the system was a nightmare. The number of offices created bore no relation to function or need. The public business was intolerably delayed, and the king's own edicts were lost in the maze of clerkships. Once entrenched, the officeholders resisted any attempt at accountability or reform. In return for short-term financial relief, the crown had traded long-term political paralysis.

In contrast to this bloated bureaucracy, Louis XIV gathered around him a tiny nucleus of advisers. Besides Colbert, the only important ministers were Lionne for foreign affairs and Le Tellier for war. The king made all decisions of state with these three. Another 30 councillors of state and fewer than 100 masters of requests prepared material and executed orders, assisted by scribes, ushers, and other minor functionaries. All in all, the royal executive consisted of fewer than 1,000 persons.

By streamlining his government at the top, Louis was able to act swiftly and in secret and to keep all major threads of policy in his own hands. If there was chaos at the extremities of the state, the king was determined to counteract it by command at the center.

The key to the royal strategy was the revived use of intendants, who were handpicked from among the masters of requests. At first, as under Richelieu, they were sent out on specific assignments to the provinces. Later, however, they took up permanent residence. Their commissions were all-embracing, and their powers superseded those of all other officials, including the provincial governor. Not since Roman times had central authority exerted such continuous and effective control at the local level.

By such means Louis was able to cut through his own bureaucracy and impose his will on France. To be sure, he often met stubborn resistance. Local noblemen, jealous of their independence, made common cause with local officials to frustrate his intentions. Proud Brittany did not submit to the yoke of an intendant until 1689. But in the last analysis, there could be no disputing the command of a divinely anointed king. As God's representative on

On the Nature of Majesty

Jacques-Bénigne Bossuet (1627–1704), bishop of Meaux and tutor to the royal family, was the foremost spokesman for the divine right of kings in seventeenth-century France and its last great apologist in Europe. In this characteristically titled work, Politics Derived from the Words of Holy Scripture *(published posthumously in 1709), Bossuet describes the quality of "majesty" in kingship as the reflection and transmission of the power and glory of God on earth.*

By majesty, I do not mean that pomp which surrounds kings, or that show of brilliance which dazzles the vulgar. This is but the reflection of majesty, and not majesty itself.

Majesty is the image of the glory of God in the prince. God is infinite; God is all. The prince, in his capacity as a prince, is not considered an individual man: he is a public person, the whole state is in him, the will of the whole people is contained within his own. As all perfection and all virtue are united in God, so is the entire power of individual persons united in the person of the prince. What greatness is it for a single man to hold such power!

God's power makes itself felt in an instant from one end of the world to the other. Royal power acts simultaneously throughout the realm. It keeps the whole realm in its proper state, just as God does for the whole world. Let God withhold his hand, and the world would collapse again into nothingness; let authority cease in the realm, and everything would be in confusion.

Source: K. M. Baker, ed., *Readings in Western Civilization*, vol. 7 (Chicago: University of Chicago Press, 1987), p. 39.

earth, his will was supreme. Bishop Bossuet (1627–1704), Louis' chief spiritual adviser, went so far as to declare that the king was God himself. It is not recorded that Louis denied it.

Versailles: The Sun King Enthroned

For the king's power to be felt, it had to be visible. Louis had his architects and decorators turn the royal hunting lodge at Versailles, 10 miles from Paris, into the most splendid palace in the Western world. Surrounded by formal gardens and artificial lakes, it stretched in a great semicircle for more than a quarter of a mile. Fountains and statues adorned it on all sides. Inside, a hall of mirrors lit by thousands of candelabras led to the main apartments. Louis himself was portrayed in triumph everywhere, ruling over Europe, Asia, and the Americas in the frescoes that lined the halls of state or garbed as a Roman emperor surrounded by classical gods and goddesses. The king had taken the sun as his personal emblem early in the reign, and every aspect of Versailles, from the smallest decorative details to the long, tree-lined avenues that spread out from the palace like the rays of a great orb, reflected the solar theme. An army of workmen and engineers the size of a city—36,000 were counted on the site at one time—toiled to construct this ultimate monument to *gloire*, digging trenches and canals, erecting pagan temples, stocking the game parks, and trimming the gardens to create a perfect world where nature as well as man obeyed an absolute ruler.

This artificial paradise enclosed one of the most artificial societies ever created. The most distinguished noblemen of France vied for the honor of living in the cramped and squalid conditions of an overcrowded court. Proximity to the king determined one's status. Personal attendance on him was the most coveted honor of all. Great dukes fought for the right to serve as his footmen, adjusting his livery or holding his candlestick. Louis lived in Versailles not as a man but as an idol, displaying himself to the privileged few permitted to worship him in person. In this way, he tamed his nobility. Absorbed in etiquette, obsessed with their own vanity, they neglected the most important aspect of status: power.

As Voltaire remarked, "Louis liked the ladies, and it was reciprocal." The prominence of women in the court life of Versailles reflected the general softening of manners that had come to the French court with its increasing refinement and sophistication of taste. But royal favor, once withdrawn, could be devastating. Louis' first mistress, Louise de la Vallière, had to endure the ignominy of watching him pass through her apartments to visit his new favorite, Madame de Montespan, until she was permitted to retire to a Carmelite nunnery.

The king was finally tamed by a remarkable woman, Madame de Maintenon (1635–1719). Born Françoise d'Aubigné, she was taken to the Caribbean island of Martinique as a child and left penniless at her father's death. She struggled back to France with her mother and, soon

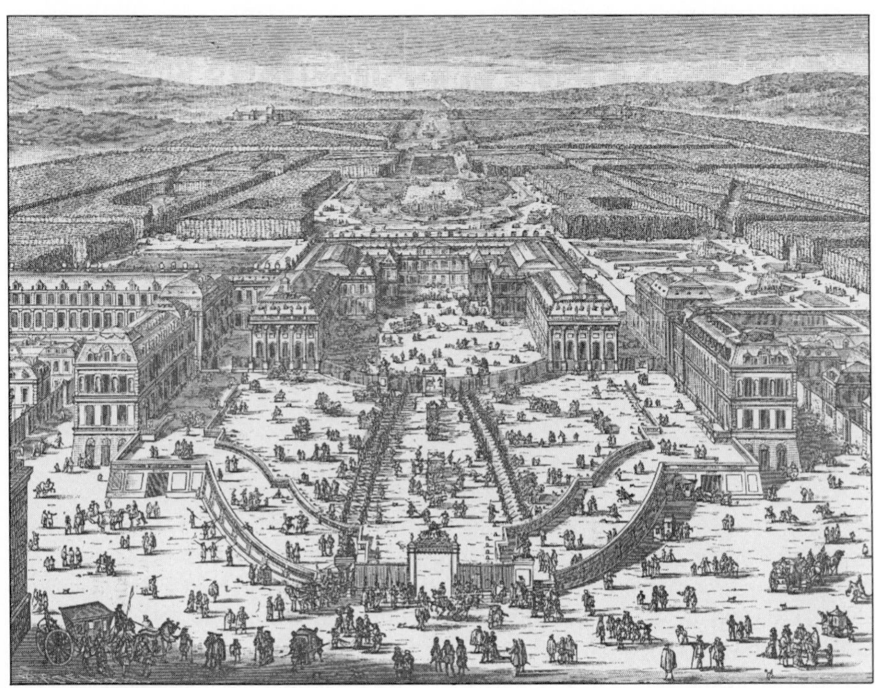

This contemporary engraving of the palace at Versailles gives a good idea of the vast extent of the royal complex and grounds and the throngs of courtiers, suitors, officials, and ladies of fashion that made up its daily traffic. [Bettmann Archive]

orphaned, escaped the fate of a poor relation by marrying the poet Paul Scarron. After Scarron's death, a chance connection brought her the estate of Maintenon and a position at court, where she became governess to Madame de Montespan's bastards and eventually the king's confidante. When Queen Marie-Thérèse died in 1683, Louis secretly married the woman now called Madame de Maintenon, and although the wedding was never acknowledged, she was the dominant presence at Versailles until his death.

Under Maintenon's influence, the court, still brilliant, took on a more pious and sober tone. Remembering the hardships of her own life, Maintenon had begun to educate poor children as early as 1674, and in 1686 she opened a school exclusively for the daughters of impoverished nobility, St. Cyr. For the remainder of her life she visited it nearly every day, directly overseeing the development of its curriculum and the welfare of its pupils. St. Cyr was an immense success, a training college whose graduates spread the spirit of reform into old-fashioned convent schools and a milestone in the history of women's education. Maintenon was buried in the school's chapel, beside her beloved children. St. Cyr itself was closed during the French Revolution, and in 1794 some workmen, engaged in demolishing the chapel, discovered her grave, pulled out her preserved body, dragged and kicked it about the grounds, and threw it into a pit.

The Wars of Louis XIV

If Versailles was the image of *gloire*, war was the practice of it. Louis waited until Colbert had filled the treasury before embarking on his first military adventure, an attack on the Spanish territories of Flanders and the Franche-Comté, which he claimed by right of inheritance through his wife, Marie-Thérèse. This brief contest, the so-called War of Devolution (1667–1668), gained him a dozen towns, including the important commercial centers of Lille and Tournai. It also provoked an alliance between England and the Netherlands, which had only recently completed a war of their own.

The Dutch War (1672–1678)

For Louis, the Dutch were both commercial rivals, whose defeat would open up their lucrative carrying trade to French shipping, and religious heretics, whose Calvinism he was planning to suppress among his own Protestant subjects, the Huguenots. The Dutch had personally offended him at the end of the Flanders campaign with a cartoon that portrayed his sun emblem eclipsed by a wedge of Dutch cheese. More important, the Dutch alone stood between Louis and his long-range goal to dominate the Low Countries and Germany, and even—as a book published under royal sponsorship in 1667 declared—to revive the empire of Charlemagne in the West.

Louis struck in the spring of 1672. The French occupied three of the seven Dutch provinces, and Amsterdam was saved only by opening the dikes and flooding the province of Holland. The Dutch offered to concede all their strongholds in Flanders and to pay an indemnity of 10 million livres. This would have given Louis victory and left the Dutch frontier defenseless. But Louis demanded a virtual surrender of sovereignty: major territorial concessions within the seven provinces themselves, French commercial and religious penetration, an indemnity of 24 million livres, and most insulting of all, an annual embassy to present a medal in tribute to Louis, like a Roman satellite acknowledging its emperor.

These humiliating demands may have been the worst mistake of Louis' career. The Dutch dug in, determined to resist to the end. The republican Regime of True Liberty that had governed the Netherlands since 1650 was overthrown; its leader, Jan de Witt, was torn to pieces by an angry mob, and the 22-year-old Prince William of Orange was summoned as stadholder and captain general of the army. Louis thus raised up his own worst enemy, for

William of Orange, stadholder of the Netherlands and later, as William III, king of England, was the heart and soul of European opposition to Louis XIV for thirty years. [Scala/Art Resource]

the dour but capable William was to be the heart and soul of European resistance to Bourbon France for the next 30 years. With French troops stalled by the floodwaters, he gained support from Spain and Austria. By 1674 the French had withdrawn from Dutch soil. The Treaty of Nijmegen (1678) not only affirmed Dutch independence but forced the French to lower their own tariffs against Dutch goods. Louis had lost the war.

Aggression Without War: Louis Against Germany

Despite this check, the French state, with its army of 250,000 men, was the strongest not just in Europe but probably in the world. The Dutch were exhausted, the Spanish enfeebled under their last Habsburg king, the ailing and incompetent Charles II, and the Austrians preoccupied by a new Turkish advance along the Danube that brought Ottoman armies under the grand vizier, Kara Mustafa, to the gates of Vienna by 1683 for the first time in a century and a half. Only a relief army commanded by the king of Poland, Jan Sobieski, saved the imperial capital. Louis, meanwhile, continued his war of nerves along the Rhine. He claimed any area on or near his borders that had ever been French by law or custom, a tactic not unlike the one Hitler employed in Germany in the 1930s. Accordingly, French troops occupied large parts of Flanders, Luxembourg, Alsace, and the Saarland after 1680, as well as the free city of Strasbourg. Even Casale Monferrato in northern Italy admitted a French garrison.

Louis insisted that these actions were in accordance with the treaties of Westphalia and Nijmegen. He certified each claim in special courts set up for that purpose, the Chambers of Reunion. In the absence of any international court of arbitration, what better title could be established? But as his courts and armies pushed farther and farther into the heartland of Germany, the princes of the Holy Roman Empire became alarmed. Alarm turned to panic when, in 1685, Louis revoked the Edict of Nantes, which had guaranteed freedom of worship to French Protestants. If the French king's worst diplomatic miscalculation was to have rejected the Dutch peace terms of 1672, the revocation of the Edict of Nantes was his greatest domestic blunder. The thousands of refugees who fled across the border with their tales of persecution were among Louis' most productive subjects, and their skills were soon enriching his enemies. Meanwhile, under Habsburg leadership, the German princes hastily formed a defensive alliance, the League of Augsburg (1686).

The War of Five Continents

When Louis entered the Rhenish Palatinate in September 1688 to support his claims in the region, he began a war that was to outlast all the protagonists but himself. Ranging over five continents and lasting 25 years, it was the first truly global war in history. No war of comparable scale was to be seen again until the twentieth century. For the first time, the quarrels of Europe became the affair of the world.

The 1683 siege of Vienna, here depicted in a composite view, marked the last great Muslim advance in Europe, although the Turks remained a presence on the continent until the early twentieth century. [Austrian National Library, Vienna]

The conflict had two distinct phases. The Nine Years' War (1688–1697) was fought largely along the disputed frontiers of Flanders and Germany, though it reached as far afield as North America, where it was known as King William's War. At first the French had the advantage. But Louis had too many enemies now to win a decisive victory. The Anglo-Dutch alliance was revived in the most dramatic way when William of Orange, responding to a secret invitation from a coalition of English lay and religious leaders, sailed to England in November 1688 and deposed James II. William became king of England (as William III), reigning jointly with his wife Mary (1689–1695), James' elder daughter, while continuing to govern the Netherlands through his able regent, Antonius Heinsius. With such a base, William soon brought Spain, Austria, and Savoy together in a grand anti-French alliance. By the end of the war virtually all of Europe east of the Elbe was fighting France. Louis could not be dislodged from his strong defensive position. But the war took a terrible toll within France itself. Poor harvests, soaring grain prices and military requisitions caused a devastating famine in 1694–1695. Before it had run its course, 2 million French subjects—one-tenth of the population—had died. It was a man-made disaster comparable in its effects on France only to World War I.

The Treaty of Ryswick (1697) compelled Louis not only to restore almost all the territories he had occupied since 1678 but also to withdraw recognition from his hapless guest and pensioner, the former James II, and to acknowledge his archenemy William III as king of England. But a new round of warfare was in the offing, for even higher stakes. For a third of a century, the dynastic politics of Europe had swirled about the fate of the Spanish throne, whose feeble and childless occupant, Charles II, had presided helplessly over the ruin of a once-great power. When Charles died at last in 1700 his government was so impoverished that it could not pay for masses for the repose of his soul. Yet Spain still held much of the southern Netherlands and most of Italy, as well as its great empire in the Americas. In the hands of a competent ruler, it might still regain its former glory; in the hands of a foreign one, it was an incomparable asset.

So thought both Louis XIV and his Habsburg contemporary and anatagonist, the Austrian emperor, Leopold I (1658–1705). Since neither was willing to concede control of the whole Spanish patrimony, either by themselves or through dynastic proxies, they had begun to negotiate for Spain's division as early as 1668. As Charles II's death at last became imminent, an effort was made to find a compromise candidate for the throne. This failed, however,

The Disasters of War

In 1695, at the height of the great famine, which had been induced by a combination of bad harvests, wartime requisitions, soaring inflation, and speculation and hoarding, a remarkable open letter circulated among elite circles in France. Addressed to Louis XIV, it was probably the work of an outspoken clergyman, François Fénelon (1651–1715). Its view of the king's pursuit of gloire *is a very different one from that offered by Bossuet.*

Your people, Sire, whom you should love as your children, and who up to this time have been so devoted to you, are dying of hunger. The land is left almost untended, towns and countryside are deserted, trade of all kinds falls off and can no longer support the workers; all commerce is at a standstill. . . . For the sake of getting and keeping vain conquests abroad, you have destroyed half the real strength of your own state. Rather than take money from your poor people, you ought to feed and cherish them. . . . All France is now no more than one great hospital, desolate and unprovided. . . . And it is you, Sire, who have brought these troubles on yourself. . . . Little by little the fire of sedition catches everywhere. The people believe that you have no pity for their sufferings, that you care only for your own power and glory. They say that if the king had a father's heart for his people, he would surely think his glory lay rather in giving them bread and a little respite after such tribulations than in keeping hold of a few frontier posts which are a cause of war.

Source: P. Goubert, *Louis XIV and Twenty Million Frenchmen* (New York: Pantheon, 1970), p. 220.

and when Charles died, he unexpectedly willed his throne and all his dominions to the Bourbon claimant Philip of Anjou, Louis' grandson, who became Philip V of Spain (1700–1746).

Britain and France: The Contest for Empire

The result was the second phase of the great war of France against Europe, the War of the Spanish Succession (1701–1713). Louis moved quickly to consolidate his hold on Spain and its possessions. It was a foregone conclusion that Austria would resist. England and the Netherlands were even more directly menaced. With the occupation of the Spanish Netherlands, the last buffer between French and Dutch territory had been stripped away. The English found their access to the Mediterranean cut off and their empire in the New World threatened.

William III swiftly organized a new Grand Alliance against Louis. It was his last accomplishment. In March 1702 he died following a fall from his horse, to be succeeded in England by James II's younger daughter, Anne (1702–1714), while in the Netherlands Heinsius remained the dominant figure until his death in 1720. The Anglo-Dutch alliance held, though England was now decidedly the senior partner. The English general John Churchill, duke of Marlborough (1650–1722), the greatest soldier of his age, turned back Louis' thrust into Bavaria at Blenheim (1704) and crushed French armies at Ramillies (1706) and Oudenaarde (1708) in Flanders. Meanwhile, the superior Anglo-Dutch fleet kept France at bay in the New World and Africa. By 1709 Louis' position was desperate. Allied armies were poised on the borders of France itself, the treasury was empty, and famine ravaged the land. A bitter parody of the Lord's Prayer circulated at court: "Our father who art at Versailles, whose name is no longer hallowed, whose kingdom is no longer large, give us our daily bread. . . ."

Louis held out, stiffened by demands not only that he surrender all the conquests of his reign but that he help drive his grandson from the Spanish throne as well. At Malplaquet, the bloodiest battle on European soil up to that time, he blunted the allied advance. Thereafter, the Grand Alliance dissolved and the war wound down. The cluster of treaties known as the Peace of Utrecht (1713) left Spain and its overseas dominions to Philip V, though on condition that his throne never be united with that of France. Spain's possessions in the Netherlands and Italy were given to Austria, partly to compensate it for the lost Spanish throne and partly as a buffer against French expansion, though the Dutch received so many concessions in the former area that they actually dominated it. England's prizes reflected its increasing concern with empire. Gibraltar and Minorca gave it control of the Mediterranean, Nova Scotia and Newfoundland entrenched it on the North American coast, and trading concessions offered a foothold in the lucrative slave trade of Spanish America.

The wars of 1688–1713 were fought to contain the territorial ambitions of the French in Europe. In retrospect, however, they marked the first stage in the great contest of empire between England and France that, resumed in the war cycles of 1740–1763 and 1792–1815, would end only with Wellington's defeat of Napoleon at the Battle of Waterloo. They marked as well the final eclipse of Spain as a great power. The Austrians gained the most territory in Europe itself, but their greatly distended borders were to prove more of a burden than an asset in the long run.

Louis XIV and the Climax of Absolutism

Despite its defeat, France was still the greatest power on the European continent. When Louis XIV died on September 1, 1715, he had reigned longer than anyone else in the history of the world and had dominated his time more completely than anyone since Charlemagne. If he had failed ultimately to impose his will on Europe, it had taken the united strength of his adversaries to contain him. Yet the sum of Louis was more than his parts. He was neither a great soldier nor a genuine innovator. His economic views were firmly rooted in the rigidly protectionist doctrines of mercantilism, and his persecution of the Huguenots drove away many of his most productive subjects. Although he personified divine right kingship, his religion was conventional and often opportunistic. Even his administrative reforms looked backward to the traditions of personal monarchy rather than forward to the modern bureaucratic state. If he showed what could be accomplished by a determined royal absolutism, he showed the limitation of such a system as well. It was left to his arch-rivals, the English, to develop on a large scale what the Dutch polity had already suggested: that a politically stable oligarchy with a moderate representative base could be a far more effective instrument of government than an absolute monarchy dependent on the will and energy of a single man.

Peter the Great and the Emergence of Russia

As forceful as Louis XIV and far more despotic, Peter I (1682–1725), called the Great, consolidated autocracy in Russia and brought his country into the European state system. From its modest beginnings in the fourteenth-century duchy of Muscovy, Russia had become the largest

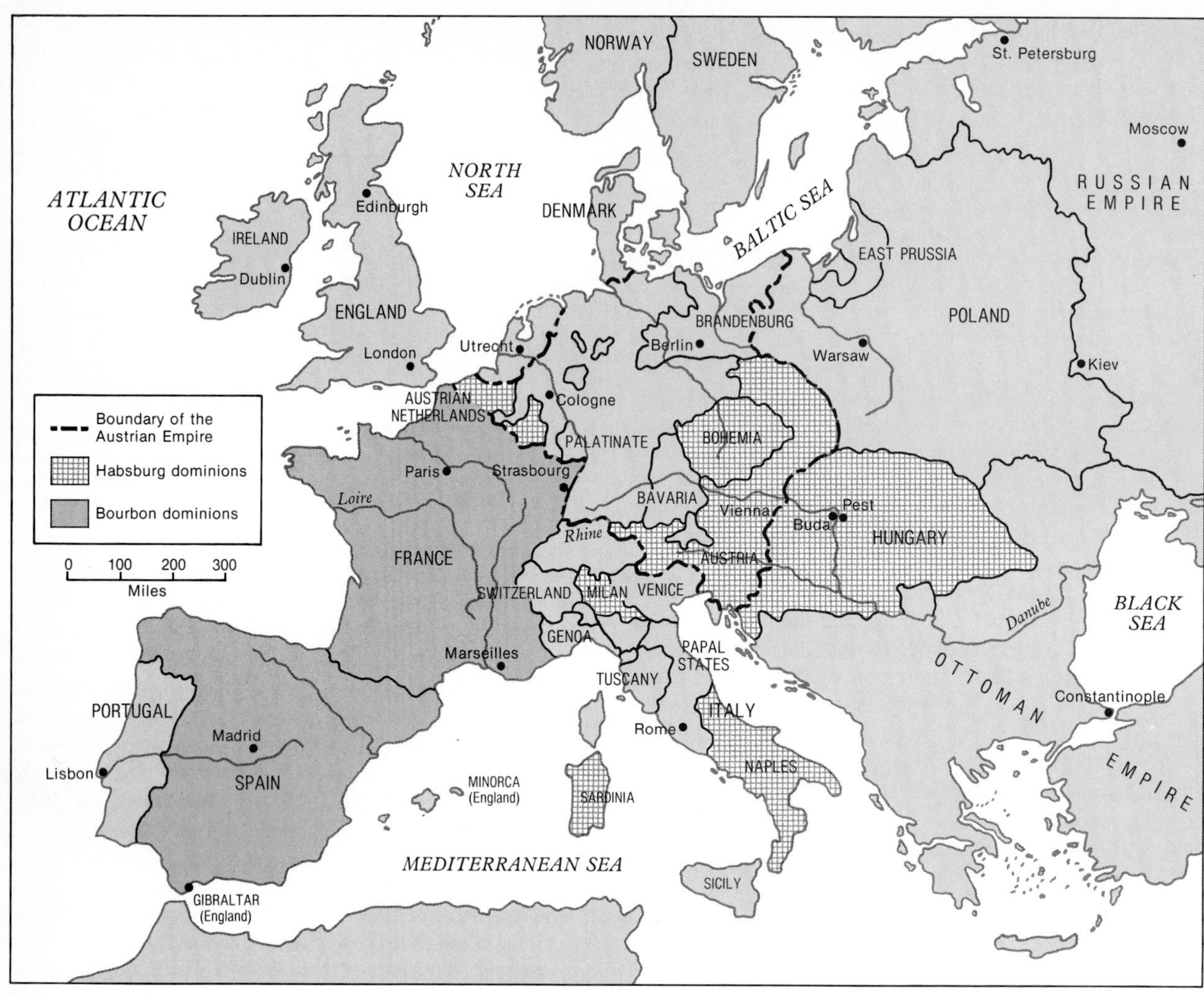

22.2 Europe in 1714

state in the world by Peter's time. Three times the size of Europe, it spanned the Eurasian landmass from the Polish steppe to the Pacific Ocean, embracing some 5.7 million square miles. Much of this expansion had taken place in the seventeenth century, culminating in the first Russian settlement on the Pacific (1647), the reconquest of the ancient Rus' capital of Kiev (1654), and the pacification of the Siberian tribes.

The Tsarist State

This vast land had a population of only 14 million, only one-fortieth the density of France or Italy. Grain yields were comparable only to those of pre-Carolingian agriculture in the West, compelling almost the entire population to farm; only 2 percent lived in towns. The tsarist state and its nobility had undertaken to control this scarce labor supply since the late fifteenth century, first restricting and at last completely eliminating all freedom of movement. By the seventeenth century the Russian peasantry had been fully enserfed except in some frontier areas, and for all practical purposes enslaved. The great law code, or *Ulozhenie,* of 1649, which served as the basis of Russian society for the next 200 years, formalized its rigid, castelike divisions. Each person's status was fixed by law down to the last detail. Townsmen as well as peasants were bound to their dwellings and occupations. The nobility had become a civil service class since, apart from the clergy, only those who performed state service were permitted to own land. Few societies have ever been more tightly controlled. The concept of personal rights, so important to the development of the West, simply did not exist. Authority could be questioned only by authority. Only the tsar was free, and his freedom—that is, his power—was absolute. What an Austrian ambassador to Russia said in the early sixteenth century was if anything even more true at the end of the seventeenth:

> **In the sway the tsar holds over his people, he surpasses all the monarchs of the whole world. . . . He uses his authority as much over ecclesiastics as laymen, and holds unlimited control over the lives and property of all his subjects; not one of his counsellors has sufficient authority to dare to oppose him, or even differ from him, on any subject. They openly confess that the will of the prince is the will of God, and that whatever the prince does he does by the will of God.[2]**

Peter and the West

This was the throne that passed to Peter the Great. Like Louis XIV, he experienced a turbulent minority. At the death of his father, Alexis (1645–1676), his half brothers Feodor (1676–1682) and Ivan (1682) succeeded, but both were incompetent, and in 1682 the nobility proclaimed the 9-year-old Peter tsar instead. The country was saved from civil war only by Peter's sister, Sophia, who ruled in his name until 1689. The Peter who came to young manhood then needed no help from anyone. Nearly 7 feet tall and with strength and appetites to match, he was no less ambitious than the ruler of Versailles but far less prudent. All but one of his 36 years of active rule were spent at war. Military expenditures consumed more than 80 percent of his revenue. Even church bells were melted down into cannon. The Russian state was turned into a gigantic battering ram, and it was aimed west.

At the same time, Peter was deeply impressed by the advanced technology and warcraft of the West. He studied tactics and fortifications and built a standing army of 300,000 that, despite Russia's acute manpower shortage, was made up largely of his own subjects, whom he conscripted for life. In 1697–1698 he became the first Russian prince to visit the West, where he and his entourage made a sensation. A bemused William III was his host in Holland and England, where he ignored protocol by touring and even working in foundries and dockyards. The ruler of the world's largest landmass was fascinated by the sea and proudly flourished a certificate declaring him a master shipwright. William invited him to attend a session of England's Parliament. Peter was impressed by the sight of subjects speaking openly to their sovereign, but constitutional monarchy was not one of the Western innovations he brought home with him.

Peter's first military efforts were directed against the Ottoman Turks, from whom he wrested Azov on the Black Sea in 1696. His attention than turned to the Baltic. Here, 1,000 miles from Moscow, he built a new capital, St. Petersburg, whose royal residence, the Winter Palace, rivaled Versailles in its splendor.

But Peter still lacked a secure northern seaport except at Archangel (Arkhangelsk) on the White Sea, whose harbor was frozen nine months a year. Access to the Baltic was blocked by Sweden, whose territory enclosed it on three sides. The eastern end of the Swedish triangle included the traditionally Russian Karelian peninsula, which Sweden had occupied during the Time of the Troubles. Tsar Alexis, Peter's father, had failed to recapture it. The time now appeared ripe. Sweden's hardy but scattered population of 1.5 million seemed insufficient to defend it against a concerted attack. Its new ruler, Charles XII (1697–1718), was still a boy. With Denmark, Poland, and Brandenburg-Prussia as allies, Peter declared war.

The result was the Great Northern War (1700–1721). After swiftly dispatching Denmark, the warlike Charles, not yet out of his teens, humiliated Peter at Narva (1700), crushing an army five times the size of his own. Muscovy lay defenseless before him. But Charles turned to secure his rear in Poland, giving Peter time to rebuild. By 1704 Peter had retaken Narva. Not content merely with fighting a major war, however, he was simultaneously building his new capital and attempting to join the Don and Volga rivers by a canal, thus giving full access to his port at Azov.

Peter's insatiable demands on the country at last provoked revolt. Invoking the name of the rebel Stenka Razin, the Cossack chieftain Kondraty Bulavin rose in 1707. He burned villages along the whole length of the Don, and cannon were mounted on the Kremlin walls. At the same time, Charles began his long-awaited invasion, striking south into the Ukraine. Peter himself lay ill. Desperately seeking help, he turned to his old ally, England. But the English, fighting their own war with Louis XIV and fearing that Charles might turn against Austria if not otherwise occupied, sent Marlborough the length of Europe personally to persuade the Swedish king to attack Russia.

Victory at Poltava (1709) saved Peter. While Charles was forced to seek refuge in Turkey, Peter overran Karelia and the Baltic provinces of Ingria, Estonia, and Livonia, securing the ports of Revel and Riga. These gains were confirmed by the Treaty of Nystad (1721), which established Russia as the major power in the Baltic. Peter celebrated by assuming the titles of father of his country and emperor and accepted formally the appellation of "the Great." "By our deeds in war," he exulted, "we have emerged from darkness into the light of the world."

The Reforms of Peter

Peter dreamed of yoking the great rivers of Russia together by a system of canals, thereby linking the vast expanses of his realm to his new outlets on the sea. Azov was lost to the Turks in 1711, and with it ten years' labor on the Don-Volga canal. Undaunted, Peter linked the

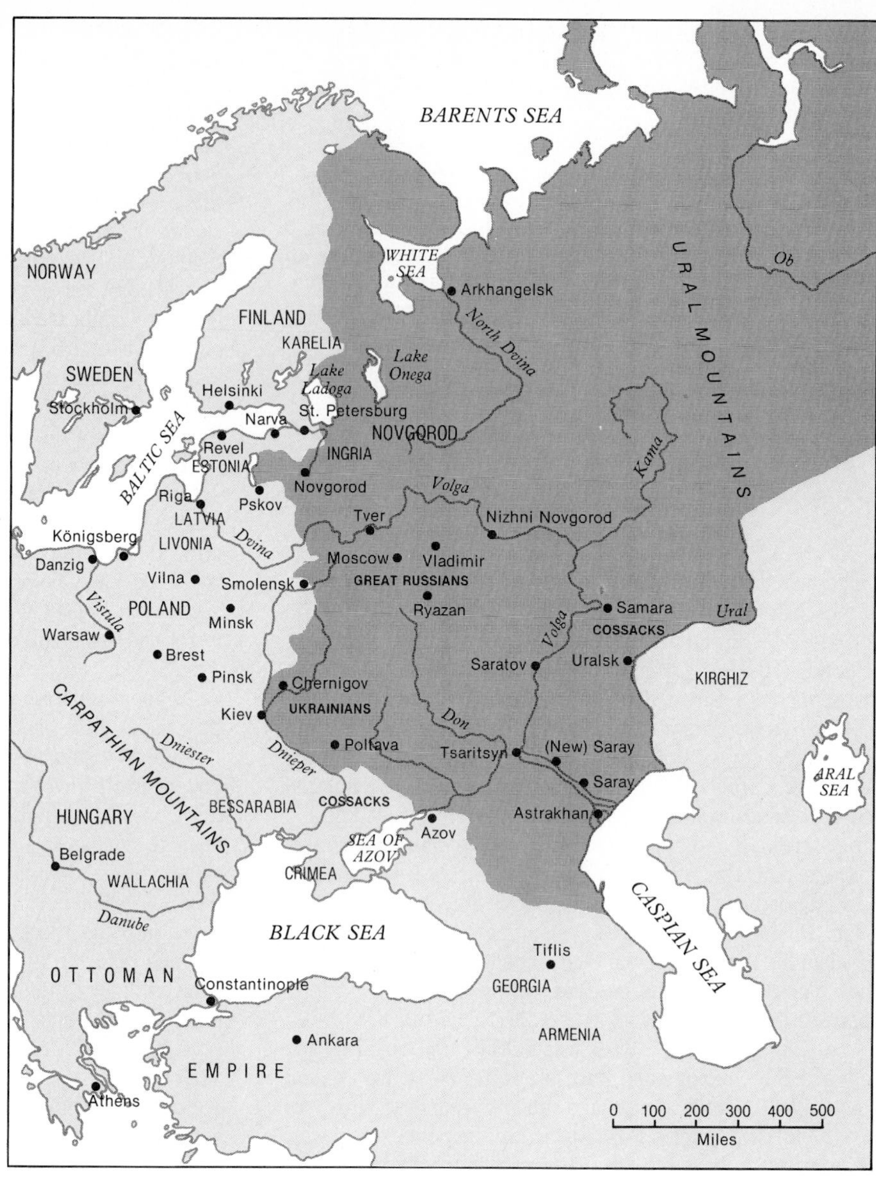

22.3 Russia in the Age of Peter the Great, 1689–1725

Volga to St. Petersburg's river, the Neva, thus uniting the Caspian Sea with the Baltic. Thousands of lives were lost on the project, but within a decade of Peter's death flotillas of flat-bottomed barges were moving the grain and oak timber of central and southern Russia steadily to market.

Peter reorganized his government on the latest Western models. He replaced the old boyar duma (council of nobles) with a nine-member senate, in effect a supreme council of state, and reduced the 40-odd ministries to 12, each headed by a "college" of senior officials reporting to the senate. The countryside was also divided into new provinces and districts. The purpose of the whole, as Peter straightforwardly told the senate, was "to collect money, as much as possible." In this it was successful; tax revenues tripled over the course of the reign.

Foreigners were at first brought in to coordinate the new system and even to staff it. But Peter had always intended that his boyars be bound, as before, to state service. To learn Western ways, he compelled them to adopt Western food and dress and to shave their beards, personally shearing off any he saw in his presence. There were grislier acts of submission as well. When his palace guard, the *Streltsi*, rebelled in his absence, Peter forced the palace nobility to participate in their executions.

In 1722 Peter capped his administrative reforms with the Table of Ranks, which created a new hierarchy of 14

Law and Justice Under Peter the Great

Ivan Pososhkov (1652–1726) was a Russian merchant and entrepreneur who was frequently in trouble with the law and ultimately died in prison. This passage reflects both his own frustration with an often arbitrary and capricious judicial system and the horrific abuses to which it could easily give rise.

There is no man more excellent and judicious than Prince Golitsyn, yet in 1719 I petitioned him for permission to build a distillery and for a license to supply vodka for sale, but he had me put under arrest for no known reason. I remained in custody for a whole week and began to get impatient at being there so long without knowing why. On the eve of the Lady Day fast I asked the corporal of the guard to inform the Prince of my case and Prince Golitsyn said: "Has he been in custody long?" And the corporal said: "A whole week, Sir." And he at once ordered my release. Now I am not entirely without position, I think, and Prince Golitsyn knows me personally; yet I was detained for a whole week for no reason at all. How much worse is the case of a man of no account who will be arrested and forgotten about? In this way a great number of innocent folk languish in prison and die there before their time. . . . I am truly astounded that judges are in the habit of holding men in prison for five or six years or more. If judges and governors were to inspect the new prisoners daily this would no longer happen and there would be no possibility of an innocent man being imprisoned or kept in custody.

Source: I. Pososhkov, *The Book of Poverty and Wealth* (Stanford, Calif.: Stanford University Press, 1987), p. 207 (modified slightly).

military and civil service grades. It permitted commoners as well as nobles to enter state service, ennobling them either upon receiving an officer's commission or attaining the civilian rank of collegiate assessor. In this way Peter broadened the base of the landowning class and gave room to talent from below, though the most privileged positions were still reserved for the old nobility. This system remained essentially intact down to 1917.

The church was also thoroughly restructured. The office of patriarch, assumed by the metropolitan of Moscow in 1589, had in the hands of such men as Philaret (1619–1633) and Nikon (1652–1666) rivaled the power of the tsar, as Peter himself complained. In 1700 he permitted it to lapse, and in 1721 he replaced it with the Holy Synod, a body closely tied to the state. He reduced the number of monasteries and nunneries as well and diverted much of their income into his own coffers, though they were too much a part of the fabric of Russian life to be done away with altogether, as he would probably have wished. For Peter, all idle hands were useless, and praying hands were idle.

Peter the Great, himself clean-shaven after the fashion of the West, decreed that his nobility must shear off the beards that were a traditional mark of their status. Recalcitrant nobles were fined or, as here, subjected to compulsory barbering. [Granger Collection]

There were perhaps 3,000 foreigners in Russia at the beginning of Peter's reign, many of whom lived in the so-called German suburb of Moscow. Peter brought in many more to staff his ministries and run his new technical schools and fledgling industries. Their heathen mores aroused the ire of churchmen and nobles, and native merchants resented their privileges; they even sometimes inspired actual panic in the countryside. At one point a wild rumor circulated that Russian men would be forbidden to marry for seven years so that foreigners imported by Peter (himself viewed by many as the Antichrist) could take their women instead. One of the rallying cries of the Cossack rebellion was a demand for the expulsion of all foreigners.

Despite this, Peter persisted in his attempts to westernize Russia. He reformed the calendar and redesigned the alphabet, ordered translations of the Greek and Roman classics, and hired a German troupe to perform French comedies in the Kremlin Square. In 1703 he introduced the first newspaper into Russia, which he edited himself. He built the first Russian greenhouses and laboratories and in 1724 established the Russian Academy of Sciences, though its first members were all Germans.

Peter died in February 1725, leaving an unsettled succession and an exhausted realm. But he had created the foundations of a modern state and economy and made Russia a permanent part of Europe. The Western powers were not slow to recognize this. Peter's ambassador in Vienna reported after Poltava, "It is commonly said that the tsar will be formidable to all Europe, that he will be a kind of northern Turk." By 1711 Prussia was already proposing an anti-Russian alliance, and the British fleet appeared in the Baltic to challenge Peter's presence.

In many ways, Peter's life was a struggle to tame himself as well as Russia. The young tsar who loved to trick his courtiers by signing decrees with pseudonyms became the statesman who introduced orderly, bureaucratic government to his realm. The man who corresponded on politics with the great philosopher Leibniz had ungovernable fits of rage and beat his ministers. As a foreign visitor observed, "He is a prince at once very good and very bad; his character is exactly that of his country." In his passionate contradictions, Peter mirrored the conflicts of a Russia torn between the isolation of its past and the world presence of its future.

Austria: The Dynastic State

After the division of the Habsburg crown in 1555 between its Spanish and Austrian branches, the Austrian monarchy consisted of three major units, the hereditary provinces of Austria itself; the so-called crown of St. Wenceslas, comprising Bohemia, Moravia, and Silesia; and the crown of St. Stephen, including Hungary, Transylvania, and Croatia. Bohemia and Hungary had become part of the Habsburg dominions in 1527 after the Battle of Mohács, though much of Hungary was still contested. Indeed, only the continuing threat of the Turks in southeastern Europe could have united so disparate a group of peoples—Germans, Czechs, Magyars, Croats, Slovaks, Slovenes, Italians, Romanians, Ruthenians—under a single head. Turkey may in this sense be said to have engendered the Austrian monarchy; nor was it a coincidence that the final expulsion of Turkey from Europe in the early twentieth century should have been followed shortly after by the collapse and dismemberment of the Habsburg empire. The histories of Turkey and Austria rose and fell together.

Austria in the seventeenth century might be described as a power but not a state. The imperial title was recognized only in the Austrian provinces proper; the Habsburg emperor was separately king of Bohemia and Hungary. The chief unifying factor in this strange entity, whose ruler lacked a single title and whose lands lacked a common name, was the person of the monarch himself. His government was actually a series of ongoing negotiations with the provinces of his realm, whose noble estates possessed extensive powers, including the right to veto imperial taxes and, in Hungary, even to rebel.

After the failure of Ferdinand II's attempt to reassert his power as Holy Roman Emperor in the Thirty Years' War, his successors, Ferdinand III (1637–1657) and Leopold I, concentrated on achieving internal consolidation. The Counter-Reformation in Austria was, in its political dimension, a struggle against the Protestant nobility who were dominant in Bohemia and Hungary. Bohemian Protestantism had been ruthlessly suppressed after 1620, and the native nobility was replaced by Catholic loyalists. A similar policy was applied in Hungary after 1671 following an abortive rebellion. While the zeal to root out heretics tended to diminish in states that had achieved political stability, the Habsburgs continued their efforts to impose religious uniformity and, with it, centralized control. Such persecution fell most heavily on the Jews, who were expelled from all of Lower Austria as a pious act by Leopold I despite the fact that his principal financier, Samuel Oppenheimer, was and remained a Jew.

Religious orthodoxy was linked to what the Habsburgs saw as their special mission: the defense of Christian Europe against the menace of the Ottoman Turks. After a period of quiescence following the Treaty of Sitva-Torok (1606), the Turks crossed the Danube in strength in 1663, ravaging Hungary, Moravia, and Silesia. Repulsed at St. Gotthard by a papal-sponsored and Austrian-led army, they acceded to the Truce of Vasvar (1664). This treaty formally divided Hungary, which, though nominally a Habsburg principality, had long enjoyed semi-independence as a border region between the two great powers. When the Turks renewed the war in 1683 with an army of 200,000 men, the Hungarians, preferring the Ottoman yoke to what they had seen of the Habsburg, joined forces with the invaders. The Turks were also assisted by Louis XIV, who saw the attack as a welcome opportunity to divert Leopold's attention from his own aggression on the Rhine, though he temporarily suspended aid as a gesture to European public opinion when the Turks stormed up to the very gates of Vienna, subjecting it to a two-month siege.

The relief of the Habsburg capital by John III Sobieski of Poland (1673–1696) was hailed throughout Europe as a miraculous deliverance. It was a historic moment, for it marked the last great thrust of Muslim power that had threatened Europe for nearly 1,000 years. In the war that ensued, climaxed by Prince Eugene of Savoy's great victory at Zenta (1697), the Turks were driven permanently from the Danube basin and back upon the Balkans. They might have been expelled completely from Europe had France heeded the appeal of Pope Innocent XI to join the Habsburg alliance. But the bitter rivalry between Bourbon and Habsburg prevented any such union, leaving a significant Turkish presence on the continent for more than two centuries.

The Treaty of Karlowitz (1699) gave the Habsburgs possession of virtually all of Hungary, Transylvania, and Croatia. Hungary's crown of St. Stephen was declared hereditary in the Habsburg family (1687). The Magyar nobility was not purged, as in Bohemia, and it was permitted to retain its provincial assemblies and national diet. But its power was curbed, and non-Magyar nobles were settled in the new lands, as well as German and Slavic peasants. The result was a new Magyar rising under Prince Ferenc Rakoczi, which lasted from 1703 to 1711. The defiant Magyars, with their proud sense of isolation among the surrounding Slavic populations, remained the most refractory of the Habsburg empire's many peoples.

The Habsburgs thus faced three major problems during the long reign of Leopold I and after: in Germany, to contain Louis XIV and to restore the influence if not control of the emperor; in the east, to defend the frontier, first against Turkey and later Russia; and at home, to assert the imperial authority over a fractious and independent nobility. Each of these tasks seemed beyond their strength. French influence appeared well on the way to replacing Austrian in Germany. The timid Leopold had fled Vienna at the approach of the Turks, and only the courage of a foreign prince had saved the empire. The monarchy's plight at home was symbolized by the efforts of Charles VI (1711–1740) to gain support for the Pragmatic Sanction, which tried to establish the principle of a common succession in all Habsburg lands and thus ensure a single rule.

Yet the unwieldy Habsburg state continued to grow. Its victories against the Turks had doubled its effective size during the reign of Leopold I. The Treaty of Rastadt (1714) brought it the Spanish Netherlands and most of Italy. Another brief war with Turkey (1716–1718) pushed its borders into the Balkans. Even Prince Eugene, who conducted this campaign, expressed misgivings about the acquisition of so much territory. A swollen empire now stretched from the Carpathian Mountains to the North Sea. The Habsburgs had multiplied their subject populations but had devised no strategy for integrating them.

Prussia: The Garrison State

A very different course was pursued by Prussia, which emerged from the rubble of post-Westphalian Germany to become a major European power and the ultimate unifier of Germany as a whole. Prussia had its origin in the electoral mark of Brandenburg, a flat, sandy terrain south of the Baltic coast that passed in 1417 to the princely house of Hohenzollern. In 1618 the elector of Brandenburg acquired the duchy of Prussia, then a fief of Poland, giving the dynasty its first access to the sea. At about the same time (1614) he fell heir to Cleves, a small duchy on the Rhine. These three entities were widely separated on the map. Their populations, half German and half Pole, half Lutheran and half Catholic, half serf and half free, had nothing in common but their ruler. During the Thirty Years' War, all three territories were overrun by foreign armies. Brandenburg was occupied between 1627 and 1643, and the population of its capital, Berlin, fell from 14,000 to 6,000. Many towns were destroyed completely.

Under these circumstances 20-year-old Frederick William (1640–1688), later known to history as the Great Elector, succeeded to the Hohenzollern legacy. By 1648 he had built up an army of 8,000, a small force but one sufficient to obtain for him a part of the coastal region of Pomerania and the ecclesiastical principalities of Magdeburg and Halberstadt at the Conference of Westphalia. Frederick William had the means of a prince but the ambition of a great dynast. When Pomerania and East Prussia were menaced by a war between Sweden and Poland in 1655, he ignored the refusal of the Brandenburg estates to vote new taxes and collected them by force. Though he lacked a royal title, he considered himself as much a divine right ruler as Louis XIV, demanding recognition of this from the estates of Prussia and landing 2,000 troops in its capital, Königsberg, to enforce his claim. Frederick William found the key to state-building in the maintenance of a standing army, which he swelled to 30,000. The army was both his excuse for raising taxes and his means of compelling payment. His soldiers collected taxes directly and exercised police powers as well. Thus from the first, the Great Elector broke down the distinction between civilian and military functions.

Frederick William was not uniformly successful. He made no further territorial gains after 1648 despite participating in two major wars and was thwarted in his lifelong goal of connecting Prussia with the rest of his dominions,

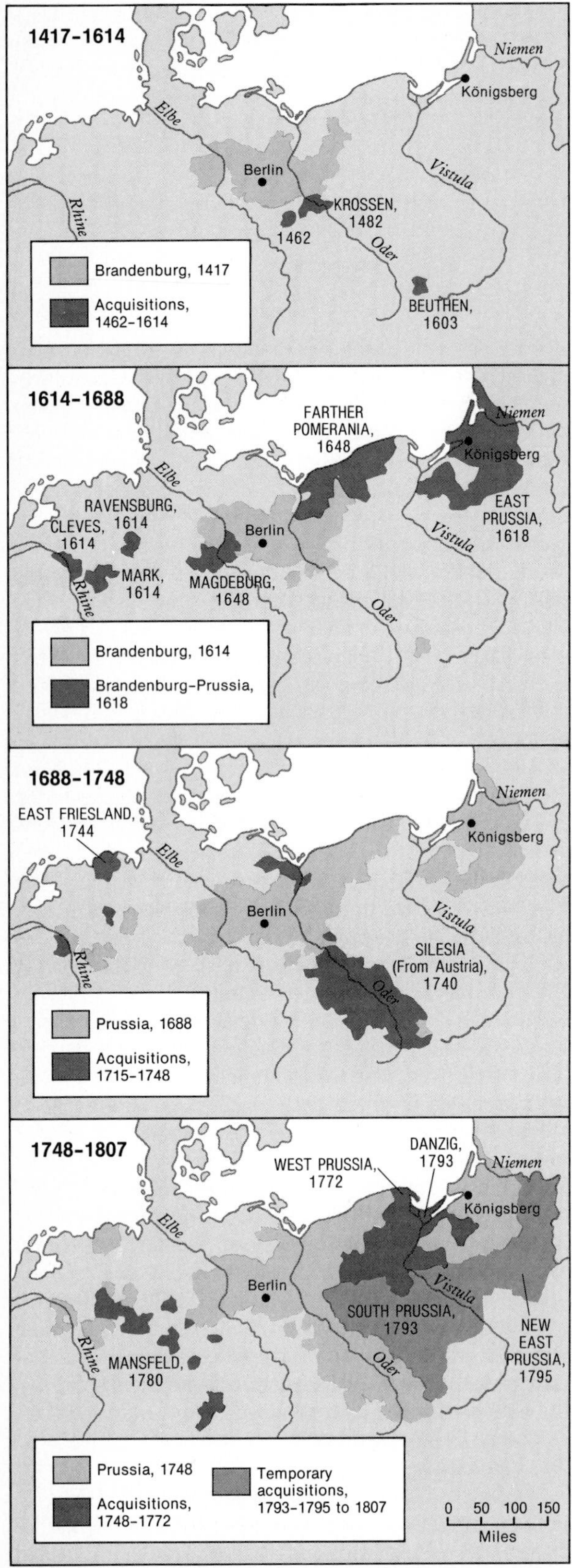

22.4 The Rise of Brandenburg–Prussia

a task not accomplished until 1772. Though he tripled his tax revenues, he remained dependent on foreign subsidies to maintain the army. To conciliate the nobility, he exempted them from his new taxes. These fell mainly on the towns instead, thereby frustrating his goals of commercial and industrial development. Like Peter the Great, however, he required service of the nobility, particularly in the army. Thus while curbing the nobility's privileges on a political level—that is, their power to obstruct him—he confirmed their social preeminence and integrated them into his absolutist state.

The elector Frederick III (1688–1713) was recognized as King Frederick I of Prussia in 1701 in return for his participation in the War of the Spanish Succession against Louis XIV, though Prussia contributed little. The task of state-building was resumed by his eccentric but capable successor, Frederick William I (1713–1740). The Great Elector had seen the army as an instrument of state power; under his grandson and namesake, the army to all intents and purposes became the state. With the establishment of the General Directory in 1723, which combined the functions of the war and finance councils, the entire governing apparatus down to the lowliest tax collector or quartermaster in the provinces revolved about the needs of the army. Frederick William divided the country into recruitment districts and regimental cantons. The army was not segregated in barracks but billeted among the general population, so that civilians, particularly in the towns, were continuously exposed to the impress of military discipline and drill. No sight in Prussia was more common than a parade. In addition to the regular career army, every Prussian male was subject to three months of military service a year. By this means Frederick William was able to maintain a standing army of 80,000 men on a population base of only 1.5 million. Not since ancient Sparta had a society lived so completely by the military ideal.

Under Frederick II (1740–1786), also called "the Great," Prussia reached the full status of a great power. Frederick was the most impressive monarch of the eighteenth century, and at least for the first half of his reign he dominated continental politics almost as completely as Louis XIV had done. Frederick broke with the personal austerity and Calvinist piety of his father. He was a son of the Enlightenment who flirted with atheism and entertained the philosopher Voltaire; a soldier-king whose armies, like Louis XIV's, held off half of Europe. In his social policies, however, he adhered closely to the practice of his father. Each class was assigned its duties from above. The higher ranks in the army and the state bureaucracy were reserved for the nobility. Merchants and townsmen were obliged to accept a subordinate position. They could neither purchase noble land nor aspire to noble status. Frederick had kind words for the peasantry, which, he declared, deserved the greatest respect because it carried the heaviest burdens. He did little to relieve those burdens however, even in East Prussia, where peasants were enserfed and in many respects little better than enslaved by the local nobility, known as Junkers.

Eastern European Absolutism in Context

Vast Russia, divided Austria, and militarized Prussia took different routes after 1650 toward a common goal: the centralization of authority. All three were landlord states where peasant labor was largely unfree and trade and industry were largely undeveloped. All three lacked suitable outlets to the sea until the eighteenth century, and despite the efforts of Peter the Great to build a Russian navy, none became a true maritime power. Thus the commercial pressures that spurred the development of centralized (though not necessarily absolutist) authority in western Europe were not directly present. But the impressive wealth and power of the Atlantic states—England, France, and the Netherlands—were very much on the minds of Romanov, Habsburg, and Hohenzollern sovereigns. Peter the Great's visit to the West in 1697–1698 determined him to modernize his country. The Great Elector had been educated in the Netherlands and dreamed, though in vain, of emulating its commercial success. The Habsburgs, too, sought to encourage mining and industry and even attempted to establish overseas trading companies as the Dutch and English had done. Mercantilist doctrines that equated the amassing of treasure and the increase of state power took hold in the east just as they had begun to give way to more sophisticated models in the west. In England, particularly, a more flexible political and financial system emerged in the wake of a second rebellion to give it a signal advantage in the new global context of European state competition.

England: The Triumph of Parliamentary Government

The Stuart monarchy had been restored in 1660 under a formula that defined the government as consisting of king, lords, and commons. But it was not clear where the balance of authority lay among these three elements. A newly constituted Convention Parliament, composed chiefly of nobles and other great landowners, compelled the new king, Charles II (1660–1685), to accept its terms. The crown could no longer create special courts outside the jurisdiction of the common law, nor could it collect taxes not authorized by Parliament. The king was obliged to issue a general amnesty for all but those directly responsible for his father's death. In all, 13 persons were executed, an astonishingly small number in view of the scale of the rebellion and the customs of the age. Finally, Charles agreed to exchange his traditional feudal revenues for a permanent grant of customs and excise taxes, thus freeing the magnates from all restrictions on the ownership of their estates and shifting the tax burden from the landed classes toward the towns.

Charles was not even able to reward those who had supported him. Royalists whose estates had been confiscated during the revolution were permitted to sue for their recovery, but those who had sold them, even under duress, received no compensation. This too confirmed the rebel gentry in their gains and accelerated the tendency toward concentration of land ownership. Charles' promise of religious toleration was swept away by his first elected parliament. This "Cavalier" Parliament, as it was nicknamed for its initially reactionary tone, restored the supremacy of the Anglican church and placed severe restrictions on all other forms of worship. Some 1,200 ministers were ejected from their parishes for refusing to accept a new prayer book and to take an oath of conformity, creating a schism within English Protestantism that persists to the present day.

Charles' return was generally popular at first, though a republican underground persisted. But his honeymoon was short-lived. An unsuccessful war with the Dutch resulted in the fall of his chief minister, the earl of Clarendon (1667), and a similar fate befell his successor, the earl of Danby (1678). Charles' most persistent problem was money. The grant of taxes he had received in 1660 was calculated to meet his expenses. It proved insufficient, however, and he remained financially and therefore politically dependent on Parliament. Charles sought to escape this dependence by obtaining a French subsidy in return for supporting Louis XIV's war against the Netherlands (Treaty of Dover, 1670). But Charles also agreed secretly to announce his conversion to Catholicism and, if necessary, to accept French troops to impose it on the country. The rumor of this agreement poisoned the remainder of his reign. Parliament responded in 1673 by passing the Test Act, which barred all religious dissenters from public office. The real object of attack was the king's younger brother and prospective heir, the openly Catholic duke of York. After a wave of anti-Catholic hysteria following allegations in 1678 of a Jesuit plot to assassinate Charles, three successive parliaments attempted to ram through an act excluding the duke of York from the throne. The country seemed again on the verge of civil war. But the opposition party, called the Whigs, was divided in its aims, some members favoring alternative candidates to the throne and some the establishment of a republic. The king was able to rally his own supporters, the Tories, behind the principles of direct hereditary succession and divine right. The leading Whigs were banished or executed, and, on his deathbed, Charles was finally received into the Catholic church.

The Glorious Revolution and the Revolutionary Settlement

The duke of York succeeded peacefully as James II (1685–1688). He promised to preserve the constitution and the supremacy of the Church of England. He was already 51, and without a male heir. The country hoped that his brief Catholic reign would pass without serious incident.

But James soon revealed his true intentions. He placed Catholics in key civil and military positions. This violated the Test Act, but James claimed that he was not bound by former acts of Parliament. He camped Irish troops above London, allowed Jesuits to proselytize freely, and imprisoned seven Anglican bishops for refusing to read a proclamation giving freedom of worship to Catholics and Protestant nonconformists. When James reported the birth of a son in June 1688, thus opening the possibility of a Catholic dynasty, Whigs and Tories swiftly united. They called on William of Orange to free the country.

William's invasion was one of the great gambles of history. Victory meant the possibility of combining England and the Netherlands into a force capable of resisting Louis XIV; defeat meant the loss of his fleet and, most likely, his country. Landing on the coast of Devon in the southwest on November 5, William was hailed as a liberator. Most of James' army deserted him, and James was forced to flee into exile.

William summoned a parliament, which declared him jointly sovereign with his wife, Mary. Over the next dozen years they built a new constitutional order that, much modified by time and circumstance, has remained both the basis of English government itself and the primary model of representative government the world over. The Bill of Rights (1689) declared the supremacy of all law passed by Parliament. Henceforth, no king could levy taxes, maintain an army, or create new organs of government without

The Right to Alter Government

In 1688 England deposed a king for the second time in 40 years. Writing to justify the right of a sovereign people to alter its institutions of government, John Locke (1632–1704) offered what would become a classic defense of revolution.

The reason why men enter into society is the preservation of their property, and the end why they choose and authorize a legislature is that there may be laws made and rules set as guards and fences to the properties of all the members of the society. For since it can never be supposed to be the will of the society that the legislative should have a power to destroy that which everyone designs to secure by entering into society and for which the people submitted themselves to the legislators of their own making: whenever the legislators endeavor to take away and destroy the property of the people or to reduce them to slavery under arbitrary power, they put themselves into a state of war with the people. . . . By this breach of trust they forfeit the power the people had put into their hands for quite contrary ends, and it devolves upon the people, who have a right to resume their original liberty and the establishment of a new legislative (such as they shall think fit), to provide for their own safety and security, which is the end for which they are in society. . . . What I have said here, concerning the legislative in general holds true also concerning the supreme executor, who having a double trust put in him, both to have a part in the legislative, and the supreme execution of the law, acts against both when he goes about to set up his own arbitrary will as the law of the society.

Source: J. Locke, *Two Treatises of Government,* ed. P. Laslett (Cambridge: Cambridge University Press, 1964), pp. 430–431 (spelling and punctuation modernized).

Parliament's consent. No Englishman could be arrested without legal warrant, detained by excessive bail, or subjected to "cruel and unusual punishments"—a phrase incorporated directly into the American Bill of Rights a century later. Though they lacked the phrase for it, the framers of this new order—which came to be known as the Revolutionary Settlement—worked to contain executive authority by a separation of powers. The king might not tamper with elections or interfere with free speech in Parliament, nor might royal officials sit in the House of Commons. Similarly, judges could no longer be removed by the king, only through parliamentary impeachment. Some of these ideas proved unworkable, such as the ban on electioneering and the exclusion of officials from Parliament, and others were modified in practice. But the essential principles of legislative and judicial independence remained.

The new system worked awkwardly at first. With the threat of James removed, Whigs and Tories fell out with each other over the spoils of power. There were genuine differences between them as well, however. Though both derived from the landed gentry, the Whigs tended to embrace the great London merchants who believed in commercial and colonial expansion and eagerly supported parliamentary supremacy. The Tories, by contrast, were reluctant revolutionaries, rural and isolationist, who regarded 1688 as a tragic necessity rather than a brilliant opportunity. William naturally tended to rely on the Whigs, and with their support he chartered the Bank of England (1694). Private banks had been in operation in England since the 1650s, and the Bank of Amsterdam (1609) was the most important commercial institution in Europe. The Bank of England, however, represented a new kind of marriage between private capital and government. It was established for the specific purpose of lending William £1.2 million—nearly a year's ordinary revenue—to help finance the war against Louis XIV. By borrowing rather than taxing, William was able to tap an almost limitless source of funds. Thus was born the idea of a permanent national debt and with it the power of modern government.

By 1713 the public debt stood at £54 million, nearly 100 times more than in 1688. This was the money that defeated Louis XIV. Some feared that without the need to rely on Parliament for taxation, the monarchy would soon become independent of any control. But the Whig magnates who funded William through the bank were the same men who supported him in Parliament. The struggle between crown and Parliament had ended in the discovery of common interests: war, empire, and profit.

The only thing that threatened this new partnership was the fragility of the Stuart line in England, represented by Queen Mary. At William III's death, he was succeeded by Mary's sister Anne (1702–1714), none of whose 16 children had survived. Parliament settled the succession on the electoral house of Hanover in Germany, distantly related to the Stuarts through the daughter of James I. At the same time, it declared that no Catholic could ever sit on the throne of England, thus barring James II and his son, James Edward. As a further precaution, the Whigs united Scotland with England in 1707, thus creating the modern Great Britain. When Anne died, some Tory leaders, unwilling to relinquish divine right, rashly backed an invasion attempt by James Edward. The Whigs, who staunchly supported the new dynasty, were more firmly entrenched than ever and remained the dominant political force in the country until 1760.

LATE STUART AND HANOVERIAN LONDON

If Paris was the cultural capital of Europe and Amsterdam its financial center, London's time was fast approaching in the late seventeenth century. With a population of about 500,000 to 600,000 by 1700, it was, with Paris and Edo (Tokyo), one of the three largest cities in the world. Whereas only one of every 40 or 50 Frenchmen was a Parisian, however, one of every ten Englishmen lived in London, fully half the urban population of the country.

The magnet of London was trade. People engaged in commerce and manufacturing averaged four times the income of those who farmed. The wealth and produce of the entire country flowed daily into the city: great droves of turkeys who walked the roads from Norfolk and Suffolk, sheep from Lincoln and Leicester, cattle from Wales and the Scottish Highlands, corn from the midland counties, cheese from Cheshire, fish from Kent, coals from Newcastle, stones from Dorset. London "sucks the vitals of trade in this island to itself," wrote Daniel Defoe, the author of the immensely popular *Robinson Crusoe* (1719). Daily, 3,500 boats and barges plied London's river, the Thames; in 1700, 77 percent of England's foreign trade and nearly 60 percent of its shipping passed through the city.

By the late seventeenth century a lively business culture had grown up around a new London institution, the coffeehouse. Over 500 of them flourished in the reign of Queen Anne. Merchants wrote maritime insurance at Lloyd's, and brokers traded stocks and securities at Jonathan's and Garraway's in Exchange Alley (a formal stock exchange was finally licensed by the government in 1697; the first crash followed in 1720). Noblemen and men of fashion, artists and scholars had their favorite houses too. Here men exchanged news and gossip; read the daily newspapers, which, beginning with *The Daily Courant*, had reached a circulation of 67,000 by 1714; and avidly consumed political pamphlets and the popular periodicals, *The Tatler* and *The Spectator*. But the new climate of business so evident after 1688 predominated. As Defoe, himself the editor of an influential journal, *The Review*, put it

***Gin Lane*, William Hogarth's devastating portrayal of the poverty and degradation that lay at the heart of Britain's imperial capital and their consequences. A besotted, pox-ridden mother is oblivious as her infant falls over a wooden rail; an emaciated drunk is on the brink of death by starvation, while another hangs himself in an exposed tenement; and the very walls of the city begin to topple. *Gin Lane* was one of the earliest examples of the power of social propaganda; a year after it was published, the consumption of cheap gin was sharply curtailed by law. Little was done, however, about the underlying squalor and despair of which gin drinking was only a symptom. [Lauros-Giraudon/Art Resource]**

simply, "the main affair of life" appeared to be "getting money."

The face of London also changed in this period. The Great Fire of September 1666 burned down 13,000 of the city's old timbered houses. Most were rebuilt with brick and mortar, many in the classical style popularized by Sir Christopher Wren (1632–1723), England's greatest architect. The new West End suburbs of Bloomsbury, Piccadilly, and St. James' were marked by splendid squares and esplanades down which the rich and fashionable paraded or were carried in coaches or sedan chairs. But the vast majority of the population lived quite otherwise, in one-room tenement apartments without water or sanitation on streets so crowded and obstructed by carts, overhangs, basements, and open sewers that movement was next to impossible. The working poor of the city—porters, coal heavers, dockworkers, scavengers, domestics—lived hand to mouth in squalor and filth. An underworld of thieves and cutthroats preyed on this population, their activities all but uncontrolled in a world where life was cheap, riot common, and policing virtually nonexistent. (By contrast, Paris had instituted an effective police force as early as 1667.) The introduction of cheap gin in the second quarter of the eighteenth century sent the death rate soaring, particularly among the destitute. The London magistrate and reformer Henry Fielding observed that gin was "the principal sustenance . . . of more than a hundred thousand people in this metropolis." A man too poor to eat could drink himself into a stupor for a penny. Even after an act of Parliament regulated the consumption of gin, 1,000 people a year starved to death in the richest city of the world.

The state system of Europe in the second half of the seventeenth century and the first half of the eighteenth century was characterized by the tension between monarchies that attempted to extend and centralize their authority, often by appeal to divine right, and landed aristocracies that generally resisted them, seeking to reassert traditional privileges. In most cases the monarchies prevailed to a greater or lesser extent, sometimes by coercion, sometimes by cooptation, and sometimes with the assistance of a new elite of merchants, bankers, and bureaucratic office-holders. In France, the leading power on the Continent throughout the period, this process was clearly visible in the policies of Louis XIV, who placed men of bourgeois origin in the most important offices of state and kept his nobility in opulent idleness at Versailles.

In England, by contrast, the landed and mercantile elites united to create through revolution a uniquely successful partnership between limited monarchy and a broad governing class. In Russia the absence of constitutional tradition enabled Peter the Great to subordinate his nobility and to replace Sweden as the major power in the north, while the retreat of Turkish power left Habsburg Austria, despite its diffuse political structure, dominant in southeastern Europe. The most extraordinary example of state building was in Prussia, where a series of able and determined rulers welded a scattered and unpromising patrimony into a formidable military machine. These new patterns of power produced a Europe more politically complex, competitive, and interdependent than ever before.

Notes

1. G. Treasure, *Seventeenth Century France* (New York: Barnes & Noble, 1966), p. 334.
2. R. K. Massie, *Peter the Great* (New York: Knopf, 1980), p. 177.

Suggestions for Further Reading

Anderson, P. *Lineages of the Absolutist State*. London: N.L.B., 1974.

Baxter, S. B. *William III and the Defense of European Liberty, 1650–1702*. New York: Harcourt, Brace & World, 1966.

Blum, J. *Lord and Peasant in Russia from the Ninth to the Nineteenth Century*. Princeton, N.J.: Princeton University Press, 1961.

Carsten, F. L. *The Origins of Prussia*. Westport, Conn.: Greenwood Press, 1981.

Clark, G. N. *The Later Stuarts, 1660–1714*. 2d ed. Oxford: Clarendon Press, 1958.

——. *War and Society in the Seventeenth Century*. Cambridge: Cambridge University Press, 1958.

Evans, R. J. W. *The Making of the Habsburg Monarchy, 1550–1700*. New York: Oxford University Press, 1979.

Goubert, P. *Louis XIV and Twenty Million Frenchmen*. New York: Pantheon, 1972.

Greaves, R. L. *Deliver Us from Evil: The Radical Underground in Britain, 1660–1663*. New York: Oxford University Press, 1986.

———. *Enemies Under His Feet: Radicals and Nonconformists in Britain, 1664–1677*. Stanford, Calif.: Stanford University Press, 1989.

Hatton, R. M., ed. *Louis XIV and Absolutism*. Columbus: Ohio State University Press, 1977.

Hellie, R. *Slavery in Russia, 1450–1725*. Chicago: University of Chicago Press, 1982.

Kamen, H. *Spain in the Later Seventeenth Century*. London: Longman, 1980.

Kann, R. A. *A History of the Habsburg Empire, 1526–1918*. Berkeley: University of California Press, 1974.

Kenyon, J. P. *Revolution Principles: The Politics of Party, 1689–1720*. Cambridge: Cambridge University Press, 1977.

Laslett, P. *The World We Have Lost*. London: Methuen, 1965.

Massie, R. K. *Peter the Great*. New York: Knopf, 1980.

Plumb, J. H. *The Growth of Political Stability in England, 1675–1725*. London: Macmillan, 1967.

Riasonovsky, N. V. *The Image of Peter the Great in Russian History and Thought*. New York: Oxford University Press, 1985.

Rosenberg, H. *Bureaucracy, Aristocracy, and Autocracy: The Prussian Experience, 1660–1815*. Boston: Harvard University Press, 1958.

Rude, G. *Paris and London in the Eighteenth Century*. New York: Viking Press, 1971.

Rule, J., ed. *Louis XIV and the Craft of Kingship*. Columbus: Ohio State University Press, 1970.

Spielman, J. P. *Leopold I of Austria*. London: Thames & Hudson, 1977.

Sumner, B. H. *Peter the Great and the Emergence of Russia*. New York: Macmillan, 1951.

Wolf, J. B. *Louis XIV*. New York: Norton, 1968.

CHAPTER · 23

Europe's Century of Genius

Science is the systematic attempt to understand the world and to adapt it to human uses. As such, it is as old as culture itself. The establishment of the first major civilizations was concurrent with the Neolithic revolution that occurred about 8000 B.C. The advances made in China between the third and thirteenth centuries A.D. may be considered a second scientific revolution. But the development of modern science that began in Europe in the sixteenth and seventeenth centuries and, having spread across the globe, continues today at an accelerating pace has transformed not only our relation to the environment but the environment itself. It thus stands as one of the most momentous changes in human history.

This illustration from Vesalius' *De Fabrica* (1543), the first great textbook of modern anatomy, shows the sheaths of muscle beneath the skin. The body is posed upright against a typical Renaissance landscape, as if to emphasize the relationship between a human's natural elements and those of the world. [Lynn Mooney/College of Physicians and Surgeons]

From Ancient Science to the Copernican Revolution

It is often assumed that the scientific revolution was a sudden breakthrough that cleared away the mists of legend, superstition, error, and ignorance with which the human imagination had cloaked the world and revealed the physical universe in its true light. Nothing could be further from the truth or indeed further from the nature of modern science itself. The scientific revolution was the product of particular historical circumstances and imperatives and the culmination of a rich and varied intellectual tradition. Without the circumstances and the tradition, its achievement would have been impossible.

The Legacy of Antiquity

Classical antiquity had bequeathed a rich scientific heritage to Western civilization. Mathematics, astronomy, biology, and medicine were all highly developed. Much about the physical world was accurately known, and many modern theories had their origin in Greek science. Pythagoras had deduced that the earth was a sphere in the sixth century B.C., and Eratosthenes in the third century B.C. measured its diameter to within 90 percent accuracy. Anaximander, a contemporary of Pythagoras, offered the first theory of the earth's evolution, based on his discovery of fish fossils in mountain areas far removed from the sea. A century later, Leucippus and Democritus put forward the first atomic theory of matter. These theories were not universally accepted however. Aristotle put the great weight of his authority behind the rival theory of Empedocles that matter consisted not of complex structures of atoms but of compounds of the four primary elements of earth, air, fire, and water. Similarly, the third-century B.C. speculation of the astronomer Aristarchus that the sun rather than the earth was the center of the universe was rejected in favor of the geocentric view Aristotle sponsored, and given its classical expression in the work of Ptolemy of Alexandria (second century A.D.).

The Romans made little contribution to scientific theory, although their technological achievements—dams, irrigation, road building, engineering, plumbing, and heating—were unequaled in the West until the Renaissance. The period after the fall of the Roman Empire in the West, with its erosion of civic life and loss of records, interrupted the literate culture and the social and state patronage on which scientific development depended. The heritage of Greek science was continued in Byzantium, however, and even more intensely in the Arab world. Following the Arab conquests of the seventh century, Islam served as a focal point for Greek, Egyptian, Persian, and Indian traditions of thought. The introduction of paper from China provided the means of transforming the largely oral Arab culture into written form. The result was an enormous diffusion of knowledge. Whereas the sixth century Roman historian Cassiodorus had access to only one treatise by Galen (c. 130–200), the greatest physician of the ancient world, by 900 the Arabs had translated some 129 of his works. Arabic science improved on Greek measurements and astronomical calculations and built the world's first observatories in the ninth century. It culminated in the career of Ibn Sina or Avicenna (c. 980–1037), whose breadth of interest and learning in philosophy, medicine, natural history, physics, chemistry, astronomy, mathematics, and music rivaled that of Aristotle. (See Chapter 8.)

The Medieval World Picture

By the twelfth century Arab science had begun to decline, in part because of the breakup of what had been a unified empire into warring principalities. Shortly after, however, a revived and expanding western Europe began to cull its fruits. Arab scientists and their Greek predecessors were both translated into Latin. Aristotle's prestige was so great in the medieval West that he was referred to simply as "the Philosopher," as if no rival could exist, and indeed none challenged him until the sixteenth century.

Reassimilating Greek science into the western tradition meant reconciling it with Christian doctrine. Fortunately, Ptolemy's geocentric model of the universe proved readily compatible with Christian notions about man's central position in the divine order. The cosmos was held to consist of an arrangement of ten concentric spheres rotating around a fixed, motionless earth. The first two of these spheres carried the moon and the sun. The next five were occupied by the known planets, and the eighth, like a giant diadem, carried all the stars. The last two spheres were dark, but their rotation was held to account for apparent changes in the positions of the stars. Beyond the tenth sphere, whose distance from the earth was estimated by Campanus of Novara (c. 1205–1296) at 73 million miles, was the throne of God, surrounded by his angels and the souls of the righteous. The spheres themselves were moved by angels, since according to Aristotle all bodies not activated by a constant external force would come to rest. In keeping with the perfection of the heavens, the celestial bodies were composed of a pure, unchangeable substance, the quintessence. For this reason any alteration among the celestial bodies, such as the appearance of a comet or the great explosion of the Crab nebula in 1054, was looked upon as a divine portent, since they could not naturally alter by themselves. On earth, humans were locked in the prison of time and decay, but when they looked up, what they saw was the picture of eternity.

This view of the heavens was deeply satisfying. It combined a credible explanation of the natural world with a religious view of the cosmos as the theater of human redemption, in which humankind was the center of God's concern just as the earth was the center about which the heavens revolved. Medieval maps showed Jerusalem as the center of the earth and therefore of the universe, completing the perfect symmetry of the cosmos. It was true that certain details refused to fit in. Some physical bodies, such as projectiles, failed to behave as the Aristotelian theory of motion said they should. Some of the planets and fixed stars appeared to be wayward in their orbits. But these problems did not seem enough to shake an edifice built up over the centuries, hallowed by tradition, and deeply entwined with the belief and value systems of Christianity.

But new currents were running beneath this placid surface. The fourteenth and fifteenth centuries saw serious challenges to the authority of the church during the Babylonian captivity and the Great Schism. The French philosopher and bishop Nicholas of Oresme (c. 1323–1382) observed that it was fortunate that faith instructed people that the earth could not rotate on its axis and that there could be no bodies beyond the fixed stars, for it could not be demonstrated either by argument or observation. Oresme's comment illustrated the loss of confidence in the belief of men such as Thomas Aquinas that reason and revelation both disclosed the same truth about the world. A century later, the German Nicholas of Cusa (1401–1464) asserted the rotation of the earth despite official doctrine. With the Reformation, there was no longer a single authority to interpret the Christian faith. By the early seventeenth century the Jesuit Cardinal Robert Bellarmine (1542–1617) felt obliged to concede that in cases where reason and the Bible differed about the natural world, reason must be accepted. For the first time in the history of the church, faith was no longer the final arbiter of knowledge.

This mosaic from the cathedral in Siena, Italy, depicts the legendary lawgiver of ancient science, Hermes Trismegistus, with a figure who is probably meant to be Moses, giver of the moral law. The paired sphinxes in the lower-right-hand corner represent Hermes' allegedly Egyptian origins. The mosaic dates from the 1480s, when the Neoplatonic revival that so influenced Copernicus was at its height. [Alinari/Art Resource]

The Hermetic Challenge

At the same time, the authority of Aristotle was being questioned as well. The Greek scholars who fled after the fall of Byzantium in 1453 brought with them texts not previously known in the West. Prominent among these were the writings of Hermes Trismegistus ("thrice-great"), believed to be an Egyptian who had received divine revelations about the physical world at the time Moses had been given the Ten Commandments. In fact, Hermes was fictitious, and his texts were the product of third-century A.D. Neoplatonists working in Alexandria. The so-called Hermetic doctrine viewed the material world as an emanation of divine spirit. All objects were related to each other by sympathy or antipathy through the energies of this spirit, which could be released and manipulated by those who knew how to pair the right objects. Humans, the highest compound of matter and spirit, were destined to command the forces of the natural world by learning to read the book of nature and to decipher its hidden codes.

The Hermetic doctrine greatly stimulated interest in chemistry, botany, metallurgy, and astronomy, since the celestial bodies were believed to be the agency by which the divine spirit was transmitted. The sun, as the most important of these, was held to be at the center of the universe, rather than the earth, as in Ptolemaic theory. Hermeticism thus revived the heliocentric theory of Aristarchus, although on a mystical rather than a mathematical or mechanical basis. But mathematics was crucially important for the Hermeticists too. They believed, as Plato and Pythagoras had, that the universe was ultimately constructed in terms of mathematical proportions and harmonies. As the medieval mystic had sought to know the God of love by prayer and meditation, the disciples of Hermes sought to understand the Divine Mind through the mathematical harmonies by which it expressed itself. Mathematics was the highest form of understanding, both of the physical world and of the God who manifested himself in it.

Much of Hermeticism tended to degenerate into the cruder forms of magic, alchemy, and astrology. But the image of man as a natural magician calling forth the hidden powers of the world had great appeal. It suggested that there was still much to be learned about the world beyond the categories of Aristotelian science. Shakespeare's hero Hamlet reflects this new sense of possibility when he tells his loyal but conventional friend, "There are more things in heaven and earth, Horatio, than are dreamt of in your philosophy," and Prospero, the hero of his last play, *The Tempest* (1611), is a portrait of the Renaissance man as a Hermetic magician.

The Neoplatonic revival was only one element that contributed to the crisis of knowledge and belief in the sixteenth century. The Reformation had deeply unsettled people's assurance about the nature of grace and salvation and undermined their faith in those who had interpreted spiritual knowledge. The discovery of the New World shattered their faith in the adequacy of their knowledge of the physical world as well. The scientific revolution was a product of this upheaval and shared in its difficult birth the tensions and contradictions of the age.

The New Order of Knowledge

The most important convert to the Hermetic doctrine was the Polish astronomer and mathematician Nicholas Copernicus (1473–1543). Born in Toruń on the Polish-German frontier, he imbibed Hermeticism in the course of a ten-year sojourn in Renaissance Italy. Copernicus was convinced that the majesty of the cosmos demanded that the sun be at its center rather than the earth. As he explained his conception:

> **In the middle of [the cosmos] sits the Sun enthroned. . . . Could we place this luminary in any better position from which he can illuminate the whole at once? He is rightly called the Lamp, the Mind, the Ruler of the Universe; Hermes Trismegistus names him the visible God. . . . So the sun sits as upon a royal throne ruling his children, the planets which circle around him.**[1]

This engraving, from Johannes Hevelius' *Cometographia* (1608), shows the excitement generated by Copernican astronomy. In the foreground, three scholars compare their calculations; in front of them is an armillary sphere representing the celestial globe, together with a sextant, while on the roof of the building in the background observers train a telescope and measuring devices on the heavens and the comet coming into view. Comets were of intense interest for both scientific and superstitious reasons, as they were held to portend great events. [Department of Special Collections and University Archives, Stanford University Libraries]

Copernicus devoted the rest of his life to proving not only that the heliocentric theory of the Hermeticists was preferable to that of Ptolemy on aesthetic and religious grounds but also that it offered a better account where Ptolemy's theory was weakest, in explaining celestial motion. This claim was reflected in the title of his treatise, *On the Revolution of the Heavenly Spheres*, whose publication he authorized only on his deathbed in 1543. Copernicus assumed that only the earth and the five planets actually moved. The sun was motionless at the center of the universe as the fixed stars were at the periphery, their apparent motion being accounted for by the rotation of the earth. This was a great theoretical simplification, although the mathematics necessary to calculate the actual position of the stars relative to a moving earth were hardly less complex than Ptolemy's. Copernicus was also able to dispense with the idea of giant crystalline spheres moved by angels, which Christian doctrine had superimposed on Ptolemy's original theory. Heavenly bodies moved and rotated because it was their nature to do so; put a globe in space, Copernicus argued, and it will spin. Such an idea contradicted the Aristotelian notion that bodies not externally propelled would come to rest, but it did not explain why some bodies—the earth, the moon, and the planets—were in motion, while the sun and the stars were not.

The Copernican theory offered a credible but not compelling alternative to the Ptolemaic system. Its calculations of the celestial orbits were no less complex, and it created as many mathematical and physical problems as it solved. Martin Luther's reaction was typical. "That is how things go nowadays," the great German reformer said. "Anyone who wants to be clever must not be satisfied with what others do. He must produce his own theory as this man does, who wishes to turn the whole of astronomy upside down."[2] No other astronomer accepted Copernicus, and his theory was kept alive only in Hermetic circles. One such convert, the Italian philosopher Giordano Bruno (1548–1600), argued that the sun around which the earth revolved was only one of innumerable suns in an infinite universe, each of which might harbor planets and species like our own. Bruno fell into the hands of the Inquisition and was burned at the stake. Such were the perils of unguided speculation on the basis of Copernicus' theory. Catholics and Protestants alike condemned it. The greatest astronomer of the late sixteenth century, Tycho Brahe (1546–1601), explicitly rejected it.

But the Copernican theory did not die. The appearance of a bright new star in the sky in the 1570s, followed by a brilliant comet, reminded people that there were phenomena not explained by Ptolemy's static system. Tycho Brahe's meticulous celestial observations served a young German astronomer, Johannes Kepler (1571–1630), who had come to Copernicus through his own Hermetic beliefs. Kepler made the crucial discovery that the orbits of the planets were not circular, as both Ptolemy and Copernicus had assumed, but elliptical. This enabled him to simplify

On the Infinity of the Universe

The Copernican displacement of the earth from the center of the universe led the Italian philosopher Giordano Bruno to question the very notion of a "center" in space and to contend for the idea of an infinite universe that reflected the infinite power and glory of God.

How is it possible that the universe can be infinite? . . . I say that the universe is entirely infinite because it has neither edge, limit, nor surfaces. But I say that the universe is not all-comprehensive infinity because each of the parts thereof that we can examine is finite and each of the innumerable worlds contained therein is finite. I declare God to be completely infinite because he can be associated with no boundary and his every attribute is one and infinite. And I say that God is all-comprehensive infinity because the whole of him pervades the whole world and every part thereof comprehensively and to infinity. . . . What argument would persuade us that the Agent capable of creating infinite good should have created it finite? And if he has created it finite, why should we believe that the Agent could have created it infinite, since power and action are in him but one?

The influence of Bruno's daring hypothesis can be seen in the work of a contemporary scientist, William Gilbert.

Who has ever made out that the stars which we call fixed are in one and the same sphere, or has established by reasoning that there are any real and, as it were, adamantine spheres? No one has proved this, nor is there a doubt but that just as the planets are at unequal distances from the earth, so are these vast and multitudinous lights separated from the earth by varying and very remote altitudes. . . . How immeasurable then must be the space which stretches to the remotest of fixed stars! How vast and immense the depth of that imaginary sphere! How far removed from the earth must be the most widely separated stars and at a distance transcending all sight, all skill, all thought!

Source: D. W. Singer, *Giordano Bruno: His Life and Thought* (New York: Schuman, 1950), pp. 66–67, 250, 257, 262.

Copernicus' calculations, giving him for the first time a decisive advantage over Ptolemy. Ironically, however, Kepler's discovery was itself rejected by the man whose work finally undermined the Ptolemaic theory, Galileo Galilei.

Galileo and the Copernican Triumph

Galileo (1564–1642) was born in Pisa, Italy. After completing studies in mathematics and natural philosophy, he joined the faculty of the University of Padua, where Copernicus had studied a century before. Galileo was the first important figure to accept Copernicus outside the Hermetic circle. His own inspiration was the ancient Greek mathematician Archimedes (287–212 B.C.), whose works had been republished in 1543. Archimedes, like Pythagoras, had attempted to describe the world in purely mathematical terms. Unlike Pythagoras, however, he attributed no mystical significance to the mathematical proportions he found in nature, and unlike the Neoplatonists, he posited no spiritual basis in matter. For him, and for his latter-day disciple Galileo, the world was best thought of as a gigantic machine operating by simple principles expressible in geometric ratios.

Galileo's espousal of the Copernican theory and his own celestial discoveries were decisive in gaining acceptance for the new astronomy, while his strict adherence to a mechanistic view of the cosmos purged it of lingering Hermetic elements. [Art Resource]

In such a world there was no room either for Aristotle's mythical quintessence or for the medieval angels who moved the stars. Galileo's own most important work was his discovery of the principle of accelerated motion, in which he brilliantly connected velocity and distance to the variable of time. But he caused a sensation when in 1609 he turned a newly invented instrument, the telescope, on the heavens. Galileo discovered four moons in orbit around the planet Jupiter, and so many hundreds of previously undetected stars that he declared them to be innumerable. This seemed to suggest a startling confirmation of Bruno's belief in an infinite universe. Galileo also demonstrated that the surface of the moon was rough and eroded, thereby demolishing the theory of a perfect and unchanging heaven.

Copernicus had disclosed his findings only with great caution during his lifetime, but Galileo, armed with his new observations, rushed boldly into print. He claimed that the truth of the Copernican theory had now been established, and when confronted with the familiar scriptural story of Joshua making the sun stand still, he retorted that the Bible might be adequate for ignorant laymen but could hardly qualify as a scientific treatise. This was too much for the Catholic church. Despite the burning of Bruno, it had never officially condemned the Copernican theory. It did so now, however (1616), and when Galileo defiantly published a further defense of Copernicus in his *Dialogue Concerning the Two Chief World Systems* (1632), he was arrested by the Inquisition, threatened with torture, and obliged to recant his belief in the heliocentric system. But though Galileo might be silenced, his challenge to received authority could not. What he represented was not the familiar problem of the heretic who challenged Christian doctrine on its own terms but a rival system of truth that bypassed it as irrelevant to the description and understanding of the physical world. For Galileo, observation was the guide, experiment the test, and mathematics the language of physical reality. No other form of understanding was necessary, no other authority acceptable.

Thus Copernicus, who believed that the sun was the lamp of nature and the image of God, was vindicated by the mystic Kepler, who believed that the planets and stars were souls who danced to the music of the spheres, and by the rationalist Galileo, who banished spirit and purpose from the world of matter and left only physical bodies obeying the mechanical laws of motion. What all three held in common was the language of mathematical proof. It was by mathematics that Copernicus turned the Neoplatonic doctrine that the sun was the center of the universe into a plausible description of the actual cosmos, by mathematics that Kepler was able to demonstrate the superiority of that description to its rivals, and by mathematics that Galileo was able to begin constructing the new physics of motion that the Copernican universe required.

Other Scientific Advances

If the common language of mathematics made astronomy and physics the cutting edge of the scientific revolution, chemistry, medicine, anatomy, and biology all advanced as well. As in the case of astronomy, the impetus for development often came from Hermetic and Neoplatonic doctrine. The Swiss-born German physician Theophrastus Bombastus von Hohenheim (1493–1541), called Paracelsus, launched a one-man crusade against the influence of Aristotle and Galen in medicine. Paracelsus was imbued with the spirit of medieval and Renaissance magic. He believed that occult forces were at work everywhere in nature and that demons could even divert the courses of the stars. It would be hard to imagine a mind further removed from the cool, rational skepticism of Galileo. Yet Paracelsus' very belief in the omnipresence of magical forces led him away from the traditional textbooks—he is said to have burned all the medical classics before delivering his introductory lecture at the University of Basel in 1527—and back to nature. In accordance with Hermetic doctrine, he believed that the structure of the human organism was directly analogous to that of the natural world and that specific organs of the body were sympathetically related to specific plants, minerals, chemical substances, and even stars. The disorders of the body came from disturbances in the natural harmony between the body and the world, and their remedies were thus to be sought in identifying and applying substances that could correct the balance. This meant constant search and experimentation. "A man cannot learn the theory of medicine out of his own head," Paracelsus declared, "but only from that which his eyes see and his fingers touch. . . . Theory and practice should together form one, and should remain undivided."[3]

The emphasis on direct observation of nature produced the first great textbook of anatomy, the *De fabrica* (1543) of the Fleming Andreas Vesalius (1514–1564), and the discovery of the circulation of the blood (1628) by the Englishman William Harvey (1578–1657). The results of these discoveries, as in the case of astronomy, proved contrary to the theories that had originally inspired them. Vesalius believed that the structure of the human head, as the temple of reason, was necessarily different from that of animals, and Harvey saw the heart as the source of spiritual as well as physical life. What they showed instead was that the anatomies of humans and animals were similar in structure and function. Harvey became an enthusiastic disciple of comparative anatomy, remarking tartly that had the anatomists paid as much attention to animals as to humans, the mysteries of the body would have been solved long before. Indeed, the last element in the circulation of the blood unsolved by Harvey himself, the transfer of blood from veins to arteries by capillary action, was discovered in 1661 by the Italian Marcello Malpighi (1628–1694), who examined a frog's lungs with the aid of another optical instrument, the microscope.

New Technology

New inventions and techniques were stimulated not merely by the requirements of scientific curiosity but also those of practical activity. The great voyages of trade and discovery that began in the late fifteenth century are a case in point. Until that time, European ships seldom ventured out of sight of land and could proceed by pilotage, or reckoning by coastal landmarks. But when they sailed out into open and uncharted seas, they required navigation, or reckoning by the sun and the stars. For this purpose seamen adapted instruments previously used by astronomers, the quadrant and the astrolabe. The problem of plotting straight-line courses on two-dimensional maps representing a three-dimensional earth was solved by the Fleming Gerhard Kremer, called Mercator, whose map was first published in 1569 and in modified form is still used today. In 1484 King John III of Portugal appointed a commission of mathematicians to work out tables of latitude, and when Gresham College was founded in England in 1597, one of its three scientific chairs was reserved for an astronomer whose duties included the teaching of navigation. Sixteenth century interest in theories of the cosmos thus had a very practical basis. In similar fashion, the development of the cannon took ballistics, the science of calculating the trajectory of missiles, out of the realm of academic theory and on to the battlefield, while the extraction of gold and silver from the Indies stimulated the development of chemical separation processes and mining technology such as subsurface ventilation and hydraulic pumps.

Science at the Crossroads

The new scientific theories were disturbing to established authority, particularly in the universities and the churches. The new ideas were often associated with political subversion and black magic, inflammatory charges in an age marked by civil unrest and witchcraft persecution. Galileo had already been driven from the University of Padua before his arrest by the Inquisition, and Kepler was expelled from the Protestant faculty of the University of Tübingen. Jewish elders were hostile to the Cabala, a system akin to Hermeticism that claimed to decode secret meanings in the Old Testament.

The authorities' concern about the new science and the esoteric doctrines that swirled about it was not unfounded. The confidence of educated laymen in the traditional picture of the world had already been eroded by the late sixteenth century. "The more I think, the more I doubt," the Jesuit Francisco Suárez confessed in 1581, and 30 years later the English poet and divine John Donne summarized the anxieties many people felt about humanity's

Pascal on Humankind's Place in the Universe

The notion of an unlimited cosmos seemed to reduce humanity to insignificance and to call into question the idea of God's love and purpose for humankind. Such feelings were given unequaled expression by the great seventeenth-century mathematician and philosopher Blaise Pascal.

When I consider the brief span of my life absorbed into the eternity which comes before and after—*as the remembrance of a guest that tarrieth but a day*—the small space I occupy and which I see swallowed up in the infinite immensity of spaces of which I know nothing and which know nothing of me, I take fright and am amazed to see myself here rather than there: there is no reason for me to be here rather than there, now rather than then. Who put me here? By whose command and act were this time and place allotted to me? . . .

The eternal silence of these infinite spaces fills me with dread.

Source: B. Pascal, *Pensées*, trans. A. J. Krailsheimer (Baltimore: Penguin Books, 1966), pp. 48, 95.

loss of its privileged place in the cosmos in "An Anatomy of the World" (1611):

And new philosophy calls all in doubt;
The element of fire is quite put out,
The sun is lost, and the earth, and no man's wit
Can well direct him where to look for it
And freely men confess, that this world's spent
When in the planets and the firmament
They seek so many new; then see that this
Is crumbled out again to his atomies
'Tis all in pieces, all coherence gone;
All just supply and all relation.

Donne's poem is remarkable in demonstrating the speed with which scientific ideas were circulating, since Galileo had announced his discovery of new celestial bodies only a year before. His familiarity with the dispute about "the element of fire" (challenged by Paracelsus and his followers) and with the revival of interest in Democritus' theory of atoms can also be glimpsed in his lines.

Doubt and Faith: Descartes and Pascal

More extreme reactions to the new science can be seen in the Frenchmen René Descartes (1596–1650) and Blaise Pascal (1623–1662). As Descartes himself related his experience, he was assailed one night by a sudden, paralyzing doubt about the possibility of knowledge. The senses, he felt, deceived us, faith was undermined by doubt, and the authorities were only people like ourselves. How could one be sure of the existence of the world, of God, or even of oneself? Descartes' famous reply—"I think, therefore I am"—was the starting point of his extraordinary attempt to reconstruct all knowledge from the ground up on the basis of simple, self-evident propositions.

Pascal, a brilliant mathematician and a man of great religious sensitivity, felt the vast new spaces of the Copernican universe as a terrible silence in which humans were alone with their frailty and doubt and God had become a remote conjecture. He was one of the first men of his time to realize that the traditional conception of God no longer fit the world revealed by science. But he argued, in his famous "wager" with skeptics, that it was better to affirm the existence of a just and merciful God in whom one might no longer fully believe than to deny him, since there was everything to gain if he did in fact exist and nothing to be lost if he did not.

Conflicting Roads to Truth

Science itself had arrived at a crossroads by the mid-seventeenth century. The scientific enterprise was a Babel of languages from which no common grammar had yet emerged. The Aristotelian tradition was largely in shambles, but nothing had appeared to replace it. An English

The great French skeptic René Descartes in a confident pose by Frans Hals. Descartes' separation of mind from matter marked the beginning of a crisis in Western thought. [Lauros-Giraudon/Art Resource]

participant in an early scientific meeting has left us a catalog of the subjects discussed that suggests both the excitement and confusion of the new science:

> **We discoursed of the circulation of the blood, the valves in the veins, the *venae lacteae,* the lymphatick vessels, the Copernican hypothesis, the nature of comets and new stars, the satellites of Jupiter, the oval shape (as it then appeared) of Saturn, the spots in the sun, and its turning on its own axis, the inequalities and selenography of the Moon, the several phases of Venus and Mercury, the improvement of telescopes, and the grinding of glasses for that purpose, the weight of air, the possibility, or impossibility of vacuities [vacuums], and nature's abhorrence thereof, the Torricellian experiment in quick-silver, the descent of heavy bodies, and the degrees of acceleration therein; and divers other things of like nature.[4]**

Especially lacking was a common standard of judgment and proof. Although important discoveries had been made by scientists working from both Hermetic and mechanistic assumptions, in the last analysis they were incompatible as ways of seeing the world. The cosmos could be a living organism or an enormous machine, but not both. A similar division existed regarding scientific method. The English philosopher and jurist Sir Francis Bacon (1561–1626), Lord Chancellor under King James I, argued for the deductive or empirical method, by which knowledge was gained through systematic observation of the world and tested by experiment. The inductive method was championed by Descartes, who, as we have seen, rejected the senses as a basis for knowledge and argued that reality could be known only by reasoning from axiomatic principles. Descartes took a step that was decisive in the intellectual history of the West. He divided reality into two distinct entities, spirit, which was characterized by the power of thought but was without physical properties, and matter, which was substance extended in space and the capacity that that implied, motion. In doing so, he completely separated matter and spirit, rejecting the Hermetic vision of the world as a fusion of the two. He was thereby able to treat the material world in completely mechanical terms, while reserving an independent realm for spirit. Spirit meant in effect intelligence for Descartes, and the greatest intelligence was that of God, who had created the physical universe of matter in motion and designed the laws by which it operated. By studying and understanding those laws, humankind could understand God. Thus Cartesianism, as Descartes' philosophy came to be called, made science into a religious quest, but one that proceeded in terms not of theology but of mechanical engineering and mathematical reasoning.

The immediate importance of Descartes' work was that it gave impetus to the mechanistic conception of the world, where the most fruitful line of scientific advance actually lay, while avoiding the charge of black magic on the one hand and of atheism on the other. Cartesian science itself had serious drawbacks. It was well suited for physics but completely useless for biology, since it could provide no convincing explanation for the phenomenon of life. It relegated observation and experiment to matters of secondary detail at best, thus failing to provide an independent standard of proof for anyone who did not accept the premises of the system. Brilliant strategically as a means of breaking the impasse between Hermeticism and mechanism, it was still inadequate as a general model for science itself.

The Newtonian Synthesis

Sir Isaac Newton finally carried out the task Descartes had set: to provide a clear and comprehensive explanation of the physical universe in mathematical terms, a universe created by the will of God but fully subject to the laws of nature. Newton's work was a synthesis of all the elements of the scientific tradition. His solution to the problem of gravity, which he had made the key to his system, illustrates this. In Aristotelian physics, gravity was the inherent tendency of physical bodies to fall toward the earth as the center of the universe. The Englishman William Gilbert (1540–1603) had advanced the argument by his discovery that the earth itself acted as a magnet, drawing bodies to itself. But this left a serious problem in a Copernican universe where the sun was the center of the cosmos or (as both Descartes and Newton assumed) there was no center at all. Even granting the principle of inertia—that bodies set in motion would continue along the same path—how could it be explained that heavenly bodies did not simply drift randomly through space but described regular orbits about one another? Descartes rejected the idea of gravity as attraction at a distance because it seemed to him too close to the Hermetic idea of a force inherent in matter emanating from a divine source. Newton, however, had no trouble accepting such a notion, provided that it could be given an adequate mathematical basis—that is, provided that it could be shown to describe the actual orbits and positions of heavenly bodies. But classical mathematics, like classical physics, had always assumed the existence of a stable center. There was no mathematics capable of describing the interaction of independently moving bodies. Newton thereupon invented a new mathematics, called calculus, to deal with these relations.

Using the assumption of gravity as a universal constant, Newton was able to reduce the movement of all bodies in heaven or on earth to three basic laws. The elements of the system were as simple as the proofs were painstaking and complex. When Newton published his findings in his *Mathematical Principles of Natural Philosophy* (1687), he completed the work begun by Copernicus a century and a half earlier in replacing the Ptolemaic system. But Newton's model was even further from that of Copernicus than the latter's had been from Ptolemy's. Copernicus had still assumed that the universe had a definite center and a final boundary. Newton's cosmos was infinite and centerless. The speculation for which Bruno had been burned at the beginning of the seventeenth century had become scientific orthodoxy by its end.

The great success of Newton's synthesis was to reconcile not only the conflicting traditions of the new science but its competing methodologies as well. The conceptual simplicity of his system was a triumph of inductive logic, yet it was fully supported by the most up-to-date astronomical observations. This combination brought about ultimate acceptance of his system after the initial skepticism of men like the German mathematician Gottfried Wilhelm von Leibniz (1646–1716), who had independently worked out calculus at the same time as Newton but rejected his notion of gravity. The Newtonian model was not only mathematically convincing as Descartes' was not, but for the next 200 years every empirical observation and experiment confirmed it in detail. After Newton, scientific method was not a matter of theory or observation, but both. By his death in 1727, his prestige was so great that the poet Alexander Pope could write:

> ***Nature and nature's laws lay hid in night;***
> ***God said, Let Newton be! and all was light.***

The Scientific Method

Newton himself remarked, "If I have seen further [than others], it is by standing on the shoulders of giants." Indeed, the most impressive aspect of the scientific revolution was less an increase in knowledge about the world than the creation of a new method for understanding it. The ancient world had stressed the primacy of reason as a means of knowledge. The Middle Ages, while accepting reason, had insisted on the primacy of God's word as revealed in the Bible and interpreted by the church. The Reformation had changed that. Faith in God's word might be as strong as ever, but faith in its interpretation by the clergy was not. No longer was a single standard of truth acceptable to all.

The result, in part, was a return to reliance on reason. Descartes was a clear and radical example of this. What he wanted of reason was what he could no longer find in faith: certain and irrefutable truth. But the scientific method, as it had actually developed, offered both something less and something more. It was something less because science could not claim, even with Newton, to have arrived at a final truth about the world (though some of his eighteenth-century admirers would assert as much). It was something more because it amounted to a redefinition of truth itself. Henceforward, truth was not something to be revealed at once and in its entirety, whether by the sacred word or by direct intuition. Rather, truth was to be discovered and refined piecemeal, with each new stage in understanding serving as a step toward the next one. Through individual trial and error, collective truth was to be won.

For this reason, science became more and more a collabortive effort after the mid-seventeenth century. The first scientists had worked alone, like Copernicus and the reclusive Tycho Brahe, who built an observatory on his private island and jealously guarded the results of his work. Gradually, these isolated individuals became linked by chains of correspondence, such as the one set up in Paris in the 1630s by the friar Marin Mersenne (1588–1648), an enthusiast of the new science and friend of Galileo's. From this grew scientific meetings such as the one we glimpsed earlier, and finally formal societies. Among the first of these was the Royal Society of London for Improving Natural Knowledge, founded in 1662, of which Newton was an early member and later president. Four years later Colbert founded the French Academy of Sciences under state patronage, and similar societies were soon established in Berlin, Uppsala, Stockholm, Copen-

The Scientific Method

As received ideas of truth and knowledge were cast into doubt by the scientific revolution, a new method for ascertaining truth slowly evolved, stressing the importance of observation, experiment, and mathematical reasoning. The English philosopher Sir Francis Bacon stressed the importance of controlled experiment.

But by far the greatest impediment and aberration of the human understanding proceeds from the dullness, incompetency, and errors of the senses; since whatever strikes the senses preponderates over everything, however superior, which does not immediately strike them. Hence contemplation mostly ceases with sight, and a very scanty, or perhaps no regard is paid to visible objects. The entire operation, therefore, of spirits enclosed in tangible bodies is concealed, and escapes us. . . . Again, the very nature of common air, and all bodies of less density . . . is almost unknown; for the senses are weak and erring, nor can instruments be of great use in extending their spheres or acuteness. All the better interpretations of nature are worked out by instances, and fit and apt experiments, where the senses only judge of the experiment.

Of equal importance, the Frenchman René Descartes stressed the use of deductive reasoning.

By [deduction] we mean the inference of something as following necessarily from some other propositions which are known with certainty. . . . This distinction had to be made, since very many facts which are not self-evident are known with certainty, provided they are inferred from true and known principles through a continuous and uninterrupted movement of thought in which each individual proposition is clearly intuited. This is similar to the way in which we know that the last link in a long chain is connected to the first: even if we cannot take in at one glance all the intermediate links on which the connection depends, we can have knowledge of the connection provided we survey the links one after the other, and keep in mind that each link from first to last is attached to its neighbor.

Sources: F. Bacon, *Novum organum*, in *Great Books of the Western World*, vol. 30 (Chicago: Encyclopaedia Britannica, 1952), p. 111; *The Philosophical Writings of Descartes*, trans. J. Cottingham, R. Stoothoff, and D. Murdoch, vol. 1 (Cambridge: Cambridge University Press, 1985), p. 15.

hagen, and St. Petersburg. By the last decades of the seventeenth century we can speak of a scientific world, international in scope and cosmopolitan in character, in which knowledge could be systematically communicated, new theories debated, and new talent recognized.

Philosophy: The Age of Reason

In the seventeenth century no strict distinction was made between philosophy—inquiry into the limits of human knowledge as such—and science, the branch of knowledge that addressed itself to the natural world. In that sense, the attack on Aristotle, Ptolemy, and Galen that characterized the scientific revolution was part of a wider movement in European thought that questioned traditional authority in general. But there can be no doubt that the success of science in dethroning medieval cosmology gave impetus and urgency to the development of critical philosophy as a whole.

The two traditions of philosophy that were most influential in the seventeenth and eighteenth centuries were the English and the French. German philosophy, which began its modern career with Leibniz and Samuel Pufendorf (1632–1694), began to dominate European thought only in the late eighteenth and nineteenth centuries. In English and French philosophy, speculation adhered to the norms set down respectively by Bacon and Descartes. The English tended to begin from concrete observation of the world, the French from a priori assumptions about it.

Another broad distinction between English and French philosophy can be drawn in terms of subject matter. The English, preoccupied with the revolutions of 1640 and 1688, concentrated on the problem of people's relation to the civic orders of state and society, whereas the French, inheriting the skepticism of Descartes, focused on humanity's relation to the cosmos.

Thomas Hobbes and the Natural Man

The Englishman Thomas Hobbes (1588–1679), writing in the tumultuous 1640s, produced in *Leviathan* (1651) the most important work of Western political philosophy since Machiavelli's *The Prince*. Hobbes argued that human beings are social by necessity rather than by nature, as Aristotle had thought. He started from the mechanistic assumption that humans, like all other entities, could be described in terms of matter and motion and that their thoughts, feelings, and desires could be explained as responses to external stimuli, differing in degree but not in kind from those of animals. Even reason, the glory of the mind, was only a complex form of calculation, and the will, which attested to human freedom, was defined simply as the last appetite before choice. Hobbes professed to believe in God, the soul, and the workings of Providence, but, like Descartes (whom he knew and admired), he separated the realms of matter and spirit so sharply that his view of society appeared purely secular. That, combined with the fierce anticlericalism that ran through all his political writings, led to his condemnation as an atheist.

In Hobbes' view, human beings strive to maximize pleasure and minimize pain. This brings them into conflict with others who, acting on the same principle, compete for scarce goods. The result, Hobbes declared, was a "war of all against all," a condition in which the life of men was, in his pithy phrase, "solitary, poor, nasty, brutish and short." To avoid this, they gave up their natural freedom and entered society, as rational animals might enter a zoo. Hobbes' zookeeper was the sovereign, who had absolute power to order all social arrangements, allotting each person a share of goods and duties. Only in this way, he believed, could order be guaranteed and the anarchy of the natural human condition avoided. Society was in effect a contract in which freedom was exchanged for security, or at least the hope of security, since the subject, in surrendering all natural rights, had also surrendered the means to enforce the bargain. To critics who complained that this created a license for tyranny, Hobbes replied that it was better to be subject to the arbitrary will of a single individual than to the potential violence of all.

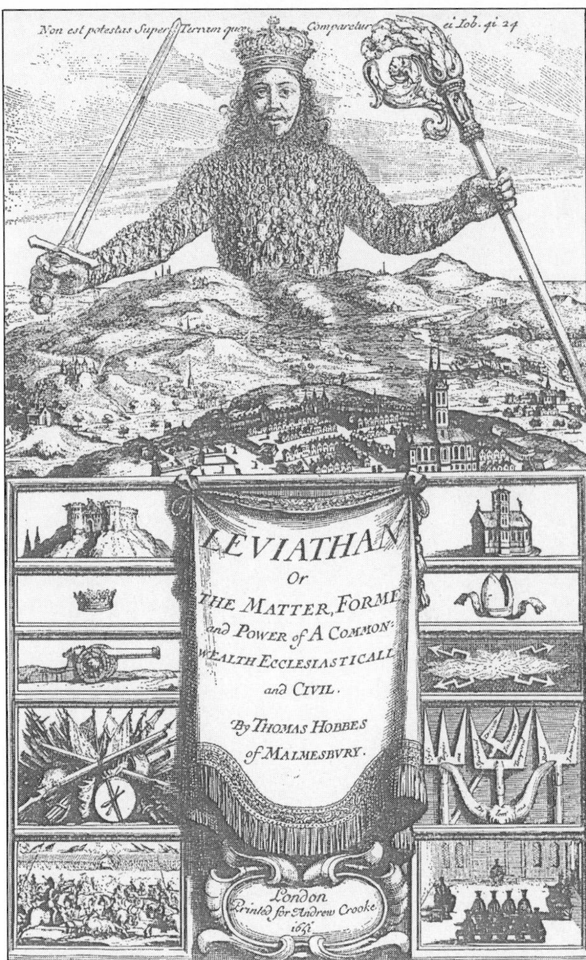

The famous frontispiece of Hobbes' book *Leviathan* shows his absolute sovereign as a giant who incorporates the entire body politic. The Latin quotation at the top, from the Book of Job, reads: "There is not his like upon earth." [Granger Collection]

Hobbes insisted that his theory was not an abstract blueprint but an actual description of power in society. Whether monarchy, aristocracy, or democracy, the core of every government was an absolute, unchallengeable sovereignty that could not be divided or infringed without destroying the state and consequently the social order. He therefore rejected all theories of "mixed" government or separation of powers as a confusion between real and delegated powers.

Hobbes' theory scandalized everyone. Liberals rejected it because it left no place for political dissent. Conservatives liked it no better because, although Hobbes condemned rebellion as the greatest of political evils, he accepted all changes of government in a spirit of pure pragmatism. The only test of a regime was its ability to

The Institution of the Commonwealth

The English philosopher Thomas Hobbes described the origin of the state in the agreement of sovereign individuals to merge their natural rights in a single person acting in the name of all.

It is manifest, that during the time men live without a common power to keep them all in awe, they are in that condition which is called war, and such a war, as is of every man, against every man. For war consisteth not in battle only, or the act of fighting; but in a tract of time, wherein the will to contend by battle is sufficiently known. . . . The only way to erect such a common power, as may be able to defend [individuals] from the invasion of foreigners, and the injuries of one another . . . is to confer all their power and strength upon one man, or upon one assembly of men, that may reduce all their wills, by plurality of voices, unto one will: which is as much as to say, to appoint one man, or assembly of men, to bear their person. . . . This is . . . a real unity of them all, in one and the same person, made by covenant of every man with every man, in such a manner, as if every man should say to every man, *I authorize and give up my right of governing myself, to this man, or to this assembly of men, on this condition, that thou give up thy right to him, and authorize all his actions in like manner*. This done, the multitude so united in one person, is called a commonwealth. . . . This is the generation of that great Leviathan, or rather (to speak more reverently) of that mortal God, to which we owe under the immortal God, our peace and defense.

A very different view of the state as originating in force and fraud was offered by Hobbes' contemporary Gerrard Winstanley (c. 1609–c. 1676).

In the beginning of time, the great creator Reason, made the earth to be a common treasury, to preserve beasts, birds, fishes, and man, the lord that was to govern this creation; for man had domination given to him, over the beasts, birds, and fishes; but not one word was spoken in the beginning, that one branch of mankind should rule over another. . . . But . . . selfish imagination taking possession of the five senses, and so ruling as king in the room of Reason therein, and working with covetousness, did set up one man to teach and rule over another, and thereby the spirit was killed, and man was brought into bondage, and became a greater slave to such of his own kind, than the beasts of the field were to him.

Sources: T. Hobbes, *Leviathan*, ed. A. R. Walter (Cambridge: Cambridge University Press, 1904), pp. 83, 118–119 (modernized); G. H. Sabine, ed., *The Works of Gerrard Winstanley* (Ithaca, N.Y.: Cornell University Press, 1941), pp. 251–252.

provide security. A government that could not do so forfeited all claim to loyalty, while any government that could possessed a sufficient title to be obeyed.

John Locke and the State of Nature

Writing 40 years later, John Locke (1632–1704) took a very different view of human society. Locke started from the premise that human beings in their natural condition—what had come to be called the state of nature—were not competitive but cooperative. Such persons entered society to gain the benefits of communal organization. Their natural rights were not surrendered but rather enhanced in society. Government on this view was merely an instrument of common social purpose, and the ruler was entrusted with such powers as were necessary to provide for the general welfare but no more. Should he abuse this trust, he might be replaced or deposed without doing violence to the constitution and certainly without dissolving society as Hobbes had thought. This was what had happened to James II in 1688, and English society, far from being destroyed or hurled back into anarchy, had been strengthened and renewed.

Locke's view of politics derived from his assumptions about human psychology, expressed in the *Essay Concerning Human Understanding* (1690). Taking a radically empirical stance, he argued that the mind at birth was a *tabula rasa,* or blank slate, on which experience inscribed itself. It followed from this that careful education could develop the mind in almost any desired direction. Thus, although reason in the state of nature suggested the desirability of human cooperation, people could easily be trained to obey the far more complex rules of society.

French Skepticism

In France a vein of skepticism ran through philosophy from the essayist Michel de Montaigne (1533–1592) to Descartes to Pierre Bayle (1647–1706). Descartes dealt with his own crisis of belief by asserting the power of reason to validate the world, including the existence of God. The idea of an infinite being, he argued, is spontaneously present in the human mind; yet since it would never have occurred of itself to a finite, limited consciousness, it could only have been placed there by God. But Descartes insisted on excluding God from any direct responsibility for the material universe, remarking that his readers could substitute "the mathematical order of nature" for "God" wherever he used the latter term.

For Pascal the absence of God from the material universe was the very source of human despair. Descartes' cool, rational conception of a God who made himself known as an idea but could not be reached as a person had no interest for him. The force of Pascal's argument was that Descartes, by exalting the powers of the mind, had excluded God, reducing him to a meaningless abstraction. It was only by admitting one's frailty and need that it was possible to reach the Christian God who had extended himself to humankind by his own suffering.

Pascal was closely associated with the religious circle at Port-Royal, a Cistercian abbey a few miles southwest of Paris that had embraced the teachings of the Dutch theologian Cornelius Jansen (1585–1638). Jansenism was a reaction against the scholastic tradition maintained by the Jesuits. Stressing individual piety and personal election rather than outward good works and conformity to church doctrine, it was viewed as a "protestant" heresy within Catholicism, although Jansen claimed his inspiration from St. Augustine rather than Calvin. Opposed by Richelieu and Louis XIV no less than by a succession of popes, it maintained itself as a religious and political counterculture well into the eighteenth century.

The skeptical tradition nonetheless continued to gain ground in France. In his *Critical History of the New Testament* (1678), the Oratorian priest Richard Simon subjected the Bible to an exhaustive textual scrutiny, exposing hundreds of errors and discrepancies. Shocked by the audacity of anyone—no less a priest—treating Holy Writ by the standards of ordinary literature, Bishop Bossuet ordered the book burned. Simon protested that his aim was not to cast doubt on the essential truth of the Bible but to purge it of human error. No such redeeming purpose could be attributed to Pierre Bayle, who satirized biblical and pagan figures side by side in his *Historical and Critical Dictionary* (1697). For Bayle, whose book profoundly influenced such eighteenth-century skeptics as Voltaire, reason and religion were mortal enemies fighting "for possession of men's souls."

THE LENS GRINDER OF AMSTERDAM, BARUCH SPINOZA

The philosophical and religious issues of the seventeenth century were perhaps nowhere better epitomized than in the life of Baruch Spinoza. Spinoza was born in Amsterdam in 1632, the son of a prosperous Jewish merchant whose family had emigrated from Portugal at the end of the sixteenth century. The Amsterdam of his youth was the most cosmopolitan city in Europe. The Jewish community mixed freely with the general population, adopting its manners and dress (as the portraits of Rembrandt show), intermarrying, and imbibing liberal social and religious ideas. This freedom created great tension within the Jewish community itself, which conservative members feared would soon lose its identity. The brilliant young Spinoza was a case in point. While the elders of the community supported the House of Orange and the Dutch East and West India companies, Spinoza backed the republican revolution of 1650 and advocated the dissolution of the trading companies and the abolition of their privileges. Above all, he rejected his Jewish heritage, abjuring the synagogue and denying that the Jews were a chosen people. The Amsterdam synagogue responded by excommunicating him in 1656. He was formally cursed, and Jews were forbidden all contact with him. Spinoza renounced the career in commerce he had begun and earned his living by grinding and polishing lenses, a job of deliberately low status but symbolically appropriate for a man determined to see the world by no light but his own.

In his major work, the *Ethics*, Spinoza proposed a radical solution to the central seventeenth-century question of the relation between God and nature. Traditional philosophy had distinguished between substance, the stuff of the universe, and cause, the external agency that acts on it and shapes it. Spinoza rejected this distinction as false. There could be no separation between God as cause and nature as substance. It followed that God *was* the world,

The great Jewish philosopher Baruch Spinoza saw God and nature as indivisible. Contemporaries found his ideas "frightening," but he was a hero to later generations. [Collection Haags Gemeentemuseum, The Hague]

which was contained in him though he was not confined by it. It is hard to imagine an idea more calculated to give offense. Religious thinkers had speculated that the human soul might be regarded as a spark of divinity within humankind. Spinoza denied the existence of the soul, since there could be no distinction between matter and spirit; but on the other hand he asserted that God was present not only in humans but in the lowest and most degraded phenomena of the world as well. To accept God was to accept everything, and once that was done, false categories such as sin and salvation, which separated man from God, lost all meaning and fell away. Descartes, daring as he was, never left the Catholic church. Spinoza's metaphysics made all religious doctrine irrelevant.

Spinoza's political ideas were equally radical. Like Hobbes, he argued that sovereignty was absolute and indivisible and denounced clerical influence in the state; unlike Hobbes, Spinoza demanded complete freedom of thought. "The rights of the individual," he declared, "extend to the utmost limits of his power," and freedom was the final, indispensable human value:

> **He that knows himself to be upright does not fear the death of a criminal, and shrinks from no punishment; his mind has no remorse for any disgraceful deed: he holds that death in a good cause is no punishment, but an honor, and that death for freedom is glory.[5]**

Spinoza was not entirely isolated. He had friends and even disciples in the Netherlands and carried on a wide correspondence. Leibniz, who visited him, professed admiration for the rigor of his thought but finally concluded that the *Ethics* was "a frightening work" and spoke of the "monstrous opinions of this Jew expelled from the Synagogue." When Spinoza died from a longstanding tubercular condition in 1677, he had no defenders, and his work fell into obscurity until Goethe rediscovered it in the eighteenth century and the Romantics made him a hero in the nineteenth. Since then he has found his place among the great Western philosophers and the champions of freedom—honored at last, but still alone.

Literature: The Triumph of the Vernacular

Latin was still the language of educated Europe in the sixteenth and seventeenth centuries, the language of international diplomacy, of scholarship, and of the Catholic church. As late as the early eighteenth century, when the elector of Hanover came to Britain to reign as King George I with no knowledge of the English language, he conversed with his chief minister, Sir Robert Walpole, in Latin. But the sixteenth century saw the beginning of a sustained tradition of vernacular literature, that is, literature in the popular spoken tongue. It began in Italy with the immensely popular chivalric poems of Ludovico Ariosto (1474–1533) and Torquato Tasso (1544–1595); in France with the prose epics of François Rabelais (1494–1553), *Gargantua* and *Pantagruel*; and in Germany with Luther's translation of the Bible, which went through 377 printings in his own lifetime. But the development of vernacular literature was particularly associated with the theater, the most popular of all art forms. The late sixteenth and seventeenth centuries were a golden age of theater in England, France, Spain, and the Netherlands, unrivaled from the time of ancient Greece and unequaled since.

The first of these national theaters was the English, where licensed companies of actors appeared from 1574. Two years later James Burbage built the first public theater in London, a roofless wooden amphitheater similar to the open spaces in inns and bull and bear-baiting arenas. Large enclosed theaters were built in the 1590s, of which the most famous were the Swan (1596) and the Globe (1599), which boasted seating capacities of 3,000. The basic price of admission was a penny for "groundlings" or standees; a seat in the lower galleries cost 2 pence, one in the upper ones 3, and a private box, usually reserved for a nobleman, was 6. The audience thus represented every element of Elizabethan society, and what it saw was the reflection of its own world, from cobblers to kings: Thomas Dekker's *Shoemaker's Holiday* (1599) depicted an upwardly mobile craftsman who becomes Lord Mayor of London; Thomas Middleton's *Chaste Maid in Cheapside* (1613), a goldsmith; Ben Jonson's *Bartholomew Fair* (1614), Puritans and pickpockets. Well might the greatest of these playwrights, William Shakespeare (1564–1616), whose imaginative world was perhaps larger than that of any person who ever lived, boastfully declare:

> ***All the world's a stage,***
> ***And all the men and women merely players.***
> ***They have their exits and entrances,***
> ***And one man in his time plays many parts.***[5]

The English stage exhibited not only great variety but also astonishing boldness and freedom. Topical and political satire abounded. Jonson was in trouble early in the reign of James I for attacking the vices and corruption of the court, and Middleton later on for a thinly veiled attack on the king's foreign policy. Shakespeare himself was paid to perform *Richard II*, his play about the fall of the fourteenth-century English tyrant, on the eve of the earl of Essex's rebellion against Queen Elizabeth in 1600. Actors, authors, and producers were often just a step ahead of the censor, until at last the Puritan revolutionaries, so often the butt of the London stage, closed it down in 1642.

Civic theater also flourished in the Netherlands, where it produced a major figure in Joost van den Vondel (1587–1679), a committed republican who protested against the rigidities of Dutch Calvinism. The playwrights of the Spanish school—Lope de Vega (1562–1635), Tirso de Molina (1571–1648), and Pedro Calderón de la Barca (1600–1681)—were immensely prolific; Lope claimed to have written over 1,500 plays, and the titles of nearly 1,000 survive. Performances were held outdoors in the public square, with seats arranged around the stage and rooms rented in private houses to provide the equivalent of boxes for noblemen and ladies. Male and female spectators were strictly segregated, and though the monarchy was often the subject of the Spanish theater, it was considered improper for the king and queen to attend. The French theater of Pierre Corneille (1606–1684) and Jean Racine (1639–1699), in contrast, was court-sponsored and reflected its patronage in its choice of classical themes, its emphasis on honor and the renunciation of the passions, and its formal, chiseled verse line. But the French produced their comic genius too in Jean-Baptiste Poquelin, called Molière (1622–1673), who mocked the social pretensions of his own bourgeois class, although he stopped carefully short of satirizing his aristocratic audiences.

The seventeenth century saw the entry of women into literature for the first time, particularly in France. Women writers of note, such as Christine de Pisan, Marguerite of Navarre, and the English mystic Juliana of Norwich, had occasionally emerged before, as had even the stirrings of a feminist literature in Elizabethan England, but not until the accession of the Bourbon dynasty in France did women begin to occupy an important place in literature and literary life. Madeleine de Scudéry (1607–1701) created a new genre with her *Grand Cyrus* (1649–1653), a historical romance that portrayed the protagonists of the Fronde in the fictional guise of ancient Persians. Similarly, Marie de Sévigné (1626–1696) established letter writing as a literary art; her volumes of correspondence, ranging in their description from court life at Versailles to peasant rebellion, are the most rounded portrait we possess of life in the age of Louis XIV. No less important to the emerging cultural prominence of women was the literary salon, pioneered by the elegant Catherine de Rambouillet (1588–1665), at whose private gatherings aspiring writers came to establish their reputations. Even so, however, literature was not yet a respectable pursuit for women; Scudéry's *Grand Cyrus*, certainly the most popular and influential French novel of its time, was published under the name of her brother George, a mediocre playwright.

The last of the great epic poets was the Englishman John Milton (1608–1674), a lonely figure despite his service in the revolutionary regimes of the 1650s. Milton's *Paradise Lost* (1667), a poem not surpassed since in any language for its breadth and ambition, looked back to the model of Dante in its account of the fall of Adam and Eve, although its powerful portrayal of the character of Satan anticipates the rebellious Romantic hero of the nineteenth century. A new medium for narrative had begun to emerge, one that would dominate the literature of the West: the novel. The rambling adventure tales of Rabelais had anticipated the form in the sixteenth century, but the first true example is Miguel de Cervantes' *Don Quixote*. Cervantes intended to satirize the chivalric tales still popular in his native Spain, but he accomplished much more. His two wandering heroes, the idealistic nobleman Don Quixote and his worldly but faithful servant, Sancho Panza, are not mere stock figures on which a tale of adventures can be strung but living, individual characters whose success arises from their vivid contrast of temperament. The English drama was accomplishing much the same thing at the same time, but 100 years were to pass before anyone was able to capture the necessary balance of character and plot again in prose. With Daniel Defoe's enormously popular *Robinson Crusoe* (1719), however, a story not for the old world of chivalry but the new one of capital formation and commercial enterprise, the age of the novel had begun.

The Age of the Baroque

The origin of the term *baroque* is obscure, but may come from the Portuguese *barroco,* an irregularly shaped pearl. It has come to define the very distinctive art of the seventeenth century, though originally, like the adjective *Gothic,* it was a term of derision. Certainly, to those whose ideal was the serene beauty of a Raphael or the monumentality of a Michelangelo, the dramatic, swirling lines of baroque architecture and the darkened palette of baroque painting, with its abrupt contrasts of light and shadow and the brooding intensity of its portraits, could not but seem strained, distorted, and profoundly disturbing. Yet the baroque, like every major art style, had complex and subtle affinities to the wider culture of the age. In its restless, probing, and essentially theatrical nature, it reflected a period of conflict, exploration, and doubt, while in its bold redefinition of space, it suggests a response to the vision of Copernicus, Bruno, and Galileo.

The baroque originated as a style in Italy. Its first patrons were the Jesuits, and Gesù, the church of the order in Rome, is commonly accepted as the first full-fledged example of baroque architecture. Certainly the sense of spiritual quest and renewal emphasized by the Jesuits can be seen in such works as the *St. Theresa in Ecstasy* of Gianlorenzo Bernini (1598–1680) or the somber ecclesiastical portraits of Francisco de Zurbarán (1598–1664), but the baroque soon stepped across national and religious frontiers. The spiritual and the sensual, moreover, often blended into one another, as Bernini's *St. Theresa* vividly illustrates, or settled down happily side by side, as in the fleshily exuberant biblical scenes of the Flemish painter Peter Paul Rubens (1577–1640).

Dutch painters carried the new chiaroscuro style of the Italian Michelangelo Merisi, called Caravaggio (1573–1610), back from Rome. Caravaggio's work, with its dramatic interior lighting, often from no visible source, was soon reflected in the work of artists all over Europe, including Diego Velázquez (1599–1660) in Spain and George de la Tour (1593–1652) in France, but it found its apotheosis in the Dutch Mennonite artist Rembrandt van Rijn (1606–1669). Rembrandt was the greatest of a remarkable series of painters who captured the variety and vitality of seventeenth-century Dutch society, leaving an unmatched record of the everyday life of their time. Rembrandt's own work reveals this same curiosity about the unusual and even (by classical standards) the bizarre, as in his *Anatomy Lesson of Dr. Tulp* (1632), in which an anatomist dissects the cadaver of an executed criminal before the Surgeons' Guild of Amsterdam. But his genius was too impatient for the landscape and genre scenes preferred by his contemporaries; as his drawings reveal, he could capture the essence of a landscape more surely in a few quick strokes of brush or pen than most of them in elaborate and painstaking canvases. He spent his own immense gifts of color and composition on individual portaits, including a series of self-portraits that, begun in a vigorous and commercially successful youth, continued up to the year of his death when, unfashionable and destitute, he painted largely for himself alone. In Rembrandt's portraits, something of what Spinoza may have meant by the "soul that lives in all things" is visible, for no other artist has ever revealed so much of our common humanity.

The music of the baroque, like its art and architecture, tended toward the dramatic. Sung texts and spoken words had largely existed apart before Claudio Monteverdi (1567–1643), who fused them into a new theatrical form, the opera. By the 1630s Italian opera had become a lavish spectacle; Cardinal Barberini sponsored one performance at his palace in Rome before an audience of 3,500, with stage designs by Bernini. Much of seventeenth-century music remained dominated by Italian models, particularly in the secular forms of the oratorio, the cantata, and the concerto. In Germany the tradition of church music introduced by the hymns of Martin Luther produced a series of important composers, including Heinrich Schütz (1585–1672). Later baroque music developed in the direction of elaborate ornamentation and contrapuntal complexity, reaching its climax in Johann Sebastian Bach (1685–1750), in whom the Lutheran tradition achieved a universality that, like the art of Rembrandt, reaches across all ages and cultures.

The state gradually superseded the Catholic church in the role of patron of baroque art. Rubens was commissioned to paint a series of allegorical portraits glorifying Marie de' Medici of France and her son, Henry IV, and he was also employed (with his younger colleague Anthony van Dyck) in making equestrian portraits of the ill-fated Charles I of England, who took the extraordinary step of knighting him for his services. It was Louis XIV, however, who saw most clearly the possibilities of bringing art to the service of the state. In Versailles the dramatic, heaven-storming qualities of baroque art (suitably refined by French taste) and the pomp of divine right monarchy came together in an image of absolute secular power. Other rulers rushed to follow his example—Leopold I in Austria, Charles XII in Sweden, Peter the Great in Russia, Frederick the Great in Prussia, Augustus the Strong in Saxony, and a host of lesser princelings, neither great nor strong, who felt that no reign could be complete without a palace to attest to its *gloire*.

ROME: THE REBIRTH OF A CAPITAL

Rome, for most of the population of Europe still the center of Christendom, recovered slowly from the sack of 1527 and the subsequent Spanish occupation. With the new energies of the Counter-Reformation, however, the city began to revive. Work on St. Peter's, still without a facade or dome, was the first order of priority. Pope Sixtus V, working men around the clock for 22 months, finished Michelangelo's dome in 1590. The architect Carlo Maderna (1556–1629) designed the new facade, and Bernini spent nearly a decade (1657–1666) completing the great colonnaded square in front. Maderna departed radically from Michelangelo's original designs, widening and opening the central nave and replacing Michelangelo's facade with columns whose variable spacing produced a fluid effect. Bernini's undulating columns in the nave and his daringly open square—the first such space in any European city—completed with baroque exuberance and novelty the great edifice that had been begun in the High Renaissance. In no other building is the contrast between the aims and aspirations of the two epochs more strikingly visible.

With St. Peter's in progress, Popes Paul V (1605–1621) and Urban VIII (1623–1644) undertook the reconstruction and beautification of Rome, giving it the squares and fountains—many designed by the ubiquitous Bernini—that still distinguish it today. With these came new churches as well, notably Bernini's San Andrea al Quirinale (1658–1670) and Francesco Borromini's San Carlo alle Quattro Fontane (1638–1641), whose interior represents the first completely undulating wall space since the reign of the Roman emperor Hadrian. In Borromini (1599–1666), the greatest Italian architect of the century, the flowing space of the baroque—like the post-Copernican universe, itself never defined by any single perspective—achieves its most characteristic form.

By the early eighteenth century the rebuilt city had become a major tourist attraction for Protestants and Catholics alike, an obligatory stop on the grand tour by which elegant young ladies and gentlemen put the finishing touches to their education. One such traveler, the French magistrate Charles de Brosses, declared that Rome was "the most beautiful city in the world." St. Peter's was "the finest thing in the universe." Like a jewel, its facets were endlessly fascinating: "You might come to it every day without being bored. . . . It is more amazing the oftener you see it." Most impressive of all, he thought, were the fountains and firework displays that played constantly and

The revival of Rome was marked by completion of the colonnaded square of St. Peter's, the masterpiece of the greatest architect and sculptor of the baroque, Gianlorenzo Bernini. The church of St. Peter's, seat of the Vatican, appears at the left rear. [Granger Collection]

The restless, aspiring spirit of the baroque is well illustrated in this detail of the curving facade of Borromini's church of San Carlo at the Four Fountains in Rome. Massive but supple form and a dramatic use of interior space characterized the architecture of the baroque. [Wim Swann, New York]

gave the city an air of perpetual festivity. This impression was not far from wrong, as Rome celebrated no fewer than 150 holidays a year, not to mention occasional pageants, local processions and fairs, and weekly summer festivals that included water jousts and mock sea battles in the flooded Piazza Navona.

Rome's population grew steadily during this period, from approximately 80,000 in 1563 to 118,356 in the census of 1621 to about 150,000 by 1709. This included some 8,000 priests, monks, nuns, and other religious who staffed the almost 400 churches of Rome and a nearly equal number of monasteries, convents, and seminaries. The papacy dominated the political and economic life of Rome just as the dome and square of St. Peter's did its skyline. It governed the city as the capital of the so-called Papal States, a band of territories that stretched across the middle of Italy, and was far and away its chief employer, dispensing charity and relief as well to the poor. What the papacy did not provide directly it did indirectly, in the services that were needed for the hordes of pilgrims, estimated at 100,000 per year in 1700, that formed the bulk of the tourist trade. The result was that Rome's was almost entirely a service economy, living on papal wealth and foreign income. Life was casual if not indolent; even at the Vatican, washing was hung out to dry from the windows. At the bottom of the social scale, Rome's easygoing ways tailed off into squalor, and its poor, favored at least by the climate, spent as little time as possible in their wretched hovels. The very openness of life acted as a safety valve for discontent; there was always distraction in the street, even for the most extreme misery, and, in a city full of wealthy strangers, always opportunity as well.

One group that stood apart from the ministrations of the church was the Jewish community. Yet it, too, was noted in the papacy's ubiquitous accounts, and when Paul V planned his new fountains for Rome, one was duly provided for the city's synagogue. A more curious and less benevolent example of Rome's uneasy relationship with its Jews was in the ceremony that opened the Roman Carnival, the eight-day pre-Lenten celebration that was the most elaborate and tumultuous holiday of the year. The Jews were taxed the cost of the prize money for the horse races and, assembled as a group, were thanked for their "gift" to the city by a pretended kick in the small of the chief rabbi's back.

The seventeenth century has rightly been called the century of genius. Shakespeare, Milton, Cervantes, Rembrandt—these men shaped the image of humankind in the West and still stand at the frontier of its cultural heritage, their works undimmed by time. Bacon, Hobbes, Descartes, Pascal, and Spinoza shaped the modern quest for knowledge, and the questions they posed, about humankind and the cosmos, about freedom and government, are still alive today. Copernicus, Kepler, Galileo, Newton, and many others of lesser ability created the scientific revolution and with it transformed humankind's capacity to know, to create, and to destroy.

The effects of the changed intellectual climate were visible by the end of the century. The triumph of the mechanistic vision of nature over Aristotelian physics and cosmology and the rival tradition of Hermetic natural magic had a decisive influence on popular superstition as well as educated thought. The beginning of the century had seen the last upsurge in witchcraft persecution, affecting some 100,000 persons between 1580 and 1650. By the end of the century belief in witchcraft itself was largely extinct, and faith in astrology and magic healing had declined sharply. The view of the cosmos as a web of hidden affinities and powers on which such beliefs depended was no longer credible, and so they silently faded away.

The cultural shock that greeted man's dethronement from his position at the center of the universe gradually gave way to a new pride in the power of human knowledge. Until the nineteenth century the scientific revolution had little practical consequence, and few of the technological advances of the

1700s owed themselves to the abstruse physics of Newton. Nonetheless, the new science came to symbolize faith in the improvement of the human condition, a faith that for some in the eighteenth century took on the quality of religious conviction itself. At the same time, the mathematized God of Newton and Descartes was gradually detached from science. For them, God had still been the ultimate guarantor of the truth of their universe. A century later, asked why he had omitted God from his system, the French astronomer Pierre Simon de Laplace (1749–1827) would answer coolly, "I have no need of that hypothesis."

Notes

1. T. S. Kuhn, The *Copernican Revolution* (Cambridge, Mass.: Harvard University Press, 1957), p. 128.
2. H. F. Kearney, *Science and Change, 1500–1700* (New York: McGraw-Hill, 1971), p. 101.
3. A. R. Hall, *The Scientific Revolution, 1500–1800* (Boston: Beacon Press, 1956), p. 132.
4. Martha Ornstein, *The Rôle of Scientific Societies in the Seventeenth Century* (Chicago: University of Chicago Press, 1938), p. 95.
5. *The Chief Works of Benedict de Spinoza*, ed. R. H. M. Elwes, 2 vols. (London: G. Bell, 1917, 1919), vol. 2, p. 263.
6. *As You Like It,* act 2, scene 7.

Suggestions for Further Reading

Butterfield, H. *The Origins of Modern Science*. New York: Macmillan, 1957.

Cohen, I. B. *The Birth of a New Physics*. New York: Norton, 1985.

Feuer, L. S. *Spinoza and the Rise of Liberalism*. Boston: Beacon Press, 1966.

Friedrich, C. J. *The Age of the Baroque*. New York: Harper, 1952.

Gillespie, C. C. *The Edge of Objectivity: An Essay in the History of Scientific Ideas*. Princeton, N.J.: Princeton University Press, 1960.

Hall, A. R. *The Scientific Revolution, 1500–1800*. Boston: Beacon Press, 1956.

Kearney, H. F. *Science and Change 1500–1700*. New York: McGraw-Hill, 1971.

Koyre, A. *From the Closed World to the Infinite Universe*. Baltimore: Johns Hopkins University Press, 1957.

Krautheimer, R. *The Rome of Alexander VII, 1655–1667*. Princeton, N.J.: Princeton University Press, 1985.

Kuhn, T. S. *The Structure of Scientific Revolutions*. Chicago: University of Chicago Press, 1970.

MacPherson, C. B. *The Political Theory of Possessive Individualism: Hobbes to Locke*. New York: Oxford University Press, 1964.

Mesnard, J. *Pascal, His Life and Works*. New York: Philosophical Library, 1952.

Nash, J. M. *The Age of Rembrandt and Vermeer: Dutch Painting in the Seventeenth Century*. New York: Holt, Rinehart and Winston, 1972.

Ornstein, M. *The Role of Scientific Societies in the Seventeenth Century*. Chicago: University of Chicago Press, 1928.

Palisca, C. V. *Baroque Music*. Englewood Cliffs, N.J.: Prentice-Hall, 1981.

Popkin, R. *History of Scepticism from Erasmus to Spinoza*. Berkeley: University of California Press, 1979.

Santillana, G. de. *The Crime of Galileo*. London: Heinemann, 1958.

Spear, R. E. *Caravaggio and His Followers*. Cleveland, Ohio: Cleveland Museum of Art, 1971.

Strauss, L. *The Political Philosophy of Hobbes*. Chicago: University of Chicago Press, 1966.

Thomas, K. *Religion and the Decline of Magic*. New York: Scribner, 1971.

Warnke, F. J. *Versions of Baroque: European Literature in the Seventeenth Century*. New Haven, Conn.: Yale University Press, 1972.

Westfall, R. S. *Never at Rest: A Biography of Isaac Newton*. Cambridge: Cambridge University Press, 1980.

Wilson, M. D. *Descartes*. Boston: Routledge & Kegan Paul, 1978.

Yates, F. A. *Giordano Bruno and the Hermetic Tradition*. Chicago: University of Chicago Press, 1964.

PART · FOUR

Toward the Modern World

The modern world that came of age in the eighteenth century was marked by rapid and revolutionary change. In Europe a century of imperial expansion and development abroad and unprecedented social criticism at home was climaxed by the French Revolution, which at a stroke abolished feudal tenures and the hierarchy of orders in the continent's most powerful state. The French Revolution paved the way for economic modernization and political centralization throughout Europe, the latter also assisted by the rising sentiment of nationalism. By the second half of the nineteenth century the two largest territorial blocks in central Europe, Germany and Italy, had been unified politically for the first time since the Middle Ages, while the growing power of Russia, the protracted collapse of the Ottoman Empire, and the increasing demands for national independence among the minorities of the Austrian empire had created an unstable zone of contending powers and client states. These complex power realignments, tied to imperial and commercial rivalry, resulted in a conflict of global magnitude, World War I.

While these changes were taking place, a far wider transformation of the human situation was under way. Beginning in the mid-eighteenth century, the number of humans began to expand at an increasing rate, a phenomenon, uninterrupted and accelerating to the present day, known as the population explosion. At the same time, new sources of mechanized power exploiting steam, coal, and other natural elements were being devised on the island of Britain, which, closely tied to the imperatives of capitalism and state power, produced the most significant development in human technology in 10,000 years, the Industrial Revolution. That process, like the population explosion, has now become a global phenomenon that continues to transform our material culture.

The decisive advantage lent to Europe by its aggressive organization and superior technology was translated into global hegemony in the nineteenth century. The European states claimed large portions of Africa and Asia as colonies, protectorates, or spheres of interest. The British completed a conquest of India begun in the mid-eighteenth century and fanned out from there to dominate much of Southeast Asia and the Middle East, creating the largest empire the world had ever known. China was forced to accept humiliating infringements of its economic and territorial sovereignty. Weakened by a terrible civil war in the mid-nineteenth century that undermined the declining Manchu dynasty, it took the first painful steps toward modernization. Only two major states remained outside the European orbit: the United States of America, founded by rebellion in the late eighteenth century and, by the end of the nineteenth, the dominant force in the Western Hemisphere and the world's greatest industrial power, and Japan, which, startled from feudal isolation by the imperial challenge, rapidly transformed itself into first the equal and ultimately the superior of any European state.

These changes in politics and technology were accompanied by far-reaching transformations of the social order. Slavery was formally abolished in Africa and the Americas, although other forms of labor coercion remained. In Europe and later in the Western Hemisphere the industrial working force began to organize in its own behalf under the banner of a new doctrine, socialism, which consciously opposed itself to the capitalist and imperialist order. The great movement for gender equality known as women's liberation began in the industrial nations and spread rapidly across the globe. In Europe the Jews were emancipated after centuries of enforced isolation, and other minorities began to claim their rights to equality and free expression. By 1900 a majority of the population in the leading industrial nations lived in cities, creating a new and distinctive urban culture, and despite the continuing economic struggle of many, improvements in sanitation and health care had begun dramatically to increase the average life expectation in the developed countries. ■

CHAPTER · 24

Europe and the Americas

By the eighteenth century the economy of western Europe had become worldwide in scope. Large regional economies, integrated by trade patterns and dominated by strong states, had existed since ancient times. China had long been the center of such an economy in East Asia. The Indian Ocean and Red Sea area constituted another large system. In Europe itself, the Mediterranean had provided a natural focus of economic integration under the successive dominion of Egyptians, Phoenicians, Greeks, Romans, Arabs, Venetians, and, most recently, Spaniards.

But Spain had begun to decline in the seventeenth century, and by the early eighteenth the Mediterranean was dominated for the first time by a power not based geographically in the region, Britain. At the same time, the center of European gravity had shifted to the Atlantic states. Britain, France, and the Dutch Netherlands were not merely the dominant economic powers of Europe, but their scattered overseas possessions, a source of persistent though relatively peripheral rivalry in the seventeenth century, became the focus of a much more intense competition in the eighteenth. Those possessions, increasingly consolidated in political terms and increasingly

William Pitt the Elder, Britain's choleric but brilliant statesman and architect of its North American empire. A contemporary described him as "imperious, violent ... implacable [and] ... despotic," yet also as "a man of veracity and a man of honor." [National Portrait Gallery, London]

valuable in economic ones, became themselves the springboard for further expansion and conquest. The slave trade directly linked four continents—Europe, Africa, and North and South America—in a complex and highly coordinated relationship. After 1750 India and to a lesser extent Indonesia were drawn more and more into the web of European-dominated exchange, and by the end of the century the British were knocking at the gates of China. As the importance of the world market grew, Britain and France clashed repeatedly for control of it. After three major cycles of warfare spread across 125 years, the British emerged victorious, though shorn of what had been their largest New World colony, the newly independent United States of America.

The Old Colonial System

The new global economy consolidated by Europe in the eighteenth century had its roots as far back as the crusades, when the potential for profit in overseas trade first became apparent. This economy was based on the establishment of colonies, used both as forward bases for trade, exploration, or further conquest and as passive markets and sources of raw materials. The crusader colonies in Palestine, Cyprus, and Greece were prototypes of the later and much larger Spanish, Portuguese, Dutch, and English colonies in the New World, Africa, and Asia. A second type of colony, developed by the Genoese in the fourteenth century, was based on control by a private trading company operating under a government charter. The English and Dutch East India companies, founded in 1600 and 1602, respectively, administered large territories under such arrangements, as did the Virginia and Massachusetts Bay companies on the Atlantic seaboard of North America. Yet a third type of colony was based on an agreement between individuals for the settlement of a territory; the Mayflower Compact was an example.

The nature of a given colonial enterprise depended on the territory to be settled and the general approach of the colonizing center, or "metropolis." In the New World tiny bands of adventurers such as those commanded by Cortés in Mexico and Pizarro in Peru, exploiting native rivalries, were able to conquer vast areas through mobile tactics, skillful use of Indian auxiliaries, and technological superiority. The urban civilizations of the Aztecs in Mexico and the Incas in Peru were in many respects the equal of Europe's, but their weapons were those of the Stone Age. Elsewhere in the Americas, Europeans confronted only scattered tribes which were quickly exterminated, enslaved, or driven into wilderness areas.

The peoples of Africa were nearly as vulnerable to European penetration as those of the Americas. The Portuguese established their influence along the Congo and Zambesi rivers in the early sixteenth century, but the unattractiveness of the climate for Europeans deterred large-scale settlement except at the Cape of Good Hope on the southern tip of the continent, where Dutch colonists arrived in the seventeenth century. For the most part, Europeans were content to barter for slaves, gold dust, and ivory with African middlemen, and apart from establishing coastal bases for commerce they made little attempt to explore the continent.

In Asia, where Europeans possessed no significant technical or military advantage except in ship design, conquest and hence colonization were out of the question. Here the Portuguese and the Dutch competed with Asian and Arab merchants for a share of the lucrative spice trade, often financed by piracy. At the beginning of the eighteenth century, however, the European presence in Asia was still marginal.

Spain and the New World

Spain ruled its colonies in the New World through its Council of the Indies, although its powers were gradually dispersed among other ministries in the eighteenth century. With the immense bureaucratic patience typical of the Spanish Old Regime, it attempted—for the first time in Europe in 1,000 years—to govern a territory and population far exceeding its own, a challenge compounded by the distance of several thousand miles of ocean. From Madrid it sent out an endless stream of edicts covering the minutest details of colonial life; by 1700 more than 400,000 of these were still technically in force, and a digest of the more important ones contained 11,000 laws.

To ensure conformity with its regulations, the council relied on the *residencia*, a review of all senior colonial officials at the end of their service, and the *visita*, irregular inspections that might produce temporary improvements but more often, as one viceroy put it, did little more than raise the dust on the streets. The empire was formally divided into the viceroyalties of New Spain and Peru, the former encompassing Mexico and most of the western two-thirds of the present-day United States. In addition, there were three captaincies general, Santo Domingo, Guatemala, and New Granada, the last of which, centered in what is now Colombia, became a viceroyalty in 1739. The viceroyalties were divided into provinces, but the basic unit of administration, as in Spain itself, centered on the municipality, governed by an official usually called the *corregidor*. The corregidor was the backbone of the colonial system, and the day to day lives of most of the population depended on his performance.

The primary purpose of the empire was the exploitation of its wealth. This required the mobilization of its inhabitants. In the early years of the sixteenth century the Spaniards enslaved the island populations of the Caribbean and worked them literally to extinction in the gold mines; by midcentury the population of Hispaniola had been reduced from several hundred thousand to a few hundred. The inhabitants of Cuba and Puerto Rico suffered a similar fate, while smaller islands, which the Spanish did not bother to settle, were stripped of their populations by raiding parties. Reports of these atrocities, and the complaints of Spanish priests that the native population was dying off before it could be converted to Christianity, prompted the Spanish government to issue an edict regarding its treatment:

> **Because of the excessive liberty the Indians have been permitted, they flee from Christians and do not work. Therefore they are to be compelled to work, so that the kingdom and the Spaniards be enriched, and the Indians Christianized. They are to be paid a daily wage and well treated as free persons, for such they are, and not slaves.**[1]

These instructions had no discernible effect on the extermination of the Caribbean Indians. In Mexico labor was at first directly enslaved. This was modified by the introduction of the *encomienda,* a type of manorial system whereby Spanish settlers were given responsibility for protecting and "civilizing" native communities in return for their labor. As mining developed in Mexico and particularly in Peru, the system proved inadequate to the demands for a mobile labor force that could be transported from site to site and was supplemented by a conscript system, the *repartimiento,* in which Indian community chiefs were required to provide a stipulated amount of labor to the authorities, who distributed the workers to Spanish contractors. Nominal wages were paid, but they were so low that they were often a mere pretext to force Indian workers into debt and peonage. Although conditions varied from region to region with the requirement of a work force (being worst where economic activity was most intense), the *repartimiento* tended to become indistinguishable from forced labor. In its brutally efficient regimentation of labor, it became the prototype of colonial capitalism, and its techniques eventually found their way home to the metropolis with the advent of the Industrial Revolution.

Gold and silver brought Europeans to the Americas in the sixteenth century. The great silver mountain at Potosí, 10,000 feet above sea level, gave rise to a city whose population eventually reached 160,000, rivaling at one point the size of London and exceeding Madrid, Paris, and Rome. Its 36 churches, with their splendid baroque ornamentation, were matched by 36 gambling casinos, no less grandly adorned. Its mines consumed the lives of an estimated 8 million Indian workers before they gave out.

Gold and the Expansion of the European Economy

The importation of massive quantities of precious metals, ferried home by an annual treasure fleet, had a profound

Conscript Labor in Spanish Mexico

A seventeenth-century Spanish commentator, António Vásquez de Espinosa, describes the operation of a textile mill in the city of Puebla.

There are in this city large woolen mills in which they weave quantities of fine cloth, serge, and grogram, from which they make handsome profits. . . . To keep their mills supplied with labor . . . [the operators] maintain individuals who are engaged and hired to ensnare poor innocents. Seeing some Indian who is a stranger to the town, with some trickery or pretext, such as hiring him to carry something, like a porter, and paying him cash, they get him into the mill. Once inside, they drop the deception, and the poor fellow never again gets outside that prison until he dies and they carry him out for burial. In this way they have gathered in and duped many married Indians with families, who have passed into oblivion here for 20 years, or longer, or their whole lives, without their wives and children knowing anything about them. . . . And although the Royal Council of the Indies . . . has tried to remedy this evil with warrants and ordinances . . . and the Viceroy of New Spain appoints mill inspectors to visit [the Indians] and remedy such matters, nevertheless, since most of those who set out on such commissions aim rather at their own enrichment . . . and since the mill owners pay them well, they leave the wretched Indians in the same slavery . . . as if it were not a most serious mortal sin.

Source: A. V. de Espinosa, *Compendium and Description of the West Indies* (Washington, D.C.: Smithsonian Institution, 1942), pp. 133–134.

effect on the European economy. The Mediterranean region, whose weak bullion base had been further eroded by the decline of imports from its previous supplier, the Sudan, suddenly burgeoned. From Seville to Antwerp, the ports of western Europe teemed with new shipping and trade, presaging the great shift of power to the Atlantic economies that occurred within the next two centuries. Transatlantic trade multiplied eightfold between 1510 and 1550 and tripled again between 1550 and 1610. Through trade and smuggling, a considerable quantity of the new bullion found its way to Asia and the Levant, and at one time a direct transpacific trade developed between Acapulco and Manila in the Philippines. Gold and silver from the New World created a network of worldwide commerce on a scale and of a complexity never seen before.

The gradual exhaustion of the mines of Mexico and Peru brought this first, precocious global economy to an end. Asia had no interest in Western goods comparable to the European demand for silks and spices, which therefore had to be paid for almost entirely in bullion. As new supplies tapered off, the Asian trade dwindled. At about the same time, the European economy, so powerfully stimulated by the influx of precious metals, began to contract. European states blamed the prolonged depression that set in between 1619 and 1622 on their shrinking bullion reserves, although this was only one factor in a complex process of overproduction, diminished population growth, and a long-term pattern of severer climate. The anxiety of states to protect their bullion supplies led to import restrictions, thus hindering trade and deepening the slump. This in turn heightened the tensions surrounding the Thirty Years' War, which itself produced ruin in much of Europe.

A woman weighing gold looks thoughtful in this painting by Rembrandt. Gold was vital to commercial and industrial expansion in early modern Europe and the chief spur to exploration and colonization in the Americas. [Marburg/Art Resource]

Merchant Capitalism and the Growth of the State

Nonetheless, the great sixteenth-century boom had permanent effects. The sharp rise in profits and prices enriched the merchant bourgeoisie, whose new political importance was clearly manifested in Britain, France, and the Netherlands. The value of estates and rents tended to fall, thus putting pressure on the landed nobility. In eastern Europe the demand for foodstuffs and raw materials to stoke the expanding Atlantic economies stimulated the enserfment of scarce peasant labor, an apparently "backward" step that was, like the regimentation of Indian labor in the Americas, in significant part a response to growth in the core economies of the West. The results of this were profound. It immobilized the peasant population, stunting urban growth and confirming the power of the landed nobility at a time when it was under challenge in the West. From the sixteenth century onward, the development of eastern and western Europe increasingly diverged; their present political and economic divisions are a consequence.

The growth of the economy was linked to that of the state. The expansion of the latter was most visible in palace building and the development of a court-based culture, which reached their climax in the Versailles of Louis XIV. These self-conscious displays of power were accompanied by a proliferation of state offices and the gradual transformation of royal attendants serving the king's pleasure into bureaucratic functionaries performing regular and prescribed duties. At the same time, the state took a greater interest in economic development, which provided it with a larger tax base. The fiscal demands of the state stimulated the growth of banking and credit, and these in turn expanded the state's capacities further.

The development of merchant capitalism and of centralized political authority was thus reciprocal. The establishment of centralized authority was essential to peaceful commerce at home and the protection of colonial ventures abroad. Often, as in the development of the silk and glass industries in France or of mining in Austria and Hungary, the state allied itself directly with business interests, and the entire process of exploration and colonization in the sixteenth century may be considered as a partnership between the state and private entrepreneurs in which the state provided venture capital in return for a fixed share of the profits. War itself took on a more overtly commercial tone, as states fought over trade routes, commercial privileges, and control of profitable or potentially profitable territories.

This did not mean that the interests of rulers and merchants were necessarily harmonious. Their partnership was always an uneasy one, and by the eighteenth century some merchants felt that the state had become unduly restrictive and even oppressive, hampering rather than fostering economic development with its rigid controls and regulations. On balance, however, the state and merchant capitalism were mutually supportive during the first stages of global economic growth in the West. If the merchant bourgeoisie had developed to the point where state intervention was perceived as a handicap, it was only because state power had nurtured it to the point of self-generating growth.

The Economy of the Americas

The principal economic activity of Spanish America, even in the headiest days of gold and silver production, was agriculture. Spanish colonial society quickly reproduced the patterns of the home country, with large estates worked by native labor. The government made land grants of immense size as a means of encouraging new settlements, and great cattle herds pushed the frontiers of New Spain beyond Mexico into what is now the southwestern United States. The Spaniards supplemented the native crops of maize, beans, and squash with wheat and a variety of fruits. Sugar was grown from early on in the Caribbean islands and on the Mexican lowlands, and olive and vine culture was successfully established in Peru. Cortés, seeking a profitable crop, introduced the silkworm into Mexico in 1523. The most successful export over the next three centuries of Spanish dominance in America, however, was cochineal, an insect used in red dyes.

In Portuguese Brazil, where no precious metals were discovered until 1690 and the native population was inadequate as a labor force, a plantation society quickly developed based on sugar, tobacco, cocoa, and cotton, employing black slave labor. This pattern was repeated by the British, French, and Dutch in the Caribbean and the southern colonies of North America, where similar climatic and demographic conditions prevailed. Farther up the North American coast and along the rivers of the interior, notably the Mississippi and the St. Lawrence, a settler society developed in the absence of readily exploitable labor or natural resources. The most populous of these settlements were the British colonies along the Atlantic seaboard, although the most far-flung geographically was the long arc of French trading stations and fortifications that extended from the Gulf of Mexico to Hudson's Bay. The principal Dutch base on the North American mainland was New Amsterdam, at the mouth of the Hudson River. From here the Dutch conducted a lucrative fur trade and an even more profitable smuggling operation until the settlement was conquered by the British in 1664, who renamed it New York.

The Settlement of North America

British settlement in North America proceeded fitfully. After several false starts, a small colony was established at Jamestown on the Potomac River in 1607. By 1733 the number had grown to 13 colonies along the coast and the adjacent river valleys from New England to Georgia. The northernmost of these colonies, particularly Massachusetts, Rhode Island, and Connecticut, were essentially subsistence economies of slight value to the mother country. They served, together with the Quaker colony of Pennsylvania, primarily as a dumping ground for religious and political dissidents, some 20,000 of whom migrated to New England between 1629 and 1642 in the wave of repression that preceded the English revolution. In the Middle Atlantic and southern plantation colonies, indigents and convicts (frequently transported as an alternative to hanging) joined religious exiles as settlers, together, of course, with imported slave labor.

Since Britain's mainland colonies were at first perceived largely as a safety valve for excess population or unwanted social groups, the crown exerted relatively little control over them. The French, in contrast, never thought of allowing their colonies to be peopled by paupers, felons, and dissidents. Great efforts were made to procure suitable migrants, down to the provision of tools, seed, stock, and even free passage to Canada for women willing to marry settlers. The crown first subsidized and controlled the companies formed to plant settlements and then, under Jean-Baptiste Colbert, relieved them of all administrative responsibility, placing each colony under a military governor. Nonetheless, the combined French and British presence in the New World in the seventeenth century was only a fraction of Spain's in size, population, and wealth—and that in spite of the loss in Spanish America, mostly to epidemic disease, of some nine-tenths of its preconquest population of 20 million or more, one of the greatest demographic extinctions in history. It was not, however, the vast expanses of the North American continent that were to make the New World profitable for Britain and France in the late seventeenth and early eighteenth centuries but the small sugar-producing islands of the Caribbean.

Sugar and Slavery

Sugar had been grown in the New World almost from the beginning of European colonization. As early as the 1510s sugar cultivation had been introduced into the Caribbean islands, where it was harvested by black slaves imported from Africa to replace an Amerindian population already decimated by white settlers. The Portuguese were the first to introduce sugar on a relatively large scale in Brazil, where some 60 mills were in operation by 1580. Most of the export trade was carried on by Dutch merchants, one of whose spokesmen, Willem de Usselincx, farsightedly pointed out that plantation crops such as sugar had a far greater long-range profit potential than the Spanish bullion that so dazzled his contemporaries. The Dutch themselves were driven out of Brazil by 1654, but their role in spreading the sugar trade in the West Indies by means of shipping and selling the product, introducing the processes that turned brown sugar into the much more popular white variety, and supplying African slaves, was crucial.

The replacement of the Dutch as middlemen and their defeat as competitors marked the coming of age of the British and French imperial systems. The British moved swiftly to consolidate control of their colonial trade. The Navigation Acts of 1651 and 1660 provided that colonies could trade certain "enumerated" products—sugar, tobacco, cotton, indigo, ginger, and dyewoods—only with the mother country or other British colonies and only on British ships. In return they were to accept manufactured goods from Britain. This closed system of trade exemplified the economic theory of mercantilism, which sought to enhance the wealth of the mother country by acquiring a captive source of supply for its commodity needs and a compulsory outlet for its manufactures. The French were never able to develop a system as fully integrated as that of the British, partly because of the absence of a mainland population sufficient to promote intercolonial trade, but as commodity suppliers alone their major West Indian possessions—Guadeloupe and Martinique, settled in 1635, and Santo Domingo, acquired from Spain in 1697—had an increasing impact on the metropolitan economy.

The phases of sugar harvesting and processing are shown here in a print representing a slave plantation in the West Indies. At right raw cane is being brought in from the fields; it is crushed in a roller mill, mixed with lime and egg white, and left to crystallize. The profitability of sugar, and of the slave trade that supplied the labor it demanded, resulted in one of the greatest forced migrations in history. [Bettmann Archive]

Of all British and French colonial products, sugar was by far the most important. Its cultivation required not only suitable colonies but also a heavy investment in land and labor. Wealthy royalist exiles from the English civil wars provided this in the 1640s and 1650s, driving out poorer white settlers and consolidating their land into large plantations. By 1673 sugar production on tiny Barbados was one-quarter that of Brazil's, and by 1700 the economic value of the West Indian islands exceeded that of all the mainland colonies combined. Jamaica, acquired by Britain in 1655, did not develop into a major supplier until the early eighteenth century, but by 1770 it was producing half of all British sugar and was incontestably the single most valuable colonial territory in the New World. Despite some price fluctuation, the demand for sugar remained extraordinarily high for well over a century, particularly in Britain itself, where per capita consumption was eight times that in France. Overall, the production of sugar in the Americas rose from 20,000 tons per year in 1600 to 200,000 tons on the eve of the American Revolution.

The Slave System

The labor required for sugar cultivation on this scale could have come only from slaves, and as the pace of importation quickened, the free white population of the West Indies fell dramatically; some 30,000 whites left Barbados alone between 1650 and 1680. Seen in this perspective, the "settlement" of the New World in the seventeenth, eighteenth, and much of the nineteenth century was overwhelmingly by African blacks. A million blacks had been imported into the Americas by 1700, and 6 million more arrived in the course of the eighteenth century, a number nearly equaling both the partially recovered remnant of the original Amerindian population and that of white settlers combined. Half of this number was funneled into the West Indies alone, where the permanent British and French population was less than 100,000. Yet despite the 3 million black men, women, and children who entered the Caribbean during this period, the net population increase was only 700,000. The vast majority of slaves perished within ten years of arrival. In part this may be accounted for by disease, the major factor in the destruction of the native population in the sixteenth century. But the primary reason was exploitation. Blacks were systematically worked to death.

At first glance this appears difficult to explain. Slaves were an expensive investment; they accounted for 90 percent of the capital value of Jamaican plantations in the eighteenth century, exclusive of land. Nonetheless, in the calculus of profit, they were expendable. It was cheaper to replace than to maintain them, which meant supporting those too young and too old to work.

The Slave Trade

The mechanism of replacement, the great wheel that turned all of eighteenth-century colonial commerce, was the slave trade. Slaving was a textbook example of what mercantilist economists called the "triangular trade." Ships from Liverpool or Nantes exchanged cheap textiles, gunpowder, or gin for slaves provided by native traders at stations on the West African coast. As new cargo, the slaves were transported to the West Indies. Allowing for a 15 to 20 percent mortality rate en route, the survivors would sell for approximately five times their original purchase price. The ships would then fill up with sugar and return home.

The transatlantic voyage, known euphemistically as the "middle passage," took two months. The slaves were segregated by sex and packed together below decks in chains, helpless amid vermin and rats. In fair weather they were exercised on deck, under the lash; when seas were rough, they were kept below with the portholes shut. The tensions of the voyage provoked insane acts of cruelty. The captain of one ship flogged a 10-month-old child with a cat-o'-nine-tails for refusing to eat, then plunged it into scalding water, tied it to a log, flogged it again to death, and forced its mother to throw it into the sea.

Once ashore, the slaves in Britain's Caribbean colonies possessed neither legal nor moral rights. A planter who flogged a 14-year-old girl to death was actually tried for murder in Jamaica but was acquitted on the ground that "it was impossible [that] a master could destroy his own property." The Spaniards had tried to justify their conquest of the Americas by the necessity to convert the heathen, but eighteenth-century missionaries were forbidden to proselytize among blacks, and one slave caught going to church in Grenada was given 24 lashes.

In assessing the mutual dependency of sugar and the slave trade and its overall economic impact, it would be a mistake to focus too narrowly on the calculations of the plantation owner, crucial though they were. Only by bringing profitable cargo into the New World on a large scale and a regular basis could the European sugar market be developed, since merchant fleets would not risk the journey across the Atlantic with empty hulls, and the sugar islands were hardly major consumers of manufactured products. Thus slaves were vital not only to the production of the tropical economy but also to its marketing process. If black mortality in the New World had not exceeded reproduction, a saturation level would have been reached, and the slave trade would have died. From this perspective, the sugar market could only have been sustained by genocide.

Much attention has been focused on the economic marginality of the slavers themselves. It is true that while the opportunity for great profit existed, the risk of great loss was also present, as on any long-distance voyage. The

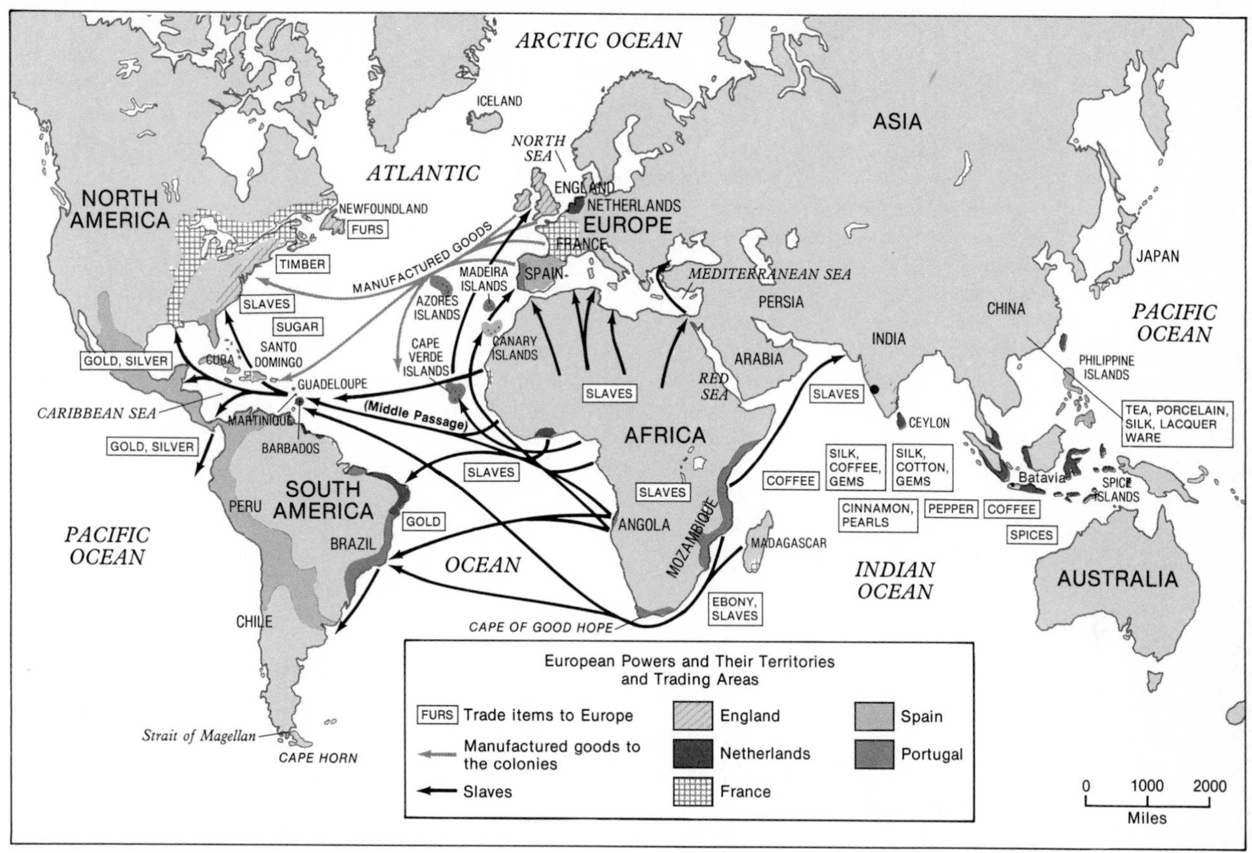

***24.1** Overseas Trade in the Seventeenth and Eighteenth Centuries*

significance of the triangular trade itself, however, did not lie in the reliability of profit in any single component but in the profit-generating capacity of the whole. The existence of the trade meant a steady demand for shipping; the feeding and clothing of millions of slaves was a major stimulus to textiles and agriculture. The capital spinoff into the European economy was therefore of considerable importance; and it was with the mechanization of the textile industry, financed in part by the slave trade, that the Industrial Revolution began.

LIVERPOOL IN THE AGE OF SLAVERY

Even before industrialization, the influx of slave-generated wealth was very evident. Liverpool, an English coastal town on the Irish Sea with a population of barely 500 in the sixteenth century and only 28 streets in the late seventeenth, became the chief slave port of Europe, carrying at its height almost two-thirds of the British and nearly half of the total European slave trade. The town's rise to success was in part the result of the bankrupting of the London slave merchants in the South Sea Bubble of 1720. Enterprising Liverpudlians soon took over from them, taking advantage of the port's westerly location. The profitable War of the Austrian Succession in the 1740s also enabled trade, in the words of a local merchant, "to spread her golden wings." By 1750 a flotilla of nearly 200 ships directly served the slave trade, and four years later a splendid new exchange opened on Castle Street—as if to emphasize the alliance of commerce and government, it also housed the town hall. No expense was spared, as the town fathers sought to emulate the Greek columns and the imposing cupola of the Royal Exchange in London. A week of boat races, public breakfasts, and balls celebrated its opening. An observatory and an academy of arts came soon after, a regular stagecoach run to London, and in 1768 representation in Parliament, the final mark of new status.

Fourteen banks graced the town by midcentury as well, none with fewer than £200,000 in assets. Most banks were founded by the slave merchants, who also operated their own insurance companies, collected the excise, and

A Slave's Experience

Olaudah Equiano (c. 1745–1797), an Ibo born in eastern Nigeria, near Benin, was abducted into slavery at the age of 10. He survived a transatlantic crossing and a series of masters, eventually bought his own freedom, worked as a barber, a domestic servant, and a sailor, and in 1789 published, in English, a two-volume memoir of his life as a slave, from which these excerpts are taken.

The first object which saluted my eyes when I arrived on the coast was the sea, and a slave ship which was then riding at anchor and waiting for its cargo. These filled me with astonishment, which was soon converted into terror when I was carried on board. I was immediately handled and tossed up to see if I were sound by some of the crew, and I was now persuaded that I had gotten into a world of bad spirits and that they were going to kill me. Their complexions too differing so much from ours, their long hair and the language they spoke (which was very different from any I had ever heard) united to confirm me in this belief. . . . When I looked round the ship too and saw a large furnace or copper boiling and a multitude of black people of every description chained together, every one of their countenances expressing dejection and sorrow, I no longer doubted of my fate. . . .

The stench of the hold while we were on the coast was so intolerably loathsome that it was dangerous to remain there for any time, and some of us had been permitted to stay on the deck for the fresh air; but now that the whole ship's cargo were confined together it became absolutely pestilential. The closeness of the place and the heat of the climate, added to the number in the ship, which was so crowded that each had scarcely room to run himself, almost suffocated us. This produced copious perspirations, so that the air soon became unfit for respiration from a variety of loathsome smells, and brought on a sickness among the slaves, of which many died. . . . This wretched situation was again aggravated by the galling of the chains, now become insupportable, and the filth of the tubs, into which the children often fell and were almost suffocated. The shrieks of the women and the groans of the dying rendered the whole a scene of horror almost inconceivable.

Source: P. Edwards, ed., *Equiano's Travels: His Autobiography* (New York: Praeger, 1967), pp. 25, 28–29.

guaranteed the municipal finances. They were, in fact, Liverpool. The city maintained its traditional trade with Ireland, chiefly in cattle, and it produced pottery, glassware, and salt. But these activities were dwarfed by the slave and sugar trade and gradually strangled by it. The banks, the warehouses, and the dockyards formed a commercial trinity that dominated the city's life as it did its skyline. Until 1772 it was also possible to see slaves in their iron collars being sold for domestic use at the city market, but in that year Lord Chief Justice Mansfield ruled in the court of King's Bench that no person could be subjected to slavery in Britain. Liverpool's slave market disappeared, but not its slave trade; it was to be 61 years before the slaves in Britain's colonies were likewise freed.

From Liverpool the prosperity produced by the slave and sugar trade spread visibly across the English landscape in the form of great country houses and the merchant mansions of London and Bath. As early as 1729 the pamphleteer Joshua Gee noted that "all the great increase in our treasure proceeds chiefly from the labor of negroes in the plantations." But conspicuous consumption by the rich was not the principal result of the commerce in human lives. The new wealth was to lay the ground for Britain's rise to world power.

From the sixteenth century on, the European economy had become significantly entwined for the first time with that of a region thousands of miles away that provided it with the means of capital expansion, first through the importation of bullion from Spanish America and later primarily through the trade in sugar and slaves. The importance of this new global economy was great. So, too, was its human cost. It destroyed by direct or indirect means much of the native population of two continents and substantially depleted that of a third.

Liverpool was the chief port of terminus for the sugar and slave trades, and it prospered accordingly. The corner of Tithebarn Street is shown, with the back of the Town Hall at right. Behind the hall, space is being cleared for the erection of a new commercial exchange, in which the man with the wheelbarrow is presumably employed. [Herdman Collection, Liverpool Public Library]

The First Age of Global War

"It is a notorious fact that the history of colonial expansion is also the history of incessant warfare," the historian Walter Dorn observed.[2] The wars of the early modern period, particularly in what has sometimes been called the era of the second Hundred Years' War (1689–1815), were fought for a variety of reasons, including religion, dynastic rivalry, and positional advantage on the European continent. Increasingly, however, the major wars of Europe involved conflict in four overseas areas as well—North America, the West Indies, Africa, and India. By the time of the Seven Years' War (1756–1763) these external theaters had become more important than the European struggle itself.

The wars of Europe were, then, in part the effect of expansion; but they were a cause of it as well. The use of firearms and cannon in European warfare became decisive between 1460 and 1540, and during that time iron production rose by as much as 500 percent and copper by even more. The mechanization of war made it the monopoly of the state. As heavy field pieces replaced horses, armor, and crossbows as the major capital investment in warfare, private noblemen could no longer afford the personal armies that had been the hallmark (and often the bane) of the late medieval period. A modern arsenal containing furnaces, forges, foundries, gunpowder mills, and saltpeter shops might employ, as the French arsenal at St. Étienne in the early seventeenth century did, 700 workers or more. The building of warships, which carried two or three banks of cannon and often exceeded 1,000 tons, was an even more complex activity, requiring specialized skills and materials that might come from halfway around the world. The state alone possessed the resources for such investment, and this in turn spurred its own growth. The increasing scale of warfare, the expanding role of the state, and the widening arc of commerce

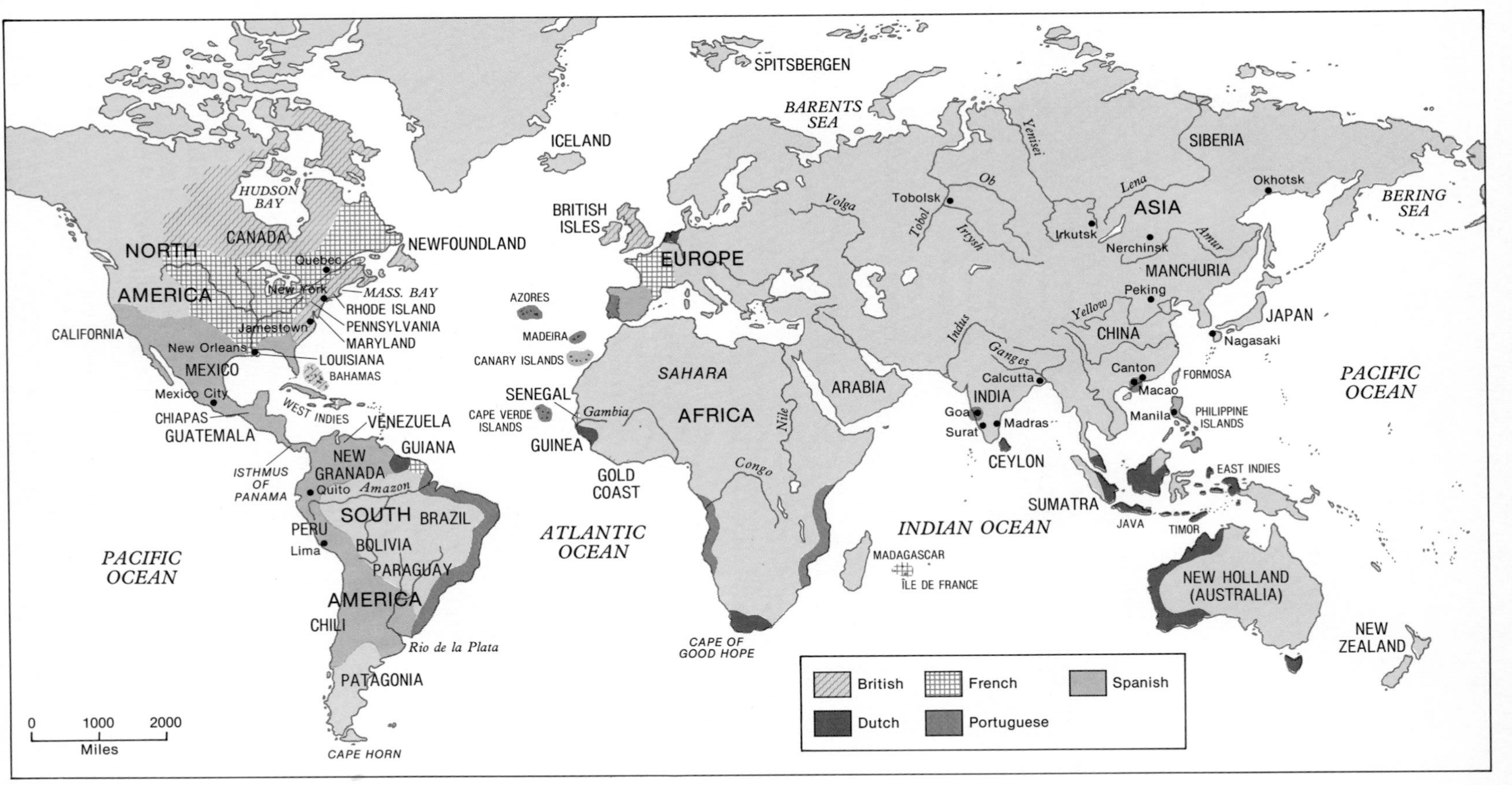

24.2 The Expansion of Europe, 1715

were all part of the dynamic that made Europe's wars, as well as its economic activity, worldwide.

The New Balance of Power

The wars of Louis XIV marked a turning point in the European balance of power. France remained, as it would for the next century and a half, the dominant land power on the Continent. Its main rival, however, was no longer Spain, its great antagonist in the Thirty Years' War, or Austria, the chief barrier to its expansion in Germany, Italy, and the Low Countries, but Britain. Britain owed its new international prominence to its naval supremacy, its commercial wealth, and, perhaps most important, its access to that wealth through the working partnership of the landed elite, the financial community, and the organs of government.

Walpole, Britain's First Prime Minister

The stability of the new system was epitomized by the man who made it function for two decades, Sir Robert Walpole (1676–1745). The son of a prosperous Norfolk squire, Walpole rose steadily through the Whig hierarchy. He sat in Parliament for 40 years, held high office for 30, and for some 20— from 1722 to 1742—was the effective ruler of the country, the first prime minister of Britain in fact if not in name.

Walpole grasped the fact that the Glorious Revolution of 1688 had settled the basic issues of seventeenth-century British politics, creating a limited monarchy firmly subject to the wishes of the landed gentry. What remained, with rising prosperity and a stable dynasty on the throne, was to organize the division of spoils. Walpole's command of the system was based on his control of its three major components, the crown, Parliament, and patronage. The support of the first two Hanoverian kings, George I (1714–1727) and George II (1727–1760), was his anchor. He consulted their wishes, cultivated their prejudices, and flattered their mistresses; through them, he consolidated and controlled all honors, promotions, offices, and contracts, scrupulously rewarding his friends and punishing his enemies. This monopoly of favor enabled him in turn to ensure a comfortable majority in Parliament, for although the principle of ministerial responsibility—that the king's ministry must retain a working majority in the House of Commons—was not firmly established until the nineteenth century, it was already true that no government could survive for long without such support. That this support was based more or less openly on bribery and corruption did not bother Walpole. If corruption was required to ensure stable government and general prosperity, he argued, then corruption was a political virtue, if not a moral one.

The Triumph of the Elite

The real stability of the British system, however, was in the unchallenged dominance of the landed elite, particu-

In this contemporary print, the way to favor under Sir Robert Walpole's rule is graphically illustrated. [Culver Pictures]

larly its uppermost stratum. The government of eighteenth-century Britain, superficial political scrimmaging apart, rested securely with some 400 families, who independently controlled one-quarter of the arable land in the country. This striking concentration of ownership, which had been achieved largely since the Restoration of 1660, was the result of several interrelated factors. Large estates were protected from partition by laws that required that they be passed on to a single heir, who was prohibited from selling off parcels except under strict conditions. The value of land had been enhanced by increased productivity, in part the result of agricultural improvements, in part of laws that encouraged the cultivation of grain for export. This spurred the process known as enclosure, by which common grazing land and individual farm plots were fenced in by wealthy landowners armed with sheriffs' writs or private acts of Parliament. By 1840 fully 6 million acres had been enclosed in this fashion, bringing another quarter of Britain's farmland under elite control. The small independent farmer or yeoman, once the backbone of English agriculture, had become an endangered species by the eighteenth century and virtually extinct by the nineteenth, disappearing into the mass of wage laborers and tenant farmers who worked the great estates of the few.

Such a far-reaching and traumatic centralization of ownership might have been expected to produce unrest and even rebellion, yet Britain's countryside was for most of the eighteenth century among the most peaceful in Europe. This was partly due to the unique nature of its aristocracy. Only about 200 families in England held formal titles of nobility (as opposed to half a million each in France and Spain), and the only distinct advantage such titles conveyed was the right to sit in the House of Lords. It entailed no other significant legal privileges such as marked off Continental elites from the mass of the population, particularly exemption from taxation. Indeed, the difference between Britain and the other European monarchies might be summarized by saying that whereas on the Continent the landed elite tolerated royal control of taxation on the condition that it fall chiefly on others, in Britain it accepted the burden of taxation in return for the right to control it through Parliament.

The absence of a status system based primarily on graded titles of nobility and distinguished by special privileges meant that wealth itself was the basic criterion for membership in the British elite. This encouraged entrepreneurship and investment in mining, industry, canal building, and urban real estate as well as colonization and agriculture, and the ever-expanding wealth of this elite provided the sinews of empire. At the same time, it was a true governing class that controlled and unified the instruments of social order from the pay of the local justice of the peace to the provision of the Royal Navy. Few aristocracies in history had exercised so clear and thorough a dominion over their societies as that of eighteenth-century Britain.

France Under Louis XV

The situation of France was quite different. Louis XIV had devoted much of his energy to reducing the nobility to political impotence. He had worked all his life to create a system of government dependent on the will and capacity of the sovereign, only to leave his throne to a 5-year-old boy, Louis XV. Power devolved upon his elder cousin, Philip, duke of Orléans, as regent. With a nobleman heading the government, the aristocracy reasserted its claims to power, with disastrous results for central authority. By 1723 Louis XV had proclaimed his majority; but in a real sense he never grew up. Though rather bright and served by some able ministers—Cardinal Fleury, the duke of Choiseul, and René de Maupeou—he lacked the discipline and the character to impose his will on the government, and so faint was his impress on the history of his long reign (1715–1774) that the age is better remembered for a shrewd and vivacious royal mistress, Madame de Pompadour, than for its titular ruler. Without forceful leadership, the bureaucracy became slack and unresponsive, the intendants pursued policies at variance with those of the government, and the parlements openly defied the crown, supporting opposition groups such as the Jansenists and successfully resisting all efforts to raise taxes.

Taxation and Finance

A pair of similar incidents early in the reigns of Louis XV and George I demonstrated the growing difference between the pace of development in France and Britain. In 1716, while Orléans was regent, he gave permission to a Scottish speculator, John Law (1671–1729), to found a private bank whose notes could be used as legal tender to pay taxes. Orléans hoped in this way to centralize tax collection and to avoid the rapacity of the tax farmers, who even under Louis XIV had kept a third of all receipts for themselves. At the same time, Law was given a chartered monopoly of all overseas French commerce, the Mississippi Company, whose profits were to secure the bank's notes. Wild reports of gold and diamonds in French Louisiana, some deliberately fabricated, drove the price of Mississippi stock up from 500 to 15,000 livres. By 1720 Law had been appointed controller general of France, with virtual control of the nation's economy. His fall was as dramatic as his rise. The profits of overseas trade lagged behind expectations, and the rumor of a bonanza in Louisiana was soon dispelled. Mississippi stock plummeted, Law's bank collapsed, and by the end of the year he had fled the country, leaving French finances as before in the hands of the tax farmers.

What the French had sought in Law's bank was to emulate the success of the Bank of England in providing regular, low-interest credit to the crown. It failed in part because of opposition by the tax farmers, who preferred to siphon off one-third of French tax revenues rather than settle for the 8 percent per annum paid by the Bank of England, and in part because of the suspicion of the nobility that Law's scheme was simply a device to abolish their tax privileges. In Britain, where the landed elite controlled the taxing power and taxes were collected directly instead of through farmers, there were no vested interests to overcome or privileges to be protected.

What did concern Britons, however, was the size of the public debt, which had risen from £644,000 in 1688 to £54 million in 1713. This represented more than the gross annual product of the economy, and many Englishmen wondered how they could owe more than they were worth. It was at this point that the South Sea Company, a trading company set up to exploit the South American slave trade, put forward an audacious proposal to assume the entire public debt from the Bank of England on the strength of its anticipated profits and to pay it off by establishing a sinking fund equivalent to 2 percent of the value of the debt per year. For a time it appeared that the company might replace the bank as the leading credit institution of the country. Its board of directors included prominent Whig politicians, and George I himself consented to become its honorary head. But as with Law's Mississippi Company, the profits on which its scheme was to be capitalized proved illusory, and after a similar run-up, the value of its stock collapsed in the spring of 1720. The company went into receivership, and a number of smaller firms set up by using its stock as collateral failed, ruining thousands of investors. Thus the first two great financial panics of modern times occurred almost simultaneously in Paris and London. Their consequences, however, were far different. The Bank of England, having weathered the challenge to its supremacy, emerged stronger than ever, and the expanding British economy absorbed the effects of the panic with relative ease. In France, the failure of Law's bank set back the development of modern credit for 70 years, condemning the crown to an escalating spiral of debt.

The Wars of Midcentury

Europe enjoyed a generation of relative calm after the Peace of Utrecht. But the death of two kings brought war again in 1740. Frederick II succeeded to the throne of Prussia, where his father, Frederick William I, had drilled and perfected an army he had never used. Maria Theresa (1740–1780) became empress of Austria and queen of Hungary, the first female sovereign in the history of the

The First Stock Market Crash

The rage for speculation and the lust for profit, which at its height inflated stock values on the London Exchange to five times the estimated cash reserves of the entire continent of Europe, was well described by a contemporary observer, William Chetwood. Shortly after, the South Sea Bubble collapsed, ruining thousands and threatening the Bank of England itself.

The whims of the stocks in this kingdom [are] of late so far cultivated and improved from a foreign example [Law's Mississippi Company in France], that one might reasonably conclude the numerous inhabitants of this great metropolis had for the most part deserted their stations, business, and occupations; and given up all pretensions to industry, in pursuit of an imaginary profit.

If your occasions are never so urgent for a mercer, a tailor, a shoemaker, etc., they are nowhere to be met with but at the Royal Exchange. If you resort to any public office or place of business, the whole enquiry is, How are the stocks? If you are at a coffee-house, the only conversation turns on the stocks. . . . If you repair to a tavern, the edifying subject (especially to a philosopher) is the South Sea Company; if you wait on a lady of quality, you'll find her hastening to the House of Intelligence in Exchange Alley. . . . Even smocks are deposited to help make up the security for cash; jewels pawned to raise money for the purchase of ruin—and, perhaps, wives and daughters have been mortgaged for the very same purpose.

Source: L. Melville, *The South Sea Bubble* (London: O'Connor, 1921), pp. 78–79.

Habsburg dynasty. Her father, Charles VI (1711–1740), had spent the better part of his reign trying to get the princes of Europe to recognize her right to succeed him through the document known as the Pragmatic Sanction. Their promises were worthless. Charles Albert, the elector of Bavaria, immediately claimed the Austrian throne. Bavaria, in turn, was considered a mere stalking-horse for Austria's arch-rival, France. At the same time, Frederick II sought to take advantage of Austria's disarray by seizing the rich province of Silesia, which Prussia had long coveted. This was the signal for a general conflict, the War of the Austrian Succession (1740–1748).

The war soon turned into another chapter in the great imperial war of the century between Britain and France. Britain entered it on the side of Austria, while France supported Prussia and Bavaria. The Anglo-French conflict once again extended to North America, where fighting ranged from the isthmus of Panama to Cape Breton Island off the coast of French Canada. In Europe the chief battles were fought in Flanders, where the French sought to dislodge Austria. In the end, France's success on land was checked by Britain's supremacy at sea. The Treaty of Aix-la-Chapelle (1748) restored Britain and France to their original positions, as the British surrendered Fort Louisburg, taken by colonial militia, in return for their trading station at Madras on the east coast of India. The only belligerent to come out ahead was Frederick of Prussia, who, having realized his objective in the conquest of Silesia, had dropped out of the war six years before.

The Seven Years' War

The absence of a clear winner ensured an early resumption of the conflict. The Seven Years' War (1756–1763) marked the decisive triumph of the British Empire over that of France on all fronts, in North America, Africa, and India. It also marked the end of the rivalry between Habsburg and Bourbon that had been the polestar of European politics for the previous $2\frac{1}{2}$ centuries. This was the achievement of the brilliant, eccentric Count Wenzel von Kaunitz, who was to direct Austrian foreign policy until his death in 1794. Kaunitz' chief objective was the recovery of Silesia from Prussia. Austria's former allies, Britain and the Netherlands, had forced it to give up Silesia and to fight instead for Flanders, a policy that suited their interests but not Austria's. The solution was simple. In return for French troops and money against Prussia, Austria would cede Flanders, a territory it could neither usefully exploit nor properly defend. Thus the alignment of the previous war was completely reversed. All former friends were now enemies, all former enemies friends.

Kaunitz completed the diplomatic isolation of Prussia by entering into an alliance with Russia, which thus joined the European concert of powers for the first time. For five years Frederick fought a war of survival against apparently hopeless odds, earning the appellation "the Great." Each year defeat seemed inevitable; each year—at Rossbach, Leuthen, Zorndorf, Leignitz, Torgau—he staved it off with a last-ditch victory. The toll on Prussia, fighting virtually alone against the three largest powers in Europe, was immense. The Prussian army was reduced from 150,000 in its first campaign to 90,000 in its last. Frederick himself despaired of the final outcome. "To tell the truth," he wrote a minister, "I believe all is lost. I will not survive the ruin of my country."

For Britain, too, the war at first went badly. The French began their drive into the Ohio valley in North America two years before the formal outbreak of hostilities in Europe. They built a line of forts to block British expansion in the region and repelled expeditionary forces sent against them under General Edward Braddock and the young colonial colonel, George Washington. While Indian raids harassed the British frontier, the French seized Oswego on Lake Ontario and captured the strategic Mediterranean island of Minorca when Admiral John Byng abandoned its defense. The British hanged Byng, "to encourage the other admirals," as Voltaire remarked dryly, and in June 1757 replaced the inept ministry of the duke of Newcastle with one headed by William Pitt (1708–1778).

Pitt, the son of a great merchant in the Indian trade, was a leader born for crisis. Magnificent in debate, possessed by his vision of Britain's imperial destiny, he had been for 20 years the most dominant personality in the House of Commons. Yet power had eluded him. Harsh and uncompromising, often ill and frequently unstable, he had none of Walpole's managerial skills, and George II despised him. In the crisis of 1757, however, no one else would do. For the next four years he ruled with almost dictatorial powers and brought Britain victory.

Pitt's strategy was to keep Frederick the Great in the field against the French and the Austrians while he applied Britain's naval superiority against France's North American empire and plundered its trade. In effect, while the French refought the Hundred Years' War in Flanders, Britain would fight for everything else. The French fleet was bottled up in Brest and Toulon and was destroyed at Quiberon Bay and at Lagos off the coast of Portugal when it attempted to break out. Relief expeditions to North America were turned back, and the sheer weight of numbers—the 13 colonies now had a combined population of 2.5 million, against only 70,000 permanent French settlers—told at last. The French forts on the Great Lakes and the St. Lawrence River fell, and the Ohio valley was evacuated. Quebec was captured after a daring campaign in 1759, and with the fall of Montreal in 1760, the last French army in North America surrendered. The West Indian island of Guadeloupe was taken too, as well as the African slaving stations of St. Louis and Gorée. French aggression also backfired in India, where the British found themselves after their victory at Plassey in 1757 not only in possession of the rich Carnatic coast but of the entire hinterland of Bengal.

Pitt resigned in 1761 when his cabinet balked at his plans to conquer the whole of the French West Indies. The Peace of Paris (1763) reflected the view of more cautious men that Britain could not hold on to all it had conquered (which now included Havana and Manila, taken from Spain in 1762) and that any attempt to do so would shortly provoke another war. Guadeloupe was restored, its sugar having proved a glut on the British market, and the French were permitted again to trade in India and to fish off Newfoundland, though not to maintain garrisons. Havana and Manila were returned to Spain in exchange for Florida. From his back bench seat, Pitt denounced the treaty as a betrayal of Britain's blood and treasure. Nonetheless, victory over France was complete and decisive. Britain had gained all of Canada, doubling the size of its American territories. France would never, as it seemed, pose a threat to its hegemony in the New World again. The significance of the unexpected British victory in India would prove even greater, as Britain's wealth provided much of the capital for the Industrial Revolution a generation later. If Britain had not achieved all that Pitt desired, it had accomplished more than anyone but Pitt would have thought possible.

With the hope of winning Flanders gone, the French deserted their Austrian allies. Russia too pulled out in 1762. With no hope of accomplishing alone what it had failed to do with two powerful allies, Austria reluctantly made peace with Prussia (1763). Frederick the Great retained Silesia, although it had cost him the near-destruction of his country to do so, and the remainder of his reign was spent largely in rebuilding it. The transfer of this single province from the Habsburg to the Hohenzollern crown was the only territorial result of two great wars in Europe. Those wars were the last to be fought over questions of dynastic succession and among the first to be fought for the high stakes of overseas empire.

The Birth of the American Republic

If the map of Europe had been little altered by the Seven Years' War, that of North America had been substantially redrawn by the British capture of Canada from France and

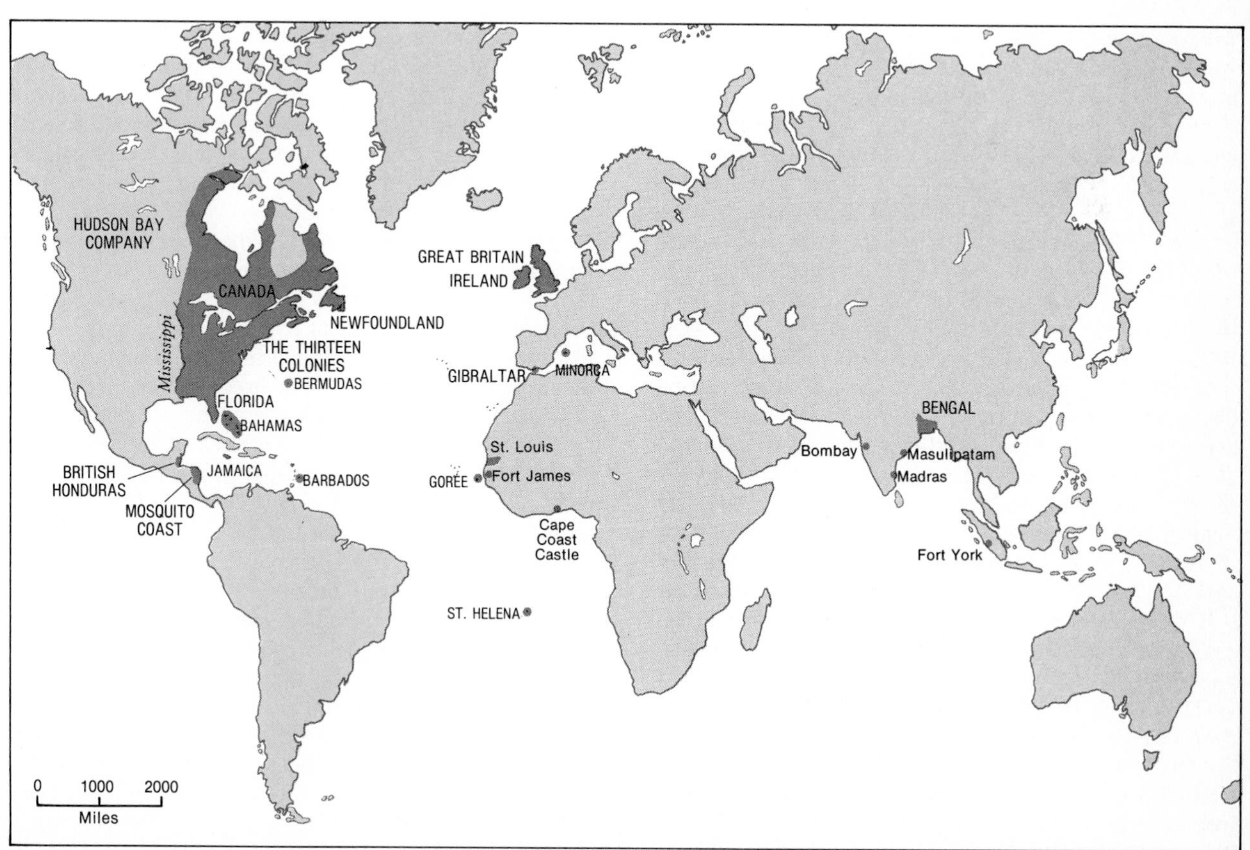

24.3 The British Empire in 1763

Florida from Spain. The British prepared to exploit and extend their new conquests, but they failed to take into account the existing colonies, whose inhabitants, themselves largely of English and Scots-Irish stock, had reached a point of economic and political maturity at which they were no longer prepared to subordinate their interests to those of the mother country, with which they had already begun aggressively to compete. The result was rebellion and the creation of the first independent nation in the New World, the United States of America.

The American Colonies and Britain

By 1763 the 13 colonies of the Atlantic seaboard had become an important market for British manufactures, and if they could not yet compete with the West Indian sugar islands in sheer profitability, their size and the potential for expansion opened up by the conquest of Canada ensured that they would eventually dominate Britain's American empire. Yet within 13 years those colonies would begin the first successful rebellion in the New World, within 13 more they would have established the first indigenous non-European republic in history, and little more than three decades later, with their example and in part with their support, the whole of the Western Hemisphere south of Canada would have thrown off the European yoke brought in with the Spanish conquest.

In might be said with justice that the cause of the 13 colonies' rebellion was Britain's attempt actually to govern them. Until 1763 they had enjoyed an extraordinary degree of independence. Though theoretically subject to the British Parliament, they were exempt from British taxation and had their own assemblies, legal systems, and finances. Instead of serving the home economy as envisioned by mercantile theory, the colonists competed with British ships in the Newfoundland fisheries, built their own vessels in competition with British shipyards, and carried on a lively smuggling trade with the West Indies. The crown had made sporadic attempts between 1685 and 1714 to revoke colonial patents and charters with a view to governing the colonies more directly, but these had foundered on the refusal of Parliament to tamper with what it regarded as property rights. The American colonists saw this as a vindication of their autonomy. They considered themselves not a subject people but Britons with the same rights and entitlements as anyone living in Britain itself.

The crown viewed matters differently. It regarded the colonies as a dominion or possession, united to it like Ireland but distinct from the realm of Britain itself, which after 1707 had consisted of England, Wales, and Scotland. Ireland too had its own lawmaking assembly, the Irish Parliament, but its subservience to the acts of the British Parliament had been spelled out in the Declaratory Act of 1719. But whereas Ireland was a plantation economy in which an Anglo-Scottish minority ruled a subject population of Catholic tenantry, the Middle Atlantic and New England colonies in particular consisted largely of independent freeholders and a mobile class of wage earners. And while Ireland was geographically in Britain's shadow, the American colonies were 3,000 miles away.

America's distance from Britain made it difficult not only to control but also to defend. Even after the defeat of the French, the western frontiers were insecure, as the general rising of Indian tribes under Pontiac in May 1763 made clear. In theory, the colonial militias could have looked to their own defense, but their performance in the war against the French had been reluctant and halfhearted. Moreover, the British government was anxious to prevent uncontrolled settlement beyond the Appalachian Mountains, which was certain to provoke further Indian attacks. Accordingly, it placed the trans-Appalachian west under direct royal control, although several of the colonies had already claimed the Mississippi River as their border. At the same time, it proposed to maintain a permanent army of 10,000 to guard the frontier and levied new taxes, notably on all stamped or licensed paper, to help pay for it.

Protest and Rebellion

The British were quite unprepared for the explosion of protest that greeted these acts. Rioters burned the official stamps and formed resistance groups called the Sons of Liberty, merchants boycotted British wares, the colonial assemblies passed resolutions denouncing taxation without representation in Parliament, and nine colonies sent representatives to a Stamp Act Congress in New York. The British reacted uncertainly. On the one hand, they affirmed parliamentary control of the colonies, arguing that the colonists were "virtually" represented in Parliament in the same way as Britons at home who lived in boroughs that lacked a parliamentary franchise. On the other hand, they repealed the Stamp Act and reduced the much hated customs levy on sugar to a token penny per gallon.

Britain's policy continued to vacillate in the next several years, in part because of a rapid turnover of ministries until 1770, when the new king, George III (1760–1820), finally settled on the conciliatory but ineffective Frederick Lord North to serve as prime minister. The American colonies were importing almost £2 million more in British goods by 1770 than they were shipping back across the Atlantic. If they could not recoup that sum in trade with the West Indies, legally or illegally, their economy, particularly that of the mercantile Northeast, could not survive. Britain's vague but alarming gestures in the direction of new taxes and import duties as well as its sweeping assertions of jurisdiction over colonial trade threatened America's economic viability. Concern for prosperity merged with concern for legal rights. The closing of the western frontier and the policing of the Caribbean menaced two freedoms that Americans valued highly indeed: freedom of movement and freedom of trade.

A clash between British soldiers and a mob in Boston that left five colonists dead sobered both sides momentarily. North withdrew all British taxes except that on tea and announced that no further ones would be levied. When, however, in 1773 he permitted the East India Company to dispose of a tea surplus in America, it was promptly interpreted as a new attempt to raise revenue. The Bostonians dumped the company's tea in their harbor. North responded by closing it and imposing martial law on Massachusetts. At the same time, Parliament passed the Quebec Act, extending the Canadian frontier southward to the Ohio River. Unrelated in British eyes, these actions signaled a new campaign of repression to the colonials. As a sympathetic Englishman, Edmund Burke, observed, "Any of these innumerable regulations, perhaps, would not have alarmed alone; some might be thought reasonable; the multitude struck them with terror."[3]

Events now moved swiftly. An assembly of all the colonies calling itself the Continental Congress met in Philadelphia in September 1774. Although it still acknowledged the authority of the crown, its very meeting was regarded as an act of rebellion in Britain. Sporadic fighting broke out in Massachusetts in the spring of 1775, and in May the Continental Congress voted to raise an army in defense of the colonies. Much of the hardening on the British side came from George III himself. Burke and others opposed the drift to war, but North, who lacked the stomach to fight it, found himself without a politically acceptable way to back down.

The Revolutionary War

On July 4, 1776, the Continental Congress declared the independence of the 13 colonies in a document, drafted largely by Thomas Jefferson of Virginia, whose tone was more of sorrow than anger. The colonials had little choice but resistance or surrender. Strong forces had already landed from Canada, with reinforcements from Britain. Inferior in numbers and training, with British troops in possession of Boston, New York, and Philadelphia, the colonial army fought at first merely to survive. But in October 1777 a British army unit of 7,000 men under General John Burgoyne, intended as part of a pincer movement to cut the northern colonies in two, blundered into a trap in the wilderness near Saratoga, New York, and was forced to surrender.

This defeat changed the character of the war. Until Saratoga, France and Spain had limited themselves to offering aid and financial credits to the rebels. Now they entered the war actively, France in 1778 and Spain a year later. America's war for independence had become an international struggle in which Britain found itself rapidly isolated. Control of not only the Atlantic seaboard but also the West Indies, the Mediterranean, and even India was at stake. Gibraltar withstood a three-year siege (1779–1782) that was, militarily, the largest operation of the war, and a French thrust at Jamaica was repelled by Admiral George Rodney in the great naval Battle of the Saints (1782). But the French fleet, temporarily gaining control of the waters off Virginia, forced the surrender of another large British army at Yorktown in October 1781.

With their empire threatened on all fronts, the British could no longer continue the luckless and draining struggle in America. The independence of the colonies was recognized in the Treaty of Paris (1783); Minorca and East Florida were returned to Spain, and the French recovered some West Indian islands and their former strongholds in Senegal. A shattered Britain was left to redirect its imperial energies toward India and the Far East, where in 1788 it began to colonize Australia. The French could now reflect that the loss of Canada had at least been balanced by the separation of the 13 colonies from Britain. But victory would prove dear. France's habitually insolvent treasury, taxed by the demands of another major war while still burdened with the debts of previous ones, soon tottered into bankruptcy, bringing the French state, and with it the entire Old Regime in Europe, to crisis.

Forming a Nation

Having won their independence, the 13 colonies set about the task of forming themselves into a nation. The Declaration of Independence had boldly asserted that "all men are created equal"—a revolutionary sentiment in a world ruled by monarchy and nobles, although America had never had a hereditary aristocracy—yet the new nation was clearly dominated by a landed and mercantile elite, and one-fifth of its total population (one-third in the plantation states of the south) consisted of black slaves. But the revolution liberalized white American society to a significant degree. Primogeniture and entail, which protected large estates from division, were swept away; Anglican and Congregationalist churches lost their privileged positions, paving the way for the complete separation of church and state that would be one of the most radical features of the American constitution; and the electoral franchise was widened in a number of states. These represented concessions won by workers, farmers, frontiersmen, and religious dissidents in return for support of the rebellion.

Though America was far from having achieved true egalitarianism and though the cloud of slavery, already troubling to many, hung over its future, it was incontestably the most democratic state in the world and the first since the short-lived English Commonwealth of the 1650s to proclaim the sovereignty of the people, or at least those who were free and male. As such, it was a potent inspiration for reformers in Britain and elsewhere in the Old World, a unique experiment that embodied much of the advanced political thought of the century.

From Confederation to Commonwealth

At first the 13 states were individually sovereign entities that associated themselves loosely under the so-called Articles of Confederation. Each state had its own constitution, civil laws, militia, and currency. The Continental Congress continued as a national organ, but it lacked the power to tax or to raise an army and could order nothing without the approval of all 13 states. There were no central courts to resolve disputes between the states, most of which had rival territorial claims, and no agency existed to provide for common trade policy, diplomacy, and defense. As John Adams of Boston remarked, trying to provide for any collective interest was like trying to get 13 clocks to chime at once. In addition, the elites feared that continued popular pressure on weak state governments for political and economic reform would lead to anarchy. In 1786 farmers threatened by foreclosure rebelled in Massachusetts under a former militia captain, Daniel Shays. To men such as the Virginia patrician Edmund Randolph, Shays' rebellion was a perfect example of "the turbulence and follies of democracy."[4]

The result was a convention that met in Philadelphia in the summer of 1787 with the approval of the Continental Congress to amend the Articles of Confederation. The leading members of the convention, including George Washington (1732–1799), the former commander in chief of the revolutionary army, who chaired it, and James Madison (1751–1836), a brilliant young lawyer and fellow Virginian, scrapped the articles completely and, defiantly exceeding their mandate, devised an entirely new constitution. This created a new federal entity, the United States of America, with a bicameral legislature composed of a House of Representatives and a Senate empowered to levy taxes, raise an army, regulate commerce, fix a uniform national currency, and, in a sweeping grant of authority, "make all laws necessary and proper for carrying into execution" these powers. A strong executive was also provided, consisting of a president and vice-president, as well as the foundation of a national court system. In a frankly revolutionary gesture, the convention discarded the requirement that any act at the national level have unanimous consent, declaring that approval by any nine states would ratify the constitution. If there had been a national government worthy of the name, the actions of the convention would have constituted a coup d'état against it.

Historians of the American Revolution have been divided ever since the publication of Charles A. Beard's *Economic Interpretation of the Constitution* in 1913 over whether the U. S. constitution was a betrayal of the democratic promise of the new republic by a cabal of rich men anxious to protect their property through a strong government. Unquestionably, the new system reflected suspicion if not hostility toward popular democracy. It was warmly welcomed by the elites and viewed with skepticism by wage earners and small farmers. But the inconveniences of the Articles were real, and some of the more drastic proposals at the convention—such as the abolition of the states altogether and life terms for the president and the members of the Senate—were rejected. Madison, the constitution's most articulate defender, argued that no lesser degree of centralized authority would suffice to govern a state larger than any in Europe except Russia and larger than any republic in history. After turbulent debate, the constitution was ratified (in the event by every state), and the new republic was inaugurated in 1789 with George Washington as its first president.

American and Canadian Expansion

The United States contained 3 million persons at its first census in 1790, including 600,000 Afro-American slaves. Approximately three times as many American Indians were dispersed within its borders and across the remainder of the North American continent. The new nation was expansionist from the start. As early as 1787 plans were laid in the Northwest Ordinance for the development of new states in the territory west of the Alleghenies, and new land was systematically acquired, by purchase (Louisiana, Florida, Alaska), annexation (Texas), settlement and negotiation (Oregon), and conquest (New Mexico, California). By the mid-nineteenth century Americans had fulfilled what they called their "manifest destiny" of becoming a transcontinental power with a larger territorial mass than any other nation save Russia and China.

The chief obstacle to the expansion of the United States was the native Amerindian population. Although less sophisticated than the Mayans, Aztecs, and Incas of pre-Columbian America, the Indians of North America were far from primitive: they farmed as well as hunted, formed complex political and commercial networks, and often lived in towns. The Iroquois Confederation under Pontiac had allied with the French in an effort to resist British expansion during the Seven Years' War, and 50 years later the Shawnee chieftain Tecumseh (1768–1813) allied with the British during the Anglo-American War of 1812 to resist the United States. Tecumseh dreamed of a united Indian nation strong enough to drive whites off the continent altogether, but the withdrawal of the British ended all practicable hopes of resistance. The Indians were largely decimated by war, forced migration, disease, and starvation, and by 1890 only a million were left in the territorial United States.

Visiting the United States in the 1830s, the French observer Alexis de Tocqueville ventured the bold prediction that the United States would have a population of 100 million within 100 years and would be, with Russia, the great power of the twentieth century. America, Tocque-

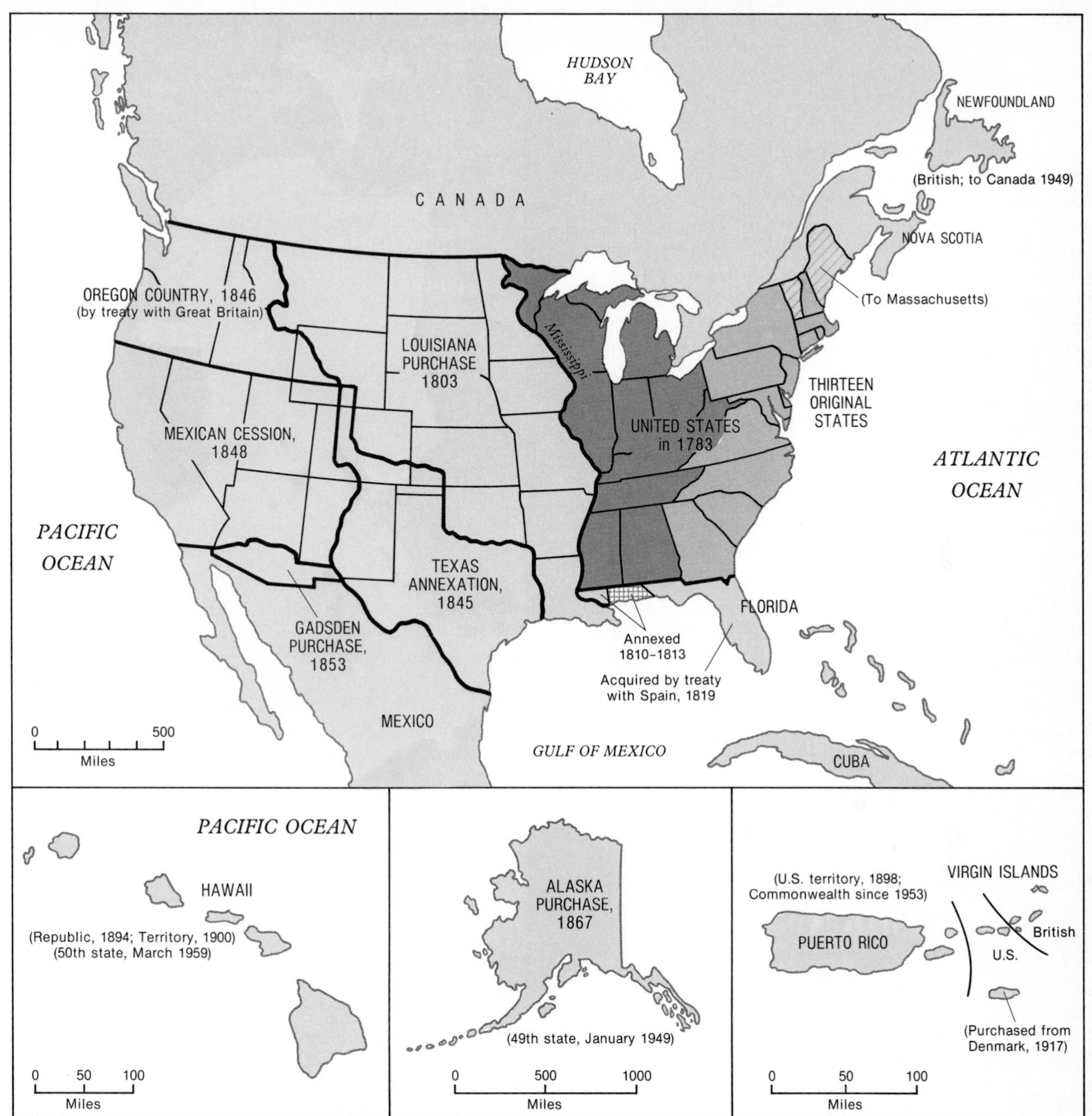

24.4 The Expansion of the United States

ville asserted, represented the triumph of equality and of the democratic revolution that he believed was destined to sweep the globe. By almost every yardstick, the new society appeared to be a success: "While all the nations of Europe have been ravaged by civil strife," he wrote, "the American people alone in the civilized world have remained pacific. Almost the whole of Europe has been convulsed by revolutions; America has not even suffered from riots."[5] But sectional antagonisms between the urban north and the plantation society of the south, particularly over the issue of the westward expansion of slavery, undermined the seeming tranquillity of the Union. By 1861 it collapsed, following the secession of the ten southern states, in a civil war that left more than 600,000 dead.

Many former Loyalists—supporters of the British cause in the American Revolution—had fled to Canada at the conclusion of that war. The British, attempting to deal with a still preponderantly French population, divided Canada into two jurisdictions in 1791. English-speaking Upper Canada, the future province of Ontario, retained English laws and institutions, while French-speaking Lower Canada, now Quebec, kept French law, seigneurial land tenures, and an officially recognized Catholic church. An invasion by the United States during the War of 1812 united the inhabitants of both Canadas briefly, but a steady stream of immigrants from Britain aroused French fears of cultural submergence. Following the Durham Report in 1839, Britain reunited Upper and Lower Canada over the latter's opposition, and the British North America Act of 1867 created the Dominion of Canada, a fully self-governing entity within the British Empire. This voluntary granting of independence, called "devolution," was to be applied later to Australia (1901), New Zealand (1907), the Union of South Africa (1910), India and Pakistan (1947), and the other former colonies in the Caribbean, Africa, and Asia that remain associated in what is today the British Commonwealth of Nations.

Canada expanded rapidly westward after 1867, linking both oceans by rail in 1885. Comparable in size to the United States, its population has never been more than a tenth as large, with most of it clustered in the more temperate coastal regions and the southern plains. Generally stable and prosperous, its chief problems have been intercommunal tensions with the French-speaking minority of Quebec and the economic and cultural dominance of the United States.

Toussaint L'Ouverture, the leader of the second successful colonial rebellion in the Americas and the first great black revolutionary of modern times. [Mansell Collection]

The Abolition of the Slave Trade and the Emancipation of Spanish America

The last quarter of the eighteenth century witnessed a revulsion against the Atlantic slave trade. Testimony before the British Parliament in 1788 laid bare the inhuman conditions under which millions of slaves had been transported, and revolutionary France in the 1790s found slavery incompatible with its professions of universal brotherhood. The slaves, for their part, were unwilling to wait for the enlightenment of their masters; a major rebellion broke out in Jamaica in 1760, and in 1791 half a million blacks under Toussaint L'Ouverture drove the French out of Haiti. At the same time, the profitability of the slave trade declined sharply with the collapse of sugar prices in the 1790s. The framers of the American constitution agreed to abolish the slave trade after 1807, and Britain outlawed it as well in that year, soon to be followed by most other European states. Slavery itself, however, remained legal in the British Empire until 1833, in the United States until 1863, and in Brazil and Cuba until 1886 and 1888, respectively. The slave trade continued to flourish illegally for most of the nineteenth century, and a British commission reported in 1844 that more slaves were being transported than at any time in the previous century.

What doomed the slave trade—at least in the West Indies, where the advanced economies of Britain and France predominated—was the obsolescence of the old colonial system itself. As the Scottish economist Adam Smith argued persuasively in *The Wealth of Nations* (1776), free trade was far more profitable to a state such as Britain than a rigid protectionism that tied down capital, engendered pointless wars, and leaked away profits in smuggling. With the loss of the 13 colonies by Britain and of Haiti by France, the futility of a closed labor and commercial system became apparent.

The economy of Spanish America had gradually been reorganized in response to pressures from the more advanced imperial powers, but politically it was as tightly ruled from Madrid as before. Despite earlier rebellions in Peru and Colombia and the spread of republican ideas among some of the Creole (American-born) class, however, disaffection was not widespread until disaster struck the mother country itself. That disaster was Napoleon's conquest of Spain in 1808. For the next six years the American colonies refused to recognize the occupation ruler, Joseph Bonaparte, and were left to fend for themselves. When the Bourbon ruler Ferdinand VII was restored in 1814, most of the colonies swore renewed allegiance to him. In the six years of Ferdinand's absence, however, they had come of age politically. Competing parties and improvised organs of government, or *juntas*, had been formed, the latter often based on extensions of the municipal councils traditionally dominated by Creoles. The experience of self-government had changed the chemistry between Spain and its colonies. When Ferdinand, blind to the new situation, attempted to reimpose royal government and commercial monopoly in its old form, there was widespread resentment.

SIMÓN BOLÍVAR, THE LIBERATOR

Disillusionment with Ferdinand was exploited by republican nationalists, who had staged several abortive revolts during the interregnum of 1808–1814, notably in Mexico, Venezuela, and Argentina. Though formally professing loyalty to Spain, the Argentines refused to readmit the old royal officials and declared independence under their leader José de San Martín (1778–1850) in 1816. By 1821 San Martín had occupied Lima and declared Peru liberated. Royalist forces soon retook it, however, and the real work of revolution was left to another Creole leader, Simón Bolívar.

Bolívar was born in Caracas, Venezuela, in 1783, the fourth child of one of the oldest and wealthiest noble families in the city. Orphaned at an early age, Bolívar was fired as a young man by the republican ideals of the American and French revolutions. Like most Creole aristocrats, he completed his studies in Europe and was present in Paris when Napoleon was crowned emperor. He brought a young wife, Maria Teresa del Toro, back with him from Madrid, but she died of yellow fever. Bolívar kept his vow never to marry again, although it did not prevent him from enjoying a number of passionate love affairs.

Bolívar began his revolutionary career in an abortive uprising at Caracas in 1810, in which he played a leading role. After toying with the idea of accepting a commission in the British army in Spain, he raised a new rebel army, declaring war to the death against the Spanish empire. By

Bolívar's Message to the Congress of Angostura

Simón Bolívar's message to the congress that had gathered in 1819 to consider a proposed constitution for the new state of Venezuela reflects the disillusionment he already felt for the revolution he had led and his foreboding for the future stability of the South American republics.

America, in separating from the Spanish monarchy, found herself in a situation similar to that of the Roman Empire when its enormous framework fell to pieces in the midst of the ancient world. Each Roman division then formed an independent nation in keeping with its location or interests; but this situation differed from America's in that those members proceeded to reestablish their former associations. We, on the contrary, do not even retain the vestiges of our original being. We are not Europeans; we are not Indians; we are but a mixed species of aborigines and Spaniards. Americans by birth and Europeans by law, we find ourselves engaged in a dual conflict: we are disputing with the natives for titles of ownership, and at the same time we are struggling to maintain ourselves in the country that gave us birth against the opposition of the invaders. Thus our position is most extraordinary and complicated. But there is more. As our role has always been strictly passive and our political existence nil, we find that our quest for liberty is now even more difficult of accomplishment; for we, having been placed in a state lower than slavery, had been robbed not only of our freedom but . . . we were deliberately kept in ignorance and cut off from the world in all matters relating to the science of government.

Source: V. Lecuna, comp., and H. A. Bierck, Jr., ed., *Selected Writings of Bolívar*, vol. 1 (Caracas: Banco de Venezuela, 1951), pp. 175–176.

Proud, imperious, and mercurial, Simón Bolívar liberated a continent from three centuries of foreign rule and lived to regret his own work. [Granger Collection]

January 1814 he had returned to Caracas, declaring Venezuela a republic with himself as its head. Rather than choosing a more conventional name as head of state, he adopted the title of "liberator," symbolizing his commitment to the freeing of all of New Granada. Driven out by the Spaniards six months later, he fled to Jamaica but returned to Venezuela in 1817 and, raising an army of native forces and British soldiers of fortune, staged a daring invasion of Colombia. By August 1819 the entire province was in his hands, and three months later he proclaimed a constitution for the United States of Colombia, including Venezuela, where the last pro-Spanish resistance was extinguished in 1821. Ecuador fell in 1822, and Peru was conquered in 1824.

Bolívar hoped to unite this entire area—virtually all of South America apart from Brazil, Argentina, and Chile—into a single great republic. His enemies attacked him for his apparently boundless ambition; "I am tired," he complained to Bernardo O'Higgins, the liberator of Chile, "of hearing men call me tyrant, that I wish to make myself King, Emperor, the Devil." But his brutal methods of conquest, the indiscipline of his armies, and his undoubted dictatorial tendencies ultimately defeated what remained a noble if tarnished dream. By his death in 1830 the provinces of what he called "Gran Colombia" had splintered again into their old imperial configurations. "He who serves a revolution," he wrote in one of his final letters, "ploughs the sea."

The End of Empire

Backward Brazil, a slave society with few cities worthy of the name, had an even more passive revolution. The regent John came to it in exile after Napoleon's conquest of Portugal, and when he attempted to recall his son Pedro home again in 1822, the Brazilians refused to let him go, raising him to the position of emperor and driving Portuguese troops out of the country. In the viceroyalty of New Spain, a rebellion that had broken out in Mexico in 1810 under the leadership of a Creole priest, Father Hidalgo, was brought to completion in 1821 by a renegade royalist, Agustín de Iturbide, who proclaimed himself emperor. The remaining provinces of New Spain—Honduras, Nicaragua, San Salvador, and Costa Rica—all became independent at the same time, rejecting union with Mexico or each other.

Within ten years Spain had been divested of an empire it had ruled with remarkable equanimity for three centuries, retaining only Cuba and Puerto Rico of its former possessions in the New World. Unlike the newly fledged United States of America, Spain's colonies were neither prepared for independence nor particularly desirous of it. External events had weakened Spain's grip on the New World, and when it attempted to reimpose it without suitable consideration for the developments that had taken place in the interim, it was easily shaken off. The Spanish were never able to send large forces to combat the rebels, and the wars of liberation were essentially fought between native loyalists and republicans. The factor that tipped the balance in favor of the latter was the support of the British, who, seeking to break up Spain's commercial monopolies for good and for all, permitted irregular land and naval forces to assist Bolívar and San Martín openly and threw up a virtual blockade against the feeble Spanish navy. Britain, having lost its own most important American colonies in a bitter and protracted war, thus emerged, ironically, as the patron of liberation. But the new societies of Central and South America, where a 20 percent white minority continued to perpetuate oligarchic rule over a majority population of native and mixed (*mestizo*) blood, subsided into a period of political oppression, governmental instability, and economic exploitation from which they began to emerge only in the twentieth century.

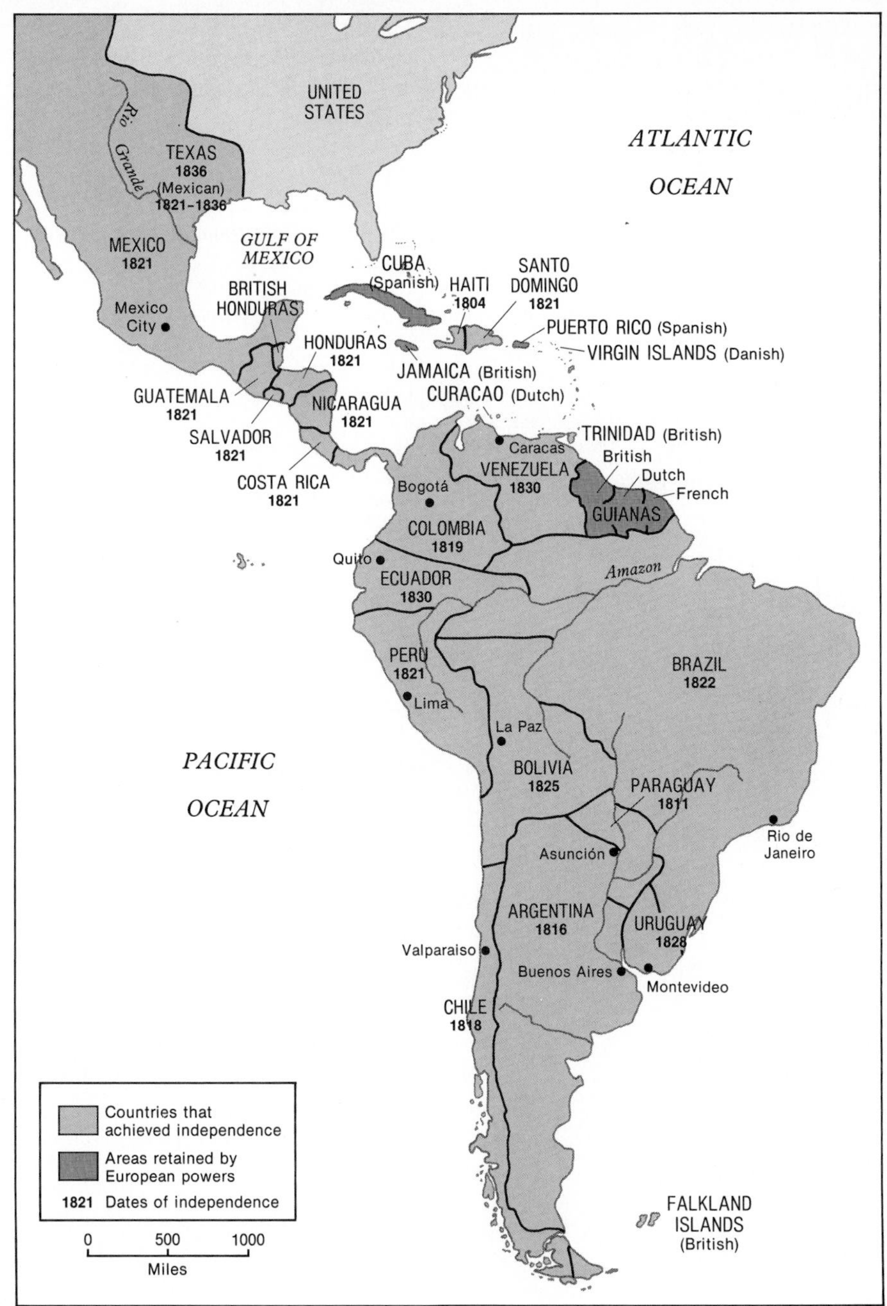

24.5 Latin American Independence

The colonies of the New World became a critical element in the advanced European economies of the eighteenth century, and the character of European warfare was gradually reshaped by the struggle for possession of them. By the end of the first quarter of the nineteenth century, most of those colonies had gained their independence, and what remained in European hands—Canada and most of the West Indies—had become relatively insignificant in economic terms.

Nevertheless, the wealth derived from them was a crucial factor in the development of the new global economy and of capitalist enterprise, particularly in Britain. The transportation of millions of blacks across the Atlantic constituted the largest involuntary migration in human history up to this time, and their settlement throughout North and South America profoundly altered the demographic and social structure of the New World.

Notes

1. R. Davis, *The Rise of the Atlantic Economies* (Ithaca, N.Y.: Cornell University Press, 1973), p. 43.
2. W. D. Dorn, *Competition for Empire, 1740–1763* (New York: Harper, 1940), p. 13.
3. D. K. Fieldhouse, *The Colonial Empires* (New York: Delacorte Press, 1967), p. 109.
4. W. U. Solberg, ed., *The Federal Convention and the Formation of the Union* (Indianapolis: Bobbs-Merrill, 1958), p. xc.
5. A. de Tocqueville, *Democracy in America* (New York: Anchor Books, 1969), p. xiv.

Suggestions for Further Reading

Brown, P. D. *William Pitt, Earl of Chatham: The Great Commoner*. London: Allen & Unwin, 1978.

Butler, R. *Choiseul*. New York: Oxford University Press, 1981.

Curtin, P. *The Atlantic Slave Trade: A Census*. Madison: University of Wisconsin Press, 1969.

Davis, D. B. *The Problem of Slavery in the Age of Revolution*. Ithaca, N.Y.: Cornell University Press, 1966.

de Vries, J. *The Economy of Europe in an Age of Crisis, 1600–1750*. Cambridge: Cambridge University Press, 1976.

Dickson, P. G. M. *The Financial Revolution in England: A Study in the Development of Public Credit, 1688–1756*. London: Macmillan, 1967.

Dorn, W. D. *Competition for Empire, 1740–1763*. New York: Harper, 1940.

Fieldhouse, D. K. *The Colonial Empires: A Comparative Survey from the Eighteenth Century*. New York: Delacorte Press, 1967.

Fox-Genovese, E., and Genovese, E. D. *Fruits of Merchant Capital: Slavery and Bourgeois Property in the Rise and Expansion of Capitalism*. New York: Oxford University Press, 1983.

Frank, A. G. *World Accumulation, 1492–1789*. New York: Monthly Review Press, 1978.

Heckscher, E. *Mercantilism*. New York: Macmillan, 1955.

Lynch, J. *The Spanish American Revolutions, 1808–1826*. London: Weidenfeld & Nicolson, 1973.

McDonald, F. *We the People: The Economic Origins of the Constitution*. Chicago: University of Chicago Press, 1958.

McKeown, T. *The Modern Rise of Population*. New York: Academic Press, 1976.

Madariaga, S. de. *Bolívar*. New York: Farrar, Straus & Cudahy, 1956.

Mintz, S. W. *Sweetness and Power: The Place of Sugar in Modern History*. New York: Viking, 1985.

Morgan, E. S. *Birth of the Republic, 1763–1789*. Chicago: University of Chicago Press, 1977.

Nef, J. U. *War and Human Progress*. New York: Russell & Russell, 1968.

Parry, J. H. *Trade and Dominion: European Overseas Empires in the Eighteenth Century*. New York: Praeger, 1971.

Plumb, J. H. *Sir Robert Walpole*. 2 vols. Boston: Houghton-Mifflin, 1956, 1960.

Shennan, J. H. *Philippe, Duke of Orléans, Regent of France, 1715–1723*. London: Thames & Hudson, 1979.

Wallerstein, I. *The Modern World System*. 2 vols. New York: Academic Press, 1974, 1980.

Wood, G. S. *The Creation of the American Republic, 1776–1787*. Chapel Hill: University of North Carolina Press, 1969.

CHAPTER · 25

The Enlightenment

The eighteenth century was characterized by a wide-ranging critique of the social and intellectual bases of European culture to which contemporaries gave the name of the Enlightenment. Unlike other movements of renewal and reform in the West since the advent of Christianity, the Enlightenment did not take the form of a religious revival. It grew instead out of the new methods of inquiry bequeathed by the scientific revolution and the questions that its view of the cosmos posed to traditional religion. The thought of the Enlightenment was frankly secular and rationalist, and this, in a society where all art, science, morality, and political authority had acknowledged the primacy of religious truth for 1,500 years, posed a revolutionary challenge to the social order. At the same time, the Enlightenment was a response to economic and political changes at work in European society. Some of the most influential thinkers of the Enlightenment were men of bourgeois origin. Unattached to church or court, they heralded the coming of a new secular society, and their demands for freedom and toleration, their conception of a worldwide human community, and their contempt for inherited privilege echoed the interests of free trade, unfettered enterprise, and an expanding global economy.

REFLECTIONS

ON THE PRESENT CONDITION OF THE

FEMALE SEX;

WITH

SUGGESTIONS FOR ITS IMPROVEMENT.

BY

PRISCILLA WAKEFIELD.

LONDON:
Printed for J. JOHNSON, in St. Paul's Church-yard;
and DARTON and HARVEY, in Gracechurch Street.

1798.

The cover of an early treatise on women's rights, dated 1798. [Library Company of Philadelphia]

The Roots of the Enlightenment

The scientific revolution gravely undermined a set of closely interlocked assumptions on which the traditional social order rested. According to the traditional view, all created things had their place on the universal ladder of existence that ultimately led to God. The angels were subordinate to God as humankind was to the angels, beasts to persons, and inanimate matter to living, in a descending scale of natural value. Each order of being had its own internal hierarchy as well. There were superior and subordinate angels, higher and lower animals, and nobler and baser persons. The human order was part of the harmony ordained by God for the universe, and anyone who attempted to disturb it was defying God as well as humankind. The historian Arthur O. Lovejoy has named this complex of ideas the "great chain of being."

In social terms, the great chain of being entailed a general principle of subordination, by which women and children were subject to the authority of men, commoners to noblemen, and all subjects to their rulers. This notion culminated in the idea of the divine right of kings. Monarchs received their authority directly from God as a means of enforcing his will on earth. Since kings had no superior but God, their actions could not be questioned by anyone on earth, and their commands must be treated as if coming directly from God. If a king were a tyrant, he should be regarded as a scourge sent by God to chastise people for their sins. God would hold the tyrant accountable, but subjects could not.

In practice, the absolute power of kings was often subject to challenge. The church of the Counter-Reformation insisted that heretical rulers might be deposed or even killed; in 1570 Pope Pius V absolved Queen Elizabeth I's English subjects of their allegiance to her, and in 1610 Henry IV of France was assassinated by a deranged priest. The English in 1649 had executed their own king, Charles I, after trying him before an extraordinary tribunal, and even Louis XIV had known rebellion in the early years of his reign. Further down the social scale, desperate peasants rebelled frequently against oppressive taxes and other burdens, and such customs as the English practice of ducking scolds who beat or abused their husbands in the local pond or river showed that women did not always passively accept the roles imposed on them.

Although resistance might be offered in particular cases, most women continued to regard their subservience to men, and peasants to their lords, as part of the natural order of things. This pattern of submission, called *deference,* was instilled in the lower orders of society from an early age. Here is the journalist Richard Steele's description of the proper attitude of the tenant farmer, written in 1672:

> **A just fear and respect he must have for his landlord, or the gentleman his neighbor, because God hath placed them above him and he hath learnt that by the father he ought to honor is meant all his superiors.[1]**

These words were written in England. Even there, where the attempt to impose absolute monarchy had been curbed by the revolutions of 1640 and 1688, the social supremacy of the nobility was not merely undiminished but greater than ever. This was generally true of the privileged orders throughout eighteenth-century Europe. Beneath the surface, however, the Old Regime was not only being reshaped by the stresses of imperial competition and the emerging global economy but also being undermined by the intellectual consequences of the scientific revolution.

The most immediate of these consequences was a weakening of faith in the traditional Christian God of salvation, at least among the more educated classes. It was true that nothing in the new science directly contradicted the tenets of Christianity. But it was difficult to reconcile the biblical God who regularly manifested his presence in the world through signs, wonders, and miracles with the expanded Newtonian universe of self-regulating mechanical motion. Such a God seemed not so much incompatible with this universe as irrelevant to it.

The revolution in the Western concept of space was soon matched by a corresponding revolution in the concept of geologic time. Just as the cosmos had been thought to be contained within the ten heavenly spheres of the Ptolemaic universe, so its age, reckoned by the creation of Adam and Eve, was thought to be no more than 6,000 years. A seventeenth-century English theologian, James Ussher, calculating by biblical genealogies, had even announced the precise date of creation to have been October 23, 4004 B.C.

The God of Reason

As scientists began to turn their attention to the natural history of the earth, it was soon apparent that a far longer span was necessary to account for the evolution of its features. The God who had already been exiled to the outer edges of a vast and perhaps boundless universe now seemed to recede as well from the intimate scale of human history to that of a remote, geologic time. Such a God might be conceived of as a creator, but in what sense was he still a father? Yet if the idea of a paternal God had begun to lose its credibility, what would become of the divine right monarchs who ruled in the name of that God? The theories of Newton might have seemed very far removed from the glitter and pomp of Louis XIV's court, but their implications for royal absolutism and noble privilege were serious and ultimately fatal. In pulling the linchpin of a traditional Christian God from the great chain of being, the new mechanical universe had called into question the entire justification for the social order that rested on it.

For some thinkers, such as Pascal, the erosion of faith in a personal God of salvation was profoundly disturbing. But for many others in the late seventeenth and eighteenth centuries, the biblical God died a natural death with the view of nature and the cosmos of which he had been part, to be replaced by one more in keeping with the rational world of the new physics. Thus was born what was called "natural religion," or Deism. Deism rested on a variant of the old scholastic argument from design. The rational universe revealed by science, the Deists contended, could never have organized itself by accident and was thus necessarily the product of a rational, divine mind. Having created an orderly and self-perpetuating universe, this intellectual God had no need to intervene in it, and his apparent absence from it reflected merely his repose in its perfection. What God did in the world, in effect, was to contemplate it. He had no need to force notice of himself on it, since his presence was implicit throughout its design. It followed that the proper way to worship such a God was to study the world itself.

Deism appeared on the surface to reject and even scorn Christianity. For the cultural outsider Spinoza or for a cool, rationalist skeptic such as the third earl of Shaftesbury (1671–1713), this was a matter of indifference if not pride. But many people anxious to embrace Deism wished to save as much as possible of Christianity within it. They found their spokesman in John Locke, who argued in *The Reasonableness of Christianity* (1695) that Christian ethics reflected divine reason. What Christianity could not claim to possess was an exclusive revelation of truth. All religions reflected the "natural religion," which recognized and worshiped the divine intelligence in the world. This was the valid core of each religion, underneath the impurities of dogma and superstition. For this reason, as Locke argued in *An Essay on Toleration* (1689), all religions were worthy of respect, none of priority. Toleration thus emerged as a positive virtue, not merely a truce in a war to the death between rival systems of belief.

The argument that each religion should be sifted for the truth it possessed was akin to the method of science in testing different theories by experiment. Common to both was the assumption that truth was not discovered all at once through external revelation but rather acquired slowly by applying reason to the facts of experience, in the manner of fitting together the pieces of a jigsaw puzzle. The scientific revolution itself was the most triumphant demonstration of this process. Newton's synthesis, "the true system of the world," as an eighteenth-century admirer called it, had been built on the earlier theories of Copernicus, Galileo, and Kepler, each of which had contributed its partial truth to the final discovery of the whole. If the truth about the physical cosmos, obscured even to the greatest minds of antiquity, had been disclosed at last by this method, what mystery could not be made to yield to it? Reason, perfected by the method of science, seemed poised to unlock the final secrets of heaven and earth.

The Idea of Progress

The upshot of these developments was the idea of progress, a notion that changed an entire civilization's conception of itself. For more than 2,000 years, the West had thought of its world as the shrunken remnant of a glorious past. The Greeks had looked back to a mythical world of gods and heroes, the Romans of the empire to the virtue of the republic, the Middle Ages to the sanctity of the apostles, and the Renaissance back again to Rome. Most important of all was the Judeo-Christian myth of humankind's fall from grace in the Garden of Eden. In the Jewish version of the fall, redemption was still conceived in secular terms as a return to the promised land. But for Christians, human sin could not be eradicated in historical time; indeed history, time itself, was the punishment inflicted on humanity for its sins.

The notion of secular progress, the improvement of the human condition in the world through human effort alone, thus required a radical transformation in Western thinking. The scientific revolution, and the Deist faith in a rational God to which it gave rise, provided the basis of this transformation. The success of the scientific method in explaining the cosmos generated great confidence in its ability to resolve social, political, and even moral problems as well. If humankind could unlock the secrets of the natural world, why should it be unable to master its own human one? At the same time, the God of Deism freed humankind from the Christian preoccupation with sin, and it became possible to think of human nature positively. The human race was not born with an innate propensity to sin, but it could be animated, even in the absence of divine grace, by feelings of benevolence and a disinterested desire for the welfare of others. "I have seen some take on the feelings of others," declared the French poet Saint-Lambert, "espouse the interests of others, and enter into their situation to the point of losing their own feelings, of forgetting their own interests and situation."[2] A Deist, Saint-Lambert believed that contemplating the goodness of God was necessary to the cultivation of moral sentiments. Established churches, however, were actually harmful to them, since they substituted formal duties and barren rituals for natural and spontaneous feeling.

The possibility of progress was the subject of a famous literary debate in late seventeenth-century France, the so-called quarrel of the ancients and the moderns. The ancients upheld the view that modern man could never duplicate the achievements of classical Greece and Rome, while the moderns asserted that the age of Louis XIV was the equal if not the superior of any previous period in history. The most persuasive of the moderns' spokesmen, Bernard de Fontenelle (1657–1757), argued that whereas great works of art required only individual genius, the

The idea of progress spawned a number of amusing fantasies, such as this alleged flight from "Plazentia" to "Coria" in Spain. By the end of the eighteenth century, balloon flights had already been made and observation balloons were being used in battle. [Musée Carnavalet, Paris; Photographie Bulloz]

growth of knowledge was a collaborative effort and thus cumulative over time. Although history suffered periods of reversal as well as advance, the attainments of the past always remained to be built on and surpassed by the present. An enthusiastic popularizer of the new science, Fontenelle believed that his own time represented a new peak of human achievement. In the perspective of centuries to come, he declared, the fifth century before Christ and the seventeenth after would both be seen as points on a line of ascending progress. The time of Christ himself was pointedly absent from this reckoning.

If each period could build on the past, each individual represented a new and untested set of possibilities. The traditional Christian view had assumed that the individual was born in a state of sin and that the primary task of education was to control a natural inclination to evil. In the view suggested by Deism, however, humankind was morally neutral if not instinctively good, and the proper function of education was to maximize society's potential for progress by developing each individual talent to the fullest. Once again, John Locke provided the most popular account of this new psychology. In *Essay Concerning Human Understanding* (1690) he argued that the mind at birth was a blank slate that registered the experience of the senses passively. These sensations were organized by simple categories and processed by reflection. The result was a product called knowledge or understanding. Locke viewed the mind of the child as fluid and malleable. Bombarded by sense impressions and relatively unorganized, it was, he said, "as easily turned this way or that, as water itself." This meant that education was critical in determining human development. Properly guided, the mind could realize its full powers, both for its own benefit and that of society. Deprived of such guidance, or purposely misled, it was prey to superstition, intolerance, and tyranny.

Locke and Liberty

John Locke (1632–1704) was a member of the Whig opposition to Charles II and James II and for a time went into exile under an assumed name. After the Glorious Revolution, he published *Two Treatises of Government* (1690), intended to defend the deposition of James II and to refute the theories of Thomas Hobbes.

Hobbes had argued that people contract with a sovereign whose unchallengeable authority erects a society that protects them from one another. Although Hobbes, like Locke, explained human psychology from a materialistic standpoint, his view of the antagonism between individuals reflected traditional Christian pessimism about the depravity of human nature. For Locke, by contrast, reflecting the new Deism, humans were innately peaceful, rational, and gregarious in the state of nature, enjoying their natural rights to life, liberty, and the fruit of their own labors. They entered society not from fear but from the desire to increase their wealth and happiness by cooperation with their fellows. The social contract thus involved not a surrender of natural rights but the protection and enhancement of them. Society itself was the voluntary association of free, equal, and separate individuals into the free, equal, and united members of a group.

The first task of society was to establish a rule-making authority or government. Locke rejected Hobbes' assertion that sovereignty must reside in a single person or institution. As each individual had been sovereign over himself or herself in the state of nature, so all were now jointly sovereign over the society they had created together. This was the very meaning of their union as a people. It followed that government was first and foremost an instrument of the people's will. If the particular government they had chosen proved tyrannical or otherwise defective, they might amend it or cast it off. Thus the right of rebellion was implicit in the formation of society itself. Far from dissolving the social order, as Hobbes had argued, rebellion was a means of renewing and reaffirming the ends for which it had been instituted. Nothing could dissolve the union of a free people as long as they elected to remain together.

Locke's *Treatises* provided what still remains the classic foundation of the liberal state, with its emphasis on associative community, representative government, and natural rights. His view of society as an act of collective decision making by free and unconstrained individuals reflected both the Deist vision of man as a rational being and the values of an emerging secular society with its emphasis on choice and satisfaction. His influence on the American Revolution, with its claim to a people's right to rebel on behalf of their inalienable rights, was obvious, and the convention of the founders who drafted a constitution for the 13 former colonies might almost have stepped from the pages of the second *Treatise* as an illustration of society in the making.

Locke's views remained open to objection however. His picture of the human mind as a bundle of sensations acted on by "reflection" did not explain how the capacity to reflect could arise. By locating political sovereignty in the people as a whole, he begged the question of how power is actually exercised in society. In asserting that natural rights disclosed themselves intuitively, he assumed that everyone would agree what they were. But the English revolutionary Gerrard Winstanley had already rejected one of Locke's rights, the right of property, as incompatible with true liberty, and the abuse of property was to be denounced by Jean-Jacques Rousseau and others in the eighteenth century as well.

Philosophy in Action

The Enlightenment was a broadly based intellectual movement whose avowed goal was to apply reason to society for the purpose of human betterment. It was led by the *philosophes,* a loose coalition of thinkers and critics who were not philosophers in the traditional sense but social activists for whom knowledge was something to be converted into reform. Many of the leading philosophes were French, but they came from virtually every country in Europe, and their ideas carried everywhere. The philosophes saw themselves not as subjects of a particular country but as citizens of the world, or, in Peter Gay's phrase, as "the party of humanity." They claimed to speak on behalf of all oppressed by tyranny or blighted by ignorance, and their goal was nothing less than a world where reason alone was sovereign.

The philosophes prided themselves on their political and intellectual independence. The bible of their movement, Denis Diderot's *Encyclopedia,* defined the philosophe as one who, "trampling on prejudice, tradition, universal consent, authority, in a word all that enslaves most minds, dares to think for [himself] . . . [and] to admit nothing except on the testimony of his experience and his reason." The philosophes did not seek specific political reform so much as fundamental changes in values and attitudes that would bring reform about. Their motto, coined by the German philosopher Immanuel Kant, was "Dare to know," and their object, Diderot boasted, was to make "a revolution in men's minds."

Voltaire

The most famous and influential of the philosophes was François-Marie Arouet (1694–1778), known to history by his pen name of Voltaire. Born in Paris, Voltaire was, like many of the philosophes, of bourgeois origin; his father was a notary. He began his career as a satiric playwright but ran afoul first of the regent, who imprisoned him for 11 months in the Bastille, and then of a prominent nobleman, the Chevalier de Rohan, who had him caned in the street and imprisoned again when he protested. Forced into exile, Voltaire spent three years in England. This experience was the turning point of his career. Voltaire was deeply impressed by the relative freedom he found in England, and his *Philosophical Letters on the English* (1734) praised that nation's institutions. He was influenced as well by Lockean psychology and Newtonian physics, and his *Elements of the Philosophy of Newton* (1738) is one

Frederick II of Prussia visits Voltaire in his study during the latter's residence at Frederick's court. In this extraordinary image, it is Voltaire, pen in hand, who remains seated while his royal host bends forward in greeting. Only the rearing horse outside conveys the image of bridled majesty and hints at the stormy rupture that was to part the two men later. [Bettmann Archive]

of the clearest and most direct links between the scientific revolution and the thought of the Enlightenment.

Unable to publish freely in France, Voltaire accepted an invitation from an admirer, Frederick the Great of Prussia, at whose court he spent two years (1749–1751). He then retired with his niece and mistress, Madame Denis, to an estate at Ferney, just over the French border in Switzerland, where he spent the last third of his life. There he functioned as a one-man republic, entertaining a steady stream of visitors, firing off as many as 30 letters a day, and carrying on a tireless series of campaigns for justice. The most famous of these was to clear the name of Jean Calas, a French Protestant put to death on the trumped-up charge of having murdered his son to prevent his conversion to Catholicism. As a Deist, Voltaire had no more use for one form of Christianity than another; his interest was in exposing the consequences of bigotry. *"Écrâsez l'infame!"*—crush the infamy!—he cried, and no one did more, by anger or ridicule, to expose intolerance and to undermine the authority of established religion in Europe. The compliment was returned: his last major work, the *Philosophical Dictionary* (1764), was burned in Paris, Geneva, and Rome, and Voltaire observed wryly that the authorities would gladly have burned the author as well.

Satire was Voltaire's special forte, and his wit was turned against his friends as well as his enemies. His novel *Candide* (1759), the most popular and enduring of all his works, was a satire on the faith of his contemporaries in automatic or unlimited progress. There was a dark side to Voltaire; that God was good, he believed, did not protect humankind from evil. What people could do was to minimize the evil they inflicted on one another, and they could do this best by coming to understand their common heritage. In a sense Voltaire is the father of this book; his *Essay on Custom* (1756) was the first survey of the history of world civilization, beginning with that of ancient China. As always, Voltaire's purpose was didactic, to show that no culture had a monopoly on beauty or value, just as no religion had a monopoly on truth. In his last years he was able to return to Paris in triumph. He described himself as bowed down with every infirmity of old age; but nothing, he added, "can deprive me of hope."

The Enlightenment and Society

When the philosophes put their own society under the lens of reason, they found it seriously wanting. Superstition abounded; free thought was stifled; education was in the hands of the established churches. Idleness had been elevated to a way of life by the aristocracy, while the efforts of the most productive class, the bourgeoisie, were for the most part scorned.

At the same time, the idea that the structure of society reflected the hierarchical order of the universe was under attack. "No society can exist without justice," Voltaire had written; yet could a God of reason have created a society where justice was so perverted? Some of the more radical philosophes had already gone beyond Deism, however. For such openly avowed atheists as the Frenchmen Denis Diderot (1713–1784) and Julian La Mettrie (1707–1747) or the Baron d'Holbach (1723–1789), a wealthy German nobleman living in Paris, the idea of God itself was the last superstition. Humankind, they declared, was alone in the universe, the author of its own destiny. Society, its own creation, should respond to its needs. If it did not, the answer to the problem had to be sought in humankind itself, for the only law to which humanity was subject was that of its own nature.

Rousseau and the Social Contract

These questions led the philosophes to investigate the origins of society. The most radical analysis was offered by Jean-Jacques Rousseau (1712–1778). Born in Geneva, Rousseau was, unlike most of the philosophes, poor and ill-educated. He ran away from home at the age of 16 and remained a misfit all his life, betraying friends and even abandoning his own children. Rousseau's personal discontents were reflected in his view of society. "Man is born free," he declared, "yet everywhere we find him in chains." Society had not fulfilled human nature but perverted it. In his *Discourse on the Origin of Inequality* (1755), he found the origin of injustice in the institution of property:

> **The first man who, having enclosed a piece of ground, bethought himself of saying *This is mine*, and found people simple enough to believe him, was the real founder of civil society. From how many crimes, wars and murders, from how many horrors and misfortunes might not someone have saved mankind, by pulling up the stakes and filling in the ditch, and crying out to his fellows, "Beware of listening to this impostor; you are undone if you once forget that the fruits of the earth belong to us all, and the earth itself to nobody."**

Rousseau depicted the state of nature as an idyllic primitive communism, corrupted by the sin of possession. That original transgression created the basic institution of society, property. This in turn led to greed, the source of all oppression. The love of gain made sons wish for the death of their fathers and helped speculators profit from plague, famine, and war. Far from being an absolute natural right, as Locke had thought, property, when perverted by greed, was the evil that usurped and destroyed all other rights.

The solution, Rousseau argued in *The Social Contract* (1762), was to create a society in which private interest was subordinated to the common good. This, he asserted, could be accomplished only if each individual agreed to give up the final determination of his interest to the collective whole. Rousseau saw in this not loss but a gain of freedom. Since each person, while giving up his own rights, received at the same time the surrender of everyone else's, his original rights were actually returned many times over. Yet since everyone had made the same exchange, all persons remained exactly equal to one another. This was the true meaning of the social contract. In Hobbes' version of it, all persons were equal in their subordination to an absolute ruler, but none were free. In Locke's version, all persons were free to pursue their private interests, which led inevitably to inequity, oppression, and the loss of freedom. Only by guaranteeing both freedom and equality, Rousseau believed, could the conditions for a just society be met.

Rousseau called the collective entity in which all individual rights were vested the *general will.* Rousseau took the general will (as opposed to the will of any segment, including a majority) to mean both the permanent interest of the entire community and the course of action that represented its best interest at any given moment.

Ideally, the general will would be enacted by the unanimous consent of the entire community. In practice, however, it could not be expected that all citizens would be able to transcend their private interests, and to wait for unanimity on every question would, Rousseau admitted, reduce the social contract to an empty formula. It would therefore be necessary at some point to oblige dissenters

Rousseau on the Social Contract

Rousseau, agreeing with Hobbes that society had been founded by compulsion but with Locke that it ought to be founded on consent, argued that a properly constituted social order was the instrument for converting natural into civil freedom.

Man is born free, and everywhere he is in chains. One thinks himself master of others, but is himself the greater slave. How did this change take place? I do not know. What can render it legitimate? I believe I can answer this question.

If I were to consider nothing but force and its effects, I should say: "As long as a people is compelled to obey, and does so, it does well; as soon as it can shake off the yoke, and does so, it does even better; for in recovering its liberty on the same grounds on which it was stolen away, it either is right in resuming it, or was wrongly deprived in the first place." But the social order is a sacred right which serves as the basis for all others. And yet this right does not come from nature; thus it is founded on conventions.

Source: J. J. Rousseau, "The Social Contract," in *Rousseau: Political Writings,* trans. and ed. F. Watkins (Edinburgh: Nelson, 1953), pp. 3–4.

to comply with the general will, for their own good as well as the community's. In the last analysis, Rousseau declared, citizens who could not recognize where their real freedom lay must "be forced to be free."

State and Utopia

Rousseau's insistence that freedom and equality were inseparable was echoed in the famous assertion of the American Declaration of Independence that all men were created free and equal. But Rousseau never clearly explained how the general will was to be recognized. The American founders therefore turned instead to the ideas of another philosophe, the Baron de Montesquieu (1689–1755), who argued in *The Spirit of the Laws* (1748) that liberty was best secured by a separation of the powers of government. Montesquieu's influential notion found its way not only into the checks and balances of America's constitution but into the French constitution of 1791, the Prussian Code of 1792, the Spanish constitution of 1812, and the short-lived revolutionary constitutions of 1848.

If Montesquieu had the more practical effect on political reform, Rousseau expressed the more fundamental tension that lay at the heart of Enlightenment thought. If men were created equal in rights and yet unequal in the wealth, power, and interest by which those rights were to be enjoyed, how was society to achieve justice and promote the common welfare? For the Abbé Morelly, author of the *Code of Nature* (1755), the only answer was to abolish all property and commerce and to establish a rigidly egalitarian society in which each individual was allotted a specific quota of production and consumption. The late Enlightenment figure Simon-Henri Linguet, a lawyer disbarred for his attacks on the property system, predicted a widening gap between rich and poor that would lead to general revolution: never, he wrote, "has Europe been nearer to a complete upheaval."

The majority view, expressed by Bernard de Mandeville (1673–1733) and Adam Smith (1723–1790), remained optimistic. In his *Fable of the Bees* (1714), Mandeville argued that just as bees building a hive contributed to the greater good without being aware of it, so even vices such as vanity, envy, and pride were useful because they promoted commerce and industry and gave employment. Adam Smith, expounding a similar view more systematically in *The Wealth of Nations* (1776), asserted that public wealth (and thereby private benefit) was maximized by allowing each individual to pursue his or her own selfish interest. Just as the Newtonian universe produced balance and harmony by obeying its own laws without the need of special divine intervention, so the market was a self-regulating mechanism that functioned best when left alone. As Alexander Pope expressed it in verse, "God and Nature link'd the gen'ral frame, / and bade Self-love and Social be the same."

The Philosophes and Their Public

The philosophes spoke to and largely for the new commercial classes and their interests. But their ideas were also disseminated in the salons of the liberal aristocracy. At these large and semipublic social gatherings, where wit rather than birth was the criterion for admission, they held forth as the guests of such influential tastemakers as Madame du Deffand and Madame Geoffrin. The salons served

A lively conversation among the philosophes, dominated as usual by Voltaire, whose arm is raised. International celebrities, the philosophes are each identified by number. Diderot, the editor of the *Encyclopedia,* is seated at Voltaire's left. [Mansell Collection]

to domesticate the ideas of the Enlightenment and also to make them more acceptable. These ideas in turn undermined the social dominance that the French court had enjoyed in the days of Louis XIV and thus some of its power as well. The salons gave the leading figures of the Enlightenment both a prestige and entrée into circles of the highest influence they could not have attained without them, a point ruefully acknowledged later by the conservative Joseph de Maistre when he remarked that "an opinion launched in Paris was like a battering ram launched by thirty million men."

Literacy and Censorship

The principal vehicle of Enlightenment thought, however, was the printing press. In the 100 years before the French Revolution, 18 more men and 13 more women in every 100 became literate in France, and comparable increases were recorded in England, Austria, Denmark, and parts of Germany. The philosophes rode the crest of a great wave that created a new kind of public in Europe: the reading public. For the first time, literature had not merely a circulation but a market, and this market created a new profession, that of the independent writer. Newspapers and periodicals flourished, among them the remarkable *Journal des dames* ("Ladies' Journal"), whose feminist tone was ringingly set by its first female editor, Madame de Beaumer: "Be silent, all critics, and know that this is a *woman* addressing you!"

One indication of the burgeoning appetite for serious discussion, particularly in France, was the emergence of provincial literary academies that sponsored essay competitions on such subjects as the nature of the passions, the influence of Christianity, and the condition of philosophy. Rousseau himself first gained recognition through a competition offered by the Dijon Academy, and the future revolutionary Robespierre was secretary of the one at Arras in the 1780s. Lower down on the social scale, but still appealing primarily to a bourgeois audience, were less formally organized reading clubs and social groups such as the Freemasons, a social brotherhood dedicated to celebrating human dignity whose members included figures as diverse as Mozart and Benjamin Franklin.

The governments of the Old Regime tried vainly to stem the spread of new and seditious ideas through the licensing of printers and booksellers, censorship, confiscation, and in the case of notorious figures such as Voltaire, burning books by the common hangman. In Austria under Maria Theresa, even foreign ambassadors had their luggage searched for forbidden books, and Prussia under Frederick William I exiled its foremost philosopher, Christian Wolff. Nor did governments alone exercise censorship; the Catholic church maintained its *Index of Prohibited Books,* and such bodies as law courts and universities could also order the suppression of printed works. Universities, with few exceptions, played little part in the Enlightenment. The Austrian reformer Joseph von Sonnenfels lamented that the universities in his country were a century behind the times, but the same could be said for Paris, Cambridge, and Oxford.

The philosophes used great ingenuity in getting around the various forms of censorship. Some of them used the device of the fictional reporter, as Montesquieu did in his *Persian Letters,* or science fiction, as Voltaire did in his Utopian fantasies *Zadig* and *Micromegas* and the satirist Jonathan Swift (1667–1745) in *Gulliver's Travels.* A large underground book trade also flourished, fed by presses in Switzerland and the Low Countries that supplemented their business in serious social criticism with scandal, gossip, blasphemy, and pornography. One enterprising Spanish editor even established a journal called *El Censor.*

The Encyclopedia

The most important and embattled publishing project of the Enlightenment was the great *Encyclopedia,* conceived and edited by the versatile Diderot. The son of a provincial artisan and himself the author of philosophical and mathematical treatises as well as plays, essays, and novels, Diderot commissioned a veritable Who's Who of the Enlightenment, including Voltaire, Rousseau, and Montesquieu, to contribute thousands of articles on every aspect of human knowledge. The result was the largest publishing venture up to that time in Western history. The first volume, containing controversial articles on atheism and the human soul, appeared in 1751. It was pounced on by the censors, who first suspended and later revoked the publisher's license. The attorney general of France denounced it as a conspiracy against public morals, and the pope declared anyone buying or reading it to be excommunicated. When the coeditor, Jean d'Alembert, dropped out, Diderot continued alone, issuing further volumes despite the ban, filling in the gaps when contributors defaulted, and even setting up the plates himself. By 1765 the 17 volumes of text were complete, and in 1772 the last of 11 volumes of illustrations appeared. In the end, the *Encyclopedia* was a great commercial success, although Diderot himself saw little of its profits. By 1789 an astonishing 20,000 full sets had been sold, and many more circulated in abridgments, extracts, and pirated editions. Modern public opinion—the reaction of an audience too large and too independent to be controlled by any institution of church or state—was born in the eighteenth century. No single book did more to create and mold it than Diderot's *Encyclopedia.*

The Enlightened Despots

One of the most remarkable aspects of the Enlightenment was the adoption and espousal of many of its ideas and

In addition to its often provocative articles, Diderot's *Encyclopedia* offered hundreds of unique illustrations of the industrial and mechanical arts of the eighteenth century, such as the brass foundry pictured here, whose workers seem dwarfed by the giant machines and implements they ply. The horse pictured at left turns wheels that crush crude zinc. The workmen in figure 6 crank a barrel that mixes the zinc with copper to make the brass alloy. The brass is then stamped in a mold and cut by giant shears. [Granger Collection]

From Diderot's *Encyclopedia*

Denis Diderot, whose multivolume Encyclopedia *was the largest, most daring, and most influential single work of the Enlightenment, here defends his project against the censors.*

We have already remarked that among those who have set themselves up as censors of the *Encyclopedia* there is hardly a single one who had enough talent to enrich it by even one good article. I do not think I would be exaggerating if I should add that it is a work the greater part of which is about subjects that these people have yet to study. It has been composed with a philosophical spirit, and in this respect most of those who pass adverse judgment on us fall far short of the level of their own century. I call their works in evidence. It is for this reason that they will not endure and that we venture to say that our *Encyclopedia* will be more widely read and more highly appreciated in a few years' time than it is today. . . . Some . . . were once praised to the skies because they wrote for the multitude, following the prevailing ideas, and accommodated their standards to those of the average reader, but they have lost their reputations in proportion as the human mind has made progress, and they have finally been forgotten altogether. Others, by contrast, too daring for the times in which their works appeared, have been little read, hardly understood, not appreciated, and have long remained in obscurity, until the day when the age they had outstripped had passed away and another century, to which they really belonged in spirit, overtook them at last and finally gave them the justice their merits deserved.

Source: D. Diderot, *Encyclopedia,* ed. and trans. S. Gendzier (New York: Harper & Row, 1967), p. 95.

principles by some Old Regime rulers themselves, a phenomenon known as "enlightened despotism." This was less surprising than it might seem. The Enlightenment was a general movement that penetrated the most entrenched bastions of tradition and privilege; even rulers were not immune to new ideas. Moreover, some monarchs saw the philosophes as potential allies in their struggles with the nobility, which almost everywhere resisted the centralizing tendencies of royal governments. Thus it was that Voltaire could be the guest and companion of one king at the same time that his works were being burned by order of another.

For their part, the philosophes welcomed enlightened despotism as the most efficient means of realizing their objectives. Although Locke and Rousseau had championed popular sovereignty, neither was a democrat; Rousseau, despite his humble origins, scorned the masses. Most philosophes were ready enough to welcome a despot, provided that he was willing to use his power in the service of reason and reform.

Catherine the Great

Russia, still in many respects on the margins of European society, seemed a particularly unlikely setting for enlightened despotism. In the 37 years following the death of Peter the Great, it had had six rulers, including a boy of 12, an infant, and a half-wit. Some observers believed that the country was headed toward the kind of aristocratic anarchy that had befallen Poland, whose elective king was a mere figurehead. The Russian nobility had largely emancipated itself from the code of state service Peter imposed on it, and the status of the peasantry had deteriorated even further. The criminal code of 1754 listed serfs only under the heading of property; they had lost even the legal status of human beings.

Strong rule returned to Russia in 1762 when Catherine the Great (1762–1796), the German-born wife of Tsar Peter III, organized his assassination and seized the throne for herself. Few rulers have ever matched Catherine's blend of cosmopolitan charm, instinct for publicity, and ruthless opportunism. She described herself, somewhat disconcertingly, as "every inch a gentleman," but certainly there were at least a few that were not; she had 21 attested love affairs during her reign, and doubtless more of briefer duration.

In the early years of her sovereignty, Catherine was oriented almost wholly toward the West. She founded new schools and stimulated the nascent publishing industry. While neighboring states were banning the philosophes, she read Voltaire openly and admiringly, and she subsidized the publication of the *Encyclopedia*. In 1767 she summoned a legislative commission of 560 delegates, of whom half were commoners, including peasants, to revamp the Russian legal code. Catherine herself drafted an elaborate "instruction," including long passages cribbed from her favorite philosophes, expressing her commitment to reform.

The Instruction was a remarkable document in many ways, although some of its more liberal provisions, especially concerning the reduction of serfdom, were cut out of the final draft. The sections on legal procedure were particularly novel. Catherine declared that all persons should be equal before the law. Reflecting her reading of the seminal reform treatise by Cesare Bonesana, marquis de Beccaria, *Of Crimes and Punishments* (1764), she called for the abolition of torture and the reduction of capital punishment. The Instruction was translated into the major languages of Europe; Voltaire received a personal copy. Catherine's fellow enlightened despot, Frederick the Great, was so delighted with it that he made her a member of the Berlin Academy. The most flattering response came from France, where it was banned as subversive.

Despite this fanfare, the legislative commission was a disappointment if not a fiasco. The delegates, most of them inexperienced in public affairs, were bewildered as to what was expected of them, as well they might have been, since Catherine's proposals would have stood much of Russian society on its head. The commission divided bitterly over the issue of serfdom, with the peasants and a few of the liberal nobility opposed stoutly by the landed interest, and produced only minor reforms in provincial administration. It was adjourned at the outbreak of war with Turkey in 1768 and never reconvened.

The Russo-Turkish war of 1768–1774 marked a turning point in Catherine's reign. Her dalliance with reform was now over, and she devoted herself instead to the more familiar business of power politics. In this and a subsequent war with Turkey (1787–1792), Catherine annexed the north shore of the Black Sea, although her goal of conquering Constantinople itself—the oldest and hardiest of all Russian imperial dreams—remained unfulfilled. The false hopes of reform Catherine raised were also largely responsible for the great rebellion of Emilian Pugachev (1773–1774), a Cossack chieftain who declared himself to be the murdered Tsar Peter, set up a court with the "true" Catherine, and promised an end to serfdom, taxation, and conscription, as well as the abolition of the landed aristocracy. For a time much of southern Russia was aflame, and refugees streamed into Moscow; but Pugachev was defeated at last in a series of pitched battles, brought to Moscow in a cage, and, like Stenka Razin a century before, quartered in the Kremlin Square.

Pugachev's Rebellion confirmed the mutual dependence of Catherine and her nobility. As the nobility needed the strength of absolute despotism to protect their privileges, so they alone stood between the empress and peasant anarchy. Their common interest was sealed in the Charter of the Nobility (1785). The charter completely freed the nobility from imperial service, giving it instead sole responsibility for provincial administration. In this way the nobility, in looking after their own interests as landowners, exercised direct political control of the countryside on behalf of the state. Content with their powers, they ceased to meddle in palace affairs, while the imperial government no longer concerned itself with serfdom, human and political rights, and other unpalatable subjects. The few intellectuals who still did, such as the educational reformer Nikolai Novikov (1744–1818) or Alexander Radischev (1749–1802), author of the bitterly critical *Journey from Moscow to St. Petersburg* (1790), soon found themselves in exile or in prison. It was of no avail for Radischev to point out that he had said nothing that Catherine herself had not affirmed in her days of Enlightenment. In the end, she even banned her old friend Voltaire.

Frederick the Great

A far more sophisticated example of enlightened despotism was Frederick the Great of Prussia. Frederick was the most admired monarch of the eighteenth century. He dominated it, by reputation if not by the actual strength of his country, much as Louis XIV had dominated the Europe of his time. Frederick liked to encourage the parallel, although he was certainly Louis' superior both as a soldier and as a man of intellect. Not only did Frederick speak the rhetoric of the Enlightenment, but he was a philosophe of sorts himself. He scorned divine right kingship, declaring that his power rested on his service to the people; a ruler, he said in a famous phrase, was only "the first servant of the state." In effect, Frederick replaced the divine right notion of a mystical relation between the ruler and God with an equally mystical relation between the ruler and his people. He identified the king with what Rousseau was to call the general will, for the monarch alone, he argued, standing above all parties and interests, could legislate for the common good. For that reason too, although the monarch's power derived from the people and was exercised solely on their behalf, they could never recall or revoke it. Their interests being partial, they could never be in a correct position to judge the whole; only the ruler could see the common interest.

Such a ruler, restrained by neither God nor man, might turn tyrant with impunity. But, Frederick argued, having already all the power he could desire and all the wealth he could consume, he was beyond ordinary temptation. Frederick himself seemed the perfect illustration of this. He built a palace at Potsdam in imitation of Versailles but found little time to enjoy it. No breath of scandal ever touched him; he had no private vices and, it almost seemed, no private life. His energies, apart from philosophy, literature, and music, were wholly absorbed in Prussia. He drained its swamps, encouraged its industry, and expanded its agriculture. Within the country, he promoted education, welcomed religious refugees of every stripe, and undertook a codification of the laws. "My chief obligation," he wrote, "is . . . to make [my people] as happy as human beings can be, or as happy as the means at my disposal permit."

The people Frederick wished to serve were not the free and equal citizens of Rousseau's commonwealth, however, but the hierarchically divided subjects of an Old Regime society. Prussians were not free; although Frederick, like Catherine, was opposed to serfdom in theory, he did little to alleviate it. Nor were Prussians equal. Frederick favored the nobility even more than his father had, reserving the officer corps of the army and the upper levels of the civil service exclusively for them. Because the army and the bureaucracy dominated Prussian society

Frederick the Great on the Enlightened Despot

Frederick here offers the classic justification for the traditional sovereign who, by comprehending all interests, is alone qualified to promote the common interest.

The sovereign is attached by indissoluble ties to the body of the state; hence it follows that he, by repercussion, is sensible to all the ills which afflict his subjects; and the people, in like manner, suffer from the misfortunes which affect their sovereign. There is but one general good, which is that of the state. . . . The sovereign represents the state; he and his people form but one body, which can only be happy as far as united by concord. The prince is to the nation he governs what the head is to the man; it is his duty to see, to think, and act for the whole community, so that he may procure it every advantage of which it is capable. . . . Such are in general the duties imposed upon a prince, from which, in order that he may never depart, he ought often to recollect that he himself is but a man, like the least of his subjects. If he be the first general, the first minister of the realm, it is not so that he should shelter in the shadow of authority, but that he should fulfil the duties of such titles. He is only the first servant of the state, who is obliged to act with probity and prudence; and to remain as totally disinterested as if he were each moment liable to render an account of his administration to his fellow citizens.

Source: Frederick the Great, *An Essay on Forms of Government,* trans. T. Holcroft, in E. Weber, ed., *The Western Tradition,* 3d ed. (Lexington, Mass.: Heath, 1972), pp. 539, 544.

between them, this meant that little initiative and less authority was left for the fledgling merchant class. At Frederick's death, Prussia was the most aristocratically controlled society in Europe. The long-term consequences of this, for Prussia and for Germany, were severe.

If Frederick believed in service to inferiors, he had few behavioral scruples toward his fellow monarchs. Even Louis XIV had attempted to rationalize his aggressions by legal claims, but when Frederick attacked Silesia in 1740, he blandly justified it on the grounds that it was in the nature of states to expand up to the limit of their ability. In 1772 he joined Catherine and Maria Theresa of Austria in carving up a helpless Poland in order to "adjust" the balance of power in eastern Europe in the wake of Catherine's gains against Turkey. Poland lost a third of its territory and half its population in this so-called Partition Treaty. Despite desperate attempts to strengthen itself by constitutional reform, it was wholly swallowed up by the subsequent partitions of 1793 and 1795 and ceased to exist as an independent nation. Enlightened despotism might sometimes aim at making states more rational and efficient; it did not make them more peaceful.

Joseph II: The Revolutionary Emperor

If Catherine and Frederick were essentially conservative rulers who used the rhetoric of the Enlightenment to maintain traditional autocracy, the Austrian emperor Joseph II (1780–1790) was the one sovereign who seriously embraced its principles and unreservedly attempted to put them into effect. The eldest of Maria Theresa's 16 children, Joseph grew up unhappily in the shadow of a court whose dull and devout propriety was far removed from the witty, urbane skepticism of the philosophes. In 1765 he became Holy Roman emperor and coregent of Austria, but his desire for reform was frustrated during his mother's lifetime. When he succeeded her at last, he had a 15-year backlog of frustrated projects and ambitions.

The empire Joseph inherited was a crazy quilt of territories and populations that spread across Europe from Flanders on the North Sea to the borders of Russia and Turkey. Its various peoples—Flemish, Italian, German, Czech, Croatian, Magyar, Polish—had little in common, and their loyalty to the Habsburg throne had been purchased only by conceding a large measure of self-rule, especially in Hungary and Bohemia. Joseph set out to compress this explosive mixture into a single political and social order and to transform some of the most backward regions of Europe into instant models of progress and enlightenment.

In her quiet way, Maria Theresa had done much to put the Austrian empire on the path to modernization. Administration had been centralized in Austria proper and Bohemia, creating a model for the whole empire. Guild monopolies and tariff barriers had been overthrown, establishing the largest free trade zone in Europe. Church

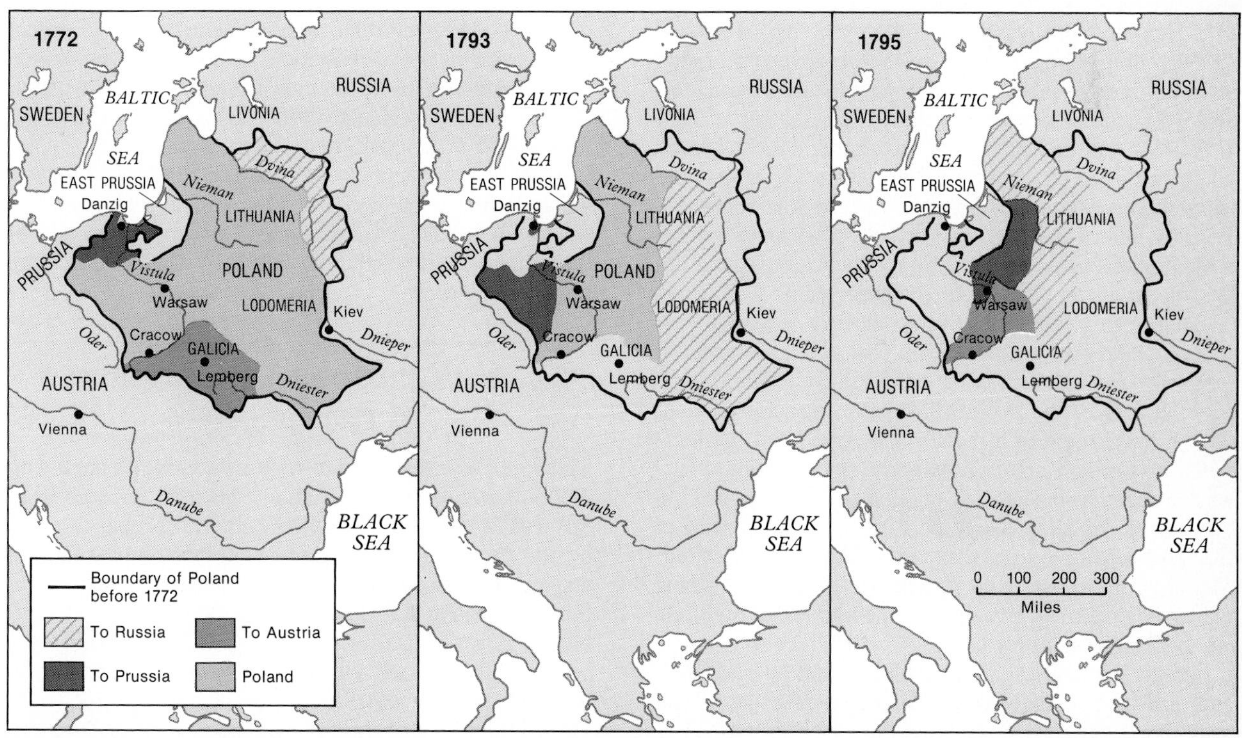

25.1 The Partitioning of Poland, 1772–1795

Joseph II and Catherine the Great, two of the Enlightened Despots and rivals in power politics as well as reform, met in 1787. By this time Catherine had long abandoned her liberal pose, while Joseph's attempt to remodel the Austrian Empire had driven many of its provinces to the verge of revolt. [Historisches Museum der Stadt Wien.]

land had been expropriated, and despite Maria Theresa's own hostility to secularism, the church's grip on education had been broken. For Joseph, however, the work of reform had barely begun with these steps. In ten years of ceaseless activity, he issued 6,000 edicts covering every aspect of life in the empire. What Catherine and Frederick had only talked of doing, Joseph decreed with the stroke of a pen. Serfdom was abolished, censorship lifted, and freedom of religion instituted. Jews were given civil rights and permitted to intermarry with Christians. Marriage itself was declared a civil contract, to the horror of conservatives and the outrage of the church. Apostasy and witchcraft were stricken from the legal code. Capital punishment was limited, and judicial torture was abolished. Equality before the law was not only proclaimed but enforced; Vienna was shocked by the sight of a young nobleman sweeping the streets in a chain gang.

There can be no doubt of the sincerity of Joseph's intentions. Although many of the changes he introduced were similar to those of other centralizing eighteenth-century monarchies, he regarded his power as an instrument for the betterment of humanity. He considered the existence of serfdom an "incredible and inexpressible evil," was outraged by bigotry and intolerance, and regarded the task of reform as an almost holy calling. "The service of God is inseparable from that of the state," he declared, and he wrote to one of his ministers, "Hasten everything that brings me nearer to the accomplishment of my plans for the happiness of my people."

Joseph brushed privilege, tradition, and special interests aside in the spate of his reform, boasting that he had made philosophy alone the legislator of his empire. The result was to unite the nobility, the church, and the provincial estates against him. Even the peasants, bewildered by the mass of edicts meant for their benefit and often sympathizing with the local priest or noble whom Joseph declared to be their oppressor, failed to support him.

Faced with almost universal opposition, Joseph redoubled his efforts. He reimposed censorship in an effort to dampen criticism, suspended due process, and set an army of spies on the population. The reactionary Count Pergen, his minister of police, became the most powerful man in the government and ultimately the only one he trusted. Rebellion flared in Hungary, the Tirol, and Flanders, and by the end of Joseph's reign, large parts of the empire were held down only by force. He died a broken man at 48, and within a few years the entire edifice of his reforms collapsed. Serfdom was restored, to survive in parts of the empire as late as 1867, and the nobility and clergy resumed their sway.

Enlightened Despotism in Perspective

The creed of enlightened despotism was best summed up in the motto of another reforming monarch, Charles III of Spain (1759–1788): "Everything for the people, nothing by the people." The enlightened despots represented a stage in the transformation of the personal monarchy of the old dynastic states to the impersonal rule of modern bureaucracies. Their very success in consolidating the power of the central state proved to be their undoing. It was true that the nobility and the church had frequently stood in the way of their ambitions. But in the long run absolute monarchy depended on these institutions as much

Jacques-Louis David's remarkable portrait of a woman of Paris' working class shows the anxiety and suffering but also the dignity and determination of those who struggled in the French Revolution, not merely for survival but also for justice. [Musée des Beaux-Arts, Lyon]

Horace Vernet's portrait of Napoleon in battle at Jena catches the intensity and concentration that made him a great field commander, but also the arrogance that presaged his ultimate downfall. [Château de Versailles/Réunion des Musées Nationaux]

Christianity's major rival, Islam, shared its belief in life after death. This illustration from the Khamsa of Nizami, a Persian manuscript of the mid-sixteenth century, shows Muhammad, astride his mare, being guided into heaven by the archangel Gabriel. [Bridgeman/Art Resource]

A Durbar (celebratory festival) in formal procession, in the traditional Indian style, in Calcutta. Note that Indians are the only ones who are walking (or carrying arms), although some Indian notables and guests are riding on the elephants with the top-hatted British. [India Office Library of the British Library]

The East India Company Docks in London by Samuel Scott. This deceptively quiet scene actually teems with activity. Cargo is drawn up and lowered from an upper-story window as an agent makes out his bill of lading; barrels are rolled and caulked; crowded ships maneuver in the harbor. In the foreground, a twist of calico cloth and packets of tea symbolize the goods prized by British consumers, while the cocker spaniel stamps the scene as unmistakably English. [Victoria and Albert Museum, London]

Burgeoning global trade in the eighteenth and nineteenth centuries influenced both East and West. Japanese woodblock prints of the late Tokugawa period, for example, had a marked impact on Western art. One of the best known was *A Sudden Shower at Ohashi* by Hiroshige (1797–1858), a contemporary of Hokusai. [The Metropolitan Museum of Art, purchase, 1918, Joseph Pulitzer Bequest]

The artists of the Romantic era sought not only to understand nature but also to commune with it. This classic image of the Romantic solitary—*The Traveler Above the Sea of Clouds* by Caspar David Friedrich, the leading German painter of his time—shows a climber on a mountaintop, above the material strife and illusion of the world, at peace with himself and nature. [Kunsthalle, Hamburg]

Eugéne Delacroix, *Liberty on the Barricades.* In this famous depiction of the 1830 French revolution, perhaps the most celebrated of all images of revolution, an idealized woman of the people leads a charge of workers whose ranks include a single bourgeois. [1830, oil on canvas, 10′10″ × 8′6″ (300 × 259 cm.); Louvre/Réunion des Musées Nationaux]

inseparably linked to it. In this respect, its most characteristic figure is perhaps Rousseau, who dreamed of an ideal community yet found himself always an outsider and insisted on the submission of the individual to the general will while exalting the rights of personal feeling and a liberated human nature. If the eighteenth century has with justice been called the age of reason, it was also a time that knew, in the words of Pascal, that "the heart has its reasons, that reason knows nothing of."

The Emancipation of the Jews

The decline of traditional Christian faith among the elite, the general questioning of the political and social order, and the concept of a secular brotherhood that animated the Enlightenment at its best led to a gradual reassessment of groups that had long been on the margins of European society. Prominent among these were the Jews. There were perhaps a million Jews in eighteenth-century Europe. The overwhelming majority were the Ashkenazim, who lived mainly in the small towns and villages of eastern Poland and Lithuania and spoke the mixed German-Polish dialect called Yiddish. Confined in ghettos, shunned and subjected to periodic outbreaks of looting and massacre known as pogroms, and for the most part desperately poor, they lived in almost complete isolation from the surrounding Christian community, marked off by their distinctive dress, beards, and speech, striving to live by their ancient biblical and rabbinical precepts, and nourishing the secret, never-extinguished hope of a messiah who would lead them out of exile and back to the Holy Land.

By contrast, the Sephardim, mostly the descendants of Jews expelled from Spain and Portugal in the sixteenth century and settled largely in such urban centers as Amsterdam, Venice, London, Frankfurt, and Bordeaux, were more prosperous and cosmopolitan. But Jews everywhere, still commonly blamed for Jesus' death and disliked for their distinctive practices, were subjected to restrictions and prohibitions of every kind. They were periodically driven from anyplace where their numbers seemed alarming, as in Vienna in 1421 and 1669 and Prague in 1557 and 1744. Elsewhere they were restricted by quota; the city of Ulm permitted exactly one Jewish family to reside there. In central and eastern Europe, Jews were forbidden to engage in agriculture and most ordinary trades and were confined to banking, commerce, moneylending, and peddling. They were subject to special taxes and assessments and often pure blackmail: Maria Theresa forced the Jews of Bohemia to pay 3 million florins to spare the community from expulsion. They were barred everywhere from public office, and a bill to naturalize British-born Jews in 1753 was withdrawn in the face of a violent public outcry.

A few Jewish financiers attained great wealth and on occasion political influence. The so-called court Jews of the seventeenth century were merchants and bankers who played a vital role in raising credit, supplying armies, and serving as financial advisers to rulers in Spain, Germany, and Austria. Samuel Oppenheimer (1630–1703) of Heidelberg organized the defense of Vienna against the Turks in 1683. The river fleet he constructed enabled the Austrian army to besiege Budapest and Belgrade, and when the victors brutally sacked the Jewish communities there, he provided for their relief. During the 1690s, as imperial armies fought both Louis XIV in Germany and the Turks in Hungary, Oppenheimer was given the title of director general of war supply. This so scandalized the Viennese that a mob was permitted to attack and loot his mansion, though not, to be sure, until the war was over.

The Sephardic Jews in the west were spared the more horrific experiences of their eastern brethren, such as the pogrom at Uman near Kiev in 1762, when 20,000 Poles and Jews were massacred by peasants and Cossack tribesmen. But all Jewish communities lived in perpetual fear and anxiety. When in 1665 a charismatic Jew of Syrian origin, Sabbatai Zevi (1626–1676), proclaimed himself the messiah, a wave of millennial fervor swept over European Jewry. It gripped not only the poor and downtrodden Ashkenazim of eastern Europe but the wealthiest Jewish families of Amsterdam and Hamburg as well. Tens of thousands of Jews sold their belongings and prepared to march east. Their hopes were tragically disappointed. The Turkish sultan, alarmed at the commotion Zevi's activities had aroused in his dominions, forced him to convert publicly to Islam on pain of death, and his movement collapsed.

Traditional anti-Semitism was at first reinforced by the Enlightenment. Christian anxiety at the weakening of faith was easily deflected toward the Jews; the Hebraic scholar Johann Andreas Eisenmenger (1654–1704) published a 2,000-page anti-Semitic tract in 1699, *Judaism Discovered,* a source frequently mined by later authors. Many of the philosophes were unsympathetic toward the Jews as well, taking up Spinoza's attack on their adherence to the Mosaic law as an enslavement to a dead past. But others, such as Locke and Montesquieu, promoted their cause as victims of the church. In *The Persian Letters,* Montesquieu's fictional correspondent upbraided the conduct of Christian Europeans: "You Christians complain that the Emperor of China roasts all Christians in his dominions on a slow fire. You behave much worse toward the Jews, because they do not believe as you do." The German playwright and critic Gotthold Ephraim Lessing (1729–1781) made a Jew the hero of his drama *Nathan the Wise* (1779). Joseph II saw toleration in more practical terms: "It is our purpose," he wrote, "to make the Jews more useful and serviceable to the state." Though even this most enlightened of despots did not grant Jews full equality, he removed most of the customary disabilities against them, encouraged them to enter agriculture and the crafts, and permitted them to enroll at academies and universities. The poll tax levied against Jews was remitted in France in 1784 and in Prussia in 1787, and the marquis de Pombal, the reforming minister of Joseph I of Portugal, promulgated the first laws against anti-Semitism.

Jewish emancipation was a special case of the more general extension of religious toleration in eighteenth-century Europe. After a long crusade, French Protestants regained in 1787 the civil rights and freedom of worship they had lost by the revocation of the Edict of Nantes in 1685, while in England the first legal Roman Catholic chapel since the mid-sixteenth century opened in Westminster in 1792. The Prussian Law Code of 1794 summed up the fruits of a century of agitation by declaring that "every inhabitant of the state must be granted complete freedom of conscience and religion."

But toleration was a two-edged sword for the Jews. Some embraced it fully, such as the philosopher Moses Mendelssohn (1729–1786), a colleague of Kant's and reputedly the model for *Nathan the Wise.* Mendelssohn founded the Haskalah movement, which attempted to reconcile Enlightenment thought with Jewish tradition. Conservatives, however, viewed such overtures with horror. They feared that what centuries of persecution had failed to do, toleration would at last achieve instead: the destruction of the Jewish community and its assimilation into the dominant Christian culture. The fear of losing Jewish identity also stimulated the growth of Hasidism, a popular religious movement akin to Pietism that emphasized the *aliyah,* or return to Israel. But neither tradition nor nostalgia nor the revival of Judaism's most ancient dream could prevent the incursion of the new secularism into even the most closed quarter of European society. After centuries, the Jews were being forced out of their isolation into a future of uncertain promise.

The assimilation Mendelssohn favored was the main goal of the Reform movement of the early nineteenth century. The first Jewish Reform temple was founded in 1810 in Brunswick, in northern Germany; the service was conducted in German as well as Hebrew, and an organ was used, a musical instrument hitherto associated with Christian churches.

The aim of the Reform movement was to demonstrate that the Jews had lost any sense of nationalism and had become a purely religious sect. Within the movement itself there was considerable debate about the authority of the Hebrew Bible and the Talmud, together with the value of retaining the use of the Hebrew language in religious worship. This challenge to tradition provoked strong reactions, with those who upheld the traditional point of view becoming known as Orthodox. In its present form, Orthodox Judaism combines a strict observance of traditional beliefs and observances with an awareness of their applicability to modern living.

An attempt at compromise inspired the development of the Conservative movement, which began in the United States at the end of the nineteenth century. Both Reform and Conservative Jews worship in synagogues in which the sexes are not segregated and in which prayers in the vernacular are used. Conservative Jews follow the Orthodox tradition of accepting the entire rabbinic tradition of the Talmud, although they interpret it more flexibly; they also promote Jewish aspirations to be recognized as a nation.

An offshoot of the practical aims of Conservatism was the development of the Reconstructionist movement, whose members interpret Jewish traditional practices as folkways acquired over the centuries and religion as only one aspect of the Jews' existence as a people. The Reconstructionist God, far from being the supreme creator and legislator of the Old Testament, is perceived as a cosmic process. Like other splinter movements, Reconstructionism has generally failed to establish itself on a widespread basis, and most practicing Jews today are either Orthodox or Reform, except in the United States, where Conservatism has a large number of followers.

The Abolitionist Movement

The contradiction between the ideals of freedom and equality expressed by the Enlightenment and the reality of eighteenth-century practice was most glaringly evident in the case of slavery. This contradiction was explained away by the assumption of black inferiority. Blacks, it was held, were less developed than whites both biologically and intellectually; thus they felt physical and mental hardships far less keenly. Perpetual children, they were incapable of taking independent responsibility for their lives and hence of genuine liberty. Their management by whites was actually a kindness; one slave ship was piously named the *Social Contract.*

The myth of the happy slave ran aground on the fact of black rebellion. The critic Samuel Johnson shocked a literary gathering at Oxford by offering a toast to the next slave revolt in the colonies. The pamphleteer Thomas Paine asked Americans in 1775 how they could rebel against the British while still keeping slaves themselves. But it was not until nearly the end of the century that a movement to abolish slavery and the slave trade gathered force. Significantly, it was led not by the philosophes but by dissenting English Protestant groups such as Quakers and Baptists as well as a group of Anglicans seeking to revitalize their church, the Clapham sect. The sect's leaders, William Wilberforce (1759–1833) and Thomas Clarkson (1760–1846), lobbied Parliament and campaigned vigorously in the press and in the pulpit, demonstrating again the growing importance of popular opinion. Clarkson, the first reformer to make abolitionism a professional career, interrogated seamen on the Liverpool docks and tracked down witnesses who could testify to the evils of the slave trade. Not to be outdone, the republican leaders of France's National Convention declared slavery abolished

The Revulsion Against Slavery

The opposition to slavery, muted at best in the writings of the philosophes, gained ground in the late eighteenth century and culminated in the abolition of the slave trade in the early nineteenth. The new revulsion was well expressed in this letter of 1778 describing a slave auction in Kingston, Jamaica.

Early this morning a Negro went through all the streets ringing a little bell. He had a slip of paper in his hand and called out something for sale. I asked what he was calling out, and someone answered: "People."

I got dressed and went to the market. There a whole mass of black people was standing about, old and young, men and women, all stark naked, just as God had made them. Each had a card hung around his neck with a number written on it.

Dear God, I thought, here people sell human beings just as we sell geese and pigs.

By nine o'clock, everything was sold, and everyone made his preparations to carry off his newly acquired goods. The little black girl kissed her little brother once again and cried; the old Negroes embraced one another and howled their goodbyes. As they were going, there suddenly started up a dull roaring among them. At first I thought it was just more howling. Then I realized they were singing a song in their Guinea language which would go something as follows:

Far from my homeland
I must languish and die,
Without comfort, amidst struggle and shame.
O the white men, so clever and handsome!
Yet I have done these pitiless white men no harm.
You, there, in heaven, help me, a poor black man!

Source: A. L. von Scholzer, "A New Year's Letter from Jamaica," trans. R. Gay, in P. Gay, ed., *The Enlightenment: A Comprehensive Anthology* (New York: Simon & Schuster, 1973), pp. 688–689.

Am I Not a Man and a Brother? **This medallion, struck by Josiah Wedgwood and adopted as the seal of the Slave Emancipation Society, may be regarded as a prototype of the modern political issue button. It was a powerful propaganda weapon in the abolitionist campaign of the late eighteenth century. [Culver Pictures]**

outright and all former slaves citizens in 1794, although this edict was never put into effect, and Napoleon later reestablished slavery in the colonies. British abolitionism proved a longer-lasting cause. It gave religious dissenters their first major social cause in 100 years and a chance to show that Christianity too could take its place in the vanguard of progress. If the actual achievement of abolition owed more to the decline of slavery's profitability than anything else, the abolitionist role in forging the political consensus necessary to act was a crucial one.

The Rights of Women

John Adams, replying in 1776 to a suggestion from his wife, Abigail, that the American revolutionaries "remember the ladies" in their new charter of rights, observed with uneasy humor that her letter "was the first intimation that another tribe more numerous and powerful than all the rest were grown discontented." The debate on the rights and status of women already had a long history when Abigail Adams spoke up to her husband. As early as 1589, a woman suitably named (or calling herself) Jane Anger had written a spirited defense of women. During the English revolution some women had preached from the pulpits of Independent congregations, and the colonist Anne Hutchinson (1591–1643) was expelled from Massachusetts Bay for demanding religious freedom; she and five of her children were later murdered by Indians. By the end of the seventeenth century a number of women, including Aphra Behn, Susan Centlivre, Mary de la Riviere Manley, and Eliza Haywood had begun to earn independent livings as writers. Catherine Macaulay (1731–1791) wrote an eight-volume *History of England* as well as pamphlets denouncing the British monarchy and defending the French Revolution, and the educational reformer and abolitionist Hannah More (1745–1833) earned more than £30,000 by her writings. These, however, were exceptions to the norm. Although Daniel Defoe had urged wives to participate actively in their husbands' businesses and a remarkable article in *The Gentleman's Magazine* in 1739 by an anonymous woman writer deplored the fact that the economic helplessness of women forced them to marry against their will, respectable tradesmen preferred to keep their spouses at home, and working women were severely stigmatized.

As we have noted, some women played important roles as hostesses of salons during the Enlightenment, and writers such as Locke, Montesquieu, and Voltaire occasionally commented on the legal disabilities of women. Significant changes were also taking place in the most important institution that touched on women, the family. The emphasis on romantic love and companionship first advanced by writers such as the poet John Milton had become general by the late eighteenth century, and with it, women's expectations in marriage had begun to rise. At the same time, the attack on divine right hierarchy shook traditional notions of male dominance in the family. The entry for "Women" in the *Encyclopedia* pointed out that marriage was a legal contract with mutual rights and responsibilities. The extension of the idea of a contract to marriage and the family had profound social implications. Its consequences are still unfolding today.

But the status of eighteenth-century women, even of the most privileged classes, is better summarized in the careers of two Englishwomen, Lady Mary Wortley Montagu (1689–1762) and Mary Wollstonecraft (1759–1797). Montagu, a woman of great energy and independence, associated on terms of equality with such leading literary figures as Alexander Pope and edited a journal supporting Sir Robert Walpole. Her husband was British ambassador to Constantinople, and in her "Turkish letters," which she circulated only in manuscript, she contrasted the freedom of Turkish women to carry on adulterous affairs under their veils with the restraints on women of her own class and nation. Montagu's intention, like Montesquieu's in *The Persian Letters,* was of course satiric, but she had a serious purpose underneath. Before her marriage she had written to her fiancé that wealthy young women were sold by their fathers into marriage "like slaves, and I cannot tell you what price my master will put upon me." Montagu's father had in fact attempted to force her to marry a man she could not love. She had educated herself against his wishes, and when she eventually separated from her chosen husband, she was forced to live the remainder of her life in Italy. Her own experience of oppression gave her sympathy for that of others, and she praised the Roman critic Longinus for having chosen as examples of the best writing of antiquity the work of "a Jew . . . and a woman."

MARY WOLLSTONECRAFT, FEMINIST

Mary Wollstonecraft was the daughter of a tradesman who squandered an inheritance and abused his wife. From an early age she showed signs of rebellion against the conventions of dress and behavior expected of respectable girls. She was also precociously aware of the ill treatment of servants, widows, and the poor generally. Leaving home, first as a lady's companion and then as a schoolmistress, she struck up a passionate friendship with a girl two years her senior, Fanny Blood. It was the first of her many attempts to find the affection and understanding that had been so painfully absent in her family.

At this time too, Wollstonecraft began to find the first adult role models with whom she could identify herself. Respectable society had been shocked by the elopement of Lady Eleanor Butler and Sarah Ponsonby, who set up house together in a remote Welsh valley where they received selected visitors in an exquisitely arranged house and garden. For Wollstonecraft and for many other young Englishwomen, they represented an ideal of companionship and personal freedom.

Escape to Wales was impracticable, but in the London suburb of Newington, Wollstonecraft met the Unitarian minister and political radical Richard Price, whose circle included women writers such as Ann Jebb and Anna Barbauld. Like Lady Montagu, Wollstonecraft soon found her professional outlet in writing. Her first essay, *Thoughts on the Education of Daughters,* was largely conventional in tone, but it contained a bitter complaint against the lack of occupations open to women that clearly echoed her own situation. This was followed by an autobiographical novel that she called simply *Mary.* In it the author advocates both social reform and sexual liberation, and in an uncompleted second novel, *Maria, or the Wrongs of Women,*

John Opie's portrait of the great English feminist Mary Wollstonecraft shows a powerful, mature woman in her mid-thirties whose introspective expression is tinged with sadness and disillusion. Mary may have been pregnant with her second child when this portrait was painted. [National Portrait Gallery, London]

Wollstonecraft makes the latter point even more strongly: "When novelists and moralists praise as a virtue a woman's coldness of constitution and want of passion, I am disgusted."

Like many other British radicals, Wollstonecraft placed great hopes in the French Revolution. Her eye, however, was as much on what could be done in Britain as on what was happening in France. In *A Vindication of the Rights of Man,* written in answer to Edmund Burke's attack on the revolution, she called for the breakup of large estates as a means of relieving urban poverty and denounced Burke's notion of liberty as a cloak for the defense of property interests. She traveled alone to Paris in December 1792 to observe the revolution at first hand and returned to publish a defense of it. "The will of the people," she declared, "is always the voice of reason."

Wollstonecraft's most famous and most important work, however, was *A Vindication of the Rights of Woman,* published in 1792 and now regarded as the true beginning of the modern women's movement. The *Vindication* is a work of passionate indignation; Wollstonecraft declares that women have been as brutalized as black slaves and degraded almost beneath the status of reasonable beings:

> **The *divine right* of husbands, like the divine right of kings, may, it is to be hoped, in this enlightened age, be contested without danger . . . . I love man as my fellow, but his sceptre, real or usurped, extends not to me, unless the reason of an individual demands my homage; and even then the submission is to reason, and not to man.**

It was time, she asserted, not to make place for "a small number of distinguished women" in society but to demand liberation for all.

Wollstonecraft won support in radical circles, but Horace Walpole's denunciation of her as "a hyena in petticoats" was typical of conservative reaction. Her personal life also shocked respectable opinion. She bore a daughter out of wedlock in 1794 and lived openly with the anarchist William Godwin (1756–1836), who opposed marriage on philosophical grounds but agreed to a wedding upon learning of her second pregnancy. Wollstonecraft died ten days after the birth of another daughter, Mary. These scandals, revived by the publication of Godwin's memoirs, led nineteenth-century feminists such as Harriet Martineau to shun her as an unsafe example for the women's movement. It was not until 1889, when Susan B. Anthony and Elizabeth Cady Stanton published the first volume of their *History of Woman Suffrage,* that Mary Wollstonecraft's name was redeemed, and given first place among the pioneers to whom the book was dedicated.

The Arts: From Rococo to Neoclassical

The dramatic style of the baroque gave way in the eighteenth century to the smaller-scaled and more refined rococo. With its often elaborate ornamentation, rococo was most effective in intimate, interior forms, and it is for the elegance of its aristocratic drawing rooms, furniture, and porcelain that the period is best remembered. The hold that French culture had taken on Europe during the reign of Louis XIV continued up to the French Revolution. French painting at last displaced Italian and Spanish in the work of Antoine Watteau (1684–1721), Pierre Chardin (1699–1779), François Boucher (1703–1770), and Jean-Honoré Fragonard (1732–1806) and in the vogue enjoyed by the earlier landscape painter Claude Lorrain (1600–1682). Watteau, Boucher, and Fragonard have left us a pictorial record of what Baron Talleyrand meant when he said that no one who had not lived before 1789 had tasted the true sweetness of life. Their aristocratic lords and ladies disport themselves against a pastoral background from which all hint of those on whose labor they existed has been removed. French, too, was the language of the Enlightenment. By the end of the seventeenth century, it had already begun to replace Latin as the language of diplomacy and learning, and it was a disgrace to be unable to speak it in society. Its influence was particularly strong in countries such as Poland, Russia, Sweden, and the German states, whose national literatures were just beginning to develop.

The chief rival to French culture was that of Britain. The brilliant satirist of London life, William Hogarth (1697–1764), showed a world in all its strength and brutality that the French court painters had so carefully eliminated, although Britain's aristocracy too had its chroniclers in Thomas Gainsborough (1727–1788) and Sir Joshua Reynolds (1723–1792). Defoe's *Robinson Crusoe* was translated into French, German, and Swedish, and the novels of Samuel Richardson (1689–1762), Henry Fielding (1707–1754), Laurence Sterne (1713–1768), and Tobias Smollett (1721–1771) had great success. Italy was still regarded as the ultimate finishing school for the cultured European, and a fresh revival of interest in antiquity led to the first excavations of Herculaneum and Pompeii and the beginnings of modern archaeology. European taste was growing more sophisticated and for the first time conscious of artistic history as a sequence of styles and traditions, each with its own value. This led to the emergence of a new kind of literary authority, the critic, whose task was to give perspective to cultural experience and to shape public taste. The critics Lessing, Johann Joachim Winckelmann (1717–1768), and Johann Gottfried von Herder (1744–1803) did much to shape an emerging national consciousness in Germany, while Samuel Johnson (1709–1784), whose life, faithfully chronicled by his admirer James Boswell, is one of history's best-known biographies, reigned for more than two decades as the literary dictator of London. Johnson, stung by the rejection of an early aristocratic patron, exemplified the new bourgeois man of letters who made his own way and owed his position to his own wit and force.

The heroic period of European exploration was largely over, to be replaced by an age of travel. One of the fruits of this was the great enthusiasm for China and its civilization displayed by Leibniz, Voltaire, Diderot, Christian Wolff, and others, a compliment, to be sure, that the Chinese did not return. On an artistic level this expressed itself in a craze for all things Chinese, particularly fine silks and porcelain, that went by the name of *chinoiserie.* Wallpaper and watercolor paints were also introduced from China, and the influence of Chinese painting was particularly evident in the work of Watteau. The European conception of China, based on reports by earlier Jesuit missionaries, was hardly an accurate one; Confucius, who was translated and widely admired, was read as a kind of philosophe. Nonetheless, the fascination with China marked a stage in Europe's expanding consciousness of the outside world; a global culture, as well as a global economy, was taking its first uncertain steps.

Vienna and the Golden Age of Western Music

Of all the forms of art, the only one that produced names to rank with the greatest figures of the seventeenth century was music. The baroque forms that had culminated in Bach and George Friedrich Handel (1685–1759), who adapted the Italian forms of the opera and the oratorio to northern tastes with great success, gave way to a more linear, less ornamental style in the works of Jean-Philippe Rameau (1683–1764) in France and Christoph Willibald von Gluck (1714–1787) in Germany. Bach's eldest son, Carl Philipp Emanuel (1714–1788), in his lifetime far better known than his father, was a crucial link in the development of what came to be called the classical style. This style, which came to fruition in the latter half of the century, was based on the elaboration of an old seventeenth-century form, the sonata. As applied in the orchestral forms of the symphony and the concerto, it produced a music that combined wit, elegance, and formal symmetry in a manner that reflected the balance of intellectual thrust and emotional restraint characteristic of much of eighteenth-century culture. Yet it was capable, too, in the hands of its greatest masters, of achieving extraordinary poignancy and depth.

The leading exponents of the new style were the Austrians Franz Joseph Haydn (1732–1809) and Wolfgang Amadeus Mozart (1756–1791), the latter an astounding prodigy who composed musically mature works from the age of 9 and works of profound originality from his teens. Haydn, slower to develop but immensely prolific in every form of the period, was employed by the greatest noble family of Hungary, the Esterhazys, who maintained a private orchestra for his use. Haydn remained with the Esterhazys all his life, although in later life he traveled widely and accepted commissions from all over Europe. Mozart's patronage was much less secure, and he depended for his living on a fickle public, for whom he turned out music with astonishing speed.

For both men, the Viennese public was the ultimate test of success. The growth of the bourgeoisie in the later reign of Maria Theresa and that of Joseph II had stimulated the development not only of music halls and theaters but also of a very lively salon culture. What verbal display and wit were to the salons of Paris, music was to those of Vienna. There were thousands of amateur musicians and singers in the city, and a British traveler remarked on provincial schools full of young children learning to read, play, and write music. The young Ludwig van Beethoven (1770–1827) came to Vienna at the age of 16, returned to stay permanently at 21, and dominated Viennese musical life for 30 years. His death, and that of Franz Schubert (1797–1828), the only native Viennese among these composers, marked the end of the golden age of Vienna's music. For Beethoven, who burst the bounds of classical tradition to forge the new Romantic style and who commanded an audience throughout Europe, Vienna was merely a stage; but Schubert, who lived his short life in the shadow of his great elder contemporary, was nurtured by the salon culture and the small circle of friends and admirers for whom he wrote his songs, sonatas, and chamber works.

The Enlightenment had a profound and lasting effect on Western culture. It called into question the basic institutions of European society, subjecting them to the test of reason and condemning whatever fell short by its measure. On the surface, it seemed the work of a small, self-appointed band of critics, the philosophes, who for the most part lacked status and position and were frequently hounded, censored, and even imprisoned. Yet the philosophes themselves represented only the cutting edge of the great transformation of Western thought that had begun with the Reformation, the commercial expansion of Europe, and above all the scientific revolution. If they succeeded despite such apparent odds, it was largely because their conservative opponents had capitulated to their values and ambitions or found it imprudent to resist. This was most evident in the phenomenon of enlightened despotism. If the seventeenth century had marked the triumph of a new order of the universe, the eighteenth produced a new vision of humanity to complement it. To many, this vision was troubling. But even those who continued to seek comfort in a traditional Christianity were forced to redefine it in terms of achieving secular progress on earth.

Notes

1. R. Zaller, *Europe in Transition, 1660–1815* (New York: Harper & Row, 1984), p. 12.
2. L. G. Crocker, *An Age of Crisis: Man and World in Eighteenth-Century French Thought* (Baltimore: Johns Hopkins University Press, 1959), p. 328.

Suggestions for Further Reading

Beales, D. *Joseph II,* vol. 1. Cambridge: Cambridge University Press, 1987.

Bernard, P. P. *Joseph II.* New York: Twayne, 1968.

Besterman, T. *Voltaire.* New York: Harcourt, Brace & World, 1969.

Cassirer, E. *The Philosophy of the Enlightenment.* Boston: Beacon Press, 1951.

Comini, A. *The Changing Image of Beethoven.* New York: Rizzoli, 1987.

Crocker, L. G. *An Age of Crisis: Man and World in Eighteenth-Century French Thought.* Baltimore: Johns Hopkins University Press, 1959.

Darnton, R. *The Business of Enlightenment: A Publishing History of the Encyclopedia, 1775–1800.* Cambridge, Mass.: Belknap Press, 1979.

———. *The Literary Underground of the Old Regime.* Cambridge, Mass.: Harvard University Press, 1982.

Ferguson, M., ed. *First Feminists: British Women Writers, 1578–1799.* Bloomington: Indiana University Press, 1984.

Gay, P. *The Enlightenment: An Interpretation.* 2 vols. New York: Knopf, 1966, 1969.

Gelbart, N. R. *Feminine and Opposition Journalism in Old Regime France: le Journal des dames.* Berkeley: University of California Press, 1987.

Gough, J. W. *The Social Contract,* 2d ed. Oxford: Clarendon Press, 1957.

Hazard, P. *The European Mind, 1680–1715.* New Haven, Conn.: Yale University Press, 1935.

Israel, J. I. *European Jewry in the Age of Mercantilism, 1550–1750.* New York: Oxford University Press, 1985.

Jacob, M. *The Radical Enlightenment: Pantheists, Freemasons and Republicans.* Boston: Allen & Unwin, 1980.

Jones, R. E. *The Emancipation of the Russian Nobility, 1762–1785.* Princeton, N.J.: Princeton University Press, 1973.

Krieger, L. *An Essay on the Theory of Enlightened Despotism.* Chicago: University of Chicago Press, 1975.

Lough, J. *The Encyclopedia.* New York: McKay, 1971.

Madariaga, I. de. *Russia in the Age of Catherine the Great.* London: Weidenfeld & Nicolson, 1981.

Manuel, F. *The Eighteenth Century Confronts the Gods.* Cambridge, Mass.: Harvard University Press, 1959.

Rendall, J. *The Origins of Modern Feminism: Women in Britain, France and the United States, 1780–1860.* New York: Macmillan, 1984.

Ritter, G. *Frederick the Great: A Historical Profile.* Berkeley: University of California Press, 1968.

Rogers, K. *Feminism in Eighteenth-Century England.* Urbana: University of Illinois Press, 1982.

Shklar, J. *Men and Citizens: A Study of Rousseau's Social Theory.* London: Cambridge University Press, 1969.

Spencer, S. I., ed. *French Women and the Age of the Enlightenment.* Bloomington: Indiana University Press, 1985.

Tomalin, C. *The Life and Death of Mary Wollstonecraft.* New York: New American Library, 1974.

Wade, I. O. *The Intellectual Origins of the French Enlightenment.* Princeton, N.J.: Princeton University Press, 1957.

Wilson, A. *Diderot.* 2 vols. New York: Oxford University Press, 1957, 1972.

CHAPTER · 26

The French Revolution and Napoleon

Great transformations had taken place in Western society between the beginning of the sixteenth century and the end of the eighteenth. The Reformation had shattered the unity of Christendom, and the Enlightenment had challenged the roots of Christian belief itself. The European economy had acquired a global dimension through the conquest and exploitation of the New World and the expansion of its markets in Asia and Africa. The scientific revolution had reordered Western people's views of the cosmos and themselves. Yet the political order of Europe had remained relatively static. The nations of Europe were still governed by kings and princes. The nobility was still predominant, its privileges seemingly more entrenched than ever.

The French Revolution challenged all that. Within a matter of weeks in the summer of 1789, a social and political edifice that had stood for 1,000 years was torn down, and for a generation all of Europe was caught up in the convulsive changes that ensued. From the very beginning, the revolution was recognized as the most important event of the age. In its turmoil and agony the shape of the modern world first became visible. Two centuries later, historians are still debating its nature and its impact.

An engraving of the pamphleteer and power broker Abbé Sieyes, who was a major force in the atmosphere of intrigue that surrounded the Directory in its last days. [Granger Collection]

The Crisis of the Old Order in France

The revolution began as an uprising not by the poorest segment of French society but by its richest and most privileged one. It was inevitable that the nobility would react against the autocratic rule of Louis XIV and seek to reassert their power. The long reign of the indolent Louis XV (1715–1774) provided them with an opportunity to do so. Thus while in most other places the privileges of the nobility were being reshaped and in many cases curtailed by enlightened despots, in France they remained unchecked. The intendants whom Louis XIV had sent to break the nobles' control of the provinces had been neutralized. The nobility's monopoly on the best and most lucrative offices in the church, the army, and the government was growing more and more restrictive; by the 1780s, for example, it required four generations of noble blood to qualify for an army commission. The parlements, the chief courts of the realm, had regained much of their old power to challenge and obstruct royal edicts, claiming broad powers of judicial review. By the 1760s they had grown bold enough to imprison provincial governors and military commanders who attempted to execute royal orders that they held to be illegal.

Of all their privileges, the one the nobility defended the most stubbornly was their exemption from most forms of taxation. Attempts to levy even token amounts in 1726 and 1749 met with furious resistance and had to be dropped. For the nobleman, taxation was the ultimate insult: like public flogging, it was something properly inflicted only on commoners. The bourgeoisie or upper merchant and professional class—a steadily expanding group in the eighteenth century—also sought to avoid taxation as a mark of status and in large part succeeded. The result was that while the privileged classes grew richer, the state became poorer, obliged as it was to rely on the poorest and most depressed sectors of the economy for support.

Reform and Reaction

Stung by the open defiance of his authority, Louis XV at last attempted to act. Guided by a reforming minister, René Charles de Maupeou (1714–1792), he took the daring step of abolishing the parlements outright and exiled their former judges to remote parts of the country. In their place he created new courts whose members would no longer have life tenure in office but could be removed at pleasure. At the same time, he undertook reforms to reduce the public debt to manageable proportions and to put the state's finances in order.

These measures were greeted by a storm of protest. Louis and Maupeou were attacked as despots bent on overthrowing the constitution. The king, however, remained firm. After nearly 60 years, he had finally decided to govern. It was too late. His death in 1774 brought his 20-year-old grandson, Louis XVI (1774–1792), to the throne. Louis was an affable, pious young man, fond of hunting and gardening and eager to please. He was soon persuaded to abandon his father's reforms and to restore the old parlements.

The Fiscal Crisis

The new king was ably served by his chief ministers, the philosopher Turgot (1774–1776) and the banker Necker (1776–1781). Both sought to relieve the chronic indebtedness of the crown by easing trade restrictions, abolishing guild monopolies, and raising new taxes. The need for reform was clear and had now become urgent. The 26 provinces of France represented a hopeless tangle of conflicting laws and jurisdictions. Taxes levied in one were prohibited in another. Commerce was impeded everywhere by customs and tolls; even a uniform system of weights and measures was lacking. But Turgot and Necker found themselves stymied. The revived parlements rejected their proposals out of hand, and factional intrigue undermined their position at court. Each in turn was forced from office, having accomplished nothing of substance.

The crown's plight was worsened by its participation in the American War for Independence, which added considerably to the debt burden. By 1786 interest payment on the existing debt amounted to half the royal budget, and the treasury was borrowing to meet that. At last it could obtain no further credit at any price. The king's comptroller, Charles de Calonne, informed his master that the state was bankrupt.

A new tax was the only possible solution. To circumvent the inevitable opposition of the parlements and to appeal directly to the more liberal nobility, Calonne proposed that Louis call a handpicked Assembly of Notables. This body convened in February 1787, but, suspicious of Calonne's motives and unwilling to bypass the parlements, it refused to support his program. Louis dismissed Calonne and dissolved the assembly.

The Constitutional Crisis

The financial crisis now became a constitutional one. The parlements now insisted that new taxes could be granted only by the representative assembly of the whole realm, the Estates General. This ancient feudal body had not met since 1614, but the judges made it into a symbol of popular liberty. Adopting the language of the Enlightenment, they insisted that law was the expression of reason, the general will, and the rights of man. It could no longer be accepted as the will of a single individual.

The crown found itself isolated, the natural focus of all discontent. The nobility feared it as the usurper of its privileges. The peasantry, ground under by taxes, resented it as the expropriator of its labor. The bourgeoisie saw it as a barrier to wealth and status. Its problems were blamed not on genuine need but on the extravagance of the court. Whereas the pomp of Versailles under Louis XIV had reflected the glory of France, it now symbolized the decadence of personal monarchy.

Louis finally attempted to suppress the parlements as his father had done and set up new courts in their place. But the tide of reform could no longer be stopped by a show of force. Rioting and near-rebellion broke out in the provinces, and committees of correspondence were formed on the model of the American Revolution. The clergy threatened to reduce their annual "gift" to the treasury, and the king's own courtiers opposed him. Louis backed down. In July 1788 he recalled the parlements, whose judges returned as heroes, and agreed to summon the Estates General. The revolt of the nobility had triumphed.

Progressive opinion now looked for a system of constitutional government to emerge, with the Estates General evolving into a more or less modern representative body like the British Parliament or the American Congress. But the progressives were in for a shock. The judges of the parlements may have spoken the language of Rousseau and Thomas Jefferson, but they had no intention of sharing the powers they had pried from the crown. The Parlement of Paris ruled at once that the new Estates General must have the same form as the old, with three separate chambers representing the clergy, the nobility, and the commoners of the realm. Because each chamber voted as a separate unit, the two privileged orders could always outvote the Third Estate of the commons, which in fact was made up of merchants, financiers, petty officials, and members of the professions, the group loosely referred to as the bourgeoisie. Except in theory, none of these groups represented the actual majority of peasants and workers who made up four-fifths of the population.

The Bourgeoisie and the Third Estate

The situation now boiled down to a three-cornered struggle among the king, the nobility, and the bourgeoisie. The resentment of this last group was of long standing. The bourgeoisie regarded themselves as the most productive element in society. They chafed at economic restrictions which they saw as largely designed to protect the interests of the nobility and, though some of them had acquired fortunes as great as any nobleman's, they were bitter at their exclusion from the highest echelons of status and power. As the political debate widened, they also came to

France on the Eve of Revolution

The English traveler Arthur Young gives a vivid impression of the ferment in pre-revolutionary France in his account of a dinner party in 1787.

Dined today with a party, whose conversation was entirely political. . . . One opinion pervaded the whole company, that they are on the eve of some great revolution in the government: that everything points to it: the confusion in the finances great; with a deficit impossible to provide for without the states-general of the kingdom, yet no ideas formed of what would be the consequence of their meeting: no minister existing, or to be looked to in or out of power, with such decisive talents as to promise any other remedy than palliative ones: a prince on the throne, with excellent dispositions, but without the resources of a mind that could govern in such a moment without ministers: a court buried in pleasure and dissipation . . . a great ferment amongst all ranks of men, who are eager for some change, without knowing what to look to, or to hope for: and a strong leaven of liberty, increasing every hour since the American revolution; altogether form a combination of circumstances that promise ere long to ferment into motion, if some master hand, of very superior talents, and inflexible courage, be not found at the helm to guide events, instead of being driven by them.

Source: A. Young, *Travels in France During the Years 1787, 1788, and 1789*, ed. C. Maxwell (Cambridge: Cambridge University Press, 1950), pp. 84–85.

see themselves as speaking, through the Third Estate, for the nation as a whole. Their position was eloquently summarized in a pamphlet circulated early in 1789 by a liberal clergyman, the Abbé Sieyès (1748–1836), which asked:

> ***What is the Third Estate? Everything.***
> ***What has it been thus far in the political order? Nothing.***
> ***What does it demand? To be something.***[1]

The Third Estate's discontent was the king's opportunity. If he could exploit it properly, he could outflank the opposition to tax reform and break the back of the nobles' revolt. Urged on by Necker, who had been restored to power, Louis decreed that the Estates General be popularly elected: nobles by nobles, clergy by clergy, and the Third Estate by all other males over 25 whose names appeared on the tax rolls. With a stroke of the pen, the king had enfranchised millions of Frenchmen for the first time.

In deference to this greatly expanded electorate, Louis agreed to "double the Third," that is, to permit twice as many representatives to be chosen for the Third Estate as for the other two orders. But this did not affect the voting balance of the three estates. Each order would still vote as a separate unit. In terms of actual power, therefore, the Third Estate's position remained that of a minority.

Louis' position was bound to leave the Third Estate unsatisfied. But the concessions he had made also aroused fierce opposition from the nobility, the Parlement of Paris, and even the royal family. The king was caught between a bourgeoisie he dared not trust and a nobility he dared not abandon.

In the meantime, an election fever swept over France. In 40,000 electoral districts all over the country, lists of grievances were compiled to be sent along with the delegates; the lists revealed widespread dissatisfaction with the social system. The same demands were repeated insistently: popular representation, legislative control of taxation, and a limitation of the monarchy. Also bitterly attacked were church tithes; traditional payments by peasants to the local lord, which ranged from a tenth to a third of the value of their crop; and hunting rights that enabled the nobility to trample across fields and vineyards in pursuit of game. The lists of the Third Estate were virtually unanimous in demanding full civil equality for all Frenchmen.

In these grievances and demands lay the seeds of a social revolution. The nobility had wanted to protect its privileges, the bourgeoisie to share them. What arose from the countryside was a cry of protest at the exploitation that the peasantry had suffered at the hands of both. Throughout the eighteenth century noble and bourgeois landholding increased, as the peasants were squeezed onto smaller and smaller plots and sometimes entirely off them. In the region of Toulouse in the south, for example, where a capitalist, market-oriented agriculture had developed, wage-earning laborers made up a majority of the rural population 50 years before the revolution. Many of those peasants who still owned land could not produce enough on it to feed themselves and their families, and they too depended on wage labor for survival. This meant that more Frenchmen were vulnerable to a subsistence crisis—crop failure compounded by price rises and hoarding—than ever before.

As it happened, the worst political crisis in the nation's history coincided with the worst subsistence crisis of the eighteenth century. Following a period of expansion in midcentury, France had entered a long cycle of depression after 1770. This was aggravated by a series of bad harvests, culminating in that of 1788. Starving peasants fled to the towns, swelling the urban unemployment rate to as high as 50 percent. Even people who had work found up to 80 percent of their earnings consumed by the price of bread. By the spring of 1789 there were violent uprisings against grain prices and shortages, and wandering bands roved the countryside, attacking the castles of the nobility.

The Revolution of 1789

France had known periods of disorder before, but the circumstances that now converged on it—a constitutional crisis that was a thinly veiled struggle for power among contending political and economic groups, a monarchy enfeebled not only by an incompetent ruler but also by attacks on its fundamental legitimacy, a widespread sense of social injustice and an assumption that radical change was inevitable—all combined to bring about the collapse of the government, the destruction of the manorial order, and the replacement of a society based on the division of estates and orders into one predicated, at least in theory, on the legal and political equality of all citizens. This was the revolution of 1789.

From the Estates General to the National Assembly

The 1,165 delegates to the Estates General were the focus of all hopes when they came together at Versailles on May 5, 1789. The First Estate of the clergy consisted of 291 delegates, of whom 46 were bishops; the majority were hardworking and underpaid parish priests, close to the peasantry they served and sympathetic to reform. The 270 nobles of the Second Estate also included a vociferous reform group. Among its number was the marquis de Lafayette (1757–1834), already celebrated as a hero of the American Revolution. Of the 578 commoners who com-

Louis XVI presides from his raised throne at the opening of the Estates General on May 5, 1789. Louis' failure to provide a credible reform program or to resolve the issue of whether the estates would vote by number or by order ended the last royal hope to control events. [Photographie Bulloz]

prised the Third Estate,* well over half were lawyers, most of whom also held government jobs, and another quarter were merchants, businessmen, and rentiers, persons who lived off the profits of feudal dues. Despite the wide franchise, not a single worker or peasant had been elected. This was partly because the final selection of delegates took place at only 200 district assemblies, where the influence of local notables predominated, and partly because of the traditional deference of the electorate to its social superiors. The result was that the full Third Estate was represented only by its narrowest elite, although an elite angry and embittered at its rebuff by the nobility.

Had the crown been able to assert itself at this point, a compromise might still have been found. But Louis and Necker had no program to present, no solution to offer. The king spoke of caution, his minister of deficits. Leaderless, the Estates General fell to wrangling over the question of voting by orders, with the Third Estate insisting that the three orders merge into a single body. As this not only would have given the Third Estate a numeric voting majority but would also have abolished the principle of separate orders on which the privileges of the clergy and the nobility rested, it was stoutly resisted. On June 17, after weeks of deadlock, the Third Estate took the decisive step toward revolution: it declared itself an independent body, the National Assembly, with the right to legislate alone in the public interest. Three days later the members of the Third Estate found themselves locked out of their chamber. They gathered in a nearby indoor tennis court, where in great passion and excitement they vowed not to disband until they had given France a constitution.

Louis now acted. He told the Estates General that he would give it a permanent place in the state, with wide though unspecified rights over the administration and the budget. In this he seemed to accept the principle of a limited monarchy that had been demanded on all sides. But he also declared the self-created National Assembly (whose numbers had now been swollen by dissident clergy and nobility) null and void and ordered the Estates to return to their separate chambers. The nobles were elated. The king had come down for the principle of blood privilege on which his own throne ultimately rested. But the Third Estate remained defiant. Facing mutinous soldiers and an angry populace, Louis backed down. On June 27 the first two Estates united with the Third. The National Assembly was now a fact.

*The remaining 26 delegates were unclassified.

The Popular Revolution

The revolution now moved into the streets. The workers and tradesmen of Paris, fearing both rural mobs and military repression, broke into the civic arsenals and armed themselves. On July 14 they stormed the ancient fortress of the Bastille and seized its weapons after a pitched battle in which 98 of the attackers were killed. This event, still celebrated annually in France, was of enormous symbolic significance. It gave the revolution its baptism of blood and resulted in the final collapse of the king's authority. Riots broke out and arsenals were pillaged in Bordeaux, Lyons, and other large cities. In some eastern towns, such as Sedan, Nancy, and Troyes, there were violent clashes, but elsewhere, as in Strasbourg and Rennes, the army defected en masse. In many places the intendants and municipal officials simply fled, leaving the local population to organize citizen militias and revolutionary committees, or *communes,* on the model already established in Paris.

Disorder broke out simultaneously in the countryside, often triggered by a wave of rumor and hysteria, the so-called Great Fear, which centered around reports of advancing royalist or bandit armies. From town to town the cry went up, "The brigands are coming!" Since there were enough bandits in the best of times, these fears were not without foundation. They soon became a pretext for looting, and by late July a full-scale agrarian insurrection was in progress. Peasants broke into the manor houses of the nobility, systematically destroying the legal records of debts and feudal dues. What went up in flames was more than paper. In the high summer of 1789 the Old Regime itself was dying in a thousand bonfires throughout France.

The Abolition of Privilege and the Declaration of the Rights of Man

The bourgeois members of the National Assembly were far from pleased with this wholesale destruction of property rights. But they quickly moved to ratify what they were powerless to prevent. On the night of August 4 two liberal noblemen, coached by leaders of the Third Estate, moved to abolish all compulsory labor service, such as road maintenance, and to offer redemption for all other dues and obligations. What can only be described as a

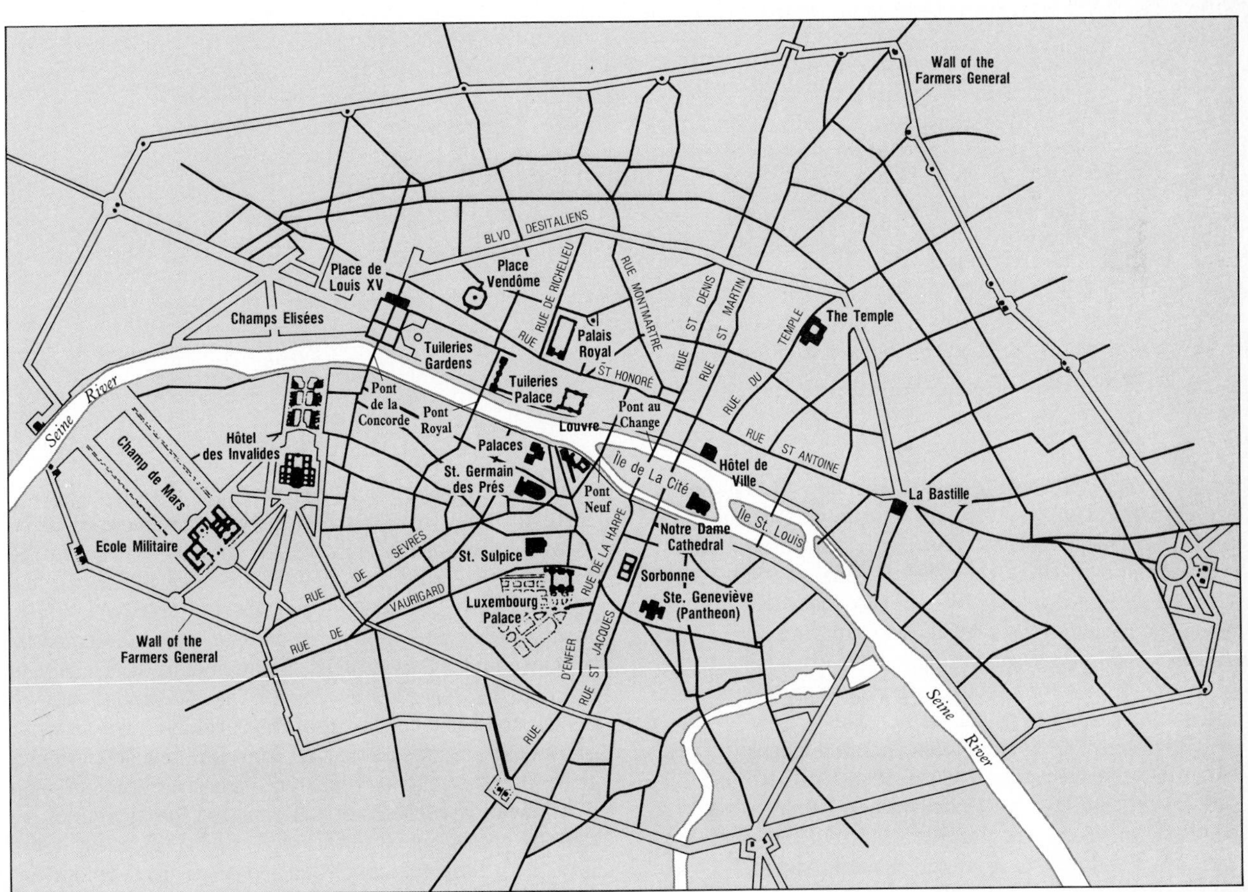

26.1 Paris at the Outbreak of the French Revolution

The Fall of the Bastille: An Eyewitness Account

Jean-Baptiste Humbert, a Parisian watchmaker who claimed to have been the first to scale the walls of the Bastille on July 14, 1789, provides a vivid account of the excitement and confusion of that day.

I followed the crowd, to get to the cellar where the arms were kept. On the staircase leading to the cellar, seeing a man armed with two muskets, I took one from him, and went up again; but the crowd at the top of the stair was so great that all those who were climbing up were pushed down again, and fell right into the cellar. . . . In spite of this horrible tumble, the crowd persisted in going down the stairs, and as nobody could get up again, there was such a crush in the cellar that people were shrieking and gasping for breath. . . . Afterwards I went to the cannon that stood just above the drawbridge of the Bastille, in order to push it off its guncarriage and render it unusable. But as I stood for this purpose with my shoulder under the mouth of the cannon, someone in the vicinity fired at me, and the bullet pierced my coat and waistcoat and wounded me in the neck; I fell down senseless; the Swiss soldier whose life I had spared dragged me on to the staircase, still clutching my gun, so he told me. . . . On my way home I remembered some friends who lived in the rue de la Ferronnerie; I had left them that morning, and they had seemed anxious about the dangers which they foresaw my zeal might lead me into. I went to their house, and four armed bourgeois escorted me to the rue du Hurepoix. I was greeted with praise wherever I went; but when we reached the Quai des Augustins, we were followed by a crowd of people who mistook me for a malefactor, and twice attempted to put me to death. As I could not explain things to everyone, I was about to be seized, when I was recognized by a bookseller on the Quai, who rescued me from the hands of the crowd and took me into his own home. . . . I rested until about midnight, when I was woken by repeated cries of *to arms! to arms!* Then I could not resist my longing to be of some further use. I got up, armed myself, and went to the guardroom, where I found M. Poirier, the Commanding Officer [of the National Guard], under whose orders I remained until the following morning.

Source: J. Godechot, *The Taking of the Bastille, July 14th, 1789,* trans. J. Stewart (New York: Scribner, 1970), pp. 281–286 passim.

psychological stampede ensued. Member after member arose to volunteer renunciation of his own privileges and those of cities, corporations, and provincial estates. Hoarse and exhausted, the delegates adjourned at 2 A.M. with the declaration, "Feudalism is abolished." By morning many had repented their enthusiasm and tried to reinstate various qualifications and exemptions. It was too late. The people of France took them at their most generous word and simply ceased to pay all former dues.

The assembly's next step was to issue a constitutional blueprint, the Declaration of the Rights of Man and the Citizen (August 26). Its 17 brief articles summarized the political principles of the Enlightenment. All men, it stated, "are born and remain free and equal in rights." Those rights were defined as "liberty, property, security, and resistance to oppression," which it was the duty of every state to preserve. Sovereign power was declared to be vested in the nation as a whole, and law was to be the expression of the general will. Freedom of speech and religion were guaranteed, and liberty—the right "to do anything that does not harm another person"—could be abridged only by due process of law, before which all men were to be regarded as equal. The declaration was to remain the basic document of the revolution, however far subsequent regimes departed from its principles in practice. At one stroke it eliminated the archaic, cumbersome divisions of French society. It replaced the system of orders by one based on formal civil equality and cleared the ground for the modern political and economic development of France. It also made devastating propaganda. Trans-

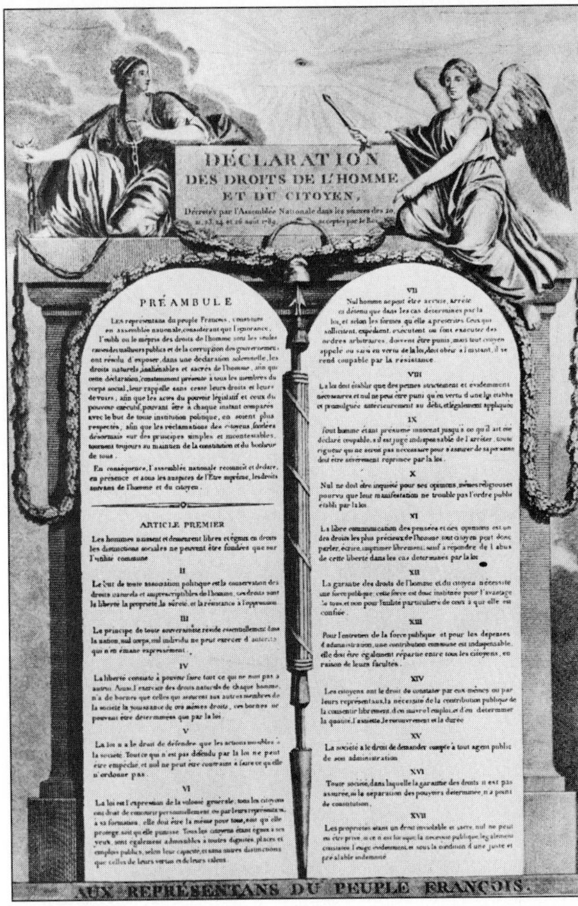

Classical and biblical symbols entwine in this engraved representation of the Declaration of the Rights of Man. The preamble and the seventeen articles of the document are depicted as the tablets of a new Mosaic law, while two female deities appear against a sky whose parting clouds reveal the light. The figure on the left holds the broken chains of privilege, while the winged figure on the right holds the staff of popular sovereignty. A luminous eye representing the God of Reason completes the trinity. [Historical Pictures Service, Chicago]

lated into every major European language, it shook the established order and galvanized demands for reform across the Continent.

The king alone remained passive and aloof in the face of these developments. This led to the last of the revolutionary tremors of 1789. On October 5 a contingent of Parisian housewives, having previously invaded the mayor's office to protest food shortages and the continuing high price of bread, marched to Versailles and demanded that Louis return to the capital. They were soon backed up by the arrival of the newly formed National Guard under Lafayette, 20,000 strong. Virtually defenseless, the royal family was forced to accompany this motley procession back to Paris, where they took up residence in the Palace of the Tuileries. The National Assembly followed a few days later, and Louis gave his unhappy consent to the August 4 decrees and the Declaration of the Rights of Man.

The New Order, 1789–1791

The poet Chateaubriand was later to remark that the nobility had begun the revolution and the people had finished it. But despite the slogan that now epitomized the goals of the Revolution—"Liberty, fraternity, equality"—there was no single "people" of France, only groups with divided and often bitterly contending interests. On one extreme were the 20,000 people, mostly aristocrats, who had left the country and rejected the revolution. On the other were those, especially the *sans-culottes** or working class of the towns, who had gained theoretically but not materially from it and continued to demand both relief from high prices and scarcity and representation of their interests. In between were the great mass of the peasants, who wished chiefly to consolidate the fruits of their rebellion in July, the destruction of the manorial regime and the freeing of their title to the lands they farmed.

The Bourgeoisie in Power

Actual power was in the hands of none of these groups, however, but rather those of the bourgeoisie, the unexpected beneficiaries of the collapse of royal authority and the abolition of the order of the nobility. The bourgeoisie dominated the National Assembly or, as it called itself from October 1789, the Constituent Assembly. The assembly had two crucial tasks: to write a new constitution for France and to govern the nation while doing so. Having achieved power and control of the king by mass action, it wanted no further interruption of its business by the sans-culottes. Its first acts from its new base in Paris were to declare martial law and censorship of the press, and on October 21 a young laborer, Michel Adrien, was hanged for sedition. The honeymoon of the Third Estate was over.

---

*Literally, "without breeches." For practical reasons, workingmen wore long pants instead of the silk or muslin stockings and breeches of the nobility and the bourgeoisie.

The assembly's desire to insulate the new government against undue popular influence was reflected in the constitution of 1791. Contrary to Article 6 of the Declaration of the Rights of Man, the constitution distinguished between "active" and "passive" citizens. Both groups enjoyed full civil rights, but only the actives, those meeting a minimum property qualification, had the right to vote for some 50,000 electors, who in turn chose the 500 representatives of the Legislative Assembly. About two-thirds of the adult male population qualified for active citizenship and fewer than half of it for nomination as electors. This was still a far wider franchise than in England, and the property qualification for voting was lower than in some states in America. But since the electors were obliged to spend several days choosing representatives at their own expense and often at a considerable distance from home, the process ensured that they would necessarily be men of means and leisure—in short, men of the bourgeoisie.

The Reorganization of Church and State

The most pressing issue before the Constituent Assembly was the unresolved crisis of the public debt. The simplest recourse was to repudiate it as a legacy of the discredited Old Regime. As a substantial portion of the debt was owed to members of the bourgeoisie, however, there was no question of doing that. Instead, the assembly decided to pay the debt off by selling the lands of the church, which it declared to be confiscated in the name of the nation. A special currency called *assignats* was issued to facilitate the purchase of these lands. In this way some 10 percent of the real estate of France was redistributed to deserving—that is, chiefly bourgeois—revolutionaries.

This massive transaction destroyed the financial independence of the church and made it a ward of the state. Clergymen became salaried officials, chosen from a qualified slate by popular election like other state functionaries. Archbishoprics were abolished, and the number of bishops was reduced from 135 to 83. Monasteries and nunneries were dissolved, and the taking of religious vows was prohibited. The pope was to be informed as a matter of courtesy when a bishop was installed, but his authority was in no other way recognized.

These changes were embodied in the Civil Constitution of the Clergy (1790). They were less drastic than they seemed, for the Gallican church might have been expected to respond favorably, since clergymen's salaries were to be nearly doubled under the new dispensation. The problem was ratification. The church wanted to adopt the Civil Constitution on its own authority, thereby affirming its continued identity as a corporate body. To the assembly, this would have been tantamount to recognizing the existence of a First Estate again, when all estates and orders had been abolished. It therefore promulgated the new constitution alone and backed it up with an oath of allegiance that all clergy were required to swear.

The assembly perhaps could not have acted otherwise, since Pope Pius VI, whose antagonism to the revolution was fanned by émigré agents in Rome, was preparing to denounce the Civil Constitution. The result, however, was to divide the French church. Half the lower clergy refused to take the new oath, and all but seven of the bishops as well. The "refractory" or "nonjuring" clergy, as they were called, emigrated or went underground, where, protected by loyal parishioners, they formed a natural focus of resistance to the revolution. Far from becoming an obedient servant of the state, the church would henceforth be its bitterest enemy.

Equally far-reaching was the assembly's reorganization of administration and government. All former courts and jurisdictions were abolished. A uniform code of administration was instituted for the 44,000 rural and urban districts of the country. The 26 old provinces, many of them rich with history (and memories of previous rebellions), were replaced by 83 "departments," all newly named and democratically equal in size. An independent judiciary was established, with elected judges and juries for criminal trials. Yet, although the administration was thus radically standardized, it was actually less centrally controlled than under the Old Regime. Local and regional officials were to be elected from below rather than appointed from above, and they were left essentially on their own in the work of government. In this respect, the Constituent Assembly's reforms did not go nearly far enough. Anxious to avoid the charge of despotism leveled at the Old Regime, it left the implementation of its decrees in the hands of officials over whom it had little effective control. Had the revolution been securely established, such a system might have been workable. As matters stood, with an embittered nobility, a divided church, a suspicious peasantry, and an unsatisfied proletariat, it was an open invitation to resistance. Counterrevolutionary disturbances broke out in the region of the Midi around Toulouse, Nîmes, and Montauban in the spring of 1790, precursors of full-scale rebellion to come.

The status of the king posed a difficult question. It was inexpedient to depose Louis, as republican members of the assembly wished. He was the only remaining link between the old France and the new and the only valid symbol of authority for millions of French citizens. At the same time, despite his grudging approval of the Declaration of the Rights of Man and the Civil Constitution of the Clergy, his hostility to the revolution was plain. His powers were therefore restricted to a three-year suspensive veto over the Legislative Assembly.

But Louis refused to play the role assigned him. On June 20, 1791, he attempted to flee the country with the royal family. Captured by peasants at the border town of Varennes, they were forced to return to Paris in a humiliating procession. The assembly accepted the fiction that the king had been "kidnapped." It was clear to all, however, that even before its formal adoption, the new constitution had been repudiated by the man intended to serve as its head of state.

In the long run, the work of the Constituent Assembly was of great importance. It dissolved and replaced the institutions of the Old Regime and laid the foundations of the modern French state. But it failed to solve almost all the immediate problems before it. It passed out of existence on September 30, 1791, leaving behind a sharply polarized nation, mounting political and economic chaos, and a constitution that, satisfying no one, survived it by barely ten months.

The Revolution and Europe

At first many people outside France greeted the revolution with enthusiasm and even rapture. "How much the greatest event that has happened in the world, and how much the best!" exulted the British politician Charles James Fox. The poet William Wordsworth later recalled the sense of liberation and almost limitless hope inspired by the French revolution:

> ***Bliss it was in that dawn to be alive***
> ***But to be young was very heaven!***

Elsewhere, too, the reformers rejoiced. In Germany the elderly philosopher Kant and the young nationalist Johann Fichte both sang the revolution's praises, and the bourgeoisie of Hamburg turned out to celebrate the first anniversary of the fall of the Bastille. Societies and clubs in support of the revolution were founded in Switzerland, Savoy, the Netherlands, and Britain, and many of them engaged in revolutionary activities themselves. An uprising in the Austrian Netherlands drove the imperial army out of Brussels in December 1789, while in the Rhineland peasants refused to pay seigneurial dues to their lords. Not content to admire from afar, many activists gathered in Paris to participate directly in the revolution, including the American pamphleteer Tom Paine and the Prussian Anarchasis Cloots, who styled himself the "representative of the human race."

Not all reaction was favorable, however. The British statesman and orator Edmund Burke (1729–1797), who had supported the American Revolution, wrote a highly effective rebuttal in his *Reflections on the Revolution in France* (1790), which remains to this day a classic statement of the conservative view of history. Burke argued forcefully against the assumption that all men possessed identical natural rights. Not men, he contended, but nations were the basic units of history. Each nation was a unique cultural entity shaped by its distinctive historic experience. Reforms that respected the time-tested institutions of the nation were right and proper. But for a single generation to destroy those institutions and to attempt to substitute some abstract formula of justice for the collective wisdom of all its predecessors was an act of folly and arrogance, a "fond election of evil" that could bring only ruin.

The émigrés who fled France brought their own tales of horror, and the monarchies of Europe were soon alert to the danger the revolution posed. Bavaria, Sardinia, Spain, and Portugal took steps to suppress all expressions of revolutionary solidarity within their own borders, and Spain posted troops along its frontier to keep out the "French plague." Not until August 1791 were the two largest Continental powers able to agree on a joint statement of policy toward France. The Declaration of Pillnitz, issued by Frederick William IV (1786–1797) of Prussia and Leopold II (1790–1792) of Austria, stated as its goal the restoration of the French monarchy, by force if necessary. A declaration without an act of war, it served only to strengthen the republicans in France, who argued that the revolution would never be complete or secure as long as Louis remained king.

PARIS AND THE FALL OF THE MONARCHY

Paris was the nerve center of the revolution, the seat of national government and the home of the volatile sansculottes, who comprised half its population of 600,000. The city had enjoyed its own revolution in July 1789 when it overthrew its royal administration and improvised, almost on the spot, a new governing authority, the Commune, based on representation from the electoral districts set up to choose delegates to the Estates General. These districts, subsequently reorganized into 48 "sections," remained the heart of the city's political activity. Although the Constituent Assembly attempted to restrict the franchise to the communal assembly, which was the city's official governing body, to so-called active citizens, the section assemblies themselves, open in practice to all comers, were at their best schools of democracy in which, in the words of a contemporary petition, "there reigns that equality, that fraternity of the golden age that our benevolent laws are seeking to restore."

Political activism in the city spilled over into numerous popular clubs and societies, of which the most famous, the Jacobins,* had more than 400 provincial affiliates by 1791 and debated before audiences of up to 2,000. By 1793 half a million people were enrolled in such clubs. Some of them

*So named from their original meeting place in the former convent of the Jacobin order.

functioned as interest groups or embryonic political parties; the Jacobins themselves had originated as a caucus of liberal members of the National Assembly. To such groups were added the *fédérés,* or "federations," spontaneous unions of the municipal councils and militias of the provinces that converged on Paris on the first anniversary of the fall of the Bastille to affirm their loyalty to the revolution. When not gathered in the large crowds and assemblies so characteristic of the revolution, Parisians themselves avidly consumed the scores of newspapers, pamphlets, and petitions that poured forth daily from the press.

One of the first newspapers, *l'Ami du peuple* ("The Friend of the People"), was founded by Count Mirabeau (1742–1791), who, boycotted by his fellow noblemen, had won election as a member of the Third Estate and emerged as a leader of the National Assembly. Other journalists such as Camille Desmoulins and Jean-Paul Marat (1743–1793) won wide public followings and often exercised considerable political influence. Thus was born the modern power of the press, whose nickname, the "Fourth Estate," still attests to its revolutionary origins.

The Parisian sans-culottes were the most radical element in the revolution, in part because of the idealism with which they embraced their first experience of politics and self-government, in part because their concrete interests clashed with those of the bourgeoisie who dominated the Constituent Assembly. The assembly, as we have seen, had sought to deny sans-culottes the vote; by the Le Chapelier law (1791) it had outlawed all workers' unions, and, in a direct confrontation, 15 sans-culottes had been killed in an antimonarchical demonstration on the civic parade ground, the Champs de Mars, in July 1791.

By the summer of 1792 the revolution had reached a new flashpoint. Swept on by a combination of ideological fervor and traditional anti-Habsburg sentiment, the new Legislative Assembly had declared war on Austria in April. It was a disastrous decision. The army was bereft of commanders, two-thirds of its officers (all former nobles) having deserted or quit. The country was in the grip of renewed inflation, in part the result of the government's failure to remove assignats from circulation as church lands were sold off. As their value depreciated, peasants refused to accept them as payment for their crops, creating food shortages and riots. When the war proved a fiasco, the public mood turned grim. Amid a general breakdown of order, there were rumors of counterrevolutionary plots. The Jacobin republicans blamed the failure of their crusade on Louis. How, they demanded, could a war against all kings be led by a king?

By the end of July, 47 of the 48 Paris sections had declared against the monarchy. The city was in an uproar as military recruits from the provinces mingled with the sans-culottes. Agitation was particularly severe in the district of St.-Antoine, whose working-class inhabitants had led the assault on the Bastille. The Jacobin leadership, alarmed by the prospect of a new popular insurrection, now backtracked and offered Louis support. But a more radical faction, led by Maximilien Robespierre, threw its lot in with the crowd. On August 10 Louis and his entourage were driven from the Tuileries by an armed mob, with heavy loss of life. It was an event as crucial as the fall of the Bastille. A new revolutionary council, composed largely of sans-culottes and lesser bourgeoisie, seized control of Paris. The constitution was suspended, the Legislative Assembly was dispersed, and a new National Convention was summoned to create a republic.

The Radical Revolution, 1792–1794

The National Convention, elected by all French males, met on September 20 in an atmosphere of near anarchy. Earlier in the month hysterical mobs had rampaged through the prisons of Paris in search of "counterrevolutionaries," killing between 1,100 and 1,400 inmates, including 37 women. A Prussian army had penetrated deep into northern France and was stopped at Valmy, only 200 miles from Paris, on the very day of the convention's first meeting. The convention had deliberately taken its name in reference to the American constitutional convention, which had written the modern world's first democratic constitution. But Paris in the early autumn of 1792 bore little resemblance to Philadelphia in the summer of 1787.

Reform and Regicide

Nevertheless, the convention set to work undaunted. It not only abolished the monarchy but the calendar, declaring September 22 the first day of Year I of the republic. Later it scrapped the entire Christian calendar of months and days, commissioning a poet, Philippe Fabre d'Églantine, to rename them. Fabre decided to call his months by their seasonal characteristics; thus July 27 was to be the ninth of Thermidor, the month of heat; November 10 became the eighteenth of Brumaire, the month of fog; and so on. The year was to consist of 12 equal months of 30 days each, with five leap days at the end to be celebrated as revolutionary holidays. Each month consisted of three weeks or "decades" of ten days each, which meant, among other things, a nine-day workweek. Saints' days, used for festivity and rest, were eliminated as well. This calendar remained in effect until 1804, although it was never adopted beyond official circles.

The convention's faith in the future was soon repaid. French armies, fired by patriotic ardor and reorganized under officers promoted from the ranks, drove the Austro-Prussian invaders out and swept across the border, occupying Frankfurt and Brussels. In two months they conquered more territory than Louis XIV had in 50 years.

The convention decreed feudal dues and services abolished in all areas occupied by French forces and offered "liberation" to any people wishing it. On February 1, 1793, war was declared on Britain, Spain, and the Dutch Netherlands.

The king remained to be dealt with. Alive, he was a magnet for counterrevolution, and his incriminating correspondence with the Austrians had been discovered. Placed on trial for treason, he was condemned to death by a single vote in the convention, 361 to 360. On January 21, 1793, Louis went to the guillotine. Ten months later, his Austrian queen, Marie Antoinette, followed him.

The revolution now entered its climactic phase. It was a time of great passions and great excesses. The men who ruled France often worked around the clock, facing political, military, and economic crises all at once. At the same time, they were conscious of living at a historic moment and making decisions that would stamp generations to come. Out of what they did, and what they failed to do, came much of the shape of the modern West.

The condemned queen, Marie Antoinette, dressed in a prisoner's smock and ironically crowned with a liberty cap, was sketched by Jacques-Louis David on her way to execution. [Photographie Bulloz]

A satirical print entitled "Exercise of the Rights of Man and of the French Citizen" depicts the violence that erupted at the fall of the monarchy in September 1792. Murder by every means is attempted: shooting, hanging, stabbing, clubbing. The victims in the foreground include a gentlewoman, a bishop, and a child; in the background, a nobleman's house and a church are burning. [Photographie Bulloz]

The center of this activity was the National Convention. Only 286 of its 750 members had served in the previous two assemblies of the revolution, although socially they had the same predominant makeup of lawyers, merchants, businessmen, and officials. Despite the fact that the convention had been created by the insurrection of the sans-culottes, it contained only two workers, a munitions maker and a wool comber. The peasants, who comprised 80 percent of the population, had no representative at all.

Politically, the convention was divided between what had emerged as the two warring factions of the Jacobin club, with the great mass of delegates in the middle. The Girondins, so called because many of their leaders came from the southwest department of the Gironde, had been the war party of the Legislative Assembly, but in the eyes of their opponents their revolutionary purity had been compromised by their attempt to deal with the king the previous summer. The more radical faction was the Montagnards (the "mountain men"), so called because they sat in the upper tiers of the convention, whose base of support was among the sans-culottes of Paris. Their leaders were Robespierre, the journalist Marat, and the worldly politician Georges Danton. The two parties were separated by no great issues or principles. Both accepted the republic, both had shed the king's blood, and both believed in the mission of the revolution to liberate Europe. But the Montagnards proved more adept at riding the tiger of mass politics that the second revolution of August 1792 had unleashed. On June 2, after a spring of military reverses, renewed inflation, and a major royalist uprising in the western region of the Vendée, Robespierre led a purge of Girondist leaders by the sans-culottes.

The Montagnards were now in power, though largely at the sufferance of their working-class allies, who came daily to the convention to harangue them. The sans-culottes demanded, and for the first time got, price controls on bread, flour, and other commodities, as well as a general increase in wages. The speech of the radical street leader and ex-priest Jacques Roux on June 25 was typical:

> **Liberty is nothing but a figment of the imagination when one class can deprive another of food with impunity. Liberty becomes meaningless when the rich exercise the power of life and death over their fellow creatures by means of monopolies. . . . Have you outlawed speculation? No. Have you decreed the death penalty for hoarding? No. Have you defined the limits to the freedom of trade? No. . . . Deputies of the Mountain, why have you not climbed from the third to the ninth floor of the houses of the revolutionary city? You would have been moved by the tears and sighs of an immense population without food and clothing . . . because the laws have been cruel to the poor, because they have been made only by the rich and for the rich . . . [but] the salvation of the people . . . is the supreme law.[2]**

The deputies of the convention were shocked by this oration, because Jacques Roux was telling them that their revolution had accomplished nothing of substance and that liberty without bread was a fraud. Roux was removed bodily from the convention and later committed suicide in prison. But his challenge would remain to haunt the politics of liberal democracy.

Robespierre and the Terror

Maximilien Robespierre now emerged as the most conspicuous figure of the revolution. Robespierre was born in 1758 in the coastal town of Arras, the son of a lawyer and a brewer's daughter. Abandoned by his father at the age of 8, he was raised by aunts and educated in the school of the Oratorian order. Robespierre was nicknamed "the Roman" by his classmates, for both his gravity of manner and his command of Latin. He grew up a reserved and serious young man, followed his father's profession, and became a judge in the local episcopal court. Fond of pets, he kept pigeons but had no close friends. He remained unmarried, and his sister Charlotte kept house for him. Elected to the Estates General in 1789, he caught the eye of Mirabeau, who remarked cynically, "He will go far; he believes everything he says." Above all, Robespierre believed in himself: "You have no idea," he said, "of the power of truth or the energy of innocence when sustained by an imperturbable courage."

Maximilien Robespierre, the leading figure in the National Convention and the principal architect of the Terror. [Mansell Collection]

Robespierre's ability to formulate and even personify the ideals of the revolution brought him to prominence. He lived for the revolution and had no life apart from it. By the end of 1792 he was the dominant figure in the Jacobin club; by the following summer he stood at the forefront of events. The convention had just finished drafting the new Constitution of the Year I. It provided for the most democratic system of government since that of ancient Athens, with a broader definition of natural rights, a ballot based on universal manhood suffrage, and a popular referendum. As Robespierre himself declared, it contained "the essential basis of public happiness." But with foreign armies still pressing against French borders and armed resistance to the government flaring across three-quarters of the country, there was no question of putting it into effect. The convention, like the Constituent Assembly before it, had attempted to govern the country by a system

Robespierre on the Principles of Revolutionary Government

In this, one of his many speeches to the National Convention, Robespierre attempts to define the nature of the revolutionary government.

The defenders of the Republic must adopt Caesar's maxim, for they believe that *nothing has been done as long as anything remains to be done. . . .*

The object of constitutional government is to preserve the Republic; the object of a revolutionary government is to establish it.

Revolution is the war waged by liberty against its enemies; a constitution is that which crowns the edifice of freedom once victory has been won and the nation is at peace.

The revolutionary government has to summon extraordinary activity to its aid precisely because it is at war. It is subjected to less binding and less uniform regulations, because the circumstances in which it finds itself are tempestuous and shifting. . . .

Under a constitutional government little more is required than to protect the individual against the abuses by the state, whereas revolutionary government is obliged to defend the state against the factions that assail it from every quarter.

To good citizens revolutionary government owes the full protection of the state; to the enemies of the people it owes only death.

Source: G. Rudé, ed., *Robespierre* (Englewood Cliffs, N.J.: Prentice-Hall, 1967), pp. 58–59.

of councils and committees. To one of these, a body with rather vague supervisory functions called the Committee of Public Safety, Robespierre was elected on July 27. Galvanized by his presence, it soon became the focal point of the revolution.

Steps were now rapidly taken to put down the revolts in the Vendée and elsewhere. Draconian punishment was meted out to rebels, as at Lyons, where nearly 2,000 people were executed in the wake of a Girondist uprising. So-called representatives on mission, armed with almost unlimited authority, struck terror into the provinces. At the same time, a *levée en masse,* or general conscription of all able-bodied men, was decreed. Of all the acts of the convention, this was perhaps the most significant. War was no longer to be the sport of kings and nobles but the sacred cause of the nation, a mass mobilization of all human and material resources. Young men who could not fight were to make weapons, munitions, clothing, and banners; women were to serve as nurses; elderly men were to make patriotic speeches.

Out of this fevered atmosphere was born the Terror, a systematic attempt to root out and destroy all enemies of the revolution. To catch these enemies, special tribunals were set up and new categories of counterrevolutionary offense established so broad as to include almost everything. A certain Monsieur Blondel was arrested, for example, for "thoughtlessness and indifference," a Citizen Lachapelle because he "did not lose much sleep over the revolution." These denunciations were made not by secret police but by zealous sans-culottes who were genuinely puzzled that anyone could lack enthusiasm for the revolution. Who but an enemy of the republic would not lose sleep over it?

Robespierre defended the Terror in a famous speech: "If the basis of popular government in time of peace is virtue, the basis of popular government in time of revolution is both virtue and terror: virtue without which terror is murderous, terror without which virtue is powerless." Terror was merely inflexible justice applied to the enemies of the people, and so "an emanation of virtue." As Robespierre's young colleague Saint-Just put it more succinctly, "Between the people and its enemies there is only the sword." In the ten months between September 1793 and July 1794 perhaps 300,000 people were arrested and 40,000 executed. Of these, only 15 percent were ex-aristocrats or priests and another 15 percent bourgeois, mostly members of the Girondist resistance in the south. The overwhelming majority were ordinary workers and peasants caught up in the whirlwind of revolutionary self-purification.

The Terror had another aim: to centralize all authority in the revolutionary government and to eliminate all opposition and dissent. By the law of 14 Frimaire (December 4, 1793), all subordinate authorities were placed under the direct control of the Committee of Public Safety, to which they were ordered to report every ten days. All local officials became "national agents," subject to immediate removal by Paris. Committees of surveillance—that is, teams of spies—were placed over government functionaries at every level. The law of 14 Frimaire became the real constitution of France.

The Republic of Virtue

The revolution produced not only a new political apparatus but a new political culture as well, the "Republic of Virtue." Styles of dress, which had indicated differences of social position under the Old Regime, now proclaimed differences of political position as well. The color of one's clothes or the length of one's trousers might touch off a quarrel or even a riot. Even common objects such as plateware, calendars, or playing cards became ways of displaying commitment, and the popular symbols of the revolution—the red, white, and blue ribbons or "cockades" worn on the hat, the liberty trees planted in the tens of thousands all over France—became enduring badges of republican affiliation that long outlived the revolution itself. The government soon began to channel spontaneous activities such as dances and celebrations into organized festivals. These centered at first around mass loyalty oaths but soon became replacements for the old religious festivals on which the regime now frowned. Thus the veneration of the Virgin Mary was deflected into that of the goddess of Liberty, popularly called Marianne, and the worship of the Christian God became that of a Deist supreme being or, even more abstractly, Reason itself. As patriotic outlets, as propaganda forums, and as a means of surveillance, the festivals were no less important than the guillotine in maintaining political discipline.

By the spring of 1794 order had been restored and the armies of the *levée en masse*, 850,000 strong, poured victoriously again into the Low Countries. Yet the Terror, like a mindless machine, ground on. Danton and Desmoulins went to the guillotine for suggesting that too much blood had been shed, the ultra-left Enragés and their leader, Hébert, for complaining that there had been too little. The Enragés were to get their wish. The law of 22 Prairial (June 10) declared spreading rumors and defaming patriots to be capital crimes and limited the Revolutionary Tribunal to two verdicts: acquittal or death. In the next six weeks more people were guillotined in Paris than in the entire preceding year. Even the members of the all-powerful Committee of Public Safety walked in fear of one another, especially of Robespierre. A group of them conspired to denounce him before the convention on 9 Thermidor (July 27). Robespierre attempted to defend himself but was shouted down and arrested. The next day he and Saint-Just were executed.

His enemies called Robespierre a tyrant who sought supreme power for himself. When he participated in the Festival of the Supreme Being, an attempt to set up a Deist god of reason as a revolutionary religion, many were convinced that he aimed to be not merely the dictator of the revolution but its high priest. Yet he never held any title but delegate to the convention, and his estate at his death came to barely 100 livres. A disciple of Rousseau, he believed that he embodied the general will. Among the corrupt and disillusioned, and even at last the horrified, he retained absolute faith in the justness of the revolution. As its tragedy unfolded, he foresaw his own martyrdom. "The founders of the Republic," he wrote, "can only find peace in the tomb."

MADAME ROLAND: A WOMAN IN THE REVOLUTION

Few women not of royal blood came closer to the center of political power in the eighteenth century than Marie-Jeanne Phlipon (1754–1793), better known by her married name, Madame Roland. The daughter of a Parisian engraver, Manon—as family and friends called her—exhibited her gifts early and was taught to read before the age of 4. Profoundly influenced by Rousseau, she found a

Madame Roland, a woman of the revolution. [Photographie Bulloz]

kindred feminine spirit as well in the writings of Madame de Sévigné. The American Revolution fired her enthusiasm as a war against kings, and she followed its progress eagerly. At about the same time, she composed an essay deploring the gulf between the rich and the poor in France, the absence of representative government, and the monarchy's use of force to stifle dissent, which, in a prophetic phrase, she denounced as a "reign of terror." In revolution alone did the 20-year-old Manon see any hope for her country's future.

In 1780 Manon married Jean-Marie Roland de la Platière, the inspector of manufactures for the province of Picardy, 20 years her senior. With characteristic frankness, the young bride described her wedding night as "surprising and disagreeable," but a daughter, Eudora, soon resulted from the union. Madame Roland threw herself into her husband's career, collaborating on his technical studies and polishing his awkward literary style. When Roland was transferred to Lyons, she was appalled at the condition of the local peasantry, tending so assiduously to the sick among them that Roland feared for her own health.

From the moment the revolution began in 1789 Madame Roland lived for little else. She chafed at her provincial isolation, wrote to warn her friends in Paris of the reactionary tendencies of the smaller cities, and urged from the beginning the abolition of the monarchy. The Rolands returned to Paris in 1791, where Manon, with her vivacity, ambition, and charm, created a salon that attracted such figures as Robespierre and Tom Paine. Roland became minister of the interior and a member of the war party led by his patron, Jacques Brissot. In June 1792 he delivered a letter to the king, actually written by Manon, demanding that he revoke his veto of the legislation against nonjuring priests. Louis responded by dismissing Roland, and the entire Girondist ministry soon fell. This triggered an attack on the royal palace and, following a summer of heated intrigue in which Madame Roland took an active part, the fall of the monarchy, the September massacres, and the summoning of the National Convention.

When it was moved in the convention that Roland be invited to resume his ministry, Georges Danton, a political opponent, suggested that the invitation be extended to Madame Roland as well. The convention, knowing her influence, burst into laughter. But Roland's star was already on the wane, while Manon, appalled by the September massacres and now deeply distrustful of Robespierre, began to waver for the first time in her belief in the revolution. She so triumphantly acquitted herself of charges of conspiring with royalist émigrés that she received a standing ovation from the convention, but six months later she was arrested in the coup of May 31, 1793. Imprisoned for five months, she hastily composed her memoirs, knowing that she would be permitted no other defense. Condemned and executed on the same day, November 8, she showed great courage and composure on the scaffold, and uttered before the guillotine fell what have come down as the most famous words of the French Revolution: "O Liberty, what crimes are committed in thy name!" Roland, who had gone into hiding, committed suicide at the news of her execution.

Madame Roland was a heroic figure to nineteenth-century historians, with their tendency to idealize women of passion and character. Her powers were not always matched by her judgment, but her integrity was unquestioned, and her career was astonishing and unprecedented. Not until the emergence of organized feminist politics in the late nineteenth century would any woman put a comparable stamp on the events of her time.

Conquest and Reaction, 1795–1799

The fall of Robespierre was followed by a sharp swing to the right, known as the Thermidorian reaction. Men were tired of terror and virtue alike. Political opportunists, money men, and speculators abounded. Aristocratic styles and even sentiments returned to fashion among the *jeunesse dorée,* or "gilded youth," of the bourgeoisie. Ex-Robespierrists in the provinces were purged by a semiofficial White Terror that rapidly degenerated into a brutal settling of scores with radicals in general. The democratic Constitution of the Year I was shelved for good, and with surviving Girondists readmitted to the convention, a new constitution was devised in 1795 that reinstated the old system of electors, with a property qualification so high that only 20,000 men in France met the test. The electors chose all department officials and a new Legislative Assembly, which in turn chose a five-member executive, the Directory, from which the new regime was to take its name. As a precaution against future reprisal, the convention decreed that two-thirds of the new assembly must be made up of its own members.

These events spelled final defeat for the sans-culottes. The convention removed economic controls, prices skyrocketed, and the bread ration was cut to 2 ounces a day. Concluding not unreasonably that they were being deliberately starved into submission, the sans-culottes stormed the convention in May 1795, crying, "Bread or death!" It was less a demand than a simple statement. But loyal units of the National Guard dispersed them, and, leaderless, they were henceforth spent as a political force.

Despite this, however, the Directory was inherently unstable. It had neither the ideological attraction of Jacobinism nor the traditional appeal of monarchy. It was particularly vulnerable to attacks from royalists, who denounced its bourgeois leadership as a would-be aristocracy without the courage to choose its king. A royalist uprising in October was put down only by the presence of mind of a decommissioned young brigadier of artillery named Napoleon Bonaparte who happened to be in Paris at the time, but the threat remained. When elections in April 1797 produced startling gains for the right, the results were annulled, and the Directory declared that anyone advocating either the monarchy or the democratic constitution of 1793 would be shot on sight. With this, it shed its last pretense to legitimacy. What remained was simply a cabal in search of a strongman.

Despite its difficulties at home, the revolution went militarily from success to success abroad. Its conquering armies annexed the Austrian Netherlands, the left bank of the Rhine, and the Mediterranean principalities of Nice and Savoy to France outright and turned the proud Dutch republic into a satellite state after exacting an indemnity of 100 million livres. A daring foray by Napoleon in 1796 produced a string of new satellite republics in Italy, all grandiloquently named: the Cisalpine (Milan), the Ligurian (Genoa), the Roman (the Papal States), and the Parthenopean (Naples). The Swiss cantons were also herded into a so-called Helvetic Republic. Austria was compelled to recognize these conquests, as well as the annexation of its province in the Netherlands, by the Treaty of Campo Formio (October 1797). As a sop, the Austrians received Venice, thus extinguishing the independence of Europe's oldest republic.

Propped up by this success, the Directory drifted on for two more years. But the outbreak of war again in 1799 made a strong government imperative. A group led by the Abbé Sieyès put forward Napoleon Bonaparte, whose rapid rise to military prominence seemed to make him an ideal front man for a reorganized and strengthened executive. A coup in November 1799 ousted the Directory and dispersed the Legislative Assembly. It was the eighth major change of power in the revolution. Napoleon rapidly dispensed with his civilian allies and assumed complete power. For the next 15 years he governed France alone as first consul, consul for life, and finally emperor of the French. The revolution was over.

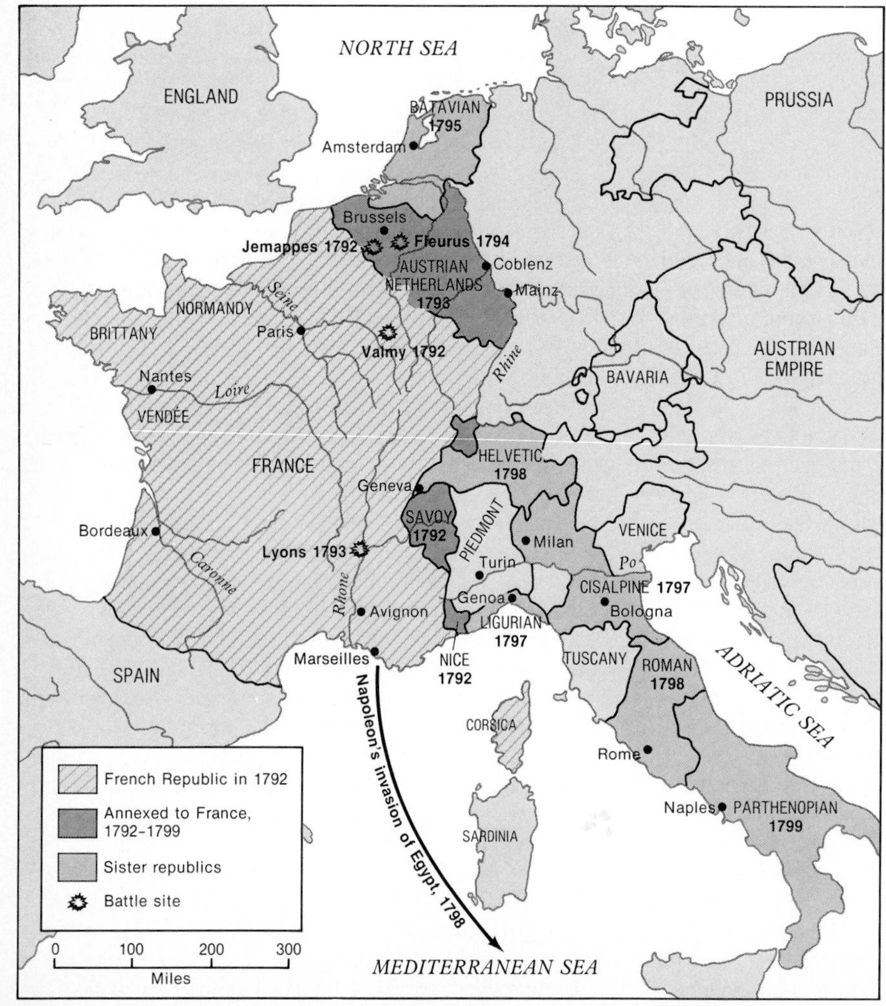

26.2 The Expansion of Revolutionary France, 1792–1799

The Legacy of the Revolution: Conflicting Interpretations

The men and women who experienced the French revolution can be broadly classified into three groups. Some wished it had never occurred and wanted only to turn the clock back before 1789; some were satisfied with their gains at a given point and wished it to go no further; and some felt that it had not yet accomplished its task. The first group was composed chiefly of the nobility and the nonjuring clergy, the second of the peasants and the bourgeoisie, and the third of the sans-culottes and their allies among the liberal nobility and bourgeoisie. From these differing attitudes emerged the right, center, and left of nineteenth-century European politics.

Historians too, depending on their own political sympathies, have seen in the revolution either a great calamity, a necessary adjustment to changing circumstances, or a vision of social justice as yet unrealized. The first view was best represented in the nineteenth century by Hippolyte Taine (1828–1893), who feared a new revolution in his own time and wished to warn his fellow countrymen of the evils he felt it would unleash, and in more modern form by J. L. Talmon, who saw in the revolution a false dream of secular salvation that could lead only to tyranny. The second view is identified with Alexis de Tocqueville (1805–1859), who argued in his highly influential *The Old Regime and the French Revolution* (1856) that the revolution was not so much a break with the Old Regime as a development of the tendencies toward centralization and bureaucracy already inherent in it. From this perspective, the constructive work of the revolution was essentially complete by 1791, and the radical or Jacobin phase was an aberration caused by the instability of the constitutional monarchy that the Constituent Assembly had attempted to set up.

The third view, associated with the work of Jules Michelet (1798–1874) and, later, Albert Mathiez and Albert Soboul, argues to the contrary that the Jacobin republic was the climax of the revolution, which by exposing the hollowness of a formal political equality unaccompanied by a redistribution of the wealth on which actual political power depends set the agenda for modern mass politics and the demand for social justice. This view was first put forward during the revolution itself by the left-wing ideologue and conspirator Gracchus Babeuf (1760–1797), who predicted in his *Manifesto of the Equals* (1796) that "the French Revolution is but the forerunner of another, far more grand, far more solemn, which will be the last."

The group least satisfied by the revolution was women, particularly those of the urban working class. Although women bore the brunt of the revolution's hardships at all times and at least at one point, in the march on Versailles in October 1789, played a critical role in events, their interests were not addressed by any of the dominant factions of the revolution. Very few were in the position of Madame Roland, whose salon was a center of revolution-

A Revolutionary's Plea for the Rights of Women

In On the Admission of Women to the Rights of Citizenship, *the marquis de Condorcet, one of the few French noblemen to give his unqualified support to the revolution, chided the authorities for failing to provide for the rights of women as well as those of men.*

Is there a stronger proof of the power of habit, even among enlightened men, than to hear the principle of equality invoked in favor of 300 or 400 men deprived of their rights by an absurd prejudice [against counting all votes in the Estates General equally] and forgotten in the case of some 12 million women? . . .

Women are superior to men in the gentle and domestic virtues. Like men, they know how to love liberty, although they do not share all its advantages; and in republics they have often been known to sacrifice themselves for it. They have demonstrated the virtues of citizens whenever chance or civil troubles have brought them upon a scene from which the pride and the tyranny of men have excluded them in all nations.

Source: Marquis de Condorcet, *Selected Writings*, ed. K. M. Baker (Indianapolis: Bobbs-Merrill, 1976), pp. 97, 99.

ary intrigue; most spent their days on ration lines, often to receive spoiled or unpalatable goods, or nothing at all. Women and children were the first to succumb to starvation or malnutrition, as local records clearly show, and one can only imagine the desperation of the mothers of Masannay who in May 1794 demanded the elimination of all people over 60 so that the young might be fed enough to survive. When the women of Paris tried to organize their own clubs, they were shut down by the procurator of the Commune, who observed that sans-culottes had a right to expect their wives to keep house while they attended political meetings.

The legacy of the revolution remains a matter of debate among historians as they continue to discuss the precise composition of the groups we call "bourgeois," "aristocratic," and "sans-culotte," to study the complex interactions and alliances among these groups, and the relationship between Paris and the countryside and between France and Europe. There are still many questions to be answered about the actual redistribution of land, wealth, and power in the revolution; about the functioning of revolutionary institutions, especially outside Paris, and the effect of those institutions on conquered territories abroad. Some conclusions, however, seem unlikely to be seriously modified.

The revolution destroyed the localism of Old Regime France, welding it into a single political and economic unit and opening it to the forces of market capitalism while giving impetus to similar developments elsewhere. It produced the first citizen army of modern times and showed for the first time what an entire society mobilized for war and driven by ideology could achieve. It introduced modern mass politics and made the sovereignty of the people, already proclaimed in America, the fundamental legitimating principle of Western governments. It also introduced in the name of the people the suspension of all legal rights and forms and the elimination of all dissent by genocide, a practice that began with the Jacobins but was equally characteristic of the Directory and has since become an increasingly casual weapon of modern regimes. In that respect the revolution may be said to have opened up the Pandora's box of modern politics in which, as the Russian novelist Feodor Dostoevsky remarked, "everything is permitted." But it also, like Pandora, gave the great mass of the human race what it had never had before except from religion: hope.

The Napoleonic Era

It was not immediately clear that Napoleon's coup d'état would be very different from the previous changes of government of the past ten years, let alone that it would usher in a new era both for France and for Europe. As Napoleon slowly but firmly drew the reins of power into his own hands, however, and as his campaigns of conquest brought more and more of the continent under French sway, it became apparent that France had a master, and Europe a ruler, such as neither had known before.

From Republic to Empire

The Abbé Sieyès had brought Napoleon to power under the slogan, "Confidence from below, authority from above." Napoleon took the slogan and dropped his ally. Born in 1769 into a family of impoverished minor nobility on the island of Corsica, he was barely 30 when he became master of France. Italian by descent (Napoleon dropped the *u* in the family name Buonaparte when he invaded Italy in 1796), he was French only by virtue of Corsica's annexation to France in 1768, and his first adventure was fighting for his island's independence in 1789. Soon swept up in the revolution on the mainland, he gained notice by taking the royalist port of Toulon in 1793, and after the stroke of luck that put him in Paris during the revolt of October 1795, he became a central figure in the political upheavals of the Directory. His brilliant campaign in Italy made him the man of the hour, and despite the failure of a campaign against the British in Egypt in 1798, his reputation was undimmed.

Napoleon promulgated a new constitution, which created an enfeebled legislature whose three chambers could respectively debate, enact, and veto laws but do nothing together and centralized executive authority in the hands of three "consuls." Napoleon took the title of first consul, with full authority to appoint all officials and magistrates, conduct diplomacy, declare and wage war, and protect the public safety. Napoleon had vowed to keep the republic, but all that remained of it was a facade. The powers he gave himself made him an uncrowned king. In a masterful stroke of public relations, he submitted the constitution to a popular referendum, although he had already proclaimed it in effect. The result was predictably lopsided, with 3,011,007 votes counted for and 1,562 against. Napoleon could now claim his "mandate" from the people. In 1802 he extended the term of his consulship from ten years to life, and in 1804, after making peace with the church, he assumed the title of emperor. Both acts were ratified by popular referendum, but for his coronation Napoleon summoned Pope Pius VII to Paris, and in a gesture deliberately reminiscent of Charlemagne's at his coronation as Holy Roman emperor 1,000 years before, he took the crown from the pontiff's hands and placed it on his own head. Shortly afterward he created an aristocracy, mostly from the upper bourgeoisie. The revolution against kings, priests, and nobles had come full circle.

Napoleon ruled through propaganda, press censorship, a highly efficient secret police, and, on occasion, acts of political terrorism such as the kidnapping and execution of the young Bourbon duke of Enghien in 1804. Yet his popularity was genuine, and he enjoyed the broad support of all classes almost to the end. Only diehard royalists and

Napoleon on Himself

Napoleon's boundless ego and lack of ethical principles are clearly reflected in his many statements, a sample of which follow.

My policy is to govern men the way the great majority wants to be governed. This, I believe, is the only way in which it is possible to acknowledge the sovereignty of the people. By making myself Catholic I brought the war in the Vendée to an end. By becoming a Muslim I established myself in Egypt. By acting ultramontane I won the minds of the Italians. If I governed a nation of Jews, I should restore the temple of Solomon. Thus I shall talk freedom in the free part of Santo Domingo; I shall confirm slavery in the Île de France and even in the slave part of Santo Domingo—with the reservation that I shall soften and limit slavery wherever I maintain it and shall restore order and discipline wherever I maintain freedom.

You must know that I am not in the least afraid of committing an act of cowardice if it were useful to me. Look here, at bottom there is nothing either noble or base in this world. My character possesses all those qualities that are capable of strengthening my power and of deceiving those who imagine that they know me. Frankly, I am a coward, indeed I am—essentially a coward. I give you my word of honor that I would not experience the least repugnance toward committing what the world calls a dishonorable action.

Don't talk to me of goodness, of abstract justice, of natural law. Necessity is the highest law; public welfare is the highest justice. Unto each day the evil thereof; to each circumstance its own law; each man according to his own nature.

Source: J. C. Herold, ed. and trans., *The Mind of Napoleon* (New York: Columbia University Press, 1955), pp. 79, 160.

republicans refused to accept him. Simply stated, Napoleon gave the rich what they wanted, the poor what they would accept, and, through an unprecedented career of conquest, a measure of glory to everyone such as Louis XIV had only dreamed of.

Napoleon centralized political control as thoroughly as the Jacobins had ever done in the days of the Terror. All officials from the lowest level were responsible to the national state and ultimately the emperor himself through a clear chain of command. The judiciary, declared independent in 1791, was brought back under executive control. The economy was similarly taken in hand. Napoleon applied price controls as he saw fit, promoted new industry, and built an extensive network of roads and canals. The Bank of France was chartered in 1800 to free the government from reliance on private credit. Thus the French began to catch up with the fiscal system developed by the English more than a century before.

Napoleon capped his reforms with the Civil Code of 1804, known, with later additions and modifications, as the Napoleonic Code. The code was the culmination of efforts to produce a digest of French legal and administrative principles dating back to the sixteenth century, and it became the most influential code of secular law outside the Anglo-Saxon tradition since Roman times. The main principles of the early revolution—civil and legal equality, religious toleration, and the abolition of feudal obligations and legally privileged orders—were confirmed. Beneath the veneer of formal equality, however, the code envisioned a hierarchical society based on subordination to wealth and gender. The emphasis, as in the Old Regime, was on the flow of authority downward from the state to the patriarchal family. Women were enjoined to obey their husbands and prevented from acquiring property without written consent and from administering joint property. Children might be imprisoned for up to six months on the mere word of their father and had to gain his consent to marry up to the age of 30. A similar hierarchy was established in the workplace; for example, the word of an employer automatically prevailed over that of a worker in court. The code was extremely detailed in its guarantees of property rights and its provisions for contracts and debts, but as for labor, denied as before the right of association, it was merely "free"—free to survive or perish as market conditions might dictate.

Napoleon's other major settlement was with the church. By the Concordat of 1801, the Vatican recognized the confiscation of its lands and tithes as permanent, thereby accepting the role of the clergy as salaried employees of the state. It even consented to a catechism in which disobedience to Napoleon was declared to be grounds for eternal damnation, something no divine right monarch had ever succeeded in making a part of religious instruction. Napoleon himself had no religious convictions whatever. "I was a Muslim in Egypt," he remarked in a famous moment of candor; "I shall be a Catholic here for the good of the people . . . and had I to govern a nation of Jews I would rebuild Solomon's temple." In return for his concessions, the pope was recognized as head of the church, and Catholicism was declared to be the religion "of the majority of Frenchmen." By this careful formulation, Napoleon stopped short of making Catholicism the official state church, thus preserving the principle of religious toleration; yet it served that function in effect. With the Concordat, the empire, and the code, his structure of authority was complete.

France Against Europe

Napoleon inherited command of the war France had been fighting since 1792, which by 1815 ranged over the entire globe and brought such consequences as the conquest of India, the liberation of South America, and the doubling of the size of the United States. Despite its complexity, however, it had, like the wars of Louis XIV a century before, a single dominant element: the containment of France.

The French had gone to war in 1792 to extend the revolution abroad and to maintain its momentum at home. By 1795 this initial enthusiasm was largely spent, and the French pursued the war for more traditional imperial and commercial goals. They were opposed by a shifting coalition whose only stable member was Great Britain. The Continental powers were slow at first to react to the French threat. Informed military opinion, far from considering France a menace, dismissed the revolutionary army as a leaderless mob. It was a measure of their preoccupation with more important matters, such as the partition of Poland, that Austria and Prussia did not even think this defenseless France worth attacking and confined themselves at first to diplomatic gestures such as the Declaration of Pillnitz.

The success of French forces took Europe wholly by surprise. No one had ever seen an army like this, which broke all the rules of military practice yet kept on winning. New recruits picked up their training on the march, discipline was negligible, and supplies were always short. Promotions were made on the basis of merit rather than birth: Napoleon's marshals included former coopers, millers, masons, and stable boys. Their average age was about 30; most of Prussia's generals were over 60.

But Europe could not long tolerate a French frontier that ran from the North Sea to the Ionian. Backed by British money and Russian troops, a second coalition drove the French back on a broad front in 1799. If the original revolutionary impetus of the French army was exhausted, however, it was now replaced by an equally powerful force: Napoleon's own dream of world empire. Napoleon smashed the Austrians at Hohenlinden and Marengo, forcing them to sue for peace (Treaty of Lunéville, 1801) on even worse terms than at Campo Formio, and with the fall of the 18-year ministry of William Pitt the Younger, the son of the hero of the Seven Years' War, the British made a reluctant peace at Amiens in 1802.

Full-scale war resumed in 1805 with Britain, again under Pitt, subsidizing Russian troops to the tune of £1,250,000 per each 100,000 recruits. But at Ulm on October 15 an Austrian army, completely outgeneraled, surrendered without firing a shot, and six weeks later, on the first anniversary of his coronation (December 2), Napoleon won the greatest of all his battles over a combined Austro-Russian force at Austerlitz. Prussia, neutral since 1795, blundered into war alone in 1806, only to have its reputedly invincible army destroyed in two simultaneous battles 12 miles apart at Jena and Auerstadt. The French now pursued Russia along the Baltic shore into East Prussia, where after bloody battles at Eylau (February 1807) and Friedland (June), Tsar Alexander I (1796–1825) too offered peace. Napoleon was unsuccessful only at sea, where his plan for invading Britain was dashed by the fleet under Lord Horatio Nelson at Cape Trafalgar off the coast of Spain. Nelson sank or captured 18 French ships without the loss of a vessel but was himself slain in the battle.

The Grand Empire

European politics had long been predicated on maintaining a balance of power between its major states. This principle was formally incorporated into the Peace of Utrecht (1713), and it appeared so self-evident to eighteenth-century commentators that one even likened it to gravity as a law of nature. The French Revolution had challenged it with the idea that all states might be compelled to respect natural rights, if necessary by force. Napoleon openly rejected the balance of power. "Europe," he declared, "cannot be at rest except under a single head who will have kings for his officers." Clearly he saw himself as that head.

After the defeat of the Third Coalition in 1805, Napoleon began to construct his Grand Empire. The debris of petty German principalities was swept away, to be replaced by the Confederation of the Rhine, a satellite entity whose 38 members acknowledged Napoleon as their protector and agreed to furnish troops for his army. The 1,000-year-old Holy Roman Empire, once the symbol of German nationality and latterly of Austrian domination, was summarily abolished in 1806. Only Prussia retained its nominal independence, but shorn of half its territory and with its army reduced to a mere 42,000 men. Prussian Poland was reconstituted as the Grand Duchy of Warsaw, another satellite. Napoleon created a kingdom of Italy for his stepson Eugène, later annexing some of it to France and imprisoning Pius VII when he objected to the occupation of the Papal States. Similarly, a kingdom of Holland was created for Napoleon's brother Louis but absorbed outright four years later. Using his siblings essentially as prefects, Napoleon made his brother Jérome king of the German satellite of Westphalia in 1807 and his brother Joseph king of Spain in 1808, deposing the reigning Bourbon dynasty.

By the time this structure of satellite kingdoms was complete, however, Napoleon considered it obsolete. National entities, even ruled as the private preserve of the emperor's own family, were still too insubordinate, too conscious of their separate historical identities. As the Constituent Assembly had abolished the old provinces of France, so Napoleon decided to abolish the nations of Europe, replacing them with a single imperial administration. But events overtook him, and this last design was never carried out.

The Napoleonic Code was used as the basis of administration in the Grand Empire, from whence its influence spread throughout Europe and beyond, reaching places as far distant as Bolivia, Egypt, and Japan. By abolishing serfdom, dissolving the Old Regime system of orders, and introducing public education, it opened careers in commerce, industry, and government to men of talent. If the code represented the revolution at its least liberal, it was still often startlingly new and progressive elsewhere in Europe, and its importance as a solvent of feudal structures and as a model of modern society can scarcely be exaggerated.

Despite the order and prosperity Napoleonic government introduced, it provoked reactions ranging from passive resistance to outright rebellion everywhere. The chief common grievance was the Continental System, an attempt by Napoleon to close the ports of the empire to British commerce. This exposed such ports to reprisals by the British, who wholly dominated the seas, as well as to a counterblockade that had a crippling effect on European commerce. The deeper reason for resentment, however, was the suppression of national culture in the subject territories, the dominance of French officials and the presence of French troops and police, and the exploitation of the wealth and resources of a continent for the benefit of a single nation and ultimately a single family. In the Dutch Netherlands, where French aggression had been resisted for centuries, the occupation was particularly severe. The use of Dutch was discouraged, and all books were rigidly censored. Unhappy Westphalia rebelled no fewer than seven times against Napoleonic rule, while Rome bitterly resented the humiliation of the papacy. But by far the most serious resistance came from Spain. Spaniards of all classes rose up spontaneously against the French occupation and waged a fierce guerrilla war for six years whose atrocities were recorded for all time by the painter Francisco Goya. Spain was the stanchless wound in Napoleon's side. He thought that 20,000 men could hold the country; ten times that many failed. A British army under Arthur Wellesley, later duke of Wellington, linked up with the Spaniards through Portugal in what came to be known as the Peninsular War. By early 1814 southern France itself was under attack. The war ended with the British in Toulouse.

A more lasting effect of the Napoleonic occupation was the stimulation of national feeling, particularly in Italy and

"And They Are Like Wild Beasts." Spanish women, virtually unarmed, give battle to Napoleon's troops in this print from Goya's series of etchings *Disasters of War*. No other artist has ever captured so directly the naked ferocity of war. [Metropolitan Museum of Art, Rogers Fund, 1922]

Germany. Passed from hand to hand since the sixteenth century, Italy had been parceled out in bits and pieces to in-laws and even cabinet ministers by Napoleon. But despite heavy taxes and a general distaste for the French presence, Italian commerce and industry benefited from the abolition of tariff barriers, the building of new roads, and the introduction of uniform weights and measures. It is significant that many of the future leaders of the movement for Italian unification were descended from families that became rich under Napoleon. These new industrialists and financiers were not prepared to return to the inefficiencies of the traditional economy after 1815, and they chafed under its reimposition.

National consciousness had been promoted in eighteenth-century Germany by the philosopher Johann Gottfried von Herder, who argued that each people had a separate and unique historical destiny shaped by its *Volksgeist,* or inner spirit. But most German intellectuals of the Enlightenment prided themselves on a lofty cosmopolitanism instead. Their ideal was the tiny, idyllic dukedom of Weimar, whose ruler, Karl August (1775–1828), had gathered around him a brilliant court crowned by the great poet Goethe. They despised Prussian militarism in particular, and many initially welcomed the Napoleonic invasion; on the eve of the Battle of Jena the philosopher Hegel, himself a Prussian, wrote, "As I [did] formerly, now everybody wishes success to the French army."

The collapse and dismemberment of the Prussian state changed all that. Defeat brought Prussia what victory never had: a sense of nationhood. As French troops paraded through the streets of Berlin, the philosopher and publicist Johann Gottlieb Fichte (1762–1814) delivered a series of "addresses to the German nation" in which he argued that the German Volksgeist was intrinsically superior and must protect itself from contamination by outside cultures. Fichte denounced the petty sectionalism of German politics and called for a national movement to drive out the French oppressor. The dramatist Friedrich von Schiller also preached national liberation in his patriotic odes and plays, and freedom from oppression was the thinly veiled message of Beethoven's opera *Fidelio*. In Prussia itself, meanwhile, the crown ministers Baron Stein and Prince Hardenburg initiated significant land reforms, including the abolition of serfdom, liberalization of land tenures, and the reform of the bureaucracy.

For the moment, however, liberation seemed far away. From the Atlantic to the Polish steppe, from the Baltic to the Mediterranean, Napoleon ruled or dominated the whole of Europe. A swollen France itself stretched from the north German port of Lübeck to south of Rome. When Austria, which like Prussia had been reduced to dependent status, rebelled in 1809 and called on the former states of the Holy Roman Empire to assist it, not a single one responded. The Habsburg army was quickly crushed at Wagram, and it was now Vienna's turn to entertain a triumphal parade of French troops.

Yet Napoleon's empire was inherently unstable. As the flush of idealism and reform it had borrowed from the revolution wore away, the cynical and exploitive nature of its administration was increasingly apparent. It preached human equality but demanded permanent subjection. It violated the entire history and tradition of the European state system. It was not even in the interest of France, whose distended borders now resembled a jaw open on the whole continent. As early as 1808 Napoleon's foreign minister, Talleyrand, had made secret overtures to Tsar Alexander. Even at the height of the empire, Talleyrand did not believe it would last.

Napoleon himself was aware of the weakness of his position. He became obsessed with founding a dynasty. When his first wife, Joséphine de Beauharnais, failed to provide him with an heir, he divorced her in favor of Princess Marie-Louise of Austria. In 1811 she bore him a son, whom Napoleon grandly called the king of Rome. But nothing could obscure the fact that Napoleon, who had so often humiliated Austria, felt compelled to buy legitimacy by mixing his blood with that of the Habsburgs.

The Collapse of the Napoleonic Order

Of the major states of Europe, only Britain and Russia remained outside the Grand Empire. Britain continued its struggle with Napoleon alone, resulting in a war with the United States over its naval blockade of the Continent in 1812. Russia, by contrast, was formally a French ally. By the Treaty of Tilsit (1807), which the tsar and the emperor had negotiated in person on a barge in the middle of the Niemen River, Alexander agreed to join the Continental System if his efforts to mediate between Britain and France failed, and he also accepted French intercession in his conflict with the Turkish sultan. Superficially, this seemed to be an agreement between equals to assist each other in disputes with their neighbors; in reality, it obliged the tsar to recognize the Napoleonic order while giving Napoleon an entrée into a traditional Russian sphere of interest.

An uneasy truce prevailed for the next five years, as both sides probed for each other's weaknesses. Alexander attempted to gain control of the Grand Duchy of Warsaw, which under Napoleonic rule was a dagger pointed at Russia itself. Napoleon in turn sought influence in Constantinople, which he regarded as the "center of world empire," an empire presumably to be controlled by himself.

When Russia reopened trade with Britain and erected tariffs against French goods, Napoleon resolved on war. In June 1812 he crossed the Niemen into Russia with over 600,000 men, the largest army ever assembled for a single campaign. Napoleon envisaged a quick victory. His troops carried only four days' rations and the supply convoys

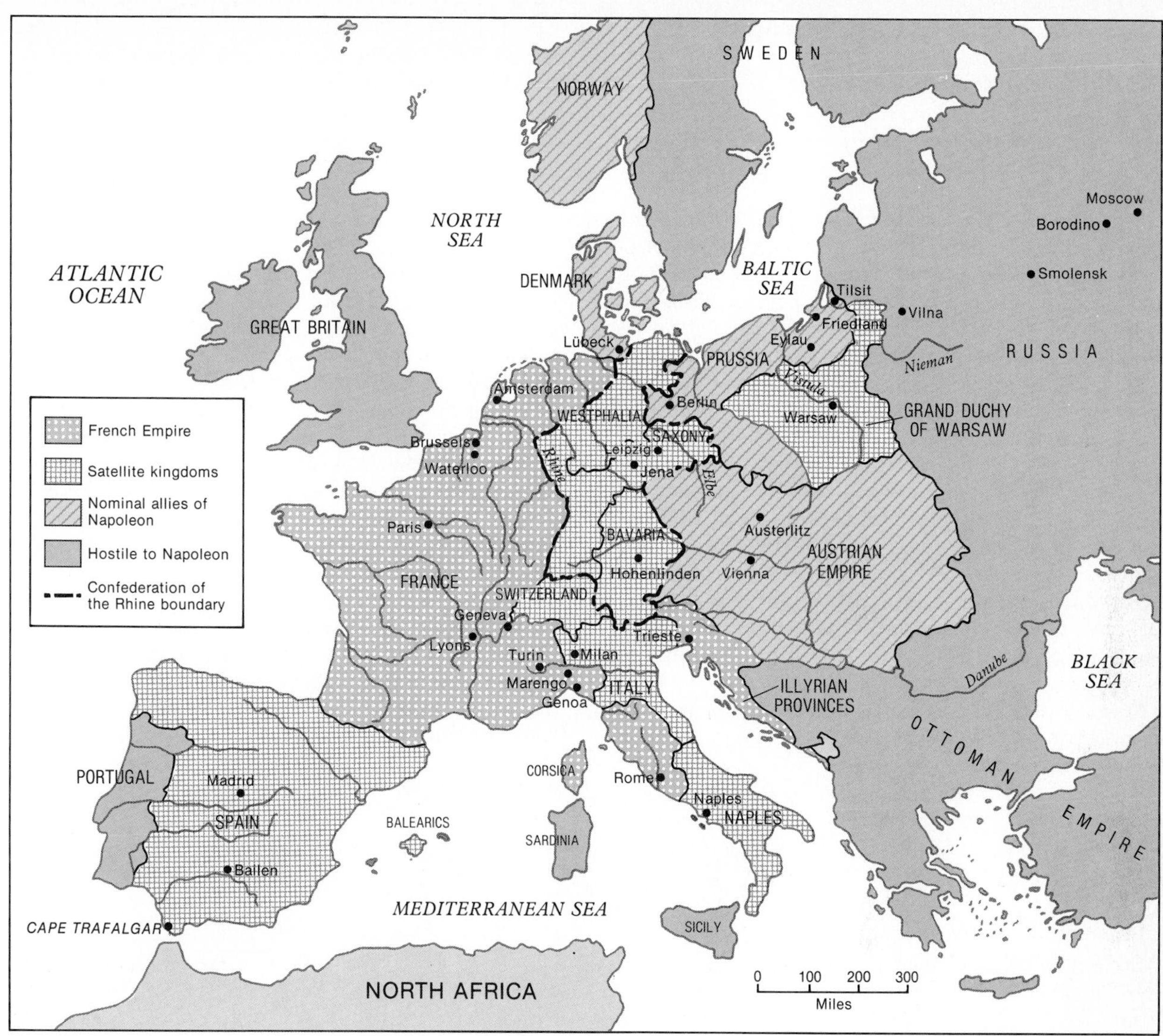

26.3 Europe in 1810

three weeks' more. But the Russians gave ground instead of fighting, leaving behind only scorched earth. They surrendered Moscow after an indecisive but bloody battle at Borodino, and Napoleon entered it unopposed on September 14. What had been a city of 300,000 was all but deserted. Fires had already begun, and within a week three-quarters of it had burned down. Without food or shelter, Napoleon could not winter in the devastated city. On October 19 he began a retreat. Mired in snow and mud, dogged by Russian sappers, his army laid a 1,000-mile track of corpses along its way. More than half a million men died, deserted, or disappeared.

Abandoning his army to its fate, Napoleon raced back to Paris. He raised a new army of 250,000 to face a revived coalition of Russia, Prussia, Austria, and Sweden, with Britain as usual footing the bill. After several indecisive victories, he was defeated outside Leipzig in the great three-day Battle of the Nations (October 1813) and thrown back upon France. The Austrian foreign minister, Count Klemens von Metternich, alarmed at Prussia's new nationalism and eager to have the Russians out of Europe, offered to guarantee the French borders of 1792, including the former Austrian Netherlands and the left bank of the Rhine. Napoleon refused. For the emperor of the French, the only stakes were all or nothing. Allied armies now poured into France from Belgium, the middle Rhine, and Switzerland, with Wellington attacking from the south. Napoleon's defensive campaign was the most brilliant of his career, but the result was foregone. On April 4, 1814, he abdicated as emperor in favor of his 3-year-old son, a day after his Senate had deposed him.

The Bourbon Restoration

The victorious allies, aided by Talleyrand, restored the Bourbon dynasty in the person of Louis XVIII, count of Provence,* who signed the Treaty of Paris on May 30 that ended France's 22-year war with Europe. Wishing to support the new monarch, the allies demanded no indemnities or reparations. France was simply required to return to its prewar boundaries. Even Napoleon was treated leniently. He was exiled to the island of Elba off the west coast of Italy but permitted to retain the title of emperor and granted a pension of 2 million francs a year.

Louis XVIII was in theory an absolute king, but he confirmed the revolutionary land settlement and the Napoleonic Code and issued a Constitutional Charter that provided for a bicameral assembly chosen by a restricted suffrage of large landowners. But thousands of vengeful émigrés returned with him who would be satisfied by nothing less than a complete restoration of the Old Regime.

*The son of Louis XVI, who died in prison at the age of 10 without ever reigning, was recognized as Louis XVII.

The activities of these Ultraroyalists, or Ultras, as they were popularly called, together with economic depression and the inevitable letdown from the excitement of Napoleon's reign, cost the Bourbon regime whatever credibility it had. Napoleon, sensing his opportunity, returned with a small flotilla and with 1,000 veterans marched unopposed on Paris. The Bourbons fled to Belgium, and the emperor declared himself restored "by the unanimous wish of a great nation."

The allies, who had gathered in Vienna to discuss the settlement of postwar Europe, promptly declared Napoleon a public outlaw. Napoleon himself, courting support at home, made conciliatory gestures both to the right and to the left. But only a trial by battle could reestablish him. Raising an army, he crossed into Belgium, where on June 18, 1815, he met a combined force under the duke of Wellington and the Prussian general Gerhard von Blücher at Waterloo on the road to Brussels and was defeated in daylong combat. Returning to Paris, he was met with a stony demand for abdication. His second reign had lasted exactly 100 days.

Napoleon was now exiled to St. Helena, a bleak, tiny island in the south Atlantic, 4,000 miles from Europe, where in 1821 he died of stomach cancer. His legend lived on in France, where a veritable cult grew up around him that was climaxed by the return and reentombment of his body in 1840.

Napoleon himself said that the man of genius is a meteor who illuminates his time but does not transform it. Talleyrand, who knew him as well as anyone, thought that he had squandered an opportunity to create a lasting political equilibrium in Europe. Yet Napoleon did leave a permanent legacy. His code became the basis of modern French society. His conquests stimulated both anti-French nationalism and aspirations for a liberal society on the French model. His suppression of the Holy Roman Empire was the first step toward the unification of Germany. If the ideas he spread were those of the revolution rather than his own, they might never have traveled as far as they did without him. Napoleon failed to make Europe a province of France, but he did much to make the French Revolution European.

Notes

1. J. H. Stewart, *A Documentary Survey of the French Revolution* (New York: Macmillan, 1951), p. 42 (modified slightly).
2. R. Zaller, *Europe in Transition, 1660–1815* (New York: Harper & Row, 1984), p. 130.

Suggestions for Further Reading

Bergeron, L. *France Under Napoleon.* Princeton, N.J.: Princeton University Press, 1981.

Blanning, T. C. W. *The Origins of the French Revolutionary Wars.* London: Longman, 1986.

Cobb, R. C. *The People's War.* New Haven, Conn.: Yale University Press, 1987.

Cobban, A. *The Social Interpretation of the French Revolution.* Cambridge: Cambridge University Press, 1964.

Doyle, W. *Origins of the French Revolution.* Oxford: Oxford University Press, 1980.

Furet, F. *Interpreting the French Revolution.* New York: Cambridge University Press, 1981.

Geyl, P. *Napoleon: For and Against.* New Haven: Yale University Press, 1967.

Godechot, J., Hyslop, B., and Dowd, D. *The Napoleonic Era in Europe.* New York: Holt, Rinehart, and Winston, 1971.

Hampson, N. *A Social History of the French Revolution.* Toronto: University of Toronto Press, 1963.

Hunt, L. *Politics, Culture and Class in the French Revolution.* Berkeley: University of California Press, 1984.

Jones, P. M. *The Peasantry in the French Revolution.* Cambridge: Cambridge University Press, 1988.

Jordan, D. *The Revolutionary Career of Maximilian Robespierre.* New York: Free Press, 1985.

Kennedy, M. *The Jacobin Clubs in the French Revolution.* 2 vols. Princeton, N.J.: Princeton University Press, 1981, 1988.

Lefebvre, G. *The French Revolution.* 2 vols. New York: Columbia University Press, 1962, 1964.

———. *The Great Fear of 1789: Rural Panic in Revolutionary France.* New York: Pantheon, 1973.

———. *Napoleon from Tilsit to Waterloo, 1807–1815.* New York: Columbia University Press, 1969.

May, G. *Madame Roland and the Age of Revolution.* New York: Columbia University Press, 1970.

Palmer, R. R. *The Age of the Democratic Revolutions.* 2 vols. Princeton, N.J.: Princeton University Press, 1959, 1964.

———. *Twelve Who Ruled: The Year of the Terror in the French Revolution.* Princeton, N.J.: Princeton University Press, 1970.

Rose, R. B. *The Making of the Sans-Culottes: Democratic Ideas and Institutions in Paris, 1789–92.* Manchester: Manchester University Press, 1983.

Rudé, G. *The Crowd in the French Revolution.* Oxford: Oxford University Press, 1959.

Schama, S. *Citizens: A Chronicle of the French Revolution.* New York: Knopf, 1989.

Soboul, A. *The Sans-Culottes and the French Revolution.* Princeton, N.J.: Princeton University Press, 1980.

Thompson, J. M. *Napoleon Bonaparte: His Rise and Fall.* New York: Oxford University Press, 1969.

Death and the Human Experience (II)

Throughout history, every society has grappled with the fact of death and speculated about what may lie beyond the grave. Thus death is a common human bond, linking the most primitive societies with the most advanced. While all of the major world religions have offered explanations of death and hypotheses about subsequent existence, each has, in practice, been forced to accommodate its tenets to folk customs and popular mores. In so doing, religion has borne witness to the universal human effort to find a satisfying way to cope with death and dying. Reformers, in their quest to purify religion, have periodically attempted to purge funeral rituals of these culture-bound practices, thereby forcing their followers to rethink the question of death. Missionaries made similar efforts, attempting to replace folk customs with their own conceptions of death and the afterlife. Thus history is in part the story of conflicting attitudes about the common human experience of mortality.

The fundamental need to render death less fearful led orthodox Muslims to embellish the tenets of the Koran. Gradually Muslims came to believe that as a believer neared death, white-faced angels descended and sat before him. When he died, the Angel of Death gently extracted his soul from the corpse and gave it to other angels (see the third color insert). They in turn carried the soul, wrapped in a perfumed shroud, to the seventh heaven, where the beliefs and deeds of the deceased were recorded. The soul then rejoined the body in the grave for an interrogation on those beliefs and deeds by two blue-eyed, black-faced angels named Munkar and Nakir. To prepare the dead person for this Trial of the Grave, mourners sometimes whispered advice—the Instruction of the Deceased—to the corpse at the funeral. After the Trial of the Grave, the soul was comforted by Munkar and Nakir and allowed to enjoy a virtually limitless garden before its resurrection from the grave.

For an unbeliever the routine was superficially similar, though the angels attending him were black-faced and his soul could only be dragged from his body with enormous difficulty. The soul was borne only to the gate of the lowest heaven, bound in haircloth that reeked like rotting flesh. Following the questioning by Munkar and Nakir, this soul would be sentenced to a period of torment in a grave filled with heat and smoke. The point of adding these details was to help the living deal with the demise of others as well as to prepare for their own deaths. Such details made the account more memorable as well as more familiar in experiential terms.

A comparable phenomenon occurred in Japan as traditional folk belief was blended with Buddhism. According to folk religion, death occurred when the soul left the body; hence as a person lay dying, his or her friends beseeched the soul not to depart. Following death, a bowl of cooked rice for sustenance and a sword or other sharp object for protection were placed beside the corpse. As happens occasionally in the West, family members sat with the corpse the night before the funeral. The service itself was conducted by Buddhist priests, one of whom gave the deceased a new name for use in the afterlife seven days after his or her death. Formal mourning lasted 49 days, on the last of which a commemorative service was held. As in Roman Catholicism, requiem masses were observed for the deceased at specified intervals. The last of these, held 33 or 49 years after the person's death, marked the point at which the spirit lost its individuality and merged with the ancestral diety (*kami*), following which reincarnation in a newborn child could occur. The family of the deceased could take comfort that through its ritual observances the soul of the dead could enhance its status until it united with the ancestral *kami*. Thus not only was death familiarized, but the bereaved could find comfort in their efforts to aid the soul in the afterlife, much as Roman Catholics pray for the speedy passage of souls through purgatory.

While many sought to familiarize death by blending spiritual tenets with folklore, reformers periodically tried to purge religion of these customs. In Europe, for example, the Protestant reformers of the sixteenth century denounced requiem masses, prayers for the dead, monthly and yearly "minds" (commemorative services for the dead), purgatory, and extreme unction on the grounds that they were superstitious and without foundation in the Bible. In India the bhakti movement, a religious renewal in the fifteenth and sixteenth centuries, similarly deemphasized ritual in favor of devotion to the Godhead. The poet-reformer Kabir (died 1518), for instance, criticized traditional Hindu death rituals, holy places, and the doctrine of reincarnation. Taking a less extreme position, devotional cults in northern India retained simplified funeral rites but insisted that they were meaningful only if infused with love for God.

Colonial expansion brought Europeans into contact with many new perceptions of death and, to them, exotic burial customs. But there were also some striking resemblances. African folklore, for instance, included numerous myths to explain the origin of death, some of which were similar to Judeo-Christian concepts. As in the ancient Hebrew belief in a fall from a pristine state, some Africans suggested that death was the consequence of a fall from morality or disobedience to specific commandments. A number of African myths

This mask from the Ikoi tribe in Nigeria illustrates death (the dark male face to the left, with eyes closed) and life (the lighter female face to the right). This was a way of expressing belief in life after death. [Werner Forman Archive]

are essentially variations of the "forbidden fruit" theme of Genesis, but others attribute the origins of death to such things as family discord, disease, sexual intercourse, or a natural longing to die.

The spread of Western imperialism starkly juxtaposed Christian beliefs and funeral rites with those of other religions. In northern India the imposition of British rule beginning in 1763 actually sparked a revival of Hindu funerary practices, including pilgrimages to holy places associated with death rituals. But the British in turn tried to prohibit "unnatural" funerary customs. Among them was suicide at holy places, which could be undertaken for a variety of reasons, including a desire to be reincarnated in a higher state or, for Muslims, entry into paradise. British authorities also tried to limit the practice of *sati,* insisting that a widow could not be forced to cast herself into the flames of her husband's pyre. British Baptist missionaries in Bengal attempted to stop the Hindus from leaving the terminally ill beside a river without food or shelter. From a Hindu perspective, to allow such a person to die in a home would mean lengthy and expensive purification rites. Though in some respects colonial rule brought modifications in burial customs, Indians who resented imperialism clung resolutely to traditional rites, at least in part to defy their colonial overlords.

The Indonesian island of Sumba provides another illustration of the conflict between Christian and native burial customs. Like the Chinese, the Sumbanese believed that the dead engaged in social relations with the living; in fact, the dead enjoyed greater power because they could enforce supernatural sanctions in dealings with their descendants. Missionaries discouraged such beliefs, especially when Sumbanese diviners began reporting that deceased converts to Christianity were demanding reburial according to traditional customs, including interment of their corpses in megalithic tombs. The diviners buttressed their claims by blaming illness and hardship among descendants on their failure to bury their ancestors in the traditional manner. Numerous converts finally left the church in order to reinter their forebears in their ancestral villages.

Sometimes the customs associated with death

An eighteenth-century illustration of the Hindu practice of *sati.* [Granger Collection]

shocked Westerners. In the seventeenth century French Jesuits were scandalized by the practices of the Huron Indians of southeastern Canada. According to the Hurons, at death the soul is separated from the body and enters an afterlife akin to the world of the living. It was therefore important to participate in a ritual known as the Feast of Courage to enable one's soul to be powerful in the afterlife. In this feast the Hurons drank the blood and ate the flesh of an enemy warrior who had died valiantly after being cruelly tortured; by this act, they believed, they incorporated his courage within themselves.

The Hurons also observed the Feast of the Dead, which was held every 10 or 12 years with the intent of binding the people together. At heart, the ritual entailed a second burial. Family members began by retrieving the bodies of deceased relatives that had been stored on scaffolds in a cemetery, after which the women cleaned any remaining skin and flesh from the bones. The bones were then wrapped in furs and taken back to the village houses, where the families dined in their presence. Only then were the bones taken to a circular burial pit, over which they were suspended on poles for as long as a week while the people played games, gambled, danced, and feasted. After an elaborate ritual, the bones were buried in the pit along with various gifts. When the Hurons were defeated by the Iroquois, they began to lose faith in the Feast of Courage, and when, in the nineteenth century, they were forced to move to reservations in Oklahoma, they left behind their dead and thus their sense of identity as a people.

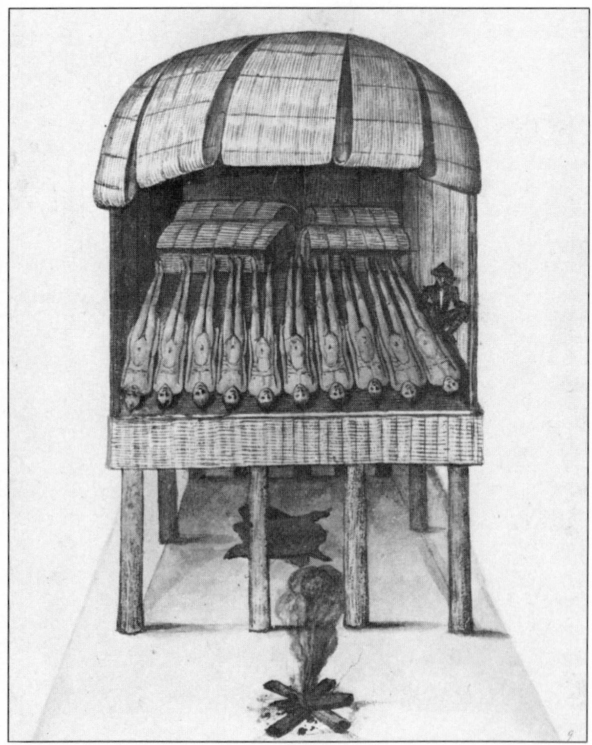

Like the Hurons, the Natchez Indians dried their corpses on frames. [Watercolor by John White; British Museum]

The use of death to heighten the sense of community is present in other cultures. This is true, for example, of the Christian community's commemoration of the death and resurrection of Christ, a ceremony sometimes linked to passion plays and realistic reenactments of the crucifixion. Among Shi'ite Muslims, the annual performance of rites to commemorate the death of Muhammad's grandson, Husein, underscores the historical continuity of the Shi'a movement and deepens its sense of community.

In the Iraqi cities of Nejev and Karbala, pilgrims honoring Husein annually crowd the streets. Their buildings are draped in black, and the cafés, bars, and theaters are closed, as religious processions command attention. As in Christian lands, there are dramatic reenactments of the last days and death of the religious leader. The public ceremonies climax with a procession reputedly bearing Husein's head, followed by flagellants, bare to the waist, thrashing themselves with chains. Other ritual sufferers bear swords, periodically striking themselves on the forehead or scalp until blood gushes forth. Some worshipers have died, among them actors who, for the sake of realism, had depicted Husein's decapitation by burying their own heads or bodies in the scorching sand. Others engage in knifing rituals, the object of which is to stab oneself in the stomach without bleeding, thereby demonstrating a higher spirituality.

The ultimate self-punishment is, of course, suicide, as sometimes occurred among Hindus in India or by believers in other countries who burned themselves to death to dramatize their message. The public suicide of Buddhist monks in Vietnam helped bring about the fall of the American-sponsored Diem government in 1963. Closely related to these practices is the deliberate courting of martyrdom. In Islam this has been a means of immediate entry to paradise and has been fairly common among such diverse groups as modern terrorists and Iranian soldiers willing to sacrifice themselves in the Iran-Iraq war. From time to time Christianity too has experienced this phenomenon, particularly during the period of the church's persecution in the late Roman Empire and again during the crusading movement that commenced in the 1090s. Thus many have courted death at the hands of others to advance their cause or obtain spiritual rewards.

Martyrdom of a different sort has been practiced among the Jews, who, though in no sense seeking death, have confronted a death inflicted by others with a commandment known as the *Kiddush Hashem,* the sanctification of God's name. During the Holocaust there were numerous instances of Jews going to their death singing religious songs, radiating spiritual ecstasy, or performing ritual dances. As one rabbi wrote in 1939, "Every Jew [is prepared to] be killed for *Kiddush Hashem,* happy in the privilege of sanctifying, by his own means, the Name of Heaven."[1]

For many modern Westerners, death has become something to shun or even deny. The roots of this attitude can be found in a number of complex changes that occurred in the early modern era. During the Reformation, Catholics, Lutherans, and Puritans called for simple funerals and greater attention to the spiritual truths involved in death and resurrection; physical death was deemphasized. At the same time, artists and writers began consciously linking death and love, sometimes in an openly sensual way, making death at once a thing of beauty and a sudden rupture between this world and an alluring afterlife. In the seventeenth century Baroque playwrights staged love scenes in tombs, and Bernini's statue of St. Theresa's mystical union with God simultaneously depicted physical death and a spiritual ecstasy suggestive of sexual fulfillment. Death and resurrection, death and ecstasy—the tendency of the new sensibility was to play down the cruder physical aspects of dying by associating death with life and especially pleasure.

During the Enlightenment this trend culminated in attempts to suppress the awareness of death. Mourning, said the Abbé Coyer, a French priest, only encourages a cruel image of death, when in fact dying is "agreeable." Some chose to speak not of death but of a journey, a voyage, a refuge, a harbor, or sleep. Efforts were made to halt burials in churches and churchyards within the cities, partly for health reasons, thus symbolically expelling the dead from the community of the living. Corpses were to be interred in public cemeteries, enabling families to visit specific grave sites as distinct from vaguer burials under church floors or in charnel houses. The grave plot became in effect a piece of family property, keeping the deceased "at home." In rare instances this was carried to the point that bodies were preserved for viewing in huge containers of alcohol or as mummies in the home. More often, loved ones contented themselves by keeping an embalmed heart at hand; it was the wish of one Frenchman that his be kept in his mother's sewing basket.

Attitudes shifted again in the late eighteenth and nineteenth centuries, primarily due to the rise of the modern nuclear family with its heightened sense of personal affection. Concern now focused more on the family survivors than on the deceased. Even wills changed, becoming merely a record of the disposition of property, as in our time; the more personal elements, such as expressions of religious faith or decisions about burial, were discussed with family members, who thus became more intimately involved in the process of dying.

A change also occurred with respect to the manifestation of grief. From the late medieval period to the eighteenth century, mourning was socially controlled: excessive grief was frowned upon, but some manifestation of sorrow was expected even if it was not genuine. In the nineteenth century the restraints were dropped, sometimes leading to hysterical mourning. Unleashed feeling was but one manifestation of the emotion so fundamental to Romanticism. Another was the exaltation of death as a thing of eerie beauty, a means to attain reunion with loved ones, a path to eternal peace. The English author Emily Brontë wrote:

> Oh, not for them should we despair,
> The grave is drear, but they are not there;
> Their dust is mingled with the sod,
> Their happy souls are gone to God![2]

The age of Romanticism also produced the cult of the hero, and this too was reflected in funerary practices, including the Pantheon in Paris and the monuments to George Washington, Thomas Jefferson, and Abraham Lincoln in Washington, D.C., to Victor Emmanuel II in Rome, and to Lord Nelson in London.

The Romantic vision of death as at once emotional, beautiful, and perhaps heroic could not survive World War I. Death in the trenches was indescribably ugly, as reflected in soldiers' memoirs:

> Each body was covered, inches deep, with a black fur of flies which blew up into your face, into your mouth, eyes, and nostrils, as you approached. The bodies crawled with maggots. . . . We worked with sandbags in our hands, stopping every now and then to puke.[3]

It was again time to rethink death. Dying became ugly, death itself a taboo. Efforts were made to protect the dying person from a knowledge of her or his condition, and the place of death was transferred from the home to the hospital or sanitarium. As belief in life after death declined, there was a growing tendency to downplay the reality of death itself. Mourning was sharply curtailed as too upsetting, a sign perhaps of mental instability; tears were banished to the privacy of solitude. The practice of cremation, which had revived amid considerable controversy in the late nineteenth century, became popular. As the founders of the Cremation Society of England candidly asserted, this method of disposing of corpses did not offend the living and rendered the remains "innocuous." Especially in America, people began to "depart" rather than die; their corpses became "remains" taken to "funeral homes" or "parlors," from thence to be placed in "memorial parks" for their "eternal rest." But the effort to hide from death is simply one more manifestation of the diverse human experience in coping with an inescapable fact of nature.

The Funeral of Attala **by Girodet illustrates the Romantic tendency to make death both sensual and a thing of beauty. [Art Resource]**

The tendency to romanticize death made no sense in the trenches of World War I. Shown here is a German corpse from the battle of the Somme. [Imperial War Museum, London]

Notes

1. F. E. Reynolds and E. H. Waugh, eds., *Religious Encounters with Death: Insights from the History and Anthropology of Religions* (University Park: Pennsylvania State University Press, 1977), p. 174.
2. P. Ariès, *The Hour of Our Death,* trans. H. Weaver (New York: Knopf, 1981), p. 438.
3. S. Cloete, *A Victorian Son: An Autobiography, 1897–1922* (Collins: London, 1972), p. 237.

Suggestions for Further Reading

Abrahamsson, H. *The Origin of Death: Studies in African Mythology.* New York: Arno Press, 1977.

Ariès, P. *The Hour of Our Death,* trans. H. Weaver. New York: Knopf, 1981.

———. *Images of Man and Death,* trans. J. Lloyd. Cambridge, Mass.: Harvard University Press, 1985.

———. *Western Attitudes Toward Death: From the Middle Ages to the Present,* trans. P. M. Ranum. Baltimore: Johns Hopkins University Press, 1974.

Gillon, E. V. *Victorian Cemetery Art.* New York: Dover, 1972.

Gorer, G. *Death, Grief and Mourning in Contemporary Britain.* Garden City, N.Y.: Doubleday, 1965.

Greaves, R. L. *Society and Religion in Elizabethan England.* Minneapolis: University of Minnesota Press, 1981.

Harrah, B. K., and Harrah, D. F. *Funeral Service: A Bibliography of Literature on Its Past, Present and Future, the Various Means of Disposition and Memorialization.* Metuchen, N.J.: Scarecrow Press, 1976.

Kipp, R. S., and Rodgers, S., eds. *Indonesian Religions in Transition.* Tucson: University of Arizona Press, 1987.

McManners, J. *Death and the Enlightenment.* Oxford: Oxford University Press, 1981.

Miller, A. J., and Aeri, M. J. *Death: A Bibliographical Guide.* Metuchen, N.J.: Scarecrow Press, 1977.

Mitford, J. *The American Way of Death.* New York: Simon & Schuster, 1963.

Morley, J. *Death, Heaven and the Victorians.* Pittsburgh: University of Pittsburgh Press, 1971.

Reynolds, F. E., and Waugh, E. H. *Religious Encounters with Death: Insights from the History and Anthropology of Religions.* University Park: Pennsylvania State University Press, 1977.

Stannard, D. E. *The Puritan Way of Death.* Oxford: Oxford University Press, 1977.

———, ed. *Death in America.* Philadelphia: University of Pennsylvania Press, 1975.

Watson, J. L., and Rawski, E. S., eds. *Death Ritual in Late Imperial and Modern China.* Berkeley: University of California Press, 1987.

Whaley, J., ed. *Mirrors of Mortality: Studies in the Social History of Death.* London: Europa, 1981.

Wolf, A. P., ed. *Religion and Ritual in Chinese Society.* Stanford, Calif.: Stanford University Press, 1974.

CHAPTER · 27

Early Modern India and Iran

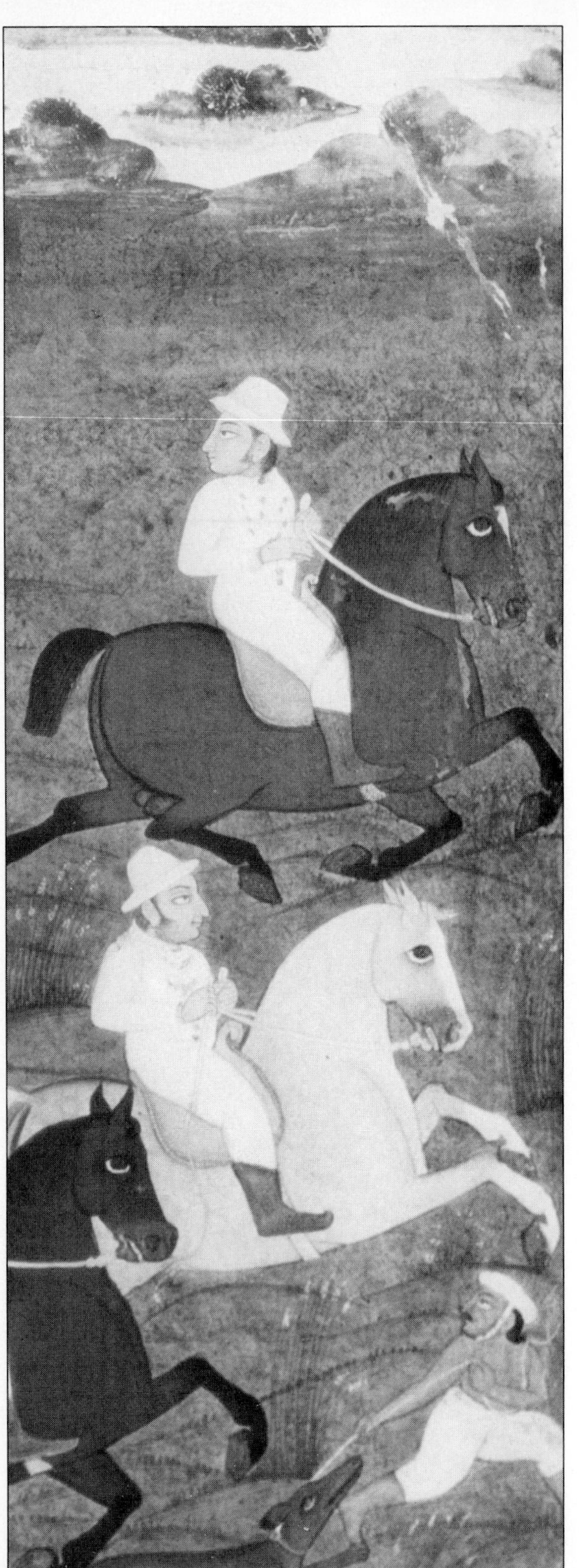

Colonel James Todd, an East India Company official, on tour "upcountry" c. 1800, by an Indian artist. Many Company officials took on the trappings of traditional Indian potentates and performed many of their functions, such as hearing cases and settling disputes. [E. T. Archive]

The collapse of Mughal power in India after 1707 was not followed by the rise of a new Indian order. The subcontinent's legacy of cultural diversity and intergroup rivalry worked against unity, and there was no single effective successor to the Mughals. In this confused setting, the English East India Company began to extend the position it had slowly built up as a trading agent on both coasts, first to protect its merchants, trade partners, and goods against banditry and civil war, then to take on the actual function of government. By 1800 or so the Company was the most powerful single force in the country, and it had become the real sovereign over most of India. In the course of the next half century, a series of military campaigns, more peaceful takeovers, and treaties with local Indian rulers left the Company as the direct administrator of about half the subcontinent and indirectly the dominant power in the rest. The development depended to a large degree on Indian collaboration, but in 1857 dissidents joined forces in supporting a mutiny by some of the Indian troops in the Company's army. This was put down after much bloodshed, and the British asserted dominance over the whole of India.

Iran in the eighteenth century had to withstand powerful Ottoman efforts to conquer the country, which the orthodox Sunni Ottomans considered a stronghold of heretical Shi'ite Islam. After early Ottoman successes, Nadir Shah came to the Iranian throne in 1736 and regained the lost territories but presided over a bloody period of internal repression. His successor, Karim Khan, restored peace until his death in 1779, when Iran was again torn by internal rivalries.

The Mughal Collapse

India had been left in chaos at the death of Aurangzeb in 1707. His military campaigns in the south and his continued persecution of Hindus and Sikhs had brought most of the country to rebellion. His successors on the throne at Delhi were far weaker men. Aurangzeb's three sons fought each other in the usual battles of the Mughal succession. After $2\frac{1}{2}$ years of civil war, the victor was then virtually besieged by a Sikh uprising that swept the Punjab and by guerrilla warfare to the west and south. His death in 1712 brought on another struggle for the throne among his sons. They were outmaneuvered by a cousin, who captured and killed the Sikh leader only to be poisoned by his own courtiers in 1719.

The authority of the once great Mughals was by now irretrievably lost, and it no longer mattered to most people what feckless creature sat on the Peacock Throne, dreamed away his days in the imperial harem, or smoked opium. But even Aurangzeb could never have reestablished control over Rajasthan, Maharashtra, Gujarat, Punjab, or Bengal, let alone the Deccan or the south. Only a remnant of the former empire remained around Delhi and Agra. Most of the rest of India was also torn by factional fighting, civil war, and local banditry, with widespread raiding by Maratha cavalry all over the Deccan and into the north.

Aurangzeb's immediate successors had officially recognized the Maratha Confederacy (so called, although it never really achieved unity) and its extensive conquests in Mysore and on the southeast coast. The Marathas were made nominally tributary allies of the Mughals but controlled their own territories and revenues. They were in effect given thus both the means and the license to extend their raids or conquests into still more of central, southern, and eastern India, whose revenues could further augment their power. They continued to nibble away at the

India in Turmoil

The Muslim Indian historian Khafi Khan, writing in the 1720s, gives a vivid picture of the chaos following the death of Aurangzeb in 1707.

It is clear to the wise and experienced that . . . thoughtfulness in managing the affairs of state and protecting the peasantry . . . have all departed. Revenue collectors have become a scourge for the peasantry. . . . Many townships which used to yield full revenue have, owing to the oppression of officials, been so far ruined and devastated that they have become forests infested by tigers and lions, and the villages are so utterly ruined and desolate that there is no sign of habitation on the routes.

This is matched by English descriptions of late seventeenth-century Bengal, which had broken away from Mughal control.

Bengal is at present in a very bad condition by means of the great exactions on the people. . . . There are no ways of extortion omitted . . . [which] makes merchants' business very troublesome. . . . The king's governor has little more than the name, and for the most part sits still while others oppress the people and monopolize most commodities, even as low as grass for beasts . . . nor do they want ways to oppress people of all sorts who trade, whether natives or strangers.

Sources: I. Habib, *The Agrarian System of Mughal India* (New York: Asia Publishing House, 1963), p. 186; H. Yule, ed., *Diary of William Hedges*, vol. 2 (London: Barlow, 1887), pp. 237, 239.

remaining shreds of Mughal authority in the north and Hindustan, ultimately raiding Agra and Delhi itself as well as deep into Bengal as far as Calcutta, though English defenses kept them out of the city.

For a time it looked as if the Marathas might inherit the former Mughal position, but they proved incurably divided into contending factions, and no leader emerged who might have welded them into a coalition. The Maratha cavalry operated more and more as bandits and plunderers, rarely attempting to set up any administration in the areas they swept for loot and then left in chaos. In the south, Hyderabad became a large and wealthy kingdom independent of both the Mughals and the Marathas, while in the central Ganges valley the independent kingdom of Oudh with its capital at Lucknow also emerged from the breakup of the once great empire. In many parts of India cultivated areas were abandoned by peasants unable to defend their crops or their homes against raiders and bandits. Trade dwindled, famine increased, and India slipped further into impoverishment and anarchy.

The last shreds of Mughal power were swept away when a Persian army sacked and looted Delhi in 1739, massacred its inhabitants, and took back with them the famous Peacock Throne. Iran's powerful ruler, Nadir Shah, upon seizing the Persian throne in 1736, asked for Mughal help to crush Afghanistan, formerly a part of the Mughal Empire. But the Mughals were by now hard pressed to defend even Delhi against Maratha raiders. In 1738 Nadir Shah, acting alone, conquered Afghanistan and went on to Lahore and Delhi, leaving them in smoldering ruins. The dynasty continued in name, and successive Mughal emperors sat in state in Delhi's Red Fort until 1858, when the last of them was banished by the British.

After 1739 few people in India or elsewhere took the Mughals seriously. This was the harvest of Aurangzeb's cruel reign, which had condemned most of India to chronic civil war, local disorder, and impoverishment. Unfortunately, Rajputs, Marathas, Sikhs, Gujaratis, Bengalis, and other regional groups who had fought against the Mughals saw each other as rivals and indeed as enemies rather than as joint Indian inheritors of power. Their languages, though related like those of Europe, were different, and they differed culturally as well. Their divisions now made it possible for the English and French to make a place for themselves and to increase their commercial and political power.

Westerners in India

The story of the Portuguese arrival in India and their establishment of a major base at Goa on the west coast has been briefly told in Chapter 17. For about a century after Vasco da Gama's voyage to Calicut in 1498, the Portuguese dominated Western trade with India, as well as with Southeast Asia, China, and Japan. In India they competed with Indian and Arab traders and increasingly after the end of the sixteenth century with Dutch and English merchants and their ships. But no Westerners even thought about contending for political power in India for another 250 years, until the latter half of the eighteenth century. Although the Portuguese arrived well before the establishment of the Mughal Empire in 1526, they were a tiny handful with no effective means of confronting any of the Indian states of the south, let alone the soon-triumphant Mughals.

Westerners fought among themselves for control of the sea routes, but their objectives in India were purely commercial, except for the early Portuguese interest in converting the few Indians they encountered to Catholicism. In their competition for trade, the Europeans offered local rulers guns and naval help for use against their neighbors, together with a share of their profits, in exchange for commercial privileges or the use of a port. Small numbers of Europeans might involve themselves on opposite sides of such inter-Indian conflicts, seeking further influence or advantage. Once the Mughals became the dominant force in India, such power brokering largely subsided, and European merchants became humble petitioners before the Peacock Throne, whose influence was so much greater than their own.

The Portuguese were first in India and hence obtained the largest number of concessions, including a base at Goa. Concessions elsewhere included the rights to warehouses, residences and commercial rights of way at small ports on both east and west coasts, as well as at sites inland in Bengal, source of the finest cotton textiles for export and the richest and biggest market. By the early seventeenth century, however, the Portuguese were rapidly losing ground to Dutch and English traders. Their ships were outclassed in size, speed, maneuverability, firepower, and numbers, and their poor and tiny home base could no longer sustain the effort of maintaining an overextended commercial empire. The Portuguese also suffered from political miscalculations. Vijayanagar, for example (see Chapter 10), actively sought Portuguese help in its efforts to fight off its ultimate conquest by a coalition of Muslim sultanates in the northern Deccan. The Portuguese had earlier provided Vijayanagar with imported horses and cannon and had benefited commercially from their association with this dominant state of the south, but the ruler's urgent request for more aid in his greatest hour of need was shortsightedly refused. After the defeat of Vijayanagar in 1565, Portuguese trade and the Portuguese position in India rapidly declined.

The Dutch and later the English were able to move into the Indian market by making their own agreements with local rulers or with the Mughals and to begin to establish their own trade bases. The interest of the Dutch in Asia was from the beginning centered on the spice trade and its sources in the Indonesian archipelago, but they established several bases in small ports along the east coast of

India, retaining many of them until late in the eighteenth century. There they competed vigorously against the Portuguese and later the English. The Dutch involvement in Ceylon, however, was far more extensive. The Portuguese had fortified a base at Colombo some years after arriving there in 1502 and controlled large parts of the lowland west coast of the island, including the profitable trade in cinnamon bark from the Colombo area. Their efforts to extend their control inland were repelled by the Sinhalese* kingdom of Kandy in the central highlands, which had become the chief power in Ceylon after the collapse of the classical and medieval state based at Anuradhapura and Polonaruwa (see Chapter 10). But the Portuguese did succeed in converting many of the west coast Sinhalese to Catholicism, at first often by force, and Portuguese surnames remain widespread there, as in parts of Southeast Asia.

The Dutch drove out the Portuguese between 1640 and 1658 and established their own more extensive position in Ceylon, including bases on the east as well as the west coast. Although they too failed in several attempts to conquer the mountain-girt Kandyan kingdom, they made Ceylon an even more profitable commercial enterprise, setting up a plantation system for coconuts and later for coffee, imported from their territories in Java. Like the Portuguese, they often intermarried with the Sinhalese, producing a Eurasian group still known as "Burghers." By the 1630s Dutch ships dominated the Indian Ocean and its approaches and were even able to blockade Goa. Ceylon was an obvious prize, both for its trade profits and for its strategic role along the route eastward from India, in sight of the southern tip of the subcontinent and only three or four days' sail from Goa. The Dutch were to remain in control of the trade of Ceylon from their several coastal bases until the Napoleonic wars, when the British took over the island and in 1815 finally conquered the Kandyan kingdom.

The Early English Presence

England, like other European trading nations, learned about Portuguese profits in India and began to seek a northeast passage to India by sea around Russia and Siberia in 1553. The expedition was found two years later frozen into the Arctic ice, all aboard dead. A later effort to run the Portuguese blockade in 1583 in the ship *Tiger* ended in Portuguese capture of the vessel, but one of the English merchants aboard, Ralph Fitch, escaped and went on to India, where he visited Akbar's capitals of Agra and Fatehpur Sikkri as well as Goa, returning to London in 1591 with firsthand accounts of India's wealth. Portugal was dynastically united with Spain in 1580, but this tended to weaken rather than strengthen the Portuguese effort in Asia, and with the defeat of the Spanish Armada in 1588 the way eastward was more open to England.

The English East India Company was founded in 1600. Its first two ventures were aimed at the spice trade in Southeast Asia, but the third went to India, reaching Surat, the major port of Gujarat, in 1608. Gujarat had been absorbed into the Mughal Empire in 1573, and Captain William Hawkins, who commanded the fleet of three English ships, carried presents and a letter from King James I to the Mughal emperor, Jahangir, requesting a trade treaty. Hawkins claimed that the Portuguese, especially the Jesuits who were already ensconced at the Mughal court, conspired against him, but in any case he was kept waiting for over two years and was finally obliged to return home empty-handed. A second English envoy reached Agra in 1612 but was sent away even more summarily after the Jesuits there urged the emperor not to deal with him.

However, later in 1612 a single English ship defeated and dispersed four Portuguese galleons and a number of frigates off Surat, in view of those on shore, a feat that was repeated in 1615. Indians now saw that the English were more valuable clients than the Portuguese and better able to defend Indian shipping and coasts from pirates and from rival Europeans, whose tactics were often indistinguishable from those of pirates. The Indian market had little or no interest in trade with England and was not impressed by the samples of goods it was offered from what was, after all, a much less advanced economy.

The lack of goods attractive to the Eastern market was indeed to hamper European and American trade in India until the British conquest and trade with China and the rest of Asia until well into the nineteenth century. The Mughals, however, had no navy and had to depend on foreigners for protection against piracy; of these, it now seemed clear, the English were the least troublesome and the most effective. In 1616 King James sent another ambassador, Sir Thomas Roe, who finally won permission from Jahangir for the East India Company to build a warehouse in Surat. Seven years later the Dutch massacred ten English merchants who had been sharing the spice trade of eastern Indonesia, signaling the end of the Netherlands' willingness to allow any European competition in what thus became their private preserve. The English were obliged to abandon their effort to penetrate Dutch territory and to concentrate on India.

Territorial Bases

From Surat, English ships completed the elimination of Portuguese power at sea, and English merchants became the main traders in the port. They then sought bases on

*The Sinhalese are the dominant inhabitants of Ceylon (Sri Lanka), having invaded and settled the island, probably from northern India, in the seventh century B.C.

the east coast and in Bengal, where they could buy the finest-quality cottons more directly as well as the indigo and saltpeter produced in the lower Ganges valley. After their early attempts had been driven off by the Dutch, English negotiations with a local ruler to the south led to their purchase of land in 1639 around a small harbor that later became the city of Madras. Here they immediately built Fort St. George. Madras became their chief base in eastern India, from which they had access to south Indian cottons and other goods. From Madras they made repeated efforts to trade directly in Bengal and finally established a warehouse up river near the provincial capital. They found, however, that such proximity to the Mughal and Bengali authorities exposed them to arbitrary taxation and even sometimes expropriation, and on at least one occasion the Company's agent was publicly whipped and expelled. Accordingly, they sought a more secure position. They had traded periodically at a small market half a day's sail up the Hooghly River, one of the lesser mouths of the Ganges, and in 1690 decided to make a settlement there where they felt their ships could protect or rescue them if needed. There they were also more distant from Indian authority. Soon thereafter they received permission to build a fort. The new settlement, called Fort William (after the English monarch William III), was shortly to be known as Calcutta.

At Surat the English remained among many merchant groups and were dependent on the fickle pleasure of Mughal and Gujarati powers. But Bombay, originally a chain of small islands enclosed in a large bay, was ceded to the English crown by Portugal in 1661 as part of the marriage contract of the Portuguese princess Catherine of Braganza and Charles II. The Portuguese had built no settlement there and used it only occasionally, since it was vulnerable to piracy, cut off from landward access to markets by the rampaging Marathas, and had a harbor too big for the small ships of the time. But the quite different drawbacks of Surat and the attractions of a more nearly independent and protected base, as at Madras and Calcutta, led the Company to move its western India headquarters to Bombay in 1687.

With the founding of Calcutta in 1690, the English now

Why Calcutta?

Before the founding of Calcutta, the English had tried to use several other harbors on the seaward edge of the Ganges delta. Here is a 1689 description of the problems at Ballasore, one of those harbors, and of the plan to make a base instead at Calcutta.

Our ships in Ballasore road do generally ride in a hard and dangerous roadstead and many of our men come to sickness and death by the constant labor of rowing so far in such a rough sea, which we would willingly prevent all that in us lies, and therefore if the Moors [Mughals] will allow us to fortify ourselves at Chutanutee [the village that became Calcutta] where our ships may go up and ride within the command of our guns it would be much better for us, though it should cost us a bribe of thirty or forty thousand rupees to the great men to be paid when we are possessed of the Mughal's Phirmaund [charter of trading privileges] for that and for the twelve articles made with Mr. Charnock [the Company's chief agent in Bengal], but the confirmation of these articles we insist on in right and will not purchase them.

But Calcutta had other problems. Here is a description in 1703.

[Mr. Charnock chose the site] for the sake of a large shady tree, though he could not have chosen a more unhealthful place on all the river, for three miles to the northeast is a salt water lake that overflows in September and October and then prodigious numbers of fish resort thither, but in November and December when the floods are dissipated those fishes are left dry and with their putrefaction affect the air with thick stinking vapors which the northwest winds bring with them to Fort William [where] they cause a yearly mortality.

Sources: C. R. Wilson, *Old Fort William in Bengal* (London: Murray, 1906), p. 5; J. N. Das Gupta, ed., *India in the Seventeenth Century* (New Delhi: Associated Publishing House, 1976), p. 232.

had three small territorial footholds, well placed to tap the trade of India in each of its major segments, west, south, and east. But like all other foreigners in India, they remained petitioners, dependent on the favors of the Mughal state or of local rulers and liable to be driven out, expropriated, or denied trading privileges. No one as yet anticipated the imminent collapse of Mughal power.

Even after the death of Aurangzeb, there was little recognition of the changed situation. The East India Company sent an embassy to the by then virtually powerless Mughal emperor in 1714; the embassy's leader prostrated himself before the throne as "the smallest particle of sand" giving "the reverence due from a slave," asking for additional trade privileges. Significantly, however, the agent also sought the right to collect revenues in the immediate areas around Madras and Calcutta, where the Company was by now the de facto government. The embassy was largely ignored and would probably never have been even acknowledged if the emperor had not fallen ill and asked for treatment from the embassy's English doctor. His success led to the embassy's reception, and in 1717 all its requests were granted.

The Mughal and Post-Mughal Contexts

The Mughals, like many premodern states, were used to such arrangements with various groups or individuals to whom they in effect farmed out the collection of taxes and the administration of local areas that the taxes supported. In their view, the English were little different from scores of others who had long been granted such rights, equivalent to the Mughal *jagir* or *zamindari* (see Chapter 19), and Delhi attached little importance to the 1717 concession. Indeed, it seems important now only because we know what followed and can recognize it as the first step toward English territorial sovereignty in India.

After the death of Aurangzeb, the Mughals as well as local and provincial authorities had ceased to maintain order. In this context, the English East India Company was at least able to keep up a semblance of government in its fortified bases, and, with the help of small private armies, in the areas immediately around the bases as well. The embassy to Delhi in 1714 had to fight off large armed robber bands even on the imperial road from Agra. Most of the rest of India was in even worse condition. The Company could survive and prosper only if it could create security for trade goods in storage and in transit and could offer its Indian partners similar security. Areas of production could generate trade commodities also only if they could be kept orderly. The main consequence of the fading of Mughal power was thus not that the English rose politically in India, but that they were driven increasingly to provide their own defense, policing, revenue collection, and local government. They did this well enough to survive and to attract Indian merchants to deal with them and even become residents of the English bases, where their profits and property could also be secure.

Within a few years Madras, Calcutta, and Bombay were overwhelmingly Indian in population, home to many laborers and servants as well as numerous merchants, artisans, bankers, and agents, all having selected the still tiny English-dominated world of the fortified ports over any Indian alternative. Apart from the Mughals, who counted for little in any case, local states and rulers were often also willing to have the Company manage trade, collect taxes, and keep order. Civil order and healthy conditions for trade, which the English offered, were more than enough to ensure the cooperation of most Indians.

The Company prospered, and Indian cottons became so popular in England that Parliament in 1701, concerned to protect English textiles, prohibited their import. When that ban was ignored, a parliamentary ruling in 1720 prohibited their use or wear, but reexport to the Continent continued and even domestic consumption could not be prevented. Indian cottons were clearly superior to Western products, and the finest of them have never been surpassed. A widely repeated story told how the emperor Aurangzeb had reproved his daughter for appearing naked at court, to which she is said to have replied that she was wearing seven thicknesses of Dacca muslin.

Bombay Green in 1767, with the buildings, servants, and troops of the East India Company. Note the Western-style architecture of the buildings, including the church in the center. [Granger Collection]

The Company was not alone in its prosperity. From the first factory at Surat to Indian independence in 1947, Indians found employment in the expanding economy of what became the colonial ports and later their inland equivalents, as well as in the colonial bureaucracy. English and Scots who prospered were greatly outnumbered by Indians, but most of the biggest gainers were British. Most Indians remained poor, and most of those who prospered did so as junior partners, especially after 1830, despite British economic and social discrimination against them. For most peasants the gradual spread of Company rule meant at least protection against banditry or Maratha raids and a growing new market within India and abroad for their commercial crops. Commercialization of agriculture proved ruinous to some but profitable to many. In any case, the Company could never have succeeded without extensive Indian collaboration, particularly the connections with domestic trade networks and production provided by Indian merchants, agents, and bankers. All were dependent on the Company's ability to maintain order.

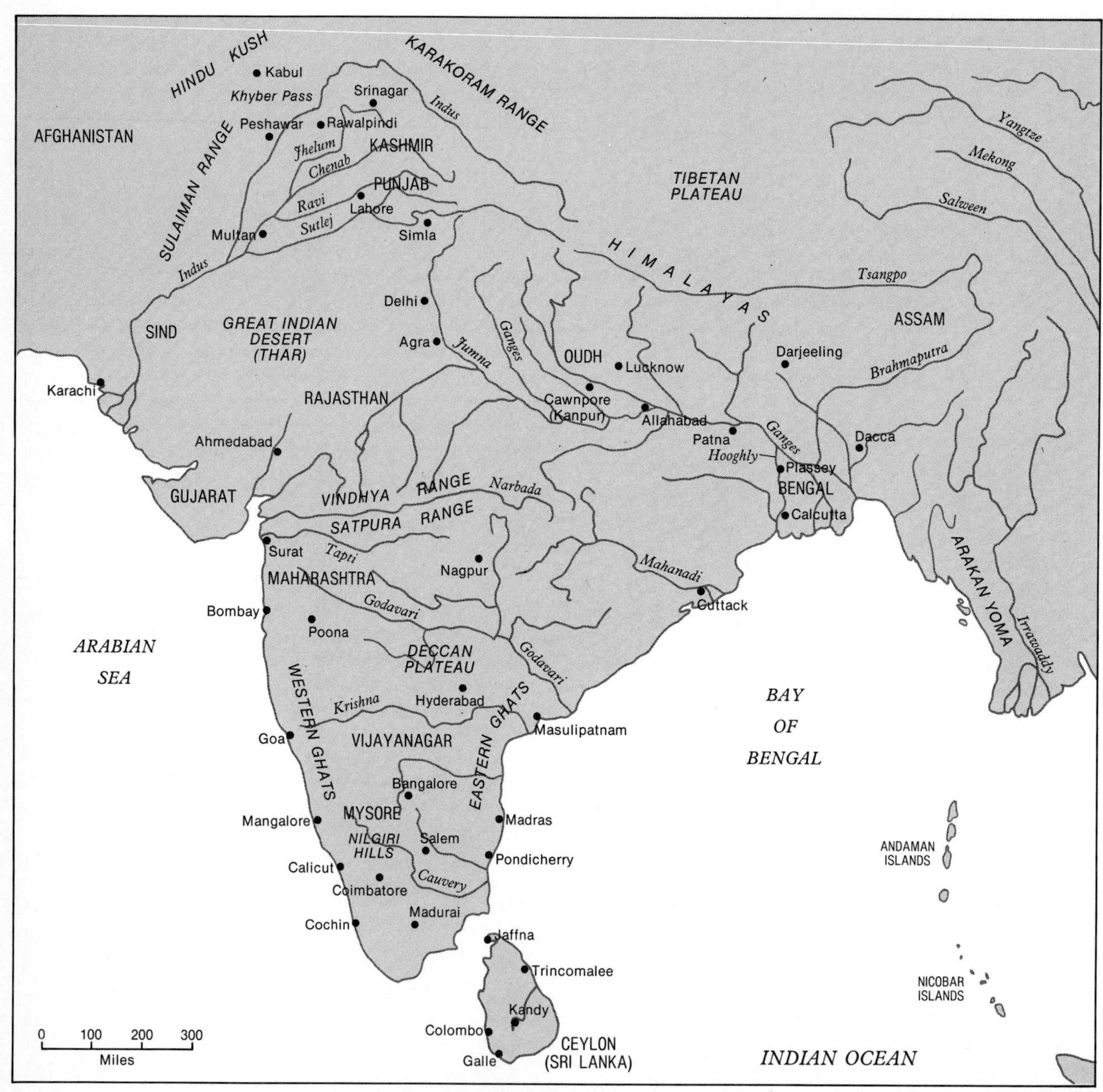

27.1 India

Anglo-French Rivalry and the Conquest of Bengal

The French had also been active contenders for the trade of India since the founding of the French East India Company in 1664 and had established a warehouse of their own at Surat, an east coast base at Pondicherry, south of Madras, and another warehouse just up river from Calcutta. The French bases, in India as in all their overseas ventures, were government-sponsored and controlled. They had the advantage of superb leadership under Joseph Dupleix (1697–1764), who favored an expansionist policy. He was supported by able military and naval commanders. Their forces captured Madras in 1746 and went on to defeat the local Indian ruler of the southeast, becoming the dominant power in the whole of south India. Unfortunately for them, they got little support from home, and the Treaty of Aix-la-Chapelle in 1748 restored Madras to the English. Two years later the English trader Robert Clive defeated both the French and their southern Indian allies with a small force.

When the Seven Years' War (1756–1763) erupted in Europe, fighting spread to India as well as North America, and the British and French provided troops and ships to supplement the Indian forces who did most of the actual fighting. Now deprived of the leadership of Dupleix, who had been called home for allegedly spending too much of the French company's resources in "unprofitable adventures," the French lost out in this struggle. A major lesson of the conflict was that very small numbers of European troops, operating with somewhat larger numbers of Indian soldiers trained in Western methods, could repeatedly defeat enormously larger Indian armies. Those on the European sides were disciplined to fire regular volleys on command and to plan and coordinate their actions. Their guns and cannon were better, but organization and leadership made them more effective, as did morale enhanced by regular pay and uniforms.

Western military power was, however, tested most severely by a Bengali challenge to the growing English position in and around Calcutta. As their local authority increased, the English became less deferential to the still technically sovereign rulers of Bengal, now independent of the Mughals. No longer humble petitioners who had regularly kissed the feet of the *nawab* (king) of Bengal, their independent behavior and their addition to the fortifications of Fort William offended the new nawab, Siraj-ud-Dawlah, who came to the throne in 1756. In a last flash of imperial fire, his army and war elephants overwhelmed Calcutta and its small corps of defenders in June 1756. Some escaped in boats and fled to Madras, but about 60 were left behind, to be thrown into the fort's tiny, airless dungeon. Next morning two-thirds of them were dead of suffocation. The incident of the so-called Black Hole of Calcutta became infamous. It seemed the end of the English position in Bengal, but appearances were deceiving. Within four months an expedition sailed from Madras under the same Robert Clive who had earlier ousted the French from the south. In January 1757 he retook Calcutta and then drove the French from their remaining bases in Bengal. With support from Indian groups, he defeated the huge army of the nawab at the battle of Plassey in June, some 75 miles northwest of Calcutta.

Although no one seemed fully to realize it at the time, the English were now masters of Bengal. They had no effective rivals, nor were there viable alternatives to British rule. Their military victory was, however, due in large part to Indian collaboration, including, perhaps most important, bankers who had lent money to both sides and who calculated that an English victory was more desirable on practical grounds. The English paid their debts, as the nawab did not, and as a merchant group the English East India Company furthered trade rather than preying on it. The leading Indian banker in fact paid very large sums to troops on the nawab's side to persuade them not to fight; the reserves, which were to have swept the field at Plassey when the battle hung in the balance, never came. But the traditional Indian armies of the day were usually composed of different groups who were often rivals and were rarely effectively led. Contingents often deserted, failed to appear, or decided to throw their lot in with another side.

ROBERT CLIVE AND THE BEGINNINGS OF BRITISH INDIA

Robert Clive (1725–1774) had shipped out to Madras as an East India Company clerk but he soon developed a reputation as an adventurer. He found his clerk's job so boring that he tried unsuccessfully to blow his brains out with a pistol that misfired. Adventure soon came when the French captured Fort St. George in 1746 and he was taken prisoner. He escaped and took a commission in the Company's small army. His first military expedition, against a powerful southern kingdom allied with the French, was won by brilliant strategy even though his opponents outnumbered his forces 20 to 1. Clive was acclaimed as a hero and repeated his success by driving out the French and their Indian allies in the major Deccan kingdom of Hyderabad. Still only 27 years old, he was praised as a deliverer and granted two years' home leave. Sent out again with the rank of colonel in 1756, he reached Madras just as Calcutta was being overwhelmed by the armies of the nawab of Bengal.

Already known to Indians by a nickname roughly translatable as "He Who Is Daring in War," Clive sailed north with a small force. He recaptured Calcutta, defeated the greatly superior army that tried to stop him just north of

Robert Clive accepting tribute from Mir Jaffar, the puppet whom he had placed on the throne of Bengal after the battle of Plassey, as depicted in an oil painting by Francis Hayman, c. 1760. [National Portrait Gallery, London]

the city, and four months later met the main Bengali contingent at Plassey. By this time he had just over 1,000 British troops and about 2,000 Indians under his command. The Bengali army totaled 18,000 cavalry and 50,000 foot soldiers, with more than 50 field guns managed by French artillerymen. Again Clive's tactical genius won the day, confusing, outmaneuvering, and finally routing the enemy. He then marched to the Bengali capital, where he installed his own Indian client and ally as ruler.

Clive and his English and Indian colleagues helped themselves to the provincial treasury, and the Company too was richly repaid in reparations and new revenues now under its control. After consolidating his conquests with further victories against Indian and French forces, Clive devoted his enormous energy to strengthening the Company's army, refortifying Calcutta, and administering the new domains. Four years of incessant activity broke his health, and he spent five years in England. He was sent back to India in 1765 to try to check the plundering excessses of his successors and to reorganize what now amounted to the Company's government of Bengal.

Two years later he was back in England to face charges in Parliament that he had defrauded the Company and enriched himself by extortion. The accusations were brought by many of the same people whom he had tried to restrain from similar behavior and who were jealous of his successes. Although in the end he was cleared, he brooded over his grievances, and still suffering from poor health, he shot himself in 1774 at the age of 49. The same mercurial temperament that had made him try suicide as a young man and then carried him to the heights of success proved his undoing. Yet more than any one person, he began the process that was to end in British rule in India. He was far more than a brilliant field commander and was concerned about the implications of British policy in India. His immediate successors were more interested in personal enrichment.

The Establishment of British Rule

With Bengal now in their hands, many of the English turned to plunder as well as trade, extorting silver and jewels from the rich and also demanding what amounted to protection money. After a few years this brought severe criticism from home, parliamentary inquiries, and finally, in 1784, the India Act, which created a board of control for India in London. Meanwhile, beyond Bengal, the rest of India remained in turmoil. Afghan armies repeatedly laid waste the northwest and looted Delhi again in 1757, slaughtering most of the inhabitants. A huge Maratha army gathered to repel yet another Afghan invasion in 1760 was crushed in a great battle near Delhi early in 1761. The Afghans then withdrew, but they had in effect removed the only Indian power able to contest the English. Three years later outnumbered Company forces soundly defeated a final Indian coalition organized by leading Bengalis, ending the last serious challenge to their power in the north.

From this point on the policy of both the Company and its London supervisors was to acquire no more territory but to achieve their ends through alliances with Indian princes, offering them military protection in exchange for trading rights. In Bengal as in the smaller areas around Madras and Bombay, they continued to collect taxes and run the administration as nominal agents of the local or regional Indian rulers. Administration was expensive and distracted from the Company's main business, trade. The collection of rural taxes was farmed out to Bengali agents, or *zamindars*. The zamindars, with British encouragement, seized land from defaulting taxpayers, thus allying themselves with the new company administration. Calcutta was made the capital of all of British India; after 1785 the Company, under parliamentary supervision from London, concentrated on promoting trade but also administered justice and defense. Indian agents were necessarily employed in the lower echelons of government; all higher administrative and military posts were reserved for the British.

Cultural blending in colonial India: an Indian ruler in Rajasthan in British uniform, by an Indian artist. [Victoria and Albert Museum, London]

The official policy of discouraging further direct conquest yielded in the 1790s to the strategic pressures of the Napoleonic wars. The French still had small footholds in South India and a history, like that of the English, of alliances with various Indian rulers. Successive heads of state in Mysore had had some dealings with the French and had also periodically threatened Madras. In 1799 Mysore was overwhelmed by Company troops. Half of it, including the commercially important coastal strip, was annexed outright, thus linking the Madras area to the west coast. Most of the rest of it was given to a loyal Indian ally, the neighboring state of Hyderabad, which was to remain nominally independent until 1947. The peninsular south was now firmly under Company control, but the Marathas remained a formidable power, and their home base in Maharashtra blocked Bombay's access to inland markets. Taking advantage of internal Maratha division, the Company signed a treaty with one side in 1802 promising military support in exchange for territorial rights. When the Maratha puppet the British had installed tried later to revive his power, the Company defeated his forces and took over all Maratha domains in 1818, soon joining them to Bombay Presidency, the major British territory in western India.

The central Ganges valley west of Bengal, through which India's major trade route ran, was too important to be left uncontrolled. In 1801 the ruler of the state of Oudh was forced to accept British protection, although he remained nominally sovereign. The same arrangement was made with the Mughal emperor for his domains in the Delhi-Agra area. Southern Gujarat, including the commercially important port of Surat, was also brought under Company control. Only Rajasthan, the Indus valley and Sind, Kashmir, and Punjab remained outside the British sphere. Much of what the British controlled was, however, nominally ruled by allied Indian princes.

The British, troubled by the French threat and reminded of French naval successes in the Bay of Bengal 50 years earlier, moved on Dutch-held Ceylon after Napoleon's occupation of Holland. Their first concern was to take over the fine natural harbor of Trincomalee on the east coast of Ceylon, where they could base their naval vessels. There were no harbors safe to enter or leave during the northeast monsoon or winter anywhere on the Indian east coast, nor were any of them large enough for the fleet, which had to be withdrawn to winter haven in distant Bombay. Trincomalee filled this urgent need, and the British occupied it in 1795, subsequently taking over all of the other Dutch holdings in Ceylon.

As the French threat faded, British attention shifted to the far more productive southwestern lowlands of Ceylon, and the colonial capital was fixed at Colombo. From there roads were built crisscrossing the island and, after the final conquest of the Kandyan kingdom in 1815, into the central highlands, followed by railways after 1858. Coffee plantations spread rapidly with this improved access to export markets, as did coconut production, and by midcentury Ceylon had the plantation economy it retained until after independence. Tea was introduced after a disastrous coffee blight in the 1870s, and rubber was added at the end of the century. Tamil laborers were brought in from overpopulated South India to build roads and railways and to provide labor for the new plantations. Ceylon was designated a crown colony separate from British India and was administered as such despite its long and close Indian connections.

The conquest of India by a relative handful of British settlers, merchants, and troops, at first almost a private venture, could not have happened without native support or without the factional divisions that fatally weakened Indian resistance. Most people accepted Company control either because they benefited from it as merchants, bankers, collaborators, agents, or employees or because they saw it as preferable to control by the Mughals, the Marathas, or any of the local rulers, whose record was not attractive. Most contemporary Indian states were oppressive, taxing merchants and peasants unmercifully and often arbitrarily, while at the same time failing to keep order, suppress banditry, maintain roads and basic services, or administer justice acceptably. Revenues went disproportionately to support court extravagances and armies, which spent their energy more in interregional conflict than in genuine defense. This was partly the legacy of the Delhi sultanate and particularly of the Mughals. It became clear to most Indians that, in fact, only the British were both willing and able to protect them from banditry, ensure the security of life and property, and foster conditions under which trade and agriculture could again prosper. That was enough to win their support or at least ensure their acquiescence. At any rate, nearly a century was to pass between the last Bengali resistance in the mid-1760s and the first major uprising against British rule in 1857.

The Indians accommodated themselves to the British as they had to foreign conquerors in the past. Mindful of the early English rapacity in Bengal, the Company generally tried as much as possible to avoid displacing or offending Indians or disrupting local customs except for slavery and *sati* (widow burning). This maturation of policy was illustrated in a letter from the directors to the company offices in Bombay in 1784:

> **By the exercise of a mild and good government people from other parts may be induced to come and reside under our protection. Let there be entire justice exercised to all persons without distinction, and open trade allowed to all.[1]**

Such a plan reflected the original exclusive aim of trade profits, more bluntly stated almost a century earlier: "Merchants desire no enemies, and would create none."[2]

The Orientalists and the Bengal Renaissance

As British administration was extended, more and more company employees were not merchants or clerks but officials and magistrates. British and Indian merchants had obvious common interests, and many even appreciated each other's culture. Some Company traders and officials, such as Sir William Jones (1746–1794), found themselves fascinated by the rich variety of the Indian tradition. Jones, a judge in late eighteenth-century Bengal, had the usual classical education in England and then had to learn Persian (still used for Mughal law), Sanskrit (the classical language of India and of Hindu texts, which were often cited in law cases), and the modern languages of North India spoken by those who appeared in court: Bengali, Hindi, and so on. He began to realize after his arrival in 1783 the close connections among them and between them and Greek, Latin, and the languages of modern Europe, including English. In 1786 he published a paper that convincingly made the case for an Indo-European language family, thereby earning himself the nickname "Oriental" Jones. Other Englishmen studied and translated the Indian classics and the great traditions of Indian religion and art and carried out archaeological work of great importance, including the later rediscovery of Harappa, Mohenjo Daro, and the Mauryan empire.

British scholars of Indian culture and history founded the Asiatic Society of Bengal in Calcutta in 1784, whose *Journal* published Jones' paper and many others on a wide variety of Indian topics. Most of the members and contributors were Company employees or officials who pursued their research on the side, but some found their Indian studies so engrossing that they retired to devote all their time to what was now known as Indology. Many took Indian wives, though few brought them home in retirement.

These British Orientalists, as they were called, were matched by Indian scholars who learned perfect English, studied Latin and Greek, wrote in the English literary and academic tradition, and also produced what is labeled both the Hindu Renaissance and the Bengal Renaissance, begun primarily by the work of the Bengali Ram Mohun Roy (1772–1833). Roy and others who followed him—some Company employees, others private scholars—sought their own cultural identity as well as Western learning and helped to restore the pride of educated Indians in their rich religious, philosophical, and literary heritage.

Roy founded a society in Calcutta to pursue these efforts, which made a deep impact on successive generations of Bengalis and Indians everywhere. Members of the society and like-minded Indians studied India's classical texts and led a revival of interest in the power and virtue of the Indian cultural tradition. H. L. Derozio

The British Indicted

In 1772 one of the early Orientalists, Alexander Dow, criticized the English.

Posterity will perhaps find fault with the British for not investigating the learning and religious opinions which prevail in those countries in Asia into which either they or their commerce or their arms have penetrated. The Brahmins of the East possessed in ancient times some reputation for knowledge, but we have never had the curiosity to examine whether there was any truth in the reports of antiquity upon that head. . . . Literary inquiries are by no means a capital object to many of our adventurers in Asia.

But William Jones was soon to join Dow and others. This is what he wrote in 1783.

It gave me inexpressible pleasure to find myself . . . almost encircled by the vast regions of Asia, which has ever been esteemed the nurse of science, the inventress of delightful and useful arts, and scene of glorious actions, fertile in the production of human genius, . . . abounding in natural wonders, and infinitely diversified in the forms of religion and government, in the laws, manners, customs, and languages as well as in the features and complexions of men. . . . [Later he wrote:] It was my desire to discharge my public duties with unremitted attention, and to recreate myself at leisure with the literature of this interesting country. . . . I am no Hindu, but I hold the doctrine of the Hindus concerning a future state to be incomparably more rational, more pious, and more likely to deter men from vice than the horrid opinions inculcated by Christians on punishments without end.

Sources: A. Dow, *History of Hindoostan* (1772), p. 107; P. Mudford, *Birds of a Different Plumage* (London: Collins, 1974), pp. 88–90 passim.

(1809–1831), of mixed Indian and British parentage, became in his short life a brilliant teacher and poet, inspiring young Bengalis to pursue, as he had done, learning in both the Indian and the Western or British traditions. He thus served to promote a true meeting of East and West, as his British counterparts among the Orientalists also attempted to do.

One prominent member of the society was Dwarkanath Tagore (1794–1846), an outstanding Western-style entrepreneur, banker, merchant, and industrialist who became,

An East India Company official studying an Indian language with a *munshi* (a native language teacher), c. 1813. Especially after 1800, the Company began to require all of its officials to learn at least one Indian language fluently, an obvious necessity for those who dispensed justice and managed administration as well as traded. [British Library]

Nadir Shah drove the Ottomans out of the Iranian territories they had occupied and even sacked and looted Delhi, but his ruthlessness and repression led to his own assassination and to civil war. His ultimate successor, Karim Khan, restored peace, but on his death, fighting resumed, and Iran never recovered its former glory. Similar bloody struggles over the succession to the Mughal throne in India deeply marred the century after Akbar, whose successors also plundered and neglected the empire while building their gorgeous palaces. Aurangzeb exhausted the country in his fruitless efforts to conquer the south and to persecute Hindus, leaving India at his death in 1707 torn by civil war and economic devastation.

In this critically deteriorating situation, the English East India Company, which had established small trading positions on both west and east coasts in the seventeenth century, began after 1700 to fortify and develop its bases at Bombay, Madras, and Calcutta, becoming the de facto rulers of small areas around each base. As India sank ever deeper into chaos, the Company's small army of mixed Indian and British forces began to acquire control over more territory, primarily to protect trade routes and the storage of trade goods. Clive's victory at Plassey in Bengal in 1757, in retaliation for the Bengali capture of Calcutta the previous year, opened a new phase in which the Company began to take over larger areas in both the north and the south. By 1800 the foundations of a British Indian empire had been laid, in part as the result of the British defeat of French ambitions and the rivalries of the Napoleonic wars. Imperial aims were accompanied by considerable blending of British and Indian cultures and interests, especially on the part of the Orientalists, as they were called, and of the Indian response in the Bengal Renaissance. But as British power and confidence rose, fed by growing industrialization, wealth, and technological progress at home, British arrogance in India increased, culminating in the mutiny of 1857, exactly a century after Plassey. The mutiny was not yet a national war of independence, but it did express long-standing grievances and foreshadowed the later rise of an Indian nationalist movement that would demand the country's freedom. The nation's political, economic, legal, and cultural institutions would evolve substantially within the patterns worked out during the colonial period.

Notes

1. From Company records, in S. N. Edwardes, *By-ways of Bombay* (Bombay: Tara Porevala, 1912), pp. 170–171.
2. From Company records, reproduced in C. R. Wilson, ed., *Old Fort William,* vol. 1 (London: Murray, 1906), p. 33.
3. R. Kipling, "Song of the Cities," in *The Five Nations and the Seven Seas* (New York: Doubleday, 1915), p. 183.
4. From T. B. Macaulay's "Minute on Education," in S. Wolpert, *A New History of India* (New York: Oxford University Press, 1982), p. 215.
5. G. Moorhouse, *India Britannica* (New York: Harper & Row, 1983), p. 89.
6. Ibid., p. 84.
7. Ibid., p. 97.

Suggestions for Further Reading

India

Bearce, G. D. *British Attitudes Towards India, 1784–1858.* Oxford: Oxford University Press, 1961.

Bhattacharya, S. *The East India Company and the Economy of Bengal, 1704–1740.* London: Luzac, 1954.

Broehl, W. G. *Crisis of the Raj: 1857 Through British Eyes.* Hanover, N.H.: University Press of New England, 1986.

Chaudhuri, K. N. *The Trading World of Asia and the English East India Company, 1600–1760.* Cambridge: Cambridge University Press, 1978.

Das Gupta, A. *Malabar in Asian Trade, 1740–1800.* Cambridge: Cambridge University Press, 1967.

Farrell, J. G. *The Siege at Krishnapur.* London: Weidenfeld & Nicolson, 1973. (A lively novel of India in 1857.)

Fawcett, C., ed., *The English Factories in India.* Oxford: Clarendon Press, 1952.

Furber, H. *Bombay Presidency in the Mid-Eighteenth Century.* New York: Asia Publishing House, 1965.

Hibbert, C. *The Great Mutiny: India 1857.* New York: Viking, 1978.

Kincaid, D. *British Social Life in India, 1608–1937.* London: Routledge & Kegan Paul, 1973.

Kling, B. *The Blue Mutiny: The Indigo Disturbances in Bengal.* Philadelphia: University of Pennsylvania Press, 1966.

———. *Partner in Empire: Dwarkanath Tagore and the Age of Enterprise in Eastern India.* Berkeley: University of California Press, 1976.

———, and Pearson, M. N., eds. *The Age of Partnership.* Honolulu: University Press of Hawaii, 1979.

Kopf, D. *British Orientalism and the Bengal Renaissance, 1773–1835.* Berkeley: University of California Press, 1969.

Laird, M. A. *Missionaries and Education in Bengal, 1793–1837.* Oxford: Clarendon Press, 1972.

Marshall, P. J. *East Indian Fortunes: The British in Bengal in the Eighteenth Century.* Oxford: Clarendon Press, 1976.

———, ed. *Problems of Empire: Britain and India, 1757–1813.* New York: Barnes & Noble Books, 1968.

Mudford, P. *Birds of a Different Plumage: A Study of British and Indian Relations from Akbar to Curzon.* London: Collins, 1974.

Mukherjee, S. N. *Sir William Jones: A Study in Eighteenth Century British Attitudes to India.* Cambridge: Cambridge University Press, 1968.

Murphey, R. *The Outsiders: The Western Experience in India and China.* Ann Arbor: University of Michigan Press, 1977.

Raychaudhuri, T. *Jan Company in Coromandel, 1605–1690*. The Hague: Nijhoff, 1962.

Sinha, D. P. *The Educational Policy of the East India Company in Bengal to 1854*. Calcutta: Punthi Pustaic, 1964.

Sinha, N. K. *The Economic History of Bengal*. Calcutta: K. L. Mukhopadhyay, 1956.

Spear, P. *Master of Bengal: Clive and His India*. London: Thames & Hudson, 1975.

———. *The Nabobs: A Study of the Social Life of the English in Eighteenth Century India*. London: Oxford University Press, 1963.

———. *Twilight of the Mughals*. Cambridge: Cambridge University Press, 1951.

Stokes, E. *The English Utilitarians and India*. Oxford: Clarendon Press, 1959.

Tripathi, A. *Trade and Finance in the Bengal Presidency, 1793–1833*. Bombay: Orient Longmans, 1956.

Watson, F. *A Concise History of India*. London: Thames & Hudson, 1979.

Iran

Armajani, Y. *Iran*. Englewood Cliffs, N.J.: Prentice-Hall, 1972.

Perry, J. R. *Karim Khan Zand: A History of Iran, 1747–1779*. Chicago: University of Chicago Press, 1979.

Ramazani, R. K. *The Foreign Policy of Iran: A Developing Nation in World Affairs*. Charlottesville: University of Virginia Press, 1966.

CHAPTER·28

Manchu China and Tokugawa Japan

On the eve of the modern world, China and Japan both emerged, in their separate ways, from periods of decay, rebellion, and civil war to found vigorous new orders. In China this occurred with the beginning of the Ch'ing (Qing) or Manchu dynasty, which took power in 1644 and ruled the empire until 1911. Under Manchu rule, China became once again the greatest power in the world as well as its richest and most sophisticated society. Despite their nomadic origins in northern Manchuria and their role as alien conquerors, the Manchus quickly adopted Chinese culture. This began even before 1644 as they built their power base in southern Manchuria, which had long been part of the Chinese system. They called their new dynasty Ch'ing, meaning "pure," in an effort to give legitimacy to their rule; in fact they governed China completely in the Chinese mode and with widespread Chinese cooperation.

Under Ch'ing government, China prospered. The commercialization and urbanization begun under the Sung and the Ming dynasties developed still further, while agricul-

Official court painting of the emperor Kang Hsi (1661–1722) by an unknown artist. Note the imperial dragon robes. [Metropolitan Museum of Art, New York]

ture became far more productive, with total output at least doubling. But population growth, in itself a result of prosperity, began to exceed production, and in the nineteenth century the Ch'ing regime also slowly lost its effectiveness. Peasant poverty bred rebellion, while China was at the same time unable to resist foreign pressures for trade concessions. In the early 1840s the Chinese were humiliatingly defeated by the British in the so-called Opium War. With the 1850s China entered a steep decline that left it largely at the mercy of Western incursions.

In Japan centuries of conflict among rival clans degenerated into open civil war in the sixteenth century. In 1600 a strong new centralized government, the Tokugawa shogunate, emerged to unify the country for the first time. Under Tokugawa control, Japan enjoyed more than two centuries of order, prosperity, and economic growth. But the regime rested on a revived system of feudal ties, and as the economy matured and a new merchant class became more prominent, pressure for change increased. Foreign demands for trade concessions, as in China, finally broke down Japan's self-imposed isolation in 1853. This Western pressure revealed Japan's weakness while feeding domestic discontent with the Tokugawa rulers. The shogunate was ended in 1868 by what is called the Meiji Restoration; although it ostensibly did restore the emperor, it is more accurately seen as a nonviolent revolution that brought to power a new group of radical reformers who set Japan on a course of rapid modernization, while China continued to flounder.

China Under the Manchus

Manchu rule, established in 1644, was only slowly consolidated. Scattered groups of Ming loyalists and others, including former Manchu allies who had been granted fiefs in the south, fought the new conquerors until the 1680s. Once resistance had been crushed, however, the new dynasty made a genuine effort to win not just Chinese support but actual partnership, a far more successful approach than that of the Mongol dynasty four centuries earlier. With Chinese collaboration, the Ch'ing gave the country order and tranquillity under which it prospered as never before.

Like the Mongols, the Manchus, who totaled only a little over a million people, or some 2 percent of the empire, could not hope to rule without the cooperation of the Chinese, who filled about 90 percent of all official posts throughout the dynasty. Manchu aristocrats dominated the top military positions, but the body of the army, militia, and police were predominantly Chinese, as were many generals. Provincial administration was headed by two-man teams of Chinese and Manchu governors working in tandem—and, of course, checking on each other. The gentry, who provided unofficial leadership and authority at all local levels, remained almost entirely Chinese. The gentry continued to supply nearly all of the officials through the imperial examination system, which the Manchus retained and expanded. At the capital in Peking (Beijing), the Grand Secretariat, the various ministries, and the imperial censorate were staffed equally by Chinese and by Manchus. The Manchu spoken language continued to be used, but all Manchus were by now equally at home in Chinese.

The Manchus succeeded also because they had become, even before 1644, as thoroughly Sinified as their "subjects"—indeed, they had long been an outlying part of the Chinese empire themselves. They came from an area of Manchuria where pastoral nomadism merged with Chinese-style intensive agriculture in the Liao valley and where Chinese cultural dominance dated back at least to the Han dynasty. To protect their homeland and their identity, they discouraged further Chinese emigration to Manchuria until around 1870, and kept northern Manchuria as an imperial hunting preserve.

In their administration of China itself, however, they maintained continuity with the now long established imperial structure and its institutions. The emperor appointed all officials down to the level of the county magistrates and presided over a mobile body of civil and military servants who owed direct loyalty to the throne. These officials were rotated as a rule every three years to emphasize their imperial rather than local or regional roles. The emperor was accessible to all his officials, who could send confidential memoranda (known as "memorials") for the emperor alone and to which he could reply in confidence to the sender only. The emperor personally had to approve all policy matters, to sign all death sentences, and to hear appeals.

The Chinese imperial structure was top-heavy, but on the whole it worked at least as well as the administration of other large empires and better than most. Each official had an extensive unofficial staff to help with the otherwise unmanageable burden of administrative routine and paperwork. But even so, it was a thinly spread system and grew progressively more so as a relatively static number of about 30,000 imperially appointed officials served a growing population. Most of China, still over 90 percent rural, continued to govern itself through the Confucian system of the "self-regulating society." But there was a huge amount of imperial administrative business too. Communication was essential among the widely scattered provinces and districts of this enormous empire, considerably larger than the modern United States and far more populous, and between each of them and the capital, where most important decisions had to be made or approved. The Ch'ing established some 2,000 postal stations along the main and feeder routes of the imperial road system, much of which was paved. The network extended into Manchuria, Mongolia, Sinkiang, and Tibet. Less urgent communications and shipments traveled by water wher-

28.1 China Proper Under the Ch'ing

ever possible, but for emergency messages or documents mounted couriers using relays of fast horses could cover 250 miles a day or more. This still meant nearly a week of travel from Canton to Peking, but it was almost certainly faster than anything in the West and was rivaled, at least before the end of the eighteenth century, only by the courier system of the Roman Empire at its height.

We know more about Ch'ing China than about any previous imperial period, partly because its recency means that far more of the documentation is still available. But we also have a great many foreign accounts, especially after the late eighteenth century. The Europeans were fascinated by China, and they can give us a perspective, and a comparative dimension, lacking for earlier periods. Their accounts help to establish a picture of Manchu China as the largest, richest, best governed, and most sophisticated country in the world of its time. European thinkers of the Enlightenment, including Leibniz and later Voltaire

Adam Smith on China

The founder of classical Western economics and advocate of the free market, Adam Smith, commented on China in his Wealth of Nations, *published in 1776, which was based on the accounts of Europeans who had been there.*

The great extent of the empire of China, the vast multitude of its inhabitants, the variety of climate and consequently of productions in its various provinces, and the easy communication by means of water carriage between the greater part of them, render the home market of that country of so great extent as to be alone sufficient to support very great manufactures, and to admit of very considerable subdivisions of labor. The home market of China is perhaps in extent not much inferior to the market of all the different countries of Europe put together.

Source: A. Smith, *The Wealth of Nations,* vol. 2 (New York: Dutton, 1954), p. 217.

and Quesnay, were much influenced by what they knew of Ch'ing China. They were struck in particular by its emphasis on ethical precepts as opposed to the commands of revealed religion and on selection for office through competitive examination. China, they thought, avoided the evils they ascribed in Europe to a hereditary officeholding nobility. To them China seemed close to the Platonic ideal never achieved in the West, a state ruled by philosopher-kings.

The Ch'ing compiled a vast new law code, dealing mainly with criminal offenses; most civil disputes continued to be handled locally through family, clan, and gentry networks. It too impressed European philosophers and legal scholars for its grounding in Confucian ethics. Admiration of China led also to a European vogue for Chinese art, architecture, gardens, porcelains, and even furniture and wallpaper (another Chinese innovation), all of which became the height of fashion for the upper classes, especially in France and England. The foreign perspective on China began to change in the nineteenth century as China declined and the West entered its steep modern rise. But traces of the original admiration long remained, for those less blinded by Victorian imperialist arrogance.

Prosperity and Population Growth

The first 150 years of Ch'ing rule were an especially brilliant period, marked by the long reigns of two able and dedicated emperors, Kang Hsi (Kang Xi, 1661–1722) and Ch'ien Lung (Qian Long, 1735–1796). As a direct consequence of the order and prosperity they established, population began an increase that continued until about 1850, probably nearly tripling over two centuries. Until late in the eighteenth century production and the growth of commerce more than kept pace. Even by the 1840s and 1850s, when per capita incomes had probably been declining for two generations or more, British observers agreed that most Chinese were materially better off than most Europeans. Robert Fortune, a well-informed traveler and resident in China, writing in 1853, succinctly summarized the prevailing view by saying that "in no country in the world is there less real misery and want than in China."[1] Fortune wrote from the perspective of industrializing England, with its repressed proletariat, but his judgment about China was probably accurate and is corroborated by other Western observers.

The massive growth of population and production is a good measure of the success of Ch'ing rule and the confident spirit of the times. Government officials diligently promoted improvements in agriculture, new irrigation and flood prevention works, roads, and canals. More new land was brought under cultivation to feed the rising population, and more new irrigation projects were constructed than in the whole of previous Chinese history. The Ch'ing period also saw the Chinese agricultural conquest of the cultivable areas of the south and southwest, at the expense of the remaining minority non-Han inhabitants (see Chapters 3 and 11). Much of the new tilled land was in the hilly south, where terracing was often pushed to extremes, driving the indigenous population into still more mountainous areas, especially in the southwestern provinces of Szechuan (Sichuan), Yunnan, and Kweichou (Guizhou). Large new acreage was also brought under the plow in the semi-arid margins of northern China. Yields everywhere rose with new irrigation, increased fertilization, better seeds, and more intensive cultivation.

Merchants were also allowed a broader scope under the Ch'ing even than under the Ming. Trade with Southeast Asia grew still further, and permanent settlements of Chinese merchants grew with it. Domestic commerce and urbanization reached new levels and remained far more important than overseas connections. Merchant guilds proliferated in all of the growing Chinese cities and often acquired great social and even political influence. Rich merchants with official connections built up huge fortunes and patronized literature, theater, and the arts. Fleets of junks (Chinese-style boats) plied the coast and the great inland waterways, and urban markets teemed with people and goods. General prosperity helped to ensure domestic peace. Silver continued to flow in to pay for China's exports to the West, now including tea and silk, leaving a large favorable trade balance. Cloth and handicraft production boomed with the sophisticated division of labor and an increasing market.

Along with silver, other New World goods entered the China market through Manila. These included new and highly productive crops from the Americas, including sweet and white potatoes, maize, peanuts, and tobacco. All had been unknown in Asia before, and in many cases they supplemented the staple agricultural system of rice, wheat, and the other more drought-tolerant cereals, such as millet and sorghum, grown in the drier parts of the north. Potatoes could be raised in sandy soils unsuited to cereals, white potatoes in the colder areas, sweet potatoes in the south. Both produced more food energy per unit of land than any cereal crop. Corn yielded well on slopes too steep for irrigated rice. Peanuts and tobacco filled other gaps and added substantially to total food resources or to the list of cash crops, such as cotton.

Early-ripening rice introduced from Southeast Asia in the Sung and Ming periods was further developed under the Ch'ing, and the period from sowing to harvest was progressively reduced. In the long growing season of the south, this meant that more areas could produce two crops of rice a year and some could manage three. The practice of transplanting rice seedlings in spaced rows set in irrigated paddies became universal in the Ch'ing period. This greatly increased yields and shortened the time to harvest.

Food and nonfood crops were now treated with the kind of care a gardener uses for individual plants, fertilized by hand, weeded at frequent intervals, with irrigation levels precisely adjusted to the height and needs of each crop as the season advanced. The use of human manure now also became universal, and the amounts increased as the population rose, providing both the source and the need for more intensive fertilization. Rice yields were more than doubled by a combination of all these methods, and the total output also rose as the result of double and triple cropping and the addition of newly cleared land. Improvements in rice cultivation, China's major crop since Han times, as well as new irrigation and other techniques, were probably the chief source of food increases. Rising population provided both the incentive and the means for improved crop yields under the management of local magistrates and gentry. The irrigation of rice was finely engineered, permitting the alteration of water levels and the draining of the paddies in the last few weeks before harvest. These improvements required immense amounts of labor and organization, but they paid handsomely in increased yields.

These changes, improvements, and additions to the system help to explain how an already large population could double or triple in two centuries and still maintain or even enhance its food and income levels. Agriculture remained the heart of the economy and the major source of state revenue, but its surpluses created a growing margin for both subsistence and commercial exchange. The population figures the Ch'ing compiled, like those of earlier

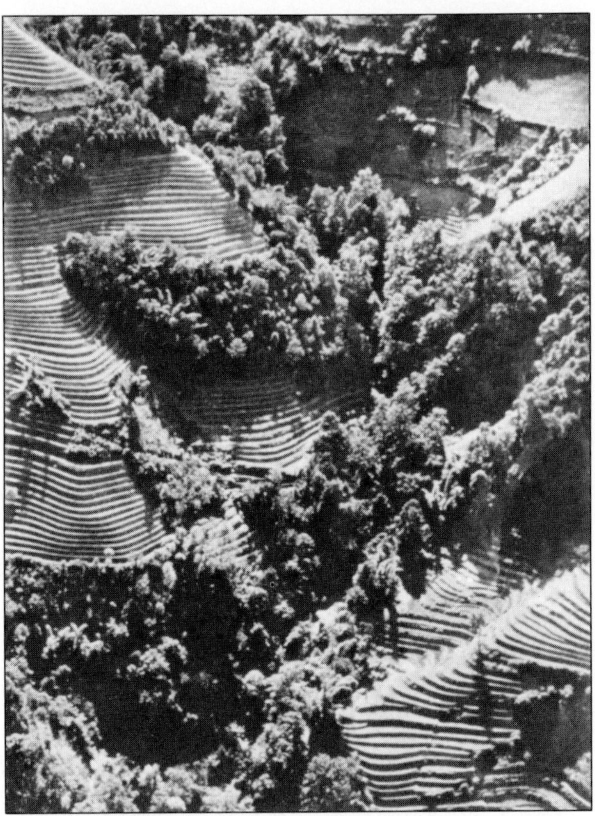

As population increased and demand for food rose, agriculture was pushed up onto steeper and steeper slopes, as in this photograph from the southwestern province of Yunnan. Terracing required immense labor but could create only tiny strips of level land, and water for irrigation was a major problem. Terracing was necessary because by the late Ch'ing period all gentler slopes had been occupied, while the population continued to rise. This is an extreme example, but such terraces were not uncommon. [Rhoads Murphey]

dynasties, were not designed as total head counts and were based on local reports by village headmen enumerating households and adult males fit for military service. Land ownership and output were also recorded for tax purposes, and for a time, as in previous centuries, there was also a head tax. Since everyone knew that population figures were used for calculating taxes and for conscript labor, there was an understandable tendency for local headmen and households to understate the true numbers.

Early in the dynasty it was announced that the head tax would never be raised, and it was later merged with the land tax and a levy on crops. At the same time, the Ch'ing made it plain that reports of population increase were welcome evidence of the prosperity of their reign. Reports showing little or no gain would reflect on the effectiveness of the local magistrate. For these and other reasons having to do with the imprecision, inconsistency, and incompleteness of the count (which often but not always excluded women, servants, infants, migrants, and non-Han people), Ch'ing population figures must be used cautiously, but the long-term trend is clear. From roughly 150 million in the late seventeenth century, the population had reached 400 or possibly 450 million by 1850. The official figures, almost certainly an undercount at first and possibly an overcount after 1750 or so, show 142 million in 1741 and 432 million in 1851. The rising population was indeed strong evidence of the success of Ch'ing rule, but in time it became a burden that the system could no longer carry successfully, leading to increasing poverty, disorder, and bureaucratic breakdown.

The Reigns of Kang Hsi and Ch'ien Lung

The emperor Kang Hsi, completely Chinese in culture and even an accomplished poet in that language, encouraged literature, art, printing, scholarship, and artisan production. He revived and enlarged the Imperial Potteries, which with other centers turned out great quantities of beautiful porcelain for the palace and court, the rich merchant elite, and the export trade. A patron of learning, Kang Hsi studied Latin, mathematics, and Western science with Jesuit tutors at his court and corresponded with European monarchs. Toward the end of his reign he lost patience with the sectarian quarreling of the Catholic missionaries and was incensed that a foreign potentate, the pope, should presume to tell the few Chinese Christian converts what they should and should not believe. He remained interested in a wide variety of things, however, and is described by his Jesuit tutors as insatiably curious.

Kang Hsi was a conscientious and able administrator of boundless energy who tried to ensure honesty in government and a harmonious partnership among Chinese and Manchu officials. He went on six major state tours around the empire and showed a great interest in local affairs. He commissioned an ambitious new encyclopedia of all learning, updated and greatly expanded from Yung-lo's compilation under the Ming dynasty. Running to 5,000 volumes, it was probably the largest such work ever written anywhere. The huge dictionary of the Chinese language that Kang Hsi also commissioned, which still bears his name, remains the most exhaustive and authoritative guide to classical Chinese up to his own time. He also supervised the compilation of a voluminous administrative geography of the empire. He encouraged the further spread of private academies for the sons of the gentry and state-supported schools for worthy but poorer boys, to spread classical learning and to open the way to office for those who mastered it. Older scholars and retired officials were sent around the empire at government expense to lecture to the populace on morality and virtue.

Kang Hsi was equally effective in military affairs. He supervised the reconquest of Taiwan, restored Chinese control over Mongolia and eastern Sinkiang, and in 1720 mounted an expedition to put down civil war in Tibet, where he established firm Chinese authority. His armies had earlier chased the Russians out of the Amur region of northern Manchuria. He then negotiated the Treaty of Nerchinsk in 1689 with the tsar's representatives, confirming Chinese sovereignty in the Amur valley and southward. This was both China's first significant engagement and its first treaty with a Western power. The Ch'ing clearly emerged as victors, successfully defending China's traditionally threatened landward frontiers. The Russian negotiators were kept on the frontier and not received in Peking; Nerchinsk was a minor border post, and relatively minor Chinese officials were sent to deal with them, assisted by Jesuit interpreters.

Far less attention was paid to the Westerners already attempting to trade at Canton and to extend their efforts farther northward along the coast. These traders, mostly Portuguese, Dutch, and English, were regarded as a minor nuisance in the same category as bandits or pirates. They were certainly not perceived as representatives of civilized states with whom China should have any dealings. The difference in response to the Russians reflected the perennial Chinese concern about their continental borders, the source of so much trouble in the past, as compared with the maritime frontier, which had never presented any major security problem. Their defenses, their front doors, and their military priorities faced westward toward the great Eurasian landmass whence the Mongols and other invaders had come.

Ch'ien Lung, Kang Hsi's grandson, succeeded him in 1735. He might have reigned officially until his death, but filial piety prompted him to retire in 1796 after 60 years so as not to stay on the throne longer than his grandfather. However, he remained the real power until his death three years later at the age of 89. Less austere and more extroverted than Kang Hsi, Ch'ien Lung, with his grand manner, has often been compared to King Louis XIV of France. Until his last years Ch'ien Lung was a diligent and

Ch'ing glory: the Altar of Heaven, just outside the Forbidden City in Peking, originally a Ming structure but rebuilt by the Ch'ing. Here the emperor conducted annual rites to intercede with Heaven for good harvests. The temple roofs are covered with magnificent colored and glazed tiles. [Bildarchiv Foto Marburg]

humane ruler who continued his grandfather's administrative and patronage model in all respects; comparison with Louis XIV does him less than justice. He commissioned the collection and reprinting of an immense library of classical works in over 36,000 volumes. But his support for learning was marred by the destruction of more than 2,300 books that he thought were seditious or unorthodox.

Ch'ien Lung was, of all Chinese emperors, probably the greatest patron of art. He built up in the imperial palace a stupendous collection of paintings and other works of art from all past periods as well as his own. Most of it is still intact. Ch'ien Lung also spent huge sums on refurbishing, embellishing, and adding to the imperial buildings inherited from the Ming.

Militarily, too, he was an aggressive and able leader. Despite Kang Hsi's expeditions, the Mongols had remained troublesome. Ch'ien Lung completely and permanently destroyed their power in a series of campaigns in the 1750s, after which he reincorporated the whole of Sinkiang into the empire. A revolt in Tibet shortly afterward led to a Ch'ing occupation that fixed Chinese control there even more tightly. Punitive expeditions were launched against Nepal, northern Burma, and northern Vietnam to compel tributary acknowledgment of Chinese overlordship.

Until the 1780s Ch'ien Lung, like the men who preceded him on the Dragon Throne, dealt personally with an immense mass of official documents and wrote his own comments on them. One of the Grand Council secretaries remarked in wonder at his diligence: "Ten or more of my comrades would take turns every five or six days on early morning duty, and even so would feel fatigued. How did the Emperor do it day after day?"[2] But as Ch'ien Lung grew older, he became more enamored of luxury and surrounded himself with yes-men. In old age he left matters of state increasingly in the hands of his favorites. His chief favorite, the unscrupulous courtier Ho-shen (He shen), entered the palace in 1775 as a handsome young bodyguard of 25 and, becoming Grand Councillor within a year, built up a clique of corrupt henchmen and plundered the empire. At his fall after Ch'ien Lung's death, the private wealth Ho-shen had extorted was said to be worth the equivalent of a $1.5 billion, an almost inconceivable sum for that time and probably a world record for corrupt officials. He concentrated all power in his own hands, holding in time as many as 20 different positions simultaneously. He betrothed his son to the emperor's daughter and clearly intended to take over the dynasty.

Ho-shen's rise was symptomatic not only of Ch'ien Lung's growing senility but also of the deterioration of the administrative system as a whole. The army, too, was neglected. A major rebellion by the White Lotus sect (see Chapter 20) erupted in 1796. The rebels were finally put down only after Ho-shen's fall by the new emperor, Chia Ch'ing (Jia Qing). In 1799 he quickly moved against Ho-shen, stripping him of his power and wealth.

Ho-shen's career illustrates the importance of personal connections in imperial China (and to some degree in China now), despite the merit system of examinations. Corruption, connections, and nepotism (favoring one's relatives) were aspects of China, and of Asia generally, that Westerners criticized as more widespread than in their own political and economic systems. Westerners were at least embarrassed by it at home; Asians supported it as proper. Family loyalties and the ties of friendship were valued as the highest goods. Anyone with wealth or power who did not use it to help relatives and friends was considered morally deficient. The family was the basic cement of society and with its support system of mutual aid was regarded as a microcosm of the empire as a whole, in which the emperor was seen as the nurturing father of his people as well as his officials. The connections of friendship were also part of the Confucian-sanctified "five relationships" (see Chapter 7) and took precedence over other considerations. In addition, political office was relatively poorly paid, and it was expected that officials would use their position to provide for their families and friends by diverting funds or receiving "presents." People of rank were expected to live well, in keeping with the dignity of their position. Even now one hears repeated the traditional saying, "Become an official and get rich." Ho-shen was only the most extreme example of a normal practice that was grossly abused.

The Later Ch'ing: Symptoms of Decline

By the 1750s the Ch'ing dynasty was already well into its second century. The eighteenth century saw the pinnacle of its glory, prosperity, and harmony, but even before the death of Ch'ien Lung, decline had begun. Prosperity remained widespread, accompanied by a major output of art and literature. This included new popular novels such as *The Dream of the Red Chamber* (also known as *Story of the Stone*), which prophetically dealt with the decline and degeneracy of a once great family and is still widely read.

Part of the government's problem was the failure of its officialdom to keep pace with the growth in population. Despite the rapid increase in overall numbers, there was only a small increment in the number of official posts, perhaps 25 percent versus a 200 to 300 percent boost in the population as a whole. This had an obviously negative effect on both governmental effectiveness and morale. A prestigious career in the bureaucracy, once a reasonable ambition for able scholars, became harder and harder to obtain. At the same time, the imperial examinations became still more rigidified exercises in old-fashioned orthodoxy and the memorization of traditional texts. These were to be commented on in the infamous eight-legged essays (see Chapter 20), allowing no scope for imagination or initiative. "Men of talent," as the best of the scholar-gentry had been called since the Han period, were often weeded out by this process. The examination failure rate climbed rapidly, and only students who lacked or suppressed all creativity could hope to pass.

Disappointed examination candidates and others who passed but were not called to office became a larger and larger group of alienated intellectuals. Paradoxically, the problem was only made worse by the earlier Ch'ing efforts to expand education and to open it to larger sections of the population. Learning had always been the key to advancement. Now, however, it was far from necessarily so. The system had hardened just when flexibility was most needed. Instead of preserving the Great Harmony, it bred discontent. One result was new corruption. Degrees, once attainable only by examination, and occasionally even offices, began to be sold. Failed candidates and disappointed office seekers provided the leadership for dissident and ultimately rebellious groups, whose numbers increased rapidly after 1785.

The lack of firm leadership and virtuous example, under Ho-shen and again after the death of the emperor Chia Ch'ing in 1820, aggravated the burdens of overworked officials. A magistrate of the Sung dynasty 500 years earlier had been responsible for an average of about 80,000 people in his county. By the end of the eighteenth century the average county, still administered by a single magistrate and his staff, numbered about 250,000; many were larger, and the average rose to about 300,000 in the nineteenth century. Local gentry, landlords, merchant guilds, and sometimes dissident or even criminal groups began to fill the vacuum. This led to a revival of anti-Manchu sentiment, for the Ch'ing was, after all, an alien dynasty of conquest.

The most basic and intractable problem the dynasty faced was a product of its own earlier success. By the last quarter of the eighteenth century population growth had probably outrun increases in production. Per capita incomes stabilized and then began slowly to fall. The poorest areas suffered first, and local banditry started to rise. By the end of the century open rebellions were breaking out. The secret society of the White Lotus, revived from a long quiescence, reemerged in a major uprising in 1796. Its reappearance tended to suggest to many Chinese that once again the ruling dynasty was perhaps losing the Mandate of Heaven. The secret and semi-Buddhist rituals of the White Lotus and its promise to overthrow the Ch'ing attracted many followers, including distressed peasants. Until 1804 the rebels defied the imperial army from mountain strongholds in the upper Yangtze valley along the borders of three provinces. The enormous expense of suppressing the White Lotus bled the treasury and fed corruption in the military. The unnecessarily long campaign also revealed the decline in the effectiveness of the army, which ultimately prevailed only with the help of some 300,000 local militiamen.

New Barbarian Pressures: The Westerners

Despite these mounting problems, China was still able to awe Westerners, who now appeared in unprecedented numbers and who tried to deal with the Dragon Throne as an equal and to obtain trading privileges. Like all foreigners, they had from the beginning been fitted into the tributary system, the traditional Chinese way of dealing with outsiders. At Canton, the only port where Westerners were permitted to trade, they could stay only for the trading season of about six months and were forbidden to bring in firearms and women, to enter the city proper, or to trade elsewhere on the China coast. They were obliged to deal only with the official monopoly that controlled all foreign trade, a restraint that they found galling in view of the huge potential market that China represented. Westerners were seen as potential troublemakers and perverters of Chinese morality. They should, it was felt, be kept on the fringes of the empire and walled off from normal contact with its people.

Various attempts by the British and the Dutch to trade elsewhere or with other merchants were rebuffed. In 1755 the English trader James Flint had sailed into several ports north of Canton, including Shanghai and Tientsin (Tianjin), in an effort to establish trade there. He was jailed and then deported, but the emperor ordered execution for the Chinese who had served as his interpreter and scribe. By the 1790s the restrictions at Canton seemed intolerable, especially to the British, then in their own view the greatest mercantile and naval power in the world and tired of being treated like minor savages.

In 1793 Britain's King George III sent an embassy to Ch'ien Lung led by a British nobleman, Viscount Macartney, to request wider trading rights and to establish relations with China as an equal power. He brought with him samples of British manufactures as presents to convince the Chinese of the benefits of trade with the West; these articles were not yet refined enough to impress the Chinese, though they included samples of the contemporary pottery of Josiah Wedgwood—hardly likely to appeal to the inventors of porcelain. The Chinese could still make most of the things Macartney brought better and cheaper and saw no need for British goods. The mission was a comedy of errors on both sides, since both were still profoundly ignorant of each other and lacked any standard of comparison. The Chinese interpreted the visit and the presents as a standard tribute mission, although from an especially distant and hence backward group of people, too far from China to have picked up any civilization. Chinese politeness obliged them to accept the presents, but with the kind of tolerance a kindly parent might display for the work of children.

The Chinese expected Macartney to perform the *k'e t'ou* (kowtow), or ritual submission, as all tribute missions did, before the Son of Heaven. Macartney, a typical Georgian aristocrat in his satin knee breeches who also suffered from gout, refused. He offered instead to bend one knee slightly, as he would to his own sovereign. Macartney further offended his hosts by pompously saying that he was "sure the Chinese would see that superiority which Englishmen, wherever they go, cannot conceal." One can almost hear him saying it! As a result, he never had a real audience with Ch'ien Lung, although he was kept waiting in Peking for over a month. Instead Ch'ien Lung sent him a letter for George III that was a masterpiece of crushing condescension:

> **I have already noted your respectful spirit of submission. . . . I do not forget the lonely remoteness of your island, cut off from the world by intervening wastes of sea. . . . [But] our Celestial Empire possesses all things in abundance. We have no need for barbarian products.[3]**

One can imagine the reaction of George III and Macartney.

In 1793 it was still possible for China to get away with such haughty behavior, and it was true that China was happily self-sufficient. A Dutch embassy of 1795 that also asked for better trade conditions was similarly rejected, even though the Dutch, perhaps less concerned with power or dignity than with profits, vigorously performed the kowtow several times as they lined up at court with other representatives from other countries sending tributary missions. A later British embassy under Lord Amherst in 1816 had a similarly humiliating experience. Amherst had the bad luck to turn up just when the British in India were fighting the Gurkhas of Nepal, a Chinese tributary since 1792, and was ordered out of the country by the emperor without an audience.

Nevertheless, the accounts of China given by members of the Macartney and Amherst parties as they traveled south from Peking to Canton, nursing their rage at the way they had been treated, were still strongly positive. They found China prosperous, orderly, and agriculturally productive, with an immense commerce and numerous large cities. Here are a few samples from the diary kept by a member of the Amherst mission in 1816:

> **Tranquility seemed to prevail, nothing but contentment and good humor. . . . It is remarkable that in so populous a country there should be so little begging. . . . Contentment and the enjoyment of the necessities of life [suggest that] the government cannot be a very bad one. . . . The lower orders of Chinese seem to me more neat and clean than any Europeans of the same class. . . . Even torn, soiled, or threadbare clothing is uncommon. . . . All the military stations are neatly whitewashed and painted and kept in perfect repair, and instead of mud cabins the houses of peasants are built in a neat manner with brick. The temples are also handsome and numerous.[4]**

Stagnation and Vulnerability

China may have declined from its eighteenth-century peak, but it was far from collapse. Although the emperors after Ch'ien Lung fell short of his level of brilliance, they were conscientious and honest. The corruption that had marred Ch'ien Lung's last years was greatly reduced, his scheming favorites were disposed of, and a renewed atmosphere of responsibility and service was established. The official salt monopoly, which had become semiparalyzed by corruption, was totally reformed in the 1830s. This was one indication that the imperial bureaucracy still had resilience and the power to correct weaknesses.

Omens of Crisis

For all his pompousness and the failure of his mission, Viscount Macartney was an astute observer. Though he was impressed by China's productivity and its well-ordered society, he accurately saw political trouble ahead.

The empire of China is an old first-rate man of war, which a succession of vigilant officers has continued to keep afloat for these 150 years past, and have overawed their neighbors merely by her bulk and appearance. [Here, of course, he spoke also from his own humiliating experience.] But whenever an insufficient man happens to have command on deck, adieu to the discipline and safety of the ship. She may perhaps not sink outright; she may drift for a time as a wreck, and then be dashed to pieces on the shore; but she can never be rebuilt on the old bottom.

But the economy continued to flourish well into the nineteenth century. Here is part of the account of a French traveling priest, the Abbé Huc, written in 1850.

European productions will never have a very extensive market in China. . . . China is a country so vast, so rich, so varied that its internal trade alone would suffice abundantly to occupy that part of the nation which can be devoted to mercantile operations. . . . Foreign commerce cannot offer them any article of primary necessity which they do not already produce themselves, nor even of any real utility, and they would see it stopped altogether . . . with a certain feeling of satisfaction.

Sources: J. L. Cranmer-Byng, ed., *An Embassy to China* (London: Longman, 1962), pp. 212–213; E. R. Huc, *The Chinese Empire* (London: Longman, 1855), p. 365.

At its best Ch'ing art remained magnificent, although much of later Ch'ing painting, decoration, and ceramics lacked originality and toward the end became overly ornate. Like much of the scholarship and philosophy of the time, it was technically accomplished but without the exuberance or imagination of earlier periods. Urban culture continued to thrive as merchant wealth was more widely diffused and city dwellers could read the new vernacular literature, enjoy the art of the time, and attend popular plays. China remained a sophisticated society as well as a prosperous one, still generally confident, even complacent. Imperial slights to barbarian upstarts like the British were in keeping with what most Chinese thought.

Yet the state really had no adequate long-run means to respond to the relentless pressures of increasing population. Decline was slow at first. China was immense, and its society and economy, largely independent of state management except for the official monopolies, took time to decay. Signs of trouble here and there did not mean that the whole system was rotten—not yet. Nor did governmental or military inefficiency or corruption among some officials mean that the whole administration was in trouble. Most of the Chinese world was only indirectly affected by the political sphere and continued to flourish after political decay was far advanced. Government was a thin layer on top of traditional controls.

Both foreign and Chinese critics were often misled by signs of administrative weakness into concluding that the whole country was falling apart. But the basic problem of growing rural poverty, especially after 1850, remained, as population continued to rise faster than production. Traditional agricultural technology had reached its limit of productivity, and all usable land had been pressed into cultivation. Only new technology could break this jam. Chinese agriculture, only a century before the most advanced in the world, was now rapidly falling behind the West's but showed no readiness to adapt. There was little interest in the now superior technology of Europe, and especially not in the disruption that would inevitably have accompanied its spread. China continued to protect itself against any ideas or innovations of foreign origin that might disrupt traditional ways. A different sort of response might have come from a new and vigorous dynasty, but the Ch'ing was now old, rigid, and fearful of change. Always sensitive about their alien origins, they feared to depart in any way from their self-appointed role as the guardians of the ancient Chinese way in all things.

The growing wealth of commercial elites did not fuel other kinds of growth or change, as it did in Europe. Individual or family wealth came not so much from increasing production as from acquiring a greater share of what already existed, through official connections or through managing the state monopolies. Merchants and their guilds never became an independent group of entrepreneurs or sought to change the system to their advantage, as their European counterparts did. In the Chinese view, they prospered by working within the existing system and had few incentives to alter it. For long-term investment, land was the preferred option since it was secure and offered social prestige as well. Capital earned in trade went into land, moneylending at usurious rates, or luxurious living but rarely into manufacturing or new technology.

Leisure and gracious living in gentry style were more valued in China than in the modern West, and there was less interest in further accumulation for its own sake. The gentry and the scholar-officials dominated Ch'ing China as they had since at least the Han dynasty, leaving little separate scope for merchants, who were still looked down on as parasites and who depended on their gentry or official connections to succeed. They neither could nor wished to challenge the Confucian bureaucracy but were content to use it for their own ends. All of this discouraged or prevented the rise of private capitalism and the kinds of new enterprise and investment that were basic to the commercial and industrial revolutions in the modern West.

Until the eighteenth century China had been in most respects the world's most technically advanced society. Iron-chain suspension bridges, canal locks, mechanical threshers, water-powered mills, looms, clocks, and the basic technology of the motor—crankshaft, connecting rods, and piston rods for converting rotary to longitudinal motion and back—all originated in China and were still spreading under the Ch'ing. But Chinese accomplishments, like those of earlier periods, were primarily a catalog of cumulative empirical discoveries rather than the result of systematic or sustained scientific inquiry. Confucianism offered little scope for abstract theorizing or empirical investigation. Learning concentrated on the Confucian classics and on records of the past as the proper guide for the present and the future.

The tradition of the learned man as a gentleman also created a deep division between those who "labored with their minds," as Mencius put it, and those who worked with their hands. Chinese craftsmen were highly skilled and ingenious but rarely engaged in theory or experiments, and most were not even literate. Scholars regarded all manual work, even experimental work, as beneath them, whereas the joining of theory, design, experiment, and practice from the time of Leonardo da Vinci produced the achievements of modern science and technology in the West. No such fusion occurred in China, which rested on its already high level of development.

It seems easier to understand why China did not become capitalistic or move on from its early achievements in science and technology than to understand why Europe did. The abrupt break with its own past that the transformation of the modern West involved and the explosion of modern science are harder to explain. China remained sufficiently successful not to seek or require such fundamental change. To a poorer and less developed Europe, change was more compelling, as the means to "progress." By the nineteenth century, however, China had fallen critically behind the insurgent West and was ruled by a dynasty old in office and suffering from complacency and loss of efficiency. The weakened government faced a population bigger than ever before and now sliding into economic distress, as well as a threat posed by militant Westerners. Neither was adequately dealt with.

Corruption is endemic in all systems; its seriousness is only a matter of degree. As the nineteenth century wore on, corruption in China became a growing cancer sapping the vigor of the whole country. Confucian morality began to yield to an attitude of "devil take the hindmost." People and families with connections had their lands and fortunes removed from the tax rolls, as in the last century of all previous dynasties. This put a heavier burden on the decreasing number who had to provide the state's revenue, mainly peasants. The strain on their already marginal position led many of them into banditry and rebellion. In all of these respects, late Ch'ing China was especially unprepared to meet the challenge of an aggressive, industrializing West. It was hard also to readjust Chinese perspectives, which had always seen the landward frontiers as the major area of threat. China was slow to recognize that external danger now came from the sea and along the coast.

The Opium Wars

China's resources, and those of the economy as a whole, were also depleted by a reversal of the earlier flow of silver that accounted for its favorable export balance. Exports of tea, silks, porcelain, and other wares continued, but imports of opium rose dramatically after 1810, mostly from India, where the British East India Company encouraged its cultivation as a cash crop for exchange on the Chinese market. By the 1820s opium imports exceeded China's total exports in value, and a heavy drain of silver flowed out, disrupting the economy.

Opium had been imported from Persia and was later grown in China for many centuries. It was widely used medically, but it began to be smoked as a recreational drug on a large scale in the late eighteenth century. Chinese addicts and their merchants and middlemen created the booming market for imported opium, which was thought to be superior to the domestic variety. No foreign pressure was necessary to encourage its use.

Although the imperial government declared opium smoking and traffic a capital offense, the profits of the trade were high, and the ban was ineffective. Westerners, including American as well as European traders, delivered opium to Chinese smugglers on the coast, who distributed it throughout the country through a vast network of dealers. Most of the fortunes won by early American traders to China rested on opium. Its growing use in China was a symptom both of the growing despair of the disadvantaged and of the degeneracy of a once proud and vigorous system, including many of its now self-indulgent upper classes.

Meanwhile, opium provided the occasion for the first Anglo-Chinese war of 1839–1842, popularly called the Opium War. Nearly 50 years had passed since Ch'ien Lung's rebuff of Macartney and his trade requests. Opium was the immediate issue that sparked the outbreak of hostilities, but much larger matters were involved. British patience was wearing thin; the British wanted freer access to the huge Chinese market as well as diplomatic recognition, as equals, by its government. They saw China as out of step with a modern world where free trade and regular diplomatic relations were the common ground of all "civilized" nations. China's resistance to such demands was taken as proof of its backwardness, and as India had been brought under the blessings of Western civilization, now, they thought, it was China's turn. China's arrogance toward the West was now matched by the West's toward China.

In 1838 the Chinese sent an imperial commissioner, Lin Tse-hsu (Lin Zexu), to Canton to stop the traffic in opium. Lin ordered stocks of the drug burned as contra-

The Opium War: the British steam-powered paddle wheeler *Nemesis* destroying a Chinese fleet in a battle on January 7, 1841, near Canton. The *Nemesis* was one of the first iron-hulled steam vessels; it was designed with a shallow draft so that it could attack inland shipping. Its guns had far greater range and accuracy than those of Chinese ships or shore batteries, and its name as well as its devastatingly easy success made it a symbol of Western naval and military ascendancy. [Bettmann Archive/BBC Hulton]

band. The British regarded their lawful property as having been destroyed and used the incident as a pretext to declare war. A small mobile force sent mainly from India soon destroyed the antiquated Chinese navy, shore batteries, and coastal forces. With the arrival of reinforcements it attacked Canton, occupied Shanghai and other ports northward on the coast, and sailed up the Yangtze River to Nanking (Nanjing) to force the Chinese government to grant what the British wanted. Because of distances, supply problems, and the stubbornness of the Chinese government, the war dragged on fitfully for more than three years. Each encounter ended in a Chinese rout that demonstrated the overwhelming superiority of Western military technology. The Chinese finally capitulated in the Treaty of Nanking (1842). Signed on board a British naval vessel, the agreement was the first in a long series that the Chinese came to call "the unequal treaties." Western imperialism had come to China.

Reunification and the Tokugawa Shogunate in Japan

Late medieval Japan under the Ashikaga shogunate had been marked by the rise of regional feudal lords and their armies, as summarized in Chapter 11. Ashikaga rule from Kyoto became increasingly ineffective in the sixteenth century. Although the shogunate had never been in control of more than central Japan, even areas beyond the immediate vicinity of Kyoto became more and more independent under their own *daimyo* (feudal lords), each with an army of *samurai* based in impressive fortified castles. Fighting between such armies became chronic, and with the final collapse of the Ashikaga shogunate in 1573, Japan dissolved into civil war.

Japan was still a small, poor, relatively backward country on the edge of the major Asian stage, divided among warring clans. The settled area of the country was only a fraction of the whole, and its total population was about 15 million, the size of a single Chinese province. The refined court and urban culture of Kyoto was luxurious, and technologically Ashikaga Japan had made much progress, even surpassing China in such fields as steelmaking and the production of fine swords.

Trade with the rest of East Asia was extensive, and Japanese shipping by the fifteenth century dominated the East China Sea. Japan's relatively small size and population and its weak central government worked to its advantage in this respect, making it easier to develop a national commercial system and a strong and semi-independent merchant class, unlike China or India. Foreign trade was proportionately more important than in China or India, more nearly on the scale of European countries. Most rural areas, by contrast, were isolated and lagged culturally and economically behind the urban centers. The political chaos of the late sixteenth century tore Japan apart once more, but it was to emerge from its troubles to find a new national unity.

The rising power of the daimyo destroyed the Ashikaga. The continued growth of their feudal domains, each more and more like a state in miniature, needed only common leadership to turn Japan into a national political unit. That was essentially the nature of the Tokugawa regime. The Tokugawa founders started out as daimyo like any of

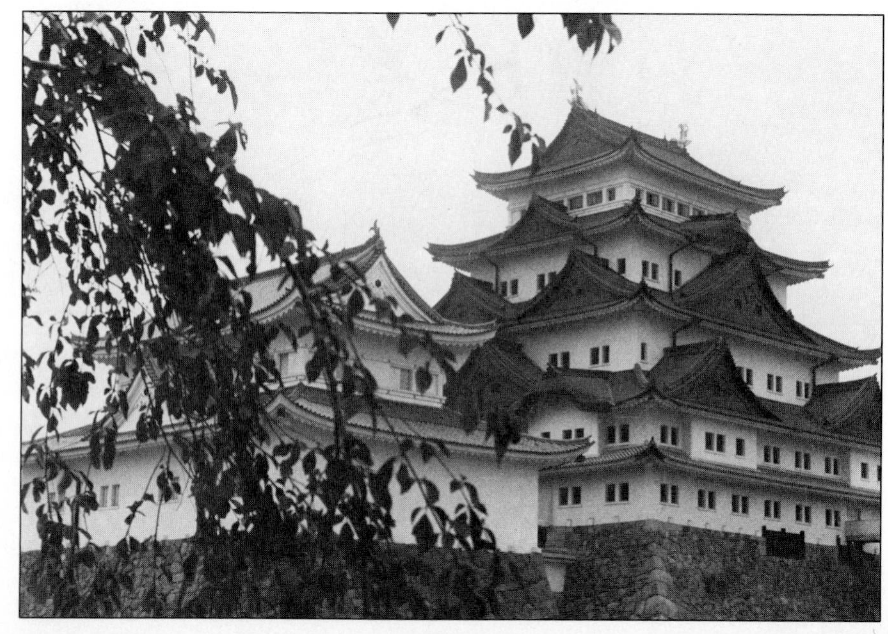

Daimyo castle, Nagoya. This is a typical example of the fortresses built during the last troubled decades of the Ashikaga dynasty and in the early Tokugawa period by local lords who then were conquered by or swore allegiance to the Tokugawa shogunate. The massive wall was surrounded by a moat. Such castles could usually be taken only by a long siege leading to the surrender of the starving defenders. [Wim Swann]

the others. Over about a generation a series of three exceptionally able leaders progressively conquered all their daimyo rivals and superimposed their dominance on an essentially unchanged feudal order. The subject daimyo were given substantial authority in their areas in return for formal submission to the Tokugawa shogun and periodic attendance at his court. Tokugawa central authority was far stronger and extended over a much larger area than any government in previous Japanese history. Despite its feudal trappings, it was in many respects in a class with the emerging national states of contemporary Europe. Samurai served not only as military officers but also as administrators. The flourishing merchant group provided revenue to add to land or agricultural taxes and also transported troops and supplies.

The Era of the Warlords

The process of unification began even before the formal end of the Ashikaga shogunate when Oda Nobunaga (1534–1582), a powerful daimyo who ruled the area around Nagoya, seized Kyoto in 1568 and became supreme in central Japan. He later captured the great temple-castle of Osaka, until then the independent seat of the militant Shin Buddhist sect. Nobunaga was murdered by a vassal in 1582, but his place was assumed by his chief general, Toyotomi Hideyoshi (1536–1598), born a peasant, who rose to the top through his ability and driving ambition. Hideyoshi soon eliminated the remaining faction of Nobunaga's family, subdued its vassals, and rebuilt the castle at Osaka as the base of his military government. In a campaign westward, he crushed the Satsuma clan on the

28.2 Tokugawa Japan

Hideyoshi Writes to His Wife

Hideyoshi wrote to his wife while he was besieging a daimyo castle in the spring of 1590.

Now we have got the enemy like birds in a cage, and there is no danger, so please set your mind at rest. I long for the Young Lord [his son], but I feel that for the sake of the future, and because I want to have the country at peace, I must give up my longing. So please set your mind at rest. I am looking after my health. . . . There is nothing to worry about. . . . Since as I have thus declared it will be a long siege, I wish to send for Yodo [his concubine]. I wish you to tell her and make arrangements for her journey, and tell her that next to you she is the one who pleases me best. . . . I was very glad to get your messages. We have got up to within two or three hundred yards and put a double ditch around the castle and shall not let a single man escape. All the men of the eight eastern provinces are shut up inside. . . . Though I am getting old, I must think of the future and do what is best for the country. So now I mean to do glorious deeds and I am ready for a long siege, with provisions and gold and silver in plenty, so as to return in triumph and leave a great name behind me. I desire you to understand this and to tell it to everybody.

Source: G. B. Sansom, *Japan: A Short Cultural History,* rev. ed. (New York: Appleton-Century-Crofts, 1962), p. 410.

island of Kyushu. In 1590 all of eastern and northern Honshu submitted to him after he had defeated the chief daimyo in the Edo (Tokyo) area. Hideyoshi scorned the title of shogun (the emperor's military adviser) and ruled instead as a dictator, although warlord is probably a more appropriate title.

With a large and unified army of professional fighters, Hideyoshi now looked abroad for more worlds to conquer. China was an obvious target, but to reach it he needed passage through Korea. When this was refused, he invaded Korea in 1592 and made rapid progress until a joint Korean and Chinese army forced him back almost to the coast.

Hideyoshi's death in 1598 ended this wasteful and destructive adventure, and his troops welcomed the chance to return home. His place was soon taken by one of his leading vassals, Tokugawa Ieyasu (1542–1616). Ieyasu had already built a castle-headquarters at Edo, where he had served as Hideyoshi's deputy. In 1600 he won a great victory in the battle of Sekigahara, near Nagoya, over a coalition of rivals. This established his power as Hideyoshi's successor, and he solidified it by capturing Osaka Castle in 1615.

Tokugawa Rule

Ieyasu wanted to build a strong, centrally controlled political system. He and his able Tokugawa successors largely achieved this, creating stability and peace for the next 250 years. They did so by enforcing a set of rigid controls on society as well as on political behavior and by repressing change. Tokugawa feudalism was even more hidebound than that of earlier eras, and the shoguns also tried to control dangerous thought with the help of a fearsomely efficient secret police. They themselves administered the central core of the country, from the Edo area to Kyoto, Osaka, and the peninsula south of Osaka, placing members of their own clan in the key centers of Mito, Nagoya, and Wakayama. This was, then as now, the economic heart of Japan, containing most of its best farmland and most of the commercial towns and cities. Other loyal allies and early supporters of Ieyasu were given fiefs in the rest of this central area. Beyond it, to the north and to the west, the Tokugawa bound other daimyo to them by feudal ties, helping to ensure their loyalty by requiring them to leave members of their own families, including wives and sons, in Edo as hostages. Daimyo were required to keep a permanent residence in Edo and to alternate their time between attendance at court and service in their distant fiefs, but armies were not permitted to leave their fiefs. The expenses of this required travel, with their retinues, and of maintaining two residences, which were often luxurious, put the daimyo increasingly in debt to merchants, whose unofficial power thus slowly rose.

A close eye was kept on the construction or repair of daimyo castles to keep them from becoming potential bases for rival military power, as they had been in earlier centuries. The shogunate created a new group of officials who acted as censors, on the Chinese pattern, and the secret police watched for any threats to Tokugawa rule. At Edo a new castle was built as the shogun's headquarters, a vast fortress inside massive walls and moats arranged in a series of concentric rings about 2 miles across. The innermost ring, with its moat and walls, remains as the imperial palace in the center of downtown Tokyo to-

The procession of a daimyo and his retainers along their journey from his local domains to take up the required period of residence at Edo. [Bildarchiv Foto Marburg]

Tokugawa Ieyasu: Instructions to His Successor

Tokugawa Ieyasu was a careful planner, a good judge of men, and one who understood the virtue of patient waiting until the time was right for action. Here is one of the instructions he left to his successors.

The strong manly ones in life are those who understand the meaning of the word patience. Patience means restraining one's inclinations. There are seven emotions: joy, anger, anxiety, love, grief, fear, and hate, and if a man does not give way to these he can be called patient. I am not as strong as I might be, but I have long known and practiced patience. And if my descendants wish to be as I am, they must study patience.

Source: A. L. Sadler, *The Maker of Modern Japan* (London: Allen & Unwin, 1937), pp. 389–390.

day. The emperor was left in place with his court at Kyoto, and the ancient fiction of imperial divinity and supremacy was preserved. Technically, the shogun was only the emperor's military chief of staff; in reality, he was the acknowledged ruler of the country.

By the time Ieyasu died in 1616, having prudently transferred power to his son so as to avoid a dispute over the succession, the new feudal order was firmly established. It is called feudal because it preserved many feudal forms, but the new central authority of the Tokugawa makes the label only partly appropriate. A new post of prime minister was created, assisted by a council of state, in part to ensure that the system would not weaken or collapse under a less effective shogun. In time a relatively complex central administration grew up, with posts filled first largely by able members of the Tokugawa clan or from the families of loyal daimyo and later from the expanding group of gentry in the central area.

Merchant groups and other commoners had begun to acquire new power and even some independence as Ashikaga rule deteriorated. Large-scale trade centered in the Osaka area. The neighboring commercial center of Sakai, now part of greater Osaka, was actually a self-governing city run by merchants with their own army, like a Renaissance city-state in Italy. The Tokugawa suppressed the rising political power of the middle and lower classes as a threat to their authority. Merchants were restricted and supervised in their activities and were made subservient to the new aristocratic order. Sakai's walls were demolished, its armies were dissolved, and its government was absorbed into the Tokugawa system.

The same order was brought into the countryside. Peasants were made to surrender their swords and other weapons to the government, and the hereditary warrior class of samurai was left in complete charge of military affairs. Swords became the badge of the samurai and came to symbolize their dual role as "gentlemen warriors" and as administrators. Firearms, which the Japanese knew of both from the Chinese and from the Portuguese and Dutch, were also seen as potentially disruptive. They too were successfully outlawed, and Japan remained free of them for the more than two centuries when foreigners were also excluded. Swords became even more an exclusive hallmark of the aristocracy, not easily challenged by unarmed peasants. In isolation from the world, Japan prolonged a medieval technology and the social system that went with it.

Peasants and artisans were essential producers, but merchants, despite their obvious accomplishments, literacy, cultivation, and wealth, were regarded as parasites and put into the lowest social order of all. This reflected classic Confucian values, revived by the Tokugawa, which admirably suited their feudal and hierarchical system. Merchants were forbidden to wear the fine clothes or materials of the upper classes, to ride in sedan chairs, or to omit the groveling and subservient bowing also required of peasants and artisans to samurai or other aristocrats whom they encountered. Those who did not bow low enough might have their heads chopped off by samurai guards.

The Expulsion of Foreigners

The Portuguese had reached Japan by 1543, and for nearly a century they and later the Spanish and the Dutch carried on an extensive export and import trade. Catholic missionaries came too and made numerous converts. Japan was more curious about Westerners than China was, having long understood the value of learning from others. But the Tokugawa grew irritated by the factional bickering among the different missionary orders and the allegiance converts had to give to a distant and alien pope. The foreigners and their intrigues were disturbing to the smooth order the Tokugawa had worked so hard to establish. In the years after Ieyasu's death in 1616, all missionaries were killed or expelled and converts executed or forced to recant. The persecution culminated in the suppression of a rebellion by impoverished Christian peasants in the area of Nagasaki, which had been the chief trade port for Westerners, in 1638. The survivors were slaughtered and thousands were crucified, but a few escaped and kept Christianity alive on an underground basis until the reappearance of Western missionaries in the 1860s.

All Western merchants were expelled by 1638, and Portuguese envoys who came in 1640 to ask for a reopening of trade relations were executed. Japanese were forbidden to go abroad, and no ships capable of overseas trade were built. In order not to lose complete touch with what was happening in the rest of the world, one Dutch ship a year was permitted to come for trade, on the island of Deshima in Nagasaki harbor, remote from the main centers of Japanese population.

Culture and Nationalism

With such an array of controls over people's lives, the Tokugawa did indeed ensure peace and stability. For about two centuries they also largely succeeded in retarding most change, especially in social or political matters. Economically, however, Japan continued to develop, and now, under the long Tokugawa peace, more rapidly than ever before. Production and internal trade grew, and with it, despite their low status in Tokugawa society, an expanding

Japanese Women: An Outsider's View

From the early accounts of the Dutch at Deshima, some American authors in 1841 compiled this account of the state of women in Japan.

The position of women in Japan is apparently unlike that of the sex in all other parts of the East, and approaches more nearly their European condition. The Japanese women are subjected to no jealous seclusion, hold a fair station in society, and share in all the innocent recreations of their fathers and husbands. The minds of the women are cultivated with as much care as those of men; and amongst the most admired Japanese historians, moralists, and poets are found several female names. The Japanese ladies are described as being generally lively and agreeable companions, and the ease and elegance of their manners have been highly extolled. But, though permitted thus to enjoy and adorn society, they are, on the other hand, during their whole lives, kept in a state of tutelage: that is, of complete dependence on their husbands, sons, or other relatives. They have no legal rights, and their evidence is not admitted in a court of justice. Not only may the husband introduce as many unwedded helpmates as he pleases into the mansion over which his wife presides but he also has the power of divorce, which may be considered unlimited, since he is restrained only by considerations of expediency. The Japanese husband, however, is obliged to support his repudiated wife according to his own station, unless he can allege grounds for the divorce satisfactory to the proper tribunal; among which, the misfortune of being without children takes from the unhappy wife all claim to maintenance. Under no circumstances whatever can a wife demand to be separated from her husband. At home, the wife is the mistress of the family; but in other respects she is treated rather as a toy for her husband's amusement, than as the rational, confidential partner of his life. She is expected to please him by her accomplishments, and to cheer him with her lively conversation, but never suffered to share his more serious thoughts, or to relieve by participation his anxieties and cares. She is, indeed, kept in profound ignorance of his business affairs; and so much as a question from her in relation to them would be resented as an act of unpardonable presumption.

Source: P. F. Siebold, *Manners and Customs of the Japanese in the Nineteenth Century* (London: Murray, 1852), pp. 122–124.

merchant class. A truly national market developed for many basic commodities, aided by the use of a system of paper credit. None of this fit well with the formally feudal arrangement of the social and political systems, and in the long run it had the same disruptive effects on Japanese feudalism as the revival of trade, towns, and merchants had in late medieval Europe. As rich merchants began to lend money to needy or extravagant noblemen and then to marry their daughters, they could no longer be treated as beneath the notice of daimyo and samurai. The cultural life of Tokugawa Japan was largely urban, and merchants came to dominate it as a new bourgeoisie.

The amusement quarters in the cities, especially Edo, were patronized mainly by merchants and by occasional samurai who sought relaxation from the stiff conventions of aristocratic society. This was the great age of the geisha, women carefully trained to cater to a male clientele as entertainers who specialized in singing, dancing, lively conversation for male patrons, and sometimes sex. Artists and novelists loved to depict geisha scenes, which became a distinct genre of refined eroticism.

Tokugawa splendor: a view of the main audience hall at Nijo Castle, Kyoto. The superb screen paintings, beautifully set off by the plain *tatami* (rush mat) floor, are a fine example of early Tokugawa decorative art for the elite. [Anne Kirkup]

The arts, too, produced relief from a highly conventionalized society. These included popular puppet plays and, from the seventeenth century, a new dramatic form, *Kabuki*, which is still popular in Japan. Kabuki catered to less refined tastes than the classical *Noh* theater and emphasized realism, comedy, and melodrama. Classical poetry, based on Chinese models, was reduced to three-line miniatures, the *haiku*, which at their best were superb snapshots of a moment of thought or feeling. Painting became more flamboyant, colorful, and grand, but still in keeping with the remarkable Japanese sense of good taste. Magnificent decorated screens and wall panels were produced for the palaces of the shogun and of noblemen, who wore gorgeous silk brocades and furnished their tables with beautiful lacquer ware and porcelain. In time, much of this splendor could also be found in the houses of rich merchants, but popular art became more important, and commoners' houses were more often decorated with woodblock prints. This is probably still the Japanese art best known abroad; it reached the climax of its development in the work of Hokusai and Hiroshige in the last decades of the Tokugawa regime early in the nineteenth century.

A good deal of information about the outside world continued to filter in by way of the Dutch at Nagasaki, including Western advances in medicine, shipbuilding, and metalworking. A few Japanese scholars began to study Western science; they compared Dutch texts on anatomy with traditional Chinese medical texts, for example, and through their own dissection of the corpses of executed criminals, demonstrated as early as 1771 that the Dutch version was accurate, whereas the Chinese was not. The Chinese rejected dissection, taboo in light of Confucian respect for the body. The Japanese also acquired a new national consciousness, thanks to the Tokugawa unification. They were able to adopt ideas and techniques from foreign sources, as they had long done from China, without in any way diluting their own cultural and national identity. Japan's separateness as an island nation further reinforced its sense of uniqueness.

Together with a renewed interest in things foreign, the late Tokugawa period saw a nationalist-inspired revival of Shinto, the ancient Japanese worship of natural forces. Shinto legends and naive myths about the divine origin of the emperor, and through him of the Japanese people, appealed more to the new nationalist attitudes, although Shinto never replaced Buddhism or the Confucianism of the upper classes and intellectuals as the dominant religion. These and other developments were slowly transforming Japan, despite its unchanging surface, toward modernity, including a commercial economy and society that would soon be ready to burst the artificial restraints imposed on them.

EDO AND THE "FLOATING WORLD"

By 1770 it is probable that the population of Edo and its immediate environs had reached a million, rivaled only by Peking and larger than any city in Europe. This urban concentration (the population of Japan by then was about 30 million) resulted from a combination of administrative centralization under the shogunate and the rapid commercialization of the economy. Edo and Osaka were the major centers of a national trade system and the headquarters of large merchant groups. The requirement that all daimyo had to maintain households in Edo, where they left their wives and family members as hostages, further swelled the population, as did their regular formal visits with their large retinues. Daimyo family estates, the large court of the shogun, and rich merchant families employed very large numbers of servants and artisans who provided them with luxurious furnishings and works of art.

Edo was also a major port; much of Japan's coastal trade passed through it, in addition to the trade that came by land. Much of the site had originally been swampy or prone to flooding, and large new tracts were drained and reclaimed as the city grew. Areas were set aside for daimyo and merchant residence and for shops, open-air markets, temples, and amusement quarters around the landward sides of the huge new castle built by Ieyasu. Thousands of soldiers based in Edo added to the numbers, as did the even more numerous laborers whose work supported the huge population.

Merchants dominated the bourgeois culture of Edo. Rich commoners wore forbidden silk under their plain outer clothing. The arts and amusements centered around what was called the Floating World, a pleasure quarter of theaters, restaurants, baths, and geisha houses. The main pleasure quarter was at the northern edge of the city, outside the official limits. Lesser aristocrats and their retainers, and even artisans, frequented this quarter, mingling with merchant patrons on a temporary basis of equality.

Rapid growth and crowding made for many problems, not the least of which was fire. Except for the shogun's castle and a few daimyo mansions, Edo was built almost entirely of wood, like all Japanese cities of the time, and fires often could not be controlled. The city burned down almost completely several times, but on each occasion it was rebuilt, larger and grander.

This was a new urban age of great cultural vigor, reminiscent in some ways of Sung dynasty Hangchow but increasingly dominated by bourgeois tastes. Culture was not necessarily vulgarized; merchants in fact often insisted on high aesthetic standards.

HOKUSAI, MASTER ARTIST

Probably the best known of Japanese woodblock printmakers under the Tokugawa was the man called Hokusai (1760–1849), whose astonishingly fertile career spanned eight decades. He was born in Edo of unknown parentage and was adopted at age 3 by a craftsman named Nakijima, who made mirrors for the shogunate. The boy seems to have shown a talent for drawing by the time he was 5, and by the age of 13 he had been apprenticed to an engraver of woodblocks. Hokusai was a devout Buddhist and chose the name by which he is known, which means "north studio," to honor a Buddhist saint who was thought to be an incarnation of the North Star. His early work centered on book illustration, and he also made many portraits of contemporary actors. His prints are very Japanese in style but had become enormously popular in the West even before the end of Japan's seclusion policy.

Hokusai emerged at a period when Japan's arts had again begun to penetrate an international market. Japanese craftsmen had begun to copy the Chinese blue-and-white porcelain ware, so popular with Westerners that it became, together with silk and tea, an important Japanese export. It did not occur to the Japanese that Westerners would find their art desirable, although the woodblock prints in which their artists specialized were turned out in large numbers, sold very cheaply, and could easily be duplicated from the original block. But the freshness, color, and simple lines of Hokusai's work, like that of many of his contemporaries, appealed strongly to a Europe already impressed and influenced by Chinese art. The European craze for chinoiserie in the late eighteenth and early nineteenth centuries was joined by an enthusiasm for "japonoiserie." Many Japanese prints in fact arrived in Europe as wastepaper, used for wrapping porcelain and other export goods, but they soon became prized and collected. Return trade to Japan brought, among other things, the color and materials for Prussian blue, which Hokusai and others soon used to brighten and enliven their work.

Perhaps the best known of Hokusai's prints in the West is his *Thirty-six Views of Mount Fuji.* His style and that of his contemporaries had a great influence on Western artists, especially in late-nineteenth-century France. Most of the impressionists acknowledged their debt to Hokusai, and many of them painted pictures in an avowedly Japanese style during the craze for things Japanese after 1870, including Vincent van Gogh's careful copy of a print by Hokusai's great contemporary Hiroshige (1797–1858). Thus while Meiji Japan was busily adopting Western ways as fast as it could, Western artists were returning the compliment.

Hokusai: "The Breaking Wave," from *Thirty-six Views of Mount Fuji*: perhaps the woodblock print best known outside Japan. Note Mount Fuji in the background. [Metropolitan Museum of Art, Henry L. Phillips Collection]

Foreign Pressures and Domestic Unrest

The political system controlled so tightly from Edo ran relatively smoothly through the first half of the nineteenth century, and there were few outward expressions of dissent. In time the pressures building up behind the orderly facade of Tokugawa life would probably have forced basic change. As it happened, an outside force provided the impetus that destroyed the shogun's power and compelled Japan to face the world fully. It is not surprising that, having been so long suppressed, the change that resulted was on a truly revolutionary scale.

Among the outsiders, Americans were most eager to open Japanese ports to foreign trade. First American whalers, then clipper ships plying the China trade, then steamships in need of coal supplies sought permission to obtain provisions in Japan. The Tokugawa response was sharply negative. American and European sailors shipwrecked on Japanese shores were often handled roughly. American, British, and Russian expeditions after 1800 were repelled by the Edo government, and their requests were rejected. Finally, the American government took matters in its own hands. In 1853 it sent a small but powerful naval force under Commodore Matthew Perry with a letter to the shogun demanding trade relations and better treatment of foreign castaways.

Perry's squadron anchored in Tokyo Bay, in full view of Edo. The government was duly impressed by the size and the guns of the Americans' steam-powered "black ships," against which they realized Japan was defenseless. The Japanese tried to stall, and conservative forces, which dominated the Tokugawa, urged that the foreigners be refused and ejected. When Perry renewed the show of force the next year, the government capitulated. It signed a treaty, opening two ports and allowing a limited amount of regulated trade. Similar treaties ensued with European powers, and in 1858 a set of more detailed commercial treaties followed.

Foreigners could now reside in five ports as well as Osaka and Edo and could trade with whom they liked. The political backlash was severe. Many Japanese still felt strongly that the foreigners must be expelled before they further sullied the sacred soil of Japan. The official who had signed the trade agreements was assassinated by conservative elements in 1860. Other extreme nationalists murdered an Englishman near Yokohama, a former fishing village that had become the main foreign settlement. There were, of course, reprisals, and the Tokugawa government was caught in a dilemma. It was neither able to resist foreign pressures nor to control its own subjects, who increasingly felt that the government had failed them and revealed its impotence. The outer daimyo domains in western Japan had always been restless under Tokugawa domination and now saw their chance to challenge it. They and others began to intrigue at the court in Kyoto and finally confronted Edo's forces militarily.

When the emperor died in 1867, the shogun, bowing to the general pressure, formally handed over power to the new boy emperor, Meiji, and his advisers, among whom samurai from rebellious western Japan had a prominent place. A little over a year later they persuaded the outer daimyo to offer their domains to the emperor, and feudal lords in the rest of Japan followed suit. The emperor moved to the more modern Edo, which thenceforward was known as Tokyo ("eastern capital"). This largely nonviolent revolution of 1868 is known as the Meiji Restoration, for technically the emperors of Japan had never surrendered their sovereign powers. But it was a revolution nonetheless, and it brought to power new forces bent on rapid and radical change. The daimyo were compensated for their surrendered lands, and some remained as governors and other officials of the new government. Feudalism in Japan was over; the way was clear for the wholesale remaking of the nation as a modern industrial power.

The growth of cities, trade, and merchants and the rise of a strong centralized government helped make it possible for Japan to modernize itself rapidly along Western lines while Manchu China floundered. Tokugawa rule had been profoundly conservative, even hidebound in its feudal forms, but its often harsh political controls had created the stability that made economic development possible. Antiquated though the feudal forms seemed, late Tokugawa Japan, like late medieval Europe, was a society on the eve of economic revolution.

In China late Ch'ing rule was also conservative, but its central administrative controls weakened after 1800, and Western penetration accelerated its collapse. The economy remained dominated by peasant agriculture, and urban life was never more than a small part of a basically agrarian system. China was too big to be affected by new trends except very slowly. The inherent conservatism of both the peasants and their rulers worked against change. But none of this was clear as of 1860 or even 1870. Most foreign observers still looked to China as the dominant force in the East Asian economy. Within the next century, however, Japan, with a population still less than a tenth of China's, was to outstrip its neighbor in productivity, wealth, and power.

Notes

1. R. Fortune, *Three Years' Wanderings in the Northern Provinces of China* (London: Murray, 1853), p. 196.
2. J. K. Fairbank, E. O. Reischauer, and A. Craig, *East Asia: Tradition and Transformation* (Boston: Houghton Mifflin, 1978), p. 228.
3. J. L. Cranmer-Byng, ed., *An Embassy to China* (London: Longman, 1962), pp. 212–213.
4. G. Stanton, *Notes of Proceedings During the British Embassy to Peking in 1816* (London: Murray, n.d.), pp. 153–225 passim.

Suggestions for Further Reading

China

Fairbank, J. K., ed. *The Cambridge History of China*, vol. 10: *Late Ch'ing*. Cambridge: Cambridge University Press, 1978.

Fay, P. W. *The Opium War*. Cambridge: Cambridge University Press, 1975.

Greenberg, M. *British Trade and the Opening of China, 1800–1842*. Cambridge: Cambridge University Press, 1951.

Ho, P. T. *Studies on the Population of China, 1368–1953*. Cambridge, Mass.: Harvard University Press, 1959.

Kahn, H. L. *Monarchy in the Emperor's Eyes: Image and Reality in the Ch'ien Lung Reign*. Cambridge, Mass.: Harvard University Press, 1971.

Lach, D. *Asia in the Making of Europe*. 2 vols. Chicago: University of Chicago Press, 1965, 1978.

Metzger, T. *The Internal Organization of Ch'ing Bureaucracy*. Cambridge, Mass.: Harvard University Press, 1973.

Miyazaki, I. *China's Examination Hell: The Civil Service Examinations in Imperial China*, trans. C. Schirokauer. New York: Weatherhill, 1976.

Perkins, D. *Agricultural Development in China, 1368–1968*. Chicago: University of Chicago Press, 1969.

Rawski, E. *Education and Popular Literature in Ch'ing China*. Ann Arbor: University of Michigan Press, 1978.

Rozman, G. *Urban Networks in Ch'ing China and Tokugawa Japan*. Princeton, N.J.: Princeton University Press, 1973.

Spence, J. *Ch'ing Sheng-tsu, Emperor of China*. New York: Knopf, 1974.

Van der Sprenkel, S. *Legal Institutions in Manchu China*. London: University of London Press, 1962.

Wakeman, F. *The Great Enterprise: The Manchu Reconstruction of Imperial Order in Seventeenth-Century China*. Berkeley: University of California Press, 1986.

Wong, R. B., Will, P. E., and Lee, J. *State Granaries and the Food Supply of China, 1650–1850*. Ann Arbor: University of Michigan Press, 1987.

Japan

Barr, P. *The Coming of the Barbarians*. London: Macmillan, 1967.

Bix, H. P. *Peasant Protest in Japan, 1590–1884*. New Haven, Conn.: Yale University Press, 1986.

Bolitho, H. *Treasures Among Men: The Feudal Daimyo in Tokugawa Japan*. New Haven, Conn.: Yale University Press, 1974.

Dore, R. P. *Education in Tokugawa Japan*. Berkeley: University of California Press, 1965.

Dunn, C. J. *Everyday Life in Traditional Japan*. London: Batsford, 1969.

Elison, G., and Smith, B. *Warlords, Artists, and Commoners: Japan in the Sixteenth Century*. Honolulu: University Press of Hawaii, 1981.

Michener, J. A. *The Floating World*. Honolulu: University Press of Hawaii, 1983.

Reischauer, E. O. *Japan: The Story of a Nation*. New York: Knopf, 1970.

Storry, R. *A History of Modern Japan*, rev. ed. New York: Penguin Books, 1982.

Totman, C. *Politics in the Tokugawa Bakufu, 1600–1843*. Cambridge, Mass.: Harvard University Press, 1967.

———. *Tokugawa Ieyasu: Shogun*. San Francisco: Heian, 1983.

CHAPTER · 29

The Industrial Revolution

From the beginning of history to the nineteenth century, all physical labor was accomplished by human hands, either directly or with tools held or rigged by human hands or with animals guided by human hands. Power was supplied by muscle reinforced by levers, pulleys, and weights and supplemented by running water, moving air, or fire. Since then, work has been performed increasingly, and in the more developed regions of the world predominantly, by machines powered by steam, electricity, combustible gases, and the exploding atom. The use of new power sources to drive increasingly complex machines is still developing, as may be seen in such contemporary devices as computers and lasers. The enormous consequent increase in productive capacity and technical mastery of the resources of the globe has transformed work, society, and the face of the planet itself more than any single development since the introduction of agriculture. This process is still known by the name given to it by the nineteenth-century British historian Arnold Toynbee: the Industrial Revolution.

An early steam-powered engine, based on English design and built in 1727, pumps water from a Swedish mine. Impressive in scale, it could pump 100 gallons a minute out of flooded shafts. [Trustees of the Science Museum, London]

The Background: Population, Energy, and Technology

The Industrial Revolution began in western Europe, specifically in Great Britain. Europe had achieved an aggregate growth of population, commerce, and energy between the fifteenth and the eighteenth centuries. Such growth, at an even faster relative rate, had been experienced between the eleventh and thirteenth centuries, only to be succeeded by the demographic catastrophe of the fourteenth. Some observers, such as the Englishman Thomas Robert Malthus (1766–1834), feared at the end of the eighteenth century that Europe was on the brink of such a catastrophe again. In his *Essay on Population* (1798), Malthus noted with alarm the surge in Europe's population, apparent since the middle of the century. Asserting that population tended to increase geometrically while production grew only arithmetically, he calculated that Europeans would soon outstrip their resources. The result would be scarcity, famine, and war.

Had the Industrial Revolution not transformed Europe's productive capacity, Malthus' dire prophecy might have come true. By the end of the eighteenth century, its once

Malthus on Population

The English clergyman and economist Thomas Malthus, writing at the beginning of the population explosion, concluded that the permanent pressure of population would frustrate all efforts to achieve a more perfected society, and that only sexual abstinence could prevent widespread misery.

In plants and irrational animals, the view of the subject is simple. They are all impelled by a powerful instinct to the increase of their species; and this instinct is interrupted by no doubts about providing for their offspring. Wherever therefore there is liberty, the power of increase is exerted; and the superabundant effects are repressed afterwards by want of room and nourishment.

The effects of this check on man are more complicated. Impelled to the increase of his species by an equally powerful instinct, reason interrupts his career, and asks him whether he may not bring beings into the world for whom he cannot provide the means of support. If he attend to this natural suggestion, the restriction too frequently produces vice. If he hear it not, the human race will be constantly endeavoring to increase beyond the means of subsistence. But as, by that law of our nature which makes food necessary to the life of man, population can never actually increase beyond the lowest nourishment capable of supporting it, a strong check on population, from the difficulty of acquiring food, must be constantly in operation. This difficulty must fall somewhere, and must necessarily be severely felt in some or other of the various forms of misery, or the fear of misery, by a large portion of mankind.

That population has this constant tendency to increase beyond the means of subsistence, and that it is kept to its necessary level by these causes, will sufficiently appear from a review of the different states of society in which man has existed. But, before we proceed to this review, the subject will, perhaps, be seen in a clearer light if we endeavor to ascertain what would be the natural increase of population if left to exert itself with perfect freedom; and what might be expected to be the rate of increase in the productions of the earth under the most favorable circumstances of human industry.

It will be allowed that no country has hitherto been known where the manners were so pure and simple, and the means of subsistence so abundant, that no check whatever has existed to early marriages from the difficulty of providing for a family, and that no waste of the human species has been occasioned by vicious customs, by towns, by unhealthy occupations, or too severe labor. Consequently in no state that we have yet known has the power of population been left to exert itself with perfect freedom.

Source: T. Malthus, *An Essay on Population* (London: Dutton, 1914), pp. 6–7.

abundant forests had been seriously depleted by industrial demand and agricultural clearance. The average Parisian, for example, was consuming 2 tons of fuel per year by 1789, almost all of it wood, and French forests had already shrunk to their present-day size. At that rate, the exhaustion of France's major energy source and chief industrial material seemed inevitable.

The solution was the replacement of wood by coal. Coal had become an important fuel source in the sixteenth century in Liège, where it was mined in the surrounding basin, and even more so in Newcastle on the Tyne basin in England, where after 1600 it was used extensively in the production of salt, glass, bricks, and tiles, in metal and sugar refining, and in baking and brewing. But its more general use was restricted by the difficulty and danger of mining it, the lack of overland transportation to distribute it, and the foul-smelling sulfur released in burning it.

One of the chief hazards of coal mining was subsurface water. At the beginning of the eighteenth century, Thomas Savery, a London inventor, and Thomas Newcomen, a Dartmouth blacksmith, developed a steam-powered pump that Savery called "the Miners' Friend." The efficiency of this pump was increased fourfold by the introduction in the 1770s by the Scotsman James Watt (1736-1819) of a condenser that kept the steam from being dissipated into the atmosphere, and demand for it jumped. Dissatisfied with what was still essentially a simple pump, Watt continued to experiment until by 1782 he had converted it into a double-action rotary engine capable of turning heavy machinery. By 1800, 500 such engines were in use in Great Britain.

Just as industrial progress was limited by the use of wood as its primary source of energy, so too was it limited by its dependence on wood and stone as its chief construction materials. Running a poor third to these, though indispensable for such everyday products as nails, needles, wire, spurs, buckles, and rings, as well as heavier implements such as stoves and weapons, was iron. Smelting iron, which involved separating it from its ore, was a complex, labor-intensive process (the Italian city of Brescia, a major iron center, was said to employ 60,000 people to manufacture iron in the late fifteenth century), requiring heavy machinery and great amounts of fuel. The product itself, like coal, was difficult to transport, and most iron for domestic use was produced in small quantities on the village level.

Smelting was accomplished by the use of charcoal, which required that all large ironworks be located near forest areas. The search for an alternative fuel as the forests dwindled led to coke, a waste product obtained from coal essentially as charcoal is from wood. Its high sulfur content resulted in an unacceptably brittle product, however, until the Quaker ironmaster Abraham Darby was able to produce a coke-smelted iron suitable for heavy utensils and military ordnance in 1709. The demand for munitions during the Seven Years' War led to a considerable expansion of coke-fed blast furnaces in Great Britain. But it was not until 1784, when Henry Cort introduced the puddling process for converting crudely cast pig iron into the lighter and more tensile wrought iron necessary for most domestic products, that the iron industry was freed from its dependence on wood.

The result of these technical innovations was that by the 1780s Europe stood on the verge of a great breakthrough in its industrial capacity. The use of steam facilitated the extraction of coal; the use of coal made possible the increased production of iron; and iron (with other metals) was first to supplement and then to replace wood and stone as the prime industrial material. At the same time, transportation was improved by new highways called turnpikes that could bear far heavier loads and by canals that turned Britain's waterways into an integrated transport system. The symbol of the new age was the great iron bridge that Abraham Darby III built across the Severn River in Shropshire in 1779; 50 years later, the first phase of the Industrial Revolution was to culminate in the locomotive, which, made of iron and powered by steam and coal, was to provide industry with an incomparably cheap and efficient method of transportation.

These neatly interlocking developments suggest that the Industrial Revolution was a more or less straightforward consequence of certain technical improvements in mining and metallurgy, prompted by a threatened scarcity of traditional resources. But such an explanation by itself would be misleading. Other societies, including previous European ones, had faced scarcity without finding a key to increased productivity. Other societies had achieved technical levels comparable to those of eighteenth-century Europe without an industrial breakthrough. The Chinese had used coal for domestic heating for several thousand years and for metalworking from about 500 B.C. Their smelting processes were far more sophisticated, and they were able to produce wrought iron and steel of far higher quality. The swords forged with this steel, proceeding westward along the trade routes, had enabled Persian cavalrymen to rout Roman legions in the third century A.D. Western metalworking, despite considerable advances between the eleventh and eighteenth centuries, was still in fact inferior to that of China and India; and when in 1591 the Portuguese captured a cargo of Indian steel, no blacksmith in Lisbon or Spain was able to forge it. Yet at the same time the fine silks and cottons of China and India, so much in demand in eighteenth-century Europe, were woven on looms whose crudeness astonished Western visitors. Clearly, the relation between craft and technology was complex; nor do we fully understand the social processes that inhibited technology in China after the thirteenth century at just the moment it had begun to advance in what had only recently been one of the most backward sectors of the globe, western Europe.

The technical breakthrough of eighteenth-century Europe should therefore be seen not as the beginning but as

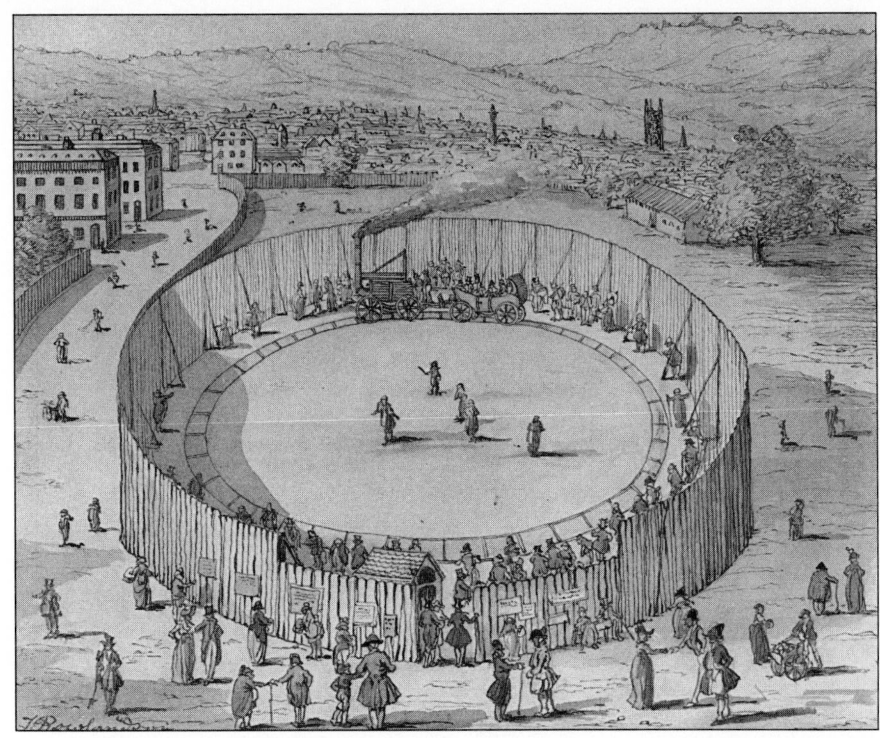

The first railway track was laid inside this circular enclosure near what is now the site of the great Euston train station in London to demonstrate Richard Trevithick's steam locomotive in 1808. The first commercially practical engine was built in the 1820s, and by the 1840s rail networks had begun to span Europe and the United States. The enormous capital outlays forced business, industry, and the state into partnership on an unprecedented scale. The drawing is by Thomas Rowlandson. [Trustees of the Science Museum, London]

the end product of a complex process of social change. That process had at least three distinguishable components: commercial, agricultural, and scientific.

Commerce and the Formation of Capitalist Society

Before the term *Industrial Revolution* had been coined, the nineteenth century social critics Karl Marx (1818–1883) and Friedrich Engels (1820–1895) had identified the banking and commercial classes of Europe—the bourgeoisie—as critical in the development of the new industrial society. "The bourgeoisie," they wrote,

> **has subjected the country to the rule of the towns. It has created enormous cities, . . . agglomerated population, centralized means of production, and has concentrated property in a few hands. . . . [It] has created more massive and more colossal productive forces than have all preceding generations together.[1]**

Marx and Engels saw the bourgeoisie as a group unique to modern Western society, differing from merchant elites in all previous societies in its ability to grasp, organize, and exploit the basic elements of production: capital, land, and labor. Exaggerated though this view may be, it is certainly true that the development of business and commerce had become critical to the prosperity and expansion of Europe.

Commerce becomes a specialized economic function when consumers no longer obtain their goods directly from producers. In commercial economies, producers and consumers typically consummate their exchange through a person appropriately called a *middleman,* or merchant. In the simplest case, the commercial exchange involves a seller (the producer) and a buyer (the consumer) linked by a person who both buys (from the producer) and sells (to the consumer). By extending the links in this chain—by adding more intermediaries—goods can be shipped around the world, joining producers and consumers who share no common language or currency or even knowledge of one another's concrete existence. In such a case, the producer produces for a wholly abstract market, the size and nature of which is defined by the number of men in the middle.

What expands this number, and hence the economy itself, is capital. Capital can be defined in stocks of goods or resources, in warehousing and shipping facilities, in command or control of a labor supply. But its simplest form is money, since money is freely interchangeable into all the other elements. The term *capital* in this sense was first used in the West in the twelfth and thirteenth centuries. A *capitalist,* as the term emerged by about the mid-

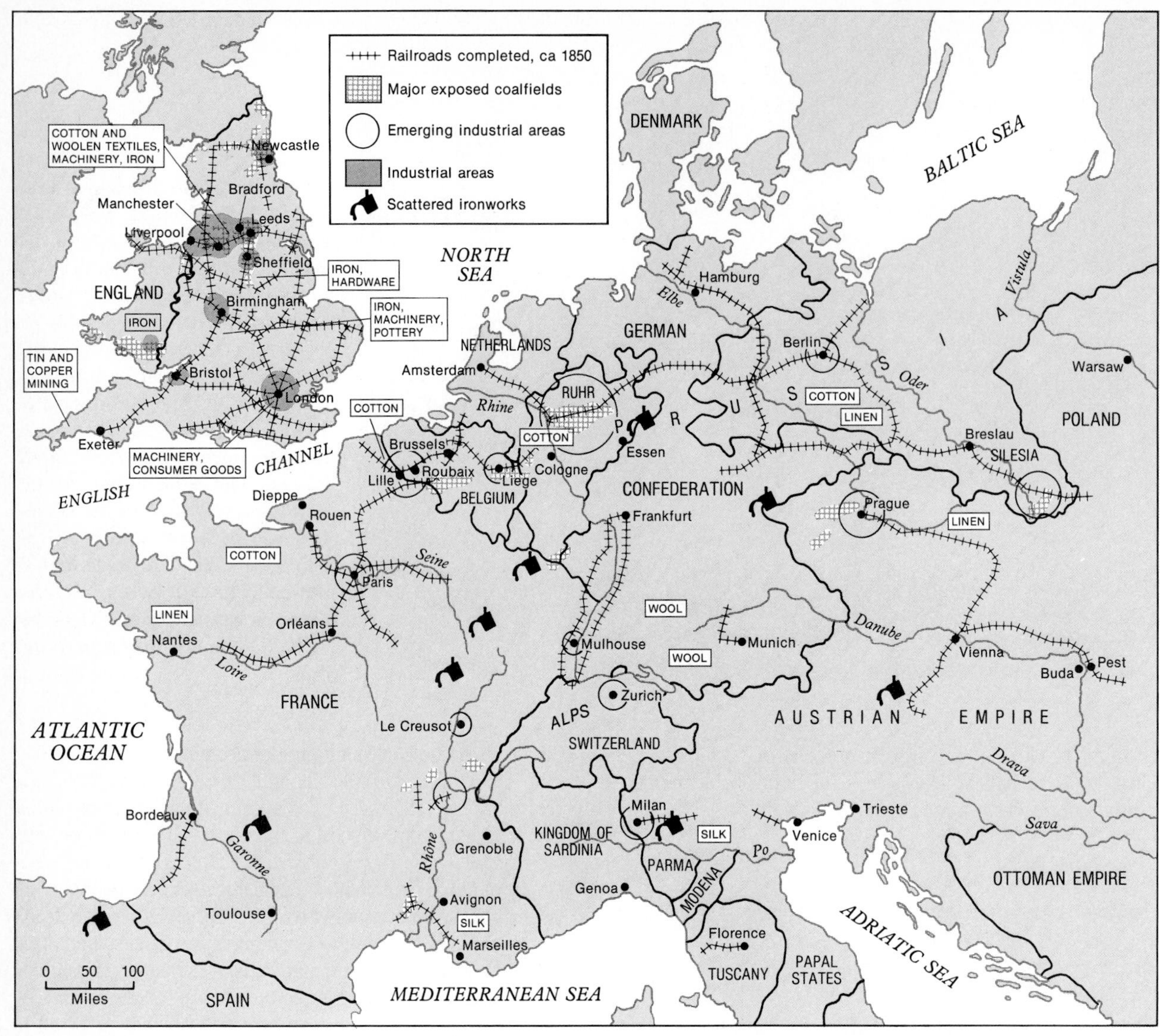

29.1 European Industrialization, c. 1850

seventeenth century, was someone who possessed a large stock of money, whether or not he chose to invest it. Although the term *capitalism* can be found as early as 1753, it emerged as a description for an economic system characterized by control of the means of production (capital in its modern sense) by a distinct group of private individuals (capitalists) only in the early twentieth century. Marx himself never used the term.

Capitalist society—the distinctive form of the modern West—may then be understood as one in which economic relations are integrated by those who possess, as personal or corporate property, the means of production, through which they command both the labor force and the range of consumer choice. In this sense, capitalism as a fully developed system cannot be said to have existed before the transformation of European society by the Industrial Revolution in the nineteenth century. Yet if the Industrial Revolution made capitalism possible as a distinctive economic system, the capitalist element in the preindustrial economy—the activity of the bourgeois or merchant class—was the most dynamic element in that economy, the activity that enabled it to grow.

Preindustrial capitalism was, in short, commercial capitalism, a capitalism not of producers but of distributors. The two states of eighteenth-century Europe where this capitalism was most advanced were Great Britain and the Netherlands. Dutch prosperity, the envy of Europe in the previous century, was chiefly the result of commercial activity. The Dutch had been merchants and seafarers since the Middle Ages. The Bank of Amsterdam was the greatest commercial institution on the Continent. Through joint-stock companies—limited-liability partnerships of merchants and investors—it financed a worldwide traffic; at its height, Dutch shipping carried half of the world's trade, exclusive of China. Though Dutch industry and agriculture were also advanced, it was the trading of other people's goods that gave the Netherlands the highest standard of living in the seventeenth-century West and enabled it to enjoy great power status with a population barely an eighth the size of France's, and a land area—largely barren of resources—no more than a twentieth that of France.

The culture of early modern capitalism was nowhere better displayed than in the Netherlands. The Dutch republic was dominated by its town life; as early as 1500, more than half the population of its largest province, Holland, was urban. Dutch towns, with their meandering waterways, humpbacked bridges, and the mellow red brick of their pavements and houses, were connected by a web of canals plied constantly by barges, ferries, and flyboats. Their harbors were crammed with the treasures of the Americas and the Indies—sugar, silks, spices, cocoa, tobacco; its shipyards launched 2,000 new seagoing vessels each year. Cloth manufacture and finishing remained the staple industry, as it had been since the Middle Ages, but there were hundreds of other industries and specialized trades such as diamond cutting, lens grinding, and bookmaking (Amsterdam alone had between 40 and 50 presses). Business was serviced by a host of bankers, factors, jobbers, and commodity and discount brokers.

The great commercial families, the so-called regent class, ruled with all the aplomb of the traditional European aristocracies. As their city grew, the merchant oligarchs of Amsterdam conceived the bold plan of virtually quadrupling its area by constructing three new concentric canals linked by a system of cross canals and streets. They carried out this extraordinary project in the midst of their war of independence against Spain, and with their own profits on it built sumptuous houses for themselves along the new canals. But population pressure on the towns was continuous. A shantytown arose beyond the northern boundary of Haarlem, where, it was reported in 1643, there was "much disorder and mischief not only by night, when the gates of this city are closed, but at all times."[2] The modern problems of overcrowding, poverty, and violence were already in evidence.

The Dutch had had a miniature Industrial Revolution of their own in the sixteenth and seventeenth centuries. The introduction of a movable cap to the windmill, traditionally an important power source in the Netherlands, meant that the central drive shaft no longer had to be turned, only the sails. Windmills and their sails could henceforth be much larger, making them both more powerful and responsive to lighter airs. In the 1590s Cornelis Cornelisz attached a crank to the drive shaft that transformed the rotary motion of the sails into a reciprocating motion driving a series of vertical saw blades. This enabled the Dutch to hew the giant Baltic timbers they used in shipbuilding with far greater precision and efficiency. By adapting the crank to other kinds of implements—hammers, rams, paddles—they were able to convert the windmill to a host of industrial uses: hulling, oilseed crushing, fulling, boring, and paper and dye preparation, among many others. Even more significant was the development of the water-pumping mill, which enabled the Dutch to drain lakes and marshes and thus to add significantly to their land-poor country. Such large-scale reclamation projects were financed by groups of wealthy merchants, particularly Amsterdammers; thus once again commercial capital, industrial innovation, and economic development went in tandem.

The British were slower to develop as a commercial power, but during the eighteenth century their growing naval and imperial supremacy, their control of the lucrative slave trade, and the systematic creation of capital and credit through the expansion of the national debt enabled them to outstrip the Dutch. In 1688, before the creation of the Bank of England, the public debt was £688,000; by 1713, after the wars against Louis XIV, it had grown to £54 million; in 1815, after the defeat of Napoleon, it stood at £861 million. At first much of this expansion was financed by the Dutch themselves, who as late as 1776 held 43 percent of the British debt, but this share rapidly declined thereafter. By 1815 it was held almost entirely by the British upper classes themselves: noblemen, gentry, and well-to-do merchants. This oligarchy not only determined the expenditure of the debt through their control of the government but also reaped a direct return through the payment of interest on it, estimated in 1815 at nearly a tenth of the government's revenue. In effect, the British state itself had been converted into a giant corporation paying dividends to its wealthy shareholders. This great capital, the spoil of commercial profit, war, and empire, was a fuel that stoked the engines of the Industrial Revolution no less than coal and steam.

The Agricultural Revolution

The backbone of European society was the traditional peasant village, typically structured around open fields divided into narrow, unfenced strips. These strips were worked by individual peasants, but since they comprised a single large field, the strips were all plowed, sown, and harvested as one. These rhythms enforced the communal cooperation and solidarity that characterized peasant society. The peasants' life was the life of their villages: traditional, conservative, immemorial as the soil and the seasons, and highly resistant to change. But that life was soon not only to change but within a few generations actually to disappear.

The two necessities of the peasant's life were to feed his family and to pay his dues and taxes—to his lord, the church, and the state. These two necessities constituted the task of subsistence—survival—since peasants who could not meet their obligations to the lord would lose the use of the land. Subsistence was difficult in the best of times, and only the wealthiest of peasants could think of producing for the market. The majority dared not experiment with new crops or techniques that promised greater productivity. Their existence held no margin for error.

But changes in both demography and the structure of land ownership undermined these traditional patterns. The general surge in population in the sixteenth century had put great pressure on the food supply, driving up land and food prices. This made life harder for the average peasant, whose increased cost for seed was not compensated by higher food prices, since he did not produce for the market and indeed was often a purchaser of food himself. But it opened great opportunities for those able to speculate in land and sell grain. In England this class of substantial landowners, the gentry, had already been enriched by the purchase of church lands at the time of the Reformation. In the seventeenth and eighteenth centuries they set out to maximize their profits, partly through land acquisition and enclosure and partly through the importation of new techniques developed by the Dutch and the Flemish.

Simply defined, enclosure was the process of appropriating a portion of the village commons, usually by the manorial lord or chief local landowner, by erecting a fence or a hedge. Enclosure removed pastureland and sometimes plowland from the community. The result was hardship and sometimes devastation. Resistance was often violent. A major rebellion in 1549 following a period of heavy enclosure climaxed in an attempt to set up a communistic peasant community in Norfolk under the leadership of Robert Kett.

Most enclosure before the seventeenth century was for the purpose of pasturing sheep, which the gentry raised for market. Thereafter it was increasingly justified as a means of raising agricultural productivity to feed a growing population through the introduction of crops and fertilizers on land that peasants lacked either the means or the desire to "improve." But when the increase in population temporarily leveled off, as it did in the late seventeenth century, the lure of profit did not. Agrarian capitalism—the replacement of small-scale farming for subsistence by large-scale farming for the market—had begun to transform the traditional village; it would end by destroying it.

The improvement of enclosed land involved a variety of new techniques. As in the Low Countries, marshland was extensively drained and filled in. Marl and clay were mixed in sandy soils to make them more productive. Jethro Tull (1674–1741) introduced the planting of seeds in straight, even rows in place of the wasteful old method of sowing them at random (broadcast), while Lord Charles Townshend—"Turnip" Townshend, as he came to be nicknamed—demonstrated that yields could be significantly improved by rotating crops and planting with turnips and clover fields that had previously lain fallow. Both plants replenished the soil and provided winter fodder to sustain animals that would otherwise have been slaughtered for lack of feed. Not only did this substantially increase the size of herds, but thanks to the tireless experiments of the Leicestershire breeder Robert Bakewell, they became larger and heavier as well: between 1710 and Bakewell's death in 1795 the average weight of sheep had trebled and cattle doubled. By the mid-eighteenth century, a veritable craze for agricultural improvement had swept the country. More than 1,000 books, pamphlets, and journals on agricultural subjects had been published by the end of the century, 250 of them alone by Arthur Young, at whose urging the governmental Board of Agriculture was established (1793). King George III himself contributed to Young's journal under the pen name "Farmer George."

Spurred by personal competition and the quest for profits, improving landlords hastened to acquire and enclose more and more land. The unquestioned control of Parliament by the gentry facilitated a policy of legalized confiscations. Between 1760 and 1815 some 3,600 acts of Parliament enclosed 6 million acres of land, or roughly a quarter of the arable land in England. By 1840 the communally farmed open field had ceased to exist.

What emerged in its place was a system of great estates worked by tenant farmers and hired laborers—no longer a peasantry but an agricultural work force. This system, with its vastly greater productivity and efficiency, enabled Britain to feed a population that had begun to grow at an unprecedented rate. In 1700 the population of England was about 5.5 million; by 1801 it had increased to 9 million and by 1851 to 18 million. This growing population provided both the work force and the primary market for the products of the Industrial Revolution, while at the same time the profits of the new agricultural economy, together with those of commerce and empire, constituted yet another major source of capital.

A New Prosperity?

Analysts have vigorously debated whether Britain's new wealth resulted in a higher general standard of living. Certainly the disparity between the immense wealth of the propertied few and the mass of the population had never been greater. Even more significant was the sense of dispossession many English men and women felt from their own country. The small independent proprietor or yeoman sank with the more ordinary village peasant to the status of a mere laborer, no longer owning the land he worked or entitled, even in part, to its fruits. The poet Oliver Goldsmith caught the popular sense of alienation and bitterness in "The Deserted Village," which went through five editions in the year of its publication, 1770:

> ***Ill fares the land, to hastening ills a prey***
> ***Where wealth accumulates and men decay.***
> ***Princes and lords may flourish, or may fade***
> ***A breath can make them, as a breath has made***
> ***But a bold peasantry, their country's pride***
> ***When once destroyed, can never be supplied.***

Even Arthur Young, the foremost propagandist of the new agriculture, came at last to deplore its human cost. "I had rather," he wrote at the end of the eighteenth century, "that all the commons were sunk in the sea than that the poor should in future be treated as they have generally been hitherto."

Apart from Britain, the Low Countries, and Denmark (where Dutch methods were also introduced), the agricultural revolution was slow to spread. Enthusiasm for agricultural improvement ran high in France, particularly among the group of reformers called the Physiocrats, led by François Quesnay (1694–1774); Louis XV wore a potato flower in his lapel in an attempt to popularize the plant. But the French aristocracy was not eager to disturb the system of seigneurial dues that constituted its chief profit from the peasantry, and the peasant insurrection of July 1789 (see Chapter 26) that led to the abolition of the manorial regime left France a nation of small proprietors and delayed the introduction of large-scale capitalist agriculture for a century. Elsewhere, despite some interest in the new methods, change was retarded by the ingrained conservatism of lords and peasants, especially in eastern Europe where serfdom was still widespread. The agricultural revolution was bound up with the existence of commercial capitalism and the habits of a developed market economy; where these were lacking, little headway was made.

The agricultural revolution was a revolution in soil management and animal husbandry rather than mechanization. The scythe gradually replaced the sickle in the eighteenth century, but it was not until the nineteenth that threshers and reapers were introduced, and their use spread slowly. The abundance of cheap labor—and the necessity to absorb a rapidly growing population—made the introduction of laborsaving machinery in agriculture not only less necessary but also politically dangerous. No similar inhibitions were at work in industry, where machines created more work than they destroyed. But if the agricultural revolution was not in this sense a part of the Industrial Revolution, at least until the introduction of combine harvesters in the 1880s, it was an indispensable precondition of it.

Science, Technology, and the State

The last major element in the Industrial Revolution was the development of machine technology itself. As will now be clear, the new technology was not a cause but rather an effect of conditions that favored and to some degree compelled an attempt to expand productive capacity—the extension of a market economy and the pressure of a growing population.

Technology itself must be viewed not as the mere sum of new methods and inventions but as the outcome of a complex social process in which need precedes opportunity and opportunity precedes design. Time and again in history, seeming technological breakthroughs had failed to yield significant results for lack of sustained economic demand; even in Britain itself, the Newcomen steam pump and Darby's coal-smelting process had little impact for half a century until the need for new energy sources spurred further development.

Nonetheless, cooperative interest in new industrial processes and techniques was growing. The Royal Society (1662), which served as a general clearinghouse for scientific ideas, provided the model for bodies such as the national Society of Arts, which sought improved methods of production. Informal groups of scientists and manufacturers in England and Scotland coordinated efforts to find solutions for specific industrial problems and sponsored prize competitions. Each such solution set a potential agenda for the next.

A case in point was the mechanization of the textile industry. Textiles were the most important element of the European economy after agricultural products. In the early eighteenth century they accounted for three-fourths of all English exports. Traditionally, England had specialized in woolens, but the leading edge of the industry was in cotton, stimulated by the popularity of fine calicoes from India and by the supply of raw cotton provided by slave labor in the colonial plantations. Raw materials were thus available, and a market was waiting, but productive capacity lagged. The first breakthrough occurred in 1733 when a Lancashire clockmaker, John Kay, invented the flying shuttle. This device enabled weavers to drive the shuttle across their looms by pulling strings attached to hammers. At one stroke it doubled the capacity of the loom. Yet the weavers could produce their cloth no faster than spinners could provide them with thread. The Royal Society offered a prize for a spinning machine, but not until James Hargreaves startled his wife at work on her wheel one day in 1764 was a solution found. Jenny Hargreaves' wheel overturned, but it continued to revolve on its side even though the spindle remained upright. Hargreaves envisioned a set of spindles driven by a single wheel, and thus the "spinning jenny" was born. A former barber, Richard Arkwright, attached the jenny to the water frame, a system of rollers that drew the thread taut before it was spun. The supply of thread now exceeded loom capacity until the clergyman Edmund Cartwright invented a power loom that could be operated by water or steam. Arkwright made a fortune and was rewarded with a knighthood in 1786, the first ever given to an industrialist, while Cartwright was voted £10,000 by a grateful House of Commons.

The official recognition given these men of humble status indicated the importance the state attached to commercially viable inventions. Yet the British government was far less directly involved in promoting industrial development than mercantilist France, with its state-sponsored factories, or the Prussia of Frederick the Great. The British concentrated instead on seeking raw materials, opening markets, and securing naval supremacy. From the age of the Navigation Acts (1651–1660), designed to ensure control of the colonial trade, the government pursued a consistent policy of commercial advantage. Britain's wars were fought not for *gloire* but for trading posts and privileges; what it sought above all from the wars against Louis XIV was penetration of the rich market of Spanish America, and when, 70 years later, it obtained logging rights along 300 leagues of wooded Mexican coastline, a British diplomat noted sagely, "If we manage this area wisely, there ought to be enough wood for eternity." If free enterprise and laissez-faire, the gospel so compellingly preached by Adam Smith in *The Wealth of Nations,* were to prove the formula for industrial expansion at home, it was within the framework of unfettered access to world markets and vital resources opened up by a century and a quarter of conscious government policy.

The Transformation of Britain

Between about 1780 and 1830 Great Britain was transformed more profoundly than any nation in recorded history. This transformation affected the size of the population and the distribution and living conditions of the vast majority. It altered the nature and in some respects the very notion of family life, work, and leisure. It profoundly affected the bonds of social organization and even the physical face of the land itself. From Britain the effects of this transformation rippled outward, first to the rest of Europe and then, through the mechanism of imperialism, to the furthest corners of the globe.

During this same period, the eyes of all Europe were fixed not on Britain but on the revolutionary upheavals in France—the great revolution of 1789, the meteoric career of Napoleon, the Bourbon restoration, and finally, in 1830, yet another round of revolution (discussed in Chapter 30) that overthrew the ruling dynasty once more and shook European politics as far away as St. Petersburg. Yet economically and even socially, France in 1830 was still in many respects the France of 1780, a nation of peasant proprietors tilling the soil much as their ancestors had done for hundreds of years.

The events in France were significant, certainly, and indeed they were broadly related to the great transformation in Britain. But if we can in the last analysis see the same fundamental change at work in both countries—the triumph of the capitalist mode of production and its integration with the powers of the state—the method of this change was very different in each. In France, owing to the survival of the seigneurial regime until 1789 and the relative underdevelopment of commercial capitalism, the drama was played out as a contest for control of the state, while in Britain, where the interests of the commercial classes and the state had been completely harmonized, a social transformation of unprecedented magnitude was achieved with relatively little political disturbance, and virtually none at all at the level of national authority. Britain saw only two monarchs between 1780 and 1830, George III and George IV, and even more remarkably, the office of prime minister was occupied for 35 of those 50 years by only two men as well, the brilliant William Pitt the Younger and the colorless Lord Liverpool.

The magnitude of economic change in Britain can best be suggested by statistics. In 1700 Britain produced 2.5 million tons of coal; in 1815 it mined 16 million. Pig iron production rose from 17,000 tons in 1740 to 125,000 in 1796 and then doubled again to 256,000 tons in 1806. Much of this production went to service the booming cotton industry, where output rose from 21 million yards of cloth in 1796 to 347 million by 1830. During this period cotton cloth rose from ninth to first place in the value of British manufactures, accounting for almost half of all exports. Even after 1830 textiles in general and cotton in particular constituted the essential product of the Industrial Revolution.

The Organization of Labor

The enormous increase in production attested by these figures entailed not only new energy sources and new machines but also new methods of commercial and industrial organization. Thus arose the two distinctive institutions of the Industrial Revolution: the bank and the factory. The function of banks was to concentrate capital; of factories, to concentrate labor. There were still only 12 banks in Great Britain outside London in 1750; by 1793 there were nearly 400, and by 1815 about 900. The intimate connection between banking and industrialization was demonstrated by the fact that some of the leading inventor-industrialists of the period—Richard Arkwright and James Watt among them—formed banks of their own as their business expanded.

The modern factory was the result of the machine. Previously, production had been carried on by four more or less distinct means of organization: the small workshop; the "cottage" or "domestic" system of home labor; the urban "manufactory" (to use Marx's term), which concentrated large numbers of workers under the same roof; and the preindustrial factory, or "arsenal," which assembled workers on an open-air site such as a mine, dockyard, or foundry.

Of these four, the first two were by far the most important. The small workshop, consisting typically of a master craftsman, two or three journeymen, and a like number of apprentices, had been characteristic of the medieval city. The workshops were organized on the basis of craft or trade into guild associations, which set general conditions of work and wages and standards of production. The guild system was in decay in the eighteenth century and in Britain had been legally abolished, although the workshop itself, with its distinction among master, journeyman, and apprentice, still remained. The result was that journeymen increasingly tended to organize in defense of their working conditions and wages, a phenomenon noted with deep disapproval by the German Imperial Diet in 1731.

The cottage or domestic system was particularly widespread in the clothing trade, although it was common as well in metalworking and other pursuits. Under this arrangement the clothier provided the yarn and the looms to spinners and weavers who worked at home and whose product the clothier then collected and marketed, thus combining the function of capitalist and merchant in one. On his travels in the English countryside in the 1720s Daniel Defoe noted that the population of whole villages was engaged in cloth production, "so that no hands being unemployed, all can gain their bread." Cloth-producing centers on the Continent were similarly organized. At its most developed, the domestic system converted rural hamlets into integrated productive units in which the workers were separated only by walls.

The urban manufactory was typical of more specialized textile production such as hat, lace, and tapestry making; the Gobelins tapestry works established by Colbert was perhaps the most famous example. The manufactory concentrated as many as 500 workers under a single roof, thus making possible a greater division of labor and a closer supervision of the productive process—both typical of the nineteenth-century factory. The manufactory differed from a factory in the modern sense, as the etymology of its name implies, in that machinery was still directly hand-operated and hand-powered; human muscle still supplied the energy.

The eighteenth century reserved the term *factory* itself for industrial or mining operations in which human energy was supplemented by wind, running water, or fire. Iron foundries, arsenals, and shipyards were typical examples, while large-scale water-powered mining was well established in central Europe by the sixteenth century. Yet even though the concentration of labor and the increasing sophistication with which it was organized laid the basis for an industrial breakthrough, it could not of itself bring it about. Far greater concentrations could be found in China, for example, where in Songjiang south of Shanghai

Coal-mining operations such as the one depicted here in the county of Northumberland, belching their black smoke for miles around, transformed much of the British landscape in the early nineteenth century. [Trustees of the Science Museum, London]

over 200,000 workers were employed in the cloth trade. What made the difference was the development of iron machinery powered by coal and steam and the expanding market economy prepared by commercial capitalism. China had neither. Its immense productive base was turned inward on primarily domestic consumption, and its unexcelled craftsmanship had been developed at the expense of its technology.

The factory system of the Industrial Revolution was essentially an adaptation of the urban manufactory to the new machines. These machines doomed the domestic system. The engines that powered them required buildings of unprecedented size and complexity of design. Andrew Ure described one such factory at Stockport:

> **The building consists of a main body, and two lateral wings, the former being three hundred feet long, and fifty feet wide, the latter projecting fifty-eight feet in front of the body. There are seven stories, including the attics. The moving power consists of two eighty-horse steam-engines, working rectangularly together, which are mounted with their great gearing-wheels on the ground floor . . . and are separated by a strong wall from the rest of the building. This wall is perforated for the passage of the main horizontal shaft, which, by means of great bevel wheels, turns the main upright shaft, supported at its lower end in an immense pier of masonry, of which the largest stone weighs nearly five tons.[3]**

Ure described the steam engines as the "two-fold heart" of the factory, whose alternating pulsations caused "an uniformity of impulsive power to pervade every arm of the factory." As this language suggests, the factory was conceived as a giant organism whose lifeblood was the surging force of its engines and whose vital activity—production—depended on the coordination of all its parts. This was why the factory was, much more than a gigantic enclosure for heavy machinery, an integrated system of production. Ure himself defined the nature of this system: "The term *Factory System* . . . designates the combined operation of many work-people, adult and young, in tending with assiduous skill a series of productive machines continuously impelled by a central power."[4]

Industrial Discipline

Ure's words reflected a profound transformation in attitudes toward work itself. The work patterns of an agrarian society had been dictated by the rhythms of nature. People satisfied with subsistence quit when they had achieved it. But production for the market was open-ended, and long before the advent of the modern factory, entrepreneurs such as the Scotsman John Law had deplored the fact that many agricultural laborers were "idle one half their time." From this equation of leisure time with idleness it was only a short step to regarding the typical worker as lazy and unwilling to work—especially for his employer's profit—except when goaded by necessity. Daniel Defoe was irked when "strolling fellows" refused his offer of day labor, replying that they could earn more money by begging. This did not suggest to prospective employers the desirability of offering better wages; rather, most agreed with Samuel Johnson that "raising the wages of day laborers is wrong for it does not make them live better, but only makes them idler."

In fact, few workers could afford "idleness" in the market-oriented British economy of the eighteenth century, where most of the rural population could make ends meet only by entering the cottage system. But the productivity of workers in their own homes could be imperfectly supervised at best; only in factories could a genuine work discipline be enforced. Long before such discipline came to Britain, Colbert had applied it to his state factories in France. Overseers pounced on every defect; at the third mistake, a worker would be put in irons for two hours next to a sample of the faulty work. No swearing or idleness was permitted; only hymns might be sung, in a low voice that would not disturb the other workers.

The mechanized factory carried this process to its logical conclusion. Instead of assigning one class of worker, the overseer, the task of imposing discipline on the rest of the work force, such discipline was now imposed by the rhythm of the machine itself. No longer did the laborer work a machine; rather, the machine worked the laborer. The penalties for slackness were savage. "Idlers"—often women and children, who comprised the majority of the work force in the textile mills—were flogged, tortured, and hung with weights, had vises screwed to their ears, or were tied three or four at a time "on a crossbeam above the machinery, hanging by our hands," as a witness told an investigating commission in 1835. Sixteen-hour workdays were not uncommon, and many workers toppled from weariness into their machinery: the grisly image of a worker falling into a vat of lard and becoming a part of the product in Upton Sinclair's novel *The Jungle* (1906) had its counterpart in fact. Some commentators compared the treatment of factory workers unfavorably to that of West Indian slaves, and conditions were even worse in the mines.

Family Life: A Tale of Two Cultures

The early Industrial Revolution had a devastating effect on traditional patterns of child rearing and family life among the rural poor. Child labor among the poor had been common in preindustrial Europe, but parents maintained direct supervision of their children in the field or, in the cottage system, at the wheel or loom. Once families were brought under the discipline of the factory, however, it was no longer the father but the overseer who determined the nature, duration, and rhythm of work. Adult males were indeed a minority in the typical textile mill. Employers preferred women and children, the younger the better; Andrew Ure confessed that it was "near impossible to convert persons past the age of puberty . . . into useful factory hands." At the factory of Samuel Greg, seven workers in ten were under the age of 18, one in six under the age of 10. Children entered the factory at the age of 5 or 6, as they enter school today; in some mills children as young as 3 were employed, and in one recorded case a child of 2. Ure depicted these children as "lively elves" whose work "seemed to resemble a sport." Unfortunately, the elves seemed not to live very long; the child mortality rate among Britain's working poor in the mid-nineteenth century was two to three times that of the suburban middle class, and the average life expectancy of the poor in the working-class district of Bethnal Green in London was two years lower than that estimated for Cro-Magnon man. Children who emerged from what the poet William Blake (1757–1827) called the "dark Satanic mills" of early industrialism were so puny and stunted that they seemed to many observers to belong to a separate race.

The relative underemployment of adult males in the factories left many fathers to serve as "house-husbands" while their wives and children worked. Many young women went into domestic service in middle- and upper-class households; by the middle of the nineteenth century, female servants made up the second largest occupational category in Britain, after farmworkers. Such women were often sexually exploited by their employers; others went into prostitution in the new factory towns. Under these circumstances the male-dominated family unit that had been characteristic of early modern Europe at all social levels was gravely undermined among the new working class. Many of what we regard as typical family problems of the modern poor—single-parent, female-headed households, high rates of illegitimacy and child delinquency, participation in the underground economies of prostitution and theft—were already in evidence in early industrial Britain. The Poor Law of 1834 was the culmination of this process. The assumption behind it was that unemployment and destitution were the result not of low wage rates and violent fluctuations in the industrial economy but of personal idle-

Child Labor

This testimony was given by Joseph Hebergam, age 17, before a select committee of Parliament in 1832.

Q.: You had fourteen and a half hours of actual labor at 7 years of age?
A.: Yes
Q.: What means were taken to keep you at your work so long?
A.: There were three overlookers; there was a head overlooker, and then there was one man kept to grease the machines, and then there was one kept on purpose to strap.
Q.: Was the main business of one of the overlookers that of strapping the children up to this excessive labor?
A.: Yes, the same as strapping an old restive horse that has fallen down and will not get up.

* * *

Q.: How far did you live from the mill?
A.: A good mile.
Q.: Was it very painful for you to move?
A.: Yes, in the morning I could scarcely walk, and my brother and sister used out of kindness to take me under each arm, and run with me to the mill, and my legs dragged on the ground. . . .
Q.: Were you sometimes too late?
A.: Yes; and if we were five minutes too late, the overlooker would take a strap, and beat us till we were black and blue.

Source: "Report of the Select Committee on the Factories Bill," in *Industrial Revolution: Children's Employment*, vol. 2 (Shannon: Irish University Press, *British Parliamentary Papers*, 1968–1972), 2: 157–159.

ness and unwillingness to work. Paupers were herded into workhouses where husbands were separated from wives, as if in jail, and parents from children. Those who died there were denied church burial. For the first time, poverty itself was made a crime.

In contrast to the working-class family, the bourgeois household was becoming more closely knit. It was also more child-centered than ever before. Children had been viewed traditionally as miniature adults. They were neither the object of family life nor the prime focus of its concern. In peasant families children were put to work as soon as they were able; in aristocratic ones they were boarded out at the age of 7 or 8. But in the wake of such reformers as Rousseau and Pestalozzi childhood was not only defined negatively as the absence of such adult traits as size, strength, and rationality but also seen as distinct phase of life with its own experiential value. Rousseau and Pestalozzi were succeeded by a torrent of popular manuals on child rearing with titles such as *The Parents' Handbook.* "The child," declared the poet Wordsworth, "is father to the man," and the bourgeois household was gradually redefined as a kind of factory whose product the child was, an attitude still reflected in our language today when we speak of children as "products" of either good or broken homes.

While thus internalizing the values of industry within the home itself, the bourgeois household was also viewed as a refuge from the competitive pressures of society, "a tent pitch'd in a world not right," in the picturesque phrase of Coventry Patmore. The influential Victorian poet and critic John Ruskin called it "the place of peace; the shelter, not only from all injury, but from all terror, doubt, and division." This idealized vision of "home, sweet home" implied a domestic division of labor between a male breadwinner and a woman whose function as wife and mother was to maintain a secure and idyllic refuge. This reinforced the patriarchal dominance of the bourgeois household just when it was being shattered in the working-class one.

The bourgeois wife and mother was expected to subordinate herself totally to her husband and to have no thought or interest beyond his welfare and comfort. Such subordination began in the bedroom. The Victorian woman was taught not merely to put her husband's pleasure before her own but to experience no pleasure at all. As one physician wrote, "A modest woman seldom desires any sexual gratification for herself. She submits to her husband, but only to please him; and, but for the desire of maternity, would far rather be relieved of his attentions."

In every respect then, the working-class and bourgeois family experience was as different as possible. In the bourgeois home the husband was the master and sole provider; in the working-class one it was often the wife who found employment while the husband maintained whatever home life was possible. The bourgeois family exalted the child as the "product" for which it existed, while the children of the working class were expendable units in the dredging of coal or the making of textiles. The result, wrote the novelist and later statesman Benjamin Disraeli, was that Britain had become

> **two nations between whom there is no intercourse and no sympathy; who are ignorant of each other's habits, thoughts and feelings, as if they were dwellers in different zones, or inhabitants of different planets, who are formed by a different breeding, are fed by a different food, are ordered by different manners, and are not governed by the same laws.[5]**

Capital, Labor, and the Rights of Man

Disraeli's two nations might also be given another name: capital and labor. Writing in the 1830s, the French novelist Honoré de Balzac (1799–1850) remarked that the three orders of Old Regime society "have been replaced by what we nowadays call classes. We have lettered [professional] classes, industrial classes, upper classes, middle classes, etc." Balzac's *etc.* would include the growing army of industrial laborers, which Marx would call the proletariat and others, more simply, the working class.

The very different thing about the new social division between classes instead of orders was that it no longer assumed a harmony but rather a conflict of interests between the various groupings, particularly between the two broad categories known as capital and labor. The traditional medieval distinction among those who work, those who fight, and those who pray—the peasantry, the aristocracy, and the clergy—was based on the ideas that each order had a distinctive function that was essential to the good of the whole and the glory of God and that if the role of the fighters and prayers included command over the bodies and souls of the workers, it was on behalf of a common welfare that embraced all. Martin Luther, whose revolution shattered the unity of the priesthood, reinforced the idea of subordination when he preached that each man had a vocation prescribed by God in which it was his duty to labor and to remain content. But the Enlightenment brought with it a fundamental change of attitude. The Declaration of the Rights of Man asserted the political equality of all men, even as the economic inequality between them continued to widen. Adam Smith declared that the public interest was not something that could be determined in advance and hence worked toward as a common goal but the result of each person pursuing his or her private interest in an arena of competitive equality.

Taking this a step further, Smith's successors, notably David Ricardo (1772–1823), argued that capital and labor were governed by natural laws as fixed and immutable as the laws of physics. Those laws enshrined the clash of interests at the heart of society. Competition, not cooperation, was the law of social life.

These horrific images of work in a British coal mine of the 1840s, recorded by a French visitor, speak for themselves. Women and children were preferred for work in the coal galleries because of their smaller stature and greater docility. Notice that the woman in the left frame is chained to her cart so that she can drag it forward on all fours. The height of the galleries was approximately that of the holds on slaving vessels. [Mansell Collection]

For anyone unable to compete, there could be only a struggle to survive. Long before the new proletarians began to perceive their employers as class antagonists, however, the spokesmen of the new industrial order had portrayed them as enemies of progress. In effect, the working class was defined negatively as having no interests and hence no social existence. Its only desire, according to writers such as William Temple, was to be as idle as possible. "Great wages and certainty of employment render the inhabitants of cities insolent and debauched," Temple declared. He concluded that "the only way to make [the poor] temperate and industrious is to lay them under a necessity of laboring all the time they can spare from meals and sleep, in order to procure the common necessities of life." Ironically, both Adam Smith and David Ricardo regarded labor as the source of all economic value, an idea that was to be crucial to the thought of Karl Marx. But Smith and Ricardo failed to relate the abstract value of labor to the actual toil of the laborer. In effect, labor was seen as something to be extracted from the recalcitrant body of the worker as coal was hacked out of the side of a hill.

At first workers' resistance to the new industrial order was directed chiefly at the introduction of new machinery or the importation of foreign labor or products. As early as 1675 the silk weavers of East London smashed 35 mechanical looms imported from Holland. In 1719 the weavers rose again to protest the importation of cheap calico fabrics from India and secured an act of Parliament against them. The use of Irish immigrant labor occasioned the riots of 1736, which included a bomb blast in the houses of Parliament. Anti-Irish feeling also sparked the great Gordon riots of 1780, when London burned for six days.

The most sustained violence occurred between 1811 and 1817, a period marked not only by an intensive mechanization of textile production that threw tens of thousands of traditional weavers out of work but also by the general depression that set in with the end of the Napoleonic wars. A destitute rioter in East Anglia summed up the plight of many in 1816: "Here I am between Earth and Sky, so help me God. I would rather lose my life than go home as I am." The rioters were called Luddites after a legendary figure, Ned Ludd, who may have destroyed stocking frames in Yorkshire in the 1780s. *Luddism* has gone into the dictionary as a synonym for mindless opposition to change. In fact, the Luddites were chiefly artisans and skilled workers who put forward a platform of political grievances and demands, including the right to organize. More generally, machine breaking was often used as a bargaining tool in industrial disputes, and workers were surprisingly sophisticated in targeting machines that threatened their livelihood.

Industrialists opposed worker organization for obvious reasons of self-interest, but also on the grounds that it interfered with the working of the "objective" laws of economics to the detriment of productive efficiency and hence general prosperity. The doctrine that the free interplay of private market interests produced maximum public benefit in the form of wealth and happiness was known generally as economic liberalism or, in a phrase borrowed from the French, *laissez-faire* (roughly, "leave it alone").

The philosopher Jeremy Bentham (1748–1832) argued that it was actually possible to calculate social benefits on an arithmetic scale and thereby determine objectively what constituted the public good, which Bentham defined as "the greatest happiness of the greatest number." Bentham agreed with Smith and Ricardo that this happiness could be achieved only by noninterference in economic activity, especially by the state. "Every law is an evil because every law is a violation of liberty," he wrote, "so that the government can only choose between evils."

But if nonintervention was enjoined on the state, it applied equally to organizations, such as guilds or unions, that attempted to raise wages artificially or to reduce working hours. The chief economic role allotted the state in the laissez-faire dispensation was to prevent such organizations from arising to do mischief, and the only good laws the state could enact in the economic sphere were those suppressing them. The government did indeed act, spurred in the 1790s by fear of political clubs organized on

Luddism

This declaration by framework knitters, a formerly prosperous class of artisan workers who possessed a royal charter regulating their production of hosiery, illustrates the grievances of skilled craftsmen, which included complaints about the inferior quality of machine-made goods as well as fears of depressed wages and unemployment. "Ned Ludd" was a symbolic signature, referring to an already mythic figure, and "Sherwood Forest" was meant to evoke not only the legend of Robin Hood but also the freedom and independence traditionally associated with England's woodsmen.

Whereas by the charter granted by our late sovereign Lord Charles II, by the Grace of God King of Great Britain, France, and Ireland, the framework knitters are empowered to break and destroy all frames and engines that fabricate articles in a fraudulent and deceitful manner and to destroy all framework knitters' goods whatsoever that are so made. . . . And we do hereby declare that we will break and destroy all manner of frames whatsoever that make the following spurious articles and all frames whatsoever that do not pay the regular prices heretofore agreed to by the masters and workmen—All print net frames making single press and frames not working by the rack and rent and not paying the price regulated in 1810: warp frames working single yarn or too coarse hole—not working by the rack, not paying the rent and prices regulated in 1809. . . . All frames of whatsoever description the workmen of whom are not paid in the current coin of the realm will invariably be destroyed. . . .

Given under my hand the first day of January 1812. God protect the Trade.

Ned Ludd's Office
Sherwood Forest

Source: A. Aspinall and E. A. Smith, eds., *English Historical Documents*, vol. 11: *1783–1832* (Oxford: Oxford University Press, 1959), p. 531.

the Jacobin model by the London shoemaker Thomas Hardy and by tracts such as Tom Paine's *The Rights of Man*, which demanded popular rights, including reform of the House of Commons and abolition of the monarchy and the House of Lords. In 1799 and 1800 it passed the Combination Acts, which forbade workers to organize for any purpose whatever. However, it did nothing about industrial lobbies such as the General Chamber of Manufacturers, organized by Matthew Boulton and Josiah Wedgwood. Nor did most advocates of laissez-faire seem to regard the thousands of enclosure acts passed by Parliament on behalf of private interests as state intervention.

As the catastrophic effects of industrialization on the working class became apparent, however, widespread demand arose for government regulation of at least the conditions of child and female labor. "A feeling very generally exists," the conservative Thomas Carlyle remarked, "that the condition and disposition of the Working Classes is a rather ominous matter at present; that something ought to be said, something ought to be done, in regard to it." That "something," largely the work of reformers such as Francis Place (1771–1854) and the earl of Shaftesbury (1801–1885), was a series of Factory Acts, of which the most significant included the Factory Act of 1833 and the Mines and Collieries Act of 1842, which prohibited the employment of children under the age of 9 in textile mills and children under 10 and women underground in mines, and the Factory Act of 1847, which established a ten-hour day for women and children. Slowly, the pulverizing conditions of industrial labor were relaxed, and its devastating impact on the working-class family was mitigated.

ROBERT OWEN, INDUSTRIAL REFORMER

The most sustained opposition to laissez-faire economics came from Robert Owen (1771–1858), industrialist, philanthropist, and founder of British socialism. "Under this system," he declared,

> **there can be no true civilization; for by it all are trained civilly to oppose one another by their created opposition of interests. It is a low, vulgar, ignorant and inferior mode of conducting the affairs of society; and no permanent, general and substantial improvement can arise until it shall be superseded by a superior mode of forming character and creating wealth.**[6]

The strength of Owen's attack was that it rejected the claim of laissez-faire economics to scientific status. Far from being, as its disciples argued, an objective conformity to the immutable laws of economics, it was only one possible means among many for ordering society, in fact a "low" and "inferior" one that created not wealth and harmony but misery and conflict. It was possible to do much, much better; and, being possible, it was morally obligatory.

Owen was born in a small Welsh town, the son of a saddler and ironmonger and a local farmer's daughter. At the age of 15 he migrated to Manchester. Here he shared rooms at one point with Robert Fulton, the inventor of the steamboat, whom he lent £100 out of his first savings. Shy and diffident, Owen was nonetheless manager of a cotton mill employing 500 people by the age of 19. In 1794 he became a partner in the Chorlton Twist Company, one of Manchester's principal textile firms, and five years later he persuaded his fellow partners to purchase the New Lanark spinning mills near Glasgow from the industrialist David Dale, whose daughter Caroline he married.

Thus far Owen's career resembled that of many of the other self-made industrialists of the era. But he was already a member of the Manchester Board of Health and keenly interested in reform. New Lanark, with its 2,000 employees, one-fourth of them children, was well run by the standards of the day, and David Dale was considered an enlightened employer. But Owen had plans that went far beyond Dale's kindly paternalism. He was horrified by child labor and refused to employ anyone under the age of 10. He rebuilt the workers' houses, cleaned and paved their streets, provided cheap coal for heating, and opened a company store that sold goods at cost.

As Owen's views grew more radical (and his profit margins lower), his business partners became restive. In 1813 he bought them out and formed a new company whose partners, including Jeremy Bentham, agreed to limit themselves to a 5 percent return. This enabled him to carry out the educational theories he had gradually developed, which he first spelled out in *A New View of Society* (1813). Owen argued that people were wholly the products of their environment and education; this alone, he said, made the difference between judges and the persons they sentenced to be hanged or deported. He built a large educational complex at New Lanark, characteristically named the Institute for the Formation of Character, the heart of which was the first nursery school in Great Britain. Owen's theories anticipated much of progressive education. His school was run on the principle of play; no child was forced to do anything against his or her wishes, and no punishment was ever imposed. New Lanark became a mecca for reformers of every stripe and a major tourist attraction as well: between 1816 and 1826 nearly 20,000 visitors streamed through its gates.

Owen himself had meanwhile turned his interests to reform on a national level. His agitation was largely responsible for the passage of the early (though ineffective) Factory Act of 1819. By now he had become convinced of the radical injustice of contemporary society. Always a religious skeptic, he openly denounced the clergy from 1817, thus parting company with mainstream reformers such as William Wilberforce, who sought to mitigate the evils of the Industrial Revolution by an appeal to Christian ethics. Owen shocked a meeting of his fellow magnates by declaring that it would be better for the cotton industry to perish altogether than to be carried on under conditions that destroyed the health of its workers.

Between 1817 and 1820 Owen put forward a sweeping plan to reorganize society on the basis of small, cooperative communities. Each community would contain 500 to 2,000 members and would be both agriculturally and industrially self-sufficient. The major buildings, suitably spaced and landscaped, would be contained in a large rectangle, giving everyone access to light and air. Production for profit was prohibited; goods were to be distributed on the basis of labor performed, an anticipation of Marx's formula, "From each according to his abilities, to each according to his needs." Each community was to be completely self-governing. Owen suggested that such communities might be set up by private philanthropists, by parishes or counties seeking relief from the burden of their poor, or by associations of tradesmen, workers, and farmers who wished to escape "the evils of the present system." He envisioned such communities as establishing regional and national federations and, ultimately, a worldwide one. It was, he fervently believed, the social, economic, and political form of the future.

Owen traveled widely over the next several years in Ireland and on the Continent to promote his plan, and in 1825, convinced that the New World was a more fertile ground for his ideas than the Old, he set up the model community of New Harmony on a 20,000-acre site in Indiana. Despite initial enthusiasm, it collapsed after three years, having cost Owen himself the bulk of his fortune.

Owen returned to England in 1829 to find that in his absence he had become a hero to the nascent British labor movement, which, coming into the open after the repeal of the Combination Acts in 1824, had adopted his call for worker self-governance. Owen once more threw himself into reform agitation. He now saw that the potential for organizing a great federation of the producing classes actually existed in the trade union movement, and in October 1833 he launched what was to become the Grand National

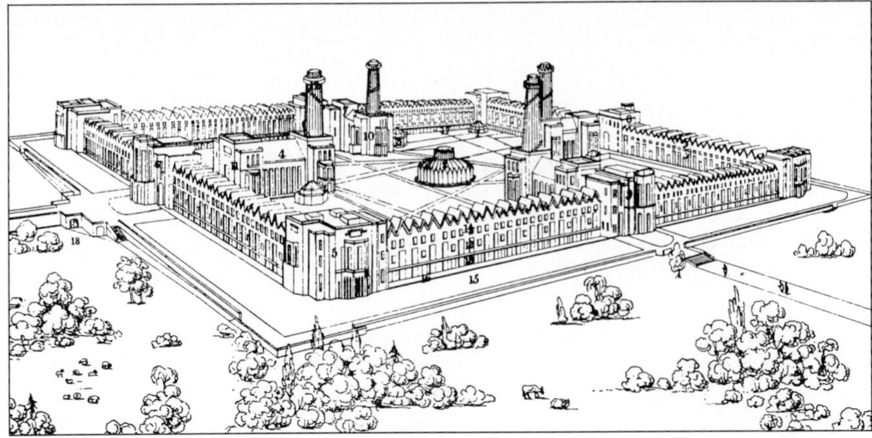

Stedman Whitwell's conception of one of Robert Owen's utopian communities is a cross between a medieval fortress and a planned city, with its fanciful architecture and rigidly straight thoroughfares. The idyllic pastoral scene in which it is so incongruously set emphasizes its rejection of commerce and the corrupt world beyond. Such communities were designed as self-sufficient living systems for 500 to 2,000 persons. [Granger Collection]

Consolidated Trades Union, the first nationwide confederation of labor in history. For a few heady months Owen was the acknowledged leader of the worker movement, and as local unions and associations rushed to join, the Grand Union claimed no fewer than 500,000 members by the spring of 1834. Thoroughly alarmed, employers initiated lockouts of workers who joined the Union, and the government cracked down as well, hastily deporting seven Dorset workers who went down in labor history as the Tolpuddle martyrs. What doomed the Grand Union, however, was the very speed at which it had grown, outstripping both its organizational resources and its agreed-on goals. Owen himself was disillusioned as the Union, far from evolving peacefully toward communal living, appeared bent on a bloody confrontation with capital. By late 1834 it had ceased to exist in all but name, and embittered labor militants turned their backs on socialism in Britain for the next 50 years.

Owen continued to travel and speak widely on behalf of his ideal communities (seven more were founded in Britain between 1825 and 1847). An exchange founded by the flannel weavers of Rochdale in 1844 became the basis of the modern cooperative movement, which still flourishes in the midwestern United States. Owen himself continued to see America as the best hope for the realization of his principles. All four of his sons became U.S. citizens; the eldest, Robert Dale Owen, served in Congress and had a distinguished career as an advocate of educational reform and women's rights. Active to the end, Owen addressed public meetings into his eighty-eighth year. Carried home to die in his native town, he spent the last day of his life planning the reform of education in the parish. The liberation of women was an abiding concern as well, and it is appropriate that the best summation of Owen's character and influence should have come from a pioneer feminist, Harriet Martineau. He was, she said,

> **always a gentle bore in regard to his dogmas and expectations; always palpably right in his descriptions of human misery; always thinking he had proved a thing when he had only asserted it in the force of his conviction; and always really meaning something more rational than he had actually expressed.[7]**

The Population Explosion

An observer visiting our planet about 250 years ago and returning today would probably be struck by two things: first, by how many more human beings were inhabiting it, and second, by how densely concentrated they were in specific areas. The first of these phenomena goes popularly by the name of the population explosion; the second is called urbanization. Both of them are related to the Industrial Revolution, though they are by no means simply its result.

The human population of the earth was probably well under 10 million at the time of the neolithic revolution—the cultivation of plants and the domestication of animals—about 10,000 years ago. Agriculture made historical civilization possible, and civilization, from a very early point, was marked everywhere it developed by city-dwelling. Thus a continuous rise in population and a propensity to urbanization have been characteristic of civilization from the beginning. What has been unprecedented is the steady rise and concentration of population since about the mid-eighteenth century. In 1750 the world population was under 800 million. It reached 1 billion by about 1830, 2 billion in 1930, 3 billion in 1960, 4 billion in 1975, and 5 billion in 1986. At the same time, the number of persons engaged in agriculture has been steadily diminishing. In most places, at least 80 percent of the population was engaged in agriculture in 1750; in most industrialized nations today, the percentage is less than 5 percent.

These numbers suggest some obvious conclusions. The population explosion began before the advent of the Industrial Revolution, and it was well under way as a worldwide phenomenon long before the effects of industrialization reached beyond Europe. However, its continued rate of increase has unquestionably been sustained by the Industrial Revolution, including the continuous transformation in the productive capacity of agriculture known today as the "green revolution." Despite the fears of Malthus and of many neo-Malthusian commentators today, the food supply has kept pace with population growth; indeed, most of the industrially developed nations suffer at present from excess productive capacity, which has led them to warehouse enormous quantities of food and to subsidize farmers to keep large portions of their acreage fallow—a development that would no doubt have seemed like a world turned upside down to "Turnip" Townshend. It remains true that world nutritional levels are declining as a whole and that patches of famine have even broken out in places like the Sahel region of Africa, but it is quite clear that this is the result of unequal economic development and wealth and not of inadequate productive capacity as a whole.

Although there is much debate about the causes of the population explosion, it has everywhere been associated not with an increase in fertility but with a decrease in mortality. The difference may be summarized by a single statistical comparison. In 1700 only 475 of every 1,000 persons born live would reach the age of 20; by the mid-twentieth century 960 would do so. The sharp decline in the death rate was essentially the result of a reduction in mortality from infectious diseases and (after the introduction of modern contraceptive devices) infanticide. At the same time, increases in agricultural capacity enabled more developed nations to sustain population growth. The population of England and Wales increased from 5.5 million to 18 million between 1700 and 1850, yet, thanks to the agricultural revolution, food production kept pace. Emigration and the settling of new lands also relieved population pressure; some 60 million Europeans left the continent between 1846 and 1924, mostly for the Western Hemisphere, the Siberian hinterland of Russia, and Australasia. Not all of this resulted in net population gain. White settlers in Australia completely exterminated the native population of the large island of Tasmania, and four-fifths of the Maori population of New Zealand and three-fourths of the Indian population of the United States had been destroyed by the 1870s.

The first great surge in population was to a large extent a European phenomenon. In the absence of reliable data (only Sweden kept mortality statistics before 1800), we can only speculate that a cyclic remission in the incidence of microbic diseases combined with the increase in agricultural productivity in northern Europe generated sufficient thrust to trigger growth. Given the enormously high level of mortality, even a marginal increase in the survival rate could have had a significant impact on population.

Not until after 1850 was control of infectious diseases made possible by the introduction of hygiene and sanitation, particularly in the purification of water supplies and the disposal of waste. These two measures did (and continue to do) more to reduce mortality rates than any others, including the development of vaccines and so-called wonder drugs (the sulfa family in 1935 and antibiotics, most notably penicillin, in the 1940s). The concern for sanitation was at first provoked by the appallingly high mortality rates among workers in early industrial towns, but it was extended systematically only after the scientific connection between dirt and disease had been established by the research of Pasteur in France, Lister in Scotland, and Koch in Germany in the 1860s and 1870s. The results were dramatic. Typhoid deaths fell by more than 85 percent in England over a 35-year period, malaria by nearly as much in Italy over 20 years. It was not the ability to cure infectious disease but the simple reduction of exposure to it that accounted for this progress.

The population of Europe (including Russia) roughly quadrupled between 1650 and 1900, from about 100 to some 430 million, exclusive of emigration. From less than a fifth of the world's population in the mid-seventeenth century, Caucasians had become a third of it by the dawn of the twentieth. This was the high-water mark of European demographic advance. The introduction of Western standards of sanitation to other areas of the globe—essential to preserve the health of European colonizers in the heyday of imperialism—ignited a similar population explosion in Asia and Africa. By the 1980s non-Western peo-

POPULATION GROWTH, 1750–2000 (IN MILLIONS)

	1750	1800	1850	1900	1950	2000 (projected)
Asia (excluding Russia)	498	630	801	925	1,381	3,458
China	200	323	430	436	560	1,200
India and Pakistan	190	195	233	285	434	1,269
Africa	106	107	111	133	222	768
Europe (including Russia)	167	208	284	430	572	880
North America	2	7	26	82	166	354
South and Central America	16	24	38	74	162	638
Australasia and Pacific Islands	2	2	2	6	13	32
World	**791**	**978**	**1,262**	**1,650**	**2,515**	**6,296**

ples again accounted for approximately four-fifths of the world's population.

Perhaps the most significant and far-reaching effect of the Industrial Revolution was the urbanization of Western society. The city had occupied a distinctive place in the West since the Middle Ages. With its walls and towers, it stood off boldly from the surrounding countryside. No less important were the charters and privileges, often won by long struggle, that gave it a unique degree of self-government and political importance. The late medieval city-states of Italy and the free imperial cities of Germany were the finest flowering of this proudly independent civic culture, and neither the Renaissance nor the Reformation would have been conceivable without them. But the new state-centered global economies that had begun to develop by the late sixteenth century were inimical to them, and their decay was shortly evident. Machiavelli had written with admiration of the vigor and independence of the German cities of his time; 200 years later Frederick the Great could reply that a word from the emperor sufficed to control them.

The great eighteenth-century cities of London, Paris, and Amsterdam, with their worldwide commercial and financial connections, were prototypes of a new kind of city, the global metropolis. But such cities were still exceptional. With nearly a million inhabitants by 1800, London was ten times larger than the next British city and 100 times or more the size of the majority of Britain's towns, which still served as they had for hundreds of years primarily as markets for the local countryside. Although urbanization had reached 50 percent or more in some highly commercialized regions of the Low Countries, in Britain less than a third, and in France less than a quarter of the population lived in towns.

The Industrial Revolution changed all that. Factory towns like Huddersfield sprang up overnight near the coalfields and iron mines of Britain's industrial heartland. The pulse of manufacture turned regional marketing centers like Northampton into points on a nationwide distribution grid and old coastal towns like Bristol into international seaports. These in turn were now linked by a new mode of transportation ideally designed for hauling large quantities of goods, the steam locomotive. The British census of 1851 distinguished between manufacturing, mining, and hardware towns, regional centers and seaports, and spas and coastal resorts. Like everything else, the city was now a specialized category, a part of the universal division of labor.

And it was to the city that the rapidly growing British population now came. To London above all: from under a million inhabitants in 1800 it swelled to 2.5 million by mid-century and 4.5 million by the early 1900s. Half again as many people lived in its suburbs. No city of its size had ever been seen before in the world. No other British city approached it, but many others achieved rates of growth that were proportionally no less impressive; Sheffield, for example, grew from 111,000 to 285,000 over a 40-year period, Nottingham from 52,000 to 187,000. By 1851 half the population lived in urban areas, and that number would grow to three-quarters by 1900. The percentage of farm laborers declined correspondingly. In 1851 only two of every nine working Britons were engaged in agriculture; 30 years later that number was 2 of every 16; and on the eve of World War I fewer than two out of 25 members of the work force remained on the farm. As the British commentator Robert Vaughan wrote as early as 1843, "If any nation is to be lost or saved by the character of its great cities, our own is that nation."[8]

A river of humanity streams up this impossibly congested street in Gustave Doré's depiction of nineteenth-century London. The vividly gesturing porters and drivers suggest the vigor and tumult of a great commercial metropolis, and the Dickensian fat boy asleep on the pile of cargo in the center adds a touch of humor, but the picture recedes darkly into a sea of anonymous human faces and forms—an ominous comment on the mass society Doré already saw taking shape in his time. [Mansell Collection]

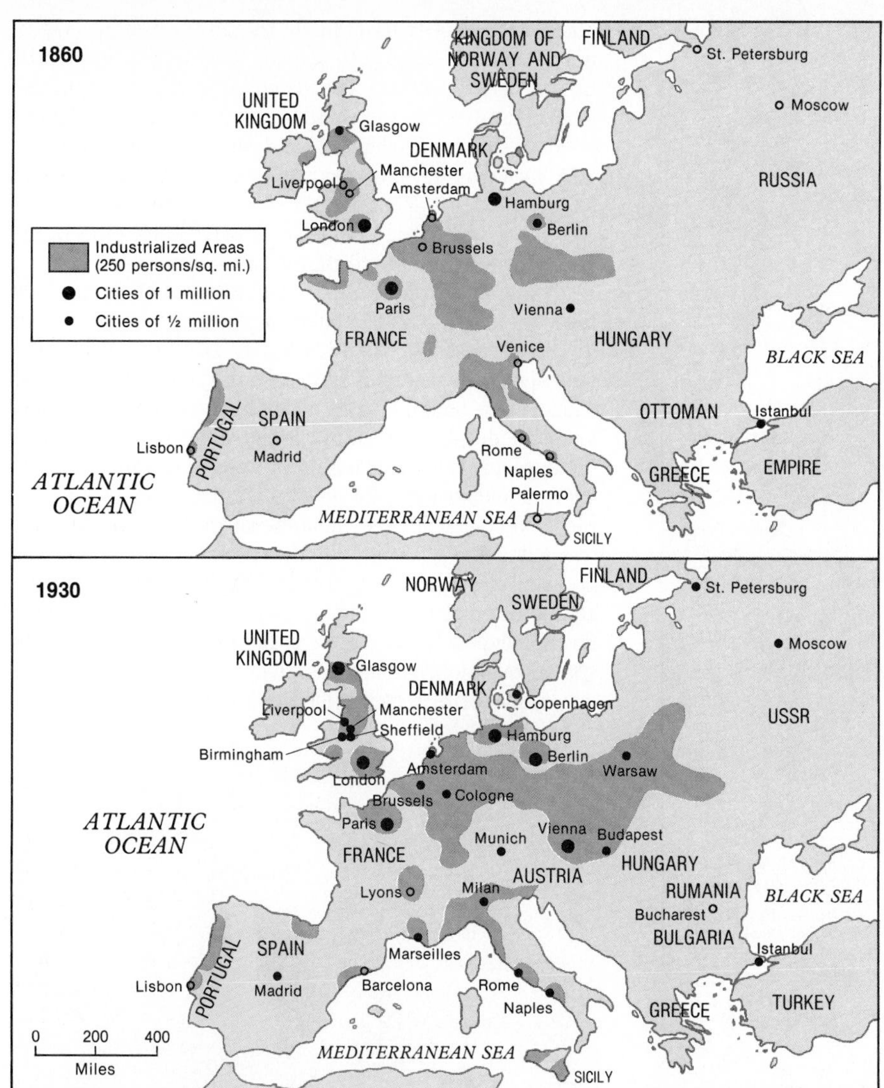

29.2 Urbanization in Europe

MANCHESTER, THE FACTORY TOWN

If any city might have served as a test case for Vaughan's assertion, it was industrial Manchester. Situated in Lancashire west of the Pennine mountains and connected to the port of Liverpool by the river Mersey, Manchester had long been a modestly prosperous regional marketing center whose population on the eve of the Industrial Revolution was about 17,000. The cotton industry transformed it in the 1770s and 1780s, and the grim, grime-blackened factories with their surrounding slums, which seemed to mushroom overnight, made it the prototype of the new industrial city. By the 1780s its population had grown to 40,000, by 1801 to 70,000, and by 1831 to 142,000: an eightfold increase in 80 years. Visitors commented on the new appearance of what had once been described as the "fairest" town in the region, and as late as 1784 it had seemed attractive to a French tourist. By 1814, however, a Prussian visitor noted the pall that hung over the town. "The cloud of coal vapor may be observed from afar. The houses are blackened by it. The river . . . is so filled with waste dye-stuffs that it resembles a dyer's vat." Another visitor proclaimed it "abominably filthy" and obnoxious to the senses: "the Steam Engine is pestiferous, the Dyehouses noisesome and offensive, and the water of the river as black as ink or the Stygian lake." The Frenchman Alexis de Tocqueville summed up contemporary opinion in 1835 when he wrote of Manchester, "Civilization works its miracles, and civilized man is turned back almost into a savage."

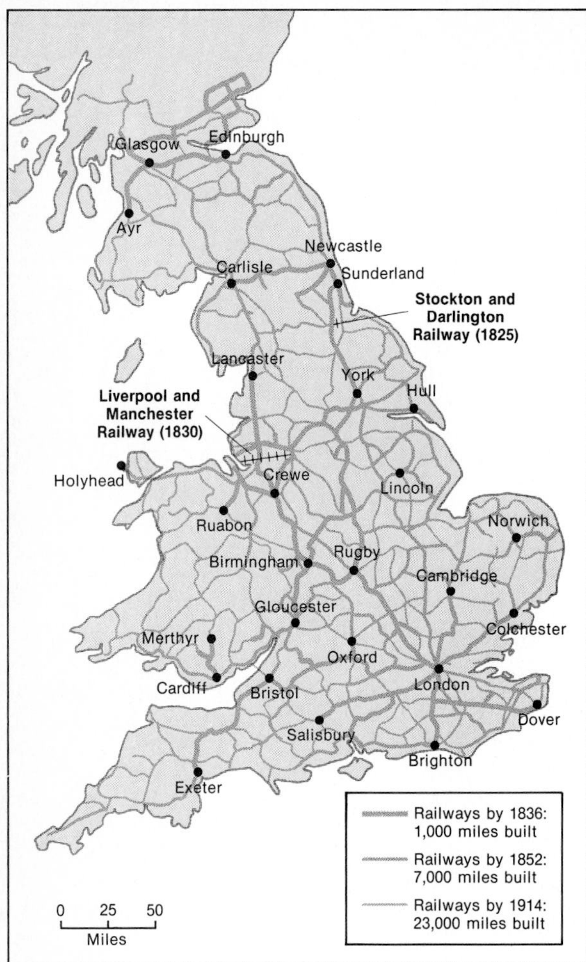

29.3 Railways in Great Britain, 1825–1914

Nowhere else was the confrontation between the classes more starkly posed. A local clergyman noted:

> **There is no town in the world where the distance between the rich and the poor is so great. . . . There is far less *personal* communication between the master cotton spinner and his workmen . . . than there is between the Duke of Wellington and the humblest laborer on his estate.**

When Friedrich Engels, the colleague of Karl Marx and himself a Manchester industrialist, tried to engage a "middle class gentleman" in conversation about the condition of the city's slums, he received the brusque reply, "And yet there is a great deal of money made here. Good morning, sir."[9] It was no doubt the existence of such attitudes that made an American visitor "thank Heaven that I am not a poor man with a family in England."

Such despair, as the reformer Francis Place noted, had turned large sections of the Manchester working class into potential revolutionaries. In 1817 a band of destitute weavers set out for London to protest their wages, only to be turned back by force. Two years later, in August 1819, troops fired point-blank into a mass rally at St. Peter's Field in the city, killing 11 persons and wounding some 400, including 113 women and children. It was the first battle of modern labor history, and the "Peterloo Massacre," as it was called in mocking comparison to the Battle of Waterloo, symbolized the threat of class war.

In the 1830s and 1840s Manchester often seemed on the verge of anarchy. Popular unrest exploded again with the economic slumps of 1829 and 1836. These were compounded by devastating outbreaks of typhoid and cholera, which were added to the normal toll of respiratory and intestinal diseases taken by air and water pollution and by the appalling lack of sanitation: it was estimated that there was one indoor toilet for every 212 inhabitants of the city. Moreover, despite its phenomenal growth, Manchester was still being governed as if it were a village. There was no regular police force, no provision for social services, and no attempt to regulate growth. Not until 1853, when the population, now in excess of 300,000, had begun to sprawl over into suburbs as chaotic as the center itself, was Manchester formally incorporated as a city.

Raw industrial waste was dumped directly into Manchester's river, the Irwell, whose still and blackened waters are captured in James Mudd's 1854 photograph. [The Manchester Public Libraries]

Two Views of Manchester

Two highly contrasting views of Manchester were provided by John Aikin and, some 40 years later, by James Kay.

The prodigious extension of the several branches of the Manchester manufactures has likewise greatly increased the business of several trades and manufactures connected with or dependent upon them. The making of paper at mills in the vicinity has been brought to great perfection, and now includes all kinds, from the strongest parcelling paper to the finest writing sorts, and that on which banker's bills are printed. To the ironmongers' shops, which are greatly increased of late, are generally annexed smithies, where many articles are made, even to nails. A considerable iron foundry is established in Salford, in which are cast most of the articles wanted in Manchester and its neighborhood. . . . The tin-plate workers have found additional employment in furnishing many articles for spinning machines; as have also the braziers in casting wheels for the motion-work of the rollers used in them; and the clockmakers in cutting them. . . . To this sketch of the progress of the trade of Manchester, it will be proper to subjoin some information respecting the condition and manners of its tradesmen, the gradual advances to opulence and luxury. . . . Within the last twenty or thirty years the vast increase of foreign trade has caused many of the Manchester manufactures to travel abroad. . . . And the town has now in every respect assumed the style and manners of one of the commercial capitals of Europe.

The township of Manchester chiefly consists of dense masses of houses, inhabited by the population engaged in the great manufactories of the cotton trade. Some of the central divisions are occupied by warehouses and shops, and a few streets by the dwellings of some of the more wealthy inhabitants; but the opulent merchants chiefly reside in the country. . . . Manchester, properly so called, is chiefly inhabited by shopkeepers and the laboring classes. . . . The rapid growth of the cotton manufacture has attracted hither operatives from every part of the kingdom, and Ireland has poured forth the most destitute of her hordes to supply the constantly increasing demand for labor. . . . The population . . . is crowded into one dense mass, in cottages separated by narrow, unpaved, and almost pestilential streets, in an atmosphere loaded with the smoke and exhalations of a large manufacturing city. . . . The houses . . . are too generally built back to back, having therefore only one outlet, no yard, no privy, and no receptacle for refuse. Consequently the narrow streets, in which mud and water stagnate, become the common receptacle of offal and ordure.

[These] districts . . . are inhabited by a turbulent population, which, rendered reckless by dissipation and want, . . . has frequently committed daring assaults on the liberty of the more peaceful portions of the working classes, and the most frightful devastations on the property of their masters. Machines have been broken, and factories gutted and burned at mid-day. . . . The police form . . . so weak a screen against the power of the mob, that popular violence is now, in almost every instance, controlled by the presence of a military force.

Sources: J. Aikin, *A Description of . . . Manchester* (London: John Stockdale, 1795), pp. 176–184 passim; J. Kay, *The Moral and Physical Condition of the Working Classes Employed in the Cotton Manufacture in Manchester,* 2d ed. (London: Cass, 1970), pp. 20–43 passim.

As the historian Asa Briggs explained:

All roads led to Manchester in the 1840s. It was the shock city of the age, and it was just as difficult to be neutral about it as it was to be neutral about Chicago in the 1890s or Los Angeles in the 1930s.[10]

Reformers focused on it and novelists such as Mrs. Gaskell in *Mary Barton* and Charles Dickens in *Hard*

Times depicted it, as Mrs. Gaskell said, to "give utterance to the agony" of the poor. Manchester's mill owners, protesting the unflattering portraits of themselves in such social novels, complained that their services to the nation in creating new wealth and new opportunity were unfairly disparaged. But whichever side one took in the great class debate, all agreed that Manchester was the crucible of an unprecedented phenomenon, as prodigal of energy and power as it was of misery and despair: the industrial city.

Ironically, Manchester itself had already passed the peak of its industrial importance. Its factories were obsolescent in comparison to newer models elsewhere, and its prosperity rested increasingly on its importance as a trading center. The Manchester Exchange, first opened to the public in 1809 and greatly expanded in 1838, was the largest brokerage facility in Europe. With economic maturity came at least the beginnings of civic responsibility. A local sanitary code, one of the first in the country, was drafted in 1845. The next year Manchester got its first public parks and a bequest to found what became the greatest of the early civic universities. In 1857 it held an exposition that drew more than 1.3 million visitors and led to the founding of an orchestra. By late Victorian times the city that had been described as "the entrance to hell" by the commander sent to quell its disturbances in 1839 had become respectable and almost staid.

The Spread of the Industrial Revolution

The rest of Europe was not economically idle while Britain was undergoing its great revolution. Population and production, both agricultural and industrial, was rising on the Continent between 1780 and 1830, and cities were growing as well. Arthur Young was impressed with the progressive nature of farming in parts of France on his travels in the 1780s, while German farmers introduced a variety of new crops into their country, including potatoes, beets, hops, and tobacco. Nor were industrial improvements confined to Britain. In France new methods of iron and steel production were developed, and Joseph-Marie Jacquard invented a silk loom. In Germany the world's first sugar-beet refinery began operation. Moreover, interest in the new developments in Britain was intense. British factories drew thousands of foreign visitors, and details about British inventions and techniques spread rapidly. In other respects, too, much of the infrastructure of the Industrial Revolution was in place on the Continent. Swiss and Dutch banking were highly developed, and the eighteenth century saw major improvements in roads, bridges, and harbors and extensive canal-building projects in northern France and Prussia. An observer looking for the likeliest place for the Industrial Revolution to begin would probably have suggested the Netherlands in 1700 or France in 1750.

Exploitation and Resistance

Nonetheless, it was in Britain that the spark caught fire. In France a largely parasitic aristocracy drained off capital investment, a top-heavy governmental bureaucracy often crushed the initiative it was trying to promote, and the absence of a central banking system hampered the flow of credit. Germany suffered from its division into hundreds of tiny principalities and the chaos of internal customs barriers and road and river tolls that this engendered. The Dutch republic, the great commercial success of the seventeenth century, had exhausted itself in struggles with Louis XIV. In eastern Europe, including Prussia, Austria, and Russia, the persistence of serfdom hamstrung the movement of labor so critical to industrial development.

Thus it was not until about 1830 that industrialization per se—the use of power-driven machinery and the organization of labor and production in factories—came to the Continent. It appeared first along a belt that included the Low Countries, northeastern France and western Germany, and northern Italy, where the concentration of a skilled and urbanized work force, plentiful deposits of coal and iron, good road and river communications, and access to seaports were most favorable. Its spread, however, was notably uneven. It advanced most rapidly in Belgium, which profited not only from its commercial connections with the Netherlands but also from its rich deposits of coal, which the Dutch lacked.

France, despite its partial development, remained primarily a nation of small farmers throughout the nineteenth century; in 1881 its population was still two-thirds rural. A key variable was social attitude. French capital, long sheltered behind government subsidies and high tariffs, was far more timid and less entrepreneurial than its British counterpart; the Parisian banker Seillière was all too typical when, returning from a visit to an ironworks in 1836, he was reported "scared out of his wits by the investment going on." Large-scale financing was still a novelty in France, and much of it was introduced by foreign firms, such as the great international banking house of Rothschild. French industry, which specialized in luxury items—silks, carpets, tapestries, porcelain, fashion clothing, vintage wines, and brandies—was craft-oriented and not easily adaptable to mass production. A British visitor at a French industrial exhibit in 1802 remarked that there was not a single item of ordinary consumption on display.

In fact, it was British entrepreneurs who introduced the first power machines into France. William Wilkinson set up the first coke furnace in the country at Le Creusot in 1785; not until 1819 was another built. John Holker, who settled in France in the mid-eighteenth century, was almost single-handedly responsible for setting up a modernized textile industry in Rouen, and as late as 1840 it was observed that the majority of foremen in its plants were from Lancashire. The pace of British investment stepped up considerably in the 1820s. Aaron Manby and Daniel Manton set up a large ironworks plant at Charenton in 1827 that became an industrywide model, and the same partners introduced the first gas lighting in Paris two years later.

As in Britain, industrial expansion in France was at first largely confined to textile manufacture; cotton production doubled between 1830 and 1846. A railway building boom in the 1840s brought increased demand for iron and steel as well. At the same time, high tariffs and other barriers to trade began to give way before the increasingly direct control of the levers of government exercised by the commercial bourgeoisie and, especially, banking interests. The ascendancy of such interests was even more open after the revolution of 1848. In the two decades that followed, the French economy entered the industrial era, although many small-scale enterprises continued to flourish. The value of industrial production doubled, foreign trade trebled, internal commerce quadrupled, and railway mileage and total industrial horsepower quintupled.

As in Britain, industrialization was accompanied by ruthless exploitation of the work force, including women and children. Conditions in France had never been idyllic; in 1776 the bookbinders of Paris had struck to *win* a 14-hour day. But the regime of the factory intensified the worst abuses of the preindustrial workshop. An observer in the department of Nord described working conditions in 1826:

> **The greed of the manufacturers knows no limits; they sacrifice their workers to enrich themselves. They are not content with reducing these poor creatures to slavery by making them work in unhealthy workshops from which fresh air is excluded, from 5 A.M. to 8 P.M. (and sometimes 10 P.M.) in the summer, and from 6 A.M. to 9 P.M. in the winter; they force them to work a part of Sunday as well. From bed to work and from work to bed—that sums up the life of their victims. . . . They never have a moment for their private affairs; they always breathe a polluted atmosphere; for them the sun never shines.**[11]

France, too, had its outbreaks of machine breaking, as at Viennes in 1819, and the industrial riots in Lyons in 1831 and 1834 paralleled those in Manchester. In Charles Fourier (1772–1837) it had its own utopian reformer as well. Fourier, a mathematician who had been head of the statistical office in Lyons during Napoleon's Hundred Days in 1815, proposed a network of small, self-contained communities called phalansteries similar to Owen's experiments at New Lanark and New Harmony; like Owen's, attempts to found such communities were short-lived. More modest goals of reform lagged behind the British example. Despite official concern about the high rate of physical rejection among French army conscripts, the only industrial legislation passed in the first half of the nineteenth century was the Factory Law of 1841, which prohibited the employment of children under the age of 8 in factories.

The German Giant

The Napoleonic wars had been a watershed in German economic development. They had caused serious dislocation, but German industry, sheltering behind the Continental System, had benefited by a respite from competition with British products. They had also radically simplified Germany's political geography, reducing its hundreds of principalities to 39 states, of which an enlarged Prussia, now in control of the coalfields of the Ruhr and the Saar, the main river systems of the north, and the prosperous cities of the Rhineland and Westphalia, was the most important. The most important single item on the economic agenda was the removal of internal tolls and tariff barriers. Under Prussian leadership, a great free trade zone, the Zollverein, or Customs Union, had been established by 1834, embracing some 34 million people. This formed the basis for a sustained industrial expansion whose rate of growth was unsurpassed on the Continent.

Textiles and metallurgy flourished, and new mining techniques opened up the great coal deposits of the Ruhr. Railways were introduced in 1835, eight years after the French had built their first line; by 1850 there were twice as many miles of track in Germany as in France. Private and public capital were symbiotic in Germany to an extent unparalleled except in tiny Belgium, which was for all practical purposes an extension of Germany's western frontier. By the 1820s and 1830s the great industrial pioneers—Krupp, Stinnes, Mannesmann—had already made their mark. Major capital construction, such as railways, was financed by joint-stock ventures underwritten in part by government funds, and by the late 1840s the first state railways were built. By virtually every measure—population, production, urbanization—Germany was the most economically powerful nation on the Continent by 1850, and within a generation it would be challenging the lead of Britain itself.

Industrial Development After 1850

The wealth and productivity of the West increased exponentially after 1850. In part this increase was stimulated by the same factor that had fueled the economic boom of the sixteenth century: the discovery of gold in the New World. The discovery of gold in 1848 at Sutter's Mill in California (and sizable deposits later in Australia) added as much gold to the world's stocks in the next 20 years as in the preceding 350. As the new supply leveled off, the European economy contracted in the 1870s and 1880s,

Flags fly proudly over the Crystal Palace, built to house the world's first international industrial exhibition in London in 1851, while a festive bourgeois crowd takes its ease outside the monument. The palace itself, constructed of cast iron and glass, was a triumph of the new technology. [Bettmann Archive/BBC Hulton]

only to surge forward again with fresh supplies from South Africa and the Klondike. A second source of capital, particularly for Britain and, to a lesser extent, France, was the profits of trade and empire. The traffic of European commerce had constituted 75 percent of the world's trade by 1800. The volume of that trade now skyrocketed, increasing at least 1,200 percent between the 1840s and 1914.

Much of this trade was with the United States, which, already a major economic force by 1860, had become the world's leading industrial power by 1900. The industrialization of the United States marked the triumph of Alexander Hamilton's vision of an America founded on commercial and industrial prosperity over Thomas Jefferson's dream of a pastoral democracy based on independent yeomen. Numerous factors created an ideal climate for expansion: vast deposits of iron, coal, and petroleum, which, with a plenitude of gold and silver, provided an unsurpassed source of both raw materials and specie; a domestic labor and consumer market continually fed by immigration; and a political system firmly controlled by northern banking and industrial interests after the Civil War. By 1890 American iron and steel production had surpassed that of Britain; by 1900 the United States was making more steel than Britain and Germany combined; by 1910 its rail network was carrying a billion tons of freight per year. Huge trusts and monopolies dominated the economy, exploiting the cheap labor drawn primarily from southern and eastern Europe. When the United States Steel Corporation was organized in 1901, it was capitalized at $1.4 billion—a sum greater than the total wealth of the country a century before.

The Harnessing of Science

At the same time, new technological developments greatly extended the scope of the Industrial Revolution. A new age of steel resulted from the refining processes introduced by Sir Henry Bessemer in the 1850s, Werner von Siemen in the 1860s, and the cousins Percy Gilchrist and Sidney Thomas in the 1870s, which permitted both much higher temperatures in blast furnaces and the use of lower grades of ore. In the last three decades of the nineteenth century world steel production increased fiftyfold, as steel, both lighter and more tensile than iron, began to replace it everywhere in rail, ship, and building construction.

For the first time as well, applied science and engineering began to feed directly and systematically into technological development, creating new products, processes, and sources of energy. The age of the amateur inventor, the inspired tinkerer working alone, was rapidly drawing to a close; the American Thomas Alva Edison (1847–1931) was the last and greatest of the type. Large firms began to employ their own scientists and engineers, working directly on product development and production improvement. At the same time, the lag time between basic scientific discovery and its technological application was sharply diminished. As crucial to the nineteenth century as steam had been to the eighteenth was electricity, which as a natural phenomenon had attracted the interest of a host of scientists from Benjamin Franklin to Alessandro Volta. Following the conversion of mechanical motion into electric current by Michael Faraday in 1831, the American Samuel F. B. Morse produced the first practical telegraph in the 1840s. The telegraph was the beginning of a communications revolution that paralleled that of the steam locomotive in transportation. The telephone followed in 1879, and in 1896 the Italian Guglielmo Marconi adapted radio waves, discovered by Heinrich Hertz a decade before, to a new mass communications device.

The development of electromagnets, the electrolytic process, and the modern dynamo paved the way for the use of electricity in public places such as railways, docks, theaters, and markets, as well as in some factories. The incandescent light bulb, invented independently by Edison in America and Sir Joseph Swan in Britain, brought electrical illumination into the home and the office in the 1880s. In the same decade the steam turbine began to replace the old reciprocal-action engine. It was soon adapted to coal and then to the fuel source that would power the twentieth century, petroleum. The combustion engine followed in 1886, the airplane in 1903. By the early 1900s, European and American cities were lit electrically by huge generating systems, and their streets were crowded with trams and, increasingly, automobiles. At the same time, organic chemistry (the chemistry of carbon compounds), developed especially in Germany, produced a whole range of synthetic dyes, textiles, paints, and other products. No longer were humans confined to working, blending, crushing, and refining the given raw materials of nature; by manipulating the basic organic components of these materials, new, artificial products could be created.

By every measure—energy produced, goods and services distributed, miles of railway track and telegraph, telephone, and cable line laid—industrialization and the new, unprecedented standards of living it made possible increased by quantum leaps in Europe and the United States during the nineteenth century. But industrial development remained unevenly distributed geographically, and industrial wealth was even more unequally shared socially. Moreover, the disparity between worker and owner in Europe and the United States was greater still between colonizer and colonized as capital penetration and imperial expansion brought the mines, factories, technical processes, and industrial discipline of the West to the far corners of the globe. As this process intensified during the last decades of the century, social and political dislocation, and in some cases devastation, occurred on a scale that dwarfed the changes that had taken place in Britain and on the Continent. Only a few places outside Europe achieved industrialization on their own before 1900. Chief among them was North America, and particularly the United States, where, with a population nearly equal to that of France or Germany by 1850 and a role as the principal supplier of raw cotton to the European market, integration with the new industrial economy was a foregone conclusion. Beyond the North Atlantic trade circuit, however, only Argentina in the Western Hemisphere and Japan in the Far East had developed a significant industrial base on their own. As the twentieth century dawned, European economic and political hegemony in the world was at its zenith.

The Industrial Revolution and the population explosion that accompanied it both began, independently, in the middle of the eighteenth century, and both continue unabated the processes of change and upheaval that have transformed the globe. Population pressure spurred agricultural and industrial development, at first in Britain and then elsewhere, and success in sustaining an ever-expanding population generated the market and product demand that fed technological growth. When in 1851 Britain celebrated its role as the "workshop of the world" with a great international industrial exhibition at the Crystal Palace in London, the most important technological advance in humanity's recorded history was already an accomplished fact. The windmill and the waterwheel had given way to the steam engine, the domestic workshop to the factory, the horse and cart to the locomotive and the telegraph. Metals had replaced wood in the construction of harbors, bridges, buildings, and machinery, as coal had replaced it as the source of power. Petroleum in turn was soon to supplement and then largely replace coal, as petroleum itself, having succeeded animal and vegetable oils for lighting, was soon to be replaced by electricity. At the same time, the nature of work and of the social organization that revolved around it was no less radically transformed. The artisan who saw a job through from start to finish was replaced by the skilled factory worker who was confined to a single part of a process and integrated into a complex market structure that dictated the wages, conditions, and availability of employment. The family circle, the primary preindustrial work unit the world over, began to give way to an impersonal industrial discipline that reshaped and often shattered traditional relationships and modes of living at the most basic level. Inexorably, these changes radiated outward from their European origins to embrace the entire world and to create not merely a new global economy but a new global culture as well.

Notes

1. K. Marx and F. Engels, *The Communist Manifesto* (New York: New York Labor News Co.), pp. 13-14. First published in 1848.
2. A. M. Lambert, *The Making of the Dutch Landscape* (New York: Seminar Press, 1971), p. 195.
3. A. Ure, *Philosophy of Manufactures* (New York: Kelley, 1967), p. 109. Originally printed in 1861.
4. Ibid., p. 13.
5. B. Disraeli, *Sybil, or, the Two Nations.* In *The Works of Benjamin Disraeli,* (New York: M. W. Dunne, 1904–1905), Book II, Chap. 5.
6. R. Owen, *Life of R. Owen, by Himself* (London: Bell & Sons, 1920), pp. 122–123.
7. M. Cole, *Robert Owen of New Lanark* (New York: Oxford University Press, 1953), p. 152. First published in 1857.
8. A. Briggs, *Victorian Cities* (London: Odhams Books, 1965), p. 55.
9. Ibid., p. 102.
10. Ibid., pp. 92–93.
11. W. O. Henderson, *The Industrial Revolution in Europe, 1815–1914* (Chicago: Quadrangle Books, 1961), p. 107.

Suggestions for Further Reading

Ashton, T. S. *The Industrial Revolution 1760–1830.* London: Oxford University Press, 1961.

Braudel, F. *Civilization and Capitalism.* 3 vols. London: Collins, 1979–1985.

Briggs, A. *Victorian Cities.* London: Odhams Books, 1965.

Chambers, J. D., and Mingay, G. E. *The Agricultural Revolution, 1750–1850.* New York: Schocken Books, 1966.

Clapham, J. H. *The Economic Development of France and Germany, 1815–1914.* Cambridge: Cambridge University Press, 1928.

Cipolla, C. M., ed. *The Industrial Revolution, 1700–1914.* London: Penguin Books, 1973.

Cole, M. *Robert Owen of New Lanark.* New York: Oxford University Press, 1953.

Crafts, N. F. R. *British Economic Growth During the Industrial Revolution.* New York: Oxford University Press, 1986.

Dennis, R. *English Industrial Cities of the Nineteenth Century.* Cambridge: Cambridge University Press, 1984.

Harrison, J. F. C. *The Early Victorians, 1832–1851.* New York: Praeger, 1971.

Henderson, W. O. *The Industrial Revolution in Europe.* Chicago: Quadrangle Books, 1961.

Hobsbawm, E. J. *Industry and Empire.* London: Penguin Books, 1970.

Landes, D. *The Unbound Prometheus: Technological Change and Industrial Development in Western Europe from the Seventeenth Century to the Present.* London: Cambridge University Press, 1969.

Mathias, P. *The First Industrial Nation: An Economic History of Britain, 1700–1914.* New York: Scribner, 1969.

McKeown, T. *The Modern Rise of Population.* New York: Academic Press, 1976.

Perkin, H. *The Origin of Modern English Society, 1780–1860.* London: Routledge & Kegan Paul, 1969.

Thompson, E. P. *The Making of the English Working Class.* Harmondsworth, England: Penguin Books, 1964.

Weber, A. F. *The Growth of Cities in the Nineteenth Century.* Ithaca, N.Y.: Cornell University Press, 1969.

Wilson, C., and Parker, G. *An Introduction to the Sources of European Economic History, 1500–1800.* London: Weidenfeld & Nicolson, 1977.

Zaretsky, E. *Capitalism, the Family, and Personal Life.* London: Pluto Press, 1976.

CHAPTER · 30

The Age of Ideology

In the wake of the French Revolution and the Napoleonic conquests, Europe experienced some of its most turbulent and troubled decades. The statesmen of the victorious allies, meeting at Vienna, sought to restore the Old Regime and to find an antidote to revolution. Their attempts foundered on the continuing demands for representative government, free competition, and social justice, often expressed through a fervent desire for national independence or unity. This was in turn linked to the wider cultural movement of Romanticism, which, in its emphasis on the free expressive powers of the individual, questioned traditional values and undermined traditional authority. By 1830 the fragile détente between the old noble elites and the increasingly powerful bourgeoisie had broken down, and a new wave of revolutionary disturbance swept Europe. This was only the precursor of the far more widespread and violent revolutions of 1848, in which the industrial proletariat, fired by the doctrines of socialism, played for the first time a leading role. These revolutions ended largely in apparent failure, but they confirmed the ascendancy of the bourgeoisie as the only barrier to the demand for a new social order.

Detail from Honoré Daumier's *Les Divorceuses*. At an impassioned meeting of women, one of many such during the Revolution of 1848, a feminist spokeswoman, probably Jeanne Derain, demands reform of the divorce laws. Daumier's portrayal typified the derisive reaction of the press to the new and disturbing phenomenon of feminist activism. [Musée Carnavalet/Photographie Bulloz]

The Legacy of Revolution

The American Revolution, in declaring all men born "free and equal," and the French Revolution, in asserting liberty, equality, and fraternity to be the goals of a just society, had propounded new political values to the Western world. Freedom or liberty, as the Old Regime understood these terms, meant not general rights applicable to all but franchises or exemptions enjoyed by particular individuals or corporate groups: the right of a town or locality to charge bridge, river, or road tolls, for example, or the exemption of the clergy from the jurisdiction of secular courts. The foundation of Old Regime society was not equality but hierarchy and subordination; its members were not citizens but subjects.

Even more foreign to the old order was the new revolutionary ideal of fraternity, the voluntary solidarity of all citizens with one another and their patriotic identification with the nation and, beyond borders, with all humanity. In America these principles had inspired the first nation ever created on the basis of citizen equality, though it still excluded women and blacks. The founding of the United States had in turn been a powerful inspiration to the French revolutionaries of 1789. But whereas the United States, an ocean away, had been able to export its revolution only by precept and example, the armies of the French republic, crossing the Alps and the Rhine, had brought theirs by force to much of Europe.

The champions of the old order, led by Britain—whose own revolutions of 1640 and 1688 had been the antecedents of both the French and American ones—had fought and finally defeated the armies of France. Long before Waterloo, however, the ideals of freedom and equality had been tempered both in revolutionary France and democratic America. In the United States the election of senators by state legislatures and of the president and vice-president by an electoral college represented a barrier to direct citizen control of the legislative and executive branches of government. In France a similar retreat was visible as early as 1791 in the distinction between active and passive citizens, and by the time of Napoleon, passive acquiescence in a dictatorial regime was the only function left to citizenship.

Despite this, the ideals of representative government and an egalitarian society remained alive. No longer could the rulers of Europe rely on obedience to authority based on the unquestioned subordination of subject populations to their natural masters, and political agitation everywhere now took the form of demands for basic rights and representation. Of no less importance were the values of freedom and equality to dissolve the traditional barriers to state centralization. The reduction of many particular and individual freedoms was a tedious and sometimes impossible task; the removal of a single set of generalized freedoms required only the suspension of constitutional guarantees by an emergency decree, as first Robespierre and then Napoleon had shown. Liberties extended to all and tyranny exerted over all lay uncomfortably close together as the legacy of the democratic revolutions of the late eighteenth century.

The demand for liberty and equality was often linked to another pervasive political sentiment of the early nineteenth century, nationalism. In its simplest terms, nationalism was a sense of cultural and political identity among a given people. Cultural identity was manifested in shared traditions and the possession of a common language; political identity was expressed in the association with or residency in a particular region or territory. The ultimate expression of a people's identity was the possession of a state.

Nationalism first expressed itself in Germany. The philosopher-critic Johann Gottfried von Herder (1744–1803) argued in the 1770s and 1780s that each people had its own organic development and must pursue its own individual destiny. This contention, like many other early manifestations of Romanticism, went counter to the Enlightenment ideal of a universal reason that would bring an identical justice to all. Herder urged his compatriots to look to their own cultural heritage for meaning and direction, rather than to an imported French model that could only be valid for the French, not the Germans.

Herder's work stimulated a cultural nationalism that was displayed in patriotic literature; research into German philology, folklore, and legend (including the famous collections of the brothers Jacob and Wilhelm Grimm); and attempts to define the German "soul." The Napoleonic conquests galvanized political nationalism in Germany as well. Johann Gottlieb Fichte (1762–1814) called on the people of Prussia to regenerate the lost honor of their fatherland, while his fellow Prussian, the philosopher Georg Wilhelm Friedrich Hegel (1770–1831), claimed that the historical dichotomy between the individual and the community was overcome in the unity of the modern nation-state. The highest manifestation of this unity was not, as Fichte expressed it, in the securing of particular benefits such as life, liberty, and personal well-being, as in the Anglo-American tradition, but in a noble patriotism and love of country.

This almost mystical sense of the union, or perhaps submersion of the individual in the nation, suggests that nationalism was not an essentially liberal cause, even though liberals often expressed their aspirations through it and used it as a vehicle of rebellion against the established order. In Russia nationalism would be invoked in the 1840s both by liberal Westernizers who wished to see Russia become modern and competitive by adopting western European values and institutions and by conservative Slavophiles who believed that Russia could fulfill its mes-

The Mystique of Nationalism

The nationalist fervor that Napoleon stimulated and that ultimately overthrew him was powerfully fed by the antirationalist elements that also produced the Romantic movement. In this passage, the French philosopher Joseph de Maistre (1753–1821), a conservative opponent of the Enlightenment and of the French Revolution, expresses his sense of the "national soul" inherent in all peoples.

Human reason left to its own resources is completely incapable not only of creating *but also of conserving any religious or political association*, because it can only give rise to disputes and because, to conduct himself well, man needs beliefs, not problems. . . . Religion and political dogmas, mingled and merged together, should together form a *general* or *national mind* sufficiently strong to repress the aberrations of the individual reason which is, of its nature, the mortal enemy of any association whatever because it gives birth only to divergent opinions. . . .

What is patriotism? It is this national mind of which I am speaking; it is individual *abnegation*. Faith and patriotism are the two great wonder-workers of the world. Both are divine. All their actions are miracles. Do not talk to them of scrutiny, choice, discussion, for they will say that you blaspheme. They know only two words, *submission* and *belief*; with these two levers, they raise the world. Their very errors are sublime. These two infants of heaven prove their origin to all by creating and conserving; and if they unite, join their forces, and together take possession of a nation, they exalt it, make it divine and increase its power a hundred-fold.

Source: J Lively, ed., *The Works of Joseph de Maistre* (New York: Macmillan, 1965), pp. 108–109 (modified slightly).

sianic destiny in the world only by remaining true to its traditions. In short, nationalism appealed across the spectrum from economic rationalists, who saw the nation-state as an efficient market mechanism, to religious enthusiasts, who saw it as a communal salvation; from Friedrich List, who dreamed of a tariff-free greater Germany, to Adam Mickiewicz, a Polish poet who identified the history of his nation with the passion of Christ and its longed-for independence as the resurrection.

The result of these conflicting ideologies—civil freedom against local and traditional rights, a society conceived as a body of equal citizens or as a patriotic community versus one conceived as a set of hierarchical orders—was a new and uncertain age in which, for the first time, the very basis of the social order was in dispute. In the aftermath of Napoleon's defeat, the victorious allied powers set about to restore the world they had known before 1789 as far as they could. Their attempts to do so, against not only the countervailing forces unleashed by the French and American revolutions but the as yet unreckoned ones of the Industrial Revolution, determined the course of European politics to the middle of the nineteenth century and beyond.

The Congress of Vienna

The major European powers met in Vienna in September 1814 to try to untangle 20 years of war and revolution. It was the first such general congress of the powers since the one that had settled the Thirty Years' War at Westphalia in 1648. Every state on the Continent sent representatives, including defunct members of the old Holy Roman Empire seeking reinstatement. But only five parties really counted—Austria, Britain, Prussia, Russia, and France, represented, respectively, by Prince Metternich, Viscount Castlereagh, Baron Hardenberg, Tsar Alexander I (the only sovereign taking direct part in the proceedings), and the ubiquitous Baron Talleyrand, who after deserting Napoleon had brokered the return of the Bourbon dynasty to France.

The Congress of Vienna, which redrew the map of Europe in the wake of the Napoleonic era. Metternich stands in the left foreground; Castlereagh is seated in the center with his legs crossed; Talleyrand is seated to the right with his right arm on the table. [Photographie Bulloz]

Collective Security

What the allies wanted at Vienna, broadly speaking, was to restore the old order of kingship and aristocracy, to prevent the domination of Europe by any single state, and to contain the virus of revolution wherever it might spread. To accomplish this, they created a structure of collective security that was essentially a classical balance-of-power system tinctured by the agreement to suppress all forms of radical activity. This meant that collective security would be brought to bear not only against states that threatened the stability of the system by external action but also against those whose internal stability was threatened by domestic discontent.

The framework for this sytem was already in place in the wartime coalition that had defeated Napoleon; formalized as the Quadruple Alliance in 1815 and extended, after a suitable period of probation, to include France in 1818, it formed the basis of the so-called Concert of Europe, which kept the peace of the Continent, or at any rate took the credit for doing so, down to 1914. The novelty of the system was the recognition that war, because it had the potential to unleash revolution, had become too dangerous a luxury for Europe to afford. Alexander I, for whom it represented not merely a political instrument but a spiritual compact, managed to bully his fellow sovereigns (with the exception of the pope, the Turkish sultan, and the regent of Britain) into signing a "holy alliance" against war and for Christian concord. On a more mundane level, Prince Metternich conceived it as a sanction to intervene in the affairs of any state threatened by revolution. The British were suspicious of the uses to which such an unlimited warrant might be put, however. Reverting to a lone hand after years of marshaling coalitions on the Continent, they refused to commit themselves to any joint command. Prussia, too, was skeptical of any rapprochement between its two powerful eastern neighbors, Austria and Russia.

The Diplomatic Settlement

The strains among the allies at Vienna came into the open over the Polish-Saxon question, which nearly torpedoed the congress. Napoleon had taken away almost all the territory gained by Austria and Prussia in the partitioning of Poland to create a satellite entity, the Grand Duchy of Warsaw. Its collapse with the defeat of his empire again left a power vacuum in eastern Europe. Alexander I insisted on restoring the original prepartition Poland, with himself as king. To win Prussia's support, he offered to cede it Saxony, which had become vulnerable as the last German state to desert Napoleon. Metternich, appalled, sought out Castlereagh and Talleyrand, who agreed to resist the Russian plan, if necessary by force.

The Polish-Saxon question was finally settled by compromise. Alexander received a reduced "congress" Poland that was roughly equivalent to Napoleon's Grand Duchy, and Prussia was compensated with two-fifths of Saxony. But the whole episode pointed up the inherent contradiction of the congress system, which presupposed lasting cooperation between historical rivals whose interests were fundamentally opposed.

The Congress of Vienna did, however, decide a wide range of issues, which set the diplomatic framework of the nineteenth century. Uppermost in the minds of the allies was the creation of buffer zones, primarily against France but more subtly against Russia as well, whose steady westward encroachment had become a major concern over the preceding 100 years. A new Belgo-Dutch kingdom of the Netherlands was erected as a barrier on France's northern frontier, and Prussia was given a solid bloc of territory along the Rhine to perform a similar function. With the acquisition of the Rhineland—which, with the Saxon strip, made it the largest territorial gainer at the congress—Prussia now overarched all of northern Germany, facing France to the west and Russia to the east. Austria was reinstalled in northern Italy and expanded

***30.1** Europe After the Congress of Vienna (1815)*

along the Dalmatian coast, where, from a southern vantage, it could serve as a check against Russian designs on Turkey and French ones on Italy. The British, following the policy they had adopted at the Peace of Utrecht a century before, sought no territory on the Continent but added several key islands and stations in the West Indies and the Far East to their unrivaled sea empire. They now controlled the Mediterranean through Gibraltar, Malta, and the Ionian islands, the South Atlantic through the West Indies and the Cape of Good Hope, and the Indian Ocean and the South China Sea through Ceylon, Mauritius, and Singapore. Bestriding the major ocean arteries of the world, they were uniquely situated to exploit the productive expansion of the Industrial Revolution and to enjoy a century of extraordinary world dominion.

The thorniest single issue facing the powers was the settlement of Germany. Beset by the rival demands of nationalists who dreamed of a unified German state and the claimants of liquidated states who wanted a return to the benevolent chaos of the Holy Roman Empire, they chose to preserve the states carved from the empire by Napoleon, loosely linked in a federation whose main function was to keep the smaller states from gravitating toward France. It was a pragmatic solution that left Prussia in a position of greatly augmented influence and postponed for 50 years the final confrontation between Prussia and Austria for control of Germany.

France itself was treated leniently in an attempt to shore up the restored Bourbon monarchy, whose representative, Talleyrand, was treated nearly as a partner in the peacemaking. The dramatic return of Napoleon from Elba and the ensuing Hundred Days compelled the allies to harsher sanctions. The Congress took away some snippets of French territory, imposed an indemnity of 700 million francs, and posted an army of occupation in France for three years. Nevertheless, France's treatment was exceedingly lenient. Events bore out the wisdom of the allies' moderation; the age of French aggression and French preponderance in Europe was over.

By their lights, the diplomats at Vienna accomplished a good deal. They cleared away the debris of a generation of war and converted a wartime coalition into a permanent instrument for maintaining order. The instrument was flawed, and the values it sought to defend—monarchy, aristocracy, and hereditary privilege—were already in eclipse, but the goal of regulating interstate conflict was a first step toward the recognition of the historical obsolescence of war.

What the men at Vienna were unwilling to recognize was the change of their own time. Formed under the Old Regime, their conception of society was still patriarchal; in the words of the Holy Alliance, the sovereigns of Europe were "as fathers of families towards their subjects and armies." In redrawing the map of the Continent, they acted in the high-handed manner of old, parceling out peoples and territories solely according to the abstract scales of power. It would never have occurred to them to ask the Belgians whether they wanted to be under the Dutch, the Venetians under the Austrians, or the Poles under Russia. They rightly calculated that nationalism, the new sentiment that a land belonged to its people and not to its ruler, was incompatible with the preservation of the existing order; they wrongly concluded that they could contain it with treaties, armies, and spies.

Reaction and Revolution

The notion of collective security against revolution—what came to be known as the Congress System—was the brainchild of Prince Klemens von Metternich (1773–1859), who as foreign minister of Austria from 1809 to 1848 put his stamp on the diplomacy of the age. Metternich envisioned the system operating through periodic meetings of the great powers that by monitoring developments in each state could scotch any activity that threatened either internal or external stability. As the Troppau Protocol of 1820 put it,

> **States which have undergone a change of government due to revolution, the results of which threaten other states, *ipso facto* cease to be members of the European alliance. . . . If owing to such alterations immediate danger threatens other states, the powers bind themselves, by peaceful means, or if need be by arms to bring back the guilty state into the bosom of the Great Alliance.**

The opportunity soon arose to test the system. The restored regimes in Spain and the Kingdom of the Two Sicilies were violently unpopular. The Spanish had waged a heroic resistance against Napoleon on behalf of the Bourbon regime to which, after a century, they had transferred their loyalty. When King Ferdinand VII returned to Madrid in 1814 after a six-year exile, he was welcomed rapturously. But enthusiasm for the symbol of Spanish monarchy was not the same as a desire to turn back the clock. The Enlightenment had penetrated Spain, particularly during the reign of Charles III (1759–1788), and the Napoleonic administration, however despised on nationalist grounds, had left its mark in the form of greater tolerance and bureaucratic efficiency. An elected national body, the Cortes, meeting in the free city of Cadiz in 1812, had adopted a liberal constitution on the basis of which Ferdinand had been recalled. But the king swiftly dissolved the Cortes, nullified its acts, scrapped its constitution, and threw its chief leaders and supporters into jail. Restoring the Inquisition and the lands of the church and the aristocracy in full, he proclaimed a return to divine right absolutism. It was a formula for revolution. The economy languished; Seville and Cadiz were full of merchants ruined by the long

Metternich's Plea for the Old Order

Count Metternich, the preeminent figure in European politics between 1815 and 1848, here forcefully expresses his conservative credo.

Drag through the mud the name of God and the powers instituted by his divine decrees, and the revolution will be prepared! Speak of a social contract, and the revolution is accomplished! The revolution was already completed in the palace of kings, in the drawing-rooms and boudoirs of certain cities, while among the great mass of the people it was still only in a state of preparation. . . .

The first and greatest concern for the immense majority of every nation is the stability of the laws, and their uninterrupted action—never their change. Therefore let the governments govern, let them maintain the groundwork of their institutions, both ancient and modern; for if it is at all times dangerous to touch them, it certainly would not now, in the general confusion, be wise to do so.

Source: K. von Metternich, *Memoirs*, trans. Mrs. A. Napier, vol. 3 (London: Richard Bentley & Son, 1881), pp. 461, 474.

wars and the revolts of the American colonies, against which the regime seemed helpless to respond. Discontent spread to the military, and secret societies sprang up in defiance of the censorship. Rebellion broke out in early 1820, and Ferdinand, made a virtual prisoner, was compelled to summon the Cortes and to reinstate the constitution of 1812.

Portugal, Spain's Iberian neighbor, was soon touched by an uprising as well when rebels demanded the return of King John VI, who was still in exile in Brazil, but also a constitutional government. At the same time, a series of revolts and disturbances broke out on the Italian peninsula aimed against both Spanish and Austrian rule. They began in Naples, where King Ferdinand I, like his nephew Ferdinand VII in Spain, had abrogated reforms and alienated both the army and the bourgeoisie. Sardinia next attempted to depose its reactionary monarch, Victor Emmanuel I, and there were threats of rebellion in the Papal States as well.

The Overthrow of Ottoman Rule in Greece

A more complex—and far more broadly based—rebellion broke out in Greece in 1821, which soon became a revolution against 3½ centuries of Ottoman rule. Within the space of a year, insurrection had sparked across the entire Mediterranean coast from Cape Finisterre to the eastern Aegean.

Metternich called for action but met a divided response. The British dissented from the Troppau Protocol, and the French, unwilling to serve as the agent of Austrian interests in Italy, sat idle. Metternich was more successful with Prussia and Russia, with whose assent an Austrian army descended on Italy and speedily crushed the rebellions in Naples and Sardinia. France was more amenable to action in Spain, where it was anxious to restore its influence, and when the revolutionary government in Madrid rejected an ultimatum to modify its reforms in 1823, it sent troops across the Pyrenees to restore the king it had deposed 15 years before. Despite promises of clemency, Ferdinand VII carried out a bloody purge and plunged Spain back into a civil and clerical autocracy that left a bitter legacy.

The case of Greece was more complicated. The Ottoman Empire had revived in the seventeenth century to make a last great assault on Europe, only to be driven back from the walls of Vienna and deep into the Danube basin (see Chapter 19). Battered by the southward expansion of Russia in the eighteenth century, it now faced revolt among the subject peoples within its own borders. The Serbians had risen in 1804 in the beginnings of a struggle for nationhood that was to have profound consequences for all of Europe. Their rebellion aroused little interest, but when the Greeks of the southern Peloponnesus raised the flag of independence in 1821, the Continent took sudden notice. The so-called Phanariot Greeks of Constantinople had become effectively the governors of Turkey's Balkan provinces, where their suppression of native culture had been bitterly resented and had indeed contributed to the Serbian rebellion. Greek merchants dominated the trade of the eastern Mediterranean, sometimes flying a Russian flag. At the same time, the Greeks were engaged in a great revival of their own culture, largely dormant since the conquest of Crete in 1669. The Society of Friends, a secret organization supported by Alexander I (whose horror of rebellions stopped short at those that advanced Russian interests), engineered an uprising after a number of false starts.

Under heavy pressure from his alliance partners, Alexander withdrew his support from the rebels, and the powers waited for the Greek insurrection to burn itself out. But they failed to take into account both the resolve of the Greeks and a new force that the very idea of collective security had helped create—public opinion. A new classical revival had begun in the mid-eighteenth century, spurred chiefly by German scholars and archaeologists, that merged with the nascent Romantic movement to produce a fascination with things Greek. The British government paid £35,000 to acquire the friezes of the Parthenon known as the Elgin marbles, and the French installed the Venus de Milo in the Louvre. "We are all Greeks," the poet Shelley enthused, and his great Romantic contemporary, Lord Byron, putting the fervor of many thousands of "philhellenes" (lovers of Greece) into practice, fought and died beside the Greek rebels. Committees to support the Greek cause sprang up spontaneously all over western Europe and the United States, furnishing desperately needed funds and supplies. In the face of this, the calculated indifference of the powers could not be kept up. Britain, France, and Russia attempted to impose an armistice on Turkey in 1827 and, that failing, sent out a squadron that first blockaded and then destroyed the Turkish fleet at Navarino in the Peloponnesus. King George IV of Britain apologized to the sultan for this attack on "an ancient ally," but Russia reverted to its open support of the Greeks and soon declared war. The Turks, galvanized by new nationalist and religious energies of their own, put up surprising resistance but were compelled to recognize Greek independence by the London Protocol of 1830. Two German princes refused the crown of the new kingdom before it was finally accepted by Otto, the son of King Ludwig of Bavaria, in 1832.

The poet Byron in Greek dress. His struggle on behalf of Greek independence symbolized the Romantic quest for freedom and the recovery of the heroic ideal. [National Portrait Gallery, London]

The Troubled 1820s

The revolt of the Greeks was the political cause célèbre of the 1820s. It gave heart to nationalist movements everywhere, although it showed too that such movements could not hope to succeed merely on the basis of elite elements such as the bureaucracy and the officer corps but required mass support. It left the Congress System in ruins as well. The spectacle of an allied fleet playing midwife to a revolutionary state demonstrated that Metternich's dream of a perpetual status quo could not withstand a united demand for change and that in a crisis each power would consult its own interest first and its treaty obligations second. What emerged was a looser, more informal understanding, the Concert of Europe, by which the great powers would attempt to resolve their major differences and attempt to avoid general war.

While only Russia among the major powers underwent an actual rebellion within its borders between 1815 and 1830—the Decembrist revolt of 1825—all experienced significant unrest. We have touched on the Luddite attacks and urban agitation in Britain. In retrospect, it was remarkable that unrest was contained as well as it was in Britain, given the unprecedented social transformation of the Industrial Revolution, whose maximum impact was being felt in these years. It seemed serious enough, however, to the Tory government of Lord Liverpool. In the wake of the Peterloo Massacre, the government passed a series of repressive measures through Parliament, the Six Acts, which suppressed public meetings, curbed the press, and speeded up procedures for prosecuting offenders against the public order. Waterloo's hero, the duke of Wellington, expressed the hope that Britain's example of firmness would be followed by others so that the world might escape "the universal revolution which seems to menace us all." Three months later, in February 1820, a plot to assassinate the entire cabinet and seize control of the government was "discovered," although the conspirators' arms had actually been supplied by the government. It was not until the late 1820s that a less hysterical atmosphere began to prevail.

In France, Louis XVIII (1814–1824) sought a middle ground between the reactionary Ultraroyalist party, which wanted to turn the clock back literally to 1789, and the ex-Bonapartists and republicans, whom Louis knew he would have to conciliate to stabilize his regime. He offered a charter that in essence preserved the structure of the Napoleonic code and set up a bicameral assembly that could veto royal legislation. The Hundred Days brought a violent Ultra reaction in which hundreds of suspected Jacobin and Bonapartist sympathizers were massacred. No sooner had Louis regained a measure of control than the assassination in 1820 of the duke of Berry, the heir to the throne, set off a new wave of reaction. As Louis' reign ebbed, power passed to his intransigent brother, the count of Artois, who succeeded him as Charles X (1824–1830). A new spate of legislation enacted the program of the Ultras. The Law of Indemnity (1825) compensated nobles who had lost their estates during the revolution by devaluing government bonds held by the bourgeoisie, and the Law of Sacrilege, passed in the same year, imposed the death penalty for the theft of sacred objects and other vaguely defined offenses against the church. When members of the Jesuit order, still officially banned in France, appeared openly in Catholic schools, liberals concluded that they were now directing the government.

Despite its greatly strengthened geopolitical situation, Prussia was content to allow Metternich to play ideological policeman to the rest of Germany, a role he assumed with relish. By the Carlsbad Decrees of 1819, Metternich suppressed the student societies that had taken up the aspirations for national unity thwarted at the Congress of Vienna. These societies were in turn the successors of the quasi-military gymnastic clubs founded by Friedrich Ludwig Jahn (1778–1852) during the Napoleonic wars, whose members, wearing gray-shirted uniforms and imbued with a hatred of "foreign" (including Jewish) influence, strikingly foreshadowed elements of Nazi ideology and practice. Student groups that gathered at Wartburg Castle near Eisenach to commemorate the tricentennial of Luther's Ninety-five Theses in 1817 toasted unity and freedom but also burned conservative and antinationalist books after a torchlight procession, a rather dubious way to protest censorship.

In Austria itself Metternich's chief concern was to suppress nationalist stirrings among the many minority groups that comprised the Habsburg empire. The very name *Austria* had been adopted no less recently than 1804 to describe the patrimonial lands of the emperor, and whereas the yearning for national identity might encourage a sense of unity in such regions as Germany and Italy and strengthen it in states such as Britain, France, or Spain already established on the basis of a common language and heritage, it could only foster division and separatism in such an amalgam of peoples and tongues as the Habsburg state represented. By skillfully playing rival minorities off against one another, Metternich delayed his day of reckoning for more than 30 years; by failing to provide a genuine accommodation for nationalist aspirations within the framework of the empire, he ensured that that day would come.

Russia was still by far the most autocratic of all European states. Like Catherine the Great, the eccentric Alexander I (1801–1825) began his reign with a flourish of reform. Men of all classes were legally entitled to hold land for the first time, and masters were encouraged to free their serfs. New schools were founded, including six universities, and new ideas entered the country, particularly through the medium of the Freemasons and other secret fraternities, much in vogue at the time. Leo Tolstoy has left a vivid picture of liberal ferment among the early nineteenth century urban aristocracy in his novel *War and Peace* (1869). The reforming Count Speransky even drafted plans for a system of representative bodies culminating in a national assembly, though without real legislative power. But the Napoleonic invasions blew away these fair hopes like petals before a storm, and a chastened Alexander, regarding his country's disaster as a providential judgment, lapsed into a reactionary mysticism that made him Metternich's most zealous if not always most reliable ally in the war against reform.

Frustrated liberal aspirations among the officer corps in conjunction with a succession crisis in December 1825 provoked Russia's first attempt at revolution. Alexander's heir, the Grand Duke Constantine, had secretly resigned his claim to the throne in favor of his brother Nicholas, but when the tsar died suddenly, each brother proclaimed the other. In the resulting chaos, some of the disaffected officers raised the standard of "Constantine and constitution," which some of the soldiers apparently thought referred to the tsar and his wife.

Whatever the comic overtones of the Decembrist uprising, it was ruthlessly suppressed. Hundreds were imprisoned or exiled, and five officers were executed; these officers' courageous bearing made them symbols of resistance under the dreary and despotic reign of Nicholas I (1825–1855). The latent genius of the Russian people flowered in an extraordinary literary generation that included the poets Alexander Pushkin (1799–1837) and Mikhail Lermontov (1814–1841) and the novelists Nikolai Gogol (1809–1852) and Ivan Turgenev (1818–1883). Gogol in particular caught the spirit of Nicholas' Russia in his comic novel *Dead Souls* and his play *The Inspector General*, while the young Feodor Dostoevsky (1821–1881), later one of the century's greatest novelists, began his career by facing a mock firing squad in Siberia for allegedly "socialist" activities. Others, like the journalist Alexander Herzen (1812–1870), sought haven abroad, thus initiating the long tradition of the Russian exile.

Goethe; the Brontë sisters, Charlotte and Emily; and Mary Anne Evans (1819–1880), known by the pen name of George Eliot, whose novel, *Middlemarch*, is rivaled only by the major works of Charles Dickens. At the same time the reclusive New Englander Emily Dickinson (1830–1886) was writing some of the finest lyric poetry since Sappho.

Nevertheless, the disabilities faced by women attempting to compete in what was still a man's world were obvious. Elizabeth Gaskell was never known by her own forename but simply as "Mrs. Gaskell"; Dupin and Evans both adopted masculine pen names in an effort to gain more serious attention for their work; and Emily Dickinson's poems were never published in her own lifetime. If, moreover, a place in literature and to a lesser extent in the other arts was reluctantly conceded to women, it served only to confirm age-old prejudices against them in the fields of philosophy, politics, and the professions. The German nationalist philosopher Johann Gottlieb Fichte (1762–1814) argued that women lacked the "speculative aptitude" for either philosophical inquiry or public office. Hegel made what was to be the fundamental nineteenth-century bourgeois distinction between a public world of work and struggle, in which only men were fit to compete, and the private sphere of "piety and domesticity," for which women were intended by nature. The Frenchman Auguste Comte (1798–1857) doubted that women could be entrusted even with running a household except under male supervision. If women excelled in literature, it only confirmed the prevailing stereotype of them as creatures in whom the imagination prevailed at the expense of the intellect.

The rejection of marriage by women like Mary Wollstonecraft and George Sand and their demand for free sexual companionship reinforced the widespread male belief that women should be confined as tightly within the bounds of "piety and domesticity" as possible. Yet the image of woman had come to stand allegorically for revolution itself. In 1792 the new French republic decreed that it was to be represented officially by a seal that bore the likeness of a woman dressed in ancient style holding a pike. This popular figure of "Marianne," which blended the image of Roman virtue and Joan of Arc with secular allusions to the cult of the Virgin Mary, reached its apotheosis in Delacroix's famous painting of the revolution of 1830, *Liberty on the Barricades*. The painting shows a semiallegorical female figure leading a charge over the bodies of fallen sans-culottes, a top-hatted bourgeois at her side. Her bared breast recalls the classical image of the Amazon warrior, but the realistic touches—the stained petticoats, the hair under the arms—proclaim her as well to be a woman of the people. At the same time, her nudity carries an implicit message of sexual aggressiveness that is only partly offset by her averted, impassive gaze. Far more powerfully than the seal of Marianne, Delacroix's figure conveys the conflicting impulses behind the early Romantic image of woman: the idealized warrior-goddess and the available woman of the street, the symbol of liberation who remains chained in her petticoats, who leads a battle that will be fought by the sans-culottes but won by the bourgeoisie.

The Liberal Revival and the Revolutions of 1830

By the late 1820s dissatisfaction with the reactionary Bourbon dynasty in France and the slow pace of reform in Britain had reached the flashpoint of revolution. A neutral observer, asked to predict where it would actually occur, would probably have chosen Britain. The British political system, unreformed since 1689, had refused even a token accommodation to the new social reality created by the Industrial Revolution. The great new cities, half-anarchic, had virtually no representation in Parliament and no access to central government. Yet Britain alone, of all the major states of Europe, was to avoid revolution in 1830 and the years to come. Not London but Paris was to provide the impetus for the next wave of insurrection.

The July Revolution in France

The new revolutionary crisis began in March 1830 when the French Chamber of Deputies, led by the bankers Jacques Lafitte and Jean-Paul Casimir-Perier, voted no confidence in the government of Charles X and its policies of censorship, suffrage restriction, and clerical control of education. Charles dissolved the assembly, but new elections, even though limited to an electorate of 100,000, produced a decisive opposition majority. The king wavered, but spurred on by his chief minister Polignac, the archbishop of Paris, and Metternich, he responded on July 26 by dissolving the just-elected Chamber before it could meet, imposing new press censorship, reducing the electorate to a hard core of 25,000 aristocrats, and announcing fresh elections on this basis.

The target of these edicts was the regime's bourgeois opposition, but the reaction came from the working-class sections of Paris. The very next day barricades appeared spontaneously in the streets, and the army, called out to clear them, refused to do so. Faced with anarchy, Charles abdicated two days later in favor of his grandson and fled into exile. France was left without a government.

The sudden vacuum of power revealed the clear-cut divisions of the French political spectrum. The bourgeois opposition—bankers, industrialists, and merchants—wanted not the overthrow of the Bourbon monarchy but greater favor within it for themselves. The Parisian workers, students, and radical intellectuals who had taken to the barricades and made the revolution wanted a republic, headed by the venerable marquis de Lafayette as president. A compromise was hastily brokered behind the scenes. The duke of Orléans, a collateral relative of the Bourbons but a republican soldier in the army of 1792, was put forward as a constitutional monarch by a coalition consisting of Talleyrand, the liberal journalist Adolphe Thiers, and Lafitte, the duke's personal banker. When Lafayette publicly endorsed him, the republican opposition melted away. Louis-Philippe, as the new king was called, promised to abide by the charter of 1814, flew the tricolor flag of the 1789 revolution rather than the Bourbon lily, and was the first monarch to wear the contemporary equivalent of a business suit in public. With his paunch and umbrella, he was indistinguishable from the bourgeois interests that had brought him to power and whose interests he faithfully served.

Revolution East and West

The three-day revolution in France was the signal for major uprisings across the border in Belgium and, for far different reasons, in Poland. The union of Belgium and the Netherlands, arranged at Vienna, had much to recommend it in theory, as the two nations formed a natural economic and geographic unit. The Catholic Belgians, however, long accustomed to relative autonomy under the rule of Spain and Austria, chafed under the domination of a Protestant Dutch king, William I. Heartened by the French example, they rose up in August 1830 and, after fruitless efforts at conciliation, proclaimed independence under a liberal monarchy of their own. When Dutch troops failed to quell them, a hastily arranged big power conference in London recognized the new government to forestall French intervention.

The Polish rebellion was triggered by the news that Tsar Nicholas I, who was also king of Poland, was planning to send Russian troops through that country on its way to help suppress the Belgians. Russian rule was desperately unpopular, however, and almost any pretext might have served. The Polish Diet declared Nicholas deposed, but the tsar's army speedily crushed the revolt. Poland was absorbed directly into the Russian empire and ruled under a state of military emergency that lasted technically from 1833 until the First World War. Thousands of Poles were executed, imprisoned, or banished to Siberia, and many more fled to the West, among them Chopin.

Mazzini's Call to Revolution

Despite the failure of the revolutions of 1830, young nationalists took heart at the year that had rocked the kings of Europe on their thrones. Giuseppe Mazzini, the leader of Young Italy, an organization dedicated to the liberation and unification of Italy, here declares both the faith and the method of his revolutionary band. The emphasis on education and guerrilla tactics sounds a particularly modern note.

Young Italy is *Republican*. . . . Republican—because theoretically every nation is destined, by the law of God and humanity, to form a free and equal community of brothers; and the republican is the only form of government that insures this future. . . .

The means by which Young Italy proposes to reach its aims are—education and insurrection, to be adopted simultaneously, and made to harmonize with each other.

Education must ever be directed to teach by example, word, and pen the necessity of insurrection. Insurrection, whenever it can be realized, must be so conducted as to render it a means of national education. . . .

Insurrection—by means of guerrilla bands—is the true method of warfare for all nations desirous of emancipating themselves from a foreign yoke. This method of warfare supplies the want—inevitable at the commencement of the insurrection—of a regular army; it calls the greatest number of elements into the field, and yet may be sustained by the smallest number. It forms the military education of the people, and consecrates every foot of the native soil by the memory of some warlike deed.

Source: N. Gangulee, ed., *Giuseppe Mazzini: Selected Writings* (London: Lindsay Drummond, 1945), pp. 129–134 passim.

Lesser disturbances also shook Germany, Italy, Switzerland, Spain, and Portugal, though for the most part without significant result. Yet liberals could, with the tragic exception of Poland, count 1830 as a year of victory. The bourgeoisie had reclaimed political primacy in France and, no longer dependent on a dictator such as Napoleon to retain it, had cut a king to their own measure. The powers had been forced to acquiesce in an independent Belgium, nominally a monarchy, whose constitution acknowledged its origin in the sovereignty of the people and provided what was to be for many years the widest electoral franchise in Europe. The autocratic William I was forced to embrace reform in the Netherlands, and liberal gains were made in Switzerland. Above all, 1830 marked the year when history seemed to move again in Europe. The liberal triumph was far from complete, but its outlines at last seemed visible.

Britain: Revolution Averted

Britain accomplished revolutionary change without revolution. The settlement of 1689 had confirmed the supremacy of Parliament over the king. But neither the size of the electorate—less than 4 percent of the population—nor the distribution of seats had changed in nearly a century and a half, and both were now profoundly unrepresentative of the urban, industrialized society that Britain had become. The long and almost unbroken Conservative domination of British politics from 1760 to 1830 had hardened the nation's rulers in their belief that, as the duke of Wellington put it, the British constitution was already more perfect than any human intelligence could contrive to improve.

In fact, reform had already begun during the ascendancy of George Canning, Castlereagh's successor as foreign minister in Lord Liverpool's government. Tariff duties and colonial trade restrictions, some in effect since the seventeenth century, were relaxed, and the Test Act, which had barred Catholics and Dissenters from public life since 1673, was at last repealed (1829). A gesture was even made toward the lower orders; unions were recognized, and the number of offenses punishable by death was cut by 100—which nevertheless left another 100 on the books. But the one issue that had become symbolic of the liberal cause as a whole—parliamentary reform—remained unaddressed.

The reformers' moment came in 1830, when Wellington's government fell and a Whig ministry under Lord Grey came to power. Despite bitter Tory opposition, Grey at last steered a parliamentary reform bill through both houses in 1832, although the Lords acquiesced only when faced with the king's threat to create enough Whig peers to override them. It was just in time; riots had broken out all over the country, a tax strike was being organized, and radicals urged a run on the Bank of England as a means of bringing the propertied classes to their knees.

The Reform Bill was as important for the revolution it averted as for the rather modest alterations it produced. It changed the image but not the reality of power in Britain. Some 143 seats in the House of Commons, about a quarter of the total, were redistributed. Slightly fewer than half of these went to new industrial towns, such as Manchester, which had previously lacked representation of any kind. Some, but by no means all, of the "rotten boroughs"—decayed constituencies that continued to return members to Parliament with a largely phantom electorate—were eliminated. The franchise was extended from slightly under 500,000 to just over 800,000 voters, still little more than 5 percent of the population. The net effect was a token recognition of the industrial bourgeoisie

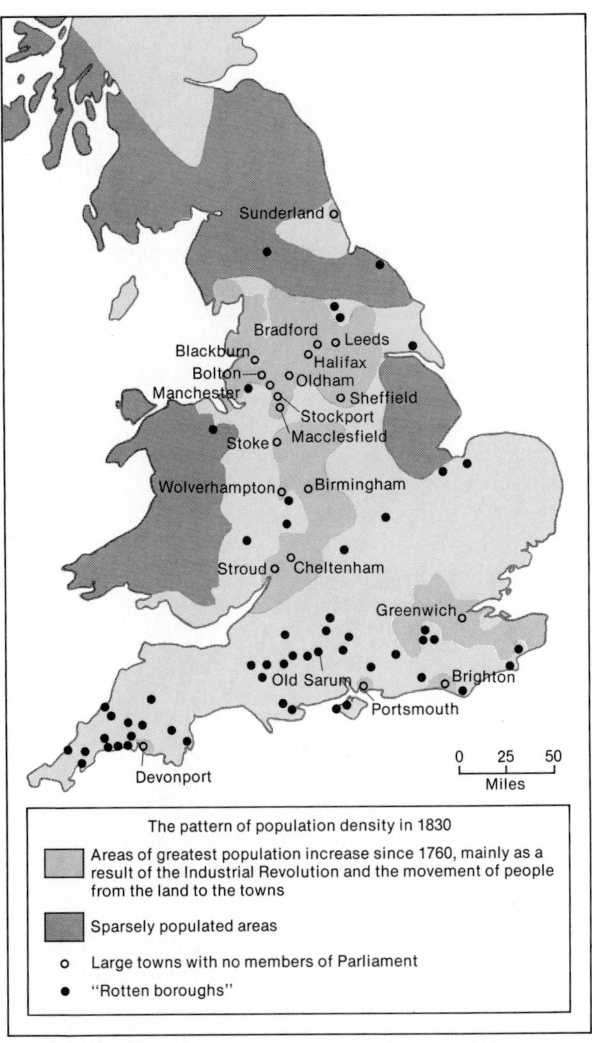

***30.3** Parliamentary Representation in Britain Before 1832*

that kept the balance of electoral power safely in the hands of the gentry and nobility. But while on some issues the interests of the two groups were genuinely divided, it would be a mistake to see them as fundamentally opposed. The new magnates of industrial capitalism, like their eighteenth-century predecessors in commerce and finance, had little need of parliamentary representation to make their weight felt. The propertied classes in town and country had adjusted their mutual relations in a manner that more adequately represented the influence of the former. Both agreed that the reins of government would continue to rest with them to the exclusion of the vast majority. The Reform Bill of 1832, like the regime of Louis-Philippe in France, reflected that broad consensus.

The Socialist Challenge

It would be accurate to say that the working classes had fought the revolutions of 1830 and the bourgeoisie won them. The sans-culottes on the barricades in Paris, the workers who defied the Dutch king in Brussels and Antwerp, and the British laborers who seized Bristol and threatened other towns in their demand for parliamentary representation had all taken an initiative that their betters were quick to convert to their own advantage. Nothing could symbolize the irony of mass politics in the early industrial age more than the spectacle of elderly aristocrats like Lafayette and Lord Grey stage-managing the transference, or at any rate the sharing of power between the traditional nobility and the industrial bourgeoisie at the behest of the workers.

The Demand for Reform

The experience of the 1830s and 1840s taught at least the more advanced elements of the working class that their interests could not be encompassed by those of the bourgeoisie. The mass movement that Robert Owen led briefly from 1833 to 1834 (see Chapter 29) was prompted in part by disillusion with the Reform Bill, and by the end of the 1830s the first sustained workers' movement had emerged in Britain, the Chartists. It began in 1836 when a small shopkeeper, William Lovett, founded the London Workingmen's Association. The association's relatively modest initial demands were presented in the tradition of social deference to one's superiors. Its tone, however, soon grew more radical. In 1838, with the assistance of the veteran reformer Francis Place, it drew up the first People's Charter. This document rejected the piecemeal reform of Parliament, which was all conventional politics could offer. It demanded a secret ballot, equal electoral districts, annually elected Parliaments on the basis of universal manhood suffrage, the removal of property qualifications for office, and payment for all members of Parliament. The effect of this would have been fully to democratize the political system (at least for men) and to enable workers themselves to stand for and occupy seats in Parliament. Here was a genuine break with the politics of deference, with its assumption that the interest of the working class could be represented satisfactorily by its social betters.

In February 1839 a self-styled workers' convention met in London to press for the People's Charter, now attached to a petition that had gained a million signatures. The delegates called themselves "Members of the Convention," both in evident allusion to the French National Convention of 1792 and to Parliament itself. When the House of Commons rejected the charter, a general strike was proposed. Lacking organization and experienced leadership, it petered out in sporadic agitation from which many existing unions held aloof. Unlike Owen's Grand Union however, the Chartist movement did not collapse with its first defeat but remained a powerful force throughout the 1840s.

A similar rethinking of worker interests was going forward in France, where, having consolidated its position, the government of Louis-Philippe set its face against even token reform. In 1839 the journalist Louis Blanc (1811–1882) argued in a widely read book, *The Organization of Labor*, that the state should socialize all major economic services, including banking, transportation, and insurance, and establish "social workshops," or cooperative factories operated by and for workers. Blanc's reformism derived from the Saint-Simonians, followers of the influential Count de Saint-Simon (1760–1825), who had advocated control of public services and enterprises by a technocratic elite of scientists and engineers. What both Saint-Simon and Blanc ignored, however, like more "utopian" socialists such as Owen and Fourier, was the problem of actual political power. The state, whether controlled by aristocrats, by bourgeoisie, or, as in much of western Europe, by an uneasy combination of both, was highly unlikely to cede authority to either workers or engineers.

From Reform to Revolution

Such was the conclusion drawn by revolutionaries such as Louis-Auguste Blanqui (1805–1881) and Pierre Proudhon (1809–1865), who in turn derived from the martyred Gracchus Babeuf (see Chapter 26) and his Italian disciple, Filippo Maria Buonarotti (1760–1837). Proudhon, unwilling to compromise with any scheme of state ownership, declared roundly that all property was a theft of the value created by labor. He envisioned the abolition of the state in favor of a system of decentralized cooperative enterprises that would produce and exchange goods noncompetitively on the basis of social need. For Blanqui, such an arrangement, however desirable in principle, begged the fundamental question of power: how was such a peaceful system to be established against the resistance of the propertied classes and the state machinery they controlled? Blanqui's answer was armed revolution aimed at establishing a "dictatorship of the proletariat," a phrase he coined. Like his mentor Buonarotti, Europe's first professional revolutionary, Blanqui spent most of his life in jail or on the run; Tocqueville, observing him in 1848 at a rare moment of liberty, said that he had the appearance of a man who had passed his life in the sewers. But with Buonarotti and Blanqui, a new kind of person had appeared on the European scene, convinced of the inevitable struggle between the classes and dedicated to revolution at any cost.

All the thinkers and political activists just considered subscribed to a common critique of the capitalist system. They accepted Adam Smith's definition of labor as the source of all productive value and believed (as Smith did not) that the wealth produced by this labor should be owned socially or collectively: hence the name *socialism* applied to their ideas and demands. The socialists' beliefs were clear-cut: private ownership was the appropriation by force of an excess share of the common social wealth (in the pithy formulation associated with Proudhon, "property is theft"), and unregulated capitalism was the equivalent of unrelieved exploitation. But they disagreed about the remedy. Owen, Fourier, and Proudhon put their faith in small, collectively owned enterprises linked voluntarily into cooperative associations; Saint-Simon and Blanc believed that only state power could break up existing concentrations of private capital and ownership; and Blanqui added that only revolution from below could give the proletariat access to that power. What they all lacked was a theory of social action or, more simply, a credible plan for overthrowing the existing order.

Karl Marx

Karl Marx supplied the theoretical basis for socialism. Until Marx, the socialists had produced no thinker who could conceptually challenge the defense of capitalism put forward by Adam Smith and David Ricardo. For both Smith and Ricardo, private enterprise—economic competition for individual profit—maximized the production of wealth and hence the aggregate social good. Ricardo in particular was sensitive to the high social cost of capitalism: the exploitation of child and female labor, the tendency of worker income to remain at subsistence level, and the "business cycle"—the abrupt spasms of boom and bust to which the industrial system had already shown itself to be vulnerable. These costs were regrettable but, Ricardo felt, for the most part unavoidable. This was particularly true for income stagnation, which Ricardo formulated as the "iron law of wages." In times of industrial expansion when the demand for labor exceeded the supply, Ricardo argued, wages would tend to rise above subsistence level; but the result of relative prosperity was a higher birthrate, which produced excess labor capacity, depressed wages, and caused starvation and misery. For this reason, worker demands for higher wages were self-defeating. Marx was the first socialist thinker to challenge this and similar "laws" of economics on their own ground and in his major work, *Capital*, to advance a comprehensive countertheory to demonstrate that capitalism was not merely unstable but inherently self-destructive as well.

Marx was born in Trier in the rapidly industrializing Rhineland. He was descended on both sides from a long line of rabbis, but his father, like many other Jews of the time, had submitted to Christian baptism to gain entry into the legal profession. Marx studied philosophy at Bonn and Berlin, drank and dueled, and wrote bad poetry, a comic novel, a tragic play, and a doctoral dissertation on the

The founder of modern communism, Karl Marx, in a photograph taken in the mid-1870s. [Globe Photos]

difference between the atomic theories of Democritus and Epicurus. He also became part of a circle of young radicals who were attempting to extend Hegelian philosophy in a leftward direction. As a correspondent for the *Rheinische Zeitung*, he exposed the wretched poverty of the winegrowers of the Trier region in an article that helped lead to the suppression of the newspaper. Quitting Germany in disgust, he settled in Paris, where he produced a series of extraordinary and prophetic essays on worker alienation and shed his last attachments to Hegelian idealism. With his friend and lifelong collaborator, Friedrich Engels, he hailed the coming of a new socialist order in *The Communist Manifesto*, but the failed revolutions of 1848 led him into exile instead.

Marx took refuge in London with his large and needy family, living under the watchful eye of the local police and the spies of a dozen nations and on the bounty of Engels, who owned a factory in Manchester. Marx was not embarrassed to live on the profits of capital and himself speculated on the stock market. The task of philosophy, he said, was not to understand the world but to change it, and the man who meant to make that philosophy was not worried about being judged by the rules of the world that would be left behind.

Dismissing his predecessors and rivals, Marx declared his work to be the only "scientific" socialism. It was founded on a grand theory that, arguing humanity's intellectual and social development from its material struggle to wrest the necessities of life from nature, proceeded to describe the stages of history in terms of a social struggle for control of the technical means of production—land, labor, and machinery. Marx described ancient society as founded on slavery, the medieval West on feudalism, and capitalism on wage labor, which he saw as a modern form of slavery. Since, like other socialists, Marx regarded labor as the only source of productive value (capital itself, whether in the form of money, machinery, or tilled lands, was only labor in objectified or symbolic form), all profit extracted from labor by means of the wage system was "surplus" or appropriated value.

Marx praised the bourgeoisie for having greatly expanded the material base of civilization by industrialization and urbanization, even as it simultaneously debased its human content by forcing the great mass of the population to live in conditions of unparalleled exploitation and misery. The contradiction between the prosperity of the few and the poverty of the many would, however, ultimately be too evident to ignore. At the same time, the inherent tendency of capitalist competition to contract and profit margins to shrink would lead to ever shorter and severer contractions of the business cycle and the growth of monopoly, until the conditions for socialist revolution were ripe.

But revolution could be neither prepared nor accomplished without active class struggle. Marx collaborated (and ultimately quarreled with) all the leading social activists of his day, including the Frenchman Proudhon, the Russian anarchist Mikhail Bakunin (1814–1876), and the German trade unionist Ferdinand Lassalle (1825–1864). Yet he continually stressed the cooperative nature of the proletarian struggle across all borders, rejecting nationalism as a bourgeois phenomenon that reflected the divisive, competitive nature of capitalism itself. In 1864 he was instrumental in founding the International Workingman's Association, later known as the First International, to promote the proletarian cause throughout Europe and America. At his death in 1883, he was clearly the foremost figure of European socialism, as both a thinker and an activist.

Marx never managed to put his mature ideas into finished, comprehensive form. Half his manuscripts lay unpublished at his death, many to remain unknown for decades; even his masterpiece, *Capital*, the first part of which was published in 1867, was only a torso. In part this reflected his own refusal to settle into any mold, even his own; as he once wittily remarked, "I am not a Marxist." Yet, though always controversial and frequently misinterpreted, his thought has been more decisive than anyone else's in the shaping of the modern world, and in the universality of his influence he may be regarded as the first nonreligious thinker of world significance. Certainly he takes his place as one of the most important figures in the Western tradition. Before Marx no theory of societal development had advanced much beyond Plato and Aristotle 2,000 years before. There was no theory of historical change that dealt adequately with the concrete problems of subsistence, organization, or technological innovation. There was no theory of the Enlightenment that portrayed humanity as anything more than orphans of reason or suggested the possibility of a truly just society. As with all revolutionary thinkers, time continues to winnow away what was local and circumstantial in his thought from what remains of continuing significance and value. The Russian émigré Annenkov described Marx as unkempt, domineering, and very nearly offensive in manner; but, he added, "he looked like a man with the right and power to demand respect, no matter how he appeared before you and no matter what he did," a man with "the firm conviction of his mission to dominate men's minds and prescribe them their laws." More than a century later, the world still responds to that force.

The Revolutions of 1848

When late in the year 1847 the young Marx warned of the imminence of revolution in *The Communist Manifesto*, he may have been the only person in Europe to expect it. Yet within the first four months of 1848 the Continent was rocked by almost 50 separate revolutions in France, Prussia, Austria, and almost all the lesser German and Italian states. Surveying the wreckage of monarchies, Tsar Nicholas I wrote to Queen Victoria that Russia and Britain seemed to be the last two states standing in Europe. The exaggeration in that statement was slight.

The Causes of the Revolutions

Some general causes of the revolutions can be discerned, although they differed with the circumstances of each state or region. The Industrial Revolution, which had begun in earnest on the Continent after 1830, had shaken social and demographic patterns and profoundly altered political ones. Unfulfilled nationalist aspirations were a primary impetus in Germany, Italy, and eastern Europe. These tensions and grievances were also exacerbated, as before 1789 and 1830, by hard times. Harvests were poor in the three years preceding 1848; the Prussian peasantry, lacking bread, survived on potatoes, while in Ireland, the failure in 1845 of the potato crop—the last resort of the poor—led to mass starvation and emigration, which between them reduced the population of the country from 8.5 million to 6.5 million in five years. Urban workers were also squeezed by the rising price of food, and the agricultural crisis soon produced industrial depression as well. The integration of agricultural and industrial markets through capitalist development meant that any disturbance in one sector of the system had immediate repercussions in the rest of it, while the new concentration of population in towns and cities provided natural foci of discontent.

The single most pervasive element in the revolutions of 1848, however, was a general questioning of the existing political order. The monarchs of the Old Regime had based their authority on appeals to divine right and a traditional social order, but divinity no longer shielded a ruler who could be forced off his throne by a three-day riot as Charles X had been in 1830 or set up like Louis-Philippe by a backstairs cabal consisting of a diplomat, a journalist, and a banker. Nor could such a ruler appeal to traditional values or deference in a society where the most basic relations of property, production, and authority were being transformed and a new financial, commercial, and industrial elite was busily accumulating power. Still less could rulers legitimate themselves where, as in most of Italy, they served not a native but a foreign interest.

The new bourgeois or quasi-bourgeois regimes established by the events of 1830–1832, though based explicitly or implicitly on popular sovereignty and constitutional guarantees, had proved singularly unwilling to embrace the vast majority of the people in the political process. In no European nation with a representative system did the electorate exceed 5 percent of the population. The Chartists pursued their demand for universal manhood suffrage in Britain with petitioning campaigns of 3 million signatures in 1842 and five million in 1848, only to meet with continuing rejection in Parliament, while in France, with only 300,000 electors in a population of 30 million, the government of François Guizot set itself resolutely against even a token extension of the franchise. After two revolutions and 60 years, the French Assembly was a less representative body than the Estates General of Louis XVI had been.

The Collapse of the Old Order

The revolutions began with a stirring in Italy, where on January 12 the people of Sicily rose against Ferdinand II. By the end of the month Milan and Venice had proclaimed their ancient independence as republics and called on King Charles Albert of Piedmont and Pope Pius IX to help unify the entire peninsula. The French were not far behind. Liberal reformers, blocked from public demonstrations, had adopted the British tactic of holding banquets that were in effect mass political rallies on behalf of a modest extension of the franchise. When the authorities sought to ban one such banquet in Paris in late February, the events of 1830 swiftly repeated themselves. Riots broke out, barricades went up, and the National Guard, called out to quell the disturbances, joined in instead. Louis-Philippe dismissed the unpopular Guizot in a bid to regain middle-class support. But the Parisian workers were not to be duped a second time. Breaking into the Chamber of Deputies, they forced the proclamation of a republic, and Louis-Philippe fled into exile in London.

The news from Paris galvanized dissidents in Germany and Austria. In Berlin the irresolute Frederick William IV (1840–1861) found himself a virtual prisoner of nationalists who demanded that Prussia take the lead in unifying Germany under a liberal constitution. Student rebels and workers joined in Vienna to extract a promise of reform from the emperor, Ferdinand I, and the aged Metternich fled the city in disguise to join Louis-Philippe in exile. More serious were nationalist uprisings by the Bohemians in Prague and the Hungarians in Budapest. The latter, under the leadership of the fiery journalist and orator Louis Kossuth (1802–1894), demanded virtual independence from Austria, with a separate army, government, and system of finance. In addition, the Hungarian Diet, composed exclusively of noblemen and long one of the most reactionary assemblies in Europe, voted for constitutional government, the abolition of serfdom, and the imposition of taxes on the nobility. By the end of March the Austrian empire was prostrate, while in Germany a group of liberals, meeting spontaneously in Heidelberg, called for the election of an all-German parliament on the basis of universal manhood suffrage and under the supervision of an electoral body, the *Vorparliament*, summoned directly by them. So great was the enthusiasm for unity throughout the country, and so paralyzed were the existing governments, that the election was duly carried out, and on May 18 the 830

***30.4** Europe's Revolutions of 1848*

delegates of the new parliament convened in Frankfurt to make Germany a nation.

The single most evident fact about this whirlwind of revolutions was the weakness and prostration of the established governments. As Charles X had fallen at what seemed the merest touch in 1830, not only had his successor been toppled, but what seemed the most rock-solid thrones in Europe, Prussia and Austria, had shaken in their foundations before relative handfuls of protesters who made up their demands as they went along. Nothing could have more conclusively demonstrated the ideological bankruptcy of these regimes and their helplessness in the face of even the most disorganized challenge. At the same time, however, the revolutionaries, united for the moment in the flush of success, were soon as divided from one another as they had been from the kings who served as the common target of their discontent.

Counterrevolution in Central Europe

Among the first of the revolutions to unravel occurred within the Austrian empire. In Italy, Charles Albert had no sooner assumed leadership of the anti-Habsburg coalition when it began to collapse; a counterrevolution restored Ferdinand II in Sicily, while the Venetians made it clear that they had no intention of abandoning their republic to merge with the House of Savoy. In July, Austria badly defeated Charles Albert's forces at the battle of Custozza, and a last attempt to resuscitate the cause ended in disaster at Novara in March 1849. The Italian conflagration was not quite over; in November 1848 Pius IX fled Rome after the assassination of his chief minister, and a republic was proclaimed in February headed by Giuseppe Mazzini (1805–1872), whose impassioned vision of a united, democratic Italy had made him a hero to a generation of young nationalists. Mazzini's government immediately announced the confiscation of church lands and their redistribution to the peasantry, as well as a program of public housing for the urban poor. Although it controlled only the city of Rome and its immediate environs, the republic declared itself the nucleus of a united Italy. But it fell to a French army in July despite stubborn resistance, and with the fall of Venice a month later, the collapse of the revolutionary cause was complete.

In Hungary the Magyar majority under Kossuth rapidly alienated the various minorities under its control by proclaiming what amounted to racial hegemony: it abolished local assemblies in non-Magyar provinces and prescribed that Hungarian be the exclusive language of all higher education as well as of the Diet. This stimulated Slavic nationalism, which culminated in a pan-Slav congress that convened in Prague in June, only to be suppressed by troops under General Alfred Windischgratz still loyal to the Habsburgs. This victory emboldened the court party to attempt the liberation of Vienna. In October, Windischgratz occupied the city after a bombardment and executed or exiled its radical leaders on the spot. Two months later the feebleminded Ferdinand I was induced to step down in favor of his 18-year-old nephew, Franz Joseph I (1848–1916), who, unhampered by his predecessor's promises to the liberals, completed the process of restoration the following summer by crushing the Hungarian revolt with the aid of 140,000 Russian troops.

In Germany, meanwhile, the Frankfurt Assembly set to its task of providing the country with a national government and a constitution. The fundamental anomaly of its position, however, was soon apparent. Almost all the delegates were university-educated members of the upper bourgeoisie: lawyers, doctors, scholars, ministers, bankers, merchants, and manufacturers. Their vision was of a world made safe for bourgeois opportunity: free trade, untrammeled growth, an end to the political monopoly of the aristocracy, and a liberal regime presiding benignly over a swelling gross national product. But the masses, whose rebellion had cleared the ground for them, wanted none of these things. They were peasants clamoring for land, artisans demanding protection for their trades, and workers who wanted higher wages and industrial regulation. Free enterprise only meant new chains to them, and free speech was less important than bread they could afford to eat.

While the Frankfurt delegates attempted to thrash out their own manifold differences—whether the new Germany should be a federation or a unitary state, a monarchy, an empire, or a republic, and above all whether it should seek to incorporate German-speaking areas of Austria, Denmark, and Poland within its borders—the existing governments of the German Confederation, supposedly waiting for final extinction but still in control of their armies, slowly recovered their authority. By the time the Assembly had drafted its constitution, which included provisions for freedom of speech, assembly, and the press, religious toleration, and public education, both Prussia and Austria had become strong enough to reject it out of hand. When Frederick William IV, no doubt with memories of being forced to ride through the streets of Berlin with a revolutionary tricolor in his hat the previous spring, was approached in April 1849 to become "emperor of the Germans," he replied loftily that he would not pick up a crown from the gutter. At that the Frankfurt Assembly began to collapse. The more moderate delegations, unwilling to contemplate a republic, went home, and the radical remnant was dispersed by force in June. The revolution in Germany was over.

The June Days

The French liberal Alexis de Tocqueville describes the June Days of 1848.

I come at last to the insurrection of June, the most extensive and the most singular that has occurred in our history, and perhaps in any other: the most extensive, because, during four days, more than a hundred thousand men were engaged in it; the most singular, because the insurgents fought without a war-cry, without leaders, without flags, and yet with a marvellous harmony and an amount of military experience that astonished the oldest officers.

What distinguished it also, among all the events of this kind which have succeeded one another in France for sixty years, is that it did not aim at changing the form of government, but at altering the order of society. It was not, strictly speaking, a political struggle, in the sense which until then we had given to the word, but a combat of class against class. . . .

It must also be observed that this formidable insurrection was not the enterprise of a certain number of conspirators, but the revolt of one whole section of the population against another. Women took part in it as well as men. While the latter fought, the former prepared and carried ammunition; and when at last the time had come to surrender, the women were the last to yield.

Source: A. T. De Mattos, trans., *The Recollections of Alexis de Tocqueville* (New York: Columbia University Press, 1949), pp. 150–151.

France: From Revolution to Empire

In France the course of events was quite different. Here alone (apart from Mazzini's short-lived Roman republic), the monarch of an independent state had actually been deposed and a new provisional government established. A hasty compromise among revolutionary factions, it consisted of seven moderate and three radical (socialist) republicans. Among the latter was Louis Blanc, who urged immediate relief for the unemployed through a Ministry of Progress that would establish his workshop system. Behind Blanc was the specter of Blanqui, white-haired and black-clad, "the most complete revolutionary of his time,"[1] who showed his power by mounting a demonstration of 100,000 workers in Paris in March 1848. When Blanc failed to win them the concessions they demanded, one of the marchers denounced him as a traitor. The revolution had already been split.

Most of the wealthier bourgeoisie and nobility had already fled Paris, and the United States was the only foreign power to recognize the French republic. The moderates in the government placed their hopes in speedy elections, which they expected to produce a conservative majority that would isolate the radicals. A Constituent Assembly, elected by universal manhood suffrage in April, convened on May 4 and immediately replaced the provisional government with a five-man executive of its own that contained no socialists. On June 22, following an abortive coup led by Blanqui, the government announced the dissolution of the workshop program, which had been set up as a sop to Blanc but had provided only ill-paid road work for the 200,000 unemployed of Paris. The reaction was immediate. The workers took up arms, the government proclaimed martial law, and the class war heralded only six months before by Marx in *The Communist Manifesto* became bloody reality in the streets of Paris. Ten thousand people were killed or wounded in a three-day struggle without quarter (June 24–26) until troops under General Louis Cavaignac regained control of the city. Capping victory with vengeance, the Assembly decreed that the 15,000 prisoners taken be deported. An army of 50,000 occupied the French capital until October.

The so-called June Days sent a shudder of terror throughout bourgeois Europe; one woman likened the strife in Paris to the siege of Rome by the barbarians. The feeling was reciprocated, and not by French workers alone. "Every proletarian," wrote the editor of *Red Revolution* in London, "who does not see and feel that he belongs to an enslaved and degraded class is a *fool.*" The ideological breach between the classes was complete, and that division remains the formal posture of western European politics to this day.

Looking back on the revolutions of 1848, Karl Marx observed wryly that history repeats itself: the first time as tragedy, the second as farce. There was more than a touch of farce about many of them, but there was much tragedy too, and in the June Days of Paris, an ominous portent of the future. But perhaps the dominant emotion was frustration. For a glorious moment, liberals had dreamed of constitutions, nationalists of unification, and radicals of a classless society in which the workers of every land could embrace as comrades. These dreams were not as yet to be.

The European elite of the mid-nineteenth century—an amalgam of the upper bourgeoisie and the traditional landed aristocracy—was still powerful enough to maintain itself, while its opponents were too diffuse in their aims, too divided among themselves, and too little rooted in the political and social realities of the mass of the population they claimed to represent. Yet the demands they made—political equality, national consolidation, and social justice—reflected deeply felt ideological contradictions within European society. Inherited privilege, the basis of political dominance in Europe for centuries, was no longer self-justifying, while acquired privilege—the accumulation of wealth and capital by the bourgeoisie—was equally suspect as a mandate to rule. If the revolutionaries of 1848 had failed to topple the existing order, they had exposed the essential hollowness and vulnerability of any authority not based on popular consent.

Notes

1. P. Robertson, *Revolutions of 1848* (New York: Harper & Row, 1960), p. 61.

Suggestions for Further Reading

Abrams, M. H. *The Mirror and the Lamp: Romantic Theory and the Critical Tradition.* New York: Oxford University Press, 1953.

Artz, F. B. *Reaction and Revolution 1814–1832.* New York: Harper & Row, 1963.

Chevalier, L. *Laboring Classes and Dangerous Classes in Paris During the First Half of the Nineteenth Century.* New York: Fertig, 1973.

Clark, K. *The Romantic Rebellion.* New York: Harper & Row, 1973.

Dakin, D. *The Greek Struggle for Independence.* Berkeley: University of California Press, 1973.

De Ruggiero, G. *The History of European Liberalism,* trans. R. G. Collingswood. Boston: Beacon Press, 1959.

Droz, J. *Europe Between Revolutions, 1815–1848.* New York: Harper & Row, 1967.

Friedenthal, R. *Goethe. His Life and Times.* Cleveland: World Publishing Co., 1965.

Hammond, J. L., and Hammond, B. *The Age of Chartism.* Hamden, Conn.: Archon Books, 1962.

Hobsbawm, E. J. *The Age of Revolution: Europe, 1789 to 1848.* New York: New American Library, 1962.

Kohn, H. *The Idea of Nationalism.* New York: Collier Books, 1967.

Krieger, L. *The German Idea of Freedom.* Boston: Beacon Press, 1957.

Lichtheim, G. *A Short History of Socialism.* New York: Praeger, 1970.

McLellan, D. *Karl Marx: His Life and Thought.* New York: Harper & Row, 1973.

Manuel, F. E. *The Prophets of Paris.* Cambridge, Mass: Harvard University Press, 1962.

Nicolson, H. *The Congress of Vienna.* London: Constable, 1946.

Pinkney, D. H. *The French Revolution of 1830.* Princeton, N.J.: Princeton University Press, 1972.

Pointon, M. "Liberty on the Barricades: Women, Politics and Sexuality in Delacroix," in S. Reynolds, ed., *Women, State and Revolution.* Brighton: Wheatsheaf, 1986.

Robertson, P. *Revolutions of 1848.* New York: Harper & Row, 1960.

Stearns, P. N. *1848: The Revolutionary Tide in Europe.* New York: Norton, 1974.

Taylor, A. J. P. *The Habsburg Monarchy, 1809–1918.* New York: Harper & Row, 1965.

CHAPTER · 31

The Triumph of Nationalism in the West

The failure of the 1848 upheavals represented at once a crushing blow to the ideals of romantic revolution and the last desperate stand of the conservative order established by the Congress of Vienna. In the decades that followed, the forces of order gave way to those of change as a powerful, rapidly spreading nationalism triumphed in Europe.

As the dominant theme of European history over the next half century, nationalism had a powerful appeal to a broad cross section of society, from workers to industrialists and from merchants to aristocrats. Many factors explain the success of nationalism in the post-1848 period. Unlike the abortive nationalist movements of the 1820s and 1830s, it now combined the Romantic celebration of the past and its tortured search for self-identity with a new realism based on the understanding and use of power. Moreover, artists, writers, and musicians explored nationalistic themes in their work, while both higher literacy rates and more skillful propaganda made ever-larger numbers of the middle and lower classes sensitive to nationalist

Princess Victoria of Hohenzollern, the wife of Emperor Frederick William IV of Germany, was at the center of liberal opposition to Bismarck's domestic policies. [Mansell Collection]

symbolism. Most important, in regions where nationalistic aspirations were frustrated by foreign domination, a new generation of practical, tough-minded leaders came into power. Raised during the turbulent days of the Napoleonic empire, these men admired the methods of modern warfare and diplomacy, appreciated the benefits of efficient government, and understood the principles of liberal economics and industrial development. Cavour in Italy and Bismarck in Germany were the two most outstanding examples of this marriage between nationalism and power politics. In an age increasingly under the influence of science and technology, Bismarck and Cavour successfully translated the ideals of an earlier generation into the concrete action of the new.

Although all-pervasive, nationalism reflected local conditions. In Italy and Germany it assumed the form of nation building. Where centralized states already existed, as in Britain, nationalism merged with liberalism to forge a new ruling elite dedicated to industrial and commercial expansion through overseas empire or, as in the case of France, to economic development under a restored empire. In the Austrian, Russian, and Ottoman empires, despotic but ineffectual monarchies struggled to control ethnically diverse populations clamoring for independence or self-determination, while the young republic of the United States struggled to restore unity after a destructive civil war. Finally, the international Zionist movement added a new element to nationalism as it sought to give expression to the centuries-old quest for a Jewish homeland.

The emergence of nationalism in the second half of the nineteenth century is a development of immense importance. As a worldwide phenomenon, its long-range repercussions would be felt in the national antagonisms that twice in the twentieth century erupted into global war, in the twisted ideas that fed the ideologies of fascism between the wars, and in the national rivalries over which the United States and the Soviet Union have fought a dangerous ideological war. Ironically, nationalism also inspired the revolt of former colonies against Western rule, which was itself partly a consequence of nationalism.

The Politics of National Grandeur: Napoleon III in France

Nowhere after 1848 was the beguiling appeal of nationalism stronger than in France. In December 1848, partly as a result of the gruesome violence of the June insurrection, French males overwhelmingly chose as the president of their new Second Republic Louis-Napoleon Bonaparte, the enigmatic nephew of Napoleon I. Much to everyone's amazement, General Louis-Eugène Cavaignac, the conservative republican hero who had crushed the June riots, received only 1.5 million votes, the socialist Alexandre Ledru-Rollin and the poet Alphonse de Lamartine even less, whereas the virtually unknown Louis-Napoleon won the trust of more than 5.5 million Frenchmen.

Louis-Napoleon (1808–1873) had almost no political experience, but the magic of his name was irresistible. For years he had lived abroad, a dreamy youth caught up in the euphoria of revolutionary romanticism. Implicated in the 1831 revolt in the Papal States and in two ludicrous plots to overthrow Louis-Philippe, he spent time in exile and then in prison until his escape to England in 1846. French and English reactionaries funded his return to Paris in the midst of the 1848 revolution, whereupon he campaigned for the presidency by invoking the theme of national unity.

Louis-Napoleon's platform, designed to appeal to a strife-torn society, argued that the country needed an authoritarian leader. Like many modern politicians, however, Louis-Napoleon was duplicitous. While appealing to Catholics and other proponents of authority, he also cultivated the support of the working classes.

He proposed to eliminate a corrupt Parliament and political parties to open the way to a direct relationship between the citizens and himself through plebiscites based on universal male suffrage. Unlike the role of the aristocratic Old Regime or the upper-middle-class government of Louis-Philippe, the proper role—indeed, the duty—of government was, in Louis-Napoleon's mind, to wipe out poverty and provide prosperity for all citizens.

These views, first expressed in two pamphlets he wrote while in prison, *On Napoleonic Ideas* and *The Extinction of Poverty*, formed the core of Louis-Napoleon's political thought. But his popularity was derived in large measure from the memory of national greatness attached to Napoleon I. Despite a stocky build and an exaggerated mustache and goatee, Louis-Napoleon had a charismatic appeal that transcended class and social status. He also realized that public opinion could be a powerful instrument of authority. He knew almost by instinct what later, twentieth-century dictators would discover, that an authoritarian state based on nationalist pride and popular consensus and promising both social tranquillity and economic prosperity had a strong appeal in times of stress.

The Second Republic lasted three years. Although its constitution provided for a strong president, the chief executive could serve for only one term. Louis-Napoleon therefore played to the conservatives who dominated the National Assembly by enacting measures in favor of the Catholic church, reducing the suffrage, and restricting freedom of education and the press. When the legislature refused to amend the constitution to permit him a second term, Louis-Napoleon seized power. On December 2, 1851, he illegally dissolved the Assembly and proclaimed a temporary dictatorship in the name of the people. With the support of the army, he arrested his opponents and crushed an uprising of the workers. In a plebiscite held that same month, 92 percent of the voters gave him the power to draft a new constitution that made him president for ten years. A second plebiscite a year later confirmed by an even greater margin the hold of the Napoleonic legend on the national psyche: Louis-Napoleon was proclaimed Napoleon III, emperor of the French.*

The Second Empire

The structure of imperial government, inspired by the constitution of Napoleon I, was designed to give the impression of a regime responsive to the popular will. An appointed senate was balanced by an assembly chosen every six years by carefully manipulated elections based on universal male suffrage. Parliament could, however, only discuss items submitted by the emperor and had to debate behind closed doors. Napoleon personally controlled the army and the budget and conducted foreign affairs, advised by a handpicked Council of State.

Napoleon's domestic policies, resting on vigorous government intervention in the economy, produced unparalleled prosperity. The emperor deliberately strengthened the middle class by encouraging investment and the modernization of industry. The state-owned railroad increased its mileage fivefold during the first decade of imperial rule, thus stimulating industrial development and commerce. A law passed in 1865 introduced the concept of limited liability to protect corporate stockholders from excessive risk. Investment capital was raised through the *Crédit Mobilier*, a banking institution that sold shares to the public. A free trade agreement with Britain in 1860 resulted in an increase in French exports and eventually a favorable balance of trade. In an effort to advance commerce with the East, French capital financed—and a French engineer, Ferdinand de Lesseps, constructed—the Suez Canal in the decade between 1859 and 1869. These measures bound

*Napoleon II, son of Napoleon I, died in 1832 without having served as emperor.

The Napoleonic Myth

In 1839, while living in exile in Great Britain, Louis-Napoleon wrote a pamphlet titled On Napoleonic Ideas. *Praising the reign of his uncle as having been founded on the will of the people, Louis-Napoleon contributed to the popularization of the Napoleonic myth on which he was to base his own rise to power.*

The Emperor Napoleon has contributed more than any other person to hasten the reign of liberty, by preserving the moral influence of the revolution, and diminishing the fears which it inspired. . . .

The government of Napoleon, better than any other, could have sustained liberty, for the simple reason that liberty would have strengthened his throne, though it overthrows such thrones as have not a solid foundation.

Liberty would have fortified his power, because Napoleon had established in France all that ought to precede liberty; because his power reposed upon the whole mass of the nation; because his interests were the same as those of the people; because, finally, the most perfect confidence reigned between the ruler and the governed. . . .

There is no longer any necessity to reconstruct the system of the emperor; it will reconstruct itself. Sovereigns and nations will concur in re-establishing it; because each one will see in it a guaranty of order, of peace, and of prosperity. . . .

In conclusion, let us repeat it, the Napoleonic idea is not one of war, but a social, industrial, commercial idea, and one which concerns all mankind. If to some it appears always surrounded by the thunder of combats, that is because it was in fact for too long a time veiled by the smoke of cannon and the dust of battles. But now the clouds are dispersed, and we can see, beyond the glory of arms, a civil glory greater and more enduring.

Source: L. N. Bonaparte, *Napoleonic Ideas*, trans. J. Dorr (New York: Appleton, 1859).

Napoleon III and the Empress Eugenie with their son. Napoleon III dreamed of imperial grandeur, but this photograph shows the Bonapartes as a proper bourgeois family. [Culver Pictures]

the middle class to the government, for industrial production had doubled and the vitality of the economy seemed to confirm the wisdom of the French people in putting another Bonaparte on the throne.

Working-class support for Napoleon III was almost as strong as middle-class enthusiasm, for wages kept pace with inflation and the emperor sponsored government health programs, low-cost housing, and numerous public works projects. Despite the fears of many businessmen, in the 1860s he even permitted the formation of trade unions and legalized the right to strike.

The vigorous economic life of the Second Empire was accompanied by a deliberate effort to drape the public image of France in a grand, if at times gaudy, style. The results were most stunning in the imperial capital, where Napoleon appointed Baron Georges Haussmann to direct a massive rebuilding program. Narrow but picturesque medieval streets and unattractive neighborhoods were demolished to make way for 85 miles of broad boulevards and tree-shaded pavements. Along with large squares and stately new buildings, Haussmann also built sewers to provide drainage. Although costly and controversial, these projects not only created jobs but also gave the emperor better security because the wider avenues made it difficult to erect barricades against government troops, as the Parisians had done so often in the past. This experiment in urban renewal transformed Paris into a well-ordered and elegant city. It also created a vast stage on which Napoleon and his consort, the empress Eugénie, performed lavish public ceremonies befitting the renewed splendor of France.

Born Eugénia de Montijo (1826–1920), Eugénie was the beautiful, ambitious daughter of a Spanish father and a Franco-American mother. When she met the French president in 1850, she judged him a man of greatness and offered to finance his *coup d'état* the next year. They were married in January 1853, after Napoleon became emperor, in a sumptuous ceremony in Notre Dame Cathedral. Together they presided with great elegance over the Second Empire. Just as Napoleon dreamed of the reemergence of his nation as a great power, so Paris was to become once again the arbiter of Europe in matters of taste and culture. After the drab years of Louis-Philippe's bourgeois monarchy, the new imperial court gave at least the appearance of grandeur.

Despite the considerable domestic achievements of the Second Empire, the economic conditions of the working class were depressed and Napoleon III did nothing to improve the condition of French women. Although his uncle's civil code had declared the equality of all French citizens, women were not included in the definition of citizenship, with the result that the power of men over them was actually strengthened. For example, after marriage, women could not control their own property, engage in a business or profession, or administer children's financial affairs without the consent of their husbands. Divorce laws favored men, and adultery had significantly more serious consequences for wives than for husbands. The law codes thus reinforced women's legal inequality and subordination.

Uniting with the utopian socialists in the 1830s and with the republican socialists in 1848 and 1849, the French feminist movement had been one of the most vigorous and advanced in Europe, pushing hard for women's rights and social reform in general. But the censorship and restrictive domestic policies of the Second Empire repressed the feminists along with other opponents of Napoleon III's rule. Feminist views were therefore restricted largely to the liberal salons of Paris and the underground press, where women writers—notably Juliette Lamber and Jenny Héricourt—fought against conservative patriarchy and the equally antifeminist views of former socialist and republi-

Renovation of a Paris neighborhood, as ordered by Baron Haussmann. [**Granger Collection**]

can allies such as Pierre-Joseph Proudhon and the historian Jules Michelet. Lamber and Héricourt argued for women's rights in education, the professions, and government and exposed the contradictions implicit in the prevalent attitudes toward marriage, divorce, and the double sexual standard. They and women like them kept social debate alive until the repressive phase of the empire came to an end in the 1860s.

The Liberalization of the Empire

Napoleon III protested that he was a man of peace, but foreign entanglements often threatened to disrupt the stability of the Second Empire. Almost unavoidably, the invocation of the Napoleonic legend raised the specter of war, although Napoleon III had neither the military genius nor the diplomatic astuteness of his uncle. French participation in the Crimean War had been popular, and colonial forays in Africa and Indochina had limited success. But his intervention in Italian affairs backfired when it resulted in the loss of papal territory. More damaging was the disastrous attempt in the 1860s to impose French control over Mexico; even worse was Napoleon's failure to obtain territorial gains from the unification of Germany. The cumulative effect of these mistakes gave rise to domestic criticism, and Napoleon's sensitivity to public opinion led him to make reforms intended to soothe the discontent.

This process of liberalizing the empire, against which Eugénie counseled her husband, began by granting the Assembly increased powers and permitting his political enemies—especially liberals, republicans, and legitimist monarchists—to criticize the government openly. He next lifted the restrictions on parliamentary debate and freedom of the press, a move that encouraged the opposition. The lifting of censorship also led to the emergence of a reinvigorated feminist movement. Women such as Maria Deraismes debated the issue of inequality before large audiences, published feminist newspapers, and established the Association for the Rights of Women. Although Deraismes and her friends were few in number and it would be many decades before their movement scored significant victories, they contributed much to the quality of French political life in the last years of the Second Empire. By 1869, when national elections were held, it became clear that the emperor had lost control of the political situation—almost half of the voters supported opposition candidates and elected 30 republicans to the assembly. Early in 1870 Napoleon institutionalized these changes in a new constitution that for all practical purposes created a parliamentary government with the emperor serving as head of state. In May the last of Napoleon's plebiscites showed 7.5 million citizens in favor of the new regime but only 1.5 million against.

Whether these sweeping changes reflected Napoleon III's desire to bring France closer to democracy is uncertain, but his days as emperor were numbered. In the summer, drained and in ill health, he went to war against Prussia, and before it was over the Second Empire had collapsed in defeat and the French people had once again turned to a republic.

Material progress made the first decade of Louis-Napoleon's reign among the best years economically in the history of modern France, at least for the bourgeoisie, yet the price of prosperity was the suppression of political freedom. The second half of his rule saw the gradual restoration of liberty accompanied by imperialism and war. Once admired as one of the great rulers of the mid-nineteenth century, he died a broken man, scorned by European opinion and repudiated by the French people. He was the victim of the very Napoleonic legend that he represented.

Power Politics and the Unification of Italy

If nationalist pride had made and then destroyed an emperor in France, its impact was even more dramatic in central and southern Europe. There, by 1871, two new nation-states, Italy and Germany, appeared. Italy, in Metternich's famous phrase, had been merely a "geographical expression." The Italian peninsula comprised a dozen or so independent states; Germany was, at the same time, little more than a name used to describe the region between France and Austria that consisted of some 38 separate kingdoms, principalities, and duchies. Both had had glorious pasts, Italy as the center of the ancient Roman empire and the land of the Renaissance humanists, Germany as the core of the medieval Holy Roman Empire and the site of Luther's Protestant Reformation. But circumstances and history combined to keep each divided and subject to foreign intervention and manipulation.

Nationalism in Italy and Germany was aroused by the French invasions and the wars of Napoleon I. Bonaparte had reduced and rearranged the states in each region and thereby suggested the possibilities of national unification to Italians and Germans, but their nationalism was in part a reaction against foreign occupation. After Waterloo, the Congress of Vienna restored almost all the original rulers of these states to their thrones and replaced French occupation with Austrian influence. In the 1820s and 1830s

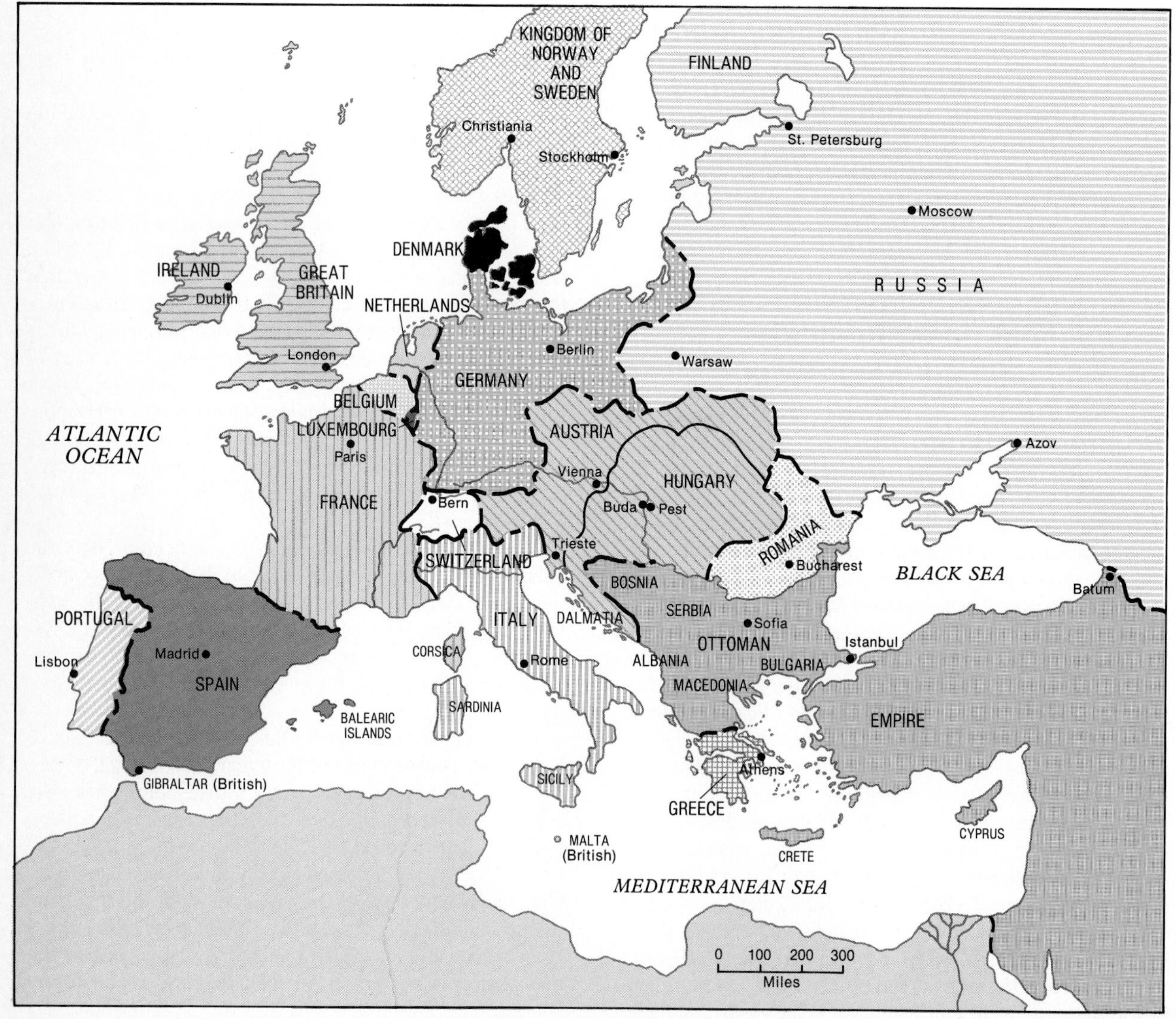

31.1 Europe in 1871

revolutionary Romanticism failed to bring down the status quo so anxiously guarded by Metternich, although national feeling continued to mature during the next decade. As we have seen, the 1848 revolutions gave rise to the first serious attempts to achieve unification in Italy and Germany, but again Austrian military intervention crushed nationalist hopes.

Out of the defeats of 1849 came one positive result: Piedmont-Sardinia emerged as the only viable Italian state to champion national independence, while Prussian leadership became the focus of the unification effort in Germany. In the 1850s Cavour as prime minister of Piedmont and in the 1860s Bismarck as chancellor of Prussia gave their national movements strong leadership that easily matched Napoleon III in cunning and ambition and, by substituting the principles of power politics for Romantic idealism, achieved unification at last.

Nation building in Italy and Germany demonstrated that midcentury nationalism had secured the consensus of large portions of the middle classes and eventually the nobility. By 1871, when the process was complete, the entrance of Italy and Germany into the European state system profoundly altered the balance of power on the Continent.

The Italian Risorgimento

Strong local traditions and competition characterized the politics of the Italian peninsula since the appearance of city-states in the Middle Ages. Despite some changes wrought at Vienna in 1815, the congress restored the overall structure of the Italian state system. In the south the Kingdom of the Two Sicilies (including Naples and Sicily) was ruled by a branch of the Bourbon dynasty related through marriage to the Austrian Habsburgs. In central Italy the Papal States remained the temporal possession of the Catholic church and were ruled from Rome by the popes. The north-central region consisted of a patchwork of small states dominated from Florence by the Grand Duchy of Tuscany, where dynastic and political arrangements also gave the Habsburgs considerable influence. In northeastern Italy the Vienna settlement gave the Habsburgs direct control over the provinces of Lombardy and Venetia, which were ruled from Milan by an Austrian viceroy. Finally, in the strategically important northwest corner lay the Kingdom of Sardinia, consisting of the Piedmont and Savoy regions and the island of Sardinia, ruled by the House of Savoy. This ambitious dynasty had pursued a long-standing policy of expansion in Italy, and in the first half of the century Charles Albert had made two dramatic but unsuccessful bids to oust Austria from the peninsula.

Italian nationalists debated a variety of programs that shared the common goal of an Italian "resurgence," or *Risorgimento*, as the movement for independence and unity was known. Giuseppe Mazzini (1805–1872), one of the great European theorists of nationalism, preached a revolution aimed at creating a united Italian republic based on popular sovereignty and universal suffrage. Mazzini's idealistic propaganda, which educated a generation of Italians to the cause of freedom, posed a radical democratic alternative to the more conservative programs of his contemporaries. The Neo-Guelph* movement, founded by the Piedmontese priest Vincenzo Gioberti, advocated a federation of Italian states led by the papacy and protected by the king of Sardinia. The election of Pope Pius IX in 1846 gave brief impetus to Gioberti's plan, but ultimately his effort to reconcile Italian unification with the temporal interests of the church proved unrealistic. The third alternative, known as the moderate program, was the work of a group of liberal Piedmontese noblemen. Opposed to the revolutionary tactics and democratic principles of Mazzini, the moderates championed a unification imposed from above by Piedmontese armies and a constitutional monarchy under the House of Savoy. The Risorgimento was the climax of Italian nationalism, but from another perspective it was also an ideological civil war fought between radicals and moderates deeply divided over the form and purposes of the unified state that all desired.

*In the Middle Ages the Guelphs were supporters of the papacy against the ambitions of the Holy Roman Emperor.

Cavour the Realist

Charles Albert's valiant war against Austria in 1848 and 1849 had given credibility to the moderate program. De-

Count Cavour, whose shrewd policies ultimately unified Italy, is depicted here in a photograph taken at the Congress of Paris in 1856. [Mansell Collection]

spite his abdication in 1849, the hapless monarch had left his kingdom a constitution that became the symbol of Italian liberal hopes and that his son, Victor Emmanuel II (1849–1878), refused to rescind despite Austrian pressure. In 1850 the young king appointed to the cabinet Count Camillo Benso di Cavour (1810–1861), a brilliant statesman into whose hands the leadership of the Risorgimento passed.

Although born into the nobility, Cavour was also the epitome of the nineteenth-century businessman. Portly, nearsighted, and a dull orator who spoke French better than Italian, Cavour was nonetheless crafty and steel-willed. Above all, he was a master of power politics, unwilling to allow principle to interfere with objectives and capable of outwitting Europe's shrewdest diplomats. With a successful background in agriculture, industry, and banking, he developed an abiding belief in economic liberalism. First as minister of agriculture and commerce in 1850 and then as prime minister from 1852, he modernized Piedmont's economy and forged an alliance of moderate forces within parliament that was responsible for progressive legislation. He understood fully that Piedmont lacked the strength to rid Italy of the Austrians alone, and his policy hinged on securing the support of powerful foreign allies. Nevertheless, Cavour's view of unification was more limited than Mazzini's, for his goal was originally the creation of a large Piedmontese kingdom covering northern Italy but excluding the Papal States and the Bourbon south.

Cavour's first step in the realization of his plan was a masterstroke of political cynicism. Although Piedmont had no apparent interest in the Near East, in 1854 he intervened in the Crimean War on the side of Britain and

31.2 The Unification of Italy, 1859–1870

France, thus securing a place for himself at the Paris peace talks that followed. Cavour not only succeeded in raising the "Italian question" at the conference but also won the admiration of Napoleon III. The French emperor, who in his youth had developed a strong affection for Italy, believed that his sponsorship of the Italian cause would further his own prestige. In July 1858 he and Cavour negotiated the secret Treaty of Plombières. The agreement pledged French military support for a war against Austria, the goal of which would be Piedmont's annexation of Lombardy and Venetia. Victory was to result in the creation of a kingdom of upper Italy and an Italian federation under the presidency of the pope. For its help, France would receive from Piedmont the provinces of Savoy and Nice. Cavour and Napoleon further agreed to manufacture a suitable pretext for war with Austria, and they promised not to make a separate peace until their goals had been reached.

In the tension-filled months that followed, efforts to settle the Italian problem peacefully threatened to wreck Cavour's plans. In April 1859, however, the Austrians played into his hands by issuing an ultimatum demanding that Piedmont demobilize its armies. The French declared war and, taking advantage of Austrian delays, quickly moved into Italy to join their Piedmontese allies. Lombardy was liberated, but as the allies prepared to press into Venetia the unpredictable Louis-Napoleon suddenly announced the conclusion of an armistice at Villafranca with the Austrian emperor, Franz Joseph. It clearly violated Napoleon's agreement with Cavour, for the Austrians were forced only to surrender Lombardy. Nevertheless, Victor Emmanuel accepted the terms, and the outraged Cavour resigned in protest.

Yet all was not lost. During the fighting in Lombardy, moderate nationalists and liberal businessmen secretly worked in cooperation with Cavour to stage a series of revolts that unseated the rulers of the central Italian duchies. Then, in the wake of the armistice of Villafranca, they engineered popular demonstrations in favor of union with Piedmont. Returning to office in January, Cavour suppressed his anger and struck a bargain with Napoleon that permitted the Piedmontese annexation of these territories. Borrowing one of Napoleon's favorite political tactics, Cavour engineered plebiscites to confirm popular enthusiasm for his territorial aggrandisement. Thus by 1860 Piedmont had been considerably enlarged by the addition of Lombardy and the duchies of central Italy. The first step in the unification of Italy was over.

The Crisis of Italian Unification

Until the plebiscites in central Italy, the astute Cavour had managed to shape the course of events, but now the initiative was seized by Giuseppe Garibaldi (1807–1882). A hero in the age of power politics, a determined Romantic in the face of Cavour's cynicism, Garibaldi was nevertheless the greatest guerrilla fighter of the century. Although he believed in Mazzini's republican doctrines, he was above all a patriot determined to see Italy free and united. With a death sentence on his head for having taken part in a Mazzinian plot, Garibaldi fled to South America in 1834 and fought against authoritarian government in the jungles of Uruguay. He returned to Italy in 1848 to fight along with Charles Albert and then went to Rome to lead the dramatic defense of Mazzini's republic against the French troops sent there by Louis-Napoleon to restore the pope. By 1859, when Garibaldi again commanded a volunteer army against Austria, he was a popular figure with a rapidly growing following.

Garibaldi's vision of unification encompassed the entire Italian peninsula. In 1860 he decided to complete the process begun by Cavour with a daring military expedition against the Kingdom of the Two Sicilies. Cavour not only mistrusted Garibaldi's republican sentiments but also feared that Napoleon III would intervene if Garibaldi attempted to seize Rome. He therefore played a double game, secretly encouraging Garibaldi's 1,000-man army of "Red Shirts" while simultaneously preparing to stop the guerrilla leader with force should he threaten Rome. Landing in Sicily in May, Garibaldi outmaneuvered the Bourbon armies, recruited additional volunteers among the disaffected peasants, and captured the island. By September he had crossed to the mainland and taken the Neapolitan capital, declaring a provisional dictatorship over the entire Italian south. In the meantime, a worried Cavour had persuaded Napoleon III to agree to the passage of Piedmontese troops through the Papal States in order to protect the pope. Instead, Victor Emmanuel seized all the papal lands except for the area around Rome. In October, as the Risorgimento reached its climax, Victor Emmanuel and Garibaldi met just south of Naples, thus bringing the moderate and the radical forces face to face. Determined to make Italy a nation rather than plunge it into civil war, Garibaldi relinquished his conquests to the king. In March 1861 the Piedmontese sovereign was proclaimed Victor Emmanuel II, king of Italy. Two months later Cavour died.

The euphoria of the Risorgimento quickly faded as the Italians encountered the problems of nationhood. Indeed, the kingdom was still incomplete—Venetia was not incorporated until the Austro-Prussian War of 1866, and Rome itself was not seized until the Franco-Prussian War in 1870. When it did occur, the annexation of Rome produced deep hostility between the Catholic church and the new state that plagued Italian affairs for the next half century. Regional differences and local loyalties remained strong, and the gap between the developing industrial interests of the north and the depressed agricultural economy of the south widened. A host of vital public policy issues that included illiteracy, disease, and extreme poverty, placed

Cavour Versus Garibaldi

Throughout 1860, while Garibaldi's volunteer army seized the island of Sicily and then the mainland portion of the Kingdom of Naples, Count Cavour, the Piedmontese premier, tried to prevent Garibaldi from seizing control of the Italian unification movement. In this letter Cavour describes his political calculations and his efforts to stop Garibaldi.

If Garibaldi proceeds to the mainland of southern Italy and captures Naples just as he has already taken Sicily and Palermo, he will become absolute master of the situation. King Victor Emmanuel would lose almost all his prestige in the eyes of Italians. . . .

We would be forced to go along with his plans and help him fight Austria. I am therefore convinced that the king must not receive the crown of Italy from Garibaldi's hands. . . .

I have no illusions about the grave and dangerous decision I am advocating, but I believe it is essential if we are to save the monarchic principle. Better a king of Piedmont should perish in war against Austria than be swamped by the revolution. The dynasty might recover from a defeat in battle, but if dragged through the revolutionary gutter its fate would be . . . sealed.

Although I have made up my mind how to act if Garibaldi reaches Naples, it is nevertheless my first duty to the king and Italy to do everything possible to prevent his success there. My only hope of foiling him is if I can overthrow the Bourbon regime before Garibaldi crosses to the mainland—or at least before he has had time to reach Naples. If the regime falls, I would then take over the government of Naples in the name of order and humanity, and so snatch out of Garibaldi's hands the supreme direction of the Italian movement.

Source: C. B. di Cavour, letter to Costantino Nigra, August 1, 1860, in D. Mack Smith, ed., *Garibaldi* (Englewood Cliffs, N.J.: Prentice-Hall, 1969), pp. 44–45.

enormous pressure on a national debt already burdened by the costs of the wars of unification. Added to these difficulties was an often corrupt parliamentary regime that remained unresponsive to the needs of the largely unenfranchised poorer classes and a ruling elite bent on making Italy a great power. The challenge for Cavour's successors, then, would be to resolve these problems of national development and move Italy toward political democracy.

Iron and Blood: The Making of the German Empire

In Germany, as in Italy, the Congress of Vienna mandated a restoration designed to prevent national unification as well as to guarantee Austrian preponderance in German affairs. The creation of the German Confederation, with a diet, or parliament, at Frankfurt representing 38 sovereign states, recognized the irreversibility of Bonaparte's destruction of the Holy Roman Empire and his simplification of the German state system. The new German Confederation included small states with only a few hundred square miles of territory, such as the Thuringian principalities, and much larger units such as the Kingdom of Bavaria, which comprised more than 10,000 square miles. Religious differences reinforced political divisions, for while northern Germany was Protestant, the predominantly Catholic South tended to regard Austria as a bulwark against Protestant Prussia. In these circumstances, Austria dominated the divided German states.

Nationalism and the German State System

The Kingdom of Prussia, with considerably enlarged territories and a formidable army, was the second most powerful state in the German Confederation. Its autocratic and

31.3 The Unification of Germany, 1866–1871

unstable monarch, Frederick William IV (1840–1861), aspired to expand the Hohenzollern position in Germany. Just as Piedmont vied with Austria for mastery in Italy, so Prussian-Austrian rivalry was the heart of the German power struggle after 1815. The stronghold of German nationalism, however, was not the Prussian monarchy, whose motivation was largely one of dynastic power, but the rapidly growing liberal middle class. The Prussian-sponsored *Zollverein* (customs union) that developed after 1818 not only stimulated trade throughout Germany and underscored the economic advantages of unification but also anticipated the so-called *kleindeutsch* (small German) solution that sought to exclude Austria from German affairs.

By 1848 these middle-class elements hoped that Prussia would provide the leadership to unify Germany and give it a constitutional monarchy. Twice during the revolutions of 1848, however, these expectations were dashed by the military-aristocratic forces that ruled Prussia. In the fall Frederick William, encouraged by the army and reactionary elements in his court, withdrew his promise to allow an elected constituent assembly to draft a liberal constitution. In March 1849, when the Frankfurt assembly elected him emperor of Germany, he rejected the "crown from the gutter," later issuing a more conservative constitution of his own. This royal document provided for a two-chamber parliament, an appointed upper house and a lower house elected by an unequal and indirect system of universal male suffrage. Although the constitution was ambiguous about the role of the lower house (*Landtag*) in formulating budget laws, it was clear that the king retained extensive authority. Yet Frederick William's efforts to unify Germany failed. In 1850, when he attempted to solicit an imperial crown from his fellow German monarchs, Austria and Russia coerced him to abandon the plan in a humiliating confrontation at Olmütz.

Bismarck and the Liberals

Despite its commerical and industrial primacy, Prussia's repressive domestic policies, together with Frederick William's timidity in foreign affairs, cast doubt on its ability to bring about German unification. These tendencies were reinforced when William, the monarch's brother, became regent in 1858 and then king in 1861. William I (1861–1888) precipitated a constitutional crisis in Prussia that changed the course of German history.

In February 1860 William presented a bill to the Prussian Landtag that proposed to double the size of the regular army and increase compulsory military service from two to three years. Most controversial, perhaps, was the fact that the king, himself a professional soldier, wished to reduce the role and independence of the civilian militia, whose lack of discipline he regarded with contempt. The liberal middle classes—who, because of the elitist nature of the suffrage law, dominated the Landtag—saw these measures as a constitutional challenge, for they wished both to assert the power of parliament over the king and to reduce the influence of the military in Prussian society. As a result, the military bill was eventually withdrawn. When a later version of the same bill was voted down in 1862, William dissolved the Landtag, but the new elections only increased the liberal majority. Torn between abdicating and forcing a showdown with the liberals, the king appointed Count Otto von Bismarck (1815–1898) as his new minister-president.

Bismarck, who forged the modern German state, is shown in 1871, the year the new empire was proclaimed. [Culver Pictures]

Bismarck ranks as one of the dominant figures in modern German history. Although a member of the conservative *Junker* class of aristocratic landowners, he was neither provincial in his outlook nor ideologically wedded to the past. He cut an imposing figure, stubborn, fiercely combative, and oblivious to the constraints of tradition and constitutional theory. Bismarck was also a master political strategist. His early career had given him wide experience in diplomacy, first as a Prussian delegate to the Frankfurt Diet and then as ambassador in St. Petersburg and in Paris. While he disdained the parliamentary demands of the liberals, he recognized that they had embraced nationalism and that Prussia needed their industrial skills and wealth. Bismarck's view of unification was at first limited—the imposition of Prussian mastery over largely Protestant northern Germany, a goal he eventually came to believe would require the expulsion of Austria from the German state system.

For Bismarck, the German question and the conflict with the Landtag were linked, for a strong army was needed to deal with Austria. When he found that compromise with the liberals over military reform was impossible, he reorganized the army with funds earmarked for other purposes. The liberals denounced Bismarck's high-handed tactics, and the issue was further complicated by public criticism from Frederick, the heir to the throne, who had been influenced by his liberal-thinking wife, Victoria (1840–1901), the oldest daughter of Britain's Queen Victoria and Prince Albert. Victoria envisioned a unified Germany ruled not by the military but by the best traditions of German culture. Her role in the constitutional crisis resulted in her exclusion from public life for many years.

Not only was Bismarck oblivious to the protests of the liberal opposition, but he lectured them on *Realpolitik*. In blunt speeches before the Landtag, he declared that only a policy of "iron and blood" would yield results, that power rather than principle determined the outcome of conflict, and that results justified means. A vigorous program in foreign affairs, he believed, would win over many liberals and critics of his violation of constitutional procedure. Moreover, since the defeats of 1848, the German intellectuals had either emigrated or abandoned politics. Bis-

Bismarck on Power Politics

On September 30, 1862, Bismarck made the following remarks before the Prussian Landtag in order to secure approval of the military reorganization bill proposed by King William I. His words were the quintessential statement on the nature of power politics.

While it is clear that we cannot avoid complications in Germany, we do not seek them. Germany does not look to Prussia's liberalism but to her power. Because the southern states of Germany—Bavaria, Württemberg, and Baden—would like to indulge in liberalism, Prussia's role will not be assigned to them! Prussia must gather her forces and hold them in reserve for the right moment, which we have already missed several times. Since the Treaty of Vienna, our borders have not been designed to ensure a healthy body politic. Not by speeches and majorities will the great questions of the day be decided—that was the mistake of 1848 and 1849—but by iron and blood.

Source: H. Kohl, ed., *Die politischen Reden des Fürsten Bismarck* (Stuttgart: Cotta, 1892–1905). Translated by P. Cannistraro.

marck thus set the terms on which German unification would be achieved, for just as Cavour's actions intensified the ideological struggle between Italian moderates and radicals, so Bismarck polarized the German unification movement between liberals and the advocates of power politics.

The Showdown with Austria

Bismarck's determination to extend Prussian authority over northern Germany made a military confrontation with Austria all but inevitable. The showdown evolved between 1863 and 1866 and resulted from a situation involving Schleswig and Holstein, two northern duchies controlled by the king of Denmark although not an actual part of his kingdom. Holstein, inhabited almost entirely by Germans, was part of the Confederation, whereas Schleswig's mixed population of Danes and Germans fought bitterly over the issue of membership. When Denmark moved to annex Schleswig in 1863, Bismarck persuaded the Austrians to join Prussia in what proved to be a short and successful war to reclaim the two provinces. The Peace of Vienna that ended the war against Denmark provided that Austria and Prussia would administer the provinces jointly. Discussion as to their future resulted in a deadlock when the Austrians insisted that the provinces become a single state ruled by a German prince, while Bismarck demanded extensive commercial rights that would have made them virtual Prussian provinces. A temporary agreement was established in 1865 according to which Holstein would be run by Austria and Schleswig by Prussia. This awkward arrangement led to continued quarrels between the two allies and eventually gave Bismarck the excuse to provoke a war with Austria.

Like Cavour, Bismarck understood that *Realpolitik* required careful diplomatic preparation among the other European powers. Prussia needed assurance that other nations would not come to Austria's assistance. Because he had offered to help Russia put down a Polish uprising in 1863, Bismarck was fairly certain that Tsar Alexander II would not interfere, but Napoleon III was the unknown element. In the fall of 1865 Bismarck and Napoleon held a secret meeting reminiscent of the Plombières encounter between Napoleon and Cavour. Bismarck secured Napoleon's promise of neutrality in the event of an Austro-Prussian war with vague promises of territorial compensation for France along the Rhine. The following year he negotiated an alliance with Italy that promised Italian military assistance in return for the Austrian-held province of Venetia. After years of preparation, the war came suddenly. On June 1, 1866, the Prussians sent troops into Holstein in protest over what Bismarck claimed was an Austrian violation of their agreement. In response, the Austrians persuaded the German Confederation to vote military action against Prussia. Bismarck's answer was to declare the Confederation dissolved and order Prussia's armies into action.

The Austro-Prussian War was important for several reasons. Bismarck tried to make the point that the "national development of Germany" was at stake, although in truth Prussian aggression was the real issue. After seven weeks of fighting, Austria was defeated at the Königgratz in Bohemia. The Prussian victory was due to the ability to deploy troops rapidly by railroad, to the use of a new breech-loading gun, and to the brilliant strategist Count

Helmuth von Moltke. The king's controversial military reorganization bill had proved itself. Although the war was fought against the other states of the German Confederation as well as Austria, the latter had been poorly prepared and had to fight on both the German and the Italian fronts. By imposing deliberately moderate peace terms on Austria in the Treaty of Prague (August 1866), Bismarck demonstrated once again his mastery of *Realpolitik*. No reparations were extracted from Austria, and a separate agreement forced it only to cede Venetia to the Italians. Bismarck's real goal was achieved by the dissolution of the Confederation and Austria's withdrawal from German affairs. The Austrians also had to recognize Prussia's annexation of Schleswig-Holstein and a number of German states in the north. While the southern Catholic states remained independent, they had to pay indemnities and sign military alliances forcing them to fight on Prussia's side in any future war.

After the war, Bismarck presided over the creation of the North German Confederation. Dominated by Prussia, it included all German states north of the river Main. A constitution made the king of Prussia its president and Bismarck its chancellor. Local affairs remained in the hands of each state, but foreign policy and military authority were controlled by the central government. The parliament of the North German Confederation consisted of the *Bundesrat*, or upper house, representing each of the states, and a *Reichstag*, or lower house, elected by universal male suffrage. This system, which later provided the model for the constitution of united Germany, reflected the wide powers of the Prussian king and limited such parliamentary principles as ministerial responsibility. But the liberalized franchise created the sense that wide strata of the people, not just the middle class, now had a stake in Germany's future.

The Franco-Prussian War and the Forging of German Unification

It is difficult to say just how long Bismarck intended the North German Confederation to remain in place. As a Prussian rather than a German nationalist, his vision of unification may well have remained limited despite the events of 1866. But just as Garibaldi had forced Cavour to broaden his view of Italian unification in 1860, so now the diplomatic blunders of Napoleon III pushed Bismarck to complete the process he had begun.

Austria's defeat at the hands of Prussia shocked Napoleon, who had underestimated Prussian power. The suddenness of the Austrian collapse prevented him from intervening, and Prussia's victory had been so complete that Bismarck did not grant the territorial rewards that he had vaguely promised Napoleon. Napoleon's failure to extract concessions from Bismarck, compounded by fiasco in Mexico, stimulated the emperor's opponents at home, who argued that the war represented a severe blow to French prestige. Napoleon became convinced that the consolidation of German strength on France's borders had to be stopped. For his part, Bismarck came to realize that a war with France would inflame German nationalism and push the southern states, where business circles already favored unification, into a united Germany.

Friction between the two countries mounted steadily, with both Napoleon and Bismarck contributing to the tension. The pretext for war arose from a dispute over whether a German prince related to William I would become king of Spain. The immediate cause for the outbreak of the Franco-Prussian War was the so-called Ems dispatch. When William I agreed to withdraw his support of the Hohenzollern candidate, Napoleon demanded that the Prussian king apologize and promise not to raise the Hohenzollern candidacy again. Meeting with the French ambassador at Ems in July 1870, the Prussian ruler refused to give such a promise and telegraphed the details of the talk to Berlin. Bismarck had the dispatch published in the press after changing the wording to create the impression that William had insulted the French. Newspapers in Paris and Berlin sensationalized the telegram and enraged public opinion. On July 19 the French declared war.

As in the case of the struggle with Austria four years earlier, the swiftness of the Franco-Prussian War and the superiority of Prussia's military forces stunned Europe. Thanks to Bismarck's lenient treatment of Austria in 1866, it remained neutral, as did the other great powers; moreover, the military treaties he had forced on the southern German states brought them into the war on the side of Prussia, so that the war became, at least in name, a "national" one. On September 1 the Prussian armies captured Napoleon III along with more than 100,000 French soldiers at Sedan. The news of Napoleon's surrender was followed a few days later in Paris by the proclamation of a republic. The republican forces continued to fight for five additional months despite the siege of the capital and the outbreak of an uprising in March known as the Paris Commune. While Paris held out against starvation and the violence sparked by the Commune, Bismarck consolidated Germany. On January 18, 1871, in the Hall of Mirrors in the palace of Versailles, William I was proclaimed German emperor, and all of Germany was at last unified under a political system virtually identical to the one that had governed the North German Confederation.

At the end of the month the French republic capitulated, and in February a National Assembly was elected and the liberal monarchist Adolphe Thiers chosen as chief executive. Thiers, who made peace with the Germans, had little room to negotiate, for Bismarck was in no mood to be generous. The peace of Frankfurt, signed on May 10, was harsh—France had to pay an indemnity of 5 billion francs and accept German occupation until it was paid.

Most distressing to the French, however, was the loss of Alsace and most of Lorraine to Germany. These provinces, which contained iron deposits and a prosperous textile industry, were inhabited by German-speaking people who preferred the French to the Prussians, and their annexation remained for the next half century a source of bitterness between Germany and France.

The Franco-Prussian War had profound repercussions. Along with the unification of Germany came the victory of Bismarck's political strategy, which had wedded German nationalism to the conservative-aristocratic forces that ruled Prussia and cowed the liberals into abandoning their opposition in the face of unification. The completion of Italian territorial unity was an unexpected by-product of the Franco-Prussian War, for when Napoleon III brought home the troops stationed in Rome to protect the pope, King Victor Emmanuel III seized the city and made it the capital of Italy. Most immediately the war led to the collapse of Napoleon's Second Empire. Perhaps its most far-reaching result was the shift in the balance of power. By 1871 Italy was demanding recognition as a great power, and the collapse of Austria and France demonstrated that Germany had emerged as the most powerful European state. The Treaty of Frankfurt confirmed the end of the Concert of Europe created by the Vienna peace settlement in 1815, for not only had Austria and France been defeated by the new German colossus, but Britain and Russia had remained aloof from the wars. Napoleon III, Cavour, and Bismarck, each in his own way an embodiment of the nationalist doctrines that dominated the age, had wrought profound changes in the structure of the European state system.

Eastern Europe and the Ottomans

Austria's role in Italian and German affairs after 1815 was symptomatic of its status as a multiethnic empire in an age of rising nationalism. This last dynastic state, ruled by the Habsburgs since the Middle Ages, survived the waves of Romantic nationalism of the 1820s and 1830s, as well as the upheavals of 1848, but its existence was seriously challenged in midcentury as its many nationalities clamored for independence. Twelve million Germans controlled political power and enjoyed special status in a state that reached 50 million by 1914 and included 24 million Slavs to the south, 10 million Magyars and 4 million Romanians to the east, as well as Czechs, Slovaks, Poles, Croats, Serbs, Italians, and a variety of other ethnic groups. The Habsburgs made a number of attempts to bring the forces of nationalism under control, but neither reforms, the granting of limited provincial autonomy in 1859, nor the new constitution of 1861 was effective.

The Austro-Prussian War of 1866 demonstrated just how divided and weak the Austrian Empire was, and defeat provoked still one more effort at reform. After difficult negotiations, the emperor Franz Joseph reached a compromise (*Ausgleich*) with Hungarian leaders. The new constitution created the Dual Monarchy, in which Franz Joseph was both king of Hungary and emperor of Austria. Foreign affairs, finance, and military matters were conducted by common ministers, but otherwise the two parts of the monarchy were autonomous, each with its own constitution, official language, and parliament.

The *Ausgleich* did not, of course, eliminate the serious problems facing the empire but merely enabled the Hungarians to share with the Germans in its rule. The other nationality groups continued to demand their freedom. Some industry and a middle class thrived in Bohemia and the area surrounding Vienna, and serfdom had been abolished in 1848. However, in both halves of the Dual Monarchy most inhabitants were landless, backward peasants burdened by conservative landowners and heavy taxes. Despite the ancient lineage of the Habsburgs and the importance of its strategic position in Europe, the Dual Monarchy remained an anachronism in a Europe rapidly dividing along national lines.

VIENNA IN THE AGE OF FRANZ JOSEPH

As the capital of Austria, Vienna was a microcosm of the empire, reflecting its strengths and weaknesses, its brilliance and its contradictions. Since 1278, when the Habsburgs selected the town on the banks of the Danube for their capital, the city was a center of bureaucracy and aristocratic splendor. Vienna grew rapidly in the modern period, and by the opening of the nineteenth century it contained more than a quarter of a million people. Yet although the Habsburg capital was the government center for a vast multiethnic empire, it remained an essentially German city in language and culture.

Because its economy was built around the court and the government, Vienna had little industry or industrial proletariat until the mid-nineteenth century. It collected and spent tax revenues, and its economic life centered on banking, crafts, and the production of luxury goods, including silk and porcelain. Similarly, the social structure of the city included a wealthy aristocracy, a variety of civil servants, artisans and shopkeepers, a small but prosperous business class, and workers. With the coming of the Industrial Revolution to Vienna in the 1830s and 1840s, tens of thousands of peasants streamed into the city, and by the eve of the revolutions of 1848 its population had increased to 400,000.

As long as Austria remained a great European power, Vienna was a center of European diplomacy, a role it played never more splendidly than as host of the great peace settlement following the Napoleonic wars. In the generation before the revolutions of 1848, the city of Metternich became the capital of the European conservative order, crowded with diplomats, reactionary politicians, and police agents bent on uncovering revolutionaries. Metternich's office, and therefore the nerve center of the bureaucracy, was housed in the Ballhaus chancery, built in the early eighteenth century, but the true grandeur of the Habsburg empire was displayed in the rich array of luxurious royal palaces. The emperor Franz Joseph, who died in 1916 after 68 years on the throne, was installed in the vast Hofburg Palace and moved in the summer months to the ornate Schönbrunn Palace. The important aristocratic families of the realm built lavish residences, of which the most remarkable was the Belvedere, the summer palace of Prince Eugène of Savoy. While the bulk of the population lived in middle-class housing and ugly tenements, much of the European nobility that visited Vienna saw only the splendors of the ruling class. In the 1860s Vienna's beauty was enhanced still further by the demolition of the city's medieval wall and the building of the Ringstrasse, a majestic tree-lined boulevard encircling the city that rivaled Haussmann's work in Paris.

Vienna's importance to Western culture was unequaled in the sphere of music. The city nurtured the greatest concentration of musical brilliance in modern times, for the patronage of the Habsburgs and the nobility attracted the musical giants of Europe—Mozart and Haydn, Beethoven, Schubert and Schumann, Johann and Richard Strauss, Brahms and Mahler. Although the second half of the nineteenth century was a period of crisis and decline for the Habsburg empire, its capital thrived as a refined city basking in sentimentality. The light operatic themes of Franz Lehar's *Merry Widow* (1905), together with the late Romantic lushness of the music of Anton Bruckner and Gustav Mahler, had wide popular appeal. The aging emperor Franz Joseph, who stood stiffly in uniform braced by his sword while the imperial court danced to the waltzes of Johann Strauss, was the symbol of a fragile and once great empire.

In this time of unabashed nostalgia, Vienna also gave birth to avant-garde movements that challenged the values of the past. Richard Strauss' *Der Rosenkavalier* (1911) represented the swan song of Romantic opera in the classical style—a young composer, Arnold Schönberg, had already broken from the Western tradition of tonality, and two young followers, Alban Berg and Anton Webern, were pushing the revolution in music even further by abandoning the standard conception of keys. Painters and writers were experimenting with new forms of expression that would later lead to the movement in the arts known as the Vienna Secession. But it was perhaps in the study of a Viennese physician named Sigmund Freud that the most profound transformation was taking place. Freud's investigations suggested that deep-rooted instincts struggled for release and dominance within the human psyche, and the popularization of his work shattered nineteenth-century rationalism.

Vienna also saw the emergence of political movements that challenged the roots of European liberalism, among them the Christian Socialist party of Karl Lüger and the Social Democratic party led by Victor Adler. But whereas the Social Democrats appealed to the city's growing industrial working class, Christian Socialist membership came largely from the petty bourgeoisie. Lüger and his followers identified closely with a growing anti-Semitic sentiment in the city. Lüger was mayor of the city when, in 1907, a teenage German first came to Vienna to study painting. In Vienna the young man discovered anti-Semitism and came to loathe the mixing of nationalities that he saw in the capital. His name was Adolf Hitler.

Russia Between Reaction and Reform

The dilemmas facing a multiethnic empire such as Austria were perhaps more serious still in Russia, where the problems of national minorities were compounded by the vast size of its territory and the complexity of its population. Stretching thousands of miles across two continents, the peoples of the Russian empire included a wide diversity of Europeans and Asians, and for centuries Russia struggled unsuccessfully to define its national identity between the pulls of two civilizations.

Despite its complexity, the social structure of Russia's population was rigidly divided between a small and highly privileged nobility and a huge, impoverished peasant population. Perhaps 95 percent of Russian subjects fell into the peasant category, the great majority of them serfs with no civil rights or property who owed heavy dues and services to the landowning masters. The wealthy nobility owned almost all the land and were exempt from taxes and military service. Because Russia's economy was predominantly agricultural throughout most of the nineteenth century, a small middle class existed only in the larger cities.

In an age when autocracy was disappearing in Europe, the Russian tsar remained an absolute monarch. His will was law, and only the poverty, backwardness, and ineffective bureaucracy of imperial Russia limited his authority. Because no legitimate forms of protest existed, conspiracy and local insurrection were frequent. When faced with such threats, the Romanov dynasty swung between extremes of enlightened reform and brutal repression.

Tsar Alexander I (1801–1825), who recognized that the political and social structure of the empire needed to be modernized, had experimented with constitutionalism and

Tsarist Russia on the Edge of Revolution

In 1881 Tsar Alexander II was assassinated by an anarchist group known as "The Will of the People." In March of that same year the terrorist organization addressed an open letter to the new tsar, Alexander III, of which the following is an excerpt.

A dispassionate glance at the grievous decade through which we have just passed will enable us to forecast accurately the future progress of the revolutionary movement, provided the policy of the government does not change. The movement will continue to grow and extend; deeds of a terroristic nature will increase in frequency and intensity. Meanwhile the number of the discontented in the country will grow larger and larger; confidence in the government, on the part of the people, will decline; and the idea of revolution—of its possibility and inevitability—will establish itself in Russia more and more firmly. A terrible explosion, a bloody chaos, a revolutionary earthquake throughout Russia, will complete the destruction of the order of things. Do not mistake this for a mere phrase. We understand better than any one else can how lamentable is the waste of so much talent and energy—the loss, in bloody skirmishes and in the work of destruction, of so much strength which, under other conditions, might have been expended in creative labor and in the development of the intelligence, the welfare, and the civil life of the Russian people. . . .

These are the reasons why the Russian government exerts no moral influence and has no support among the people. These are the reasons why Russia brings forth so many revolutionists. These are the reasons why even such a deed as killing a Tsar excites in the minds of a majority of the people only gladness and sympathy. Yes your Majesty! Do not be deceived by the reports of flatterers and sycophants; Tsaricide is popular in Russia.

Source: J. H. Robinson and C. Beard, eds., *Readings in Modern European History,* vol. 2 (Boston: Ginn, 1909), pp. 364–366.

federalism before reverting to autocracy. His brother, Nicholas I (1825–1855), was so obsessed by the fear of revolution that he appointed secret police to hunt down subversives. Nicholas proclaimed the principles of "autocracy, Orthodoxy, and nationalism," by which he meant obedience to the Romanov dynasty, adherence to the Russian Orthodox church, and the advancement of Russian national interests. Censorship and restrictions on intellectual life were combined with the exile of political prisoners to Siberia.

The tsar also ordered a program of Russification of ethnic minorities and supported the Slavophiles, who believed that Russia should live according to its traditional Slavic values in an agrarian society based on Orthodoxy, mysticism, and despotism. Opposed to this position were the Westerners, who argued that Russia should modernize by adopting the European model of industrial society built on rationalism. This debate split the *intelligentsia,* Russian intellectuals who wanted to achieve political goals.

Alexander II and the Dilemma of Russian Reform

The great issues confronting Russian society in the mid-nineteenth century came to a head after Russia's defeat in the Crimean War. The crisis began when Russia and Turkey went to war in 1853 over the Balkan territories of Moldavia and Wallachia. The next year Britain and France, concerned over Russian attempts to control the Christian holy places in Jerusalem and Palestine and to expand into the eastern Mediterranean, came to the aid of the Turks by invading Russia's Crimean peninsula in the Black Sea. Eventually Piedmont and Austria also sided against Russia, thus involving most of the European powers in a military conflict for the first time since the Congress of Vienna. The Crimean War ended in 1856 with Russia's defeat on the battlefield and diplomatic losses at the Paris peace conference.

Nicholas I died during the war. Like many other Russians, his more liberal son, Alexander II (1855–1881), realized that the Crimean disaster was due in part to the country's military and industrial backwardness, and he at last gave in to demands for reform. In 1861 he issued an imperial edict that emancipated more than 22 million serfs and gave them communal title to a portion of the land on which they worked. A system of local government was begun at the level of the village commune (*mir*), which held the land in common. District councils administered the courts and collected taxes, while indirectly elected provincial councils (*zemstvos*) acted as forums for open discussion of political and social issues and provided elementary education. But the emancipated serfs were forced to compensate their former lords and their land parcels were generally too small for profitable cultivation. The emancipation edict was thus a step forward in relative terms only, for most of the former serfs quickly fell into debt and wound up as agricultural laborers on the estates of their former masters. Moreover, Alexander began to doubt the wisdom of some of his measures after an assassination attempt in 1866, and in the mid-1870s he reimposed censorship on the press and the universities and curtailed freedom of debate in the *zemstvos*.

The new wave of repression sparked widespread discontent. Socialists such as Alexander Herzen (1812–1870) inspired many of the radical intelligentsia to live in the small villages in an attempt to raise peasant political consciousness. But as these so-called *Narodniki* (from the Russian word *narod*, "people") became disillusioned by the obstacles they faced, many began to proclaim themselves "nihilists," who believed in nothing. In the face of Alexander's return to repression, some of the nihilists came under the influence of the anarchist Mikhail Bakunin (1814–1876), who preached the destruction of the government through "propaganda of the deed," by which he meant individual acts of violence. In 1881 Alexander II was assassinated by such a terrorist act.

Russia descended into deep reaction during the reigns of Alexander III (1881–1894) and his son, Nicholas II (1894–1917). The only positive developments were the economic reforms carried out in the 1890s by Count Sergei Witte (1849–1915), a tough finance minister bent on modernizing the Russian economy along Western lines. Under Witte's leadership, government initiative rather than private capital stimulated industrialization. Until reactionary agrarian interests forced his dismissal in 1903, Witte succeeded in attracting Western investments by putting Russia on the gold standard, launching the trans-Siberian railroad, and stimulating industry. The French, eager for an alliance with Russia, poured capital into the empire. According to one estimate, industrial production doubled in a decade. Yet Witte's programs did not begin to come to grips with the monumental social and political problems the country faced.

Turkey: "The Sick Man of Europe"

By the start of the nineteenth century, the Ottoman Empire still ruled an estimated 40 million people, but corruption and administrative chaos were rife and, as in the Austrian Empire it bordered, the nationalist aspirations of its subject populations were already threatening to tear it apart. Revolts by Serbs and Greeks were followed later in the century by Bulgarian and Romanian uprisings, while some of the sultan's ambitious regional commanders, such as Muhammad Ali, governor of Egypt, pursued independent policies. The Western view of the Ottoman Empire was summed up by Tsar Nicholas I, who during a state visit to England in 1844 referred to it as a "dying man."

While nationalist movements challenged the unity of the Ottoman Empire, the great powers posed a more serious threat to its existence. By 1830 the Russians had occupied the Danubian principalities of Moldavia and Wallachia, the French had seized Algiers, and with the help of foreign intervention the Greeks had won their independence. As the internal decay of the Turkish system accelerated and the territorial ambitions of the European states grew, the so-called eastern question emerged. Although on one level it involved the interaction between the Ottoman Empire and the great powers, the eastern question may more clearly be understood as the conflict among the great powers over the future of the sultan's domains. One major complication arose from the growing competition between Austria and Russia for predominance in the Balkans; another was due to the centuries-old Russian ambition to gain control over the Turkish Straits in order to have free access from the Black Sea into the Mediterranean. The fate of the Ottoman possessions in the Middle East interested both Britain and France, for the British regarded the area as the gateway to India and the French were concerned over the protection of Christian holy places. Similarly, in North Africa the French were intent on expanding their foothold in Algiers into Morocco and Tunisia at the same time that the British consolidated their interest in Egypt following the completion of the Suez Canal.

The web of competing interests that comprised the eastern question made the Ottoman Empire a sensitive issue in European diplomacy. The Crimean War and the Paris peace conference of 1856 confirmed the neutrality of the Black Sea, ended the Russian occupation of Moldavia and Wallachia—the provinces were merged into the Kingdom of Romania a few years later—and left the protection of the Christian populations of the Middle East to the sultan. But if the peace conference basically preserved the Ottoman Empire, succeeding events speeded its disintegration. In 1875 revolts against Turkish rule in Bosnia led to a declaration of war against Constantinople by the semiautonomous states of Serbia and Montenegro, which

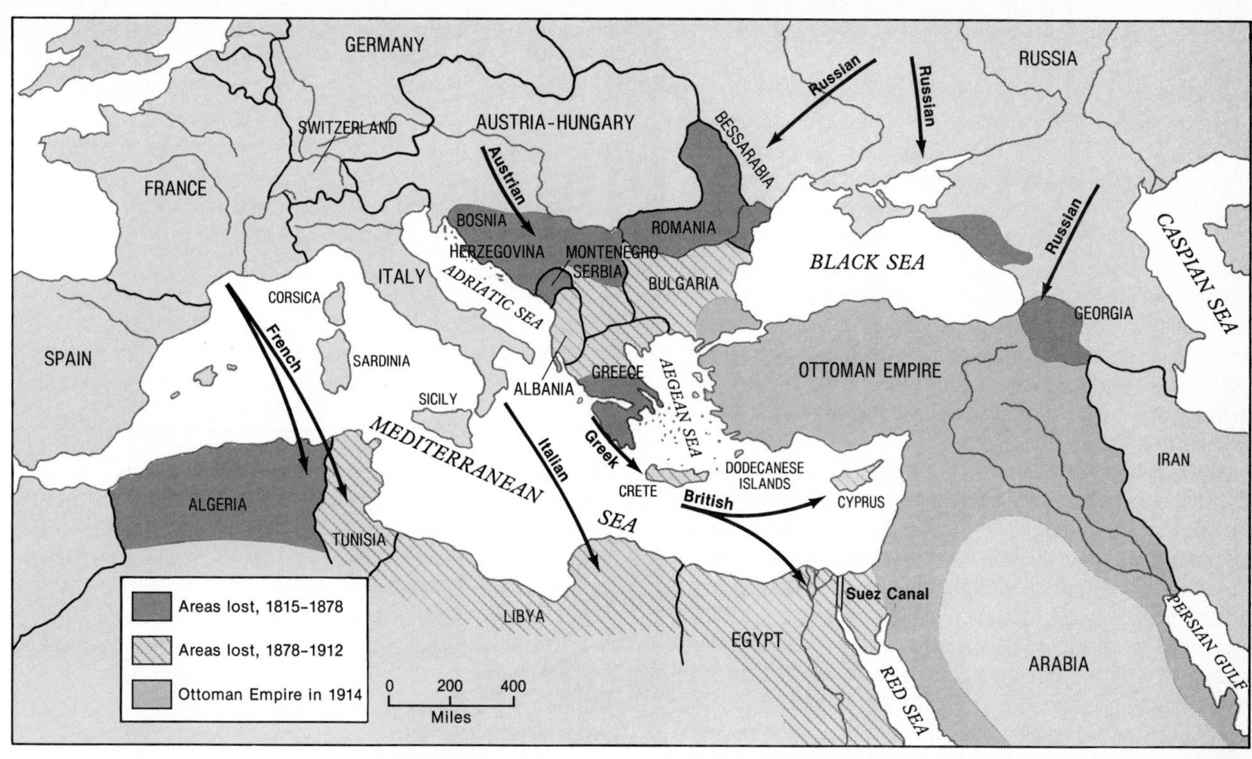

***31.4** The Decline of the Ottoman Empire to 1914*

were eventually assisted by Russia. When the resulting Treaty of San Stefano (1878) threatened to shift the balance of power in the Balkans in favor of Russia, Austria and Britain became alarmed. That summer, therefore, the Russians were forced to the conference table at the Congress of Berlin. Despite Bismarck's claim that he would act as an "honest broker" at the conference, Russian gains from the Treaty of San Stefano were severely reduced. Serbia, Montenegro, and a new state, Bulgaria, were recognized as fully independent from Turkish rule, while the provinces of Bosnia and Herzegovina were placed under Austrian administration. The Ottoman Empire lost half of its European territory. During the next 30 years European powers would strip Turkey of its remaining possessions in North Africa.

The dismemberment of the Ottoman Empire aroused discontent among the sultan's younger, Western-educated subjects and in the army, where opposition to the inefficient rule of the sultans was growing. In 1856 a far-reaching reform edict, the Hatt-i Humayun, established a progressive political structure for the empire, but a new sultan, Abdul Hamid II (1876–1909)—known for his brutal tyranny as "Abdul the Damned"—crushed the hopes of the reformers. After issuing a new constitution, Abdul Hamid reimposed tyranny. In the Ottoman Empire, as in Russia, the weight of centuries of repression seemed to move toward revolution.

Abdul Hamid II, a cruel despot, ruled the Ottoman Empire until the Young Turks deposed him in 1909. [Bettmann Archive]

The Jewish Question and the Birth of Zionism

The Enlightenment had significantly advanced the theoretical equality and the actual emancipation of the Jews, and during the nineteenth century the remaining legal restrictions on them were eliminated in virtually every major country of Europe, although quasi-official sanctions such as educational and professional quotas remained. Despite the fact that religious and social prejudices against them were still deeply rooted in Europe, most Jewish populations were being assimilated into Europe's social, economic, and cultural life.

In an age of self-conscious nationalism, however, the Jewish question grew increasingly complicated. The development of "scientific" theories of race in the late nineteenth century and the resulting merger of nationalism and racism stimulated anti-Semitic discussion. In countries where Catholic and Christian influence blended with political conservatism, anti-Semitism emerged as a political movement with widespread appeal. In Germany, Adolf Stöcker's Christian Socialist Workingman's Union, the Conservative party, and even an Anti-Semitic League advocated an end to Jewish influence in national life, and in 1882 an international anti-Semitic congress was held in Dresden. In France, Edouard Drumont's book *La France juive* (1886) inflamed popular attitudes, and the shocking Dreyfus affair revealed the depth of anti-Semitic sentiment. In the Dual Monarchy, the Christian Socialist party elected Karl Lüger mayor of Vienna on a distinctly anti-Semitic platform.

It was in Russia, where the partitions of Poland in the late eighteenth century had made millions of Jews subjects of the tsar, that systematic repression became state policy. Anti-Semitic measures coincided with the reactionary policies of Alexander I and Nicholas I, and in the wake of the assassination of Alexander II in 1881, violent anti-Semitic campaigns, or pogroms (*pogrom* is Russian for "devastation"), were unleashed, often with official connivance, as Jews were killed and beaten and their homes and shops burned and looted. The infamous May Laws of 1882 provided the basis for the expulsion of Jews from villages and rural centers outside Poland, and even fiercer pogroms broke out in 1902 and 1903. In the period from 1881 to 1910, millions of Russian Jews fled, most of them to the United States.

As a reaction to these persecutions and a defense against the assimilation and secularization of Jewish life, the end of the century saw the development of an organized movement of Jewish nationalism called Zionism. Advocates of Zionism argued that Jews would never find justice and equality until they returned to their biblical homeland and formed their own national state. Rabbi Zevi-Hirsch Kalischer and a number of other Jewish thinkers had already proposed the establishment of a homeland in Palestine, and in 1869 an agricultural colony named Mikveh Yisrael ("Hope of Israel") was founded there. In 1882 Leo Pinsker, a Russian Jewish physician, published an influential pamphlet, *Autoemancipation,* advocating a similar program.

THEODOR HERZL AND THE QUEST FOR A JEWISH HOMELAND

The founder of modern political Zionism was Theodor Herzl (1860–1904). Against overwhelming odds, and at times almost singlehandedly, Herzl set in motion the movement that years after his death resulted in the establishment of the state of Israel.

The founder of the modern Zionist movement, Theodore Herzl, was driven by the revival of anti-Semitism in the late nineteenth century as well as by the centuries-old aspirations of Jews for a homeland in Palestine. [Granger Collection]

On Anti-Semitism

The reemergence of anti-Semitism assumed new and more virulent forms in the late nineteenth century and led Jewish leaders such as Theodor Herzl and his friend Max Nordau to found the Zionist movement. Here are two moving statements by them on the nature of anti-Semitism.

Stunned by the hailstorm of anti-Semitic accusations, the Jews forget who they are and often imagine that they are the physical and spiritual horrors which their deadly enemies represent them to be. The Jew is often heard to murmur that he must learn from the enemy and try to remedy the faults ascribed to him. He forgets, however, that the anti-Semitic accusations are meaningless, because they are not a criticism of facts which exist, but are the effects of a psychological law according to which children, wild men, and malevolent fools make the persons and things they hate responsible for their sufferings.

I believe that I understand Anti-Semitism, which is really a highly complex movement. I consider it from a Jewish standpoint, yet without fear or hatred. I believe that I can see what elements there are in it of vulgar sport, of common trade jealousy, of inherited prejudice, of religious intolerance, and also of pretended self-defense. I think the Jewish question is no more a social than a religious one, notwithstanding that it sometimes takes these and other forms. It is a national question which can only be solved by making it a political world-question to be discussed and controlled by the civilized nations of the world in council.

We are a people—One people.

Sources: M. Nordau, speech to the First Zionist Congress, 1897, in A. Hertzberg, ed., *The Zionist Idea* (Garden City, N.Y.: Doubleday, 1959), p. 241; T. Herzl, *The Jewish State: An Attempt at a Modern Solution of the Jewish Question* (New York: Maccabaean Publishing Co., 1904), pp. 4–5.

Herzl was born in Budapest in a merchant family of assimilated Jews. After taking a law degree from the University of Vienna, he turned to writing, immersing himself in the world of sentimental, bourgeois culture that characterized the Austrian capital in the 1880s. Although he wrote successful plays, journalism was Herzl's real talent, and he made an international reputation as foreign correspondent for the prestigious *Neue Freie Presse*. A handsome man with a Romantic, narcissistic personality, he moved in literary and aristocratic circles. But in 1891 his Viennese paper sent Herzl to Paris, where his life took a sudden and dramatic turn. In Paris, Herzl discovered his identity as a Jew. France was then in the throes of the Dreyfus scandal, and Herzl witnessed the anti-Semitic frenzy firsthand. Thereafter, Jewish issues began to preoccupy him. The result was his famous pamphlet, drafted in a few intense months in late 1895 and published the following year as *Der Judenstaat* (*The Jewish State*).

Written in a powerful, crisp style, *The Jewish State* was a radical analysis of the Jewish question. Herzl argued that although many Jews had attempted to assimilate into European society, anti-Semitism had made this impossible. "I consider the Jewish question," he wrote, "neither a social nor a religious one, even though it sometimes takes these and other forms. It is a national question." His solution, therefore, was that Jews all over the world should organize to obtain a land of their own. In his mind, Palestine was the natural site for a Jewish state. But unlike earlier leaders, he insisted that Palestine should be secured not through unofficial immigration and infiltration but rather through an international charter.

Herzl threw himself into the task. Sacrificing his marriage, his wealth, and eventually his health, he spent the rest of his life in a tireless campaign to convince his fellow Jews and to secure the support of world opinion. His efforts resulted in the establishment of the World Zionist Organization. In 1897 he presided over the First Zionist Congress, in Basel, Switzerland, which proclaimed that "Zionism seeks to establish for the Jewish people a publicly recognized, legally secured home in Palestine" and to strengthen "Jewish self-awareness and national consciousness." By 1901 there were local Zionist organizations throughout the world, including 1,034 in Russia and 135 in the United States, and branches as far afield as New Zealand, Chile, and India. Herzl gained the help of influential Jewish leaders and met with heads of state, including Kaiser William II and the Turkish sultan, in efforts to realize the Basel program. In 1903 the British government offered part of its East African possessions as the basis for a Jewish state. Through the work of Herzl's successor, Chaim Weizmann (1874–1952), and the support of the British statesman Arthur Balfour, the British government became increasingly sympathetic to the Zionist cause, but not until World War I did it support a Jewish homeland in Palestine.

Herzl's program provoked great controversy, even within the ranks of the Zionist movement. Some biographers have portrayed him as a man with a messianic complex—he demanded blind obedience from his followers, and everywhere he traveled, especially in eastern Europe and Russia, throngs of poor Jews greeted him with adulation. His argument that assimilation had failed suggested to many that he despaired of liberalism, yet his vision of the new Jewish state was so grounded in tolerance and progressive ideals that it often provoked resentment from cultural Zionists who saw nothing specifically Jewish about it. Similarly, he failed both to understand the importance of socialism within the Zionist ranks and to anticipate the clash between Jews and Arabs that would result from the occupation of Palestine. Yet his methods yielded results, and he galvanized millions of Jews the world over. His despondency over the failure of assimilation, together with his warnings about the dangers of anti-Semitism, gave an urgency to his search for a solution to the Jewish question. Some of his critics charged that he was obsessed by the Zionist program, but his forebodings about the fate of Europe's Jews would prove tragically prophetic.

The United States from Civil War to National Unity

The struggle for national identity in the nineteenth century was by no means limited to Europe, and similar developments were occurring as far away as China and Japan. Perhaps the closest parallels were to be found in the newly formed United States, for the American government had been set up by people who considered themselves European in culture and values and who were inspired by the same Enlightenment principles that nourished the French Revolution.

Even after the American union had adopted its constitution in 1787, the United States continued to wrestle with ideological issues concerning the nature of its democracy. Indeed, the struggle between the Federalists, who represented the conservative northern landowners and the commercial classes, and the southern landowner Democratic-Republicans, who championed the small yeoman farmers of the young republic, was not unlike the European conflict between liberalism and conservatism. The passage of the Bill of Rights in 1791 and the subsequent election of Thomas Jefferson (1801–1809) as president signaled the rejection of a powerful central government dominated by privilege and wealth, a tendency later confirmed in the democratic principles of Andrew Jackson (1829–1837).

The advance of democratic attitudes in the United States went hand and hand with its territorial expansion. In less than half a century huge tracts of land, each larger than most European countries, were added to the United States. The Louisiana Purchase in 1803, the settlement of the old northwestern territories, and the conquest of Texas and California in the Mexican-American War, all fulfilled what Americans came to call their "manifest destiny," an attitude first expressed by the Russians in their expansion across Siberia. As more settlers pushed westward into the frontier territories, the pioneer values of hard work, individual worth, and self-reliance were deemed more valuable than birth and status. The seemingly unlimited American continent, with its fertile farmland and natural resources, gave Americans self-assurance and unbridled optimism.

Yet the American experience was not without serious problems. Sectional disputes, particularly between the agricultural south and the industrializing north, threatened to disrupt the republic. By the 1850s the institution of slavery, on which the southern economy depended, had become a deeply divisive issue. The test of nationhood came in the bitter civil war between 1861 and 1865, waged by Abraham Lincoln (1861–1865) to preserve national unity just when Cavour had forged an Italian state and Bismarck was striving to create a united Germany. The defeat of the secessionist Confederacy not only ended slavery in the United States long after it had been abolished in most other places in the Western world but also preserved the American union.

In the decades following the civil war, the United States entered a period of unrestrained economic development and industrialization. By the end of the century almost 200,000 miles of railroads crisscrossed the continent, and American mills produced a third of the world's steel. The population of the nation, swelled by almost 30 million immigrants from Europe and Asia between 1860 and 1914, settled hundreds of millions of acres of land in the west and swarmed into the burgeoning cities. On the eve of World War I almost half of the nation's 100 million people lived in urban centers. The rapid transformation of the American continent from a frontier society to an industrial giant, and the resulting leap in America's status to global power, was to have profound consequences for the world.

In the second half of the nineteenth century European history was largely shaped by triumphant nationalism, which underwent a profound transformation. In midcentury a proponent of nationalism such as Giuseppe Mazzini saw no contradictions between his demands for Italian national liberation and the aspirations of other nationalities. Indeed, Mazzini had cast his nationalist ideas in broad international terms, envisioning an interdependent Europe in which free, equal, self-governing peoples cooperated in a spirit of harmony. Mazzini, who died in 1872, lived to see nationalism triumphant in Italy and Germany, yet by the end of the century he would hardly have recognized the concept as the same idealistic doctrine he had once preached.

Nation building had been a complex interaction in which patriotism and middle-class liberalism had first joined forces against conservatism. Ironically, however, success subverted nationalist movements, for as military, industrial, and conservative aristocratic elites embraced nationalism, many liberals subsumed or abandoned their political values to the more immediate goal of unification. Once national unity was achieved under the leadership of men such as Bismarck and Cavour, the Mazzinian vision of a new European civilization nurtured by a spirit of freedom and equality gave way to an aggressive chauvinism that perceived history as the struggle between nations for power and dominance. Bitter national rivalries resulting from the wars of unification gave concrete form to the larger political and intellectual changes taking place in Europe. The nationalists of the postunification period absorbed and twisted the theories spawned by the Darwinian revolution in science, substituting the doctrine of supremacy for belief in equality, rejecting cooperation in favor of competition, and preaching imperialist expansion instead of self-determination. By the end of the century nationalism, which once had promised a new age of peace and security for Europe, pointed to an unstable and dangerous future.

Suggestions for Further Reading

Binkley, R. C. *Realism and Nationalism, 1852–1871*. New York: Harper, 1935.

Crankshaw, E. *Bismarck*. New York: Macmillan, 1981.

Emmons, T. *The Russian Landed Gentry and the Peasant Emancipation of 1861*. Cambridge: Cambridge University Press, 1968.

Florinsky, M. T. *Russia: A History and an Interpretation*. New York: Macmillan, 1953.

Griffith, G. O. *Mazzini: Prophet of Modern Europe*. London: Hodder & Stoughton, 1932.

Hamerow, T. S. *The Social Foundation of German Unification, 1858–1871*. 2 vols. Princeton, N.J.: Princeton University Press, 1969.

Hertzberg, A., ed. *The Zionist Idea*. Garden City, N.Y.: Doubleday, 1956.

Kohn, H. *The Idea of Nationalism*. New York: Macmillan, 1944.

Mack Smith, D. *Cavour*. London: Weidenfeld & Nicolson, 1985.

———. *Garibaldi*. London: Hutchinson, 1957.

Mosse, W. E. *Alexander II and the Modernization of Russia*. London: English Universities Press, 1958.

Pflanze, O. *Bismarck and the Development of Germany*. Princeton, N.J.: Princeton University Press, 1963.

Schorske, C. E. *Fin-de-Siècle Vienna*. New York: Knopf, 1979.

Seton-Watson, H. *The Decline of Imperial Russia, 1855–1914*. New York: Praeger, 1952.

Shaw, S. J., and Shaw, E. K. *History of the Ottoman Empire and Modern Turkey*. 2 vols. Cambridge: Cambridge University Press, 1977.

Stavrianos, L. S. *The Balkans, 1815–1914*. New York: Holt, Rinehart, & Winston, 1963.

Taylor, A. J. P. *Bismarck: The Man and the Statesman*. New York: Knopf, 1955.

———. *The Habsburg Monarchy, 1809–1918*. New York: Harper & Row, 1965.

———. *The Struggle for Mastery in Europe, 1848–1918*. Oxford: Clarendon Press, 1960.

Thompson, J. M. *Louis Napoleon and the Second Empire*. New York: Norton, 1967.

Williams, R. L. *Gaslight and Shadow: The World of Napoleon III*. New York: Macmillan, 1957.

Woolf, S. *A History of Italy, 1700–1860*. London: Methuen, 1979.

Wright, G. *France in Modern Times*. Chicago: Rand McNally, 1960.

CHAPTER · 32

Industrial Society and the Liberal Order

In the years from 1871 to 1900 Europe achieved a higher level of material well-being than any previous civilization. Its population was healthier, more nutritiously fed, better educated, and longer-lived, and it enjoyed more physical comforts than any other people in history. Europeans of this generation made remarkable progress in understanding and controlling the physical world. By the end of the century they moved themselves and the products of their industrial culture efficiently not only by steam but by the internal combustion engine; they turned machines with steam turbines and electrical energy, communicated rapidly around the globe with the telegraph, underwater cable, and telephone, and illuminated the darkness with the light bulb.

These astonishing advancements in science and technology, together with unprecedented prosperity, determined how the post-1871 generation thought about itself. Most Europeans looked at the world with a faith in the limitless capacity of reason to solve problems. "Progress," inexorable and continuous, was their religion. Believing

The British naturalist Charles Darwin revolutionized science with his theory of evolution. [National Portrait Gallery]

that they were moving steadily toward an ideal future, Europeans were self-assured about the achievements and superiority of their civilization.

The materialist culture of the era reflected the fact that the middle class had become an influential elite in European life. Liberal doctrines shaped the governments of most Western nations, while entrepreneurs and industrialists extolled unregulated, growth-driven capitalism. As the middle class achieved status and political power, bourgeois notions of order and respectability defined public attitudes toward family, sexuality, the roles of men and women, and social behavior. Middle-class values also set standards of style and comfort as well as artistic taste.

Still, the age was by no means as well ordered as many contemporaries believed. Industrial capitalism spawned unanticipated problems. Beneath the surface of middle-class prosperity lay widespread poverty and dehumanizing drudgery in the workplace, loudly denounced by social critics. Some demanded social and political reforms and a wider suffrage. As the right to vote spread, radical opponents of liberalism, inspired by the Marxist critique of capitalism, joined industrial workers in forming labor unions and socialist parties in an effort to wrench power from the bourgeoisie.

The social implications of the industrial system were enormous. By the end of the century factories had drawn millions of farmers from the countryside and had transformed a once rural and agricultural Europe into a predominantly urban civilization with pressing problems of public welfare. Higher factory wages had also attracted women to the workplace in large numbers, altering the pattern of family life, modifying sexual behavior, and challenging traditional models of male-female relationships.

Industrial Development and Monopoly Capitalism

In the last third of the nineteenth century, Europe's economy was transformed in three important ways: the Industrial Revolution spread more widely to other European nations, new sources of energy and products were developed, and business elites evolved new forms of control over industry and capital. These trends brought the earlier industrialization process to a climax and shaped Western economic life for generations.

The Second Industrial Revolution

The first phase of industrialization led by Great Britain had been marked by the application of steam power in the manufacturing of two important commodities—iron and textiles. Subsequent changes in science and technology led to a "second industrial revolution." Although steam remained the major source of industrial energy until 1914, electric power and internal combustion engines fueled by petroleum products increasingly replaced steam-driven machinery. The new energy sources led to the development of more sophisticated machines that greatly expanded efficiency and output and lowered production costs.

During the second industrial revolution, steel replaced iron as the basic metal and the chemical industry grew rapidly. Both developments resulted from the application of scientific discoveries to industry. Through the process developed by Henry Bessemer (1830–1898) at midcentury, steel could now be manufactured in large quantities. The greater strength and flexibility of steel had a profound impact on construction, manufacturing, and transportation. As railroad networks spread across the European and American continents, the production of locomotive engines, cars, and tracks became a major impetus to industry and capital investment and opened significant new markets. In Europe the rail network doubled between 1890 and 1914. In addition, methods for the mass production of chemical substances revolutionized industry by allowing for the creation of such new products as fertilizers, dyes, explosives, plastics, synthetic fabrics, and medicines such as aspirin.

Germany, France, Italy, Russia, the United States, and Japan became industrial nations. Coal and steel provided useful indices of the growth of production during the second industrial revolution. Between 1870 and 1913 world output of coal had risen from 230 million to more than 1.5 billion metric tons, while steel production rose from 550,000 to more than 80 million tons. By 1914 the "inner zone" of Britain, Germany, and France produced 80 percent of Europe's coal, steel, and machinery and 70 percent of its manufactured products. Germany soon emerged as Europe's industrial giant and rapidly outdistanced Britain. By 1900 German steel production had outpaced Britain's, and on the eve of World War I it was more than double that of Britain and second only to the United States, which manufactured almost twice as much as Germany. Germany also led the field in the cast-iron and chemical industries. In the four decades after 1870 Britain's annual growth rate was 2.2 percent, compared to 2.9 percent for Germany and 4.3 percent for the United States.

The sharp increase in productivity that characterized the post-1870 period was made possible not only by new energy sources and the spread of industrialism but also by more efficient machines that reoriented production techniques toward standardized parts and specialized tasks. Pioneered by the American automobile manufacturer Henry Ford (1863–1947), the division of labor on assembly lines made cheaper, mass-produced consumer goods available on a wide scale. Although these trends contributed

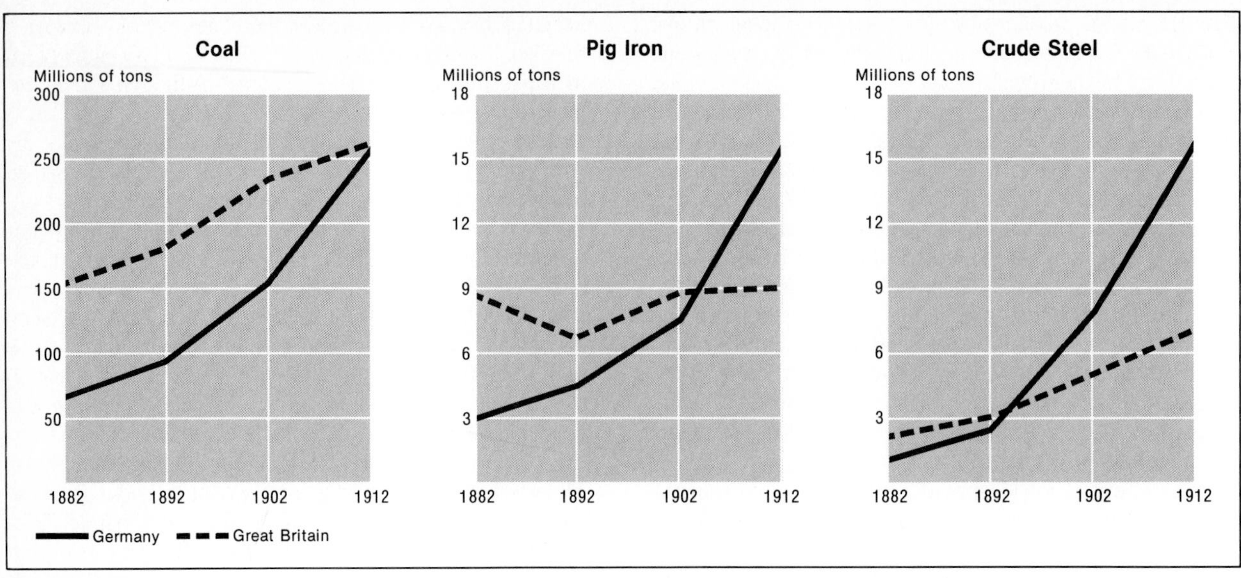

32.1 German and British Industrial Production, 1882–1912

to the material improvement of daily life, they also resulted in overproduction, the further dehumanization of the work process, and a decline in the quality of many products.

The Rise of Big Business

The second industrial revolution bore out Karl Marx's prediction of a trend toward the concentration of wealth in fewer hands. The large numbers of small factories and businesses characteristic of early industrialization gave way to fewer, larger concerns. Business legislation encouraged the trend by extending the concept of "limited liability," which insured the personal assets of investors against business losses. The pattern was not, however, due simply to competition such as took place in retail sales, where department stores forced many independent shopkeepers out of business by buying in large quantities and selling at lower prices. As the cost of such large-scale operations as steel foundries and chemical refineries increased, entrepreneurs required enormous capital, which smaller producers could not afford. Partly for this reason, but largely because competition drove down the margin of profit, investors created monopolies.

Entrepreneurs often operated through a process known as "horizontal integration," whereby they achieved control over a sector of industry or business such as steel, coal, or oil. Such huge combinations—called amalgamations in

The giant Krupp manufacturing complex at Essen, Germany (1912), reflected both the new era of early-twentieth-century industrialization and the industrial power of Germany. [Brown Brothers]

Britain, cartels in Germany, and trusts in the United States—dominated industry by the end of the century because they absorbed or drove out competitors and could limit production, fix prices, divide markets, and control labor. By means of "vertical integration," steel manufacturers could buy up coal and iron mines, chemical plants, blast furnaces, and rail companies to ensure manufacturer control over the entire industrial process.

Unregulated, monopoly capitalism had long-range implications. Investment banking grew in importance, especially with the adoption of the international gold standard for all major currencies. John Pierpont Morgan (1837–1913), the famous American banker, financed governments as well as railroads and steel companies through his firms in New York and London. Industrial monopolies were the work of "captains of industry" such as Andrew Carnegie (1835–1919), who controlled the United States Steel Corporation, and John D. Rockefeller (1839–1937), owner of the Standard Oil trust, or Alfred Krupp (1812–1887) and August Thyssen (1842–1926) in Germany. Such men were ruthless in their pursuit of profit and accumulated vast fortunes that enabled them to wield unprecedented economic and political power. The social ramifications of the second industrial revolution were far-reaching, especially as the emergence of the private-sector bureaucracy enlarged the white-collar class.

The Social Hierarchy

The political and economic changes that transformed Europe in the nineteenth century profoundly affected society. Despite unprecedented material progress, social and economic differences remained sharp, and the quality of life varied greatly between classes.

The Aristocracy: Adjustment and Change

The aristocracy had been the dominant elite before 1789. Most nobles, whose wealth and status had been determined by land ownership, failed to make the transition to modern capitalist agriculture or industrialization. Although land continued to be important, the real wealth of the aristocracy declined along with their income and access to liquid capital. In countries that remained predominantly agricultural, competition from cheaper overseas grain further reduced farm income. Yet in Britain the aristocracy remained stable well into the nineteenth century. The declining influence of the aristocracy appeared sharper than it actually was because of the rapid rise of the middle class. Liberal constitutions gave the bourgeoisie political power, but aristocrats dominated the upper chambers in parliaments. While the spread of civil service examinations and higher education opened administrative positions to the middle classes, there was little competition with the aristocracy for such positions. Ancient lineage and access to royal courts sustained the status of nobles, who remained the point of reference in matters of social prestige and style.

After 1870 the line separating the aristocracy and the upper middle class began to blur, as it had in the sixteenth and seventeenth centuries, as industrial wealth and noble titles sometimes came together through mutually advantageous marriages. Businessmen with surplus capital often bought sumptuous estates as symbols of their rising status. Increasingly, the upper levels of the industrial class copied the living standards of the aristocracy.

The Growth of the Middle Classes

While the aristocracy underwent adjustment in the late nineteenth century, the middle classes enjoyed expansion, though not uniformly. Grouping economic interests and social strata so diverse that they were often mutually antagonistic, the middle classes included wealthy industrialists and bankers as well as shopowners and white-collar workers. In industrialized countries the middle classes represented perhaps one-fifth of the inhabitants, although the powerful industrial and banking families formed a very small percentage of the general population. This elite reaped great benefits from expanded industrial production, earning a third of all national income. Consisting of no more than several hundred families in any given country, this group tended to merge with the old aristocracy, aping their manners and elitist attitudes.

Most middle-class Europeans were members of less wealthy and powerful subgroups: the middle middle class of small entrepreneurs, professional experts, and managers or the lower middle class of shopkeepers and white-collar workers. The ranks of the middle range swelled after 1870 with scientists, engineers, lawyers, and accountants—whose occupations grew more professional—as well as with corporate managers and bureaucrats.

The number of shopkeepers and small business owners grew along with teachers, nurses, and other salaried, nonpropertied members of the lower middle class. The most dramatic increase, however, was among the white-collar employees—clerks, salespeople, secretaries, and low-ranking bureaucrats, most of whom came from the ranks of the working class. White-collar wages were sometimes less than those of skilled workers, but the status of carrying a briefcase, wearing a tie, or having uncallused hands was often seen as compensation for low salaries. The lower middle class expanded rapidly between 1870 and 1900, doubling in Britain to 20 percent of the population.

Although middle- and lower-middle-class groups did not control great wealth, they tended to lead comfortable lives that reflected the values and aspirations of the upper-class bourgeoisie. Yet the status of most of the middle class was precarious in comparison to other groups. Easy social mobility encouraged the lower ranks to strive for greater status and income, but tensions were equally strong. Economic pressure from large industries and corporations threatened small businessmen and shopkeepers, while people living on fixed incomes from savings and pensions feared that business cycles and recessions could suddenly wipe them out. For white-collar employees, who made every effort to distance themselves from the workers, the greatest fear was that economic adversity would force them back to their working-class origins.

This photograph of an upper-middle-class English family at tea reveals the Victorian ideal of social and domestic propriety. [Culver Pictures]

The Decline of the Working Class

Most people—four-fifths of them—lived by physical labor. Industrialization made Europe a predominantly urban civilization, so by the end of the nineteenth century agricultural workers were a distinct minority in most western and central European countries. The agricultural crisis that began in 1873 as a result of huge imports of wheat from the United States reduced the price of European grains. Landowners cut wages and pushed peasants, many of whom already lived close to subsistence, into more extreme poverty. The decline in agricultural earnings, compounded by natural disasters in the 1870s and 1880s, also struck peasant owners, whose land decreased in value.

Behind the exuberant prosperity of Victorian London lay the poverty of much of Britain's working class. This photograph shows an alley in a working-class section of the city. [Snark/Art Resource]

The rural standard of living improved after 1890 with changes in crops and cultivation methods, as well as the introduction of protective tariffs, but agricultural wages remained less than half the average of factory rates.

In industrialized countries the urban working class represented the largest single social stratum and was even more diverse in composition than the middle classes. Among skilled workers, industrialization brought stressful changes as artisans gave way to factory workers who required less skill. Yet there was also a growing need for new kinds of skilled jobs, including metalworkers, machine tool makers, and locomotive engineers. Skilled workers, whose wages were at least twice as high as those of unskilled laborers, saw themselves as an elite with middle-class pretensions. Semiskilled and unskilled workers vastly outnumbered the artisans and the skilled elite. The semiskilled, such as masons, carpenters, plumbers, and some factory workers, earned less money, while the unskilled workers, among whom the largest number were domestic servants, were the lowest paid.

Between the years 1873 and 1896 the West experienced a series of economic crises known collectively as the Long Depression. Primarily an agricultural phenomenon sparked by competition from North American farms, the Long Depression nevertheless affected industry and trade. Rising costs, increased competition, and shrinking markets reduced profits and triggered stock and bank panics. Periods of high unemployment resulted. In Britain, for example, unemployment among unionized workers rose from 1 percent in 1872 to 11 percent in 1879, from 2 percent in 1882 to 10 percent in 1886, and again from 2 percent in 1890 to 7.5 percent in 1893. Such sharp cycles of unemployment not only caused severe hardships among working-class families but also fanned enthusiasm for militant labor unions. Yet even though fluctuations in wages accompanied the crises, during the three decades after 1870 real wages rose by about 37 percent, increasing by a third in France and Germany and by more than half in Britain.

Urban working-class diets improved and became more varied as food prices declined and purchasing power increased, and health conditions in the cities improved with the development of sewage systems, clean water supplies, and the scientific control of disease. Industrial productivity reduced the cost of clothing, so workers were better dressed. The expansion of urban construction made less cramped housing available, and the development of inexpensive railway, subway, and tram services gave workers access to better housing in the suburbs, although they still had to devote large portions of their budgets to rent.

Despite advances in the standard of life for urban workers, production outpaced wages. Although working-class purchasing power expanded and living standards improved for all social groups, the gap between workers and the middle classes widened.

THE URBAN LANDSCAPE

The urbanization of European society—the movement of people from country to city, the growth in the number of urban centers, and the dense concentration of huge populations in them—continued well beyond 1900. Between 1871 and 1911 England's urban population rose from 62 to 78 percent of the whole and France's from 33 to 44 percent. In Germany, which was rapidly industrializing, the increase was spectacular—from 36 to 60 percent. Moreover, 90 percent of Germany's population growth in the same period was in cities. The culture of western Europe had become predominantly urban.

Improved transportation, particularly the railroad, spurred urban growth, and most important cities became hubs of rail lines or port facilities, and frequently both. In large cities the basic infrastructure—drainage systems, water supply, police and fire protection—had already been established by midcentury, and these services were expanded.

Baron Haussmann's redevelopment of Paris during the Second Empire provided the model for a similar project in Vienna, whose Ringstrasse was inspired by Haussmann's grand boulevards. London and Berlin permitted the reconstruction of inner-city zones in the 1870s, when town planning revived. By the end of the nineteenth century

POPULATION OF THE MAJOR CITIES
OF CONTINENTAL EUROPE AROUND 1910

City	Population	City	Population
Paris	2,888,000	Turin	428,000
Berlin	2,071,000	Rotterdam	418,000
Vienna	2,031,000	Frankfurt	415,000
St. Petersburg	1,908,000	Lodz	394,000
Moscow	1,481,000	Düsseldorf	359,000
Hamburg	931,000	Lisbon	356,000
Budapest	880,000	Stockholm	347,000
Warsaw	781,000	Palermo	342,000
Naples	723,000	Nuremberg	333,000
Milan	599,000	Riga	318,000
Madrid	598,000	Charlottenberg	306,000
Munich	596,000	Antwerp	302,000
Leipzig	590,000	Hanover	302,000
Barcelona	587,000	Bucharest	295,000
Amsterdam	568,000	Essen	295,000
Copenhagen	559,000	Chemnitz	288,000
Marseilles	551,000	Stuttgart	286,000
Dresden	548,000	Magdeburg	280,000
Rome	539,000	Genoa	272,000
Lyons	524,000	The Hague	270,000
Cologne	517,000	Bordeaux	262,000
Breslau (Wroclaw)	512,000	Oslo	247,000
Odessa	479,000	Bremen	247,000
Kiev	469,000		

advances in engineering, building materials, and construction techniques began to change the face of cities. Reinforced concrete and steel permitted multistory office and apartment buildings, and both the American skyscraper and the metal tower designed by French engineer Gustav Eiffel in the 1890s became symbols of the new, aggressive city. Sewers, sidewalks, and electric lights made urban centers more pleasant places to live and work.

France led the way with other distinctive features of the modern city. Using wrought iron and steel, Parisian developers built large, glass-covered galleries in which independent shops and cafés were situated, and by the 1880s Moscow had followed the example. The first major department store was the Bon Marché in Paris. By buying in quantity, department stores could sell a wide range of mass-made goods inexpensively, thus making the products of industrial civilization available to workers and the lower middle class.

Working-class housing, which in the early industrial revolution had consisted of squalid, crammed tenements, improved considerably in this period as a result of health and welfare legislation. The French pioneered middle-class apartment complexes, New York exploited that concept, and British cities added the notion of garden apartments. As urban transportation systems grew, more people escaped urban living for tranquil suburbs, and the city became the metropolis.

Everywhere cities adopted from each other, equipping themselves with London-style parks and suburbs, Paris-style boulevards and cafés, and New York–style office blocks and gridded street plans. All of them acquired grand public buildings and cultural centers such as opera houses, concert halls, museums, and public libraries, and all were afflicted with pollution, noise, and overcrowding. By the end of the century the urban landscape had assumed its modern appearance.

Sexuality, Women, and the Family

The Industrial Revolution and the consequent movement of populations from the country to the cities had significant repercussions on the relationship between men and women, as well as on the family. Urban life tended to erode moral codes and traditional forms of courtship and marriage that were more easily enforced in small villages. At the same time, the employment opportunities and higher wage scales that drew workers to the factories often enabled young men and women to escape family supervision. In the period before 1850 the result had been a dramatic increase in premarital sex (among partners who intended to marry), illegitimate births, and common-law marriages, but this pattern diminished by the last third of the century.

The spread of birth control information contributed to the decline of the birthrate. The French took the lead in contraception, and such traditional methods as the sponge, sheepskin condoms, and the vinegar douche were widely used among the upper classes. In Britain laws prohibited the publication or distribution of contraceptive information until Annie Besant, a socialist, and Charles Bradlaugh, a radical, won a celebrated court case in 1878. Between 1880 and 1900 they distributed more than a million copies of birth control pamphlets that advocated the use of the sponge, syringing with zinc or alum solutions, cervical caps, and rubber condoms. Although Besant aimed her information at the poor, it was the middle class that first made widespread use of these methods, and only by the end of the century did they spread among urban workers. Moreover, middle-class men could more easily afford recourse to brothels, where they found women who were often driven to prostitution by unemployment and poverty.

Industrialization brought mixed results. During the nineteenth century roughly two-thirds of all single women and more than a quarter of married women worked. Life was especially difficult for working women, for most also had to function as mothers and wives. Married generally in their early and mid-twenties after experiencing the relative independence derived from their jobs, working women subordinated themselves to their husbands. The men ate better food, dressed better, went out without their families in the evenings, and often abused their children and wives. Yet despite the grueling physical and psychological pressures, working mothers managed to keep the basic family structure intact.

The principal female employment categories—domestic service, textile work, and garment making—remained fairly constant into the early twentieth century, but the female work force consisted increasingly of single women; by 1911 only 9.6 percent of married women were employed. The notion that women should "retire" when they married was a product of urban industrial culture. In the cities domestic service employed more women than any other activity in the nineteenth century. Because it promoted such virtues as hard work, cleanliness, and obedience, domestic service was regarded as ideal training for future wives of the working class.

Bourgeois Respectability

The expanding demand for domestic servants reflected both the growing prosperity of the middle class and the new ideal of womanhood that it cultivated. The separation between the male sphere of work and business and the female sphere of home and family reached its most fully developed form among the middle class. Bourgeois respectability required that the home be comfortable, well

The Cult of Domesticity

The development of the cult of domesticity, which limited women largely to home maintenance and child rearing, contributed greatly to the social construction of gender roles. In this nineteenth-century handbook for housewives, Mrs. Isabella Beeton explains the principles of household management.

Of all those acquirements, which more particularly belong to the feminine character, there are none which take a higher rank, in our estimation, than such as enter into a knowledge of household duties. . . .

Early rising is one of the most essential qualities which enter into good household management, as it is not only the parent of health, but of innumerable other advantages. Indeed, when a mistress is an early riser, it is almost certain that her house will be orderly and well-managed. . . .

Cleanliness is indispensable to health, and must be studied both in regard to the person and the house, and all that it contains. Cold or tepid baths should be employed every morning, unless, on account of illness or other circumstances, they should be deemed objectionable. . . .

Frugality and economy are home virtues, without which no household can prosper. . . . The necessity of practising economy should be evident to every one. . . .

The treatment of servants is of the highest possible moment, as well to the mistress as to the domestics themselves. On the head of the house the latter will naturally fix their attention; and if they perceive that the mistress' conduct is regulated by high and correct principles, they will not fail to respect her.

After this general superintendence of her servants, the mistress, if the mother of a young family, may devote herself to the instruction of some of its younger members, or to the examination of the state of their wardrobe, leaving the latter portion of the morning for reading, or for some amusing recreation.

Source: I. Beeton, *Book of Household Management* (London: Beeton, 1861), pp. 2–9 passim.

furnished, and characterized by an atmosphere of warmth and safety from the outside world. Middle-class sensibilities idealized women as gentle and virtuous creatures devoted to bearing and raising children and looking after their husbands. The Victorians evolved a "cult of domesticity" for women that stressed duty, submissiveness, and devotion. A close and emotionally intimate family life was extolled as the social bedrock of the age.

The middle-class family concentrated legal power in the hands of the husband and father. Until midcentury contracts were often used in upper-class families to safeguard the property rights of daughters about to be married, for a husband ordinarily gained control of a wife's property. Most states in America passed married women's property acts, as did Britain in 1882, but these were designed largely to enable fathers who had no sons to pass inheritances to their daughters. Widows almost always had to defer to the relatives of their deceased husbands regarding such matters as their children's education and upbringing. Similarly, divorce was still generally obtainable only by women who could prove that their husbands were impotent or unfit fathers; in most countries husbands could gain a divorce on the grounds of adultery, but women could not. Educational patterns perpetuated the inferior status of women. While middle-class boys usually went to school to receive classical education or professional training in law, medicine, or accounting, girls stayed home to learn painting, needlework, and religion.

Sexual Attitudes

The ideology of bourgeois respectability had a powerful impact on attitudes toward sexuality, though not on its practice. Sexual pleasure was regarded as a male preserve. The assumption that women were not supposed to enjoy sex was a powerful form of male dominance. Public attitudes toward sexuality encouraged a double standard according to which men might, with proper discretion, visit brothels and maintain mistresses to fulfill their "natural" needs. Victorian moral strictures were also imposed on children, whose clothing and physical activities were regulated to repress masturbation and sensations that might lead to sexual arousal. Menstruation—known as "the curse"—was little discussed, and pubescence was regarded as a profoundly disturbing and disagreeable experience.

Diaries and letters, the proliferation of sex manuals and pornography, and the literature of the period demonstrate that despite the strictures fostered by middle-class sexual codes, men and women continued to enjoy sex. The sensational trial and imprisonment in 1895 of the writer Oscar Wilde (1854–1900) because of his love affair with Lord Alfred Douglas made Victorians uncomfortably aware of other sexual orientations. Wilde's account of this experience, *The Ballad of Reading Gaol* (1898), had to be published anonymously, and his "open letter" to Douglas, *De profundis* (1905), did not appear until after his death. The tension created by the dissonance between moral theory and behavior produced a pyschological anxiety that pervaded the late Victorian age.

Liberalism and the Political Order

The middle class had been a driving force behind the political upheavals that stretched from the American Revolution in 1776 to the revolutions of 1848. They had reacted strongly against the excesses of the French Revolution, but their demands for a share in political power, expressed through the doctrine of liberalism, had made them the foe of absolutism and aristocracy. After 1815 the bourgeoisie stood in sharp opposition to the conservative political principles of the Restoration. In France they brought the "bourgeois king" Louis-Philippe to power in 1830, while in England, where the 1832 Reform Bill had enfranchised the industrialists, the propertied classes enjoyed significant political influence. In 1848 and 1849 they came close to establishing constitutional regimes in central and eastern Europe.

The political triumph of the middle classes came after 1850, when they joined forces with elements of the aristocracy in supporting unification movements in Germany and Italy and Napoleon III in France. Thereafter, as the middle classes gained power, they reversed their historical role—whereas once they had acted as a powerful force for change, now they emerged as the champions of order. Liberalism, the doctrine that expressed middle-class aspirations, changed as well.

Over the course of the nineteenth century liberalism had proved to be a flexible doctrine capable of encompassing a wide range of objectives, from the Enlightenment belief in individual rights to romanticism, and from nationalism to Bismarck's *Realpolitik*. After 1870 the industrial and financial bourgeoisie began to appropriate political liberalism as their special preserve, making it the philosophy of the capitalist establishment.

Though liberalism underwent a transformation after 1870, it continued to stand for the basic premise that government should be based on a written constitution—except in Britain, where an unwritten agreement prevailed—with the middle classes and aristocracy represented in parliamentary institutions elected by limited male suffrage. Liberal parliamentary systems reflected a number of trends: a widening suffrage that eventually encompassed most of the working classes, the appearance of modern political parties representing a range of class and special interests, free elementary education, compulsory military service, the secularization of national culture, and the growing role of the state in social legislation and public policy. Individual countries produced variations in this pattern, but as the century drew to a close, liberalism had permeated the political culture of western Europe almost everywhere. By 1900 all but one of the great European states were part of the "liberal" order; Russia alone stood outside the system.

Britain in the Victorian Age

No nation more completely represented the liberal order than Britain, and no European monarch symbolized that ideal more completely than Queen Victoria (1837–1901). She inherited the throne from her uncle, William IV, at the age of 18. In 1840 she married a German cousin, Prince Albert of Saxe-Coburg-Gotha, who had a formative influence on her character. She learned to express her wishes and opinions forcibly to her ministers and had a strong though discreet influence on politics. After Albert's death in 1861, Victoria lapsed into seclusion as the "widow of Windsor." Her 64-year reign as queen (she was also crowned empress of India in 1876), together with the fact that she was the grandmother of both Kaiser William II of Germany and Tsar Nicholas II of Russia, made Victoria the venerable matriarch of Europe's royalty. But as the symbol of Britain's political stability and industrial power, she was no glittering incarnation of imperial splendor—when she reappeared in public in the 1880s, it was as a matronly icon of bourgeois virtue, dressed in black and wide in girth.

Midway through Victoria's reign, British politics underwent a crucial transformation that resulted in the emergence of new leaders at the head of modernized political parties. Under William Gladstone (1809–1898), the old

Queen Victoria and her husband, Prince Albert, were the ideal royal couple, in love with each other and serious about their duties. [Victoria and Albert Museum, London]

Whig-radical coalition evolved into the Liberal party. An eloquent orator, Gladstone, the pious son of a merchant, was trained as a classical scholar before entering politics. As chancellor of the exchequer, he had pushed for a policy of free trade as well as reforms that included a postal savings and insurance system widely used by workers and a reduction in taxes. In 1864, when only one adult male out of six had the right to vote, Gladstone pressed for an extension of the franchise, which had not changed since 1832.

At this time Benjamin Disraeli (1804–1881) was molding the aristocratic, agrarian-based Tories into the new Conservative party. More flamboyant than Gladstone, the brilliant Disraeli was the descendant of Spanish Jews and the author of political novels. He was convinced that the Conservatives needed to broaden their support by appealing to the middle classes. After a successful record of leadership in the House of Commons, he overcame the suspicion of his colleagues, who regarded him as opportunistic, and eventually won the support of Queen Victoria, who preferred the Conservatives to the Liberals.

Gladstone and Disraeli made possible the passage of the Reform Act of 1867. After Gladstone had tried without success to secure passage of a similar bill in 1866, Disraeli—who saw an opportunity for the Conservatives to reap the political credit—maneuvered the measure through the House of Commons. By giving the vote to all middle-class males and the highest-paid urban workers, the second Reform Act doubled the size of the electorate by adding almost a million voters to the rolls.

From 1868 to 1914 the Liberal and Conservative parties alternated in power. First Disraeli and Gladstone, and then their successors, outdid each other in sponsoring political and social legislation. Competitive civil service examinations were introduced in 1870, the secret ballot a year later. After 1884, when Gladstone passed another reform bill that increased the electorate by the addition of 2 million agricultural laborers, Britain continued to evolve toward parliamentary democracy, at least for men.

Before the end of the century the great mass of British workers and farm laborers benefited from a range of reforms— largely modeled on similar legislation introduced in Germany by Bismarck—that included free elementary education; minimum-wage laws; accident, health, and unemployment insurance programs; old-age pensions; and a graduated income tax. Marxist socialism, which was gaining a foothold in less democratic Continental states, had little appeal in Britain. By the eve of World War I, England's upper bourgeoisie believed that their country offered compelling testimony of the wisdom of the alliance between political liberalism and industrial capitalism. Still, as late as 1892 a report found that almost a third of the inhabitants of London—Britain's largest city and the hub of the British empire—lived in poverty.

The Third Republic in France

For 70 years after 1870 France was governed by a republic born out of military defeat and civil war. The French surrender following the battle of Sedan had resulted in the overthrow of Napoleon III and the proclamation of a republic (see Chapter 31). The National Assembly chose the liberal royalist Adolphe Thiers (1797–1877) as president. Thiers negotiated the humiliating peace terms with Bismarck that ended the Franco-Prussian War.

In March 1871 the National Assembly moved the government to Versailles, the traditional seat of the French monarchy. There the liberal-monarchist majority further aroused the fury of the Parisians by canceling the debt

After toppling this column bearing a statue of Napoleon I in Paris, the communard rebels erected the red flag of revolution in its place. [Musée Carnavalet/Photographie Bulloz]

moratorium and the pay of the civilian National Guard, measures that had kept tens of thousands from starvation during the Prussian siege of the capital. Thiers then tried to confiscate the 200 cannon that had been cast by public subscription during the siege. Angry mobs dragged the cannon to safety and drove off government troops.

Civil war erupted. Extremists in Paris took control of the rebellion and established a "Commune," modeled on the revolutionary government of 1792. When the regular army broke through the city's defenses in May, the Communards executed hostages, including the archbishop of Paris, while the Assembly's soldiers summarily shot everyone found with weapons. By the time government troops had secured the city, as many as 20,000 Communards had been executed and twice that number were deported to penal islands. The repression of the Commune had been bloodier than any civil clash in modern French history. It left a permanent legacy of class bitterness that polarized French politics and intensified social division.

The Third Republic proved both politically unstable and unpopular. Although the monarchists had a majority in the National Assembly, they could not agree on a suitable candidate for king and continued the republic in effect by default. The constitution of 1875 created a democratic government in which the prime minister and his cabinet were fully responsible to Parliament, whose lower house, the Chamber of Deputies, was elected by universal male suffrage.

Unlike the British, the French failed to develop modern political parties until the end of the century. Poorly organized political groups were held together only by immediate concerns. Royalist sentiment, which remained strong, was the focus of opposition to the Third Republic, but the monarchists remained divided on whether to support the Bourbon, Orléanist, or Bonapartist claimant to the throne. Republican supporters were equally divided. Radical republicans, led by Georges Clemenceau (1841–1929), were anticlerical and anti-German. Moderate republicans were more willing to compromise on major issues. Together, the moderate royalists and the republicans represented the liberal tradition in French politics. The left, which took more than a decade to recover from the disaster of the Commune, was also split into factions. In Parliament, majorities were difficult to form and still more difficult to maintain. More than 50 coalition cabinets governed France during the first 40 years of the republic.

The republic was no friend of social revolution. Reform legislation was slow in coming, and it was 1910 before earlier work and health laws were complemented by accident and social insurance programs. Still, moderates established the supremacy of Parliament and a system of secular state education that slowly engendered republican values in the post-1870 generation.

The strange career of General Georges Boulanger (1837–1891) mirrored the discontent that beset the Third Republic. Originally a radical republican and protégé of Clemenceau, Boulanger became war minister in 1886. He was a popular figure who made a habit of riding a magnificent black horse through the streets of Paris. Chafing under the humiliation of defeat in the Franco-Prussian War, royalists and patriotic admirers saw him as a symbol of French glory. Boulanger lost his cabinet position in 1887 and was sent to the provinces, where he drummed up support for a new constitution and a more authoritarian regime. With the help of right-wing politicians, he planned a coup d'état in 1889 but lost his nerve at the last minute and fled to Brussels.

More serious in its repercussions was the dramatic Dreyfus affair. In 1894 Captain Alfred Dreyfus (1859–1935), a Jewish officer attached to the French General Staff, was court-martialed for treason on charges that he had supplied military secrets to the Germans. A military court ignored evidence that another officer had been the guilty party. This aroused the radical republicans, who believed the military had falsely condemned Dreyfus while protecting the real traitor. While Dreyfus languished in prison on Devil's Island, the notorious penal colony, Clemenceau and the novelist Émile Zola (1840–1902) took up his cause and accused the General Staff of harboring clerical, royalist, and anti-Semitic prejudices. In 1899 the army found Dreyfus guilty "with extenuating circumstances" and pardoned him, but his supporters continued to demand a full acquittal, which came only in 1906.

The episode widened the wedge that already separated radicals, socialists, and intellectuals from army leaders, monarchists, and the Catholic church. The crisis unleashed a wave of anti-Semitism that fueled right-wing forces. The Dreyfus case, like the Boulanger affair, revealed that the enemies of the government were strong. Yet the legacy of the French Revolution was equally powerful, and the Third Republic survived for another half century.

Germany Under the Reich

Liberalism in Germany was weaker than in Britain or France because it had been tied so closely to the triumph of Bismarck's unification program. Bismarck had been appointed minister of Prussia to overcome a deadlock between the king and the liberals in the Landtag, which he did by circumventing its control of the budget. In September 1866, however, after his stunning victory over the Austrians, the liberals and others sanctioned his violation of the Prussian constitution.

While Bismarck cowed the liberals, he also forged a powerful alliance between bourgeois industrialists and aristocratic landowners that enabled him to impose political unity on the German states. Prussia ran the federal structure of the German empire through its monarchy, bureaucracy, and army, and, with 236 of 397 seats in the lower house of parliament, the Reichstag, dominated the national assembly. Outwardly, the German parliament conformed to the liberal formula: the Reichstag was elected by universal male suffrage. The Reichstag approved laws and budgets, but it had no real authority over foreign affairs or the imperial ministers. The upper house, the Bundesrat, represented the 26 federated units of the empire and could initiate laws and block measures proposed by the Reichstag. The powers of the emperor were extensive, for he was commander in chief of the army and, in his role as king of Prussia, remained an absolute monarch. Moreover, the kaiser appointed the imperial chancellor, who was responsible to him alone.

Bismarck presided over the empire as chancellor for 19 years. Distainful of his critics, the "iron chancellor" rammed his programs through parliament with the support of the conservative landowners and the upper middle class. The interests of the industrialists and bankers were represented by the National Liberals, while the great landowners backed the Conservatives. The Progressives, who spoke for the more radical liberals who had initially opposed Bismarck; the Center party, which spoke for the Catholics; and the Social Democrats, representing the socialist party, were Bismarck's chief sources of opposition.

Bismarck's ruthless methods and high-handed policies were designed to forge a single nation out of the patchwork of states that made up the new empire. He tried to extinguish local loyalties and crush opposition to the central state.

The first target of this policy was the Catholic church, against which he unleashed the so-called *Kulturkampf*, or "battle for civilization"—a campaign to make loyalty to Germany supreme over devotion to the Catholic church. Although the *Kulturkampf* was an extreme example of a growing trend toward secularization all over Europe, Bismarck saw it essentially as a political issue. Germany was predominantly Protestant, but Catholics comprised a third of the population and were strong in Alsace-Lorraine. Bismarck clashed with the church when he sponsored laws that abolished religious orders, imposed state supervision over Catholic education, made civil marriage compulsory, and required government approval of ecclesiastical appointments. When he removed bishops and hundreds of

The headstrong Kaiser William II dismissed Bismarck in 1890 and assumed personal direction of German affairs. [Mansell Collection]

priests, Bismarck succeeded only in making political martyrs of them and found that German Catholics rallied to their church. In the next elections, the Catholic-oriented Center party nearly doubled its representation in the Reichstag. Always the realist, Bismarck eventually reached an accommodation with Pope Leo XIII (1878–1903).

Bismarck also dealt with what he considered the other major national problem, the threat of socialism. The formation of the Social Democratic party in 1875 led him to fear that the socialists would capture the loyalties of workers for the cause of revolution and internationalism. He persuaded the Reichstag to pass legislation restricting socialist activities. Denied an open forum, the socialists organized support underground and elected their candidates to the Reichstag in ever larger numbers. Faced with another political disaster, Bismarck switched his tactics in the 1880s by sponsoring social welfare programs designed to wean the workers away from the socialists while keeping the antisocialist laws intact. Bismarck's social security laws, the most advanced in Europe, provided workers with accident and health insurance and retirement benefits. After 1890 workers were given additional rights, including labor arbitration and better working conditions. These measures failed to reduce working-class support for the socialists, but they did demonstrate that organized political pressure could win substantial material benefits for workers without revolution. As a result, the Social Democratic party grew enormously in electoral strength and by 1912 was the largest party in the Reichstag. At the same time, however, it lost much of its revolutionary impetus.

Bismarck virtually ruled the German empire until 1890, when Kaiser William II (1888–1918) forced him to retire. As erratic as Bismarck was strong-willed, William had come to the throne when he was 29. Strict training had made him deeply attached to military discipline and the spirit of manly virtue that infused the aristocratic Prussian officer corps. Determined to rule Germany himself and unwilling to be dominated by Bismarck as his predecessors had been, William proclaimed, "There is only one master in the Reich, and that is I." Heaping honors on Bismarck, the kaiser retired the man who had created the German empire.

In assuming command of the Second Reich—German nationalists considered the medieval Holy Roman Empire to have been the first—William II now ruled the most powerful state in Europe. Its population was large and growing rapidly, and its modern industrial plant was outpacing other nations in the production of coal, steel, chemicals, and electrical energy. Spectacular economic growth combined with a system of higher education that stressed technical training and produced the most literate and scientifically advanced population in Europe. The German army was the most efficient military force in the world. Stridently nationalistic, the kaiser launched Germany on a new and dangerous course in world affairs.

The Liberal State in Italy

Britain and Germany offered examples of the liberal order at its extremes, one strong and stable, the other weak and shallowly rooted. Italian liberalism evolved between the two extremes. As in the case of Germany, Italian unification owed a great deal to the efforts of one man, Count Cavour. Unlike Bismarck, however, Cavour had been an admirer of British political traditions and was a moderate liberal by conviction.

Much as Prussia had done in Germany, Piedmont had essentially imposed its traditions and institutions on the Italian states along with unification. The king was commander in chief of the armed forces and had the authority to declare war and make treaties. He also appointed the prime minister, who was declared to be "responsible," although whether to the king or to parliament remained unstated. The Chamber of Deputies, or lower house of the Italian parliament, was elected on the basis of limited manhood suffrage, with only 2 percent of the population able to vote. The Chamber controlled budget appropriations and could initiate legislation. The Senate, or upper house, could veto measures passed in the Chamber, and its members, appointed by the king for life, tended to be conservatives, nobles, and public officials.

As in France, organized political parties did not emerge in Italy until after the turn of the century.* Instead, parliamentary deputies considered themselves members of either the right or the left. These were largely meaningless labels that had been used during the unification struggle to describe, respectively, the supporters of Cavour's program of constitutional monarchy and Mazzini's republican followers. After 1870 the terms denoted degrees of liberalism, although the differences in outlook were often more a matter of emphasis than substance. In the first years of the kingdom, when the Right was in power, the government pursued a fiscally conservative program of high taxation and low expenditure for social reform. When the Left came into power in 1876, it repealed some of the more onerous taxes, widened the suffrage, and instituted compulsory elementary education. Significant social and economic progress came slowly. The lack of clearly defined political parties and programs contributed to the practice of *trasformismo*, whereby prime ministers formed coalitions that changed constantly, depending on the specific issue and the patronage to be distributed.

The euphoria that had accompanied unification quickly faded as Italians faced the problems of nationhood. The annexation of Rome in 1870 produced deep hostility between the Catholic church and the new state that was to plague Italian politics for the next half century. Through the Law of Guarantees, parliament recognized papal sovereignty over Vatican City and offered financial compensation to the church. But Pius IX, who declared himself a "prisoner of the Vatican," would not compromise. He refused to recognize the kingdom and prohibited Italian Catholics from taking part in political life. The stalemate, known as the "Roman question," weakened the legitimacy of the new state in the eyes of Italy's overwhelmingly Catholic population.

Regional differences and local loyalties remained strong in Italy after unification. The gap between the industrial interests of the north and the depressed agricultural economy of the south widened after 1870, and illiteracy, disease, and poverty put pressure on a national debt already burdened by the costs of the wars of unification. Despite the reforms of the left after 1876, the ruling liberal elite remained unresponsive to the needs of the unenfranchised poor for many years. Unemployed migrant workers turned increasingly to brigandage in the south, while peasant anarchism was widespread in Sicily and central Italy. In the industrial centers of Milan and Turin, workers turned to socialism.

The last two decades of the century were a period of crisis that tested liberalism. From 1887 to 1891 and again from 1893 to 1896 leadership was in the hands of Francesco Crispi (1819–1901). Like Bismarck, Crispi was determined to stem the rise of socialism by suspending constitutional rights and smashing the Socialist party with massive arrests and police harassment. He was also anxious to make Italy a great power through military alliances and colonial conquest, but scandals and military defeat in Africa brought him down. Vigorous action against socialists and anarchists by Crispi's successors climaxed in the bloody suppression of labor demonstrations in 1898. The liberal state in Italy demonstrated its deep hostility to working-class movements.

The accession of Victor Emmanuel III (1900–1946) to the throne in 1900 brought Giovanni Giolitti (1842–1928) to the forefront of national politics. Giolitti served off and on as prime minister for most of the years before World War I. A shrewd politician, he toned down the level of confrontation with labor, coopted moderate socialists into the parliamentary system, and ended strikes through negotiation. Giolitti sought a reconciliation with the church, presided over the development of industry, and sponsored significant factory and social legislation. Finally, in 1911 Giolitti introduced near-universal manhood suffrage. The liberal state had begun its first tentative steps toward democratic reform when the First World War interrupted its progress.

Spain and the Smaller Powers

Instability and unrest, due largely to intrigues surrounding the succession to the throne, marked Spanish political life in the mid-nineteenth century. After a revolution unseated Queen Isabella II (1833–1868), a number of governments—first under the Cortes, then under a king imported from Italy, and finally as a republic—failed to find support and encouraged the church and the army to interfere in politics. Only when Alfonso XII (1874–1885) became king under a liberal constitution did a measure of stability return.

Thereafter, Spain struggled with the problems of social and economic modernization. Small areas of industry existed within an agrarian nation dominated by conservative landed interests. Anarchist and regionalist movements were strong, especially in the Basque region and Catalonia, while industrial growth in Barcelona prompted the rise of socialism. In 1890 universal male suffrage was in-

*The Italian Socialist party, founded in 1892, was the exception.

stituted, but the constant struggle between the Liberal and Conservative parties made social reform difficult.

Events in Spain's colonies added to the nation's problems. When a combination of repressive policies and ineffective administration led to the outbreak of guerrilla resistance in Cuba in 1898, the United States seized the opportunity to wage war with Spain over its possessions. The Spanish-American War resulted in the loss of Cuba and the cession of the Philippines, Puerto Rico, and Guam to the United States. By the end of the century intellectuals known as the Generation of 1898 were engaged in reassessing Spain's culture and turned increasingly to mystical nationalism in their search for national purpose.

Belgium, the Netherlands, Denmark, Sweden, and Norway followed a more stable pattern. All were constitutional monarchies that by 1914 had introduced universal manhood suffrage. Belgium was the most industrialized region on the Continent, but the other states underwent rapid economic development that enlarged the middle class.

By 1900 Britain, France, Italy, and Germany represented the range of liberal experience in the European political order. Almost without exception, other nations were variants on the liberal theme. The pace of social and political change differed, depending on the strength of liberalism and the ability of elites to maintain their authority against the emerging political challenge of the working class. As widening suffrage laws involved larger numbers in political life and as governments assumed a greater responsibility for social welfare, the state also claimed more loyalty from its citizens.

The Rise of Feminism

In 1879 the Norwegian dramatist Henrik Ibsen (1828–1906) published a play, titled *A Doll's House*, which exposed the frustration of a wife who felt trapped in what appeared to be a "perfect" marriage. The play ends with Nora, the wife, walking out of her husband's house and slamming the door. Nora became a symbol of female independence for women who sought to escape patriarchy and the middle-class family.

Modern feminism has its roots in the social transformations caused by industrialization as well as in the rebellion against the constraints imposed on women by the ideology of bourgeois respectability. The gulf separating lower-class from middle-class women widened, and not simply because of differences in income and status. Prosperity increased the leisure of middle-class females, who were relieved of household tasks by servants and labor-saving devices. Yet many bourgeois women resented their removal from the workplace, their inferior education, and their confinement in the home.

Social Activism and Women's Rights

To escape their constricted lives, bourgeois women sought outlets in such activities as philanthropy, church work, and temperance drives. British and American women were zealous proponents of abolitionism, although they were forced to take second place to males in abolitionist groups. In the second half of the nineteenth century they did volunteer duty in workhouses, hospitals, and urban tenements, thereby opening up new professions for women in nursing and teaching. After Jane Addams (1860–1935) had established Hull House, Chicago's famous social welfare center, and Beatrice Potter Webb (1858–1943) had disguised herself as an unemployed worker in order to investigate poverty in London's slums, social work also gave women employment opportunities.

Women could not help but be struck by the bitter irony of their efforts to combat racial and industrial slavery while they themselves remained oppressed, and many turned from social activism to feminist militancy in an effort to secure political equality. The beginnings of the modern women's liberation movement can be traced to the world antislavery convention that met in London in 1840, where Elizabeth Cady Stanton (1815–1902) and other women delegates were forced to sit in a curtained galley, separate from the men. In July 1848 Stanton organized a women's rights convention in Seneca Falls, New York, which issued an 18-point Declaration of Sentiments demanding the vote, property and divorce rights, and equal employment opportunities.

In Europe feminists found support in the British reformer John Stuart Mill (1806–1873). Mill was a disciple of the philosopher Jeremy Bentham, who had argued that the best government was one that gave its citizens access to the greatest pleasure and the least pain. In 1859 Mill published *On Liberty*, which posited that society should permit every individual the fullest degree of liberty consistent with the freedom of others. Government, argued Mill, may restrict freedom only to protect society. Conversely, Mill's democratic sentiments led him to urge government action to eliminate poverty, the exploitation of child labor and economic injustice, and the repression of women.

During the debate over the Reform Act of 1867, Mill, a member of the House of Commons, introduced an amendment to give women the vote. Though defeated 194 to 73, the minority vote was surprisingly large. With contributions from his wife, Harriet Taylor (1807–1859), Mill incorporated the women's rights issue into his theory of liberty in a ground-breaking essay, *The Subjection of Women* (1869). The principle of utility, said Mill, demanded that society eliminate inequality and prejudice, which had prevented women from bringing their talents to bear on public issues. Mill had been arrested in his youth

The Principle of Utilitarianism

The philosophical basis of nineteenth-century Liberalism owed much to the work of John Stuart Mill, whose "utilitarian" theories were based on the principle of the greatest good for the greatest number of people. Here Mill explains what he meant by "good."

The creed which accepts as the foundation of morals, Utility, or the Greatest Happiness Principle, holds that actions are right in proportion as they tend to promote happiness, wrong as they tend to produce the reverse of happiness. By happiness is intended pleasure, and the absence of pain; by unhappiness, pain, and the privation of pleasure. To give a clear view of the moral standard set up by the theory, much more requires to be said; in particular, what things it includes in the ideas of pain and pleasure; and to what extent this is left an open question. But these supplementary explanations do not affect the theory of life on which this theory of morality is grounded—namely, that pleasure, and freedom from pain, are the only things desirable as ends; and that all desirable things (which are as numerous in the utilitarian as in any other scheme) are desirable either for the pleasure inherent in themselves, or as means to the promotion of pleasure and the prevention of pain.

Source: J. S. Mill, *Utilitarianism,* 15th ed. (London: Longman, 1907), pp. 9–10.

for advocating birth control methods and was convinced that women were the victims of sexual domination. His essay pointed out that men had convinced women of their own inferiority. Later the social scientist Lester Ward (1841–1913) extended Mill's arguments by asserting in *Dynamic Sociology* (1883) a theory of the natural superiority of women.

The Suffrage Struggle

The women's movement spread throughout Europe in the nineteenth century. Often divided over tactics and goals, feminist leaders nevertheless constituted a kind of women's international as they fought against male privilege, government and church policy, and tradition. In 1868 British women founded the National Society for Women's Suffrage. The following year Susan B. Anthony (1820–1906) and Elizabeth Stanton established the National Woman Suffrage Association, which merged with other groups in 1890 to form the National American Woman Suffrage Association. By the 1870s unmarried propertied women received the municipal franchise in Britain, Sweden, and Finland, and American women gained the suffrage in a few states.

On the European continent, especially where the Catholic church was strong, the women's movement generally incorporated the suffrage into broader campaigns. In France two generations of feminist activism had been repressed after the 1848 revolutions, but the women's rights struggle revived during the Third Republic under the leadership of Hubertine Auclert, who demanded the vote on the principle of "perfect equality of the sexes before the law and before customs and morality."[1] Anna Maria Mozzoni translated Mill's essay on women into Italian and published a women's journal, while Luise Otto-Peters, who had fought for women's rights during the 1848 revolutions, cofounded the General Association of German Women in 1865. Efforts to forge unity among suffrage forces climaxed in 1902 in the International Alliance of Women, which held congresses in Berlin, Copenhagen, Amsterdam, London, Stockholm, and Budapest.

EMMELINE PANKHURST AND THE POLITICS OF CONFRONTATION

The suffrage movement captured public attention in Britain after the turn of the century under the fiery leadership of Emmeline Pankhurst (1858–1928). She was a woman of immense determination and eloquence. The daughter of a Manchester textile printer, Pankhurst was educated in Paris and was influenced by French feminists. In 1879 she married Richard Pankhurst, an advocate of women's suffrage with whom she promoted the Women's Property Act.

After working with suffrage groups in Manchester, Pankhurst became convinced that women had to use confrontational, and at times violent, tactics to publicize their cause and win the right to vote. In 1886 she participated in a strike of female workers in a London match factory, an experience that taught her the advantages of direct action. Three years later she helped establish, in affiliation with the Liberal party, the Women's Franchise League. Because it met with resistance from the Liberals, she subsequently switched her political allegiance to the Independent Labour party. When the death of her husband in 1898 left her alone to raise a son and three daughters, she took a civil service job but was fired because of her suffrage work.

Inspired by her daughter Christabel, also an ardent feminist, in 1903 Pankhurst created the Women's Social and Political Union (WSPU), a London-based suffrage organization without party affiliation. The WSPU opposed candidates for elected office who did not support the women's vote. Together with her daughters Sylvia and Christabel, Pankhurst led an army of women—called "suffragettes" to distinguish them from the "suffragists" of the moderate National Union of Women's Suffrage Societies—in public meetings, marches to Buckingham Palace, and demonstrations before Parliament.

In 1911, after the government's continued refusal to adopt a prosuffrage platform, Pankhurst took control of the WSPU and, with Christabel, directed a window-smashing campaign along fashionable shopping streets, for which Emmeline received a nine-month prison term. Nevertheless, the WSPU's tactics grew more violent. One woman chained herself to the railings at 10 Downing Street, the residence of the prime minister, while shouting "Votes for women!" Some resorted to bombings and arson; one woman smashed the Rokeby Venus, a painting in the Na-

The Suffragette Revolt

The radical suffragettes of the pre–World War I period declared a feminist war against middle-class society in their efforts to win the vote for women. In this speech, made in London in 1912 after having been released from prison, the British suffragette Emmeline Pankhurst delivered her challenge in no uncertain terms.

Ladies and gentlemen, the only recklessness the militant suffragists have shown about human life has been about their own lives and not about the lives of others, and I say here and now that it never has been and never will be the policy of the Women's Social and Political Union recklessly to endanger human life. We leave that to the enemy. We leave that to the men in their warfare. It is not the method of women. . . . There is something that governments care far more for than human life, and that is the security of property, and so it is through property that we shall strike the enemy. From henceforward the women who agree with me will say, "We disregard your laws, gentlemen, we set the liberty and the dignity and the welfare of women above all such considerations, and we shall continue this war as we have done in the past; and what sacrifice of property, or what injury to property accrues will not be our fault. It will be the fault of that government who admits the justice of our demands, but refuses to concede them. . . ."

Be militant each in your own way. Those of you who can express your militancy by going to the House of Commons and refusing to leave without satisfaction, as we did in the early days—do so. . . . Those of you who can express your militancy by joining us in our anti-government by-election policy—do so. Those of you who can break windows—break them. Those of you who can still further attack the secret idol of property, so as to make the government realize that property is as greatly endangered by women's suffrage as it was by the Chartists of old—do so.

And my last word is to the government: I incite this meeting to rebellion! . . . Take me, if you dare, but if you dare I tell you this, . . . you will not keep me in prison.

Source: E. Pankhurst, *My Own Story* (New York: Hearst's International Library, 1914), pp. 264–266.

Emmeline Pankhurst, whose radical strategies emboldened British suffragists, was repeatedly arrested. [Culver Pictures]

tional Museum, and another tried to strike the Tory Winston Churchill with a horse whip. Following an attempt to bomb the house of Lloyd George, Pankhurst was sentenced to three years' penal servitude. During repeated jail terms, she and her daughters went on hunger strikes to dramatize their cause and had to be force-fed. In 1913 Emily Davison was killed after flinging herself in front of King George V's horse at the Epsom Derby. As the American suffrage leader Carrie Catt observed, the Pankhursts were "in a state of insurrection" against the British government.[2]

The efforts of Emmeline Pankhurst and other courageous women contributed to the development of feminist consciousness as well as to the vote issue, but the women's movement achieved only limited success before World War I. Pankhurst threw herself into war work after 1914 despite her fading health. Her lifelong struggle for women's suffrage bore fruit in 1918 with the passage of the Representation of the People Act.

Science and the Doctrine of Progress

The worship of science and the belief in progress that marked European attitudes in this period weakened the eighteenth-century emphasis on the efficacy of human will. In broad terms, the Enlightenment had taught that people could shape their own destinies and mold society to their needs. Nineteenth-century developments, by contrast, reinforced the view that the scientific method could merely reveal the laws governing the physical and social environment. The process of discovery offered the promise of unending material improvement, but the laws of science could not be changed or suspended. Hence the optimism of the eighteenth century was replaced by a vision of perfectability that portrayed humans as part of a larger process of change.

The Darwinian Revolution

Scientific discoveries and technological advances had made possible Europe's Industrial Revolution and the improvement in its standard of living. The growth of literacy encouraged the popularity of science and the spread of its methods to other disciplines. The French philosopher Auguste Comte (1798–1857) was the first major figure to apply scientific principles to the study of society. In his *System of Positive Philosophy*, worked out in the 1830s, Comte argued that laws of social behavior paralleled the physical laws governing the universe and that both were discoverable through the study of specific data. Observation of individual phenomena, he believed, would demonstrate the similarities between them, which would in turn reveal natural laws. Comte described human thought as having moved from an early "theological" stage in which it was believed that the world operated by divine action to a "metaphysical" phase that sought to understand nature through abstract principles. Comte saw the thought of his own day as the final, "positive" stage, when observable data rather than metaphysical forces explained human behavior and the physical world.

Although Comte rejected theories of evolution, his work dovetailed with that of a number of natural scientists. Jean-Baptiste Lamarck (1744–1829) had tried to show that plants and animals—including humans—had evolved by adjusting to the environment. Sir Charles Lyell (1797–1875), in his *Principles of Geology* (1830–1833), explained the formation of the earth as the result of a slow process of geologic evolution rather than a sudden cataclysm or act of creation. Lamarck and Lyell relied on the painstaking accumulation of evidence in the development of their theories.

These theories formed the intellectual climate in which the British naturalist Charles Darwin (1809–1882) formulated his theses about evolution. His famous book *On the Origin of Species by Means of Natural Selection* (1859) was not the first work to posit a theory of evolution, but it explained in unprecedented detail how the evolutionary process worked. Darwin's principle of natural selection involved a number of points. Because every species produced more individual life forms than could survive, a struggle for existence took place within and between species. Variations, he asserted, gave some organisms advantages in the competition, so that only the fittest survived. But changing environmental conditions demanded alterations in the definition of fitness. In *The Descent of Man* (1871), Darwin argued that, like other forms of life, humans also evolved—from an ancestral type common to anthropoid apes—by the same principle of natural selection.

Darwin's theory was startling because it challenged both the deistic notion that the universe had been designed by God as well as the biblical account of creation. By claiming that the survival and development of organisms was a mechanistic process, Darwin rejected the notion of divine purpose in nature. His vision of a constantly changing world in which humans were simply another form of animal life seemed to support the spirit of materialism.

Science and Society

Darwin had been influenced by social theorists, including Thomas Malthus, whose *Essay on the Principle of Population* (1798) had predicted that population growth would outstrip food supplies. Social scientists, in turn, used Darwin to support their arguments, but in doing so they took evolution far beyond Darwin's intent. The British political philosopher Walter Bagehot (1826–1877) applied natural selection to politics, asserting the superiority of nations that conquered others. His fellow countryman Herbert Spencer (1820–1903) made the classic case for what, ironically, came to be called Social Darwinism—Darwin himself never endorsed this doctrine. In his *Synthetic Philosophy,* Spencer contended that the economic competition of individuals advanced social progress by eliminating the weak. His arguments reflected an extreme form of laissez-faire liberalism that opposed state assistance to the poor and similar social legislation. By the end of the nineteenth century the Darwinian concept of the survival of the fittest had even been used to justify imperial conquest and racism.

Culture and Industrial Society

European artists and writers were profoundly affected by the new culture of science and industry. The contradictions of industrial civilization gave rise to two opposing trends in the arts during the second half of the nineteenth century. The idealistic fervor of Romantic painting was replaced by an "academic" style descended from the official canons of seventeenth- and eighteenth-century painting that deemphasized the individual's quest for meaning through an encounter with nature. Academic portraits conveyed the values of the middle class, while bucolic landscapes presented orderly treatments of nature.

Other artists responded to industrial society with a powerful "realism" that rejected an idealized version of industrial civilization. The call for a new artistic conscience was sounded by critics such as John Ruskin (1819–1900), who, like many of the realists, was influenced by socialist critiques of industrial capitalism and sought to make painting and literature responsive to the problems of the age.

Painting: New Visions of Reality

Scientific developments affected culture profoundly. Some artists saw the development of the camera in the early decades of the century—the first photograph dates from around 1826—as a threat to painting, especially if they defined art as the reproduction of observable experience. But artists such as the Frenchmen Édouard Manet (1832–1883) and Edgar Degas (1834–1917) and the American Thomas Eakins (1844–1916) used photography to study form and motion. Moreover, the realist painters found inspiration in daily life and approached their subject matter with sensitivity.

The British artist J. M. W. Turner (1775–1851) had taken an important step in this direction with his controversial *Rail, Steam and Speed, The Great Western Railway*

(1845). Although Turner claimed that the scene represented a literal depiction of a train in a snowstorm, the public rejected his energy-charged treatment of a locomotive as subject matter unsuited to true art. The French painters Gustave Courbet (1819–1877) and Honoré Daumier (1808–1879) were the major proponents of realism. Courbet believed that the search for truth required the artist to reveal the ugly as well as the beautiful. Influenced by socialism, Courbet made the working class the focus of his work because modern life relied on its labor. He was a realist not in the sense that he rendered the details of every object but in that he portrayed the harsh reality of workers and peasants without idealizing his subjects. *The Stonebreakers* (1849) depicts two workers whose hidden faces speak to the anonymity of grueling labor. Daumier, who had been a cartoonist for a radical newspaper, executed watercolors and drawings of common people that deliberately avoided a romanticized vision of poverty.

In the last third of the nineteenth century some artists moved beyond realism under the impact of scientific theories. From recent discoveries in optics, artists learned that air and light are waves of color joined by the human eye into patterns. Their use of short, broken brushstrokes and specific hues captured the way in which changing sunlight affected objects. In doing so, these artists rejected a frozen rendering of reality in favor of a view that was at once scientific and subjective.

The painting by the Frenchman Claude Monet (1840–1926) titled *Impression: Sunrise* (1873) inspired a hostile critic to dub the new style "Impressionism." Monet's fellow Impressionists, including Camille Pissarro (1830–1903), Auguste Renoir (1841–1919), Henri de Toulouse-Lautrec (1864–1901), and Edgar Degas, were similarly committed to these concerns. The Impressionists depicted subject matter that varied from Monet's early railroad station, *Gare Saint-Lazare, Paris,* to the chorus girls of Lautrec's posters and Manet's *Bar at the Folies-Bergères*. While their vision still concerned how the world appeared to the human eye, it was sharply different from that of realists such as Courbet and Daumier.

The Literary Response

If poetry was the major literary mode of the Romantic era, the novel best suited the industrial age. By midcentury an older generation of writers such as Honoré de Balzac (1799–1850) and Victor Hugo (1802–1885) was already making a transition from romanticism to realism to express injustice. Whereas Hugo's *Les Misérables* (1862) combined political radicalism with emotionally evocative social criticism, Balzac and Gustave Flaubert (1821–1880) shaped a consciously unromantic form. Balzac launched the realist movement with a series of novels collectively entitled *The Human Comedy*, while Flaubert's *Madame Bovary* (1857), which was prosecuted for its candid treatment of adultery, revealed the sordid underside of bourgeois life. One of the most powerful works in this genre was Émile Zola's *Germinal* (1885), a portrayal of socialist hopes among French miners. Flaubert and Zola led the way from realism to naturalism by applying the principles of scientific observation to the human condition. Influenced by Darwin, the naturalists demonstrated the effect of social environment on personality.

The works of two Russian writers, Ivan Turgenev (1818–1883) and Leo Tolstoy (1828–1910), and of the Norwegian dramatist Henrik Ibsen revealed the universal character of realism. Flaubert had a pronounced influence on Turgenev. Turgenev's first important work, *A Sportsman's Sketches* (1852), was a strenuous protest against serfdom. His novel *Fathers and Sons* (1862) introduced the term *nihilism* to express his protagonist's rejection of all forms of authority. In the tragic story of *Anna Karenina* (1877), Tolstoy depicted a character similar to Flaubert's Madame Bovary, but his masterpiece was *War and Peace* (1869). Set against the background of the Napoleonic wars, this monumental novel reflected his sense of Russian nationalism as well as the detailed analysis of characters and events many realists employed.

Ibsen's plays explore the conflict between individual freedom and the bourgeois, materialist culture of the late nineteenth century. While Flaubert and Tolstoy examine the theme of adultery, *A Doll's House* (1879) portrayed a wife who suddenly realizes that she has been living for years with a distant husband who considers her simply a precious possession. Like Mill, Ibsen believed in the obligation of society to further individual freedom, but he was disillusioned by political theories. In *An Enemy of the People* (1882), Ibsen lashed out at the cupidity of the majority who, because their income is endangered, refuse to accept a physician's discovery that the mineral waters of their town are polluted.

The greatest popular success of the realist genre was achieved by the British writer Charles Dickens (1812–1870). His novels were widely read through serialization in newspapers and magazines. His grotesque characters and often improbable plots took Dickens beyond the realm of conventional realism. Yet his novels vividly portrayed the social problems of his times, and his most compelling plots were set in the cities, where social classes played out the contradictions of industrialism. The protagonist of *Oliver Twist* (1838) is an orphan brought up in a workhouse for pauper children, where he is mistreated by a cruel master. Dickens reveals how poverty leads to injustice, crime, and tragedy. In *Hard Times* (1854), Dickens deals with the human consequences of aggressive economic individualism in an industrial city called Coketown, where a selfish businessman obsessed with sales and money destroys the lives of his children.

From industrial Britain to agrarian Russia, nineteenth-century novels and plays came to grips with the harsh realities of industrial capitalism and bourgeois society, adding a powerful voice to the protests of the working class.

Socialism and the Labor Movement

Working-class militancy in Europe struggled against the misery and alienation of industrial capitalism. The sans-culottes of the French Revolution and the Luddites of eighteenth-century Britain, like the utopian idealism of Robert Owen and Saint-Simon or the British Chartists and the revolutionaries of 1848, had been expressions of worker rebellion against exploitation. As liberalism triumphed after 1850, some of the harsher aspects of industrialism were blunted by reforms. Nevertheless, laborers devised strategies aimed at improving working conditions, and some advocated the elimination of capitalism itself.

In the second half of the nineteenth century the working-class movement focused around three traditions: trade unionism, anarchism, and the scientific socialism derived from the principles of Karl Marx and Friedrich Engels. Unionism accepted industrial capitalism as a permanent feature of modern life but sought to mitigate its impact by improving wages, benefits, and working conditions. Unionists gradually won a legal basis for organizing and the right to strike. Anarchism and Marxist socialism, by contrast, rejected the permanency of capitalism and saw private property as a source of repression and inequality that could not be reformed. Although Marx himself in later life advocated a political path to socialism, many of his followers continued to believe in violent revolution. Anarchists and Marxists were divided in their attitudes toward the state. Anarchists, rejecting all forms of authority, sought to destroy government, while Marxists wanted to seize control of the state and install the proletariat in power, leaving the destruction of the state for a later stage. These divisions weakened the working-class movement.

Socialism, Anarchism, and the Paris Commune

Initially, socialists, anarchists, and other radicals collaborated in the creation of the International Workingmen's Association, founded in London in 1864. The First International, as it was generally known, tried to coordinate labor activities throughout Europe and provide a vehicle for socialist debate. Marx, who gave its inaugural address and was its dominant figure, clashed with Mikhail Bakunin (1814–1876), the exiled Russian anarchist, and eventually drove nonsocialists from the International.

Marx's triumph came a year after the the Paris Commune, a pivotal event in international socialism. Marx contributed to the legend surrounding the Commune with a pamphlet titled *The Civil War in France*, in which he argued that it represented the first clear-cut case of proletarian violence. A few international socialists and anarchists had been involved in the Commune uprising, along with large numbers of radicals and ordinary citizens who had no clear program, but the Commune was by no means a Marxist revolution. Yet socialists everywhere came to regard it as a symbol both of the class struggle and of the bourgeois determination to crush worker agitation. Throughout Europe liberal governments reacted to the Commune by imposing restrictions on the working-class movement.

The First International dissolved in 1876 in the wake of the Commune and the socialist-anarchist split. For two decades thereafter, militant action remained largely in the hands of the anarchists, who increasingly adopted terrorist tactics, which they termed "propaganda of the deed." Anarchists tried twice in the 1870s to assassinate Kaiser William I and succeeded in killing a number of statesmen and heads of state, including Tsar Alexander II of Russia (1881), the French president François Sadi-Carnot (1894), the Spanish prime minister Antonio Cánovas del Castillo (1897), the empress Elizabeth of Austria-Hungary (1898), King Umberto I of Italy (1900), and the American president William McKinley (1901). Despite these acts of terrorism, many anarchist leaders repudiated violence. Prince Peter Kropotkin (1842–1921), a Russian noble exiled in London, argued for peaceful cooperation among workers, and the Italian anarchist Errico Malatesta (1853–1932) stressed the humanitarian nature of anarchism and saw himself as an antiauthoritarian socialist.

Trade Unions and the Labor Movement

Although Marx had predicted the growth and concentration of capitalist wealth, the condition of the working class itself did not worsen. Indeed, the general prosperity that began in the 1850s improved the standard of living of most workers, moderating the attitudes of labor and slowing the growth of unions. By the latter part of the century, however, craft unions, representing skilled trades, were again organizing. In the 1870s the Liberal ministry of Gladstone recognized such unions and legalized the strike. The London dockworkers' strike of 1889 provided the impetus for the organization of unskilled laborers and gave rise to industrial unions representing both skilled and unskilled workers throughout an entire industry. By the end of the century Britain's 2 million union members represented the largest and most successful union experience in Europe.

Beyond Britain, modern unions developed largely during the two decades of economic depression that stretched into the 1890s, largely under the banner of socialism. Napoleon III had permitted unions in 1864 in France, but they were suppressed after the Commune, and only in 1884 did the Third Republic grant them legal status. In Germany, Bismarck's antisocialist campaign retarded their formation until the Imperial Industrial Code of 1891 permitted the right to strike. By 1900 organized labor counted some 850,000 members in Germany and 250,000 in France, while in Italy and Austria-Hungary unions were slower to develop.

In the 1890s unionism on the Continent took a more radical turn under the influence of syndicalist leaders. The Frenchman Georges Sorel (1847–1922) was the major proponent of syndicalism (from the French word *syndicat*, "trade union"). He argued that unions rather than political parties were the logical institutions through which working-class leaders could take power from the middle class and reorganize society. In 1895 syndicalists formed the General Confederation of Labor, a union umbrella organization that undertook strike action and rivaled the socialists for leadership of the labor movement. Syndicalism spread to Italy, where leaders attempted an unsuccessful general strike in 1904. After the 1905 Russian revolution, Rosa Luxemburg (1870–1919), a Polish Jew active in politics, published a pamphlet titled *The Mass Strike, the Party, and the Trade Unions* (1906) in which she defined the strike as a political weapon. In *Reflections on Violence* (1908), Sorel proclaimed the general strike as the only means of achieving socialism. The general strike, he argued, would provoke violent state repression, which would incite the workers to revolt.

Socialist Parties: Between Reform and Revolution

Socialist parties grew rapidly in the years after the Paris Commune. Despite Bismarck's efforts to crush it, German socialism flowered. In 1869 two Marxists, August Bebel (1840–1913) and Wilhelm Liebknecht (1826–1900), founded the Social Democratic Labor party, which elected several deputies to parliament. In 1875 the Social Democrats joined forces with the more moderate followers of Ferdinand Lassalle (1825–1864) to issue the so-called Gotha program, combining Marxian theory with pragmatic Lassallian reforms. Although Marx denounced the mixture of revolutionary doctrine and reformist objectives, the resulting German Social Democratic party (SPD) became the strongest socialist party in Europe.

The German example inspired socialists elsewhere. In Belgium socialists founded a party in 1879. A non-Marxist Italian Worker party developed in 1882, although the socialists did not develop an organization of their own until ten years later. Meanwhile, Russian exiles in Switzerland formed the Russian Social Democrats in 1883. In both Italy and Russia police repression against socialists and anarchists was particularly severe and forced many radicals to spend years in exile. In France doctrinal disputes led to the creation of separate parties that did not unite until 1905.

Women were active in organizing labor unions and in strike activity. Here is a women's labor parade in New York City, 1913. [UPI/Bettmann Newsphotos]

Socialist Women

The Russian-born Angelica Balabanoff (1869–1965) was one of the most important figures in the prewar socialist movement. After leaving her wealthy family, she studied and worked in the movement throughout Europe, serving on the executive committee of the Second International for many years. Here she describes her early collaboration with Maria Giudice, an Italian socialist, while both were in St. Gall, Switzerland, in 1904.

One day . . . I received word that a young Italian teacher, an ardent propagandist for Socialism, was coming to St. Gall. She had only recently fled from Italy to escape imprisonment for an article she had written. I wrote the comrades at St. Gall that Maria was to have the use of my room. When I returned I found . . . Maria was experiencing her first pregnancy. She eventually became the mother of seven children and the object of considerable gossip. . . . Several years later, in Italy, the editor of a clerical journal made slurring remarks about Maria's morals. Meeting him in the marketplace one day, Maria, in a loud voice that all round her could hear, inquired of a vegetable woman if this was the man who had gossiped about her. The startled woman . . . nodded her head affirmatively. Maria then stepped in the path of the astonished editor and, before the crowd which had already assembled, gave him a resounding slap in the face. There was little more talk of Maria and her children after that. . . .

At the time Maria lived with me in St. Gall, the Italian Socialists had no special propaganda paper for women. We conceived the notion that one should be started. . . . Both Maria and I were hostile to any form of "feminism." To us the fight for the emancipation of women was only a single aspect of the struggle for the emancipation of humanity. It was because we wanted women, particularly workingwomen, to understand this, to learn that they had to fight not *against* men but *with* them against the common enemy, capitalist society, that we felt the need of this paper. Moving to Lugano, Maria and I founded *Su', Compagne! (Arise, Comrades!)*. It was an almost instant success. . . .

Source: A. Balabanoff, *My Life as a Rebel* (New York: Harper, 1938), pp. 34–35.

British socialism followed the same moderate path as its unions. In 1884 a group of middle-class intellectuals founded the Fabian Society.* Led by the Irish playwright George Bernard Shaw (1856–1950), Sydney Webb (1859–1947), Beatrice Webb, and the novelist H. G. Wells (1866–1946), the Fabians rejected violent revolution. In 1900 socialists formed the Labour party.

As socialist parties gathered strength throughout Europe, their leaders attempted to reawaken international solidarity with the creation in 1889 of the Second International. It served largely to organize congresses, coordinate May Day celebrations, and provide a forum for consultation. National parties continued to provide the impetus for the socialist movement.

In the two decades before World War I the international working-class movement was dominated by the opposing models offered by German and French socialists. In 1899 Éduard Bernstein (1850–1932) published a theoretical work titled *Evolutionary Socialism*. Bernstein, who had been influenced by the British Fabians, was both a revisionist and a reformist. His revisionism derived from his conviction that Marxist doctrine had to evolve as social, political, and economic conditions changed. In the context of a parliamentary system and an expanding industrial economy such as prevailed in Germany, Bernstein challenged Marx's beliefs in the coming crisis of capitalism, the increasing polarization of classes, and the certainty of working-class revolution. This position led him to abandon revolutionary tactics in favor of achieving concrete gains

*Named after the ancient Roman general Quintus Fabius Maximus, who avoided pitched battles with the Carthaginians in favor of harassing operations.

for workers through parliamentary reform and collaboration with non-Marxist parties. In effect, Bernstein's arguments reflected German socialist policy since the 1870s, although his reformism was bitterly denounced by orthodox Marxists. Indeed, the reformist-revolutionary controversy split socialist parties everywhere.

Bernstein's counterpart in France was Jean Jaurès (1859–1914), a fiery speaker and humanist scholar who urged socialist collaboration with middle-class governments to secure reforms. Under pressure from the International, which condemned revisionist "opportunism" and urged French socialists to unite into one party, Jaurès reverted to orthodoxy.

Women of the Left

The development of socialist political parties gave added impetus to the women's movement. Although women experienced resentment even within socialist parties and did not often rise to top positions in labor organizations, they found more acceptance from male comrades than in other parties. Socialists eschewed civil marriage as a bourgeois institution and practiced free love in radical circles. Most socialist parties eventually advocated universal suffrage, divorce laws, and birth control.

Despite German laws that prohibited women from engaging in political activity, the SPD took the lead in organizing women. After the party accepted their right to work, a law forced the creation of separate groups for women. In 1878 Bebel issued his *Women in the Past, Present, and Future*, the first sustained study of the women's question from a socialist perspective. Six years later Engels published *The Origins of the Family, Private Property, and the State*. The core of their arguments remained the idea that the suppression of women evolved as the concept of private property developed.

The party's major theoretician of Marxist feminism was Clara Zetkin (1857–1933), who pioneered female militancy within the SPD as well as in the Second International and edited the magazine *Equality*. Zetkin's theories of female emancipation started out from Marx and Engels' position concerning the nature of the middle-class family. She argued that housework and child rearing represented exploitation in the form of unpaid labor. Bourgeois morality had made women little more than property controlled by men. Hence women's liberation was impossible in isolation but had to take place as part of the broader socialist struggle against capitalism. Because Zetkin believed that female labor was a precondition for the liberation of women from sexual slavery, she urged them to participate in the work force as well as in socialist politics.

The Gotha Program of 1875 had advocated universal suffrage but refused to support more radical feminist views. Zetkin and other women eventually forced the SPD to adopt a broader feminist position. In 1894 SPD deputies in the Reichstag first proposed a bill for women's suffrage, although it was defeated.

Together with Rosa Luxemburg, Zetkin opposed Bernstein's revisionist principles. Their denunciations of reform socialism separated them from other women in the SPD as well as from nonsocialists because they argued the incompatibility of the socialist women's movement and bourgeois feminism. Nonsocialist feminists, they argued, sanctioned capitalism, a system of exploitation that repressed men and women alike. While Zetkin made the feminist cause the center of her professional life, Luxemburg subsumed women's issues into the larger question of revolution. The hostility of the revisionist leadership drove Zetkin and Luxemburg further to the left, and on the eve of World War I they were among the extremists who formed the German Communist party.

The rise of feminism and socialism after 1870, like the work of realist painters and novelists, revealed the deep contradictions that beset the liberal order in Europe. The political order moved toward democracy, while advances in education, health, and communications contributed to the modernization of a society in which workers and peasants were more fully integrated into national life. Yet industrial capitalism, which had produced remarkable prosperity, also engendered economic and cultural oppression in the organization of work, gender and family relations, and the accumulation of unprecedented wealth by a new business-financial elite. Nor was the prosperity of the period evenly distributed. Workers' wages rose except during the Long Depression, but poverty was still widespread. Illiteracy, infant mortality, and illness remained higher among the workers than in the middle classes.

Constitutional monarchies and parliamentary regimes based on universal male suffrage had replaced absolute monarchy almost everywhere in Europe by the opening of the twentieth century. Nevertheless, in some Western states lib-

eral governments proved no less vigorous than the old autocrats in preserving a stable social order and protecting the interests of industrial capitalism and patriarchy. While Europe remained generally at peace for almost a half century, the international order spawned by liberalism also produced militarism and new forms of nationalism, racism, and imperialism.

Notes

1. C. G. Moses, *French Feminism in the Nineteenth Century* (Albany: State University of New York Press, 1984), p. 213.
2. E. F. Hurwitz, "The International Sisterhood," in R. Bridenthal and C. Koonz, eds., *Becoming Visible: Women in European History* (Boston: Houghton Mifflin, 1977), p. 337.

Suggestions for Further Reading

Bridenthal, R., and Koonz, C., eds. *Becoming Visible: Women in European History*. Boston: Houghton Mifflin, 1977.

Burrow, J. W. *Evolution and Society: A Study in Victorian Social Theory*. Cambridge: Cambridge University Press, 1966.

Clark, M. *Modern Italy, 1871–1982*. London: Longman, 1984.

Girouard, M. *Cities and People: A Social and Architectural History*. New Haven, Conn.: Yale University Press, 1985.

Harrison, F. *The Dark Angel: Aspects of Victorian Sexuality*. New York: Sheldon Press, 1977.

Hayes, C. J. H. *The Generation of Materialism, 1871–1900*. New York: Harper, 1941.

Joll, J. *The Second International, 1889–1914*. New York: Harper & Row, 1966.

Landes, D. *The Unbound Prometheus: Technological Change and Industrial Development in Western Europe from 1750 to the Present*. Cambridge: Cambridge University Press, 1969.

Milward, A. S., and Saul, S. B. *The Development of the Economies of Continental Europe, 1850–1914*. Cambridge, Mass.: Harvard University Press, 1977.

Mosse, G. L. *The Culture of Western Europe*. Chicago: Rand McNally, 1961.

Pugh, M. *The Making of British Politics, 1867–1939*. Oxford: Basil Blackwell, 1982.

Rewald, J. *The History of Impressionism*. New York: Museum of Modern Art, 1961.

———. *Post-Impressionism*. New York: Museum of Modern Art, 1978.

Sheehan, J. J. *German Liberalism in the Nineteenth Century*. Chicago: University of Chicago Press, 1978.

Stearns, P. N. *European Society in Upheaval: Social History Since 1800*. New York: Macmillan, 1967.

Thoennessen, W. *The Emancipation of Women: The Rise and Decline of the Women's Movement in German Social Democracy, 1863–1933*. London: Pluto Press, 1973.

Thompson, D. *Democracy in France Since 1870*. New York: Oxford University Press, 1969.

Vicinus, M., ed. *Suffer and Be Still: Women in the Victorian Age*. Bloomington: Indiana University Press, 1972.

Writing and Communication (II)

Throughout the ancient and medieval world, literacy was relatively uncommon, but in time improved printing techniques encouraged its spread. In the Arab world and in Europe the production of books was limited by two factors: each copy of a text had to be written by hand, and the material used for manuscripts was generally either parchment, made from split sheepskins, or vellum (calfskin), both of which were expensive. These limitations were first overcome in China, where paper had been manufactured since the first century A.D. Around the eighth century the Chinese invented a system of printing using blocks of wood. The idea of binding several sheets of paper together followed shortly; the first printed book, consisting of six pages, was published in 868.

The notion of movable type originally had little appeal to the Chinese, whose script is made up of thousands of different characters. But in the eleventh century the Chinese developed movable type in wood, a technique later adopted by the Koreans, who were the first to use it on a large scale. Both the Chinese and the Koreans soon made metal type, which obviously lasted longer and made mass printing possible.

By the eighth century the Arabs had borrowed the Chinese method of manufacturing paper, but they had little interest in block printing, perhaps because the art of writing had become an important skill in itself. Toward the end of the twelfth century the Arabs introduced papermaking into Spain, from where the technique spread slowly into northern Europe; by the beginning of the fifteenth century it had reached Germany and Switzerland. There is no evidence, however, that the Europeans knew anything about Chinese printing methods, since almost their only contacts with Chinese culture were through Arab traders.

The invention in Europe of movable type occurred much later than in China and Korea, in the mid-fifteenth century. The material used for the type was metal, since medieval craftsmen were skilled at engraving medals and coins. The first printed book, the so-called Gutenberg Bible, was published in 1455 at Mainz.

In China the production of books had generally been limited to works for the educated classes. The first major printing project was an edition of the Confucian classics in the tenth century, followed by the Buddhist scriptures, and during the Sung period books on art, literature, science, and philosophy appeared in large numbers. Literacy remained primarily an elite preserve, given the difficulty of the written language, but popular fiction began to grow, and literacy rose among the urban merchants, themselves an expanding group.

The effects of printing in Europe may have been more widespread or immediate than in Asia, especially as universities and other schools enlarged their enrollments to educate the children of merchants and craftsmen. The demand for texts could now be met. Furthermore, the process was self-reinforcing: the more books there were, the more people learned to read. Thus the impact of printing was not merely to facilitate the circulation of ideas among educated people but also to make available on a popular level a vast range of material to which access had formerly been difficult, such as almanacs, herbals, and prophecies.

It soon became apparent that the new technology could be employed in conducting political, religious, and scholarly debate, and controversial positions were circulated quickly. Among the first masters of the medium was the Protestant Martin Luther, who published a series of printed tracts on church reform in 1520, and a German translation of the Bible (New Testament in 1522, Old Testament in 1534) that became a cornerstone of the Reformation. The Reformation introduced printed pamphlets, hymns, religious texts, and sacred pictures to much of northern Europe, calling not only for religious changes but social ones as well. Subsequently, debate in the Western world has been conducted in large measure in print, now supplemented by radio and television. Print has not been replaced for scholarly, scientific, or religious debate, and access to the media on social issues (except for talk shows) is generally limited to those who have established their positions in print. Only political debate has partly replaced print as the medium of prime communication, and even here it remains indispensable.

Between the Reformation and the French Revolution mass literacy began to develop in Europe and spread among European colonizers elsewhere in the world. The first battleground for printed texts had been a sacred one, but pamphlets could now be distributed and books published to advocate or even galvanize social and political change, and the spread of popular literature had an enormous impact on the English, American, and French revolutions. Not only did pamphleteers advance specific causes or claim individual wrongs; they also served to make accessible at a popular level ideas that had hitherto been limited to intellectuals.

The pamphleteers of the French wars of religion at the end of the sixteenth century and the English Revolution in the mid-seventeenth argued fundamental religious and political ideas, and their works, often cheaply printed, attracted wide circulation. The London bookseller George Thomason collected nearly

This web press, which was capable of printing on both sides of the paper, was featured at a Philadelphia exhibition in the 1870s. [Granger Collection]

30,000 books, pamphlets, broadsides, and newssheets published in England between 1640 and 1661, an astonishing output in a country of only 5 million people. The appetite for news persisted, and the seventeenth century saw the first newspapers established in Augsburg, Strasbourg, London, and Paris. The role of print expanded in the eighteenth century, making it possible for growing numbers of Westerners in particular to keep abreast of public events and political issues. "Every Englishman, nowadays," said Samuel Johnson, "expects to be promptly and accurately informed upon the condition of public affairs." But not until the advent of the "penny press" in the next century were newspapers fully accessible to the masses. Such exposure required not only literacy and the availability of an extra penny to spend for a paper but also a desire to use the money to acquire the news rather than other goods.

The Enlightenment would have been unthinkable without the printing press, which enabled the philosophes to appeal over the heads of established authority for fundamental reform. Often, however, the most radical thought became available on a popular level only in times of crisis. Tom Paine crystallized revolutionary attitudes in America with a pamphlet appropriately titled *Common Sense,* and the ideas of Jean-Jacques Rousseau became crucial to the thinking of French revolutionaries when they were expressed in popular form by Sieyès in his pamphlet *What Is the Third Estate?* published in January 1789. In China, with its far greater population, there was from the eleventh century a major increase not only in popular fiction but also in printed manuals and pamphlets, although, unlike their European counterparts, they were rarely critical of the established order.

At the same time, the growth of knowledge and its relatively easy transmission were fundamental to the sudden surge of scientific development in the West. In the eyes of thinkers such as Francis Bacon and René Descartes, it was pointless to continue to depend on ancient writers and their books: new research was needed, and fresh ideas had to be circulated. In medicine and astronomy, chemistry and physics, the basis of modern scientific practice was laid in books published as early as the sixteenth and seventeenth centuries.

Popular literacy was also responsible for something less awesome in scope but equally valuable: instruction and pleasure. From the beginning, many of the most popular books were horoscopes and prophecies, cookbooks, collections of tales, and reports of extraordinary events. New literary forms such as the novel, the short story, and science fiction were created to meet popular demand for fiction and to express new social values and aspirations. All of these forms, including manuals, novels, and even detective stories, appeared in print in China several centuries earlier than in the West, although total literacy in China probably lagged behind after A.D. 1600. In the nineteenth century, the great age of the novel in the West, New

York's dockside was often crowded with readers eagerly awaiting the arrival of the latest installment of a Charles Dickens book from England.

If the invention of writing and the discovery of printing represent two giant steps in the development of world civilization, the mass communication systems of the twentieth century represent a third. The virtually instantaneous global communication that is possible today was foreshadowed in a series of nineteenth-century inventions that did much to change the role of the written word. A government postal system was introduced in Britain in 1840, which was much facilitated by the rapid growth of the railway system. Four years earlier, in 1836, the stamp tax on newspapers had been reduced, and by the middle of the century press circulation was three times its former level. The American Samuel Morse invented the telegraph, first used in 1844, and it soon became a valuable means of communication for Julius Reuter's news agency, the first international news service. The Prussian chancellor Otto von Bismarck effectively combined the telegraph and the press in 1870 when he edited a captured French telegram, the Ems dispatch, for publication, knowing that it would probably provoke the French to declare the war he sought; he was right, and the way was prepared for the completion of German unification.

The laying of the first permanent transatlantic cable in 1866 and Alexander Graham Bell's invention of the telephone a decade later made direct, instantaneous communication between Europe and North America possible. During World War II British prime minister Winston Churchill and American president Franklin Roosevelt conferred frequently by telephone, using the undersea cable. In the aftermath of the 1961 Cuban missile crisis, Soviet and American leaders approved the creation of a direct communications link, or "hot line," between the Kremlin and the White House to facilitate rapid discussion in the event of future crises.

Another revolutionary development in communications involved the technology of the camera and film. Graphic materials, of course, had been reproduced on printing presses for centuries, but beginning in the 1830s it was possible to transmit, through the new process of photography, the immediate pictorial image of an event. Photographs were vehicles of emotion as well as information, reaching the illiterate as well as the educated. The photographs of Mathew Brady (c. 1823-1896) enabled Americans to grasp the horrors that were occurring on the Civil War battlefields; his work laid the foundation for modern newsphoto services. Cameras could do more than record battles; they could shape them, particularly after aerial photography became practicable. Although the first aerial shots (from balloons) dated from 1858, the development of the airplane half a century later permitted extensive use of aerial photographs for military purposes, a vital advantage in World War I. Aerial photography has also played an important role in mapping and surveying natural resources, thus facilitating communication about our physical environment.

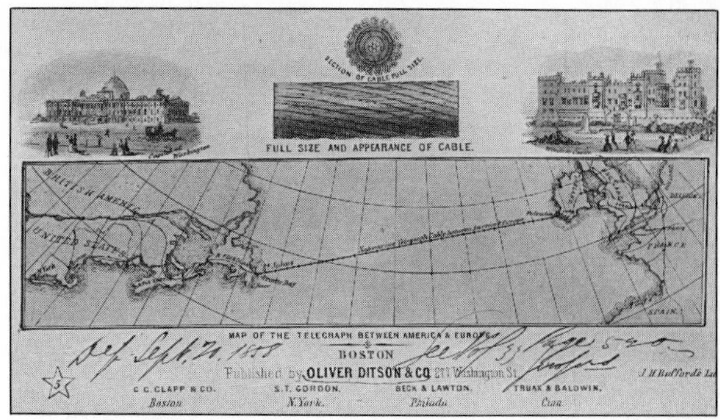

This detail from a sheet music cover commemorated the laying of a transoceanic telegraph cable in 1858. The cable failed after operating only one month. [Granger Collection]

The initial impact of these changes was limited to Europe and North America, but they were spread elsewhere in part by the Western colonial powers. In India the British founded universities in Calcutta, Bombay, and Madras, and public opinion expressed itself through newspapers. In China the foreign-run Maritime Customs Service began an efficient Western-style postal and telegraph system after 1860, while missionaries published huge numbers of tracts and founded Western-style schools, colleges, and universities. The Dutch colonial administration of Indonesia, the British in Burma and Malaya, and the Americans in the Philippines did much the same. Japan was first widely exposed to Western influence in 1853 and soon began to employ Western technology.

In Africa the principal beneficiaries of technological progress were the colonial powers themselves. Many parts of Africa had a rich tradition of song and story that went back centuries, but little of it became known beyond the immediate oral range until the twentieth century. In general the African communicative tradition was a spoken one; some of the works of Somali and Swahili poets of the eighteenth and nineteenth centuries were written down, but virtually everything else that is known of earlier times was collected by modern anthropologists. With the arrival of European colonizers and missionaries, a limited number of Africans learned the languages and writing systems of their conquerors, but only the liberation struggles of the twentieth century produced any level of general

Alexander Graham Bell demonstrates the telephone by calling Boston from Salem, Massachusetts, on March 15, 1877. [Granger Collection]

literacy. Many African writers were thus faced with the dilemma of deciding whether to produce works in an alien language for the outside world or use their own tribal language. The same problem still confronts writers in other areas whose native languages and cultures—Basque, Gaelic, and Welsh for example—struggle to survive in the face of more widely spoken rivals.

The appearance of new inventions—radio, movies, the phonograph—combined with earlier changes to enhance the ability to communicate. In the case of sound transmission, war was again crucial in accelerating the technological development that had begun in the mid-nineteenth century. The transmission of sound using light waves rather than wires was discovered by the Italian Guglielmo Marconi in 1895, and within 20 years transmission was possible across both the Atlantic and the Pacific. After World War I, the radio came into common use, bringing with it revolutionary possibilities for political leaders to communicate directly with the masses of their people. Among the early masters of this medium were Franklin Roosevelt, who used the radio for his "fireside chats," and Josef Goebbels, Hitler's propaganda minister. The integration of sight and sound in the cinema was achieved in 1927, when Al Jolson spoke and sang in the first "talkie," *The Jazz Singer*, and by 1930 silent pictures were antiquated. The stage was set for the filming of not only movies for entertainment but also the massive spectacles staged by Hitler at Nuremberg and the patriotic newsreels shown in movie theaters that bolstered morale during the Second World War.

The phonograph also had roots in the mid-nineteenth century, though only in the 1890s did serious manufacturing commence. Improved electrical reproduction came in the 1920s and fine-grooved records in the following decade. Culturally, it was now possible for people in one part of the world to hear and appreciate music from other continents. Perhaps there is no better example of this than the present Japanese fondness for Beethoven's Ninth (Choral) Symphony, performances of which are widespread in Japan each year. Moreover, Japanese and Korean conductors and soloists are now some of the best performers of Western music.

Perhaps the most revolutionary development in communications has been television. Although development of electronically transmitted images was under way as early as 1924, only after World War II was intercity network television launched, using coaxial cables. Microwave radio transmission began the same year, 1946, and in 1951 microwave relay made possible the first coast-to-coast television broadcast. The historical ramifications were enormous. In addition to the educational and cultural possibilities television afforded, the medium's ability to provide viewers with virtually immediate coverage of major events created new pressures as well as opportunities for political leaders. Mounting American anger over military involvement in Vietnam in the 1960s resulted at least in part from what people saw on their television screens. The widespread outpouring of sympathy and aid for famine-stricken areas in North Africa in the 1970s and

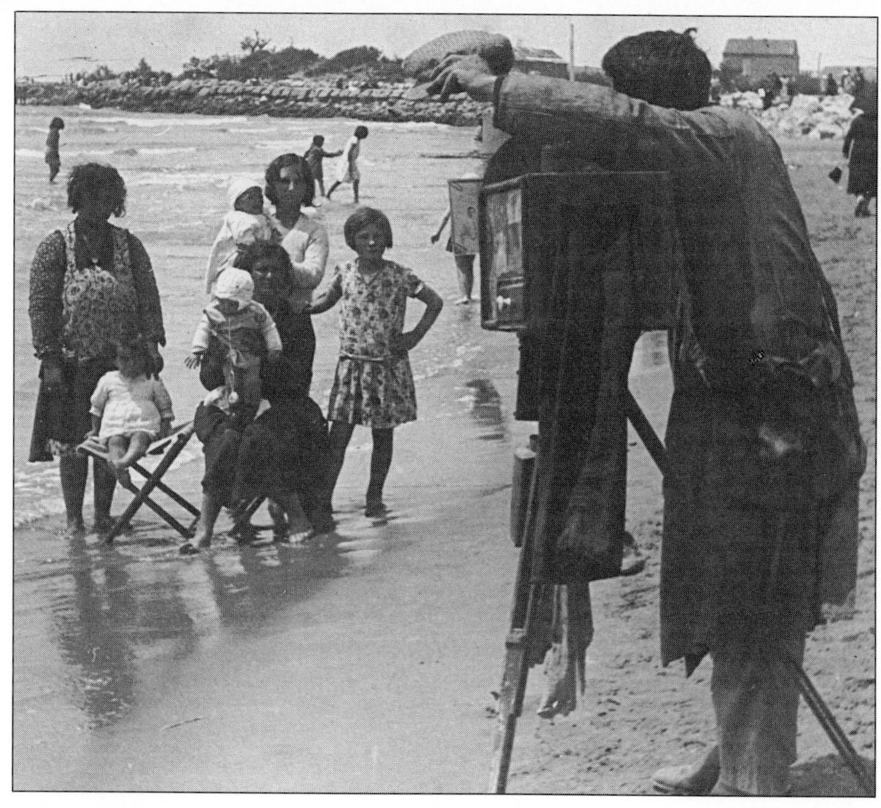

Roving photographers such as this one provided valuable documentation for social historians. This photograph was taken at a summer resort in France. [Culver Pictures]

early 1980s was triggered by television pictures of the victims.

Improved communications are changing modern society. Radio and especially television have substantially altered industrial societies by creating mass markets, which have in turn altered labor-management relations and created a greater homogeneity of manufactured goods. Mass communications also facilitate the creation of a consensus for action, while simultaneously providing minorities—in the absence of censorship—with the means to alter majority thinking and behavioral patterns, as Martin Luther King, Jr., demonstrated in the civil rights movement of the 1960s. Through modern technology, ideas and tastes can be increasingly homogenized, yet it is also possible to use the same means to facilitate the rapid acceptance of new styles and ideas. Television and the movies have even intensified urbanization by popularizing the lure of the cities, which are increasingly attractive not only because of their employment possibilities but also for their culture and lifestyle.

The pace of the communications revolution still varies considerably from region to region. For every 1,000 people in the United States, for example, there were 408 televisions and 1,417 radios in 1968, compared to 208 and 255, respectively, in Japan and 3 and 74 in South Korea. Indonesia and India lagged even further behind, with only 14 and 13 radios per 1,000 people, respectively; Nigeria had only one television set for every 1,000 persons in 1968. Such countries are only now experiencing the full brunt of the print revolution. In the period between 1948 and 1968 the number of daily newspapers declined slightly in the Western industrial countries of the United States, Great Britain, France, Italy, and the Netherlands, while they doubled in India, nearly tripled in Pakistan, and jumped nearly sevenfold in Turkey. There are, of course, exceptions to these patterns, often because of political factors such as the rise or fall of authoritarian regimes. The main problem facing developing countries seeking to implement new communications technology is the extraordinary capital outlay required, a problem that will perpetuate the communications gap in the forseeable future.[1]

Nevertheless, the introduction of communication satellites in the 1970s made possible an operational communications network that is worldwide. Even in areas without electricity, a transistor radio can enable people to hear the news, political messages, and cultural events. But instantaneous communications can complicate international relations. In the nineteenth century reports of hostile action on another continent could take a week or more to reach a concerned government, but at least that provided time for a consid-

In the early 1920s the radio became very popular. Primitive sets required the use of headphones. [Culver Pictures]

ered response. With the advent of the telegraph, and now communication satellites, the pressure for rapid decisions at the expense of deliberate analysis is increased, thereby intensifying the risks of war.

The ability of computers to store and retrieve information is a recent technological advance with major implications for communications. Computers can be programmed with artificial languages to facilitate high-speed transmission of information. Used responsibly, computers are valuable for uses ranging from complex mathematical calculations to scientific experiments. But computers can also be programmed to act in the absence of human reflection, as in the case of the massive computer-generated trading that triggered enormous losses on the New York Stock Exchange in 1987 and the computer-geared nuclear arsenals of the superpowers. Ironically, revolutionary advances in communications technology, often generated by wartime research, have simultaneously presented the world with possibilities both deadly and visionary.

Notes

1. Statistics in this paragraph from W. P. Davison, "The Media Kaleidoscope: General Trends in the Channels," in *Propaganda and Communication in World History*, ed. H. D. Lasswell, D. Lerner, and H. Speier, vol. 3 (Honolulu: University Press of Hawaii, 1980), pp. 191–248.

Suggestions for Further Reading

Abel, E., et al. *Many Voices, One World: Communications and Society*. Paris: UNESCO, 1984.

Craig, J. *Thirty Centuries of Graphic Design: An Illustrated History*. New York: Watson-Guptill, 1987.

Frawley, W. *Text and Epistemology*. Norwood, N.J.: Ablex, 1987.

Lasswell, H. D., Lerner, D., and Speier, H., eds. *Propaganda and Communication in World History*, vols. 2 and 3. Honolulu: University Press of Hawaii, 1980.

Logan, R. K. *The Alphabet Effect: The Impact of the Phonetic Alphabet on the Development of Western Civilization*. New York: Morrow, 1986.

Lowenthal, L. *Literature and Mass Culture: Communication in Society*, vol. 1. New Brunswick, N.J.: Transaction Books, 1984.

Schiller, H. I. *Information and the Crisis Economy*. Norwood, N.J.: Ablex, 1984.

Siegel, L., and Markoff, J. *The High Cost of High Tech: The Dark Side of the Chip*. New York: Harper & Row, 1985.

Whalley, J. I. *Writing Implements and Accessories: From the Roman Stylus to the Typewriter*. Detroit: Gale Research, 1975.

CHAPTER · 33

The Age of Western Domination

Contemporary world history began during the last three decades of the nineteenth century, when a handful of European countries imposed their domination over huge portions of the globe. Britain, France, Germany, and to a lesser extent Italy and Belgium completed control of a large proportion of the earth's land surface and population. Russia continued to push its borders eastward into Asia, while the United States and Japan extended their presence into the Pacific region. One result of this sudden grab for colonial possessions was the establishment of complex forms of interdependency among world civilizations that still shape our lives. This first major phase in the creation of a "global village" as a product of imperialism is the background of the contemporary age.

The battle of Omdurman (1898), in which General Kitchener's army decisively defeated a Muslim force in the Sudan. [The Mansell Collection, detail from a painting]

The New Imperialism

The process by which this transformation took place is known as the new imperialism, to distinguish it from the previous phase of European colonial expansion that took place between the sixteenth and eighteenth centuries. This newer form of imperialism was characterized not only by its rapid and intense pace but by other unique features as well.

The earlier overseas empires lay chiefly in the Americas and included extensive European-run areas in India and Southeast Asia as well as footholds on the East Asian and African coasts. After 1870 the Western powers moved deep into the interiors of Asia and Africa. Although the older empires traded with local populations, they were generally regarded as sources of direct revenue for the home country—tribute from native rulers, taxation from the local populations, and the expropriation of gold and silver.

Because the new imperialism was the work of advanced industrial-capitalist nations rather than of mercantile economies, it involved the commitment of significant financial investment as well as the deliberate exploitation of the material and human resources of the colonial areas. The economic function of the new imperialism, whether real or perceived, led in turn to the establishment of direct political control over the colonies, administered through elaborate bureaucracies. By the opening of the twentieth century, therefore, a new and direct relationship of unequal exchange had been established among the civilizations of the world, marked by a vast difference between the industrial and technological power of the West and the relative weakness of less technologically developed cultures.

Conflicting Interpretations

Scholars debate the causes and consequences of the new imperialism. One basic fact appears to be generally accepted: by 1870 conditions in Europe were ripe for overseas expansion. The breakdown of the Concert of Europe and the creation of nation-states in Germany and Italy heightened aggressive national rivalry. Moreover, power status was increasingly equated with the possession of overseas colonies, so empire became a matter of national honor. The Long Depression of 1873–1896 convinced some business and government leaders that overseas colonies would solve the problems caused by shrinking European markets and increasingly higher wages. Though policymakers often used economic arguments to explain the necessity for expansion, imperialism had support among all classes, including workers. Even trade union leaders and some socialists were enthusiastic about colonial expansion.

Economics and Empire

Economic rivalry between older industrial states such as Britain and France and newly industrializing states such as Germany and the United States added to the competition for colonies, especially as tariff barriers restricted European markets after 1880. Unprecedented prosperity and military-industrial power produced by the second industrial revolution and advances in science, technology, and industrial organization gave Europeans confidence in the superiority of their civilization. The climax of European development in the last decades of the century thus brought together a growing concern over national pride and security, the desire for continued economic expansion, and an appetite for cultural dominance.

The connection between economics and imperialism is hardly in doubt, although its exact nature is debated. The economic slump that began in the 1870s had increased unemployment, pushed prices for manufactured goods down, and diminished exports, making industrial nations compete fiercely over markets for their manufactured goods at a time when the abandonment of free trade limited the European market. This competition prompted some observers to argue for sheltered colonial markets limited to trade with the home country. An additional stimulus to imperialism arose from the demand for raw materials unavailable in Europe, especially copper, rubber, tin, cotton, jute, and petroleum, as well as foodstuffs such as coconut, coffee, and tea, on which Europeans had come to rely. Not only raw materials were necessary to the new industrial products, but their value was enhanced because cheap colonial labor made mining, extraction, and agriculture especially profitable.

The debate over economic factors centers on accumulated surplus capital. This argument, which later became the major interpretation of Marxist writers, was first proposed in 1902 by the British economic liberal John A. Hobson (1858–1940) in *Imperialism: A Study*. Hobson believed that capitalism suffered from underconsumption—that is, wealth in capitalist societies was poorly distributed as a result of overaccumulation by the rich. The business and financial interests that controlled such surplus capital soon discovered that it could be more profitably invested overseas, where cheap labor and raw materials made a greater return possible. Hobson saw imperialism as the effort of capitalists to find investment outlets for their surplus wealth. He argued that surplus capital could be eliminated if workers were paid higher wages and the rich taxed more heavily; because these measures would result in greater purchasing power for the working class, the need for new markets—hence imperialism—would disappear.

In 1916 V. I. Lenin (1870–1924), the future Communist leader of the Russian Revolution, wrote the classic Marxist analysis of the subject, *Imperialism: The Highest Stage of Capitalism*. The scramble for colonies, Lenin noted, coincided with the change in Europe's economy from a phase of free competition to one of intense monopoly through combines, trusts, and the control of finance capital. Imperialism emerges from this "highest" stage of capitalism when business and financial interests in each country seek to extend their monopolies overseas in the search for greater profits. Imperialism was therefore an inevitable response to the "internal contradictions" of monopolistic capitalism. For Lenin, imperialism would result in the breakdown of the capitalist system.

Hobson and Lenin were partly correct. Between 1860 and 1900 the value of British capital invested abroad grew from $7 billion to $20 billion. By the eve of World War I, a fifth of the foreign investments of France and Germany was in colonial regions, while about half of Britain's overseas investments were in the colonial world. In many instances, however, foreign rulers needed and requested Western capital, and financial investment hardly explained the imperialist expansion of less developed nations such as Italy and Russia, which had little surplus capital. Nor does colonialism explain the equally large British investments in non-colonial areas, such as Latin America and the United States. Finally, although some colonial possessions were profitable, the military and bureaucratic costs of occupation sometimes exceeded the financial return.

However important the economic motives behind imperialism, it caught the imagination of the European mind and responded to a popular thirst for the exotic. Scientists, missionaries, hunters, and adventurers poured into Africa and Asia in the late nineteenth century. Yet even the humanitarian instincts of the missionaries, intent on bringing Christianity and modern medicine to "heathens," involved a conviction about the superiority of their own civilization. When the British writer Rudyard Kipling spoke of the "white man's burden," he reflected the view of many Europeans that the civilizing mission was a sacred duty of more advanced races—a view supported in more ruthless fashion by those who believed in Social Darwinism.

Imperialism and Economics: The Debate

Among analysts of the economic causes of the new imperialism, two major authors stand out: Hobson and Lenin.

By far the most important economic factor in imperialism is the influence relating to investments. The growing cosmopolitanization of capital is the greatest economic change of this generation. Every advanced industrial nation is tending to place a larger share of its capital outside the limits of its own political area, in foreign countries, or in colonies, and to draw a growing income from this source.

Imperialism is capitalism in that stage of development in which the dominance of monopolies and finance capital has established itself; in which the export of capital has acquired pronounced importance; in which the division of the world among the international trusts has begun; in which division of all territories of the globe among the great capitalist powers has been completed.

More recent students of imperialism, however, have questioned these earlier views.

In the second half of the twentieth century, it can be seen that imperialism owed its popular appeal not to the sinister influence of the capitalists, but to its inherent attractions for the masses . . . and the adoption of a creed based on such irrational concepts as racial superiority and the prestige of the nation. . . . Imperialism cannot be explained in simple terms of economic theory and the nature of financial capital.

Sources: J. A. Hobson, *Imperialism: A Study* (New York: Pott, 1902), p. 30; V. I. Lenin, *Imperialism: The Highest Stage of Capitalism* (New York: International Publishers, 1939), p. 89; D. K. Fieldhouse, "Imperialism: A Historiographical Revision," *Economic History Review*, 2d ser., 14 (1961): 209.

Africa and the Colonial Powers

The most intense phase of the new imperialism unfolded in Africa, a continent four times the size of Europe. For centuries Westerners had viewed sub-Saharan Africa as the "Dark Continent," a vast, unexplored expanse where inhospitable climate, diseases, and geography conspired to keep them out. Muslim traders criss-crossed much of West Africa and the Sahara, but as late as the mid-nineteenth century only the coastal settlements and a few interior regions were represented on European maps. Despite Western ignorance, however, Africa had undergone major transformation in the centuries before the new imperialism. Iron metallurgy, agricultural techniques, and the introduction of new crops had spread across the continent, and a large increase in population had caused migrations into central and southern Africa. Diversity of geography and ethnocultural patterns determined development. Sophisticated cultures and effective states marked some regions, especially in the savannah zone of West Africa, where the kingdoms of Ghana, Mali, and Songhai had once flourished, and in Zimbabwe and the Swahili city-states of Southeast Africa. In the rain forests and southern regions, inhabited mainly by San, Pygmies, and Khoikhoi, political organization revolved around village communities that relied on primitive food-gathering techniques.

Changes in military techniques and weaponry also affected conditions in Africa. The earliest of these innovations were the tactics developed by the Zulu, a warlike

Military Revolution in Africa: The Zulu Warrior

In the 1820s African warfare underwent a major transformation that altered the balance of power among the Bantu-speaking peoples of the southeast. Shaka, the ruler of the Zulu, introduced highly disciplined infantry regiments that were protected by shields and used short, stabbing spears instead of the traditional throwing type. Here is an account of these warriors by Robert Moffat, a British missionary who visited the Zulu a number of years after Shaka's death.

Some thousands of the Matabele [Zulu], composing several regiments, are distinguished by the colour of their shields, as well as the kind and profusion of feathers which generally adorn their heads, having also a long feather of the blue crane rising from their brows, all which has an imposing effect at their onset. Their arms consist of a shield, short spear, and club. The club, often made of the horn of a rhinoceros or hard wood, they throw with unerring precision, so as even to strike dead the smaller antelope. The spear is not intended for throwing, but for close combat, and such being their mode of warfare, the tribes accustomed to throw their light javelins to a distance, are overtaken by these organized soldiers and mowed down. They must conquer or die, and if one return without his shield or spear, at the frown of his sovereign he is instantly despatched by another. They look best in their war dress, which is only worn on great occasions, and without which they are like the Kafir tribes in a state of nudity. They rarely use a war axe, which distinguishes the Bechuana warrior, and which he only uses when brought into embarrassed circumstances, when his spears are expended, or when butchering the vanquished enemy. Their shields, made of the thickest part of the ox hide, are very different in size and shape. That of the Matabele is sufficiently long to cover the body, while the other is light, and easily manoeuvred so as to throw off the missles of the enemy. That of the Basuto is smaller still, and seems only capable of defending the left hand, which grasps the spears, and a rod bearing a plume of black ostrich feathers.

Source: R. Moffat, *Missionary Labours and Scenes in Southern Africa* (New York: Carter & Brothers, 1855), p. 351.

Bantu-speaking people in the southeast. Under their ambitious leader, Shaka (1817–1828), the Zulu steadily conquered new territory. Shaka armed infantry troops with spears designed for fighting at close range. The subsequent introduction of firearms by the British and the Muslims had even more serious consequences. The breechloading rifle and the Gatling gun, for example, enabled the British to subdue the Zulu in a series of bloody wars in the 1870s. In the hands of Westerners and Africans, modern weapons unsettled the political life of numerous African states, which were either consolidated under new native rulers or subjugated by foreigners. Thus Sayyid Said, a Muslim contemporary of Shaka, became sultan of Zanzibar in 1806 and for 50 years controlled a vast commercial domain in East Africa. Similarly, the rifle enabled the Boer settlers in South Africa to push into the interior in the face of British and Bantu resistance.

Explorers and Missionaries

Western interest in Africa intensified in the early nineteenth century as a result of the debate over the abolition of the slave trade. Curiosity about the interior of the Dark Continent combined with humanitarian concerns to bring a host of explorers and missionaries to Africa. Exploration focused on two unsolved geographic mysteries: the source of the Niger River in West Africa and the source of the Nile in East Africa. As early as 1795 Mungo Park, a Scottish doctor, led an expedition up the Niger, but not until 1830 was the river fully traced. Successive British adventurers made their way from the coast of East Africa in search of the sources of the Nile, including Sir Samuel White Baker and his wife, Lady Florence Baker. In 1864 the Bakers at last arrived in the vicinity of Lake Albert, which they discovered and named. The most famous African explorer of the period was David Livingstone, whose humanitarianism and courage caught the imagination of Europe. His expeditions in the 1850s sparked public interest. From 1857 to 1863 Livingstone explored the Zambesi River region and in 1866 set out on his last journey, intending to settle the question of the source of the Nile. When no word reached the outside world for five years, an American newspaper sent Henry M. Stanley, a well-known correspondent, to find the lost missionary. The two men met in 1871, but Livingstone, sick and exhausted, refused to return to Britain. When Stanley returned to the Congo in 1878 on behalf of King Leopold of Belgium, he paved the way for a new phase in the history of Western imperialism.

The Scramble for Africa

Portugal had held Angola and Mozambique since the age of exploration, but before 1870 European powers had seized only a few footholds along the coast. France had occupied Algeria and portions of the Senegal, and Britain already controlled the Cape of Good Hope, Gambia, and Sierra Leone and had imposed its commercial influence on the Niger River region and Zanzibar. Following the mid-century explorations, the pace of expansion became intense as Western powers scrambled for territory.

The race for colonies was sparked by King Leopold, who planned to exploit the Congo through the privately financed International Congo Association. Establishing a pattern that would be used by other entrepreneurs, hundreds of tribal chieftains were tricked into signing treaties granting the association some 900,000 square miles of land. Karl Peters, founder of the German Colonization Society, followed suit in East Africa, and the Germans seized Southwest Africa; the French army officer Pierre de Brazza secured control over vast tracts north of the Congo.

In 1885 Bismarck called a conference in Berlin to establish international guidelines for the acquisition of African territory. The conference recognized the Congo Free State as a neutral region. Although the Congo was to be governed by the Belgian King, all nations were to have free access to trade and navigation, and the slave trade was to be suppressed. The diplomats agreed that henceforth a power with coastal possessions had a right to the adjacent hinterland only if it effectively occupied the territory. Future disputes were to be settled by arbitration.

The Congo under Leopold's rule suffered unimaginable exploitation. Private firms used forced labor to squeeze maximum profit out of the rich rubber and ivory resources. Atrocities committed by the labor overseers, together with the toll of disease and climate, claimed more than 10 million lives during the next 20 years. Conditions did not improve until Leopold turned his private ownership of the Free State over to the Belgian government in 1908, when it became the Belgian Congo.

Following the Berlin conference, nine-tenths of the African continent was rapidly divided among the European powers. Italy and Germany joined the scramble. When France blocked Italy's ambitions in Tunisia, Italy instead occupied Eritrea and Somaliland, desolate areas along the Red Sea. In 1896 the Italians attempted to conquer the Christian state of Abyssinia (Ethiopia), but the emperor Menelik's forces, four times the size of the Italian army, defeated the invaders at Adowa. By the end of the century Abyssinia and the American-sponsored nation of Liberia on the west coast remained the only nominally independent states on the continent. Although Bismarck was personally opposed to African colonization, he yielded to domestic pressure. Germany proclaimed a protectorate over Southwest Africa and German East Africa (Tanganyika) and eventually added Togoland and the Cameroons to its empire. When Kaiser William II dismissed Bismarck in 1890, German colonial activities intensified.

Britain, France, and the Perils of Empire

The largest empires in Africa were acquired by France and Britain, whose conflicting ambitions at times brought the two powers to the brink of war. The de Brazza expedition had enabled France to claim a huge portion of Equatorial Africa, and by 1896 France had occupied Madagascar as well. The focus of French efforts, however, was in the Sahara. From Algeria, Senegal, and the Ivory Coast the French pushed south, east, and north across the great desert, establishing military outposts while fighting nomads. In 1881 they occupied Tunisia, and by the end of that decade they had gone beyond Lake Chad to the borders of the Sudan. Eventually the French hoped to reach the Nile and perhaps the Red Sea, a plan that brought them into conflict with British aspirations.

By the time the Berlin conference convened, Britain held the Cape Colony in southern Africa and had imposed its control over Egypt. In 1875 Ismail, Egypt's ruler, was unable to repay huge loans from French and British bankers. When, as a result, he was forced to sell his stock in the Suez Canal Company, representing 44 percent of all shares, British prime minister Benjamin Disraeli bought them, giving Britain a vital stake in the strategic waterway. The next year Ismail suspended interest payments on Egypt's foreign debts, and France and Britain assumed joint control of its finances. Foreign intervention sparked nationalist reaction among Egyptian intellectuals and army officers, and in 1882 riots in Alexandria led to a British bombardment of the city and the establishment of a protectorate over the country. For the next 25 years Egypt was ruled by a British governor.

The British next moved to secure the Sudan, an Egyptian dependency to the south. In 1885 a British garrison at Khartoum under General Charles ("Chinese") Gordon was massacred by the armies of the Mahdi, the leader of fierce Muslim tribesmen. Not until 1898 did the British send an expeditionary force, commanded by General Horatio Kitchener, to retake the Sudan. This time the nationalist fervor of the Muslims was no match for the new British machine guns—more than 10,000 tribesmen were wiped out at Omdurman. A few months earlier a French expedition under Captain Jean-Baptiste Marchand had arrived at Fashoda, where it planted the French flag. On September 18, only a few weeks after Omdurman, Kitchener, with a superior force, met Marchand there. An open clash was avoided only when the French government backed down.

British and French imperial plans ran directly counter to each other, for while France sought to create an east-west empire that stretched from the Atlantic to the Red Sea, Britain dreamed of a north-south domain that reached from Egypt to Cape Town. Along with Egypt and the Sudan, they already controlled Uganda and British East Africa (Kenya), and a determined British push north from the Cape might connect the parts.

South Africa and the Boer War

The British Cape-to-Cairo scheme was the brainchild of Cecil Rhodes (1853–1902), who had become fabulously wealthy in diamond and gold mining. A fierce nationalist and social Darwinist, in 1890 Rhodes became prime minister of the Cape Colony and began to formulate a scheme to bring more of Africa under British rule.

The other European powers represented less of an obstacle to Rhodes than did internal conditions in South Africa. The Cape had been settled in the seventeenth century by Dutch immigrants, staunchly independent Calvinist farmers and cattlemen. When Britain annexed the colony after the Napoleonic Wars, these Afrikaners—the British called them Boers, from the Dutch word for farmer—migrated north in the Great Trek, eventually establishing the Orange Free State and the Transvaal Republic. As they carved out new settlements, the Boers encountered opposition from the Bantu and Zulu populations as well as from the British, and more than 30 years of continuous fighting ensued. Just when a compromise appeared possible, the discovery of gold and diamonds

Paul Kruger, prominent Boer politician and President of the Transvaal. [Bettmann Archive]

intensified the conflict between the British and the Boers. In the 1880s and 1890s hundreds of thousands of Englishmen poured into the mining towns of the Transvaal, Bechuanaland, and the area later known as Rhodesia, overwhelming the Boers and making open conflict all but inevitable.

The principal Boer spokesman was Paul Kruger (1825–1904). As president of the Transvaal, Kruger pressured

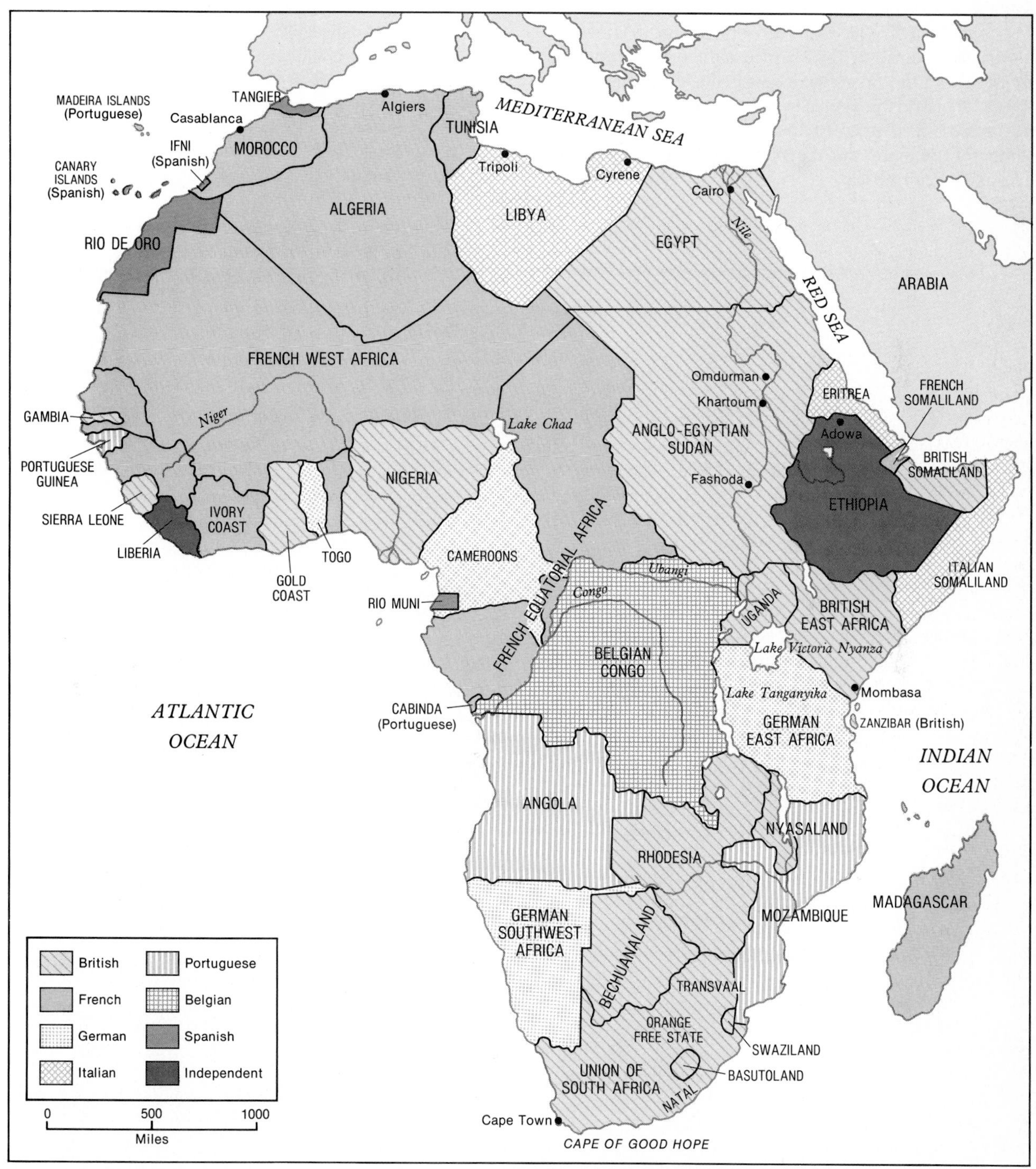

***33.1** Africa on the Eve of World War I*

the *Uitlanders* ("foreigners") by levying discriminatory taxes on them, curbing the use of English, and curtailing the exercise of political rights. In 1895 Rhodes and his agents attempted to overthrow Kruger when a small British force invaded the Transvaal under the command of Dr. Leander Jameson. The Jameson raid failed, but public opinion in Europe condemned the British, and Kaiser William II telegraphed Kruger that the Germans had been ready to help the Boers. In 1899 Britain and the Boer republics went to war; the Boers were defeated and surrendered in 1902. The British eventually granted self-government to the region, and in 1910 the Cape Colony, Natal, the Orange Free State, and the Transvaal were joined as the Union of South Africa.

Imperialism and Its Consequences

Imperialism affected both the European conquerors and their colonial subjects. Economic and industrial development in the West responded to the influx of raw materials and the opportunities for overseas investment, and it is probable that the resulting lower prices had a positive effect on the real wages of some European workers. On the diplomatic level, however, competition for colonies increased tensions among the great powers. The impact on Africa was incalculable as the full weight of Western technology descended on the continent, which for centuries

Women and African Society

Travelers in precolonial Africa encountered long-established social customs that appeared alien to them and that their own cultural arrogance or ethnocentrism made them perceive as primitive. Even David Livingstone, who had a deeper respect for African traditions than most Westerners of his day, sometimes misunderstood the import of what he found. This anecdote, which Livingstone's Victorian mind found humorous, revealed the strength of women's roles in one African community.

The person whom Nyakoba appointed to be our guide, having informed us of the decision, came and bargained that his services should be rewarded with a hoe. I showed him the article; he was delighted with it, and went off to show it to his wife. He soon afterward returned, and said that, though he was perfectly willing to go, his wife would not let him. I said, "Then bring back the hoe"; but he replied, "I want it." "Well, go with us, and you shall have it." "But my wife won't let me." I remarked to my men, "Did you ever hear such a fool?" They answered, "Oh, that is the custom of these parts; the wives are the masters." . . . When a young man takes a liking for a girl of another village, and the parents have no objection to the match, he is obliged to come and live at their village. He has to perform certain services for the mother-in-law, such as keeping her well supplied with firewood; and when he comes into her presence he is obliged to sit with his knees in a bent position, as putting out his feet toward the old lady would give her great offense. If he becomes tired of living in this state of vassalage, and wishes to return to his own family, he is obliged to leave all his children behind—they belong to the wife. This is only a more stringent enforcement of the law from which emanates the practice which prevails so very extensively in Africa, known to Europeans as "buying wives." Such virtually it is, but it does not appear quite in that light to the actors. So many head of cattle or goats are given to the parents of the girl "to give her up," as it is termed, i.e., to forego all claim on her offspring, and allow an entire transference of her and her seed into another family. If nothing is given, the family from which she has come can claim the children as part of itself: the payment is made to sever this bond.

Source: D. Livingstone, *Missionary Travels and Researches in South Africa* (New York: Harper, 1858), pp. 667–668.

had been relatively undisturbed by outside influences. In less than a generation Africans found their social and political structures shattered, their agrarian economy transformed, and their values undermined. Europeans exploited the natural and mineral resources of Africa, extracting huge quantities of gold, diamonds, ivory, rubber, and copper. White settlers seized fertile agricultural land formerly occupied by tribal communities, especially in southern and eastern Africa. The construction of roads, railroads, and telegraph lines stimulated internal trade across long distances and, together with the introduction of a wage-earning structure, transformed the barter economy into a monetary system. Yet enormous manpower was needed to reshape the African economy and build an infrastructure, and the labor supply, poorly paid, was often conscripted by force and treated brutally.

The "modernization" of the continent took a terrible toll on the cultural and political pattern of African life. Broken family and kinship patterns often resulted as workers were required to move over wide distances and tribal communities were stripped of their land. Moreover, imperialism resulted in artificially drawn political boundaries that divided many tribes and merged hostile groups. Even Western humanitarian programs had a mixed impact on local populations. The missionary efforts improved sanitation and agricultural methods and provided Africans with Western education. But these benefits also subverted African identity and undermined traditional values and social mores, for young Africans exposed to Western education or converted to Christianity often rejected family and tribal authority.

The speed and relative ease of European conquest obscures the fact that Africans resisted imperialism. The nomads of the Sahara, the Muslims of the Sudan, and the Zulus of southern Africa fought vigorously against Europeans. After the conquest, resistance took more subtle forms. A new class of Westernized Africans, many trained in European universities and then appointed to posts in the colonial administrations, eventually emerged. Ironically, these Africans, having absorbed Western political attitudes and values, returned home to provide leadership for their people and sometimes spearheaded the drive for independence.

The West in Asia

Many of the same trends were set in motion by the pressures for Westernization in Asia. This was most true in the countries incorporated in Western colonial systems—India, Ceylon, Burma, Malaya, Indochina, Indonesia, and the Philippines—but similar trends were evident in China and even in Japan. Traditional Asian cultures and states were, however, more highly developed than in Africa and could more readily resist or choose from among Western ideas and institutions. For example, a major Christian missionary effort was made, but it produced few converts, although as in Africa it was an important means of introducing Western medicine and education. Much of traditional Asian culture remained vigorous, especially the family system. At the same time, many Asian institutions were remade under Western influence or were augmented by new ones introduced by Westerners.

The arrogance as well as the success of Western imperialism was galling to most Asians, especially given their own pride in their ancient traditions of greatness. Western colonialism, and the unequal treaties forced on Siam (Thailand), China, and Japan, stimulated a renewal of the national Asian traditions and an effort to make them relevant to a world dominated by the West and its standards. Thus India saw the Hindu Renaissance and related movements (often under British pressure) to eliminate or restrict institutions now seen as unacceptable, such as *sati* and child marriage. In China similar movements arose against footbinding, chaste widowhood, and concubinage, in Japan against premarital promiscuity, class-based restrictions on clothing, and more or less open pornography (known as "spring pictures").

Asians found this forced reexamination of much of their cultural heritage under the eyes of an alien conqueror deeply disturbing. Now more than ever they needed to hold their heads up, convinced that to be Indian or Chinese or Japanese or Southeast Asian was something to be proud of. Many convinced themselves that while the West might have a temporary material advantage, the East was still superior spiritually and in the arts of civilization.

Industrialization was in time pursued vigorously, first in India, then in Japan, and finally in China, although it lagged in Southeast Asia. At least as important as technological change were institutions such as banking and joint-stock companies and the particularly Western idea of nationalism. The great Asian empires and states of the past had been cultural and bureaucratic structures different from the nation-states of modern Europe, whose national coherence and drive Asians rightly saw as a source of strength that they lacked but that they must have if they were again to be masters in their own house.

British Imperial India

A divided and weakened India had progressively fallen under the domination of the English East India Company (as described in Chapter 27), and by 1857 most of it was being administered, directly or indirectly, as a single unit. Most Indians exposed to the new British model of Western-style progress admired it, but in the long run being united for the first time yet treated as second-class citizens in their

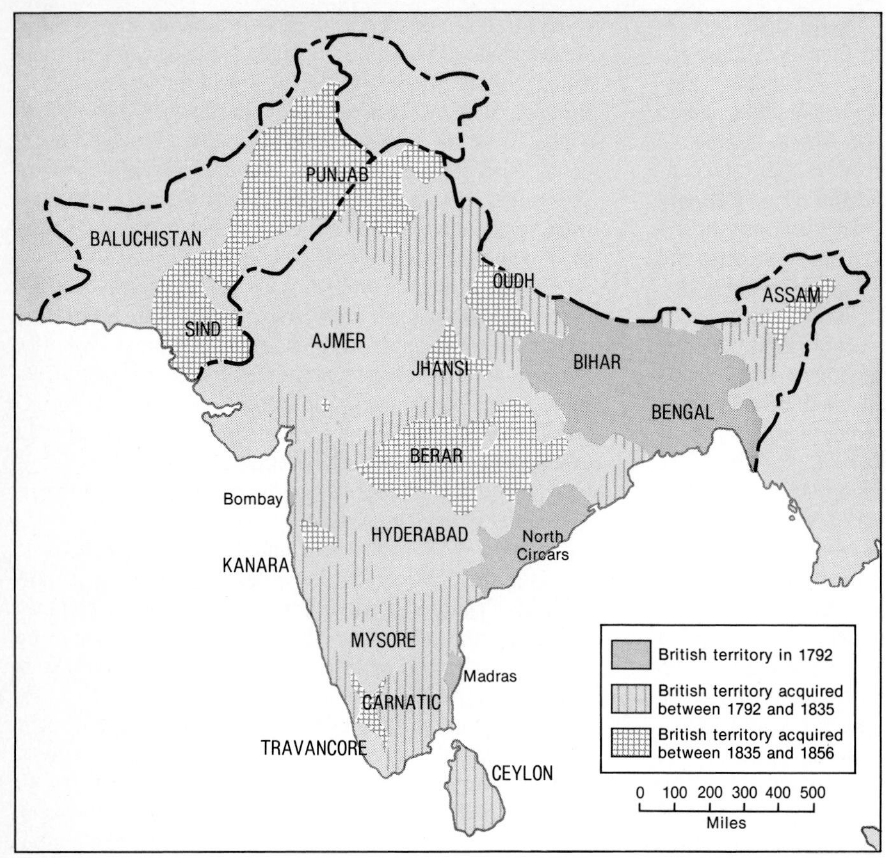

33.2 Growth of the British Empire in India

own country led to the emergence of Indian nationalism. The insurrection of 1857 was not yet a war of independence, but it marked the beginning of Indian response to a foreign control increasingly tinged with arrogance. In the wake of the insurrection, the English East Company was dissolved and the so-called Dual System abolished.

The mutiny marked a watershed between the earlier stages of company rule, which saw considerable racial and cultural mixing, and the rise of full-blown imperialism. The British crown assumed direct imperial authority under the Government of India Act (1858), although the facade of Indian principalities was maintained until independence. To complete the transformation, Queen Victoria adopted the title Empress of India in 1877. She took a special interest in her new dominions, which her prime minister, Benjamin Disraeli, called "the brightest jewel in the crown," and is said to have prayed nightly for her Indian subjects. Although she never went there, many Indians revered her as their own empress, part of the long Indian imperial tradition even under alien rulers, and her picture was widely displayed in people's homes.

The British were careful not to displace any more of the native rulers or to take over more territory, a policy kept until Indian independence in 1947. British residents were placed in each of the hundreds of small and a few large Indian-ruled states, but intervention or threats were rarely needed to keep the roughly half of India still formally in native hands in line with British policy. The army remained largely Indian, but the proportion of British officers and troops was increased, and elite regiments of Sikhs, Rajputs, and Gurkhas (from Nepal) were formed. Indians joined the colonial civil service as well and held responsible positions in all fields under overall British supervision.

Modern Growth

The opening of the Suez Canal in 1869, the shift to steam navigation, and the rapid spread of railways brought India much closer to Europe, greatly accelerating the commercialization of the economy. By the end of the century India had by far the largest rail network (25,000 miles) in all of Asia, on a par with many European countries but on a far bigger scale. This too had obvious commercial consequences, but there were social ones as well. British women could now join their husbands more easily in India and raise their families there, thus creating another wedge of separation between the races and cultures. Colonial social life centered in the buildings and grounds of the British

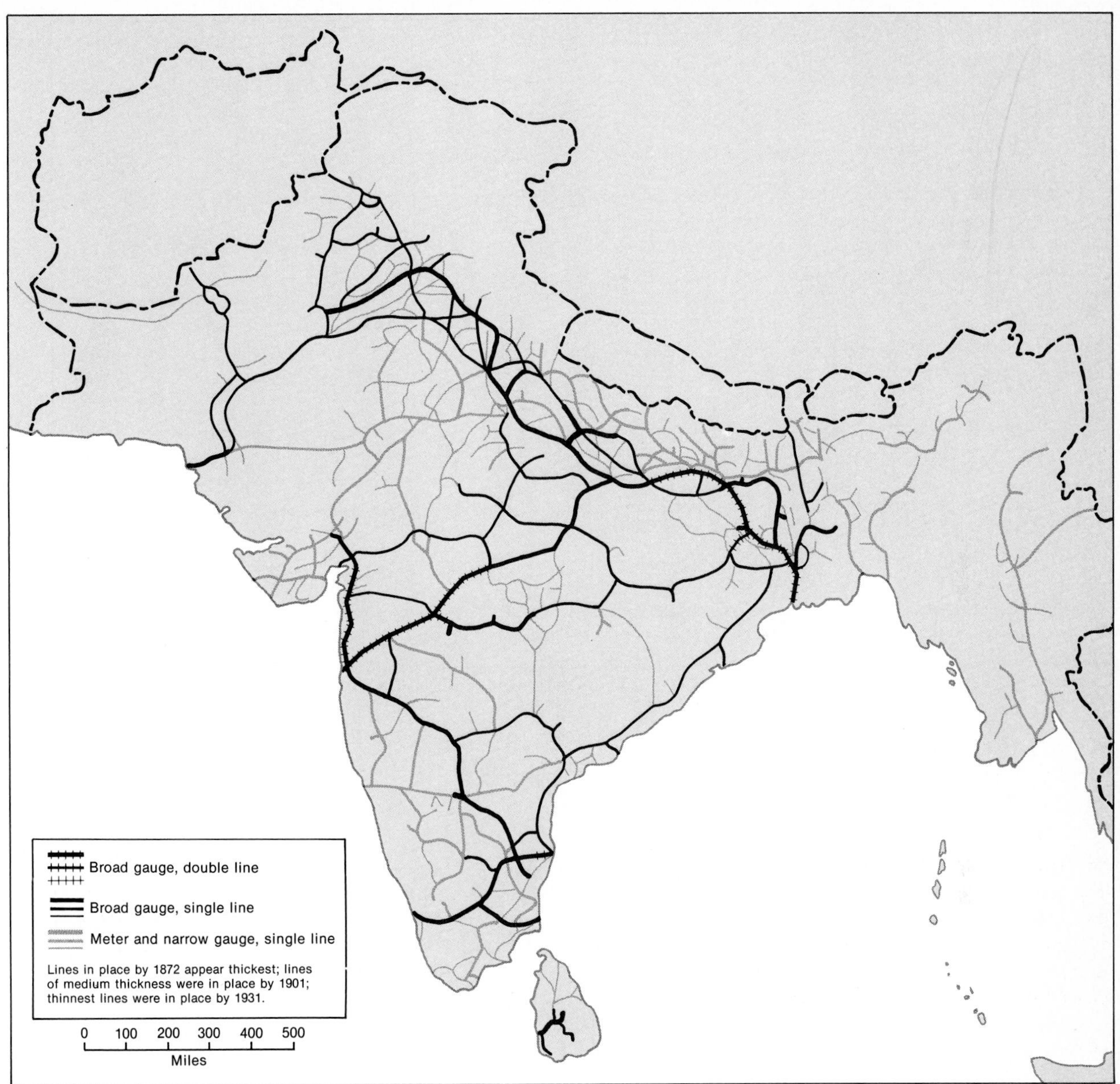

33.3 Growth of India's Railway Network

Club in each city or town, from which Indians were excluded. This social barrier not only delimited the Indians' inferior status but also kept many of the British in a kind of prison of their own making, cut off both from the subjects they ruled and from fresh ideas and attitudes from home. Thus developed what came to be called the colonial mentality, which preserved a mid-Victorian code of conduct and mores well into the twentieth century.

Indians were the first Asians to experience the impact of Western capitalism and industrialization in their country on a large scale. Many of them were quick to respond as entrepreneurs to the new economic opportunities in commerce and machine manufacturing. As in Britain, industrialization began first with machine-made textiles in Bombay and Calcutta, then in a widening range of other manufacturing. Railways stimulated the growing commercialization of agriculture, especially in industrial crops such as jute (fibers), cotton, indigo, and new plantation production of tea, grown mainly in the hills of Assam, which captured most of the world market. New irrigation projects, especially in the semiarid Punjab and the Indus valley, opened productive farming areas to feed India's booming cities, and increased output elsewhere. By 1900 India had the world's largest irrigation system.

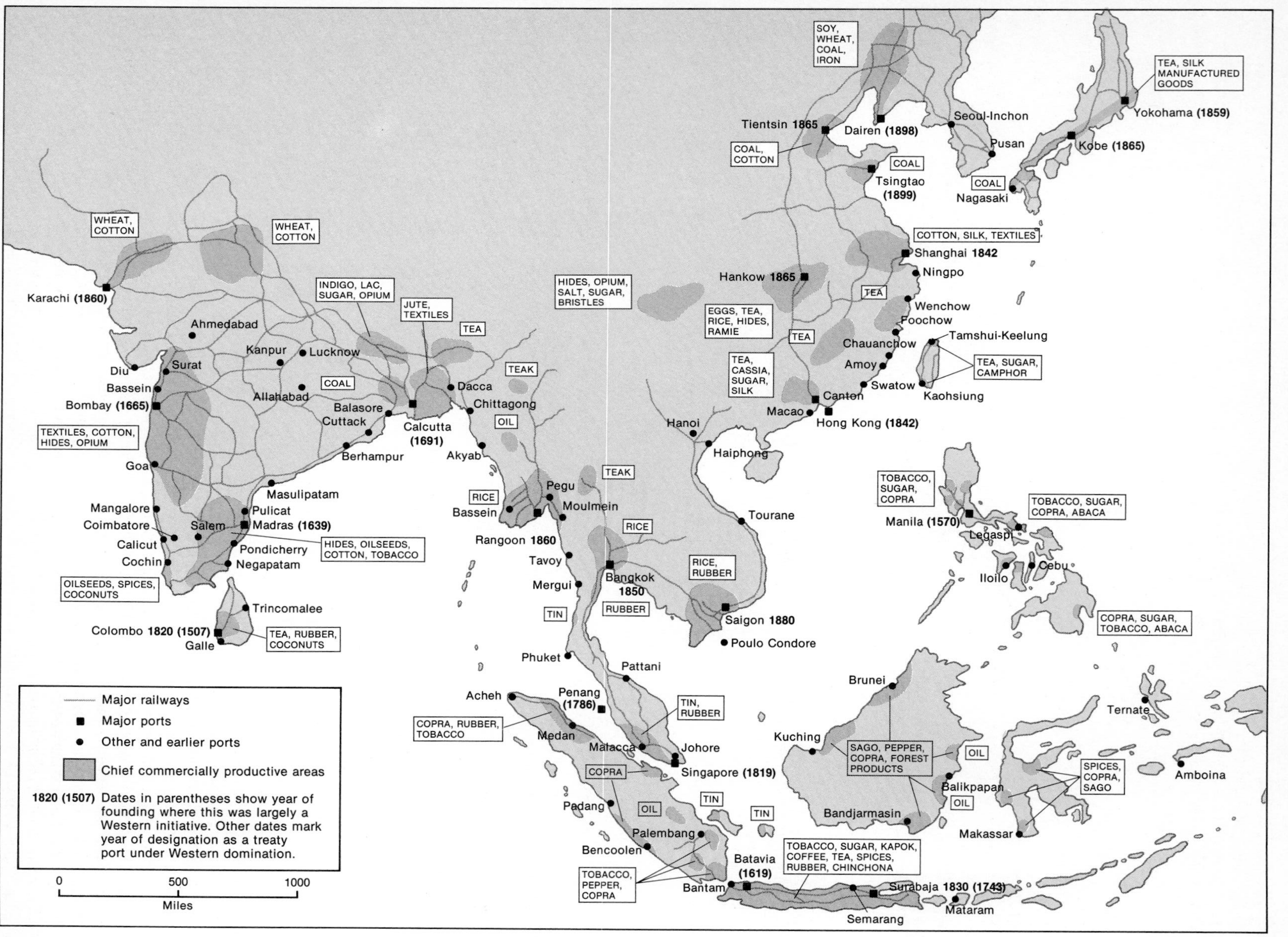

33.4 Major Ports and Commercially Productive Areas in East Asia, 1600–1940

Calcutta remained the country's largest city, closely followed by Bombay and then by Madras. Bombay, with its magnificent harbor and its closeness to cotton-growing areas in Gujarat and Maharashtra, became the premier port and the chief center of Indian-owned textile manufacturing. Large new industrial cities also grew inland as the railway linked most of the country in a single market: Ahmedabad in Gujarat, Lucknow, Kanpur, and Allahabad in the central Ganges, Salem and Coimbatore in the south, and many more. Karachi became the port for cotton and wheat from the Indus valley. British industrial and commercial investors, managers, and traders made money and sold goods in this vast new market, but Indians were increasingly prominent as well in the growing modern sector. Indians also entered and in time dominated the new Western-style professions such as law, medicine, engineering, and education. By 1900 India had the world's fourth largest textile industry and by 1920 the biggest steel plant in the British Empire, both, like many other industries, owned and managed largely by Indians.

Colonial Government

The British saw themselves as the bringers of order and "civilization" to their empire, a role that many of them likened to that of the Romans 2,000 years earlier in Europe. Britain was the greatest power in the world from the mid-eighteenth century to the early twentieth. It was also the nursery of industrialization and modern representative government. These things bred a sense of pride and greatness. Britons were fond of describing theirs as an empire on which the sun never set, since it stretched almost around the globe. Indians, they felt, should be grateful to be included, and indeed many were.

British-style education, conducted in English, continued to shape most Indian intellectuals and literate people to a large degree in the British image. The law of British India, based on English common law, was practiced and administered overwhelmingly by Indians themselves. Nonetheless, the British retained firm control of all senior positions. The prestigious Indian civil service (ICS), staffed until the twentieth century almost entirely by Britons trained in Indian affairs, long remained an exclusive supervisory group under the viceroy, the effective head of state in India appointed by London. The ICS was referred to proudly as the "steel framework" whose roughly 900 members ensured the smooth operation of the colonial government.

Despite colonial achievements in agriculture, public health, education, and transportation, however, most Indians remained poor, illiterate, and powerless. Occasional regional famines continued, as in China. Tenancy and landlessness grew with the increasing commercialization of agriculture, and industrial growth was far too slow to absorb or produce adequately for the rising population.

Between 1800 and 1947 the total population of India probably at least doubled, in itself a sign of order and greater economic opportunity, as in eighteenth-century China. The official census begun in 1871 showed a more or less continuous growth of population together with a falling death rate. But this surge in population was barely matched by overall economic growth, which was in any case unbalanced. There was thus little new margin for improved living standards, and while some commercial, professional, and landed groups prospered, much of the peasantry sank deeper into poverty. India remained poor in part because it was poor to begin with after the extravagances, exploitation, and collapse of the Mughals. Industrialization and commercialization directly impoverished some groups and benefited others, as happened in the West too. The hand spinners of cotton, India's single largest manufacturing work force, were devastated by factory production and British imports, although hand weavers benefited from the cheaper machine-spun yarn. The widening market also gave new employment to many farmers, craftsmen, factory or railway workers, and laborers. The pattern in textiles was repeated in other industries and markets and occurred in China as well.

The colonial government was chronically pinched for funds; London insisted that all expenses had to be covered from Indian revenues. The army took much of these, in part for the conquest of Burma, and there was little to spare. Planning was thus difficult, and problems were addressed piecemeal or not at all. Reformers accused the government of playing the role of night watchman while most Indians remained in poverty. Even so, the colonial administration required indirect support, costs that were necessarily borne by ordinary British taxpayers. Thus the imperial system was supported by the middle and lower classes of both countries for the benefit of British and Indian elites.

It would have been impossible for the relative handful of British in India to control the subcontinent and its 350 million people by the 1930s without the support or the active help of most Indians. The British officer contingent in the Indian army reached 40,000 only in the special circumstances of World Wars I and II. The total number of Britons of all levels and in all branches of the civil service, including district officers, judges, and police, was never more than 12,000. In short, colonial India was run mainly by Indians, who until relatively late willingly supported the British raj or government. By 1910, for example, the police force comprised about 5,000 Britons and over 600,000 Indians. The rest of the civil service employed about 600,000 Indians with only some 5,000 Britons, and the army consisted of about 150,000 native troops and approximately 25,000 British officers.

In contrast, the higher echelons of government remained a British preserve. As if to show their aloofness from the country, they governed in the blazing hot months of summer from hill stations in the Himalayan foothills,

Social life in the hill stations: a fete at Simla, in a glade nostalgically named "Annandale," painted by A. E. Scott c. 1845. [India Office Library of the British Library]

first at Darjeeling in northernmost Assam and later from Simla, north of Delhi. From both they enjoyed spectacular views of the snow-covered mountains, cool, bracing air, Western-style lodges and cottages that reminded them of home, and a round of parties, picnics, and receptions.

As more colonial officers served longer, young British women came or were sent out to India to find a husband, an annual migration at the beginning of the cool weather in autumn irreverently referred to as the "arrival of the fishing fleet." Those who remained unspoken for by the time the hot weather resumed in mid-March often went back to England as "returned empties." As the British community grew, many families by the twentieth century had lived in India for several generations and thought of it as home. They called themselves Anglo-Indians, and they lived in separate residential areas built for them some distance from the Indian town where they worked. These were known as "civil lines" or "cantonments," since many of them had begun as quarters for troops or garrisons. Each of their households was waited on by large numbers of Indian servants, whose labor was extremely cheap.

Another group was also known as Anglo-Indians. These were the products of intermarriage, which had been common in the eighteenth and early nineteenth centuries and still occasionally took place in later years. These Anglo-Indians were rejected by both the Indian and British communities, but they usually tried to pass as English and spoke wistfully of "home," meaning an England that most of them had never seen. Many of them became Christians in an effort to raise their status, as did many untouchables. Missionary efforts made few converts otherwise, although mission schools remained an important means to Western education for many non-Christians as well as for the few Christians.

NEW DELHI: INDIAN SUMMER OF THE RAJ

Calcutta had long seemed inappropriate as the capital of a British India that had expanded to cover the subcontinent, thousands of miles from Bengal. Although now a thoroughly Indian city, it had been founded by the British themselves and had no indigenous roots or history. Its marginal coastal site further emphasized the foreignness of British rule. For several years after 1900 alternative capital sites were considered, and Delhi, the former Mughal capital, was chosen. At the head of the Ganges valley, Delhi controlled routes from both east and south to the heart of India. Successive invaders had to capture Delhi first, mounting their campaigns and ruling their empires from there. The British raj moved too in 1911 to rule from where so many others had before.

It was decided to build a new planned city as an imperial statement, adjacent to the old city and with open space around it but still well within sight of Shah Jahan's Red Fort (see Chapter 19). The remains of other imperial Delhis of the past also showed on the skyline. An artificial hill was built as the setting for the monumental residence and gardens of the viceroy, flanked on each side by two large and stately government buildings known as the Secretariat. From this low rise, broad boulevards and wide vistas led to other buildings and monuments to empire, including the parliament house, by the 1920s filled with mainly Indian members.

Like Paris and Washington, New Delhi was planned before the age of mass transit and the automobile. It was essentially built in a star-shaped pattern with broad tree-lined streets intersecting at angles and punctuated by circles of green area around which traffic had to move. The plan included a large separate commercial and shopping district, with buildings in neoclassical and Anglo-Indian styles, grouped around an immense circle, still called Connaught Circus. Related enterprises lined the streets leading into it at various angles. Pleasant shaded avenues with British names occupied most of the rest of the new planned city, most of them filled with gracious residences and beautiful gardens for civil servants, Indian princes (most of whom maintained extensive establishments in New Delhi), and other members of the upper classes. Lesser officials, workers, and servants commuted the mile or so from Old Delhi, mainly by bicycle, or were housed in the unplanned developments that soon grew around the edges of New Delhi.

The ambitious building plans of 1911 and 1912 were delayed by World War I, but by 1930 the new imperial capital was complete. The architects of New Delhi were of course British, but they made a generally successful effort to combine Western and Indian monumental and imperial traditions, consciously using the same red sandstone of which the Red Fort had been built and creating buildings that fit their Indian setting far better than the earlier Victorian extravagances in Calcutta and Bombay. Old Delhi remains a traditional Indian city, centered around the Red Fort. A confusing maze of tiny streets and alleys surrounds the bazaar near Shah Jahan's great mosque, the Jama Masjid. The large unbuilt area in front of the Red Fort remains a vast open-air market and a frequent scene of political rallies. New Delhi became almost automatically the capital of independent India, with no sense of inappropriateness for the world's largest parliamentary democracy, still based on British colonial foundations. Since 1947 Delhi has boomed and become a major industrial center. But Old and New Delhi represent different strands in India's varied past and now also show the two faces of contemporary India, traditional and modern.

An example of colonial architecture: Victoria Station, Bombay, with a statue of Queen Victoria on the top of its dome. [Rhoads Murphey]

The Rise of Indian Nationalism

British-educated Indians, despite their prosperity, were increasingly resentful of the racial discrimination to which they were subject. Many began to demand a larger role in their country's government. Gradually a movement for independence developed. Liberal Englishmen agreed, contending that alien rule was contrary to the British tradition of representative government and political freedom. Gestures toward increasing the participation of Indians in the administration and civil service and elections for some officials and advisers came too slowly to satisfy either Indian or British critics.

The Indian National Congress, which was to become the core of the independence movement, was actually founded by an Englishman in 1885. Indian political leaders made nationalist appeals, among them highly effective and articulate figures such as M. G. Ranade (1842–1901), B. G. Tilak (1856–1920), G. K. Gokhale (1866–1915), and Motilal Nehru (1861–1931), the father of Jawaharlal Nehru (1889–1964), independent India's first prime minister. Their language, culture, and education were as much English as Indian, and they could speak eloquently in terms of British tradition itself against the colonial rule of their country.

Meanwhile, fear of the still expanding Russian empire in central Asia prompted yet another disastrous invasion of Afghanistan in 1878 to install a British puppet on the throne of Kabul. The Afghans murdered the British resident and his entire staff and military escort within a year, and guerrilla fighters stalemated a second invasion until it was withdrawn in 1880 and the Afghans again were "permitted" to choose their own ruler. Opinion in Britain was outraged by both the brutality and the cost of this futile military adventure, and the Disraeli government fell as a result.

The colonial government in India spearheaded other costly ventures as well. In addition to the conquest of Burma, it launched an armed reconnaissance against Tibet in 1903 and 1904 to forestall illusory Russian influence there. The mission showed the flag and obtained an agreement about the frontier. While imperial posturing preoccupied the colonial government and drained the country's resources, poverty in India remained largely unaddressed. Indian nationalists blamed the severe economic distress in many areas on colonial rule. Boycotts of British imports were begun, cutting their value by 25 percent between 1904 and 1908. The government's response was often repressive, and many political leaders were jailed. There were still many British in government with more liberal ideas, and many more outside government, who strove to reduce racial discrimination and urged Indian self-government as Britain's ultimate goal. In 1883, for example, it was agreed that Indian judges could preside over cases involving Europeans. But imperialist attitudes and bureaucratic inertia retarded the giving of Indians a larger and more appropriate role in their own government.

The Amritsar Massacre of April 1919 was followed by further repression in the wake of renewed protests and demonstrations. Here British police officers in Amritsar watch while their Indian assistants search a demonstrator. [Bettmann Archive/BBC Hulton]

Over a million Indian troops and noncombatants served the British effort in World War I in Europe and the Middle East. Many hoped that this would speed progress toward self-government. When change lagged after the war, civil disobedience movements spread, now led by Mahatma Gandhi (1869–1948), among others, only to be met by more government repression. In 1919 Indian troops under British command, called in to put down rioting in Amritsar near Lahore, fired on a peaceful and unarmed crowd celebrating a festival, leaving 400 dead. The massacre was a watershed in Anglo-Indian relations. It turned most Indians away from the idea of reform and toward the goal of full independence, creating almost overnight a greatly expanded nationalist movement.

In 1907 the British Parliament had declared that independence was Britain's objective in India, a point the British government reaffirmed in 1917 and 1921, but the colonial administration remained slow to move. Although the electoral system was greatly broadened in the 1920s and 1930s and Indian legislatures and officials were given far more power and responsibility, it was too little, too late. Time had run out for British rule in India.

Colonial Regimes in Southeast Asia

The Dutch came to control the largest amount of territory and population in Southeast Asia, incorporating the whole of what is now Indonesia in their colonial empire, from which they largely excluded other Western trade or investment competition. Large numbers of Chinese were already there, however, and their numbers increased to some 3 million as they expanded their control of smaller-scale domestic trade and retailing. The British, along with other Westerners, had been trading in Burma since the seventeenth century, but as their Indian empire, and their imperial ambition, grew, they progressively annexed Burma to their colonial holdings. Malaya was thinly settled and unimportant in trade until the tin and rubber boom of the late nineteenth century, but the British hoped to use bases there in an effort to tap the trade with Southeast Asia and with China, a role ultimately performed by Singapore. By the end of the nineteenth century all of Malaya was under British colonial administration, but primarily on an indirect basis through local Malay sultans. French and

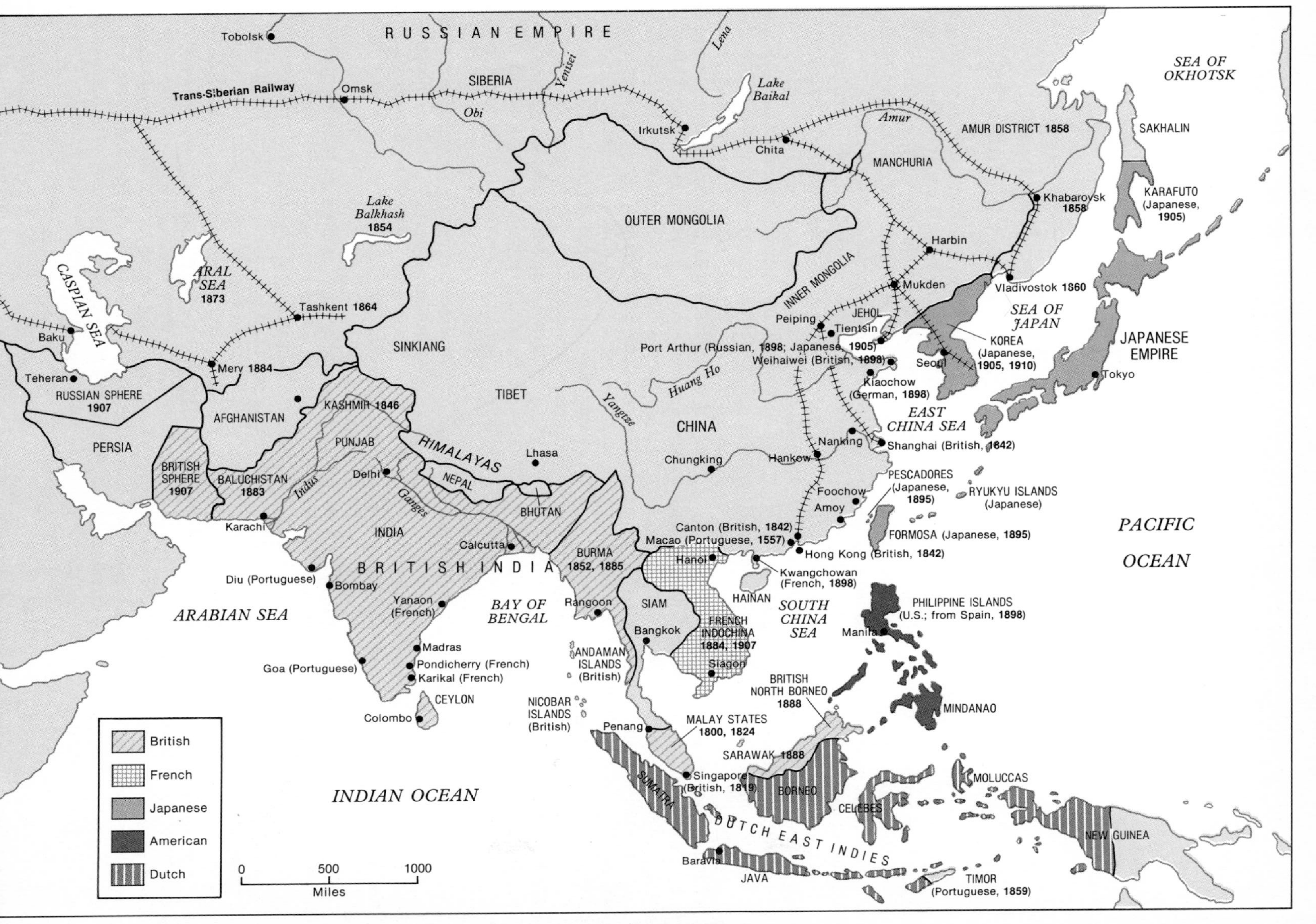

33.5 Colonial Empires in Asia

American colonialists arrived late on the scene. France acquired the Indochinese states of Vietnam, Cambodia, and Laos through conquest by 1885, and the Americans inherited control of the Philippines as a consequence of their defeat of Spain, the former colonial master of the area, in 1898. Each of these Western colonial regimes followed policies with many similarities and some differences. Siam (now Thailand) remained independent as a buffer between rival colonial empires but had to accept the same set of "unequal treaties" as was imposed on China and Japan.

The British in Burma and Malaya

Britain's activity in Southeast Asia had been incidental to its concerns in India and its efforts to break into the China market. It was at first confined to founding bases on the fringes of Dutch power in Malaya. In 1786 a settlement was made at Penang on the northwestern Malay coast, where the British hoped to attract Chinese traders. This was only moderately successful, and they established what soon became their major Southeast Asian trade base at Singapore in 1819.

From the start, Singapore was a commercial center for all of Southeast Asia. Malaya itself remained thinly populated and largely undeveloped until the end of the nineteenth century. Burma was India's immediate geographic neighbor to the east. Its antiquated monarchy periodically made difficulties for British merchants and ignored or insulted British representatives. A brief war from 1824 to 1826 added the important coastal provinces of Burma to the East India Company's territories. Two more minor wars in 1852 and 1885–1886, largely provoked by the British, annexed the rest of the country. Burma was then administered as a province of British India until it was granted separate colonial status in 1937.

Burma and Malaya were rapidly commercialized after 1880 under British rule. Railways were built and steam navigation developed. The Irrawaddy delta in lower Burma, including much newly cultivated land, became a major exporter of rice. Upper Burma produced timber, especially teak, for export, and the central valley yielded oil from wells drilled by the British. All this moved out for export through the port of Rangoon, which served as the colonial capital. In Malaya were found rich deposits of tin, a metal in great demand in the industrializing West, and toward the end of the century Malaya also became the world's major producer of plantation rubber. Labor for tin mining and rubber tapping had to be imported, since the local Malays, subsistence farmers, were not interested in such work. The gap was filled mainly from overcrowded South China, and Chinese settlers soon comprised nearly half the population of Malaya. In time many of these Chinese immigrants, who also entered the booming commercial economy of Singapore, became wealthy. The Malays increasingly resented Chinese domination of the commercial economy. Indians also entered, as both laborers and merchants, and with the Chinese and the British controlled the commercial production and foreign trade of both Burma and Malaya. The colonial government of Malaya ruled as much as possible through local sultans and tried to preserve traditional Malay culture, but both countries were economically transformed.

French, Dutch, and American Colonialism

Largely eliminated from India by the end of the eighteenth century, the French sought their own colonial sphere in Asia. They used the persecution of French Catholic missionaries in Vietnam as a pretext for conquering the southern provinces in 1862, including the port of Saigon. Later they annexed Cambodia and Laos, and in 1885 took over northern Vietnam after defeating Chinese forces sent to protect their tributary state. Under French control, southern Vietnam became a major exporter of rice and rubber grown in the delta of the Mekong River. They were exported through the chief port of Saigon, which was made the colonial capital. Cambodia and Laos remained little developed commercially. Northern Vietnam was already too densely populated to produce surpluses for export, but there was some small industrial growth around the city of Hanoi and in the northern port of Haiphong. The colonial administration tried to impose French culture on these territories, collectively called Indochina.

French rule was oppressive and often ruthless in suppressing all gestures toward political expression. The army was augmented by special security forces and had much of the apparatus of a police state, which executed, jailed, or drove into exile most Vietnamese leaders. These included the young Ho Chi Minh (1890–1969), later the head of the Vietnamese Communist party, who went to Europe in 1911 and later from Paris to Moscow and Canton.

The Dutch left most of Indonesia to native rulers until late in the nineteenth century, content with controlling trade from Batavia (now Djakarta), their colonial capital. Batavia was situated on the tropical island of Java, which produced a variety of plantation crops the Dutch promoted after 1830, including sugar, coffee, tea, and tobacco. By the early 1900s rubber was an important commodity, and Indonesia was second only to Malaya in its production. Oil was also found and exploited. The discovery of more oil and tin and the cultivation of prime land for rubber and tobacco prompted the Dutch to increase their control, first of the neighboring island of Sumatra, and then of Borneo, Celebes, the Moluccas, Bali, and the hundreds of smaller islands in the archipelago south of the Philippines. New railways and ports were built to expedite trade.

Dutch rule was fiercely contested on some of the islands, especially Sumatra, and it never penetrated effectively into the mountain and jungle interior of Borneo. The northern coast of Borneo was controlled by the British. Dutch rule became increasingly oppressive. Indonesians were excluded from participation in government and the exercise of political rights and were denied access to more than elementary education. Java was systematically exploited by forcing its peasants to grow export crops for Dutch profit. Production and population grew very rapidly, but living standards and the quality of life declined.

In 1898 the United States went to war with Spain over Cuba and acquired the Philippines as its first overseas colony. The 43 years of American control had a greater effect on the culture and economy of the islands than 450 years of Spanish rule. The Americans built roads and hospitals and established an education system up to the university level. Literacy and public health rose to levels second only to Japan in Asia. But America's economic impact was exploitive. In partnership with rich Filipinos, it concentrated on growing commercial crops for export, especially sugar, and often neglected the basic needs of the people as a whole. Manila, the colonial capital, became a rapidly growing commercial center and the chief base of the Filipino middle class and educated elite. The Americans declared as their goal the creation of a democratic society in their own image. To a degree this was achieved, but Philippine politics remained under the control of a landed elite supported by others who profited from the American connection and paid little attention to the dominantly peasant population, who remained exploited. The country had been subjugated only by a brutal war against Filipino nationalist resistance from 1899 to 1902 in which the Americans pursued policies that foreshadowed their later misadventures in Vietnam. Most peasants, still largely illiterate, could hardly take advantage of free public education and free expression. The United States granted independence to the Philippines in 1946 on terms that ensured its continuing influence and left huge American military bases there.

Independent Siam

While the rest of Southeast Asia was being taken over by imperialist powers, the Thais kept their independence. This was in part the result of geography. Siam lay between the British in Burma and Malaya and the French in Indochina. Neither was willing to let the other dominate the country. British preponderance in Thai foreign trade and investment was balanced by French annexation of territory claimed or occupied by Siam in western Cambodia and Laos. British Malaya detached Siam's southern provinces. Nonetheless, the Thais benefited from a series of able kings who adroitly played the French off against the British and urged the advantages to both of leaving at least part of their country as a buffer state. They had to grant special trade, residence, and legal privileges to the colonial powers, a system like that imposed on China, but there was no foreign effort to take over the government. Nevertheless the Thai economy developed along the same lines as colonial Southeast Asia, with a big new export trade in rice from the delta area, followed later by rubber and tropical hardwoods. Bangkok, the capital, grew rapidly as the chief port for foreign trade and spreading commercialization.

Overseas Chinese

Western development had important demographic consequences for Southeast Asia. Immigrant Chinese began to flood into all the commercially developed parts of the region in growing numbers after 1870, as plantation and mining labor and as traders. They soon largely monopolized the retail trade in all the cities of Southeast Asia, although they shared it with immigrant Indians in Burma and Malaya. In Bangkok they constituted over half the population and, as in Burma and Vietnam, controlled most of the large export trade in rice. Southeast Asians resented them, especially since they also served as moneylenders and owned most of the shops, but they were often welcomed by the colonialists as useful labor and commercial agents. In Siam, unlike the rest of Southeast Asia, most Chinese were quickly assimilated into Thai society through intermarriage and acculturation. Elsewhere they tended to remain confined to their own quarters and suffered discrimination from the local people. Altogether, Chinese settlers in Southeast Asia totaled about 15 million by the outbreak of World War II.

China Besieged

The Treaty of Nanking, which ended the Anglo-Chinese Opium War of 1839–1842, granted Britain most of its demands for trading rights and concessions. The port of Hong Kong was ceded outright, and five mainland ports, including Shanghai and Canton, were opened to British trade and residence. Other Western powers, including the United States, negotiated similar treaties the following year. These included the right of extraterritoriality, whereby foreign nationals in China were made immune from Chinese jurisdiction and were dealt with according to their own laws. The war had finally cracked China's proud isolation.

Foreign trade immediately began a rapid increase that continued until the world depression of the 1930s. Tea and silk remained the dominant exports and opium the main import, although it was overtaken after 1870 by cotton yarn, textiles, kerosene, and a variety of other foreign

Opium

The imperial commissioner sent to Canton in 1839 to stop the opium trade wrote a letter in the same year to the young Queen Victoria that read in part as follows.

Magnificently our great emperor soothes and pacifies China and the foreign countries. . . . But there appear among the crowd of barbarians both good and bad persons, unevenly. . . . There are barbarian ships that come here for trade to make a great profit. But by what right do they in return use the poisonous drug [opium] to injure the Chinese people? . . . Of all that China exports to foreign countries, there is not a single thing which is not beneficial. . . . On the other hand, articles coming from outside China can only be used as toys; they are not needed by China. Nevertheless, our Celestial Court lets tea, silk, and other goods be shipped without limit. This is for no other reason than to share the benefit with the people of the whole world.

Source: S. Y. Teng and J. K. Fairbank, *China's Response to the West* (Cambridge, Mass.: Harvard University Press, 1954), pp. 24–26.

manufactured goods. The treaties further impinged on China's sovereignty by limiting the import tariffs it might impose to 5 percent. This had the effect of giving Western goods virtually unrestricted access to the vast Chinese market. Although China continued to provide most of its own needs, the treaties reduced the country to semicolonial status.

Peking's reluctance to abide by the terms of the treaties led to a second war from 1858 to 1860. British and French troops captured Tientsin (Tianjin) and Peking and burned the imperial summer palace. They saw this as retaliation for Chinese "treachery"—the breaking of successive agreements to observe earlier treaties and to receive the British ambassador in Peking, as well as firing on British forces and imprisoning their representatives.

Traders and Missionaries

The Treaty of Tientsin, which ended this second war, opened still more ports to residence and trade and allowed foreigners, including missionaries, free movement and enterprise anywhere in the country. Missionaries often served as a forward wave for imperialism, building churches and preaching the Gospel in the interior and then demanding protection from their home governments against Chinese protests or riots. Trouble missionaries or foreign traders encountered might be answered by sending a warship to the nearest coastal or river port to threaten or shell inhabitants, a practice known as "gunboat diplomacy." When antiforeign mobs assulted missionaries or their converts, Western governments often used this as a pretext for extracting still more concessions.

Most Chinese were not receptive to the Christian message, especially in the evangelical form of most missionary preaching, and they resented foreigners with special privileges and protection encroaching on their country. Nor did they understand the missionary practice of buying or adopting orphans for charitable and religious purposes and so assumed the worst motives for these practices. Stories circulated that they ate babies or gouged out their eyes for medicine. In 1870 a mob destroyed a French Catholic mission in Tientsin and killed 10 nuns and 11 other foreigners; gunboats and heavy reparations followed.

Unlike the British, the French had no important trade with China and often used protection of their missionaries as a means of increasing their influence. In 1883 they went to war with China over Vietnam when Chinese troops crossed the border to eject them. The French destroyed part of the new Western-style Chinese navy and the dockyards at Foochow on the South China coast, which they had earlier helped to build. China was humbled again.

The Taiping Rebellion

Meanwhile, the greatest of all uprisings against the Ch'ing government erupted in 1850, the Taiping Rebellion. Westerners tend to overemphasize their own role in China as the major influence on events after 1840. China was huge, Westerners were few, and their activities were limited to the treaty ports and outlying mission stations. China con-

Through Each Other's Eyes

After the Opium War, foreign arrogance increased. Here is a sample from 1858.

It is impossible that our merchants and missionaries can course up and down the inland waters of this great region and traffic in their cities and preach in their villages without wearing away at the crust of the Chinaman's stoical and skeptical conceit. The whole present system in China is a hollow thing, with a hard brittle surface. . . . Some day a happy blow will shiver it [and] it will all go together.

But the Chinese returned the compliment.

It is monstrous in barbarians to attempt to improve the inhabitants of the Celestial Empire when they are so miserably deficient themselves. Thus, introducing a poisonous drug for their own benefit and to the injury of others, they are deficient in benevolence. Sending their fleets and armies to rob other nations, they can make no pretense to rectitude. . . . How can they expect to renovate others? They allow the rich and noble to enter office without passing through any literary examinations, and do not open the road to advancement to the poorest and meanest in the land. From this it appears that foreigners are inferior to the Chinese and therefore must be unfit to instruct them.

Sources: G. W. Cooke, *China: Being the Times Special Correspondence from China in the Years 1857–58* (London: Routledge, 1858), p. v; "A Chinese Tract of the Mid-Nineteenth Century," in E. P. Boardman, *Christian Influence on the Ideology of the Taiping Rebellion* (Madison: University of Wisconsin Press, 1952), p. 129.

tinued to respond primarily to its own long-standing internal problems, chief among which was a burgeoning population. Having outstripped production, it was falling into poverty and distress in many areas. The Taiping leader, Hung Hsiu-Ch'uan (Hong Xiuquan), was a frustrated scholar who had failed the rigid imperial examinations several times and then espoused an idiosyncratic version of Christianity adapted from missionary teaching. Hung became the leader of a largely peasant group from the impoverished mountain region of southern China, which resented its exclusion from the treaty ports and sought the overthrow of the Manchus. The rebels picked up massive support as they moved north and captured Nanking (Nanjing) in 1853. A northward thrust from there was turned back later that year near Tientsin, but rebel forces won at least a foothold in 16 of China's 18 provinces and dominated the rich Yangtze valley.

The efforts of the Taiping rebels to govern were relatively feeble. Large-scale fighting against the imperial forces continued without significant breaks until its final suppression in 1864. The cost in destruction and loss of life was horrendous. As many as 40 million people died, and much of the productive lower Yangtze region was laid waste. During the same period the Ch'ing also faced three other mass uprisings, in the north, the southwest, and the northwest. The latter two were primarily Muslim rebellions against Ch'ing rule, which lingered until 1873. As one Ch'ing official said, these revolts were like a disease of China's vital organs. In contrast, the activities of the Western powers were a marginal affliction only of the extremities.

Attempts at Reform

One foreign power, however, was still advancing by land: the Russians. Sensing China's weakness, they penetrated the Amur valley in northern Manchuria, from which they had been excluded in 1689. In the treaties following the war of 1858–1860 they detached the maritime provinces of eastern Manchuria and added them to their empire; among their acquisitions was the port of Vladivostok. Muslim rebellion in the northwest after 1862 served as a pretext for Russian intervention in northern Sinkiang (Xinjiang). The Ch'ing government decided that this threat must be met head on, marched an army 2,500 miles from its base in eastern China, and to general surprise defeated both the rebels and the Russians by 1878.

Survival of the Ch'ing regime against the appalling challenges it faced showed that it was still capable of successful action. After 1860 it undertook a policy of "self-strengthening," which included the establishment of new Western-style arsenals, gun foundries, and shipyards. These and other efforts to modernize were handicapped by government red tape, but they achieved some progress. Several outstanding senior officials who realized the need for change rose to power. For a decade or two the Ch'ing seemed to have a new lease on life and to show surprising vigor.

It was not to last. The reformers never won full support from the still archconservative throne or from most of the people. Both remained essentially antiforeign and opposed to adopting Western tactics even to fight Westerners. In 1862 a weak boy-emperor came to the throne, dominated by his scheming mother, Tz'u Hsi (Cixi, 1835–1908), a former imperial concubine who had plotted her way to the top. When the emperor died in 1875 at the age of 19, she put her 4-year-old nephew in his place, retaining all real power for herself as the empress dowager until her death in 1908. Tzu Hsi was clever and politically masterful but narrow-minded and deeply conservative. She had no understanding of what was required to cope with the foreign threat to Chinese sovereignty.

China's first tentative efforts at change were thus for the most part aborted. The Confucian reactionaries, who with few exceptions again dominated the government, grudgingly acknowledged the potency of Western arms but insisted that there could be no abandoning or even altering the traditional Chinese view of the world to deal with them.

The empress dowager Tzu Hsi (Cixi). She was a powerful and unscrupulous ruler, but in keeping with the degeneracy of the late Ch'ing period favored the over-ornate style in which she decorated many rooms in the imperial palace in Peking, as shown here. [Freer Gallery of Art, Smithsonian Institution]

Treaty Ports and Mission Schools

Meanwhile the treaty ports, which numbered over 100 by 1910, grew rapidly, attracting Chinese as merchants, partners, and laborers. Manufacturing also began to grow in the treaty ports, especially after 1895 when the Japanese imposed a new treaty that permitted foreign-owned factories to operate in the ports; these produced mainly textiles and other consumer goods. This was the real beginning of modern industrialization in China.

Chinese entrepreneurs and industrialists, many of whom had been blocked or discouraged by the conservative government, welcomed the more enterprising world of the treaty ports. As elsewhere in Asia, imperialist arrogance was growing, and the Chinese found themselves excluded from foreign clubs and parks and treated as second-class citizens in their own cities. Many of them were torn between their ancient cultural pride and their sense of humiliation by Westerners on the one hand and their reluctant admiration for the West's power and success on the other. As with their Indian counterparts in colonial Calcutta and Bombay, these conflicts produced the first stirrings of modern nationalism.

The most widespread Western influence on Chinese society came through the efforts of missionaries. The total number of Chinese Christians remained discouragingly small, and many, perhaps most, of them were so-called "rice Christians," who attended church for handouts. Most Chinese looked down on Christian converts as traitors or simply as the dregs of society. Many of the missions came to realize that education and medical help were more attractive than Christian doctrine and might pave a smoother path toward the goal of conversion. Mission-run schools spread rapidly, as did their hospitals. The schools drew many students, in time most of the young Chinese who wanted to study English and Western learning or science. Although most graduates did not become converts, they adopted Western ways of thinking in many respects. Most twentieth-century Chinese nationalists were influenced by mission schools, and nearly all of China's universities were founded by missionaries.

Government schools that included Western curricula were also established, and in 1905 the traditional examination system was abolished. Missionaries and others translated a wide range of Western works, which were read avidly by the new generation of Chinese intellectuals. Many of them began to call for the overthrow of the Ch'ing regime. Ironically, they used the treaty ports, notably Shanghai, as their base, where they were protected from Ch'ing repression by living under foreign law.

The Boxer Rebellion

Missionaries in rural areas continued to provoke antiforeign riots as their activities spread. In the late 1890s the empress dowager adroitly turned a group of impoverished bandits and rebels in eastern North China against the missionaries instead of against the dynasty, and by extension against all foreigners. By early 1900 this group, which called itself the "fists of righteous harmony" but was known more simply to Westerners as the Boxers, went on a rampage, burning mission establishments and killing missionaries and Chinese converts. Converts were resented for their use of foreign intervention in their disputes with other Chinese. By June 1900, with covert imperial support, the Boxers besieged the foreign legations in Peking, which barely held out until relieved by a multinational expedition in mid-August. Having earlier declared war officially against all the foreign powers, the court fled to Sian (Xian). After brutal reprisals, the Western powers (now including a large Japanese contingent) withdrew, and a peace was patched up a year later. A staggering indemnity was forced on China, on top of one already extracted by Japan in 1895. The empress dowager and her reactionary councillors, who had seen the Boxers as the final solution to the "barbarian problem," were left nominally in power.

The Ch'ing dynasty was moribund, but no workable alternative was yet at hand. China had still to learn the lessons of national unity and shared political purpose, which had been unnecessary in the past when the empire controlled "all under heaven" and China had no rivals. The government finally fell in 1911, more of its own weight and incompetence than because of the small, disorganized group of revolutionaries whose uprising joined the defection of disgruntled troops. The fall of the Ch'ing dynasty was hardly a revolution, but it ended the imperial rule by which China had been governed for more than 2,000 years and opened the way for fundamental change.

Japan Among the Powers

As indicated in Chapter 28, the antiquated Tokugawa shogunate was toppled in 1868 and 1869 by a new group of reformers. Their goal was the rapid modernization and Westernization of Japan in order to save their country from colonialism and to remove the unequal treaties that had been forced on it. That effort was spectacularly successful. By 1895 new Western-style technology and industry had progressed far and had given Japan new power. With power came new ambition. In a conflict over dominance in Korea, Japan's new navy and army easily defeated China's poorly coordinated forces in 1894–1895 and detached both Korea and Taiwan from Chinese control, adding them to what was now the Japanese colonial empire. In 1904–1905 Japan's new strength enabled it to win early victories against a more formidable opponent, Russia, and then to conclude a treaty that replaced Russian dominance in Manchuria with Japanese. Confidence was high, as Japan was clearly established as a major power in East Asia, and by the early years of the twentieth century Japan was able to get rid of the unequal treaties and to deal with Western powers as an equal. But imperial ambition and military adventuring led the nation into what the Japanese call the "dark valley," beginning with their efforts to take control of much of eastern China in 1915, their formal takeover of Manchuria as part of their empire in 1931, and the morass of their full-scale invasion of China from 1937, a road that led to Pearl Harbor and Hiroshima. Nevertheless, the Meiji period, from 1868 to 1912 (the death of the Meiji emperor), was one of great and constructive progress that laid the foundation of modern Japanese society and economy.

The Meiji Restoration: Response to the West

In contrast to China, the Meiji Restoration in Japan ushered in a period of rapid change and wholesale Westernization. Meiji was the reign title of the young emperor, who moved to Tokyo ("eastern capital") in 1869 as the restored head of state, although his role remained symbolic only. He and his successors served as a rallying point for new nationalist sentiment, and most Japanese took inspiration from the fact that their country was once again under imperial rule.

The goal of the new government was to strengthen and modernize Japan and thereby to free it from the unequal treaties (see Chapter 28). Like China, Japan had suffered loss of control over its tariffs and had been forced to concede extraterritoriality and other special privileges to the Western powers. In contrast to the Chinese, however, Japan's leaders realized that regaining their independence depended on mastering Western technology. They also saw that military technology could not be separated from overall industrialization or from the institutional structures that had produced and accompanied it in the West.

Whereas pride rendered these truths unacceptable to the Chinese, Japan showed little hesitation after 1869 in transforming or abolishing traditional institutions. Many Japanese urged wholesale Westernization, arguing, "If we use it, that will make it Japanese." Some radical enthusiasts in the early years of Meiji actually tried to destroy traditional temples in their zeal to sweep away the old and make way for the new Japan. Japanese national pride did not rest so much in the culture as in the people's sense of themselves. Although change proved largely bloodless and was accompanied by relatively minor political reorganization, Meiji Japan produced in many ways a real revolution.

Economy and Government

The first priority was rapid industrialization, especially in heavy industries and armaments. Foreign advisers were hired to expedite this growth—from Britain for a modern navy, from Germany for a modern army and armaments industry, and so on. Railways were quickly built to link the major cities, and new ports and facilities were created. The machinery of government and law was wholly remade, modeled on a judicious combination of Western systems. What emerged was a modified constitutional monarchy with a parliament and a largely Western-derived legal system. Such change was important also to demonstrate that Japan was a "civilized" country where foreigners did not need extraterritoriality to protect them.

All Western institutions, and even such details of Western culture as dress and diet, were seen as sources of strength. Samurai discarded their swords and picturesque garb, put on Western business suits, learned to waltz, and dominated the new bureaucracy. Some samurai found careers as officers in the new army, and others went into business or manufacturing. The ranks of the army were filled with peasant conscripts; war was no longer a gentlemen's preserve.

The Japanese were rapidly mobilized toward the new goals. They were accustomed to direction, from daimyo, samurai, or other hierarchical superiors, and most came to share the national objectives with genuine enthusiasm. Japan's almost ready-made nationalism, the fruit of an island country with a long history of separateness, was a strong asset. Its people were also racially and culturally homogeneous (as the Chinese and Indians were not), and the country was small and more easily integrated as a unit. In landmass and population, approximately 50 million by 1910, it was about the size of one of China's larger provinces, and some 90 percent of its people were concentrated in the corridor between Tokyo and Osaka. What was decided in Tokyo was quickly carried out everywhere as national policy. Farm output tripled between 1870 and 1940 with the use of new Western technology as well as hard work. In many ways it was the latter that accounted for Meiji Japan's astounding success.

Japanese Imperialism

By the 1890s Japan had a modern navy and army and a fast-growing industrial base. Japanese steamships had won a major place in East Asian trade, and Japanese merchants had acquired a rising share of the China market. In 1894 Britain agreed to relinquish the unequal clauses of the old treaty with Japan by 1899, and other nations soon followed suit.

Having followed the Western lead in modern development, Japan now joined the other imperialist powers in colonial conquests. Korea was the handiest target, and in brief campaigns in 1894 and 1895 the new Japanese fleet and army demolished Chinese forces sent to protect China's tributary dependency. The peace treaty made Japan dominant in a still nominally independent Korea; the Chinese also ceded to them the island of Taiwan (Formosa), a huge indemnity, and the right to operate factories in the China treaty ports.

At the same time, the Russians were extending their influence, railways, and concession areas in Manchuria, whose southern tip they leased from China. The Japanese saw this as a threat to their position in Korea, but in any case they had their own plans for Manchuria. They struck there in 1904 without declaring war, winning a rapid series of land and naval battles against Russia by a combination of dash and willingness to take heavy casualties. The Russians were far from their home base and inadequately prepared; in time, their much greater resources would have prevailed, but the Japanese persuaded the American president, Theodore Roosevelt, to arrange a peace at Portsmouth, New Hampshire, in 1905. The Russians were concerned by then with the first stirrings of revolution at home, and the war was expensive and unpopular in Russia. Japan inherited Russia's position in Manchuria and tightened its grip on Korea, which in 1910 became an outright colony in a growing Japanese empire.

Japan's first steps toward empire profited from the tacit support of the Western powers, who saw it as a counterweight against Russia's geographic advantage in the Far East. Japan had been encouraged to attack Russia by the Anglo-Japanese treaty of alliance and friendship signed in 1902, which was welcomed in Japan as a mark of international equality. Theodore Roosevelt saw the Japanese as promising allies, "bully fighters," as he called them. The Russo-Japanese War of 1904–1905 inaugurated a period of new pride, confidence, and continued economic progress.

Japan joined the Allies in World War I, ostensibly as an equal partner, although it took no part in the fighting in Europe apart from sending a few destroyers to join the British Mediterranean fleet. The opportunity was instead used to take over the German concession areas in China, centered in the province of Shantung in eastern North China. In 1915 Japan presented China with a list of 21 demands that would have made it in effect a Japanese colony. By such bullying tactics, Japan quickly lost the admiration and goodwill built up by its progress since 1869. The Twenty-one Demands also infuriated Chinese patriots and more than any other event spurred the rise of broad-based Chinese nationalism. The Demands were rejected, although Japan hung onto the German concessions in Shantung. Meanwhile, the Japanese continued to develop Taiwan, Korea, and Manchuria.

Taiwan offered rice, sugar, and tropical crops to feed Japan's booming population. Korea had rich resources of coal, iron ore, and timber, which Japan appropriated. The Japanese drained the country of every useful commodity, including food crops, to support their growth, leaving the Koreans as an impoverished and exploited labor force. Koreans were forced to adopt Japanese names, and most were denied even elementary education; the public use of their own language was forbidden. Manchuria, still formally part of China but in effect a Japanese sphere, was a storehouse of coal, ores, timber, productive agricultural land, and potential hydroelectric power. Japan exploited all these resources while building an infrastructure of railways, mines, irrigation systems, dams, port facilities, and a colonial administration. In Korea too, railways, mines, factories, and roads were built and basic economic growth begun, although for Japanese benefit. In Taiwan the infrastructure for economic redevelopment was also laid, primarily in agriculture, leading to new prosperity.

In Manchuria the Japanese built the largest single industrial complex in Asia, including closely integrated mines and factories in the Mukden (Shenyang) area, a dense rail network, and a highly productive commercialized agriculture that generated large surpluses of wheat and soybeans for export to Japan and to world markets through the port of Dairen. Large power dams were built on Manchuria's rivers. The population increased by nearly a million a year from 1900 to the outbreak of the Pacific war in 1941, consisting almost entirely of Chinese who migrated from a disordered and impoverished North China in search of new economic opportunity. Japan's huge investment in Manchuria laid the basis for China's industrialization after Japan's defeat in 1945. But Japan's record as a colonial power, despite the constructive achievements, was marred, as in Korea, by an exploitive approach as well as a disregard for local interests or aspirations.

ITO HIROBUMI: MEIJI STATESMAN

The leading statesman of Meiji Japan, Ito Hirobumi, was born in one of the outer daimyo domains of southwestern Japan in 1841. As a youth, he wanted passionately to save his country from the foreign threat, and at the age of 21 tried to burn the newly established British embassy in Tokyo. But when he visited Britain the next year, he realized that it was impossible to drive the Westerners out by such tactics, and he returned to work for Japan's modernization. After the Meiji Restoration, he went with government missions to Europe and America to learn how to make his country strong and in 1881 became Japan's first prime minister under the new Western-style government. A later visit to Prussia convinced him that a constitutional monarchy was best suited to Japan. Ito was the chief architect of the new constitution proclaimed by the emperor in 1889, which contained many elements of the German imperial constitution. He understood, however, that constitutional government, and the cooperation of the new parliament, could not be made to work without political organization and popular support. In 1898 he left office to form a political party for that purpose, which was dominant in Japan until 1941.

After the Russo-Japanese War in 1905, Ito became the first Japanese resident-general in Korea. The Koreans deeply resented Japanese control, but Ito saw a civilian-based policy as preferable to the complete military occupation urged by powerful voices at home and hoped, against the odds, that he could win the Koreans' goodwill and cooperation in developing their country. In 1909 he was assassinated by a Korean patriot while on a visit to northern Manchuria—an abrupt end to the career of a man who might have played a vital moderating role in subsequent Japanese policies. Ito was an enthusiastic modernizer, especially after his visits to the West, but he also understood the need for compromise in politics and for adapting Western ways to Japanese traditions, circumstances, and values. In some ways he remained at least as traditional as he was modern. His objective was the preservation and development of his country, and Westernization was only a means to that end. He believed deeply in the restoration of the emperor's personal rule and aimed to accomplish his goals by working through the throne. But he also understood the rising yearning for a less authoritarian form of government, the need for political parties, a constitution, and a parliament. These aspirations he served well, never letting personal ambition or power cloud his judgment or his dedication to the public welfare.

Australia and the Pacific Islands

Western expansion came late to the Australian continent and most of the Pacific islands. Australia, however, had been inhabited by aborigines for some 50,000 years, and more recently peoples from Southeast Asia had migrated to Australia and the myriad islands of the Pacific. The culture of these peoples varied from that of the aborigines, who lived until Western colonization very much as their paleolithic ancestors had, to the Maori of New Zealand, skilled seamen whose delicate, filigreed woodcarving was the equal of craftsmen in any part of the world. Western explorers called this region Oceania. In addition to Australia and New Zealand, Oceania included Melanesia, extending from New Guinea to Fiji; Micronesia, to the north, embracing the islands from the Marianas to the Gilberts; and Polynesia, the easternmost islands, encompassing Samoa and Hawaii.

Australia: Convicts, Wool, and Gold

Although Spanish explorers and traders had plied the Pacific throughout much of the sixteenth century, the Dutch were the first Westerners to reach Australia, which they called New Holland, in the early 1600s. The English displayed some interest late in the same century, but not until 1770 did a British expedition under James Cook discover land suitable for settlement and claim Australia for Britain. Because the great island continent was not astride the trade routes, it had hitherto been ignored, but the British soon found a use for the latest acquisition to their empire. Having lost the war with the American colonists and having failed to establish penal settlements in West Africa, they could dump unwanted convicts in Australia.

The first British colony was founded at Sydney on the southeast coast in 1788 by Captain Arthur Phillip, who became the first governor. Because the colony was so distant from Britain and so difficult to supply, it was slow to attract free settlers. Many of the earliest free colonists were soldiers who decided to stay in Australia after serving in the British garrison, notwithstanding the fact that the land was described by one officer as "very barren and forbidding." By the mid-nineteenth century it had become the home of some 160,000 transplanted convicts, many of whom were assigned to work a specified number of years for the free colonizers. New South Wales, as the region around Sydney was called, was difficult to farm, especially because of insufficient water, but in the early 1800s the woolen industry developed rapidly, aided by the British government's termination of import duties on colonial wool. Between 1821, when wool was first shipped to Britain, and 1845, wool export increased from 175,000 to 24 million pounds.

By that point exploration was moving rapidly forward, and there were key settlements at Melbourne in the south, Perth in the southwest, and Brisbane to the north. Interest in Australia increased substantially when gold was discovered in New South Wales and its southern neighbor, Victoria, in 1851, two years after the great rush had begun in California. In the ensuing decade the population of New South Wales jumped from 200,000 to 350,000, while Victoria's rose from 77,000 to 540,000. As the population of the continent as a whole passed 1 million, more attention had to be given to food production, especially when the supply of gold dwindled. As in the American west, bitter conflicts arose between ranchers and farmers, with the latter additionally plagued by water shortages and inadequate transportation facilities. The crisis was gradually resolved only as roads, railways, and irrigation systems were built and as farmers learned to dry-farm and apply chemical fertilizers.

During the late nineteenth century interest grew in uniting the six Australian colonies, each of which had been given its own legislature by an 1850 British statute. Federation would not only eliminate internal economic barriers but also enhance Australia's ability to withstand potential aggression from one or more of the imperial powers. The resulting commonwealth of Australia, founded in 1901, was a constitutional federation, with the central government, as in the United States, possessing only limited authority.

New Zealand: Maori and Missionaries

The Australian aborigines had been spread too thinly and were too pacific to have posed a serious threat to colonizers. In New Zealand, however, the native Maori were not only relatively more populous, considering New Zealand's smaller size (one-thirtieth the size of Australia), but much better organized and temperamentally more militant. Although Captain Cook had claimed New Zealand for Britain in 1769, interest in settling the island was slow in developing. Missionary efforts to the Maori, begun in 1814, made striking progress by midcentury. Simultaneously, however, some of the Maori began acquiring European guns, which they turned against rival tribes in an orgy of violence. The island also became a battleground in a different kind of war—one fought ideologically and politically between missionaries, who wanted the land preserved for Christianized Maori, and imperial colonizers, who envisaged a country dominated by white settlers.

Matters came to a head in 1840, thanks largely to the colonizing schemes of Edward Gibbon Wakefield and his New Zealand Land Company. The island, he truthfully told a parliamentary committee, was "the most beautiful coun-

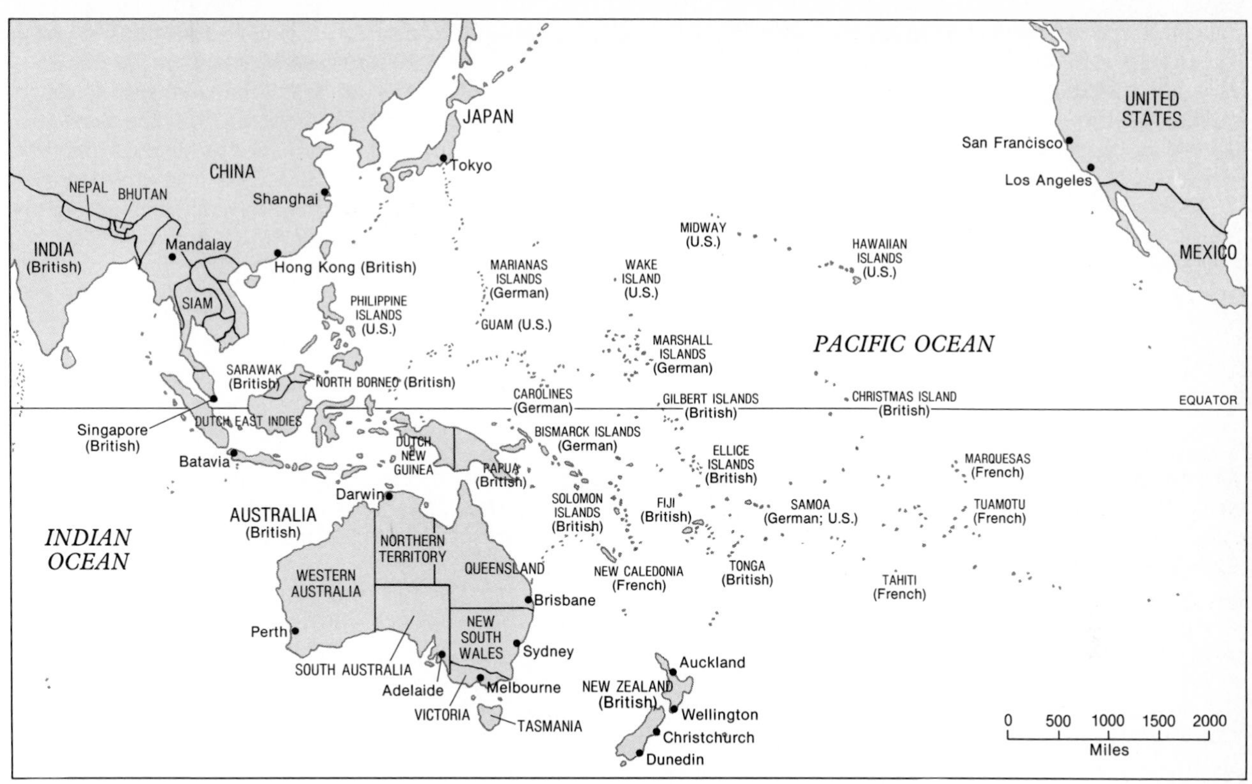

33.6 Colonial Empires in the Pacific, c. 1900

try" with a fine climate and productive soil. The British decision to annex New Zealand may have been stimulated as well by a French show of interest in the island nation. The British government formally annexed New Zealand in 1840; the newly appointed governor negotiated a treaty with the Maori, obtaining their recognition of British sovereignty and promising them secure land tenure. But many of the Maori were soon disillusioned as whites from Australia and Britain poured into the island, and fighting was frequent until 1872, when the Maori finally accepted defeat. By that point the population of the island was approximately 250,000, of whom less than 40,000 by one estimate were Maori. They were victims not only of the fighting but, like the Australian aborigines and the Amerindians, of the new diseases transmitted by Europeans. Peace provided fresh opportunities for growth, and in the next 30 years the population more than tripled, modern transportation and communications systems were developed, and a democratic political constitution evolved that in 1893 extended suffrage to women.

Islands of the Pacific

Although Spanish and Dutch explorers had discovered some of the islands of Melanesia, Micronesia, and Polynesia, it was not until the late eighteenth century that Europeans began to show serious interest in them. At first their motives were largely economic: whalers and sealers from America, Britain, and France used some of the islands as bases, while merchants traded tools, cloth, and guns for the sandalwood that found a ready market in China. As in New Zealand, much of the early interest in the islands was also religious. Spanish missionaries sought converts in the Marianas, while British Protestants in 1797 launched their campaign in Tahiti, and American Protestants began working in Hawaii in 1820. Where the missionaries went, the political interests of their home governments were usually quick to follow. In Tahiti, however, the English Protestants who virtually ran the island were ousted by the French navy in 1843, after which Catholic missionaries taught the natives their version of Christianity.

As imperial rivalry intensified among the great powers in the late nineteenth century, the Pacific islands were increasingly coveted. The interest in converting the native populations continued but was clearly subordinate to economic considerations and imperial advantage. Britain, France, the United States, and Germany competed for the spoils, toppling native states, such as the kingdom of Fiji, in the process. The most notorious example of this occurred in 1893, when American planters, aided by a contingent of 150 marines, overthrew Hawaii's Queen Liliuokalani (1891–1893). Despite the fact that the United

States had recognized Hawaii's independence in 1842, the American government waited only until 1900 to annex it, as it had annexed the Philippines and Guam two years earlier. "We need Hawaii just as much and a good deal more than we did California," insisted President William McKinley; "it is manifest destiny."

Thus in 1900 every island in Polynesia, Micronesia, and Melanesia was a colonial possession of Britain, France, Germany, or the United States. Once-mighty Spain, after losing the Philippines and Guam, had sold its remaining Pacific islands—the Carolines, Marianas, and Marshalls—to Germany the previous year. The Germans, however, would lose those islands to Japan in 1914, the same year they lost northeastern New Guinea to Australia and their part of Samoa to New Zealand. Less than three decades later, conflicting Japanese and American ambitions in the Pacific resulted in the attack on Pearl Harbor that propelled the United States into World War II.

The age of domination saw European powers take control of most of Africa, India, Ceylon, Burma, Malaya, Indochina, Indonesia, and the Philippines, while they and the Americans exercised a strong influence and enjoyed special concessions in Thailand, China, and Japan. The Japanese, taking a lesson from their Western teachers, created their own colonial empire in Korea, Taiwan, and Manchuria.

Imperialism radically challenged the traditional values and structures of the societies it conquered or dominated. The result was dislocation, suffering, and cultural trauma. Much of value was weakened or destroyed. But the West also brought advances in technology, productivity, and medicine that raised the standard of living and increased life expectancy. For better or worse, the colonial impulse united most of the globe in a broad, overarching web of economic and political interdependency for the first time in history. Some of the West's values would be adopted, some contested, some rejected. Many of them would be accepted only after being assimilated to the older cultural patterns that reasserted themselves as the yoke of Western dominance was shaken off. The four great civilizations of Asia each responded differently to the Western challenge. British dominion in India stimulated the development of a nationalist movement that created a modern state on the subcontinent. Similar developments came later in Southeast Asia and were retarded by repressive French and Dutch colonial policies. China, too large to be conquered, would find its own path to modernity after a century of confusion and anarchy. Japan made the most rapid and apparently the easiest transition from a traditional society to a modern, industrial one and in mere decades achieved the status of a world power.

Suggestions for Further Reading

Imperialism and Africa

Curtin, P. D. *Africa and the West: Intellectual Responses to European Culture*. Madison: University of Wisconsin Press, 1972.

Fieldhouse, D. K. *Economics and Empire, 1830–1914*. Ithaca, N.Y.: Cornell University Press, 1973.

Hallett, R. *Africa Since 1875*. Ann Arbor: University of Michigan Press, 1974.

Langer, W. L. *The Diplomacy of Imperialism, 1890–1902*, 2d ed. New York: Knopf, 1965.

Oliver, R. and Atmore, A. *Africa Since 1800*, 3d ed. Cambridge: Cambridge University Press, 1981.

Perham, M., and Simmons, J., eds. *African Discovery: An Anthology of Exploration*. London: Faber & Faber, 1961.

India

Embree, A. T. *1857 in India: Mutiny or War of Independence?* Boston: Heath, 1963.

Forster, E. M. *A Passage to India*. New York: Harcourt, Brace, 1924. (Fiction)

Mason, P. *The Men Who Ruled India*, rev. ed. New York: Norton, 1985.

Seal, A. *The Emergence of Indian Nationalism*. Cambridge: Cambridge University Press, 1968.

Southeast Asia

Bastin, J., and Benda, H. J. *A History of Modern Southeast Asia*. Englewood Cliffs, N.J.: Prentice-Hall, 1968.

Hall, D. G. E. *A History of Southeast Asia*, 4th ed. New York: St. Martin's Press, 1984.

Harrison, B. *Southeast Asia: A Short History*. London: Macmillan, 1968.

Orwell, G. *Burmese Days*. New York: Harcourt, Brace, 1934.

Steinberg, D. J., ed. *In Search of Southeast Asia*. Honolulu: University Press of Hawaii, 1987.

China

Fairbank, J. K. *The Missionary Enterprise in China and America*. Cambridge, Mass.: Harvard University Press, 1974.

Gasster, M. *China's Struggle to Modernize*. New York: Knopf, 1972.

Hsu, I. *The Rise of Modern China*. New York: Oxford University Press, 1975.

Murphey, R. *Shanghai: Key to Modern China*. Cambridge, Mass.: Harvard University Press, 1953.

Pruitt, I. *Daughter of Han*. New Haven, Conn.: Yale University Press, 1945.

Schrecker, J. *Imperialism and Chinese Nationalism*. Cambridge, Mass.: Harvard University Press, 1971.

Japan

Beasley, W. G. *The Meiji Restoration*. Stanford, Calif.: Stanford University Press, 1972.

Borton, H. *Japan's Modern Century*. New York: Ronald Press, 1955.

Myers, R. *The Japanese Empire*. Stanford, Calif.: Stanford University Press, 1984.

Storry, R. *A History of Modern Japan*, rev. ed. New York: Penguin Books, 1982.

PART · FIVE

The Twentieth Century

In 1910 King Edward VII of Great Britain died. At his funeral a stately procession of Europe's reigning monarchs—including George V, Edward's successor; Tsar Nicholas II of Russia; Kaiser William II of Germany; Crown Prince Karl of Austria-Hungary; and King Albert of Belgium—paraded on horseback, their helmets and swords glittering in the sun. Looking back on it from the perspective of the present, we are tempted to see great symbolism in the event—the mourning, as it were, for a world that was dying. Within four years the monarchs who had posed so congenially with each other, many of whom were related by marriage or blood, were at war with each other. When that struggle—the "Great War"—was over, some of them had lost their thrones, and those who remained would reign over states with sharply diminished power and prestige.

The world changed rapidly after the Great War of 1914–1918. Revolutionary upheavals in Russia and new ideologies in Italy and Germany proclaimed the entrance of the masses onto the stage of history and the demise of the old liberal order. These Western transformations were accompanied by equally momentous events in India, China, and the Middle East, where anticolonial movements sought both liberation from Western domination and national regeneration. Within twenty years economic crisis and a second world war had completed the decline of Europe as the center of world power. The influence of the traditional European powers was quickly replaced by the emergence of the Soviet Union and the United States as "superpower" states whose military-industrial strength has dominated world affairs ever since.

By 1945 the twentieth century had assumed the broad contours that we now find familiar. A fundamental shift had occurred in the relationship between the West and the rest of the world as Asia, Africa, and Latin America completed the transition from colonialism. If the first half of the century began with a few European states controlling huge colonial empires across the globe, the second half draws to a close with a world community consisting of more than 150 independent nations. Indeed, those newer states today play an increasingly more prominent role in shaping a common destiny through a joint international posture of nonalignment, seeking thereby to mitigate the effects of superpower hegemony.

If, then, there is a sequel to the funeral of Edward VII that vividly symbolizes this dramatic change, it is perhaps to be found in the gathering of nonaligned states that met in New Delhi, India, in 1983, where Cuba's Fidel Castro, dressed in guerrilla fatigues, passed the gavel of the meeting to India's Indira Gandhi, resplendent in the silk sari of her country.

While the twentieth century saw the end of European political supremacy, it also witnessed the extension of Western technology, institutions, and ideas to these very same newly independent nations. The adoption of Western models of development was both a deliberate weapon in the struggle against colonialism and a legacy of their former subordinate status. But as traditional societies experience the disruptive stresses of modernization, developing nations are searching for alternatives more appropriate to their own cultures.

As we move toward the twenty-first century, a host of vital issues—social and political justice, peace, human rights and equality, and economic well-being—loom ever larger as the joint responsibility of an increasingly interdependent global community. ■

CHAPTER · 34

Culture, Society, and the Great War

Until a second global conflict erupted in the 1930s, modern memory recalled only the "Great War" of 1914–1918. World War I was called "great" because its toll on human life, its monetary cost and physical destruction, and the human trauma it caused made all others pale in comparison. It started because rulers and government officials blundered in the summer of 1914, but a half century of diplomatic and cultural history lay behind the immediate events. Many artists and writers had rejected traditional moral and social values, and some glorified violence as a catharsis that would strengthen what they believed was a civilization in decay. Such views anticipated the political breakdown of Europe by creating a climate in which war seemed acceptable, even desirable.

Although the fighting stopped in November 1918, its impact was felt for decades. Four empires disappeared as a result of the conflict—Hohenzollern Germany, Habsburg Austria-Hungary, Ottoman Turkey, and Romanov Russia. This last was replaced by the world's first state to describe itself as socialist with the goal of transforming itself into a communist society. The shock of the war experience, no less than the conditions of peace imposed on the vanquished, helped shape the twentieth century.

Women served at or near the front lines in a number of capacities during World War I. Here a British ambulance driver is shown in France. [Bettmann Archive]

The Great War was not the first worldwide war, for earlier struggles had also been waged on several continents and oceans. In this war military engagements took place in Africa, Asia, and the Middle East, but the fighting was concentrated in Europe. Although imperialism formed part of the background to the war, its causes were almost entirely in the West. Nevertheless, the Great War had worldwide repercussions. In its aftermath, Europe's overseas empires disintegrated as its global supremacy collapsed.

The Crisis of European Culture

In the three decades preceding World War I, European culture underwent a revolution that transformed thought: antirationalists challenged the optimism inherited from the Enlightenment and the materialism of the nineteenth century, while the literary and artistic avant-garde experimented with new ways of experiencing time and space. Philosophers increasingly favored instinct over reason to explain human behavior, while students of the mind proclaimed that beneath the fragile veneer of civilization lurked dark forces. Scientists, who had previously explained the physical world through the observation of recordable data, confronted a universe in which measurement itself was relative to the observer. Literary narrative, which once expressed motives and character, spoke increasingly in the language of ambiguity. The crisis also overturned aesthetic values as artists questioned conventional expressions of reality. Most disturbing, new strains of antidemocratic and racist thought were introduced into politics.

The Revolt Against Positivism

The intellectual rejection of materialism and reason is known as the antipositivist revolt. Its most outspoken proponent was the German Friedrich Nietzsche (1844–1900). A philosopher repelled by the hypocrisy and pettiness of his time, Nietzsche assaulted traditional morality. His scathing criticism of bourgeois values extended to the roots of Western culture, from Greco-Roman rationalism to the Judeo-Christian belief in compassion, sin, and humility—concepts he said were more suitable to slaves and weaklings than the free and the strong.

To realize freedom and human potential, Nietzsche urged the abandonment of these traditions in favor of instincts and emotions. He called on heroic leaders to guide the masses: "All gods are dead," he proclaimed, "so we now want the superman to live." While he condemned democratic liberalism and equality, he also repudiated nationalism, militarism, and anti-Semitism, although apologists for Nazism later seized on his writings as justification for their doctrines of national and racial superiority. These justifications were part of the philosophical underpinning for European anti-Semitism. Misunderstood during his lifetime, Nietzsche's ideas had a profound influence on European culture. Literary and artistic rebels drew inspiration from his attack on the establishment, and in the 1920s political demagogues were influenced by his concept of the superman.

Nietzsche's stress on the irrational was echoed by the French philosopher Henri Bergson (1859–1941). Distinguishing between the rational intellect and intuitive understanding, Bergson believed the former a useful tool for analyzing knowledge but not for understanding reality. Only intuition could grasp the "life force," which informed all experience and expressed itself in a continuum, or "duration," that instinct alone could describe. Bergson's chief influence lay in underscoring nonrational experience. Although he did not reject science, he undermined the scientists' claim to a monopoly on knowledge.

Sigmund Freud (1856–1939), a Viennese physician, confirmed Bergson's arguments about the limits of reason. Freud's treatment of psychiatric disorders, based on clinical data, convinced him that behavior is the result of powerful and primitive desires such as aggression and sex. These drives usually remain in an irrational unconscious, which he called the *id.* Freud believed that the id struggles constantly against the *ego,* which rationalizes and channels these desires according to the constraints of reality and the socially implanted values of the *superego.*

The superego functions as a kind of conscience, but instead of reflecting absolute moral values or rational truths, it is the product of social conditioning. Because the mind tends to repress the id, the conflict generally remains unconscious. Nevertheless, the resulting tensions can cause crippling experiences of guilt and fear or even mental breakdown. Freud's theories, particularly those concerning infantile and childhood sexuality, shocked bourgeois notions of human nature. Moreover, by positing the notion that some people live emotionally in a frozen past, Freud and other psychoanalysts altered human perception of time as a forward-moving concept.

Like Nietzsche, Freud emphasized the irrational basis of human behavior and social values. For Freud, civilization is built on the repression of powerful individual urges, particularly sexual ones. Socialization, and hence "progress," rests not on reason but on the frustration of instincts that, held continually in check, threaten to overwhelm it. Nietzsche had questioned whether civilization was worth its cost in terms of human fulfillment. Freud assumed that repression and self-denial are the necessary price of society. World War I seemed to bear out his pessimism about human nature and the stability of civilization, and his influence on postwar thought was enormous.

Freud's leadership within the movement he founded for the study and treatment of the human psyche—psychoanalysis—was challenged by his former disciple, Carl Jung (1875–1961), who elaborated his own theory of a collective unconscious. In recent decades Freud's theories have been sharply challenged. Nonetheless, he has remained one of the most influential thinkers of the century, and his indirect impact on sexual attitudes, artistic expression, and the concept of mental illness has been incalculable. Perhaps no one has done more to change the modern conception of human nature.

The Dilemmas of Science

Ironically, advances in the realm of physical science seemed to reinforce antirationalist arguments. Since the days of Newton, science had sustained the idea that the physical world operated according to immutable laws and predictable mechanical processes. The modern scientific age, which began with investigations into the nature of matter following the discovery of X-rays in 1895 by Wilhelm Röntgen (1845–1923), shattered these illusions. Experiments by Marie Curie (1867–1934) and her husband, Pierre (1859–1906), showed that the atomic weight of elements such as radium changed as they emitted energy in the form of "subatomic" particles. These findings suggested a relationship between matter and energy. By the end of the 1920s a radical revision of the basic assumptions of classical physics had totally recast scientific understanding of the universe.

Early in the twentieth century the German physicist Max Planck (1858–1947) conducted studies of radiation that revealed that contrary to earlier theories, light energy moves not in steady waves but in discontinuous yet calculable spurts, which he called *quanta.* Working independently, Albert Einstein (1879–1955) also began to revolutionize physics. His "Special Theory of Relativity," published in 1905, rejected the notion that space and time were absolutes, suggesting instead that both were relative to the position of the observer. Einstein showed that light moves through space in particles known as photons and calculated that the energy contained in a photon was equal to its mass multiplied by the square of the speed of light—a concept expressed in his famous formula, $E = mc^2$. Hence not only do mass and time vary with velocity, but energy and mass are interchangeable. In 1915 Einstein's "General Theory of Relativity," which explained gravitation, further shook standard views of the physical world: it described the universe as curved, so that when light waves are deflected as they pass through a gravitational field, they eventually return to their point of origin. Einstein's universe was a four-dimensional one in which length, breadth, and height also had to be conceived in terms of time.

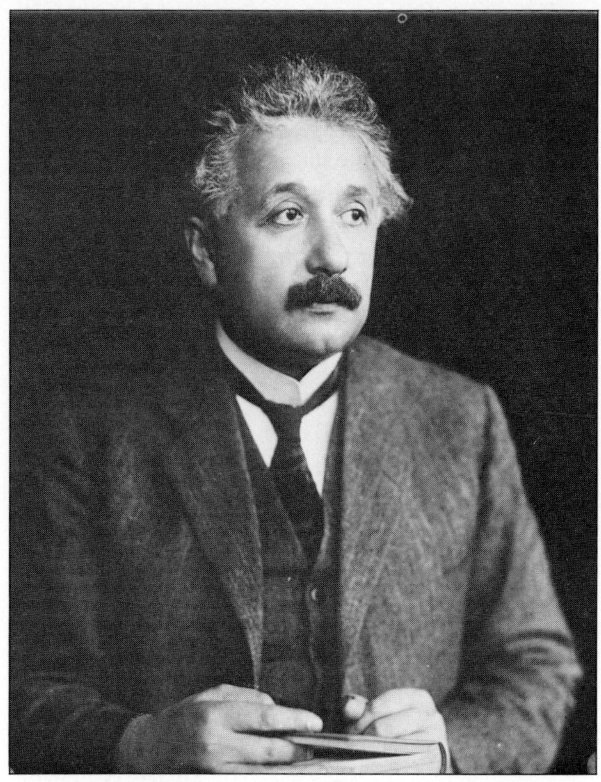

Albert Einstein, whose theories of relativity revolutionized our concepts of the universe, is shown here in his middle years. He received the Nobel Prize for physics in 1921. [Granger Collection]

In the years between the evolution of Einstein's theories of relativity, Ernest Rutherford (1871–1937) forced contemporaries to abandon still another basic assumption about matter. Rutherford theorized that the atom, which since ancient times had been regarded as a solid, indivisible mass, was actually an arrangement much like a solar system, consisting of a central particle (the nucleus) with a positive electrical charge, surrounded by orbits of negatively charged electrons. He demonstrated that by bombarding substances with subatomic particles, the structure of atoms could be changed.

In the popular mind these theories and findings led to a doubly disturbing conclusion about the physical universe: that it was not unchangeable but shifting and uncertain, and that perhaps knowledge of it lay beyond human comprehension. While almost all countries, in an effort to coordinate wireless communications and transportation schedules, were adopting World Standard Time at the beginning of the twentieth century, scientists such as Einstein were shattering the concept of a uniform public time into the infinite variations of private times relative to each individual.

Realism Abandoned: Literature and Art

The revolt against positivism was reflected in literature and painting. Writers and artists not only expressed the social criticism that rejected the values of materialist culture but also probed beyond the conscious mind. Alienation impelled literary figures to take refuge in obscure symbolism, decadence, or aestheticism, while artists provided visual evidence of the breakdown of traditional forms.

The rebellion in literature had begun at midcentury with the publication of *Flowers of Evil* (1857) by the French poet Charles Baudelaire (1821–1867). Like the British poet Algernon Swinburne (1837–1909) and others, Baudelaire was hostile to bourgeois values and deliberately shocked conventional morality. The 1880s saw the birth of the Decadents and Symbolism, two literary movements derived in part from these earlier sources. The Decadents were sophisticated aesthetes such as Oscar Wilde (1854–1900), J. K. Huysmans (1848–1907), and Gabriele D'Annunzio (1863–1938), who extolled the idea of art for art's sake and cultivated exoticism and artificiality.

The Symbolists, represented by Stéphane Mallarmé (1842–1898) and Paul Verlaine (1844–1896), sought to express the inexpressible in experimental verse that relied on symbols to convey images that logic alone could not fathom. They rejected conventional perception in favor of a subjective, inner world. Often proclaiming the values of aestheticism and decadence, the Symbolists portrayed emotions derived from immediate experience, much as Bergson had urged.

In the 1870s Impressionism assaulted both realism and academic art by depicting the disintegrative effects of light. By the 1880s Impressionism was under attack by Postimpressionists, who, like the Symbolists, were moving away from the outer world of visible reality to an inner realm of the individual artist. In his later years, Claude Monet (1840–1926), the leading Impressionist, painted huge canvases depicting waterlilies. These shimmering pools of color, almost devoid of form, represented a transition between the perceived reality of Impressionism and the emotion of Postimpressionism.

One of the most powerful Postimpressionists was Vincent van Gogh (1853–1890), whose works conveyed an imaginative vision of the world. Like Paul Gauguin (1848–1903), who left the materialistic society of France to settle in Tahiti, van Gogh was interested in using the formal, abstract elements of art—line, color, and form—to express an intensely personal view of truth. Paul Cézanne (1839–1906), however, wanted to free art of subjectivity and emotionalism. Following classical principles, he used color to stress the underlying weight and volume of objects. His landscapes define objects only in the most general sense by using contour, color, and mass to convey abstract equivalents for conventional objects.

BARCELONA AND THE MODERN TEMPER

No city better reflected the cultural ferment of turn-of-the-century Europe than Barcelona. Located on Spain's northeastern plain at the edge of the Mediterranean Sea, Barcelona was the center of Catalan regionalism. In many ways the capital of Catalonia province represented the outstanding example of a modern European city, an innovative, rapidly modernizing enclave in a traditional, agrarian nation. By the late nineteenth century Barcelona had become a city marked by bold cultural experimentation.

Founded at the end of the first century B.C. as a Roman administrative center, the town had grown up in the Middle Ages around a military fortress. Its location on the sea made it a natural focus of trade and shipbuilding. The Industrial Revolution reached Spain through Barcelona, where an enterprising middle class emerged in the late eighteenth century. By the 1850s chemical and machinery manufacturers had joined bankers, shipping magnates, and textile producers in forming a powerful liberal oligarchy. Although its members pressed for urban development and economic modernization, they also fought the labor and socialist movements with support from the government.

At midcentury greater Barcelona had a population of several hundred thousand that exhibited the class characteristics of an advanced capitalist society. Demographic growth forced the adoption in 1859 of a new town plan, similar to the plans followed in Paris and elsewhere, that consisted of a square grid pattern of streets and parks cut across by broad diagonal avenues. Less than a generation later, when more than 500,000 people lived there, Barcelona hosted the Universal Exhibition of 1888. The project, which incorporated a huge complex of exhibition halls, hotels, apartment buildings, factories, and urban services into the city plan, gave a strong thrust to construction and the arts.

Despite their reactionary politics, the economic elites that sponsored the Universal Exhibition encouraged an atmosphere of cultural innovation that made Barcelona synonymous with the most avant-garde trends in Europe. Brilliant local architects, working in the so-called *modernista* style, designed new buildings in a wide range of exciting idioms. This eclectic movement found inspiration in Moorish, Romanesque, and Gothic patterns, in the strong craft tradition of Catalonia, and in the international Art Nouveau style of the period.

The most creative architect of the period, Antonio Gaudí (1852–1926), developed a unique style that reconciled form with function and expressed his militant Catholic beliefs. Gaudí's creations, such as the Guell Palace, incorporated organic forms that resembled sculptural modeling. While his designs were derived from both Gothic and Art Nouveau styles, they represented an original architectural vocabulary that was a reaction against what he saw as the falsity of *fin-de-siècle* design. Many of his ambitious creations remained unrealized or only partially complete; a society exists even to this day that seeks to finish his most famous project, the Church of the Holy Family.

While Gaudí and other architects gave the city a bold new face, Barcelona also became a haven for the avant-garde, which included some of Europe's major artists and writers. Four important Spanish-born artists lived and exhibited in Barcelona in the early years of the twentieth century: Pablo Picasso (1881–1973), usually associated with Paris, executed his first mature works in Barcelona, along with Joan Miró (1893–1983), pioneer abstract painter and a native of the city, Julio Gonzalez (1876–1942), a craftsman turned sculptor, and Salvador Dalí (1904–1989), the famed Surrealist painter. The economic boom that Barcelona experienced during World War I drew many foreign artists from war-torn countries to neutral Spain. The French Dadaist and Surrealist painter Francis Picabia (1879–1953) came into contact with Dalí, and worked in Barcelona, and was later joined by the Belgian Surrealist René Magritte (1898–1967). In the 1930s the American photographer and painter Man Ray (1890–1976), the Italian sculptor Alberto Giacometti (1901–1966), and the German painter Max Ernst (1891–1976) all exhibited there.

While these and other creative talents pushed art and design toward modernism, the Spanish writer Eugenio d'Ors (1882–1954) founded a more conservative cultural movement known as *Noucentisme* ("Twentieth Century"), which stressed a revival of Mediterranean classicism in the arts. Nevertheless, as Spain headed toward dictatorship and conflict in the 1920s, Barcelona remained a bastion of cultural discourse. The International Exhibition of 1929 was the last symbol of Barcelona's cultural primacy. The brilliant architect Mies van der Rohe designed the exhibit's German pavilion in the Bauhaus style, which had come to stand for internationalism and modernity. Ironically, his "Barcelona chair," a pivotal example of modern furniture design, was intended as the official seat for King Alfonso XIII.

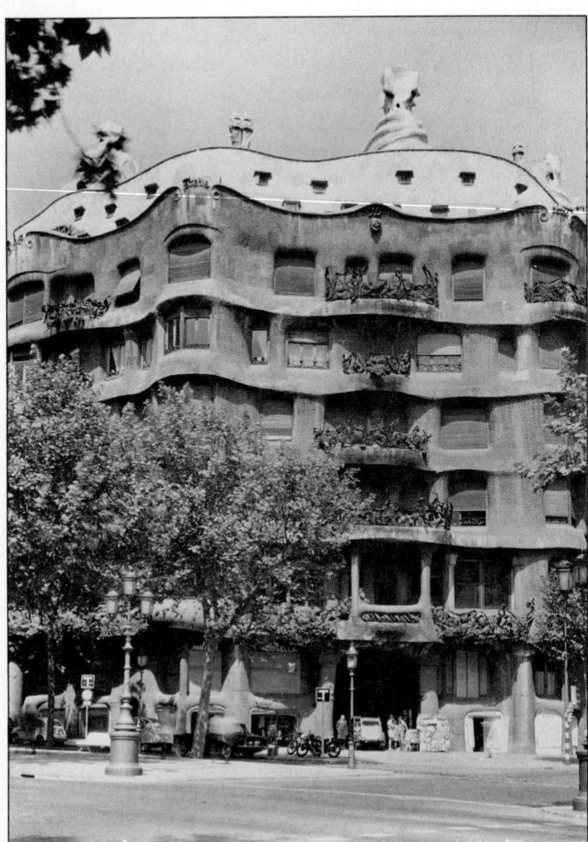

The highly original talent of the Barcelona architect Antonio Gaudí is seen here in a photograph of the Casa Milá, an apartment house completed in 1910. [Giraudon/Art Resource]

Postimpressionists, Cubists, and Futurists

Postimpressionists such as Cézanne brought painting to the edge of modernism. At the Paris Salon of 1905, the works of a number of Postimpressionist artists—Matisse, Rouault, and others—were hung together because of certain common characteristics. Their distortions, flat patterns, and preoccupation with line and form rather than objective reality, combined with violent, bold colors and stark contrasts, earned these men the title of *fauves* ("wild beasts"). Closely related to Fauvism were two German Expressionist groups, the Bridge and the Blue Rider, formed between 1905 and 1911, whose proponents emphasized bold colors and psychological portraiture.

The most significant step away from the traditional portrayal of reality came with Cubism, launched in Paris by the Spaniard Pablo Picasso and the Frenchman Georges Braque (1882–1963) in 1907. Influenced by Cézanne, Picasso and Braque developed a concept of form and context that enabled them to render the whole structure of an object as well as its position in space. Abandoning the bright colors and striking contrasts of the *fauves*, they focused on the subtleties of intersecting lines and angles and the reduction of objects to abstract forms. The Cubists not only set in motion the revolution in abstract painting, but by fracturing objects into separate elements and fixing them in time-space relationships, they transformed traditional views of reality.

The only major prewar art movement to develop independently of Paris was Futurism, founded by Filippo T. Marinetti (1876–1944) and a group of young Italian writers and artists in 1909. In contrast to most of the avant-garde of the period, the Futurists rejected humanist culture in the name of the machine and industrial civilization. Exalting the speed and energy of modern life, painters such as Umberto Boccioni (1882–1916) and Carlo Carrà (1881–1966) moved toward the elimination of traditional forms. Futurists advocated the destruction of libraries and museums and, influenced by the ideas of Nietzsche, Sorel, and Bergson, preached violence as an act of liberation.

The Futurist Manifesto

The Futurists were symptomatic of the crisis of prewar European culture. Not only did they rebel against reason, tradition, and conventional standards of beauty, but they also demanded a new civilization based on the aesthetic of the machine. Here is the first Futurist manifesto, drafted by Filippo T. Marinetti and originally published in Paris on February 20, 1909.

We want to praise the love of danger, the attitude of energy and fearlessness.

Courage, audacity, and revolt will be essential elements of our poetry.

Until now literature has exalted pensive immobility, ecstasy, and sleep. We want to exalt aggressive action, a feverish insomnia, the racer's stride, the mortal leap, the punch, and the slap.

We assert that the beauty of the world has been enriched by a new beauty: the beauty of speed. A racing car . . . is more beautiful than the *Victory of Samothrace*.

We want to praise the man at the wheel, who hurls his spiritual lance across the earth, along the circle of its orbit.

The poet must give himself with ardor, splendor, and generosity, to swell the enthusiastic fervor of the primordial elements.

There is no beauty except in struggle. No work without an aggressive character can be a masterpiece. Poetry must be conceived as a violent attack on unknown forces, to reduce and prostrate them before man.

We stand on the last promontory of the centuries! . . . Why must we look back, when what we want is to break down the mysterious doors of the impossible? Time and space died yesterday. We already live in the absolute, because we have already created eternal, omnipresent speed.

We want to glorify war—the world's only hygiene—militarism, patriotism, the destructive gesture of liberators, beautiful ideas worth dying for, and scorn for woman.

We want to destroy museums, libraries, academies of every kind, and want to fight moralism, feminism, every opportunistic or utilitarian cowardice.

We will sing of great crowds excited by work, by pleasure, and by riot; we will sing of the multicolored, polyphonic tides of revolution in modern capitals; we will sing of the vibrant nocturnal fervor of arsenals and shipyards blazing with violent electric moons; of hungry railway stations that devour fire-breathing serpents; factories hung on clouds by the twisted lines of their smoke; bridges that stride the rivers like giant gymnasts, gleaming in the sun with a glitter of knives; adventurous steamers that cut the horizon; deep-chested locomotives whose wheels gallop along the tracks like the hooves of huge steel horses bridled by tubing; and the sleek flight of planes whose propellers flutter in the wind like banners and seem to cheer like an enthusiastic crowd.

Source: L. De Maria, ed., *Per conoscere Marinetti e il futurismo* (Milan: Mondadori, 1973), pp. 5–7. Trans. P. Cannistraro.

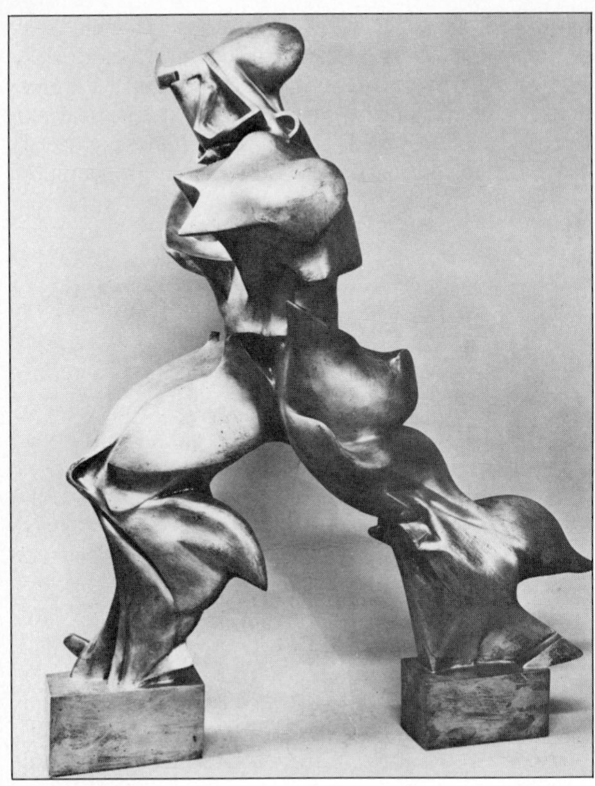

Umberto Boccioni's sculpture *Unique Forms of Continuity in Space* (1913) typifies the Futurist concern for motion and action. It is bronze and measures $43\frac{7}{8} \times 34\frac{7}{8} \times 15\frac{3}{4}$ wide. [Museum of Modern Art, New York; acquired through the Lillie P. Bliss Bequest.]

Futurism found other disciples in art and literature, notably in the English painter Wyndham Lewis (1882–1957) and the Russian poet Vladimir Mayakovsky (1893–1930).

Nationalism and Racism

The Futurists may have been the most extreme example of the crisis of European culture, but such disturbing concepts also affected public affairs. Some political theorists and social critics rejected the positivist doctrines on which both liberalism and socialism were based. Georges Sorel founded his syndicalist theories on the belief that the working masses could be stimulated to violent action by the idea of the general strike. Sorel's ideas were reinforced by the psychologist Gustav Le Bon (1841–1931), whose book *The Crowd* (1895) argued that mobs responded to pathological suggestion, and by others who maintained that instinct determined social conduct.

The characterization of mass behavior as essentially irrational led the Italian sociologist Vilfredo Pareto (1848–1923) to assert the need for government by an elite rather than by the people. The French monarchist Charles Maurras (1868–1952) founded a reactionary political organization known as *Action française* on the theory that "the mob always follows determined minorities." Such thinking would influence important political leaders of both the right and the left, from Benito Mussolini to V. I. Lenin.

A further manifestation of these trends was the rise of racism and a new form of nationalism. Whereas nationalists of the 1830s and 1840s fought oppression on behalf of subjected peoples, a chauvinistic nationalism now pitted races and nation-states against one another. Influenced by Social Darwinism, the virulent nationalism of the late nineteenth century preached aggression and dominance. In the 1870s the pan-Slav movement proclaimed Russia's historic mission to unite all Slavic peoples into a great federation for an inevitable struggle against the West, while the Pan-German League, founded in 1893, demanded territorial expansion and a German-dominated central Europe.

The exaggerated nationalism of the period was linked to racist doctrines, which owed much to the Frenchman Arthur de Gobineau (1816–1882), author of "An Essay on the Inequality of the Races." Gobineau argued that the white races—especially the "Aryans" descended from Germanic tribes—had created civilization but had degenerated as a result of intermingling with "inferior" races. His theories impressed the German musical genius Richard Wagner (1813–1883), who condemned "Jewish" influence in music and whose cycle of four powerful operas in *The Ring of the Nibelungen* (1848–1876) glorified Germanic mythology. Wagner's son-in-law, the British expatriate Houston Stewart Chamberlain (1855–1927), espoused the creation of a superior race through genetic breeding. Chamberlain's *Foundations of the Nineteenth Century* (1899) blamed Europe's racial "degeneration" on the Jews.

Although anti-Semitism had existed for centuries, it reappeared in the vicious Russian pogroms of the late nineteenth century and as the basis for political movements spawned by racial doctrines. In Germany political parties inspired by Adolf Stöcker (1835–1909) elected deputies to the Reichstag on anti-Semitic platforms, while the mayor of Vienna, Karl Lüger (1844–1910), used anti-Semitism to generate popular support for his Christian Socialist party. In France, Charles Maurras led a campaign against the Jews during the Dreyfus affair. Nazi anti-Semitism was rooted in the racist atmosphere of the 1890s.

The Breakdown of the European Order

Few topics in modern history are more controversial than the causes of World War I. During and after the conflict, governments on both sides issued volumes of documents to justify their positions. In the wake of the Allied victory, a defeated Germany was forced to accept the blame. Since then, historians have taken a more balanced view of the war's origins, separating the long-range developments in which all European nations had participated from the immediate circumstances that led to its outbreak. The controversy erupted again in the 1960s when a German scholar, Fritz Fischer, maintained that his country had deliberately planned a far-reaching program of conquest before 1914. The response to Fischer's thesis has been heated, and today most historians would argue that his explanation focused too narrowly on Germany and underemphasized the broader European causes of the war.

For decades historical antagonisms, colonial rivalries, economic competition, and expansionist aspirations, all fueled by chauvinistic nationalism, had propelled Europe into an arms race and hostile alliances. Diplomatic confrontations increased tensions among the powers, so that most nations came to believe that only military alliances provided safety. When the final crisis came in the summer of 1914, the diplomatic order collapsed through a combination of fear and miscalculation. Science and technology, the twin sources of power and pride that had enabled the West to dominate the globe, made what most statesmen hoped would be an easy war a long and agonizing ordeal from which Europe never fully recovered.

Bismarck and the Concert of Europe

For more than half a century after the defeat of Napoleon in 1815 Europe's international system had been based on the notion that the great powers would act "in concert" to keep the peace established by the Congress of Vienna. The system worked remarkably well until the creation of the German empire in 1871 drastically altered international politics. Bismarck's triumph, won on the ruins of the second French empire, gave birth to a powerful state whose unsurpassed military strength was quickly equaled by its industrial and economic power.

The rapid emergence of Germany upset the European balance of power. Upon achieving unification, Bismarck denied having any further territorial ambitions. For the next 20 years his foreign policy goals remained the preservation of the concert of Europe and the protection of Germany. Bismarck saw two potentially troublesome situations. On the western frontier the French were obsessed with achieving revenge against Germany after their humiliating defeat in the Franco-Prussian War. For the Iron Chancellor the worst scenario was a military pact between France and Russia that would sandwich Germany between them in a two-front war. To avoid such a "nightmare," as he described it, Bismarck sought to keep France isolated from diplomatic alliances with other powers.

The east presented a more complicated security problem. The rise of nationalism threatened to destabilize east-central Europe and the Balkans by pulling apart both Austria-Hungary, which had been severely weakened by Prussia's lightning victory in 1866, and the deteriorating Ottoman Empire. The Balkans became the focus of this regional instability, for there Austria-Hungary and Russia competed for territory and influence at the expense of the Turks. Conflict between Vienna and St. Petersburg over the Balkans could drag Germany into a major war in the east and allow France to invade from the west. Bismarck responded by creating secret and often mutually contradictory diplomatic and military pacts. His strategy placed Berlin at the center of a complicated web of alliances that exploited competing national interests and fears.

Bismarck took his first step in 1873, when he concluded a mutual consultation treaty, the League of the Three Emperors, with Russia and Austria-Hungary. The league faced a serious crisis in 1877 and 1878. Russia, motivated by a desire for expansion, joined Serbia, Montenegro, and Bulgaria in a war against Turkey. The Treaty of San Stefano freed the Balkan states from Turkish control and gave the tsar a foothold in the region. Assuming the self-professed role of an "honest broker," Bismarck tried to engineer peace at the congress of Berlin and redress the balance of power. Austria secured the right to administer the provinces of Bosnia and Herzegovina, which technically remained Ottoman possessions, and the size of Bulgaria was reduced. Nevertheless, the Berlin congress aroused Slavic hostility against Germany and Austria-Hungary, for the Russians were angered by what they considered Bismarck's perfidy, while Serbia and Montenegro were bitter over Austria's occupation of Bosnia and Herzegovina. Romania and Greece were disappointed at not having gotten territories from the Turks. The Balkans had become a powder keg.

Bismarck moved immediately to protect Germany from reprisal. In 1879 he concluded the Dual Alliance with Austria-Hungary, a defensive military pact. The Russians, sensing their isolation, responded in 1881 by agreeing to a mutual-security pact with Germany. Not only did this ease Russia's fears of encirclement, but it also gave Germany a measure of security by reducing the possibility of a joint attack by France and Russia. Bismarck had successfully played off Austria and Russia.

Two additional treaties closed the circle of Bismarck's diplomatic policy. In 1882 the Triple Alliance drew Italy into a defensive agreement with Germany and Austria. Finally, in 1887 Bismarck secretly negotiated the Reinsurance Treaty with Russia, guaranteeing neutrality by one power if the other were attacked. Thus Russia did not have to worry about Germany in the event of a war with Austria, while Germany no longer feared what Russia would do in case of a war with France. Bismarck could now be confident that German interests were protected—at least as long as he managed German affairs.

The Triple Entente

When Kaiser William II forced Bismarck into retirement in 1890, German foreign policy changed drastically. The new emperor rejected the necessity of an alliance with Russia and friendship with Britain, two vital premises of Bismarck's diplomacy. Convinced that Austria was Germany's natural ally, William refused Russian requests to renew the Reinsurance Treaty. The inevitable happened: in 1894 France and Russia signed a defensive military agreement that created the "nightmare alliance" Bismarck had dreaded.

Britain had remained aloof from Continental alliances, adhering instead to its traditional "balance of power" policy. But the kaiser, who resented Britain's preeminent world position, was determined to raise German prestige by winning colonial territories and brandishing German power. Britain, whose industrial growth had fallen behind Germany's, grew alarmed at the kaiser's hostility. Abandoning Bismarck's opposition to imperial conquest, William attempted to block the consolidation of British interests in Africa and in 1896 enraged London by expressing pro-Boer sentiments. Between 1898 and 1900 British security interests were again put at risk when Germany began constructing a powerful fleet that challenged Britain's goal of maintaining a two-to-one margin over Germany's naval forces.

German aggressiveness forced Britain to end its diplomatic isolation. An Anglo-Japanese agreement in 1902 was followed two years later by the Entente Cordiale ("friendly understanding") with France, which settled colonial disputes between the two nations. France agreed to a British sphere of influence in Egypt in return for French predominance in Morocco. Outraged by this, Kaiser William visited Tangier to support Moroccan independence. The Algeciras conference of 1906 affirmed the Entente agreements, rebuffing Germany.

In 1906, in the wake of the Moroccan crisis, the British launched the first of a series of battleships known as dreadnaughts, with greater range, speed, and firepower than any previous type of military vessel. The next year the Germans followed suit, unleashing a costly naval race between the two powers. Tensions increased as German plans to construct a Berlin-to-Baghdad railroad made Britain, France, and Russia uneasy over their interests in the Middle East. Encouraged by the French, Russia and Britain negotiated a treaty in 1907 that settled colonial rivalries in Tibet, Afghanistan, and Iran and, like the Entente Cordiale, made possible closer cooperation in Europe.

In the 20 years after Bismarck's retirement, Europe's great powers had aligned themselves into two blocs. Germany, Austria, and Italy were bound by the terms of the Triple Alliance, while Britain, France, and Russia were tied less formally by treaties that together formed a Triple Entente. Separating these military and diplomatic blocs was a pattern of growing hostility. Disputes between members of the rival blocs heightened tensions and made the alliance systems more rigid, for the fear of being left without the protection of friends led nations to support their partners, regardless of the merits of the issue. The most dangerous consequence of this development was that in times of crisis the alliances limited the options available to each power.

The Arms Race

Even before the division of Europe into opposing blocs, firms such as Krupp in Germany, Schneider in France, and Armstrong-Whitworth in Britain reaped enormous profits from the sale of weapons and exercised great influence on the defense policies of their governments. International rivalries over colonies and markets stimulated armaments industries and were used to justify huge military expenditures. French per capita arms spending more than doubled between 1870 and 1914, while Germany's increased more than sixfold. By the eve of World War I both countries were spending almost 5 percent of their national income on weapons.

Improvements in weapons advanced rapidly, yet the nature of technological development made permanent advantage impossible. Reinforced concrete and steel alloys improved defensive systems. Nevertheless, the enormous firepower of heavy artillery—especially long-range howitzers—and more powerful explosives made impregnable fortresses a thing of the past. The British dreadnaughts, designed to revolutionize sea warfare, were mounted with ten 12-inch guns, each capable of hurling an 850-pound shell 10 miles. But the thick armor plating and turbine engines of the dreadnaughts were vulnerable to enemy guns as well as to torpedoes from newly developed submarines and destroyers. Military planners were convinced that the outcome of warfare on land and sea would be determined by artillery.

Despite the technology, infantry soldiers were the basis of war strategy. By 1874 all of the great powers except Britain had introduced compulsory military service. France and Germany doubled their standing armies between 1870 and 1914, each keeping almost half a million men under arms in peacetime. The function of the infantry was modified in the 1880s with the introduction of the magazine rifle and the machine gun, which gave great advantage to defensive positions and guaranteed huge casualties to attacking armies. Despite these changes, European tactics were still based on the Prussian campaigns of 1866 and 1870, with their emphasis on speed, mobility, and surprise. Military plans, based on elaborate transportation networks and exact timetables, contributed to the possibility of war, for generals insisted on rapid mobilization during international crises.

Such was the case with the Schlieffen Plan, worked out

in 1905 by the German general staff. Based on the likelihood of a two-front war against France and Russia, the strategy assumed that the Russians would take longer to mobilize than the French. Hence, Schlieffen proposed that while Germany remained on the defensive against Russia, two armies—a powerful one sweeping through Luxembourg and Belgium and a weaker force moving from the south to lure the French away from the real attack—would swing rapidly around a central "hinge" and crush the French in a giant pincer. Having defeated France, the Germans could then concentrate their military strength against Russia.

With mass conscription came the introduction of the general staff, also based on the German model, and the growing prestige of a professional officer caste. Although strongest in Germany, the link between the landed nobility and the military command was present in every country. Their aristocratic lineage gave high-ranking officers special access to and influence over their sovereigns, even in representative governments, while their conservative outlook in domestic politics weakened the position of liberal civilians in government circles.

Government propaganda, the sensationalism of the press, and the nationalism imbued in citizens by universal elementary education conditioned the public to conscription and the high cost of armaments. Compulsory military training in turn convinced the public to accept the possibility of war.

Europe on the Brink

Relations between the Triple Alliance and the Entente deteriorated as one international crisis succeeded another. The Austro-Russian struggle for hegemony stirred nationalist fervor in the Balkans, where Serbian nationalists sought to create a united Slavic state and looked to Russia—the Slavic "big brother"—for support. Austria-Hungary, which regarded Slavic nationalism as a threat to its multinational empire, opposed Serbia. These forces came to a head in 1908 when Austria attempted to prevent Serbian expansion to the Adriatic Sea by annexing Bosnia and Herzegovina. The angry Serbs, who had hoped to incorporate Bosnia into their greater Slavic state, could do little without Russia, which felt too weak to respond in the face of British and Austrian pressure.

European aggression speeded the disintegration of the Ottoman Empire. In 1911 the kaiser dispatched the *Panther* gunboat to the Moroccan port of Agadir under the guise of protecting German nationals, but his real purpose was to challenge French and British domination in Africa. The crisis dissipated when the French agreed to cede part of the Congo to Germany, but it had the effect of alarming British opinion and solidifying the Anglo-French Entente. Later that year Italy went to war against the Ottoman Empire and wrested Libya from the Turks.

Encouraged by these events, the Balkan states attacked Turkey in 1912. The Balkan League, consisting of Serbia, Bulgaria, Greece, and Montenegro, easily defeated the Turks. Bulgaria emerged with the lion's share of the spoils. Austria intervened again to prevent the Serbs from gaining access to the Adriatic Sea, and when Russia protested, an international conference resolved the dispute by creating the state of Albania and compensating Serbia with inland territory. No one was satisfied. A month later, in June 1913, a second Balkan war erupted in which Serbia, Romania, Greece, and Turkey stripped Bulgaria of many of its territorial gains.

The Serbs, who had now doubled the size of their country, reoccupied parts of Albania, but their Russian protectors again failed to back them when an Austrian ultimatum forced their withdrawal. In fact, both Vienna and St. Petersburg remained deeply anxious. Throughout 1912 and 1913, the Austrians were bitterly critical of Germany, to whose lack of support they attributed Serbia's expansion. The Russians simultaneously blamed Britain for having prevented Serbia from gaining access to the sea. On both sides an uneasy feeling prevailed that neither the Triple Alliance nor the Entente could survive further internal tensions.

Sarajevo: The Failure of Diplomacy

On June 28, 1914, three students assassinated Archduke Franz Ferdinand (1863–1914), nephew of the emperor of Austria-Hungary and heir to the throne, while he attended military maneuvers in Bosnia. The three terrorists—members of Young Bosnia, a Slavic nationalist group—had been trained by Serbian army officers in a secret organization called Unity or Death (also known as the Black Hand). The Austrians did not know that Serbian cabinet members had been aware of the plot for some weeks, although they had not approved of it. Nevertheless, the Austrians expressed outrage and accused Serbian officials of complicity in the assassination. Some officials pushed for quick military action, hoping to crush Serbia permanently. The danger lay in the probability that conflict with Serbia would spark Russian intervention. Austria thus sought the support of Germany before acting.

In response, Kaiser William gave Austria-Hungary a "blank check" on July 5—that is, clear assurance of military support, along with advice to strike while world opinion was still hostile to Serbia. His chancellor, Theobald von Bethmann-Hollweg, acknowledged the risk of a general European war but believed that decisive Austrian action supported by Germany would deter Russia. Britain, he assumed, would not intervene. On July 23 Austria presented Serbia with a stiff ultimatum, including a demand that Austria be permitted to hunt for Franz Ferdinand's assassins on Serbian territory. Although Belgrade's reply

One of the conspirators responsible for the assassination of Archduke Franz Ferdinand is shown here being taken into police custody. [Granger Collection]

was conciliatory, the Serbians refused to accept this provision, which would have undermined their independence. On July 28 Austria declared war on Serbia.

When a reluctant Tsar Nicholas II ordered partial Russian mobilization on July 30, General Helmuth von Moltke, the kaiser's chief of staff, appealed for an immediate German mobilization in order to put the Schlieffen Plan into operation. Bethmann-Hollweg belatedly tried to persuade the Austrians to negotiate, to no avail. The Austrians announced mobilization against Russia on July 31, and Nicholas responded in kind. The Germans immediately demanded that the tsar pull back, but before he could reply, Germany declared war on Russia on August 1.

The elaborate diplomatic calculations continued to go awry. On August 2 the German ambassador in Brussels delivered an ultimatum demanding free passage through Belgian territory, presaging a preemptive strike against France. The British foreign secretary, Sir Edward Grey (1862–1933), intimated to Berlin that a violation of the international treaty guaranteeing Belgian neutrality would be regarded as a serious matter, but Bethmann-Hollweg ridiculed the idea that Britain would fight over "a scrap of paper." Two days later Germany declared war on Belgium and France and set the Schlieffen Plan in motion. On August 4 Britain declared war on Germany. "The lamps are going out all over Europe," Grey is supposed to have said, and "we shall not see them lit again in our life-time."[1]

The Ordeal of the West

Most countries greeted the coming of war with relief and even enthusiasm, and almost no one thought it would last for very long. Within a few weeks, however, these expectations proved illusory. Europe found itself locked in a prolonged ordeal that brought unprecedented death and destruction.

War of Attrition

The rapid war of movement and assault anticipated by military planners turned into a bloody stalemate almost at once. The German armies crossed into Belgium on August 4, but unexpected resistance and last-minute changes in strategy threw off their timetable. By September they advanced to within 25 miles of Paris, but the French halted them at the Marne River and forced retreat. With the Schlieffen Plan in shambles, the Anglo-French allies and Germany then tried to outflank each other; the line of battle soon reached from the Swiss border to the sea.

Once the Germans failed to strike a death blow against France, their dream of a rapid victory vanished. Instead, the equally matched combatants now faced each other in a war in which defense proved stronger than attack. On either side of the front, the combatants dug hundreds of miles of trenches, protected by barbed wire, land mines, and machine guns, in which millions of infantry soldiers lived and died. After preparatory artillery barrages, soldiers were ordered to charge the enemy trenches and cross the "no man's land" that separated them, only to be cut down by deadly machine gun fire and artillery. The first four months of fighting alone resulted in 1,640,000 casualties, yet after the first battle of the Marne the front line hardly moved. Generals clung stubbornly to the same tactics for 3½ years, squandering the lives of their men. The conflict had become a war of attrition in which the

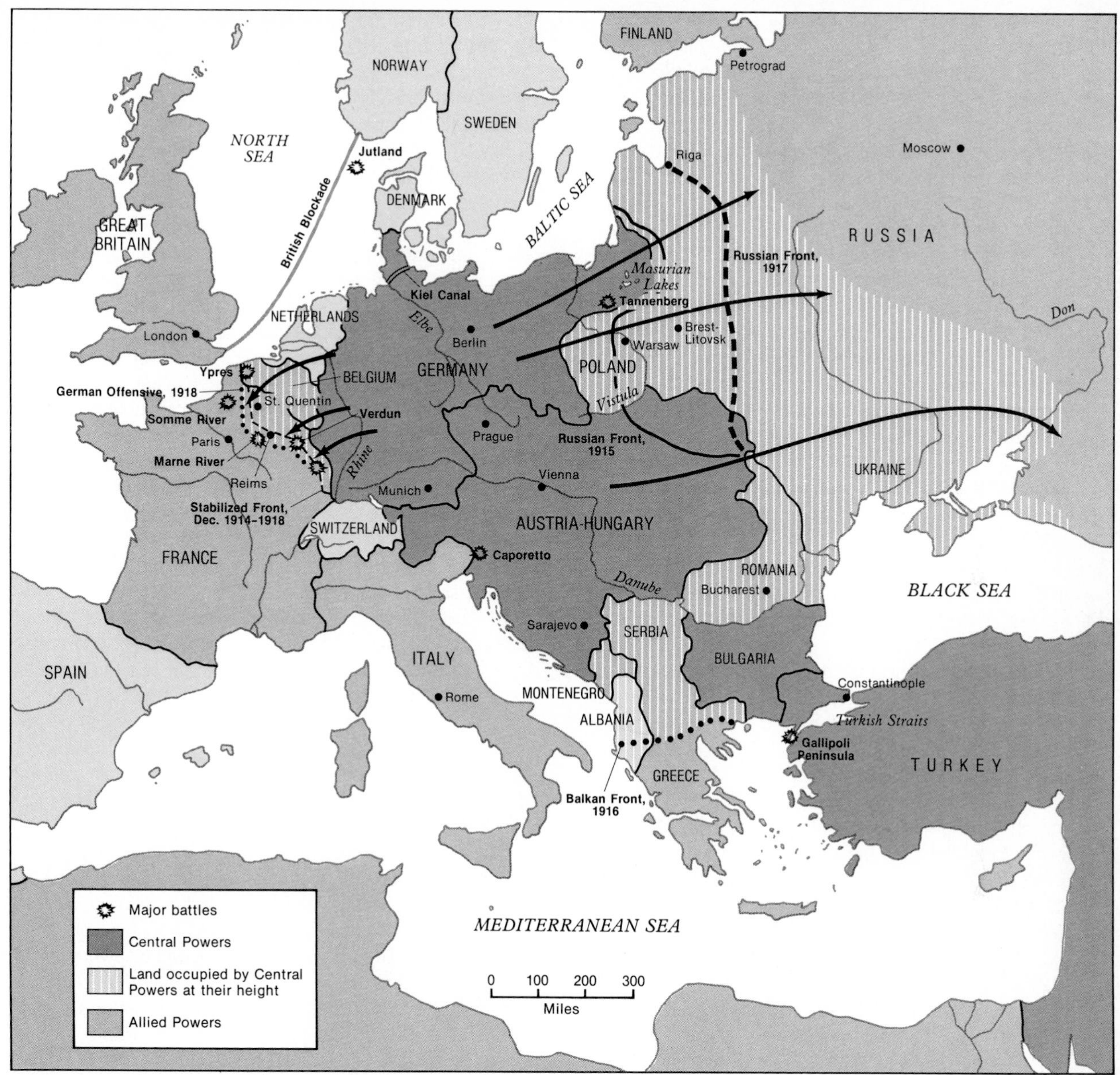

34.1 World War I, 1914–1918

infliction of casualties rather than the capture of terrain became the measure of success.

The Eastern Front and Italian Intervention

Conditions were far different on the eastern front, where men and supplies had to move over vast distances. In August the Russians won unexpected victories by moving two separate armies deep into East Prussia. The Germans panicked and withdrew four divisions from Belgium, while the kaiser put the retired general Paul von Hindenburg (1847–1934) in charge of operations and made the major general Erich Ludendorff (1865–1937) his chief of staff. By dealing separately with each of the Russian armies Hindenburg and Ludendorff won major victories at Tannenberg and the Masurian Lakes, and by mid-September the Russians had lost 250,000 men.

Russia fared better against the Austrians, overrunning Galicia and driving into Hungary. The Austrians suffered further setbacks in the Balkans, where the Serbs twice repelled their armies. But Russian fortunes declined with the entrance of Turkey into the war on the side of the

Central Powers, for the closing of the Dardanelles straits cut Russia off from critical supplies. Winston Churchill (1874–1965), Britain's First Lord of the Admiralty, conceived a daring plan to force the straits open, but a joint Anglo-French fleet failed to break through in March 1915. This effort was followed by landings on the Gallipoli peninsula, which were commanded by Mustapha Kemal (1881–1938), the future dictator of Turkey. By January the British had withdrawn.

The war widened further in 1915. The Germans struck, advancing some 200 miles against Russia, inflicting more than 2 million casualties and capturing or destroying almost a third of its industries. Allied reverses on the eastern front were mitigated in part by Italy's entrance into the war in May in return for promises of territory on the Italo-Austrian border and on the Dalmatian coast. In September, Bulgaria joined Germany and Austria.

The War Beyond Europe

Although military activity beyond Europe was of little importance to the outcome of the war, in the Middle East the fighting was to have a direct bearing on postwar events. Arab nationalists meeting in Paris in 1913 had insisted on autonomy within the Ottoman Empire, but during World War I the British deliberately encouraged the Arabs to revolt, thus foiling Turkish efforts to mobilize them against the Allies. When the Ottoman Empire joined the Central Powers in November 1914, the British Indian army sent an expeditionary force to the Persian Gulf and Iraq, nearly reaching Baghdad before being driven back by Turkish forces. Another Indian force guarded the Suez Canal. During the Gallipoli and Dardenelles campaigns, British diplomats pledged to support an Arab revolt and gained the cooperation of Abdul-Aziz ibn-Saud (1880–1953), the sultan who ruled the Nejd region of south-central Arabia.

British promises to the Arabs were designed to help the war effort, not to bring independence to the region. In 1916 Hussein ibn-Ali (1856–1931), a proclaimed descendant of the prophet Muhammad and protector of the holy city of Mecca, instigated a revolt against the Turks, frustrating efforts to launch a holy war against the Allies. With British approval he declared himself king of the Arabs, claiming control over a vast area stretching from the Hejaz along the Red Sea to the Persian Gulf. That same year the British and French concluded the Sykes-Picot Agreement, which divided much of the region into spheres of influence; France would get Syria and Lebanon while Britain obtained Iraq and Palestine. Throughout 1917 and 1918, T. E. Lawrence (1888–1935), a British archaeologist and soldier—later known as Lawrence of Arabia—assisted Prince Faisal (1885–1933), Hussein's son, who commanded the Arab forces that seized Damascus and Jerusalem.

The dual nature of British policy in the Middle East became clear in November 1917 when Foreign Secretary Arthur James Balfour formally supported Zionist aspirations for a Jewish homeland in Palestine. The Balfour Declaration did not specifically promise Jewish control over all of Palestine, but it contradicted other statements on behalf of Arab nationalist interests.

Elsewhere in the world the war posed a long-range threat rather than an immediate military danger for the West, for Britain and the Dominions feared Japanese expansionism. Allied with Britain since 1902, Japan declared war against the Central Powers in 1914 and swept over the German Pacific islands north of the equator. Australia occupied New Guinea and New Zealand took German Samoa in order to forestall Japanese expansion in the South Pacific. China declared war against Germany and Austria-Hungary only in 1917, but a 200,000-man Chinese labor batallion served with the Allies in Europe. Yet the Japanese seized the German holdings in China's Shantung province and presented China with the infamous Twenty-one Demands (see Chapters 33 and 35). Unlike China or India, Japan took no part in the war in the West beyond sending several destroyers.

In Africa, British colonial armies, made up of Indian, African, and Afrikaner troops, had little difficulty in taking German Togoland and Southwest Africa. But the German commander in East Africa, Paul von Lettow-Vorbeck, matched the daring exploits of T. E. Lawrence in organizing native resistance and conducting guerrilla warfare. He stopped an assault led by the South African general Jan Smuts and invaded Kenya, successfully defending German East Africa until the end of the war.

The British feared German attempts to foment rebellion in Afghanistan and Japanese propaganda in India, but, with minor exceptions, the Indian army remained loyal. More than a million Indian troops and support personnel fought with the British army in France and elsewhere, and India was notified that it was automatically at war as part of the empire. Most Indian nationalists, including Gandhi, supported the war, hoping that a British victory would hasten India's freedom. Yet the contributions made by the colonies, together with Allied promises of "liberation" both in the Middle East and in the German possessions, raised questions about the future.

Agony on the Western Front

In 1916 and 1917 the killing on the western front intensified. In February 1916 the Germans massed their forces for an assault against Verdun, hoping the French would make a costly defense. They were not disappointed. On the first day of the battle the Germans fired about 1 million artillery shells, and when the siege was over months later, 700,000 French and German soldiers were dead. Verdun held, but the bloodletting left deep scars on France. Oblivi-

The Trauma of Trench Warfare

As millions of young men poured into the trenches during World War I, the unimagined horrors of modern warfare crushed both the values and the optimism of a generation of Europeans. Here two British soldiers describe their experiences during the battle of the Somme in the summer of 1916.

There was a terrific smell. It was so awful it nearly poisoned you. A smell of rotten flesh. The old German front line was covered with bodies—they were seven and eight deep and they had all gone black. The smell! These people had been laying since the first of July. Wicked it was! Colonel Pinney got hold of some stretchers and our job was to put the bodies on them and, with a man at each end, we *threw* them into that crater. There must have been over a thousand bodies there. I don't know how many we buried. I'll never forget that sight. Bodies all over the place. I'll never forget it. I was only eighteen, but I thought, "There's something wrong here!"

As far as you could see there were all these bodies lying there—literally thousands of them. . . . Some without legs, some were legs without bodies, arms without bodies. A terrible sight. . . . It didn't seem possible. It didn't get inside me or scare me, but it just made me wonder that these could have been men. It made me wonder what it was all about. And far away in the distance we could see nothing but a line of bursting shells. It was continuous. You wouldn't have thought that anybody could have existed in it, it was so terrific. And yet we knew we were going up into it, with not an earthly chance.

Source: L. Macdonald, *Somme* (London: Michael Joseph, 1983), pp. 113–114.

ous to the lessons of Verdun, the British embarked on an offensive at the Somme River in June. Despite a massive preliminary bombardment, 60,000 British soldiers were cut down the first day. The British introduced primitive tanks into the battle with minimal effect, and by November this offensive too was over with little result but slaughter—600,000 British and French and 500,000 German soldiers had been killed or wounded.

In the spring of 1917 the Allies suffered a major blow in the east. On March 12 St. Petersburg erupted in revolution, and three days later Tsar Nicholas abdicated. While awaiting what they now regarded as an inevitable Russian defeat, the Germans retired behind the Hindenburg Line, a fortified defensive position in the west. The French vainly attacked it in April, suffering 250,000 casualties. From July to November the British fought the Germans at Ypres in the fields of Flanders, despite the new horrors of poison gas. The British suffered another 300,000 casualties.

Europeans could hardly grasp the fearful toll that the fighting had taken—more than 2.5 million dead and wounded alone in the four major western engagements of 1916 and 1917. The enthusiasm of 1914 turned to shock and a sense that civilization had reached the point of collapse. "The higher civilization rises," observed a German general, "the viler man becomes."[2] Churchill, writing about the war a few years later, was equally bleak: "When all was over, Torture and Cannibalism were the only two expedients that the civilized, scientific, Christian States had been able to deny themselves: and these were of doubtful utility."[3]

The Social Consequences of Total War

The futility of the war brought opposition and sometimes revolt. During the spring 1917 offensive in Champagne, some French units had refused to leave the trenches, and the Russian army was rife with mutiny long before the revolution. The shock of the war also spread defeatism among civilians. In Turin, Italian socialists staged an abortive uprising, and in July the German Reichstag passed a peace resolution.

The collapse of morale on both sides raised serious concerns about the home front, for in a war of such gigantic proportions, industrial production was as important as front-line fighting. Attrition created huge shortages not only of manpower but also of food, clothing, and munitions. To cope with the economic and political strains, leaders formed cabinets of national unity, representing in some cases even socialist parties. Governments instituted rationing, placed controls on prices and wages, restricted union activity, and set up planning boards to coordinate production of war matériel.

The trend toward the greater militarization of society that had begun in the late nineteenth century accelerated sharply. The military assumed more authority in civilian affairs, and governments imposed censorship on the press and suspended constitutional procedures. Official propaganda called for a "total" war effort that demanded the regimentation of civilian life. Soldiers and civilians were regarded as one in the struggle. To dehumanize the enemy, Allied propaganda spread stories of "Huns" committing barbaric atrocities in Belgium and northeastern France. As civilian morale fell in the face of mounting casualties at the front, propaganda increased the stakes in victory so as to justify the enormous sacrifices. Both sides claimed to be fighting not just for national defense but in the name of civilization and democracy.

The ceaseless demands of war resulted in full employment, an unprecedented situation that provided wages for women and the poor. Hundreds of thousands of women left the home for the factories, and by the end of the war they comprised more than a third of all industrial workers in most countries. Women also filled white-collar jobs ordinarily occupied by men. Their independence grew with their importance to the war effort, and they broke social customs that had previously restrained them in behavior and dress. Women also contributed to the war effort by serving as nurses, orderlies, and ambulance drivers. The huge number of casualties created a serious shortage of medical facilities and overwhelmed trained personnel, so that thousands of volunteers staffed field hospitals along with professional nurses. The primitive conditions under which they worked exposed these women not only to infection and disease but also to the dangers of artillery bombardment and the threat of capture, for nursing and Red Cross units were often immediately behind the front.

The most famous nurse of the war was Edith Cavell (1865–1915), a Briton in charge of a Red Cross station in Belgium. She remained at her post to care for the wounded while Germans overran the area. When they learned that she was also helping captured British and French soldiers to escape, they shot her for espionage. Although her nonnursing activities had removed her from the protection of international law, Allied propaganda made her death a symbol of enemy "barbarism."

Class distinctions tended to break down under the impact of the common struggle for survival. Aristocratic ladies volunteered for nursing duties along with working women, and union leaders worked side by side with industrialists on government boards. Moreover, although the enlisted ranks of the armies were filled overwhelmingly with workers and peasants, young aristocrats and educated middle-class men made up the lower officer corps. The dynamics of trench warfare, in which the junior officers led the charges over the top, meant that the upper classes actually spilled a larger proportion of their blood on the battlefields.

Total war targeted civilians as part of an overall military strategy that sought to break morale. German zeppelins dropped bombs over British cities, and Austrian artillery shelled Venice. More effective, however, were efforts to starve entire populations into submission through naval blockades. Britain and France continued to receive food and supplies from the United States and the British Empire, while Russia and the Central Powers, virtually cut off from overseas trade, felt the shortages acutely. Germany instituted rationing as early as 1915. During the bitter winter of 1916–1917, the German people suffered from hunger and cold, subsisting on turnips and synthetic products.

The British violated international agreements by interfering with neutral shipping to Germany. The Germans responded with a major innovation in naval warfare, the U-boat or submarine. To be effective, submarines had to fire on ships by surprise from below the surface, without being able to ascertain whether they were enemy or neutral vessels or whether they were carrying war contraband. Submarine warfare antagonized American opinion, especially after the sinking of a commercial liner, the *Lusitania*, in May 1915 with the loss of over 1,000 lives, 128 of them American. That summer U-boat commanders were given restricted orders.

American Intervention and the German Collapse

The submarine was a devastating weapon, sinking 750,000 tons of shipping in 1915 alone. After the stalemate of Verdun and the Somme, the Germans believed it might be decisive as well, despite the risk of bringing the United States into the war. Unrestricted submarine warfare was unleashed on February 1, 1917, and President Woodrow Wilson broke diplomatic relations with Germany two days later. Allied and neutral shipping losses more than doubled in 1917. The U-boats, together with German diplomatic intrigue, Allied propaganda, and the influence of American munitions manufacturers and other trading and banking interests, influenced Congress to declare war against Germany on April 6.

American supplies began to tip the balance in favor of the Allies, but before the end of 1917 they suffered two serious setbacks. In October the battle of Caporetto nearly knocked Italy out of the war. In March 1918 the new Bolshevik government in Russia signed the Treaty of Brest-Litovsk with Germany, taking Russia out of the war. The events of 1917 were partially offset when Wilson seized the political initiative by announcing American commitment to war aims he hoped would bring "peace without victory." His Fourteen Points, issued in January 1918, included a proposal to end secret diplomacy, freedom of the seas, unimpeded international trade, disarmament, self-determination for the peoples of eastern Europe, the adjustment of imperial claims based on the interests of colonial peoples as well as those of the powers, and the creation of an international peacekeeping organization, the League of Nations.

The last year of the war saw a desperate effort by the Germans to win a military victory. In March, Ludendorff regrouped German troops from the former Russian front and made a massive assault against France, driving once again to the Marne River but failing to break through the Allied lines. On July 18 the Allies, reinforced by some 300,000 American soldiers, began their counteroffensive. By the end of September the German armies, having lost another million men, were in retreat, and civilian morale was on the point of collapse. Convinced that victory was impossible, Ludendorff advised the kaiser to sue for peace.

Germany's request for an armistice on the basis of the Fourteen Points met with a stiff response from Wilson, who demanded that the Germans first make political reforms. In the meantime, Bulgaria, Turkey, and Austria-Hungary collapsed. On November 3 the German fleet at the port of Kiel mutinied, setting off revolutions in Munich and Berlin. Six days later socialists proclaimed a republic in the capital, and the kaiser abdicated. The armistice, signed on November 11, officially ended the fighting.

The Reordering of Europe

At the close of the Great War people knew that Europe would never be the same. Thirty-four nations had been engaged in the struggle. Vast tracts of once productive land lay in ruins, and the populations of cities such as Berlin and Vienna were at the edge of starvation. More than 10 million fighting men and at least 1 million civilians had been killed and 20 million wounded. The war had also bled Europe's financial resources of $3.3 billion, turning a continent that had once exported huge amounts of capital into a debtor to the United States. Disillusioned by the experience of total war, Europeans were hopeful that the peace would bring a better world.

The Paris Peace Conference

In January 1919 representatives from 27 victorious nations assembled in Paris to draw up peace treaties with five vanquished states—Germany, Austria, Hungary, Bulgaria, and Turkey. Two reasons accounted for the air of expectancy that surrounded the conference. First, Wilson's presence suggested that the treaties would be equitable, since both sides had accepted his Fourteen Points as the basis for peace. Second, each nation brought a delegation of technical experts who promised to arrange the

The leaders of the principal Allied powers gather at the Paris peace conference (1919): (left to right) David Lloyd George, Vittorio E. Orlando, Georges Clemenceau, and Woodrow Wilson. [Brown Brothers]

settlements according to objective, "scientific" principles instead of old-fashioned power politics.

Like the Congress of Vienna 100 years earlier, the Paris peace conference was an impressive gathering of national leaders. Britain was represented by its prime minister, the Welsh Liberal David Lloyd George (1863–1945); France by the Republican premier, Georges Clemenceau (1841–1929); and Italy by its prime minister, Vittorio E. Orlando (1860–1952). Most of the major decisions were the result of negotiations among the "Big Three," Wilson, Lloyd George, and Clemenceau.

Operating in the shadow of the Bolshevik revolution in Russia and the fear that its example would spread, the Big Three excluded Lenin's government from the deliberations. Moreover, public opinion among the victors demanded harsh peace terms for the defeated enemy. Unlike the Congress of Vienna, where France was accorded full diplomatic representation, Germany was permitted to have only observers at the conference and to await terms dictated by the Allied Powers.

The Treaty of Versailles

The most pressing problem was what to do with Germany. Three issues were paramount: French insistence on future security against Germany, the disposition of German colonies, and the reparations the Germans would pay. Because France had twice been invaded within 50 years, Clemenceau demanded the creation of a separate buffer state in the Rhineland between his country and Germany. Wilson objected that such a plan would violate the principle of self-determination, and his debate with Clemenceau became so acrimonious that the American president threatened to leave the conference. In the end, Clemenceau compromised: the Rhineland would be demilitarized and occupied by Allied troops for 15 years, during which time the coal-rich Saar region was to be administered by the League of Nations for the economic benefit of France and Britain, and the United States promised to conclude a defensive military alliance with France.

France, Britain, and Japan all coveted German colonies. The "mandate principle" offered a solution under which these powers were each given control over some of the territories under League supervision, with the object of preparing them for independence. The principle did not apply, however, to China's Shantung peninsula, which came under full Japanese authority. Reparations were another contentious issue. Britain and France insisted that Germany be responsible for all damage done to civilians, including pensions and family support. As a result, the Allies drafted Article 231, which held German aggression responsible for the war. The exact amount was fixed two years later at the staggering sum of $33 billion.

John Maynard Keynes (1883–1946), an economist attached to the British delegation, believed the peace treaty put Germany in an untenable position that spelled future disaster. In *The Economic Consequences of the Peace* (1919) he argued that the enormous reparations anticipated were impossible in view of the other economic provisions of the treaty. Large amounts of German coal were allocated to France, many of Germany's ships were given to Britain, and billions of dollars of its foreign assets were confiscated. Territorial losses stripped Germany of half its iron mines and a fifth of its iron and steel industries. The treaty forced Germany to return Alsace and Lorraine to France; on its eastern borders, Germany ceded parts of East Prussia and Upper Silesia to a revived state of Poland, lost the city of Danzig to League control, and gave up territory to newly independent Czechoslovakia. *Anschluss*, or union, was forbidden between Germany and Austria.

Determined that Germany would be in no position to wage another aggressive war, the Allies reduced its army

The War Guilt Principle

The harsh treaty the Allies imposed on Germany at the Paris peace conference contained a unique principle that forced Germany to accept responsibility for having caused World War I. Article 231 of the Treaty of Versailles is known as the "war guilt clause."

The Allied and Associated Governments affirm and Germany accepts the responsibility of Germany and her allies for causing all the loss and damage to which the Allied and Associated Governments and their nationals have been subjected as a consequence of the war imposed upon them by the aggression of Germany and her allies.

Source: U.S. Congress, Senate, *Treaty of Peace with Germany*, 66th Cong., 1st sess., S. Doc. 49 (1919).

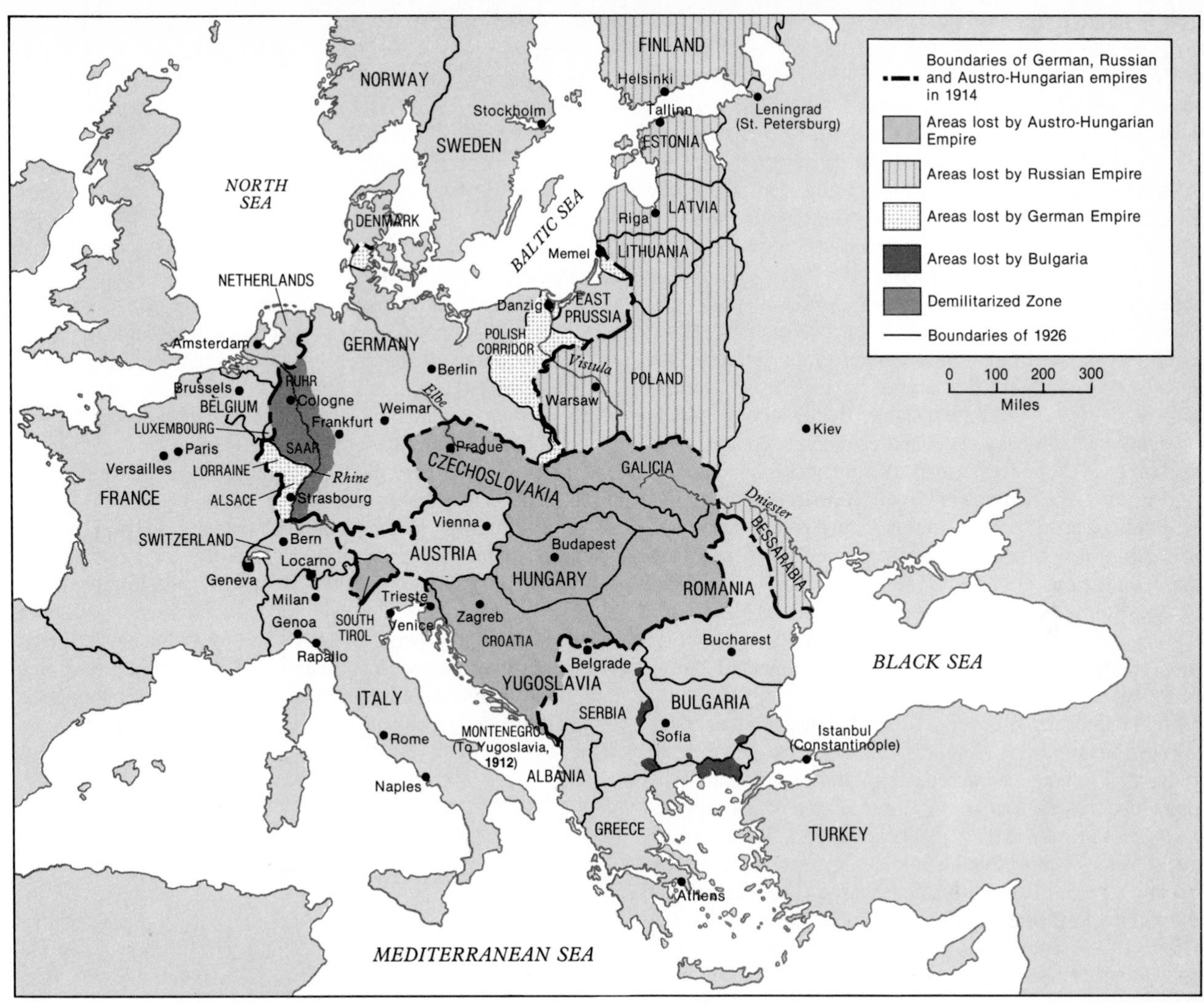

***34.2** Territorial Settlements in Europe, 1919–1926*

to a 100,000-man volunteer force and limited its navy to a handful of small ships. They also prohibited all offensive weapons, including submarines, airplanes and zeppelins, heavy artillery, tanks, and poison gas. Finally, the treaty provided for the trial of the former kaiser as a war criminal, but the Netherlands, to which he had fled, refused to extradite him. The threat of renewed war forced representatives of the new German government to sign the treaty on June 28, 1919.

The peace terms with Germany's allies were hardly less severe. Austria was reduced to a third of its former size, while Hungary was left with a fourth of its former territory. Bulgaria, too, lost land, and all three states had to reduce their armies. Turkey remained only with Asia Minor and a small strip of territory around Constantinople, and the Turkish straits were demilitarized and opened to international shipping.

The Search for Security

Wilson had insisted that permanent peace rested on the creation of an international body known as the League of Nations. The Covenant, or constitution, of the League was incorporated into each of the peace treaties. It provided for a system of "collective security" by which the League would encourage disarmament and prevent war by arbitrating disputes and applying economic sanctions. The Covenant also established a system of mandates by which the European powers assumed the right to rule a number of non-Western areas that they argued were incapable of self-government. Granting self-determination to some European states, such as Poland and Yugoslavia, while denying the same right to the colonized peoples of Asia, Africa, and the Pacific reflected racist assumptions. Because it had no armed force to coerce violators, the

League lacked the power to enforce its principles. Moreover, when Congress refused to ratify the Treaty of Versailles, the United States itself failed to join the organization; neither Germany nor the Soviet Union was to become a member for years.

France and Germany sought alternatives to the League of Nations to ensure their security. American withdrawal from European diplomatic affairs denied France the defensive treaty that Britain and the United States had promised. Consequently, France created a "little entente" by aligning itself with Czechoslovakia, Romania, and Yugoslavia, hoping thereby to encircle Germany on its eastern borders. Isolated from the community of nations, Germany made common cause with Soviet Russia, another outcast nation. In 1922 they signed the Treaty of Rapallo, opening diplomatic relations and pledging economic cooperation as well as secret military contacts.

France remained uneasy over German intentions, and when the Germans failed to meet their reparations quota in 1923, French and Belgian troops occupied the Ruhr Basin on the eastern bank of the Rhine. Passive resistance among Ruhr factory workers and miners and British and American protests eventually forced a withdrawal, but the fear and hatred between the nations remained deeply rooted.

In 1925 German Foreign Minister Gustav Stresemann (1878–1929) proposed that Germany, France, Britain, Italy, and Belgium guarantee the western European status quo. The result was the Locarno Pact, which relieved some of the international political tension. In 1926 Germany finally joined the League of Nations. In 1927 the French foreign minister, Aristide Briand (1862–1932), and the American secretary of state, Frank Kellogg (1856–1937), sponsored a treaty renouncing war as an instrument of national policy. The Kellogg-Briand Pact of 1928, eventually signed by 65 states, "outlawed" war.

Society and Culture: The Impact of War

A decade after World War I, José Ortega y Gasset (1883–1955), a Spanish philosopher, wrote, "Today, by the very fact that everything seems possible to us, we have a feeling that the worst of all is possible: retrogression, barbarism, decadence."[4] Ortega's irony revealed how deeply disturbed his generation had been by the war. Yet his pessimism makes little sense unless we remember that even as Europeans rebuilt their cities and mourned their dead, they were haunted by the memory of their former confidence in the superiority of their civilization. This explains why the West experienced a profound crisis of belief after 1919 despite the victory of the democracies and the return of peace.

Ultimately, Ortega's foreboding proved justified. Although European intellectual and cultural life in the postwar period was creative and varied, it was marked by a mood of anxiety. The sense of futility was particularly acute among the veterans who returned to a civilian society beset with political and economic problems and intent on getting back to "normalcy." To these dashed hopes was added the horror of modern warfare. The German author Erich Maria Remarque (1898–1970) captured the shock experienced by soldiers in two best-selling novels, *All Quiet on the Western Front* (1929) and *The Road Back* (1931). The mood of despair seemed to confirm the prewar intuitions of Nietzsche and Freud that civilized society was irrational and that humans were unable to control their "primitive" instincts. This atmosphere of skepticism stimulated a transformation of Western culture. A decade after the war's end, the "modern" temper of twentieth-century life had been established.

Distrust of established beliefs, uncertainty about the meaning of life, and anxiety about the future produced what the author Gertrude Stein (1874–1946) termed a "lost generation." The triumph of communism in Russia and the rise of fascism in the 1920s suggested a willingness to abandon democracy. Frustrated material expectations added to the disorientation, for the economic boom after 1919 proved to be only a prelude to the Great Depression.

Social Change and Economic Crisis

The impact of the war was felt differently in each country and class. Everywhere the status and power of the old nobility were seriously weakened, especially in the new states of eastern Europe. The aristocracy had been systematically eliminated in Russia after the Bolshevik revolution, and a large number of young British nobles had been killed in the war. Peasants had been conscripted into military service more heavily than any other class, so the toll in death and disablement among them was also high. After the war many peasants refused to go back to their villages and often formed the rank and file of militant veterans' groups in the cities. When they did go back to the countryside, they frequently led protest movements.

Postwar society in western Europe was predominantly urban. In France, the most agrarian of the industrialized nations, the percentage of the working population engaged in agriculture fell from one-half before 1914 to one-third by 1931. Nevertheless, the number of industrial workers remained fairly stable over the following decades as advances in technology and assembly-line processes made labor more productive. During the first years of the war severe labor shortages had produced higher wages and a modicum of prosperity for the working classes, but government controls and inflation eventually forced wages to lag behind prices, resulting in significant discontent. The support and cooperation socialist parties and unions gave to the war effort had conditioned many labor leaders to moderate policies. Some working-class leaders, however, reverted to more radical doctrines after the war, and many looked to the Russian Revolution for inspiration. As real wages rose between 1924 and 1929, particularly for the unskilled, worker discontent was once again mitigated, a trend reinforced by new social welfare measures in many countries.

The war affected the middle classes most severely. Greater educational opportunities and the growth of the service sector increased the number of white-collar workers, many of whom came from working-class families. The economic slump of the 1920s, however, slowed middle-class mobility. The pressure was particularly acute on the lower middle class, whose opportunities for advancement into managerial positions in the private sector shrank as the economy slowed. Inflation also limited the earning power of this group and threatened its status. The most extreme distress occurred in Germany, where by 1925 inflation had eaten up more than 50 percent of the capital held by the lower middle class. Retirees, widows, and others living on fixed incomes were hit especially hard, as were property owners whose incomes were frozen by rent regulations. Lower-middle-class earnings fell markedly in the 1920s, and millions of workers were forced back into the factories, where salaries equaled or exceeded those of white-collar employees. Hence the lower middle class felt squeezed between two groups: the wealthy capitalists, whose income was still increasing, and the workers from whose ranks many of them had risen. Lower-middle-class resentment of big business and labor often found political expression in radical right-wing groups.

The New Morality: Women, Work, and Sex

The middle class, which had experienced prewar optimism most fully, now found its values under assault. Wartime conditions disrupted social arrangements and family structures: husbands at the front, women in the factories, strangers crowding into the cities, and the uncertainty of survival had loosened the restrictions of bourgeois society and contributed to the breakdown of traditional morality. Psychological and social stress encouraged a new style of life that celebrated "liberation" from conventional behavior. In the 1920s Europeans were caught up in the spirit of the "jazz age," a name reflecting the popular perception that American life was more modern and less tradition-bound.

Public manifestations of the new morality appeared everywhere. Women's skirts were shorter and dresses more revealing, slinky adaptations of the "flapper" style made famous in Prohibition America. Young people drank and smoked in public, bars and nightclubs proliferated, and dancing took on more expressive—and suggestive—forms. Motion pictures, perhaps the most popular mass entertainment of the period, created the cult of the "vamp," and the private lives of film stars were spread across the front pages of the popular press. The use of chaperons and arranged marriages declined sharply, while illegitimacy and divorce rates rose. Such changes produced a more open attitude toward sexual matters.

Social developments reflected the new morality. Greater tolerance toward sexual minorities evolved. Events once thought sensational, such as Oscar Wilde's trial in the 1890s, seemed quaint to Europeans of the 1920s who openly professed their differing sexual orientation. Paris and Berlin, the two centers of postwar avant-garde culture, were havens for artists, writers, and musicians that included homosexuals as well as American blacks. Gertrude Stein and Alice B. Toklas, the most famous lesbian couple of the period, presided over a brilliant artistic and literary scene in Paris. Sexual minorities still faced formidable obstacles to equality and acceptance, but the more tolerant attitudes of the 1920s brought the issue into the open.

The emancipation of women was another result of the social transformation. An earlier generation of feminist agitation had made important advances in raising the consciousness of women and calling public attention to their demands for equality. Yet despite the work of the middle-class suffragists and the socialist women's movement, Finland and Norway were the only Western nations in which women had won the right to vote before 1914.

Wartime labor shortages created a situation in which women made significant progress toward equality in the workplace. As women crowded into the munitions industries and the service sector, governments made propaganda appeals to them, thus raising expectations for change. Some nations granted women the right to vote: in 1918 the British Parliament extended suffrage to women over 30, and the next year both the United States and the new German republic gave the vote equally to men and women. Austria, Poland, and Czechoslovakia joined Belgium, the Netherlands, Sweden, and Denmark in following suit.

While these were crucial gains, the suffrage was not made universal in Spain, France, Switzerland, and Italy until after World War II. Moreover, in many countries marriage and property laws favoring husbands also remained largely intact. After 1919 more women gained access to educational opportunities and a wider range of jobs, although many were forced out of their wartime work by returning soldiers, and in practice some professions remained closed to women. Nor was progress in regard to the status of women and sexual minorities permanent, for serious setbacks occurred in the interwar years when right-wing regimes repressed both with renewed vigor.

Postwar Sexual Mores

In the decade after World War I, many aspects of nineteenth-century codes of social behavior were abandoned in the West as religious belief, defined gender roles, and public morality were consciously rejected by the "lost generation." Here Walter Lippmann (1889–1974), an American social critic, sees changes in the status of women and advances in birth control as the principal reasons for the freer sexual conduct that marked the 1920s.

Until quite recently the main conventions of sex were enforced first by the parents and then by the husband through their control over the life of the woman. The main conventions were: first, that she must not encourage or display any amorous inclinations except where there was practical certainty that the young man's intentions were serious; second, that when she was married to the young man she submitted to his embraces only because the Lord somehow failed to contrive a less vile method of perpetuating the species. All the minor conventions were subsidiary to these; the whole system was organized on the premise that procreation was the woman's only sanction for sexual intercourse. . . . The virtuous man, by popular standards, was one who before his marriage did not have sexual relations with a virtuous woman. . . . These conventions were not perfectly administered. But they were sufficiently well administered to remain the accepted conventions, honored even in the breach. It was possible, because of the way people lived, to administer them.

The woman lived a sheltered life. That is another way of saying that she lived under the constant inspection of her family. . . . She met young men under the zealous chaperonage of practically the whole community. No doubt, couples slipped away occasionally and more went on than was known or acknowledged. But even then there was a very powerful deterrent against an illicit relationship. This deterrent was the fear of pregnancy. That in the end made it almost certain that if a secret affair were consummated it could not be kept secret and that terrible penalties would be exacted. In the modern world effective chaperonage has become impracticable and the fear of pregnancy has been virtually eliminated by the very general knowledge of contraceptive methods.

The whole revolution in the field of sexual morals turns upon the fact that external control of the chastity of women is becoming impossible. . . .

For when conception could be prevented, there was an end to the theory that woman submits to the embrace of the male only for purposes of procreation. She had to be persuaded to cooperate, and no possible reason could be advanced except that the pleasure was reciprocal.

Source: W. Lippmann, *A Preface to Morals* (New York: Macmillan, 1929), pp. 286–291 passim.

JOSEPHINE BAKER: AN AMERICAN IN PARIS

One of the most celebrated figures in Europe between the wars was the black American entertainer Josephine Baker. Born in St. Louis in 1906 to a black mother and a father reputedly of Spanish descent, Baker left school at the age of 8 to help support her family. While living in East St. Louis, she witnessed the race riots that broke out there in 1917, and the sight of white bands burning and killing with impunity left an indelible mark on her.

Baker's talent soon surfaced. She starred in basement musicals as a child and ran away with a vaudeville troupe at the age of 13. Four years later she appeared at Radio City Music Hall in New York in a musical featuring black performers titled, stereotypically, *Shuffle Along.* In 1925

The blues singer and dancer Josephine Baker was a great celebrity in Paris during the years between the wars. [Granger Collection]

she went to Paris with a show called *La revue nègre,* which sought to capitalize on the topical vogue for jazz and for "exotic" black entertainers. The show failed and the company was stranded, but Baker caught on with the Folies Bergère, a club famous for its lavish sets and its scantily dressed performers. She created a sensation in her debut, in which she appeared clad only in a tutu made of rhinestone-studded bananas and three bracelets.

Baker's multiple talents as a singer and dancer, wed to a style of inimitable comic abandon, soon made her an international celebrity. Billed only as Josephine, the former slum child earned and spent enormous sums of money; mimicking her own exotic image, she strolled down the streets of Paris with a pet leopard. After a hugely successful world tour, she appeared in films opposite such French stars as Jean Gabin and ventured into light opera as well.

In 1937 Baker married a wealthy industrialist, Jean Lion, converted to Judaism, and became a French citizen. At the outbreak of World War II she joined the Red Cross and was later recruited into the French Resistance, gathering intelligence and also entertaining Free French forces. At the end of the war she was awarded France's highest decorations, the Croix de Guerre and the Légion d'Honneur, as well as the rosette of the Resistance. Baker's wide travel and her experience of poverty and discrimination led her in 1947 to found what she called a World Village at Les Milandes, her estate in southwestern France. Here, she and her second husband, Jo Bouillon, adopted a "rainbow family" of 12 children of all races and religions. She became a center of controversy in 1951 after she protested the refusal to serve her at the Stork Club in New York, but the National Association for the Advancement of Colored People (NAACP) named her its Woman of the Year. Baker began a crusade against segregation in her native country and succeeded in integrating theaters and nightclubs from Las Vegas to Miami. In 1963 she stood with Dr. Martin Luther King, Jr., at the climax of his march on Washington, D.C., and delivered an impassioned speech in front of the Lincoln Memorial.

Bankrupted finally by her debts at Les Milandes, Baker was provided a villa for herself and her children by Princess Grace of Monaco. In 1973 she triumphed at Carnegie Hall in another comeback tour, and despite failing health she repeated her success in Paris in a performance commemorating her fiftieth anniversary in France on April 10, 1975. Two days later, she died of a stroke.

On or off the stage, in or out of controversy, Josephine Baker was for half a century a uniquely vivid symbol of glamor, vitality, compassion, and commitment to the struggle for human equality. At the end of her life a film biography was planned, but, as she told reporters in a 1973 interview, "I would like to meet the woman who has the courage even to play my life story in a film. . . . I do not believe the woman exists who could have had the courage to have *lived* it as I have done." Certainly, few women of the twentieth century have combined careers and interests so daringly, served the human cause so passionately, and triumphed so indomitably.

Science, Literature, and Art

The postwar crisis of belief was especially acute among artists and writers, whose search for meaning led to creative ferment and experimentation. Proclaiming a "crisis of the mind," the French poet and critic Paul Valéry (1871–1945) articulated the state of anxiety and pessimism. His gloomy prognosis of the future was echoed by the German scholar Oswald Spengler (1880–1936). Spengler's immensely popular book *The Decline of the West* (1918) compared the development of Europe with the historical pattern of other civilizations. He argued that the West had entered a period of decay that could be reversed only by an authoritarian "Caesar" capable of imposing peace and order on a chaotic world. In a similar vein, Ortega y Gasset's *The Revolt of the Masses* (1930) warned that democratic society would result in the decline of education and culture.

Science offered no antidote to these laments. Building on the advances in physics at the turn of the century, the Danish physicist Niels Bohr (1885–1962) had formulated a theory of the atom in 1913 that attempted to reconcile Max Planck's quantum theory with Ernest Rutherford's view of atomic structure. By the mid-1920s, however, more complex ideas challenged Bohr's conclusions. The abstract language of differential equations took the place of concepts such as orbits, while Bohr and others revised their earlier hypotheses. In 1927 the German physicist Werner Heisenberg (born 1901) announced his "uncertainty principle": the behavior of atomic particles did not conform to the laws of cause and effect. The futility of attempting to find a comprehensive explanation of physical phenomena to replace the old Newtonian model became increasingly apparent.

Postwar developments in philosophy both reflected and reinforced the findings of science. Ludwig Wittgenstein (1889–1951), the most forceful advocate of the movement called logical empiricism, maintained that traditional ethical and metaphysical systems were meaningless because philosophy was nothing more than statements of fact clarified by logic. Logical positivists asserted that unless such concepts as "freedom" and "God" could be reduced to the precise language of mathematics and symbolic logic, they were meaningless. Similarly, existentialism, derived from the Danish philosopher Søren Kirkegaard (1813–1855) and later associated with the French philosophers Jean-Paul Sartre (1905–1980) and Albert Camus (1913–1960), presented an image of human helplessness and despair in the face of an existence devoid of meaning and a supreme being. Although the existentialists argued that humans exist without a predetermined purpose, they still asserted the necessity of responsible moral action.

In the world of literature, a no less startling revolution took place. Language and structure gave way to experiments that reflected new theories of the human personality as well as a conscious desire to break away from traditional forms. Authors extended the path opened by Marcel Proust (1871–1922), the French author of *Remembrance of Things Past*, with a new "stream of consciousness" of subjective experience. The year 1922 saw the publication of two influential works in this genre, *Ulysses* by the Irishman James Joyce (1882–1941) and *Jacob's Room* by the Englishwoman Virginia Woolf (1882–1941), followed in 1929 by *The Sound and the Fury* by the American William Faulkner (1897–1962). Each of these works probed the random thoughts and emotions of everyday consciousness and the obscure sources of human motivation that Freud had suggested.

D. H. Lawrence (1885–1930), whose controversial *Lady Chatterley's Lover* (1928) was censored for its explicit description of sexual desire, exemplified the postwar liberation from bourgeois mores. The German Thomas Mann (1875–1955), in *The Magic Mountain* (1924), evoked the collapse of meaning. Franz Kafka (1883–1924), a German Jew who lived in Prague, wrote frightening tales of nightmares that haunt the imagination, most notably *The Trial* (1925) and *The Castle* (1929).

While much of the literature of the period between the world wars was so innovative as to confuse and repel readers, the poetry of the Irishman William Butler Yeats (1865–1939) had a more direct appeal, for he combined traditional lyricism with a stoic view of the world. In a similar manner, the German Rainer Maria Rilke (1875–1926) attempted to evoke harmony with nature.

The Italian dramatist Luigi Pirandello (1867–1936) and the poet T. S. Eliot gave the most representative expression to the concerns of the period. In Pirandello's *Six Characters in Search of an Author* (1918), two sets of players, a family and a group of actors, appear on stage at the same time, with the family members asking actors to portray their roles. Both family and actors present versions of the truth peculiar to their own viewpoints. Much as in Einstein's theories, Pirandello's play offered relative truths from which the observer—or the audience—could choose. The absurdity of a world without fixed guideposts was a pervasive theme of interwar European culture. Eliot, in *The Waste Land* (1922), captured most poignantly the sense of desolation that so many creative thinkers of the postwar world felt. Eliot portrayed the spiritual emptiness of modern London and brought the mood of Symbolism into English poetry. He eventually resolved his personal crisis by joining the Anglican church.

The plastic arts, like literature, caught the spirit of the period. As early as 1915 the horrors of the war had begun to produce the deliberately nonsensical anti-art movement known as Dada (from the French meaning "hobbyhorse").

Other artists embraced a "return to order" that restored representational forms to painting so as to express human alienation and isolation. Surrealism drew from a variety of sources, including the new realism, prewar Cubism, Dadaism, and Freudian psychology. Surrealists such as Salvador Dalí and Giorgio de Chirico (1888–1978) created visions of a dream world and hallucinatory landscapes according to the irrational dictates of the subconscious. Other artists, such as Wassily Kandinsky (1866–1944) and Paul Klee (1879–1940), moved from their earlier Expressionist concerns toward greater abstraction, a trend that Piet Mondrian (1872–1944) brought to its extreme in rigidly nonobjective paintings.

Klee and Kandinsky taught at the Bauhaus, the most famous school of architecture and design in modern times. Founded in Weimar by the architect Walter Gropius (1883–1969), the Bauhaus sought to reconcile art with science and technology. It advanced an architectural style emphasizing functionalism, the use of glass and prefabricated concrete, and a rejection of ornamentation. The Bauhaus "international style," also championed by the French architect Le Corbusier (1887–1965) and the American Frank Lloyd Wright (1869–1959), testified to the triumph of the modern temper.

The generation that grew to maturity between 1890 and 1919 experienced the stress and excitement of living through the end of one historical era and the birth of another. The second half of the nineteenth century had been generally a period of material growth, optimism, and self-confidence. Science and technology had made life in the West more comfortable and had enabled the Western powers to impose their rule over much of the globe.

Many of the same factors that caused European expansion contributed, however, to a mounting crisis among the Western states. To a litany of old grievances were added new rivalries and competition for increasingly limited resources. While political leaders and capitalist entrepreneurs in one nation worked to outmaneuver their counterparts elsewhere, military officers and ideologues planned strategies of defense and domination. Once the crisis erupted, the West discovered that it had become much better at waging war than it had imagined. But unlike the wars of imperial conquest, the great European powers were more or less evenly matched, and the war consequently became an exercise in self-destruction.

The strain of total war had produced major change. Socialists shared power in wartime governments, and monarchies were overthrown in three states. In some countries the bloodletting decimated the ruling classes, while in others revolution eradicated or severely wounded traditional elites. Prewar social arrangements were further altered as a result of the massive conscription of peasants, the mobilization of women into the work force, and the disruption of family life.

The postwar age was a new world. Not only had the European map changed with the shifting of frontiers, but new states appeared on the ruins of old empires. Positive thinkers saw liberal democracy installed in central and eastern Europe for the first time; the more pessimistic questioned the chances for its survival. New forms of political extremism arose everywhere and, in Russia and Italy, soon came to power and threatened to spread. Nor did Europe's world supremacy survive much beyond the war. As the forces of nationalism took hold in the colonies, Western control of the subject peoples of Asia, Africa, and the Middle East weakened.

Science, literature, and art undermined the optimism of an earlier age, expressed the despair of a generation that had experienced shattering trauma, and forged new directions. Some intellectuals turned back to religion as a source of hope and comfort. Even Carl Jung rejected the teachings of Freud, his intellectual mentor, by advocating the therapeutic value of religious faith. In 1934, with the world in the throes of the Depression, the British historian Arnold Toynbee published the first of a series of volumes, entitled A Study of History, *which likened the development of civilizations to the biological process of life, with cycles of birth, growth, and decline. Unlike Spengler, however, Toynbee entertained the prospect that Western civilization might revive itself. In the search for meaning, others turned instead to political movements of protest and violence.*

Notes

1. Viscount Grey of Fallodon, *Twenty-five Years, 1892–1916,* vol. 2 (New York: Stokes, 1925), p. 20.
2. K. Robbins, *The First World War* (New York: Oxford University Press, 1984), p. 88.
3. W. S. Churchill, *The World Crisis* (New York: Scribner, 1923), p. 3.
4. J. Ortega y Gasset, *The Revolt of the Masses* (New York: Norton, 1957), p. 45.

Suggestions for Further Reading

Calder, N. *Einstein's Universe*. New York: Penguin Books, 1980.

Cantor, N. F., and Wertman, M. S., eds. *The History of Popular Culture Since 1815*. New York: Macmillan, 1968.

Ellenberger, H. F. *The Discovery of the Unconscious*. New York: Basic Books, 1970.

Fussell, P. *The Great War and Modern Memory*. New York: Oxford University Press, 1975.

Hughes, H. S. *Consciousness and Society: The Reorientation of European Social Thought, 1890–1930*. New York: Knopf, 1958.

Hughes, R. *The Shock of the New: Art and the Century of Change*. New York: Knopf, 1981.

Joll, J. *The Origins of the First World War*. London: Longman, 1984.

Kern, S. *The Culture of Time and Space, 1880–1918*. Cambridge, Mass.: Harvard University Press, 1983.

Lafore, L. *The Long Fuse: An Interpretation of the Origins of World War I*. Philadelphia: Lippincott, 1965.

Martin, M. W. *Futurist Art and Theory, 1909–1915*. Oxford: Clarendon Press, 1978.

Masur, G. *Prophets of Yesterday: Studies in European Culture, 1890–1914*. New York: Macmillan, 1961.

Mayer, A. J. *The Politics and Diplomacy of Peacemaking*. New York: Knopf, 1968.

Mosse, G. *The Culture of Western Europe*. Chicago: Rand McNally, 1969.

Pulzer, P. G. *The Rise of Political Anti-Semitism in Germany and Austria*. New York: Wiley, 1964.

Rewald, J. *The History of Impressionism*. New York: New York Graphic Society, 1980.

Robbins, K. *The First World War*. New York: Oxford University Press, 1984.

Sontag, R. V. *A Broken World*. New York: Harper & Row, 1971.

Stearns, P. N. *European Society in Upheaval: Social History Since 1800*. New York: Macmillan, 1967.

Williams, J. *The Other Battleground: The Home Fronts, Britain, France, and Germany, 1914–1918*. Chicago: Regnery, 1972.

Wohl, R. *The Generation of 1914*. Cambridge, Mass.: Harvard University Press, 1979.

The Human Image (II)

Since the primitive carvers of the Old Stone Age some 25,000 years ago, the human figure has been a central theme of artistic representation. Each civilization has accorded it a different emphasis, and artists of every culture have interpreted it from the aesthetic and religious points of view of their times and societies. Throughout much of the ancient period and during the first millennium A.D., the human figure served a number of important purposes, principally as the embodiment of religious themes, as a means of representing notions of beauty, or as a general commentary on the human condition.

While these functions continued to be served by the human image, important changes began to occur in the modern age. The sixteenth century saw a more secularized portrayal of the human figure in cultures as diverse as Europe and India, together with greater stylistic naturalism. At the same time, an exceptionally active artistic patronage began to emerge throughout much of the world. From the court of Ming China to the Mughal Empire in India and the Medici of Florence, rulers turned to painters and sculptors to produce memorials to the greatness of their regimes. Artists had, of course, always served political purposes, but in some cases rulers now developed a new respect for their creative powers. Figures such as Michelangelo achieved the stature of a culture hero in the late European Renaissance, a phenomenon enshrined in Giorgio Vasari's *Lives of the Painters.* Moreover, while patronage elsewhere in the world remained largely in the hands of rulers, in the West private parties began to commission artists to paint their portraits, so in European art the human figure increasingly represented the wider elite.

Mughal culture in India revealed the diversity of Muslim artistic response to figurative art. The court of Akbar and his successors was the center for the production of portrait miniatures, exquisitely delicate works that meticulously recorded their subjects in a narrative style. Unlike Persian miniatures of earlier times, with their fairy-tale decorations, these paintings display an almost unnerving detachment, as in the portrait of a courtier dying of opium addiction. They testify as much to the virtuosity of the artist as to the representation of an individual.

The emperors of Ming China treated artists with less respect than the court of Akbar: Chinese artists worked in palace workshops under tight supervision, a custom that drove many of the more progressive among them to flee the capital for the cities of the south. Free from the demands of the emperors, many painters of the period seem to have deliberately avoided the depiction

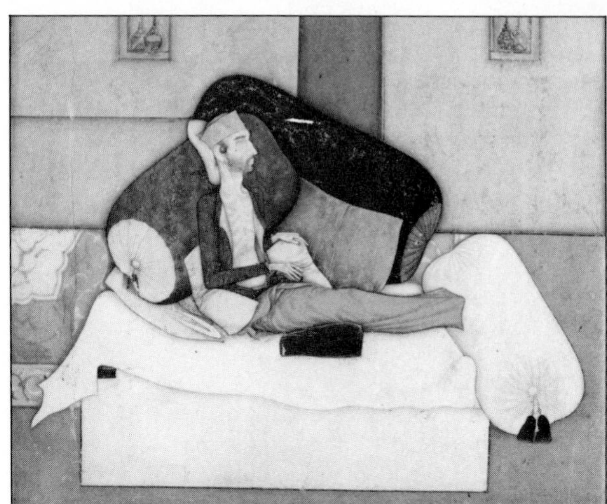

Dying Courtier, c. 1618. [Bodleian Library, Oxford]

of human beings, thus reinforcing the Chinese preference for landscapes.

During the Ch'ing dynasty (1644–1912) sculptors reverted to smaller-scale works in porcelain, exceeding the technical skill of earlier Chinese ceramists. A small white porcelain statute of Kuan-yin (the Chinese goddess of compassion) from the seventeenth century reveals the softness of form and the deeply humanized rendering of a goddess achieved in this medium. Large quantities of such ceramics were exported to Europe in the eighteenth century, and to this day the term *china* is used to describe fine ceramic wares, especially porcelain.

In contrast to the detached aestheticism of the Mughal image and the refined delicacy of later Chinese porcelains, artists of the early Edo period in Japan depicted the human figure as a means of preserving historic events. Chinese travelers observed that like their own painters, their Japanese neighbors tended to use scroll paintings to narrate events, often without philosophical meaning. A pair of painted Japanese screens from 1610 depict Westerners playing music. These are among the interesting works that show Portuguese and Dutch influences on Japanese painting as well as Japanese curiosity at the appearance of the "southern barbarians," as the Jesuit missionaries were known. The figures show little interest in the individuals represented but rather depict their customs, together with their costumes, so drab to Japanese eyes.

Toward the end of the seventeenth century the principal artistic medium in Japan shifted from scroll paint-

White porcelain statue of Kuan-yin, the Chinese goddess of compassion. [Barlow Gallery, University of Sussex, England]

Ivory portrait mask, Benin, West Africa. [Trustees of the British Museum]

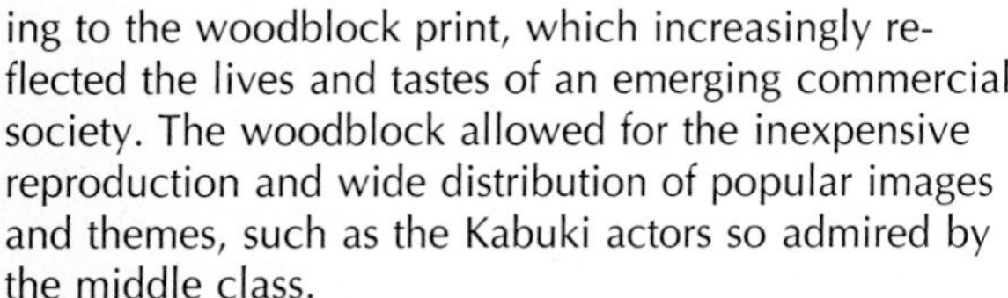

ing to the woodblock print, which increasingly reflected the lives and tastes of an emerging commercial society. The woodblock allowed for the inexpensive reproduction and wide distribution of popular images and themes, such as the Kabuki actors so admired by the middle class.

When the Portuguese arrived at Benin, West Africa, in the fifteenth century, they found a rich and sophisticated kingdom, whose sculptural tradition may well have been related to that of the earlier civilization of the neighboring city of Ife. Climatic conditions in sub-Saharan Africa have not favored the survival of early wooden carvings, but sculptures made of ivory and metal reveal skillful renderings of the human form both realistically and in more abstract styles. A fifteenth-century zinc brass head is a delicate and idealized portrait of a king. Like the Japanese, Benin artists recorded the appearance of the newcomers, though in a much more symbolic and stylized form. An ivory portrait mask made for a ruler is topped by a crown composed of a band of long-haired, bearded Portuguese. The carver of this piece is more interested in hairstyles than in dress but shows the same curiosity at strange customs and appearance. The ruler's portrait expresses elegance and power out of all proportion to its size.

No such record survives of the arrival of Westerners in the Americas. The art of the last Aztecs retains a strong element of decoration, as in the statues of deities carved to embellish temples. Yet the last period of Aztec art provides at least one outstanding example of an artist's use of the human figure to depict a primal event: the carving of a woman (perhaps a goddess) giving birth. The realism of the straining and the cold, damp look of the skin, produced by a careful working of the stone, are powerfully contrasted with the stylized miniature adult emerging from the womb.

From the sixteenth to the late nineteenth century European art was molded by the principles of the Italian Renaissance style, which flourished in the fifteenth and early sixteenth centuries. In their efforts to combine the splendors of classical antiquity with Christian values, Renaissance artists turned to the human figure as an image of the highest form of beauty. The face and body reemerged in a way that has been as important for the subsequent development of Western art as its appearance in ancient Greek art in the fifth century B.C. The Renaissance stress on mental and physical prowess and on the ability to control and change environment resulted in the triumph of the human figure as the chief focus of artistic representation in the Western world. Its treatment of the body may best be understood by examining two categories of painting and sculpture: the nude and portraiture.

After centuries of neglect, the female nude was reemphasized in European art in the late fifteenth century. Several of Sandro Botticelli's paintings, including his *Primavera,* were inspired by Hellenistic statuary, especially depictions of Venus, yet they also reflect the early Renaissance philosophical interest in ideal beauty. The classical Venus figure offered the artist an opportunity to depict the female nude, something that could not be done with the Virgin Mary, hitherto the most popular female subject in European art. Titian, the brilliant Venetian painter, displayed the female nude in the reclining form that would remain popular for centuries. His *Venus of Urbino,* vividly and sensuously colored, reflects the Renaissance artist's interest in rendering the human figure in a wholly natural condition, in contrast to the late medieval renditions of naked bodies, often shown at the Last Judgment or in hell. Donatello's famous statue of a virtually nude David is a particularly fine example of the combination of Christian and pagan elements in the Renaissance. The subject is a figure from the Old Testament, but the classical stance and the provocative nudity are Greek.

In portraiture Renaissance painters combined an interest in personality and the external world. Leonardo da Vinci's *The Last Supper* is both the re-creation of a famous biblical episode and a masterpiece of psychological study in which the viewer is implicitly invited to interpret the emotional responses of Christ's disciples through expressions and physical gestures when they learn one of them is a traitor. No less psychological were the late works of Donatello and Michelangelo, both of whom rejected external beauty in their quest to understand the depths of the penitent soul. A half century later, when the art of the late Renaissance had begun to give way to the sophisticated Mannerist style, the Florentine artist Bronzino brilliantly depicted the individualized Renaissance man in his *Portrait of a Young Man.* Here is an elegant, affected youth whose aloof demeanor, handsome face, and elegant hands reveal the haughty arrogance of an educated gentleman of high social position. While Mannerists such as Bronzino emphasized the neck and hands to convey a sense of grace, others, such as El Greco, distorted their figures to highlight the spiritual values of the Counter-Reformation.

Bronzino, *Portrait of a Young Man.* [Metropolitan Museum of Art, Bequest of Mrs. H. O. Havemeyer, 1929. The H. O. Havemeyer Collection.]

The baroque art of the seventeenth century in Europe was characterized by the expression of strong emotions, often religious, and a virtuoso technique. These characteristics can be seen in the works of the Italian sculptor Bernini. In his *St. Theresa in Ecstasy,* the body of the enraptured saint, her robes, and the cloud on which she rests combine to create the illusion of mystical drama. Unlike Michelangelo, Bernini uses the facial expression of his subject, suffused with a passion at once mystical and sensual, to enhance the dramatic effect. Rubens, the Flemish baroque master, concentrated on the human figure as the epitome of the animal body straining against the physical forces around it, whether in the form of soft, luminous female flesh or muscular, tanned male bodies. Unlike the bodies of El Greco or the late works of Donatello and Michelangelo, those of Rubens vividly represent the zest for physical life that was a dominant element of the baroque spirit.

A more traditional use of the human figure as political icon appears in Hyacinthe Rigaud's portrait of Louis XIV (see color insert 3), painted at a time when the grandeur of the baroque style was beginning to yield to the more graceful, intimate rococo. Much rococo art was more concerned with shallow aristocratic pastimes than the use of the human form to explore deeper values. However, a strong interest in portraiture, firmly rooted in the Renaissance, continued throughout the period, especially in Britain.

By the late eighteenth century a similar kind of style had developed in Japan, which depicted day-to-day human activities with a directness that marks a distinctly independent school. Much of earlier Japanese art was strongly influenced by Chinese traditions, but no Chinese artist would have produced prints of the kind known as *ukiyo-e* ("pictures of the floating world") or even recognized them as works of art. One print depicts the scene in a bathhouse, with both naked and dressed figures casually going about their business. In strong contrast to the imposing image of Louis XIV, these figures are given an intentional anonymity, expressing as they do the universality of human experience. This and other prints of the kind made a great impression in Europe when they were first seen there in the nineteenth century. Their influence was strongly felt by the Impressionists.

The later years of the Mughal court saw an increasing informality in the treatment of the human figure, although eighteenth-century Indian art never approached the candor of the *ukiyo-e* prints. The paintings often deal with romantic themes, as in the depiction of a prince embracing his favorite mistress. Lacking the precision of earlier Mughal art, the work remains within the same framework of stylistic refinement, and a common human experience becomes transformed into an episode of elegance and grace: it hardly seems to matter that the faces of the women in the scene are virtually indistinguishable.

Most of the works discussed so far either commemorated an individual or used the human figure to symbolize universal human experience or values. These traditions continued during most of the nineteenth century. The austere Neoclassicism of Jacques-Louis David, as reflected in *The Death of Marat,* glorified the French Revolution. But by the end of the century Euro-

Detail from bathhouse scene, c. 1800, Japan. [Museum of Fine Arts, Boston; William Sturgis Bigelow Collection.]

Muhammad Yusuf al-Husaini, love scene, c. 1630. [Pierpont Morgan Library, New York]

pean artists had begun to employ human images to express anxiety about the state of their world. There are few more disturbing images of tension and neurosis than *The Scream,* by the Norwegian Edvard Munch, in which the distortions of the human body in the painting are reflected in the cosmic upheaval of land and sky.

The years preceding World War I produced traumatic changes throughout the world, in politics and society as well as in cultural life. Munch's attempt to unify figure and landscape to express a transcendent emotion characterized much of the art of the late nineteenth and early twentieth centuries in Europe. In many respects Munch's projection of human emotion onto landscape recalls fourteenth-century Christian art in Italy, but now devoid of religious context.

Years before Munch, the Frenchman Paul Cézanne had begun the effort among modern Western artists to reduce visual experience to simple, abstract forms. This movement was in turn influenced by European contact with the art of Asia, Africa, and Oceania. Western artists found universal messages in the highly stylized art forms of these regions, an impact that may be clearly seen in the paintings of Picasso and Gauguin and the sculptures of Constantin Brancusi. The brutally stylized representations of prostitutes in Picasso's *Les Demoiselles d'Avignon* caused a great scandal and presaged his even more radical experiments in abstraction a few years later, in which recognizable images disappeared altogether.

The so-called Expressionist style of Munch, which was taken up by German and Austrian artists shortly before World War I; the flat, abstracted style perfected by Picasso and his colleague Georges Braque and known as Cubism; and the wholly abstract canvases and watercolors of the Russian Wassily Kandinsky all foreshadowed a crisis in the representation of the human image in Western art. The cultural shock of World War I and the impact of Freudian psychology brought further distortions of the image in the form of Surrealism, a movement that dominated European art between the world wars. Seeking to penetrate psychological states, Surrealist art was, like Expressionism, an attempt to probe beyond the image into inner realms of feeling, and much of it was overtly erotic. But, although it was often accused of being obscure, Surrealism was also capable of powerful political statement, as in Salvador Dalí's *Soft Construction with Cooked Beans—Premonition of Civil War.*

At the same time, Soviet Russia and Nazi Germany were demanding a new official art that would represent their propaganda objectives—the depiction of happy and contented workers in the first case, racially pure Aryans in the second. Hitler banned all abstract or Expressionist art in the Third Reich, and in 1937 he organized a notorious exhibit of "degenerate" art,

Edvard Munch, *The Scream*, 1893. [Nasjonalgalleriet, Oslo]

which showed the work that had been purged from German museums. The exhibition backfired, as audiences streamed in not to mock but to admire some of the finest German painting of the century.

Some artists of the period, such as the British sculptor Henry Moore (1898—1986), continued to represent the human figure in simplified, monumental forms of great power (see color insert 4), and Picasso, the most protean and prolific painter of the human image in history, returned to it after World War I. The image was banished again when Abstract Expressionism became the dominant international style after World War II, only to return with the Pop Art of the 1960s. Pop Art, whose images were derived largely from advertising and comic strips, sought to satirize consumerism and both cinematic and political cults of personality, as in the portraits of Marilyn Monroe and Mao Tsetung (see color insert 4) by the American Andy Warhol (1928–1987). Pop Art was soon assimilated into a new style of "magic realism," which aimed for photographic illusion, while the former Abstract Expressionist Philip Guston (1913–1980) returned to the image with an effect at once comic and chilling, as in the disembodied head that rolls up an inclined plane in

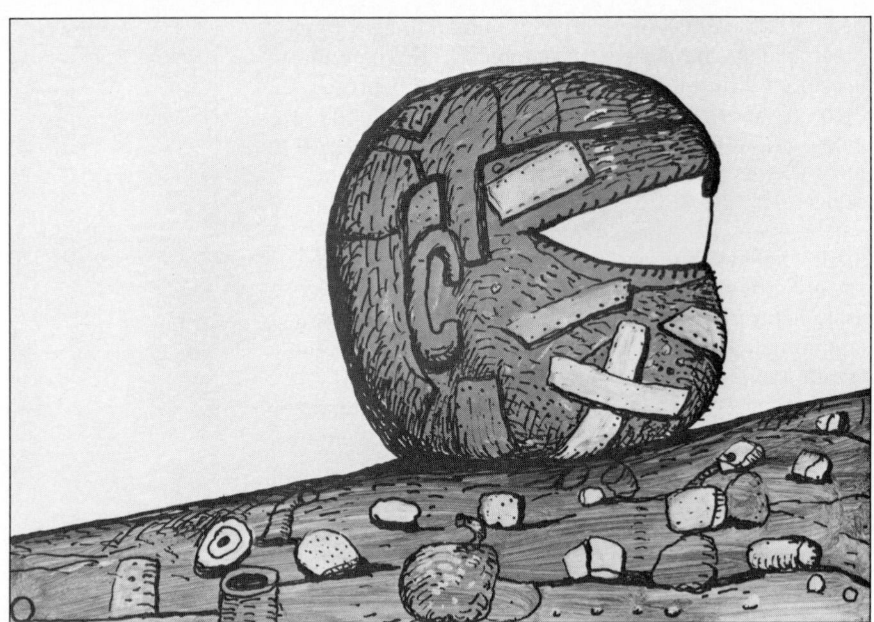

Philip Guston, *Untitled*, 1980. [David McKee Inc./photo by Bevan Davies]

Untitled. More recently, the German Anselm Kiefer (born 1945) has turned to the long-disfavored genre of historical portraiture in his remarkable representations of German cultural history.

It is hardly surprising that the history of art has been marked by a continual recourse to the human figure as a source of expression and communication. The range of treatment reflects the diversity of human experience. Works have served religious, political, and aesthetic purposes, have documented events, and sometimes have tried to control them, as in fascist and Soviet art. Differences between cultures seem stylistic rather than reflective of profound divergences: the statue of an Egyptian pharaoh and the portraits of a European, Indian, Chinese, or African sovereign reflect a similar political aim, the exaltation and commemoration of the ruler. If anything seems unexpected, it is that at the end of the twentieth century, a period of unprecedented upheaval both in life and in the arts, naturalistic depictions of human beings continue to fascinate us. Such works suggest that the need to "see ourselves as others see us" remains constant.

Suggestions for Further Reading

Clark, K. *The Nude: A Study in Ideal Form.* Princeton, N.J.: Princeton University Press, 1956.

De Dilva, A., and Von Simson, O. *Man Through His Art,* vol. 6: *The Human Face.* New York: Graphic Society, 1968.

Garland, M. *The Changing Face of Beauty.* New York: Barrows, 1957.

Lee, S. *A History of Far Eastern Art.* New York: Abrams, 1974.

Man: Glory, Jest, and Riddle—A Survey of the Human Form Through the Ages. San Francisco: M. H. de Young Memorial Museum, California Palace of the Legion of Honor, and San Francisco Museum of Art, 1965.

Mayor, A. H. *Artists and Anatomy.* New York: Artist's Limited Edition, 1984.

Mode, H. *The Woman in Indian Art.* New York: McGraw-Hill, 1970.

Neumeyer, A. *The Search for Meaning in Modern Art,* trans. R. Angress. Englewood Cliffs, N.J.: Prentice-Hall, 1964.

Relouge, I. E., ed. *Masterpieces of Figure Painting.* New York: Viking, 1959.

Rowland, B. *The Art and Architecture of India.* Baltimore: Penguin Books, 1967.

Segal, M. *Painted Ladies: Models of the Great Artists.* New York: Stein & Day, 1972.

Selz, P. *New Images of Man.* New York: Museum of Modern Art, 1959.

Smart, A. *The Renaissance and Mannerism in Italy.* New York: Harcourt Brace Jovanovich, 1971.

Walker, J. *Portraits: 5,000 Years.* New York: Abrams, 1983.

Wentinck, C. *The Human Figure in Art from Prehistoric Times to the Present Day,* trans. E. Cooper. Wynnewood, Pa.: Livingston Publishing, 1970.

Willett, F. *African Art: An Introduction.* New York: Praeger, 1971.

CHAPTER · 35

Upheaval in Eurasia and the Middle East

The twentieth century has been characterized by rapid change, particularly in the transformation of the world's biggest countries, China, Russia, and India, and the similar transformation of the Middle East. Together the four regions hold half the world's population. In China and Russia this change has appropriately been called revolutionary, entailing not only the overthrow of old governments by violence and civil war but also a radical restructuring of social, economic, and political systems in a short period of concentrated effort. The upheavals in each country were engineered and directed by native Communist parties, which made use of mass support by workers and peasants,

Leon Trotsky ariving in Paris in 1929, an exile from the Bolshevik USSR he helped to create a decade earlier. ["L'Illustration"/Sygma]

groups that previously had been excluded from power. Each revolution also created a new set of ideological values.

Like the French and American revolutions, those in Russia and China inspired others and served as models for change elsewhere in the world. The Chinese Revolution did not prevail until 1949, but its early stages from 1919 to 1934 were strongly influenced and for a time directly guided by Russian communists. When these early revolutionary efforts failed, China left the Soviet path. The ultimate success of the Chinese Revolution in 1949, and its later development, was far more an indigenous phenomenon than a response to the Russian experience.

Although strong differences marked the struggles for independence in India and the Middle East, neither can properly be viewed as a revolution. The Arabs fought Ottoman control with arms during World War I but then came under British and French authority. Indian protests against the British emphasized a nonviolent strategy. In both regions political power was eventually handed over peacefully to nationalist leaders. In the Middle East the League of Nations mandate system and the influx of Jewish settlers into Palestine, negligible until the rise of Nazism but significant thereafter, stimulated resistance from the native Arab population. Yet in the interwar years Arab nationalism failed to become a genuine mass movement as it did in India. There, the independence effort, as in China and Russia, involved peasants and workers under the direction of political organizers. While the nationalist regimes in Turkey and Iran attempted to modernize their countries after World War I, little effort went into radical restructuring of Indian society or its values.

Nevertheless, the changes that took place in India and the Middle East were in some ways revolutionary, for the awakening of nationalism and the end of the colonial system were to have long-range repercussions. India is the outstanding case of a drive for change that used traditional vehicles and symbols to attract support and to accelerate transformation, a pattern that repeated itself in the form of Muslim fundamentalism among Arab states after World War II.

In all these regions powerful leaders played a key role in planning and directing change, among them Lenin and his successor Stalin in the USSR, Mao Tse-tung (Mao Zedong) in China, Gandhi and his successor Nehru in India, and Faisal, ibn-Saud, Mustapha Kemal, Chaim Weizmann, and Reza Shah Pahlavi in the Middle East. Each of these leaders could claim to have made an enormous impact, not only on his own country but on states far beyond its borders as well. The twentieth century has been called the century of revolution primarily because of the massive upheavals in Russia, China, India, and the Middle East. The ripples that each revolution sent around the world helped to spawn fundamental changes in Asia, Africa, and Latin America. The century of revolution began with dramatic events in Russia in 1917.

The Russian Revolution

In March 1917* the first of two revolutions erupted in war-weary Russia, shattering 300 years of history in the space of a few days: the Romanov dynasty, the last absolute monarchy in Europe, was toppled from the throne it had occupied since 1613. Though laden with drama, the events of March were only a prelude to an even farther-reaching transformation. As if one revolution was insufficient to shift the weight of Russian history, with its virtually unbroken pattern of political and social repression and economic hardship, a second revolution erupted in November. The communist state that arose out of the November revolution became a major force in shaping the twentieth century.

The Twilight of the Romanovs

That the people of Russia were deeply discontented should have come as no surprise to Tsar Nicholas II (1894–1917), for the 1905 uprising had been a clear symptom of crisis. Although Nicholas had given in to demands for the creation of a Duma, the protection of individual liberties, and a broad franchise, within two years imperial decrees undid most of these reforms. Convinced that his power was divinely ordained, Nicholas was determined to restore his absolute authority. After 1911, following the assassination of Peter Stolypin, a reformist minister who had tried to repress terrorists and reactionaries, he further alienated the educated and professional classes by surrounding himself with conservative advisers. By 1914 some ministers even saw a European war as a positive catalyst for national unity.

Nicholas was an indecisive and not very intelligent leader. After the outbreak of war, he took direct command of the Russian armies—the only European head of state to do so—despite his lack of military training. At first his gesture had a positive symbolic value for the millions of peasants who rallied to the call for arms, but as the imperial armies suffered defeat after defeat, even the least sophisticated Russians began to hold the tsar personally responsible. However, most military officers had been poorly trained in modern strategy. Soldiers sent to the German front were among the worst-fed and equipped in Europe. Tens of thousands lacked even a rifle and were told to take one from a fallen comrade or a dead enemy; thus their greatly superior numbers failed to compensate for the country's lack of preparedness. Every setback in

*Russia still used the ancient Julian calendar, which had been abandoned in the West centuries earlier. By this time it was 13 days behind the modern Gregorian calendar. Throughout this chapter Gregorian dates will be used.

Tsar Nicholas II and his five children a few years before the revolution that overthrew the Romanov dynasty. [Bettmann Archive]

the field brought greater disenchantment among the troops. In addition to the incompetency of the generals and the enormous logistical problems stemming from Russia's vastness, Russian society was not sufficiently modernized to organize effectively for or sustain a major war effort. The Romanov dynasty collapsed in part because of the retarded development of the country's industries and infrastructure.

While Russia's war effort deteriorated, Nicholas left the government in the hands of his wife, Tsarina Alexandra (1872–1918), a religious zealot and absolutist. Her harsh, uncompromising attitudes were in part shaped by Grigori Rasputin, an eccentric Russian Orthodox monk whose great influence derived from his ability to convince Alexandra he could relieve her son's hemophilia. Rasputin's power over the tsarina and his manipulation of official policy outraged officials and members of the imperial court who hoped that political reforms would defuse popular discontent. Between September 1915 and November 1916 the Duma was suspended, while severe shortages of food and fuel provoked massive resentment in the cities. In December, hoping to free the royal family from his influence, liberal aristocrats murdered Rasputin. By then, however, the domestic situation had deteriorated so severely that revolution was imminent. Within the reconvened Duma even conservatives and constitutional monarchists opposed the royal family.

The March 1917 Revolution

On March 8, 1917, disorder erupted in Petrograd.* Food riots led by women spread to the workers, and both a factory lockout and a socialist-inspired Woman's Day celebration filled the streets with protesters. The crisis came when the tsar, still at the front, ordered the revolt suppressed. On March 11 troops fired into a crowd, but the government's inexperienced reinforcements then mingled with the demonstrators. As cries of "Down with the tsar!" rang out, officials found their orders unenforceable. The next day the Duma proclaimed a provisional government under Prince Georgi Lvov and called on Nicholas to step down. With the generals unable to assure him of the army's loyalty—indeed, military leaders supported his stepping down—the last of the Romanov tsars abdicated.

After centuries of absolutism and repression, Russia experienced a sudden liberalization. The provisional government planned the election of a constituent assembly on the basis of universal male suffrage and introduced civil liberties. It also implemented the eight-hour workday, ended the persecution of the Jews, and released thousands of political prisoners, although it maintained that only a legally constituted government could resolve the land problem. The new regime enjoyed the support of Western-educated Russians as well as the business and professional classes, while the Duma was dominated by liberals who favored a constitutional monarchy. Even the Entente Powers generally preferred the provisional government to the rule of the tsar, hoping that it would reinvigorate the Russian war effort.

From its inception, however, the provisional government was challenged by the more radical Soviet ("council") of Workers' and Soldiers' Deputies, formed in March. Modeled after the organization that had led the 1905 general strike, the Petrograd soviet was in the hands of workers' representatives who had served on the tsar's War Industries Committee. Its executive committee quickly became a barometer of public sentiment. While hundreds of similar groups soon sprang up in army units, industrial centers, and the countryside, the Petrograd soviet maintained its preeminence because of its location in the capital, where power had traditionally been concentrated.

In contrast to the Duma, led by liberal elements, membership of the soviets consisted largely of socialists of var-

*The tsar had changed the name of the city from St. Petersburg to the Russian form, Petrograd, to emphasize the patriotic nature of the war.

ious types. The Social Revolutionaries looked to the Russian peasants and their traditional village councils for instituting fundamental change and favored the use of violence. The Mensheviks and the Bolsheviks, factions within the Social Democratic party, were both Marxist in ideology, though sharp differences divided them. The reform-minded Menshevik ("minority") faction sought to build a large party organization along the lines of the Western social democratic movements. They hoped to achieve their goals through peaceful evolution but did not expect to establish socialism in Russia until industrial development was more advanced.

The Bolshevik ("majority") group accepted Marxist goals but followed the teachings of Vladimir Ilyich Lenin (1870–1924), their exiled leader. Lenin rejected Marx's idea that socialist revolution was premature in an underdeveloped country like Russia, where the industrial proletariat was small. He also opposed the evolutionary strategy of the Mensheviks, arguing that peaceful methods were impossible in the tsarist autocracy and that only violent revolution would achieve socialism. Lenin argued for a "vanguard" of professional revolutionaries that would control a disciplined party, educate the workers and peasants, and prepare to seize the initiative.

The soviets, composed of these competing factions and without a clearly articulated ideology, supported the spontaneous actions of the urban crowds and landless peasants. By so doing, they competed with the provisional government for the people's loyalty. As this struggle progressed, the provisional government found itself at a growing disadvantage. The Bolsheviks, the only major group of the left not represented in the government, remained free of responsibility for unpopular policies.

The weaknesses of the provisional government proved to be fatal. The new leaders made no attempt to address the demands of the urban proletariat or to satisfy the land hunger of the peasants. Of more immediate significance, however, was its war policy. Despite the desperate unpopularity of the conflict, the Duma felt duty-bound to honor the alliance with the Entente against Germany. When the government renewed its pledge to support the war effort in May, popular opposition forced many ranking members to resign.

Lenin and the Bolshevik Coup

The Bolsheviks skillfully exploited the shortsightedness of the provisional government as Lenin began to dominate events. A short, stocky man, mostly bald, with a mustache and a goatee, he did not look charismatic. But John Reed, a young left-wing American writer, understood that although Lenin was a "colorless" man, he had a gift for "explaining profound ideas in simple terms" that any unschooled Russian peasant could understand. He led, said Reed, "purely by virtue of his intellect."[1] Born Vladimir Ilyich Ulyanov, Lenin had been a radical since age 17, when the government had executed his older brother for plotting to assassinate Alexander III. During his twenties he became a Marxist, and his revolutionary activities brought him nearly five years of imprisonment and exile in Siberia. In 1900 he found refuge in western Europe, where he led the Bolshevik break from the Mensheviks.

When the March revolution erupted, Lenin, still in exile in Switzerland, persuaded the German government to grant him passage to Russia. The Germans, hoping that the Bolsheviks would disrupt the Russian war effort, transported him in a sealed train across their lines to the border, and Lenin arrived in Petrograd on April 20. His famous April Theses declared total opposition to the provisional government and instructed his followers to work for a second revolution in Russia, one that would eventually spread to the more industrialized countries of Europe. A communist victory, he said, would contribute to Russia's industrial base and help sustain Marxist socialism permanently.

Early in July soldiers and sailors led a massive uprising in Petrograd. The provisional government put down the revolt and blamed the Bolsheviks. Lenin, disguised as a locomotive fireman, fled to Finland, while a number of his followers—among them Lev Kamenev and Leon Trotsky—were arrested. When the provisional government launched a final military offensive against the Germans in July, soldiers deserted en masse, while in the countryside millions of peasants seized large estates. In an effort to broaden its support, the provisional government replaced Prince Lvov with Alexander Kerensky (1881–1970), a moderate Social Revolutionary. Kerensky's refusal to negotiate a withdrawal from the war served only to discredit him and his Menshevik allies. The final blunder came in September, when Lavr Kornilov, a reactionary military officer, attempted to crush the soviets. Kerensky appeared to welcome the general's action, but he came to believe that Kornilov intended to turn against him as well; he therefore armed the Red Guards, volunteer units from the Petrograd soviet. Prosoviet railway workers refused to transport Kornilov's equipment, and many of his troops fraternized with the Red Guards.

While Kerensky had prevented a military coup, his power now depended to a great extent on the soviets, which bitterly opposed his determination to continue the war. In the meantime, Bolshevik strength grew rapidly. Lenin's program of "peace, land, and bread" presented a compelling alternative to the provisional government's promises, and his slogan of "all power to the soviets" was a shrewd appeal for popular support. In late October, as the Bolsheviks gained a majority in the Petrograd soviet as well as in Moscow, Lenin secretly returned to Russia.

With Trotsky, now freed from imprisonment, Lenin planned the seizure of power. Trotsky (1879–1940), born Lev Bronstein, was a brilliant intellectual and strategist

The Bolshevik Strategy

Lenin's revolutionary theories formed the basis for Bolshevik action during the Russian upheaval of 1917. Here Lenin describes the need for a "professional" revolutionary vanguard.

I assert: (1) that no revolutionary movement can endure without a stable organization of leaders maintaining continuity; (2) that the broader the popular mass drawn spontaneously into the struggle, which forms the basis of the movement and participates in it, the more urgent the need for such an organization, and the more solid this organization must be (for it is much easier for all sorts of demagogues to sidetrack the more backward sections of the masses); (3) that such an organization must consist chiefly of people professionally engaged in revolutionary activity; (4) that in an autocratic state, the more we confine the membership of such an organization to people who are professionally engaged in revolutionary activity and who have been professionally trained in the art of combatting the political police, the more difficult will it be to unearth the organization; and (5) the greater will be the number of people from the working class and from the other social classes who will be able to join the movement and perform active work in it.

Source: V. I. Lenin, "What Is to Be Done?" in D. N. Jacobs, ed., *From Marx to Mao and Marchais* (New York: Longman, 1979), p. 45.

who had spent some of his own political exile in the United States. He was the real architect of the Bolshevik coup. He secured control of military power by persuading the Petrograd soviet, which he headed, to appoint him commander of a military revolutionary committee to protect the city. After winning over the soldiers in the Petrograd garrison, his forces captured the telephone exchange, railroad and electric stations, bridges, and government buildings on the night of November 6. Sailors from the Kronstadt naval base brought the cruiser *Aurora* up the Neva River to within firing range of the Winter Palace, seat of the provisional government. The Bolshevik majority in the Congress of Soviets, meeting the next morning in Petrograd, proclaimed that power was now in the hands of the soviets and announced that Lenin was the head of the new government. On November 8 Kerensky fled the city. With almost no bloodshed, the Bolsheviks had won control of Russia. Holding that power, however, would prove a formidable task.

Lenin and Trotsky planned the Bolshevik revolution and won the Russian civil war. They are shown here in a doctored photo. [Bettmann Archive]

Building the Communist State

The seizure of Petrograd and the overthrow of the Kerensky government by no means guaranteed the Bolsheviks a lasting victory. Lenin still had to extend his control to the rest of the country. Setting up an enduring Bolshevik regime would require three more years of bitter struggle amid civil war, political opposition from anti-Bolshevik groups, and invasion by the troops of 14 foreign countries.

Lenin's immediate strategy was to achieve popular support and a measure of stability by ending war, hunger, and peasant unrest. The Social Revolutionaries had the largest following among Russia's landless rural population, but Lenin stole their thunder by declaring the nationalization of all land and its distribution to the peasants. Although in theory the soviets were to keep the large estates intact as collective farms, in practice the peasants, who were already seizing land on their own initiative, were permitted to keep what they had taken. As revolutionary as these actions were, they failed to solve the hunger crisis. Small property holders jealously withheld their crops from urban consumers. Hoarding increased as a result of the civil war and poor harvests; for years starvation plagued millions.

The promise of peace proved costly to keep. The Germans now sensed victory in the east. German peace terms, however, were so harsh that some Bolshevik leaders, including Trotsky and Nicolai Bukharin, wanted to continue the war as a revolutionary struggle. Lenin's insistence on ending the hostilities ultimately prevailed, and on March 15, 1918, his representatives signed the Treaty of Brest-Litovsk. It ceded to Germany all its wartime conquests as well as eastern Poland, the Ukraine, and the formerly Russian areas of Finland, Estonia, Latvia, and Lithuania. Not until the Nazi-Soviet Pact of 1939 would Russia recover its 1914 frontiers, but the treaty provided Lenin with the much needed opportunity to solidify his authority. Lenin quieted opposition to it within the Communist party—the new official name the Bolsheviks adopted in March 1918—by arguing that the spread of "world revolution" into western Europe would eventually render Russia's losses meaningless.

Despite the euphoria that had greeted the reforms and promises of the provisional government following the March revolution, political liberalism had shallow soil in which to grow. Initially the revolutionaries took democracy far beyond conventional practice, with popular choice entering virtually every area of life. In the soviets a kind of direct democracy prevailed, while in army units soldiers elected officers and in the factories workers organized management councils. Yet there was no tradition of self-government above the village level in Russia. The revolution left a vacuum that inexperienced local councils of semiliterate peasants could hardly fill. Into this void Lenin moved his disciplined organization after the November revolution. Yet his own forces were small and lacked administrative experience.

Lenin's victory destroyed the possibility of democratic government. The Bolsheviks had never pretended to value democracy, and Lenin's program demanded peace and economic well-being, not freedom in the traditional Western sense. He knew, too, that after the distribution of land, universal suffrage would produce a majority representing small landowners. In fact, when the elections for a constituent assembly previously scheduled by the provisional government were held in late November, the Social Revolutionaries won nearly twice as many delegates as the Bolsheviks. When the assembly met in January 1918, Lenin swiftly demonstrated his intention to create a Marxist-style "dictatorship of the proletariat," disbanding the assembly after only one day of deliberation. For several months Lenin governed in a coalition with left-wing Social Revolutionaries, but when the latter withdrew their support in June, Russia came under the one-party rule that still governs it today.

During 1918 and 1919, the Bolsheviks began to implement their political and economic policies. Grass-roots government yielded to centralized state administration by the Communist party, soldiers' councils were replaced by appointed officers, and factory committees gave way to trade unions controlled by party officials. In the countryside previously independent peasants now had to deliver their "surplus" produce to hungry urban populations. Advances toward self-determination for ethnic minorities and border peoples were eventually replaced by Russian-dominated centralization thinly disguised as a federal state. Lenin believed this system of "war communism" to be necessary under the dual pressure of civil war and foreign invasion. The pressing need for industrial production was not being met by the factory committees, which often lacked necessary technical skills and sometimes resisted state efforts to coordinate labor. Moreover, Lenin saw industrial cartelization as the basis of a socialist economy. Each branch of industry was therefore nationalized and centralized into state trusts. By 1920 about 90 of these trusts existed, all subordinated to the Supreme Council of National Economy, which attempted to direct industrial production throughout the country.

Revolution Under Siege

Early Bolshevik policies and Leninist authoritarianism were shaped in large part by the return of war and strife to Russian soil. The infant Communist regime had to fight for its survival against an array of domestic and foreign enemies: counterrevolutionary legions made up of conservatives, moderates, and even some Social Revolutionaries, known collectively as the White Army; border nationalities seeking independence from Russia; more than 100,000 troops from 14 foreign nations, including the United States, Britain, France, and Japan; and peasants waging a so-called green revolution against the Reds who requisitioned their crops. Between 1918 and November 1920 the Red Army defended Russia's borders in a desperate effort to save the Communist regime.

A combination of military and ideological motives led to the Allied invasion of Russia. The Entente Powers had supported Kerensky's government in order to bolster the war on the eastern front. Lenin's demands for a separate peace aroused Allied suspicion that he was a German agent, but they failed to convince the Bolsheviks to reject the German peace terms. With their troops no longer tied down on the Russian front, the Germans broke through Allied lines in the west and marched to a position less than 40 miles from Paris. The German advance was repulsed, but the Allies, fearful that the Bolshevik revolution might spread to their own war-weary population, determined on a preemptive strike.

In June 1918 the Allies decided on military intervention.

The French and British sent nearly 24,000 soldiers to Murmansk and Archangel. On July 16 the Bolsheviks, worried that the Allies might try to liberate the tsar, executed the entire royal family. In Siberia 40,000 Czech prisoners of war, formerly Austro-Hungarian conscripts, revolted against their Russian guards and commandeered the trans-Siberian railroad in an attempt to reach their homeland, where they hoped to fight for Czech independence. To assist the Czech legion, President Wilson approved a landing at Vladivostok, where 72,000 Japanese and 8,000 American troops eventually arrived. During the winter of 1918–1919 two British divisions seized the rail lines that connected the Black and Caspian seas along the oil-rich Russo-Turkish border. French units, joined by Greek forces, also landed at Odessa on the Ukraine's Black Sea coast.

Allied soldiers remained in Russia after the armistice was signed in November, giving support to the White Army. Against difficult odds, the Bolsheviks possessed a number of advantages. Party discipline and Lenin's leadership kept their forces together while the White Army factions, united only in their opposition to the Communists, were rent with political division. The Bolsheviks also controlled the Russian heartland and could wage war along interior lines, whereas their enemies were scattered along the periphery. Moreover, the Red Army generally had the support of the peasants, who knew the Bolsheviks would never restore the power of the large landowners. Finally, in ethnically Russian areas Bolshevik propagandists shrewdly combined revolutionary rhetoric with a patriotic appeal in the face of foreign invasion.

Bolshevik military operations were commanded by Leon Trotsky, whose abilities as a speaker and Marxist theoretician were matched by brilliant organizational talent. Trotsky raised, equipped, trained, and directed the Red Army, rushing from one front to another in a special train outfitted as a mobile headquarters. He kept troop morale high by means of political propagandists, called commissars, who were attached to Red Army units. His forces repulsed assaults from Siberia, the Ukraine, and the newly independent state of Poland. Late in 1920 Allied ships evacuated more than 100,000 soldiers from Odessa. By the end of the struggle the Bolsheviks had recovered much of the old imperial lands on the western front, except for the Baltic states and the territory lost to Romania and the new states of Czechoslovakia and Poland. With the civil war won, they also regained control over Azerbaijan, Russian Armenia, and Georgia, which separatist forces had threatened to make independent. These and other nominally autonomous states were eventually incorporated into the Union of Soviet Socialist Republics (USSR), established in December 1922. After two years of desperate fighting against invasion, civil war, and famine, the Communist regime was secure but exhausted.

What Price Revolution?

The great loss of human life during the Russian Revolution and the civil war, criticized by the enemies of bolshevism, was defended by Leon Trotsky as a necessary price for great historical change.

But the misfortunes which have overwhelmed living people? The fire and bloodshed of civil war? Do the consequences of a revolution justify the sacrifices it involves? The question is teleological and therefore fruitless. It would be as well to ask in the face of the difficulties and griefs of personal existence: Is it worth while to be born? Melancholy reflections have not so far, however, prevented people from bearing or being born. Even in the present epoch of intolerable misfortune only a small percentage of the population of our planet resorts to suicide. But the people are seeking the way out of their unbearable difficulties in revolution.

Is it not remarkable that those who talk most indignantly about the victims of social revolutions are usually the very ones who, if not directly responsible for the victims of the world war, prepared and glorified them, or at least accepted them? It is our turn to ask: did the war justify itself? What has it given us? What has it taught?

Source: L. Trotsky, *The Russian Revolution* (Garden City, N.Y.: Anchor/Doubleday, 1959), p. 483. (Originally published in 1930.)

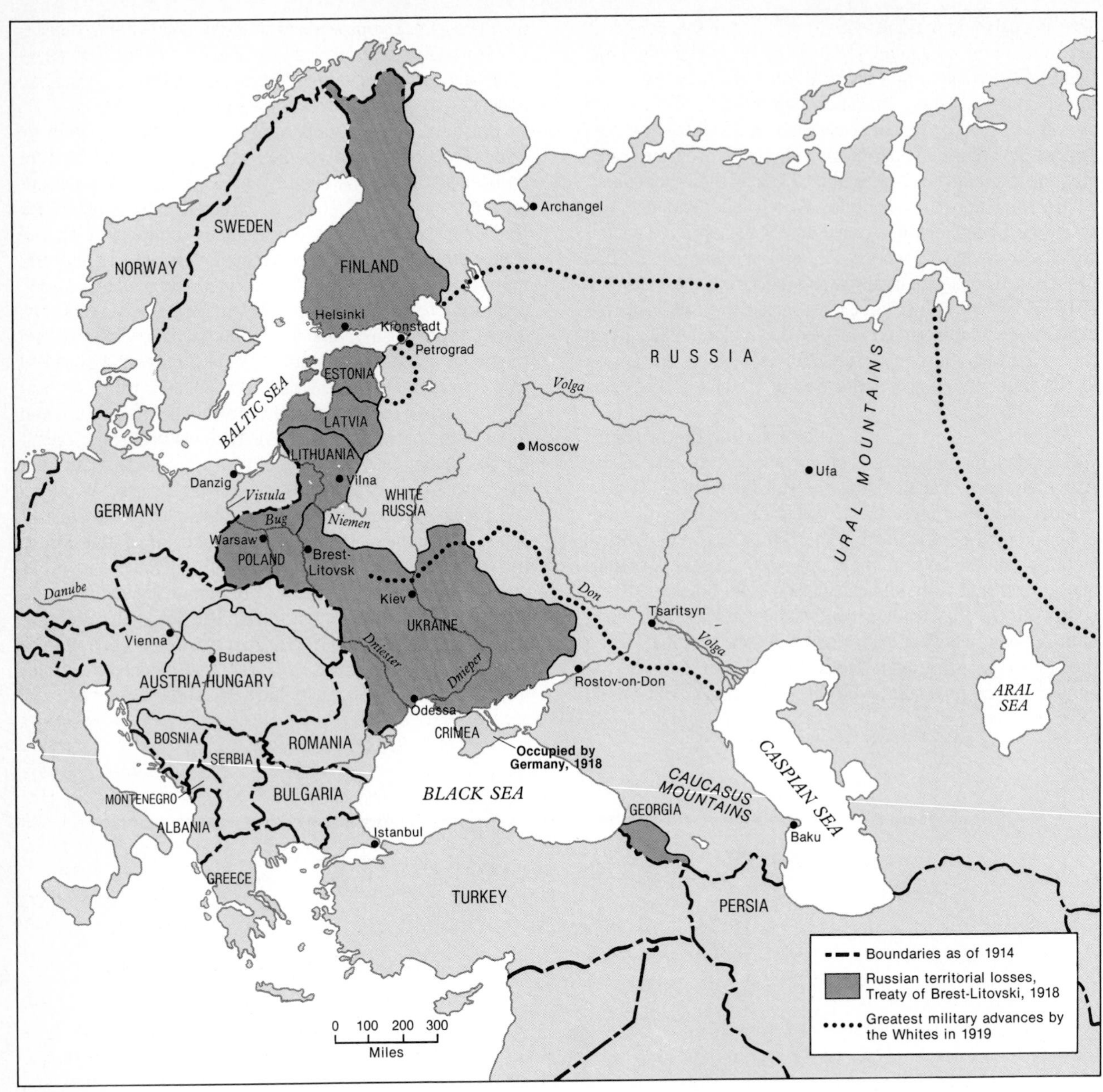

35.1 Russia in War and Revolution, 1917–1921

ALEXANDRA KOLLONTAI AND THE WOMEN'S QUESTION

In Russia, as elsewhere in Europe, women had long played an important role in radical movements. Daring women such as Vera Zasulich, who assassinated a cruel provincial governor in 1878, and Olga Liubatovich, who was exiled in Siberia and conspired in St. Petersburg, were but two of the many Russian women active in the revolutionary underground. Others, such as Angelica Balabanoff and Anna Kulischiov, achieved prominence as exiled socialist militants, Balabanoff as secretary to the Second International and Kulischiov as a leader of the Italian socialist women's movement. The career of Alexandra Kollontai (1872–1952) illustrates both the role of women in the anti-tsarist movement and the tense relationship between women's liberation and the Bolshevik revolution.

Born into a wealthy landowning family as Alexandra Domontovich, she married a young engineer but after

An early Bolshevik and ardent feminist, Alexandra Kollontai took part in the first stages of Lenin's government. [Novosti from Sovfoto]

three years left her husband, who viewed her sympathies for the working class as willful defiance of his authority. After studying in Zurich, she returned to St. Petersburg and joined the Menshevik wing of the Social Democratic party. At the time of the 1905 revolution Kollontai recognized "how little our Party concerned itself with the fate of women of the working class and how meager was its interest in women's liberation." She also came to believe that liberation for women "could take place only as the result of the victory of a new social order and a different economic system."[2] Forced into exile because of her radical activities, she lived in western Europe and the United States from 1908 to 1917. In 1915 she broke with the Mensheviks over the war issue and began to correspond with Lenin, returning to Russia at the outbreak of revolution in March 1917.

As a member of the Bolshevik Central Committee, Kollontai supported Lenin's call for an armed uprising. After the November coup she was appointed commissar for social welfare in Lenin's cabinet. Within the party and the government she argued that the revolution would be betrayed unless it destroyed bourgeois moral standards and the authoritarian family. These ideas and her efforts to establish a state-supported system of maternity and infant care drew sharp criticism from her male comrades, who accused her of wanting to "nationalize" Russian women. Her position was undermined when she joined the anti-Leninist faction and pushed to democratize the Communist party through direct worker participation in policymaking. In March 1918 she resigned from the government and later joined the Workers' Opposition movement. Following the civil war, during which she worked as a propagandist with the Red Army in the Ukraine, Kollontai bitterly criticized the new marriage laws established by the Soviet (Bolshevik) regime, which she felt maintained inequality, and demanded full rights for women. Her controversial ideas on women's liberation and sexual freedom were explained in *The New Morality and the Working Class* (1920), the publication of which alienated her still further from the Communist leadership. Although Kollontai's advocacy of sexual relationships based on affection and equality rather than on socially imposed codes offended her more conservative comrades, many others—especially young urban middle-class Russians and intellectuals—agreed.

When Joseph Stalin became general secretary of the Communist party in 1922, the Workers' Opposition movement was purged and Kollontai's lover, Alexander Shylapnikov, was killed. Kollontai herself was virtually banished for the next two decades: from 1924 until her retirement in 1945 she served as Russian ambassador to Norway, Mexico, and Sweden and as a representative to the League of Nations. In her last lonely years Kollontai suffered from the knowledge that the revolution she had helped to make had fallen short of her hopes.

Stalin Versus Trotsky: The Struggle for Power

Even without the military struggles of the 1918–1920 period, chaotic economic and social conditions would have threatened the Bolshevik regime. Millions of Russians had died as a result of war, epidemics, and famine. Cities and villages lay in ruin, and the transportation system barely functioned. A lack of managers, technicians, and raw materials had brought factories to a virtual standstill, and industrial production had fallen to about 20 percent of its prewar level. Hoarding and drought continued to cause severe food shortages. In the face of these problems, popular support for the Bolsheviks eroded. A wave of peasant uprisings and factory strikes preceded a military revolt, in March 1921, when sailors at the Kronstadt naval base, once a pro-Bolshevik bastion, seized the Winter Palace and proclaimed a "third revolution" against Lenin's regime. The Red Army crushed the movement with much bloodshed, and Lenin knew he had to act swiftly to restore control.

In March 1921 Lenin announced the New Economic Policy (NEP), a retreat from Marxist orthodoxy. The NEP permitted a degree of private enterprise in small industries and the retail trade, ended food requisitioning, and allowed peasants to sell their produce on the open market after paying a small tax. The state, however, continued to own and operate major industries, banking, and transportation and to control wholesale and foreign trade. The NEP slowly achieved success, and by 1928 agricultural and industrial production had returned to prewar levels. The policy, much debated among Communist leaders, resulted in the revival of the rural middle class of kulaks ("large peasants") that ran counter to the Marxist goal of a classless society.

As long as Lenin lived, he and the Old Bolsheviks—the group that had made the revolution in 1917—retained control of the Communist party, but he was concerned over the increasing number of bureaucratic careerists entering its ranks. The Soviet constitution of 1923 created the All-Union Congress of Soviets, a representative body in which the highest power theoretically resided. The Congress—its name was changed to the Supreme Soviet in 1936—elected a Council of People's Commissars (changed to the Council of Ministers in 1946), the Executive Committee, and the small Presidium, which acted for the Congress between sessions. In reality, however, the Communist party ran the country through its Central Committee, composed of just under 50 members, which met several times each year. The Central Committee in turn elected a ten-member Politburo, which convened weekly and chose a Secretariat of from one to three members to perform executive duties.

In 1922 two strokes removed Lenin from day-to-day leadership. Trotsky appeared to be the logical choice to succeed Lenin, but party members began to unite against him. A temporary *troika*, or three-member leadership, emerged late in 1922 to carry on Lenin's work, consisting of Grigori Zinoviev, party leader in Petrograd (later named Leningrad); Lev Kamenev, the Communist boss of Moscow; and Joseph Stalin, general secretary of the party and the least known of the three.

Tough, clever, and power-hungry, Stalin (1879–1953) was the only Old Bolshevik of lower-class origin. Born Joseph Djugashvili in the province of Georgia, he was the son of a shoemaker and the grandson of serfs. After being expelled from a theological seminary, he joined the Bolshevik movement at the turn of the century and took the underground name of Stalin, meaning "man of steel." He performed some of the party's most reprehensible tasks, including the robbing of treasury transports to acquire operating funds. Hardened in the tsar's prisons and Siberian exile, Stalin possessed none of the broader culture of his colleagues, most of whom had lived in western Europe during the worst years of tsarist repression. As general secretary he dispensed patronage to build a personal following and came to that office at a time when a new generation of bureaucrats was developing within the party.

Lenin recognized Stalin's power at the very time that the other Old Bolsheviks were growing suspicious of Trotsky. After his second stroke in December 1922, Lenin began to consider the problem of succession. With the help of his wife and closest political assistant, Nadhezhda Krupskaya (1869–1939), he dictated a "testament" in which he reviewed the credentials of possible successors, chiefly Trotsky and Stalin. Although he seemed to favor Stalin, he expressed doubts as to whether Stalin knew how to use his power wisely. Less than two weeks later Lenin added a "codicil," or supplement, to these notes denouncing Stalin as "too rude" and advising the party to appoint someone "more tolerant, more loyal, more polite and more considerate to comrades, less capricious, etc."[3]

While Lenin had always held reservations about Stalin, his opinion hardened when he learned that Stalin had tried to intimidate Krupskaya. Following Lenin's death early in 1924, the testament and the codicil were read before the party's Central Committee. That summer Krupskaya attempted to have the documents presented before the entire party congress, but Stalin managed to have only minor commissions hear them. Krupskaya survived Stalin's brutal purges and remained on the Central Committee for the rest of her life, but her husband's denunciations of the man who became the dictator of Soviet Russia went unpublished until after Stalin's death.

In 1924 Stalin, who was never known for his mastery of Marxist theory, put forward the novel concept of "socialism in one country." He argued that the Soviet Union could create the industrial economy necessary to sustain socialism without exporting revolution to the rest of Europe. Against this position Trotsky offered the doctrine of "permanent revolution," an unceasing struggle aimed at the elimination of capitalism everywhere. Stalin believed that the extension of communist revolution to all capitalist societies required resources that Russia did not have and meant continual armed strife with the West. Stalin eventually won the struggle with Trotsky because he secured control over the party apparatus and won the support of other party leaders. Even leftists such as Zinoviev and Kamenev, whose views corresponded more closely to the permanent revolution theory, feared Trotsky's ambitions, and in 1925 they helped the supposedly safer Stalin to strip him of his position as war commissar. In 1929 Trotsky fled into exile, where, after years of opposition to Stalin's regime that won an often sympathetic hearing from Western socialists, he was murdered by a Soviet agent in 1940.

Stalin's skill at maneuvering was consummate. Having used the support of the party's left to weaken Trotsky, he then joined forces with Nicolai Bukharin, leader of the right. Together they removed Stalin's opponents, one by one, from the Central Committee while Stalin increasingly controlled the smaller Politburo. He then turned against his former allies. After the failure of a communist uprising in Bulgaria in 1925, he secured the dismissal of Zinoviev as head of the Communist International and then destroyed Kamenev's authority by having the Moscow party apparatus placed in the hands of the Politburo. In 1928, having crushed the party's left wing, Stalin broke with the right. He did this by favoring the collectivization of agriculture and forced industrialization, positions long associated with the left. When Bukharin opposed these policies, Stalin drove him from office. With Trotsky in exile and the old-guard Bolsheviks outmaneuvered, Stalin emerged as the unchallenged master of the Soviet state.

The Comintern: Russia Between East and West

Stalin's formula for one-country Socialism rejected not only Trotsky's insistence on the need for continuing revolution but Lenin's legacy as well. In March 1919 Lenin had invited the world's socialist leaders to Moscow to create a new global organization known as the Communist International, or Comintern. The purpose of this so-called Third International was to convert the Russian Revolution into a world struggle. The instability of the immediate postwar period, marked by the fall of the monarchies in Austria-Hungary and Germany, riots in China, India, and Japan, the seizure of factories by Italian workers, and the establishment of a Communist regime in Hungary under Béla Kun, gave Comintern leaders hope, for they saw in such events proof that capitalism and imperialism were about to collapse everywhere. Their optimism was, however, premature, for except in the Soviet puppet state of Mongolia, communism failed to seize permanent power beyond Russia. The Comintern sent agents to every corner of the world to organize and strengthen indigenous communist movements, but in the long run Stalin's policies and the organization's internal limitations hampered its effectiveness.

The Comintern had a divisive impact on the European left. Demanding disciplined followers among the socialists in other countries, Lenin established 21 conditions for foreign parties seeking membership in the Comintern. These included purging themselves of reformists, restructuring their organizations along Bolshevik lines, supporting all communist governments, preparing for the seizure of power in their own countries, and fighting social democrats as well as capitalists. Lenin believed the moment for world revolution had arrived, but many Western socialist leaders were reluctant to gamble their previous gains on the chance of revolution. Social democrats preferred to achieve socialism without resorting to dictatorship. The result was that socialist parties outside the USSR split into two camps between 1920 and 1921, with most rejecting Lenin's demands in favor of achieving socialism through parliamentary reform. Lenin accused them of wasting a historic opportunity.

Despite these divisions, the Comintern caused panic in Western countries. In the United States a "Red scare" in 1919 led to a government witch-hunt for radicals of every kind. In Europe many frightened members of the middle class abandoned liberalism in favor of fascism and other anti-Communist movements.

The hysteria the Comintern aroused in the West was ironic in view of the fact that revolutionary communism was so unsuccessful elsewhere in the world. The early socialists were essentially Eurocentric in outlook, a characteristic derived in part from Marx's belief that revolution was likely only in advanced capitalist societies. "The founders of Marxism," noted one scholar, "judged non-European civilizations through the prism of European civilization. The road to progress for the backward peoples they saw as the road of Europeanization, not only from the socio-economic standpoint but also culturally."[4]

Comintern leaders gave little attention to the needs and aspirations of non-Western communists. At the third congress of the Comintern in 1921, the Indian Marxist M. N. Roy attacked the meeting for allowing him only five minutes to report on revolutionary activities in the subcontinent. The next year the Indonesian communist Tan Malaka condemned the Comintern for opposing the pan-Islamic movement, which he said had isolated his party from the Muslim peasants of his country. At the 1924 congress Mexican representatives warned Soviet leaders that they were ignoring potential allies in Latin America, while Sen Katayama of the Japanese Communist party assailed Zinoviev for hardly mentioning the Eastern question. Ho Chi Minh (1890–1969), the Vietnamese activist, complained bitterly that Westerners were ignoring revolutionaries in colonial areas and misunderstood the liberation movements.

When the Comintern did support revolutionary activities in the Third World, its approach reflected Soviet concerns. In 1924 the Comintern sent the able but inexperienced Michael Borodin to China to establish a Communist military college at Whampoa, near Canton. The principal of the college was young Chiang Kai-shek (1887–1975), recently returned from a visit to Russia. Despite Chiang's involvement in the Chinese Nationalist party (Kuomintang) and his close ties to bankers, the Comintern ordered the Chinese Communists to integrate themselves into the Kuomintang. On April 12, 1927, Chiang's troops, aided by gangs hired by Shanghai businessmen, launched a surprise attack against Borodin, the Communists, and the trade unions, murdering thousands and imprisoning many more. Nevertheless, for a time the Comintern attempted to mend the ill-fated alliance with the Kuomintang.

Of all the factors that undermined the Comintern, none was more important than Stalin's rise to power. His one-country socialism was essentially a defensive strategy designed to protect the Soviet state. His concern lest revolutionary activities elsewhere endanger the USSR resulted in his using the Comintern only to keep foreign Communist leaders in line. Under Stalin the Communist International became an anachronism, and in a gesture to antifascist unity during the Second World War, he disbanded it in 1943.

The Comintern: East Versus West

At the Congress of the Peoples of the East, called by the Communist International in 1920, the representatives of non-Western countries complained bitterly that their concerns were being ignored by Russian leaders. One of the most vocal critics was M. N. Roy, an Indian Communist, who argued that the official report on colonial questions maintained that the fate of the revolutionary movement in Europe depended entirely on the course of the revolution in the East.

Without the victory of the revolution in the Eastern countries, the Communist movement in the West would come to nothing. . . . This being so, it is essential that we divert our energies into developing and elevating the revolutionary movement in the East and accept as our fundamental thesis that the fate of world Communism depends on the victory of Communism in the East.

Here is Lenin's response to Roy's arguments.

Comrade Roy goes too far when he asserts that the fate of the West depends exclusively on the degree of development and the strength of the revolutionary movement in the Eastern countries. In spite of the fact that the proletariat in India numbers five million and there are 37 million landless peasants, the Indian Communists have not yet succeeded in creating a Communist Party in their country. This fact alone shows that Comrade Roy's views are to a large extent unfounded.

Source: F. Claudin, *The Communist Movement: From Comintern to Cominform,* vol. 1, trans. B. Pearce (New York: Monthly Review Press, 1975), pp. 247–248.

The inability of the Comintern to establish Communist regimes beyond the Soviet Union should not obscure the profound impact of the Russian Revolution. The Bolshevik seizure of power shook the West to its foundations and altered international relations. Stalin was shortsighted only in failing to recognize the Russian Revolution as the first of a series of momentous upheavals that would transform the world.

China: Rebels, Warlords, and Patriots

In contrast to the Russian Revolution, the upheaval in China began almost tentatively, then sputtered and apparently died, and finally broke out in full force only after nearly 40 years of false starts and setbacks. In China too there were perhaps revolutionary implications in the Taiping Rebellion of 1850–1864. All revolutions have their antecedents, but China's was particularly slow in the making. China had first to develop a national political consciousness and a political organization that could pursue revolutionary change, both of which were lacking in its historical experience. The Chinese were accustomed to the overthrow of dynasties grown old and ineffective and their replacement by a new group, which would then administer the traditional system more successfully. The system itself, however, enshrined by the Mandate of Heaven, appeared to be beyond challenge.

But by the twentieth century the traditional model had lost its ability to deal with the now overwhelming problems of mass poverty, technological backwardness, and political weakness. These problems were vividly symbolized by China's helplessness in the face of the imperial powers of the West. It was to take another century to create a new set of solutions and a political structure to pursue them. Meanwhile, China's material welfare and ancient pride continued to suffer.

The Ch'ing dynasty collapsed in 1911, with the gentlest of shoves from a small and poorly organized group of revolutionaries (see Chapter 33). It was widely seen as a failure and was equally resented as an alien dynasty of conquest. Most of the revolutionary support rested on one or both of these grounds rather than on the still only half-formed plans for change. The end of Manchu rule is considered a revolution because the government was overthrown in an armed uprising by people who called themselves revolutionaries and had some new and radical ideas. But they were too few and too politically inexperienced to establish an effective government of their own, and to make matters worse, they were split into factions. The most important revolutionary organization was the Kuomintang (Guomindang), founded around the turn of the century and led by Sun Yat-sen (1866–1925), an idealist with great personal charisma but little sense of practical politics.

Sun Yat-sen and the 1911 Revolution

Sun was born to a peasant family near Canton (Gwangzhou), traditionally a hotbed of separatism and political ferment. At the age of 13, like many Cantonese, he emigrated, joining his older brother in Honolulu, where he went to a church boarding school and became a Christian. At 16 he returned to study in Hong Kong and finished a medical degree there in 1892 at a British mission hospital. After practicing only briefly in Macao, he founded a secret society to overthrow the Manchus, drawing support from overseas Chinese. In 1895 he was forced to flee to Japan, from where he made repeated trips to build Chinese contacts in the United States, Britain, and Hawaii. Other radical leaders and groups in China were also active, and several abortive attempts were made to seize power until an uprising at Wuhan in 1911 was joined by some troops among its garrison. Its successful defiance brought the fall of the imperial government. Sun returned from abroad and became the first president of the newly proclaimed republic. The last Ch'ing emperor, a 6-year-old boy, abdicated early in 1912, marking the end of an imperial tradition more than 2,000 years old.

China was still hopelessly divided, and even Sun saw that he could not provide unity and strong central government. He agreed to step down in 1912 as president in favor of Yuan Shih-kai (Yuan Shikai, 1859–1916), a leading Ch'ing military man who had thrown his lot in with the republicans. Sun had earlier put together a set of guidelines for a new government called the Three Principles of the People. These were nationalism, democracy, and the people's livelihood, none of which was clearly defined. Nationalism in the modern sense was still a new idea to most Chinese, but they could at least make common cause against the foreign Manchu dynasty in the name of Chinese self-determination. Sun's notion of democracy was heavily indebted to Western models. It implied but did not spell out social and political equality, a notable departure in itself from the hierarchical forms of Confucianism. Democracy was to be assured by a constitution largely on an American pattern, while "livelihood"—a partial redistribution of wealth on behalf of the poorer peasantry—was to be achieved through tax reforms.

China was far from having the requisite basis for democracy, however. There were no true political parties as yet, only a variety of elite or intellectual groups, divided among themselves. When the new Kuomintang won national elections in 1913, Yuan Shih-kai, who had busily concentrated real power in his own hands, arranged the assassination of its leading organizer, Sung Chiao-jen (Song Jiaoren), who had pressed for constitutional government. Sun again fled to Japan, while Yuan tightened his grip as military dictator by force, bribery, and intimidation. In 1915 he had himself declared president for life and took to riding around in an armored car for fear of attack by frustrated revolutionaries. Meanwhile, he dared not confront Western and Japanese imperialism in China because he was dependent on foreigners who looked to him as a strongman who could ensure order. The revolution had been betrayed.

Several southern and western provinces, where disgruntled military men and revolutionaries were active, broke away from Yuan's control. In 1916 he died suddenly after failing to have himself declared emperor. Political and ideological change had gone much too far to permit any return to such traditional forms, although there was still neither a consensus on what should succeed them nor a semblance of national unity. During the next 12 years China dissolved into virtual anarchy, divided among a number of regionally based warlords and other local military leaders. The Kuomintang and the early revolutionaries had a political ideology of sorts but no army; the warlords had armies but little or no program or party organization. Their troops marched around the countryside like a scourge on the peasants, while a bewildering variety of short-lived regimes or political cliques succeeded each other in Peking as the nominal government of China.

In 1917 Sun returned to Canton, formed a rival government, and began building a more effective political organization. He complained that trying to get the Chinese people to work together was like trying to make a rope out of sand. But although he tried to arouse mass support, he appealed mainly to intellectuals and the few Chinese who were as yet politically conscious. What began to spark Chinese nationalism more effectively were new Japanese encroachments on the nation's sovereignty and spontaneous popular protests against them.

The May Fourth Movement

Japan's Twenty-one Demands on China, issued in 1915, provoked immediate protests from patriotic Chinese, especially after Yuan Shih-kai accepted most of them. China joined the Allied side in World War I in 1917, sent labor battalions to the Western front, and hoped thus to get a hearing at the Paris peace conference. But Japan had secretly obtained Allied agreement to keep what it had taken in China's Shantung province, and it soon appeared that the lofty talk about self-determination did not apply to Asia.

When news broke that the warlord government in Peking had also signed secret agreements with Japan, mass demonstrations erupted on May 4, 1919. Chinese nationalism boiled over in what came to be called the May Fourth movement. A new and increasingly radical generation of students in government and mission schools and universities emerged, imbued with Western ideas and dedicated to building a new China. Student protesters beat up a pro-Japanese official and burned a cabinet minister's house. They went on to organize a union and to seek support among the large group of Westernized businessmen, industrialists, and shopkeepers in the treaty ports. Strikes and boycotts of Japanese goods attracted widespread support. The cabinet resigned, and China refused to sign the Versailles Treaty.

The May Fourth movement stimulated renewed intellectual ferment as well, especially in Peking and Shanghai, where hundreds of new political and literary periodicals attacked traditional culture, deplored China's weakness, and advocated a variety of more or less radical solutions. The model of the Confucian scholar steeped in the classics gave way to that of "progressive" thinkers who wrote in the vernacular and tried to appeal not only to fellow scholars or intellectuals but to the people as a whole. Parental and family controls, arranged marriages, and the subjugation of women and the young became targets of attack. Women, especially students, played a prominent part in the May Fourth movement; they and their male colleagues urged full-scale female emancipation and an end to the rigidity of the traditional system as a whole. Lu Hsun (Lu Xun, 1881–1936), the greatest modern Chinese writer, voiced bitter indictments of the old society, whose supposed ideals of "benevolence" and "virtue," he alleged, were hypocritical masks for oppression and exploitation. Foreign imperialism was deeply resented, but such critics as Lu Hsun saw it as the result of China's weakness rather than as the cause. The May Fourth movement sought to build a new China in which modern Western ideas of democracy, equality, science, and nationalism would have a prominent place. The example of Meiji Japan was much admired, despite Japanese aggression against China. Like the Meiji leaders, China's new voices called for a clean slate and a national renewal that would incorporate Western ideas.

China and the Marxist Model

Among the Western concepts with particular appeal was Marxism, especially after the success of the Russian Revolution in 1917. Russia too had been a relatively undeveloped country that had embraced the Marxist-Leninist doctrine of centralized organization and collective effort. The Soviet formula seemed to fit China's circumstances, and Marx himself had suggested the relevance of his ideas to China many years earlier. In 1921 a small group of intellectuals, including Mao Tse-tung (Mao Zedong, 1893–1976), then a young student, founded the Chinese Communist party. Representatives from the Comintern helped the new party to set up its organization. Soviet experience in political mobilization was also attractive to the Kuomintang, which, like the Communist party, remained largely without any mass base. Sun Yat-sen, still head of the Kuomintang, agreed to an alliance with the Communist party under Comintern direction. Sun's military assistant, Chiang Kai-shek, was sent to Moscow to study Soviet methods. Party dictatorship was seen as necessary in the early stages of national unification, but Sun's Three Principles of the People and some form of representative government were reasserted as the ultimate goal. Sun may have been moving in the direction of socialism during his last years, but he died suddenly in 1925, and party control passed to Chiang Kai-shek. Chiang, despite his Soviet experience, was a far more conservative, even reactionary, figure. With his military background, Chiang saw China's first priority as the achievement of national unity, through force if necessary. He began promisingly by mounting a military and political campaign with Communist help. Moving north from the Kuomintang base in Canton with his Communist allies to defeat the warlords, he established a new national capital at Nanking (Nanjing) in 1927.

The Nanking Decade

Chiang never completely eliminated warlord power in several of the outlying provinces, and although he dominated the Kuomintang, he led it far from its radical origins and progressively lost support. He tried to wipe out his Communist allies in a military coup in Shanghai in 1927 and then in a series of campaigns from 1930 to 1934. Some of the Communists, including Mao, were not in Shanghai in 1927 but in rival areas trying, without success, to organize peasant rebellion. Their small remaining forces retreated to a mountain stronghold in the southeast. Chiang's forces finally drove them out in 1934, forcing them into a retreat known as the Long March. An increasingly ragged column of Communists dodged ahead of Chiang's troops in a zigzag route across western China. The precariously few survivors finally reached a new base area in the remote and mountainous northwest in 1935, centered on Yenan (Yanan). Relatively safe from Chiang's army, they pursued land reform policies and slowly extended their support base in this border area, from which they were to emerge after the Second World War in 1945 to lead a victorious revolution.

The decade of the Nanking government between 1927 and 1937 was, despite its repressive aspects, a period of at least modest recovery and growth. Chiang permitted no genuine democracy, with the excuse that order and

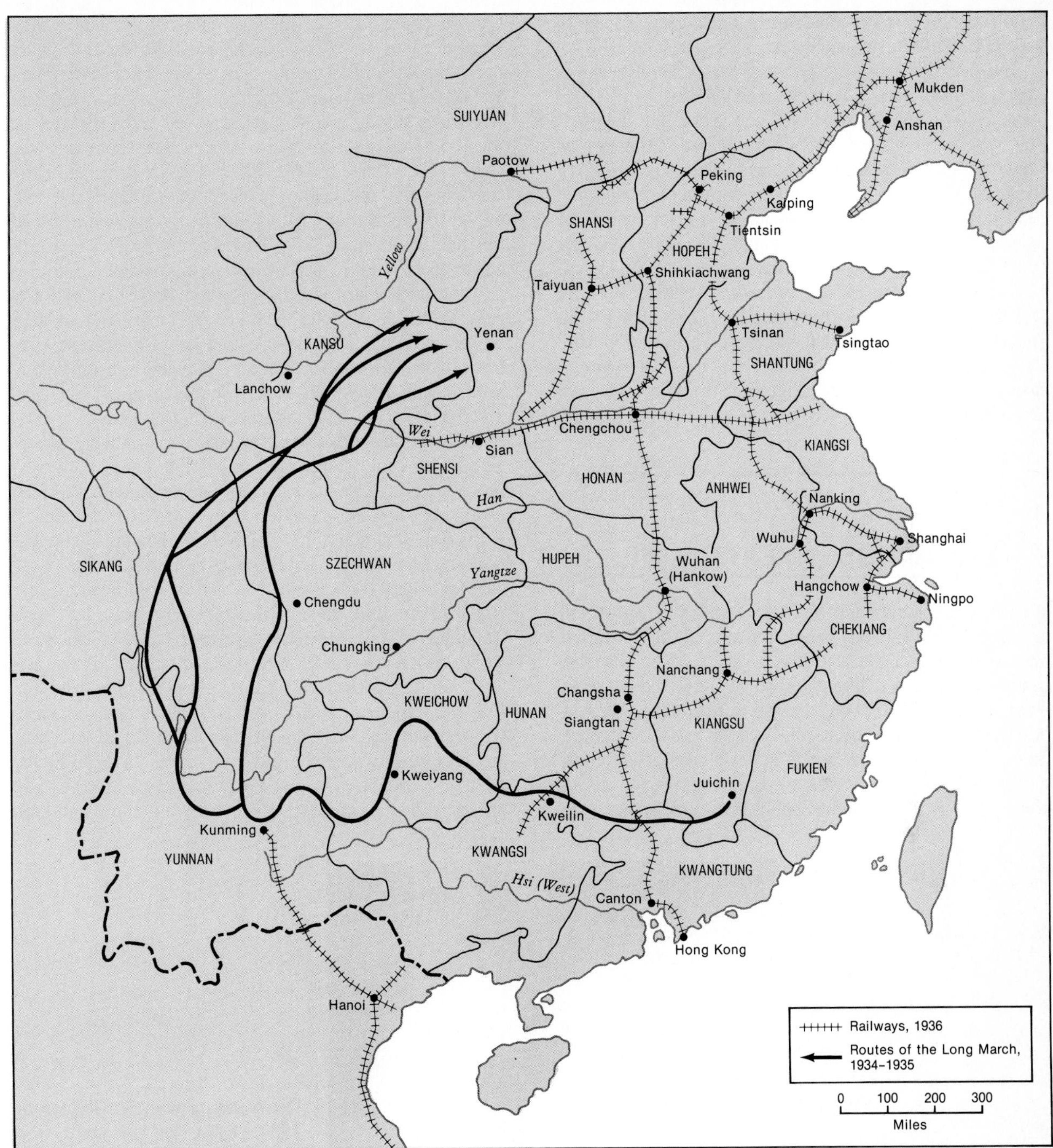

35.2 China in the 1930s

unity must come first. But at least the forms of constitutional government existed, and the economy underwent considerable modernization. Western-trained Chinese developed a central banking system, and a national rail network began to take shape. Industrial growth was still confined almost entirely to the treaty ports but increasingly under Chinese management.

These developments, however, were on a small scale compared to the needs of the country and had little or no impact on most of its predominantly peasant population. Poverty grew in the countryside. The Kuomintang's political base had become largely a coalition of businessmen from the treaty ports and rural landlords, which sought to suppress agrarian reform and prevent the rise of a politicized peasantry. The Communists, meanwhile, clung to their small base in the northwest, biding their time.

The situation was transformed by Japan's invasion of China. The Japanese, having reduced Manchuria to an economic colony, invaded it in 1931 and annexed it outright. They watched with concern as Chiang made progress toward national unification and began to build China's military strength. When the militarists who controlled Japan after 1930 saw their hopes for dominance in China and East Asia threatened, they launched a general assault on China in 1937, attacking first at Peking and then at Shanghai; later in the year they moved on to sack Nanking. With its capital in flames, the Kuomintang retreated up the Yangtze, largely to sit out the rest of the war, while the Communists in the north perfected a guerrilla strategy against the invaders and captured the leadership of Chinese nationalism.

SHANGHAI: THE MODEL TREATY PORT

While the Communists retreated to remote Yenan behind its mountain barriers and began to work out their program for a new China under the leadership of Mao, Shanghai remained a bastion of foreign privilege and Chinese collaborators. But it also harbored the growing group of Chinese dissidents, radicals, and revolutionaries who lived there under the protection of foreign law. Chinese police could not pursue suspects in the foreign settlements, which were ruled by a foreign-dominated municipal council with its own police. The Chinese Communist party had been founded there in 1921 for that reason, by a small group of revolutionaries and writers, part of the much larger number of political refugees living in the city, many of whom were periodically hounded or captured and executed by the Kuomintang secret police. Chiang Kai-shek's military coup in 1927 killed many of them and drove some of the survivors out, but many remained underground and continued to produce literary and political magazines with titles like *New China, New Youth,* and *New Dawn,* which were avidly read by intellectuals in the rest of China.

After Shanghai passed Peking as China's biggest city about 1910, it became the country's chief center of literature, publishing, and cultural and political ferment. The May Fourth movement spread immediately from Peking to Shanghai; student organizers persuaded many Shanghai merchants to boycott Japanese, and later British, goods. Shanghai joined Peking as a major base for the New Culture movement, sometimes called the Chinese Renaissance, and its efforts to remake Chinese society. Lu Hsun and many other New Culture writers lived in Shanghai.

At the same time, Shanghai remained by far the largest port and commercial center in China, through which over half its foreign trade passed. It also housed over half the country's modern industry. Chinese entrepreneurs, both traditional and Westernized, competed and collaborated with foreigners in trade, banking, and manufacturing, and many of them adopted a Western style of living. The foreign settlements at Shanghai were replicas of the modern Western city and looked physically much like Manchester or Chicago. The muddy foreshores of the Huangpu River, a Yangtze tributary that ran along one edge of the city and constituted the harbor, were covered in the nineteenth

Cosmopolitanism in Shanghai, 1933: from left to right, the American journalist Agnes Smedley, the playwright George Bernard Shaw, Mme. Sun Yat-sen, Ts'ai Yuan-p'ei (a leading intellectual), and Lu Hsun. Shaw was on a visit to China and is here being welcomed by the founders of the China League for Civil Rights. [Eastfoto/Sovfoto]

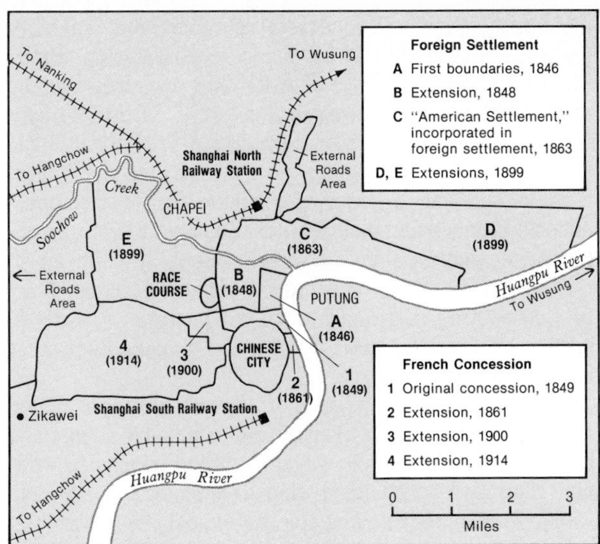

35.3 The Growth of Shanghai

century by an embankment known as the Bund. It became Shanghai's main thoroughfare, lined with imposing Western banks and hotels. Nanking Road, the main shopping street, ran at right angles to it, away from the river, and extensive residential areas featured houses in the Western style. The foreign population peaked at about 60,000 in the 1930s, in a city which by then totaled about 4 million, many of whom lived outside the foreign concession areas in sprawling slums or in the walled Chinese city next to the concessions. But the commercial and industrial heart of Shanghai was largely run by foreigners (the Japanese had edged out the British as the majority interest by the 1930s), and they built it in the Western image. They spoke of it as a beacon of "progress" in a vast Chinese sea of "backwardness."

Shanghai was described as "in China but not of it." The city brought silk, tea, and other agricultural goods from the Chinese hinterland for export in return for metals, machinery, and manufactured goods. Overall, however, Shanghai's economic example made relatively little impact, except in the other treaty ports. Elsewhere, it was largely rejected as alien and unsuited to China. The Communists labeled Chinese collaborators in Shanghai and the other treaty ports "running dogs" of the imperialists and were contemptuous of their departure from Chinese ways in favor of Westernization.

Shanghai and the other treaty ports cut a deep wound of humiliation in the Chinese psyche, but they also offered an example of the kind of industrial and organizational strength without which China could not hope to chart its own destiny. Shanghai played a major role in stimulating the rise of modern Chinese nationalism and with it a determination to rid the country of its foreign oppressors. The foreign way was rejected, but its technological and industrial achievements were to be adapted to serve Chinese needs. The residents of Shanghai were, of course, the most affected by its example, and it was primarily there that China's modern revolution began. In the end, all foreign privileges were swept away by the revolution, but Shanghai remains China's biggest city and its most advanced industrial and technological center. Shanghai's modernity thus survived the expulsion of the foreigners and shaped basic aspects of the new China.

India: Toward Freedom

In India the pressures for change were narrowly concentrated on winning freedom from colonial rule. Like China, India suffered from mass poverty, technological backwardness, and foreign domination. Indian nationalists tended to blame colonial oppression for their problems and to see the solution as getting rid of their British overlords. But as in China, a new national consciousness had first to be developed and a national political organization built. India had functioned throughout most of its past not as a national political unit but rather, like China, as a cultural tradition. It took time to get Indians or Chinese to work together for a common political goal. The Indian independence movement did respond to the need for attacking poverty and injustice and for pursuing modern development, but the immediate objective was political freedom. While its final achievement was in some ways a revolutionary change, most Indians saw no need to reject either their own tradition or aspects of the British colonial experience that could help the new nation adapt to the modern world.

India's progress toward freedom is in large part the story of the careers of two men, Mohandas K. Gandhi (1869–1948), often called the Mahatma, or "Great Soul," and Jawaharlal Nehru (1889–1964). Gandhi gave the independence movement what it had not yet had, mass appeal and a mass following. Nehru, in close cooperation with Gandhi, gave practical leadership but acknowledged the charismatic power of Gandhi's example. In the years after World War I the Congress party was transformed under Gandhi's direction from a small group of intellectuals into a truly national party representing a wide range of regional interest groups and mobilizing millions of Indians. Gandhi proved adept at using aspects of the Indian tradition as vehicles of protest against British imperialism and as rallying points for nationalist sentiment and organization.

Gandhi and Mass Action

The son of a minor official in commercial Gujarat, Gandhi followed the path of many upwardly mobile Indians in a rapidly changing society. At 19 he went to London to study law and there became thoroughly Westernized. Soon after his return to India, he took a job with an Indian law firm in South Africa, where he spent the next 20 years defending Indian merchants and other immigrants against racist oppression and developing tactics of nonviolent protest and noncooperation.

Back home in 1913, he supported Indian participation in the First World War on the Allied side, hoping, as many Indians did, that loyalty to Britain in its hour of need would be rewarded by self-government. The British secretary of state for India announced in 1917 that the government's policy was "the gradual development of self-governing institutions" and an increase of Indians in responsible positions, but with the end of the war it became clear that such change would be painfully slow. Meanwhile, peasant economic suffering and distress among exploited industrial workers were growing. Gandhi traveled through India dressed as a poor peasant, reaching out to the masses and gaining a reputation for personal sanctity. But he also organized and led successful strikes and protest movements, using nonviolent methods with great effect. These and other signs of ferment appeared to members of the government as "seditious conspiracy." Repression followed, culminating in the Amritsar Massacre of 1919 when Indian troops under British command fired on an unarmed and peaceful crowd, leaving 400 dead.

From then on, few Indians saw accommodation to colonialism as acceptable. The Congress party began to press for independence, and Gandhi's weapon of nonviolent protest and noncooperation attracted more and more followers. Gandhi based his tactics on the ancient Hindu idea of *ahimsa*, or reverence for life, and drew on the redemptive power of love to convert even brutal opponents by its "soul force," or *satyagraha*. Traditional Indian values stressed the avoidance of conflict and the importance of self-control, seeking resolution through compromise and consensus. Nonviolent action was also a practical means for unarmed and powerless people to confront an oppressive state. As the American civil rights leader Martin Luther King, Jr., was later to demonstrate, it worked, both to build a dedicated following and to make its protest against injustice effective.

Gandhi organized boycotts of British imports, an action that caught the popular imagination, as it had in China, and helped build a larger following. He urged Indians to wear only their own cottons and wherever possible to spin and weave for themelves. The spinning wheel became a powerful nationalist symbol, linked also to 5,000 years of the country's history. Some of the Congress party's intellectual elite were scornful of Gandhi's methods, the style of a traditional saddhu, or holy man, he adopted, his embrace of the poor, and his personal asceticism. But as both an astute politician and a saintly figure he attracted more support and got more results than the party's politicians had ever done. Gandhi gave the Indian people a sense of their own national identity and inspired them to action through traditional methods and symbols. He succeeded where others had failed in attracting Muslims, Sikhs, Christians, and agnostics to his cause, thus creating India's first truly

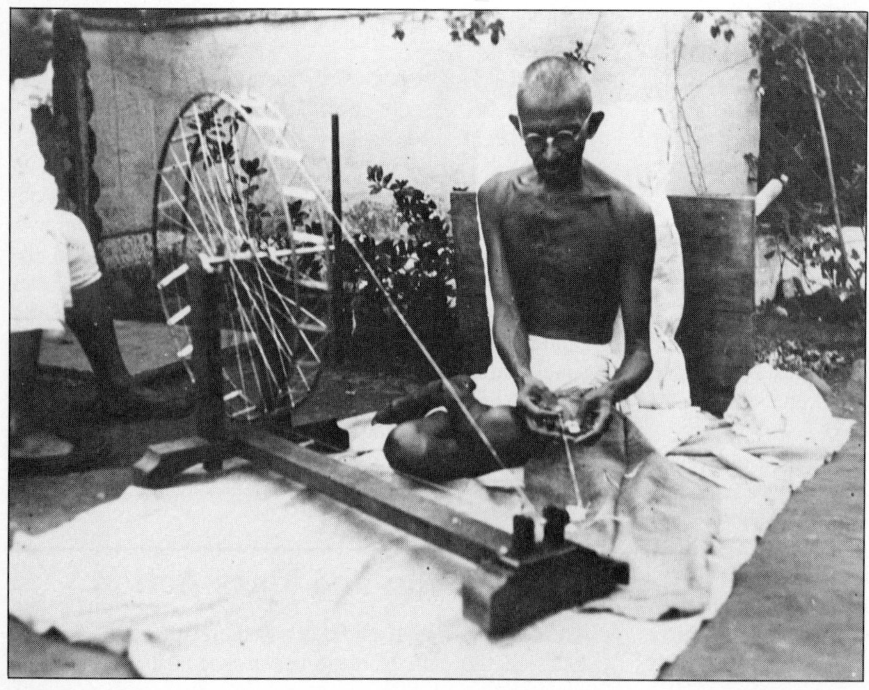

Gandhi the ascetic, spinning cotton yarn. He made it a point to spin 200 yards of yarn every day as a symbolic act, no matter how busy he was. ["L'Illustration"/Sygma]

national movement. He urged his fellow Indians to "get rid of our helplessness" and stand together. As Nehru said of him, "He has given us back our courage, and our pride."

Strikes, boycotts, and demonstrations spread in the early 1920s, but with millions of people now involved, Gandhi could not always guarantee nonviolence. Thousands were jailed, violence occurred on both sides, and in 1922 Gandhi was sentenced to prison for six years. He was released for medical reasons after two but did not resume political agitation until 1929, distressed that his nonviolent campaign had gone astray.

Hindus and Muslims

Meanwhile, the government, affected by Gandhi's popular movement, began to implement many of the reforms previously demanded by the Congress party. It greatly increased the number of Indian officers in the civil service and the army and moved toward the abolition of the tax on cotton. By 1937 all of the British Indian provinces had become self-governing, with legislatures elected by Indian voters. Nehru became mayor of his home city of Allahabad. During this time, rioting between Muslims and Hindus broke out in many areas, a symptom of the general atmosphere of turmoil but also of the efforts of special groups to ensure a better place for themselves in the independent India that was now clearly coming. Hindus and Muslims had worked together for many years in the Congress party. Now Muslims were warned that they had to safeguard their interests against the Hindu majority and that their own party, the Muslim League, led by Mohammed Ali Jinnah (1876–1948), was their only sure protector.

Jinnah pressed for a separate Muslim electorate to vote for candidates for the new posts being opened to Indian

Gandhi's Message to the British

Gandhi knew England and British culture well, in part from his time there as a student, and he had many British friends. In his Hind Swaraj *(Independent India), he addressed them.*

I admit you are my rulers. . . . I have no objection to your remaining in my country, but . . . you will have to remain as servants of the people. . . . We do not need any European cloth. We shall manage with articles produced and manufactured at home. . . . This is not said to you in arrogance. You have great military resources. . . . If we wanted to fight with you on your own ground, we should be unable to do so but [we must] cease to play the part of the ruled. . . . If you act contrary to our will, we will not help you; and without our help, we know that you cannot move one step forward. . . . You English who have come to India are not good specimens of the English nation, nor can we, almost half-anglicized Indians, be considered good specimens of the real Indian nation. If the English nation were to know all you have done, it would oppose many of your actions. . . . If you will search into your own scriptures, you will find that our demands are just. Only on condition of our demands being fully satisfied may you remain in India; and if you remain under those conditions, we shall learn several things from you and you will learn many from us. So doing we shall benefit each other and the world. But that will happen only when the root of our relationship is sunk in a religious soil.

Gandhi's ideas and personal qualities are well brought out in that passage. Nehru said the following of him in 1935.

I have never met any man more utterly honest, more transparently sincere, less given to egotism, self-conscious pride, opportunism, and ambition. . . . It has been the greatest privilege of our lives to work with him and under him for a great cause. To us he has represented the spirit and honor of India.

Sources: W. T. de Bary, ed., *Sources of Indian Tradition*, vol. 2 (New York: Columbia University Press, 1964), pp. 265–266. J. Nehru, "Mahatma Gandhi," *L'Europe* (February 1936), p. 21.

officeholders and Indian voters. Meanwhile, Nehru increased his organizational control of the Congress party, although he maintained his loyalty to Gandhi as India's spiritual and symbolic leader. Nehru insisted that the Congress party was the party of all Indians, including Muslims, and that the independence movement would be weakened by factionalism. He was proved tragically right.

The worldwide depression that began in 1929 bore heavily on India and greatly increased its economic distress. When Gandhi resumed political action in 1930, he chose as his targets the tax the government imposed on salt and the official ban on private saltmaking from the sea, arguing that the tax and the monopoly especially hurt the poor. He led a protest march on foot across India to the coast, where he purposely courted arrest by picking up a lump of natural salt and urging Indians to do likewise, as many thousands did. Gandhi, Nehru, and many others were jailed, and there was a wave of strikes. Gandhi had again stirred the conscience of the nation. After eight months in prison, he was released to meet with the viceroy in New Delhi. Gandhi agreed to discontinue civil disobedience; in return, the government sanctioned a movement to promote the use of Indian-made goods and invited Gandhi to a London conference on India later in 1931, together with Jinnah as a representative of the Muslims.

The conference ended in stalemate, and Gandhi was taken back to jail a week after his return. Boycotts, strikes, and violent demonstrations erupted again without Gandhi to restrain them. Meanwhile, economic distress deepened as world markets for India's exports shrank, and a new, more conservative viceroy was appointed. In England, however, popular and parliamentary opinion was turning more and more toward self-government for India. In 1935 a new constitution for India was announced, followed by nationwide elections in 1937 in which nearly 40 million Indians voted. Congress candidates swept the election, and the Muslim League did not even win most of the seats reserved for Muslims. The new constitution granted "safeguard" powers to the colonial government, but Congress ministries took over the provinces. Jinnah was outraged, and until his death devoted his energies to building first an effective party for Muslims and finally a separate state. Nehru pointed out in reply that the Congress party was a national, not a special interest, party, and that over 100,000 Muslims belonged to it.

By the outbreak of war in 1939, India was well along the road to self-government, but the war brought the pro-imperial Winston Churchill to power in Britain and postponed all talk of independence until fascism could be defeated in Europe and Asia. Indians were informed that they were automatically at war with Germany, and later with Italy and Japan. Neither the Congress party's representatives nor other Indian leaders were consulted. Nationalists once again felt betrayed. The Congress party's provincial ministries resigned in protest, leaving the political field to Jinnah and his Muslim League. A belated British offer, reduced at Churchill's insistence from independence to dominion status once the war was over, was rejected. Gandhi called it "a postdated check on a failing bank." He began a series of nonviolent campaigns, culminating in the "Quit India" movement of 1942, a slogan that was scrawled on walls all over the country and shouted at Britons. Nehru spent most of the war in jail, and Gandhi was confined periodically. Jinnah exploited their absence to

The Declaration of Indian Freedom

Nehru, as president of the Congress party, declared January 26, 1930, a special day for the assertion of India's right to independence and issued this pledge, which was recited throughout India by millions of nationalists. Note the close similarity, quite conscious on Nehru's part, with the American Declaration of Independence.

We believe that it is the inalienable right of the Indian people, as of any other people, to have freedom and to enjoy the fruits of their toil and have the necessities of life, so that they may have full opportunities of growth. We believe also that if any government deprives a people of these rights and oppresses them, the people have a further right to alter it or abolish it. The British government in India has not only deprived the Indian people of their freedom, but has based itself on the exploitation of the masses, and has ruined India economically, politically, culturally, and spiritually.

Source: S. Wolpert, *A New History of India* (New York: Oxford University Press, 1982), pp. 314–315.

press for a separate state for Muslims, to be called Pakistan. Independence would come too late to avoid the bloody tragedy of partition.

The British had begun in India as a small group of merchants competing with Arabs, Portuguese, Dutch, French, and Indians for a share of the trade and a few ports. Trading and maintaining the security of routes and warehouses led imperceptibly to more and more political influence and control in an India that lapsed into chaos after 1707. In time the lure of imperial glory captured the British imagination, but there was a kernel of truth in the observation some made that the Indian empire was acquired in "a fit of absentmindedness." After 1784 Parliament began to supervise the governance of India, and by 1858 virtually the whole of the subcontinent had been brought under direct or indirect British control.

As early as the 1830s, most Britons agreed that India would one day be independent, and long-term British policy should prepare for this. Indians were quick to learn Western ideas and techniques wherever they saw them as useful, including business and industrial methods and British-style education, law, and parliamentary government. India is still governed today by institutions derived from Britain. The assimilation of British ways also greatly enhanced and accelerated the growth of the independence movement, which Indians saw as itself within the British tradition of political freedom.

If independence had come in 1907, when Parliament first declared it to be Britain's objective, or in the 1920s, when the policy was reaffirmed, it would have been possible to look back on the British era in India in relatively positive terms, though marred in the late eighteenth century by plunder and by the arrogance which led to the 1857 mutiny and its bitter aftermath. But however one assesses the balance or weighs it with other aspects of British rule, especially the failure to combat the fundamental modern Indian problem of poverty, Britain's clearest political error was its delay in giving India independence. The bloody consequences that followed might have been avoided had independence come earlier and had the Second World War and Winston Churchill not intervened. Nevertheless, there is little bitterness over the colonial legacy in India, in contrast to much of the rest of Asia, which underwent a harsher rule under the Japanese, French, or Dutch. Many originally British institutions are now firmly a part of South Asian civilization. India has much in common today with other former British colonies, including the United States and Canada, as joint inheritors of many aspects of a common culture.

The Nationalist Awakening in the Middle East

The same nationalist forces that challenged European imperialism in India and China had an equally pronounced impact on the Middle East. Despite ethnic disunity and traditional theological differences within Islam, Arab consciousness had been stimulated by the common experience of Turkish and European exploitation. By the eve of World War I, independence movements, often used as an entering wedge for Western interests, had already dismembered large portions of the weakened Ottoman Empire. The Greeks and most of the Slavic peoples of the Balkans had either freed themselves from Turkish rule or had fallen under Austro-Hungarian control. In North Africa, France had taken Algeria and established protectorates in Morocco and Tunisia, Britain had imposed a sphere of influence over Egypt and the Sudan, and Italy had occupied Libya and Somalia. Besides Turkey proper, only Iraq, Syria, Palestine, and Arabia still remained within the Ottoman sphere.

The Mandate System and the Palestine Question

British success in arousing Arab hostility against the Turks during the war, together with the success of the British adventurer T. E. Lawrence in coordinating Arab resistance, had helped to free most of the Middle East from Ottoman control by 1918. When the war was over, Faisal of Iraq and Lawrence lobbied the Paris peace conference for Arab rights, while Chaim Weizmann, who had succeeded Theodor Herzl as the leader of the Zionist movement, continued to push for the creation of a Jewish state. Neither party succeeded. After Faisal's appeals were rejected, an Arab congress declared him ruler of Syria, Palestine, and Lebanon.

While Faisal and Lawrence were in Paris, Abdul-Aziz ibn-Saud took to the deserts with his troops, extending his control over central Arabia. In 1925 he finally forced Hussein to abdicate as ruler of the Hejaz, which he united with his own Nejd sultanate. The British quickly recognized these conquests, and in 1932 ibn-Saud formally changed the name of his realm to the Kingdom of Saudi Arabia. Vast oil deposits were soon discovered, and ibn-Saud's hereditary absolute monarchy eventually grew wealthy through the concessions granted to Western oil companies.

Although the Saudi dynasty was successful in Arabia, Arab nationalism continued to be frustrated elsewhere. Faisal's rule over Syria was short-lived, for in 1920 the Allies tacitly recognized the terms of the Sykes-Picot Agreement by approving the League of Nations mandate system, and Turkish control formally gave way to Western domination. The French ejected Faisal from Syria, engendering bitter resistance from the Arab population, and created Lebanon as a separate mandate. In 1926 Lebanon was made a republic, with borders similar to those of the now independent state. The roads, buildings, and irrigation systems constructed under French occupation did not make up for the suppression of civil liberties and the divisive efforts to gain the allegiance of the Christian Arabs of Lebanon. The Lebanon mandate had a rich religious diversity, for in ancient times it had been a place of refuge for religious sects of all kinds. The Maronite Christians, a Roman Catholic group that followed Eastern Orthodox rites, had roots that went back to the seventh century; it comprised about 40 percent of the population, while Muslims of various sects made up the bulk of the remaining inhabitants. When the French eventually evacuated the area after World War II, they left behind a legacy of deep hostility.

The British were more successful in their mandate areas. Following an Iraqi rebellion in 1920, which they put down with much bloodshed, they made the popular Faisal king of Iraq, although they continued to run his financial and military affairs for another decade and supervised the creation of a constitutional monarchy. In 1922 Britain granted nominal independence to Egypt but refused to withdraw its troops from the country, and it followed a similar path in Iraq, where independence was recognized in 1930 in exchange for a military alliance that maintained British influence there. Nor did the discovery of rich oil fields in Iraq benefit the population of the region, for foreign companies secured lucrative concessions, further enflaming Arab resentment against the West.

The Palestine problem remained another source of anti-Western hostility as well as a cause of regional unrest. Britain's contradictory policies in the Middle East satisfied neither Arab nor Jewish demands, and throughout the interwar period British governments continued to shift between the two. Arab riots erupted in Palestine immediately after the creation of the British mandate over the area, prompting London to issue assurances that the Balfour Declaration would not be implemented in a way that would damage Arab interests. Yet British statesmen agreed with the Zionist position that the anguished history of the Jews made the creation of an independent Jewish homeland in Palestine a moral necessity. The Jewish community there—the Yishuv—had had a nearly uninterrupted residence since biblical times. It increased as a result of Zionist efforts in the late nineteenth century. By 1919 Jews in the mandate numbered around 60,000, or less than 10 percent of the population. In the early 1920s Britain permitted many Jews to join the Yishuv; by 1939 it had grown to 450,000, almost a third of the total.

Serious violence against Jews, provoked in part by aggressive settlement and the exclusion of Palestinians from newly established factories, broke out in 1929. When Nazi racial policies in Germany and anti-Semitism elsewhere caused another large wave of illegal Jewish immigration in the 1930s, the violence escalated to a virtual state of civil war. The British responded with proposals to create two separate states in the area, but both sides rejected the plan. The bitter struggle between Arab and Jew would reemerge after World War II with far-reaching results.

Despite overwhelming obstacles, Jewish immigrants achieved remarkable success. Although most came from European cities, they adjusted quickly to the rural conditions in Palestine, buying up Arab farmland as well as turning formerly arid terrain into fertile farms and citrus orchards through irrigation, much as the Arabs themselves were doing. The socialist beliefs of many of the early settlers encouraged collective agricultural labor through a farm unit known as the *kibbutz*, where men and women worked on an equal basis and shared nurseries, dining facilities, and schools as well as the defense of the community. Another form of enterprise was the *moshav*, a mixture of capitalist and socialist economic features. By 1939 the Jews had created, on socialist principles, an economic infrastructure that encompassed transportation networks, irrigation schemes, and other forms of industrial and agricultural productivity unique in the Middle East at that time. They also built new and prosperous cities, such as Tel Aviv, where a rich intellectual life thrived, based on the Hebrew language. This intellectual revival was facilitated by a Hebrew-language publishing industry and theater. Other institutions that elaborated biblical and medieval Jewish cultural themes in a twentieth-century context included art and music academies, a philharmonic orchestra, and the Hebrew University of Jerusalem and its Jewish National Library. By the late 1930s Jewish claims to Palestine, both biblical and historical, were reinforced by their achievements in constructing the foundations of a modern society.

The Modernization of Turkey and Iran

In the second half of the nineteenth century internal problems had made it difficult for the Ottoman Empire to deal effectively with external challenges. The reactionary excesses of the Sultan Abdul Hamid (1876–1909) stimulated opposition among Western-educated reformers and army officers (see Chapter 31). These groups formed the Young Turk movement, which in 1908 forced Abdul Hamid to restore the constitution and the parliament. When the sultan attempted a counterrevolution, the Young Turks unseated him. They soon imposed rigid centralization based on Turkish supremacy on a state that included substantial Arab, Armenian, and Slavic minorities. Wooed by German agents, who trained their army, the Young Turks brought Turkey into the First World War on Germany's side.

Military defeat precipitated the final demise of the Ottoman Empire. While the subject Arabs were breaking away from Istanbul, the Allies imposed a harsh peace treaty on Turkey that provided for the partition of its empire. In these circumstances, patriotic Turks turned to Mustapha Kemal (1881–1938), who had defended Gallipoli against the British in 1915. The Western-educated Kemal, charismatic and strong-willed, became the focus of a nationalist movement that revolutionized Turkish life. Setting up a new capital at Ankara, in central Anatolia—a site chosen as deliberately remote from European influence—he won popular acclaim by defying the Allies, abolishing the privileges that foreigners once had in Turkey, and repelling the Greek armies that attempted to wrest further territory from the Turks. While recognizing the inevitability of Arab independence, he was unwilling to surrender Asia Minor, eastern Thrace, or the Dardanelles. In 1923, after creating a republic and defeating a Greek thrust against Asia Minor, he forced a revised peace treaty on the Allies that permitted Turkey to keep Asia Minor and a small strip of territory around Istanbul on the European side of the Turkish Straits.

Kemal—who was given the name Atatürk, or "Father of the Turks"—embarked on a program of massive change designed to bring Turkey into the modern era. Although technically president of the republic, he governed as a dictator under a one-party system with a national assembly elected by indirect vote of a limited electorate, made universal only in 1934. His ability to introduce far-reaching change stemmed in part from an appeal to Turkish nationalism. As the Japanese had done so successfully in their own drive for Westernization, Kemal now played on the fear and resentment that Western imperialism had provoked while simultaneously stressing Turkey's historic role as the dominant force in a region of lesser states. With ruthless determination, he abolished ancient customs and swept away cultural patterns he felt impeded Turkish modernization. Outwardly, the most visible signs of Kemal's revolution were the changes in dress that he decreed. Government officials were required to substitute Western business suits and hats for robes and fezzes. Western-style family names were introduced, and place names were altered to symbolize the break from an archaic past. But other changes had a more profound impact. Kemal, who professed no religious beliefs, struck deeply at Islamic tradition by separating church from state and secularizing the nation's educational and legal systems. A simpler, more phonetic alphabet replaced the intricate Arabic script as the written language, and the government launched a far-reaching educational campaign among millions of previously illiterate Turkish citizens.

Mustapha Kemal Atatürk, the architect of modern Turkey and its first president. [Culver Pictures]

Kemal's vigorous social reforms inspired a similar modernization experiment in Iran. In a move much like the revolt of the Young Turks, nationalistic Iranian reformers forced the despotic and backward shah to grant a constitution in 1906. The reform momentum was shattered the next year when the British and the Russians divided Iran into spheres of influence and assumed substantive control of the country. When the British tried to impose their authority over the entire country after the war, Reza Khan Pahlavi (1877–1944), a colonel in the Persian Cossack Brigade, took power and assumed the title of shah in 1925.

Reza Shah Pahlavi greatly admired Kemal Atatürk and imitated his modernization program, though with less success. The shah's secularization efforts met with fierce opposition from the powerful Islamic religious leaders, who resented all Western influence and were as strong as the small group of European-trained reformers. Like Kemal, Reza Shah Pahlavi changed place names and Westernized dress. He built an efficient army and encouraged trade and industry, but he was personally corrupt, and his government proved tyrannical.

In Turkey, Kemal's reforms radically altered the status of women. Polygamy, still practiced by a minority, was abolished in 1926, and marriage laws were modeled after Western examples. Wealthy women began to attend universities and abandoned their veiled costumes in favor of modern European dress. In 1934 women were enfranchised and made eligible for election to the National Assembly. Reza Shah Pahlavi introduced similar policies in Iran, although there Islamic influence kept a stronger hold on women. These and other changes marked a sharp departure from tradition, whose tribal and Islamic practices had kept women in bondage to men, secluded from public life, and confined by strict codes of behavior. The older customs continued to prevail in the Kingdom of Saudi Arabia and elsewhere. Nevertheless, the new social norms fostered by Kemal Atatürk and Reza Shah Pahlavi, together with the emergence of a cohesive Jewish community in Palestine where women labored on an equal basis with men, broke the centuries-old pattern of female subservience in the Middle East.

Early in the twentieth century the largest and oldest societies in the world broke sharply with the patterns of the past. In Russia, China, India, and the Middle East, half of the world's people rejected the political systems that had governed them and strove to remake their societies.

In Russia, a corrupt, ineffective, and repressive regime was toppled by an alliance of workers and intellectuals under the charismatic leadership of Lenin. In November 1917 his Bolsheviks swept away the provisional government that had replaced the Romanov dynasty and began a radical experiment in economic and social mobilization. They instituted a program of forced modernization that would enable the Soviet Union, as Russia was now called, to catch up with western Europe and improve the economic condition of its people. On Lenin's death in 1924, leadership passed to the more ruthless, power-conscious Stalin. Lenin's dream of a workers' democracy quickly faded, but Russia's industrial and military power grew rapidly, and the Soviet example of successful revolution and modernization exerted worldwide influence.

In China the revolutionary Kuomintang party succeeded the antiquated Ch'ing dynasty, which collapsed in 1911, but the revolutionaries were too few and too divided to form an effective government. The revolution was betrayed by a military strong man, Yuan Shih-kai, and upon his death in 1916 China disintegrated into a civil war among rival warlords. Under the leadership of Chiang Kai-shek, the Kuomintang managed to form a national government in 1927 but failed to unite the country or to eliminate the rival Chinese Communist party. The Japanese invasion of 1937 mortally weakened the Kuomintang, and civil war after 1945 soon brought the Communists to power with their radical solutions to China's urgent problems of poverty and weakness.

In India the long struggle for independence from British rule made real progress only after 1919, when Mahatma Gandhi greatly widened the movement's support by appealing to mass sentiment. Gandhi restored Indians' pride in their own tradition and identity. With the help of Jawaharlal Nehru, he forged a political instrument, the Congress party, into a successful vehicle for freeing India from colonialism and addressing its inherited problems of economic backwardness and inequality.

In the Middle East both Turkish and European colonial domination was also rejected, and new regimes were created in each country. In 1919 the League of Nations replaced the centuries-long rule of the Ottoman Empire in the Middle East with British and French mandates, designed to provide a transition to independence. The seeds of Arab nationalism grew slowly in the interwar period, for rulers such as Faisal in Iraq and ibn-Saud in Saudi Arabia remained heavily dependent on the European powers, while leaders such as Kemal Atatürk in Turkey and Reza Shah Pahlavi in Iran attempted to modernize their countries according to Western models. The colonization of Palestine by Jewish settlers under British patronage further exacerbated Arab nationalism. Only in the post–World War II era did true independence develop, when several factors combined to bring the new Arab states together against the lingering dominance of the West: the enormous financial strength achieved through the regional coordination of oil resources, a new-found cultural identity inspired by a return to Islamic fundamentalism, and common opposition to the Jewish state of Israel.

Each of these regions linked approaches based on its individual historical experience to the goal of creating new national strength and development. Each swept away unacceptable political systems and built in their place new governments designed to be more effective in responding to urgent national needs. Taken together, the revolutionary changes in these four major regions did indeed shake the world, by fundamentally transforming the half of it that they governed and by inspiring millions in the other half to do the same.

Notes

1. J. Reed, *Ten Days That Shook the World* (New York: Random House, 1960), pp. 170–171.
2. A. Kollontai, *The Autobiography of a Sexually Emancipated Communist Woman*, trans. S. Attanasio (New York: Herder & Herder, 1971), p. 13.
3. D. N. Jacobs, ed., *From Marx to Mao and Marchais: Documents on the Development of Communist Variations* (New York: Longman, 1979), pp. 104–105.
4. F. Claudin, *The Communist Movement: From Comintern to Cominform*, vol. 1, trans. B. Pearce (New York: Monthly Review Press, 1975), pp. 72–73.

Suggestions for Further Reading

Balfour, Baron J. P. *Atatürk: The Rebirth of a Nation*. London: Weidenfeld & Nicolson, 1964.

Bondurant, J. *The Conquest of Violence: The Gandhian Philosophy of Conflict*. Berkeley: University of California Press, 1969.

Carr, E. H. *The Russian Revolution: From Lenin to Stalin*. New York: Free Press, 1979.

Chamberlin, W. H. *The Russian Revolution, 1917–1921*. New York: Macmillan, 1952.

Chen, J. T. *The May Fourth Movement in Shanghai*. Leiden, Netherlands: Brill, 1971.

Daniels, R. V. *Red October: The Bolshevik Revolution of 1917*. New York: Scribner, 1967.

Deutscher, I. *The Prophet Armed: Trotsky, 1879–1921*. New York: Viking, 1965.

Eastman, L. E. *China Under Nationalist Rule, 1927–1937*. Stanford, Calif.: Stanford University Press, 1974.

Edwardes, M. *The Last Years of British India*. London: Cassell, 1963.

Fischer, L. *The Life of Lenin*. New York: Harper & Row, 1965.

Gasster, M. *Chinese Intellectuals and the Revolution of 1911*. Seattle: University of Washington Press, 1969.

Irving, R. G. *Indian Summer: Luytens, Baker, and Imperial New Delhi*. New Haven, Conn.: Yale University Press, 1982.

Iyer, R. *The Moral and Political Thought of Mahatma Gandhi*. New York: Oxford University Press, 1986.

Low, D. A., ed. *Congress and the Raj: Facets of the Indian Struggle, 1917–47*. Columbia: University of Missouri Press, 1977.

Majumdar, R. C. *History of the Freedom Movement in India*. Calcutta: K. L. Mukhopadhyay, 1962.

Pandey, B. N. *Nehru*. London: Macmillan, 1976.

Reed, J. *Ten Days That Shook the World*. New York: Random House, 1960.

Sachar, H. M. *The Emergence of the Middle East, 1914–1924*. New York: Knopf, 1969.

Sheridan, J. E. *China in Disintegration: The Republican Era*. Glencoe, Ill.: Free Press, 1975.

Trotsky, L. *The Russian Revolution*. Garden City, N.Y.: Anchor/Doubleday, 1959.

Ulam, A. B. *The Bolsheviks*. New York: Macmillan, 1965.

———. *Lenin and the Bolsheviks*. London: Collins, 1969.

Upton, J. M. *The History of Modern Iran*. Cambridge, Mass.: Harvard University Press, 1960.

Von Laue, T. H. *Why Lenin? Why Stalin?*. London: Weidenfeld & Nicolson, 1966.

Wilbur, C. M. *Sun Yat-sen: Frustrated Patriot*. New York: Columbia University Press, 1976.

Wolfe, B. D. *Three Who Made a Revolution*, rev. ed. New York: Dial Press, 1964.

Wright, M. C. *China in Revolution: The First Phase, 1900–1903*. New Haven, Conn.: Yale University Press, 1968.

Young, E. P. *The Presidency of Yuan Shih-kai*. Ann Arbor: University of Michigan Press, 1977.

C H A P T E R · 3 6

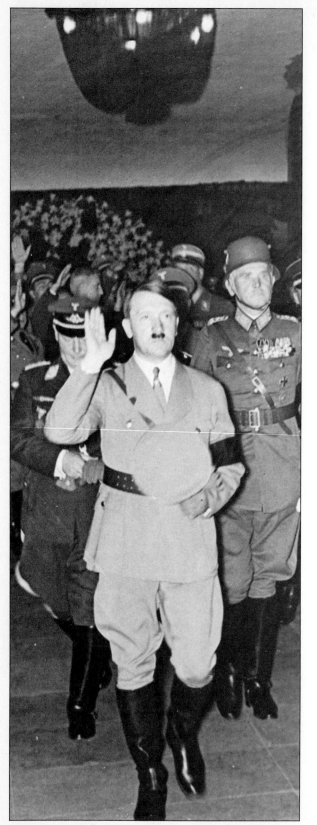

Fascism and the Crisis of Democracy

The year 1919 opened with general optimism about the prospects for democracy on the Continent. Widespread confidence prevailed that the leaders of the victorious Allied powers who assembled at Paris in January would not only arrange a lasting peace but would also fulfill President Wilson's dream of making the world "safe for democracy." Indeed, the collapse of the imperial autocracies in Russia, Germany, and Austria-Hungary was followed by the creation of parliamentary governments throughout central and eastern Europe. Within two decades, however, liberal ideals and democratic governments were in crisis as fascist movements developed in almost every country and authoritarian regimes emerged in many. By 1933 fascists had seized power only in Italy and Germany, but their appeal was so pervasive that one historian has characterized the entire interwar period as the "epoch of fascism."*

*The spelling *Fascism* refers to Italian Fascism, *fascism* to the generic variety.

Adolf Hitler salutes upon emerging from a meeting with his diplomatic corps. [FPG]

Fascism, in contrast to communism, proclaimed itself a spiritual rather than a materialist philosophy, but its appeal nevertheless increased dramatically during periods of economic hardship. The financial crisis that began in 1929 plunged the world into an economic collapse of unprecedented dimensions, causing extreme social distress and challenging capitalism itself. The political consequences of the Great Depression were equally disastrous. The political systems of Britain, France, and the United States, where democracy was deeply rooted, were threatened, though without succumbing to fascism. In the newer states of central and eastern Europe, however, where democracy had been largely the product of the 1919 settlements, liberal governments often fell victim to dictatorship and spawned native fascist movements. Together, fascism and the Great Depression posed a deadly challenge to democracy.

The Nature of Fascism

Many Europeans, dissatisfied with liberal governments but unwilling to adopt communism, regarded fascism as an alternative, a "third way" capable of solving the problems of industrial society. Fascists claimed their system would overcome class struggle and transform society. Over the next two decades, however, fascism inflicted suffering and destruction on millions and collapsed only after the most devastating war in history.

Scholars continue to debate the nature of fascism. Some regard it as a universal phenomenon that transcended national borders and possessed a core of similar characteristics in all countries. Yet most experts concede that despite some similarities, Italian Fascism and German Nazism had deep ideological differences and that each system in turn differed from fascist movements elsewhere. It may be possible to understand fascism only in the context of a particular nation during a specific time. Although the term *fascist* continues to be applied to noncommunist authoritarian regimes, some doubt that we can speak of fascism outside the European setting and beyond the chronological period 1919–1945.

Nor is it easy to classify fascism according to traditional political categories. Was it a movement of the Right or of the Left? Was it a revolutionary, a conservative, or a reactionary force? Some experts suggest that these questions may be resolved in part by recognizing the distinction between fascism as a movement before it came to power and fascism as a regime after it seized control of a government. This approach is based on the fact that once in office, fascist leaders often compromised with traditional power elites in order to consolidate their authority, and these compromises changed the original aims of their movements.

General Characteristics

However difficult it is to define fascism precisely, it is possible to identify characteristics found in virtually all such movements. The fascists rejected the concept of liberty inherited from the French Revolution and nineteenth-century liberalism. They argued that democracy corrupts the human spirit with greed, sacrifices national interests for the sake of party and class concerns, and replaces heroism and honor with alienation and a loss of community. Fascists claimed they would eliminate the materialism and class conflict implicit in Marxism, which divided the national community. The fascist claim that forces of will could create a new age of heroism had its roots in the Romantic rejection of Enlightenment rationalism. In its place they proclaimed the superiority of instinct, feeling, and blood, and they glorified violence and action. The fascists promised to restore idealism, youthful activism, and the spirit of sacrifice and to integrate every class and citizen into the all-embracing "totalitarian" state. As distinct from traditional authoritarian governments, totalitarian regimes attempt to shape minds and attitudes, indoctrinating people and turning them into loyal supporters. To achieve its goals, the totalitarian state employs terror and propaganda.

Dictators such as Benito Mussolini and Adolf Hitler played crucial roles in fascist regimes. These were sustained in large part by the cult of the charismatic leader, whose authority was unquestioned and to whom all loyalty and obedience were directed. Propaganda and public rituals instilled in the population a fanatical faith in the infallible leader, who, with an elite party, ruled in the name of a single national will. Future leaders would be trained through the party, which acted as a link between the people and the state.

The mass base of fascism came chiefly from the lower middle class. White-collar workers, civil servants, artisans, and shopkeepers resented the wealthy, powerful capitalists just as they feared the working classes. This lower-middle-class group, from which the early movements filled their ranks, hoped that fascism would solve the postwar economic crisis and restore traditional values—respect for authority, family, and nation. It shared the fascists' alienation from the existing social and political order, whose elites monopolized power and restricted advancement. Support for fascism was not limited to the lower middle class, however. Fascist programs were tailored to attract diverse interests so that segments of the aristocracy, big business, urban labor, and the peasantry found them appealing.

While fascism incorporated some aspects of socialist thought, its major appeal was to nationalism or racism. Such appeals cut across class lines and economic interests, and fascist propaganda played successfully on the popular desire for national greatness and ethnic dominance. Mussolini's dream of re-creating a Roman empire and Hitler's prophecy of a "thousand-year Reich" reflected the fascist thirst for expansion, and the foreign policies of both dictators were aggressive. For some fascist movements—particularly the German National Socialists—racism was the core of their ideologies, but for others—such as the Italian Fascists—racism represented a later addition. Nevertheless, many fascists emphasized the biological or spiritual distinctiveness of their national "races" and exalted the unity of "blood and soil" in their national histories. Ethnic minorities are usually suppressed in authoritarian regimes, but fascism systematically eliminated entire populations as the extreme logic of its racism unfolded: hundreds of thousands of North African natives were slaughtered by Italian Fascist armies, and millions of Jews were murdered by the Nazis in central Europe.

The Origins of Fascism

In the broadest terms, fascism was the product of crisis—economic, political, social, and cultural. Some historians regard fascism as a reaction against ruling elites, while others consider it as a strategy adopted by those elites to forestall revolution from below. Although a few scholars insist that its origins must be traced back hundreds of years, many agree that we must look for its sources in the nineteenth century. In Italy and Germany the manner and circumstances in which national unification was achieved may have had an important bearing on the origins of fascism. Unification was the work of political and economic elites who excluded the masses from the process of nation building and used the instruments of power politics—war and diplomacy—to achieve their purposes. These elites shaped the new national states according to their own interests to secure power. Large segments of the populations of these countries were therefore unintegrated into national life and looked to fascism as a response to the elitist nature of national unification.

The Marxist interpretation argues that fascism is the product of the class struggle that takes place in all capitalist societies. As the counterrevolutionary form adopted by the capitalist classes to suppress the workers in an effort to prevent the proletarian revolution, fascism, according to the Marxist interpretation, is the last, desperate attempt by the industrial and financial interests to save dying capitalism. While there are many variations of this interpretation, most Marxists now consider fascism an independent force distinct from capitalism itself. In this view, capitalists supported and used fascism as a weapon in their struggle against the working classes. The "Red scare" that spread throughout Europe following the Russian Revolution provided the atmosphere in which fascism rose to power, and the anticommunist thrust of fascism was the capitalist response to that revolutionary threat.

Other scholars defend national unification as the triumph of nineteenth-century liberalism. They argue that the origins of fascism are to be found in the moral and cultural crisis that Europe experienced at the turn of the century. The late nineteenth-century "revolt against positivism" undermined many of the ideals inherited from the Enlightenment and the French Revolution and challenged the underlying Judeo-Christian ethical principles on which Western civilization was based. The decline of these values affected political behavior and produced social disintegration, and World War I was seen as an irrational triumph over reason. Accordingly, fascism emerged out of the dislocation of the postwar period as an extreme revolt against positivist values.

Marxist and non-Marxist scholars agree that fascism was an immediate result of World War I. In the postwar crisis, a number of elements—the presence of numerous unemployed and alienated veterans, thwarted lower-middle-class aspirations, capitalist fears of revolution, the outrage of nations defeated in the war or in the peace settlements—were skillfully manipulated by fascism.

Italy: The Fascist Triumph

The life of Benito Mussolini and the history of Italian Fascism were inextricably linked. Italian Fascism and its regime bore the indelible stamp of his personality and ideas, but he never dominated his movement as Hitler did Nazism.

Benito Mussolini

The founder of Fascism was born in 1883 in a small village in northeastern Italy. Mussolini's father, a blacksmith, was a socialist from whom he inherited a radical, anticlerical bias. He displayed a violent personality but a keen intelligence. His mother, a devout schoolteacher, sent him to a Catholic seminary, from which he was expelled for having stabbed another pupil. By 1901 Mussolini was teaching elementary school and active in local socialist politics. The next year he fled to Switzerland to avoid the draft, remaining there until 1904. As a center for revolutionary exiles from many countries, Switzerland afforded Mussolini the opportunity to develop his socialist ideas. He read widely and worked as a propagandist for the Italian Socialist Party (PSI). After his return to Italy, he distinguished himself as a revolutionary socialist, a public speaker, and a journalist. During the Italo-Turkish War (1911–1912) he appeared as a staunch pacifist and anti-imperialist, serving a prison term for inciting antiwar riots. In 1912 he helped the revolutionary socialist faction seize control of the PSI and was made editor of *Avanti!,* the official Socialist party daily.

By the outbreak of World War I, Mussolini had become

a prominent socialist leader. During the "interventionist crisis" (1914–1915), in which Italy remained neutral while arranging to enter the war on the Allied side, he rejected some of his socialist principles, particularly his antiwar stance. Concluding that the war could act as a catalyst for revolution, he advocated Italian intervention and as a result was expelled from the PSI in 1915. That year, with money from industrialists and foreign sources, he founded his own newspaper, *Il Popolo d'Italia*, which became the official Fascist organ.

Following a brief stint as a soldier, during which he was wounded and made a sergeant, Mussolini returned to political agitation. He had meanwhile absorbed nationalist ideas from Cesare Battisti (1875–1916) and abandoned his belief in the class struggle. By the end of the war Mussolini was a revolutionary without an ideology, a leader in search of a movement.

Postwar Crisis in Italy

Peace produced a crisis in Italy. To bolster wartime morale the government had promised land for peasants, jobs for workers, and political and social equality. These promises created heady expectations among Italians of all classes, but postwar realities brought swift disillusionment. Italy's national debt had risen dramatically, the value of its currency had fallen sharply, and foreign trade had been seriously curtailed for more than three years. The spiraling cost of living hit the working and middle classes hard. Demobilized soldiers demanded jobs, many of which had been filled by women during the war, and the difficulties of converting the economy to peacetime production resulted in more than 2 million unemployed by the end of 1919.

Theory of the Fascist State

Fascist political theory rejected nineteenth-century liberalism, which held that government's function was to guarantee the rights and freedoms of individuals. Instead, Fascists argued that service to an all-powerful state was the highest moral goal. In these passages, written in collaboration with the philosopher Giovanni Gentile, Mussolini explained the essence of what he called the totalitarian state.

Against individualism, the Fascist conception is for the State; and it is for the individual in so far as he coincides with the State, which is the conscience and universal will of man in his historical existence. It is opposed to classical Liberalism, which arose from the neccessity of reacting against absolutism, and which brought its historical purpose to an end when the State was transformed into the conscience and will of the people. Liberalism denied the State in the interests of the particular individual; Fascism reaffirms the State as the true reality of the individual. And if Liberty is to be the attribute of the real man, and not of that abstract puppet envisaged by individualistic Liberalism, Fascism is for liberty. And for the only liberty which can be a real thing, the liberty of the State, and of the individual within the state, and nothing human or spiritual exists, much less has value, outside the State. In this sense Fascism is totalitarian. . . .

The Fascist State, the highest and most powerful form of personality, is a force, but a spiritual force, which takes over all the forms of the moral and intellectual life of man. It cannot therefore confine itself simply to the functions of order and supervision as Liberalism desired. It is not simply a mechanism which limits the sphere of the supposed liberties of the individual. It is the form, the inner standard and the discipline of the whole person; it saturates the will as well as the intelligence. . . .

Fascism, in short, is not only the giver of laws and the founder of institutions, but the educator and promoter of spiritual life. It wants to remake, not the forms of human life, but its content, man, character, faith. And to this end it requires discipline and authority that can enter into the spirits of men and there govern unopposed. . . .

Source: B. Mussolini, "The Doctrine of Fascism" (1932), in M. Oakeshott, ed., *The Social and Political Doctrines of Contemporary Europe* (Cambridge: Cambridge University Press, 1939), pp. 166, 168.

Economic hardships were compounded by a crisis of national prestige. The Treaty of London (1915) that brought Italy into the war had committed the Allies to extensive territorial concessions for Italy, including the Trentino and southern Tirol, the port of Trieste, the Istrian peninsula, the Dalmatian coast, and the Dodecanese islands, which the Italians had occupied since 1912. But at the Paris peace conference Woodrow Wilson and Lloyd George not only gave Dalmatia to the new Yugoslav state but also refused to compensate Italy with the port city of Fiume, which Prime Minister Orlando demanded. The Italians felt betrayed, and a patriotic frenzy swept the country. Nationalists blamed Orlando's liberal government for what they termed the "mutilated victory," and Fiume became the symbol of Italy's frustrated hopes.

In September 1919 the nationalist writer and adventurer Gabriele D'Annunzio (1863–1938) invaded Fiume with a group of veterans and set up an independent state. Although the Italian government drove him out after a year, the Fiume adventure set a dangerous precedent for military coups and demonstrated the extent of nationalist sentiment. While he ruled Fiume, D'Annunzio adopted symbols and techniques that Mussolini later copied, including the Roman salute, fiery rhetoric, mass torch-lit rallies, and the title of *Duce* ("leader").

The frustration most Italians felt was directed against the liberal regime. In the postwar elections of November 1919, held on the basis of universal male suffrage, the liberals, who had enjoyed a large majority of seats in the Chamber of Deputies since the unification of Italy, suddenly found themselves reduced to the third-ranking party in Parliament, behind the Socialists and the Italian Popular Party, which combined progressive Catholic principles with demands for social and economic reform. The Socialists and Catholics together held enough seats to control the Chamber of Deputies, but each failed to form a coalition with the other, and King Victor Emmanuel III (1900–1946) continued to select his prime ministers from the ranks of the discredited liberals.

Against this background, industrial and agrarian unrest reached major proportions, with more than 1,600 strikes in 1919 alone. In the impoverished south, landless peasants led by veterans and socialists seized uncultivated land, and in September 1920 a major factory sit-in in the northern industrial centers threatened to develop into a revolution. This "occupation of the factories" helped push the industrialists into the arms of the Fascists.

Mussolini (left) leading the Fascist march on Rome in the fall of 1922. [Brown Brothers]

The Fascist Movement

In this tumultuous context Mussolini founded the Fascist movement. At a meeting of about 100 followers in Milan in March 1919, he established the first *Fascio di Combattimento* ("combat group"), a mixture of nationalist intellectuals, former socialists and syndicalists, and war veterans. The name of the movement was derived from the Latin word *fasces*, a bundle of rods tied around the shaft of an ax, which had been used by the ancient Romans to symbolize unity and authority. As Fascist groups spread throughout northern and central Italy, membership grew from less than 1,000 in the summer of 1919 to 20,000 by late 1920 and to more than 250,000 by 1922. The rank and file were veterans who sought to forge a sense of community based on the "spirit of the trenches"—comradeship, loyalty, bravery, and action. These alienated young men formed Mussolini's paramilitary squads, whose members came to be known as *Squadristi*. Their parades and rallies, black-shirted uniforms, and nihilistic slogans vividly symbolized Italy's postwar crisis.

The *Squadristi* unleashed a reign of terror across the nation under the command of local Fascist chieftains. They launched "punitive expeditions" against socialist and trade union offices, urban strikers, and peasant protesters. By 1921, in the aftermath of the factory occupations, the antisocialist campaign was bringing Fascism financial backing from industrialists and landowners, while the liberal government took no steps to halt Fascist violence. Fascist

Mussolini's Seizure of Power

In late 1924 Mussolini was accused by the opposition of having ordered a secret Fascist police to assassinate socialist deputy Giacomo Matteotti. After weeks of hesitation, during which pressure from both his enemies as well as from radical Fascist leaders mounted, he assumed full authority and declared a dictatorship in a speech on January 3, 1925.

It is I who in this chamber make accusations against myself. . . . If I had founded a secret police, I would have done so through the kind of violence that is an integral part of history. I have always said . . . that violence, to be effective, must be surgical, intelligent, and high-minded. . . .

I declare here, before the entire Chamber and before the Italian people, that I and I alone assume political, moral, and historical responsibility for everything that has happened.

If this surprising statement is sufficient to indict me, then bring forth the scaffolds! If Fascism has been only castor oil and clubs instead of the superb passion of Italy's best youth, the fault is mine. If Fascism has been a gang of criminals, then I am their leader.

If all the violence in this country has been the result of a special historical, moral, and political climate, I am responsible for that climate because I created it. . . .

When two elements are in inevitable conflict, the solution is force. History has never known another solution.

I tell you now that the problem will be solved. Fascism, the government, the party, are all in working order.

You are all under an illusion. You believed that Fascism was finished because I compromised it, but this is not at all the case. Italy wants peace, tranquility, and calm labor. We will give it these things, with love if possible, but with force if necessary.

Rest assured that within the next twenty-four hours the situation will be clarified in every way.

Source: E. Susmel and D. Susmel, eds., *Opera omnia di Benito Mussolini*, vol. 21 (Florence: La Fenice, 1953), pp. 235–241. Trans. P. V. Cannistraro.

assaults were extended to city halls and provincial officials and were followed by open threats to take over the state.

The March on Rome

While the Blackshirts' violent tactics weakened the Socialist party and created the impression that Fascism possessed a strength beyond its actual numbers, Mussolini maintained the profile of a respectable politician. In 1921 he signed a peace pact with the Socialists, which he promptly violated. That same year the Fascist movement, which had been converted into the National Fascist party (PNF), won 35 seats in Parliament. Mussolini now had the prestige of being a deputy. The Liberal premier, Giovanni Giolitti, sought to lure him into a coalition of moderate and conservative parties with offers of a ministerial post, hoping thereby to co-opt the Fascists into the established order. Like most other liberals, the premier failed to understand that Fascism was not a conventional political force.

In 1922 Mussolini marched on Rome to frighten the government into conceding power to Fascism. Between October 26 and 28, tens of thousands of Blackshirts moved toward the capital while Mussolini waited in his headquarters in Milan. King Victor Emmanuel III, uncertain of the army's loyalty and fearful of civil war, refused to sign a decree of martial law. On October 29 he asked Mussolini to become prime minister. Mussolini arrived in Rome the following day, dressed in top hat and tails, and took the oath of office. Only then did the Blackshirts enter Rome, but now to cheer Mussolini before the royal palace. The liberal state had collapsed in the face of a bluff.

Mussolini took office by legal means, but with only 35 Fascist deputies in a chamber of more than 500, he moved cautiously to consolidate his strength. Over the next year

Under the influence of these sources, Hitler became obsessed with the idea of race. He came to see Judaism and Marxism as twin forms of degeneracy and to identify the Jews as the principal source of moral and cultural decline and corruption in Europe. From Schönerer's pan-German ideology he concluded that Germany and Austria must be united into a "greater Germany," while Lüger's political success suggested that the key to a radical movement was the ability to generate and channel the enthusiasm of the masses.

When World War I broke out, Hitler volunteered in a Bavarian infantry regiment, for he considered himself a German. He fought at the front, was promoted to corporal, and was twice awarded the Iron Cross. The end of the war found him recuperating in a hospital from the effects of poison gas.

At the end of World War I, Hitler worked in Munich as a political informant for the army. In this capacity he joined a small group known as the German Worker's party, one of many such organizations that sought to stimulate German patriotism and infuse the working class with the spirit of nationalism. Hitler spent the next five years developing his political talents and leadership within the party. Like Mussolini, he had a natural oratorical ability and spoke frequently in public squares, in beer halls, and in the streets, expounding the views he had evolved in Vienna. He was unimpressive in appearance, yet he projected a personal magnetism that gripped a nation. To a far greater degree than Mussolini, Hitler had an uncanny ability to sway the masses and evoke worship. These qualities enabled the Nazi *Führer* ("leader") to convert his small group into a mass party.

In 1920 the German Workers' party was renamed the National Socialist German Workers' party (NSDAP), shortened in popular usage to "Nazi." It acquired its own newspaper, and its 25-point program called for a Greater Germany incorporating all German-speaking peoples, annulment of the Treaty of Versailles, denial of citizenship to Jews, and socioeconomic reforms to benefit the workers and the middle class. Although Hitler himself regarded the socialist provisions as propaganda, some Nazi leaders—such as Gregor and Otto Strasser—took them seriously.

The party also developed a paramilitary wing of storm troopers called the *Sturmabteilung* (SA), with its brown shirts and outstretched arm salute, "Heil Hitler!" greeting, and swastika symbol. Rallies, marches, songs, and banners provided the techniques that Hitler's propaganda machine later developed on a massive scale. The SA membership, like that of Mussolini's Blackshirt squads, consisted of disaffected veterans and Free Corps volunteers, rootless young men, and thugs and criminals. Ernst Röhm, the SA leader, believed that violence and terror would bring about the Nazi revolution.

In 1923 Hitler determined to seize power by force. Inspired by Mussolini's march on Rome, he planned a putsch in Munich with the connivance of local officials and the backing of a popular World War I general, Erich Ludendorff. On the evening of November 8 the Brownshirts surrounded a beer hall in which a political meeting was scheduled. Hitler rushed into the room, jumped onto a table, and fired a pistol in the air, shouting, "The National Socialist revolution has begun!" The putsch ended in fiasco the next day as the police scattered the participants and arrested Hitler. The abortive revolt brought Hitler a five-year prison term, of which he served less than nine months. In jail he wrote his famous testament *Mein Kampf* ("My Struggle"), outlining his racial theories, domestic policies, and plans for world conquest. He also concluded that violence alone would not assure the Nazi conquest of Germany and that the party must combine the legal methods of the election process with the violence advocated by Röhm and the SA.

After the failure of the Munich uprising, Röhm attempted to wrest control of the party from Hitler. Röhm wanted his SA, which he believed would be the instrument for the conquest of the state, to dominate the party. But in Hitler, who wanted to subordinate the SA to the party, Röhm met his match in duplicity. Using murder, blackmail, and slander to reassert his position, Hitler defeated Röhm, who went into exile in Bolivia in 1925. Hitler had become the undisputed leader of the movement.

The inner core of the Nazi leadership, attached to Hitler by bonds of loyalty and fear, began to take shape. The hierarchy included the gluttonous Hermann Göring, future air marshal; the tireless party organizer Rudolf Hess; the brilliant propagandist Joseph Goebbels; the rabid ideologue Alfred Rosenberg; and the chilling technocrat of police terror, Heinrich Himmler. The party also developed its organizational apparatus, creating youth groups and the infamous *Schutzstaffel* (SS), an elite defense corps later used in the mass exterminations of World War II. In 1929 Himmler took control of the SS and turned it into one of the principal instruments of Hitler's power. The black uniforms and death's-head insignia of the SS became synonymous with the Nazi terror state.

BERLIN, CAPITAL OF WEIMAR CULTURE

In contrast to the political and economic turmoil that beset the Weimar Republic, German cultural life between 1919 and 1933 was marked by a feverish brilliance. In theater, cinema, art, architecture, and literature, Germany exploded with a creative energy that was at once modern, experimental, and tormented. Berlin emerged as the center of Weimar's cultural ferment.

Little in Berlin's past suggested that it would be the center of a revolutionary culture. Founded in the thir-

The Nazi State

Although Hitler, like Mussolini, wanted an all-embracing totalitarian government, the Nazi state was to fulfill a special diabolical function—to form and propagate a "master race" that would dominate the world. Hitler explained his view in the pages of Mein Kampf, *which he dictated while in prison in 1925.*

The folkish [*völkisch*] philosophy finds the importance of mankind in its basic racial elements. In the state it sees in principle only a means to an end and construes its end as the preservation of the racial existence of man. Thus, it by no means believes in an equality of the races, but along with their difference it recognizes their higher or lesser values and feels itself obligated, through this knowledge, to promote the victory of the better and stronger, and demand the subordination of the inferior and weaker in accordance with the eternal will that dominates this universe. Thus, in principle, it serves the basic aristocratic idea of Nature and believes in the validity of this law down to the last individual. It sees not only the different value of the races, but also the different value of individuals. From the mass it extracts the importance of the individual personality, and thus, in contrast to disorganizing Marxism, it has an organizing effect. It believes in the necessity of an idealization of humanity, in which alone it sees the premise for the existence of humanity. But it cannot grant the right to existence even to an ethical idea if this idea represents a danger for the racial life of the bearers of a higher ethics. . . .

And so the folkish philosophy of life corresponds to the inner-most will of Nature, since it restores that free play of forces which must lead to a continuous mutual higher breeding, until at last the best of humanity, having achieved possession of this earth, will have a free path for activity in domains which lie partly above it and partly outside it.

We all sense that in that distant future humanity must be faced by problems which only a highest race, become master people and supported by the means and possibilities of an entire globe, will be equipped to overcome.

Source: A. Hitler, *Mein Kampf*, trans. R. Manheim (Boston: Houghton Mifflin, 1943), pp. 383–384.

teenth century along the east-west trade routes, the Hohenzollerns made it the capital of their Prussian domains in 1411. Berlin's importance grew as the ambitious dynasty extended its power, but culturally it remained a dull garrison town. Frederick the Great and his successors improved the appearance and cultural climate of the city by building an opera house, the Tiergarten Park, and Unter den Linden, a magnificent mile-long boulevard planted with lime trees and ending at the neoclassical Brandenburg Gate. Friedrich-Wilhelm University, opened in 1810, boasted the largest student body in Germany and attracted famous scholars that included J. G. Fichte, Georg Hegel, and the Grimm brothers. When Berlin became the capital of the Second Reich in 1871, it was already a city of some 825,000 inhabitants. The huge government bureaucracy and the teeming economic life of the German empire pushed its population to 2 million by the eve of World War I and made it the greatest industrial-commercial city on the Continent.

In 1919 Social Democrats Friedrich Ebert and Philip Scheidemann vied with Spartacists such as Rosa Luxemburg and Karl Liebknecht to seize the revolutionary initiative in Berlin. Although the Weimar Republic represented the triumph of the more moderate Social Democrats, postwar Berlin retained a hectic atmosphere. War, defeat, and revolution had combined to transform the grim solemnity that had once marked the capital into an irreverent spirit that made the city a mecca for young, talented Germans in search of a faster-paced, modern life. By the early 1920s restaurants, bathhouses, dance halls, and nightclubs—including the dozens of gay and lesbian bars described by British writer Christopher Isherwood in his *Berlin Stories*—gave the city a rowdy allure that rivaled even the attractions of Paris. American jazz became the rage, and the iconoclastic atmosphere also gave rise to a peculiar Berlin institution, cabarets in which political and social satire took the form of musical comedy. The air of unreality became starker in the aftermath of the terrible inflation

Nazism: The Philosophy of Domination

The Nazis viewed life—and therefore history—as a Darwinian struggle for existence in which the fittest triumphed over the weak. Hitler's call for German rearmament was therefore only the first step in a plan for world domination. Hitler preached his brutal message in a speech in Munich on March 15, 1929.

If men wish to live, then they are forced to kill others. The entire struggle for survival is a conquest of the means of existence which in turn results in the elimination of others from these same sources of subsistence. As long as there are peoples on this earth, there will be nations against nations. . . .

There is in reality no distinction between peace and war. Life, no matter in what form, is a process which always leads to the same result. Self-preservation will always be the goal of every individual. Struggle is ever-present and will remain. This signifies a consistent willingness on the part of man to sacrifice to the utmost. Weapons, methods, instruments, formations, these may change, but in the end the struggle for survival remains. . . .

One is either the hammer or the anvil. We confess that it is our purpose to prepare the German people again for the role of the hammer. For ten years we have preached, and our deepest concern is: How can we again achieve power? We admit freely and openly that, if our Movement is victorious, we will be concerned day and night with the question of how to produce the armed forces which are forbidden us by the peace treaty. We solemnly confess that we consider everyone a scoundrel who does not try day and night to figure out a way to violate this treaty, for we have never recognized this treaty. . . .

We confess further that we will dash anyone to pieces who should dare to hinder us in this undertaking. . . . Our rights will never be represented by others. Our rights will be protected only when the German Reich is again supported by the point of the German dagger.

Source: G. W. Prange, ed., *Hitler's Words* (Washington, D.C.: American Council on Public Affairs, 1944), pp. 10–11.

that struck in 1923 and put a quarter of a million Berliners out of work.

No artist better symbolized Berlin's cultural life than George Grosz (1893–1959). Drafted into the army in 1914, Grosz's hatred of authority had led to his court-martial for insubordination. In Berlin he was a founder of the German Dada movement and was active among the Expressionists. In 1919 he joined the Spartacists and designed illustrations for a communist publisher. Inspired by the bitter irony he saw in the cabarets, Grosz produced political drawings—in series such as *Ecce Homo* and *Café*—that satirized fat industrialists and war profiteers, Junkers, militarists, and corrupt politicians. Grosz gradually rejected Expressionism and joined other artists in the search for a "new objectivity." He continued to assault bourgeois standards of morality and relentlessly indicted the reactionary forces that dominated German society and politics. Grosz detested the Nazis and in 1923 executed a startlingly prescient drawing of a monocled officer with a swastika, the first of many anti-Nazi works depicting storm troopers and other symbols of the political reaction stalking Germany.

BERTOLT BRECHT AND THE THEATER OF COMMITMENT

Grosz's counterpart in theater was Bertolt Brecht (1898–1956), whose plays and poems explored the agony of human isolation and the dilemma of moral and political commitment. A pacifist repelled by the horrors of World War I, Brecht's first critical success came in 1922 with a play titled *Spartacus* (later renamed *Drums in the Night*),

In his stunning painting *Rain, Steam, and Speed: The Great Western Railway,* the English artist J. M. W. Turner used swirling colors to evoke a Romantic vision of a train churning across a bridge. A closer look reveals a rabbit racing ahead of the engine, a scene that symbolizes technology's threat to the environment. [1844, oil on canvas, 3′ × 4′ (91 × 122 cm.); National Gallery, London]

THE VISUAL EXPERIENCE

The Modern World

Artists have been simultaneously fascinated and repelled by the industrialization and technological achievements of the modern world. On the one hand, these developments have made possible improved transportation and communication, better medical care and diet, and physical comforts undreamed of by past societies. On the other hand, they have created the setting for totalitarian dictatorships and unparalleled human destruction even as they have failed to eradicate hunger and homelessness. Not suprisingly, artists have responded to these enigmas by exploring anew the age-old questions of human nature and our relationship to the world in which we live. No single work more fittingly evokes the common human experience than Henry Moore's *Family Group.*

The iron horse in Japan. Early Meiji woodblock artists were fascinated by the new railways, as most Japanese were intrigued with the artifacts of the modern West that flooded into their country. [Asian Art Museum of San Francisco]

William Prinseps' watercolor of the Calcutta waterfront in the early nineteenth century graphically illustrates the link between the old and the new. The small sampan-like boats in the foreground were used as barges to ferry goods to and from the oceangoing ships in the background, which usually had to anchor in deeper water in the Hooghly River. Note the completely European late-eighteenth-century architecture of the buildings. [Spinks & Sons Ltd., London]

Despite its dangerous potential, nationalism could be a constructive force. The meeting of Victor Emmanuel II and Garibaldi at Teano in 1861 was a major step in the process of Italian unification. [Scala/Art Resource]

The works of Gustave Courbet epitomized a new realism that reflected social commentary as well as an aesthetic departure from academic realism. Courbet focused not on the aristocracy and the bourgeoisie but on the proletariat, as in this painting, *The Stone Breakers,* which shows two men building a road. [1849, c. 63″ × c. 102″ (160 × 259 cm.); Oskar Reinhart Collection, Winterthur, Switzerland]

Cezanne's search for meaning led him to impose order on nature. He attempted, he once said, to "treat nature in terms of the cylinder, and the sphere, and the cone," an approach reflected in this painting of Mont Sainte-Victoire. [1905, oil on canvas; Giraudon/Art Resource]

Like Courbet, Pablo Picasso often painted humble people, but in increasingly abstract forms. In this work, the angular figures, three of whom wear African masks, were prostitutes on Avignon Street in Barcelona. Cezanne's interest in geometric forms was carried much farther by Picasso. [1907, oil on canvas, 8′ × 7′8″ (243.9 × 233.7 cm.). Collection, The Museum of Modern Art, New York. Acquired through the Lillie P. Bliss Bequest.]

This allegorical painting by American artist Peter Blume, titled *The Eternal City* (1934–1937), was intended as a bitter satire on Mussolini's claim that Rome would be the new capital of a glorious Fascist empire. Mussolini's head is the jack-in-the-box. [Oil on composition board, 34′ × 47′$\frac{7}{8}$″ (86.4 × 121.6 cm.). Collection, The Museum of Modern Art, New York: Mrs. Simon Guggenheim Fund.]

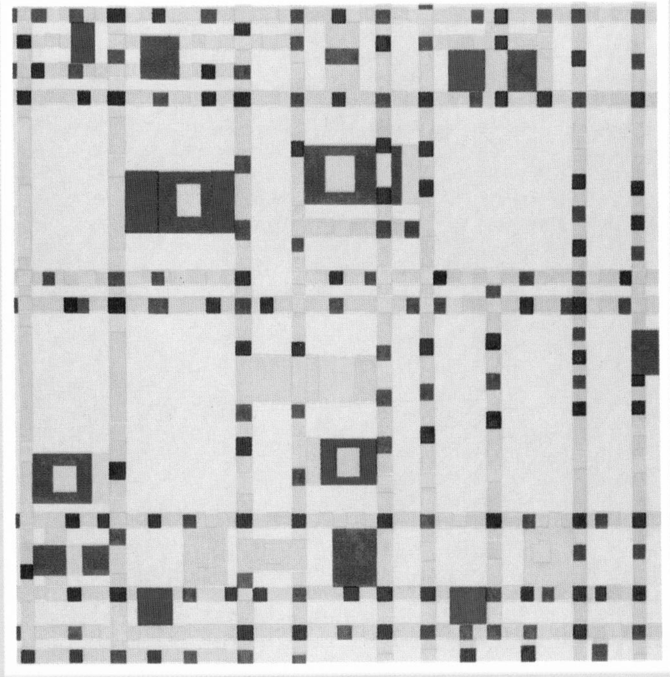

The Dutch painter Piet Mondrian was fascinated by the growth of modern urban centers such as New York City. "The new style," he predicted, "will spring from the metropolis"; its characteristics were broad planes of primary colors dissected by rigid horizontal and vertical lines. This, he claimed, was "pure reality." Shown here is his *Broadway Boogie-Woogie.* [Oil on canvas, 50 × 50″ (127 × 127 cm.). Collection, The Museum of Modern Art, New York.]

No modern artist more effectively merged the classical Western sculptural tradition of Donatello and Michelangelo with the styles of Africa and Latin America, Oceana and the Etruscans, than Henry Moore. His absorption with the human form—as in this sculpture, *Family Group*—stems from his belief in its dignity. [Bronze, $59\frac{1}{4}$ × $46\frac{1}{2}$ × $29\frac{1}{4}$″ (150.5 × 118 × 75.9 cm.). Collection, The Museum of Modern Art, New York; A. Conger Goodyear Fund.]

If Mondrian embraced the great metropolises, the American artist Andy Warhol not only made peace with their blatant commercialism but capitalized on it, in part with his portraits of cinematic and political celebrities. Here he portrays the Chinese revolutionary Mao Tse-tung, a hero of the radical left in the 1960s. [1973; Bruce C. Jones/Leo Castelli Gallery]

One of the leaders of the reaction against abstractionism was Jasper Johns, who, beginning in the 1950s, made distinctive studies of such commonplace objects as beer cans, toothbrushes, and the American flag. His *Target with Four Faces* was completed in 1955. [Collection, The Museum of Modern Art, New York; gift of Mr. and Mrs. Robert C. Scull]

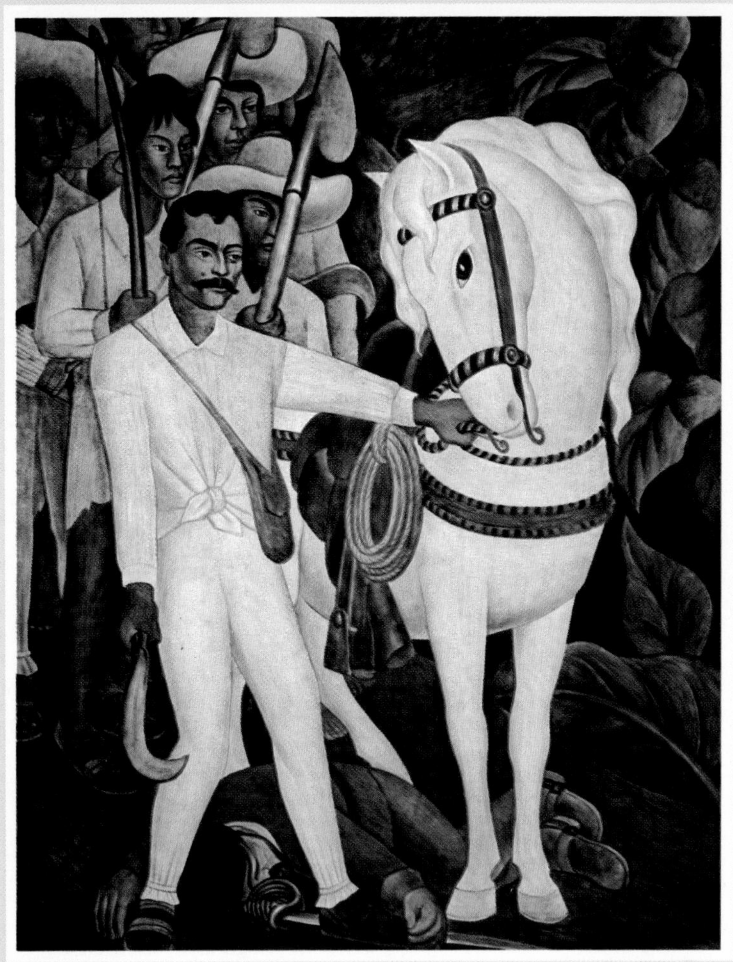

The Mexican painter Diego Rivera, having studied both classical Italian frescoes and Picasso's cubist paintings, developed his own lyrical style in murals featuring the proletariat. Among his best work is this fresco titled *Agrarian Leader Zapata,* which depicts a rebel in the Mexican revolution who seized haciendas and distributed the land to the poor. [7′9$\frac{3}{4}$″ × 6′2″ (238.1 × 188 cm.). Collection, The Museum of Modern Art, New York; Abby Aldrich Rockefeller Fund.]

In both the Soviet Union and the People's Republic of China, efforts were made to encourage "socialist realism" in art. This slightly idealized but traditional-style Chinese painting depicts a new oil refinery complex. [Shio-yun Ken and Anna Merton, London]

A detail from one of George Grosz's satiric drawings contrasts sober working men with partying "fat cats." [Bildarchiv Preussischer Kulturbesitz]

about a veteran who chose a comfortable life instead of joining the Spartacist uprising.

In 1924 Brecht moved to Berlin, where theatrical producers quickly recognized his genius. Before long he was writing for Max Reinhardt's experimental Deutsches Theater and collaborating with the composer Kurt Weill. In his plays as in his personal life, he struggled to detach himself from the irrationality of violence, sex, and aggression and strove to understand how modern society transformed individuals into groups. In *Man Is Man* (1927), he recognized the powerful forces at work in Germany as he described how a worker had been changed into a bloodthirsty soldier.

After 1929, Brecht's work revealed a growing commitment to Marxism, which he believed to be the only solution to the nihilism of his age. But he saw Marxism as a scientific method of analysis, not as a faith. *The Three Penny Opera* (1928) expressed his cynical distaste for bourgeois materialism by taunting his audiences for their gluttonous appetites and lack of ethical values. Under the growing influence of the German Communist party, Brecht shifted to an austere didactic style. His rigorously controlled language and aesthetic precision urged self-discipline and self-denial in the interests of mankind—he was, he said, interested in the ideas his characters represented rather than in the characters themselves. These influences led him to the development of the Epic Theater, in which plays were conceived on a grand scale and the audience kept at a distance through the use of signs, posters, and light.

In 1932 his full-length play *St. Joan of the Stockyards*—based in part on Upton Sinclair's novel *The Jungle*—depicted the Great Depression as the story of greedy speculation in the Chicago stock market. Despite his Marxism, Brecht never made himself a blind servant of party discipline. *The Measures Adopted* (1930) brought criticism from German Communist officials because he depicted the murder of a young comrade by party militants. He refused to dramatize revolutionary events, believing that "to requisition the theatre for the purposes of the class struggle is to endanger the true revolutionizing of the theatre."[2]

Darker forces began to encircle Brecht in the early 1930s. The air of creative genius that had given Berlin's cultural life its brilliance seemed unreal in the midst of the Great Depression, which by 1932 had raised unemployment in the city to 636,000. The ironic contrast between Berlin's cabaret culture and Germany's political realities grew sharper as Hitler's storm troopers spread violence and bloodshed. Brecht left Berlin in 1933, living for several years in Denmark and traveling in Europe before emigrating to the United States. He earned a precarious living working on film scripts in Hollywood and on plays in New York. Even after the war, trouble followed him. In 1947 the House Committee on Un-American Activities called him to testify in its investigation of communism in Hollywood.

The day after his testimony, Brecht returned to Europe. He supported the communist German Democratic Republic and worked during his last years for the revived Berliner Ensemble; he was an honored but controversial figure who kept his independence to the end.

The Nazi Seizure of Power

At first the Nazi party's electoral prospects were not promising. When the economy began to recover in 1924, the Weimar Republic's political instability seemed to abate. The next year the country elected a new president, the revered Field Marshal Paul von Hindenburg (1847–1934), who provided middle class Germans with a sense of security. Although Nazi membership increased in 1925 from 27,000 to 178,000 in 1929, the number of Nazi deputies in the Reichstag fell from 32 to 12. By the end of the decade the future of National Socialism was by no means clear. It required the economic shock of the Great Depression to create the mass base Hitler needed to seize power.

No other country suffered greater hardship as a result of the Great Depression than Germany—by 1932 production had fallen by 39 percent and unemployment hit 6 million. The economic collapse encouraged the rapid rise of extremist movements. Although other factors enhanced the appeal of Nazism to many Germans, the severe hardship and pervasive fear generated by the financial crisis produced the ideal environment for Nazi success. The depression polarized German politics. In parliamentary elections held between 1929 and 1932, Nazi representation rose to 230 seats, while the Communist delegation increased from 54 to 89. Moderate elements stepped aside as these two sworn enemies battled physically in the

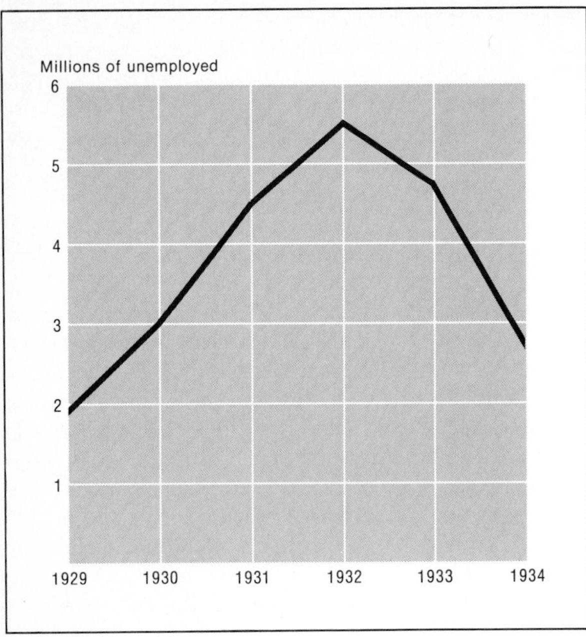

36.1 Unemployment in Germany, 1929–1934

streets and meeting halls and verbally in speeches, posters, and handbills. When the 85-year-old Hindenburg decided to run for a second term as president in 1932, Hitler and Communist leader Ernst Thälmann opposed him. Hindenburg and Hitler faced each other in a runoff, but although the now senile field marshal won, Hitler had received more than 13 million votes. The Nazis slipped to 196 seats in the November 1932 elections as the Communists raised their total to 100, encouraging some to believe that the radical left would assume control of a government that was helpless in the midst of economic, political, and social chaos.

Hitler's followers urged him to seize control of the government forcibly in a coup d'état, while conservative antidemocratic forces—aristocratic landowners, army officers, industrialists, wealthy merchants, and financiers—were both terrified at the prospect of a Communist victory and attracted to Hitler's nationalist slogans. Hoping to manipulate him to stem mass discontent and advance their own interests, some began supplying funds to the Nazis.

On January 30, 1933, Hindenburg, fearful of civil war and pressured by his advisers, appointed Hitler chancellor of the German Republic. The new Nazi-dominated cabinet included some members of the Nationalist party. Hitler promptly dissolved the Reichstag and called for new elections, but the parliament building was destroyed in a fire of unknown origin. The Nazis blamed the Communists and conducted the balloting in an atmosphere of anti-Communist hysteria and intimidation. Although the Nazis won only 44 percent of the vote, their Nationalist partners added another 8 percent to give the coalition a legislative majority. Declaring a national emergency, Hitler expelled the Communist deputies from the Reichstag, which then voted him dictatorial powers for four years. After using this authority to outlaw all other political parties, he completed the transition from democracy to dictatorship when he combined the office of president with that of chancellor following the death of Hindenburg in August 1934. Hitler destroyed the short-lived Weimar Republic and became

A group of young Nazis confiscating books to be taken to the Operplatz in Berlin for burning in May of 1933. [UPI/Bettmann Newsphotos]

Hitler as Demagogue

Hitler was unequaled as a public speaker. His ability to hold huge numbers of people in his spell, to arouse their passions and whip them into a frenzy of adulation, made him a master of political demagogy. Although he was a skillful actor on the political platform, his charisma also derived from his conviction of his own destiny. Konrad Heiden, who witnessed many of Hitler's public speeches, provides a vivid description of his ability to sway audiences.

Hitler's special trait is his concentration on greatness. This is the source of his power. When suddenly this man, who has been awkwardly standing around, now and then muttering a remark that by no means dominates the conversation, is seized with determination and begins to speak, filling the room with his voice, suppressing interruptions or contradictions by his domineering manner, spreading cold shivers among those present by the savagery of his declarations, lifting every subject of conversation into the light of history, and interpreting it so that even trifles have their origin in greatness; then the listener is filled with awe and feels that a new phenomenon has entered the room. This thundering demon was not there before; this is not the same timid man with the contracted shoulders. He is capable of this transformation in a personal interview and facing an audience of half a million. The magic power of this image of greatness emanating from human nullity greatly appealed to the German people after the World War, when this people, oppressed by their own nullity, longed for greatness; but a far deeper and more decisive explanation of Hitler's effect is the soul state of modern man, who, in his pettiness, loneliness, and lack of faith, longs for community, conviction, and greatness. Here he sees greatness emerging from a creature who as a man is smaller than you or I—that is what made Hitler an experience for millions.

Source: K. Heiden, *Der Führer: Hitler's Rise to Power* (Boston: Houghton Mifflin, 1944), pp. 377–378.

the unchallenged ruler of a Germany that was anxious to restore its economy and regain its place in international affairs.

Fascism as a World Phenomenon

In the years after 1919 it appeared to many Europeans that the world was rapidly being divided into two antagonistic systems—communism and fascism. In every European country a struggle unfolded between left and right, between "revolution" and "reaction," that ultimately polarized around these extreme ideologies. Because of their long-range consequences, Italian Fascism and German Nazism were the most serious instances of the triumph of the right in this struggle. But no European nation escaped the trauma of ideological divisiveness or the specter of fascist radicalism. Societies as advanced as Britain's and as underdeveloped as Romania's experienced their own peculiar brands of fascism: in each state segments of the population looked to extreme solutions for seemingly unmanageable problems.

Varieties of European Fascism

In the strongholds of liberal democracy, France and Britain, fascism was not a genuine threat to the established order, for right-wing movements failed to establish a mass base. But France produced fascistlike political groups that challenged the country's democratic tradition: radical "leagues" proliferated in the 1920s and 1930s, some of which modeled themselves after Mussolini's or Hitler's example—the *Jeunesses patriotes* ("Patriotic Youth"), for instance, and the infamous CSAR, or *Cagoulards* ("Hooded Men"). During the depression the *Parti populaire français* ("French Popular Party") had perhaps as many as a half million members, but it was unable to unify the right. France also produced more traditional conservative movements that capitalized on nationalism and adopted antidemocratic, anti-Semitic principles. Such groups included

Charles Maurras' *Action française* ("French Action") and Colonel de la Rocque's veterans' movement, the *Croix de feu* ("Cross of Fire").

In Britain as well, where Mussolini was a popular figure in the 1920s, fascist organizations were established. In the early 1930s the wealthy aristocrat Sir Oswald Mosley founded the British Union of Fascists. An admirer of Mussolini, Mosley modeled his union, a band of armed thugs, on the Blackshirts. Like Hitler, to whom he gravitated after 1933, Mosley dreamed of a "Greater Britain" in which all citizens were integrated into a regimented society to revive national glory. Mosley's advocacy of political violence resulted in the outlawing of the movement, and during World War II he was imprisoned.

In Spain, where the struggle between right and left was largely the result of a government unable to solve national problems, a military dictatorship under Miguel Primo de Rivera (1870–1930) emerged after 1923. His son, José António Primo de Rivera, created a fascist movement called the *Falange*. In the mid-1930s Spain became the bloody battleground in the conflict between communism and fascism. The Spanish civil war was marked by the military intervention of Hitler and Mussolini on the fascist side as well as that of the Soviet Union on the side of the republican government, and ended with the installation of the dictatorship of General Francisco Franco.

Other varieties of fascism developed in Belgium, Romania, and Austria. In Belgium, a nation bitterly divided between Dutch- and French-speaking ethnic groups, the Rexist movement of Léon Degrelle aimed at national unification in a spiritual and racial sense. A different form of fascism developed in Romania, an agrarian society with a strong Orthodox tradition rooted in peasant society. There Corneliu Codreanu's Iron Guard movement appealed to the traditional associations of soil and religion. In Austria two armed organizations, the urban Social Democratic *Schutzbund* ("Alliance for Defense") and the rural Christian Socialist *Heimwehr* ("Home Guard"), vied with each other and with the Austrian Nazi party. Led by Prince von Starhemberg, the reactionary *Heimwehr* opposed democracy as bitterly as it did Hitler's attempts to Nazify the country. Under the Austrian chancellor, Engelbert Dollfuss, the *Heimwehr* was given representation in the government, which forged a "Fatherland Front" to block the union (*Anschluss*) of Austria and Germany. These movements, together with the Nazis, gained ground with the assassination of Dollfuss in 1934.

Fascism in Asia

Whether or not European fascism had counterparts elsewhere in the world is problematic. In the 1930s there appeared to be at least superficial evidence to justify Mussolini's prediction that fascism would be the dominant political philosophy of the twentieth century, for admirers of fascism were to be found the world over. Demagogues who modeled themselves after Mussolini and Hitler were so popular in the United States that Anne Morrow Lindbergh, wife of the famous aviator Charles Lindbergh, spoke of fascism as "the wave of the future." In India and the Arab countries of the Middle East some nationalist leaders gravitated to fascism in the hope that it would lead to independence from colonial rule. Fascist influence may even have inspired a group of radical army officers in China to establish the so-called Blue Shirts (more properly, the "Cotton Cloth People"), although their militaristic, authoritarian program was little more than a variant of the nation-building doctrine of the Kuomintang regime of Chiang Kai-shek, itself often called fascist.

The most compelling evidence may have been in Japan, where as early as 1934 Marxist writers identified the authoritarian, militaristic, expansionist tendencies of the country as a form of fascism. The code of the samurai and emperor worship also suggest that the roots of a native fascism were to be found in Japanese history. Young army officers and small ultranationalist groups pressed for radical changes in politics and the economy, and the leading nationalist ideologue of the period, Kita Ikki (1883–1937), seemed to be a Japanese counterpart of Mussolini. Kita was a former Marxist socialist who called for nationalization of some industries, state regulation of the economy, authoritarian government under the emperor, and the creation of a greater East Asian empire. Yet unlike Italian Fascism or German Nazism, none of the Japanese groups became a significant party or movement capable of seizing power, and Japan's constitution and political system remained largely unchanged. When Kita Ikki and some of his followers staged a revolt in Tokyo in 1936, they were rounded up and executed. The continuity of Japan's political and cultural traditions proved stronger and more entrenched than the new fascistlike ferment. Moreover, the military aggression of the 1930s was not due to an indigenous Japanese fascism but was rather the result of a broad nationalist consensus in favor of expansion among Japan's traditional political and military leaders.

Brazil's Estado Novo

In Latin America fascistlike military dictatorships were widespread in the years between the wars. The rule of Getulio Vargas (1883–1954) in Brazil offers the best example of a regime strongly influenced by European fascism but shaped largely by local conditions.

The Brazilian republic, founded by the military in 1889 when the emperor Dom Pedro II was overthrown, had proved itself unable to deal with problems of national development. The federal government, in effect a federation of autonomous states, was weakened by regionalism and the power of local bosses. Because the agrarian economy rested largely on coffee production, the conservative plan-

Although technically not a fascist government, Brazilian dictator Getulio Vargas' Estado Novo bore close similarities to the Italian Fascist state. [UPI/Bettmann Newsphotos]

tation owners dominated Brazil's society and its politics. Poverty and illiteracy afflicted the rural population, while the government repressed the labor movement. Only the small Brazilian middle class, represented chiefy by intellectuals and a group of young military officers known as the *tenentes*, wanted industrialization and agrarian reform.

The Great Depression, which ruined the coffee market and made it impossible for the government to repay its staggering foreign debts, brought down the republic. In October 1930 a military coup suspended the legislature and put Vargas in power as provisional president. He was to rule Brazil, with one interval, for almost 20 years.

Vargas came from a wealthy ranching family in the state of Rio Grande do Sul and had run unsuccessfully for president. Vargas had few interests in life other than acquiring and exercising power. A shrewd leader, his enemies denounced him as an unprincipled dictator while his followers revered him as the "father of the poor."

Vargas strengthened the central government by virtually destroying state autonomy. He tried to create worker consensus through labor legislation and government-controlled unions while simultaneously encouraging the development of a strong middle class. Vargas stimulated the economy by diversifying agriculture, limiting coffee production, and extending tax incentives and government loans to business. Like Mussolini, Vargas expanded his personal power by balancing the conflicting economic and political interests that dominated the country. The left-wing *tenentes* pushed for basic reforms, while the conservatives, resenting his centralization efforts and alarmed by his economic reforms, made an unsuccessful attempt to seize power. On the surface, his reforms seemed to point the way toward greater democracy and social justice—the electorate was expanded and given the secret ballot, women received the vote, social security laws and educational reforms were enacted, and labor unions were formed. In 1934 Vargas pushed through a new constitution that reduced state autonomy and established government authority over the economy. The new Chamber of Deputies reflected Mussolini's corporatist doctrine by providing for the election of representatives not only by population and area but also by class and profession. The Chamber appointed Vargas president for a four-year term.

Vargas thereupon shifted to the right. He gradually stripped the *tenentes* of their influence and suppressed the National Liberation Alliance, a popular-front coalition dominated by the communists. At the same time, he encouraged the growth of *Integralismo*, a fascist movement secretly financed by Mussolini. The Integralists, who adopted green-shirted uniforms and a paramilitary organization, railed against democracy, communism, and Jews while preaching rabid nationalism and "Christian virtues."

Vargas could not succeed himself as president, but as the 1937 elections approached, he dropped all pretense of constitutional rule. Claiming that the army had uncovered a communist plot, he canceled the elections and assumed dictatorial power in November. From 1937 to 1945 Vargas ruled Brazil under the *Estado Novo* ("new state"), a totalitarian government that strongly resembled European fascist regimes. The Estado Novo abolished political parties, imposed rigid censorship, established a special police force to combat "enemies of the state," and filled the prisons with political dissidents. Vargas offered Salgado, the Integralist leader, a cabinet post.

Although Vargas did not attempt the kind of mass mobilization that Mussolini and Hitler had undertaken, he denounced democracy as "decadent" and courted the workers with populist rhetoric. Vargas permitted no alternate sources of power to exist—in 1938 he banned all paramilitary groups, and when the Integralists tried to seize power, he crushed them.

The economic policies of the Estado Novo revealed an affinity to Mussolini's fascist programs. Vargas banned both strikes and lockouts and joined labor laws into a single code that stripped workers of the right to organize independently of the government. The regime set wages and hours, but although industrial workers benefited from some legislation, Vargas appeased the landowners by excluding agricultural workers from the new laws. He succeeded in industrializing Brazil through a policy of economic planning and government investment in development ventures that combined public and private ownership. State technocrats expanded and rationalized Brazilian business, while Vargas preached an economic nationalism designed to free Brazil from dependency on foreign capital. In the end Vargas succeeded too well—he had forced Brazil through a period of rapid social change and economic modernization, and his efforts eventually antagonized the traditional elites as well as his supporters.

During World War II, Vargas attempted to liberalize his regime, but in 1945 the army deposed him in a bloodless coup. Vargas, who kept his popularity among Brazilians, was elected president in 1950. Four years later, when the army tried to force him out of office again, he committed suicide.

The Estado Novo in Brazil, as well as other fascistlike regimes, demonstrates that fascism can be regarded not only as a political movement in individual countries but also as a model for resolving social and economic problems. The spread of the Industrial Revolution and its alteration of traditional society created immense tensions. In such cases fascism was seen as either a means for speeding up the pace of modernization or a method whereby old power elites could retain their authority and status. On still another level, fascism provided an example of how expanded government authority could alter the nature of society. Fascism offered new and brutally direct methods for social organization and control.

While fascism may have been a response to these problems, the question remains why it was so appealing and why it succeeded in some cases in destroying its liberal enemy. In Italy and Germany the answer seems clear. Liberalism was in crisis at the end of World War I in Italy and poorly rooted in Germany, and traditional leaders were incapable of understanding both the new social forces unleashed by the war and the fascist response. On a more general level, the success of fascism was due to the fear and despair among people whose lives and values were threatened by economic collapse and loss of social status. This sense of desperation that led ordinary people to join fascist movements is aptly expressed in the title of the 1932 novel by the German author Hans Fallada, *Little Man, What Now?*

The Great Depression and the Crisis of Capitalism

By the eve of World War I the capitalist system had grown complex and global in scope. In theory, a free international market set the prices of most basic commodities, although imperialism had long since made the law of supply and demand obsolete in many sectors of the world economy. Moreover, some regions enjoyed special status as the sole producers of specific items sold to the rest of the world. Traditionally, industry and commerce were financed through a system of credit resting on the assumption that lenders or investors could collect the money owed them and that borrowers could earn enough income to repay their loans while continuing to purchase agricultural or industrial products. It was a resilient system, having weathered numerous financial crises—what today might be termed recessions—prior to 1914. But the crisis that erupted in 1929 and lasted in some respects until the outbreak of World War II was more than simply an adjustment in the world economy. Along with major changes in economic theory and practice, it brought untold suffering to millions and raised serious doubts about the viability of capitalism and the liberal political systems on which it rested.

The Economic Collapse

After an initial postwar slump, the 1920s exhibited a surge of economic vitality that brought prosperity to more people than ever before. Much of this growth derived from international trade, construction, and the development of new industries such as the automobile, radio, and motion pictures. While many people believed that the prosperity would last forever, the economic expansion had been financed largely by personal, corporate, and international credit—a shaky foundation whose flaws were exposed in the October 1929 stock market crash. Securities purchases relied heavily on margin trading, whereby investors bought stocks and bonds by putting up only a fraction of the purchase price; the remainder was borrowed from brokers, who in turn obtained credit from banks. Such unregulated practices led to widespread speculation in stocks, whose market value was often many times higher than their actual worth. With installment credit readily available, consumers were encouraged to buy houses, automobiles, and other major items without having the cash to pay for them. Here, too, retailers and wholesalers borrowed funds from banks to pay their suppliers. Manufacturers, in turn, easily obtained credit for plant expansion, and small nations received foreign loans far beyond their ability to repay. If one link in this credit chain suddenly demanded immediate repayment, the others would be forced to produce large amounts of cash to meet their debt obligations.

The availability of easy credit concealed other serious flaws in the post–World War I economy. The new prosperity was not evenly distributed, for profits far surpassed wages for nearly all working people, and farm prices continued to lag far behind those charged for manufactured goods and basic services. Consequently, despite the abundance of credit, mass purchasing power based on solid financial ground never really existed. Furthermore, the economic optimism of the day resulted in high levels of production and huge inventories, with the possibility that unsold goods could force cutbacks and eventual job layoffs. On the international level, the appearance of new states in central and eastern Europe introduced further volatility into the world economy. Since the economies of these states were immature and their finances precarious, their

Anxious crowds gather outside the New York Stock Exchange in October 1929, following the crash. [UPI/Bettmann Newsphotos]

vulnerability to credit difficulties weakened the global economy in times of trouble.

Strictly speaking, the Great Depression began with the financial collapse touched off by the sudden deflation of the New York Stock Exchange in October 1929. In reality, the world agrarian sector had already been experiencing severe hardship as the prices of basic agricultural goods followed an unchecked downward spiral. The stock market crash produced a sudden rush by creditors to call in loans at all levels, and the consequent failure of a major European lender (Austria's *Creditanstalt*) in 1931 gave the crisis an international dimension. The panic soon passed to industry, and even large corporations were forced to halt production as the markets for their goods dried up. By 1933 world production had declined 38 percent and world trade had dropped to one-third its pre-1929 level. When farmers who had escaped previous difficulties were hit by the lack of credit and customers, the collapse of the modern capitalist economy appeared complete.

The resulting Great Depression caused mass suffering, desperation, and fear to an extent hitherto unknown in the modern West. Unemployment reached epidemic proportions—Great Britain reported 3 million unemployed in 1933, Germany 6 million, and the United States 13 million. Worldwide, some 30 million people were without jobs when the depression reached its depth in 1932. People living on fixed incomes or running marginal businesses saw their savings disappear, often literally overnight. Skilled and productive employees were reduced to supporting families on what meager welfare was available. As the depression dragged on, demoralization turned to frustration and resentment. Families disintegrated, suicides rose dramatically, and the very fabric of society seemed torn apart.

Government Response

Nations dealt with the crisis in various ways. The reactions of Britain, France, Germany, Italy, the United States, and the Soviet Union are considered elsewhere in this and the following chapters, but some general observations will prove useful here.

At first governments pursued deflationary policies that made the problem worse but then switched to pump-priming strategies, including deficit spending, in order to stimulate economic revival. All states, whether democratic or totalitarian, undertook measures to generate work for their citizens and limit the economic hardship as much as possible: public works programs, spending cuts, currency controls, and tariffs were among the most widespread efforts. Governments assumed a greater degree of control over economic and social life than ever before as they attempted to come to grips with the immediate consequences of the economic collapse and its long-range implications.

The Great Depression affected the future in ways that were not immediately apparent but had a lasting impact. What had once been an integrated world economy disintegrated into highly competitive national economic systems. Economic competition bred distrust between countries and fostered a spirit of nationalism that shattered postwar dreams of international cooperation. Extremist political movements that promised quick solutions to the crisis spread rapidly. While representative government survived in long-established Western democracies, even France, Britain, and the United States experienced profound trauma that altered their political and social traditions.

Britain, France, and the United States: The Trial of Democracy

The Great Depression challenged liberal democratic systems, yet the problems facing each of the three major democracies were unique. Common to Britain, France, and the United States, however, were an extension of state welfare measures, stronger government control over the economy, and the basic survival of democratic institutions.

Politics and Society

After 1919 Britain had to cope with a serious economic slump brought about by the end of the war and the reorientation of the global economy. In the 1920s British governments, led in succession by the Liberals, Conservatives, and finally by the Labour party, grappled with two closely related issues: chronic unemployment—18.5 percent between 1930 and 1935—and a growing deficit produced in part by social welfare programs. Despite serious labor unrest, most notably a 1926 coal miners' work stoppage that grew into a full-fledged general strike, in periods of severe crisis the Labourites and the Conservatives tended toward ideological convergence. Moreover, the currency policies of successive governments sheltered the British population, particularly its middle class, from the devastating inflationary cycles that ruined other countries.

The postwar period in the United States saw the economic boom of the so-called Roaring Twenties, especially in the construction and automobile industries, and America became obsessed with material success. Under Republican presidents Warren G. Harding (1921–1923) and Calvin Coolidge (1923–1929), the country pursued a "return to normalcy" that aimed at a nostalgic re-creation of the atmosphere of the prewar era. Although Americans were suspicious of foreign political entanglements, government policies spread U.S. economic influence into Latin America and the Pacific. The labor movement found organized action increasingly difficult in the face of government hostility, and the rapid economic growth that produced nearly full employment and better wages undercut the appeal of unions. Only farmers seemed excluded from the prosperity. Facing declining prices and rising costs well before the depression, farmers received little support from the government, and hard times had begun to grip rural America in the early 1920s.

The difficulties experienced by the farmer were often obscured by the glare of Jazz Age life in the big cities. Despite the Eighteenth Amendment to the U.S. constitution, which introduced Prohibition, popular culture was indulgent and iconoclastic. Flashy automobiles, speakeasies, gangster heroes such as Al Capone, and "flappers"—women who wore flimsy dresses and led uninhibited lives—became symbols of America's frenzied modernism, while the election of Republican president Herbert Hoover (1929–1933) epitomized the belief in uninterrupted prosperity.

Aside from the contrasting tone of life in Britain and the United States, both represented relatively stable political states with two-party systems. In France, by contrast, chronic instability had long appeared to be the rule. This was due in part to the tremendous financial investment needed to rebuild the economy after the wartime destruction the country had suffered. Successive cabinets advanced—and then under fierce opposition retreated from—plans for tax increases and other measures designed to finance reconstruction. The result was a large deficit and a serious inflationary spiral. In addition, the electoral system, based on proportional representation, stimulated political factionalism with a multiparty system that necessitated coalition government.

One of the few islands of stability in the period came with the "government of national union" formed in 1926 by Raymond Poincaré (1860–1934). A careful and temperate man, Poincaré governed for three years, during which time he restored a measure of equilibrium to the country. He stabilized the franc, halted the deficit spending programs of previous administrations, and introduced social legislation that rejuvenated the economy and eased social tensions. As living standards improved by the end of the decade, France reestablished its reputation for cultural leadership. Although Paris again became a thriving center of avant-garde artists and writers, its fame in the 1920s rested largely on its large colony of brilliant expatriates, which included the writers James Joyce, Ernest Hemingway, and Gertrude Stein.

Toward the Welfare State

The Great Depression shattered the complacency that had permeated life in the three major democracies. Britain, with the apparatus of the modern welfare state well in place by 1930, endured the economic crisis with the least shock to its political system. British Labour prime minister Ramsey MacDonald (1929–1935) converted his cabinet into a national coalition government in 1931 to eliminate partisan policy disputes. He reduced unemployment compensation in 1931 and sought to stimulate economic recovery by raising taxes, reducing the budget, lowering interest rates, and changing currency and tariff policies. The Conservative governments that followed under Stanley Baldwin (1935–1937) and Neville Chamberlain (1937–1940) continued this approach. Britain weathered the crisis and experienced an economic revival in the late 1930s, based largely on the continued low prices of raw materials from abroad. However, conditions in northern England, Scotland, and Wales remained far more depressed than in the south, encouraging a flight of capital and population from what had once been Britain's industrial heartland that has continued ever since.

Although unemployment in France was not as severe as in other countries, the depression had a critical impact on the country's political system. The government failed to deal effectively with the economic collapse, so as prosperity disappeared after 1932, political tensions resurfaced. The radical right in particular posed such a serious threat that the socialists, communists, and other leftist elements formed a coalition government under socialist Léon Blum (1936–1937), the so-called Popular Front. Social reforms aimed chiefly at the working and lower classes appeared to reduce social stress, but concerted resistance from the financial and business communities halted the recovery program. By the end of the decade France was economically worse off, more bitterly divided, and more politically unstable than any other leading European power.

The United States underwent the greatest transformation as a result of the depression. Firmly committed to the principles of a free enterprise market economy, the Hoover administration did little to halt the financial collapse of the stock market. By 1932 unemployment had reached 25 percent. Yet the mounting despair of the American people, who increasingly demanded action, did not turn against the fundamental principles of the economic and political system. Hence, when Democrat Franklin D. Roosevelt (1933–1945) was elected president by a large majority, he assumed he had received a mandate for fundamental change that would reform capitalism in order to save it.

Roosevelt rejected both socialism and fascism in favor of forceful intervention by the federal government in economic life. Along with regulating the economy and stimulating business recovery through deficit spending, Roosevelt's New Deal introduced several basic social welfare programs. The result was a resurgence of industrial, commercial, and agricultural activity that, while never attaining predepression levels, stimulated significant recovery and partially cushioned the impact of the economic crisis. By 1938, when deficit spending was reduced, a recession had set in, and it required the massive production needs of World War II to pull the nation completely out of its economic slump. Some critics accused Roosevelt of introducing socialism or fascism. Yet except for persistent unemployment, the economic turnabout his policies induced was so successful that most Americans were willing to accept them.

The United States, Britain, and France thus retained both the form and essence of their democratic systems in the face of severe trials. Although fascistlike demagogues developed followings in all three countries, their citizens did not succumb to dictatorship.

President Franklin D. Roosevelt inaugurated major changes in America's economic and social life. [UPI/Bettmann Newsphotos]

Central and Eastern Europe

The strength of liberal institutions in the United States and western Europe was not duplicated in most of eastern Europe. New states had arisen after 1919 out of the remnants of the shattered German, Austro-Hungarian, Russian, and Ottoman empires. These "successor states" were Poland, Czechoslovakia, Yugoslavia, Hungary, Austria, Turkey, and the Baltic republics of Estonia, Latvia, and Lithuania. In these nations democracy proved less resistant to the political and economic stress of the postwar period.

The Successor States

Together with the already independent countries of Bulgaria, Greece, Romania, and Albania, the successor states formed a bastion of small nations in the strategic heartland of Europe. They were governed either by constitutional monarchies with representative institutions or by republican systems modeled after Western democracies. The new democracies were considered important in London and Paris as barriers against the spread of communism and the revival of German power. Most of these states eventually abandoned democracy for authoritarian dictatorship. Although a genuinely fascist regime never ruled in any of these nations prior to World War II, the reactionary right came to dominate the political and economic systems throughout the region. The special circumstances of the successor states demanded unique approaches to governing and to socioeconomic organization that the liberal system often could not manage.

In retrospect, it is surprising that there was such confidence in eastern Europe as a proving ground for democracy. Without exception, these nations faced problems that would have staggered wealthier, well-established states. A variety of factors retarded economic development. Before 1918 the region had functioned, directly or indirectly, as colonial territory for larger powers, which had supplied it with investments and manufactured goods in return for agricultural products and raw materials. When the war ended, the area faced the sudden loss of secure markets and the inexpensive resources necessary for industrial modernization. To these problems were added a lack of native investment capital, outmoded commercial and agricultural structures, and inadequate communication and transportation systems. Indeed, except for portions of Czechoslovakia, Poland, and Austria, the economies of eastern Europe resembled those of colonial areas in Asia, Africa, or the Middle East.

Social weaknesses contributed to the economic difficulties in eastern Europe. These societies had been dominated by landowning or entrepreneurial nobility and a religious hierarchy that ruled peasants who lived as virtual serfs, despite the formal abolition of serfdom in the nineteenth century. Again with the exception of Austria, Poland, and Czechoslovakia, there was no substantial middle class of merchants, financiers, or managers to provide the expertise and resources needed for modern industrial and commercial development. A small but influential intelligentsia provided the real leadership on a local level. Much of the middle class that did exist was German or Jewish. Finally, these nations were beset with problems common to underdeveloped societies. Illiteracy, high birth and death rates, primitive health conditions, and poor nutrition combined to retard modernization and undermine the democratic systems.

In addition to the clash of interests between landowners and peasants or between the emergent urban dwellers and the much larger rural population, these states were characterized by enormous ethnoreligious diversity. For historical reasons, nearly all of them had a heterogeneous population composed of groups whose ethnic and religious affiliations were different from those of the ruling majority. In some cases, notably Poland, Czechoslovakia, Yugoslavia, Hungary, and Romania, these minorities formed a substantial proportion of the inhabitants. Except for Greece and Turkey, which solved this problem by exchanging minority groups, governments faced ongoing challenges from the minorities. The minorities' reluctance to accept the supremacy of national states, coupled with the failure of most governments to treat their minorities fairly, was a major barrier to the formation of integrated societies.

The Decline of Liberalism

Liberal democracy in eastern Europe also suffered from political liabilities. The lack of experience in representative government meant that the normal give-and-take and compromise of parliamentary systems were absent from local and national politics, with the result that policymaking was often paralyzed. Many states had a multiplicity of political parties, which made legislative activity difficult. Perhaps the most serious political liability was the intense nationalism that pervaded the region and colored the perceptions of leaders and common people alike. Some areas, such as Poland, Hungary, and Bohemia, had long-established nationalist traditions, but national animosities were deepened by the wartime experience. Those on the losing side—Austria, Hungary, Turkey, Bulgaria—were determined to regenerate patriotic pride and regain lost territory; the victors who were already independent—Romania, Greece, Albania—viewed nationalism as a device to keep the hard-won spoils of war. In the states formed from territory of the defeated empires—Poland, Czechoslovakia, Estonia, Latvia, Lithuania—an uncompromising nationalism was seen as the basis for protecting their newly won sovereignty. Nationalism in eastern Europe produced aggressive international behavior that impeded cooperation among the countries and rendered impossible the formation of regional organizations that might have resolved economic problems.

It is hardly surprising that parliamentary democracies often failed to cope with these difficulties and gave way to authoritarian dictatorships. The first nation to adopt a dictatorial government was Hungary, which turned to Admiral Miklós Horthy after a short-lived communist regime under Béla Kun in 1919. Authoritarian leaders soon came to power elsewhere: Marshal Józef Pilsudski in Poland (1926), Antanas Smetona in Lithuania (1926), King Zog in Albania (1928), and King Alexander in Yugoslavia (1929). The Great Depression intensified the problems these nations faced and accelerated the trend toward dictatorship. King Carol began to assume dictatorial power in Romania in 1931, and within three years Engelbert Dollfuss in Austria, Konstantin Päts in Estonia, and Karlis Ulmanis in Latvia had followed suit. In 1935 and 1936 King Boris of

Bulgaria and General John Metaxas of Greece completed the transformation to authoritarianism in the region. Only Czechoslovakia, under the leadership of Tomáš Masaryk and Edvard Beneš, managed to retain its democratic government, despite authoritarian tendencies and serious internal problems.

Whether they were royal, civilian, or military dictatorships, these regimes shared certain characteristics. All retained the facade of democratic institutions, but all developed secret police systems, curtailed civil liberties, suppressed political opposition, and relied on centralized bureaucracies to enforce dictatorial decisions. Fascist movements appeared throughout the region, although none came to power before World War II. Instead, the dictators claimed that their regimes represented protection against exploitation, revolutionary unrest, or the persecution of minorities and posed as the embodiment of the national will. The appeals to nationalism and stability in an area beset with competition, mistrust, and insecurity ultimately proved too strong for the democratic experiment in eastern Europe.

As an ideology, fascism drew on the elitist, antidemocratic radicalism and nationalist-racist doctrines that emerged out of Europe's cultural ferment at the turn of the century—although fascist ideologues often claimed descent from prominent intellectuals, such as Nietzsche and Wagner, who had no direct connection with their movements. At the same time, modern concepts of political communication and social mobilization provided skillful leaders with the techniques for developing a power base and a new style of authoritarian leadership. The impact of World War I and the subsequent economic crisis helped to discredit democratic systems and enable these leaders to channel popular discontent into mass movements.

By the mid-1930s the world appeared to be engaged in a series of ideological struggles: for some, the battle was between democracy and fascism, while others saw it as one between capitalism and communism. Fascist victories in Italy and Germany made the prospects for democracy seem dark. The Western democracies came through the economic crisis with their political institutions changed but fundamentally intact. Yet little of the democratic experiment in eastern Europe survived the decade. More dangerous still, in Italy, Germany, and the Soviet Union the totalitarian restructuring of political, social, and economic life offered compelling alternatives to the liberal order. Finally, the spread of totalitarianism had important foreign implications. Both in Europe and in Asia militarism and the thirst for expansion began to undermine peace. With Mussolini and Hitler in power, one of the compelling forces behind the rise of fascism—nationalist frustration over the 1919 settlements—drove the dictators relentlessly toward the destruction of the postwar international order.

Notes

1. P. N. Stearns, *European Society in Upheaval* (New York: Macmillan, 1967), p. 339.
2. K. Völker, *Brecht: A Biography*, trans. J. Nowell (New York: Seabury Press, 1978), p. 116.

Suggestions for Further Reading

Arendt, H. *The Origins of Totalitarianism*, 2nd ed. Cleveland, Ohio: World Publishing, 1958.

Bullock, A. *Hitler: A Study in Tyranny*. New York: Harper & Row, 1964.

Cassels, A. *Fascism*. New York: Crowell, 1975.

De Felice, R. *Interpretations of Fascism*. Cambridge, Mass.: Harvard University Press, 1977.

Dulles, J. W. F. *Vargas of Brazil: A Political Biography*. Austin: University of Texas Press, 1967.

Gay, P. *Weimar Culture*. New York: Harper & Row, 1968.

Greene, N. *From Versailles to Vichy*. New York: Crowell, 1970.

Kindleberger, C. P. *The World in Depression, 1929–1939*. Berkeley: University of California Press, 1973.

Laqueur, W., ed. *Fascism: A Reader's Guide*. Berkeley: University of California Press, 1976.

Larsen, S. U., et al., eds. *Who Were the Fascists?* Oslo: Universitetsførlaget, 1982.

Lyttelton, A. *The Seizure of Power: Fascism in Italy, 1919–1929*. London: Weidenfeld & Nicolson, 1973.

Mack Smith, D. *Mussolini*. London: Weidenfeld & Nicolson, 1981.

Maruyama, M. *Thought and Behaviour in Modern Japanese Politics*. London: Oxford University Press, 1963.

Morris, I., ed. *Japan, 1931–1945: Militarism, Fascism, Japanism?* Boston: Heath, 1963.

Payne, S. G. *Fascism: Comparison and Definition*. Madison: University of Wisconsin Press, 1980.

Seton-Watson, H. *Eastern Europe Between the Wars, 1918–1941*. Cambridge: Cambridge University Press, 1962.

Shannon, D. A. *Between the Wars: America, 1919–1941,* 2d ed. Boston: Houghton Mifflin, 1979.

Taylor, A. J. P. *English History, 1914–1945*. New York: Oxford University Press, 1965.

Toland, J. *Adolf Hitler*. Garden City, N.Y.: Doubleday, 1976.

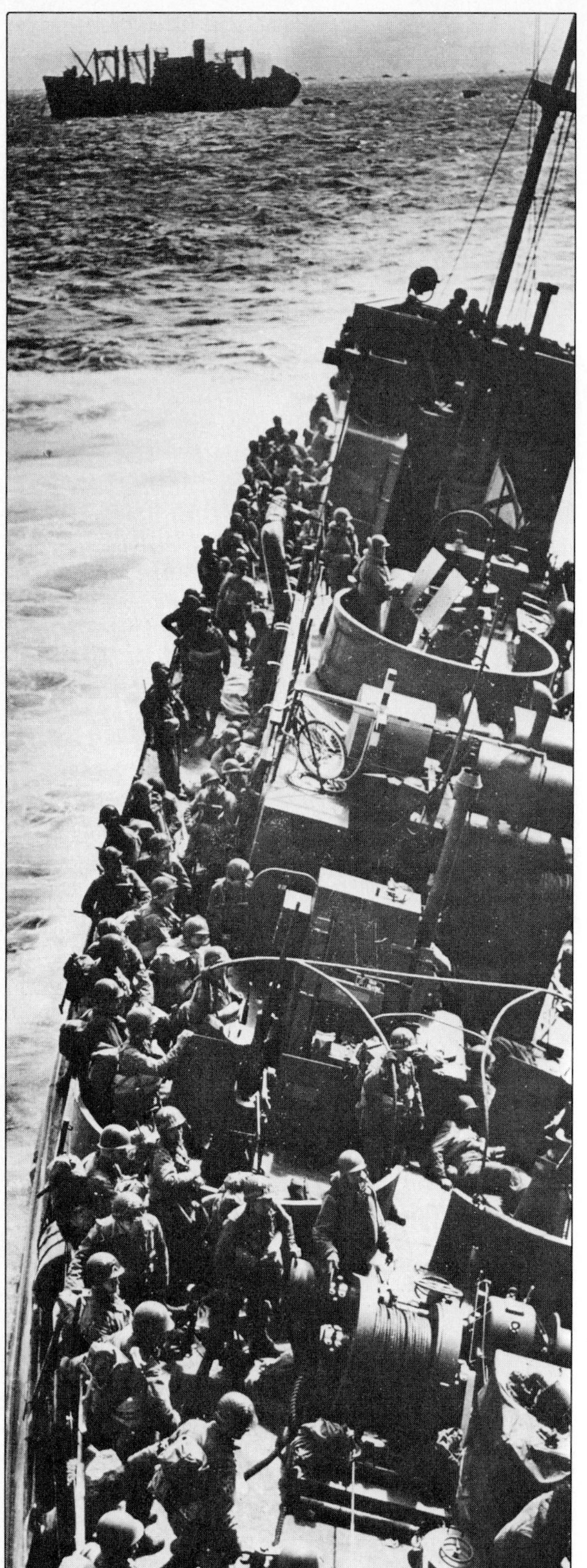

CHAPTER · 37

Totalitarianism and War

Some historians see the 20 years separating the two world wars as little more than a pause in an ongoing conflict. Yet two unique developments made the interwar period different from the years leading up to 1914—the rise of fascism and the emergence of a new form of political organization, the totalitarian state. Experiences as different as Nazi Germany and Soviet Russia demonstrate no causal link between fascism and totalitarianism. Totalitarianism as a form of government imposes complete control over its citizens in order to implement an ideology that seeks to transform society according to supposedly immutable historical laws. Both fascism and communism are totalitarian.

Totalitarian governments are single-party dictatorships in which constitutional rights are severely restricted or eliminated. All political organizations but the official party are outlawed, and in totalitarian states the bureaucracy and the party are closely intertwined. Such regimes are characterized by state terrorism, coercion, police surveillance, government monopoly of the communications media, and strong state economic control. Educational sys-

D day: American soldiers head for the beaches of Normandy as Allied troops assault Fortress Europe. [Brown Brothers]

tems indoctrinate citizens from an early age, while social and leisure organizations are designed to mobilize the masses.

Totalitarian rulers are ideological dictators. Men such as Lenin and Mussolini, Stalin and Hitler were driven by a determination to put their doctrines into practice. While they often compromised for expediency, ideological goals took precedence over traditional moral values. These dictators relied on modern technology—loudspeakers, radio, motion pictures—to achieve social control as well as to reinforce their leadership. In the hands of Mussolini and Hitler the totalitarian state became the instrument for the mobilization of huge industrial, economic, and military resources to unleash wars intended to reshape human life.

Mussolini's Italy

In the two years following the March on Rome in 1922, Benito Mussolini laid the foundations of his totalitarian state. He abolished all political organizations except the Fascist party, censored the press, set up a political police force, instituted loyalty oaths for civil servants, created a military court to prosecute anti-Fascists, and secured power to rule by decree. Once Fascists were installed in key government posts, he set out to forge a broad popular consensus.

On the surface Italy was still a parliamentary state with a monarch. The 1861 constitution remained in force, and Mussolini supposedly held office as prime minister at the pleasure of the king. Imposed above this system was the Fascist Grand Council, which in theory combined party and state functions. The council, appointed by Mussolini, selected candidates for election to the Chamber of Deputies and approved policy decisions. In 1939 this Chamber was replaced by the Chamber of Fasci and Corporations, which represented trades and professions rather than parties. Traditional institutions therefore coexisted with new Fascist bodies, and the totalitarian state never fully superseded them.

Economic Policy

The Fascists established strong state control over the economy while preserving capitalism. Mussolini compromised with the industrialists by agreeing to abolish the non-Fascist unions, prohibit strikes, and recognize the rights of industrial associations. In return, the industrialists supported his regime and dealt only with Fascist unions. Having abolished the economic rights of workers, Mussolini established the "corporate state" in the late 1920s by combining unions and employer associations into "corporations" for each major economic sector and industry. The corporate system was touted as an original form of economic organization, in which state-supervised cooperation between capital and labor would replace class conflict. In reality, private business continued largely unhindered, and the corporate structure had little impact on economic life, except to control workers.

Mussolini failed to solve Italy's economic problems or temper the long-range effects of the Great Depression. Efforts to impose autarchy, or economic self-sufficiency, made matters worse. Marshlands were drained and cultivated, and farmers were coerced into growing more wheat and less of other crops. Nevertheless, overall agricultural production declined. Higher tariffs to stimulate industry increased consumer prices and shortages. Despite welfare programs and subsidies to large families, the standard of living of industrial and farm workers declined throughout the 1930s.

The Church and Fascism

Mussolini was more successful in relations with the Catholic church. Though an atheist, he understood the importance of Catholicism in Italian life and saw the church as a bulwark against communism. He thus ended the hostility that had existed between church and state since 1870, when the Kingdom of Italy seized Rome from the papacy. The Lateran Pacts of 1929 recognized the independence of Vatican City, which became a separate state within the city of Rome; anticlerical laws were repealed; Catholic youth groups were to be free from interference; the Vatican was to have its own newspaper and radio station; religious instruction in state schools became compulsory; and the government paid the Vatican an indemnity. The Lateran Pacts represented a triumph for Mussolini, for they secured the church's cooperation and gave the regime a respectable image. Most important, Mussolini won the support of many devout Italians. Pope Pius XI (1922–1939) proclaimed him "the man sent to us by Providence."

Regimentation and Propaganda

The regimentation of life under Fascism affected both thought and behavior. Mussolini created a secret police agency (called OVRA), spied on anti-Fascists, and introduced a new penal code. Nevertheless, a variety of circumstances—Mussolini's penchant for compromise, a long tradition of Italian resistance to bureaucratic authority, and the more limited ideological goals of Fascism—combined to make his system of terror less severe than that in Nazi Germany or the Soviet Union.

Control of the media and cultural life was placed under the Ministry of Popular Culture. Young people were trained in the party's youth organization, which included separate groups for males and females aged 6 through 17. They provided military training, sports, and political indoctrination and by the mid-1930s had over 3 million members. Leisure activities for workers and peasants were controlled through the party's *Dopolavoro* ("afterwork") organization. By 1940 the party, once an elite vanguard, had been opened to practically all Italians, many of whom viewed membership as a career necessity.

Although Mussolini's early movement had included several female Blackshirts, Fascism held a rigidly chauvinist attitude toward females, who were viewed exclusively as housewives and "mothers of the race." The Duce's highly publicized mistresses enhanced his reputation as a virile lover, and Fascists in general regarded women as objects to be "conquered" by men. The regime fostered conservative social values that reinforced traditional mores. The party trained young females to be wives and mothers, while state agencies provided maternity assistance, hygiene instruction, and child care information. Mussolini had supported giving the vote to women, but once in power he buried political equality. During the Fascist period the percentage of women making up the working population dropped as the depression affected both agriculture and industry.

The party glorified the leader. Mussolini was virtually deified as the farsighted "man of destiny." His skills as an orator, combined with his studied poses and facial expressions, captivated huge throngs. Slogans glorified the Duce and the achievements of Fascism: "Mussolini is always right," "A minute on the battlefield is worth a lifetime of peace," "Believe! Obey! Fight!"

In the mid-1930s the party introduced programs designed to alter Italian customs. Males were to be molded into the Fascist "new man"—obedient, virile, ruthless, efficient, and selfless. The military salute supplanted the handshake, black shirts were to be worn instead of business suits, and bourgeois pastimes such as golf and tennis were replaced with team sports. Many Italians privately scoffed at such measures, which were observed only superficially. The Fascists idealized imperial Rome as their inspiration, and Mussolini promised to create a new empire in which his people would recapture the Roman traditions of sacrifice and discipline. Mussolini was to be Italy's new Caesar.

MARGHERITA SARFATTI AND FASCIST CULTURAL POLICY

The first Italian biography of Mussolini, published in 1926 with the Latin title *Dux*, was the work of Margherita G. Sarfatti (1880–1961). It is ironic that the antifeminist Fascist regime owed a considerable debt to a woman, for the

Margherita Sarfatti, Italian art critic and the author of a popular biography of Mussolini, was the Fascist dictator's lover and cultural mentor for twenty years. [Photograph by Ghitta Carell, 1931, in possession of P. V. Cannistraro]

best-selling biography promoted the legend of Mussolini as the new Caesar. Born Margherita Grassini, Sarfatti was the daughter of a prominent Venetian Jewish family. Intelligent and sophisticated—she was fluent in five languages—Sarfatti began her career as a socialist art critic. After marrying Cesare Sarfatti, an attorney, she moved to Milan, the center of modern Italian cultural life and socialism. There she was attracted to the Futurist movement, which she encouraged, and became a lifelong advocate of Italy's avant-garde painters and writers.

In 1909 Sarfatti began writing for *Avanti!,* the socialist daily of which Mussolini became editor. The two were immediately attracted to each other and began a passionate romance that lasted for many years. Sarfatti introduced Mussolini to her artistic and literary friends, including the Futurists, and gave the crude revolutionary a veneer of respectability and social grace. Together they agitated for intervention in World War I. The death of Sarfatti's 17-year-old son at the front in 1918—he was the youngest Italian to win the gold medal for bravery—made her personally committed to Mussolini's goal of vindicating Italy's wartime sacrifices. When Mussolini founded the Fascist movement in 1919, Sarfatti became art columnist for his official paper, *Il Popolo d'Italia*. During the March on Rome, she was his constant companion and adviser.

With Mussolini in power, Sarfatti emerged as the most influential woman in Italy, although she held no formal government post. She wrote books on modern art, edited Mussolini's official monthly, and drafted his articles for the foreign press. An international array of prominent writers paid court at her salon in Rome, and she patronized intellectuals and painters, for whom she secured commissions and arranged exhibits. Because of her influence in the art world, she came to be known disparagingly as the "dictator of culture." After World War I many artists had begun to turn away from the abstractionism that had marked prewar artistic modernism. Sarfatti supported this "return to order," advancing painters who remained committed to a modern style while appreciating older Italian traditions, especially perspective, portraiture, and classical landscape.

Sarfatti believed that this transformation could form the basis for an artistic revival that suited the Fascist emphasis on nationalist values. While she championed the cult of Rome, she also promoted modern art, architecture, and literature. In 1922 she organized the artists whose work combined modernism and classical motifs into a movement called the Twentieth Century and persuaded Mussolini to inaugurate its first group exhibit. Until the early 1930s the movement came close to representing Fascism's official artistic style, and thus Mussolini's regime encouraged the kind of avant-garde culture that Hitler condemned as "decadent." In promoting the Twentieth Century, Sarfatti struggled against anti-intellectual Fascists who viewed modernism as a product of a corrupt civilization and wanted a "social realist" art that was little more than posterlike propaganda.

By the mid-1930s Sarfatti's star began to wane. Not only had her physical relationship with Mussolini ended, but the Duce had come to believe in his own charismatic abilities. When Mussolini imitated Nazi racial policy by adopting anti-Semitic measures in 1938, Sarfatti (who had converted to Catholicism on the eve of the Lateran Accords) fled to Latin America. She returned to Italy in 1947, after Mussolini had been killed and Fascism destroyed. She spent the rest of her life writing art criticism, never making any public comment about the man she had once loved or the regime she had helped to build.

ROME, THE FASCIST CAPITAL

Sarfatti inspired Mussolini to redesign Rome as the capital of the Fascist state. With its ancient grandeur and rich archaeological remains, Rome was ideally suited for Mussolini's imperial dreams. Its history spanned 2,000 years. A city with a complex physical appearance, its ancient ruins and monuments stood against medieval buildings, Renaissance palaces, and Baroque churches. Fountains and squares provided relief from the winding, dark streets and bustling shopping districts.

Besides its role as a cultural center, Rome was a seat of government. After the collapse of the ancient empire, the city became the site of the papacy and the Catholic church, dominated by the Vatican and St. Peter's Basilica. When Rome became the capital of Italy in 1870, it began to assume its modern appearance. The influx of white-collar workers to staff the bureaucracy increased the size of the urban community significantly. Rome's population of 200,000 in 1870 doubled by the turn of the century, and by 1936 had reached almost 1.2 million. During the reign of King Umberto I (1878–1900) the city underwent a construction boom to accommodate its growing population, and elaborately ornate "Umbertine" architecture took its place alongside older styles.

Like emperors and popes before him, Mussolini determined to redo Rome in order to accent its imperial past, thus making the city the capital of the new Fascist empire. He ordered archaeological excavations and the renovation of ancient sites. He demolished entire residential districts of the inner city to build a grand concourse, the Via dell'Impero ("Imperial Way"), running from the Colosseum along the Forum to the Piazza Venezia, where his office was located. On the walls of the Basilica of Maxentius he placed massive marble maps of the ancient Roman conquests, followed by one showing the Fascist domain. The Piazza Venezia, dominated by the huge monument to Victor Emmanuel II, was the core of Fascist Rome. From the balcony of the Palazzo Venezia, Mussolini harangued enormous crowds. Mussolini also gave the city a modern appearance by constructing monuments and buildings in a modernized classical style characteristic of the regime's taste in architecture. In the 1930s a new complex for the University of Rome was built, as was the Italic Forum, a stadium surrounded by statues of nude athletes intended to symbolize Fascism's emphasis on physical strength. After the Lateran Pacts of 1929, Mussolini again destroyed residential districts to build a wide boulevard from the Tiber River to St. Peter's.

By the end of the decade plans had been laid for a new minicity in the suburbs between Rome and the ancient port of Ostia. Here modern public buildings were designed in the Fascist style for a world's fair in 1942, but the coming of World War II ended the project.

The Anti-Fascist Opposition

In spite of the enthusiasm Mussolini engendered, many Italians opposed Fascism. Mussolini's enemies came from all political parties and walks of life. By 1926 most of the well-known anti-Fascists who escaped Blackshirt brutality had been forced into exile, where they established groups with such names as Justice and Liberty. In the early 1930s an underground Communist network had been set up in

Italy and, together with Justice and Liberty, kept the hope of freedom alive while refuting Fascist propaganda. Mussolini's irresponsible foreign adventures gave anti-Fascism an added impetus, and his anti-Semitic laws alienated many Italians, who regarded the small Jewish population of 50,000 as loyal and productive. The degree to which Italians were repulsed by Mussolini's anti-Semitic policies reflected their humanist traditions.

Nazi Germany

A decade after Mussolini's seizure of power, Adolf Hitler became chancellor of Germany. With greater self-assurance and with clear policies already formulated, Hitler embarked on a total reshaping of German life, thereby establishing the second—and even more brutal—fascist totalitarian state in Europe.

The Nazi State

Hitler created new political and administrative systems. The former states of the German Republic, such as Prussia and Bavaria, were abolished, and a highly centralized government replaced the federal structure established in 1871. Hitler christened his new regime the Third Reich and proclaimed that it would last 1,000 years. He was the *Führer,* the supreme commander who embodied the sovereignty of his nation. Nazi party members replaced high-ranking officials in the central and local bureaucracies. The party itself was reorganized so that local leaders occupied positions equivalent to their bureaucratic counterparts in government. Although the Reichstag remained intact, it served only to provide Hitler with a forum for public declarations and the legitimation of Nazi programs.

The new German legal system also conformed to Nazi philosophy. Law was defined as the will of the German people acting in the interests of the state and its Führer. "People's courts" replaced the regular judicial system to dispense Nazi justice arbitrarily. To enforce compliance, Hitler established a secret political police—the dreaded *Gestapo*—and, six months after the Nazi seizure of power, concentration camps—the first one was at Dachau, outside Munich—to hold political prisoners. Under the command of SS leader Heinrich Himmler (1900–1945), ten or more such centers were built in Germany. Prisoners were used as slave labor, while others were beaten, tortured, or starved to death. Medical personnel performed fiendish experiments on living inmates. The Nazi state deliberately abandoned all traditional moral values.

Hitler was more cautious in dealing with the armed forces. The officer corps, drawn largely from the elite of Prussian society, had been a powerful and independent force in German life. The generals regarded Hitler and his followers as rabble-rousers who could be cast aside once they had generated a renewed sense of patriotism and crushed the communist threat. Hitler brought the generals under his control by compromising his own movement and agreeing to preserve the army's independence.

In 1930 Hitler had persuaded Ernst Röhm, the exiled leader of the SA, to return to Germany and resume command of the Brownshirts. After Hitler became chancellor, Röhm pressed him to eliminate the regular army and turn the SA into a revolutionary people's force. But Hitler needed the army both to consolidate his power and to realize his larger plans for world power. In April 1934 he cut a deal with the officer corps: they would support his policies in exchange for the elimination of the SA. The result was a violent end to a major chapter in the history of National Socialism and a dramatic demonstration of Hitler's ruthlessness. On June 30—the "Night of the Long Knives"—Hitler unleashed a bloody purge of the SA in which Röhm and scores of associates were murdered.

Economic Policy

To pull Germany out of the depression and make it economically self-sufficient, Hitler launched extensive public works programs that changed the appearance of Germany through reforestation, swamp drainage, and the construction of superhighways and housing. Farmers received subsidies and protection against debt foreclosure. To avoid dependence on imported raw materials, German scientists developed artificial rubber, plastics, synthetic textiles, and other substitute products.

While unemployment virtually disappeared and living standards began to rise, both employers and workers lost much of their economic freedom. Strength through Joy, an organization similar to Mussolini's *Dopolavoro,* offered low-income citizens entertainment, vacations, and travel. Industry and commerce remained privately owned but were placed under strict government control. In 1936 Hitler proclaimed the first of two four-year plans that regimented economic life, including wages, profits, and production decisions. Business and professional associations became arms of the Nazi economic system, and independent labor unions were replaced with the National Labor Front, in which membership was compulsory. Strikes were prohibited, and all labor relations were regulated by the state. Hitler's economic policies and rearmament program did pull Germany out of the worst aspects of the depression, restoring relatively full employment. Yet workers paid a heavy price—the destruction of their liberty and a devastating war.

Society and Culture

State coordination also affected social and cultural affairs. Conscious of the need for future soldiers and workers,

Hitler promoted the enlargement of German families through a rising birthrate and improved health care. Some 20 percent of Nazi party members were women in the early 1920s, but once in power Nazi ideologists, like the Fascists in Italy, limited the role of women in national life. In *Mein Kampf,* Hitler had written that for women "the chief emphasis must be laid on physical training, and only subsequently on the promotion of spiritual and finally intellectual values. The goal of female education must invariably be the future mother."[1] Official propaganda projected women as symbols of Germanic female virtue in contrast to the warrior image of men.

Nazi women were generally enthusiastic about restoring traditional social values, and Hitler established a large corps of female officials to organize women in local communities. After 1937, when he began to prepare for war, women were encouraged to work in industry, agriculture, and the service sector.

For males, Hitler removed many of the social barriers that had previously limited economic or political opportunities. Most middle-class citizens perceived the Nazi regime as a promoter and guardian of this social transformation.

Organized religion posed a challenge to the new order and hence came under growing pressure to accept government control. Catholic and Protestant clergy alike were prohibited from criticizing official policies and found it difficult to maintain ties with churches outside Germany. The state discouraged children from attending religious schools while supporting the revival of anti-Christian movements that worshiped ancient Teutonic gods.

The cultural sphere drew special attention both as a means to promote the cult of the *Führer* and to construct the Nazi world view. Under the vigilance of the minister of propaganda, Joseph Goebbels (1897–1945), every facet of intellectual and artistic life was harnessed to generate enthusiasm for Nazi doctrine and its leader. Publishing houses came under the control of the government, which eliminated all literature not conforming to officially endorsed ideas; "offensive" books were publicly burned. The government assigned themes to writers, artists, architects, and musicians. As in Fascist Italy, sports were seen as physical demonstration of Nazi virtues. Radio and film, whose potential for shaping mass opinion was immense, were perhaps Goebbels' most powerful propaganda weapons. Leni Riefenstahl, a talented film director, won international acclaim for the seductive power of her visual imagery in such films as *Triumph of the Will* (1935).

Hitler took a keen interest in art and architecture. Viewing modern styles as alien to the "Germanic spirit," he dismissed modern-minded artists and museum curators and in 1935 regimented artists under Nazi party orders. In his inaugural address at the opening of the House of German Art in Munich in 1937, Hitler denounced Impressionism, Futurism, and Cubism as Jewish-inspired "cultural bolshevism." He demanded an art that reflected German values. To illustrate the "depravity" of modernism, the government set up a permanent Exhibition of Degenerate Art. Nazi painting and sculpture reflected a Romantic hero worship inspired by the themes of Nordic mythology made famous by Wagner's operas. This official art lacked originality or creative expression, let alone aesthetic

Seamstresses sew Nazi flags in 1933. [Landesbildstelle Berlin]

value. Instead, it glorified the *Führer* as a Germanic warrior, extolled the concept of "blood and soil," idealized the image of mothers and children, and depicted muscle-bound nudes as the embodiment of German strength. The Nazis also attacked modern architecture, closing down the Bauhaus and driving its architects out of Germany. Hitler and his architectural consultant Albert Speer planned to erect in Berlin monumental buildings designed in a pseudo-Greek classicism.

Underpinning all these efforts was the educational system. Schools and universities underwent a thorough reconstruction of their curricula and faculties to ensure that all students received indoctrination and only carefully screened information. The Nazi party formed a comprehensive youth movement—the *Hitlerjugend,* or Hitler Youth—that reinforced intellectual, psychological, and political conformity.

Hitler and the Jews

The ultimate horror of the Nazi regime began to reveal itself soon after Hitler came to power. More than any other authoritarian or totalitarian movement, National Socialism was based on racial and ethnic hatred. Nazi ideologues considered the Germans a superior race who deserved to be masters over such "undesirables" as Slavs, gypsies, and Latins. But Hitler, whose anti-Semitism had been formed during his Vienna days, reserved his special animosity for the Jews, whose persecution and ultimate annihilation became his obsession.

The Nuremberg Racial Laws

Hitler incorporated the principles of Nazi anti-Semitism into a series of laws introduced between September and November 1935. The so-called Nuremberg Laws captured the essence of Nazi racism. The following selections are from these infamous measures.

I. The Reich Citizenship Law of September 15, 1935:

A citizen of the Reich may be only that subject who is of German or kindred blood, and who, through his behavior, shows that he is both desirous and personally fit to serve loyally the German people and the Reich.

II. The Law for the Protection of German Blood and Honor, September 15, 1935:

Any marriages between Jews and citizens of German or kindred blood are herewith forbidden. Marriages entered into despite this law are invalid. . . .

Extramarital relations between Jews and citizens of German or kindred blood are herewith forbidden.

Jews are forbidden to employ as servants in their households female subjects of German or kindred blood who are under the age of 45 years.

Jews are prohibited from displaying the Reich and national flag and from showing the national colors.

III. Supplementary decree of November 14, 1935:

A Jew cannot be a citizen of the Reich. He cannot exercise the right to vote; he cannot occupy public office. . . .

A Jew is an individual who is descended from at least three grandparents who were, racially, full Jews. . . .

A Jew is also an individual who is descended from two full-Jewish grandparents if:

(a) he was a member of the Jewish religious community . . . ;

(b) when the law was issued he was married to a person who was a Jew . . . ;

(c) he is the issue from a marriage with a Jew . . . ;

(d) he is the issue of an extra-marital relationship with a Jew. . . .

Source: Reichgesetzblatt (1935), No. 100 (September 15, 1935), 1: 1142–1147.

Hitler swiftly launched a campaign of official persecution against the Jews. In April 1933 the government barred Jews from the civil service, while racial laws forbade them to study or teach in the universities or to practice medicine, law, and other professions. In 1935 the notorious Nuremberg Laws deprived Jews of all civil rights, including the freedom to marry non-Jews. A campaign of terror against German Jews followed. "Jewish" became the characteristic term of official disapproval for everything considered negative in Nazi eyes—democracy, communism, liberalism, or individual rights.

As the anti-Semitic drive intensified, thousands of Jews fled Germany. The assassination of a German diplomat in Paris by a young Polish Jew in 1938 was the pretext for the infamous *Kristallnacht* ("Night of Broken Glass"), a coordinated wave of violence that destroyed Jewish homes, businesses, and synagogues and took many lives; later the Jews were heavily assessed to pay for the damage. The Western democracies, unwilling to assume the burden of caring for millions of refugees, refused to accept mass Jewish immigration. Although some international protests were lodged against these outrages, most Germans either approved or accepted them.

The Jews still in Germany now found it virtually impossible to leave, having become an imprisoned humanity for whom the worst of the horrors still lay ahead. Nazi anti-Semitism drew on a long tradition of persecution, prejudice, and superstition, but the Nazis went far beyond that tradition in their effort to impose the domination of the German "master race" on the "inferior" peoples of Europe. During World War II the fate of Germany's Jews would be tied to that of Jews throughout the Continent as Hitler drove anti-Semitism to its ultimate conclusion: the planned extermination of European Jewry.

Stalin's Russia

Unlike Hitler or Mussolini, Stalin inherited an established, if not completely shaped, revolutionary system. He had several goals, the first of which was the consolidation of his hold over the country and its Communist party. He also wished to make Russia economically independent of the hostile capitalist powers, particularly by modernizing industry. In part he was motivated by ideological considerations. Committed to socialism as they perceived it, Stalin and his supporters were uneasy about the NEP policies introduced by Lenin, which had created a kind of market socialism based on nationalized industry, mixed private retail trade and state distribution, and capitalistic agriculture strongly influenced by state prices and quotas. Eliminating the vestiges of capitalism and introducing a new model of development became a priority, now that the economy had recovered from its wartime prostration and Stalin's political power was secure.

Stalin as the genial leader; a photo of a painted portrait. [Mansell Collection]

The Five-Year Plans

Stalin's device to attain these objectives was the five-year plan. This strategy sought to replace private property and economic activity with a system of production quotas formulated and administered by a central authority under the party's direction. The plan established production goals for every citizen. Heavy industry and transportation received most of the resources at the expense of consumer-oriented manufacturing and agriculture. The quotas were unrealistic—projected increases of 250 percent for heavy industry, 300 percent for steel production, and 150 percent for agriculture. Workers and managers who met or exceeded their targets received bonuses; stiff penalties awaited those who fell short. A new government agency, GOSPLAN, became the vehicle for translating party directives into performance. In sum, the plans attempted to impose centralized state control on resources and manpower that capitalism regulated through such market forces as supply and demand or changes in wages, prices, and interest rates.

The initial plan (1928–1932) had mixed success. Frequent breakdowns in planning and implementation caused waste, surpluses, or shortages, and quotas rarely were met. Moreover, the emphasis on quantity resulted in shoddy products. Nonetheless, due in part to the substantial importation of machinery, skilled workers, and technicians from the advanced industrial countries, production doubled in five years.

Agriculture was another story. Stalin was determined to gain control over the countryside and punish the land-owning peasants who had resisted state authority. Moreover, he wanted to collect grain efficiently and pay for his industrialization programs by controlling grain prices. The method adopted was to consolidate the thousands of small family farms into a few hundred large agricultural enterprises that could use the latest mechanization and management techniques. Each huge farm would focus on a specific crop, which could be grown more efficiently. This would result in agricultural surpluses for sale abroad to finance industrialization.

In 1929 Soviet peasants were ordered to surrender their land and farm animals to the state and to become members of cooperative farms known as collectives. Under state control, each collective would receive quotas, much like factory workers or coal miners. Except for their houses and personal belongings, members were to turn over their property to the collective and to share the work and whatever profit or loss the farm recorded. Much of the peasantry—especially the well-to-do kulaks—rebelled against this system, burning crops and seed reserves or slaughtering livestock rather than surrendering them to the collectives. Across rural Russia detachments of police and, occasionally, Red Army troops attacked villages that resisted collectivization. The most capable farmers were either killed or dispatched to labor camps. The scheme was disastrous for Soviet agriculture. Livestock declined by over one-half, and the output of grain barely increased between 1928 and 1938, when it finally reached the prewar level. A famine swept the country in 1932 and 1933, the direct result of forced collectivization. Together Stalin's agrarian policy and the famine killed between 5 and 8 million persons in the Ukraine alone.

In addition to its social and economic impact, collectivization had important political implications. The systematic and brutal intrusion into the countryside saw a significant extension of the Communist party's power, for until then its direct control over the vast majority of Soviet citizens had been limited. Stalin's radical measures represented a vital step toward totalitarian control.

Declaring the five-year plan a success, Stalin announced a second in 1932 and a third six years later. In the later versions, steps were taken to improve quality and eliminate shortcomings in production and distribution. The results in industry were impressive. During the first two plans, the output of iron and steel expanded fourfold, that of coal 3½ times; by 1938 the Soviet Union had become the world's largest producer of tractors and locomotives. Many of the new plants featured the latest equipment from America or western Europe. Agriculture, however, continued to present major problems. Grain production crept upward very slowly, and the country faced constant shortages of meat, fruits, vegetables, and dairy products. By the end of 1932 some 60 percent of all surviving peasant families had joined collective farms; by 1938 the proportion reached 93 percent. The government could count on a reasonably steady supply of basic goods for the cities. Collectivization provided Stalin with at least a political triumph.

Industrial expansion coincided with urbanization, as modern cities rose up in previously isolated areas of Siberia and central Asia. To populate them and meet the demand for labor, millions migrated from rural regions to the new manufacturing centers. Workers lost most of their independence as their unions became instruments of the state and their employment was decided by the central authorities.

Life in Stalin's Russia was harsh. Adequate housing was scarce, and wages failed to keep pace with prices—in 1937 a nonagricultural worker could buy about 60 percent of what he could have purchased in 1928. To material hardships was added the psychological strain of political indoctrination. Everyone was required to attend lectures by party activists, who extolled the virtues of Soviet socialism while warning of capitalist plots. Artists, writers, film producers, playwrights, musicians, and other communicators took seriously Stalin's command that they become "engi-

In the Soviet Union women were mobilized into virtually all sectors of the labor force. Here a female tractor driver leads a procession to the fields. [Sovfoto]

neers of human minds" and competed as composers of Communist propaganda.

By the mid-1930s another major propaganda theme was added: virtual deification of Stalin. Unlike other dictators, Stalin shunned public appearances at mass rallies and similar functions. Yet his presence, in the form of portraits, statues, and books, was inescapable. Indeed, he became the focal point of a cult of personality comparable to that in Nazi Germany and Fascist Italy.

Social Policy

Stalin's regime offered positive incentives to labor. Unemployment virtually disappeared, and the basis was laid for free state medical services, old-age pensions, subsidized housing, and day-care facilities for children. Perhaps the most meaningful benefit to many was the extension of free education to all, a policy begun in the 1920s. The government declared war on illiteracy, bringing basic schooling to even the most isolated portions of the Soviet Union. Advanced education was provided free to students demonstrating superior aptitude and ability, and a reward system of high salaries, bonuses, and privileges awaited successful graduates. Indeed, a managerial and technocratic class soon emerged that, together with the political and artistic elites, formed a new aristocracy in this supposedly classless society. The welfare system, combined with fear of the consequences of any criticism, effectively muted discontent among the masses.

The status of women underwent significant change during the Stalinist period. The hopes of early Bolshevik feminists such as Alexandra Kollontai that the revolution would achieve equality for women were never fully realized. In 1918 the *Zhenotdel,* or Party Women's Bureau, was established to educate and recruit women for the Communist party. The Zhenotdel also acted as an advocate for women's interests in the workplace and sponsored women candidates for local elections. Even though it had no powers of enforcement, the Zhenotdel had an uneasy relationship with party officials, and Stalin abolished it in the 1920s.

In that decade, however, Russian women were given legal access to abortion and divorce, and although Stalin minimized the rhetoric of sexual equality, industrial policy and economic necessity resulted in wider opportunities for women. The collectivization of agriculture brought women into the fields in greater numbers, while subsistence salaries for male workers pushed millions of wives and daughters into factory jobs, public works projects, and heavy construction. The most significant change, however, came in educational opportunities, which were now open to women, especially in science, technology, and medicine. Despite the advances in education and employment, the Soviet mobilization of women increased their physical and psychological burdens, for most women were expected to care for children and do housework while working or going to school. Nevertheless, unlike the fascist regimes in Italy and Germany, which relegated women to the roles of wives and mothers, Soviet totalitarianism at least proclaimed the goal of female equality and made important strides in breaking the pattern of traditional roles for women.

The Great Purges

Stalin's development programs had employed totalitarian mechanisms of state control that made wide use of police terror against the peasants. But as uneasiness over his brutal methods mounted, the internal security forces—known as the NKVD—were soon turned against the Communist elite. Between 1936 and 1938 Stalin unleashed an immense reign of terror that engulfed eminent party members, high-ranking administrators, and military leaders. Eventually it expanded to include ordinary citizens, many of whom fell victim to sudden arrest and summary execution or exile to a remote labor camp without apparent reason. The reasons behind these "great purges" remain obscure. There is evidence of at least one serious plot against Stalin; paranoia may have so consumed him that he struck out blindly against presumed enemies.

The terror began with the assassination in December 1934 of Sergei Kirov, a close associate of Stalin's and, according to some, his chosen successor. Claiming that Kirov's murder was part of a vast conspiracy led by supporters of the exiled Trotsky, Stalin, who had in reality arranged for the murder himself, ordered mass arrests. In 1936 there began a series of public trials that captured world attention. Sixteen "Old Bolsheviks"—activists who had joined the party prior to 1917—were charged with conspiring to topple Stalin and restore Trotsky to power. Led by Grigori Zinoviev and Lev Kamenev, all confessed and were executed. Similar trials claimed other Old Bolsheviks, including the theoretician Nikolai Bukharin; all offered identical confessions followed by summary execution. Next the purge reached the army. A secret court-martial in 1937 found Marshal Mikhail Tukhachevsky and other officers guilty of conspiring with the Germans and the Japanese as well as with Trotsky, and all were executed. In addition, thousands of prominent party members, union officials, business executives, and intellectuals lost their liberty or their lives. Stalin culminated the purges by executing the leaders of the very police force that had implemented his program of terror. When the purges were over, millions had fallen victim to his obsession.

The great purges served to remove upper and middle-level officials in the party, state, military, and economic institutions, and Stalin replaced them with younger functionaries who would dutifully obey him. Yet they also had the effect of halting the revolutionary changes that had been going on in the Soviet Union since the early 1920s.

Thenceforth the regime would follow the path set by Stalin's totalitarian dictatorship.

The Rising Sun: Japanese Expansion in East Asia

The Japanese had come to view the large but internally weak Chinese territory as their sphere of interest and had taken advantage of World War I and the Russian civil war to extend their influence on the mainland. In addition to providing an opportunity to seize territory, the war in Europe had also quickened the pace of Japanese industrial growth and enabled Tokyo to capture many regional markets from the Western powers. In the postwar period Japan became the main source of textiles and other consumer products for the rest of Asia.

But this thriving economy rested on a precarious base. Lacking essential raw materials, Japan's chief asset was its highly motivated, well-disciplined work force. Indeed, Japanese leaders were able to mobilize workers even more effectively than Europe's totalitarian dictators, producing a modern industrial machine along with a series of related commercial and financial institutions, largely controlled by a few great family trusts known as the *zaibatsu*. Political and economic leaders realized that their nation would continue to prosper only if it had a guaranteed flow of raw materials from abroad, together with secure foreign markets for its finished products. A disruption of this balance would halt the growth of Japanese power and expose its vulnerability to forces beyond its control.

The Japanese political system vigorously pursued the interests of the nation's economic elite. On paper Japan possessed a government strikingly similar to that of many European powers—a written constitution adopted in 1889, universal male suffrage since 1925, and modern parliamentary and judicial systems. But this institutional structure was largely misleading. The Diet (parliament) had sharply limited powers, and ministers governed in the name of the supreme and holy emperor, to whom they were completely responsible. A spirit of militarism pervaded Japanese life and gave the professional officer corps a political influence comparable to that enjoyed by the German military caste prior to World War I. In the 1930s Japan was the only modern nation that required its war and naval ministers to be generals and admirals on active-duty status. Many of its younger officers, influenced by the national revival that had begun in the mid-nineteenth century, were drawn from a segment of the small landowning nobility that followed the warrior code of the old samurai. The powerful combination of nationalism, militarism, and authoritarianism that dominated Japanese politics determined that in time of crisis, ultimate authority passed to the military leaders.

After World War I, Chinese tariff barriers and the Great Depression threatened Japan's access to raw materials and markets. Younger army officers proposed the conquest of nearby territory from which materials could be obtained and to which manufactured goods—as well as surplus population—could be sent. Military spokesmen added a messianic tone to these arguments by insisting that the prosperity and progress of all Asia depended on the Japanese, who would liberate Asia from Western exploitation. Japan's imperial program thus assumed the guise of a broader campaign in defense of Asian interests.

Manchuria was the first target of Japanese expansionism. Russia, whose territory bordered Manchuria on the north and east, had dominated the area until its defeat in the 1905 war. Thereafter, although it remained nominally part of China, Manchuria became a Japanese sphere. In September 1931 Japanese colonels took advantage of a minor incident involving the South Manchuria Railway at Mukden to invade Manchuria. The civilian government reluctantly approved the army's initiative, and by early 1932 the Japanese conquest of Manchuria was complete.

When the Chinese responded with a boycott against Japanese goods, Tokyo landed 70,000 troops at Shanghai, then withdrew them under pressure from the Western powers. Japan nonetheless renamed its conquered Manchurian territory Manchukuo ("Country of the Manchus") and proclaimed it an independent state under Henry Pu Yi, the last Manchu emperor, who remained a Japanese puppet. Condemned by the League of Nations, the Japanese withdrew their membership, presenting the League with the first real test of its ability to stop aggression. The League failed to meet the challenge, imposing neither economic nor military sanctions. Japan's ambitions were emboldened by the signing of the Anti-Comintern Pact with Germany in 1936, which bound both partners to withhold aid from Russia should either party go to war with the Soviets.

Aggression and Appeasement in the West

Japan's success in defying the League of Nations encouraged Hitler's and Mussolini's quest for territorial expansion. Mussolini's emphasis on the virtues of war, combined with his dream of creating a new Roman Empire, impelled him toward conquest. Hitler was even more outspoken about his plans for a "Greater German Reich" in Europe, the corollary of a racial policy that aimed at bringing the "inferior" peoples of the Continent under the domination of the "master" Germanic race.

Europe and Africa: The Axis Advance

Hitler laid the groundwork for expansion while rebuilding German military strength. In October 1933 Germany withdrew from the League of Nations and the following July instigated a coup in Austria aimed at bringing about the union (*Anschluss*) of Austria and Germany. The conspirators murdered Austrian chancellor Engelbert Dollfuss but were halted by Mussolini, who intervened to protect Austrian independence, which he considered vital to Italy's security.

In January 1935 Hitler won a huge majority in the Versailles-mandated plebiscite that returned the Saar region to Germany. In March he openly defied the postwar settlement, declaring that Germany had formed an air force and had reinstituted the military draft. Despite protests, Britain tacitly endorsed Hitler's actions in June 1935 by signing a naval agreement with Germany.

In the summer of 1934 Mussolini had begun preparations for the conquest of Ethiopia, one of the two remaining independent nations in Black Africa (the other was Liberia). Arousing enthusiasm with a propaganda campaign at home, the Duce launched his invasion in October 1935. The League of Nations promptly imposed economic sanctions, but it omitted oil from the list of products that member nations could not sell to Italy. This important exception, together with the abstention of the United States, Japan, and Germany from the boycott, virtually assured Italy of victory. In May 1936, when Mussolini proclaimed the incorporation of Ethiopia with Italian Somaliland and Eritrea into a new empire called Italian East Africa, the collective security system created at Versailles crumbled.

Hitler took full advantage of these developments. In March 1936, while the conquest of Ethiopia was under way, he ordered German troops into the Rhineland, which the Versailles treaty had established as a demilitarized zone. At the same time, he repudiated the 1925 Locarno treaties that guaranteed Germany's frontiers with Belgium and France and recognized the demilitarized status of the Rhineland. Although the French mobilized their troops, Britain refused to act. Hitler and Mussolini had shown that the democracies were unwilling to preserve the postwar settlement. In October 1936 the Führer and the Duce agreed to coordinate their foreign policies in what Mussolini called the Rome-Berlin Axis.

The Spanish Civil War

The Axis partnership demonstrated its military capacity during the Spanish civil war. When Spain became a democratic republic after the collapse of the Bourbon monarchy in 1931, the new government launched a campaign of social and economic reform. Conservative elements, especially the military, the Catholic church, and the aristocracy, opposed the reforms and gained control of the government in 1933. In response, leftist and democratic groups formed the Popular Front, which regained power in the 1936 elec-

Franco's victory in the Spanish civil war forced thousands of civilians to seek refuge across the border in France. [UPI/Bettmann Newsphotos]

Guernica

The aerial bombardment of the town of Guernica during the Spanish civil war became a symbol of the horror of modern warfare and inspired Pablo Picasso to paint his wrenching painting by that name. Here a British correspondent described the event.

Guernica, the most ancient town of the Basques and the center of their cultural tradition, was completely destroyed yesterday afternoon by insurgent air raiders. The bombardment of this open town far behind the lines occupied precisely three hours and a quarter, during which a powerful fleet of airplanes . . . did not cease unloading on the town bombs weighing from 1,000 lb. downwards and, it is calculated, more than 3,000 two-pounder aluminum incendiary projectiles. The fighters, meanwhile, plunged low from above the centre of the town to machine-gun those of the civilian population who had taken refuge in the fields. . . .

At 2 A.M. today when I visited the town the whole of it was a horrible sight, flaming from end to end. The reflection of the flames could be seen in the clouds of smoke above the mountains from 10 miles away. Throughout the night houses were falling until the streets became long heaps of red impenetrable debris. . . .

In the form of its execution and the scale of the destruction it wrought, no less than in the selection of its objective, the raid on Guernica is unparalleled in military history. Guernica was not a military objective. . . .

The rhythm of this bombing of an open town was, therefore, a logical one: first, hand grenades and heavy bombs to stampede the population, then machine-gunning to drive them below, next heavy and incendiary bombs to wreck the houses and burn them on top of their victims.

Source: The Times (London), April 28, 1937.

In 1937, after the German bombing of the village of Guernica during the Spanish civil war, Pablo Picasso produced this painting by that name to express the agony. [A&R MAS]

tions. Unwilling to accept this, army officers under the leadership of General Francisco Franco (1892–1975) revolted in July. Franco was soon joined by extreme nationalists and Spanish fascists, known as the Falange, and the nation was plunged into civil war.

The Spanish civil war was a major barometer of the willingness of democratic and totalitarian forces to act. Hitler and Mussolini poured tanks, planes, and military personnel into Spain on behalf of the Nationalists. Stalin countered by shipping equipment and military advisers to the republican Loyalists. Fearful of escalation, the British and French adopted a policy of nonintervention. Thousands of liberals, socialists, communists, and anarchists from Europe and America who viewed Spain as an ideological battleground fought as volunteers in international brigades against the Franco forces. The agony of the Spanish people was exemplified by the German bombing of the town of Guernica on April 26, 1937. By the beginning of 1939, the Nationalists had won, and Franco became dictator of Spain.

The Czech Crisis

Emboldened by the timidity of the Western powers, Hitler annexed Austria, occupying it with German troops in March 1938. He then turned to Czechoslovakia. The 3 million ethnic Germans who lived in the Sudeten border region had never been reconciled to Czech rule. In the aftermath of the Austrian *Anschluss*, the Czech Nazi leader, Konrad Henlein (1898–1945), demanded autonomy for the Sudetenland, a move that Hitler promptly endorsed. The democratic Czech government, headed by President Edvard Beneš (1884–1948), appealed to France and the Soviet Union, with which it had defensive alliances, and mobilized its own forces. Hitler responded by threatening an invasion. War appeared imminent.

The French, unprepared to fight, yielded the diplomatic initiative to Britain's prime minister, Neville Chamberlain (1869–1940). Determined to avoid war, Chamberlain held a series of meetings with Hitler. A final conference, held in Munich with Mussolini and French premier Edouard Daladier (1884–1970) on September 29 and 30, settled the fate of Czechoslovakia. Chamberlain and Daladier accepted the demand for German annexation of the Sudetenland and forced the Czechs to acquiesce. Chamberlain then returned to London to proclaim "peace in our time." Six months later Hitler violated the agreement, moving German troops into Prague and dismembering what was left of Czechoslovakia. It, like Austria, had ceased to exist as a sovereign state.

The Munich settlement represented the culmination of the Western policy of appeasement. The strategy of appeasement had been calculated to eliminate the dangers of war by satisfying the demands of aggressor states through peaceful negotiation. At the time the policy did not seem as shortsighted as it does in retrospect. Many agreed with Hitler and Mussolini that some aspects of the

Hitler's War Plans

On November 5, 1937, Hitler held a secret meeting with his military leaders in which he sketched his plans for aggression and war. Hitler's comments were recorded by his aid, Colonel Hossbach.

The aim of German policy is to make secure and to preserve the racial community and to enlarge it. . . .

Germany's future was therefore wholly conditional upon the solving of the need for space. . . .

Germany's problem could only be solved by means of force. . . .

If the *Führer* was still living, it was his unalterable resolve to solve Germany's problem of space at the latest by 1943–45.

Our first objective, in the event of our being embroiled in war, must be to overthrow Czechoslovakia and Austria simultaneously. . . . Our agreements with Poland only retained their force as long as Germany's strength remained unshaken. . . .

Actually, the *Führer* believed that almost certainly Britain, and probably France as well, had already tacitly written off the Czechs. . . .

Military intervention by Russia must be countered by the swiftness of our operations. . . .

Source: Documents on German Foreign Policy, 1918–1945, Series D, I (Washington, D.C.: U.S. Government Printing Office, 1949), Document No. 19.

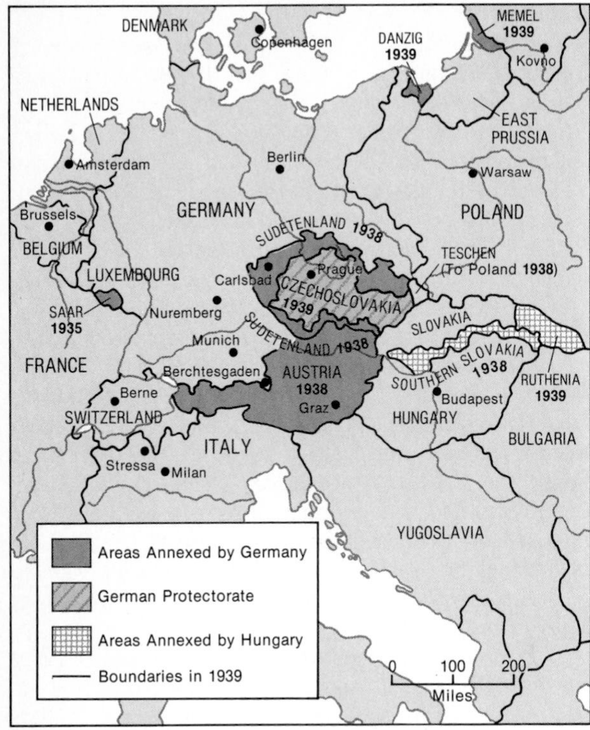

37.1 Central Europe, 1939

postwar peace settlements had been unfair, while others saw the instability of the new states in eastern Europe as proof of the failure of Wilsonian self-determination. Appeasement was the policy of people who had survived the horrors of World War I and were determined to avoid another at almost any cost.

Appeasement was all the more compelling because some European statesmen, still haunted by the specter of the Russian Revolution, believed that the upheavals of war would unleash communism in the West. The Great Depression had seriously weakened the economic and social order of capitalism and had shaken Western faith in democratic political systems. The lack of military preparedness in Britain and France reflected these post-1919 developments, whereas for some Western leaders the armed strength of the aggressors made appeasement seem necessary. The policy, however, only whetted the territorial appetites of Mussolini and Hitler.

World War II

At the end of March 1939—when it was already clear that Poland would be Hitler's next victim—Chamberlain publicly assured Warsaw that Britain and France would defend Polish independence. By then, the dictators had no reason to believe the Western powers meant what they said. On April 3 Hitler secretly ordered the invasion of Poland in September, and five days later Mussolini invaded Albania. In May, after Britain and France extended guarantees to Greece and Romania, Hitler and Mussolini signed the Pact of Steel, a formal military alliance.

In preparation for his assault against Poland, Hitler sought to guard against two possible contingencies: the intervention of Russia and, in the event that the Western powers did fight, a two-front war between Russia in the east and an Anglo-French campaign in the west. The Soviet Union had been negotiating with both sides since early spring, but mutual mistrust in Moscow, London, and Paris ultimately prevented an agreement. From Stalin's perspective, while an alliance with Britain and France might mean a war against Germany with no prospect of gain, Hitler offered him tangible benefits—neutrality in the event of war between Germany and the West and a division of eastern European territory. For Stalin the choice was clear. On August 23 Germany and Russia announced a nonaggression treaty, which contained a secret protocol that divided Poland into German and Russian spheres, gave Lithuania to Germany, and ceded Finland, Latvia, and Estonia to the Soviet Union, thereby almost restoring Russia's 1914 frontiers. The Nazi-Soviet Pact was a consummate act of *Realpolitik* concluded by two bitter ideological enemies. It shattered the loyalty of many Communists and supporters of the Soviets around the world. On September 1 German planes and armored columns attacked Poland. Two days later Britain and France declared war on Germany. World War II had begun in Europe.

The Nazi Onslaught

Poland fell in less than four weeks, in what the Germans called *Blitzkrieg* ("lightning war"), which coordinated air and ground forces in a sudden furious attack. Before the collapse of Warsaw, Stalin rushed troops into eastern Poland to secure the territory promised him in the Nazi-Soviet Pact. Poland, too, was obliterated.

Unable to launch an offensive before the onset of winter, Hitler held back from an all-out assault on the West. Between the end of September 1939 and April 1940, this "phony war" was interrupted only by German-British naval engagements. In the meantime, the Soviet Union moved troops into Estonia, Latvia, and Lithuania and on November 30 invaded Finland, conquering it by March 1940 after unexpected resistance. In April, Hitler suddenly struck at Norway and Denmark. The latter fell in less than a day, Norway by the end of the month. Then, on May 10, the full weight of the German war machine was flung against Belgium and the Netherlands. The same day, Chamberlain resigned and was replaced as prime minister by Winston Churchill (1874–1965).

Secret Protocol of the Nazi-Soviet Pact

The nonaggression pact Hitler and Stalin signed on August 22, 1939, contained a secret clause that divided Poland and Lithuania between the two powers in the event of a war.

The territory of the Lithuanian state falls to the sphere of influence of the U.S.S.R., while, on the other hand, the province of Lublin and parts of the province of Warsaw fall to the sphere of influence of Germany. . . . As soon as the Government of the U.S.S.R. shall take special measures on Lithuanian territory to protect its interests, the present German-Lithuanian border, for the purpose of a natural and simple boundary delineation, shall be rectified in such a way that the Lithuanian territory situated to the southwest of the line marked on the attached map shall fall to Germany.

Source: R. J. Sontag and J. S. Beddie, eds., *Nazi-Soviet Relations, 1939–1941: Documents from the Archives of the German Foreign Office* (Washington, D.C.: U.S. Government Printing Office, 1948), p. 107.

Although the combined British, French, Belgian, and Dutch forces matched Germany's 134 divisions, the Allies were deficient in planes and antiaircraft power, and overwhelmed by German *Blitzkrieg* tactics. By the end of May the Germans had pushed the Allied armies to the English Channel, where more than 330,000 French and British troops were evacuated from Dunkirk to England. Bypassing the Maginot line, a system of static fortifications that ran north from Switzerland, the Germans pushed rapidly through Belgium into France, outflanking French forces. On June 10 Mussolini, who had kept Italy neutral but now feared that the war might be over before he could act, declared war. French premier Paul Reynaud turned over the government to 84-year-old Marshal Henri Pétain (1856–1951), the hero of Verdun. Determined to salvage what he could, Petain sued for terms. The armistice, signed on June 22, 1940, granted the Germans occupation of more than three-quarters of France, leaving the southern portion of the country to Petain, who established a puppet regime in the city of Vichy. A small resistance group led by General Charles de Gaulle (1890–1970) escaped to London and formed the Free French organization. In less than two months, France, the mainstay of democracy in continental Europe, had fallen.

Allied Resistance and Axis Setbacks

With France defeated, Hitler was certain that Britain would finally seek an accommodation. To hasten this, he unleashed his air force against Britain in July to wreck civilian morale by terror bombing. Churchill, Britain's new leader, was a veteran of its imperialist wars, having been First Lord of the Admiralty during World War I, and a stirring orator. A convinced anticommunist, he had once expressed admiration for Mussolini but since 1936 had strongly opposed appeasement. Now he personified the British will to resist. Outnumbered by more than two to one, the Royal Air Force (RAF) fought in the skies over London and other cities, inflicting unexpected casualties

Prime Minister Churchill inspects the damage from a German air raid. [Brown Brothers]

on the German *Luftwaffe*. In London, St. Paul's Cathedral remained almost alone in the midst of devastated streets as a symbol of survival, while Churchill rallied the nation in eloquent speeches. Unable to launch an amphibious invasion against a superior navy and facing mounting air losses, Hitler broke off what came to be called the Battle of Britain.

Stymied in Britain, the Axis turned to eastern Europe and North Africa. The Italians assaulted the British stronghold in Egypt in September and were repulsed into Libya, but Hitler salvaged the operation and pushed to within 100 miles of the Suez Canal. The pattern was repeated in October, when Mussolini invaded Greece. Valiant Greek resistance, British aid, and poor Italian equipment required Hitler to intervene again. Together with Hungarian and Bulgarian troops, the Germans overran Yugoslavia and defeated Greece.

As early as July 1940, Hitler ordered preparations for an invasion of Russia. Despite the Nazi-Soviet Pact, Hitler remained obsessed by the desire to destroy Bolshevism and to gain control of the grain-rich fields of the Ukraine. Once Russia was defeated, he believed, Britain would be forced to capitulate. The Russian invasion began on July 22, 1941. "Operation Barbarossa" moved the mightiest army in history—some 175 German divisions—against a vast, unfortified front. The Germans took the Soviets by surprise and, shattering their weak defenses, killed or captured 2 million soldiers in the first months of the campaign. By late October, Russia appeared about to collapse. But instead of allowing his generals to make a concentrated push against Moscow, Hitler insisted on dispersing his forces along the front. An early winter brought the German offensive to a halt, just as it had Napoleon's Grand Army in 1812. When Stalin's troops counterattacked, first

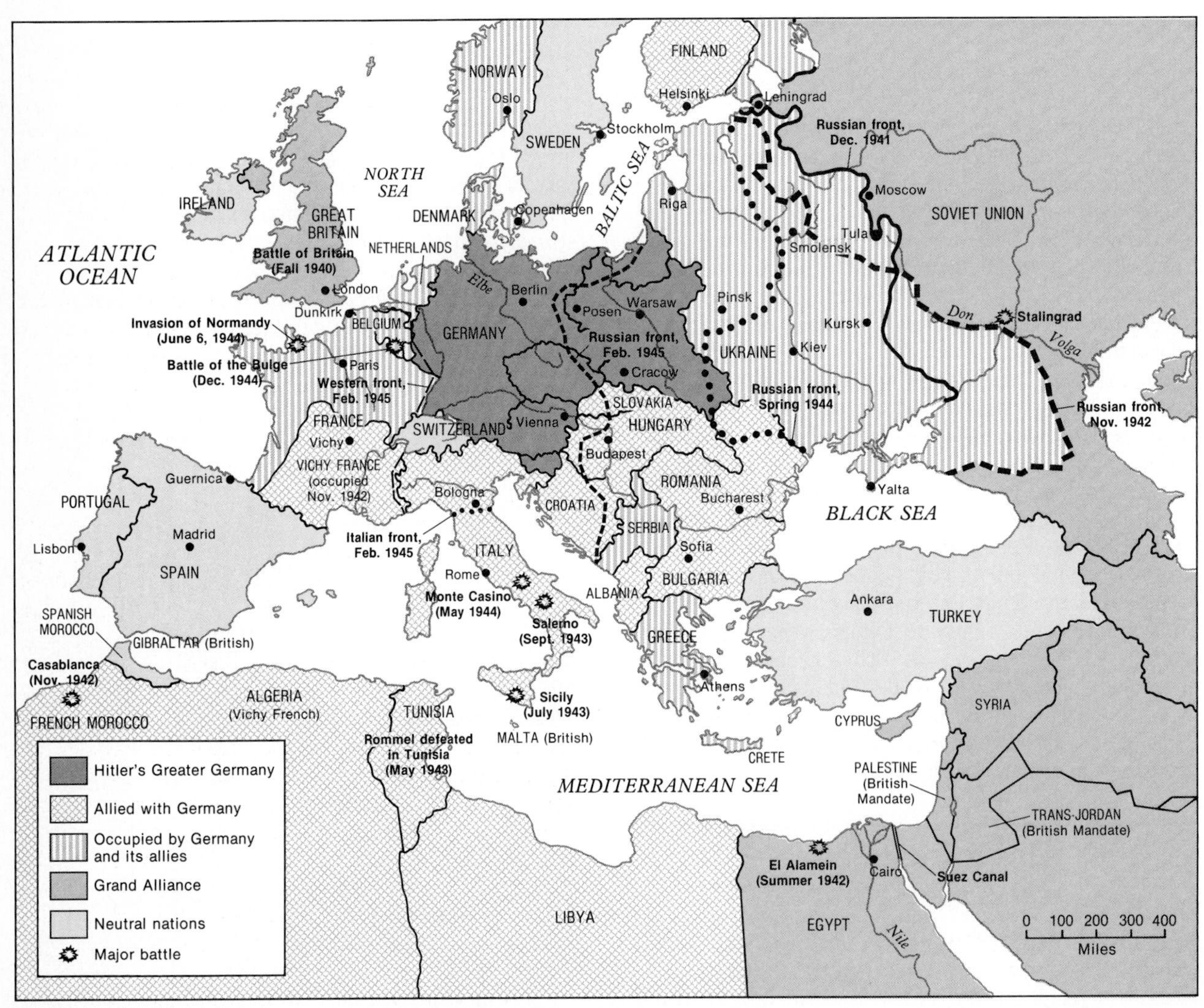

37.2 World War II in Europe

in November and again in December, the Nazi war machine suffered its first setbacks. With Britain holding out in the west and Russia having survived in the east, Hitler now faced the prospect of a two-front war.

The United States and Japan: The Road to Pearl Harbor

Among the great powers of the world, only the United States remained at peace. Disillusionment over the outcome of World War I had nurtured isolationist sentiment among many Americans, and when President Franklin Roosevelt came into office, he moved cautiously to make the nation aware of the precarious state of world affairs. Roosevelt wanted the United States to exert its influence against fascist and Japanese expansionism. But as the threat of war mounted, isolationists in Congress passed neutrality laws that prohibited the export of arms. Nevertheless, the Japanese drive into northern China in the summer of 1937 moved the American government into an openly anti-Japanese position. That October, Roosevelt, in a public statement known as the Quarantine Speech, declared that war was a contagion that had to be contained.

The outbreak of war in Europe found the American public sympathetic to Britain and France but unwilling to become directly involved. Roosevelt, determined to supply France and Britain with weapons, secured a revision of the neutrality laws that enabled the Allies to buy arms on a cash-and-carry basis. As the Nazis stormed across western Europe, he obtained a $1 billion defense appropriation. Public opinion began to rally behind the president during the Battle of Britain, and in September 1940 Congress implemented the first peacetime draft in American history. Two months later, as British resources neared exhaustion, Roosevelt devised the lend-lease program, which extended unlimited goods, instead of credit, to Britain. In the wake of the Nazi invasion of Russia, munitions were also sent to the Soviet Union under the same plan. America had become, in Roosevelt's words, "the arsenal of democracy."

In August, Roosevelt and Churchill met on a cruiser off the Newfoundland coast to sign a statement of principles tantamount to war aims. This Atlantic Charter not only called for national self-determination, disarmament, and "freedom from fear and want" but also looked forward to "the final destruction of the Nazi tyranny" and unconditional German surrender.

Asian events finally brought America into the war. United States policy toward Japan had already hardened over China. Now, with the Western powers fighting in Europe, Japanese expansionists saw their opportunity. In September 1940 Japan signed a defensive Tripartite Pact with Germany and Italy, extending the Axis alliance to Asia. America responded by banning the sale of essential raw materials, including iron, steel, and aviation fuel, to Japan. Negotiations initiated with the United States in the spring of 1941 by Prince Konoye, the Japanese premier, resulted in deadlock. Hitler's invasion of Russia freed Japan to move without fear of Soviet interference, and in July it occupied Indochina. Roosevelt immediately froze Japanese assets and joined with Britain in imposing economic sanctions. The failure of negotiations, together with the stiff American response to Japan's conquest of Indochina, played into the hands of the extremists in Tokyo. In October, General Tojo Hideki (1885–1948), a militarist, became premier. On the morning of December 7— without a declaration of war and while Japanese envoys were meeting with American officials in Washington—two waves of Japanese planes attacked the United States naval base at Pearl Harbor, striking a devastating blow at American power in the Pacific. The next day the United States declared war or the Axis.

The War in China

The Second World War was far more a global conflict than the first, and the major theater outside Europe was Asia. More territory and people in Asia were involved in the fighting than in any other part of the world. Asia experienced the first and so far the only use of nuclear weapons, by the Americans against the Japanese, and China suffered the greatest number of war casualties of any nation.

For China the war had actually begun in 1931 with the Japanese invasion of Manchuria and escalated to an all-out battle for survival when the Japanese attacked Peking and Shanghai in 1937 and fought their way to the Kuomintang capital of Nanking. Japanese troops, with the full knowledge of their commanders, went on an orgy of killing when Nanking fell, vowing to punish the Chinese for holding up the imperial army by their resistance in Shanghai and on the route to Nanking. Chiang Kai-shek had committed most of his best soldiers and modern weapons to slowing the Japanese drive for Nanking, but it was innocent civilians—probably as many as 300,000 dead—who suffered in the so-called Rape of Nanking once the Japanese entered the city. Survivors described horrifying sights of raped women impaled on stakes and children sliced in two.

Chiang's government and the remnants of his army retreated westward to Chungking (Chongqing). The Kuomintang war effort was largely spent, its best troops and equipment gone. New conscription drives in the western provinces brought the army to some 5 million men, but they were poorly clothed and fed, often virtually starved, and tyrannized by their officers; they had few or no weapons and very poor morale. The Japanese invasion was stalled by the mountains of western China, by overextended supply lines, and by the effective guerrilla resistance of the Communists in the north, who pinned down 1 million enemy troops but were never themselves eliminated. Japanese planes bombed the cities left under

Chinese control almost at will after 1937 but had little military effect except to kill many thousands of civilians.

A few small battles took place, largely ineffective retreating actions by demoralized and poorly led Chinese forces easily brushed aside by Japanese columns probing westward. Near the Burma border in the far southwest, periodic artillery duels across the gorge of the Salween River broke out, but no real battles. In the north a different kind of war hurt the Japanese far more. Chinese Communist guerrillas controlled most of the countryside at night, especially west of the coastal plain, bombing bridges, roads, and railways and ambushing Japanese patrols but avoiding pitched battles, given the vast Japanese superiority in equipment. They confined the invaders to the cities and towns, and as the war progressed, they won control of much of the rural north while they too depended on mountains and distance to limit enemy occupation to urban areas in the east. When Japan surrendered in August 1945, its armies still held most of the eastern half of China, from which the Chinese never had the strength to drive them.

But although there were only skirmishes rather than major battles after 1937, more than 20 million Chinese died at Japanese hands from 1937 to 1945, most of them civilians. The occupying army was at least as ruthless as the Nazis in Europe, exterminating whole villages as part of a policy of terror and slaughtering noncombatants indiscriminately. Their officially sanctioned slogan was "Kill all, burn all, loot all!" In the occupied territories the Japanese forced Chinese to bow or even kneel to their officers and beat or shot them if they were not sufficiently deferential. The record of the Japanese was equally bad elsewhere in Asia, but in China they began much earlier and made no real effort to win local support. Like Nazi terror, Japanese brutality stemmed also from a conviction of their own cultural and even racial superiority and from their contempt for those they conquered. It was a grim period in the history of East Asia. At the end of the war, the Kuomintang had been fatally weakened, and the Communists had grown from a tiny and hunted band to a major military presence in the north. Their effectiveness against the Japanese had won them a broad base of popular support even among many in the Kuomintang-controlled areas, and by mid-1945 they were the real government of much of the north.

CHUNGKING: BELEAGUERED WARTIME CAPITAL

Just before the fall of Hankow (one of the three cities now part of Wuhan) on the central Yangtze in October 1938, China's capital moved farther upriver to Chungking, where

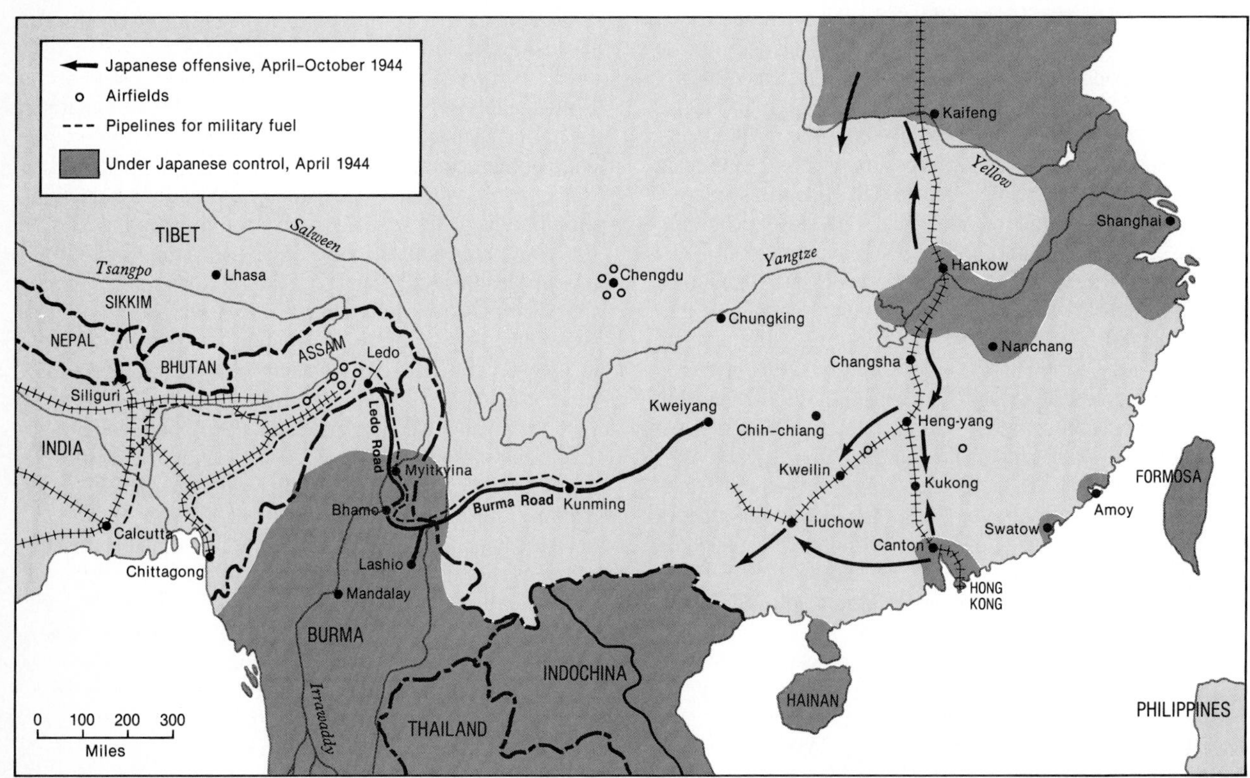

37.3 The China–Burma–India Theater in World War II

it remained for the rest of the war. Chungking sprawled over steep hills at the junction of the Chialing (Jialing) River and the Yangtze near the center of the generally hilly Red Basin of Szechuan (Sichuan), which was in turn surrounded on all sides by mountains. The steep and narrow gorges of the Yangtze about halfway between Hankow and Chungking along the provincial border were easily blocked by a boom. These natural defenses kept Chungking secure from the Japanese army, but it had few defenses against air attack, and Japanese bombing caused great destruction and loss of life. By 1941, before Pearl Harbor, an unofficial American group, the Flying Tigers, paid by the Chinese but with their own fighter planes, had greatly reduced the bombing raids. Chinese morale was high for the first two or three Chungking years, and the wartime capital was a symbol of patriotic resistance. Whole arsenals and factories had been disassembled and carried on the backs of workers to Chungking and elsewhere in Szechuan to escape the Japanese; university faculties and students made the same journey, carrying what they could of their libraries and laboratories. America's entry into the war against Japan in late 1941 gave morale another boost.

But disillusionment spread as the Kuomintang army largely sat the war out while the increasingly corrupt government of Chiang Kai-shek and his cronies stockpiled arms for use against the Communists. Chungking was also notorious for its gray, cloudy weather, its drizzle, its suffocatingly hot summers and cold, damp winters, and its painful overcrowding. More than a million people from all parts of China, including officials and army personnel, were added to the originally smaller population, with too few additions to housing, water supply, and other basics. Fires set by Japanese bombs often burned out of control, and air raid shelters were grossly inadequate. Chungking's main link with the outside world was the extension of the Burma Road through mountainous southwest China and, after the Japanese took Burma, the American airlift from India over the "hump" of the Himalayas. The main airport was a sandbank in the Yangtze hemmed in by steep hills on both sides, flooded every spring and summer by rising river levels, and obscured most of the time by heavy low clouds. The summer airport was on the edge of a cliff above the river, which was equally dangerous. There were no railways anywhere in Szechuan. People understandably felt isolated. Prices for everything skyrocketed through a combination of wartime shortages, government ineptitude, and a swollen population. The Szechuanese blamed it on "downriver people," who in turn were contemptuous of "ignorant provincials."

Tight "thought control" and the secret police suppressed all free political expression, and people with "dangerous thoughts" or caught with "improper" books in their dwellings were jailed or executed. Those with money and connections lived luxuriously in guarded villas with American-made limousines, but most people in Chungking lived in poverty, mud, and squalor. By 1940 inflation began to rise at about 10 percent per month, accelerating wildly after 1943. Currency might lose half or more of its value between morning and afternoon. The government printed more notes of larger denominations, while its finance minister, H. H. Kung, brother-in-law of Chiang Kai-shek, obtained gold from the United States for his own accounts in overseas banks, as did other Kuomintang officials. Salaries and wages fell hopelessly behind inflation, and malnutrition, tuberculosis, and other diseases of poverty were widespread. Furniture, clothing, books, and heirlooms were sold in a vain attempt to stay afloat. Nearly all officials succumbed to bribery and other forms of corruption, whatever their original principles, if only to save their families. By the end of the war the Chinese were universally demoralized and had lost faith in the Kuomintang. The Chungking years saw the death of Kuomintang hopes to remain the government of a China now sick of its ineffectiveness, corruption, and reaction.

India and Southeast Asia

India was only marginally involved in the war, although 2 million Indian troops fought under British command in several theaters, and India itself became a major military base and supply center for the Allied war effort in Asia. A few Japanese bombs fell on Calcutta but the big invasion push through northwestern Burma was stopped by British and Indian troops at Imphal, just inside the Indian border, in the spring of 1944, followed by the accelerating collapse of the Japanese position in Burma as British and Indian forces advanced. Ceylon (Sri Lanka) served as a major Allied base and became the headquarters of the Allied Southeast Asia Command under Lord Louis Mountbatten (1900–1979), who directed the reconquest of Burma and Malaya.

A frustrated Bengali and Indian nationalist, Subhas Chandra Bose (1897–1945), who had been passed over for leadership in the Congress party, saw his chance for power in alliance with the Japanese. Bose had visited Mussolini and Hitler in Europe. He escaped from British arrest in 1941, made his way to Berlin, and in 1943 went by German submarine around Africa to Singapore, where the Japanese gave him command of 60,000 Indian prisoners of war. He called them the Indian National Army for the "liberation" of their homeland, but they were used as cannon fodder in the advance wave for the bloody and fruitless assault on Imphal. Bose escaped and was later killed in an air crash, but he remained a national hero to some Indians.

Japan and the Pacific Theater

The chief military action in Asia took place in the Pacific. Following the attack on Pearl Harbor, the Japanese conquered Malaya, Burma, Indonesia, and the Philippines in rapid succession. This was assisted by Japanese use of French bases in Indochina, granted by the Vichy government in mid-1940 and vital to the assault on Southeast Asia.

The speed of the Japanese advance paralleled that of the Nazis in Europe. Japanese dive bombers destroyed the major ships of the British Asian fleet off Singapore as they had sunk most of the American fleet at Pearl Harbor. The Americans now lacked the naval capacity to defend or supply the Philippines, where much of their air force had been destroyed on the ground a few hours after the Pearl Harbor raid. The Japanese had developed a light, fast, maneuverable fighter plane, the Zero, which gave them air supremacy. The Dutch East Indies (Indonesia) were weakly defended, and no help was available for the greatly outnumbered Dutch. Thailand remained neutral, but at the price of granting Japanese use of bases there. By early 1942 Japan had occupied all the smaller islands in the western Pacific and installed garrisons even in the western Aleutians off Alaska.

Japan's thrust southward had long been planned as part of the "Greater East Asia Co-prosperity Sphere." Japan claimed that it would liberate Asia from Western colonialism, but the real aim was to combine its technological, industrial, and organizational skills with the manpower and resources of the rest of East Asia, thereby creating a single economic unit dominated by Tokyo. Poor in natural resources, especially oil, Japan sought access to the oil, rubber, tin, and rice of Southeast Asia and the iron ore and coal of the Philippines and China. But Japan ignored the rising force of nationalism, first in China and then in its Southeast Asian conquests. Almost from the beginning, Japanese racist arrogance and brutality made a mockery of "co-prosperity" and earned the Japanese bitter hatred everywhere. Western prisoners, including the defeated American forces in the Philippines, were treated with special cruelty. Japan was now master of Asia, and its warrior tradition had only contempt for soldiers who surrendered even when their position was hopeless.

The Price of Victory

The brutality of Japanese rule in Asia occurred on a massive scale, but it lacked the carefully organized, systematic scope of Nazi atrocities in Europe. As the year 1942 opened, Hitler controlled, directly or indirectly, a huge empire that stretched from the English Channel to the gates of Moscow and from Norway to North Africa. His goal, after victory, was to create out of this area a "New Order" with Germany as its center and around which Europe and the world would revolve. Hitler never developed detailed plans for his empire. Yet the war provided ample evidence of what the New Order would have entailed.

Descent into the Abyss: The Holocaust

Hitler's plans derived from his notions of race, which he believed held the key to world history. Nazi racial ideologues divided Europe's population into three broad categories: the master "Aryan" race of German-speaking or related peoples, below which stood the Latins, and at the bottom the Slavs, Jews, and gypsies. Hitler dealt with the conquered territories according to this scale of values. The inferior populations of the eastern regions would provide Germany with *Lebensraum* ("living space") and a huge supply of cheap or slave labor. Immediately after the conquest of Poland, pockets of German colonists were established there, while more than 1 million Poles were brought to Germany as forced workers. Later even greater numbers of Russian prisoners suffered the same fate.

Nazi policy in eastern Europe was a vital part of Hitler's geopolitical scheme, but the Jews were at the core of his obsession about race. He spoke repeatedly of making Germany *Judenrein*, or free of Jews, and in *Mein Kampf* he described how the Nazi state would breed a population of Aryans free of the sick, the weak, and, most important, the Jewish "contagion." As early as 1919, Hitler had written that "the final objective" of anti-Semitism must "unswervingly be the removal of the Jews altogether."[2]

After the seizure of power, Nazi policies had forced the vast majority of German Jews to emigrate, so that by 1939 few were left in the Reich. Once the war began, large-scale emigration became impossible, and Nazi officials evolved barbaric plans to deal with the millions of Jews in the conquered territories of Poland and eastern Europe. They first schemed to concentrate Europe's Jews in "reservations" in the Lublin district of Poland or on the island of Madagascar. As plans for the invasion of Russia progressed, the removal policy gave way to the Final Solution—the extermination of European Jewry.

Hitler gave SS leader Himmler orders for the Final Solution in the spring or early summer of 1941. As the German army pushed eastward, special SS units—*Einsatzgruppen* ("special-duty groups") commanded by police chief Reinhard Heydrich—herded Jews into ditches behind the front lines and shot them. Mobile gassing vans were also used. By fall the extermination process had been organized on a massive scale as Jews and other victims were transported by rail from all over the Continent to death camps in Poland.

The SS murdered millions in extermination camps such as Auschwitz, Treblinka, and Bergen-Belsen, where tens of thousands of men, women, and children were gassed to death each day. A precedent for the killing had been set earlier by the gassing of 70,000 mentally ill Germans. The bodies of the victims were stripped of clothing, hair, and gold teeth. Corpses were either processed for soap and fertilizer or burnt. Outside the camps, in Poland and

A group of Polish Jews are marched to the death camps flanked by German Gestapo agents. [UPI/Bettmann Newsphotos]

Russia, SS squads continued to slaughter many thousands more, shooting and burying their victims in mass graves.

The Nazis murdered a startling range of victims in their effort to purge Europe of "undesirable" elements, including gypsies, the infirm and mentally ill, Jehovah's Witnesses, and some 60,000 known German homosexuals. But their primary focus remained the Jews. Some estimates suggest that more than 6 million Jews perished in the Holocaust, more than three-fourths of Europe's Jewish population. Beyond the statistical enormity of the Holocaust lies the memory of the planned elimination of entire categories of human beings by a modern, technologically advanced society. Modern history has known no more heinous example of human barbarism.

ISABELLA KATZ AND THE HOLOCAUST: A LIVING TESTIMONY

No statistics can adequately render the enormity of the Holocaust, and its human meaning can perhaps only be understood through the experience of a single human being who was cast into the nightmare of the Final Solution. Isabella Katz was the eldest of six children—Isabella, brother Philip, and sisters Rachel, Chicha, Cipi, and baby Potyo—from a family of Hungarian Jews. She lived in the ghetto of Kisvarda, a provincial town of 20,000 people, where hers was a typical Jewish family of the region—middle-class, attached to Orthodox traditions, and imbued with a love of learning.

In 1938 and 1939 Hitler pressured Hungary's regent, Miklós Horthy, into adopting anti-Jewish laws. By 1941 Hungary had become a German ally, and deportations and massacres were added to the restrictions. Isabella's father left for the United States, where he hoped to obtain entry papers for his family, but after Pearl Harbor, Hungary was at war with America and the family was trapped. In the spring of 1944, when Hitler occupied Hungary, the horror of the Final Solution struck Isabella. On March 19 Adolf Eichmann, as SS officer in charge of deportation, ordered the roundup of Jews in Hungary, who numbered some 650,000. On May 28, Isabella's nineteenth birthday, the Jews in Kisvarda were told to prepare for transportation to Auschwitz on the following morning. Isabella recalled:

> **And now an SS man is here, spick-and-span, with a dog, a silver pistol, and a whip. And he is all of sixteen years old. On his list appears the name of every Jew in the ghetto. . . . "Teresa Katz," he calls—my mother. She steps forward. . . . Now the SS man moves toward my mother. He raises his whip and, for no apparent reason at all, lashes out at her.**

En route to Auschwitz, crammed into hot, airless boxcars, Isabella's mother told her children to "stay alive":

> **Out there, when it's all over, a world's waiting for you to give it all I gave you. Despite what you see here . . . believe me, there is humanity out there, there is dignity. . . . And when this is all over, you must add to it, because sometimes it is a little short, a little skimpy.**

Isabella and her family were among more than 437,000 Jews sent to Auschwitz from Hungary.

When they arrived at Auschwitz, the SS and camp guards divided the prisoners into groups, often separating family members. Amid the screams and confusion, Isabella remembered:

We had just spotted the back of my mother's head when Mengele, the notorious Dr. Josef Mengele, points to my sister and me and says, "Die Zwei" [those two]. This trim, very good-looking German, with a flick of his thumb and a whistle, is selecting who is to live and who is to die.

Isabella's mother and her baby sister perished within a few days.

The day we arrived in Auschwitz, there were so many people to be burned that the four crematoriums couldn't handle the task. So the Germans built big open fires to throw the children in. Alive? I do not know. I saw the flames. I heard the shrieks.

Isabella was to endure the hell of Auschwitz for nine months.

The inmates were stripped, the hair on their heads and bodies was shaved, and they were herded into crude, overcrowded barracks. As if starvation, forced labor, and disease were not enough, they were subjected to unspeakable torture, humiliation, and terror, a mass of living skeletons for whom the difference between life and death could be measured only in an occasional flicker of spirit that determined to resist against impossible odds. Isabella put it this way:

Have you ever weighed 120 pounds and gone down to 40? Something like that—not quite alive, yet not quite dead. Can anyone, can even I, picture it? . . . Our eyes sank deeper. Our skin rotted. Our bones screamed out of our bodies. Indeed, there was barely a body to house the mind, yet the mind was still working, sending out the messages "Live! Live!"

In November, just as Isabella and her family were lined up outside a crematorium, they were suddenly moved to Birnbäumel, in eastern Germany—the Russians were getting nearer and the Nazis were closing down their death camps and moving the human evidence of their barbarism out of reach of the enemy. In January, as the Russians and the frigid weather closed in, the prisoners were forced to march through the snows deeper into Germany, heading toward the camp at Bergen-Belsen. Those who could not endure the trial fell by the side, shot or frozen to death. On January 23, while stumbling through a blizzard with the sound of Russian guns in the distance, Isabella, Rachel, and Chicha made a successful dash from the death march and hid in an abandoned house. Two days later Russian soldiers found them. Philip had been sent to a labor camp, and Cipi made it to Bergen-Belsen, where she died.

Isabella later married and had two children of her own, making a new life in America. Yet the images of the Holocaust remain forever in her memory. "Now I am older," she says, "and I don't remember all the pain. . . . That is not happiness, only relief, and relief is blessed. . . . And children someday will plant flowers in Auschwitz, where the sun couldn't crack through the smoke of burning flesh."[3]

The Grand Alliance: Victory in Europe

By 1942 the Grand Alliance of Russia, Britain, and the United States had been formed against Hitler's New Order. From the first the Allies were plagued by mutual distrust: Churchill feared Soviet territorial designs in Europe and what he believed was America's ignorance of European affairs; Roosevelt suspected Churchill's imperialist ambitions in the Mediterranean and Stalin's political motives; and Stalin suspected both Western statesmen, who hated communism, of wanting to deny the Soviet Union the fruits of victory. Nevertheless, they agreed to make military objectives—defeating first Germany and Italy, then Japan—their immediate goal, postponing political issues until the war was won. In January 1942 the three powers joined with 23 other nations in a United Nations declaration that reaffirmed these goals as well as the principles of the Atlantic Charter.

The tide of battle began to turn in favor of the Allies in 1942. In May and June, American forces stopped the Japanese advance in the Pacific in crucial battles in the Coral Sea and at Midway Island. In November the United States and Britain launched Operation Torch, the invasion of North Africa.

Under the pressure of the gigantic battles that were consuming Russian manpower on the eastern front, Stalin had repeatedly insisted on the opening of a major second front in the west. No nation sustained a greater burden of physical destruction and death than the Soviet Union, which lost some 20 million men, and no nation contributed more to the defeat of Germany. Since the winter of 1941 the German armies had continued to batter the Russians along an 1,800-mile front, but in August 1942 the German war machine was flung at the southern zone in a protracted battle for Stalingrad. The situation appeared hopeless when the Germans stormed the city in September. But Stalin's armies, circling around from the south and north, caught Hitler's forces in a gigantic pincer movement. Although winter fast approached, Hitler refused to withdraw his soldiers. On February 2, 1943, the last of the 500,000-man Sixth German Army surrendered. That July, German and Russian forces fought bitterly along the Kursk salient, southwest of Moscow, in the biggest tank battle of the war. A clear victory for the Russians, the engagement cost another half million German casualties and spelled ultimate defeat for Hitler.

Churchill and Roosevelt had met in January 1943 in Casablanca, where they made plans for opening the second front. To forestall the Soviets in central Europe, they chose Italy as the target, and in July, Allied troops landed in Sicily from their base in North Africa. The Sicilian in-

The female labor force in the United States more than doubled during World War II. Here women riveters work on an airplane. [UPI/Bettmann Newsphotos]

vasion precipitated a coup d'état against Mussolini by dissident Fascists and involved King Victor Emmanuel III and Marshal Pietro Badoglio. The king arrested Mussolini and appointed Badoglio prime minister, but Hitler quickly moved German troops into northern Italy and rescued the Duce. By early September, when the Italians signed an armistice and joined the Allies as a cobelligerent against Germany, the Allies had crossed to the mainland. In the north Mussolini established a puppet regime, the Italian Social Republic, under German auspices. Thereafter, for 18 months Italy became the scene of bitter fighting, not only between Allies and the Axis but also between Fascist loyalists and a massive partisan resistance movement.

In October, Allied foreign ministers meeting in Moscow reiterated their demand for unconditional surrender. They also agreed to the joint occupation of Germany, the purge of Nazism, and the creation of a United Nations organization. A month later Churchill and Roosevelt met with Stalin in Teheran for their first face-to-face conference. The talks focused on plans for the final attack against Hitler's "Fortress Europe." The three agreed to an invasion of western Europe in the spring of 1944.

Operation Overlord began on June 6, 1944—"D day." Under the supreme command of General Dwight D. Eisenhower (1890–1969), the Allies carried out the greatest amphibious landing in history on the coast of Normandy. More than 2 million men and millions of tons of equipment poured into northwestern France over the next few months. By the end of August, Allied armies had driven the *Wehrmacht* to the frontiers of Germany, but the drive stalled. In a desperate effort to stave off defeat, Hitler launched a counteroffensive in December, driving deep into the Allied sector in Belgium and Luxembourg, but the bloody Battle of the Bulge proved to be Germany's last major effort. From the east, Soviet armies poured into Germany in January, coming within 100 miles of Berlin, while British and American troops pushed toward Germany from the west, crossing the Rhine in March.

While the Allies were closing the ring around Germany, Churchill, Roosevelt, and Stalin met in February 1945 at Yalta, on the Black Sea. The Yalta conference revealed the growing tensions that would divide the Allies after the war. Roosevelt, eager to secure Soviet entry into the war against Japan, conceded some of Stalin's demands regarding the future governments of Europe. Soviet armies were already in Poland, Germany, eastern Europe, and the Balkans. Churchill, who had made a secret arrangement with Stalin regarding Soviet and British influence in the Balkans, joined Roosevelt in agreeing to a larger Russian role in eastern Asia and the transfer of Poland's eastern territory to Russia while compensating the Poles with German land. In return, Stalin promised to permit democratic elements in the postwar governments of Poland, Yugoslavia, and eastern Europe.

Three days after American and Russian soldiers met on the Elbe River on April 25, Mussolini was executed by Italian partisans. On April 30 Hitler committed suicide in a secret bunker beneath the ruined streets of Berlin. German representatives signed the surrender in Eisenhower's headquarters on May 7, 1945.

The Atomic Bomb and the Defeat of Japan

With the European conflict at an end, American strategists turned their attention to the Pacific theater, where Japanese defeat was imminent. The naval battle of Midway in

37.4 World War II in Eastern Asia

June 1942 had been won mainly by American aircraft carriers, which had been on patrol when Pearl Harbor was bombed, and by use of British-developed radar. A long island-hopping campaign began in which American and Australian troops retook the fiercely defended islands of the western Pacific one by one. Bloody battles in the jungles of New Guinea, the Solomon Islands, and the Bismarck Archipelago were followed by a slow northward advance, with hand-to-hand fighting and heavy losses on both sides. The Allies captured Saipan, within bombing range of Japan's big cities, in June 1944, and in October the Japanese suffered a major defeat in the Philippine Sea. By early 1945 the Philippines themselves were retaken, and in June the Allies seized Okinawa, part of Japan's home territory. Fanatical Japanese defenders often fought to the last soldier. Japanese pilots began to make suicidal *kamikaze* ("divine wind") attacks in planes loaded with bombs that purposely crashed into enemy ships. American losses, though serious, were soon replaced. Japan's fleet was by now almost entirely sunk, and American submarines had destroyed the majority of its supply and merchant ships. Meanwhile, American and Chinese forces had joined British and Indian troops in the liberation of Burma, while Allied naval dominance had cut the Dutch East Indies off from Japanese supply lines.

Japan was ready to surrender by the spring of 1945 and had begun peace feelers through the still neutral Russians. American bombers had destroyed nearly all of Japan's cities, using incendiary bombs to start giant firestorms. In one horrible night in Tokyo, fire bombing killed an estimated 100,000 people, the same number slain throughout the war in air raids over Britain. Many of the survivors in the gutted cities starved.

Events in the United States cut short plans for the final assault against the Japanese mainland. Working in secret laboratories on the so-called Manhattan Project, American, British, and European refugee scientists developed a primitive atomic bomb. The weapon was successfully tested on July 16 at Alamogordo in the isolated desert of New Mexico. Harry S Truman (1884–1972), who became president in April on Roosevelt's death, decided to use the awesome new weapon against Japan, a decision that subsequently aroused great controversy. On the one hand, some strategists argued that an invasion of Japan would cost heavy American casualties, although Eisenhower did not believe that the atomic bomb was needed to force Japan's surrender. On the other hand, at Yalta, Stalin had agreed to attack Japan within three months after the defeat of Germany, and Truman, with a decisive weapon at hand, may have been anxious to forestall the Russians. On August 6 an American plane dropped an atomic bomb on the medium-sized town and army base of Hiroshima, obliterating the city and killing over 78,000 civilians. Radiation fallout and other injuries eventually claimed thousands of additional victims. Truman called it "the greatest thing in history." Russia declared war on August 8 and swept into Japanese-occupied Manchuria. The next day the Americans leveled the city of Nagasaki with a second atomic device, with another large loss of life. On August 15 Emperor Hirohito announced the Japanese surrender.

The war had cost the lives of 2.5 million Japanese soldiers and sailors, and an additional million civilians had died in air raids. The country was in ruins. But the Japanese defeat of colonial regimes in the early years of the war had destroyed the myth of Western invincibility, and Japanese brutality had further stimulated Asian nationalism. Despite

The End of Emperor Worship

On August 15, 1945, after the atomic bombing of Japan by American planes, Emperor Hirohito spoke to his people for the first time over the radio and declared the war lost. Here is how one listener, 10 years old at the time, recalled the impact of the news.

The adults sat around their radios and cried. The children gathered outside in the dusty road and whispered their bewilderment. We were most confused and disappointed by the fact that the Emperor had spoken in a *human* voice, no different from any adult's. None of us understood what he was saying, but we had all heard his voice. One of my friends could even imitate it cleverly. Laughing, we surrounded him—a twelve year old in grimy shorts who spoke with the Emperor's voice. A minute later we felt afraid. We looked at one another; no one spoke. How could we believe that an august presence of such awful power had become an ordinary human voice on a designated summer day?

Source: O. Kenzaburo, *A Personal Matter*, trans. J. Nathan (New York: Grove Press, 1968), pp. vii–viii.

the Western victory in Asia, the old Western empires were irretrievably gone.

The United Nations

Allied plans for establishing a secure peace were based on the conviction that the fascist regimes had been responsible for the war and should be destroyed. The Allies imposed democratic and educational reforms on Germany, Italy, and Japan and removed compromised officials from positions of influence. They also supervised the drafting of new constitutions establishing parliamentary governments and civil liberties. Furthermore, the discovery of the Nazi death camps led to the establishment of the Nuremberg military tribunal to punish prominent Nazis for "crimes against humanity." Similar trials, on different grounds and sometimes under local jurisdiction, were held in Japan and Italy.

As in 1919, the victors in World War II placed great significance on the creation of an international organization to maintain the peace. Roosevelt, a Wilsonian idealist, was an ardent advocate of a new world body empowered to prevent aggression. The Allies dissolved the League of Nations and in its place created the United Nations, with headquarters in New York City. The formal charter, drafted at a meeting in San Francisco in April, was signed by 50 nations in June 1945.

The UN charter gave one vote to each member state in a General Assembly, which has since grown to more than triple its original size. But real power lay in the Security Council, whose permanent members were the United States, the Soviet Union, Britain, France, and China. Because each could veto Council decisions, the organization was mired in controversy from the start. Subsidiary agencies, such as the World Health Organization and the Food and Agricultural Organization, have, however, made important contributions in noncontroversial areas such as combating disease and starvation.

As the world began to recover from the ashes of destroyed cities and the loss of some 50 million lives, it could look back on a generation of economic depression, brutal dictatorship, ideological strife, and the bloodiest war in history. But even as the postwar recovery got under way, signs of further strife appeared. The peace settlements and the structure of the United Nations reflected the growing tensions that had already begun to divide the former Allies. Nations such as Britain, France, and Germany would never return to the positions of power they once commanded. Instead, two superpowers—the United States and the Soviet Union—would predominate in the postwar world. Moreover, the birth of the atomic age, mirrored in the ruins of Hiroshima and Nagasaki, suggested the possibility that humans could one day destroy civilization.

Yet people everywhere could celebrate the triumph over European fascism and Japanese militarism. At the time, opportunity for rebuilding presented the world with a more immediate challenge. Moreover, out of the tragic and sobering legacy of the war, only the prospect of an end to the vast colonial empires that had once held in their grip the peoples of Asia, Africa, and Latin America, augured well for the future.

Notes

1. A. Hitler, *Mein Kampf*, trans. R. Manheim (Boston: Houghton Mifflin, 1962), p. 414.
2. L. S. Dawidowicz, *The War Against the Jews, 1933–1945* (New York: Holt, Rinehart and Winston, 1975), p. 153.
3. I. K. Leitner and I. A. Leitner, *Fragments of Isabella* (New York: Dell, 1988), pp. 18–19, 28, 31–32, 46–47, 102–103.

Suggestions for Further Reading

Boyle, J. H. *China and Japan at War, 1937–1945*. Stanford, Calif.: Stanford University Press, 1972.

Bracher, K. D. *The German Dictatorship*. New York: Praeger, 1970.

Butow, R. *Japan's Decision to Surrender*. Stanford, Calif.: Stanford University Press, 1954.

Calvocoressi, P., and Wint, G. *Total War*. London: Penguin Books, 1972.

Campbell-Johnson, A. *Mission with Mountbatten*. New York: Dutton, 1953.

Deutscher, I. *Stalin: A Political Biography*, 2d ed. New York: Oxford University Press, 1967.

Divine, R. A. *The Reluctant Belligerent: American Entry into World War II*. New York: Wiley, 1979.

Eubank, K. *The Origins of World War II*. New York: Crowell, 1969.

Friedrich, C. J., and Brzezinski, Z. *Totalitarian Dictatorship and Autocracy*. New York: Praeger, 1956.

Gilbert, M., and Gott, R. *The Appeasers*. Boston: Houghton Mifflin, 1963.

Havens, T. *The Valley of Darkness*. New York: Norton, 1978.

Hildebrand, K. *The Foreign Policy of the Third Reich*. Berkeley: University of California Press, 1973.

Hinz, B. *Art in the Third Reich*. New York: Pantheon Books, 1979.

Hsi-sheng Chi. *Nationalist China at War*. Ann Arbor: University of Michigan Press, 1982.

Ienaga, S. *The Pacific War*. New York: Pantheon Books, 1978.

Langer, W. L., and Gleason, S. E. *The Undeclared War, 1940–41*. New York: Harper & Row, 1953.

Lebra, J., ed. *Japan's Greater East Asia Co-prosperity Sphere in World War II*. Kuala Lumpur, Malaysia: Oxford University Press, 1975.

Myers, R. H., and Peattie, M. R., eds. *The Japanese Colonial Empire, 1895–1945*. Princeton, N.J.: Princeton University Press, 1984.

Robertson, E. M. *Mussolini as Empire Builder*. London: Macmillan, 1977.

Schoenbaum, D. *Hitler's Social Revolution: Class and Status in Nazi Germany*. New York: Anchor Books, 1967.

Tannenbaum, E. R. *The Fascist Experience: Italian Society and Culture, 1922–1945*. New York: Basic Books, 1972.

Taylor, A. J. P. *The Origins of the Second World War*. New York: Wiley, 1972.

Thomas, H. *The Spanish Civil War*, rev. ed. New York: Harper & Row, 1977.

Ulam, A. *Stalin: The Man and His Era*. New York: Viking, 1973.

White, T., and Jacoby, A. *Thunder Out of China*. New York: William Sloane Associates, 1946.

Wright, G. *The Ordeal of Total War, 1939–1945*. New York: Harper & Row, 1968.

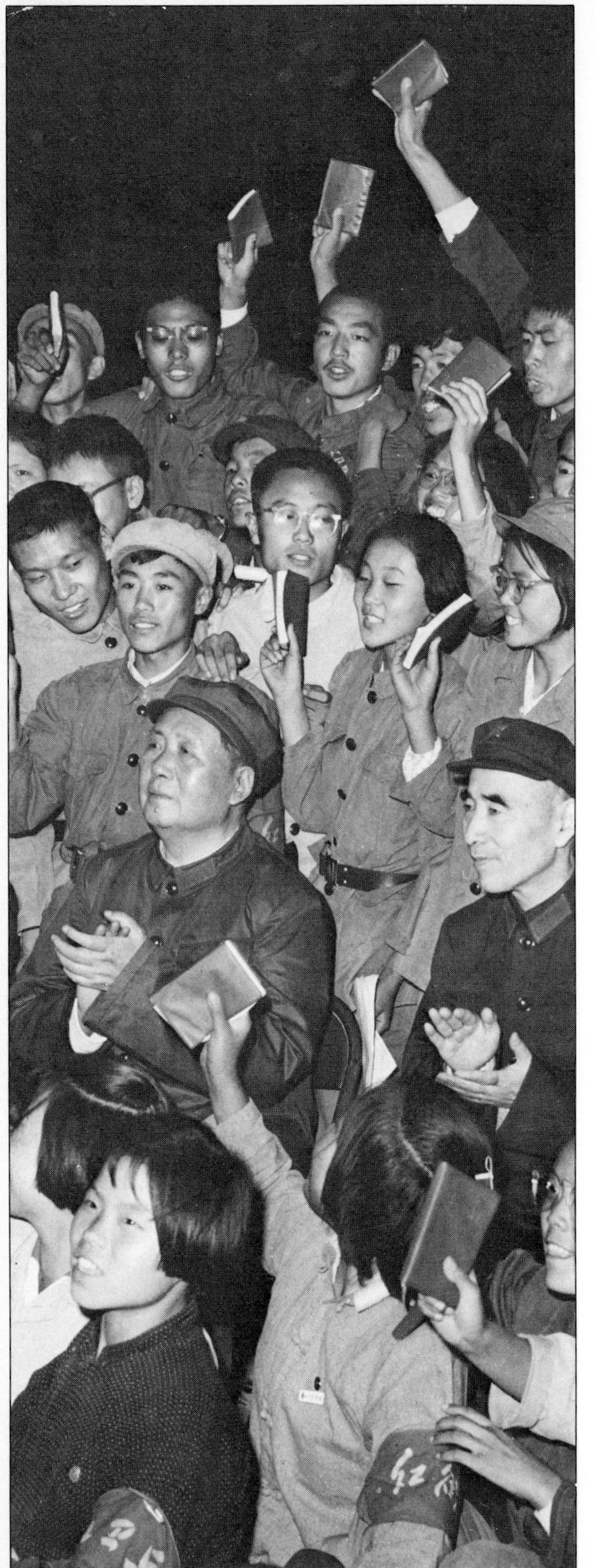

CHAPTER · 38

Revival and Revolution in East Asia

Much of Asia was devastated by World War II, and no part of it was unaffected. There were more war casualties in Asia than in all of the rest of the world. The heavy human and economic losses were, however, accompanied by the end of colonial rule and Western dominance in Asia. The Japanese conquest of Southeast Asia destroyed the image of Western superiority, while the war in Europe weakened both the power and the desire of the European powers to resume their former positions in Asia. The Japanese economy was destroyed by the war, and almost all of its cities were bombed to rubble. Japan lived under American military occupation from 1945 to 1952, but by 1950 the damage to the economy had been largely repaired and rapid new growth that would continue for decades had begun. By 1965 Japan had become the world's third industrial power, after the United States and the Soviet

The Cultural Revolution: Mao Tse-tung at a Peking University rally in 1966 where frenzied students wave their "Little Red Books." [Eastfoto/Sovfoto]

Union, and in the 1970s and 1980s it won a commanding position in world markets for its manufactured exports.

In China long-pent-up pressures for change resulted in civil war, from which the Communists emerged victorious over the Kuomintang (Guomindang) government in 1949. The new revolutionary government quickly repaired war damages, but in 1957 Mao Tse-tung, the Communist leader, launched the Great Leap Forward, a radical economic program that ended by plunging the country into mass starvation. It was followed in 1966 by the Cultural Revolution, a destructive effort to revive flagging revolutionary ardor, which ended only with Mao's death in 1976. China began to reopen its contacts with the West in the 1970s and to rejuvenate its economy. Korea was split by the Cold War into rival states; Vietnam, similarly divided, was unified by a successful war against the United States; and in Southeast Asia a number of new nations emerged, each following a different path.

The Recovery of Japan

Japan had been more completely destroyed by the war than any of the other belligerents. In addition to Hiroshima and Nagasaki, which had been leveled by the first atomic bombs, virtually all of Japan's cities, especially Tokyo and Yokohama, had been flattened and burned by massive conventional and incendiary bombing. A notable exception was Kyoto, the old imperial capital, which had been preserved by the intervention of American art historians. The government and what remained of the army in the home islands were still, however, in good order, and there was a smooth transfer of power to the American military government of occupation under General Douglas MacArthur. Japan had surrendered to the Allied forces, including Britain, China, Australia, Canada, New Zealand, and the Soviet Union, although the Soviets had intervened only in the last week of the war. But MacArthur permitted only token representation from each of the other allies in his SCAP (Supreme Commander Allied Powers) regime of occupation, over which he presided like a virtual emperor.

With very few exceptions, the Japanese people, including officials, officers, and troops as well as other civilians, accepted Emperor Hirohito's pronouncement of surrender and his call to "endure the unendurable." Most felt relief that the disastrous war was over. They soon found that the occupying Americans were not the devils some had feared and vented their bitterness on the now discredited military leaders who had so nearly destroyed the nation they were sworn to serve. In general, the occupation, which lasted from late August 1945 to late April 1952, was a period of peaceful reconstruction, with the Japanese doing most of the work of government under American supervision, except at the highest level.

38.1 Modern Japan

The American Occupation

Relief on finding the occupying forces bent on reconstruction rather than revenge was soon joined by gratitude for American aid. Most Japanese had lived at best on an austerity diet during the last years of the war, and many were half starved, living in makeshift shelters in the bombed-out cities. The winter of 1945–1946 would have been far harder if the Americans had not flown in emergency supplies of food and got the main rail lines working again to transport fuel and essential building supplies. Having expected far worse from their new rulers, the Japanese were pleasantly surprised. Many were even enthusiastic about the institutional changes that SCAP began to decree to root out the remnants of militarism and implant American-style democracy.

The big prewar industrial combines were broken up, although they subsequently re-formed. Thousands of political prisoners who had been accused of "dangerous thoughts" and jailed by the military-controlled government

The Japanese emperor Hirohito photographed with General MacArthur at the U.S. Embassy in 1945. [Bettmann Archive]

of the 1930s and 1940s were released. Other Japanese who were identified—sometimes wrongly—as having been too closely associated with Japanese fascism or militant imperialism were removed from their posts, including a number of senior officials. Several hundred Japanese were identified as suspected war criminals, and most were tried by a special tribunal in Tokyo that included Allied representatives. Seven were executed, including the wartime prime minister, Tojo, and 18 others were sentenced to prison terms. Nearly 1,000 minor war criminals in Japan and Southeast Asia, largely military men, were executed for gross cruelty to prisoners or to the inhabitants of conquered countries. This contrasted with the far more lenient treatment and in some cases even protection of all but the most major Nazi leaders by the United States and its allies in Europe.

A victor's justice in the aftermath of a bitter war is easily criticized, especially when racially tinged, but most Japanese accepted the tribunal's verdict as inevitable and perhaps even appropriate punishment. Most blamed their failed leaders rather than their new masters. The flexibility and adaptability of the Japanese in turn impressed the Americans, who had expected a sullen and resentful populace and found instead that they were to a surprising degree both liked and admired. Having fought ruthlessly and with immense dedication, the Japanese proved quite ready to accommodate to a relatively benign new order. Americans were admired because they had won and also because not only their relief and reconstruction program but also their efforts to democratize Japan were generally popular. The Japanese, after all, had suffered terribly under a militaristic police state and were ready to follow new paths. American ways were imitated uncritically by many, but the basic political reforms of the occupation sent down firm roots.

Most of the changes were reaffirmed after the occupation or, perhaps more accurately, were grafted onto earlier Japanese efforts to adopt Western institutions prior to the years of military government (1931–1945). In addition to a revitalization of electoral and party democracy, government was decentralized by giving more power to local organs. Public education, formerly supervised closely by the central government, was also decentralized and freed as much as possible from bureaucratic control. One of the most successful and permanent changes was the program of land reform, which compensated the large owners whose property was expropriated and sold the land to former tenants, thus ending the last surviving traces of the Tokugawa order. Japanese society began to evolve rapidly toward its present social system, in which status results from achievement rather than birth.

The new constitution drafted by SCAP officials retained the emperor as a figurehead but vested all real power in a legislature and prime minister elected by universal suffrage. There was a detailed bill of rights for the protection of individuals against arbitrary state power. Article 9 of the constitution forbade Japan to have any armed forces except for police and denied it the right to go to war. To most Japanese this was not only reasonable but welcome, given the ruin that arms had brought them and the aftermath of atomic warfare, of which they were the living witnesses. Japan, many felt, should set an example of the folly of war for the rest of the world. What disillusioned the Japanese about the occupation was the shift in American policy beginning in 1948 toward rebuilding Japan's military capacity and using it as a base of American strategic operation.

The goal of making Japan a Cold War ally of the United States soon took precedence over reform and reconstruction. The Berlin blockade, the final Communist victory in China in 1949, and the Korean War all further hardened the American line. Although President Harry Truman fired MacArthur in 1951 for his irresponsible management of the Korean War, Cold War considerations continued to dominate American policy. When the occupation ended in 1952, Japan was bound to the United States by a security

MacArthur: An Assessment

Most observers described General Douglas MacArthur as a vain man, ever conscious of his public image. Here is a leading Western historian's assessment of MacArthur in his role as the head of SCAP from 1945 to 1951.

A tendency toward complacent self-dramatization was encouraged by the adulation of a devoted wartime staff that he took with him to Japan. . . . They took almost ludicrous care that only the rosiest reports of the occupation should reach the outside world. In their debased opinion the slightest criticism of S.C.A.P. amounted to something approaching sacrilege. MacArthur took up residence in the United States Embassy in Tokyo. Each day at the same hour he was driven to his office in a large building facing the palace moat; at the same hour each day he was driven home again. . . . He never toured Japan to see things for himself. . . . The irreverent were heard to say that if a man rose early in the morning he might catch a glimpse of the Supreme Commander walking on the waters of the palace moat. There is no doubt that this aloofness impressed Japanese of the conservative type. . . . But it may well be doubted whether this kind of awed respect was compatible with the healthy growth of democratic sentiment. . . . The Japanese perhaps learned more about democracy from MacArthur's dismissal than from anything he himself ever did or said.

Source: R. Storry, *A History of Modern Japan*, rev. ed. (New York: Penguin Books, 1982), pp. 240–241.

treaty that permitted the buildup of a Japanese "self-defense force," the stationing of American troops, and American use of several major bases in Japan. U.S. pressures for Japanese rearmament have continued, and the bases remain, but Article 9 of the constitution still has the support of most Japanese.

Economic and Social Development

Whatever the political shifts as the occupation wore on, economic reconstruction was almost miraculously rapid. By 1950 the shattered cities, factories, and rail lines had been largely rebuilt, and by the end of 1951 industrial production was about equal to what it had been in 1931, now from new and more efficient plants. The Korean War provided an additional economic boost as Japan became the chief base and supplier for American forces in Korea. By 1953, with reconstruction complete, personal incomes had recovered to their prewar levels, and Japan was entering a new period of rapid development. Some credit is due to American aid in the hard years immediately after the war, but the "Japanese miracle" was overwhelmingly the result of the nation's own hard work, organization, and the pursuit of economic success through group effort. The growth of production and income in Japan from 1950 to 1975 was faster than has been measured in any country at any time; in those 25 years, output and incomes roughly tripled. Yet the Japanese continued to maintain a very high rate of personal savings.

At the same time, production quality also rose impressively, and in many respects Japanese goods, notably automobiles, cameras, sound reproduction equipment, optics, and many electronic items, became the best in the world market. This was a tribute to advanced Japanese technology and design, as well as to the efficiency of an industrial plant rebuilt with the latest design and equipment. Similar factors were active in the postwar recovery of Germany, while the victorious Allies, including the United States, were saddled with their older and less efficient plants. After 1953 Japan dominated world shipbuilding, although it gave ground increasingly to South Korea in the 1980s. By 1964 Japan had become the world's third largest producer of steel, and by 1980 it had overtaken both the USSR and the United States in steel output while also becoming a major producer and exporter of automotive vehicles. Japan also invaded European and American markets on a large scale with its "high-tech" and industrial goods.

Japanese democracy has retained healthy growth, although politics continue to be dominated by a conservative coalition with no effective rival parties. High school education is virtually universal, and literacy among the Japanese is the highest in the world. The press is of high quality and is avidly supported by a public that also buys and reads more books than in any other country. Over half of young Japanese continue with postsecondary education in a great variety of colleges, universities, and other institutions. Overall, the Japanese are now probably the best-educated population in the world.

Education was a major reason for Japan's spectacular economic success. Economic growth largely eliminated the nation's poverty and unemployment. With the postwar disappearance of aristocratic values, Japan became largely a nation of prosperous middle-class people in an orderly society. Despite crowded conditions—population density in its central urban corridor is the highest in the world—there are few slums, little violent crime, and few signs of social malaise. By 1980 Japan achieved the world's highest life expectancy and its lowest murder rate, less than one two-hundredth that of the United States.

Japanese disarmament, a condition at first imposed by the American occupation but now for many an ingrained social value, has also paid handsome dividends. Japan has thus been largely free of the crushing economic burden of maintaining the huge military establishment undertaken by most other large countries in the postwar world. Money was invested instead in economic growth, new technology, full employment, education, and a wide range of social services. Japan is virtually alone in the world in having escaped from most of the cankerous problems that breed in poverty, such as violence, hopelessness, and drugs. The national ethic of work, achievement, and high standards, now in the service of personal and group goals of economic advancement rather than imperial ambition, has produced a new and more constructive society.

Nevertheless, Japanese society has significant problems. The drive for achievement exacts a toll on schoolchildren as well as on adults. Pressures begin for admission to the "right" kindergarten and continue through elementary school, middle (high) school, and college or university. Each stage of schooling is accompanied by fiercely competitive examinations. Childhood, after the age of 5, is a stressful time for most Japanese. Extreme urban crowding and cramped living space add further burdens. Commuting time for people who work in downtown Tokyo *averages* nearly two hours each way and is only slightly less in other big Japanese cities. Parks and recreation facilities are extremely limited. Housing is fearfully expensive, and most urban Japanese, who constitute over 80 percent of the population, live in tiny apartments with minimal amenities. Yet as one of the best-informed and widely traveled people in the world, most Japanese know they are generally very well off despite their cramped quarters.

Notwithstanding the newer values of social equality and status based on achievement, traditional patterns remain, especially the subordinate status of women. Deference to superiors or elders, and of all women to men, is still expected by older Japanese. New generations may well reshape their society on somewhat freer lines, but most would agree that it will be a long time before women achieve anything close to equality. In the workplace women are in subordinate or service roles, with very few exceptions. At the same time, women are often the real powers within the family and household. They usually have control of the family finances and have the preponderant role in the upbringing of children; most fathers work long hours, and their long commute usually gets them home only after the children are in bed. Nevertheless, about half of adult Japanese women work outside the house, close to the current American figure, often managing a small family business or neighborhood store. Equality in the professions remains a distant goal.

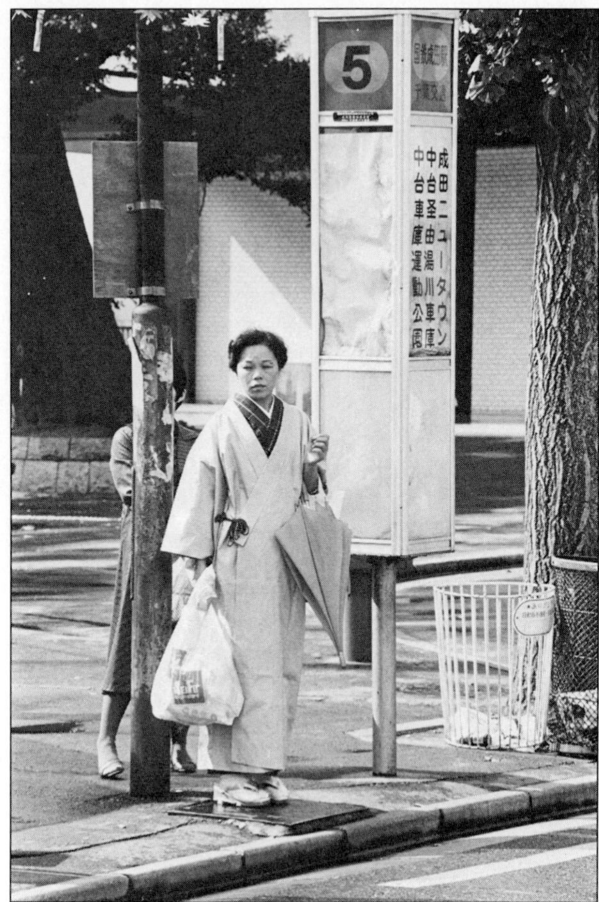

Tradition meets modernity: woman at a bus stop dressed in the traditional kimono. [Ira Kuschenbaum/Stock, Boston]

Modern Japanese women still learn traditional arts, and playing the *koto* is one. Koto players, including learners, must wear the traditional kimono, and usually practice in a thoroughly traditional setting such as that shown here, kneeling on a tatami (grass and bamboo mat) in a traditional-style room. [Shashinka Photo, Inc.]

Japan's International Role

Despite their global economic stature, the Japanese have been reluctant to assume the role of a world power in political terms, a role that has brought them tragedy in the past. They have often been uncomfortably aware of this disparity between their economic power and their more hesitant political stance abroad. On a number of occasions they have felt their interests ignored in the maneuverings of Cold War diplomacy. As an American client and a bulwark against neighboring communist states, Japan was dumbfounded when in 1971 Washington, reversing a 22-year policy, suddenly renewed contact with China without informing Tokyo in advance. The Japanese still refer to this event as the "Nixon shock," and on many other occasions as well, U.S. actions have caused the Japanese to feel slighted or ignored.

It seems likely that in time Japan will come to play an international diplomatic role more in keeping with its economic power, but most Japanese continue to hope that this can be done without adding new military power. Some Japanese have openly favored rearmament to compete in a world dominated by nations with the greatest military power, a policy that deeply concerns Japan's neighbors and former victims of its imperialism. Although the Americans have pressed for it, a rearmed Japan would no longer be their client, which is indeed why some Japanese support rearmament. More positively, by 1988 Japan had become the world's largest donor nation of foreign aid.

Modern Japan has been a leader in other nonmilitary directions, notably in the control of industrial pollution. Japan is small, and most of its population, cities, and industry are crowded into a narrow coastal corridor only about 400 miles long. Industrial concentration is higher there than anywhere in the world, and hence Japan was the first to notice the lethal effects of air and water pollution as one consequence of its postwar industrial growth. Many deaths and many more health casualties derived from heavy metal toxins and air pollution, traced to specific plants and their poisonous discharges into the water or the atmosphere. Once this became clear and public opinion had been mobilized, national and municipal governments quickly passed stringent legislation, beginning in 1969 with the city of Tokyo, to limit emissions and effluents from industry and vehicles. As industrial growth continues, concentration and crowding will go on generating the same problems, and pollution levels are building up again, while controls have remained incomplete. But Japanese organization, efficiency, and technology have demonstrated that the problems can be managed, given the willingness to confront them. The technology needed to control or even eliminate pollution was developed quickly, and the added expense was extremely modest, estimated at between 1 and 2 percent of total production costs.

Japan has also led the way in reducing energy use through more efficient plants and better engine design. Nearly all Japanese trains are electrified, including the heavily used high-speed line that connects Tokyo with the major cities to the south and southwest and Hokkaido to the north. Trains leave Tokyo every 15 minutes for Osaka, making the 310-mile trip in three hours, including stops at Nagoya and Kyoto, running at speeds up to 140 miles per hour.

Urbanization is higher in Japan than anywhere else in the world, and the coastal area from Tokyo to Osaka and on to northern Kyushu is rapidly becoming a single vast urban-industrial zone. Although the rural Japanese landscape, especially the mountains that cover much of the country, is very beautiful, a good deal of the remaining countryside is increasingly empty as people have flocked to the cities in search of wider economic and cultural opportunity. On weekends and holidays urbanites rush to natural beauty spots, temples or shrines, and resorts, which are often excessively crowded. Crammed onto overloaded trains or buses, most passengers must stand

Schoolchildren in front of the Heian Shrine in Kyoto. Japanese students wear uniforms, the boys' dating from Meiji times. [Steve Elmore]

for hours, while many others are locked into gigantic traffic jams on the highways. Much of traditional Japanese culture has been lost or discarded in this avalanche of change. Although many Japanese regret the price they have paid for development, their sense of national identity has remained strong, bound together with many symbolic survivals of traditional culture: customary food and rituals, aesthetic sensitivity, and the commitment to order, self-discipline, and group effort in the pursuit of excellence.

TOKYO AND THE MODERN WORLD

By about 1965 Tokyo had become the world's largest city and a symbol of Japan's new economic leadership. The urban area had grown outward to merge with that of previously separate cities in the same lowland basin, including Kawasaki and Yokohama. By the 1980s this vast, unbroken conglomeration of dense settlement, commerce, industry, and government measured 50 miles across and included over 30 million people linked by the world's largest and most efficient subway system. Almost nothing is left of the Edo described in Chapter 28, most of which had been in any case periodically destroyed by fires. Modern Tokyo was also largely ruined by a catastrophic earthquake in 1923 and then again by American bombs and firestorms in 1944 and 1945.

The only part of the city that has survived all of these cataclysms unscathed is Tokugawa Ieyasu's massive shogunal castle, surrounded by its moats and stone walls, originally built in the early seventeenth century and since 1869 used as the imperial palace. In the middle of a huge and strikingly modern city of glass, steel, skyscrapers, and expressways, with traffic flowing around it, the palace still stands as a symbol of Japan's traditional past, both as a Tokugawa monument and as the home of a still enthroned emperor whose lineage goes back to before the dawn of Japanese history. Among Japan's many big cities, Tokyo still plays the role of the brash modernist, the focus of change, the center of everything new; but even in Tokyo the Japanese do not forget their past. The palace, though an anachronism, is nevertheless an appropriate focal point for the capital of Japan. For all its apparent emphasis on the streamlined or frantic present and future, Tokyo is also a city of the Japanese tradition.

That aspect of the city's character becomes clear beyond the immediate downtown and government areas. Except for the industrial clusters around the fringes of each originally separate municipality, Tokyo is primarily a vast collection of neighborhoods. Many are grouped around a surviving or rebuilt temple, shrine, former daimyo estate, or parklike garden. Wandering through the back streets and alleys of these neighborhoods, it is easy to imagine oneself in Tokugawa Edo. Clouds of steam escape from public bathhouses, enveloping the patrons, who include many dressed in traditional kimonos and walking in wooden clogs, especially in the evening after work. Inside countless tiny restaurants and teahouses with their tatami (bamboo mats), low tables, and wall scrolls, little seems to have changed since Ieyasu's time, including much of the food. Many inhabitants of the tiny houses or apartments maintain miniature Japanese-style gardens the size of a small tabletop or lovingly tend potted plants set out by the doorway or on small balconies to catch the sun. Street vendors, singing traditional chants, peddle roasted sweet potatoes, chestnuts, or *yakitori* (Japanese shish kebab).

Crowds of kimono-clad worshipers, or people simply on an outing, throng the courtyards of rebuilt temples and shrines, especially on festival days. Similar crowds fill the narrow streets and patronize street vendors or shops selling traditional as well as modern goods: fans both manual and electric, silks and nylons, horoscope fortunes and stock market guides, tea and beer, lacquer and plastic, scrolls and comic books. Like Japan itself, Tokyo is both very modern and very traditional, very Japanese and very Western.

China in Revolution

The cataclysmic changes that transformed twentieth-century China constitute the largest revolution in human history, measured by the numbers of people involved and the radicalness and speed of the changes. Although the events of 1911 leading to the overthrow of the Manchu dynasty are called a revolution, the pace of change was slow for many years, and the dominant political party, the Kuomintang, became in time largely a supporter of the status quo rather than a force for radical reform. The Chinese Communist party barely survived Kuomintang efforts to eliminate it, but during the anti-Japanese war from 1937 to 1945 it rapidly gained strength and support in the course of its guerrilla resistance to the invaders. The final contest between the two parties ended in Communist victory in 1949, and fundamental revolution began under a radically new set of ideals.

Postwar China and the Communist Triumph

The Japanese invasion and occupation of China from 1931 to 1945 fatally eroded the power and legitimacy of the Kuomintang government of Chiang Kai-shek. Buttressed by massive American military and economic support, it clung to a nominal authority while American representatives under General George C. Marshall tried to arrange a coalition with the Communists. When this effort predictably failed in 1947, China was torn by full-scale civil war. The Communist forces, meanwhile, had perfected a guerrilla strategy in their long struggle against the Japanese and had attracted millions of Chinese by their defense of the nation and their program of peasant-oriented reform.

Their leader, Mao Tse-tung (Mao Zedong, 1893–1976), offered a return to the simple virtues of hard work and self-sacrifice in order to build a new China, free from foreign influence and humiliation and free also from the now discredited and reactionary elitism of Confucianism and the old order it represented. The Confucian society had deteriorated sadly as China had sunk deeper into poverty, demoralization, and unwillingness to face drastically changed circumstances. People necessarily concentrated on ensuring their own survival rather than on responsibility for others or on group welfare. In their remote frontier base at Yenan (Yanan) in the northwest, where they were centered from 1934 to 1947, the Communists under Mao's direction had worked out a number of ideas for China's regeneration, while at the same time appealing broadly to the masses.

Mao himself, like several other Communist leaders, came from peasant stock, and their program emphasized peasant welfare and peasant values, as the Kuomintang had not. Landlordism and oppression of the peasantry were popular issues in the face of widespread rural poverty and mass suffering. Chinese who collaborated with foreign businessmen in the treaty ports prospered in league with a government that was prone to favor foreign influences. The cities, nearly all of which were foreign-dominated treaty ports as well as centers of Kuomintang strength and the home of "running dogs" (collaborators with the foreigners), were obvious targets for a peasant-oriented revolutionary movement.

Success depended, however, on building a mass support base in the countryside, where most Chinese lived. The Communists initiated land reform programs in the areas they controlled—most of the north—as well as campaigns to politicize and organize the peasants. Intellectuals were also involved in an effort to create a new ideology that could appeal to peasants. Mao himself, though the son of a rich peasant turned grain merchant, was primarily an intellectual as well as a gifted poet in the tradition of the Confucian scholars and emperors. His prescriptions for art and literature that would "serve politics" and "serve the masses" attracted growing numbers of fellow intellectuals disillusioned with the corruption and spiritual bankruptcy of the Kuomintang. As an intellectual organizing peasant rebellion, Mao consciously followed an old Chinese tradition.

The civil war that broke out in 1947 soon became a rout, despite heavy American support for the Kuomintang. The Communists had few weapons except what they could capture from their opponents or make themselves, but their strength quickly multiplied as growing numbers of Kuomintang troops and officers surrendered to them, often voluntarily, with all their equipment. The close American connection, with its connotation of foreign dominance, probably weakened rather than strengthened the Kuomintang in its fight against the Communists and left a legacy of anti-American bitterness when the civil war ended. On October 1, 1949, Mao announced the inauguration of the People's Republic of China from a rostrum in front of the Forbidden City in Peking (Beijing), conscious, as always, of the tradition of China's imperial greatness, to which he was now the heir. "China has stood up," he said, and the great majority of Chinese responded with enthusiasm.

The revolution was the culmination of a long process that began with the overthrow of the old Ch'ing (Qing) dynasty in 1916. After the failure of Sun Yat-sen and the corruption of the Kuomintang, the Communists, originally appealing largely to intellectuals, had finally succeeded in creating a mass political base, with a peasant army forged in the fires of the Japanese war. They called their program "the mass line," claiming to represent the more than 80 percent of the Chinese people who lived in the countryside.

Reconstruction and Consolidation

Chiang Kai-shek and the remnants of the Kuomintang government and army fled to the offshore island of Taiwan (Formosa), where American aid helped them in time to build a prosperous economy and gain firm control of the island's population. From this tiny base, sheltered only by

38.2 Modern China

American power, Chiang continued to claim sole legitimate authority over China. The United States supported the Kuomintang until the desire to exploit the split between the Chinese Communists and their erstwhile Soviet allies led belatedly to official American recognition of the government in Peking in 1979. Unofficial ties with Taipei (the Taiwan capital) remained, however. On the mainland the new government moved quickly to repair the physical damage of the long years of war and to extend its land reform and political education programs into the newly conquered south and southwest. All over the country what was still called land reform became more violent as party organizers, in an effort to create "class consciousness," encouraged peasants to "speak bitterness" and to identify their landlord-oppressors. Many thousands of the latter were killed by angry mobs, and their land was distributed among the poorer peasants.

Firm central government control was reestablished in all of the former empire, including Manchuria (now called simply "the northeast"), southern or "Inner" Mongolia, Sinkiang (Xinjiang), and Tibet, and a major program of industrialization was begun. War with the United States in Korea from late 1950 to mid-1953 and an American-sponsored embargo on trade with China slowed these efforts but also helped to radicalize the country and to strengthen dedication to the goals of self-reliance and reconstruction. By 1957 Mao judged that support for the new government was wide and deep enough to invite criticism. In a famous speech, he declared: "Let a hundred flowers bloom; let a hundred schools of thought contend." Many intellectuals and others, including many of China's ethnic minorities such as Tibetans and Muslims, responded with a torrent of criticism aimed at rigid party or government controls. Most of it was pronounced counterrevolutionary, and many of the critics were punished, jailed, or even executed.

The Great Leap Forward

Despite the evidence of dissent, Mao still felt secure enough in the support of the majority of his people that he moved swiftly to collectivize the land. By 1958 he moved beyond the Soviet model of collectivization as China's farms and fields were organized into new communes; private ownership was abolished, and all enterprises were managed collectively. The communes varied widely in area and population but averaged about 25,000 people, frequently incorporating large numbers of previously separate villages. Several villages made up a "production team," several teams a "production brigade," and several brigades a commune. Communes were supposed to include manufacturing enterprises as well, to bring industrialization to the rural areas. Communes were also set up in the cities but added little to existing factories, departments, or offices, and the experiment was short-lived.

Mao announced that 1958 would be the year of the "Great Leap Forward" in which China would overtake Britain in industrial output by united efforts within the commune structure. Communal dining halls were set up so that families need not lose work time by preparing meals. Backyard steel furnaces sprang up all over the rural landscape, using local iron ore and coal or other fuel. Communes were given quotas for production of specific agricultural and industrial goods, but too little attention was paid to the nature of local resources or to rational organization more generally.

The Great Leap was a dismal failure, and the country collapsed into economic chaos in 1959. Peasants had been driven to exhaustion in pursuit of unrealistic goals and by inefficient combinations of tasks and resources. Nearly all of the iron and steel from the backyard furnaces was of unusable quality, and the same was true of much of the other commune industrial output. Crops failed as labor was shifted arbitrarily between different tasks, and for at least three years food was scarce and famine widespread. Probably about 30 million people died of starvation or malnutrition in one of the worst famines in world history. Mao's radical policies had brought disaster, and for several years more moderate leaders such as Chou En-lai (Zhou Enlai, 1898–1976) and Liu Hsiao-chi (Liu Xiaoqi, 1894–1971) eclipsed him, although he remained the party chairman.

The Sino-Soviet Split

The Russians were alarmed by what they saw as the radical excesses of the Great Leap and its departure from the Soviet pattern. They were annoyed also by Mao's assertion that his version of socialism was superior to theirs, his continued support of Stalinist policies after they had been discredited in the USSR, and his accusations that Russia had now become ideologically impure, or "revisionist." The Russians saw Mao's bellicose stand on the reconquest of Taiwan, for which he requested Soviet nuclear aid, as a threat to world peace, and inevitable tensions arose out of the large-scale Soviet aid program and Soviet advisers in China. In 1959 the Russians withdrew their aid and advisers and moved toward a more antagonistic relationship with China. The next 15 years saw revived territorial disputes and armed border clashes between the two former allies on the long frontier between them, especially in the Amur region of northern Manchuria and along the northern border of Sinkiang.

Each claimed to be the true heir of Marx and Lenin and hence of the correct path to socialism, and in this ideological context long-standing historical conflicts between them surfaced. These dated back to the period of early tsarist expansion into Northeast Asia and to Russia's exploitation of Manchuria and its role as one of the Western imperialist powers during China's years of political weakness. On the other side, China's billion people, bordering thinly settled

Attack on the "Revisionists" and "Imperialists"

At the Tenth Party Congress in 1973, Vice-Chairman Chou En-lai gave a long address in which he castigated the Russian "revisionists" and lumped them together with the American "imperialists."

There were many instances in the past where one tendency covered another and when a tide came, the majority went along with it, while only a few withstood it. . . . We must not fear isolation and must dare to go against the tide and brave it through. Chairman Mao states: "Going against the tide is a Marxist-Leninist principle. . . . The West always wants to urge the Soviet revisionists eastward to divert the peril toward China, and it would be fine so long as all is quiet in the West. China is an attractive piece of meat coveted by all. But this piece of meat is very tough, and for years no one has been able to bite into it. . . . The U.S.-Soviet contention for hegemony is the cause of world intranquillity. . . . They want to devour China but find it too tough even to bite. . . . U.S. imperialism started to go downhill after its defeat in the war of aggression against Korea. . . . [Khrushchev and Brezhnev in Russia] made a socialist country degenerate into a social imperialist country. Internally it has restored capitalism, enforced a fascist dictatorship and . . . exposed its ugly features as the new tsar and its reactionary nature, namely 'socialism in words, imperialism in deeds.' . . ."

If you are so anxious to relax world tension, why don't you show your good faith by doing a thing or two—for instance, withdraw your armed forces from Czechoslovakia or the People's Republic of Mongolia and return the four northern islands [the Kurile archipelago north of Hokkaido] to Japan? China has not occupied any foreign countries' territory. Must China give away all the territory north of the Great Wall to the Soviet revisionists in order to show that we favor relaxation of world tensions? . . . The Sino-Soviet boundary question should be settled peacefully through negotiations free from any threat. We will not attack unless we are attacked; if we are attacked, we will certainly counterattack.

Source: I. Hsu, *The Rise of Modern China* (New York: Oxford University Press, 1975), pp. 878–879.

Siberia and Russia's maritime provinces, were seen as an alarming threat to Soviet Asia. The rhetoric of accusation mounted on both sides; troops were stationed along the frontiers, and small clashes occurred. But China could not stand alone against the entire world, and its leaders began indirect overtures to the United States. More than a decade later, with the end of their misadventure in Vietnam in sight, the Americans finally responded. A cautious restoration of contact began when President Richard Nixon visited Peking late in 1971. This led to the establishment of diplomatic relations, with full U.S. recognition and an exchange of ambassadors with the People's Republic in 1979.

The Cultural Revolution

During the decade from 1966 to 1976, however, China passed through an unprecedented social cataclysm, the so-called Cultural Revolution, in which hundreds of millions of people suffered. The failure of the Great Leap Forward had necessitated more moderate policies and a period of recovery from economic disaster. By 1966 Mao judged the recovery to be complete, and he launched a new campaign designed to renew a revolution that he saw as having slipped into bureaucratic complacency and opportunism.

Mao remarked that he felt like "an ancestor at his own funeral and at the burial of his hopes." His cure was a purge, though his message was the old one of "serve the people," with its clear echoes of Confucian responsibility. The chief targets of his purge were the members of the elite: party managers and officials, teachers, writers, and intellectuals, as well as others who were allegedly tainted by foreign influence or bourgeois lifestyles or whose class origins were not appropriately peasant or proletarian.

The results were devastating. Millions were hounded out of their jobs. Artists and musicians who showed any interest in Western styles were attacked. Many intellectuals and other "counterrevolutionaries" were beaten or killed, and others were jailed, sent to corrective labor camps, or assigned to the lowest menial tasks as a means of "reeducation." Opera stars, writers, and concert violinists were set to cleaning latrines. All foreign music, art, and literature and the expression of all ideas not approved by the state were banned. Most books disappeared or were burned, to be replaced by the ever-present works of Mao himself and the *Little Red Book* of his sayings. Chinese who had studied abroad were particular targets. People were encouraged to inform on friends, colleagues, and even family members, causing deep trauma and division in a society based on traditional family ties. The accused were often jailed or condemned to corrective labor without evidence. Few people had the courage to try to help them, for fear that they too would meet the same fate. The ensuing turmoil affected the lives of hundreds of millions of people and paralyzed the country. Nor were the rural communes exempt, for there, too, many were obliged to confess ideological sins and subjected to punishment and corrective labor.

During the height of the Cultural Revolution all universities and colleges were closed, as breeding grounds for a new elite. When they slowly began to reopen, it was only to the children of peasants, workers, and party loyalists still in power. The new curriculum concentrated on "political study." Most high school graduates in the decade after 1966, particularly those in the cities, were assigned to productive labor in the countryside, where, Mao felt, they would learn the value of simple toil and peasant virtues. This was partly a leveling alternative to the universities, partly a means to ease unemployment and housing shortages in the cities, and partly a way to reeducate

Mao: The Revolutionary Vision

The Communist revolution in China was in large part a peasant-based movement against the vested power of the cities. Mao Tse-tung put it dramatically.

Since China's key cities have long been occupied by the powerful imperialists and their reactionary Chinese allies, it is imperative for the revolutionary ranks to turn the backward villages into advanced consolidated base areas, . . . bastions of the revolution from which to fight their vicious enemies.

This equally famous statement of Mao's was published in the periodical Red Flag.

China's 600 million people have two remarkable peculiarities; they are first of all poor, and secondly blank. That may seem like a bad thing, but it is really a good thing. Poor people want change, want to do things, want revolution. A clean sheet of paper has no blotches, and so the newest and most beautiful words can be written on it, the newest and most beautiful pictures painted on it.

Still driven by his revolutionary vision, Mao the poet wrote in 1963, in traditional classic verse:

So many deeds cry out to be done,
And always urgently.
The world rolls on,
Time passes.
Ten thousand years are too long;
Seize the day, seize the hour,
Our force is irresistible.

Sources: Mao Tse-tung, *The Chinese Revolution and the Chinese Communist Party* (Peking: Foreign Language Press, 1954), p. 17 (written in 1939); *Red Flag*, June 1, 1958, pp. 3–4; "Reply to Kuo Mo-jo" (dated February 5, 1963), in *China Reconstructs* 16 (March 1967): 2.

Chinese too young to have shared the early years of hardship and sacrifice.

Some 17 million young people were sent down in this program by the time it was discontinued in the late 1970s. Most of them saw it as ruinous to their own ambitions and career plans, for which their urban origins and education had prepared them. Nor were most of them very helpful in agricultural or other development work. Their training had not in most cases been relevant, and indeed it had tended, as in China's past, to make them think of themselves as an educated elite who looked down on peasants and manual labor. The program was understandably unpopular with peasants too, since they had to feed and house disgruntled city youth who, with their higher level of education, were unprepared for farmwork. All white-collar workers were required to spend at least two months each year doing manual labor, mainly in the countryside, which not surprisingly met with resistance from professionals and others.

Mao called on teenagers and students to serve as shock troops for the Cultural Revolution. Like young people everywhere, they had little stake in the status quo, were filled with idealism, and were easily diverted from their studies. They welcomed their exciting new role and the opportunity to exercise authority over their elders. Mao called them "Red Guards" and permitted them to roam the country freely, ferreting out "rightists" and harassing everyone in responsible positions. Millions rode free or commandeered trains and buses to the cities, including Peking, where Mao addressed cheering crowds of Red Guards at mass rallies. Mao and his supporters promoted a personality cult; huge pictures and statues of the "Great Helmsman" and copies of his *Little Red Book* appeared everywhere. Rival factions quickly emerged among the Red Guards, each claiming to be followers of the true line. Many welcomed the opportunity to pay off old grudges and to denounce others, often anonymously. Uncontrolled violence broke out in many cities.

To halt the mounting chaos, Chou En-lai prevailed on Mao to call in the army in 1968. The Red Guards were suppressed, thus creating yet another embittered and dislocated group; the Guards felt they had been betrayed, a "lost generation." But the nightmare went on even after the Red Guards had been sent to the countryside. Even politicians at the top, except for Mao himself, were attacked for alleged deviations from the party line, which changed unpredictably. Liu Hsiao-chi (Liu Xiaoqi), a revolutionary comrade Mao had originally picked as his successor, was purged and accused of "rightist revisionism" because of his efforts to rebuild the economy after the disaster of the Great Leap Forward. He died under arrest after public humiliation and beatings. Other high officials suffered similar fates. Professionals in all fields were scrutinized for their political views and activism. Absence from the endless daily political meetings or silence during them was evidence of "counterrevolutionary tendencies." One of the many slogans of the Cultural Revolution was "Better Red than Expert." No one at any level felt safe.

The Chinese Revolution remained primarily a peasant movement, a Chinese rather than a foreign-style answer to China's problems. This was appealing also on nationalist grounds, especially since nearly all the cities had been tainted by semicolonial foreign dominance. There was thus both a pronounced antiurban bias to the revolution and a determination to exalt the countryside, to put the peasants in charge, and to concentrate efforts at development in the rural areas, the supposed source of all revolutionary values.

This was the theme of both the Great Leap Forward and the Cultural Revolution. All movement of people was controlled, especially to the cities, where housing and ration books for food and household supplies were allocated only to those with assigned employment. Individuals could not chose jobs; they worked wherever the state sent them. In the 1970s a growing number of illegal migrants to the cities lived underground or on forged papers. Most of them are still there, their numbers apparently greatly increased; urban unemployment has become a major problem. Despite the official denigration of cities, they remained the places where most people wanted to be.

In the countryside each commune was designed to be self-sufficient as far as possible. The Cultural Revolution promoted a particularly extensive growth of small-scale rural industry, especially in what were labeled the "five smalls": iron and steel, cement, fertilizer, agricultural goods (including tools, machinery, and irrigation equipment), and electric power. There was also considerable production of light consumer goods for local use. Local manufacture did reduce the load on an already overburdened road and rail system and saved transport costs while providing employment and experience to the masses of rural people. But in most cases such production was considerably more expensive than that in larger-scale and better-equipped urban-based plants and of much lower quality. Decentralized industry has been considered as an alternative to the crowding, pollution, and dehumanization of industrial cities since the eighteenth century, but it has seldom proved economically practical. Mao's utopian vision of rural development was appealing as an attempt to alleviate the real poverty of the countryside, but it was pursued at dreadful cost. China, meanwhile, lagged farther and farther behind the rest of the world, technologically and educationally.

Mao had said that the major goals of the revolution should be the elimination of the distinctions between city and countryside, between intellectuals and manual workers, and between elites and common people. In pursuit of these aims, workers or janitors became plant managers and university officials; peasants were elevated to power in the communes' "revolutionary committees"; professors, technicians, and skilled managers were humiliated or reduced to the most menial jobs. Even "rich peasants"

Revolution, Chinese Style

From the beginning of their revolutionary victory, the Chinese asserted that their principles and experience should be the guide for the rest of the world, not the Russian way. Here is Liu Shao-ch'i in 1949.

The road taken by the Chinese people in defeating imperialism and in founding the Chinese People's Republic is the road that should be taken by the peoples of many colonial and semi-colonial countries in their fight for national independence and people's democracy. . . . This is the road of Mao Tse-tung. . . . This is the inevitable road of many colonial and semi-colonial peoples in the struggle for their independence and liberation.

Lu Ting-i, director of propaganda of the Central Committee, added in July 1951:

Mao Tse-tung's theory of the Chinese revolution is a new development of Marxism-Leninism in the revolutions of the colonial and semi-colonial countries. . . . It is of universal significance for the world Communist movement. . . . The classic type of revolution in colonial and semi-colonial countries is the Chinese revolution.

The Russians replied, in the words of Y. Kovalev, a leading propagandist:

The decisive prerequisites for the victory of the Chinese revolution were the October Socialist Revolution and the victory of socialism in the U.S.S.R., and the defeat of Japanese and German imperialism by the Soviet Union in World War II. . . . Stalin's analysis of the peculiarities of China as a semi-colonial country was taken as the basis for the working out of the strategy and tactics of the struggle for an independent and democratic China by the Chinese Communist Party.

Stalin's successor, Nikita Khrushchev, lectured Mao in 1958, after Mao suggested that the combined numbers of China and Russia could overcome the capitalist West.

Comrade Mao Tse-tung, nowadays that sort of thinking is out of date. You can no longer calculate the alignment of forces on the basis of who has the most men. Back in the days when a dispute was settled with fists and bayonets it made a difference who had the most men. . . . Now with the atomic bomb, the number of troops on each side makes practically no difference.

But the Chinese stuck to their insistence that theirs was the only true way. This editorial, in characteristic Cultural Revolution style, appeared in Liberation Army Daily *in May 1966.*

The thought of Mao Tse-tung is the sun in our heart, the root of our life, and the source of all our strength. Through it one becomes unselfish, daring, intelligent, and able to do anything; no difficulty can conquer him, while he can conquer any enemy. The thought of Mao Tse-tung transforms man's ideology, transforms the fatherland. . . . Through it the oppressed people of the world will rise.

Source: I. Hsu, *The Rise of Modern China* (New York: Oxford University Press, 1975), pp. 810–813, 859.

The leaders of Communist China in 1965: from left to right, Chou En-lai, Chu-Teh, Mao Tse-tung, and Liu Hsiao-chi. [Eastfoto/Sovfoto]

became targets. All those with any claim to expertise were suspect and were often hounded out of their positions in angry "struggle meetings"; those who refused to join in the denunciations risked being denounced themselves. The moral virtue and practical wisdom of the peasants and the countryside were extolled.

Mao drew heavily on traditional ideas in emphasizing the duty of those in positions of power and responsibility to serve the masses, and he, like the Confucians, used moral examples and slogans to inspire and mold group behavior. He also relied on the new technique of mass campaigns to galvanize people into action. Some were constructive, like the campaigns to eliminate flies or to build new dams and irrigation canals. But most were politically inspired and were aimed at "rightists" and "counterrevolutionaries." The Chinese revolution's radical phase lasted longer and went to greater extremes than similar phases of earlier revolutions, but in time it too faded, if only because the Chinese people were exhausted by constant political campaigns and by the terror itself. Mao's death removed the chief obstacle to a return to more normal conditions, and China turned with relief from its long ordeal.

China After Mao

As Mao lay dying in 1976, a few months after his old comrade-in-arms Chou En-lai had died of overwork and exhaustion while trying to hold the country together, a radical faction led by Mao's widow, Chiang Ch'ing (Jiang Qing), tried to continue his extreme policies. But in 1978 a more moderate leadership emerged under Hua Kuo-feng (Hua Guofeng), whom Mao had designated as his successor. Chiang Ch'ing and three of her associates, the so-called "Gang of Four," were tried and convicted of "crimes against the people" and sentenced to jail. China began to emerge from its nightmare and to resume cautious interchange with the rest of the world after 30 years of isolation. The universities and their curricula were slowly restored, and students now had to pass entrance examinations rather than merely to demonstrate proper "class origins." Efforts were made to provide somewhat greater freedom for intellectuals, writers, teachers, and managers.

Hua Kuo-feng was peacefully replaced by an old party pragmatist, Teng Hsiao-p'ing (Deng Xiaoping, born 1904), who returned to power in 1981 as the real head of state and chief policymaker. Most of Mao's policies were progressively dismantled. The new government acknowledged that China was still poor and technically backward, that it needed foreign technology and investment, and that to encourage production its people needed material incentives rather than political harangues and "rectification campaigns."

The communes were quietly dissolved in all but name. Agriculture, still by far the largest sector of the economy, was largely organized into a "responsibility system" whereby individual families grew the crops that they judged most profitable in an economy that was now market-oriented. The commune still nominally owned the land and the state still appropriated a share of farm output, but peasants were free to sell the rest in a free market. Those who did well under this system, and urban entrepreneurs who prospered in the small private businesses now permitted, felt free once again to display their new wealth. Expensive houses with television aerials sprouted here and there in the countryside, and in the cities motor scooters, tape recorders, and refrigerators became more common. The new rich and even party officials began to indulge personal tastes in clothing, including Western-style and fashionable outfits, which replaced the drab uniforms decreed in earlier years.

Rural industry remained where it had proved practical, but renewed emphasis was placed on large-scale and urban-based industrial production and on catching up with world advances in technology to make up for the lost years. Many factory and office managers and workers were now rewarded on the basis of their productivity. Technological, managerial, and educational elites also reappeared, and with them the bourgeois lifestyles denounced by Mao as the antithesis of revolutionary socialism. The new pragmatism was illustrated by Teng Hsiao-p'ing's pithy remark: "I don't care if a cat is red [socialist] or white [capitalist] as long as it catches mice." At the same time, he affirmed that China was still a socialist country under a Communist government that planned and managed the economy and aimed to provide social justice.

The decade after Mao's death saw a reappraisal of his legacy. The new leadership permitted controlled public criticism of the excesses of the Cultural Revolution and acknowledged the failures of Mao's economic policy. But much had also been accomplished. China remained poor, but there was some growth in agriculture (except for the period 1958–1964), thanks in part to irrigation, better seeds, and fertilization. Industry grew rapidly, if unevenly, from what had been a very small and limited base. In 1964 China tested a nuclear bomb and thereby joined the ranks of the major powers. Thousands of miles of new railways and roads were built. China became a major industrial power. One of China's greatest successes was in delivering basic health care to most of its people, including for several years the system of "barefoot doctors" who traveled even to remote villages to provide basic care and the clinics established in every commune.

Building an earthen dam for flood control on the Veniu River not far from Peking, 1971. Note the hand labor and absence of heavy machinery. [Sovfoto]

As in India, this greatly reduced the death rate, while the birthrate remained high. The result was a rapid growth in population, which nearly doubled between 1949 and 1982, when the first real census was taken. This growth placed great pressure on agriculture, where gains in production barely exceeded population increase. As long as such growth continued, China could expect little progress in terms of the per capita welfare, by which real economic growth must be measured. In the 1970s the government began an attempt to control population growth. Beginning in 1983 families were penalized for having more than a single child, a policy seen as necessary for perhaps a generation if China was to escape from poverty.

Chinese socialism has also reduced gross inequities in wealth. Poverty at the bottom has not yet been eliminated, but increased production, better distribution, and the collective welfare system of communes and factories have benefited nearly everyone; recent inflation, however, has hurt many. Health levels, thanks in part to better nutrition as well as improved medical care, are in general high. Literacy has more than doubled since the revolution, and about half the population now gets as far as the early high school grades, although there are places for only about 3 percent in the universities.

Despite Mao's efforts, living standards in the cities have risen far more rapidly and substantially than in most rural areas. The growing division between urban and rural lifestyles and levels of affluence is a particular problem for the heirs of a peasant revolution, although it is shared by the rest of the developing world. China's cities are not yet disfigured by masses of visibly homeless and unemployed persons, as are many elsewhere in the developing and even the industrial world, but only because rigid controls on all movement and employment still prevent most rural people from migrating to the cities. Progress in other respects too has been won at the cost of state and collective social controls and the suppression of personal choice. This is not as disturbing to most Chinese as it might be to many Westerners, since the subordination of individualism to group effort and welfare has long been central to Chinese tradition.

China's past achievements and its revolutionary progress were due in large part to the primacy of responsibility and the pursuit of common goals over privilege and self-interest. Nevertheless, there have been protests and even student demonstrations against the continuing controls on free expression and choice of employment. As China opened its doors to more normal interchange with the rest of the world, more Chinese have come to see their political system as repressive. The political grievances resulting from this, along with the effects of Western cultural influence, led to remarkable demonstrations in Peking, Shanghai, and other major cities in the spring of 1989 that shook the party hierarchy. Most would argue that the system has other important virtues and that some controls remain necessary. Nearly all Chinese share a pride in their modern accomplishments as a nation. China has indeed stood up. Now it must make up for the years of isolation and move ahead with what it calls "modernization," recognizing that this must include a large infusion of foreign technology and perhaps also a greater scope for individual initiative and creativity.

Taiwan and Hong Kong

Taiwan had been taken over by the Japanese in 1895 as part of their colonial empire, but with Japan's defeat in 1945 the island was returned to Chinese sovereignty. In 1949 it became the sole remaining base for the defeated Kuomintang. Some 2 million mainland Chinese, including units of the Kuomintang army and government, fled to Taiwan, where they largely excluded the Taiwanese from political power.

The island had originally been settled by Chinese from Fukien (Fujian) province, just across the narrow strait that separates it from the mainland, beginning on a significant scale in the seventeenth century. They had retained their Chinese culture while developing some regional feeling, especially when the island was under Japanese control. They welcomed the mainlanders in 1945, but after repressive actions in 1947, and especially after the mass influx of 1949, they tended to regard them as oppressors.

Nevertheless, Taiwan in the 1950s began a period of rapid economic growth, at first with heavy American aid and then, by the early 1960s, on its own. A land reform program gave farmers new incentives as well as increased supplies of fertilizer, new crop strains, and new irrigation. Growing rural prosperity was matched and, by the 1970s, exceeded by industrial growth as Taiwan experienced a small-scale version of the Japanese "economic miracle." Taiwanese developments followed much the same path in technological achievements and both light and heavy manufacturing. Taiwan's trade with the rest of the world quickly exceeded that of mainland China. Taipei, the capital, became a large city and was joined by other rapidly growing industrial centers and ports.

Prosperity, wider relations with the rest of the world, and an unspoken acceptance of political realities in China and East Asia began by the 1980s to soften the harsher aspects of Kuomintang control. Taiwan remained a police state, but more representation and positions were offered to the Taiwanese along with a little more freedom of expression.

The tiny and rocky island of Hong Kong, just off the mouth of the West River, which leads to Canton, had been ceded to Britain by the Treaty of Nanking, which ended the Opium War in 1842. Additional territory was later leased on the adjacent mainland peninsula to supply Hong Kong with food and water as well as to provide room for expansion. Hong Kong grew rapidly in the nineteenth and twentieth centuries. Although under British control as a crown colony, it remained an overwhelmingly Chinese city, peopled by immigrants from overcrowded southern China who brought with them their interest and skill in commerce and their capacity for hard work. With the Communist victory in China, Hong Kong was isolated from its major market, for which it had served as a leading port for foreign trade. At the same time, it was flooded by waves of refugees from the mainland. The city and its resourceful people survived the crisis by developing a highly successful array of light industries, including textiles and electronics. Although dependent on imported raw materials, they were made profitable by inexpensive labor and efficient factories.

Hong Kong became even more prosperous than it had been before World War II. As China began to resume some trade outside the Communist bloc, Hong Kong regained its former role as a major distribution, commercial, and financial center, a function it also came to perform for much of Southeast Asia. By the 1980s the city and its adjacent territories had a population of nearly 6 million. But the Chinese government announced that when the lease on those territories expired in 1997, they and all of Hong Kong would be reclaimed. To this the British agreed. It remains to be seen how this citadel of capitalism will be integrated with the socialist system of the People's Republic.

Divided Korea

Korea had suffered perhaps more than any colonial country in the world under the exceptionally harsh Japanese rule that lasted from 1910 to 1945. Living standards fell sharply during this period as Japan milked Korea of much of its raw materials and food (see Chapter 33). Virtually all nonmenial jobs were filled by Japanese. All efforts at political expression were ruthlessly suppressed, and activists were jailed, killed, or exiled. When the Pacific war ended in

1945, almost no Koreans had the educational or administrative experience to form a viable government.

In the confused weeks after the Japanese surrender, an ad hoc arrangement left Russian troops to occupy the northern half of the country above the 38th parallel while American troops occupied the southern half. The Cold War resulted in both a hardening of this division into a political boundary and the emergence of rival political regimes. A Russian-dominated government emerged in the north with its capital at Pyongyang, and an American client-state was formed in the south, headquartered at Seoul. The conservative, American-educated politician Syngman Rhee (1875–1965) became the first president of the Republic of South Korea, while the Communist leader Kim Il Sung (born 1912) headed the Democratic People's Republic of North Korea. When American and Russian troops withdrew from their respective areas, they left a United Nations commission to keep the peace but also left their two client regimes heavily armed with modern weapons.

On June 25, 1950, the North Koreans launched an invasion across the 38th parallel, although the South was clearly preparing its own strike. Because the Russians were then boycotting the United Nations Security Council, the United States was able to push through a motion condemning North Korea, which the government of the North ignored. A special United Nations emergency force was raised to combat North Korea, but the United States had already committed its soldiers to action, and the United Nations force was almost entirely American. By September the North Korean forces had overrun the entire peninsula except for a small section in the southeast. General Douglas MacArthur counterattacked behind enemy lines at Inchon. Ignoring his instructions from Washington, he pushed deeply into North Korea, bombed the bridges linking it with China, and massed troops near its frontier. The Chinese entered the war almost immediately, driving back MacArthur's forces and retaking much of the peninsula. At this critical point, MacArthur openly advocated attacking military bases in Manchuria and using atomic weapons against the Chinese. Enraged by this insubordination, President Harry Truman relieved him of duty, touching off a bitter domestic debate. Dwight Eisenhower, Truman's successor, ended the hostilities. Campaigning for the presidency in 1952 on a pledge that he would bring peace, he approved an armistice signed at Panmunjom in July 1953.

Most of Korea was devastated by the fighting, as the armies of both sides surged back and forth over the country. A million Koreans and a million Chinese (as compared with 150,000 Americans) died, and 3 million Koreans were made refugees from their shattered homes and villages. Coming on top of the ruthless exploitation of Japanese rule after 1910, the war further reduced Korea to poverty. Korea suffered as a pawn in the Cold War rivalries between the superpowers. Korea was left divided, its economy further disrupted by the separation of its two halves, which were interdependent. The superpowers continued to supply the police-state regimes in both North and South with arms and economic aid, as their puppets, and the risk of another war between them remains, despite the fervent desire of most Koreans to see their country reunited.

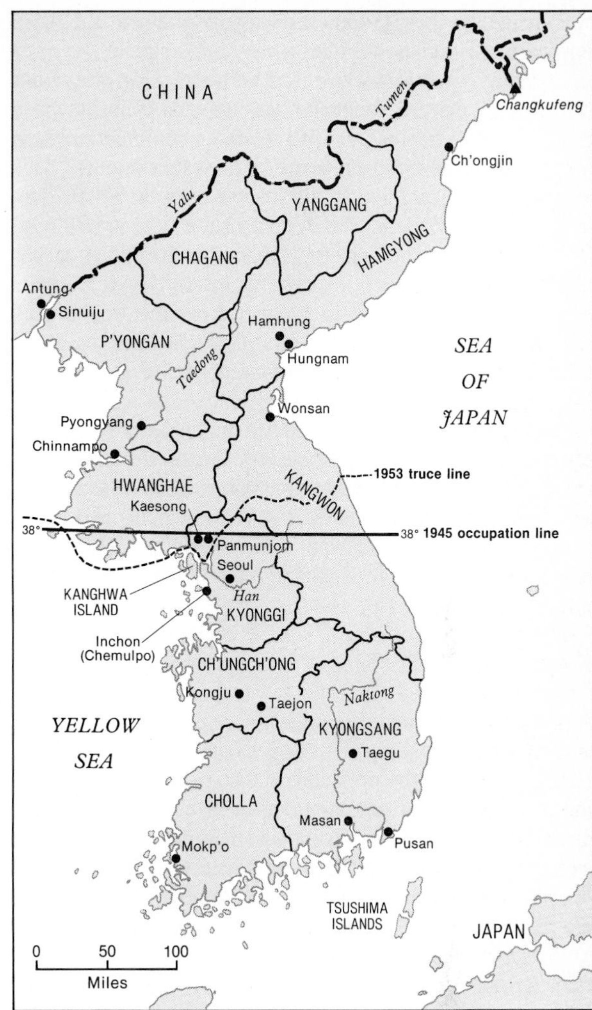

38.3 Modern Korea

American intervention in 1950 under its United Nations cloak was thus responsible for a fundamental worsening of the welfare of all Koreans. The alternative would have been a takeover of the entire country by the Communist government of the North, which, of course, is what prompted the American action. But the United States has belatedly come to accept a Communist government of China, among others, and it is not easy to argue that a Communist but unified Korea would be substantially worse, especially for Koreans, than the present situation, including its built-in tensions. American intervention in Korea formed the background for a similar policy in Vietnam, now generally acknowledged as a tragic mistake.

Although the war devastated both halves of the country, Korean culture, language, and national consciousness nevertheless remained one. Both states continued to pour scarce resources into their military establishments. This was a greater sacrifice in the less developed North than in the South, which included most of the best agricultural land and much of the industry, which the North had earlier supplied with most of its raw materials. By the 1960s South Korea had begun to recover from the war and by the 1970s to leap ahead economically, following the same path of rapid industrial development earlier pursued by Japan.

Syngman Rhee was forced to resign as president in 1960 after his dictatorial style had alienated many of his rivals, to be succeeded by a military junta and from 1963 by equally dictatorial rulers. President Chung Hee Park took office in 1963 but was assassinated in 1979 by his own Korean Central Intelligence Agency. His policies continued under Chun Doo Hwan, while the North remained under the tight control of Kim Il Sung. Both halves of Korea were police states in which free expression was savagely repressed. In 1987 a wave of student protests erupted in Seoul, and the government of Chun Doo Hwan was obliged to make a few concessions, among them the direct election of the president and somewhat more scope for political parties, including those in opposition. In the first direct presidential election in 16 years, the government's handpicked candidate, Roh Tae-woo, was chosen president in December 1987 amid charges of massive voting fraud, although he benefited from a split opposition.

Meanwhile Korean economic growth continued to produce growing prosperity for most people in the South. Rising incomes were spread widely among the population, and the gap between rich and poor was smaller than in most societies. South Korea began to invade world markets in a number of advanced manufacturing sectors, including automobiles. North Korea was largely closed to non-Communist outsiders, but economic development there was substantial, including industrial growth, although less impressive than in the South. As long as Korea remains divided between two implacably hostile governments supported by the United States and the Soviet Union, respectively, the peace of this chronically troubled part of the world will continue at risk, and the welfare of its people will suffer.

Southeast Asia Since World War II

China's revolutionary resurgence sent shock waves through Southeast Asia, where some 15 million Chinese resided. The Japanese had helped to destroy European colonialism in Asia before World War II, but the Chinese revolution now offered a new set of ideas. In neighboring Vietnam the Chinese government aided the Communist party under Ho Chi Minh (1890–1969) in its struggle first against French colonialism and then against an American invasion in support of a puppet government in the South (see Chapter 41). In the Philippines the Chinese example helped to inspire a peasant Communist uprising, the Hukbalahaps, whose successors still challenge the American-backed regime. In Indonesia reports of an alleged coup by Indonesian Communists and Chinese led to an American-supported counterstrike in 1965. Mass killings of innocent Chinese and suspected Communists resulted, and the toll of victims was probably over half a million. Malaya faced an insurrection between 1943 and 1957 by a small group of native Chinese guerrillas, but most Malayan Chinese refused to join it. The rebellion was suppressed by the outgoing British colonial administration when help from China did not materialize.

Neighboring Thailand was wary, but Thai Chinese, who had been assimilated into Thai society much more completely than in any other Southeast Asian country, remained peaceful. In Burma chronic tension existed between the majority Burmans and the numerous minority groups in the mountains around the Irrawaddy plain, and the small Chinese minority in Rangoon was expelled. The military government, which came to power in 1962 under General Ne Win (born 1911), however, modeled its policy in part on the Chinese example by cutting nearly all of Burma's ties with the rest of the world and attempting to promote domestic development through state-directed socialism.

The Philippines and Indonesia

The major event of the years after 1945 in Southeast Asia was the coming of independence to former colonial states. The Philippines in 1946 were the first to achieve it, as the Americans handed over the reins of government, although their continued presence was such that the country remained a virtual protectorate. The first two decades saw some token efforts at land reform. But in 1965 Ferdinand Marcos (1917–1989) became president and soon assumed dictatorial powers, which he used to favor the rich and to suppress free expression. For some 20 years his rule was firmly supported by successive American administrations. He was finally voted out of office in 1986, and a reformist government under Corazon Aquino began to attempt to repair the damage he had done.

Neighboring Indonesia won its armed struggle for freedom against the Dutch in 1949, who left the country unprepared for independence. Like the Koreans, few Indonesians had any administrative or technical experience, and the new government was unable to control inflation and corruption or to spur economic development. The outlying islands resented the dominance of Java, which contained the capital at Djakarta, and regional rebellion became chronic. President Achmed Sukarno (1901–1970), the leader of the independence movement, suspended the ineffective parliamentary government in 1956 and gradually took personal control, together with the army, in the name of what he called "guided democracy." This too failed to deal with Indonesia's mounting problems, and in 1966 General T. N. J. Suharto (born 1921), fresh from his CIA-supported purge of suspected Communists and Chinese, took over, confirming his rule by stage-managed elections in 1973 and 1978. The Suharto regime has made slow progress toward more orderly development despite its repressive nature, but this vast island country of some 175 million people stretched over a 3,000-mile-long archipelago has yet to evolve into full nationhood or to emerge from widespread poverty.

Indochina and the Vietnam War

When Japan surrendered in 1945, Ho Chi Minh, the head of Vietnam's Communist party, declared the independence of all Indochina. From the northern city of Hanoi, he began a war of liberation against French occupation. Under the leadership of General Vo Nguyen Giap, the Communists perfected guerrilla fighting techniques and conducted a war of attrition. Although the French retook southern Vietnam, Ho's forces controlled much of the north. In 1954, after the French-occupied fortress of Dien Bien Phu fell to Giap's forces, a hastily arranged summit conference in Geneva brought together French, Vietnamese, British, American, Soviet, and Chinese representatives. They agreed to break up Indochina temporarily into separate states and to hold national elections to reunify Vietnam within a year. The government under Ho Chi Minh in the north of Vietnam was balanced by an American-backed dictatorship set up in the south under Ngo Dinh Diem based in Saigon, the old French colonial capital. Laos and Cambodia became independent nations.

Diem and the Americans, fearing a Communist victory, refused to permit the national elections agreed to at Geneva. Guerrilla warfare broke out in South Vietnam in 1957, but President Eisenhower limited American involvement to matériel and military advisers. The Kennedy administration escalated the local civil struggle into a major international conflict on the basis of the "domino theory" that a Communist victory in Vietnam would threaten all governments in Southeast Asia. Some 17,000 American military personnel were assigned to Vietnam, but the Communist-led National Liberation Front (NLF) succeeded in capturing most of the countryside. In 1963 Vietnamese generals abetted by the United States killed Diem and ushered in a succession of military regimes.

Under President Lyndon Johnson the conflict became a full-scale war. He ordered air strikes against the Communist North and in August 1964, following a staged naval incident in the Gulf of Tongking (Tonkin), secured passage of a resolution from Congress that gave the president carte blanche to enlarge America's role in the war. By the spring of 1965 the United States was carrying out massive bombardment of North Vietnam and had committed its soldiers to offensive operations. The number of American troops grew steadily, from 184,000 in 1965 to more than 500,000 by the end of 1968.

Indonesian rice fields, Sumatra. Rice remains the major crop of lowland Southeast Asia, and much of Java and Bali resemble this scene, as do the lowland rice-growing areas of Burma, Thailand, Vietnam, Malaysia, and the Philippines. [Henri Cartier-Bresson/Magnum]

38.4 Southeast Asia

Despite this buildup, victory eluded the United States and its allies. The attempt to secure territory in the South by so-called search-and-destroy operations against the enemy proved futile, and the administration, fearing Chinese intervention as in Korea, declined to invade the North. Unable to gain victory on the ground, the United States dropped more explosives on Vietnam than the Allies had dropped on all fronts during World War II, and American troops killed thousands of civilians in fruitless efforts to prevent villagers from hiding Communist guerrillas.

The turning point in the war came in February 1968, when the NLF launched a wave of attacks against towns and cities in South Vietnam, the Tet Offensive. In April peace talks between the United States and North Vietnam opened in Paris, and in November, American voters elected the Republican Richard M. Nixon (born 1913) to the presidency. Nixon began the secret bombing of Communist supply routes in Cambodia and Laos in early 1969, concealing the operation through false reports. When Congress learned of the Cambodian bombings, it repealed the Tongking Gulf Resolution. In 1971 the publication of classified war documents heightened antiwar sentiments by revealing earlier deceptions by both Johnson and Nixon. Protests mounted as the 1972 presidential elections approached, but Nixon neutralized them by removing the last American ground troops. The Paris Accords, signed in January 1973, officially ended American involvement in the war. In April 1975 the North Vietnamese captured Saigon, ousted the government of President Nguyen Van Thieu, and unified the country.

The Americans claimed that the struggle was an example of "Communist aggression." Most Vietnamese saw it as a patriotic "war of national liberation" against French colonialism and U.S. imperialism. Peasants came to fear and hate the repressive policies of the puppet government of the South and of their American supporters, as they and most Vietnamese intellectuals had hated French oppression. There were some Vietnamese anti-Communists, including Catholic converts who fled the North, and some who supported the United States–backed government, but they were mainly relatively well-to-do elites and others who benefited from the widespread corruption of the Saigon government or who profited in various ways from the American presence. The war's outcome was ultimately decided by the support of most Vietnamese, including the peasants in this predominantly rural country, for the forces of the National Liberation Front, which they saw as a national rather than as a partisan effort.

In many ways the Vietnam war was a repeat of the long

struggle of the Chinese Communists against the Kuomintang. In Vietnam, too, the Communist party under Ho had captured the leadership of Vietnamese nationalism by the end of the Second World War. Like the Chinese, Vietnamese nationalists strove to free their country from foreign domination, and like them, they drew support against a corrupt and repressive regime domestically, which was further weakened politically by its subservience to foreign interests. Between 1.5 and 2 million Vietnamese gave their lives in the struggle; perhaps as many as 4 million were wounded, and over a million were refugees. The Americans suffered 57,000 dead and some 300,000 wounded.

As in Korea but to a far greater extent, American intervention produced in the end nothing but destruction and death. Official policy was based on almost total ignorance of Vietnam, its history of repeated success in repelling vastly superior Chinese armies, and the strength of Vietnamese nationalism. The small nation's guerrilla fighters humbled the military might of the world's greatest superpower, as the Chinese Communists had earlier defeated another United States client, the Kuomintang. But Vietnam suffered terribly. Its people and its economy have not recovered from what has been called the "endless war" from 1945 to 1975, although for many Vietnamese the struggle against the French had begun in the second half of the nineteenth century. The United States merely prolonged that struggle and, far from preventing a Communist victory, had the effect of hardening the determination and the political rigidity of the government of the North. Since 1975 Vietnam has continued to suffer not only from the effects of unprecedented devastation but also from ideological tension and repression augmented by the long ordeal of conflict. If Ho had been allowed to prevail against the French in 1945 or 1946, as he clearly would have done without massive United States support for the French, most of these tragic problems would have been avoided.

Recovery from the war damage to the economy was slow. As after any civil war, bitterness remained between the Communist victors and those in the south who had opposed them. Many Vietnamese fled the country, including a large group who emigrated to the United States. But continued political and ideological tensions further slowed the recovery of Vietnam, which lagged behind much of the rest of Southeast Asia.

Vietnam's war of independence spilled over into neighboring Laos and Cambodia, with appalling human consequences. The overthrow of the neutralist ruler of Cambodia (now Kampuchea), Prince Norodom Sihanouk (born 1919), led to a civil war and subsequently to the genocidal Communist regime of Pol Pot, who was responsible for the deaths of perhaps a third of the country's people from 1976 to 1979 by forced labor, execution, or starvation. Vietnamese military intervention helped a more moderate rival government to win control of most of the country in 1979, but Pol Pot's Khmer Rouge forces remain active in

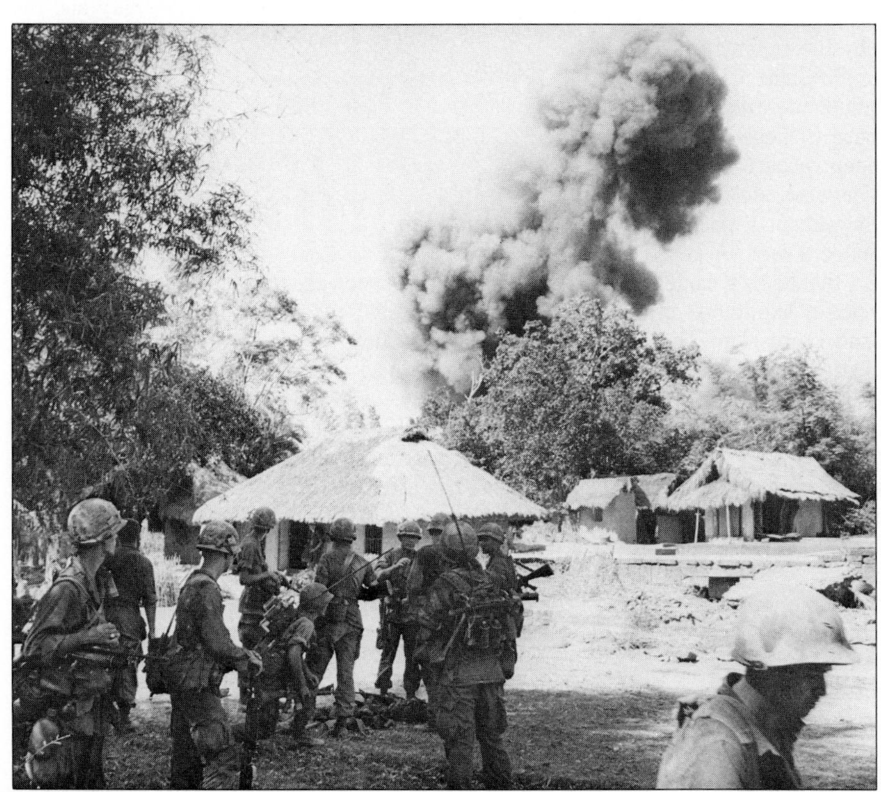

South Vietnam, 1967: a squad of American soldiers stops to watch as a target in a village burns. [Philip Jones-Griffiths/ Magnum]

their northern bases, supplied by China and the United States. Vietnam was still seen as the enemy of America and now again of China, and its move to eliminate Pol Pot was therefore resisted by both countries for political reasons. Those reasons included Russian support for Vietnam, which helped to sustain it in its war with the United States and which the Chinese also saw as a threat to themselves. Continuing Cold War rivalries in Indochina have thus prolonged its agony.

Malaysia, Singapore, and Thailand

Malaya's independence was delayed by the Communist insurgency, but once order was restored, the British quickly handed over power to the new state in 1957. Its major problem has been the diversity of its people. The Malays constituted a bare majority in their own homeland, thanks to massive Chinese immigration since the late nineteenth century. Most Malays were not interested in wage labor, and the booming growth of tin mining and rubber plantations brought in a wave of Chinese workers and entrepreneurs from overcrowded southern China. Many of them went on to become the dominant figures in the commercial life of Malaya and were joined by wives and families from China, as well as by immigrant laborers and merchants from India. By the time of independence Malays were only about half of the population.

This problem was eased in 1965 by the separation of the island of Singapore, overwhelmingly Chinese, as an independent city-state, and by the addition of former British colonies in northern Borneo, where Chinese were a minority. Since then the state has been called Malaysia, but there have been chronic conflicts between Malays and Chinese. The Chinese are effectively without a political voice, but Malays resent their economic power. A generally stable parliamentary system on the British model was marred in the 1980s by tendencies, like those in Singapore, toward authoritarianism and repression. The economy has remained relatively vigorous and has expanded from its colonial foundations in tin and rubber to include important palm oil production and a rapidly growing light industrial sector.

Independent Singapore continues as a high-income and high-growth center of trade for much of Southeast Asia and has become the world's fourth largest port in volume of traffic.

Thailand, just north of Malaya, was the only nation of Southeast Asia to retain independence throughout the colonial period. Since 1945 it has also enjoyed precarious political stability under democratic forms and has shared in the prosperous commercial growth of Malaya and Singapore through its port and capital of Bangkok, now a rapidly growing Western-style city.

Burma

Burma won its freedom from Britain in 1948 in the wake of India's independence, but it has been troubled by violence between the dominant Burmans and the diverse minorities who occupy the mountain fringes of the country. Chronic guerrilla-style civil war existed between government forces and rebel groups. General Ne Win's military government was not able to resolve this problem fully, and his policy of isolation from the rest of the world had the effect of further slowing Burma's already sluggish economic growth. Burma has begun to move cautiously toward resuming some external contacts and trade. A new and more responsive government may be able to build a more equitable and consensual national partnership among Burmans and non-Burmans, but the country still has far to go to attain viable nationhood.

For Southeast Asia as a whole, the transition from colonialism has been a hard one. Only Singapore and Thailand can be called fully successful states, and both may be regarded as special cases: Thailand never underwent colonial occupation and contains few non-Thai minorities. Singapore is in essence a creation of Western colonialism and capitalism. In the 1980s government policies in Singapore were often repressively applied and free expression curtailed or silenced. The countries of Southeast Asia are too scattered and too different from each other to work together as a unit, even for common economic purposes. It is a major sector of the world, but its diversity and the legacy of its colonial domination continue to retard its development.

Women Leaders in Modern East Asia

Several women have been prominent in positions of power in East Asia since 1945. Most traditional Asian societies were noted for the low status accorded to women, although Southeast Asia was a relative exception. In the modern period, however, some women have risen to great prominence, becoming heads of state in India, Sri Lanka, and the Philippines and political powers in Pakistan and China. Japan has produced notable women writers.

Chiang Ch'ing (Jiang Qing, born 1914), Mao Tse-tung's third wife, had been a minor movie star before she married him in Yenan in 1939. She assumed a prominent role in shaping party cultural policy, and with the Cultural Revolution in 1966 she emerged publicly as a member of the party's Central Committee in charge of cultural affairs. She was personally responsible for the persecution of writers and artists and for decreeing what was acceptable in music, art, literature, and drama. She reportedly used her power to pay off old scores against professional rivals and increasingly ignored or countermanded her husband's advice. She was often vituperative and spiteful in her personal style and ruthless in carrying out the policies she favored. Both traditional and foreign works were banned in favor of a rigid "socialist realism" whose overtly political message was designed to appeal to the masses of peasants and workers.

During Mao's last years, when ill health and advancing senility obliged him to withdraw from the day-to-day management of affairs, Chiang Ch'ing and her radical colleagues appear to have greatly enhanced their power, and they were probably the chief architects of the Cultural Revolution as a whole after 1968. They made a bid for full power after the death of Prime Minister Chou En-lai in January 1976 and while Mao was in his final illness. After Mao's death in September, Chiang and her colleagues were arrested and denounced. At her trial she insisted that she alone had been faithful to Mao's vision, but most Chinese had come to fear and hate her, and she is still seen as the archvillain of China's dark years.

Imelda Marcos (born 1930) acquired great political power as the wife of President Ferdinand Marcos of the Philippines. She became notorious for her ludicrously extensive wardrobe, including, reputedly, the world's largest personal collection of shoes and a huge hoard of jewelry. Far more important, however, was the worldwide real estate and investment empire she and her husband built for themselves with the help of Filipino tax money, American aid, and open corruption.

Mrs. Marcos played a prominent public role, opening public housing projects that proved to be shams, raising money to build a hospital in Manila that only the very rich could afford to enter, and speaking on behalf of her husband at rallies and functions. Ferdinand Marcos suffered periodic bouts of illness with advancing years, and it was rumored that his wife intended to succeed him.

But the Marcoses lost the elections of 1986, and a quite different woman, Corazon Aquino (born 1933), became president. Her husband, Benigno Aquino, had been the principal opposition leader until his murder in 1983 by guards assigned to him by Marcos on his return from exile. Assuming the leadership of his party, Mrs. Aquino ran a vigorous election campaign against Marcos and was elected and installed in office with belated American support.

As president she began the long task of rebuilding responsible government and countering the appeal of entrenched Communist rebels. This required a reduction in the great power of the rich landed and business families; but Mrs. Aquino, herself a member of this elite, needed their support. Continuing Communist insurgency, defections from her coalition by ambitious rivals, and plots by former Marcos loyalists have made her task difficult, although she has remained personally popular with most Filipinos. Her political power base remains precarious, like her tenuous control over the army.

Chiang Ch'ing and Imelda Marcos did not advance the cause of women's liberation in Asia, but many other women did, and the movement gathered new strength in all of Asia after 1945. Mao Tse-tung said that "women hold up half the sky," and although China has not yet approached gender equality, great strides have been made there, and even in Korea and Japan, away from traditional female subservience and toward greater recognition of women's rights and their coequal role in society.

Women in East Asian Society

The position of women in contemporary East Asia varies widely. In China life for women remained essentially unchanged from the time of Confucius to the beginning of the twentieth century. The Chinese woman was considered a temporary member of her parents' household, to be transferred to her husband's control at marriage. She adopted her husband's surname, only then followed by her own. Upon her death, only her husband's family surname was recorded in her husband's genealogy, so that her personal identity was permanently effaced. Despite the achievement of some women of rank in scholarship and the arts, the average woman was, at least until she bore a son, near the bottom of the status hierarchy.

The impact of Western imperialism in the late nineteenth century brought the first challenge to the traditional system. Mission schools and colleges began to educate women and added support to the movements against footbinding, chaste widowhood, and the general subjugation of women. After the revolution of 1911, the first women's magazines began to appear, and the demand of the younger generation for greater freedom from parental control opened up new secondary and university education to girls. Pioneer feminists became doctors, lawyers, teachers, and active revolutionaries; there were even banks staffed entirely by women and serving a female clientele. Missionary boarding schools provided an important avenue of mobility for aspiring village girls, while in the cities they offered daughters of the merchant class a Western-oriented education and social contact with foreigners. World War II, with its increased demand for labor power and its dislocation of families, also increased social and economic opportunities for women.

After the revolution of 1949, women in the People's Republic were given basic legal rights for the first time. The Marriage Law of 1950 not only gave women the right freely to choose their husbands and equal responsibility for the raising of children but also established the right of women to own property and to choose an occupation. The effect of this legislation was galvanic. A newspaper estimated in 1953 that 2 million persons had been affected by divorce in Shanghai, Peking, Tientsin, and Wuhan alone.

In the same year the Ministry of Justice reported that 70,000 to 80,000 women were being murdered or forced into suicide each year as a result of family conflict or oppression. This backlash presaged a long struggle for genuine equality. By 1958 women comprised 50 percent of the agricultural labor force but were far from equally compensated with men; nor had they advanced far in penetrating the manufacturing sector, where they were still largely confined to the textile and tobacco industries. The commune movement of the late 1950s also had the effect of regimenting women. The top political and professional echelons were still almost entirely reserved for men. Twenty years after the revolution, only 10 percent of the members of the Communist party itself were women.

Official policy toward women in the early decades of the revolution reflected the drive to mobilize labor in general. The traditional extended family was drastically affected by land reform, forced resettlement, and the commune system. Not until 1974, as part of a campaign against the Confucian ethos, was the position of women systematically addressed, particularly the residual dominance of the patrilocal family. Even then, however, the primary impetus was economic rationalization and increased productivity.

The other major prong of social policy affecting women has been the campaign for birth control. Since the late 1970s women have been under extreme pressure to reduce the birthrate, in many cases through late-term abortions. At the same time, the economic and social importance of male offspring remains very high, since daughters still join their husbands' families and family welfare depends critically on the number of working members, with males almost always better paid. The result has been a revival of female infanticide, which, though condemned by the government, is nonetheless a direct result of the combination of its demographic policies with a still largely unreformed social system.

The status of women in the newly industrialized nations of Taiwan and Korea, the city-state of Singapore, and the British colony of Hong Kong displays the tension between traditional Chinese or Chinese-influenced family culture and the needs of market capitalism, which tends to treat workers in isolation from the family or other social unit. On the one hand, wage remuneration has given women in these labor-intensive, export-oriented societies some potential economic independence; on the other, they are still expected to remain firmly under family control.

In Southeast Asia, where women have long had independent property rights and have been as active as men in the economy, the primary change in the past several decades has been the increasing differentiation between town and country life. The postwar constitutions of Burma, Thailand, and Indonesia gave legal equality to women, and in South Vietnam the Family Law Bill of 1958 spelled out such equality in detail. In the Islamic states of Malaysia and Indonesia, the special problem of women, apart from the general Islamic subordination of them, is the persistence of polygamy and the ease of divorce, which has mounted in some areas as high as 60 percent.

The situation of Japan is unique in that it is the only East Asian nation in the front rank of the world's industrial powers. Before the twentieth century, women had been subservient to men, as in Confucian China, and unable to inherit property even when male descendants were lacking. As elsewhere in East Asia, a feminist movement had arisen early in the century, led particularly by Hiratsuka Raicho (1886–1971), who founded the first Japanese women's magazine, *Blue Stockings*, in 1911, and Ichikawa Fusae (1893–1981), who was later to serve in the House of Councillors almost continuously from 1953 until her death. A feminist organization, the New Women's Association, was founded after World War I, although it was not until the American occupation that women were able to win formal legal equality and the right to vote. Traditional patterns of deference continued to prevail, however. In 1980 fully 75 percent of the eligible women voted in the nationwide elections, as opposed to 53 percent of the male electorate; yet only 3 percent of the members returned to the Japanese Diet were women.

Social and economic inequality between the sexes continues to characterize Japan. The introduction of coeducation in 1950 led to a doubling of girls in secondary schools during the next decade and more than tripled the number of female university students. Yet university women are still regarded as exceptional in Japan. Women now comprise 35 percent of the work force but still lag far behind their male counterparts in earnings and benefits. They are exploited in every sector, including agriculture, where they constitute the majority of the labor force but are almost entirely unpaid workers on family farms. Most working women leave their employment upon marriage, only to reenter 10 to 15 years later at the bottom of the pay scale. Laws have recently been passed, however, providing child care and other benefits for working women. Japanese feminists are particularly active in such causes as consumer and environmental protection, peace and nuclear disarmament movements, and the fight against job discrimination.

Rewards and Problems of Modernization

East Asia as a whole had the highest economic growth rate of any part of the world in the decades following World War II, a pattern that still continues. Hong Kong, Taiwan, and South Korea rapidly developed in the wake of Japanese economic success after the mid-1950s. Much of this development was on the Japanese model, beginning in light industry and consumer goods and continuing into heavy manufacturing and precision goods. Singapore's growth paralleled that of Hong Kong; both were tiny Chinese city-states that had originally prospered as trade centers and then moved into "high-tech" industrialization and processing. In China, despite the drag exerted by antiurbanism and revolutionary ideology, industrial growth was impressive, and after 1980 overall economic development was rapid. In Southeast Asia several of the major cities besides Singapore, notably Bangkok in Thailand and Manila, the Philippine capital, grew enormously as booming commercial and light industrial centers.

Much of this growth rested on the East Asian tradition of disciplined hard work and organized group effort, but it was striking enough to attract world attention and speculation about its causes. East Asia does share, to varying degrees, an originally Chinese culture, which has for centuries stressed education, hard work, and group effort, perhaps enough to override other differences in the pursuit of advancement.

But modernization has brought new problems. These include the rapid erosion of traditional cultures (to the distress of many East Asians), the rise of huge cities inadequately supplied with basic services or housing, and fearsome pollution of urban and rural environments. Japan was only the first to suffer dramatically from industrial pollution as a result of the unprecedented concentration of cities and manufacturing in its lowlands. As a high-income and technologically developed society, Japan was also the first to deal successfully with at least some of those problems.

For the rest of East Asia, as in the developing world as a whole, largely unchecked pollution is still increasing, with deeply worrisome long-term consequences for human welfare. Other East Asian countries have passed environmental legislation too, but in most cases it is not effectively enforced. Chinese, Korean, Taiwanese, and Southeast Asian cities are dangerously polluted, their air heavy with soot and fumes, and their water supplies, often inadequate to supply their mushrooming populations and factories, are loaded with poisonous industrial residues. In rural areas heavy applications of chemical fertilizers, the use of largely unregulated chemical pesticides, and the development of factories cause additional environmental damage. Massive cutting of trees to feed the demand for new construction has exposed slopes to erosion, and silt chokes rivers and irrigation systems. In large parts of Southeast Asia the tropical rain forest that covers much of the area is rapidly being depleted to provide lumber for both domestic and world markets, with potentially serious effects on local and world climate.

Most of these countries are bent on rapid industrial and economic growth; they are reluctant to slow that growth or add to its costs, even by limiting the worst of the environmental damage. Such controls, many of them argue, are for rich countries. It may take more human disasters such as Japan experienced to persuade them that their own welfare is at stake. Japan, lacking most industrial raw materials and having to import nearly all of its oil, has invested proportionately more heavily in nuclear power than any country in the world, ignoring its location in one of the world's major earthquake zones. China has huge domestic supplies of coal, most of it with a high sulfur content, which supplies about three-quarters of the nation's energy. These problems may become future disasters as East Asia continues to modernize.

Urban growth in East Asia has taken place very rapidly and with minimal planning, especially outside China. Even in China industrial and residential areas have not been adequately separated; housing, water supply, and other urban services lag seriously behind demand; Peking has grown uncontrollably. These problems are equally pronounced in urban centers such as Seoul, Taipei, Bangkok, Manila, and Djakarta, where unchecked migration from rural areas has swollen city populations without a substantial increase in basic services.

While the problems of modernization seem especially serious in the cities, it is there also that the chief forces for economic growth are centered. The cities are the major industrial bases, educational centers, commercial and financial hubs, and centers of intellectual and cultural ferment, as they were in the history of the West. So far Asia has tended to repeat the Western experience of economic and industrial development, which in its early and middle stages was unpleasant and unhealthy for most people. As the process has gathered momentum in Asia after the Second World War, one may hope that the rest of the Western experience will be repeated too, as the cities become, like those in Japan, centers of improved welfare. Their advances can then spread more widely over each country.

The years after 1945 were momentous for East Asia. New nations were born out of the former colonial regimes in Southeast Asia. Korea regained its independence, only to be torn by war and split by superpower tensions. China underwent the largest revolution in history, measured by the numbers of people involved, the scope of its change, and the length of both its gestation and its active course, including the convulsive struggles of the Cultural Revolution. A shattered Japan rebuilt its economy and rose to world industrial leadership. But although each of these major areas had its own internal problems, the dominant trend in all of them was economic growth and industrialization. East Asia as a whole, led by Japan, became the world's largest and most rapidly expanding commercial and industrial network, as it had long been its most populous geographic region. It remains to be seen whether the area's new economic power will be reflected proportionately in new political power on the world scene.

Suggestions for Further Reading

Japan

Dore, R. *City Life in Japan: A Study of a Tokyo Ward*. Berkeley: University of California Press, 1967.

Hane, M. *Modern Japan: A Historical Survey*. Boulder, Colo.: Westview Press, 1986.

Immamura, H. E. *Urban Japanese Housewives*. Honolulu: University Press of Hawaii, 1986.

Kawai, K. *Japan's American Interlude*. Chicago: University of Chicago Press, 1960.

Lebra, T. S. *Japanese Women: Constraint and Fulfillment*. Honolulu: University Press of Hawaii, 1984.

Minear, R. *Victor's Justice*. Princeton, N.J.: Princeton University Press, 1971.

New, C. *The Troubled Encounter: The United States and Japan*. New York: Wiley, 1975.

Reischauer, E. O. *The Japanese*. Cambridge, Mass.: Harvard University Press, 1980.

Stockwin, J. A. *Japan: Divided Politics in a Growth Economy*. London: Weidenfeld & Nicolson, 1975.

Storry, R. *A History of Modern Japan*, rev. ed. New York: Penguin Books, 1982.

Vogel, E. *Japan as Number One: Lessons for America*. Cambridge, Mass.: Harvard University Press, 1979.

China

Bonavia, D. *The Chinese*. New York: Harper & Row, 1984.

Ch'en, J. *Mao and the Chinese Revolution*. Oxford: Oxford University Press, 1967.

Dietrich, C. *People's China: A Brief History*. New York: Oxford University Press, 1986.

Fairbank, J. K. *The Great Chinese Revolution*. Cambridge, Mass.: Harvard University Press, 1986.

Johnson, K. A. *Women, the Family, and Peasant Revolution in China*. Chicago: University of Chicago Press, 1983.

Lee, H. Y. *The Politics of the Chinese Cultural Revolution*. Berkeley: University of California Press, 1978.

Leeming, F. *Rural China Today*. London: Longman, 1985.

Liang, H., and Shapiro, J. *Son of the Revolution*. New York: Knopf, 1984.

Murphey, R. *The Fading of the Maoist Vision*. New York: Methuen, 1980.

Nathan, A. *Chinese Democracy*. Berkeley: University of California Press, 1986.

Riskin, C. *China's Political Economy: The Quest for Development Since 1949*. New York: Oxford University Press, 1987.

Schram, S. *Mao Tse-tung: A Preliminary Reassessment*. New York: Simon & Schuster, 1984.

Selden, M. *The Yenan Way in Revolutionary China*. Cambridge, Mass.: Harvard University Press, 1971.

Terrill, R., ed. *The China Difference*. New York: Harper & Row, 1983.

White, M. K., and Parrish, W. *Urban Life in Contemporary China*. Stanford, Calif.: Stanford University Press, 1985.

———. *Village and Family in Contemporary China*. Chicago: University of Chicago Press, 1978.

Woronoff, J. *Asia's "Miracle" Economies*. New York: Sharpe, 1986.

Korea

Clough, R. N. *Embattled Korea*. Boulder, Colo.: Westview Press, 1987.

Lee, K. B. *A New History of Korea*, trans. E. W. Wagner. Cambridge, Mass.: Harvard University Press, 1985.

Southeast Asia

Greene, G. *The Quiet American*. New York: Viking, 1957. (A novel about the Vietnam War.)

Martin, L. K., ed. *The Asian Success Story*. Honolulu: University Press of Hawaii, 1987.

Steinberg, D., ed. *In Search of Southeast Asia: A Modern History*, rev. ed. Honolulu: University Press of Hawaii, 1987.

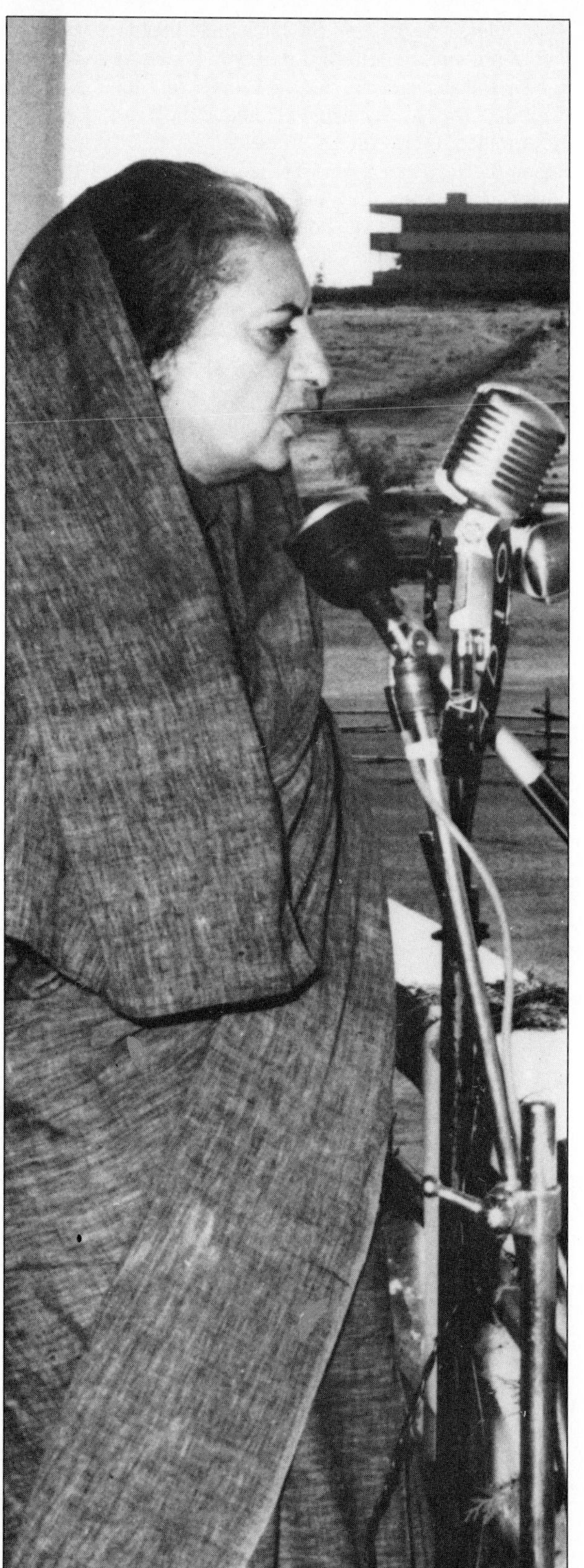

CHAPTER · 39

Nationalism and Revolution: India, Pakistan, Iran, and the Middle East

The postwar period was a time of rapid and radical change throughout the Middle East and central Asia. Britain and France withdrew or were forced from their colonial dominions, and a host of new nations emerged, some with ancient roots in the area, others the product of modern nationalism. Among the former, India and Egypt regained their old independence, one as a constitutional democracy, the other as a revolutionary socialist state. Among the latter, Pakistan, the world's third largest Islamic state (after Indonesia and India), emerged from the Muslim-majority regions of pre-1949 India. Some states, such as Jordan, were created primarily as buffer zones or as acts of political compromise, while in other cases nationalist movements, such as those of the Palestinians and the Kurds, remained frustrated. The most controversial new nation to emerge in the region was the state of Israel, where a powerful modern nationalism sought to revive the heritage of a kingdom that had flourished nearly 3,000 years before. Throughout the postwar decades, however,

Indira Gandhi in 1972, addressing a crowd at Kolhapur, India. [UPI/Bettmann Newsphotos]

the region as a whole has been characterized by turmoil and instability, culminating in the 1980s in a war between Iran and Iraq that now ranks as the fourth bloodiest conflict of the twentieth century.

South Asia: Independence and Political Division

The Indian subcontinent, known since 1947 as South Asia, is composed of the separate states of Pakistan, India, Bangladesh, Nepal, and Sri Lanka and contains well over a billion people, one-fifth of the world. British colonialism died in the ashes of the Second World War, and the British were in any case unwilling to continue their rule of an India determined to regain its freedom. Gandhi, Nehru, and other Indian political leaders had spent most of the war years in jail after they had refused to support the war without a promise of independence. Their example inspired many new followers, and by 1945 the independence movement was clearly too strong to be denied by a Britain now both weakened and weary of colonialism. The conservative wartime leader Winston Churchill was voted out of office. Churchill had been rigidly opposed to Indian independence. During the war he had declared, "I was not

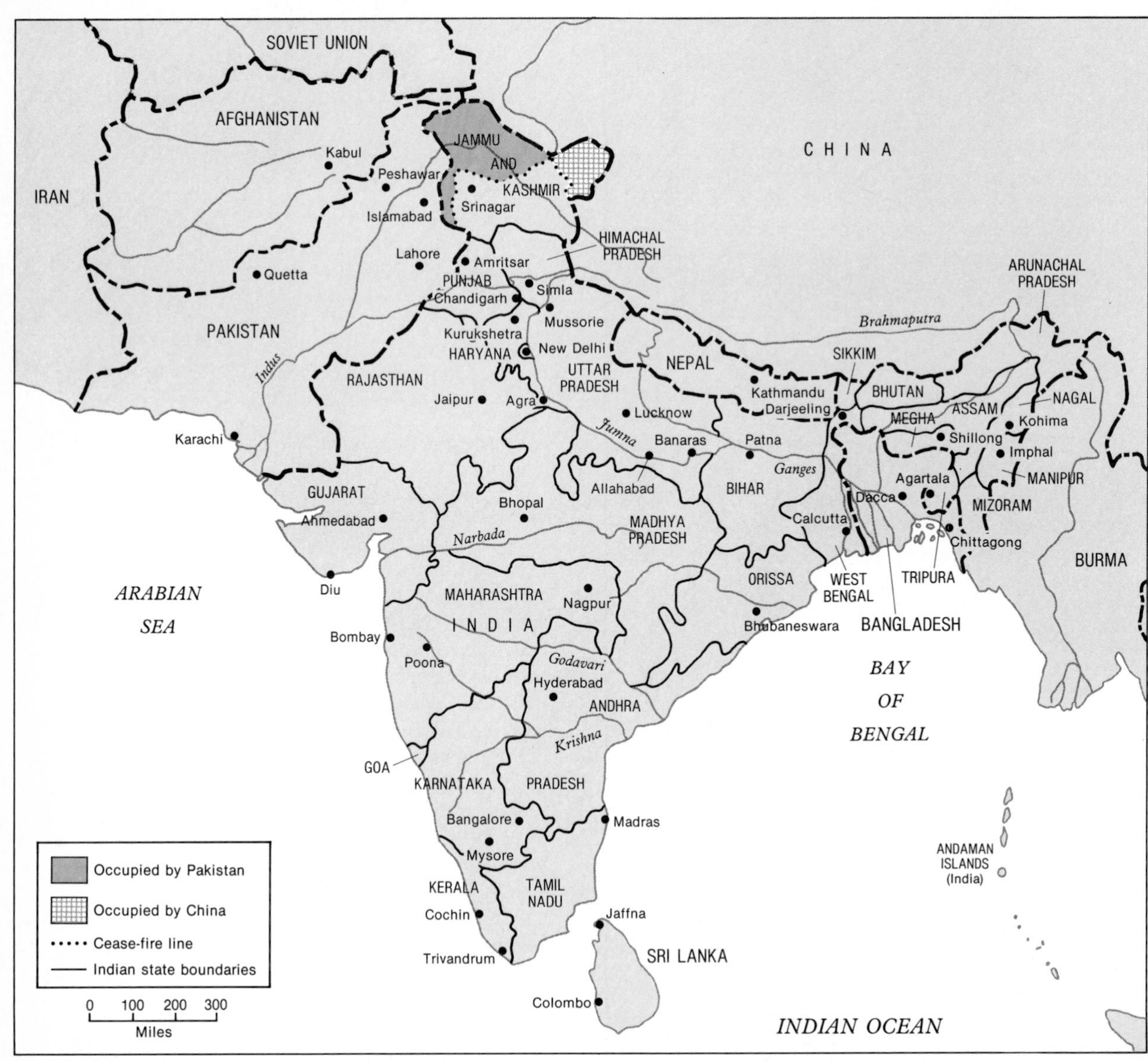

39.1 South Asia Today

made His Majesty's first minister in order to preside over the liquidation of the British Empire," and he was contemptuous of Gandhi. Lord Wavell, military commander in India and the first postwar viceroy, wrote in his diary: "Churchill hates India and everything to do with it. He knows as much of the Indian problem as George III did of the American colonies. . . . He sent me a peevish telegram to ask why Gandhi hadn't died yet."

The new Labour government under Clement Attlee moved quickly toward giving India its freedom. Elections were held in India early in 1946, but by then it had become clear that support for a separate state for Muslims had gained strength. The Muslim League, the chief vehicle for this movement, had been founded as early as 1906, but until 1945 it was supported by only a few Muslims, most of whom remained willing to work with the Congress party as the main agent of politically conscious Indians. The Muslim League's president, Mohammed Ali Jinnah (1876–1948), had earlier been a member of the Congress party and was even for a time its president. He and a few other Muslim leaders became dissatisfied with the Congress party's plans for a secular independent state that deemphasized religious identity and with the party's leaders' unwillingness to reserve what Jinnah regarded as adequate positions and representation for Muslims. Hindus and Muslims had lived together peacefully for most of nine centuries, even at the village level. Persian Muslim culture had blended in with indigenous elements to form modern Indian civilization. Both groups were long-standing parts of the Indian fabric. It was hard to see them as irreconcilable.

Mohammed Ali Jinnah in 1946. Note his totally Western dress. [India Office Library of the British Library.]

Jinnah, like Nehru, was British educated. In his earlier career as a British-trained lawyer, he had paid little attention to Islam, and he knew no Urdu, the language of Islam

Muslim Solidarity: Jinnah's Call

Jinnah made a number of speeches during the Second World War in his effort to promote Muslim solidarity and political action. Here are excerpts from a 1943 speech.

The progress that Muslims, as a nation, have made during these [past] three years is a remarkable fact. . . . Never before has a nation, miscalled a minority, asserted itself so quickly and so effectively. . . . We have created a solidarity of opinion, a union of mind and thought. . . . Let us cooperate with and give all help to our leaders to work for our collective good. Let us make our organization stronger. . . . We, the Muslims, must rely mainly upon our own inherent qualities, our own natural potentialities, our own internal solidarity, and our own united will to face the future. . . . Train yourselves, equip yourselves for the task that lies before us. The final victory depends upon you and is within our grasp. You have performed wonders in the past. You are still capable of repeating history. You are not lacking in the great qualities and virtues in comparison with other nations. Only you have to be fully conscious of that fact and act with courage, faith, and unity.

Source: W. T. de Bary, ed., *Sources of Indian Tradition*, vol. 2 (New York: Columbia University Press, 1964), pp. 286–287.

in India. But as he saw his political ambitions threatened by the success of Gandhi and Nehru, he shifted his allegiance to the Muslim League and began to use it to persuade Muslims that a Hindu-dominated India would never, as he put it, give them "justice." He found support among some of the communal-minded (those who put separate group loyalty above national feeling) and also from Muslim businessmen, especially in the port city of Karachi, who saw a possible way of ridding themselves of Hindu competition. Nehru and others insisted that communalism had nothing to do with religion and that the exploitation of religious differences by a few politicians for their own ends fueled communal tensions. Hindus were often more active and more successful in business than Muslims, they were generally more educated, and as the great majority in India they also dominated politics and the professions. But they did not generally discriminate against Muslim intellectuals or professionals. Some other Muslim political figures, like Jinnah, saw greater opportunity for themselves if they could have their own state and supported the League in its campaign to convince Muslims that "Islam was in danger." When such relatively peaceful tactics did not produce enough result, Jinnah and the League began to promote terror and violence, urging Muslims to demonstrate and to attack Hindus in order to call attention to their cause.

The Congress party was slow to respond or to offer Muslims or the League a larger share in an Indian future. Gandhi and Nehru in particular were reluctant even to consider partitioning India just as it was about to win freedom. This tended to increase the League's fear of a Hindu threat to Muslims and its resort to tactics of violence. In the later stages of the long negotiations during 1946 and 1947 Jinnah offered to give up the demand for Pakistan (as the separate Muslim state was to be called) if he could be guaranteed the position of first prime minister of independent India. That demand was rejected, and Jinnah remained adamant in insisting on a separate state, of which he could be the head. Successive British representatives tried to work out a solution in sessions with the Congress party and the League, ending with the special mission in 1947 of Lord Louis Mountbatten (1900–1979), the wartime supreme commander in Southeast Asia. Mountbatten was appointed viceroy of India, with the sole charge of working out the terms for independence as quickly as this could be done.

If independence had been granted at any time before 1939, as most Indians and most British had wanted, the issue of partition would not have arisen. Jinnah was able to use the war years, while the Congress party leaders were in jail, to build his political base and then to spread the fear of cultural engulfment and oppression among his followers. Muslim-Hindu violence, once stirred up by the Muslim League, acquired its own dreadful momentum on both sides, especially in regions that were nearly evenly divided between the two religious communities, such as Punjab and East Bengal. Mob riots and mass killing spread widely. Although Mountbatten, like Nehru and Gandhi, hoped to avoid handing over power to a divided India, by July he as well as the party leaders recognized that partition and the creation of Pakistan were inevitable. Nehru

Nehru and Mountbatten in New Delhi, 1947. The two men developed an immediate liking for each other, which greatly eased the transition to independence. [UPI/Bettmann Newsphotos]

remarked bitterly that "by cutting off the head we will get rid of the headache," while Gandhi continued to regard partition as "vivisection."

Lines were drawn to mark off the predominantly Muslim northwest and western Punjab and the eastern half of Bengal as the two unequal halves of Pakistan, separated from each other by nearly 1,000 miles. At midnight on August 14, 1947, the Republic of India and the Islamic state of Pakistan officially won their independence. Gandhi boycotted the independence day celebrations in New Delhi, going instead to Calcutta to try to quell fresh outbreaks of mass violence there as refugees streamed in from eastern Bengal.

The first months of independence were tragically overshadowed by perhaps the greatest mass refugee movement in history as over 10 million people fled from both sides in 1947 alone, about a million of whom were victims of mob massacre along the route. When it was all over, 50 million Muslims continued to live in India much as before, and India still has more Muslims than Pakistan. For those who chose to migrate to Pakistan, including further millions after 1947, life in the new state (with an initial population of 70 million), was hard in the first chaotic years as Pakistan struggled to cope with the flood of refugees. Hindus remaining in Pakistan soon found that they had little place in an Islamic state that explicitly discriminated against all non-Muslims, and within a few years most of them had migrated to India, depriving Pakistan of many of its more highly educated and experienced people. For the educated elite of both countries, including the army officers who soon faced each other across the new boundaries, partition divided former classmates, friends, and professional colleagues who had shared a common experience, training, and values.

The partition lines also split the previously integrated cultural and economic regions of densely populated Punjab

India and the Sense of History

On the eve of independence, Nehru addressed the Constituent Assembly in 1946 with his characteristic eloquence, stressing the sense of history that many Indians share.

As I stand here, . . . I feel the weight of all manner of things crowding upon me. We are at the end of an era and possibly very soon we shall embark upon a new age. My mind goes back to the great past of India, to the 5000 years of India's history, from the very dawn of that history which might be considered almost the dawn of human history, until today. All that past crowds upon me and exhilarates me, and at the same time somewhat oppresses me. Am I worthy of that past? When I think also of the future, the greater future I hope, standing on this sword's edge of the present between the mighty past and the mightier future, I tremble a little and feel overwhelmed by this mighty task. We have come here at a strange moment in India's history. I do not know, but I do feel, that there is some magic in this moment of transition from the old to the new, something of that magic which one sees when the night turns into day and even though the day may be a cloudy one, it is day after all, for when the clouds move away, we can see the sun again. Because of all this I find a little difficulty in addressing this House and putting all my ideas before it, and I feel also that in this long succession of thousands of years, I see the mighty figures that have come and gone and I see also the long succession of our comrades who have labored for the freedom of India. And we stand now on the verge of this passing age, trying, laboring, to usher in the new. . . .

I think also of the various constituent assemblies that have gone before and of what took place at the making of the great American nation when the fathers of that nation met and fashioned a constitution which has stood the test for so many years. . . . [He then mentions the French and Russian revolutions also.] We seek to learn from their success and to avoid their failures. Perhaps we may not be able to avoid failures, because some measure of failure is inherent in human effort. Nevertheless we shall advance, I am certain . . . and realize the dream that we have dreamed so long.

Source: W. T. de Bary, ed., *Sources of Indian Tradition,* 4th ed., vol. 1 (New York: Columbia University Press, 1964), pp. 350–352.

and Bengal and caused immense disruption. Since the division was by agreement based solely on religion, nothing was considered except to separate areas with a Muslim majority, often by a thin margin. Many districts, villages, and towns were nearly evenly balanced between the two religions, which were deeply intertwined over many centuries of coexistence. The partition cut through major road and rail links, divided rural areas from their urban centers, and bisected otherwise uniform regions of culture and language.

The Kashmir Conflict

The still nominally independent native states, under their own Indian rulers, were technically given the choice to join India or Pakistan, but there was really no choice for the few Muslim-ruled states or smaller Muslim-majority areas surrounded by Indian territory, which were absorbed or taken over, including the large state of Hyderabad in the Deccan, Muslim-ruled but with a Hindu majority.

Kashmir, which lay geographically between the two rivals, had a Muslim majority but a Hindu ruler and its own hopes for independence. The ruler, Hari Singh, delayed his decision until his state was invaded by "volunteer" forces from Pakistan, and he agreed to join India in return for military help. Indian paratroops arrived just in time to hold Srinagar, the capital, and the central valley, the only economically important and densely settled part of the state. The cease-fire line, which still stands, gave roughly the western quarter of Kashmir to Pakistan, but the larger issue of which state Kashmir should belong to has never been resolved.

The Kashmir dispute has continued to poison relations between the two states and has sparked three inconclusive wars. Thus to the tragedy of partition and the violence following it has been added chronic Indo-Pakistani tension instead of the cooperation that would be more appropriate between two developing nations born out of the same context and sharing a common cultural tradition. Mahatma Gandhi, who had prayed and labored so hard to stop Hindu-Muslim violence, ironically became one of its victims when he was murdered on January 30, 1948, by a Hindu extremist who considered him too tolerant of Muslims. Nehru saw his death as "the loss of India's soul" and commented, "The light has gone out of our lives and there is darkness everywhere."

India After Independence

In the Republic of India, parliamentary democracy and British-style law have survived repeated tests and remain vigorous. Jawaharlal Nehru, who became prime minister at independence and served until his death in 1964, was a strong and revered leader who effectively dominated the new nation. He presided over the creation of 16 new language-based states within a federal structure. Federalism was necessary in any case given India's size and diversity, and language was the single most obvious basis of regional differences. Although Nehru and others were reluctant to acknowledge the importance of language-based regionalism, it became clear after several years of debate and negotiation that such a concession would have to be made. The states created by 1956 were the size of France, Germany, or Italy in population, and each coincided approximately with the distribution of what were officially declared to be "major" languages out of the many hundreds spoken. Each of these major languages had its own proud history and literary tradition, older, more extensive, and with more speakers than most European languages.

Hindi, the language of the Delhi area and the upper Ganges valley, was declared the official national language, to be used in national government and taught to all Indians in every region, while leaving each state its own regional language in its schools and legislatures. English, familiar to educated people in all the states, was retained as an "associate language" at the national level and continued to be taught in nearly all schools. Indian English has more speakers than American English, and it too has diverged from its British origins. Hindi is the mother tongue of only about 30 percent of the population, and even so consists of several mutually unintelligible dialects. No other native Indian language comes close. Hindi was therefore the obvious choice for a nationwide language, but for most Indians it remains a foreign tongue. It is resented especially by Dravidian-speaking southerners as yet another example of "northern domination" and the "oppression of Delhi."

India Under Nehru

Nehru saw India well launched on the path of economic development, both agricultural and industrial, but he acknowledged the Gandhian legacy by providing special government support for handicraft production and for small-scale rural industries, especially the hand weaving of cotton cloth. As in China, these were often not economically practical, but symbolically they were important because of their long association with the nationalist movement, and they also offered employment in rural areas, where most Indians still lived. Traditional village councils were revitalized and used as channels for new rural development in agriculture as well as other village enterprises.

But the most rapid growth was in the expanding cities, where industry and new economic opportunity were concentrated for the fortunate and which attracted streams of rural immigrants. Housing and other basic human services

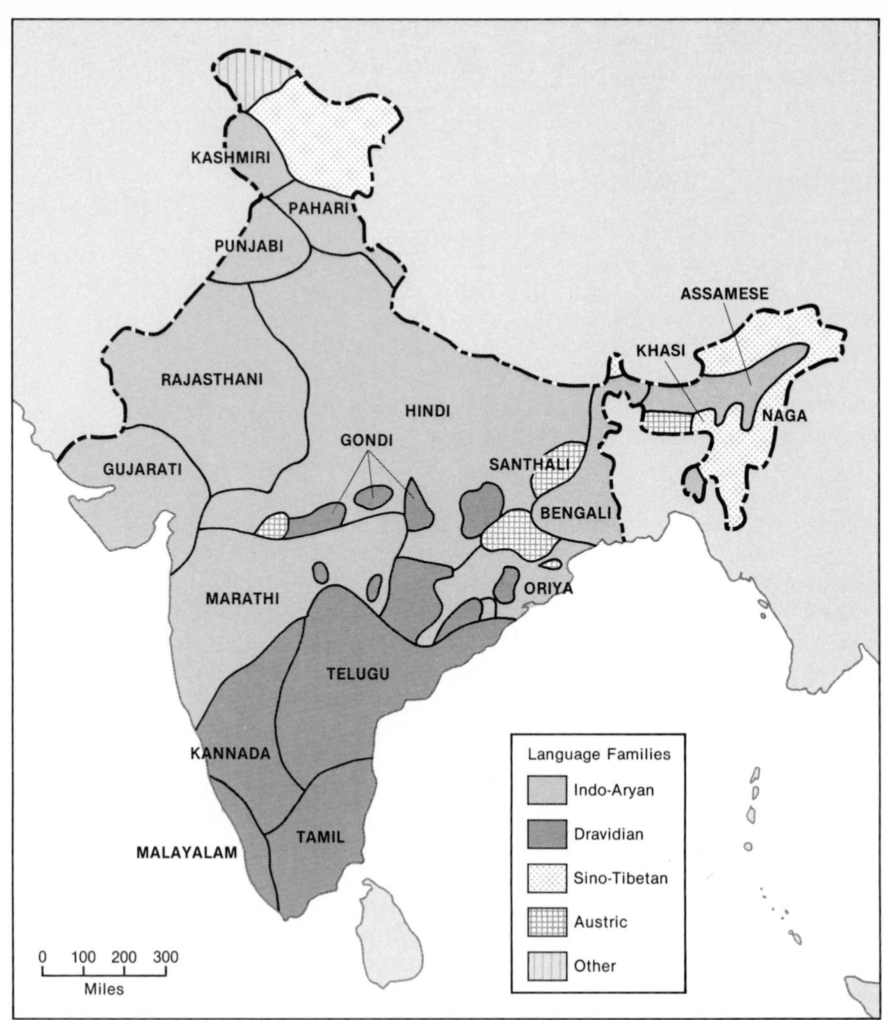

39.2 Major Languages of India

such as water, sewers, power, education, health care, and urban transport could not keep up with a mushrooming population, including many still unemployed, a familiar problem throughout the developing world. New immigrants took time to make a place for themselves and lived, or squatted, in slums or in the open air, but the wider opportunity that the cities potentially offered continued to draw them despite the squalor and hardships with which most of them had to contend. Calcutta, Bombay, and Delhi–New Delhi, the three largest cities, are among the largest in the world, but like most, including big American cities, combine luxurious lifestyles for a few and ragged poverty for many.

Despite government efforts to slow it down, India's population continued to grow, owing primarily to improved nutrition from agricultural gains and advances in public health that largely eliminated epidemic disease; life expectancy rose and death rates fell. But rising production, including new industrial output, more than kept pace, and per capita incomes began a slow and steady rise, which still continues. A third or more of the population, however, remained in severe poverty as the top third won new wealth.

The Nehru years were marred by a border dispute with China, in the remote Himalayas, which erupted in brief hostilities in 1962. Fresh from their armed reoccupation of Tibet, the Chinese won a quick victory. The Chinese retained control of the small border area they had claimed, which they needed for access into western Tibet, where they were concerned to put down rebellion against their rule. India had refused to discuss the Chinese claim and foolishly tried to eject the Chinese troops, an effort for which the Indian army was poorly prepared. Nehru had attempted, with much success until then, to build pan-Asian friendship and cooperation in partnership with China as the other major Asian power and to promote India as the leader of the nonaligned nations. His death was hastened by the failure of relations with China, which he took

India's World Role

Nehru saw India as an emerging power in the modern world and as a major Asian leader. He wrote about this and about East-West relations.

One of the major questions of the day is the readjustment of the relations between Asia and Europe. . . . India, not because of any ambition but because of geography and history . . . inevitably has to play a very important part in Asia . . . [and is] a meeting ground between the East and the West. . . . The Middle East and Southeast Asia both are connected with India. . . . You cannot consider any question concerning the Far East without India. . . . In the past the West ignored Asia, or did not give her the weight that was due her. Asia was really given a back seat . . . and even the statesmen did not recognize the changes that were taking place. There is considerable recognition of these changes now, but it is not enough. . . . I do not mean to say that we in Asia are in any way superior, ethically or morally, to the people of Europe. In some ways, I imagine that we are worse. There is however a legacy of conflict in Europe. . . . We might note that the world progressively tends to become one. . . . [We should] direct [our] policy towards avoiding conflict. . . . The emergence of India in world affairs is something of major consequence in world history. We who happen to be in the government of India . . . are men of relatively small stature. But it has been given to us to work at a time when India is growing into a great giant again.

Source: W. T. de Bary, ed., *Sources of Indian Tradition,* 4th ed., vol. 1 (New York: Columbia University Press, 1964), pp. 352–353.

as a personal failure, calling it "a Himalayan blunder" (*Himalayan* is understandably used in India to mean "enormous").

With his passing, India felt it had been left leaderless and was fearful about finding an adequate successor. Nehru had been the symbol and architect of the new India and its dominant political figure for more than a generation. But the gap was filled through normal democratic processes by the old Congress party moderate Lal Bahadur Shastri as prime minister. His promising start, including an agreement with Pakistan to reduce tensions, was cut short by his death after only a year and a half. The party then chose Nehru's daughter, Indira Gandhi (no relation to the Mahatma), who quickly established her firm leadership and vowed to continue Nehru's and Shastri's policies.

India had maintained its political stability and democratic system through successive crises, despite a still largely illiterate electorate and the multiple problems of new nationhood, wars, internal and external tensions, and poverty, a record matched by few other new nations. Illiterate voters demonstrated a surprising grasp of political issues, and a far higher proportion of those over 18 voted than in the United States. The Indian press remained freely critical of government shortcomings and offered an open forum for all opinions. India's faithfulness to the system it inherited and has continued to cultivate stands in contrast to the failure of parliamentary democracy and the rise of totalitarianism, dictatorship, censorship, and the police state in so much of the rest of Asia and the world. American policy toward India has been slow to recognize the importance of this major democratic state, second only to China in total numbers.

INDIRA GANDHI

Like her famous father, Indira Gandhi (1917–1984) was British-educated and widely traveled and came to office with long experience as her father's confidant after her mother's death in 1943, acting as hostess to streams of Indian and foreign visitors who sought Nehru's counsel or favors. Mrs. Gandhi had separated from her husband, Firoze, a journalist, a few years after their marriage, and she reared her two sons in her father's house. She impressed all who knew her with her razor-sharp mental powers and her keen grasp of political affairs, but during her father's lifetime she modestly eschewed any public role. After his death in 1964, she accepted the cabinet post of minister for information in Shastri's government, but only as one of many able women who had already held cabinet rank and who had been prominent earlier in the long struggle for independence.

The Ministry of Information gave her new public visibility, and when Shastri suddenly died, she entered the contest for Congress party leadership, which ended in her overwhelming victory and subsequent endorsement by the national electorate. She was a consummate politician within the Congress party, and many accused her of becoming merely a power broker, but without her father's charisma or deft diplomacy. Indira Gandhi shared her father's commitment to Western values but drew her political strength mainly from left of center. During her years as prime minister, from 1966 to 1977 and from 1980 to her death in 1984, she was a commanding figure.

Drought in 1965 and 1966, which caused much suffering but relatively few deaths, led India to become one of the first countries to launch a major campaign in the so-called green revolution, an agricultural policy that achieved higher yields with improved seeds and expanded irrigation and fertilizer production. By the end of the 1960s there had been a real breakthrough in production, and by 1975 India was again self-sufficient in grains and had a surplus for export, a situation it has since maintained. Industrial growth also continued, but the gap between rich and poor widened. The green revolution benefited farmers with enough land and capital to use and pay for the new seeds, irrigation, and fertilizers. Small farmers and people in nonagricultural areas sank further into relative poverty, and tenancy and landlessness rose. Upwardly mobile urban workers, managers, professionals, and technicians were more than matched by rising numbers of urban and rural poor. These growing pains were typical of economic development everywhere, including the nineteenth-century West.

In part to quash charges of corruption and to weaken her political opposition, Mrs. Gandhi in June 1975 proclaimed a state of national emergency in the name of "unity" and "reform." Civil rights were suspended, the press was controlled, opposition leaders and "troublemakers" were jailed, the constitution was amended to keep the courts from challenging the government, and a series of measures was announced to control inflation, inefficiency, hoarding, and tax evasion. It seemed the end of India as the world's largest parliamentary democracy, but Mrs. Gandhi miscalculated her people's judgment. When she finally permitted a national election in January 1977, she and her party were defeated. The Indian democratic system and its tradition of free expression were soundly vindicated, but the coalition government of non-Congress parties that emerged under the aged Morarji Desai floundered and finally dissolved into bickering, paving the way for Mrs. Gandhi's return to power in the elections of January 1980.

Although she made no effort to reestablish the "emergency," Mrs. Gandhi's response to tensions and protests by disaffected regions and groups became increasingly rigid and authoritarian. Meanwhile, economic growth continued in agriculture and industry. By 1983 over a third of India's exports were manufactured goods, many of them from high-tech industries that competed successfully on the world market. India had become a major industrial power, and its pool of trained scientists and technicians, products of the British-inherited education system, was exceeded only by those of the United States and the Soviet Union. In 1974 its own scientists completed the first Indian nuclear test, though the government continued to insist it would not make nuclear weapons but would instead concentrate on the production of nuclear energy for peaceful purposes. Indian satellites joined American and Russian

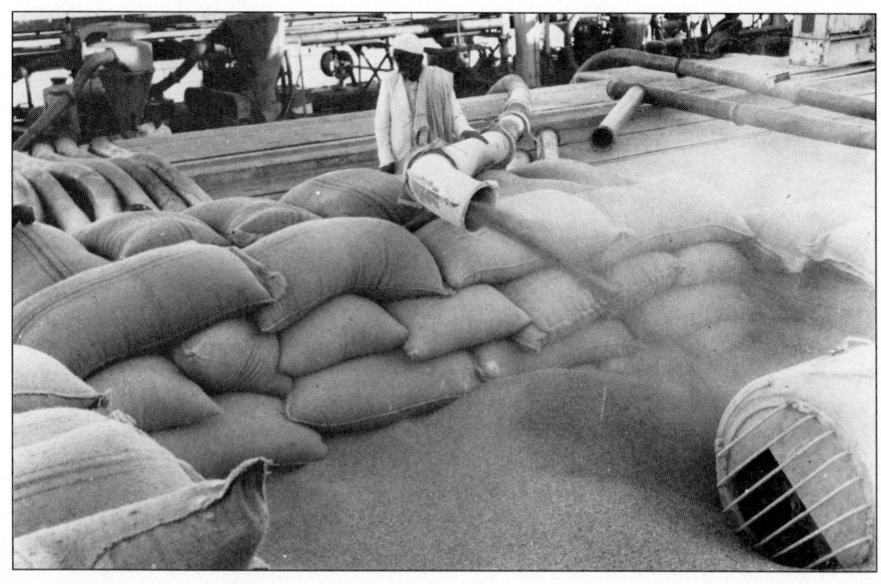

Grain being fed into a storage silo in New Delhi: one of the fruits of the green revolution. [UPI/Bettmann Newsphotos]

ones in space, and Indian-made microchips began to revolutionize industry. At the same time, many rural sectors remained in the bullock cart age, and the urban poor slept under bridges near the new luxury apartments of those who had done well in the rapidly growing economy.

The Sikhs

Of the many groups that felt disadvantaged, the most continuously and effectively organized were the Sikhs of Punjab. Ironically, Punjab had led the nation in agricultural progress under the green revolution, and although not all Sikhs were well off, as a group they had prospered more than most others. Part of their discontent was no doubt related to the rising expectations common to periods of development. Having put the green revolution to work with their traditional entrepreneurial talents and hard work, the Sikhs grew increasingly angry at government controls on agricultural prices imposed by Mrs. Gandhi's fight against inflation, which severely restricted farmers' profits. A religious community founded in the fifteenth century as a reformist offshoot from Hinduism, the Sikhs also wanted greater recognition, increased political status, more control of Punjab state (where they were in fact a minority), and greater provincial autonomy.

Sikhs comprised only about 2 percent of India's population, and Mrs. Gandhi was reluctant to favor them or to make concessions on provincial autonomy when she had to confront so many similar demands from other discontented groups and protest movements. But her stance on the Sikhs was rigid to a fault; she met violence with more violence, capped by the storming of the Golden Temple in Amritsar, sacred to Sikhism, which a group of extremists had fortified. Four months later, in October 1984, she was gunned down by two of her Sikh guards in the name of Indian freedom. Many others had come to see her as corrupted by power.

India After Indira Gandhi

The Congress party chose Gandhi's son Rajiv (born 1944) to succeed her, and in January 1985 this choice was overwhelmingly confirmed in a nationwide election. Rajiv Gandhi offered peace to the Sikhs, granted many of their more reasonable demands (including new borders for Punjab that created a state with a Sikh majority), and in other ways as well showed himself to be a sensitive and responsible leader. As the grandson of Jawaharlal Nehru, Rajiv Gandhi had many of the same qualities of personal charm, ability, and diplomacy. He had never sought power and was accordingly trusted, but the reservoir of popular support for him began to decline as critics claimed that the Congress party under his leadership remained more interested in power-brokering than in serving all the needs of the people. India, in fact, has been a largely one-party democracy since independence, although the Congress party was defeated in 1977 and after Nehru's death became increasingly split into rival factions. Many Indian voters have felt that they were not offered adequate alternatives and that government was often insensitive to their needs.

Three basic problems still resisted solution: miserable poverty for the bottom third or more of India's people, a population still growing too rapidly (one root of poverty), and continued outbreaks of violence among many of the groups in its highly diverse population. Caste continued to weaken slowly, especially in the cities, but most Indians remained in traditional village worlds, where caste connections still served an important function. Higher or "dominant" castes, as they were often called, resented and tried to suppress the rise of Untouchables. Hindus and Muslims fought one another in some areas. Sikh terrorism and Hindu reprisals threatened to plunge Punjab and Delhi into civil war.

Nationalism grew among Indian intellectuals late in the nineteenth century, but it did not stimulate a mass movement until the 1920s. Even Gandhi did not reach all Indians, and the country since independence in 1947 has been moving toward creating a single overriding sense of Indian identity that can take precedence over regional, religious, caste, and other group loyalties. India well illustrates the dictum of the British historian Lord Acton (1834–1902): "The nation is not the cause but the result of the state. It is the state which creates the nation, not the nation the state." To many—perhaps most—Indians it remains more important that they are Bengalis or Marathas or Tamils, Hindus, Sikhs, or Muslims, Brahmins or Untouchables, than that they are fellow Indians. It will take more time before such group loyalties can be merged into common "Indianness" through common experience in a single national state. This problem is shared with most new nations, many of which have difficulties comparable to India's. The difference is partly the scale of India's problem—some 800 million people with a diversity greater than all of Europe—and partly in the recency of its modern experience as a nation-state after 5,000 years of regional and group separatism. Since 1949 the traditional world of the village and its ties has expanded to include considerable integration with the modern world of the cities and with the larger world of regional states sharing a common language and culture.

Within India's federal political structure, central economic planning and an expanding national civil service also help to join people in mutual self-interest. Regular bus services on all-weather roads link every village with these wider worlds and with a national network. The sense of nationhood needs time to grow, but while it cannot come about in a single generation, that is clearly the hope of India's future.

The war against poverty, as the government called it, is of course related to communal and intercaste tensions

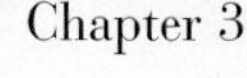

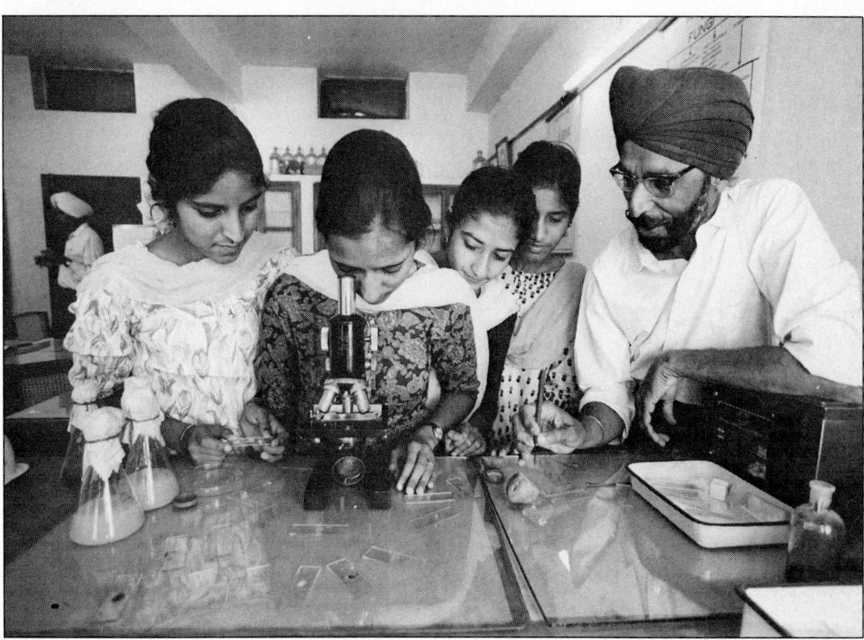

Women botany students at Ludhiana Agricultural University in Punjab. [© Marc and Evelyne Bernheim, 1981/Woodfin Camp]

and is the greatest challenge of all developing countries. India has done better economically than most of the so-called Third World, perhaps overall better than China, whose record has been praised by many economists in the West. But India's new wealth has not been well distributed. The hope is that as development proceeds and as efforts to limit population growth succeed, the fight against poverty may make significant headway. This is the same path followed by the West a century earlier as the fruits of the Industrial Revolution eventually raised the economic level of most people. Life expectancy rates and living conditions for most inhabitants are in fact better for modern Calcutta and Bombay than for nineteenth-century Manchester and New York. In India, as in most of Asia, the economic trends are strongly positive, and literacy is growing fast as universal free education spreads. This oldest of world civilizations still keeps much of its ancient tradition alive and draws strength from it as it also pursues the path of modernization.

Bangladesh and Pakistan

East Bengal, which became East Pakistan in 1947, was one of the subcontinent's poorest areas and had virtually no industry of any kind. It had been heavily dependent on Calcutta as its educational, cultural, commercial, industrial, and shipping center, through which its exports and imports moved and where nearly all transport lines were focused. East Bengal contained over half of Pakistan's population and produced three-quarters of its exports, mainly jute, but much of the profit went to Karachi. Moreover, East Bengal was strikingly underrepresented in and underfunded by the national government. Even its language, Bengali, was not officially recognized.

Pakistan continued to be run by and for the small clique of Karachi and Punjabi businessmen and politicians who had pushed for its creation, although the faltering effort at parliamentary government was swept aside by a military dictatorship in 1958. When elections, finally held in late 1970, produced a victory for the East Pakistan party on a platform of greater autonomy, the military government in West Pakistan responded by arresting the party's leader, Sheikh Mujibur Rahman, and then turning its army and tanks against demonstrators in East Pakistan in a mass slaughter. About 10 million refugees poured across the nearby Indian border by the end of 1971, mainly to already overcrowded Calcutta. Guerrilla actions by Bengalis against the terrorism of the West Pakistani forces finally brought in the Indian army, which in ten days ended the slaughter.

With the Pakistani army defeated, East Pakistan became the new People's Republic of Bangladesh in December 1971. Sheikh Mujib, as he was called, became prime minister and the refugees returned home, but Bangladesh proved unable to achieve political stability or even effective government. Mujib was murdered by his own army in 1974, following charges of corruption. His military successor was assassinated in 1981, and no clear or successful political order has since emerged. Bangladesh remains one of the world's poorest nations, despite the agricultural productivity of its rice lands, burdened by a still too rapidly growing population and hampered by the lack of forceful planning and leadership. Periodic flooding caused in part by deforestation has compounded Bangladesh's problems.

What remained of Pakistan, in the west, continued to be governed by a military dictatorship, although there was some respectable economic growth in both agriculture and manufacturing. Jinnah died within a year of independence, and in 1958, after a series of corrupt and ineffective prime ministers, the country came under martial law, as it has been much of the time since. The army commander in chief, General Zia-ul-Huq, seized power in a 1977 coup d'état, dissolved the politically corrupt parliamentary system, and in 1979 executed the American-educated former prime minister, Zulfkar Ali Bhutto, after he was found guilty of conspiring in the murder of a political opponent. In an effort to break the connection with the "Karachi clique," the capital had been moved in stages between 1961 and 1965 to a new planned site called Islamabad ("City of Islam"), about 10 miles from the city of Rawalpindi in the northwest; the two cities operate as an urban unit, linked by commuting workers and civil servants, and now rival Karachi in size. Lahore, an older and larger city and the chief center of Muslim culture, was more central, but it was thought to be too close to the border with India to be safe. Pakistan lacks most industrial resources, except for some recently discovered oil, and it began in 1947 well below the all-Indian average economic level. Nevertheless, it has avoided major famine, greatly increased irrigation in Punjab and the Indus valley, and built a basic industrial structure. As in India and China, however, economic gains continue to be retarded in per capita terms by a growing population. As an Islamic state, Pakistan has been reluctant to promote family planning or to limit the growth of its population. Islamic fundamentalism similar to that in Iran has also won some support in Pakistan.

More recently the government became deeply involved in aiding and providing refuge for the Afghan guerrilla resistance to the Soviet-supported government in Kabul, the Afghan capital, only about 100 miles from the Pakistani frontier. Such activity further strengthened Pakistan's role as a Cold War client of the United States and produced a new flow of American military supplies. But such aid had little relevance to Pakistan's domestic problems and again prompted Indian complaints that the arms were being stockpiled for use against India. The two states have fought two small wars, in 1965 and 1971, in both of which Pakistan's military power came virtually exclusively from U.S. equipment. Pakistan has seemed useful to the United States as a regional anticommunist bulwark against the Soviet Union and as a friend and intermediary with China, particularly during America's resumption of relations with the People's Republic in the early 1970s.

When China became a Soviet rival instead of an ally and soon thereafter came into conflict with India over a border dispute, Pakistan took the Chinese side. American surveillance flights over the Soviet Union took off from bases in northwestern Pakistan, and in 1971 Washington used the Pakistan-China connection to respond to Chinese overtures, leading to President Richard Nixon's visit to Peking. But these international power ploys had little or nothing to do with Pakistan's people or their needs. Indeed, they put the Pakistanis at serious risk both by exposing them to the threat of war, the suffering resulting from further conflict with India, and the massive diversion of resources from urgently needed development into military expenditures. India and Pakistan, with so much history and so many problems in common, have more recently begun to move cautiously toward a less antagonistic relationship, but only after 40 years of tragic tension and conflict. This process has been helped by Soviet withdrawal from Afghanistan and by the death of General Zia in a plane crash in 1988. Bhutto's daughter, Benazir, was elected prime minister as Zia's successor in an open contest, thus becoming the first woman to govern an Islamic state, and Pakistan returned to a more democratic path.

Pakistan is a diverse state, resembling India on a smaller scale. It includes a majority whose mother tongue is not the official national language, Urdu, and many groups who feel unrepresented, neglected, or oppressed by the government. Outside the Indus valley and western Punjab, where most of the population is concentrated, Pakistan encompasses arid mountains along its western and northern borders, inhabited by people like the Baluchis and Pathans whose cultures and histories have little in common with those of the lowlands. A truly national state that can include them as partners has not yet emerged. The partition of India has become a permanent fact of life, but Pakistan has still to develop into a nation.

Sri Lanka

The island nation of Ceylon (which changed its name officially to Sri Lanka, an old precolonial name for the country, in 1975) lies across the Palk Strait from India. It made a relatively easy transition to independence in 1948, primarily as a consequence of Indian independence rather than of any strong nationalist movement on the island itself.

Sri Lanka had been under Western domination since the first Portuguese bases there early in the sixteenth century, and its small size and population were easily overwhelmed by foreign influences. Many of the elite were more British than Sinhalese (the majority inhabitants) in language and culture, and many regretted the end of their membership in the British Empire. But in the mid-1950s Ceylon was swept by what has been called "second-wave nationalism," a belated but emotional determination to rediscover and assert its own identity. In the elections of 1956 self-serving politicians stirred up communal feelings among the dominant Sinhalese against the minority Tamils, originally immigrants from nearby South India, who form about a fifth of the population. Approximately half of them had lived there, at the northern tip of the island, for over

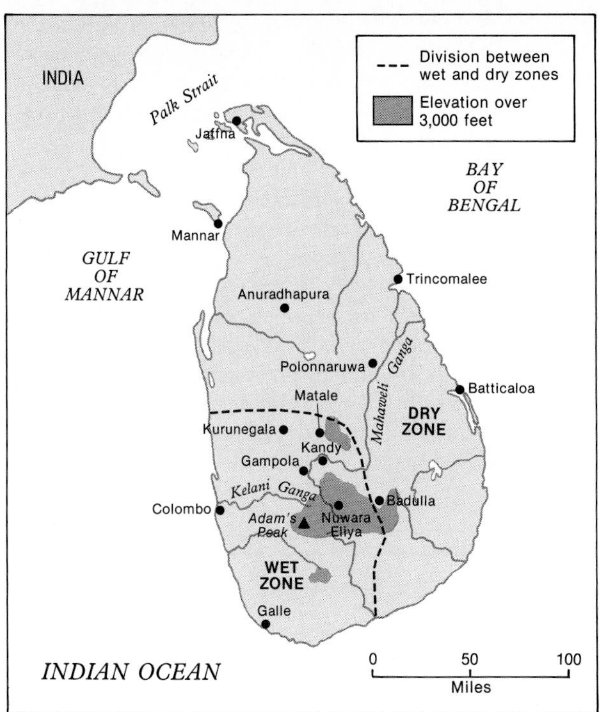

39.3 Sri Lanka

1,000 years, but the other half were more recently arrived laborers recruited to work the tea plantations in the central highlands. The Tamils are Hindu and speak primarily their own language, which has heightened their distinction from the Buddhist (or for the elite, nominally Buddhist) Sinhalese. They became a convenient scapegoat to stimulate the sense of Sinhalese nationalism, like the Chinese in many Southeast Asian countries.

The tragic pattern of communal violence between Sinhalese and Tamils began with the 1956 election of S. W. R. D. Bandaranaike, on a platform of Sinhalese-only nationalism. Like Jinnah, he had been educated in Britain and was thoroughly Westernized; his personal ambition and his keen mind turned to communalism, until then of little interest to him, as a means of creating a new political base for himself. Once called into existence by his campaign of discrimination, it could not be laid to rest, and he was assassinated in 1959 by a Sinhalese Buddhist who felt he had not gone far enough.

His place was taken by his widow, Sirimavo Bandaranaike (born 1916), the world's first woman prime minister. She continued most of his policies and ruled with a firm hand for two terms, 1960–1965 and 1970–1977. Like her husband, she was British-educated, sophisticated, and extremely able, showing a talent for both international and domestic diplomacy. Her authoritative rule restored order and relative stability at a time of domestic crisis. Tamils felt more and more excluded and oppressed and took to terrorism as a weapon, finally demanding a separate state.

The Sri Lankan economy was disrupted by chronic fighting, which retarded its generally healthy growth after 1948. Nevertheless, Sri Lanka became self-sufficient in rice by the late 1970s, thanks to major investments in new irrigation and agricultural technology, and at the same time maintained the profitable plantation sector in tea, rubber, and coconuts, which continued to dominate its exports. Education, literacy, and public health were improved still further from the relatively high levels established under British colonial control, and per capita incomes remained somewhat higher than in any of the other South Asian states, thanks in part to the government's success in limiting population growth. But violence and terrorism on both sides, in an atmosphere close to civil war, eroded the British-inherited system of parliamentary government and the rule of law. In 1987, with Indian mediation and commitment to prevent clandestine support from South India to Tamil terrorists in Sri Lanka, an agreement was reached that gave some local autonomy to areas in which the Tamils were a majority and which aimed to end the fighting. But much bitterness and tension remained.

Sirimavo Bandaranaike is an example of the improving status of women in South Asia. Like China and Japan, South Asia traditionally accorded women a relatively low status, especially during the centuries of Muslim dominance in the north. There were exceptions, including even women military figures and heads of state among the Marathas and other groups and dominant figures at court such as Nur Jahan (see Chapter 19). The Westernization that accompanied British control led to increasing education for women; many educated women were prominent in the independence movement, and in government and the professions after 1947. In general this was a relatively small group, an intellectual and Westernized elite, while most South Asian women, especially in the villages, remained uneducated and subservient to their husbands to a degree that seemed extreme to Westerners. There were exceptions, particularly in South India and in the southern state of Kerala, where ancient matriarchal and matrilocal* social forms persisted to some degree. Husbands in this region commonly walk behind wives and defer to them, while property and family names often descend through the female line. Elsewhere in South Asia, women such as Sirimavo Bandaranaike and Indira Gandhi have achieved great prominence on the national scene since independence.

The Turbulent Middle East

When World War II ended, Britain was still the paramount power in the Middle East, directly controlling Egypt, Pal-

*In a matrilocal society, a husband joins the wife's family.

estine, Transjordan, Iraq, southern Arabia, and the Persian Gulf. In the next decade, however, it withdrew almost completely from the region, leaving a vacuum of power that was filled by Arab nationalism, superpower rivalry, and the emergence of the state of Israel.

The Establishment of Israel

Britain's first withdrawal was from Palestine, where the conflict between Palestinian Arabs and Jewish settlers, compounded by an influx of refugees and Holocaust survivors, had reached a flashpoint. That conflict, in turn, represented a clash between the traditions of two great religions and the aspirations of two nascent nationalisms.

A small number of Jews had always lived in Palestine, to which the faithful believed their people would someday return to reestablish the ancient nation of Israel and await the coming of the messiah. In the mid-seventeenth century a messianic pretender, Sabbatai Zevi, had led an ill-fated expedition of thousands of Jews to Palestine. The serious immigration to the region that commenced two centuries later was spurred, however, not by millennial fervor but by a secular nationalist movement, Zionism.

The Zionist Movement

Zionism was a historic response to Jewish circumstances in nineteenth-century Europe. Emancipation had eliminated most of the civil restrictions that had confined Jews to the ghetto for centuries past without offering them a clear role or place in European society. Many Jews simply attempted to assimilate themselves into the larger nationalities among whom they lived, preserving their religious and cultural traditions while identifying themselves as Frenchmen, Germans, or Russians. To Zionist writers, however, as for other nineteenth-century nationalists, political identity as a nation was the final and necessary goal of every people's development. The Zionist position was supported negatively by anti-Semitic writers such as Count Gobineau (1816–1882), who argued that the Jews were an alien, unassimilable element that threatened the racial and cultural integrity of any nation that harbored them. The increasing tempo of anti-Semitic incidents in the late nineteenth century, culminating in the pogroms of Russia and, in the West, in the long, drawn-out agony of the Dreyfus affair (see Chapter 32), suggested to many that assimilation was a mirage. The result was a mass exodus of European Jews, particularly from Russia, from which 3 million emigrated between 1882 and 1914.

The great majority of Jewish emigrants went to the United States, Canada, South America, and Australia; scarcely 1 percent joined the trickle of earlier settlers in Palestine. The real impetus for creating a Jewish state in the Holy Land came from Theodor Herzl, the founder of modern Zionism. Herzl realized that the large-scale settlement necessary to provide a critical mass of population in Palestine would require both organization and capital. His solution was the Jewish National Fund, which undertook the purchase of all land to be occupied by the settlers. He envisioned a society whose growth would be rationally planned rather than subject to the vagaries of speculators and profiteers. New towns would be erected, carefully spaced and separated by belts of collective farmland and linked by express trains and superhighways. In short, the Zionist state was to be a utopian society in which mutualistic socialism was combined with technological progress and centralized planning.

Conflict over Palestine

Herzl's vision and Hitler's persecution combined to increase the Jewish population of Palestine tenfold between the end of World War I and the end of World War II. From less than a tenth of the total population of the territory in 1917, it had increased to a third by 1947. The Arab majority greeted the Jewish influx first with suspicion and then alarm. The entry of Western powers into the formerly Ottoman-controlled lands of the Middle East after World War I stimulated Arab nationalists. For such nationalists, the Jews were a spearhead unit of Western colonization. Their fears were underscored by the report of an American commission Woodrow Wilson sent to the area, which concluded that the Jewish National Fund intended the eventual purchase of the entire territory of Palestine, thereby dispossessing its Arab population. From an Arab perspective, Jewish socialism was simply the handmaiden of British imperialism.

Confronted by bitter and sometimes violent Arab resistance, the British government decided in 1939 to cap Jewish population in Palestine at one-third of the whole and to limit future land purchases severely. These new controls had broader implications, as Britain, the United States, and other powers sought to restrict Jewish emigration from Nazi-held Europe in general. When the dimensions of the Holocaust were discovered at the end of World War II, there was general humanitarian pressure to establish Palestine as a refuge for the remnants of European Jewry. The British Labour party, soon to be in power, endorsed Zionist demands for the immediate creation of a Jewish commonwealth and in December 1944 called for the transfer of Palestinian Arabs to neighboring countries. Nothing came of these or more moderate postwar proposals for a federated Jewish-Arab state, which were rejected by both sides. The British, unwilling to maintain their trusteeship in the face of mounting Jewish terrorist attacks and unable to contain the flood of illegal immigrants who ran their blockade, laid the problem before the United Nations in April 1947. After months of lobbying and debate, the General Assembly adopted in November a proposal to divide Palestine into three Jewish and three Arab sectors forming a Jewish and an Arab state, with Jerusalem as an international zone. All seven areas were to be linked in an economic union.

The General Assembly resolution was greeted with rejoicing by the Jews but unanimous rejection throughout the Arab world. The British refused to implement it on the grounds that it had not been accepted by both sides and withdrew their troops without making provision to transfer authority to either one. When the last units departed on May 14, 1948, the Jewish communal government proclaimed the state of Israel. A general struggle immediately ensued for control of Palestine. Armies from Egypt, Syria, Lebanon, Jordan, and Iraq poured across the frontiers to assist the Palestinian Arabs, but the better-organized Jewish forces more than held their own. When a United Nations armistice halted the fighting in 1949, Israel controlled a third more territory than had been granted the Jews under the partition plan, while nearly 750,000 Palestinian Arabs had taken refuge in Lebanon, Syria, Jordan, and the Egyptian-occupied Gaza strip in southern Palestine.

While still fighting, Israel held its first elections in January. The fiery socialist David Ben-Gurion (1886–1973), founder of the first Jewish agricultural cooperative, or *kibbutz*, became Israel's first prime minister and its dominant political figure until his retirement in 1966, and the veteran Zionist leader Chaim Weizmann (1874–1952) was installed in the ceremonial office of president.

Israel or Palestine?

Two rival nationalisms with ancient roots in the same land put forward their claims to modern sovereignty over it.

The land of Israel was the birthplace of the Jewish people. Here their spiritual, religious, and political identity was shaped. Here they first attained statehood, created cultural values of national and universal significance, and gave to the world the eternal Book of Books. . . .

On the 29th November, 1947, the United Nations General Assembly passed a resolution calling for the establishment of a Jewish state in the land of Israel; the General Assembly required the inhabitants of the land of Israel to take such steps as were necessary on their part for the implementation of that resolution. This recognition by the United Nations of the right of the Jewish people to establish their state is irrevocable. This right is the natural right of the Jewish people to be masters of their own fate, like all other nations, in their own sovereign state.

THE PALESTINIAN NATIONAL CHARTER

Article 1: Palestine is the homeland of the Arab Palestinian people; it is an indivisible part of the Arab homeland, and the Palestinian people are an integral part of the Arab nation.

Article 2: Palestine, with the boundaries it had during the British mandate, is an indivisible territorial unit.

Article 3: The Palestinian Arab people possess the legal right to their homeland and have the right to determine their destiny after achieving the liberation of their country in accordance with their wishes and entirely of their own accord and will.

Article 4: The Palestinian identity is a genuine, essential, and inherent characteristic; it is transmitted from parents to children. The Zionist occupation and the dispersal of the Palestinian Arab people . . . do not make them lose their Palestinian identity and their membership of the Palestine community, nor do they negate them.

Sources: Declaration of the Establishment of the State of Israel, May 14, 1948; Decisions of the National Congress of the Palestine Liberation Organization, July 1–17, 1968.

DAVID BEN-GURION, ISRAEL'S FOUNDER

The single most important figure in the establishment of modern Israel was David Ben-Gurion. Born David Gruen in Plonsk, Poland (then a part of the Russian empire), he was the son of a local Zionist leader. At 17 he startled the local Jewish community by calling for armed resistance against the state-backed pogroms. Three years later, in 1906, he emigrated to Palestine, where he worked as a farmer in Jewish settlements and adopted the Hebrew name Ben-Gurion ("son of the lion"). Expelled by the Ottoman Turks for his political activity at the outbreak of World War I, he eventually reached New York, where he met and married Pauline Munweis, his wife until her death in 1968.

Ben-Gurion responded to the Balfour Declaration by joining the British-sponsored Jewish Legion. Returning to Palestine after its capture from the Turks, he threw himself ardently into political organization and over the next two decades forged the institutions that were to become the nucleus of the Jewish state. In 1920 he founded the Histadrut labor confederation and ten years later its political arm, the Mapai, or Israeli Workers party, which later merged into the Labour party. Besides leading both organizations, he was elected chairman of the Zionist Executive, the supreme directive body of the Zionist movement, and head of the Jewish Agency, its executive branch.

When Britain, responding to Arab pressure, abruptly pulled back on its commitment to a Jewish homeland in 1939, Ben-Gurion urged and later led armed resistance to it. In May 1942 he assembled an emergency meeting of Zionists in New York that decided on the establishment of a Jewish state as soon as the war in Europe was ended. With the proclamation of Israel six years later, Ben-Gurion became simultaneously its first prime minister and minister of defense, welding its disparate and often conflicting resistance forces into a national army.

With a single brief interval, Ben-Gurion remained Israel's prime minister from 1948 to 1963, firmly shaping Israel's identity as a modern industrial state and a bulwark of Western influence in the Middle East. To critics of his frank espousal of Western interests, including the acceptance of $800 million in reparations from West Germany for Nazi war crimes, he replied characteristically, "What matters is not what Gentiles will say but what the Jews will do." Never wavering in his belief that modern Israel was the direct and legitimate heir of the ancient Jewish state, he was determined at all costs to establish it and to give no quarter to anyone who opposed it. This led him into an assault against Egypt's President Nasser in 1956 that brought about the fall of the Eden government in

A 1955 photo of Israeli leaders. David Ben-Gurion is on the right; from the left, the others are General Moshe Dayan, Premier Moshe Sharett and President Itzhak Ben-Zvi. [UPI/Bettmann Newsphotos]

Britain and contributed to the demise of the Fourth Republic in France, but left Ben-Gurion himself stronger than ever at home. Yet in his last years in office he attempted, though unsuccessfully, to institute peace talks with Arab leaders.

Ben-Gurion resigned abruptly in June 1963, in part because of dissension within the Labour party. He founded a new opposition party as a vehicle for his views, but it won only ten seats in the Knesset (parliament). Spent as a political force, he nonetheless remained a charismatic and controversial elder statesman, and to a world public the short, rotund man with the familiar pugnacious features and the halo of white hair remained the image of Israel itself. In failing health, he retired from all political activity in 1970 to spend his last years at the kibbutz of Sde-Boker in the Negev, writing his memoirs. He lived just long enough to see the twenty-fifth anniversary of the founding of Israel in 1973 and to experience the Yom Kippur War, which revealed how vulnerable, and how far from peace, the new nation still was.

Israeli Society: Challenge and Conflict

The new state chose a system of proportional representation rather than electoral districting for the Knesset, so each member represented the nation as a whole. This meant full representation for minority views but entailed coalition government as well; no single party has won a majority to date. Nevertheless, the Labour bloc, strongly Zionist, social-democratic and secular in character, controlled the government until 1977.

Despite its unity in times of crisis, Israel has been beset by contradictions from the beginning. The ideologically active left wing of the Labour bloc remained attached to the early Zionist ideal of social regeneration through physical labor and communal living exemplified in the kibbutz. The new Jewish man and woman, purged of the effects of centuries of ghettoization and bonded to the soil, would constitute the basis of a genuinely egalitarian society. What emerged instead, however, was an urbanized, consumer-oriented society that bore considerable resemblance to the social-democratic regimes of the West. Class divisions within the Jewish population intensified, particularly between the well-to-do eastern European settlers who dominated the Labour bloc and the so-called oriental Jews who flocked to Israel from the Arab states and Iran in the first two decades of independence and now comprise 65 percent of its Jewish population. This poorer and less literate group, wooed by the conservative Likud coalition of Menachem Begin (born 1913), turned the Labour coalition out of office after nearly three decades.

The tension between old socialist ideals and the reality of a consumer society is paralleled by that between religious fundamentalists and secular liberals. The fundamentalists, a hard core constituting 15 percent of the Jewish population, retain Orthodox diet, dress, and observance and have successfully insisted on religious controls over marriage, divorce, inheritance, and other social arrangements. Often confrontational, their influence derives not merely from their unity as a single-issue pressure group but from the unresolved debate over the nature of a "Jewish" state.

From its inception, Israel has advertised itself as the homeland of Jews the world over, and under the Law of Return, any Jew emigrating to it is automatically entitled to citizenship. Nonetheless, there is no generally accepted criterion of what defines a Jew, and a prolonged debate in the Knesset in 1960 and 1961 failed to produce one. Originally Semitic, the Jews have become racially heterogeneous through the long centuries of the Diaspora, and fair-haired Scandinavians mix today on the streets of Tel Aviv and Jerusalem with brown-skinned Indians, black Ethiopians, and even Chinese. Still more problematic is the attempt to define them as a "people," since they share few common customs, and fewer than half the population speaks the official language, Hebrew, as a native tongue. Least of all can they be distinguished on the basis of a common faith, since many secularized Jews in Israel and elsewhere no longer keep up religious observances. The fundamentalists alone have developed a clear standard, excluding anyone whose mother was not Jewish or who had not undergone Orthodox conversion. In practice, however, the authorities have simply accepted as a Jew anyone professing to be one. Even Israelis converting to Christianity have continued to be accorded the rights of citizenship.

The unresolved question of what defines a Jew goes to the heart of the central contradiction of present-day Israeli society: the situation of its Arab minority. Although enjoying formal equality, including the right to vote and to sit in the Knesset, the Arabs are clearly second-class citizens in the Jewish state, and their movements and activities are subject to regular military scrutiny and interference. Moreover, while Israelis can justifiably point to levels of health, literacy, and material prosperity among Arabs within their borders considerably higher than those of neighboring countries, they remain far below the national norm as a whole. The problem was compounded by Israeli occupation of the West Bank of the Jordan River as a result of the 1967 war; this doubled the number of Arabs under Israeli jurisdiction. For 20 years the occupation was relatively benign, but since late 1987 popular rebellion has repeatedly erupted.

Whether or not the Arabs under Israeli rule would be prepared to accept integration into a multiethnic state remains part of the larger question of Palestinian self-determination and the future of Arab-Israeli relations in general. In either case, their presence poses a challenge to an Israel defined, by whatever standard, as a purely Jewish state.

The Arab-Israeli Wars

The more immediate questions in the Middle East involve the general nonrecognition of the Israeli state by the other powers in the region apart from Egypt and the insistence of Palestinian Arab nationalists that Palestine be restored to them. Four wars have been fought to date over this question. All have resulted in military victories by the Israelis, none in settlement. The Palestine War of 1948–1949 established Israel as an independent state while creating a major refugee problem. The Israelis refused to allow the 750,000 Palestinians who had fled their homes to return without guarantees of security from their neighbors, a point that became moot as their abandoned homes and lands were occupied by the almost equal number of Jewish immigrants, mostly from the other countries of the Middle East, who flocked to the new state in the first two years of its existence. In effect, the massive population transfer envisioned by Zionists had taken place. But neighboring Arab states were both unable and politically unwilling to accept the tide of Palestinian refugees who crowded at their borders. Instead, the refugees were interned in squalid camps along the narrow Gaza strip and on the West Bank of the Jordan River, previously part of Palestine but now annexed by Jordan. The Palestinian Arabs thus became a people without a country.

Arab nationalists regarded Israel not only as a usurper in the region but also as an agent of Western interests. These suspicions were dramatically confirmed in October 1956 when Israel joined an amphibious Franco-British force in an invasion of Egypt, whose new president, Gamal Abdel Nasser (1918–1970), had nationalized the French- and British-owned Suez Canal Company in response to a cutoff of Western aid. For the British in particular, Egypt's control of the canal threatened important interests in the Far East, while Israel, alarmed at an Egyptian arms buildup, felt that a preemptive strike was essential to its security. With British air support, the Israelis swept across the Sinai peninsula to join assault troops at Port Said. But the war ended in fiasco. The United States, furious at the independent action of its allies, joined the Soviet Union in calling for an immediate cease-fire and withdrawal. Faced with the threat of ruinous economic sanctions, the British and French capitulated. Israel too withdrew, the damaging identification with colonial interests only partly compensated by the opening of the Gulf of Aqaba to Israeli shipping.

The long-term effects of the episode were profound. Nasser emerged as a hero and became the recognized leader of the Arab world until his death. The government of Sir Anthony Eden was forced from office in Britain, and with the assassination of the Iraqi king, Faisal II, and his prime minister, Nuri-es Said, in 1958 the British were forced from their last bases in the Middle East. The United States entered the breach to forestall Soviet influence, and in 1958 its own forces invaded Lebanon in support of pro-Western leadership. With Nasser and other Arab radicals looking to the Soviet Union for aid and the crucial oil resources of the region at stake, the Middle East became an important new area of superpower rivalry.

In the meantime, a new war brewed between the Arabs and the Israelis. In 1964 Israel began to divert water from the Jordan River to irrigate its southern Negev desert. Jordan protested, and an Arab summit conference in Cairo set up a command force that would coordinate guerrilla activities against Israel and serve as a provisional government for the refugees, the Palestine Liberation Organization (PLO). Terrorist attacks and retaliatory raids increased, while Egypt, Syria, and Jordan announced plans to attack Israel. When Nasser ordered United Nations peacekeeping forces to leave the Sinai in May 1967 and closed the Gulf of Aqaba, the Israelis struck first. In a campaign lasting only six days, Israel swept again across the Sinai, seized the West Bank, including the contested city of Jerusalem, and drove Syria off the strategic Golan Heights on the borders of eastern Galilee. Israel had occupied some 28,000 square miles, three times the size of its own territory. It was one of the swiftest and most decisive military victories in history. In November the United Nations Security Council adopted a resolution demanding Israel's withdrawal from the areas it had conquered but also calling for a settlement that would recognize its right to exist.

Humiliated by the Six Day War, Egypt rearmed with Soviet assistance and planned a new attack with Syria. This time preparations were secret. Israel was caught napping by the Yom Kippur War of 1973, so called because it began with a surprise attack on the annual Jewish day of atonement. Initially repulsed, Israeli forces quickly recovered and with American tactical assistance had regained the offensive when fighting was halted after 18 days on October 24. But they had suffered heavy losses on the ground and in the air, and the conflict brought the superpowers closer to confrontation in the Middle East than ever before.

The Yom Kippur War underlined the dangers posed by continued instability in the Middle East. It brought in its wake a threatened cutoff of oil exports that struck at the very heart of the Western economy. Accordingly, the American secretary of state, Henry Kissinger, conducted arduous "shuttle diplomacy" between the major Arab capitals and Jerusalem in an attempt to find a basis of accommodation. These efforts bore fruit in the Camp David accords of September 1978 between Egypt and Israel. The two parties agreed to a phased withdrawal of Israeli troops from the Sinai and a vaguely defined autonomy for the West Bank and the Gaza strip. President Sadat had ended the humiliating occupation of Egyptian territory and gained a major American subsidy for his ailing economy. Prime Minister Begin had won diplomatic recognition for the first time from an Arab state, secured Israel's western frontier, and divided its two principal antagonists, Egypt and Syria. Both men shared a Nobel peace prize. But Sadat was denounced in the Arab world for having made a separate peace with Israel and for failing to secure Palestinian rights. Egypt lost the position of leadership it had enjoyed for the previous quarter century, and Sadat himself was assassinated by Muslim fundamentalists in October 1981.

JERUSALEM: A CITY DIVIDED

The divisions of the contemporary Middle East are nowhere more vividly symbolized than in the historic city of Jerusalem. Today, with its population of around 300,000, it reflects both a rich past and a divided present. The New City, to the west, is a modern capital, with fashionable shops, a convention center, and a Kennedy memorial. It also houses the Knesset, Israel's parliament, and the Israel Museum. The Old City, once shared by Arabs and Jews, is in the Arab quarter, a labyrinth of bazaars, market alleys, and narrow, winding streets. Administratively, the New and Old City are now one; politically, they are as far apart as ever.

After a long history as a religious center first of Judaism and then of Christianity, Jerusalem was conquered by the Muslims in 629. Unlike previous conquerors, they treated the city with great respect. It was sacred to Islam because the Jewish temple was the place to which Muhammad had been carried in his famous vision prior to ascending the seven heavens into the presence of the Almighty. Accordingly, the caliph Omar built a wooden mosque in the temple compound, above which rises today the gold-domed, octagonal structure known as the Haram el-Sharif (Dome of the Rock), still much as it was when completed in 691. For several centuries Christian and Jewish worship was permitted side by side with Islamic. As unrest increased in the Arab world, however, particularly after the ninth century, access to the holy sites became hazardous.

Crusader Europe recaptured Jerusalem and established Christian control of the city again for most of a century (1099–1187) and briefly from 1229 to 1244, expelling Jews and Muslims. Thereafter for nearly 700 years the city again reverted to Islam, first under the Mameluke Turks (1250–1517) and then under their Ottoman successors (1517–1917). It reached a low point in the seventeenth and eighteenth centuries as Ottoman rule decayed, but European influence began to revive it in the nineteenth century, and with the advent of Zionism it became a focus of Jewish immigration.

The British capture of Jerusalem in 1917 inaugurated its modern period. Extensive rebuilding took place, and access to the holy places was given to the three faiths, although at Muslim insistence the ban on Jews entering the Dome of the Rock on the site of the temple mount was maintained. Communal violence between Arabs and Jews erupted as early as 1929, and when the British withdrew from Palestine in 1947, the city (whose population was by now more than 60 percent Jewish) was besieged by the Arab Legion. The armistice of 1949 divided it into an Israeli and an Arab (Jordanian) sector, separated by barbed wire, sandbags, and sniper fire. The Six Day War gave Israel full control of the city, which was itself a major battlefront.

Jerusalem continues to house its three faiths. Its Christian community is particularly variegated, with Protestant, Catholic, Greek Orthodox, Armenian, Abyssinian, and Coptic churches represented. The city's shrines are once again open to all, but its future remains clouded by the Arab-Israeli controversy. As in the days of the prophet Ezekiel, it can be said of the city: "This is Jerusalem; I have set her in the midst of nations."

Arab Nationalism

Until the late nineteenth century communal identity among the various Arab peoples of the Middle East had little to do with political self-determination or territorial units. Under the Ottoman system members of each religious faith—Muslim, Christian, and Jewish—lived in an independent community governed according to its own law by its clerical hierarchy. Communal consciousness was therefore awareness of religious values and customs rather than ethnic differentiation. Although religious rivalries often had a territorial dimension, not until the final breakup of the Ottoman Empire and the arrival of Western imperialism did such rivalries become identified with control of political entities with discrete boundaries. The idea of nationhood in its modern meaning was, as in so many other parts of the world, a Western import that cut across religious, cultural, and tribal affiliations.

Despite a major Arab cultural revival in the nineteenth century centered in Cairo, Beirut, and Damascus, there was no serious call for Arab separation from the Ottoman Empire until Neguib Azouri, a Palestinian Arab living in Paris, published *The Awakening of the Arab Nation* in 1905, in which he envisioned a united Arab state stretching from the Persian Gulf to the Suez Canal. The revival of Turkish nationalism after the Young Turk revolution of 1908 galvanized its Arab counterpart. Moderate Arabs who had been content with the idea of greater political autonomy within the Ottoman framework rather than independence now faced a regime in Istanbul bent on more rigorous controls. When Turkey allied itself with the Central Powers in World War I, Britain, already in quest of oil for its modernized navy in the region, promised support for a united Arab state to the sharif of Mecca, Hussein ibn-Ali, in return for military assistance.

This promise was not kept. In 1920 Britain and France

divided the Arab provinces of the former Ottoman Empire between them as mandates under the League of Nations, with Britain adding Palestine, Transjordan, and Mesopotamia (Iraq) to its former protectorate in Egypt, and France gaining Syria and Lebanon. Although ibn-Saud united the vast interior of the Arabian peninsula as Saudi Arabia in the 1920s and proclaimed a kingdom in 1932, Britain remained in firm control of most of its coastline. At the same time, American companies began a vigorous exploitation of oil resources in Saudi Arabia and Iraq. World War II saw the Middle East turned into a major theater of operations, with Germany's failure to gain access to the oil fields a crucial factor in its defeat.

The status of some of the Arab trust territories evolved during the interwar period. Iraq had achieved at least enough of the appearance of a state to be admitted to the League of Nations in 1932, although British influence remained strong. In Transjordan a strongman who ruled with British backing, the Amir Abdullah, was recognized as a king in 1946, but British control was still so transparent that not until 1955 was the renamed kingdom of Jordan, including the West Bank area seized in the Palestine War, admitted to the United Nations. The pace of change was even slower in Syria and Lebanon, where the French showed little inclination to prepare their territories for statehood. French control lapsed during the Nazi occupation, however, and in 1946 both became independent. Although far more advanced economically than Britain's mandates, both countries faced special challenges. Lebanon had no sectarian majority; a variety of Muslim and Christian groups vied for dominance. Syria, despite its proud heritage, was fragmented by religious and tribal divisions among both its majority Muslim and minority Christian populations. In Syria these tensions remain barely under control; in Lebanon they erupted in 1975 in a civil war that precipitated anarchy, invasion, and foreign occupation.

The end of World War II brought rapid changes. In 1945 the League of Arab States was formed under British auspices, consisting originally of Egypt, Syria, Lebanon, Iraq, Transjordan, Saudi Arabia, and Yemen. Although many of these states were as yet in no credible sense independent, they rapidly became so as British influence waned, and it was the league that coordinated the 1948 invasion of Palestine. Defeat at the hands of the tiny Jewish army provoked a military coup in Syria, an upsurge in anti-Western sentiment, and an agonizing reassessment of the wider problems of Arab development and unity.

Nasser and the Egyptian Revolution

The most significant result of this ferment came in Egypt, where in 1952 the military revolution led by Gamal Abdel Nasser drove out the corrupt, British-supported King Farouk, spelling the end of Britain's role in the Middle East and hence of the last direct Western presence in the region.

Nasser was born in 1918, the son of a postal clerk in upper Egypt. Like many young Egyptians of modest origin, he joined the army as a means of gaining educational opportunities and career advancement. His fellow graduates in the 1938 class of the military academy were mostly of similar background, the sons of minor officials, petty merchants, commercial agents, and small landowners. They shared a common sense of frustration at Egypt's continued dominance by Britain and a sense of alienation from the older and wealthier officer corps. Under Nasser's leadership they began to meet on a regular basis to discuss the nation's problems and to plan for its future. By 1942 this group had evolved into a central committee with smaller cells throughout the army. Contacts were also established with religious organizations and foreign Arab leaders. The army's humiliation in the Palestine War strengthened the resolve of the young officers to reform the nation. Now banded together as the Free Officers' Society, they staged a virtually bloodless coup on July 23, 1952, that brought a revolutionary council to power. At first the council attempted to govern the country through its civilian institutions and bureaucracy. When the latter refused to implement the council's directives on land reform, a military dictatorship was proclaimed.

The council's nominal head was a senior general, Muhammad Naguib, but Nasser remained its true leader. It was he who decided on the policy of "guided democracy." Political parties and parliamentary institutions remained the goal of the regime, he declared, but until the masses had been prepared for active political life by reform and education, these could only serve the interests of the few. The press was brought under government regulation, and political activity was exercised through a single mass party, the Arab Socialist Union. In 1954 Nasser assumed direct control of the revolution as prime minister, and two years later he unveiled a constitution guaranteeing basic rights, including racial, religious, and sexual equality.

Nasser's revolution was as much social as political. While most of Egypt's 25 million people lived on an annual per capita income of $60, an elite of 12,000 owned 37 percent of its arable land. Nasser broke up the great estates and distributed them among the peasantry, with the smaller lots subsumed into cooperative farms. The Permanent Council for National Production was established in 1953 to draft first a five- and then a ten-year plan for integrated industrial and agricultural development. Crucial to the success of these plans was the Aswan Dam, which aimed to increase cultivated land by a third by harnessing the Nile River. When the United States, alarmed at Nasser's rising popularity in the Arab world and irked by his lack of enthusiasm for an American-sponsored regional alliance, the Baghdad Pact, announced that it would not help fund the dam, Nasser responded dramatically. He nationalized the Suez Canal, with the stated purpose of using its income to build the dam, which had now become symbolic not only of his revolution but of Third World hopes in general for independent development. Launched in 1959 with a $300 million loan from the Soviet Union, the dam was completed in 1974 at a cost of more than $2 billion. Although its projected goals for irrigation and hydroelectric power were not fully met and ecological problems such as silting and stagnation continue to plague it, the dam enabled Egypt nearly to double its agricultural output.

Equally significant strides were made in the industrial sector, although much of it remained in handicraft and small-scale production. Nasser's record of accomplishment in one of the world's poorest nations, though politically and economically blemished by the disaster of the Six Day War, was impressive. Nonetheless, these gains were all but negated by unchecked population growth, running at some 3 percent a year. By the late 1970s Anwar el-Sadat had accepted a new client relationship with the United States as the price of economic survival, a policy continued since 1981 by his successor, Hosni Mubarak. The heroic age of Nasser had ended.

The Middle East in the Postwar World

Nasser's revolution was a model for many emerging nations in the postwar period, but its influence was most direct on Egypt's North African neighbors. By 1956 the French protectorates of Morocco and Tunisia and the British-occupied Sudan had achieved full self-government, largely under the impetus of Egypt's example, and the former Italian colony of Libya was also granted independence under a feudal monarch, King Idris. However, the French refused to consider withdrawal from Algeria, where a strong settler interest prevailed. A war of national liberation ensued between 1954 and 1962, marked by savagery on both sides and resolved only when Charles de Gaulle, whom the war had brought back to power, arranged a plebiscite.

The rapid formation of new states in the immediate postwar period failed to give definitive shape or stability to Arab nationalism. Tribal groups dispersed over various borders, such as the Kurds of Turkey, Syria, Iran, and Iraq, demanded a homeland of their own. Radical nationalist parties, such as the Ba'ath movement in Syria and Iraq, remained dissatisfied with the conservative, pro-Western regimes left behind in the wake of the imperial powers. Pan-Arabic pressures for political unification between separate states also remained strong. In 1958 Syria and Egypt combined to form the United Arab Republic, with Nasser as president. Ardent Arab nationalists, particularly Syrian Ba'athists, saw this union as the precursor of a grand Islamic federation but were soon disillusioned when the Egyptians moved to take complete control of Syria's government and economy. Following a Syrian army rebellion in September 1961, the union was dissolved by mutual consent. Similar experiments with other partners have proved equally short-lived, but the dream of a single, unitary state remains deeply embedded in Arab nationalism.

OPEC and the Politics of Oil

The history of the modern Middle East has been to a large extent determined by oil. Otherwise sparing in its gifts, nature has endowed the region with 60 percent of the proven world oil reserves. Britain was already dependent on Iranian oil to power its fleet by the first decade of the twentieth century, and as the West converted rapidly from coal to oil-based energy, the strategic importance of the Middle East grew apace. The discovery of vast new reserves in the desert wastes of Arabia in the 1930s was immediately exploited by the California Arabian Standard Oil Company (later called Aramco) on concessions granted by King ibn-Saud. Almost overnight Saudi Arabia was transformed from a poverty-ridden principality of nomadic tribes to a nation with one of the highest per capita incomes in the world.

In 1960 the Saudis took the initiative in forming the Organization of Petroleum Exporting Countries (OPEC). Originally composed of Saudi Arabia, Iran, Iraq, the tiny and newly independent emirate of Kuwait, and Venezuela, it subsequently expanded to include Algeria, Ecuador, Gabon, Indonesia, Libya, Nigeria, Qatar, and the confederation of small Persian Gulf sheikhdoms known as the United Arab Emirates. At first OPEC confined its activities chiefly to gaining a larger share of the revenues produced by Western oil companies and greater control over levels of production. The persistence of the Arab-Israeli conflict, however, turned it from a simple cartel into a formidable political force. After the Six Day War the Arab members of OPEC formed a separate, overlapping group (OAPEC) for the purpose of concerting policy and exerting pressure on the West over Israel. Egypt and Syria, negligible oil producers but populous and militarily powerful, joined the latter group to underline its intentions.

The Yom Kippur War of 1973 galvanized Arab opinion. Furious at the emergency resupply effort that had enabled Israel to withstand the Egyptian and Syrian assault, the Arabs imposed an oil embargo against the United States, western Europe, and Japan. This was followed by a more than fourfold price increase in the price of oil, causing sudden inflation and economic recession in the noncommunist industrial world and even greater hardship among the underdeveloped nations. At the same time, the Saudis acquired operating control of Aramco, fully nationalizing it in 1980. As other OPEC nations followed suit, the cartel's

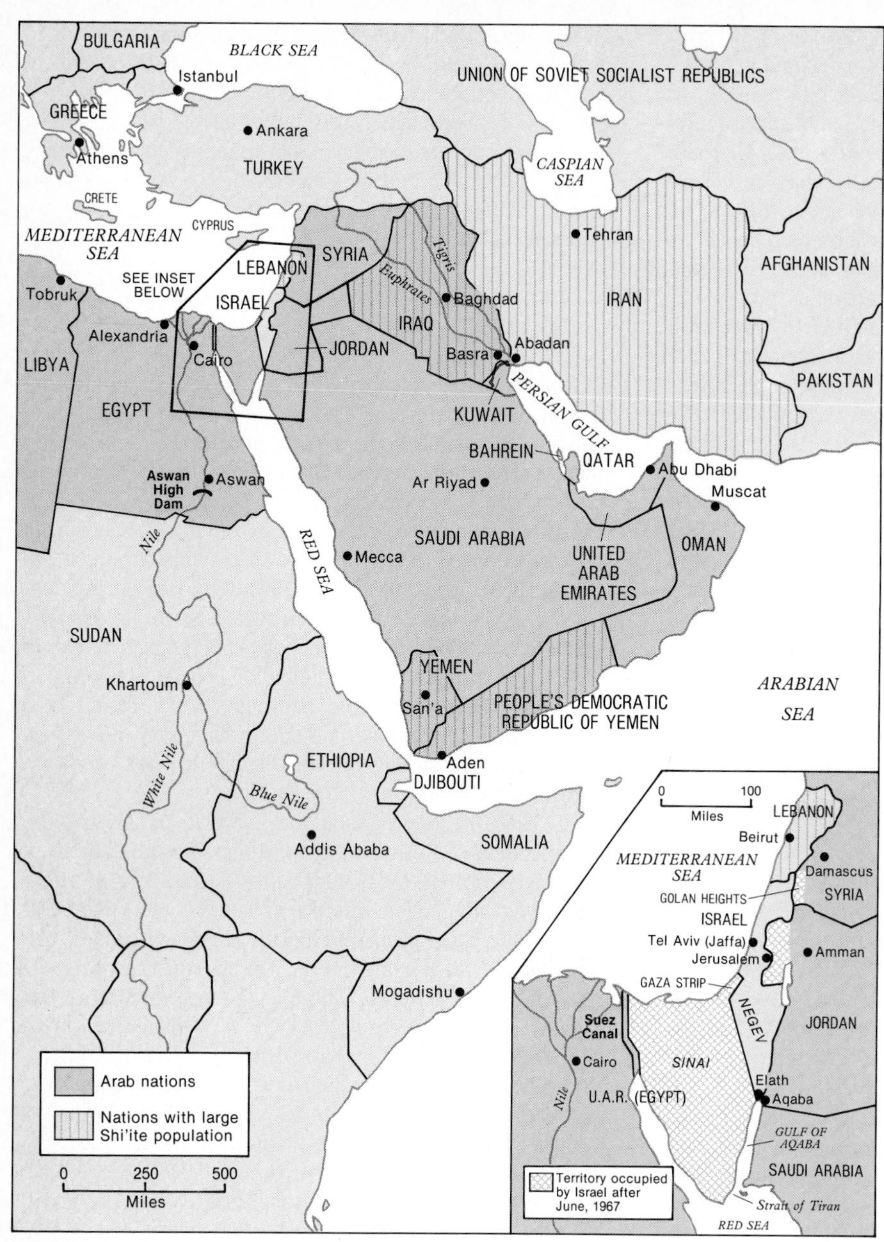

39.4 The Modern Middle East

income soared. Saudi Arabia, awash in profits, undertook a series of five-year development plans, of which the most ambitious, begun in 1980, called for the expenditure of $250 billion. Other cartel members also undertook major economic programs. For the first time, Third World nations whose resources and labor had long been exploited by the industrial giants had acquired control of a vital commodity, reversing the flow of capital. Some of this income was dispensed in the form of aid to other underdeveloped nations whose economies had been caught between higher prices for oil and the lower prices for their own commodities and raw materials caused by shrinking Western demand. Much of it, however, was reinvested in the West or absorbed in massive arms purchases that exacerbated political tensions, particularly in the Middle East. When reduced demand and overproduction produced a glut on the world market in the mid-1980s, oil prices plummeted and the cartel lost its unity. Producers such as Mexico, Nigeria, and Venezuela, whose economies had expanded recklessly, were plunged into near-bankruptcy, and even Saudi Arabia felt the pinch. The enormous reserves and relative underpopulation of the leading Middle East producers guaranteed the region its continuing strategic importance, but the politics of oil had proved dangerous for all concerned.

Modernization and Revolution in Iran

Iran, though ethnologically and linguistically distinct from its Arab neighbors in the Middle East, has shared its geographic destiny. As elsewhere in the region, social and political controls on the local level were traditionally exercised by the clergy on behalf of tribal landowning elites, with civil law and custom derived directly from religious precepts, although the merchant class of the larger towns had some independent influence. Patriarchal and hierarchical in structure, Iranian society was based on the absolute control of fathers over their families, khans or leaders over their tribes, and the shah as ruler over all, subject only to the ultimate authority of Shi'ite religious principles.

Iran's modernization began with its penetration by two conflicting imperial powers, Russia and Great Britain. In the 1860s and 1870s the first telegraph lines were set up with British assistance, thus ending the country's virtual isolation from the world. Concessions were given to build railroads and develop the country's resources. By 1907 the Russians and the British had formally divided Iran into spheres of influence, but a nationalist uprising in 1921 led by Reza Shah Pahlavi produced a modernizing dictatorship that, like Kemal Atatürk's in Turkey, attempted to introduce Western cultural and industrial models and to reduce the power of the clergy by stressing the nation's pre-Islamic past. New schools and industries were begun, and a conscript army was raised. A trans-Iranian railroad from the Caspian Sea to the Persian Gulf was built from the profits of state monopolies. Wide new avenues were cut through the major towns and named for national folk heroes. Sumptuary laws mandated the wearing of Western dress, and the traditional women's veil, the *chadar,* was made obsolete. In 1935 Reza Shah Pahlavi changed the country's Hellenistic name of Persia to Iran, meaning "land of the Aryans."

This last change was meant to reflect Iran's Indo-European roots but had contemporary significance as well. Reza Shah Pahlavi, dictatorial and often terroristic in his methods, was an ardent admirer of Hitler, and when an Allied force occupied Iran in August 1941, he was forced to abdicate in favor of his son, Muhammad Reza Pahlavi. For the next decade the country was once again a battleground of foreign interests, with the United States replacing Britain soon after World War II and the Soviet Union trying to regain its traditional foothold in the north. A new nationalist insurrection brought Muhammad Mossadegh, a prewar opponent of Reza Shah Pahlavi, to power as prime minister in 1951. Mossadegh nationalized the British-owned Anglo-Iranian Oil Company, thereby reasserting the country's independence. The West retaliated with a boycott of Iranian oil, and a CIA-led army coup deposed him in August 1953.

The shah, who had been briefly forced to flee the country by pro-Mossadegh crowds, returned with American blessing and remained a Western client thereafter. Like his father, however, he harbored grandiose ambitions. A "white revolution" was launched in the early 1960s to complete the process of modernization begun under Reza Shah Pahlavi, although the traditional landed elite remained firmly in control of the countryside. Using the massive oil profits of the 1970s, the shah attempted to turn Iran into the major military power of the Middle East, purchasing $15 billion worth of American arms between 1972 and 1978. But by the latter part of the decade his regime was under general assault. The land hunger of the peasantry remained unsatisfied despite promised reform, while the middle classes cultivated by the shah were frustrated by their exclusion from real power. Showy industrial projects and exotic weapons could not be operated without foreign advisers and technicians, reinforcing a painful sense of dependence on the West. Even the aristocracy, which had never accepted the Pahlavi dynasty, offered little support.

The Ayatollah Khomeini in 1979, addressing an adoring crowd from his home. [Alain Dejlan/Sygma]

The shah's most serious opposition, however, came from the Shi'ite clergy, which bitterly opposed what it took to be his promotion of corrupt Western values and mores. By raising a culturally sensitive issue that cut across class lines and evoked powerful religious and nationalist sentiment, the clergy brought to focus a general sense of grievance. Their exiled leader, the Ayatollah Ruhollah Khomeini (1900–1989), became the symbol of popular resistance.

The shah responded at first with repression and then, when crippling strikes brought the economy to the verge of bankruptcy, by desperate concessions. In January 1979 he fled into exile, and on February 1 Khomeini returned to Teheran as head of a revolutionary council, which proclaimed an Islamic republic. Real authority, however, emanated from Khomeini himself, who eliminated all political competitors and, armed with nearly absolute powers, embarked on a program of fundamentalist religious reform.

Khomeini's appeal reached far beyond the Shi'ites of Iran. His call to all Muslims to overthrow corrupt and tyrannical rulers and to return to the purity of Islamic law and ritual was particularly attractive to the migrant workers who maintained the economies of Saudi Arabia, Kuwait, and Bahrain. His order to seize 52 American em-

Militant Islam

The view of Islam as historically beleaguered by alien and hostile forces from the West is put forward by the Ayatollah Khomeini in his book, Islamic Government.

At its inception, the Islamic movement was afflicted by the Jews, who initiated a counteractivity by distorting the reputation of Islam, by assaulting it, and by slandering it. This has continued to our present day. Then came the role of groups which can be considered more evil than the devil and his troops. This role emerged in the colonialist activity which dates back more than three centuries ago. The colonialists found in the Muslim world their long-sought object. To achieve their colonialist ambitions, the colonists sought to create the right conditions leading to the annihilation of Islam. They did not seek to turn the Muslims into Christians after driving them away from Islam, because they do not believe in either. They wanted control and domination because during the Crusades they were constantly aware that the greatest obstacle preventing them from attaining their goals . . . was Islam with its laws and beliefs and with the influence it exerted on people through their faith. . . . Islam is the religion of the warriors who fight for right and justice, the religion of those seeking for freedom and independence, and those who do not want to allow the infidels to oppress the believers.

The role of women under revolutionary Islam is stated in the constitution adopted by the Islamic Republic of Iran on December 3, 1979.

In creating Islamic social foundations, all the human forces that had up to now been in the service of foreign exploitation will be accorded their basic identity and human rights. And in this regard it is natural that women, due to the greater oppression that they have borne under the idolatrous order, will enjoy more rights.

The family unit is the foundation of society and the main institution for the growth and advancement of mankind. . . . It is the principal duty of the Islamic government to regard women as the unifying factor of the family unit and its position. They are a factor in bringing the family out of the service of propagating consumerism and exploitation and renewing the vital and valuable duty of motherhood in raising educated human beings. . . . As a result motherhood is accepted as a most profound responsibility in the Muslim viewpoint and will, therefore, be accorded the highest value and generosity.

Source: T. Y. Ismael, *Iraq and Iran: Roots of Conflict* (Syracuse, N.Y.: Syracuse University Press, 1982), pp. 101, 147.

bassy officials and workers in November 1979 was the most dramatically popular act in the Middle East since the nationalization of the Suez Canal. Depicting the United States as a "great Satan" (while at the same time firmly repressing Iran's Communist party and doing pragmatic business with Israel, America's principal surrogate in the area), Khomeini skillfully combined Islamic revivalism with appeals to regional nationalism. In September 1980 Iraq's Saddam Hussein launched an ill-judged invasion of Iran that bitterly divided the Arab world, with Syria, Libya, and South Yemen backing Khomeini and Saudi Arabia and Jordan supporting Iraq. The war enabled Khomeini to keep revolutionary fervor high in Iran while consolidating a theocratic regime that may well outlast him and to burnish his image as the leader of Islam's *jihad,* or holy war, against the corrupting influence of the West. It was militarily inconclusive, however, and hostilities were halted by a truce in the summer of 1988.

Women and the Islamic Revolution

The resurgence of Islam has not been confined to Iran. From the Atlantic coast of North Africa to the islands of the Indonesian archipelago, across the great east-west belt where most of the world's 1 billion Muslims live, a major reawakening of Islamic culture has occurred since 1945. In part this has been associated with the emergence of new nation-states along this belt and the consequent testing of one of the world's most important religious traditions with the essentially secular ideology of modern nationalism. In part as well it reflects a struggle for identity in a region whose people are skeptical of both Western materialism and Soviet atheism and are reluctant to align themselves with either of the superpower blocs. But it also has great significance for the social position of one-fifth of the world's women.

Koranic law continues to assign women a subordinate position in society. In the more conservative Middle Eastern states the law has continued to deny them equality in the public sphere and even access to it; in Saudi Arabia women were still not permitted to drive automobiles as late as 1980. In contrast, women had made significant strides in the postwar period in countries either heavily subject to Western influence or unified by socialist revolution. Tunisia, under the presidency of the strongly pro-Western Habib Bourguiba (born 1903), became in 1956 the first Islamic nation to replace the Koranic law on marriage, divorce, and childbearing by a civil code and the first Arab state to ban polygamy. Egypt under Nasser promulgated a constitution giving women full civil equality for the first time, and the socialist governments of Algeria and Yemen have included women's groups within their ruling party organizations. Such developments, however, have tended to affect only the urban middle class, with rural, tribal, and nomadic life continuing along traditional lines. The Iranian revolution of 1979 had a dramatic effect on women; Western attire vanished almost immediately, replaced by the traditional black or gray veil and a shapeless garment covering the entire body. Elsewhere too in the Middle East the *chadar* has again become the norm, sometimes as a symbol of resistance to Western mores, but often a matter of compulsion. Thus while Arab radicalism in the 1950s was at least rhetorically receptive to women's liberation, the fundamentalist revival of the 1980s has

Iranian demonstrators burn the American flag. [Jean Gaumy/ Magnum]

tended to consign women to their former roles, encouraging domesticity, public anonymity, and male dominance.

The Middle East Today

The hope of Camp David, that the Israeli-Egyptian accord would pave the way to a general settlement in the Middle East, has not been realized. No other Arab nation has moved toward recognition of Israel, while the Palestinian issue remains unresolved. During the 1970s the PLO was recognized as the legitimate government of the Palestinian people by many Arab, Soviet bloc, and Third World nations, and its leader, Yasir Arafat (born 1929), addressed the United Nations as a head of state. His influence declined precipitously in the early 1980s as the PLO's more militant factions fell under Syrian influence. In 1987, however, a popular uprising, the *intifada,* broke out on the West Bank against the Israeli occupation. Seizing this opportunity to reassert his leadership, Arafat began an intensive diplomatic campaign that climaxed in an address before the United Nations in 1988 and the initiation of direct bilateral talks with the United States.

The tragic clash between the Israelis and the Palestinians has become, for much of the international public, emblematic of the continuing appeal of nationalism in a globally interconnected world. The Palestinian poet Mahmoud Darwish spoke perhaps best for the common feeling on both sides of the conflict when he wrote:

> ***Where shall we go, after the last frontier?***
> ***Where will birds be flying, after the last sky? . . .***
> ***We will cut off the hand of song, so that our flesh can complete the song.***
> ***Here we will die. Here in the last narrow passage. Or here our blood will plant—its olive trees.***[1]

Legacy of Violence: The Lebanese Civil War

A tragic by-product of the Arab-Israeli conflict has been the civil war in Lebanon. On the surface, Lebanon had been one of the most successful of the states to win independence following World War II. Its thriving commercial economy had given it one of the Middle East's highest standards of living, and the political coexistence of a varied community of Christian, Jewish, and Muslim groups had made it a model of religious pluralism. Lebanon's equilibrium was, however, precarious. Urban prosperity masked rural poverty in the central valleys, a rising Muslim birthrate threatened the traditional Christian hegemony, and the country's semiofficial neutrality in the Arab-Israeli conflict brought it under increasing pressure from Arab nationalists. The sudden influx of some 300,000 Palestinian refugees after the Six Day War, followed by others expelled from Jordan in 1971, greatly exacerbated these tensions. The PLO made Lebanon its main base of operations, drawing retaliatory fire from Israel. The Lebanese divided sharply over the Palestinian presence, with Christian groups tending to regard them as unwelcome intruders and Muslims seeing them not only as victims seeking to regain their homeland but as patriots fighting in the common Arab cause against Israel. By 1975 the country had slid into full-scale civil war. When Syrian troops finally enforced a cease-fire 19 months later, 60,000 lives had been lost and nearly a third of the population displaced.

Syria's presence diminished the bloodshed but did nothing to restore stability. The PLO intensified its raids and attacks against Israel, while the Israelis sought to cultivate Christian allies in Lebanon. By 1980 there were approximately 40 separate armed groups in the country. Two years later the Israelis invaded Lebanon, driving the PLO from Beirut and occupying the southern third of the country. This defeat marked the temporary eclipse of Arafat, but the Israelis, now a target for all forces, soon withdrew after heavy losses. An American intervention in 1983 ended even more disastrously, with the death of 241 marines in a commando attack. By the late 1980s Lebanon had vanished as a nation in all but name, the epitome of sectarian anarchy and of the collapse of multiethnic community in the Middle East.

The increasing polarization of the Middle East was reflected in the prominence of revolutionary Iran; Syria, a state widely linked to support of terrorism; and Libya, whose ruler since 1969, Muammar al-Qaddafi (born 1942), has pursued a policy of military adventurism in North Africa while proclaiming the virtues of Arab unity. At the same time, the influence of militant Shi'ism has grown apace, particularly in countries with large Shi'ite populations, including (besides Iran) Iraq, Yemen, Bahrain, and Lebanon. In addition, economic pressures have intensified on many Middle Eastern countries that overextended themselves financially during the boom years of the 1970s and now face serious problems of unemployment and social unrest. The Iran-Iraq war demonstrated the fratricidal tendencies within Islam. Above all, the Arab-Israeli conflict continues to jeopardize hopes for the peaceful development of the region and, on a wider scale, international stability as well.

The forces of religion and nationalism created powerful tides in the postwar period along the great arc stretching from the Middle East to south-central Asia. The new states of India and Pakistan were born in an agony of civil war between their Hindu and Muslim populations, while the state of Israel was created in an equally bitter confrontation between Arab and Jew. Within Islam itself, divisions between Sunni and Shi'ite Muslims produced bloody conflict as well, most visibly in the Iran-Iraq war. At the same time, the unfulfilled national aspirations of the Palestinians and of the Kurds, the vulnerable oil economy, the problems of poverty and rapid social change, and the continuing unrest in Afghanistan and elsewhere all combine to make this region perhaps the most volatile in the world.

Notes

1. M. Darwish, "Earth Scrapes Us," in *Modern Arabic Poetry: An Anthology,* ed. S. K. Jayyusi (New York: Columbia University Press, 1987), p. 208.

Suggestions for Further Reading

India, Pakistan, and Sri Lanka

Azad, M. *India Wins Freedom*. London: Longman, 1961.

Brown, J. *Modern India: The Origins of an Asian Democracy*. New York: Oxford University Press, 1985.

De Silva, K. M. *A History of Sri Lanka*. Berkeley: University of California Press, 1981.

Franda, M. *India's Rural Development*. Bloomington: Indiana University Press, 1980.

Gold, G. *Gandhi: A Pictorial Biography*. New York: Harper & Row, 1986.

Joshi, R., and Rindle, J. *Daughters of Independence: Gender, Caste, and Class in India*. London: Zed Books, 1986.

Kohli, A. *The State and Poverty in India*. Cambridge: Cambridge University Press, 1987.

Lamb, B. P. *India: A World in Transition*, 4th ed. New York: Praeger, 1975.

Mellor, J. *The New Economics of Growth: A Strategy for India and the Developing World*. Ithaca, N.Y.: Cornell University Press, 1976.

Moon, P. *Divide and Quit*. Berkeley: University of California Press, 1962.

Rosen, G. *Democracy and Economic Change in India*. Berkeley: University of California Press, 1966.

Swamy, S. *Economic Growth in China and India, 1952–1970*. Chicago: University of Chicago Press, 1974.

Tirtha, R. *Society and Development in Contemporary India*. Detroit: Harlo Press, 1980.

Wolpert, S. *Jinnah of Pakistan*. New York: Oxford University Press, 1984.

Ziegler, P. *Mountbatten*. London: Collins, 1985.

The Middle East

Abdulghani, J. *Iran and Iraq*. London: Croom Helm, 1984.

Ajami, F. *The Arab Predicament: Arab Political Thought and Practice Since 1967*. Cambridge: Cambridge University Press, 1981.

Anderson, J. N. D. *Islamic Law in the Modern World*. Westport, Conn.: Greenwood Press, 1975.

Avineri, S. *The Making of Modern Zionism: Intellectual Origins of the Jewish State*. New York: Basic Books, 1981.

Bakhash, S. *The Reign of the Ayatollahs*. New York: Basic Books, 1984.

Devlin, J. *Syria: Modern State in an Ancient Land*. Boulder, Colo.: Westview Press, 1983.

al-Fassi, A. *The Independence Movements in Arab North Africa*, trans. H. Z. Nuseibeh. New York: Octagon, 1970.

Kurzman, D. *Ben-Gurion: Prophet of Fire*. New York: Simon & Schuster, 1983.

Lacouture, J. *Nasser: A Biography*. New York: Knopf, 1973.

Mortimer, E. *Faith and Power: The Politics of Islam*. New York: Faber & Faber, 1982.

Rabinovitch, I. *The War for Lebanon, 1970–1983*. Ithaca, N.Y.: Cornell University Press, 1984.

Reich, B. *Israel: Land of Tradition and Conflict*. Boulder, Colo.: Westview Press, 1985.

Said, E. W. *The Question of Palestine*. New York: Times Books, 1979.

Salibi, K. *A History of Arabia*. Delmar, N.Y.: Caravan Books, 1980.

Sampson, A. *The Seven Sisters*. New York: Bantam Books, 1979.

Taryam, A. O. *The Establishment of the United Arab Emirates, 1950–85*. London: Croom Helm, 1987.

Waterbury, J. *The Egypt of Nasser and Sadat*. Princeton, N.J.: Princeton University Press, 1983.

CHAPTER · 40

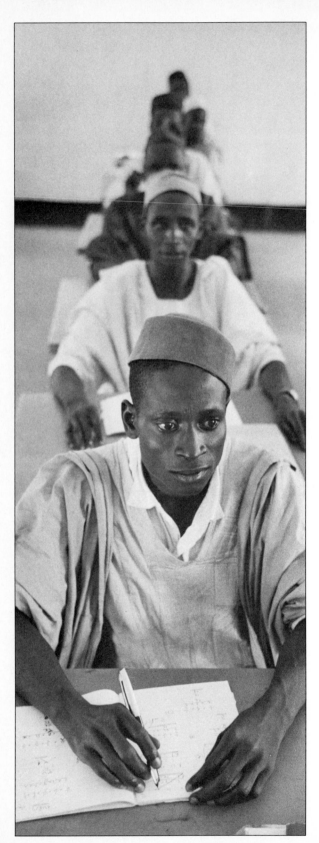

Decolonization and Development: Africa and Latin America

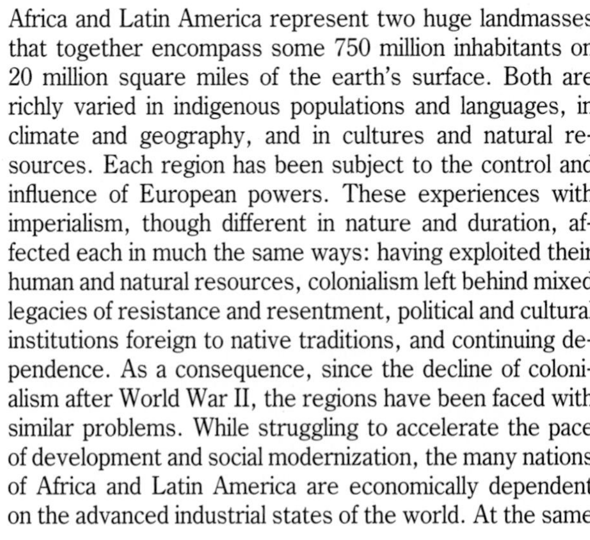

Africa and Latin America represent two huge landmasses that together encompass some 750 million inhabitants on 20 million square miles of the earth's surface. Both are richly varied in indigenous populations and languages, in climate and geography, and in cultures and natural resources. Each region has been subject to the control and influence of European powers. These experiences with imperialism, though different in nature and duration, affected each in much the same ways: having exploited their human and natural resources, colonialism left behind mixed legacies of resistance and resentment, political and cultural institutions foreign to native traditions, and continuing dependence. As a consequence, since the decline of colonialism after World War II, the regions have been faced with similar problems. While struggling to accelerate the pace of development and social modernization, the many nations of Africa and Latin America are economically dependent on the advanced industrial states of the world. At the same

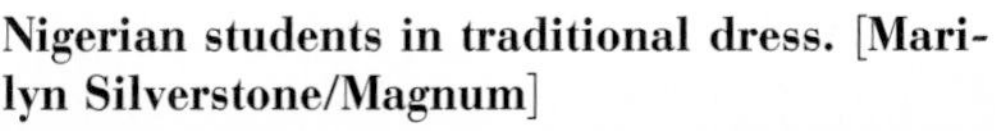

Nigerian students in traditional dress. [Marilyn Silverstone/Magnum]

time, the political record has been marked in many cases by instability and a pattern of repeated military-authoritarian governments. Most daunting of all remain the stark conditions of poverty and social inequality in which the vast majority of Africans and Latin Americans continue to live.

Europeans maintained control over their African territories in the decades before World War II. Few Africans held positions of influence or responsibility in their own lands. The Italian conquest of Ethiopia in 1935 and 1936 seemed yet again to demonstrate the Africans' helplessness in the face of Western power politics. Yet the colonial system in Africa disintegrated rapidly after 1945.

Conditions in Central and South America were different. Although unaffected directly by the fighting of the two world wars, Latin American economic strength was seriously undermined by the interruption of world trade. Equally serious were the effects of the Great Depression in the United States, which reduced the prices of Latin American exports. Thus whereas in Africa the years following World War II saw the Africans asserting a newfound strength over their exhausted European rulers, the same period in Latin America was marked by a precipitous economic decline. Outside influences grew, moreover, as the United States, fresh from victory in World War II, came increasingly to oversee developments throughout the Western Hemisphere.

Africa: The Seeds of Revolt

A prime factor in the early stages of the African independence movements was, paradoxically, the firmness with which European rule was enforced. Further, it was increasingly clear to the Africans that the colonial powers were not prepared to stimulate the economies of the countries they ruled. Railway networks, for example, had been constructed earlier in the colonial period, in the late nineteenth and early twentieth centuries; those of German East and Southwest Africa were built in the years before 1914 and that of the Gold Coast had been completed by 1903. By the 1920s, however, work and investment had virtually ceased. With the slump in works projects came a rapid decline in European emigration to Africa; most unskilled European workers preferred to seek a new life in North America.

Thus Africans found themselves increasingly responsible for performing work for governments over which they had no control and which were seemingly unconcerned for the present and future welfare of their subjects. The consequence was the formation throughout Africa of nationalist movements that sought complete independence and self-government. One of the first examples of this phenomenon occurred in North Africa, where Habib Bourguiba helped to found a Tunisian liberation party in 1934. Four years later the party was banned and Bourguiba was thrown into jail, but the foundations of an autonomous Tunisian government had been laid.

The first political protest movements south of the Sahara developed in West Africa, where European rule had produced a class of Africans who were Western-educated but shut out from any control over their own destiny. In the British colonies African political associations such as the West African National Congress, formed in 1918, began to push for the conversion of legislative councils, which were generally made up of colonial officials and a few token Africans, into true African parliaments.

In the French territories, whose rule remained firmly based in Paris, would-be nationalist leaders found it necessary to spend time in France. Léopold Senghor (born 1906), the nationalist leader of Senegal, first established himself as one of the leading French poets of the period; J. B. Danquah, the founder of the movement to free the Gold Coast, published works on anthropology and religion. Inspiration came from similar movements in the United States and the West Indies, where figures such as W. E. B. Du Bois (1868–1963) and Marcus Garvey (1887–1940) were leading movements of black consciousness. These Europeanized African intellectuals tried to establish the concept of an African personality and to assert the intrinsic aesthetic beauty of African culture, which drew its strength from tribal roots. With this intellectual and moral foundation, they hoped to construct a new political status for people dominated by Europeans.

The main exception to this gradual stirring of independence was South Africa, although even there an organized opposition to white domination had been formed among the black labor force by 1912. The discovery of diamonds and gold there in the 1870s and 1880s led to the establishment of mining operations on a massive scale. Townships grew up around the mining camps, populated by unskilled African laborers who were recruited by the white-owned mining companies. Although in comparison with their skilled and unionized white coworkers black laborers were underpaid, their incomes were significantly higher than those elsewhere in black Africa. This had two consequences: black labor began to collect in shantytowns around the large South African cities, and the whites began to produce goods that could be sold to this new class of African consumers. The South African industrial revolution thus led to the appearance of a black proletariat rigidly governed by white masters. The profound racial tensions that followed have marked the history of South Africa to this day.

World War II hastened the process of resistance to colonial rule that had already begun. The bitter divisions of the European powers were plain for all to see. Indeed, some of the fiercest fighting of the British, French, and American forces against the Italians and Germans occurred on North African soil. In sub-Saharan Africa the colony of French Equatorial Africa, under the leadership of Félix Éboué, sent soldiers to fight against the Germans, even though the Vichy-dominated French West African administration supported Germany.

With the end of hostilities and the resumption of international trade, outside investment in Africa, both public and private, began to increase. In part this was due to the innate value of many of the continent's raw materials, including oil, copper, and cocoa. At the same time, the scale of foreign development projects reflected an increasing concern among the governing powers for the moral welfare of their subjects. Britain and France initiated colonial development schemes that involved the investment of large sums of public capital.

The independence movements that emerged after World War II were conditioned in large measure by the differences that had marked colonial rule among the great powers. The British supported Western-style education for Africans and involved them in the processes of colonial administration; after 1945 at least, most British politicians saw independence as the ultimate goal, for which they should prepare the people of their colonies. The French were less inclined to surrender control, preferring to assimilate their colonial populations with that of the motherland by offering access to French culture, including education in France itself.

Even by these standards, however, Portuguese and Belgian colonial policies were unenlightened and repressive. The Portuguese administrators did almost nothing to encourage, let alone finance, local economic or social development plans and concentrated instead on trade, and the standard of living of their subjects remained probably the most depressed in Africa. The Belgians ruthlessly exploited the Congo and provided almost no higher education or managerial experience for Africans.

It is not surprising, therefore, that the most successful of the new African states are mainly former British colonies, such as Kenya and Tanzania, even though not one has avoided disruptive problems and conflicts. Among the most strife-torn and chaotic have been Zaïre (the former Belgian Congo) and Angola (formerly Portuguese); Niger, Chad, and the Central African Republic, all former French colonies, have remained economically and militarily dependent on France.

In addition to economic improvements, the colonial powers began, partly in response to pressures from liberation movements, to improve living conditions in their African territories. In fields such as health and housing, sanitation and water supply, new developments were aimed at social as well as economic improvement. These were accompanied by an expansion in education. Beginning in 1943 Britain had formulated a scheme to set up universities in the colonies. Other colonial powers were less enlightened; in the Belgian Congo money was invested only in primary and vocational schooling, since the Belgians feared that it would be dangerous to allow their subjects to advance too quickly.

Postwar colonial Africa, then, was marked by a sense of transition. The stagnation of the previous decades gave way to an improvement in communications produced by road and air travel and a new social mobility. Many Africans benefited from the work of the teachers, welfare officers, surveyors, and other skilled professionals who came from Europe, but these outsiders reaped the major rewards of African economic progress. The imported planners, advisers, and researchers often earned large salaries; the Africans for whom they planned did not.

Black Africa: The Challenges of Nationhood

In the process of decolonization that marked the period from 1957 to 1975, the holdings of the four colonial powers that survived World War II—Britain, France, Belgium, and Portugal—acquired independence. Each of the colonial empires had combined a great variety of areas and peoples. By 1975 they had become 51 separate countries, very few of them with an understanding of nationhood and most of them uniting a variety of peoples, cultures, languages, and traditions. The first decades of independence were accordingly fraught with problems for most of them, some of which are still unresolved. The new states were relatively poor, although some had major natural resources awaiting fuller development. The progress of public health and medical care produced a rapid increase in population and a decline in infant mortality. Population in Africa is still growing faster than in most of the rest of the world, while economic development is only beginning.

In most African states today, tribal groups are still the most meaningful cultural and political units. Although most African nations were originally based on Western models, the majority of their citizens think of themselves as Kikuyu, Ibo, or Masai rather than as Kenyans, Nigerians, or Congolese. Even the relatively small state of Ghana in West Africa, about the size of Oregon, harbors ethnic groups speaking more than 35 languages, each with origins in long-standing tribal communities. The population of Nigeria, at nearly 100 million the largest in Africa, is split into some 200 similarly tribal-based language and cultural groups. Many of the new African communities, struggling with problems of poverty and internal diversity, have seen formal parliamentary democracy replaced by military or dictatorial regimes.

Most African nations began their independence under the leadership of charismatic figures such as Kwame Nkrumah (1909–1972) in Ghana, Patrice Lumumba (1925–1961) in the Congo (now Zaïre), Jomo Kenyatta (1891–1978) in Kenya, and Julius Nyerere (born 1922) in Tan-

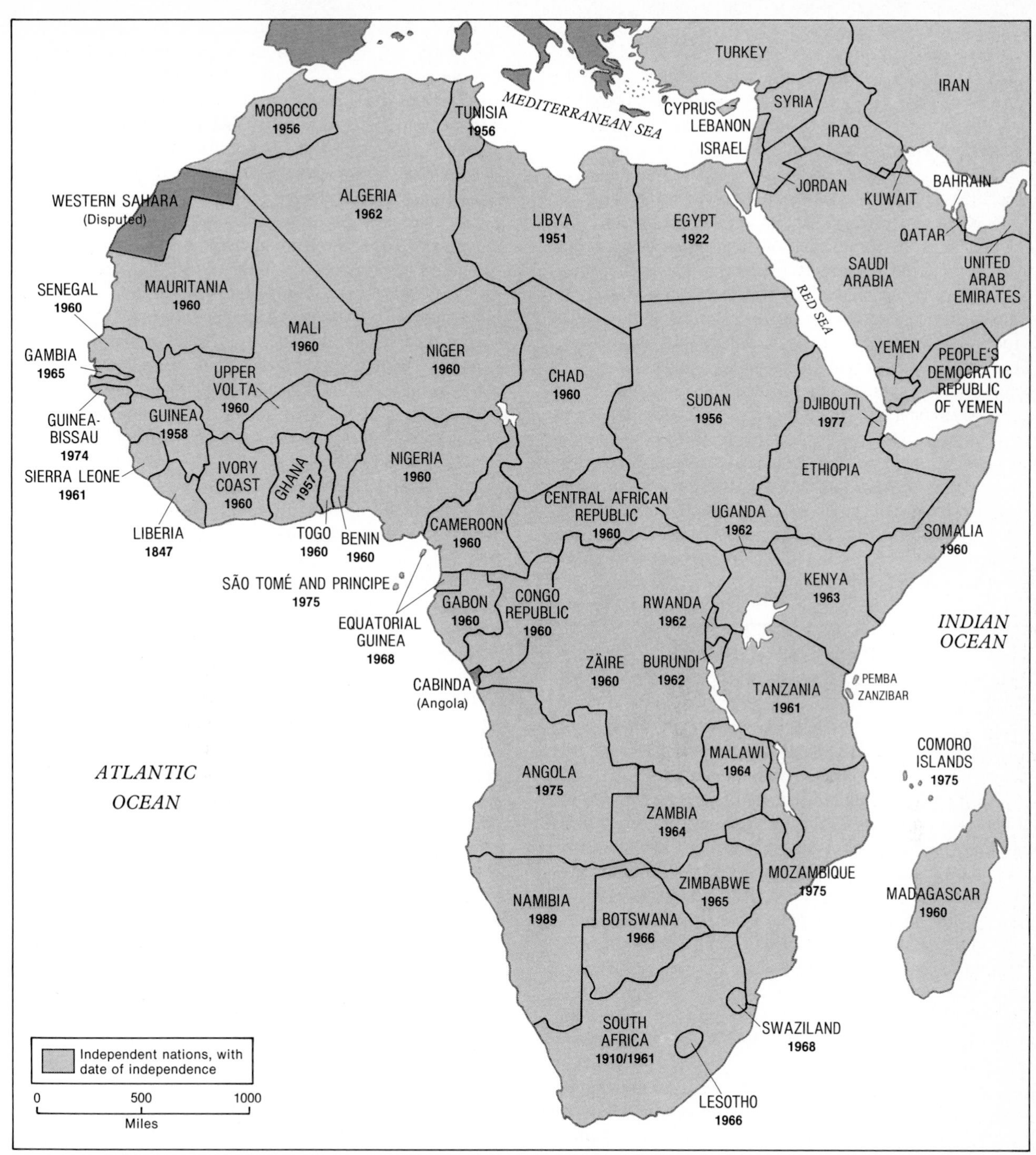

***40.1** Africa Today*

zania. Others relapsed after independence into one-man rule; the cruelest and most gruesome example is probably Idi Amin's dictatorship in Uganda from 1971 to 1979, when political opponents were brutally tortured and murdered. Traditional tribal government, however, has its own democratic forms based on consensus, a process apparent even in many of the one-party states of contemporary Africa. Indeed, some of the new states, notably Kenya,

Tanzania, Senegal, and Zambia, have achieved considerable domestic stability based on well-established negotiating techniques between various interest groups. The success of this return to African tradition demonstrates that Western forms of government may not be the most appropriate vehicles of political stability.

The sheer number and diversity of the African states precludes all but the broadest generalizations about them. Throughout its history, Africa's physical geography has played a large part in establishing and reinforcing cultural patterns, and this remains true today, in spite of improvements in communications and transport. The Sahara remains a formidable barrier between northern and central Africa, although the new states of Mauritania, Mali, Niger, Chad, and Sudan straddle its southern limits. North and south of the Sahara are different worlds. To the north lies the Arab-dominated Mediterranean coastal plain known as the Mahgreb. South of the Sahara stretches a succession of semiarid savannah, rain forest, and mountain country. As we have seen, Islam crossed the great desert and spread into parts of black Africa, but the central rain forest area—the "big bush," as Africans still call it—repelled nearly all outside contacts until the imperialist rush of the late nineteenth century.

The Achievement of Independence

Ghana was the first African colony to win independence in 1957. It had been the British colony of Gold Coast, so named for the early coastal trade in gold. Its American-educated leader, Kwame Nkrumah, began to win a reputation as an oppressive dictator and in 1966 was overthrown. The effects of his mismanagement and his squandering of Ghana's resources outlasted his disappearance. The parliamentary democracy that was established in 1969, to the initial satisfaction of both the armed forces and the people, had little chance to show whether it could improve on the record of Nkrumah's one-party state, since it inherited the debts and empty treasury of its predecessors. In 1972 the army took control, and in succeeding years Ghana has yet to achieve effective cohesion or sustained economic growth.

Like Ghana, Nigeria was plagued by conflicts among its many tribal and cultural groups after achieving independence in 1960. Northern Nigeria extends into the savannah borders of the Sahara, while the southern and coastal areas are in the rain forest. Different cultures had evolved in each, breaking down in turn into distinct local or regional districts. The major rival groups were the Hausa of the north, who had been converted to Islam by the Mali traders of the fourteenth century, and the southern and coastal Ibo. These latter had benefited from the fact that Nigeria's colonial capital was at Lagos, on the coast. The effects of British administration were more pronounced in the coastal region than in the interior, and the Ibo were thus in general better educated and more involved in the contemporary world.

When an Ibo army officer murdered the Hausa prime minister and seized power in 1966, Hausa tribesmen massacred Ibo living in northern Nigeria. In response, in 1967 the Ibo east of the Niger River seceded as the Republic of Biafra. The central government fought a long campaign against them, which dragged on with great suffering and bloodshed until the rebels surrendered in 1970 and were reincorporated into the Nigerian state. New discoveries of large coastal and offshore oil reserves brought a welcome infusion of revenues and general prosperity, helping to heal the internal divisions; in 1979 civil government was restored. Nigeria's economy has become one of the fastest-growing in Africa, although the fluctuating international price of oil has introduced elements of instability; it remains to be seen whether domestic differences can be managed in the long run.

In contrast to the more laissez-faire style of the British, the French attempted to mold the future destinies of their colonies by controlling the terms of their independence. The de Gaulle government offered to all French black African territories the choice of independence or autonomy as separate self-governing states within a French "community." This federation, presided over by France, would deal with matters of common interest such as foreign policy and defense. In the referendum that followed, France's technique for protecting its own self-interest seemed to have worked, since every territory except Guinea voted for autonomy within the community. By the end of 1960, however, virtually all of France's African possessions had followed Guinea's example and negotiated their independence.

Perhaps the most stable state to emerge from the French colonial empire has been Senegal, whose country's first leader, Léopold Senghor, retained power into the mid-1970s. Its stabilization was made easier by its relatively small size and by the fact that its capital, Dakar, the former capital of French Africa, was a modern center whose port provides access to international markets.

In 1960 Belgium abruptly pulled out of the Congo. Regional rivalries erupted into civil war, and the copper-rich southern province of Katanga seceded under its own leader, Moise Tshombe. After United Nations troops had helped to restore order, and following the CIA-sponsored assassination of Patrice Lumumba, the military regime of General Joseph Mobutu established firmer control and changed the country's name to Zaïre. Its subsequent history has been troubled by the conflicts of rival groups. Economic development has lagged, although Zaïre temporarily benefited from a rise in copper prices in the 1970s.

Trouble in the Congo spilled into neighboring Angola, where prolonged guerrilla warfare finally forced the Portuguese to withdraw in 1975 without establishing a fully effective government. The consequence was a civil war in which three separate liberation movements fought for control of the country. At first the right-wing Union for the Total Independence of Angola (UNITA), whose forces were reinforced by South African troops, seemed victorious, but the South African contingent provoked further intervention. The rival People's Movement for the Liberation of Angola (MPLA) received support from Communist countries, especially Cuba. With this help, the MPLA extended its control over the greater part of Angola, defeating both the forces of UNITA and of a third group, the National Liberation Front (FNL), whose main support came from across the border in Zaïre. The MPLA is generally recognized as the successor of the Portuguese governing authority, and a settlement of the fighting has been negotiated.

In East Africa, Tanganyika won independence in 1961 and in 1964 merged with the nearby island of Zanzibar to form the state of Tanzania. Its gifted leader, Julius Nyerere, attracted Chinese aid in railway building while adhering to the same neutralist course followed by many non-Western countries. Following Chinese and Indian models, he promoted cooperative schemes on a village basis to stimulate agricultural growth. Lacking Kenya's resources, Tanzania was further plagued by drought and poor soil. Nyerere retired from national politics in 1986; it remains to be seen if his country can survive its natural weaknesses and maintain a stable government.

Nyerere's generally high reputation was due in part to his style of rule. Unlike many of his fellow African leaders, he and his party maintained broad contact with Tanzanian society, avoiding the ostentatious paraphernalia of presidential palaces and limousines seen elsewhere. The moral authority gained from his concern with popular welfare buttressed Nyerere's main external concern: opposition to white oppression in southern Africa and help to black resistance there.

In Kenya the last years of British rule were rent by bitter conflict with the Mau Mau, a secret terrorist society among the dominant Kikuyu tribe sworn to kill or drive out all white settlers. By 1960 the movement was suppressed, and Jomo Kenyatta, the first president of independent Kenya, emerged from 11 years of prison and detention imposed for his involvement in the Mau Mau society. In power, Kenyatta proved moderate and led one of the most stable of African governments. By retaining the presence and support of at least some of the Europeans and Asians who had controlled Kenya's businesses during the colonial period, he avoided serious economic breakdown. By the time of his death in 1978, the country was sufficiently secure to allow for a peaceful transfer of power to his successor, Daniel arap Moi.

JOMO KENYATTA: KENYA'S FOUNDING FATHER

The grandson of a Kikuyu medicine man, Kenyatta, who was himself uncertain as to the day and year of his birth,

Black Power

The aspirations of African blacks to direct their own destiny was eloquently stated in 1960 by Rashidi Mfaume Kawawa, who would later succeed Julius Nyerere as prime minister of Tanganyika.

The demand for Africanization is made by the black people and means a replacement by them of those of different origin. Despite the wider meaning that the term African has acquired today, the blacks are still at the bottom of every ladder and identify themselves completely and practically with the struggle for change. To ask the indigenous Africans to forget the agony of their past is to ask them to ignore the lesson that their experience has taught them. Asians and Europeans are crying in Tanganyika today for non-racial parties, but just how practical is this? Those non-racial political parties which have been formed in Tanganyika have never succeeded, for they never aimed at emancipating the African, but only at deluding him into satisfaction with the lowest rung. It is the experience of the present that will constitute African reaction in the future; and the place that the Asian and the European will build for themselves in Africa will be governed by the degree of sacrifice they are prepared to make in the cause of a life in joint advancement and dedication with and amongst the Africans.

Source: R. Segal, *African Profiles* (Baltimore: Penguin Books, 1962), pp. 113–114.

was probably born in 1891. The name by which he is known is a nickname: *Kenyatta* refers to the beaded belt, or *kinyata,* that he always wore, and *Jomo* means "burning spear" in the Kikuyu dialect.

Much of Kenyatta's youth was spent traveling in Europe. When he returned to Nairobi in the 1920s, he joined the Kikuyu Central Association and began to involve himself in his country's future. In 1929 and again in 1931 he went to London to argue his tribe's rights to the land on which it had settled. The British government refused to grant his request but allowed the Kikuyu to establish their own schools. Over the following years Kenyatta spent much of his time in Britain, studying at the London School of Economics and writing anthropological studies of his people, as well as an autobiography, *Facing Mount Kenya* (1938), that became a bible of the independence movement.

In October 1945 Kenyatta was one of the organizers of a pan-African congress in Manchester. The theme of the congress was "Africa for the Africans," and among the participants was Kwame Nkrumah, the future leader of Ghana. The congress emphasized the common goals of the independence movement for all Africans. When Kenyatta returned to Kenya, he was elected president of the Kenya African Union, a political party that sought to combine and unify Kenya's tribes. While urging his people to act with discipline and integrity, he fought for African voting rights, the elimination of discrimination based on race, and the return of land to its original owners.

Jomo Kenyatta, first president of independent Kenya. [© Jason Laure 1977/Woodfin Camp]

In the face of British resistance to these demands, the Mau Mau movement developed. Kenyatta tried to dissociate himself and his party from the terrorists, but in 1952 he was accused of masterminding the Mau Mau and was put on trial. Despite questionable evidence, Kenyatta was convicted and sent to jail. Although much of his political base was drawn from Mau Mau support, he himself always professed his innocence.

By the late 1950s it became clear that Kenya would follow the example of Ghana and obtain independence. The principal political party, by now known as the Kenya African Nationalist Union, refused to make any moves to form a government as long as Kenyatta was imprisoned, and in 1961 he was finally freed from detention. Returning in triumph to his home territory, he became the first president of the new Republic of Kenya in 1964.

Avoiding recriminations or resentment against white Kenyans, Kenyatta aimed at forging a broad consensus of support among blacks and whites alike. He firmly rejected Communist efforts to gain a base in Kenya, declaring that his country would not "exchange one master for a new master." Although his government made every effort to involve native Kenyans in the economic and administrative organization of his country, it also encouraged European and Asian settlers to remain, as long as they accepted African leadership. For the first decade or so of Kenya's independence, Europeans continued to occupy key government posts. In neighboring Uganda, by contrast, non-Africans were expelled and their land was confiscated.

Kenyatta was married four times. A man of enormous vitality, he came to represent the new Africa on the international stage. Never losing his contact with his origins—while president he lived on a farm outside Nairobi, the capital, and regularly worked on the land—he was a familiar figure at international conferences and world assemblies such as the United Nations. Wearing alternately the finest of tailored suits and resplendent tribal robes, he represented not only his country but also the ideal of an African unity that combined modernity and tradition. A British administrator who worked with him described him as a man with "a sense of destiny but also a sense of humility." He died, still in office, in 1978.

South Africa

The tormented history of South Africa is bedeviled not only by conflict between black and white but by division among the white ruling class as well. The British and the Dutch-descended Boers were the primary European settlers in the region, although the discovery of gold in the

1880s drew an influx of immigrants from eastern Europe, many of them Jews who founded important communities in and around Johannesburg. By the 1920s subsequent waves of immigration had swelled the Jewish population of South Africa to 100,000.

At the beginning of the twentieth century "race relations" referred to dealings between the British and the Boers. By the time the four British colonies that formed the Union of South Africa came together in 1910, the only nonwhite Africans permitted to vote were those of the former territory of the Cape of Good Hope, a right that was subsequently abolished. The division between the Afrikaners, as the Boers came to be called, and the English settlers effectively blocked any chance of the nonwhite population's obtaining political rights. Furthermore, although the Afrikaners led the opposition to nonwhite participation in government and in the country's social and economic management—all of South Africa's prime ministers from 1910 to the present have been Afrikaners—the British community did little to promote nonwhite interests. The United party, the main political opposition movement to the white Nationalists, advised moderation while never contesting the guiding principle of Nationalist policy, segregation.

By the end of World War II white South Africans made up less than a fifth of the country's population. Nonwhites included over a million Indians who had settled there since the nineteenth century and the descendants of mixed European and African parentage, officially called "Coloureds." The largest black groups were of the Bantu and Hottentot tribes. South African policy centered on *apartheid* ("separateness"), which segregated whites and nonwhites in separate living areas and denied nonwhites access to any but the most menial jobs. Black Africans were assigned to drought-ridden and sparsely populated areas, first called "reserves" and then in the 1960s and 1970s nominally independent states, or "homelands," such as Bophuthatswana, Venda, and the Transkei.

The Afrikaners, who still speak a version of Dutch called Afrikaans, have retained their Calvinist religious beliefs, coupled with the conviction that the superiority of whites over blacks is God-ordained. African efforts at political expression are suppressed, the press is heavily censored, and "emergency laws," renewed at frequent intervals, have created broad police powers and subverted the constitutional system of justice. The largest black African resistance organization, the African National Congress (ANC), founded as early as 1912, helped to organize strikes, boycotts, and mass demonstrations. In 1959 a more radical alternative appeared in the Pan-African Congress, but antigovernment demonstrations led to reprisals by the whites, symbolized for many by the massacre of black demonstrators by white forces in 1960 at Sharpeville. The active black struggle for independence may be dated from that event. The violent suppression of political demonstrations, including a bloody police action in the black township of Soweto in 1976, has characterized the official South African response to the black demand for freedom.

The South African regime has persistently refused to accept the authority of the ANC to represent black interests. In 1983 nonwhites of Indian descent and Coloureds were admitted to a limited form of franchise with the formation of a "lower house of parliament," but black South Africans remain unrepresented and generally excluded from South Africa's economic prosperity. The ANC's leading spokesman, Nelson Mandela (born 1918), has been in jail for almost two decades; his wife, Winnie, kept his

Casualties of South Africa's brutal attempts to maintain apartheid: Sharpeville, 1960. [UPI/Bettmann Newsphotos]

Apartheid and the Oppression of Women

The brutality of apartheid is particularly apparent in its effects on black family life.

Widowhood—a life of void and loneliness; a period of tension, unbalance, and strenuous adjustment. And what can it be to those thousands of African women—those adolescent girls married before they reach womanhood, thrown into a life of responsibility before they have completely passed from childhood to adulthood; those young women in the prime of early womanhood left to face life alone, burdened with the task of building a home and rearing a family; those young women doomed to nurse alone their sick babies, weep alone over their dead babies, dress and bury alone their corpses? What can it mean to those young brides whose purpose has been snatched away, overnight, leaving them bewildered and lost, leaving them with a thirst and hunger that cannot be stilled?

And yet this is the daily lot of tens of thousands of African women whose husbands are torn away from them to go and work in the cities, mines, and farms—husbands who because of the migratory labor system cannot take their wives with them and, because of the starvation wages they receive, are forced to remain in the work centers for long periods—strangers in a strange land—but equally strangers at home to their wives and children.

These women remain alone in the Reserves to build the homes, till the land, rear the stock, bring up the children. They watch alone the ravages of drought, when the scraggy cows cease to provide the milk, when the few stock drop one by one because there is no grass on the veld, and all the streams have been lapped dry by the scorching sun. They watch alone the crops in the fields wither in the scorching sun, their labor of months blighted in a few days. They witness alone the hailstorm sweep clean their mealie lands, alone they witness the wind lift bodily their huts as if they were pieces of paper, rendering them and their children homeless. Alone they bury their babies one by one and lastly their unknown lovers—their husbands, whose corpses alone are sent back to the Reserves. For the world of grinding machines has no use for men whose lungs are riddled with . . . miner's phthisis [tuberculosis of the lungs].

Source: P. Ntantala, in *The Africa Reader: Independent Africa*, ed. W. Cartey and M. Kilson (New York: Vintage Books, 1970), pp. 306–307.

name—and his views—alive by her frequent public statements and appearances until the violence associated with her followers removed her from the scene. The main white opponent of apartheid throughout the 1960s and 1970s was also a woman, Helen Suzman. In the 1980s a new leader of moderate black African resistance appeared in the person of the Reverend Desmond Tutu, who was awarded the Nobel peace prize in 1984 for his efforts in the struggle against apartheid.

If there is any immediate sign of hope in the face of the regime's intransigence, it can perhaps be found in the informal dialogue between the ANC and some of the most prominent of South Africa's business leaders. The talks, begun in 1986, have continued sporadically. By far the richest and most industrially developed country in Africa, as well as the world's principal supplier of gold and diamonds, South Africa remains the last white-ruled state in sub-Saharan Africa.

North Africa

The world of North Africa was vastly different from that of the rest of the continent. Because it had been a center of Arabic culture for centuries, many of the newly emerging states either returned to earlier forms of government or at least had a single predominant cultural group formed by the native Arab population.

The independent nations of North Africa have been plagued by many of the same problems. Despite the predominance of Islam, tribal and religious divisions have ob-

Helen Suzman, a member of the South African Parliament, has been an outspoken opponent of apartheid. [William Campbell/Sygma]

structed the effectiveness of national governments. Most are dependent on the fluctuations of international commodity prices. Although population growth is unchecked, chronic food shortages and disease have caused widespread poverty and suffering. In addition, many nominally independent states continue to be dominated and manipulated by their former colonizers. The phenomenon of neocolonialism is particularly obvious in the case of France's former possessions.

The former French North African colonies have witnessed the triumphant revival of Islam. In Morocco and Tunisia the process of decolonization was relatively peaceful. Tunisia was allowed local autonomy in 1954 and became a republic in 1957, with Bourguiba as its president. The Islamic monarchy of Morocco was restored to its full powers in 1956. In Algeria, by contrast, the independence struggle was among the bitterest in Africa. Its liberation movement, the FLN, was openly aided by Egypt, Tunisia, and Morocco. Against the background of violent public division at home, the French army in Algeria revolted, and in 1958 France's wartime hero, General de Gaulle, was placed at the head of the French state.

De Gaulle confounded the expectations of his military supporters by negotiating Algeria's independence. In 1962 the country became an independent Muslim republic, threatened in its first years by the attempts of the former Algerian colonists to undermine its existence as well as by divisions within the FLN. The combined wars of the French against the Algerian nationalists and the subsequent struggles of both French and Algerians to repress the colonists' resistance have left inevitable scars. In the late 1960s the Algerians retreated into a period of isolation from international affairs from which they emerged as an active neutralist state.

The French withdrawal from North Africa, together with the creation of the state of Israel and the resulting hostility of the Arab world, led to the disappearance of the Jewish communities that had flourished there under colonial protection since the nineteenth century. A large number of the Jews of Tunis and almost the entire Jewish population of Algeria migrated to France and Israel. The Jewish settlement in Morocco, which at 250,000 had been the largest in Africa, was reduced to a fifth of its former size.

The most extreme appearance of fundamentalist Islam in North Africa has been in Libya, a former Italian colony, which was administered by Britain from 1942 to 1951. With its independence it became a conservative Muslim kingdom, whose ruler was the spiritual leader of the Sanussi, a Muslim sect whose opposition to Mussolini's rule had resulted in brutal Fascist repression in the 1920s. In 1969, however, the monarchy was overthrown in a coup led by Colonel Muammar al-Qaddafi.

Qaddafi's histrionic ability to command world attention has depended on three factors: the vast revenues accumulated by Libya from its oil supplies, Soviet attempts to gain control in the region by providing Libya with military and financial aid, and Qaddafi's underwriting of terrorist groups operating in many parts of the world. The results have won Libya the hostility of much of the Western world, together with uncomfortable acceptance by many Arab neighbors. Since 1980 the Libyans have been embroiled in a civil war in neighboring Chad, a former French colony, that has brought them into open conflict with French forces. Skirmishes in 1985 and 1986 resulted in both sides retreating and the informal negotiation of an uncertain peace.

Libya's most dramatic, or at least most publicized, international activity has been the encouragement of terrorism on a worldwide scale. Much of this may well have been vocal rather than practical, principally intended to make headlines. In 1986, however, American planes bombed Libya in reprisal for alleged Libyan involvement in terrorist incidents and narrowly missed killing Qaddafi himself. The subsequent retaliation threatened by Libya did not materialize, and Qaddafi's own position may well have been shaken by the American attack, although the long-term consequences are impossible to foresee.

In Ethiopia, with the expulsion of the Italians in 1941, Haile Selassie returned to power. Unlike its neighbors, Ethiopia was Christian by tradition, although many of its customs, including slavery, had been adopted from Muslim practice. Ethiopia's geographic position at a key location on the Red Sea gave it an increasing importance following World War II, but imperial rule did little to modernize the country. After a period of growing chaos, characterized by student demonstrations, army mutinies, and reports of corruption in high circles, a serious famine brought the regime to crisis. In 1974 the emperor was deposed and replaced by a group of army officers; united only in their opposition to Haile Selassie, they ranged from moderates to extreme radicals.

Within a short time the radicals had gained control, and since then they have dismantled Ethiopia's traditional feudal system and replaced it with a repressive one-party state. The resulting disruption in food production has been only partly offset by Soviet aid after 1978. Soviet weapons and Cuban troops have been used against two of Ethiopia's long-standing enemies, Somalia and insurgents in the Ethiopian province of Eritrea. The latter staged a rebellion in the mid-1970s with the help of Arab states; by 1980 the revolt was firmly suppressed. The Somalis, meanwhile, have been forced to abandon their attempts to "liberate" the Ethiopian province of Ogaden, whose principal inhabitants are Somali nomads.

Throughout the Sahel region, which includes much of Ethiopia and Somalia, an already difficult situation was made even worse by a widespread famine that took a large toll of life in the mid-1980s. Western attempts to provide aid were in large measure frustrated by local bureaucratic inefficiency and corruption.

From the time it attained political independence in 1956, the Sudan was divided between its Muslim north and Christian south. The threat of an Egyptian attack, coupled with the increasing ineffectiveness of party government, provoked a military coup in 1958. Subsequent years have seen an alteration of democratic and military rule and the short-lived secession in 1974 of the southern part of the country. The deposition of the Sudan's military head, Colonel Gaafar Nimeiri, in 1985 has yet to lead to the secure return of democracy in a country devastated by famines in the mid-1980s.

In the decades following the end of World War II every part of the continent except for South Africa underwent significant political and social change. Despite modernization, however, women remain largely confined to traditional roles. Poverty and illiteracy continue to afflict the women of sub-Saharan Africa, who are also still subject to clan-arranged marriages and, in many places, polygamy. Drought, starvation, forced migration, civil war, and the AIDS epidemic have compounded these problems in recent years, as has the urbanization that has broken up old communal relationships in which men and women worked side by side. In sub-Saharan countries a large proportion of women are involved in subsistence farming. In the cities female underemployment is particularly acute and paid jobs are the exception. Legal equality has gradually emerged, as elsewhere, and Ghana in 1960 took the unprecedented step of reserving ten seats in the national assembly for women. Women have long been active in handicraft production and trading, and when organized they have been formidable: thousands of Ibo women staged a tax rebellion in eastern Nigeria in 1923 that left 50 people dead.

Economic growth and political stability have proved hard to achieve and harder still to maintain, and the future of many African countries remains uncertain at best. If one cause unites so diverse a range of nations, it is opposition to continued white domination in South Africa. The Organization of African Unity, first formed in 1963, has articulated this common African concern while serving a broader, less tangible ideal, African "community," which inspired many of the leaders who guided their nations to independence.

South America: Reform and Revolution

Throughout most of Latin America the mood at the beginning of the twentieth century was one of confidence and optimism. But as the century nears its end, the economic and political progress of the early decades of independence after 1821 has been checked and, in some places, even reversed. Few Latin American governments, democratic or not, have found lasting solutions to the basic social and economic problems that beset the region.

Poverty and overpopulation remain endemic. Wealth and land continue to be concentrated in the hands of a privileged elite that sometimes represents as little as 2 percent of the population and has often protected its own landed and commerical interests by supporting undemocratic regimes. The deep-rooted social ills that afflict Latin American society are revealed in huge cities such as Buenos Aires and Mexico City, where millions live in overcrowded squalor. The Catholic church has maintained its influence throughout the region. Although at a local level pastoral workers have sought to improve living conditions for the poor, the official image of the church has been compromised in places by its lack of public opposition to repressive regimes.

The main force behind the maintenance of political repression has been the military. Since the mid-nineteenth century Latin American political life has been dominated by an endless series of crises and coups provoked by the

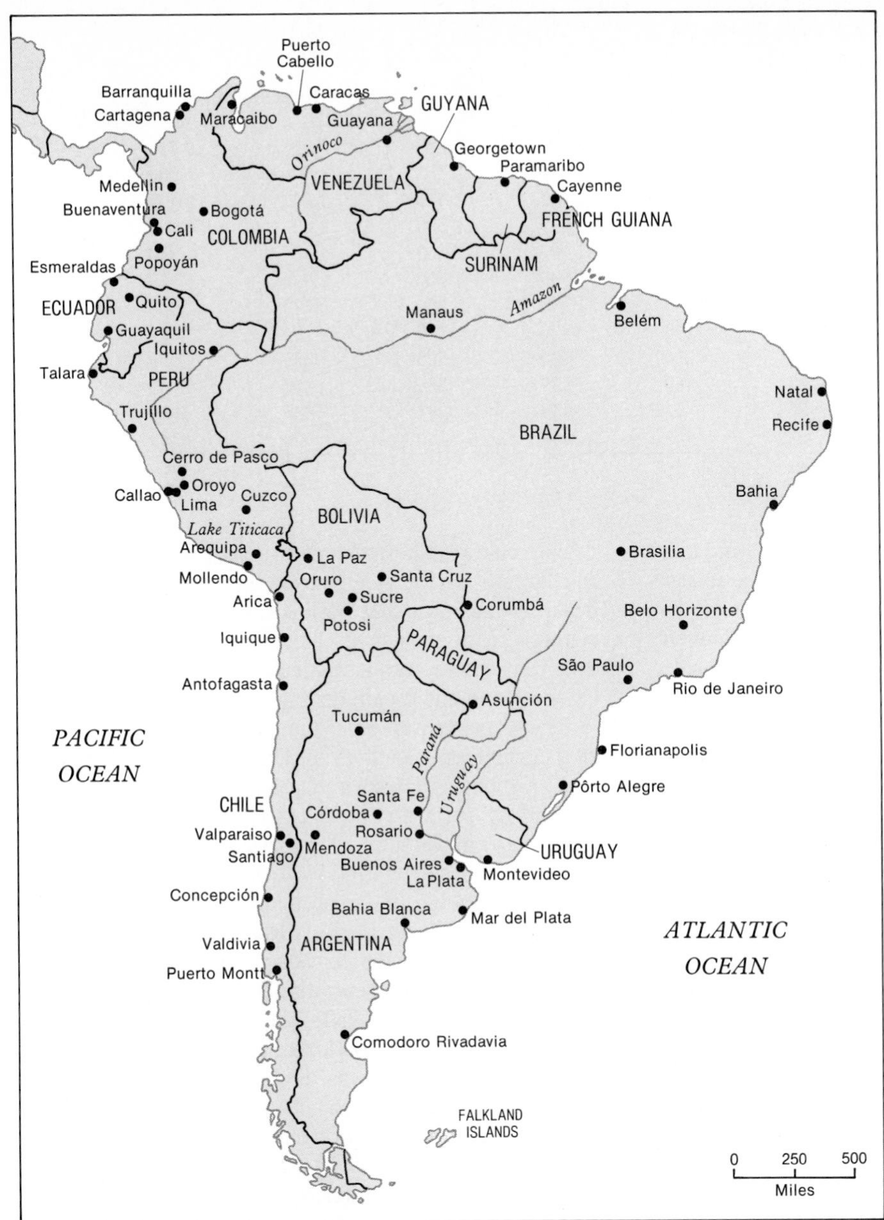

40.2 Modern South America

intervention of the army in civil affairs. Once in power, military leaders have retained control by co-opting the support of the landed and business classes. With the notable exception of Perón in Argentina, these so-called *caudillo* figures have lacked both charisma and broad-based popular support.

In economic terms, most Latin American countries are dependent on the export of raw materials and therefore at the mercy of world prices and demand. Continuing political instability has impeded the consistent development of natural resources and industrial production for the benefit of the population at large. The problems of financial instability have been further compounded by the inability of countries such as Mexico and Brazil to repay the vast loans made to them by international organizations and foreign banks.

Each nation in Latin America faces its own special problems, in some cases created by its history and in others by its natural environment. Yet for the most part political life has been determined by a single basic principle: revolution, or sudden changes of authority, that merely redistribute power within the old elite. Only in a few instances has the new leadership produced significant change. In Chile a military coup overthrew a left-wing gov-

THE GROWTH OF LATIN AMERICAN CITIES

	Population (in thousands)					
	1940	1950	1960	1970	1980	Mid-1980s
Buenos Aires (Argentina)	2,410	5,213	7,000	9,400	9,927	10,728
Mexico City (Mexico)	1,560	2,872	4,910	8,567	12,000+	17,000
Rio de Janeiro (Brazil)	1,159	3,025	4,692	5,155	5,542	5,615
Lima-Callao (Peru)	—	947	1,519	2,500	4,601	6,000
Santiago (Chile)	952	1,275	1,907	2,600	4,309	4,750
Havana (Cuba)	936	1,081	1,549	1,700	1,935	1,970
Guayaquil (Ecuador)	—	259	450	800	1,279	1,387
Guatemala City (Guatemala)	186	294	474	770	754	1,800
La Paz (Bolivia)	—	300	400	500	635	950
San Salvador (El Salvador)	103	162	239	375	400	—[a]
Tegucigalpa (Honduras)	86	72	159	281	485	550
Managua (Nicaragua)	63	109	197	350	608	730

[a]*No accurate figures available after 1980.*

ernment in 1973 and installed a repressive right-wing dictatorship. In Bolivia the 192 changes of government that had taken place by 1985 only worsened its problems.

Since the days of the Monroe Doctrine, the United States has assumed an important and often decisive role in Latin American affairs. In its quest for territorial expansion in the 1840s, the United States seized huge tracts of Mexican territory that later became Texas and California, and in the 1890s it stripped Cuba and Puerto Rico from Spain. Thereafter, a combination of economic and security interests led Washington not only to limit the influence of European powers in Latin America but also to intervene unilaterally in the region. Yet the role played by the United States has varied greatly from one country to another. American involvement in Central American politics increased in the 1980s, and in more repressive regimes such as Chile, the United States has sometimes encouraged their leaders to mitigate the harsher effects of military rule. Direct U.S. intervention established and supported dictatorial regimes in Nicaragua, Haiti, Guatemala, and the Dominican Republic. Successive American administrations have never accepted a left-of-center regime except in Mexico or done more than tolerate centrist governments. When Argentina became embroiled with Britain in 1982 over the Falkland Islands (Islas Malvinas), Washington secretly supported its European ally while professing neutrality. In all cases, American authorities carefully monitor, influence, and often determine events throughout Latin America.

Brazil: The Unstable Giant

Brazil, which occupies almost half of the South American continent—some 3 million square miles—and has a population of more than 140 million, is a far more varied nation than its neighbors. Whereas the other countries in Central and South America speak the Spanish of their conquerors, Brazil's cultural inheritance is mixed. The official language and culture derive chiefly from Brazil's Catholic Portuguese colonizers. That heritage is supplemented by the cultures of the indigenous Indian population and the Africans whose ancestors were imported as slaves in the seventeenth and eighteenth centuries.

The waves of European immigrants who came to Brazil in the nineteenth century included a sizable number of Jews. Continuing Jewish immigration was brought to a halt in 1930 by restrictive legislation, and in 1937 a secret order was circulated to all Brazilian consulates to reject visa applications submitted by Jews. In spite of official discrimination, however, small numbers of skilled workers and professionals escaped to Brazil from Nazi Germany. After World War II the Jewish population rose gradually to about 150,000, concentrating in the larger cities.

In Brazil during the 1930s and 1940s the rule of Getúlio Vargas introduced a period of relative economic and political stability. When Vargas died in 1954, the alliance between nationalism and capitalism that he had forged and maintained for a quarter of a century collapsed. The same forces that produced conflict elsewhere in South America now pitted themselves against each other in Brazil: the working class and the peasants on the one hand, and the landowning elite and the military on the other. This conflict unfolded against uncontrolled economic expansion based on foreign loans, used mostly for grandiose public works projects that resulted in profiteering and disastrous inflation.

Expensive public projects took an enormous toll in foreign exchange and political stability. The consequence was growing inflation and an increase in social tension. In 1964 a military government seized power, holding it for a generation. Successive military governments held occasional elections but refused to relinquish control. Although the country has made progress toward economic stability, the gap between the prosperous business class and the poor continues to widen. Uncontrolled development and specu-

The *favelas* of Rio de Janeiro: slums where a quarter of the city's people live in squalid shanties without water or sewers. [Bruno Barbey/Magnum]

lation have led to the spoliation of much of Brazil's land, especially in the Amazon basin. Political repression produced the familiar pattern of rigid censorship, police brutality, and human rights abuse.

By 1975 serious strains had developed in relations between Brazil and the United States. In addition to concern over Brazil's public image as a police state, Washington was alarmed at its growing involvement with nuclear technology. When the Carter administration reduced military aid, the Brazilians retaliated by canceling their military pact with the United States.

From 1979 to 1985 Brazil's military rulers slowly moved toward the reestablishment of civilian government. After parliamentary elections in 1982, a coalition of opposition groups, the Democratic Alliance, chose as its candidate for the presidency Tancredo Neves, a trusted and popular figure. His successor, José Sarney, lacked the ability to command a consensus, and the rest of 1985 was marked by a series of paralyzing strikes. Coming on top of a disastrous drought that devastated Brazil's coffee crop, a major source of exchange, the industrial unrest forced Sarney's government into action. Prices and wages were frozen, and negotiations with the International Monetary Fund and private banks rescheduled Brazil's debts.

Economically, Brazil's future seems unclear. A major steel industry has emerged; exports of goods such as chemicals, shoes, and automobiles are increasing; and minerals such as iron and bauxite are bringing in foreign currency. Nonetheless, the repayment of its foreign debts—the largest in the world—reached the breaking point in 1987, when Brazil suspended payments as inflation reached 365 percent per annum. The democratic government has yet to deal with the country's social inequities and has failed to implement land reform. Yet the spirit of optimism that led to the creation of Brasilia is characteristic of Brazilian popular culture and may help the country weather its current crisis.

BRASILIA: THE PLANNED CITY

While Brazil faced financial collapse in the 1950s, its president, Juscelino Kubitschek, inaugurated the country's most ambitious public undertaking, a new capital city, Brasilia. The scheme, commissioned in 1957, was designed to give visible form to the government's faith in Brazil's future. The new capital was situated in the plains of the state of Goias, 600 miles inland. Within three years the master plan of Lucio Costa and the buildings of the architect Oscar Niemeyer had taken sufficient shape for the government to move there. As in Chandigarh, the Indian planned city designed by Le Corbusier, a major city was laid out from the beginning with an eye to its total physical and architecture design, as well as a concern for the day-to-day needs of its inhabitants.

The central part of the city, set on two main axes, north-south and east-west, is surrounded by an artificial lake that divides it from the suburbs. Most of the public buildings are set on the east-west—or "monumental"—axis. At its east end, in the Square of Three Powers, are the legislative, judicial, and executive buildings of government. Given the region's relative inaccessibility, it was necessary to construct a new highway system to connect

Brasilia with Rio de Janeiro, the former capital and Brazil's largest city. Brasilia boasts huge water and waste disposal systems and is entirely electrified.

Additional building projects were undertaken in the following decades. The University of Brazil is the center of the city's cultural life, with its auditorium and public library. Public services such as hospitals and clinics and fire and police departments are extensive and modern. By the late 1980s the population had reached about 1.4 million. Many of the original inhabitants came from economically depressed areas of the country to work on the construction of the city, but they have now been supplemented by those employed in local industries, which include printing, furniture, and services.

Brasilia has proved both daring and controversial. The notion of moving Brazil's capital to the interior goes back to the days of Portuguese rule and had been discussed again in the 1820s. Rio de Janeiro certainly exercised a cultural and social monopoly that many Brazilians found stifling. Moreover, the new city is a prosperous one. However, the architectural plans have been criticized as an example of utopian controlled design derived from a Bauhaus aesthetic with totalitarian overtones.

The artificial nature of the project has produced a city that is an exception to most great urban centers throughout the world, which have been almost always the result of a long period of human habitation, the products of accumulated human experience. Diplomats "exiled" to Brasilia complain of its arid climate and the shantytowns that have sprung up around it. Other countries that have followed Brazil's example, such as Nigeria with the construction of a new capital at Abuja, have met with mixed success. Yet the daring speed with which the scheme has been executed, together with the breadth of the concept, compels admiration. Certainly the creation of Brasilia has marked a commitment to urban living as the future basis of a nation that is still predominantly agrarian.

Argentina: Dictatorship and Democracy

Ever since Argentina's first struggles to win freedom from Spain in the early nineteenth century, political stability has proved elusive. The second largest country in Latin America, after Brazil, Argentina covers an area of just over 1 million square miles and is home to 30 million inhabitants.

Unlike Ecuador, which has a large Indian population, or Colombia and Paraguay, which have mestizo (mixed Spanish and Indian) majorities, Argentinians are overwhelmingly of European origin. The waves of immigrants, mainly Spanish and Italian, who flocked to Argentina in the nineteenth century produced conflicting interest groups that have proved difficult to reconcile. The industrialists of the capital city of Buenos Aires, the ranchers who control the great coastal estates, the farmers of the interior, and radical populists all vie for political recognition and power.

Among the European immigrants were large numbers of Jews attracted to Argentina by its relatively early industrialization. The Jewish community there, almost half a million in number, remains the largest in Latin America. The country's once liberal immigration policies changed, however, in the 1930s, when Argentina became a center of anti-Semitism. This trend continued after World War II as Argentina became a haven for escaped Nazi war criminals.

From the time of its rebellion against Spain in 1810, Argentina's history has been dominated by a series of caudillo rulers, most of whom were wealthy landowners or generals devoted to power and money. Only in 1916 were democratic radicals able to defeat the landowners and industrialists in Argentina's first open election and govern the country until 1930. But the Great Depression wrought havoc with the economy and induced the army to replace the government with a conservative coalition of bankers, landowners, and generals. This combination of interests has constituted the single most powerful force in Argentine politics ever since.

By the end of World War II the charismatic Colonel Juan Domingo Perón (1895–1974) had come to dominate the ruling clique. The archetypal caudillo, Perón's ability to mesmerize his fellow citizens owed much to the charm and brilliance of his wife Eva (1919–1952), once a popular radio announcer. By the time of her death, "Evita," who sponsored much of the regime's social reform programs despite her own opulent lifestyle, had become a popular folk heroine to her people. Her memory still remains a powerful force in Argentine politics.

With Eva's encouragement, Perón realized that his personal rule could not continue without the backing of the middle classes and the poor. Gaining control of the trade unions, he was elected president in 1946 with a large majority. Through skillful propaganda and careful attention to interest groups such as the church and the army, the Peróns retained the reluctant support of the right. At the same time, they introduced health and welfare benefits for the poor and stimulated jobs for the unemployed. These measures resulted in increased taxation, which brought a drop in agricultural production and export revenues. Financial chaos and corruption, together with the death of Eva, undermined support for Perón, who was deposed by the army in 1955.

A series of military regimes followed, alternating with brief periods of civilian rule. By 1973 Perón decided to end his exile in Spain and run for the presidency again. When the army refused to allow his candidacy, he put forward Hector Campora, a Peronist party worker, as his representative. Although Campora won, the Peronist victory led to a bloody civil struggle. In less than two months Campora was compelled to resign, Perón's opponents were forced into retirement, and new elections were

Eva Perón on Peronism

Juan Perón's dictatorship combined populism and nationalism into a political regime that in many ways resembled European fascism. Here Eva Perón, his wife and adviser and herself an important political figure, extolls Peronism with the kind of rhetoric that made the phenomenon so popular among Argentinians.

This is why we, the *peronistas*, may never forget the people; our heart must always be with the humble, the comrades, the poor, the dispossessed, for this is how to carry out best the doctrine of General Perón; and so that the poor, the humble, the working forces, and we ourselves, do not forget, we have pledged to be missionaries of Perón; to do this is to expand his doctrine, not only within our own country, but to offer it to the world as well, as a hope of the rewards always wished for by the working classes. . . .

General Perón has defeated internal capitalism, through social economy, putting capital at the service of the economy, and not vice versa, which only gave the workers the right to die of hunger: the law of the funnel, as it is called, the wide part for the capitalists and the narrow part for the people.

Perón has suppressed imperialist action. Now we have economic independence. He knows well all the insults he will receive for committing the "crime" of defending the country. Some Argentines allied themselves with foreigners in order to slander him, because General Perón was the first to make foreign powers respect Argentina, and treat it as an equal.

Source: E. Perón, *Historia del Peronismo* (Buenos Aires: Presidencia de la Nacion, 1951), trans. in R. Cameron, *Civilization Since Waterloo* (Itasca, Ill.: Peacock, 1971), pp. 529–531.

called. With his new wife, Isabel, as his running mate, Perón won by a large majority.

Perón's solutions to Argentina's massive problems were contradictory and self-defeating. While courting Communist countries such as Russia and Cuba, he instituted a repressive domestic policy. Liberal government officials and teachers were dismissed, and the left-wing opposition was crushed. Perón's failures may have been the result of ill health, which prevented him from controlling the conflicting forces within his coalition.

Isabel attempted to take her husband's place after his death in 1974, but the task proved impossible. Many Argentinians resented her efforts to portray herself as Evita's successor. Occupying the highest position ever held by a woman in the Western Hemisphere, the reclusive Isabel found herself unable to control her conspiring ministers. In the 21 months that she held office, she reorganized the cabinet ten times. Nor was she able to rectify Argentina's trade deficit or maintain a policy of economic

Juan and Eva Perón, who established a political system in Argentina that combined dictatorship with populist rhetoric and wide appeal. [Bettmann Archive]

austerity. Finally, the social life of the country was paralyzed by a rash of kidnappings and assassinations carried out by terrorists of both the left and the right. In 1976 yet another military coup—the sixth in 21 years—installed an army junta.

The army restored some order to the economy, increasing agricultural and industrial production and reducing inflation. The junta raised taxes and froze wages. In the face of mounting foreign debt, however, the value of the peso, the Argentine currency, fell, and the government devalued it by 70 percent. Thousands of political opponents were rounded up, tortured, and murdered. In protest, the United States suspended military aid to Argentina.

By 1982, with inflation and unemployment again increasing rapidly, the trade unions began a series of strikes, and the banned political parties called for a return to constitutional government. The regime, led by General Leopoldo Galtieri, sought to generate nationalist sentiment by challenging Britain for control of the Falkland Islands, a British Crown Colony. The Malvinas, as they are called in Latin America, are a group of barren, windswept islands off the southeast tip of Argentina inhabited mainly by sheepherders. In April 1982 Galtieri became an instant national hero when he ordered an invasion of the islands, but the government of British prime minister Margaret Thatcher, assisted by the United States, defeated Argentina.

The military government's popularity plummeted in the wake of its military defeat. The 1983 presidential campaign was won by a political moderate, Raúl Alfonsín. Despite his efforts to prosecute Galtieri and his associates for human rights violations, pressure from the army frustrated the process. Nevertheless, Alfonsín's election helped to restore international confidence in his country, and in 1986 he succeeded in negotiating loans from private banks in the United States and from the International Monetary fund. But lasting democratic solutions to the problems facing Argentina still remain an unrealized goal.

Chile and Peru: Socialism and the Military

Peru and Chile comprise most of South America's west coast. Both contain wide variations in climate and geography and have a population that is overwhelmingly mestizo. In Peru a left-wing military regime has given way to an unstable democracy, while in Chile a democratically elected socialist leader was replaced by a right-wing military dictatorship.

Throughout the nineteenth and early twentieth centuries Chilean politics were marked by continual struggles between the Liberal party, which first came to power in 1861, and the Conservatives, who represented the army and wealthy landowners. In 1920 the middle classes joined with the workers to bring the populist Arturo Alessandri Palma to power. While his government was ousted and reestablished, left-wing political parties continued to develop. In the 1930s the Radical party replaced the Liberals, while the Socialists and Communists grew in importance. Indeed, by the end of World War II the Communists were the focus of parliamentary opposition.

From 1946 to 1964, as coalitions formed by smaller parties replaced one another, public support for the left increased as a result of a well-organized labor movement. In 1970 Salvador Allende (1908–1973), a Marxist, came to power with a left-wing coalition government. Continuing support for Allende was demonstrated by large victories for his supporters in local elections the next year.

In his three years of power, Allende sought to redress many of Chile's social and economic inequities. Farms were distributed to peasants, who were provided with a wide range of social benefits. But Allende lacked the resources to pay for his programs, and deficit spending finally produced uncontrolled inflation.

Allende's government was isolated from abroad. His nationalization of American copper mines, together with other industries, led to the suspension of U.S. aid and trade. The United States even refused to sell food to Chile. The Soviets and the Chinese provided some help but not enough to offset a general boycott by non-Communist countries. Finally the army, with assistance from the American CIA, seized control in September 1973 and has remained in power ever since. Allende was slain during the coup.

Since the overthrow of Allende, Chile, one of South America's pioneers in democracy, has been governed by a repressive military dictatorship. Its leader, General Augusto Pinochet, proclaimed himself president. His well-documented policies of arbitrary arrests, torture, and executions led to a temporary suspension of American aid in 1979, although President Reagan restored it in 1981. Pinochet's constitution provided for his continued rule until 1997. Demonstrations of public opposition that marked 1985 and 1986 provoked brutal reprisals. Pinochet's presidential rule was repudiated in the elections of 1988, but he remains head of the armed forces and the effective head of the country. It is difficult to imagine a country more different from the revolutionary republic envisioned by its founders.

Like Chile, Peru was the scene of an experimental socialism, but under the unlikely direction of the army. A liberal reformist movement developed among the Peruvian educated classes in the early twentieth century. In 1924 this progressive coalition crystallized in the creation of the American Popular Revolutionary Alliance (APRA). Although anti-Communist, the APRA borrowed socialist ideas from Russia and western Europe and became the focus of an Indian rights movement. Most of Peru's history from the appearance of the APRA to 1968 consisted of periods of liberal government interrupted by army coups and military regimes.

The 1968 coup was unusual. The military leaders proclaimed a policy of "social democracy," intending to follow a middle way between capitalism and communism on the basis of a mixed economy. Banks, mines—some of them U.S.-owned—and other key industries were nationalized, and many large estates were distributed to peasants. Educational programs were expanded and social benefits introduced. The regime suppressed political opposition movements and censored the press.

The international effects of these policies were predictable. Russia sent money, weapons, and advisers, while in 1974 the Peruvian government expelled U.S. officials on charges of spying for the CIA. Peru became one of the leading advocates of Third World causes and an outspoken critic of American policies. As a result, foreign investment declined and Peru's economy began to collapse. Some industries were returned to their owners after 1975, but the damage had been done. By 1978 the regime returned the country to civilian rule.

Both of Peru's subsequently elected presidents have been drawn from the APRA. Their problems—a declining economy, massive debt, drug trafficking, and industrial unrest—have been compounded since 1983 by bands of guerrilla fighters in the countryside of southern Peru. Calling themselves *Sendero Luminoso* ("shining path," a quotation from Lenin), they are a splinter group of the Peruvian Communist party. In 1984 they were joined by another revolutionary movement, the *Tupac Amaru*, named after an eighteenth-century Indian who revolted against the Spaniards. The former group is active in rural areas; the latter operates primarily in the cities, including Lima, the capital. Together with the terrorist activites of cocaine traders, the guerrilla groups present serious problems. In 1987 President Alan García survived mutinies and public outrage against police and army brutality, but the future of his country remains troubled.

Bolivia: Land of Revolutions

Although the history of Bolivia, with its succession of military coups, superficially resembles that of Argentina, fundamental social differences prevail. The overwhelming majority of Bolivia's population is either of pure Indian or of mixed European and Indian descent. In the early days of independence after 1825 no educated middle class existed to run the state bureaucracy. Wealthy landowners were interested only in protecting their own interests. The military filled the vacuum with 50 years of misrule.

By the end of the nineteenth century political parties led by Bolivia's landed aristocracy had developed. The Liberal party exploited Bolivia's major resource, tin, and constructed road and rail networks throughout the country. The proceeds from these modernization programs further enriched the wealthy, who became known as the "tin barons," instead of improving living conditions for the poor.

By the 1930s most of Bolivia's mineral wealth had been sold to American investors, and the Great Depression devastated the economy. In 1932 conflict broke out between Bolivia and its southern neighbor, Paraguay, complicating an already difficult situation. The so-called Gran Chaco War ended in 1935 with Bolivia losing a sizable chunk of its territory.

Military governments continued into the postwar period. A brief attempt was made between 1937 and 1939 to introduce social reform for the workers, but its sponsor was murdered, and protests were brutally suppressed. Nevertheless, with great difficulty, Victor Paz Estenssoro managed to unify various urban protest groups into the National Revolutionary Movement (MNR) in 1941. A decade later the MNR won the national elections, but the army refused to allow Estenssoro to take power. Their action finally prompted a revolution that put Estenssoro in office as president.

In 1952 the new government took over the tin mines and raised workers' wages and benefits. Unfortunately, these moves coincided with a fall in tin prices on the world market, pointing up the danger of dependence on a single export. Not until 1966 did the mines return to their former profitability. Estenssoro also tried to redress the grievances of the Indians, most of whom lived in a condition of servitude that had changed little since the sixteenth century. The urban rebellion of the MNR had been accompanied by widespread uprisings and Indian land seizures in the countryside. The government recognized the claims of the Indians in 1953 and distributed land to the farmers.

The democratic government brought genuine social and economic improvement to Bolivia, but it failed to reduce the domination of the military, which seized power once more in 1964. Estenssoro returned to office in 1985 after 20 years marked by a succession of military coups. Most of the regimes were repressive and reactionary, although the pattern was briefly broken by General Juan José Torres, who seized power in 1970. Known for his left-wing sentiments, Torres relied on peasant, worker, and student support and convened a "people's parliament" to represent their views.

In 1972 he was deposed by Colonel Hugo Banzer, who remained in office for six years, a record in Bolivia's political history. Banzer attempted to introduce a coherent economic policy but also sold off the country's natural resources, including oil and natural gas, to foreign business interests. Although these measures stimulated economic growth, the rich gained most of the benefits. Another bewildering succession of coups marked the post-Banzer period. As unfavorable international reaction to drug trafficking and human rights violations grew, the United States broke diplomatic relations with Bolivia, forcing elections in 1982.

The new moderate government of Hernan Siles Zuazo appealed to foreign banks and the International Monetary Fund for help. The aid did little, however, to reduce inflation or satisfy worker demands. In the ensuing chaos, Estenssoro emerged once again, at the age of 77, as president. He promised economic and social reform, but lacking coherent political forces, or even a single charismatic figure such as Perón, Bolivia's history, already witness to 192 changes of government, persistently fulfills gloomy expectations.

Central America and the Caribbean

Private American businesses, especially the United Fruit Company and sugar, coffee, and tobacco firms, had entered Central America and the Caribbean in the late nineteenth century. The United States has maintained a more direct presence in the region since the Spanish-American War. In the wake of its victory over Spain in 1898, the United States declared a protectorate over Cuba and annexed Puerto Rico. Five years later, when Panamanian rebels revolted against Colombia, which claimed the territory of Panama, Washington supported the rebels and quickly imposed its control over the newly formed republic. Americans then built the Panama Canal on land leased from its new dependency. The strategic importance of the canal for the United States, together with extensive economic interests, have maintained the U.S. presence in the area ever since.

The Cuban Revolution

Cuba has been one of the most prominent nations in Latin America since 1959, when the country experienced a dramatic political upheaval that has challenged America's sway over the Central American region.

Fidel Castro (born 1927), a charismatic leader and brilliant propagandist, united forces opposed to the corrupt dictator Fulgencio Batista, who had ruled the island since 1936. Yet when Castro's guerrilla campaign overthrew Batista in 1959, his goals were unclear. Although he had plans to hold elections, he quickly suspended them. By 1961 he had begun introducing state economic and social controls and declared himself a Marxist-Leninist.

Castro's revolution aimed at a radical transformation of Cuba's social and economic structure. His socialist pro-

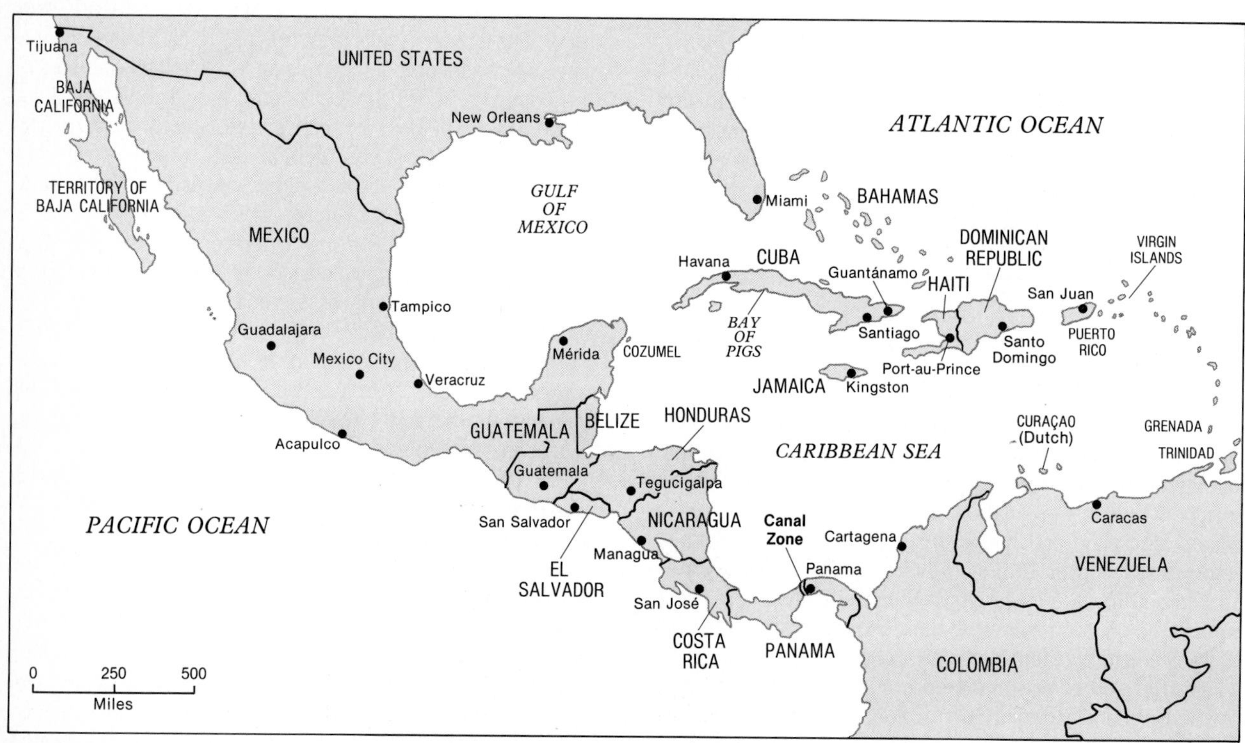

40.3 Mexico and Central America

grams drove much of the middle class—some 750,000 people—from the island, and many opponents who stayed were silenced by means of firing squads or imprisonment. Collective farms replaced the estates once owned by large landowners, and the government nationalized the sugar and tobacco industries. Moreover, significant social and educational reforms have improved the lives of Cuba's citizens, and today Cuba's infant mortality and illiteracy rates are the lowest in Latin America. Castro's reforms also gave women equality before the law and open access to education and the professions.

In many ways Cuba's history embodies the dilemma created by America's dealings with its southern neighbors. Batista's rule collapsed only after the withdrawal of informal American support in 1958. Yet Castro anticipated that his radical economic and social policies might bring American intervention. He therefore turned to the Soviet Union, which he hoped would serve as a counterweight to the United States. The Soviets proved powerful and willing patrons in return for a base of operations only 90 miles from the coast of Florida.

In April 1961 the United States sponsored a badly organized invasion by Cuban exiles at the Bay of Pigs on the southern coast of Cuba. The United States, reluctant to engage Cuban forces directly, refused air cover at the last moment, and the invaders were routed. The fiasco confirmed Castro's belief that American imperialism was poised to undermine him and encouraged the Russians to exploit their foothold in Cuba. Weapons, including intercontinental missiles, were deployed on the island, only to be withdrawn in 1962 when an alarmed American government confronted the Soviet Union.

In the 1960s Castro's Cuba served as a center for revolutionary aspirations throughout Latin America. Castro's chief aide in seizing power and organizing the new state had been Ernesto ("Che") Guevara (1928–1967). Guevara now became the principal theorist of guerrilla insurgency as a technique for bringing revolution to the rest of the Americas, personally encouraging rebel forces there and elsewhere. He was killed in Bolivia in October 1967 by U.S.-trained counterinsurgency forces, setting back Castro's policy of exporting revolution.

Despite this retrenchment, the Cuban regime has continued to defy American trade boycotts and the loss of the lucrative U.S. market. The stability of the Cuban economy is maintained largely by Soviet aid. In the 1980s Cuba began to involve itself in revolutions beyond Latin America, including those in Angola and Ethiopia. An apparent easing in relations with the United States in 1984 was reversed the following year, when a private American-based radio station, Radio Martí, began to transmit anti-Castro propaganda to Cuba. Castro himself has been elected president three times, and in 1986 he proclaimed a new emphasis on women, blacks, and young people and

Ernesto "Che" Guevara and Fidel Castro greet Soviet leader Anastas Mikoyan in 1961. [Sovfoto]

Che Guevara on Guerrilla Warfare

In the course of the revolution against the Batista dictatorship in Cuba, Che Guevara found it necessary to transform Marxist doctrine and Leninist strategy to meet the conditions prevailing in the agrarian societies of Latin America. Here he explains the fundamental principles of guerrilla warfare.

The armed victory of the Cuban people over the Batista dictatorship . . . forced a change in the old dogmas concerning the conduct of the popular masses of Latin America. . . .

We consider that the Cuban Revolution contributed three fundamental lessons to the conduct of revolutionary movements in America. They are:

(1) Popular forces can win a war against the army.

(2) It is not necessary to wait until all conditions for making revolution exist; the insurrection can create them.

(3) In underdeveloped America the countryside is the basic area for armed fighting.

Of these three propositions the first two contradict the defeatist attitude of revolutionaries or pseudorevolutionaries who remain inactive and take refuge in the pretext that against a professional army nothing can be done. . . .

Naturally, it is not to be thought that all conditions for revolution are going to be created through the impulse given to them by guerrilla activity. . . . People must see clearly the futility of maintaining the fight for social goals within the framework of civil debate. . . .

The third proposition is a fundamental of strategy. It ought to be noted by those who maintain dogmatically that the struggle of the masses is centered in city movements, entirely forgetting the immense participation of the country people in the life of all the underdeveloped parts of America.

Source: C. Guevara, *Guerrilla Warfare*, trans. J. P. Moray (Lincoln: University of Nebraska Press, 1985), pp. 47–48.

appointed his sister-in-law as the first female member of the party council.

Patterns of Violence

Military dictatorships have dominated Central American politics since the turn of the century. In the 1970s elections in Guatemala, El Salvador, and Nicaragua were subverted by military intervention. In Guatemala, where half the arable land is owned by 2 percent of the population, each military regime tried to outdo its predecessor in violently repressing popular discontent. The result was some of the bitterest guerrilla warfare in Latin America.

Haiti, which achieved independence from France in 1804 following a slave revolt, has been racked by violence ever since. In 1957 François Duvalier established a police state, which his family maintained for two generations by a combination of brutality and superstition. After Jean-Claude Duvalier succeeded his father, his wife exhausted the country's treasury with extravagant shopping trips to Paris while the people suffered the worst social conditions in the Caribbean. When rioting broke out in 1986, the Duvaliers fled the country, taking millions of dollars with them. Family rule proved equally unstable in the Dominican Republic, where with American support General Rafael Trujillo maintained a harsh but efficient dictatorship from 1930 until his assassination in 1961. His son failed to retain power and, together with his family, fled the island. United States troops occupied the country between April

1965 and September 1966, thwarting the reformist candidacy of Juan Bosch and installing a rightist regime.

El Salvador, a coffee-producing country in which a tiny oligarchy controls three-fifths of the land, remains torn by a civil war that has claimed thousands of civilian casualties. In 1984 a moderate president was elected and negotiations were opened between the regime and the guerrillas, but no satisfactory end to the strife appears in sight. As in Guatemala, American aid, rationalized by a fear of communism, helps to finance the government's battle against the guerrillas.

The Nicaraguan Revolution

If fear of Castro's Cuba had earlier dominated American policy in Central America, the Nicaraguan revolution of 1979 set the tone for the 1980s. Like prerevolutionary Cuba, Nicaragua was harshly ruled for more than 30 years by a corrupt and stubborn dictator under American protection. When Anastasio Somoza García was finally ousted, the new revolutionary government and the United States confronted each other with mutual suspicion. Little has happened to dispel that mistrust.

The new ruling party, the *Sandinistas* (named for César Augusto Sandino, a guerrilla leader of the late 1920s and early 1930s), created a "national reconstruction government" under the presidency of Daniel Ortega. It has vastly improved public health, education, and food production through land reform. Sandinista economic policy contains a mix of capitalist and socialist elements. Nevertheless, much government spending has been devoted to fighting the U.S.-sponsored *contra* rebels in a war that has claimed over 30,000 lives to date. Much to the displeasure of Washington, the Ortega regime has not implemented Western-style democracy or guaranteed a free press. Whereas America has provided aid to the *contras*, Nicaragua has accepted Cuban, Soviet, and Swedish assistance. Nicaragua has undoubtedly aligned itself with Third World and Communist countries. Fears of intervention in the region were heightened by the American invasion of the Caribbean island of Grenada in 1983 and the installation of a pro-American government there.

At the beginning of that year, four Latin American

A Sandinista Woman

The revolutionary movement that toppled the repressive government in Nicaragua in 1979 drew dedicated militants from all walks of life, men and women who worked in the underground against difficult odds for years. Here a Sandinista woman leader, Dora Maria, explains the nature of her revolutionary commitment.

Sometimes I wonder, I ask myself why, given the brutal repression in 1973, when the people didn't yet support us, when they informed on comrades who carried out various actions, when they pointed them out on the streets, when the repression shattered us, when thousands of people fell—why did we keep on believing? And why in 1960, in 1961, in 1963, and in 1967 did the militants keep believing that one day the people would rise up?

What makes a man believe in his own potential as a man? What makes a woman believe that she is capable of anything? No one taught us. That is one of the great mysteries about the Revolution. They don't teach it to you at school. You don't learn to believe in humanity on the streets. Religion doesn't teach it. It teaches us to believe in God, not in men and women. So it's difficult to awaken that belief in yourself and in others. But in spite of all that, many women and men did develop that commitment.

It becomes an obsession—the people must rise up, they must. It begins with a vision, an imaginary idea. . . . We had to understand that people are historically capable of making revolutions. . . . But I never understood it as historical law. I think many people didn't. . . . All we knew was that we were going to make the Revolution, however long it took.

Source: M. Randall, *Sandino's Daughters: Testimonies of Nicaraguan Women in Struggle* (Vancouver, Canada: New Star Books, 1983), pp. 53–54.

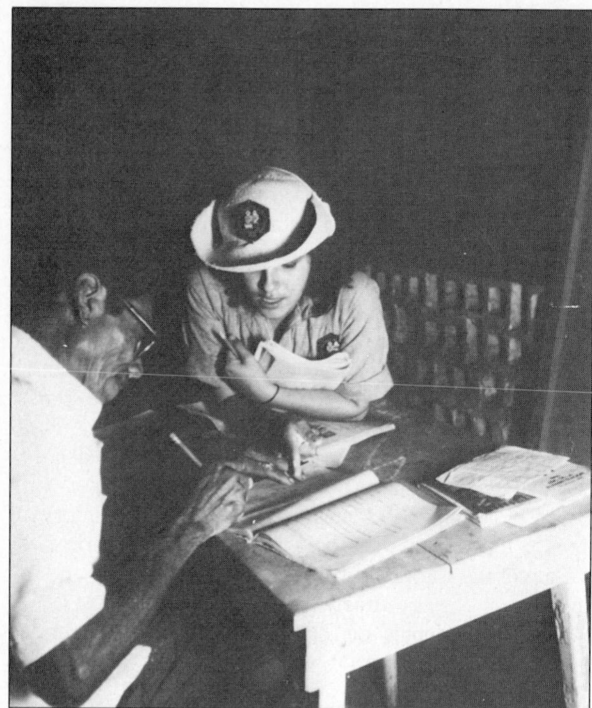

A literacy campaign in Nicaragua. [Owen Franken/Stock, Boston]

countries—Venezuela, Colombia, Panama, and Mexico—met on the island of Contadora off the coast of Panama to develop a peace plan for Central America. The revelation late in 1986 that arms sales to Iran had secretly been used to fund *contra* forces caused a major scandal in the Reagan administration and undermined America's credibility as an opponent of international terrorism. Unlike Castro's Cuba, where the revolution developed in relative peace after 1962, Nicaragua's new regime has not had the opportunity to establish its domestic programs on a peaceful footing.

Mexico in the Twentieth Century

Although 300 years of Spanish control over Mexico ended in 1821, the modern republic was not inaugurated until 1920. The intervening century saw continuous conflicts between Mexico and the United States, culminating in the American annexation of Texas following the Mexican-American War. Attempts by Benito Juárez (1806–1872) to better the conditions of the Indian poor by a program of land reform from 1855 to 1876 were briefly interrupted by the intervention of the French emperor Napoleon III, who installed his relative Maximilian as emperor of Mexico. After the death of Juárez, Porfirio Díaz (1830–1915) ruled despotically for nearly 35 years. By 1910 popular discontent had united peasants, workers, and intellectuals. The opposition was led by Francisco Madero (1873–1913), supported by bandit revolutionaries such as Pancho Villa and Emiliano Zapata. When Díaz fled in 1911, Madero assumed the presidency but was murdered in a military uprising openly encouraged by the United States ambassador to Mexico. The subsequent revolution led to the establishment of a republic.

Although since 1920 Mexico has had a parliamentary government, in practice the chief political force, the Institutional Revolutionary Party (PRI), has dominated the country, winning every election since 1929 and providing all of Mexico's presidents. Virtually every aspect of Mexican life is under PRI control, including political patronage, education, the economy, and cultural activities. Lázaro Cárdenas, who served as president from 1934 to 1940, introduced ambitious plans for the redistribution of land, causing confrontation with the Catholic church, and expropriated foreign-owned oil properties in 1938.

Mexico's population, currently more than 75 million, has doubled since 1960. Initial attempts to improve the lives of its vast and underprivileged peasant population gave way after World War II to a drive to industrialize. The result was the creation of large modern cities and an incipient middle class. Yet there has been little change in the lot of the urban or rural poor, whose numbers continue to swell. By the late 1960s the postwar economic boom had begun to decline, and in 1975 inflation had reached 40 percent. Following the killing of some 300 university students during a demonstration in 1968, unrest beset the country. In the 1970s the political leadership did little to arrest the erosion of public confidence, borrowing heavily from foreign investors attracted to Mexico's huge oil reserves, the fourth largest in the world.

With the fall of oil prices in 1981, Mexico's economy collapsed. The currency was drastically devalued, and the prices of electricity and gasoline increased. In the 1982 elections—which featured the candidacy of Rosaria Ibarra de Piedra, the first woman to run for president in the nation's history—the PRI presidential candidate, Miguel de la Madrid, won 74 percent of the votes, a small victory by Mexican standards. The challenge to PRI control was confirmed by a bitterly contested election in 1988.

Mexican society is beset by a wide range of natural and human problems. In 1985 a massive earthquake rocked the capital, Mexico City, leaving thousands dead or homeless. Even with international aid, the damage left irreparable wounds in a city already on the verge of collapse. The plight of Mexico City was, in fact, already one of the country's most serious problems. With more than 17 million people, many living in hovels, and plagued by pollution, it embodies the worst aspects of urbanization, with day-to-day difficulties in energy and public services. Like other Third World urban centers such as Calcutta, Mexico City symbolizes the crisis of city life in the late twentieth century.

Mexico's relations with the United States, always strained, deteriorated in the 1970s. Illegal immigration into America, formerly tolerated by both nations, was more tightly checked. Mexican drug trafficking, a national industry in which even the PRI was implicated, added to these tensions along with a rash of kidnappings and murders of Americans by Mexican bandits posing as policemen.

Mexico's immediate hope must be that oil prices will rise again. The elimination of the harsher inequities that pervade Mexican society represents the major challenge Mexico faces as one of Latin America's most populous countries.

Society and Culture in Latin America

It is difficult to generalize about so vast and varied a region as Latin America, but certain broad principles have applied during the twentieth century. The first is that democratic participation in the political process has been the exception rather than the rule. Paradoxically, because most citizens have been excluded from an active role in government, they have turned to direct political action far more than Americans or Europeans. The abuses of the secret police in Chile or Guatemala and the massive protests of the "mothers of the disappeared" (missing political prisoners) in Argentina have demonstrated how political realities affect the daily lives of Latin Americans in a direct and often violent manner.

The Catholic church has played an important, if inconsistent, role in Latin American society. Catholicism is deeply rooted in virtually every country of the region, although its external manifestations are often affected by indigenous Indian traditions and its influence varies from country to country. Hence whereas the church occupies an important position as a force for national unity in Argentina, Bolivian Catholicism represents only a thin veneer of European culture on an Indian civilization that goes back to pre-Columbian times. In Mexico the church has almost no influence in public affairs. In the 1970s Latin America saw the growth of so-called liberation theology, a philosophy of social activism that condones the use of violence to promote change in extreme circumstances. Generally developed by worker-priests closely involved in social reform in local communities, this philosophy met with a mixed reception from Catholic religious leaders, both in Latin America and in the church hierarchy. It was condemned by Pope John Paul II, most notably in his 1987 visit to Chile and Argentina.

The reactions of individual national clergy have been determined in part by local conditions. Whereas the archbishop of El Salvador played an important part in negotiations there before his assassination in 1979, the confiscation of church property by Nicaragua's Sandinista regime generated official Catholic protests. Yet even though Catholic influence varies throughout Latin America, the phenomenon of secularization that has swept Europe and North America has yet to make serious inroads there.

A third characteristic common to many Latin American countries has been the vitality and persistence of their popular cultures. With the possible exception of Mexico, more directly influenced by its powerful northern neighbor, Latin America shows less cultural conformity than Europe, where American influence has produced a degree of uniformity in popular music, television entertainment, and fast food. The folk songs and dances of Brazil's Carnival, the "reggae" music of Jamaica, the traditional pottery and weaving of Peru, all are manifestations of living and thriving cultural traditions.

Latin American achievements in the arts have also maintained a sense of national character. The Argentinian novelist Jorge Luis Borges (1899–1986) captured the blend of Spanish and Indian mysticism that pervades the life of his country while constructing parables of universal significance. Pablo Neruda (1904–1973), the Chilean writer and diplomat, is probably Latin America's best-known poet and one of four of the region's writers to win the Nobel prize for literature—the others being his compatriot Gabriela Mistral, the Guatemalan novelist Miguel Angel Asturias, and the Colombian novelist Gabriel Garcia Marquez (born 1928). If there is a feature common to the work of these writers, it is the use of fantasy and magic that provides an escape from reality: Marquez' novel *One Hundred Years of Solitude* describes life in an imaginary town in a remote region of Colombia, where extraordinary events are the order of the day.

Mexico has produced a number of major painters, including Diego Rivera (1886–1957), whose Communist sympathies influenced much of his work. Rivera's murals in Rockefeller Center, New York City, were removed after fierce controversy. Among his associates was José Clemente Orozco (1883–1949), famous for the bold realism of his frescoes. By contrast, Rufino Tamayo (born 1899) created a more cosmopolitan style that invokes a magical world comparable in painting to that of Borges' and Marquez' novels. On the whole, realistic depictions of the lives of workers and peasants have dominated Latin American painting, as in the moving frescoes of Rivera and the Brazilian Cândido Portinari (1903–1962), whose work can be seen at the United Nations building in New York.

Latin American composers have frequently been inspired by the folk music of their homelands. The Brazilian musician Heitor Villa-Lobos (1887–1959) wrote a series of works titled *Bachianas Brasileiras*, in which he treated

Brazilian folk motifs in a style reminiscent of Johann Sebastian Bach. Among the works of the Mexican Carlos Chávez (1899–1978), who founded the Mexican Symphony Orchestra, is the *Sinfonia India,* which uses folk motifs to evoke the country's Indian past. The generally underdeveloped state of musical conservatories in Latin America has forced most performing artists, including the famous Chilean pianist Claudio Arrau (born 1904), to study abroad. Yet many capital cities in the region have a thriving operatic tradition that goes back to the nineteenth century. The most famous and beautiful opera house in South America is the Teatro Colón in Buenos Aires, where performances meet international standards.

The best film production unit in Latin America is the Cuban Film Institute, where young directors and performers are encouraged to develop their skills at government expense. Elsewhere, filmmakers have used their works to document their country's history. The Argentinian film *The Official Story,* which describes events in Argentina after the fall of the military dictatorship in 1983, won an Academy Award as the best foreign film of 1985.

The thriving arts and popular culture of Latin America represent both a reminder of and an escape from the grim realities of everyday life. Unlike much of the rest of the world, the twentieth century has seen little change in age-old social patterns in the region anywhere but in Cuba and Nicaragua. Apart from Mexico, and to a lesser extent Argentina and Brazil, the population remains split into the wealthy few and the many poor, with little sign of a developing middle class. For example, in Brazil, Colombia, and Peru half or more of the households live in absolute poverty, defined as the ability to purchase the barest necessities for subsistence. Yet Latin America has the fastest-growing population in the world, increasing about 3 percent each year. In these same countries approximately one out of five adults is illiterate, and infant mortality remains high. Despite huge potential resources, most of the region is still predominantly agricultural. Industrial production is unequally distributed: as late as 1970 three nations—Argentina, Brazil, and Mexico—accounted for 80 percent of all industrial production in Latin America, and a third of that was confined to the cities of Buenos Aires, São Paulo, and Mexico City.

Women and the Culture of *Machismo*

Women in Central and South American society have only recently begun to regain the position they held in most communities before the Spanish conquest. Among the Aztecs, for example, women came close to legal equality with men. They could possess property, enter into contracts, testify before tribunals, seek divorce, and remarry freely. At the age of 50 they were accorded full equality and enjoyed equal status with men as elders.

Under the colonial regime, women lost most of their rights. The law presumed them to be mentally inferior, and the style of male bravado and presumption known as *machismo* that produced such laws became deeply ingrained in the culture. Yet in colonial times women were allowed to own property and to sign for mortgages in their own names. Independence brought little but lip service to the idea of greater equality for Latin American women. Not until the Mexican revolution in the early twentieth century was legal equality recognized. Argentina, Uruguay, and Chile followed suit in the 1920s and 1930s. Yet women in Argentina did not get the vote until 1947 and in Mexico only in 1953; with the passage of a female suffrage law in Paraguay in 1961, all women in the Americas had won the right to vote.

Despite progress, the goal of full equality remains elusive. Men are still recognized as head of the household in many Spanish-American countries, with the legal right to choose the place of domicile, direct the education of children, administer their property, and retain custody in case of divorce. *Machismo* enforces a double standard of sexual morality, with men permitted and even encouraged to form extramarital liaisons as proof of their virility. The result is a very high incidence of rape and illegitimacy, particularly marked in Brazil.

As elsewhere, the position of women is greatly affected by the variables of class, status, and income, by residence in town or country, and by skin color. The women of the elite are in many respects indistinguishable from their counterparts in the industrial West; for those trapped in rural poverty or urban squalor, the still-halting steps toward equality have had little effect. Eva and Isabel Perón notwithstanding, until recent years few women have played a visible part in public life. Beginning in the 1970s, however, more and more women have held appointed or elected positions in government. In Venezuela and Mexico women have served in presidential cabinets, and one woman became governor of the Mexican state of Colima.

Differences in education and training have generally relegated women to lower-paying jobs in the work force, and men usually displace women as a result of technological and unemployment cycles. Thus although women have been part of agricultural labor in Latin America for centuries, mechanization has made it difficult for them to obtain work in that sector. Similarly, ever larger numbers of Latin American women have moved into factory work, but they are generally paid less than men and hold less skilled jobs. Nevertheless, some exceptions hold out the promise of future change. In Brazil, for example, where the proportion of economically active women is lower than that of men, more women actually hold professional positions. Moreover, the number of working women doubled in the decade after 1970.

Experience has shown that when organized, women can exert a powerful force for change, as in the case of the Argentinian mothers of the disappeared. More revealing still, it has been estimated that women comprised as much as a third of the Sandinista People's Army in Nicaragua, where women now hold important government positions. In Cuba legislation passed in 1976 actually provided a legal basis for the sharing of housework and child care. Despite such transformation, however, the pattern of custom and prejudice dies slowly, and *machismo* continues to exert a powerful influence on male attitudes toward women.

The myriad of problems facing the global community as the second half of the twentieth century draws to a close can be seen as two broad challenges: the avoidance of a nuclear war that could destroy human society—an issue that will be examined in Chapter 41; and the securing of economic, social, and political well-being for the bulk of the world's inhabitants—an issue symbolized by the status of Africa and Latin America.

Both regions have undergone significant political change since the end of World War II as their peoples struggled against colonialism and continue to work to free themselves from dependency on the more advanced industrialized states. Yet the political systems under which many African and Latin American nations operate have been fraught with instability and a marked tendency toward authoritarianism. In part this political experience has been the result of the massive problems of development that each faces. The economic potential of the regions is vast, but immediate financial resources are limited. In most cases the small, privileged elites that control much of the wealth of these countries have neither directed resources toward the people nor been willing to extend democracy to them. In many areas racial and ethnic tensions contribute to political and social instability. Inefficiency, corruption, and the lack of appropriate technological capacity have combined to retard development, and despite productive agricultural soils, many states cannot feed their rapidly growing populations. Africa and Latin America are burdened with the fastest-growing populations in the world, high illiteracy, daunting health problems, and widespread poverty. Only far-reaching changes in the social and political structures of these regions can, in the long run, resolve such dilemmas.

Though these and other challenges appear at times insurmountable, the future holds substantial promise. Africa and Latin America possess not only extensive natural resources and rich cultural heritages but also populations that have repeatedly proved their creativity and resilience.

Suggestions for Further Reading

Africa

Bairoch, P. *The Economic Development of the Third World Since 1900*. London: Methuen, 1975.

Breese, G., ed. *The City in Newly Developing Countries*. Englewood Cliffs, N.J.: Prentice-Hall, 1972.

Elliott, C. *Patterns of Poverty in the Third World*. New York: Praeger, 1975.

Emerson, R. *From Empire to Nation: The Rise of Self-assertion of Asian and African Peoples*. Cambridge: Cambridge University Press, 1960.

Giliomee, H., and Elphick, R., eds. *The Shaping of South African Society*. Capetown: Longman, 1979.

Goode, W. J. *World Revolution and Family Patterns*. New York: Free Press, 1970.

Legum, C. *The West's Crisis in Southern Africa*. New York: Africana, 1978.

———, et al. *Africa in the 1980s: A Continent in Crisis*. New York: McGraw-Hill, 1979.

Lloyd, P. C. *Africa in Social Change*, rev. ed. Harmondsworth, England: Penguin Books, 1972.

Mazrui, A. A. *Protest and Power in Black Africa*. London: Oxford University Press, 1972.

Suckling, J., et al. *The Economic Factor of External Investment in South Africa*. London: Africa Publications Trust, 1975.

Wallerstein, I. *Africa: The Politics of Independence*. New York: Random House, 1963.

Latin America

Blasier, C. *The Hovering Giant: U.S. Responses to Revolutionary Change in Latin America*. Pittsburgh: University of Pittsburgh Press, 1985.

Booth, J. A. *The End of the Beginning: The Nicaraguan Revolution*, 2d ed. Boulder, Colo.: Westview Press, 1985.

Burns, E. B. *A History of Brazil*. New York: Columbia University Press, 1971.

———. *Latin America: A Concise Interpretive History*, 4th ed. Englewood Cliffs, N.J.: Prentice-Hall, 1986.

Keen, B., and Wasserman, M. *A Short History of Latin America*, 2d ed. Boston: Houghton Mifflin, 1984.

Meyer, M. C., and Sherman, W. L. *The Course of Mexican History*. New York: Oxford University Press, 1979.

Randall, M. *Sandino's Daughters: Testimonies of Nicaraguan Women in Struggle*. Vancouver, Canada: New Star Books, 1981.

Stepan, A., ed. *Authoritarian Brazil: Origins, Politics, and Future*. New Haven, Conn.: Yale University Press, 1976.

Thomas, H. *The Cuban Revolution*. New York: Harper & Row, 1977.

Maps and Their Makers (II)

The attempt to map the environment began with the earliest human societies. By the middle of the first millennium B.C., the first world map had been produced in Babylonia. Maps of considerable sophistication were drawn in the ancient West and China, but not until the discovery of the Americas and of the Pacific by Columbus and his successors in the late fifteenth and sixteenth centuries were the true dimensions of the earth known with any accuracy.

The discovery of the New World coincided with the development of movable type in the West. Printed maps circulated rapidly, facilitating trade and exploration. In 1570 Abraham Ortelius, a Flemish contemporary of Gerardus Mercator, published his *Theater of the World*, a collection of 70 maps covering the entire globe and incorporating the latest discoveries. It became a traveler's bible, going through 40 editions; a French reader enthused that it was the greatest work in the world after the Holy Scriptures.

Globes came into fashion too, and as Aristophanes had unfolded a map of the world on the ancient Greek stage, so William Shakespeare referred to the first English globe in *The Comedy of Errors*. Shakespeare remarked that "all the world's a stage," and it was no accident that the most important theater of his time was called the Globe. The European imagination of the late sixteenth century was as fascinated with the idea of a knowable world as it was soon to be with its conquest.

The discovery of a new earth stimulated speculation about a new heaven as well. In 1595 the great Mercator's final work was published, called *Atlas*—the first collection of maps to bear this title—and subtitled *Cosmographical Meditations upon the Creation of the Universe, and the Universe as Created*. As this subtitle made clear, Mercator envisioned the mapping of the earth as only a first step toward a new understanding of the cosmos. Fourteen years later, in 1609, Galileo Galilei trained his telescope on the heavens and saw the four largest moons of Jupiter, the first new objects, apart from comets, to be observed in the heavens in thousands of years.

The discovery of these new celestial objects had a very different import from Columbus' discovery of the New World. Although pre-Columbian maps, based on Ptolemy, had underestimated the size of the globe, it was known and accepted that there were places on it where no humans lived and perhaps none had ever gone. The Ptolemaic heavens, however, for all their greater size, were believed to be fully mapped; nor

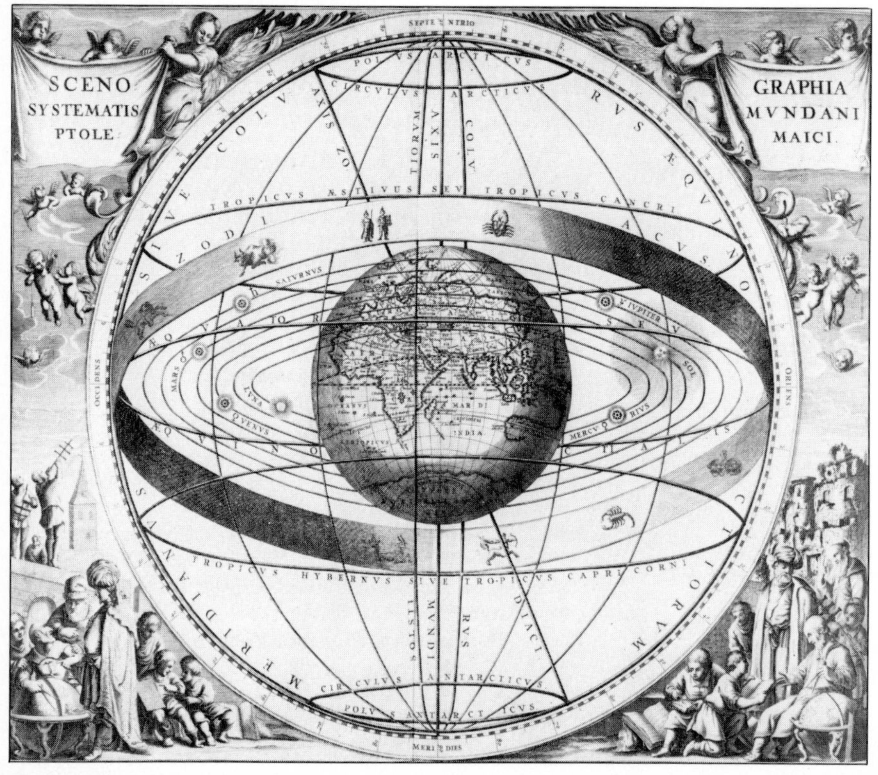

This elegant illustration of the Ptolemaic theory by Pieter Schenk and Gerard Valk dates from 1706, indicating that Ptolemy's model still had advocates into the eighteenth century. The earth is at the center, surrounded by a fiery atmosphere, while the sun, the moon, the five planets then known, and the heavens are represented by mythological figures and cherubs riding on a bed of clouds. At the edge of the system are the divisions of the Zodiac. [American Philosophical Society]

had the Copernican system, in transposing the earth and the sun, enlarged them. Galileo's four moons changed all that. The cosmos had begun to be explored; as much might be hidden as was known.

If the real exploration of the heavens had to await the development of radio astronomy in the twentieth century, the telescopes of the seventeenth were able to bring at least one celestial body within reach of the cartographers: the moon. Although only one side of it was visible from earth, some 48 craters had been located and named (mostly after ancient philosophers and modern scientists), as well as eight so-called seas. Celestial globes, depicting the sun, the earth, the planets, and the stars, became almost as popular as terrestrial ones. Such representations suggested an attempt to domesticate the cosmos. Europeans began to speculate whether beings like themselves might not inhabit other celestial bodies, and in 1639 the Italian friar Thomas Campanella published one of the earliest works of science fiction, *The City of the Sun*. With the publication of Sir Isaac Newton's *Mathematical Principles of Natural Philosophy* in 1687 (see Chapter 23), the distinction between celestial and terrestrial mechanics that had been maintained since the time of Aristotle collapsed, and it was soon generally accepted that the same physical laws governed both the earth and the heavens.

At the same time, cartography became a weapon in the struggle for commercial advantage and empire. As the imperial initiative passed in the seventeenth and eighteenth centuries from Iberia to England and France, both nations realized the crucial importance of reliable maps. Under Louis XIV mapmaking became a state enterprise. Astronomers were sent to Egypt, South America, and the West Indies to make the celestial observations essential for accurate mapping. The explorer La Salle was commissioned to survey the newly established colony of New France in North America, and a team under Jean-Dominique Cassini, director of the Royal Observatory, set out to produce a true map of France itself. Using the moons of Jupiter as a point of reference for sighting latitude, they discovered that previous maps had placed the port of Brest too far west, in what was actually open sea, and Marseilles too far south. When Louis XIV was shown these results, he exclaimed, "Your work has cost me a good part of my state!"

What France itself lost, however, its colonies regained in Guillaume Delisle's maps of Canada (1703) and Louisiana (1718), which extended French claims in the New World at the expense of England's. The British were not slow to respond, and a veritable war of maps ensued in fixing the boundaries of Nova Scotia, ceded by the French at the end of the War of the Austrian Succession (1748), with Britain ironically citing French maps to substantiate its claims to more of the coastline with its rich fisheries and the French citing British maps to limit them.

Despite these conflicts, however, the two nations were able to cooperate occasionally in a common scientific interest. In the 1730s French expeditions to Lapland and Peru confirmed Newton's hypothesis that the earth was not a perfect sphere but, because of its variable motion, a prolate one, bulging at the equator and flattened at the poles. This was important to navigation, because it meant that degrees of latitude and longitude were not uniform but lengthened as they approached the equator and shortened as they receded. Fifty years later a joint team of British and French geographers measured the precise distance between Greenwich, England, and Paris, using French techniques of triangulation and a new British instrument, the theodolite, a 200-pound device consisting of telescopes, reflectors, and angle registers. One hundred years later, in 1884, an international conference established Greenwich as the prime meridian, that is, the point of 0 degrees of longitude from which all divisions of east and west would thenceforth be measured. Among other things, this made it possible to divide the earth into its present 24 time zones, each 15 degrees of longitude apart. Greenwich thus became, as Babylon, Jerusalem, and Ch'ang An had once been, the center of the earth.

Magellan had crossed the Pacific, but for the next 250 years little was reliably known about its western expanses. It found its geographer at last, however, in James Cook (1728–1779), the son of a Yorkshire laborer who worked himself up to a naval commission, driven by a passion for discovery that, as he confessed, "leads me not only farther than any man has been before me, but as far as I think it possible for man to go." Cook's three voyages set out in search of those will-o'-the-wisps of cartographers, a navigable shortcut to Asia through the Americas called the Northwest Passage and a great southern continent called Terra Australis, hypothesized by the ancient Greeks, popularized by Marco Polo, and still a standard feature of eighteenth-century maps. Cook found neither, but he did map thousands of miles of northwestern American coastline and virtually every island in the Pacific, and he did go farther than any man had been, sailing to within a few hundred miles of both the north and south poles.

Cook's voyages put a third of the world on the map, although it remained for others to complete his work. The Norwegian Roald Amundsen (1872–1928) finally traversed the chain of bays, straits, and sounds across northern Canada to the Beaufort Sea in 1903–1906. Antarctica, the true southern continent, was first sighted in 1820; the name Australia was given to the great landmass that the British explorer Matthew Flinders was the first to realize in 1801 was not an archipelago but a continent in its own right. Cook himself was tragically murdered in Hawaii, another of his discoveries, while preparing to make a fourth voyage.

The efforts of Cook, Flinders, and two other Englishmen, George Vancouver and Francis Beaufort, had given a tolerably good idea of the coastal contours of the six habitable continents by the mid-nineteenth century. It remained to map the equally challenging interiors of the Americas, Africa, and central Asia.

One of the first native surveyors of North America was George Washington, who as a young man charted the region between the Potomac River and Lake Erie, and, failing to persuade Congress of the urgency of a full geographic survey of the young American republic, left his countrymen at his death a full set of surveying instruments, including parallel rules, compasses, and a theodolite. The acquisition of the Louisiana Territory from France in 1803, however, provided the needed incentive. No one knew exactly what the country had bought. Some people speculated that the Missouri and Columbia rivers might provide a passage to the Pacific. Others imagined the West, as the Greeks had once imagined Terra Australis, as a land of milk and honey. The actual barrier of the Rocky Mountains was barely guessed at.

In 1804 the government dispatched a party of 45 men under Meriwether Lewis and William Clark that two years later, guided by Indian maps, reached the Pacific, laying claim to the western territories beyond Louisiana. They were followed by settlers, adventurers, and, after 1838, by the systematic surveys of the Army Corps of Topographical Engineers. In the 1870s John Wesley Powell rafted down the Colorado River, mapping much of the plateau and desert West, and in 1879 the United States Geological Survey was instituted. Its work continues today.

The British mapped India rapidly after its final conquest in 1818, proceeding northward to the Himalayas, where a Bengali clerk surmised that the mountain known as Peak XV, and called in Tibetan Chomolungma, or "Goddess Mother of the World," was the tallest in the world. It was named, however, after an Englishman, George Everest. Similarly, the mapping of Africa awaited its intensive colonization after 1870. In contrast, the Jesuits who reached China and Japan in the sixteenth century found an ancient and sophisticated cartographic tradition in both countries. When Matteo Ricci presented a world map to the Chinese emperor in 1602, he tactfully placed China in the center. The Italian Jesuit Martino Martini published the first European atlas of China in 1655, based on Chinese sources. But the Chinese, with their proud isolation, were slow to adopt Western mapping techniques or to accept the results of Western discoveries. The consequence was to place them at a considerable disadvantage in dealing with European imperialism in the nineteenth century.

While the true dimensions and contours of the earth were slowly yielding to exploration and measurement, a similar process was taking place with regard to the heavens. One of the stumbling blocks to the acceptance of the Copernican theory in the seventeenth century was that it suggested a far greater distance to the fixed stars than that of Ptolemy. By the latter part of the century, however, Copernicus had won the day, and French astronomers had calculated the distance between the earth and the sun with better than 90 percent accuracy.

A better appreciation of the scale of the cosmos, however, awaited one of the most important conceptual breakthroughs in history: the realization that the sun itself was a star. Only by means of this could even a rudimentary notion of the immensity of interstellar space be achieved. If any single individual may be credited with it, it was perhaps the martyred Giordano Bruno, who had argued—at the cost of his life—for the idea of an infinity of worlds and hence of an infinite space. A century later the great Dutch astronomer and mathematician Christiaan Huygens (1629–1695), hypothesizing that the star Sirius was a body as bright as the sun, calculated its distance as 27,664 times that of the earth from the sun. Sirius was in reality nearly 20 times farther away, but Huygens' estimate was at least a beginning. William Herschel (1738–1822) took a quantum leap by suggesting that the universe was a sea composed of great galactic islands, of which the sun's island, the Milky Way, was but one. Since Herschel had calculated the equatorial plane of the Milky Way at 7,000 light-years, and since the distance between galaxies must necessarily be far larger than their internal dimensions, he was faced with a universe that was, if not infinite, then perhaps ultimately incalculable.

Herschel was the first to realize that the light from the stars he gazed at had traveled so far—millions of years, he thought—that the bodies that had emitted them might no longer exist. At the same time, his slightly older contemporary James Hutton (c. 1726–1797) was suggesting, on the basis of his observation of geologic strata, that the earth itself was not (as had been thought only a century before) only a few thousand years old but many millions. The universe was receding in time as it was expanding in space.

These twin conceptions may have led to a fresh attempt to humanize space by populating it with intelligent life. In 1877 the Italian astronomer Giovanni Schiaparelli observed a network of fine symmetrical lines on the surface of Mars. An American, Percival Lowell, argued that these were elaborate canals built by a race of technologically advanced beings. This theory had wide credence in scientific circles and en-

A sketch of Herschel's 20-inch telescope. Later Herschel built a giant reflecting telescope with funds provided by Britain's King George III. [Yerkes Observatory]

tered popular culture as well; in 1938 millions of Americans were panicked by a radio hoax that announced that Martians had landed in New Jersey. Not until the Mariner 9 orbiting of Mars in 1971 and the unmanned Viking landing of 1976 were these fantasies laid to rest.

If the period from Columbus' discoveries and Copernican astronomy to Newtonian physics had seen an enormous advance in human knowledge of the earth and the heavens, and that from Newtonian to Einsteinian physics a similar one, the twentieth century marked the beginning of an era of unprecedented exploration and discovery. In 1909 Robert Peary reached the North Pole, and in 1911 Roald Amundsen reached the South Pole. Aerial photography of the Antarctic began in 1928, but not until the postwar period, particularly the International Geophysical Year of 1957–1958 and the U.S. Geologic Survey of 1961–1962, did the continent's true outlines begin to emerge.

At the same time, the oceans and their depths were at last surveyed. Magellan, having probed the depth of the Pacific to about 2,300 feet in 1521, pronounced it immeasurable, and many sailors indeed believed the seas to be bottomless. Not until 1856 was the Pacific's depth roughly ascertained (using tidal wave measurements), and only in the 1950s was the first map of the ocean floors produced. It revealed a planet beneath the planet, with mountain ranges greater than the Himalayas, chasms deeper than the Grand Canyon, and plains broader than the Russian steppe.

The discovery of the ocean's great topographic diversity, particularly of the earth's largest single feature, the Midocean Ridge in the Atlantic, led to the realization that the earth was dynamic and the continents themselves in motion. A theory of "continental drift" had been proposed 50 years earlier, to wide ridicule, by the German meteorologist Alfred Wegener. As the discovery of deep space had opened up the geographic dimension of time—as Herschel and his successors had realized that the image of the heavens was a record of past events—so the present generation of cartographers has begun to work backward to reconfigure the continents of past geologic ages. As Wegener had hypothesized, there may have been a single landmass or supercontinent, Pangaea, from which the present seven continents have emerged over the past 200 million years. Such projections may ultimately read forward too, enabling us literally to ascertain the shape of things to come.

At the beginning of the twentieth century the size of the universe was still estimated at no more than 10,000 light-years, and the existence of other galaxies was still an unproven hypothesis. The picture was rapidly transformed by the development of powerful new telescopes, the analysis of light spectra, and the discovery of stars whose variable luminosity enabled astronomers to use them as cosmic yardsticks, like beacons at sea. By 1930 Edwin Hubble (1889–1953) had demonstrated not only that other galaxies existed but also that they were receding at a velocity proportional

Kingdoms of space: the great spiral galaxy Andromeda, known as M 31, is roughly similar to our own Milky Way in shape although rather larger in size, with a diameter of about 180,000 light years. About 4 billion galaxies, each consisting of billions of stars, lie within reach of modern telescopes. [Observatories of the Carnegie Institution of Washington]

to their distance from our own. Hubble's law, as this discovery was called, suggested both that cosmic magnitudes were far greater than had been hitherto supposed and that those magnitudes were indefinitely expanding. Estimates of the present size of the universe have been extended continuously since then. Hubble calculated the edge of the universe as 500 million light-years away, but by midcentury that estimate had doubled, and with the introduction of radio telescopes after World War II and the consequent discovery of quasars (quasi-stellar discrete radio sources), it was soon revised tenfold upward again. In the farthest reaches of space, stars may be beaming their light toward us while simultaneously receding from us at a speed nearly equal to that of light itself, and it appears certain that light has reached the earth that was propagated before our planet existed.

It has only been some thousands of years since humans first attempted to mark the distance between here and there on stone, skin, and sand, but our maps have now led us billions of years back in time and billions of light-years outward in space. As astronomers and geologists pursue their visions, the variety, utility, complexity, and sophistication of the mapmakers' art continues to increase. Maps are now indispensable for such diverse projects as weather prediction, flood control, agricultural and urban planning, mining, and—a sad commentary on the human adventure—arms control. At the same time, satellite photography, electronic data processing, and computer simulation have greatly increased the range and precision of mapping. The hand-drawn map, in use for scientific purposes until only a few years ago, may soon go the way of the hand-lettered book. Yet the caution of a nineteenth-century British surveyor remains valid: "All observations are liable to error; no telescope is perfect; no leveling instrument is entirely trustworthy; no instrumental gradations are exact; no observer is infallible."

Suggestions for Further Reading

Bagrow, L. *A History of Cartography*. London: Watts, 1964.

Bricker, C., and Tooley, R. V. *A History of Cartography: 2500 Years of Maps and Mapmakers*. London: Thames & Hudson, 1969.

Brown, L. A. *The Story of Maps*. Boston: Little, Brown, 1980.

Harley, J. B., and Woodward, D., eds. *The History of Cartography*. Chicago: University of Chicago Press, 1987–.

Kopal, Z. *Widening Horizons: Man's Quest to Understand the Structure of the Universe*. New York: Taplinger, 1970.

Schlee, S. *The Edge of an Unfamiliar World: A History of Oceanography*. New York: Dutton, 1973.

Sullivan, W. *Continents in Motion*. New York: McGraw-Hill, 1974.

Thrower, N. J. W. *Maps and Man*. Englewood Cliffs, N.J.: Prentice-Hall, 1972.

Wilford, J. N. *The Mapmakers*. New York: Knopf, 1981.

CHAPTER · 41

The Age of the Superpowers

The meeting of Soviet and American troops on the Elbe River in April 1945, amid the rubble of a continent, symbolized the eclipse of Europe as the dominant force in international politics. Germany had been decisively defeated and occupied. An exhausted Britain found itself the world's greatest debtor nation. France, overrun and occupied by Hitler's armies, had only de Gaulle's Free French and the internal resistance of the Maquis to remember with any pride. Few could deny that the Soviet Union and the United States had been the principal architects of victory or that their military strength would determine the future of the globe. The hegemony once exercised by western Europe was now to be shared by the two superpowers.

The Second World War transformed both nations, and each saw its role in a different light. Stalin, though a brutal dictator, represented the views of most Soviet peoples when he adopted a defensive posture toward postwar geopolitics. Since coming to power in 1924, his foremost concern in foreign affairs had been Soviet national interests. From that viewpoint, he saw the spread of communism primarily as an extension of Soviet influence and only secondarily as the success of an ideology. Three times in as

Leading Polish workers in a union movement of great political importance, Lech Walesa speaks to a crowd of strikers outside the Lenin shipyard in Gdansk in 1988. [Reuters/UPI Bettmann Newsphotos]

many decades Western powers had invaded his country, and the savage war fought on Soviet soil against the Nazis had taken an enormous toll on the Soviet Union's people and resources. Now he was determined to strengthen the USSR against a rearmed Germany and a hostile United States.

The American people emerged from World War II with a vastly different outlook. Attacked directly only at Pearl Harbor, the United States had lost some 390,000 soldiers in the war as compared to 20 million Soviet deaths. Wartime spending had brought full employment after more than a decade of economic depression. In 1945 a wealthy America towered above its devastated allies. In the face of shattered European economies, the United States could look eagerly toward the opening of vast new markets for the products of its businesses and farms. Secure behind the world's only nuclear capability, most Americans wanted rapid demobilization, lower taxes, more consumer goods, and an end to foreign political commitments. Only the Soviet Union threatened the global aspirations of American policymakers.

The Cold War

The conflict between Soviet and American national interests came to be known as the Cold War. As it grew in intensity after 1945, the Cold War assumed the public guise of a clash of ideologies. Many Americans saw themselves as defending capitalist democracy against communist totalitarianism, while the Soviets portrayed themselves as opponents of Western imperialism. In both instances the rhetoric obscured the reality of the Cold War as a struggle for dominance between the world's strongest nations.

Potsdam and the Origins of the Cold War

Historians disagree as to when the Cold War began and who was responsible for breaking Soviet-American wartime collaboration. Some scholars place the beginnings as early as 1918, when American troops invaded northern Russia at Archangel to try to topple the Bolshevik regime. Others argue that the growing antagonism between the United States and the Soviet Union, already revealed in wartime discussions among the Allies, did not become irreversible until 1947 or 1948, when anticommunism became the guidepost of American policy. The consensus, however, is that the Cold War emerged out of the conflict between Stalin and Truman over the future of eastern Europe during the Potsdam Conference in the summer of 1945.

Stalin had made it clear at Yalta that he wanted a readjustment of borders and an extension of the Soviet frontier into Polish territory. In return, he promised to allow free elections in eastern Europe after the war. Between February and July, however, the situation had changed drastically, for the Red Army had overrun Poland, Romania, Hungary, Bulgaria, and most of Czechoslovakia and Yugoslavia, and pro-Soviet governments dominated by the Communists were installed. At Potsdam, with Truman now representing the United States and Clement Attlee, Churchill's successor, Great Britain, the issue resurfaced.

The Big Three at Potsdam, 1945: Churchill, Truman, and Stalin confer on post–World War II settlements. [Imperial War Museum, London]

Truman took an aggressive stance, charging that Stalin had betrayed the Yalta agreement. Stalin's goal was to establish a line of buffer states between Germany and the Soviet Union. With eastern Europe under Red Army occupation, the Soviet leader remained adamant in the face of what some historians believe was Truman's attempt to use America's atomic monopoly to blackmail the Russians into making concessions.

In any case, the division of Europe into Western and Soviet blocs was an accomplished fact when, in March 1946, former prime minister Winston Churchill set the tone for Cold War rhetoric by declaring that the Soviets had lowered "an iron curtain" across the continent, a term quickly adopted by Western cold warriors as a symbol of the division between East and West in Europe.

The Soviet-American clash soon took on a more global character. The United States blocked Soviet efforts to secure a foothold in Iran, and in August, when Stalin demanded a voice in controlling the Dardenelles straits, Truman sent an aircraft carrier to the eastern Mediterranean. The future promised a pattern of repeated and dangerous confrontations.

From the Truman Doctrine to the Berlin Blockade

While relying increasingly on the nuclear deterrent to safeguard American security, Truman insisted that the United States had to counter a growing communist challenge throughout the world, especially in Greece, China, and Indonesia, where communist movements were attempting to overthrow local governments. The Greek situation provided the president with an opportunity to arouse American public opinion. Since the liberation of Greece from the Axis in 1944, Britain had stationed troops there in support of a corrupt monarch in order to keep Soviet influence out of the Mediterranean. A civil war, led by procommunist wartime resistance fighters, now threatened the political stability of the country. Although Stalin abided by his wartime agreement to recognize Greece as an Anglo-American sphere of influence, the communist government of Yugoslavia was aiding the rebels, and the British could no longer sustain their effort on behalf of the rightist regime.

The Iron Curtain

As Cold War tensions with the Soviet Union grew, Western leaders adopted the powerful image of the "iron curtain" to describe the Soviet-controlled areas of Europe. The phrase originated in a speech given by British prime minister Winston Churchill while on a visit to the United States in 1946.

From Stettin in the Baltic to Trieste in the Adriatic, an iron curtain has descended across the continent. Behind that line lie all the capitals of the ancient states of Central and Eastern Europe. Warsaw, Berlin, Prague, Vienna, Budapest, Belgrade, Bucharest, and Sophia, all these famous cities and the populations around them lie in the Soviet sphere, and all are subject, in one form or another, not only to Soviet influence but to a very high and, in many cases, increasing measure of control from Moscow. . . .

The Communist parties, which were very small in all these Eastern states of Europe, have been raised to preeminence and power far beyond their numbers and are seeking everywhere to obtain totalitarian control. Police governments are prevailing in nearly every case, and so far, except in Czechoslovakia, there is no true democracy. . . .

Whatever conclusions may be drawn from these facts—and facts they are—this is certainly not the Liberated Europe we fought to build up. Nor is it one which contains the essentials of permanent peace. . . .

Last time I saw it all coming, and cried aloud to my fellow countrymen and to the world, but no one paid any attention. . . .

We surely must not let that happen again.

Source: R. R. James, ed., *Winston S. Churchill: His Complete Speeches, 1897–1963,* vol. 7 (New York and London: Chelsea House, in association with R. R. Bowker), pp. 7290–7293.

On March 12, 1947, Truman announced that America must assist nations that were "resisting attempted subjugation by armed minorities or by outside pressures. . . . The free peoples of the world look to us for support in maintaining their freedoms."[1] Urging Congress to appropriate $400 million in military aid to bolster the Greek and Turkish governments, the president inaugurated the Truman Doctrine, the cornerstone of American foreign policy for the next two decades. Soon the word *containment* was being used to describe the basic principle of the Truman Doctrine, according to which the United States should restrict communism to areas already under Soviet control. That July, Congress also passed a measure establishing the National Security Council, which was to coordinate military and diplomatic policy for the president with the assistance of the newly formed Central Intelligence Agency (CIA). Truman was especially concerned about Third World areas, where professed Marxists often led national anticolonial movements. Soviet propagandists answered the Truman Doctrine by accusing the United States of seeking to preserve colonialism and asserting that the Soviet Union spoke for national liberation.

Containment had its economic as well as its military side. The United States attempted to draw all European states into the American orbit through a massive program of economic development. In June 1947 Secretary of State George C. Marshall offered economic assistance to any European nation that promised to consult with the American government to determine its needs. Although Czechoslovakia, Poland, and Hungary were interested, the Soviet Union vetoed their participation in the Marshall Plan, fearing that Western economic penetration would weaken its hold on the eastern European states. In western Europe, however, the United States pumped $13 billion into Britain, France, Italy, Germany, and other countries. The Marshall Plan proved a huge success, inaugurating a sustained era of European prosperity that helped combat the growth of socialist and communist parties.

In response, the Soviet Union strengthened its hold on eastern Europe. In 1946 Stalin already controlled Poland, Romania, Bulgaria, and Albania, and over the next two years he consolidated Russian influence over Hungary and Czechoslovakia. The Soviet counterpart to the Marshall Plan was COMECON, an economic organization that claimed to integrate the economies of the eastern European states and the Soviet Union. Under the program, some nations, such as Czechoslovakia, were assigned industrial goals, while others, such as Bulgaria, were given agricultural quotas. In place of the old Communist International (Comintern), abolished during the war in the name of Allied cooperation, Stalin created the Communist Information Bureau (Cominform), designed to reassert Moscow's control over the world communist movement.

As the United States and the Soviet Union consolidated their respective positions in Europe, Germany assumed major importance. The future of Germany had been debated since Potsdam, when Stalin had insisted on moving Russia's borders westward at the expense of Poland, which in turn would receive portions of East Prussia as well as the city of Danzig, renamed Gdansk. Germany's eastern border was set at the Oder and Neisse rivers, and the country was broken into four occupation zones to be governed separately by Britain, France, the United States, and the Soviet Union. Berlin, inside the Russian zone, was similarly divided among the four powers. Yet no formal peace treaty or final resolution of Germany's status ever came, for disputes between Russia and the West left Germany broken into two separate states. The Soviet Union, which had suffered such massive casualties and destruction at the hands of Germany, preferred to see it permanently divided.

After 1946 the Western powers agreed to combine the three Western occupation zones into a single economic unit as a prelude to political sovereignty for a "West German" government. In 1948 self-government was instituted on a local level, and the Germans were permitted to write a new constitution. No postwar American action antagonized the Soviet Union as much as these efforts to reestablish a German nation, for Stalin feared both the industrial revival and the remilitarization of a new German state. That June, Stalin restricted access to West Berlin. The Americans promptly closed their sector to Soviet traffic. When Stalin blockaded all road, rail, and water access to Berlin, Britain and the United States followed suit with a counterblockade against goods moving from East to West Germany. Amid fear of war, the United States began to supply West Berlin by air, moving huge quantities of food, fuel, medicines, and other vital goods to the beleaguered city for almost a year until Stalin conceded defeat.

The Berlin blockade hastened the creation of a separate West German government, formally proclaimed on May 21, 1949, as the Federal Republic of Germany, with its capital at Bonn. Parliamentary elections brought to power as chancellor the Christian Democrat Konrad Adenauer (1876–1967), a former mayor of Cologne who had been imprisoned by Hitler. In contrast to Kurt Schumacher, the Social Democratic candidate who advocated nationalization of industry and banks, Adenauer represented America's Cold War position: cooperation with the West, rapprochement with France, and vigorous anticommunism. Five months after the creation of the Bonn government, the Soviet Union formed a Communist regime in the eastern sector, known as the German Democratic Republic, with its capital in East Berlin.

As the decade drew to a close, Cold War tensions heightened. In April 1949 the United States sponsored the North Atlantic Treaty Organization (NATO), a mutual-defense pact in which most Western nations, including Greece and Turkey, pledged to treat an armed attack against one nation as an assault against all. Although Soviet ground strength at the time outnumbered Western troops by about ten to one, in 1955 the Soviet Union established a similar defense system, dubbed the Warsaw Pact.

The relationship between the superpowers changed dramatically in September 1949 with news that the Soviet Union had detonated an atomic bomb. Several months later Communist forces under Mao Tse-tung (Mao Zedong) defeated the Nationalist armies of Chiang Kai-shek and seized power in China (see Chapter 38). The end of nuclear monopoly and the Communist takeover in China replaced confidence with uncertainty in American foreign policy.

The Cold War and American Politics

For Americans, the Cold War had powerful repercussions at home. In February 1950 Senator Joseph R. McCarthy (1908–1957) of Wisconsin claimed to have a list of Communists who held important positions in the State Department and accused Secretary of State Marshall of protecting them by inaction. McCarthy never produced the name of a single Communist and repeatedly changed the number of alleged "traitors" he had discovered in the government. But his message was clear: the Truman administration had bred and coddled the Communist enemy within the government.

That a senator could make such accusations against Truman appears incongruous in retrospect, for the president had shown himself to be an enthusiastic cold warrior, had imposed a loyalty program on federal employees, and had jailed most leaders of the small and nearly impotent Communist party of the United States. Yet a wave of anti-Communist hysteria swept the country. It lasted for four years, and in some areas of American life, pools of suspicion lingered far longer.

McCarthy's "Red scare" campaign made him a national figure. Despite the election of a Republican president, Dwight D. Eisenhower (1953–1961), he continued to claim conspiracy in high places. The witch-hunt spread from Communists to other groups, including homosexuals. In televised hearings that ended in mid-1954, McCarthy finally overextended himself when he charged that the army itself was riddled with Communist spies. In December the Senate censured McCarthy, ending his influence. Yet imitators perpetuated his methods, especially in monitoring schoolteachers and blacklisting actors.

The Soviet Union and Eastern Europe

In the postwar period Stalin's immediate concerns were to establish a Soviet presence in eastern Europe and to undertake the domestic reconstruction of the Soviet Union. These goals were linked, for he regarded eastern Europe as a region whose economic resources could be used to rebuild Soviet strength.

The Cold War at home: Senator Joseph R. McCarthy of Wisconsin (seated) and his two chief aides, G. David Shine (left) and Roy Cohn (right). [Eve Arnold/ Magnum]

Postwar Reconstruction in the Soviet Union

The Soviet Union faced an enormous task of reconstruction in the wake of a war that had destroyed much of its industry, many of its cities, and 30 percent of its national wealth. Not satisfied to restore conditions to the 1941 level, Stalin was determined to build an industrial base worthy of the USSR's new role as a world power. The Cold War increased the burden by adding massive expenditures for arms.

Stalin forced the USSR to return to the policies of the 1930s—extracting surplus capital for the development of heavy industry from the work of Soviet men and women. Although the exploitation of eastern Europe aided the work of reconstruction, most Soviets had to sacrifice their living standards again. Between 1946 and 1950 another five-year plan poured more resources into capital investment than had been spent during the 13 years after 1928, yet the economy produced only a minimum of consumer goods and began to stagnate by 1950. Housing remained so scarce that couples had to postpone marriage for years or live with in-laws in a single room.

Stalin's policies had a grimmer side. To meet the demand for workers, he deported huge numbers of people to labor camps, or *gulags*, across Siberia and central Asia, where thousands died from inadequate food, primitive conditions, and exhaustion. The inhuman conditions of life in the labor camps were brought to the attention of the Western world through the writings of Alexander Solzhenitsyn (born 1918), especially in his monumental work *Gulag Archipelago*. Harsh censorship policies and the repression of intellectuals remained a hallmark of Stalinist rule.

But Stalin's policies produced dramatic economic results. Tremendous increases were achieved in the production of iron, coal, steel, oil, chemicals, and electrical power, and science and technology moved ahead at an impressive rate. The USSR exploded an atomic bomb in 1949, tested a hydrogen bomb in 1953, and built high-quality fighter planes that proved themselves against American models during the Korean War (1950–1953). Most impressive, in 1957 the Soviet Union shocked the West by launching *Sputnik*, the world's first unmanned space satellite.

The war had relaxed social controls, but during Stalin's final years he reimposed ideological conformity. Secret police chief Lavrenti Beria began massive roundups of "enemies of the state" and transported them to the labor camps. There is also evidence that Stalin was planning another major purge, this time of Jews. He had already accused Soviet Jews of harboring pro-Western and anti-socialist views, and in January 1953 he ordered the arrest of nine Jewish physicians on charges that they had attempted to shorten the lives of Soviet officials. Before the alleged "doctors' plot" could unfold, however, a stroke took Stalin's life on March 5. His successors released the physicians and buried Stalin beside Lenin in the Kremlin's mausoleum.

From National Fronts to People's Democracies

The full extent of Stalin's plans for eastern Europe became apparent soon after the war. Unlike the Allies at the end of World War I, Stalin did not attempt to adjust frontiers along ethnic or national lines. Instead, he forcibly relocated entire populations to fit his notions of Soviet security. This entailed the removal of 13 million ethnic Germans, including families that had resided in the Czech Sudetenland, Silesia, and areas east of the Oder and Neisse rivers for centuries. He also moved about 4.5 million Poles westward, replacing them with Russians and Ukrainians, and about 600,000 Balts from their homelands in Estonia, Latvia, and Lithuania, sending half to East Germany and half deep into Russia.

Because most eastern European states had provided troops for Hitler's legions, Stalin forced those countries to pay reparations. The Soviet Union aligned the entire region with its economic system, chiefly as a source of raw materials that satellite states were compelled to sell to the USSR at low prices.

The Soviet Union constructed new governments in states occupied by the Red Army, setting up "national front" coalitions of Communist, Social Democratic, and peasant parties. Each coalition enjoyed a degree of autonomy that varied from country to country. Where Stalin feared a serious threat to Soviet security, as in Poland and Romania, the national fronts were a sham. Bulgaria fared better, since after the arrival of Russian troops in 1944, the Bulgarian army had joined in the war against Germany. Thus Stalin demanded no reparations from Bulgaria. However, when non-Communist members of the Bulgarian government sought assistance from the Western allies after the war, Stalin manipulated the regime to suit his aims. By contrast, between 1945 and 1947 the national front governments of Hungary and Czechoslovakia were true coalitions in which parties possessed a wide degree of freedom.

The national front regimes lasted less than three years, but they brought about fundamental changes. The Communists joined their coalition partners in breaking up the large, quasi-feudal estates that had characterized eastern European agriculture for centuries, distributing land to millions of peasant families. In addition, between 1945 and 1947 these governments nationalized the coal, steel, banking, and insurance industries.

In the late summer of 1947 Communist parties throughout the region began a concerted attack on their main rivals for popular support, the agrarian parties. Within six months all the national front regimes vanished. In their places appeared one-party Communist governments called "people's democracies." Two pressures probably led to the Soviet crackdown: the desire to use the area's wealth to support reconstruction at home and the decision to impose more direct control on the eastern European states in the face of the Marshall Plan.

The people's democracies geared their economic programs to meet Russia's needs. Governments forced the collectivization of small farms, thus releasing significant numbers of peasants for work in factories under a series of five-year plans. The Soviets intensified their policy of sending high-priced exports to the region while paying low prices for imports. In essence, eastern Europe, an area containing some 90 million people, became an adjunct to the Soviet system. This policy postponed eastern European recovery, leaving the region bleak for many years.

The Yugoslav Model

Direct Soviet hegemony stopped at Yugoslavia, which proved to be an important exception to Russian dominance in eastern Europe. Under the leadership of the Communist leader Marshal Tito (Josip Broz, 1892–1980), the Yugoslav resistance had liberated the country from the Nazis without significant aid from the Red Army. In the postwar period Tito rejected Stalin's claim to preeminence in the Communist world, engaging in a bitter confrontation with Stalin over national sovereignty and Communist strategy.

Tito had aided leftist rebels in Greece against Stalin's orders. When Tito urged Communist leaders in the region to follow his example and ignore Russia's strategic needs, Stalin vowed to discredit him and bring Yugoslavia into the Soviet orbit. In September 1947 Stalin located the headquarters of the newly created Cominform in Belgrade, the Yugoslav capital, hoping to use it to spy on Tito and undermine his support. When this tactic failed, Stalin responded in 1948 and 1949 by expelling Yugoslavia from the Cominform, placing an embargo on its economy, and isolating the country from its neighbors.

Within months the resourceful Tito applied for and received American economic assistance, simultaneously abandoning his support for world revolution while proclaiming the need for separate paths to socialism. In 1950 he initiated a policy of political decentralization by transferring authority from Belgrade to workers' councils and communes. These reforms gave workers a larger voice in the management of factories than anywhere else in the world. Tito had not only maneuvered Yugoslavia into a position of nonalignment between the Soviet Union and the West but had also made his country the major world model of independent Marxism.

De-Stalinization and the Rise of Khrushchev

Stalin groomed no successor. In the power struggle that broke out after his death, his closest followers lost out. Beria, dismissed from his posts and expelled from the party, was executed. A collective leadership soon emerged that abolished the office of general secretary of the Communist party, Stalin's base of power for 30 years, and established party secretaries in its place. At the top of this group was Nikita Khrushchev (1894–1971), a miner's son who as party boss had governed the Ukraine from 1939 to 1950. By 1955 he was joined by Nikolai Bulganin and Vyacheslav Molotov, Stalin's longtime foreign minister, to form a three-man *troika.*

Khrushchev came to personify post-Stalinist Russia. Though he would never wield the arbitrary power that Stalin had, he stood out from his rivals. Illiterate until his twenties, his bald, rotund appearance and outgoing personality belied a keen intelligence. Khrushchev solidified his position in a speech before the Twentieth Congress of

Nikita Khrushchev, who emerged as the leader of the Soyiet Union after Stalin's death, initiated a new stage in domestic development and confrontation with the West. [Sergio Larrain/Magnum]

Martin Luther King, Jr., who popularized the passive resistance strategy that led to victories in the civil rights movement, leads a march from Selma to Montgomery, Alabama in 1965. To his left is Coretta Scott King, his wife. [Bob Adelman/Magnum]

of nonviolent disobedience was the answer to the civil rights struggle. In 1960 King became copastor with his father at the Ebenezer Baptist Church in Atlanta but devoted his energies to the SCLC and to a concerted drive against racial injustice. While protesting segregation at a lunch counter, he was arrested and sentenced to state prison on a pretext. The case aroused the interest of then–Democratic presidential candidate John Kennedy (1917–1963).

King's influence reached its peak in the years between 1960 and 1965. The nonviolent strategy of "sit-ins" and protest marches drew a huge following of blacks and whites and put pressure on President Kennedy, who proposed a comprehensive civil rights bill intended to end legal segregation. King's success also made him the subject of covert FBI surveillance. In the spring of 1963 his efforts to end segregation in Birmingham, Alabama, resulted in national attention as police turned dogs and fire hoses on the demonstrators and arrested King along with hundreds of schoolchildren. From jail King wrote a letter of great eloquence explaining his nonviolent philosophy. In August 1963 King and other civil rights advocates marched on Washington. Before the Lincoln Memorial, his moral passion captivated some 200,000 peaceful demonstrators as he recounted his "dream" that one day blacks and whites would be brothers and sisters.

Kennedy's legislative proposal was blocked in Congress by a coalition of Republicans and southern Democrats and remained stalled in committee when he was assassinated in 1963. His more politically astute successor, Lyndon B. Johnson (1908–1973), obtained passage of the 1964 Civil Rights Act, which prohibited discrimination in public places and in the use of federal funds. For his contributions to civil rights, King was awarded the Nobel prize for peace.

In his final years King's leadership came under increasing pressure from more militant blacks, who faulted him for being too cautious. Riots in the Watts district of Los Angeles in 1965 brought attention to the enormous problems of blacks in northern and western cities, where his nonviolent tactics were questioned. King began to broaden his work to include housing discrimination in Chicago, and in 1967 he strongly opposed the war in Vietnam. In April 1968, while in Memphis, Tennessee, to support a strike of sanitation workers, he was gunned down by a white racist.

King's great contribution to civil rights had been his ability to turn regional protests into a national crusade. He had galvanized the black masses into action, and although complex racial problems continued to plague the nation, America would never quite be the same again.

The New Activism and American Women

The same year as the passage of the Civil Rights Act, Johnson ran for election on a platform calling for a "Great Society" made possible by a war on poverty. The voters returned him to office along with 40 additional Democratic members of Congress, giving the House of Representatives a progressive majority for the first time since 1938. The dramatic triumph of liberalism reflected a new social activism that had been stimulated by the struggle for racial equality.

Since the early 1960s university students in America had been in the forefront of social and political militancy, as they were in Europe. In June 1962 about 60 young people, members of a group known as Students for a Democratic Society (SDS), met at Port Huron, Michigan, to discuss civil rights, foreign policy, education, and welfare. The statement of principles they issued—the Port

Letter from Birmingham Jail

After the arrest of Martin Luther King, Jr., in 1963, eight fellow clergymen published a statement calling his actions "unwise and untimely." In April he wrote a lengthy response—scribbled in the margins of a newspaper and on scraps of paper—explaining "why we can't wait."

Perhaps it is easy for those who have never felt the stinging darts of segregation to say, "Wait." But when you have seen vicious mobs lynch your mothers and fathers at will and drown your sisters and brothers at whim; when you have seen hate-filled policemen curse, kick, and even kill your black brothers and sisters; when you see the vast majority of your twenty million Negro brothers smothering in an airtight cage of poverty in the midst of an affluent society; when you suddenly find your tongue twisted and your speech stammering as you seek to explain to your six-year-old daughter why she can't go to the public amusement park . . . and see ominous clouds of inferiority beginning to form in her little mental sky, and see her beginning to distort her personality by developing an unconscious bitterness toward white people; when you have to concoct an answer for a five-year-old son who is asking: "Daddy, why do white people treat colored people so mean?" . . . when you are humiliated day in and day out by nagging signs reading "white" and "colored"; when your first name becomes "nigger," your middle name becomes "boy" (however old you are) and your last name becomes "John," and your wife and mother are never given the respected title "Mrs."; when you are harried by day and haunted by night by the fact that you are a Negro, living constantly at tiptoe stance, never quite knowing what to expect next, and are plagued with inner fears and outer resentments; when you are forever fighting a degenerating sense of "nobodiness"—then you will understand why we find it difficult to wait. There comes a time when the cup of endurance runs over, and men are no longer willing to be plunged into the abyss of despair. I hope, sirs, you can understand our legitimate and unavoidable impatience.

Source: M. L. King, Jr., *Why We Can't Wait* (New York: Harper & Row, 1963), pp. 83–84.

Huron Statement—focused on the concept of "participatory democracy," the notion that people should take part in the decisions that affect their lives. SDS organized an interracial movement of the poor in northern cities, took part in sit-ins and demonstrations in the south, and became increasingly militant over the Vietnam War. By the late 1960s SDS had begun to split apart, one faction forming the Weathermen, an extremist group devoted to violent action. Yet the Port Huron Statement left its mark on an entire generation of Americans.

The civil rights movement and student activism transformed American society in other ways. The gay rights movement, born in 1969 when a police raid in New York's Greenwich Village sparked violent protests from men in the Stonewall Bar, raised important issues about sexual oppression and coincided with the emergence of a powerful new impetus toward women's liberation.

Many women who had left the home for the factory during World War II sought job opportunities traditionally closed to them. Feminists were encouraged by the controversial arguments of Betty Friedan (born 1921), whose book *The Feminine Mystique* (1963) argued that women should seek fulfillment beyond their ties to husbands and children. After the war the number of women who worked for pay outside the home rose dramatically, so that by 1960 twice as many women worked as in 1940. Equally significant was the fact that whereas only 15 percent of all wives worked in 1940, the figure exceeded 50 percent by 1980.

Two separate movements took up the challenge of feminism in the 1960s. The National Organization for Women (NOW), representing older professionals, worked for women's rights through the political and legal systems. Friedan was elected president when it was formed in 1966. The women's liberation movement, which attracted many younger women who had been involved in antiwar and civil rights efforts, was more confrontational. Beginning in 1968 it identified the patriarchial family and socially formed gen-

The new feminism began in the 1960s and has continued ever since. Here, at a 1970s fund-raiser for the equal rights amendment, are Betty Ford, wife of former president Gerald Ford (speaking), with Bella Abzug on the far right and Betty Friedan on the left. [Alex Webb/ Magnum]

der patterns as causes of oppression. Not only did feminists demand legal equality with men, but they also encouraged women to seek power through female solidarity and "gender consciousness."

Affirmative action regulations designed to enforce equal opportunity brought about improvement in employment patterns and wage scales for minorities and women. Yet in the 1970s a woman earned only 59 cents for every dollar earned by a man. In 1972 Congress passed the equal rights amendment to the constitution, but the measure failed when a number of state legislatures did not ratify it. Racial, ethnic, and sexual prejudice remains deeply entrenched in some segments of American society.

Canada: Economic Expansion and Social Change

Canada and the United States together make up most of the North American continent.* The two nations share a common 3,000-mile border that stretches from the Pacific to the Atlantic and along the eastern frontier of Alaska. Nevertheless, Canada possesses unique historical and cultural traditions and, since World War II, has undergone its own social and economic transformation.

Despite an expanse of nearly 4 million square miles—making it, after the USSR, geographically the world's second largest nation—60 percent of Canada's 25 million people live in the Quebec-Windsor corridor, an industrialized region that hugs the U.S.-Canadian border from Detroit to the Atlantic. The remainder of the country represents a vast, sparsely populated territory of thick forests, productive agricultural prairies, and rich mineral deposits.

Canada's modern history has shown a gradual distancing from Great Britain, its traditional "mother country." The British North America Act of 1867 had defined its political and constitutional structure as a dominion within the empire. In 1931, however, the Statute of Westminster conceded full sovereignty to Canada, Australia, New Zealand, and the other dominions, which then became members of the voluntary Commonwealth of Nations. Today Elizabeth II serves as Canada's queen, but an elected prime minister and parliament actually govern. In 1947, after Canadian participation in World War II heightened national self-identity, parliament passed the Canadian Citizenship Act, which ended the granting of automatic citizenship to British subjects. Only in the mid-1980s did growing national sentiment result in the "patriation" of the constitution to Canada, that is, the replacement of the constitutional provisions of the British North America Act with a new constitution. The new Charter of Rights and Freedoms reinforced basic civil liberties. Throughout this

*Mexico, though geographically part of North America, is usually grouped, for linguistic and historical reasons, with the other nations of Latin America.

century three major parties have dominated the political system. The Liberals, the largest party, have been in power for most of the modern period. The Progressive Conservatives, or "Tories," have a large following that is less inclined to support an extension of the welfare state. The left-of-center New Democratic party follows a social democratic program.

Persistent and at times violent tension has marked relations between Canada's chief linguistic groups, the English- and French-speaking populations. The abiding nationalism of Quebec province, where most French Canadians live, has grown into stiff political resistance against the nation's dominant English element. As a result of pressure from the Parti Québécois and other groups, in 1963 the Royal Commission on Bilingualism and Biculturalism was given a mandate to redress French grievances. The Official Language Act, passed in 1969, established both French and English as the official languages of the nation. Nonetheless, in 1970 the so-called October Crisis erupted in Quebec when a British trade commissioner was abducted and a provincial minister was murdered by the extremist Quebec Liberation Front. Martial law was imposed on the country, but French nationalism did not abate. Several years later the Parti Québécois won control of the provincial government on a separatist platform.

Despite such tensions, the Canadian economy expanded greatly. In the 1960s the diversified manufacturing sector spurred unparalleled prosperity, with the production growth rate reaching 7 percent in 1973 and the GNP jumping by 15 percent. Trade expanded, and agricultural exports soared with massive grain sales to China and the USSR. The discovery of large oil reserves in the western province of Alberta increased the nation's economic promise further. Real income rose as much as 6.5 percent a year. Indeed, Canada's growth was so rapid that it had negative consequences by the next decade. The problem, still to be resolved, centers on the fact that the greatly increased manufacturing sector is too large for the small size of the domestic market, which means that continuing prosperity relies too heavily on the vagaries of foreign exchange and economic conditions elsewhere.

Canada's growth in recent decades has been driven in large part by ever-increasing economic ties with the United States. American investments began pouring into Canada in the 1920s. Today about 70 percent of its manufacturing industries are owned and controlled by U.S. companies—the automobile industry, for example, is almost completely American-owned, and the oil and gas concerns are 80 percent foreign-owned. This pattern has meant that major decisions regarding Canadian subsidiaries, especially ones affecting labor and employment conditions, are made abroad. The integration of the two economies has recently been advanced by the signing and ratification of a free trade treaty that aims at creating a single market for the movement of goods across borders.

To the unequal economic relationship has been added the Americanization of the country's culture, increasingly resented by Canadian intellectuals, who are striving to create a unique cultural life of their own. From Canada's point of view, one of the most pressing issues of the future will be coming to grips with the pervasive feeling that the United States, with far greater wealth and population, is an overshadowing influence.

Canada's widening prosperity has had social consequences, especially in the growth of an affluent middle class, most of which lives in burgeoning urban centers. Toronto and Montreal, each with some 3 million people, symbolize the Canadian experience. While most of the nation's wealth is still controlled by the English population and centers on the modern financial network of Toronto, the French middle class has risen rapidly in recent years. Montreal, a sophisticated and cosmopolitan city, is the hub of a province, Quebec, that is now 70 percent urban and home to an ambitious entrepreneurial class. Although unemployment has been high in recent years, Canada's population has had since the 1960s one of the most advanced welfare states in the world, providing cradle-to-grave health care, social security insurance, and an array of other benefits. Canada's future, though faced with serious challenges, remains bright.

From Brinkmanship to Détente

By the early 1950s the superpowers were enmeshed in a struggle for hegemony. For 25 years the pattern of conflict set in 1947 remained fairly consistent: with American influence predominant in Latin America and western Europe and the Soviet Union supreme in eastern Europe, each power challenged the other in peripheral regions of the globe. The danger lay in the possibility that diplomatic confrontations would lead to local military conflict, which could in turn escalate into nuclear war. The Korean War (1950–1953) proved to be the first of several such situations (see Chapter 38).

Confrontation and Crisis

Eisenhower delegated exceptional authority to his secretary of state, John Foster Dulles (1888–1959). A man who combined a brilliant legal mind with righteous moralism, Dulles had been part of Wilson's delegation at the Paris peace conference in 1919. During his long tenure as secretary of state, he was one of the most strident voices of the Cold War, denouncing Truman's containment policy and advocating an offensive program to "liberate" areas under communist control. Dulles emphasized America's nuclear strength, basing foreign policy on repeated warnings that local communist aggression would lead to "massive retaliation" by the United States. The Dulles policy of rattling nuclear missiles whenever international crises erupted was dubbed "brinkmanship," but the eastern European revolts of the 1950s revealed the hollowness of these threats. America stood by in 1956 while anti-Soviet fighters in Hungary battled Soviet tanks with cobblestones and rifles.

The Eisenhower administration never abandoned containment. Using marines or covert operations directed by the CIA, the United States played a key role in overthrowing supposedly procommunist governments around the world, including those in Iran (1953), Guatemala (1954), and Chile (1973). The CIA also plotted the assassination of Congolese leader Patrice Lumumba in 1961 and, with the aid of American gansters, made several attempts against the Cuban leader Fidel Castro.

Under Kennedy, American Cold War strategy shifted again, but only in emphasis. Kennedy undertook a huge buildup of conventional and nuclear weapons. In his effort to close the "missile gap" with the Soviet Union, he accelerated the nuclear arms race, to which Russia responded in 1961 by detonating a hydrogen bomb in the atmosphere. Kennedy was fascinated with "counterinsurgency" operations, by which he meant the use of limited warfare against communist infiltration of Third World countries. One result of this was the Bay of Pigs fiasco in Cuba (see Chapter 40).

Encounters between Kennedy and Khrushchev brought the world to the edge of nuclear disaster. In the summer of 1961 Khrushchev tried to stem the flow of refugees from East Berlin to the West and threatened to sign a treaty with East Germany that would terminate Western rights in the city. Kennedy ordered reservists on military alert and urged Americans to build fallout shelters. This sharp response may have persuaded Khrushchev to back down, for on August 13 the East Germans sealed off their portion of the city by erecting a wall between the two sections of Berlin.

A year later Khrushchev intruded into the American sphere of influence in Latin America by constructing nuclear missile bases in Cuba. Khrushchev argued the need to prevent another American attempt to overthrow the Castro government, but Kennedy considered the action a direct military threat. In October 1962, when American air reconnaisance found Soviet missiles in Cuba, the president imposed a naval quarantine around the island and demanded the missiles' removal. For six tense days Soviet ships sailed toward Cuba and American forces went on war alert. Khrushchev finally drew back by sending Kennedy a letter deploring the horrors of nuclear war and offering a face-saving compromise. The Soviets agreed to withdraw their missiles in return for a public pledge from America not to invade Cuba; unofficially, the United States agreed to dismantle its own offensive missiles in Turkey.

Brezhnev and the Return to Repression

The turbulent Kennedy-Khrushchev era soon came to an end. Kennedy was assassinated in Dallas, Texas, on November 22, 1963. The following summer, while Khrushchev was vacationing in the Crimea, the Communist party's Central Committee stripped him of his power, charging him with a host of errors that included the Cuban crisis, the rift with China, and setbacks in Russia's agricultural and industrial growth. After a brief period of collective leadership, a veteran bureaucrat, Leonid Brezhnev (1906–1982), took Khrushchev's place. Brezhnev served as both Soviet president and Communist party secretary.

During the almost two decades that Brezhnev ruled, the Soviet Union underwent a return to government repression, although not to the extremes of the Stalin era. Party officials agreed on the need for stability and retrenchment after the changes wrought by Khrushchev. Restraints were reimposed on Russian intellectuals, symbolized by the expulsion of Alexander Solzhenitsyn in 1974. Despite Moscow's acceptance of the human rights provisions of the Helsinki Accords, criticism of government policy by prominent dissidents such as Andrei Sakharov, an internationally acclaimed physicist, brought persecution and long periods of Siberian exile. Recalling Russia's wartime sacrifices, Soviet leaders stressed nationalist traditions and the unity of the Soviet Union, crushing regionalism in the Ukraine and elsewhere.

The new wave of repression also affected the Soviet Union's 1.8 million Jews, who suffered from a long tradition of repression. In the Soviet system, state atheism discouraged Judaism along with all other religions, but the government also claimed that Jewish cultural identity and Zionism undermined the unity of the nation. Khrushchev's liberalization program had hardly affected the Soviet Union's Jews. In the 1960s they formed underground networks to keep Jewish tradition alive, circulating typewritten translations of books such as Leon Uris' novel *Exodus* (1958), which traced the emigration of the Jewish people to Palestine and the founding of the state of Israel. The Brezhnev regime, preoccupied with nationality problems within the Soviet Union and political dissidence, stepped up persecution of the Jews. Emigration to Israel, which had been virtually impossible before, was loosened as a result of international pressure in the 1970s. The exit rate reached a peak in 1979, when over 51,000 Jews left the Soviet Union, but declined steadily thereafter. Only in 1987, under Mikhail Gorbachev's more liberal policies, did the number begin to increase again. Western sources estimate that perhaps as many as 25 percent of Soviet Jews wish to emigrate.

The Cuban Missile Crisis: Two Views

The discovery by the United States in the fall of 1962 that the Soviet Union was installing missile bases in Cuba brought the world to the edge of nuclear war. The first of the following accounts of the crisis is by special White House assistant Arthur M. Schlesinger, Jr., who described President Kennedy's speech of October 19.

Then at seven o'clock the speech: his expression grave, his voice firm and calm, the evidence set forth without emotion, the conclusion unequivocal—"The purpose of these bases can be none other than to provide a nuclear strike capability against the Western Hemisphere." He recited the Soviet assurances, now revealed as "deliberate deception," and called the Soviet action "a deliberately provocative and unjustified change in the status quo which cannot be accepted by this country. . . ." He then laid out what he called with emphasis his *initial* steps: a quarantine on all offensive military equipment under shipment to Cuba; an intensified surveillance of Cuba itself; a declaration that any missile launched from Cuba would be regarded as an attack by the Soviet Union on the United States, requiring full retaliatory response upon the Soviet Union . . . and an appeal to Chairman Khrushchev "to abandon this course of world domination, and to join in a historic effort to end the perilous arms race and to transform the history of man."

Here is Soviet Premier Khrushchev's account.

I want to make one thing absolutely clear: when we put our ballistic missiles in Cuba, we had no desire to start a war. . . . In October, President Kennedy came out with a statement warning that the United States would take whatever measures were necessary to remove what he called the "threat" of Russian missiles in Cuba. . . . In our estimation the Americans were trying to frighten us, but they were no less scared than we were of atomic war. . . .

President Kennedy issued an ultimatum, demanding that we remove our missiles and bombers from Cuba. I remember those days vividly. I remember the exchange with President Kennedy especially well because I initiated it and was at the center of the action on our end of the correspondence. I take complete responsibility for the fact that the President and I entered into direct correspondence at the most crucial and dangerous stage of the crisis. . . .

The climax came after five or six days, when our ambassador to Washington, Anatoly Dobrynin, reported that the President's brother, Robert Kennedy, had come to see him on an unofficial visit. Dobrynin's report went something like this:

"Robert Kennedy looked exhausted. One could see from his eyes that he had not slept for days. He himself said that he had not been home for six days and nights. 'The President is in a grave situation,' Robert Kennedy said, 'and he does not know how to get out of it. We are under very severe stress. In fact we are under pressure from our military to use force against Cuba.' " . . .

We could see that we had to reorient our position swiftly. . . . We sent the Americans a note saying that we agreed to remove our missiles and bombers on the condition that the President give us his assurance that there would be no invasion of Cuba by the forces of the United States or anybody else. Finally Kennedy gave in and agreed to make a statement giving us such an assurance.

Sources: A. M. Schlesinger, Jr., *A Thousand Days: John F. Kennedy in the White House* (Boston: Houghton Mifflin, 1965), pp. 812–813; N. Khrushchev, *Khrushchev Remembers*, trans. S. Talbott (Boston: Little, Brown, 1970), pp. 496–498.

MOSCOW: RUSSIAN CITY AND SOVIET CAPITAL

One of the world's great cities, Moscow is not only the political capital of the Soviet Union but also the center of its industrial and cultural life. It embodies the sense of continuity that links the country's history from its early development to its status as superpower.

Moscow stands on the Moscow River, in the center of the vast plain of European Russia. Its origins stretch back to the twelfth century, when an early Russian prince built fortifications around an area known as the Kremlin ("Citadel"). The town gradually became a thriving trading site, and in 1326 the head of the Russian Orthodox church transferred his seat there. Moscow's rulers incorporated more of the surrounding countryside and provided defense against repeated Mongol invasions. By the fifteenth century it had become the undisputed core of a unified Russian state under Ivan the Great, who enlarged and strengthened the Kremlin with the crenelated red brick walls and towers that still give it its characteristic appearance.

The establishment of the Romanov dynasty in 1613 added employment in state administration to craft manufacturing. Commercial activity in Moscow centered in a large open market area called Red Square (in Russian, the word meaning "red" also means "beautiful"). In the second half of the eighteenth century Moscow University was founded, and architects from France and Italy were imported to design public buildings. Even after Peter the Great moved the capital to his new city of St. Petersburg, Moscow's industries continued to grow. By 1812, when Napoleon invaded Russia and occupied Moscow, its population had surpassed 275,000.

Following a disastrous fire during the occupation and Napoleon's withdrawal, a great program of rebuilding was undertaken that reconstructed the interior structures of the Kremlin and the Bolshoi Theater. The emancipation of the serfs in 1861 brought many of them to Moscow, whose population had increased to more than 600,000 by 1870. As new rail lines linked the city to the rest of the country during the 1890s, heavy engineering and metal industries developed. The number of inhabitants expanded rapidly, reaching almost 2 million before the outbreak of World War I.

The Soviets have given Moscow much of its modern appearance. Lenin moved the capital back to the city in 1918, and despite the ravages of the civil war its population had doubled by 1939 to more than 4 million, creating serious overcrowding and housing shortages. During World War II, Moscow withstood the onslaught of the German armies, which reached to within 25 miles of the city in late 1941. With Stalin remaining as a symbol of Russian resistance, the citizens of Moscow built antitank defenses, and the Red Army repulsed the *Wehrmacht*.

Recovery was rapid. In the late 1940s and early 1950s Stalin added ornate "wedding cake" skyscrapers to the Moscow skyline, and in the 1960s Khrushchev began the construction of extensive suburban apartment complexes to relieve the chronic housing shortage. Much of the country's modern industry is concentrated around the periphery.

The eclectic mix of Moscow's architecture reflects the richly diverse history of Russia. The Kremlin still dominates the city. Within its walls is one of the most striking and beautiful architectural ensembles in the world, over which rise the five golden onion-shaped domes of the fifteenth-century Cathedral of the Assumption and the white bell tower built by Ivan the Great. The nineteenth-century Kremlin Great Palace is now the seat of Soviet political power, while the Palace of Congresses, completed in 1961, is used for Communist party meetings. Along the east wall of the Kremlin lies Red Square, the ceremonial center of the capital. Today marchers in the annual May Day and the October Revolution parades pass by the squat bulk of the Lenin Mausoleum, as well as the domed sixteenth-century Cathedral of St. Basil the Blessed and GUM, the state department store. These sites symbolize the contradictions that mark Soviet life, while Moscow itself represents that peculiar combination of historical tradition and the legacy of revolution that is the Soviet Union.

Coexistence and Détente

In the 25 years following the clash over Cuba, American-Soviet disagreements remained sharp. Yet since the mid-1960s superpower relations have been partially clarified as both sides came to realize that nuclear confrontation would be a common disaster. Summit meetings and disarmament talks have formed the backdrop to a more fundamental trend toward the recognition of political realities that had been obscured by ideological rhetoric. If, in the 1960s, Cold War propaganda gave way to a public discussion of peaceful coexistence, so in the 1970s the United States and the Soviet Union began to define their relationship in terms of *détente,* literally a "relaxation of tensions."

American involvement in Vietnamese affairs (see Chapter 38) sparked a political and social crisis at home. The escalation of the war under President Johnson resulted in more than 500,000 American troops' being sent to Vietnam by the end of 1968. Unable to gain victory on the ground, the United States dropped more explosives on Vietnam than the Allies had used on all fronts during World War II, while American troops killed thousands of civilians in fruitless efforts to prevent villagers from hiding Communist guerrillas. By the mid-1960s a vigorous antiwar movement had begun to emerge in America. The protests started on college campuses, but outspoken opponents soon emerged in Congress and in the press. In 1967 demonstrations spread throughout the country, while thou-

South Vietnam's national police chief executes a Viet Cong officer on a Saigon street. Such scenes aroused opposition to the war in the United States and abroad. [Wide World Photos]

sands of young Americans declared themselves conscientious objectors or fled the United States to avoid the draft. Senator Eugene McCarthy (born 1916), campaigning on an antiwar platform, challenged President Johnson for the Democratic nomination. In March 1968, following McCarthy's strong showing in an early primary, the president announced that he would not seek another term.

After the Tet offensive in February 1968, peace talks with North Vietnam opened in Paris, and in November voters elected the Republican Richard M. Nixon (born 1913) to the presidency. Nixon began the secret bombing of Communist supply routes in Cambodia in early 1969, concealing the operation through false reports. In 1971 the publication of classified war documents heightened antiwar sentiments by revealing earlier deceptions by both Johnson and Nixon. Protests mounted as the 1972 presidential elections approached, but Nixon neutralized them by removing the last American ground troops. The Paris Accords, signed in January 1973, officially ended American involvement in the war.

The 1962 Cuban crisis and the Vietnam War provided the superpowers with an unstated but important lesson in international relations. In withdrawing Russian missiles from Cuba, Khrushchev had tacitly recognized America's predominance in Latin America. Vietnam had forced the United States to accept the limitations of its military strength. The leaders who followed Johnson and Khrushchev spoke increasingly of tempering Soviet-American relations with détente. Détente actually defined the process by which the superpowers agreed to formalize the dominance that the postwar settlements had given them.

This rapprochement was the work of an unlikely pair: Richard Nixon, a lifelong anticommunist, and Leonid Brezhnev, who had opposed Khrushchev's revisionist policies. Nixon repudiated the Dulles doctrine, which had demanded a rollback of Russian communism, while Brezhnev fell back on Lenin's notion that direct confrontation with the West was unnecessary in light of the inevitable decay of capitalism and the overthrow of colonialism by wars of national liberation.

The so-called Watergate crisis ended Nixon's presidency but not the era of détente. It was revealed that Nixon and his aides had illegally manipulated the campaign and had authorized surveillance and espionage against his political opponents. The crisis, which climaxed in 1974, exposed Nixon's efforts to cover up illegal White House operations. In August, faced with the possibility of impeachment, the president resigned in disgrace. Nixon's successor, Gerald R. Ford (born 1913), continued the policy of détente.

Détente contributed to the Helsinki Accords. In 1973 the United States and the Soviet Union joined Canada and almost all the European nations at the Conference on Security and Cooperation in Europe, held in Helsinki, Finland. In the final treaty, signed two years later, the Soviets endorsed political and human rights statements and agreed to encourage closer relations with the West. In return, the signatories guaranteed Europe's political boundaries, including the division of Germany into two states. Russia thus obtained formal recognition of the territorial adjustments in eastern Europe that had been arranged at Yalta and Potsdam. In effect, détente had served to achieve permanent agreement on the postwar settlements that had established the Russian—and, by implication, the American—sphere of influence in Europe.

American foreign policy remained basically unaltered under Ford's successor, Jimmy Carter (born 1924). Carter denounced repressive governments that violated basic human rights and decried the plight of political dissidents in the Soviet Union, but he continued to support dictatorships in Chile and Iran. He also cited the Soviet military buildup to justify an increase in American arms spending.

The Superpowers Challenged

In November 1979, after toppling Shah Muhammad Reza Pahlavi in Iran, Shi'ite Muslims under the leadership of the Ayatollah Ruhollah Khomeini seized the American embassy and captured 52 staff members. The unsuccessful American attempt to free the hostages was a major factor in determining the outcome of the 1980 American presidential elections, leading to the defeat of President Carter by Republican Ronald Reagan.

The hostage crisis demonstrated that the postwar world hegemony jointly exercised by the United States and the Soviet Union had not gone unchallenged. Smaller states have continually sought to mitigate superpower dominance and exert autonomy. In Europe and the non-Western world national leaders have employed a variety of techniques to maneuver between America and the Soviet Union. Within the Communist world ideological nonconformity has proved a powerful means of asserting independence, while in both western and eastern Europe nationalism has been used as a lever against Washington and Moscow.

Outside the immediate areas of superpower hegemony, states often exploited Cold War rivalries to extract economic and political concessions from each side. Neutralism and ideological nonalignment, especially among former colonies, have achieved the same results. The balance of nuclear terror actually enhances such possibilities, for to avoid mutual self-destruction over issues that do not threaten their vital interests, the superpowers are forced to act with restraint. Regional and economic organizations have exercised a moderating influence through the control of vital natural resources and markets. The revival of religious fundamentalism among Islamic states, so dramatically demonstrated in the United States–Iran crisis, suggests the availability of still other alternatives.

The Growth of European Autonomy

European efforts toward economic unity led to a subtle undermining of American influence. In 1950, against the background of the Marshall Plan, French foreign minister Robert Schuman (1886–1963) proposed a plan for cooperating in the production of steel and coal. Belgium, Luxembourg, and the Netherlands joined France, West Germany, and Italy in forming the European Coal and Steel Community (ECSC), which quickly tripled iron and steel output and increased coal production almost 25 percent. By 1957 the ECSC concluded that further cooperation could strengthen Europe's economies and enable its members jointly to influence the superpowers. As a result, ECSC members created the European Economic Community, better known as the Common Market. Through the elimination of tariff barriers and the free exchange of labor and capital, the Common Market achieved remarkable success in economic integration. After years of French objection, Britain, Ireland, and Denmark became members in 1973. Although the United States still exercises a major influence in European economic life, Europe has escaped the direct dependency it once had on America. Indeed, while the Common Market brought an increase in American business in Europe, in the 1980s the flow of capital began to move in both directions as European products and investments entered the United States.

Charles de Gaulle, president of France from 1958 to 1969, led a more direct challenge to American hegemony. Proud and intensely nationalistic, he wanted to put France at the center of a Europe that would reassert its autonomy between the United States and the Soviet Union. For that reason, de Gaulle pulled French forces out of NATO, twice vetoed the entry of America's closest ally, Great Britain, into the European Common Market, and condemned America's escalating role in Vietnam. More grating still to Washington, the French leader tried to weaken the American economy by demanding gold for the large quantity of U.S. dollars held in Paris.

West Germany also demonstrated more autonomy. When the socialist Willy Brandt became federal chancellor in 1969, he embarked on a policy of reconciliation with the Communist bloc countries of eastern Europe. In exchange for guarantees of West Berlin's freedom and a mutual renunciation of force, Brandt concluded treaties with the Soviet Union, Czechoslovakia, and Poland that formally recognized existing frontiers. Of equal importance, he also began the normalization of relations with East Germany.

The success of the Common Market, together with the experience of de Gaulle and Brandt, led to Europe's increasing political independence from Washington. Although some Europeans have expressed anxiety at the prospect of an American missile withdrawal, since 1968 powerful grass-roots peace movements have challenged American nuclear policy. Moreover, most European states refused to follow the American lead in applying sanctions against the Soviet Union in 1979 after the Russian invasion of Afghanistan. A similar request was rejected in 1981 following the suppression of the Polish trade union movement, and in 1986 European states refused an American request for overflight permission during the bombing raid against Libya.

In eastern Europe the trend toward autonomy has been slower. Although the open revolts against Soviet authority in East Germany (1953) and Hungary (1956) were swiftly crushed, cautious ideological divergence from orthodox Communist policy drew many eastern European regimes away from Moscow. Combining Yugoslav nationalism with doctrinal innovation, Marshal Tito steered his country into a quasi-neutral position even during the Stalinist period. Tito's example no doubt contributed to the harsh Soviet reaction against similar efforts in Czechoslovakia. In Jan-

41.1 Europe Since World War II

uary 1968 reformists within the Czech Communist party installed Alexander Dubček (born 1921) in office. Dubček lifted censorship and permitted local decision making in factories, unions, and the Communist party itself. The Czech example aroused demands for similar reforms elsewhere in eastern Europe. In August 500,000 Soviet and Warsaw Pact troops poured into Czechoslovkia and arrested Dubček and his reformist supporters. Brezhnev subsequently asserted the Soviet Union's right to intervene in the affairs of any socialist nation whenever necessary—the so-called Breshnev doctrine. By the 1970s a subtle shift in Soviet policy was introduced as Moscow sought to reduce the need for military intervention by stimulating economic integration with the eastern European region.

Efforts to achieve autonomy within the Communist world climaxed a decade later in Poland. In 1980 a rash of illegal strikes led to a massive work stoppage at the Gdansk shipyards and inspired the formation of the Solidarity movement, headed by Lech Walesa (born 1944), a tough but moderate organizer. With support from almost 10 million workers and the Catholic church, Solidarity won major concessions from the government before party leader General Wojciech Jaruzwelski (born 1923) imposed martial law and arrested union leaders. Walesa was eventually freed and Solidarity recognized. In the midst of a deepening economic crisis, partially free elections were held in 1989, leading to the formation of a coalition government headed by Tadeusz Mazowiecki of Solidarity.

The desire for ideological autonomy has also been linked to the growing identification of Communist parties with the idea of an independent Europe free from the influence of both superpowers. This trend gave rise to the phenomenon known as Eurocommunism, which found its first example in Italy, whose Communist party was inspired by the theoretical writings of Antonio Gramsci (1891–1937). Italian Communists have adopted considerable tactical flexibility based on Gramsci's notion that the history of a nation should guide the development of its Communist movement. Not unlike the European popular front policies of the 1930s, Italian Communist leaders have accepted both democratic principles and the possibility of sharing power in a coalition with bourgeois parties. The Communists of France, Spain, and most other Western countries have moved in the same direction, at times breaking with Moscow over international issues. In 1968 the Italian Communist party, together with its French counterpart, attacked the Soviet Union's invasion of Czechoslovakia.

The Nonaligned World

The colonial territories that gained nationhood after World War II found themselves economically dependent on the industrialized, wealthier Western states. Much-needed developmental resources came through assistance programs sponsored by the United States and the Soviet Union, which vied with each other to capture the political support of the newly independent countries. Yet, rather than becoming pawns in the East-West competition, underdeveloped states devised a strategy that turned the Cold War into what they called "creative confrontation"—playing off the superpowers to their own advantage while maintaining nonaligned status. India's Jawaharlal Nehru saw neutralism as a means of forging a "third force" among nonaligned nations, much as de Gaulle would attempt to do in Europe in the 1960s. The Egyptian leader Gamal Abdel Nasser maneuvered skillfully between the superpowers in pursuit of his goals.

In 1955 a large number of neutralist states convened the Afro-Asian Conference in Bandung, Indonesia, to discuss mutual interests and strategy. The United Nations soon became a focus of Third World nonalignment. The ranks of the General Assembly swelled rapidly as former colonies won independence, thus forming a substantial voting bloc with members from Latin America. Anticolonial sentiment, reinforced by the Soviets, often translated into anti-Western positions, but the primary agenda among nonaligned countries was to secure passage of social and economic assistance measures. Superpower refusal to fund such programs has often undermined the effectiveness of the neutralist coalition.

The Bandung conference symbolized continuing efforts to establish regional organizations designed to forge unity of policy and economic cooperation among Third World nations. The Organization of African Unity (OAU) was established because African leaders believed that disunity played into the hands of the superpowers. Founded in 1963, the OAU required a policy of nonalignment from each of its 30 member states and spawned a number of subregional economic groups similar in concept to the European Common Market. The OAU has also pursued a policy of political cooperation with other Third World regional coalitions, especially with Arab countries.

Much of the frustration expressed by nonaligned nations stemmed from the vastly unequal relationship separating rich and poor states. The resentment, strongest where key resources and local economies have been exploited by multinational Western corporations, has had a major impact on recent world events. The formation of the Organization of Petroleum Exporting Countries (OPEC) in 1960 reflects these concerns. OPEC devised the strategy of counterpenetration, whereby it hoped to make industrial economies that relied heavily on oil imports vulnerable to Third World pressures. Initially, the strategy had astounding success. Dwindling foreign aid from the United States and its allies, coupled with the West's pro-Israeli policy in the Middle East, angered the Arab nations in OPEC. In 1973 the group quadrupled the price of crude oil in one year. The sudden rise in fuel costs intensified inflation and recession in the West and underscored the interdependency of world societies. The next year the nonaligned bloc in the UN passed a resolution demanding the creation of a "new international economic order" in which resources, trade, and markets would be equally distributed.

Nonaligned states have forged still other forms of economic cooperation as leverage against the superpowers. OPEC, the OAU, and the Arab League have overlapping members, and in the 1970s the Arabs began extending huge financial assistance to African nations in an effort to reduce African economic dependency on the United States and the Soviet Union. At a 1977 Afro-Arab summit conference in Cairo, oil producers pledged $1.5 billion in aid to Africa. Recent divisions within OPEC have made concerted action more difficult. Nevertheless, the 1973 oil crisis provided dramatic evidence of the limitations of superpower hegemony.

The Nuclear Peril

Despite a history of ideological conflict and Cold War confrontations since the end of World War II, the United States and the Soviet Union have remained at peace with each other. Indeed, relations between the superpowers grew less tense in the 1980s, and efforts at political cooperation and disarmament held out the promise of a more peaceful world.

The Quest for Disarmament

Nuclear arms limitations talks have been a feature of diplomatic relations for more than 40 years. Some progress has been made; the superpowers have been forced to be sensitive to the demands of the international community, and their monopoly over nuclear arms has ended.

In 1946, when it still had the world's only atomic weapons, the United States suggested the creation of an international atomic development authority with the power to inspect all countries to prevent the manufacture of nuclear weapons. America proposed turning its research data and facilities over to the agency. The Soviet Union, in the midst of developing its own atomic capability, vetoed the proposal and in 1949 detonated an atomic weapon. Since then the United States and the Soviet Union have been engaged in a costly and dangerous nuclear arms race. Each now possesses enough nuclear weapons to exterminate most of the life on the planet.

During the height of the Cold War the superpowers developed their nuclear arsenals and delivery systems and conducted unrestrained testing of atomic weapons that threatened to destroy the environment. In 1952 the United States exploded a hydrogen bomb, an even more destructive weapon. The following year the Soviets announced their own hydrogen device, and in 1961 they tested a 50-megaton bomb, the equivalent of 50 million tons of TNT.

The first important step in nuclear disarmament came in 1963 with the signing of a test ban treaty that permitted only underground explosions. Although more than 100 nations signed the treaty, some states, hoping to achieve their own nuclear capability, refused. In 1968 the United States and the Soviet Union jointly sponsored a nonproliferation treaty that sought to restrict nuclear weapons to the five nations already in possession of them—the United States, the Soviet Union, Britain, France, and China. The pact called for international inspections to ensure that nuclear energy facilities would be used only for peaceful purposes. Eight countries (Argentina, Brazil, Egypt, India, Israel, Pakistan, Spain, and South Africa) did not sign the agreement. A similar pact in 1977 secured the agreement of 90 nations, but again, those approaching nuclear capacity refused. The limited success of the nonproliferation effort has not only made disarmament more difficult but also reflects the sobering failure of the superpowers to reach their own accord.

Little progress was made in American-Soviet disarmament until the 1972 SALT I treaty, which froze the number of offensive "strategic" intercontinental missile launchers for five years. The antiballistic missile (ABM) provisions of SALT I limited the number of ABM sites. In theory, ABMs could provide a nuclear defense by intercepting attacking missiles, although the cost would be prohibitive and decoys could make the system ineffective; in a nuclear exchange, even a small margin of error could result in tens of millions of fatalities. The ABM accord was based on the notion of deterrence, which argues that each side would not attack the other because it feared counterattack. By contrast, an unrestricted ABM race might tempt the nation that acquired an effective defense to consider a first strike against the other if nuclear war seemed "winnable."

The SALT I pact was imperfect. The United States possessed a manned nuclear bomber fleet that the Soviets could not match. Moreover, nothing prevented either side from equipping its missiles with multiple warheads (MIRVs), and no restrictions were placed on technical improvements in either missiles or warheads. The 1979 SALT II treaty limited each superpower to 2,400 nuclear launchers, of which only 1,320 could have MIRVs. But the U.S. Senate refused to ratify SALT II because of conservative opposition and the difficulty of maintaining true parity in the face of continued weapons research. The treaty was observed informally until President Reagan exceeded SALT II limits in 1986. Both the United States and the Soviet Union have continued to test nuclear weapons.

The Gorbachev Era

Recent changes in Soviet-American relations have further reduced superpower tensions. Brezhnev died in November 1982, only to be replaced in rapid succession by former secret police chief Yuri Andropov (1904–1984), the Politburo veteran Konstantin Chernenko (1912–1985), and, in March 1985, Mikhail Gorbachev (born 1931). Representing a younger generation, Gorbachev was reformist in outlook. He took symbolic steps to liberalize Soviet rule at home by permitting more open discussion—a policy known as *glasnost* ("openness")—releasing some prominent political dissidents, and establishing a commission to review censorship policies. In 1987 came news that *Dr. Zhivago*, Boris Pasternak's sweeping novel of love broken by the Russian Revolution, would be published, three decades after its appearance in the West.

The real focus of Gorbachev's domestic program concerned the Soviet economy. Administered through a central planning system that had originated with Stalin, economic policy was beset by a maze of bureaucratic processes that resulted in inefficiency, low-quality consumer goods, and outdated technology. Under Stalin the economy had grown rapidly until 1950 through an "extensive" method of expanding output by manipulating labor and capital. Growth slowed further in the 1970s, and the annual rate of the Soviet GNP dropped by half in the early 1980s. Gorbachev's reform program, which he has called *perestroika* ("restructuring"), called for an "intensive" growth fed by technological progress and efficiency and the cautious introduction of market incentives.

The climate for change stimulated by Gorbachev's reform program elicited a favorable response from the Soviet people. In the spring of 1989 elections were held for membership in the Supreme Soviet. For the first time in 70 years, citizens were free to vote for representatives from a long list of candidates, not all of whom had been nominated by the party or were party members. The results, dramatic in their implications, demonstrated popular discontent with party bureaucrats. Among those elected was Boris Yeltsin, a strong critic of the old party machine who had been ousted from his post as Moscow party boss because of his open criticism of bureaucratic vested interests. The elections, which strengthened Gorbachev's hand in his struggle with the older Communist party leadership, appear to have confirmed the impetus behind *perestroika*.

The early 1980s saw a steady buildup in the arms race. President Reagan increased military spending from one-fourth to one-third of the federal budget. The Soviets threatened to match the weapons escalation. The Reagan administration's arms policy aimed at achieving two goals: nuclear superiority over the Soviet Union and the development of the Strategic Defense Initiative (SDI). Dubbed "Star Wars" by the media, the SDI plan called for research and development of satellite-mounted lasers capable of destroying offensive enemy missiles in flight. SDI critics feared that the system might be intended to enable the

President Ronald Reagan and Soviet leader Mikhail Gorbachev meet in Moscow, May 1988. [Blanche/Gamma-Liaison]

United States to win a nuclear war, while advocates have argued that it would reduce the threat of war. Extensive research in space-based offensive weapons systems was simultaneously carried on under classified military budgeting.

Nevertheless, Gorbachev's reformist attitudes have had a positive impact on superpower relations. Beginning with a Geneva meeting in 1985, Gorbachev and Reagan held four summit meetings. At Reykjavik, Iceland, in 1986 the two leaders agreed in principle to a reduction of missile systems. Two years later, in Moscow, they signed documents that put into effect a treaty eliminating Soviet and American medium and shorter-range land-based missiles. Between 1985 and 1988 the two nations concluded more than 40 other treaties concerning a variety of issues from cultural exchanges to fishing rights. Still, they have made no headway on space-based defense systems, and the issue of long-range missiles remains unresolved.

Perestroika: Reform in Gorbachev's Russia

In April 1985 Mikhail Gorbachev announced a policy of far-reaching reform that he called perestroika *("restructuring"). Gorbachev claimed that this policy of delegating more responsibility to the people, of encouraging initiative and openness, is the next natural stage in the development of the Soviet system. Here he describes his goals as a phase in the continuing revolution.*

We have come to the conclusion that unless we activate the human factor, that is, unless we take into consideration the diverse interests of people, work collectives, public bodies, and various social groups, unless we rely on them, and draw them into active, constructive endeavor, it will be impossible for us to accomplish any of the tasks set, or to change the situation in the country. . . .

It is wrong, and even harmful, to see socialist society as something rigid and unchangeable, to perceive its improvement as an effort to adapt complicated reality to concepts and formulas that have been established once and for all. The concepts of socialism keep on developing. . . .

Perestroika is a word with many meanings. But if we are to choose from its many possible synonyms the key one which expresses its essence most accurately, then we can say thus: perestroika is a revolution. A decisive acceleration of the socioeconomic and cultural development of Soviet society which involves radical changes on the way to a qualitatively new state is undoubtedly a revolutionary task. . . .

In accordance with our theory, revolution means construction, but it also always implies demolition. Revolution requires the demolition of all that is obsolete, stagnant and hinders fast progress. . . . Perestroika also means a resolute and radical elimination of obstacles hindering social and economic development, of outdated methods of managing the economy and of dogmatic stereotype mentality. . . .

And like a revolution, our day-to-day activities must be unparalleled, revolutionary. Perestroika requires Party leaders who are very close to Lenin's ideal of a revolutionary Bolshevik. Officialdom, red tape, patronizing attitudes, and careerism are incompatible with this ideal. On the other hand, courage, initiative, high ideological standards and moral purity, a constant urge to discuss things with people, and an ability to firmly uphold the humane values of socialism are greatly honored. . . . We still have a long way to go to achieve this ideal. Too many people are still "in the state of evolution," or, to put it plainly, have adopted a wait-and-see attitude.

Source: M. Gorbachev, *Perestroika: New Thinking for Our Country and the World* (New York: Harper & Row, 1987), pp. 29–55 passim.

Despite a record of slow and often interrupted disarmament negotiations, the superpowers have moved closer to the goal of reducing the nuclear peril. Indeed, the agreements reached in the 1970s and 1980s are far more hopeful than all previous disarmament efforts undertaken since the Great War. This advance must surely reflect the lessons derived from a century of war and strife and a realization that the world of tomorrow must rest on the basis of common purpose.

Notes

1. F. Freidel, *America in the Twentieth Century* (New York: Knopf, 1960), pp. 475–476.

Suggestions for Further Reading

Brzezinski, Z. K. *The Soviet Bloc: Unity and Compromise*. Cambridge, Mass.: Harvard University Press, 1967.

Crankshaw, E. *Khrushchev*. New York: Viking Press, 1966.

Dawisha, K. *Eastern Europe, Gorbachev and Reform: The Great Challenge*. Cambridge: Cambridge University Press, 1988.

De Porte, A. W. *Europe Between the Superpowers*. New Haven, Conn.: Yale University Press, 1979.

Epstein, W. *The Last Chance: Nuclear Proliferation and Arms Control*. New York: Free Press, 1976.

Fejto, F. *A History of the People's Democracies: Eastern Europe Since Stalin*. New York: Praeger, 1971.

Freedman, L. *The Evolution of Nuclear Strategy*. New York: St. Martin's Press, 1982.

Gaddis, J. L. *The United States and the Origins of the Cold War, 1941–1947*. New York: Columbia University Press, 1972.

Herken, G. *The Winning Weapon: The Atomic Bomb in the Cold War, 1945–1950*. Princeton, N.J.: Princeton University Press, 1988.

Kolko, G. *The Politics of War*. New York: Random House, 1969.

Kriegel, A. *Eurocommunism*. Stanford, Calif.: Stanford University Press, 1978.

Laqueur, W. *Europe Since Hitler*. London: Weidenfeld & Nicolson, 1972.

Lovenduski, J. *Women and European Politics*. Amherst: University of Massachusetts Press, 1986.

Mastny, V. *Russia's Road to the Cold War*. New York: Columbia University Press, 1979.

Mazrui, A. A. *Africa's International Relations: The Diplomacy of Dependency and Change*. Boulder, Colo.: Westview Press, 1977.

Milward, A. S. *The Reconstruction of Western Europe, 1945–51*. Berkeley: University of California Press, 1984.

Pinkus, B. *The Jews of the Soviet Union: A History of a National Minority*. Cambridge: Cambridge University Press, 1988.

Ulam, A. *Expansion and Coexistence: The History of Soviet Foreign Policy, 1917–1967*. New York: Praeger, 1974.

Van der Wee, H. *Prosperity and Upheaval: The World Economy, 1945–1980*. Berkeley: University of California Press, 1988.

Von Laue, T. *The World Revolution of Westernization: The Twentieth Century in Global Perspective*. New York: Oxford University Press, 1987.

Civilization and the Dilemma of Progress

History, Time, and Progress

In the modern era, the prevailing view of historical process has been defined by the concept of progress, which sees history as a steady advance toward a better world. A century ago one proponent of progress, the American writer Edward Bellamy (1850–1898), wrote a popular novel that embodied this belief. In *Looking Backward,* Bellamy imagined a man who fell into a hypnotic sleep in 1887 and awoke in the year 2000. The man discovered a perfect world of universal peace and happiness in which all people shared equally in the wealth and benefits of a society freed from conflict, greed, and even the need for laws.

Repelled by the social evils of his own day, Bellamy believed that the future had to be better than the past and that it would inevitably lead to an ideal civilization. His

A powerful symbol of twentieth-century technology, the United States space shuttle *Discovery* roars off the launch pad in September of 1988. [UPI/Bettmann Newsphotos]

work belongs to a long utopian tradition that stretches back to Plato's fourth-century B.C. *The Republic.* Bellamy's optimism for the future stemmed from a prejudice against the past, for his vision of progress did not permit him to see the mixture of good and bad that is present in every period of history. Like many others then and now, he assumed that the passage of time automatically brought with it improvement over what had been before. Those who embrace this view generally assume that the closer in time to our own day, the better human life has been, that the present is superior to the past because it is now rather than then. Yet in his letter from Birmingham Jail, written in 1963, the American civil rights leader Martin Luther King, Jr., pointedly rejected the "strangely irrational notion that there is something in the very flow of time that will inevitably cure all ills."[1] The notion of progress has often obscured the fact that even at moments of relative peace and prosperity, certain groups without power or status—such as workers, racial minorities, and women—have not shared in the broad advances made by society at large.

Bellamy's understanding of progress reflects a relatively modern, peculiarly Western world view that broke with older Western and non-Western traditions alike. Earlier civilizations had viewed progress chiefly in spiritual or theological terms and tended to see history as cyclical rather than progressive. The ancient Greeks of the classical age believed that their ancestors of the archaic period had been more "heroic" and thus better. Confucius, whose ethical philosophy dominated Chinese thought, accepted the notion of social improvement through education and good example, but he also inculcated a respect for the knowledge and wisdom of the past and a measured view of the present and future. The Judeo-Christian and Islamic religions prophesied salvation and the attainment of a heavenly paradise through spiritual rectitude but had no place for a secular conception of progress. The Hindu and Buddhist concept of reincarnation, which stressed "progress" from lower to higher states of being, aspired to the ultimate spiritual state of Nirvana that would transcend the material world. Indian conceptions of history were decidedly cyclical; the period since about 900 B.C., in which we still live, the *Kali-yuga,* was conceived as one of decline and chaos.

Nineteenth-century Western thinkers were thus a minority in viewing progress in secular terms, based on belief in the material perfectibility of society. In this sense the human adventure is measured in terms of our ability to master the physical environment through scientific and technological advances and to improve the level of material well-being and comfort through the ever-increasing accumulation of wealth. Advocates of this conception of progress claimed that improvement would come through the application of knowledge to political, social, and economic problems. History, according to this view, would unfold as the natural laws that governed the universe were discovered and manipulated in the interest of human improvement. The ethos of liberal capitalism sought to unfetter the laws of economics in order to achieve the greatest material good for the greatest number of people.

Even while this conception gained ascendancy in the West, a variety of reform-minded thinkers recoiled against the effects of industrialism by experimenting with socialist utopias in which private ownership of capital was replaced by communal property in rural egalitarian societies. Some utopian socialists even conceived of a technocratic society in which scientists and industrialists governed on behalf of the general populace. Then, in the mid-nineteenth century, "scientific" socialists explained history as the product of class conflict: categories of human beings—classes—competed for ascendancy by seeking control over the means of production and distribution. The Marxist utopia looked forward to the inevitable triumph of the working class over the capitalists and the ultimate creation of a classless society.

Bellamy's utopia was a combination of these visions. It imagined a highly organized industrial society in which a secular state exercised complete authority and evoked voluntary compliance from its citizens because it provided them with material comfort and well-being. Though repelled by the poverty and exploitation that characterized the expanding industrialization of his time, Bellamy remained a believer in the ability of technology to resolve the ills of modern society.

More than a century after the publication of *Looking Backward,* modern writers have become less sanguine about the benefits of a technological society. In 1932, in the midst of the Great Depression, the British author Aldous Huxley published *Brave New World,* a novel that depicted a totalitarian society in which people lacked no bodily comfort but were without freedom or creativity. In 1949, following World War II, George Orwell portrayed a dehumanized totalitarian society of the future in his book *1984.* The appalling nature of such totalitarian regimes as those of Hitler and Stalin and the specter of the atomic bomb provided the impetus for Orwell's novel and its bleak vision of the future. Orwell's message, in the words of the psychologist Erich Fromm, was intended to awaken us to the common "danger of a society of automatons who will have lost every trace of individuality, of love, of critical thought, and yet who will not be aware of it."[2]

Global Implications of Progress

The materialist theory of progress provided a powerful rationale for the imperialism that conquered much of the non-Western world in the late nineteenth century. Many

Europeans believed that they were bringing the benefits of their technologically superior civilization to unfortunate primitive peoples. Western science and industry, on which the theory of progress was based, in turn made possible imperialist domination over much of the rest of the world.

As we have seen, the reaction of the non-Western world to the Western intrusion has been mixed. The Chinese effort to keep all Western influences out of their country was by no means the norm, for the Japanese aggressively adopted Western-style industrialization and technology, both to resist Western domination and to extend their own hegemony over East Asia. Similarly, some southern African tribes conquered their neighbors with European firearms, and Arab traders used Western weapons to capture Africans for the slave market. In the early twentieth century Turkish and Iranian admirers of Western technology attempted to "modernize" their countries along the Western model, but more recently Islamic fundamentalists, particularly in Iran, have strenuously repudiated Western influences.

The Western idea of progress continues to influence both Western policies toward the nonindustrialized nations and Third World thinking about how to solve the immense social, economic, and cultural problems endemic to their own countries. Since World War II, industrialized nations have systematically exported their notion of progress to underdeveloped states as they emerged from colonial status to independence. In 1961 President John F. Kennedy announced a massive program of economic assistance for Latin America that he called the Alliance for Progress.

As Western developmental strategies for "modernization" replaced imperialism as the basis of the global dynamic, new forms of dependency have been substituted for older forms of subjugation. During the struggle for India's independence from the British, Mahatma Gandhi—who recognized the relationship between imperialism and the materialist notion of progress—rejected the Western model of development by urging his fellow Indians to adopt the traditional spinning wheel as the symbol of freedom and national regeneration.

Despite Gandhi's rejection of modern technology, his successors embraced Western-style industrialization, making India one of the first Third World countries to develop not only conventional electrical energy sources but a nuclear capability as well. Most other underdeveloped nations followed suit, generally adopting an enthusiastic attitude toward technology, with its capacity to enhance health as well as material comforts. Thus agricultural societies often seek to build huge dams, hydroelectric plants, and nuclear energy stations in order to electrify and industrialize their economies, but sometimes at the expense of destroying millions of acres of irreplaceable forests in the process of extracting raw materials and constructing factories. The problem is clearly one of balance; industrialization and conservation need not be mutually antagonistic.

Reliance on Western technology has at times been seriously disruptive to the Third World. The technology of advanced industrial nations and the accompanying infrastructures of such technology are not necessarily ideal or suited for developing countries. Historically, modern technology has been marked by its complex and large-scale character, and its success has depended on extensive national markets, skilled labor, and substantial investment capital. Because developing countries generally lack these resources, simple and inexpensive machinery that does not require extensive education and training may be more appropriate to agrarian societies. Moreover, since 1945 most technological development in the Third World has been undertaken with extensive loans borrowed from Western nations; the resultant economic dependency has crippled the debtor nations, most of which are unable to repay their huge obligations.

In recent years a rethinking of the Western notion of material progress has been unfolding. Not only has the idea of "appropriate technology" gained currency, but it is now increasingly recognized that Third World nations need not necessarily undergo the same stressful stages of development experienced by earlier industrial societies. It is probable, nonetheless, that the rapid transformation of the globe and of its human societies will continue, driven by technological change and its political ramifications.

Facing the Future: History as Freedom

As the twentieth century draws toward a close, civilization appears to be beset with a host of unparalleled problems. There is irony in the fact that science and technology have made the lives of many millions of people more comfortable, yet they have also been the source of unanticipated dilemmas. Advances in health care have resulted in a global population explosion that threatens to engulf the poorer societies of the Third World in a relentless cycle of poverty and social despair. Although new agricultural methods have increased food productivity, natural disasters and political upheavals periodically create crises of starvation and malnutrition for millions. The demands of industrialization have despoiled much of the earth's seas, rivers, forests, and air. Now that the depletion of finite energy resources looms as a distinct possibility, the harnessing of atomic power as an energy alternative is fraught with other dangers, as dramatized by the 1979 meltdown at the Three Mile Island nuclear power plant in Pennsylvania and the 1986 disaster at the Soviet plant in Chernobyl. And the entire human race faces the ultimate challenge of avoiding the folly of nuclear war.

Despite advances achieved in the struggle for human

rights by racial minorities, women, and other oppressed groups, vast inequities in economic justice and political freedom continue to exist—in Third World countries, in Communist-bloc nations, and in the Western world. These and other issues are compelling and dangerous, but the problems of our age are unique only in the particular forms they now assume. If nothing else, history provides us with perspective: war and conflict, disease and hunger, prejudice and exploitation, torture and state repression are some of the less pleasant features of history that our age has in common with all civilizations of the past. Over the course of 5,000 years, all societies have at times perceived the challenges facing them as insurmountable. Yet history also suggests that while the problems recur with relentless repetition, determined people have continued to seek durable solutions to them.

Change, often rapid and unpredictable, has been the hallmark of history. Even the most conservative of cultures, as in ancient Egypt or medieval China, underwent sudden and dramatic shifts in social and religious belief and political structure. Later generations do, of course, inherit traditions and values from the past, but they sometimes choose to discard them in the light of new circumstances. Those moments when men and women have successfully overcome adversity represent recurrent evidence of the open-endedness of history. Perhaps the only constraint under which our own age operates is the fact that as the world develops into a truly global community, we increasingly share the same human experience and thus equal responsibility for the world we make.

Notes

1. M. L. King, Jr., *Why We Can't Wait* (New York: Harper & Row, 1963), p. 89.
2. E. Fromm, "Afterword," in G. Orwell, *1984* (New York: New American Library, 1961), p. 267.

INDEX

	SOUTH ASIA	EAST ASIA	AFRICA	MIDDLE EAST	EUROPE	AMERICA
1600–1620	Death of Akbar	Founding of Tokugawa Shogunate	Slave Trade to North America	Peak of Safavid Culture	Shakespeare	Jamestown and Quebec
1620–1640	Taj Mahal	Japan Expels Westerners	Dutch Settle West Africa	Death of Shah Abbas	Thirty Years' War	Massachusetts Bay
1640–1660	Overthrow of Shah Jahan	Fall of Ming Dynasty	Dutch Base at the Cape		English Revolution	Navigation Acts
1660–1680	Aurangzeb		English Royal Africa Company		Rembrandt	English Acquire New York
1680–1700	Aurangzeb	Treaty of Nerchinsk			Glorious Revolution	
1700–1720	Mughal Collapse				War of Spanish Succession	
1720–1740				Safavid Dynasty Collapses		Great Awakening
1740–1760	Clive's Victories	Ch'ien Lung in China		Nadir Shah in Iran	Seven Years' War Begins	French and Indian War
1760–1780	Afghans Invade India	Ch'ien Lung in China		Karim Khan in Iran	"Spinning Jenny"	American War of Independence
1780–1800	British Seize Ceylon	White Lotus Rebellion	British Occupy Cape Colony	Founding of Qajar Dynasty	French Revolution	American Constitution
1800–1810			British Abolish Slave Trade		Napoleon	Louisiana Purchase
1810–1820					Fall of Napoleon	War of 1812
1820–1830	Bengal Renaissance		Zulu Expansion		Independence of Greece	Independence of Brazil and Mexico
1830–1840		Hokusai, Master Artist	French Occupy Algiers		Revolution of 1830 in Paris	Age of Jackson
1840–1850	Conquest of Kashmir	Opium War			Revolutions of 1848	